The Reader's
Encyclopedia of
WORLD DRAMA

The Reader's Encyclopedia of
WORLD DRAMA

Edited by
JOHN GASSNER
&
EDWARD QUINN

THOMAS Y. CROWELL COMPANY
New York / Established 1834

Copyright © 1969 by Thomas Y. Crowell Company, Inc.

Manufactured in the United States of America

L. C. Card 69-11830

1 2 3 4 5 6 7 8 9 10

Throughout the encyclopedia, the dates of plays are those of first production, unless otherwise labeled.

Permission to reprint the following copyright materials is gratefully acknowledged.

Excerpt from *The Theatre and Its Double* by Antonin Artaud, translated from the French by Mary Caroline Richards, is reprinted by permission of Calder and Boyars, Ltd., from *The Collected Works of Antonin Artaud,* volume four, to be published by Calder and Boyars, Ltd., in 1970; and by permission of Grove Press, Inc. Copyright © 1958 by Grove Press, Inc.

Coislinian Tractate, from *An Aristotelian Theory of Comedy* (1922), translated by Lane Cooper, is reprinted by permission of Basil Blackwell & Mott, Ltd.

Excerpt from *Problems of the Theatre,* from the Preface to *Four Plays* (1965) by Friedrich Dürrenmatt, translated by Gerhard Nellhaus, is reprinted by permission of the author; of Jonathan Cape, Ltd.; and of Grove Press, Inc. Copyright © 1957 by Peter Schifferli, Verlags AG 'Die Arche, Zurich.

Excerpt from *Discourse on Tragedy* by Pierre Corneille and excerpt from *Correspondence with Nicolai and Moses Mendelssohn* by Gotthold Ephraim Lessing, from *Dramatic Essays of the Neo-Classical Age* (1950), edited by Henry Hitch Adams and Baxter Hathaway, pp. 2–34 and 329–340, are reprinted by permission of Columbia University Press, New York.

"The Argument of Comedy," from *English Institute Essays* (1948) by Northrop Frye, is reprinted by permission of Columbia University Press, New York.

"A Fragment on Comedy and Tragedy" by Aelius Donatus and excerpt from "The Comic Art" by Antonio Riccoboni, both translated by George Miltz, from *Theories of Comedy* edited by Paul Lauter, are reprinted by permission of Doubleday & Company, Inc. Copyright © 1964 by Paul Lauter.

Excerpt from *The Philosophy of Fine Art* by Georg Wilhelm Friedrich Hegel, translated in 1920 by F. P. B. Osmaston, is reprinted by permission of G. Bell & Sons, Ltd.

Excerpt from *Feeling and Form* by Susanne Langer, pp. 301–325, is reprinted by permission of Routlege & Kegan Paul, Ltd., and of Charles Scribner's Sons. Copyright 1953 by Charles Scribner's Sons.

Preface

It is singularly appropriate that one of the last books to bear John Gassner's name as author or editor should be an encyclopedia. Few men had a more encyclopedic knowledge of world drama than he and fewer still the capacity to organize and synthesize that knowledge. Thus in a very real sense this book is an extension of the man. But it is only a partial extension. It could never adequately represent the warmth and charity, the graciousness and good humor, that were so much a part of John Gassner. Nor can it hope to convey the depth and understanding of the relationship he shared with his wife and collaborator, Mollie. The personal dimensions of this man, as of all men, are immeasurable.

What this book can reflect is what John Gassner knew about drama. To assert that is to make a very large claim indeed. Its perspective is that of drama as a universal phenomenon, deeply rooted in the culture of the community and the experience of the individual. Evolving from that primitive past, drama has consistently provided the form in which men explored the ultimate problems of human existence, problems as fundamental as those related to the experiences of terror and death, laughter and rebirth. Thus a considerable portion of our limited space has been devoted to dramatic theory in the attempt to establish a theoretical context for the factual and interpretative material that comprises the major portion of the book.

As for the scope of the work, its province is the drama as literature, not as theater. It contains no entries on actors, theatrical troupes, costumes, scenery, or playhouses. We have not forgotten that the overwhelming majority of the works mentioned in this book were designed to be performed on a stage. Commentary on the staged drama should never lose sight of that essential fact—indeed it should incorporate it wherever possible. But the dramatic experience need not be limited to the theater. The existence of drama as literature testifies to the existence of that larger theater of the mind in which one is both the actor and the audience, the created and the creator. It is on this stage—long after the insubstantial pageant of an "evening at the theater" has faded—that a play achieves its final reality. This was John Gassner's vision of drama, dominated by the image of *homo ludens*—man the actor playing his fantastic tricks before high heaven. It is hoped that this volume is an expression of that vision.

In the production of this volume we—both editors and contributors—owe a large debt to the Reference Department of the Thomas Y. Crowell Company: To Victoria Simons and Nancy Goldner, ruthless enemies of the inaccurate and the inelegant; to Joan Cenedella, who combines superbly the two essential qualities of a good editor, taste and tact; and to Edward Tripp, the prime mover and sustaining force of this enterprise from its inception to its completion.

We would also like to thank Cedric H. Whitman and James Mirollo for some excellent translations and some invaluable advice, and Evert Sprinchorn, Albert Bermel, and Jack D. Zipes for helpful suggestions. My personal gratitude to Dorothy Quinn, a tireless typist.

A special note of thanks to Mollie Gassner for her continued interest and assistance in every phase of this project.

EDWARD QUINN

Contents

Contributors

L. R. N. A.   Leonard R. N. Ashley
Brooklyn College of the City University of New York

S. A. A.   S. A. Ashraf
University of Karachi

A. B.   Anna Balakian
New York University

J. B.   Jean Basile
Drama Critic, *Le Devoir*

G. B.   Gordon Beck
Cornell University

K. B.   Karl Beckson-
Brooklyn College of the City University of New York

E. B.   Eric Bentley

A. C. B.   Albert C. Bermel
Columbia University

H. M. B.   Haskell M. Block
Brooklyn College of the City University of New York

J. R. B.   James R. Brandon
University of Hawaii

D. B.   Douglas Bush
Harvard University

M. M. B.   Sister Mary Marguerite Butler, RSM
Mercy College of Detroit

K. C.   Kenneth Cavander
Yale University

F. Č.   František Černý
Charles University, Prague

R. C.   Ruby Cohn
California Institute of the Arts

E. C.   Emilie Colahan
Graduate Center of the City University of New York

R. D.   Rae Dalven
Ladycliff College

F. D.   Frank Dauster
Rutgers, The State University

G. E. D.   George E. Duckworth
Princeton University

A. M. E.   A. M. Elmessiri
Ein Shams University, Cairo

M. E.   Martin Esslin
British Broadcasting Corporation

W. E.   Walter Eysselinck
University of Sussex

S. L. F.   Seymour L. Flaxman
City College of the City University of New York

W. F.   Wallace Fowlie
Duke University

J. G.   John Gassner
Yale University

F. G. G.   Frederick G. Goldberg
City College of the City University of New York

M. G.   Malcolm Goldstein
Queens College of the City University of New York

T. G.   Thomas Gould
University of Texas

S. G.   Stephen Grecco

W. G.   William Green
Queens College of the City University of New York

G. M. A. G.   G. M. A. Grube
Trinity College, Toronto

Ja. G.   Jacques Guicharnaud
Yale University

A. H.   Alfred Harbage
Harvard University

W. E. H.   William E. Harkins
Columbia University

C. J. H.   C. J. Herington
University of Texas

B. H.   Barnard Hewitt
University of Illinois

E. H.	Edwin Honig Brown University		C. R. M.	Carl Richard Mueller University of California, Los Angeles
R. H.	Richard Hosley University of Arizona		M. K. N.	Martin K. Nurmi Kent State University
M. J.	Maya Jamil University of Karachi		N. O.	Nüvit Özdoğru
J. K.	John Kardoss Long Island University		C. R. P.	Charles R. Pilditch Rutgers, The State University
B. K.	Bernard Knox The Center for Hellenic Studies		J. P.	Joel Pontes University of Pernambuco
D. K.	David Krause Brown University		H. v.d. P.	Helen van der Poorton University of New South Wales
F. K. K.	Filip Kalan Kumbatovič Academy of Theater, Radio, Film, and Television, Ljubljana		H. P.	Henry Popkin State University of New York at Buffalo
J. F. L.	James F. Lacey Eastern Connecticut State College		E. Q.	Edward Quinn City College of the City University of New York
J. C. L.	Joseph C. Landis Queens College of the City University of New York		R. Q.	Ricardo Quintana University of Wisconsin
J. H. L.	John Howard Lawson		J. R.	Joseph Raben Queens College of the City University of New York
D. J. L.	Daniel J. Leary City College of the City University of New York		Z. R.	Zeev Raviv Tel-Aviv University, Israel
H. L.	Harold Lenz University of Houston		I. R.	Irving Ribner State University of New York at Stony Brook
M. L.	Milton Levin Trenton State College		G. R.	Gordon Rogoff Yale University
A. W. L.	Asta Willmann Linnolt		H. R.	Hansjuergen Rosenbauer
G. L.	Glenn Loney Brooklyn College of the City Univer- sity of New York		J. E. R.	James E. Ruoff City College of the City University of New York
L. L.	Luigi Lunari Società Storica del Teatro, Milan		R. K. S.	Robert K. Sarlos University of California, Davis
R. E. L.	Robert E. Lynch Newark College of Engineering		H. S.	Heinrich Schnitzler Stage Director and Artistic Adviser, Theater in der Josefstadt, Vienna
A. MacA.	Andrew R. MacAndrew University of Virginia		H. B. S.	Harold B. Segel Columbia University
L. M.	Louis Marder University of Illinois at Chicago Circle		S. S. S.	Stephen S. Stanton University of Michigan
K. N. M.	Kenneth N. McKee New York University		D. S., Jr.	Donald Stone, Jr. Harvard University
C. A. M.	Carol A. Melillo New York University		L. S. S.	Lowell S. Swortzell New York University
B. M. M.	Barney M. Milstein Princeton University		N. F. S.	Nancy S. Swortzell New York University
W. M.	Worthington Miner American Academy of Dramatic Arts		W. S.	Wylie Sypher Simmons College
C. M.	Charles Moser The George Washington University		M. T.	Michael Tait University of Toronto

M. T.	Michael Timko Queens College of the City University of New York (England: nineteenth century and Edwardian)	H. W.	Herbert Weisinger State University of New York at Stony Brook
		H. W. W.	Henry W. Wells Columbia University
T. T.	Timo Tiusanen Helsinki University	G. E. W.	George E. Wellwarth Pennsylvania State University
R. B. V.	Richard B. Vowles University of Wisconsin	C. H. W.	Cedric H. Whitman Harvard University
E. W.	Eugene M. Waith Yale University	J. A. W.	Joseph A. Withey Hanover College
I. W.	Irving Wardle Drama Critic, London *Times*	E. Y.-S.	Ehsan Yar-Shater Columbia University
B. W.	Bruce Wardropper Duke University	J. D. Z.	Jack D. Zipes New York University
G. W.	Gerald Weales University of Pennsylvania		
A. W.	Albert Weiner State University of New York at Albany		
A. A. W.	Arnold A. Weinstein		

John Gassner, who died in 1967, was Sterling Professor of Playwriting and Dramatic Literature at Yale University. Edward Quinn, Ph.D., is a professor of English at the City College of the City University of New York.

The Reader's
Encyclopedia of
WORLD DRAMA

A

Abbey Theatre. See IRELAND.

Abdülhak Hâmit [Tarhan] (1852–1937). Turkish poet and playwright. Abdülhak Hâmit was born in Istanbul. After spending a few years abroad with his ambassador father, he returned to his native town and became a civil servant and later joined the foreign service. After the declaration of the republic in Turkey Hâmit became a member of parliament. Generally recognized as the greatest poet of the *Tanzimat,* or reform, period, Hâmit helped free Turkish poetry of its traditional narrow confines of form and subject matter and wrote lyrical, epic, and philosophical poems dealing with love, nature, patriotism, death, and metaphysics.

Hâmit's plays, numbering about twenty, deal with Turkish, Arabic, Assyrian, and Greek history and imaginary subjects. They are influenced mainly by the works of Shakespeare, Pierre Corneille, and Victor Hugo. Written to be read rather than to be performed, the plays have many scene changes, long tirades, and difficult and artificial diction. Although in an article on the theater Hâmit stressed the point that characters should speak in a style appropriate to their personalities, he did not apply this rule in his own plays. Usually writing in verse—either in *aruz,* the classical Turkish meters, or in more modern syllabic meters—Hâmit had his characters speak in imaginative but artificial dialogue filled with forced rhymes and difficult Arabic and Persian words and rules of grammar that are almost impossible for the layman to follow. In recent years, several of Hâmit's plays, including *Sabr-ü Sebat* ("Patience and Endurance," 1875) and *Finten* (written 1886, pub. 1917), have been rewritten in simplified Turkish and have been successful with audiences. *Finten* was strongly influenced by *Othello* and *Macbeth.*

Although Abdülhak Hâmit's plays are generally dated today and his poetry seldom read, he was considered by many generations to be the greatest Turkish poet and playwright.—N. O.

Abell, Kjeld (1901–1961). Danish playwright and man of the theater. Born in Ribe, southern Jutland, Abell found his first theatrical excitement at a Max Reinhardt production of Strindberg's *The Ghost Sonata.* He subsequently studied scene design and worked with choreographer George Balanchine in Paris, where he came to admire dramatist Jean Giraudoux and director Louis Jouvet as well. From 1935 until his death Abell was an active playwright and designer. He was elected to the Danish Academy in 1960.

Abell made his debut as playwright with *Melodien der blev væk* (*The Melody That Got Lost,* 1935), which deals in revue fashion with the suffocations of everyday conformity. The same theme preoccupies Abell in *Eva aftjener sin barnepligt* ("Eve Serves Out Her Childhood," 1936), in which the biblical Eve is allowed the dubious indulgence of being brought up in a Danish middle-class home, surfeited with over-stuffed chairs and aspidistra. The title character of *Anna Sophie Hedvig* (1939) is a mild-mannered schoolteacher who has committed a justifiable murder. In this play-within-a-play, Abell argues the need of resistance to the gathering threat of Nazism. Another in Abell's fine gallery of female characters is Mirena Pritz of *Dronning går igen* (*The Queen on Tour,* 1943), who, dressed as the Gertrude of *Hamlet,* defends herself against accusations of murder.

The literary fruits of Abell's wartime resistance activity are visible in *Silkeborg* (1946), a study of an

KJELD ABELL (DANISH INFORMATION OFFICE)

ordinary Danish family's life under the German occupation. In *Dage på en sky* (*Days on a Cloud,* 1947) Abell places a modern scientist in a classical mythological setting where his responsibilities to society are argued in witty, trenchant fashion. The title animal of *Den blå pekingeser* ("The Blue Pekinese," 1954), an expressionist fantasy, represents the life impulse in Abell's peculiarly whimsical symbolic language. Working on four levels in *Skriget* ("The Scream," 1961)—the fabulous (talking birds in a church tower), the everyday, the surreal, and the biblical—Abell accomplishes an extraordinary synthesis in his persistent quest after a meaning in life that transcends conformity to easy custom.

Abell's seriocomic theater owes much to Hans Christian Andersen, as he in effect admits in the festival play *Andersen* (1955). This play also represents an imaginative extension of the best of the expressionist heritage.

Days on a Cloud is in *The Genius of the Scandinavian Theatre* (1964), edited by Evert Sprinchorn, with an essay on the play by Elias Bredsdorff, pp. 466–535. *The Queen on Tour* is in *Contemporary Danish Plays* (Copenhagen, 1955).—R. B. V.

Acharnians (Acharnēs, 425 B.C.). A comedy by ARISTOPHANES. The play revolves around the central idea of a privately negotiated peace treaty. The hero, Dicaeopolis ("Set-the-City-Straight"), is an Athenian who decides, after watching the war between Athens and Sparta drag on for six years, that his only hope of recovering his farm and the blessings of peace is to make his own independent arrangements with the enemy. This he does, and the entire action of the play flows from his decision. Dicaeopolis must first encounter the hostility of the old, rigidly patriotic veterans of Marathon, represented by charcoal burners from Acharnae (a district of Attica), then the opposition of the young general Lamachus, a ferociously militant anti-Spartan, and finally, the type of private citizen who exploits the war for profit by laying information with the authorities. With the help of a costume supplied by the playwright Euripides, Dicaeopolis is victorious. He wins over the old Acharnians to his side, celebrates for the first time in years the festival of the Rural Dionysia, trades with hitherto forbidden states, and decisively repudiates Lamachus.

The play contains many of the themes that occupied Aristophanes throughout his career: youth versus age; peace versus war; and the old values (in particular, the old drama) versus the new (in particular, Euripides). It is interesting that the two groups with most to lose from the war are shown in this play to be the very people most enthusiastic for it—the young men, and the old peasants. The youth of Athens, personified by Lamachus, were excited by the prospect of personal glory and power. The older generation were swept along by politicians' rhetoric and appeals to blind patriotism. Aristophanes saw himself as a lonely voice of clarity and sanity; his task was to bring his countrymen to their senses. The conversion of the charcoal burners from hot, fiery hostility to gentle peacefulness makes the play a brilliant demonstration of the role of the poet and dramatist in Athenian society.

Translations of the play are listed under Aristophanes.—K. C.

Adamov, Arthur (1908–). Russian-born French playwright. Born of Armenian parents at Kislovstock in the Caucasus, Adamov left Russia in 1912. He was educated in Geneva, Mayence, and Paris.

La Parodie ("The Parody"), Adamov's first play, was written in 1947 and performed in 1950 in Paris at the Théâtre Lancry. The idea for this play appeared to Adamov in a street scene he happened to observe. He decided to demonstrate as blatantly as possible the subject of man's solitude, the impossibility of communication between men. For Adamov the meaning of tragedy lies in the fact that, although the world does have a meaning that man must search for, this meaning is inaccessible to man. In this sense Adamov's world is a "parody" of man's search for meaning, his helplessness before the unknown and the inevitability of his death.

One of Adamov's most ambitious plays, *Paolo Paoli,* was first performed in Lyons at the Théâtre de la Comédie in 1957. The subject of the play is the egoism and narrow-mindedness of French society between the years 1900 and 1914. The world of the play is a microcosm of the bigger world moving steadily and fatalistically toward war. The associations of a false or materialistic nature existing among the prewar characters of *Paolo Paoli* serve as premonitions for the selfish alliances among peoples and nations that followed the war.

Beginning with *Ping-Pong* in 1954, political themes have been of prime importance in Adamov's plays. But it would be false to classify him solely as a political dramatist, because he has also continued with experimental dramaturgy and the techniques of SURREALISM and the THEATER OF THE ABSURD in all of his plays since *Ping-Pong: Paolo Paoli, Le printemps 71* ("Spring 71," 1961), and *La politique des restes* (*The Politics of the Left-overs,* 1963). See also PROFESSOR TARANNE.

In the preface to his second volume of plays, *Théâtre II* (1955), Adamov comments on his career, on the origins of his plays, and on his dissatisfaction or satisfaction with them.

For information on Adamov see Peter Lennon, "An Interview with Adamov," *Plays and Players,* Vol. 7, No. 6 (March 1960).—W. F.

Adelphoe (The Brothers, 160 B.C.). A comedy by TERENCE, considered the Roman playwright's masterpiece. *Adelphoe,* based on a play by the Greek playwright Menander, is primarily a study of human nature and, more than any other Roman comedy, is a play with a purpose—to show the proper method of bringing up young men. The results of two opposing systems are clearly and amusingly portrayed. Demea rears his son Ctesipho with harshness, while his brother, Micio, who has adopted Demea's other son, Aeschinus, believes in kindness and leniency. Neither system produces frankness between father and son, and Demea's astonishing reversal at the end, a sudden change to generosity at Micio's expense, points up the desirability of an avoidance of extremes.

Numerous comedies in the seventeenth and eighteenth centuries were based on *Adelphoe,* either wholly or in part. Among them are George Chapman's *All Fools* (1604?), Beaumont and Fletcher's *The Scornful Lady* (c. 1609), Molière's *L'École des*

ILLUSTRATION FROM A MANUSCRIPT OF A SCENE FROM *Adelphoe* BY TERENCE (BIBLIOTECA APOSTOLICA VATICANA)

Maris (1661), Thomas Shadwell's *The Squire of Alsatia* (1688), Richard Steele's *The Tender Husband, or The Accomplished Fools* (1705), Denis Diderot's *Le Père de Famille* (1758), George Colman's *The Jealous Wife* (1761), Richard Cumberland's *The Choleric Man* (1774), and Henry Fielding's *The Fathers, or The Good-Natured Man* (1778).
—G. E. D.

Aeschylus (525/24–456/55 B.C.). Greek tragic playwright. The only assured dates and facts in Aeschylus' career are those relating to the productions of his plays, which were noted in the contemporary Athenian archives; but various later Greek works (especially the anonymous ancient *Life of Aeschylus*) also preserve information which, although mixed with legendary material, seems to be reliable. From these sources the following outline of the poet's life emerges.

Aeschylus was the son of an Athenian noble, Euphorion, and spent part of his childhood at Eleusis, the Attic town which was the seat of the Eleusinian Mysteries. In 499 B.C. he competed for the first time in the tragic contest at the Athenian Great Dionysia, but not until 484 B.C.—the traditional date of Euripides' birth—was his genius recognized by an award of the first prize. By then Aeschylus had fought with distinction as an infantryman against the Persians at Marathon (490 B.C.). During the second Persian invasion of 480 B.C. he served with the Athenian fleet, and was present at the great victory of Salamis. He produced his first extant tragedy, THE PERSIANS (which centers on that victory), in 472 B.C. with such success that he was invited to restage it in Syracuse by the brilliant Sicilian dynast Hieron. By the Dionysiac Festival of 468 Aeschylus had returned from Sicily to Athens, for on that occasion he was beaten in the tragic contest by Sophocles, who was competing for the first time. Just one year later, however, Aeschylus won first prize with the tetralogy containing SEVEN AGAINST THEBES, and within the next few years his Danaid tetralogy, which contains THE SUPPLIANT MAIDENS, again earned him the first prize, this time over Sophocles. In 458 he produced the ORESTEIA (containing *Agamemnon, Choephori, Eumenides,* and *Proteus*). Soon after, he left for Sicily, where he died.

The family of Aeschylus continued to produce tragic writers of more or less distinction for nearly two centuries; his nephew Philocles, for instance, won first prize over Sophocles' *Oedipus the King.*

Beyond these bare facts, little is known about Aeschylus' personal life. If the joyful caricature of him in Aristophanes' *Frogs* (405 B.C.) bears any relation to reality, Aeschylus was a man of simple nobility and fiery instincts—qualities which in fact reappear in other ancient anecdotes about him and (some may think) in his extant poetry. Several Greek writers repeat a story that "he composed his tragedies while drunk," but it is hard to know whether this is a biographical truth or a subtle form of literary criticism, or both. As literary criticism it would compare with his near-contemporary Gorgias' remark that "all Aeschylus' dramas are packed with Dionysus," and Aristophanes' description of him as "the Bacchic King" (*Frogs*, line 1259). These ancient writers, like many moderns, seem to have recognized the intoxicated, hallucinatory quality of Aeschylus' dramatic vision. His plays are "Dionysiac" in both the ancient and the Nietzschean senses.

Aeschylus probably composed some ninety dramas, of which only seven survive complete, all dating from the last sixteen years of his long career. Of the rest some seventy are known by title and by varying numbers of short fragments, which permit the general subject matter (but rarely the dramatic quality) of many of the lost plays to be reconstructed. Since all of Aeschylus' extant plays except *The Persians* were composed as parts of thematically connected tetralogies (three tragedies followed by a satyr play), it is reasonably surmised that the bulk of the lost plays also were grouped in the same way. On this assumption about half a dozen such super-dramas can be discerned, dealing with Achilles, Odysseus, Ajax, the Argonauts, and (at least twice; in one case the collective title *Lykourgeia* is recorded) with the terrible power of Dionysus. None of these lost tetralogies can be dated, but on statistical grounds the majority must probably have been produced before any of the extant plays, that is, between 499 and 472 B.C. Recently published papyrus fragments of two satyr plays, *Theoroi* ("The Pilgrims") and *Diktyoulkoi* ("The Net-Haulers"), make it possible, to some extent, to verify Aeschylus' ancient reputation as the finest of all composers in that virile seriocomic genre. Otherwise, the remains of the lost plays unfortunately provide little further insight into Aeschylus' dramaturgy. But the poetic power and imaginative range of the extant tragedies can already be glimpsed in them; so, too, can a certain indifference to what later generations would consider the conventions proper to tragedy. In *Myrmidons* (probably the first play of the Achilles tetralogy), the love of Achilles for Patroclus was frankly homosexual; and Jason with his Argonauts appeared drunk onstage in *Kabeiroi.*

Viewed as a whole, Aeschylus' extant plays present an almost bewildering versatility. More than any other ancient playwright, Aeschylus was prepared to adapt his entire technique and dramatic form to the precise requirements of mood and content, with the result that *The Suppliant Maidens* and *Seven Against Thebes,* or even *Choephori* and *Eumenides* might hardly seem to be the work of one man. Even so, certain generalizations can be made about Aeschylus' dramatic art. More tentatively, an overall development can be observed in it.

The *external* features of Greek tragedy as we know it were, by all ancient accounts, the almost single-handed creation of Aeschylus. Before he began his forty-year-long career, tragedy was an affair of a chorus and a single actor, and also (if Aristotle's *Poetics* is reliable) of "small plots and laughable diction." The text of *The Persians* shows that by 472 B.C. Aeschylus had already added a second actor, thus making possible a true stage dialogue. He is also credited with the introduction of more imposing costumes and tragic buskins for the actors, the use of elaborate stage machinery (he certainly employed a crane in the lost *Psychostasia* [*Weighing of Souls*] and apparently did so in PROMETHEUS BOUND), and even with some form of painted scenery. Aristophanes and others say that Aeschylus also created the characteristic tragic diction—an astounding style of utterance, as different from colloquial Athenian speech as the robed, masked actor was from the living figures of the Athenian streets. Again, this development had clearly taken place by the time of *The Persians*. Whether Sophocles or Aeschylus took the final step of adding a third actor was uncertain even to the ancient writers, but three actors are demonstrably needed for the performance of the *Oresteia* and for the Prologue of *Prometheus Bound*. Thus, by the last years of Aeschylus' career, Greek tragedy had acquired its definitive external shape and also the immense prestige as an art form which it has never since lost. In these senses Aeschylus fully deserves to be called the creator of Greek tragedy—and, in consequence, the pioneer of European drama.

In other such external aspects, however, Aeschylus differs immensely from any later tragedian, even from his rival and successor, Sophocles. The most crucial difference may be stated as follows: In Sophocles' and later tragedy, however profound the spiritual or moral issues at stake, the immediate dramatic interest is focused on a few sharply defined individuals. Out of their actions and passions, out of the interplay between their characters, emerges a complex and steadily developing plot. The dramatic interest in Aeschylus, however, is never concentrated exclusively on the individual masked actor; sometimes (as in *The Suppliant Maidens*) he hardly seems even to pause over him. In all the extant tragedies of Aeschylus the fates of communities are as directly involved in the dramatic action as are the fates of any individual visible on the stage: a family and a city in *Seven Against Thebes*, a mighty empire in *The Persians*, the entire community of men and gods in the culminating masterpieces, the *Oresteia* and *Prometheus Bound*. In the Danaid tetralogy, so far as it can now be reconstructed, the collective fate of the Chorus (itself a community) involved in turn the fate of the city of Argos and—it seems—the fate of the sexes in the entire universe.

Visions on such a scale were simply not expressible theatrically by Sophoclean or Aristotelian means, and perhaps the worst mistake that has been made in the criticism of Aeschylus is to assume that he could or should have employed them. For an evaluation of Aeschylus' theater Antonin Artaud (1895–1948) is probably a better guide than Aristotle. Long before Artaud, however, the anonymous compiler of the ancient *Life of Aeschylus* had comprehended the essence of Aeschylus' technique in one word: *ekplēxis*, "shock."

The very texture of Aeschylus' poetry in Greek (he is one of the most powerful of Greek iambic and choral poets in his own right) consists of a series of tiny verbal shocks. "Smoke" to him, for instance, is "spindrift of fire"; the fishes nibbling at Persian corpses off Salamis are "silent sons of the Unpollutable." The shock extends to situations: Eteocles' appalling collapse at the crisis of *Seven Against Thebes;* the prophetess Cassandra's nightmare description of her own and Agamemnon's murders just before they happen in *Agamemnon* ("this part of the drama is marveled at for its effect of shock," says the ancient Argument to the play); and the Chorus of Persian Lords howling and scraping at the earth to conjure the ghost of Darius in *The Persians*. Without exaggeration, one might say that shock extends to entire plays; each of the extant seven, in its very different way, is a violent assault on the audience's imagination and emotions.

To carry the impact of his vision Aeschylus neglects none of the available media. First, there is the superbly contrived poetry and rhythm of the great choral odes. In Greek, at least, the total rhythmic reversal in the entry song of *The Persians*, at the moment where the Chorus realize the "jealousy of God," is unforgettable. He also uses visual means, such as the purple tongue of tapestry protruding from the palace door to Agamemnon's chariot, the bloody murder-robe raised aloft near the end of *Choephori*, and the physical tortures in the *Prometheus* Prologue. He even uses mechanical contraptions. Again, to quote the author of the ancient *Life,* who evidently knew far more of Aeschylus' work than we do: "he utterly shocked the vision of the spectators with his brilliance—with paintings and stage-machinery, altars, tombs, trumpets, phantoms, Furies." Finally, the overpowering effects obtained by Aeschylus'

AESCHYLUS (VATICAN MUSEUM. COURTESY ANDERSON-ART REFERENCE BUREAU)

manipulation of supernumerary crowds, and by choreography, can be only faintly imagined from the bare texts of the plays. We know, however, that Aeschylus (like the other early tragedians) was his own choreographer as well as his own musical composer. Aristophanes' brief, but apparently trustworthy, account of Aeschylus' choreography in action describes the Trojan Chorus of *Phryges* (*Phrygians, or The Ransom of Hector,* the third play of the lost Achilles tetralogy) as "throwing themselves again and again, now into this posture, now into that!"

By the severe canon of Aristotle few of these media are relevant to drama. Yet by the canon of Artaud—or of the modern cinema—they are very relevant indeed. To the unprejudiced reader of today, Aeschylus somehow contrives to melt them into a unity which, whatever label it may be given, is certainly theater at its most powerful. Whether it reaches "tragedy" in the sense in which that word is understood by readers of Sophocles and Shakespeare is more debatable.

Aeschylus' theatrical development (so far as the accidents of survival allow it to be traced at all) divides into two distinct phases. In the earlier phase (*The Persians* and especially *Seven Against Thebes*), the cosmic background is very like the cosmic background implied in canonical tragedies such as Sophocles' *Oedipus the King* or Shakespeare's *Macbeth.* Here, therefore, Aeschylus may be said to pioneer, or at least foreshadow, "tragedy" in its generally accepted sense. The second phase, however, comprising the Danaid tetralogy, the *Oresteia,* and probably the *Prometheia* trilogy, meets no such criteria; for in them the cosmos advances from the background into the foreground. In plays where the universe itself is divided and finally reunited in a greater harmony (as it certainly is in the *Oresteia,* and conjecturally in the other two, fragmentary, trilogies), "tragedy" is hardly applicable. The fragments of the lost plays, as well as the seven that survive, indicate that Aeschylus was at all periods of his life an innovator, a free experimenter in the art of theater. After hitting on "tragedy" in the earlier group of the extant plays, he tried at the end of his career, in the *Oresteia,* a majestic theatrical—and spiritual, and mythological, and political—experiment which resists precise categorization.

The most comprehensive and exact edition of Aeschylus in English is by Herbert W. Smyth, *Aeschylus* (2 vols.; 2nd ed., 1953), with an appendix by Hugh Lloyd-Jones. This includes the Greek text, facing prose translation, and translation and discussion of the more significant fragments of the lost plays. The most recent running commentary in English is by H. J. Rose, *A Commentary on the Surviving Plays of Aeschylus* (2 vols., 1957). Since an inseparable and powerful element in Aeschylus' dramaturgy is his poetry, the reader without a knowledge of Greek must also consult a verse translation if he is to gain a fair idea of the total effect. From the later eighteenth century onward many attempts have been made to translate Aeschylus into English verse. The most recent is by Richmond Lattimore, S. G. Benardete, and David Grene, *Aeschylus* (2 vols., 1956). Though this edition succeeds, on the whole, in rendering the plays into a modern poetic idiom, the pre-

cision, delicacy, and force of Aeschylus' style are sometimes lacking. More old-fashioned versions may be compared with profit, especially George Thomson's *Prometheus* (1932) and *Oresteia* (rev. ed., 1966). Aeschylus' life, work, and sociopolitical significance are fully discussed in Thomson's *Aeschylus and Athens* (3rd ed., 1966). Thomson's discussion is heavily influenced by Marxism. Some other points of view are represented by Gilbert Murray, *Aeschylus: the Creator of Tragedy* (1940, reprinted 1962); E. T. Owen, *The Harmony of Aeschylus* (1952); and H. D. F. Kitto, *Form and Meaning in Drama* (1957), chapters I–III, and his *Poiesis* (1966), chapters I–II.
—C. J. H.

Africa. Two types of drama are indigenous to the African continent below the Sahara. One is the ancient rite of man in his natural world, a drama reaching back perhaps two hundred million years. The other is a drama of man in contemporary society, full of the complexities of emerging and changing nations mixed with economic, political, and racial strife. Both types are found in Africa today and combine to form a distinctive African dramatic literature.

To ancient Africans the most important art was dance because it fused the two central concerns of African life: religion and community. The dances were ceremonial, ritual, festive, or recreational, but all were dramatic. A dance could mark the beginning of the hunt, the end of the harvest; it could commemorate birth and death, puberty and marriage; it could honor gods and spirits; it could celebrate through the direct language of the body the joy of man, woman, and child in harmony with earth, sky, and spirits.

The dances were not merely aesthetic; rather, they were based on function and necessity. Mimetic performances were designed to guarantee success in hunt or harvest, to educate children, to celebrate the heroic exploits of African history, and to calm fears in the face of the unknown.

Most mimetic performances utilized some sort of storyteller who recited a folk tale, the traditional literature of Africa that was a vital force in the community life and was kept alive through an oral tradition. From storyteller to storyteller the tales became dialogues and eventually drama. In Europe and America drama developed similarly, but it has in large part been supplanted by formal written dramatic literature. In Africa, however, the ritual, the dramatic ceremony, the dance, the mimetic performance all take place today in the village, the city street, the open field, the edge of the rain forest, and even, occasionally, in theaters recently constructed in populated centers throughout the land. Significantly, the native oral dramas have not been obliterated by the new African drama.

Side by side with both African dramatic forms, there stands the imported theater presenting Shakespeare, Molière, Sophocles, Ibsen, Kālidāsa, Samuel Beckett, Richard Sheridan, Bernard Shaw, Rabindranath Tagore, Jean-Paul Sartre, Jean Cocteau, Arthur Miller, and Tennessee Williams, along with the latest fashionable dramas from Broadway, the West End, and Paris. These dramas are performed most often in European languages but increasingly are being translated or adapted into native African tongues. It is not uncommon to find elements of African oral literature and local character names combined with the major plot of a European classic drama. Among these adapted dramas, Shakespeare and the Greek classics are the most often used.

It is impossible to speak of African drama without mentioning the problems of race. The apartheid policy of South Africa has drawn a growing protest from English-language playwrights who are refusing to allow performances of their works in countries where such policies persist. Such playwrights as Edward Albee, Tennessee Williams, Arthur Miller, Lionel Bart, Graham Greene, John Osborne, J. B. Priestley, and Terence Rattigan have not only forbade the performance of their works in South Africa, but they have publicly objected to their plays being presented before segregated audiences. Indeed, the movement has been joined by some of the best-known English-speaking actors with the result that many South African theaters normally supported by touring productions have had to close. Among African theater personnel, there is a widespread reluctance to spend time on performing European or American dramas if a native African drama is available. Indeed, Bakary Traore of Senegal and Felix Morisseau-Leroy of the National School of the Arts in Accra, Ghana, have both argued convincingly that theater and drama should be created by Africans strictly for Africans. Critical works abound with discussions of "the African personality" of the dramas and the "negritude" of their thought.

There are a great many dangers in assessing the value and even the true existence of a total body of African drama. While many dramas are written and performed, a relatively small percentage are published. Still fewer are those available in European languages, although most published works appear in either French or English. Some plays that are published have been written as radio dramas and never performed. Finally, it is unsettling to report that some playwrights have for various reasons denied their authorship; indeed, several cases are reported in which the manuscript of a play has been sold to a publisher, who in turn brings out the drama under his own name!

Basutoland (Lesotho). Most of these dramatists were trained at the University College of Roma and write in the South Sotho tongue: Joseph Sebata Tsephe, who wrote *Ha dinyamatsane* ("Home of the Wild Animals," 1962); Bennett Makalo Khaketla, *Moshoeshoe le baruti* ("Moshesh and the Missionaries," 1947); Ntšeliseng 'Masechele Khaketla, *Mosali eo u 'neileng eena* ("The Woman You Gave Me," 1954); Mallane Libakeng Maile, *Pitso ea liphoofolo* ("A Meeting of the Animals," 1956) and *Boiphetetso* ("Revenge," 1962); and Twentyman M. Mofokeng, *Sek'hona sa joala* ("A Calabash of Beer," 1939).

Bechuanaland (Botswana; formerly part of Republic of South Africa). The two known dramatists writing in Tswana are Samson A. Moroke, who wrote *Lobisa Radipitse* (1962), and L. D. Raditladi, who wrote *Dinšhontsho tsa loratô* (*The Many Deaths of Love*, 1956).

The Cameroon Federation. Theatrical activity is centered in the capital, Yaoundé. Notable dramas are *L'Agent spécial* ("The Special Agent," 1964) by Jacques Muriel Nzouankeu, *Trois pretends . . .*

un mari ("Three Suitors, One Husband," 1965) by Guillaume Oyono-Mbia, *Le Jugement suprême* ("The Crowning Judgment," 1963) by Benjamin Matip, *I Am Vindicated* (1963) by Andrew Sankie Maimo, and *La Langue et le Scorpion* ("Speech and the Scorpion," 1966) by Eugène Dervain.

Central African Republic (formerly Ubangi-Shari). The lone dramatist known is Makombo-Pierre Bamboté, who is represented by one play, *Le Grand Etat central* ("The Great Central Country," 1965).

Congo Republic (Congo Léopoldville; Congo Kinshasa; formerly Belgian Congo). Dramatic activities take place mainly in Léopoldville and Elisabethville. Notable Congolese playwrights are Joseph Kiwele (*Chura na Nyoka*, "The Toad and the Serpent"; 1953); Christophe Makonga (*Tumbako ya mu Mpua*, "Tobacco for Snuffing"; 1959); Albert Mongita (*Mangenge*, 1956); and Catherine Mostkova, whose *Au son du gong* ("At the Sound of the Gong," 1939) is based on the life of Joseph Adidanga, the Congolese patriot.

Dahomey. The French influence continues to be very strong here with two playwrights, Paul Fabo, who wrote *Ombrages* ("Shades," 1948), and Anatole Coyssi, who wrote *La honte plus meurtrière que le couteau* ("Scandal Is Deadlier Than the Knife," 1947).

Ghana. Of all of the African nations, excepting Nigeria and South Africa, Ghana has the most active theater and one of the richest dramatic literatures. Under Professor J. H. Kwabena Nketia of the School of Music and Drama of the University of Ghana, a truly national theater is developing. Together with Efua Sutherland, head of the Ghana Drama Studio of the Institute of Art and Culture, theater and drama have been made a vital part of life in Accra. A true Ghanaian native drama has grown from the tales of Ananse, the wily spider whose search for wisdom typifies the ideals of Ghana's former president, Kwame Nkrumah. Outstanding among these native dramas are *Ananse and the Glue Man* (1961), a version of the tar baby story, and *Old Kweku* (1965), both by Joe C. DeGraft; *Nyankonsɛm* ("Fables of the Celestial," 1941) and *Biribi wɔ baabi* ("There Is More Beyond," c. 1943), both written in the Twi language by Joseph Boakye Danquah; *Mpuaasa ntiamoa* ("A Man with Three Tufts of Hair," 1950) and *Ɔsabarima* ("The Warrior," 1961), written in Twi by E. Owusu Koranteng; and Efua Sutherland's *Anansegoro, Tu prêtas serment* ("Anansegoro, You Swore an Oath," 1964).

Among the plays best known to Europeans are Mrs. Sutherland's *Foruwa* (1961) and *Adufa* (1962); *Obadzeng* (1961), a musical drama by Adali-Mortty and Saka Acquaye; and Félix Morisseau-Leroy's *Awoye, Ama, Afram* (1965), based on a Twi poem by Andrew Opoku.

Other plays are Michael Francis Dei-Anang's *Cocoa Comes to Mampong* (1949) and *Okomfo Anokye's Golden Stool* (1963); F. Kwasi Fiawoo's *Tɔkɔ atɔlia* ("The Fifth Landing Stage," 1937), written in Ewe; Henry Ofori's *The Literary Society* (c. 1950); H. K. Bidi Setsoafia's *The Tragedy of Nana Kwame Dzuato II, Omanhene of Kokoroko State* (c. 1955); Kobena Gyate Akawa's Twi drama *Hwer Nyame* ("Look to God," 1959); N. A. Odoi's Ga drama *Gbomɔ kɛ wala* ("Man and Life," 1953); C. K. Nyomi's Ewe drama *Munyala enelia* ("The Fourth Wise Man," 1959); and Joseph Hanson Kwabena Nketia's Twi drama *Ananwoma* (1952).

Guinea, The Republic of. Guinea's outstanding playwright is Keita Fodeba, who is also its leading director, impresario, and sometime minister of defense. His dance troupe, Les Ballets Africains, is justly world famous. His plays *Chanson d'Joliba* ("Song of Joliba," 1960), *Aube Africaine* ("African Dawn," 1965), and *Minuit* ("Midnight," 1952) extol the beauty of Guinea and tell of Africa's struggle against colonialism.

Other playwrights are B. Holas, whose play *La creation du monde cosmologique* (*The Creation of the World: A Cosmological Comedy, 1958*), a comic treatment of the origin of life and death using African creation myths, was performed in Paris at the Théâtre des Nations in 1960; M. Verdat (*La Bataille de Bongoye*, "The Battle of Bongoye"; 1952); and M. Diallo Midaou (*L'Aveugle Amoureux*, "The Blind Lover"; 1953).

Ivory Coast. A national theater in the Ivory Coast is being developed with technical advice of an American, Thomas Skelton. Its two main playwrights are Bernard Binlin Dadié and François Joseph Koutoua Amon d'Aby. Dadié's plays are *Assémien Déhylé, roi du Sanwi* ("A. D., King of Sanwi," 1937) and *Les villes* ("The Cities," c. 1955). Amon d'Aby's plays are *Kwao Adjoba, ou Procès du régime matriarchal en Basse Cote d'Ivoire* ("K. A., or the Trial of the Matriarchal System of Lower Ivory Coast," 1965), *Entrave* ("Shackles," 1955), and *La Couronne aux Enchères* ("The Auction Ring," 1956).

Kenya. Four known playwrights of Kenya are B. Tejani, who wrote *Babalola* (1967); Kuldip Sondhi, *Devil in the Mixer* (1967) and *Undesignated* (1964); James Ngugi, *The Black Hermit* (1962) and *This Time Tomorrow* (1966); and Rebecca Njau, *The Scar* (1963).

Liberia. Most of the theatrical activity occurs in Monrovia, the capital, where three plays by Roland Tombekai Dempster, *The Office Genius, The Search for Truth,* and *Shadows in Darkness,* were performed between 1947 and 1963.

Malagasy Republic (formerly Madagascar). Strictly speaking, the peoples of the Malagasy Republic do not like to be thought of as Africans. The Mozambique Channel is ten times wider than the English Channel and they prefer to be called a separate island nation. Their culture is also related to that of India, and their drama is strongly influenced by Indian classical drama. The confluence of Indian and African traditions is clearly seen in Jacques Rabemananjara's works: *Les deux malgaches* ("The Two Malagasys," 1947), *Agapes des Dieux* ("Feast of the Gods," 1962), and *Les Boutriers de l'Aurore* ("The Edge of Dawn," 1957).

Malawi (formerly Nyasaland). *Come to Tea* (1960) by David Rubadiri demonstrates the bitter reaction against white domination by setting the scene in a British colonial officer's drawing room in which he and his wife entertain his African clerical assistant. Realistic dialogue is interspersed with chants and poems of African culture to develop a powerful cry of protest against the white man's rule.

Two other dramatists are Aubrey Kachingwe, who wrote *The Serpent* (1966), and C. C. J. Chipinga, who wrote *Atambwali sametana* ("Cockerels Never Give Each Other a Haircut," 1961), written in the Nyanja dialect.

Mali Republic (formerly French Sudan). This landlocked nation has two dramatists of consequence, Seydou Badian Kouyaté (*La Mort de Chaka*, "The Death of Chaka"; 1962) and Mamadou Ouattara (*La Rencontre secrete de l'Almany Samary et de Tieba, Fama du Kenedougou,* "The Secret Meeting Between A. S. and T., F. of K."; 1957).

Nigeria. Easily the largest coastal country of West Africa, Nigeria has a population larger than all the other West African nations put together. Small wonder that Nigeria has the most active theater of the continent. Indeed, Nigeria has three of the four or five truly outstanding playwrights on the continent in Wole Soyinka (1934–   ), John Pepper Clark (1935–   ), and James Henshaw (1924–   ). Although this nation is now undergoing severe political strife, this report covers the region as it existed in 1966, before the Biafran separation.

With several transfusions from foundations, most notably from the Rockefeller Foundation, the University of Ibadan founded a drama school. The presence of the school and the gifted actor-manager-dramatist Kola Ogunmola has made Ibadan's civic repertory Théâtre des Arts the focus of attention for artistic standards of African drama.

The leading dramatist of Nigeria, perhaps of Africa, is Wole Soyinka. His most important play to date is *A Dance of the Forest* (1963), which was written especially to commemorate Nigerian independence. This play explores Nigeria's relationship with its past by presenting Nigerian ancestors in a great ceremony celebrating Nigerian independence. But

WOLE SOYINKA (ANN ELMO AGENCY)

the people of the present are disillusioned by the ancestors, and in a symbolic struggle using dance and mime, a previously unborn child of the past is brought forth who refuses direct interference with the past but knows that he cannot escape tradition completely. Soyinka's other plays are *The Strong Breed, The Swamp-dwellers, The Trials of Brother Jero, The Lion and the Jewel,* all published in 1963, *Camwood on the Leaves* (1965), *Kongi's Harvest* (1967), and *The Road* (1965). All of Soyinka's works deal with modern problems and are conceived upon ritualistic patterns.

John Pepper Clark, like Soyinka a product of the University of Ibadan, is more traditionally formal in his plays. *The Song of a Goat* (1961) is Clark's first major piece and contains many of the characteristics of classic Greek drama. *The Raft* (1964) deals with the plight of four lumbermen drifting helplessly downriver to a tragic death. A Nigerian *Oresteia, Masquerade* (1964) portrays a family suffering under a curse. *Ozidi* (1966) is an epic of a son born and raised to avenge his famous father, who was cut down in war by his own comrades. Clark's themes are classic, his language is poetic, but mime, ritual, music, and dance dominate his work.

Writing in the Efik tongue, James Henshaw is an example of a writer who utilizes African themes in conventional dramatic forms. In *Un homme de temperament* ("A Man of Character," 1956) Henshaw's actors speak to the audience in the manner of the eighteenth century. In *Les Joyaux de la Couronne* ("The Jewels of the Shrine," 1956) he eschews European techniques completely and tells a typical village folk tale. However, his later work, *Children of the Goddess, Companion for a Chief, Magic in the Blood,* and *Medicine for Love,* all published in 1964, utilizes conventional European dramatic techniques.

Other notable playwrights include Ernest Edyang, who wrote *Emotan of Benin* (1963) and *Sidibe* (1965), which won the International Theatre Institute's Rosamund Gilder Prize for African Drama; a series of playwrights writing in the Yoruba tongue: S. Olanipekun Esan (*K'a S'oto k'a ku,* 1964), Herbert Ogunde (*Yoruba ronu,* 1964), J. F. Odunjo (*Agbàlowõmeri bãlè Jòntolo,* 1958), and Duro Ladipo (*Oba Ko So,* 1966); and a group of playwrights writing in English: B. S. Awogbajo (*Accidents,* 1959), Joseph O. O. Okpaku (*The Virtues of Adultery,* 1966), Obotunde Ijimere (*The Fall of Man, According to an Ancient Manuscript Discovered in the City of Ife and Believed to Belong to One of the Lost Tribes of Israel,* 1966), and N. O. M. Mac Jajah (*Trial of the Wizard,* 1951).

Finally, it is impossible to end this note on Nigerian drama without mentioning the existence of a large body of drama written for the most part in English but not intended for theatrical production, namely, Nigerian "market drama." These are primarily written by hacks and are paperbound tracts in dialogue form with conventional acts and scenes. Their purpose is to communicate history, political attitudes, advice to the lovelorn, instruction in social amenities, and practical hints for attracting the opposite sex. Some representative titles are: *The Trials of Lumumba, Jomo Kenyatta and St. Paul; The Joy of Life and Its Merriments; The Right Way to Approach Ladies and Get Them in Love; Sufferers of Africans, A Complete History of White Imperialism towards African Nationalism; My Seven Daughters Are After Young Boys; Rose Only Loved My Money; Why Okafor Sacked His Wife; The Last Days of Lumumba; Why Men Never Trust Women; The Big Treason Felony Trial of Chief Awolowo Enahoro and 23 Others; Caroline the One Guinea Girl;* and *Return of Evelyn in a Drama on How I Was About Marrying My Sister.*

Niger Republic. Niger's sole known dramatist is Mahamane Dandobi, who wrote *L'aventure d'une chèvre* ("The Adventure of a Goat," 1955) and *La légende de Kabrin Kabra* ("The legend of K. K.," 1956).

Rwanda. This tiny nation with the densest population in Africa has as yet produced only one published playwright, J. Saverio Naigiziki, who wrote *L'Optimiste* (1954).

Senegal. The port city of Dakar has long had an active theatrical life, mostly of French derivation. Before World War II, the students at the Ecole William Ponty wrote and performed plays on African subjects in French: *Les triomphe du griot* ("The Triumph of the Witch Doctor," 1935), *Sokamé* (1937), *Un mariage au Dahomey* ("A Marriage in Dahomey," 1934), and others. Indigenous playwrights of Senegal are Abou Anta Ka, who wrote *La fille des dieux* ("The Daughter of the Gods," 1955), *Fouta Sobel* (c. 1955), and *Kaloka* (c. 1955); Cisse Dia, *La mort du Damel* ("The Death of D.," 1947); the poetic Léopold Sédar Senghor, *Elégie a Aynina Fall* ("Elegy to A. F.," 1957) and *Tchaka* (1951); Lamine Diakhatē, *Surzan* (1955); and Massata N'Diaye, *Les Débuts du Règne* ("The Debuts of the Queen," 1956).

Sierra Leone. The leading dramatist of Sierra Leone is a physician, R. Sarif Easmon. His most recent plays, *Dear Parent and Ogre* (1964) and *The New Patriots* (1965), have attracted attention in London's West End. The latter deals with the new popular chiefs whose values clash violently with the petit bourgeois. Although his dramatic technique is Victorian, his subject matter conveys a sense of doubt about both the "new patriotism" and the "liberalism" of former times. Other plays are *Vallée sans écho* ("Valley Without Echo," 1946) by John Akar; *De Man Way de Play Gyambul wit God* (1961), written in Krio by Abdul Karim Ghazali; and *Judas die don tidday* (1965), written in a mixture of Krio and English by an unknown dramatist.

South Africa. Theater has flourished in South Africa from the earliest days of colonization, drawing its traditions from the English and Dutch theaters. In the early 1950's a truly indigenous drama arose in Afrikaans and in English. At present, the specter of racial strife hampers the development of a vital national drama. Despite this, undoubtedly the best-known African play outside of Africa is Athol Fugard's *The Blood Knot* (1961). Regarded by many as the finest play in English yet produced in South Africa, the plot deals with two brothers, one white and one black, whose routine existence in an ugly tin shack in Korsten, Port Elizabeth, is measured by fish and chips in tin plates, foot salt baths after work, and a strident alarm clock. To relieve the monotony, they begin a pen-pal relationship with a woman in Oudtshoorn who turns out to be white. In the emotional conclusion of the piece the brothers act out the societal forces and terrors of the apartheid world in which they live. Fugard's other plays, *No Good Friday* and *Nongogo* (both dates unknown), deal with the problems of modern South African life.

Other notable dramatists writing in English are Basil Warner (*Try for White*, 1954), Lewis Sowden (*Kimberly Train*, 1957), and Harry Bloom (*King Kong*, 1959). Dramatists writing in Xhosa are E. J. Ouless (*Iziganeko Zom-Kristu*, 1966), Amos Mtingane (*Inene, nani isibhozo*, "Truly, It Shall Be Done"; 1961), Henry Masila Ndawo (*U-Nolishwa*, 1931, and *U-Nomathamsanqa*, 1937), Marcus A. P. Ngani (*Umkhonto ka'Tshiwo*, "The Spear of Mr. So and So"; 1959), Witness K. Tamsanqua (*Buzani kubawo*, "Ask My Father"; 1958), and Aaron Mazambana Mmango (*U-Dusha*, 1958, and *Law'ilahle*, "The Glowing Coal Has Fallen"; 1960). Those writing in Zulu are Nimrod N. T. Ndebele, who wrote *UGubudele namazimuzimu* ("Gubudele and the Cannibals," 1941); Elliot Zondi, *Ukufa kuka Shaka* ("The Death of Shaka," 1960); Hilda Kuper, *Inhliziyo Ngumthakathi* (1965); B. B. Ndelu, *Mageba Lazihlonza* (1962); N. P. J. Steyn, *Mvulane* (1941); K. E. Masinga and Hugh Tracey, *Chief Above and Chief Below* (1944); Andries Jeremiah Blose, *Uqomise mina nje uqomisa iliba* ("Falling in Love with Me Is Falling in Love with the Best," 1960); L. M. Mbulawa, *UMamfene* (1962); and Leonhard L. J. Mncwango, *Kusasa umngcwabo wakho nami* ("Tomorrow Is Your Nemesis and Mine," 1959), *Ngenzeni?* ("What Have I Done?" 1959), and *Mhla iyokwendela egodini* ("The Day She Married the Grave," c. 1955). Those writing in Sotho are Francis More Segwe, who wrote *Sebabet-sane* ("The Ice Plant," 1957); E. K. K. Matlala, *Thsukudu* (1941); and G. H. Franz, *Maaberone* (1940). Writing in Venda are U. M. Ramaite (*Muofhe*, 1961) and Titus Ntsiene Maumela (*Tshililo*, 1957). M. S. Mogoba wrote *Nnang* ("Not Me," 1961) in Pedi.

Others writing in English are Herbert I. E. Phlomo (*The Girl Who Killed to Save*, 1935); Lewis Nkosi (*The Rhythm of Violence*, 1964); and Alfred Hutchinson (*The Rain Killers*, 1964).

Tanzania (formerly Tanganyika and Zanzibar). The primary theatrical activity is in Dar es Salaam, where playwrights write in Swahili and occasionally in English. Notable are Gerishon Ngugi, who wrote *Nimelogwa! Nisiwe na mpenzi* ("I Have Been Bewitched! I Haven't Got a Lover," 1961), J. A. C. Blumer, *Not Guilty* (1953), and Ebrahim Hussein.

Togo. Theatrical activity occurs in Anécho and in Lomé, the capital. The American actor Arnold Moss recently assisted the national theater there. The single outstanding playwright is Toussaint Viderot, known as "Mensah," whose 1960 play, *Pour toi, Négre, mon frère . . . 'Un homme comme les autres'* ("For You, Negro, My Brother . . . 'A Man Like Others' "), was highly acclaimed in Europe.

Uganda. The Uganda National Theatre at Kampala is the principal theatrical center there. In 1966 two significant new playwrights drew widespread attention. The first is E. C. N. Kironde, whose play *Kintu* deals with the mythology of the earth's creation. The other is James Kariara, whose *Le plant de haricots verts* ("The Green Bean Plants") is a symbolic drama of the Mau-Mau uprisings. His language and style have drawn critical comparisons with J. M. Synge's *Shadow of the Glen*.

Other dramatists are Timothy Wangusa (*The Journey Back*, 1966); Elvania Namukwaya Zirimu (*Keeping Up with the Mukasas*, 1965); Ganesh Bagchi (*The Deviant*, 1961); and Madelein Githae (*A Problem for the Young*, 1965).

Upper Volta. Theatrical activity here is connected to the neighboring coastal countries of Ghana, the Ivory Coast, and Dahomey. However, four dramatists of significance have appeared: Moctar Fofana, who wrote *L'Appel du Fétiche* ("The Appeal of the Fetish," 1955); Anoumou Pedro Santos, *Fâsi* (1956); Moussa Sawadogo, *Fille de le Volta* ("Daughter of the Volta," 1961) and *L'oracle* ("The Oracle," 1961); and Ouamdégré Ouedraogo, *L'avare Moaga; comédie des mœurs* ("Miser Moaga; a Comedy of Manners," 1961).

Zambia. An auditorium providing an arena stage in Kitwe is the principal theater of Zambia. Both the theater and the Zambia Arts Trust have been established through government and industrial grants. The Theatre Association of Zambia has assisted local theater groups throughout the country and holds an annual performing arts festival. The three known dramatists here are I. Braim Nkonde, who wrote *Supuni alete misoka* ("Supuni Commits a Crime," 1961) in the Bemba tongue; Kwalombota Mulonda, who wrote *Milelo ya lifolofolo* ("The Animals' Plans," 1957) in Lozi; and Elijah H. K. Mudenda, whose *Milimo* (1961) is written in the Tonga tongue.

Although these reports from several African nations would seem a meager output for so large a continent, they must be regarded as a signal of dramatic potential only now beginning to appear.

The two best bibliographies of African drama are Anthony Graham-White, "A Bibliography of African Drama," *Afro-Asian Theatre Bulletin*, III, 1 (1967), and Jahnheinz Jahn, *A Bibliography of Neo-African Literature: from Africa, America, and the Caribbean* (1965). Others are Margaret Amosu, *Preliminary Bibliography of Creative African Writing in European Languages* (1964); Bernth Lindfors, "A Preliminary Checklist of Nigerian Drama in English," *Afro-Asian Theatre Bulletin*, II, 2 (1967); Herbert L. Shore, "African Theatre and Drama," *African Studies Bulletin*, V, 2 (1962); R. Silbert, *Southern African Drama in English 1900–1964* (1967).

Two excellent surveys of African theatrical activity are Herbert L. Shore, "African Theatre, an End and a Beginning," *Players Magazine*, XXXIX (1963) and "Drums, Dances . . . and Then Some. An Introduction to Modern African Drama," *Texas Quarterly*, VII (1964). For a complete understanding of the sociology of drama in Africa, the works of Bakary Traore are indispensable: *Le Théâtre négro-africain et ses fonctions sociales* (1958) and "Le Théâtre negro-africaine et ses fonctions sociologiques," *Presence Africaine*, XIV–XV (1957). Other articles of interest are Athol Fugard, "African Stages," New York *Times*, 20 September, 1964; Felix Morisseau-Leroy, "The Ghanaian Theatre Movement," *World Theatre*, XIV, 1 (1965); and Arnold Zeitlin, "Ghana's Young Theatre," *Theatre Arts*, XLVII (1963).—G. B.

Agamemnon. See ORESTEIA: *Agamemnon*.

Ağaoğlu, Adalet (1929–   ). Turkish play-wright. Born near Ankara, Mrs. Ağaoğlu completed her formal education in that city and joined the Ankara radio, supervising the selection of plays. She also wrote some plays of her own. After her return from the United States in 1957, she established the first private theater in Ankara. Leaving that theater in 1963, she devoted herself to playwriting for one year. Both *Evcilik Oyunu* ("Let's Play House," 1964) and *Çatıdaki Çatlak* ("The Crack in the Skeleton," 1965) are products of that period.

Evcilik Oyunu is perhaps the most daring play in Turkish history to be written about the repressive sexual customs in Turkey. This hilarious farce with serious overtones was hailed in liberal circles and condemned by conservative elements in the press. Mrs. Ağaoğlu's second important play, *Çatıdaki Çatlak,* is a portrayal from a sensitive and feminine point of view of some of the absurdities in the economic *status quo* in Turkey and their effect on common people.

To Mrs. Ağaoğlu, the theater is a school where the shapers of society should be criticized.—N. O.

agon. See GREECE: *classical period;* and OLD COMEDY.

Aiken, George L. See UNCLE TOM'S CABIN.

Ajax (Aias, date unknown; probably written before 442 B.C.). A tragedy by SOPHOCLES. The scene is the hero's tent at Troy. Ajax, furious at the award of Achilles' arms to Odysseus, has made a night attack on the tents of Odysseus and the Greek commanders. The goddess Athena tells Odysseus that she drove Ajax mad so that he fell upon herds of cattle instead of his enemies. We see Ajax exposed in his madness, boasting of the murder of the commanders and promising torture for Odysseus, who, he imagines, is a prisoner inside the tent. The Prologue closes with Odysseus' expression of pity for his enemy and a warning from Athena that man must respect proper limits. The Chorus (sailors of Ajax) hear from Tecmessa, the captive and concubine of Ajax, an account of the events of the night; they learn the meaning of it when Ajax, now sane, appears to lament his failure and his shame. In the first of a series of great speeches he decides to kill himself. Tecmessa's appeal is harshly rejected and, with a farewell to his son, Eurysaces, Ajax goes into his tent. But he comes out again, carrying a sword, and announces in a speech which is shot through with sinister ambiguities that he will go off to a lonely place on the shore and make his peace with the gods. Though the audience can have little doubt of his meaning, Tecmessa and the Chorus both think he has decided to live. When, in the next scene, a messenger tells them that Athena's anger will pursue Ajax all day and that he must be kept at home, their fears revive and they go off with Tecmessa to look for him. Ajax appears on the empty stage. (This is one of the rare scene changes in Attic tragedy; the stage now represents the lonely place by the shore.) After a bitter speech calling down vengeance on his enemies, Ajax throws himself on the sword. Tecmessa and the Chorus find the body. Their laments are interrupted by the arrival of Teucer, Ajax's brother, who mourns his loss and prepares to bury Ajax in defiance of the edict of the commanders. Menelaus arrives to see the order carried out but retires after Teucer's violent denuncia-

tion, to be followed by Agamemnon himself, who is ready to use force against Teucer's continued defiance. But Odysseus enters and persuades Agamemnon to allow the hero's burial. *Ajax* ends with the funeral procession.

The character of Ajax, a striking amalgam of harshness and obstinacy, of courage and nobility, is typical of all the Sophoclean heroes; many of his attitudes and even his characteristic expressions reappear in Antigone, Oedipus, Philoctetes, and Electra. The main problem of the play is the interpretation of Ajax's ambiguous speech. It has been taken as a genuine submission to the commanders and gods (later canceled out by a fresh access of madness), as a deceptive speech designed to prevent any interference with his suicide by Tecmessa and the Chorus, and as a soliloquy in which, unconscious of the presence of others, he reconsiders his decision but decides again for death.

See R. C. Jebb's *Sophocles, the Ajax* (1907) and W. B. Stanford's *Sophocles' Ajax* (1963). —B. M. W. K.

Aksal, Sabahattin Kudret (1920–   ). Turkish playwright, poet, and short-story writer. After graduating from the philosophy department of the University of Istanbul, Aksal taught in Turkish lycées and, subsequently, held such posts as director of the Conservatory of Istanbul, instructor in psychology and aesthetics, and artistic director of the Istanbul Opera. Between 1954 and 1959, Aksal served as drama critic of *Varlık,* a literary periodical. Currently, he is the director of publications at the Municipality of Istanbul.

Aksal has written eight plays, the first of which was produced in 1947 in Istanbul. Aksal has received prizes for his poetry, short stories, and his play *Kahvede Şenlik Var* ("There Is Festivity in the Coffeehouse," 1966). His plays are primarily psychological studies of man's aspirations and his conflict with reality. Touched with poetry and sometimes having abstract characterizations, the plays require stylized productions. Aksal's intention is to concentrate on writing stylized and poetical plays.—N. O.

Albee, Edward (1928–   ). American playwright. Two weeks after his birth he was taken out of a foundling home in Washington, D.C., adopted by Reed and Frances Albee, the heirs to a celebrated vaudeville fortune founded by Reed Albee's father, Edward Franklin Albee, and named Edward Franklin Albee III. He rather unenthusiastically attended various fashionable private schools—Lawrence, Valley Forge Military Academy, and Choate—and he was briefly (1946–47) a student at Trinity College. On receiving a bequest from his grandmother (to whom he later paid graceful compliments in *The Sandbox* and *The American Dream* and to whom he dedicated the former play) in 1950, he left home, worked at odd jobs (as an office boy, a counterman, and a Western Union messenger) in New York, tried to write poetry and fiction, attended innumerable plays, and, for nine years, shared extremely modest living arrangements with a young composer, William Flanagan.

Just before turning thirty, Albee decided to prove himself by taking a few weeks to write his first play, *The Zoo Story,* a one-acter that was first performed in German at the experimental branch of the Schiller

Theater of West Berlin, the Werkstatt, in the fall of 1959. Early the next year, it opened Off-Broadway in New York, on the same bill with Samuel Beckett's *Krapp's Last Tape;* a warm endorsement from Tennessee Williams stimulated business and helped to avert a threatened closing, and the two plays ran for nineteen months. In this compelling little drama, two strangers with nothing in common meet on a park bench and discover how nearly impossible it is for them to communicate with each other. The older, Peter, is a moderately successful bourgeois family man; the other, Jerry, who presses the conversation, is an outsider, a lonely bohemian rebel. Illustrating by his example the problem of communication, Jerry keeps promising to tell what happened to him at the zoo, but, instead, he talks about an old hostility between himself and a dog, a hostility that turned into mutual respect only when he nearly succeeded in poisoning the dog. For Jerry and Peter, too, violence is the only possible way of communicating, as Jerry demonstrates when he compels Peter to kill him; at last he has become unmistakably real to Peter. Some found signs of Beckett's influence and THEATER OF THE ABSURD, but it was clear that the moving anecdote and the pungent dialogue were uniquely Albee's.

In April 1960 a second one-act play, *The Death of Bessie Smith,* had its world première in German at the Schlosspark Theater in West Berlin. It was not seen in New York until its production Off-Broadway early in the following year. Set in Memphis in 1937, it has to do with the death in an automobile accident of the Negro blues singer Bessie Smith, but she never appears onstage. Instead, the emphasis falls upon her rejection by white hospitals and upon the portrait of a vicious white nurse who likes Bessie Smith's music but remorselessly teases her admirers and is obviously incapable of the love embodied by the singer and her songs. *The Death of Bessie Smith* is memorable chiefly for being the only Albee play to offer, however obliquely, any liberal social comment and for containing the first of Albee's characterizations of malicious, compulsive women.

A very short play, *The Sandbox,* opened Off-Broadway in May 1960. It shows the death of a perky grandmother, the only sympathetic member of an otherwise tiresome family. Another one-acter, *Fam and Yam,* was first presented at Westport, Connecticut, in August 1960. In *The American Dream* (1961) the little family of *The Sandbox* reappears: a dominating Mommy, an emasculated Daddy, and a saucy, rebellious Grandma whom the others bully. A neighbor comes calling and so does a handsome young man who identifies himself as the American Dream; he is the identical twin of a child previously adopted and destroyed by Mommy and Daddy. What is most effective in this play is its devastating parody of American small talk, which Albee originally intended as an American equivalent of Eugène Ionesco's parody of bourgeois conversation in *The Bald Soprano. The American Dream* is a stunning satire on average American life, until it turns sentimental in its last moments. Albee himself commented: "Is the play offensive? I certainly hope so; it was my intention to offend—as well as amuse and entertain."

Albee's first full-length play, WHO'S AFRAID OF VIRGINIA WOOLF?, proved to be a very considerable

EDWARD ALBEE (WIDE WORLD PHOTOS)

critical and popular success, ran for nearly two years, and won both the Drama Critics Circle Award and the Antoinette Perry Award as best play of the season. The Pulitzer Committee's two advisers on drama recommended it for the Pulitzer Prize, and, when the award was withheld, they publicly resigned. Apparently the Pulitzer trustees had objected to the play's frank sexual references.

Thereafter, Albee wrote full-length plays for Broadway. The next to be staged was actually written before *Virginia Woolf—The Ballad of the Sad Café,* a dramatization of Carson McCullers' novella. This drama about the strange attachment that binds a strapping, self-reliant woman, her rather feckless husband, and a dwarf is climaxed by a wrestling match between husband and wife that is essentially a contest for the dwarf's affections. It opened in the fall of 1963, ran for approximately four months, and did not notably contribute to Albee's fame. *Tiny Alice* opened at the end of 1964, with Sir John Gielgud playing a lay brother who is summoned to a mysterious house, marries a wealthy but equally mysterious lady whom he meets there, and finally is deserted by her and her strange followers. It was a puzzling and controversial play. The protagonist resembles Christ, Job, and Faust, and his martyrdom seems to be a cruel cosmic joke. The dramatist was clearly hostile to religion and the church, and students of the play delighted in finding little bits of church tradition embedded in it. An antifeminine bias was equally obvious, for the lay brother's primary error was to put aside his pledge of chastity. *Tiny Alice* was much talked about, but even the controversy kept it on Broadway for only a little more than five months. Early in 1966, *Malcolm,* adapted from the novel by James Purdy, opened and, after seven performances, closed. This was an antifeminine parable with a vengeance, about an innocent young man who is destroyed by his encounters with women and dies worn out. Albee, who had warmly defended *Tiny Alice* against all comers, accepted this failure stoically.

The dramatist's reputation was somewhat restored by *A Delicate Balance* (1966), concerning a family disrupted by a sudden visit from two lifelong friends fleeing a sudden, strange, and indescribable feeling of fear that they call "the terror." The visited are made to see themselves—the husband and wife who still feel guilt over the small son who died (recalling the lost son of *The American Dream*); their frequently divorced daughter, homeless herself, and so resenting the idea of giving a home to the intruders; and the wife's sister, who has taken refuge in drink and speaks the best lines in the play. *A Delicate Balance* ran a little more than four months in New York, but a subsequent tour made it a commercial success. When it won the Pulitzer Prize, the Pulitzer Committee was widely assumed to be responding to feelings of guilt over its failure to honor *Who's Afraid of Virginia Woolf? Everything in the Garden,* which opened late in 1967, was adapted by Albee from a British play of the same name by the late Giles Cooper. Albee had Americanized Cooper's cynical black comedy about suburban wives who become prostitutes to earn extra money and made it more serious and less entertaining. Originally, it was a satire on universal venality; in Albee's version, it became the tragedy of a tormented husband who discovers his wife's secret, and so it was one more comment on women's wickedness.

Albee's next plays were experimental one-acters that recalled his early writing—*Box* and *Quotations from Chairman Mao Tse-tung,* staged early in 1968 at the Arts Festival in Buffalo, New York. The first is a monologue by an unseen speaker about the decline of civilization. In the second, we hear this monologue again, and we listen to three others as well— an old lady reciting a tiresome, hackneyed poem; a middle-aged lady describing her racy life to a sleepy clergyman; and Chairman Mao reading from his little red book maxims that comment upon the decline of the West. Mao surely has the best of it, thereby reinforcing the impression that the two plays together constitute a nonpolitical comment upon the state of our decay. The interleaving of the monologues recalls the technique of Beckett's *Play.* Neither play is a major addition to Albee's total work, but each possesses a certain interest.

Albee's talent, especially in creating a distinctively waspish sort of dialogue, is very great; in addition, he established himself in his early plays as the master of a particular incident—the collision between the self-satisfied square and the self-questioning outsider. The question of his career is no more than the question of the use to which he will put his abilities.—H. P.

Alcestis (**Alkestis**, 438 B.C.).   A play by EURIPI-DES. Alcestis' husband, Admetus, is doomed to death unless he finds someone to die for him. His father, Pheres, wants to live his own life to its end, but Alcestis quietly offers her life for her husband's. Heracles, ignorant of what is going on in the palace, carouses as Admetus' guest until he learns the truth. He makes up for his gaucherie by waylaying Death at the tomb and bringing Alcestis back to her husband.

Alcestis is said to have been the fourth play of a tetralogy: that is, it took the place of the satyr play that customarily provided comic relief at the end of each group of three tragedies performed at the Athenian dramatic festivals. The play certainly has a happy, indeed a comic, ending as Heracles, having

snatched Alcestis from death, restores her to Admetus. Yet Alcestis herself, in the sorrow and love of her farewell scene, is completely tragic. So is Admetus. True, he has accepted her sacrifice—not a heroic attitude—and his expressions of sorrow at first are somewhat stylized and stilted. But when Alcestis is really gone and he has had a violent quarrel with the old father who has refused to die for him, Admetus' laments are sincere and deeply felt. Admetus comes to realize that there was truth in his father's strictures, and this change in him seems the main theme of the play as a tragedy. The Chorus sympathize with Admetus, though, in the usual manner of tragedy, they admire the nobility of Alcestis.

The Heracles of this play, on the other hand, is the jovial hero of comedy, both in the scene in which he learns of Alcestis' death and is embarrassed at his seeming callousness and in the final scene, in which he teases Admetus mercilessly. *Alcestis* is the most curious mixture of tragedy and comedy in all of Euripides' plays. Perhaps the poet set out to write an ironic satyr play based on two impossible miracles, but as he created Alcestis and Admetus, the tragic possibilities of his own creations took control of him, tragic poet that he was. The result is a play a part of which is truly tragic and the other part simply comic. The two remain emotionally separated side by side.

Translations of the play are listed in this book under Euripides.—G. M. A. G.

Alchemist, The (1610).   A comedy by Ben JON-SON. *The Alchemist* is an account of the gulling of an assortment of dupes by two gifted confidence men. Subtle and Face pose as alchemists in order to capitalize on the credulity of a group who believe in the

DAVID GARRICK AS ABEL DRUGGER IN BEN JONSON'S
The Alchemist (THEATRE COLLECTION, NEW YORK
PUBLIC LIBRARY AT LINCOLN CENTER)

ability of alchemists to transform base metals into gold. Using as their headquarters Lovewit's house during his absence, the cozeners are visited by an assortment of knaves and fools representing a broad cross section of London life. Chief among these are Sir Epicure Mammon, a sensualist; Tribulation Wholesome and Ananias, two hypocritical Puritans; Abel Drugger, a naïve young tobacconist; Kastrill, an "angry boy"; and Dame Pliant, his sister. Victimized more by his own blindness than by the machinations of Subtle and Face, each visitor is easily duped into handing over gifts and money to the con men and their sluttish colleague, Doll Common. Eventually, the rascals are exposed when the master of the house, Lovewit, returns unexpectedly. The cozeners escape, although they are forced to leave behind their booty, and Lovewit wins the hand of the lovely and rich Dame Pliant.

The play has been celebrated for the rapidity of the action and the expressiveness of the verse, but primarily for the perfection of the plot, described by Samuel Coleridge as among the three greatest in all of literature. Equally notable is the character of Sir Epicure, the grandiose voluptuary. The soliloquies in which he verbalizes his dreams of glory achieve a kind of hyperbolic grandeur that quite belies the satiric context in which they are framed.—E. Q.

Alfieri, Vittorio (1749–1803). Italian writer and playwright. Born in Piedmont of a noble family, Alfieri spent his youth at the Military Academy of Turin. Between 1767 and 1773 he traveled extensively throughout Italy and Europe, passing intolerantly through a world that seemed to him divided between two equally despicable groups: slaves and tyrants. Only in England did he find mature, urbane liberty.

From 1775, he fervently devoted himself to dramatic creation, writing twenty-one tragedies, two of which were published posthumously (one of the latter, *Abele,* he described as a *tramelogedia,* a word he coined to indicate the fusion of two genres, tragedy and musical drama); six comedies; and an autobiography that he finished in the year he died. Influenced by the Enlightenment but also animated by a romantic spirit devoid of languor and sentimentality, Alfieri turned to tragedy because it was the form most consonant with his own feelings. He employed a rigorous classical structure without being disturbed by the incongruities that sometimes arise from close observation of the Aristotelian unities. In plot, speeches, and even in number of characters, he limited himself to whatever was strictly necessary to the fundamental dramatic conflict, creating a theater that is lean and stripped to its essentials and, because of its brevity and compression, often severe in expression. As plots for his tragedies he particularly favored historical events and classical myths.

Among Alfieri's most important tragedies are *Filippo* (1781), *Antigone* (1777), *Oreste* (1778), *Virginia* (1778), and *Saul* (1782). (The dates given here are dates of composition.) His characters are figures of superhuman dimension who struggle among themselves or against a fate stronger than they. They possess grandeur and the "Roman" virtues, which Alfieri saw as positive ideals and which he contrasted with the servile softness of his society. After the

French Revolution—which Alfieri had looked upon first with great hope, then, after the excesses of the Terror, with angry disillusionment—he wrote four political comedies, which do not have the same value as his tragedies: *L'Uno* ("The One"), *I Pochi* ("The Few"), and *I Troppi* ("Too Many"). All were written in 1802 and satirize, respectively, monarchical, oligarchical, and democratic forms of government. In the fourth comedy, *L'Antidoto* ("The Antidote," 1802), he presents a moderate constitutional regime. Two other comedies—*La Finestrina* ("The Little Window," 1802) and *Il Divorzio* ("The Divorce," 1803)—are of minor importance, as are the two posthumous tragedies.—L. L.

Allegory. The continuous representation of moral or intellectual abstraction (moral allegory) or political, historical events (historical allegory) by means of the characters, setting, and action of a play. The first type is historically identified with the morality plays of MEDIEVAL DRAMA, such as *Everyman.* This form is closely allied to a doctrinal drama, the purpose of which is to inculcate in the audience particular moral and religious values. The technique employed in these plays is that of personification. Thus, *Everyman* features characters with such names as Good Deeds, Fellowship, and Worldly Goods. A modern example of moral allegory is Ibsen's *Peer Gynt.*

There is a tradition of historical allegory in many countries where existing governments forbid the direct expression of political or historical positions. What distinguishes allegory from a play that contains pointed topical allusions is that the allegory is continuously developed throughout the play. An example of this type of allegory is Thomas Middleton's *A Game of Chess* (1624), a satiric allegory about the attempt to secure through marriage the union of the English and Spanish thrones. In modern times Arthur Miller's *The Crucible* is frequently described as an allegory of the McCarthy investigations of the 1950's.

All for Love (1677). A tragedy in blank verse by John DRYDEN. The first performance of *All for Love, or The World Well Lost* was given at the Theatre Royal in Drury Lane in December. For this play Dryden rewrote Shakespeare's *Antony and Cleopatra,* condensing the action by beginning after the defeat at Actium. In Act I Ventidius persuades Antony that he should leave Cleopatra and resume the fight against Octavius Caesar. In Act II Antony is reconciled to Cleopatra but goes off to battle. After a temporary victory over Caesar in Act III, Antony is welcomed back by Cleopatra but again determines to leave her after an encounter with his wife, Octavia, who is given an unhistoric confrontation with Cleopatra. Antony is made to suspect Cleopatra's loyalty in Act IV, but his concern angers Octavia, who leaves. After her departure the lovers are again reconciled. In the last act, faced with capture by the victorious Caesar, they both commit suicide.

In this play Dryden abandoned heroic couplets for blank verse in order to "imitate the divine Shakespeare." The arrangement of the action shows the neatness of his neoclassical reordering of Shakespeare's play. As his contrasts are more clear-cut, his characters are less subtle and complex than Shake-

ALL FOR LOVE:

O R, T H E

World well Loft.

A

T R A G E D Y,

As it is Aated at the

T H E A T R E-R O Y A L;

And Written in Imitation of *Shakefpeare's* Stile.

By *John Dryden*, Servant to His Majefty.

Facile eft verbum aliquod ardens (ut ita dicam) notare : idque re- ftinatis animorum incendiis irridere. Cicero.

In the S A V O Y:

Printed by *Tho. Newcomb*, for *Henry Herringman*, at the Blew An- chor in the Lower Walk of the *New-Exchange.* 1 6 7 8.

TITLE PAGE OF THE 1678 EDITION OF JOHN DRYDEN'S
All for Love

speare's, but more obviously heroic (see ENGLAND: *Restoration drama*). Though comparison with Shakespeare's tragedy is inevitable, it does not do full justice to Dryden's play, which, considered purely on its own merits, is very impressive.

David Vieth is editing the play with introduction and notes for the Regents Restoration Drama Series. It has been edited by L. A. Beaurline and Fredson Bowers in *John Dryden: Four Tragedies* (1967).—E.W.

All's Well that Ends Well (c. 1602–1603). A comedy by William SHAKESPEARE. *All's Well that Ends Well* was first published in the 1623 First Folio. Its main plot comes from the ninth novella of the third day in Boccaccio's *Decameron* (written 1348–1358), translated in William Painter's *The Palace of Pleasure* (1566, 3rd ed. rev. 1575). The subplot is Shakespeare's invention. The earliest recorded performance dates from 1741.

The plot revolves around Helena, orphan daughter of a distinguished physician and now ward of the countess of Rousillon. Helena has fallen in love with Bertram, the countess' son, who, as the play opens, leaves for Paris to serve the French king. The king is suffering from what seems to be an incurable fistula. Drawing upon the medical knowledge her father im- parted to her, Helena travels to Paris hoping to cure the king and thus prove herself worthy of Bertram, whose station is far above hers. She succeeds, and as her reward, the king permits her to choose a husband from among the courtiers. She, of course, selects

Bertram. Initially demurring, but under threat of in- curring the king's disfavor, Bertram consents to the marriage. Immediately after, he secretly leaves for the Florentine wars but first dispatches Helena to Rousillon and then sends her a brutal letter telling her he will never be her husband until she can get a certain ring from his finger and become, in their separation, pregnant with his child. Blaming herself for Bertram's departure from France, Helena sets out on a pilgrimage to the shrine of Saint Jaques le Grand. Once in Florence, she meets by coincidence Diana, whom Bertram has been trying to seduce, and her widowed mother. Helena convinces the women to aid her in an intrigue whereby she can fulfill the conditions of Bertram's letter. The plot succeeds. At Rousillon, where all the principals—including the king—have gathered, the intrigue is revealed and Helena and Bertram are reunited. Furthermore, Parolles, Bertram's companion, is exposed as a cowardly windbag.

The play has been classified a bitter or "dark comedy"—the label scholars have affixed to the comedies of the period 1601–1604. In its satiric tone, its passages dealing with sex, and its use of the "bed-trick" (a device that though disturbing to later audiences was perfectly acceptable to the Eliza- bethans), it strongly resembles *Measure for Measure*. Like this work, *All's Well that Ends Well* appears to be a play of education, for in the end Bertram real- izes he was wrong and Parolles is exposed and cured. But it is not a well-wrought play and has never been popular with theatergoers or critics. Bertram emerges as a thoroughly unpleasant character. The Helena of the latter portion appears more as a ma- nipulator than as the charming young woman of the first half. Though integrated, the Parolles subplot is thematically only tenuously linked to the main plot. Even the verse—which through the maturity of its style has helped date the play in the absence of exter- nal facts—is uneven. The comedy may represent the unsuccessful attempt of Shakespeare to write in the new style coming to the fore in the private theaters of the time, one in which the scripts contained a great deal of sex and satire.

An outstanding edition of *All's Well that Ends Well* is the New Arden Edition (repr. 1962), edited by G. K. Hunter.—W. G.

Aloni, Nissim (1926–   ). Israeli playwright, short-story writer, and translator. Aloni was born in Tel-Aviv in 1926 and is today Israel's only play- wright whose sole occupation is playwriting and the theater. As one of the founding members of a theater ensemble, the Theatre of the Seasons, he worked with the group until 1966, primarily directing and experi- menting. Like most of Israel's dramatists, Aloni started as a writer of short stories, immediately draw- ing the attention and praise of the critics. He soon abandoned the realm of the short story and devoted himself completely to the drama. In 1953 the Habi- mah Theater produced his first play, *Achzar Mikol Hamelech* ("Cruelest of All, the King"), which soon became not only a significant play in itself but also a cornerstone for Israeli drama. The most fruitful period came soon after, in the early sixties, when three more of his plays were produced at the Habimah: *Bigdei Hamelech* ("Emperor's New Clothes," 1961), a modern "theater of the absurd" rendering of Hans Christian

Andersen's story; *Hansicha Ha' Amerikait* ("The American Princess," 1962); and *Hamahapeicha V'hatarnegolet* ("The Revolution and the Hen," 1964). All three were highly experimental in theme and form, an exceptional characteristic for an Israeli drama.

During his years of theatrical activity at the Theatre of the Seasons, Aloni did not write any plays, but in 1967 he wrote *Hakalah V'tsayad Haparparim* ("The Bride and the Butterfly Hunter"), which he subsequently produced and directed himself. It is a short drama in which an amateur butterfly hunter and a bride meet in a public park. The play was inspired by a painting of the Israeli artist Josel Bergner. Like many of the plays of the theater of the absurd, it deals with the problems of communication. A subsequent play, *Doda Liza* ("Aunt Liza," 1969), contains themes that have occupied Aloni in previous plays. This play, however, is more localized than the others in its treatment of three generations of an Israeli family. After wandering in abstract or exotic worlds in other plays, Aloni seems here to be returning home to the landscape and color of Israel. —Z. R.

Alterman, Nathan (1910–   ). Polish-born Israeli poet, translator, and playwright. Alterman was born in Warsaw, Poland, and immigrated to Israel in 1925. One of modern Israel's foremost poets, Alterman is a master of modern Hebrew, and he has created numerous new words, forms, and idioms. His poetry has influenced many younger poets and created an "Alterman school," marked by its distinct rhythms and rhymes. Initially, and perhaps primarily, a lyric poet, he is known to theatergoers as the brilliant translator of many classics. A collection of his translations of Molière was published in 1967, and among his ingenious translations of the lighter dramatic forms are found works by Shakespeare, Eugène Labiche, and others.

In 1961 Alterman wrote his first play, *Kineret, Kineret . . .* ("Kineret" is the Hebrew name for the Sea of Galilee), a nostalgic play about the life of Israeli pioneers at the beginning of the twentieth century. It was produced by the Chamber Theatre, and, because it was the first modern Israeli drama written in poetic prose, it was a milestone in the development of Israeli drama. The following year his next play, *Pundak Haroochot* ("The Inn of Ghosts"), was produced by the same theater group and the play soon became the highlight of that season, the talk of the theater community. It dealt poetically and symbolically with the problems of the artist and the meaning of life, sacrifice, and happiness. It was one of the first plays of a poetic form and vision written by an Israeli and produced in Israel. His third play, *Mishpat Pitagoras* ("The Trial of Pythagoras," 1966), contained obvious allusions to the political scene in Israel. Although the play was unsuccessful, it was still head and shoulders above the mediocre, "true-to-life" plays that make up so much of Israeli drama.— Z. R.

Aminta (1573). A "sylvan fable" in five acts and in verse by Torquato TASSO. The story concerns the love of the shepherd Aminta for the reluctant Sylvia. Tirsi, Aminta's friend, counsels the unhappy lover to meet Sylvia while she is at the spring; but before the shepherd appears, Sylvia is surprised there by a satyr. Arriving opportunely, Aminta intervenes and saves her. Sylvia flees, and her veil is subsequently found covered with blood near a group of wolves intent on tearing to pieces a shapeless mass of meat. Aminta, believing Sylvia dead, goes off to take his own life. Sylvia, however, reappears and begins to lament Aminta's fate. Fortunately, the shepherd, in throwing himself from a cliff, is saved by a bush, and the fable concludes with the marriage of the pair.

The fable is written in regular dramatic form with choral interludes that exalt simple and spontaneous love in a state of nature. Far more interesting than its dramatic development are the poetic and musical powers of the verse, the moving and lyrical description of the varying states of mind of the lovers, and the suffused, pathetic nostalgia—which was Tasso's sincere sentiment—for a lost and mythical innocence, which here takes on the forms and tones of a terrestrial paradise. *Aminta* is a masterpiece of the dramatic pastoral literature that flowered in Italy in the sixteenth and seventeenth centuries.—L. L.

Amphitryon (Lat., **Amphitruo**, 186 B.C.?). A comedy by PLAUTUS. Like all extant Roman comedies, *Amphitryon* is based on an earlier Greek play, but the author of the original is unknown. He is considered by some to be a writer of Greek Middle Comedy, but such an assumption seems unnecessary, since the technique of the play is that of New Comedy. Plautus' *Amphitryon* is unique among Roman comedies as the sole surviving specimen of a mythological parody (a *tragicomoedia*, as stated in the Prologue). Jupiter and Mercury, disguised as Amphitryon and his slave, Sosia, visit Amphitryon's house during his absence, and Jupiter spends the night with Alcmena, Amphitryon's wife. The play becomes a comedy of errors, with two pairs of "twins," when the real Amphitryon and Sosia return. Alcmena, devoted to her husband and innocent of wrongdoing, is Plautus' noblest character.

One of Plautus' most successful comedies, *Amphitryon* has been translated and adapted by many later dramatists, among them Jean de Rotrou (*Les Sosies,* 1638), Molière (*Amphitryon,* 1668), John Dryden (*Amphitryon,* 1690), Heinrich von Kleist (*Amphitryon,* 1807), and Jean Giraudoux (*Amphitryon 38,* 1929; "38" meaning that it is the thirty-eighth treatment of the Greek myth). Shakespeare based *The Comedy of Errors* on Plautus' *Menaechmi,* but derived from *Amphitryon* the two sets of twins and the episode of master and servant excluded from their home. C. D. N. Costa, "The Amphitryo Theme," in T. A. Dorey and Donald R. Dudley, *Roman Drama* (1965), analyzes the versions by Molière, Dryden, Kleist, and Giraudoux.—G. E. D.

Anagnorisis ("recognition"). Aristotle's term for the discovery of a character's true identity. This "change from ignorance to knowledge" is according to Aristotle best represented when it is "co-incident with the Reversal of the Situation." Thus, in *Oedipus Rex,* Oedipus' discovery of his identity is in fact his tragedy. Recent critics have broadened the use of the term to embrace any significant perception about himself or others that a character may come to. Thus, Macbeth's "Tomorrow and tomorrow . . ." speech is the expression of his recognition of the meaning of his life. A modern example of recognition in the stricter sense is Cuchulain's discovery that the man he killed is his son in Yeats's *On Bailie's Strand.*

The comic equivalent of tragic anagnorisis is represented by the technique of the discovery of the true identity of a young lover which makes him or her marriageable. This technique is a standard feature of NEW COMEDY and is parodied in the conclusion of *The Importance of Being Earnest.*

Anday, Melih Cevdet (1915–   ). Turkish poet and playwright. Anday was born and raised in Istanbul and studied sociology for a while in Belgium. Returning to Turkey, he worked for the ministry of education and as a journalist. Currently, he teaches. Anday is recognized along with Orhan Veli and Oktay Rifat as a leader of the "new poetry" movement in Turkey, which began in 1936 and continued for more than a decade as a reaction to over-ornate poetry. So far, Anday has published five books of poetry and a novel; three of his plays have been produced.

Anday's two major plays—*İçerdekiler* ("Those Inside," 1965) and *Mikado'nun Çöpleri* (*The Mikado Game,* 1967)—are for three and two characters respectively. The characters argue and philosophize for two hours, and yet, aided by elements of suspense, hold the interest of the audience. Because the plays do not discuss the problems of present-day Turkey in particular, but rather universal conflicts and problems, they have been criticized by some critics and hailed by others, who welcomed them for their freshness, wide scope, and intellectual content. —N. O.

Anderson, Maxwell (1888–1959). American playwright. Anderson was born in Atlantic, Pennsylvania, the son of a Baptist minister. The family moved frequently throughout Anderson's boyhood. After graduation from the University of North Dakota in 1911, Anderson taught English at Stanford University and Whittier College for a few years. He shortly turned to newspaper work, first in San Francisco, later in New York. Although he had tried his hand at playwriting before, it was not until he collaborated with Laurence Stallings (1895–1968), a colleague on the New York *World,* that Anderson had his first Broadway success and began one of the most distinguished careers in the American theater.

MAXWELL ANDERSON (WALTER HAMPDEN MEMORIAL LIBRARY AT THE PLAYERS, NEW YORK)

What Price Glory? (1924), which grew out of Stallings' experiences in World War I, introduced to the American stage profane dialogue and a bitter view of war. Other collaborations with Stallings were unsuccessful, and Anderson spent most of his career working alone. He made some notable attempts to create a modern verse drama. In *Elizabeth the Queen* (1930) and *Mary of Scotland* (1933) battles of will were vividly treated in a blank verse that echoed the Renaissance settings. In *Winterset* (1935) Anderson treats as tragedy a modern story of injustice based on the Sacco-Vanzetti case. Though highly regarded when it first appeared, *Winterset* now confirms Anderson's own conclusion that great tragedies have always had the "advantage of a setting either far away or long ago."

Anderson demonstrated his skill in dealing with the past in *Knickerbocker Holiday* (1938), a musical comedy about early New York, with a score by Kurt Weill; *Joan of Lorraine* (1947), a study of Joan of Arc, which uses the device of a group of actors rehearsing a play about the saint; *Anne of the Thousand Days* (1948), a tragicomic picture of Henry VIII and Anne Boleyn; and *Barefoot in Athens* (1951), a dramatization of Socrates' career as a critic of the state.

Contemporary events and concerns formed the subjects of *Key Largo* (1939), the tragedy of a young American who had deserted his post in the Spanish Civil War but regains his sense of purpose in a struggle against Florida gangsters; *Candle in the Wind* (1941), *The Eve of St. Mark* (1942), and *Storm Operation* (1944), studies of conditions during World War II; and *Lost in the Stars* (1949), a musical (with score by Kurt Weill) based on Alan Paton's novel *Cry the Beloved Country* (1948). In all, Anderson wrote more than thirty plays, and in most, he dealt with serious subjects, but a tendency to reduce issues to a simple struggle between good and evil left too little room for the complexity and richness that distinguish the greatest drama.

There is no standard edition of Anderson's plays, but the most important are frequently anthologized. An early, valuable study is Barrett H. Clark's *Maxwell Anderson; The Man and His Plays* (1933); the most comprehensive study is Mabel D. Bailey's *Maxwell Anderson: the Playwright as Prophet* (1957). Also see Martha Cox's *Maxwell Anderson Bibliography* (1958).—M. L.

Andrade, Jorge (1922–   ). Brazilian playwright. The childhood of Jorge Andrade was marked by the coffee crisis, which impoverished a great number of Paulista families (those from the state of São Paulo, Brazil), some of whom were descendants of the empire. The pride of the proprietors fell with the price of coffee on the international market. At the same time the large landed estates began to break up and European immigrants or large international combines seized the lands by purchase or by foreclosure of mortgages. The death of the aristocracy was accompanied by a crisis in human values. Born in this rural environment, Andrade preserved images and facts that he later would interpret with a tragic greatness until then unknown in the Brazilian theater of social observation.

Moving to the city of São Paulo, capital of the state, Andrade matriculated in the School of Dra-

JORGE ANDRADE (BRAZILIAN EMBASSY)

matic Art, where he was an apprentice playwright. His career started in 1955 with the performance of *A moratória* ("The Moratorium"). Until then he had written only one comedy, *Os ossos do barão* ("The Bones of the Baron," 1963), signifying the union between the rich immigrants and the poor representatives of the ancient aristocracy through the marriage of the son of an Italian with a Brazilian granddaughter of an old baron. As in this play, it is in the past that Andrade encounters the roots of the new society, to be composed of the workers or of the ruined nobles who accept starting over as farm hands. The family and the land, in spite of the ruin, continue to join men together and lead them toward hope. Other plays are: *O telescópio* ("The Telescope," 1955), *Pedreira das almas* ("Quarry of the Souls," 1960), *Vereda da salvação* ("Path of Salvation," 1963), *A escada* ("The Staircase," 1964), and *Rasto atrás* ("Footprint Behind," 1967).

All the plays of Andrade have been published, but they have not been translated into English.—J. P.

Andreyev, Leonid [Nikolaevich] (1871–1919). Russian short-story writer, novelist, and playwright. Andreyev was a poor law student, an unsuccessful lawyer, an undistinguished portrait painter, and a struggling newspaper reporter. Disgusted with the tsarist regime, he voiced his scorn for lower-middle-class smugness in his short stories and sympathized with various revolutionary movements. Later he became disgusted with revolutionaries too, and when the Bolsheviks took over the revolution, Andreyev openly declared his loathing for them. Thus, politically, he fell between two stools.

Maxim Gorky started Andreyev on his literary career. In 1900, already at the peak of his own literary fame, Gorky introduced the strikingly handsome young man at a meeting where young writers read their own works. Andreyev read a story entitled "Silence," which impressed his audience, and within a year his first collection of short stories appeared. It was sold out almost at once. Andreyev's fame rose

suddenly and, during the first years of the twentieth century, he was one of the best-selling authors in Russia. After the revolution, however, he was dismissed.

Although greatly influenced by other writers (Chekhov, Maeterlinck, Dostoyevsky, Tolstoy), Andreyev was just as congenitally a non-joiner of literary movements as he was of political ones. And so, while Soviet critics reproach him for having so lamentably neglected the social content of his plays and stories, for not having been a true "critical realist" under the tsar, and for having ignored dialectical materialism as a means of solving his metaphysical doubts, many émigré scholars seem to hold it against him that he never really joined the symbolists, although he did use all their paraphernalia. Here again, he seems to have fallen between two stools.

Somehow, however, although he was a "nonperson" for decades in the Soviet Union and was dismissed by the émigré exegetes as a period piece belonging to the gaudy Russian contribution to the turn-of-the-century affectations, it must be admitted by both his admirers and his detractors that Andreyev is faring quite well today, both at home and abroad. Most of his plays and stories have recently been republished in the Soviet Union, while abroad any really representative collection of Russian plays must include HE WHO GETS SLAPPED.

Among the more than thirty other plays Andreyev wrote, three should be mentioned. In *K zvezdam* (*To the Stars,* 1906) Andreyev develops the theme of the tragic gap between the intellectual, personified by the astronomer, and the ignorant crowd. *Zhizn cheloveka* (*Life of Man,* 1906), a symbolist account of the life of a man from his birth to his death, emphasizes the whimsical and senseless twists of fate (represented by a character called Someone Dressed in Gray who is always present in a dark corner). For writing this play, Andreyev was attacked first by the Russian Church (for blasphemy) and later by the Communist Party (for "petit-bourgeois negativism"). *Milye prizraki* ("Cherished Ghosts," 1916), based on an early episode in Dostoyevsky's career, sheds interesting light on Andreyev's feeling about this great writer (he loved him and was greatly influenced by him) and thus helps to explain much of Andreyev's Dostoyevskian view of the world.

Some information on Andreyev can be obtained from D. S. Mirsky's *Contemporary Russian Literature* (1926).—A. MACA.

Andromache (430–424 B.C.). A tragedy by EURIPIDES. In this play the often-heard criticism of Euripides' lack of dramatic unity seems justified, for *Andromache* falls into three parts only flimsily connected by the theme of the future of the house of Achilles.

The first part covers two-thirds of the whole. Its heroine, the captive Trojan princess Andromache, now the slave of the Greek prince Neoptolemus, has borne her master a son. For this fact his young, sterile, and jealous wife, Hermione, hates her. In the absence of Neoptolemus (who never appears except at the end of the play, as a corpse), Hermione seeks to destroy both mother and child, with the help of her father, Menelaus. At the end of this section of the play Andromache is saved by Neoptolemus' grandfather, old King Peleus, and leaves with him—never to reappear.

The second part begins with a hysterical and irrational Hermione terrified that Neoptolemus will kill her on his return. When Orestes (who was once betrothed to her) appears, she begs him to save her. He declares his intention to kill Neoptolemus and she departs with him. Hermione, too, will not reappear.

With both of the principal characters gone, the play turns its attention to Peleus. A messenger vividly describes to him the death of Neoptolemus at the hands of a crowd of Delphians. In the midst of the old king's lamentations the goddess Thetis, who was once his wife, appears to console him with a promise of eternal life with her. Andromache's son, the only surviving issue of her house and that of Peleus, will rule over Molossia with his descendants.

Although *Andromache* lacks dramatic unity, the play is remarkable for the characterization of the two women. From the first words of her monologue until she leaves the stage, Andromache is, even in slavery, still the proud widow of the great Hector. She is one of Euripides' most successful and endearing characters. Hermione is equally successful, but, true daughter of Helen that she is, she is not endearing. *Andromache* is memorable too for the vitriolic attacks of Peleus and Andromache upon the Spartan character, which, in this play, Menelaus and Hermione certainly deserve. The choral odes, though not direct commentaries on the action, are appropriate, for they sing of the Trojan War, of which the present events are an aftermath.

Translations of the play are listed in this book under Euripides.—G. M. A. G.

Andromaque (1667). A tragedy by Jean RACINE. Oreste is in love with Hermione, who is in love with Pyrrhus, who is in love with his prisoner Andromaque, who is faithful to the memory of her dead husband, Hector. Since the Greeks ask that Andromaque's son be given over to them, Pyrrhus presents her with the choice of either marrying him or having her son killed. Andromaque decides to marry Pyrrhus and then kill herself. But Hermione has Pyrrhus killed by Oreste, then commits suicide, and Oreste loses his mind. Andromaque's agonized struggle and the frenzied, murderous passions of the other three characters create a climate of true tragic fate.

This play has been translated into English verse by Kenneth Muir in *Five Plays* (1960).—Ja. G.

Anna Christie (1921). A play by Eugene O'NEILL. A "slice-of-life" drama, *Anna Christie* is a sympathetic portrayal of a prostitute. Anna is early neglected by her father, a sea captain incapable of resisting the seductions of seafaring life, and sent to a farm to live with cousins, becoming an object of their passions. She flees to the city, only to enter a house of prostitution, and after an illness is reunited with her father. Unable to understand his own behavior and overwhelmed with his sense of failure as a father, the sea captain blames everything on the sea, speaking of it as a demon and equating it with diabolic fate. Anna, however, finds the sea cleansing as she travels with him on a barge and is able to love the burly Irish stoker Mat Burke. When he discovers her sordid past, he rejects Anna and signs up for a long sea voyage with her father, although ultimate reunion of the two lovers is hinted at, a flaw in an otherwise thoroughly realistic play. This wry tragicomedy, enriched with fully flavored naturalism in dialogue and background, proved satisfying to playgoers in the United States and abroad and won for its author a second Pulitzer Prize.—J. G.

Anouilh, Jean (1910–   ). French screenwriter and playwright. Born in Bordeaux, Anouilh was the son of a skilled tailor. He went to Paris to study law, earned a living by writing advertisements, and for a short time was secretary to the director Louis Jouvet. He wrote his first play, a one-act farce, at the age of nineteen.

All the plays of Anouilh are characterized by a fundamental bitterness of tone that seems to come, especially in the earlier plays, from a noble, philosophical kind of despair. There have always been traces of the popular novel and melodrama in the Anouilh plays, but they were usually offset by an imperious spiritual suffering, a new kind of *mal du siècle,* a romantic longing. Anouilh is purely a playwright, and because of this characteristic, he has been followed with close attention as the potential representative French playwright today who best continues the tradition of Molière in being solely a man of the theater.

In a metaphysical sense, Anouilh is constantly rewriting the same comedy. Technically, he introduces innovations. He takes every liberty possible in arranging and choreographing the play, and he employs every device, from farce and vaudeville to tense, somber tragedy. The central figure in an Anouilh play is the one who says "no," who contradicts life. His heroines are all fundamentally the same character, whose purity of being and purpose are contaminated by a corrupting family relationship, by some social pressure, or by the memory of family and social entanglements.

Anouilh has created his own genres for his plays:

JEAN ANOUILH (FRENCH CULTURAL SERVICES)

pièces noires ("dark plays"), *pièces roses* ("rosy plays"), *pièces brillantes* ("sparkling plays") or *grinçantes* ("grating plays"). The dark-colored plays have been his greatest successes: *Eurydice* (*Legend of Lovers*, 1941), *La Sauvage* (*Restless Heart*, 1934), ANTIGONE, and THE LARK, while the light-colored plays are more complex: *L'Invitation au chateau* (*Ring Round the Moon*, 1947), *Ardèle ou la Marguerite* (*Ardèle*, 1948), and *La Valse des toréadors* (*The Waltz of the Toreadors*, 1952). These plays reflect some of the serious psychological problems of our period. The "brilliancy" in les *pièces brillantes*, such as *Colombe* (1951) and *La Répétition* (*The Rehearsal*, 1950), is a mixture of thematic seriousness and lightness of touch and style.

For critical studies on Anouilh, see the following works: Philip A. Benson, *The Dramaturgy of Jean Anouilh* (1958); Robert Champigny, "Theatre in a Mirror: Anouilh," *Yale French Studies*, No. 14 (Winter 1954–1955); John E. Harvey, *Anouilh: A Study in Theatrics* (1964); and Leonard C. Pronko, *The World of Jean Anouilh* (1961).—W. F.

Ansky, S. Pen name of **Shloyme Zaynvl Rappaport** (1863–1920). Russian-born Yiddish playwright, folklorist, essayist, and short-story writer. Ansky was born in Tchasnik, White Russia. He received a traditional Jewish education but while still a youth turned to secular literature. He began to study Russian and Russian literature and was much influenced by the populist spirit of the Narodnik movement, following its dictum "Go to the people!" by living among peasants, miners, and workers of all kinds. He began to publish short stories and articles in Russian on Russian folklore. In 1892 Ansky left Russia for Paris, where he served as secretary to Piotr Lavrov, the highly influential social-democratic leader, and continued his research in Russian folklore. He returned to Russia in 1905 and thereafter became increasingly involved in the Yiddish cultural movement, studying Yiddish folklore and becoming active in the Jewish Historical and Ethnographic Society of St. Petersburg. From 1912 to 1914 he led a field expedition, visiting about seventy Jewish communities in the Ukrainian provinces of Volyn and Podolia and collecting a substantial body of Yiddish folk material, some of which he incorporated into his play THE DYBBUK. (Most of this material is still in the Soviet Union.) With the outbreak of World War I, Ansky threw all his energies into war relief. Apparently exhausted by the strain, he died suddenly in Warsaw on November 8, 1920.

Ansky's dramatic output constitutes a very small part of his fifteen volumes in Yiddish and five in Russian. Besides *The Dybbuk*, he wrote only three short comedies and the unfinished *Tog un Nakht* ("Day and Night"). *The Dybbuk*, which embodies Ansky's conception of Jewish folklore as representing the triumph of the spirit, is undoubtedly the most frequently performed Yiddish play, and it is certainly the most unusual. It has been performed in at least ten languages, has been turned into an opera by several composers, and was made into a film. It is also the basis of a reputation much wider than any he would have gained from his substantial achievements as a folklorist.—J. C. L.

Antigone (442 B.C.?). A tragedy by SOPHOCLES. The scene is Thebes, at dawn, after the defeat of the assault on the city led by Antigone's brother, Polyneices. Antigone informs her sister, Ismene, of Creon's edict forbidding Polyneices' burial and of her decision to defy it; in spite of Ismene's remonstrances she goes off to bury the body. The Chorus, old men of Thebes, celebrate the city's escape and then listen to C᠁on's announcement of the principles which justify his edict: The city's interest prevails over private loyalties. A guard reports that someone has sprinkled dust on the body of Polyneices; Creon threatens him with torture and death if he does not produce the culprit. After a famous choral ode on the miracle of man's progress from savagery to the civilized life of the city, ending with a reminder of the limits to man's ingenuity, the guard reappears with Antigone, who has been captured as she tried to complete the burial. She proudly admits her deed and defends it in the name of the gods below and the eternal unwritten laws. Creon condemns her to death, in spite of the fact that she is betrothed to his own son, Haemon. Haemon's conciliatory pleas are ineffective, and the scene ends with a bitter quarrel between father and son. Antigone is to be left to die in an underground cell; after a strange speech of self-justification she is led off to her punishment. But Creon's punishment is now at hand. The prophet Tiresias tells him the gods demand the burial of Polyneices' body, and when Creon blasphemously rejects his advice, Tiresias prophesies deaths in Creon's family as retribution for his crime. Creon loses his nerve and reluctantly decides to bury Polyneices and free Antigone. But a messenger comes back to report that after the burial Creon went to Antigone's prison only to find her hanging, a suicide, and Haemon mourning her death. The son, after an attempt to kill his father, turned the sword against himself. Creon's wife, Eurydice, who has heard this report, exits and kills herself. When Creon returns with the body of his son, he finds the corpse of his wife and hears of the curses she has called down on him. The king who exalted the claims of the city over those of the family and the gods finds himself appropriately punished; his family is destroyed together with his reputation as a statesman. The man who kept a corpse in the realm of the living becomes, as he says himself, a "living corpse."

The most discussed problem of the play is Antigone's final speech. The core of it, the statement that she would not have defied the state on behalf of a husband or a son, is clearly based on a story in Herodotus, and the adaptation leaves something to be desired in the way of relevance and congruity. Her statement also clearly conflicts with her earlier championship of the universal unwritten laws. For these reasons some influential critics have condemned the lines as the work of an interpolator. Against this drastic solution stands the great authority of Aristotle, who quotes the crucial lines and attributes them to Antigone. In their defense it has been argued that Antigone is no longer pleading her case before the world; like Ajax in his ambiguous speech, she is trying in the face of imminent death to clarify and justify her action to herself and finds her true motive in loyalty to the closed circle of her family, whom she now goes to join in Hades.

See R. C. Jebb, *The Antigone* (1900), and I. M. Linforth, *Antigone and Creon* (1961).—B. M. W. K.

Antigone (1944). A tragedy by Jean ANOUILH. The character of Anouilh's Antigone is one of such innate pessimism and difficult willfulness that this in itself may be a sufficient explanation for her fate. In the opening scene between Antigone and her uncle, Creon, everything seems settled in advance, and she is able to taunt her uncle with these words: "I knew you would have me killed." When Creon asks her for whom she performed the act of disobedience of trying to bury her brother's body, she answers, "For no one. For myself." With these caustic words, she sets herself off at some distance from the Sophoclean Antigone. The French heroine rejects hope, and this theme of renunciation is repeated by the Chorus, which defines tragedy as something restful and clean because it is stripped of all elements of hope.

In opposition to Antigone, Creon is the politician concerned with imposing and maintaining order. Anouilh's Creon has no illusions about the stupidity of his edict, but he thinks it is good enough for the populace. The type of human being his nature cannot tolerate is the anarchist Antigone. In her search for truth she is as unbending as Creon in his upholding of the law. In this tragedy Anouilh presents not only two strong individuals, but a pattern of temperamental conflict, a clash of a psychological nature between a man and a woman.

Antigone has been translated by Lewis Galantière in *Antigone and Eurydice* (1956).—W. F.

antimasque. A comic interlude inserted into the main MASQUE and designed to function as a parody of it. In this respect the antimasque is similar to the comic subplot of many Elizabethan tragedies. The antimasque was introduced in England in the early years of the seventeenth century. It was not, as is sometimes asserted, first used by Ben Jonson, although the Preface to his *Masque of Queens* (1609) marks the earliest recorded use of the term and he was the most accomplished writer to use the antimasque.

Antony and Cleopatra (c. 1607). A tragedy by William SHAKESPEARE. *Antony and Cleopatra* was published initially in the First Folio of 1623. It closely follows the account of the "Life of Marcus Antonius" in Plutarch's *Lives of the Noble Grecians and Romans,* as translated into English (2nd ed., 1595) by Sir Thomas North from Jacques Amyot's French translation (1559). No early record of performance survives. *All for Love* (1678), John Dryden's version of the story, drove *The Tragedy of Antony and Cleopatra* off the stage for almost one hundred years.

Historically, the play picks up the career of Mark Antony about five years after the events depicted in *Julius Caesar.* In the division of the Roman Empire among the triumvirs—Antony, Lepidus, and Octavius Caesar—Antony has become ruler of the East. When the play opens he is in Alexandria, completely under the spell of Cleopatra. He has given himself over to a life of idleness and feasting, ignoring his administrative responsibilities to Rome. Finally, under the combined pressure of news of the death of Fulvia, his wife, who had been leading a rebellion against Octavius Caesar; a report that the Parthian army is on the march; and letters telling that Sextus Pompeius, son of Pompey the Great, is in revolt against Caesar by sea, Antony returns to Rome. At a meeting of the triumvirs, Caesar and Antony trade recriminations. To reestablish amity, Agrippa, a general, suggests that Antony marry Octavia, Caesar's sister. Antony agrees and Caesar approves the match. In spite of his marriage, Antony determines to return to Egypt. But first, peace is made with Pompey, and Ventidius, Antony's general, succeeds in overcoming the Parthians. Enmity again flares up between Caesar and Antony when the latter, now in Athens with Octavia, learns that Caesar has resumed his war against Pompey and has seized Lepidus. At Octavia's request, Antony permits his wife to go to Rome to restore harmony. In the meantime Antony returns to Cleopatra, which gives Caesar an excuse for marching on him. In the battles that follow, Antony, under the influence of Cleopatra psychologically, makes wrong judgments leading to his defeat. Afraid of his wrath, Cleopatra sends Antony a false report that she has killed herself. He resolves to join her in death. Learning before he expires that she lives, he requests to be taken to her and dies, reunited, in her arms. Cleopatra, out of love for Antony and out of pride that she not be paraded as a captive in Rome, takes her own life.

In contrast to the four great tragedies that precede it, *Antony and Cleopatra* does not concern itself with the problem of evil. Instead, in compressing Plutarch's narrative account, Shakespeare dramatizes the struggle between personal desire and public duty in a great man. Although the title stresses the importance of both Antony and Cleopatra, the emphasis, as the

ILLUSTRATION FROM A 1790 EDITION OF SHAKE-SPEARE'S *Antony and Cleopatra* (NEW YORK PUBLIC LIBRARY)

opening lines reveal, is on "The triple pillar of the world transform'd / Into a strumpet's fool." Thus the conflict may be said to center on government versus love. The settings of the play reinforce this conflict, for, as the action moves back and forth from Egypt to Rome, Egypt—the world of love—is portrayed as a sensual land of idleness and pleasure, whereas Rome—beset by internal and external strife—is a stern world where duty is paramount.

It is against this political background that Shakespeare presents his story of middle-aged romance. In choosing love over duty, Antony's emotions overcome his reason, leading not only to his own death but to the deaths of innocent persons—among them his devoted followers Enobarbus and Eros—and to a power struggle that destroys the triumvirate. Yet Shakespeare does not mock that love; he portrays it as all-consuming, time- and space-shattering. Although Cleopatra is a coquette and a completely sensual woman, she loves Antony as much as he loves her. By the end of the play (the last act focuses on Cleopatra) her love has become purified, and her physical death becomes unimportant as she envisions an afterlife with Antony.

Of particular importance in *Antony and Cleopatra* is the poetic diction. Not only is it used to infuse sexuality into a Cleopatra played on the Elizabethan stage by a boy actor, but it is employed through imagery patterns emphasizing great space, distance, and the gigantic, godlike qualities of Antony to give insight into the vastness of a love for which Antony would "Let Rome in Tiber melt, and the wide arch / Of the rang'd empire fall."

An outstanding edition of *Antony and Cleopatra* is the New Arden Edition (1954), edited by M. R. Ridley.—W. G.

Anzengruber, Ludwig. See GERMANY: *nineteenth century.*

Aoi-no-ue (fourteenth century). A Japanese NOH play in two parts by Zeami MOTOKIYO. *Aoi-no-ue* has long been held in special favor in Japan and is possibly the most familiar specimen of the *noh* among Western readers. It belongs to the category in the noh canon called "revengeful ghost pieces." The boldness of the stage symbolism doubtless accounts for some of the peculiar fascination it has held for Western eyes. The person for whom the play is named and certainly one of the chief figures in its story nowhere appears as a live actor. Lady Aoi is imagined as gravely ill, indeed almost unconscious. She is represented by an embroidered kimono folded and placed to the front of the stage. Here she is considered as present on her sickbed. The story concerns the evil charm that the revengeful ghost of Princess Rokujo, Aoi's rival for the love of Prince Genji, has inflicted on Aoi. In Part I Princess Rokujo, though dead, is seen in the form of a noblewoman. In Part II she appears as the ghost of a woman transformed into an evil spirit. Thus both protagonist and antagonist are symbolically presented. The prayers of a priest effect cures in both the natural and supernatural worlds. Lady Aoi is revived, wholly delivered from her sinister incubus, while the ghost of the Princess Rokujo is delivered from the evil spirit haunting her and her salvation in the Buddhist paradise is assured.

This play relies for its effectiveness more heavily on dance and mime and less on poetry than is the case in most major works for the noh stage. Nonetheless, it shows the noh theater in one of its most effective moments.

For the best comment and translation in English, see *Japanese Noh Drama,* selected and translated by the Special Noh Committee, Japanese Translation Committee (Vol. II, 1959).—H. W. W.

Apollinaire, Guillaume. See THE BREASTS OF TIRESIAS.

Arab drama. That there were many dramatic elements in ancient Middle Eastern, Assyrian, and Phoenician religions and legends is a fact that cannot be contested. A good example of these legends is that of Osiris, god of good and life, who is murdered by Set, god of evil and nothingness. Isis, Osiris' wife, gathers the flesh of her husband, until he is finally resurrected. Horus, their son, helps his father bring life and good back to the world. The idea of conflict between good and evil and the incarnation of ethical and natural principles into a human form, so essential for any dramatic literary form, are all present in the legend. The story has also found its way into an Egyptian form of dramatic performance quite similar to medieval mystery plays. The most ancient pharaonic play, composed in 3200 B.C., deals with the theme of the creation of the world by Betah, god of Memphis. The Isis-Osiris-Horus legend is introduced later in the play, which is concluded with the coronation of Horus as king of Egypt.

Though primarily religious in content, some plays that achieved a degree of freedom from the religious ritual and mysteries were performed for the people outside the temples. Nevertheless, the plays stayed highly ritualistic in form and specifically religious in content. Ancient Egyptian drama never developed in a way even remotely similar to ancient Greek drama. Various reasons have been cited to account for this phenomenon. It is believed that the anthropomorphism of ancient Greek legend helped liberate ancient Greek drama from the strictly religious ritual. Although the gods of ancient Middle Eastern legends may have some human attributes, they are still primarily superhuman. Osiris never becomes a bull to rape Europa, nor does the Egyptian trinity engage in some of the gross activities of the Olympians. The gap between the human and the divine was too wide to be bridged, and therefore the ancient Egyptian theater remained and died in the temple.

Be that as it may, the spread of Arab Islamic culture brought whatever there was of dramatic performances to an end. Like Judaism, Islam frowns upon any form of representation or impersonation. Moreover, the Arab literary tradition in poetry is, first and foremost, a lyrical tradition. The ancient Arab poet, when he sang of the heroic warfares of his tribe, preferred the personal and the lyrical mode to the narrative, epic, or dramatic one. What helped reinforce this lyrical, antidramatic bias was the absence of a body of legends or myths similar to those of ancient Greece. These factors may perhaps help account for the fact that the ancient Arabs rather accurately and creatively translated, commented upon, and interpreted most of Aristotle's works; yet when it came to his *Poetics* Arab translators missed the whole point of the critical work. They were so perplexed with the contents of the *Poetics* that the terms "tragedy" and "comedy" were translated with the terms *madḥ* ("eulogy") and *hija'* ("satire"), respectively. The dramatic form being so alien to the Arab imagination, it is no wonder that the ancient Arabs had no dramatic literature of their own; nor did they translate any plays from other cultures, be it Greek or Persian.

If the ancient Arab literary tradition was hostile to drama and dramatic performances, the folk Arab imagination proved more hospitable and fertile. The Arab people, as opposed to the Arab literati, knew various forms of dramatic or semidramatic forms.

Arab storytellers, in order to impress their audience, acted out some of the situations of the stories they were narrating. The Arabic *hakawātī* ("storyteller") performed amusing imitations of behavior and speech. He often used a handkerchief and a cudgel and at times even changed his headgear in order to enliven his mimicry.

The term *qaragūz* ("the black eye") designates a type of dramatic performance in which hand puppets stood for certain human types or characteristics. The manipulator of the puppets hid himself behind a curtain and mimicked the supposed human voice of the character. The main protagonist of the play was called Qaragūz—a type of a proletarian Everyman, who complained about everything and never missed a chance to rant against fate. The qaragūz is still popular all over the Arab world, and there are some modern Arab popular artists, such as Shukūkū, who have tried successfully in the 1950's to revive the art. Salāḥ Jahīn, the contemporary Egyptian poet, wrote for the marionette theater of Cairo several plays that are modernized versions of the ancient qaragūz.

A shadow play is a short one-act play called *bāba,* performed by puppets made of paper or leather. The puppets were moved either with the help of sticks inserted in holes previously made for the purpose or with the help of strings attached to the puppets. A piece of white linen was hung up, and the shadows of the puppets were cast upon it. The *muqaddam* moved the figures and mimicked the voices of some of the characters with the help of an assistant.

The shadow plays were performed throughout the Arab world, and they date as far back as the thirteenth century, perhaps earlier. The shadow play, like most folk dramatic performances, has a strong comic element brought about by puns, the stress laid on obscene elements, and by the introduction of typically funny characters, such as Afyuni (the opium addict).

A good example of a shadow play is the one written by Muhammad Ibn Daniyāl (c. 1248–c. 1311), an Egyptian physician, entitled *Taif al-Khayāl* ("The Spirit of Imagination" or "The Spirit of the Shadow"). Prince Wiṣāl is appointed a nominal caliph by the ruler of Egypt, who wants to give some kind of moral support to his regime. When Wiṣāl appears, he is dressed as a soldier and describes himself in the most heroic language (as cunning as a serpent, as ferocious as fire, more thirsty than sand). His clerk enters to read a royal decree appointing Wiṣāl king of all the lunatics and making his kingdom include all the relics of ancient Egypt and all its hills and tombs. When he decides to get married, Prince Wiṣāl is not any luckier. Upon learning that Wiṣāl has been re-

duced to poverty, the matchmaker gets him an ugly wife. At the end of the play Wiṣāl goes on a pilgrimage to atone for his sins!

Rustic plays of comical nature were not uncommon in Egypt in the eighteenth century. Carsten Niebhur, a Danish traveler, saw such a rustic play in Cairo in 1780. The plot of the play centered around one episode repeated over and over again. Some travelers are attracted to the tent of a pretty lady who robs them of their money, strips them naked, and finally drives them away. Another performance, less crude in content but not in structure, was attended a few years afterward by E. W. Lane. An Egyptian peasant is beaten and is finally sent to jail because he could not pay his debts. His wife liberates him after bribing the village chief and other influential persons.

The *ta'zia* ("consolation") plays, a Persian genre, deal with the murder of Ḥasan, Ḥusain, and other members of 'Ali's family. Some ta'zia plays were translated and performed in Arabic. The ta'zia is the only folk genre that deals with tragic subject matter. Although the qaragūz does deal with the darker aspects of life, the hero is both fatalistic and submissive, and therefore there are no tragic dilemmas or suffering.

Whether tragic or comic, crude or sophisticated, such folk dramas as the shadow play, the dramatized mimicry, the qaragūz, the rustic plays, and the ta'zia helped keep alive an interest in drama in the Arab world.

The folk tradition, however, never produced a full-fledged drama in the real sense of the word. Modern Arab drama is a wholly foreign art transplanted onto virgin soil. It is significant that the first theatrical performance in the Arab world was an adaptation of Molière's *L'Avare.* It was adapted and performed in 1848 by Marūn al-Naqqāsh (1817–1855), who had spent a few years in Italy. His second play, *Abū'l-Hasan al-mughaffal* ("Abu'l-Hasan, the Fool," written 1850), is an adaptation of Molière's *L'Etourdi* mixed with material from the *Arabian Nights* and is more creatively adapted than his first play. Al-Naqqāsh's career tells in a nutshell the story of the modern Arab theater. A child of the Western cultural tradition, the Arab theater has striven toward an assertion of an Arab identity through a return to, and a rediscovery of, the Arab heritage.

Though Arab drama made its start in Syria, it had to flee Turkish oppression to survive. Many Syrian troupes settled in Cairo and performed there. Salīm Khalīl al-Naqqash (Marūn's nephew) wrote the first entirely Arab play: a five-act drama entitled *al-Ẓalūm* ("The Tyrant," 1878). It deals from a critical viewpoint with the intrigues and life in an Oriental court.

Besides the various Syrian troupes and playwrights, a Jewish Egyptian named Ya'qūb ibn Ṣanū' (1839–1912) made a significant contribution toward the creation of Arab drama with his comedies and operettas. Many of them were performed in the spoken dialect of Egypt rather than in classical Arabic, thereby revolutionizing the theater. One of his most important plays, and the only one that has survived, is *Molière Miṣr wa-mā yuqāsīh* ("Egypt's Molière and His Troubles," pub. 1912). It is modeled after Molière's *L'Impromptu de Versailles* and its characters are as fixed and as "typical" as those in the *commedia dell'arte*. The play tells of the problems that face a pioneering figure such as Ṣanū' in his attempts to found a new Arab theater.

The contribution of Sheikh Salāma Ḥijāzī (1855–1917) was to move songs to the very center of Arab drama and make them an integral part of the dramatic action. Mention should also be made of Najīb al-Rīhānī (1891–1949), another talented Syrian. Like many other Arab playwrights of this period, he started with translations and adaptations and passed on to original creations. In *Ḥukm Qarāqūsh* ("The Reign of Qarāqūsh," 1945) a simple man is put on the throne of the tyrant Qarāqūsh for one day. This gives him the chance to demonstrate the relevance of a common-sense philosophy of life and the emptiness of power and its trappings. Al-Rīhānī, like Sanū', made the theater a popular art by dealing with social problems in a comic way. The *ancien régime* in Egypt was so threatened by Al-Rīhānī's plays that it banned some of them.

Finally, it was due to the efforts of George Abyaḍ (1880–1962) that classical drama was introduced to the Arab world. He proved, through his brilliant performances in plays such as *Oedipus Rex* and *Macbeth* the possibilities of the classical theater.

The initial stage of dependence on the Western theater came to an end when Aḥmad Shauqī (1868–1932), the leading Arab poet of his time, wrote in 1893 the first version of his first tragedy, '*Ali Bek al-Kabīr* (" 'Ali Bey the Great," 1932), while studying in France. The play takes place in the court of 'Ali Bey, the Mamlūk ruler of Egypt. One of his slave girls, Amāl, is torn between her duty to 'Ali Bey and her love for his son. Besides its inherent interest as one of the first Arab plays, '*Ali Bek al-Kabīr* reveals Shauqī's interest in Arab history and his genius for socio-historical reconstruction.

Shauqī's *Majnūn Lailā* ("The Madman of Lailā," translated into English with Arabic title; written 1916, prod. 1927) deals with the ancient Arab legend of Qais, who was so enamored of Lailā that he went mad when his beloved refused to marry him. Lailā's refusal was based on the belief that Qais dishonored her by making their love public. The play contains some of Shauqī's best love poetry and also demonstrates his ability to create characters who have a measure of psychological truth.

Maṣra' Cleopatra (*The Fall of Cleopatra*, 1930) focuses on the relationship between Cleopatra and Antonius and its tragic aftermath. The main plot is coupled with a subplot that tells of Helena's love for her Egyptian guard, Ḥabī. Though Helena commits suicide with Cleopatra, she is saved in the nick of time, and the play closes with Helena's marriage to Ḥabī.

All of Shauqī's plays, with the exception of his comedy *al-Sitt Hudā* (pub. 1936, prod. c. 1957), are written in rhymed Arabic poetry and deal with historical or semihistorical material. (*Amīrat al-Andalus* ["The Princess of Andalusia," 1932] is in prose, yet it deals with ancient Arab history.) Rhymed verse, used brilliantly by Shauqī in his lyrical poetry, did not prove an adequate tool for his verse dramas, however. It forced him to subject dramatic action and characterization to the requisites of the rhyme. Moreover, trained in the tradition of ancient Arab poetry, Shauqī could not break away from

the merely rhetorical and lyrical. His characters show a propensity toward declamation and lyrical outbursts, which have a tenuous relationship, if any, with the main dramatic movement. Many of Shauqī's plays have two plots, which are seldom well integrated. Besides making it difficult for the spectators to get fully involved in the action, it also reduces the poignancy of dramatic conflict. Shauqī's dramas also are studded with unnecessary details that divert the attention from the main plot. Yet it was largely due to Shauqī's efforts that writing for the theater became a respectable literary activity. His dramatic achievement, tenuous as it is, encouraged younger playwrights to realize the possibility of creating an indigenous Arab theater.

The contemporary playwright 'Azīz Abāza is an heir of the Shauqī tradition, seen, for example, in his play *Al-'Abbāsa* (1947). Like Shauqī's plays, it is written in fully rhymed verse and deals with an ancient Arab subject. In 1957 Abāza wrote and produced *Awrāq al-Kharīf* ("Autumn Leaves"), in which he turned to modern Egypt to develop a more modern form of his verse line. Many critics do not consider his attempts quite successful. Like Shauqī's plays, Abāza's are more lyrical than dramatic.

It was not until the 1960's that Arab poetic drama emerged as a literary genre completely independent from Arab lyrical poetry. This became possible only after technical innovations were introduced in the late 1940's in the Arab *qaṣīda* ("poem"). The long, rigid verse line was divided according to the structural need of the poem. Uniformity of rhyme throughout the poem was also abandoned in favor of a more flexible, casual rhyme scheme. The new verse line made it possible for Arab playwrights to write verse dramas that are not necessarily declamatory and lyrical. The revolution in form corresponded to a revolution in content. The poets could now turn to less traditional subjects than those dealt with by Shauqī and Abāza.

'Abdul-Raḥmān al-Sharqāwī wrote two verse dramas in this new tradition: *Jamīla Bū-ḥrid* (pub. 1962) and *Al Fata Muhran* (pub. 1966). The first play deals with the heroic struggles and agonies of the Algerian freedom-fighter Jamīla. Salāḥ 'Abdul-Ṣabūr, the leading living Arab poet, turned to the classical tradition only to deal with the life and passions of the sufi heretic al-Ḥalāj, in his only verse drama, *Maṣra' al-Ḥalāj* ("The Fall of al-Ḥalāj," pub. 1965).

Najīb Surūr tried to model his verse drama *Yāssīn wa Bahiya* ("Yāssīn and Bahiya," pub. 1965) on the folk verse tale. The narrator of a short folk song asks Bahiya who killed Yāssīn. The answer, provided by the play, is that the feudalist pasha is the culprit, because Yāssīn tried to protect his beloved Bahiya from being dishonored. Though he wrote the play in classical Arabic, Surūr used a few colloquial words. The long narrative parts of the play are sung or narrated by a minstrel with the help of a chorus; the dramatic parts are acted out. The outcome of this successful experimentation with form and content is a totally Arab play of which the source can be said to be local folk tradition and the imagination of the playwright. The mingling of the dramatic and the narrative is of particular interest because it solves the problem of trying to write a play for a people not very accustomed to seeing purely dramatic performances.

Though there is an impressive tradition of modern verse Arab drama, most modern Arab plays are in prose. Until 1920, the Arab theater was mainly musical and lyrical, but after that date prose dramas became more common. *Al Sulṭān Ṣalāḥ al-Dīn wa-mamlaket Urushalīm* ("Saladin and the Kingdom of Jerusalem," pub. 1923) by Faraḥ Anṭūn (1874–1922) is a good example of early prose drama. The play tells of the life of Saladin before his preparation for the final battle with the Crusaders. The historical event is embedded in a web of romantic intrigues. The language Anṭūn uses is basically classical Arabic, though his diction is so simple that it could be easily understood by the illiterate. The choice of subject matter and the didactic way the playwright treats it is a manifestation of the resurgence of pan-Arab feelings.

Taufiq al-Hakīm (1898–   ), however, is the towering genius of Arab prose drama. He was sent to Paris early in life to study law but spent his time there attending theatrical and musical performances. Back in Egypt, he practiced law, though again he had his heart in the world of letters, especially the theater.

Al-Ḥakīm is a very prolific writer whose genius is still quite impressionable and hospitable to change. Some of his plays are labeled "theater of ideas" for lack of a better term. Such plays were not written for performance. The action takes place in the minds of the characters, more or less. The philosophical interest, as in a Platonic dialogue, supersedes the dramatic interest. Every play is based on an "as if" hypothesis. In *Shahrazād* ("Scheherazade," pub. 1934, prod. in Paris 1955), for instance, the hero, Shahryār, becomes literally a pure mind liberated from the heart and the body. Shahrazād, the eternal woman, tries to win him back to his humanness. *Ahl al-Kahf* (*People of the Cave*, pub. 1933) is another good example of this genre. The main theme is man's relation to time. The plot is derived from a Koranic story. Three Christians fleeing Roman persecution take refuge with their dog in a cave and sleep for three hundred years. When they go back to their city, they cannot adjust themselves to the new conditions and prefer to return to their cave and die. The abstract confrontation between man and time is made highly dramatic and concrete through the careful manipulation of specific details of character. Al-Ḥakīm wrote several other closet dramas, such as *Pygmalion* (pub. 1942) and *Riḥla ila al-Ghad* ("A Trip to the Future," pub. 1957), but none of them comes even remotely close to the quality of *Ahl al-Kahf*.

Al-Ḥakīm wrote many plays of social interest also. However, in 1952, after the Egyptian revolution, the interest was given a new impetus. His play *Al-Aidī al-nā'ima* ("The Soft Hands," pub. 1954) gives a comic picture of social classes, which, since the Egyptian revolution, have ceased to play any role in society. *Al-Ṣafqa* ("The Bargain," pub. 1956) tells of the peasant's love of the earth, his determination to fight for it, and his common-sense logic. Though the play is written in classical prose, al-Ḥakīm used many colloquial idioms and even syntax. He also borrowed some dramatic devices from the popular theater, such as folk songs and dances.

Ya Tāli' al-Shagara (*The Tree Climber*, pub. 1962)

is *sui generis*. Like al-Ḥakīm's closet dramas, this play deals in a sense with a philosophical hypothesis, yet unlike them it is quite dramatic and proved a popular success. The hero of the play is an artist so dedicated to the tree of art that he neglects his fertile wife, who stands for life. His hostility to his wife leads him to murder her. The philosophical conflict between art and life is made concrete through the use of many folk symbols and situations. The title of the play itself is taken from a nursery rhyme.

Maḥmūd Taimūr (1894–   ) is the second most important dramatist in the Arab world. Like al-Ḥakīm, he was born and raised in Egypt. Though he has an aristocratic background. Taimūr's characters have a certain lifelike quality and seem to be honest imitations of everyday society in Egypt. His prose is a mixture of colloquial and classical Arabic. One of his best known plays is *Al-Makhba' Raqm 13* ("Shelter No. 13," pub. 1941). When a heterogeneous, socially mixed group of people find refuge in an air-raid shelter, the value of each person is determined by his usefulness rather than his social class. The cake vendor, who has food with him, becomes the most powerful as well as the most important figure. When the rescue party approaches, social differences become distinct again.

Like Taimūr and al-Ḥakīm, Yūsif Idrīs, an Egyptian physician, is a story writer turned dramatist. His play *Jumhūriyat Faraḥāt* ("Faraḥāt's Republic," pub. 1963) was written first as a short story and was later adapted to the stage by the author himself. In the play, a police sergeant, oppressed by his work, dozes in his office and dreams of a new world. He dreams that a rich Indian merchant loses a very expensive ring, which is returned to him by a poor worker named Faraḥāt. The merchant rewards Faraḥāt for his honesty with a large sum of money. Faraḥāt invests the money in industry, builds factories, makes the desert green, and brings prosperity to all his people. When the sergeant wakes up, he discovers to his sorrow that his dream hero is nothing but a leftist militant under arrest, whom the sergeant must transfer from the police station to a prison. The sergeant looks at the real Faraḥāt for a moment and then takes the necessary steps for transferring the prisoner.

In his latest play, *Al-Fārāfir* ("The Servants," pub. 1964), Idrīs has tried to evolve a new technique independent of any Western dramatic traditions. His characters are no longer the realistic individuals of domestic drama, but rather embodiments of a complex mixture of social and philosophical principles. His characters achieve, however, a high degree of credibility, even human specificity. The plot unfolds through the conflict revealed during the characters' long philosophical discussions and through their conversations with the audience. The use of allegory, the simultaneously didactic and fatalistic tone, and the deep sense of the basically comic nature of the human condition are testimony of the play's indigenous roots.

Studies on Arab drama, in the Western world, are quite meager. Jacob M. Landau's *Studies in the Arab Theater and Cinema* (1958) is a good, comprehensive introduction to the subject. The book deals with the awakening of dramatic interest among the Arabs prior to and during the nineteenth and twentieth centuries and with the works of the major Arab play-

wrights. The book has a very good bibliography.—
A. M. E.

aragoto. One of the most popular and long-established styles in Japanese acting, *aragoto* derives its name from a word signifying violence in speech and action. As a deliberately cultivated manner in the theater it was both invented and perfected by the great *kabuki* actor Ichikawa Danjuro I (1660–1704). One view of its historical background is that it derived from the manner of portraying in songs and popular plays the legendary hero and giant Kimpira. In developing this style to its ultimate, Danjuro I deliberately pitted his own Yedo theater against the tender and romantic style favored in the houses of Kyoto and Osaka. Japanese taste in regard to its heroes, as in so many other respects, went to extremes. On one hand was the warrior hero, a superman, robust and swashbuckling; on the other was the effeminate young lover, as devoted to the tender aspect of life as his counterpart to the violent.

Actors trained in aragoto make their entrances and exits along the *hanamichi,* or bridgeway to the stage, in a sequence of bounds, turning in six directions. They have lurid make-up, wear ponderous, gaudy costumes with large-scale designs, strut rather than walk, shout at the top of their lungs, and frequently break into exclamations unknown to the dictionary. They are leaders in violent melodrama, much as actors in the *sewamono,* or common people's plays, are masters in pathetic melodrama. Actors using the aragoto became favorite subjects for Japanese artists; thus many of the best-known theatrical prints represent a favorite actor assuming a melodramatic pose, or *mie.*

Descriptions of aragoto may be found in *The Kabuki Theatre of Japan* (1955) by A. C. Scott and in *Japanese Theatre* (1952) by Faubion Bowers.—
H. W. W.

Architecte et l'empereur d'Assyrie, L' ("The Architect and the Emperor of Assyria," 1966). A play by Fernando ARRABAL. This drama of two characters makes such demands upon the actors that their skill and power in sheer performance dominate everything else. In his short comment at the end of the published text, Arrabal says that he had hoped to fuse in this play humor and poetry, panic and love, and thereby create a text that would recall the fantasies of Don Quixote, the nightmares of Alice, the delirium of K, and the dreams of an IBM machine.

The architect and the emperor meet on a desert island, where they create endless dramatic situations wherein one affronts the other. They constantly exchange roles: the emperor becomes the architect and the architect becomes the emperor in a series of duets imposed upon them by their life together. They are mother and son, husband and wife, tyrant and victim, judge and criminal. They are condemned to being together in love and hate. Finally, one ends by devouring the other, thus realizing the dream of unity and communion that obsessed both of them.

The language of this text has the fury, aggressiveness, and provocation that is associated with Arrabal. The playwright is doubtless dramatizing his personal obsessions, but he succeeds in giving them a meaning that goes far beyond any personal interpretation.—
W. F.

Arden, John (1930–   ). English playwright. Arden was born in Barnsley, Yorkshire, and received his early education at the local elementary school. Subsequently he studied architecture at Cambridge and at the Edinburgh College of Art and worked as an architectural assistant from 1955 to 1957. Since then Arden has been a full-time playwright.

Arden began writing plays at about the age of sixteen and continued while at Cambridge and Edinburgh. His first professional production was a radio play called *The Life of Man,* broadcast in 1956. In 1957 *The Waters of Babylon* was given a one-night production at the Royal Court Theatre, and it was with the support of this theater that Arden gained his foothold in the profession. *Live Like Pigs* (1958) and SERJEANT MUSGRAVE'S DANCE both appeared at the Royal Court. In 1959–1960 he received the Fellowship in Playwriting at Bristol University and wrote *The Happy Haven* (1960). Since then Arden has maintained a steady output of large-scale plays: *Ironhand* (1961), adapted from Goethe's play *Götz von Berlichingen; The Workhouse Donkey* (1963); *Armstrong's Last Goodnight* (1964); and *Left-Handed Liberty* (1965). In collaboration with his wife, Margaretta D'Arcy, he has also produced a series of pieces for student or amateur casts to be performed in community conditions. These include: *The Business of Good Government* (1960); *Ars Longa Vita Brevis* (1964); *Friday's Hiding* (1966); and *The Royal Pardon* (1966). There are also two television plays: *Soldier, Soldier* (1960) and *Wet Fish* (1961).

This is the most varied body of work to have come from any of the new English playwrights, but—and perhaps for that reason—Arden has not proved a box-office author. He has been much played by amateur and student groups, but up to the end of 1967, he has not been produced in the West End. The first critical reaction to him was one of bewilderment. *The Waters of Babylon* is a grotesque satire on a financial scheme of the Macmillan government; then came *Live Like Pigs,* a harsh social comedy showing the conflict between a lower-middle-class family and a tribe of vagabond squatters on a housing estate; and then *Serjeant Musgrave's Dance,* a colonial war fable with a late Victorian setting; and finally *The Happy Haven,* a comedy about senility, set in an old folks' home and played in masks. The sheer diversity of these plays was one source of confusion. Others were Arden's refusal to show a preference for the issues presented in his plays, and the fact that a supposedly avant-garde playwright was lacing his work with great naked chunks of poetry, this in the immediate wake of the verse drama movement.

Arden is more cooperative than most playwrights in explaining his intentions. In the first place, he says, it is not the playwright's job to support causes or to judge character; it is to show conflict. Audiences are not convinced by sermons, but if a situation were presented to them "to hold, as it might be a ripe apple, so that they could look at it all round and decide for themselves by touch and feel whether it is sound or not—then one might have some hope of effecting a change in somebody's heart." In this respect, Arden is more Brechtian than Brecht. Where verse is concerned, he rejects T. S. Eliot's prescription for smuggling it in unobtrusively in favor of making clear divisions between prose and verse by analogy with the old Celtic bards, whose practice was to improvise most of the story in prose and draw on fixed traditional poems at moments of emotional tension.

As this analogy suggests, Arden's stylistic models are not confined to theatrical tradition. He uses past literature as a source of creative power and has drawn much from epic poetry and from ballads. (*Live Like Pigs* could best be described as an expanded ballad.) Arden has also sought to revive the old comedy of intrigue and the Jonsonian "comedy of humours." This eclecticism derives in part from his dissatisfaction with existing theatrical models and in particular with existing theatrical speech. To enrich itself, Arden says in a magazine article, "drama has to go out into the hedges and ditches like the man in the parable in search of the lame, halt, and blind." As in his handling of language and form, so in his choice of subjects, Arden aims to use the past as a source of vital meaning for the present. *Serjeant Musgrave's Dance*, for instance, comments on Britain's military presence in Cyprus from a vantage point of the Crimean War. In *Armstrong's Last Goodnight*, the history of a sixteenth-century Scottish border chieftain is related to Lumumba's Congo.

The objections to Arden are that he is a cold writer; that he adopts comic forms without displaying much personal sense of fun; and that, for all his concern with structure, audiences tend to get lost inside his plays. None of these objections diminishes his importance. He occupies a unique position on the postwar English scene as a major dramatist pledged to the ideal of community theater and as an artist whose imagination operates in harmony with his social purpose.

There is no collected edition of Arden's plays. Most of them are available in isolated volumes, published from 1957 on.—I. W.

Arden of Feversham (pub. 1592). An anonymous Elizabethan tragedy generally ascribed to Thomas KYD. Based upon the case history of the murder of a husband by his wife and her lover in 1551, the play is the earliest extant example of domestic tragedy, a genre whose characters are drawn from the middle or lower class and which emphasizes realism rather than heroism.

The action focuses on the repeated attempts of Mistress Alice Arden and Mosbie, her lover, to murder Mistress Arden's husband. The couple is finally successful, but they are soon caught and brought to justice.

The play is coarse and uneven but it contains several scenes of intense emotional power and an extraordinary dramatic character in Mistress Arden.

WOODCUT FROM THE 1633 EDITION OF *Arden of Feversham*

Lacking in subtlety and total credibility, her characterization has a strength and vigor that is nevertheless dramatically memorable.—E. Q.

Aretino, Pietro (1492–1556). Italian writer and playwright. Of humble birth, Aretino was a painter in his native Arezzo and in Perugia before he moved to Rome. In Rome, thanks to his lively satiric wit, he was well known in papal court circles and came under the protection of Leo X. In his journalistic writings, *Pronostici* ("Prognostications," issued annually from 1527) and *Lettere volanti* (*The Letters*, published in six volumes from 1537 to 1557), he bragged that he would "tear apart the names of the great with the fangs of truth." These publications gained him not only influential support but also mortal hatred, and he was forced in 1526 to leave Rome forever. In 1527 he went to Venice, putting his pen to the service of the Venetian Republic. He remained there until his death, leading a life equally divided between literature and vice.

Besides the very lively and obscene *Ragionamenti amorosi* (*Ragionamenti, The Harlot's Dialogues,* 1534–1539) and various moral and edifying treatises with which he attempted to gain the cardinal's hat, he wrote five comedies: *La Cortigiana* (*The Courtesan,* 1526), *Il Marescalco* ("The Captain," 1527), *La Talanta* (1534), *Lo Ipocrito* ("The Hypocrite," 1527), and *Il Filosofo* ("The Philosopher," 1544). In 1546 he wrote *Orazia,* a tragedy in verse, variously judged by posterity but regarded today as not in harmony with his true satiric gifts. Viewed as part of the Italian Renaissance, Aretino's comedies represent the best attempt to oppose the literary comedy that imitated classical Latin models. His is a comic theater completely free in its form, reflecting with great spontaneity and immediacy contemporary life and customs. His attempt succeeded only in part, for with the exception of *Il Marescalco,* which retraces the plot of Plautus' *Casina,* Aretino's plots lack solid structure and are sometimes arbitrary in their development. It is, however, his very indifference to models and to formal preconceptions that allows him to exercise freely his satiric spirit. It enables him to paint with extraordinary realism a world of swindlers, go-betweens, pedants, and courtiers. Out of the real world of the sixteenth century he gathers together characters unknown in traditional lists of character types. One of them is the protagonist of *Lo Ipocrito,* who has been justly labeled a precursor of Molière's Tartuffe.—L. L.

Argentina. See SPANISH AMERICA.

Arichandra (tenth century). The most highly esteemed of classical plays in the Tamil language, a tongue long spoken in southern parts of India. *Arichandra* is also one of the chief examples of Indian Buddhist drama. Based on a popular legend concerning the life and trials of Buddhist sainthood, it depicts the adventures of a king suddenly converted from a life of pleasure to a life of religious services, charity, and meditation. The play is anonymous and its ascription to the grammarian and scholar Regna Pillay has little or no significance since he is clearly no more than the reviser of one of its versions. Its English translator, Mutu Coomara Swamy, explains that he consulted several manuscripts in addition to printed texts. The work is presumed to derive from the period of decadence in

PIETRO ARETINO (NEW YORK PUBLIC LIBRARY)

the Sanskrit drama following the tenth century.

The play tells the story of Arichandra, of all kings the most powerful and least corruptible. His integrity produces jealousy on the part of the divine sage Wis Wamitra, who holds that there is no completely just man on earth. The god Indra, who questions this sardonic view, permits the sage to tempt Arichandra, much as God allowed Satan to tempt Job. The sage takes full advantage of the rule that compels any man of pious mind to comply with a brahman's request. Applying this test to the king, characters in various disguises force him to renounce in turn his kingdom, his wealth, his queen, his son. Arichandra sinks at last to the state of a *chandala,* or public executioner. He refuses to burn the body of his own son because the queen cannot pay the required burial fee. Through an error the queen is later accused of murdering their child. She is brought to Arichandra for decapitation. Obedient to the law, he is about to perform his gruesome function when his sword is transformed into a string of pearls and the gods descend to right all wrongs. The dead son is restored to life and the king and his queen to their kingdom. It is revealed that his tormentors have been deities in disguise.

The play is skillfully written, similar in scope and narrative method to the classics of the Sanskrit stage but free from many of the conventions of the Sanskrit theater. The play was revived with unusual success in the latter part of the nineteenth century by the playwright and producer Visnudas Bhave, founder of the Marathi theater, performing for the community in the neighborhood of Bombay. When his version was given before the raja of Sangli, the raja was so moved that he himself rushed onto the stage to stop the tormenting of the king. Plays dealing with the same Buddhist legend have formed an important part in the living theater in Tibet. See TIBET.

Descriptions of modernized versions of the play as performed in India may be found in *Theatre in India* (1962) by Balwant Gargi. A critical analysis is contained in *The Classical Drama of India* (1963) by Henry W. Wells.—H. W. W.

Ariosto, Lodovico (1474–1533). Italian poet and playwright. The son of a courtier of the dukes of Este at Ferrara, Ariosto abandoned his legal studies in 1494 in order to dedicate himself to letters and to his favorite classics. In 1503 he entered the service of Cardinal Ippolito d'Este, to whom he dedicated in 1516 the first edition of his chivalric poem *Orlando Furioso.* Content with his studies and the simple life, Ariosto remained all his life in the service of the Este family, undertaking various diplomatic and administrative chores, but refusing in 1523 to accept an ambassadorial appointment to the papal court of Clement VII. Instead, he spent most of his time correcting *Orlando Furioso,* completed in 1532, as well as composing other poetic works. The passion that the dukes of Ferrara had for festivities and for plays made that city the theatrical capital of Italy at the time. Ariosto directed the construction, within the ducal palace, of one of the first Italian theaters. Thus endowed with a permanent stage, he was able to present, between 1508 and 1528, his own comedies. He sometimes took part in the plays as an actor and also participated in their preparation.

Ariosto wrote five comedies: *La Cassaria* (*The Strong Box,* 1508); *I Suppositi* (*Supposes,* 1509); *Il*

LODOVICO ARIOSTO (THEATRE COLLECTION, NEW YORK PUBLIC LIBRARY AT LINCOLN CENTER)

ARIOSTO.

Negromante (The Necromancer, written 1520, prod. 1530); La Lena; and *Gli Studenti* ("The Students"), which was never completed. The definitive versions of all these plays, which Ariosto provided in the final years of his life, are in verse, but *La Cassaria* and *I Suppositi* were first written in prose.

Ariosto shared with other Renaissance literary men an admiration for the Latin dramatists. He sought a classic elegance of style and form and attempted to imitate the six-foot iambic line of Plautus by employing a hendecasyllabic line ending in a *sdrucciolo.* His plots follow the normal outlines of the Latin theater. They depend on events surrounding frustrated lovers, misunderstandings, injuries inflicted on covetous old men through jokes, and final recognitions. Indeed, in *La Cassaria* the imitation of classical types and situations is evident, and the action takes place on the Greek island of Metellinus. In *I Suppositi, Il Negromante, Gli Studenti,* and *La Lena,* however, the action is set in the cities of Ferrara or Cremona. Thus, Ariosto manifests—always within the confines of his artistic technique and classical structure—a growing attention to characters and dialogues drawn from lively contemporary reality and endows his characters with a spontaneous vivacity. He can be called, therefore, the first writer of regular Italian comedy, that is, comedy in the vernacular following the "rules" of classical form and structure.—L. L.

Aristophanes (c. 445 B.C.–c. 385 B.C.). Greek comic playwright. The only surviving writer of Attic Old Comedy (see GREECE: *the classical period*), Aristophanes is credited with more than forty plays, of which eleven are extant. Very little is known about his life. He was the son of a wealthy man, Philippus, and identified himself with the interests and outlook of the "knights," the prosperous, generally conservative stratum of society between the rich aristocracy and the peasants and urban proletariat. Aristophanes' first known play, *Daitalēs (Banqueters),* a satire on the latest fashions in educational methods, was produced in 427 B.C., when he was still a young man, and took second prize in an unknown contest. From that time on Aristophanes was an established author. The following year he presented *Babylonioi (Babylonians),* and then ACHARNIANS, the earliest of his plays to survive intact. For the first seven years of Aristophanes' career, the comedies themselves provide some biographical clues. In *Acharnians* the main character, speaking on behalf of the author, says that he has offended the powerful political leader Cleon by satirizing him in *Babylonioi* the year before. Cleon, the leading exponent of an aggressive policy in the war against Sparta, and a skillful manipulator of mass sentiment, had accused Aristophanes of "slandering the state." The accusation failed to produce a conviction, but it started a lifelong feud between the two men. The Chorus of the same play, speaking in the *parabasis,* connect Aristophanes to the island of Aegina, which, they say, Sparta is anxious to acquire "because of the author." The statement is enigmatic; possibly Aristophanes or his family had an estate there, since the island had been expropriated by Athens at the beginning of the war. From KNIGHTS we learn that Aristophanes normally handed his scripts over to a producer-director because he did not feel qualified to stage his own works.

He produced *Knights* himself, but of the other plays known to us five were produced by a certain Callistratus, two by someone called Philonides, and the last two by the playwright Ararus, one of Aristophanes' three sons.

Aristophanes' first failure (in the sense that it took third prize at the festival of Dionysia) was CLOUDS. In the version that survives, a rewritten but never reproduced script, Aristophanes rebukes the audience for not appreciating the play when it first appeared; he criticizes his rivals, who play blatantly for coarse laughs; he reminds the audience of the way he braved the wrath of Cleon; finally, he gives an interesting clue to his popularity by complaining that his plots and ideas are plagiarized. Aristophanes returned to critical success with WASPS, and in this, as well as in his next play, PEACE, he repeats his claim to be a reformer of theatrical taste and an intrepid Cleonbaiter. After *Peace,* Aristophanes ceased to use the Chorus as a mouthpiece for himself, and the plays retreated somewhat into innuendo and allusion for their effects. Perhaps, in the end, the politicians won.

Except for his own description of himself as bald, no more reliable information about Aristophanes has come down to us. He continued to write and compete at the dramatic festivals with great success, and his next three surviving plays—BIRDS, LYSISTRATA, and THESMOPHORIAZUSAE—show him at the height of his powers. He lived through the long war between Athens and Sparta, two revolutions, the defeat of Athens in 404 B.C., and the trial and execution of Socrates, which is taken up in *Clouds.* He saw the evolution of a new style of comedy, to which he successfully adapted his talents in PLUTUS. One last vignette about Aristophanes survives in Plato's *Symposium,* in which he is shown out-drinking and out-talking all the other guests at an all-night party. As dawn breaks he is left alone with Socrates, debating the question of whether the same man can write both tragedy and comedy.

Aristophanes was probably a member of the group of intellectuals attracted to Socrates at the end of the fifth century B.C. Two of the plays of this period, FROGS and ECCLESIAZUSAE, deal with the same questions of a social and political order that occupied the philosophers of the day. Sometime after the production of *Plutus* Aristophanes died, having won more first prizes at dramatic contests than any of his rivals.

Aristophanes' dramatic style is a medley of music, dance, personal lampoon, luxuriant wordplay, portraits of contemporary Athenian domestic life, political satire, lyric poetry, and surrealistic fantasy. How much of this was typical of the Old Comedy as a genre, and how much was unique to Aristophanes, we cannot know. Many of the stock types and situations of later comic forms are present, or already emerging, in Aristophanes' work. What sets him apart from later ages is his completeness. He was fortunate enough to be writing for an entire culture, and his appeal was to all elements in that culture. In consequence, his plays have a wholeness and wholesomeness that has perhaps never been equaled.

Because of the social role of the artist in Athenian society, Aristophanes is a sensitive refractor of the shifting attitudes of his times. All the conflicts of the period are reflected in his plays: the struggle between Athens and Sparta that was exhausting the energies of

ARISTOPHANES (NEW YORK PUBLIC LIBRARY)

dary, although *Clouds* and *Thesmophoriazusae* prove that Aristophanes was perfectly capable of handling a story line and creating suspense. The nearest comparison is to the traditional vaudeville show, where the audience never expected a coherent connection between the song-and-dance act, the monologue, the *corps de ballet,* the juggler, the animal act, and the political and topical satire. The comparison may be taken a step further. In both Aristophanes and vaudeville there are strict rules of style and form, extending even to the kind of jokes the audience expects to hear and see. Thus, we find Aristophanes, while disclaiming any intention of sinking to the level of his rivals' wit, slyly introducing the very joke he pretends is beneath him. It is the conclusive proof that he belonged to a truly popular theater and that his instinct, above all, was to please.

Aristophanes, A Study (1933, reprinted 1964), by Gilbert Murray, reviews Aristophanes' life and work in the light of the available evidence, according to the traditional approach of classical scholarship. *Aristophanes and the Comic Hero* (1964), by Cedric H. Whitman, gives a play-by-play analysis of the works, relating them to the political and social movements of their day and to a general theory of comedy as a literary genre.

It is hard to find truly funny and theatrical versions of the plays in English. For convenience, *The Complete Plays of Aristophanes* (1962), edited by Moses Hadas, provides the quickest reference. A more up-to-date series is under way from the University of Michigan Press. Titles in print so far are: *Acharnians, Wasps, Clouds, Birds, Lysistrata, Ladies' Day* (*Thesmophoriazusae*), *Congresswomen* (*Ecclesiazusae*), and *Frogs.*—K. C.

Greece; the controversy over education, which pitted the new Sophistic thinking against the traditional values embodied in myths (see *Clouds*); the ambivalent feelings toward Persian power and wealth; the new consciousness of feminine individuality; the rise of a politically active middle class—in short, all the intellectual and moral turmoil that found its serious dramatic expression in the plays of Euripides. Euripides, in fact, is constantly parodied and mocked by Aristophanes, and yet there is no comedy of Aristophanes in which a line or scene of Euripides does not enter, sometimes only half consciously. So fascinated was he by Euripides' ideas and style that a contemporary comic playwright, Cratinus, coined the word "Euripidaristophanizein" to describe the phenomenon.

In translation, Aristophanes' plays are often a disappointment, and not merely because so many of the jokes and allusions are lost or because the conflicts are no longer relevant. More specifically, it appears to a modern reader that Aristophanes has hit upon a brilliant comic idea, exploited it briefly, and then allowed it to fizzle out. The plays always seem to degenerate into a series of loosely related episodes and scarcely ever develop the main plot. But the comedies should be regarded as fanciful variations on a theme, rather than as "well-made plays." Aristophanes begins with a central idea derived from a particular social or political fact of his day and then develops a series of arabesques around this idea in accordance with the conventions of Old Comedy. "Plot," in the modern sense of the word, is secon-

Aristotle (384–322 B.C.). Greek philosopher. Aristotle is the author of the earliest extant philosophical defense of tragedy. His treatise is called *Peri Poietikes* ("On Poetry") in the Greek manuscripts, and it is often referred to in English as the *Poetics;* but it is in fact devoted almost entirely to tragic drama. From the sixteenth century to the present it has enjoyed much prestige. Today it is available in many editions and translations, and is read—with respect, though not always with understanding—by almost all students of Greek tragedy and many students of the nature of tragedy as such.

Aristotle was born in Stagira, a village far to the north of Athens, the home of tragedy. His father was court physician to the king of Macedon. In 367 B.C., when Aristotle was seventeen, he was sent to Athens to study with the philosopher Plato (428–348 B.C.), in his school called the Academy. He remained at the Academy for twenty years, until Plato died. By that time he had begun to publish philosophical works himself. At first these works were gracefully composed defenses of his teacher's philosophical system, but gradually—perhaps at quite an early point—he found it necessary to introduce "improvements," which Plato and some of his more orthodox students could not have accepted. After Plato's death, Aristotle spent some thirteen years away from Athens, including five years in the East (Lesbos and Asia Minor) and at least three years in Macedon as the tutor of Alexander the Great (356–323 B.C.). He returned to Athens in 335 and set up his own school, called the Lyceum after the sanctuary of Apollo

Lykeios in which it was located. He appears to have published no more, but to have devoted himself instead to lecturing and research. His interests ranged over the whole of philosophy as Plato understood it, though his devotion to certain sciences, especially biology, is peculiarly his own. In 323 B.C. Alexander died, and a wave of anti-Macedonian feeling swept Athens. Aristotle said he wanted "to prevent Athens from sinning a second time against philosophy" (the first time being the execution of Plato's teacher, Socrates, in 399 B.C.); he left the city for a nearby island, but then died within a year, of a chronic digestive trouble.

The works that survive are mostly notes for lectures—or so it would appear. They seem never to have been prepared for publication. They reveal a superb intelligence, daring, and originality, but, because they were intended for use only within the philosophical world in Athens, they are often technical, parochial, repetitive, and obscure. The *Poetics* is no exception: It is crabbed in style, inconsistent, and probably incomplete. (These qualities are often disguised in translation.) Like almost all that Aristotle wrote, the figure of Plato and what he had said on the subject looms over everything. Many of the terms and arguments cannot be understood without a thorough acquaintance with terms and arguments used by the master.

The age of the great tragedians was long past when Aristotle first came to Athens in 367 B.C. When he talks about the right and wrong ways of constructing a tragedy, therefore, he is not to be thought of as offering practical advice for his contemporaries or for some future generation of playwrights. He says (1449a15) that tragedy had already reached its highest development, meaning with Sophocles and Euripides. Though he would not rule out the possibility of a later revival of tragedy writing, this hope is not what motivates his work. His examples are drawn from the generation of tragedians, all dead before he was born, that was the subject of intense philosophical interest to Plato and possibly also to Socrates. Nor does Aristotle approach tragedy out of any special literary zeal. To judge from the way he quotes from poets, his feeling for poetry was rather naïve and not overly strong. Tragedy was for him a challenging philosophical problem, set by his master.

Plato had made the understanding of the true nature of tragedy an important part of his philosophical system. But his studies had led him to conclude that tragedy was a dangerously irrational phenomenon and one of the most pernicious instruments by which a culture perpetuated unenlightened theories about life. According to Plato, a society in which all its members were brought up to have only those values that would lead them, individually and collectively, to the highest happiness possible for man would not be able to tolerate the performance or publication of the tragedies of Aeschylus, Sophocles, or Euripides. He backs up this alarming conclusion with many pages of carefully worked-out analyses. (See especially *Republic*, Bks. II–III and X, though poetry is attacked in many other dialogues as well.) Aristotle could hardly have avoided making a stand on so large and controversial a part of his master's philosophy.

It is probable that Aristotle defended the harmlessness of tragedy against Plato's charges, not because an independent and unbiased reconsideration of the tragedies themselves persuaded him that Plato must have misread them, but because philosophical considerations convinced him that he had to vindicate the writing and witnessing of tragedies as rational activities. For one thing, some of Plato's complaints rested on features of his system that Aristotle had revised. Also, if Plato's analysis of tragedy as something inimical to philosophy and the rational pursuit of happiness had been allowed to stand unchallenged, certain very important features of Aristotle's version of Platonism would have fallen.

Plato argued that tragedies involve us emotionally by appealing to the irrational, thus properly unconscious, part of our psyches—a part that plays a role in the lives of good men only when they sleep but that can make a less good man incontinent, compulsive, criminal, or even insane in his waking hours as well as in his dreams. This, Plato suggested, is why, in order to move us, tragedians must show us stories like those of Oedipus and Thyestes, in which appallingly irrational fantasies are acted out before the audience. Aristotle makes no direct comment on this theory in the *Poetics* because his analysis of the "irrational" parts of the psyche was by now quite different from Plato's. Aristotle had argued (*Nicomachean Ethics,* Bks. I–II) that the drives of the lower parts of our psyches are actually motivated by necessary goals and that they are not inimical to rational pursuit of happiness in the way that Plato thought. Such lower drives always come in mutually exclusive pairs, such as cowardice and rashness, and rationality consists in finding the proper compromise between them. In order to reconcile tragedy and rationality, therefore, all that Aristotle had to argue in the *Poetics* was that the arousal of irrational passions in the theater helped, rather than hindered, the achievement of a balance between such natural drives. Plato had argued (*Republic* X) that performances of tragedies increase men's susceptibility to things like pity and fear. Aristotle insists (ch. 6), on the contrary, that they rouse pity and fear only to flush them out. (His term *katharsis* could mean a religious purification, as from a pollution, or a flushing out, as in a medical purgative. From his discussion of katharsis at *Politics* 1341b, ff., it would appear that the latter is uppermost in his mind.) The fact that the arousal of pity and fear is pleasurable seemed sinister to Plato, but Aristotle argues that it is merely the pleasure that accompanies any return to balance and health.

More important still is Aristotle's answer to Plato's assertion that tragedies teach men disastrously misleading things about all the most important questions—good and evil, reality, the gods, success, happiness, excellence, and so forth. Plato, like Socrates, believed that all good men and only good men are happy, that all bad men and only bad men are wretched, and that the gods are always good and just when they interfere in human destinies. Yet tragedies, Plato pointed out, must employ *mythoi* like those of Oedipus and Thyestes, stories of men who are represented as being excellent and deserving of good but who suffer, nevertheless, the most extreme wretchedness—with the consent or even connivance of the gods.

In this context the word *mythos* (plural *mythoi*)

means an emotionally charged representation of men acting or being acted upon and experiencing as a consequence success or defeat. A mythos, Plato argued, always implies something about life, whether the author is consciously using his tale to teach something or not. Thus the mythos of Oedipus implies that the gods can trick an excellent man into committing the most polluting of errors. But is that not precisely the kind of perverted view of life, Plato asks, that leads men to misunderstand what it is to be good and why they should be good? (See especially *Republic* II–III.)

Aristotle accepts Plato's definition of a mythos and the judgment that this is the truly important thing in tragedy (chs. 2 and 6), but he plays down the importance of the moral implications of tragic mythoi. (Though mythos is generally translated as "myth" in Plato, it usually comes out as "plot" in translations of the *Poetics*. Both English words are misleading.) On the other hand, Aristotle does admit (ch. 13) that a mythos about an exceptionally good man who comes to a catastrophic fate through no fault of his own would be "polluting" (*miaron,* often misleadingly translated as "shocking": 1452b36). In other words, he accepts the Socratic and Platonic theory that good men are by reason of their goodness happy, and he admits, therefore, that a Socratic would find a mythos of innocent suffering a defiling experience. He boldly challenges Plato's reading of the tragedies, however. In all successful tragedies, he asserts, there is a major flaw (*hamartia*) in the actions of the protagonist that prevents the play from being "polluting" in this way.

One of the most momentous of the changes that Aristotle introduced into his master's vision of phenomena was his denial of the existence of genuinely irrational energy anywhere in the universe. ("Irrational" energy is truly random, and not directed toward any good.) According to Aristotle, an irrational emotion in human experience, for instance, is actually directed toward a true good, even if a rational man must find a compromise between that urge and another equally good-directed urge. This innovation in theory, as we have seen, made it easier for Aristotle to dismiss Plato's charge that tragedy, since it appeals to the lower urges, must necessarily be destructive to rationality. It raised a new problem for him, however. Aristotle had to give an account of the witnessing of tragedy that would fit with his general description of how all energy is in fact directed toward good.

Aristotle argued (*Physics* I–II) that all motion is caused by "forms." These are of three kinds: crude matter (fire, air, earth, and water); the species of plants and animals; and the goals sought by men (houses, tools, speeches, constitutions, and so forth). All of these forms are perfect (they are "what it is to be" each of these things), exist for all time, and are the causes of all change in phenomena. Aristotle had to define the form of tragedy—that is, what it is to be a tragedy, its essence or the definition of its being, and explain how this form must always have affected human life as a genuine good being pursued by all men. What made this an especially difficult problem was the fact that the phenomenon of tragedy would therefore have to be shown to be a permanent and necessary part of man's existence, despite the fact

that tragedies were known to have been a strictly Athenian tradition and a fairly recent development.

Once more Aristotle finds a solution that departs as little as possible from Plato's terms and analyses. He accepts a watered-down version of Plato's theory that "imitation" is an inevitable and powerful instrument in the passing on of a culture's (usually mistaken) values from generation to generation, and also his theory that tragedy is a quintessential example of "imitation." He also accepts Plato's suggestion (*Republic* 598d–e) that Homer, in composing epics, was really doing the same thing as the later poets did in writing their tragedies. Aristotle concludes that "tragedy" is a species of the genus "imitation," that Homer's epics are merely earlier, less well realized attempts to actualize the same species, and that the function (form) of both epic and tragedy is therefore the same, namely, to produce a katharsis of pity and fear. Tragedy is a better realization of the form than is epic because it utilizes more modes (melody, dance, spectacle) and because, being direct and brief, it produces its characteristic effect with more concentrated power (chs. 24–26). Tragedy differs from comedy, the other major species of "imitation," by reason of its seriousness and the general admirableness of the protagonists—and, of course, by having a different characteristic function. Aristotle does not say what the characteristic function of comedy is; as with tragedy, it would presumably be some kind of pleasure (a fact used by Plato to damn both species), but it would not be the pleasure that accompanies the flushing out of pity and fear (see ch. 14, 1453b10–11).

Although the manuscript of all of Aristotle's notes was discovered in the first century B.C., his influence throughout antiquity was largely confined nevertheless to his earlier, more Platonic publications. Thus the *Poetics* was not generally known or studied in the intellectual circles of Greece and Rome. Aristotle as a philosopher, rather than as a literary critic, became an important influence on European thought only in the twelfth century, due in part to Europe's contact with Arabic writers who had come to admire him earlier. Even then, however, the *Poetics* played no important role in the attitudes either of philosophers or of poets. It was not until the sixteenth century, when a strong and broadly based reaction had already set in against the Aristotelians, that the *Poetics* received any attention, first in Italy and then in the rest of Europe. (See TRAGEDY.) The attention came, therefore, from literary men who were really attracted to Plato rather than to Aristotle but who were distressed by Plato's hostility to literature. They tended to welcome the *Poetics* as an obvious and necessary correction of the master. (See Plato's suggestive challenge for just such a defense at *Republic* 607d.) This is the case even today. It is a fact that must be kept in mind if one is to understand the role played by the *Poetics* in modern European and American letters. Rarely do the admirers of the *Poetics* understand Aristotelian philosophy and even more rarely do they understand or take seriously Plato's objections to tragedy.

Thus Aristotle's treatise was read, not as a philosopher's rejoinder to another philosopher, but either as the words of a wise Greek who was telling us what "the Greeks" felt about their own tragedies, or as the report of a great empirical investigator who had made an impartial analytical study of the best tragedies he could find. As a result, peculiar errors were made and futile arguments were sustained, sometimes over generations. For instance, Aristotle's observation (ch. 5) that, unlike epics, tragedies tend to show actions that take place in a single day was elevated into a law ("the unity of time") by many poets and critics from the sixteenth to the nineteenth centuries. Another law, "the unity of place," which is not even hinted at in the *Poetics,* also found adherents, beginning with Lodovico Castelvetro in 1570. (In fact, most surviving Greek tragedies do confine themselves to one scene and a single day, but that is because, without curtains or a way to get the chorus on and off rapidly, scene changes or the passage of time were hard to indicate.) And Aristotle's assertion that all good tragedies show the fall of men who, though excellent in the main, have some flaw in their actions is still bitterly defended as necessary by many critics today. This idea really is presented as a law in the *Poetics* (ch. 13), but it was dictated by Aristotle's need to defend Platonic ethics and yet avoid the Platonic condemnations of drama. It is a highly destructive way to read Greek tragedy.

Many incidental details in the *Poetics* have, however, had a constructive influence in literature and criticism over the last four centuries. Most of these concern the notion of organic form in a story. For example, the action, not merely the protagonist, should be single; actions should have satisfactory beginning and ending points; events should follow one another in apparently necessary sequences. These are ideas common in Greek literature, and statements of them as ideals can be found in Plato. But the fact remains that the prestige of Aristotle's *Poetics* was important in their dissemination.

The best translations are those by Ingram Bywater, *Aristotle on the Art of Poetry* (1909), which has a learned commentary, and G. M. A. Grube, *Aristotle on Poetry and Style* (1958). Next best are those by S. H. Butcher, *Aristotle's Theory of Poetry and Fine Art* (1951), which has a number of long essays on various problems of interpretation, and Gerald F. Else, *Aristotle's Poetics* (1967).

Several standard works on the history of literary criticism have good chapters on the *Poetics,* especially J. W. H. Atkins, *Literary Criticism in Antiquity,* Vol. I (1934), and G. M. A. Grube, *The Greek and Roman Critics* (1965). Humphry House, *Aristotle's Poetics* (1956) is an intelligent analysis and defense of Aristotle's theory, as is A. O. Prickard, *Aristotle on the Art of Poetry* (1891), which has much on the influence of the *Poetics* in later times. Gerald F. Else, *Aristotle's Poetics, The Argument* (1957) is very full and ingenious but is radical in its interpretations. *Aristotle's Poetics and English Literature* (1965), edited by Elder Olson, is a collection of appreciations by various critics, including some modern Aristotelian critics. Leon Golden's new translation, *Aristotle's Poetics* (1967), is accompanied by a very long commentary by O. B. Hardison, which is naive and should be used with caution.

There are a number of studies on the influence of the *Poetics* in later times. In addition to the volumes by Prickard and Olson, the following should be consulted: Ingemar Düring, *Aristotle in the Ancient Literary Tradition* (1957); J. E. Spingarn, *A History of Literary Criticism in the Renaissance* (1912); Marvin T. Herrick, *The Fusion of Horatian and Aristotelian Literary Criticism* (1946); and Herrick, *The Poetics of Aristotle in England* (1930).

There is a full but uncritical bibliography in Lane Cooper and Alfred Gudeman, *A Bibliography of the Poetics of Aristotle* (1928), supplemented by Herrick in *The American Journal of Philology* (1931). See also Else's "A Survey of Works on Aristotle's Poetics 1940–54," in *Classical Weekly,* now called *Classical World* (1954–1955).—T. G.

Arouet, François Marie. See VOLTAIRE.

Arrabal, Fernando (1933–   ). Spanish-born French playwright. Arrabal, a Spaniard by birth who writes in French, is better known abroad than in France. Within a few years he has become one of the leading avant-garde playwrights in Germany, England, and the United States. Three volumes of his plays have already appeared (pub. 1958, 1961, and 1965) containing thirteen plays in all. As a young man Arrabal came in contact with the civil war in Spain, terrorism, police torture, and concentration camps, and his plays are dominated by elements of shock and ferocity.

The Arrabal hero, who appears in almost all his plays, is the unadjusted modern man, reminiscent of the tramp figure in early Chaplin films, who speaks in a language of childhood and of poets. Arrabal's play *Pique-nique en campagne* (*Picnic on the Battlefield,* 1959) is an antimilitary satire written in the style of the THEATER OF THE ABSURD. Its style, like that of the other plays, *Le Tricycle* (1961) and THE CAR CEMETERY, is a combination of the comic and the oneiric, of innocent and sadistic tendencies in man. His most recent plays, which he calls *théâtre panique* ("panic theater"), draw upon SURREALISM, pop art, and happenings.

During the summer program of 1966 at the Théâtre de Poche-Montparnasse, Arrabal's play *La Communiante* ("The Communicant") was produced. In this startling shock drama, a young girl is dressed for her first communion by her man-hating grandmother, a man brings in a coffin containing a dead woman, and the girl stabs the man in the back. The play recalls *Doctor Caligari* and necrophiliac scenes by the Marquis de Sade.

Arrabal's world is one of victims, of voyeurs, sadists, and innocent children pounding against the bars of the world of adults. Yet in *Oraison* (*Orison,* 1958), and especially in *The Car Cemetery,* Arrabal proposes a gospel of gentleness and kindness. See also L'ARCHITECTE ET L'EMPEREUR D'ASSYRIE.

For information on Arrabal, consult Ann Morrissett, "Dialogue with Arrabal," *Evergreen Review,* No. 15 (Nov.–Dec., 1960).—W. F.

Artaud, Antonin (1895–1948). French director and playwright. Artaud's cherished dream was to found a new kind of theater in France that would be not an artistic spectacle, but a communion between spectators and actors. As in primitive societies, it would be a theater of magic, a mass participation in which the entire culture would find its vitality and its truest expression.

At the age of eighteen, Artaud was cared for briefly

in a sanatorium for mental disorder; there were other attacks in 1916, 1918, and 1940. In 1927 he founded the Théâtre Alfred-Jarry, which remained open for two seasons. He wrote the first manifesto of his THE-ATER OF CRUELTY in 1932 and the second in 1933. In 1944 he published his most important writing on the theater, *Le Théâtre et son double* (*The Theater and Its Double*). Artaud acknowledged that in his conception of the theater, he is calling upon an elementary idea in magic that is used in modern psychoanalysis: the patient is cured by making him assume a role and act out his problem. By plastic, graphic means, the stage production should appeal to the spectators and even bewitch them and lead them into a trance.

Theater in the West is associated with literature, whereas certain Balinese productions Artaud had seen in Paris in the Colonial Exposition of 1931 were addressed to the entire being of the spectator and the words used in them were incantatory. Artaud wanted to see stage gesticulations elevated to the rank of exorcisms. In keeping with the principal tenets of SUR-REALISM, Artaud claimed that art is a real experience that goes far beyond human understanding and attempts to reach a metaphysical truth. See also LES CENCI.

C. Richards' translation of Artaud's *The Theatre and Its Double* (1958) gives the playwright's dramatic theories. For critical studies of Artaud's work, see Mary Ann Caws, "Artaud's Myth of Motion," *French Review,* XLI (February 1968); Leonard C. Pronko, *Avant Garde* (1962) and *Theater East and West* (1967); Eric Sellin, *The Dramatic Concepts of Antonin Artaud* (1968); *Tulane Drama Review* (Winter 1963 and Spring 1963); and George E. Wellwarth, "Antonin Artaud: Prophet of the Avant-Garde Theatre," *Drama Survey* (Winter 1963).—W. F.

Asch, Sholem (1880–1957). Polish-born Yiddish novelist and playwright. Asch was born on January 1, 1880, in Kutno, Poland. Though educated for the rabbinate, he became interested in secular literature after reading modern Hebrew and German writers. He began writing in Hebrew but soon turned to Yiddish under the influence of the Yiddish writer Yitskhok Leybush Peretz, whom he visited in Warsaw in 1900. His first notable piece of fiction was *Dos Shtetl* (*The Town*), which, on its appearance in 1904, gained him widespread recognition as a novelist of great promise. The same year Asch published his first play, the two-act *Tsurikgekumen* ("Returned"), which was performed in Polish translation in Kraków that December and in 1907 in Yiddish by the Peretz Dramatic Studio of Warsaw, with Asch himself playing the lead. The subject of *Tsurikgekumen,* as of his second play, *Meshiakhs Tsaytn* ("The Time of Messiah"), is the conflict between the traditional Jewish life pattern and the new mood of emancipation that was beginning to stir in the younger generation. His one-act play *Winter* was published in 1906, and in 1907 he published GOD OF VENGEANCE, a work that was to gain him a leading position as a Yiddish dramatist as well as much notoriety because of its setting in a brothel and its motif of lesbianism. A German production by Max Reinhardt gained Asch an international reputation.

A restless man, Asch traveled much and lived in

SHOLEM ASCH (YIVO INSTITUTE FOR JEWISH RE-SEARCH)

many places. In 1914 he settled in the United States, where he became a naturalized citizen. After the 1920's Asch's work was mainly in fiction, in which he attained a position of preeminence in the Yiddish world as well as great international recognition. His subjects ranged from Palestine to America and from romantic re-creations of the Jewish past to realistic studies of contemporary Jewish life in Europe and America. He nevertheless often found himself at odds with Jewish public opinion, especially over such issues as his acceptance of a medal from the Pilsudski government of Poland (1933) and his authorship of three Yiddish novels centering around Jesus, especially *The Nazarene* (1939). The 1940's and 1950's were years of increasing estrangement from his Yiddish audience, a disappointment that his international reputation did not wholly assuage.

Asch wrote over twenty plays, most of which were performed in Yiddish as well as in other languages. He had even greater success with his own dramatizations of about a half-dozen of his novels. Especially popular were the dramatizations of *Motke Ganev* ("Mottke the Thief," 1917) and *Der T'hilim Yid* ("Salvation," 1939). Asch's drama, like his fiction, contains a fusion of idyllic romanticism and hard realism. More than any Yiddish writer before him, he relished nature's beauty for its own sake. He was also the first Yiddish writer to write sympathetically, even admiringly, of the muscled and ignorant roughnecks and of the thieves, toughs, and prostitutes of the demimonde. He portrayed them as essentially decent, and, despite their simplicity, deeply loyal

Jews who yearn for piety and morality. It is this idyllic perception of his characters that connects the brothel owner of *God of Vengeance* at one extreme to the selfless Hassidic rebbe of *Salvation* at the other.

Though most of Asch's fiction is available in English (seventeen volumes of stories and novels), only two of his plays have been translated, *God of Vengeance* and *Sabbatai Zevi*.

Sabbatai Zevi (1930) was translated from the Russian version by Florence Whyte and George Rapall Noyes. *God of Vengeance* appears in *The Dybbuk and Other Great Yiddish Plays* (1966), translated and edited by Joseph C. Landis.—J. C. L.

Asena, Orhan (1922–). Turkish playwright. Born and raised in Diyarbakır, Turkey, Asena had no opportunity to see any plays until he came to Istanbul to enroll in the medical school of the University of Istanbul. After receiving his degree in medicine, he worked for the government as a physician and also wrote plays. Asena's first produced play, *Gilgameş* (1954), was a huge success and was later rewritten as a libretto for an opera by the Turkish composer Nevit Kodallı. Asena's third major play, *Hurrem Sultan* (1959), was also a great success, and the State Theater of Ankara took it to Paris. Asena's other plays were generally unsuccessful, partly because of faulty productions.

Not bound by any set rules, Asena has employed various forms and styles, including the epic, depending upon the demands of his subject and material. An avowed individualist, Asena firmly believes in man's vast ability to change his environment. To him society is a living organism in which man both acts and is acted upon. For these views Asena has been assailed by critics who think that environment is the cause of all action. Socially conscious, but never propagandistic, Asena's better plays are likely to enjoy longevity. —N. O.

Asmodée (1937). A play by François Mauriac (1885–). *Asmodée*, the first of Mauriac's four plays, was presented at the Comédie-Française under the direction of Jacques Copeau in November 1937. The central character, Blaise Couture, a former seminarian, has become the spiritual director of a provincial family in which he is employed as a tutor. He exercises an unusual power over the mistress of the house, Mme. de Barthas, a widow for eight years. The seventeen-year-old daughter of the family, Emmanuèle, falls in love with a young Englishman, Harry. Couture encourages this marriage in order to remain alone with Marcelle de Barthas. The unfolding of Marcelle's personality dominates the lesser dramas in the play: the rivalry between Emmanuèle and her mother for the love of Harry and the struggle between divine love and human love in the heart of Emmanuèle.

The title of the play is taken from the name of a character in the eighteenth-century novel *Le Diable Boiteux* (sometimes translated in English as *Asmodeus*) by Alain René Lesage. In that book, the devil Asmodeus flies over Madrid and removes the roofs in order to observe domestic scenes. Blaise Couture is not literally a Tartuffe, because he is not a religious hypocrite. He recalls Molière's hypocrite only insofar as he has retained the manner, the speech, and the subleties of thought of a seminarian.

Asmodée has been translated by Beverly Thurman (1954).—W. F.

Aspenström, Werner (1918–). Swedish poet and playwright. Aspenström's impressions of his farming background in Dalarna are recorded in his prose sketches *Bäcken* ("The Brook," 1958). He studied in Stockholm, where he now prefers to live and work. He made his debut as a poet in 1943 and came to attract considerable attention with the luminous lyrics of *Snölegend* ("Snow Legend," 1949) and *Litania* ("Litany," 1952). Since 1948 Aspenström has been increasingly interested in the brief expressionist play, frequently written for radio and usually conceived as modern allegory with a strong social argument.

Platsen är inhöljd i rök ("The Place Is Wrapped in Smoke," 1948) and *Arken* ("The Ark," prod. 1955; pub. 1959) both image world destruction, and *Det eviga* (*The Apes Shall Inherit the Earth,* 1959) provides a retrospective view of what the world was like, by means of projector and tape recorder in the hands of the apes. Two other plays, *Snaran* ("The Noose," prod. 1954; pub. 1959) and *Poeten och kejsaren* ("The Poet and the Emperor," 1956), deal with the role of the poet in society. Moving even further into the realm of fantasy, *Den ofullbordade flugsmällan* ("The Unfinished Flyswatter," 1963) concerns an invasion of Martians, and *Spindlarna* ("The Spiders," 1966), a colony of men on the moon after the collapse of the world.

Aspenström, who once considered acting as a career, has a strong sense of dramatic moment. He is essentially a lyricist in the "theater of the absurd."

The Apes Shall Inherit the Earth and "The Poet and the Emperor" are discussed in *Tulane Drama Review* (November 1961). See also Egil Törnqvist, "Poet in the Space Age: A Theme in Aspenström's Plays," in *Scandinavian Studies* (February 1967), pp. 1–15. —R. B. V.

As You Like It (c. 1599–1600). A comedy by William SHAKESPEARE. *As You Like It* is largely a dramatization of Thomas Lodge's pastoral novel *Rosalynde* (1590). Changes in names, tone, and incident have been made, and six characters added—notably Jaques and Touchstone. The facts that the play was entered in the Stationers' Register, on August 4, 1600, to prevent unauthorized publication and that there is no printed version before the First Folio of 1623 suggest that *As You Like It* was popular in its own day (and it has so continued). Tradition has it that Shakespeare acted the part of Adam.

The plot tells how Rosalind and Orlando, who fall in love at first sight when Orlando comes to wrestle at her uncle's court, are both driven from their homes —Orlando by a villainous elder brother, and Rosalind by her usurping uncle. Independently they seek shelter in the Forest of Arden, Orlando accompanied by Adam, his old retainer, and Rosalind by her cousin Celia and the jester Touchstone. The girls disguise themselves as brother and sister, with Rosalind posing as the youth Ganymede. Residing in the forest are Rosalind's exiled father and his men, among them the malcontent Jaques. Also present are some country folk. Various love affairs ensue. These take comical turns, primarily through Rosalind's male disguise. The play ends with a wedding of four couples and with reconciliation between the villains and their kin.

As the title implies, the play is a romantic comedy as *you* like it: the setting for four of its five acts is in an idyllic forest where lovely songs fill the air, where a handsome young man and a beautiful, witty young lady—deeply in love—are united, and where villains are reformed. Beneath this world of "good in everything," Shakespeare, through mingling for the first time elements from PASTORAL DRAMA with those of comedy, explores further the nature of appearance and reality. The court, the civilized world, is cruel. But the beautiful country too has its villains, both human and natural. To comment on his themes, Shakespeare employs contrast, ranging from the coarse wooing of the country folk to the idealized love-making of the pastoral romance characters to the realistic romancing of Rosalind-Ganymede and Orlando. There is also direct commentary on the ways of man by Touchstone and Jaques, characters extraneous to the plot. The forest emerges as the environment in which honest responses engendered by love can grow within the individual. Yet civilization with its social institutions, such as the formal marriages with which the play ends, is also necessary for the total well-being of mankind.

An outstanding edition of *As You Like It* is the New Cambridge Edition (1926), edited by Arthur Quiller-Couch and J. Dover Wilson.—W. G.

Ataka. A Japanese *noh* play by Kwanze Kojiro Nobumitsu (1435–1516). *Ataka* is the most celebrated of the noh plays and its author was one of the chief successors to the founder of the noh tradition as we know it today, Zeami Motokiyo. The play belongs to the class of noh dramas known as "living persons play."

The source of *Ataka* is *Gikeiki* ("Life of Yoshitsune," c. 1400), a half-epic, half-historical narrative. Although technically regarded as among the one-act noh dramas, the play is in two episodes. It tells of the difficulties of the defeated leader Minamoto-no-Yoshitsune and his followers in passing through a barrier erected by their victorious enemies at the mountain pass Ataka. The defeated men are believed to be in the neighborhood and, to disguise themselves, have assumed the robes of traveling Buddhist monks.

The real leader is not Minamoto-no-Yoshitsune but his faithful and wily general Benkei, the play's *shite*, or hero. Benkei's plan to escape is based on the pretense that the group is traveling through the country collecting funds for a shrine. To make things doubly sure, he dresses the leader as a luggage-carrier. The guards at Ataka are suspicious. They require Benkei to read a proclamation with a subscription list to show that the men are what they pretend to be. He has no such list, of course, but successfully mimes the action. The guards remain suspicious and even believe that in the person of the luggage-carrier they have detected the leader. Once more Benkei saves the day by thrashing his leader, whom he reviles as a laggard. The scene of the second episode is farther along the road. The chief of the guards overtakes the royal party, which he still suspects, but is disposed to pardon them out of profound admiration for their courage and cunning. He plans nevertheless to outwit them by offering them wine in quantity. Benkei drinks the wine, yet even in his state as a half-drunken dancer retains secrecy, and the heroes ultimately escape.

Few plays afford actors more opportunities to reveal their skill in miming. Tension and excitement are held to the highest pitch. The play has been adopted by the *kabuki* theater under the title *Kanjincho* ("Subscription List"), rewritten but not materially altered. Indeed, there are many kabuki versions, one by nineteenth-century playwright Namiki Gohei (1789–1855). In an early kabuki version by the great actor Ichikawa Danjuro I (1660–1704), it was performed with great success. The last version was performed by Ichikawa Danjuro IX (1838–1903) before the emperor in 1887. As A. C. Scott, in his *Kabuki Theatre of Japan* (1955) observes: "In its dignity and power and the qualities of its dancing, *Kanjincho* is entitled to rank among the dramatic masterpieces of the world." But it should at no time be forgotten that in substance this is itself the noh drama *Ataka*.

For the best English rendering of *Ataka,* see *The Noh Drama,* selected and translated by the Special Noh Committee, Japanese Classics Translation Committee (Vol. III, 1960).—H. W. W.

Atay, Cahit (1925–   ). Turkish playwright. Atay is the son of a teacher of religion. Desiring to be a professional actor, he spent much time as an amateur actor with the dramatic branches of Halkevleri ("Peoples' Houses"), which were established by Atatürk, the first president of Turkey, as cultural centers. Because of these extracurricular activities, Atay never finished his secondary education. He has also worked as a lawyer's apprentice, a village schoolteacher, and since 1951 as a civil servant.

All of Atay's plays are about Turkish village life, which he knows intimately. The characters and the general atmosphere, often touched with fantasy and almost always with poetry and unforced humor, have an authenticity that gives immediacy to his plays. His *Pusuda* (*In Ambush,* 1962) has already become a classic through its vital theme, poetical charm, and penetrating social satire.

Other Turkish playwrights have borrowed Atay's themes on false values, mock heroes, and landlord-peasant relationships. By using native characters and themes and, lately, by emphasizing forms based on popular Turkish theater, Atay strives toward a national Turkish theater with universal appeal.—N. O.

Athalie (1691). A tragedy, with chorus, by Jean RACINE. Athalie, murderer of her own grandchildren and worshipper of Baal, is a queen who has usurped the throne. She discovers in the temple of Jerusalem the child Joas, the real king of Judah, and she tries to seize him. But the great priest Joad succeeds in having her killed by the Levites. A tragedy devoid of love, *Athalie* is entirely dominated by God, and the contrast between the raptures of faith and the violence of the action is striking.

This play has been translated into English verse by Kenneth Muir in *Five Plays* (1960).—Ja. G.

Atsumori (14th century). A Japanese play in two parts by Zeami MOTOKIYO. *Atsumori* is widely recognized as one of the most typical and deeply moving of the Japanese *noh* plays. In Part I a traveling priest meets a band of reapers among whom is a youth of great beauty and dignity. The priest is in reality the veteran warrior Kumagai, who has repented his life of violence and assumed that of religion. Years before, in the battle of Ichi-no-Tani, beside the Bay of Suma, he had killed the young warrior Atsumori. The young reaper is in fact an apparition assumed by Atsumori. Their conversation is full of tragic overtones. The reaper recognizes Kumagai, but Kumagai, though uncomfortable, does not recognize the reaper. Yet there is a possible clue. The reaper is playing a flute similar to that which Kumagai found on Atsumori's body after the youth had been slain. Kumagai gave this flute to his own son. In Part II Atsumori's ghost appears to Kumagai dressed in the armor of the young warrior. They recall the fatal encounter of earlier years. Atsumori, rising from the ground, advances towards the priest with raised sword. The concluding lines chanted by the chorus are among the most moving in noh drama:

> "There is my enemy," he cries, and would strike,
> But the other is grown gentle
> And calling on Buddha's name
> Has obtained salvation for his foe,
> So that they shall be reborn together
> On one lotus seat.
> "No, Rensei is not my enemy.
> Pray for me again, oh pray for me again!"

The legend on which the play is based is one of the most famous in Japanese epic or historical literature. The audience at the noh play understood certain ironic conditions in the relation between the two warriors which Zeami found unnecessary to specify. For a modern reader an ampler version of the same story, contained in the KOWAKA drama *Atsumori*, may be even more moving than Zeami's work.

For the best English rendering of Zeami's play, see Arthur Waley, *The Noh Plays of Japan* (London, 1921; New York, 1957).—H. W. W.

At the Hawk's Well (1917). A one-act verse play by William Butler YEATS. The first work that Yeats wrote under the influence of the fourteenth-century Japanese *noh* drama, *At the Hawk's Well* is a heroic account of Cuchulain's attempt to drink the waters of wisdom or immortality from a sacred well that is guarded by a mysterious Hawk Woman. The play is one of Yeats's "plays for dancers" and, like the noh plays, is performed against a patterned screen; the curtain is represented by the unfolding of a ritualistic cloth by three Musicians, who serve as the chorus and also accompany the stylized movements of the characters with drum, gong, and zither. Three masked characters take part in the "one lofty emotion," as Yeats described the event, a single dramatic situation that occurs at the well. An Old Man is already there, having wasted his life in vain pursuit of the miraculous waters. Then the young warrior-hero Cuchulain comes in to compete with him, but both of them must contend with the fierce Hawk Woman, who begins her wild dance just as the water flows from the well. Like a magical spell, her dance puts the Old Man to sleep and places Cuchulain in a trance, so that they are both frustrated. The Old Man remains doomed to his enervating pursuit of eternal

wisdom, but Cuchulain suddenly hears the cries of battle in the distance, and taking up his spear, he goes off to fight in the hills. Thus, in his ironic defeat Cuchulain has been released from the illusory quest for immortality, because it is his greater destiny to lead a mortal and heroic life of action. The Hawk's well represents the unattainable ideal, the deceptive abstraction in the pursuit of which men can only be robbed of their manhood and destroyed.—D. K.

Audiberti, Jacques (1899–1965). French novelist, poet, and playwright. During the 1930's, when Audiberti was working as a newspaper reporter in Paris, his first book of poetry appeared, titled *Race des hommes* (1937). His poetry received greater praise and achieved more success than his novels.

Audiberti made his debut in the theater with *Quoat-Quoat* in 1946. The action of this play takes place on a Second Empire boat on its way to Mexico, and the play is distinguished by its verbal ornateness, its anachronisms, and its coarseness. The following year *Le Mal court* ("Evil Runs") was produced in the Théâtre de Poche and revived with marked success in 1956. In this play, a kind of half-comic, half-tragic fairy story, Alarica's promised marriage with the prince is cancelled. Married off to a worthless spy, Alarica turns away from the good and chooses evil.

Between 1946 and 1965 Audiberti wrote twenty plays, all of them truculent texts in their verbal opulence. They are not innovations in the sense of structure or theme, and they involve the same implacable subject: the conflict between good and evil, between man's spirit and his flesh. Audiberti has called this obsession "the incarnation," because he believes that although evil is something permanent in a man's life, man has never lost his memory of his former greatness when he shared with God some of the divine qualities. Typically, *Le Mal court* is filled with innocence and sensuality. The embittered Alarica of this play is not unlike the idealistic hero of Audiberti's *La Fête noire* ("The Black Feast," 1948). *La Hobereaute* ("The Small Falcon," 1958) is an example of the many attacks on religion in Audiberti's work. The action of the play is the struggle between the good, represented by nature in *la hobereaute*, and evil, represented by the Church. —W. F.

Augier, [Guillaume Victor] Émile (1820–1889). French playwright. The greatest French writer of comedies of manners in the nineteenth century, Augier has left one of the richest collections of portraits of middle-class people in French dramatic literature. During the Second Empire (1852–1870), he championed the virtues and ideals of the middle class, chiefly the home and the family. His best plays come alive with unforgettable characterizations of scoundrels and weak individuals who have succumbed to the temptations of material prosperity—luxury, marital infidelity, venality—as well as virtuous people who embody and exemplify the traits and values Augier felt would unify and strengthen French society. The most outstanding characteristic of Augier's work, in contrast to that of his contemporary Alexandre Dumas fils, with whom he is often compared, is his unaltering balance and perspective, his broad outlook, and his clearheaded good sense.

Reared in a good bourgeois family in southern France, Augier was brought to Paris at an early age and there received a sound classical education and studied law. In general his life was uneventful. He was interested in the theater from his youth, and his first play to be successfully produced was *La Ciguë* ("Hemlock," 1844), a two-act comedy in verse about a repentant debauchee. His next several plays were also in verse. *L'Aventurière* ("The Adventuress," 1848) and *Gabrielle* (1849) are the most striking and suggest two themes Augier used later, the former showing how an adventuress can destroy a family, the latter, in a related theme, how a family gains in strength when the wife decides to remain faithful. *Gabrielle,* in contrast to Romantic plays, took a serious attitude toward marital fidelity. *Le Mariage d'Olympe* (*Olympe's Marriage,* 1855) and *La Contagion* ("Corruption," 1866) carry *L'Aventurière* two steps further. Olympe Taverny, an unforgettably scheming demimondaine, marries into an aristocratic family to enhance her social position. In the last act, when she refuses to give up her stolen title of countess, she is fatally shot on the stage. This play (which failed) was Augier's angry reply to Dumas's rehabilitation of the courtesan in *La Dame aux camélias* (1852). In Augier's *La Contagion,* however, the diabolically clever Navarette ruins her lover and brings his noble family to her feet; the unregenerate courtesan has triumphed. *Les Lionnes pauvres* (*A False Step,* written in collaboration with Edouard Foussier, performed 1858) negatively develops the situation presented in *Gabrielle.* Séraphine Pommeau, unrepentant, no longer loving her husband, and afraid of poverty, prefers to remain a kept woman.

Another major theme in Augier's plays is the effect of money on the welfare of the family and the home. In fact, many of the stronger plays reveal the power of money to corrupt. In his best play, *Le Gendre de M. Poirier* (*Monsieur Poirier's Son-in-Law,* written in collaboration with Jules Sandeau, performed 1854), Poirier (meaning "pear tree"), a wealthy businessman who wants a title, marries his daughter Antoinette to a prodigal marquis, Gaston de Presles, in a mercenary deal from which both men hope to benefit. Poirier is insensitive, selfish, pigheaded, and vulgar, but the marriage, despite its vicissitudes, is ultimately a happy one because of Antoinette's strong character and capacity for love. The good qualities latent in Gaston also emerge. Not the least of the play's merits is its sensitive probing of the conflict between the moral values of the declining aristocracy and those of the new bourgeoisie. The characterizations of Poirier, Antoinette, and Gaston are superb. Three minor plays also treat the general theme that marrying for money is undesirable: *Ceinture dorée* ("Tainted Money," 1855), *La Jeunesse* ("Youth," 1858), and *Un Beau mariage* ("A Fine Marriage," 1859).

Four major plays revealing Augier's later antiroyalist feeling demonstrate the corrupt uses of money. The trilogy consisting of *Les Effrontés* (*Faces of Brass,* 1861), *Le Fils de Giboyer* (*Giboyer's Son,* 1862), and *Lions et renards* ("Lions and Foxes," 1859) employs many of the same characters. In the first play the power of the press, backed by an unscrupulous journalist, is shown. Vernouillet is the prototype of the modern political or social villain, influential and rich, whose tyrannical power and dishonesty have contaminated the newspaperman Giboyer, who sold his talents to his corrupt employer. Witty, but cynical and without convictions, Giboyer represents venality, the danger of one's having a college education without the moral character to go with it. *Lions et renards* completes another evil portrait, that of the Baron d'Estrigaud, first introduced in *La Contagion.* He stops at nothing to undermine the morals of the bourgeoisie. The fourth of the mature plays is *Maître Guérin* (1864), which offers one of Augier's most devastating character studies. Guérin is an unscrupulous lawyer and miser reminiscent of Molière's Harpagon in *L'Avare* (1668).

Augier's last plays—*Jean de Thommeray* (1873), *Mme Caverlet* (1876), a plea for a divorce law, and *Les Fourchamboult* (1878)—contain in some measure the excellencies of theme, style, and characterization already considered.

Augier's plays, like those of the younger Dumas, are "well-made," employing the structure developed by Eugène Scribe. But Augier was not a pioneer in the development of the "thesis play," as was Dumas; rather, he was the defender and preserver of middle-class ideals. Augier probed many social and moral evils of the Second Empire stemming from the phenomenal economical prosperity of the period, and in his best plays, he makes his characters speak sincerely, naturally, convincingly.

Four Plays by Émile Augier (1915), translated by B. H. Clark, contains *Olympe's Marriage, M. Poirier's Son-in-Law, The House of Fourchambault,* and *The Post-Script. Camille and Other Plays* (1957), edited by S. S. Stanton, contains a bibliography of other translations. There is no biography in English. Critical treatment may be found in Clark's Introduction to *Four Plays,* H. A. Smith's *Main Currents of Modern French Drama* (1925), C. C. Webster's Introduction to *Le Gendre de M. Poirier* (1936), and Stanton's Introduction to *Camille and Other Plays.* —S. S. S.

Aulularia (The Pot of Gold, 194 B.C.?). A comedy by PLAUTUS. *Aulularia,* based on a lost play by the Greek playwright Menander, is primarily a play of character. The aged Euclio discovers a pot of gold and attempts to keep its existence a secret. He is less a true miser than a poor man unable to adjust to his change of fortune, but when the gold is stolen, his anguish and despair know no bounds. Among those accused of the theft is the young neighbor who has seduced his daughter. Although the ending is lost, we can assume that the young man forces the thief to return the gold and receives Euclio's permission to marry his daughter. Euclio apparently gives her the gold as a dowry, thus proving that he is not a miser.

Aulularia is considered one of Plautus' most lively and delightful comedies and has influenced several later plays: QUEROLUS, Giovanni Battista Gelli's *La Sporta* (1543), Ben Jonson's *The Case Is Altered* (1609), and Pieter Hooft's *Warenar* (1617). Harpagon, in Molière's *L'Avare* (1668), which is the most famous adaptation of *Aulularia,* is a real miser whose avarice ruins his own life and the lives of those about him.—G. E. D.

Aureng-Zebe (1675). A tragedy in rhyming couplets by John DRYDEN. *Aureng-Zebe* was first performed late in the year at the Theatre Royal in Drury Lane by the King's Company. While several of the sons of the old emperor struggle for his throne, Aureng-Zebe loyally defends his father. His chief foe is Morat, the ambitious son of the old emperor's second wife, Nourmahal, who almost personifies the extravagant passions of the emperor and his sons. These passions are displayed, not only in the struggle for power, but also in complicated love affairs. Both the emperor and Morat try to take Indamora from Aureng-Zebe, to whom she is engaged, and he becomes violently jealous. Meanwhile, he fends off the advances of his stepmother Nourmahal. Aureng-Zebe is ultimately successful in defending his father's throne, Morat is killed, Nourmahal takes poison, and the emperor repents of his treatment of his son. The play ends with reconciliation between father and son and confirmation of the love of Aureng-Zebe and Indamora.

Dryden makes these passionate entanglements into a far more compact version of the themes he had treated at large in *The Conquest of Granada* (see ENGLAND: *Restoration drama*). Morat's ambition is effectively contrasted to Aureng-Zebe's loyalty, and Indamora is used to reveal the genuine greatness in Morat as well as the flaw of jealousy in Aureng-Zebe. As a courageous but gentle proponent of order, she is strikingly opposed to Nourmahal, whose symbol is fire. The often trenchant verse and several powerful scenes make *Aureng-Zebe* one of Dryden's best plays.

Frederick Link is editing this play with introduction and notes for the Regents Restoration Drama Series. It is available in the Mermaid Dramabook *John Dryden. Three Plays* (1957), George Saintsbury, ed., and in *John Dryden: Four Tragedie* (1967), L. A. Beaurline and Fredson Bowers, eds.
—E. W.

Australia. Theatrical activity in Australia began a mere eighteen months after the first white settlers arrived in 1788. The actors were, of course, the convicts transported from England to Botany Bay (Sydney), New South Wales, and the fact that theatrical presentations began so soon after their arrival (as compared with the United States, where it took 140 years) is less a tribute to the convicts' yearning for their lost cultural heritage than to the need for a touch of social pleasure in the midst of unspeakable hardships and deprivation. The English playwright George Farquhar's *The Recruiting Officer* was performed on June 4, 1789, the only theatrical appurtenances being "three or four yards of stained paper, and a dozen farthing candles stuck around the mud walls of a convict's hut." Captain Walkin Tench, in his journal (pub. 1793), said that a prologue and epilogue written by one of the performers were spoken but that they were "not worth" including in the account. This may have been the famous George "Barrington Prologue," which includes those deathless lines: "True patriots all, for be it understood, we left our country for our country's good."

There were fairly regular performances and even a theater until 1800, at which time, by official order, all stage productions stopped. This hiatus lasted until 1832 when Barnett Levey (1798–1837), the self-proclaimed father of the Australian stage, opened the Theatre Royal, George Street, in Sydney. Probably the first attempts at playwriting were small skits that Levey himself adapted for entertainments that he

called "at homes." In 1835 Levey retitled the English farce *No. 23 John-Street, Adelphi,* to *No. 23 George-Street.* The Sydney text no longer exists, but all indications point to the fact that Levey rewrote the piece as a local farce. In 1838 Morris (also Morrice) Phillips arrived in Sydney with a play, *Fidelio,* he had written and produced in England at the Royal Pavilion in 1837. He wrote a play in Sydney, *The Massacre of Jerusalem,* which, performed at the Victoria in 1838, may be considered the first play both written and produced in Australia. Unfortunately, the manuscript is lost.

The year 1842 can be considered the first year during which original Australian plays appeared with any regularity. Many of these plays were written by Sydney actors, notably Conrad Knowles' *Salathiel* (1842). Produced in Sydney in that same year were *The Queer Client* by Charles Dibdin and *Isabel of Valois* by Henry O'Flaherty, the husband of Eliza Winstanley, the first Australian actress to make a success abroad. Other actor-dramatists were Francis Nesbitt (*Ravenswood,* 1843) and Joseph Simmons (*The Duellist,* 1844). Edward Geoghegan, about whom little is known, was the first Australian who was at all prolific. During 1844/45 at least six of his plays were produced on the Sydney stage, the most successful being the tragedy *The Hibernian Father* and the musical comedy *The Currency Lass,* perhaps the first play with an Australian subject to be produced in Australia. Charles Nagel achieved some success as Australia's first comic playwright. In 1842 he wrote Australia's first burletta, *The Mock Catalani;* in 1844 he wrote the burlesque *Shakespiriconglommorofunnidogammonae;* and in 1851, with the composer Isaac Nathan, Nagel wrote Australia's first *opera buffa, Merry Freaks in Troublous Times,* a piece not at all lacking in talent and skill. Each work was performed in the same year it was written.

During these formative years of the Australian stage, there were only two authors with any claim to literary excellence: David Burn (1799–1875) and Charles Harpur (1813–1868). Although born in Edinburgh, Burn may be considered Australia's first dramatist. In 1828, while en route to Britain, Burn wrote *The Bushrangers,* his most interesting play, although not his best. Produced at the Caledonian Theatre in Edinburgh in 1829, *The Bushrangers* deals with an actual band of convicts, captained by the notorious bushranger Matthew Brady, and their life at Macquarie Harbour, one of the most inhuman penal settlements imaginable. The inspiration for this play was an interview that Burn had had with Brady on the gallows just before the bushranger was "launched into eternity." In 1843 Burn published a volume entitled *Plays and Fugitive Pieces,* which contained four dramas and a farce, only two of which —*Our First Lieutenant* (1844) and *The Queen's Love* (1845)—were produced on the stage.

Charles Harpur deserves mention, not because of his contribution to Australian drama—Burn's influence was much greater—but because of his stature as Australia's first poet. In 1835 in a Sydney newspaper, Harpur published a serial of fourteen scenes from a five-act tragedy entitled *The Tragedy of Donohoe.* In 1853 he published the complete play under the title of *The Bushrangers.* In spite of the fact that Harpur's play, like Burn's *The Bushrangers,* deals with real people, there is no basis for comparison between the two plays. Burn's play is notable for its tendency toward realism in language, while Harpur's play is written in stilted (but not embarrassing) Elizabethan verse. In spite of the urgings of Sydney's literati, Harpur's play was never produced.

There is perhaps only one observation to be made about Australian dramatic activity before 1850: plays *were* being written. It is inappropriate and indeed irrelevant to speak about these plays as plays, for they were imitations of, and indistinguishable from, plays being written in Britain at that time and before. One possible exception might be Burn's *The Bushrangers,* but if we are seeking an Australian play with a subject treated as only an Australian could possibly treat it, there are no exceptions. Burn's play is certainly a social document, but it is a work that any English playwright could have written after having read a sufficient number of travel books about Australia. Harpur, who was a native and who unquestionably *felt* Australian, might have written a play in an Australian idiom—might even have made his *Bushrangers* truly Australian—but he chose instead to write in that language native to all lands but foreign to all ears—*literary.*

Practically all dramas written before the last quarter of the nineteenth century were written by amateurs. Not until after 1880 was it possible for a playwright to make money in the theater, and when that time came there was no dearth of playwrights and no small number of plays about Australian conditions. Yet it should be stressed that if they succeeded at all in capturing the elusive essence of Australia, it was the shadow they captured, not the substance. The image of Australia as shown in some of these early plays is as naïve as that image that foreigners hold today. Australia meant kangaroos, aboriginals, bushrangers, and gold diggers, with no hint that beneath all that there was a large and growing middle-class, urban society. Therefore, it should not surprise us that the form that these plays took was melodrama, and that their "Australian-ness" is less dependent upon character than upon *mise en scène.* For example, in Walter Cooper's *Foiled, or Australia Twenty Years Ago,* the Australian setting is less important than the story about a man who is tied to a log in a lumbermill and is about to be cut in half but is saved at the last minute. Francis R. C. Hopkins' *Reaping the Whirlwind* (1909) is worthy of note only because it is probably the first dramatic utterance of Australia's fear of the "Asiatic Peril." The last line of the play is, "The Asiatics will enter this country without firing a shot. Oh, my God!" George Darrell, equally well known as an actor and playwright, made a great deal of money in the 1880's with his plays. One of them, *Transported for Life* (England, 1880), was a play about convicts, a popular Australian theme. Another play that reiterated the convict theme was *It's Never Too Late To Mend* (1893), by Charles Reade, which included in its cast "forty Queensland Aboriginals." Alfred Dampier (1847–1908), actor, playwright, and entrepreneur, is responsible for a group of Australian melodramas, some of which he wrote himself or in collaboration, others of which he commissioned. *For the Term of His Natural Life* (1886) was adapted from Marcus Clarke's excellent convict novel of the same title. Dampier's *Robbery*

Under Arms (1890) treated bushranging, and *Miner's Right* (after 1890) dealt with the problems of the early gold diggers.

A favorite theme of Australian playwrights then and now is that of the stockman's constant battle with nature on Australia's vast sheep and cattle stations. One of the most spectacular nineteenth-century plays on this theme is Bland Holt's *The Breaking of the Drought* (1893), which included not only the bleached skeleton of a horse onstage but also trained crows, which flew down from the gridiron to pick at the bones. This play is, perhaps, simultaneously the high point and the epitome of Australian drama until the twentieth century.

Not until the first decade of this century were there Australian playwrights who possessed both dramaturgical and literary skill; but by the time such important talents as Louis Esson (1879–1943) and, to a lesser degree, Vance Palmer (1885–1959) were making their presences felt, it was too late. The future of native Australian drama was, if not decided, then markedly influenced by the advent of J. C. Williamson (1845–1913), an American actor who became, in the 1880's, the most powerful entrepreneur in the history of the Australian theater. His organization became hugely successful, and to this day it is Australia's richest, most successful production company. Since its establishment, the Williamson organization has been dedicated to commercial success and has looked only to London and New York for its productions. Indeed, with the exception of the farce by Steele Rudd, pseudonym for Arthur H. Davis (1868–1935), *On Our Selection* (1912), which immortalized the Australian stereotypes of Dad and Dave, local efforts have been completely ignored. Even Arthur H. Adams' Australian political comedy, *Mrs. Pretty and the Premier,* which was produced in the West End in 1916, has never been performed professionally in Australia. Because of Williamson's complete domination of the Australian theater, the line between the commercial and the noncommercial has become a rigid, impregnable wall. The most palpable result of this separation is that the finest dramas written before the 1950's, when a minor renaissance began to take place, were little plays (one-act plays) written for little theaters and radio dramas.

The exact effect of Australia's very popular little theater movement on the formation of indigenous drama has been disputed. Plays written for the little theaters tended sometimes to be precious and literary. The first loud and clear call for a native Australian drama came from Leon Brodsky. To accomplish that goal, he founded the Australian Theatre Society in 1904 in Melbourne. Brodsky was deeply impressed both with the Irish Abbey Theatre and his meetings with William Butler Yeats and John Millington Synge, and he complained that "Many of us are in deep despair when we see how little relation the theater in Australia bears to the national life of the country." He started his society with the intention of producing local drama, but in its four years of existence not a single Australian play was presented. Similarly, the Adelaide Repertory Company, formed by Bryceson Treharne in 1908, concentrated on G. B. Shaw, John Galsworthy, Maurice Maeterlinck, and Arnold Bennett. The Adelaide company did, however, present the one-act play *The Minstrel*

(1908) by A. H. Adams, and his Sydney drama *The Wasters* (1910); but Adams, a slick, professional writer, relied heavily on the stock constructions of the well-made play rather than experimenting with new possibilities for an Australian drama.

Art critic William Moore organized the first playwright's theater with his Annual Drama Nights in Melbourne, held from 1909 to 1912 and again in 1919. From 1910 to 1917 Gregan McMahon managed a repertory theater in Melbourne, producing thirteen plays by Australian authors, including Esson's *Dead Timber* (1911) and his political comedy *The Time Is Not Yet Ripe* (1912).

In this early period of the twentieth century, the important thing to note is that playwrights were gaining proficiency in creating authentic Australian urban settings. Adams' *The Wasters,* for example, is set in suburban Sydney, while his *Mrs. Pretty and the Premier* satirizes contemporary Australian politics. Moore's one-act *Tea Room Girl* (1909) is a Melbourne café piece, and Esson's *The Woman Tamer* (1909) is set in a downtown-Melbourne slum. Esson's most effective dramas, however, were set in the Australian outback, as in *Dead Timber* and, his most admired piece, *The Drovers* (1923). In *The Drovers,* set near the desolate Barkly tableland, a critically injured drover must be left to die, a fate quietly accepted no less by the victim than by his comrades who must leave him. Esson struggled to avoid sentimentality by using simple and direct language, casual

repetition of phrases, and by juxtaposing a quiet humor with a sad, if not tragic, situation; yet the story is so intrinsically sentimental (it is by now a Hollywood cliché) that one wonders indeed whether, as one critic put it, a "lonely death [is lifted] into the realm of universal mourning."

While overseas, Esson met Yeats and Synge, both of whom advised the young Australian dramatists to keep to their own background and disregard current, overseas developments in the theater. Esson came away thinking that the early attempts to create a native drama had been too derivative. "They don't lead to anything. Nothing's being built up," he wrote to Vance Palmer. "We'll never get anywhere until we have half a dozen dramatists working together in a movement." Esson, Palmer, and Dr. Stewart Macky decided to create such a movement by forming the Pioneer Players in Melbourne in 1921.

Vance Palmer was not primarily a dramatist, though he wrote plays throughout his career as a novelist, short-story writer, and poet. He lacked Esson's ability to catch the natural cadence of Australian speech. His best work, for example, *The Black Horse* (1923), was in the genre of one-act plays and was set in the outback. The Pioneer Players lasted until 1923, presenting only Australian plays. The organizers were not able to sustain outside interest in their productions, but they succeeded in creating a favorable climate for the writing of indigenous drama. Although there were other attempts to create

SCENE FROM DOUGLAS STEWART'S *Ned Kelly* (AUSTRALIAN NEWS AND INFORMATION BUREAU)

playwrights' theaters (notably at the Community Playhouse in Sydney in 1929, which in a year presented thirty one-act and forty-three full-length plays), no significant or vigorous drama was written until rather recent times.

During the 1930's and 1940's, the extremely popular medium of radio drama provided an outlet for the production of new plays. Australia can claim a comparatively large number of good radio plays. Australia's best radio dramatist is perhaps Douglas Stewart (1913–   ), who, in such plays as *The Fire on the Snow* (1943) and *The Golden Lover* (1944), wrote in a theatrical, if heavy-handed, verse. Stewart is best known, however, for his stage play *Ned Kelly* (1956), a highly praised verse tragedy, which, as most highly praised verse tragedies, has spent more time in the classroom than on the stage.

Sumner Locke-Elliot (1911–   ) added to the development of Australian speech in drama with his play *Rusty Bugles,* first produced in 1948 amid one of the stormiest openings in the history of the Australian stage. The first Australian playwright to attempt a nonidealized reproduction of common speech pattern, Locke-Elliot dramatized the boredom of soldiers in Australia's tropical Northern Territory at the close of World War II. The Sydney Vice Squad, which has a near perfect record in protecting the public from itself, decided that Mr. Locke-Elliot's language was too bawdy, and so the squad forbade further presentation of *Rusty Bugles.* In his exploitation of the comic possibilities of the Australian temperament and speech, Locke-Elliot was the dramatic forerunner of Ray LAWLER.

Lawler's *Summer of the Seventeenth Doll* (1955) can be seen as the realization of the early twentieth-century dramatists' aspirations. Not only was it a great success in Australia, but it also won recognition abroad and was a commercial success; it was, perhaps, the most successful Australian play ever written. Instead of setting the play in the outback, as

Esson might have done, Lawler brought two off-season sugar-cane cutters into the city; and thus he was able to contrast the harshness of outback life with the softness of city life and at the same time debunk the image of the indomitable, leathery, Australian bush hero.

Lawler influenced Richard Beynon (*The Shifting Heart,* 1957) and Alan Seymour (*The One Day of the Year,* 1960) in their renditions of Australian speech, and, but for his own inability to sustain his powers in his next play, *The Piccadilly Bushman* (1959), Lawler could have led a lively school of local playwrights. Lawler's use of language, however, has led to a number of slum plays exploiting the sensational quality of language for its own sake. He and Seymour left for London after their initial successes (Yeats and Esson might have predicted their deterioration as dramatists).

With the exception of Hal Porter and Patrick White (1912–   ), Australia's best literary minds have not been attracted to the theater. White, perhaps the best novelist Australia has produced, began writing plays as early as 1947 (*The Ham Funeral*), but he did not have his first professional production until 1961. *The Season at Sarsaparilla* (Sarsaparilla is White's capital of suburbia) was produced in 1962, *A Cheery Soul* in 1963, and *Night on Bald Mountain* in 1964. White is at his best with comedy, which usually runs between the grotesque and the bawdy. He likes the big scene, which works well in his novels but seems merely ponderous in his plays.

In 1966 an experimental playwrights' theater, the Jane Street Theatre, was born with the backing of the University of New South Wales Drama Foundation and the Gulbenkian Foundation. It is too early to tell how deep an impression this will make on Australian drama, but at least the signs are good. Previous playwrights' theaters have been very weak in production; the Jane Street Theatre, however, under the able direction of Robin Lovejoy and Alexander Hay,

SCENE FROM RAY LAWLER'S *Summer of the Seventeenth Doll* (AUSTRALIAN NEWS AND INFORMATION BUREAU)

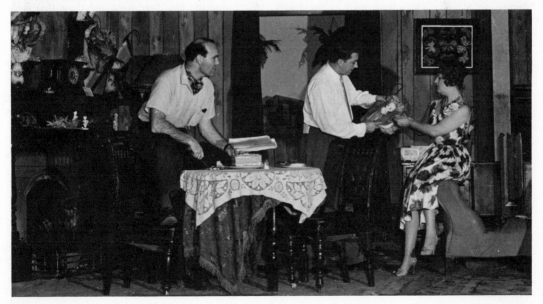

is offering aspiring young playwrights the opportunity to have their work performed by professionals. If this experiment is successful, it may prove to Australians that there are few hazards in breaking with Broadway and the West End; that in spite of the handicap of not having a language all their own, they may yet invent a national drama.

Clearly the best and most comprehensive history of Australian drama is Leslie Rees's *Towards an Australian Drama* (1953). Vance Palmer's *Louis Esson and the Australian Theatre* (1948) displays an intimate and profound knowledge of the subject; see also Keith Macartney, "Louis Esson and the Australian Drama," *Meanjin Quarterly* (No. 2, 1947). For the more recent drama see *Meanjin Quarterly* (No. 3, 1964), which was a special issue given over entirely to drama; see also R. F. Brissenden's "Some Recent Australian Plays," *Texas Quarterly* (Summer 1962) and H. G. Kippax, probably Australia's most astute critic, in his Introduction to *Three Australian Plays* (1964). A good short introduction to Australian drama is Eunice Hanger's "Australian Drama" in *The Literature of Australia* (1964). H. M. Green's *A History of Australian Literature*, 2 vols. (1961), is monumental without being intelligent. For more specialized studies see Paul McGuire's *The Australian Theatre* (1948) and Albert B. Weiner's "The Hibernian Father: The Mystery Solved," *Meanjin Quarterly* (No. 4, 1966).—A. W. and H. v. D. P.

Austria. In Austria drama as a high art begins with the work of Franz Grillparzer, yet there was a depth of tradition behind him that not only nurtured him but without which he might not have developed into the dramatist he eventually became. Most significant in this tradition are the Jesuit drama, the theatrical activity of Josef Anton Stranitzky (1676–1726), and the Viennese folk play, which reached its heights in the plays of Ferdinand Raimund and Johann Nestroy, and perhaps its apotheosis in some of the plays of Grillparzer.

The acting of Jesuit plays dates from 1551, three years after the first Jesuit college was established in Europe, in Messina. Plays were used by the Jesuit order as an aid for the secular student in his study of the humanities. At first, no excessive elaboration was countenanced, but this dictum did not last long; indeed, the history of Jesuit drama is its progress from classroom exercise to elaborate spectacle and great technical proficiency.

In the mid-1500's Jesuit colleges were established in all the countries of Europe, including Austria. Being of strict religious orientation, the colleges performed plays based for the most part on biblical stories or on the lives of the saints or martyrs. Originally there were only two types of plays: the tragedy and the comedy of serious intent. Originally, too, the plays were performed by classes of students, to provide them exercise in the Latin language, gesture, deportment, and declamation. Generally, the play was written by the professor of rhetoric, although occasionally the pupils collaborated in its composition.

The casts of the plays were usually large, and in order to utilize those who had no major roles, choruses and arias were composed that they might somehow be fitted in. The fact that the plays were based primarily on the classical five-act structure allowed the introduction of such formal and generally interlude-like choral passages. That these choruses and arias were sung owes no small thanks to the influence of the Italian opera, especially in southern Germany and Austria. With such influences working upon the Jesuit play, in addition to that of the Baroque era in which it was conceived—an era of excessive elaboration in art, music, and architecture, as well as an age in which morals and manners suffered considerable codification—it is no wonder that in Vienna, in 1659, a play called *Pietas Victrix* ("The Victory of Devotion") was given an ornate and spectacular mounting. It engaged thirty-six leading characters, plus ten characters who portrayed abstractions, an entire senate, an army, a fleet, masks, *gloriae*, and a chorus of soldiers, boys, Roman citizens, naiads, tritons, and angels.

No matter how elaborate the performance, however, the plays were meant to teach a moral lesson to the spectator. The themes chosen for such plays were always in some way related to the Church, and numerous plays were written about Herod, Joseph, Esther, Judith, and Holofernes. The effect of these plays was often praiseworthy, as in Stefano Tuccio's *Christus Judex* ("The King of the Jews"), played at Messina in 1569. It was said to have reduced the audience to tears, with the result that contrition and conversions were the rule, not only at that performance, but wherever the play was presented.

No less important to the Austrian tradition, and especially to the eventual folk play of that country, was the rise of the Jesuit comedy of serious intent. The comic form was at first approached with some scholastic hesitation, for it seemed not entirely consistent with the teaching of pious morality as was evinced in the Jesuit tragedy. Guided by extreme discretion, the Jesuits did compose some most cautious comedies, because the comic spirit could not be fettered indefinitely in Austria. From roughly the middle of the seventeenth century, various short comic pieces began to make their appearance. At times they were interludes related to the main action of the tragedy; but there were also those that were independent of the main play, autonomous comic interludes and entr'actes, which were written in the vernacular. The influence of the vernacular became so great that soon adaptations from the Latin were made and became popular as early as 1582.

As regards the other arts in Jesuit drama, not only was music used, in the form of choruses and arias, but ballet became an elaborate staple. In Austria the influence of the Italian opera, from the early years of the 1600's, and the often simultaneous appearance of the popular troupe from England known as the English Comedians had a great and important effect upon the development of the Austrian drama.

What emerged from these influences was the typical Viennese folk comedy, an indigenous and unique form of play that leads directly into the mainstream of modern Austrian drama. It is this form that found its ultimate development in Mozart's opera *Die Zauberflöte* (*The Magic Flute*, 1791). Important, too, in the development of the Viennese folk comedy is the tradition of the Italian *commedia dell'arte*, which greatly influenced the founder of the folk comedy in Vienna, Josef Anton Stranitzky. His creation of Hanswurst, a Salzburg peasant, eventually appeared in some form or other in most of the folk comedies, with their down-to-earth humor.

Out of the folk comedy there developed in the early eighteenth century an intermediary form known as the *Zauberposse* ("burlesque fairy tale"). It is the link between the folk comedy and the Viennese folk play, which developed in the skillful hands of Ferdinand RAIMUND and Johann NESTROY.

Franz GRILLPARZER is the first great dramatist of the Austrian theater. A native of Vienna, he is the direct product of the tradition discussed above, in addition to the classical Weimar tradition of Goethe and Schiller, and the intense Spanish influence that came from the Hapsburg Empire.

His first produced play, *Die Ahnfrau* (*The Ancestress,* 1817), is a fate drama that transcends that popular genre. Though it deals with the working out of a curse, it rises above that form in the careful technical aspects of its plot. Grillparzer's second play, SAPPHO, proves that he was not only a master of technique but a genuine dramatic poet as well. His lines in this play are consciously measured against the accomplishments of Goethe and Schiller. *Sappho* deals with the Greek poetess' desire and failure to achieve a lasting sexual relationship with her young admirer, Phaon. No longer are Grillparzer's characters manipulated by fate; they are free agents, capable of shaping their own destinies.

In his trilogy *Das goldene Vliess* (*The Golden Fleece,* 1821) Grillparzer gave modern drama one of its principal landmarks. He treated the main characters of the Medea legend in psychoanalytic terms, which to a great extent anticipated Freud's eventual theories. His verse in this trilogy is roughhewn and uninhibited, a successful attempt to unite form and content. *König Ottokars Glück und Ende* (*King Ottokar, His Rise and Fall,* 1825) is the first of a series of historical tragedies to come from Grillparzer's pen. It dramatizes on a vast and panoramic scale the struggle between Rudolf I, the first Hapsburg emperor, and his vassal Ottokar of Bohemia. It is a study of the conflict between virtue and arrogance and exemplifies Grillparzer's lifelong desire to respect the house of Hapsburg. The play is a masterpiece in its harmonization of language, thought, and action.

In *Ein treuer Diener seines Herrn* (*A Faithful Servant of His Master,* 1828) Grillparzer utilizes and exalts the Kantian categorical imperative that duty is all. Bancbanus is made coregent of the realm during the king's absence and is so morally determined to carry out his duty that his entire life and family collapse around him. Much the same obsession dominated Grillparzer's own life and typified his devotion to the imperial house.

HERO AND LEANDER is to a great extent the author's most successful escape from his personal psychological problems. It is a simple, classically beautiful love story based on the ancient legend of the two lovers and the tragic end of their scarcely realized love. Most splendid is the achievement of Grillparzer's verse and imagery, as well as the human depth of his characters.

In *Der Traum, ein Leben* (*The Dream Is Life,* 1834) Grillparzer demonstrates his desire for a life of passivity and retirement. In this play, most of which is a dream sequence of remarkably fast-paced scenes,

SCENE FROM FRANZ GRILLPARZER'S *The Dream Is Life* (VIENNA, BILDERGALLERIE)

Rustan dreams of the dangers that a life of action entails, and upon waking decides to remain at home, a simple undemonstrative being. *Weh dem, der lügt* (*Thou Shalt Not Lie!,* 1838), like the serious comedy of the Jesuit tradition, preaches a solid moral: inner truth is greater than literal truth. It is the story of a kitchen boy whose utter truthfulness wins the release of his master's son from the barbarians. A failure at its première, because it seemed to attribute unacceptable characteristics to aristocrats, the play is now considered one of the few genuine comedies of the German-speaking stage.

Grillparzer's three final plays were written for himself rather than for the public. It was his wish that they be destroyed at his death. They were not. Today they are considered the most mature examples of his art.

In the first of these final plays, *Libussa* (1874), he reveals his sorrow and disappointment in the state of man and man's development. Libussa represents a golden age of rule, an age when man is so good that he needs no government and no law. But man has slipped from that ideal state and has become evil. The play shows the death of the ideal in the face of terrible, but truthful, reality.

Ein Bruderzwist im Habsburg (*Family Strife in Hapsburg,* 1872) is far more personal than Grillparzer's previous plays. It depicts the reign of the weak, morose, and psychologically and emotionally ill Hapsburg emperor Rudolf II, and the political turmoil, leading to the outbreak of the Thirty Years' War, brought on by his lack of leadership in the face of his personal problems. It is a bitter and totally disillusioned play, and an incisive portrait of its author.

The same may be said for the last of the completed plays, *Die Jüdin von Toledo* (*The Jewess of Toledo,* 1873). In this story, taken from Lope de Vega, of a king who uses his duty to his state as an excuse to bring about the death of the beautiful Jewess Rahel, and thus his desired escape from her, Grillparzer is actually lashing out at his own life's history and his own inability to maintain a satisfactory heterosexual relationship. Just as the king of this play takes refuge in his duty to the state, so Grillparzer took refuge in his art as an excuse for backing out of life and love. The play brings almost full circle the problem that confronted the young Grillparzer in his second play, *Sappho:* the inability to love.

A romantic only on the surface, Grillparzer brought into modern drama an incisive awareness of human psychology, psychosis, and neurosis.

Ludwig Anzengruber (1839–1889) brought to the Austrian and German-speaking drama a thorough-going realism and an insistence upon dealing with the contemporary scene. He limited himself almost exclusively to dealing with the Austrian peasant and did so in a solid, colloquial prose style. He divested the Viennese folk play and Zauberposse of their fairy-tale elements and brought them back to reality and life. A critic of his time, he launched out against false conventions and, in particular, against the Catholic Church for destroying man's natural instincts. His play *Das vierte Gebot (The Fourth Commandment*, 1878) demonstrates the invalidity of the commandment to honor father and mother when they do not always justify that honor. He also shows how the young are spoiled by the sins of their parents toward them.

In a way a successor to Anzengruber, Karl Schönherr (1867–1943) continued to write about the Austrian peasant, though he was less an outright critic of his age than was Anzengruber. He attained his full maturity in plays such as *Mutter Erde* ("Mother Earth," 1908), which deals with an old father who refuses to die and release his son to marriage and happiness; and *Glaube und Heimat (Faith and Fireside*, 1910), set in the time of the Counter Reformation, which presents the conflict between religion and patriotism.

Hugo von HOFMANNSTHAL was the first of the truly great giants of contemporary Austrian drama. He represents the total fusion of the Austrian tradition and, along with Arthur Schnitzler, is one of the peerless recorders of the fall of an age, imperial Vienna, which was to collapse with the outbreak of World War I, in 1914. During the lifetime of these two writers Vienna was the ghost of the Paris of the Second Empire and the seat of the oldest and most degenerate dynasty of Europe. The thirst for pleasure ran high. Love and death were Vienna's dramatic motifs, and worldly weariness colored all.

Essentially, Hofmannsthal is a symbolist very much of the Stefan George school, both of them esthetes in taste and manners; yet Hofmannsthal's works are infused with a depth that is not always discernible at first sight. His early play *Gestern* ("Yesterday," written 1891) is a formal masterpiece, despite the fact that Hofmannsthal was only seventeen when he wrote it. It treats a theme that was to be his throughout his lifetime: there is no escaping the past, for it is forever part of the present. *Der Tod des Tizian (The Death of Titian*, written 1892) records the conflict between the world of pure art and the ugly world of reality. Yet Titian to his end remains a man of action. *Der Tor und der Tod (Death and the Fool*, written 1893) carries the earlier play further. It states that a divorce from life is the action of a fool, an escape into unreality, with the eventual realization that such a fool never actually lives at all. These are interior plays, probing the human soul, as are his *Das kleine Welttheater (The Little Theater of the World*, written 1897), *Der Kaiser und die Hexe (The*

Emperor and the Witch, written 1897), *Die weise Fächer* ("The White Fan," written 1897), and *Die Frau am Fenster* ("The Woman at the Window," written 1897).

In *Der Abenteurer und die Sängerin* ("The Adventurer and the Singer," written 1899) Hofmannsthal gives greater attention to the dictates of the stage. Here he deals with a favorite figure of Hofmannsthal's Vienna, Casanova. As he is presented in the play, Casanova's life has shaped the life of his former mistress, and her love for him has transformed her into the supreme artist she has become. *Die Hochzeit der Sobeide (The Marriage of Zobeide*, written 1899) is concerned with the self-destruction of a girl who marries a man of her parents' choosing and on her wedding night confesses to her husband her love for a poor man. She is allowed immediately to go to him, but finds him in the arms of a whore.

A turning point in Hofmannsthal's life came with his *Das Bergwerk zu Falun (The Mines of Falun*, written 1899; prod. 1951), in which he directed his attention more toward real life than he had done previously. The play, his first full-length drama, tells the story of a miner who on his wedding eve disappears forever down a shaft with the Mountain Queen. It demonstrates the greater strength of the spiritual world at the expense of reality.

Hofmannsthal's second period was devoted to re-writing the classics. His *Alkestis* ("Alcestis," 1893), based on Euripides' play; ELECTRA, after Sophocles; *Das gerettete Venedig (Venice Preserved*, written 1905); *Ödipus und die Sphinx (Oedipus and the Sphinx*, written 1906), a play that deals with the time prior to the start of Sophocles' work; and finally his *Ödipus Rex* (written 1909)—each is a free adaptation that alters the total complexion of each of the originals.

His third period consists largely of the comedies and the operatic librettos for the composer Richard Strauss. *Cristinas Heimreise (Cristina's Journey Home*, pub. 1910) is his first comedy, and one of the most charming in the Austrian theater. During a first trip to Venice, Cristina meets Florindo, another manifestation of one of his earlier figures, Casanova. Like the earlier prototype, Florindo is an intriguing but irresponsible young adventurer. Cristina's common sense, however, and a right instinct lead her into a marriage with a sincere and honest man.

Perhaps Hofmannsthal's greatest success was with his opera librettos, for it was with these that he gained international fame during his lifetime. *Der Rosenkavalier (The Cavalier of the Rose*, written 1911), *Ariadne auf Naxos (Ariadne on Naxos*, written 1912), his monumental symbolic drama *Die Frau ohne Schatten (The Woman Without a Shadow*, 1919), *Die Ägyptische Helena (The Egyptian Helen*, written 1928), and the attempt to duplicate the outstanding success of *Der Rosenkavalier*, his *Arabella* (1933)—each of these works represents a high-water mark in operatic literature.

Hofmannsthal's JEDERMANN was adapted from the English morality play *Everyman*, but it is in effect an original work, borrowing scarcely a hundred lines from its original. He brought the play up to date in its allusions and its significance by directing it against the materialistic society that Hofmannsthal saw in decay. This served as the first of what may be called his festival plays, works generally written for the summer festivals held in Salzburg, Austria. Another such play is *Das Salzburger grosse Welttheater* (*The Salzburg Great Theater of the World*, written 1922), adapted from Calderón's *El gran teatro del mundo*. The new play deals with the King, Wisdom, Beauty, The Rich Man, The Peasant, and The Beggar, who are summoned by God to play out the drama of Man's life. As in *Jedermann*, the significance of the new play is totally modern in its application.

Borrowing again from Calderón, Hofmannsthal wrote *Der Turm* (*The Tower*, written 1925; second version 1927), based on the Spaniard's *La vida es sueño* (*Life Is a Dream*). It is a play that pits love and nonviolence against brute force, and in the end there is a vision of hope with the establishment of a kingdom of innocent children. It is generally conceded that *Der Turm* is Hofmannsthal's masterpiece for the stage.

A contemporary of Hofmannsthal, Arthur SCHNITZLER is very unlike him in most ways. Schnitzler's feat lies in his minute, almost miniaturist depiction of Vienna between the 1880's and the dissolution of the empire in 1914. Schnitzler may be regarded as the apotheosis of naturalism, as well as the road out of it; some may call him an impressionist. His work is typified by psychoanalytical probing into the human mind and soul and by an acute understanding of the nature of sexuality. His plays are stages in the demise of a degenerate, pleasure-loving society.

One of his earliest works for the stage was a series of seven one-act plays called *Anatol* (1893) after its main character. They consist of scenes from the love life of a world-weary, melancholy Viennese gentleman, whose only escape is to live solely for the moment, to flit from one amorous adventure to the next, thinking that therein lies happiness. In a final scene, not published but produced in 1932, called *Anatols Grösswahn* ("Anatol's Megalomania"), the aged lover is made a veritable fool of, thus attesting to Schnitzler's own attitude toward him.

THE GAME OF LOVE was his next major work, and one of his most popular and enduring. It was after this play that Schnitzler left his medical practice and turned his whole energies to literature and the theater. The word *Liebelei*, the German title of *The Game of Love*, means not love, but flirtation, the only thing that was acceptable in sophisticated Viennese society at the time. In many respects the play is an extension of *Anatol*. In it flirtation and love meet head on and each destroys the other. *Freiwald* (*Free Game*, 1896) treats much the same situation: the stupidity of dueling over a ridiculous point of honor (an important element in *The Game of Love*) and the practice of baiting young actresses as free game.

LA RONDE has been called a "death dance of love." In a series of ten scenes, each between a man and a woman, we see the attempt to escape from life's weariness through sex, but even sex to the people of this play becomes dull and tedious. It is a bitterly sad and poignant indictment by Schnitzler of his age.

In THE GREEN COCKATOO he displays one of his major themes, the struggle between the ambiguous identities of appearance and reality, a theme that caught the imagination of numerous Viennese playwrights. What seems fabrication in this play on the night of the storming of the Bastille suddenly turns into terrible truth.

In a somewhat romantic verse play, *Der Schleier der Beatrice* ("The Veil of Beatrice," 1900), Schnitzler probes deeply into the unfathomable nature of woman. The play concerns a woman who drives two men to their deaths and then takes her own life.

In another series of one-act plays, *Lebendige Stunden* (*Living Hours*, 1902), he again delves into the problem of appearance and reality. In each of the plays in this series he confronts false emotions with the truth of life. The same holds true of his one-act play *Paracelsus* (1897), in which a famous doctor who has played with human lives learns that the line between truth and appearance does not exist, nothing is certain, and that we know nothing of ourselves or others: we are always playing—and only the man who realizes this is wise.

In *Der einsame Weg* (*The Lonely Way*, 1903) Schnitzler returns to the *Anatol* theme, except that now the Anatol figure is old and able to live only on the nostalgia of past pleasures. Rejected and alone, von Sala realizes that we all go the downward way alone. *Das weite Land* (*The Vast Domain*, 1911) is another picture of Vienna just before World War I.

Professor Bernhardi (1912) is unique among Schnitzler's plays in that it is not concerned with the sexual impulse. Rather, it deals with anti-Semitism and the theme of science versus religion. Bernhardi, the head of a Viennese hospital, refuses to allow a Catholic priest to visit a dying girl. He believes that the euphoric state of the girl would be shattered by the knowledge of her impending death, which the priest's visit would announce to her. A scandal is occasioned and Bernhardi is imprisoned. The play is a bitter criticism of a growing anti-Semitic attitude, which Schnitzler included among the illnesses of his society.

Other more characteristic plays followed, until Schnitzler's death in 1931. In the 1930's it seemed he had outlived his time. The Vienna of his plays was long dead; his plays were out of date. Today, however, Schnitzler's achievement is being reevaluated and new generations are becoming aware that his true greatness lay in his deep and humanitarian understanding of the human mind and soul.

Richard Beer-Hofmann (1866–1945) was a neoromantic who became the spokesman for his Jewish people. His two most famous plays are *Der Graf von Charolais* ("The Count of Charolais," 1904) and *Jaakobs Traum* ("Jacob's Dream," 1918). *Der Graf von Charolais*, like Hofmannsthal's *Das gerettete Venedig*, is based on a seventeenth-century English drama. Beer-Hofmann took *The Fatal Dowry* of Philip Massinger and Nathan Field and turned it into a play of modern significance, with a new psychological depth and an abundant poetic spirit. Impressionistic techniques replace much of the more forceful directness of the original. *Jaakobs Traum* is his acknowledgment of his racial heritage. It foretells the mission as well as the tribulations of the Jews. The play is a turning point in German-speaking drama, for it is filled with a new spirit closely akin to that of the German expressionists. Transcendental issues become paramount, religion is at its core, and its insistence on culminating on a universal note are all attributes of the expressionist movement. The play proved one of the major postwar successes.

Karl Kraus (1874–1936) was one of Austria's most important satirists. In *Die Fackel* (*The Torch*), a periodical run by him singlehandedly, he lashed out against corruption in public and private life, one of the chief causes of which he felt was the press, which, he said, incited the masses to war. Kraus's main dramatic work is one that has never been produced, *Die letzten Tage der Menschheit* ("The Last Days of Mankind," pub. 1918). Written between 1914 and 1918, the play is so vast it would require ten full evenings for production. In it the author, through the voice of the Grumbler, cries out against the way in which man is being brutalized. The play is a nightmare based to a great extent on documents, newspaper reports, letters, and interviews. Historical figures appear and enact scenes from their lives. Fatalism permeates the whole, for man cannot be made better. The drama ends with the voice of God saying: "I did not want this to happen!" The only possible solution in Kraus's eyes is demonstrated in the versified, frenzied visions that constitute the Epilogue: total destruction and the fall of man.

Kraus wrote other plays that are also extremely personal: *Traumstück* ("Dream Play," 1923) and *Traumtheater* ("Dream Theater," 1924). In still others, *Literatur* ("Literature," 1921), and *Wolkenkuckucksheim* ("Cloud-Cuckoo-Home," 1923), he attacked literary and political events. One of his major accomplishments was to translate the complete Shakespeare into German.

Max Mell (1882–   ) has achieved a reputation of high esteem in Austria. Taking the example of

FRANZ WERFEL (GERMAN INFORMATION CENTER)

Hofmannsthal's *Jedermann,* he has written a series of three religious plays in simple rhymed verse. *Das Apostelspiel* (*The Apostle Play,* 1923) tells the story of a peasant girl who, upon the intrusion into her hut by two rakes, converts them with her purity and naïveté and with her message of love. *Das Schutzengelspiel* ("The Play of the Guardian Angel," 1923) preaches the moral dictum that only humility in the face of adversity will be rewarded by God. *Das Nachfolge Christi Spiel* (*Imitatio Christi,* 1927) tells of a nobleman, attacked by robbers, who gives up his own life to save the lives of those who attacked him. Mell has written plays along the lines of high classical tragedy also, such as *Sieben gegen Theben* ("Seven Against Thebes," 1932), a modern version of the Oedipus and Antigone story. His latest play is *Jeanne d'Arc* (1957).

Despite his enormous output in biography and other branches of literature, Stefan Zweig (1881–1942) had a fairly distinguished career in the theater. His *Tersites* (1907) tries to demonstrate the spiritual superiority of the physically inferior, but it was with his *Jeremias* (*Jeremiah,* 1917) that Zweig produced his most significant work for the stage. In this expressionist play, he, like Kraus, denounces the folly of war. The form of the play, its humanitarian message, and its concentration on the single character of the prophet, with the other characters scarcely more than accompanying voices, stamp the work as manifestly expressionist. He is also widely known for his translation and adaptation of Ben Jonson's *Volpone* (1926), which, retranslated back into English, had considerable success on the New York stage.

Essentially a poet and novelist, Franz Werfel (1890–1945) has contributed some of the most significant theatrical pieces of the twentieth century. He was born in Prague of Jewish parents and was strongly influenced by the mystical traditions of his native land. This is seen especially in his expressionist poetry, which calls on all mankind to unite in love and brotherhood.

STEFAN ZWEIG (GEORGES SCHREIBER DRAWING PUBLISHED IN NEW YORK *Herald-Tribune,* JUNE 19, 1932)

His first important play was *Die Troerinnen* ("The Trojan Women," 1915), freely adapted from Euripides. Like Hofmannsthal's adaptations, this work is infused with the problems and insights of the author's time. Written just prior to World War I, the play is expressionist in its plea for peace and love, as well as in its lament for the death of the individual. It implied that a new moral center must be found.

More specifically expressionist was his trilogy *Der Spiegelmensch* ("The Mirror Man," 1920), with its Faustian overtones. It depicts the struggle between man's true and his assumed nature, between appearance and reality. Thamal is lured into evil by his mirror image, his alter ego, the manifestation of his evil instincts. Thamal is Faust, or Everyman, who is tired of life and retires to a monastery but learns that he is not yet ready for that life. He lacks the maturity that comes only with spiritual development. He goes out again into the world, like Faust and Peer Gynt, accompanied by his alter ego, appoints himself the people's leader, and promises them wealth and happiness. Later he submits willingly to a trial and is sentenced to death. As he drinks the cup of poison, his mirror image rejoins its mirror, which becomes a window showing the perfect life. One of the major works of expressionism, this play is also one of the few manifestations of this movement in Austrian drama.

Bocksgesang (*Goat Song*, 1921) uses fantastic symbolism to arrive at a picture of the time in which it was written. Two eighteenth-century peasants have a goat as their offspring, which they try to hide. But it escapes and is worshipped by the revolting peasants as if it were a god. Both the monstrous goat and the peasant uprising betoken the revolt of man's primitive instincts against the established order. Eventually the revolt is curbed and the goat killed; but in the end we learn that a peasant girl has given birth to the goat's offspring. The primitive in man is not to be quelled so easily.

Juarez und Maximilian (*Juarez and Maximilian,* 1925) shows the Austrian archduke Maximilian as the emperor of Mexico in 1864. An idealist, he cannot comprehend the political necessities occasioned by his position. His dreams are shattered by Juarez, and Maximilian is shot by a firing squad. He dies happy, not having succumbed to the demands that to him were symbolic of chaos.

Oskar Kokoschka (1886–   ), principally a painter, was the writer of probably the first expressionist drama: *Mörder, Hoffnung der Frauen* (*Murderer, Hope of Women,* 1907). (See EXPRESSIONISM.) This nightmarish play lays bare the eternal struggle between the sexes, a theme that was to dominate the expressionist movement. *Der brennende Dornbusch* (*The Burning Bush,* 1910) is perhaps even more fully expressionist. In it the Man and the Woman, after running the whole gamut of passion and torment, emerge washed clean of their suffering: the expressionist resurrection is accomplished; the New Man is born. *Hiob* (*Job,* 1917) depicts woman as the core of evil, and *Orpheus und Eurydike* (*Orpheus and Eurydice,* 1918) restates the eternal battle of the sexes.

Richard Billinger (1893–   ) is one of the most interesting of Austria's modern playwrights. His basic themes, which have been discussed by many Austrian playwrights, are the conflict between town and country and the antagonism between Christianity (especially Catholicism) and man's pagan instincts. His custom is to mingle a thoroughgoing realism with poetic mysticism. The peasant figures large in his plays, a preoccupation also not unusual in Austrian drama. The peasants of Billinger's plays are filled with an exuberance of life and primitive instinct, so that their sexual nature often leads them into criminal acts.

In *Raunacht* (*Hallowe'en,* 1931) Billinger depicts the peasant tradition that on the eve of December 23 all pagan spirits are set free to lead the people into confusion and misfortune. Simon has recently returned from Africa, where he noted the same pagan forces in the natives that he sees in his own country's peasants. That night he succumbs to an African ritual and in the process rapes and kills a girl he has lured into his house. *Rosse* ("Horses," 1931) tells of an old farm hand who loves his horses with such passion that, when a tractor salesman tries to sell him one of his machines, the farm hand feels his horses being threatened and kills the salesman. This play is perhaps the culmination of the town and country conflict in Billinger's plays. *Der Gigant* ("The Giant," 1937) tells of how the city works as an evil and destroys what is honest and good. The giant in this play is the city of Prague, which has lured into it and damaged a young girl to the point that she is rejected by her parents as well as by her village. She can now seek only death on the moors.

Austrian drama holds a unique position in European theater and is by no means a second cousin to German drama. Its uniqueness derives from the richness and breadth of its cultural heritage. Fortunately, Austria was vitally influenced by a variety of outlying cultures that were one with it during the days of the Hapsburg Empire, especially Czechoslovakia and Hungary, whose mystical traditions have had no little effect on Austrian drama. Perhaps its chief attribute over the German drama is its grace and easy nature. Austrian drama is not turgid and is seldom moralistic in a didactic manner but is devoted to action, which is not always the way with German drama. Above all, it never gave itself over fully to a particular movement, as did Germany. Naturalism, expressionism, neoromanticism never fully conquered Austria's spirit. Rather, Austria chose and filtered out what it found useful and to a profound degree maintained a continuity of cultural expression in the drama that is rare in modern times. (For Austria's place in German drama, see GERMANY.)

There exists no history of Austrian dramatic literature in English. What material is available must be culled from anthologies and collections, some of the best of which are as follows. Jethro Bithell's *Modern German Literature, 1880–1938* (1939), though not complete, does discuss several of the Austrian playwrights. Frank Chandler's *Modern Continental Playwrights* (1931) contains an individual chapter on Austrian drama. Solomon Liptzin's *Germany's Stepchildren* (1944) contains good chapters on half a dozen Austrian playwrights. H. F. Garten's *Modern German Drama* (1959) deals at some length with the Austrian dramatic tradition, in addition to brief mentions of isolated major playwrights. Martin Lamm's *Modern Drama* (1952) contains a separate chapter on Austrian drama, which discusses mainly Hofmannsthal and Schnitzler. See also *A Study of the Modern Drama* (1938) by Barrett H. Clark. —C. R. M.

auto sacramental ("sacramental act"). A peculiarly Spanish dramatic genre. An *auto sacramental* is a one-act play in verse presenting, with personified abstractions as characters, an allegorical dramatization of ideas related—closely or loosely—to the sacrament of the Eucharist. Autos were performed in the open air, as part of the celebration of Corpus Christi, from the sixteenth to the eighteenth centuries, but reached their apogee in the seventeenth century with the work of Calderón, the acknowledged master of this genre.

The main feature of the Feast of Corpus Christi was the parading of the Host through the streets as part of a joyous procession. In Spain the parade included not only clergy and civic dignitaries but also comic and symbolic masqueraders and *tableaux vivants* on floats. The tableaux vivants, at the stations of the procession, eventually became animated with choreographic movements and, finally, with simple dramatic actions, embryonic autos. The custom soon arose of isolating the floats from the procession. Autos were then performed on carts, in one plaza after another, by professional actors and actresses who were paid by the municipality. In view of the magnificence of the occasion no expense was spared. While each troupe of actors received a substantial payment for its services from the city council, the best one was awarded a lavish monetary prize. The splendid costumes and sets, paid for by the city, became the property of the troupe and were used later in performances of secular plays. The proceeds from the autos thus greatly assisted the development of the secular drama.

The auto form arose, like the secular drama, from the simple liturgical drama for Christmas. The Nativity plays presented the Bethlehem shepherds receiving the angel's message of Christ's birth; in some plays the shepherds' questions about the significance of the birth were answered by the angel. As the Christmas play was adapted to Corpus Christi, the angel was first replaced by a learned hermit or friar who might be expected to know the answers to the increasingly subtle theological questions about the sacraments. The next step was to substitute for the informant a personified abstraction, such as Faith. In time the shepherds themselves gave way to such allegorical characters as Paganism, Hypocrisy, World, Grace, or Penitence. The dramatist who did the most to create an allegorical drama at this early stage was Diego Sánchez de Badajoz (died before 1550).

Because dogma—the abstract idea derived from an historical event, for example, the Incarnation from the Nativity—is inextricably linked to the Communion, it follows that autos sacramentales are set in a timeless, eternal world and that allegory is their natural mode. A sacrament, in St. Thomas Aquinas' definition, is a sign of a sacred thing insofar as it is designed for the sanctification of man; and he defines a sign as a means of proceeding from the known to the unknown. The allegory of the autos is thus a way of penetrating some of the mystery surrounding the Communion; the central mystery of transubstantiation is usually not in question.

In the second half of the sixteenth century a great many allegorical plays related to the Eucharist were written anonymously, perhaps by village priests. Usually called *farsas sacramentales* ("sacramental farces"), many were collected in the so-called *Códice de autos viejos* ("Codex of Ancient Acts"). Some of these rough, primitive plays were revised, polished, and modernized by the sophisticated bookseller Juan de Timoneda for presentation before the hierarchy of Valencia, as well as before the common people. Timoneda gave prestige and dignity to what had previously been a rustic form of drama. José de Valdivielso (1560?–1638) and Lope de Vega were the first dramatists to recognize the potential of the genre. Valdivielso, for example, not only adapted to the glorification of the Eucharist such obvious themes as the parable of the prodigal son but also had the daring to adapt allegorically such secular subjects as the tale of a female brigand and the analogy between the world and a lunatic asylum. Increasingly, farfetched analogies were drawn in the autos between profane tales of adventure or love and divine mysteries. Valdivielso and Lope stressed above all the need for penitence. Their autos were designed not simply to enlighten but also to create the proper spiritual condition of a communicant.

The audacity of Pedro CALDERÓN DE LA BARCA in his choice of subjects exceeded that of his predecessors. He was not afraid to allegorize—giving them a quite different sense—his own secular plays, such as *La vida es sueño* (*Life Is a Dream*: secular version, 1635; final draft of the auto, 1673) or *El pintor de su deshonra* ("The Painter of His Dishonor": comedia, 1650; auto, date unknown). He could write *El verdadero dios Pan* ("Pan, the True God," 1670) on the basis of a pun (*pan*, "bread" and the mythological god Pan); on another occasion he might reinterpret an Old Testament passage—as in *La cena de Baltasar* (*Belshazzar's Feast*, 1634?)—to create a new analogy between the events and the characters of the biblical narrative and the abstract, eternal world of the sacraments. Because the Eucharist is the keystone of the structure of all seven sacraments, and because the sacraments impinge on a great deal of nonsacramental religious thought, the dramatist was free to range over many subjects without neglecting his primary obligation to the Communion. So, for example, Calderón chose a sociological theme for his treatment of distributive justice in *El gran teatro del mundo* (*The Great Theater of the World*, written 1633–1635?) and *No hay más Fortuna que Dios* ("There Is No Fortune Other Than God," written 1652–1658). Calderón's over seventy autos, commissioned by the city of Madrid, raised the sacramental art to heights previously unimagined.

Inevitably unsympathetic to the autos, the rationalists of the eighteenth century leveled charges of irreverence against them, to secure their disfavor in court circles. In 1765 a royal decree prohibited their performance. In the twentieth century, however, there has been some renewed interest in the autos. There are occasional revivals of Calderón's sacramental plays and the well-known twentieth-century poets Rafael Alberti (1902–   ) and Miguel Hernández (1910–1942) have written modern, secularized imitations of the old autos.

Few autos sacramentales have been translated into

English. An acting version of Lope de Vega's *Nuestro bien,* entitled *For Our Sake,* is included in Richard Barnes's *Plays and Fugitive Essays 1963–1966* (1966). Calderón's *The Great Theater of the World* may be read in Angel Flores, ed., *Masterpieces of the Spanish Golden Age* (1957). A selection of the six most popular autos in Spanish, edited with notes by Angel Valbuena Prat, is available in the Clásicos Castellanos series, Vols. 69 and 74.

The evolution of the auto before Calderón is traced in B. W. Wardropper, "The Search for a Dramatic Formula for the *Auto Sacramental,*" *PMLA,* LXV (1950), and, at greater length, in *Introducción al teatro religioso del Siglo de Oro* (rev. ed., 1967). An excellent critical study of three autos by Calderón, with a discussion of the aesthetic and theological problems they raise, may be found in A. A. Parker's *The Allegorical Drama of Calderón* (1943). —B. W.

Avare, L' (The Miser, 1668). A comedy in prose by MOLIÈRE. The actual plot of *L'Avare* is based both on the rivalry between Harpagon and his son Cléante for the young Mariane and on the secret love of Valère, Harpagon's steward, and Elise, Harpagon's daughter, whom Harpagon wants to marry off to the old Anselme. The ending is romanesque: generous Anselme discovers that Mariane and Valère are, in fact, his children, who had once been lost in a shipwreck. At the center of the plot is Harpagon, a sly, tyrannical father who has been monstrously perverted by his incurable and profound avarice, which is the motive for all his acts and is responsible for his children's and servants' dishonest maneuverings. The interest of *L'Avare* lies in the suspense created by the apparently insuperable force represented by Harpagon, in the very dramatic situations (for example Harpagon discovers that he is his own son's usurer) and in the farcical accumulation of innumerable traits resulting from avarice, some of which border on madness.

This play has been translated as *The Miser* by Francis Fergusson in *Plays* (1950).—Ja. G.

Awake and Sing! (1935). A tragicomedy by Clifford ODETS. The play is the story of an American Jewish family, the Bergers of the Bronx, New York, caught in a struggle for economic security in the Great Depression of the 1930's. By default of the weak father, Myron, the household is a matriarchy. Bessie, the autocratic mother, sees to it that the family has food, clothing, and shelter, but her obsession with money has virtually destroyed her feeling for humanity. Learning that her daughter Hennie is pregnant by a man who cannot be located, she forces the girl to marry another man, letting him think the child is his own. Learning that her son Ralph has become interested in a girl, she breaks up the relationship lest he want to marry and take his weekly salary away from the family. These heartless actions make it possible for her to hold up her head before her neighbors, who will never have an opportunity to gossip about the family's morals or to see it moved out into the street for failing to pay the rent. Hennie's marriage is, to be sure, unhappy, and after a year she tells her husband the truth. This precipitates the climax of the play. Ralph learns of the deception and is outraged. Bessie, angered by Ralph's recriminations, turns in furious temper on her old immigrant father, Jacob, who commits suicide. In the final scene, attention focuses upon Ralph, to whom Jacob has left three thousand dollars in insurance. Should he take the money and go off on his own, or should he turn it over to the family for everyone's benefit? He decides on the unselfish course and declares that with the help of other young men, such as those with whom he works, he will fight to make a better world —one in which the possession of money is not man's only goal.

Odets' keen ear for urban speech and his social sympathy resulted in the creation of a cast of robust, unfailingly interesting characters. Despite moments of obvious Marxist propagandizing, the exposition of the family's plight in the midst of economic dislocation rings true. However, the last-act speeches in which Ralph reveals himself as a "young leader" in the tradition of leftist agitational drama show the playwright floundering in his search for an optimistic conclusion to his characters' problems.—M. G.

Axel. See SYMBOLISM.

Ayrer, Jacob. See GERMANY: *middle ages.*

Azevedo, Artur (1855–1908). Brazilian journalist, poet, short-story writer, and playwright. The Brazilian theater was dominated by translations of French texts when Artur Azevedo arrived in Rio, in 1873, from his native state of Maranhão. Author of plays since he was nine, he began to show his comedies to theatrical companies, and his success was so rapid that he soon was receiving continuous commissions. He was successful at writing in accordance with the tastes of his end-of-the-century audience: comedies, dramas, vaudevilles, parodies, musical comedies, and operettas. He also translated and adapted works according to the needs of the impresarios. At the same time Azevedo was a journalist in charge of theatrical criticism. He was one of the first critics to recognize the talent of the actress Eleonora Duse. He was also an organizer of campaigns, including the one that resulted in the construction of the Municipal Theater in Rio de Janeiro.

Although Azevedo was writing to make a living, he also tried to write what he himself called "serious theater," but without much success. His talent revealed itself more in plays written hastily, based on Carioca (Rio) life or gossip gathered from actors just arriving from small cities during periods of theatrical excitement. *A capital federal* ("The Federal Capital," 1897) and *O mambembe* ("The Second-Rate Traveling Theater," 1896), both musical comedies, are his best works. Optimistic and lively, written in the vivid language of the streets, they are in the best tradition of the theater of manners.

Since Azevedo often wrote in collaboration with friends, it is difficult to distinguish in some plays exactly what his contribution was. Some of the principal titles that bear his signature alone are: *O dote* ("The Dowry," 1907), *A jóia* ("The Jewel," 1879), *Casa de orates* ("House of Madmen," 1882), *O retrato a óleo* ("The Portrait in Oils," 1906), *A fonte castália* ("The Castalian Fountain," 1904), *O major* ("The Major," 1880), and *Vida e morte* ("Life and Death," 1908).

There is no complete edition of Azevedo's works. For the most part, they are in separate editions, published in Brazil. No edition has been translated into English.—J. P.

B

Bacchants (Bakchai, c. 405 B.C.). A tragedy by EURIPIDES. *Bacchants* is universally acclaimed a great masterpiece. There is complete unity of plot. The poetry is very beautiful. The choral odes are clearly relevant. Yet the play has been interpreted by some as an attack upon the Olympian religion, and by others as the recantation of an aging atheist.

The story is of a type well known in Greek legend: a triumph of Dionysus, god of wine and ecstasy, over those who refuse to permit the observance of his worship. In this case, the god has come to Thebes, which is ruled by the arrogant and straitlaced Pentheus. The Theban women have joined in the god's ecstatic rites. Pentheus' grandfather, Cadmus, and the sophisticated prophet Teiresias try to persuade the young king to acknowledge the god, but he is beyond all persuasion. He has already flung some of the women into prison; those worshipping on Mount Cithaeron will soon join them. Pentheus suspects them, without justification, of sexual promiscuity. A young priest who has been imprisoned—Dionysus in disguise —makes a spectacular escape. A messenger describes the peaceful worship of the women but adds that, when provoked by Pentheus' men, they put them to flight and began to tear apart cattle. This ominous news merely strengthens the king's determination; he will call out the army.

At this point Dionysus changes. From a smiling god he becomes a spirit of vengeful cruelty. Still in the guise of his own priest, he first establishes his power over the king's mind, then leads him, dressed as a woman, to spy upon the women. When they reach the mountain, Dionysus drives the worshipping women, his bacchants, into a mad frenzy. Led by Pentheus' mother, Agave, they mistake the king for a lion and tear him limb from limb. The scene in which Agave gradually comes to her senses and realizes that she has killed her own son is praised by all critics.

Bacchants is obviously the tragedy of King Pentheus, but the main character is the god: he speaks the monologue, appears in all his power at the end, and, as the priest, directs the action throughout. The Chorus reflect the changing moods of the god from the joyful and gracious worship of their first odes to the devilish triumph of their last. In the last lamentations and the epiphany of Dionysus there are regrettable lacunae. Enough remains, however, to show the god completely unforgiving and ruthless. His power is vindicated. He lays no claim to justice.

Bacchants is the work neither of a worshipper nor an atheist, but of a great poet who dramatizes life as he sees it. Since he is not a theologian, he need do no more. This much is clear: Dionysus is a great power in the lives of men. He symbolizes and personifies those passions and desires that can be the source of loveliness and joy, but which, if denied and suppressed, will tear man to pieces and will themselves become evil and destructive.

Translations of the play are listed in this book under Euripides.—G. M. A. G.

Bajazet (1672). A tragedy by Jean RACINE. In a seraglio in seventeenth-century Constantinople, the sultana Roxane is in love with Bajazet, young brother of the sultan Amurat, who is away. Having discovered through guile and blackmail that Bajazet and the princess Atalide are in love, Roxane has Bajazet killed. She herself is assassinated by order of Amurat, and Atalide commits suicide. *Bajazet* is a tragedy of guile and lies serving the ends of frenzied passion.

This play has been translated into English rhyming verse by Samuel Solomon in *Complete Plays* (1967). —Ja. G.

Bald Soprano, The (La Cantatrice Chauve, 1950). A play by Eugène IONESCO. *The Bald Soprano,* which Ionesco calls an "antiplay," was first produced in May 1950 at the Théâtre des Noctambules by the young director Nicolas Bataille. The theme of the play, which occurs in other works of Ionesco, is that of the aging married couple who made a failure of living together and are incapable of communicating or even knowing the person they have spent their life with. The blandness of their automated life blows up as the banality of their speech and their commonplace existence become exaggerated and frighteningly grotesque. Things that seemed self-evident are no longer sure; people are unsure of their identity and can even become interchangeable, such as the Bobby Watsons—a whole family with the same name. As the nonsensical dialogue continues, a pathos slowly emerges and the tragedy of the married couple is faintly sketched.

The Bald Soprano is a parody of our conversations, of the so-called dramatic situations of our lives, and of our inability to remain silent. Three scenes in particular are models of burlesque parody: the domestic conversation between Mr. and Mrs. Smith, the recognition scene of Mr. and Mrs. Martin, and the unexpected visit of the fireman. In the deepest sense, *The Bald Soprano* is a parody of the theater. By a deliberate, stark use of the banal and a repetition of the worn-out clichés of language, Ionesco generates an unusual, fresh atmosphere.

The Bald Soprano (1965) has been translated by Donald M. Allen.—W. F.

Bali. See INDONESIA: *Bali.*

Barker, James Nelson (1784–1858). American playwright and public servant. Barker was born in

Philadelphia, the son of General John Barker, who was the mayor. Barker saw active service as a captain of artillery in the War of 1812, was mayor of Philadelphia in 1819, and collector of the port from 1829 to 1838, when President Martin Van Buren appointed him first Comptroller of the United States Treasury. He was connected with the Treasury for the rest of his life. Although not a writer by profession, Barker was the author of ten successful plays, largely on American themes.

Tears and Smiles (1806), obviously inspired by Royall Tyler's play *The Contrast,* is a sentimental comedy of manners set in contemporary Philadelphia. *The Embargo, or What News?* (1808), which has not survived, expressed American resentment of British and French encroachments on American shipping. *The Indian Princess, or La Belle Sauvage* (1808), an "operatic mélodrame," is the earliest surviving play about Pocahontas. It was widely performed in the United States and in London in 1820. His dramatization of Sir Walter Scott's *Marmion,* first produced in 1812, was revived as late as 1846. A romantic comedy, based on Pigault-Lebrun's novel *How to Try a Lover* (1817), was produced in 1836 under the title *The Court of Love.* In 1837 he wrote *The Armourer's Escape, or Three Years at Nootka Sound,* a melodrama that has not survived. Barker's most interesting play, *Superstition* (1824), dealing with religious intolerance and persecution for witchcraft in seventeenth-century New England, is important as a successful early blank-verse tragedy based on American history.

The best source is Paul H. Musser's *James Nelson Barker* (1929).—B. H.

Barnes, Barnabe (1571–1609). English playwright and poet. A native of York, Barnes attended Brasenose College, Oxford. Later he became one of the legion of literary hangers-on in the entourage of the earl of Essex. In 1598 he was arrested on a charge of attempted murder. While awaiting trial, he escaped, and the charges were subsequently dropped.

Barnes's only extant play is *The Divils Charter* (1607), a tragedy based on the life of the Renaissance pope Alexander VI. Closely modeled on Christopher Marlowe's *Faustus, The Divils Charter* pictures Alexander as one who owes his worldly success to having sold his soul to the devil. Extravagant and overwritten, the play nevertheless has some effective moments.—E. Q.

Barrie, James Matthew. See CHILDREN'S DRAMA; ENGLAND: *nineteenth century and Edwardian;* and ENGLAND: *post-Edwardian drama.*

Barry, Philip (1896–1949). American playwright. The youngest child of a successful Irish Catholic businessman in Rochester, New York, Barry grew up in a large family that both petted him and overwhelmed him. As a boy, he found escape from family and parochial school pressures in writing stories and, though he entered Yale as a political science major, he enjoyed most his writing courses. He interrupted his college career in 1917 to serve with the State Department, but by 1919 he had decided to devote himself to playwriting. After completing his work at Yale, he studied at George Pierce Baker's 47 Workshop at Harvard. There he wrote *You and I,* which was produced in New York in 1923. He wrote some two dozen plays before his death at fifty-three.

Barry's work falls roughly into two categories. The

A SCENE FROM EUGÈNE IONESCO'S *The Bald Soprano* (FRENCH CULTURAL SERVICES)

larger group consists of plays dealing with serious religious, moral, and psychological questions, often developed in symbolic and fantastic forms. The most important among them are *Hotel Universe* (1930) and *Here Come the Clowns* (1938). In the former, the characters are permitted to relive the most traumatic moment of their lives in order to exorcise their personal demons. In the latter, a stagehand at the symbolically named Globe Theatre searches for God; after escaping the spell of a satanic pessimist, he comes to recognize God's goodness and to accept man's free will and responsibility. Other plays dealing with similar themes are *John* (1927), *Tomorrow and Tomorrow* (1931), *The Joyous Season* (1934), and *Second Threshold* (produced posthumously in 1951). In all of these plays, Barry succeeded only sporadically in giving his thoughts dramatic force.

Ironically, his most accomplished works are a small group of comedies that he created with comparatively little effort and that he considered ephemeral. All deal wittily and elegantly with the nature of true marriage. In *Paris Bound* (1927) a husband and wife come to realize that a brief, merely sexual attraction to someone else need not disrupt their happy marriage. In *Holiday* (1929) Barry presents a rich young man planning to retire so that he can live more fully; his social-climbing fiancée abandons him, but he discovers a young lady who shares his Thoreauvian ideals. The hero of *The Animal Kingdom* (1932) marries the girl who rouses him sexually but later leaves her for the woman whose mind and spirit are like his. On the eve of her second marriage, the heroine of *The Philadelphia Story* (1939) discovers in herself the hedonistic strain she had rejected in her first husband, and the play concludes with her remarrying him. Without strain or sermon, always with wit and grace, Barry succeeded in questioning conventional ideas about marriage and in challenging American materialism.

There is no standard edition of Barry's plays. The fullest critical discussions are Gerald Hamm's *The Dramas of Philip Barry* (1948) and J. P. Roppolo's *Philip Barry* (1965).—M. L.

Bartholomew Fair (1614). A comedy by Ben JONSON. The play deals with the annual fair held in Smithfield, a suburb of London, on Saint Bartholomew's Day (August 24). To the fair comes an assortment of characters. A group of Puritans is led by Zeal of the Land Busy, a hypocritical, scripture-quoting preacher. Another group centers around Bartholomew Cokes, a free-spending, harebrained young country squire. He is accompanied by his servant, Wasp, and his unwilling fiancée, Grace Wellborn. In pursuit of Grace are two rival suitors, Quarlous and Winwife. Still another visitor is Adam Overdo, a local justice of the peace, determined to spy on the various activities of the fair in order to uncover its "enormities." At the fair itself is an assortment of con men, rogues, and pickpockets who congregate at the booth of Ursula the pig-woman, whose aromatic roast pork attracts them all. The various characters undergo a variety of experiences designed to purge their folly or enhance their fortunes. The resolution is achieved in a concluding puppet show, which offers a microcosmic rendering of the play's major themes and, incidentally, a notable refutation of the Puritan opposition to the popular stage.

While *Bartholomew Fair* is peripherally satiric, it is more strongly characterized by the spirit of saturnalia. It is, like the fair itself, the symbol of the principle of festivity, of joyous participation in the physicality, folly, and interrelatedness of all men. —E. Q.

Baruffe Chiozzotte, Le (The Squabbles at Chioggia, 1762). A comedy by Carlo GOLDONI. The play is set among the fishermen of Chioggia, a town at the extreme south of the Venetian lagoon, and is written in the dialect of that town. It concerns the jealousies and grudges that arise from misunderstanding and unfounded slander, which result in the separation of Lucietta from her fiancé, Titta Nane, and of Beppo from Orsetta. The ensuing hatred between the lovers' families causes them to be brought before the law, represented by the bourgeois Venetian youth Isidoro, who is coadjutor of the criminal chancery. Isidoro undertakes to clear up the misunderstandings, cure the petty jealousies between the various lovers, reestablish peace between the families, and so contrive that the comedy end with the necessary weddings.

Written in a delicious style and with poetic realism, the comedy is among the first works of the modern European theater in which the life of the people is the subject matter. Goldoni does not merely look at these fishermen from the outside, although he describes the hard, pitiless conditions in which they live, but he conveys both their inexhaustible and joyous imagination and their authentic feelings. The work has a particular attraction in the character of Isidoro, in whom Goldoni obviously adumbrates himself, for in 1729 he had indeed filled the office of coadjutor at Chioggia. His own personality as a good-humored *deux ex machina* thus appears thinly veiled. —L. L.

Başkut, Cevat Fehmi (1905–). Turkish comic playwright and journalist. Başkut began his career as a journalist in 1928 and for many years was the managing editor of the influential Istanbul daily *Cumhuriyet,* which he left in 1963. Başkut's first comedy was produced in 1942. Since then he has written about twenty plays, almost all of which have been produced. *Küçük Şehir* ("Little Town," 1945) won a prize in 1948 and *Paydos* ("Break," 1948), produced in Athens the same year, became the first modern Turkish play to be produced outside Turkey. This play also became the first Turkish play to be commercially recorded (1968), and it has been made into a film.

Başkut's plays are broad, social satires, often with long moralistic scenes. Although hastily written and generally lacking in sound dramaturgy, Başkut's plays have been box office successes and have contributed a great deal to popularizing the theater in Turkey.—N. O.

Basutoland. See AFRICA: *Basutoland.*

Bathhouse, The (Banya, 1930). A drama in six acts with a circus and fireworks by Vladimir MAYAKOVSKY. In this satire on red tape and corruption, the scene is set in a Soviet government office run by bureaucrats: Chief Coordinator Pobedonosikov, who is always busy writing speeches and signing resolutions; his secretary Optimistenko, whose job is to keep petitioners away from his superior; and the bookkeeper Nightkin, who embezzles public moneys. In opposition to these Soviet officials, who swagger, bully people, take bribes, and spout meaningless phrases, are the ordinary, hard-working Soviet citizens: Crankov, an inventor who builds a time machine; Velocipedkin, a vigilante of the Young Communist League who fights to have the time machine accepted; and Underton, a typist who is fired from her job by Pobedonosikov. When the time machine, under the direction of an emissary from the future, the Phosphorescent Woman, is ready to take them into the future (the communist millennium), the bureaucrats climb hopefully aboard. They are violently ejected, however, by a sort of extra-dimensional force of inertia, while the ordinary, humble people travel on to an unknown land of synthetic milk and honey.

In calling this big spoof *The Bathhouse,* Mayakovsky had in mind a much more common way of getting rid of vermin than the use of a time machine: that of steaming them out in a bathhouse.

The concept of time, of course, is the main element in a revolution, which is supposed to be a short cut to a desired society. Thus, the compression of time—the function of the time machine—is the goal of the revolutionary communist regime. The time machine could rush society through years of hardship in a matter of minutes and could make the millennium, looming as a remote, almost theoretical haven on the horizon, an immediate reality. This change turns out to be most unwelcome to Mayakovsky's highest Soviet official, Pobedonosikov, who fails completely to understand that time is the essence of the revolution. When, however, the emissary from the future forces him to accept the machine, he claims it for his administration, by a sort of bureaucratic reflex, and asserts that he personally has always taken a great interest in it. In the last act he makes a speech in which he admits that "the current moment is . . . static," as his secretary, Optimistenko, on behalf of his subordinates, presents him with a watch—a piece of machinery declared obsolete by the inventor of the time machine.

In this comedy satirizing the world of Soviet officialdom, Mayakovsky shows the uncomfortable effects of ubiquitous bureaucratic interference penetrating into every cranny of people's souls. He pleads that this constant intrusion not only retards the march toward communism—the main grudge voiced by Mayakovsky here—but also poisons the lives of individuals by imposing upon them an idiotic, petty conformism. Thus, Pobedonosikov's abject fear of unorthodoxy makes him at one point attempt to drive his wife to suicide because of her "religious outcries" (such as "For God's sake") and her consorting with members of the Young Communist League, who are below her because of her husband's rank.

The exposure of corrupt bureaucrats is carried out through the introduction of an outsider, just as in Nikolai Gogol's *Inspector General.* But whereas Gogol chose a very ordinary, practical young man, Mayakovsky's Russia is so tightly entangled in the bureaucratic network that he has to go all the way to an imaginary world to get his gleaming apparition, the Phosphorescent Woman.

The Bathhouse by Vladimir Mayakovsky, translated by Andrew R. MacAndrew, appears in *20th Century Russian Drama* (1963).—A. MacA.

Battles of Coxinga, The (Kokusenya Kassen, 1715). Japanese play by CHIKAMATSU MONZAEMON. Commonly considered the masterpiece in the heroic style of Japanese drama, *The Battles of Coxinga* was first performed on November 26, 1715, in the puppet theater at Osaka under the direction of the celebrated chanter, or *jōruri,* Takemoto Gidayu. The play was an unprecedented success, running for seventeen consecutive months. Adaptations of it were later made for the *kabuki* theater, where performance is by live actors. In this form it has been successful, though less brilliantly so. It remains a literary classic, displaying much of its author's gifts as a poet to great advantage.

Its triumph on the puppet (or BUNRAKU) stage was the result of its fitness in that medium. Chikamatsu provides many scenes of magic and exotic wonder, considerably more feasible to perform with dolls than with live actors. Episodes that embarrass actors liberated the playwright's fancy as poet. Considered in terms of a symbolic medium, the style is not only acceptable but moving and profound.

Both the setting and much of the plot derive from the Chinese theater. The quasi-historical narrative is based on the history of a military expedition made by Japanese warriors into China. All is exaggerated in melodramatic proportions. Blood, murder, and sudden death fill the stage. The playwright blithely scales the highest pinnacles of the heroic. One of the most celebrated and often imitated scenes depicts two Chinese sages with supernatural powers seated on a misted mountaintop quietly playing a game of *go,* symbolic of the wars and perturbations vexing the mortal world below them.

The best English translation and general introduction to Chikamatsu is Donald Keene's *Major Plays of Chikamatsu* (1961).—H. W. W.

Batu, Selâhattin (1905–). Turkish playwright and poet. Batu was born in Gelibolu, Turkey. After receiving a doctor's degree in veterinary medicine in Germany, he returned to Turkey in 1931 to join the faculty of the University of Ankara, where he is currently a professor. Batu was a member of parliament for one term and the editor of the newspaper *Ankara.* He has published many articles on medicine, two books of original poetry, a book of essays on art and man, several translations of poems and plays, and four original plays.

All of Batu's plays are in verse and deal either with Turkish or Greek mythology. He treats the myths of antiquity from a humanistic point of view and attempts to shed light on current themes and problems in Turkey and the world in general. Batu's *Güzel Helena* ("The Beautiful Helena," 1954) was translated into German by the German poet Bernt von Heiseler in 1957. The same year it received the second prize in an international drama contest and was produced in German in Vienna in 1959. Batu rewrote his *Kerem and Aslı* (1943) as a libretto for an opera by the Turkish composer Adnan Saygun.

Batu was the first Turkish dramatist to utilize antique material with a humanistic approach. His plays have helped pave the way for the works of the next generation of writers, such as Orhan Asena, Güngör Dilmen, and Turan Oflazoğlu.—N. O.

Beaumarchais, [Pierre Augustin] Caron de (1732–1799). French playwright, essayist, inventor, and spy. Pierre Augustin Caron took the name Beaumarchais from property belonging to the first of his three wives. He began his career as a watchmaker (inventing an escapement device still in use) and as a music teacher to the daughters of Louis XV. After several speculations involving him in lawsuits, he traveled to Spain in 1764 to complete certain business deals and to help his sister, who was entangled in an unhappy love affair.

In 1767 he made his debut in the theater with the serious play *Eugénie,* written according to Denis Diderot's theories of DRAME BOURGEOIS, then gaining favor. Beaumarchais defended this new genre in his Preface to the revised edition of the play, *Essai sur le genre dramatique sérieux* ("Essay on the Serious Drama," 1767), acknowledging Diderot's *Le Père de famille* (written 1758) and Michel Jean Sedaine's *Le Philosophe sans le savoir* (1765) as having inspired his own work. Despite its clarity and good sense, the essay lacks the vigor and wit found in his best work. His second play, *Les Deux amis, ou le négociant de Lyon* ("The Two Friends, or The Merchant of Lyon," 1770), was not successful.

From 1770 to 1775 Beaumarchais was involved in several lawsuits, including the Goëzman affair, involving attempted bribery of a judge. Beaumarchais replied to slanderous accusations in a famous series of *Mémoires* (1773–1774), which, although not ultimately favorable to his reputation, made him a popular hero because of his style and humor, his eloquent protest against injustice, and his searing ridicule of his enemies.

Meanwhile, *Le Barbier de Seville* (*The Barber of Seville,* 1775) had been gradually evolving from a light musical play with Spanish airs (it was later adapted for Gioacchino Antonio Rossini's well-known opera) into a finished comedy based on the old theme of the tyrannical guardian being outwitted in his attempt to marry his beautiful young ward by a

BEAUMARCHAIS (FRENCH CULTURAL SERVICES)

gallant young lover aided by a clever, intriguing servant. Beaumarchais skillfully combined materials from Molière and later French dramatists to create a complex, fast-moving comedy sparked by the biting, satirical vitality of the character Figaro. After a long delay indicating the anxiety of the censors over the rebellious, outspoken nature of Figaro, it was at last performed in February 1775. An indifferent reception caused Beaumarchais, with sure dramatic instinct, to cut his five acts to four and eliminate certain speeches, some of which were later incorporated into *The Marriage of Figaro.*

As one of the most formidably talented and versatile eighteenth-century French authors, Beaumarchais had a sense of justice and human dignity that he most passionately expressed in his masterpiece, THE MARRIAGE OF FIGARO. He probably began to write the comedy around 1776 and finished it a couple of years later, although it was not performed until 1784. Though he went on to write an opera, *Tarare* (1787), and a sentimental play, *La Mère Coupable* ("The Guilty Mother," 1792), his fame rests upon the two Figaro comedies.

By 1789 Beaumarchais's wealth aroused the suspicions of the revolutionaries who thought him sympathetic to the old regime. Resourceful as always, he spoke and wrote in his defense. He was imprisoned several times during the revolution and finally forced to leave France until 1796, but he did escape the guillotine. His final years were uneventful. Although deaf, he retained his imposing manner and persuasive tongue and pen until the end.

It should be remembered that although Beaumarchais's two great plays suffered greatly from the censorship that he condemned, his exposure of dishonesty and incompetence in high places and especially his favoring of an aristocracy of talents rather than of families were not really new ideas, except in the theater. Voltaire, Diderot, and Jean Jacques Rousseau had already prepared the upper middle class to regard the portrait of Figaro as a timely and appropriate, rather than a subversive, characterization.

There is no known English edition of Beaumarchais's works. *Le Barbier de Seville* has been translated by Albert Bermel and included with "A Letter from Beaumarchais to the Reader" and selected bibliography in *The Genius of the French Theater* (1961), edited by Bermel. The most recent biography is Cynthia Cox's *The Real Figaro: The Extraordinary Career of Caron de Beaumarchais* (1962). J. B. Ratermanis and W. R. Irwin's *The Comic Style of Beaumarchais* (1961) should be consulted on the plays.—S. S. S.

Beaumont, Francis (c. 1584–1616). English playwright. A native of Leicestershire, Beaumont attended Oxford and studied law at Inner Temple. He began playwriting about 1606, when he wrote his earliest extant play, *The Woman Hater,* for the boys' acting company Children of St. Paul's. A Jonsonian humour play, liberally sprinkled with social satire, it is a derivative but effective comedy. The only other extant play solely by Beaumont is *The Knight of the Burning Pestle* (1607). Modeled on Cervantes' *Don Quixote,* which had been translated into English in 1605, Beaumont's play is a delightful burlesque of the historical romances that were a popular staple of the

Elizabethan stage. But the play's satire is directed less at the romances themselves than at the audience who flocked to see them. Beaumont pokes considerable fun at the typical London audience, which he represents in the play-within-a-play format of the comedy.

About 1608 Beaumont began his famous collaboration with John Fletcher, an association that lasted about five years. During that time the playwrights produced jointly at least six plays. The establishment of a Beaumont-Fletcher canon has been complicated, however, by the fact that a collected edition of the plays published in 1679 describes no fewer than fifty-two plays as being "by Francis Beaumont and John Fletcher." Although Fletcher probably had a hand in all or most of the fifty-two, Beaumont, who retired from the stage in 1613, could have had a share in only a small portion. Scholars estimate that the Beaumont-Fletcher combination produced the following plays: *The Woman Hater* (1607), *Philaster* (c. 1610), *The Maid's Tragedy* (c. 1611), *A King and No King* (c. 1611), *The Captain* (1612), *Cupid's Revenge* (1612), *The Coxcomb* (1608–1610), *The Noble Gentleman* (1613), and *The Scornful Lady* (c. 1613). For a discussion of the Beaumont-Fletcher plays, see John FLETCHER.—E. Q.

Beaux' Stratagem, The (1707). A comedy by George FARQUHAR. The last of Farquhar's comedies, *The Beaux' Stratagem* was first produced less than two months before the author's death. It was successful then, and with frequent revivals has proved so ever since.

The scene is Litchfield. Two young men, Aimwell and Archer, have just arrived at the local inn, kept by the unscrupulous Boniface with the help of Cherry, his pert young daughter. Aimwell and Archer, in hope of bettering their fortunes, are traveling in disguise, the former under the name of his brother, Lord Aimwell, the latter posing as that lord's servant. They learn about the family that resides at the manor house: Lady Bountiful; Dorinda, her unmarried daughter; her son, the ill-tempered Sullen; and his discontented wife. Archer amuses himself with the engaging Cherry, and Aimwell meets and charms Dorinda, having gained admittance to Lady Bountiful's house by feigning illness. In the meantime Mrs. Sullen, weary of a country life and an impossible spouse, plots a harmless meeting with a French officer, held in Litchfield as a prisoner of war. But later on, with the appearance of Archer, Mrs. Sullen finds herself genuinely attracted to the latter. There are amusing episodes involving Boniface, the highwayman Gibbet, and the latter's two companions, Hounslow and Bagshot. Scrub, Sullen's servant, and Gipsy, maid to the ladies of the manor house, introduce moments of diverting low comedy. At Lady Bountiful's there is attempted robbery, there are rescues, there are bedroom scenes bordering on the farcical. The untangling of the various complications is skillfully managed, and the ending is altogether unusual. Aimwell, having won the hand of Dorinda, confesses that he is an impostor and chivalrously releases the lady from her promises, but he has no sooner done so than he receives word that his brother

DRAWING OF A SCENE FROM GEORGE FARQUHAR'S *The Beaux' Stratagem* (WALTER HAMPDEN MEMORIAL LIBRARY AT THE PLAYERS, NEW YORK)

has died suddenly and that he is in truth Lord Aimwell. So he claims Dorinda. But what of Archer and Mrs. Sullen, who by this time have discovered that they were meant for one another? Two turns of good fortune serve to assure them of their future happiness together, for Archer gets £10,000 from Aimwell and Mrs. Sullen is promised a divorce by her husband, who is already persuaded that they are not one flesh but "rather two carcasses joined unnaturally together."

The setting in a provincial town rather than London, the characters who provide the scenes of low comedy, and the youthfulness and high spirits of Aimwell and Archer—not to mention Cherry— give the comedy its freshness of atmosphere. The energies of the young people find free but not coarse expression, their natural desires the promise of rational fulfillment. Such promise has as background the argument voiced so emphatically by Mrs. Sullen: unhappy marriage violates the law of nature, and that very law makes divorce lawful. It is especially this concept of rational freedom—from Milton, it would seem—that makes the play memorable.

The Beaux' Stratagem (1967), edited by Eric Rothstein, contains an excellent critical introduction.—R. Q.

Bechuanaland. See AFRICA: *Bechuanaland*.

Beckett, Samuel (1906–   ). Irish-born French playwright. As an Irishman who was educated and taught at the University of Dublin, Beckett wrote his first poems, essays, and novel (*Murphy*, pub. 1932) in English. After traveling extensively on the Continent for several years, he settled permanently in France in 1938. After the war he wrote directly in French the works with which his name is associated today: the novels *Molloy* (1951), *Malone meurt* (*Malone Dies,*

SAMUEL BECKETT (FRENCH CULTURAL SERVICES)

1951), and *L'Innommable* (*The Unnamable*, 1953); and two plays, WAITING FOR GODOT and ENDGAME.

Among the leading works of revolt in our age are Beckett's novels and plays, which contain a simple, lucid indictment against our civilization and its industrialization. The style that Beckett uses is that of the THEATER OF THE ABSURD. Similar indictments had been made by Arthur Rimbaud, Le Comte de Lautréamont, Friedrich Hölderlin, and Antonin Artaud, but in each case such attacks resulted in madness or flight. Beckett's vision of man, however, is comparably grim and absolute, but he seems to have maintained a personal serenity of outlook.

By the power of his style, Beckett transforms his plays into a kind of circus and his characters into clowns. Appearing as couples—the victim and the tyrant, the simpleton and the crafty character— these clowns need each other: Vladimir needs Estragon, Pozzo needs Lucky, Hamm needs Clov. Even Krapp, in the monologue play *La Dernière Bande* (*Krapp's Last Tape*, 1958), listens to a former self. Their clowning is a kind of ceremony in which they use a few indispensable props. These clowns pretend to play in order to pass the time and forget themselves, and all their activities are diversions, amusements which comprise the daily occupation of living. In these games, which are not illusions, Beckett stresses the tragic theme in his work. See also HAPPY DAYS. For a critical study of Beckett's work, see the following: Richard Coe, *Samuel Beckett* (1966); Ruby Cohn, *Samuel Beckett: The Comic Gamut* (1962); Hugh Kenner, *Samuel Beckett* (1961) and *Flaubert, Joyce and Beckett, the Stoic Comedians* (1963); Nathan A. Scott, *Samuel Beckett* (1966); and W. Y. Tindall, *Samuel Beckett* (1964).—W. F.

Becque, Henry [**François**] (1837–1899). French playwright and critic. While he was revolutionizing French dramatic art with his two great naturalistic plays, *The Vultures* and *La Parisienne* (*Woman of Paris*, 1885), Becque was ignored by Émile Zola, the loudest of naturalism's advocates. On the other hand, Becque had little use for Zola's long-winded precepts and disassociated himself from the latter's scientific view of dramatic art: that the theater must present the degrading effects of environment and heredity. Yet Zola and Becque were destined, with their very different talents, to become the acknowledged leaders of the naturalistic movement in France, the former being a theorist, the latter a great and original, if not a popular, playwright.

Graduating from the Lycée Bonaparte in Paris, Becque became secretary and tutor in the household of a Polish diplomat. He met the composer Victorin Joncières and wrote the libretto for *Sardanapale* (1867). In 1868 his farce *L'Enfant prodigue* ("The Prodigal Son") was produced. Since his decision to write plays for a living resulted in nothing but quarrels with directors and he was in need of money, he reviewed plays for various newspapers. He himself directed his first serious play, *Michel Pauper*, and produced it at his own expense in 1870 after another disagreement with the theatrical establishment. A mixture of romanticism and crude realism with a socialistic slant, the play failed initially but fared better when revived in 1886. The failure of *L'Enlèvement* ("The Elopement") the following year forced Becque to seek employment in a stockbroker's office.

In 1877 he wrote his most famous play, THE VULTURES, whose dissimilarity to the established plays of the time delayed its performance until 1882. Meanwhile, a modest success greeted *La Navette* ("The Shuttle") in 1878, a cynical one-act farce which anticipated *La Parisienne,* and *Les honnêtes femmes* ("The Virtuous Women") in 1880. His second real success came in 1885 when *La Parisienne* was performed, after more rejections, at the Théâtre de la Renaissance.

Success had come too late, and Becque's inspiration had dried up. He wrote only a few short sketches before his premature death and left unfinished a scathing satire of the stock exchange that was to have been his masterpiece: *Les Polichinelles* ("The Puppets," Act I performed 1924). Of the sketches, two one-acters written in 1897 are interesting: *Veuve!* ("Widowed," not performed) and *Le Départ* ("The Start," 1924). The first is a sequel to *La Parisienne* with the adulterous Clotilde now a widow, but her character unchanged. The second is a naturalistic sketch of a shopgirl's moral deterioration.

Becque's two best plays virtually eliminate the traditional plot structure of the popular "well-made plays" of Eugène Scribe and Alexandre Dumas fils (withheld secret, exposition, seesaw, reversal, *scène à faire,* and logical denouement). They present without comment a photographic close-up of commonplace characters and events (the *tranche de vie,* or slice of life, of naturalistic drama). The playwright's dispassionate ridicule results from the disparity between the characters' righteous opinion of themselves (appearance) and the audience's recognition of what they are (reality). The immorality of the characters is revealed by the discrepancy between their unconscious pose of virtue and propriety and their truly selfish and dishonest lives, making them ludicrously hypocritical in their concern for decorum and respectability.

With even greater economy of characterization, structure, and dialogue than he had used in *The Vultures,* Becque attained the summit of his creative powers with *La Parisienne,* regarded as the established prototype of the *comédie rosse,* or cynical comedy, which became the vogue in the last years of the nineteenth century. It is his most simply constructed play: a *ménage à trois* ends where it began —in emotional bankruptcy. The playwright has refrained from comment and does not permit his feelings to intrude on the action. His play devastatingly parodies Parisian marital relations. Du Mesnil, a complacent cuckold, blissfully trusts his wife, Clotilde, and accepts her lover, Lafont, as one of the household. To help her husband obtain a coveted position, she momentarily takes another lover. Lafont appears as ridiculous as the husband, because he is wracked by jealousy and suspicion and is a pompous preacher of respectability. Clotilde is frivolous but wily, extravagant but calculating—and charming. Her obsession with presenting a respectable appearance is revealed when she criticizes her lover's lack of religion. Yet she sheds genuine tears in the last act for the disillusionment and the regrets her folly has brought upon her.

Freeman Tilden's translation of *The Vultures* is in *A Treasury of the Theatre* (1960), edited by John Gassner. There have been four English versions of *La Parisienne.* Jacques Barzun's is in *The Modern Theatre,* Vol. I (1955), edited by Eric Bentley. No biography has been published in English. Comment on Becque may be found in James Huneker's *Iconoclasts* (1905), H. A. Smith's *Main Currents of Modern French Drama* (1925), S. M. Waxman's *Antoine and the Théâtre-Libre* (new ed., 1964), and Gassner's *A Treasury of the Theatre.*—S. S. S.

Before Dawn (Vor Sonnenaufgang, also translated as **Before Sunrise,** 1889). A social play by Gerhart HAUPTMANN. In this play the reader is confronted with a typical Hauptmann dramatic formula: A messenger, in this case the socialist and idealistic reformer Alfred Loth, arrives to stimulate reform in a morally corrupt community. However, his attempts fail, and instead of his healing message he brings confusion, which ends in catastrophe.

Loth tries to lend his strength and support to the Silesian coal miners in their struggle against the decadent parvenus of the community. Helene, the daughter of one of these parvenus, turns to Loth for help to free herself from this existence and hopes through her marriage to him to escape the dreaded curse—drunkenness—that has corrupted her family. However, when Loth is confronted by this superior hereditary force, he is frightened and refuses to marry her: Helene, in despair, commits suicide.

One finds here in Hauptmann's first drama the typical naturalist themes and stylistic characteristics: the problems of heredity (compare with Ibsen's *Ghosts*), sympathy for the workers, detailed description of the milieu. However, Hauptmann proves himself capable of breaking through the confines of dry naturalist style as, for example, in the lyrical love scenes between Loth and Helene.—C. A. M.

Beggar's Opera, The (1728). A ballad opera by John GAY. Gay's ballad opera—the first play of its type—opened at Lincoln's Inn Fields Theatre, having previously been refused by playwright-actor Colley Cibber for production at Drury Lane. The public instantly fell in love with it, and it remained a favorite for the rest of the century. It was revived in the 1920's and again in 1963. There is a film version (1954) of *The Beggar's Opera,* and from the play has sprung Bertold Brecht's *The Threepenny Opera* (1928).

The action is simple enough. Peachum is a fence for a group of London thieves whom he controls. He and his wife are shocked to learn that their daughter, Polly, has committed the folly of marrying Captain Macheath, the highwayman she loves. They would persuade Polly to betray her husband to the authorities for a reward, but she warns Macheath of his danger. He, however, delays his flight to safety in order to pay his respects to a group of his women acquaintances, thanks to one of whom he is taken into custody by Peachum and imprisoned in Newgate. The worst of it is that Lockit, the Newgate turnkey, has a daughter, Lucy, and Lucy has been wronged by Macheath, who has refused to marry her as agreed. But Lucy aids Macheath to escape. He is again betrayed, is again apprehended, and now is condemned to instant hanging. At this point one is reminded that *The Beggar's Opera* is actually a play-within-a-play, for it has begun with an Introduction in which the playwright, a beggar, has explained certain details to one of the players. Player and beggar-playwright now reappear, the former protesting that to allow Macheath to be executed is to turn the opera into "a downright deep tragedy." The beggar yields, and so a reprieve is cried and Macheath is brought back to the stage alive to acknowledge Polly as his lawful wedded wife.

The reasons for the play's extraordinary success were several. For some time London had been enjoying Italian opera and at the same time making fun of it. Here was a different and surprising version of opera, one with sixty-nine "airs," that is, Gay's new words, with many *double-entendres,* set mostly to old tunes familiar to everyone. And the story itself was overlaid with political satire, which Gay, carrying on the Tory campaign against the Whig administration, was leveling at Sir Robert Walpole and his notorious methods of controlling elections. Then, too, romantic and sentimental themes were both given a ridiculous turn. Finally, Gay's irony—more properly his multiple ironies—runs through it all, and in the device of a play-within-a-play with the discussion of the inner play by playwright and actor there is an anticipation of the Brechtian alienation effect.

Of the many modern editions of *The Beggar's Opera,* one of the best is that appearing in 1961. In his *Gay's Beggar's Opera, Its Content, History and Influence* (1923), William E. Schultz gives an excellent general introduction to the play.—R. Q.

Behan, Brendan (1923–1964). Irish playwright. A native Dubliner, Behan was the son of a member of the conspiratorial Irish Republican Army. Continuing the family tradition, he joined the IRA while still in his teens and was imprisoned at the age of sixteen for attempting to blow up a British battleship. He subsequently served two more prison terms, the last of which resulted in his being deported to France. Interned in Dublin during World War II, Behan was released in 1946 only to be arrested again in 1947 for violating a deportation order. After a few months' imprisonment he was released and shortly thereafter began his career as a journalist and playwright. With the successful production of *The Hostage,* Behan caught the public attention as the embodiment of the wild Irishman—profane, witty, irreverent, and

BRENDAN BEHAN (IRISH TOURIST BOARD)

above all, hard-drinking. His drinking bouts won him a notoriety that far outdistanced his reputation as a playwright. The excessive drinking, however, took its toll, and he died early of complications resulting from a diabetic and liver condition.

Ironically enough, Behan found his most sympathetic audiences in the English, not the Irish, theater. His earliest play, *The Quare Fellow* (1954), although first produced in Dublin, achieved its greatest success in London in 1956. Set in a prison on the night of a scheduled execution, *The Quare Fellow* deals with the effect of the impending execution on various prisoners and jailers. Into this somber theme, however, is interwoven a rich vein of ribald comedy conveyed largely by the sparkling, vital speech of the play's many characters.

Behan's second play, *The Hostage* (1956), was originally written in Gaelic and was later translated and enlarged by the author. The play is set in a local brothel where an English soldier is taken as hostage by the IRA in an attempt to prevent the execution of a young Irishman convicted of murder. The brothel soon becomes the scene of a wild assortment of characters and incidents that are hurtled along on the wings of Behan's roistering, swaggering prose. The play has the quality of a tragic farce, its vital racy language complementing in paradoxical fashion the pervasive undertone of death. Behan's only other extant play is *The Big House* (1958), a radio drama. Another play, *Richard's Cork Leg,* remained uncompleted at his death.

In the United States *The Quare Fellow* and *The Hostage* have been published by Grove Press. A biography, *Brendan Behan: Man and Showman,* has been written by Rae Jeffs.—E. Q.

Behrman, S[amuel] N[athaniel] (1893–   ). American playwright and biographer. The son of Jewish immigrants, Behrman grew up in Worcester, Massachusetts, in a milieu totally unlike the elegant, sophisticated settings he was to use for his plays. Glimpses of his early days constitute the autobiographical sketches in *The Worcester Account* (1954). Following his graduation from Clark University, he went on to work with George Pierce Baker at Harvard. It was not until he was thirty, and had spent many years as a journalist and short-story writer, that he had a play produced, *The Second Man* (1927).

Behrman's most productive years were the late 1920's and the decade of the 1930's. He wrote a series of distinctive comedies of ideas in which he explored the role of the comic spirit—usually embodied in a lovely, detached, witty woman who is intolerant of pretentiousness, yet sensitive to human weakness, and painfully caught in a world of ideological polarities. In *Biography* (1932) a painter who has been mistress to many important men refuses to have her memoirs used for political purposes, even though she loves the young man who wants to publish her book and sympathizes with his aims. In *Rain from Heaven* (1934) the heroine rejects her lover, a distinguished explorer, because he is being used as a figurehead by a fascist organization, yet she also refuses to accept fully the militancy of the anti-Nazi position. In *End of Summer* (1936) the wealthy heroine is in the middle of a symposium on the uses of money but commits herself to no one position, though sensitive to the claims of all. And in *No Time for Comedy* (1939) a playwright, who thinks he should write protest plays about the Spanish Civil War, is convinced by his actress-wife that his true talent lies in creating life-enhancing laughter. Less directly concerned with such questions are *The Second Man* (1927), the portrait of a suave seducer painfully aware of his lack of real emotion, and *Amphitryon 38* (1937), adapted from Jean Giraudoux's play, which argues that human love, suffering, and death are preferable to the gods' bland, painless immortality.

Since 1940, Behrman's dramatic work has consisted mainly of adaptations, such as *The Pirate* (1942), from the German comedy by Ludwig Fulda; *I Know My Love* (1949), a chronicle of marriage based on *Auprès de ma Blonde,* by Marcel Achard; and *Jacobowsky and the Colonel* (1944), based on Franz Werfel's comedy about a Jew and an anti-Semitic Polish officer during the fall of France. More important has been Behrman's shift to biography. *Duveen* (1952), a study of the influential art dealer, and *Portrait of Max* (1960), a profile of Max Beerbohm, are beautifully controlled pictures.

There is no standard edition of Behrman's plays. Critical discussions can be found in the major volumes on modern American drama.—M. L.

Belasco, David (1853–1931). American producer and playwright. Belasco was born in San Francisco and grew up in Victoria, B.C. Returning to San Francisco in 1865, he worked in the theater as actor, stage manager, and writer. In 1879 he collaborated with playwright-actor James A. Herne on *Chums,* a domestic melodrama which, retitled *Hearts of Oak,* was in Herne's repertory for many years. Belasco went to New York in 1882, became a producer in 1890, and by 1900 was a power in the theater. Between 1887 and 1890, he collaborated with William C. De Mille on four successful plays: *The Wife,* a drama of marriage; *Lord Chumley,* a comedy; *The Charity Ball,* a family drama; and *Men and Women,* a melodrama of high finance and high society. For the opening of his Empire Theatre in 1893, Belasco collaborated with Franklyn Fyles on *The Girl I Left*

DAVID BELASCO (WALTER HAMPDEN MEMORIAL LIBRARY AT THE PLAYERS, NEW YORK)

Behind Me, a stirring melodrama in which an army post, besieged by Sioux Indians, is saved at the last moment by the arrival of the United States cavalry. For the actress Mrs. Leslie Carter, he wrote *The Heart of Maryland* (1895), a Civil War melodrama. He collaborated with playwright John Luther Long (1861–1927) on *Madame Butterfly* (1890), which Puccini made into the well-known opera; *The Darling of the Gods* (1902), a romantic drama laid in old Japan; and *Adrea,* a romantic tragedy set in the fifth century A.D. In *The Return of Peter Grimm* (1911) he made clever use of the supernatural.

Belasco, best known for the meticulous realism of his productions, was a practical man of the theater; he knew what would be effective on the stage. As author, co-author, or adapter of some seventy plays, the best of them he combined in sentiment, romance, and sensational action under a veneer of realistic dialogue and stage business.

The best source is Craig Timberlake, *Life and Work of David Belasco, Bishop of Broadway* (1954). —B. H.

Belgium. Belgian drama is essentially Flemish, whether written in that language (that is, Dutch, bearing in mind minor differences such as exist between English and American) or in French. This is the case at each of the significant stages in its development, in much the same way as Belgian art, until fairly recently, has been predominantly Flemish. With the advent of Belgian independence in 1830, the Flemish tradition in drama became the basis, however shaky at the time, of the new national dramatic tradition.

This Flemish character is reflected in temperament and atmosphere; its strongest trait is to be found in a fascinating, at times bewildering, ability to combine realism and mysticism, to combine an obsession with the supernatural and a shrewd sense of reality. In the Flemish tradition these two spheres are almost inseparable; there is no distance between earthy exuberance and piety, no gap separating the reckless pursuit of the supernatural from a stubborn fascination with the material dimensions of life, whether revealed in hard-jawed stinginess or boisterous generosity. What is unique about Flemish culture is not so much this duality in itself but the extremes to which the two approaches are pushed, making for an art that both capitalizes on, and at times suffers from, the excesses and contradictions inherent in a dual vision of the world.

middle ages and Renaissance. An important contribution to world drama was made by the Flemish medieval theater in its religious and, perhaps even more, its secular forms. The earliest mystery plays— plays dramatizing largely biblical material—have been lost. Of interest are the *Eerste* and *Sevenste Bliscap van Maria* (*The Joy of Mary*), the former dealing with the Annunciation, the latter with Mary's Ascension. Dating back to about 1440, they are the only extant plays in a series of seven, one of which appears to have been staged in Brussels every year for almost a century. Moving away from Church and ritualistic functions and increasingly incorporating secular elements, religious drama also turned to the lives of saints, concentrating on the miracles they performed. Great freedom was taken with the material of these saints' legends. They were frequently a mere excuse for elaborate spectacle and an anachronistic, colorful sequence of fantastic adventures in which devils—funny and appealing rather than frightening—figure prominently. One outstanding example of the genre has been preserved: *Mariken van Nieumeghen* (*Mary of Nijmegen*). Probably written by an Antwerp author toward the end of the fifteenth century, the play deals with the story of a young girl who, after having been seduced by the devil and having lived with him for seven years, is saved by the Virgin Mary. Skillful use is made of the device of a narrator. Obviously, this frequently revived play is the work of a gifted poet. Not only has he created living characters and given some of the scenes real poignancy, but he has also succeeded in combining psychological motivation and the tender expression of pure faith with a vivid evocation of the society of his day.

Developing out of mystery and miracle plays, and reflecting the didacticism of the increasingly powerful citizenry, were morality plays. The outstanding Flemish contribution to this type of allegorical drama is *Den Spyeghel der Salicheyt van Elckerlyc,* ascribed to Pieter van Diest and dating from the second half of the fifteenth century. The play is widely known in its English version, *Everyman,* but a number of American, British, and Flemish scholars seem to have proved that the English play is but a weak translation of the Flemish original.

The richness of the Flemish secular tradition precludes tracing back medieval drama exclusively to religious origins. The early Church was never able to eradicate a tradition of itinerant actors; its own schools soon turned to Latin drama for educational purposes, its teachers adapting Senecan drama or writing new religious plays in Latin verse. Play elements abound in tournaments, processionals, and other public events of the feudal age; as soon as religious drama developed, it absorbed secular passages that pushed it out of the Church. The range of secular drama is remarkable. Flanders contributed its share of crude farces (called *sotternyen, boerden,* or *kluchten*) in which the Flemish flair for relentless caricature is evident. Short, usually anonymous plays, such as *Lippijn* (c. 1350), *De Buskenblaser* ("The Box-Blower," c. 1350), *Die Hexe* ("The Witch," c. 1350), *Drie daghe Here* ("A Lord for Three Days," c. 1350), and the popular *Ghenoechlike Cluyte van Nu Noch* ("The Enjoyable Farce of Come on Now," c. 1350), usually center around marital crises, with cuckolds, henpecked husbands, gossips, and young wives in most cases making up the predictable cast of three or four. The buskenblaser lets himself be talked into getting a magic box that will rejuvenate him. All he has to do is blow into it. But the box is filled with soot and by blowing into it he only succeeds in making his face black. His hardhanded young wife does not hesitate to reward him for his efforts with a sound thrashing. In *Rubben* (c. 1350) a young, gullible husband ends up by finding it totally normal that he should become a father after a mere three months of marriage. Although these colorful, crude farces are written according to a formula, they still contain aggressively revealing social comments about medieval society. Among these farces, the *Cluyte van Playerwater* ("The Farce of Playerwater," c. 1350) is psychologically better motivated and just a little subtler than the others.

These farces were often performed after a religious play or with another type of secular drama; in either case the programming points to a Flemish obsession with extreme contrasts. Indeed, nothing in Flemish drama could be farther removed from the realm of boisterous farce than the sophistication of the *abele spelen* (literally, "beautiful" or "skillful" plays). The four abele spelen contained in the Hulthem manuscript—*Esmoreit, Gloriant, Lanseloet van Denemarken* (*Lancelot of Denmark*), and *Van den Winter ende van den Somer* (*Of Winter and Summer*)—all dating back to the middle of the fourteenth century, are truly unique in European drama. Furthermore, the first three of these plays are beautiful and exciting, ranking with *Mariken van Nieumeghen* and, perhaps, *Elckerlyc,* among the best of European drama in the middle ages. *Van den Winter ende van den Somer* is a rather drawn-out, allegorical dramatization of the struggle between the two seasons. The other plays are more deeply rooted in a romantic, chivalric tradition. *Esmoreit* seems quite rudimentary in its psychological motivation and at times clumsy in the development of its action, but its very simplicity and blunt directness make the play most appealing and refreshing. Esmoreit, the very young son of an aging king, is kidnapped by the king's brother, who has already taken the throne for granted. Esmoreit is sold to an astrologer and taken to an oriental court where he grows up as the king's son and falls in love with the ruler's daughter. Eventually, the girl reveals his true identity to him, and Esmoreit decides to wander back to his native Sicily. Arriving there, he comes across a jailed woman who, in the course of a touching recognition scene, turns out to be his own mother, accused of having murdered her child. His mother is freed, the villainous uncle hanged, and Esmoreit can marry the girl he loves. *Gloriant* and *Lanseloet van Denemarken* are far more ambitious and much subtler. *Gloriant* deals with a woman-hater who, once he has been confronted with the incarnation of ideal womanhood, the beautiful Florentijn, will risk his life and do anything to win her. The most poignant of these plays, and also the most modern, is *Lanseloet van Denemarken.* Lanseloet, a young knight, is torn between his love for Sanderijn and the rigid class-consciousness of his environment that would keep him from marrying someone below his rank. Urged by his mother, he seduces the young girl. She flees into the forest, where she meets a knight whom she tells what happened to her. In spite of this, the knight takes her along and marries her. But Lanseloet is overcome with sorrow and shame and wants Sanderijn to come back. Rather than report to Lanseloet that she refuses to return, his messenger tells him that she died. The news kills Lanseloet.

Little more needs to be said about the fifteenth century. Apart from *Mariken van Nieumeghen* and *Elckerlyc,* it produced virtually nothing of artistic merit. While the Burgundian era is synonymous with peaks in the development of Flemish painting, it is also synonymous with a decline in literature and drama that continued throughout the sixteenth century. By 1450 virtually the entire literary output had become the monopoly of the chambers of rhetoricians—subsidized civic groups officially in charge of organizing the countless festivities that were so typical of this age. One of the key figures in each of the chambers was the *factor,* the poet who wrote the plays and occasional poems. Considering drama the highest form of art, the chambers organized annual national contests (*landjuwelen*) in which the invited groups wrote and performed a play based on an assigned subject. In most of these plays incredible pomp, didacticism, and mysticism are carried to their furthest extremes. More often than not they are devoid of dramatic action and consist of endless, dull debates between allegorical figures—lessons or sermons in the form of dialogue. A typical author is Cornelis Everaert (1485–1556), a weaver from Bruges. Thirty-five of his plays have been preserved. Frequently they were commissioned for a political celebration, a religious ceremony, or, simply, a party. The best among them, *Maria Hoedeken* (1509), is basically a miracle play, but unfortunately it has been given the full allegorical treatment, with abstract characters like Good Companionship and Inner Remorse and other conventions of the morality play.

One begins to detect some sporadic influence, however slight and superficial, of the Renaissance. The Greek and Latin heritage was rediscovered, names and legends were used, and mythological episodes appeared, but all of this was mixed in with the conventions of the morality play. Thus, in *Pyramus ende Thisbe* by Matthijs de Castelein (1488–1550), Pyramus embodies the Passion of Christ and Thisbe the devout soul. More significant was the role that many of these allegorical efforts increasingly played in the promulgation of Protestantism, a role that was to lead to the temporary suppression of the chambers and their competitions during the religious wars.

seventeenth and eighteenth centuries. In most of Western Europe toward the end of the middle ages, the activities of the chambers and similar organizations coincided with a period of decline. But whereas for most countries it was also a period of preparation, a transition eventually leading to a golden age of the theater, unfortunately in Flanders any chance of growth and development in the vital period of roughly 1560 to 1610 was obliterated by uninterrupted war. The Spanish rule marked the beginning of an endless sequence of battles and occupations that drained the country of its intellectual and economic resources. The Inquisition and Counter Reformation provoked a mass exodus to the United Provinces (over 80,000 left Antwerp), and in the violent chaos and clatter they kept Flanders—Belgium—completely cut off from all the new ideas and influences that were decisive in the shaping of great seventeenth-century drama. Moreover, the occupying forces viewed the national language and its main defenders, the chambers of rhetoricians, with distrust and disdain. It must be remembered that however low their artistic standards these chambers provided the only semblance of cultural activity. The ruling classes continued to disassociate themselves from the native tongue; for all official intents and purposes Flemish was the secondary language, the dialect of the uneducated masses. The few writers who were left or who returned in the early part of the seventeenth century tried to continue where drama left off some fifty years earlier. They worked in a vacuum; Belgian drama seemed unaware of vital developments elsewhere. Its

authors were unable or unwilling to set new standards; they hung on to medieval allegorical traditions. When they turned to foreign plays, it was to imitate their external conventions and miss their spirit, to attempt cheap imitations of the most popular types of drama, such as the romantic Spanish cloak-and-dagger plays and revenge tragedies. Their preference went to the successful but mediocre authors of the era and in their clumsy adaptations of some of the great plays the originals tended to be virtually unrecognizable. The number of plays written, at least in the seventeenth century, remains quite impressive. Every type of drama is represented, from plays about Christ to pastoral dramas, from mystery plays or the dramatizations of the lives of patron saints to melodramas and crude farces. An author like Cornelis de Bie (1627–1711) is typical of the period. His dramatic output—some forty-five plays —is a veritable anthology of different forms and styles, a melting pot of national traditions and foreign influences, thrown together in the most unlikely combinations with undeniable ease and even gusto. Two authors stand out: Willem Ogier (1618–1689) and, above all, Michiel de Swaen (1654–1707). Ogier's genuine talent for comedy and realism and his perfect ear for the language of the lower classes in his native Antwerp are amply demonstrated in seven coarse but vivid farces published in one volume under the title *The Seven Deadly Sins* (1682). Michiel de Swaen is best remembered for his *De Verheerlijckte Schoenlappers of de gecroonde leersse* ("The Glorified Cobblers or the Crowned Boot," 1688), an effective farce which is still occasionally revived, and for his *De mensch–wordingh van het eeuwigh Woort* ("The Incarnation of the Eternal Word," 1686). The purity of expression, the depth of feeling, and the genuine poetry of this mystery play can hardly fail to impress.

But Ogier and De Swaen were isolated cases. From a prominent position in European theater, Flemish

MICHIEL DE SWAEN (BELGIAN INFORMATION SERVICE)

drama slipped back further and further into obscure provincialism, where it remained until well into the nineteenth century. Holland took over as the cultural center of the Low Countries. Flemish refugees met and founded new chambers there; authors of Flemish descent contributed significantly to the brilliant Dutch Renaissance and Baroque that were to produce Pieter Cornelisz(oon) Hooft, Gerbrand Adriaanszoon Bredero, Constantijn Huygens, Thomas Asselyn, and, above all, Joost van den Vondel, the greatest dramatic poet of the Netherlands. (See DUTCH AND FLEMISH DRAMA.)

nineteenth century. As Belgium gained independence in 1830, Flemish culture reached its nadir. The subordinate position of the Flemish language was confirmed by laws making French the official language in Flanders. There were no audiences left and the language of those trying to write plays for audiences of analphabets often was as clumsy as their dramatic technique. Theater societies, descendants of the old chambers of rhetoricians, immediately occupied a key position in the struggle to rediscover a language and a culture; they became a major weapon in the fight for Flemish rights. Naturally, a theater so poorly prepared and so heavily committed could hardly be expected to yield results that were artistically rewarding. Catering to the crudest of tastes and producing fervent propaganda are two extremes that leave little room for art, and the plays written in the first decades in the life of the young Belgian state prove this. Invariably, they were sentimental melodramas, highly colored, romantic, historical plays, or farces by authors like Hyppoliet van Peene (1811–1864), Karel Ondereet (1804–1868), Emmanuel Rosseels (1818–1904), or Napoleon Destanberg (1829–1875). Attempts at realism and naturalism, while they brought the dialogue onstage closer to natural speech patterns, remained steeped in pathos and romanticism with authors like Domien Sleeckx (1818–1901) and, above all, Nestor de Tière (1856–1920). The daring of some of de Tière's themes—at least by the standards of his day—his skill, and refreshing vitality account for the enormous popularity his often coarse peasant dramas enjoyed, among them *Roze Kate* (1893), *Liefdedrift* ("Love Passion," 1892), and *Wilde Lea* (1894). Lodewijk Scheltjens (1861–1946) (*Wildstroopers,* "Poachers," 1899; *Rina,* 1903; *Visscherseer,* "Fisherman's Honor," 1901) and Edmond Roeland (1873–1929) were less romantic, more socially oriented, but seldom capable of generating quite the same theatrical excitement. Brief mention should also be made of the effective farces of August Hendrikx (1846–1918). The most mature and lasting contribution in the realistic-naturalistic tradition was made when the great novelist Cyriel Buysse (1859–1932) wrote *Het Gezin van Paemel* ("The van Paemel Family," 1903) and *Driekoningenavond* ("Twelfth Night," 1903), works of somber intensity and taut economy that dramatize the economic and moral decay of the Flemish rural population. Their moments of tart humor barely conceal the author's compassion.

In the meantime, the Flemish fight for national identity had been quite impressively symbolized in *Gudrun* (1878), a heroic verse drama written by the young Albrecht Rodenbach (1856–1880). This fervent play has been overrated—at one time it was

turned into a myth—but these exaggerations should not blind one to the fact that *Gudrun,* for all its flaws and overstatement, definitely is the work of an inspired, talented young poet. Flemish drama again was reaching out for stature and nearly attaining it when Alfred Hegenscheidt (1866–1964) wrote *Starkadd* (1897). Here again lyrical overstatement tends to make the play all too stridently romantic and to obscure its dramatic structure. A trend can be detected here; what applies to Rodenbach and Hegenscheidt is also true—and to an even more damaging degree—of Cyriel Verschaeve (1874–1950), a poet and priest who only occasionally (most of all in *Judas,* 1919, and *Maria-Magdalena,* 1930) managed to rescue the drama in his historical or biblical plays from impassioned but decidedly self-indulgent oratory.

twentieth century. More names could be added to this record of slow revival, but the Flemish heritage and character, at this stage, found a much more compelling expression in the work of a number of playwrights who wrote in French. The Ghent-born poet Charles van Lerberghe wrote one of the first symbolist plays, *Les Flaireurs* ("A Sense of Death," 1892). It was another Ghent-born author, Maurice MAETERLINCK, who, with *La Princesse Maleine* (pub. 1890), put Belgian drama into the vanguard of European theater. More than any other single event the production of this violent, brooding play signaled the victory of symbolism over naturalism. The play's eerie atmosphere, its obsession with the supernatural, with occult powers shaping the destiny of man to the accompaniment of wind and thunderstorms, lightning and shooting stars, its roots in nameless fear heightened by evasive signs and ominous symbols, constantly promise more than this story actually sustains. What was meant to be tragic comes across merely as macabre; the tone and atmosphere throughout seem somewhat inflated, artificial, and decorative. Greater concentration and discipline made *L'Intruse* (*The Intruder,* 1890) and *Les Aveugles* (*The Blind,* 1890), the shorter plays which followed *La Princesse Maleine,* infinitely more rewarding. It would seem that short plays were more ideally suited to Maeterlinck's dramatic approach, and these compelling mood pieces fully justified his sudden fame. His reputation kept mounting as he wrote *Pelléas et Mélisande* (1892), *L'Intérieur* (1894), *La Mort de Tintagiles* (*The Death of Tintagiles,* 1894) and began defining his dramatic theories, especially in *Le Trésor des humbles* (*The Treasure of the Humble,* 1896). Maeterlinck was haunted by the inescapableness of dimensions of existence beyond rational control—blind, mysterious forces, eternal laws of life that keep invading man. The presence of these forces, Maeterlinck felt, could best be sensed in absolute stillness, by observing total inactivity. The highest degree of dramatic tension he found in an old man sitting in his armchair at night "giving unconscious ear to all the eternal laws that reign about his house, interpreting, without comprehending, the silence of doors and windows and the quivering voice of the light, submitting with bent head to the presence of his soul and his destiny." Hence, Maeterlinck reflected a tragic sense of life and a kind of static drama, not in violent action, but in contemplation and, indeed, in the absence of action or conflict.

Hence the significance of pregnant silences meant to convey more than spoken words. Hence also attempts to capture in dialogue snatches of unconscious thought. This concern with the mystic poetry of "soul states" encouraged Maeterlinck to look upon the actor's contribution to dramatic art with great suspicion and to advocate the suppression of his personality through the use of masks, highly stylized speech and movement patterns, and, ultimately, the introduction of a Gordon Craig-like "Ueber-Marionette," a kind of superpuppet that would replace the subjectivity, the individuality of the actor. Theory and practice reach a near-perfect balance in plays like *Les Aveugles* or *L'Intérieur.* Maeterlinck's later plays tended to contradict his theories. His pessimism was subsiding, the somber mists of his earlier landscapes were clearing, but plays like *Monna Vanna* (1902) or *Marie Magdeleine* (1913) seem ponderously commonplace in comparison with his first plays. For all its exquisite moments, even his charming *L'Oiseau bleu* (*The Blue Bird,* 1911) wears a little thin as one keeps waiting in vain for developments in the action that would vitalize and enrich the play's basic theme, happiness in the home, and make it less banal and sentimental. Judgment of Maeterlinck's work has changed considerably; nowadays even his best plays are largely neglected. But whatever the critical response may be to his excesses and qualities, his preciousness and real insight, Maeterlinck's influence on contemporary drama has been profound and wide-ranging.

Outstanding among Maeterlinck's contemporaries was Émile Verhaeren (1855–1916), the great poet of the Flemish landscape, of its rivers, its villages, and its people. His most important play, *Le Cloître* (*The Cloister,* 1900), is a taut, forceful drama set in a monastery and centering upon the rebellion of a monk who becomes obsessed with a desire for punishment for a crime committed in his youth. The absolution he received no longer satisfies him, and in his relentless insistence upon humiliation he not only disrupts the established order and pattern of life of his religious community but instigates a reexamination of its relationship to the lay world. Verhaeren's other plays, among them *Les Aubes* (*The Dawn,* 1904) and his original *Hélène de Sparte* (*Helen of Sparta,* 1912), lack the intensity and concentration of *Le Cloître.*

In 1918 Fernand Crommelynck (1885–   ) wrote *Les Amants puérils* ("The Puerile Lovers," 1923). While the qualities of this haunting confrontation between youth and old age, love and barrenness of the heart became more apparent when the play was revived a few years ago, it was *Le Cocu magnifique* (*The Magnificent Cuckold,* 1920) that—deservedly —established Crommelynck's international reputation. Torn between extremes, frequently violent and visionary, Crommelynck's work is typically Flemish, not least in its obsession with sin. *Le Cocu magnifique* is a study of jealousy, jealousy which leads the play's protagonist to doubt his young wife's fidelity and, subsequently, in the course of increasingly cruel tests he imposes upon her, her infidelity as well. The climate is one of shrill exuberance, of joy that turns sour and becomes ugly fear as jealousy reaches its fever pitch of destructiveness. It is a magnificently written play, rich in its imagery and in the sound of

FERNAND CROMMELYNCK (BELGIAN INFORMATION SERVICE)

its language. Influences of expressionism have been noted in Crommelynck's work, but in his major plays—among them *Carine ou la jeune fille folle de son ame* ("Carine or the Young Girl Madly in Love with Her Soul," 1930), *Une Femme qu'a le coeur trop petit* ("A Woman Whose Heart Is Too Small," 1934), and *Tripes d'or* ("Golden Tripe," 1925)—he is a fierce and fascinating poet who defies classification.

Likewise, it is impossible to categorize the work of Michel de GHELDERODE. In his visionary prodigality, in the range and starkness of his extremes, he is the most Flemish of Belgian authors. There are moments of tenderness (*Beeldekens uit het Leven van Sint-Franciskus* ("Images from the Life of St. Francis," 1927, a play published and produced only in Flemish) and moments of nostalgia (*Sortie de l'acteur,* "The Actor Makes His Exit," 1930), but in most of his work, Ghelderode created a merciless, hallucinating Hieronymus Bosch–like world in which the sane and the insane, the grotesque and the sublime, the tragic and the burlesque, the sensual and the mystical meet and mix and clash. It is a world of cosmic width and haunting detail, of garish contrasts in color, rhythm, and sounds, a delirious world inhabited more by living incarnations of obsessive single passions than by real people. Ghelderode's plays constantly stretch the resources of the theater and its audiences; their very relentlessness at times defeats the author. He wrote some fifty plays, and even a short list of some of his major works should definitely include *Hop Signor!* (1935), *Escurial,* (1927), *Magie rouge* (*Red Magic,* 1931), *Mademoiselle Jaïre* (1934), *La Balade du grand macabre* ("The Ballad of the Great Macabre," 1934), *Christophe Colomb*

A SCENE FROM GHELDERODE'S *Pantagleize* (ASSOCI-
ATION OF PRODUCING ARTISTS REPERTORY COMPANY)

(*Christopher Columbus,* 1929), *Pantagleize* (1930), *Masques Ostendais* (*The Ostend Interviews,* 1956), *Barabbas* (1928), and *La Mort du Docteur Faust* (*The Death of Dr. Faust,* 1928).

The importance of Crommelynck and, above all, of Ghelderode should not make one overlook the work of a number of their contemporaries, most prominent among them Henry Soumagne (1891–1951) and Herman Closson (1901–   ). With the exciting *L'Autre Messie* ("The Other Messiah," 1923), a desperate search for God by a group of drunks in the Warsaw ghetto, and also *Madame Marie,* a highly original interpretation of Christ's passion, Soumagne added new scope and depth to the religious tradition in Belgian drama. Closson's work, on the other hand, centers around historical themes, which the author, constantly in search of greatness in the human condition, approached with uncompromising lucidity. Boldly conceived, epic in structure, his plays include *Godefroid de Bouillon* (1933), *L' Épreuve du feu* (*Ordeal by Fire,* 1944), *Shakespeare ou la comédie de l'aventure* ("Shakespeare or the Comedy of Adventure," 1938), and *Les Quatre Fils Aymon* ("The Four Aymon Sons," 1941).

The work of George Sion (1903–   ) ranges from such plays as *La Matrone d'Ephèse* ("The Matron of Ephèse," 1942), an original, spirited adaptation of a classic tale, and *La Malle de Pamela* (*Key to My Heart,* 1955), an exquisite fantasy, to more serious drama. In 1947 the production of Suzanne Lilar's *Le Burlador* won the Ghent-born author the unanimous praise of the Paris theater critics. The play is a penetrating, brilliant reexamination of the Don Juan figure. Emotional and intellectual depth, skill and originality are revealed again in her mystical *Tous les chemins mènent au ciel* ("All

the Roads Lead to Heaven," 1949) and *Le Roi lépreux* ("The Leper King," 1951). Paul Willems (1912–   ) combined delicate poetic feeling with whimsical humor and enchanting ingenuity. His *Le Bon Vin de Monsieur Nuche* (*The Good Wine of Mr. Nuche,* 1952), *Peau d'Ours* ("Bearskin," 1953), *Off et la Lune* ("Off and the Moon," 1955), and, especially, *Il Pleut dans ma Maison* (*It Rains Inside My House,* 1962) are among the most genuine and endearing fantasies and fairy tales in the contemporary theater.

Jean Mogin (1921–   ) wrote *A Chacun selon sa faim* ("To Each According to His Hunger," 1950), an outstanding religious drama dealing with a young abbess who is obsessed with purity and determined not to let anything or anybody stand between God and herself. While Mogin's subsequent *Le Rempart de coton* ("The Rampart of Cotton," 1952) and the beautiful *La Fille à la fontaine* ("The Girl at the Fountain," 1951) did not meet with the success of his forceful first play, they were further evidence of his rich talent.

Contemporary drama written in Flemish gained momentum largely through the efforts of the Vlaamse Volkstoneel, a touring company that sought to combine national identity and tradition with the new styles in the theater, primarily expressionism. The troupe built up an enviable international reputation, helped to establish Ghelderode as a major dramatist, staged medieval Flemish plays, and produced the major works of the contemporary foreign dramatists. The name of the troupe was synonymous with all that was original and exciting in acting style and production during the 1920's. Although the Vlaamse Volkstoneel had an enormous influence, it did not directly contribute any great plays. The best work especially written for it was perhaps *Tyl 1* (1926) by Anton van de Velde (1895–   ). This was a striking example of pure "constructivism," using the Till Eulenspiegel legend as a mere starting point for a many-faceted scenario. In spite of the interest of Van de Velde's work, it is uneven, and, like much of the avant-garde work of the period, it rapidly became dated.

It was left to Herman Teirlinck (1879–1967) to write the best Flemish expressionist drama: *De Vertraagde Film* ("The Slow-motion Film," 1922), *Ik Dien* ("I Serve," 1924), his stunning adaptation of the medieval Beatrice legend, and *De Man zonder Lijf* ("The Man Without a Body," 1925). Later plays such as *De Ekster op de Galg* ("The Magpie on the Gallows," 1937), *De Oresteia* (1946), and *Taco* (1958) reflect his constant search for new forms. Teirlinck, one of Flanders' greatest novelists, was also its most brilliant theater theoretician and teacher. He had a decisive influence on the development of contemporary Flemish drama.

The most successful Flemish plays belong to a more popular tradition. The leading exponent of regional drama was Gaston Martens (1883–1967), whose plays include *Leentje uit het Hemelrijk* ("Leentje from the Kingdom of Heaven," 1919), *Derby* (1920), *De Prochievrijers* ("The Parish Lovers," 1924), *De Grote Neuzen* ("The Big Noses," 1925), and *Het Dorp der Mirakelen* ("The Village of Miracles," 1932). All of these comedies, partly written in dialect, capture the color and flavor of village life in the Ghent region. Martens was a keen observer, who, however, frequently dealt in types and helped to perpetuate the view of the Flemish peasant as a Pieter Breughel-like festive pig. His most popular play, *Paradijsvogels* (*The Hopeful Travelers,* 1932), was widely translated and performed and was made into a French film, *Les Gueux au paradis.*

Johan Daisne (1906–   ), by the end of World War II, was to introduce "magic realism" in both his novels and his plays. His trilogy, consisting of *Veva* (1946), *Het Zwaard van Tristan* ("The Sword of Tristan," 1944), and *Tine van Berken* (1945), is an ambitious attempt to embody the theme that human love is an objective correlative for unattainable divine love. Some critics have tended to overemphasize the artificiality of his language and to overlook the subtlety of his ideas. Like Daisne's, the theater of Herwig Hensen (1917–   ) is highly literary but is much more diverse in form and content. There are philosophical themes underlying both the plays and the poetry of this perceptive and prolific author, but he is also capable of writing a spirited comedy like *Niets zonder de Proef* ("Nothing Without Proof," 1947), as well as mercilessly examining the motives of Lady Godiva and her brutal husband in *Lady Godiva* (1948). Among his other plays are *Agamemnoon* (1952), *Polukrates* (1951), and *Het Woord Vrijheid* ("The Word Freedom," 1965).

In the postwar generation Jozef van Hoeck (1922–   ) won acclaim for his *Voorlopig Vonnis* ("Provisional Sentence," 1957), which dramatizes the dilemma of an atomic scientist who doubts whether his work is justified and so eventually betrays his government. The avant-garde found imaginative spokesmen in Piet Sterckx and Jan Christiaens and above all in Tone Brulin, who has moved from the abstractions of the absurd toward increasing involvement with political themes.

The most significant writer to emerge in the last two decades is Hugo Claus (1929–   ), novelist, poet, painter, playwright, and film producer. This young writer is remarkable for the range of his expression and for the many forms in which he casts his recurrent theme of the search for purity. His plays include *Kijk Mama, zonder Handen* ("Look, Mama, Without Hands," 1959), *Getuigen* ("Witnesses," 1956), *Een Bruid in de Morgen* ("The Bride in the Morning," 1955), *Het Lied van de Moordenaar* ("The Song of the Murderer," 1957), *Suiker* ("Sugar," 1958), and *Het Goudland* ("The Goldland," 1966).

Dr. Theo De Ronde's *Het Tooneelleven in Vlaanderen* (1930) is still one of the most complete surveys of Flemish theater and drama, especially on the periods that have usually been neglected. Marnix Gijsen's *De Literatuur in Zuid-Nederland sedert 1830* (1945) is one of the best short surveys of Flemish literature from Belgian independence to World War II, with some interesting comments on the drama. Dr. C. Godelaine's *Het Vlaamsche Volkstooneel* (1939) deals with the history of this famous company, one of the few Belgian companies to have had an impact on the theater outside Belgian borders. One of the best and most complete introductions to the modern Belgian theater is Suzanne Lilar, *The Belgian Theater since 1890* (1957), which deals not only with Flemish but also with French playwrights.

Miss Lilar, the distinguished playwright, considers the Belgian theater, whatever language it is written in, to be essentially Flemish.—W. E.

Benavente [y Martínez], Jacinto (1866–1954). Spanish playwright. Benavente, who was born and lived in Madrid, gave up a career in law to write for the stage. His life was active but uneventful, except for his winning the Nobel Prize for literature in 1922. He traveled in Europe and the Americas, supervising the production of his plays. From 1894 until his death his works were in constant production in the theaters of the Spanish capital, and several were presented in New York. His popularity in Spain has been unequaled in the twentieth century.

Many of Benavente's plays are social comedies, light in tone and concerned with nothing more transcendental than the topics of drawing room conversation. A few deal with rural life, which he presents in all its picturesqueness, especially the dialect spoken by the peasants. Still others are based on the presentation of the fantastic, occasionally with a half-hearted attempt to handle symbolism. There are also some plays for children.

Benavente wrote above all for the smug but intelligent middle class of the capital. Inveterate playgoers, the members of the Spanish bourgeoisie liked to see their own petty concerns translated into drama, satirized with a light, indulgent touch, and always resolved with a happy irony. In providing this fare, Benavente discourses on politics, education, love, and human nature. His remedy for all problems is sympathy, self-sacrifice, and stoic acceptance of the inevitable. As he asserts in *Rosas de otoño* (*Autumnal Roses,* 1905), his drama of the struggle between good and evil in love and marriage, these virtues are best represented in woman. One of his three masterpieces, *Los malhechores del bien* (*The Evil Doers of Good,* 1905), is a plea for moral tolerance, disguised as an arraignment of misguided charity. Viewed as antireligious propaganda, this play created a scandal at its première. Another masterpiece, *Los intereses creados* (*The Bonds of Interest,* 1907), is unique in the Benavente corpus, for it is set in the old world of the *commedia dell'arte.* In this masquerade modern society is seen as a puppet show in which men are moved by the strings of passion, selfishness, and ambition. Men are alleged to be a compound of vileness and idealism, capable of redemption only through love. *La mal querida* (*The Passion Flower,* 1913) is a rustic tragedy that descends into melodrama. It studies the transformation of a peasant girl's inhibitions into an evil love.

Benavente, long regarded as the brightest luminary in contemporary Spanish drama, has been in considerable eclipse since his death.

Many of the plays have been translated into English by J. G. Underhill in Jacinto Benavente, *Plays,* 4 vols. (1917–1924). Reflecting the early uncritical enthusiasm for Benavente in his own country and abroad, Walter Starkie wrote the only book-length study in English, *Jacinto Benavente* (1924).—B. W.

Benelli, Sem.   See LA CENA DELLE BEFFE.

Bengali drama.   See PAKISTAN: *Bengali drama.*

Beolco, Angelo.   Called **Il Ruzzante** (1502–1542). Italian playwright and actor. The son of a rich Paduan doctor, Beolco grew up in a cultivated and refined circle. He enjoyed the friendship and protection of the nobleman Alvise Cornaro, whose villa boasted a stone theater with a permanent stage constructed in imitation of classical theaters. Given the task of organizing festivities for the Cornaro family, Beolco appeared on the stage at the head of a company of youthful Paduan dilettantes in dialogues and comedies he himself had written. In these plays he assumed the character of a peasant called Ruzzante, a name that means "playful" or "frisky," and it is, of course, from this character that he came to be called Il Ruzzante. The plays soon enjoyed wide fame among the best society of the area. Various festivities between 1520 and 1542 attest to the productions of Beolco and his comic troupe; on these occasions they performed in the ducal court at Ferrara or in the palaces of Venetian noblemen.

Beolco's activity as a playwright extends from 1520 to 1533. His first play was *Pastoral* (1520). Its aristocratic pastoral action, constructed on the model of Angelo Poliziano's *Favola d'Orfeo*, is contrasted with its other action, recounted in the crude dialect of the peasants of the region. Among his works the following are outstanding: *L'Anconitana* ("The Woman of Ancona," 1522); *Il Reduce* ("Ruzzante Come Back from the War," c. 1528); *La Moschetta* ("The Coquette," 1528), his masterpiece; and *La Fiorina* ("The Comedy of Flora," 1530). In these works Ruzzante completely abandoned the use of the cultivated language of the literati and employed dialect, creating a society of common folk and peasants and dramatizing the fundamental feelings of love, jealousy, hunger, and fear of war. The character of Ruzzante is particularly vivid in this society, for he is the symbol of its simple love of life, of its sanguinity and robustness.

Beolco's refined literary learning is indeed visible in his work, sometimes in the classic construction of the plots, sometimes in the monologues and dialogues of love. These dialogues are often no more than translations into popular terms of the elegant, amorous fencing of literary comedy and Petrarchan lyricism. It is perhaps for this very reason that his plays attracted the favor of the aristocratic public. In his presentation of uncouth common folk, however, Ruzzante does not merely ape their external aspects. Instead, he enters intimately into that simple and primitive world, picturing it with crude realism, yet at the same time with poetic understanding suffused with irony. Beolco was almost completely ignored up through the nineteenth century, precisely because of his interest in peasant life and language. Recent criticism, however, has recognized him as one of the greatest and most unusual playwrights of the Italian stage.—L. L.

Bérénice (1670). A tragedy by Jean RACINE. The Roman emperor Titus is in love with Bérénice, queen of Palestine, and is loved by her. For reasons of glory and the state, he is forced to leave her. Antiochus, king of Commagene, is also in love with Bérénice. The play is based on the hesitations and distress of the three characters confronted by an impossible love, and it ends with their majestic separation. With *Bérénice*, Racine succeeded in writing a perfectly simple tragedy in which the action and the catastrophe take place within the characters.

This play has been translated into English verse by Kenneth Muir in *Five Plays* (1960).—Ja. G.

Bergman, Hjalmar Frederik (1883–1931). Swedish novelist, playwright. and scenario writer. Bergman fused his birthplace, Örebro, and the town of his schooling, Västerås, into the Wadköping of his regional fiction, which he produced voluminously, like some latter-day Balzac. While he was deeply rooted in Sweden, he traveled widely in southern Europe and made one abortive trip to Hollywood (1923–1924) at the behest of the distinguished Swedish film maker Victor Sjöström. Bergman married Stina Lindberg, of a well-known theater family, and was otherwise close to the theater, though he was not involved in the practicalities of it. He turned his talents compulsively to film and radio as those media developed. Clownen Jac ("Clown Jack," 1930), a radio serial that he himself read, turned out to be a kind of confessional swan song. He died in Berlin shortly after.

Of Bergman's early *Marionettspel* ("Marionette Plays," pub. 1917), written under the influence of Maeterlinck, *Herr Sleeman kommer* (*Mr. Sleeman Is Coming*, 1918), a lyrical treatment of youth and old age (June and January), remains a classic in the one-act repertory. Another, *En skugga* ("A Shadow," 1918), deals imaginatively with the *Doppelgänger* theme. Bergman is best known for his realistic comedies *Swedenhielms* (1925), about the eccentric family of a Nobel Prize winner, and *Patrasket* (literal translation, "The Rabble"; *Joe & Co.*, 1928), a folk comedy about Jews, as well as a series of adaptations of his regional chronicles, such as *Hans Nåds Testamente* (*The Baron's Will*, 1930) and *Markurells i Wadköping* (*Markurells in Wadköping*, 1930). Bergman's diversity is obvious in *Ett experiment* (*Strange Opportunity*, 1918), a Shavian exercise in class inequity; *Sagan* (*The Legend*, written 1919–1920; prod. 1942), a pleasant arabesque after the fashion of Musset; and *Vävaren i Bagdad* ("The Weaver of Bagdad," 1923), an expressionist by-product of his translation of Richard Burton's *One Thousand and One Nights*. The best films to come from his more than thirty scenarios are *Fire On Board* (1921), *Love's Crucible* (1921), and *Charles XII* (1925), though the film made from *Patrasket* after his death is possibly the best known.

Aside from the superb evocations of Swedish small-town life in the regional plays, Bergman's work frequently suggests a Noel Coward adaptation of Dostoyevsky. But his kind of comic grotesqueness is really all his own. He wrote urgently, abundantly, and, at best, in an opulent high style.

The only Bergman available in English is *Four Plays* (1968), Introduction by Stina Bergman, edited by Walter Johnson. It contains *Markurells of Wadköping, The Baron's Will, Swedenhielms*, and *Mr. Sleeman Is Coming*. Useful articles are Agne Beijer, "The Swedish Dramatists," in *World Theatre*, Vol. IV (1955), and Evert Sprinchorn, "Hjalmar Bergman," in *Tulane Drama Review*, Vol. VI (1961). —R. B. V.

Bertolazzi, Carlo (1870–1916). Italian playwright. Bertolazzi was born of a bourgeois family near Milan and lived all his life in that city. For some time he was a drama critic, and in the last years of his life he was a notary public. He began his career as a playwright at a very early age with fast-moving,

CARLO BERTOLAZZI (ITALIAN CULTURAL INSTITUTE)

realistic sketches in Milanese dialect. He then wrote numerous dramas, partly in the Italian language, partly in Milanese dialect. In these the protagonists are the Milanese bourgeoisie and proletariat. Bertolazzi made no concessions to either the facile optimism of the Italian bourgeoisie or the public's sentimentality and, as a result, enjoyed scant popularity among his contemporaries. His work, however, has recently been revived on the stage and has been amply reevaluated by critical opinion. Today he is seen as the best and most coherent Italian representative of European naturalism.

Among his most noted dramas are the two parts of *El nost Milan: La Povera gent* and *I sciori* ("Our Milan": "The Poor Ones" and "The Rich Ones," 1893); *La Gibigianna* ("The Reflection," 1898); *L'Egoista* ("The Egoist," 1900), a pitiless denunciation of bourgeois egoism; and *Lulù* (1903), a traditional but vivid feminine portrait.—L. L.

Betti, Ugo (1892–1953). Italian poet and playwright. A volunteer in World War I, Betti was imprisoned by the Austrians. During his imprisonment he wrote his first collection of poems, *Il Re pensieroso* ("The Pensive King," pub. 1922). In 1920 he entered the magistracy. He became a judge in 1930 and was transferred the following year to Rome, where he rose to the rank of counselor in the court of appeals. He remained in Rome from 1931 to the end of his life.

In 1927, Betti won a national competition for his first play, *La Padrona* ("The Landlady"), a somber, symbolist drama. Then followed in close succession twenty-five intensely dramatic works. Outstanding among them are *Un Albergo sul porto* ("A Hotel on the Port," 1930), *Frana allo scalo nord* ("Landslide," 1932), *Ispezione* (*The Inquiry*, 1942), *Irene innocente* ("Innocent Irene," 1946), and *La Regina e gli insorti* (*The Queen and the Rebels*, 1949). COR-RUZIONE AL PALAZZO DI GIUSTIZIA is the work in which Betti's principal themes are best fused and most concretely expressed.

His dominant theme in this play as in others is that of the inquest, during which an attempt is made to determine responsibility for some incident. The investigation takes in ever widening circles of people and classes until finally society as a whole and the very conditions of human existence figure in the ultimate responsibility for the event. This theme, unpleasant and desperately pessimistic, is expressed through a symbolism that becomes, particularly in the later plays, heavy and abstract. His works are sometimes lightened, however, by a serenity that arises, not from hope, but from resignation, from the acknowledgment of evil and the need for expiation. —L. L.

Beyond the Horizon (1920). The first full-length play by Eugene O'NEILL. The principal character in this ironic drama of fate is Robert Mayo, a country lad who longs to go to sea. His dreamy, romantic personality attracts a farm girl and he is condemned by an unsuitable marriage to a routine life on the farm for which he is utterly unfit. Meanwhile, his practical-minded brother and disappointed rival in love, Andrew, who was cut out to be a farmer, departs for strange lands and leads an adventurous life that he does not seek. The thwarted romanticist is an absolute failure on the farm and his marriage is destroyed by poverty and domestic recriminations while, ironically, his unromantic brother prospers, though briefly, in the romantic surroundings that Robert yearns for. Only death holds the prospect of sailing "beyond the horizon" to the dying Robert.—J. G.

Bharata. See NATYASASTRA.

Bhasa. See TRIVANDRUM PLAYS.

Bhavabhuti (c. 750– ?). Sanskrit dramatist. Born in Padmapura, in the province of Vidarbha in central India, Bhavabhuti is known as author of three works: *Malati and Madhava,* a melodrama presenting lovers beset by difficulties natural and supernatural; *Ramayana (The History of Rama)*, depicting leading episodes in the adventurous life of the young hero Rama, culminating in his consecration as king; and RAMA'S LATER HISTORY, which, taking its subject matter from the last book of the *Ramayana*, depicts the hero's bitter experiences immediately following his consecration and his temporary repudiation of his wife, Sita.

Plausible information on the dramatist's life is supplied by the introductory passage of *Malati and Madhava.* In this passage his father is said to have been versed in religious and philosophical literature, his mother to have been a poet associated with actors. Allusions in his plays, as well as his style in general, show him to be of a scholarly temperament. He appears to have encountered formidable difficulties, smarting under adverse criticism. In *Malati and Madhava* he declares: "How little do they know who speak of us with censure! This entertainment is not for them. Possibly someone exists, or will exist, of similar tastes with myself, for time is boundless, and the world is wide." However difficult his career as court poet may have been, by the time of his death his fame was firmly established and his plays have remained second only to those of Kalidasa in Indian esteem.

Bhavabhuti's work is in several respects radical when seen in the context of the development of Sanskrit drama. He dispenses with the clown, or *vidushaka,* a character conspicuous in most important Sanskrit plays. Endowed with uncommon ethical and moral sensibility, he frequently amends the harsh or even brutal epic stories used as subject matter for his major plays. In *Malati and Madhava* he conceives characters with greater initiative and also with more marked human weaknesses than the figures in the highly idealistic plays of his predecessors. His rhetoric and imagery are opulent to an unprecedented degree even in Sanskrit drama, the same being true for his use of the pathetic sentiment. A contemporary, Govardhanacharya, observed that his monumental rhetoric reduced language to stone but added that the playwright made the stone itself weep.

Malati and Madhava became one of the most widely known of Sanskrit plays. It abounds in supernatural scenes and sensational effects. There are sinister witchcraft, somewhat like that in *Macbeth,* and an extraordinarily terrifying scene in a graveyard. The lover, maddened by grief, appears more romantic than the afflicted protagonists in Kalidasa's chief plays. Here, as in all Bhavabhuti's works, are striking passages evoking images from natural scenery, especially forests, mountains, and streams. Nevertheless, the play approaches the meretricious. It is unusual in Sanskrit drama in possessing both a major and a minor action.

Decidedly more distinguished as dramatic poems are the two works dealing with the life of Rama. The first, *The History of Rama,* reveals Rama's heroic stature, depicting his wars and triumphs. The story follows the general outlines of the epic on which it is based, concluding with a splendidly imagined aerial journey from the scene of his victories to Ayodhya, the capital city, where he is consecrated king. In keeping with their subject matter both the Rama plays are celebrations of Hindu mythology, Rama himself being a manifestation of the god Vishnu.

Bhavabhuti's masterpiece is *Rama's Later History,* where many passages of psychological subtlety, impressive iconography, and poetic elevation are found. Pathos predominates in the first part of the play, whereas the second part moves forward with much artfulness to a happy conclusion, gathering in some epic sentiment on its way. The happy ending marks one of Bhavabhuti's chief departures from the epic story. His temperament led to a much more kindly and humane philosophy than that of Valmiki's *Ramayana.* The vital role of children in sustaining the tie of marriage is the most insistent and moving theme in the play's morality. A vast and innumerable group of works in poetic drama, dance drama, mime, pantomime, and fiction deals with the Rama story, not only in India itself but throughout Indonesia and the island civilizations of the South Pacific; Bhavabhuti's masterpiece is unquestionably the most remarkable among them.

Rama's Later History has been many times translated. One of the best renderings is by Shripad Krishna Belvakar (1915). There is a fluent but somewhat old-fashioned rendering by C. H. Tawney (1874). J. N. Joshi's translation, which is both faithful and forceful, appeared with P. V. Kane's com-

mentary in 1928; it is reprinted in H. W. Wells's *Six Sanskrit Plays* (1964). The rendering by P. Lal in *Great Sanskrit Plays* (1964) is considerably abridged, presumably with modern production in mind. *The History of Rama (Mahaviracarita)* has been conscientiously translated by Todar Mall (1928). *Malati and Madhava* is rendered, with abridgments, by H. H. Wilson in *Select Specimens of the Theatre of the Hindus* (1871). A more literal but less eloquent version is that by M. R. Kale (1928). The best general study of Bhavabhuti is R. G. Harshé, *Observations sur le vie et l'oeuvre de Bhavabhuti* (1938). A critique of the dramatist's philosophy is given by L. Kretzschmar in *Bhavabhuti der Dichter des Dharma* (1938).—H. W. W.

Bibbiena, Bernardo Dovizi da. See LA CALANDRIA.

Billetdoux, François (1927–   ). French director, journalist, novelist, and playwright. At age twenty-two Billetdoux was director of the French Radio-Television (R.T.F.) in Martinique. In addition to being a playwright, his career includes such occupations as actor, stage director, journalist, scenario writer, novelist, and cabaret performer.

In 1966 his play *Il faut passer par les nuages* ("You Must Pass Through the Clouds") received an ovation at the Théâtre de France. As a synthesis of some of the best characteristics of the postwar theater and some of the more enduring elements of the earlier French theater, Billetdoux's sixth play was written especially for actress Madeleine Renaud. The leading character in this play, Claire Verduret-Balade, is an immensely rich old lady who has suddenly realized that she has become the victim or the prey of those around her: sons, stepsons, and her first and second husbands. She liquidates her wealth in order to liberate her dependents and recapture, if possible, a saner, more human relationship with the members of her family. The experiment is a failure and the old lady remains alone with the small bag of diamonds into which her wealth and hopes had been transformed. This example of the "new theater" was intelligently directed by Jean-Louis Barrault in one of the national theaters.

In all of Billetdoux's plays, in his extremely successful *Tchin-Tchin* (1959) as well as *Va donc chez Torpe* (*Chez Torpe,* 1961), the principal theme is man's desperate search for an impossible love. The impossibility comes not from some exterior obstacle but from the impossibility of any real communication between human beings. His plays are both the affirmation and the negation of love.—W. F.

Bird, Robert Montgomery (1806–1854). American playwright, novelist, journalist, and politician. Bird, the most successful American playwright of the first half of the nineteenth century, was born in New Castle, Delaware, educated in Philadelphia, and received a degree in medicine from the University of Pennsylvania in 1827. He soon gave up medicine for literature, publishing stories and verse and writing several plays. In 1830, actor Edwin Forrest accepted Bird's *Pelopidas,* but it was not produced. Subsequently, however, Forrest did act in Bird's THE GLADIATOR, *Oralloosa* (1832), and *The Broker of Bogota* (1834). In 1837 Bird revised John Augustus Stone's *Metamora* for Forrest, but dissatisfied with the payment he received, ceased to write for the stage. Bird was editor of the Philadelphia *North American,* published several novels, was active in the Whig party, and ran a farm in Delaware.

Bird's plays are romantic tragedies in blank verse, obviously influenced by Shakespeare. *Pelopidas, The Gladiator,* and *Oralloosa* all deal with the revolt against tyranny, the first in ancient Thebes, the second in Rome, and the third in sixteenth-century Peru. Like *Oralloosa, The Broker of Bogota* is set in Peru, but it is a domestic tragedy about a good and noble merchant who, through the weakness of his son, falls victim to a scheming villain. The broker is a sentimentalized King Lear.

In three of his plays, Bird gave highly theatrical expression to the love of liberty, and in all four he provided excellent roles for virile stars. *The Gladiator* and *The Broker of Bogota* were two of the most popular plays of the nineteenth-century American stage.

The best sources are Clement E. Foust's *Life and Dramatic Works of Robert Montgomery Bird* (2 vols., 1919), and Mary Bird's *Life of Robert Montgomery Bird* (1945).—B. H.

Birds (Ornithes, 414 B.C.). A comedy by ARISTOPHANES. Two average Athenian citizens, Peithetaerus ("Friend-Persuader") and Euelpides ("Hopefulson"), decide to opt out of Athenian life, with all its trials and tribulations, and search for an ideal state. Their search leads them to the king of the birds, the Hoopoe, whereupon Peithetaerus has a sudden inspiration and suggests that the birds found their own utopia. The birds, who form the Chorus, are skeptical and hostile at first. But eventually Peithetaerus' arguments win them over, and they begin to fortify the sky. Their power is based on the strategic position they occupy, midway between earth and heaven, perfectly placed to intercept sacrifices on their way up to the gods and to control the success of crops on earth. Mankind soon transfers its homage from the gods to the birds. Indeed, a line of applicants, mostly Athenian, begins to form, begging for citizenship. Each of them has to be scrutinized by Peithetaerus, but most fail to gain entry; they are too much like the kind of people Peithetaerus was escaping from. The gods hold out a little longer, but when a deputation arrives that includes the glutton Herakles, the sight and smell of the food being cooked by Peithetaerus is too much for the famished gods, and they quickly come to terms. Peithetaerus, as part of the bargain struck with the gods, marries Zeus's bride, Sovereignty.

Birds echoes Aristophanes' *Acharnians* (425 B.C.) in its central idea of a private abdication from the everyday realities of Athenian life, but the passage of time since the earlier play has made a flight from earthbound actuality even more urgent. The historical context reveals why. The year before *Birds* was produced the Athenian public, seduced by dreams of gold and grandeur, had voted to equip an enormous expedition to conquer the island of Sicily. The expedition was an attempt to recoup Athens' fading fortunes in her long struggle with Sparta and was doomed to abject failure. Aristophanes' comedy is full of images of flight, escape, and transcendence of worldly cares. Most notable are the explicit fantasy of

omnipotence and the usurpation of Zeus. The exceptionally long list of minor characters who enter but are thrown out of Cloudcuckooland provides a complete rogues' gallery of the elements in Athenian life which Aristophanes most deplored. Thus *Birds* fulfills on the level of fantasy the wishes and aspirations that could never be realized in fact—utopian longings, hopes of immortality, desire for the riches that lie to the west, the challenge thrown down by a humble citizen to the father of the universe—all fused in a combination of ancient dream and contemporary illusion.

Translations of the play are listed under Aristophanes.—K. C.

Bjørnson, Bjørnstjerne (1832–1910). Norwegian poet, playwright, and novelist. The son of a minister, Bjørnson grew up in Romsdalen, the scene of many of his rural stories. After schooling in Molde and Oslo, he began to make a name for himself as a journalist and drama critic. His first major play, *Mellem slagene* ("Between the Battles," 1857), which deals with the times of King Sverre (1150–1202), inaugurated a series of historical dramas in which he explored and celebrated the identity of Norway. *Maria Stuart i Skotland* ("Maria Stuart in Scotland," 1863) marked an extension of his skills in structure and characterization.

From 1857 to 1859 Bjørnson was a stage director in Bergen, where he met the actress Karoline Reimers, whom he married in 1858. Later, from 1865 to 1867, he was director of the Oslo Theatre, with no diminution of his output of poetry and liberal-minded journalism. Bjørnson went into temporary retreat in Rome in 1873 and there began to write a series of realistic plays. *En fallit* (*A Bankruptcy,* 1875) argues the need for a responsible ethic in business, and *Redaktøren* (*The Editor,* 1875) calls for decency and moderation in the polemic press. *Kongen* ("The King," 1871) not only attacks the idea of monarchy but deplores a Christianity that is made of "dogmas and formulas instead of ideals." *Det ny system* ("The New System," 1879) marked Bjørnson's break with the established church in favor of a larger kind of humanism. In 1883 came *En handske* ("The Gauntlet"), which made a case for premarital chastity in the male and thereby incurred the displeasure of the bohemian community.

Over ævne I (*Beyond Our Power I,* written 1883; prod. 1899), probably Bjørnson's finest play, deals with the risks of excessive idealism in the "miracle worker" of whatever dispensation. *Geografi og kærlighed* ("Geography and Love," 1885), in its comic treatment of rampant pedantry, showed that Bjørnson had the capacity for self-caricature. In *Over ævne II* (*Beyond Our Power II,* written 1895; prod. 1899) Bjørnson turned to labor strife and the nature of the anarchistic movement.

Bjørnson frequently lived and traveled abroad. He lectured in the United States during 1880–1881 and spent much of his later years in Paris, where he died. He was, in 1903, the first Scandinavian to be awarded the Nobel Prize. Bjørnson's plays are infrequently played today, even in Scandinavia, but he is remembered as a great patriot of Norway and an outspoken foe of oppression and social inequity wherever he found them, at home and abroad.

BJØRNSTJERNE BJØRNSON (THEATRE COLLECTION, NEW YORK PUBLIC LIBRARY AT LINCOLN CENTER)

For translated plays of Bjørnson, see *Three Comedies* (1914), translated by R. Farquharson Sharp; also see *A History of Norwegian Literature* (1956), edited by Harald Beyer and translated by Einar Haugen. —R. B. V.

Blood Knot, The.   See AFRICA: *South Africa.*

Blood Wedding (Bodas de sangre, 1933). A folk tragedy by Federico GARCÍA LORCA. *Blood Wedding* is the first play of a trilogy concerning the frustrations of instinct that end in tragic pathos. The plays (including YERMA and THE HOUSE OF BERNARDA ALBA) are all set in rural Spain and are presented mainly through the female point of view. *Blood Wedding* tells of a fatally disrupted wedding that takes place in the hills of Castile. The mother's only remaining son plans to marry a girl living beyond the hills with her father. The mother is preoccupied with death as a result of the recent feud-murder of her husband and several sons. The prospective bride, a strong, silent girl, was once engaged to Leonardo, who is now married to her cousin. It is Leonardo's family who are responsible for the feud-murders.

A SCENE FROM FEDERICO GARCÍA LORCA'S *Blood Wedding* (FRENCH CULTURAL SERVICES)

Wild and unappeased, Leonardo still wants the girl he did not marry, and he becomes furious when he hears about her approaching marriage. The groom and his mother visit the betrothed and her father. The conversation is clipped and stark; financial details are discussed and the marriage date is set. Later, the betrothed is told about a mysterious rider who appeared the previous night. Now a sudden sound of a horse startles her. She looks out; it is Leonardo.

The second act opens on the morning of the wedding. The betrothed has uneasily resisted an early visit from Leonardo. As the wedding party arrives singing, the groom enters, and the betrothed, plainly desperate, pleads to have the nuptials take place at once. As the house fills with guests, there is ominous talk of murder and death. Leonardo's wife discovers her husband missing; the betrothed is also gone, and the groom's mother spurs on her son to pursuit and vengeance.

The symbolism of song and the strategy of spectacle dominate the third act. Three woodsmen, like three fates, wander through the forest and are met by the moon, dressed as a woodsman. A beggar woman, personifying death, appears opportunely to lead the groom to Leonardo. The subsequent fatal encounter and double murder of the groom and Leonardo occur offstage. The betrothed herself is spared. A short final scene, largely in verse, sums up the tragic statement. Four girls, winding out a red skein, objectify the grief in delicate poetic lines. This scene is swiftly followed by the appearance of all the women involved: Leonardo's mother-in-law, the beggar woman, the mother of the groom, and the betrothed. They emerge to speak and listen against a backdrop of anonymous neighbors. The dominant voices are those of the beggar woman ("It was just. Over the golden flower, dirty sand") and the groom's mother, who gives the final summary of the play's tragic view in these words: "Blessed are the leaves of grain because my sons are beneath them; blessed is the rain because it washes the faces of the dead; blessed is God, who lays us down together to rest."

Blood Wedding was translated by J. Graham-Lujan and R. L. O'Connell in *Three Tragedies* (1947).—E. H.

Bohemia. See CZECHOSLOVAKIA: *Bohemia and Moravia.*

Boker, George Henry (1823–1890). American playwright, poet, and diplomat. Boker, born into a wealthy and cultured Philadelphia family, was graduated from Princeton University. He published his first volume of verse in 1849, and in the same year his first play, *Calaynos,* a tragedy in blank verse based on Spanish prejudice against Moorish blood, was produced. Between 1849 and 1855, he wrote seven plays, all but two of which were successful on the stage. As tension grew between North and South over the slavery question, Boker was drawn into politics as a strong supporter of the Union, and in 1864 he published his *Poems of War.* While he was minister to Russia, from 1875 to 1898, he wrote two more plays, which were not produced.

Two of Boker's plays, *The World a Mask* (1851) and *The Bankrupt* (1855), had contemporary settings, but his strength lay in romantic verse dramas set in the past. These plays included *Ann Boleyn* (1849), *The Betrothal* (1850), *Leonor de Guzman*

(1854), FRANCESCA DA RIMINI, *Nydia* (1885), and *Glaucus* (1886). The last two were based on incidents in Bulwer-Lytton's historical novel *The Last Days of Pompeii.*

Boker's best play, *Francesca da Rimini,* a tragedy in blank verse, is the first play in English dealing with the ill-fated lovers immortalized by Dante, and it is the best romantic tragedy written by an American in the nineteenth century. Boker was one of the first American playwrights to receive a royalty on each performance of his plays.

The best source for Boker's life is E. S. Bradley's *George Henry Boker, Poet and Patriot* (1927). Six of the plays are in Boker's *Plays and Poems* (1857), three in *America's Lost Plays* (1940).—B. H.

Bolt, Robert [**Oxton**] (1924–). English playwright. Bolt was born at Sale, near Manchester, the son of a shopkeeper. He had a solid middle-class education, beginning at Manchester Grammar School and continuing at Manchester University, where he graduated in history in 1949. Bolt then became a schoolmaster. Meanwhile he was also writing radio plays for the British Broadcasting Company and his first two stage pieces, *The Last of the Wine* (1957) and *The Critic and the Heart* (1957).

Bolt gave up his teaching career for full-time writing after the West End success of *Flowering Cherry* in 1957. This play, often described as a British equivalent of Arthur Miller's *Death of a Salesman,* tells the story of a failed insurance man who compensates for his professional and domestic inadequacies by nourishing a pastoral dream of happiness as a fruit farmer. There is nothing slick about this piece; like all of Bolt's work, it is the product of moral honesty and a firm technique. But from the viewpoint of the West End management, its big advantage was that it did not go too far. Illusion remained illusion, reality remained reality; there was no questioning of the social pressures that had driven Bob Cherry into his fantasy life. As a work of genuine quality that did nothing to discomfort the traditional audience, *Flowering Cherry* was a rare godsend to the dominant commercial management of H. M. Tennent Limited, who elected Bolt into the position of reigning favorite and gave lavish productions of his subsequent plays: *A Man for All Seasons* (1960), *The Tiger and the Horse* (1960), and *Gentle Jack* (1963). The last of these was a spectacular failure with the public, and since then Bolt has returned to the theater only with *The Thwarting of Baron Bolligrew* (1965), an excellent CHILDREN'S DRAMA, and an exhumed early piece, *Brother and Sister* (1967).

Bolt's career illustrates the predicament of the traditional playwright in the modern English theater. However dissatisfied he may be with established forms or establishment politics (Bolt has served a prison sentence as a result of his anti-establishment politics), he feels obliged to work within the existing range of public taste; anything else, Bolt says, is "just a private game." His plays represent a continuous effort to bend the inherited theatrical categories to fit modern experience, as in *A Man for All Seasons* (about Sir Thomas More), a chronicle play in a style he described as "bastardized Brecht"; and in *The Tiger and the Horse,* a thesis play on nuclear disarmament. But when this effort reached its limit in *Gentle Jack* the public bewilderment was such that

Bolt might almost as well have been playing a private game.

Two years later, in *Baron Bolligrew,* one senses his relief at being able to work within the firm conventions of a play for children. But by that time Bolt had also written the screenplays for *Lawrence of Arabia* and *Dr. Zhivago,* leaving one to conclude that for a playwright such as Bolt the summit of the profession is now as likely to be the cinema as the theater.

Bolt's plays have been published in separate editions.—I. W.

Borchert, Wolfgang (1921–1947). German playwright, actor, and poet. Though Borchert wrote only one drama in his lifetime, *Draussen vor der Tür* (*The Man Outside,* 1947), it is most significant because it was the first outstanding play to be written by a German following World War II. It was also the first drama that captured the mood and experience of a country that had devastated itself. Borchert was the perfect spokesman for that country. He had fought as an infantryman on the Russian front and had been imprisoned for criticizing the Nazi leaders. He wrote *Draussen vor der Tür* a year after his escape from a POW camp with the realization that he was dying from an incurable liver illness incurred during the war. As fate would have it, the première of Borchert's play took place in Hamburg on November 21, 1947, the day after his death.

Borchert's drama is a tragic, surrealistic Everyman play, which portrays the experiences of the infantryman Beckmann, who returns home to find that he has no home. Not only has Beckmann's wife deserted him, but his parents have killed themselves. Beckmann, too, wants to commit suicide, but the yes man and the River Elbe will not permit this because he has not tried hard enough to find his place in postwar Germany. Beckmann earnestly tries to secure a job, to find love, and to accept the responsibility of his actions as a soldier. However, he is a mutilated being who encounters mainly savages in a wasteland. In the end, he refuses to live in a society that demands that he be a murderer and accept being murdered at the same time. Like many of the expressionist dramas written after World War I, Borchert's *Draussen vor der Tür* is a passionate protest against the corruption and decadence in German society. Borchert's use of surrealistic elements and his terse, exalted, repetitious language endow the play with a compelling intensity and seriousness. Still performed in repertory, *Draussen vor der Tür* has proved to be a key link in the German drama tradition between the expressionist work of the 1920's and 1930's and the "absurd" and parable plays of the 1950's and 1960's.—J. D. Z.

Boris Godunov (1870). A tragedy by Alexander PUSHKIN. Written in 1825, the play was banned by the censors and not produced until 1870. *Boris Godunov,* Pushkin's most important dramatic work, is written in Shakespearean iambic pentameter, with some passages in prose and others, such as songs, in rhyming verse. It is the story of Tsar Boris, a strong and complex man, who accedes to the throne through the assassination of Prince Dmitry. Confident that he can bring peace and order to Russia, Boris is forced, instead, to use terror like his predecessor Ivan the Terrible, albeit in a more subtle way. A runaway monastery novice, Gregory Otrepiev, poses as Prince Dmitry, who, he claims, has escaped from the hired assassins. The pretender enlists Polish and Lithuanian support against Boris and immediately gains popularity with the Russian masses. Although the pretender's armies suffer a series of military defeats, Boris Godunov's regime collapses from within. Tsar Boris dies of a heart attack; his son, the heir presumptive, as well as his wife and daughter, are murdered. The play ends as a courtier announces that Boris is dead and all the members of his family have poisoned themselves.

Pushkin's uncanny ability to bring to life various historical characters—Boris, Gregory Otrepiev as the false Dmitry, Prince Shuisky, the ruthless politician Basmanov, and the Polish lady Marina with whom Gregory falls in love—set *Boris Godunov* apart from the Russian historical drama of its time, which was simply an imitation of French classical tragedy in a Russian setting, whose only popularity was due to the fact that the characters called each other by familiar Russian names. Pushkin disregarded the rules of French classical tragedy, which demanded that the action take place within twenty-four hours; indeed, his play starts in 1598 and ends in 1604.

It is sad that *Boris Godunov,* a major tragedy in its own right, should be known in the West only through Modest Moussorgsky's opera with Feodor Chaliapin's bass in the title role.

The text of *Boris Godunov,* translated by Alfred Hayes, appears in *The Poems, Prose and Plays of Alexander Pushkin* (1943), edited by Avrahm Yarmolinsky.—A. MacA.

Boucicault, Dion (1820–1890). Irish-American playwright, actor, and manager. Boucicault was born in Dublin, Ireland. He attended London University but left in 1837 to become an actor in the provinces. In 1840, he returned to London determined to succeed as author and actor. His play *London Assurance* was produced with great success at Covent Garden in 1841. After his return from France, where he had been adapting French plays for the English stage, Boucicault made his London debut as an actor in his own melodrama, *The Vampire* (1852). The same year another melodrama, *The Corsican Brothers,* which he adapted from the French, provided actor Charles Kean with one of his most popular vehicles.

In 1853 with his wife, Agnes Robertson, a charming and talented actress, Boucicault accepted an engagement in the United States, where he spent the next nine years writing, acting, and managing. Successful plays of this period were *The Poor of New York* (1857), a melodrama that made use of the financial panic of that year; *The Octoroon* (1859), which made dramatic capital of slavery; *Dot* (1859), adapted from Dickens' Christmas tale *The Cricket on the Hearth; The Colleen Bawn* (1860), adapted from Gerald Griffin's novel *The Collegians;* and, in collaboration with Joseph Jefferson, RIP VAN WINKLE, an adaptation of Washington Irving's story.

After a successful run in New York, Boucicault took *The Colleen Bawn* to London, where it was equally popular. With this play, he is said to have initiated the traveling company. In 1864, *Arragh-na-Pogue,* a second very popular Irish melodrama, had its première in Dublin.

In 1872, Boucicault returned to New York, where he remained most of the rest of his life, writing, acting, managing, and coaching actors. In 1874 he had a great success with *The Shaughraun,* a melodrama, in which he played Con, an irresponsible, drink-loving, but goodhearted wanderer.

Boucicault was the author of between 100 and 150 plays, most of them adaptations, among which were some of the most popular plays of the nineteenth century. He had a shrewd eye for drama in contemporary novels and events, and he was adept at constructing fast-moving plots designed to arouse suspense, tears, and laughter.

The best source is Townsend Walsh's *The Career of Dion Boucicault* (1915).—B. H.

Bound East for Cardiff. See S. S. GLENCAIRN.

Bourgeois Gentilhomme, Le (The Would-be Gentleman, 1670). A comedy-ballet, in prose, by MO-LIÈRE. Monsieur Jourdain, son of a rich merchant, dreams of being a gentleman and tries to imitate the aristocracy in his outward appearance and general ways: he has a music master, a dancing master, a fencing master, and a master of philosophy, and dresses in what he believes to be the latest fashion at the court, while his wife and his maid continually poke fun at him. Moreover, he is in love with a marquise, Dorimène, who takes advantage of him with

ROBERTO BRACCO (ITALIAN CULTURAL INSTITUTE)

ENGRAVING OF A SCENE FROM MOLIÈRE'S *Le Bourgeois Gentilhomme* (NEW YORK PUBLIC LIBRARY)

LE BOURGEOIS
GENTILHÓME

the help of her suitor Dorante, a count. Monsieur Jourdain will not allow his daughter Lucile to marry young Cléonte until, with the help of his valet, Cléonte passes himself off as the son of the Great Turk and confers upon him the exotic title "mamamouchi."

The farcical portrait of an egotist who is ready to sacrifice everything to his illusions, *Le Bourgeois Gentilhomme* is also the satire of a society in which the bourgeoisie's aim is to become aristocratic and in which penniless noblemen are not beyond fraud.

This play has been translated by Morris Bishop in *Eight Plays* (1957).—Ja. G.

Bracco, Roberto (1861–1943). Italian playwright. Bracco was born in Naples and became known as a dialectical poet and writer; he later dedicated himself to the theater, establishing himself among the most successful Italian authors between the end of the nineteenth century and the First World War. In 1924, having been elected a member of parliament, he sided with the adversaries of the fascist regime and was consequently forced to abandon all political activities. In 1928 he was relieved of his seat and his writings were practically banished from the Italian theaters. Refusing always any compromise with fascism, Bracco abandoned even his theatrical activity and retired to Sorrento, where he spent the last years of his life in precarious financial circumstances.

Bracco was an impassioned follower of Ibsen and of naturalism and did his utmost to create in Italy a theater of ideas. It was with this in mind that he wrote *L'Infedele* (1894), *Tragedie dell'anima* (1899), and *Maternità* (1903), works that are sustained by brilliant dialogue and by an unquestionable technique but characterized at the same time by a limited capacity for psychological probing. Beyond the programmatic preoccupations that forced him to attempt certain works perhaps above his abilities, he obtained the best results, on the one hand, in ample veristic sketches inspired by Neapolitan reality (*Don Pietro Caruso*, 1895) and, on the other hand, in works (such as *Il Piccolo Santo*, 1912) that anticipate *intimismo*, a dramatic movement of the 1920's that presented detailed analyses of a particular sensibility expressing mute pain of the soul.—L. L.

Braggart Warrior, The. See MILES GLORIOSUS.

Brazil. Although there is some evidence of other playwrights in Brazil during the sixteenth century, the only texts known today are those of Father José de Anchieta (1534–1597), a Jesuit born in the Canary Islands. Sent to Brazil at nineteen, he remained there until his death, teaching in the schools of the Jesuit Society, acting as conciliator between the Indians and the colonists, writing poems and plays, directing performances, and occupying positions of great importance in ecclesiastic administration. For him, the theater was a means of converting the Indians to Christianity and encouraging good habits among the Europeans. He wrote, therefore, in Portuguese, Spanish, Latin, and Tupi, mixing two or more languages in each play. Thus, if the theme was directed particularly to the Indian, Anchieta used Tupi, but in the more complicated theological passages he preferred Latin, which the Jesuits of various nationalities living in Brazil could understand. The parts in Tupi were played by the Indians themselves, using their music, dances, costumes, and body paint. This sensible method of including Indians in the theatrical productions gave value to certain elements of the native culture, saving them from the destruction that was the general rule. As for the passages in Portuguese and Spanish, they are justified by the fact that these languages were generally understood by all the Europeans living in Brazil.

Because Anchieta was concerned with spreading Catholicism, he used medieval sources, especially the miracle plays. He mixed, anachronistically, historical and fictitious characters and used the most naïve procedures to move and frighten. Considering his drama from an aesthetic point of view, his technique was crude; yet if we take into account the complicated psychology of the Indian, we can appreciate the skill with which he reached his goals. Among Anchieta's *autos* ("acts") are *Na festa de São Lourenço* ("At the Feast of St. Lawrence," 1583), *Na aldeia de Guaraparim* ("In the Village of Guaraparim," 1589), and *Na visitação de Santa Isabel* ("At the Visitation of St. Elizabeth." 1595).

During the seventeenth century the situation is the same: there is evidence of several plays and the names of a few authors, Jesuits or laymen, but no play has survived. Only in 1705 did new texts appear, published in Lisbon. They are comedies written in Spanish, set in Europe, with no connection whatsoever with Brazilian reality. The author, who boasts in the Preface of being the first writer born in Brazil to have his works published in book form, is Manuel Botelho de Oliveira (1636–1711). His work, called *Música do Parnasso* ("Music from Parnassus") includes poems in Portuguese, Spanish, Italian, and Latin, some with native themes, and two Baroque comedies in Spanish: *Hay amigo para amigo* ("There Is a Friend for a Friend") and *Amor, engaños, y celos* ("Love, Deception, and Jealousy"). There is nothing to indicate they were ever performed. Another example of the Baroque theater is *O Parnaso obsequioso* ("Courteous Parnassus," 1768) by Cláudio Manuel da Costa (1729–1789), a poet born in the state of Minas Gerais, Brazil, with a degree in law from the University of Coimbra, Portugal. He does not reveal in his plays the transition from the Baroque to the neoclassical style, which is so marked in his poetry. *O Parnaso obsequioso* is a commissioned work, written to be performed on the birthday of the governor. It is full of exaggerated praise, poured out in excessively ornate language, and its characters are nothing less than the gods of Olympus, who gather to celebrate the sociopolitical occasion for which the play was written. It is interesting to note that, some years later, the playwright was one of the conspirators in the abortive revolution of the state of Minas Gerais, which would have made Brazil independent of Portugal. He committed suicide in prison.

It was only in the nineteenth century that printing was permitted in Brazil and schools for advanced study were founded. Immediately after independence (1822) a great cultural spurt occurred, especially notable for its effort to make the theater more national, on the part of both playwrights and actors. To replace the repertory of Portuguese works, a Brazilian poet and diplomat, Gonçalves de Magalhães (1811–1882), wrote verse tragedies, beginning with one that he considered as having "a national theme": *Antônio José ou O poeta e a Inquisição* ("Antônio José or The Poet and the Inquisition," 1838). Although his poetry introduced Romanticism in Brazil, his plays still observed the neoclassical rules. The theme of this first tragedy was not national, since it is about the Portuguese playwright and poet Antônio José da Silva, and neither was the dialogue. These defects were repeated in Magalhães' *Olgiato* (1838). Historians of Brazilian theater emphasize only the historic importance of Magalhães' tragedies.

On the other hand, some of the comedies of Martins PENA are still being performed and applauded by critics and public. Martins Pena had no official patronage such as Magalhães had and was without the latter's opportunities to see the best of the European theater of the time. His comedies of daily life constitute a complete picture of Brazilian life between 1815 and 1848, the dates of his birth and death. He was able to re-create natural speech, create a rapid succession of comic episodes and a variety of character types, both urban and rural, and to express the thoughts of the new urban middle class in relation to the social problems that were beginning to arise. Not wanting to imitate anyone (Magalhães claimed to be a disciple of Alfieri and Corneille), Martins Pena remained faithful to his time and to the city where he spent almost his entire life, Rio de Janeiro. Among his best comedies are *O juiz de paz na roça* ("Justice of Peace in the Country," 1838), *O noviço* ("The Novice," 1845), and *As casadas solteiras* ("The Wedded Spinsters," 1845).

Although he has been acclaimed as a poet, Antônio Gonçalves Dias (1823–1864) began his literary

MARTINS PENA (BRAZILIAN EMBASSY)

career with the intention of being the best playwright in Brazil. Born in Maranhão, he studied at the University of Coimbra in Portugal and, once back in Brazil, submitted a play to the National Dramatic Conservatory, a society of playwrights backed by the government and in charge of censorship and grammatical review of the texts to be performed. When the conservatory imposed some restrictions on his play, Dias haughtily lost interest in the theater. By this time he had written *Patkull, Beatriz Cenci,* and *Leonor de Mendonça,* and would afterward write *Boabdil.* After his death a friend published these texts in 1909, which reveal a new direction in the Brazilian theater: the study of historic characters portrayed as moral beings superior to their environment, because of the strength of their convictions. Dias had a special admiration for Friedrich von Schiller, having translated *The Bride of Messina* into Portuguese. He is most famous, however, for his poetry, which brought the romantic cult of the Indian into Brazilian literature.

Around the middle of the nineteenth century, a strong French influence began to be felt in Brazilian theater, through visiting companies and translations performed by Brazilian groups. It would be more accurate to say that theatrical activity was a minor reflection of that influence, for, with independence, the entire cultural axis upon which Brazil turned

changed from Lisbon and Coimbra to Paris. To speak French, travel to France, read her authors, and follow her fashions in clothing and manners came to be a sign of good taste. Some Brazilian authors, however, although aware of this influence, fought against it, insisting on a theater of characters and problems peculiar to Brazil.

Echoes of Alexandre Dumas fils can be found in the dramas of Joaquim Manuel de Macedo (1820–1882) and José de Alencar (1829–1877). Macedo wrote several comedies in the tradition of Martins Pena, such as *O fantasma branco* ("The White Phantom," 1850) and *A tôrre em concurso* ("The Bids for the Tower," 1861). He considered the problem of prostitution in *Lusbela* (1863), while Alencar actually incurred journalistic polemics against himself with his *As asas de um anjo* ("The Wings of an Angel," 1860), on the same subject. Alencar was the most important romantic novelist of Brazil, whose novels are still read and studied with great interest today for their epic and lyrical qualities and for their delicacy of psychological perception. Alencar was a well-known politician, an advocate of a parliamentary process in Brazil in the English manner. As a journalist he was a vigorous defender of liberal ideas, which conflicted with certain measures of Emperor Pedro II, whose minister he was before their final break. In the theater, he wrote two comedies (among others) that still have something to say to us: *O demônio familiar* ("The Family Demon," 1858) and *Rio de Janeiro, verso e reverso* ("Rio de Janeiro, Front and Back," 1857). His sentimental drama, famous in its time—*Mãe* ("Mother," 1862)—treats the problem of slavery, not in a general way, but with an intentionally emotional approach, suitable to the plot line. It was a great hit with the public, especially the women.

Machado de Assis (1839–1908) is the most important novelist and short-story writer of the Portuguese-speaking world, but his reputation as a dramatist has remained linked to small literary societies of the salon. He wrote short, cold, and elegant comedies, really without attraction when performed. Two or three—*Quase ministro* ("Almost a Statesman," 1864) and *Lição de botânica* ("The Botany Lesson," 1906)—when acted in a style combining equal parts of caricature and sophistication *à la* Musset (certainly not what their author intended), can still reach an intelligent audience.

Returning to the theater that portrays daily life, França Júnior (1838–1890) and Artur AzevEDO began to write in a realistic vein. Júnior resembles Martins Pena in his one-act comedies, in which the telling of the anecdote leaves him no time for more ambitious efforts. When his characters are at odds only with their little problems, Júnior attains a type of comedy much appreciated by an audience that wants to be amused. At the same time he reveals peculiarities of the psychology of the middle classes of his time, sharply defined and still interesting today from any point of view. The same is not true when he tries to moralize directly or when he takes pains to attain special effects of stagecraft. The French influence has a banalizing effect and makes his work seem more out of date than it might be. *O barão de Cutia* ("The Baron of Cutia," 1862), *Caiu o ministério* ("The Ministry Has Fallen," 1882), and *As doutôras* ("The

ARTUR AZEVEDO (BRAZILIAN EMBASSY)

Learned Women," 1889) are Júnior's best-known works.

Azevedo was a man of the theater in the widest sense: critic, a member of societies, translator, author (alone or in collaboration) of comedies, dramas, and operettas, adapter, and producer. He sought a high literary level in some plays, while writing others merely to make money, with no great care. In spite of his hopes for fame on the strength of the literary plays, his least carefully wrought works are the ones that had, and continue to have, the most success. For example, his *O mambembe* ("The Second-Rate Traveling Theater," 1896) and *A capital federal* ("The Federal Capital," 1897) are comedies with music and well-defined character types, with incidents taken from real life. Their dialogue is even today quite efficacious for comedy. Azevedo was one of the creators of the *revista*—productions containing music and satirical sketches, using characters who represent sometimes quite clearly the main political figures of the country. The revista or *revista do ano* ("yearly revista") maintained its popularity after Azevedo's death, beginning to decline in 1937 under the Vargas dictatorship. Today it is merely an imitation of French and American revues, and the critical spirit of the "man in the street" has been lost.

In the twentieth century tendencies toward realism as well as symbolism appeared. The latter predominated at first, in a generation that preferred to express itself through poetry. The dramatic poem, to be read aloud, was very popular. Poetic dramas are not strikingly different from the poems, because of the excessive value given to the word and the lack of interest in the plays' effectiveness in performance. Graça

Aranha (1868–1931), author of *Malazarte* (1911), written in French and Portuguese versions, was influenced by Ibsen's *Peer Gynt,* but the play is without theatrical effectiveness. Another poetic dramatist, Roberto Gomes (1892–1922) was a sensitive musician and writer, strongly influenced by French culture and the plays of Maurice Maeterlinck, and in many ways unadapted to Brazilian life. *Canto sem palavra* ("Song Without Words," 1912) and *Casa fechada* ("Closed House," pub. 1942) are timid questionings about love and death, from a man who appears not to live among others. Gomes killed himself, reaffirming on this tragic note the feelings of pessimism and perplexity of the characters in his plays.

Falling between symbolism and realism is Henrique Coelho Neto (1864–1934), author of more than 120 books, although part of his work is still found only in the newspapers to which he contributed. Even so, he left little of note to the theater. Only *Quebranto* ("Exhaustion," 1908) and *Ao luar* ("In the Moonlight," pub. 1913) are partially exempt from the preciosity and intoxication with words that are typical characteristics of this author.

The advent of modernism in 1922 was in no way similar to the movement of the same name in Hispanic literature. In Brazil, modernism embraced futurism, surrealism, cubism, and other postwar trends, stabilizing itself finally in an adaptation of Brazilian folk traditions. There was nevertheless, a certain attraction toward foreign models and, soon after, a search for native solutions. At this time there was a reformulation of opinions and criteria in all areas, begun by a condemnation of everything of the most recent vogue. In the theater, the effects of this aesthetic revolution arrived very late, if we compare it with what took place in poetry and fiction. The decade of the 1920's was dominated by comedies about daily life, irritatingly subjected to conventional rules and more and more hackneyed in its character types and situations. In 1932 appeared the play *Deus lhe pague* ("God Recompense You"), by Joraci Camargo (1898–   ), structured in the old technique of French realism, with a *raisonneur* and a thesis. Although thesis drama was a style of the past, the play's "communist" motif attracted general attention, even though it presented a pseudo philosophy that denied rather than affirmed its motifs. Successive official bannings and approvals of its performances increased the popularity of *Deus lhe pague,* which became for many years a sure commercial success in Brazil and neighboring countries. It was not, however, the start of a trend by which the theater would reach the level of the other arts and by which its writers would become as well known in their field as did Portinari in painting and Villa-Lobos in music.

It was only after World War II, when modernism was exerting only little influence, that the theater really came to life. Several factors contributed to this: the creation of schools of dramatic art, which produced professional actors; the presence of European directors, either refugees or attracted by the renewed theatrical vitality in Brazil; large investments in theatrical companies; and the amateur movements among university students, who participated in national festivals and were sent on scholarships to study drama in France, England, and the United States.

For years the critics had been calling for the appearance of a play that would explode the theater's unhealthy stability. The explosion came in 1943 with *Vestido de noiva* ("The Wedding Dress") by Nélson RODRIGUES. An exceptionally creative moment, it was repeated, although with rather less success, in the works that Rodrigues continued to produce year after year, such as *Senhora dos afogados* ("Our Lady of the Drowned," 1954), *Anjo negro* ("Black Angel," pub. 1946), and *A falecida* ("The Deceased," 1953).

In the 1940's and since, the best poets have done translations of plays, and the dramatic repertory alternates between works of new Brazilian writers and such authors as Lorca, O'Neill, Anouilh, and Giraudoux. In the following decade Sartre, Miller, Williams, Albee, Osborne, and, especially, Brecht have become familiar to theater audiences. Brecht, as a theorist and dramatist, is most influential at present. For three centuries, Brazilian folk theater had used demystificational techniques, so that there was a kind of convergence between German theories and the unconscious practices of Brazilian people.

New playwrights have constantly appeared in the postwar era, either independently or in small groups with a common interest in theme or technique. An independent is Guilherme FIGUEIREDO, as well as Jorge ANDRADE and Pedro Bloch (1910–   ), who wrote *As mãos de Eurídice* ("The Hands of Eurydice," 1945), a famous monologue that has traveled around the world as a challenge to the dramatic talent of the great stars. In this play, which is an apparently incoherent confession of a mentally disturbed man of his involved love life, Bloch does not develop themes to which he later adhered. His succeeding works are criticisms of Brazilian urban life, the misguided upbringing of present-day youth, and the false values of modern family life. Henrique Pongetti and Abílio Pereira de Almeida follow these trends, without any well-defined ideology, either religious, political, or philosophical.

The theme of poverty and hunger in the northeast of Brazil interests other playwrights. Ariano Suassuna (1927–   ) converted to Catholicism shortly before writing *Auto da compadecida* ("The

GUILHERME FIGUEIREDO (BRAZILIAN EMBASSY)

Rogue's Trial," 1956). His point of departure is the classical concept that the world is a puppet show and God is its puppeteer. He utilizes the folk material of his region, giving it a poetic treatment and a theological direction entirely new to Brazilian theater. Osman Lins (1924–   ) is the author of, among others, *Lisbela e o prisioneiro* ("Lisbela and the Prisoner," 1960) and *A guerra do Cansa-Cavalo* ("The War of Cansa-Cavalo," 1966). He holds various prizes for plays, novels, and short stories. João Cabral de Mello Neto (1920–   ) has written a Christmas play, first published as a poem: *Morte e vida Severina* ("The Death and Life of Severino," 1958). It is concerned with a poor man deprived of his land by one of the large landholders. He emigrates to Recife, the largest city of the region, finds the same poverty he left, and is about to kill himself when a child is born, symbolizing Christ and hope.

A group with a common political ideology (and in part a common aesthetic one) is formed by Dias Gomes (1924–   ), Augusto Boal (1928–   ), and Gianfrancesco Guarnieri (1936–   ). Gomes is the author of *O pagador de promessas* ("The Given Word," 1960), which was later a film given a first prize at the Cannes Film Festival. Among his other plays are *A invasão* ("The Invasion," 1963) and *O santo inquérito* ("The Holy Inquest," 1965). Although he uses northeast Brazil and its abject poverty as a theme, his socialist point of view transfigures and interprets the events, giving them an epic value of social protest, most evident in the first two mentioned works. The last play deals with a little-known episode of the Brazilian Inquisition and contrasts the innocence of a young girl with the casuistry of the Inquisitors. Guarnieri began to write independently and afterward associated himself with the Teatro de Arena ("Theater in the Round"), at São Paulo, in 1956. There he met Boal, who had also created independently *Marido magro, mulher chata* ("Thin Husband, Tiresome Woman," 1959) and *Revolução na América do Sul* ("Revolution in South America," 1961). The two came to direct together the Teatro de Arena in 1962 and write together for their company of players, combining Guarnieri's more lyrical interpretation of social protest with the Brechtian techniques and the greater aggressiveness of Boal. They have also turned to the Brazilian past, in which they seek parallels with present political realities and justifications for their Marxist doctrines. Depending upon the theme being handled and the political conditions of any given moment, they choose literary and theatrical techniques along the lines of Brecht or Stanislavsky, frequently mixing folk music and folk theater with these foreign-derived elements. Their latest works are *Arena conta Zumbi* ("Arena Tells Zumbi," 1965) and *Arena conta Tiradentes* ("Arena Tells Tiradentes," 1966). Both plays glorify historical figures: Zumbi, chief of an armed uprising of a group of slaves to gain their liberty, who are paralleled with modern guerrillas; and Tiradentes, hanged in 1789 after having assumed sole responsibility for a plot to effect the independence of Brazil.

Books on Brazilian drama have not been translated into English.—J. P.

Break of Noon (Partage de Midi, 1948). A poetic drama by Paul CLAUDEL. The first performance of this play, in December 1948, was given in honor of

Claudel by Jean-Louis Barrault's company at the Théâtre de Marigny. The play is about Claudel's personal experience as a diplomat in China and Japan from 1895 to 1909. He did not allow the play to be presented until, in 1948, almost half a century after the personal experience and the first version (written 1906), he acceded to Barrault's request to produce the play. At that time he reworked many passages in the play but always referred to the "author of the play," never to himself.

In *Break of Noon* Claudel focuses on the meaning of separation, of reaching a turning point. The life of each of the four characters in the play has come to the point of noon in a symbolic sense. They come together on the deck of a boat, but each is isolated from the others and on the verge of understanding a very profound aspect of his existence. The fact that the boat itself is in the middle of the Indian Ocean is significant.

The three acts take place in three different settings and in three different "climates." The woman Ysé dominates all three acts but plays different roles in each one. Three men surround her on the deck of the ship: her husband, De Ciz; a former lover, Amalric; and Mesa, whom she has just met and who is to become her lover. In Act II, in the old cemetery of Hong Kong, Ysé plays the role of lover and seductress. In Act III, she is the woman characterized by fidelity, even if this fidelity is to her lover.

The play is about the meaning of love and especially about the role of woman in the experience of love. A carnal experience is not sufficient to join a man and a woman. Ysé, instead of bringing happiness to Mesa, is there in place of happiness. Up to the ending of the play, *Break of Noon* (in the words of Amalric) resembles a poker game in which four players are around a table with an additional invisible player. This drama of passion finds its conclusion in suffering, death, and something beyond death.

Break of Noon has been translated by Wallace Fowlie (1960).—W. F.

Breasts of Tiresias, The (Les Mamelles de Tirésias, 1918). A surrealist play by Guillaume Apollinaire (1880–1918). Apollinaire was a friend of Alfred Jarry, and his play *The Breasts of Tiresias*, when it was produced in 1917 at the Théâtre Maubel, recalled the scandal of Jarry's *Ubu Roi* (1896). Apollinaire called his play *un drame surréaliste*. The word "surrealist" was invented for the occasion, and later SURREALISM was applied to an entire literary-artistic movement.

When Thérèse, the heroine of the play, loses her breasts, which rise up to heaven in the form of colored balloons, she is transformed into the prophet Tiresias. But her husband, wanting to repopulate France, gives birth through a pure act of will power to 40,049 children, as he is being observed by a mute, unmoved citizen of Zanzibar.

In the thirties, some years after the first performance of this play, Antonin Artaud claimed that there already were signs of a new kind of theater characterized by freedom, surrealism, and mystery. Artaud saw the beginnings in Stéphane Mallarmé, Maurice Maeterlinck, and Jarry. He found an instance of it in Apollinaire's *The Breasts of Tiresias*, which was the antithesis of the then popular "well-made plays" of Henry Bernstein and François de Curel.

The Breasts of Tiresias has been translated by Louis Simpson in *Modern French Theatre* (1966). —W. F.

Brecht, Bertolt (1898–1956). German poet, theorist, stage director, playwright. Bertolt Brecht was born on February 10, 1898, the son of a Protestant father (Berthold Brecht) and a Catholic mother (*née* Sophie Brezing). He was christened Eugen Berthold Friedrich. Berthold senior worked at the Heindel paper factory in Augsburg and was eventually to be its managing director. Both parents hailed from Achern in the Black Forest. Brecht attended Volksschule from 1904 to 1908 and the Royal Realgymnasium from 1908 to 1917. His account of those years is in a letter to the critic Herbert Ihering:

> Elementary school bored me for four years. During nine years of being lulled to sleep at the Augsburg Realgymnasium I didn't manage to be very much help to my teachers.

But by 1913 he was a published writer of remarkable accomplishment, as both prose and verse printed in the school paper *Die Ernte* ("The Harvest") attest. His first play, *Die Bibel* ("The Bible"), appeared there in January 1914. In this year, Brecht came before a general public, starting to publish in the *Augsburger Neueste Nachrichten*. Some of the Brecht items in this paper are nationalistic. The young poet steps forth as the patriot of Kaiser Wilhelm's war. Yet at least one commentator has questioned the sincerity of the nationalism, in view both of poems stating other attitudes and of the greater sophistication of the standpoint in items written earlier. By 1916, certainly, the profile of the Brecht the world knows is clearly seen in such a poem as "The Song of the Fort

BERTOLT BRECHT (WALTER HAMPDEN MEMORIAL LIBRARY AT THE PLAYERS, NEW YORK)

Donald Railroad Gang," as remarkable a work as any eighteen-year-old, except Rimbaud, has ever been known to write.

Graduating from high school in 1917, Brecht continued to live at home while beginning to study medicine in nearby Munich. He was even able to stay in Augsburg when inducted into the army in 1918, his service being limited to the duties of a medical orderly in the local barracks. (The story that he acted as a surgeon and actually amputated limbs is a legend created by Brecht himself.) His famous poem "Legend of the Dead Soldier" dates from this period; it was to be the only work of his cited by the Nazis as their reason for depriving him of German citizenship in 1935. It was also in 1918 that he wrote his first mature play, *Baal*. It was too indecent to find any immediate producer. Brecht's father offered to pay for it to be printed but only on a condition his son did not accept: that the family name not appear in the volume.

Though peace had come to the world, 1919 was a year of the greatest storm and stress—for Germany and for Bertolt Brecht. It was in this year that he had his first taste of politics and his only direct contact with revolution, the unsuccessful revolution that his native Bavaria underwent. He belonged for a time to the Augsburg Soldiers Soviet and to the Independent Social Democratic Party. That bitter disenchantment followed is indicated in the play that grew out of this chapter in his life, *Trommeln in der Nacht* (*Drums in the Night,* 1922), as also in the poem "Ballad of the Red Army Soldier," the Red Army of this work almost certainly the Bavarian, not the Russian. This was also the time of a love affair with a girl called Bie

Banholzer, who bore him a son. (He was named Frank, after Wedekind, but was later consigned to an orphanage and was finally killed in an air raid in World War II.) For Bertolt Brecht the poet, 1919 was an *annus mirabilis*. Though not all the products of his pen from this time have survived, many of the poems published later in *Die Hauspostille* (*Manual of Piety*, 1927) were written then.

In 1920 Brecht's mother died. His poem on the event expresses heartbreak in a remarkably direct way. It was at this point that he moved from Augsburg to Munich. The Munich years were marked by a close friendship with the playwright Arnolt Bronnen (later a Nazi, later still a communist sympathizer), by marriage to Marianne Zoff, daughter of a Munich theater man, and by the birth of Brecht's first legitimate child, Hanne (today the actress Hanne Hiob, an occasional guest artist with the Berlin Ensemble). In these years, too, Brecht not only wrote plays but had them produced. Here the principal event was the production of *Trommeln in der Nacht* at the Munich Kammerspiele in 1922, which led to Brecht's being awarded a national prize (the Kleist Prize) through the influence of the critic Herbert Ihering. The first productions of *Im Dickicht der Städte* (*Jungle of Cities,* also called *In the Swamp*) in 1923, and of *Leben Eduard des Zweiten von England* (*Edward II*) in 1924, were less successful with the public and the critics but equally important for the young playwright.

In 1924 Brecht settled in Berlin. His first marriage fell apart, and in 1926 Brecht had a son (Stefan) by the actress Helene Weigel, whom he married two years later and stayed married to for the rest of his

A SCENE FROM BERTOLT BRECHT'S *Jungle of Cities* (FRENCH CULTURAL SERVICES)

life. It was in this period that Brecht found his way to the kind of drama he intended to create, the play *Mann ist Mann* (*A Man's a Man,* 1926) making the decisive breakthrough from his early manner (lyric, balladesque, expressionistic) to what he was to call "epic theater" (narrative, objective, political, didactic). And this achievement was by no means a purely aesthetic matter. In October 1926 he wrote to a friend: "I am eight feet deep in *Das Kapital.*" It was also his habit to seek out personal mentors, and two such were important at this stage: the left-wing, but not strictly Marxian sociologist Fritz Sternberg and the Marxian, but anti-Communist Party Karl Korsch.

The early plays and the publication in 1927 of his book of poems *Die Hauspostille* gave Brecht a solid reputation in literary circles. His work reached a wider public for the first time with the Berlin production of THE THREEPENNY OPERA at the Schiffbauer-damm Theater (première: August 28, 1928). The now world-famous "musical" not only stayed in the repertoire of that theater until the advent of Hitler (when all such works were banned) in 1933 but was played all over Germany and Central Europe generally. Two successful films were made from it, one French, one German. But success stopped at the water's edge. *The Threepenny Opera* was not to be done in London until after World War II. In 1933 it ran briefly (twelve performances) at the Empire Theatre in New York and was not even a *succès d'estime.*

The money Brecht made from *The Threepenny Opera* bought him the time to write less successful works. *Happy End* (1929) was a flop, but it was also the starting point of a major Brecht play, which the author worked on intermittently for the next three years: *Die Heilige Johanna der Schlachthöfe* (*Saint Joan of the Stockyards*). Meanwhile there were three more important premières: *Aufstieg und Fall der Stadt Mahogonny* (*The Rise and Fall of the City of Mahogonny,* Leipzig, March 9, 1930), *Die Massnahme* (*The Measures Taken,* Berlin, December 10, 1930), and *Die Mutter* (*The Mother,* Berlin, January 15, 1932). (See also CHILDREN'S DRAMA.)

It was especially the two last-named works that stamped Brecht as a communist, for in them he very forthrightly identified himself, not only with Marxist philosophy in general, but with the Communist Party in particular. It did not, of course, follow that the party accepted the attentions of this enthusiastic wooer. This was, moreover, the era of Stalin's ascendancy in world communism: there was no friend-liness in the movement toward any form of modernism in art. And style was not the only stumbling block. Party critics of *Die Massnahme* had grave reservations about its content. For, like other young converts, Brecht had a tendency to be "more royalist than the King."

How the tension between Brecht and the party critics would have worked out will never be known. Hitler's rise to power (1932–1933) ended such luxuries. On January 28, 1933, a performance of *Die Mass-nahme* in Erfurt was broken up by the police, and proceedings for high treason were instituted. The burning of the Reichstag on February 27 precipitated a period of terror. Brecht had seen it coming and slipped across the frontier, with Helene Weigel, on the following day. Their two children, Stefan and

Barbara, were smuggled out later. After a few month in Switzerland, Brecht was enabled, by the well-to-do writer Karin Michaelis, to make his home in Denmark for the next six years. Black years for Europe, they were highly creative ones for Brecht. Compulsory withdrawal from politics left him all the more free to write. He completed a big play he had begun in Berlin, *Die Rundköpfe und die Spitzköpfe* (*Roundheads and Peakheads,* 1936); wrote THE PRIVATE LIFE OF THE MASTER RACE, MOTHER COURAGE AND HER CHILDREN, *Das Verhör des Lukullus* (*The Trial of Lucullus,* 1939), and GALILEO; and began THE GOOD WOMAN OF SETZUAN.

Hitler invaded Poland on September 1, 1939. Already in the summer of that year Brecht had considered Denmark too hot to hold him. The German embassy had long been harassing him there, and a Nazi invasion of Denmark was already talked of. He moved his family and collaborators to Stockholm, where another well-to-do lady offered aid. This was Naima Wifstrand, an actress whom Brecht had picked as a likely Mother Courage. (Dumb Kattrin was a role for Helene Weigel, since she wouldn't be able to speak Swedish.) When Sweden too feared a Nazi invasion, the Brecht "ensemble" moved on to Finland and the estate of a third wealthy lady, Hella Wuolijoki. The play *Herr Puntila und sein Knecht Matti* ("Mister Puntila and His Man Matti," written 1940) was originally written in collaboration with Miss Wuolijoki, who, indeed, continued to regard herself as its co-author to the end—possibly with justification. *Der aufhaltsame Aufsteig des Arturo Ui* (*The Resistible Rise of Arturo Ui,* 1941) was written on Miss Wuolijoki's estate in March 1941.

Marxist refugees from Hitler had gone off in various directions: some to fight in the Spanish war, some to live in the "Socialist Fatherland," a compact and rather important group to settle in Mexico City. It would not seem that Brecht seriously considered the first two possibilities—either one might easily have meant death—but he would probably have found his way to Mexico had not one member of his entourage, Margarete Steffin, been refused entry. In May 1941 the whole group obtained visas to enter the United States and proceeded to cross the Soviet Union, but Miss Steffin never made it beyond Moscow, where she died of tuberculosis. On July 21 the group—Brecht, his wife, the two children, and Ruth Berlau, who was both his mistress and an invaluable collaborator—landed in San Pedro, California. With a little money from the actor Fritz Kortner and the composer Kurt Weill, the family settled down in a small frame house in Santa Monica.

Brecht was in America over six years and seemed fully prepared to stay longer, yet he sank no real roots in American life. For one thing, America did not welcome his works. (As for the talents of Helene Weigel, a great actress, she was used in exactly one American film, for the space of about ten seconds, in a nonspeaking role.) But again, exclusion from social activities left Brecht free to write, and to the American years belong *Die Gesichte der Simone Machard* (*The Visions of Simone Machard,* 1942), *Schweyk im zweiten Weltkrieg* ("Schweyk in World War II," 1959), and, above all, THE CAUCASIAN CHALK CIRCLE. He made strenuous efforts to get this last produced on Broadway, but there were to be no Broadway

A SCENE FROM BERTOLT BRECHT'S *Schweyk im zweiten Weltkrieg* (FRENCH CULTURAL SERVICES)

productions of Brecht plays till the sixties (and then only unsuccessful ones). The only productions Brecht had anything to do with while he was in America were a small Off-Broadway production of *The Private Life of the Master Race* (1945) and a limited run of *Galileo,* first in Hollywood, then in the Maxine Elliott Theater, New York (1947). But meanwhile his works had begun to appear in print in America. The books led to college productions of the plays. And, after he had returned to Europe, an American audience for Brecht, located mostly in the universities, did grow up.

When *Galileo* opened at the Maxine Elliott on December 7, Brecht was already in Europe. There had taken place on October 30 a grotesque little tragicomedy, but not on the stage of any theater—on the floor of the Caucus Room of the Old House Office Building in Washington, D.C. Here Bertolt Brecht was cross-questioned by the Committee on Un-American Activities. It was a case, as one wit put it, of the biologist being studied by the apes. Brecht found himself in this position, less because he was a "Hollywood writer" at a time when Hollywood was being combed for "conspirators" than because he was a friend of the Eisler brothers, one of whom (Gerhart) was an agent of the German and/or Russian Communist Party. And someone in American "security" suspected a connection between the Eislers and the J. Robert Oppenheimer case. (Since the committee broadcast the hearings on the radio, the "Brecht program" could easily be recorded by any listener who possessed the right sound equipment; and today it can be heard on a Folkways recording.)

Bertolt Brecht's next resting place was the upper floor of a pleasant, chalet-like Swiss house overlooking the Lake of Zurich. From this spot (Feld-

meilen) he tried to orientate himself in a Europe that offered him various opportunities. One possibility was to buy a house in Salzburg and write for a much refurbished Salzburg Festival. With this in mind, he acquired Austrian citizenship—never relinquished. He was also in touch with Benno Frank, cultural officer of the United States Army in Germany, and it seems Frank would have placed Brecht back in his native Bavaria had the State Department not suddenly issued a warning against promoting communists. Frank then commended Brecht to the attention of the Russian cultural officer, Colonel Dymshitz. Dymshitz arranged for Brecht to be made welcome in East Berlin, which is where he then spent his last half-dozen years, with historic and by now well-known results.

In January 1949, *Mother Courage* opened at the Deutsches Theater in East Berlin with Helene Weigel in the title role. Brecht and Erich Engel directed it with a "scratch" company of actors. At this point the Berlin Ensemble was just a group within the larger organization of the Deutsches Theater. Not until 1954 were they to have their own building, the Theater am Schiffbauerdamm (today the full title would be "Das Berliner Ensemble am Bertolt Brecht Platz"). But during the first years of the fifties, Brecht and Helene Weigel converted their group into the most impressive theatrical ensemble in the Western world. Possibly Brecht's writing suffered; but possibly, too, it was worth it. In any case he still did some writing: poems, theoretical prose, adaptations, and one full-length play, barely finished at his death, *Turandot oder Der Kongress der Weisswäscher* ("Turandot or The Congress of White-washers," pub. 1967).

If people had raised political questions about

Bertolt Brecht in 1932 and in 1947, they were obviously going to raise them during the fifties. His conduct on June 17, 1953, became a storm center of controversy and has remained so. (Günter Grass came out with a play on the subject in 1965.) On that day, the workers of East Berlin rose in revolt against their government. Brecht wrote the party chief, Walter Ulbricht, an expression of his loyalty. According to one account, his letter to Ulbricht also contained much criticism of the regime, but Ulbricht struck it out when giving the letter to the press. This account is denied by Käthe Rülicke, who was acting as Brecht's secretary at the time. Another witness states that Brecht did propose to include such criticism in the letter but that Miss Rülicke herself persuaded him not to. Certainly he did not express solidarity with the rebels.

Nineteen-fifty-six was another year of decision. The leader of the intracommunist revolt against Ulbricht, Wolfgang Harich, named Brecht as someone who was sympathetically close to his group. That was in October. But Brecht had died in August and could not testify. His widow has stuck by Ulbricht through thick and thin, and would not wish anyone to think her husband ever did otherwise. Brecht kept a journal in which, it is said, he wrote down various unpublishable criticisms of Ulbricht and others. In the widow's view they remain unpublishable to this day, although it is also said she has taken the precaution of stowing a copy or two in the vaults of banks in the West.

Again, the main fact is that Brecht did *not* take a public stand against the East Berlin regime. On the contrary, he chose, finally, if for a mixture of reasons, to live in the East and to give the regime some very solid support. His attacks, quite naturally, were on Western misdeeds. In January 1953, for example, he sent off telegrams to Albert Einstein, Ernest Hemingway, and Arthur Miller asking them to do something about Ethel and Julius Rosenberg. He was concerned with the threat to world peace presented, in his view, by the United States, and he was happy to receive (1954–1955) the Lenin Peace Prize (then still called the Stalin Peace Prize). Ironically, his acceptance speech, delivered in Moscow, was translated into Russian, at Brecht's request, by Boris Pasternak.

Brecht's life ended with some theatrical triumphs. In July 1954 the Berlin Ensemble played *Mother Courage* at the Théâtre des Nations in Paris and in June 1955 played *The Caucasian Chalk Circle* under the same auspices. These prize-winning events laid the foundation of that international success that Brecht's work was to meet with all over Europe in the late fifties and in the sixties.

The Bertolt Brecht described by friends who saw him in his last year—the film director Erwin Leiser, the playwright Max Frisch—was a sick man. Knowing the trouble was with his heart, he said to Leiser: "At least one knows that death will be easy. One tap on the window and . . ." The tap came a little before midnight on August 14. One of the doctors who signed the autopsy was Müllereisert, a boyhood friend whose name is familiar to readers of *Die Hauspostille* (*Manual of Piety*). Brecht lies buried today beneath the windows of his last home, in the same cemetery as the remains of his second-favorite philosopher, Hegel.

Bertolt Brecht was nothing if not the creator of a new theater. New in all departments. Lighting, for instance. One of the first things the stranger notices in the Brecht theater in East Berlin is that the lighting is different. There are no gelatins on the lamps. All the light is "white." So a Brecht play has a different look even before we see *what* is on the stage. Costume, for instance. No one had ever seen a costume play that looked like *Mother Courage* or *Galileo*. Nor was the difference the accidental one of a guest designer or a special brainstorm. A view is taken of costumes that extends from one play to another. For one thing they are not seen as costumes at all, but as clothes, which have been worn before. Or stage design. "This is neither naturalism nor any of the departures from naturalism that we know about," students say who have examined the stage created by Brecht's designers (chiefly, Caspar Neher and Teo Otto). These designers usually started from a bare stage and placed on it whatever objects the action of the play required. Art? The art is in (1) the design of each object and (2) the placing of the objects. Spectators were often surprised how drastic the logic was. For example, if the action, though set in a room, makes no use of walls, you present a room without walls. Not naturalism; but Brecht called it realism.

Sometimes the setting, instead of creating the mood (which in Brecht it is never supposed to do), is in direct contrast with the mood. This is not a new idea in itself, but not an exhausted one either, and most people felt they *had* seen something new when they witnessed the interaction between setting and actor in the Pope scene of *Galileo*. Here there was the added piquancy that the setting is actually the costume. More precisely, what had been "setting"— the Pope's robe on a dummy—becomes costume as it is transferred to the Pope's body; and when he is fully dressed, it becomes "setting" again, because he is submerged under it.

Music, too, is used as comment and therefore is often in direct contrast to the moment and the word. In his book *Composing for the Films* (1947), Hanns Eisler suggests that this should be a principle of movie music, replacing the present assumption, which is that music is mood music and always either reinforces or embellishes. Eisler composed his best music for Brecht, and his idea is an application of Brecht's most famous idea, *Verfremdung* ("alienation").

Fremd is German for "alien." Hegel and Marx had made a very important principle out of *Entfremdung*, the normal German word for alienation or estrangement. *Verfremdung* is Brecht's word for the process of *making* alien or strange. Now since it is well known that alienation, especially in the writings of Karl Marx, is an appalling phenomenon—the estrangement of the worker from the ownership and meaning of what he works at—it will be asked: How can the Marxist Bertolt Brecht actually call for alienation?

But already in Hegel alienation is a positive as well as a negative thing. More important, perhaps: it is necessary. As Herbert Marcuse likes to put it, Hegel proved the power of negative thinking, proved, in-

deed, that thinking *is* negative by virtue of being analytic—it takes apart. Conversely, "positive thinking" blurs distinctions, dissolves meaning in a perhaps inspiring fog. In which fog we live our lives. To
use a metaphor that brings us back to Brecht, we
need to step *away* from a picture to come *closer* to
seeing it.

In what Brecht called the bourgeois theater, an author's aim is to make the audience think: "This man
is brilliant: he sees such things as I never saw." It was
Brecht's ambition to make his audience say: "What
this man shows me is no creation of his brilliance, it
is the real world, which I realize I was a bit out of
touch with till he reminded me." This kind of "reminder," in Brecht's view, is not—is no longer—
effected by naturalism. It requires the *alienation effect.* (Here the word "effect" [German, *Effekt*] also
gives trouble. The right sense is suggested by our use
of the plural, "effects.") In order that the buzz and
blur of the circumambient world should become defined sound and image, the world itself has to be
pushed away a little, even pushed to one side a little,
and looked at askew—as Hogarth and Daumier
knew. In this way, the world is "made alien" in order
that it may be "made known." The logic is paradoxical, but what is involved is not a trickiness in reasoning but complexity in the experience of discovery
and realization. Colloquially, we say "I suddenly realized," but the suddenness comes at the end of a
process, and the process does not resemble driving
straight ahead on a highway. Rather, after a sharp
turn left, immediately followed by a sharp turn right,
one "suddenly realizes," with a jolt, that one is still
moving ahead in the original direction. The jolt has
defined the direction one is moving in for one's emotional system. It is an alienation effect.

Brecht often addressed himself to the topic of the
"A Effect" (in German, *V-Effekt)* in acting, and it
may well be that the most radical changes he demanded in the theater, other than in the writing, were
in the acting. "Three devices," he wrote, "can contribute to the alienation of the words and actions of
the person presenting them: 1. the adoption of the
third person, 2. the adoption of the past tense, and 3.
the speaking of stage directions and comments." This
means that, in early rehearsals or classroom exercises, the dialogue of a scene should be translated
from the first to the third person and from the present
to the past tense and that an actor should read all
stage directions aloud as they occur. A Brechtian
playwright will sometimes even write scenes in the
third person and the past tense, in which case no such
translation is called for. An example is to be found in
Brecht's own play *The Caucasian Chalk Circle,* and
it will be noticed that the narration also includes
what would normally be considered "stage directions
and comments":

. . . And she rose, and bent down, and, sighing,
took the child
And carried it away.
As if it was stolen goods she picked it up.
As if she was a thief she sneaked away.

It is Brecht's thesis that, if an actress will practice en-
acting such an incident, while another performer

reads the lines, she will eventually find she has acquired another *way* of acting, another *style,* the style
of the new theater.

How does this differ from the style of the old theater? Precisely by alienating the narrative—and
with it the character the actor is presenting. The difference has sometimes been understood thus: "In the
pre-Brechtian theatre, and notably in the Stanis-
lavskyan theatre, the actor is completely identified
with the character: he *is* the character, and *we* can
completely identify ourselves with *him, we* are the
character. In the Brechtian theatre, on the other
hand, the actor openly disowns the character, shows
both himself *and* the character. By not identifying
himself with the character, he prevents *us* from making the identification. Hence, instead of losing ourselves in the character, we look at it from the outside." Which is correct, except for being highly
exaggerated. In no theater could there be *complete*
identifications, or spectators would be rushing onstage to save the Desdemonas from the Othellos. In
no theater could there be complete detachment, or
the spectator would simply be excluded—and
would detach himself from the whole occasion by
going to sleep or walking out. A degree of identification is contained in the very idea of enactment. It is a
question of what degree. And the whole difference of
opinion on the matter represents a concern with *degree.* Brecht experimented to the end of finding out
what *degree* of identification is needed and for what.
If the aim is pathos, you must make the identifications as nearly complete as theater art will permit,
and this has been done in all the pathetic domestic
dramas, from Victorian melodrama to radio soap
opera, of the past hundred years. Conversely, if the
aim were comedy, there would be nothing new (in
that sense, nothing Brechtian) about resisting identifications. A traditional way of resisting identifications is for a comedian to break out of any role he may
be playing and talk to the audience. If Brecht was an
innovator in this area, it was because he introduced
this principle into dramaturgy itself: his characters
often "break out" of a scene and address the audience. Generally, the songs, too, represent such a
break, in contrast to the songs of the American "musical," which are continuous with the dialogue.

Lighting, costume, stage design, music, acting, and,
last but not least, playwriting itself: Brecht wanted to
"make it new" in all these departments and took
steps to do so both as writer and as stage director.
One could even add directing to the list of departments, except that what it primarily means is the co-
ordination of all the others. "Audience" is not, in
this sense, a department, either. You wouldn't expect
a section on "the people who eat" in a recipe book,
and audience is not a category parallel to the theater
arts themselves. On the other hand, just as cooking
exists for eaters and no one else, so theater exists for
spectators and no one else, and if a theater theoretician does not speak of them at *one* time, it is because
he has them in mind (in the back of his mind, perhaps) *all* the time. Every kind of theater represents a
particular kind of operation performed upon the audience, and Brecht's originality consisted in his determination to perform a different operation on
them.

What operation? In Brecht's pronouncements of the late twenties and early thirties, there is heavy emphasis on the didactic: the theater is to instruct. In his essay "A Little Organon" (1948) the emphasis is shifted to pleasure: the theater must please. Brecht's shift in emphasis has sometimes been taken as a mellowing or even as simply a retreat to a more traditional position, as if his earlier preoccupation with teaching was later regarded as a waste of time. But this is to ignore much of what Brecht said in the later theoretical writings, as well as his later practice as a playwright. And of course the change of theory reflects a development in the practice. It is the development from plays of the period 1928–1934, which he himself labeled didactic (*Lehrstücke*), such as *Die Ausnahme und die Regel* (*The Exception and the Rule,* 1948), to plays of the period 1938–1944, such as *Galileo, Mother Courage,* and *The Caucasian Chalk Circle.* And of these latter, it could be said that, while they are less didactic in form, they are more instructive in effect. Brecht's development was from a rather puritanical and perhaps even undialectical didacticism to a much fuller presentation of the dialectics of living. Correspondingly, he became dissatisfied with the name he gave his kind of work in the late twenties—"epic theater"—and at the end of his life was toying with the term "dialectical theater."

There comes a point at which the distinction between pleasing and instructing does not help us any more, for what Brecht wishes to do is not flatly either to please people or to instruct them. It is something closer to waking them up. In the eighteenth century already, Schiller had complained that in the theater the Muse "takes to her broad bosom the dull-witted teacher and the tired businessman and lulls the spirit into a magnetic sleep by warming up the numbed senses and giving the imagination a gentle rocking." This describes just what the German theater was still doing in Brecht's youth, and while the older playwrights continued to purvey sleeping pills, the young Brecht manufactured an alarm clock.

The bedroom he planned to place it in was not that of the businessman. The positive emotional content of the new theater has to do with productivity and corresponds to the joy of planners and builders. Indeed, in a society where the planning and building is rational, the worker on these tasks will find them reflected—jubilantly taken up in symbolic form—in the drama. The new theater will also have a negative emotional content. It will show impatience with whatever impedes the planning and building, anger at whatever opposes or wrecks it. These two bodies of emotional content will produce their own characteristic rhythm in the theater, will outcrop in plays that have a characteristic movement. First, there is the rhythm of joy, the movement toward fruition and achievement, best exemplified in Brecht's own work by *The Caucasian Chalk Circle.* Second, there is the rhythm of rage, the movement toward defiance and resistance, best exemplified by *Mother Courage.*

Anger and defiance were, of course, commonplaces of the social drama even before Brecht. But they seldom worked: that is to say, they only touched the surface. Millionaires could be roused to cry "Strike!" from their seats in the orchestra, but their zeal had subsided before they reentered their waiting limousines. What Brecht, on the other hand, says about anger in the scene devoted to the subject (*Mother Courage,* scene 4) reveals what he has in mind for the theater. Getting worked up for an hour or two has no value. We need to generate enough anger to last a lifetime. Or rather, since we probably have that much already, we need to tap it, to make it available. This, as psychoanalysts know, can only be done by indirection. The indirections of Brechtian theater—its devices and "effects"—are ways of doing it. There could therefore be no greater error than to imagine that the purpose of Brecht was to exclude emotion. He sweeps aside facile tears because his concern is with deep passion, and he shares with religious thinkers the assumption that deep passion is seldom neutral but tends to be tied to convictions, to belong, as it were, either to God or the devil. The Brechtian drama taps those deeper springs of feeling that, like the sentiment of faith as described by St. Paul (an allusion found in *Mother Courage,* scene 4), can move mountains.

None of the innovations listed above (or any others that could be added) was to Brecht in the first instance an aesthetic matter. In that respect, he was not an "avant-garde" writer at all: none of his idiosyncrasies claims any interest in itself. And even his later homage to pleasure brought with it no innovations that had the purveying of pleasure as their specific purpose. So what *is* he doing with his audience? It would be a fair summary of what has been reported here to state: He is helping the audience to *see* certain things and to *feel* certain things. But to this must now be added that the help is not extended because the "certain things" are interesting in themselves, let alone because they are "there." It is extended because, in Dr. Samuel Johnson's words: "It is always the writer's duty to make the world better."

When, little more than a year before his death, Brecht was asked, "Can the world of today be represented on a stage?" he replied in the affirmative, "but only if it [the world] is regarded as transformable." For him, the stage is concerned with what men do to men and nothing else. And, unlike Jesus Christ, he believed that they do know what they do. They have chosen to do what they have done—and could choose otherwise. A description of their activities "makes no sense"—would have no point—if this were not true. Therefore even the most descriptive-seeming episode in a play must really be, not descriptive at all, but normative. It implies either praise or blame. It moves history along, if only by a minute, invisible step, toward a different future. It is likely that, to Brecht, the most important statement in all history was this:

> The philosophers have only interpreted the world in various ways; the point, however, is to change it.

It is the eleventh thesis on Feuerbach of his favorite philosopher, Karl Marx.

Brecht has long been the despair of bibliographers and librarians, because his books (in the original German) have come out in overlapping series: to have certain titles once, one had to buy others several times over. But in 1967 the collected works were issued in a single set of twenty volumes; published by

Suhrkamp Verlag in Frankfurt am Main, this will be an essential item from now on. Not that it is complete. The above-mentioned journal is not included; Brecht's letters have not yet been collected; alternate versions, variant readings, etc., are taken no cognizance of. Yet it represents a welcome change indeed for old Brechtians who often couldn't lay their hands on as much as half the material as the new set contains.

Listed here are only book titles of works by Brecht published in English in the United States. For further bibliographical help, the reader is directed to the various books on Brecht, for example, the convenient paperback edition of Martin Esslin's *Brecht: the Man and his Work* (1960).

A Penny for the Poor (1938), translated by D. I. Vesey and Christopher Isherwood, later reissued as *Threepenny Novel; The Trial of Lucullus* (1943), translated by H. R. Hays; *The Private Life of the Master Race* (1944), English version by Eric Bentley; *Selected Poems* (1947), translated by H. R. Hays; *Parables for the Theatre* (1948), translated by Eric and Maja Bentley, and containing *The Good Woman of Setzuan* and *The Caucasian Chalk Circle; Seven Plays by Brecht* (1961), edited by Eric Bentley and containing *In the Swamp, A Man's a Man, Saint Joan of the Stockyards, Mother Courage, Galileo, The Good Woman of Setzuan,* and *The Caucasian Chalk Circle; Mother Courage and Her Children* (1963), English version by Eric Bentley; *Mother Courage and Her Children* (1963), adapted by Eric Bentley; *Baal, A Man's a Man,* and *The Elephant Calf* (1964), edited by Eric Bentley; *The Threepenny Opera* (1964), English book by Desmond Vesey, English lyrics by Eric Bentley; *Brecht on Theatre* (1964), edited by John Willett; *The Mother* (1965), translated by Lee Baxandall; *The Visions of Simone Machard* (with Lion Feuchtwanger, pub. 1965), translated by Carl R. Mueller; *The Jewish Wife and Other Short Plays* (1966), in English versions by Eric Bentley; *Edward II* (1966), English version by Eric Bentley; *The Good Woman of Setzuan* (1966), revised English version by Eric Bentley; *The Caucasian Chalk Circle* (1966), revised English version by Eric Bentley; *Jungle of Cities and Other Plays* (1966), containing *Drums in the Night,* translated by Frank Jones, *Roundheads and Peakheads,* translated by N. Goold-Verschoyle, and *Jungle,* translated by Anselm Hollo; *Galileo* (1966), English version by Charles Laughton; *Manual of Piety* (1967), English text by Eric Bentley, Notes by Hugo Schmidt, a bilingual edition.—E. B.

Bredero, Gerbrand Adriaanszoon (1585–1618). Dutch playwright. Born in Amsterdam, the son of a middle-class family, Bredero was trained as a painter, but he did not have the classical education that was the privilege of some of his contemporaries in the Dutch Academy. For the rest of his short life he remained a man of the people, yet he became the greatest writer of Dutch comedy. The popular note in his comedies is also evident in his lyric poetry, both in the religious poems and the love poems.

Bredero wrote the first Dutch romantic plays and his sources were the Spanish romances of chivalry. Thus, he created *Rodd'rick en Alphonsus* (1611), *Griane* (1612), and *De Stomme Ridder* ("The Dumb Knight," 1618) in this genre. The best of these three plays is *Griane,* which is an excellent example of a

GERBRAND ADRIAANSZOON BREDERO (NETHERLANDS INFORMATION SERVICE)

romantic drama of the Renaissance. *Lucelle* (1616) was based on a French model, a play written by Louis le Jars. In spite of his early efforts and his romance sources, his real achievement lay in his realistic style. He was a master of the language of the people and his characters were sharply drawn. Thus, the most successful parts of these plays were the comic intermezzi, where the realistic figures Bredero drew from everyday life appeared among the knights.

Bredero's realism appears most clearly in his farces and comedies. The most famous of his farces are *Klucht van de Koe* ("Farce of the Cow," written 1612), *Klucht van Symen sonder Soeticheyt* ("Farce of Playing a Trick on Oneself," written 1612/1613), and *Klucht van den Molenaer* ("Farce of the Miller," written 1613). Bredero based the best of these, *Klucht van de Koe,* on a Dutch chapbook that is a translation of a German original. But he breathed life into this old story of a sly thief who tricks a peasant into selling his own cow and giving him the money, and the spirit, the dialogue, and the humor are all his own.

Bredero's attempt to transform a Roman comedy into a Dutch play resulted in *Het Moortje* ("The Moorish Girl," 1615), a comedy in five acts derived from a French translation of Terence's *Eunuchus.* He was much more successful in putting the everyday life of Amsterdam upon the stage in *De Spaansche Brabander* ("The Spanish Brabander," pub. 1618). His principal source was the third chapter of the Spanish novel *Lazarillo de Tormes* (1554), which he had read in a Dutch translation. He changed the

Spanish hero of his model into a Brabanter, a native of one of the Flemish provinces, in revenge for the fact that the Flemings were pro-Spanish in the Dutch struggle against Spain. Bredero created two worlds upon the stage, that of the pretentious, but penniless, nobleman Jerolimo and that of the ordinary people of Amsterdam, the old men, the prostitutes, the women who spin, and the street urchins. Bredero still remains the greatest writer of Dutch farces.—S. L. F.

Breton, André. See SURREALISM.

Bridie, James. Pen name of **Dr. Osborne Henry Mavor** (1888–1951). Scottish playwright. Bridie was born in Glasgow, where he spent much of his life as a physician and a dramatist. Though it was not until he was fifty that the demands of playwriting forced him to take down his doctor's shingle, Bridie's interest in dramatic writing goes back at least to the years when he was qualifying as a medical practitioner. His dramatic ambitions seem to have been whetted by the Abbey Theatre Players as well as various touring theatrical troupes. Even when serving as a doctor in the army, 1914–1918, Bridie was beginning to try his hand at dialogue and plot structuring.

Bridie's forty-two plays, including his one-act pieces, were written in the last twenty-five years of his life. A number of them are now very much a part of British repertory, but it was specifically Scottish drama to which Bridie wished to devote himself. Encouraged by Scottish playwright James Brandane, Bridie first wrote *The Sunlight Sonata* (1928), under the pseudonym Mary Henderson. The play was dedicated to Tyrone Guthrie, who was its director. Throughout Bridie's career the influence of Guthrie is noticeable, for the dramatist seems to have written a number of his plays with the larger-than-life, nonnaturalistic style of Guthrie in mind.

As with George Bernard Shaw, to whom he has been compared, Bridie wrote mainly comedies, but comedies that dealt with oftentimes fearsome themes. *The Sunlight Sonata,* for example, was subtitled *The Seven Deadly Sins,* and the plays that followed it focused on such harsh realities as death, damnation, disease, and drunkenness. These themes, however, are in some way transcended through his use of fantasy and his fundamental delight in the human being. His last play, *The Baikie Charivari* (1951), was subtitled *The Seven Prophets,* which suggests the serious religious concern of his comedies. Certainly, his absorption in the values of religion was every bit as complete as that of Shaw's, though less formulated. Bridie's major tenet was the primacy of the individual, and his plays sometimes approached the "extravaganza" exuberance of Shaw's final plays in their almost ungoverned enthusiasm for the bizarre, even supernatural, hero. Bridie distrusted the establishment in any of its forms and had a lifelong suspicion of the true believer in politics or religion.

After Bridie's first play, the rest of his dramatic works streamed from his pen at the rate of two and frequently three plays a year, except during the early 1940's, while he was a major in the Army Medical Corps. Among the more famous of Bridie's plays are *The Anatomist* (1930), *Tobias and the Angel* (1930), *Jonah and the Whale* (1932), *A Sleeping Clergyman* (1933), *Storm in a Teacup* (1936, an adaptation of Bruno Frank's play *Sturm in Wasserglass* with a Scottish setting), *Susannah and the Elders* (1937), *The King of Nowhere* (1938), *What Say They?* (1939), *Mr. Bolfry* (1943), *Dr. Angelus* (1947), and *Daphne Laureola* (1949). In addition to the plays, Bridie wrote an engaging autobiography, *One Way of Living* (1939), and two books of essays. He was also an accomplished graphic artist.

Throughout his dramatic career Bridie was dedicated to the Scottish theater. He played a leading part in the founding of the Glasgow Citizens' Theatre, lectured frequently, wrote a number of witty pieces on the state of modern drama, and read countless plays sent to him by aspiring playwrights. In 1950 Bridie founded the College of Drama in the Royal Scottish Academy of Music, Glasgow, the first officially recognized school of drama in Scotland.

It was, of course, in his dramatic writings that Bridie made his major contribution to Scotland's theater. His biblical plays are probably his best known and at present most widely performed works. However, plays such as *Tobias and the Angel* from the Apocrypha, *Jonah and the Whale* (which he rewrote as a radio play in 1942), and *Susannah and the Elders* reveal Bridie to be more interested in the free play of ideas than in dogma. In the final analysis, it is unfair to compare Bridie to Shaw, as has often been done. At times he seems more like an adjusted Strindberg whose awareness never prevents him from seeing the relentless vigor of women, or from accepting the physical comfort of matrimony. Bridie does share Shaw's "both/and" inclusiveness rather than the standard "either/or" attitude (to borrow from Eric Bentley's Shavian commentary), but his liberal political, religious, and social views do not have the fixed, driving quality of Shaw. The delight found in Bridie is in the constant tossing up of an idea to see how it will appear to still another character. And the fascination in Bridie is in the pervading and most unShavian sense of mystery that adds a distinctive fourth dimension to his best work. This characteristic interplay of lightness and mystery often resulted in unresolved plots and the accusation that, though lively and stimulating, his plays fall apart in the last acts. But in this lack of resolution Bridie was only reflecting his lifelong devotion to the greatest "wellmade" playmaker of them all, Henrik Ibsen. Bridie's greatest plays reveal uncannily articulate, splendidly alive human beings outlined in the verbal pyrotechnics produced by the friction of their spirits against the unresolvable questions that face all men.

As yet there has not been a great deal of critical work done on James Bridie. Winifred Bannister's *James Bridie and His Theatre* (1955) offers a summary description of Bridie's complete works and attempts to relate the dramatist through biographical facts to the rather narrow scope of the Scottish theater. Helen L. Luyben's *James Bridie: Clown and Philosopher* (1965) provides a critical analysis of twelve of the plays, illustrating that throughout Bridie's work there exists a philosophical continuity. Gerald Weales also devotes an interesting section to Bridie in his *Religion in Modern English Drama* (1961), in which he briefly traces pervading religious themes in Bridie.—D. J. L.

Brieux, Eugène (1858–1932). French playwright and journalist. The best known and most prolific but one of the least artistic of the French naturalistic playwrights, Brieux was concerned with social and moral problems needing reform. Although most of his thirty-odd pieces are propagandist "thesis" plays lacking in imagination and poetry, a few live today and have plausible characters and moving situations. In 1879 *Bernard Palissy* was performed—a one-act verse drama, written in collaboration with Gaston Salandri. For several years Brieux, who had had only cursory schooling, was a newspaperman in Rouen. Here he observed many social and political abuses and acquired the intimate knowledge of provincial life and characters that would figure prominently in his plays. The theme of six of his plays is a sympathetic concern for the upbringing of children, especially when complicated by the tension and insecurity of parental separation. Several other plays attack the causes of marital incompatibility, chiefly the conventional dowry marriage.

In his early period (1879–1896) he groped for a serious medium of expression. *Ménages d'artistes* ("Artists' Households"), an immature satire of the symbolist movement, was performed by actor-manager André Antoine at the Théâtre-Libre in Paris in 1890. *Blanchette,* the comedy of manners that made Brieux famous, was produced there two years later and shows a remarkable advance. It effectively dramatizes the demise (or salvation, in another version) of an overeducated peasant girl and criticizes government handling of higher education. Political corruption is the theme of *L'Engrenage* ("The Cogwheels," 1894). Two years later *Les Bienfaiteurs* ("The Benefactors") was performed, demonstrating the inhumanity of a coldly mechanical system of organized charity. Staged at the Comédie Française in 1896, *L'Évasion (The Escape)* attacks pseudo science and some kinds of doctors.

The works of the second period (1897–1903) are more impassioned. *Les Trois Filles de M. Dupont (The Three Daughters of M. Dupont,* 1897), Brieux's finest comedy of manners, ruthlessly exposes and indicts the dowry marriage as a cold-blooded business deal that dooms many middle-class girls to marital unhappiness, spinsterhood, or even prostitution. Two rather good comedies were performed in 1898: *Résultat des courses!* ("The Evils of Race-Track Betting") and *Le Berceau* ("The Cradle"). The second is Brieux's first real attack on divorce and the resultant suffering of children. *La Robe rouge (The Red Robe),* his greatest play, had its première at the Théâtre du Vaudeville on March 15, 1900. Without preaching, the author dramatized the temptation of men to misuse authority. After this play, however, the didactic gradually replaced the truly dramatic in Brieux's plays. Some rhetoric and exhortation dilutes *Les Remplaçantes* ("The Substitutes," 1901), an attack on wet-nursing. Still more didactic is *Les Avariés (Damaged Goods,* written 1901, but not performed in Paris until 1905 because of censorship). More like an illustrated medical report than a play, this courageous but ineffective drama broke the silence surrounding venereal disease. *Maternité* (1903) is a somewhat better play about abortion and birth control.

Few of the plays of the last period (1904–1932) have the impact, freshness, or charm to transcend the topical limitations of their subject matter. Interesting but of uneven quality is *Les Hannetons* ("The Dizzy Ones," 1906), which presents an unromantic picture of free love. *La Foi (False Gods,* 1909) makes a qualified plea for religious faith. *La Femme seule (Woman on Her Own,* 1913) exposes the prejudices against women making an independent living. Brieux's penchant for realistic rural characters is again happily displayed in *Le Bourgeois aux champs* ("The City Man in the Country," 1914). *Les Américains chez nous (The Americans in France,* performed in Paris and New York, 1920) and *L'Avocat* ("The Lawyer," 1922) were among his last plays.

Except for the alternate ending of *Blanchette,* in which Blanchette becomes a prostitute, Brieux's plays are not *comédies rosses* (at the cynical extreme of the naturalistic movement). *Les Trois Filles de M. Dupont, La Robe rouge, Le Bourgeois aux champs,* and parts of *Blanchette* and *Les Hannetons* are outstanding because Brieux compassionately breathed life into convincing lower-middle-class characters and believable human situations of injustice and degradation. *La Robe rouge* will probably remain his most powerful drama because of its passionate plea for mercy in legal justice and its relentless exposure of trial lawyers in the act of destroying an innocent and helpless peasant family. Lacking a polished wit and a brilliant comic style, he judged life from the humane perspective of social pity, of sentiment tempered with common sense. He was equally removed on the naturalistic scale from the morbidity of Henry Becque and from Émile Zola's clinical analysis of heredity and environment.

Bernard Shaw wrote a eulogistic preface to six of Brieux's plays translated by Mrs. Bernard Shaw, St. John Hankin, and others: *Three Plays by Brieux* (1910) includes *Maternity, The Three Daughters of M. Dupont,* and *Damaged Goods. Woman on Her Own* (1916) includes *Woman on Her Own, False Gods,* and *The Red Robe.* F. Eisemann translated *Blanchette* (1914) and *L'Évasion* (1896). Worthwhile but dated studies of the plays are included in H. A. Smith's *Main Currents of Modern French Drama* (1925), P. V. Thomas' *The Plays of Eugène Brieux* (1915), and W. H. Scheifley's *Brieux and Contemporary French Society* (1917).—S. S. S.

Britannicus (1669).   A tragedy by Jean RACINE. The young emperor Néron no longer wants to be dominated by his mother, Agrippine, and is beginning to hate his half brother Britannicus. Both brothers love Junie, but she loves Britannicus. Néron forces Junie to reject Britannicus and, hidden from sight, listens while she does. However, he subsequently overhears her assure Britannicus of her love. In spite of his mother and his tutor, and encouraged by the freedman Narcisse, Néron finally has Britannicus poisoned. This tragedy shows the beginnings of a monstrous criminal instinct unleashed by jealousy.

This play has been translated into English verse by Kenneth Muir in *Five Plays* (1960).—Ja. G.

Broken Jug, The (Der zerbrochene Krug, written 1806, perf. 1808).   A comedy by Heinrich von KLEIST. The historical background of this play is interesting. In 1802, when Kleist was in Bern, Switzerland, with the writers Ludwig Wieland, Heinrich Gessner, and Heinrich Zschokke, they decided to have a play competition among them, and each had to interpret an etching based on Debucourt's painting *La cruche cassée.* Kleist finished his comedy in 1806, and in 1808 it was produced by Goethe in Weimar without success. Kleist accused Goethe of destroying the play's momentum by dividing it into three acts. However, the comedy probably failed, not because of this division, but because Goethe had no real sense for humor. Kleist's drama is loaded with farcical elements that demand subtle treatment. The character of Judge Adam, a preposterous liar, is one of the great comic figures of the German stage. He has such extraordinary confidence in his ability to hoodwink others that he is unaware of the actual ridiculous impression he makes on those around him. In attempting to find a young man named Ruprecht guilty of breaking a villager's jug after an unsuccessful attempt to seduce a charming young woman named Eva, Adam proves the opposite: Ruprecht actually tried to save Eva from the real culprit, none other than Adam, who promised to keep Ruprecht out of the army if Eva would sleep with him. Once this truth comes to light before the district inspector, Adam flees as though the devil himself were after him. Though the form of the drama is farcical, Kleist has a serious intention: to break down the barriers of deception to come to the truth. Here he renders an original interpretation of paradise and original sin. Adam and Eva are expelled from paradise, not because they eat from the tree of knowledge, but because they refuse to acknowledge what they know. —J. D. Z.

Brome, Richard (c. 1590–1652). English playwright. The earliest reference to Brome is in the Preface to Ben Jonson's *Bartholomew Fair* (1614) in a context that indicates that Brome was Jonson's servant. Brome was writing for the stage as early as 1623 when he collaborated on a play, unfortunately now lost, with Jonson's son. Most of Brome's plays were acted by the King's Men, the most successful company in London, and this is an index of their popularity. With the suppression of the theaters in 1642 Brome's fortunes declined and at the time of his death he described himself as "poor and proud."

Fifteen of Brome's plays are extant. Among them is *The Northern Lass* (1632), a tale of a country girl who comes to London to win her lover. Popular in its own day, the play owed much of its success to the novelty of the North Country heroine's dialect. A more successful comedy is *The Antipodes* (1638), an unusual and imaginative play centering on the attempt of a kind of seventeenth-century psychoanalyst to mend the marriage of a quixotic daydreamer and his neglected wife. Brome's best play, *A Jovial Crew* (1641), involves two daughters' desertion of their father and their subsequent joining up with a band of gypsy beggars, led by their father's steward, Springlove. The depiction of the hardships and rewards of vagabond existence provides an interesting background to the complicated developments of the main plot. The play also has a motif of social criticism that is a recurrent feature of Brome's plays.

The standard edition of Brome is *The Dramatic Works of Richard Brome* (1873) in three volumes. R. J. Kaufmann's *Richard Brome: Caroline Dramatist* (1961) provides an excellent critical study. —E. O.

Browning, Robert (1812–1889). English poet and playwright. The son of middle-class parents residing in a London suburb, Browning was educated largely through private tutoring at home and his own constant reading in his father's 6,000-volume library. At an early age Browning had determined to become a poet, and after the publication of his first poem, *Pauline,* in 1833, his life was dedicated to writing. With the publication of such volumes as *Men and Women* (1855) and *Dramatis Personae* (1864), both of which contain many of his greatest dramatic monologues, he became known and admired by a large public. The most important personal event in his life, however, and the one that has held great interest for many people who have never read any of his works, was his elopement with Elizabeth Barrett in 1846. They lived in Italy until her death in 1861, after which Browning returned to England. The crowning achievement of his later years was his long poem *The Ring and the Book* (1868–1869).

Browning is associated principally with the dramatic monologue, but he also deserves recognition for his poetic dramas, some of which were written because of the great interest expressed by the actor William Charles Macready, who saw in Browning, for a time at least, great promise as a dramatist. From 1837 to 1846 Browning was actively concerned with writing for the theater, and it was Macready who was largely responsible. It was at Macready's urging that Browning wrote *Strafford,* which was produced at Covent Garden in 1837 and ran for four nights. Browning then devoted much of his energy and thought to the theater, and for the next ten years he wrote verse dramas, some composed expressly for production, some for the closet. *Strafford* was followed by *Pippa Passes* (pub. 1841), *King Victor and King Charles* (pub. 1842), *The Return of the Druses* (pub. 1843), *A Blot in the 'Scutcheon* (produced in 1843 by Macready), *Colombe's Birthday* (pub. 1844, produced 1853), *Luria* (pub. 1846), *A Soul's Tragedy* (pub. 1846), and *In a Balcony* (written 1853, pub. 1855 in *Men and Women*).

All of Browning's dramas display certain characteristics—long, involved speeches, lack of any real dramatic action, and occasional obscurity of language—that worried Macready and caused him to reject two of them, *King Victor and King Charles* and *The Return of the Druses.* These qualities are prominent features of Browning's closet dramas— *Pippa Passes, Luria, A Soul's Tragedy,* and *In a Balcony*—but they are also sometimes present and succeed in detracting from the positive dramatic qualities in the dramas written expressly for the theater. The thematic concern with and the presentation of liberal and humanitarian attitudes (evident especially in *Strafford, King Victor and King Charles, Colombe's Birthday,* and *The Return of the Druses*), the striking and at times brilliant depiction of character chiefly by means of stressing the conflict between love and honor (*A Blot in the 'Scutcheon* and *Colombe's Birthday*), and the many impressive poetic passages are weakened and almost overshadowed by the poet's overriding interest in the subtleties of motivation at the expense of dramatic action and effective dialogue. Paradoxically, the very qualities that enabled Browning to write such excellent dramatic monologues prevented him from realizing the great potential that he seemed to possess to write drama.

For information about Browning's life and works see William Clyde DeVane, *A Browning Handbook* (2nd ed., 1955). Three articles devoted specifically to Browning as dramatist are H. B. Charlton, "Browning as Dramatist," *Bulletin of the John Rylands Library,* XXIII (1939), 33–67; Arthur E. DuBois, "Robert Browning, Dramatist," *Studies in Philology,* XXXIII (1936), 626–655; and J. P. McCormack, "Robert Browning and the Experimental Drama," *PMLA,* LXVIII (1953), 982–991. The titles of the following two articles indicate their content and direction: J. M. Purcell, "The Dramatic Failure of *Pippa Passes,*" *Studies in Philology,* XXXVI (1939), 77–87; and G. H. Clarke, "Browning's *A Blot in the 'Scutcheon:* A Defence," *Sewanee Review,* XXVIII (1929), 213–227.—M. T.

Bruno, Giordano.   See IL CANDELAIO.

Büchner, Georg (1813–1837). German playwright and doctor. Caught in the revolutionary tide of his times, Büchner did not find it easy to follow in his father's footsteps when he began studying medicine at the University of Strasbourg in 1831. Instead, he became interested in the Young Germany (*Junges Deutschland*) movement, which sought great social and political reforms. Büchner himself differed from the followers of Young Germany, since he believed that the impetus for change must come from the lower classes, not from the educated. Shortly after he moved to the University of Giessen in 1834, he formed the Secret Society for the Rights of Man, which aimed at improving social conditions in Hesse. Büchner formulated his ideas in a controversial tract, *Der Hessiche Landbote* ("The Hessian Courier," 1834), advocating that the peasants rebel with force to gain their rights. Such a document was not tolerated by the Hessian government, and Büchner was forced to flee to his home near Darmstadt, where he was kept under surveillance. It was at this time that he began working on his first drama, DANTON'S DEATH, which incorporated both his passionate ideas on freedom and his pessimistic view of society. Danton, the great leader of the French Revolution, becomes its victim, and the people are no better for

GEORG BÜCHNER (GERMAN INFORMATION CENTER)

the change in society than they were before they broke their shackles. Büchner's pessimism stemmed from his own experiences of deprivation in Germany. Because he was considered politically dangerous, he was not allowed to travel and was obliged to receive his doctorate from the University of Zurich *in absentia.* Finally, in October 1836, Büchner was given permission to journey to Zurich, where he held a position as university lecturer on comparative anatomy. Without the fear of German censorship, he could now finish his comedy *Leonce und Lena* (*Leonce and Lena,* written 1836, pub. 1850), which, despite its fairy-tale quality, has strong political overtones. Prince Leonce of Popo and Princess Lena of Pipi are forced to enter into a marriage of convenience without having seen one another. Both decide to run away from their respective kingdoms, which repel them. They meet accidentally at an inn, fall in love, and marry without knowing each other's true identity. The world is for a moment topsy-turvy, and Leonce and Lena decide to reform their kingdom into an ideal fairy-tale realm in opposition to the decadence and corruption of the old regime. While composing this drama, Büchner was influenced by Shakespeare, Brentano, and Musset. However, the political thesis is all Büchner's, and it also shapes the action of his last play, WOYZECK. Here a simple soldier is driven to kill his wife and himself because he cannot cope with the injustices in life. Büchner saw history from a deterministic viewpoint: One incident can set off a chain reaction, which governs man's fate and allows him little choice. The structure of all his dramas reflects Büchner's philosophy, and the protagonists must be prepared to resign themselves to a destiny they did not ordain. Büchner found himself in that very same position when he was overcome with typhoid fever at the age of twenty-three. He died on February 19, 1837, never having seen one of his plays performed, while today he is acclaimed as one of Germany's greatest dramatists. A good critical analysis of Büchner's life and works is *Georg Büchner* (1951) by A. H. J. Knight.—J. D. Z.

bugaku. The word *bugaku* literally signifies dance music. It stands for a considerable number of allied, semidramatic dance forms brought from Korea and Manchuria to Japan in the tenth century A.D. These were court ceremonies that have on this account been preserved with notable fidelity. Though the costumes and musical instruments indicate their continental origin, they nevertheless became an important part of Japanese artistic life. Color schemes stress a deep red. The dance is extremely ceremonious, as a rule unhurried in its pace and stately in movements. The dancers, like the musicians, keep strict alignment. Symmetry provides for one group to the left of the stage, another to the right. Special dances are assigned to each, thirty-seven surviving for those to the left and twenty-four for those to the right. Some are highly stylized military dances, executed with spears. Only men take part. The orchestra may have as many as twenty players.—H. W. W.

Bulgakov, Mikhail [Afanasievich] (1891–1940). Russian novelist, short-story writer, and playwright. A physician by training, Bulgakov abandoned medicine after two years of practice to become a newspaper correspondent in a provincial town. In 1921 he moved to Moscow and collaborated on the magazine *Gudok* ("The Whistle"), where he developed close friendships with Valentin Katayev, Isaak Babel, Yuri Olesha, Ilya Ilf, and Evgeny Petrov—all of whom were to become prominent in Soviet literature.

In 1925/26, Bulgakov used the same subject in writing both his first full-length novel, *The White Guard* (1925), and his most famous play, *Dni Turbinikh* (*The Days of the Turbins,* 1926). The play, like the novel, was based on his personal recollections of the events he had witnessed in Kiev in 1918 and 1919: the German occupation; the creation of a synthetic Ukrainian state under the German-sponsored (and later abandoned) hetman Skoropadsky; the capture of the city by Petliura's bands after a futile defense by the "Whites"; and finally the arrival of the "Reds." Bulgakov's play, staged in 1926, was immediately attacked by the communist critics for not portraying the Whites as complete villains but showing them instead as ordinary human beings with good and bad characteristics. After a few performances, the play was banned and Bulgakov's next play, *Beg* ("The Flight," 1928), set in the same period, was never allowed to be performed.

Krasnyi ostrov ("The Red Island") a comedy he wrote in 1928, hardly fared any better: it was taken out of the repertory of the Kamerny Theater after only a few performances. When Stalin expressed a personal dislike for Bulgakov's plays, they could no longer be staged and, in order to earn his living, Bulgakov had to work as assistant stage manager at the Moscow Art Theater.

Bulgakov, who had from the start been on the side of the revolution, soon found out, like so many others, that the new regime was even harder on the writer than its tsarist predecessor had been. He expressed his views on censorship and pressure on artists in his play about Molière, *Kabala svyatosh* ("The Cabal of Saintly Hypocrites," 1936), which he tried for four years to have produced at the Moscow Art

MIKHAIL BULGAKOV (TASS FROM SOVFOTO)

Theater. After years of reworking and rewriting the play to make it acceptable, Bulgakov finally felt it had been too emasculated and was about to give it up altogether. At that point it was finally produced, but it survived only seven performances. The picture of the conflict between talent (Molière) and authority (Louis XIV) was still unacceptable to the authorities.

Among other plays by Bulgakov should be mentioned *Poslednie dni* ("The Last Days" [of Pushkin], 1935), *Don Kikhot* ("Don Quixote," 1938), and *Ivan Vasilievich* ("Ivan the Terrible," 1936). All these plays were soon removed from production because they contained elements displeasing to the regime.

Bulgakov died in 1940, one of the talented writers who could not survive the stifling regime.—A. MACA.

Bulgaria. The history of Bulgarian literature—and thus of Bulgarian drama—is one of relatively slow development. After the fall of the Second Bulgarian Empire before the Turkish onslaught in 1393, the Bulgarians entered upon a period of nearly five centuries of vassalage to the Ottoman Empire, down to their political liberation through the Russo-Turkish War of 1877–1878. Bulgarian literature in the sixteenth and seventeenth centuries approaches a total blank. The beginnings of the so-called renaissance of Bulgarian culture are usually dated from 1762, the year in which there was written a history of the Bulgarian people by the Bulgarian Orthodox monk Paisii Khilendarski. For all Paisii's heroic efforts to rouse the Bulgarian people from their cultural lethargy, it was not until about 1840 that something approximating an original literature in the modern sense of the word began to be produced. The history of the Bulgarian drama traces its beginnings to around 1840 as well, to certain didactic and moralistic "dialogues" composed by scholarly ecclesiastics. But it was not until 1856, after the disheartening conclusion of the Crimean War, that the first full-length play was staged in Bulgaria and theatrical life started up in a few Bulgarian cities. The history of the Bulgarian drama, then, especially in its first decades, must be studied in the light of that Bulgarian backwardness that was in large measure the fruit of Turkish political, and Greek cultural, oppression. Though the Bulgarians boast an ancient and glorious Slavic culture, they were late in entering the stream of modern intellectual life.

The investigator of Bulgarian drama should be further aware that it forms a weak link in a minor European literature. Justly or unjustly, no Bulgarian writer has so far achieved genuine international distinction, and most non-Bulgarians are hardly conscious that there exists such a thing as Bulgarian literature. Within this minor literature the drama is appreciably less developed than lyric poetry, the short story, or even the novel (a statement that is especially true of the last half-century), and this in spite of the fact that certain outstanding Bulgarian authors have written for the stage.

From the point of view of Bulgarian society as a whole, the theater was most vital in its earliest stages, during the years immediately preceding the Liberation. The extremist, revolutionary wing of the intelligentsia regarded it as a powerful instrument of propaganda, useful in stirring Bulgarian national feeling and agitating for a popular uprising against the Turks, in view of the impossibility of employing the printed word for such purposes at all extensively. Even the more moderate members of the intelligentsia thought that the theater had an important educational role to play as a "general school" for the entire population, although there were malcontents who grumbled that Bulgaria was ill-advised to invest any of her scant resources in such frivolity. As it turned out, the presentation of translated and original plays in the Bulgaria of the 1860's and 1870's had great historical significance.

The person most notably associated with the Bulgarian theater in its infancy was Dobri Voinikov (1833–1878). After staging some amateur theatricals in his native town of Shumen, he moved on to the Rumanian city of Braila, where in 1865 he organized the first formal Bulgarian theatrical troupe for the purpose of giving performances for Bulgarian émigrés residing in Rumania. A goodly portion of the troupe's repertory had to be created by Voinikov himself, who started out in 1866 with a stage adaptation of *Raina kniaginia* ("Princess Raina"), a tale of medieval Bulgaria by the minor Russian author A. F. Vel'tman, which was immensely popular in Bulgaria. Voinikov then continued with a string of mediocre historical melodramas drawn from the period of Bulgaria's medieval might and designed to remind his audiences that their country had a glorious historical past and deserved fully as glorious a future. This category of plays included *Pokrushtenie na preslavskyi dvor* ("The Christianization of the Court at Preslav," 1868); *Velislava, bulgarska kniaginia* ("Velislava, Princess of Bulgaria," 1870); and *Vuztsariavaneto na Kruma Strashnyi* ("The Enthronement of Krum the Terrible," 1871). Voinikov is perhaps best remembered, however, for his comedy *Krivorazbranata tsivilizatsiia* ("Civilization Wrongly Understood," 1871), an attack on the widespread Gallomania in the country at that time. The play's heroes are persuaded that only through speaking French and living in France can one be fully civilized, and they exhibit the most thoroughgoing contempt for all things Bulgarian. "I don't want to be a Bulgarian," proclaims one of them, "because there is nothing lower than a Bulgarian." Of course at the end all the characters with as much as a grain of good in them are brought to their nationalistic senses.

An important play in pre-Liberation Bulgaria was a dramatization, done in 1870, of the story *Izgubena Stanka* ("Lost Stanka," first published in 1866) by Iliia Bluskov (1839–1913). *Izgubena Stanka* is a tearjerking melodrama chronicling the vicissitudes of a fair maiden kidnapped by the Tartars but ultimately rescued. Replete with unveiled sentimentalism and characters easily tagged as either good or evil, *Izgubena Stanka* has little to recommend it artistically. However, this was precisely the sort of thing that Bulgarian audiences of the day were capable of appreciating, and *Izgubena Stanka* was received enthusiastically as an emblem of the unbearable sufferings of the Bulgarians at the hands of their Turkish overlords.

The most worthwhile play of the pre-Liberation period and the only one that has retained sufficient vitality to be staged occasionally even now was another historical drama, *Ivanko ubietšut na Asenia I* ("Ivanko the Assassin of Asen I," pub. 1872), written by Voinikov's rival Vasil Drumev (c. 1840–1901). *Ivanko* is based upon the same type of historical subject that Voinikov had made so popular, but Drumev's superior literary gifts enabled him to create a nicely constructed play with well-motivated characters, which for all its faults—for instance, the author's use of his native dialect instead of something closer to the in any case chaotic literary language—was promptly greeted as a masterpiece by contemporary critics. History has confirmed this judgment even though at the time the discomfited Voinikov maintained that the play was perhaps excellent as *poetry*, but not as *theater*.

Although the theater thus contributed much to the stimulation of the Bulgarian national consciousness (a publicistic and patriotic aim pursued, not only in the drama, but in all of Bulgarian literature at the time), the drama shared in the general literary doldrums in the period of political and cultural adjustment immediately following the Liberation. In the 1880's hardly any plays of significance were created. Ivan Vazov (1850–1921), who is now considered the classic Bulgarian writer and who was almost all that Bulgarian literature could boast of in that decade, produced a couple of minor efforts: *Mikhalaki chorbadzhi* (pub. 1882 [a *chorbadzhiia* was a member of the native aristocracy of wealth]) and *Ruska* (a proper name, pub. 1883). In the 1890's Vazov turned his attention more seriously to the theater, adapting in 1894 an earlier story of his to the stage under the title *Khushove* (*khush* was the name for a vagabond revolutionary of the immediate pre-Liberation years operating in Rumania). The play describes the unenviable lot of the impoverished revolutionaries—their conflicts with the wealthy

IVAN VAZOV (REPRINTED WITH THE PERMISSION OF FARRAR, STRAUS & GIROUX, INC., FROM *Bulgaria and Her People* BY WILL SEYMOUR MONROE. COPYRIGHT 1914 BY THE PAGE CO., RENEWED 1942.)

Bulgarian émigrés in Rumania who can only with difficulty be induced to make financial contributions to the revolutionary cause, the delirious welcome afforded by the Bulgarians to two Russian volunteers, and so forth. In its patriotic naïveté *Khushove* cannot be fully appreciated by foreigners, but it is a favorite play and remains a staple of the repertory to this day.

The broadest artistic flowering of the Bulgarian drama, given a powerful boost by the founding of the National Theater in Sofia in 1907, did not commence until roughly 1900. Vazov was a major contributor to this flowering even though from the aesthetic point of view his plays are rather weak. He began the decade with comedies such as *Vestnikar li?* ("A Newspaperman?", 1900) and *Sluzhbogontsi* ("Jobseekers," 1903), in which he attacked the blatant careerism that had become a prominent feature of contemporary Bulgarian life. The opening of the National Theater stimulated Vazov's productivity as a playwright: after 1907 he wrote five plays in six years, of which three, it is true, were merely dramatic adaptations of certain of his own novels. All five plays were historical dramas of the immediate or more distant past. *Pod igoto* ("Under the Yoke," 1910) and *Kazalarskata tsaritsa* ("The Czarina of Kazalar," 1911), based upon novels with the same titles, dealt with the more immediate past, the first treating of the famous April uprising of 1876 against the Turks. *Kum propast* ("Toward the Precipice," 1907, adapted from the novel *Ivan Aleksandur*), *Borislav* (1909), and *Ivailo* (1914), on the other hand, utilized subjects from the history of medieval Bulgaria. (Ivailo, for example, was a great peasant revolutionary who succeeded in ascending the throne temporarily in the late 1270's.) As had been the case before the Liberation, historical dramas continued to appeal to Bulgarian audiences, and between 1907 and 1912 Vazov's plays were presented 154 times at the National Theater; he was thus by far that theater's most popular playwright, his nearest rival being Shakespeare, with sixty-six performances.

Though Vazov preferred to adhere to the literary tradition of several decades before, modernistic currents in the drama were introduced by members of the younger literary generation, prominent among whom was Anton Strashimirov (1872–1937). Two plays of his have become classics of the Bulgarian stage: *Vampir* ("The Vampire," 1901) and *Svekurva* ("The Mother-in-Law," 1907). The first of these is set amidst what Strashimirov regarded as the stifling moral darkness and corruption of country life in Bulgaria; the plot involves unreasoning hatred, adultery, and murder. Though overdramatized, the play achieved renown as a distillation of the tragedies occurring in the unenlightened rural milieu. The scene of the action is switched to the city in Strashimirov's second play, *Svekurva*, which won a national competition marking the opening of the National Theater. The piece is an attempt at describing the sway that women in general, and mothers-in-law in particular, had theretofore exercised in Bulgarian society (although according to the author their power had been broken at the time of writing). In *Svekurva* the mother-in-law's despotic power, which she employs in an effort to destroy her son's marriage, is ultimately overcome when she herself realizes that she has overstepped the bounds of her authority.

Measures are taken to resurrect the marriage and the play ends happily. *Svekurva* is now considered one of the best comedies of morals in the native repertoire.

Following the success of his first plays, Strashimirov turned to an assault against the corruption of high government officials and important persons generally in plays like *Kushta* ("The House," 1909) and *Pred Vlakhernskite vrate* ("Before the Blachernae Gates," 1909) as well as the writing of plays incorporating highly modernistic currents, such as *Reveka* ("Rebecca") and *Kum sluntseto* ("Toward the Sun"), in which the characters tend to be maniacs or mystics. Since these pieces exhibit the influence of "decadents" like Maeterlinck, Nietzsche, and Przybyszewski, they are not republished in communist Bulgaria.

An original synthesis of modernistic attitudes and national folklore motifs was effected at the beginning of the century by Petko Todorov (1879–1916), whose plays mingled the fantastic and the realistic in curious ways. The first example of this dramatic subgenre was *Zidari* ("The Builders," written 1899; pub. 1902). Starting from the old folk tradition that the stability of a large building may be ensured by the expedient of walling up a human sacrifice within it, Todorov devises a complex intrigue in which love rivalries lead to the enticing of a beautiful young girl to the construction site of a church, where she is murdered so that she may be immured and the church completed on time. The church is finished on schedule, but the local population studiedly avoids it because of the tragedy with which it is associated, and the man most directly responsible for the girl's death commits suicide.

In subsequent years *Zidari* was followed by several other plays based on folk motifs, including *Samodiva* ("The Woodsprite," pub. 1904), *Neviasta Boriana* ("Young Wife Boriana," 1909), and *Zmeiova svatba* ("Zmei's Wedding," 1911). *Zmeiova svatba* is of especial interest as a study in the interrelationship between the real and the fantastic in Todorov's work. Zmei (the common noun means "serpent") is the name of a fantastic folk figure whose main function is to enchant young maidens and lure them to destruction. In Todorov's play, however, the hero Zmei seems in most respects to be a quite ordinary individual, a good-natured sort whose chief idiosyncrasy is that he lives in a cave. Any supernatural traits he may possess are no more than hinted at. Todorov's failure to combine the supernatural with the natural successfully is reflected in the ambivalent attitude of the inhabitants of the surrounding countryside toward Zmei: though in some ways they seem to fear him for the powers he should have, at the same time they mock him as a feckless character. In any event, the heroine Tsena arouses Zmei's love. Through persuasion alone he induces her to spend the night in his cave, after which she falls in love with him and decides to remain with him. However, when her fellow villagers appear before the cave to reclaim her, she is accidentally killed while shielding Zmei from an attack by her brother, and Zmei is left to mourn her. The combination of the characters' realistic psychology with the semifantastic setting in which they move bestows a unique quality upon *Zmeiova svatba*.

In his early youth Todorov was an ardent socialist. In spite of the fact that he later rejected many of his former beliefs, he occasionally treated social problems in his works. Elements of social conflict occur in *Zidari*, but Todorov's chief contribution to social drama was *Purvite* ("The First," pub. 1907; substantially revised 1912), which depicts in stark outline the split between the common people with their aspirations toward equality and justice, led by the schoolteacher Dimitur, and the chorbadzhii who hold economic and political power in the village. As the play ends, the chorbadzhii are shown as conscious that their period of hegemony is drawing to a close, a situation symbolized by the defection of the daughter of the leading chorbadzhiia from the parental camp to join her life with Dimitur's.

However good certain of Strashimirov's and Todorov's plays of the time may have been, genuine pride of place as a playwright belongs to Peio Yavorov or Iavorov (1878–1914). Although principally a poet, toward the end of his life Yavorov seemed to be moving toward the abandonment of poetry for the theater: he served for several years as the artistic director (*dramaturg*) of the National Theater and wrote two plays: the classic *V polite na Vitosha* ("In the Foothills of Vitosha" [a mountain that looms over Sofia], 1911) and *Kogato grum udari —kak ekhoto zaglukhva* ("It Thunders, The Echo Dies Away," 1912). As a dramatist, Yavorov was a close student of Chekhov and Ibsen and his plays reflect their influence—especially in the choice of personal or family tragedies as subjects—but he had a strong creative personality of his own that would not subordinate itself to "influences," however mighty.

V polite na Vitosha, which was largely based on Yavorov's own life and was thus a fascinating instance of literary catharsis, was also linked in an uncanny way with the author's fate subsequent to its publication. The play's hero, Khristoforov, is an idealistic type active in politics and journalism and in love with a young woman named Mila, whose family is on opposite sides of the political fence from him. Mila in her turn is utterly devoted to Khristoforov: as she remarks, he has his work in addition to his personal life, but she has only him to live for, and therefore her passion is more intense than his. After a stormy scene with her brother, who is determined to prevent any marriage between Mila and Khristoforov, she runs from the house and is crushed by a streetcar. Khristoforov, stunned, arrives at her bedside and, after a vain attempt to communicate with her, shoots himself with a pistol an instant before she dies so that they will be joined in death as in life. In *V polite na Vitosha* Yavorov displays occasional lapses of taste, especially in the finale where the death scene is accompanied first by thunder and then, after all is over, by the sun breaking through the clouds; but in spite of this the work must stand as the greatest Bulgarian drama to date. The dialogue is composed in some of Yavorov's most concise prose; the plot line is clearly delineated and holds the spectator's interest from beginning to end. The development of the action is completely logical if one does not balk at the credibility of such all-engrossing passion as that displayed by Mila and Khristoforov. Indeed, Yavorov himself demonstrated that such passion may exist in reality: only two years after the play's publication, in 1913, Yavorov's wife, an insanely jealous and possessive woman, impulsively ended her life in his presence with a pistol. Yavorov attempted to follow suit upon the spot but succeeded only in partially blinding himself; roughly a year later he tried again and this time did not fail. The abnormally intense passion so important in *V polite na Vitosha* was something of which the author had personal knowledge.

The lesser, though later, of Yavorov's two plays, *Kogato grum udari,* was initially conceived under the direct inspiration of a reading of Chekhov's *Uncle Vanya* and was to have been a domestic drama centered on the destruction of a supposedly normal and happy family through the exposure of a dread secret suppressed for some twenty years. In the play as it finally emerged the secret is that the son of the family is actually the fruit of an adulterous liaison between the wife and a close friend of the husband's who had been compelled to hide out in their house for political reasons and while at it gave her the child her husband was incapable of bestowing upon her. Twenty years later the friend returns for a visit and the revelation of the secret of the son's birth leads to the destruction of the family. In *Kak ekhoto zaglukhva,* a sequel to *Kogato grum udari,* the infidelity of many years before that led to the dissolution of one family is reenacted in detail, this time with the son, the son's wife, and the son's friend as participants: the echo is a reprise of the original thunderclap. At the core of both parts of *Kogato grum udari,* then, as well as of *V polite na Vitosha,* there lies the concept of demonically possessive sexual passion, the psychological ramifications of which Yavorov undertook to work out in dramatic action. Social and political considerations impinge only peripherally upon the plays, for Yavorov is primarily a psychological dramatist who deals with the wellsprings of human character.

The years from 1900 to 1913 were artistically the most fertile in the history of the Bulgarian drama. However, none of the period's four major dramatists was known primarily as a playwright: Vazov was first and foremost a poet and prose writer, Strashimirov a novelist and prose writer, Todorov a writer of prose idylls, and Yavorov a poet. Only in the 1920's did there appear on the scene an important author who wrote mainly for the stage: Stefan L. Kostov (1879–1939). Although the years between the First and Second World Wars, both of which ended disastrously for Bulgaria, saw a quantity of dramatic writing, few plays from the era have survived, and the period must be regarded as inferior to the preceding one. Kostov came into his own as a playwright—more precisely, a writer of comedies—only in the 1920's and faded in the following decade even though he continued to compose for the stage over that period. He had gained some repute before the war with his *Muzhemrazka* ("The Manhater," written about 1910 and staged about 1914), which describes the intrigues of a manhater named Androfoba who attempts to incite her female associates against men but is exposed as a hypocrite who is herself secretly involved with one of them. Another unconventional character is the hero of *Pred izgrev sluntse* ("Before Sunrise," 1921), an individual known only as "the teacher," who preaches occult doctrines and theories of free love. At the conclusion he is denounced by a disillusioned disciple, but such is the gullibility of his remaining followers that their faith in him rests unshaken.

Kostov's greatest fame as a writer of comedies, however, is based on two plays with more immediate social relevance than those described above: *Golemanov* (written in 1920, first performed in 1927) and *Zlatnata mina* ("The Gold Mine," 1926). Of the two, *Zlatnata mina,* which treats subjects closer to Kostov's usual ones, is probably the better: the plot is easy to follow and the entire play quite entertaining. The central character, Khadzhiev, succumbing to a transparent swindle, begins investing heavily in a gold mine which he falsely believes will bring him great riches. After delineating the psychology of the *nouveau-riche*-to-be—he is quite insufferable—the author deflates him cruelly by revealing the fact that he has been taken for all he has. Deserted by those who had been so attentive when they thought him a future millionaire, Khadzhiev is rescued from destitution only through a variant of the *deus ex machina* device: his future son-in-law promises to salvage his finances if he will recognize the folly of his former yearning after quick riches, which he promptly and improbably does in most earnest fashion.

Kostov's *Golemanov* harks back to Vazov's social comedies of twenty years before. The hero, Golemanov, thinking he is in line for a ministerial post (it hardly matters which, for he is equally unqualified for any of them), begins behaving like a petty tyrant until he is informed that the government has abandoned the attempt to form the cabinet in which he would have been included. At the conclusion he rants on, refusing to yield the power and authority which in actuality he has never possessed. Kostov's comedies, then, dealt with social types that most contemporary spectators would have regarded as humorous and perhaps instructive exaggerations. Since the plays were usually equipped with suitably inspirational endings, the proper theatergoing public welcomed his work.

The sole playwright of the 1930's worth a detailed discussion is Yordan Yovkov or Iordan Iovkov (1880–1937), though his plays form the weakest segment of his literary production, which consisted mostly of short stories and novels: his talent was such that even his poorer production was superior to the best that most of his contemporaries could do. Yovkov continued the line of Kostovian comedy with his play *Milionerut* ("The Millionaire," 1930), in which he casts a jaundiced but still not completely negative eye upon the foibles of established society. The hero, the veterinarian Dr. Kondov, is not the sort whom the best society is anxious to admit into its ranks until the false rumor spreads that he has suddenly become a millionaire. Dr. Kondov thereupon miraculously finds himself eagerly sought after and discovers that the way is open to a marriage with a girl of good family with whom he is in love. He convinces his parents-in-law that he is no millionaire only after the marriage, when they must make the best of an unpleasant situation. *Milionerut* is an entertaining comedy in which the greedy hypocrites of the higher social circles are merely ludicrous, no more.

Two of Yovkov's plays, *Albena* (1929) and *Boriana* (1932), deal with deeper social and family conflicts in the Bulgarian countryside but suffer from the author's compulsion to resolve them all in a spirit of Christian love. A central theme of *Albena,* the more successful of the two, is the unwitting evil that physical beauty, in this case Albena's, can cause. Albena is married to an unattractive husband, Kutsar, and is having an affair with the miller Niagul. When Kutsar discovers the lovers' relationship, Niagul decides that he must be removed and sees to his murder. Albena is arrested on suspicion of the crime, although even here her beauty moves the villagers present at the scene to call for her release, until Niagul, likewise moved, steps forward to confess his guilt and relieve Albena of responsibility for Kutsar's demise. The heroine of *Boriana,* on the other hand, though beautiful, is also thoroughly good. The plot involves a family conflict caused by greed and hatred: the father, Zlatil, hoards the treasure that he gained unlawfully from his own father and refuses to admit to his three sons that he is wealthy at all. The sons' cupidity leads to conspiracies to steal the old man's money and, when one of them succeeds at this, to the brink of bloody strife among the brothers. At this point Boriana, prospective wife of one of the sons, intervenes and by the force of her moral authority persuades Zlatil to agree to the division of the spoils among his sons and the brothers to forgive one another. By his action Zlatil salves his bad conscience over what he did to his father and the brothers are brought to see the evil of their ways. The play thus ends in a general spiritual renovation wrought by Boriana.

If the line of the comedy of manners in the 1920's and 1930's was continued by Kostov and Yovkov and the psychological drama further developed, though very much in his own unique way, by Yovkov, the historical drama also had a place in the theater of the period. A major example of this was *Zlatnata chasha* ("The Golden Chalice," 1922) by Ivan Grozev (1872–1957), a symbolist treatment of a medieval subject drawn from the time of the Bogomils, dualistic Christian heretics who flourished in Bulgaria and spread their doctrines as far as southern France and who have since exerted a peculiar fascination over the student of medieval Bulgarian history.

Mention might also be made of *Maistori* ("Master Craftsmen," pub. 1927), a superbly constructed drama of personal and professional rivalry by Racho Stoianov (1883–1951), a *homo unius libri* who never made any further significant contributions to Bulgarian literature.

No especial renaissance in Bulgarian dramaturgy has been observable since the communist takeover of September 1944; the drama has continued to be the stepchild of Bulgarian letters as it has been all along, except possibly for the 1860's, 1870's, and the first decade of this century. As in the 1920's and 1930's, quantities of plays are produced but almost all are unmemorable, something that the Bulgarians themselves will often admit. The most prominent playwright now working is Kamen Zidarov (born 1902), who came into the limelight after 1944 and whose best work to date is *Ivan Shishman* (1960), a historical play in verse describing that most absorbing period of medieval history, the years before Bulgaria's fall to the Turks in 1393.

Separate studies of facets of the Bulgarian drama

in Western languages do not exist. The single most comprehensive study in a language other than Bulgarian is in Russian: Konstantin Derzhavin, *Bolgarskii teatr* ("Bulgarian Theater," 1950). This is a thorough, if pedestrian, survey of the Bulgarian drama, including the musical theater and opera, from its beginnings until after 1944. Those interested in Vazov's plays may consult Petr Christophorov, *Ivan Vazov: La formation d'un écrivain bulgare (1850–1921)* (1938).—C. M.

bunraku. The name by which the classical puppet theater of Japan is popularly known today, *bunraku* is an historical misnomer that nevertheless serves its purpose. During a period when the puppet art had fallen into decline, Uemara Bunrakuken, a puppet manager, opened a theater in 1871 in the traditional capital of the puppet world, Osaka. The theater was named the Bunraken za. So surprisingly successful was his venture that the entire Japanese puppet theater was shortly designated by this word. The better name, strictly speaking, would be *ningyo shibai,* or doll theater.

The use of dolls in theatrical performance, known in Japan for over a thousand years, remained of minor importance until the burgeoning of Japanese arts in the late seventeenth century. The chief school was established at Osaka by Takemoto Gidayu (1650–1714). It was known as *jōruri,* after the term used to designate the narrator or chanter who spoke in the puppets' behalf. This elocutionary art was immediately brought to a state of high development, which with inevitable fluctuations has been maintained up to the present time. The words jōruri and *gidayu* have further been employed to denote the classical style in the puppet theater and at times even to signify the theater itself.

Gidayu was fortunate to attract the admiration of the ablest playwright in Japan since the rise of the *noh* theater in the fourteenth century, namely CHIKAMATSU MONZAEMON, who was experiencing considerable difficulties in writing for the *kabuki* stage. The tendency of this stage was to favor its popular actors at the expense of its playwrights. Accordingly, Chikamatsu joined forces with Gidayu, finding a major artist at work as jōruri in a theater where puppets could cause the dramatist no embarrassment. Chikamatsu actually found his powerful imagination liberated by the puppets, and wrote his most famous plays for them. Later, most of these plays were adapted for the kabuki theaters, always with changes materially diminishing their literary value.

The art of puppetry in Japan reached a degree of sophistication seldom, if ever, surpassed elsewhere. The Japanese use of the dolls is also unique. In its present form it springs directly from the period of Gidayu, having passed through several important transitions. At first only small dolls were employed and these were manipulated by comparatively simple devices. By the end of the eighteenth century, however, the dolls had become about half life-size, each doll requiring three persons, clearly visible on the stage, to manipulate it. The leading manipulator today appears in formal, old-fashioned dress, and his assistants are clad in black with their faces masked. The

SCENE FROM A JAPANESE PUPPET SHOW, OR *bunraku* (CONSULATE GENERAL OF JAPAN, NEW YORK)

leader manipulates the head, eyebrows, and right arm. His first assistant manages the left arm and body, while, in the case of a male puppet, the second assistant has charge of the legs. Female dolls do not have legs; expert care must be taken in producing the illusion of their walking or dancing. Some scenic effects are used. A samisen player accompanies the narrator, their joint efforts being known as the *chobo*. No aspect of Japanese art has been brought to a higher state of refinement.

The plays themselves readily fall into two major categories: the heroic or romantic plays, often with stories from Japan's epic or feudal age, and "domestic tragedies," as a rule overflowing with pathos, broad farces, and mythological fantasies. The latter lend themselves especially well to the artificial medium of the dolls. Several of Japan's leading playwrights of the seventeenth century and later wrote for the puppets, none, however, seriously rivaling Chikamatsu. For over fifty years the puppet theater, in a country where fashions are enthusiastically received and quickly dropped, may properly be said to have been the rage. It spread from its chief home and center at Osaka to all parts of the land. Yet after this all-too-brief triumph, it lost ground rapidly before the rise of the popular kabuki. Live actors borrowed their best plays and much of their best style from the puppets, at the same time enjoying with a popular audience the obvious advantages of a "live" theater. By the beginning of the nineteenth century the vogue of the puppets had passed. They seemed, in fact, quite out of date. Even Bunrakuken's revival proved more an aesthetic than a lasting success. This manner of entertainment was recognized by discerning critics as Japan's most original contribution to the theater arts since the rise of the *noh* in the fourteenth century. But the skills required in manipulating are truly prodigious and only a few manipulators have proved equal to the task. Well before the modern Western theater and the film invaded Japan, this great native art stood on the verge of extinction. Its sole remaining theater of importance, that in Osaka, was first supported by Japan's affluent theater industrial trust, the Schochiku Company, and has since enjoyed a small government subsidy. The group has even been taken for performances abroad, appearing in the United States in 1965. Its future, however, stands seriously in doubt. Yet no doubt remains that the Japanese puppet stage provides one of the most brilliant and astonishing chapters in the history of the theatrical arts.

Several specialized manuals on the subject have been written in Japan. It is hardly surprising that there is no authoritative book in a Western language devoted exclusively to it. One of the best descriptions of the puppet technique is in A. C. Scott's *The Kabuki Theatre of Japan* (1955), Chapter IV, pp. 53–65.—H. W. W.

Burghers of Calais, The (Die Bürger von Calais, pub. 1914). A play by Georg KAISER. In this drama, which was written the year World War I broke out, Kaiser approaches a concrete portrayal of the characteristics of the expressionist "new man." The action takes place during the siege of the city of Calais by the English. The English king agrees to spare the city if six of its citizens offer themselves as hostages. Ironically, seven citizens volunteer. Eustache, the citizen who had initially persuaded the burghers to

reject the alternative of futile defense, commits suicide in order to point the way for the other six and to give them strength in their self-sacrifice. There is a further significance to his death. His suicide underscores the idea that this offer of sacrifice cannot be revoked by the intrusion of chance. None of the seven can escape his commitment; if in fact one is superfluous, in essence he is not. Although the six are ultimately freed by a fortunate turn of fate, the value of Eustache's actual sacrifice and the potential sacrifice of the other six is illustrated by the final dramatic gesture. The position of Eustache's coffin above the altar before which the English king is kneeling portrays symbolically the spiritual victory of the pacifist over the conqueror.—C. A. M.

burlesque. A theatrical entertainment providing a ludicrous imitation of a dramatic form. The word is derived from the Italian *burlesco,* meaning mockery or raillery. Unlike satire, to which it is closely allied, burlesque does not have any serious moral purpose. Its aim is simply to provoke laughter at the absurdity of a certain type of drama—not necessarily to correct or reform. It adheres only to the first half of the satirist's dictum to expose and to propose.

One of the earliest burlesques in English drama is Beaumont's *The Knight of the Burning Pestle* (1607), a burlesque of the chivalrous romances popular in Shakespeare's time. Other notable burlesques include *The Rehearsal* (1671) by George Villiers, duke of Buckingham, *Tom Thumb* (1730) by Henry Fielding, and *Savonarola Brown* (1919) by Max Beerbohm. The latter is a delightful burlesque of Elizabethan tragedy.

In America the term "burlesque" has come to be associated with a type of variety show that throws a heavy emphasis on sex, featuring broad comedians and strip-tease dancers.

For a critical study of this genre, see V. C. Clinton-Baddeley, *The Burlesque Tradition in the English Theatre After 1660* (1952).

Burma. The origins of Burmese drama remain obscure. Not until the second half of the eighteenth century is there evidence of the performance of plays based upon a dramatic text. In 1767 King Hsinbyushin of Burma and his armies seized the Siamese capital of Ayuthia. To ensure that Siam would remain subject to Burma, the king took many hostages, among them court entertainers who customarily performed the Siamese dramatization of the Indian epic poem *The Ramayana of Valmiki.* The Burmans considered this story of Prince Rama and his consort Sita to be one of the *jatakas* (birth stories of Buddha). Consequently, they considered the Rama play a *zat* (a story based upon history or legend). Before the end of the century a version in Burmese, called *Yama,* was written to add to the enjoyment and comprehension of the court. At about the same time the court minister U Sa wrote a dramatization of a Siamese court romance, which the Burmans called *Inaung,* a tale of the romantic intrigues and heroic adventures of a young prince. *Yama* and *Inaung* both influenced the two great playwrights of the court period (1767–1866), U Kyin U and U Pon Nya.

U Kyin U (?–1853) wrote during the reign (1819–1837) of King Bagyidaw. His three plays that are extant (*Dewagonban, Papahein,* and *Mahaw*) were all written after the Burmese defeat in the first Anglo-

DRAWING OF A *zat* PERFORMED BEFORE THE KING AND QUEEN OF BURMA IN THE NINETEENTH-CENTURY OUTDOOR
GROUND CIRCLE STYLE (COURTESY JAMES A. WITHEY)

Burmese War in 1823. In their attitude toward human conduct, the plays mirror the shock of this national catastrophe. They also show the workings of a mind educated in the languages of Pali and Siamese, in the literature of the jatakas, in the history of the Burmese dynasties, and in the Siamese epic style of writing.

Mahaw, written in the form of an historical drama, is an adaptation of one of the jataka tales. Mahaw, young minister to the king of a province, tricks Kaywut, an elder minister to a neighboring king, into losing an important battle. Seeking revenge, Kaywut devises a plan to offer to Mahaw's king a beautiful princess in marriage. If the king accepts the girl, he must, by tradition, visit the home of the bride-to-be for the marriage ceremony. Kaywut then plans to attack the king and his retinue with superior forces and slay them. Unfortunately for him, Kaywut discusses this plan in the presence of a pet magpie, and Mahaw, suspicious of the proposal, learns of the plot through his own pet parrot, which he sends to spy upon Kaywut. Mahaw begs his king to reject the marriage proposal, but the king is overcome with the beauty of the princess and refuses to credit the parrot's information. Mahaw then requests permission to precede the king in order to make proper arrangements for the ceremony. Once inside the palace he will contrive to hire men to dig an underground tunnel from a point outside the palace walls to the chamber of the queen mother, whom he plans to kidnap to ensure the safety of his king. Here the play ends, leaving the

audience to imagine the workings of Mahaw's plan. Though U Kyin U develops the character of Mahaw satisfactorily, the play is deficient because it presents a plan for action rather than the action itself.

Dewagonban, an historical fantasy first published in 1873, has as its central character the elder of two sons of the king of Zayabomi. When still a child this young man is captured by an ogre king's sister. Instead of eating him, the ogress raises him with loving care; unaware that he is a human prince, he eventually inherits the ogre throne under the name of Dewagonban. As children, both he and his younger brother were betrothed to the two beautiful daughters of the king of Thiyizaya. But now, since the elder prince has disappeared, one marriageable elder daughter remains in the king's household. Though she is very beautiful and has many suitors, the king is reluctant to marry her to one of them lest the remainder make war on him. Finally he decides to give her to the young prince, along with his younger daughter, reasoning that it is the responsibility of the king of Zayabomi to find her a husband. Dewagonban finds his brother and the two girls traveling through the forest and, struck by the beauty of the elder girl, kidnaps her. The young prince pursues them, but Dewagonban wounds him with an arrow, and, after a forest god heals him of his wound, he chooses to become a hermit. However, his young bride persuades him to find her sister, with the result that he enlists the aid of a friendly dragon and rescues the girl from a dungeon where Dewagonban has imprisoned her. Infuriated at the girl's escape, Dewagonban searches the forest and tracks both girls to a tree, where the forest god has disguised them as ogresses. Dewagonban permits the two to go, but seizes the hermit prince, his brother, in whose possession he finds the jeweled casket in which the captive girl had been imprisoned. About to kill his brother, Dewagonban is prevented from doing so by the appearance of the king of the gods, who presents him with a magic sash that permits him to realize his true identity. A reconciliation takes place, but both brothers, despite the pleadings of the two princesses, decide to retire to the hermitage to avoid the storm and stress of daily living.

Whereas in *Mahaw* U Kyin U shows the influence of the jataka storyteller, in *Dewagonban* he uses the episodic structure of many short scenes as found in the epics. He achieves unity of effect, nonetheless, by skillfully employing dramatic tension. Moreover, *Dewagonban* holds a strong place in the affections of the Burmese public because it expresses the Buddhist view that only through the ascetic life may one become content.

Papahein, often considered the best of the three plays, takes the beginning of its story from the *Ramayana.* An elderly king wants to relinquish his throne. He has three sons: Zayathein, the eldest and legitimate heir to the throne; Athumbain, the youngest, by the senior queen; and Papahein, the second-born, by the junior queen. Ordinarily Zayathein would succeed to the throne, but at one time the junior queen had cured the king of a deadly disease, and in gratitude he had promised that her son would be the heir. The king discusses the problem of succession with his council of ministers and, because Papahein has been leading an unruly and dissipated life, elevates Zayathein to the throne. Papahein refuses to accept this decision and will not pay homage to his brother; as a result, he is arrested and condemned to work as a common laborer. Attempting to escape, he encounters Zayathein outside the palace walls, where the new king has ventured in disguise to mingle with the people and learn their problems. Zayathein seizes Papahein and orders his execution, but the youngest son, Athumbain, solicits a pardon, which the king grants on condition that Papahein go into exile. Papahein agrees, but instead of leaving the kingdom goes to a frontier province and raises an army to march against Zayathein. During the march Papahein encounters Athumbain on a mission for the king. Realizing his younger brother, as a son of the senior queen, is a threat to his accession to the throne, Papahein slays him. Zayathein escapes in time to avoid the attack of the rebel army and discovers the body of Athumbain in the forest. He is overcome with grief, but a sorcerer appears and restores Athumbain to life and then offers to return Zayathein to the throne. However, the two brothers decide they have had their fill of the secular life and retire together to a cave to become religious recluses, an ending that invites comparison with *Dewagonban* in its emphasis on the futility of conflict.

Though U Kyin U depicts a fantasy world inhabited by gods, demons, and talking animals intermixed with humans of royal blood, it should also be noted that his plays center upon a struggle for power, a theme prompted perhaps by the bitter war fought by the Burmans against the British. His style as developed in *Dewagonban* and *Papahein,* with their many brief scenes unified by a continuously moving action, suits this theme. The resolution in each case is also appropriate, thought of in the Buddhist context: When one realizes the futility of struggle, one will retire to a life of contemplation and seek enlightenment. U Kyin U formed a model of dramatic technique that many later dramatists were to imitate.

The other great dramatist of the court period, U Pon Nya, grew up, according to available sources, as a member of the entourage of Prince Tharrawaddy, brother to King Bagyidaw, at whose court his father was a retainer. Tutored to become a monk, Pon Nya continued as a court pundit and poet during the reigns of Tharrawaddy, Pagan, and Mindon. In 1865 he became involved in a plot to assassinate Mindon, was sentenced to life imprisonment, but was executed in 1866 for further indiscretions. A prolific writer, Pon Nya turned out poems, essays, and sermons as well as plays. His principal dramatic works were *Kawthala, Paduma, Wethandaya, Wizaya,* and *Yethè* (*The Water Seller*).

Paduma, an early Pon Nya play, was probably written in the decade of the 1850's and not published until 1949. The play has a conventional beginning derived from the *Ramayana.* A king banishes his seven sons with their consorts because of his fear that they might rebel against him. The group becomes lost in a forest and cannot find food or water. Six of the princes, in desperation, plead with the eldest, Paduma, to permit them to slay their princesses so that they may have food. Paduma, horrified, flees with his own consort, whose thirst he quenches by piercing his skin with a sword and allowing her to drink the blood. At last the two reach a riverbank where food grows and where they rescue a thief who, as punishment, has had his hands and feet amputated

DRAWING OF THE DEMON KING RAVANA IN THE BURMESE VERSION OF *The Ramayana* (COURTESY JAMES A. WITHEY)

before being set on the raft that has brought him floating down the river. Paduma's princess becomes infatuated with the man, and the two plan to dispose of the prince by pushing him off a cliff. However, a bush breaks Paduma's fall, and he is rescued by a crocodile. The prince then finds his way back to the capital, where he eventually becomes king. Meanwhile, the princess accompanies the thief from city to city of the kingdom as they eke out a living by begging. Arriving in the capital, they are recognized by Paduma, who orders the pair imprisoned to await execution. However, the prince's love for the girl makes him merciful, and he changes the sentence to one of banishment.

Though an early play, *Paduma* displays several characteristics that prevail in Pon Nya's later works. One discovers that he is a realist, that he gives dimension to female characters, and that he concerns himself with reflecting the life of the court, for in *Paduma* he is warning the ladies of the court to avoid deception.

Wizaya, published in 1872, is an historical fantasy based on the legendary history of the origin of Ceylonese Buddhism. The king of a country in southern India sentences to death his elder son, Wizaya, for looting and pillaging the countryside. The queen mother succeeds in commuting this sentence to banishment, and Wizaya, with seven hundred followers and their families, is set adrift on the ocean. Wizaya accepts responsibility for the safety of his men and succeeds in bringing them all to Ceylon, an island ruled till then by ogres and demons with magic powers. The king of the gods, knowing that Wizaya is destined to found a Buddhist kingdom on the island, sends charms to protect him against the forces of evil. Wizaya meets the ogress princess, who has trapped some of his men. The two fall in love, and the ogress helps Wizaya release the men and kill the king of the ogres. Wizaya then proclaims himself king and takes the ogress as his bride, from which union issue a son and a daughter. Since Wizaya wants his kingdom to be recognized by other countries so that he may spread the Buddhist faith, he seeks and gains a mainland princess in marriage, forcing his ogress wife to leave with their children for another island. His second wife, however, bears him no children and Wizaya, hoping to ensure a ruling dynasty with offspring, sends a message to his father asking that his younger brother be sent to assume the throne of Ceylon, only to find that the brother has become king of his native land following the father's recent death. The brother remedies this situation by sending his eldest son to Wizaya. The son, in turn, finds a queen when a princess escaping from overardent suitors lands on the island. At the end of the play we know that Ceylon will have a productive ruling dynasty and that Buddhism will flourish. *Wizaya* differs from other plays by Pon Nya, not only in the excessive multiplicity of events, but in the characters, who act, not out of personal interest, but out of a sense of duty to establish a permanent Buddhist kingdom in Ceylon. Also of prominent interest in *Wizaya* is a characteristic found in several of Pon Nya's plays: Though the gods may assist, humans must take the initiative.

In *The Water Seller* Pon Nya returns to the realistic mode and, moreover, centers the action of his play, not upon royalty, but upon two of the common folk. A prince, just returned from study at an Indian university, rests for a moment at the gates of the capital before returning to the life of the court. He observes first a male, then a female, water seller as they set down their pots, lament their poverty, and finally resume their burdens to solicit customers within the city. On entering the palace, the prince finds that his father has died in his absence and that the throne is now his. Meanwhile, the two water sellers, exhausted from their rounds, meet at the city gates, fall in love, and decide to join fortunes, each possessing a silver coin. The man, however, has hidden his coin in a crack in the wall at the other side of the city. Wishing to obtain the coin and marry at once, he runs through the streets across the city. The new king, standing on his balcony, sees the man running exuberantly past the palace and, wanting to discover the source of such happiness, asks that the runner be brought to him. Recognizing the water seller who had a short time ago lamented his poverty, and admiring his spirit, the king offers the man a fortune and also the title of crown prince. The water seller accepts but only after he obtains his own small coin and secures his bride, who becomes his princess. Later in the day at a garden party the princess goes off with some of the court ladies to admire some flowers, leaving the king and the new prince alone. Fatigued, the king falls asleep with his head in the man's lap. Seeing the king at his mercy, the former water seller finds himself tempted to kill his benefactor but overcomes his desire for power. When the king awakes, the water seller informs him of his thoughts. Impressed by the honesty and integrity of the man, the king offers him his throne. By this time, however, the water seller has realized what changes wealth and power have caused in him and decides to become a religious recluse. On learning what has happened, the princess joins him in this resolve, and they retire to the forest together.

J. A. Stewart provides a translation of a portion of the speech of the female water seller at the beginning of the play. It is worth noting because it exemplifies Pon Nya's style and because at one point the lines direct the actor to speak to the drummer, one of the musicians accompanying the play.

> Complaining brings a meal of rice no nearer.
> The price of millet's got by sale of water,
> So I'll tuck up my tattered old tamien
> Glossy with wear, a thing all seams and stitches,
> So patched and parti-colored it might be
> A checkerboard. And then with pot on head
> See me go mincing it along the street
> Crying my wares. Now strike me up a tune
> You, brother, there amid the jewelled drums,
> To help me lift my water pot and speed me
> Well on my way before the sun is high.

Acknowledged as the best of Pon Nya's plays, *The Water Seller* requires only three settings and confines the action of its characters to one day. Besides its unity of composition, it also has a dramatic climax and a central character, the male water seller, who develops psychologically while making three important decisions.

Wethandaya and *Kawthala,* the other major works of U Pon Nya, are of some interest but lack the dramatic quality found in the three plays described above.

Both U Kyin U and U Pon Nya wrote their plays in verse, employing a style called *pyo,* which, based upon that of the teller of epic tales, may be traced back to the fifteenth century. The metrical structure of these tales consisted of groups of three rhyming lines of four syllables each, the fourth syllable of the first line rhyming with the third syllable of the second, and with the first or second syllable of the third. In the fourth syllable of the third line the versifier introduced a new rhyme, which made this line the first in a new grouping as well as the last of the original group of three.

Inaung provided the first known example of the use of the four-syllable line in the dramatization of a story. However, neither U Kyin U or U Pon Nya adhered rigidly to the pattern of the pyo, Pon Nya deviating from it particularly in his use of double and triple rhymes in successive lines. Further, Pon Nya makes frequent and effective use of the link rhyme, which consists in omitting a rhyme where it is expected and inserting it later. Also, he sometimes employs a three-syllable line toward the end of a sentence, following it with a final phrase of six or seven unrhymed syllables, a device known as the *thanbauk.* Pon Nya's freer style of versification was much imitated by the playwrights of the middle period (1867–1885), which is dated from the year of his execution.

The dramas of the middle period came, not from the court, but from the city, principally Rangoon, in the hands of the British since 1853. Urban playwrights brought to their plays a new perspective and a new content. Though they continued to employ plots based upon the jatakas, upon mythology and legend, and upon history, as had Kyin U and Pon Nya, the dramatists began to reflect the contemporary scene as well. And since they realized their plays would be performed mostly to audiences in villages, the scene they depicted was that of village life. The central character was likely to be a village girl or a rustic youth, with a merchant or farmer for a father and a practical, shrewish mother. Fishermen, boatmen, village headmen, monks, and fakirs filled out the picture. Only as a sop to convention did the king and his court or a royal prince appear. These plays of contemporary life were called *pya zats.*

Another major change in content showed the impact of Western civilization upon Burmese life. The marvels of an industrial society in the form of trains and steamships, telescopes and cameras, newspapers and telegrams jostled the magic of the ogres and the tree gods, producing many anachronisms of the kind that might show an alchemist encountering a British hunter in the forest.

A third change saw an increase in the use of comedy, and particularly in comedy based upon incongruity, for it was in the middle period that a superb jester, the Burmese clown, came into his own. Comic subplots alternated with the serious main plots. Unfortunately, most of the comic scenes relied heavily upon improvisation, so that we have for the most part only sketchy scenarios, rather than actual dialogue, to tell us what took place.

The playwright U Pok Ni (1849–?) was typical of the new breed. Born in Rangoon, he was a lawyer by profession and pled cases in the courts of lower Burma. He wrote for the popular audience of his time, seeking to hold interest by melodramatic situations and by dialogues that used puns, spoonerisms (*sagalein*), and ornate rhyme schemes for comic effect. His hermits, Brahmins, hunters, and noblemen all speak in the vulgar idiom rather than in the more courtly Pali. Pok Ni's first play, *Konmara,* was published in two editions in 1875 and 1879. The second edition provides the more skillfully constructed play.

A rich merchant couple have a lovely daughter, Kun Me, who has three suitors: a servant of the family, a wealthy but ugly farmer from a nearby village, and Konmara, the crown prince of the realm. Kun Me's parents have arranged her marriage to the farmer, Kun Ti, but when the girl sees the man, she refuses to go through with the ceremony. Meanwhile, the prince has employed a go-between, Ma Aung, to obtain Kun Me as his bride. Ma Aung arranges a rendezvous between the two, at the same time delaying Kun Ti en route to the marriage ceremony by plying him with liquor. Kun Me arranges to run away and meet the prince in the forest, but Kun Ti takes his grievances to the king, and the prince is banished because of his conduct. After searching the forest for Kun Me without avail, the prince accepts the throne of a nearby kingdom. Kun Me, in the meantime, has become desolate in her forest home. She seeks entrance to a nunnery but is denied admission, lacking her parents' permission. The situation is resolved by the guardian spirits of the prince and Kun Me, who bring their souls together while both sleep. When Kun Me awakes, she finds herself pregnant, but her guardian spirit assures her that in the near future she, the prince, and their son will be happily reunited. The early scenes of *Konmara* are comic, almost farcical, but the forest scenes turn the play into a romantic pastoral with a contrived ending.

Another popular playwright of the middle period was U Ku (n.d.), who either wrote on his own or collaborated upon at least ten plays, the most well-known of which is *The Orangoutan Brother and Sister,* written and published in 1875. The play has for its central characters a brother and sister of mixed human and animal descent, whose father is the king of the country. The two were born in the forest, and the king has put them from his mind. A hunter deceives the boy and girl into leaving their forest home and eventually takes the girl, who is beautiful, to the king. The king makes her his queen, but later, discovering her identity, has her executed, not however, before she gives birth to a son. Discovering the injustice done his sister, the orangoutan brother abducts his nephew, and a tree god transforms the child into a young man. The king dies and by accident his latest wife comes upon the young prince sleeping apart from his uncle. The two fall in love and the prince becomes the new king. When his uncle goes to him, the young man, in his new status, repudiates his orangoutan relation and orders his execution. At this point, however, the spirit of the executed orangoutan queen appears to save her brother from her son's edict. The story is an original one, and the plot sustains a strong dramatic tension. Moreover, U Ku creates intense feelings of sympathy for the orangoutan brother and sister through the use of *ngo-gyin* ("crying songs").

The influence of *Konmara* on other plays of the

period is most evident in *Saw Pe Saw Me*, published in 1880 by U Su Tha (n.d.). Saw Me, the daughter of a rich courtier, has three suitors: a doltish family retainer, the son of a village chief (Saw Pe), and the king of the country. The girl runs away with Saw Pe, whom she really loves, but becomes separated from him in the forest. The king's men find her, and the king is about to order her to be executed for rejecting him but is persuaded by a forest god to free her. Meanwhile, Saw Pe has wandered into another kingdom, where he eventually becomes king through his marriage to the widowed queen. Later Saw Me finds him, and Saw Pe takes her as his second wife.

As one examines the texts of the popular pya zats of the middle period, one is struck by the presence of passages to be sung along with the passages to be spoken. When the plays of Kyin U and Pon Nya were presented, it is true that songs were included as part of the performance, but these were not written by the playwrights and, indeed, bore little or no relationship to the dramatic action. They were traditional, folk, or patriotic songs that were often sung apart from the dramatic entertainments. In the middle period, however, Pok Ni, U Ku, and other lesser talents wrote songs, or had songs written for them, which were an integral part of the action, though there were still some, such as the songs actors sang in praise of their birthplaces, that continued to be irrelevant.

Because the playwrights wrote songs to be sung by certain kinds of characters and at particular points in the plays, the songs began to fall into certain established categories. In addition to the ngo-gyin and *myaing da* (duets), there was the *tha-phyan*, a short song of a thoughtful or contemplative nature; the *than-cho*, a song permeated with emotion; the *te-tat*, a repeating song made up of three sections, most often dealing with a love theme; and the *bongyi-than*, an ancient type of folk song, sung by two groups of characters to the accompaniment of a drum. More general types were the *yodaya* (Siamese style), the *kayathan* (English style), and the *pyigyithan* (Chinese style).

Before leaving the middle period, it is appropriate to refer to another play by U Pok Ni, *Beinbon Yaza Kwambon Konma* ("The Vice of the Kingdom," pub. 1883), which verges on parody of the older drama. In this play Pok Ni employs only unsavory characters. Some are opium eaters; others are drunkards, bearing such names as Brandy and Rice Beer. *Beinbon* helped prepare the way for the dramas of the modern period, for it drew upon both the folkways of the common people, which had contributed so much to the popularity of the middle period plays, and upon the jesting view of life, prompted in part perhaps by the loss of sovereignty in 1885, that was to characterize the pya zats of the new era.

During the modern period (1886–1962) Burmese drama has taken two distinct forms. At the same time there has occurred a shift in meaning of the descriptive terms zat and pya zat in order to accommodate the newly distinguished types.

What has been called the pya zat, which had its origins with U Kyin U and U Pon Nya and developed into a play of mixed legendary and contemporary content with characters of differing social status, became the traditional play. It is called simply a zat, because of its strong antecedents in the jataka tales.

Taking its place beside the more traditional drama was the play devoted exclusively to contemporary events, which excluded entirely the royal court from its setting and persons of noble birth from its cast of characters. It also rejected courtly language for the colloquial idiom. This modern genre took the name of pya zat.

The itinerant players of the modern era found a demand for both dramatic types. The older people in their audiences took pleasure in a nostalgic remembrance of the days of the Burmese kings. The younger generation, confronted with the encroachments of Western society as exemplified in the British way of life, sought new insights into their contemporary culture, even though the wit of the modern playwright might be tinged with the bitterness of defeat and occupation.

The zats, almost all dramas of a serious nature, were for the most part available in manuscript and ready for performance. But the demand for pya zats could not wait upon the development of playwrights of literary quality. Consequently, each *pwe* ("show") troupe attached to itself one or more writers to create the contemporary plays and songs for the season. On the whole these journeymen playwrights, who were paid for each play they wrote, have remained anonymous. It is this mixture of serious traditional drama and satiric farce that has characterized the modern period. In a typical night at the Burmese theater (lasting from about 9 p.m. to 5 a.m.) one would see a pya zat, then an interlude of song and dance, followed by a zat.

In the modern era new developments in the drama

THE GREAT PO SEIN AND NGWE SEIN IN A SCENE FROM THE DANCE-DRAMA *Maurasekkya* (COURTESY JAMES A. WITHEY)

came chiefly through the efforts of Po Sein (1882–1952), Burma's most versatile theater artist. His innovations ranged through all aspects of the theater: dance, costumes, scenery, lighting, song, and the drama itself. A serious student of the ancient marionette theater of Burma, believed by some to antedate dramatic performances by live actors, he observed that only in this form were the jatakas performed with authenticity. The live performers presented only fragments or adaptations of the revered birth stories of Buddha. Po Sein resolved to present the stories as they were originally recorded in the Sutta Pitaka (one of the three sections of the Pali canon), obtained the support of the Buddhist clergy, and in 1912 presented *Shin-Thu-Dain* as the first in a series of dramatized jatakas. Other producers followed his lead.

Though the modern pya zat reflected the contemporary life of Burma, we cannot think of it as a drama of realism. The fabric of village life was still interlaced with belief in magic and spirit worship. Po Sein and others who influenced the work of the journeymen playwrights knew their audiences well; consequently the supernatural element often played a prominent part in the popular drama of the period.

Zawgyi (1961) by Kenneth Sein (1918–   ) provides an example of a modern pya zat, which combines the supernatural and the real, while featuring the antics of a Burmese clown. A *zawgyi* is a man striving to obtain supernatural powers. At the beginning of the play the zawgyi appears onstage beside a large caldron and tells the audience in song that he can obtain magical powers only if he is able to find a man who is brave, abstemious, and continent. He will know this man by his birth date and by a mark he will bear on his body. Several villagers then walk across the stage, each questioned by the zawgyi. Finally, a clown walks by, and the zawgyi discovers he has the necessary qualifications. Overjoyed, the zawgyi explains that the man must take three capsules and one by one throw them into the caldron. After each capsule dissolves, he will be put to a test. If he passes all three tests, the zawgyi will give him whatever he asks. The clown, after many humorous questions and hesitations, accepts the capsules, while the zawgyi exits.

The clown tosses the first capsule into the caldron, and a huge papier-mâché monster emerges. Though absurdly frightened, the clown finally chases the beast away. The second capsule produces a line of waiters who bring to him tray after tray of delicious food; however, the clown remembers his ulcer and regretfully declines all the dishes. The third capsule brings a trio of beautiful girls who try to drag the clown off to bed with them; he barely succeeds in resisting. Having found a man brave, abstemious, and continent, the zawgyi reappears, now possessed of supernatural powers, and tells the clown he will grant him three wishes. The clown, regretting his previous foolishness, asks for the food he had refused, the three girls, and lastly an automobile, in which they all drive off together eating and drinking.

Two further developments require comment. In 1947 U Nu (1907–   ) became prime minister of Burma. Educated at Rangoon University, Nu was well acquainted with Western literature and, during his tenure, wrote two plays in the Western mold—prose dramas without song, dance, or musical accompaniment. *The People Win Through* (1950), a lengthy play with eight scenes and as many changes of locale, tells how Nu's party, the Anti-Fascist People's Freedom League, succeeded in defeating the communists in their bid to seize the government after Burma had gained its independence from Britain. *The Wages of Sin* (1961) adheres more closely to Western conventions; it has three acts of conventional length, each with a different setting: a home, a communist classroom, and an office. The protagonist of this drama is a corrupt minister whose son turns to communism. It is an original work concerned with the idea that corruption in government can lead to a communist coup.

Lastly, credit must be given an ambitious project commissioned by Kenneth Sein, son of Po Sein and inheritor of his father's troupe of players. Aware of his people's interest in their history, as evidenced by their continued support of the zats, Sein conceived the idea of producing a trilogy of plays, cast in the form of the zat, dealing with the last years of the Burmese kings, specifically King Mindon and King Thibaw. He wanted to combine an authentic story, based upon scholarly research, with the conventional song, dance, and music of the zat. When completed in 1960, the trilogy was presented by the Sein troupe on three successive nights. The first play centers on Crown Prince Kenaung, younger brother of Mindon and heir to the throne, and the successful plot to assassinate him. The second features the dying King Mindon and ends with Thibaw's accession to the throne. The third play has Thibaw as its protagonist and ends with the capture of Mandalay by the British. The last is the best of the series, not only because its cast of characters includes Thibaw, last of the kings; Supayalat, his influential queen; Kinwun Mingyi, a famous minister of foreign affairs; and the British officers Sladen, White, and Prendergast, who accepted the surrender, but also because every action leads inevitably to the emotion-laden final scene of surrender and the song of lament for the loss of the Golden Land.

The *Trilogy of the Burmese Kings* may mark a turning point in the history of the serious drama in Burma, a point where the zat of historical fantasy becomes the zat of authentic historical drama, where a respect for factual representation is combined with the conventional lyrics, music, and dance to effect an amalgam of the modern and the traditional.

Because the style of a performance is not always revealed by the dramatic text, it is difficult for a reader to create in his mind's eye a true picture of the dramatic action as it occurs in a Burmese play. Particularly is this the case when one reads the dramas of the court and middle periods. Fortunately, there are several publications to assist the reader.

In *The Konmara Pya Zat* (1952), as an introduction to his translation of *Konmara,* Hla Pe provides a succinct account of the formal development of Burmese drama. A further boon is Maung Tin Aung's *Burmese Drama* (1937), which contains 150 pages of theater history, synopses, and criticisms, as preface to the author's translations of *Dewagonban, Papahein, Paduma,* and *The Water Seller.*

Even more likely to provide the general reader with clues to better appreciation are the perceptive and often witty accounts by two British observers of the Burmese colonial scene: J. A. Stewart in "The Burmese Stage," *Journal of the Royal Society of Arts* (June 9, 1939), and Sir J. George Scott in *The Burman, His Life and Notions* (1963).

Finally, in a firsthand report, Faubion Bowers conveys the flavor of the post-World War II Burmese drama in *Theatre in the East* (1963). Kenneth Sein and J. A. Withey, in a biography entitled *The Great Po Sein,* which covers the years from the days of the last Burmese king to the modern era, reveal the contributions of Po Sein to the drama. Combine these readings with the texts of the traditional dramas, as they continue to be published by the Burma Research Society in Rangoon, and one begins to see the true picture.—J. A. W.

Bussy D'Ambois (pub. c. 1607). Historical tragedy by George CHAPMAN. A considerably different text was published in 1641, which caused a great deal of controversy, but it is now regarded as most likely that the revisions and emendations in the later text were made by someone other than Chapman and that it thus affords the inferior of the two versions. Although we cannot be certain of when the play was written, most scholars tend to date it around 1604. At that time Chapman was writing for the acting company the Children of the Queen's Revels, which may have been responsible for the play's initial performance. The play is based roughly upon the career of the French courtier Bussy D'Ambois, who was born around 1550, acquired a reputation as a savage duelist and illicit lover during his brief but hectic career, and was murdered in 1579 by the husband of his mistress, with the probable connivance of both the duke of Guise and King Henry III of France. Since no account of Bussy's career had been published by 1604, it is likely that Chapman relied upon oral tradition for his information. He departed widely from the historical facts that are available today.

Critics have been strongly divided as to the meaning of Chapman's play. Some have seen in Bussy the conventional portrait of an errant sinner falling from power through his own excesses. Others have seen in him Chapman's attempt to embody his concept of the ideal man, one who might have lived in a mythical "golden age," when human laws and restrictions had not yet begun to impinge upon man's free, heroic nature. Still others have seen in Bussy a Renaissance analogue to the classical tragedy of Hercules, and they have pointed to Chapman's use in the play of lines roughly translated from the *Hercules Oetaeus* of Seneca. Another group of critics has found the play obscure in its language, confused in construction, and generally ambiguous and contradictory in its moral view. Clearly, it is a play with which every reader must come to terms in his own way.

Although none of Chapman's plays has ever been popular on the stage—and *Bussy D'Ambois* is no exception—this play has usually been regarded as Chapman's greatest achievement, probably because of the dynamism of the central character, which comes through in spite of the ambiguity of the author's intentions, and because of the poetry, which, in spite of its density, is probably the greatest that Chapman ever wrote.

There is an excellent edition of the play by Nicholas Brooke in *The Revels Plays* (1964).—I. R.

Byron, George Gordon [Noel], sixth baron **Byron**

(1788–1824). English poet. Byron was born in London in 1788 but moved to Aberdeen, Scotland, in 1790 with his mother, who was alternately affectionate and harsh, after she had been deserted by his father. A deformity of his foot at birth caused him to wear a special shoe and to limp. At the age of ten Byron inherited the title of sixth Baron Byron, after which he moved to Newstead Abbey and attended Dr. Glennie's Academy in Dulwich and later Harrow. He went to Cambridge in 1805, receiving his M.A. in 1808. In 1809, upon achieving his majority, he took his seat in the House of Lords and in the same year published his first major work, *English Bards and Scotch Reviewers,* an attack on both contemporary English poetry and on *The Edinburgh Review.* He set out for a grand tour through Portugal, Spain, Albania, Greece, and Turkey, returning to England in 1811 with the first two cantos of *Childe Harold's Pilgrimage.* He published the poem, resumed his seat in the Lords, made a few liberal speeches, and found himself famous overnight, the toast of Regency society and especially its women. Byron had several intrigues before he married Annabela Milbanke in 1815. His cruel behavior after his marriage caused his wife to leave him shortly after the birth of a daughter, and lost Byron his public admiration. He left England in 1816, never to return, traveling to Italy through Switzerland, where the Alps made a profound symbolic impression on him that was to bear fruit in *Manfred.* In Italy, which he was to make his home until his departure for Greece, he associated with the Shelleys, Leigh Hunt, and other literary figures and formed an enduring liaison with the Contessa Guiciolli. Early in 1824 he went to Greece to assist in the war for independence, made badly needed if unheroic contributions in money and administration, and shortly after died of fever.

Byron's contemporary reputation properly rests mostly on his verse satires, but about one-fourth of the total body of his work consists of eight plays. Some of them, like *Manfred* (pub. 1817), *Cain* (pub. 1821), *Heaven and Earth* (pub. 1823), are speculative closet dramas hardly suitable for staging. But his other tragedies, *Marino Faliero* (pub. 1821), *The Two Foscari* (pub. 1821), *Sardanapalus* (pub. 1821), and *Werner* (pub. 1822), as well as the "Faustish" fragment *The Deformed Transformed* (pub. 1824), simply called "a drama," seem conceived for the stage, showing a good deal of familiarity with theatrical convention, a desire to write dialogue in natural though rhetorical language that would get across the footlights, and an interest in practical theatrical spectacle. Actually, most of his plays were staged after his death, though evidently, to judge from prompt-copies, they required considerable cutting to be effective with early nineteenth-century audiences and, in one at least, the addition of much spectacle, music, and trumpet flourishes. But Byron kept insisting in preface after preface that his plays were "not for the stage"—despite his professed interest in "reforming the stage." His ambivalence toward the stage has been interestingly explained by David V. Erdman as a kind of stage fright: he wanted to succeed gloriously but feared he would not and so kept writing potentially actable plays, all the while protesting that they were not to be acted.

Though written speedily, Byron's plays were not

casual efforts and were written during the period when he produced his best, most mature work, including his masterpiece, *Don Juan.* In his speculative dramas, he gave dramatic, or pseudodramatic, form to some of his most important philosophical and theological ideas. In *Manfred* the Byronic hero is developed to a point where he is scarcely recognizable as a hero in the ordinary sense and becomes, as Nietzsche first recognized, an "Übermensch," an overman, a Promethean rather than a Faustian man. And in this "dramatic poem" Byron introduced a theme that he was to develop in a biblical context in his "mystery" plays, *Cain* and *Heaven and Earth,* as well as in the more nearly Faustian *The Deformed Transformed:* the conflict of the overman, with his desire for knowledge and freedom from "the ruling principle." These plays gained the admiration, even adulation, of Goethe, for their meaning and poetry but provoked vigorous attacks by pious English critics, especially of course *Cain* and *Heaven and Earth. Manfred* is often taken to be autobiographical, Byron brooding remorsefully over his incestuous relationship with his half-sister, but this is a very superficial view of it. The remorse motif popular in drama of the time is not the main theme but only a part of the material through which the larger theme is developed. Though *Manfred* is called a "dramatic poem," it has had a number of productions, characteristically with music by Robert Schumann, as a sort of dramatized oratorio, a form in which it works very well.

Byron's most objective, most theatrically regular plays are the historical dramas on Venetian subjects: *Marino Faliero,* a play whose hero is a noble, proud, but liberty-loving Doge who is crowned and then decapitated, and *The Two Foscari,* in which the elder of the two Foscari is compelled to sit in judgment of his son, who is exiled but wants to return to his beloved Venice. Though these are historical tragedies, Byron was not scrupulous about historical accuracy. He was more interested in the development of fresh dramatic characters and fresh dramatic passions, with the result that some critics have not found his characters entirely believable. But *Marino Faliero,* the only play of his produced in his lifetime, was, though not a great success, not a failure either. *The*

Two Foscari was more successful, being acted with great effect by Macready in 1838 to a standing ovation with "waving handkerchiefs." Verdi made it into an opera. A more interesting play in many ways is *Sardanapalus,* in which Byron develops the character of a voluptuous but morally ideal king of Assyria, who is less concerned with conquest than with peace and building cities but who is able to fight when called upon. Unfortunately, a good deal of the moral motivation—and therefore much of the thematic interest—of the play is diminished when cut and otherwise fitted for the stage, as it was in Charles Kean's elaborate production of 1838. The king becomes merely soft, and his transformation into a fighting leader therefore comes as a surprise. *Werner, or The Inheritance* is a dramatized version of a tale that had engaged Byron very much from the age of fourteen. In a staged version, as acted by Macready, the drama had to be cut almost in half to make it play. But it became Byron's greatest theatrical success, being produced all over England, Scotland, and America throughout the nineteenth century, though it is of little interest to students of Byron the poet. This may be the point: in *Werner* Byron was able to achieve the dramatic objectivity he did not get in the other plays. But Byron said even of this obviously theatrical play, an actor's play: "The whole is neither intended, nor in any shape, adapted for the stage."

The standard edition of Byron's poems and plays is *The Works of Lord Byron, Poetry* (7 vols., 1898–1904), edited by E. H. Coleridge. This contains excellent notes and, for the plays, stage histories. Filling out the rest of Byron's writings and included with the preceding in a uniform edition is *The Works of Lord Byron, Letters and Journals* (6 vols., 1898–1901), edited by Rowland E. Prothero. The standard biography is Leslie A. Marchand's *Byron: A Biography* (3 vols., 1957), which draws on every scrap of information known to exist and still remains readable. Samuel Chew's *The Dramas of Lord Byron* (1915) is an old but still useful study of the plays, which, besides giving a perceptive analysis of the plays, summarizes the considerable body of German scholarship on them. David V. Erdman's article in *ELH,* VI (1939), gives a concise account of Byron's writing for the stage.—M. K. N.

C

Caecilius [Statius] (c. 219–168 B.C.). Roman comic dramatist. Caecilius was considered by some ancient critics as superior to Plautus and Terence. None of his comedies has survived, except for about forty titles and almost three hundred lines of fragments, quoted by Cicero, Aulus Gellius, Festus, Nonius Marcellus, and others.

Caecilius was an Insubrian Gaul, said to have been brought to Rome as a slave and later freed. He was a friend of Ennius, epic poet and dramatist, and apparently, like his successor Terence, aimed at a more artistic and restrained type of comedy than Plautus had written. More than half of his titles are identical with those of Menander. Aulus Gellius quotes fragments of Caecilius' *Plocium* ("The Little Necklace") with the parallel Greek passages from the Menandrian original. We see here the freedom with which Caecilius treats the Greek comedy, introducing new ideas, adding jokes, and transforming a passage of iambic trimeter into a lyrical *canticum*.—G. E. D.

Caesar and Cleopatra (1899). A play by George Bernard SHAW. An unidentified Roman gentleman is musingly addressing a sphinx when interrupted by a frightened teen-age girl, Cleopatra, rightful but unthroned queen of Egypt. Calming her superstitious terror of Romans, he gently instructs her on the privileges and responsibilities of monarchy. Charmed, Cleopatra does not realize until other Romans arrive that her instructor is Julius Caesar. Cleopatra's young brother Ptolemy rules Egypt, but he is completely dependent on the powerful eunuch Pothinos. Ptolemy, in timidly reciting a prepared defiance of Rome, clearly has been instructed in a speech, not a way of life. When Caesar arrives in Alexandria, he calmly dismisses the pro-Ptolemy Egyptians from the palace and enthrones Cleopatra, thus causing much political intrigue.

Six months later, besieged in her palace, Cleopatra has grown much wiser and more adult from her constant association with Caesar, though still she dreams of another Roman, Antony, whom she saw as a girl. Pothinos denounces Cleopatra to Caesar in her very presence, but Caesar accepts her ambitions philosophically. However, Cleopatra furiously gives orders that Pothinos be secretly killed before he leaves the palace. When the news of Pothinos' murder breaks, Caesar is coldly disgusted with her; this will now turn all the indifferent citizens against them. Vengeance is always futile, Caesar tells her in an eloquent speech. Only the news that outside help is on the way saves the situation that Cleopatra's vindictiveness created.

In the final scene, almost like an epilogue, Caesar says his farewell to Egypt and consoles Cleopatra by promising to send Mark Antony to her in his place.

Written in 1898, *Caesar and Cleopatra* was clearly Shaw's most ambitious work up to that time. With its colorful historical setting, frequent physical violence, and sweeping pageantry, the play might seem to resemble the romantic costume dramas so popular throughout the nineteenth century. But one has only to compare it with Edmond Rostand's *Cyrano de Bergerac* (1897), for instance, to recognize, despite occasional flashes of melodrama, the play's bracing, astringent tone, the constant play of ideas that are uniquely Shaw's own. If anything, the play deromanticizes the facts, for Caesar's relationship to Cleopatra is purely paternal, to train her in the responsibilities of rulership; no hint is given of the affair that in history produced their son, Caesarion. Shaw replaced the bedroom with the schoolroom.

A truly convincing portrait of greatness, Caesar is the first of several superior beings who were to appear in Shaw's plays. Caesar's vision is dramatically realized in large part through the candor of his statements and the directness of his actions. Admittedly, his willingness to apply his views in a practical way often appears as ruthless despotism in his dealings with those who are hopelessly committed to the closed, egocentric morality of society, but the best human beings around him realize that through Caesar's open cosmic morality they can achieve the personal salvation of greater self-development. In his notes following the play, Shaw maintains that generosity, magnanimity, and freshness when associated with the great man are only by-products of his "originality," for it is this virtue that enables him "to estimate the value of truth, money, or success in any particular instance quite independently of convention and moral generalization." Thus Caesar is benevolent not because of Christian kindness but because he can anticipate that monstrous chain reaction of revenge that takes place in the wake of violence. One minute Caesar is elevated, poetic, generous, the next he is hard, civil, prosaic; but as qualities these are only instances of the inevitable functioning of his clear-seeing nature. They are forms, one might say, of biological intelligence.

Arthur H. Nethercot writes perceptively of the unresolved paradox of Caesar's character in his *Men and Supermen* (1954). Shaw's theory and practice of the comic mode is analyzed in G. W. Couchman's "Here was a Caesar: Shaw's Comedy Today" in *PMLA*, LXXII (1957). Among a number of far-ranging articles in *George Bernard Shaw: A Critical Survey* (1953), edited by Louis Kronenberger, John Mason Brown has an appreciative piece on *Caesar and Cleopatra*, which suggests that Shaw's strength in this as in other plays was that he could present a hero without being a hero-worshipper.—D. J. L.

Çağan, Sermet (1929–   ). Turkish playwright and director. Çağan began his career in the theater as an amateur actor. After a period as a journalist, he became active as a director, actor, and set designer in private and government-subsidized theaters. In 1966 Çağan established the theater TÖS and toured Anatolia for a year to bring the "theater of ideas" to the general masses. Çağan's full-length play *Ayak-Bacak Fabrikası* ("The Feet and Legs Factory," 1964) and *Savaş Oyunu* ("The War Game," 1964), a one-act play, have won prizes in theater festivals. Besides plays for the stage, he has written several plays for radio.

Çağan's plays are among the most politically charged in Turkish history. The recurrent theme is the exploitation of the working classes through the compradors in underdeveloped countries by the military, industrial, and political complexes in the ruling nations. So far, Çağan has used the epic style to express his political ideas. In fact, *Ayak-Bacak Fabrikası* is the most Brechtian play in Turkish drama. Çağan utilizes as much as possible the forms and spirit of traditional Turkish theater, which has common elements with the theater of Bertolt Brecht, and transmits his sociopolitical ideas to the population at large.—N. O.

Calandria, La (1513). A comedy by Bernardo Dovizi da Bibbiena (1470–1520). The protagonist, the elderly Calandro, is enamored of the beautiful Santilla, the twin sister of Lidio, who, in turn, is the lover of Fulvia, Calandro's wife. The sensual and overwhelming love of Fulvia and Lidio is contrasted with the silly credulity of the old Calandro. Calandro is led astray by the inventiveness and the tricks of Fessenio, a servant, who convinces him to be shut up in a coffin, thus to be able to meet at ease with the young girl. Fessenio subsequently arranges for an old prostitute to lie alongside Calandro. Other amusing misunderstandings arise from the resemblance between the twins, especially when Calandro encounters Lidio who, dressed up like a woman, is on his way to meet Fulvia.

Calandria, which stands among the very finest comedies in the Italian language, is derived from Plautus' *Menaechmi* and *Casina,* as well as from certain situations in Boccaccio's writings. The influence of these sources is limited, however, only to the nature of the incidents involved; for the play is rich in witticisms and observations drawn from the lively reality of the sixteenth century. The play possesses an agile and vividly realistic language and a mocking, joking attitude, which, unrestrained by any prejudice or moral preoccupation, is typical of the Italian Renaissance.—L. L.

Calderón de la Barca, Pedro (1600–1681). Spanish Golden Age poet and playwright. The most significant dramatist ever to write in Spanish, Calderón de la Barca was the author of over two hundred full-length plays, better than half of which are extant. In addition, he wrote more than seventy one-act sacramental dramas (*autos*), a good number of mythological plays, musical plays, even several librettos. A masterful poet—his powerful religious poem *Psalle et sile* ("Sing and Be Still") is an insufficiently appreciated example—as well as a consum-

PEDRO CALDERÓN DE LA BARCA (BIBLIOTHÈQUE NATIONALE, PARIS)

mate dramatic craftsman, Calderón refined the *comedia* (a generic term in Spanish for "play") while perfecting its astonishing variety of verse forms. He has to his credit as many masterworks as Shakespeare and somewhat more than Racine and Sophocles.

The son of Don Diego, the secretary of the council of the Royal Treasury, Pedro Calderón de la Barca was born on January 17, 1600, in Madrid. Following the court, his family moved to Valladolid and back to Madrid before Calderón attended a Jesuit college in 1608. At the age of fourteen Calderón enrolled at the University of Alcalá to study rhetoric and logic. Until 1620 Calderón divided his time between Alcalá and Salamanca, while residing in Madrid. In a poetry contest he entered that year in honor of San Isidro, Calderón's work attracted favorable comment from Lope de Vega, one of the judges.

Calderón's first great period of productivity began in 1623 with the performance of three plays: *Amor, honor y poder* (*Love, Honor and Power*), *La selva confusa* (*The Tangled Forest*), and *Judas Macabeo* (*Judas Maccabeus*); this period culminated in 1637 with the publication of the first two volumes of his plays, nominally edited by his brother José. By this time Calderón had written sixty-six plays, including all those that have since become world-famous, except *The Mayor of Zalamea.* When Lope de Vega died in 1635, Calderón succeeded him as theater director at court. He became knight of Santiago two years later, after directing his own magnificent *zarzuela* ("music drama"), *El mayor encanto amor* (*Love, the Greatest Enchanter*), to inaugurate the new palace in the Buen Retiro Park of Madrid. This became the setting of scores of spectacular open-air plays by Calderón.

Favorable as the 1630's were, in the next decade Calderón's fortunes were overcast by national and personal misfortunes. In 1640 he joined the army that was sent to Catalonia to put down a rebellion; two years later he was compelled to leave the service due to illness. Then, with the closing of the public and court theaters, Calderón was forced to join the duke of Alba's household, where he stayed from 1646 to 1650. Suddenly, in a short period, both his brothers were killed and his mistress died, leaving him a son. Resigning from his post with the duke, Calderón took religious orders and was ordained a priest in 1651. By 1653 he had written thirty-three more plays and twenty-one autos—the particular sort of allegorical play to which he devoted the rest of his life. He served as a chaplain in Toledo until the king recalled him to his former post at court in 1663; there he remained until his death. Between 1664 and 1677, the third, fourth, and fifth volumes of his collected plays were issued under the editorship of friends. In 1677 Calderón himself published and wrote the Preface for his collected autos. At the request of the duke of Veraguas, Columbus' great-grandson, Calderón wrote out the titles of his plays. He listed 111 secular plays and seventy sacramental dramas. The following year, on May 25, 1681, Calderón died in Madrid. According to one report, he collapsed while writing a new auto.

Among his best-known plays are LIFE IS A DREAM, THE MAYOR OF ZALAMEA, DEVOTION TO THE CROSS, THE PHANTOM LADY, and SECRET VENGEANCE FOR SECRET INSULT. To this list may be added at least a dozen other plays, some not as widely read, which may be said to rank with the best of the better-known group. These include *El pintor de su deshonra* (*The Painter of His Dishonor*, pub. 1650), *El médico de su honra* (*The Surgeon of his Honor*, c. 1629), *No hay cosa como callar* ("There's Nothing Like Keeping Still," written 1639), *El magico prodigioso* (*The Wonder-working Magician*, 1637), *El príncipe constante* (*The Constant Prince*, written 1629), and *El galán fantasma* ("The Ghostly Lover," written by 1635, pub. 1637).

Calderón grew up in a highly authoritarian country when the Spanish empire was crumbling and the nation was losing its identity as a world power. These conditions are imaginatively reflected in his "honor" plays, expressing the near-hysteria of a caste society struggling in vain to force new experiences into the molds of old shibboleths. The son of a successful court official who seems to have been a harsh autocrat, Calderón often dramatized violent family situations rising from the sins of a hypocritical father and, when not reconciled, leading to multiple murders, incest, and a sort of self-immolation that resembles suicide.

But the range of Calderón's dramatic subjects is richer than this summary suggests. He wrote of contemporary wars and adapted chronicle histories that go back to classical times. He has plays on legendary and folkloric subjects—Irish and Italian as well as Spanish—on the Moorish wars, Old Testament stories, miracles, martyrs, and saints. There are comedies of romantic intrigue (giving rise to the term "cape-and-sword" dramas) and honor plays that enact the virtues of free conscience and personal sacrifice in opposition to the cruel fixation of preserving one's reputation. Always scrupulously structured, his best plays share the culminating effect of first-rate detective stories: they bring problems of character, narrative, and theme together at the end with a single click. This sort of satisfaction is missing in the plays of his great predecessor Lope de Vega, and only one or two other Golden Age playwrights strike home so tellingly that artistic effect is indistinguishable from the profound articulation of the problem.

Since Calderón had already mastered dramaturgy as a young man while his interest in symbolic expression continued to deepen, it is fortunate that he had somewhere further to go as a dramatic artist. This was toward the greater condensation—and not only simplification—of imagery, plot, and thematic resolution required by the one-act structure of the AUTO SACRAMENTAL. Released in mid-career from servitude to the public theater and provided with an ideal outdoor stage, both by the court and by the religious brotherhoods responsible for the two annual dramatic productions at the Feast of Corpus Christi, Calderón contrived subtle dramatizations of basic human problems, drawing on popular biblical and classical tales.

A typical aspect of his style supporting greater dramatic concentration was his particular way of building images: piling up trope after trope to serve a single idea, then ingeniously resolving them all in a few concluding lines. Disparate and paradoxical elements that have been held in suspension in a long speech are thus suddenly brought together with great effectiveness. Occasionally, in his dramatic effort toward concentration, Calderón went back to the sources and themes of his best-known plays (such as *Life Is a Dream* and *El pintor de su deshonra*) and rewrote them as religious allegories that were quite distinct, in characters, plots, and even situations, from the plays from which they were adapted. His most famous autos are *El gran teatro del mundo* (*The Great World Theatre*, 1649) and *La cena de Baltasar* (*Baltassar's Feast*, probably 1634). But even finer are those written in his old age: *El pastor fido* ("The Faithful Shepherd," probably 1678), *No hay más fortuna que Dios* ("There Is No Greater Fortune Than God," 1653), and *El día mayor de los días* ("The Greatest of All Days," written 1678). But if his later autos are neglected, so are his other plays written after Calderón had become a priest. The best are the mythological plays, *La estatua de Prometeo* ("The Statue of Prometheus," pub. 1677) and *Eco y Narciso* ("Echo and Narcissus," 1661), and the religious plays *Los dos amantes del cielo* ("Two Lovers of Heaven," written by 1651) and *El José de las mujeres* ("The Women's Joseph," pub. 1660).

A. A. Parker's *The Allegorical Drama of Calderón: An Introduction to the Autos Sacramentales* (1943) is a deep, appreciative study and analysis of the best autos. A. E. Sloman's *The Dramatic Craftsmanship of Calderón* (1958) is a close study of the best-known plays. *Critical Essays in the Theatre of Calderón* (1965), edited by Bruce W. Wardropper, is also valuable. For translations of the plays see Edward Fitzgerald's translations *Eight Dramas of Calderón, Freely Translated* (1961); Edwin Honig's

A SCENE FROM ALBERT CAMUS'S *Caligula* (FRENCH CULTURAL SERVICES)

Calderón: *Four Plays* (1961); D. F. MacCarthy's *Calderón de la Barca: Six Plays* (1961); and Roy Campbell's *The Surgeon of His Honour* (1960). —E. H.

Caligula (1945). A play by Albert CAMUS. Camus's first play, *Caligula* was performed at the Théâtre Hébertot in 1945 and later translated and performed in New York. Caligula is the handsome young Roman emperor. A single grief, unexpected and swift, caused by the death of a sister whom he loved, is sufficient to change the universe for him and to reveal a truth almost stupid in its simplicity: "Men die and are not happy." The emperor's powers are limitless, and he claims the will to change the order of the universe. This is the beginning of an experiment during which he ridicules the patricians, tortures countless victims, and blasphemes and strangles his mistress. Caligula watches himself as he performs these horrors. Before he is slain, he experiences a nameless solitude and the approach of hatred and conspiracy.

When it was first performed, *Caligula* stimulated interest and reflection, and it revived the fresh memories of the German occupation. But the play is not a dramatic conflict, because we do not see any moral crisis in the character of Caligula. We witness, instead, a comment on a rather elaborate spectacle that is the result of a moral crisis.

Caligula has been translated by Stuart Gilbert in *Caligula and Three Other Plays* (1958).—W. F.

Cambises (c. 1560–1570). A tragedy by Thomas Preston (1537–1598), about whom nothing is known. An early and apparently very popular Elizabethan tragedy, *Cambises* relates the story of Cambises, king of Persia, whose reign was marked by bloodshed and tyranny. The scenes in which the wicked king engages in his "shameless deeds" are alternated with knockabout comic scenes presided over by Ambidexter, the comic Vice. The play, described on its title page as "A Lamentable Tragedie,

mixed full of pleasant mirth," makes no attempt to present a coherent dramatic structure. Each scene is an independent episode, unrelated to the rest of the play. The mixture of Cambises' villainous rant with the low-comic scenes must have proved popular, for thirty years after it was first presented, Shakespeare made a satiric allusion to it in Falstaff's remark "For I must speak in passion, and I will do it in King Cambises' vein." (*1 Henry IV*, II, 4, 425).—E. Q.

Cameroon Federation, The. See AFRICA: *Cameroon Federation, The.*

Camille. See LA DAME AUX CAMÉLIAS.

Camões, Luís de. See PORTUGAL.

Campistron, Jean Galbert de (1656–1723). French playwright. Born in Toulouse, Jean Galbert de Campistron was a young man when he entered the theatrical world, where he was encouraged by actors and perhaps by Racine. After Racine's retirement, a whole clique of noblemen, desperately in search of a successor to Racine in tragedy, launched Campistron, who remained in the forefront as a dramatist from 1683 to 1693. He then took a high administrative post in the navy, became a member of the French Academy in 1701, and finally, in 1713, retired to Toulouse.

Campistron wrote three opera librettos and two comedies, but mostly tragedies. Of his seven existing tragedies, the first, *Virginie,* was a triumph in 1683. The most renowned and the best, *Andronic,* was performed in 1685.

Written at a time when tragedy proved to be very poor indeed, Campistron's works are not negligible. They are filled with imitations or echoes of Pierre Corneille and especially Racine, and the style, essentially elegiac, is often perfectly insipid. Nevertheless, they consist of "well-made plays," peopled with original characters, and written in a dialogue that does not always lack vigor.—Ja. G.

Camus, Albert (1913–1960). Algerian-born French philosopher, novelist, and playwright. As a

ALBERT CAMUS (LEFT) AND DIRECTOR JEAN-LOUIS
BARRAULT (FRENCH CULTURAL SERVICES)

student in Algiers, Camus studied philosophy. Attracted by the theater, however, he organized the avant-garde drama group Théâtre de l'Équipe in 1935 and worked with it until 1938. Then, until the beginning of World War II, he worked in both North Africa and Paris as a journalist. During the war, Camus was a leader in the Resistance movement, and in 1943 he founded and worked as editor on the underground newspaper *Combat*. In 1957 he was awarded the Nobel Prize for literature.

Today Camus's high position in French letters is due not to his plays but to his roles as polemicist and chronicler. The plays represent, in the unfolding of his thought, a moment of tragic lucidity. His first two plays, *Le Malentendu* (*The Misunderstanding*) and CALIGULA, were performed in 1945. The last two plays, *L'État de siège* (*State of Siege,* 1948) and *Les Justes* (*The Just Assassins,* 1950), represent a definitive break by Camus with the lies and the compromises he discovered in the composition of our society. A deep-seated will to revolt against injustice, humiliation, and fear of death created the psychoses of both Marthe (*Le Malentendu*) and Caligula. The scorn they manifest for their fate is an almost Nietzschean will to power. The "misunderstanding" grows into a study of political tragedy when it is applied to more than individual life, to a nation, for example, and to all of mankind.

Despite some admirable elements, notably its strong lyric accent, *L'État de siège* was a failure. The characters are abstractions, the speeches are a potpourri of ideas, the allegory is too transparent, and the form is too rhapsodic. For both Camus and the director, Jean-Louis Barrault, it was an experi-

ment in combining many theatrical forms (lyric monologue, dialogue, movement of large groups on the stage, farce, chorus, pantomime) to give a dramatic expression to the theme of pestilence.

For critical studies of the work of Camus, see Germaine Brée, *Camus* (1961); Adele King, *Camus* (1964); Thomas Hann, *The Thought and Art of Albert Camus* (1958); Albert Sonnenfeld, "Albert Camus as Dramatist," *Tulane Drama Review,* V (June 1961); and Philip Thody, *Albert Camus 1913–1960* (1961).—W. F.

Canada: *drama in English.* It must be acknowledged at the outset that drama has not developed on a par with the other arts in Canada. From the earliest years the English-Canadian playwright has been confronted with a uniquely unpropitious set of circumstances. The problem of creating a national dramatic literature meaningful to a cross section of the population is intensified in a vast, sparsely inhabited country comprised of two main national stocks. In addition, the amorphous nature of Canadian society, its lack of distinctive features that may be readily projected onstage, has presented a particularly elusive challenge. Moreover, the pioneer conditions of Canada's early history, conditions which made energetic work an end in itself, left little place for the theater or any drama that sought to define significant social conflicts. The communal indifference to the theater was reinforced by the twofold puritan heritage of Scotland and New England, which perpetuated a view of the theater as a suspect, or at any rate an expendable, commodity. It was not until the 1920's that widespread interest in the creation of a distinctively Canadian drama began to take root. But by this time the films were changing the entertainment routine of the nation, depriving the potential playwright of most of his audience at the moment he was beginning to find his voice.

The position of Canadian drama is that of a cultural colony. From before Confederation in 1867 most theatrical fare has been imported from abroad. Canada has so much in common with both England and the United States that the dramatists of these latter countries can offer immediate entertainment to Canadian audiences. When the distinctive qualities of one group of playwrights begin to pall, a second group is available.

Such authors as Charles Heavysege (1816–1876), J. Hunter-Duvar (1830–1899), Charles Mair (1838–1917), and Wilfred Campbell (1858–1918), writing in the last decades of the nineteenth century, were drawn in the main to biblical or historical subjects, which they dramatized with high-minded energy. Their works have a certain historical interest and are occasionally redeemed by an effective passage, but as plays their merit is minimal. The reasons are not far to seek. In the first place, these dramas were composed in a pseudo-Shakespearean verse measure, which was the fashion for much English literary drama of the time. Although Ibsen and then Shaw were creating revolutionary concepts of theater, their influence did not extend to Canada.

Moreover, these Canadian writers were imprisoned, not only by a dead linguistic convention, but also by the rigid moral attitudes of a provincial society. They clearly aspired to elevated art but the pat moral formulas and pasteboard characterizations of melodrama appear everywhere in their work. Finally, and most significantly, their complete separation from the practical stage and the conditions of performance deprived them of the chance to learn the essentials of their craft.

The efforts of Canada's nineteenth-century verse playwrights, then, proved a false start and a dead end. The history of Canadian drama properly begins with the rise of the little theater movement, with the rapid growth of amateur, community theaters in the years after the First World War. The optimistic excitement that attended this development prompted the composition of numerous plays. Would-be dramatists throughout the country essayed a wide variety of genres, but unfortunately the great mass of this writing was without literary or theatrical distinction. In almost every case, originality, intensity, and technique were absent.

The only playwright of merit to emerge from this ferment was Merrill DENISON, whose plays were performed at Hart House Theatre at the University of Toronto in the active years immediately following its foundation in 1919. A group of his plays collected in a volume entitled *The Unheroic North* (pub. 1923) range from somber, rural tragedy to satirical farce contrived to puncture idealistic notions about life in the Ontario northland. The various other collections of plays published during this period illustrate, for the most part, the dangers of trying to create a national drama through earnest, self-conscious determination.

In the early years of the 1930's, Canadian plays continued to appear in profusion, although as the Depression wore on, their numbers diminished. Various associations and little theaters continued to encourage writers through competitions and prizes, such as the Dominion Drama Festival's award for the best performance of a native play. But in spite of all inducements, few first-rate dramas were forthcoming.

A considerable number of the plays that appeared during these years were directly inspired by the Great Depression. Most have sociological interest only, but the pity and anger they reflect, rare emotions on the Canadian stage, are often impressive. The chief drawback of almost all these plays is a confusion of art with propaganda.

Two figures of the period who stand somewhat apart are Gwen Pharis Ringwood (1910–   ) and John Coulter (1888–   ). Mrs. Ringwood is the author of several plays, most of them set in her native province of Alberta. They dramatize with considerable power the relation between the inhabitants of the prairies and their harsh but compelling environment. Some of Mr. Coulter's best plays are set in Ireland, the country of his birth, and show the influence of Ireland's celebrated group of dramatists, Lady Gregory in particular, Synge less often. In addition to his Irish settings, Coulter has also used Canada's northwest for a background in *Riel* (1950), the best Canadian historical drama.

The Second World War interrupted many of the country's dramatic activities, and after it far fewer plays appeared, in published form at least. It is as if the first optimistic experiments had been tried and it had become discouragingly clear to all that playmaking is a difficult and elusive craft. In addition, devel-

ROBERTSON DAVIES (ASHLEY AND CRIPPEN)

opments in radio and later in television had the effect of diverting the energies of potential playwrights to these remunerative media.

During the 1940's, however, Canada's most prolific dramatist, Robertson DAVIES, made his appearance. Davies' plays display a large measure of theatrical invention, satiric flair, and refreshingly literate dialogue. Among his preoccupations are the widespread philistinism, narrowness, and prudery of life in Canada, the conflict between the many who would confine the human spirit and the few who would liberate it, and the fate of the creative imagination in an inhospitable climate, which is home and hence inescapable. What distinguishes Davies from his predecessors is the greater insight, energy, and technique with which he explores these themes.

During the 1950's and 1960's, such dramatists as Norman Williams, Patricia Joudry, Lister Sinclair, John Reeves, and most notably James REANEY wrote for the stage with varying degrees of success. Reeves's *A Beach of Strangers: An Excursion* (pub. 1959), an allegory about human solitude and the precarious reprieve from isolation that love accomplishes, won an international award in 1959. One continuing problem for these playwrights is that the publication of plays in Canada is a very haphazard process. Merit is not by any means always the criterion.

It is hard to discern any significant continuity or pattern of development in the course of English-Canadian drama beyond some tenuous points of contact between such figures as Denison and Davies and certain recurrent themes. As one might expect, several of the plays set in a rural context have at their center the struggle with an intimidating natural environment, while many of those set in the city present in some form the conflict between the exuberant, creative individual and a censorious, life-denying society. In both cases it is the precise quality of this conflict that gives these plays, the better ones at least, their distinctively Canadian character. However, the overriding impression one receives from a review of drama in Canada is of a group of playwrights, some with considerable gifts, separated primarily not by space and time but by the absence of a native dramatic tradition, a tradition that may be accepted or challenged but within which action produces reaction. In an important sense the Canadian playwright has hardly anything to follow or repudiate. He must begin each time to build from the bottom, and in such circumstances it takes a dramatist of formidable energy and skill to build very high. The spectacular success, however, of the Ontario Stratford Festival, the building of the National Arts Centre in Ottawa, and the growth of professional theater in various regions of the country offer increasing opportunity for the native playwright. Measured by international standards of excellence, the achievement of English Canadian dramatists is not great, but the future holds promise.

There is as yet no comprehensive history of Canadian drama. Useful articles and studies include: J. Ball, ed., "Theatre in Canada: A Bibliography," *Canadian Literature,* XIV (Autumn 1963), 85–100; N. Cohen, "Theatre Today: English Canada," *Tamarack Review,* XIII (Autumn 1960), 24–37; J. M. Moore, "The Theatre in English-Speaking Canada," *The Arts in Canada: A Stock Taking at Mid-Century* (1958), edited by Malcolm Ross; A. L. Phelps, "Canadian Drama," UTQ, IX, 82–94; M. S. Tait, "Theatre and Drama," *Literary History of Canada* (1965), edited by C. F. Klinck; H. Whittaker, "The Theatre," *The Culture of Contemporary Canada* (1957), edited by J. Park.—M. T.

Canada: *drama in French.* Although just beginning, the French-Canadian theater is nevertheless an accomplished fact. Its birth is marked by the creation of *Tit-Coq* by Gratien GÉLINAS in 1948. Since then, an increasing number of writers have devoted theii talents, in whole or in part, to the theater. In addition to Marcel DUBÉ, the most prolific French-Canadian dramatist, these writers include the poet Anne Hébert and the novelists Françoise Loranger, Marie-Claire Blais, Réjean Ducharme, and Jean Basile.

French-Canadian playwrights have found a source of inspiration in the work of Americans Eugene O'Neill and Tennessee Williams and the French contemporary theater of Eugène Ionesco and Samuel Beckett. Worthy of notice is the almost total absence of *pièces de boulevard,* the light, comic, popular plays.

Television, for which most of the French-Canadian dramatists have worked, seems to have largely influenced the formal composition of the plays. Baneful according to some, television has, according to others, permitted the playwrights to "try their wings."

Solicited by theater troupes, aided financially by the Conseils des Arts, which distributes grants, and followed by an ever-increasing public, lately the French-Canadian playwrights have found sufficient reason to write for the theater. To provide young French-Canadian authors with an audience before whom they can try their plays, a cooperative group of these young dramatists formed the Dramatic Authors' Centre d'Essai in Montreal in 1960. Open to all, the Centre organizes public readings of unpublished works and periodically publishes the magazine *Theatre Vivant,* which includes the texts of works presented at the readings. Of the organizers of the Centre, some have seen their works produced on the professional stage: Robert Gurik, Michel Trembley, and Claude Levac.

Stemming from a *populiste* inspiration, French-Canadian drama is actually directed toward political debate. Because numerous plays explore the facets of French-Canadian nationalism, the theater has a limited audience—French-Canadian. After some unsuccessful attempts at exportation, it is enough that, for the moment, it holds the attention of the local public.

The most celebrated poet of French Canada, Anne Hébert (1916–   ), has written one play—*Le Temps sauvage* ("The Wild Days," 1953). This work portrays the conflict between a mother and her children and presents one of the most fair and severe portraits of the traditional French-Canadian mother as she expresses her will and strength.

Another writer who became interested in the theater is novelist Françoise Loranger, who turned to drama by way of radio and television. Her plays are Chekhovian because of their refined dialogue and psychological portraits. Her dramatic comedy *Une Maison, un jour* ("A House, A Day," 1965), about a middle-class family obliged to sell the family home, would be a bourgeois drama except for the finesse of the writing and the author's ability to create a soft and sensitive atmosphere. Her other comedy, *Encore cinq minutes* ("Five Minutes More," 1967), portrays a woman of about forty who finds herself face to face with her own life, a prosaic husband, and children whose existence escapes her. This feminine world is the one that Loranger explores most successfully.

Both novelists Jean Basile (1932–   ) and Marie-Claire Blais (1939–   ) have written one play each. Basile's comedy *Joli Tambour* ("Pretty Drum," 1967) is Brechtian inform and tells the story of a young soldier who becomes, in spite of himself, the first hangman in New France. While Basile drew his subject from the annals of Canadian history, Blais based her drama, *L'Execution* (1968), on a news item. Her play, about a crime committed without any apparent motive by two eighteen-year-old college students, was not successful. Another French-Canadian novelist who also writes for the theater is Réjean Ducharme (1945–   ). In *Le Cid maghané,* a parody of Corneille's *Le Cid* in French-Canadian slang, and *Ines Pérée et Ina Tendu,* a verbal exercise making wide use of puns, Ducharme severely criticizes the state of language in French Canada.

Jaques Languirand (1930–   ) uses language in the same repetitive way used by the avant-garde playwrights in France. All his plays have an element of absurdity similar to that found in the work of Ionesco and Jean Vauthier: The comedy *Les Insolites* ("The Unusual Ones," 1956) has a vaudeville, impromptu quality; and the tragedy *Les Violons d'automne* ("The Violins of Autumn," 1961) has a cyclical theme. Languirand's *Klondike* (1965), on the gold-rush theme, ends with a poetic, musical fresco.

His tragedy *Les Grands Departs* ("The Big Departures," 1957), about a family who decides to move in the false hope of somehow escaping themselves, is considered one of the best plays of the Quebec theater.

Also influenced by French dramas is the work of Paul Toupin (1917–), the French-Canadian essayist and playwright. His major tragedy, *Brutus* (1952), about Brutus' plot and assassination of Caesar, has a haughty tone, concision, and severity that are reminiscent of the works of Henry de Montherlant and the classical French drama of the seventeenth century. Toupin's *Le Mensonge* ("The Lie," 1952), dealing with medieval courtly love, is set in Brittany, France, in 1480 and is distinguished by the harshness of its language. The bourgeois comedy *Chacun son amour* ("Each His Love," 1955) presents a new variation of the Don Juan theme and creates a disenchanted, cynical atmosphere reminiscent of Montherlant's work. Toupin's dramas have a certain cerebral coolness, but there is no sense of nationalism, as appears in the work of other French-Canadian playwrights, such as actor-director-playwright Jean-Louis Roux. In *Bois-Brûlés* ("Burnt-Wood," 1968) Roux presents a political fresco of French-Canadian nationalism that is centered on the life of a French-speaking half-breed who rebels against the central government of Canada. Written in Brechtian style, this work was conceived from historical documents.

Nationalism is also the central concern in the dramas of Jacques Ferron (1921–), one of the masters of irony in French Canada. His historical drama *Les Grands Soleils* ("The Great Suns," 1968) is set within the framework of the French-Canadian rebellion against the English regime and opposes the audacity and self-confidence of the hero with the emptiness and indifference of the clergy and peasantry.— J. B.

Candelaio, Il ("The Candle-Maker," 1582). A comedy by Giordano Bruno (1548?–1600). Divided into five acts and preceded by a dedication and three prologues, *Il Candelaio* narrates the trick played by a sorcerer on Bonifacio, an elderly miser who takes pleasure from both women and young boys (*candelaio* in this play means sodomite). Bonifacio had trusted the sorcerer to help him win the love of the courtesan Vittoria. Believing that he is going to bed with Vittoria, Bonifacio instead lies with his own wife, Carubina, who ultimately obtains revenge by hastening to meet her lover. Interwoven with this action are the tricks played on the pedant Manfurio by Ottaviano and on the credulous Bartolomeo by an alchemist, while Bartolomeo's wife is amusing herself with her lover. The conclusion of the three actions seems to conform to the cynicism and customary amorality of the Renaissance; in fact, however, it arises from a profound moral sense that manifests itself in violent but tolerant sarcasm when coming to grips with a distasteful world. Typical of the philosophic attitude of Bruno and of his distaste for stupidity and cultural and moral indifference, *Il Candelaio* wittily exposes and criticizes three things: vapid credulity, enslaving superstition, and ignorant rascality. The play is considered today a witty and violent manifestation of a proud and superior spirit, although critics have at times accused it of gratuitous

vulgarity. Written in somewhat difficult language, it has necessarily been adapted, sometimes in language, sometimes in plot, when it has been presented on the stage.—L. L.

canticum. Any scene in a Roman comedy not composed in the six-foot iambic line known as senarius. (See DIVERBIUM.) The cantica, accompanied by flute music, fall into two groups: scenes of monologue or dialogue recited in longer iambic or trochaic lines, the most common meter being the trochaic septenarius, a line of seven and one-half feet; and lyrical songs in a variety of meters, usually monodies but sometimes sung by two or more characters. The second type of canticum is common in Plautus, especially in his later plays, and produces an occasional effect of musical comedy. The origin of these polymetrical songs is not known, but they may have been derived from earlier dramatic entertainments in Italy. There is no evidence for them in the extant Greek New Comedy, and cantica of the second type are very rare in Terence.—G. E. D.

Čapek, Josef (1887–1945) and **Karel** (1890–1938). Czech dramatists, novelists, and essayists. The brothers Capek collaborated in the composition of several plays (though each of them also wrote plays separately).

Born in northeastern Bohemia, a country doctor's sons, the brothers were almost inseparable for most of their lives. As a young man, Josef went to Prague to study painting, while Karel soon followed to enroll in Charles University as a student of philosophy. Their first story, written jointly, was published in January 1908 and was followed by a stream of stories, causeries, aphorisms, and reviews of books and paintings, for the most part written together and published in various Prague journals and newspapers. Their first play, published in 1910, was an erotic comedy in blank verse. The same year Josef left for Paris to continue his art studies, while Karel went to Berlin to attend the university there. But they were reunited the following year in Paris, where Karel acquired a strong interest in French avant-garde literature and painting and in the philosophy of Henri Bergson, who, together with the American pragmatists, was to constitute the principal philosophic influence on his work. They returned the same year to Prague, where Karel resumed his studies at the university, taking his doctorate in 1915. Poor health exempted the brothers from military service during the war, and they continued to publish throughout the war years. With the end of the war and the independence of the newborn Czechoslovak state, they embarked on careers as journalists, eventually working on the liberal paper *Lidové noviny*, which supported the new president, Thomas Masaryk. Meanwhile, two of Karel's plays were produced with great success: *Loupežník* ("The Brigand," 1920) and *R.U.R.* The latter work, which presented robots on the stage, soon made his reputation all over the world. The success of *R.U.R.* was quickly followed by that of *Ze zivota hmyzu* (*The Insect Comedy,* 1922), written by both brothers; it too soon found a place in the world repertory.

Each of the brothers now wrote a play separately: *Věc Makropulos* (*The Makropulos Secret,* 1922), by Karel and *Země mnoha jmen* (*The Land of Many Names,* 1923) by Josef; though less successful than

R.U.R. and *The Insect Comedy*, these plays also gained some success abroad. Meanwhile, Karel was employed from 1921 to 1923 as a director at the Prague Municipal Theater, while Josef, who had become a well-known painter, worked as a stage designer.

A new utopian comedy, *Adam stvořitel* (*Adam the Creator,* 1927), represents the final joint effort of the brothers. It failed to gain the success of the earlier plays, and Josef gave up writing for the stage, while Karel abandoned it for ten years.

The staid domesticity of the two brothers, their jointly occupied villa in the suburbs of Prague, and their gardens became symbols of their work and their philosophy. Karel's humorous collection of essays *Zahradníkův rok* (*The Gardener's Year,* pub. 1929), illustrated by Josef, deepened this association, and their critics, especially the communists, viewed this domesticity as petit bourgeois. Their writings of the 1920's glorify a pragmatic, relativistic philosophy that seems to imply an apolitical view and a certain lack of concern with social or political causes, and with this too their enemies reproached them. But in fact Karel's newspaper essays frequently treat social and political questions, and by the end of the 1920's he rejected a superficial relativism in favor of a deep comprehension of the tragedy of the individual, alienated from nature and the social order. Josef moved further to the political left, and during the 1930's both brothers played an active part in trying to inspire their countrymen to resist Nazi aggression. Josef published a famous series of political cartoons savagely caricaturing the Nazis, while Karel directed his last two plays, *Bílá nemoc* (translated as *Power and Glory,* 1937) and *Matka* (*The Mother,* 1938), against fascism. The Munich agreement of September 1938, giving the Sudentenland to Hitler, bitterly disillusioned the brothers. Advised to emigrate from their own country, where the new rightist regime was hostile to them, they steadfastly refused. Falling prey to depression, Karel developed inflammation of the lungs and died on December 25, 1938. On March 15, 1939, German soldiers entered Prague, and Gestapo agents, unaware of Karel's death, came to arrest both brothers. Josef was taken to a concentration camp and died in Bergen-Belsen, probably of typhus, only a few weeks before the end of the Second World War.

The early writings of the brothers consist chiefly of satirical and parodic stories, causeries, and aphorisms. These use the manner of symbolism and decadence to ridicule the *Weltanschauung* of the Czech symbolist school with which the Capeks were breaking as members of a younger, avant-garde generation. Among these works is a one-act comedy in blank verse, *Lásky hra osudná* ("The Fateful Game of Love," pub. 1910; prod. 1930), a stylized imitation of the *commedia dell'arte*. The symbolist poets and playwrights were attracted to the Italian commedia, but it is hard to say where the Čapeks found a precise model, if any, for their play, which is actually a parody on the cult of illusion in the symbolist theater. There is also a lively parody of stage conventions.

Karel's first full-length play, *Loupežník* ("The Brigand," 1920), mixes symbolist and realist styles somewhat in the manner of Anton Chekhov, August Strindberg, or Frank Wedekind. It is a drama of the conflict between the rights of young love and the prudery of the older generation. Most of the play is in prose, but the love dialogue is in verse. The setting is a staid professor's country house, which has been turned into a fortress for the purpose of keeping his younger daughter a prisoner. This fortress is besieged and taken by a young wanderer, a partly symbolic figure, who seduces the daughter. But he is outwitted and chased away by the maidservant, a harpy envious of young love, and the parents again make their daughter a prisoner. The atmosphere of the play's outdoor setting is poetic, and Čapek provided the work with directions for an open-air performance. In accordance with his typical relativistic point of view, none of the characters appears as entirely right or wrong; hence, the natural tragedy that might ensue from such a subject is replaced by comedy. The play was for many years Čapek's favorite and is perhaps his strongest from the point of view of dramatic construction.

Loupežník was soon followed by the utopian "collective drama" R.U.R.: ROSSUM'S UNIVERSAL ROBOTS. The title and subtitle are in English and are the names of an international trust for the manufacture of robots that so closely resemble humans that it is almost impossible to tell them apart. The robots rise up to overthrow the human race, which is exploiting them. In the ensuing struggle the secret of their manufacture is lost, and they lack the power to reproduce themselves. In the end a miracle occurs: the robots become human and two of them fall in love, thus regenerating the human race. The robot is an effective dramatic and expressionistic symbol of the threat of modern technology's potential to destroy man; Čapek fears that technology, in making possible a life without struggle, will debilitate man and imperil his survival. But a strong vitalist faith is reasserted at the play's close: man will not perish but will survive in spite of all threats of his extinction. The construction of the play is by no means perfect, and the brilliant conception of the robot symbol is scarcely matched by the dramaturgy, which, in spite of the expressionistic character of the main symbol, suffers from a rather banal realism full of improbable details. The eloquence of the play's theme is unrealized in terms of eloquence of dialogue, as Kenneth Burke has observed in *Counter-Statement* (1931). Still, the play has dramatic force, and the stiff, marching movements of the robots can be effective on the stage. The word "robot" is of Czech coinage (from *robota,* "hard labor" or "servitude"); introduced in a story by Josef Čapek, it was Karel's *R.U.R.* that spread the term all over the world.

Meanwhile, the brothers had written a kind of theatrical revue from the insect world, *The Insect Comedy*. The conception of the play came from reading the works of the French entomologist Jean Henri Fabre, while much of its technique derived from the allegory of the medieval mystery and morality play. The central figure that holds the various scenes of the play together is that of a wanderer, a tramp, who observes life among the insects and comments on it. The main play consists of three distinct scenes. The first, set in the world of butterflies, shows the triviality and ephemeral quality of love. The second, among the beetles, parodies the family and shows up its insularity: love of family may actually be a form of

KAREL ČAPEK (WIDE WORLD PHOTOS)

selfishness, for it may shut out the rest of the world. Finally, the third scene, among the ants, attacks the modern monolithic state and its readiness to wage war. In an epilogue illustrating the ephemeral character of life itself, the tramp dies. When critics found this epilogue too pessimistic, the brothers provided a second, "optimistic" ending (the director was to choose between them), in which the tramp dies but an infant is born. Thus, they left the meaning of their play ambiguous. No doubt it has often been taken for gloomy pessimism, but the authors insisted on its essential comedic quality; satire of vice, they argued, is a traditional literary and dramatic theme and need not imply that all life is vicious or without value. Though the dramatic line of the play is inevitably weak (it is essentially more of a revue than a play), its theatricality is very strong, and it draws on the techniques of such theatrical media as the ballet, revue, film, and pantomime.

Karel Čapek's next play, *Věc Makropulos,* is again on a utopian theme: the dream of immortality. The heroine, Elena Makropulos, is the daughter of the Greek physician to Emperor Rudolf II; he has discovered the elixir of life and tested it on his daughter. At the play's opening she has been living for over three hundred years but now requires the lost formula in order to rejuvenate herself. After a complex plot based on a legal melodrama, she recovers the formula, but disgusted and profoundly bored with life, she allows it to be destroyed. The play employs certain elements of melodrama, but actually it is more of a philosophic comedy. The critics received it as a polemical reply to Shaw's *Back to Methuselah,*

which had appeared the preceding year and which asserted that increased longevity would benefit mankind. Čapek denied any knowledge of Shaw's play when he wrote his own, but in a philosophic sense the play is, of course, an answer, and Čapek opposes Shaw's evolutionary cult of the superman as a form of absolutism of potential harm in a relativist world. The play has had considerable success in the theater and also as the basis for the libretto of Leos Janáček's opera of the same name.

Josef Čapek wrote only one play of his own, *Země mnoha jmen,* also on a utopian theme. A new continent arises out of an earthquake, is settled, and becomes the occasion for a whole series of wars before it is finally divided among the powers. But by the time peace is won, the new continent has again disappeared.

The next play of the brothers, *Adam stvořitel,* another utopian allegory, was their final joint effort. Adam destroys the world, using the "cannon of negation," but God commands him to create it again. Adam's creations turn out just as imperfect as those of God, which he had criticized, and the world he fashions is no better (if perhaps no worse) than God's. In the end Adam learns the lesson that the world, with all its faults, is essentially good. This message is impaired by the fact that a more literal reading would rather suggest the conclusion that any conscious attempt by man to improve the order of things will only worsen it, a pessimistic message indeed. In spite of the humor of certain details, the play has never been a success.

Bílá nemoc, Karel Čapek's first antifascist play, is also an allegory. The "white plague" of the title is a mortal disease, something like leprosy, which attacks only persons over forty. A pacifist physician, Dr. Galén, discovers a cure but will reveal it only on condition that the powers agree to make peace. The dictator of the land rejects Galén's proposal as "unheroic" but finally yields when he himself contracts the disease. His change of heart comes too late, however, for a crowd dominated by war hysteria kills Galén as he is on his way to the dictator's bedside. The plague itself is, of course, an expressionist symbol of war, but it is poorly incorporated into the realistic matrix of the play: one fails to see how Galén, once his secret is revealed, could have continued to enforce permanent peace.

Karel Čapek's final play, *Matka,* is also an antifascist work. In the light of contemporary events—the Spanish Civil War and the Nazi threat to Czechoslovak independence—Čapek now exchanges pacifism for belief in a nation's right to defend itself against aggression; thus, in place of his earlier faith in philosophical relativism he now gives us a new, ethical absolute: not so much the right of self-defense, but man's duty to defend others who are attacked. The play depicts the tragedy of a mother whose husband and sons have all been sacrificed on the altar of careerism. Left with only one son, her youngest, she hides him at home when their land is invaded by a foreign aggressor, but, hearing that the enemy is killing helpless women and children, she sends him off to fight. The play is no doubt sentimental, but in its fundamental opposition between the mother's nature, dedicated to the preservation of life, and that of her menfolk, who risk their lives in the service of masculine ideals of honor and courage which she cannot understand, Čapek has created an effective dramatic conflict.

It is still difficult today to assess the ultimate significance of the work of the Čapeks. Their drama is very much a drama of ideas, and no doubt they failed to develop a form or technique capable of adequately representing these. Yet in Karel Čapek's conception of the robot as a dramatically expressive symbol of technology's threat to mankind, *R.U.R.* is certainly original. *The Insect Comedy,* in its return to the form of the medieval morality play and its use of the techniques of a variety of theatrical forms, is also richly inventive and achieves a balance between technique and idea. As a more conventional play, Karel's *Loupežník* is also dramatically strong.

The influence of the Čapeks' drama has not been great, either in Czechoslovakia (where perhaps only *Loupežník* has had some influence) or abroad. Probably the weakness of their dramatic technique and the utopian character of their subjects, which were rapidly dated, are responsible. The brothers' ideas, too, were partly vitiated by the limitations of a rather superficial philosophical relativism. Thus, the thesis of *R.U.R.* that technology will rid human life of conflict is simply untrue, and even in the world of today's technology man's life is still beset by struggle. Only in their fiction, which, though less popular abroad, is probably greater, did the Čapeks transcend the ideological limitations of their relativism.

The communist take-over in Czechoslovakia in 1948 placed the work of the brothers, particularly Karel's, under a cloud; in spite of his antifascism, he was criticized for his friendship with President Masaryk and his supposed petit-bourgeois sympathies. But, after several years, his high standing was restored and today he is secure in his position as a leading Czech writer of fiction and essays, as well as plays.

All the Čapeks' plays except *Lásky hra osudná* and *Loupežník* have been published in English translations, in some cases several times. Paul Selver translated *R.U.R. (Rossum's Universal Robots)* (1923). *Ze Života hmyzu* (literally, "From the Life of Insects") is known under several English titles, including *And So Ad Infinitum,* translated by Paul Selver (1923) and *The World We Live In (The Insect Comedy),* adapted and arranged by Owen Davis (1933). *Věc Makropulos* (literally, "The Makropulos Case") has been translated by Paul Selver as *The Makropulos Secret* (1927). Josef Čapek's *The Land of Many Names* has been translated by Paul Selver (1926). *Adam the Creator* was translated by Dora Round (1930). *The White Plague* was rendered by Paul Selver and R. Neale as *Power and Glory* (1938), while *The Mother* was also translated by Paul Selver (1939).

On the Čapeks, in particular Karel, see William E. Harkins' *Karel Čapek* (1962); Alexander Matuska's *Karel Čapek: An Essay* (1964); and René Wellek's "Karel Čapek," in *Essays on Czech Literature* (1963). On Josef Čapek see René Wellek's article in *The Columbia Dictionary of Modern European Literature,* edited by Horatio Smith (1947). —W. E. H.

Captivi (The Captives). A comedy by PLAUTUS, usually dated in his middle period (200–192 B.C.). Based on a lost Greek play, *Captivi* is a comedy that combines mistaken identity and deception but is unique in its serious tone and elevated theme of loyalty and devotion. Instead of the usual young man in love, tyrannical father, and braggart soldier, we have a master and slave, both prisoners of war, who exchange roles to enable the master to escape. The resultant complications provide humor and pathos and irony.

Gotthold Ephraim Lessing, the eighteenth-century German critic, considered *Captivi* the finest play ever produced, an estimate undoubtedly based on the play's high moral tone. Later comedies largely derived from *Captivi* include Lodovico Ariosto's *I Suppositi* (1509), adapted by George Gascoigne in *The Supposes* (1566) and by Philip Massinger in *A New Way to Pay Old Debts* (1625); Ben Jonson's *The Case Is Altered* (1597), which combines the plots of Plautus' *Aulularia* and *Captivi;* Calderón's *El principe constante* (1629); Jean de Rotrou's *Les Captifs* (1638); and G. P. Clerici's *I Prigionieri* (1881). —G. E. D.

Car Cemetery, The (Le Cimetière des Voitures, 1959). A play by Fernando ARRABAL. Arrabal's characters are impoverished wretches, childlike, cruel at times, and hungry for kindness and justice. In this play the character Emanou tries to practice kindness and gentleness in the *bidonville* ("shanty town") of abandoned autos where he lives. He is betrayed by one friend, disowned by another, tied to a police bicycle, and put to death by a gas jet. Without realizing it, he has lived through Christ's passion. As a "beat" character resembling Christ, he remains steadfastly innocent.

The Car Cemetery is full of energy and black humor, bitterness and terror. It depicts the despair of children who cannot fathom what they are going through. The spirit of the play is closer to a nightmare than a dream, but it also has the clear lines of an obsession, of a fable that owes something to the Marquis de Sade, Carl Jung, and Samuel Beckett. In their actions, the characters exist in some unnamed land midway between a recognizable way of life and an apocalyptic life.

The Car Cemetery has been translated by Richard Howard in *Car Cemetery and The Two Executioners* (1960).—W. F.

Caretaker, The (1960). A play by Harold PINTER. *The Caretaker* won the London *Evening Standard* award as the best new play of the year. In 1962 a film version was made with the screenplay by Pinter.

As in much of Pinter's work, the situation is territorial. The conflict arises from the characters' unrelated attitudes to a shared environment, that of a derelict house owned by Mick, who has entrusted it to his brain-damaged brother, Aston, who, in turn, engages a tramp as caretaker. So far as underlying motives are concerned, Pinter, as usual, covers his tracks. (The one speech in which character and past history become clear, when Aston unequivocally describes his experience of electric-shock treatment, stands out as idiomatically foreign to the rest of the play.) But it appears that Mick's principal aim is to regain contact with his brother, and as the tramp changes from a servile scavenger to a greedy aggressor, so he becomes a rival who is finally thrown back on the street. The dialogue explores three types of evasiveness: Mick's calculated intrigue, Aston's mental impediment, and the tramp's compulsive lying. *The Caretaker* is a perfect example of Pinter's mastery of the poetic comedy of common speech. —I. W.

Caroline drama. See ENGLAND: *Caroline drama.*

Carroll, Paul Vincent (1900–1968). Irish playwright. A native of County Louth, Carroll began his career as a schoolteacher, a profession he abandoned in 1937 as a result of the success of his best-known play, SHADOW AND SUBSTANCE. Carroll's first play was *The Watched Pot* (1930), written, as he later said, "under the baleful influence of Tolstoy." His first success was scored in *Things That Are Caesar's* (1932), an intense domestic drama about the conflict between a husband and wife for the soul of their daughter. After *Shadow and Substance,* Carroll's best play is *The White Steed* (1939). Based on an old Irish folk legend, it depicts a spirited young girl's battle against the forces of prudery and puritanism in a small Irish town. When produced in New York in 1939, the play won the New York Drama Critics' Circle Award as the most distinguished foreign play of the year.

During this early phase of his career Carroll was employed as a schoolmaster in Glasgow, Scotland, to which he had moved in 1921. His residence there evoked in him a sincere affection for, and interest in, the Scottish people. These qualities are displayed in a number of his plays. The best of these are: *The Strings My Lord Are False* (1942), a description of the heroism of the people of Glasgow during the bombing of that city in 1942, and *Green Cars Go East* (1951), a sympathetic and moving picture of life in the Glasgow slums. Carroll's imaginative commitment nevertheless still lay with his native land. He was a consistent critic of modern Ireland but he was always been numbered among the loyal opposition. His ambivalence is reflected, for example, in *The Old Foolishness* (1940), which opposes the deeply sensuous romanticism of Ireland's pagan heritage to the life-denying realities of its contemporary life. A similar theme is expressed in *The Devil Came from Dublin.* Described by its author as "a satirical extravaganza," it celebrates the victory of human life over repressive institutions. One notable feature of most of Carroll's plays is his satiric but sympathetic and perceptive analyses of the Irish Catholic clergy. In his plays a priest always figures prominently, lending a delicate air of wit-seasoned spirituality to the action. More importantly, however, the clerical point of reference effectively emphasizes the pervasive presence of Catholicism and clericalism in every aspect of Irish life.

In addition to individual publications of his plays, a collection of Carroll's work is to be found in his *Irish Stories and Plays* (1958). Drew Pallette provides a critical survey of his later work in "Paul Vincent Carroll: Since *The White Steed,*" *Modern Drama,* VIII (1965), 375–385.—E. Q.

Cartwright, William (1611–1643). English poet and playwright. Educated at Oxford, where he later served as reader in metaphysics, Cartwright won considerable acclaim in his lifetime as a dramatist, poet, and preacher. The 1651 edition of his *Works* contains no less than fifty-one commendatory poems by his fellow writers, including Henry Vaughan and Izaak Walton.

Cartwright's four extant plays were written either for academic or private productions. Ben Jonson's influence is clearly discernible in Cartwright's most realistic play, *The Ordinary or The City Cozener* (1634), a comedy modeled on Jonson's *The Alchemist.* His three other plays, *The Lady Errant* (produced between 1628 and 1643), *The Royal Slave* (1636), and *The Siege* (produced between 1628 and 1643) are highly mannered and artificial exercises. They are representative examples of the attempt among Caroline court dramatists to dramatize the abstract principles of Neoplatonism, which came to be known as "Platonic drama."—E. Q.

Cathleen ni Houlihan (1902). A verse play by William Butler YEATS. Yeats's most nationalistic play, written for Maud Gonne, who played the title role, this patriotic allegory in one act is a folk drama set in a peasant cottage at the time of the ill-fated rebellion of 1798. The day before Michael Gillane's wedding coincides with the beginning of the rebellion, when insurgent Irishmen are preparing to join the French ships in the bay to fight against the British and liberate Ireland. The wedding preparations are interrupted when an Old Woman comes into the cottage, "the strange woman that goes through the country whatever time there's war or trouble coming," and she speaks as the traditional symbol of Ireland, "Cathleen, the daughter of Houlihan." She talks about all the courageous men who have died for her, and many more soon to give their lives, trying to drive the strangers out of her house and regain her "four beautiful green fields" (the four provinces of Ireland). Then she leaves, singing of her brave martyrs, "They shall be remembered for ever, / They shall be alive for ever . . ." Confronted by a difficult choice, Michael makes the only possible decision, tears himself away from his weeping bride-to-be, and rushes out after the Old Woman, who now is described as "a young girl, and she had the walk of a queen." In this work Yeats made one of his infrequent attempts to re-create the peasant dialect, and though Lady Gregory helped him with the idiomatic dialogue, he knew he could never capture the rich poetry of John Millington Synge's peasant language. Looking back on his play, he wrote: "The dialect of *Cathleen ni Houlihan* is, I think, true in temper but it has no richness, no abundance."—D. K.

Caucasian Chalk Circle, The (Der kaukasische Kreidekreis). A play by Bertolt BRECHT. Written in 1944/45, *The Caucasian Chalk Circle* was first performed in an English translation in 1948. The play was not produced in German until 1954. It opens with an introductory prologue: After the end of World War II members of two Soviet collective farms meet in the ruins of a Caucasian village. They try to settle the dispute about a valley formerly owned by the goat-breeding collective, and they finally agree to let the fruit- and wine-growing farm use the land, since the farm has developed an irrigation plan that would make the land more productive. To honor the visitors, the fruit farmers call upon the local ballad singer Arkadi Tscheidse to perform a play that has some bearing on the problem just settled. The five episodes, including twelve songs, are connected by the narrator's comments.

The governor of a province in feudal Georgia is killed during the revolt of the princes against the grand duke, who has been losing a war with Persia. The governor's wife, mainly concerned with her wardrobe, flees the city, leaving her young son, Michael, behind. Grusha, a kitchen maid, who has just gotten engaged to the soldier Simon, rescues the child from the burning palace. During her flight into the mountains, Grusha has to pay excessive prices to get milk for the child; further, she knows it is dangerous for her to keep the governor's child. In despair she tries to abandon it at a farm, but when two soldiers in search of the missing Michael threaten the child, she insists that she is the mother and in desperation knocks one of them down. She then escapes across a rotten bridge.

Reaching her brother's farm, Grusha collapses. Fearful of his wife's objections and the gossip of the neighbors, he arranges a deathbed marriage between Grusha and a peasant, whose "fatal" disease disappears when he hears that the war is over. Grusha's fiancé returns from the war and finds her married. When soldiers come with a warrant for the son of the governor, Grusha again insists that it is her own child. Michael is taken to the capital anyway to be returned to his mother. Grusha follows them and prepares to contest the governor's wife in court.

The judge who will decide the case is Azdak, a village scribe, who had unwittingly hidden the grand duke. Realizing that he has aided the "Grand Butcher," Azdak brings himself to trial, but the city judge has just been hanged. Azdak then, in a mock trial, plays the grand duke and defends himself admirably, showing by implication that the princes and the grand duke are all the same where the people are concerned. The soldiers, amused by Azdak's peculiar sense of justice, make him the new judge. For two years he breaks the laws to help the poor. When Grusha's case comes up, Azdak is about to be hanged by the soldiers of the grand duke, who has been restored to power. But in the last minute a letter from the grand duke, because Azdak had hidden him, saves Azdak and reappoints him to his judgeship. The trial reveals that the governor's wife wants her son only because he has inherited his father's fortune. To decide the case, Azdak orders a circle of chalk to be drawn on the ground. The child is put in the center, and both women are told to try to pull the child out of the circle. Twice the governor's wife violently drags Michael out of the circle, while Grusha is unwilling to use force for fear of injuring the child. Because Grusha showed more love, Azdak declares her to be the true mother, grants her a divorce, and disappears, never to be seen again. The storyteller concludes the play by noting "that what there is shall go to those who are good for it, thus: the children to the motherly, that they prosper . . . and the valley to the waterers, that it bring forth fruit."

As a source, Brecht used the ancient Chinese play by Li Hsing-tao, also adapted by the German poet Klabund in 1925. But in the original story it is the real mother who gets the child. By reversing this, Brecht emphasizes that social ties are more important than biological. *The Caucasian Chalk Circle,* Brecht's last major play, is based on one of his earlier stories, "The Augsburg Chalk Circle." Victor Lange (in a 1966 edition of the play) writes that "in no other play of Brecht's are his unfailing sense of the theatre, his poetic power, and his ethical convictions blended with equal skill." Some of Brecht's notes can be found in *The Drama Review,* T 37 (1967), together with drawings by Kulisiewics. An excellent collection of materials has been published under the title "Materialien zu Brechts *Der Kaukasische Kreidekreis* (1968).—H. R.

Cena delle beffe, La ("The Banquet of Jests," 1909). A dramatic poem by Sem Benelli (1877–1949). Inspired by one of Lasca's short stories from *Le Cene* and set in Florence in the second half of the fifteenth century, *La Cena delle beffe* narrates the story of the ferocious struggle between the weak and ungraceful Giannetto Malaspini and two brothers, Neri and Gabriello Chiaromontesi. Neri takes the beautiful and frivolous Ginevra away from Giannetto, making him suffer cruel mockeries and outrages. Giannetto pretends that he is suffering his plight while actually he is figuring out his revenge: during a banquet, where, at the initiative of the lord of Florence, the reconciliation of the two families is to take place, Giannetto leads Neri into a trap by goading his self-respect to the point where he becomes violent and is imprisoned as a madman. When he comes out of jail, realizing that he has been fooled by Giannetto, who has in the meantime rewon Ginevra, Neri runs to the Malaspini house intent upon killing his rival; instead he kills his own brother Gabriello, who during the night has come to see the fickle Ginevra and was sleeping with her.

La Cena delle beffe was greeted with exceptional public approval, for it is marked by a scenic construction of undoubted effectiveness, by a powerful —even if only exterior—melodrama of characters and situations, and by the violence of strife. Its period of success was brief, but it remains among the most significant documents of that taste—which reached its height at the turn of this century—for setting tragedy in the middle ages; it represents also an attempt to create an historical Italian play outside the conventional classical and Roman environment. —L. L.

Cenci, Les (1935). A play by Antonin ARTAUD. The one experiment by Artaud in his THEATER OF CRUELTY is *Les Cenci,* his adaptation of texts by Shelley and Stendhal. With this play Artaud initiated the fundamental notion of a "theater in the round," thus bringing the actors and spectators into closer contact than in the regular theater. In this production a visible and audible frenzy was created by such mechanical devices as strident and dissonant sound effects, whirling stage sets, and the effect of storms by means of light. This performance in 1935 marked a return in the French theater to a complicated stage production, which has since been specially developed by Jean-Louis Barrault (who had a role in the original performance of Artaud's play). Although the production was a failure, some of the discerning critics praised the stage set of Balthus and the direction of Artaud.—W. F.

Central African Republic. See AFRICA: *Central African Republic.*

Cervantes [Saavedra], Miguel de (1547–1616). Spanish novelist, playwright, and poet. Cervantes, who belonged to an earlier generation than the Golden Age playwright Lope de Vega, the inventor of the Golden Age *comedia,* remains outside the main line of development of Spanish drama. He was formed intellectually under the Humanist influence of Erasmus, before the Council of Trent (1545–1564) imposed its reaffirmation of Catholic orthodoxy on Spanish literature. When, in the latter half of his life, Cervantes turned from soldiering to writing, he approached his task with a more open mind than his younger colleagues. His experiments and innovations in drama, however, bore little fruit in the works of other writers.

Born in Alcalá de Henares, he studied in the academy of the Humanist López de Hoyos. He wrote some poetry before going in 1569 to Italy in the service of a cardinal. He enlisted in the army in 1570 and saw service at the battle of Lepanto (1571), where he received a wound that maimed his left hand. After spending some months in a hospital at Messina, he took part in expeditions to Corfu and Tunis. In 1575, on the return voyage to Spain, he was captured by Barbary pirates and taken as a prisoner to Algiers. During the five years of his captivity, which involved several attempted escapes, his conduct was heroic. Finally ransomed by a religious order, he returned to Spain and a life of poverty. He wrote a few plays, including *El cerco de Numancia* ("The Siege of Numantia," written sometime between 1580 and 1590), with no great success. In 1584 he married and the following year published his pastoral romance *La Galatea*. He obtained a post as purveyor of provisions to the Invincible Armada. Because of financial irregularities in his accounts, he was jailed in 1597 and again in 1602. Residing in Valladolid from 1603 to 1604, Cervantes was once more jailed as a result of a murder committed in front of his house. From this time on, he devoted himself to writing. He published his works in rapid succession: *Don Quixote* (Part I pub. 1605; Part II pub. 1615); *Novelas ejemplares* ("Exemplary Short Stories," pub. 1613); *Viaje del Parnaso* ("Journey to Parnassus," pub. 1614), a survey in verse of the state of literature; *Ocho comedias y ocho entremeses* ("Eight Plays and Eight Interludes," pub. 1615); and *Persiles y Sigismunda* ("Persiles and Sigismunda," a Byzantine romance, published posthumously in 1617).

El cerco de Numancia and *El trato de Argel* ("The Business at Algiers") are the only two surviving plays of the score or so Cervantes claimed to have written between 1580 and 1590. Patriotic in spirit, these dramas are four-act discursive pieces. In the Algiers play Cervantes draws on his personal experience to present the vicissitudes undergone by Christian captives in the slave market and prisons of the Moorish city. A slight love story gives a modicum of unity to the work, which ends with the ransoming of the prisoners. In *La Numancia,* a Senecan tragedy with witchcraft, a bloodbath, and a holocaust, the Spanish city is under siege by the cold, calculating Roman general Scipio Africanus. Scipio rejects both the military grandeur that would accrue from a frontal attack on the walls and the chance to show his magnanimity by accepting the Numantians' offer to settle the dispute by single combat. With what Cervantes considers a ruthless "sanity," Scipio proposes to starve out the population. Faced with imminent defeat, the Numantians, in a fit of "sublime madness," destroy the city and every living thing in it, thus depriving Scipio of his general's right to a triumphal march through Rome, because he has not conquered a city that has chosen to annihilate itself. *La Nu-*

mancia has inspired resistance at critical moments of history: in Spain during the French invasion, and in Paris during the German occupation.

In 1615 Cervantes published a set of eight more mature plays, written in three acts in an apparent challenge to Lope de Vega's hegemony. *Pedro de Urdemalas* (*Pedro, the Artful Dodger*), centering around the rogue named in the title, is one of his best plays. *El rufián dichoso* ("The Blessed Pimp") presents a blackguard from the Sevillian underworld who becomes religious and ends his days as a saintly friar in Mexico. It is an example of the saints-and-bandits cycle that was so popular among classical Spanish dramatists. An allegorical Prologue to Act II consists of a discussion between Curiosity and Play in which the drama's emancipation from neo-Aristotelian rules is justified: the shift of scene from Seville to Mexico need present no problem for the spectator, because his imagination can fly swiftly and tirelessly across the Atlantic. Cervantes was greatly concerned with the neoclassic rules legislating the unity of time, place, and action. In *Don Quixote* (Part I, Chapter 48) he has a canon of the Church make a determined plea for the regulation of Spanish dramas under these neoclassic rules. Critics often assume that the canon is the author's mouthpiece for expressing his disapproval of Lope de Vega's type of drama, with its emancipation from traditional dramatic theory. It should be remembered, however, that the canon is illogical and pompous and that Cervantes is anything but dogmatic in his views; he is always ready to entertain both sides of a question. The Prologue to the *Ocho comedias* contains Cervantes' interesting reminiscences about the stage as it was in his boyhood.

Cervantes' greatest contribution to the Spanish theater took the form of *entremeses* ("interludes" or "sketches"), eight of which were published in the volume of 1615. In all but two he used prose, the medium he handled best. Cervantes forced into the farcical mode of the entremés some momentous questions and a kind of satire that reflected his fearless political and social thinking. In *El retablo de las maravillas* (*The Wonder Show,* pub. 1615) he presents an interior duplication in the form of a nonexistent puppet show. A village is swindled by a confidence man and his assistants: they announce a puppet show that can be seen only by those whose ancestry is untainted with Jewish blood or bastardy. Since the puppet show does not exist, no one sees anything, but all pretend to. The girls pull their skirts tight against the mice alleged to be onstage; everyone fears he will get wet at the presentation of the Great Flood; one of the young men dances with a purely imaginary Salome. When, expecting to find billets for his troops, a quartermaster bursts in and frankly admits that he can see no show, the villagers maliciously turn on him with the words addressed by the maid to Peter after he has denied Christ: "This is one of them." No other writer so savagely showed up the sham in the racialism that was then so rampant in Spain. In another interlude, *El juez de los divorcios* (*The Divorce-Court Judge,* pub. 1615), Cervantes speculates about what might happen if divorce courts existed in seventeenth-century Spain. After the sordid revelations of the misery that reigns in many marriages, the entremés reaches the wry conclusion that "the worst reconciliation is better than the best divorce." *El viejo celoso* (*The Jealous Old Husband,* pub. 1615) is a sardonic comment on the consequences of marriage between a lusty young girl and an overprotective old man. The wife surreptitiously introduces her lover into the closely guarded house, makes love to him in a locked inner room loudly enough for her husband to overhear her ecstasy, and then spirits the lover out of the house. The husband never knows whether his wife playacted the adultery in order to punish him for his distrustfulness or whether she in fact betrayed him. The interlude called *La cueva de Salamanca* (*The Cave of Salamanca,* pub. 1615) presents a resourceful student who invents an *ad hoc* "magic" to enable the mistress of the house in which he is staying to deceive her husband and get away with it. In a sense all Cervantes' entremeses exploit and pillory human credulity. No one has excelled him in this genre. His longer plays of 1615, however, were regarded so lightly that they were never performed in his lifetime and seldom have been since.

The only full-length play by Cervantes accessible in English is *Pedro, the Artful Dodger,* in *Eight Plays of the Golden Age* (1964), translated by Walter Starkie. Two excellent translations have been made of the entremeses. *The Interludes of Cervantes* (1948), edited and translated by S. Griswold Morley, is scholarly and contains the Spanish text on pages parallel with the English text. Miguel de Cervantes, *Interludes* (1964), translated by Edwin Honig, is a racy but accurate translation for the common reader.

While most general books in English on Cervantes contain some discussion of his drama, the best analysis is in Spanish: Joaquín Casalduero, *Sentido y forma del teatro de Cervantes* (rev. ed., 1966). —B. W.

Césaire, Aimé (1913–   ). Martinique-born French poet and playwright. As a poet, Aimé Césaire remains close to the experience of SURREALISM. *Et Les Chiens se taisaient* ("And the Dogs Were Silent," pub. 1956) is a long dramatic poem in which the fate of a single individual coincides with the destiny of a community or race. It is almost a call to the Negro islanders to take up arms against the white colonialists. The play *La Tragédie du roi Christophe* ("The Tragedy of King Christophe," 1964), produced at the Venice festival in 1964 by J. M. Serreau and performed a few times at the Théâtre de France in 1965, is about the king of Haiti, Christophe, who, between 1811 and 1820, lived through the experience of decolonization. In this drama Césaire is very concerned with the temptations besetting the Africans after the white colonials leave: the traps of tyranny, magical rites, and intolerance. In a word, it is on the difficulty of recovering human dignity after centuries of slavery.

In 1966 Césaire published a new play, *Une Saison au Congo* ("A Season in the Congo"), about Lumumba, the martyred hero of the Congolese struggle for freedom. Produced by the Théâtre de l'Est Parisien in 1967, this play, far more than a biography, is a moving, lyrical commentary on African conscience.

For a critical study of Césaire, consult Helmut Hatzfeld, *Trends and Styles in Twentieth-Century French Literature* (1966).—W. F.

Chairs, The (Les Chaises, 1952). A tragic farce by Eugène IONESCO. In this ingenious play Ionesco's obsessive theme of the husband and wife is fully developed. They are the only characters and the setting is a bare, circular room at the top of a tower that is surrounded by water at its base. After a long life of emptiness and mediocrity, the husband and wife, Le Vieux and La Vieille, attempt to justify their failure. They stage an imaginary reception for a large number of guests who come to hear a speech by the old man. They arrange the chairs, seat the invisible guests, talk with them, and revive memories, dreams, and mistakes. In her need to admire and protect her husband, the woman wishes above all to express maternal tenderness, and the man is determined to play the part of a misunderstood intellectual who has had a great message for the world, a message of freedom. These two characters are not deceived by the sinister game they are playing, and when it becomes too complicated and burdensome to continue, they jump out the window into the water below.

The Chairs has been translated by Donald M. Allen in *Three Plays* (1958).—W. F.

Changeling, The (1622). A tragedy by Thomas MIDDLETON and William ROWLEY. Middleton is generally thought to be the author of the chief plot of the play, Rowley of the comic subplot. The main story concerns the unholy alliance between Beatrice Joanna and the villainous De Flores, obsessed by his desire for her. Beatrice commissions De Flores to murder her intended husband, in return for which he demands possession of her body. Although she considers him loathsome, she capitulates, thus involving herself in an inextricable web of intrigue that eventually exposes the two of them. The subplot concerns the efforts of two young gentlemen to seduce the beautiful wife of an aged and jealous doctor who runs an institution for the insane. They disguise themselves as madmen in order to become patients in the institution, thereby hoping to gain access to the wife. Here, also, there is a servant who attempts to blackmail his mistress, but the dilemma is resolved comically. The power of the play derives primarily from the intensity with which it reveals the evil lying at the heart of its two main characters. Beatrice is utterly transformed from a spoiled, capricious child into a hardened villainess. De Flores remains unchanged, ruthless, cynical, and unrepentant. Their moral degeneracy, however, is more than offset by their formidable dramatic stature. The tone of the play is marked by the tight restraint of its language, understated but remarkably effective. The subplot, in its bizarrely comic mirroring of the main theme, reinforces and intensifies the impact of the play.—E. Q.

Chapman,   George (1559?–1634). English playwright, poet, and translator. A handsome engraving of Chapman on the title page of his translation of *The Whole Works of Homer,* published in 1616, includes an inscription around its borders that tells us that he was fifty-seven years old at that time, making his date of birth 1559 or 1560. We also know that he was born in Hitchin, Hertfordshire, but otherwise his early life is obscure. Nothing is known of his family or his early education. His considerable classical learning might indicate that he had attended

GEORGE CHAPMAN (NEW YORK PUBLIC LIBRARY)

a university, but no record of his presence at either Oxford or Cambridge has survived. In his time he was known chiefly for his translation of Homer, an enterprise to which he devoted many years, publishing the first seven books of *The Iliad* in 1598 and the complete works in 1616. There is some reason to believe that he served as a soldier in the Low Countries sometime before 1594, when his earliest known composition, a long and somewhat obscure poem in two parts called *The Shadow of Night,* was published in London. A second volume of poems, called *Ovid's Banquet of Sense,* appeared in 1595, and in 1596 he dedicated *De Guiana, Carmen Epicum* to Sir Walter Raleigh. At around this time he seems to have become involved with the theater, for we know from Philip Henslowe's diary that he was writing plays for the acting company the Lord Admiral's Men by 1596. During his long career he also wrote comedies and tragedies for the stage, both alone and in collaboration with Ben Jonson, James Shirley, and Richard Brome, of which a considerable number have survived.

The dedicatory epistles of Chapman's volumes of poetry and the subject matter of some of his poems have served to connect him with a group of intellectuals sometimes called "the school of night." This group was associated with Sir Walter Raleigh, who may have been the first of Chapman's various patrons. Although evidence for the existence of a formal organization is extremely tenuous, the group, which included the earls of Derby and Northumberland, Matthew Royden, Thomas Harriott, and Christopher Marlowe, supposedly involved men of similar intellectual concerns who were acquainted with one another. That Chapman knew these men and was influenced by them seems certain. Most important probably was the influence of Marlowe, who seems to have had a considerable effect upon the direction Chapman was to take as a dramatist and whose poem *Hero and Leander* Chapman completed after Marlowe's death and published in 1598.

Chapman's career was marked by poverty and constant struggle against debt that often involved him in legal litigation, the most extensive being a long and involved chancery suit that lasted from 1617 to 1622. Earlier, in 1603, he was obliged to give evidence in chancery with regard to his play *The Old Joiner of Aldgate* (now lost), which the rejected suitor of an heiress paid him to write in order to ridicule the behavior of her father in his various negotiations with prospective sons-in-law. He was imprisoned along with John Marston and Ben Jonson in 1605 when *Eastward Ho,* an excellent comedy on which they had collaborated, offended King James I. And in 1608 he was in trouble again when his *Byron* plays gave offense to the French ambassador, although this time he escaped imprisonment. He also seems to have been exceedingly unfortunate in his choice of patrons, starting with Raleigh, who was imprisoned and sentenced to death in 1603, and ending with the earl of Somerset, who was tried for murder in 1615. His last days appear to have been spent in poverty and gloom. He quarreled with his old friend Ben Jonson, supposedly because of Jonson's criticism of his Homeric translations. He died in May 1634 and was buried in the churchyard of St. Giles in the Fields, London, where a monument designed by his friend, the architect Inigo Jones, was erected.

Chapman's earliest known play is *The Blind Beggar of Alexandria,* acted at the Rose Theatre by the Lord Admiral's Men in February 1596. It is a kind of hybrid tragicomedy in which a disguised ruler manipulates a whole series of episodes by rapidly changing disguises. In *An Humorous Day's Mirth* (1597), he pioneered in the "comedy of humours," using a single character to manipulate and control three situations, each of which is dominated by the "humour" of suspicion or jealousy. He also portrayed the humours of the melancholy scholar and the gull. The humour of the scholar he exploited again in *Sir Giles Goosecap* (written 1601–1603). As might be expected, Chapman was profoundly influenced by neoclassical critical theory as well as by classical models. But his comedies, although they subject the follies of mankind to derision, do not carry so great a burden of moral instruction as do his tragedies. Often he was concerned with re-creating Plautine and Terentian situations in modern setting, as in *All Fools* (1604), one of the best of his comedies, based upon two plays of Terence. Here, as in his *May Day* (c. 1609), translated from the Italian *comedia erudita* of Alessandro Piccolomini, we have the cheerful but unrelenting gulling of the foolish. Sometimes, as in *The Gentleman Usher* (1602?) and *Monsieur d'Olive* (1604), Chapman uses tragicomedy as a vehicle for his own philosophical preoccupation, and in *The Widow's Tears* (written 1603–1609), probably Chapman's bitterest and most profound exercise of this kind, there is a searching examination of the hollowness of all human pretensions. The comedies of Chapman that have survived cover a vast range, from the lighthearted and jocular to the deeply moving and pessimistic.

Although Francis Meres had referred to Chapman as a writer of tragedy in his *Palladis Tamia* of 1598, the earliest of his tragedies that has come down to us is his greatest and most widely celebrated: BUSSY D'AMBOIS. Of uncertain date, it was almost certainly acted after the accession of James I, probably in 1604. It took its subject matter from the career of a hero of fairly recent French history, and although there has been considerable dispute among scholars as to the precise meaning of the play, it is clear that Chapman shaped his story to give expression to his own philosophical concerns. In the Preface to a sequel, *The Revenge of Bussy D'Ambois,* performed by the Children of the Queen's Revels sometime between 1609 and 1612, Chapman gave his own definition of tragedy:

> Poor envious souls they are that cavil at truth's want in these natural fictions; material instruction, elegant and sententious excitation to virtue, and deflection from her contrary, being the soul, limbs and limits of an authentical tragedy.

This moral concern is evident in all of his tragedies. In *Bussy D'Ambois* he depicted the plight of the Herculean hero in a corrupt society; in *The Revenge* he explored the implications of stoicism in the face of evil; in his two-part play *The Conspiracy and Tragedy of Charles Duke of Byron* (1608), he turned again to French history to depict the fall of an heroic spirit; and in *Caesar and Pompey* (c. 1613), he was concerned with Cato of Utica, the greatest of the classical exemplars of Stoicism. His final play seems to have been *The Tragedy of Chabot, Admiral of France,* a first version of which must have been completed around 1613, although the text that has come down to us is one that was later revised by James Shirley. Here again Chapman turned to the recent history of France to present perhaps the most probing exploration of the meaning of human justice in the entire Jacobean drama. In all of Chapman's tragedies, varied in form and method as they may be, we witness the destruction of isolated and heroic man. His greatness may be in heroic vitality as in Bussy and Byron, in greatness of mind as in Cato, or in a profound sense of inner virtue as in Chabot, but always Chapman is concerned with alienated man destroyed by a world of lesser beings of whom he can never be a part.

The standard edition of Chapman's plays, *The Plays of George Chapman,* edited by Thomas Marc Parrott, is in two volumes: *The Tragedies* (1910, reprinted 1961); *The Comedies* (1914, reprinted 1961). For editions of his poetry, see Phyllis B. Bartlett, *The Poems* (1941), and Allardyce Nicoll, *Chapman's Homer* (2 vols., 1956), Bollingen Series XLI. The most comprehensive treatment of Chapman's life and work is by Jean Jacquot, *George Chapman, sa vie, son poesie, son théâtre, sa pensée* (1951). Other important studies include Paul V. Kreider, *Elizabethan Comic Character Conventions as Revealed in the Comedies of George Chapman* (1935); Millar MacLure, *George Chapman: A Critical Study* (1966); Marcello Pagnini, *Forme e motivi nella poesie e nelle tragedie di George Chapman* (1958); Ennis Rees, *The Tragedies of George Chapman, Renaissance Ethics in Action* (1954); E. M. Waith, *The Herculean Hero in Marlowe, Chapman, Shakespeare and Dryden* (1962); and J. W. Wieler, *George Chapman—The Effect of Stoicism upon His Tragedies* (1949).—I. R.

Chekhov, Anton [Pavlovich] (1860–1904). Russian short-story writer and playwright. The son of a small-town grocer from Taganrog on the Sea of Azov, Chekhov started writing to pay for his medical education. Later, however, the means became an end in itself and instead of practicing medicine, he continued writing short stories and plays and became, in the opinion of many, the world's foremost short-story writer and Russia's greatest playwright.

Chekhov's first efforts at playwriting date from the early 1880's, when he produced several one-act comedies strongly influenced by Nikolai Gogol's farces. These comedies include two monologues: the farcical lecture *O vrede tabaka* (*The Harmfulness of Tobacco,* 1886) and the pathetic *Lebedinaya pesnya* (*Swan Song,* 1886), in which in a play-within-a-play an old provincial actor holds forth on his grim existence to empty theater seats. Some of the one-act comedies are very funny and are often performed to this day. The best are *Svadba* (*The Wedding,* 1889), *Yubilei* (*The Jubilee,* 1891), *Predlozhenie* (*The Marriage Proposal,* 1888), *Medved* (*The Bear,* 1888), and *Tragik ponevole* (*The Tragedian in Spite of Himself,* 1889).

Chekhov's first major play, IVANOV, was produced in 1887 and was followed by THE SEA GULL, UNCLE VANYA, THE THREE SISTERS, and his last work, THE CHERRY ORCHARD.

Chekhov was acclaimed as a great dramatic innovator and he had considerable influence both in Russia and abroad. Many critics, Russian and foreign, have tried to pinpoint Chekhov's unique ability as a playwright. His plays, it has been said, have no plots, no dramatic climaxes, and what little action there is occurs offstage; his characters, instead of talking to one another, deliver a series of parallel monologues reflecting their individual dreams, aspirations, and delusions. Chekhov, it is often repeated, is a "realist," a "psychological realist," and "a master of understatement."

While Chekhov did exert some influence on the playwrights who came after him, his uniqueness does not seem to lie in the above points. Some of these points and terms are debatable in themselves. In the first place, his plays do tell a story, although the plot is not traced with a simple neat India-ink line, but is rather loosely drawn, like a charcoal sketch. How carefully Chekhov plotted and composed his plays can be gauged by his famous piece of advice to a beginning playwright: "If a gun is hanging on the wall in the first act, it must fire in the last." And although the fighting, dying, and violent wooing do, as a rule, take place offstage, this offstage device has been used by innumerable playwrights, including Shakespeare.

Chekhov's realism—psychological or otherwise (meaning probably that he showed people "as they are" in "all the grayness of their everyday life")—could as easily be called symbolism or impressionism, because of his use of symbols and sound effects, which was exploited to the utmost by the Moscow Art Theater. And as to the assertion that Chekhov is a master of understatement, this remark must be based on the fact that the inner voices of his characters tend to drown out the words of their interlocutors, resulting in a breakdown of communications. It is true, therefore, that Chekhov does not make his point explicitly through the words of his characters. However, this

ANTON CHEKHOV (THEATRE COLLECTION, NEW YORK
PUBLIC LIBRARY AT LINCOLN CENTER)

technique is not so much understatement as it is the *implicit* expression of the author's point, which, perhaps, is the measure of his artistry. As to Chekhov's characters themselves, their moaning and groaning is so overstated that, to the spectator, assertions about understatement may seem quite absurd. Indeed, while the sighs, tears, and exclamations of Chekhov's characters are often accepted by foreigners as a charming Russian feature, many Russians wince and feel acutely embarrassed at performances of Chekhov's plays, especially foreign productions in translation in which the emotional outbursts are further amplified by too literal a rendering.

It is something much less obvious, much more subtle, that makes Chekhov a great dramatist. It is his deep sense of tragic human destiny (not just the special doom hanging over the Russian gentry before the impending revolution), conveyed by the hopeless stutterings and mumblings of its victims, in a masterfully created atmosphere of futility and stagnation which, nevertheless, is charged with lyricism as heavy gray air is charged with electricity.

Curiously, immediately after the 1917 revolution, Chekhov's plays were discarded as unsuitable for performance in a proletarian society. After a few years, however, the Bolsheviks decided to accept him as a "critical realist" (almost any writer who had criticized the preceding tsarist regime) and interpreted him as one of the prophets of the revolution.

Among the biographical and critical assessments of Chekhov may be mentioned Ernest J. Simmons' *Chekhov: A Biography* (1962) and David Magarshak's *Chekhov the Dramatist* (1960).—A. MacA.

Cherry Orchard, The (*Vishnevyi sad*, 1904). A comedy in four acts by Anton CHEKHOV. Lyubov Ranevskaya and her daughter Anya return after five years in France to their heavily mortgaged estate. It is May and the cherry orchard is in bloom, but they are told that in August the orchard must be sold to pay the interest. Lopakhin, a self-made local man, suggests that they cut down the orchard, tear down the old family house and the other buildings, divide the estate up into lots, and rent them to summer vacationers. Mme. Ranevskaya, her brother Gaev, and her daughters Anya and Varya indignantly reject such a solution. Gaev decides to try to raise the money by some other means. Nothing is done, however, and the estate is sold at auction. The surprise buyer and new owner is Lopakhin, who will now carry out his scheme of cutting down the orchard and dividing the estate into lots for rental. In the end Mme. Ranevskaya, Anya, and Gaev are moving out, and, as Lopakhin somehow fails to propose to Varya as he was supposed to, she also leaves to become a governess. In the final scene Firs, the ancient butler who sighs for "the good old days of serfdom," dies as the sound of the ax felling the cherry trees can be heard offstage.

This play, which Chekhov calls a comedy and which many consider his masterpiece, is generally interpreted as a picture of the delicate and nostalgic moods of Russian landowners sighing over the passing era of graceful living, symbolized by the cherry orchard about to be cut down by a practical, unrefined "new man." Indeed, such a narrow social interpretation made one authority, D. Sviatopolk-Mirsky, predict that Chekhov's plays would soon lose their interest because they reflected a specific social situation that was gone forever and could no longer move anyone, either in Soviet Russia or abroad. Since Chekhov's plays are still performed, however, both in the Soviet Union and the West, it would seem that their themes are more general and permanent. Besides, it is probable that Chekhov never really intended to say what, to this day, he is supposed to have said. Thus, Mme. Ranevskaya and Gaev are by no means elegant vestiges of a refined past. Gaev is a sentimental, slobbery old bore ("Here we go again, please, uncle, the best thing you can do is to keep your mouth closed," he is constantly reminded) and Mme. Ranevskaya is an enamored old hussy who is really more concerned with rushing off to her wicked gigolo in Paris than preserving her family estate. Indeed, all the members of the impoverished family seem relieved when the estate is finally sold and they are all quite happy to leave, including the seventeen-year-old Anya, who is in love with a young, eternal student. The man who most regrets losing the past is the old flunky Firs, for whom things have never been the same since the accursed year of 1861, the year of the emancipation of the serfs. Chekhov certainly felt no nostalgia for the institution of serfdom and, despite the sentimentalism typical of the period and the great amount of weeping, kissing, and embracing that takes place in this play, it was not an accident that he chose to describe it as a comedy. Indeed, what makes *The Cherry Orchard* still a classic today is Chekhov's extraordinary knack for breathing warm life into a set of characters, whatever the intrinsic value of their preoccupations.

The Cherry Orchard by Anton Chekhov has been translated by Constance Garnett in *Great Russian Plays* (1960).—A. MacA.

Chester Plays, The (c. 1375). A Corpus Christi cycle of twenty-five scriptural plays of unknown authorship. The text (running to over 11,000 lines of verse) is found in five manuscripts, preserved in the Bodleian Library, the Huntington Library, and the British Museum. There are also extant a number of manuscripts containing fragments. F. M. Salter's date of c. 1375 for original composition of the cycle challenges the date of c. 1325 maintained by earlier scholars. Chester was produced during three successive days on pageant wagons proceeding successively from stop to stop throughout the city. Plays 1 through 9 were performed on the first day, Plays 10 through 18 on the second, and Plays 19 through 25 on the third. Probably, an earlier version of the cycle had been produced in accordance with the Place-and-scaffold method—rather than at a series of stops.

The Chester Cycle consists of the following plays (elements absent from the York, Wakefield and N-Town Cycles are starred).

From narratives of the Old Testament:
    (1) Fall of Lucifer
    (2) Creation, Fall of Man, Cain and Abel
    (3) Noah and His Wife, the Flood
    (4) * Lot, * Melchisedek, * Order of Circumcision, Abraham and Isaac
    (5) Moses (Ten Commandments), * Balak, Balaam, the Ass, and Prophets.
From narratives of the Nativity:
    (6) Annunciation, Visit to Elizabeth, Suspicions of Joseph about Mary, * Caesar Octavian and the Sibyl, Birth of Christ
    (7) Adoration of the Shepherds
    (8) Coming of the Magi, Herod
    (9) Adoration of the Magi
    (10) Flight into Egypt, Slaughter of the Innocents, * Death of Herod's Son, Death of Herod
    (11) Purification of the Virgin; Christ and the Doctors.
From narratives of the Public Ministry:
    (12) Temptation, Woman Taken in Adultery
    (13) * Healing of the Blind Chelidonius, * Attempt to Stone Christ, Raising of Lazarus
    (14a) Entry into Jerusalem, * Cleansing of the Temple.
From narratives of the Passion:
    (14b) Conspiracy of the Jews with Judas
    (15) Last Supper, Betrayal
    (16) Trial before Caiaphas (the Buffeting), Peter's Denial
    (17) Procession to Calvary, Casting of Lots, Crucifixion, Longinus, Joseph of Arimathea.
From narratives of the Resurrection and Doomsday:
    (18) Harrowing of Hell, * Arrival of the Virtuous Damned in Paradise, * Alewife
    (19) Guarding of the Sepulcher, Resurrection, Compact of Pilate with the Soldiers, Marys at the Sepulcher, Appearance to Magdalen, * Appearance to Mary Salome, Mary Jacobi, and Peter
    (20) Pilgrims to Emmaus, Doubting Thomas
    (21) Ascension
    (22) Choice of Matthias, Descent of the Holy Spirit (Pentecost), * Institution of the Apostles' Creed
    (23) * Prophets of Antichrist, * Signs of Judgment
    (24) * Coming of Antichrist
    (25) Last Judgment.

Chester differs from the other three English scriptural cycles in treating the apocryphal legend of the Antichrist and in omitting the Baptism of Christ and the Death of Judas. It is the oldest and simplest of the four cycles, relatively serious in tone, and peculiarly concerned (through Expositor and other choral characters) with religious formularies such as the Apostles' Creed. It is also unusual in having a few speeches in French. The relatively small number of plays in the cycle results from the relatively greater length and complexity of individual plays. Records indicate that the cycle once included a play of the Assumption of the Virgin performed by "the worshipful Wives of this City." Chester begins with a set of banns describing the cycle to a prospective audience.

Part One of *The Chester Plays*, Plays 1–13, has been edited by H. Deimling, Early English Text Society, Ext. Ser., No. LXII (1892); Part Two, Plays 13–25, has been edited by J. Matthews, Early English Text Society, Ext. Ser., No. CXV (1916). (In this edition, because of a peculiarity of the manuscript used as copy-text, Plays 19 and 20 of the synopsis given above appear as Play 19, Plays 21 to 25 accordingly as Plays 20 to 24.) For a critical study, see F. M. Salter, *Mediaeval Drama in Chester* (1955). —R. H.

Chettle, Henry (c. 1560–c. 1607). English playwright. Chettle began his career as a printer and editor. In the latter capacity he edited Robert Greene's deathbed repentance pamphlet *Greene's Groats-worth of Wit* (1592), containing the famous attack upon Shakespeare as "an upstart crow beautified with our own feathers." Chettle apologized for the attack in the epistle to his *Kind Heart's Dream*, published a few months later in 1593.

By 1598 Chettle had become associated with the stage as a playwright for the producer Philip Henslowe. Most of the forty-eight plays on which he worked were collaborative efforts commissioned by Henslowe and few of them have survived. The only extant play attributed solely to him is *The Tragedy of Hoffman* (c. 1602), a revenge tragedy. The action focuses on the career of Hoffman, who, motivated by the desire to avenge the death of his father, engages in a series of diabolical plots against the family of the duke of Luneberg. The play is crowded with lurid incidents of torture, murder, and lust. Nevertheless, it frequently reveals a powerful theatrical effectiveness, and its avenging villain-hero anticipates the more successful presentation of the type in *The Revenger's Tragedy*.

Among the plays written by Chettle in collaboration are *The Death of Robert Earl of Huntington* (1598), written with Anthony Munday; *Patient Grissill* (1600), written with Thomas Dekker and William Haughton; and *The Blind-Beggar of Bednal-Green* (1600), written with John Day.

A facsimile edition of *Hoffman* was edited by J. S. Farmer as a volume in the series *Old English Plays: Students' Facsimile Edition* (1914). The best critical and biographical treatment of Chettle is Harold Jenkins' *The Life and Work of Henry Chettle* (1934). —E. Q.

Chiarelli, Luigi. See LA MASCHERA E IL VOLTO.

Chikamatsu Monzaemon (1653–1725). Japanese playwright, known simply as Chikamatsu. Chikamatsu is the chief of his country's dramatists to flourish after the creative period of the *noh* plays three centuries before him. From the earlier drama he inherited a few important conventions, such as the stage journey (*michiyuki*) and the traditions of musical accompaniment and intermittent offstage commentary, but in general he established drama on a thoroughly new basis, reaching out to new forms and invariably altering whatever he borrowed from the old. He is today granted a place among the world's leading playwrights.

Chikamatsu was born in the province of Echizen, his father being of a minor samurai family, the Sugimori. He wrote of himself: "I was born into a hereditary family of samurai but left the martial profession. I served in personal attendance on the nobility but never obtained the least court rank. I drifted in the market place but learned nothing of trade." Behind these deprecating comments may lie the explanation of his firsthand acquaintance with the different ranks of Japanese society. His breadth of outlook upon Japan was to become comparable with Shakespeare's comprehensive outlook on England or Molière's on France.

Chikamatsu's first published work is in the favorite form for the Japanese short poem, the *haiku*. During the decade following 1684 he wrote many plays for the KABUKI theater, the chief form of theater popular at the time. Nevertheless, throughout his entire career he wrote for the puppet theater (see BUNRAKU) and it is by his work in this field that his fame was established. Hand puppets had long been known in Japan and comparatively crude plays written for them. During Chikamatsu's lifetime and in large part through his own efforts and those of the great *jōruri*, or chanters, these plays became the chief literary drama of Japan. Gradually, however, the theater with live actors gained the ascendancy in popular favor. Chikamatsu's major plays for the puppet theater were commonly rewritten for the kabuki during the nineteenth century. The original texts were at all times cherished as literature and are today viewed with the highest esteem. Yet they are seldom performed as written, either by puppets or live actors. Chikamatsu's role in the history of drama is, accordingly, a peculiar one. Although differences in playwriting between Chikamatsu's puppet plays and works for live actors may seem to the reader surprisingly slight, they were in practice sufficiently formidable to relegate his works to a category of their own.

The first play that can unquestionably be established as his is *The Soga Successors* (*Yotsugi Soga,* written 1683), written for the chanter Uji Kaga-no-jo. It is in no respect an outstanding work. In 1685, however, he wrote for the celebrated chanter in Takemoto Gidayu's theater the heroic drama *Kagekiyo Victorious* (*Shusse Kagekiyo,* written 1685), described by the American scholar Donald Keene as "so important a work that it is considered the first 'new' puppet play." From this time on, Chikamatsu's work in the field of puppet drama unquestionably possessed serious literary value. It is significant that at about this time the playwright moved from his family home at Kyoto to Osaka, which had recently become the chief center for the puppet stage.

His plays fall into two clearly marked groups: the heroic or quasi-historical plays, such as THE BATTLES OF COXINGA, and the "domestic" plays, such as *The Love Suicides at Sonezaki* (*Sonezaki Shinyū,* 1703). The historical dramas are loosely constructed presen-

CHIKAMATSU (COLLECTION OF TAKANO MASAMI, TOKYO, COURTESY COLUMBIA UNIVERSITY PRESS)

tations of idealized episodes drawn from the chronicles of Japan. The scene occasionally shifts from Japan to a foreign land, such as China or Formosa, but never departs in essential character from an idealized representation of feudal life with its thoroughly romantic code of values. Such plays abound in military pageantry and interventions of the supernatural. The imagination is vigorous and occasionally the writing has high poetic value, but as a rule these works appear to modern taste as meretricious and extravagant, both in their images and emotional tone. Their ethical content, also, is restricted to a code long outmoded even in Japan itself.

The contrary holds true for most of the so-called domestic plays. These have small commerce with the manners and actions of the Japanese aristocracy but give a remarkably naturalistic picture of the middle classes and even of the lower orders in Japanese society as it was at the close of the seventeenth and the early years of the eighteenth centuries. The samurai, or warrior class, is represented only by its minor figures. More conspicuous are the tradesmen and average citizens of the fast-growing mercantile towns. Many scenes are laid in the quarter of the courtesans or prostitutes, where the theaters themselves flourished, along with the arts giving Japanese life its peculiar elegance—music, dance, colorful costume, and the crafts of decoration. Several of the plays depict scenes of holiday rejoicing, festivals, and religious pilgrimages that instead seem rather to be excursions for secular entertainment.

Against this lively background are depicted the precarious and, as a rule, unhappy adventures of young lovers and families torn asunder by passionate encounters. Actions that depend on money transactions occur in the larger number of the plays. Thus a rich but disagreeable lover wishes to "ransom" a courtesan from her contract at a house of pleasure at the same time that she has fallen deeply in love with an impecunious and weak-willed tradesman. The hero of the domestic plays is usually drawn with the most unheroic qualities imaginable, partly in defiance of samurai standards. His infatuation ruins his business and destroys his honor. When he cannot repay, he borrows or deliberately steals to effect his ends. His family is deserted. Devotion on the part of his loyal wife fails to reclaim him. Driven into a desperate impasse, the two lovers escape from their entanglements only by hastening at night to some appropriate scene in the country outside the city limits where together they commit suicide. Plays on this theme became so popular that in 1722 the government banned all with the term "love suicides" in the title. Actual suicides of lovers had become prevalent and are, indeed, still surprisingly frequent in Japan.

THE LOVE SUICIDES AT AMIJIMA is the most celebrated of Chikamatsu's plays in this category. Other domestic dramas of exceptional power are *The Woman-Killer and the Hell of Oil* (*Onnagoroshi Abura Jigoku,* 1721), *The Uprooted Pine* (*Nebiki no Kabumatsu,* 1718), and *The Courier for Hell* (*Meidono Hikyatu,* 1711). Especially notable for Chikamatsu's skill in suggesting the bustle of crowds are the early scenes in *The Woman-Killer and the Hell of Oil,* and *Yosaku from Tamba* (*Tamba Yosaka,* 1708). Brilliant in their picture of wives tempted to illicit relations during the absence of their husbands are *Gonza the Lancer* (*Yari no Gonza,* 1706) and *The Drum of the Waves of Horikawa* (*Horikawa Nami no Tsuzumi,* 1706).

Japanese concepts of honor (*giri*) notwithstanding, many actions in the plays and repeated outbreaks of violent weeping raise obstacles to cordial appreciation by readers outside Japan and removed from the Japanese traditions of feudal obligations and fanatical patriotism. The ideals often appear strained, the expressions of emotion lachrymose. The sacrifices seem unreal; the pathos, a species of self-pity. The union of noble courtesan and ignoble hero may seem uninspiring or unconvincing. Yet Chikamatsu's art, both in poetic speech and dramatic gesture, is highly perfected and the presentation of human nature proves on the whole to be masterly and warm. Although at times episodes come close to the banalities of melodrama and its gratuitous violence, a high level of seriousness and poetic imagination is generally attained. The virtuosity and violence that the plays indisputably possess have not as yet sunk into the dubious extravagance later to mar the kabuki stage, which owed much of its initial impetus to Chikamatsu's puppet plays.

Chikamatsu's writing is an extraordinary mixture of sensational journalism and highly conscious, sophisticated art. Several plays dramatize crimes that occurred barely a month before the work was staged. Yet the stylistic elaborations, often taking the form of puns and various plays on words, are truly ingenious. Emotions that appear primitive are expressed in an art verging on preciosity or even decadence and an extreme of aestheticism. Much of Chikamatsu's ambivalence is explained by the audience for which he wrote. The aristocratic culture voiced three hundred years earlier in the noh plays was losing its force; the clichés of the period synchronous in Japan with Victorianism in England had not as yet become dominant. The audience was prevailingly middle class but still inspired with much of the aesthetic culture of an earlier age. It was a less diversified audience than Shakespeare's, although in many ways the two are comparable. It discouraged work of the highest finesse at the same time that it relished work of substantial artistic force. Chikamatsu has been facilely compared with Shakespeare. Possibly he is closer to such a baroque dramatist as Marlowe or to such a spokesman for middle-class London life as Thomas Dekker. His *Kagekiyo Victorious* may be likened to Marlowe's *Tamburlaine,* his *Love Suicides at Amijima* to Dekker's *The Honest Whore.*

Donald Keene's *The Major Plays of Chikamatsu* (1961) is a masterpiece of translation. The Introduction supplies by far the best account in English of the dramatist's life and art.—H. W. W.

Children of Heracles, The (Herakleidai, date uncertain). A tragedy by EURIPIDES. The children of the dead hero Heracles, together with his mother, Alcmene, and his nephew and former companion, Iolaus, have come to the Athenian town of Marathon seeking refuge from Heracles' old enemy Eurystheus, king of Argos. Heracles' former allies have been powerless to help them, but Demophon, king of Athens, grants them asylum. Eurystheus' arrogant herald, Copreus, tries to make them leave their haven so that they can be executed. Failing, he goes off threatening war. An oracle says that only the sacrifice of a noble maiden will give the Athenians victory in the ensuing struggle. Macaria, a daughter of Heracles, goes willingly to her death. Heracles' son Hyllus unexpectedly brings reinforcements. Old Iolaus, suddenly rejuvenated in battle, captures Eurystheus. Alcmene insists that the prisoner must be killed, though this is contrary to Athenian custom.

The Children of Heracles is clearly a patriotic play. The glorification of Athens is the main theme, though there is an ironic twist when the Athenians finally acquiesce in the killing of a prisoner. There are some good dramatic scenes—that with the herald, the Macaria scene, the confrontation of Alcmene and Eurystheus—but as a whole the play is disappointing. Although the Chorus' odes are relevant to the action throughout, they are undistinguished. There are a good many abrupt shifts: the brave, even noble, conduct of Eurystheus is unexpected, and the rejuvenation miracle is the more incredible because we have just seen Iolaus comically tottering off to war. One feels that the play was hastily composed for some occasion, yet the topical references are as obscure as the date is uncertain.

Translations of the play are listed under Euripides. —G. M. A. G.

children's drama. Until the twentieth century, playwrights seldom wrote for juvenile audiences, even though youngsters from the Greeks onward regularly attended theatrical performances. In the middle ages children helped in the preparation of plays associated with Christmas, Easter, and other religious holidays. Nativity plays, then as now, introduced countless children to drama both as spectators and participants. Sometime between 1553 and 1558 the first known play expressly intended for youngsters was written by an anonymous dramatist; *A New Interlude for Children to Play, Named Jack Juggler, both Witty and Very Pleasant* mixes classic and native elements, taking for its basic structure a Plautine farce of mistaken identity and adding characters of the English countryside.

As early as 1903, The Children's Educational

Theatre established its programs in New York City, offering five seasons of plays. Under the direction of Alice Minnie Herts Heniger, this theater played to thousands of city children, many of whom were immigrants confined to ghettos with only the culture of the streets available to them. Financial problems brought on by an ordinance forbidding Sunday performances ended this endeavor which, however short-lived, proved the worth of professional theater for children. Also at this time, the American writer John Jay Chapman (1862–1933) turned his attention to children's drama in several volumes of plays published in 1908 and 1911. Today, these moralistic dramas prove of interest largely for the information they reveal about the author during a particularly troubled time of his life and as examples of an oddly pious concept of children's literature that is now totally out of fashion.

Peter Pan, by J. M. Barrie (1860–1937), the play seen in England and America by more children than any other in this century, first took flight in 1904 and has been revived regularly ever since, in stage, film, and television versions. A fantasy celebrating youth, this modern classic tells of the adventures of the Darling children in the Never-Never-Land home of Peter Pan, a boy who refuses to grow up. After encounters with Indians, pirates, a crocodile, and the menacing villain Captain Hook, the children return to their parents and former life, leaving Peter to go on forever as the epitome of boyhood. In one famous passage, Peter enlists the aid of the audience to save the life of his friend, the fairy Tinker Bell, by clapping their hands if they believe in fairies. Leonard Bernstein contributed music to the 1950 revival; Jule Styne, assisted by five others, created the score for the Mary Martin musical adaptation seen by millions on television. Barrie created other plays of sentiment and whimsy, but none comes close to rivaling *Peter Pan* in the affection of children. *The Little Minister,* based on his novel, became popular in 1897. His last play, the widely overlooked *The Boy David* (1936), is a poignant portrait of the biblical David, his slaying of Goliath, his musical soothing of Saul, and, finally, his visionary dreams of the future Israel.

George Bernard Shaw, looking back in his old age, said he had written *Androcles and the Lion* (1912) as an antidote to *Peter Pan,* in order, he insisted, "to show what a play for children should be like. It should never be childish; nothing offends children more than to play down to them . . . ." *Peter Pan* appeared to him to be "a sample of what adults think children like." The short two acts of *Androcles* require a jungle, the emperor's box at the Coliseum, and a Roman arena to tell, in Shavian terms, the ancient tale of a lasting friendship formed when a meek slave removes a thorn from the paw of a lion. To this plot Shaw adds his own invention, an examination of the principles of sainthood and martyrdom from the points of view of Androcles, his fellow Christians, and their Roman captors. In spite of its scenic demands, the play has been produced on several occasions for children, notably by the Glyndebourne Children's Theatre in the 1948 Edinburgh Festival, but it has never rivaled the steadfast popularity of *Peter Pan.*

The Belgian dramatist Maurice Maeterlinck, in his international triumph *The Blue Bird* (1908), fabri-

cated an allegorical fairy tale that appeared on the professional and amateur stages for several decades. In six acts, with a cast of over one hundred characters, the Hansel-and-Gretel protagonists, here called Tyltyl and Mytyl, seek the elusive Blue Bird of Happiness, journeying along the way to the Land of Memory, where they visit their dead grandparents, to the Palace of the Night, a graveyard, and The Kingdom of the Future. Preoccupied with themes of death, blatantly didactic, with characters bearing names such as Loving One's Parents and The Joy of Seeing What Is Beautiful, *The Blue Bird* now appears to be a dated curiosity, of interest for its extravagant theatricality and the impact it once made upon children who had not been exposed to the realism of television and films.

A large number of childhood classics were adapted for the stage and became commercial successes during the first decade of this century. The single year 1903, for example, offered elaborate productions of *The Wizard of Oz,* dramatized with lyrics by its original creator, L. Frank Baum; *The Little Princess,* an adaptation by Frances Hodgson Burnett of her book *Sara Crewes;* and *Mr. Pickwick,* a musical drawn from Charles Dickens' novel. Children's drama, by and large, continued in subsequent decades to take its inspiration from the library shelves rather than from original sources.

Until the late 1930's, when an active market was established for the publication of plays, few authors specialized in children's drama. One notable exception was the Englishman A. A. Milne (1882–1956), celebrated for his *Pooh* books for children. Milne dramatized Kenneth Grahame's *The Wind in the Willows* in a popular stage version entitled *Toad of Toad Hall* (1932). Milne's other plays for children include *Make-Believe* (1918) and the short romance *The Ugly Duckling* (1941), both widely produced in England and America.

Beginning in 1935 with her dramatization of *Jack and the Beanstalk,* Charlotte Chorpenning (1876–1955) wrote a series of over twenty full-length plays for children that were performed frequently for three decades. A former student in George Pierce Baker's famous 47 Workshop at Harvard, Mrs. Chorpenning directed student productions of her plays at the Goodman Memorial Theatre, an adjunct of Chicago's Art Institute. She recorded her experiences both as playwright and director in the fragmentary *Twenty-One Years with Children's Theatre* (1954). Her best-known plays are dramatizations of childhood classics: *The Emperor's New Clothes* (1938), *Cinderella* (1940), *The Sleeping Beauty* (1947), *King Midas and the Golden Touch* (1950), and *Many Moons* (1946), based on the James Thurber story. A contemporary American dramatist, Aurand Harris, has contributed a number of plays produced today by regional theaters for children: *Circus Day* (or *Circus in the Wind*) (1949), *Pinocchio and the Indians* (1950), *Simple Simon* (1953), and *Rags to Riches* (1966). *The Journey with Jonah* (1967), by Madeleine L'Engle, the prize-winning American writer of children's fiction, relates in poetic language the parable of the prophet Jonah and the whale. Unlike most plays for children, this one can be acted effectively by young people.

The Englishman Robert Bolt, author of the adult

A SCENE FROM *The Wizard of Oz*, DRAMATIZED BY ELIZABETH FULLER GOODSPEED FROM THE STORY BY L.
FRANK BAUM (ANTA COLLECTION, WALTER HAMPDEN MEMORIAL LIBRARY AT THE PLAYERS, NEW YORK)

play *A Man for All Seasons* (1960), wrote his play for children, *The Thwarting of Baron Bolligrew* (1965), at the invitation of the Royal Shakespeare Company, who have performed it in London during several Christmas seasons. The hero of this tongue-in-cheek adventure, Sir Oblong Fitz Oblong, is sent to the Bolligrew Islands to suppress the world's last known dragon, as well as to end the evil hold of Baron Bolligrew, an anachronistic but amusing villain. Vacillating between mock heroics and cartoon quips, Bolt was more interested in creating easy laughter than genuine suspense, yet his comedy has undeniable theatrical appeal and a robust cheer that speaks to today's youngsters, often in their own terms.

Thanks to the directorial talents of Natalia Satz, who developed the Moscow children's theater into one of the most important in the world, the Soviet Union has long been productive in the field of child drama. Yevgeny Schwartz (1897–1958), Soviet author and editor of books and plays for children, dramatized the juvenile stories *The Snow Queen* and *Little Red Riding Hood* before writing his fairy-tale fantasies *The Shadow* (1940) and *The Dragon* (1943). The seventy or more plays that comprise the repertory of Russia's thirty-six theaters for children may be divided into the following categories: fairy-tale plays for children between the ages of seven and twelve; histories, biographies, vaudeville comedies,

and dramatizations of popular books for ages twelve to fourteen; and plays for adolescents related to modern life and bearing titles such as *In Search of Joy* and *Good Luck*.

In the area of musical drama for children, Kurt Weill and Bertolt Brecht composed *Der Jasager* (*He Who Says Yes*) in 1930 as a school opera to be enacted entirely by students, with a score that calls for instruments and musical skills found in the average high school orchestra. Based on a Japanese *noh* play, *Der Jasager* tells the story of a pupil who sets forth with his teacher on a journey over high mountains in order to obtain medicine for his ailing mother. But along the way, the boy falls sick and soon is unable to continue; his fellow students recall an ancient custom that permits travelers to cast the indisposed, with their consent, into the valley. The student says "yes" and goes to his death. Seated on either side of the stage, a chorus explains the events of this forceful morality. Complying with German students who demanded an alternate version in which the hero says "no" to convention and thereby saves his life, Brecht offered *Der Neinsager* (*He Who Says No*), also in 1930. Brecht and Weill, collaborating with the German composer Paul Hindemith, wrote a radio play for children, *Der Flug der Lindberghs* (*The Flight of the Lindberghs*, 1929). Hindemith alone turned his attention to children in short pieces such as *Hin und*

Zurück (*Back and Forth,* 1927) and *Wir Bauen eine Stadt* (*We Build a City,* 1930). Benjamin Britten's *Let's Make an Opera* (1949) invites the children in the audience to participate in the creation of an opera about a little chimney sweep named Sam. In the United States *Young Abe Lincoln* (1961), a musical comedy for children pieced together by several people, became so popular Off-Broadway that it was moved to Broadway for a short run and thus inspired numerous other musicals, most of which are imitations of commercial successes in the adult theater.

American and European drama for children may be read in several anthologies. Stuart Walker edited his adaptations of the classics in *Portmanteau Plays* (1917) and *More Portmanteau Plays* (1919). Montrose Moses compiled three collections: *A Treasury of Plays for Children* (1921), *Another Treasury of Plays for Children* (1926), and *Ring Up the Curtain* (1932). A recent volume, *Twenty Plays for Young People* (1967), edited by William B. Birner, contains plays by Charlotte Chorpenning, Aurand Harris, and a number of European dramatists specializing in children's theater. Two doctoral dissertations deal significantly with the subject of writing plays for children: "The Evaluation of Plays for Children's Theatre in the United States" by Kenneth L. Graham (University of Utah, 1947); and "Five Plays: A Repertory of Children's Theatre to be Performed by and for Children" by Lowell S. Swortzell (New York University, 1963). Production of children's plays is discussed in *Theatre for Children* (1958) by Winifred Ward and *Children's Theatre* (1960) by Jed H. Davis and Mary Jane Watkins.—L. S. S.

Chile. See SPANISH AMERICA.

China. The Chinese theater as we know it is extremely diverse. Plays originating in the north differ from those produced by the south, the former being largely spectacular, the latter more poetic. Some are in the classical forms of the language, others employ the more popular dialects. Some are short farces, others are as long as full-length novels. There are plays primarily for dance, for music, for spectacle, and for poetry. Subjects range from military to civilian, historical to romantic, mythological to political. In the Yüan period the theater gained a wide and diversified audience, which it has ever since maintained (see YÜAN DRAMA). Even the farces and the most hilarious comedies show a considerable measure of nuance, yet there is no exclusive or strictly academic theater. Much as in Shakespeare's England, the best of the popular plays were performed at court, while most of the plays originating at court sooner or later reached popular audiences. Thus the Chinese theater is, sociologically speaking, one of the most democratic of all theaters. Moreover, the styles developed in the different provinces of China have in most instances been commanding enough to reach the stages of other sections as well. In spite of such diversity, the Chinese theater is singularly retentive of its traditions.

Until the Yüan dynasty (1280–1368), the records of the Chinese theater remain fragmentary. Although it is known that theatrical activity existed as early as the eighth century B.C., nothing definite or authoritative can be said about its nature. By the eighth century A.D. a school of the performing arts had been established by the Emperor MING HUANG at his luxurious and enlightened court at Chang-an (see PEAR GARDEN). To this day Ming Huang is honored by actors working in the traditional patterns as the patron of the Chinese theater. The nature of the productions at Chang-an is unclear, but presumably they emphasized dance and music rather than speech. Such plays as there were must have been dance-drama or a kind of opera rather than works of literary significance. The ceremonious modes of life in court encouraged spectacular productions, where strict stylization and aesthetic sophistication are most readily attained. Urban life and a middle class, which seem everywhere important for the development of a mature dramatic literature, were not yet firmly established. Nevertheless, a drama of such high literary merit as appears in the Yüan period must have had roots, however obscure they have become, in the preceding years.

Several conjectures have been advanced concerning this sensational rise of the Yüan drama. It has been proposed that the conquering Mongols under Kubla Khan and his successors sought to inform themselves regarding Chinese manners and language through the genial aid of theatrical productions. It has also been proposed that the Chinese literati, relieved of their official positions by the new regime, found an outlet for their literary skill in playwriting, thus making themselves useful to their new masters. Certainly, important changes in Chinese social life were at last favoring a more popular theater than had hitherto existed, providing an audience that extended well beyond the limits of the court. Plays were becoming civic rather than courtly commodities.

The chief problem the Yüan plays present their critics is the extraordinary elaborations of their technique even in the earliest specimens whose texts survive. The Chinese theater offers almost no "primitives." By the Yüan period it was already an art with a vast and intricate organism of laws, conventions, and rules. How this maturity in form came about, even in so advanced a civilization, is unknown, but it is unthinkable that such intricate patterns were developed from their genesis to their lavish proliferation within a single, relatively short-lived dynasty. The rise of this drama presents one of the more mysterious episodes in the history of civilization.

If the origins of the Yüan drama cannot be traced, at least its salient features may be described. First, we have its tenacity, for although in the course of the six or seven centuries since its rise it has undergone extensive transformations, it has also clung with Chinese conservatism to many long-established usages. Yüan drama and plays within the intervening centuries are still produced in styles by no means alien to those that must have obtained at the time of their origin. Second, and in contrast to Western attitudes, authorship, except in a few cases, must be treated lightly or ignored. The Chinese have viewed their drama with much enthusiasm but with relatively little curiosity regarding its authors. Texts are by no means sacred and are continually revised for new productions. As far as playwrights' biographies are concerned, tradition—at times imaginative—has sufficed where the West might have preferred scholarly precision. Almost all important plays have been assigned to authors, but since scholars have seldom felt inclined to scrutinize the playwrights' lives, few controversies have arisen over who wrote the plays, the Chinese putting into practice Shakespeare's words, "the play's the thing." As with all vigorous works of the imagination, the plays differ considerably from each other but fail to arrange themselves before us in terms of their creators. It must be considered part of their outstanding value that they remain the creations of the land and times from which they sprang.

Yüan drama always offered a large repertory of plays with which the public was already familiar. Any new play followed the old in subject and style; strictly speaking, there were few new plays—only occasional variations of the old. The plays are commonly divided into acts, at first generally four, but after the Yüan period, extending to fifty or sixty. (Farces, of which little need be said here, do not require act division.) Although the act is a firmly constructed unit, major plays are based on narratives that, despite their many episodes, generally provide a well-unified design. The ending is happy as a rule, though, despite a commonly held opinion to the contrary, not invariably so. Each act contains verse and prose, the verse being sung. As a rule, only one singer appears in any single act. All the lines in the lyrics of a single act have a single rhyme. This considerable importance of the act design facilitates the common

practice of giving acts rather than entire plays and of presenting parts of many plays during a single day's offering.

Each lyrical passage is sung in one of the many available musical modes. Instrumentalists accompany the play in all its parts, whether these are rendered in song, speech, or, as frequently, in mime. An enormous number of gestures and costume usages lie at the playwright's disposal. Every step, each bodily movement or vocal tone of the actor is studied and allocated appropriately to each moment of the performance. It is a learned style, acutely conscious of itself.

Type characters are well established, yet within the types surprising variety is attained. The playwriting takes in this regard a mean position between the manner of the *commedia dell'arte* and Shakespeare. In other words, types are always present, yet in conspicuous instances considerable individuation and characterization occurs. Especially in the pseudohistorical plays, individual figures are sharply drawn. There are even conventions to this effect. To the sedate yet witty master tactician, the heroic K'ung-meng, or, as he is sometimes called, Chu-ko-Liang, are assigned certain conventions in voice and costume allowed to no other role. His archantagonist, Ts'ao Ts'ao, is as no ordinary villain marked by his own peculiarities. Each of these characters appears in

SCENE FROM A CHINESE PLAY BY TANG HSIEN-TSU, SHOWING THE TYPICALLY ELABORATE COSTUMES AND SCENERY
(CHINESE INFORMATION SERVICE)

a large number of important plays, dating from several dynasties. With such strongly delineated figures on the stage, the fictional drama vied in credibility with real life.

The plays abound in scenes of pathos. Wives and servants are usually long-suffering. Villains are uncommonly villainous, stepmothers almost invariably wicked. Warriors are bold but strategists are even more admired than swordsmen. The playwriting provides long, lyrical passages sung with much formality, brisk though naturalistic dialogue, and almost constant occasion for bodily action, which at times comes to the fore in scenes of pure miming. Some plays have little intellectual content; they present spontaneous actions springing directly from emotion or fanciful scenes borrowing from folklore and magic, introducing ghosts and spirits; others are inspired by the strictest Confucian morality as applied both to public and private life. A play can be either fantastic, didactic, or both. The scope extends from the farcical to the tragic. The spaciousness of this theatrical world gives it an air of freedom almost as expansive as Shakespeare's, for it embraces with nearly equal enthusiasm the natural and the supernatural. All this diversity notwithstanding, it seems one world, the world of imagination closest to the heart of the Chinese people.

The classical Chinese theater itself is in every sense a creation without walls. In this respect it remains today as it was in its beginning. The plays can be given as occasion dictates, outdoors or indoors. An elevated platform, adequate space for the audience, and a back curtain or screen with entrance and exit for the performers, giving a boundary to the theatrical illusion, provide the only essentials for the framework. A table, a few chairs supply sufficient furniture. These might be used symbolically. Highly elaborate costumes and stage properties accord with innumerable prescriptions in color and design, with symbolism appropriate to each occasion. Dance scenes are frequent, yet the action throughout almost all scenes is so severely stylized that introduction of an episode unquestionably choreographic threatens no violent transition. Similarly, stylized speech alternates happily with song.

The extraordinary discipline of the classical Chinese stage is partly due to the singularly rigorous and prolonged training of its actors. Throughout by far the greater part of Chinese theatrical history the larger number of actors were, as Henry H. Hart in the Introduction to his translation of *The West Chamber* vigorously expresses it, "recruited from the off-scourings of the population—abandoned or stolen infants, and children purchased from their starving parents in time of flood, war or famine." Most were brought up with the theater as their foster mother, having no other education and memorizing all their parts solely through the ear. These boys barely learned to walk before they were instructed in the artificial manner of walking peculiar to the Chinese stage. Until the present century they were regarded as an inferior class. Although performances were well patronized, enthusiastically enjoyed, and held in considerable esteem, actors were viewed merely as the humble slaves and servants of a precious art. The actors themselves seem not only to have accepted their fate but to have been religiously

devoted to their profession. Exacting traditions guided them, which together with the almost incredible devotion of the Chinese to hard work resulted in a superlative measure of artistic finesse. Many of these conditions obtained in all periods of the Chinese theater of which we now possess any considerable knowledge, despite other conditions that exhibit radical changes. Women were conspicuous on the stage up to the beginning of the eighteenth century. In that and the following century all actors were male. In recent years women have once again been admitted, even in performances of the classical plays, in which originally they also appeared.

On considering the relation of this classical Chinese theater to modern theatrical innovations, the readiest word is coexistence. Contemporary China has by no means discarded its classical theater and although in important respects it may be endangered, it is far too early to foresee its demise either as a performing art or a living literature. By its side, illogically, it may appear to the West, there has risen a propagandistic theater largely inspired by Chinese communist movements, which, of course, have themselves passed through several distinct phases. During the Sino-Japanese War this theater was largely anti-Japanese; later it became anti-American. The coexistence of old and new was made possible in various ways. Patriotism obviously encourages the Chinese to treasure those aspects of their cultural heritage that do not in obvious ways conflict with new doctrines. Moreover, in the popular theater of the past a considerable number of plays are found that actually accord with much of the current political doctrine. China has repeatedly been an arena for class warfare. Several Yüan dramas themselves glorify champions of the poor who consider themselves oppressed by arbitrary and tyrannical overlords. Thus such a traditional play as THE FISHERMAN'S REVENGE needs little or no rewriting to appear as radical class propaganda. This became a favorite play with by far the greatest twentieth-century Chinese actor, MEI LAN-FANG, not merely because of its political relevance but primarily because of its high theatrical liveliness. It has pleased both a capitalist and a communist regime. So also did Mei Lan-fang, who did so much to preserve the classical theater in China at the same time that he has lived and worked without overt hostility between himself and the communist government. His career appears symbolical. Similarly, the Chinese drama itself promises to retain much of its traditional wit, pathos, and splendor while political systems rise and fall. In enigmatic China the bamboo flute bids fair to survive atomic blasts by friend or foe.

Chinese drama has met with diverse appraisal in its homeland. Ultraconservative or academic opinion has often deprecated it. There is a story that Confucius had entertainers executed because of their licentious criticism of the state. Certain phases of literary opinion, here as elsewhere, have been inclined to regard all theatrical activity as frivolous or worse. Yet over many years an extremely large number of plays in many editions has appeared and recently the literary merit of the theater as well as its undeniable brilliance in performance has been increasingly recognized. Further, its complicated patterns have been to some extent clarified by modern scholars. The plays have been performed in many communities throughout the world where Chinese people are domiciled. In the lands of Southeast Asia, such as Vietnam and Thailand, and as far east as the Philippines, theatrical activity deeply indebted to the Chinese traditions has developed. Nearly three centuries ago the Chinese theater inspired military and romantic plays written in Japan by Chikamatsu and his followers. It has in more recent times even begun to make its influence felt, though to a limited degree, on the drama of the West. The open stage with all that this conception implies has been employed by Western play producers, some with little knowledge of the East. Strindberg's *Dream Play* and *To Damascus* have seminal significance in the encouragement of these practices. Although altogether inadvertently, such a poetic dramatist as Garcia-Lorca, in his *After Five Years,* has complied with Chinese usages. Plays by Thornton Wilder, on the contrary, notably *Our Town,* show conscious borrowing of Chinese practices. It is noteworthy that Wilder spent some of his early and formative years in China. Again, with much deliberation and forethought, Bertolt Brecht wrote several plays, among them *The Good Woman of Setzuan* and *The Caucasian Chalk Circle,* in imitation of the Chinese stage. With fluctuations often dependent upon the winds of political change, the theaters of East and West have in the present century shown marked increase in mutual interrelations.

It has been shown that owing to the peculiar character of the Chinese theater, the plays themselves seem more important than their authorship. Only a few entries in this volume deal with Chinese playwrights, the most eminent of whom is KUAN HAN-CHING. Special note, however, is taken of a few representative and important works which have already been rendered into Western languages. See THE SORROWS OF HAN, THE WEST CHAMBER, THE CIRCLE OF CHALK, THE ROMANCE OF THE LUTE, THE PALACE OF ETERNAL YOUTH, SNOW IN MIDSUMMER, THE WHITE SNAKE, AN HEIR IN HIS OLD AGE, MADAME CASSIA, and LI K'UEI CARRIES THORNS.

Western scholarship and translators in both East and West have as yet done only scant justice to the Chinese theater. The Japanese and Indian drama have been far more diligently cultivated. Most studies deal with the Chinese stage rather than with its dramatic literature, revealing a predilection that springs from a fundamental misconception. A fair survey of the Chinese drama as literature makes linguistic demands that only a few scholars can sustain, even in China itself. It calls for knowledge of a number of dialects, some of them obsolescent if not actually extinct. The best studies are based on close observation of performances in China today. Especially praiseworthy is A. C. Scott's *The Classical Theatre of China* (1957). Much is to be learned from Faubion Bowers' *Theatre in the East* (1956). An appraisal of classical Chinese drama, with special comment on English translations, is found in H. W. Wells' *The Classical Drama of the Orient* (1965). The best translation of a Yüan drama is James Crump's rendering of *Li K'uei Carries Thorns,* appearing in *Anthology of Chinese Literature* (1965), edited by Cyril Birch. In this volume is also a translation by Donald Keene of *The Sorrows of Han.* Some of the best renderings are by S. I. Hsuing, notably his translation of *The*

West Chamber (1935). He has brilliantly translated *Madame Cassia* in *The T'ien Hsia Monthly,* Vol. I, 1935. The same play, with many others, will be found in *Famous Chinese Plays* (1963), translated by L. C. Arlington and Harold Acton, first published Peking in 1937. For *Snow in Midsummer* and other plays, see *Select Plays by Kuan Han-Ching* (1955), translated by Yang Hsien-yi and Gladys Yang. The same translators have given us a valuable rendering of *The Palace of Eternal Youth* (1965). For an able analysis of Chinese versification, poetry, and aesthetics, with close relation to the poetic elements in the drama, see James J. Y. Liu, *The Art of Chinese Poetry* (1962). A short but authoritative account of Chinese drama seen in the general perspective of Chinese culture may be found in *An Introduction to Chinese Literature* (1966) by Liu Wu-chi.—H. W. W.

Choephori. See ORESTEIA: *Choephori.*

Chorell, Walentin. See FINLAND.

chorus. Greek drama is a direct development of the activities of groups of singers and dancers who participated in ancient festivals and other ritualistic feasts. The immediate source of tragedy, according to Aristotle, is the choral hymn in honor of Dionysus (DITHYRAMB). In any case, early Greek tragedy and comedy were dominated by the chorus. In the development of comedy the importance of the chorus steadily diminished, so that by the time of Plautus and Terence it had completely disappeared. In tragedy the activities of the chorus at first comprised a significant portion of the play. Later, they acted as observers and commentators on the main action. By the time of the English Renaissance the role of the chorus—in Northrop Frye's words, to represent "the society from which the hero is alienated"— had been absorbed by one character, such as Horatio in *Hamlet,* or placed outside the framework of the play, as in *Romeo and Juliet.*

In the Greek theater the leader of the chorus was called *coryphaeus.* The term *choregus* (literally, "chorus leader") was used to denote the citizen who was responsible for the entire production, including the expenses, of a play performed at the Festival of Dionysus in Athens.

chronicle play. Chronicle plays are plays drawn from historical sources in which important issues of public welfare are emphasized. In addition, a chronicle play deals with the historical, as opposed to the legendary, past of the nation to which it is addressed and for whose contemporary problems it cites the past as example or warning.

Though Aristotle wrote on the relationship of history and drama, and one Greek history play, Aeschylus' *The Persians* (472 B.C.), has survived, the Greek idea of history was quite different from Renaissance and modern historiography. Accordingly, there is nothing we know of in classical drama that is comparable to the chronicle play as it emerged in England, almost in full maturity, in the 1580's. Within a decade the form had flowered in the work of Christopher Marlowe and been perfected by Shakespeare. But by 1630 it was considered old-fashioned, and though the form was often to be revived, there has never been a cluster of chronicle plays to match those produced in the Elizabethan age.

History was a natural subject for the drama as it developed in the sixteenth century. Medieval mystery plays had dramatized Bible stories, and morality plays were didactic moral allegories. As the drama passed from clerical to secular hands, secular history, though still presented for propagandistic purposes, became the obvious source for dramatic material. And the playwrights had ample material upon which to draw. The Tudor reign (1485–1603) is almost as renowned for its historical writing as for its drama. The series of chronicles began with Robert Fabyan's *New Chronicles of England and France* (1516). Then the *Anglica Historia* (1534), the fruit of thirty years of research by Polydore Vergil, appeared, sounding a distinctly modern note by rejecting Arthurian legend. Vergil's work inspired Edward Hall's influential *The Union of the Two Noble and Illustre Famelies of Lancastre and York* (1548), and Hall was followed in turn by Richard Grafton, John Stow, and Raphael Holinshed, all of whose chronicles had appeared by 1580. Another important source was *A Mirror for Magistrates* (1559), a collection of historical tales in verse, "diligently collected out of the chronicles," illustrating the downfall of many English noblemen.

Since originality of plot was no more important to Elizabethan playwrights than it had been to medieval writers, they went to history for material, not only for their history plays, but for tragedies (and sometimes for comedies) as well. It is sometimes difficult to distinguish a history from a tragedy, but some sort of distinction, even if tentative and subjective, is called for. When the playwright chose to involve the audience in the personal plight of his protagonist, relegating the issue of the commonweal to the background, his work came to be considered a tragedy. When the principal character's actions were seen as causing not so much private disaster as social or communal catastrophe, the play came to be called a history. Thus, for example, in *Hamlet,* though he does not neglect the question of Denmark's future, Shakespeare clearly stresses the personal dilemma of its prince; in *Richard III,* however, England's fate concerns us more than Richard's. In some plays, such as *Julius Caesar* and *Coriolanus,* the distinction is far less apparent.

But a chronicle play is a certain type of history play, and though many see no need for any further distinctions, there is a difference between writing about the history of another country and dealing with the past of one's native land, a difference perceptible in the tone of the play and in the response it evokes from a native audience.

Chronicle plays assume a national consciousness in their audience, and it has been chiefly in times of nationalistic feeling that they have flourished. A spirit of nationalism inspires the playwright, and his play, in turn, fosters a still stronger sense of national solidarity. Such a spirit characterized much of Elizabeth's reign. The Tudors had set out to regain the unity and prestige England had lost during the civil wars. The establishment of the Church of England was one form this movement took; another was the war with Spain and the victory of the English navy over the Armada in 1588. It has often been said that a single hero dominates all the English chronicle plays, and that hero is England itself. In virtually every Elizabethan chronicle play there is at least one fervid speech recounting the glories of the nation and calling for a renewal of patriotic zeal. The best known, of

course, is John of Gaunt's description of England in *Richard II* (II, i, 31–68). In the last few years of Elizabeth's reign this nationalistic feeling declined, and so did the popularity of the chronicle plays.

Another problem arises in the matter of plays based on ancient British history or, more accurately, legend. Plays dealing with such British kings as Gorboduc, Lear, Locrine, and Cymbeline have been considered by some as chronicle plays. A few of them are better classified as tragedies under the norms mentioned above. The rest would more appropriately be categorized as historical fables or myths. The treatment of such legends is discernibly different from that of plays based on relatively recent events, the repercussions of which were still being felt in Tudor England. The Elizabethan plays properly called chronicles cover periods from the time of Edward the Confessor (d. 1066) to that of Elizabeth herself.

Chronicle plays, as has been noted above, retained the essentially didactic purpose of the mystery and morality plays. The histories that were their sources were similarly didactic, propagating what is now called the "Tudor myth." Having come to the throne after three decades of civil war, Henry VII encouraged the English to look upon his reign as providential. Though from the Lancaster faction himself, his marriage with Elizabeth of York was to signify the reunion of those houses, a reunion to be embodied in their heirs. History was seen as the working out of a divine plan, and Henry VII (who fancied himself the spirit of Arthur come back to save England) was king by a special divine right. Thus, the chroniclers, especially Edward Hall, could denounce rebellion and usurpation even though the Tudors themselves had obtained rule by rebelling against Richard III.

This view was so widespread, in fact, that it has been said that the reading of history was a practice second in piety only to the study of Scripture itself. For the most part, the playwrights in their work adhered to the Tudor myth and to the concept of providential history. The past was called upon to provide lessons for the present. In his *Apologie for Actors* (1612) Thomas Heywood stressed this function when he noted that chronicle plays

> are writ with this ayme, and carryed with this methode, to teach the subjects obedience to their king, to shew the people the untimely ends of such as have moved tumults, commotions, and insurrections, to present them with the flourishing estate of such as live in obedience, exhorting them to allegeance, dehorting them from all trayterous and fellonious stratagems.

The theory did not always fit comfortably. Not only did it fail to justify the overthrow of Richard III, it also seemed to denounce the Scots for rejecting Mary, a rejection Protestant England applauded. The resolution of this difficulty was supersubtle. Taking their cue from the *Mirror for Magistrates,* the historians distinguished between the unjustified deposition of a merely incapable king, such as Richard II, who was perhaps sent by God to chastise the nation, and the proper defeat of a genuine tyrant, such as Richard III, or of an enemy of God, such as Mary, Queen of Scots.

Occasionally, aesthetics challenged didactics. In *Richard II* Shakespeare so artfully balanced the arguments on each side that it has long been argued whether the play ultimately supports the divine right of kings or insurrection on behalf of the public good. When Essex rebelled against Elizabeth in 1601, his followers had Shakespeare's company, the Lord Chamberlain's Men, perform *Richard II*, apparently to convince the public that rebellion could be justified sometimes. But Richard is portrayed sympathetically, at least after he loses power, and the stratagem may well have had the opposite effect. Other, more important factors were of course involved, but it is clear that Essex did not get the public support he expected, the rebellion failed, and virtually everyone connected with it was punished except the Chamberlain's Men, who were exonerated. Indeed, only a few months later Elizabeth, with no apparent shame, identified herself with the unfortunate king: "I am Richard II, know ye not that?" In practice, then, the didacticism of the chronicle play was not always so pronounced as in theory it should have been.

If aesthetic concerns sometimes overcame propaganda, they far more often superseded historical accuracy. Some of the inaccuracies of the chronicle plays can be traced to their sources, but others seem to serve distinct dramatic functions. In *Henry IV, Part One*, for example, Shakespeare sets up Hotspur as a clear foil to Prince Hal—two noblemen of apparently the same age but with differing sets of values, who meet in single combat to decide which is the more fit to rule England. The pairing off is thematically as well as dramatically meaningful. But the real Hotspur was in fact older than Hal's father, and there is no historical support for the idea that Hal himself killed Hotspur at Shrewsbury.

In addition to changes for dramatic reasons, the plays, like the chronicles they drew upon, sacrificed historicity for doctrinal convenience. King John, hardly an admirable monarch by objective standards, became the hero of a number of plays once Protestants chose to see in his defiance of Rome a prelude to the Reformation. It was John, in fact, who was the subject of the first English play based on chronicle material. In *Kynge Johan* (written c. 1536), John Bale set out to counter Polydore Vergil's pro-Catholic account of that reign. But except for the hero of the title, the characters are all allegorical— Widow England oppressed by Sedition, Private Wealth, Usurped Power, and so forth. The play is obviously more a morality play than a chronicle.

Closer to the chronicle type was a three-part Latin play, *Richard Tertius*, written by Thomas Legge of Cambridge in 1579. A group of chronicle plays written in English for the public theaters appeared in the late 1580's, plays such as *The Famous Victories of Henry V, The Life and Death of Jack Straw, The Troublesome Reign of John King of England, The True Tragedy of Richard III*, all of them of uncertain authorship. But the genre blossomed in the early nineties with the appearance of Christopher Marlowe's *Edward II* and the plays later to be called *Henry VI, Parts Two and Three* by Shakespeare. Scholars have long argued over who deserves the credit, Marlowe or Shakespeare, for purifying the genre, but it is likely that the influence was mutual. Marlowe died in 1593, but Shakespeare went on to complete two tetralogies of chronicle plays covering the history of England from 1398 to 1485. He also wrote a *King John* and had at least a hand in *Henry VIII*.

Many Elizabethan chronicle plays, of course, are lost, and many of those that are extant are unsigned, but a few of Shakespeare's most worthy contemporaries wrote chronicle plays that have survived: George Peele's *Edward I* (1590), Thomas Dekker and John Webster's *The Famous History of Sir Thomas Wyatt* (written 1607), and Thomas Heywood's *Edward IV* (1599) and *If You Know Not Me You Know Nobody* (1604), the last concerning the recently deceased Queen Elizabeth. The vogue apparently passed, for in the Prologue to his own chronicle play, *Perkin Warbeck* (c. 1634), John Ford noted that the form had by then become "out of fashion" and "unfollowed."

No subsequent period of English drama, or that of any other nation, has equaled the Elizabethan output of this type of play, but chronicle plays are still being written and produced. During the Restoration and eighteenth century in England there were a number of adaptations of Shakespeare's chronicle plays, the best known being Colley Cibber's *Richard III* (1699). Some new plays on English history were also written: Roger Boyle's *The Black Prince* (1667), John Bancroft's *Edward III* (1690) and *Henry II* (1692), Nicholas Rowe's *Jane Shore* (1714) and *Lady Jane Gray* (1715), Henry Brooke's *The Earl of Essex* (1750), to name but a few. In the Victorian period, no less a poet than Alfred Lord Tennyson wrote three plays on "The Making of England": *Harold* (pub. 1877), *Becket* (pub. 1879), and *Queen Mary* (pub. 1875). At about the same time, Algernon Swinburne was working on a trilogy of plays on Mary, Queen of Scots: *Chastelard* (pub. 1865), *Bothwell* (pub. 1874), and *Mary Stuart* (pub. 1881). And worthy of mention in the twentieth century are two plays by John Drinkwater, *Oliver Cromwell* (1923) and *Mary Stuart* (1922), and such recent works as Robert Bolt's play on Thomas More, *A Man for All Seasons* (1960); and John Arden's *Left-Handed Liberty* (1965), on the signing of the Magna Carta and his *Armstrong's Last Goodnight* (1964), about the sixteenth-century wars between England and Scotland.

In other countries, history plays based on native sources were generally produced during times of nationalistic feeling and often in periods of romanticism in literature. Few of these plays, however, correspond closely to the Elizabethan concept of chronicle, and many use the past more to escape contemporary problems than to relate to them.

In France, for example, many plays based on French history appeared in the early nineteenth century, but these plays are better classified as historical romances. Alexandre Soumet's *Jeanne d'Arc* (1825) and Dumas père's *Henri III et sa cour* (1829) and *Napoléon Bonaparte* (1831) are good examples. More recently, Jean Anouilh's *The Lark* (1953) has achieved some success. Less popular but closer to the ideals of the chronicle play is Arthur Adamov's *Le Printemps, 71* (1961).

In the Golden Age of Spanish literature, Lope de Vega wrote a number of plays on Spain's past, which he called *comedias historicas* ("history plays"). But the best-known such work of the time is Tirso de

Molina's *La Prudencia en la mujer* (pub. 1634), concerning the queen mother of Ferdinand IV. There was also a group of similar plays written during Spain's Romantic period, 1830–1845.

It was through his *Götz von Berlichingen* (1773), a play about a sixteenth-century German knight who leads a peasants' revolt, that Goethe first attracted attention. His friend Schiller wrote many historical dramas, but the ones based on German history, the *Wallenstein* trilogy (1798–1799), are closer to tragedy than to chronicle.

In Scandinavia national theaters have encouraged native historical drama and both Ibsen and Strindberg contributed. While still in his twenties, Ibsen wrote a series of such plays, the best known probably being *Lady Inger of Östrat* (1855) and *The Feast at Solhaug* (1856), both set in sixteenth-century Norway. In the tradition of playwrights such as Bernhard von Beskow and Johan Börjesson, August Strindberg, at the age of twenty-three, wrote *Master Olof* (1881) and returned to the genre toward the end of his career, writing between 1899 and 1908 eleven plays covering periods in Swedish history from the late thirteenth to the late eighteenth century. In them Strindberg was consciously constructing a cycle of chronicle plays in the manner of Shakespeare. *Gustav Vasa* and *Erik XIV* (both 1899) best manifest Shakespeare's influence. Strindberg's work in turn influenced later Swedish chronicle plays, such as Per Hallström's *Charles XI* and *Gustaf III* (both 1918).

Soviet drama has been especially concerned with the didactic use of Russian history in the theater. Under the influence of Anatoli Lunacharsky, who had written plays about other national revolutions, Michael Bulgakov (*Days of the Turbins,* 1926) and Alexander Korneichuk (*The Sinking of the Squadron,* 1934, and *Truth,* 1937) produced popular plays dealing with the Russian revolution. Another noteworthy Soviet playwright, Alexei Tolstoy, wrote a series of chronicle plays including *The Plot of the Empress* (1925), about Alexandra and Rasputin, *Peter the Great* (1934), and *The Death of Ivan the Terrible* (1943).

The Revolutionary War served as the subject of scores of generally undistinguished nineteenth-century American plays. The glories of early American history are also the subject of many works, more pageants than plays, by Paul Green (such as *The Common Glory,* 1947). Lincoln has inspired a number of plays, the best being Robert Sherwood's *Abe Lincoln in Illinois* (1938) and Mark Van Doren's *Last Days of Lincoln* (pub. 1959). James Scheville's play about Roger Williams, *The Bloody Tenet* (pub. 1965), and Sidney Kingsley's *The Patriots* (1943) also merit attention, but the finest American chronicle play is generally agreed to be Arthur Miller's *The Crucible* (1953), in which a Salem witch trial is used to protest the political purges of the fifties.

The most thorough comparison of Greek and Elizabethan notions of history is Tom Driver's *The Sense of History in Greek and Shakespearean Drama* (1960). Felix Schelling's *The English Chronicle Play* (1902) was an early attempt to define the genre. E. M. W. Tillyard treats the backgrounds of the chronicle plays in his *Shakespeare's History Plays* (1944), and Lily Campbell's *Shakespeare's Histories: Mirrors of Elizabethan Policy* (1947) stresses the didactic element in both the plays and the histories upon which they drew. M. M. Reese takes a slightly different approach, stressing literary backgrounds, especially *A Mirror for Magistrates,* in his *Cease of Majesty* (1961). Irving Ribner rejects any distinction based on national origin of subject matter in his thorough *The English History Play in the Age of Shakespeare* (1957). The best study of Strindberg's chronicle plays is Walter Johnson's *Strindberg and the Historical Drama* (1963).—R. E. L.

Chushingura. A Japanese play by Takeda IZUMO, probably the most popular of all plays for the Japanese *kabuki* theater. Its story, taken with considerable modifications from actual events, concerns the forty-seven *ronin,* or loyal retainers of their slain lord. A ronin is a masterless man, discarded through some fateful event from the service of a feudal lord and therefore left to roam among the unprivileged populace. The violent shift in Japanese social and economic life in full force during the seventeenth century rendered men in this position especially sympathetic to the emerging middle class. The heroes of Izumo's play were thus doubly sympathetic as heroes by virtue of feudal tradition and by virtue of their association with the new class in society rapidly coming into the position of dominance.

The play, in eleven acts, takes a full day or even a longer period to perform. All Japanese theatergoers, however, know the story and thus it is customary, as in many similar cases, to give only separate acts. There is a large cast of characters, a surprising number of whom attain strong individuality. The action is long and intricate. Although many episodes toward the center of the play are extremely effective and well contrived, the scenes near the commencement and the conclusion are the best known. The earlier scenes depict the callousness of an official, Moronao, who seeks to seduce the wife of the noble Hangan. Failing in this, he insults Hangan so outrageously that the latter loses patience and deals him a blow. This action, as viewed by the code of Japanese chivalry, constitutes treason, which in turn binds the doer to commit ritualistic suicide. Hangan's loyal retainers watch the scene with horror. Their leader, Yuranosuke, and his associates vow revenge. The climax in this section of the play is reached as Yuranosuke performs his exit, holding in his hand as sacred relic the dagger with which their master has killed himself. The play comes to its inevitable conclusion when Moronao is slain with the same dagger and all the ronin kill themselves as required by feudal law. Although many of the supplementary scenes are of almost equal force and show a remarkable naturalism, it is these melodramatic passages overshadowed by thoughts of death and revenge that give the play its great hold on the popular mind. Chushingura inspired an English drama by John Masefield, *The Faithful* (1915).

For an analysis of the entire play, see A. C. Scott, *The Kabuki Theatre of Japan* (1955). For an English rendering of the most famous act, see *Six Kabuki Plays* (1963), translated by Donald Richie and Miyoko Watanabe. The story was first filmed in 1942 under the direction of Kenji Mizoguchi.—H. W. W.

Cibber, Colley. See ENGLAND: *Restoration drama;* ENGLAND: *eighteenth century.*

Cid, Le (1637). A tragicomedy, later called a tragedy, by Pierre CORNEILLE. Inspired by *Las*

Mocedades del Cid (pub. 1631) by Guillén de Castro, *Le Cid* recounts the adventure of Rodrigue and Chimène, who are in love and destined for each other but are separated because of a quarrel between their fathers. The action takes place in Seville. Since Don Gormas, Chimène's father, has slapped Don Diegue, Rodrigue's father, Rodrigue, who has never fought, must defend his old father's honor. He challenges Don Gormas to a duel and kills him. Chimène is then forced to seek redress against Rodrigue. That evening Rodrigue enters Chimène's room, and the two desperate young people agree that they are merely doing what they can and must do to remain worthy of each other. During the night, when Rodrigue learns that the Moors are planning a surprise attack against the city, he takes the initiative of getting together an army and beats off the Moors, who thus consider him their conqueror and name him "the Cid." Chimène continues to seek redress against the young hero. Don Sanche, Chimène's other suitor, offers to champion her against Rodrigue, who is ready to let himself be killed; but in the course of a second meeting Chimène begs Rodrigue to defend himself. After the duel Chimène, mistakenly believing Rodrigue to be dead, publicly confesses her love for him. The king then urges Chimène to marry Rodrigue, who had in fact won the duel. They will marry eventually, after a suitable delay. A subplot serves as the gauge of Rodrigue's rise to glory: the infanta of Spain, who is in love with him, at first stifles her love, because he is unworthy of her, and then finds him worthy after his

victories, but out of generosity sacrifices herself and gives him to Chimène.

In *Le Cid* Corneille drew a portrait of youth as demanding, active, and heroic and passionately attracted by honor and glory, without which love is impossible. Ironically, the two protagonists can continue to love one another only if they remain faithful to the duty that separates them. But they go to such lengths that they transcend the obligations of the initial situation and can finally be reconciled.

This play has been translated into English blank verse by Kenneth Muir in *Seventeenth-Century French Drama* (1967).—Ja. G.

Cinna (1641). A tragedy by Pierre CORNEILLE. Emilie and Cinna, who love one another, are leaders of a plot to kill the emperor Auguste. Maxime, one of the conspirators, in love with Emilie, betrays them out of jealousy. Auguste, however, rises above his desire for revenge and pardons them all, not because it is politically expedient but out of magnanimity and a sense of glory. In addition to its suspense, *Cinna* is remarkable for its final reconciliation and the dramatic portrait of Auguste, who is at first presented as a tyrant but becomes increasingly admirable.

This play has been translated into English blank verse by Lacy Lockert in *Chief Plays,* 2nd. ed. (1957).—Ja. G.

Circle, The (1921). A comedy by W. Somerset MAUGHAM. Thirty years before, Lord Porteous, a promising young statesman, eloped with the beautiful Lady Catherine Champion-Cheney, wife of a mem-

A SCENE FROM PIERRE CORNEILLE'S *Cinna* (FRENCH CULTURAL SERVICES)

ber of Parliament and mother of a five-year-old child. Now, after living together unmarried in Florence all these years, they return to England, but they are no longer the romantic couple of sentimental legend. Kitty refuses to act her age, and Porteous is "bald, elderly . . . snappy and gruff." Kitty's former husband, Clive, on the other hand, "bears his years jauntily." Altogether, the three constitute a rather terrible object lesson for Elizabeth, Kitty's daughter-in-law, who wants to run off with her lover and abandon her stuffy husband, who is, like his father before him, an M.P. Clive advises his son to prevent his wife's flight by giving her free choice. This strategy almost works, but Elizabeth's lover is quite persuasive, and the two go away together. Kitty wonders: "Will they suffer all we suffered?" Porteous answers: "If we made rather a hash of things perhaps it was because we were rather trivial people." Maugham's cynicism is more bland here than usual, and, in fact, his principal cynic, Clive Champion-Cheney, is quite routed when his advice fails. The play is particularly admired for its symmetry and for the curious way in which the portraits of the farcical Kitty and Porteous develop and deepen.—H. P.

Circle of Chalk, The (Hui lan chi). Chinese drama, attributed to Li Ch'ien-fu, who flourished during the Yüan dynasty (1280–1368). *The Circle of Chalk* has long been popular in China and has become one of the best-known of Chinese dramas in the West. It is a full-length play typical of the most vigorous Chinese playwriting, strengthened by the

earnestness of Confucian ethics. In Act I an evil-minded woman, conspiring with her lover, kills her husband and accuses her rival—her husband's subordinate, or second, wife—of the murder. Childless herself, she even succeeds, in Act II, through the aid of lying witnesses, in claiming the son of the second wife as her own. In a trial scene reeking with perjury the unfortunate second wife is convicted and dispatched, in chains, to the provincial capital, where her execution is to take place. In Act III the evil woman and her lover impatiently pursue their victim to a country inn, making their way through a fierce snowstorm. Here they encounter the brother of the condemned second wife, once a ne'er-do-well and a prodigal, now reformed to the honorable status of an exemplary official. In the fourth and final act the first decision is wholly annulled and justice meted out to all. The judge, in trying to determine the true mother of the child, draws a circle of chalk on the floor and places the child within, saying that only the true mother will be able to draw the child out. The first wife takes his arm and withdraws him while the second refuses to tug at him, fearing that he will be hurt. Because of the second wife's concern for the child, the judge is able to discern in her the true mother. This piece of action resembles the famous "judgment of Solomon" in a similar dispute.

The play has been translated into several Western languages, although never artfully rendered. It has also been several times produced in the West. It was first translated by Stanislas Julien into French in

DRAWING OF A SCENE FROM *The City Madam* BY PHILIP MASSINGER (THEATRE COLLECTION, NEW YORK PUBLIC LIBRARY AT LINCOLN CENTER)

1832. This version, with occasional consultation of the original, was put into forthright and vigorous English by Frances Hume in 1955. It had already been translated directly from the Chinese by Ethel Van Der Veer, whose rendering appears in Barrett H. Clark's *World Drama* (1933). With many gratuitous omissions and additions, the play was put into German by "Klabund" (Alfred Henschke) in 1925. This version was produced in Germany; an English translation of it was made in 1929 by James Laver for production in London. Fresh attention has been given the play by Bertolt Brecht, who used it as the basis of departure for his inversion of its morality in his *Caucasian Chalk Circle* (1945). Brecht presumably admired the Chinese play, though he may have imperfectly understood it through bad translations, using it as a means to attack Western attitudes from which he violently dissented.—H. W. W.

City Madam, The (1632). A comedy by Philip MASSINGER. In order to cure his wife and three daughters of their pretentious haughtiness, Sir John Frugal, a prosperous London merchant, devises a plan. He leaves home under pretense of retiring to a monastery and gives over the management of his estate to his younger brother, Luke, an apparently reformed rake. Once in command, Luke demonstrates that his reformation was merely superficial. He quickly appropriates his brother's fortune, showing no mercy toward the servants and debtors of Sir John. He is particularly ruthless to the wife and daughters, whom he ridicules and humiliates. When three "Indians" approach him with a request for three women to be used as human sacrifices, he prepares to hand over his brother's family. The Indians, however, turn out to be Sir John and two loyal suitors of his daughters who have been waiting for the chance to unmask and punish the villainous Luke. Humbled and contrite, the three women acknowledge their former folly, while Luke, unrepentant to the end, is banished from Sir John's home.

The play provides an interesting analysis of middle-class values in Caroline London. Sir John represents the ideal virtues of the merchant class. One distortion of his capitalist, enterprising nature is seen in the rapacious and acquisitive Luke. The other distortion is mirrored in the proud and foolish aspirations of his wife and daughters. Between these extremes Sir John looms as a model of civic virtue: moderate, temperate, and adaptable.

A modern edition of *The City Madam* (1966) has been edited by Cyrus Hoy. An excellent discussion of the play is contained in L. C. Knights's *Drama and Society in the Age of Jonson* (1936).—E. Q.

Clark, John Pepper. See AFRICA: *Nigeria*.

Claudel, Paul (1868–1955). French poet, diplomat, and playwright. Claudel was born in a small village in Aisne. He studied law in Paris and attended the École des Science Politiques. While serving as a diplomat at various posts all over the world, Claudel composed poetry. The mystical tone of this poetry pervades his dramas, which are like dramatic poems.

The poetry of Arthur Rimbaud greatly influenced Claudel in both a literary and spiritual manner. Claudel first read Rimbaud's *Les Illuminations* in 1886, and that same year, on Christmas Day in Notre-Dame Cathedral, Claudel experienced a spiritual awakening, a revelation of faith that was immutable.

As he embarked on a long diplomatic career, Claudel continued his studies of Rimbaud, Stéphane Mallarmé, and St. Thomas Aquinas. Claudel only went to Paris for the production of his plays: THE SATIN SLIPPER in 1942, BREAK OF NOON in 1948, and THE TIDINGS BROUGHT TO MARY in 1955.

In Claudel's concept of drama the relationship between man and woman and between man and God is an eternal relationship. If salvation is the goal of each human existence, love is the means for reaching this goal. Believing so deeply in the identity of all loves, Claudel would say that human love, as it grows in intensity, will end by seeing what it really is: a divine love of God. Fundamentally, he believes that one human being cannot be the end or even the satisfaction of another human being.

The seriousness of Claudel's religious sentiment lies at the source of each poem, play, and essay, and it pervades the development of his work. The tone and lyricism of Claudel's work are always religious, even if the specific subject is secular, because for Claudel the truth of art naturally tends toward the sacred. (For a discussion of Claudel's use of symbolist techniques, see SYMBOLISM.)

For a critical study of Claudel's work, see the following: Eric Bentley, "Theater, Religion, and Politics," *Theater Arts,* XXXIV (1950); Joseph Chiari, *The Poetic Drama of Claudel* (1954); Wallace Fowlie, *A Guide to Contemporary French Literature* (1957) and *Claudel* (1957); and Henri Peyre, "The Drama of Paul Claudel," *Thought,* XXVII, No. 105 (1952).—W. F.

PAUL CLAUDEL (FRENCH CULTURAL SERVICES)

cloak-and-sword play (comedia de capa y espada).
Also known as cape-and-sword drama, this Spanish comedy of romantic intrigue takes its name from the cloaks and swords worn by the aristocratic characters. The action centers around amorous intrigues, courtly manners, and flamboyant duels. The forerunner of this genre was Bartolomé Torres Naharro's *Himena* (pub. 1517), and both Lope de Vega and Calderón wrote several cape-and-sword dramas. By the nineteenth century this term was used for any romantic costume play with a strong love interest and some swordplay.

closet drama. A play meant to be read rather than acted upon the stage. Although historians of the theater have generally considered it a bastard genre, writers from classical times to the present have been attracted to the purely literary drama.

Plato's discursive yet dramatic dialogues describing the tragic death of Socrates are the first distinguished forerunners of the form in literary history. Significantly, they were written when Greek tragedy had begun to decay. When the Roman populace lost interest in tragedy, Julius Caesar Strabo and Quintus Cicero wrote plays intended for private reading. The plays of the Stoic philosopher Seneca are considered closet dramas, although they were written to be declaimed publicly, if not acted. The genre achieved some popularity during the Renaissance, particularly among the aristocracy. The Elizabethans, for example, produced a number of closet dramas, the most notable being *Mustapha* by Fulke GREVILLE.

Milton's *Samson Agonistes* is a classic example of the closet drama. Described by its author as a "dramatic poem," *Samson Agonistes* is a verse tragedy that observes many of the conventions of the Greek drama. Milton notes in his introduction that the play was not intended for the stage, as its lengthy speeches and scant action may suggest. See John MILTON.

The term closet drama is often used pejoratively to describe the plays of English Romantic and Victorian poets, such as Byron's *Manfred*, Shelley's *The Cenci*, Browning's *Strafford*, and Hardy's *The Dynasts*. It is less frequently used to describe Goethe's classics, *Iphigenia* and *Faust*.—J. F. L.

Clouds (Nephelai, 423 B.C.). A comedy by ARISTOPHANES. Strepsiades ("Twisterson"), a petit-bourgeois Athenian who has married above his station, now finds himself saddled with the debts of his high-living, racehorse-fancying son, Pheidippides. In desperation, Strepsiades decides to have himself trained in the new discipline being offered by the "Think Factory" run by Socrates, which claims to be able to make black appear white, and right, wrong. Strepsiades hopes that a course in instruction at this school will give him the dialectical skill to wriggle out of the payment of his debts. At the school he meets Socrates himself, as well as the Chorus of clouds, misty, airy images of the vapor that is Socrates' thinking. But Strepsiades is a useless pupil and is persuaded to turn his son over to Socrates, only to find the new learning being used, not only against his debtors, but also against himself. In a fury, Strepsiades burns the whole Think Factory to the ground.

Clouds was not a success at its first performance. The version that survives is a rewritten script, never produced, so far as we know. Yet Aristophanes thought this the cleverest of his plays and did not

quickly forgive his public for rejecting it. One tribute to its effectiveness is preserved in Plato's *Apology,* in which Socrates, defending himself at his trial, mentions the part played by the comic dramatists in misrepresenting his views to the Athenian audience.

Socrates is certainly right that his own philosophical beliefs were nothing like the doctrines parodied by Aristophanes in this play. How, then, could Aristophanes hope to convince people of such a misleading picture? Parody should bear some relationship to the thing parodied. The most likely answer to this much-labored question is that Socrates was merely a convenient figure on which to hang the trappings and costumes that belonged to a whole group of intellectuals and teachers whose ideas were arousing considerable animus among the more conservatively minded Athenians. Aristophanes, writing for effect, did not care about the philosophical accuracy of his attacks.

A more interesting question raised by *Clouds* is the evidence it provides of the rise of a new consciousness in Greek life and the conflicts that ensued. All over the Mediterranean, ideas that challenged the old order were being debated and put into practice, and nowhere was the debate more fierce than in Athens. The result was a reassessment of all the accepted beliefs about political and personal relationships. In particular, the exponents of these new ideas, collectively called "Sophists," claimed that *arete* could be taught like any other subject. Arete, traditionally rendered as "virtue" or "excellence," also carried the meaning of "being good at something." By saying that arete, previously thought a trait of those with the right upbringing and background, could be taught, the Sophists were saying, in effect, that anybody could be taught to be good at anything. This was felt to be an attack on the very roots of social stability. The comic version of this revolution in thought and behavior is embodied in the scene where Strepsiades is talked into accepting the logic of being beaten by his son—this in a society where the sacred relationship between fathers and sons was protected by law.

Translations of the play are listed under Aristophanes.—K. C.

Cock-a-doodle Dandy (1949). A comedy by Sean O'CASEY. Written in his seventieth year, this comic extravaganza represents a consummation of the mythic visions that O'Casey dramatized in his late plays. The enchanted Cock, a merry figure of apocalyptic exuberance who symbolizes the life force, is a barnyard Dionysian turned loose in a joyless little Irish village where the priest-led people have been taught to fear him as an incarnation of the devil. During the same year that he wrote this play, O'Casey also published the fourth volume of his autobiography, *Inishfallen, Fare Thee Well,* which could well serve as a subtitle for the play. Both works record the reasons for his self-exile from Ireland some twenty years earlier. The theme of exile grows out of the main conflict of the play, which is presented as a mock battle between the forces of life championed by the Cock and the forces of despair led by Father Domineer. The Cock and his followers, Robin Adair and the maid Marion and the young women, are finally banished, but not before they scourge the humorless puritans. Ireland is seen as a land of thou-shalt-nots, yet the play is a comic morality with a universal theme for men of all countries. At a time when so much modern literature has been obsessed with original sin, O'Casey expressed his faith in what might be called original joy.—D. K.

Cocteau, Jean (1889–1963). French poet, novelist, director, and playwright. Cocteau was born near Paris and grew up in a family of lawyers. At the age of seventeen he had his first book of poetry published. In addition to writing in all the genres of literature, he also experimented with the cinema, ballet, and jazz. He often used music in conjunction with drama, as in *Le Boeuf sur le toit* ("The Ox on the Roof," 1920), for example, which has a jazz accompaniment, and in *Oedipus Rex* (1927), which has a score composed by Igor Stravinsky.

Cocteau had a deeply rooted, persistent need to be a part of the theater. It was the form he used most often to express and release the phantoms that peopled his imagination. He wrote in all the various genres: a Greek play (*Antigone*, 1922), a story of Greek mythology (ORPHÉE), a contemporary psychological tragedy (*Les Parents terribles, intimate relations*, 1938), a romantic drama (*L'Aigle à deux têtes, The Eagle Has Two Heads*, 1946), a French medieval myth (*Les Chevaliers de la table ronde*, "The Knights of the Round Table," 1937), a Renaissance melodrama (*Bacchus*, 1951), a surrealist fantasy (*Les Mariés de la Tour Eiffel, The Eiffel Tower Wedding Party*, 1921), and a tragic monologue (*La voix humaine, The Human Voice*, 1930).

The theater is the greatest of all literary risks. This sense of precariousness was always felt and understood by Cocteau. In fact, he encouraged this risk and worked under its domination. From his earliest *Parade* (1917) and *Les Mariés de la Tour Eiffel*, through his adaptation of Sophocles (where he practiced his scales and learned about the form of tragedy), to the major dramatic works, *Orphée*, THE IN-

PADRAIC COLUM (IRISH TOURIST BOARD)

FERNAL MACHINE, *Les Parents Terribles*, and *Bacchus*, he presented experimentations on the stage with the tireless enthusiasm of a dramatist enamored of the theater and the idea of a spectacle. (See SURREALISM.)

Cocteau always claimed that the poet's close association with death is not a terrifying experience but a necessary initiation into immortality. In both his early and late works death was for Cocteau his means of coming into contact with truth, his vehicle for understanding the ordinary objects in his life and the daily occurrences he experienced. Death is the total vision for Cocteau, the aggrandizement and the triumph over constriction.

For critical studies of the work of Jean Cocteau, consult the following: Margaret Crosland, *Jean Cocteau* (1955); William Fifield, "Jean Cocteau: An Interview," *The Paris Review*, No. 32 (Summer-Fall, 1964); Wallace Fowlie, *Age of Surrealism* (1950); and Neal Oxenhandler, *Scandal and Parade: The Theater of Jean Cocteau* (1957).—W. F.

Colombia. See SPANISH AMERICA.

Colum, Padraic (1881–   ). Irish playwright and poet. A native of County Longford, Colum moved to Dublin as a young man and went to work as a railway clerk. In 1914 he went to the United States, where he settled permanently except for periodic sojourns abroad. Since leaving Ireland, Colum all but abandoned his playwriting career, devoting most of his time to poetry, children's literature, and miscellaneous writing.

An early and active enthusiast of the Irish Literary Theatre, the forerunner of the famous Abbey Theatre, Colum had his first important play, *Broken Soil*, produced by that group in 1903. *Broken Soil*, later revised and retitled *The Fiddler's House*, centers around Maire Hourican, whose unrequited love of Brian MacConnell leads her to a recognition and understanding of the wanderlust that grips her father, an itinerant fiddler. Colum's second play, *The Land* (1905), deals with one of Ireland's greatest problems in the last century: the emigration to America of its strongest and boldest young people. Colum's *Thomas Muskerry* (1910) deals with the decline of a dignified man brought to ruin by the demands of his family.

Two of Colum's later plays are *Balloon* (1929), a comedy, and *Moytura,* a play for dancers written after the manner of Yeats and based on the life of Oscar Wilde's father, Sir William Wilde.

comedy. Dr. Johnson was seldom more judicious than when he remarked that "comedy has been particularly unpropitious to definers." At the close of Plato's *Symposium,* Socrates is found arguing that the craft (*techné*) of writing comedy is the same as the craft of writing tragedy, though in *The Republic* Plato has Socrates note snobbishly that there is something debasing in the comic impulse to play the buffoon. The classic, but in many ways unsatisfactory, definition of comedy is in Aristotle's *Poetics* (Chapters 4 and 5), asserting that, whereas tragedy presents the "noble actions" of "noble personages," comedy represents "actions of the ignoble" and was at first devoted to "invective" or what is "ridiculous." The ridiculous, he explains, is "a species of the ugly," that is, "a mistake or deformity not productive of pain or harm to others." Like tragedy, he adds, comedy arose from "improvisations"—tragedy deriving from "the dithyramb" and comedy from "phallic songs." And in his *Ethics* (II, 7; IV, 7–8) Aristotle appears to identify at least three types of comic character: the *alazon,* a boastful or pompous man; the *eiron,* a mock-modest man who understates or belittles; and a *bomolochos,* a buffoon or clownish jester.

Whatever its authenticity may be, the fragment known as the *Tractatus Coislinianus,* presumably dating from the fourth to second centuries B.C., reformulates a definition of comedy that obviously parallels Aristotle's definition of tragedy in the *Poetics:*

> Comedy is an imitation of an action that is ludicrous and imperfect, of sufficient length, [in embellished language,] the several kinds [of embellishment being] separately [found] in the [several] parts [of the play]; [directly presented] by persons acting, and not [given] through narrative; through pleasure and laughter effecting the purgation of the like emotions. It has laughter for its mother." [Lane Cooper's translation]

The problems of interpreting these Aristotelian passages have been unresolved. It is agreed that the term comedy (*komodia*) does not derive from *kome* ("village" or "quarter of a city") but rather from *komos* ("a processional celebration"), though we do not know exactly what Aristotle meant by "improvisations" and "phallic songs." Traditionally, Epicharmus of Syracuse (c. 480 B.C.) is supposed to have given Greek comedy its basic form. Arthur Pickard-Cambridge conjectures that comedy may trace back to festivals in which ithyphallic revelers masqueraded as animals and marched or danced in a simulated contest involving choruses of satyrs, giants, fat men, or actors dressed in cloaks performing a komos sequence with a *parodos-agon-parabasis* (that is, a processional celebration with a song or dance at entrance, a debate or dispute, and an address to the audience). In any event, it is clear that the Greeks associated comedy with ridiculing characters who are represented as absurd or offensive, and the savagery of OLD COMEDY is found in Aristophanes, who, in plays like *Clouds* (423 B.C.), does not hesitate to attack Socrates by portraying him as the worst kind of sophist, atheist, and faker. Old Comedy was a topical satire directed against individuals—against Euripides, for instance. Shortly after Aristotle, however, the NEW COMEDY of Menander (342 –291 B.C.) ridiculed types of characters instead of well-known persons, and this early form of comedy of manners was a model for Roman playwrights like Terence and Plautus, who had a great influence on Renaissance drama. (See ROMAN COMEDY.)

Medieval comedy arose within the Church as biblical stories were enacted first by clerics, then by various guilds. The great contribution of the miracle and mystery plays and moral interludes was the fusing of the sacred with the secular in, for example, *The Second Shepherd's Play* of the Wakefield Cycle (c. 1400), where the humble and ridiculous figure of Mak the sheep-stealer shares the stage with the newborn Christ Child. The mystery cycles treated Satan as the Vice, a comic character who is an ancestor of Shakespearean villains—Iago, for example, with his diabolic vitality. Medieval drama is "total" or "epic" in the Brechtian sense, and Shakespeare inherited from it the mingling of genres that makes it possible for him to introduce the fool in *King Lear* (c. 1605), the gravedigger in *Hamlet* (c. 1601), and the clown at Cleopatra's death. Then too, medieval comedy was affected by the carnival-like Feast of Fools, a popular festival that was really a continuation of the old Roman Saturnalia, which was in the tradition of the unrestrained prehistoric ceremonies to which Aristotle must have been referring when he spoke of the origins of comedy. As Lord of Misrule, Falstaff still presides over the revels in Shakespeare's history plays. The *commedia dell'arte,* or improvisations enacted extemporaneously by type characters like Harlequin and Pulcinella, belongs to this unbroken tradition of popular theater: so Hamlet urges the players, "let those that play your clowns speak no more than is set down for them."

Yet the Renaissance also inherited the classic mode of Roman comedy, and Nicholas Udall's *Ralph Roister Doister* (1553) is modeled upon Plautus' *Miles Gloriosus* ("The Braggart Warrior," 205 B.C.?). The Renaissance critics, especially, returned to a severely academic notion of comedy; Giovanni Giorgio Trissino, Antonio Minturno, and Lodovico Castelvetro sharply distinguished it from tragedy and developed a very theoretical standard for the genre. "Comedy imitates the lowest actions," says Trissino. "The comic play ought to represent low trifling matter," adds Francesco Robortello. Minturno confines the comic to the "low, humble, sometimes mediocre" in the ordinary life of persons like merchants. "Not all baseness is appropriate to comedy," explains Lodovico Riccoboni, "but only that which is ridiculous." Thus in Italian and French theory there occurs a strange union of classical notions along with a new sense of social class in a culture that was losing its feudal structure as the bourgeoisie was becoming dominant. This restrictive academic notion of comedy, humanistic and "cultured," was a counterforce to medieval folk comedy with its ecumenical view.

In England, academic comedy is at its best in Ben Jonson, who was a stern moralist and whose charac-

A SCENE FROM SHAKESPEARE'S *Henry IV* OF FALSTAFF AT THE BOAR'S HEAD TAVERN

ters, like Volpone, are animated by one of the "humours" in man:

> . . . in every human body
> The choler, melancholy, phlegm, and blood
> By reason that they flow continually
> In some one part, and are not continent,
> Receive the name of humours. Now thus far
> It may, by metaphor, apply itself
> Unto the general disposition:
> As when some one peculiar quality
> Doth so possess a man, that it doth draw
> All his affects, his spirits, and his powers,
> In their confluxions, all to run one way.
> This may be truly said to be a humour.
> (Induction: *Every Man Out of His Humour,* 1599)

Shakespeare's plays are filled with "humourous" characters, and he, like Jonson, transcends the theories of Renaissance critics by exaggerating oddity until it is grotesque, as in Shylock, that scorned, powerful, injured figure. Like many great playwrights, Shakespeare infuses his most appalling drama (*Lear,* for instance) with the grotesquerie of comedy, and he fits Hamlet with an antic disposition. The humourous character can be as complex as the tragic hero: witness Falstaff, who elicits pity and sympathy as well as contempt and mirth. The humours can also be used almost schematically, as in *Troilus and Cressida* (c. 1601), a comical satire or dry mockery that is Euripidean in its intellectuality and cynicism.

As the Renaissance developed, it became impossible to isolate tragic from comic effects, and the many ambiguities in John Donne's metaphysical verse are echoed in that paradoxical genre called TRAGICOMEDY, toward which *Troilus and Cressida* moves. In plays by James Shirley and Beaumont and Fletcher a melodramatic action with its tragical theme is happily, and often mechanically, concluded. The French kept their genres purer, Corneille and Molière being symptomatic of the isolation of heroic tragedy from comedy, tragedy heading toward the artificial grandeurs of *Le Cid* (1637) or the subtler anguish of Racine's *Phèdre* (1677), and comedy heading toward social satire and comedy of manners with its examination of what is fraudulent. As Molière said, "People do not mind being wicked, but they object to being made ridiculous." In its relevance to life comedy was surpassing heroic tragedy.

Molière's comedy of manners, however, is different from the Restoration comedy of William Wycherley and William Congreve, whose characters are often more finely individualized than the social types in French theater. Molière seeks a certain sanity to cure man of preciosity, hypocrisy, and the dishonesties likely to appear when society is overpious or when ambition is too pressing. The English playwrights likewise studied affectation and pretense; yet their drama is, in a sense, not directed toward actual life, as Molière's is, but, instead, retreats into what Charles Lamb properly called an artificial world "beyond the diocese of the strict conscience." With its limited but sensitive psychology, Restoration comedy is one of the most fragile illusions of all theater. L. C. Knights and others have judged that this delicate theatrical fabric is a consequence of a select audience, the circle of wits who had so lost touch with humanity that the sexuality in this comedy is only an *idea* of sexuality. The politeness and innuendo in this comedy of manners require a purely verbal action, an idiom without any lived experience behind it. The licentiousness of Restoration comedy is a highly specialized technique resembling that which appears, earlier, in Shakespeare's *Love's Labour's Lost* (c. 1594), and, later, in Oscar Wilde's drawing-room theater. Fiction though it was, this drama provoked a puritan reaction against the way of the world. Yet moralists like Jeremy Collier could have spared their wrath, for the seeming realism of Restoration comedy was so frail a construct that it could not last. William Hazlitt rightly said that this drama fed on its own dissipations until it perished.

The verbal glitter was followed by sentimentality. With Richard Steele and the eighteenth century came "weeping" comedy, along with the equally hollow emotionalism of *drame bourgeois,* both encroaching on pathos. Oliver Goldsmith contrasted this "tender" comedy with the ridicule of "laughing" comedy, saying the former represented the "virtues of private life" and misfortunes instead of faults. It was a domestic drama with the bland moralizing of novels like Samuel Richardson's *Pamela* (1740–1742), focusing on situations in average families. Molière's good sense was devalued to mere common sense, without wit or humor.

Even before comedy was sentimentalized, John Dryden had discussed the distinctions between wit and humor, a question that rather profitlessly concerned critics for more than a century. Essentially, Dryden takes humor to be eccentricity of character, as in Jonsonian comedy. Congreve took humor to be "a singular and unavoidable manner of doing or saying anything, peculiar and natural to one man only; by which his speech and actions are distinguished from those of other men." Wit, by contrast, is what Hazlitt termed "the product of art and fancy."

As sentimentalism and *drame bourgeois* enfeebled the theater during the eighteenth century, comedy reappeared in the novel. Henry Fielding's comic epic poem in prose and Tobias Smollett's roistering fiction had a vitality lost on the stage. Laurence Sterne's *Tristram Shandy* (1759–1767) united a comedy of humours with the verbal artifice of a comedy of manners and served as a parody of the novel itself. By the opening of the nineteenth century, comedy had taken lyrical form in Goethe's *Faust* (1808), a closet drama. Bypassing the theater, comedy permeated the deepest currents of literature and thought: Lord Byron's mock-epic, Stendhal's picaresque or dandaical fiction, Victor Hugo's grotesquerie, Thomas Carlyle's grim humor, Søren Kierkegaard's religious absurdism, and Herman Melville's powerful sense of the incongruous all became more significant than the official theater, with Edmond Rostand's tragicomic *Cyrano de Bergerac* (1897). Comedy, in brief, temporarily left the stage to become a mode of modern thought in all its confusion and disturbance, as is apparent in Feodor Dostoyevsky's *Notes from Underground* (1864) and Franz Kafka's hideous parables.

Toward the close of the nineteenth century, comedy did reappear in the theater in many guises. Anton Chekhov's new sentimental comedy, bringing to bear an intimate psychology and reflecting a grave social malaise, often verged on the extremes of the tragic. Henrik Ibsen's *Wild Duck* (1884) has been read as a tormented modern comitragedy. Oscar Wilde revived comedy of manners, and George Bernard Shaw's dialectic of ideas brought new vigor to a comedy that is largely rhetorical. Then came the new

philosophic and existential comedy with Luigi Pirandello, Eugène Ionesco, and Samuel Beckett.

Meanwhile, audiences in the theater had separated into classes so that in addition to Shaw's high-brow debates there was the low-brow tradition of the music hall, burlesque, and vaudeville, all exhilarating and fertile modern comedy and all in the spirit of the old *opéra bouffe.* In fact, the popular afterpiece,. the jig, and farce had never really disappeared. From the vaudeville tradition came the comedy of the early film with its exploitation of the pratfall, pantomime, and the wisecrack—the tradition that, begot Charlie Chaplin and W. C. Fields. Hollywood was the beneficiary of the Keith Circuit; Laurel and Hardy, Buster Keaton, and Harold Lloyd adapted a kind of *commedia dell'arte* to the movies. The talking film pulled cinema back toward more traditional forms of stage comedy. This injured Chaplin but led to the exuberant nihilism of the Marx Brothers and the extremely knowing performance of Mae West, who reentered the artificial world of Restoration theater on her own vernacular, but very sophisticated, plane.

During the present century, the conventional meanings of comedy have been entirely revised, and recent "black" or "sick" comedy has almost completely leveled the boundaries between the so-called tragic and the so-called comic, because we have become increasingly aware that we exist in a world ever more absurd and menacing. As Friedrich Dürrenmatt observes, tragedy "can no longer cope with" this world. By hindsight we may read new significance into Socrates' question whether the craft of comedy is not the same as the craft of tragedy. Kierkegaard noted that wherever there is life there is contradiction, and the comical is present wherever there is contradiction or incongruity. The scholasticism of Renaissance critics, based upon dubious readings of Aristotle, made distinctions between comic and tragic effects and between comic and tragic heroes that we can no longer accept.

Even Aristotle suggested that comedy and tragedy both arose from kindred improvisations, and Friedrich Schiller once remarked that a work is tragedy or comedy, not by reason of its theme, but by its effect on "the tribunal before which it is judged." Whether an action is tragic or comic depends in part, at least, on how it is taken, not on how it is given. There is also Horace Walpole's cliché that the world is tragic for those who feel and comic for those who think. It has been said that the comic hero controls his world, that comedy deals with a world man has made; that the tragic hero cannot master his world, before which he is helpless. This distinction no longer holds firmly; we are defeated by the world we have made: it terrifies us. So Maurice Regnault writes of our paradoxical condition: ". . . the absence of tragedy in a tragic world gives birth to comedy." Bertolt Brecht expresses this condition.

One of the major attainments of modern criticism and drama is this new and disconcerting notion of comedy. L. C. Knights speaks for our age by stating that ". . . comedy is essentially a serious activity." Thomas Mann endorses this view: "Broadly and essentially, the achievement of modern art is that it has ceased to recognize the categories of tragic and comic or the dramatic classifications, tragedy and comedy, and views life as tragicomedy." Ionesco repeats: "I have never been able to understand the difference that is made between the comic and the tragic." One of the consequences of such indecision is the reinterpretation of Shakespeare, a dramatist who above all others seems modern in his unwillingness to isolate tragic from comic—witness our trouble in responding simply, unequivocally, to Hamlet, to Lear, to Shylock.

In effect, the comic is for us a more immediate problem than the tragic, and Northrop Frye has ventured to interpret tragedy itself as uncompleted comedy, since the full comic cycle, originating in some archetypal fertility ritual, embraces not only death but also resurrection, tragedy being the mythos of autumn, comedy the mythos of spring. One difficulty in defining the "elusive genre" we term comedy is that compared to the tragic hero the comic hero is unspecialized. If the Aristotelian tragic hero is a great and good man at last victimized by his flaw, the comic hero can be alazon, eiron, and clown—or any of the many varieties of The Fool, who can appear as the innocent one, the saint, the idiot, the pretender, the hypocrite, the tempter or catechist, the devil himself, or else the scapegoat or the slain god sacrificed for the sins of the world. The comic hero wears many masks; all men seem eligible for one or another of the comedian's roles, only a certain few for the role of tragic hero. And sometimes the tragic hero himself, like Oedipus or Othello, is a kind of ignoramus—a fool, a pretender, and a sacrifice. Alain Bosquet has formulated thirty-six "recipes of the comic."

Thus, the contradictions in comedy are at least as numerous and as provocative as the contradictions in tragedy. Formerly it was alleged that comedy springs from incongruity; yet incongruity is as inherent in tragedy as in comedy. Once, also, mirth was explained as our response to a perception of incongruity, and comedy was presumed to stimulate laughter. But laughter is one of the most ambiguous human reactions. It results from our sense of the absurd; but it also results from ebullience, from cruelty, from hysteria or fear or relief, from a "sudden sense," as Thomas Hobbes has it, of our own superiority—or else from shame or sympathy. By contrast, tears are a simple reaction. We can, as Dostoyevsky says, laugh through clenched teeth. A difference, perhaps, between farce and comedy is indicated by the simplicity or naïveté of our laughter at farce compared to the interpenetrating moods of our laughter at comedy.

If comic laughter is somet:mes joyous, it is also anarchic, for comedy is often a revolutionary, or even destructive, art. The Marx Brothers can demolish any world in which they are let loose, and we laugh as it is annihilated. James K. Feibleman has a theory that comic laughter occurs when we detect how far actuality falls short of an ideal world, that, in other words, the deepest comedy expresses our disillusion with things as they are. We laugh our intolerable situation out of existence. By contrast, Freud was inclined to take comedy as a recovery of the "lost laughter of childhood," the eroticism that loved all the world and was committed to reality; or else it is an expenditure of impulses that are repressed by the decencies of our daily life. When the superego has its "rendezvous with madness" in comedy, all inhibitions vanish. The comic spirit is radically profane; it

parodies our cherished ideals; there is nothing it will not desecrate, whether our good opinion of ourselves, our sense of security, our fixed notions, or our stereotyped responses. It will malign what we hold most sacred, whether the piety of the puritan or the fervor of the nationalist. This very profanity is a way of reestablishing our sanity and giving us a detached or distanced view of our insufficiencies or follies.

In fact, most of the values assigned to tragedy reappear in comedy under another guise. There is comic as well as tragic irony, comic as well as tragic fatality, purgation, pathos, reversal, and recognition. The tragic view magnifies our situation to nobility; the comic vision reduces and identifies our situation by another kind of distortion—by deflation, caricature, or fantasy, as in *A Midsummer Night's Dream*. Kafka could have been defining the comic technique when he noted that we clarify things by exaggeration. Then again, caricature and the grotesque can arise from hate or rejection, and behind the comic attack is often a savagery that is almost sadistic, as it is in Harold Pinter's dramas or Jonathan Swift's chapters on the human condition. Tragedy has certain sadistic overtones and concealed motives —our wish to reduce ourselves suicidally to extremes of misery. This misanthropy sometimes makes the comic hero, like Lear's Fool, a helpless victim.

If comedy is revolutionary or nihilistic, it is likewise an affirmation of order, an order we have betrayed by our idiocies. For comedy is a corrective, a discipline, as well as an exposure of our blunders. It has its own righteousness and puritanism, even if puritan repressions are abhorrent to it. Comedy cleanses and, like tragedy, chastens the proud, the blind, the mediocre, or the complacent. This is the comic rectitude of sanity, a willingness to look at the case humbly, without delusions. The comedian has his own sense of shame at what man has made of man. It may even be a sense of guilt, as in the troubled moral comedy of Beckett or Dürrenmatt. George Santayana found that civilized man has a choice between the mask and the fig leaf. For the comedian this is not a choice: he tells us to drop both mask and fig leaf. A play like Molière's *Tartuffe* rejects one kind of puritanism for another, the false for the true, the hypocritical for the authentic. It disciplines or corrects fraudulence by mocking. Jonson asserted that comedy, like tragedy, teaches. Comedy slanders the merely conventional for the sake of integrity, and thus is profoundly conservative. Aristophanes' *Clouds*, which unfairly ridicules Socrates, is at once radical and conservative in this way. Comic irresponsibility is a means of attaining responsibility.

In spite of such ambiguities, comedy seems to differ from tragedy in at least two regards: it is often more thematic and topical than tragedy and more closely focused upon the strictly contemporaneous. *Othello* (c. 1604) is not thematic in the sense that a play by Aristophanes, Molière, or Shaw is thematic; and although Ibsen and Jean-Paul Sartre are thematic, there are relatively few tragedies of ideas, unless we are willing to call Shakespeare's *Troilus and Cressida* such. And comedy—affiliated as it is with SATIRE—is normally more local, parochial, or topical than tragedy. Comedy is likely to exploit a current situation, and if it survives its own day, it does so because it bears upon some matter of abiding interest. By contrast, tragedy is "timeless."

Nevertheless, comedy can reach beyond the present, for its spectrum is broad enough to embrace a wide range of human experience, from sacred to secular, from the obscene and the trivial or mechanical misadventures of farce, to the human distresses in Beckett's *Waiting for Godot,* which is our modern Book of Job. In this searching and pitiless reach, comic absurdity infringes upon the domain ordinarily claimed by tragedy. And conversely, we may read *King Lear* as an excursion of the tragic spirit into a realm of comedy that qualifies for sublimity.

For there is a philosophic comedy that shakes the mind, and it is an error to confine our notions of comedy to drama alone. Cervantes touches us with the pathos of our ideals; Swift writes a terrifying comedy of man as Yahoo; Sterne whimsically studies the oscillations of our sensibility; Nietzsche's Blond Beast is a frightening comic monster; Jean Genêt's derelict characters are ignoble refugees from our grotesque world. We are no longer able, like Aristotle and the Renaissance critics, to scorn characters of a base or "inferior" sort. The range of comedy has constantly expanded until the category of the comic is more suggestive of our experience than anything that in the older sense could be termed tragic. Comedy has become truly philosophic in a world where Ludwig Wittgenstein can claim that our very language, our scientific formulas, are themselves a form of nonsense. Now that we are aware of the nonsense we talk, of the insignificance of our lives, we have of necessity looked upon our existence as comic. The difference between modern comedy and older varieties is the humiliating and hopeless cast of our absurdity; so, also, the former distinctions between "low" and "high" comedy have become blurred. This change began, perhaps, with Alfred Jarry's *Ubu Roi* (1896), a play foreshadowing the anarchic temper of our comedies; and along with Jarry came Strindberg, who reduced tragedy to a form of mania tinged with nihilism. Arthur Adamov, Ionesco, Dürrenmatt, Genêt, Beckett, and Pinter have justified the prediction made over a century ago by William Hazlitt: "Comedy naturally wears itself out—destroys the very food on which it lives; and by constantly and successfully exposing the follies and weaknesses of mankind to ridicule, in the end leaves itself nothing worth laughing at."

The ebullience of the comic triumph, which expressed itself in the carnival, is gone. Our laughter is no longer an overflow of the "toxic mood of cheerfulness" Freud attributed to the comic spirit. Yet even our nihilistic comedy is a sign of a height of consciousness—a sense that we are in trouble even while we fail to rebel. Comedy has always guarded us against egoism or romanticism, showing us what we are *not.* No matter how depressing our view of ourselves may be, the comic perspective, by incongruity, abides. Our "black" comedy, however savage—or indifferent—it may be, it remains a guarantee that we are still able to disengage ourselves far enough to see, at least, where we are.

This is to say that our bleak comedy remains a form of play, for play is a mode of both engaging and disengaging ourselves, giving an extra dimension to our experience. From Aristotle onward nobody has doubted that comedy, originally set in a green world, is a way of playing. So we keep on playing out our desperate comedy now that there is nothing worth laughing at—except, possibly, at moments, and with a probably unique, sick laughter. See also TRAGEDY.

Compared to the vast amount of criticism on tragedy, relatively little has been written on comedy. Many of the basic documents on the history and nature of comedy can be found in Paul Lauter's inclusive anthology *Theories of Comedy* (1964) and in Robert W. Corrigan's equally valuable *Comedy— Meaning and Form* (1965). The history of comic forms is also sketched in Allardyce Nicoll's *The Theory of Drama* (1931) and L. J. Potts's *Comedy* (1948). Basic questions concerning the rise of comedy, its form and nature, are discussed from quite different points of view in Arthur Pickard-Cambridge's *Dithyramb, Tragedy, and Comedy* (2nd ed., revised by T. B. L. Webster, 1962) and in Francis M. Cornford's *The Origin of Attic Comedy* (1914). Lane Cooper has printed the document known as the *Tractatus Coislinianus,* modeled on Aristotle, in *An Aristotelian Theory of Comedy* (1922), and the nature of irony is the theme of J. A. K. Thomson's *Irony* (1926). The larger anthropological and mythical implications of comedy are considered at length in four significant books: Northrop Frye's *Anatomy of Criticism* (1957); Albert S. Cook's *The Dark Voyage and the Golden Mean* (1949); Johan Huizinga's *Homo Ludens* (1944, 1950); and Enid Welsford's *The Fool* (1935). Also illuminating is Arthur Koestler's *Insight and Outlook* (1949) dealing with the "bisociation" in comedy. Some of the ambiguities and contradictions in laughter are indicated in Sigmund Freud's essay *Jokes and Their Relation to the Unconscious* (1905), a matter that has been further treated in Ernst Kris's *Psychoanalytic Explorations in Art* (1952) and J. Y. T. Greig's *The Psychology of Laughter and Comedy* (1923). Also notable in this connection are James Feibleman's *In Praise of Comedy* (1939) and Marie Collins Swabey's *Comic Laughter* (1961). The special derision in irony is a topic in Alan Reynolds Thompson's *The Dry Mock* (1948), and the peculiar nature of Restoration comedy is analyzed in Kathleen M. Lynch's *The Social Mode of Restoration Comedy* (1926). Many of the complexities in modern comedy are suggested in Karl S. Guthke's *Modern Tragicomedy* (1966) and Martin Esslin's *The Theatre of the Absurd* (1961), dealing with the unresolved difficulties in reaching any orthodox theory of recent comedy. Shorter discussions of the problematic nature of comedy are L. C. Knights's "Notes on Comedy" in *Determinations* (1934), edited by F. R. Leavis, and Wylie Sypher's "The Meanings of Comedy," in *Comedy* (1956). —W. S.

comedyllion. See GREECE: *modern period.*

Comedy of Errors, The (c. 1590–1593). A comedy by William SHAKESPEARE. The first recorded production of *The Comedy of Errors,* regarded by most scholars as Shakespeare's earliest comedy, took place at Gray's Inn on December 28, 1594. The shortest of the dramatist's plays, it was published initially in the First Folio (1623). For his plot Shakespeare drew on two plays by Plautus: *Menaechmi* and, secondarily, *Amphitryon.* To these Latin farces

Shakespeare added a serious frame story derived from the tale of Apollonius of Tyre as retold in John Gower's *Confessio Amantis* (1386–1390).

The Comedy of Errors deals with the arrival in Ephesus of the Syracusan merchant Aegeon in search of his son Antipholus. Accompanied by his slave Dromio, Antipholus had left Syracuse five years earlier to seek his mother, his twin brother, and Dromio's twin, from whom he and Dromio had become separated when they were infants. While Aegeon is captured and sentenced to death as a result of hostilities between Ephesus and Syracuse, Antipholus of Syracuse also arrives in Ephesus. The action revolves around the mistakes in identity (the "errors" of the title) that occur as the Syracusan twins are confused with their namesakes, who have been living in Ephesus all these years. The complications and their eventual unraveling are spread over the one day Aegeon has been granted as a reprieve to seek someone to ransom his life.

Basically a farce, the play betrays itself as an early work of Shakespeare through its concentration on physical action, its slight characterizations, the long narrative opening scene, and the undistinguished poetry. Yet in having two sets of twins instead of the one set in *Menaechmi,* Shakespeare reveals consummate skill in plotting. The humane quality that pervades the play is also far different from the spirit of the Plautine comedies. Beneath the swift-paced action and the horseplay run themes touching on order, harmony, and the redeeming power of love.

An outstanding edition of *The Comedy of Errors* is the New Arden Edition (1962), edited by R. A. Foakes.— W. G.

comedy of humours.   See Ben JONSON.

comedy of manners.   A kind of comedy in which the manners, customs, and outlook of a particular society are depicted. The point of view is often satirical and the dialogue usually witty. In England this kind of comedy flourished mainly in the Restoration with writers such as John Dryden, Sir George Etherege, and William Congreve (see ENGLAND: *Restoration drama).*—E. W.

commedia dell'arte.   The *commedia dell'arte* was one of the most unique developments in the history of the theater in Western Europe. It originated in Italy in the sixteenth century, and its influence spread throughout Europe, becoming one of the most potent forces in shaping comedy in the seventeenth and eighteenth centuries, with echoes continuing into the twentieth century.

Basically, the commedia dell'arte (comedy of the guild or by the professionals in the "art") is improvised comedy that follows a scenario rather than written dialogue. Some six hundred scenarios are extant, about half of them accounted for in Flaminio Scala's *Il teatro delle favole rappresentative* (1611), in the Corsini miscellany, and in the Locattelli manuscripts. The rest are scattered through libraries in Venice, Naples, Modena, and other cities, as well as in the Vatican library. In some instances, set speeches and tirades are written out and directions for *lazzi* routines (a series of slapstick antics) are given.

While these scenarios provide much knowledge about the personages and staging of the plays, the actors themselves left very few records of the troupes' activities. However, scholars have found fragments of information in contracts, in licenses to play in various cities, in plans for tours to foreign countries, and in diaries and correspondence. In the early eighteenth century Luigi Ricconboni, who headed a troupe of Italian players sent to Paris at the request of the duke of Orléans, kept rather complete accounts of both the repertory and the finances of his company. From these scattered details, and in spite of dates and items that sometimes seem contradictory, it has been possible to reconstruct much of the history of the commedia dell'arte.

The commedia dell'arte is largely free of conscious imitation, but it did draw on the sources of dramatic literature that have accumulated down through the ages: ancient Asiatic mimes; the comedies of Plautus and Terence; Attelan farces; the minstrels, jongleurs, and king's jesters of medieval days; the soties and farces inserted into the mystery plays; and even the *commedia erudita.* While the presence of these various elements can be noted, still they were so transformed by the skill of the Italian artists that they lost their identity in the commedia dell'arte itself when the genre reached maturity in the hands of the notable acting companies, which came into being in the second half of the sixteenth century.

The immediate origin of the commedia dell'arte in the first half of the sixteenth century is rather shrouded in legend, but a few facts emerge with some clarity. It is known that the playwright and actor Il Ruzzante (whose real name was Angelo Beolco) and his troupe were giving some kind of improvised comedy in 1528, and it is probable that other troupes were experimenting in the same way. It is also known that troupes of Italian musicians and mountebanks were making frequent trips to the capitals of Western Europe. However, real form came to the genre shortly after 1550, when professional players began to organize themselves into companies. One of the earliest of these companies to attain recognition was the celebrated Gelosi ("zealous to please"), recruited by Francesco Andreini and his talented wife, Isabella. By the end of the century the Uniti, the Confidenti, the Desiosi, and the Fideli were all in operation; companies sprang up in Modena, Padua, Mantua (the duke of Mantua himself sponsored at least two companies), and other cities. Some companies lasted for generations as children grew up and replaced their elders; or new troupes emerged on their own. At any rate, until the mid-eighteenth century, commedia dell'arte companies prospered in Italy and on their tours.

A dozen or so stock characters were common to every company. First and foremost, there were always two or more *zannis* whose lazzis ranged from comic grimaces and intonations through acrobatics to obscene gestures. A zanni might now be a clever valet working in the interest of the hero, now a stupid lackey, but he was always a buffoon ready to make comedy whenever the opportunity occurred. Regardless of the talents of the other members of the troupe, the zannis were the very embodiment of the spirit of the commedia dell'arte. Their names have become bywords in theater history: Brighella, Arlecchino, Pedrolino, Scaramuccia, Pulcinella, Mezzottino, Scapini, Coviello, Burattino, and a whole brood of slightly less famous cousins. The zannis were often

THE STOCK CHARACTER PULCINELLA OF THE *commedia dell'arte* (NEW YORK PUBLIC LIBRARY)

the main attraction of the troupe, especially before plebian audiences, and at each performance they had to dispense a broad sampling of their tricks.

Of equal importance were a Pantalone, or *magnifico,* who was an elderly parent or guardian; Gratiano, the *dottore,* a gullible old crony of Pantalone and the butt of much of the comedy of the play; a hero and an ingenue, the latter usually the daughter of Pantalone or the ward of the dottore; a braggart Spanish captain, jealous suitor, or other secondary romantic figure; a maid for the heroine, who connived with the young couple to outwit their elders; and a throng of subordinate characters. Certain towns and villages purportedly furnished many of the characters, so that a babble of dialects added a farcical touch: Pantalone was a Venetian merchant; the dottore, a native of Bologna; the zannis Arlecchino and Brighella hailed from Bergamo; and Scaramuccia and Pulcinella were Neapolitans.

The foregoing assortment of roles remained almost constant throughout the life of the genre, although names often changed from troupe to troupe: the young hero of the Gelosi company was Fortunio or Aurelio; of the Confidenti, Ortensio; of the Fideli, Fulvio; Lelio or Ottavio or Valerio was used in a number of other companies. The names of Isabella, Flaminia, Silvia, Olivetta, and Valeria are among those that were given to heroines. Colombina was usually the name of the heroine's servant, with Violetta, Fioretta, and Smeraldina occurring from time to time.

An actor often played a character for so many years and became so famous for his interpretation of the role that he was known to the publìc, and in subsequent theater history, by his stage name rather than his real name. For instance, Francesco Andreini is called Captain Spavento. He created this enormously popular Spanish captain (who is not unlike the *miles gloriosus* of Plautus) and thereby initiated the enduring vogue for the braggart soldier in other countries.

G. B. Biancolelli was more commonly known as Arlecchino than by his own name. Zanetta Benozzi, who played the Silvias in comedies by Pierre Marivaux (1688–1763), is labeled in the annals of eighteenth-century French theater simply as Silvia.

Masks, an inheritance from the classical mimes, were worn by most of the important actors except the dashing hero and the young ingenue, yet each character was readily distinguished by his dress: the dottore, for example, always had a fulsome black cape and a broad-rimmed black hat, while Pierrot wore slack white trousers and a blouse with large pompoms down the front. The mask did not hinder an actor from playing his part; he simply made greater use of bodily movements and inflection of voice. The English man of the theater David Garrick, upon witnessing a performance of the commedia dell'arte, is said to have remarked, "See how much expression Carlino's back has."

The expertise of the Italian players is legendary. Each player had to sense the mood of a particular audience and be clairvoyant with respect to his colleagues' intentions, so that a performance of a commedia dell'arte was an exercise of interplay among the actors as they improvised the dialogue. The zannis, too, took advantage of a responsive audience to indulge in a prolonged interlude of comic antics. Yet the whole had to have dramatic coherence; in fact, each performance was a collective tour de force of ingenuity, a demonstration of superb ensemble artistry that is rare in the theater.

While these troupes excelled in the presentation of commedia dell'arte, they were equally expert in performing other types of plays with written dialogue, such as tragedies, pastorals, tragicomedies, commedia erudita, and, frequently, parodies or satires of classical masterpieces. With such a diversified repertory and with their dependence on one another to perform commedia dell'arte skillfully, it was wellnigh impossible for actors to shift from one troupe to another, and most troupes remained intact over the years.

Once the genre was established, the tours of the Italian companies carried the commedia dell'arte into every corner of Europe. Apparently language was no obstacle, for the actors were such excellent mimics that the spectators had little difficulty following the antics on the stage.

The Gelosi troupe appeared at the French court intermittently from 1571 to 1604, and after them other companies visited France with increasing frequency, until finally, in 1660, Louis XIV authorized Tiberio Fiorilli and his troupe to settle in Paris, where they stayed until 1697. Another company, under the direction of Luigi Ricconboni, was installed on the stage of the Hotel de Bourgogne in 1716. This troupe adopted the policy of adding comedies by French writers to the repertory. As a result the Italian element diminished as time went on, and eventually, in 1763, when the direction was taken over by Favart and his wife, the theater evolved into the Opéra Comique.

Italian players visited England as early as 1546 and frequently thereafter. Revels Accounts (a record of expenditures for court entertainment) for 1573/74 indicate that Italian companies performed in Windsor and Reading. Drusiano Martinelli was granted permission to appear in England in 1577. By the end of the century, visits of Italian companies were fairly common, and in 1602 Flaminio Curtesse played before Queen Elizabeth. And so on for the next hundred years.

In 1574 Alberto Naseli, known professionally as Zan Ganassa, went to Spain, where his popularity enriched him and enabled him to build a theater in Madrid. The Martinelli brothers, Tristano and Drusiano, followed him later in the century. Performances by Italian troupes are recorded in many Spanish cities, including Toledo, Seville, Valladolid, and Valencia.

Italian players began to tour the Germanic kingdoms and Slavic countries in the second half of the seventeenth century. The Calderoni couple took their distinguished company to Munich in 1687, where they played for four seasons, and they visited Vienna in 1699 and again in 1703. The Ristori troupe started an engagement in Warsaw in 1715 that lasted fifteen years, after which the company journeyed to Russia to entertain Empress Anna in 1733 and 1735. The Bertoldis spent most of their professional careers in Warsaw and Dresden from 1738 to the mid-1750's.

Wherever the touring companies went, they left their imprint. The influence is at once self-evident and intangible: self-evident, in that for two centuries dramatists universally and unashamedly borrowed the infectious gaiety and teeming action of the commedia dell'arte for their own uses; intangible, in that the usual literary comparisons cannot be made, since the Italians put no artistic value on their scenarios. The innumerable plot devices—mistaken identities; one or more characters in disguise; young people of unknown origin who turn out to be brother and sister of high birth; a friend torn between love and loyalty to his comrade; a lover posing as a servant to be near the girl he adores and to save her from marriage to a rich old man; a girl dressed as a man; the use of twins, sometimes two sets of twins; combinations of the fanciful with reality—all these and a host of other farcical inventions were exploited ad infinitum in every country in Europe by the Italian troupes.

In France glimpses of Italianate influence appeared early in the seventeenth century in the farces performed on the *tréteaux* of the Pont-Neuf. Shortly thereafter the Spanish captain caught the imagination of French dramatists and appeared in a variety of guises. Jean de Rotrou (1609–1650) used this character in the person of Rhinocéronte in *Clarice,* the extravagant Rosaran in *Agésilan de Colchon,* and the blustering Émile in *Amélie.* Pierre Corneille (1606–1684) presented the captain under the name of Matamore, this time as a Gascon instead of a Spaniard, in *L'Illusion comique.* The captain appears again in *Le Railleur* by A. Mareschal.

It is a generally accepted fact that Molière was on friendly terms with Italian actors and that, as a novice in the provinces, he probably acted in Italian farces or adapted them for his own use. When he brought his troupe to Paris in 1659, he was installed in the Hotel de Bourgogne, where he shared the stage for some years with the Italian troupe of Fiorilli. Needless to say, the contacts between the French and Italian players were inescapable. Certainly Molière's comedies are steeped in the Italian tradition. Many of his plays are based on the plot devices of the commedia: the frenetic maneuverings of a crafty servant

in the interests of his young master (*The Tricks of Scapin*); the bewildered elders outwitted by a dashing hero and an intriguing ingenue (*The School for Wives* and *The Would-be Gentleman*); the pedant doctor (*The Doctor in Spite of Himself* and *The Imaginary Invalid*); and all the wily Frontins, Scapins, and Sganarelles stem from the substance of the commedia dell'arte. To be sure, Molière endowed the material with his own genius, but the influence is unmistakable.

In the 1720's and 1730's, Marivaux wrote most of his comedies—certainly his best and most successful ones—for Ricconboni's troupe. Hence, the Arlequins, the Silvias, the Lelios, and the Colombines in his theater. His first play, *Arlequin poli par l'amour,* with its flight into Arcadian fantasy, blends French and Italian elements to perfection; *Le Jeu de l'amour et du hasard* and *Le Prince travesti* make use of disguises; in *La Surprise de l'amour* conniving servants dominate their masters; and in *La Fausse suivante* and *Le Triomphe de l'amour* the heroines pose as men. Famed though he is for his delicacy of expression, refinement of comedy, finesse in psychological probing, and excursions into fantasy, Marivaux projected these qualities through the situations and stock characters of the commedia dell'arte. At the end of the century, Bartolo and Basile of *The Barber of Seville* and *The Marriage of Figaro* by Beaumarchais (1732–1799) might well have stepped out of a number of Italian scenarios.

Elizabethan writers followed the pattern of imitating the visiting Italians. Zanni, Pantalone, and Arlecchino had their counterparts in Zany, Pantaloon, and Harlakeen. Just as the Italian braggarts were the models for the bravos in English drama, so were the English pedants fashioned after Gratiano.

Like other playwrights, Shakespeare utilized material wherever he could find it, and therefore it is not surprising to see many parallels between his plays and the Italian scenarios. The brother-sister twin situation and Viola's masquerade in *Twelfth Night* have their counterpart in a score of Italian scenarios. The trickery of Autolycus in *The Winter's Tale* and the vulgar stage business by Stephano and Trinculo in *The Tempest* derive from the bag of tricks of the zannis. The Arcadian setting and characters of *As You Like It* match the pastorals of the commedia dell'arte repertory. *The Merry Wives of Windsor* and *The Comedy of Errors* savor strongly of the materials and methods of the Italian players. The mixture of fantasy and buffoonery in *A Midsummer Night's Dream* can be found repeatedly in Italian scenarios. Like Molière, Shakespeare's genius transcended and transformed the Italianate material, but the echoes are heard nonetheless. In addition, Ben Jonson's *Alchemist* and *Volpone,* John Chapman's *An Humorous Day's Mirth,* Thomas Middleton's *The Widow,* and John Marston's *What You Will* are typical of the scores of English plays that embody elements of the commedia dell'arte.

Aside from the graciosos, which evolved from the zannis created by Ganassa and Bottarga, the Spanish theater was considerably less affected by the commedia dell'arte than were the English and French theaters. Perhaps the most important influence is to be found in timing; the Italian troupes did much to give direction to the Spanish theater toward the end of the sixteenth century as it was developing into the *comedia nueva.*

As for the impact of the commedia dell'arte on the emerging cultures of Eastern Europe, the stimulus was rather direct. According to the literary historian Allardyce Nicoll, "Without a doubt, in these three lands, Germany, Poland and Russia, the Italian comedy was a force leading towards the development of native theaters."

Critical opinion has differed on the relative impact of the commedia dell'arte, and literary historians have disputed the degree of Italian predominance in one play or another, or the influence on one author or another. Some critics have tended to minimize the influence of the commedia dell'arte on European comedy on the grounds that many situations—identical twins, for example—actually come from Plautus or other ancient sources. However, this theory overlooks the fact that the playwrights of the sixteenth and seventeenth centuries were not scholars who turned to ancient manuscripts for inspiration; rather, they were usually professional actors like Shakespeare and Molière who had to supply vehicles for their troupes. The commedia dell'arte repertory offered a rich lode in which to quarry, and the lure was irresistible. The immediacy of the commedia dell'arte performances made these Italian plays the most available, natural, and direct source of ideas. Of course, no one can say just what performances of the Italian troupes were witnessed by Shakespeare, Lope de Vega, Molière, and their contemporaries, but as has already been pointed out, most playwrights had close professional ties with visiting Italian companies. In the final analysis, one cannot survey the European theater without sensing the strong imprint of Italianate influence.

Traces of the commedia dell'arte persist in the twentieth century. The pantomime theater in the Tivoli Gardens in Copenhagen still uses the characters and plots of the commedia dell'arte. The Punch and Judy shows so popular in England and the Guignol theater that delights French children in the Luxembourg Gardens perform commedia dell'arte tricks in puppetry. The slapstick comedy of early American movies, typified by the Keystone Cops and Laurel and Hardy films, repeats the zanni tricks of Arlecchino and company. In the mid-twentieth century, such troupes as the Piccolo Teatro di Milano and the Teatro Stabile di Genova have won critical acclaim for their superb performances of plays in the commedia dell'arte tradition. See ITALY: *commedia dell'arte and Goldonian reform.*

The bibliography for the commedia dell'arte is rather limited. Allardyce Nicoll's two books, *Masks, Mimes and Miracles* (1931) and *The World of Harlequin* (1963), are excellent; the former contains reliable information regarding the sources of the commedia dell'arte from antiquity through the middle ages and traces the formation of the commedia dell'arte in mid-sixteenth-century Italy, while the latter gives a masterful summary of the genre. In her two-volume work *Italian Popular Comedy* (1934), Kathleen M. Lea presents a thorough study of the influence of the commedia dell'arte on English comedy and provides the text and translation of several scenarios. Joseph S. Kennard's *Mimes and Marionettes* (1935) offers a few details not found else-

where. For the role of the commedia dell'arte in the Spanish theater, N. D. Shergold gives the essential facts in his brief but cogent article "Ganassa and the Commedia Dell'Arte in Sixteenth-Century Spain" in *Modern Language Review* (July 1956). Henry Salerno's *Scenarios of the Commedia Dell'Arte* (1967), which is a translation of Flaminio Scala's *Il teatro delle favole rappresentative* (1611), makes available to English readers the most important single collection of scenarios, with helpful notes.—K. N. M.

commedia erudita. The term refers to the comedy of the Italian Renaissance, exemplified by such playwrights as Lodovico Ariosto (1474–1533) and Pietro Aretino (1492–1556). As distinguished from the Italian *commedia dell'arte,* which was improvisational, the commedia erudita was a written drama.

Comus. See John MILTON.

Congo Republic. See AFRICA: *Congo Republic.*

Congreve, William (1670–1729). English comic dramatist. Born near Leeds, England, Congreve was educated in Ireland, where his father commanded a garrison. He attended the Kilkenny School and Trinity College, Dublin, in both of which he knew Jonathan Swift as a fellow student. After a brief period at the Middle Temple in London, he abandoned law for a literary career. He wrote a novel, *Incognita* (1692), under a pseudonym and then turned to drama. He showed his first comedy, *The Old Bachelor,* to John Dryden, who considered it so remarkable that he and Thomas Southerne helped Congreve to put the final touches to it for its performance in 1693. The success of this play confirmed him in his desire to write for the theater, which he continued to do until 1700, when the cool reception of *The Way of the World* determined him to stop. After this time his connection with the stage was slight, though he briefly shared with John Vanbrugh the management of the new Queen's Theatre in the Haymarket; wrote words for a masque, *The Judgment of Paris,* and an opera, *Semele* (the latter probably never performed during his lifetime); and collaborated with Vanbrugh and William Walsh (1663–1708) in the translation of Molière's *Monsieur de Pourceaugnac.* With his income augmented by various minor government offices, he led an agreeable life in these years, was received in the best society, sought out by such literary figures as Pope, Swift, Steele, and Gay and visited by Voltaire. He died from injuries received in the overturning of his carriage and was buried in Westminster Abbey.

Congreve was the greatest of the English writers of comedy of manners (see ENGLAND: *Restoration drama*). He wrote four comedies: *The Old Bachelor* (1693), *The Double Dealer* (1693), LOVE FOR LOVE, and THE WAY OF THE WORLD. In all of these plays, but especially in the last, witty dialogue was brought to a degree of perfection never surpassed before or since. His one tragedy, *The Mourning Bride* (1697), was greatly admired in its own day and later by Dr. Johnson, though it now contributes little to Congreve's reputation.

The best edition of Congreve's drama is *The Complete Plays of William Congreve* (1967), edited by Herbert Davis. The standard biography is John C. Hodges' *William Congreve, the Man* (1941). —E. W.

Connelly, Marc [us Cook] (1890–   ). American playwright. Connelly, a native of McKeesport, Pennsylvania, began his career as a newspaper reporter, working for the Pittsburgh *Gazette-Times* among other papers. After a brief apprenticeship as a writer of lyrics, he achieved Broadway recognition when he collaborated with George S. KAUFMAN on *Dulcy* (1921). In addition to his playwriting, Connelly has been active as a director, actor, and film writer. In recent years, he has been a teacher of drama, notably as a member of the faculty of the Yale University School of Drama from 1946 to 1950.

Marc Connelly's collaboration with Kaufman resulted in a number of sharp satires. *Merton of the Movies* (1922), based on the book by Harry Leon Wilson, was one of the first comic portraits of Hollywood. In *Beggar on Horseback* (1924) Connelly and Kaufman explored, in farcical, semiexpressionist form, the fate of an idealistic composer who succumbs to the materialism of his fiancée's businessman father. (See EXPRESSIONISM.) Connelly also collaborated with Herman J. Mankiewicz (*The Wild Man of Borneo*, 1927), Frank B. Elser (*The Farmer Takes a Wife*, 1934), and Arnold Sundgaard (*Everywhere I Roam*, 1938), but none of these has the stature of his work with Kaufman.

Connelly's reputation rests on *The Green Pastures* (1930), which won him the Pulitzer Prize in 1930. Based on *Ol' Man Adam an' His Chillun* (1928), a collection of stories from the Old Testament retold by Roark Bradford, *The Green Pastures* dramatizes key events from the Bible as they might be imagined by Negro children in a rural church in Louisiana. Beginning with a heavenly fish fry at which God accidentally creates the earth in His determination to provide enough firmament for the cooks to use in their custard, the play traces the moral growth of the Lord as He tries to deal with man's corruptibility. At the end, after deciding to abandon His creation, God learns from a simple soldier that what man wants is a loving god, not a wrathful one. Though the people he deals with are naïve, Connelly is rarely patronizing, and the seriousness of his theme keeps the play from becoming merely quaint.

There is no standard edition of Connelly's plays. Critical discussions can be found in the major studies of modern American drama.—M. L.

Conquest of Granada, The (1670, 1671). A heroic play in two parts in rhyming couplets by John DRYDEN. Part I of *The Conquest of Granada by the Spaniards* was first performed by the King's Company at the Theatre Royal in Bridges Street in December 1670. Part II followed in January, and thereafter the two parts were given on successive nights. John Evelyn commented in his diary on the "very glorious scenes and perspectives."

The setting for the play is Granada from the last days of Moorish control to the triumph of Ferdinand and Isabella. The power of the weak king Boabdelin is undermined by the quarrels between the two factions, the Zegrys and the Abencerrages, and by the ambitious scheming of Lyndaraxa. The main plot concerns the noble stranger Almanzor, of unknown birth, who arrives in Granada and joins in the fighting, bringing victory to whichever side he aids. He falls in love with Almahide, who checks his advances, since she is contracted to Boabdelin, but exercises an increasing influence over him. After the death of

Boabdelin and the victory of the Spaniards, she agrees to marry Almanzor, who is discovered to be the son of a Spanish nobleman. A second plot deals with the rivalry of Abdalla and Abdelmelech for the love of Lyndaraxa, and a third with the ideal love of the Abencerrago Ozmyn for Benzayda, a Zegry.

The Conquest of Granada has an epic sweep, a magnification of character, and a combination of extravagance and control in its rhymed couplets that together make it one of the best examples of the heroic play. By means of his schematic organization of the complex plot, Dryden makes it into a drama of conflicting ideals (see ENGLAND: *Restoration drama*).

The Conquest of Granada will be included in the Regents Restoration Drama Series. It is available in the Mermaid Dramabook *John Dryden. Three Plays* (1957), George Saintsbury, ed.—E. W.

Conscious Lovers, The (1722). A comedy by Sir Richard STEELE. Steele's last comedy, widely publicized in advance, opened with a distinguished cast and was an overwhelming success. Upon its publication later on in the year, King George I, to whom the play was dedicated, rewarded Steele with a gift of five hundred guineas.

Bevil Junior and Myrtle are friends. Bevil has just returned from abroad to find that a marriage between himself and Lucinda has been agreed upon by Bevil Senior and Lucinda's father, the vastly wealthy Mr. Sealand. It is a marriage for which Bevil Junior has no desire, since his affections lie elsewhere, and since Lucinda is in love with Myrtle and he with her. Now, however, Mr. Sealand suddenly opposes the marriage, having learned of a recent incident that seems to indicate that the young Bevil has become involved with a girl of, as Sealand assumes, questionable character. The girl is Indiana, found in distressing circumstances in France and befriended and helped back to England, along with an aunt, by the generous Bevil, every inch a Christian hero. Bevil and Lucinda, neither of whom has as yet learned of Mr. Sealand's second thoughts, correspond clandestinely and are in agreement concerning their distaste for this impending marriage. Lucinda herself is faced with further difficulties, because her mother, Mr. Sealand's second wife, is bestirring herself to bring about the union of her daughter and Cimberton, a ridiculous suitor. Myrtle and Bevil's servant, Tom, disguised as two lawyers, wait on Mrs. Sealand and Cimberton and effectively reduce the business of a marriage settlement to a temporary state of hopeless confusion. Lucinda, however, shortly finds herself free to marry Myrtle. And a clear path likewise opens up for Bevil Junior and Indiana as a result of her meeting with Mr. Sealand. He is forthwith convinced of her virtuous character and then discovers through a bracelet of hers that she is his long-lost daughter by his first wife.

Steele's long campaign which as an essayist he had carried on in behalf of a drama purged of indecencies of speech and action came to a climax in *The Conscious Lovers*. Though some of the plot has been borrowed from Terence's *Andria,* and though Steele saw a precedent for good-natured comedy in Terence, what gave the play its novelty in the eyes of his contemporaries and what marks it as something of a landmark in eighteenth-century sentimental comedy must be credited to Steele himself. The hero, Bevil

DRAWING OF A SCENE FROM RICHARD STEELE'S *The Conscious Lovers* (WALTER HAMPDEN MEMORIAL LIBRARY AT THE PLAYERS, NEW YORK)

Junior, is exemplary in all he does. Steele was presenting him as an inspiring model of right conduct, and the public, properly inspired or not, was moved by his virtuous behavior. Indiana is almost a match for Bevil in virtue and tender sympathy, and her recital of her trials and misfortunes wrung tears from box, pit, and gallery. Today we find it regrettable that Steele allowed moralism such scope and left too little room for the genuine comedy he could command and which does in fact emerge when the action centers on Myrtle and his amusing disguises and on those two winning servant characters, Tom and Phillis.

The Conscious Lovers is included in *Richard Steele* (1903), the edition of the plays edited by George A. Aitken. There is a discussion of the play in the study by John C. Loftis, *Steele at Drury Lane* (1952).—R. Q.

contaminatio. The word *contaminari* means "to touch," "to spoil." Modern scholars of Roman comedy define contaminatio as the process of joining together material from two or more Greek originals to form one Latin play. This joining together might take the form either of adding a small section of a second Greek play to a first, as Terence did in his *Andria, Eunuchus,* and *Adelphoe,* or combining two Greek comedies to form one play. The latter type of fusion has been ascribed to Plautus to explain certain difficulties or inconsistencies in plot structure in several comedies (for example, *Amphitryon, Miles Gloriosus, Poenulus,* and *Pseudolus*), but the evidence for such interweaving is weak and has been rejected in recent years.

Terence said that he was accused of contaminating many Greek plays while writing a few Latin ones. The Greek original was spoiled if alien matter was added to it from another source, and the second original was perhaps likewise spoiled for later adaptation if a part of it was added to another play.—G. E. D.

Contrast, The (1787). A comedy by Royall Tyler. Written in three weeks and first performed in New York in 1787, this is the first American comedy to be performed by professional actors. It was a success that was repeated in New York and other cities as late as 1799.

The play revolves around Dimple, a New Yorker whose mania for everything English has turned him into a fop and a rake. Engaged to Maria, the daughter of a wealthy merchant, he pursues at the same time Maria's two fashionable friends, Charlotte and Letitia. Charlotte's brother, Colonel Manly, a plain-mannered, high-principled veteran of the Revolution, appears. He and Maria fall in love, Dimple is revealed as a villain and a coward, Charlotte and Letitia are taught a lesson, and Manly and Maria are united. Manly's servant, Jonathan, and Dimple's servant, Jessamy, provide an additional contrast between native worth and the affectation of foreign manners.

The main plot and principal characters derive from Sheridan and Vanbrugh; the hero and heroine, however, are sentimental and sententious. The play's distinction lies in the character of Jonathan: unsophisticated but shrewd, crude but warmhearted, refusing the name of "servant" but devoted to Manly,

SCENE FROM ROYALL TYLER'S *The Contrast* (MUSEUM
OF THE CITY OF NEW YORK)

Jonathan is "a true born son of liberty." The scenes
in which Jessamy tries to teach this bumpkin elegance in courtship are first-rate comedy.—B. H.

Coriolanus (c. 1608). A tragedy by William
SHAKESPEARE. *Coriolanus* was first published in the
1623 First Folio. Its main source is the account of
"The Life of Caius Martius Coriolanus" in Plutarch's *Lives of the Noble Grecians and Romans,* as
translated into English (2nd ed., 1595) by Sir Thomas
North from Jacques Amyot's French translation
(1559). No pre-Restoration record of performance
exists.

The Tragedy of Coriolanus deals with the election
to the consulship and the immediate fall from power
of Caius Marcius, a proud, aloof patrician. Rome, as
the play opens, is in a state of political unrest as a
result of a famine. Intensifying the problems is the
news of an impending attack by the Volscians under
Tullus Aufidius. Caius Marcius, regarded by the
plebians as their "chief enemy" because he scorns the
commoners, is sent as one of the commanders to repel the attack. In the battles that follow the Volscians
are defeated. For his role in capturing Corioli, the
Volscian capital, Caius Marcius receives the
agnomen of Coriolanus. Now regarded as a great
hero, he is named consul by both the patricians and
the plebians. Using Coriolanus' reluctance to perform before the plebians the customary rituals for assuming office, the tribunes Brutus and Sicinius stir
the people to revoke the election of their new consul.
In the civil discord that follows only the pleading of
Coriolanus' mother, Volumnia—who holds her son
very much under her control—persuades him to
address the populace. Baited by the tribunes,
Coriolanus flies into anger at the crowd, and is banished. He seeks out Aufidius, who is resuming hostilities, and together they march on Rome. Emissaries
fruitlessly entreat Coriolanus to spare his native city;
finally, an appeal from his mother to make an honorable peace prevails. Aufidius returns to Corioli,
where, enraged over the actions of Coriolanus, he incites his followers against the Roman. In a public

confrontation, Aufidius goads Coriolanus into an
angry outbrust against the Volscians, who, led by
Aufidius' followers, kill him.

Coriolanus differs greatly from Shakespeare's
other tragic protagonists in that he emerges as a
completely unattractive individual. He is a military
hero who is an egoist, is easily provoked to great anger, lacks insight into himself, and is dominated by
his mother. In standing for the consulship he is
placed in a position where his personality traits and
his own desires conflict with public responsibility.
Knowledge of the art of governing is a key issue in
the tragedy, for the relationships between the patricians and the plebians have seriously deteriorated,
and social and political chaos are imminent in Rome.
The play, therefore, probes the problem of political
instability made exceptionally explosive by the selection of a consul who is temperamentally unfit to rule.
The political issue would have had relevancy for
Jacobean audiences because there was great unrest in
England at the time, as manifested by the Midlands
revolt of 1607.

Structurally, the dual interest in political problems
and character analysis pulls the play in two directions, and it is this factor that lies at the heart of most
of the divided critical commentary on *Coriolanus.*
However the play was received in its own time—
and it does not appear to have been popular—it becomes a powerful drama for moderns who tend to
view it as a psychological character study with "silver cord" overtones. Viewed as a work conforming
to the patterns of great tragedy, *Coriolanus* leaves
much to be desired.

An outstanding edition of *Coriolanus* is the New
Cambridge Edition (1960), edited by J. Dover Wilson.—W. G.

Corneille, Pierre (1606–1684). French playwright and poet. Born in Rouen into a family of lawyers and administrators, Pierre Corneille, a brilliant
student, was educated by the Jesuits in his home
town. From 1624 to 1628 he trained in the practice of
law at the Parliament of Rouen, and for at least
twenty-five years thereafter, despite a very active
literary life and frequent stays in Paris, he fervently worked in law and administration in various
capacities. As early as 1624 Corneille had begun to
write verse. In 1629 he gave his first play, the comedy
Mélite, to the road company of the actor Montdory,
which was on its way to Paris and eventually took
over the Marais theater. The play's success encouraged him to continue, and before LE CID he wrote one
tragedy, one tragicomedy, and five comedies. Soon
considered the equal of the best dramatists of the
time, he was presented in 1633 to Cardinal Richelieu,
who granted him his patronage and convinced him in
1635 to collaborate with four other poets. Until
around 1639 the "Society of the Five Authors" wrote
several plays for the cardinal. Corneille, it would
seem, had difficulty bearing the constraints of work
written to order. In the meantime he had been at the
center of the most renowned dispute in French classical theater, which took place at the time of his
tragicomedy *Le Cid*'s great success, and during
which Richelieu tried to bring the talented writer to
heel. Deeply wounded by the French Academy's decision regarding his play—the academy disapproved
of the subject and of Corneille's disregard of the

PIERRE CORNEILLE (NEW YORK PUBLIC LIBRARY)

French classical tenets of verisimilitude and propriety—and at the same time involved in a trial, Corneille left the theater until 1640. From then until 1652 he contributed nine tragedies, two comedies, a "machine" tragedy, and a heroic comedy.

Corneille was then the most eminent dramatist in France. But during the same period he was also the dupe of the political maneuvers of the Fronde, and after having been entrusted by Mazarin in 1650 with a very high judiciary office in Rouen, he found himself in 1651 both jobless and with no pension. In 1652, when for the first time a play of his failed, he again left the theater and devoted himself to translating the *Imitation of Christ*. At the same time, however, he was working on a machine tragedy for a Norman nobleman: *La Toison d'or* ("The Golden Fleece"), which was not performed in Paris until 1661, but then with great success. He had thus not lost his taste for theater, and both pensioned and encouraged by the superintendent of finance, Nicolas Fouquet, in two months he wrote the tragedy *Œdipe,* which was performed in Paris in 1659 and was so successful that Corneille came back into prominence, closely followed by his brother Thomas. In 1662 both decided to move to Paris with their families (Pierre had married in 1641). And in 1663, the year that royal pensions were institutionalized, Corneille became one of the writers most richly endowed by the king.

In 1674, after eleven new plays, one of which was the tragicomedy *Psyché* (1671), written in collabora-

tion with Molière and Philippe Quinault, Corneille left the theater forever. Little by little his success had diminished. The Abbé d'Aubignac had highly criticized *Sophonisbe* in 1663. In 1666 *Agésilas,* a gallant tragedy in free verse, had been a failure. When Molière staged *Attila* in 1667, it was only a partial success. That same year Racine triumphed with *Andromaque* and began to attack Corneille indirectly in his prefaces. And in 1670 Racine's *Bérénice* was far better received than Corneille's *Tite et Bérénice.* After the unexpected success of *Pulchérie* (1672), which the troupes had at first refused, he had *Suréna* performed in 1674 with some success, but it was eclipsed by Racine's *Iphigénie en Aulide* (1674). From that year on (the year that one of his sons was killed in the war against the European coalition), Corneille attended to the publication of his plays, to his income, and to finding a place for another of his sons. He also assiduously attended the meetings of the French Academy, of which he had become a member in 1647. Comfortably off, but physically weakened, he died in 1684.

He remained, in spite of Racine's popularity, "the great Corneille" with much of the public. Indeed, the "Cornelian" clique was made up of writers and leading members of high Parisian society. And although the court's favor was granted to Racine, and from 1674 to 1682 Corneille did not receive a royal pension, his masterpieces of the 1640's and 1650's were often revived. Louis XIV himself had six tragedies of that period performed for him in 1676. That same year Racine, who was well on the way toward religious conversion, removed from his prefaces the allusions insulting to Corneille, and in 1685, on the occasion of Thomas Corneille's replacing Pierre in the French Academy, Racine made a renowned eulogistic speech in honor of "the great Corneille."

Corneille began in the theater eight years before the birth of Louis XIV and left it at the time of Louis XIV's war against the European coalition. His career as a dramatist thus covered a period of forty-four years, during which he wrote thirty-three plays—hence the variety of his works, where he tried to follow the fashion, to react against it, or to start new ones. His first plays showed great understanding of the new taste of the 1630's, both conforming to it and guiding it: *Mélite* (1630), a comedy; *Clitandre* (1631), a tragicomedy; *La Veuve* ("The Widow," 1631), a comedy; *Médée* (1635), a tragedy; *L'Illusion comique* ("The Comic Illusion," 1636), a comedy; and finally *Le Cid.* The 1640's were the time of his greatest tragedies and the best comedies of the period preceding Molière: HORACE, CINNA, POLYEUCTE, *La Mort de Pompée* ("Pompey's Death," 1643), all tragedies; *Le Menteur* (*The Liar,* 1643), a comedy; RODOGUNE, a tragedy; *La Suite du Menteur* ("Sequel to *The Liar,*" 1645), a comedy; *Théodore* (1646), a tragedy; and *Heraclius* (1647), a tragedy. With the Fronde, there was a slack in the Paris spectacles, but 1650 was the year of *Andromède,* a machine tragedy, and *Don Sanche d'Aragon* ("Don Sancho of Aragon"), a heroic comedy; in 1651 the tragedy *Nicomède* seemed to reflect the current political picture; and the season 1651/52 included the tragedy *Pertharite,* a failure for obscure reasons, which were perhaps political. When he returned to the Paris stage in 1659, Corneille, while keeping his originality, made concessions to the new ROMANESQUE fashion or experimented within the rules of classicism, with sometimes successful, sometimes disastrous, results: *Œdipe* (1659), a tragedy; *Le Toison d'or* (1661), a machine tragedy; *Sertorius* (1662), a tragedy; *Sophonisbe* (1663), a tragedy; *Othon* (1664), a tragedy; *Agésilas* (1666), a tragedy; *Attila* (1667), a tragedy; *Tite et Bérénice* (1670), a heroic comedy; *Psyché* (1671, written in collaboration), a tragicomedy-ballet; *Pulchérie* (1672), a heroic comedy; and *Suréna* (1674), a tragedy.

In the prefaces to his plays and in the three *Discours* ("Discourses") published in 1660 along with the complete edition of his works to date, Corneille affirmed his independence within the bounds of the classical doctrine—which, indeed, he had helped formulate and which he accepted but at the same time subordinated to his pursuit of "beautiful effects." For him theater was a spectacular art (hence his taste for the machine plays) that had to astound the spectator. He liked historically true but surprising situations that forced a number of characters into action and in which the individual, through his heroic and magnanimous decisions, his heinous crimes, or his renunciations, proved his powers of transcendency. Faced with a difficult choice, Corneille's protagonists take the most admirable alternative, even in crime, so that they may shine in their own eyes and in the eyes of others. This is called "the ethics of glory," by which the hero convinces himself and seeks to convince others of his self-possession and superiority. Ordinary morality is left far behind and is replaced by the elucidation of inner conflicts and the explanation of great feats by which a hero contrives to reconcile his will and his passions in order to achieve his goal. The strong heroes succeed; others are not altogether free from bad faith when they rationalize, thus making Corneille's theater rich in irony. As he grew old, Corneille created increasingly complex and increasingly ambiguous characters. The individualistic ideal of glory became more and more difficult to attain, although it remained the essential concern of his protagonists. Political decisions and even love were conditioned by it. But while love meant dazzling and being dazzled, this did not, in *Le Cid* and in certain of Corneille's last plays, exclude tenderness.

The most comprehensive book in English on Pierre Corneille is Philip John Yarrow's *Corneille* (1963), which studies the age of Corneille, his career as a dramatist, and the techniques and themes of his tragedies. For a more specialized analysis of the characters, see Robert J. Nelson, *Corneille, His Heroes and Their Worlds* (1963).—Ja. G.

Corneille, Thomas (1625–1709). French playwright. Brother of Pierre, Thomas Corneille was born in Rouen and began his career in law. He started to write for the theater in 1649, was the most prolific of the writers of the French classical period and, until around 1680, the most appreciated along with his brother Pierre, Molière, and Racine. His last play was written in 1695. A member of the French Academy after 1685, he devoted the end of his life to scholarly and encyclopedic works.

The first plays of Thomas Corneille were comedies inspired by the Spanish *comedia*: *Don Bertrand de Cigarral* (1651), based on a work by Fernando de Rojas, and *Le Geôlier de soi-même* ("His Own Jailer," 1655), based on a work by Calderón, and in which the actor Jodelet played the comic role, in a plot typical of the genre, consisting of *quid pro quos* and mistaken identities. With *Timocrate* (1656), which was the most successful play of the seventeenth century, he wrote the masterpiece of ROMANESQUE tragedy, based on the obligations of the code of love and, again, on mistaken identities. His major tragedies, sometimes very influenced by his brother, other times very similar to Racine's, were *La Mort de l'Empereur Commode* ("The Death of the Emperor Commodus," 1657), *Stilicon* (1660), *Camma* (1661), *La Mort d'Annibal* ("The Death of Hannibal," 1669), *Ariane* (1672), and *Le Comte d'Essex* (*The Earl of Essex*, 1678). He also did a verse adaptation in 1677 of Molière's *Dom Juan* (1665), wrote opera librettos, and at the end of his theatrical career collaborated with Donneau de Visé on comedies dealing with contemporary customs.

Thomas Corneille was a virtuoso in dramatic technique and very skillful in conforming to the tastes of his contemporaries. He was not unoriginal; and certain of his comedies are quite lively, while some of his tragedies, like *Camma,* which anticipated aspects of Racine's *Andromaque* (1667), show a real sense of passion. Although in *Ariane* he was clearly capable of achieving Racinian simplicity, he was more naturally drawn to complexity, imbroglios, and an often superficial but pleasing rhythm, while respecting the classical rules.

In *Thomas Corneille, Protean Dramatist* (1966), one of the rare studies of Thomas Corneille in English, David A. Collins gives a biographical sketch of him and traces his evolution through an analysis of some thirty plays.—Ja. G.

Corpus Christi play. See SCRIPTURAL PLAY.

Corpus Christi, The Play Called. See N-TOWN PLAYS.

Corruption in the Palace of Justice (Corruzione al Palazzo di Giustizia, 1944). A play by UGO BETTI. The action of *Corruzione al Palazzo di Giustizia* revolves around the investigation into the cause of death of a shady adventurer whose body has been found in the corridor of the Palace of Justice. The investigation takes a sharp turn when a house, being searched for compromising documents, is burned down. The determination of criminal responsibilities becomes almost impossible because the entire Palace of Justice—even the city itself—seems involved in a web of corrupt silence. The strongest suspicions finally fall heavily on "Great Cases," the section of the Palace where all the great interests that govern the city meet and clash. There is a particularly violent conflict between the old and sick but ambitious Justice Croz and the lucid, hypocritical Cust, against whom Croz has gathered considerable evidence. But suddenly Croz dies, and in the last moment of his life he contrives a refined vendetta: he accuses himself, thus freeing Cust of any suspicion but leaving him all alone with his remorse, at the base of a long stairway where he starts out to present himself to the "High Reviewer." This drama, considered Betti's masterpiece, is constructed with an insistent rhythm and great dramatic efficacy. It deals with the author's characteristic concerns, namely guilt, remorse, and need for expiation, in which a profound existentialist anguish is at the base of a desperate search for secure moral values.—L. L.

costumbrismo. See SPANISH AMERICA.

Country Wife, The (1675). A comedy by William WYCHERLEY. *The Country Wife* was first performed in January at the Theatre Royal in Drury Lane by the King's Company. In this comedy, Horner, a libertine, pretends to be impotent in order to disarm the suspicion of husbands. Much of the witty satire of the play is directed at the hypocrisy of seemingly virtuous women like Lady Fidget, who are only too willing to be seduced (see ENGLAND: *Restoration drama*). Pinchwife's folly in trying to protect his "country wife" is exposed most ludicrously in the scene in which he brings her, disguised, to Horner's rooms. Another butt of the satire is the gullible fop Sparkish, whose fiancée is stolen from under his nose by Horner's libertine friend. The play is concluded by a dance of cuckolds.

The humor is often uproarious and usually licentious. That it shocked some of the first spectators is shown by the scene in Wycherley's *The Plain Dealer* in which a prude is satirized for taking offense at *The Country Wife*. One of the most successful and amusing characters is Margery Pinchwife, the "country wife," whose frank delight in the pleasures of the city contrasts with the pretenses of the city ladies and the cynical debauchery of the rakes.

T. H. Fujimura has edited this play with introduction and notes for the Regents Restoration Drama Series (1965).—E. W.

Courteline, Georges. Pen name of **Georges Victor-Marcel Moineaux** (1858–1929). French comic playwright. Courteline's boyhood was divided up among three cities: Tours, where he was born and to which he frequently returned to visit his grandparents; Paris, where he lived in the Montmartre *quartier* with his father, mother, and older brother; and Meaux, to which his family moved in 1870 during the German invasion and Commune period. His father was Jules Moineaux, who made a modest reputation as the author of operettas, sketches, short stories, and

GEORGES COURTELINE (NEW YORK PUBLIC LIBRARY)

Les Tribunaux comiques, accounts of trials in a small court. Courteline himself (he took the name, an invention of his own, during his twenties) composed some verse and fiction during his school days. But he did not turn wholeheartedly to writing until after he left the Collège Rollin without graduating, spent two years in the army without promotion, and acquired a sinecure at the Ministry of Culture, where he collected a salary without working. In 1881 he helped to found a periodical, *Paris-Moderne,* to which he contributed poems and stories. When it expired in 1883, he took over a daily column of "chronicles" for a newspaper, *Les Petites Nouvelles Quotidiennes.*

Like many other Parisians, the director André Antoine read Courteline's chronicles, as well as his subsequently published tales of army life, *Les Gaîtés de l'escadron* ("A Good Time in the Squadron," 1886) and later *Le Train de 8 heures 47* ("The 8:47 Train," 1891). In 1890 Antoine suggested that Courteline adapt some of his earlier writings for the stage. Since the partnership between them on the first play, *Lidoire* (1891), proved amicable, Courteline became a leading comic playwright for Antoine's Théâtre-Libre. By 1900 he had had twenty-two plays performed and had acted in some of them. They ranged in length from brief one-acts (*saynètes*) to a long comedy, the dramatic-revue version (1895) of his *Les Gaîtés de l'escadron,* and included as well a topical revue, *Les Grimaces de Paris* ("Paris Pulls Faces," 1894), and a five-act musical fantasy, *Les Joyeuses Commères de Paris* ("The Merry Wives of Paris," 1892). These last two works were collaborations. At the same time he continued to publish prose pieces, mostly in the distinguished literary journal *L'Echo de Paris.*

After 1900 he added relatively little to his output: a small volume of personal reflections, *La Philosophie de Georges Courteline* (1917, enlarged edition 1922), and six more plays. One of them, *La Conversion d'Alceste* (1905), commissioned by the Comédie-Francaise, was a sequel to Molière's *Le Misanthrope* and was composed in faultless seventeenth-century alexandrines.

For the last twenty-five years of his life Courteline was a national celebrity, but he went into gradual retirement as his health began to fail. His first wife, Suzanne (*née* Berty), who had borne him a son and a daughter, died in 1902. Five years later he married Marie-Jeanne Brécourt, who, like Suzanne, had been an actress before her marriage.

Courteline's writings were praised by many of his greatest contemporaries, among them Alexandre Dumas fils; Maurice Barrès; Stéphane Mallarmé; Anatole France; and Pierre Loti. In 1926 the Goncourt Academy invited him to join its judges. For Courteline this proved more of an honor than an active post, for he was suffering from acute diabetes. Less than three years later, during surgery on a gangrenous leg, he died.

Courteline's plays are often said to be farces. A few of them are: *Hortense, Couche-toi!* (*Hold on, Hortense!* 1897), *Les Boulingrin* (*These Cornfields,* 1898), *Le Commissaire est bon enfant* (*The Commissioner Has a Big Heart,* 1899). The others belong more appropriately to late nineteenth-century realism. Their governing themes are serious: the tyranny of the law and of bureaucrats, and the fragility of the relationships between men and women in love. Like all comic writers Courteline freely employs exaggeration, but his comedy is full of precise detail. Many of the plays are drawn from his own experience or from stories he heard at first hand. His masterpiece, *Boubouroche* (1893), is the painfully convincing story of a middle-aged, good-natured bachelor who keeps a mistress. She, in turn, keeps a boy friend in the apartment the bachelor is paying for. The play comes out of one of Courteline's own premarital liaisons.

Courteline's satirical comedies about the ordinary citizen's tangles with the French law code or with the lower ranks of French bureaucracy are the result of his persistent attendance at law courts and his profound concern with the inequities enacted in them. *L'Article 330* presents Courteline's most famous character, Jean-Philippe La Brige, whom Georges Duhamel called "the hero of non-conformity," and who became known in France as "the friend of the law" because he out-argued lawyers and judges on legal technicalities. Indicted for deliberately showing his bare backside to thousands of witnesses, La Brige proves himself to be innocent, but he is nevertheless fined and imprisoned.

In these and other plays—*La Cruche* ("The Blockhead," 1909), *La Peur des coups* (*Afraid to Fight*, 1894), and *La Paix chez soi* ("Peace at Home," 1903)—Courteline's dialogue glides easily from the vernacular exchanges into longer outbursts and more formal speeches, though the latter always bear directly on the plot and arise from the given characterizations. Courteline wrote slowly and painstakingly, making frequent revisions. Late in life he expressed dissatisfaction with every one of his plays but *La Conversion d'Alceste*. However, they remain popular in the French repertory, and in the past decade have often been produced in England and the United States.

Les Oeuvres complètes de Georges Courteline (1925–1927) in fifteen volumes is the standard French edition. His plays are also collected (not in chronological order) in three paperbound volumes, *Georges Courteline, Theatre I, II, and III* (1947–1948). The only full biography, useful but uncritical, is *La Curieuse Vie de Georges Courteline* (1958) by Albert Dubeux. Five of the plays are available in English in *The Plays of Courteline*, Vol. I (1961), edited and with introduction by Albert Bermel: *Article 330* (translated by Jacques Barzun), *Badin the Bold, Hold on Hortense!*, *Afraid to Fight*, and *Boubouroche*, the latter four translated by Albert Bermel. Other English versions: *These Cornfields*, translated by Eric Bentley, in *Let's Get a Divorce! and Other Plays* (1958); *The Commissioner Has a Big Heart*, translated by Albert Bermel, in *Four Modern French Comedies* (1960); *The Scales of Justice, The Torn Transfer*, and *The Registered Letter*, all translated by Jacques Barzun in *Tulane Drama Review*, Vol. III, No. 1 (October 1958).—A. C. B.

Coward, Noel (1899–   ). English playwright, actor, composer, and director. Born December 16, 1899, in Teddington, England, Coward first went on the stage early in 1911 as an actor and has continued to work in the theater ever since. His first play, *The Last Trick*, a melodrama written in 1918, was bought by a producer but never staged. Of the next three plays he wrote, he later preferred to re-

NOEL COWARD (WALTER HAMPDEN MEMORIAL LIBRARY AT THE PLAYERS, NEW YORK)

member only *The Rat Trap*, which he called "my first really serious attempt at psychological conflict"; by the time it got its short London run in 1926, other Coward plays had preceded it. His first work to reach the stage was *I'll Leave It to You* (1920), a comedy about a legacy, based on an idea provided by the American producer Gilbert Miller. Coward acted in it himself, as he did in his first entirely original play to be staged, *The Young Idea* (performed in the provinces in the autumn of 1922 and in London early in 1923), about two playful teen-agers (one of them acted by the dramatist) who mend their parents' broken marriage. *The Vortex* (1924) ran for more than five months in London and securely established Coward's fame in both London and New York. This "problem play" concerning a mother who has affairs with young men and whose son (played by Coward) is a drug addict is especially remembered for the heavy drama of its closing moments, when the son compels his mother to face reality. It is curious that this relatively solemn work should be the cornerstone of Coward's reputation, because afterwards he was known primarily as the author of those light, deft comedies that are his most interesting plays and are continually being revived.

The first of the comedies belonging to the permanent Coward repertoire is *Fallen Angels* (1925), a farcical work about two married ladies who, drinking heavily, nervously await their former lover's re-entry into their lives. HAY FEVER, about an aging actress and her peculiar family, opened in London in 1925 and ran for nearly a year; it has, over the years, proved its durability on the stage. Coward has been an extremely prolific author, and therefore a selective account of his comedies will give a sufficient impression of his accomplishment. In *Private Lives* (1930) Elyot Chase and Amanda Prynne, who were formerly married to each other, are honeymooning with their new mates when they find they have all gone to the same hotel. Elyot and Amanda are a pair of quarrelsome but essentially harmonious bohemian eccentrics, while their new wife and husband are dull, conventional types: the original couple run off together and withstand the efforts of the leftover husband and wife to separate them. The principals of the comedy *Design for Living* (New York, 1933), two men and a woman, decide that for them perfect harmony is to be found in their bohemian *ménage à trois*. Of the nine one-act plays of *Tonight at Eight-Thirty* (1936), several, including *Ways and Means* and *Hands Across the Sea,* are comedies of the sort that made Coward famous. *Blithe Spirit* (1941) portrays a husband who has remarried but is haunted by the mischievous ghost of his former wife; the intervention of a fuzzy-minded medium does nothing to remedy the situation. In *Present Laughter* (1943) a brilliant actor maintains an unconventional household with the generally unacknowledged aid of the serene and all-knowing wife from whom he is separated; she is clearly more important to him than the casual flirtations in which he engages. *Relative Values* (1951), in which a countess contemplates her son's desire to marry a lowborn film star, is generally considered to be below Coward's best.

Most of these plays present witty, stylish people acting in accordance with their unconventional morality. They are in league against more ordinary folk, whose style is much less striking—the budding "serious" dramatist of *Present Laughter,* the abandoned husband of *Design for Living* and the abandoned husband and wife of *Private Lives,* the uncomprehending house guests of *Hay Fever,* and others. Furthermore, as John Russell Taylor has shrewdly observed, "Each play presents a group of people who find it impossible to live together and impossible to live apart." Convention usually requires these people, like the divorced couple of *Private Lives,* to live apart, and, in such cases, convention is cheerfully defied. Coward's stylish characters express themselves in gracefully understated language. Although Coward's dialogue does not possess the witty invention of Oscar Wilde or William Congreve, it is reality pared down, trimmed so that it reflects the casual, understated omniscience of the stylish folk who are in the know and so is significantly contrasted with the unconsidered loquacity of the unstylish.

It is for his light comedies that Coward's name will live, but he also gave an extraordinary amount of his time to other types of dramas. Following *The Vortex,* he wrote other serious plays, including *Easy Virtue* (1926), about a lady with an uncertain past; *This Happy Breed* (1942), an episodic history of a working-class family between the wars; *Peace in Our Time* (1947), about England as it would be if Hitler had conquered it; and *A Song at Twilight* (1966),

about an aged writer (generally identified with Somerset Maugham but suggested also, Coward said, by Max Beerbohm) determined to prevent an actress from publishing his old letters to her and also set on keeping his homosexuality from becoming known to the world. Coward frequently wrote or collaborated on revues, from *London Calling* (1923), of which he was co-author, to *Sigh No More* (1947), of which he was sole author. The musical shows he wrote include *Bitter Sweet* (1929), a romantic costumed period piece; *Cavalcade* (1931), "a big play on a big scale," a panorama of British life in the twentieth century; *After the Ball* (1954), adapted from Oscar Wilde's *Lady Windermere's Fan; Sail Away* (1961), about tourists traveling to Europe; and *The Girl Who Came to Supper* (1963), based on Terence Rattigan's *The Sleeping Prince.* In addition, he adapted Georges Feydeau's farce *Occupe-toi d'Amélie* as *Look after Lulu* (1959). Coward also wrote two autobiographies, *Present Indicative* (1937) and *Future Indefinite* (1945), and several books of fiction. The range of his work is so considerable that generalizations are difficult, but such works as *Bitter Sweet* and *Cavalcade,* and also *Easy Virtue* and *This Happy Breed,* display a sentimental and nostalgic strain that seems deeply rooted. The cynical, understated nonchalance of his most successful comedies can be seen as a reaction to the sentiment and nostalgia that Coward found within himself as well as in the spirit of the times. Thus, his congenial cynicism, congenial both to him and to us, is a highly successful antidote to sentiment.

Robert Greacen's *The Art of Noel Coward* (1953) briefly and sympathetically interprets Coward's accomplishment. Raymond Mander and Joe Mitchenson give a detailed history of productions in *Theatrical Companion to Coward* (1957). John Russell Taylor provides a sound estimate of Coward's work in *The Rise and Fall of the Well-Made Play* (1967). —H. P.

Crébillon, Prosper Jolyot de [born **Sieur de Crais-Billon**] (1674–1762). French playwright. Born in Dijon, Crébillon was educated by the Jesuits, studied law in Besançon, and clerked for an attorney in Paris, where he led a dissipated life. He began to write for the theater in 1705. In 1720 he lost all his money in John Law's Mississippi scheme, became a member of the French Academy in 1731, and started work as a censor in 1733, thus incurring the hostility of Voltaire, who later used the subjects of some of Crébillon's tragedies to show his own superiority. For a long time Crébillon had court patronage, and the royal treasury payed for the splendid staging of *Catilina* in 1748 and then for the publication of his works in 1750. Extremely passionate and rather strange by nature, he was nevertheless carefree, not very concerned with glory, and resolved to keep aloof from literary disputes.

Crébillon's works consist of nine tragedies performed from 1705 to 1726, the most renowned of which are *Atrée et Thyeste* (1707), *Electre* (1708), and *Rhadamiste et Zénobie* (1711). After a failure with *Pyrrhus* in 1726, he left the stage and returned to it only at the insistence of his friends in 1748 with *Catilina* and again in 1754 with *Le Triumvirat.*

Reacting against the gallantry of the tragedies of his time, Crébillon sought to give new vigor to the genre by rejecting certain proprieties and pushing tragic terror to the point of horror by choosing the bloodiest and most criminal situations. In his day Crébillon was considered by many the long-awaited successor to Racine, until he was eclipsed by Voltaire. Although his plays today seem highly melodramatic and poorly written, they nonetheless show a true sense of the tragic: the characters are preys to an often monstrous fate that blinds them and makes them commit, in spite of themselves and sometimes unknowingly, the most heinous deeds.

For detailed information on Crébillon and his theater, see Henry C. Lancaster, *Sunset* (1945) and *French Tragedy in the Time of Louis XV and Voltaire, 1715–1774*, 2 vols. (1945).—Ja. G.

criticism. See MODERN DRAMATIC CRITICISM; SHAKESPEAREAN CRITICISM; DRAMATIC THEORY.

Croatia. See YUGOSLAVIA.

Crommelynck, Fernand. See BELGIUM.

Crothers, Rachel (1878–1958). American playwright. Miss Crothers, one of America's few successful women playwrights, was born in Bloomington, Illinois, and educated at the State Normal School. She trained for the stage in Boston and at the Wheatcroft School in New York, where she later became an instructor. After two seasons of professional acting, she devoted herself to writing plays and to directing them herself. From 1906, when her first long play, *The Three of Us*, was produced in New York, until 1937, she wrote twenty-three full-length plays, most of which were successful on the professional stage, and a number of one-act plays that were popular with amateurs.

All of her plays are concerned with the moral and social problems of women, and most of these works are set in the metropolitan world of high society. *A Man's World* (1909) deals with the double standard and with the conflict between career and marriage. *He and She* (1911) presents husband and wife, both sculptors. She defeats her husband in an important competition but gives up the first prize to cope with her daughter's problems. *Mary the Third* (1923) contrasts conventional ideas of marriage with reality through the attitudes of three generations. In *Let Us Be Gay* (1929) love reclaims a marriage broken up by the husband's infidelity. *As Husbands Go* (1931) contrasts American and British conceptions of marriage. *When Ladies Meet* (1932) deals with husband, wife, and mistress. In *Susan and God* (1937), a selfish, self-deceiving woman learns the meaning of love.

Miss Crothers expressed a conservative view of women in skillfully constructed comedies of upper-class city life. Her characters, most of whom are charming, wealthy, and cultured, hide their feelings under a gay mask of smart, sometimes witty dialogue. Her plays, beneath the sophisticated surface, are essentially dramas of sentiment.—B. H.

Crucible, The (1953). A play by Arthur MILLER. This play is set in Salem, Massachusetts, 1692, and based on the history of the Salem witch trials. John Proctor has had a love affair with Abigail Williams, an adolescent girl who worked in his house and who was discharged by his wife, the coldly virtuous Elizabeth Proctor, when the affair was discovered. Now, Abigail and the Proctors' present servant, Mary Warren, are among some girls who pretend to have been bewitched. Abigail brings a charge of witchcraft against Elizabeth Proctor, who is taken to prison.

Urged by Proctor, Mary confesses that the girls were only shamming, but the girls next turn the charge of witchcraft against her. Proctor at last admits his adultery with Abigail. He is not believed, however, because his wife, testifying separately, tries to protect him by denying any knowledge of his adultery. Mary Warren charges Proctor with witchcraft. The Reverend John Hale, a learned authority on witches, is so distressed at this turn of events that he denounces the inquiry. Elizabeth is freed, but Proctor is convicted and offered an amnesty only if he will give the names of other witches. He refuses, insisting that he must keep his good name. Like other estimable citizens of Salem, he goes off to be hanged for witchcraft. Miller obviously intended his audience to recognize parallels with the political "witch-hunting" of Senator Joseph McCarthy. It was exceptionally timely, and it is still a very effective play of action and suspense. If it falls short of the highest mark as a play of ideas, that is because Miller is attacking a cause—witch-hunting—that no one can conceivably defend, although one must add that in 1953 the contemporary parallel—McCarthyism—had no lack of defenders.

This play was first published in 1953.—H. P.

Cruz, Sor Juana Inés de la (1648?–1695). Mexican nun, poetess, and playwright. The finest Spanish American lyric poet of her century, Sor Juana's devotion to learning in all forms, her scientific experiments, and the metaphysical poem *Primero sueño* ("First Dream," 1692) mark her as precursor of eighteenth-century rationalism.

Her drama is written within the conventions of her time, but its humor and verbal brilliance give it a personal stamp. The eighteen short allegorical and circumstantial *loas* are of little interest today, as is the AUTO SACRAMENTAL *El cetro de José* ("Joseph's Sceptre"), but the autos *El mártir del Sacramento, San Hermenegildo* ("St. Hermenegildo, Martyr of the Sacrament") and particularly *El divino Narciso* ("The Divine Narcissus") transcend the genre's limitations to create delicate worlds of symbolic beauty.

Sor Juana's best work is in her two *sainetes* ("interludes") and two comedies. The *First Sainete* (date unknown) is of interest for its verbal irony, but the second, which actually takes place in a playhouse between the acts of one of her own plays, elicits delightfully frank laughter at herself and the theater. The comedy *Amor es más laberinto* ("Love Is the Greater Labyrinth," date unknown), written with Juan de Guevara, is an enormously complex version of the story of Theseus and Ariadne, while in *Los empeños de una casa* ("The Zeal of a House") she uses the formula of the Spanish Golden Age comedy to construct a work of delicate complexity, unusual characterization, and subtle humor.

Sor Juana's complete works have been published in an excellent edition, *Obras completas* (4 vols.), 1957). A standard critical text is Ludwig Pfandl's *Sor Juana Inés de la Cruz: La Décima Musa de México* (originally published in German in 1946; tr. to Spanish, 1963). Irving A. Leonard's *Baroque Times in Old Mexico* (1959) is a splendid introduction to Sor Juana and her milieu.—F. D.

Cuba. See SPANISH AMERICA.

Cumalı, Necati (1921–   ). Turkish playwright, poet, short-story writer, and novelist. Cumalı was born in Florina, Greece. After the Turkish War of Independence, his family moved to a small town near Izmir, Turkey. Cumalı has worked for the ministry of education and has practiced law. Since returning to Istanbul in 1966 from Tel Aviv and Paris, Cumalı has been earning his living solely by writing. Although he established himself first as a poet and a prize-winning short-story writer, he has recently been concentrating almost entirely on playwriting. Cumalı's play *Susuz Yaz* (*Dry Summer*, 1967), which was originally written as a short story, was made into a prize-winning film.

Having spent a great portion of his life in a small town, Cumalı came to know firsthand the small-town mentality, with its narrow outlook. He unfolds the problems existing in small Turkish towns through well-drawn characters and interesting plots. Some audiences have found a few of Cumalı's plots, such as that of *Susuz Yaz,* a little farfetched. Actually, the plot of that play was drawn almost entirely from two criminal cases in which Cumalı sat as a lawyer. The harsh realities of life in Anatolia are revealed in Cumalı's sensitive, poetical, and sometimes slightly sentimental plays. Perhaps no other Turkish dramatist has understood with more depth the plight of the Turkish woman in the family and the restricting effect of a petty society.

Cumalı, although a social thinker, refrains from preaching in his plays; rather, he shocks or delights audiences by his strong characterizations and humor and by well-constructed plays.—N. O.

Cyclops (Kyklops, c. 425 or 415–409 B.C.). A satyr play by EURIPIDES. The chief interest of *Cyclops* is that it is the only extant satyr play, that curious comic farce that a tragedian by tradition composed to follow his three tragedies. We know the story from the *Odyssey:* Odysseus and his companions are captured by the man-eating Cyclops, who makes a meal of them until Odysseus manages to make him drunk, drives a stake into his one eye, and escapes. The Homeric version is followed pretty closely, with such adaptations as are necessary to stage it. In order to keep the play comic, Euripides placed less emphasis on the cannibal's meal. Even so, the weird mixture of the comic and the horrible is the most Euripidean feature.

Cyclops is a piece of burlesque, with its drunken Cyclops, wine-bibbing Silenus, cowardly satyr

A SCENE FROM EURIPIDES' *Cyclops* (VASE IN THE BRITISH MUSEUM. R. B. FLEMING & CO. LTD.)

chorus, and resourceful Odysseus. Some commentators have sought deep meanings and of course have found them; they see in the Cyclops the prototype of the fifth-century Sophists who upheld the doctrine that might is right, and in Odysseus that of the depraved fifth-century politician. This seems very fanciful. The play is merely competent, crude, and in no way distinguished. It adds nothing to our knowledge of Euripides, except a further proof, if such were needed, of his versatility.

Translations of the play are listed under Euripides.—G. M. A. G.

Cymbeline (1609–1610). A romance by William SHAKESPEARE. *Cymbeline* is based upon legendary material of early Britain. In the palace of King Cymbeline of Britain, Imogen, the king's daughter, has provoked her father's fury by secretly marrying Posthumous, a gentleman of the court. The king's anger is fed by his new queen, who had hoped to wed Imogen to her brutish son, Cloten. Posthumous is banished to Italy, while Imogen is forced to remain at court. While in Italy, Posthumous becomes involved in a wager with Iachimo, a local scoundrel. Iachimo wagers that he can seduce Imogen, whose virtue has been the subject of her husband's praise. Arriving in England, Iachimo is unsuccessful in his assault on Imogen and is forced to revert to a trick. Hiding himself in her bedroom, he manages, while Imogen is asleep, to record various details of the room and then slips from her arm the bracelet that was her husband's parting gift to her. Returning to Italy, he convinces Posthumous of his wife's infidelity. Posthumous, mad with revenge, sends a letter to Imogen asking her to meet him secretly in Wales. Accompanied by Posthumous' servant, Pisanio, Imogen arrives in Wales only to discover from Pisanio that he is under orders from his master to kill her. However, the servant devises a plan whereby Imogen will be disguised as a page while he reports that she is dead. In her new guise, she encounters two young men who are in fact her own brothers, disappeared many years ago and long presumed dead.

In the meantime, Cymbeline has declared war on Rome rather than pay tribute to the emperor. Posthumous returns to fight for Britain and teams up with the two lost princes in order to bring about a British victory. Confusion as to various identities persists after the battle, but everyone is eventually reconciled as Britain and Rome conclude an amicable peace.

The play's reliance on mythic, romantic, and fairy-tale elements has not endeared it to audiences and readers seeking psychological consistency and plausibility of action. Recent students of *Cymbeline*, however, have focused attention on the artful manipulation of the themes of death and rebirth, the relation between father and daughter, and the achievement of self-identity. Added to this is the lyric beauty of many individual passages, aided by the interpolation of some of Shakespeare's loveliest songs.

A recommended edition of *Cymbeline* is the New Arden Edition (1955), edited by J. M. Nosworthy.—E. Q.

Cyrano de Bergerac (1897). Neo-Romantic "heroic comedy" in verse by Edmond ROSTAND. The première of *Cyrano* and the subsequent universal success of the play mark one of the most enthusiastic receptions of a play in history. The discouragement that accompanied the rehearsals was turned to delirious joy on the night of December 28, 1897. At a time when the starkly realistic plays of Ibsen, Strindberg, Henry Becque, and Eugène Brieux were favored, it was little short of a miracle for an unabashedly Romantic historical drama in lyrical verse to succeed. From 1898 on, *Cyrano* was staged in many countries.

The plot is loosely based on the life of the French poet-soldier-philosopher Savinien Cyrano de Bergerac (1619–1655), but Rostand's Cyrano, affirming a heroic spirit in the face of disillusioning reality, is of course idealized. Cyrano loves Roxane, but feels he is too ugly to win her. Instead, he helps the inarticulate Christian to woo her by writing love letters for him and, in the famous balcony scene, by whispering to Christian the phrases that win Roxane's heart. Christian dies in the wars, and Roxane, now his widow, goes into mourning. Fifteen years later Roxane learns the truth from Cyrano, who is dying from a humiliating injury. Cyrano ends a barren lifetime in a final moment of ecstatic love, proudly defying cowardice, falsehood, compromise, and death.

Next to Hamlet, Cyrano is often considered the theater's most popular role. In his self-detachment and his ability to contemplate himself as a Romantic figure, he demonstrates a kind of ironical humor that counteracts the sentimental moments and gives him a unique gusto. "With Rostand," says T. S. Eliot, "the center of gravity is in the expression of the emotion, not as with Maeterlinck in the emotion which cannot be expressed." Altogether, Cyrano is more consistent than the traditional Romantic heroes of Alexandre Dumas père and Victor Hugo. His spirit of self-sacrifice also marks a transformation from the passion of the Romantic heroes to the pure realm of the ideal. And where Hugo artificially mixed the sublime and the grotesque in, for example, *Ruy Blas* (the nobleman in lackey's uniform), Rostand depicted Cyrano as ironically but plausibly combining the unselfish and the egotistical, the spiritual and the ugly, the bravura of his boastful jests and the deflating actions portrayed on the stage. Rostand also evoked the illusion and the local color of the seventeenth century, duplicated the swagger and the preciosity of seventeenth-century rhetoric—its bombast and grandiloquence, its flourish and gallantry—and, through it all, revealed the sadness and devotion of the sensitive lover and poet masquerading as a clown.

Of the many versions in English, the best is Brian Hooker's, prepared especially for Walter Hampden's production in 1923 and included in J. Gassner's *A Treasury of the Theatre* (1935). Gassner's Introduction helpfully summarizes comments of other critics. For comparison the reader might consult the Howard Kingsbury version, reprinted in *The Romantic Influence* (1963), Vol. II of *Laurel Masterpieces of Continental Drama,* edited by N. Houghton. T. S. Eliot's appraisal of *Cyrano* as literature is included in his *Selected Essays* (1932).—S. S. S.

Czechoslovakia: *Bohemia and Moravia.* The origins of the Czech drama can be found in the theatrical elements of the rites and customs of the Slavonic tribes that settled in Bohemia and Moravia after the fifth century A.D. Evidences of these rituals are preserved from a later period in history, after they had been slightly altered by the pressures of Christian ideology. Elements of these early ceremonies were used in the secular drama of the middle ages and some of them were preserved, with various modifications, up to the twentieth century.

The Czech theater as such, however, originated in the Church and secular milieus of the feudal period. Preserved from the ecclesiastical drama of the middle ages are a number of Latin, Latin-Czech, and Czech texts relating almost exclusively to Christ's death and resurrection. These dramas were of considerable significance in the development of European medieval ecclesiastical drama. The oldest extant text from this period is the Latin ceremony *Ordo ad visitandum sepulchrum,* which was put in writing toward the end of the twelfth or the beginning of the thirteenth century. In addition to the visit to Christ's sepulcher by Mary and the apostles, this play includes the biblical episode of Christ's revelation to Mary Magdalene.

Both the ecclesiastical and secular Czech dramas developed rapidly during the fourteenth century. The religious ceremony that had previously been part of the liturgy was transformed at this time into a form of drama that was occasionally performed outside the Church. These religious plays were written not only in Latin but also in a combination of Latin and Czech, with the Czech portion increasing until it dominated the work. These Latin-Czech ecclesiastical plays went through a process of secularization in which the laity became involved in the composition and production, the traditional religious themes were modified, and such secular characters as craftsmen and merchants were introduced into the texts. As the religious dramas moved out of the Church and into the secular world, the sharp distinction between sacred and profane drama was blurred.

In contrast to the written tradition of the ecclesiastical drama, the Czech secular drama was part of the oral tradition of the middle ages, and our knowledge of it today is based upon the secular texts that were incorporated into the religious dramas of the period. The most important extant secular texts from this period are two manuscript fragments called Mastičkář muzejní and Mastičkář drkolenský. The muzejní text preserves a secular scene adapted to a religious play, but the drkolenský fragment is closer to the original oral tradition. The humorous, secular "Quack scene" formed part of a Latin-Czech religious play about the three Marys, as seen in the Latin texts that are preserved in both fragments. In these a medieval doctor-charlatan, his servants, and some customers were presented for the amusement of the audience. These texts, which also included satires alluding to the immoral life of the clergy, are part of the tradition of critical literature in the middle ages that called for the reform of the Church. Several of the scenes are intentionally frivolous treatments of religious drama: for example, the scene dealing with the resurrection of Abraham's son Izaac in the muzejní fragment is actually a travesty of Christ's resurrection. The influence of the oral tradition handed down by the jugglers and students also pervades some Latin and Latin-Czech plays, such as *Hra veselé Magdaleny* ("A Play of the Gay Magdalene"), in which Magdalene is treated like a medieval harlot. Included in this text, which is a part of the drkolenský manuscript, are rare verses of an old Czech love song.

In the beginning of the fifteenth century, the

Hussite revolutionary movement obstructed the development of both secular and religious drama, because the Hussites considered the theater to be a form of idolatry. They made use of the theater only for social satires. Consequently, ecclesiastical drama in the Czech countries was never as fully developed as the religious drama of Western European countries. The Hussite movement did not succeed, however, in completely breaking off the medieval theater tradition in the Czech countries. The ecclesiastical drama of the middle ages survived until the sixteenth century, and elements of the Czech Renaissance and Baroque dramas were continuations of this medieval tradition.

A long period of isolation from the rest of Europe delayed the growth of Renaissance drama in the Czech territories. Although the first contacts with European Renaissance drama occurred as early as the fourteenth century in the Czech area, an intensive interest in this drama did not develop until the beginning of the sixteenth century. The Charles University, founded in Prague in 1348, played a major role in assimilating contemporary European culture into Czech culture. Also instrumental in this movement were the Prague University professors who used drama (namely, classical drama) as a pedagogical tool. The first public students' performance was held at the university in 1535.

The origin of the Czech Renaissance drama, created by the urban intellectuals, dates from the middle of the sixteenth century. Jan Aquila z Plavče (?–1587) imitated foreign biblical plays. The most important Czech playwright of the Latin Renaissance drama is Jan Campanus Vodňanský (c. 1572–1622), a university professor who wrote the historical play *Bretislaus, comoedia nova* ("Bretislaus, New Comedy," pub. 1614). In this play, which was historical according to the Renaissance aesthetic principles, Campanus laid the foundations of Czech historical drama that was later to become so popular. The majority of the plays of this period were written in the national tongue, rather than in Latin, and some of them were produced at various schools, especially secondary schools.

Like the Central European drama of the period, the themes of these Czech dramas were taken from the Old Testament. Concerned with the reformation of the Church, these dramatists chose biblical rather than secular themes as the most appropriate form of expression.

One of the most important Czech playwrights of the Renaissance period is Pavel Kyrmezer (?–1589), a Slovakian who lived in Moravia. In *Komedie česká o bohatci a Lazarovi* ("The Czech Comedy About a Money-bag and Lazarus," pub. 1566) and *Komedie nová o vdově* ("The New Comedy About a Widow," pub. 1573) Kyrmezer successfully dramatized the life of his time and portrayed the poor people with great sympathy. In contrast to the other biblical dramas of the period, which were merely monologues amplified to dialogues, Kyrmezer's plays were built on a sound plot structure and his dialogues revealed the personalities of his characters. Another Slovakian writing in Czech, Jiří Tesák Mošovský (c. 1545–1617), also dramatized contemporary life in a small town in his play *Komedie z knihy zákona božího, jenž slove Ruth* ("The Comedy from the Book of God's Testa-

ment Which Is Called Ruth," pub. 1604). This process of localizing biblical stories reached its peak in a play by Šimon Lomnický z Budče (1552–c. 1622) called *Triumf neb Komedie o vzkříšení Páně* ("The Triumph or Comedy of Our Lord's Resurrection"), written in the tradition of the medieval Easter plays.

During this period of Czech Renaissance drama, secular themes were presented in short comical scenes called *interludia* ("interludes") or *intermedia* ("intermezzi") that were performed between the acts of a biblical drama. These humorous scenes depicted the boorish manners of peasants. Among these texts should be mentioned the intermedium *Polapená nevěra* ("The Caught Unfaithfulness"), which is preserved in a manuscript dating from 1608, about an old merchant and his young unfaithful wife. The three-act anonymous play *Sedlský masopust* ("The Peasants' Carnival," pub. 1588) is the longest and the most courageous original attempt to write a Czech play dealing with contemporary life. Tobiáš Mouřenín z Litomyšle (?–c. 1625), who is the author of the comedy *Vejstupný syn* ("The Roguish Son," pub. 1604), also wrote *Historia kratochvilná o jednom sedlském pacholku . . .* ("An Amusing Story of One Peasant Groom . . . ," pub. 1604), which he modeled after a foreign play. In this play the motif of the magical power of a musical instrument, later a very popular theme in Czech drama, was used for the first time. Another secular drama of this period, *Tragedie neb Hra žebrací* ("The Tragedy or Beggars' Play," pub. 1573), was translated by an unknown author into Czech from an original Polish text. In this play, which has a Czech setting, the dramatist presents a very detailed, lengthy legal dispute between gay beggars who feign suffering and a rich merchant. The court decides the argument in favor of the friends of freedom—the beggars. The text, with only a few theatrical qualities, was apparently meant for reading only.

In the middle of the sixteenth century the Jesuits came to the Czech countries and made considerable use of the theater in their anti-Reformation movement. The Jesuits performed mostly their own original Latin and Czech plays. For example, the Jesuit Mikuláš Salius wrote a play in Czech about Saint Wenceslaus, the Czech king and saint, which was performed in 1567.

By the end of the sixteenth century, foreign troupes of professional actors appeared in the Czech states, but they performed only foreign plays. There were no professional theaters to support Czech drama, and the rulers of the Czech countries, a foreign and reactionary Austrian dynasty, did not offer favorable conditions for the rise of a professional Czech theater.

After the battle at White Mountain in 1620, the Czech state was temporarily destroyed and the Czech theater (which had been developing on an amateur basis) was paralyzed. This defeat and extinguishment of the Czech state ruined those classes—the middle class, intelligentsia, and aristocracy—that had previously taken part in the Czech cultural life of the country. Only the Catholic intelligentsia was not threatened by this new political situation, and their members, such as the Jesuits, became the bearers of the new culture. They wrote dramas in Latin, rarely in Czech, with religious, anti-Reformation aims. In the theaters of the new feudal lords—mostly foreigners who had confiscated the property of the local Reformation nobility—plays written by Czech authors were not performed. Czech plays were performed only sporadically by foreign troupes in the latter half of the eighteenth century, but in the same century drama in the Czech language appeared in religious circles (especially in Moravia). The most outstanding examples are the librettos of the Czech Baroque operas, which were written to entertain the priests.

The important Czech playwright of this period, Jan Amos Komenský (1592–1670), called Comenius, who had to live in exile for religious reasons, linked up with the Renaissance drama at the beginning of the Baroque period. His plays *Diogenes Cynicus redivivus* ("Diogenes Cynicus Alive Again," 1640), *Abrahamus patriarcha* ("Abrahamus, the Patriarch," 1641), and *Schola ludus* ("School as Amusement," 1654) reveal his considerable talent as a playwright, but this talent was intentionally subordinated to the pedagogical purpose of his plays, which were performed by students. In *Schola ludus* Komenský presented in dramatic form the basic philosophical, natural-scientific, and other knowledge of mankind of that time and his own ideas on various stages of education.

Because of oppressive political circumstances, the development of Czech drama in the seventeenth and eighteenth centuries was confined mainly to the economically exploited lower middle class of the towns and farmers of the Czech villages. Occasionally, the schoolmasters and priests who were more worldly took part in the development of the theater. On the whole the plays of this period were conservative in structure when compared to the Baroque European drama of that period.

The folklore of the small Czech towns formed a natural basis for the theater of this period because it was filled with rites of an explicitly theatrical kind, such as masked carnival processions, spring fertility rituals, harvest-home festivals, and weddings. The dramatic texts of the folk theater, which are known to us mostly from records dating only from the nineteenth and twentieth centuries, were based upon stories from the New and Old Testaments as well as the lives of the Catholic saints. These plays were written and performed not only for amusement but also as a protest against the social oppression of the peasants. The conflict between a pagan ruler and a Christian saint was used by playwrights to represent the conflict between a contemporary feudal lord and a serf. An example of such an anonymous folk play about a saint is *Hra o svaté panně Dorotě* ("The Play About the Holy Maid Dorothy," written in the seventeenth or eighteenth century), which was preserved in several variants. The play deals with a conflict between a pagan king and Saint Dorothy, whom the king wants to marry. Dorothy refuses the king because she does not want to give up her faith in God but prefers, instead, to be imprisoned and tortured. From this difficult situation she is saved by God, Whom she did not betray. The contemporary social situation was reflected in the Czech pastoral play *Rakovnická hra vánoční* ("Rakovnicka Christmas Play," written c. 1780–1790, probably by a priest), in which the argument between the shepherds and the kings about the ques-

tion to whom the Infant Jesus was born is decided by the angel in favor of the poor shepherds. Another group of folk Baroque plays is represented by the passion plays, which make up large dramatic units. In these plays, especially, the opinion of the common people was voiced.

In the eighteenth century, under the influence of foreign itinerant companies, folk plays with secular themes increased in number. An excellent example of this genre is the play *Komedie o Františce, dceři krále Anglického, a o Honzíčkovi, synu kupce londýnského* ("The Comedy about Frances, the English King's Daughter and about Jock, the London Merchant's Son," written in the eighteenth century), which was praised for celebrating the honest work of the common people. The main character of the play is Honzíček, a rich tradesman's son who refuses to become a tradesman and becomes, instead, an excellent joiner. During a trip he takes, he saves the English king's daughter Františka from being captured by the Turks, and after various adventures and obstacles, he marries her. *Komedie o selské rebelii* ("The Comedy About the Peasants' Rebellion," written c. 1775) is the most important text of the genre of folk drama dealing with contemporary themes dating from the end of the Baroque period. Influenced by the contemporary bourgeois drama, this play dramatized the struggle of the Czech peasants against the feudal lords and the state power, which ended in the defeat of the rebels in 1775. The texts of these folk Baroque plays were only occasionally put in writing, usually at a later date. The producers adapted the plays according to the local social conditions. The plays were written for an anti-illusionistic theater that counted upon the creative activity of the audience. These playwrights did not adhere to the unities of time and place, and they wrote their plays in verse to strengthen the audience's feeling that it was watching an artificial stage reality.

Although the Czech folk drama was subordinated to the bourgeois type of drama, some folk drama survived until the nineteenth and even into the twentieth century. In the twentieth century, these texts were revived by artists who belonged to the so-called interwar left-wing avant-garde theater, because these folk plays suited their ideological and artistic purposes. The avant-garde artists appreciated the folk plays because of their anti-illusionism and progressive ideas. One such artist was E. F. Burian, who produced some of these plays in his Prague theater called D toward the end of the 1930's. Some of these folk dramas are still performed today.

The rise of a professional Czech theater at the end of the eighteenth century contributed to the advancement of Czech drama, and there were, especially in the first half of the nineteenth century, many amateur companies in the Czech states that performed plays written expressly for them. Numerous marionette groups were also active during this period.

The period of the revival of the Czech nation in the last third of the eighteenth century and the first half of the nineteenth century was matched by a period of rapid development in Czech drama. With the development of the lower middle classes, the Czech nation began to grow toward the end of the eighteenth century, when the inner antagonisms of the feudal system became acute and the capitalist economy started to develop. An obstacle to the expansion of Czech drama was the ruling Austrian state, which for the sake of the governing feudal class censored and persecuted democratic ideas. Practically the only criticism the government allowed in the theater was a form of self-criticism: the middle class was allowed to criticize only the middle class. It was forbidden to criticize representatives of the feudal state power and the clergy, or to show a conflict of nationalities on the stage. Because the theater in the Baroque period was popular with all the social classes, the leaders of the new Czech nationalist movement, in opposition to the Austrian rulers, seized upon the theater as its tribune. In this way the Czech theater was used as a vehicle for fighting for the rights and perfection of the Czech language, for bolstering the national self-confidence by dramatizing famous events from Czech history, for spreading the political ideas of the third estate (the lower middle classes), for criticizing the negative social elements, and for championing technical progress. It was during this period that the Czech theater became closely linked to the contemporary problems of Czech society.

The various genres of Czech drama were actually formed during this period of national revival. Satirical comedy, historical plays, and dramatic fairy tales were the most successful, artistically, of the typical Czech forms. Czech plays written in a lofty, poetic style were not as successful as those plays that dealt with philosophical, moral, and other problems on the concrete level of daily (historical or contemporary) practice. In the last third of the eighteenth century, many historical plays were written that showed the strong influence of foreign, mostly German, Baroque plays and of romantic chivalrous dramas. These plays had the effect of strengthening the national self-confidence, drawing attention to the Czech language, and expressing their authors' ideas of the Enlightenment. The most significant author of these plays was Václav Thám (1765–c.1816). In the 1790's the Prague local farce also began to develop, especially under the auspices of the playwright Prokop Šedivý (1764–c. 1810). The local farce is a genre of comedy with songs and dancing that was popular on the Central European stages toward the end of the eighteenth and the first half of the nineteenth century. It showed the life of middle class and common people from a certain town, such as Prague, Vienna, or Kraków. During this time the adaptation of many foreign plays to the local milieu gave the Czech playwrights an opportunity to feature contemporary society. Also during the revivalist period several stock characters —a musician, a matchmaker, and a silly farmer's son—were introduced into Czech drama.

The first great Czech dramatists during this period were Jan Nepomuk Štěpánek (1783–1844) and particularly Václav Kliment KLICPERA, who were especially talented in writing comedies about life in small towns. They also tried to write poetic drama. In the work of both these playwrights a tension exists between the retreating classical techniques and the entering Romantic style. Štěpánek, with his plays about the life of the lower middle classes (such as *Cech a Němec,* "A Czech and a German," pub. 1816; *Berounské koláče,* "The Cakes from Beroun," pub. 1818; *Pivovar v Sojkově,* "The Brewery in Sojkov," pub. 1823), was closer to the life of the majority of theatergoers of the revival period, while Klicpera, with his interest in antique comedy (the Roman comedy of Plautus), wrote a more literary type of comedy which was appreciated mainly by the intelligentsia. Klicpera wrote several sharp satirical comedies set in provincial towns in which he inveighed against philistinism. These plays, such as *Divotvorný klobouk* ("A Magic Hat," pub. 1820), *Rohovín Čtverrohý* (pub. 1825), *Veselohra na mostě* ("Comedy on a Bridge," pub. 1828), and *Každý něco pro vlast* ("Everyone's Duty for the Country," pub 1829), are still performed today.

The principal playwright of the Czech revivalist drama is Josef Kajetán TYL. This leading Czech theatrical figure of the 1830's and 1840's belonged, according to his ideas and style, to the Romantic movement. At first he tried to write a play about contemporary life, the Prague local farce *Fidlovačka* (1834). But his most important play of the thirties was his Romantic tragedy *Čestmír* (1834), in which Tyl reconciles the conflict between the Romantic hero and society because he considered the Romantic, rebellious attitude too dangerous and destructive for Czech society. The Romantic dramatist's subjectivism is typical, and this is especially true for Tyl's play, which can be considered his personal confession, a monologue about his feelings and opinions. On the eve of the bourgeois democratic revolution and during the revolution itself, Tyl wrote several dramas that he hoped would help to destroy the negative phenomena in the life of the bourgeoisie and the common people: an example is *Pražská děvečka a venkovský tovaryš aneb Paličova dcera* ("Prague Maid and Country Journeyman or Incendiary's Daughter," 1847) and the dramatic fairy tale *Strakonický dudák aneb Hody divých zen* ("The Bagpiper of Strakonice or Wakes of Wild Women of the Woods," 1847). In his historical tragedy *Krvavý soud aneb Kutnohorští havíři* ("The Bloody Trial, or Miners of Kutná Hora," written 1847, prod. 1848), written from the impressions Tyl had of the first great workers' strike in the Czech area, he depicted with sympathy a workers' strike in a story from the fifteenth century. In the verse drama *Jan Hus* (1848) Tyl presented Hus as a fighter for the national and social rights of the Czech nation. Tyl's interest in a concrete, dramatic realism became so strong that at the height of his career his plays, such as *Paličova dcera,* formed a link between Romanticism and realism in the Czech drama. On the whole, Czech Romantic drama was not as developed as the Romantic drama in France or England. Censorship restricted the freedom to express rebellious, Romantic ideas, and many Czech intellectuals considered the Romantic attitude socially destructive. The most successful Czech Romantic dramas were those of the so-called lower genres: the local farce and the fairy tale.

After the bourgeois democratic revolution of 1848, Czech drama was created by a generation from the Romantic middle class, whose goal was the complete, free, and unlimited development of the human personality. The work of Shakespeare had the greatest influence on these dramatists, especially on Josef Jirí Kolár (1812–1896) and Vítezslav Hálek (1835–1874). They imitated Shakespeare's style in their own historical plays based on themes drawn from Czech history. In spite of the relaxing of censorship by the

Austrian rulers and the opening of the first independent Czech theater (Prozatímní divadlo, The Temporary Theater) in 1862, no great playwright appeared. Not one of the rather large number of historical plays that supported the fight for national rights from 1850 to 1880 and which could be classified as late Romantic plays is performed today. Working during that era was Emanuěl Bozděch (1841–c. 1889), who wrote quasi-historical plays, in the style of Victorien Sardou's "well-made" play, in which he depicted the intimate life of great historical figures. An example of this style is his play about Napoleon Bonaparte called *Světa pán v županu* ("Master of the World in a Dressing-Gown," 1876). Of greater value than Bozděch's plays were the poetic dramas of two late Romantic playwrights: Jaroslav Vrchlický (1853–1912) and Julius Zeyer (1841–1901). A lively value is still found today in many of Vrchlický's works, such as his lyrical comedy *Noc na Karlštejně* ("The Night at the Karlštejn," 1884). This comedy, of perfect structure, fine humor, and poetic charm, dramatizes the private life of the popular Czech king and Roman emperor Charles IV. *Soud lásky* ("The Trial of Love," 1886) is a frivolous love comedy set in early Renaissance Avignon. His trilogy *Hippodamie* (*Námluvy Pelopovy*, "Pelop's Wooing," 1890; *Smír Tantalův*, "Tantal's Conciliation," 1891; and *Smrt Hippodamie*, "Hippodamia's Death," 1891) was made by Zdeněk Fibich into a melodrama. Zeyer drew his themes from different time periods in various cultures; his dramatic fairy tale about the winning power of love—*Radúz a Mahulena* ("Raduz and Mahulena," 1898)—was drawn from Slovak folklore.

The drama dealing with contemporary life, which grew out of the work of Tyl, remained in the background from the 1850's to the 1870's. The little work that was being done in this genre can be seen in the librettos of Bedřich Smetana's operas and the farces of František Ferdinand Šamberk (1839–1904). The theatrical flair and the understanding of everyday problems of the Prague middle class and peasantry were the main attractions of the farces by Šamberk: *Jedenácté přikázání* ("The Eleventh Commandment," 1882) and *Palackého třída 27* ("27 Palacký Avenue," 1884). František Věnceslav Jeřábek (1836–1893) wrote *Služebník svého pána* ("His Master's Servant," written 1870), in which he dealt with contemporary life, examining from a progressive point of view the problem of exploiting both mental and manual work.

In 1883 the National Theater opened in Prague. It was built with money collected over many years from all strata of Czech society and it provided good conditions for the further development of Czech drama. Also at this time, itinerant companies traveled widely throughout the Czech states and performed new Czech drama of the period, and new amateur troupes appeared toward the end of the nineteenth century.

Although the Czech drama had previously lagged behind the European drama, by the 1880's, when a group of outstanding Czech dramatists created a new era of realism in the Czech theater, the development of realistic and naturalistic drama in the Czech theater was commensurate with its growth throughout Europe. The playwrights who came to the fore during this period tried to depict with great authenticity the contemporary life of the common people. These new dramatists became more objective, in contrast to the subjectivism of the Romantic and late Romantic drama, in their attempt to present a realistic picture of contemporary society. In order to dramatize the negative aspects of society, these dramatists often focused on the life of women as the best way to show what was wrong with contemporary life. Playwrights of the school of realism gave shocking testimony about their society in an attempt to reform it.

It is typical of Czech drama that the most significant themes used in the theater of realism were drawn from the Czech and Moravian village milieus. Ladislav Stroupežnický (1850–1892), in his comedy *Naši furianti* ("Our Uppish and Defiant Fellows," 1887), was the first playwright to show a village without the covering of an idyllic veil, which had formed an organic part of the Romantic and late Romantic attitude toward reality. The plays of Gabriela Preissová (1862–1946) (*Gazdina roba*, 1890, and *Její pastorkyňa*, "Jenufa," 1891), Alois Jirásek (1851–1930) (*Vojnarka*, 1890, and *Otec*, "Father," 1894), and Alois Mrštík (1861–1925) and Vilém Mrštík (1863–1912) (*Maryša*, 1894) are dramas of great personal tragedies. The causes of these tragedies involve problems of property and, in some cases, superstition and slander. During this period of great activity in the workers' movement, Matěj Anastazia Šimáček (1860–1913) and František Adolf Šubert (1849–1915) wrote realistic plays about the life of the worker. In their dramas they added to the stock of characters by creating variations of the Czech farmer type. The psychological make-up of some of these new characters was complexly drawn.

The most important Czech realistic historical drama was written by Alois Jirásek on the eve of the national independence of the Czechoslovak Republic in 1918. Jirásek's trilogy—*Jan Hus* (1911), *Jan Žižka* (1903), and *Jan Roháč* (1918)—presented a broad picture of Czech society in the Hussite age.

In the 1890's, as a reaction against realism and naturalism in the Czech theater, a new group of dramatists came to the fore who criticized both Czech society and realistic and naturalistic drama. This group is called impressionistic and was also influenced by the symbolists. Some of these dramatists, writing about the life of the intelligentsia and lower middle classes, tried to give the impression of bearing true testimony about contemporary life but in fact made use of concrete details to show certain problems and proclaim certain ideas that they personally considered important. They did not intend, like realistic and naturalistic authors, to create drama-documents, drama-photographs, or drama-copies of reality but, instead, to create artificial constructions with the help of realistic details to express their subjective relations to reality. Great attention was given to rendering the subtle psychological processes of modern, complex man. Outstanding among these playwrights were Jaroslav Hilbert (1871–1936), the author of *Vina* ("The Guilt," 1896); Jaroslav Kvapil (1868–1953), the creator of the psychological drama *Oblaka* ("The Clouds," 1903); and Jiří Mahen (1882–1939), the author of *Ulička odvahy* ("An Alley of Courage," 1917) and other plays. The poet Fráňa Šrámek (1877–1952) praised life and youth in his excellent impressionist dramas. Of his works, *Léto*

("The Summer," 1915) and *Měsíc nad řekou* ("The Moon Above the River," 1922) have survived. Šrámek's dialogue, rich in nuancès that reveal mental processes, embodies various levels of meaning. Pervading the works of Hilbert, Kvapil, Mahen, and Šrámek is a strong lyricism that is a typical feature of all Czech drama.

Czech symbolic drama was another, even stronger, reaction to the realistic and naturalistic drama. The symbolism evoked new interest in the genre of the dramatic fairy tale. In his fairy tale *Lucerna* ("The Lantern," 1905), set in an eighteenth-century Czech patriarchal village, Jirásek made use of symbols to support the Czech nation's struggle for independence. As a symbol of the Czech country, he used an old lime tree, which the village people, with the help of fairy-tale figures, defend against feudal clerks who want to chop it down. In *Princezna Pampeliška* ("The Princess Dandelion," 1897), the symbolist Jaroslav Kvapil dealt with the tragic feeling of the inevitability of death. The symbolist dramatists also used the historical play as a vehicle for exposing certain ideas and problems. The leading playwright who wrote historical dramas was Viktor Dyk (1877–1931), the author of *Revoluční trilogie* ("The Revolutionary Trilogy," written 1907–1909), *Posel* ("The Envoy," 1907), and *Zmoudření dona Quijota* ("Growing Wise of Don Quijot," 1914). This last play deals with the conflict between the great dreams and goals of a man (symbolized by Don Quijot) and the life of small, self-satisfied people. After Don Quijot recognizes the impossibility of realizing his dreams, after he grows wise, he dies because he cannot live. Otokar Theer (1880–1918) is the creator of the drama *Faethon* (written 1916). The plays of Arnošt Dvořák (1881–1933), *Václav IV* ("Wenceslaus IV," 1910) and *Husité* ("The Hussites," 1919), already show the growing influence of expressionism in the Czech theater.

The structure of the symbolic drama was also suited to the purpose of those playwrights who, shortly after the October Revolution, wanted to express their social hopes on the stage. The most significant work of that period is *Zástupové* ("The Throngs," pub. 1921, prod. 1933), written by F. X. Šalda (1867–1937). This play is set between today and tomorrow and between the West and the East in the same way that its dramatic characters (Lazarus, executioner, newspaperman, clergyman, and others) are of symbolic significance. The theme of the play is the relationship between an individual and the revolutionary masses, and Šalda is of the opinion that a great individual should serve the masses and merge with the masses.

On this period of Czech drama see František Chudoba's *Short Survey of Czech Literature* (1924), William E. Harkins' *Anthology of Czech Literature* (1953), Arthur P. Coleman's *Kotzebue and the Czech Stage* (1936), and Stanley Buchholz Kimball, *Czech Nationalism: A Study of the National Theater Movement, 1845–1883* (1964).—F. C.

Bohemia and Moravia since 1914. The period following the end of the First World War and the establishment of a free Czechoslovak state in 1918 saw the flowering of Czech drama, previously retarded in comparison to other literary genres. New theaters sprang up under the young republic, and the high level of development of the art of stagecraft and direction provided the younger avant-garde playwrights with productions that were aesthetically and stylistically congenial. In some cases, such as that of Karel Čapek, the younger writers also worked as directors.

Of the older trends that survived from the period before 1914, symbolism was stronger than realism or naturalism. The plays of Viktor Dyk emphasize the illusory character of life and of idealism. Dyk's play *Ondřej a drak* ("Andrew and the Dragon," 1919) is a parodic fairy tale in which a menacing dragon turns out to be a hoax; fraudulent too are the beauty and virtue of the maiden chosen to be sacrificed to him. Another symbolist is Fráňa Šrámek (1877–1952); his plays are remarkable for their lyricism and their intuitive comprehension of the pain of young love. Typical is the theme of his play *Léto* ("Summer," 1915), influenced by Ivan Turgenev's *A Month in the Country* as well as by the plays of Frank Wedekind: a young high school student falls desperately in love with a lady novelist who is merely conducting a flirtation; she leaves him but the boy finally finds consolation in the love of a servant girl. The play is the first in a trilogy concerned with the antagonism of the young and the old; it is followed by *Měsíc nad řekou* ("The Moon over the River," 1922) and *Plačicí satyr* ("The Weeping Satyr," 1923), in which a young girl rekindles the erotic dreams of three aging artists but leaves them unfulfilled. Less talented, but popular with the youth of their day, were Šrámek's war plays preaching pacifism: in the best of these, *Zvony* ("The Bells," 1921), the bells of a village church, requisitioned for military needs, stir a common conscience and rouse the villagers to resist.

Of the new trends that influenced Czech drama after 1918, the strongest is German EXPRESSIONISM. The plays of the brothers Josef and Karel ČAPEK employ utopian subjects to warn mankind against the destructive powers of modern civilization; in a pragmatic and relativistic spirit, they propose more modest limits for the aspirations of human life. Of these, *R.U.R.*, q.v., presents an effective dramatic symbol of modern technology in a robot, while *Ze života hmyzu* (*The Insect Comedy*, 1922) satirizes the insularity of the family and state by finding parallels in the world of insects. Though the plays of the Čapeks gained popularity all over the world, they failed to exert much influence on younger dramatists; perhaps their style and technique were too strongly associated with their utopian subjects.

Besides the Čapeks, the best modern Czech playwright is František LANGER, and his plays are particularly noteworthy for their fine dramatic construction. Langer's plays fall into two groups: his social comedies, in which the hand of George Bernard Shaw and the English writers of comedies of manners can be felt, and his more serious dramas, in which German expressionism is a dominant influence. But he is a thoroughly Czech playwright as well, and the dialogue and native manners of his comedies are especially successful. In the first group belongs Langer's comedy *Velbloud uchem jehly* (*The Camel Through the Needle's Eye*, 1923), which had considerable success on Broadway in a Theatre Guild production. It portrays the social rise of a poor young girl, who, through her wit and courage, becomes the wife of a

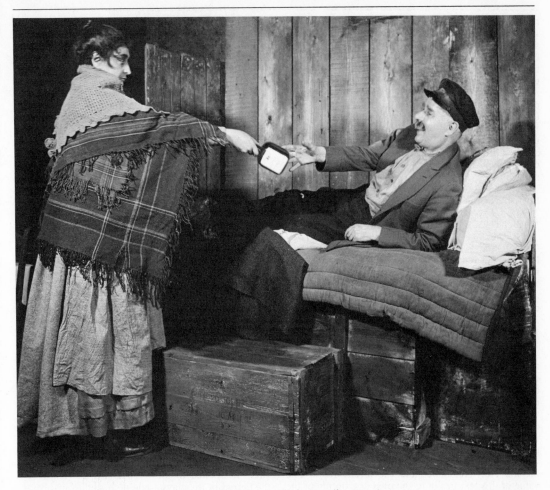

A SCENE FROM FRANTIŠEK LANGER'S *The Camel Through the Needle's Eye* (THEATRE COLLECTION, NEW YORK PUBLIC LIBRARY AT LINCOLN CENTER)

wealthy, if silly, young man. The girl's parents, proprietors of a small food shop, are depicted with wonderful humor and fidelity of speech, manners, and petit bourgeois psychology. The second type is illustrated by Langer's greatest drama, *Periferie* (*The Outskirts,* 1925), in which a man kills another in the heat of justifiable anger and is able to disguise the crime by making it appear an accident. But later he feels guilty. The police only laugh at him, however, when he tries to confess, and the dead man's wife thanks him for his deed. In the end he determines, rather like a hero of Dostoyevsky, to commit a second murder to find punishment for the first and kills his mistress, a reformed prostitute who sacrifices herself out of love for him. The play is a powerful tragedy of existential guilt.

The 1930's brought the rapid decline of Czech drama. The writers of the 1920's, such as Langer and Karel Čapek, still dominated the stage, but their work was weaker intellectually and technically. World War II, German domination, and the postwar Stalinist period hampered the theater, and no playwright of stature appeared during this period. The compulsory influence of the Soviet doctrine of So-

cialist Realism, imported after 1948 and applied to Czech drama, was particularly harmful and made for wooden and derivative plays based largely on socialist industrial themes.

In recent years censorship has loosened and several young playwrights of talent have emerged. These include Josef TOPOL and Václav HAVEL. In his play *Jejich den* ("Their Day," 1959), Topol depicts the life of young people who are unable to dedicate themselves to socialist construction or even to take it seriously. More recently he has departed farther from realism in several directions in *Konec masopustu* ("The End of Shrovetide," 1963), with its stylized use of the Czech folk ritual of Mardi Gras, and *Slavík k večeři* ("Nightingale's Dinner Invitation," 1967), a symbolic dream play in which the poet Slavík ("nightingale") comes to dine with strangers only to discover slowly that they are going to murder him. The first and leading practitioner of Czech absurd comedy is Václav Havel. Like Eugène Ionesco, he is deeply concerned with language and the possibility of meaningful communication, and like the Polish absurd playwright Sławomir Mrożek, he is specifically concerned with the fate of language threatened by the meaningless slogans of a communist bureaucracy. *Zahradní slavnost* ("The Garden Party," 1963) presents a young hero who makes his career very quickly by parroting official slogans; eventually he rises to the post of head of both the Inauguration Office and the Liquidation Office (so that he inaugurates the liquidation of the Inauguration Office). Havel's second play, *Vyrozumění* (*The Memorandum*, 1965), imagines a fantastic language, Ptydepe, developed for bureaucrats; it is too difficult to learn, however, and only lip service is paid to its use. Eventually, it is discredited in the name of common sense, but a new and equally fantastic language is at once introduced to replace it.

Only a few of the plays discussed are available in English versions. Langer's *The Camel Through the Needle's Eye* is published in a translation by Philip Moeller (1932); his *Periferie* is available in two versions: *The Ragged Edge*, translated by Frederic McConnell and Fern Long, and *The Outskirts*, translated by Lawrence Hyde. Havel's *The Memorandum* is found in the *Tulane Drama Review*, XI:3 (Spring 1967). Most of the plays of Josef and Karel Čapek are also available in English. On the most recent Czech dramatic developments, see Kenneth Tynan, "The Theatre Abroad: Prague," *New Yorker* (April 1, 1967) and *Tulane Drama Review*, XI:3 (Spring 1967).—W. E. H.

Slovakia. There is almost no record of any theatrical activity in the middle ages in Slovakia, which was part of Hungary at that time. The only evidences of a secular theater are reports about the persecution of jugglers in Hungary. The only proof of the existence of ecclesiastical drama in that same period is one extant text of a liturgical ceremony, called *Codex Prayanus* ("Pray's Codex," twelfth to fourteenth century), which originated in the Slovakian region. This work contains a short dialogue between angels guarding the Holy Sepulcher and the three Marys. The value of this text lies in its detailed description of the ecclesiastical ceremony.

The ecclesiastical drama reached a high level of development in the fifteenth century. At that time it was performed in the German towns of the Slovakian region and the texts contained many secular features. During this Renaissance period, the theatrical activity in German and Latin languages was confined to productions in schools. There is no record from this era of performances of plays written in Slovak. There were, however, two important playwrights, Pavel Kyrmezer (?–1589) and Jiří Tesák Mošovský (c. 1545–1617), who wrote in the Czech countries. The work of both these writers belongs to the drama of the Czech Renaissance. Religious themes from the Old Testament were dramatized like scenes from the contemporary life of small Czech towns. Pavel Kyrmezer evinced a strong social feeling in his short dramatic comedies *Komedie česká o bohatci a Lazarovi* ("The Czech Comedy About a Money-bag and Lazarus," pub. 1566) and *Komedie nová o vdově* ("The New Comedy About a Widow," pub. 1573). In *Komedie z knihy Zákona božího, jenž slove Ruth* ("The Comedy from the Book of God's Testament Which Is Called Ruth," pub. 1604), Mošovský gives a clear picture of the life of farmers.

During the Baroque period, the Slovak and Czech languages were used sometimes in school produc-

tions, but there is no evidence of their appearance in professional productions. At this time the theatrical creativity of the Slovaks was outstandingly expressed in various folk plays with religious themes that were performed in villages and small towns until the beginning of the twentieth century. An example of this type of highly popular theater is *Hra o svaté Dorote* ("The Play About the Holy Maid Dorothy," c. eighteenth century), produced in the Zvolen district. Also, some of the folk rites and customs had a strong theatrical character. The drama of the middle class, however, did not continue this folk tradition.

Slovakian drama was slowly developing from the end of the eighteenth century. Under very hard national and social conditions, the Slovak drama strengthened the national struggles and consciousness of the Slovak intelligentsia and lower middle class. Until the foundation of the Czechoslovak Republic in 1918, the Slovakian theatrical productions were created by amateurs only.

The most outstanding playwright of the Slovak Romantic movement was Ján Chalupka (1791–1871), who wrote excellent comedies. In his best work, the farce *Kocúrkovo* ("Gotham," pub. 1830), he ridicules the narrow-minded, unpatriotic petite bourgeoisie who seek power. Based on his familiarity with middle-Slovakian towns, Chalupka portrayed the racy characters of these small towns, and in his talented use of common Slovak speech, he proved that the Slovak language could be used in the theater.

Chalupka laid the foundation for the most successful Slovakian genre—satirical comedy. Ján Palárik (1822–1870) continued this work of Chalupka. Palárik, whose best work was written in the 1850's and 1860's, wrote comedies according to the aesthetic principles of Romanticism. He mirrored the Slovak middle class in his plays in hopes of educating and activating this social group. For the future of Slovakia he looked to the intellectuals and students—the heroes of his plays—and he hoped to involve the aristocracy in the Slovakian nationalist movement. His most significant works are the comedies *Inkognito* ("Incognito," pub. 1858), *Drotár* ("A Tinker," pub. 1860), and *Zmierenie alebo Dobrodružstvo pri obžinkoch* ("A Settlement or an Adventure at Harvest Home," pub. 1862).

Of the attempts of several Slovakian playwrights to write historical dramas, only Jonáš Záborský (1812–1876) systematically pursued this genre, and he became the founder of Slovakian historical drama. In his plays, such as *Posledné dni Veľkej Moravy* ("The Last Days of the Great Moravian Empire," date unknown), *Bitka pri Rozhanovciach* ("A Battle at Rozhanovcie," date unknown), and *D'orde Čierny* (date unknown), Záborský took only those events from Slovakian or Slavonic history that he could use as warnings for his contemporaries. Although his historical dramas, infused with a romantic spirit, were pioneer works, they were never performed during his lifetime; they remained closet dramas. The poet Pavol Országh-Hviezdoslav (1849–1921) also wrote an effective Slovakian historical play: the poetic tragedy *Herodes a Herodias* ("Herod and Herodias," pub. 1909). Using a theme from the Old Testament, Hviezdoslav in this work ponders over the ethical problems of man.

In the early twentieth century, Jozef Gregor-

Tajovský (1874–1940) developed the tradition of Slovakian comedy. In *Zenský zákon* ("Women's Law," pub. 1900) and *Statky-Zmätky* ("Estates-Confusions," pub. 1909) he created realistic images of the social life in contemporary Slovakian villages. Gregor-Tajovský struggled against considerable opposition from social conservatives to incorporate the principles of realism in Slovakian drama. With his plays, whose main characters were often plain, ordinary men, the democratization process in Slovakian drama made progress.

Gregor-Tajovský and other early twentieth-century playwrights wrote for amateur theatrical companies and had constantly to take into consideration the limited capabilities of these groups. Ferko Urbánek (1859–1934) was a popular playwright among these amateur troupes, and his works, almost forty plays, were often performed in small villages. Jozef Hollý (1879–1912) set higher creative goals for himself than Ferko Urbánek. He wrote the comedies *Geľo Sebechlebský* (pub. 1912) and *Kubo* (pub. 1904).

In 1918, when the Slovaks and Czechs formed their own state, the Czechoslovak Republic, conditions for the development of Slovakian drama improved. The development of the Slovakian drama was considerably strengthened by the establishment of professional Slovakian theaters. The leading playwright of the interwar period was Ivan STODOLA, the author of many comedies, some of which were performed abroad. Stodola's forte was his critical portrayal of the Slovakian petit bourgeois who wished to get as much as possible for himself under the new republican system. This type of character appears particularly in the comedies *Náš pán minister* ("Our Minister," 1926), *Čaj u pána senátora* ("Tea with the Senator," 1929), and *Jožko Púčik a jeho kariéra* ("Jožko Púčik and His Career," 1931). Stodola also wrote several serious dramas and historical plays.

The traditional world of Slovakian plays—the life of the petite bourgeoisie and intelligentsia—was abandoned by Július Barč-Ivan (1909–1955) during the interwar period. The main characters of his works were often people drawn from the modern world—businessmen and proletarians. In his plays Barč-Ivan always solved social problems from his religious point of view. His most important plays are *3000 ľudí* ("3000 People," pub. 1934), *Človek, ktorého zbili* ("A Man, Who Was Pummeled," pub. 1936), *Diktátor* ("Dictator," pub. 1937), *Mastný hrnec* ("A Greasy Pot," pub. 1940) and *Matka* ("Mother," 1944).

During World War II, when the Slovakian nationalists and fascists formed the Slovak State (1939 to 1945), the best dramatists—Stodola and Barč-Ivan —wrote allegorical satires directed against the fascist system. This satirical purpose is also apparent in *Tanec nad plačom* ("A Dance over Crying," 1943) by Peter Zvon (1913–1942). In the historical play *Jánošík* (1941) dramatist Mária Rázusová-Martáková deals with the legendary Slovakian folk hero who had already appeared in nineteenth-century Slovakian plays. Jánošík, a Slovak rebel, represents for the Slovaks the struggle for national and social freedom.

After the liberation of Czechoslovakia in 1945, when the country went through revolutionary social changes, a new group of playwrights appeared. In the years just after World War II, the poetic, richly philosophical work of Leopold Lahola (1916–1968) appeared. His plays during this period include *Bezvetrie v Zuele* ("Dead Calm in Zuela," 1947), *Štyri strany sveta* ("Four Cardinal Points of the World," 1948), and *Atentát* ("The Assassination," 1949). Later, while living in exile, he wrote *Skvrny na slunci* ("Stains on the Sun," date unknown). The most important postwar Slovakian dramatist is Peter KARVAŠ. Karvaš is the author of a number of comedies and serious dramas with topical themes that have a high intellectual level and a well-developed form. His most important drama is *Polnočna omša* ("A Midnight Mass," 1959) and his best comedy is *Veľká parochňa* ("A Great Wig," 1964). Another outstanding playwright of this period is Štefan Králik (1909–), who wrote *Svätá Barbora* ("Saint Barbara," 1953) and *Buky podpolianske* ("The Podpoliana Beeches," 1949). Of the younger generation of Slovakian dramatists, Igor Rusnák is the most important. In *Lísky, dobrú noc* ("Foxes, Good Night," 1964), he dramatizes the problems of the younger Slovakian generation.—F. Č.

D

Dagerman, Stig (1923–1954). Swedish novelist and playwright. Dagerman represents, better than any other writer, the intensified anguish of neutral Sweden in the 1940's. First active in syndicalist journalism, Dagerman then turned to fiction, distinguishing himself with such stories as "Open the Door, Richard," in *Nattens lekar* (*Games of Night,* 1947) and the novel *Bränt barn* (*Burnt Child,* 1948). His growing preoccupation with theater is observable in his friendship with the actor-director Bengt Ekerot and in his second marriage, to the distinguished actress Anita Björk. Although Dagerman committed suicide, after many unsuccessful attempts, he was probably less preoccupied with death than with life, which he lived on its edge.

Dagerman's first play, *Den dödsdömde* (*The Condemned,* 1947), is an expressionist study of the absurdities of human justice, somewhat after the fashion of Strindberg and Kafka. In the realistic drama *Skuggan av Mart* ("The Shadow of Mart," 1947) Dagerman is concerned with the nature of heroism and its impact on others. *Streber* ("The Upstart," 1949) has to do with the working-class experiment of syndicalism, and *Ingen går fri* ("No One Goes Free," 1949), an adaptation of his novel *Bränt barn,* with the agony and loneliness of a father-son relationship in the drabness of an urban setting.

The Condemned is in *Scandinavian Plays of the 20th Century,* third series (1951). See also A. Gustafson, *A History of Swedish Literature* (1961), and Olof Lagercrantz, *Stig Dagerman* (Stockholm, 1958).—R. B. V.

STIG DAGERMAN (SWEDISH INFORMATION SERVICE)

AUGUSTIN DALY (NEW YORK PUBLIC LIBRARY)

Dahomey. See AFRICA: *Dahomey.*

Daly, Augustin (1838–1899). American producer and playwright. Daly was born in Plymouth, North Carolina, but grew up in New York City. His various occupations of critic, press agent, and play-adapter centered around the stage, and in 1869 he established an acting company that quickly became popular. In the next thirty years Daly's company became famous for its brilliant ensemble acting in a style that approached realism and for the realistic staging that anticipated the work of David BELASCO. Exercising absolute control over every aspect of production, Daly was the first all-powerful producer-director in America.

Daly is credited with the authorship of eight original plays, ten dramatizations of novels, and between thirty-five and forty adaptations from French works. In most of his writing, however, he had the collaboration of his brother, Judge Joseph F. Daly, and hired other writers whose contributions he did not acknowledge.

Daly's first successful play was *Leah the Forsaken* (1862), which he adapted from S. H. Mosenthal's German play *Deborah.* His first original play was the melodrama *Under the Gaslight* (1867), in which the heroine rescues faithful Snorkey at the last moment from the railroad track to which the villain has tied him. *Horizon* (1871), an early romantic drama of the American West, is of interest because of its satirical portrait of Sundown Rowse, a lobbyist and crooked politician, and an unromantic Indian, Wannemucka.

Not only in his original plays but also in his adaptations, which were thoroughly Americanized, Daly added to the gallery of native characters and to the panorama of local color, thereby contributing to the development of realistic drama about American life.

The best source is Marvin Felheim's *The Theatre of Augustin Daly* (1956).—B. H.

Dame aux Camélias, La (Camille, 1852). French sentimental comedy of manners by Alexandre DUMAS fils. Greeted with mixed approval and bewilderment when it opened, *La Dame aux Camélias* (*The Lady of the Camelias*, erroneously known through a translator's error as *Camille* in America), was Dumas's adaptation of his own novel, *La Dame aux Camélias* (1847). The success of the play's first long run was largely the result of the magnificently subtle and restrained acting of Eugénie Doche, who played the rehabilitated courtesan Marguerite Gautier, and Charles Fechter, who played Armand Duval, her lover.

The plot is well known. Falling in love with Armand, Marguerite, impoverished by her extravagant life, borrows money and pawns her possessions to rent a country house for Armand and herself. Duval Sr. begs her to break off the affair to save the family name. She reluctantly complies and, writing Armand that she no longer loves him, joins De Varville, a former lover. Ignorant of the whole truth, Armand hurls money won from De Varville at Marguerite, insultingly repaying her for her sacrifice. Then, learning the complete truth, Armand goes to Marguerite, who is dying of tuberculosis, professes his love, and receives her forgiveness.

Written when Romanticism was on the wane and the "well-made plays" of Eugène Scribe were in fashion, *Camille* established a brand-new genre in France, the realistic comedy of manners. Although constructed according to the Scribean formula, its main action is less theatrically contrived than the complex mechanisms of Scribe. And Dumas's style is more flexible than Scribe's: eloquent, witty, or pathetic by turns. Whereas the Romantics sacrificed verisimilitude, often inventing plots with which to re-create characters taken from history, Dumas presented on the stage from firsthand experience the morals, manners, and conversation of the courtesan. His characters are realistic types, and their language and feelings and their relationship to society have been acutely observed by the author. He unobtrusively demonstrated that this kind of life is hollow and trivial. Despite the passion of the lovers, many of the characters are represented as avaricious or repellent. No disinterested critic would claim that *Camille* is a dramatic masterpiece. The implied thesis of a courtesan's redemption through love and suffering is exaggerated, sentimental, and to a large extent untrue. The climactic scene (*scène à faire*) in which Armand denounces Marguerite in public seems excessive because his jealousy and distrust are nothing new; indeed, no significant new truth is disclosed. His contrition in the last act seems excessive, the death scene is too long, and its dialogue artificial. Nevertheless, realistic social drama in France, England, and America began with *Camille*. It was the first of a line that continues today of realistic plays concerned with the relation of the erring woman to society.

Then, too, it is perhaps the most remarkable first play ever written: it has been performed thousands of times in many countries for well over a hundred years. The critic Clayton Hamilton once pointed out that every aspiring actress plays Marguerite to help her reputation and to be ranked among her illustrious predecessors. While spurious as a claim to literary excellence, this fact is in itself a singular achievement for a young, inexperienced playwright. For, in spite of its faults, *Camille* has the power to move any audience deeply, and the faults of the play are offset by the force of the dramatic conflict and the emotional depth of Marguerite's love for Armand.

One of the best English versions, by Edith Reynolds and Nigel Playfair, is in *Camille and Other Plays*, edited by S. Stanton, which also contains a critical introduction, notes on *Camille*'s theater history, and a bibliography.—S. S. S.

Dance of Death, The (Dödsdansen, 1900). A play in two parts by August STRINDBERG. No Strindberg play has had wider international currency. The lead male role of the Captain, Edgar, has attracted such diverse actors as Poul Reumert (1928 in French, 1937 in Danish), Erich von Stroheim (film, 1947), Oskar Homolka (1948), Jean Vilar (1948), Lars Hanson (1959), and Sir Laurence Olivier (1967).

Edgar, commanding officer of an island ("Little Hell") off the coast of Sweden, and his wife, Alice, once a promising actress, approach their silver wedding anniversary in a situation of corrosive isolation, frustration, boredom, and hatred for each other. Alice's cousin Kurt comes to the island as quarantine master and is sensually attracted to Alice, as the Captain is stricken by two heart attacks, which Alice applauds. The cumulative fury is too much for Kurt, and his departure from the bizarre fortress household precipitates a darkly comic reconciliation of the married couple.

Strindberg wrote Part II, really a second, sequel play, to alleviate the acrimony of Part I, but he was only partially successful. After conducting a merciless vendetta against Kurt, Edgar dies, and his daughter, Judith, and Kurt's son, Allan, unite to give some promise for the future.

The realism of *The Dance of Death*, written in Strindberg's expressionist period, is only illusory. His "lovers" perform their macabre dance in the shadow of the medieval iconography suggested by the title, and the overtones of Edgar Allan Poe and E. T. A. Hoffmann are manifest. This *pièce grinçante* is clearly a predecessor of Jean Anouilh's *Waltz of the Toreadors* and Edward Albee's *Who's Afraid of Virginia Woolf?*, if not of Samuel Beckett's *Endgame* and some of Eugène Ionesco's plays as well.

The text may be found in *Five Plays of Strindberg* (1960), translated by Elizabeth Sprigge. See also K. I. Hildeman, "Strindberg, *The Dance of Death*, and Revenge," in *Scandinavian Studies*, Vol. 35 (1963). —R. B. V.

Dancourt, Florent Carton [born **Sieur d'Ancourt**] (1661–1725). French playwright and actor. Born at Fontainebleau into a family of Calvinists converted to Catholicism, Dancourt studied with the Jesuits, hesitated between the priesthood and law, and eloped with an actor's daughter. From 1685 to 1718 both were actors at the Comédie Française. Af-

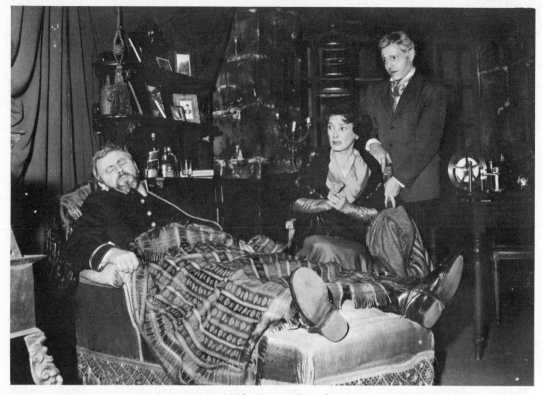

A SCENE FROM AUGUST STRINDBERG'S *The Dance of Death* (FRENCH CULTURAL SERVICES)

ter 1718 Dancourt devoted himself to a translation of
the Psalms, and in 1725 he died, surviving the wife he
worshipped by only a few months.

Some sixty plays are attributed to Dancourt, many
of which were written in collaboration with the moralist Saint-Yon. The best known of these are *Le Chevalier à la mode* ("The Fashionable Chevalier,"
1687), *Les Bourgeoises à la mode* ("The Fashionable
Bourgeois Ladies," 1692), and *La Fête de village*
("The Village Feast," 1700). But he also wrote many
one-act comedies dealing with the customs and
events of the day: *La Maison de campagne* ("The
Country House," 1688), *Les Vendanges de Suresne*
("Vine Harvest in Suresne," 1694), *Les Vacances*
("Vacations," 1696), and others.

Very lively and gay, and full of associations with
Molière's work, Dancourt's comedies are also highly
cynical: His characters are all more or less corrupt or
mutually corrupt one another. With his nonchalant
mixture of seducers, gamblers, and social climbers,
he presented a realistic mirror of an unstable, always
self-seeking, unscrupulous society. In those of his
comedies situated in the countryside near Paris,
Dancourt frequently included peasant types different
from Molière's but vigorously drawn and also caught
in the whirlpool of general corruption.

For detailed information on Dancourt and his
plays, see Henry C. Lancaster, *A History of French
Dramatic Literature in the Seventeenth Century*, 9
vols. (1952).—Ja. G.

Daniel, Samuel (c. 1563–1619).   English poet and

playwright. Chiefly known as a lyric and narrative
poet, Daniel also wrote a few plays and masques. The
son of a musician, he was born in Somerset and educated at Magdalen College, Oxford. After touring the
Continent, he became tutor to William Herbert, third
earl of Pembroke. He thus gained entry into the literary and intellectual coterie of which Herbert's
mother, Mary Herbert, countess of Pembroke, was
patron. His sonnet sequence *Delia* (1592) was dedicated to the countess, as was his long historical epic
Civil Wars (1595; revised and expanded 1609). In
1604 he was appointed licenser of plays performed by
the boys' acting company Children of the Queen's
Revels. Sometime before his death in 1619, he received the title of groom of the Queen's Privy Chamber.

Daniel's first play, *Cleopatra* (1595), was designed
as a companion piece to Mary Herbert's translation
of Robert Garnier's French tragedy *Antony* (1592).
Cleopatra is a Senecan closet drama, more declamatory than dramatic. It was revised in 1607 in a manner indicating the influence of Shakespeare's *Antony
and Cleopatra*. Daniel's other neoclassical tragedy,
Tragedy of Philotas (1605), was widely regarded as a
sympathetic, allegorical treatment of the earl of
Essex, executed for rebellion in 1601. Daniel is also
the author of a pastoral tragicomedy, *The Queen's
Arcadia* (1605), and a number of masques. Among
the latter the best known is *The Vision of the Twelve
Goddesses*, performed at court on January 8, 1604.
The leading role was played by Queen Anne, the

stagestruck wife of James I. Daniel's graceful style was well suited to the masque, within the restricted confines of which his polished verse excelled.

Daniel's *Complete Works* (1883) have been edited by A. B. Grosart.—E. Q.

D'Annunzio, Gabriele (1863–1938). Italian writer, poet, and playwright. Born in Pescara of a bourgeois family, D'Annunzio manifested a precocious literary talent when he published a collection of poems with a Latin title, *Primo vere* ("In Early Spring"), at the age of seventeen. In 1881 he moved to Rome, married a daughter of Duke Hardouin after a romantic elopement (the first of a long series of wild and noisy love affairs), and published some realistic short stories in *Terra vergine* ("Virgin Land," 1882) and the audacious *L'Intermezzo di rime* ("Intermezzo of Poems," 1884), in which he showed an extraordinary command of the language and an undoubted narrative and poetic talent. Everywhere he excited admiration and scandal, because he was snobbish and pugnacious and because his style of life strongly opposed the norms of conservative society. (He was inspired to independence and autonomous morality by Nietzsche's concept of the superman.) In 1894 he met the great actress Eleanora Duse, with whom he formed a long friendship, which he chronicled in his novel *Il Fuoco* (*The Flame of Life,* 1900). This friendship also marked the beginning of his writing for the theater. In 1911 his unrestrained and luxurious life brought him to financial ruin, and in the same year the Catholic Church put all his works on the Index. During World War I he accomplished audacious martial feats, such as his flight over the enemy capital, Vienna, to drop propaganda leaflets. At the end of the conflict he judged that Italy had been treated unfairly in the Treaty of Versailles. Therefore, against the wishes of the Italian government, he and his legionnaires occupied for fifteen months the Dalmatian city of Fiume, which he felt should have been ceded to Italy. Taking from his work its most exterior aspects, the Fascist government adopted him as poet of the regime. This attachment was, however, never more than superficial.

GABRIELE D'ANNUNZIO (WALTER HAMPDEN MEMORIAL LIBRARY AT THE PLAYERS, NEW YORK)

Among D'Annunzio's narrative and poetic works the most important are the novels *Il Piacere* ("Pleasure," 1889) and *L'Innocente* ("The Innocent One," 1892), and the four books of *Laudi* ("Lauds," 1904). He also wrote fifteen plays of which three are in French. His plays, however, are the weakest of all his writings, except for the "pastoral tragedy" LA FIGLIA DI IORIO. The plot derives from a legend of D'Annunzio's native country, the Abruzzi, and is written with great dramatic vigor and provocative poetry. The aesthetic bases of his other plays are not very clear. (D'Annunzio declared that he used as models the Greek tragedians, the madrigalists of the Baroque age, and Wagner's operas.) His theater lives above all in his medieval verse tragedies, such as *Francesca da Rimini* (1901), *La Fiaccola sotto il moggio* ("The Light Under the Bushel," 1905), and *La Parisina* (1912). In these tragedies the poet's sensuous language capably created lights and shadows, as well as a somber mood that a public of romantic temper saw as suggestive of the middle ages. See LA GIOCONDA. —L. L.

Danton's Death (Dantons Tod, written 1835, pub. 1850, perf. 1902). A tragedy by Georg BÜCHNER. Büchner wrote this four-act drama in five weeks. At the time of composition, he was under the threat of arrest for his political activities and influenced by Thiers's *History of the French Revolution.* The mood and movement of the play reflect Büchner's desperate situation and dim view of social progress. The scenes are spasmodic in nature, and the language is at times terse, sarcastic, and vulgar and, at other times, rhapsodic, tender, and mellifluous. Danton and Robespierre, the two foremost leaders of the revolution, both realize that the ideals of the movement can never be attained. Danton abandons himself to despair and pleasure while Robespierre orders more executions to save the cause. They oppose one another, and the dialectics of the play hinge on the debate between the free and aesthetic Danton and the repressed and puritanical Robespierre. Since Büchner did not believe in the movement to a new synthesis, his drama ends on a dissonant note. Danton is executed. There is no hope for freedom. This pessimistic ending is contrary to the idealism of earlier German political plays by Lessing and Schiller, and it indicates why Büchner was "rediscovered" only at the beginning of the twentieth century. His fatalism is similar to that of the naturalists, his mood like that of the *fin de siècle,* and his language typical of the expressionists. Today it is not so much the determinism of the play that is praised as its political and documentary nature.—J. D. Z.

Da Ponte, Lorenzo. Born **Emanuele Conegliano** (1749–1838). Italian poet, librettist, teacher, and adventurer. Da Ponte's fame rests on his work as the librettist of three major Mozart operas. His *Memoirs,* somewhat reminiscent of those of his friend Casanova, detail the misadventures of a man with a gift for intrigue and artistry. Born in Ceneda, near Venice, Da Ponte changed his name when he converted from Judaism to Christianity, taking the name of his patron, the Bishop of Ceneda. Consecrated a priest, the young Abbé Da Ponte taught Italian at the Seminary of Portogruaro but resigned under pressure after two years. Freethinking and free living combined to cause his banishment from Venice in 1779. Austria and Dresden were his next stops, before he settled in Vienna in 1782. He learned the lyric craft from the famed poet-librettist Metastasio, becoming poet to the Imperial Theatre through clever maneuvering. Beset with enemies after the death of Josef II, Da Ponte went to London (1792–1798) and finally to New York (1805). Failing in business, he took up teaching and was involved in attempts to establish opera in his new country (1825–1826 and 1832). In 1825 he became an Italian-language instructor at what is now Columbia University.

For Mozart, Da Ponte wrote *The Marriage of Figaro* (*Le Nozze di Figaro,* 1786), *Don Giovanni* (1787), and *Così fan tutte* (1792). That he is remembered only for these works, while his other librettos have passed into oblivion, is not only a measure of Mozart's genius as a composer but also of his ability to inspire Da Ponte to his best efforts. Mozart suggested that he use Beaumarchais' *Le Marriage de Figaro* as a libretto for a proposed opera, but Josef II had forbidden performances of that supposedly licentious play and did not consider it appropriate material for an opera. Josef, displeased with *Abduction from the Seraglio* (*Die Entführung aus dem Serail*), an earlier Mozart commission, was convinced the composer could not create a competent opera. By clever stratagems and plain speaking to the emperor, Da Ponte won approval for the forbidden scenes of Beaumarchais' plays as well as for the music. Critics generally praise Da Ponte for understanding Mozart's strengths and for providing a libretto with witty satire, well-rounded characters, and a plot which, while intricate, skillfully conveys the sense of decay in the old social order. Critic Herbert Weinstock says in *The World of Opera* that *The Marriage of Figaro* alone justifies the existence of opera. *Don Giovanni,* written in haste while Da Ponte was also fashioning two other librettos, is a less successful libretto. The Don, a strongly developed character, is surrounded by much weaker ones, which tends to weaken the conflict. *Così,* based on real events in Vienna, was ordered by the emperor. Da Ponte's wit and sarcasm are unexcelled in this *opera buffa.*

Although he is not altogether scrupulous about the truth, Da Ponte is capable of describing his sins with some gusto in his remarkably frank autobiography, *The Memoirs of Lorenzo Da Ponte* (1959), translated by Elizabeth Abbot. Illuminating introductory essays and generous notes help put this evocation of Mozart's age in perspective. April Fitzlyon's study, *The Libertine Librettist* (1955), draws upon Da Ponte's testimony but does not depend entirely on it.
—G. L.

Davenant, Sir William (1606–1668). English dramatist and theater manager. Davenant was born in Oxford and according to an unfounded legend was an illegitimate son of Shakespeare, who, in fact, was a frequent visitor at his father's inn. After a brief period at Lincoln College, Oxford, Davenant went to London, where he became a page in the service of the Duchess of Richmond and thus established a connection with the court. In 1628 he wrote a tragedy, *Albovine,* and later, in addition to plays for the public theater, wrote masques for Charles I and Queen Henrietta Maria. After Ben Jonson's death, he was made poet laureate in 1638. An active supporter of the

SIR WILLIAM DAVENANT (BRANDER MATTHEWS DRAMATIC MUSEUM, COLUMBIA UNIVERSITY)

royal cause in the Civil War, Davenant was knighted in 1643. Later, after the triumph of the Parliamentary forces, he was imprisoned in the Tower of London for over a year, during which time he completed his epic *Gondibert* (pub. 1651). Some time after his release in 1652, he began to interest himself in the theater again and, though plays were legally banned, produced several dramatic pieces between 1656 and 1660, evading the law by representing them as musical entertainments (see ENGLAND: *Restoration drama;* ENGLAND: *Caroline drama*). After the restoration of Charles II, he and Thomas KILLIGREW were given patents for the two theatrical companies that were to be allowed. Davenant had the Duke's Company—a group of young actors including Thomas Betterton.

Davenant was the most important link between the theater prior to the closing in 1642 and the theater of the Restoration. Early plays such as *Love and Honor* (1634) anticipated the heroic themes of Restoration drama, and masques such as *The Temple of Love* (1635) and *Salmacida Spolia* (1640) pointed the way to *The Siege of Rhodes* (1656), the most famous of his "entertainments," in which the use of actresses and changeable scenery for a public performance heralded a new era in the public theater. Furthermore, by treating idealized love in *The Temple of Love* and *The Platonic Lovers* (1635), he catered to the taste of the court as Restoration dramatists were to cater to the taste of their elite audience. *The Siege of Rhodes* was not only the immediate ancestor of the heroic play but has also been called the first English opera.

In addition to managing the Duke's Company, Davenant continued to write for the theater, adapting *Macbeth* (1664?) and, with Dryden, *The Tempest* (1667). It is some indication of Davenant's ability to gauge the taste of his time that Pepys, after seeing *Macbeth* in 1667, singled out for praise the "divertisement"—presumably a Davenant addition.

The standard edition of Davenant's *Works* by James Maidment and W. H. Logan, originally published in 1872, has been reprinted (1964). There are two biographies: Alfred Harbage's *Sir William Davenant, Poet Venturer 1606–68* (1935), and Arthur Nethercot's *Sir William D'Avenant, Poet Laureate and Playwright-Manager* (1938).—E. W.

Davies, [William] Robertson (1913–). Canadian novelist, playwright, and essayist. Davies is the most prolific and widely performed of contemporary Canadian dramatists. His *Eros at Breakfast* (1948; pub. 1949) is a volume of one-act plays satirizing those aspects of Canadian society—prudery, complacency, indifference to the arts—that Davies deplores. *Hope Deferred* (1948) is an especially trenchant little drama based on the banning of Molière's *Tartuffe* in Quebec in 1693. The best single play in this collection is *Overlaid*, an exuberant, poignant comedy of life in backwoods Ontario.

Davies' first three-act drama, *Fortune My Foe* (1948), is a less satisfactory play about the alienated artist. The theme, once again the philistinism of the Canadian public and the improvidence of a society that loses its talented citizens because of indifference to them, lends an angry energy to many of the scenes. However, an unassimilated residue of rancor mars the tone.

At My Heart's Core (1950), Davies' next full-length play, is a stronger work. By setting the action in Upper Canada in 1837, he more easily presents with the necessary degree of detachment the issues that concern him. The period setting also enables the playwright, who is not at ease with the amorphous idiom of modern urban speech, to exploit his gift for precise rhetoric.

The main plot of *At My Heart's Core* concerns the attempt by Cantwell, a mysterious, baleful figure, to undermine the composure of three gentlewomen whose husbands have gone to York to suppress the rebellion of 1837. Cantwell's strategy is to persuade each in turn that the development of her talents is thwarted by the social and domestic wasteland that surrounds her. All three repudiate him, cleave to their husbands, and remain in Canada. In the ambiguous ending Davies seems at the same time to assert that faith in Canada's cultural future is an admirable thing and to question whether such faith is worth the sacrifice of the rich possibilities life offers elsewhere.

A Masque of Aesop (1952), a slight but charming satirical masque written originally for a cast of boy actors, ridicules varieties of bigotry and insensitivity. Davies has written another masque, centering on the figure of Mr. Punch, and one further drama, *A Jig for the Gypsy* (1954), in which he dramatizes the clash between the intuitive wisdom of a gypsy woman and the sterile rationalism of a group of politicians who try to exploit her powers of divination.

Davies' strengths are his wide literary experience, his wit, and his ability to compose deft, literate dialogue—secondary rather than primary attributes of the playwright. His characters and themes are lacking in depth or force, and his dramatic techniques are conventional. Moreover, in the larger cities at least, the stolid Canadian society that he postulates in so many of his plays is rapidly becoming an obsolete object for his kind of satire. Nevertheless, Davies remains one of the most able and entertaining of English Canadian playwrights.

A brief but illuminating discussion of Davies' theatrical techniques is M. W. Steinberg's "Don Quixote and the Puppets: Theme and Structure in Robertson Davies' Drama," *Canadian Literature*, VII (Winter 1961), 45–53.—M. T.

Day, John (1574–c. 1640). English playwright. Day was educated at Caius College, Cambridge, from which he was expelled in 1593 for stealing a book. He began writing for Philip Henslowe's acting company, the Admiral's Men, about 1600, collaborating in that year with Henry Chettle on *The Blind-Beggar of Bednal-Green,* a folk romance imitative of the comedies of Robert Greene. Shortly thereafter he started writing for the Children of the Revels. For this troupe he wrote a series of witty, graceful comedies including *Law Tricks* (c. 1604), *The Ile of Guls* (1605), and *Humour Out of Breath* (1607/08). Of these, *The Ile of Guls* achieved notoriety because of some allegedly satirical references to prominent persons at the court of James I. Day's best-known and most unusual work is *The Parliament of Bees* (produced between 1634 and 1640), a series of twelve allegorical character sketches in dialogue form. Many of these sketches were adopted almost verbatim from plays written by Thomas Dekker, and it is possible that Dekker worked as a collaborator on the series. Whoever their author, these sketches have always been acknowledged to be superb examples of fanciful, delicate light verse.—E. Q.

Death of a Salesman (1949). A play by Arthur MILLER. The scene is Brooklyn. Willy Loman, a salesman of sixty, is undergoing a nervous breakdown. He can no longer go out on the road to make sales, and he is upset by the presence of his older son, Biff, who scorns his father's dream of achieving success by being well liked and prefers to be a cowboy out west. On the same day, Willy tries to get a transfer to his firm's home office, while Biff looks for a job. Both fail, and Willy is fired. Biff and his brother, Happy, meeting their father for dinner at a restaurant that night, pick up two girls and desert Willy. The next day, Biff argues that their failure in business has proved Willy's conception of success to be false. Willy kills himself in an automobile accident, having announced that he will do it in order to leave the insurance money that will give Biff a start in business. At his funeral, Biff asserts that Willy's best self was reflected in his work with his hands, Happy praises his father's philosophy of success, and their mother, Linda, expresses her bewilderment. The present action of the play is accompanied by Willy's recollection of the hopeful past, when Biff was growing up. He recalls also his brother Ben, who preaches aggressiveness as the means to success, and his neighbor Charley, whose son Bernard became a real success, as a lawyer, without subscribing to any myth. Willy's reminiscences culminate in the incident that, years before, ruined his close relationship with Biff: Biff found him in a hotel room in Boston with a woman.

In his use of dramatized reminiscences and of archetypal characters (some of whom, like Charley, do not have last names), Miller consciously employed the technique of expressionism. Muffled though it is by the plainness of its language, the play still states effectively the danger of failure in the land of success.

The play was first published in 1949.—H. P.

Deathwatch (Haute Surveillance, 1949). A play by Jean GENET. The action of Genet's second play, *Deathwatch,* takes place in a prison cell where a very precise and powerful hierarchy of seductiveness exists among three young men. Yeux-Verts, as the murderer of a girl, expects to be guillotined in two months' time. He loses himself in admiration over the magnitude of his own condemnation and fate. With the prestige of an exalted criminal, he dominates a second prisoner, who in his turn dominates a third prisoner, a mere thief. This is the hierarchy of the cell, where seductiveness (essentially of a sexual nature) comes from the power of evil.

The heroes of *Deathwatch,* who pace back and forth in their close cell, provide a picture of their obsessions from which they cannot escape. Theirs is a self-contained world of damnation. Genet's subject matter is that which is condemned by society; he presents evil in the form of a criminal hierarchy. Yeux-Verts, the protagonist of the play, has his own prestige and magnificence, because he is the beneficiary of a perverted kind of grace and power. Genet has methodically exploited the appeal and the prestige that vice can engender.

Deathwatch has been translated by Bernard Frechtman in *The Maids/Deathwatch* (1954).—W. F.

De Filippo, Eduardo (1900–   ). Italian playwright and actor. Born in Naples, De Filippo is one of three illegitimate sons of the famous Neapolitan actor Eduardo Scarpetta. The identity of the father was unknown until it was disclosed in 1968 by Eduardo's brother Peppino. Eduardo began as a child to act with Scarpetta's acting company, which performed in dialect. In 1932, together with Peppino and Titina, his two brothers, he established the Company of the Humorous Theater, also known as "The De Filippos." The company, under his direction, had an enthusiastic and immediate success because of the realistic sense, the profound humanity, and the extraordinary comic gifts of the three actor-brothers, who are considered to be among the greatest Italian actors of the twentieth century. De Filippo left the company in 1945 in order to establish his own company, for which he found a permanent stage in 1954 at the Teatro San Ferdinando in Naples.

De Filippo's lively dramatic work includes brief one-act plays, written by himself or in collaboration with others and inspired in part by the traditional motifs of popular Neapolitan farce, as well as more carefully completed comedies in Italian and in dialect, which, in the 1930's, formed the best part of the repertoire of "The De Filippos." Among these comedies the following stand out: *Natale in casa Cupiello* (*"Christmas at the Cupiellos' House,"* 1931), a comic and bitter contrast of reality and illusion in a setting of colorful misery; and *Uomo e galantuomo* ("Man and Gentleman," 1933), famous for a scene of proverbial comedy. These works, collected later under the title *Cantata dei giorni pari* ("Cantata for Even-Numbered Days"), were followed, beginning in 1945, by a group of plays collected in *Cantata dei giorni dispari* ("Cantata for Odd-Numbered Days"). (The two titles of collected works refer to the popular belief that even- and odd-numbered days are lucky and unlucky, respectively). These plays are concerned with the world of Naples during the crises of war, occupation, and the difficult return to normality. The following plays were written in this period: *Napoli milionaria!* ("Millionaire Naples!," 1945), *Questi fantasmi!* ("These Ghosts!," 1946), FILUMENA MARTURANO, *La Grande magia* ("Great Magic," 1948), and *Le Voci di dentro* ("Internal Voices," 1948). In these, which constitute the highest point of De Filippo's theatrical production, the focus is on the Neapolitan people, with their paradoxical humor, their dubious cunning nourished by centuries of hunger, their fantasies, and their love of life. Because De Filippo deals with the common folk, he remains an isolated man within Italy's refined theatrical world. He expresses poetic understanding and love for the people and a solid faith in man. His theatrical art has its roots in the popular Neapolitan tradition of the nineteenth century. It is descended, then, directly and clearly from the *commedia dell'arte.*—L. L.

Deirdre (1907). A tragedy by William Butler YEATS. An heroic tragedy in the Greek manner, Yeats's one-act verse play is about Deirdre, a figure in Celtic mythology parallel to Greece's Helen of Troy. The play takes place on the fated last day in the life of Deirdre and her lover, Naoise (pronounced Neesh-a). Two Musicians, serving as a wise and worried chorus, relate the background of the legend and the events that have brought the lovers to their final hour; their escape seven years ago from Conchubar, the aged High King of Ulster who had reared young Deirdre to be his Queen; their uneasy return at the invitation of the apparently forgiving Conchubar. When they realize that the King has betrayed them and will use any means to have Deirdre, the stoical lovers play a game of chess as they wait for him to strike. Fergus, the honest emissary of Conchubar, had assured them that the King would keep his word and forget the past; and when Conchubar breaks his oath Deirdre says, "We listened to the counsel of the wise, / And so turned fools." It is a recurring Yeatsian theme, the older voice of apparent wisdom and restraint that so often deceives and destroys the young and passionate. Naoise is caught in a net and slain, and the stricken yet fiercely proud Deirdre, pretending to be compliant to the jealous old King, carefully controlling the terms of her own fate, escapes by stabbing herself over the body of her dead lover. Meanwhile, outside the voices of the people cry out warnings of the imminent end of Conchubar and his kingdom. In contrast to John Millington Synge's peasant Deirdre, an impressionable child of nature who gradually takes on the dignity and strength of a romantic queen, Yeats's aristocratic Deirdre is always a noble and superior woman, an austere queen who dominates everyone and goes serenely to her death.—D. K.

Deirdre of the Sorrows (1910). A tragedy by John Millington SYNGE. Although Synge died in 1909 before he could complete the final revisions of this work, it is an outstanding three-act tragedy of love and betrayal, based upon one of the famous legends in the Red Branch or Ulster Cycle and written in the poetic idiom of the Irish peasants, a daring and successful experiment for a heroic play. The Helen of Troy of Celtic mythology, the beautiful young Deirdre is destined from birth to fall in love with the handsome Naisi (pronounced Neesh-a), but to be promised to the aged High King of Ulster, Conchubor, who by betraying her in order to win her provokes her death and the destruction of the kingdom. A wild and instinctive creature of nature, proud and passionate, Synge's Deirdre rejects Conchubor and elopes to Scotland with Naisi for seven idyllic years of love and joy. Only then, after realizing that such happiness cannot last forever, she decides they must go back to Ireland to face Conchubor, even though she suspects treachery in his invitation to return. In her intuitive wisdom she insists that since old age and death must inevitably come, she and Naisi are in a position to shape their own destiny at the peak of their love, a love so powerful that it alone can conquer death. When they return, Conchubor slays Naisi, and as he tries to take Deirdre, she calmly prepares for death on her own terms: "I have put away sorrow like an old shoe that is worn out and muddy, for it is I have had a life that will be envied by great companies." Then she stabs herself with Naisi's knife and leaves Conchubor spiritually destroyed; the flames of the kingdom have gone out.—D. K.

Dekker, Thomas (c. 1572–c. 1632). English playwright and pamphleteer. Dekker was a native Londoner of obscure and presumably humble origin. The earliest reference to Dekker, a note in producer Philip Henslowe's diary in 1598, mentions him as a playwright for the Lord Admiral's Men. Between 1598 and 1602 Dekker was among the busiest of the harried hacks employed by Henslowe, turning out —largely in collaboration with others—some forty-five plays. His prolificacy, however, could never keep pace with his profligacy. He was continually in debt throughout his career, at least six years (1613–1619) of which were spent in debtors' prison.

In addition to his dramatic activity Dekker was a busy and popular pamphleteer. Among his many pamphlets the best known are *The Wonderful Year* (1603), a description of the London plague, and *The Gull's Hornbook* (1609), a satirical picture of Jacobean London that is also a valuable source of information about prevailing theatrical conditions.

Dekker's earliest extant play is *Old Fortunatus* (1599), a condensation and revision of an older two-part play probably written by Robert Greene. His next and best-known drama is THE SHOEMAKER'S HOLIDAY, one of the most charming plays in all of English drama. In marked contrast to the tone of *The Shoemaker's Holiday* is Dekker's next play, *Satiromastix* (1601), probably written in collaboration with John Marston. It represents a belated attempt to engraft on a straightforward romantic comedy certain satirical material directed at Ben Jonson. The satire inaugurated the so-called *poetomachia* or WAR OF THE THEATERS, in which Dekker appears to have been a major participant. His next major dramatic achievement was the two-part play *The Honest Whore* (1604, 1605), written in collaboration with Thomas Middleton. Based upon the time-honored theme of the prostitute with a heart of gold, *The Honest Whore* contains an adroitly manipulated triple plot. The

denouement of Part I is set in Bedlam, Part II is resolved in a prison scene, two settings which give the play the macabre theatrical tone typical of Jacobean drama. Less typical is the warmth and sensitivity of Dekker's portrait of Bellafront, the prostitute who is converted into a virtuous wife.

Dekker collaborated with John Webster on two comedies, *Westward Ho!* (1604) and *Northward Ho!* (1605), both cynical farces of London life. He collaborated with Middleton on *The Roaring Girl* (1607/08) and with William Rowley and John Ford on *The Witch of Edmonton* (1621), a moving drama of an old woman driven to witchcraft by the ignorance and cruelty of her neighbors. Here, as in *The Honest Whore*, Dekker's intuitive sympathy for society's outcasts enables him to create a memorable character. In the last analysis it is this sympathy that distinguishes Dekker's work and gives it a compassionate quality notably absent in the work of many of his contemporaries.

The Dramatic Works of Thomas Dekker (1961), edited by Fredson Bowers in four volumes, provides an excellent old-spelling edition of the dramatist. Mary L. Hunt's *Thomas Dekker: A Study* (1911) provides a full-length critical treatment of Dekker's plays and prose.—E. Q.

dengaku. The Japanese word *dengaku* means "field music." The artform so named was developed with at least definite dramatic elements as early as the eleventh century. The investigation of it belongs, however, even more to students of folklore than of the theater. It carried the racy or earthy elements in Japanese poetic imagination into the period that witnessed the rise of the *noh* and *kyogen* forms and many of the strongest and most distinctly national aspects of Japanese arts in general. Hence its considerable importance in cultural history. —H. W. W.

Denison, Merrill (1893–   ). Canadian playwright and business historian. Denison, the first dramatist of note to appear in Canada, is the author of several plays written around 1920 and performed between 1919 and 1927: *Balm* (pub. 1926) in *Plays from Hart House Theatre*, Vol. I; *The Prizewinner* (pub. 1928), four pieces—*Brothers in Arms, From Their Own Place, The Weather Breeder*, and *Marsh Hay*—collected in a volume entitled *The Unheroic North* (pub. 1923).

In every respect the last four mentioned offer a contrast to the plays that preceded them, the unstageworthy closet dramas of the nineteenth century. They are short (most of them one act), are realistic in manner, display a nice command of dialogue, and are eminently suitable for performance. They were written to be performed separately, and except for *Marsh Hay*, which was never produced, these plays were performed between 1919 and 1923. Their content is in the main satirical, their mood in harmony with the critical temper of the period.

Denison's technique is to strike out in as many directions as possible, debunking whatever seems to him pretentious or absurd in Canadian attitudes of mind. The title, *The Unheroic North*, gives the clue to one such attitude, the notion that the northland is an environment conducive to moral uplift, inhabited by men of heroic virtue. Denison's backwoodsmen are distinguished only by their laziness and cunning.

But the playwright's satire has many dimensions, and in *Brothers in Arms,* for example, ideals of patriotism, social respectability, thrift, and industry—in effect, the shibboleths of the city—are also held up to derision.

There is evidence even in the farces that Denison is aware of the dark side of the society he depicts. This insight finds full expression in *Marsh Hay,* Denison's only three-act published drama. The theme of this play is the crippling effect intellectually and psychologically of the backwoods environment, particularly on those who must wring a living from the worthless land. Denison does not pass judgment, point to a moral, or offer any solution, yet in its intensity of mood, *Marsh Hay* is comparable to O'Neill's *Desire Under the Elms.*

Denison's characters and themes are neither subtle nor profound, and his dramatic techniques are unadventurous. He is the first Canadian playwright, however, to reflect the Canadian scene in a viable dramatic idiom.—M. T.

Denmark. With few exceptions, comedy has dominated the Danish stage from its earliest signs of life, through eighteenth-century rationalism and nineteenth-century skepticism, down to a variety of satiric practices in our time. Among the first surviving vernacular plays are such saints' legends as *Dorotheæ komedie* ("Comedy of Dorothea," 1531) and *Spillet om Hellig Knud Hertug* ("The Play of the Holy Knud," 1531), but they are not nearly so interesting as the sixteenth-century school farces *Paris' dom* ("The Judgment of Paris") and *Den utro hustru* ("The Unfaithful Wife"). These farces pave the way for more sophisticated plays of known authorship, such as the late sixteenth-century *Karrig Nidding* ("Stingy Miser"), based on Plautus' *Aulularia,* by Hieronymus Justesen Ranch (1539–1607), the Wittenberg-educated master of Viborg Cathedral School. Ranch also introduced the Fool into Danish literature in *Kong Salomons hylding* ("Allegiance to Solomon," 1584) and wrote Denmark's first musical play, *Samsons fængsel* ("Sampson's Prison," 1599). Though English companies are known to have visited Denmark at this time, indigenous drama did not take on the dimensions of Elizabethan or Jacobean drama in England, nor can there be said to be anything that approaches the best of French seventeenth-century drama, unless we assign the honor to a comedy of French classical stamp by the diplomat Mogens Skeel (1650–1694), namely *Grevens og friherrens komedie* ("The Comedy of the Count and the Baron," 1678), in which a sketchy intrigue provides the vehicle for astringent political satire.

Seldom have a man and a moment intersected so vigorously, almost explosively, as when the Norwegian-born scholar-writer Ludvig HOLBERG turned to writing plays for Denmark's first real playhouse, the Theater on Lille Grønnegade (Little Green Street). From the inception of the playhouse in 1722 to its closing in 1728, Holberg was stimulated to write twenty-eight comedies; and when a national stage was established in 1748, he wrote six more. With apparently inexhaustible fecundity Holberg summoned up practically every known comic character to his theater: the drunken peasant, the talkative barber, the pretentious scholar, the would-be politi-

cian, the braggart soldier, the wily servant, the termagant wife, the busy incompetent, and the fickle lady. Holberg borrowed with some abandon—from Plautus, Terence, Molière, and the *commedia dell'- arte*—but most such comic types had passed into the public domain and, in any case, Holberg made them his own. The result is the most impressive single body of drama in the history of the Danish stage and a concerted attack on pedantry and pretense wherever it is found. Even when the plays are little more than scenarios, as is sometimes the case, they bustle with improvisational excitement. Many of them continue to refresh the Scandinavian stage, chiefly *Den politiske kandestøber* (*The Political Tinker,* 1722), *Jeppe på bjerget* (*Jeppe of the Hill,* 1722), and *Erasmus Montanus* (written 1723; prod. 1742).

With the passing of Holberg's era and the founding of the Royal Theater in 1770, it is not surprising that tragedy displaced comedy and that the exploration of Scandinavian mythology began—first in the pre-Romanticism of Johannes EWALD and then in the high Romanticism of Adam OEHLENSCHLÄGER. The weight of Shakespeare, totally ignored by Holberg, came to be felt, largely through German intermediaries. But the tragic mode did not really thrive in Denmark, and by 1830 the lively polemic and talent for dramatic satire of Johan Ludvig HEIBERG had handed the stage back to comedy, chiefly in the French form of the vaudeville. It remained for the baroque humor of Gustav Wied (1858–1914), beginning at the end of the 1880's, to sustain a tradition that has come to dominate the modern Danish stage.

It is impossible to pass over the nineteenth century without mentioning three writers who were not—at least essentially—playwrights. Hans Christian Andersen (1805–1875) laid siege to the theater without success, but he entered by the back door. While his plays are history—and bad history—the humane humor of his fairy tales has impregnated the theater with unexpected frequency. Søren Kierkegaard (1813–1855), too, affected the course of drama, chiefly through his use of the *persona* (mask); his probing explorations of the comic, the ironic, and the nature of dramatic motivation; and the groundwork that he laid for an existential theater in the twentieth century. Georg Brandes (1842–1927), a literary historian remote from Kierkegaard in every aspect of philosophy and temperament, dramatized the shift from Romanticism to naturalism and in so doing exerted an influence on Ibsen and Strindberg that can scarcely be overestimated.

There is little comparable to Ibsenesque realism in Danish drama, except for the problem plays of Georg Brandes' brother Edvard (1847–1931), who was chiefly a drama critic and liberal journalist and the founder of the great Copenhagen daily *Politiken.* His plays are forgotten, but the time may come when the trenchant triangle drama *Et besøg* ("A Visit," 1882) is revived with appreciation. Together, the Brandes brothers created a momentum of social inquiry that prepared the way for modernism. They thought and worked in larger than Danish terms at a time when there were risks of provincialism. At the same time the theater never lost touch with a quality of wit that is essentially Danish. It found new force in expressionism, and gave to it an extrovertive quality in its use of cartoon backdrops, colorful design, revue continuity, and satiric vitality, as opposed to the introvertive expressionism of Sweden.

In 1919 Svend Borberg (1888–1947) called for a drama that was "great, symbolic, and Dionysian," and thereupon proceeded to a Freudian dissection of the identity of a post-World War I soldier in his play *Ingen* ("Nobody," 1923). With him, Bertel Budtz Müller (1890–1946), leader of the Worker's Theater from 1924 to 1928, was instrumental in introducing German expressionism to Denmark. But far more important to the 1920's was Sven Clausen (1893–1961), lawyer and language reformer, who wrote influential plays like *Nævningen* ("The Juryman," 1929), which presents three versions of a crime as they are seen in the mind of a member of the jury, and *I rosenlænker* ("Among Garlands of Roses," 1933), a playful marital comedy in which the commedia characters Pierrot, Columbine, and Harlequin are the vehicles.

The instantaneous and sustained success of Kjeld ABELL best typifies the drama of the 1930's and 1940's. It is elegant, urbane, and sophisticated, somewhat after the manner of Giraudoux. Abell's talent ranged from the witty, revue-like commentary on bourgeois smugness of *Melodien der blev væk* (*The Melody That Got Lost*, 1935) to the rather more mystical expressionism of *Den blå pekingeser* ("The Blue Pekinese," 1954). *Dage på en sky* (*Days on a Cloud*, 1947), which raises important questions about survival in an atomic age, is probably the best example of Abell's dialectic and total theater wit in action and interaction.

The playwright who goes simply by the name of SOYA has much in common with Abell, except that he takes a delight in sensation, shock, and the macabre —with about equal ease in the formats of either realism or expressionism. Soya has written a tetralogy of "problem plays" in which he explores many kinds of accident and chance convergence, as if he were asking "Is there really a law governing these things?" But he is at his best in the satiric extravaganza *Løve med korset* ("Corseting the Lion," 1950), which, without being derivative, looks like a fusion of expressionistic devices in Kaufman and Connelly's *Beggar on Horseback*, Elmer Rice's *The Subway*, and Thornton Wilder's *The Skin of Our Teeth*.

If the Soya-Abell school of playwriting lacked a soul, as Abell himself lamented, soul was present in abundance in the pastor-playwright Kaj MUNK. The fact that Munk died a martyr's death at the hands of the occupying Nazis did much to enhance his reputation as a writer, perhaps beyond just desert. But Munk called for a drama of will and passion, of high moment and great style shaped by God's flaming contradictions. He demonstrated it in *En idealist* (*An Idealist* or *Herod the King*, 1928), a study of Herod's wily maintenance of power and defiance of God, and in *Ordet* (*The Word*, 1932), in which, in the mode of rural realism, Munk explores contemporary religious belief and the power of "the Word" in an age of apathy and skepticism.

From 1936 to 1950 the communist writer Leck Fischer (1904–1956) wrote a quantity of plays of about uniform drabness; Knud Sønderby (1909–1966) enjoyed a single but impressive theater success

with his study of the oppressive mother in *En kvinde er overflødige* ("A Woman Is Superfluous," 1942); and H. C. Branner (1903–1966) accomplished interesting fusions of realism and symbolism, especially in *Søskende* (literal translation, "The Siblings"; *The Judge*, 1952), which examines the effect of the death of a stern, authoritarian father on his three children.

Among more recent playwrights, Preben Thomsen (1933–   ), a theologian, has tried to keep the biblical Munk tradition alive, and Finn Methling (1917–   ), an actor, has kept the theater from losing its sense of wonder. But the revue habit persists in *Teenagerlove* (1962) by Ernst Bruun Olsen (1923–   ), with sardonic music by Finn Savery. A good deal of promise is to be found in the jazz exercise *Udviklinger* ("Developments," 1965) by one of the most gifted of the moderns, Klaus Rifbjerg (1931–   ).

Scandinavian drama is intermittently but fairly extensively treated in the series of literary histories sponsored by the American-Scandinavian Foundation: *A History of Danish Literature* (1957), edited by P. M. Mitchell. Some of the more recent plays have appeared in the Foundation's *Scandinavian Plays of the 20th Century* series. Denmark is particularly well represented in *Contemporary Danish Plays* (1955), edited by Elias Bredsdorff.—R. B. V.

Desire Under the Elms (1924). A naturalistic drama by Eugene O'NEILL. A tragic story involving the inevitable passion between the third wife of a

SCENE FROM EUGENE O'NEILL'S *Desire Under the Elms* (ANTA COLLECTION, WALTER HAMPDEN MEMORIAL LIBRARY AT THE PLAYERS, NEW YORK)

New England farmer and his son by his deceased second wife, this work is altogether dynamic and grim. Over the developing destiny of the fateful lovers, Eben Cabot and his stepmother, Abbie Putnam, drawn irresistibly toward each other despite initial conflict of interests, brood the trees, symbolic of natural fertility and mystery, of a flourishing New England farm. O'Neill, who belonged to a generation severely critical of Victorian, especially puritan, morality, contrasted the passions of his youthful characters with the hardness and lovelessness of a Calvinist view of life. This is represented by the old farmer, Ephraim Cabot, who has nothing but contempt for sensitive individuals like his son Eben—whom he takes for one of the world's weaklings—and whose first and last truth is in the Old Testament God who tests men's strength with severe trials. Eben, who betrays his tyrannical father, is engaged in Oedipal conflict with him; and the young stepmother, who marries Ephraim because she sought security and coveted his farm, becomes tragically involved with her stepson when her suppressed hunger for love turns into reckless passion. She bears him a son, but, to cover their love, they allow the old man, in his blind vanity, to believe it is his.

Desire Under the Elms held in solution O'Neill's critical view of his milieu and his interest in Freudian psychology as well as his tragic sense of life; and in this intense play he strained the boundaries of naturalistic drama until the play verges on melodrama when Abbie strangles her baby in order to convince Eben that she gave herself to him out of love rather than out of a desire to deprive him of his heritage by producing a new heir to his father's farm. And in *Desire Under the Elms,* as in earlier naturalistic plays, O'Neill also strained toward the estate of poetry with his symbols of fertility and an enveloping atmosphere of longing, loneliness, and lust. *Desire Under the Elms* marks the peak of O'Neill's early, naturalistic period.—J. G.

Desmarets [Sieur] de Saint-Sorlin, Jean (1595–1676). French playwright, poet, and novelist. Born in Paris, Jean Desmarets de Saint-Sorlin became proficient in the arts of music, painting, and architecture. Highly appreciated by Richelieu—who enjoyed his conversation, made him a founding member of the French Academy in 1634, and entrusted him with high administrative posts—Desmarets went into theater at his request and continued in it until the cardinal's death in 1642. He was also the author of numerous poems and a historical novel. Desmarets was considered something of a mad genius. At first a libertine, he became extremely pious in 1645, devoted himself to religious works, including one Christian epic poem (*Clovis ou La France chrétienne,* 1657), and fanatically fought the Jansenists.

Of his seven plays, *Mirame* (1641), a tragedy, was written in collaboration with Richelieu for the opening of the new theater of the Palais Cardinal (later the Palais Royal). In addition to tragicomedies, Desmarets, at the request of Richelieu, wrote the comedy *Les Visionnaires* ("The Visionaries") in 1637. Although its plot is rather feeble, the play portrays a whole series of harmless lunatics typical of the period: an extravagant poet, a girl in love with Alexan-

der the Great, another girl with a wild passion for theater, a man who believes he is rich, and so forth. In five acts and in verse, this gallery of caricatures was hugely successful because of its high literary standards and originality, as well as its allusions to people living at the time. Molière not only revived the play but drew upon it when he wrote *Les Femmes savantes* (*The Learned Ladies*) in 1672.

For detailed information on Desmarets and his plays, see Henry C. Lancaster, *A History of French Dramatic Literature in the Seventeenth Century,* 9 vols. (1952).—Ja. G.

Destouches. Pen name of **Philippe Néricault** (1680–1754). French playwright. Philippe Néricault, later called Destouches, was born in Tours. As a very young man, he became an actor in a company of traveling players. He then was in the service of the French ambassador to Switzerland, who, in 1708, introduced him into Parisian society. Around 1715 he was given a post at the French embassy in London, where he married an Englishwoman. Destouches returned to France in 1723, became a member of the French Academy, and retired to a chateau near Melun, where he devoted himself to literature.

Extremely hostile to the skeptical ideas at the beginning of the Enlightenment, shocked by the "vulgar gaiety" of the writers of comedy at the time, and imbued with English sentimentality, Destouches wrote high-minded and very moralizing comedies. His best are *Le Philosophe marié* ("The Married Philosophe," 1727) and *Le Glorieux* (*The Conceited Count,* 1732).

Destouches's technique was a direct imitation of Molière's, but his conception of human nature and of the goal of comedy was quite different and pointed to the genre that was to become *drame bourgeois:* Tears alternate with laughter; a flawed protagonist is a continual object lesson; virtue is touching; and reason and the heart finally triumph.—Ja. G.

deus ex machina ("the god from the machine"). A theatrical device in Greek drama whereby a god is lowered in a crane in order to resolve the complications of the plot. It is a feature of many of the plays of Euripides, including *Hippolytus, Iphigenia among the Taurians,* and *Orestes.*

In modern times the phrase has been extended to refer to any arbitrary or externally imposed resolution of the conflict of a play. Examples of a deus ex machina in this sense are the arrival of the United States Cavalry, the reenactment in the psychoanalyst's office of the initial trauma, and the perception that any obstacle can be overcome as long as two people love each other.

Devil and the Good Lord, The. See LUCIFER AND THE LORD.

Devotion to the Cross (La devoción de la cruz, 1633). A miracle play by Pedro CALDERÓN DE LA BARCA. The main action of *Devotion to the Cross* opens with a duel in which Eusebio kills his friend Lisardo, who incited him to the duel for daring to court Julia, Lisardo's sister, without the permission of their father, Curcio, an impoverished nobleman. Eusebio presumably lacks the qualifications of nobility, though before killing Lisardo he relates at length the story of his miraculous existence. Essentially, it has been influenced by the holy cross, whose symbol appeared on his chest at birth. Before Lisardo dies, Eusebio complies with his friend's plea to be carried off and shriven. Then, before Lisardo's corpse is brought home, Eusebio appears there in order to persuade Julia to escape with him instead of complying with her father's wish that she enter a convent. When she learns of Lisardo's death, Julia cannot bring herself to hate Eusebio; but she sends him away and he goes unwillingly. She is forced by her father to enter a convent. Eusebio then becomes the leader of a brigand gang, marauding the mountains and villages, killing, and living off the spoils of his victims. One near victim, an elderly priest Alberto, is saved when a holy book he wears against his chest diverts the bullet. Eusebio lets him go free when the priest agrees to confess him before he dies one day.

Curcio, who has denounced Julia for being like her dead mother, now pursues Eusebio; these three are in the vicinity of the mountains where, in jealousy, Curcio once struck his wife Rosmira. Rosmira had given birth to twins at the foot of a cross, and one child (Julia) and the mother were then miraculously transported home, but the other child disappeared. Now Eusebio breaks into the convent and is about to rape Julia when he discovers that she too bears the cross in the flesh of her breast. He flees from her in dread; she follows, but he does not know this. Disguised as a man, Julia leads a life of crime and murder, ultimately confronting and threatening Eusebio, who disarms her. Curcio's men find Eusebio and stab him. He dies after he is acknowledged by Curcio as Julia's long-lost twin. Alberto the priest returns and Eusebio comes back to life long enough to be shriven. When Eusebio dies a second time, Julia reveals herself and publicly confesses her sins. She is about to be struck by her father when she rushes to embrace the cross at the foot of which Eusebio's corpse is lying, and both she and Eusebio are immediately borne upward to Heaven.

The tyranny of the honor code is mitigated and momentarily transcended in *Devotion to the Cross*. Upheld by a single individual's faith, the thaumaturgy of religious faith succeeds, because it is part of a mightier machine, in toppling the ratiocinative machinery of the insult-vengeance formula.

Devotion to the Cross, translated by Edwin Honig, appears in *Calderón: Four Plays* (1961).—E. H.

Diderot, Denis (1713–1784). French philosopher, essayist, playwright, and critic. Born in Langres in the province of Champagne, where his father was a well-to-do artisan, Diderot studied among Jesuits and was sent in 1728 to the Louis-le-Grand College in Paris. Rebelling against the conventionalism of his middle-class family, he became a bohemian in the Latin Quarter of Paris. There he read avidly, caroused, and wrote pamphlets. Although his unhappy marriage to a laundress was a gesture of defiance against his family's clannish conservatism, his love for his daughter, born in 1753, elicited his latent bourgeois impulses. His love of virtue and a sentimental nature had been evident since he translated the earl of Shaftesbury's *Essay on Merit and Virtue* in 1745, from which he had borrowed the motto "The good, the true, and the beautiful." He was engaged in the late 1740's and early 1750's in attacking Christianity, in defending deism (*Pensées philoso-*

DENIS DIDEROT (FRENCH CULTURAL SERVICES)

phiques, 1746) and other "progressive" ideas born of an age of rationalistic and mechanistic thought, and in editing his famous *Encyclopédie* (the completion of which was to take him twenty years).

Not until 1757 did Diderot establish any connection with the theater. When he did, he brought to that branch of the arts most of the established tendencies of the century: a rationalistic and philosophic outlook (not entirely anti-Christian in flavor) with a reformatory purpose, a point of view skeptical if not destructive of tradition, a sociological rather than a psychological approach, and a mildly artistic (but rather too subjective and sentimental) execution.

At this time three varieties of comedy had been or were still being written. Alain-René Lesage had continued the comedy of manners that Molière had brought to fruition in the mid-seventeenth century. Pierre de Marivaux had refined the sentiment and polished the dialogue into a delicate instrument of wit and sparkle. Another offshoot was the *comédie larmoyante* ("tearful comedy"), whose chief writer, Nivelle de La Chaussée, had attempted to forge a compromise between tragedy and comedy with a heavy emphasis on tears, pathos, and sentimentality. Diderot was to transform this last-mentioned form into the DRAME BOURGEOIS, which influenced Beaumarchais early in his career and, later, the German romantics Gotthold Lessing, Johann Wolfgang von Goethe, and Friedrich von Schiller.

Although *Le Fils naturel* ("The Illegitimate Son," written 1757) and *Le Père de famille* ("Father of a Family," written 1758) were written only a year apart, the former was performed but once, in 1771, while the latter, a somewhat better play, was acted with moderate success at the Comédie Française in 1761. Accompanying each published play was a long, original essay setting forth the theory of the new drame bourgeois, of which the plays themselves are the earliest models for the stage. Diderot was not a good playwright, and the plays are overly sentimental and contrived and have undoubtedly deserved their almost complete neglect. *Entretiens sur "Le Fils naturel"* (*Conversations on "The Natural Son,"* 1757) and *Discours sur la poésie dramatique* (*On Dramatic Poetry,* 1758), on the other hand, are provocative dramatic critiques and reveal that his ideas were always superior to his creative ability. In both essays Diderot views the theater as a means of social reform, and the dramatic theory he espouses is rooted in man's natural goodness and emotional response to human suffering. In these traits and in Diderot's belief in the unity and dignity of the middle-class family, he exerted a remarkable influence on such dramatists of social reform as Alexandre Dumas fils and Émile Augier.

A generous sampling of the critical essays is contained in L. G. Crocker, ed., *Diderot's Selected Writings* (1966), translated by Derek Coltman. The latest biography is L. G. Crocker's *The Embattled Philosopher* (1954). *Diderot's Writings on the Theatre* (1936), edited by F. C. Green, is in French with critical introduction and notes in English.—S. S. S.

Didone abbandonata (Dido Abandoned, 1724). A drama for music by Pietro METASTASIO. Dido does not yet know that Aeneas, whose sense of duty and mission has been reawakened, is on the point of leaving Carthage. Happy in her love for the hero, she indignantly refuses the offer—marriage or war—of Jarba, king of the Numidians, who comes to her court disguised as his own ambassador Arbace. The drama begins to unfold when Dido learns of Aeneas' decision. Her dignity and pride hurt, and menaced with war by Jarba, Dido fights desperately to prevent her lover's departure. She even persuades him—hoping thereby to arouse his jealousy—to listen in on her conversation with Jarba, in which she promises to marry him. At last Dido decides to seek her death on the pyre. Aeneas departs with his ships and Jarba assaults Carthage.

Didone abbandonata is characterized by musicality of verse, able dramatic structure, and a psychological presentation of its heroine that is summary but not ineffective. The play enjoyed a tremendous success throughout the eighteenth century and even later. Its first presentation took place in Naples with the music of Domenico Sarro (1678–1741); subsequently it was set to music by at least fifty-one composers.—L. L.

Dilmen, Güngör [Kalyoncu] (1930–   ). Turkish playwright. Dilmen was born in Tekirdağ, a small town in Turkey, and raised in Çanakkale, also a small town, by the Dardanelles. In 1950 Dilmen entered the classical philology department of the University of Istanbul, but his education was much interrupted because he had to work for a living in various parts of Anatolia. This gave him ample opportunity, however, to observe his country and his people. These were also the years of solitary apprenticeship in playwriting. Dilmen's first play, *Midasın Kulakları* (*The Ears of Midas*), was published and produced in 1959 and was widely acclaimed as a well-balanced work of art. The following year, Dilmen went to Israel and Greece to be better acquainted with the theaters of those countries, and in the same year he went to the Yale Drama School. There Dilmen wrote his satire *Canlı Maymun Lokantası,* which he translated into English as *Live Monkey Restaurant.* On his return to Turkey from the United States in 1964 Dilmen joined the Municipal Theater of Istanbul in the capacity of dramatist and play director. Two years later he accepted a position with the theater section of the Istanbul radio station but resigned in 1968 to devote his time to playwriting.

Dilmen has been an eloquent champion of poetical drama. He has captured the speech rhythms of his people and has used them in plays that are wholly or in part in verse. Dilmen stresses the visual as much as the verbal aspects of the theater. The themes and plots of his plays determine the forms of his plays. He has written dramas inspired by mythology and history. These works have been realistic, symbolical, or surrealistic. Dilmen has used a chorus and dance effectively but has stayed away from the epic theater on one end and naturalism on the other. He strives toward a dramatic theater.

Meticulously wrought as well as artistic, Dilmen's plays have been recognized as fine examples of poetical drama.—N. O.

dithyramb (Gr., *dithyrambos,* a choric hymn). Originally, the dithyramb was a passionate, impetuous Doric lyric in honor of the god Dionysus. Later, the odes were chanted in honor of other deities and also of mortal heroes.

At first, the ode was sung by a chorus. The Greek historian Herodotus says that Arion of Lesbos (c. 620 B.C.) gave dramatic structure to the dithyramb by inserting spoken lines among the lyrical songs. The leader of the chorus thus became a kind of soloist, initiating a question-and-answer sequence between himself and the chorus. This pattern is thought by many, including Aristotle, to be one of the origins of drama, with the secular dithyrambs evolving into tragedy and the Dionysiac dithyrambs into comedy, that is, dramas about gods, half-gods, and satyrs.

diverbium. A scene in Roman comedy, monologue or dialogue, written in six-foot iambic lines, called senarius rather than trimeter because of the freedom of substitutions in the second and fourth feet. The diverbium was spoken, but all other scenes were recited or sung to a musical accompaniment. (See CANTICUM.) The spoken iambic senarius is by far the most frequent meter in Terence, but Plautus favors the trochaic septenarius, used in scenes of recitative.—G. E. D.

Doll's House, A (Et dukkehjem, 1879). A play by Henrik IBSEN. The world première of *A Doll's House* took place in Copenhagen and was first performed in English (as *The Child Wife*) in Milwaukee in 1882.

Torvald Helmer, successful lawyer and bank manager, has kept his pampered wife, Nora, in a cage-like home sequestered from life. But she, the little squirrel, has her secret: Whether out of childlike daring or pure folly, she once committed a forgery to get quick funds to provide a life-saving holiday for her overworked husband. Nora is threatened with blackmail by Krogstad, the moneylender, and subsequently the threat is withdrawn, but not before the whole story is bared to Torvald. His righteous indignation, untainted by awareness of the essential magnanimity of Nora's deed, convinces Nora that the marriage has been built on false premises, and she

A SCENE FROM HENRIK IBSEN'S *A Doll's House* (NORWEGIAN INFORMATION SERVICE)

departs to find her real identity in the world outside.

From the time it was first performed, *A Doll's House* has raised controversy over whether Nora did the right thing. The protests of a German actress persuaded Ibsen to write an ending in which Nora returns, at least to her children. While Ibsen seems to have regretted that the play was, in some quarters, greeted as a militant suffragist document, he also admitted that the "happy ending" was, in his words, a "barbaric outrage" because it violated the whole drift of the play, and today that ending is rarely used. *A Doll's House*, whatever its period character, remains one of Ibsen's best realistic plays.

The text may be found in *Ibsen*, Vol. V (1961), edited by J. W. McFarlane. See also Hermann J. Weigand, *The Modern Ibsen* (1960), pp. 26–75. —R. B. V.

doll theater. See BUNRAKU.

Dom Juan ou Le Festin de Pierre (Don Juan or the Stone Guest, 1665). A comedy in prose by MOLIÈRE. Dom Juan has left his wife, Elvire, immediately after their marriage. During his subsequent adventures, and while being pursued by Elvire and her brothers, he tries to seduce two peasant girls at the same time, humiliates a beggar, and invites to dinner the statue of the commander whom he has killed. Once in his own house, his father and then Elvire try vainly to remind him of his duty. Suddenly the statue appears and, in turn, invites Dom Juan to dinner. Finally, Dom Juan commits the supreme crime—that of hypocrisy: He chooses to pass himself off as a pious man. But when the statue reappears, he does not hesitate to follow it into the flames of hell.

The interest of this "machine" comedy, of very free form, lies in the profound ambiguity of the na-

ture of Dom Juan, who is both odious and attractive. He is indifferent to divine and human values, with the exception of courage, and is in constant conflict with his valet Sganarelle, who both hates and admires his master.

This play has been translated by Donald M. Frame in *Tartuffe and Other Plays* (1967).—Ja. G.

Don Carlos, Infante of Spain (Don Carlos, Infant von Spanien, 1787). A tragic history play by Friedrich von SCHILLER, based on the life of Don Carlos, son of Philip II of Spain. The play was rewritten in Shakespearean blank verse from an earlier prose version and marks Schiller's movement toward classicism.

The play concerns the relationship of Philip and his son Don Carlos: The king, evidently fearing that he might be overthrown by his son—just as he himself had forced his own father from the throne—refuses to trust Don Carlos with any of the crown's affairs. Further, Philip marries Elizabeth de Valois, whom Don Carlos loves and was courting. The substance of the play, however, resides in the figure of Marquis Posa (a nonhistorical character invented by Schiller), whose bid for freedom of thought overrides both the political and domestic elements of the play. Marquis Posa, concerned not only over Philip's domestic tyranny with regard to his son but also his political tyranny over the Netherlands, promises to help Don Carlos and asks Don Carlos' help in trying to free the Netherlands. Marquis Posa gains the king's confidence and works in secret to save Don Carlos from his father's growing suspicion that his son and his queen are plotting against the crown through the Netherlands. The Marquis's attempts prove ultimately vain, however, and he finally draws all suspicion upon himself and sacrifices his life—he is assassinated by Philip—for Don Carlos. Don Carlos resolves to flee to the Netherlands and undermine his father's tyranny from there but is caught by Philip and handed over to the Inquisition as a heretic.

Don Juan. A legendary profligate. The dramatic and poetic legend of Don Juan has produced that rare phenomenon, a modern myth. In most respects it is the successor to the ancient myth of Venus. While the interpretations of his character and his significance are many and varied, Don Juan is usually taken to be a type of libertine, playboy, seducer, driven by an irresistible urge to destroy the female sex. The explanations for his driving force, made by both creative writers and speculative psychologists, range from onanism and sexual impotence through social rebelliousness to atheism.

It is generally held that Don Juan first appeared in literature in the play *El burlador de Sevilla y convidado de piedra* ("The Deceiver of Seville and the Stone Guest," pub. 1630, evidently several years after its composition) by Friar Gabriel Téllez (1584?–1648), known by the pseudonym Tirso de Molina. However, an undated work (wrongly attributed to Calderón and perhaps by Tirso) called *Tan largo me lo fiáis* ("You Give Me Such Long-Term Credit") is probably an earlier version of Tirso's play. Two sets of folk legends combined to produce the resolution of both plots: the tale of the living statue and ballads about inviting a dead man to supper as a jest.

At various moments in Tirso's play Don Juan attempts to seduce four women. By impersonating their lovers, he worms his way into the rooms of two ladies of the court. Dazzling them with his high rank, he also makes love to two country girls, one on the eve of her wedding. The girls yield to his advances because he is prepared to swear to each that he will marry her. On the occasion of his one failure, his attempted seduction of Doña Ana is forestalled by the arrival of her father, the venerable old Don Gonzalo, who, after accusing Don Juan of cowardice, is killed by him in a duel. In all these escapades Don Juan is abetted by the amused tolerance of his uncle and his father, both of whom are responsible for the enforcement of the law. One day, on seeing Don Gonzalo's statue on his tomb in a church, Don Juan jestingly invites the dead man to supper. To his consternation the stone statue arrives at the appointed hour and returns the invitation. Afraid to show fear, Don Juan accepts. In the church the statue seizes his hand and drags him through flames down to hell. Don Juan's victims, who have all come to court to seek redress for their grievances, are appropriately married off to one another by a somewhat rueful king.

This play, which is loosely constructed in the light of classical dramatic canons, is given unity and meaning by Tirso's dense interweaving of poetic themes. An image from banking runs through the work: the Great Banker has made man a loan of life that may be recalled at any moment; Don Juan, always counting on having more time, is surprised— when death overtakes him in his youth—to discover that it is too late for him to be shriven of his mortal sins and receive God's mercy. Another theme is basically satiric: since human justice refuses to punish the

miscreant, divine justice must intervene unnecessarily, prematurely, and awesomely. Yet another theme is that of burning Troy: a long, so-called episodic description of Lisbon (the city of Ulysses, according to a false but accepted etymology) binds together the various strands of the idea that Don Juan, having lived by fire (of passion), must in poetic justice die by fire (of hell). The fusion of many such themes gives the play its complex poetic significance. Don Juan is not thrust into hell by God's agent, the statue, because of his dissolute life, but rather because he has taken the name of God in vain. In seducing one of his rustic victims he is obliged by her to swear marriage, not (as his custom is) on her beautiful eyes or hands, but on the name of God. He makes a mental reservation in the hope of avoiding perjury: if he does not keep his sworn word he prays that he may be killed, but (as he says to himself) by a dead man. God grants this blasphemous prayer by working a miracle, causing him indeed to die at the hands of a dead man. In short, the first Don Juan play—one of Spain's great legacies to the modern world—is concerned with the punishment, not the aggrandizement, of a great sinner.

The moral and theological implications of Tirso's drama were overshadowed in later developments of the myth by what increasingly less devout playwrights regarded as the inspiring grandeur of the character of Don Juan. From the villain who gets his just deserts, he becomes the hero whose misdeeds make him superior to the pettily conventional society in which he lives.

It is possible to mention here only the most important dramatic recreations of the Don Juan legend. One of the earliest adaptations was the scenario of the *commedia dell'arte* called *Il Convitato di pietra* ("The Stone Guest," date unknown), adapted from Tirso's play. By this means the story passed to Italy and France. In France, following some earlier adaptations, Molière wrote his *Le Festin de pierre* (*The Stone Guest*, 1665), in which he presented his hero as a cynical and hypocritical freethinker. Mozart's seriocomic opera *Don Giovanni* (1787), with libretto by Lorenzo da Ponte, was inspired by another *Il Convitato di pietra* (1786), an *opera buffa* by Giuseppe Gazzaniga (librettist, Giovanni Bertati).

The Romantic movement, exalting the outcast and the social rebel, found in Don Juan the prototype of its dramatic heroes. (Byron's Don Juan, although he does not appear in a drama, is surely the best known.) Alexandre Dumas's *Don Juan de Mañara,* translated into Spanish by Antonio García Gutiérrez in 1839, inspired José Zorrilla to write the most famous Spanish version of the legend, *Don Juan Tenorio* (1844). In this Romantic drama Don Juan's catalogue of seductions and murders is immensely expanded, but he is saved from damnation by the love of one of his victims. Performances of this play, with its supernatural manifestations, celebrate All Souls' Day in cities and towns all over Spain and Spanish America. The best-known twentieth-century interpretation of the myth is George Bernard Shaw's *Man and Superman* (1905).

The ramifications of the Don Juan myth may be studied in the exhaustive list of works given by Armand E. Singer in *A Bibliography of the Don Juan Theme: Versions and Criticism* (1956). The changes it underwent across the centuries are well analyzed by John Austen in *The Story of Don Juan: A Study of the Legend and the Hero* (1939) and by Leo Weinstein in *The Metamorphoses of Don Juan* (1959). A perceptive account of Don Juan's fate at the hands of playwrights is Oscar Mandel's *The Theater of Don Juan* (1963).—B. W.

Don Juan or The Love of Geometry (Don Juan oder Die Liebe zur Geometrie, 1953). A comedy by Max FRISCH. Frisch's Don Juan is by no means the one history has come to know, the infamous seducer, the archetypal amorous adventurer. The Don Juan of Frisch's play seeks not women but solitude, not amorous indulgence but immersion in the pure knowledge of mathematics. His reputation is the result of unpremeditated action in the course of flight. At his marriage he says no instead of yes, and promptly flees the scene. In flight he seduces the fiancée of his best friend and his supposed mother-in-law-to-be; he kills his fiancée's father and is the cause of his own father's fatal heart attack. His fiancée then drowns herself, for he had seduced her on the night before the wedding.

These are the stations in his flight away from sex and toward the solitude and the freedom to indulge in pure reason. His reputation becomes such that for a woman to fail to bed down with him for a night is a sin of sexual omission. Yet the real Don Juan plays chess at a house of prostitution, to which he has been dragged.

The traditional story of the stone statue (his fiancée's father, slain by Don Juan) is treated lightly by Frisch. One thousand and three women later, Don Juan invites the bishop of Cordoba and various women to a final supper at his home. He has arranged with the bishop that in return for giving the Church a legend he be allowed to live out the remainder of his earthly days in a monastery studying geometry. Don Juan has planned a ruse, involving the statue, to put the pact into effect. The statue is impersonated by a local madame, at the sight of whom Don Juan leaps through a trap door into "hell." The women are taken in by the hell-fire performance, and the life of Don Juan is officially over. However, it is Don Juan who is actually the victim of the ruse. For the bishop is no bishop (he is a husband once cuckolded by the Don himself), and there is no monastery. But how does a man who has no official existence come by money with which to live? In the end Don Juan must marry, to a nobleman's widow who was once a prostitute. The final coup comes at the conclusion of the play: Don Juan learns that he and his wife are to have a child.

Don Juan or The Love of Geometry is an engaging and significant theatrical statement. It gains much of its originality and delightfulness from the reversal that Frisch has imposed upon the traditional legend of the great lover. It is also Frisch's committed statement that no man may exist alone. A man who believes he can suffers from *hybris* and will be punished.

Don Juan or The Love of Geometry is in *Three Plays* (1967), translated by James L. Rosenberg. The play is discussed critically in a volume by George Wellwarth, *The Theater of Protest and Paradox* (1964).—C. R. M.

dramatic theory. The whole early history (as well as much of the later history) of dramatic theory is overshadowed by Aristotle's *Poetics*. In the centuries following the *Poetics*, efforts were made to amplify and to interpret Aristotle's account of TRAGEDY, to construct a comparable theory of COMEDY, and even to transform Aristotle's treatise from an impersonal description of a genre into a stiff code of legislation binding upon all dramatists. Mighty battles have been fought over the precise meaning of such key Aristotelian terms as imitation, catharsis, and *hamartia*. (See ARISTOTLE.) In comparison with the *Poetics*, any other contributions to dramatic theory in classical times were infinitely less meritorious, less influential, and less controversial. Plato in his *Republic* condemned violent poetry as an encouragement to violence (and thereby apparently inspired Aristotle's doctrine of catharsis, purgation through pity and fear), and Aristophanes in *The Clouds* extolled the dignity of Aeschylus and deplored the debased qualities of Euripides, but the only classical author other than Aristotle who demands attention as a dramatic theorist is the Roman poet Horace (65 B.C.–8 B.C.) in the *Epistola ad Pisones* (written c. 20 B.C.), better known as the *Ars Poetica*. Horace recommended decorum, urging certain decorous principles for dramatists: Tragedy and comedy must be kept separate; words must suit the emotions being expressed; characters must be consistent (with themselves, but also with the general conceptions of stock character-types); violence must be kept off the stage; plays must have five acts; the chorus must be a relevant character; and, above all, the example of the Greeks must be studied and imitated. In particular, literature should both profit and delight, and to profit is to teach sound principles. It should be noted that Horace, in instructing dramatists by giving them rules, was doing precisely what Aristotle did not do. Horace set a precedent for rule giving, for dictatorial dramatic theorists in centuries to come, and incidentally encouraged those critics who chose to believe that Aristotle, too, was giving rules to dramatists. Also influential was the grammarian Aelius Donatus (fourth century A.D.), who drew heavily upon Horace for his highly regarded summary of the elements of comedy and quoted Cicero's definition of this genre: "a copy of life, a mirror of custom, a reflection of truth."

The ascendancy of Christianity put an end to the pagan theaters, and, in the middle ages, even the idea of drama seemed lost. Writers continued to employ the traditional dramatic terms but without any reference to the theater. Accordingly, Dante, in the fourteenth century, spoke of tragedy and comedy as different kinds of narratives and gave the title *The Divine Comedy* to his long narrative poem, which is comic by virtue of its having a happy ending in paradise. Later in the same century, the monk in Geoffrey Chaucer's *Canterbury Tales* calls tragedy the story of a man who falls from high estate, and he then proceeds to entertain the Canterbury pilgrims by reciting several narrative tragedies. At the same time that Dante and Chaucer wrote, in medieval England and elsewhere in Europe the drama was being reborn out of church ritual, but without benefit of dramatic criticism or theory. When dramatic theory was itself at last reborn in the Renaissance, it drew its primary inspiration from Aristotle and Horace, not from the example of the popular drama.

Several Italian critics of the sixteenth century

framed in their individual treatises the standard Renaissance concepts of dramatic theory. Five were especially important: Bernardino Daniello, Geraldo Cinthio, Minturno (whose real name was Antonio Sebastiano), Julius Caesar Scaliger, and Lodovico Castelvetro. They made abundant use of Aristotle and Horace, and they generally agreed on the sharp distinction between tragedy and comedy (a distinction based in part on the higher social rank of tragic characters), the didactic function of the drama (with some occasional murmurings in behalf of "delight"), and the necessity of unity. Aristotle had endorsed unity of action in tragedy and noted the common Greek practice of observing unity of time by confining action to a single day. Cinthio made unity of time a strict rule, and Castelvetro, who was obsessively concerned about a play's effect upon an audience of extremely limited credulity, formulated the new principle of unity of place, thus completing the roster of the three unities that were to haunt dramatic theory for centuries. Scaliger, who was one of the most dogmatic of this group, spent the last years of his life in France, where he won an audience for his codification of dramatic theory. French dramatic theory of the Renaissance conformed to the Italian pattern.

Unlike France and Italy, England and Spain enjoyed, in the Renaissance, a popular drama of great merit that flouted the neo-Aristotelian rules, mingled the tragic and comic genres, served a didactic end only in the most indirect way, and ignored the three canonized unities. Observing the English popular drama just before its first flowering with the work of Marlowe and Shakespeare, Sir Philip Sidney (1554–1586) assailed it for its violation of the rules in his *Defence of Poesie,* written shortly before his death. But the popular drama of Elizabethan England was under attack mainly on moral grounds, and the attacks came from those Puritans who finally succeeded in closing the theaters in 1642. Attacked on moral grounds, the theater, naturally enough, defended itself on moral grounds in such treatises as Thomas Heywood's *An Apology for Actors* (1612), which insisted upon the irresistible and even automatic didactic effect of the drama. The Elizabethan dramatist who had the most to say about dramatic theory was Ben Jonson, who was also the most "classical" of the popular writers, and so; in his *Discoveries* (1641) and in some of his prologues and inductions, he restated conventional doctrine, especially on the satirical-didactic function of comedy. Still, the popular dramatists had formulated a theory that supported their practice, and they occasionally reflected it in their prologues, epilogues, inductions, plays-within-plays, and incidental conversations on theatrical matters. For example, the chorus of Shakespeare's *Henry V* discourses at length upon the qualities of the imagination that Elizabethan playgoers were required to employ and, by means of a play-within-a-play, Philip Massinger's *The Roman Actor* (c. 1627) critically examines the opinion that comedies teach virtue.

The first formal statement of the theories governing the popular drama appeared a few years after the theaters had reopened—in John Dryden's *An Essay of Dramatic Poesy* (published in 1668 but evidently written in 1665); Neander, who obviously speaks for Dryden in this dialogue, defends the liberty of the English stage, decrying the crippling effect of the unities and praising the pleasurable contrast obtained by mixing the comic and tragic genres. (See TRAGICOMEDY.) Spain's popular drama did not have to wait so long to be defended on aesthetic grounds. One of its principal practitioners, Lope de Vega, justified it in *The New Art of Writing Plays in This Age* (1609), first exhibiting his knowledge of the neo-Aristotelian rules and his respect for them and then explaining that he combined the dramatic types and violated the unity of time to please his unlettered audience. Only a few years before, an attack upon just such violations of the rules, obviously directed against Lope himself, had been made by a less successful dramatist, Miguel de Cervantes Saavedra, in his novel *Don Quixote* (1605). France at this time contributed one notably heterodox document, a Preface (1628) by François Ogier defending the mixture of types and attacking the unity of time and, indeed, the very idea that any rules inherited from the ancients were in any way binding upon modern dramatists.

Nevertheless, neoclassicism won the day. Following the Restoration in 1660, the English drama became more decorous. Significantly, among the four participants in Dryden's dialogue *An Essay of Dramatic Poesy,* one speaks for classical practice and another for the strict French neoclassical code. English neoclassicism found its most extreme embodiment in Thomas Rymer, who, in *A Short View of Tragedy* (1693), attacked Shakespeare's *Othello* for its many absurdities, particularly its violation of the decorum of character in representing a soldier, Iago, as treacherous. Across the channel, French critics and dramatists vied to express their loyalty to neoclassical principle. A controversy erupted over *Le Cid* (1637) by Pierre Corneille, which seemed to be a tragedy of unimpeachably classical qualities. *Le Cid* was attacked for its lack of verisimilitude, since Corneille, piously observing the unities, had compressed a rather improbable amount of action into twenty-four hours. On the defensive, the dramatist represented himself as an exponent of the strictest orthodoxy, but, at the same time, he revealed the tensions created by his fidelity to the rules.

Dramatic theory of the Renaissance and the later seventeenth century had less to say about comedy. Formal criticism overlooked a distinctively English genre that Shakespeare had pioneered—the sort of play that C. L. Barber called "festive comedy" (in *Shakespeare's Festive Comedy,* 1959), a play reflecting the freedom of holidays and festivals. More formal attention was given to the comedy of humours, a genre both essayed and interpreted by Ben Jonson in *Every Man In his Humour* (1598) and *Every Man Out of his Humour* (1599). These comedies mocked eccentrics, "humour" characters whose one-sidedness provided extreme examples of ridiculous human failings. Where Jonson liked to create a symphony of idiosyncratic humours, in France, on the other hand, Molière preferred to expose a single oddity in each play and, utilizing the didactic defense that comic authors preferred, urged that ridicule was the best method of teaching virtue, asserting that people were more afraid of being ridiculous than of being considered wicked. Even the English comic dramatists of the Restoration period professed to be teaching virtue, but, like the Elizabethans, they were replying to attacks that had been made specifically on moral grounds; defending himself along these lines, George Farquhar defined comedy as "a well-framed tale handsomely told as an agreeable vehicle for counsel or reproof." William Congreve noted that he and his contemporaries had substituted a more subtle and decorous characterization for the Jonsonian humours, but a more adequate interpretation of Restoration comedy came only later, when Oliver Goldsmith, in *Essay on the Theatre* (1772), contrasted the "laughing comedy" of the past with the deplorably sentimental "weeping comedy" of his own day. Further theoretical interpretation of Restoration comedy of manners came from Charles Lamb in *On the Artificial Comedy of the Last Century* (1823), representing this genre as unrelated to morality and set in "the Utopia of gallantry, where pleasure is duty, and the manners perfect freedom." Later in the nineteenth century, George Meredith, in *An Essay on Comedy* (1877), celebrated the comic spirit, embodied in Congreve and Molière, as an element both civilized and civilizing, tolerant, sophisticated, and reflective of the new equality of women.

The weeping comedy of which Goldsmith complained was a symptom of a general reaction against neoclassical drama, both in comedy and tragedy. If, as usual, practice preceded theory, it must be added that the statement of theory, by Denis Diderot, Jean Jacques Rousseau, and, in some respects, Samuel Johnson, was more interesting and significant than most of the examples of the new drama, with the honorable exception of the plays by G. E. Lessing and Beaumarchais. While Voltaire was the dedicated foe of orthodoxy in most public matters, he was relentlessly conservative in the drama, insisting upon the three unities and exalted subjects for tragedy and excoriating Shakespeare for his gross errors of taste, notably in *Hamlet*. On the other hand, Dr. Johnson, notably conservative in most of his opinions and prejudices, defended Shakespeare against Voltaire's objections, and, in the Preface to his collected edition of Shakespeare (1765), expressed doubt that the author of *Hamlet* would have profited from a knowledge of the unities. Conceding that Shakespeare had violated the rules (as later formulated) by combining the tragic and comic genres, Johnson maintained, "there is always an appeal open from criticism to nature." Johnson was appealing to human nature, that is to say, the experience of life itself, and so he was invoking a broadly human principle more consistently applied to both art and life by Diderot, Rousseau, and Beaumarchais. Diderot objected, in his early writings, to the artificiality of the French drama and advocated a new kind of drama, the "serious drama" or DRAME BOURGEOIS, a mirror of bourgeois life inspired by the fiction of Samuel Richardson and the plays of George Lillo that would make a profoundly realistic and emotional impression upon its audience. Later Diderot apparently came to see the uses of artificiality, for, in *Le Paradoxe sur le comédien* (completed in 1778 and published posthumously), he found the good actor to be more dependent on art than on nature. The approach of the young Diderot to solve the problems of the theater had been sentimental, but Jean Jacques Rousseau employed a sentimental, emotional approach to attack the drama, arguing in his *Letter to M.*

d'Alembert on the Theatre (1758) against the founding of a theater in Geneva and demonstrating that the drama cannot teach virtue. He found comedy reprehensible for ridiculing virtuous men and chose to regard the hero of Molière's *Le Misanthrope* as a tragic hero, cruelly misrepresented by his creator. Although Rousseau's hostility to the theater is puritanical and practically categorical, his sentimentalizing of Molière's Alceste implies that he was in harmony with the states of mind that produced Lillo's sentimentalized characters and Diderot's advocacy of a sentimental drama. Beaumarchais, in his beginnings as a dramatist and in his principal critical document *Essay on the Serious Drama* (1767), followed Diderot in advocating a sentimental type of play that combined tragic and comic elements and that, he speculated, might be called "*bourgeois* tragedy" or "tearful comedy." Fortunately, he amended his principles to write *The Barber of Seville* and *The Marriage of Figaro,* genuine comedies, although they are touched by a new and more humane spirit. Lessing undertook a similar cause in Germany, reinterpreting Aristotle and the Greeks, criticizing the French worship of the rules, and leading a rebellion against the domination of the German stage by J. C. Gottsched's neoclassical principles. Johann Wolfgang von Goethe and Friedrich von Schiller continued the task of rejuvenating the German stage. Goethe extravagantly praised Shakespeare and provided in his novel *Wilhelm Meister* (published 1795 but substantially written much earlier) an interpretation of *Hamlet* that made Shakespeare's Dane seem melancholy indeed. His growing conservatism led him to conclude eventually that Shakespeare's genius was more psychological than theatrical. He became a classicist, writing tragedies on Greek models and adapting *Romeo and Juliet* to fit his new view of dramatic propriety. Schiller interpreted tragedy by reference to its moral and psychological patterns, showing little concern for those rules that had meant so much in the eighteenth century, but, like Goethe, he increasingly came to appreciate the purity of the classics.

Romantic theory and practice carried on the rebellion Goethe and Schiller had led and then partially abandoned. The Romantic attitude found its most typical embodiment in Victor Hugo, who challenged neoclassical domination in his practice (notably with his romantic tragedy *Hernani,* a *cause célèbre* of 1830) and with his theory, which is best stated in his Preface to an unproduced play, *Cromwell* (pub. 1827). Combatting the artificial simplicity and unity of classical example and neoclassical imitation, Hugo recommended a diversity derived from the truth of nature and containing "the fruitful union of the grotesque and sublime types." The novelist Stendhal joined Hugo in urging Shakespeare rather than Racine as a model for dramatists, and such English critics of this period as Charles Lamb and William Hazlitt confirmed this tendency by paying close attention to Shakespeare and his long-neglected contemporaries. It can be argued that the fullest expression of Romantic diversity occurs in the operas of the German composer-librettist Richard Wagner, who aimed at combining words, music, and spectacle for the most elaborate theatrical effect. What he achieved was the widest extension of that diversity that the English critics found in Shakespeare and his contemporaries. The dramatic contrast described in Thomas De Quincey's "Note on the Knocking at the Gate in *Macbeth*" may seem small beside the epic sweep of a Wagnerian opera, but the same Romantic diversity is reflected in both. Wagner was equally Romantic in advocating, like Hugo and Stendhal, the use of native rather than classical subjects. The German philosopher Friedrich Nietzsche set out, in his first book, *The Birth of Tragedy from the Spirit of Music* (1872), to interpret and to justify Wagner, but, in fact, he developed an independent theory of the drama, finding in Greek tragedy a combination of opposite elements—Apollonian form and Dionysian rapture. Again, diversity is the keynote, and the neglected element of Dionysian rapture is not totally divorced from the despised grotesque that Hugo celebrated.

Romantic aspiration did not transform the theater; it became a place of entertainment, dominated by the journeymen dramatists Eugène Scribe and Victorien Sardou. The alternative to their theater of agreeable suspense and happy endings was naturalism, most authoritatively expounded by the French novelist-dramatist Émile Zola, especially in *Naturalism in the Theater* (1881) and in his Preface to his play *Thérèse Raquin* (1873), based on his novel of the same name. Taking a determinist view of society, Zola traced all social phenomena to the influence of heredity and environment. On the stage he wanted to see nothing that looked like mere acting but instead the unadulterated image of human behavior. The Swedish dramatist August Strindberg wrote a Foreword to his own *Miss Julie* (1888) that made that tragic play virtually a demonstration of Zola's naturalistic principles; everything in *Miss Julie* seems traceable to entirely intelligible causes. Strindberg, however, was a versatile dramatist who, late in life, became converted to a more stylized drama, performed by the Intimate Theater that he founded in Stockholm in 1907. But the main path of the drama since Zola and Strindberg is surely that of realism, a term not always clearly distinguished from naturalism but usually taken to mean adherence to probability and the surfaces of experience, without the necessary accompaniment of the naturalistic view of society and the naturalistic reduction of human behavior to intelligible causes. The advent of realism in the theater is associated with the practice of the Norwegian dramatist Henrik Ibsen and with both the dramatic practice and the polemical criticism of the Anglo-Irish dramatist Bernard Shaw. Shaw was an advocate of the theater of ideas, and in *The Quintessence of Ibsenism* (first published 1891 but later expanded) he reduces Ibsen's plays to systematic dramatic essays on social problems (generally the question of women's rights), seldom misrepresenting Ibsen's interpretation of ideas but also seldom doing full justice to the full complexity of Ibsen's dramas. Elsewhere in his abundant writing about the drama, Shaw proclaimed the dramatist's need to attend to the life of his times and to represent recognizable human behavior on the stage. (See REALISM AND NATURALISM.)

The German playwright Bertolt Brecht was equally a realist, but of a different sort. A convinced Marxist throughout most of his adult life, he was wedded to a freer and more flexible sort of play than the conventional realistic drama of modern life. His EPIC THEATER was objective by design; it put the audience at a distance by turning Hitler into a Chicago gangster or setting an archetypal parable of modern capitalism in a primitive Chinese city. The nominal purpose of this estrangement (*Verfremdung,* usually translated "alienation" and applied to the objective style of acting that Brecht encouraged) is to keep the audience from identifying with the action and becoming emotionally involved with it; also, estrangement provided a new perspective for viewing Hitler or modern capitalism or whatever other subject the dramatist undertook. To make his drama more flexible and, when necessary, to implement his didacticism, Brecht employed some of the dramatic conventions of the Chinese and Elizabethan theaters.

Numerous dramatists and dramatic theorists have, in modern times, departed from realism. In the second and third decades of the twentieth century, EXPRESSIONISM, which flourished first in Germany, offered a stylized, simplified distortion of life, designed to represent the vision of a dream and to express submerged and subconscious feelings. The classic summary of expressionist intentions was made by a precursor of this school, Strindberg, who asserted in his brief Author's Note to *A Dream Play* (1902) that he "sought to reproduce the disconnected but apparently logical form of a dream." The Belgian dramatist Maurice Maeterlinck attempted another way of getting at submerged emotions. He advocated and strove to create a poetic theater that gave symbolic expression to subconscious thoughts. (See SYMBOLISM.) He found the greatness of tragedy "not in the actions but in the words." His efforts were related to the attempts of the Anglo-Irish poet William Butler Yeats to found a minority theater for poetic drama. Actually, Yeats did help to establish Dublin's Abbey Theatre, a deliberately nationalistic venture that interpreted Irish themes in plays of folk life (like those of John Millington Synge and Lady Augusta Gregory) or heroic plays derived from ancient legends (like those of Yeats). Yeats wanted to celebrate heroism and to dramatize Irish subjects. The poet T. S. Eliot first interpreted the poetic drama of the past (especially the Elizabethan drama) and endeavored, by his own writing, to restore poetry to the theater.

If Maeterlinck, Yeats, and Eliot believed in the word, the French director and dramatic theorist Antonin Artaud believed in the action and observed: "Dialogue—a thing written and spoken—does not belong specifically to the stage, it belongs to books." Artaud wanted to bring to the stage magic, dreams, extravagant gestures, incantation, and cruelty. (See THEATER OF CRUELTY.) *The Theater and Its Double* (1938) expresses his ideas, which were not influential in his own lifetime but later affected the English director Peter Brook, notably his production of Peter Weiss's *Marat/Sade* (1964). Artaud was a forerunner also of the THEATER OF THE ABSURD, whose most voluble spokesman, the French dramatist Eugène Ionesco, proclaimed a theater that is not topical but interprets the timeless issues of absurdity and alienation.

Still other dramatic theorists were divorced from

the drama in general and approached it only to justify an idea or apply a general concept. Is the Viennese psychoanalyst Sigmund Freud a dramatic theorist because he found in Sophocles' *Oedipus Rex* an illustration of the Oedipus complex, the phenomenon of the son's rivalry with his father for love of his mother? Are the Marxists dramatic theorists when, like Georgi V. Plekhanov, they have seen the drama in the light of economic and social organization? The Swiss psychoanalyst Carl Jung is perhaps more relevant to dramatic theory because a Canadian critic, Northrop Frye, has used the Jungian approach in working out the archetypal forms of the drama, in *Anatomy of Criticism* (1957). The British classical scholar Gilbert Murray analyzed Greek tragedy in the light of its presumed employment of inherited ritual patterns; although Murray withdrew some of his findings toward the end of his life, he and his colleagues made an indelible impression upon the criticism of drama; for example, the American critic Francis Fergusson makes ample use of the "ritual" theory in his perceptive volume *The Idea of a Theater* (1949). (See RITUAL ORIGINS OF DRAMA.) A permanently interesting theory of comedy was provided by the French philosopher Henri Bergson, who suggested in *Laughter* (1900) that, by laughing, we respond to the incongruous combination of the human and the mechanical in the human being who, accidentally or deliberately, takes on the inhuman rigidity of a machine. (For excerpts from some of these critical writings, see the Appendix.)

Many of the texts of dramatic theory are collected in *European Theories of the Drama* (1965), edited by Barrett H. Clark and newly revised by Henry Popkin; *Theatre and Drama in the Making* (1964), edited by John Gassner and Ralph G. Allen; and *The Theory of the Modern Stage* (1968), edited by Eric Bentley. Syntheses of dramatic theory are offered by Allardyce Nicoll in two books: *The Theory of Drama* (1931) and *The Theatre and Dramatic Theory* (1962). *Form and Idea in Modern Theatre* (1956), by John Gassner, is a synthesis of modern dramatic theory. —H. P.

drame bourgeois. A term used in the late eighteenth century to designate serious, and often sentimental, plays that show that man is essentially good but misled by social prejudices. *Drame bourgeois,* also called *genre sérieux,* is directed toward, and its central theme deeply concerns, the middle-class spectator. It emphasizes a moral lesson applicable, through the depiction of characters and social abuses, to the spectator's daily life. Denis DIDEROT, father of the drame, adapted it from the *comédie larmoyante,* or tearful comedy, of Nivelle de la Chaussée (1692–1754). "Conditions," rather than mere characters, were to be presented; not only the professions of the various middle-class characters, but also the varied relationships of husband, father, sister, son; indeed, these conditions were to be viewed seriously, even tragically.

In his critical essay on the theater, *Entretiens sur "Le Fils naturel": Dorval et Moi (Conversations on "The Natural Son,"* pub. 1757 with his play *Le Fils naturel*), Diderot gives the central ideas of the drame bourgeois. Rules such as the three unities are important in writing and acting plays, but a truly creative playwright should never be enslaved by them. Dialogue has tended to overshadow the subtle and infinitely expressive skills of pantomime and acting itself. The script should permit the great actor to provide the clues to great passions with his own sound patterns—even, on occasion, his own words, much as opera singers are permitted to do. "It is the actor who provides the written text with energy." Passions must be recognizable as true and universal, regardless of the social class of the character made to utter them. The strict conventions that time has dictated for the writing and acting of tragedy must be loosened and adapted to the expression of serious public and domestic themes. "The subject should be important, the plot simple, domestic, and close to everyday life." Character study should be subservient to roles played as social types. To maintain unity of interest and tone and a strong moral emphasis, mere *coups de théâtre* should give place to tableaux of mute pathos. An effective example of such a tableau is provided at the end of the third act of Sedaine's *Le Philosophe sans le savoir (The Duel,* 1765): the father tenderly reproves his son who is about to fight a duel with another aristocrat over an alleged insult to middle-class tradesmen; the son, asserting his nobler feelings, embraces his father in silence.

Selected excerpts of the *Entretiens* are included in L. G. Crocker, ed., *Diderot's Selected Writings* (1966), translated by Derek Coltman, and in F. C. Green, ed., *Diderot's Writings on the Theatre* (1936) (in French) with introduction and notes in English. —S. S. S.

Dream Play, A (Ett drömspel, written 1901; given a prologue in 1906; prod. 1907). An episodic play by August STRINDBERG. Notable productions have been those of Max Reinhardt (1921), Alfred Jarry (1928), Olof Molander (1935), and Ingmar Bergman (1961), the last for television. The play has gradually established itself on the stage as the theater has been able to rise to its extraordinary technical demands.

According to the allegory, Indra's daughter, an Indian deity, visits the earth. There she encounters the officer imprisoned in a curiously growing castle, later sees him waiting eternally and in vain at the stage door for the opera diva Victoria, tries a doomed marriage with the lawyer, witnesses social inequity on the Riviera, exchanges views with the poet by Fingal's Cave, observes an unseemly scuffle of the four traditional university faculties, and finally experiences an ascension, taking back to the heavens the message, ritually repeated through the play, that the human condition is one of misery. But the conclusion is that misery must have some meaning in the total plan of things.

"My most beloved drama, the child of my greatest suffering," Strindberg called *A Dream Play.* Its greatness lies in that it liberated the theater from the time-bound, space-bound assumptions of naturalism. To the extent that the officer, the lawyer, and the poet all represent components of a total self, the play led to dissolution of "whole character" in the theater, from EXPRESSIONISM through surrealism to the "theater of the absurd." Whatever its limitations, the influence of *A Dream Play* has been very great.

An adequate English text may be found in *Six Plays of Strindberg* (1955), translated by Elizabeth Sprigge. Probably the best analysis in any language is that of Maurice Valency in *The Flower and the Castle* (1963), pp. 321–42.—R. B. V.

droll. A short scene, usually comic, extracted from a play. Drolls were popular in England during the suppression of the theater (1642–1660) when no more elaborate dramatic presentation was permitted. The most popular performer of drolls during this period was the actor Robert Cox (1604–1655), whose repertoire included at least two adaptations from Shakespeare: "The Merry Conceits of Bottom the Weaver" (from *A Midsummer Night's Dream*) and "The Bouncing Knight, or, the Robbers Rob'd" (from *Henry IV, Part One*).

Dryden, John (1631–1700). English poet, playwright, and critic. Dryden was born in Northamptonshire and educated at Westminster School and Trinity College, Cambridge. In 1658 he published "Heroic Stanzas" in commemoration of Cromwell, but two years later he welcomed the returning Charles II in "Astraea Redux," where he expressed the conservative, monarchist view that he was to hold the rest of his life. In this poem he first demonstrated his skill with the heroic couplet. In 1668 he was appointed poet laureate, and his greatest poetic achievements, such as his satires *Absolom and Achitophel* (1681) and *MacFlecknoe* (1682), were nondramatic. Nevertheless, Dryden was the greatest of the Restoration dramatists and one of the most prolific. For some years he was a shareholder in the King's Company.

Through his marriage in 1663 with Lady Elizabeth Howard, sister of Sir Robert Howard with whom he collaborated on *The Indian Queen* (1664), Dryden was on the fringe of court society. But unlike the so-called court wits, gentlemen of means who wrote as a distraction, Dryden wrote to earn his living. Very much involved with the politics of the day, he defended the government against Shaftesbury in *Absolom and Achitophel*, a political satire in verse. He also engaged in private controversies with such literary and theatrical figures as Elkanah Settle, the earl of Rochester, and Thomas SHADWELL. He became a Catholic in 1685 and, after the Revolution of 1688, was deprived of his laureateship and of a government post he had occupied. A period of financial difficulties followed, during which he did a great deal of translating but also wrote occasionally for the theater. Throughout the latter part of his life he was recognized as the leading literary figure of the day.

Though excelled by Thomas Otway and Nathaniel Lee in the portrayal of emotion and by Sir George Etherege and William Congreve in comic wit, Dryden wrote the best heroic plays of the period and some very good comedy (see ENGLAND: *Restoration drama*). Of his more than twenty-five plays (a few written in collaboration with others), the most important are *Secret Love* (1667), THE CONQUEST OF GRANADA, MARRIAGE À LA MODE, AURENG-ZEBE, ALL FOR LOVE, and *Don Sebastian* (1689). His essays showed him to be an outstanding critic, and those that deal with the theater, many of them published with early editions of his plays, are major sources for the understanding of Restoration drama. Some of the

most important are *An Essay of Dramatic Poesy* (1668), "Of Heroic Plays" (1672), the Preface to *All for Love* (1678), and the Preface to *Troilus and Cressida* (1679), "containing the Grounds of Criticism in Tragedy."

Both in his critical writing and in his practice, Dryden was one of the chief proponents of rhymed couplets for serious plays, until he changed to blank verse in imitation of Shakespeare in *All for Love*. His firm control of the design of these plays gives the dramatic conflicts an intellectual substance not found in the heroic plays of his contemporaries. In comedy his forte was witty repartee, often, as in *Marriage à la Mode*, replete with sexual *double-entendre*. The witty lovers of the comic plot in *Secret Love* anticipate in many respects the more famous hero and heroine of Congreve's *The Way of the World*.

The definitive complete edition of Dryden, the "California" edition, edited by H. T. Swedenberg, Jr., began appearing in 1956. Until it is in print the standard edition remains that of Sir Walter Scott, revised by George Saintsbury (1882–1893). The best biography is Charles E. Ward's *The Life of John Dryden* (1961). There are two valuable studies of his drama: Arthur C. Kirsch, *Dryden's Heroic Drama* (1965), and Frank H. Moore, *The Nobler Pleasure: Dryden's Comedy in Theory and Practice* (1963).—E. W.

Dubé, Marcel (1930–   ). French-Canadian playwright. After studying literature, Marcel Dubé started writing scripts for radio and television in 1951. *Zone* (1953), created for the Dramatic Arts Festival of the Province of Quebec, is his first play.

JOHN DRYDEN (WALTER HAMPDEN MEMORIAL LIBRARY AT THE PLAYERS, NEW YORK)

Since then, many plays have followed; they are usually presented on television first and then on the stage.

Dubé is the most prolific dramatist in French Canada. He generally presents disinherited characters, ones who have lost their social position or whom society puts on trial. *Zone* portrays a group of young people who, in smuggling cigarettes between the United States and Canada, kill a customs officer. The gang leader is arrested and brought to trial. This play is valued for its simplicity, suspenseful atmosphere, and direct, popular language. In his comedy *Un Simple Soldat* ("A Simple Soldier," 1958), Dubé presents a poor soldier, recently discharged from the Canadian army, and a family divided by hate and weakness. The story of this maladapted soldier is considered Dubé's best and gives Dubé the opportunity to display his gift of observation and his love of men. In *Au Retour des oies blanches* ("At the Return of the White Geese," 1967) the unexpected arrival of a mysterious uncle creates a disturbance in a middle-class family. For the mother, the visit is the chance to remember a lost love; for the daughter, the discovery of love; and for the father, an occasion to become aware of his mediocre life and his failure. *Le Temps des lilas* ("The Time of Lilacs," 1958), in a more poetic style, is to be set apart from Dubé's other works. This play brings to the stage some old people who watch their world give way to the agitation of modern life. The old house in which they live is going to be expropriated, and they must leave. This play is valued for its simple action, Chekhovian characters, and vibrant life.

The spirit of Dubé's theater is fundamentally pessimistic. One recognizes the influence of Eugene O'Neill and Tennessee Williams. As for the form, one finds, necessarily, a strong influence from television.—J. B.

Dubillard, Roland (1923–   ). French playwright. Dubillard's two plays have already made him a part of the avant-garde theater in Paris. *Naïves hirondelles* ("Naive Swallows"), produced in 1962 by Arlette Reinerg, might have disappeared quickly if Eugène Ionesco had not publicly proclaimed his admiration for it. The charm of the play is in the language, in the use of banal, prosaic speech. There is scarcely any situation or action. Dubillard uses nonsense and plays on words; long silences are followed by platitudes. In his effort to reflect life directly, he has created a form of poetic drama.

In his other play, *La Maison d'os* ("The House of Bones"), Dubillard uses language with a more constant flow and incorporates more reflections on the subjects of life and death. Produced in 1963, the play is about an old, rich man with many servants and without a family. He dies alone in his house, and the servants are totally indifferent to him. This second text shows greater skill in dramaturgy and greater inventiveness.—W. F.

Duchess of Malfi, The (1612–1614). A tragedy by John WEBSTER. One of the most moving tragedies in the English language. *The Duchess of Malfi* deals with the disastrous consequences of the marriage of the widowed duchess to her steward, Antonio. The marriage is viewed as a disgrace to the family honor by the duchess' two brothers, the duke of Calabria

and the cardinal. The two bring about the death of the duchess, her husband, and her children through the agency of their villainous servant, Bosola. Particularly worthy of note is the famous "death" scene of the duchess (IV, 2). In it she is subjected to a series of terrifying and diabolical tableaux that include waxed representations of her children and her husband, a visitation from a group of madmen, and, finally, the entrance of her murderers bearing a coffin and tolling a bell. The scene is an extraordinary blend of the macabre and the pathetic, of realism and fantasy. Its terrors elevate the duchess' courageous acceptance of death to the level of the heroic.

Like *The White Devil,* Webster's other great tragedy, *The Duchess of Malfi* is set in Renaissance Italy and is pervaded by the sense of intrigue, deceit, and corruption that symbolized Italy to the seventeenth-century Englishman. But the vitality of the play is such that it moves beyond the confines of time and place to present a dramatic and startling picture of the intense extremes of human experience. From the suffering of its beautiful heroine and the machinations of its formidable villains, the play passionately questions the meaning of life, the presence of evil, and the fact of death. Offering no solutions, it nevertheless testifies with a mixture of horror and wonder to the depth and seriousness of those questions.—E. Q.

Dumas, Alexandre. Known as **Dumas fils** (1824–1895). French playwright, essayist, and novelist.

ALEXANDRE DUMAS FILS (WALTER HAMPDEN MEMORIAL LIBRARY AT THE PLAYERS, NEW YORK)

Dumas fils introduced French realistic social drama, or the comedy of manners, in 1852 with his first play, LA DAME AUX CAMÉLIAS. To French audiences, his fifteen major plays, mostly "problem" or "thesis" plays (*pièces à thèses*), were a welcome relief from both Romantic drama and the "well-made plays" of Eugène Scribe. Yet for thirty-five years Dumas's work drew upon the successful elements of both these genres. Following a precept of Romanticism that urged the fusion of comedy and serious drama, he combined moral instruction with entertainment. He possessed an intense emotional power but realized that to kindle in his audiences his love of moral and social reform he would need to cast his plays in the mold of the well-made play, with its clever plots, action, and suspense. He also dramatized the effects of social and physical environment and wrote in one of his prefaces: "The dramatist who knows *man* as Balzac did and the *theatre* as Scribe did will be the greatest of the world's dramatists." Dumas helped to motivate the naturalistic writers in their uncompromising search for truth in exposing moral and social evils. Noble as this accomplishment was, he himself was able to realize it in only a few plays.

Born illegitimately to the elder Dumas and Catherine Labay, Dumas was reared by his reckless father in a hedonistic environment. An unhappy boyhood and a lack of formal education inflamed his urge to rebel against what he considered a cruel and false society, but they also contributed to an exaggeration, a lack of objectivity, and a rigid attitude toward social evils in some of his plays. Nevertheless, his work reveals a keen and logical mind, a brilliant wit, and great conversational skill. The anguish of his youth is seen in his overwhelming desire to reform the morals and manners of his time, especially in the plays treating marriage and the evils of money, adultery, prostitution, and illegitimacy.

In the seven years following his first play, in 1852, Dumas had five plays produced, of which two were successful and are among his better plays: *Le Demi-Monde* (*The Demi-Monde,* 1855) and *Le Fils naturel* (*The Illegitimate Son,* 1858). Dumas coined the word *demi-monde* (which became a part of the vocabulary) to define the world he had already depicted in *La Dame aux camélias.* The second play introduced a subject with which the author was obsessed and which he treated in six plays. Unsuccessful were *Diane de Lys* (1853), *La Question d'argent* (*The Money Question,* 1857), and *Un Père prodigue* ("A Prodigal Father," 1859). In 1861 he married Mme. Narischkine after they had a daughter. He wrote nothing else until 1864, when *L'Ami des femmes* (*The Woman's Friend*) failed, and in the following seven years he had two plays performed, of which *Les Idées de Mme Aubray* ("Mrs. Aubray's Ideas," 1867) was distinctly the best. *Les Idées* shows that for most people forgiveness and charity mean only one's indifference to what does not touch him personally.

From 1871 to 1873 Dumas produced three plays on adultery and one on illegitimacy. Of these, *La Femme de Claude* (*The Wife of Claude,* 1873) is the best constructed. This bizarre but effective drama, haunted with the acerbity of "an avenging angel," announced a great but short-lived change to symbolism in Dumas's work. The other two adultery plays were less successful: *Une Visite de noces* ("A Gay Visit," 1871) is a one-act farce; *La Princesse Georges* (1871) is a more serious treatment, backed by a rather tedious preface. *Monsieur Alphonse* (1873) treats the illegitimacy theme more compactly and more objectively than does *Le Fils naturel;* again the tone is intensely didactic. Oddly enough, there is no trace of the symbolic exaggeration of *La Femme de Claude.*

After Dumas was elected to the Académie Française in 1874, he produced no important plays until *Denise* (1881). Showing the importance of engaged girls not keeping secrets from their fiancés, this play is one of his best-written thesis plays. The distorted *L'Étrangère* (*The Foreigner*), Dumas's only other symbolical work, was performed in 1876; his *Entr'actes* were published in 1878/79 in three volumes; and the melodramatic *La Princesse de Bagdad* was performed in 1881. His final play, *Francillon* (1881), lacks merit but is at least free of the rigid and inexorable preaching that was in other Dumas plays.

Dumas's talent did not lie in the creation of living characters but rather in the dramatic contrasting and balancing of characters by groups or by types. One of his main contributions to the technique of the thesis play was the use of a spokesman, known as the *raisonneur,* for the playwright's ideas. Although Dumas certainly did not invent this type of character, he developed it to its fullest possibilities. The great danger with raisonneurs in general is that they tend to become mechanical mouthpieces.

About a dozen of the plays have been translated, more or less faithfully, usually in too free or pedantic Victorian versions. Barrett Clark's version of *Le Demi-Monde* is in *World Drama* (1933, 1956 paper), edited by B. H. Clark. The authoritative biography is A. Maurois's *The Titans: A Three-Generation Biography of the Dumas* (1957), translated by G. Hopkins. A bibliography for translations and critical studies is included in *Camille and Other Plays* (1957), edited by S. Stanton.—S. S. S.

Dumas, Alexandre [**Davy de la Pailleterie**]. Known as **Dumas père** (1802–1870). French novelist and playwright. Alexandre Dumas père was the grandson of a Haïtian black woman surnamed Dumas. After a liaison with a seamstress, he fathered Alexandre fils in 1824, who would be known as a more serious literary artist than his father. Dabbling in dramatics during his teens, while a small-town clerk, Dumas père had his first play, *La Chasse et l'amour* ("The Pursuit of Love," the joint effort of several collaborators), performed in 1825.

He wrote his first serious play, *Christine,* in 1828, but it was not performed until 1830. His second ambitious attempt at playwriting was almost immediately successful. Ready in two months, *Henri III et sa cour* ("Henry III and his Court") premièred at the Théâtre Français in February 1829. The first Romantic drama to be staged, it anticipated Victor Hugo's *Hernani* by a little more than a year and actually sparked the Romantic revolution. An audience including Alfred de Vigny and Victor Hugo applauded this performance. Its triumph caused Dumas to revise with moderate success the ill-fated *Christine.* At twenty-seven he was famous. For the next thirty years his hastily written plays (about ninety in all) were popular and melodramatic, and most of them were written in prose.

Antony (1831), one of his best plays, is an excellently constructed romantic tragedy of contemporary adulterous passion, often regarded as the prototype of the genre in France. The hero of this play is a moody Byronic lover whose violent but short-lived and fatal affair with Adèle d'Hervey is based partly on the author's liaison with Mélanie Waldor, wife of an army officer. But in his Preface to *Le Comte Hermann* (1849), Dumas deprecated the earlier triumph of *Antony*. *Charles VII chez ses grands vassaux* ("Charles VII Among His Royal Subjects"), written in mediocre verse, was produced later the same year. The play as a whole lacks distinction, despite some moving lines on race prejudice. He also concocted in 1831 a poor play, *Térésa*, in which Ida Ferrier, another of his mistresses (and later his wife), acted in 1832.

If *Antony* caused a scandal about Dumas's private life—one of his mistresses had been "put into a play," and two more were acting in it—*La Tour de Nesle* (*The Tower of Nesle*, 1832) created another about his collaboration methods. His most famous play, André Maurois has called it rare vintage MÉLODRAME, "a classic of over-acting." But in adapting the unactable script of Frédéric Gaillardet, Dumas became involved in a row over the use of collaborators' names in the playbill and had to fight a duel. His enemies called him a cribber. Although only two years before he and Hugo had been hailed as joint creators of the Romantic drama, Dumas was to suffer some loss of literary stature after 1832. This kind of detraction was unjust, for he possessed brilliant powers of invention, a keen sense of dramatic situation, and great skill as a storyteller. Nevertheless, his reputation as a playwright rests solely upon the best of his plays written between 1829 and 1832. Later dramas include *Catherine Howard* (1834); *Kean, ou désordre et génie* ("Kean, or Disorder and Genius," 1836), written for the actor Frédéric Lemaître; *Caligula* (1837); *Mademoiselle de Belle Isle* ("Young Lady of Belle Isle," 1839); *Hamlet* (1847); and *La Conscience* (1854). The plays that he wrote or collaborated on occupy some 25 of the 257 volumes of his collected works.

The period of the novels began in 1839 when, with his most congenial collaborator, Auguste Maquet, Dumas launched his famous musketeers and Valois series. *Les Trois Mousquetaires* and *Le Comte de Monte Cristo* appeared in 1844. He also collaborated on many other novels of French history.

Among the few available translations of his plays is *The Tower of Nesle* (1906), translated by A. L. Gowans. André Maurois's *The Titans: A Three-Generation Biography of the Dumas* (1957) is a fascinating account, and *The Dumasian* (*The Magazine of the Dumas Association*, 1956–1960) contains many articles on the life and work of Dumas. Dumas's own account of his early career, "Comment je devins auteur dramatique," serves as a preface to his *Théâtre Complet* (1833).—S. S. S.

dumb show. Part of a play done in pantomime. Dumb shows were a feature of some Elizabethan plays, serving to symbolize a significant aspect of the play or to introduce a particular scene. When fully integrated into the action of the play, as in Thomas Kyd's *Spanish Tragedy*, they created a powerful, concrete impression of an abstract idea or moral theme. Dumb shows are featured in such prominent Elizabethan plays as *Gorbuduc* and *The Changeling*. The most celebrated dumb show in drama is that featured in the play-within-a-play scene of *Hamlet*, in which the murder of Hamlet's father is reenacted in pantomime.

Dunlap, William (1766–1839). American playwright, theater manager, painter, and historian. Dunlap, the first American to attempt to make a profession of playwriting, was born in Perth Amboy, New Jersey, the son of a former officer in the British Army. In 1787 Dunlap set up as a portrait painter, but, inspired by the success of Royall Tyler's play THE CONTRAST, he began to write plays. Dunlap's second attempt, *The Father, or American Shandyism,* was successfully produced by the Old American Company in 1789. Two more comedies, two tragedies, and an opera followed. In 1796 he bought a quarter interest in the management of the Old American Company and in 1798 became sole manager until he was forced into bankruptcy in 1805. For a year he devoted himself to miniature portrait painting, then became assistant manager of the Park Theatre, where he remained until 1811. Thereafter, he supported himself largely by painting and writing. He wrote two biographies and several histories, including *History of the American Theatre* (1832) and *History of the Rise and Progress of the Arts of Design in the United States* (1834).

Dunlap was the author or part-author of twenty-nine plays and translator or adapter of about twenty-five more, among which are examples of sentimental comedy, romantic and historical tragedy, patriotic drama, and ballad opera. His most interesting play is *André* (1798), a tragedy concerned with an episode in the Revolutionary War.

A competent if uninspired painter, Dunlap was one of the founders of the National Academy of Design. He was an ardent believer in individual liberty, a staunch patriot, and an early worker for the abolition of Negro slavery. Although none of his plays survived long on the stage, they helped to set the patterns for later American drama, and their success encouraged other Americans to write for the stage. The best source is O. S. Coad's *William Dunlap* (1917, 1962).—B. H.

Dunsany [**Edward John Moreton Drax Plunkett**], 18th baron. Known as **Lord Dunsany** (1878–1957). Irish dramatist. A member of the Anglo-Irish gentry, Lord Dunsany was educated at Eton and Sandhurst, the English military school. After service as an officer in the British army during the Boer War, Dunsany returned to Ireland. He soon became involved in the activities of the newly founded Abbey Theatre, which produced his first play, *The Glittering Gate*, in 1909. For the next thirty years he continued to write plays for the English and American as well as the Irish stage.

Dunsany's work is characterized by a skillful combination of fantasy, fable, and sharp satire. Much of his work is brief and fragile, sustained by a sharp and occasionally bitter irony. Typical of his early work is *King Argimenes and the Unknown Warrior* (1911), a short play dealing with the theme of the instinctive superiority of a true-born king. Among his longer works is *The Gods of the Mountain* (1912), a grimly ironic fable, and *The Tents of the Arabs* (1914), a tender if somewhat sentimental idealization of a simple, nomadic existence.

Dunsany's best-known play, *A Night at an Inn* (1916), is a sinister and terrifying "thriller" that tells of the supernatural vengeance wrought upon a group of thieves who have stolen a ruby from the forehead of an Indian idol. In a chilling and theatrically effective final scene, the thieves are individually summoned by the idol itself to meet their deaths on a deserted Yorkshire moor. The play has been a great favorite in America, where it was first produced.

Dunsany's other plays include *The Golden Doom* (1912), *The Lost Silk Hat* (1913), *The Laughter of the Gods* (1916), and *If* (1922). All contain the Dunsany blend of fantasy and irony.

Duras, Marguerite (1914–). French novelist and playwright. One of the plays of Mme. Duras, *Le Square* (1955), is taken from her novel with the same title, and a second play, *Des Journées entières dans les arbres* ("Days Spent in the Trees," 1966), is taken from a short story with the same title. In addition to these adaptations, Mme. Duras has written two texts directly for the stage: *Les Viaducs de Seine-et-Oise* ("The Viaducs of Seine-et-Oise," 1963) and *Les Eaux et forets* (*The Rivers and Forests*, 1965).

Le Square is about the meeting on a park bench of two strangers: a housemaid and a traveling salesman. While the twenty-year-old housemaid hates everything about her life, the older man refuses to hope for anything better. The girl tries to instill a spirit of revolt in the man, but he is unmoved. His meager existence does not permit him to change his place in society, nor would he change it if he could. He lives an isolated and neutral existence devoid of desire. "I am a coward, mademoiselle," he says at the end.

The character of the gluttonous, possessive mother in *Des Journées entières dans les arbres* is a strong creation admirably played by Madeleine Renaud in the first run of the play at Le Théâtre de France. The two original dramas, however, seem less successful than the two adaptations.

For information on Duras, see Jacques Guicharnaud, "Woman's Fate: Marguerite Duras," *Yale French Studies*, No. 27 (1961).—W. F.

Dürrenmatt, Friedrich (1921–). Swiss playwright, novelist, short-story writer, and dramatic theorist. Dürrenmatt was born in the Swiss canton of Berne in the village of Konolfingen. He is the product of divergent backgrounds, which manifest themselves in his writing. His father was a Protestant pastor, which accounts for his interest in the rural village. The source of Dürrenmatt's intellectual dissent is his grandfather, who was an eccentric nineteenth-century Swiss politician as well as a poet of satiric verse. He has said in his essay *Theaterprobleme* (*Problems of the Theater*) that the difficulties a Protestant faces are precisely those of his faith.

Dürrenmatt's primary ambition was to be a painter, and his early plays are illustrated with his own sketches. It was not until the mid-1940's that he began seriously to devote himself to literature. In 1945 he published a short story that is reminiscent of the intense style of Ernst Jünger. Dürrenmatt also wrote various other small pieces and fragments, while at the same time learning the financial perils of being a free-lance writer. But after a while he received aid in the form of stipends and help from pa-

trons. His attempt at being a theater critic failed, as did his sketches for cabaret shows, except for the fact that those sketches displayed one of Dürrenmatt's strongest interests, namely in being a critic of his time. This was apparent in his first published play, *Es steht geschrieben* ("Thus It Is Written," 1947), in which the influences of Brecht are somewhat prominent, especially the alienation techniques utilized.

Essentially, Dürrenmatt believes that life is in the last analysis insignificant and that man is most often corruptible, a line of thought that is the basis of his play *Die Ehe des Herrn Mississippi* (*The Marriage of Mr. Mississippi*, 1952). Two primary themes dominate his works: power and death, both of which play an inextricable part in his plays THE VISIT and ROMULUS THE GREAT. Death is omnipresent, a vague and amorphous something that leads man on with the belief that he can accomplish something of value. The bitter irony resides in the fact that life, as Dürrenmatt sees it, really accomplishes very little, except in the immediate present. For in the end man is reduced to a ridiculous and absurd creature because he is subject to the ultimate meaninglessness of a futile death. Death is life's culmination, but it is merely an anticlimax, a final futility. These sentiments are vital as well in his *Die Ehe des Herrn Mississippi*. Dürrenmatt intimates throughout his major work that man is ridiculous because he must die. In keeping with so bitter a view, he utilizes a bitter but vitally comedic sense of ironic implication. This gift places him in the company of the best writers in the genre: Bertolt Brecht, Frank Wedekind, Johann Nestroy, and Aristophanes.

The second major theme in his works is the corrosive, corrupting effect of power. There is always present in his works a character who by virtue of his possession of power is placed in the precarious balance of using or not using that power. Dürrenmatt's dark vision, albeit comedic, is that the result of the power to do good is evil, because man is eventually corrupted by this possession. In the midst of his philosophy of gloom, however, Dürrenmatt is remarkably aloof and detached, Olympian in his view of man and existence.

Dürrenmatt is unquestionably one of the major theatrical figures of the mid-twentieth century and quite in line with the absurdist and avant-garde schools. He is highly experimental, but in his own way. His techniques, despite the superficial influence of Brecht, are always varied and fresh. Most important, his works share with the mainstream of playwrights and thinkers of our age the view of man as an absurd and essentially pitiable creature. His vision is pessimistic, often frustrating, but never anything less than highly inventive and utterly committed to a thoroughgoing criticism of our time.

No single biography of Dürrenmatt has appeared in English, although there are various important treatments of his writings in a number of different volumes. In the *Tulane Drama Review* the following may be found: Melvin W. Askew, "Dürrenmatt's *The Visit of the Old Lady*" (June 1961); Adolf Klarmann, "Friedrich Dürrenmatt and the Tragic Sense of Comedy" (May 1960); and Gordon Rogoff, "Mr. Dürrenmatt Buys New Shoes" (October 1958). There is also an excellent chapter on him in George Wellwarth's *The Theater of Protest and Paradox* (1964), as well as in a volume by H. F. Garten, *Modern German Drama* (1959). One final study is by Peter Seidmann, "Modern Swiss Drama: Frisch and Dürrenmatt," *Books Abroad,* Vol. 34 (1960).—C. R. M.

Dutch and Flemish drama. As in many other countries, the oldest form of drama in the Netherlands and the Flemish part of Belgium may be found in the liturgy, which developed into church drama at about the beginning of the twelfth century. There are no extant manuscripts of Dutch church dramas of the thirteenth century, but it is known that such plays in the Dutch language must have existed, for there is evidence of them in later literary developments.

There may have been a parallel secular drama, which arose out of dialogues or out of dramatizations of such natural phenomena as the yielding of winter to spring, but very little is definitely known about this. The *abele spelen* (literally, "beautiful" or "skillful" plays) are dramatizations of motifs from the romances of chivalry, but they are characteristically Dutch. *Esmoreit* (mid-fourteenth century) depicts the difficulties that stand in the way of the love between Esmoreit, the son of the king of Sicily, and Damiët, the daughter of the king of Damascus. In *Gloriant* (mid-fourteenth century) the proud hero of the title looks down upon the love of women but is eventually united by the bonds of love to Florentijn, who, at first, had contempt for men. The most highly developed of these plays is *Lanseloet van Denemarken* (*Lancelot of Denmark,* mid-fourteenth century), which depicts the tragic love of Lanseloet for Sanderijn. Through his unchivalrous behavior, the hero loses not only Sanderijn but also his life. Another abel spel is *Van den Winter ende van den Somer* (*Of Winter and Summer,* mid-fourteenth century), which takes up the debate between the two seasons over who benefits mankind most. Sometimes one of these plays would be followed by a farce, or *sotternie*. The farces, which date from the second half of the fourteenth century, were dramatized anecdotes or crudely realistic scenes from the everyday life of the people. They often involved relationships between man and wife, such as *Nu noch* ("Go Ahead," c. 1350), which portrays a henpecked hero, or jokes about sex, such as *De Buskenblaser* ("The Box-Blower," c. 1350), in which an old farmer is tricked into paying a large sum of money for the privilege of blowing into a box in the belief that it will rejuvenate him. All he gets for his pains is a face full of black powder.

Only a few of what must have been a rather large number of mystery plays have survived. A good example of these is the *Eerste Bliscap van Maria* (*The First Joy of Mary,* c. 1448), which takes up the fall of man and his redemption through Christ. It is the message from the Angel Gabriel to the Holy Virgin that is the first joy. The texts of the next five joys have been lost, but the *Sevenste Bliscap* (*The Seventh Joy,* c. 1448) has survived. It portrays the last days of Mary's life and Her Assumption and its style points toward the art of the *rederijkers* ("rhetoricians"). The tendency of the rhetoricians toward allegory is evident in *Het spel van de V vroede ende V dwaeze Maegden* ("The Play of the Five Wise and the Five Foolish Virgins," written during the fifteenth century). The miracle plays and the plays based on the lives of the saints are closer to the secular drama. The oldest extant miracle play, which probably dates from the last quarter of the fifteenth century, is *Tspel vanden heilighen Sacramente vander Nyeuwervaert* ("The Play of the Holy Sacrament of Nieuwervaert"). It revolves about the finding of a host that begins to bleed when it is touched, but a comic note is added in the scenes in which the devils appear. The greatest example of Middle Dutch drama, however, is *Mariken van Nieumeghen* (*Mary of Nijmegen*), which dates from between 1485 and 1510. In this play the young heroine, Mary, enters into a pact with the devil and goes off to Antwerp with Moenen, where they lead a loose and riotous life. But after seven years Mary repents and returns to Nijmegen. She finds peace by entering a convent, and there she finds forgiveness for her sins. In the end she is saved by the Virgin Mary. The tavern scene, a masterpiece in itself, shows the author's ability to capture everyday reality. He also succeeds in giving psychological depth to his characters, especially his heroine, and the realistic dialogue makes them entirely convincing. The theme of sin, repentance, and forgiveness attests to its completely Catholic tone, yet it is not difficult to discern the spirit of the Renaissance.

The morality plays are didactic and allegorical. The most famous of all the Dutch morality plays is *Den Spieghel der Salicheit van Elckerlijc* (*Everyman*), in which Death comes to Everyman in the midst of his rejoicing and tells him that it is time to die. He must come before God and account for his life. In searching for a traveling companion, he calls upon several natural talents who help him, but only Virtue accompanies him to the grave. The allegorical figures are convincing, although the morality play

ENGRAVING OF A SIXTEENTH-CENTURY STREET THEATER IN GHENT (NEW YORK PUBLIC LIBRARY)

has a certain abstract quality. Some scholars claim that the Dutch *Everyman,* which dates from the end of the fifteenth century, is the original from which the English version arose by translation. *Van Nyeuvont, Loosheit ende Practice hoe sy vrou Lortse verheffen* ("Of Trickery, Deceit, and Duplicity and How They Take in Madam Fraud," c. 1500) is a satirical morality play.

At the beginning of the fifteenth century classical material began to make its way into the drama. At the same time the Latin school drama flourished in the Netherlands and in the Flemish-speaking part of Belgium. Terence, Seneca, and Plautus served as models during the period of Humanism. It was in this tradition that Gulielmus Gnapheus (1493?–1568) wrote his *Acolastus* (1529), which is a biblical school drama based on the story of the Prodigal Son.

An interesting cultural and theatrical development in the period between the middle ages and the golden age of the seventeenth century is the art of the rederijkers. The chambers of rhetoric were groups of middle-class citizens in the towns who were interested in the performance and even the writing of drama. They first appeared in the cities of the Flemish-speaking part of Belgium at the beginning of the fifteenth century, and the influence of the *chambres de rhétorique,* which had existed in northern France since the twelfth century, is evident in their very name. The Flemish rhetoricians were originally connected with the church, but their chambers were organized in the manner of the guilds. They entered into contests with each other, and some of these contests, such as the one that involved the whole province of Brabant, were cyclical in nature and lasted for decades. The cities and the princes encouraged and helped them. At the end of the sixteenth century most of the chambers fell into decline, although a number of them survived for centuries. There were chambers of rhetoric in the Netherlands, too, although neither their numbers nor influence were as great.

Anthonis de Roovere (c. 1430–1482) was a rhetorician who wrote morality plays and *esbatementen* ("farces"), as well as lyric poetry. Jan Smeken (c. 1450–1517) was the author of *Een Spel op hertoghe Karle, ons Keijser nu es* ("A Play about Duke Karl, Who Is Now Our Emperor," 1500). He is also supposed to have written other plays, including *Hue Mars en Venus tsamen bueleerden* ("How Mars and Venus Had a Love Affair," c. 1550), which contained classical material foreshadowing the Renaissance. Cornelis Everaert (1485–1556), like Anthonis de Roovere a native of Bruges, wrote thirty-five plays, not all of which are of equal value. He criticized the social and economic conditions of his day. *Van den Visscher* ("About the Fisherman," early sixteenth century) is a play about the wife of a fisherman who confesses her infidelity to him during a storm at sea but who manages to keep her hold over him when the storm has passed. The *spelen van zinne* ("plays of the senses," in the moral meaning of the term) are allegorical, moralizing, and didactic and critical of social and economic conditions. The anonymous *Esbatement van den Appelboom* ("The Farce of the Apple Tree," c. 1500) reveals the allegorical style of the rhetoricians, but the characters have a lifelike quality. In this play God bestows on an apple tree the miraculous power of holding fast anyone who climbs

it, if the owner so desires. It is based on an old fairy tale. There are also a number of farces that reflect the rough life of the lower classes. The plays of Cornelis Crul, who lived during the first half of the sixteenth century, show the influence of Erasmus.

De Spiegel der Minnen ("The Mirror of Love," before 1530) belongs to the period of the rhetoricians but is a remarkable play. The characters are ordinary people, and this play is thus the first middle-class drama in Dutch. It is the love story of a merchant's son and a young seamstress. The opposition of his parents to his plans for marriage leads to misunderstanding and estrangement between the hero and heroine. The tragic ending is death for both, and the moral is that one should marry within his own class. Too ardent a love, moreover, leads to disaster. While pride and jealousy are personified, the dramatist has endowed his characters with life and psychological depth. The archaic language creates a difficulty for the modern reader.

Another interesting dramatist among the rhetoricians is Jan van den Berghe (d. 1559). Even more important than his farce *Hanneken Leckertant* ("Johnny Toothsome," c. 1541) is his *De Wellustige Mensch* ("The Voluptuary," 1551), an allegorical play whose hero has something of the Renaissance spirit in his view of life. The hero falls into bad company, but he then begs God for forgiveness and is absolved. The allegorical figures have a realistic quality, so that they are human beings, rather than shadows. Matthijs de Castelein (1485–1550), one of the most famous rhetoricians of the period, is the author of *De Conste van Rhetoriken* ("The Art of Rhetoric," pub. 1555), which is the first comprehensive book on aesthetics in Dutch. Cornelis van Ghistele translated Terence and Sophocles, but adapted their work to the allegorical style of the rhetoricians.

Most of the work of Jan van Hout (1542–1609) has been lost. While he was by no means a great writer, he was the first dramatist in the Netherlands to see things from a national and Renaissance point of view. His *Loterij spel* ("Lottery," 1596), which was performed to welcome ten chambers of rhetoric that had assembled in Leiden for a celebration, is the first modern play by a rhetorician. It presents a realistic view of the classes and professions, without abstract, allegorical figures or lyrical passages. His loose, narrative rhythm foreshadowed Gerbrand Adriaanszoon Bredero, and each of his characters speaks in a language that is appropriate for him. *Numa ofte Ambtsweigeringe* ("Numa, or Refusal of Office," c. 1580) is a play by Hendrik Laurensz Spiegel in which Numa is chosen to succeed Romulus. Numa wants neither office nor glory, however, preferring piety and the search for truth, justice, and goodness. In the end, he accepts the will of the gods and recognizes that through his office he can benefit many people. This play may be an adaptation of Plutarch's *Numa,* perhaps by way of Jacques Amyot's French translation. But the ideas are those of a Humanist stoic, and the characters come to life.

In the seventeenth century the drama was considered the highest form of literary art and was thought to be closest to philosophy. In the typical Renaissance drama of Europe it was possible for the tragic and comic to come together in harmony. This modern type of drama reached its height only in England

and Spain, however, and in the Netherlands and Flanders tragedy and comedy soon went their separate ways. Tragedy was guided by classical rules, and the classical tragedy of the Renaissance involved princes or persons of equal importance, and an unhappy ending was required. The people of the middle class were the heroes of comedies, and their faults were held up to ridicule. On the other hand, certain traditional Dutch characteristics appear in the drama of the seventeenth century. These are realism, an emblematic and allegorical quality, and a moralizing tendency. The master of Dutch comedy in the seventeenth century is Gerbrand Adriaanszoon BREDERO, who died at the height of his powers. In addition to the first Dutch romantic plays, he wrote a number of excellent farces, the greatest of which is *Klucht van de Koe* ("Farce of the Cow," written 1612). He brought the life of Holland, especially of Amsterdam, into his plays. The greatest dramatist of the seventeenth century is Joost van den VONDEL, who began to write late in life but who produced a large and significant body of work. He was a deeply religious man who was sensitive to the religious conflicts of his time. Vondel may not be the most typical representative of the Renaissance, but he is the outstanding example of the Dutch Baroque.

Samuel Coster (1579–1665) produced his comedy *Teeuwis de Boer* ("Teeuwis the Peasant") in 1612, the same year that Bredero's *Klucht van de Koe* appeared. He used an old folk song as his source, and, unlike his predecessors, he was able to create a farce out of everyday life without depending on a foreign model. His hero, Teeuwis the peasant, seduces his master's wife and then tricks them both. In addition to such realistic farces, Coster also wrote several classical plays, such as *Ithys* (c. 1614), *Iphigenia* (1617), *Polyxena* (1619), and *Isabella* (1618), a dramatization of an episode from Lodovico Ariosto's *Orlando Furioso* (1532), which Pieter Corneliszoon Hooft had begun but which Coster finished. Coster also played a leading role in De Egelantier (The Eglantine), a chamber of rhetoric, and the Nederduytsche Academie (the Dutch Academy), both of which were important in the production of plays in the first half of the seventeenth century. Vondel greatly admired him.

Theodoor Rodenburg (c. 1578–1644) was a prolific dramatist and wrote a dozen plays, in the period from 1615 to 1619, in which his model was Lope de Vega. In spite of all the romantic elements he borrowed from the Spanish drama, he also put something of middle-class life into his plays and added a didactic element. Unfortunately, his work has no great literary value, for it is weak in both language and structure.

Like Coster, Jan Janszoon Starter (c. 1594–1626) incurred the opposition of the clergy. He wrote several tragicomedies and farces and is also the author of the first Dutch operetta, *Kluchtigh t'samen-Gesang van dry Personagiën* ("Farcical Chorus of Three Personages," pub. 1621), which he based on an English model. A drama in the classical style is *Achilles en Polyxena* (written 1597) by Pieter Corneliszoon Hooft (1581–1610), which he wrote at the age of seventeen. The play takes place before the walls of Troy during the siege, but in spite of its classical sources and exterior, it includes a passionate struggle between honor and love. In the end the Greek Achilles is betrayed by his Trojan lover Polyxena and murdered. In this play Hooft values the simple life more than that of the prince, who should maintain a stoic indifference to his own fate and think only of the welfare of his people. *Theseus ende Ariadne* (written 1602) is also a mixture of love and stoicism, but it is a better play. It shows that fortune does not remain the same and that misfortune can yield to happiness, for God makes everything turn out for the best. Theseus and Ariadne are in love, but Theseus is persuaded to desert Ariadne in her sleep. Ariadne is ready to kill herself in despair, but her nurse counsels stoicism and everything turns out for the best. Bacchus marries Ariadne and takes her to heaven as a goddess.

In 1598 Hooft made a trip to France and Italy, where he came into contact with French and Italian culture, which had a great influence on his literary development. It was after this trip that he wrote *Theseus ende Ariadne* and *Granida* (written 1605). The first act of the latter drama shows his debt to Battista Guarini's *Il pastor fido* (1596), but the change from sensual love to the platonic ideal in *Granida* also reflects the autobiographical element. Natural virtue and freedom from social prejudice emerge from the drama as Hooft's ideals. Princess Granida and Daifilo, a shepherd, are in love with each other. Daifilo wins her in combat for his master Tisiphernes but then abducts her. Tisiphernes' heart is softened, however, and Daifilo and Granida are married. Hooft's mastery of language and his gift for lyrical expression are strikingly evident in this play. Hooft's *Geeraerdt van Velsen* (pub. 1613), is a historical drama that is based on an old folk song and other sources. The subject is the conflict between Floris V and Gerard van Velsen, which threatens the welfare of the country and leads to civil war. Gijsbert van Aemstel is the wise statesman who attempts to restore order and harmony and whose efforts foreshadow the rise of the great city of Amsterdam. Both Floris and van Velsen are destroyed in the tragic struggle. The allegorical figures from the plays of the rhetoricians still appeared in Hooft's drama, but he understood the importance of creating living characters and allowing the play to grow out of the conflict between them. If his characters are not as great as they might have been, at least he endowed them with personalities and passions, and he had a grasp of dramatic structure and action. Although he took his ideas on form from Seneca, Hooft's style is his own, and his language and poetry assure *Geeraerdt van Velsen* an important place in Dutch literature. His other great play is *Baeto* (written 1617), in which the hero of the title chooses self-imposed exile over the destruction of his country. With his followers, whom he calls Batavians, after himself, he founds a new country in the then unoccupied territory known as Holland. Baeto is thus the ideal prince who preserves peace above all. His antagonist is the passionate and domineering villainess Penta. The relationship between the state and the church also plays an important role in this drama, and Hooft rejects the idea of a theocracy. His *Warenar* (written 1616) is based on Plautus' *Aulularia* (194 B.C.?), but he turned it into a Dutch play about Amsterdam. Hooft translated Pietro Aretino's *Lo ipocrito* (1527) as *Schijnheylich* ("The

Hypocrite," pub. 1624). For half a century Hooft exerted an enormous influence on Dutch dramatic literature. It was through him, too, that the influence of Seneca was continued and the bucolic element was strengthened.

The poet Constantijn Huygens (1596–1687), skilled in both Dutch and Latin verse, is also important as the writer of a farce, *Trijntje Cornelis* (written 1653). The heroine of the title is a boatman's wife who goes on a spree in Antwerp. When she wakes up, she finds herself sitting on a dung heap, dressed only in an old coachman's jacket. By using her wits, she is finally able to get all her things back. Its earthy scenes of everyday life offer a remarkable contrast to Huygens' neoclassical poetry. He uses dialects and knows how to build his characters out of them. The result is more than a farce and approaches comedy.

The second half of the seventeenth century did not produce any great achievements in the drama, which was dominated by imitators of Vondel and Bredero. Neoclassicism triumphed, and there was a great deal of translation. Jan Vos (c. 1620–1667) controlled the theatrical world of Amsterdam from about 1647 to 1667 and opposed Vondel's dramatic style. Vos enjoyed greater popularity with the theatergoing public. His *Aran en Titus* (1641) was a huge success, not only with the public, but with the great men of letters, including Vondel. This five-act tragedy involves several plots and counterplots by Titus Andronicus, Thamera, and her lover, the Moor Aran, and is filled with sensational action and horror. Twelve corpses fall upon the stage during the play, but there is no human feeling or psychological depth beneath the violent action. Vos is also the author of another tragedy, *Medea* (1665), in which the scenes are more important than the dialogue.

The Amsterdam society Nil Volentibus Arduum ("Nothing Is Difficult for Those Who Have the Will"), which was founded in 1669, promoted the French neoclassical dramatic style and was even inspired by the Académie Française. In the same year there appeared a little book on literary theory, *Onderwijs in de Tooneel-Poezy* ("Instruction in Dramatic Poetry"), which described the neoclassical style. Thomas Asselyn (c. 1620–1701), who was opposed to the principles of the society, wrote several tragedies that are of little importance, but his comedy *Jan Klaaz of gewaande Dienstmaagt* ("Jan Klaaz, or the Supposed Servant Girl," 1682) is a masterpiece. Jan Klaaz tricks Saartje's parents into allowing her to marry him by getting her a job as a servant girl in his parents' home, where he seduces her. There is effective social criticism in this play, and Asselyn shows great skill in characterization and in summoning up the Dutch Mennonite atmosphere of the times. He also wrote several other comedies, two of which are continuations of *Jan Klaaz*. By the end of the seventeenth century French classicism had triumphed, but the moralizing tendency had increased, and the plays had become stiff and colorless. The most important dramatist at this time was Pieter Bernagie (1656–1699), who was more creative and prolific than his contemporaries.

Although the number of translations increased, some Dutch playwrights, such as Lucas Rotgans (1654–1710), created original dramas in the French neoclassical style. His most important play, *Eneas en*

Turnus (written 1705), is based on the twelfth book of Vergil's *Aeneid*. This tragedy, in which Aeneas and Turnus fight over Lavinia, ends in the death of Turnus and the suicide of Lavinia's mother. Rotgans' *Scilla* is based on material from Ovid's *Metamorphoses*. In this tragedy, written in 1709, Scilla commits suicide after Minos spurns her love. Rotgans is more dramatic, but less literary, than Vondel. The rhetorical element has disappeared, and the verse form is simpler.

Achilles (pub. 1719) by Balthazar Huydecoper (1695–1778) is often considered the best tragedy in the French classical style in the eighteenth century. Achilles becomes a more admirable hero when his arrogant insistence upon honor yields to reason. The other important writer in the neoclassical style is Jan Harmenszoon de Marre (1696–1763), who is best known for his *Jacoba van Beieren* (pub. 1736). His source for this drama was the events of the year 1432 in Dutch history.

The comic tradition of Hooft and Bredero, continued by Asselyn and Bernagie, culminated in the work of Pieter Langendijk (1683–1756). His *Don Quichot op de bruiloft van Kamacho* ("Don Quixote at Camacho's Wedding," 1711) is drawn from Cervantes' novel, but it is a thoroughly Dutch comedy and very effective on the stage. *Het Wederzijds Huwelijksbedrog* ("The Mutual Marriage Hoax," pub. 1714), in which Lodewijk and Charlotte each pretend to be rich in order to persuade the other to enter into marriage, is the best Dutch comedy of manners of the eighteenth century. The contrast between appearances and reality is again used advantageously in *Krelis Louwen of Alexander de Groote op het poëetenmaal* ("Krelis Louwen, or Alexander the Great at the Poets' Feast," pub. 1715). *Spiegel der vaderlandsche kooplieden* ("A Mirror of Our Country's Merchants," pub. 1760) is also a comedy of manners in which Langendijk again unmasked arrogance and conceit.

The dominance of the French neoclassical style continued through the second half of the eighteenth century and into the beginning of the nineteenth, but tragedy based on middle-class life began to appear, and there were also many translations of German plays, particularly of August von Kotzebue and August Iffland. Willem Bilderdijk (1756–1831), one of the most important literary figures of the eighteenth century, did not make a significant contribution to the drama with such plays as *Floris de Vijfde* (*Floris V*), *Willem van Holland*, or *Kormak*, all of which were written in 1808. Adriaan van der Hoop, Jr. (1802–1841), a leader in the Dutch Romantic movement, adapted Adolf Müllner's German fate tragedy *Die Schuld* (1813) as *Hugo en Elvire* (pub. 1831). In this melodrama of murder and incest, Elvira commits suicide because of her feelings of guilt over the murder of her first husband. Hoop's *De Horoskoop* ("The Horoscope," pub. 1838) is an original fate tragedy, and *Johanna Shore* (pub. 1834) and *Han van Ysland* ("Han of Iceland," written 1837) reveal the influence of Victor Hugo. Another dramatist who shows the influence of Hugo, as well as that of Friedrich Schiller, is Hendrik Jan Schimmel (1823–1906), who wrote a number of historical dramas, such as *Twee Tudors* ("Two Tudors," pub. 1847), *Joan Woutersz* (pub. 1847), *Napoleon Bonaparte* (pub. 1851), and, his most important play, *Struensee* (pub. 1868). *Schuld en Boete* ("Guilt and Atonement," written 1852) and *Juffrouw Bos* (pub. 1878) are middle-class dramas. Eduard Douwes Dekker (1820–1887), who, under the pseudonym of Multatuli, became one of the greatest of all Dutch novelists, wrote one drama in verse that is worth mentioning: *Vorstenschool* ("School for Princes," 1873). It contains his social and political ideas. A political comedy, *De kiesvereniging van Stellendijk* ("The Electoral Association of Stellendijk," 1880), is the only significant play by Lodewijk Mulder (1822–1907). Marcellus Emants (1848–1923) put some of his own life and disillusionment into *Juliaan de Afvallige* ("Julian the Apostate," pub. 1874). *Fatsoen* ("Respectability," 1890) portrays the fate of a man whose family never quite forgives him for having married beneath his class, even after his wife is dead. Emants achieved popular success with *Domheidsmacht* ("The Power of Stupidity," 1904), in which a successful politician is brought to defeat by the stupidity of his wastrel son and his suspicious wife. Emants is an independent figure in Dutch literature who attempted to gain a place for realistic drama on the stage. Frederik van Eeden (1860–1932) was the only member of the Dutch literary revival known as The Movement of Eighty to achieve any success on the stage. His first important literary work was *Het Koninkrijk der Wijzen* ("The Kingdom of the Wise," written 1881), a dramatic idyll. *De Student thuis* ("The Student at Home," written 1885) is a satire and *Don Torribio* (written 1887) is a comedy. *De Broeders* ("The Brothers," written 1894) and *Lioba* (pub. 1897) both glorify women who suffer because of a guilty love. *IJsbrand* (1908), *De Idealisten of Het Beloofde Land* ("The Idealists, or The Promised Land," 1908), *Het Paleis van Circe* ("Circe's Palace," 1910), and *In Kenterend Getij* ("In the Turning of the Tide," pub. 1913) all contain idealized and misunderstood prophets. They reflect van Eeden's unhappy experiences in his attempt to set up a cooperative community, which he named Walden. The most successful of his serious dramas is *De Heks van Haarlem* ("The Witch of Haarlem," 1915), which is based on historical events of the seventeenth century. It portrays the uncertainty of a man torn by his various duties and obligations.

The only modern dramatist to achieve an international reputation is Herman HEIJERMANS. His most famous play is *Op Hoop van Zegen* (*The Good Hope,* 1900), but he also wrote a number of other dramas of social criticism. Although he was a master of the realistic drama, he made effective use of fantasy.

Josine Adriana Simons-Mees (1863–1948) reveals a sense of irony and psychological insight in her work. She achieved her first success on the stage with *De Veroveraar* ("The Conqueror," 1906), to which she wrote a sequel, *Atie's Huwelijk* ("Atie's Marriage," 1907). In these plays Atie is engaged to Willem but is fascinated by his spirited half brother, whom she finally chooses in the sequel. Her dramas often portray the conflict between the claims of family and society and the freedom of the individual. Thus, *Een Moeder* ("A Mother," 1905) is an effective portrait of a widow who has learned to fend for herself and her family so well that she dominates them, while *Levensstroomingen* ("The Currents of

Life," 1919) presents the conflict between a father who has worked his way up to a position of wealth and his children, whom he has brought up in luxury. Willem Frederik Schürmann (1879–1915) is also able to give psychological depth to family conflicts. In *Paddestoelen* ("Toadstools," 1906) a writer deserts his wife and family in what proves to be a vain quest for happiness with an "extraordinary" woman. *Veertig* ("Forty," 1909) is a drama of the love of a wealthy businessman of forty for a girl of eighteen. *Het Dubbele Leven* ("The Double Life," 1907) reveals the inner weakness of a powerful businessman who speculates with the funds entrusted to him. Schürmann's best play is *De Violiers* ("The Violiers," 1911), in which the daughter of Mark Violier, a Jewish businessman who has lavished all his affection on her, runs off with his Christian competitor.

Jan Fabricius (1871–1966) achieved considerable popular success with his dramas of life in the former Dutch East Indies: *Met den Handschoen Getrouwd* ("Marriage by Proxy," 1902), *Eenzaam* ("Alone," 1907), *Dolle Hans* ("Crazy Hans," 1916), and *Tòtòk en Indo* ("European and Half-Breed," 1915). Some of his plays, like *Onder Één Dak* ("Under One Roof," 1915) and *Ynske* (pub. 1914), are based on life in the Netherlands. Jan de Hartog (1914–   ) began his career in Amsterdam with *De Ondergang van de "Vrijheid"* ("The Wreck of the 'Liberty,'" pub. 1938), but has also gained a reputation in the United States, where he now lives, with such English plays as *The Fourposter*. The most important dramatist in Flemish Belgium in the twentieth century has been Herman Teirlinck (1879–1967), whose *De Vertraagde Film* (*The Slow-Motion Picture,* pub. 1922) shows the influence of the cinema. His interest in the medieval drama is evident in *Ik dien* ("I Serve," pub. 1924), a version of the Beatrice legend, and *Elckerlyc* ("Everyman," date unknown). Other plays by Teirlinck are *De Ekster op de Galg* ("The Magpie on the Gallows," pub. 1937), *De Man zonder Lijf* ("The Man Without a Body," pub. 1925), *Ave* (pub. 1928), and *De Boer die Sterft* ("The Dying Peasant," date unknown). The greatest Dutch dramatist of modern times, indeed since the seventeenth century, remains Herman Heijermans.

A few Dutch plays have been translated into English: *Esmoreit* (1924), *Lancelot of Denmark* (1924), *Mary of Nimmegen* (1924), *Redentin Easter Play* (1941), *Everyman* (1892), Joost van den Vondel's *Lucifer* (1898), Frederik van Eeden's *Ysbrand* (1910), Herman Heijermans' *Ahasverus* (1934), *Jubilee* (1928), *The Ghetto* (1899), *The Rising Sun* (1926), and *The Good Hope* (1912). For a study of Vondel's life and work see A. J. Barnouw, *Vondel* (1925). An account of the modern Flemish theater will be found in S. Lilar, *The Belgian Theater since 1890* (1950). For a brief account of the Dutch theater in the second half of the nineteenth century and for a biographical and critical study of Heijermans, see Seymour L. Flaxman, *Herman Heijermans and His Dramas* (1954).—S. L. F.

Dybbuk, The (1920). A tragedy by S. ANSKY. Originally titled *Tsvishn Tsvey Veltn: A Dramatishe Legende* ("Between Two Worlds: A Dramatic Legend"), *Der Dibuk: Tsvishn Tsvey Veltn* (*The Dybbuk: Between Two Worlds*) was first produced by the Vilna Troupe in Warsaw on December 9, 1920, to

A SCENE FROM S. ANSKY'S *The Dybbuk* (YIVO INSTI-
TUTE FOR JEWISH RESEARCH)

mark the end of the traditional thirty-day mourning period for Ansky, who had died on November 8.

In the play a young rabbinical scholar, Khonnon, prevented from marrying Leye because he lacks the wealth her father, Sender, seeks for her, tries in desperation to get it by invoking Satan's help, but he dies at the very moment he is triumphantly crying out, "I have won!" Leye, distraught by Khonnon's death, is possessed by a dybbuk, an alien spirit later identified as Khonnon's, just as she is to be married to another. Before the dybbuk can be expelled, a dream reveals that, as a youth, Sender and his friend Nissen had plighted their yet unborn offspring, Leye and Khonnon. The spirit of Nissen, who died shortly thereafter, now demands that Sender be brought to trial. The rabbinical court punishes Sender, expels the dybbuk, and orders that the marriage of Leye to her betrothed proceed. Before the bridegroom arrives, however, Leye dies and her spirit joins Khonnon's.

On the surface the play seems to be a romantic story illustrating the power of love to transcend circumstance. It is, however, much more than that. The love story is merely the focal point of the twin motifs of the theme—the eternal capacity of man to redeem himself and the basic justice of the universe. Man may yield to temptation and fall from virtue, but he may also by his own volition find his way back to moral conduct. The fallen soul may by his efforts rise again. The spirit of Khonnon, having finally ceased its sinful usurpation of the body of Leye, can

begin anew its struggle for redemption. The Lord of the universe, for His part, permits no wrong to go unrighted. Leye, having been plighted to Khonnon, is joined to him in spirit after her death. And Sender, who, in his thirst for wealth has forgotten the value of man, is sentenced to use his wealth for the benefit of man.

The setting and the plot of *The Dybbuk* draw heavily from the folk materials that Ansky collected during his field expedition. It is a meticulously constructed play that developed over a period of eight years through several revisions, including the addition of the key role of the messenger at the suggestion of director Konstantin Stanislavsky. In each act, prior to the movement of the plot, there is a careful exposition of the relevant Hassidic lore by the messenger to establish the mood and prepare for the ensuing events. He is both chorus commenting on the action and mysterious foreshadower suggestive of the immediate presence of the supernatural. From the death of Khonnon at the end of Act I to the final union with Leye ending Act IV, the action proceeds inexorably to the final triumph of justice and redemption.

This play has been translated by Joseph C. Landis in *The Dybbuk and Other Great Yiddish Plays* (1966).—J. C. L.

Dyskolos (The Bad-Tempered Man, 316 B.C.). A comedy by MENANDER. Cnemon, an old man embittered by the materialism and selfishness of the world, lives with his daughter and servant on a small plot of land near Athens. His estranged wife and her son by her first marriage, Gorgias, farm the plot of land next door. One day a rich young man, Sostratus, sees Cnemon's daughter and falls in love with her. Enlisting the aid of Gorgias, Sostratus sets to work to persuade Cnemon to allow him to marry his daughter. This will be difficult because Cnemon is convinced of the wickedness and dishonesty of all men. First Sostratus tries digging in the fields, to show how honest and hard-working he is; but the labor proves too much for him. Then Cnemon falls down a well, and Sostratus helps Gorgias to rescue him. Cnemon is so impressed by this act of kindness that he undergoes a conversion and agrees, though unhappily, to let his daughter marry Sostratus. Sostratus then asks his own father to betroth *his* daughter to Gorgias. A double wedding is held, to which Cnemon is invited. At first he refuses, but at last he allows himself to be led off, garlanded and dancing, to the feast.

Dyskolos is an early play by Menander. The plot is weakly constructed, for the main action is completed too early, leaving the rest of the play to be filled out with a series of episodic scenes. Running through the play, however, is an undercurrent of serious reflection. What is the effect of wealth, and the desire for wealth, on human relationships? Cnemon is the prototype of the misanthrope. His dark view of the world is explained by his disillusionment with the greed and inhumanity of man in his pursuit of material goods. At these moments Menander's psychological insight appears particularly strong and modern.

Dyskolos can be found in *Menander—Plays* (1967), translated by Philip Vellacott.—K. C.

E

Ecclesiazusae (Ekklēsiazousai, "Women in Debate," 392 B.C.). A comedy by ARISTOPHANES. Disgusted by the mismanagement of public affairs in Athens, the women of the city pack the assembly one morning, disguised as men, and pass a decree giving full powers to themselves. Among the provisions of this decree is the abolishment of private property and the distribution of all goods according to need. "All goods" includes men, and the greatest need is among the oldest and ugliest women. The rest of the action follows up the implications of this new law and shows the struggles of a young lover to avoid being raped by three old hags. In the end the law is upheld, and the play ends with a citywide orgy.

Ecclesiazusae uses some of the motifs of previous plays about women (namely, *Lysistrata* and *Thesmophoriazusae*) but carries them to macabre lengths, as, for instance, in the repeated linking of marriage and death. The best writing of the play shows the attitude of the Athenian male to his money and his domestic power. The shift from the conventions of Old Comedy is already apparent. In two places the Chorus are given no lines, merely a note in the text indicating some kind of unspecified interlude.

Translations of the play are listed under Aristophanes.—K. C.

Ecole des femmes, L' (The School for Wives, 1662). A comedy by MOLIÈRE. Arnolphe, a French bourgeois who has just taken the name of Monsieur de la Souche, is bringing up a very young girl, Agnès, whom he cuts off from the world and wants to make his wife. Agnès, however, falls in love with the son of one of Arnolphe's friends, young Horace, whom she sees from her window. Horace keeps Arnolphe informed of his hourly progress with Monsieur de la Souche's prisoner. Although the precautions he takes turn against him, Arnolphe would finally have separated Horace and Agnès forever if Molière had not, by way of a romanesque ending, brought Agnès' father back from America so that he might unite the two young people.

Through the confusion created by Arnolphe's double identity, Molière enriched that traditional plot of farce and very simple comedy—a young man stealing a girl from an elderly man. Moreover, he involves the two main characters in an insoluble conflict because of the fixity of their natures—Arnolphe being tyrannical and possessive, Agnès being altogether instinctive, leading her to love another, who is far more suitable.

This play has been translated by Morris Bishop in *Eight Plays* (1957).—Ja. G.

ENGRAVING OF A SCENE FROM MOLIÈRE'S *L'École des femmes* (NEW YORK PUBLIC LIBRARY)

Edwardian drama. See ENGLAND: *nineteenth century and Edwardian.*

Egmont (pub. 1788). A tragedy by Johann Wolfgang von GOETHE. *Egmont* is based on the downfall of a historical Count Egmont (1522–1568) who was executed in connection with the Netherlandic revolt against Spain. Like Goethe's earlier *Götz von Ber-lichingen* in his play of the same name, Egmont is upright and straightforward in his striving for freedom but is unable to survive in an atmosphere of subtle political machinations. Though Goethe was already working on the play in 1776, in his *Sturm und Drang* period, he did not finish it until 1787, when his ideas had already taken a strong turn toward classicism. This change is reflected in the play's relative polish of form and language as compared with *Götz*. Beethoven wrote his famous *Egmont* music for Goethe's play.

Egypt. See ARAB DRAMA.

Electra (Elektra, 420?–?410 B.C.). A tragedy by SOPHOCLES. The scene is the palace of Agamemnon. Orestes, accompanied by his tutor (the old man who carried him off to safety when Agamemnon was killed), has returned to carry out Apollo's command and avenge his father. The tutor is to give a false report of Orestes' death in a chariot race at the Pythian games and so gain admission to the house; he will give Orestes the signal for action when the moment comes. As they go off to make offerings at Agamemnon's tomb, Electra enters and, at first in soliloquy and then in dialogue with the Chorus of young women, gives a vivid picture of her miserable life under the rule of her father's murderers. Her sister, Chrysothemis, enters carrying offerings for Agamemnon's tomb; she has been sent by Clytemnestra, who is terrified by a dream that foretells Orestes' return. The dialogue between the two sisters shows us the time-serving acquiescence of the one and the stubborn rebelliousness of the other. Electra, encouraged by the dream, persuades Chrysothemis to make offerings, not for Clytemnestra, but for Agamemnon's children. The next scene, a bitter quarrel between mother and daughter, explores the background of Clytemnestra's crime and exposes the irreconcilable hatred between the two women. As Clytemnestra prays (in cryptic terms) for Orestes' death and an end to her fears, the tutor enters and with his detailed account of Orestes' death seems to answer her prayers. Electra is left alone with the Chorus to mourn the loss of her last hope. Chrysothemis comes back with news of offerings on Agamemnon's tomb, which, she says, can only have been made by Orestes, but Electra convinces her that Orestes is dead. She now proposes that the two of them, unaided, attack Aegisthus; when Chrysothemis refuses, Electra decides to act alone. Orestes then enters with a funeral urn, which is supposed to contain his own ashes. Electra asks permission to make a funeral lament over it and does so in a speech of such desperate sorrow that Orestes realizes who she is. He reveals his own identity and the sorrow is replaced by joy. But the rejoicing of brother and sister is interrupted by the tutor, who comes to tell Orestes that now is the time: Clytemnestra is alone. We hear, offstage, Clytemnestra's appeals for mercy as Orestes kills her. In the final scene, Aegisthus is lured to his doom by the same false story of Orestes' death. He is presented with a corpse, which, when uncovered, turns out to be Clytemnestra, and is driven into the house to be killed.

Electra is, technically speaking, Sophocles' masterpiece. The simple device of delaying the recogni-

tion between brother and sister produces a series of brilliant scenes which display Electra's heroic resolution under constant attack. It remains firm even at the news of Orestes' death and rises to its climax when she makes her heroic resolve to act alone. But the problem of Sophocles' attitude to the matricide remains controversial. It is quite clear that he has deliberately emphasized the killing of Aegisthus and played down that of Clytemnestra (mother and son do not meet onstage), but there are hints in the text that Orestes, if not Electra, doubts the wisdom of Apollo's command to murder once that command is fulfilled. Yet these hints do not obscure the main dramatic effect—the triumph of Electra's inflexible will and the punishment of Agamemnon's murderers.

See I. M. Linforth, *Electra's Day in the Tragedy of Sophocles* (1963), and C. P. Segal, "The *Electra* of Sophocles," in *Transactions and Proceedings of the American Philological Association,* Vol. XCVII (1966), pp. 473–545.—. B. M. W. K.

Electra (Elektra, 413 B.C.). A tragedy by EURIPIDES. Agamemnon, king of Mycenae, returned in triumph from the Trojan War to his wife, Clytemnestra, only to be struck down by her lover, Aegisthus, with Clytemnestra's connivance. A servant spirited away Agamemnon's son, Orestes, and Clytemnestra herself later protected their daughter Electra when Aegisthus wanted to kill her. Aegisthus then married her to a farmer, expecting that she would have baseborn sons who would be no threat to his power. The farmer, however, has respected her virginity. At the beginning of the play Orestes, now grown to manhood, returns to Mycenae with his friend Pylades. The old servant who had rescued Orestes recognizes him by a scar, and brother and sister plot the deaths of their mother and her lover. Orestes kills Aegisthus while Electra lures their mother to her hut. Orestes then kills Clytemnestra, encouraged by Electra.

Aeschylus, Sophocles, and Euripides all wrote tragedies on Orestes' double murder of his mother and her lover. In Sophocles' *Electra,* Orestes' sister became the chief character and urged her brother on to the end, but she was conscious that her obsessive hatred of her mother had debased her. In Euripides' play Electra's degradation has gone so much further that she is no longer conscious of it. This (one can imagine Euripides saying) would be the real psychological state of a woman who loved her father deeply and has loathed her mother for years, almost as much for her adultery as for the murder. Euripides' Electra is self-centered and gets a perverse pleasure from exaggerating her poverty and misery, thus forcing a contrast between herself and Clytemnestra's luxurious life among the rich spoils that Agamemnon had brought home from Troy. His Electra is the driving spirit of the revenge. When Orestes hesitates, she drives his sword into her mother's breast. It is not a pretty picture, but even those critics who cannot stomach it admit that it is brilliantly drawn and entirely convincing.

Having thus given his realism full play in his chief character, Euripides adjusts the others to her portrayal. Clytemnestra is much more human than in Aeschylus' or Sophocles' plays. Orestes is no coward (though he is often thought to be), but he hates the thought of the matricide that he (and Apollo) consider his duty. He hesitates before Electra's violence and the joy she feels at the murder to come, but she will brook no delay.

Murder by stealth is not attractive, and Euripides makes both murders most unpleasant. Aegisthus is hacked down while engaged in sacrifice to the gods, and Electra entices her mother into her house by sending a message that she has had a child, thus trading on Clytemnestra's grandmotherly affection. The one ray of light in Electra's dark soul is her appreciation of her peasant husband, who is a quite delightful character. The Chorus side with Electra, but their odes, which are few, sing of the remote past and contribute little to the drama. Although *Electra* is often distasteful, it is an undoubted masterpiece.

Translations of the play are listed under Euripides. —G. M. A. G.

Electra (Elektra, written 1904). A one-act drama in verse by Hugo von HOFMANNSTHAL. *Electra* is freely based on Sophocles' play of the same name. Agamemnon has been murdered by his wife, Clytemnestra, and her paramour, Aegisthus. Electra, daughter of Clytemnestra and Agamemnon, is determined to avenge her father's death. Orestes, her brother, absent from the palace since childhood, returns, and Electra urges him to accomplish the deed for her. When Clytemnestra and Aegisthus are dead, Electra dances ecstatically in victory and collapses in death.

Hofmannsthal's contribution to the Greek myth was a negative one: to strip from it all social, ethical, and moralistic concerns, such as were indigenous to the myth in Greek times. The result is a new conception in terms of psychosexual symbolism. His Electra is not motivated to commit the murder for any reason other than her own psychosis. In this sense Hofmannsthal's play operates in a vacuum, and this may well be its strength. The play takes place in Electra's distorted, perverted, and morbid mind, with its terrible shadows and sudden bursts of bright light and blood-red splotches. In concentrating all his energies on her, Hofmannsthal has created a figure of such terrible passion and dominance that the role virtually defies performance.

Electra, in her single-minded and solely personal desire to avenge her father's murder, has divested herself of all semblance of humanity. She is in every respect an animal. She rejects Orestes' conventional claim that it is the gods demanding revenge of him; her life is one long, tortuous swing of the death-dealing ax. The murder is a ritual, to be sure, but one that takes its form and being from the pulsing of Electra's blood and her pathological desire to see more blood flow. Upon hearing her mother's scream from the palace, she lurches into a frantic but exalted and ecstatic dance of victory. In the midst of a high and triumphal stride, head thrown back, she falls to the ground in a death of self-immolation. Revenge born of her own blood was her only will to live. That accomplished, Electra dies fulfilled.

The play is also the libretto for the opera *Elektra,* composed by Richard Strauss.

The latest translation of this play is by Carl R. Mueller, in *Masterpieces of the Modern Central European Theater* (1967), edited by Robert Corrigan. One of the most perceptive of contemporary essays dealing solely with the play is by Robert Corrigan, "Character as Destiny in Hofmannsthal's *Electra,*" *Modern Drama,* Vol. IV (1960).—C. R. M.

Eliot, T [homas] S [tearns] (1888–1965). American-born English poet, critic, and playwright. Born in St. Louis, Eliot studied at Harvard, the Sorbonne, and Oxford, specializing in philosophy. After working for brief periods as a teacher and a bank employee, he became a full-time author and editor. His first volume of verse, *Prufrock and Other Observations,* appeared in 1917, and his first book of literary essays, *The Sacred Wood,* was published in 1920. His experimental poetry and his magisterial but more conservative literary criticism made him a considerable force in the literary world. After several years of regular residence in England, he became, in 1927, a British subject.

Eliot's interest in the drama was first reflected in his critical essays on the Elizabethan dramatists and other theatrical subjects. He applauded the formal, poetic drama of the Elizabethans and deplored the relative lack of form in the modern theater. His first effort to put his theory into practice came when he wrote two dramatic fragments in verse, *Fragment of a Prologue* (pub. 1926) and *Fragment of an Agon* (pub. 1927). In 1932 the two "fragments" reappeared as *Sweeney Agonistes: Fragments of an Aristophanic Melodrama.* The play is indeed fragmentary. In the first section two prostitutes receive some cheerful callers; in the second, they entertain Sweeney, who tells the story of a man who killed a girl.

The two jazz songs in the second fragment make *Sweeney Agonistes* a melodrama in the original sense of the word. This play's casual, elliptical comment on the lower reaches of the contemporary world recalled Eliot's long poem *The Waste Land* (1922). Promising as this experiment was, Eliot never wrote another play in the same vein.

In 1934 Eliot was commissioned to write for "the Forty-Five Churches Fund of the Diocese of London" the text of a religious pageant, *The Rock.* The scenario was worked out in advance of the poet's participation; the text dramatizes, in prose and verse, the difficulty of building churches from ancient times to the present. Eliot chose to preserve only the verse choruses from *The Rock* in *The Complete Poems and Plays* (1952). This didactic play was followed by a more significant contribution to religious drama, MURDER IN THE CATHEDRAL, written to be performed at the Canterbury Festival of 1935 and concerning the assassination in 1170 of Thomas Becket, archbishop of Canterbury. This most admired of all Eliot's dramatic works owes its verse form to the medieval morality play *Everyman* and its dramatic form to Greek tragedy, medieval morality plays, and church ritual. It is not merely a presentation of an historical event but an examination of it through a variety of perspectives.

Eliot moved closer to the mainstream of contemporary drama with *The Family Reunion* (1939), a verse play of contemporary life with parallels to the *Oresteia* of Aeschylus. Harry, the son of a rather depressing English middle-class family, is, like Aeschylus' Orestes, haunted by guilt, although it is never really clear whether or not he killed his wife. Uncovering the family's secrets has the effect of liberating

Harry, and he goes off to "follow the bright angels" and to do good in some undefined way. This family and its fate possess some curious interest; the play itself represents a first step away from the formalism that had been Eliot's distinguishing characteristic as a dramatist.

Eliot successfully entered the commercial theater with *The Cocktail Party,* a verse play, which was first performed at the Edinburgh Festival of 1949 and then, beginning in 1950, ran for a year on Broadway and for ten months in the West End. An unconventional psychoanalyst abruptly intrudes into the lives of a husband, his wife, and their lovers. The intruder restores the marriage, incidentally sending the husband's mistress as a nurse to Africa, where she is crucified by rebellious natives. In this play Eliot's language, although distinguished, barely sounded like poetry, and nonnaturalistic devices were limited to a formal libation in which three family friends join. The heart of the play's interest is the character of the unpredictable psychoanalyst, and so it was curious to discover, when Eliot revealed the classical model for this play to be Euripides' *Alcestis,* that the psychoanalyst was based on Heracles.

The verse of *The Confidential Clerk* (1953) was even more prosaic. This farcical comedy, about a financier's quest for the illegitimate son who is to be his heir, was based on Euripides' *Ion.* To Euripides' story of confused and mistaken identities, Eliot added a quest for a vocation that once more sends one of his characters off (as it did in *The Family Reunion* and *The Cocktail Party*) to seek a new destiny. In *The Elder Statesman* (1958) a former prime minister, confronted by the irresponsible deeds of his youth, comes to terms with himself. It has been called Eliot's *Oedipus at Colonus,* and certainly it is a suitable valedictory for the poet-dramatist.

In *Poetry and Drama* (1951) Eliot examined his own problems as a dramatist. The best general studies of Eliot are probably F. O. Matthiessen, *The Achievement of T. S. Eliot,* 3rd edition (1958), and Grover A. Smith, Jr., *T. S. Eliot's Poetry and Plays: A Study in Sources and Meaning* (1956). Two useful studies of Eliot's plays have appeared: D. E. Jones, *The Plays of T. S. Eliot* (1960), and Carol H. Smith, *T. S. Eliot's Dramatic Theory and Practice* (1963).—H. P.

Elizabethan drama. See ENGLAND: *Elizabethan drama.*

Emfindkamseit. See GERMANY: *eighteenth century.*

Emilia Galotti. See GERMANY: *eighteenth century;* Gotthold Ephraim LESSING.

Emperor Jones, The (1920). An expressionistic play by Eugene O'NEILL. The subject of this play, a Negro dictator's flight from his oppressed subjects, was suggested to O'Neill by Haitian history. Brutus Jones, self-styled emperor of a West Indian island and former Pullman porter and jail-breaker, learns of the imminent revolt of his subjects, who have realized at last that they have been victimized by him. His attempted escape is depicted as a succession of scenes of panic. In these vignettes, Jones, fleeing through the jungle, is plagued by recollected events from his private past, such as his slaying of a prison guard, his meager knowledge of racial history, and his superstitious fears and savage rituals. Impacted into this drama of a frustrated escape and the influ-

ence of atavism was a powerful sense of theatricality that expressed itself most effectively in the incessant beat of tom-toms while the rebellious natives made magic and cast a silver bullet with which to destroy him, since he had fostered the belief that no other sort of bullet could harm him. O'Neill, having read accounts of Congo ritual, was impressed by the suggestive power of relentlessly repeated rhythms of the drum, "how it starts at a normal pulse and is slowly intensified until the heartbeats of everyone present correspond to the frenzied beat of the drum." The prostrate Jones is found in the morning by the natives, who shoot him with the silver bullet; it is not apparent to them, however, that he has already died of fright. See EXPRESSIONISM.—J. G.

Endgame (Fin de Partie, 1957). A play by Samuel BECKETT. The first production of *Endgame,* Beckett's second play, was directed by Roger Blin at the Studio des Champs-Élysées in May 1957. The title of the play is a term used in chess to designate the third and final part of the game. It was perhaps chosen to designate the end of many things, the end of life itself.

Two of the characters, Nagg and Nell, live in ash cans, the covers of which they raise from time to time in order to speak. But most of the dialogue is carried on between their son Hamm, who is paralytic, blind, and confined to a wheelchair, and his male attendant, Clov. All movement has slowed down. Hamm is immobilized, and Clov walks with difficulty. Nagg and Nell do not have legs, and they occupy little space in their ash cans. No affection joins the four characters. Nagg and Nell depend on Hamm for food. Clov, the son-slave, would kill Hamm if he knew the combination of the lock to the buffet where the last crackers are stored.

Each has the remains of a kind of dream or aspiration that he tries vainly to communicate to the others. This is the game that man plays and in which he is always checkmated. The drama is the lack of meaning that life provides. In the dialogue between Hamm and Clov there is an inverted kind of desperate intellectualism, as there is in the dialogue between the two tramps in Beckett's *En Attendant Godot* (*Waiting for Godot,* 1953).

Endgame (1958) has been translated by Beckett himself.—W. F.

England: *middle ages.* The various kinds of English medieval drama may be conveniently classified in terms of religious or secular subject matter. The class of religious medieval drama includes liturgical drama, scriptural drama, saint's drama, and the morality play. The class of secular medieval drama includes the moral interlude, the farce, minstrelsy, folk drama, and romance drama. Within the two major classes there is, of course, occasional overlapping of one particular category upon another, as in the case of scriptural drama and saint's drama or of the morality play and the moral interlude; some of the categories, such as minstrelsy, folk drama, and romance drama, can be illustrated from surviving texts only sparsely or not at all; and other of the categories, such as liturgical drama and the farce, are represented hardly at all by surviving examples from England. In addition, some of the categories, such as the moral interlude and romance drama, being represented chiefly by sixteenth-century texts, belong perhaps rather to the Renaissance than to the middle ages. In any case, religious drama is both the more important and the better represented of the two major classes of medieval drama. Moreover, the various kinds of religious medieval drama (with the exception of liturgical drama) are well illustrated by surviving examples from England.

Liturgical drama differed from other kinds of medieval drama in two significant respects. First, it was devotional—that is, liturgical drama was usually performed, as the name suggests, in connection with a church service. Thus it was usually performed within a church (hence indoors, in a highly particularized architectural situation), by clerics (hence by nonprofessional actors), and on the day of the liturgical year which commemorated the event dramatized —the Nativity, for example, would be performed on Christmas day, the Slaughter of the Innocents on Childermas (December 28), the Resurrection on Easter Sunday, and so on. Second, liturgical drama was a musical drama—the lines were sung or chanted to the accompaniment of various musical instruments; and enough of the music has survived to permit modern performances with singing and music more or less in the style of original production. Finally, unlike other types of medieval drama, liturgical drama was usually performed in Latin. The last, however, is not an essential characteristic, for isolated liturgical plays contain some vernacular speeches, and a fully vernacular play performed on the day of the year that commemorates the scriptural event dramatized is no less a liturgical play than one written in Latin and so performed. The example cited by Kolve (who makes this useful point) is the early fifteenth-century English play *Christ's Burial and Resurrection.* This is in two parts, of which the first part, dealing with the Burial, was to be performed on the afternoon of Good Friday, and the second, dealing with the Resurrection, on the morning of Easter Sunday.

Most of the liturgical drama (to judge from surviving examples) was concerned with events of Scripture —but with an emphasis altogether different from that of the vernacular scriptural drama. We have very few liturgical plays based on Old Testament narratives: extant examples include only two plays on Daniel, one on Joseph and his Brethren, one on Jacob and Esau. Thus the liturgical drama seems not to have treated a number of subjects that crop up in all of the four extant English scriptural cycles: Cain and Abel, Noah and the Flood, Abraham and Isaac, Moses (both the Ten Commandments and Exodus). No extant liturgical play treats the Creation, the Fall of Lucifer, or the Creation and Fall of Man (although there is record of a lost example that treated all three subjects). Narratives of the Nativity are well represented among extant liturgical plays. There are several plays of the Prophets, the Adoration of the Shepherds, the Adoration of the Magi, and the Slaughter of the Innocents; and some other events of the Nativity story are represented each by a single example: the Annunciation, the Presentation of the Virgin, and the Purification of the Virgin. There is no treatment of Christ and the Doctors or other Infancy narratives. Only one event of the public ministry is dramatized: the Raising of Lazarus (two examples). No event of the Passion is treated, probably because the Mass itself commemorates the Passion. Narratives of the Resurrection are represented by plays on two topics: the Marys at the Sepulcher (the famous *Quem queritis,* of which some 400 examples survive), and the Pilgrims to Emmaus (of which a few examples are extant). There is one play on the Ascension, none on the Descent of the Holy Spirit (Pentecost). Narratives of the Last Judgment are represented by two plays, one on the Wise and Foolish Virgins, the other on the Coming of Antichrist. However, no extant liturgical play treats the Last Judgment itself. Some of the most interesting liturgical plays are the Beauvais *Play of Daniel,* the Avignon *Presentation of the Virgin in the Temple,* the Benediktbeuern Christmas Play and Passion Play, and the Tegernsee *Antichrist* (though this is not, strictly speaking, a liturgical play).

A few liturgical plays are concerned with events in the lives of the saints. Extant examples include one on the Conversion of St. Paul (sometimes classified as a scriptural subject) and a number on the legends of St. Nicholas—the Three Daughters, the Three Clerks, the Image of St. Nicholas, and the Son of Getron. Presumably these are indeed liturgical plays in the sense of having been written for performance on the particular saint's day in question—but if so it is difficult to understand why no more than two saints are represented among the nine surviving plays, eight of which deal with a single saint (St. Nicholas).

Occasionally two or more liturgical plays were combined to produce a sequence of plays. Thus the thirteenth-century Benediktbeuern Christmas Play is a Nativity sequence, including plays of the Prophets, the Annunciation, the Adoration of the Shepherds, the Adoration of the Magi, the Slaughter of the Innocents, and the Flight into Egypt. The creation of such sequences of liturgical plays should not, however, be thought of as part of a development according to which liturgical plays gradually evolved into such cycles as the English Corpus Christi plays, for Hardison has recently demonstrated, through analysis of the twelfth-century Anglo-Norman *Mystère d'Adam* and *Sainte Resurrection,* the existence of a vernacular theatrical tradition in England that reached a complex level of development a century before the Latin drama of the Church.

Scriptural drama and saint's drama have long posed a problem in terminology for the student of English medieval drama. In France a scriptural play originally was (and still is) called a *mystère,* the word deriving from Latin *mysterium* (Greek *musterion,* "mystery"), that is, an event regarded as having mystical significance; and a saint's play was (and is) called a *miracle.* In imitation of this convenient terminology numerous writers in English (including, for example, Craig, Salter, and Prosser) use the terms *mystery play* and *miracle play* to designate, respectively, the scriptural play and the saint's play. However, the English word *mystery* in the term *mystery play* is sometimes confused with the different word of the same spelling which derives from Latin *misterium* (a variant of *ministerium,* "ministry"), in the sense of occupation or craft—since in England scriptural plays were commonly acted by crafts or guilds. Moreover, the term *mystery play* seems not to have been used in English before the eighteenth century. In England during the middle ages and the Renaissance both scriptural plays and saint's plays were referred to indiscriminately as *miracles,* and some modern writers (including, for example, Chambers, Wickham, and Cawley) prefer this use of the term. Consequently one never knows at first glance whether the modern term *miracle play* designates both scriptural drama and saint's drama or only the latter; and many readers mistakenly suppose that the term *mystery play* means "a play performed by a craft or gild." Since the term *miracle play* is hopelessly ambiguous, since writers who prefer the one sense of that term are unwilling to yield to writers who prefer the other, and since the term *mystery play* is also open to misunderstanding, it seems desirable (following the lead of such recent writers as Williams, Hardison, and Kolve) to avoid the terms altogether and to designate the two kinds of drama in question by the unambiguous terms *scriptural drama* and *saint's drama.*

Scriptural drama may be defined as vernacular drama dealing with the Patriarchs, the Prophets, and the life of Christ. The sources are the Old and New Testaments, the Apocrypha of both, and the liturgy of the Church. In England a few individual scriptural plays have survived from towns such as Norwich and Newcastle, but it seems clear that most of the scriptural drama was organized into historical (or "cosmic") cycles telling the story of mankind from the Creation of the World to Doomsday, with emphasis on such Old Testament figures as had predicted the Coming of Christ or might be interpreted typologically as symbolizing Christ; on the Nativity, Passion, and Resurrection of Christ; and on the Last Judgment. Such cycles were usually called Corpus Christi plays because of original performance in connection with the Feast of Corpus Christi (falling between May 23rd and June 24th). Some of the cycles took three, four, and five or more days to perform. Four full-length English cycles have survived: the CHESTER PLAYS, YORK PLAYS, WAKEFIELD PLAYS, and a traveling cycle usually called the N-TOWN PLAYS, which may incorporate parts of the cycle known to have been performed at Lincoln. Two plays on the Nativity sequence from the Coventry Cycle (late fourteenth century) are extant, as is also a full-length cycle in Cornish entitled the *Ordinalia* (fourteenth century). This is in three parts, for performance on three consecutive days: the Origin of the World, the Passion of our Lord, and the Resurrection of our Lord. Like the French scriptural cycles, the *Ordinalia* omits the story of the Nativity. It includes, however, as the four English cycles do not, the story of David and Bathsheba and the legend of the Holy Rood. In addition to the cities already mentioned, records indicate the existence of lost cycles at London, Newcastle-upon-Tyne, Beverley, Norwich, Worcester, Ipswich, Canterbury, and elsewhere in England. The Corpus Christi plays continued to be performed until the last quarter of the sixteenth century, although in the face of ever-increasing opposition from a hostile Protestant government; and by about 1580 all of the great scriptural cycles had been suppressed.

Saint's drama may be defined as vernacular drama dealing with a miracle or with a saint's life, the events of which are not directly connected with the life of Christ. Thus *The Conversion of St. Paul* (c. 1500) is usually considered an example of saint's drama rather than of scriptural drama. A frequent characteristic of saint's drama is the use of legendary material with a strong romantic coloration—readily available in the narrative lives of saints that served as sources. Thus in the Digby *Mary Magdalen* (c. 1500), Mary converts the King and Queen of Marseilles to Christianity, the three go to sea in a ship that is wheeled about the Place, the Queen gives birth to a child on shipboard, mother and child die and are set ashore on an island, Mary and the King land on a rock (obviously the Church), the ship returns for Mary and the King, they return to the island, and Mary performs a miracle in bringing the Queen and her baby back to life. This play also represents Mary's fall from virtue in a tavern scene notable for its realism and satire. Other saint's plays deal with medieval saints or miracles. The Croxton *Play of the Sacrament* (late fifteenth century) is an unusual and powerful English example, *The Life of St. Meriasek* (1504) a most entertaining Cornish one designed for performance during two days.

The morality play may be defined in a very general sense as a kind of drama that is didactic and concerned with proper and improper conduct. Usually the subject is fully generalized, in which case the allegorical mode is employed, the protagonist being a symbolic character (Everyman, Youth, Wit, Banquet). Sometimes, however, the subject is only partly or not at all generalized, in which case the allegorical mode is not employed, the characters being either representative examples of particular social classes (Merchant and Peasant, Windmiller and Gentlewoman) or particular fictional personages whose story serves as an exemplum (Lucrece, Melebea). Thus Mackenzie's definition of the morality play as a kind of drama that employs allegory (despite—or perhaps because of—its admirable clarity) is less than satisfactory. The more inclusive definition proposed at the beginning of this paragraph can be refined by classification on the basis of religious or secular subject matter. Thus it is convenient to use the term *morality play* in a narrower sense to designate plays such as *Everyman* and *The Castle of Perseverance* which deal with conduct in relation to a question of religious doctrine (the question chiefly treated in extant English examples being salvation or damnation), and the term *moral interlude* to designate plays such as *Youth, Wit and Science,* and *La Condamnation de Banquet* by Nicolas de la Chesnaye (printed at Paris in 1507), all of which deal with conduct in relation to a question of secular doctrine. The suggested usage, although arbitrary, approximates that of most modern writers on the English drama. (The fifteenth- and sixteenth-century terms *morality, moral play,* and *interlude* seem to have been used indiscriminately of both kinds of drama.) The term *interlude* or *interludium* as used in the middle ages and the Renaissance apparently had no more restricted a meaning than "a short play," whether religious or secular, allegorical or nonallegorical, serious or comic. Presumably the term bore this meaning because an interlude consisted of mimetic action involving two or more characters—that is, *play* or *game between* or *among* two or more actors. There is little evidence to suggest that the term *interlude* designated a *play* performed *between* the courses of a meal or *between* the parts of a longer play.

In a more restricted sense, then, the morality play may be defined as a kind of drama that is didactic and concerned with proper and improper conduct in relation to a question of religious doctrine. Usually the protagonist is symbolic of man (Mankind, Everyman, Humanity) and is acted upon alternately by the forces of good and evil in the persons of allegorical characters (Wrath and Patience, Reason and Sensuality, Chastity and Lechery), the issue in most cases being whether Mankind is to be saved or damned when he comes to the end of his life.

The morality play sometimes presents the ages of man in a life cycle. In *The Castle of Perseverance* (c. 1425), a play of over 3,500 lines, the action begins with the birth of Humanum Genus or Mankind, proceeds through his youth and maturity, and ends with his death, which, since he dies without receiving extreme unction, is followed by a debate among the four daughters of God (Mercy, Peace, Truth, and Righteousness) on the nature of contrition and the question of Mankind's salvation or damnation. Here Mankind is saved, as was usual in morality plays written before the influence of Calvinism (compare Marlowe's *Doctor Faustus*).

The use of personifications in writing about spiritual or psychological states was elementary to medieval thought: the battle in *The Castle* in which the Virtues conquer the Vices by pelting them with red roses (emblematic of Christ's passion) is in a long tradition going back to the fifth-century *Psychomachia* of Prudentius. In this respect the morality play can be regarded as a dramatized sermon, for the patterned bellicosity of the characters struggling over Mankind was well suited to express the ebb and flow of sin, remorse, repentance, penance, and the attainment of grace; and the expression is effected through the same allegorical technique as a preacher might use in addressing a congregation.

Despite a good deal of humor and horseplay by vicious characters such as Backbiter and Covetousness, the overarching tone of *The Castle of Perseverance* is serious if not tragical: at the humble level of the life of ordinary man (conceived of in the allegorical mode) the author succeeds in reproducing something of the grand and serious pattern of the Corpus Christi play in dealing with the life of that greater man Christ.

EVERYMAN is a short play (about 900 lines) dealing only with the moment of death. It is as though the career of Mankind in a long life-cycle play such as *The Castle of Perseverance* had been divided into parts or "ages" and one of them developed into a dramatic statement on the Coming of Death or the Art of Holy Dying (*Ars moriendi*). This statement is expressed in terms borrowed from the late-medieval Dance of Death (Death the great leveller, Man's strength and riches of no avail) and combined with the Faithful Friend story as illustrated in the legend of Barlaam and Josaphat. The theme is salvation or damnation, expressed through the opposition of such characters as Good Deeds and Confession on the one hand, Good Fellowship and Goods on the other; and the action is worked out through the various symbols of a summoning to the session of a law court, a pilgrimage on which companionship is needed, and

FIRST PAGE OF THE MORALITY PLAY *Everyman*,
c. 1500 (NEW YORK PUBLIC LIBRARY)

finally (the symbol turning into the thing symbolized) a descent into the grave. Almost entirely serious in tone, *Everyman* is a tragical play if not technically a tragedy; and it has the power of pleasing modern audiences to whom the author's theological assumptions are quite foreign. It is probably a translation of the Dutch play *Elckerlijc*, although it is possible that the indebtedness lies in the other direction. The fragmentary *Pride of Life* (c. 1400) is another morality play dealing with the Coming of Death.

As *Everyman* treats one element of the life cycle of man, so *Mankind* (c. 1466) may be thought of as treating another element of that cycle, Despair in Maturity. In this play of some 900 lines (perhaps abridged from a longer and fuller version) the form of the morality play has been corrupted by the author's catering to the tastes of an extremely lowbrow audience—presumably a crowd of peasants gathered about a booth stage near an inn. Scatology and slapstick have run away with most of the doctrine. There is only one Virtue (Mercy), and he only just succeeds in carrying the day; and the Vices (Mischief, Nought, Nowadays, Newguise, and the comic devil Titivillus) lack the force of characters based on the Seven Deadly Sins as in *The Castle of Perseverance*. In some respects *Mankind,* despite its treatment of despair and the protagonist's temptation to commit suicide, is not so much an allegory treating of man's relationship to death as an exemplum in which a hard-pressed peasant is bedeviled by a group of practical jokers. In accordance with these altered emphases, the play does not end in death.

The moral interlude, in accordance with a distinction made above, may be defined as a kind of drama that is didactic and concerned with proper and improper conduct in relation to a question of secular doctrine. Usually the protagonist is symbolic of man (Youth) or an allegory of some aspect of man's conduct (Wit, that is, man's capacity to learn) or a particular fictional character whose story is an exemplum (Lucrece), and usually the protagonist is acted upon alternately by the forces of virtue and vice in the persons either of allegorical characters (Pride and Humility, Honest Recreation and Idleness) or of particular fictional characters (Lucrece's suitors Gaius Flaminius and Publius Cornelius), the issue being whether the protagonist is to persist in (or to embrace) vicious conduct or to prefer the corresponding virtuous conduct. A majority of the extant examples of the moral interlude in English are concerned with the temptations and sins of a young man. In this respect the moral interlude, in general, duplicates the situation of the *adulescens* in the comedies of Plautus and Terence.

In the moral interludes concerned with youth, it is again as though one element of the life cycle of a long morality play, such as *The Castle of Perseverance,* has been separated from the cycle and developed independently. The subject is usually treated in the allegorical mode. In *Youth,* for example, the protagonist is influenced first by Riot (that is, dissipation), Pride, and Lechery, then by Charity and Humility. As with Mankind before him, Youth repents in the denouement, the chief departure from the older tradition being that, instead of (like Mankind) dying and achieving salvation, Youth rejects a life of dissipation and accepts the responsibility of virtuous conduct, thus demonstrating that he has reached maturity. The pattern is typical, being repeated with variations in such plays as Henry Medwall's *Nature, The World and the Child, Hickscorner, Nice Wanton, Lusty Juventus,* and others. Most of these plays and those mentioned in the following paragraph were written during the first half of the sixteenth century.

Other moral interludes deal not with Man (Youth) but with some aspect of Man's conduct. Examples are John Rastell's *Four Elements* (the kind of learning one should acquire), *Gentleness and Nobility* (the nature of true nobility); John Redford's *Wit and Science* (the learning process itself—but imaged in an allegory of Youth); *La Condamnation de Banquet* (proper diet—and of course the opposite); John Heywood's *The Weather* (a proper attitude toward the same); John Skelton's *Magnificence* (proper and improper conduct in a ruler); and Part 2 of Sir David Lindsay's *Satire of the Three Estates* (political controversy). John Bale's *King John* may be regarded as in this tradition. Still other moral interludes deal not with abstractions or types but with particular fictional characters. Extant examples, apparently in imitation of plays dealing with the temptations besetting a young man, deal with the temptations besetting what might be called Everygirl: Medwall's *Fulgens and Lucrece* (the qualities to prefer or reject in

choosing a husband) and *Calisto and Melebea* (proper behavior for a girl whose suitor attempts to seduce her). Lewis Wager's *Mary Magdalen* may be regarded as in this tradition. Probably the best of the moral interludes is Redford's *Wit and Science* (c. 1539), which in the excellence of its allegorical technique may be compared with *Everyman,* and one of the most significant is Medwall's *Fulgens and Lucrece* (before 1516), which in its double action and treatment of the wooing situation anticipates the method of Shakespeare's romantic comedies.

Another kind of secular medieval drama, the farce, may be regarded as a dramatic tradition deriving from the narrative tradition of the French *fabliau.* Many French farces of the fifteenth century are extant, and one of these, *Pernet qui va au vin,* was translated into English by John Heywood early in the sixteenth century as *John John the Husband, Tib his Wife, and Sir John the Priest.* This is a good example of the type: the wife humiliates her peasant husband while engaged in amorous dalliance with her lover the priest. Other of Heywood's plays in the farce tradition are *The Four P's* and *The Pardoner and the Friar;* these, written by a staunch Catholic on the eve of the Reformation in England, are concerned mainly with anticlerical satire. That the farce tradition was alive in England as early as about 1300 is

ENGLISH STREET THEATER

demonstrated by the existence of a fragmentary play in English entitled *Interludium de Clerico et Puella.* This, based on the *fabliau* of *Dame Siriz,* deals with a clerk's unsuccessful attempt to seduce a girl and his consequent appeal to an older woman for aid as a go-between; presumably in the lost ending he attains his goal.

Other kinds of secular medieval drama may be dealt with briefly. On minstrelsy, critics are divided, some affirming and some denying that the *histriones* and *mimi* of the late Roman empire passed on to their medieval descendants (*jongleurs, trouvères, minstrels*) dramatic traditions as well as traditions of nondramatic entertainment such as storytelling, singing, dancing, tumbling, and juggling. The question is complicated by the absence of texts and the ambiguity of records. However, it seems reasonable to suppose that something of the acting technique of late classical farce (if not something of the drama itself) was kept alive during the middle ages and contributed to the development of vernacular drama in about the twelfth century and later.

About folk drama we know much more, although this too, despite the existence of texts (mostly of late date and of course derived from oral tradition), is a controversial subject. Among the various types of folk drama are the Sword Play, the Mummers' Play, the St. George Play, and the Robin Hood Play. It seems likely that these plays reflect pre-Christian rituals of death and rebirth connected with the seasons of the year. The Feast of Fools and the holiday reign of the Boy Bishop show that traditions of folk drama were carried into the Church itself. The Marston Mummers' Play was still being performed annually (on Boxing Day) in the 1960's.

Of medieval romance drama no examples survive from England. Records indicate, however, that a play called *Eglemour and Degrebelle* was performed at St. Albans in 1444, and another on the subject of "a knight cleped Florence" at Bermondsey in the same year. A play of *King Robert of Sicily* was given at Lincoln about 1450, but this is called a saint's play by some writers. Romance drama became extremely popular in England during the second half of the sixteenth century; a good example is the anonymous *Clyomon and Clamydes,* dating from the 1570's.

A final word may be said about the production of medieval English drama. There were two methods of indoor production. One, in a church, accommodated liturgical drama; the other, in a hall, the moral interlude, a morality play such as *Everyman,* and perhaps romance drama. Of outdoor production there were three methods. The first, involving a circular *platea* or Place surrounded by "scaffolds," was used for Corpus Christi cycles performed in the open country, such as the N-Town Plays and the Cornish *Ordinalia,* saint's plays such as the Digby *Mary Magdalen* and *The Life of St. Meriasek,* and morality plays such as *The Castle of Perseverance* and *A Satire of the Three Estates.* The manuscript of *The Castle* (the famous Macro Manuscript, now in the Folger Library) preserves a most informative plan of a Place with its surrounding scaffolds and water-filled ditch; this plan, together with the Place-and-scaffold method of staging, has been studied exhaustively by Southern. The second method of production, involving successive performances of cycle plays on pageant wagons moving from stop to stop about a city, was used for the Chester, York, and Wakefield plays. The third, involving a booth stage set up in a market place or on a village green, was used for a morality play such as *Mankind,* a farce such as *John John, Tib, and Sir John,* and perhaps for some of the moral interludes.

Useful reference works on medieval drama include the *Catholic Encyclopedia* and Carl J. Stratman, *Bibliography of Medieval Drama* (1954). Texts of the plays themselves include *The Ancient Cornish Drama* (2 vols., 1859), which contains the Cornish *Ordinalia,* translated by Edwin Norris; *Chief Pre-Shakespearean Dramas* (1924), J. Q. Adams, editor; *The Digby Plays,* F. J. Furnivall, editor, Early English Text Society (ext. ser., no. 70, 1896); *Everyman* (1961), A. C. Cawley, editor; *The Life of St. Meriasek* (1872), Whitley Stokes, editor; Sir David Lindsay, *A Satire of the Three Estates,* F. Hall, editor, Early English Text Society (no. 37, 1869); *The Macro Plays,* F. J. Furnivall and A. W. Pollard, editors, Early English Text Society (ext. ser., no. 91, 1904); *Le Mystère d'Adam* (1925), Henri Chamard, editor; *The Non-Cycle Mystery Plays,* Osborn Waterhouse, editor, Early English Text Society (ext. ser., no. 104, 1909); John Skelton, *Magnificence,* R. L. Ramsey, editor, Early English Text Society, (ext. ser., no. 98, 1908); *Two Coventry Corpus Christi Plays,* Hardin Craig, editor, Early English Text Society (ext. ser., no. 87, 1902, 2nd ed., 1957); *A Fourteenth-Century Prompt Book* [the Avignon *Presentation of the Virgin*] (1958), translated by A. B. Weiner; Karl Young, *The Drama of the Medieval Church* (2 vols., 1933). General studies of drama in the middle ages include E. K. Chambers, *The Mediaeval Stage* (2 vols., 1903); Hardin Craig, *English Religious Drama of the Middle Ages* (1955); Grace Frank, *The Medieval French Drama* (1954); A. P. Rossiter, *English Drama from Early Times to the Elizabethans* (1950); F. M. Salter, *Mediaeval Drama in Chester* (1955); Arnold Williams, *The Drama of Medieval England* (1961). Studies in the liturgical drama include R. B. Donovan, *The Liturgical Drama in Medieval Spain* (1958); O. B. Hardison, *Christian Rite and Christian Drama in the Middle Ages* (1965); W. L. Smoldon, "Liturgical Drama," in *Early Medieval Music Up to 1300* (1954), Dom Anselm Hughes, editor; Karl Young, *The Drama of the Medieval Church* (2 vols., 1933). The reader interested in scriptural drama (Corpus Christi cycles) should consult H. C. Gardiner, *Mysteries' End* (1946); V. A. Kolve, *The Play Called Corpus Christi* (1966); Robert Longsworth, *The Cornish Ordinalia* (1967); Eleanor Prosser, *Drama and Religion in the English Mystery Plays* (1961). The morality play is studied in W. R. Mackenzie, *The English Moralities from the Point of View of Allegory* (1914). The moral interlude is examined in David M. Bevington, *From Mankind to Marlowe* (1962); C. F. Tucker Brooke, *The Tudor Drama* (1911); T. W. Craik, *The Tudor Interlude* (1958); Mackenzie, *op. cit.* Those interested in the farce should consult Ian Maxwell, *French Farces and John Heywood* (1946). Minstrelsy is discussed in Chambers, *op. cit.;* Allardyce Nicoll, *Masques, Mimes, and Miracles* (1931). Folk drama is discussed in E. K. Chambers, *The English Folk Play* (1933); R. J. E. Tiddy, *The Mummers' Play* (1923). Useful works on the staging of medieval plays are Craik, *op. cit.;* Richard Southern, *The Medieval Theatre in the Round* (1957); Glynne Wickham, *Early English Stages 1300–1642,* vol. I, 1300–1576 (1959).—R. H.

Tudor drama. Performances of the comedies of Plautus and Terence, as well as of imitations in both Latin and the vernacular, came into fashion in Italy during the first few decades of the sixteenth century. By the fourth decade, English scholars and teachers were drawn to the same enterprise; and since the plays were written for academic performance, they became known as "school plays." Some of these are as slight but lively as *Thersites* (1537), a sort of burlesque about the antics of a cowardly boaster, employing classical names or designations for the characters. This little piece, for example, was based on an imitation of *Miles Gloriosus* ("The Braggart Soldier") of Plautus written in Latin by the French Humanist Jean Textier, or J. Ravisius Textor as he learnedly called himself, who became rector of the University of Paris in 1520.

Two classic imitations in English rose well above the level of academic exercises. They are *Ralph Roister Doister,* written between 1550 and 1553 by the schoolmaster Nicholas Udall (1505–1556), and *Gammer Gurton's Needle,* written between 1552 and 1563 by a "Mr. S., Master of Arts," probably William Stevenson, a fellow of Christ's College at Cambridge, where the play would have been first performed. (Stevenson, ordained a deacon in London in 1552, died in 1575.)

RALPH ROISTER DOISTER is the first fully developed adaptation that is fundamentally English in spite of its dependence upon classic character types and despite its "regularity"—that is, its five-act structure, unified dramatic action, and single setting. Even Ralph Roister Doister, the impudent braggart-soldier type introduced into the Western theater by Roman comedy, is an English character, as is Ralph's hanger-on, Merrygreek, another Roman character type, the parasite who carries on the intrigue of the plot. Englishmen could recognize him as a close relative of the old mischief-making Vice of the morality plays. The familiar courtesan of Greek and Latin comedy is displaced in *Ralph Roister Doister* by a virtuous widow, and she is wooed by a worthy English merchant, who takes the precaution of assuring himself that she is an innocent party after she has been maligned. These characters represent the middle class upon which depended the prosperity and power of Elizabethan England.

GAMMER GURTON'S NEEDLE is an even livelier

SCENE FROM THE TUDOR PLAY *Gammer Gurton's Needle* (THEATRE COLLECTION, NEW YORK PUBLIC LIBRARY AT LINCOLN CENTER)

farce and even closer to the folk spirit of Elizabethan country life. It is a distinctly folksy play with its village setting, its rustic manners, and its flavorsome dialogue in rhymed verse. It has a homespun, distinctly "unrefined" yet essentially wholesome plot. Its author may have been a "Master of Arts," but he did not incur any great obligation to his classic models except in the regular five-act organization and unity of his action. If Diccon, the prankster of the play, can find some ancestors in the intriguing slaves of Roman comedy, he is nevertheless an authentic English country figure. Diccon is the "Bedlam" (a former inmate of Bethlehem Hospital) released as a harmless lunatic and licensed to wander about the countryside as a beggar. He sets Gammer Gurton at odds with her neighbor Dame Chat over the alleged theft of a needle and is not above stealing a ham in the midst of the confusion he has produced. A parish curate and a village bailiff, a pair of scolding women, and a heavy-witted bumpkin of a servant round out a country scene that Ben Jonson himself might have enjoyed creating. The extravagant action is as good a peg as any on which to hang exhibitions of human folly.

Both plays, written in somewhat cumbersome verse, are noteworthy for the authors' competence in plot construction and have been favorably contrasted with the inchoate form of most of the still medieval morality plays and interludes. The classic example of plot complication and denouement and the classic act structure plainly advanced the development of Elizabethan comedy. Another, but related, influence came to England from Italy. The queen had been on the throne of England barely eight years when George Gascoigne, then a law student at Gray's Inn, translated the poet Ariosto's comedy *I Suppositi*, loosely based on Roman comedy with its resort to confusions of plot caused by mistaken identities but set in sixteenth-century Italy. *The Supposes* (meaning "the substitutes"), first produced in 1566, won much favor in the early Elizabethan period and set a useful example in the genre of prose comedy subsequently practiced by John Lyly and Robert Greene.

Tudor tragedy reflects the literary efforts of the law students of the Inns of Court in London and their interest in history and politics. Tragedy during the Renaissance was, in fact, more or less identified with history, and history with political ambitions and struggles for power. *Gorboduc* (1561), the most famous of the Inns of Court plays, is characteristically a tragedy of considerable historical range and conveys appropriate lessons of a moral and political nature.

In GORBODUC, the five-act dramatic form, the choruses, and the reports of offstage action by a *nuntius*, or messenger, as well as the general theme of revenge, are Senecan features. To these were added allegorical pantomime or "dumb shows" derived from Italian pageants known as *intermedii;* and a general influence from Italian Renaissance tragedy, itself patterned after Seneca's works, is to be found in the play. It was written by authors who were naturally responsive to classical and Renaissance example: Thomas Sackville (1536–1608), a barrister of the Inner Temple, later the earl of Dorset and lord high treasurer of England, and Thomas Norton (1532–1584), who became a distinguished lawyer.

Sackville was a poet of some distinction and contributed the best poems, *Induction* and *The Complaint of Buckingham,* to the 1563 edition of *A Mirror for Magistrates,* a collection of narrative poems dealing with the tragedies of famous persons, first licensed for publication in 1559. It was no doubt Sackville's facility in verse writing that accounted for the most important feature of *Gorboduc*—the substitution of blank verse for rhymed verse in the English drama. Blank verse, consisting of unrhymed iambic pentameter (introduced into English versification by the earl of Surrey's translation of Books II and IV of Vergil's epic poem the *Aeneid*), displaced the doggerel of the native drama and provided a suitably sonorous yet also "natural" medium for the writing of tragedy. Within a quarter of a century, it became the standard form of versification for plays and developed into the great poetic medium of Christopher Marlowe and Shakespeare.

Gorboduc proved so successful at its première in the Hall of the Inner Temple, where both authors were students, that it was repeated before Queen Elizabeth as a command performance. It set the fashion for subsequent Senecan tragedies. No less than five young law students of the Inner Temple collaborated on another Senecan tragedy, *Gismonde of Salerne,* which was presented before the queen in 1566. Although romantic in substance—it dealt with a love story first related by Boccaccio—it had all the formal Senecan features, including a moralizing chorus. Originally written in rhymed couplets, it was rewritten in blank verse many years later by one of the authors, Robert Wilmot, in 1591, and published under a new title, *Tancred and Gismunda.* Another Senecan tragedy, *The Misfortunes of Arthur,* was written by Thomas Hughes and other law students of Gray's Inn in London as late as 1588 and performed for the queen with DUMB SHOWS conceived by the young Francis Bacon among others. King Arthur was the protagonist, but his story had none of the idealization of knighthood associated with that celebrated name in romance; the Arthur of this play commits incest with his sister and is killed by their illegitimate son, Mordred, who not only rebels against Arthur but seduces the latter's queen, Guinevere. A ghost calling for vengeance, a messenger reporting unseen action, a chorus, several confidants, sententious passages, and indeed direct quotations from Seneca's tragedies make this play one of the most Senecan to be written in the period. It marks the culmination and end of this type of pseudoclassic drama, which was already beginning to be supplanted by typically Elizabethan drama, which presented the action of a play to the audience instead of relegating it to narration by the messenger.

No early work of tragic character was, however, as impressive as *Gorboduc.* Its very action, presented with a typically British disregard of the unities of time and place, and its very rhetoric had force and relevance for the times, since it dealt with the dangers of civil war. This was becoming a subject of grave concern to Elizabeth's subjects, because problems of the succession would arise if their Virgin Queen should die without leaving an heir to the throne.

Imitations of Senecan drama had a vogue among the Renaissance-influenced gentlemen of London. Five of Seneca's plays were separately translated, as well as possibly performed, between 1559 and 1566 before the famous complete translation, *Ten Tragedies,* was published in 1581. But the tragedy of Gorboduc, the ancient king who abdicated in favor of his two sons and so allowed his kingdom to fall to pieces, was no academic exercise for Sackville and Norton. The seriousness of their play, its semiabstractness that links it with medieval morality plays, its maxim-hurling rhetoric, and the symmetrical organization of the action into parallel situations served the authors' intention of writing significant drama. They anticipated the creation of high tragedy by Marlowe, Shakespeare, and the latter's contemporaries.

Among the many collections of early Tudor drama are J. M. Manly's *Specimens of Pre-Shakespearian Drama* (1900); C. M. Gayley's *Pre-Shakespearean Comedies* (Vol. I of his *Representative English Comedies,* 1907); J. Q. Adams' *Chief Pre-Shakespearian Dramas* (1924); and Edmund Creeth's *Tudor Plays* (1966). Recommended critical studies include F. S. Boas' *An Introduction to Tudor Drama* (1933); A. P. Rossiter's *English Drama from Early Times to the Elizabethans* (1950); T. W. Craik's *The Tudor Interlude* (1958); W. Clemen's *English Tragedy Before Shakespeare* (1961); and D. M. Bevington's *From "Mankind" to Marlowe* (1962).—J. G.

Elizabethan drama. Strictly speaking, Elizabethan drama encompasses the dramatic activity during the reign of Queen Elizabeth (1558–1603). Like the Renaissance drama of which it is a part, Elizabethan drama represents a synthesis of two great traditions: the classical and the medieval. Shakespeare and his contemporaries were the fortunate heirs of two profoundly different modes of living and visions of life, embodied in two radically opposed theatrical traditions. The achievement of the Elizabethans lay in their capacity to take the best of these two worlds and to fuse them into a great and unique dramatic accomplishment of their own.

The contribution of the classical drama was essentially formal. The five-act structure was more than just an arbitrary scaffolding on which to hang a series of events. It provided the framework for what Aristotle called a complete action—one with a beginning, a middle, and an end. Its influence can be seen in the taut construction of two of the greatest plays of the period: *Macbeth* (1606) and *The Alchemist* (1610).

From classical drama (which for the Elizabethan meant only Seneca, Plautus, and Terence, the Greek dramatists being all but unknown) the Elizabethans also extracted a number of substantive features. Plautus and Terence provided popular dramatists with a whole repertory of stock comic types: the braggart warrior, the clever servant, the harried father, and the prodigal son. Occasionally, as in the case of *The Comedy of Errors* (written c. 1590–1593), classical comedy was presented virtually unchanged on the Elizabethan stage, but this was more often true of private and school performances than of those in the London theaters.

In Elizabethan tragedy the classical influence is evident in the pervasive presence of Senecan characteristics (see THE MISFORTUNES OF ARTHUR). The Elizabethans were indebted to Seneca for certain character types (the ghost, the messenger, the confidant), for certain sensational themes (revenge, in-

cest), and, most important, for conveying a sense of the inner life of a dramatic character. Although it would be far from accurate to characterize Senecan tragedy as psychological drama, his characters consistently reveal a concern for motive and self-analysis. The soliloquizing hero of Elizabethan drama is essentially Senecan.

Despite these considerable contributions of the classical theater, the Elizabethans owed a far greater debt to their own native English tradition. From the miracle and morality plays and the interludes of medieval drama they derived a host of dramatic conventions, a number of stock figures, a comprehensive picture of the ordering principles of life, and, finally, a tendency toward allegorization, which, properly restrained and transformed, lent their best plays a universality and significance that time has not diminished.

The instrument with which the Elizabethan dramatist accomplished the fusion of classical and medieval traditions was the English language, itself a product of the same two traditions. Pre-Shakespearean drama was essentially experimental, designed to test the hypothesis, till then unproven, that the English tongue could achieve the dignity and sonority of Latin. The sources of this attempt were the twin impulses of Protestantism and nationalism, both of which received resounding fulfillment in the victory over the Spanish Armada in 1588.

The defeat of the Armada signaled the emancipation at once of the English people and the English language. This new freedom was celebrated in the theater by the creation of a new form, neither comedy nor tragedy: the CHRONICLE PLAY. Designed to articulate a sense of national identity, the chronicle play also helped to establish the reputation of the young playwright who was probably the creator of the genre, William SHAKESPEARE. The form owes to medieval drama the episodic structure, the broad expanse of the action, and the didactic impulse that motivates it.

At this time, too, the vigorous native comic tradition was becoming fused with that of Plautus and Terence. Medieval comedy was an incongruous synthesis of bawdiness and didacticism. At its best, as in the plays of John HEYWOOD, it was distinguished by a liveliness and exuberance that compensated for its loose, rambling, episodic structure. The classical tradition, on the other hand, although retaining the admirable formal structure of Plautine and Terentian comedy, had tended to become fossilized. The numerous academic imitations of Roman comic drama were more scholastic exercises than explorations of the comic mode. Here again the Elizabethans borrowed the best of both worlds. Anticipated in the early comedies *Ralph Roister Doister* (c. 1553) and *Gammer Gurton's Needle* (c. 1560), the fusion of the broad humor of the popular tradition and the governing form of the classical became the hallmark of Elizabethan comedy.

A third shaping force in the development of English comedy was contemporary Italian comedy—the *commedia dell'arte* and the more formal comedies of Machiavelli, Lodovico Ariosto, and others. A prominent early example of this influence is *Supposes* (1566), a translation by George GASCOIGNE of Ariosto's *I Suppositi. Supposes* is essentially a comedy of intrigue, loosely based on classical models. It is notable, too, for the fact that it is the first English comedy written in prose. Shakespeare testified to its influence when he used the play for the subplot of *The Taming of the Shrew*. In fact, THE TAMING OF THE SHREW itself is a good example of the diverse strains that inhere in Elizabethan comedy. Its Italian and Latin lineaments are evident in the Bianca plot, while the motifs of the taming of a shrewish wife and the "Induction" (the Christopher Sly episode) are derived from popular folk humor. Shakespeare, never content merely to imitate an established pattern, added one other element—romantic love. Love and laughter had always been coupled, of course, but never before with a sense of the restorative, regenerative power that Shakespeare saw as common to both of them. Between the guffaw and the smirk, he discovered the smile.

In tragedy, the interaction of classical and English drama is less easy to trace. The medieval conception of tragedy derived less from the drama than from narratives, beginning with Boccaccio's *De casibus virorum illustrium* (1355–1360), which exemplified the inexorable movement of the wheel of fortune. The tradition initiated by this work was transmitted to England through John Lydgate's *Fall of Princes* (1431–1438) and later, in the popular collection called *A Mirror for Magistrates* (1559), it was merged with Senecan tragedy. To this tradition was added one element that, in tragic drama, was a distinctively Elizabethan innovation—humor. An early example of the native tradition is CAMBISES, described on its title page as "a lamentable tragedie, mixed full of pleasant mirth." Based upon the story of King Cambises given in *A Mirror for Magistrates,* the play reveals its essentially medieval characteristics, alternating the comic and the serious in a series of undeveloped, unrelated episodes characterized by bombastic speeches, prolific bloodletting, and a comic underplot. The mingling of tragedy and comedy was much decried by sixteenth-century classicists, and has continued to be until recently. We have come to recognize, however, that far from providing mere comic relief, the presence of comedy adds another dimension to the tragic events, placing them within a more human context and ultimately deepening the tragic experience.

The Senecan influence not surprisingly was channeled to the popular theaters through the more classical university drama. The most important of these plays is *Gorboduc* (1561), written by Thomas Norton and Thomas Sackville, the first English tragedy in blank verse. Even here, the Senecan strains have been mixed. Its subject is drawn from English, not classical, legend and it incorporates such notably non-Senecan features as the DUMB SHOW. Sackville was a contributor to *A Mirror for Magistrates,* and he brought to this work the medieval view of tragedy as a "mirror"—a warning to the high and mighty.

Another influence that partook both of the native and the classical tradition was the popular prose narrative of the day, the *novella.* Italian in origin, the *novelle* were popularized in France through the *Histoires Tragiques* (1559–1582) of Belleforest and Boaistuau and in England by William Painter's *The Palace of Pleasure* (1566), Sir Geoffrey Fenton's *Tragical Discourses* (1567), and George Pettie's *A Petite Pallace of Pettie his Pleasure* (1576). These anthologies proved to be a treasure house of source material that Elizabethan playwrights regularly ransacked for plots and characters. Primitive by most modern standards, the great virtue of these narratives was their almost exclusive devotion to telling a story and telling it well. Thus, it was within the narrative framework provided by these stories that two of the

ENGRAVING OF SHAKESPEARE AND HIS CONTEMPORARIES (THEATRE COLLECTION, NEW YORK PUBLIC LIBRARY AT LINCOLN CENTER)

Sylvester   Selden   Beaumont   Daniel   Raleigh
                          Bacon   Donne   Earl of Southampton   Dekker
                  Fletcher   Ben Jonson
Sackville, Earl of Dorset   Shakespeare   Sir Robert Cotton
Camden

world's greatest dramatic masterpieces, *Hamlet* (c. 1600–1601) and *Othello* (1604), were produced.

In adapting these stories, Shakespeare and his fellow dramatists were appealing to that other product of the native tradition, the Elizabethan audience. Elizabethan theatergoers were good listeners: they spent many hours attending sermons and conversing with friends. The popular notion of them as a mass of rowdy, noisy illiterates interested only in bloodletting and bawdy is a gross oversimplification. As Alfred Harbage (*Shakespeare's Audience,* 1941) has shown, they were a vocal but appreciative audience, made up largely of the shopkeepers and apprentices of London. Having been nurtured on the miracle and morality plays, they were used to seeing action covering wide ranges of time and space. Furthermore, they were capable of making an imaginative effort to appreciate the plays presented before them. This last feature was particularly important in view of the nature of the Elizabethan theater. The public playhouses were large, roofless buildings with a three-foot stage extending from one wall to the center of the yard. Uncurtained, employing relatively little scenery, and thrust out into the middle of the audience, this stage demanded a capacity to visualize suggested events and scenes, to view time and space symbolically—a demand that Shakespeare made explicit in the Prologue to *Henry V.* The details of the stage can only be conjectured, but it is generally agreed that it was "open," that is, surrounded on three sides by the audience. The actors made their exits and entrances through two doors at the rear of the stage and, occasionally, through a trap door in the center of the stage floor. Running the width of the stage above the stage doors was a gallery that may also have been used as an "upper stage." The question of the "inner stage," an enclosed area allegedly located at the rear of the stage between the stage doors, is still disputed by students of the subject. The majority are now of the opinion that there was no inner stage but that there was a curtained area between the doors that could be used for making "discoveries," such as the discovery of Polonius' body in *Hamlet* (Act III, scene 4). Even an interior scene such as that in Desdemona's bedroom (*Othello,* Act V, scene 3) may have been prepared for simply by thrusting out Desdemona's bed onto the main stage in full view of the audience. Thus, the audience was required to make a greater imaginative effort than do modern audiences attending a realistic drama. The rewards of the effort were greater than those that most modern audiences enjoy: an intimacy, occasionally even an interplay, that lent a sense of communion to the dramatic enterprise.

The catalysts of this relationship between author and audience were the actors. The descendants of the strolling players and vagabonds who had been a feature of the English countryside since the late middle ages, they had, by the time of Elizabeth's reign, managed to secure a measure of stability by becoming, technically at least, servants of one of the powerful noblemen or of the queen herself. This maneuver was vitally important to the survival of the acting companies, subject as they were to the harassment of the puritanical city authorities in London and to the frequent closings of the theaters because of the plague. Despite these threats to their existence, a number of the companies managed to survive a reasonable length of time and a few even prospered. Shakespeare's company (the Chamberlain's-King's Men) was by far the most successful, but it was not unique, except in the length (forty-eight years) of its continuous existence.

Precarious as was the existence of the acting companies, it was relatively secure in contrast to that of the playwright, who received very little reimbursement for his plays. Shakespeare's career as a permanent and prominent member of an acting company was an outstanding exception in an age when even some of the best playwrights, including Marlowe and Jonson, were barely able to survive. The bleak career of Robert Greene differed from that of many other dramatists only in that it was sensationally publicized. Successful literary figures like Samuel DANIEL survived through the support of patrons from the nobility. Others such as Samuel ROWLEY and Nathan FIELD combined acting with playwriting. Less resourceful figures such as Henry PORTER, Barnabe BARNES, Henry CHETTLE, and John DAY sometimes found themselves in debtor's prison. Frequently resorting to hack work that inevitably drained their creative energy, they nevertheless produced in the last fifteen years of the sixteenth century a number of plays of extraordinarily high quality and wide diversity.

The chief creators of these dramas were the so-called University Wits, a group of graduates of Oxford and Cambridge who arrived on the London theatrical scene in the 1580's. Bristling with reckless enthusiasm for life and literature, these stylistic innovators provided the necessary foundation for the achievements of the later drama. Besides Marlowe and Greene, the group included George Peele, Thomas Lodge, Thomas Nashe, and Thomas Kyd. To these should be added the name of John Lyly, who, while not a member of the group, shared many of its characteristics. Before the advent of the Wits, Elizabethan drama had consisted largely of lifeless and literal imitations of classical drama or medieval romance. The Wits developed these types, simultaneously transforming them into richer and more subtle patterns.

The forerunner of the group was John LYLY, who began writing for the theater in the early 1580's. As a playwright for the Children of St. Paul's, a boys' acting company, Lyly wrote for an aristocratic audience, and his plays—fanciful, elaborate, highly mythologized dramatizations of the courtly love tradition—are accurate reflections of that audience's taste. His best known works are *Campaspe* (1584), *Endymion* (1588), and *Love's Metamorphosis* (produced between 1588 and 1590). They are written in the highly stylized, "euphuistic" prose for which Lyly is best known. Characterized by witty dialogue, interpolated songs, and artificiality of plot, they formed the basis of the later and greater achievement of Shakespeare in *Love's Labour's Lost* and *Much Ado About Nothing.*

The Arraignment of Paris (pub. 1584), by the versatile George PEELE, is a courtly fantasy in the tradition of Lyly. Peele, however, wrote most of his plays for the public stage. The variety in his repertory is, therefore, much wider, ranging from the charming folk romance of *The Old Wives Tale* (c. 1593) to the blustering bravado of *The Battle of Alcazar* (c. 1588). Between these extremes Peele wrote a chronicle play, *Edward I* (c. 1590), and *David and Bethsabe* (1594), a reworking of the biblical story with strong influences from the medieval morality play. If we also consider, as some scholars do, Peele to be the part-author of *Titus Andronicus* (produced between 1589 and 1593), we can see that his influence as a pioneer in a variety of genres was pervasive.

Another experimenter in a variety of genres was Robert GREENE, whose brief career was marked chiefly by a talent for innovation. His *Alphonsus, King of Aragon* (c. 1587) is either a grotesque imitation or a broad parody (critics are undecided) of Marlowe's *Tamburlaine.* His *Orlando Furioso* (c. 1591) is a dramatization of Ariosto's epic, and his *James IV of Scotland* (c. 1591) is a pseudohistorical romance notable for its charming and resourceful heroine, Dorothea, who bears a strong resemblance to the heroines of Shakespearean romance. Greene is also thought to be the author of *George-a-Greene, the Pinner of Wakefield* (pub. 1599), a charming romance of the English countryside, which bears some similarities to *Friar Bacon and Friar Bungay* (c. 1590), perhaps Greene's best play.

A collaborator with Greene on one play (*A Looking Glass for London and England,* c. 1590) was Thomas Lodge, best known as the author of the prose romance *Rosalind* (pub. 1590), Shakespeare's chief source for *As You Like It.* His only other extant play is *The Wounds of Civil War* (1594), a historical drama set in classical Rome. Lodge's dramatic output was small, as was that of Thomas Nashe, whose only extant play of which he is the sole author is *Summer's Last Will and Testament* (pub. 1600), a masque-like allegory written for performance at the home of John Whitgift, archbishop of Canterbury. Nashe was also the collaborator with Ben JONSON on the *Isle of Dogs* (1596), a lost satire comedy so scandalous that it resulted in the temporary closing of the London theaters, the arrest of Jonson, and a precipitous flight from London by Nashe.

The only member of the Wits not trained in the university was Thomas KYD, whose *The Spanish Tragedy* (c. 1588) was probably the most popular play of its day. Kyd is probably also the author of *Soliman and Perseda* (c. 1589) and of the so-called *Ur-Hamlet* (c. 1588), the lost play on which Shakespeare based his tragedy. Kyd is credited as the creator of REVENGE TRAGEDY, the neo-Senecan genre that achieved great popularity in the Elizabethan theater.

Towering above Kyd in poetic genius, if not in dramatic craftsmanship, was his friend Christopher MARLOWE, the greatest artist of the group. In the course of a career tragically abbreviated by his death at the age of twenty-nine, Marlowe captured one aspect of the Renaissance. His major plays focused on the restless, inquiring spirit of an age of newly awakened individualism. His tragedies dealt with the fate of the "overreachers," individuals who assert themselves in absolute terms and who thus become symbols of excitement and danger. Thus, Faustus, Barabas in *The Jew of Malta* (c. 1589), and Tamburlaine all exhibit the impulse to defy the limiting conditions of existence. The verbal equivalent of this defiance was Marlowe's "mighty line," which transformed blank verse into expansive, majestic, dramatic speech and provided the poetic vehicle for the golden age of Elizabethan drama.

The Spanish Tragedie:
OR,
Hieronimo is mad againe.

Containing the lamentable end of *Don Horatio,* and *Belimperia;* with the pittifull death of *Hieronimo.*

Newly corrected, amended, and enlarged with new Additions of the *Painters* part, and others, as it hath of late been diuers times acted.

LONDON,
Printed by W. White, for I. White and T. Langley, and are to be fold at their Shop ouer againft the Sarazens head without New-gate. 1615.

TITLE PAGE OF THE 1615 EDITION OF THOMAS KYD'S *The Spanish Tragedy*

Significant as were the accomplishments of the Wits, however, their importance rests less in their achievements than in their innovations. Theirs was pioneer work, more valuable as raw material than as finished product. The transmutation of that material into great drama was, with the occasional exception of Marlowe, beyond their reach. That achievement belongs to their chief heir, apparently recognized as such even by them (if we are to take seriously Greene's slurring reference to "an upstart crow, beautified with our feathers"). The court comedies of Lyly, pastoral romances of Greene, revenge plays of Kyd, chronicles of Peele, and the poetic tragedies of Marlowe were to achieve their consummate expression in the Shakespearean drama of the 1590's. Too often it is assumed, implicitly at least, that Shakespeare's plays blossomed in a historical greenhouse, isolated from the work of his contemporaries. In fact, the great achievements of his early and middle periods are much closer to being syntheses of existing dramatic currents than original creations. He seemed instinctively to see the final forms that his predecessors were striving to create and built on the foundation they had laid.

Not the least of the qualities that these plays share is an ebullience of spirit that was also characteristic of the age as a whole. They were created within the framework of a world view that was essentially medieval. The universe was an ordered, harmonious, hierarchical structure whose governing principles were reproduced on every level of life—social, political, and personal. Individual man was a microcosm of this larger world, located on the great chain of being midway between matter and spirit. Radically flawed by original sin, he had nevertheless been redeemed by Christ and was therefore capable of happiness and ultimate salvation as long as he observed the natural laws of proportion and degree. However, even at the height of the celebration of this ideal, undertones of doubt and discontent were evident. Shakespeare's chronicle plays, while upholding the hierarchical principle, were at the same time subtly probing that principle, testing its viability in the light of power politics as enunciated by Machiavelli and practiced by Elizabethans such as Lord Burghley, Elizabeth's chief minister. The undertone became the dominant note in the plays of Marlowe, whose overreaching heroes defy all the laws of measure and proportion in order to assert their individual will in the absolute pursuit of power, wealth, or knowledge. As the century drew to a close, the optimism ushered in by the great victory of 1588 over the Spanish Armada began to fade and skepticism and disenchantment became more pronounced. Men became conscious of entering a new era, an undiscovered country of the mind in which the old ordering principles were no longer relevant. The stage was set for tragedy.

The standard scholarly work on Elizabethan drama is E. K. Chambers' *Elizabethan Stage* (1923) in four volumes. The best account of the medieval influence is Willard Farnham's *The Medieval Heritage of Elizabethan Tragedy* (1936). Accounts of the Elizabethan world view are given in Hardin Craig's *The Enchanted Glass* (1936) and E. M. W. Tillyard's *The Elizabethan World Picture* (1943). Excellent accounts of its relationship to drama, and specifically to Shakespeare's drama, are given in Theodore Spencer's *Shakespeare and the Nature of Man* (1943) and Alfred Harbage's *Shakespeare and the Rival Traditions* (1952).—E. Q.

Jacobean drama. The drama of England during the reign of James I (1603–1625). The closing years of Queen Elizabeth's reign (1558–1603) witnessed a profound change in the spirit of English life and English drama. By the beginning of the new century the buoyant optimism of the 1590's had given way to a profoundly pessimistic mood of uncertainty and defeat. The old queen, all but apotheosized by her subjects as the embodiment of the nation's welfare, was showing the signs of advanced age—sickness and indecisiveness. Her failure to name an heir heightened the anxiety of a people who could easily recall the strife and bloodletting that marked the reigns of her predecessors, Edward VI and Mary Tudor. Factionalism and Machiavellian intrigue were rife at court. Enclosing of farm lands and granting of monopolies to favorites were proving intolerable economic burdens for the common people. Abroad, the indomitable Irish rebels, aided and abetted by England's great enemy, Spain, were seemingly unbeatable. At home, the threat of insurrection and

civil war—always a very real and imminent danger—erupted into reality when the earl of Essex, the charismatic hero of the earlier decade, attempted to wrest control of the crown. The total failure of Essex's revolt seemed to call into question the Elizabethan ideals of chivalry, courage, and optimism that the dashing young earl embodied. Nor did the outlook improve with the accession of James I in 1603. Lacking both the charm and the intelligence of his predecessor, he widened even further the gap between the court and the people.

Added to the economic and social problems was the always-burning religious question. The growing number of religious dissidents intensified the internal divisiveness shockingly climaxed by the Gunpowder Plot (1605), the attempt by a group of Roman Catholics to blow up both houses of Parliament. The resulting fear and distrust precipitated even stricter suppression of religious nonconformity.

More directly important to the drama, however, were the intellectual developments of the period. Chief among these were the contributions of Machiavelli and Montaigne. Both men in different ways signaled the arrival of a new spirit—skeptical, analytical, interested more in man as he is than in man as he ought to be. This shift in focus called into question the great principle of order inherited from the middle ages. The idea of the hierarchical ordering of everything in the cosmos was the cornerstone of Elizabethan optimism, but the new philosophy, as John Donne had said, called all in doubt. Although the Elizabethan world view would not be overthrown until much later, the seeds of doubt and uncertainty were already being sown in the early years of the seventeenth century.

It was during this period that the MASQUE and most of the drama we identify as Jacobean was produced. Later in James's reign a sense of renewal and stability reasserted itself, a spirit reflected in the romances of Shakespeare and the tragicomedies of Francis BEAUMONT and John FLETCHER. However, it was in the earlier phase—approximately the first decade of the seventeenth century—that the clash of modern and medieval values, the conflict between the aspirations of a newly awakened individualism and the demands of carefully structured, hierarchical social organizations, found its expression in drama. The resultant tension and spiritual uncertainty provided the stimulus for the great achievement of the Jacobean dramatists.

The earliest expression of the conflict between modern and medieval world views took the form of satire. By the late 1590's a new generation of poets—inevitably reacting against the genteel romanticism of their immediate predecessors, Sidney, Spenser, and the sonneteers—arrived on the literary scene. Caustic, critical, and truculent, these Tudor ancestors of the angry young men invoked the spirit of Juvenal as they railed against the follies of the time. The young Juvenals—Joseph Hall, John Marston, the early John Donne—were soon suppressed by the authorities and their books burned in a public conflagration known as the "bishops' bonfire" (1599). However, the episcopal blaze did not consume the public's taste for satire.

At the turn of the century the children's acting

FRANCIS BEAUMONT AND JOHN FLETCHER (THEATRE COLLECTION, NEW YORK PUBLIC LIBRARY AT LINCOLN CENTER)

companies—eclipsed by the adult companies during the 1590's—were reactivated. Performing in private theaters before a more select, sophisticated audience, they provided the ideal theatrical medium for the newly awakened satiric impulse. The early popularity of the children's companies spurred the rival public theaters to competition. Satire dominated the London playhouses, and the famous WAR OF THE THEATERS broke out.

One of the generals of the "war" and one of the most influential of the satiric dramatists was John MARSTON. Whether writing comedies, tragedies, or melodramas, Marston was never very far from his central task—unmasking human folly and vice. His concentration on this theme has an obsessive intensity that occasionally lapses into hysteria. Nevertheless, in his best plays, such as *The Malcontent* (1604), he demonstrates an originality and vitality that mark him as a distinctive, if limited, dramatic artist.

Considerable as Marston's talents were, they were no challenge to the superiority of his chief adversary in the war of the theaters, Ben JONSON. Not the least aspect of Jonson's greatness is the fidelity with which he adhered to the satirist's creed, the determination to "show an Image of the times / And sport with humane follies not with crimes." For the realization of this ideal he formulated his conception of the comedy of humours. Anticipated by George CHAPMAN, whose *The Blind Beggar of Alexandria* (1596) and *An Humorous Day's Mirth* (1597) must be accounted the first humour comedies, Jonson's plays are nevertheless the classic examples of the type. The degree to

which he perfected his portrayals of obsessive human drives is evidenced by the organic unity that underlies the diverse aspects of credulity and greed in *Volpone* (1605/06). Almost all of the characters are propelled by the lust for money, but each particular lust is subtly differentiated and harmoniously related to the total dramatic structure. And the structure itself is sustained by the wit, erudition, and moral imagination of its creator.

But satire could function within a tragic as well as comic framework. As the comic satirist explored the realm of human folly, the tragic satirist sought to discover the nature of human evil. Armed with the insights of Machiavelli and Montaigne, his avowed purpose was to expose man's deeply rooted capacity for corruption without invoking as a solution the innately antitragic principles of Christianity. Like the medieval philosopher (as opposed to the medieval theologian), the tragic dramatist was required to suspend his belief. To be sure, in some cases—Chapman's for example—there was probably no belief that required suspension, but the result in any case was finally the same: violent encounter with the twin facts of evil and death, faced with stoic endurance.

An excellent representative example of the genre is the anonymous THE REVENGER'S TRAGEDY, generally attributed to Cyril TOURNEUR, although an eloquent minority claims the authorship for Thomas Middleton. As its title suggests, the play is written in the tradition of REVENGE TRAGEDY. Significantly enough, however, it dispenses with that stock character of the earlier revenge plays, the ghost who summons the protagonist to revenge. Tourneur (or Middleton) seems at pains to demonstrate that the source of blood lust lies, not in an other-worldly spirit, but in the complex impulses of the human heart.

Another powerful dramatist of the period was Thomas MIDDLETON. In understated but effective tones Middleton's work reflects the dominant concerns of the age. His realistic comedies, such as *A Chaste Maid in Cheapside* (1611), focused with unsparing clarity on the interplay of social, economic, and moral pressures in seventeenth-century London. His tragedies such as THE CHANGELING, written in collaboration with William ROWLEY, provided a piercingly ironic context for the aspirations and self-assertions of his flawed heroes.

The fascination with evil and death achieved an even more powerful artistic expression in the works of John WEBSTER. In his two great plays THE WHITE DEVIL and THE DUCHESS OF MALFI the villains Flamineo and Bosola dominate the action and the attention of the audience. No stereotyped villains, they are complexly wrought creations, passionate, self-aware, intensely alive in a world where the guilty and the innocent suffer or prosper indiscriminately.

> O, this gloomy world!
> In what a shadow, or deep pit of darkness,
> Doth womanish and fearful mankind live!

The sense of the world as a "deep pit of darkness" is forcefully conveyed in Jacobean tragedy. It is conveyed in part by the macabre humor, the rough diction, the irregular verse, the overtones of insanity, and the imagery of disease that pervade the plays. Underlying this sense of dissolution and incongruity is a steadfast refusal to accept any facile consolatory explanations. Some Jacobeans, such as Chapman and James's chancellor of the exchequer, Fulke GREVILLE, author of the closet drama *Mustapha* (1600–1603), cling to a painfully expressed classical stoicism. In the plays of others, Webster for example, heroes and villains meet their inevitable mortal fate "in a mist," without the suggestion of an ordering vision of life. The Jacobeans wrestle with the great questions of the meaning of suffering and evil, but only in the tragedies of Shakespeare do we perceive a unified design behind the images of disruption and decay. In *King Lear* (1606), for example, the evil atmosphere of *The Revenger's Tragedy* is magnified into an apocalyptic vision of the disordering of all nature. But within this catastrophic framework, we see the naked human spirit achieving a dignity that neither the malevolence of fortune, the wantonness of the gods, nor the presence of evil in human nature itself can erase. In *Hamlet* (1601/02) the same destructive forces are seen in a narrower focus, filtered through the mind and sensibility of one representative man. Hamlet's struggle to wrest a meaning from his keen sense of the anarchy of life is in itself a heroic vindication of that life. In *Macbeth* (1606) we see a capitulation to the darker forces redeemed by the heroism of defiance. For this reason alone Shakespearean tragedy towers over that of its contemporaries. However, the signature of the age is on these works and even more prominently on some of his less great but more "Jacobean" dramas, such as *Troilus*

and Cressida (1601/02), *Measure for Measure* (1604), and *Timon of Athens* (1606/07). Each of these plays embodies a significant aspect of the drama of the period. *Troilus and Cressida* is a sharply satiric account of the decline of the principle of order and the dominance of "wars and lechery" in human nature. *Measure for Measure* focuses, also with satiric intent, on religious hypocrisy and corruption in high office. *Timon of Athens,* at least in the imperfect form in which it has come down to us, is a vituperative attack on obsequiousness and greed. These plays participate in the dark Jacobean vision characterized by satire, invective, and a restless discontent.

By the end of the first decade of the seventeenth century, however, this trend had begun to reverse itself. James was settled more securely on the throne; the fires of religious dissidence were temporarily banked; the intellectual innovations were assimilated to some extent; and a brave new world on the other side of the Atlantic, opening up to colonization, began to stir men's aspirations and hopes. Appetite for the romantic, the fanciful, the exotic quickened and was quickly satisfied by the young playwriting team Beaumont and Fletcher. Shakespeare, too, now writing for the more aristocratic patrons of the Blackfriars theater, began to accommodate the new mood. But there is a world of difference between Shakespeare's romances and the entertaining but rather frivolous "tragicomedies" of his successors. Nowhere in Beaumont and Fletcher is there a suggestion of having come through a purgatorial experience to a profoundly serene vision of life that is the essence of *The Winter's Tale* and *The Tempest.*

The tragic tradition that remained at the end of the Jacobean period was similarly transformed by the romantic spirit. Responding in mellower and homelier terms were two older playwrights—Thomas DEKKER and Thomas HEYWOOD. Dekker's *The Witch of Edmonton* (1621) and Heywood's *The English Traveller* (c. 1627) are marked by a compassion and sentiment closer in tone to eighteenth-century drama than to the dark visions of Webster and Tourneur. Similarly, the comedy of Philip MASSINGER and Richard BROME is less notable as a development of the satire of Marston and Middleton than as an anticipation of Restoration comedy. The searing tragic satire of Webster gave way to the melancholy, introspective, psychological studies of John FORD. On the quiet, sensitive note sounded in Ford's plays the Jacobean age comes to an end.

The standard scholarly work on the period is G. E. Bentley's *The Jacobean and Caroline Stage* (1941–1956), in five volumes. The best general study is Una Ellis-Fermor's *Jacobean Drama* (1936). Two excellent recent works are Robert Ornstein's *The Moral Vision of Jacobean Tragedy* (1960) and Irving Ribner's *Jacobean Tragedy* (1962).—E. Q.

Caroline drama. The drama of England during the reign of Charles I (1625–1642). In 1615 Sir Walter Raleigh expressed a truth about English politics and society that had been common knowledge among intellectuals like Donne, Shakespeare, and Jonson since the last decade of Elizabeth's reign. "The heirs of the feudal past no longer hold the keys to the future," observed Raleigh, "and monarchy, if it were wise, would come to terms with the House of Commons, the organ of the gentry." The old Tudor hegemony of lands and lordships had eroded, and the new center of power no longer rested on a combine of king, bishops, and titled lords sequestered in remote estates but on a multitude of aggressively Puritan, upper-middle-class lawyers and merchants with their economic roots in industrial London, Southampton, and Bristol; their spiritual resources in militant Calvinism; and their political muscle in the House of Commons.

The disastrous reign of Charles I, collapsing as it did with civil war in 1642 and with his own execution in January 1649, can be attributed, in large measure, to his obstinate refusal to acknowledge the truth of Raleigh's dictum. Unlike his predecessor, James I, Charles Stuart was charming and gracious, a generous patron of Rubens and Van Dyck, and an avid reader of Beaumont and Fletcher and of French and Spanish romances. According to his busy master of the revels, Sir Henry Herbert, Charles actually collaborated with James Shirley in the writing of *The Gamester* in 1633. As a man, Charles was cultured, pious, and deeply patriotic. Yet his enthusiasm for romance and tragicomedy contributed substantially to the dissolution of the great Elizabethan heritage of the drama; his uncompromising piety led to the destruction of the Anglican Church and its bishops; his patriotism tore the nation into warring political factions and religious sects.

Oliver Cromwell remarked at the end of his life that he had come to realize that all the basic conflicts during the reign of Charles I and in the years immediately after the civil war were religious conflicts, and a careful reading of the Stationers' Register for the years between 1625 and 1642 reveals that, indeed, perhaps 90 percent of the matter printed during the period consisted of sermons, biblical commentary, religious polemics, and devotional tracts. This second Reformation in the first half of the seventeenth century also produced England's greatest religious poetry by men like John Donne, Richard Crashaw, George Herbert, Henry Vaughan, John Milton, Thomas Traherne, and many others, and England's most magnificent sermons by such Anglican divines as Launcelot Andrews, Donne, and Jeremy Taylor. The spiritual urgency of the times is expressed vividly in Milton's powerful *Lycidas* and in the baroque sensuousness of Crashaw's *The Flaming Heart*. "What if this present were the world's last night?" inquires a terrified Donne in his midnight of soul, but no such lyric responses to the awesome crises of the times are heard in the Caroline drama, which, instead of reflecting the tumultuous present, turned back in nostalgia to the Elizabethan past with imitations, sustained or occasional, of Jonson, Shakespeare, and Beaumont and Fletcher; or, in tragicomedies and cavalier romances, it turned forward to anticipate the Restoration comedy of manners and the heroic plays of John Dryden and the earl of Orrery.

Two dramatists in a class by themselves are Philip MASSINGER and John Ford. Massinger's A NEW WAY TO PAY OLD DEBTS, the first considerable comedy of the period, was derived from Thomas Middleton's *A Trick to Catch the Old One* (1608). Massinger based his conception of the villainous Sir Giles Overreach on an actual Sir Giles Mompesson; a notorious disciple of Buckingham, Mompesson was convicted of extortion in 1621. *A New Way* draws its characteriza-

tions from Jonson's *The Alchemist* (1610), but its social perspectives—its obsession with social class and position, with commerce, writs, land, and the other paraphernalia of middle-class power—are similar to those of Charles Dickens, Jane Austen, and Anthony Trollope. The rapacious Sir Giles Overreach, a Stuart version of Christopher Marlowe's Barabas and William Faulkner's Snopes, forces his way into respectable society by extorting money from poor widows and lands from titled gentlemen and ancient gentry. Thus, Overreach is a pure ogre in a tense, insecure society in a state of great transition; the Elizabethan usurper with his knife, rack, and mercenary sycophants is replaced by the social-climbing, unscrupulous landlord with his pen, legal parchments, and armies of lawyers, and the threat is not to "degree" in the cosmos but to a whole privileged class in society. From this perspective, *A New Way* can be seen as a Calvinist morality play, with the prodigal Wellborn—who anticipates by a generation the spendthrift gallant in such Restoration comedies as Richard Sheridan's *School for Scandal* —as Everyman standing between hell, which is clearly debt, and heaven, which is affluence, credit, and position. When Wellborn is extended credit by Lady Allworth, he is "saved" from the devil Overreach. *A New Way* is not only a fast-paced comedy of manners but a curious social document expressing some important changes in values at the twilight of the Renaissance in England.

In THE CITY MADAM Massinger modernized still another comedy from the Elizabethan period, *Eastward Ho!* (1605), by Jonson, Marston, and Chapman. This time the upstart is Luke Frugal, the scheming prodigal who is taken into the home of his brother and benefactor, kindly old Sir John Frugal, whose lands and wealth Luke attempts to usurp. Under the harsh rule of Luke, Sir John's spoiled wife and daughters are almost shipped off to Virginia as bond-slaves before they learn the virtues of humility and gratitude. To a greater extent than in *A New Way*, *The City Madam* conveys some of the graceful humor of middle-class romantic comedies like Thomas Dekker's *The Shoemaker's Holiday* (1599), but it also reveals Massinger's fundamental shortcoming in writing a comedy of manners: He never mastered Ben Jonson's techniques of exploiting a single, expanding situation rather than unraveling an episodic story. The tendency toward episodic narration had been firmly established by Elizabethans like Robert Greene, Dekker, and Thomas Heywood; like some of their plays, Massinger's seem to grope toward the novel form.

During the reign of Charles I, John FORD wrote four tragedies and four tragicomedies, including *The Lover's Melancholy* (1628), *Love's Sacrifice* (1633), 'TIS PITY SHE'S A WHORE, *The Broken Heart* (1633), and *Perkin Warbeck* (1634). In his tragedies, which are in the vein of Beaumont and Fletcher's *A King and No King* (c. 1611) and *A Maid's Tragedy* (c. 1611), Ford spoke with more authority and authenticity than any dramatist of the Caroline period. Like Beaumont and Fletcher, Ford's theme is love and honor; like John Webster, he focuses on the agony of his heroines, yet in Ford's haunting tragedies of suffering and fortitude Elizabethan clamor fades into taut whispers, solemn dirges, mute but expressive gestures; Webster's violent outbursts and savage atrocities become, in Ford's plays, ritualistic sufferings expressive of pathological wounds deeper than flesh. Ford's characters are neither good nor evil; they are enigmatic neurotics with contrasting obsessions who consume themselves in adultery, incest, or sexual frustration. Ford's guiding text is not the New Testament but Robert Burton's *Anatomy of Melancholy* (1621), which is known to have profoundly influenced his first published play, *The Lover's Melancholy*. Those who think of Shakespeare as a "psychological" dramatist must read Ford to learn how misleading that simplistic epithet can be. Ford's characters, such as Calantha, the "flower of beauty," or Ithocles, "honour of loveliness" in *The Broken Heart,* have no identity whatever in our daylight world of morality; they exist exclusively in some eternal landscape of their own minds, in totally isolated relationship to an inexplicable ideal of perfection, the silent heavens their only witness to strange rituals of self-immolation. In *The Broken Heart* Penthea, who is a chaste victim by any conventional standard, imposes upon herself death by starvation to atone for her "whoredom," and Calantha causes herself to "die smiling" of a broken heart because, as the choral dirge proclaims at the end, "Love only reigns in death." Ford's plays reiterate the Elizabethan motives of revenge, usurpation, and enforced marriage, and his characters follow the familiar Elizabethan dramatis personae of usurpers, contrasting sets of lovers, foolish old counselors, headstrong young princes; yet all the traditional landmarks have been removed. His syntax is loose and disconnected; his images turgid or facile, often deliberately obscure. To move from the Elizabethans to John Ford is like leaving a gregarious, energetic world of imminent joy and entering a lunar desolation haunted by lonely and querulous ghosts.

Shortly after the accession of Charles I a new group of dramatists appeared upon the scene whose egregious influence accelerated the decline of the popular playhouses on the Bankside and made the Caroline stage an exclusively aristocratic pastime. These were the cavalier dramatists who fashioned plays to the taste of Charles's wife, Henrietta Maria, and her ladies at court. The young queen had been raised in the care of Madame de Monglat and her daughter, Madame St. George, both frequenters of the *salon* at the Hotel de Rambouillet established in 1615 by Catherine de Vivonne in imitation of such circles of excruciating refinement as the Urbino depicted by Castiglione in *Il Cortegiano.* As Massinger observed in his *Emperor of the East,* printed in 1630, Henrietta Maria had made the court "a kind of academy" and "school of virtue" over which she reigned as "sovereign abbess." In June 1634, James Howell wrote that at court was "a love called Platonic love, which much sways there of late. . . . This love sets the wits of the town on work," and by 1638 so many courtiers had rushed forward to gorge the presses with pastoral dramas and heroic plays that William Cartwright had a character say in *The Siege:*

> I will turn
> Poet myself. It is in fashion, lady.
> He's scarce a courtier now that hath not
> Writ his brace of plays.

The court had invaded the drama. The first courtier to trigger the queen's prurient enthusiasm was Walter Montague with his *Shepherd's Paradise* (1629), a rambling pastoral in rhythmic prose that reads like an inadvertent parody of Honore d'Urfé's *L'Astrée,* the interminable pastoral romance that had served as an Arcadian textbook of love and gallantries at the Hotel de Rambouillet a generation before. With mindless garrulity, *The Shepherd's Paradise* portrays a society of delicate nymphs and "pretty boys" in a "paradise of chastity" governed by Queen Fidamira, who is, of course, Henrietta Maria. *The Shepherd's Paradise,* which Henrietta Maria and her coterie rehearsed for four months before its presentation at court, helped to establish the peculiarities of that genre of tragicomedy best described as the "cavalier romance"—witless preciosity, Platonic philosophizing, and an obsessive preoccupation with the niceties of "love and honor" between a pedantic princess and her supine royal wooer. The cavalier romance usually has its mythic setting in the aristocratic mind—in "Euboea" or "Tasminia"—and although the stage shakes with distant battles and the collapse of empires, all that really matters is the outcome of a *débat de coeur* between two painfully verbose lovers. The issues spring inevitably from an insulated culture that viewed reality as tantamount to vulgarity. Will a farewell kiss jeopardize the spiritual integrity of love? Does a mistress have the authority to release her lover to serve a friend? As Alfred Harbage has pointed out, the cavalier romance is not "decadent" because it is immoral; the genre itself is decadent for its vacuous improbabilities, its formless narration, its disregard for human values, and its brutal ignorance of life.

The chief cavalier romancers, in addition to Walter Montague, include Aston Cokain, Lodowick Carlell, William CARTWRIGHT, William Habington, Henry Glapthorne, Henry and Thomas Killigrew, Richard Lovelace, Jasper Mayne, and Sir John SUCKLING. On the periphery of this courtly group, and infinitely superior to any of those listed, were William DAVENANT and James Shirley. Davenant's career at court was launched with *The Temple of Love* in 1634, which was performed at Whitehall by Henrietta Maria, nine lords, and fifteen ladies and "set out with the most stately scenery, machines, and dresses" by Inigo Jones. Davenant followed up this triumph with *Love and Honor* (1634), *The Platonic Lovers* (1635), *The Fair Favorite* (1638), and *The Unfortunate Lovers* (1638). He wrote one comic masterpiece, *The Wits* (1636), which indicates that in a different age he might have rivaled Dekker and Massinger. Made poet laureate in 1638, later imprisoned and rendered bankrupt for his royalist loyalties, Davenant survived the wars to write the romantic epic *Gondibert* in 1651 and the immensely influential *Siege of Rhodes* in 1656. It was probably Davenant, rather than his talent-starved contemporaries in Henrietta Maria's coterie, who, in the operatic *Siege of Rhodes,* represents the truest link between cavalier tragicomedy and the heroic plays of Dryden and Orrery in the Restoration period.

In spite of Dryden's lampoon of him in *MacFlecknoe* (1682), James SHIRLEY was the last important dramatist of the Caroline stage. Unlike the cavaliers, who often wrote in rhythmic prose and had the printer set up their pages in verse, Shirley was a genuine poet capable of "strong lines," and he worked in genres more considerable than cavalier romance—tragedy in *The Maid's Revenge* (1626), *The Traitor* (1630), *Love's Cruelty* (1631), and *The Cardinal* (1641); occasionally brilliant Jonsonian comedy of humours in *The Lady of Pleasure* (1635); and one romantic comedy in the mode of Robert Greene. Shakespeare, and Dekker in *Hyde Park* (1632). His *Contention of Ajax and Ulysses* (1659) contains the two lines that are said to have haunted Oliver Cromwell; for modern readers Shirley's famous dirge, erupting out of a whole era of drolleries, recalls suddenly how much Caroline writers had fallen from their magnificent past:

> The glories of our blood and state
> Are shadows, not substantial things.

Shirley more deliberately invoked that Elizabethan past in his last play, *The Cardinal,* a revenge tragedy in imitation of Webster's great *Duchess of Malfi.* Shirley's recipe includes all the old ingredients—Machiavellian villainy, gloomy soliloquies, tortuous doubts—and yet that long-simmering Elizabethan sauce turns out to taste like catsup. *The Cardinal* attests that tragedy is not a formula but a way of perceiving the world, and by 1641 tragedy on a London stage was no longer possible because society, like the drama that had betrayed it for two decades, was spiritually exhausted.

A few disciples of Ben Jonson struggled to keep the popular stage alive—Richard BROME, Nathan Field, and Shakerly Marmion—and crisp, witty comedies like Brome's *The Antipodes* (1638) and *A Jovial Crew* (1641) helped to convey to a later generation Jonson's virile wit and realism. Another disciple of Ben Jonson was Thomas RANDOLPH, educated at Jonson's alma mater, Westminster School, and at Trinity College, Cambridge. His *Aristippus, or The Jovial Philosopher* (1630) disputes in loose dramatic form the relative merits of ale and sack, and his *Muse's Looking-Glass* (1638), set in Blackfriars, is a lively but rambling defense of the stage against such Puritan "fantastics" as Mistress Flowerdew and Bird, two characters who might have stepped out of Jonson's *Bartholomew Fair.* Although Randolph's five plays held a brief vogue during the last decade of the period, his uncertain strength was not so much in drama as in classical translations, satires, elegies, and epithalamia; he was incapable of weaving a tight plot, and his erudition found no outlet in the trivialities of feminist tragicomedy or cavalier romance. Like William Davenant, Randolph could not reconcile the tough-minded, satiric, and learned world of Jonson's London comedies with the soft-brained and humid fairyland of Platonic pastoral and heroic drama. His most popular play at court, *Amyntas, or The Impossible Dowry* (1630), an elaborate pastoral in five acts acclaimed by the king and queen when it was performed at Whitehall, demonstrates with its occasional brilliance that he perceived viable alternatives to Montague's vapid *Shepherd's Paradise.*

But for Randolph and his contemporaries the hour was late. By 1642 the popular theaters on the Bankside had fallen into disrepair, and Shakespeare's old company, the King's Men, performed exclusively for royal audiences at Blackfriars and Whitehall. When, on September 2, 1642, Parliament decreed that "public stage plays shall cease and be foreborne," the proclamation meant little more than a *coup de grâce* inflicted on what was already a corpse.

The definitive history of the period, with biographical data, stage and publication information, the records of acting companies, and so forth, is G. E. Bentley, *The Jacobean and Caroline Stage* (1941–68), in seven volumes. A good general introduction is Frederick S. Boas, *An Introduction to Stuart Drama* (1946). For the court dramatists, the best study is Alfred Harbage, *The Cavalier Drama* (1936). The political implications of the Stuart drama are analyzed in E. N. S. Thompson, *The Controversy between the Puritans and the Stage* (1903) and in numerous scholarly articles by William Haller and G. F. Sensabaugh. The chief primary source, and one comparable in value to Henslowe's diary in the Elizabethan period, is *The Dramatic Records of Sir Henry Herbert,* edited by Joseph Q. Adams (1917).—J. E. R.

Restoration drama.   English drama from the restoration of Charles II (1660) to the end of the seventeenth century. When Parliament recalled Charles II in the spring of 1660, the theaters, closed by an act of Parliament in 1642, were able to reopen. During the eighteen-year period when the theaters were closed, plays were sometimes given illegally at the public theaters of London, where they were apt to end with the arrest of the players and the confiscation of their costumes and properties. More often the illegal performances took place outside London or in the private house of some noble. A less risky form of surreptitious drama consisted in the performance of "drolls"—scenes excerpted from the most popular plays and arranged as farcical acts to be mixed with dancing and acrobatics in order to disguise somewhat the nature of the entertainment. Only at the end of the interregnum were there stirrings of new theatrical life in London. At that time Sir William DAVENANT offered "entertainments" at Rutland House, his own mansion, to which the public was admitted for an admission fee. The most famous of these entertainments, *The Siege of Rhodes* (1656), was later hailed by John Dryden as the beginning of heroic plays in England, though to avoid the ban on plays it was presented as opera. It was a landmark, not only because of its heroic theme, which had been to some extent anticipated in earlier plays, but chiefly because of the use of painted scenery, hitherto hardly seen in England except in court masques, and because the cast included actresses. Thus, though the eighteen years following 1642 had offered the theater-lover very slim pickings, continuity with the Elizabethan theater had not been totally destroyed. By the end of the period a tentative experiment had been made in an important new genre with new technical means.

Within three months of his return, Charles II granted patents to Thomas KILLIGREW and Sir William Davenant to organize actors into companies that would enjoy a theatrical monopoly. Although at various times other companies tried to gain a foothold, these two, the King's Company and the Duke's Company (under the patronage of the king's brother the duke of York), are the only important ones in the years before 1682. Killigrew formed the King's Company of older actors, some of whom, such as Michael Mohun and Charles Hart, had acted in their youth before the closing of the theaters. Davenant's younger group included Thomas Betterton, who was to become the most distinguished actor of the period. As a most attractive novelty, each company added to these men certain actresses of whom the best known today is Nell Gwyn, who began as an orange-wench in the theater and left the stage to become the king's mistress. More talented as actresses were Elizabeth Barry and Anne Bracegirdle, who appeared a few years later. In 1682, because of financial difficulties that even the monopoly did not solve, the King's Company was obliged to join forces with the Duke's to form the United Company. This organization lasted until 1695, when a group of actors, under the leadership of Betterton, seceded to form once again a second company.

When they were first formed, the King's and the Duke's companies were obliged to settle in makeshift quarters while they constructed new theaters, for most of the old ones had been torn down and would not, in any case, have suited the taste of this period. What Davenant and Killigrew wanted were indoor theaters in which spectacular effects could be produced with changeable scenery and stage machines. The most elaborate of the new theaters was the elegantly decorated Dorset Garden Theatre, designed by Christopher Wren for Davenant and opened in 1671. By this time the other company had been for several years in the theater they had built in Drury Lane, which was later destroyed by fire and rebuilt in 1674.

Although these various buildings differed from one another, they shared certain features that were characteristic of the Restoration theater. A proscenium arch divided the forestage, which projected into the auditorium, from an upstage area with scenery made of painted side wings and shutters that moved in parallel grooves. There were two or three doors on each side of the proscenium and windows over the doors. Characters usually made their entrances through these doors, unless they were "discovered" by the opening of one of the shutters, and much of the action took place on the forestage, where the actors could be in almost as intimate a relationship to the audience as were the actors on the Elizabethan stage. In such situations the "scene" area, which was approximately as deep as the forestage, merely served as an ornamental background, but in many plays action took place within the scene, as in the "picture-frame" stage of a later era. The Restoration stage was a midpoint in the change from one sort of theater to another.

The scenery, potentially an effective agent of stage realism, was more often used to suggest a world remote and marvelous, the revelation of which by moving the shutters was a marvel in itself. Consequently, the curtain was ordinarily lowered only at the end of the play, permitting changes of scene to take place before the eyes of the audience. A more familiar world of rooms or streets was easily suggested in the proscenium area with its doors and windows. Whether the stage represented contemporary London or the Mexico City of Cortes, it was lit partly by candles and partly by the daylight that came in through a skylight in the auditorium.

To some extent the styles of acting corresponded to the two kinds of stage effects just described. Excluding the style for farce, which remains essentially the same in all ages, the two chief styles required by Restoration drama were the heroic and the high comic. For the former the actors and actresses were expected to declaim their big speeches in a singing tone, somewhat in the manner of an incantation. The effect of the sweeping gestures that accompanied this sort of delivery was heightened by the costumes worn in heroic roles—the gentlemen's plumes and the ladies' trains—which in turn encouraged a stately bearing. By every means the actor sought to project a larger-than-life image in such plays. In comedies of manners, on the other hand, the aim was to imitate the behavior of polite society, as many a prologue and epilogue assured the audience. It was to be hoped that spectators would recognize this style of speaking and gesturing as their own or as what they had often observed. From the point of view of the twentieth century, even this style and the lace-trimmed clothes worn by both sexes seem exceedingly formal, and hence, compared to today's performances, all Restoration acting may be called stylized, though to the society of that age the acting in comedy may have appeared easy and natural. Some of the great actors were equally proficient in both heroic and comic parts: for example, Charles Hart was not only the ranting, heroic Almanzor of Dryden's *The Conquest of Granada* but also the comic, libertine Horner of Wycherley's *The Country Wife*. Elizabeth Barry was both the ludicrous cast-mistress of Etherege's *The Man of Mode* and the pathetic heroine of Otway's *The Orphan*.

The audience for whom Restoration dramatists wrote consisted mainly of the court and the higher levels of town society. While Charles II lived, he often went to the theater. The highest ranking spectators sat in boxes on the sides of the auditorium and in the rear. Here it was also customary for ladies to sit, wearing the "vizard masks" that became synonymous with "ladies." The fashionable young men often chose to sit in the pit, where backless benches, covered with green cloth, were set on a sloping floor. Here orange-wenches peddled their wares, and the beaux chatted with their friends, sometimes paying little attention to the play. Since they were allowed by custom to drop in free if they stayed for only an act or two, they were easily tempted to let social considerations outweigh aesthetic appreciation. Furthermore, when their attention was devoted to the stage, it was not always welcome; a standard complaint of the playwrights was against the caprice of the would-be wits who masked ignorance with self-assurance. In galleries above the boxes sat the less fashionable spectators. As the period drew to a close, these included increasing numbers of middle-class citizens. In the top galleries were the servants of the fashionable spectators. Altogether these theaters probably accommodated about five hundred people, many fewer than the Elizabethan public theaters. Despite some mixture of classes, the Restoration audience was essentially an elite one.

Some of the playwrights who catered to this coterie were part of the coterie themselves. As in the reign of the first Charles, there were courtiers who wrote plays as a gentlemanly amusement, nobles such as the duke of Buckingham, the earl of Orrery, the earl of Rochester, and gentlemen of good family such as Sir George Etherege (knighted by Charles II) and William Wycherley. All of these men, however gifted and however much in need of money, were amateurs. In contrast to them were many others like John Dryden and Thomas Shadwell, professional playwrights who lived by their pens. They derived their income mainly from the profits of the third performance of a play (set aside by custom for the author), from whatever a publisher might pay for the copyright, and from the gifts of patrons to whom they might dedicate their plays.

The two most distinctive forms of Restoration drama are the HEROIC PLAY and the COMEDY OF MANNERS, each of which bears the stamp of this period while owing much to earlier English drama and to French fiction and drama. The ultimate source of the heroic play is the classical epic, as Dryden makes clear in his essay "Of Heroic Plays," printed with *The Conquest of Granada* in 1672. In defending the character of his hero, Almanzor, Dryden writes: "The first image I had of him was from the *Achilles* of Homer; the next from Tasso's *Rinaldo* (who was a copy of the former), and the third from the *Artaban* of Monsieur Calprenède, who has imitated both." This genealogy is most instructive. Not only does it point to the archetype of heroic self-assertion, but it reminds us of the Italian Renaissance version of such a character in Torquato Tasso's *Jerusalem Delivered,* where the ideals of medieval Christian romance are superimposed on the Homeric pattern. Finally, we are referred to an immediate source of the play: the seventeenth-century French romance *Clèopâtre,* one example of a fashionable genre in which extravagant action is combined with the utmost refinement of sentiment. Growing from such stock, it is not surprising that the heroic play often presented actions of epic scope. It was, as Dryden said, "an imitation, in little, of an heroic poem" and in some instances not notably little: *The Conquest of Granada* was in two parts of five acts each.

Nor is it surprising that the characteristic themes of the heroic play were, in Dryden's words, "Love and Valour." The hero represented an exalted ideal of the potentialities of human nature—the sort of ideal to which the marvels of both the classical epic and medieval romance had contributed and which had found a philosophic base in the Renaissance in the writings of such men as Pico della Mirandola. It is not angelic virtue which distinguishes most of these Restoration supermen, but a greatness less easy to place in a moral category and having more to do with energy, imagination, and magnanimity than with strictly defined goodness. Heroes of this kind had occasionally trod the English stage in the Elizabethan era, notably in the plays of Marlowe and Chapman. Beaumont and Fletcher had exploited the themes of love and honor in contemporary French and Spanish romances to produce dilemmas that tried the souls of their extraordinary protagonists. Several dramatists had followed their lead in the portrayal of romantic heroes, among them Davenant and Killigrew, who were to play so vital a part in reviving the theater. In France Pierre Corneille had not only created a brilliant succession of great-spirited men and women but had also discussed them in his influential critical writings. The debt of the English stage to Corneille was acknowledged by Dryden in "Of Heroic Plays."

If the themes of the heroic play were derived in part from native and in part from foreign traditions, one feature of the first heroic plays came, without any doubt, from France. Shortly after his accession to the throne, King Charles, who admired the rhyming Alexandrines of French drama, asked the earl of Orrery (1621–1679) to write a play in rhyme. *The General,* in rhymed pentameter ("heroic") couplets, was the result. Written in 1661, though not performed in London till 1664, it set a fashion that reigned for some fifteen years and that has led some historians of drama to restrict the term "heroic play" to those written in rhyming verse. Here, however, the term is used more flexibly to include the plays in blank verse that present similar characters and themes. Though it is proper to consider heroic plays as variants of a tragic form, the endings of many of them, following the precedents of Beaumont and Fletcher and of Corneille, are happy, reinforcing in this way the emphasis on potentiality inherent in epic and romance.

The comedy for which Restoration drama is best known today was in some respects the antithesis of the heroic play. With a local setting rather than a remote one and a worldly rake as protagonist instead of a glorious warrior or idealistic lover, witty and satirical repartee, usually in prose, took the place of declamation in verse. Repartee had appeared in English comedy as far back as the plays of John Lyly and had been conspicuous in the dialogue of Shakespeare's Benedick and Beatrice and in Ben Jonson's *Epicene.* Satirical humor had been featured by Jonson and John Marston. John Fletcher had combined wit and a libertine attitude in *The Wild Goose Chase* and *Wit Without Money,* and James Shirley, writing shortly before the closing of the theaters, had added to the ingredients of his predecessors a greater concern for the manners of polite society in *The Lady of Pleasure* and *Hyde Park.* The characters surrounding the comic hero of Restoration comedy were usually familiar types, some of which, like the irate old father or the clever servant, derived ultimately from Greek and Roman comedy and were common in Renaissance drama. The humor inherent in this kind of characterization was often accentuated by the use of "ticket" names, such as Sir Fopling Flutter or Sir Tunbelly Clumsey, which reduce the personality to one or two conspicuous traits. Ben Jonson had made extensive use of such names, as had many other English dramatists. Thus, though the delicately pointed satire of Molière was obviously an inspiration to Restoration playwrights, who borrowed freely from his plays, the native tradition already contained almost all the elements they were to develop.

Heroic drama and the comedy of manners differ so greatly that at first it is difficult to see how the same audiences could have accepted both. Yet there are plays in which hero and rake, rant and repartee, romance and satire appear together. Again Fletcher anticipated later developments. In *Monsieur Thomas* he used libertine comedy as counterpoint to heroic tragicomedy. Dryden's *Secret Love* (1667) and *Mar-*

THE

REHEARSAL,

As it is now Acted at the

Theatre-Royal.

The third Edition with Amendments and large Additions by the Author.

LONDON,

Printed for *Thomas Dring,* at the *Harrow* at the Corner of *Chancery-lane* in *Fleet-ſtreet.* 1 6 7 5.

TITLE PAGE OF THE 1675 EDITION OF THE DUKE OF BUCKINGHAM'S *The Rehearsal*

riage à la Mode (1671) both have heroic romance in one plot and libertine wit in the other with no indication that the romance is to be taken any the less seriously. There is no doubt that Restoration audiences were well aware of the ludicrous possibilities in the extravagant postures of heroic characters, for we have the evidence, not only of comic subplots, but also of burlesques such as *The Rehearsal* (1671) by the duke of Buckingham and others, explicitly satirizing Dryden's heroic plays. But people at all times have known that anything solemn can be made to seem ridiculous, and this knowledge does not necessarily destroy belief in what they have laughed at for a moment. There is no reason to believe that the validity of the heroic ideal was seriously questioned by Restoration wit or burlesque.

What is more surprising than the juxtaposition of heroic drama and witty comedy is the existence in each form of characteristics of the other. The rake's wit is like the hero's imagination. The dullard is the antithesis of both, as Dryden states in the dedication of *Aureng-Zebe,* where dullness is opposed to the virtues that constitute true greatness. Like the hero, the rake is supremely energetic in pursuit of his goals and supremely concerned with his own dignity. He is ready with a Hobbesian laugh of "sudden glory" at the ineptitude of the fop but as determined as the hero to avoid such a disgrace himself.

If we look at heroic drama with the characteristics of comedy freshly in mind, we see what commentators from the seventeenth century to the present time

have noticed—that a libertine ethos is often present here too, and not just in the characterization of villains and wicked adventuresses. Though a hero such as Almanzor (Dryden's *Conquest of Granada*) is not a thoroughgoing libertine, his claim to superiority over ordinary morality and his longing for complete freedom of action are strikingly analogous to those of the rake. Furthermore, in Dryden's *Aureng-Zebe* the idealistic hero is given the speech "When I consider life, 'tis all a cheat . . ." which expresses a disillusionment appropriate for the most skeptical of libertines. In this play, satire with a wryly humorous twist invades several serious scenes.

From these juxtapositions and interpenetrations of the heroic and comic, it must be concluded that in some sense the idealism of one and the cynicism of the other were mutually dependent. The unresolved tension between them gave vitality to both forms, and neither one totally negated the other.

To produce an adequate picture of the dramatic fare offered by Restoration theater, these comments on the most distinctive forms of plays must be supplemented in two ways. It is necessary to know which of the old plays were performed and to examine the new plays in greater detail. Of the old plays available when the theaters reopened, those by Francis Beaumont and John Fletcher were by far the most popular. Dryden's comment in 1668 in his *Essay of Dramatic Poesy* is most revealing: "Their plays are now the most pleasant and frequent entertainments of the stage: two of theirs being acted through the year for one of Shakespeare's or Johnson's [*sic*]: the reason is, because there is a certain gaiety in their comedies, and pathos in their more serious plays, which suits generally with all men's humours. Shakespeare's language is likewise a little obsolete, and Ben Johnson's [*sic*] wit comes short of theirs." Thus, Shakespeare and Jonson followed Beaumont and Fletcher in popularity. Some of the other pre-Commonwealth authors represented by a play or two in the early years of the Restoration were Marlowe, Chapman, Webster, Middleton, Massinger, Ford, Shirley, and Brome. Occasionally a translation of Corneille was performed. In the season 1675/76, when the new companies and new playwrights were well established, nineteen plays by Restoration playwrights were performed. In this same season twelve older English plays appeared, including four by Beaumont and Fletcher, four by Shakespeare, and two by Jonson. There was also one play by Corneille in translation. Even at this time, then, more than a third of the plays were revivals of pre-Restoration plays.

The continuity between the two periods is demonstrated even more forcibly by another circumstance. Many of the new plays were heavily indebted to Elizabethan drama, sometimes to the point of being little more than adaptations. When Shakespeare was altered, the plays were usually presented as his work with the "improvements" offered, however condescendingly, as homage to his genius. Even when Thomas Otway rifled *Romeo and Juliet* for his Roman play *Caius Marius* (1679), the Prologue acknowledged the theft and thus transformed it into an allusion. With lesser-known Elizabethans the procedure was different. One of the plays of the 1675/76 season was *Abdelazer* by Mrs. Aphra Behn (1640–1689), a tragedy of monstrous villainy taken directly

APHRA BEHN (NEW YORK PUBLIC LIBRARY)

and silently from the anonymous *Lust's Dominion* of about 1600. It is less surprising to find that Mrs. Behn has updated the dialogue with a "love and honor" speech for one of the characters than to discover that some of the heroic rant of the villain is taken with the alteration of only a few words from the original play. This secondhand Marlovian rhetoric is perfectly at home in the Restoration play.

A highly successful comedy of Aphra Behn's, *The Rover* (1677), abounding in the libertine situations and sentiments that seem so characteristic of Restoration comedy, is the end result of a series of thefts. Written in a style that sometimes recalls Fletcher, it owes its plot partly to a play by Jonson's follower Brome and even more to a play by Killigrew, who had taken his basic situations from Middleton's *Blurt Master Constable* (1601). It is another indication that something more than merely the seeds of Restoration drama was present in Elizabethan drama.

A closely related phenomenon is the persistence, side by side with plays in the latest fashion, of some that patently continue or revive Elizabethan modes and styles. Tragedies of blood that were not pure thefts like *Abdelazer* continued to be written, as did comedies of humor in the manner of Jonson and comedies of intrigue based, in the Fletcherian manner, on French or Spanish romances. Especially striking examples of the revival of an old mode are the English history plays written by John Banks (c. 1650–c. 1700). The blank verse, rarely more than competent, has an oddly Elizabethan ring, and there is very little in the characterization that cannot be found in the earlier period.

Enough has been said to suggest the general character of the chief forms of Restoration drama, but individual dramatists achieved very different effects with them. In heroic drama there were vast differences in the kinds of heroes they depicted. While some pursued the line of the Elizabethan villain-

hero, Orrery, in his *Henry V* (1664) and *Mustapha* (1665), chose to present irreproachable heroes whose amazing generosity recalls the *Nicomède* of Corneille. Dryden ran the gamut in one play, *Tyrannic Love* (1669), from the virtue of a Christian martyr to the villainy of a tyrant. Although he insisted, no doubt sincerely, that his villainous Maximin was intended only "to set off the character" of his saint, both characters are heroic, and Maximin far more dynamically so.

Dryden more often depicted a hero who was neither saint nor villain but whose largeness of spirit made him admirable. Of Antony in *All for Love* Ventidius remarks that the path of virtue is sometimes "too narrow / For his vast soul." Almanzor in *The Conquest of Granada* is compared to "a wandering star, / Whose motion's just, though 'tis not regular." An irregular greatness, which is in the main beneficent, characterizes most of Dryden's heroes.

The meaning of this irregular greatness is clarified by a structure of contrasting characters. In THE CONQUEST OF GRANADA, a particularly good example, the hero Almanzor is contrasted with a weak and corrupt king; a Hobbesian adventuress who has almost as much ambition as the hero but none of his principles; an ideally good warrior and lover who lacks the spectacular force of the hero; and with the object of his affection, Almahide, who admires Almanzor's energy while adhering to a stricter concept of moral and political order. Ultimately, through her influence, a balance between energy and order is attained.

In AURENG-ZEBE, Dryden's last play in heroic couplets, the balance is suggested not only by the contrast between Indamora, a faithful woman, and Morat, whose soul is "irregularly great," but also by a division of the hero's role between Morat and his brother, the titular hero who comes far closer to the good and generous characters of Orrery. When Dryden reworked *Antony and Cleopatra* into ALL FOR LOVE, he accentuated Shakespeare's suggestions of contrasting systems of value—Roman law and Egyptian love—and contrived a final scene in which the dead lovers, enthroned side by side, "As they were giving laws to half mankind," seem to have achieved the order that eluded them in life. See John DRYDEN.

In the hands of Thomas Otway and Nathaniel LEE, both of whom began writing for the stage in the mid-1670's, serious drama became a display of overwhelming emotions. Lee's characters, in plays such as *Sophonisba* (1675) and THE RIVAL QUEENS, have the vast dimensions of Dryden's, but the essential conflict has less to do with the values for which they stand and more with the fact that they are articulately passionate. In *The Rival Queens* the major scenes are the confrontations of Statira and Roxana, the wives who vie for the love of Alexander the Great. After the rhetoric of their encounters, other scenes—even the death of the warrior-hero—seem rather tame. Dryden was quite aware of the difference between his own plays and those of his young friend, with whom he was later to collaborate. In a commendatory poem published with *The Rival Queens,* he wrote, "We only warm the Head, but you the Heart."

Thomas OTWAY, a more subtle dramatist than Lee, also achieved his greatest successes in the portrayal of emotion, especially pathos. His most famous characters are more sinned against than sinning and more acted upon than acting. Though their emotional response is intense, their stature is less conventionally heroic than that of Dryden's or Lee's characters. Like many tormented heroes and heroines of Beaumont and Fletcher, they are caught in dilemmas for which they are only partly responsible. Their agony is what Otway makes memorable.

In Otway's first great success, *Don Carlos* (1676), the hero is a noble prince whose father has deprived him of the woman he loves by marrying her himself. Though the prince is driven to the verge of rebellion by his father's cruelty, his essential goodness is so convincingly demonstrated that the king repents. In the climactic scene of the play, father and son are reconciled, but only as Don Carlos is dying of self-inflicted wounds. The pathos of goodness recognized too late is characteristic of Otway, though there are verbal echoes in this reconciliation scene of Dryden's *Aureng-Zebe,* performed the previous year. In 1668 Dryden had praised the pathos in the "more serious plays" of Beaumont and Fletcher, and in 1679 he wrote in his Preface to *Troilus and Cressida* that pity was "the noblest and most god-like of moral virtues." Now Otway was making the appeal to this virtue the mainstay of his drama.

Otway's THE ORPHAN and VENICE PRESERVED were cited with Southerne's *The Fatal Marriage* (1694) by John Downes, a contemporary man of the theater, as the three most successful plays of the period. In all of them Elizabeth Barry triumphed in the role of an innocent but fatally doomed heroine. The nature of Otway's chief concern is especially clear in his best play, *Venice Preserved,* where the prominence of political allusion leads one to expect propaganda or possibly debate between rival political philosophies (in this case revolution and authoritarianism). Though the political themes are important, and seemed especially so in the heated atmosphere of the recent "Popish Plot" of 1678, more important still is the personal dilemma of the hero, Jaffeir, married to the daughter of a heartless senator and taken into the conspiracy by a political idealist who is his best friend. The power of the tragedy is felt in Jaffeir's torment—in the conflict between love and friendship, between personal honor and patriotic duty.

John Banks's history plays, cited as examples of Elizabethan style in the Restoration, were typical of their time in one respect—in their emphasis on pathos. The very title of one of them, *Virtue Betrayed, or Anna Bullen* (1682), suggests the emotional response that many scenes in these plays sought to evoke. A thoroughly second-rate dramatist, Banks reflects clearly the shift of sensibility that was taking place.

When Dryden, after several years' absence from the theater, wrote *Don Sebastian* (1689), his treatment of tragedy was in line with this development. His main plot concerns the lovers Don Sebastian and Almeyda, who discover that they are brother and sister and who therefore renounce their love. In a position of prominence is a scene in which the renegade Dorax recognizes the goodness of Don Sebastian after years of misunderstanding. Like earlier Dryden heroes, Don Sebastian is noble and energetic, but the ultimate manifestation of his nobility is renunciation,

and his energy is seen in what Dorax describes as "this headlong torrent of your goodness."

Some dramatists, Dryden among them, explored the possibility of intensifying emotion and reinforcing the marvelous by means of operatic techniques. Music was an important feature of all Restoration theater. The Elizabethan tradition of songs in plays was continued, incidental music for atmospheric effects was used more than it had been, and the orchestra entertained the audience with an overture before the play began. In opera the contribution of music was still greater. It was the exceptional opera, however, which was sung throughout, as were Davenant's epoch-making *The Siege of Rhodes,* where music was a device for evading the ban on plays, and Purcell's *Dido and Aeneas* (1689), written for a girls' school. What was called opera in England in this period was usually a mixture of spoken and sung drama in which only the climactic scenes were musical. A good example is the Dryden-Purcell *King Arthur* (1691), in which certain tendencies of the heroic play can be studied to advantage. At important moments the action stops while the significance of the situation is projected in musical terms. The "air," or aria, takes the place of the heroic declamation, with music rather than figures of speech to produce the desired elevation. The formality of heroic drama is carried a step further; familiar behavior is a step further removed.

Lesser practitioners of heroic drama, such as Elkanah Settle, John Crowne, Nahum Tate, and John Banks (whose history plays have already been mentioned), left little imprint on the form. They were content to "elevate and surprise," as the satirical authors of *The Rehearsal* put it, and to write huffing speeches for their heroes or villains. Settle's popular *The Empress of Morocco* (1673) has a special interest, however, since it was published with engravings that show some of the settings used for the performance in the Dorset Garden Theatre. From these it is easy to see what sort of contribution changeable scenery made to heroic drama. For *The Empress of Morocco,* it provided not only exotic splendor for certain scenes but also, for a rousing finale, a shocking spectacle of the corpse of the villain impaled on iron spikes.

If serious drama became less heroic and more pathetic in plays such as Otway's *The Orphan,* it was not only pathetic but also domestic in *The Fatal Marriage, or The Innocent Adultery* (1694) by Thomas Southerne (1660–1746), the third of the plays cited by Downes as the outstanding successes of this period. Southerne used for his main plot a novel by Aphra Behn about a woman who marries for the second time when she believes her first husband to be dead. The heart of the play is the heroine's plight, after seven years of waiting for her husband's return, when the cruelty of her father-in-law forces her to accept at last the hero's offer of marriage. When her first husband reappears, the shock drives her to madness and suicide. The strong suggestions of melodrama in these situations are reinforced by the presentation of the first husband's younger brother as a singularly wicked schemer who knows his brother is alive but conceals his knowledge as part of a plot to get an inheritance. This is a tragic world far removed from the ideal perspectives and the awesome ambitions of Dryden's *The Conquest of Granada*. Appropriately, Southerne offers in his last scene an admonition to parents not to discriminate against younger brothers and thus push them toward crime. In keeping with the atmosphere of domestic and homiletic pathos, blank verse, which had been common in tragedy for fifteen years, is mixed with prose, and the language is relatively simple, if exclamatory. Truly heroic figures had not vanished from the stage, and more were to come in some of the plays of Rowe and Addison, but Southerne's tragedy is an excellent illustration of a gradual diminution of tragic stature and avoidance of extravagant language along with a marked increase of sentiment and explicit morality.

The Fatal Marriage also provides one more example of the combination of serious and comic drama, for the subplot, occupying a large portion of the first three acts, consists of the deceptions practiced by young rakes and their cooperative ladies upon an old, jealous husband who is brought to repentance for his folly. Tragic deception is thus matched by comic deception, a fatal marital imbroglio by an amusing one, and a homily against discrimination by a homily against jealousy.

The authors of Restoration comedy differed as much from one another as the authors of serious drama. The wit and libertinism of Sir Frederick Frollick in *The Comical Revenge, or Love in a Tub* (1664) by Sir George ETHEREGE pointed the way to the witty comedy that was most distinctive of the period. This play, like Dryden's *Secret Love* and *Marriage à la Mode,* had a heroic as well as a comic plot, but in his next play, *She Would If She Could* (1668), Etherege dropped the serious plot and improved upon the comic wit. In THE MAN OF MODE he wrote his best play and brought witty comedy to one of its high points. Dorimant, the libertine hero, is a superb representative of a kind of fashionable behavior that Etherege makes attractive while he also exposes it to critical examination. Occasionally we see Dorimant from the perspective of the lower-class characters to whom his behavior seems extravagant and affected, but most of the scenes are contrived to emphasize his seeming naturalness, grace, and artful refinement. When he casts off an old mistress, he maintains a witty detachment while she flies into a fury. Even when his feelings are engaged by a beautiful girl, he conceals them with urbane compliments. His control is matched by that of Harriet, the heroine, who is as witty as he and as clever at playing a part. Compared to Sir Fopling Flutter, the amusing but absurd fop, Dorimant has the perfect assurance of one to the manner born, though he is also cruel where Sir Fopling is harmless. It is not easy to be sure whether the engagement of Dorimant and Harriet at the end is another conquest for him or evidence that at last he has had to give up his libertine detachment. Thus, the venerable romance formula by which the hero finally wins the heroine is given an ambiguous meaning, and the lofty ideal of love is, if not totally negated, at least heavily qualified.

During the years between Etherege's first and last comedies, Dryden, in the comic plots of the plays already mentioned, also presented witty couples, allowing them a licentiousness of speech, chiefly in the form of sexual *double-entendre,* which goes beyond anything in Etherege. MARRIAGE À LA MODE, the better of the two plays, is one of the funniest comedies of the period. Less subtle and less complex than *The Man of Mode,* it differs also in presenting a mainly satirical view of fashionable manners.

Still more satirical are THE COUNTRY WIFE and *The Plain Dealer* by William WYCHERLEY, both of which are based in part on plays by Molière. In the first, the chief satirical agent is the hero, Horner, who pretends to be impotent so that husbands will trust him with their wives. His success with a series of ladies is used, not only as the basis for bawdy comedy, but also as a means of unmasking a corrupt and hypocritical society. Where deception and play-acting in *The Man of Mode* are part of a game played by the most admirable characters, they are made more repulsive in *The Country Wife*. The calculated deceptions of Horner are more crudely self-serving than those of Dorimant and Harriet, and the emphasis of the play falls on his stripping away of the pretenses of his victims.

Manly, the hero of THE PLAIN DEALER, is a more conventional satirist than Horner—a disillusioned idealist, suggested by Molière's "misanthrope." His stripping and scourging of society are more savage than Horner's, and the tone of the play is correspondingly more somber, sometimes to the point of bitterness. Dryden wrote in 1677 that "the author of the *Plain Dealer,* whom I am proud to call my friend, has obliged all honest and virtuous men, by one of the most bold, most general, and most useful satires, which has ever been presented on the English theatre." A typical motif of romance is found in Wycherley's presentation of the heroine Fidelia, who, disguised as a boy, follows Manly. This motif adds to the seriousness of tone while at the same time jars with the satire. The fun and high spirits of *The Country Wife* are replaced in the majority of scenes in *The Plain Dealer* by indignation or pathos, though in the subplot a more lighthearted comedy prevails.

Several years before the appearance of *The Plain Dealer* a battle was fought over the proper way to write comedy. In *An Essay of Dramatic Poesy* Dryden wrote that repartee was "one of the chiefest graces" of comedy and that "the greatest pleasure of the audience is a chace of wit." He boldly maintained that Jonson, though "the most learned and judicious writer which any theatre ever had," was "frugal" of wit. "Humour was his proper sphere." For Thomas SHADWELL, a worshiper of Jonson, the suggestion of such a limitation was heretical, and in the Preface to his comedy *The Sullen Lovers* (1668), he vigorously defended Jonson by stating that wit in comedy did not consist in repartee (which he considered a euphemism for bawdy and profane dialogue) but in the depiction of humours. In his own comedies he attempted to follow his master and demonstrate the proper method of comic composition. *The Sullen Lovers* is a parade of humour characters, some of whom were easily recognizable as satirical portraits of contemporaries. Humour characters were not absent from the plays of Etherege, Dryden, or Wycherley, but in *The Sullen Lovers* much more time is taken, as in some of Jonson's early plays, with the mere exhibition of various eccentricities. Even in a later and better play, *The Squire of Alsatia* (1688), which has a firmer structure based on the Roman dramatist Terence, much of the comedy derives from the presentation of underworld characters and their special cant. The chief virtue of Shadwell's comedies is their satirical reflection of the life of the time, yet they have neither the subtlety of Etherege nor the power of Wycherley.

A number of playwrights, competent but less talented than those just discussed, produced comedies in the first twenty-five years of the period. Aphra Behn has already been mentioned, and others succeeded, as she did, in giving a contemporary flavor to romantic or domestic drama such as had flourished before the closing of the theaters. A few attempted the newer comedy of wit, and more took advantage of the tolerance of immorality on the stage to write what would now be called bedroom farce, such as *The London Cuckolds* (1681) by Edward Ravenscroft. Entertaining as some of these comedies are, and in some respects characteristic of the period, they do not contribute much to an understanding of the distinctive developments of Restoration comedy.

In the last ten years of the seventeenth century an important new development can be seen in the midst of a continuation, or a revival, of witty comedy. In 1696 Colley Cibber (1671–1757), who was to be one of the outstanding men of the theater and eventually poet laureate, appeared as the fop, Sir Novelty Fashion, in his own play, *Love's Last Shift.* Despite the impression given by Pope's devastating satire of him in *The Dunciad,* Cibber was far from dull, and he con-

COLLEY CIBBER (NEW YORK PUBLIC LIBRARY)

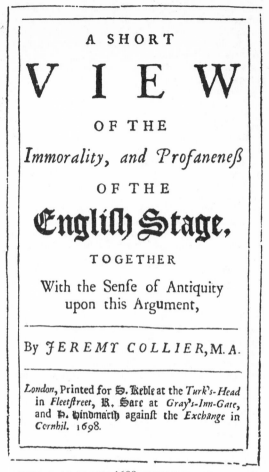

A SHORT

VIEW

OF THE

Immorality, and Profaneß

OF THE

Engliſh Stage,

TOGETHER

With the Senſe of Antiquity
upon this Argument,

By *JEREMY COLLIER,* M. A.

London, Printed for S. Keble at the *Turk's-Head* in *Fleetſtreet,* R. Sare at *Gray's-Inn-Gate,* and H. hindmarth againſt the *Exchange* in *Cornhil.* 1698.

TITLE PAGE OF THE 1698 EDITION OF JEREMY COLLIER'S *A Short View of the Immorality and Profaneness of the English Stage*

trived both clever dialogue and amusing situations for his lovers and their ladies. The new development is to be seen in the main plot where, by a trick, the libertine Loveless is brought back to the wife he deserted many years before. The conventional morality of this action contrasts strongly with *The Man of Mode* and *The Country Wife,* and the Epilogue even boasts that "There's not one cuckold made in all this play." To be sure, the device by which the married couple is reunited exposes the morality of the play to question. Loveless, returning after a long absence, is persuaded that his wife, Amanda, is dead, and he is offered an assignation with a lady who turns out to be Amanda. Her appearance has been so altered that he does not recognize her, and only after the "seduction" does she reveal her identity. The ending is repentance, the prospect of a happy future, and a brief masque in praise of marriage. Thus the spectator is given the titillation of an immoral intrigue along with the assurance that it is no such thing.

Even this compromise, however, is an indication of changing taste. Partly because of the increasing numbers of middle-class theatergoers, a movement to reform the stage was gaining impetus and was to find its most voluble and violent spokesman in Jeremy Collier, a clergyman whose *Short View of the Immorality and Profaneness of the English Stage* appeared in 1698. Early in the next century comedy was to become rigorously didactic.

Sir John VANBRUGH immediately wrote a sequel to *Love's Last Shift* called THE RELAPSE, in which Loveless again becomes unfaithful to Amanda. It is a more sparkling play than Cibber's but by no means a total rejection of Cibber's premises. Vanbrugh retained the character of the fop, now elevated to a barony as Lord Foppington and acted once again by Cibber. And though Loveless is a rake again, Amanda's virtue not only withstands the advances of a lover but converts him to a virtuous life. The subplot presents the broadly farcical scenes in which Lord Foppington's younger brother outwits him by marrying the country heiress he had designed for himself. Somewhat unexpectedly, Lord Foppington ceases to be entirely a figure of fun in these scenes and acquires some shreds of dignity and humanity in the midst of his comic misfortunes. The play is neither so immoral nor so heartless as some of the earlier comedies.

The best of all the comic dramatists of the Restoration made his entrance in this last decade. William CONGREVE was able to bring the comedy of wit to its highest point by writing a more polished prose than any of his predecessors. Both Dryden and Etherege had excelled at repartee, but Congreve achieved a rhythm, balance, and acuity that made his dialogue superior to that of even *The Man of Mode*. Of his two best plays, LOVE FOR LOVE and THE WAY OF THE WORLD, the second is the more representative of his genius, though the first had by far the greater success and is often considered even today the more playable. It has more laughable scenes and more farce mixed in with the repartee, but in brilliance of wit and consistency of tone *The Way of the World* outstrips it. Something of the special quality of Congreve's comedy may be suggested by two quotations. The first illustrates his skill with epigrammatic characterization: "An old woman's appetite is depraved like that of a girl—'tis the green sickness of a second childhood, and like the faint offer of a latter spring, serves but to usher in the fall and withers in an affected bloom." Though the character described is entertaining onstage, no pleasure she gives can surpass that of the description. The second quotation exemplifies the detachment that is characteristic not only of the author but also of the hero, Mirabell, who is speaking, and the heroine, Millamant, whom he is discussing. Fainall, the villain of the play, has just said that Millamant has wit.

> *Mirabell:* She has beauty enough to make any man think so, and complaisance enough not to contradict him who shall tell her so.
> *Fainall:* For a passionate lover, methinks you are a man somewhat too discerning in the failings of your mistress.
> *Mirabell:* And for a discerning man, somewhat too passionate a lover; for I like her with all her faults—nay like her for her faults.

From this second quotation it can be seen that Mirabell not only has the assurance and self-control of his predecessor, Etherege's Dorimant, but also has

more genuine feeling. While the edge of the witty raillery is finer than in Etherege's play, the tone of *The Way of the World* is noticeably warmer. In this respect Congreve is similar to his contemporary Vanbrugh, and both are in step with the tragic dramatists who were putting greater stress on pathos. The development in comedy was soon to lead to tearful sentimentality.

With regard to morality, *The Way of the World* is also characteristic of the period. Congreve, along with Vanbrugh, engaged in the defense of the stage against the formidable Jeremy Collier, but it cannot be said that they scored any great successes, for if Collier's premise was adopted that the stage must "recommend virtue and discountenance vice" by showing only indisputably moral characters in a favorable light, then few Restoration comedies could be justified. Though *The Way of the World* has far less libertinism than many earlier comedies, its hero is not a model of virtue, and yet he is rewarded with marriage to the woman he loves. It was unfortunate that Congreve felt obliged to defend himself on the wrong grounds. The virtue of his work is one that was never discussed in the controversy with Collier—a keen and nicely balanced view of the world, perfectly projected in the shapeliness of the prose. A sane morality is not absent from such a view, but the inculcation of morality is not the prime objective. The achievement of such a balance is an end in itself. It constitutes the perfection of high comedy.

The standard general history of Restoration drama is Volume I of Allardyce Nicoll's *A History of English Drama 1660–1900*, entitled *Restoration Drama 1660–1700* (4th ed., 1955). Invaluable for its detailed information about the theater and its day-by-day account of performances is *The London Stage 1660–1800*, edited by William Van Lennep, Emmett L. Avery, and Arthur H. Scouten; Part I (1965) covers the years 1660–1700. Various aspects of the theater are also treated by Montague Summers in his two books, *The Playhouse of Pepys* (1964) and *The Restoration Theatre* (1964). An excellent brief introduction, containing detailed accounts of many plays, is John Harold Wilson's *A Preface to Restoration Drama* (1965). There are too many special studies of Restoration comedy to mention here, but three general treatments stand out: Bonamy Dobrée's *Restoration Comedy 1660–1720* (1924); Thomas H. Fujimura's *The Restoration Comedy of Wit* (1952); and Norman N. Holland's *The First Modern Comedies* (1959). On the tragedy of the period the best is still Bonamy Dobrée's *Restoration Tragedy 1660–1720* (1929). Three recent collections of stimulating critical essays are: *Restoration Theatre. Stratford-upon-Avon Studies, VI*, edited by John R. Brown and Bernard Harris (1965); *Restoration Drama: Modern Essays in Criticism*, edited by John Loftis (1966); and *Restoration Dramatists: A Collection of Critical Essays* (1966), edited by E. Miner.—E. W.

eighteenth century. The eighteenth century, it is generally agreed, does not constitute one of the more notable periods in English drama. Although the playwrights of the time were numerous and often successful in scoring theatrical triumphs at one or another of the London playhouses, few are well remembered today or, judged solely on the basis of their dramatic work per se, really deserve to be.

However, a distinction should be made between the eighteenth-century English theater as an established institution of national importance, enjoying uninterruptedly a thoroughly vigorous life, and the dramatic literature that was produced between about 1700 and the onset of the Romantic era in the 1790's. The theatrical enterprise, taken in its inclusive aspects, possesses an importance of its own in that it directs our attention in the clearest manner to the conditions then surrounding the drama and giving it its distinctive properties. Many of the plays of this period, which otherwise hold little or no interest, acquire significance as dramatic events when they are placed in this wider setting. Such is the case regarding many of the comedies—in particular sentimental comedy as a type—and perhaps most of the tragedies.

The dramatists of genuine distinction, of whom there were scarcely as many as ten, were preponderantly writers of comedy. However, any discussion of eighteenth-century drama confined to the work of the foremost playwrights is bound to result in an inaccurate picture of the London theater as a whole. The trends and changing fashions that occurred in dramatic taste and practices ought not to be entirely overlooked, any more than should the social and moral views affecting all the literary arts of that time. Nor should the lesser dramatists be left out of account.

The theater of the Restoration had reflected the mood and interests of a small, closed society. The all-important fact about eighteenth-century theater is that it belonged increasingly to the middle class, to whose artistic preferences and sense of everyday values it was necessarily responsive. Manifestations of the new spirit were hastened perhaps by Jeremy Collier's tract of 1698 criticizing the English stage, but playwrights at the turn of the century were simultaneously reflecting the new ideas about comedy. Thomas D'Urfey (1653–1723), for instance, who had already introduced a softer note into his comedy *Love for Money* (1690 or 1691), showed further compliance with the changing mood in both *The Bath* (1701) and *The Modern Prophets* (1709), the latter comedy being described as "morally intended." George Farquhar was creating a comic world full of good nature and irresistible high spirits, refreshingly different from that provided by Restoration comedy. Richard Steele had begun to chasten the harsher notes of comedy. The close of 1704 brought the production of *The Careless Husband* by Colley Cibber, with its scenes and accompanying rhetoric of exaggerated sentimentalism.

A state of mind as different from old-fashioned moral rigorism as from the worldliness of the Restoration was emerging. Benevolence, a Divine principle, was taken to be immanent in human nature. Every man was thought to have within himself, implanted by God, the instincts of love and charity toward his fellows. This credo suited a nation that was now confident of its course, increasingly well-to-do, developing a humanitarian sense of social responsibilities, and proud of its tradition of political liberty. Something of this spirit naturally found expression in literature and, in more exaggerated forms, yielded the sentimentalism so often present in eighteenth-century drama and fiction. As for the theater, it was now, *pace* Collier, pronounced a delightful school of morality, affording the most rational and highest entertainment. Or, as Steele put it, there was no human institution "so aptly calculated for the forming of a free-born people as that of the theatre."

It is in comedy that the effects of the new attitude are most apparent. Good-natured laughter, essentially sympathetic, now began to replace satiric ridicule. The function of comedy was being redefined: Its purpose was not to reveal knaves and fools but to reform truants through an appeal to their better, that is, their true, selves. The entire comic syndrome—characters, plot development, scenes, language—was in consequence altered. A different situation governed in the theater when comedy was on the boards, for the audience was no longer invited to view the play objectively but rather to share the emotional experiences the characters were undergoing. Distance, essential for what at most other times has been assumed to be true comedy, disappeared.

The change in tragedy was not so radical. The reason lies in the fact that the kind of pathos that Nicholas Rowe, for instance, sought to evoke through "she-tragedies" like *The Fair Penitent* and *Jane Shore* had already been well established in Restoration tragedy by such writers as Nathaniel Lee, Thomas Otway, and Thomas Southerne. Sympathetic response would seem to be an inevitable part of our experience in the presence of tragic drama. Undoubtedly the increasing emphasis on feeling in general accounts in part for the fact that the eighteenth century made so much of the pathetic nature of the tragic play, but what was thought of as pathos should not be too hastily identified with the sentimentalism informing so many of the comedies. In comedy sentimentalism carried with it principles of a benevolistic stamp by no means always present in, and rarely central to, the tragedies, however pathetic. The spectacle of human suffering was believed to be in itself sufficient to stir us profoundly. Dr. Johnson, surely no friend of benevolism as a moral credo, asserted that the design of tragedy was "to instruct by moving the passions." We are no longer moved by the tragedies of Dr. Johnson's century; their idiom has dated. We find ourselves closer, really, to the comedy of the eighteenth century, despite all its shortcomings.

To trace, now, the outstanding events in the dramatic history of the period, first in regard to tragedy and then to comedy. The generic distinctions were then so sharply defined and so insistently emphasized that for many years tragedy and comedy led virtually separate lives. At the same time, however, many kinds of comedy were recognized in the repertories of the principal theaters: Shakespearean comedy, Jonsonian "comedy of humours," Restoration comedy of manners, plays of intrigue, and sentimental comedy. In tragedy there were the favored plays of Shakespeare, the tragicomedies of Beaumont and Fletcher, John Dryden's heroic dramas, pathetic tragedies, and Augustan classical tragedies. Never before or since has a theatergoing public enjoyed such varied offerings. It is to be noted that, although new fashions put in an appearance, the work of the living dramatists never stood apart from, and was never independent of, this body of time-honored drama. From the first, nevertheless, there were signs of a coming breakdown of the genres. Entertainment, supplanting art, was bringing in pantomimes, dancing, low farce, even acrobatics. After Italian opera came ballad opera, then the comic opera. The enemies of sentimental comedy were constantly pointing out that it was a bastard species, mingling tragic and comic characteristics. By the close of the century the traditional categories were disappearing. Farces, pantomimes, burlettas were enormously popular; melodrama was supplanting tragedy; the ideological play, born of a revolutionary era, was rendering comedy more serious than it had ever been.

Nicholas ROWE is still recognized as the preeminent tragic writer of the Queen Anne period (1702–1714). His earliest play, *The Ambitious Stepmother* (1700), showed the influence of heroic drama but even more clearly that of the later pathetic tragedy. It is the principles of this second kind that Rowe set forth in his prose Dedication. In later and more famous plays, like *The Fair Penitent* (1703), *Jane Shore* (1714), and *Lady Jane Gray* (1715), Rowe's powers are seen to best advantage. His blank verse is fluent, and the plots are developed with economy and concentrated force. To be sure, everything is directed to the generation of pathos, but Rowe's pathos is more serious than it had ever been. *Cato* (1713), the sole tragedy by Joseph Addison (1672–1719), was acclaimed not only when originally produced but long afterward, setting the tone and general character of an Augustan type of tragedy, which aimed at emotional effects, took its themes from classical history, and sought a measure of conformity with neoclassical decorum.

Ambrose Philips (1675?–1749), Addison's protégé; John Dennis (1657–1734), best remembered as a critic and as one of those receiving Alexander Pope's barbs; James Thomson (1700–1748) and Edward Young (1683–1765), poets respectively of *The Seasons* (1726–1746) and *Night Thoughts on Love, Death and Immortality* (1742–1747)—all contributed tragedies that, taken together, are fairly representative of the first half of the century. Dennis' *Appius and Virginia* was presented in 1709 and Philips' *The Distrest Mother,* adapted from Racine's *Andromaque,* in 1712; most of Thomson's plays appeared in the 1730's; Young's last tragedy, *The Brothers,* was produced in 1753. Meanwhile, though many of Shakespeare's tragedies were produced (some were in disgrace), it was Voltaire—how strange this seems to us today!—who throughout the mid-decades commanded highest respect.

But it is the work of the London dissenter George LILLO that has come to hold more interest for us than almost anything else in the entire body of eighteenth-century tragedy. Of Lillo's eight plays the two for which he is now remembered are *The London Merchant* (1731), predominantly in prose, and *Fatal Curiosity* (1736), in blank verse. Bourgeois tragedy was not entirely new in English drama, and Lillo acknowledged in his Prologue to *The London Merchant* that in Otway, Southerne, and Rowe tragedy had put aside pomp and had worn "a humbler dress," but Lillo was fully aware—and so were his

DRAWING OF A SCENE FROM GEORGE LILLO'S *The London Merchant* (WALTER HAMPDEN MEMORIAL LIBRARY AT THE PLAYERS, NEW YORK)

contemporaries—that, despite precedent, he was breaking new ground. George Barnwell, the central character in *The London Merchant,* is a young apprentice led to his ruin by Millwood, "a lady of pleasure." Barnwell's master, the London merchant, is both a father image and a one-man chorus, declaring the benefits of trade and strict personal morality. Despite the sententiousness and calculated pathos marking both tragedies, they are scarcely to be described as "sentimental" if that term is thought to denote, as in the case of comedy, the benevolistic view of human conduct. Lillo was a pious dissenter; his message, "Lo, poor sinner!"

During the second half of the century tragedy was all too clearly on the decline. The two plays that have most to recommend them are *The Gamester* (1753) by Edward Moore (1712–1757), in the manner of Lillo's moralities, and John Home's *Douglas.* Home, a Scot, took his theme from the old Scottish ballad "Gil Morice." The tragedy was rejected by actor and manager David Garrick but received a tremendous ovation when produced in Edinburgh (1756) and was equally successful at Covent Garden the following year. *The Mysterious Mother* (1768) by Horace Walpole (1717–1797) is of historical interest in that it was the first of those Gothic or "terrific" tragedies of which *The Castle Spectre* (1797) by Matthew Gregory Lewis (1775–1818) is the most famous example. By the last decade of the century, melodrama, with its simplistic plots, stereotyped rhetoric, and factitious stage effects was rapidly establishing itself in popular favor. Tragedy was realizing its most debased form.

In the comedy of the century there are more interesting things to chronicle. The story properly begins with Cibber's significant contribution. His first comedy, *Love's Last Shift* (1696), reached tentatively toward sentimentalism. Cibber's third play, *The Careless Husband,* proved to be of decidedly sentimental cast, with its famous scene in which Lady Easy discovers her husband's infidelity and promptly forgives him, an action that leads to the errant one's prompt amendment. Cibber's career as playwright, actor, and manager was a long and honorable one, but of his later plays it is sufficient to mention only *The Provok'd Husband* (1728), a sentimentalized version of *A Journey to London,* which had been left unfinished by Vanbrugh. *The Provok'd Husband* was a marked success, though suffering somewhat from the fact that THE BEGGAR'S OPERA by John GAY opened the same month. Two decades before this, however, George FARQUHAR had come forth with a version of comedy that, had it been taken up by succeeding dramatists as vigorously as was moralized comedy, might have given the theater a much greater vitality. Humor and liveliness of a natural and spontaneous sort run through both *The Recruiting Officer* (1706) and THE BEAUX' STRATAGEM. Here we have an alternative to the caustic comedy of manners that achieves geniality without sentimentalism. In subsequent eighteenth-century comedy there is more of this spirit than has always been perceived, but still not enough.

Joseph Addison and Richard STEELE worked together, in the periodicals *The Tatler* and *Spectator,* to bring greater propriety to the stage. They also discussed the question of humor, deprecating unsympa-

thetic, satiric laughter. Ridicule should be good-natured, they insisted, directed at the singularities of essentially lovable people. Steele's views led easily to sentimental comedy. Steele was a born dramatist, gifted with a fine sense of comic theme and situation. In his first play, *The Funeral, or Grief à-la-Mode* (1701), the sentimental accent is scarcely audible, but in the case of *The Lying Lover* (1703) and his final play, THE CONSCIOUS LOVERS, genuine comedy, though still present, goes out of its way to make room for tender moralizing.

A contemporary of Steele who is likely to be lost sight of but does not deserve to be is Mrs. Susannah Centlivre (1667?–1723), author of some nineteen plays and perhaps the most distinguished of English women playwrights. She ventured into both tragi-comedy and the play of sentiment, but her most successful pieces—*The Busy-Body* (1709), *The Wonder: A Woman Keeps a Secret* (1714), and *A Bold Stroke for a Wife* (1718)—are ingeniously plotted comedies of intrigue or ones approaching farce.

Gay's comedy entitled *The Wife of Bath* was produced in 1713, his *Beggar's Opera* in 1728. In this year Henry FIELDING began his career as a dramatist. But with the passing of the Licensing Act in 1737, which closed down all theaters except Covent Garden and Drury Lane, he virtually left off playwriting. Gay and Fielding redeem this period of twenty-five years. As dramatists they are more important figures today than they were when alive, despite Gay's immediate fame as the author of *The Beggar's Opera* and Fielding's not inconsiderable success. Their off-beat plays—both men wrote a number of these—are alive with the spirit of rough-and-ready comedy; they are irregular in form, vulgar, raucous, and wonderfully amusing, especially Gay's *The Mohocks* (printed 1712; never staged), *The What D'Ye Call It* (1715), and *Three Hours after Marriage* (1717; with Pope and John Arbuthnot assisting), and Fielding's *The Author's Farce* (1730), *Don Quixote in England* (1734), *Pasquin* (1736), and *The Historical Register for the Year 1736* (1737).

The middle years of the century, relatively uneventful, were chiefly notable for *The Suspicious Husband* (1743) by Benjamin Hoadly (1706–1757) and *High Life Below Stairs* (1759) by James Townley (1714–1778), neither one a great comedy but both great successes. By 1760, however, comedy was coming to life once more, and the period extending through the 1770's is a memorable one in the annals. The playwrights were numerous. Better still, most of them were competent, though only Oliver GOLD-SMITH and Richard SHERIDAN were blessed with genius. Garrick, responsible for a number of comedies and farces, collaborated with George Colman the elder (1732–1794) in writing one of the best "laughing comedies" of the time, *The Clandestine Marriage* (1766). Samuel Foote (1720–1777), thanks to his farces, gained a reputation as "the modern Aristophanes." *The Way to Keep Him* (1760), an attractive play by Arthur Murphy (1727–1805), had been preceded by several farces and was followed by a number of better-than-average comedies, including *All in the Wrong* (1761) and *Know Your Own Mind* (1777). Hugh Kelly (1739–1777) is remembered in connection with his *False Delicacy* (1768), a sentimental comedy that ran at Drury Lane in direct competition with Goldsmith's *The Good Natur'd Man* at Covent Garden. Isaac Bickerstaffe (1735?–?1812), William Whitehead (1715–1785), Mrs. Frances Sheridan (1724–1766; the mother of the dramatist), and Richard Cumberland (1732–1811) are other figures in the landscape, most of them associated with plays of sentiment.

It is of course Goldsmith and Sheridan who gave to this later Georgian comedy the qualities for which we remember it. Goldsmith, unfortunately, came to the drama late in his career and did not live to follow up the success of his second play, SHE STOOPS TO CONQUER. He had both the instinct for drama and a clear concept of the function of comedy. Throughout his life Goldsmith fought sentimentalism, and in his first play, *The Good Natur'd Man* (1768), he contrived to satirize the sentimental comedy, although in terms that are sometimes themselves often sentimental. Laughing comedy, however, triumphs in *She Stoops to Conquer,* and the spirit of Farquhar lives again. The play breathes geniality and good nature while preserving comic distance at all times. Goldsmith, dying in 1774, did not live to see the tradition he had done so much to restore to the English stage carried on for a few more brilliant years by the young Sheridan. Sheridan's *The Rivals* (1775) and THE SCHOOL FOR SCANDAL are witty in a way that *She Stoops to Conquer* never attempts to be and are richer in striking theatrical effects, but it may be that

TITLE PAGE OF THE 1776 EDITION OF RICHARD SHERI-DAN'S *The Rivals*

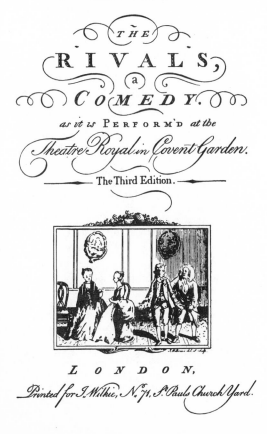

they lack the comic perspectives of Goldsmith's play. However that may be, Sheridan's plays also tell us clearly that the eighteenth century brought forth not only sentimental comedy but something different and much better—a comedy of good will.

A year-by-year record of the plays produced in London between 1700 and 1776 is given in *The London Stage, 1660–1800,* Part 2 of which (1960), edited by Emmett L. Avery, covers the 1700–1729 period, Part 3 (1961), edited by Arthur H. Scouten, the 1729–1740 period, and Part 4 (1962), edited by George Winchester Stone, Jr., the 1747–1776 period. The Critical Introductions included by the three editors are valuable. Allardyce Nicoll's *Early Eighteenth Century Drama* (3rd ed., 1952) and *Late Eighteenth Century Drama: 1750–1800* (2nd ed., 1952), constituting Vols. II and III of his *History of English Drama: 1600–1900,* are standard treatments. Vol. VI (1959) of his *History—a Short Alphabetical Catalogue of Plays Produced or Printed in England from 1660 to 1900* is of great help. Frederick S. Boas gives an interesting summary of the work of the more important dramatists in *An Introduction to Eighteenth-Century Drama: 1700–1780* (1953). Various aspects of the drama are taken up by John C. Loftis in *The Politics of Drama in Augustan England* (1963) and by James J. Lynch in *Box, Pit, and Gallery: Stage and Society in Johnson's London* (1953). Concerning tragedy, Bonamy Dobrée's *Restoration Tragedy, 1660–1720* (1929) remains of interest, although the best treatment is probably still that of Ashley H. Thorndike in *Tragedy* (1908). Michael R. Booth's *English Melodrama* (1965) deals with developments later in the century. Of the many books concerned with comedy, the following are all of importance: Bonamy Dobrée, *Restoration Comedy: 1660–1720* (1924); F. W. Bateson, *English Comic Drama: 1700–1750* (1929); Ashley H. Thorndike, *English Comedy* (1929); Ernest Bernbaum, *The Drama of Sensibility* (1915); Joseph Wood Krutch, *Comedy and Conscience after the Restoration* (1924); Arthur Sherbo, *English Sentimental Drama* (1957); John C. Loftis, *Comedy and Society from Congreve to Fielding* (1959); Leo Hughes, *A Century of English Farce* (1956); and V. C. Clinton-Baddeley, *The Burlesque Tradition in the English Theatre after 1660* (1952).—R. Q.

nineteenth century and Edwardian. In most discussions of English drama, critical or historical, the nineteenth century is usually given little attention and, more often than not, dismissed as "barren," "trivial," or "unproductive." At first glance, and particularly if the period is compared with, say, the sixteenth century, such adjectives may seem fitting; however, a closer, more searching examination of the dramatic works of the period—and of the various changes in theatrical practices and approaches—reveals a surprising amount of activity and a significant body of dramatic materials relevant to our own time. Thus, a familiarity with nineteenth-century drama is important to a thorough understanding of drama in the twentieth century. To appreciate fully the contribution of the nineteenth century, both the transitional nature of the period and its meaning for our own time must be stressed. The transitional nature is perhaps best seen, not only in the gradual evolvement of the stage and playhouse into the modern theater of today, but also in the development of the plays them-selves. In the Preface to his anthology of nineteenth-century British drama, J. O. Bailey states that his in-tention is to present plays that illustrate the evolution of English drama from the legitimate verse drama of 1800 into the new drama of the 1890's. This state-ment might well serve as a point of departure for any discussion of nineteenth-century plays and play-wrights, for the evolution is plainly to be seen; at the two poles are the "legitimate" verse plays and the serious "problem" plays. In between these two are found a number of types that cannot be so neatly classified, but for purposes of discussion they might be placed under such headings as melodrama, burletta (which would encompass farce, burlesque, and extravaganza, which are more closely connected with the "minor" or "illegitimate" theaters than with the "major" or "legitimate" ones), comedies of manners, and, finally, "Robertsonian" comedy, with its suggestion of satiric commentary.

The influence of Shakespeare on the playwrights of the period, especially those who attempted the seri-ous or "literary" plays for the legitimate theater, was great indeed, and the spirit of "Bardolotry" is par-ticularly evident in the many verse dramas of the pe-riod, especially in those of the early part. Some of these were attempted by writers known today only to literary historians, some by dramatists more closely connected to the theater, and some by such famous people as Wordsworth, Byron, Shelley, Browning, and Tennyson. The efforts of the first group demon-strate the worst excesses of these writers. Among the many works of this kind, one can cite Joanna Bail-lie's series of plays on the passions, some of which were published in the early part of the nineteenth century; Henry Hart Milman's *Fazio* (1816); Felicia Hemans' *The Vespers of Palermo* (1823); Mary Rus-sell Mitford's *Rienzi* (1828); and Thomas Noon Talfourd's *Ion* (1836). The weaknesses of Joanna Bail-lie's plays are typical of those of most of the dramas in this group: a tendency toward abstraction, diffuse construction, "romantic" characters too often unbe-lievable, and unreal dialogue and language, often overwhelmingly imitative of Shakespeare and the Elizabethans.

If Joanna Baillie and the others failed as play-wrights because of their inability to humanize their characters and subjects, the playwrights more di-rectly connected with the theater erred in the other direction. They were so intent on making their pieces capture the interest of their audiences that, in the true spirit of their day, they "domesticated" their "po-etic" dramas, emphasizing the sentimental and pathetic, bringing out the "sanctity" of such relation-ships as husband-wife, parent-child. That they suc-ceeded in this domestication is undeniable, and the audiences did respond, but this success often came at the expense of meaningful drama and vital poetry.

Two important playwrights of the period, for in-stance, James Sheridan Knowles (1784–1862) and Edward Bulwer-Lytton (1803–1873), wrote poetic dramas that illustrate their success in this direction. *Virginius,* by Knowles, was a great success at Covent Garden in 1820, but Knowles's inability to maintain verisimilitude in any aspect of the play—especially of character and language—soon becomes evident. Instead of Roman nobility and dignified poetry, we keep hearing nineteenth-century actors and senti-ments.

Richelieu (1839) and *The Lady of Lyons* (1838) by Bulwer-Lytton are somewhat better, mainly because Bulwer is a better playwright than Knowles and his plays have more substance. However, the spirit of the age is still recognizable in these pieces, especially in their sentiment, morality, and imitativeness—in this case of the French romantic-poetic tradition of Victor Hugo and Alexandre Dumas père as much as the Elizabethan and Byronic traditions. Of the two plays, *Richelieu* is the more domesticated and there-fore the poorer. *The Lady of Lyons,* written partly to restore Bulwer's reputation as a dramatic author af-ter the failure of his *The Duchess de la Vallière* (1837), exhibits more obviously, however, the banal-ity of Bulwer's poetry, especially the trite figures of speech and forced comparisons. In what is supposed to be one of the heightened love scenes of the drama, for instance, Pauline, the heroine, resorts to clichés:

Oh, as the bee upon the flower, I hang
Upon the honey of thy eloquent tongue!

We are like the insects, caught
By the poor glittering of a garish flame;
But, oh, the wings once scorch'd, the
    brightest star
Lures us no more; and by the fatal light
We cling till death!

In spite of its banal poetry and apparent deriva-tiveness, *The Lady of Lyons* nevertheless exhibits some of the qualities that made Bulwer one of the foremost playwrights of his generation, the play itself being a success in its own day and still able to hold our interest today. The plot, centering around how Pauline is tricked into thinking Claude Melnotte a prince only to discover after their marriage that he is really poor, and of her love for him in spite of this poverty, lends itself to melodrama and theatricality. Bulwer exploits both, but the melodramatic moments are played down, and the theatricality is a positive attribute in this case. In addition, *The Lady of Lyons* demonstrates both the sense of underlying energy that Bulwer could give to his plays and his excellent craftsmanship, which he learned from the experience of his previous failures and from the French. The ac-tion may be melodramatic, but it is logically devel-oped within the context of the play. The strong scenes may be sensational, but they are clearly foreshadowed and dramatically conceived. These are the reasons why Allardyce Nicoll, in his history of English drama, could write that in this play "almost for the first time, do we catch the accents of the new French style of playwriting . . . . The easy construction, the comparatively natural dialogue and the general atmosphere of the play all strike a new note." This new note is even more evident in Bulwer's *Money* (1840), a comedy of manners.

The charge against Bulwer concerning the banality of his poetry certainly cannot be brought against the third group of playwrights influenced by Shake-speare, the major poets of the time who attempted to write plays. If they failed, and they obviously did for the most part, the reason lies elsewhere. What they lacked, and what Bulwer had, was a knowledge of dramaturgy and a sense of theater. That they were interested in writing dramas (closet or otherwise, with generous portions of German Gothicism and French Romanticism as well as Shakespearean and Elizabethan lines tossed in) is evident from a listing of their more important attempts: Wordsworth, *The Borderers* (pub. 1842); Coleridge, *Remorse* (1813); Byron, *Marino Faliero* (1821), *Cain* (pub. 1821), *Werner* (1830), and *Manfred* (1834); Shelley, *The Cenci* (written 1819, prod. 1886); Browning, *Strafford* (1837) and *A Blot in the 'Scutcheon* (1843); and Tennyson, *Queen Mary* (pub. 1875), *Harold* (pub. 1877), and *Becket* (pub. 1879 and made into a personal success by actor Henry Irving in 1893). Perhaps here should also be mentioned the twentieth-century poets who, while not having the reputations of those already mentioned, attempted to write verse dramas for the Edwardian theater: Stephen Phillips (*Paolo and Francesca,* 1902, and *Faust,* 1908); Rudolph Besier (*The Virgin Goddess,* 1906); and John Masefield, whose most impressive play, *The Tragedy of Nan* (1908), though in prose, has a quality that makes it more "poetic" than his own dramas written in verse.

Of all of these poets, perhaps Byron and Browning had the greatest potential as playwrights, although John Gassner in his *Masters of the Drama* (1940) calls Shelley's *The Cenci* the "only English tragedy between the Elizabethan age and the twentieth century that possesses some genuine greatness." Be that as it may, and certainly there is a great deal of dramatic power in Shelley's portrayals of the villainous Count Cenci and the fascinating female characters Beatrice Cenci and her stepmother, the fact remains that Shelley lacked the satiric objectivity that Byron brought to his dramas and the psychological curiosity that Browning brought to his. Even these poets, however, were unable to avoid the faults found in all of the "literary" dramas, especially the verbosity, the melodramatic situations and characters, the ignorance of solid dramaturgy, and the constant tendency to reduce everything, finally, to subjectivity. The occasional passages of magnificent poetry and the infrequent brilliant dramatizations of noble characters are not enough to offset the real defects of these verse plays.

Part of the difficulty these poets had was their refusal, often implied but still evident, to subject themselves to the discipline of writing for the theater. The other difficulty was the one mentioned earlier: the heavy hand of Shakespeare. "It was," writes Nicoll, "the Shakespearian poetic play which provided the greatest hindrance to the development of prose drama in the age. The romantic poets thought that they could become a set of second Shakespeares; yet, if they only could have known it, the true representatives of the Elizabethan in the nineteenth century . . . were the writers of the melodrama and the farce." There is just a note of exaggeration in this summary, but, basically, Nicoll is absolutely correct. It is to these genres that we must turn to see the real begetters of the later new drama. See also Robert BROWNING; George Gordon BYRON; Percy Bysshe SHELLEY; Alfred, Lord TENNYSON.

Of the "illegitimate" forms of drama, it was the melodrama, farce, and burlesque that supplied the greatest quantity and vigor to the nineteenth century. With the last two modes, the names of Henry J. Byron (1834–1884) and James Robinson Planché (1796–1880) are inextricably and inevitably linked. The absence of genuine comedy during much of the first half of the century was made up for by burlesques and farces that were tailored to the audience, which liked its humor broad and its action obvious. Planché excelled in the writing of burlesque—which, in the tradition of Henry Fielding and John Gay (and, ultimately, as he himself insisted, Aristophanes), were comic treatments of serious or classical subjects—and of "burlesque extravaganzas," which Planché himself defined as "the whimsical treatment of a poetical subject" as distinct from the "broad caricature" of a tragedy or serious opera.

Neither form, however, had the biting quality of Fielding (or Aristophanes), the main point of many of the pieces seeming to be ridicule for its own sake, with punning one of the main comic attributes. Basic to both genres, of course, was the incongruous yoking of the serious with the low, a trait exploited to the full by such later masters as William S. Gilbert, Oscar Wilde, and George Bernard Shaw. Some of the titles of Planché's works indicate the nature and aim of his comic thrusts: *Amoroso, King of Little Britain* (1818); *Olympic Revels* (1831); *Olympic Devils* (1831); *The Golden Fleece* (1845); and *Orpheus in the Haymarket* (1865). It was only a step from these to the offerings of H. J. Byron—some of them, such as *La! Sonnambula! or, The Supper, the Sleeper and the Merry Swiss Boy* (1865) and *Lucia de Lammermoor; or, The Laird, the Lady and the Lover* (1865), written for Marie Wilton.

It was only another step to the world of Gilbert. Building on the foundations set up by these two predecessors, Gilbert (and later Shaw) raised the level of burlesque and extravaganza and gave respectability to both forms. What ultimately distinguishes Gilbert, Shaw, and Wilde from Byron and Planché is their irony, which was beyond most earlier nineteenth-century playwrights. Irony is not much in evidence in the farces of the period, a form even more popular than burlesque. As in burlesque and extravaganza, punning was the most important comic ingredient of farce, broad comic situations and physical buffoonery being other staples of the genre. As was also true of the other forms, the quantity of farce was great and the quality low. There are some well-known names connected with the genre—Douglas Jerrold (*Paul Pry,* 1827), Planché (*Hold Your Tongue,* 1849), and Dion Boucicault (*Used Up,* 1844)—but it was not until later in the century, when the influence of the French "well-made play" helped overcome the formlessness of the genre and authors like Gilbert and Wilde sharpened the ironic intent, that farce took on both historical importance and artistic effectiveness.

Audiences did not care for subtlety of any kind, a fact that accounts for the popularity of melodrama in nineteenth-century England. "Melodrama," writes Ernest Bradlee Watson, "in its finish is French, but in its materials and spirit truly English"; and it was Douglas Jerrold (1803–1857) who helped make both spirit and materials "truly English." Jerrold, as much as anyone, was responsible for the transformation of that genre from its German and French models to the type of "domestic" melodrama that is now inevitably linked with the nineteenth-century English theater, and of which his *Black-Ey'd Susan* (1829) is the prototype. Whether agreement can be reached about the specific origins or the precise classifications of the form, the general characteristics are easily enough recognized: a simple story easily understood, with no serious references to controversial subjects; musical accompaniment; stock characters, clearly delineated as good or bad; emphasis on action, the busier and more complicated the better; and the triumph of good over evil, brought about by a last-minute intervention. This is, of course, popular theater, and Jerrold's ability to give the audience what it wanted is attested by the lengthy initial run, frequent revivals during the century, and various burlesques and parodies of *Black-Ey'd Susan.*

The ingredients of *Black-Ey'd Susan* are found in varying degrees in all of the melodramas that span the century, from Thomas Holcroft's *A Tale of Mystery* (1802), through Tom Taylor's *The Ticket-of-Leave Man* (1863), Dion Boucicault's *The Colleen Bawn* (1860) and *After Dark* (1868), and Leopold Lewis' *The Bells* (1872), right up to Henry Arthur Jones's *The Silver King* (1882). In *Black-Ey'd Susan* we have a simple story and theme, characters that are appealing and recognizable, and sentiments that can be easily understood. In addition, there is a great deal of sentimentality and excitement, for Jerrold, who had a solid theatrical background and a great deal of dramaturgical experience, was writing for the theater, not the closet. The weaknesses of *Black-Ey'd Susan* (and of all melodramas, for that matter) are readily apparent—the fairly primitive exposition, the faulty construction, the dependence on coincidence, and the shallow characterization—but the fact remains that the direct appeal to the audience and the pervasive vitality of the play counteracted these weaknesses. Even when, later in the century, different authors, influenced by the well-made play, tightened up the structure and added their own particular touches, the basic appeal to all types of people persisted. Perhaps the reason for this unflagging attraction is found in Allardyce Nicoll's comment on the genre:

> Gazing drearily on the long array of "unacted" dramas and of "poetic" dramas put forward by well-meaning litterateurs of the age, I personally feel convinced that, had I lived in these decades, I should have loved better the struggling actors at the minor theatres than the lordly potentates legitimately wedded at Drury Lane and Covent Garden.

While melodrama and farce were the most popular forms of the time, at least up to the middle of the century, the future lay elsewhere. The prophet of the "new drama" was Thomas William ROBERTSON, whose comedy-dramas, as they have been called, were the concrete evidence of the changing nature of the drama. Drama was coming to reflect a growing concern with the essentials rather than the surface qualities of life and the social problems of the age. In the Introduction to his anthology of nineteenth-century plays George Rowell warns that it is easy to overestimate Robertson's importance "in an anxiety to detect the dawn of the New Drama in England." Yet he goes on to show Robertson's tremendous im-

portance and praises his use of original material, his pride in craftsmanship, and his "conscious attempt to discard the anecdotage which served his colleagues for plots, and let into the theatre some of the broader issues which gripped a country in the throes of social transformation." Robertson certainly pioneered in letting into the theater "some of the broader issues" of his day. While some attempts in this direction might be found in earlier plays such as Jerrold's *The Rent Day,* Bulwer's *Money,* and Taylor's *The Ticket-of-Leave Man,* the titles of which suggest their concerns, it is Robertson's plays, *Society* (1865), *Caste* (1867), *Progress* (1869), *School* (1869), *Birth* (1870), *War* (1871), that pointed the way to the future. While James Albery (*Two Roses,* 1870) and Sydney Grundy (*A Pair of Spectacles,* 1890) are often regarded as Robertson's successors, his real heirs are Jones, Pinero, Gilbert, Wilde, and even Shaw, whose major interests were those of Robertson himself. Like him, these playwrights, some of whom, it is true, also had the example of Ibsen, were interested in dramatizing the broader issues of the day. The new drama, the drama of serious artistic and realistic concern, begins with Robertson. The two plays *Society* and *Caste* illustrate the importance of thematic intent in Robertson's plays and his emphasis on discussion rather than outright moralistic platitudes. In *Society,* Robertson demonstrates in his own way what Gilbert later dealt with in *Engaged*—that is, the heavy emphasis society places on material things, on things that money can buy. Like Gilbert, but much less sharply, Robertson points out the hollowness of all things held dear by English society. In *Caste,* based on one of his own short stories ("The Poor Rate Unfolds a Tale"), the exposure is a bit more bold, and Robertson is much more blunt in his depiction of the difficulties of caste.

Robertson's success in creating atmosphere may be the reason that *Caste* is a much more successful play, thematically, than *Society.* In fact, theme and atmosphere are closely linked, for in telling the story of how Esther Eccles, a girl of low caste, marries George D'Alroy, a man of high caste, and of the subsequent difficulties and ultimate resolution, Robertson's evocation of the working-class world adds subtly but immeasurably to the thematic impact of the play. By skillful characterization, notably of old Eccles, Esther's drunken father, and Sam Gerridge, the plumber boy friend of Esther's sister, Polly, and by his accurate and sympathetic depiction of the relationship between Sam and Polly, Robertson brings to life right on stage the kind of existence that the marchioness, George's mother, and Captain Hawtree, his friend, find so difficult to understand and so easy to disparage. There may be the influence of Scribe in the form of the play, but Robertson is responsible for the English atmosphere. A comparison of Bulwer's *The Lady of Lyons,* which has somewhat the same thematic interest, with *Caste* makes clear the difference between Bulwer's suggestion of the problem and Robertson's dramatization of it. Looking ahead to Jones, Pinero, and Shaw, it is immediately apparent that Robertson is much further removed from *The Lady of Lyons* than the distance of thirty years. Robertson brought into the theater a new realism and it is for this reason that plays like *Caste* and *Society* can be called "modern" plays and

Robertson himself designated as one of the important pioneers in the rise of the new drama.

Robertson, then, leads, not to Grundy and Albery, but to Jones, Pinero, Gilbert, Wilde, and, inevitably, to Shaw and the Edwardian generation of playwrights, Harley Granville-Barker, St. John Hankin, John Galsworthy, and James M. Barrie. Excluding, for the moment, Shaw and the Edwardians, the Robertsonian influence on the other four is apparent in a number of ways, although other dramatic currents of the latter part of the century must, of course, always be kept in mind—especially those of Scribe and Ibsen. William S. GILBERT, for instance, is linked to Robertson in a number of ways; he was, in fact, a friend of Robertson's, and it was Robertson who was partly responsible for Gilbert's first produced play, the burlesque *Dulcamara,* at the St. James's Theatre on December 29, 1866. Like Robertson, Gilbert had a deadly serious approach to the theater and strongly believed in the necessity of lengthy and painstaking rehearsals and in the complete dominance of the playwright over all phases of his work. Robertson's influence is also seen in Gilbert's work, although not so much in the librettos that he wrote for Sullivan's music as in his "serious" plays: *Sweethearts* (1874), *Dan'l Druce* (1876), *Blacksmith* (1876), and *Engaged* (1877). Perhaps the satire and style are much sharper and score more direct hits in such operas as *H.M.S. Pinafore* (1878, where the target is the Admiralty); *Trial by Jury* (1875, the law); *Iolanthe* (1882, Parliament), and *The Gondoliers* (1889, social classes or castes); however, Gilbert's "serious" plays, of which *Engaged* is perhaps the best, are of great importance in determining Gilbert's place in nineteenth-century drama.

At first glance, a resemblance between *Caste* and *Engaged,* or between *Saints and Sinners* and *Engaged,* might be missed, but is not *Engaged* in many ways an even more vicious exposé of society than either of the other two? What may blind us to the viciousness is the manner, which is very Gilbertian; rather than a "serious" discussion of a problem, Gilbert, exploiting his verbal wit, topsy-turvy humor, and satiric genius, gives us a world in which all the Victorian (and thus contemporary theatrical) values are, quite logically to be sure, turned upside down. Gilbert's theme and method are perhaps most admirably summarized in Belinda's lines to Belvawney after she hears from him that he will retain his income only as long as he is able to prevent Cheviot from marrying. This makes Belvawney's financial situation rather precarious, since Cheviot is constantly proposing marriage, as a matter of course, to every woman he meets. "Belvawney," Belinda tells him, "I love you with an imperishable ardour which mocks the power of words. If I were to begin to tell you now of the force of my indomitable passion for you, the tomb would close over me before I could exhaust the entrancing subject. But, as I said before, business is business." The method was not to be seen again until the appearance of Wilde's plays; the theme, not until Jones, Pinero, and Shaw, whose "unpleasant" plays ere to carry on even more vigorously Gilbert's battle against the evils (both in the theater and in life itself) fostered by Victorian philistinism.

Oscar WILDE wrote four plays during the nineties and on these his reputation rests. Three of them, mixtures of the comedy of manners and the well-made play, are derivative of melodrama and Restoration comedy; these are *Lady Windermere's Fan* (1892), *A Woman of No Importance* (1893), and *An Ideal Husband* (1895). The fourth, his inimitable farce THE IMPORTANCE OF BEING EARNEST, has many Gilbertian overtones. Wilde's "problem" comedies are surprisingly conventional, filled with stereotyped characters (the woman with a past, the tempted wife), situations, and subjects (seduction, the double standard, past indiscretions, and blackmail). Wilde's reputation rests on what distinguishes his plays from the dreary number of sentimental comedies and thesis dramas of the time, that is, the epigrammatic wit and the Wildean tone and style, especially the apparent flippancy and hyperbolic statement that convey neatly and skillfully the satiric thrusts at Victorian philistinism, hypocrisy, and self-deception. Since *The Importance of Being Earnest* contains all of the positive qualities of Wilde's dramatic writing and since the "problems" are never treated sanctimoniously but rather farcically, this play emerges as his best. In portraying the follies of the theater of his time (especially the worst features of melodramatic writing and pompous thesis drama), Wilde, like Gilbert, succeeds in exposing the shallowness and hypocrisy of the age. Always fond of paradox, he once wrote: "I took the drama, the most objective form known to art, and made of it as personal a mode of expression as the lyric or the sonnet; at the same time I widened its range and enriched its characterisation." That he succeeded is beyond question, and *The Importance of Being Earnest* is the best proof of his success.

Jones and Pinero consciously worked at writing thesis drama of social significance. Jones was particularly vehement in his insistence that drama be more than mere entertainment, that the dramatist be free to portray "all aspects of human life, all passions, all opinions," and that he fight for largeness and breadth of view against the cramping and deadening influences of what he called "pessimistic realism." Pinero, too, wanted to write plays that were essentially serious and independent of the "predilections of the public." Of the two, Jones is the more effective because, unlike Pinero, who preferred theatrical to dramatic effect, Jones eschewed the surfaces of realism in the theater in favor of truth. Their practice illustrates their theories, to the disadvantage of Pinero.

Henry Arthur JONES was a prolific writer, and his plays may be roughly categorized as melodramas— *The Silver King* (1882), *Heart of Hearts* (1887), *The Middleman* (1889); serious problem plays—*Saints and Sinners* (1884), *Judah* (1890), *The Masqueraders* (1894), *The Triumph of the Philistines* (1895), *Michael and His Lost Angel* (1896), *Mrs. Dane's Defence* (1900); and, especially during his later years, comedies of manners—*The Liars* (1897) and *Dolly Reforming Herself* (1908). The first group gave him his experience and wealth; the last demonstrates his skill; the middle group reveals those qualities that connect Jones, in spite of his own violent objections, with Ibsen and the other significant realistic playwrights of this period, particularly in satiric approach toward accepted conventions.

It is now fashionable to sneer at Jones's timidity

A SCENE FROM OSCAR WILDE'S *The Importance of Being Earnest* (ANTA COLLECTION, WALTER HAMPDEN MEMORIAL LIBRARY AT THE PLAYERS, NEW YORK)

and willingness to compromise, and it is obvious that Jones did tend to identify his own ideas with those of his public. However, he also displayed the courage of his theoretical convictions in his desire to present truth rather than realism. His treatment of religious hypocrisy and uncontrollable passion in *Saints and Sinners* and *Michael and His Lost Angel,* of philistine materialism in *The Triumph of the Philistines,* and, inevitably, of the double standard in *Mrs. Dane's Defence* is honest enough for his own time and might even be called courageous. His incisive portrait of the middle-class philistine in *Saints and Sinners* was so accurate and damning that his contemporary viewers and readers raised objections. The skillful combination of characterization and theme is clearly seen in Jones's depiction of Hoggard, a philistine who refuses to let religion interfere with business. Hoggard, a deacon and a pillar of the church, tells his minister: "Look here, Fletcher, you're my minister, but I won't be preached to on week-days. Sunday is the day for preaching." Prabble, another deacon, also puts forth the philistine view: "If I support your chapel, I expect you to get the congregation to support my shop. That's only fair." To the objections that this portrayal was unfair, Jones replied:

> I can only urge in defence that it is impossible to suppose that God himself can have taken any great degree of pride in creating four-fifths of the present inhabitants of the British Isles, and can hardly be imagined as contemplating his image in the person of the average British tradesman without a suspicion that the mould is getting a little out of shape.

Always, too, Jones's expert craftsmanship gives formal support to his thematic purpose. In reviewing *Michael and His Lost Angel,* for instance, Shaw wrote that one of the "comforts" of reviewing any of Jones's plays was that the critic could go straight to the subject matter without troubling about the dramatic construction. The playwright's technical skill, he concluded, is taken as a matter of course.

In the case of Arthur Wing PINERO craftsmanship is also taken as a matter of course. As prolific a writer as Jones, with a solid foundation in the theater reflecting the influences of the "cup-and-saucer" realism of Robertson, the well-made dramatic construction of Scribe and Dumas *fils,* and the thesis drama of Ibsen, Pinero first gained popularity with the series of farces that he wrote for the Court Theatre—*The Magistrate* (1885), *The Schoolmistress* (1886), *Dandy Dick* (1887)—and was also very successful, as far as the public was concerned, with his Robertsonian plays of sentiment, of which *Sweet Lavender* (1888), *Lady Bountiful* (1891), *Trelawny of the "Wells"* (1898), and *Letty* (1903) are best known. His place in nineteenth-century theater, however, is based mainly on his thesis plays, which treat the problems raised by characters in conflict with their society: *The Profligate* (1889), *The Notorious Mrs. Ebbsmith* (1895), *Iris* (1901), *The Thunderbolt* (1908), *Mid-Channel* (1909), and, of course, perhaps his most famous, *The Second Mrs. Tanqueray* (1893). In all of these, the craftsmanship and technical efficiency are readily apparent. Lacking, however, the breadth of view of Jones, the reformative drive of Shaw, and the philosophical outlook of Ibsen, Pinero seemed to view the thesis play as simply another type of drama to be written for the stage; consequently, while we admire his skill of presentation, we feel the absence of profound commentary or even, on a lower level, a satisfactory or satisfying solution to the "problem" in each of his plays, whether it be that of the man with a past (*The Profligate*), the woman with a past (*The Second Mrs. Tanqueray*), the rebellious woman unable to sustain her revolt against conventions (*The Notorious Mrs. Ebbsmith*), or the weak woman unable to preserve her marriage (*Iris* and *Mid-Channel*). Pinero's failure to fuse completely substance and form is most clearly seen in *The Second Mrs. Tanqueray*. The exposition is presented through actual dialogue rather than asides or soliloquies; the foreshadowing of important events is expertly done; and the logicality of events that bring about the failure of Aubrey and Paula's marriage (the exposure of her past, her constant fear of failing to live up to her stepdaughter's expectations) is impressive but reflects deliberate craftsmanship rather than deep concern, a charge that could be brought against all his thesis plays. In the end we are forced to agree with the criticism that finds Pinero lacking vision and failing to discover a morality that lies deeper than convention and respectability.

Perhaps the chief difficulty lies in Pinero's desire to avoid giving the impression that he is writing thesis drama, that he is, instead, being completely objective in his presentation of character in conflict with society. The result is too often that he becomes a spectator, like the *raisonneurs* in his plays. For instance, Cayley Drummle's remarks about himself in *The Second Mrs. Tanqueray* describe Pinero as well: "And remember that, after all, I'm merely a spectator in life; nothing more than a man at a play, in fact; only, like the old-fashioned playgoer, I love to see certain characters happy and comfortable at the finish. You understand?" This may explain too why Pinero's later plays seem almost anticlimactic. In reviewing *The Notorious Mrs. Ebbsmith*, perhaps Pinero's best-known play after *The Second Mrs. Tanqueray*, Shaw wrote that Pinero appeared to be running away from the consequences of having presented a daring problem. If this appeared to be so in 1895, it became more, not less, apparent as the years went by, and the plays that Pinero wrote during the last twenty years of his life did not enhance his reputation. This conclusion, of course, in no way diminishes Pinero's importance as a pioneer in preparing the way for the drama of the Edwardian period and the twentieth century. He may not have been in the van, but his place in the group of new dramatists is not to be denied.

George Bernard SHAW was never one to run away from any problem, and his early career demonstrates this fact clearly and forcefully. He cannot be categorized as a realistic dramatist, but it is undeniable that during the last two decades of the nineteenth century and the first decade of the twentieth he helped further the cause of serious drama in both matter and manner, content and art. His championing of Ibsen is too well known to be dealt with at any length; his insistence that dramatic writing is an art and not a craft also needs no elaboration. This attitude is important, for it helps distinguish Shaw and other writers of the first decade of the twentieth century from dramatists

like Jones and Pinero. While it is possible, as some critics have done, to treat the period usually called Edwardian as the culmination of the Victorian theater, it is also important to remember that there was a deepening of purpose and a focusing of goals that do give a distinctiveness to the Edwardian period. In an essay on the Edwardian theater, Gerald Weales has attempted to isolate distinctive qualities by citing what he calls the three primary identification marks of Edwardian theater: a sense of expectation; a faith in the theater as an institution that might transcend its box office; and an acceptance of an implied exchange of ideas between the theater and the social, political, and psychological world in which it made its way. We can legitimately discuss the early work of Shaw, John Galsworthy, and James M. Barrie and the chief plays of Harley Granville-Barker and St. John Hankin, then, as the culmination of the movement that began with Robertson and developed through Gilbert, Wilde, Jones, and Pinero.

The dominant figure of this period was, of course, Shaw. Though he was surely indebted to his predecessors, he also pointed the way to new directions in the twentieth century. In this respect, he and his contemporaries were fortunate in having for the production of their plays J. T. Grein's Independent Theatre, which produced *Widowers' Houses* (1892); the Stage Society; and the J. E. Vedrenne–Granville-Barker Court Theatre (1904–1907). Without such organizations, as Shaw himself realized and often admitted, the way for the new drama would have been far more difficult, if not impossible, for most of the "respectable" playhouses, run by respectable actor-managers, would not have attempted any avant-garde dramas, pleasant or unpleasant. It was the pioneering spirit present in these theatrical groups and in the playwrights themselves, especially Shaw, that helped firmly to establish and maintain the new drama.

Part of this pioneering spirit is seen in Shaw's lack of reverence for cherished institutions and persons both in and out of the theater; indeed, he was not even averse to satirizing himself. Part of it lies in his view of a play as something other than a well-made vehicle for simple entertainment. "Formerly," he wrote in *The Quintessence of Ibsenism* (1891), "you had in what was called a well made play an exposition in the first act, a situation in the second, and unravelling in the third. Now you have exposition, situation, and discussion; and the discussion is the text of the playwright." Finally, Shaw's pioneering spirit is a result of his undeniable dedication to the theater and the serious purpose he felt it should have, both artistically and philosophically. Shaw always saw drama not as formula but as opportunity for the exchange of ideas.

Further evidence that Shaw's shadow loomed over Edwardian drama may be seen in the plays themselves; his own interest in offering through his dramas as well as his criticism "some recognition of the importance of social context" is echoed time and again in the plays of his contemporaries. The major concern of the serious Edwardian playwrights becomes largely the conflict of man and his society, with certain themes predominating, especially those involving economic, religious, social, and political questions. Shaw's plays of the nineties and the first decade of the twentieth century certainly demon-

A SCENE FROM BERNARD SHAW'S *Arms and the Man* (ANTA COLLECTION, WALTER HAMPDEN MEMORIAL LIBRARY AT THE PLAYERS, NEW YORK)

strate this concern. *Widowers' Houses* (1892) treats the question of slum landlordism and so-called pleasant people who either are not or simply do not want to be aware of where the money on which they live comes from. *Mrs. Warren's Profession* (written 1893; pub. 1898) has the same theme, but prostitution is the means of raising the question. *The Philanderer* (written 1893, pub. 1898), the last of the "unpleasant" plays, takes up the problem of Ibsen's "new woman" and gives it a Shavian solution. In fact, in both form and content all three of these "unpleasant" plays can be seen as Shavian variations on the problem play. *Arms and the Man* (1894), in which he satirizes the military and debunks the glamor of war and heroism, can be called his variation on Gilbertian comedy; *Candida* (1895), in which he treats the question of marital relations, can be called a variation on the old domestic comedy; and *The Devil's Disciple* (1897), in which he treats more fully marriage, war, and heroism, can be called the Shavian version of melodrama. *Man and Superman* (1905), perhaps his most philosophical play of this period, follows up much more rigorously the thematic implications of *Candida*. *Pygmalion* (1913), Shaw's commentary on caste, and *Androcles and the*

Lion (1913), his religious melodrama, are the other notable plays of this phase of his career.

The mere listing of themes and genres used by this dramatist, who insisted he was in direct apostolic succession from Aeschylus, fails to give his other qualities. Such a list cannot convey a sense of his expert craftsmanship, his brilliant characterizations, his scintillating humor, and the spirit and vivacity of the prefaces and directions that he so carefully wrote for his reading as well as his viewing public. There is enough evidence even in the listing of themes and genres, however, to demonstrate the overpowering presence of his thought and art and to show the various legacies that he left. Above all, he brought life and vivacity to the theater of his time and enriched it by providing it with wit and substance. Shaw himself indicated very early in his career what the theater was to him, stressing not only Ibsen's importance for him but also his own impact on those who followed him. Shaw wrote in *The Quintessence of Ibsenism:*

> In the new plays the drama arises through a conflict of unsettled ideals rather than through vulgar attachments, rapacities, generosities, resentments, ambitions, misunderstandings,

oddities and so forth as to which no moral question is raised. The conflict is not between clear right and wrong: the villain is as conscientious as the hero, if not more so: in fact, the question which makes the play interesting (when it *is* interesting) is which is the villain and which the hero. Or, to put it another way, there are no villains and no heroes. This strikes the critics mainly as a departure from dramatic art; but it is really the inevitable return to nature which ends all the merely technical fashions.

To Shaw, then, the theater was life itself, not mere technical facility.

Of Shaw's fellow travelers, as they have been called, perhaps the best known are Galsworthy and Barrie, although Granville-Barker and Hankin are more closely identified with Shavian drama, especially the former, a disciple of Shaw's. (Somerset Maugham is remembered more for his later plays, such as *The Circle* [1921] and *The Constant Wife* [1927], than such early ones as *A Man of Honour* [1903], *Mrs. Dot* [1908], and *Loaves and Fishes* [1911], although the last, with its focus on the worldly, materialistic, and ambitious clergyman, Canon Spratte, may be identified with the Edwardian plays of Shaw and the others.) Galsworthy and Barrie, however, in their early work are more closely connected with this tradition. The first took the problem play, especially that connected with personal and public social relationships, and made it uncompromisingly naturalistic; the second made it either sentimental fable or comedy.

With his aristocratic background and legal training, John Galsworthy, it might be argued, simply used his own keen observation and sensitive conscientiousness to portray the injustice, hypocrisy, and snobbery that he saw about him. Like Shaw, he was intent on exposing these, no matter what the form, and expose them he did, but without Shaw's wit and vivacity—in short, his genius. Galsworthy's plays are solidly built structures (sometimes too obviously so) that take up a problem, unrelentingly and objectively examine it from various points of view (as represented by various characters, some of whom verge on stereotype), and finally come to a conclusion that may at first seem unsatisfactory but on reflection appears as Galsworthy meant it to: inevitably right in terms of the dramatic circumstances and events. Thus in *The Silver Box* (1906) and *Justice* (1910) he exposes the double standard of the law; and in *Strife* (1909), a study of the clash between capital and labor, he points out, through the stubborn inability of his characters John Anthony (who represents capital) and David Roberts (labor) to understand each other's position, the inevitable results: suffering and violence. At the end, Roberts' wife is dead and both men are broken in spirit and health.

Justice, perhaps his most impressive play of this period, demonstrates Galsworthy's view of justice without mercy. Falder, a junior clerk in a law firm, driven to desperation by his love for a woman suffering from an unhappy marriage, forges a check, is caught by his employer, and sent to prison. When he is released his employer tells him he can come back only if he promises to stop seeing the woman for

whom he committed the crime. Falder's suicidal jump at the end of the play as he is being led away by a detective is predictable, but the irony of having him put in a position of being forced to give up the very thing that led him into his predicament in the first place is typical of Galsworthian drama. The same note is found in *Strife,* in which, at the end, the terms that are finally agreed on between the owners and workers are those that were submitted before the strike began. It is this heavy ironic note that is characteristically Galsworthian and, ultimately, constitutes both his chief strength and weakness, for, as logical and impressive as the ending of *Strife* is, it still retains the label of "well-made" so closely associated with his own day.

With James M. Barrie the problem of labels increases, for he is certainly not objective in his own work and critics have not been objective in their judgments of his plays. There is, of course, no doubt about his craftsmanship, which is as highly developed as that of any playwright of this period or any other. There is also no doubt concerning his appeal; in fact, at times he challenges Shaw in his ability to charm and attract, especially by means of the entertaining and whimsical stage directions in printed versions of his plays. Indeed, perhaps the most fruitful way to examine these early plays of Barrie's is to compare his work with Shaw's, not so much for the purpose of examining reputations as for perceiving Barrie's particular approach to themes common to both playwrights. Shaw himself, for instance, said that he wrote *Androcles and the Lion* partly to show Barrie how a play for children should be handled, his great objection to Barrie's *Peter Pan* (1904) being that it was childish and condescending. While it is true that *Androcles* is not so outrightly fantastical as *Peter Pan,* and therefore not so popular with children, the point made by Shaw is still valid, and the many passages of overt sentimentality and sweetness in *Peter Pan* prevent it from being as effective or affecting as *Androcles.*

Lack of philosophical depth, Barrie's greatest weakness, becomes evident in his other important plays of this period: *The Admirable Crichton* (1902) and *What Every Woman Knows* (1908). In the first, the treatment of caste is given added perspective by placing the characters on an island and having Crichton, the family butler, assume control of the family, especially of Lady Mary, the daughter of the house, thus illustrating, as did Shaw in *Pygmalion,* that social rank is merely a matter of circumstance and nature will out. Barrie undermines his point, however, by having the family go back to England, where Crichton and all the others are placed right back as they were, having occasional remembrances of times past but living in the civilized present. Says Crichton to Lady Mary at the end of the play:

> My lady, I am the son of a butler and a lady's maid—perhaps the happiest of all combinations; and to me the most beautiful thing in the world is a haughty, aristocratic English house, with every one kept in his place. Though I were equal to your ladyship, where would be the pleasure to me? It would be counterbalanced by the pain of feeling that Thomas and John were equal to me.

Shaw or Galsworthy would have made this ironic; Barrie does not. In the same way, *What Every Woman Knows* is Barrie's *Candida*, but, again, there is not the subtlety that Shaw's play contains. Maggie manipulates John Shand in every way and makes him admit her superiority to him in the end, thus justifying Barrie's own obvious feminism. Even here, with Maggie as a counterpart to Shaw's Candida and with John as Shaw's Morell, we do not have the saving grace of Shaw's poet, Eugene Marchbanks, to provide the essential choice and conflict for the drama of ideas. Maggie's rival, Sybil, is indeed a weak rival, both dramaturgically and intellectually, and this weakness detracts from the philosophical impact of the play. Without the saving Shavian wit and the merciless Galsworthian objectivity, Barrie emerges as a playwright with occasional observations on the important questions of his time but more often as the master of whimsy and sentimentality.

Perhaps the only truly legitimate Edwardian playwrights are Granville-Barker and Hankin, and it is their specifically Edwardian flavor that gives their plays more of a historical than an intrinsic appeal. Both men's works exhibit too many characteristics which "date" them. Hankin, for instance, in his three most important dramas—*The Return of the Prodigal* (1905), *The Cassilis Engagement* (1907), and *The Last of the De Mullins* (1908)—takes up the conventional themes of caste, wealth, and sex and treats them in what is by this time in the new (rapidly becoming old) drama the conventional way. *The Last of the De Mullins* demonstrates the opposition of a "new woman" to the conventions of the day. *The Cassilis Engagement* and *The Return of the Prodigal* illustrate the smugness of the middle class and various problems created by social distinctions, real or imaginary. For all of this social concern, however, Hankin's plays remain unconvincing, mainly because of the absence of any distinctive style or approach. Even disregarding the many echoes of Shaw in his plays, there still remain the conventional dramaturgical approach of the noncommercial Edwardian theater and a lack of any genuine vitality and passion.

In *The Return of the Prodigal,* in which Eustace "blackmails" his father into supporting him for the rest of his life, there is little real comic invention and, in the end, no legitimate philosophical insight. In *The Cassilis Engagement,* Geoffrey Cassilis is saved from a bad marriage by his mother's shrewd maneuver of inviting his fiancée and her mother to the Cassilis estate for a long visit in order to demonstrate their vulgarity to Geoffrey and his friends and to make Ethel, the girl of the intended misalliance, realize her own lack of enthusiasm for the dull life that the other half leads. The play has a few amusing scenes and some incisive portrayals of character, but these come too seldom. Perhaps Hankin, in his desire to avoid well-made plays, succeeded too well in simply transferring what he had seen and known onto the stage. As a "new" dramatist, he deserves recognition for his pioneering effort to make the theater a vital part of life itself. His great failure—a fatal one—is the inability to make his work exciting and, more important, dramatic. See St. John HANKIN.

Much the same can be said of Harley GRANVILLE-BARKER, except that Granville-Barker has a keener sense of the dramatic and a surer knowledge of how to make events come alive in the theater. Some of this knowledge and sense of the dramatic is due, no doubt, to Granville-Barker's careers as actor and director as well as playwright; in fact, he is probably remembered today mainly for his Shakespearean productions rather than as playwright. However, he was a "new" dramatist, and his most important plays —*The Voysey Inheritance* (1905), *Waste* (1907), and *The Madras House* (1910)—bear the stamp of the Edwardian period; like Hankin's works, Granville-Barker's seem dated in various ways. In *Waste* one of the central topics is that of disestablishment, while *The Madras House* is concerned with the living-in system at a drapery shop. Like Hankin's plays, too, Barker's chief concerns and themes are the usual ones of the new Edwardian drama of ideas, especially sexual freedom, economic and religious hypocrisy, and, of course, the class system. In *The Voysey Inheritance,* Edward, on discovering that his father has been defrauding his clients, struggles to decide whether or not to accept his father's "inheritance" and carry on the business of investment in the same fraudulent way. In the end, with the help of a Shavian young woman, Alice Maitland, who finally accepts his proposal of marriage, the young man does decide to carry on his father's fraudulent work, realizing that, paradoxically, it will be the means of his own salvation, his reason for living.

In *Waste* and *The Madras House* the Shavian life force and the battle of the sexes play a large part, and these are connected with such Edwardian concerns as economic exploitation of labor by capital, the double standard, and the proper role of the new woman in society. In *Waste* a rising politician, Henry Trebell, is brought to ruin and suicide by the death of a shallow but physically attractive married woman, who was having an abortion performed after their affair. In *The Madras House* Philip Madras sells his share in a drapery establishment and decides to go into "useful" work by standing for the County Council in order to help humanity come of age. Rebelling against what he calls the "farmyard world of sex" that his father and most Edwardian men have always supported, Philip tells his wife Jessica that he wants their relationship to be more than that; further, he wants "an art and a culture that shan't be just a veneer on savagery." When she asks what is to be done, he replies: "We must learn to live on a thousand a year . . . put Mildred to a sensible school . . . and I must go on the County Council. That's how these great spiritual revolutions work out in practice, to begin with."

Unlike Hankin, Granville-Barker succeeds in bringing some distinctive qualities to his plays, not the least of which are his mastery of dialogue and his ability to depict setting. These skills constitute Granville-Barker's strength as a playwright. In performance and in reading, there is always a note of authenticity in what is being said and in the context of actions and events. These positive attributes enabled Granville-Barker to do what Hankin could not —that is, to transcend, at times, his own period and provide meaningful commentary of significance for others. This is best seen in *Waste,* where the sudden cutting-off of the life and career of Trebell is as pertinent today as it was in Granville-Barker's own time.

Similarly, the cause of the struggle and suffering of the protagonists in *The Madras House* and *The Voysey Inheritance*—the battle between the practical and the ideal—is as vital today as it was then. Unfortunately, those moments in Granville-Barker's work when the thematic concerns become, with the aid of his positive attributes, so impressively meaningful do not happen often enough.

To say this of Granville-Barker, however, is not to detract from his achievement and from the achievement of his contemporaries and predecessors of the nineteenth century. Of all of them, only Shaw consistently wrote plays that may be said to transcend his own era and retain their interest in our own. Shaw is the only "modern" in this sense. Yet, Shaw does not stand alone, and he serves to remind us that no dramatist does. As Rowell concludes:

> By the dictate of the alphabet Shakespeare, Sheridan, and Shaw stand side by side on the library shelf, and by the dictate of the public their plays command the English repertory. Of other playwrights who shaped the course of English drama the playgoer sees and learns little. These forgotten men and the times in which they lived and worked are part of the pattern of the English theatre. To ignore them is to neglect the whole pattern as well as its parts.

It is both the parts and the pattern of the nineteenth century of which we should be aware; and once we do become aware of them, we see that it is only a very short distance in historical perspective from the beginning of the nineteenth century to the present day. In content, dramaturgy, and theatrical development, there is a close connection between the drama of the last century and this. Twentieth-century drama has its roots, not in the immediate past, but in the entire dramatic tradition of the nineteenth century, a tradition whose significance is only now beginning to be fully recognized and appreciated.

Still the best work with which to begin an examination of nineteenth-century drama is Allardyce Nicoll, *A History of English Drama,* Vol. IV, *Early Nineteenth Century Drama, 1800–1850* (1955), and Vol. V, *Late Nineteenth Century Drama, 1850– 1900* (1959). Good surveys of the period are found in George Rowell, *The Victorian Theatre, A Survey* (1956) and, less thoroughly, in Alan S. Downer, *The British Drama, A Handbook and Brief Chronicle* (1950). Ernest Bradlee Watson, *Sheridan to Robertson, A Study of the Nineteenth-Century London Stage* (1926), and John W. Cunliffe, *Modern English Playwrights, A Short History of the English Drama from 1825* (1927), supply much useful information on nineteenth-century theatrical practices and conventions. Much of the same may be found in Squire Bancroft, *The Bancrofts: Recollections of Sixty Years* (1909), with the emphasis, as might be expected, on actors and acting. The Shakespearean productions of the period are treated by George Odell, *Shakespeare from Betterton to Irving,* with a new introduction by Robert H. Ball, Vol. II (1966). Michael Booth, in *English Melodrama* (1965), and M. W. Disher, in *Blood and Thunder: Mid-Victorian Melodrama and Its Origins* (1949), discuss the various phases of melodrama in the century, while Martin Meisel, in

his *Shaw and the Nineteenth-Century Theater* (1963), places Shaw in the context of nineteenth-century theater. Gerald Weales ("Edwardian Drama and the Shadow of Shaw," *Edwardians and Late Victorians,* Richard Ellmann, ed., English Language Institute Essays, 1960) comments on Shaw's place in the drama of the late nineteenth and early twentieth centuries, but his emphasis is on Shaw's contemporaries, especially Harley Granville-Barker. Criticism of the period is found in Clement Scott, *The Drama of Yesterday and Today* (2 vols., 1899), and William Archer, *The Old Drama and the New* (1923). There are some pithy criticisms of nineteenth-century plays and playwrights in John Gassner, *Masters of the Drama* (1940). Some representative anthologies are Montrose J. Moses, *Representative British Dramas, Victorian and Modern* (rev. ed., 1931); George Rowell, *Nineteenth Century Plays,* World's Classics ,1953); J. O. Bailey, *British Plays of the Nineteenth Century* (1966); and Gerald Weales, *Edwardian Plays* (1962).—M. T.

post-Edwardian drama. The end of the Edwardian era does not in itself mark an important change in the history of drama. For more than a decade after 1910 the leading figures in the theater were playwrights who had established themselves in the preceding period: Bernard SHAW, Arthur Wing PINERO, Henry Arthur JONES, and James Matthew Barrie (1860–1937). Certain patterns seemed to be shared by the post-1910 work of these writers. Although Pinero and Jones lived on for a good many years after 1910, their new plays did practically nothing to confirm their previous reputation. The same is true of yet another playwright whose work became less interesting—and less considerable—after 1910: Harley GRANVILLE-BARKER had shown enormous promise, but soon after 1910, he was divorced from his actress-wife, became a Shakespeare scholar and a translator, and virtually gave up writing for the stage. He revised some of his earlier works, and, in his last plays, he moved in the same unexpected direction that was being taken by his more renowned contemporaries—the direction of fantasy. Curiously, although Shaw, Pinero, and Jones are the three men who generally receive the most credit for establishing the realistic "problem play" on the modern British stage, all three in their last years showed a surprising interest in dramatic experiments that departed from the realistic presentation of contemporary life, and Granville-Barker, who had been equally a realist, moved toward fantasy along with them. Barrie, who had already demonstrated in *Peter Pan* (1904) his talent for escaping from humdrum reality, also gave his primary attention after 1910 to three dramatic fantasies and a biblical play. No doubt these dramatists had, in their early plays, said most of what they wanted to say about the contemporary scene and, as older men, they ceased to have firsthand experience of the strongest currents of modern life; fantasy and history became more congenial. Their defection did not alter the main course of modern British drama; realism still dominated the scene, and a new generation continued the techniques that the older writers had pioneered.

After 1910 Shaw still produced in his familiar style such conventionally realistic plays as *Pygmalion* (1913), but his more typical writings were historical plays (*Androcles and the Lion*, 1912; and SAINT JOAN), a Chekhovian "fantasia in the Russian manner" (HEARTBREAK HOUSE), an exceedingly long play about the future (*Back to Methuselah*, pub. 1921), and two semifantasies about contemporary politics (*The Apple Cart*, 1929; and *Geneva*, 1938). No one can question that these experiments outweighed those of Pinero and Jones. The only one of the several post-Edwardian plays of Pinero that attracted much attention was *The Enchanted Cottage* (1922), a "fable" about a homely couple who are made, by the enchantment of their cottage, to seem beautiful to each other. Jones was more fortunate; he had two successes —the comedy *Mary Goes First* (1913) and the melodrama *The Lie* (New York, 1914; London, 1923), in which a virtuous older sister makes great sacrifices for an unworthy younger sister. Two other plays by Jones are of curious interest for their resistance to the main line of radical intellectual thought: *The Ogre* (1911) is an attack on feminism, and the fantasy *The Pacifists* (1917) is an attack on pacifism in which a bully disrupts the quiet life of a country town but meets no opposition from most of its leading citizens.

Barrie confirmed his attachment to sentimental fantasy in *A Kiss for Cinderella* (1916), in which Miss Thing, a slavey, does good deeds as "the penny friend." She dreams she is Cinderella, and a policeman who has been watching her turns up as the prince; their romance continues even after she awakens. If Barrie's best-known one-act play of this period—*The Old Lady Shows Her Medals* (1917) —is conventionally realistic, it still has to do with the fantasies of a charwoman who pretends she has a soldier son. *Dear Brutus* (1917) permits its characters to see what their lives would be like if they were to get a second chance. Only one discovers an essential alteration—a melancholy artist who finds himself inspired when, in his make-believe life, he has a daughter. *Mary Rose* (1920) is even more thoroughly bathed in sentiment. The girl of the title vanishes for twenty-five years while on a journey to "The Island that Likes to be Visited." Returning, she looks as young as when she left, but she vanishes again; in another reappearance she meets her fully grown son, but then she vanishes for good. One is reminded of Peter Pan's eternal youth, but the surest guide to this play's peculiar appeal is probably the element of wish fulfillment, the same element that figures also in Miss Thing's becoming Cinderella and in the second chance granted so freely in *Dear Brutus*. *Shall We Join the Ladies?*, the "first act of an unfinished play," was first staged in London in 1921; departing from Barrie's usual pattern, it is a psychological detective play. *The Boy David* (1936) presents David's encounters with Goliath, Saul, and Jonathan, and ends with David and Jonathan promising to be "friends for ever." The stage direction adds, a bit suspiciously, "They are not sentimental." In this last play, which was a failure on the stage, Barrie tried unsuccessfully to use a poetic language. Of the full-length plays written in the last half of the dramatist's career, only *Dear Brutus* has enough substance to make its sentiment bearable, and today most of Barrie's work is out of fashion.

If the older dramatists of the post-Edwardian era generally preferred to eschew contemporary reality,

the younger ones did not. In the second decade of the twentieth century the most important dramatic genre continued to be the problem play. Its most successful practitioner was the novelist John GALSWORTHY, who had begun by commenting in *The Silver Box* (1906) on the different sorts of justice society metes out to the rich and the poor. In the years that followed, he continued to examine social issues and to appeal for fair play; with JUSTICE, he actually helped to bring about some reform in the administration of prisons.

An extraordinary number of the realists of the period were associated with the repertory venture run by Miss Annie Elizabeth Fredericka Horniman at the Gaiety Theater, Manchester, from 1907 to 1914. The dramatists whose plays were performed here comprise the so-called Manchester School of drama, which includes Allan Monkhouse, Harold Brighouse, and Stanley Houghton; St. John Ervine, whose *Jane Clegg* was staged at the Gaiety in 1913, is usually not counted as one of the School, probably because he wrote prolifically for many other theaters as well. The typical plays of this group are solemn, conscientious, carefully wrought, and accurately reflective of middle-class town life. Allan Monkhouse (1858–1938) contributed *Mary Broome* to Miss Horniman's theater in 1911. Familiar though its basic situation may be, this play goes a step beyond conventional expectation; a wealthy young man is compelled to marry a girl whom he has gotten into trouble, but ultimately his self-reliant bride leaves him for another man. Oddly enough, Galsworthy (in *The Eldest Son*, 1912) and Houghton (in *Hindle Wakes*, 1912) used somewhat the same idea; in each of their plays the girl refuses the marriage that is to make "an honest woman" of her. Obviously, the emancipation of women had made this idea common coin for serious, modern-minded dramatists. Most of Monkhouse's other plays are equally in tune with the times. The most notable of them is *The Conquering Hero* (1923), in which a young man goes unenthusiastically to war, has a shattering experience in combat, and resents his hero's standing afterward. It is so cool and understated that it does not now seem very moving, but in its time it was regarded as the definitive antiwar play of World War I.

The humor of *Hobson's Choice* makes Harold Brighouse (1882–1958) now the most attractive of the Manchester School. In this comedy, first staged in New York in 1915 and then in London the following year, a bootmaker tyrannizes over his shop and his family until his equally determined daughter marries her humble but indispensable employee and makes her husband a partner in the family business. Some years after being filmed, this play was revived by the National Theater (1965) and then turned into a Broadway musical, *Walking Happy* (1966). Other plays by Brighouse, including the one-acter *The Price of Coal* (1909), have won some attention, but none of them seriously competes with *Hobson's Choice*.

The reputation of Stanley Houghton (1881–1913) rests mainly upon two plays: *The Younger Generation* (1910), concerning the conflict between a puritanical father and his rebellious children; and *Hindle Wakes* (1912), in which another authoritarian father tries in vain to compel a marriage between his son and a girl of similar social origin but less wealth with whom the young man spent a weekend. This self-reliant girl, unlike the equally self-reliant serving maids of Galsworthy's *The Eldest Son* and Monkhouse's *Mary Broome,* is not "in trouble" in the usual sense of that phrase, and so her independence may be better motivated. In all three plays, the young men are dull fellows; echoing Ibsen's and Shaw's conception of the new woman, the girls alone show some spirit.

St. John ERVINE was connected with the Manchester School only briefly—in 1913—when Miss Horniman presented his *Jane Clegg,* in which a virtuous, hard-working wife sends her weak husband off with another woman. Other plays of his equally bear the stamp of Manchester realism. Ervine, who was born in Belfast but later lived in England, briefly ran the Abbey Theater of Dublin, where seven of his plays were staged, including *Mixed Marriage* (1911), about a marriage that links a Protestant and a Catholic family, and *John Ferguson* (1915), in which a heroic old man suffers one disaster after another. Entirely divorced from the grim, spare environment and the solemn purpose of these earlier works is Ervine's successful boulevard comedy, *The First Mrs. Fraser* (1929), in which an omniscient and ultimately irresistible first wife wins back her errant husband from a designing second wife. Even this uncharacteristic work shows the author to be, like most writers of problem plays, a dedicated defender of resolute women. No doubt Ervine's turning to comedy reflected a change in the times. Although Galsworthy continued to write problem plays of some skill and variety, most of the talented writers, notably Somerset Maugham, Noel Coward, and Frederick Lonsdale, were, after 1920, going into boulevard comedy. But it must be added that the play of social comment was not, in the second decade of the century, the sole province of Galsworthy and the Manchester School. For example, *Milestones* (1912) by the novelist Arnold Bennett and Edward Knoblock chronicled the life of a manufacturing family and exhibited the continuing conflict between youth and age. The trouble with this play and with many others of its genre is its tendency to reduce itself to parable, to settle for making a point about society instead of primarily presenting people and events.

Strikingly different in this respect are the plays of the novelist D. H. Lawrence (1885–1930). They had few performances in his lifetime, but several won critical acclaim when they were staged in London in the 1960's. The most effective are realistic portraits of life among the miners of Nottinghamshire: *A Collier's Friday Night* (written c. 1909), concerning a possessive mother who finds herself in conflict with her husband and her son's girl friend, is a dramatic treatment of some of the subject matter of Lawrence's novel *Sons and Lovers; The Daughter-in-Law* (written c. 1912) shows a possessive mother in conflict with her daughter-in-law; *The Widowing of Mrs. Holroyd* (completed c. 1914), exhibiting the last stage of a bitter war between a collier's wife and her insensitive husband, shares the subject of Lawrence's short story "The Odour of Chrysanthemums"; and *Touch and Go* (written 1919), reinterpreting the struggle between capital and labor in a colliery, is a reworking of some of the material in his novel *Women in Love. David,* a play with a biblical theme, was published in 1926 and staged in the following year. In his plays of contemporary life, Lawrence had, unlike many other dramatists of the time, shown his characters' emotional lives and had not confined himself to making them automatic exemplars of their social origin or of that "new spirit" that Ibsen and his followers liked to celebrate. In their unpretentious concern for the nuances of human motivation and action, Lawrence's plays of Nottinghamshire life stand comparison with any dramatic writing of their time.

The plays of the 1920's that are least outdated are the comedies, particularly those of W. Somerset MAUGHAM, who satirized the life of wealthy and titled people and implicitly extolled cynicism in such works as THE CIRCLE and *The Constant Wife* (1927); Noel COWARD, who introduced a fresh note of bohemian irreverence in HAY FEVER and *Private Lives* (1930); and Frederick Lonsdale (1881–1954), who got good results by combining the high style of elegant ladies and gentlemen with their compulsive behavior in *On Approval* (1927) and *Canaries Sometimes Sing* (1929). The most popular of Lonsdale's plays was *The Last of Mrs. Cheyney* (1925), a romantic comedy in which a glamorous jewel thief promotes her larcenous schemes by getting herself invited into high society but becomes an honest woman at last. More lasting qualities are to be found in *On Approval,* which is less romantic and much more comic. In this bitter comedy, two couples, each consisting of one even-tempered and one difficult person, maroon themselves in rural Scotland with a view to testing their compatibility and deciding whether marriage would be a good risk. After a short stay, the two couples are sundered when the two even-tempered experimenters withdraw in dismay, leaving the quarrelsome and utterly impossible man and woman to each other. The same clever cynicism prevails in *Canaries Sometimes Sing* and in *Aren't We All?,* in which the accusations of a wronged wife are stilled by the revelation that she has been just as unfaithful as her husband. This 1923 revision of a 1909 comedy, *The Best People,* marked Lonsdale's rebirth as a dramatist and his abandonment of his previous career as a contributor of the books to such musical comedies as *The Balkan Princess* (1910) and *Monsieur Beaucaire* (1919; based on Booth Tarkington's novel).

Several authors provided milder comedies for more conservative tastes. A. A. Milne (1882–1956) won popular success with *Mr. Pim Passes By* (1920) and *The Dover Road* (1922), plays in which naïve strangers intrude upon the complex lives of others. His *Michael and Mary* (1930) is as simple in its approach but more serious in its subject. Serious or not, Milne was indefatigably sentimental. The sentimentality of Dodie Smith (1895–   ) has a more domestic bias, especially in *Dear Octopus* (1938) and *Call It a Day* (1935), her two popular celebrations of the cheerful, loyal unity of the English family. However, *Autumn Crocus* (1931), her first play to be produced, struck a less resolutely wholesome note and showed a spinsterish English schoolteacher engaged in a bittersweet flirtation on an Austrian holiday. C. K. Munro (1899–   ) wrote several plays but earned his tiny niche with one in particular, *At Mrs. Beam's* (1921), in which a pair of swindlers fleece the comic cross section of idiosyncratic residents in Mrs.

A SCENE FROM NOEL COWARD'S *Private Lives* (ANTA COLLECTION, WALTER HAMPDEN MEMORIAL LIBRARY AT THE PLAYERS, NEW YORK)

Beam's boardinghouse. All of these plays are amiable enough, and *Dear Octopus* even enjoyed some moderate success when it was revived in London in the 1967/68 season, but no one can deny that the more durable comedies are the less amiable and more outrageous ones by Maugham, Coward, and Lonsdale.

Except for the work of J. B. Priestley and James Bridie, the problem play—and, indeed, the serious play in general—went into a decline in the 1920's and 1930's. Curiously, the great problem of the period, the worldwide depression that began in 1929, had remarkably little direct impact upon the popular drama. The one memorable English drama dealing with slum life in the Depression, *Love on the Dole* (1935), by Ronald Gow and Walter Greenwood, was not written directly for the stage but was based on Greenwood's novel of the same name. The cataclysmic event that preceded the Depression, the First World War, was dealt with on the stage most notably in *Journey's End* (1928), by R. C. Sherriff (1896–), a dramatist whose subsequent life was haunted by his failure to match his initial success. *Journey's End* showed the impact of war upon character, exhibiting in particular an officer who has taken to drink. No doubt *A Bill of Divorcement* (1921), the first play by Clemence Dane (1888–1965), qualifies as a problem play, but its problem is a bit special: the question of what to do with an insane man, for whom either his divorced wife or his daughter must sacrifice her chance for personal happiness. Miss Dane later showed a flair for historical drama, with *Will Shakespeare* (1921) and *Wild Decembers* (1932), about the nineteenth-century English family the Brontës. A sensitive play on a personal crisis was *Young Woodley* (1928), about a schoolboy in love with his teacher's wife, the first play by John van Druten (1901–1957) to win serious attention. Van Druten afterwards wrote many popular plays, including such comedies as *The Voice of the Turtle* (1943). Quite a different personal crisis was dealt with by Emlyn Williams (1905–) in *The Corn Is Green* (1938), an obviously autobiographical play about a young Welsh miner who is sent to the university by a strong-willed schoolteacher. Williams had made his initial impact as a writer of thrillers, including *Night Must Fall* (1935), about a mad but charming Cockney killer. He continued to turn out a variety of plays and also to pursue his career as an actor.

Sometimes the play of character took the form of a chronicle drama. One significant instance was the solemn, hero-worshipping *Abraham Lincoln* (1919), by John Drinkwater (1882–1937), who tried in vain to repeat his success with biographical dramas about Mary Stuart, Oliver Cromwell, and Robert E. Lee. Gordon Daviot (the pen name of Elizabeth Mackintosh, who signed the name "Josephine Tey" to her mystery novels) reexamined the reign of Richard II

A SCENE FROM T. S. ELIOT'S *The Cocktail Party* (ANTA COLLECTION, WALTER HAMPDEN MEMORIAL LIBRARY AT THE PLAYERS, NEW YORK)

in *Richard of Bordeaux* (1932). Clifford Bax (1886–1962) re-created a romantic episode from the reign of Henry VIII in *The Rose Without a Thorn* (1932), but the greatest international popularity in this vein was won by Laurence Housman (1865–1939), whose long chronicle play on the reign of Queen Victoria was edited into *Victoria Regina* (1935). An equally international play was *The Barretts of Wimpole Street* (1930), in which Rudolph Besier (1878–1942) dramatized the courtship of Robert Browning and Elizabeth Barrett.

Except for the surprising popularity of *The Cocktail Party* (1949), by T. S. ELIOT, verse drama had only a small audience at this time. Drinkwater had written plays in verse, including *X = O* (1917), a play on the Trojan War, and had introduced verse choruses into *Abraham Lincoln*. A more interesting sort of verse drama was provided in the plays of social comment, part verse and part prose, by W. H. Auden (1907–   ) and Christopher Isherwood (1905–   ): *The Dog Beneath the Skin* (1935), *The Ascent of F. 6* (1936), and *On the Frontier* (1938). But the most lasting contributions to verse drama in this period were made by W. B. Yeats in a great number of plays and T. S. Eliot in MURDER IN THE CATHEDRAL.

One of the two most important playwrights of the 1930's, J. B. Priestley (1894–   ) became a dramatist when he collaborated with Edward Knoblock in

adapting his own pleasant, Dickensian novel *The Good Companions* for the stage. This dramatization opened in London in 1931 and ran for nearly a year. Encouraged by this success, Priestley persevered as a dramatist and wrote *Dangerous Corner,* which was well received in both London and New York in 1932 and has been a favorite among British repertory companies ever since. In this play a casual conversation takes a chance turn and compels the characters to unmask themselves and also to reconstruct a past event, a presumed suicide that turns out not to be a suicide at all. Each person makes new and surprising revelations about his connection with the man who died; the primary impression, however, is not so much of the depth of Priestley's characterization but of his extraordinary dramatic skill. The last minutes of the play repeat the first minutes, but at the critical moment the conversation does not take the turn that brings on all the revelations, and so the mysteries go unexplored. This last twist foreshadows a later development in Priestley's career: his "time" plays, in which his characters nostalgically contemplate past events and actively, sometimes supernaturally, speculate about the future. After his comedy success of 1933, *Laburnum Grove,* in which a counterfeiter lives a quiet life among respectable folk, Priestley resumed his serious vein with the Chekhovian *Eden End* (1934), which shows an actress revisiting her peaceful, ordinary family after a long absence, sadly recalling the past, and going away again. In this play Ralph Richardson, who was to become almost the official interpreter of Priestley on the stage, made his first appearance in one of Priestley's works, playing the actress's shallow actor-husband. A year later Richardson played the title role in *Cornelius,* a play of office life that was favorably reviewed but not popular. Richardson and Laurence Olivier co-directed and acted in the unsuccessful *The Bees on the Boatdeck* (1936), a "farcical tragedy" (in Priestley's phrase) with political implications.

Priestley's nostalgic inclinations are abundantly reflected in the first of his two time plays of 1937, *Time and the Conways.* The first and third act show a family party in 1919, celebrating the twenty-first birthday of a daughter of the family. The daughters are young and full of life, the sons are beginning promising careers, and everyone is full of hope for the future. The second act moves forward to the dismal reality of 1937; the youngest daughter has died, the prettiest one has married a mean, petty tyrant, the two brothers are failures, and the family is hard-pressed. Priestley's effect is comparable to the one attained in the last minutes of *Dangerous Corner,* but here it is deeper and more serious. The dramatist did not conceive the second act to be simply his own vision of the future, but rather the private vision of the girl whose birthday is being celebrated. In accordance with a theory that Priestley had acquired from the popular philosophy of J. W. Dunne's *An Experiment with Time* (1927), she is experiencing an authentic foretaste of future reality.

In a prefatory note to *I Have Been Here Before,* the second time play of 1937, Priestley acknowledges his indebtedness to P. D. Ouspensky's *A New Model of the Universe,* which expounds a theory of eternal recurrence in human experience. The spokesman for Ouspensky (and apparently for Priestley as well) is a refugee professor who, in an isolated English country inn, comes upon the eternal triangle—a wealthy industrialist, his young wife, and the young headmaster with whom she falls in love. The eternal pattern for these people is set: When the lovers elope, the industrialist will ruin the headmaster's career and his own as well. But this time the professor prevails upon the industrialist to act differently, for once, and be generous. Unhappily, this play is more directly connected with its time theory than is *Time and the Conways.*

Priestley's *Music at Night,* acted at the Malvern Festival in 1938, presents the internal monologues of a number of people listening to a concert. *When We Are Married* (1938), is a Yorkshire comedy about three couples who find their marriages are not legal. *Johnson over Jordan* (1939) found Priestley in a more philosophical and experimental vein; Ralph Richardson played a businessman recently dead who contemplates his life, examining in turn his business career, his pursuit of pleasure, and then his happiest memories. The dramatist called it "a biographical-morality play." Lavishly presented, it was a commercial failure. Priestley's wartime plays included *They Came to a City* (1943), which gathers a variety of characters outside a mysterious city and uses them to express Priestley's liberal social philosophy; and *Desert Highway* (1943), another play of conversation and social philosophy about British soldiers in the

desert. Later successes include *An Inspector Calls* (1946), in which a mysterious visitor calls a family to account for its moral crimes, and *A Severed Head* (1963), which might be described as a sexual round dance, adapted with Iris Murdoch from Miss Murdoch's novel of the same name. Throughout, Priestley's professionalism, both in drawing character and in constructing plays, has been impressive; while his ideas may help to give a solemn tone, it is not for them that we prize his writing.

The other best-liked dramatist of the 1930's was a more disorderly sort of writer. James BRIDIE was, in fact, a Scottish physician named Osborne Henry Mavor. In an affectionate essay Priestley recorded his astonishment that Bridie had once presumed to lecture him on play construction: "Bridie, for all his great gifts, was the last possible playwright to instruct a colleague about the mere mechanics of the drama." Bridie's main stock in trade was ingenuity, and he ingeniously embellished plots drawn from history and tradition. The first play to bring him fame, *The Anatomist* (Edinburgh, 1930; London, 1931), deals with an historical figure, a Scottish surgeon who bought fresh corpses from two unscrupulous body snatchers. *Tobias and the Angel* (Cambridge, 1930; London, 1932) amusingly retells, from the Apocrypha, the story of a humble lad who performs heroic deeds with the quiet help of the Archangel Raphael. Bridie frequently returned to biblical subjects, most notably in *Susannah and the Elders* (1937), an inventively expanded version of another story from the Apocrypha, in which Susannah remains Jewish but the hypocritical elders become members of the gentile Babylonian majority. Bridie also used the Bible as source material for *Jonah and the Whale* (1932) and *What Say They?* (1939), a comedy that transplants the story of Esther to a Scottish university in modern times. *A Sleeping Clergyman* (1933) explores the problem of heredity by tracing a crime-ridden, highly illegitimate family tree back to 1867 and then following it up to the present day; the founders of the family include a drunken rascal, a murderess, a blackmailer, and other immoral people, but their descendants turn out to be useful, decent citizens whose medical research saves many lives. Bridie's greatest popular success was *Storm in a Teacup* (1936; called *Storm over Patsy* in New York), based on a German comedy by Bruno Frank about bureaucracy baffled by a dog. In *The King of Nowhere* (1938) Laurence Olivier played the dashing role of an actor who escapes from a mental home and finds a new function as leader of a semifascist political movement. *The Golden Legend of Shults* (1939) retells the Flemish legend of Tyl Eulenspiegel, putting it into a Scottish setting. Later plays include *Mr. Bolfry* (1943), concerning one of the devil's visits to Scotland; *It Depends What You Mean* (1944), which contains a devastating parody of the brain trust type of celebrity panel; *Gog and McGog* (1948), about a wandering Scottish poet; and *Daphne Laureola* (1949), in which Edith Evans played a queenly lady of great wealth. After dedicating many years to his medical practice, Bridie made a late start as a dramatist, but he was unusually prolific. His plays reflect an inventive ebullience and a lively awareness of stories that demand to be told, but the telling itself is often sufficiently idiosyncratic to justify Priestley's criticism of Bridie as a constructor of plays. Bridie was a serious, conscientious writer, and not a mere entertainer, but he was not committed to any easily labeled intellectual position, even though he wrote in an age of ideology.

Books giving an account of the drama in this period include John W. Cunliffe's *Modern English Playwrights* (1927), Ernest Reynolds' *Modern English Drama* (1949), J. C. Trewin's *The Theatre since 1900* (1951) and *Dramatists of Today* (1953), and Audrey Williamson's *Theatre of Two Decades* (1951). A more critical approach is provided in John Russell Taylor's *The Rise and Fall of the Well-Made Play* (1967). Useful individual studies are *J. B. Priestley—The Dramatist*, by Gareth Lloyd Evans (1964), and *James Bridie and His Theatre*, by Winifred Bannister (1955).—H. P.

contemporary drama. New ages in the theater begin as obscurely as those in any other department of history, but if there is one firm date in English drama that separates the present from the past it is May 8, 1956—the day on which *Look Back in Anger* by John OSBORNE opened at the Royal Court Theatre in London.

Whether or not one describes 1956 as a year of revolution, it is a fact that most of the big names in the theater (heroic actors apart) changed after that date, and the structure of the theater underwent a radical alteration. A new generation of actors, directors, and critics moved into key positions, and throughout England the theatrical landscape was transfigured by the long-delayed arrival of subsidized companies. The change is summed up in the career of Sir Laurence Olivier, the most commanding figure in

A SCENE FROM JOHN OSBORNE'S *Look Back in Anger* (ANTA COLLECTION, WALTER HAMPDEN MEMORIAL LIBRARY AT THE PLAYERS, NEW YORK)

the postwar English theater. Before 1956 his position was that of central pillar in the star system. His first action after 1956 was to seal his alliance with the new age by playing in Osborne's THE ENTERTAINER. Since then, as director of the National Theatre (established in 1963), he has devoted himself to building up a great troupe with an antistar policy. But whatever the changes that have come about in other sectors of the theater, 1956 was above all a watershed for playwrights.

The first ten years after World War II produced some remarkable English writers, but none of them —with the exceptions of John WHITING and Denis Cannan (1919–   )—had much connection with the theater. The big names in the theater of that period had all been active since the 1930's or earlier. Two giants, George Bernard Shaw and Sean O'Casey, were still writing, but producing nothing that any London management would touch; nor had management much interest in the work of serious middlebrows like J. B. Priestley and James Bridie, of Scotland. The field really belonged to such elegant entertainers as Terence Rattigan, Noel Coward, and Emlyn Williams, and of these, only Rattigan was still in his creative prime. To say this is not to belittle them. They are as professionally accomplished as any English playwrights of the twentieth century, and sometimes their work went beyond mere professionalism. But, temperamentally diverse as they are, the one objection that can be made against them is that they had an overdeveloped sense of what their audience would or would not accept.

In this they had the full support of the then conventions of the West End, especially as embodied in the dominant management of H. M. Tennent Limited. Tennent's—which at one time after the war had six shows running simultaneously in London— had built up its empire by shrewd cultivation of budding talent and even shrewder calculation of middle-class taste. They created a theater of glitter in which playwrights such as N. C. Hunter and Enid Bagnold had the relatively humble role of showing off star actors to advantage. It was not up to playwrights to make pronouncements on society, still less to say anything that might offend a public with fixed ideas on sexual morality and the class system. West End managements traded to their customers like family grocery shops, dealing only in reputable brands and thriving on the public's trust. But the price of this trust was an internal censorship far exceeding anything imposed by the lord chamberlain.

The objection is not to the playwrights who flourished in these conditions but to the system that prevented anything better from appearing. Rattigan and company apart, the West End honored its debt to modern drama mainly by glossy importations of Jean Anouilh, Ugo Betti, and Fritz Hochwaelder. Their plays formed the high-water mark of sophistication. Below that point one descended into an amorphous zone of intimate revues, light comedies, and thrillers by such writers as William Douglas Home, Anthony Kimmins, and Agatha Christie, whose work made up much of the regular traffic of the commercial stage.

At the other end of the scale were the productions of the little theater clubs, almost all of which have now vanished. These again were largely devoted to Continental importations and classic revivals. The most famous of them, the Mercury, was the home of English verse drama, a movement to which many of the postwar poets contributed and which reached its peak with the commercial production of T. S. Eliot's plays and the discovery of Christopher Fry. Such was the desire for a theatrical revival that these often insipid pieces were greeted as a union of popular and avant-garde taste. It was one of the numerous mirages in theater history (like the English musical later in the 1950's), and it faded out with the events of 1956.

In the terminology of the time, 1956 was known as the year of the "breakthrough." This was taken to mean both that a new generation of writers had invaded a previously closed shop and that the theater itself had regained contact with the world outside. (The most celebrated line of the year was playwright Arthur Miller's statement that the English theater was "hermetically sealed off from life.")

The first meaning was undoubtedly true. The English Stage Company had been originally established in 1956 at the Royal Court Theatre with the modest aim of persuading reputable novelists and poets to give some attention to the theater. But its actual achievement was to release a body of unforeseen new talent that flooded the theater like a pent-up natural force. Works by N. F. Simpson (1919–   ), Ann JELLICOE, Arnold WESKER, Bernard Kops (1928–   ), Robert BOLT, Peter SHAFFER, Brendan BEHAN, Shelagh Delaney (1939–   ), Harold PINTER, and John ARDEN all appeared within a couple of years, mainly at the Royal Court, or at Joan Littlewood's Theatre Workshop in the East End. The center of English theatrical life decisively shifted from the actor to the playwright.

On the other hand, few of the playwrights secured transfers to the West End. In policy and performance the commercial structure withstood the breakthrough for several years. What finally dented it was less the impact of the new writers than economic competition from the new subsidized managements: the National Theatre, the Royal Shakespeare Company, and the English Stage Company in London; and the growing network of civic repertories in the provinces.

In the early days it was easy to take sides. Now it is clear that the breakthrough was not a prelude to a golden age and that it entailed losses as well as gains. The main loss is the spirit of trust between the West End and its public. One consequence of this is that playwrights have found it increasingly hard to make a living in the theater and are now inclined to begin by making a prestigious reputation in the theater and then moving on to other media, which pay better and involve less exposure to destructive criticism. Of the first wave of new writers only Arden and Osborne have remained primarily committed to the stage; the others have either spread themselves or fallen into silence.

Economics does not, of course, explain everything. What originally bound the new writers together was the sense of a common cause, and it was not until this went off the boil that the profit motive asserted itself. By 1959 the breakthrough as a social movement was dead and its members were revealed as a set of highly unclubbable individualists. Since then good new playwrights—such as Henry LIVINGS, David Mercer (1928–   ), Joe ORTON, John MORTIMER, Bill NAUGHTON, David RUDKIN, Peter TERSON, and Charles WOOD—have continued to appear, but they do not add up to an English avant-garde. And the problem remains that not only does the commercial theater treat them very gingerly but also that the subsidized theater (which plays either in short runs or repertory) can offer them less money and fewer outlets than were available in the old days.

A cynic, looking at the record of the past ten years, might say that the English theater has only been up to its old habit of catching up with the other arts: belatedly acknowledging the social consciousness of the 1930's and finding a stage equivalent for the black comic novels of Evelyn Waugh and Angus Wilson. But such a view would ignore the actual quality of the plays and the fact that the newcomers of the last decade have broken the monopoly of mere competent professionalism and have restored the trade to the artist.

There are several good books on contemporary English drama: *Anger and After* (1962) by John Russell Taylor; *The Encore Reader* (1965), edited by Charles Marowitz, Tom Milne, and Owen Hale; *Theatre at Work* (1967), containing interviews with new English dramatists, edited by Charles Marowitz and Simon Trussler; *Curtains* (1961) by Kenneth Tynan; *Tynan Right and Left* (1967); and *John Whiting on Theatre* (1966).—I. W.

Enrico IV (1922). A play by Luigi PIRANDELLO. The play has been variously translated into English as *The Mock Emperor, The Living Mask, The Emperor,* and *Henry IV.* A young man loves a woman and is not loved in return. What is more, he has a rival. In a costumed cavalcade, the rival causes the young man's horse to slip, and the young man falls, faints, and, when he comes to, is the victim of the delusion that he *is* the person whose costume he is wearing: the German emperor, Henry IV. His sister converts a villa into a replica of this emperor's palace so that the young man can live on as Henry IV undisturbed. After twelve years, however, the delusion wears off. But our man, no longer so young, decides not to let anyone know it and to stay on as emperor, though sane. After eight more years, his sister dies. But she had visited him shortly before her death and gained the impression that he might now be curable. She tells her nephew this, and soon after her death, he brings a psychiatrist to the villa to see what can be done. The psychiatrist, after seeing on the wall portraits of our emperor and the girl he loved, dating back to the time of the cavalcade, proposes a very precise form of shock treatment. He replaces the canvases with living human beings dressed up like the portraits. They make good likenesses, as one is the woman's own daughter, the other, the emperor's nephew. The doctor next makes the woman herself dress like the portrait. The idea is that the emperor will notice that the pictures have come alive, then he will see the older woman, then he will look at himself, and noting in shock the difference between the older couple and the younger will be forced out of his illusion of having remained young, of having remained Henry IV. The doctor's plan is of course bound to go wrong, since "Henry IV" has known for eight years that he is not Henry IV. And indeed everyone else finds this out now from his attendants to whom he has just released the secret. No sooner

SCENE FROM LUIGI PIRANDELLO'S *Enrico IV* (FRENCH CULTURAL SERVICES)

has he had an instant to receive the image of the two couples than in rushes everyone to announce the truth and confound confusion. But if the incident cannot have the effect on Henry that the doctor intended, it does have an effect, and the doctor's first impression is that it has reactivated the insanity, for Henry seems to take the younger woman for the elder one and later on tries to define the whole new situation in terms of this illusion, finally taking the girl in his arms. Her mother's lover—Henry's old rival—protests on the grounds that Henry is sane and able to control himself. "Sane, am I?" says Henry, and kills him on the spot.

Such is the story of the play as given in the opening paragraphs of Eric Bentley's study "Il tragico imperatore" (*Tulane Drama Review*, Spring 1966). It can hardly give a clear impression of the play as a whole, much less of the impact the play has made on the theater world since its première in 1922. Often held to be Pirandello's masterpiece, *Enrico IV* tended to be taken, at first, as a philosophical drama, expounding the Pirandellian view that what we call illusion is reality and therefore that the distinction we traditionally make between illusion and reality has broken down. Received in this way, the play reads like a demonstration. At the end Enrico is saying: "You see: my illusion is now my reality, indubitably, irrevocably." And we nod and add: *Quod erat demonstrandum.*

The emotional force of the play, however, defies any such reduction to theorem, and not all critics have been content to attribute this force, vaguely,

merely to "poetry," the author's "genius," and the like. There is a psychological depth to the play, which indeed can be seen as a distinctly realistic study in schizophrenic experience. On this view, the sanity that Enrico achieved after twelve years is dubious, and the ironical "Sane, am I?" at the end is a thought not just of Enrico's but of Pirandello's.

Whatever the correct interpretation of its meaning —if there *is* one correct interpretation—*Enrico IV* is certainly a milestone in modern drama, standing, as it does, midway between late Ibsen and early Genet.

Entertainer, The (1957). A play by John Osborne. When it first appeared, *The Entertainer* was compared with Arthur Pinero's *Trelawny of the "Wells"* (1898) as an affectionate portrait of theatrical private life. It is certainly the most affectionate of Osborne's plays and one of his most popular, due to the performance of Sir Laurence Olivier, for whom the play was commissioned. It concerns three generations of the Rice family, once a great music-hall clan but now reduced to trekking round the country, playing to near-empty provincial theaters. Grandfather Billie, a proud Edwardian survivor, still preserves his dignity; granddaughter Jean has left home for a teaching job in London. The central position is occupied by her father, Archie, a dilapidated comic with nothing left in life but drink and ancient gags. The plot involves Archie's disastrous attempt to repair the family's fortunes by putting his father back on the stage.

The play is divided between domestic scenes and

scenes of Archie's act, for which the theater is converted into a music hall with orchestra and illuminated billings. The domestic scenes are more remarkable for their delicate overlapping dialogue than for Osborne's attempt to relate the play to topical issues (particularly the Suez crisis of 1956). The play's main distinction is Archie's solo routine, partly for the sheer theatrical force of the transformation of the man and the theatrical environment and partly for the metaphor identifying modern England with the decayed music-hall tradition, as expressed in the line, "Don't clap too hard; it's an old building." —I. W.

entremés. See INTERLUDE.

Epicene, or The Silent Woman (1609). A comedy by Ben JONSON. Frequently described as Jonson's gayest and liveliest comedy, *Epicene* recounts the trials of Morose, a gentleman inordinately sensitive to noise. Displeased with the behavior of his nephew, Sir Dauphine Eugenie, Morose expresses the intention of marrying and thereby cutting off Dauphine from a sizable inheritance. The problem for Morose is to find a woman suitably silent to share his life. He believes he discovers such a woman in Epicene, a soft-spoken woman of few words. Immediately after the marriage, however, Epicene reveals herself as a loquacious shrew. As if this were not bad enough, Morose's house is then invaded by a swarm of garrulous well-wishers come to celebrate the wedding. Among these visitors are two would-be ladies' men, Sir Amorous LaFoole and Sir Jack Daw, both of whom claim to have had sexual relations with Epicene in the past. Also present are the Ladies Collegiate, a group of pretentious, superficial gossips who are there to advise Epicene how to deceive or otherwise manipulate a husband. Driven to distraction by the clamor, Morose throws himself on the mercy of his nephew, who agrees to resolve his difficulties in return for £500 a year and the eventual inheritance of Morose's estate. Morose readily agrees, and with that Dauphine removes Epicene's wig, revealing a boy trained for the part by the victorious nephew.

The almost diabolical harassment of Morose strikes some readers as cruel and not particularly humorous, but Jonson's comic vision is here, as always, relentless in its pillory of any deviations from the norm.—E. Q.

epic theater. A term used to describe a form of expressionistic drama that attempts to instruct its audience. In its more limited sense the epic theater may be identified with the dramatic techniques and principles of Bertolt BRECHT, its leading spokesman and practitioner.

Brecht believed that the drama must be non-Aristotelian if it is to deal effectively with contemporary moral problems and social realities. He therefore refused to exploit devices traditionally associated with strong plotting—suspense, reversals, revelations, and the "big scene." These devices, he argued, are actually deterrents to thinking and judgment. In their place Brecht utilizes a variety of devices intended to alienate the audience's emotions from the action on the stage. These include spoken summaries of the action to follow, dialogue contradicting the action on the stage, harangues addressed to the audience, and the open use of visible stage machinery.

Epic theater, as Brecht insisted, is aimed at the intellect, not the emotions. The spectator should not identify with the hero—ordinarily a morally ambiguous figure in Brecht. Actors should not strive for empathy with the audience, as in the Stanislavsky method, but for emotional alienation (*Verfremdung*). Nonrealistic stage devices such as posters, slide projections, and motion pictures are meant to inhibit stock emotional responses by making the familiar seem bizarre. The action moves forward episodically, or in "jerks," as Brecht put it. The audience of the epic theater is expected to gather evidence objectively, perceive the moral issue involved, and reach an intelligent verdict.

Although Brecht may have been, as he claimed, the Einstein of the new stage, various stylistic elements of the epic theater can be traced to predecessors. Georg Büchner violated Aristotelian formal conventions in didactic plays composed of brief episodes. Like Brecht, he presented ideas in a precise, clipped, and newly coined idiom. Frank Wedekind combined elements of the fantastic and bizarre with ultrarealism in a number of problem plays. Georg Kaiser's *Gas I* (1918) and *Gas II* (1920), antiwar documents aimed at an intellectual audience, were staged amid surrealistic factories and production charts. Erwin Piscator, with whom Brecht collaborated in 1927, specialized in the spectacular technical effects of the epic theater and adapted expressionism to the requirements of straightforward sociological exposition.

The most questionable element in Brecht's dramaturgy is his insistence that the epic theater must exemplify the social philosophy of Karl Marx, to which the playwright was unalterably converted before 1930. Ironically, Brecht's greatest success with critics and the public has been in the West, and his least successful plays fail largely because of their crude and partisan political propaganda. The plays upon which Brecht's reputation rests, from *The Threepenny Opera,* his first in the epic manner, to *The Caucasian Chalk Circle,* his last mature effort, are only indirectly concerned with contemporary politics. In *Die Plebjer proben den Aufstand* (*The Plebeians Rehearse the Uprising,* 1966) Günter Grass hoisted Brecht by his own petard in using the epic theater to attack Brecht's support of the communist authorities during the popular uprising of June 1953 in East Berlin.

Mordecai Gorelik's "Epic Realism," in *Theatre Workshop* (April–July 1937, pp. 29–40), is an early yet penetrating analysis of Brecht's dramatic principles. A more recent study that probes Brecht's theories and his accomplishments is Heinz Politzer's "How Epic Is Bertolt Brecht's Epic Theater?" in *Modern Drama: Essays in Criticism* (1965), Travis Bogard and William Oliver, editors.—J. F. L.

Erduran, Refik (1928–). Turkish playwright and political columnist. Erduran was born and raised in Istanbul. After spending some time in the United States, England, and France, he returned to Turkey, where he started a publishing house, made a film, and wrote a best-selling novel. In 1956 he began to concentrate entirely on writing plays. Between that time and 1967, he wrote three short and fifteen full-length plays, all but three of which have been professionally produced. Feeling that he had "things to say which should be expressed journalistically, and not theatrically," he became in 1965 the political columnist of the newspaper *Milliyet*. Now, he is concentrating on playwriting again.

Aware of the chasms between man and man, man and society, and between society and society, Erduran sees the theater as a vehicle for bettering the world by bringing men together. He writes neither for a mass audience nor for the elite but strives to please the most ignorant laborer and the most erudite intellectual in the audience, as he did with *Cengiz Hanın Bisikleti* (*Genghis Khan's Bicycle*, 1959). Erduran is specifically revolted and fascinated by the intellectual's insistence on placing his ego above everything, and the consequences thereof. This theme is explored in *Bïr Kilo Namus* ("One Pound of Virtue," 1958) and in other plays, both serious and comic.

Erduran believes that Turkish dramatists are in a particularly favorable position to open or strengthen lines of communication between peoples, since Turkey is both geographically and culturally a crossroads of the East and the West, the medieval and the ultramodern, the haves and the have-nots.—N. O.

Ervine, St. John (1883–   ). Anglo-Irish playwright and novelist. A native of Belfast, Ervine has lived most of his life in England. In World War I he served in the British army and lost a leg in battle. After the war he worked as a drama critic in London and New York. His career has spanned two theatrical worlds: native Irish drama and modern English theater. He began his playwriting career with *Mixed Marriage* (1911) and *The Magnanimous Lover* (1912), penetrating studies of religious intolerance and sexual prudery, two characteristics often attributed to the Irish.

Ervine's best play is *John Ferguson* (1915), a tragedy produced at the Abbey Theatre. The play is set in the North Ireland countryside in the year 1885 and concerns the murder of a villainous landowner by the brother of a girl the landowner had seduced. The focus, however, is on the girl's father, John Ferguson, a Job-like victim of fate who derives his moral strength from an adherence to a simple Protestant fundamentalism.

Outstanding among Ervine's other plays are *Jane Clegg* (1913), the story of a worthless philanderer, married to a woman who eventually summons up the courage to dismiss him and face life alone; *The First Mrs. Frazer* (1929), a drawing-room comedy that won considerable success in the twenties; *The Lady of Belmont* (1924), a satirical sequel to *The Merchant of Venice;* and *Robert's Wife* (1937), an Ibsenite problem play about a woman doctor's attempt to establish a birth-control clinic. One of his most recent plays, *My Brother Tom* (1952), is, like his earlier work, set in Ireland, although the mood of the play is much lighter than that of the somber and moving *John Ferguson*. Ervine has also written *Boyd's Shop* (1936), *Friends and Relations* (1941), and *Private Enterprise* (1947), all plays, and a number of biographies, notably *Bernard Shaw: His Life, Work and Friends* (1956).—E. Q.

Estonia. The history of native Estonian drama is organically linked with the Estonian national renaissance (1860–1880), of which Lydia Koidula (1843–1886) is the most revered poet and penwoman. For nearly seven centuries Estonia had suffered various foreign occupations. Annexed to Russia in 1721 and burdened by a superimposed German gentry, it was not before the middle of the nineteenth century that the Estonians, due to more progressive trends in the tsarist government, could start to buy their own land and acquire higher education. A spark for national self-realization was kindled, manifesting itself in a song festival in 1869, involving the whole nation. Capitalizing on the enthusiasm it generated, Koidula adapted Theodor Körner's comedy *Der Vetter aus Bremen* (1815) from German, refashioned it to fit rural Estonia, retitled it *Saaremaa Onupoeg* ("The Cousin from Saaremaa"), and had it produced in 1870. The play is about a poorly educated farmer who wants his daughter to marry his aged cousin but is outwitted by the resourcefulness of his daughter and her young lover. An immediate success, *Saaremaa Onupoeg* created a wide interest in drama and theater.

Although Koidula wrote three more comedies, it was Juhan Kunder (1852–1888), a teacher and literary critic, who provided the mushrooming theater groups with the next durable piece, *Kroonu Onu* (1885). *Kroonu* means the Crown, a government, or military establishment; in the context of the play, it refers to a retired infantryman, who, back in his native village, beneficially meddles in other people's affairs, particularly young lovers. The play pits the wealthy farmer against the poor leaseholder, and forced marriage against love.

During the following period of Russification, lasting until World War I, theaters were among the very few public institutions in which the use of the Estonian language was officially permitted. Perforce, they became the centers of the nation's strivings for cultural independence. With the help of various societies and small joint-stock companies, which appealed to the entire nation for funds, three impressive playhouses went up in less than a decade, from 1906 to 1913. From its beginning the drama was fashioned by Estonia's socioeconomic fabric. Thus, the leaven to original drama came from rural Estonia, though its intellectual and artistic bearings were taken from the West. The keynote was prose realism. Pillorying bigotry and pettiness, and not flinching from social satire, the Estonian dramatists managed to accentuate national individuality both in its negative and positive shadings.

August Kitzberg (1856–1927) was one of the writers who responded to the growing demand for drama. Of his eleven plays, comic and tragic, *Libahunt* ("The Werewolf," 1912) is the most outstanding. In this tragedy Kitzberg reached back to feudal times to comment symbolically on his own time. The play tells how superstition, serf mentality, and jealousy destroy a girl of free spirit, stigmatized by a general belief that she is a werewolf. Urban milieu was introduced into Estonian drama by Eduard Vilde (1865–1933), a prolific writer of novels and short stories. Of his three plays, *Pisuhänd* (a treasure-bringing goblin in Estonian mythology, 1913) soon became a classic. In this comedy Vilde lashed out against cheap literary taste as related to national self-glorification, as well as against literary climbers profiting from it.

The coming of independence as a result of the War of Liberation (1918–1920) greatly furthered the cause of drama. In the mid-1930's there were in Estonia as many as twelve professional repertory stages. The ever-growing demand for original plays had to be supplemented with adaptations of novels, of which many soon became known in their own right. Anton [Hansen] Tammsaare (1878–1940), the foremost Estonian novelist, wrote two original plays, *Juudit* ("Judith," 1921) and *Kuningal on Külm* ("The King Is Cold," 1935). Seven of his novels were made into plays, of which four, derived from his five-volume epic *Tõde ja Oigus* ("Truth and Justice," pub. 1926–1933), have become classics. Of other writers who adapted their novels to the stage, August Gailit (1891–1960), Albert Kivikas (1898–), and Oskar Luts (1887–1954) should be mentioned.

The master of Estonian low comedy is Hugo Raudsepp (1883–1951), whose social parody *Mikumärdi* (1929) is most popular. Though the plot is weak, the play derives its strength from its characters: the farmer Mikumärdi, the laborers in his household, the romantically adventurous female summer guests, and the city-slicker salesman. Through them parvenu ambitions and hollow self-esteem are relentlessly exposed.

Artur Adson (1889–), well known as a poet and drama critic, is the author of nine plays. While his comedies take place in contemporary times, his serious pieces plumb the past. For example, *Lauluisa ja Kirjaneitsi* ("The Father of Song and the Penmaiden," 1930) is a dramatically engaging exploration into the delicate relationship between the youthful Koidula and the elderly Kreutzwald (1803–1882), one of the most outstanding literary figures of the Estonian national renaissance. Mait Metsanurk (1879–1957) severely criticizes in his novels as well as in his seven plays religious hypocrisy, the various façade values of the urban proletariat, and financial corruption in newly rich societies. August Mälk (1900–), author of six original plays and also a short-story writer of quiet humor, won most fame as a dramatist with the adaptation of his novel *Õitsev Meri* ("The Flowering Sea," 1936), in which he depicts life in a fishing village, his favorite milieu. Evald Tammlaan (1904–1945) and novelists Aino Kallas (1878–1956) and Karl A. Hindrey (1875–1949) also tried their hand successfully at playwriting, and the poet Henrik Visnapuu (1890–1951) provided the Youth Theater with original plays as well as mass spectacles for national holidays. Dramatists of lesser caliber, such as Jaan Kärner (1891–1958), Christian Rutoff-Rajasaare (1879–1940), Arnold Sepp (1908–), Enn Vaigur (1910–), and August Jakobson (1904–), have also contributed to the country's dramatic tradition.

Further development was cut short by World War II, which brought to Estonia three devastating waves of foreign occupation: first Russian, then German, and in 1944 Russian again, which is still in force. Although theatrical life in Estonia proper has not abated, playwrights now must observe the well-outlined communist ideology and the normative aesthetics of Socialist Realism. August Jakobson, Johannes Semper, Mart Raud, Juhan Smuul, and Egon Rannet are now active playwrights in Estonia. Refugees have established theatrical centers in Stockholm, Toronto, and New York, where predominantly Estonian classics presented in their native language are revived.

There are no books in English about Estonian drama, although some information is available in books dealing with Estonian literature in general, such as *The Face of Estonia* (1961), translated by Hillar Kallas; and *Estonia* (1953), a reference book by Villibald Raud.—A. W. L.

Etherege, Sir George (1634?–?1691). English comic dramatist. Etherege was probably the son of a Bermuda planter, though very little is known about his birth and early life. Shortly after the return of Charles II to the throne, he was leading the life of a fashionable rake in London, where he was a frequent companion of the earl of Rochester, the model for Dorimant in *The Man of Mode*. Between 1677 and 1680 he was knighted and soon married a rich widow. In the latter part of his life he had a diplomatic post in The Hague and then at Ratisbon, which he found socially very dull, though he wrote amusingly about it in letters that have been published. He died in Paris.

Playwriting was an amusement for Etherege, as for the other "court wits" in Rochester's circle, and he wrote only three: *The Comical Revenge* (1664), *She Would If She Could* (1668), and THE MAN OF MODE. Along with John Dryden he initiated the fashion of witty repartee, which he carried to a high point in his last comedy (see ENGLAND: *Restoration drama*). His satirical and yet sympathetic portrayal of the manners of the society he knew makes excellent comedy.

The standard complete edition is H. F. B. Brett-Smith's *The Dramatic Works of Sir George Etherege* (1927). An important study of his comedy is Dale Underwood's *Etherege and the Seventeenth-Century Comedy of Manners* (1957). The best insight into Etherege as a person is to be had in *The Letterbook of Sir George Etherege* (1928), edited by Sybil Rosenfeld.—E. W.

Eumenides. See ORESTEIA: *Eumenides*.

Eunuchus (The Eunuch, 161 B.C.). A comedy by TERENCE. *Eunuchus,* produced with acclaim, is based on a Greek play of the same name by Menander, with additional scenes from Menander's *Kolax* (*The Flatterer*). Combining mistaken identity and deception, the play weaves together the love affairs of two brothers. Phaedria is devoted to the courtesan Thais, and Chaerea is smitten by the charms of Pamphila, who is supposed to be Thais' sister but is in reality a freeborn Attic citizen. To be near the girl he loves, Chaerea disguises himself as a eunuch and gains admission to Thais' home, where he seduces Pamphila. Phaedria's love affair is blocked temporarily by a rival, the braggart warrior Thraso, from whom Thais hopes to learn the secret of Pamphila's parentage. The many complications of the plot make for lively humor and the characters are well drawn, especially Thais, an unusually noble courtesan. Thraso and his parasite Gnatho provide additional buffoonery and make the play the most Plautine of Terence's six comedies.

Modern adaptations include Jean Antoine de

Baïf's *L'Eunuque* (1565), Pierre de Larivey's *Les Jaloux* (1579), William Wycherley's *The Country Wife* (1673), Sir Charles Sedley's *Bellamira, or The Mistress* (1687), and Thomas Cooke's *The Eunuch, or The Darby Captain* (1736). Nicholas Udall's famous *Ralph Roister Doister* (c. 1553) combined material from *Eunuchus* and Plautus' *Miles Gloriosus.*—G. E. D.

Euripides (480–406 B.C.). Greek tragic playwright. When Sophocles said, as reported by Aristotle, that his own characters represented men as they ought to be, while Euripides represented them as they were, he was pointing to a basic difference that distinguished Euripides from both his predecessors, Aeschylus and Sophocles. No critic would deny that Euripides' characterization is more realistic and more vivid than that of the other Greek playwrights. This applies to his minor as well as to his major characters. Electra's peasant husband, Medea's nurse, the brief appearance of Helen, that spoiled and self-centered beauty, in ORESTES—each of these characters is a little masterpiece, and there are many others in no way artistically inferior to such well-known main characters as Electra, Medea, or Hippolytus. Euripides was already famous in his lifetime for his dramatizations of the strong and violent passions of men, and especially of women. In fact most of his chief characters are women, even though he was reputed to be a misogynist. Certainly, the depth of his characterization was something quite new on the Attic stage.

Euripides' realism shocked his contemporaries, and it shocked nineteenth-century critics even more, for they felt that it debased heroic tragedy to the level

EURIPIDES (PALAZZO DUCALE, MANTUA. COURTESY OF ALINARI-ART REFERENCE BUREAU)

of everyday life. To the contrary, however, Euripides' realism is not of that bogus kind that concentrates on the sordid and the base. He has some completely noble characters, such as Alcestis and Polyxena, and in IPHIGENIA AT AULIS Iphigenia achieves nobility; he also has a few villains, such as Menelaus in *Orestes.* As a rule, however, our sympathies are divided or they switch in the course of the play, as in MEDEA: We feel great sympathy for the abandoned wife at the beginning of the play, but we loathe the witch who kills her own children at the end. No true realist would preach a black-and-white morality. Euripides gave heroism its due but he disliked heroics, and it is no wonder that he was tempted to debunk the heroic characters of legend.

Another aspect of Euripides' realism is that he boldly mixes the comic with the tragic. Sometimes he does so only for comic relief, as with Heracles in ALCESTIS and with many a minor character, such as the messenger in IPHIGENIA AMONG THE TAURIANS. But at times he uses the comic to enhance the horror, as in the scene between Dionysus and Pentheus before they set out for the mountain, or when Polymestor crawls out of the women's tent where he has just been blinded. The result is horrible grotesqueness.

Men and women as they are must live in the world as it is. When realistic characters are transported into the world of myth and legend, the legendary framework is strained to the breaking point. Euripides, as Aristophanes makes clear, was the poet of the new thought in Athens, and his characters show an awareness of the social, religious, and political problems of the fifth century. These later ideas sound strange on the lips of the personages of ancient legend, but such thought-anachronism is not objectionable provided it is not out of character or does not completely break the dramatic framework. This it very rarely does, and the charge that Euripides is frequently philosophizing on his own account through the mouth of his character is not deserved.

This accusation is most often made in connection with Euripides' attitude toward the gods, and one extreme school of critics almost reduces many plays to atheistic tracts, while the less extreme see him frequently implying that *such* anthropomorphic divinities cannot exist. This difficult subject is extremely complex, but in reading his plays we should keep in mind certain obvious truths. First, when dramatic consistency is maintained, the views of Euripides himself are irrelevant, just as is Shakespeare's belief or disbelief in ghosts or George Bernard Shaw's belief or disbelief in the miracle of the eggs at Vaucouleurs, at least *while in the theater.* Second, the Greek gods for the most part are poetic personifications of real forces in human life. Even if you deny the divinity of Aphrodite or Dionysus, the very real forces they represent are of the very essence of the drama. Third, a dramatist must use the religious symbols of his day and age, and even an atheist can do so without irony. In the case of Euripides this meant representing the gods with human shape, human minds, and human feelings. Fourth, a direct result of this is that if sexual lust can cause evil as well as good, as is obviously the case in HIPPOLYTUS, Aphrodite as a person will be evil as well as good. If it is dangerous to ignore or deny the powerful forces that the gods personify, the anthropomorphic Aphrodite or Dionysus will inevitably be represented as resenting this neglect or denial and ready to avenge themselves upon the guilty mortals, even if it involves much suffering for many who are innocent, as the punishment of the guilty always does in real life.

If we keep these points in mind, we shall find the gods of Euripides *dramatically* effective, at least in the greatest of his plays. No one would suggest that he was an unquestioning worshipper of the Olympian gods or that he wanted to send his audience away unthinkingly satisfied, about this or any other subject. There may be irony in some of Euripides' statements about the gods, when he seems to imply that the definitely anthropomorphic presentation of them is not literally true. This kind of irony, however, is more likely to occur in the more lighthearted plays, like ION; it occurs rarely, if at all, in the great tragedies. In any case, when such irony destroys dramatic consistency, it is a dramatic fault. There is one passage in HERACLES where this may well be the case, but it is very infrequent.

It is customary to recognize in Greek thought a growing tendency toward monotheism, and this is clearly true of the philosophers. Yet insofar as this was true in the fifth century, Euripides seems to stand outside such a current of thought. In plays in which the gods play an important part there is no reconciliation between the conflicting forces of heaven. Such reconciliation or peace as takes place is on the human plane, as in *Hippolytus* and *Heracles*.

A god frequently appears at the beginning or the end of Euripides' plays, though only rarely in both places. At the beginning the god or goddess speaks the introductory monologue, a device used by Euripides with much greater regularity than by his predecessors. Its minimum purpose is to tell the audience the particular version of the story adopted in the play, to give an account of the situation, and also frequently to place this situation in its legendary background. Usually, however, the monologue also expresses the feelings of the speaker and gives us, through him, our first introduction to the main characters. The monologue is then followed by a second scene, usually a dialogue between two characters, which continues the presentation of the dramatic situation or enacts part of it by bringing further news or the like. This completes the *prologos* (the part of the play before the entrance of the chorus). Then the *parodos*, or entrance song, of the chorus completes the presentation. These divisions are elaborated in various ways and are not hard and fast.

When a god appears at the end of the play (this occurs in about half the plays of Euripides), he usually prophesies the future, thus relating the story to the future just as the monologue often puts it in perspective with the past. This seems to be the god's main function, since even when no gods appear the future is often foretold. The old accusation, first made by the comic poets, that the tragedians used the *deus ex machina* to get themselves out of difficulties with their plot is quite undeserved. In four plays (ANDROMACHE, THE SUPPLIANT WOMEN, ELECTRA, and BACCHANTS) the divinity does not even profess to interfere with the course of events. In the other plays a careful reading makes it quite obvious that Euripides, had he wished, could quite easily have avoided

bringing in a god; indeed, the poet often seems to give the story a slight twist in order to justify the epiphany, such as the sudden storm in *Iphigenia among the Taurians* that brings the fugitives back to shore, or the sudden threat in *Orestes* to kill Hermione. Clearly, however, if the future was to be foretold, a god could most easily do this. There is another feature of these prophecies: They often link the drama with the contemporary scene by mentioning some contemporary ritual supposedly originating in the dramatized myth. This etiology probably pleased the audience and, as it were, brought the story more home to them. There is only one tragedy in which the epiphany does change the course of events, and that is not by Euripides; it is *Philoctetes* of Sophocles.

It is an obvious fact, reported in all textbooks, that as tragedy developed the choral odes became more detached from the action of the drama. Moreover, in contrasting the older tragedians with Agathon (c. 447–c. 400 B.C.), who began the practice of inserting choral odes that were mere interludes, Aristotle says that "the chorus should be considered one of the actors, a part of the whole play, and take part in the action not as in Euripides but as in Sophocles." We do not know what Aristotle had in mind, but this passage is usually interpreted to support the view that Euripides' odes are less relevant to the drama itself than are those of Sophocles. This is doubtful, and in any case this irrelevance in Euripides has been much exaggerated.

Generally speaking, the chorus is composed of persons who support, or at least have a great deal of sympathy with, a main character. Fourteen of Euripides' choruses are women, but then most of his main characters are women. There is a chorus of men in *Alcestis*, but then Admetus, not Alcestis, is the main character; in *Heracles* the chorus of old men provide a suitable background for Amphitryon and Heracles; and in THE CHILDREN OF HERACLES the chorus of Athenian citizens are natural, for they support Demophon, who himself typifies the virtues of Athens. In *Hippolytus* we have a male hero and a female chorus, but they support Phaedra, who dominates the first part of the play; furthermore, there is a subsidiary chorus of men. In choral odes we should recognize two kinds of relevance: a direct relevance to the dramatic action at a single point; and a relevance of ideas or background to the dramatic situation as a whole, such as the great ode on the power of Eros and Aphrodite in *Hippolytus* or the odes in THE TROJAN WOMEN. If we keep these two kinds of relevance in mind, we shall find very few odes of the detached or irrelevant kind. There are some—the ode on the shield of Achilles in *Electra* or that on the sorrows of Demeter in HELEN—but they are rare. In most odes, the subject is clearly suggested by the action, or else they provide the legendary background, which in itself contributes to a proper understanding of the drama.

We may well imagine that if Euripides had read Aristotle, with his strong insistence on unity of plot, he would have disagreed with the philosopher and argued that dramatic unity is a much broader concept. He might then have pointed to his *Trojan Women*, a play that might well be said to have no action or plot at all, but in which various incidents, though not following each other as "probable or inevitable," yet have a clear emotional pattern and unity of their own. Had Euripides felt self-critical, he might have said that his *Andromache,* the story of which is not disjointed, achieves a lesser degree of dramatic unity.

For good or ill, however, Euripides could not have read Aristotle. His was a less stringent form of plot structure and a looser kind of dramatic unity, which does not always satisfy us completely. Yet at times it is certainly we who are at fault, as with *Hippolytus,* for example, about which modern commentators have been known to say that their interest flagged after the death of Phaedra; they have misread the play from beginning to end.

Euripides was a bold experimenter and he wrote many different kinds of plays. By experimentation I do not mean his satyr play CYCLOPS, all three tragedians wrote this kind of drama, and even the serious-minded Aeschylus was apparently very successful with it. Six of Euripides' extant dramas end happily. *Alcestis* may have taken the place of a satyr play, and yet all the scenes, except the end and the scene with a drunken Heracles, are fully tragic. *Helen* is, except for the early lamentations of Helen and the choral odes, frankly comic from beginning to end. *Ion* is unusually lighthearted and ironic. *Iphigenia among the Taurians* is a romantic drama with definitely tragic scenes. *Orestes* has what must be called a happy ending, but it does not fit the characters very well; otherwise it is serious and heartbreaking tragedy.

Among the others too there are very different kinds of plays: patriotic and political plays, such as *The Suppliant Women* and *The Children of Heracles,* in which the main theme seems to be the glorification of Athens; psychological studies, such as *Electra* and *Medea;* war plays, such as *The Trojan Women,* HECUBA, THE PHOENICIAN WOMEN, and RHESUS; and then the great tragic masterpieces, such as *Hippolytus* and *Bacchants.*

Euripides' plays were very popular after his death. However, he won few dramatic prizes in his lifetime and shocked his contemporaries. Evidence in support of this view may be misleading, for, if we can believe Plutarch's story, after the defeat in Sicily in 413 B.C. many of the enslaved Athenians won their freedom by reciting from the latest plays of Euripides. Indeed, he seems to have fascinated even his detractors. Aristophanes thought him the immoral and dangerous representative of the new thought, but he was always quoting or parodying him and wrote several scenes and two whole comedies about him. Aristotle too was always ready to criticize Euripides; nevertheless, with all the fifth- and fourth-century tragedies before him, he paid the poet the very high compliment of calling him "the most tragic of the poets."

For further information on Euripides, besides the usual histories of Greek literature, consult H. D. F. Kitto's *Greek Tragedy* (4th ed., 1966) and Gilbert Norwood's book of the same title (1960), though the reader should be warned that the former has less sympathy for Euripides than for his predecessors and that the latter views Euripides as continually propagandizing against the Olympian gods.

More specifically, G. M. A. Grube's *The Drama of Euripides* (1961) contains, besides essays on the gods, the chorus, and so forth, a full analysis of every play. *Euripide* (1960), edited by O. Reverdin for the Fondation Hardt series, contains discussions by well-known scholars on various aspects of Euripidean drama. Those interested in Euripides' treatment of the myths will find the answer to many questions on this subject in D. J. Conacher's *Euripidean Drama* (1967).

The best editions of the main plays are in the Oxford series by different scholars (not yet completed); these have introductions, the Greek text, and commentaries.

As for translations, all the plays will be found in *The Complete Greek Tragedies,* edited by David Grene and Richmond Lattimore, Vols. III and IV (1959); various plays from this edition are also published in a paperback series. There are selected plays also in the Penguin Classics series, and, where available, the translations of Gilbert Murray are still well worth while.—G. M. A. G.

Everyman (c. 1495). A medieval morality play, probably a translation of the Dutch play *Elckerlijc.* Like all moralities, *Everyman*'s plot is based on the struggle of the vices and virtues for the soul of man, in this case for the soul of Everyman in the moment of death. The play is allegorical; the characters are named for the qualities they represent, such as Fellowship, Kindred, Goods. The "action" revolves around Death's summoning of Everyman to a general reckoning before God. Everyman, taken utterly by surprise, exclaims "Oh Death, thou comest when I least had thee in mind!" and proceeds to seize upon every expedient at his means to avoid the summons: the request for a delay because he isn't ready; the offer of a bribe; a feeble minimizing of the magnitude of the event; the desire for company on his journey. But Death remains firm. Everyman then asks, in turn, Fellowship, Kindred, Cousin, and Goods to accompany him, and each, with typically human, inadequate excuses (Cousin has a cramp in her toe), refuses as soon as they discover where he is going. Everyman then turns to Good-Deeds, who, weak from Everyman's neglect, lies in the cold ground. Although she is too weak to accompany him, she advises him to call upon Knowledge, and with Knowledge's advice, Everyman's salvation begins. He dons the robes of contrition and does penance, thereby strengthening Good-Deeds so that she can rise and walk with him. Everyman then calls on Strength, Discretion, Beauty, and Five Wits, who promise to accompany him but who desert him one by one as the journey nears its end. Knowledge takes him to the point of the grave, but only Good-Deeds descends with him, thereby assuring his salvation.

Everyman is a kind of sermon in allegorical form, a lesson in the preparation for the Day of Judgment. It is a warning that in the moment of death, man must give up not only his physical endowments (friends, family, worldly goods) but certain more abstract endowments (beauty, intelligence, strength) as well. Only Good-Deeds can speak for his salvation. The strength of this play lies in its vivid characterizations. The characters may stand for certain things and qualities, but they are also dramatically alive, more dramatically alive than they need be for the didactic purposes of the play. See ENGLAND: *middle ages.*

Ewald, Johannes (1743–1781). Danish poet and

JOHANNES EWALD (DANISH INFORMATION OFFICE)

playwright. Ewald grew up in Schleswig, returned to the city of his birth, Copenhagen, in 1758, and, after adventures in the Prusso-Austrian Seven Years' War, took a theology degree in Copenhagen in 1762. Ewald's personal encounter with the German poet Friedrich Gottlieb Klopstock late in the 1760's resulted in his breaking with classicism and espousing Nordic mythology. Ewald was plagued most of his life with rheumatic ill health intensified by dissipation. Probably his best years, 1773–1775, were spent at Rungstedlund, which conveyed a literary heritage to the Danish short-story writer Isak Dinesen (1883–1962), who, much later, came to occupy the inn turned manor house.

Ewald's first play, *Adam og Eva* ("Adam and Eve," 1769), is a cross between opera and tragedy, written in the French classical form with strong infusions of Milton and Klopstock. Mining the historian and poet Saxo Grammaticus (c. 1150–c. 1220) for material, Ewald wrote the Shakespearean tragedy *Rolf Krage* (1770) and the "heroic *singspiel*" *Bladers død* ("The Death of Balder, 1773), the latter supplied with music by Johan Hartmann. He culminated his life and work with another musical play, *Fiskerne* ("The Fishermen," 1778), his greatest success in the theater. From this play comes the aria "King Christian," the Danish national anthem, subsequently translated by Henry Wadsworth Longfellow ("Path of the Dane to fame and might!").

Ewald's plays seem florid today, but he was the most important of the Danish pre-Romantics and also prepared the way for bourgeois tragedy.

See P. M. Mitchell, *A History of Danish Literature* (1958).—R. B. V.

expressionism. Expressionism in drama was a movement that began in Germany in 1910 and flourished until around 1924. Examples of drama written since 1924, both in Germany and outside it, which abound in expressionist influences are numerous. But these plays are largely under the influence of expressionist technique and do not subscribe to the expressionist philosophy. One of the confusions about the term is the fact that it is used in literature, music, architecture, and art as well as in the drama. The term was apparently first used by the French painter Julien-Auguste Hervé in 1901 but did not achieve general acceptance for several years. The clearest way to arrive at an understanding of the term is to contrast it with impressionism. Impressionism is an account of how the world of reality affects the describer. It is thus a subjective account of an objective perception. Expressionism, on the other hand, is an imposition on the outside world of the describer's concept of it. It is thus a subjective account of a subjective perception. Indeed, reality per se has no meaning for the expressionist. Everything in his art is "expressed," that is to say, brought forth from within himself. Expressionism is perhaps the most completely self-centered art form ever evolved. The expressionist writer takes the whole human race and the entire cosmos as his province, but he shows it to us as it is seen through the eyes of one character, invariably an alter ego for himself. Thus, for the expressionist the world is crammed into the compass of one man's vision, and, as it is completely subjective, it becomes deliberately and purposefully distorted. This subjective distortion always emerges in the form of protest and rebellion.

The expressionist movement was the symptom of a feeling of intense unrest and dissatisfaction among the younger generation of German writers in the first decade and a half of the twentieth century. The German society that World War I destroyed had been a stifling and stultifying one based on a narrow-minded, patriarchal concept of the family with strongly pietistic overtones that, in the larger sphere, manifested itself in a rigid, political authoritarianism. Thus, the protest and rebellion that we find in the expressionist drama is almost invariably directed against family relations and the way in which these relations prevent youth from developing its individuality. This twofold intention is the key to the purpose of the expressionist drama and explains the many seemingly outrageous scenes in which children castigate their parents (even to the point of killing or raping them) as well as the intense subjectivism—the "efflorescence of the inner self," as Julius Bab, the German drama scholar, put it—that is an indirect way of asserting the writer-hero's individuality.

Intense subjectivism—the externalization of the writer's inner feelings—and an atmosphere of violence directed largely against the family as the basis of society are, then, the two chief characteristics of the expressionist drama. There are, however, several other important identifying aspects that cannot be neglected in a full description of the form. Chief of these is the lyricism of the language. All of the expressionist dramatists were also poets, and their interest in language took precedence over their interest in stage technique. The difficulty both of translating the expressionist dramas and of reviving them is directly attributable to this attitude. Most of the expressionists were primarily poets who turned to the theater as the most convenient medium for the dissemination of their ideas. Only through the theater could they hope to transmit their message to the people as a whole. Poetry rarely shocks; it is read almost exclusively by people who empathize with the poet to begin with. Hence the technique of the expressionist plays frequently strikes us as clumsy and untheatrical. It was primarily a drama that depended for its success on the writer's ability to strike a responsive feeling in his audience. This feeling—the scream of protest against the bonds imposed by the family—is now outmoded. The fight has been won and the protest directed against a different target—God and the cosmic order.

The language of the expressionist drama is also responsible for its demise, because its intensely personal and lyric quality no longer finds any response in the temper of our times and because it makes the dramas impossible to translate satisfactorily. When the critic Felix Emmel referred to the expressionist theater as "the ecstatic theatre," it was of the quality of the language that he was thinking. This language is frequently eminently untheatrical, consisting as it does of long, lyric monologues so intensely subjective in feeling as to seem almost incomprehensible. Often the expressionist dramatist uses an elliptical, telegram-like style in which syntax is compressed, often a staccato, machine-gun style abounding in stichomythic phrases, but always there is the identifying characteristic of intense feeling. The expressionist does not make a statement; he lets loose what we have come to recognize as the expressionist *Schrei* (scream).

The primacy of language over plot and action in the expressionist drama has had the further effect of removing all psychological verisimilitude from the plays. Only the author-hero is psychologically delineated. The other figures are usually puppet-like emanations of the protagonist's self-centered mind. Consequently, we find that the subsidiary characters in the expressionist drama are always types, virtually impersonal and frequently grotesque. The grotesquerie in the expressionist drama stems from the fact that the protagonist's view of people is invariably determined by his personal prejudices. These attitudes are always inimical to the other characters, who are usually either members of his own family or representatives of the authoritarian social order. As part of their criticism of these characters, the expressionists denied them psychological individuality and saw them only as marionettes jiggled around in a grotesque parody of existence through their unthinking devotion to the ideals of society. In many instances there is no attempt made to give the subsidiary characters any individuality but a symbolic one, and they then become abstractions that represent aspects of the state or society.

Expressionism, then, is characterized by intense subjectivism, a violent antipathy to society and to the family, a powerful lyricism that takes precedence over plot and character, and a lack of psychological delineation resulting in type characters and symbolic abstractions.

Prior to the advent of expressionism the chief schools of dramatic writing in Germany had been naturalism and neoromanticism. Naturalism was an attempt to reproduce reality on the stage objectively in order to show the evils of society and stimulate social reform. Neoromanticism used old-fashioned poetic language and traditional German myths in order to evoke the glory of the German past. Expressionism was, of course, a violent reaction against both schools of dramatic writing. Nevertheless, the movement was by no means the entirely clean break with the past it was thought to be at the time. The expressionist theorists, of whom the most important were Kasimir Edschmid and Kurt Pinthus, liked to think that expressionism had no links with anything that had come before in German literature. But the creation of a new literary movement without roots in previous literature is extremely rare. Expressionism is similar to naturalism in that both had a common concern with social reform, and it is related to neoromanticism in that both valued language above plot and character. In addition to these links with previous movements—movements, it should be noted, that continued concurrently with expressionism— there were plays that were clearly forerunners of the movement. Several of Strindberg's later dramas, most notably *A Dream Play,* are completely expressionist in technique and in philosophy. As its title indicates, Strindberg's play consists entirely of the emanations of the mind of a central intelligence. The whole play is a realization of the dreamer's stream-of-consciousness, and the play can be understood only if the reader or viewer identifies himself with this intelligence. The world is seen in the play as dreamt by the Daughter of Indra, who comes down to earth in order to understand the ways of men. Everything that happens in the play takes place in the boundless and amorphous realm of the dream. The daughter of the god comes to observe men and sees that they are unhappy and evil. Here, as in all expressionist drama, the atmosphere is pessimistic and angry, but there is an implicit belief in an undefined something that is better. This is the essential difference between the social criticism of Ibsen the naturalist and Strindberg the expressionist. Both saw society as bad and in need of improvement, but whereas Ibsen and the naturalists dealt with specific evils of society and showed specific ways of eliminating them, Strindberg and the expressionists bewailed the general evil of society and disseminated an evangelistic faith in a better world to come, without, however, holding out any specific hope.

Another very important forerunner of expressionism was Frank Wedekind. Wedekind's first play, *Frühlings Erwachen* (*Spring's Awakening*), which was produced in 1891, showed the direction his work was to take: criticism of society by means of an analysis of its hypocritical attitudes toward sex. This viewpoint showed the way to the later expressionists, since it indicated that the attack on society should be initiated through an attack on the family and on the education of the young. Wedekind also influenced the movement linguistically. In order to hold the attention of bourgeois audiences more firmly, he developed an elevated, unrealistic, declamatory speech that he felt would be more effective than the lackluster reproduction of everyday speech that the naturalists advocated. Wedekind also directed his own plays and acted leading parts in them, which enabled him to develop a new, unrealistic, exaggerated, puppet-like style of acting. He exercised a profound influence on the expressionists with this acting style, and with his often fleeting, barely comprehensible expositions and his numerous scenes flimsily connected by their theme rather than by their relevance to the progress of the plot. Strindberg and Wedekind both made important contributions to the technique of the expressionists, and Wedekind also helped to develop expressionist lyricism.

The influence of August Stramm was purely linguistic. Stramm, who was killed in battle in 1915, had been a member of an experimental literary group in Berlin before the war. This group put out a periodical called *Der Sturm* (*The Storm*) to which Stramm contributed poetry in which he sought to cut language down to its skeletal structure without regard to the exigencies of formal grammar. The result was that Stramm's plays have extended, monosyllabic dialogues like the following: "I!" "You?" "No," "Yes," "Who?" "How?" "Thus," and so forth. Clearly, this kind of dialogue is merely a scenario for a display of emotions rather than a vehicle for meaning. Although none of the expressionists were as radical in their linguistic usages as Stramm was, they did learn from him the value of language as an indicator of feeling. Stramm showed that language could be poetically and dramatically effective if it was purposefully vague instead of analytically descriptive.

The first drama of the expressionist movement, as opposed to the forerunners described above, was Reinhard Johannes Sorge's *Der Bettler* (*The Beggar*). It was written in 1911 and published the following year, but it was not produced until 1917, a year after the playwright's death in battle. *Der Bettler* is an extremely significant beginning for the movement because it is not only the epitome of self-centered drama but also a plea for a new theater. Sorge is himself the hero of his own drama, the plot of which concerns the Poet's efforts to find a theater willing to produce his new play. This new play, like Sorge's, is for all humanity instead of for "a little heap of intellectuals." Sorge wishes to show mankind that it is inseparably linked to the Divine Mercy. His idea seems to be that what prevents mankind from perceiving this connection is the old patriarchal order. The Poet's Father is depicted as insane, his Mother as sick. The solution is the Poet's destruction of his parents. This theme of matricide and patricide was to appear either actually or symbolically in several other expressionist plays. A graveyard scene, which Sorge probably derived from its use in Wedekind's *Frühlings Erwachen*, was also to become almost a leitmotif for the expressionist drama.

Sorge's early death prevented him from becoming an influential figure in the later development of the movement. This role was left to Walter Hasenclever, whose play *Der Sohn* (*The Son*, 1914) was the first play of the expressionist movement to be produced. Performed in Dresden in 1916, its success there was repeated in numerous theaters throughout Germany during the following years. Like *Der Bettler*, this drama was seminal in the development of expressionistic themes. The hero is a son rebelling against his father, who is depicted as being incapable of understanding the desires of youth and its strivings for freedom and self-realization. The son announces as his goal the destruction of the "medieval" tyranny of the family, which he calls a "witches' sabbath" and a

"sulphurous torture chamber." We must, he says, "recreate freedom, mankind's highest good." The Father locks the Son up, but he escapes with a Friend. The Friend is another stock figure of the expressionist drama, who stems directly from the Muffled Gentleman in Wedekind's *Frühlings Erwachen*. He is the character who shows the hero the meaning of life and the path he must take. The Son escapes with his Friend, and they attend a festival for the celebration of youth and joy. When the Son has his final confrontation with the Father, the latter threatens him with a whip, whereupon the Son brandishes a revolver and the Father dies of a stroke.

Hasenclever's other important play is *Die Menschen* (*Humanity*), which was produced in 1919. Here he specifies that the time is "Today" and the scene is "The World." The whole play is written in a series of disconnected, panoramic scenes shot through with a stichomythic, telegraphic dialogue patently influenced by the linguistic experiments of August Stramm. The story concerns a murdered man who rises from the grave carrying a sack with his head in it. He then embarks on a wild career of gambling and drinking during which he associates with madmen, prostitutes, alcoholics, and degenerates of all types. Finally, he is himself sentenced as his own murderer and returns to his grave. Hasenclever was perhaps the most self-centered writer of a movement in which that quality was the keynote. As one of his characters says, "Can't you understand? You can only live in a state of ecstasy; reality would only hamper you. How wonderful it is always to realize that you are the most important person in the whole world!"

Oskar Kokoschka is justly celebrated more as a graphic artist than as a dramatist, but his contributions cannot be ignored in a survey of expressionist drama. *Mörder, Hoffnung der Frauen* (*Murderer, Hope of Women*) was premièred in Dresden in 1916, although it had been written several years earlier and performed by Kokoschka's friends and associates in Vienna. In Kokoschka's work the struggle for a new apocalyptic freedom is translated into a struggle between the sexes. The father-son opposition of Sorge and Hasenclever becomes a man-woman opposition, so that Kokoschka is more closely related to Wedekind as far as his thematic material is concerned. *Mörder, Hoffnung der Frauen* takes place against a mythic background of knights and maidens as a Man and Woman face each other. They speak in hysterical, almost incomprehensible phrases that quickly lead to instinctive hatred and violence. The Man has the Woman branded with a hot iron, whereupon the Woman stabs him and has him shut up in a cage. She taunts him as he lies there, but he recovers his strength, walks out of the cage, and kills her. Kokoschka continues this often incoherent and ecstatic vision of the sexual conflict in such other plays as *Hiob* (*Job*), *Orpheus und Eurydike*, and *Der brennende Dornbusch* (*The Burning Bush*).

The expressionist dramatists were not, as has been frequently supposed, essentially products of the First World War. The confusion has arisen from the natural association of writers of protest with antiwar plays. It is true that the majority of the expressionists did not approve of the war, but the type of specific protest that an antiwar play demanded was opposed to their deepest feelings. They were more at home in vague, generalized protests against the nature of society and the family than in a particular dissent against the war. The only successful play concerning the war that any of the expressionists produced was Reinhard Goering's *Seeschlacht* ("Sea Battle"), produced in 1918. This play, however, is not an example of pure expressionism. Goering uses the language of expressionism, but he does not use the single-viewpoint technique. Instead, there are seven subjective standpoints—those of seven sailors trapped in a gun turret on board a German battleship just before the battle of Jutland. They are all nameless types representing various human attitudes. One of the sailors decides to start a mutiny and sacrifice himself for a higher ideal than the Fatherland: the freedom of his comrades. Before he can organize the mutiny, however, the battle begins, and he fights alongside his comrades. The play ends on an ambiguous note as one of the two surviving sailors says that the battle is still raging on. Since the speaker is the sailor who had contemplated mutiny, his remark might refer to the war for the Fatherland or the struggle for ultimate freedom.

The other prominent expressionist dramatist who dealt with the war was Fritz von Unruh. The son of a general (it is a significant fact that all of the young expressionists came from staid, middle-class backgrounds), von Unruh is best known for his expressionist trilogy about war in the abstract: *Ein Geschlecht* ("A Race of Men"), performed in 1917, *Platz* ("Place"), produced in 1920, and *Dietrich*. The last play was not written until 1936, when von Unruh was in exile in France, and thus does not belong to the expressionist movement. In *Ein Geschlecht* von Unruh deals with the fate of a Mother, four Sons, and a Daughter. He specifies that the time is any time, and the place is a cemetery on a mountaintop. The Mother, the Daughter, and the Youngest Son are burying another Son, who has fallen in battle. Meanwhile, the other two Sons are brought up to the cemetery from the valley below, where a battle is going on. The soldiers who bring them say that the Youngest Son must redeem his race by executing his two brothers, who have been sentenced to death—one for committing atrocities, the other for cowardice. When the Youngest Son refuses to do this "duty," he is dragged away to the battlefield. The two themes of the play, both typically expressionist, are the guilt of the Mother for bringing her sons into the world and the birth of a "new age," which will come about when the world is cleansed of its sins through the revolution that the Youngest Son prepares to lead at the end of the play. The second play, *Platz,* is a fantastically confused account of the Youngest Son's leadership of the revolution. Von Unruh's importance rests in his attempt to carry the themes of expressionism to their extreme, but the incoherence of his language, which is more marked than that of the other members of the movement, prevents his plays from having any lasting significance.

Paul Kornfeld was an extremely important theorist of expressionism. It was he who coined the term "seelendrama" ("drama of the soul") when he proclaimed, "Let us leave character to the everyday world, and let us be nothing but soul . . . for the soul pertains to Heaven, while character is earthbound. . . . Psychology tells us as little about man as anatomy does." Kornfeld thus disposes of the traditional dramatic elements of characterization and motivation. In 1917 his most significant expressionist drama was produced: *Die Verführung* ("The Seduction"), another of the plays in which the author-hero (here significantly named Bitterlich) seeks the meaning of life and announces an apocalyptic vision of humanity.

The themes of expressionism can be seen even more clearly in the work of Arnolt Bronnen. Like Hanns Johst, another early expressionist, whose work, however, is without value or significance, Bronnen later became a Nazi. The apocalyptic vision of mankind's emancipation could as easily lead to a belief in an authoritarian system, which promised a millennium when all men would be free under its aegis, as it could lead to individualism. Although many expressionists fled Nazism and many fell victim to it, Johst and Bronnen turned to it. Bronnen dealt with the themes of anarchy and hatred toward parents and teachers. In his *Vatermord (Patricide)* the rebellion of the son is taken to the point of stabbing his father and making love to his mother. Bronnen himself later remarked that in his early days he defined freedom as anarchy and destruction.

Expressionism was a movement that attracted many German authors of the time. In addition to the playwrights already mentioned, whose most important work was expressionist, there were others, such as Ernst Toller, Carl Sternheim, Georg Kaiser, Franz Werfel, Yvan Goll, and Ernst Barlach, who experimented briefly with expressionism but whose principal literary achievements were elsewhere. The influence of expressionism outside Germany, however, was minimal. It seems to have been a way of thinking peculiarly fitted to the ethos of the German thinkers at that particular time. Such influence as it has had outside Germany has been limited to adaptations of expressionist style rather than philosophy.

The principal non-German experimenter with this technique—the technique of writing plays from the viewpoint of one central intelligence and of showing the action as it appears through his eyes—has been the American playwright Eugene O'Neill. In *The Emperor Jones* and *The Hairy Ape,* O'Neill created two almost perfect adaptations of expressionist style, without, however, incorporating any of its philosophy. *The Emperor Jones* is, indeed, a remarkable tour de force, both as drama and as an exposition of expressionist technique. With the exception of the first and last scenes, in which Smithers is an independent intelligence, the play is pure expressionism: All action is a projection of Jones's mind. Ironically, this perfect, sustained exemplification of the expressionist manner contains no trace of the hysterical Schrei of social indignation or the fuzzy, elliptical language that characterized the German expressionists; O'Neill used only the technique of seeing everything through a central intelligence and thus made his play truly and permanently viable. In *The Hairy Ape* O'Neill again used expressionist technique skillfully, although here he used it only episodically. Unlike *The Emperor Jones,* which is essentially a psychological study, *The Hairy Ape* is an expression of social protest; the protest is specific and the language incisive. Furthermore, O'Neill makes the very effective experiment of changing the expressionist focus in this play. In the stokehole scene, the apelike traits of the workers are seen through Mildred's distorted and neurotic vision; in the Fifth Avenue scene the robot-like characteristics of the leisure class are seen through Yank's equally distorted vision. This scene has become a classic example of expressionist technique. O'Neill made occasional use of the technique in subsequent plays, but it was never as sustained as in these two plays. His most effective use of it in his later plays is in *Marco Millions,* when Marco, on his travels to the East, sees all countries and customs as the same because he is blinded by his purely commercial point of view.

By and large it may be said that although American playwrights have used expressionism, they have used it only as an auxiliary technique. In writers like O'Neill, Rice, Kaufmann and Connelly, and Hart, expressionism is a means to an end rather than an end in itself. The program of the German expressionists finds no response among the Americans they influenced. There is no protest against the family as a symbol of an authoritarian system, nor is there any feeling that society has collapsed. This attitude is, of course, understandable enough in view of the different social backgrounds of the two countries and the radically dissimilar effects of World War I. In both Elmer Rice's *The Adding Machine* and Kaufmann and Connelly's *Beggar on Horseback,* both produced in the 1920's, there is social protest, but it is not the frustrated, all-encompassing excoriation found in the German drama. The American playwrights directed their protest against the crass economic materialism of their country and its resultant cultural philistinism. It was a protest, in other words, against a remediable aspect of the community, not a blanket condemnation of society nor an attempt to replace its very underpinnings with a vaguely conceived apocalyptic new dawn. As a result, the small number of American plays influenced by expressionist technique are far more lucid and theatrically viable than their largely incoherent German counterparts.

Rice's *The Adding Machine* is a picture of a society that has become soulless and mechanical as a result of its single-minded devotion to the inverted ideal of business. The central intelligence—a courtesy term in this case—is Mr. Zero, the human adding machine who is replaced by the far more efficient mechanical one. As his name indicates, he is nothing and never will be anything. His life is meaningless, his death is meaningless, even his life after death is meaningless. Even in the afterlife Zero remains a cipher, obviously having learned nothing, since he still subscribes, ironically, to the false ideals of the society that killed him.

Beggar on Horseback is far more lighthearted. It is a basically good-humored, satiric attack on the American businessman's lack of culture. The principal expressionist device used by the authors here is the dream sequence. This is really a shortcut to expressionism, since as soon as the author has specified a dream sequence, he has postulated the central intelligence of the dreamer and is saved the trouble of dramatizing the concept for the audience. Properly used, however, as in *Beggar on Horseback* or in John Howard Lawson's *Roger Bloomer,* the dream technique gives excellent examples of expressionism. In

more recent years, expressionism seems to have faded from the American stage, its most recent use having been Moss Hart's *Christopher Blake,* a grandly conceived, incredibly banal play about the fantasies of a boy who has to choose between his parents, who are getting divorced.

To some extent expressionism has had some residual influence in other countries as well, notably Ireland. In 1928 Sean O'CASEY used it in the battlefield scene of *The Silver Tassie,* although there is no central intelligence here, unless it be O'Casey's own. The scene is essentially a re-creation of the speech and atmosphere of expressionism, with its combination of the battlefield and graveyard scenes found in so many of the original expressionist plays. The Croucher, a character symbolic of death, the staccato and dehumanized speech, and the fantastic behavior of the officer and the civilian are further signs of expressionist influence. Denis Johnston uses a bold and highly original combination of expressionist and Pirandellian technique in *The Old Lady Says "No".* Here the dream device is used in a satiric commentary on modern Irish nationalism. Johnston creates a play within a play within a play. He begins with a stilted, ultraromantic play about the Irish patriot Robert Emmett. The actor playing Emmett is "accidentally" knocked on the head, and a Pirandellian interlude ensues with stagehands coming on and a "doctor" entering from the audience to treat the "injured" actor. The bulk of the play, however, is pure expressionism, consisting of the unconscious actor's dream of himself as Robert Emmett in modern Ireland. It must be emphasized once again that here, as in the American plays influenced by expressionism, only the technique is used, and it is used for purposes other than those that inspired the original German playwrights.

The only prominent expressionist playwright of the post-World War II period in Germany was the brilliant Wolfgang Borchert, whose *Draussen vor der Tür (The Outsider)* is one of the most powerful and one of the best of all expressionist dramas. Borchert, unlike the postexpressionists in Ireland and the United States, had precisely the same reason for writing as the World War I German expressionists did: disillusionment with society and a feeling of disgust and horror at the effects of war. Borchert's reaction to postwar Germany is, like that of his predecessors, an anguished and frustrated scream. He uses the familiar *Heimkehrer*—the soldier returned from the wars to find everything reduced to rubble and ruins. In two magnificent satiric scenes, entirely expressionist in technique, he exposes the German's love of militarism and his ability to anesthetize his moral sense. In one scene, Beckmann, the returned soldier, goes to visit the colonel of his old regiment. Beckmann has been having nightmares, because the colonel once made him responsible for a group of men, eleven of whom were killed. In this nightmare, which is always the same, Beckmann is haunted by the eleven women the soldiers had left behind and by a giant skeletal figure in a general's uniform that plays on an enormous xylophone made of human bones. As Beckmann relates the dream to the colonel, Beckmann becomes more and more hysterical; the sound of the frantic xylophone fills the theater, and the colonel turns into the nightmarish figure of the skeleton in the dream. The other scene is very simple. Beckmann has stolen a bottle of liquor from the colonel's table, and in his drunkenness he savagely caricatures the army routines that in his youth had enslaved his mind and crippled his body. Almost beside himself with rage, Beckmann struts around the stage in a grotesque parody of the goosestep, shouting "Heil!" at every step. Borchert could not have written a sharper denunciation of the Nazi ritual than this furious, twisted ridicule. The most interesting aspect of Borchert's revival of the expressionist technique is the change that has taken place in the object of the rebellion. The battle against the family as a symbol of repression has now been won—indeed, has become out of date. The post-World War II expressionist does not write plays about sons struggling against fathers; he faces the conflict directly and writes of sons struggling against their country and against God.

Julius Bab, *Das Theater der Gegenwart. Geschichte der dramatischen Bühne seit 1870* (1928) and *Das deutsche Drama* (1925), edited by R. F. Arnold, are the best early accounts in German on the rise of the expressionists. Julius Bab's *Die Chronik des deutschen Dramas,* 5 vols. (1922–1926) is an excellent year-by-year account of developments on the German stage. The most comprehensive and reliable account of expressionism is to be found in Volume II of *Dichtung und Dichter der Zeit* (1963) by Albert Soergel and Curt Hohoff. Useful works in English are Walter Sokel's *The Writer in Extremis* (1959) and the pertinent sections in *Modern German Literature, 1880–1938* (1939) by Jethro Bithell and *The New Spirit in the European Theatre, 1914–1924* (1926) by Huntley Carter. Carl Dahlström's *Strindberg's Dramatic Expressionism* (1930) is a well-researched, scholarly work on the origins of expressionist technique. The best and most comprehensive work on the subject in English is *Expressionism in German Life, Literature and the Theatre* (1939) by Richard Samuel and R. H. Thomas. Several important works on the theory of expressionism were written in Germany; the most useful and authoritative are *Expressionismus* (1920) by Hermann Bahr, *Anarchie im Drama* (1928) by Bernhard Diebold, *Über den Expressionismus in der Literatur und die neue Dichtung* (1919) by Kasimir Edschmid, *Das ekstatische Theater* (1924) by Felix Emmel, *Das expressionistische Drama* (1921) by R. Frank, and *Expressionistisches Theater* (1948) by Lothar Schreyer. The only complete edition of translations of expressionist plays in English is *An Anthology of German Expressionist Drama* (1963) edited by Walter Sokel; the translations, however, leave much to be desired. *The Drama of German Expressionism* (1960) by Claude Hill and Ralph Ley is an essential bibliographical reference work.
—G. E. W.

F

fabula Atellana. An early Italian farce, deriving its name from Atella in Campania, and originally given in the Oscan dialect. Plays of this type were performed in Latin at Rome before 240 B.C., when comedies based on Greek originals were first introduced. (See ROMAN COMEDY.) The Atellan farces were short and dealt with life in the country or small towns. Masks were worn, which facilitated the representation of stock characters, of which there were at least four: Maccus, the stupid clown; Bucco, the glutton or braggart; Pappus, the gullible old man; and Dossennus, probably the cunning trickster. In the first century B.C. the fabula Atellana became a literary form, written chiefly by Pomponius and Novius. Titles of their plays and a few fragments have survived. Atellan farces continued to be presented in the early Empire but yielded in popularity to the mime. —G. E. D.

fabula palliata. See ROMAN COMEDY.

fabula tabernaria. See FABULA TOGATA.

fabula togata. Original Roman comedy in Roman dress, dealing with lower-class life in Rome or small towns in Italy, also called *fabula tabernaria.* No plays of the fabula togata have survived, but about sixty titles are known and more than six hundred lines of fragments are extant. The three chief writers of the togata were Titinius, Lucius Afranius, both of the second century B.C., and Quinctius Atta, who died in 77 B.C.—G. E. D.

Faith Healer, The (1909). A drama in three acts by William Vaughn MOODY. *The Faith Healer,* unsuccessfully performed in St. Louis and New York, had its origin in 1895 in the activities of Slatter, "the New Mexico Messiah." The play centers around Ulric Michaelis, a faith healer, and his love for Rhoda, which conflicts with his belief in his mission. His belief is further shaken by Dr. Littlewood, atheist and cynic, and by the Reverend Culpepper, who cannot accept modern miracles. Michaelis regains his faith and power to heal when he realizes that his love for Rhoda is part of the divine love for all humanity. At his command Rhoda's crippled aunt Mrs. Beeler walks again, and he goes out to the waiting crowd sure of his mission.

The simple action of the moving scenes grows naturally out of the characters and situation. The characters are vividly presented, and among them are expressed many different attitudes toward religion, so that the play has a solidity and richness of texture rare in American drama.—B. H.

farce. One of the principal classifications of the nonmusical drama, the others being tragedy, melodrama, and comedy. Farce is sometimes confused with broad comedy; the two may be separated in theory by saying that farce draws its humor from physical activity on stage arising from the given situation, whereas comedy depends on the study of characters and the attempts by these characters to be witty. The appeal of farce is therefore primarily visual and sensuous; that of comedy, auditory and intellectual. Even so, plays that are labeled or recognized as farces may steal scenes or moments from comedy, while comedy may incorporate bits of business—*lazzi* or, as they are called on Broadway, "shticks"—that are clearly farcical. In practice, especially in performance, the division is not a hard-and-fast one. Nor are there, in the history of the theater, many examples of plays that are farcical throughout.

Contemporary farce has a long antecedence. It goes back as far as the fifth century B.C., to the beginnings of the Greek Old Comedy, the farcical playlets put on in the Attic town of Megara, some of them taken piecemeal or adapted into the plays of Aristophanes. The latter contain some of the richest, most inventive farce ever devised, from the lofting of Socrates in a basket (in *Clouds*) to Philocleon's frantic efforts (in *Wasps*) to break out of his house after he has been imprisoned by his son.

In Sicily and southern Italy *phlyax* troupes that specialized in farcical mime productions came into being at about the same time as the Megaran farces. Some *phlyakes* moved north through the Italian peninsula. By the third century B.C. many of them had established themselves in Campania and were only slightly modified in form. Today they are known as Atellan farces (*fabulae Atellanae*). They in turn had detectable influences on the written drama of Plautus, which has come down to us in such plays as *Menaechmi, Aulularia, Miles Gloriosus,* and *Pseudolus,* with their outrageous coincidences, narrowly defined characters, errors of identity, and their intricate plotting.

Since the Renaissance there have been four great flowerings of farce as a dramatic medium. The first, the COMMEDIA DELL'ARTE of Italy, represented a popular, informal revival and transformation of the plays of Plautus and of the phlyakes. The commedia productions introduced their scenes in an improvised order, but their anecdotes and characters became conventional. In fact, from the commedia comes one of the basic elements of subsequent farce, the stock or typed character who is shuffled through an assortment of set situations. The commedia roles were rigid; each player adopted a particular part for life, wore a mask, and used a regional accent. Pantalone, the old merchant, talked in a Venetian dialect and was generally threatened with the loss of his gold, his daughter, or both; the Spanish Capitano mouthed splendid oaths but proved a coward when anybody stood up to him; the clownish, sometimes ingenious, sometimes scoundrelly servants, or *zanni,* such as Pulcinella or Coviello, each had their personal characteristics and costumes. Hundreds of commedia routines have survived as scenarios without dialogue.

Much as Aristophanes and Plautus had borrowed from and codified the Megaran farces and the Atellan farces, respectively, so Molière helped himself to commedia characters and incidents in writing his brief, early comedies, such as *The Flying Doctor* (164?), *Sganarelle ou le cocu imaginaire* (1660), and *Le Mariage forcé* (1664), and in his later, full-length plays, for example, *The Miser* (1668), of which the central figure Harpagon is descended from Euclio in Plautus' *Aulularia,* and *The Imaginary Invalid* (1673), in which the physicians closely resemble *dottori,* or stock pedants from Padua, in the commedia scenarios.

The second outburst of farce came about in the nineteenth century. Its center was Paris; its dramaturgical props were the "well-made play" based on the accomplished formulas of Eugène Scribe and Victorien Sardou, and on the French *vaudeville* with its sketches punctuated by little songs. The leading exponents of the French varieties of farce were Eugène Labiche in *An Italian Straw Hat* (1851), *Monsieur Perrichon's Journey* (1860), *Célimare* (1863), and *Pots of Money* (1864), among other plays; Georges Courteline in the one-act *Hold on, Hortense!* (1897), *These Cornfields* (1898), and *The Commissioner Has a Big Heart* (1899); and Georges Feydeau, who composed more than thirty of the most relentless farces in the modern repertory, some celebrated ones being *Un Fil à la patte* (1894), *The Ribadier System* (1893), *Hotel Paradiso* (1894), *A Flea in Her Ear* (1907), and *Keep an Eye on Amélie* (1908).

France, however, held no monopoly on nineteenth-century farce. In Germany Christian Dietrich Grabbe made an unorthodox contribution with his *Jest, Satire, Irony, and Deeper Meaning* (1822), an apparently disorganized collection of scenes that would later provide technical inspiration for the surrealists. In Russia Nikolai Gogol's *The Inspector General* (1836) had distinctly farcical complications. Like Gogol's one-act *Gamblers* (1842) and *The Marriage* (1842), it was populated mostly by stock characters. A half-century later Anton Chekhov's short plays, subtitled farces, showed their indebtedness to Molière, especially *The Bear* (1888), *The Proposal* (1888), and *The Wedding* (1889).

In Britain W. S. Gilbert contrived to have farcical moments in most of his plays and librettos. Oscar Wilde superimposed epigrams on farcical business in *The Importance of Being Earnest* (1895). Bernard Shaw flirted with farce in a number of his comedies, notably, *Arms and the Man* (1894), *You Never Can Tell* (1899), *The Six of Calais* (1934), and *The Millionairess* (1936). In *Passion, Poison, and Petrifaction* (1905), Shaw gave a swift, out-and-out farce treatment to themes he would deal with more contemplatively in *Heartbreak House* (1916).

Alfred Jarry's *Ubu Roi* (1896) and Guillaume Apollinaire's *The Breasts of Tiresias* (1917) became the foster parents of the surrealist drama, which continued into the 1920's and 1930's, and in which farci-

cal elements predominated. The plays of André Breton (*If You Please,* written in collaboration with Philippe Soupault, 1920), of René Daumal (*En Gggarrrde!,* 1924), and of Roger Vitrac (*The Mysteries of Love,* 1927, and *Victor, or The Children Take Power,* 1928) are notable examples of this third series of experiments in farce.

The fourth, most recent and most varied manifestation of farce has come about largely as a result of the dramatic opportunities opened up by surrealism; and like surrealism it has been affected by advances in the theater's sibling arts, particularly the modern dance, the silent movies of Charlie Chaplin, Buster Keaton, and Harold Lloyd, by the acts of vaudeville comedians and the Marx Brothers, by the film *Hellzapoppin* based on the Broadway show of the same name, as well as by those animated cartoons in which small animals behave brutally to one another. Farce occurs and recurs as a basic ingredient or as heavy seasoning in innumerable plays written since the late 1940's. It is discernible, disguised sometimes as fantasy, in *One Way for Another* (1951) by Jean Tardieu; Eugène Ionesco's *Jack, or the Submission* (1950), *The Chairs* (1951), *The Future Is in Eggs* (1951), *Maid to Marry* (1953), *Amédée* (1953), and *The New Tenant* (1957); René de Obaldia's *Edward and Agrippina* (1961), and *The Wind in the Sassafras Branches* (1965); Harold Pinter's *The Birthday Party* (1958), *A Slight Ache* (1959), *The Caretaker* (1960), *The Lover* (1963), and *The Homecoming* (1965); Sławomir Mrożek's *The Police* (1958), *Męczeństwo Piotra Oheya* (1959), and *Out at Sea* (1961); and Laurent Lourson's *Narcissus* (1960). By all odds the most thoroughgoing farce writer of the modern theater has been the British dramatist and revue writer N. F. Simpson, whose plays include *A Resounding Tinkle* (1957), *The Hole* (1957), *One-Way Pendulum* (1959), which is subtitled "A Farce in a New Dimension," and *The Cresta Run* (1965).

In the United States a great deal of the "black humor" and madcap stunts of the younger playwrights is loosely considered farcical, perhaps for want of a better adjective. But these works for the most part resolve themselves by proposing love as the analeptic for the ills of the universe. They occupy the outskirts of sentimental comedy. One of the hallmarks of farce has been its pitilessness.

As a dramatic tool, rather than as a genre, farce has frequently, almost unavoidably, gone hand in hand with satire. In the modern theater the two are so affectionately related that an underlying distinction must be drawn between them. Satire delivers critical social comments and may take on the aspect of farce in order to make the comments palatable. Farce, on the other hand, aims to be palatable—that is, funny —and may employ satire to give its humor an edge. Even when a farce is not directly satirical, though, it has a strong tinge of bitterness, even iconoclasm. In most farces there is a sense of intemperance, of "going the limit," of reaching for extreme cases and examples; the worst that can happen in a given situation will happen.

Farce not merely derides propriety, tact, and the social graces; it thrives on misrepresenting them; it strives to reduce the pillars of society to ruins. Among its customary marks are marriage, the army, the law (both police officialdom and the courts), all

A SCENE FROM EUGÈNE IONESCO'S *Amédée* (FRENCH CULTURAL SERVICES)

legislative bodies, all disciplinary institutions, and anybody with rank or a title. Nor does it spare the honest man, the beggar, or the slave.

Today playwrights and audiences alike find farce more congenial and more appropriate than tragedy as a way of looking at their world. At a time when the public is confronted by its news media with one crisis and calamity on top of another, it becomes more bearable to laugh one's way toward seriousness than to retreat into continual sorrow. Thus we see farces burrowing into tragedy's stockpile for their raw materials and producing not sublimations but caricatures of the world's cruelty. Some or all of the characters in farce undergo physical damage. Receiving or giving a beating was a standard episode in the commedia dell'arte. In the more refined modern drama, aided by superior stage machinery, walls collapse on old women; there are picnics on the battlefield; troublesome children are shot to death (and sometimes revived). Yet farce is no more cruel than it ever was, only more exaggerated. If Ionesco mocks a young lady because she has only two noses, he is being no more vindictive than earlier farce writers who ridiculed blindness, deafness, speech defects, goiters, and sundry other disfigurements and deficiencies, as well as such mental aberrations as obsessions with money, sickness, and neatness.

The plots of farces generally appear to be anarchic. Everything gets out of the characters' control, although, in French farces especially, this effect can be realized only because the dramatist has maintained a tight control over the sequence of events. Any play by Feydeau, for example, may be visualized as a series of predestined moves over a misleadingly large checkerboard.

Most farces grow into a chase or a rush. Time is of the essence; the exact time nearly always figures in the action. Somebody has to be somewhere shortly. An important visitor may walk in at any second or, worse, two visitors who must on no account meet (they invariably do). A sensation of madness is engendered as the hero gets pulled desperately—it seems, inextricably—into a catastrophe.

The pace and insanity of farce in turn create an atmosphere onstage that approximates the conditions of a dream world or, rather, of a nightmare: the terrors of humiliation—of being, say, unable to remember the simple answer to a leading question; of being found in a stranger's bedroom without pants on; of being taken for a notorious criminal or a lunatic with not a scrap of evidence to support one's identity—such typical dream fears are familiar to audiences. As they recognize them, consciously or unconsciously, they laugh; they are relieved witnesses of somebody else's nightmare.

To achieve the desired unreality of mood and to court the desired response, laughter, the playwright will generally begin his farce in commonplace, credible circumstances and surroundings. Then by means of theatrical logic he will shift it gradually into improbability and beyond that into the realm of nonsense. (In contemporary farce the progression tends to be more abrupt, while logic has given way to a blatant use of "antilogic.") By bringing in a string of fresh complications, by uncovering secrets and letting out surprising revelations, by the introduction of coincidences and accidents, he does not give his audience a chance to see quite how the action is developing, nor to find a psychological footing, until his plot maneuvers have entrapped his characters. The cast is in continual flux with new arrivals and sudden departures. The precipitous entrance and exit are the most common stage directions in farce. They enhance the instability of the action; they intensify the bustle; they foster a feeling in the onlookers of uncertainty. Anything can happen next, and probably will. Comedy, by way of contrast, remains grounded in reality. Its characters are not meant to be suspect; they are plausible reconstructions of human beings with motives that make sense to a spectator.

The events in an average farce, if taken out of their context, would probably do service as the framework for a melodrama, and vice versa. The farces of Ionesco and Pinter verge on melodrama in places; some of them actually end with a melodramatic flourish. The screenplay of any recent film by the supreme melodramatist of the twentieth century, Alfred Hitchcock, could be converted without much difficulty into a classical nineteenth-century farce. But the distinctions between the two genres remain. The principal difference is the contempt of the farceur for his characters, *vis-à-vis* the sympathy of the melodramatist for his, and this difference is responsible for the two sets of theatrical dividends that result: raucous amusement and gooseflesh.

In farce, characters are not so much villains and saint-martyrs as amoral mixtures of innocence and roguery. Frequently they are ordinary people who become caught up in extraordinary goings-on. They may have an objective (a wedding in *An Italian Straw Hat;* a meal in *The Inspector General*), but the exigencies of the plot force them to postpone it, sometimes indefinitely. It is therefore unreasonable to complain about the limited characterizations in farces compared to those to be found in comedies and tragedies. The people in Plautus, Labiche, and Feydeau have been born expressly to obey the mandates of the plot; in Gogol, Wilde, Courteline, Shaw, and Ionesco, to confirm those authors' points of view. They are mankind as primitives, or as baffled children who operate on impulse. They are not equipped for reflection; they do not appear to lead self-conscious, independent lives nor to think interesting thoughts; the author has not intended them to. They wear faces that are variants on the masks of the commedia dell'arte or the phlyax, hardly fleshed out.

If they seemed more like human beings, we would be less able to laugh at their misfortunes.

General critical literature about farce is scarce, although allusions to farcical effects, not always to farce by name, will be found in most of the standard books and essays on comedy and humor and in criticism of specific plays and playwrights. The best discussion of the psychology of farce is in Chapter 7 of *The Life of the Drama* (1964) by Eric Bentley. See also "Farce" by Vsevelod Meyerhold in *Tulane Drama Review* (Autumn 1959).—A. C. B.

Farquhar, George (1677–1707).   Irish-born English comic playwright. Farquhar was the son of a poor clergyman. He was a student at Trinity College, Dublin, for a year and a half but left without taking a degree. After acting for a while at the Smock Alley Theatre in Dublin, Farquhar went to London in 1697, resolved to be an author. Luck was with him. His first play, *Love and a Bottle,* was successfully presented at the close of 1698. This was followed by *The Constant Couple, or A Trip to the Jubilee* (1699), which took London by storm. After a trip to Holland Farquhar came forward with three more plays—*Sir Harry Wildair, The Sequel of "A Trip to the Jubilee"* (1701), *The Inconstant* (1702), and *The Twin Rivals* (1702)—all of them proving failures. But luck once more favored him. *The Stage Coach,* a short farce adapted from a minor French play, pleased London when acted in 1704. In the same year Farquhar received a lieutenant's commission in the army and was shortly sent on a recruiting campaign to Lichfield and then Shrewsbury. It was while stationed at the latter town that he is said to have written *The Recruiting Officer,* which opened triumphantly in 1706 and became one of the stock comedies of the eighteenth-century theater. What happened thereafter is not clear, but by the close of 1706 Farquhar, ill and destitute, had taken refuge in a London garret, where THE BEAUX' STRATAGEM was composed in about six weeks. Some two months after the play was produced Farquhar died.

Farquhar's two earliest plays have more than a little of the Restoration manner in them, but the elements of sex intrigue and frank speech are balanced, if not neutralized, by boisterous gaiety, characters who prove amusing even in their misdemeanors, and diverting situations. These qualities point to a substantially different kind of comedy, which informs both *The Recruiting Officer* and *The Beaux' Stratagem.* Farquhar chose to break out of the confines of the metropolitan scene and move into the provinces. He finds amusement in town marketplaces, inns, and the homes of the gentry. The characters he observes include absurd rustics and amusing scoundrels, as well as young heroes and heroines. Disclosed in these two plays are a freshness and a humanity almost unknown since the Elizabethan theater.

Charles Stonehill has edited *The Complete Works of George Farquhar* (2 vols., 1930). A good short introduction to Farquhar's work is to be found in *George Farquhar* by A. J. Farmer (*Writers and Their Work,* No. 193, 1966).—R. Q.

Fashion (1845).   A comedy by Anna Cora Mowatt (1819–1870). *Fashion* was first performed in New York and then with equal success in Philadelphia. Successfully revived by the Provincetown Players in 1924; still occasionally performed.

The play deals with a New York businessman's social-climbing wife, Mrs. Tiffany, who is determined to marry her daughter Seraphina to Count Jolimaitre. Nearly ruined by his wife's extravagance, Mr. Tiffany has forged a note, putting himself in the power of his clerk, Snobson, who wants to marry Seraphina. Contrasted with Seraphina is Gertrude, Seraphina's levelheaded governess who falls in love with honest Colonel Howard. Adam Trueman, a plain-living, sturdy American farmer, is offered as a contrast to the Tiffanys. Trueman saves Mr. Tiffany from Snobson, and Count Jolimaitre is exposed as a fraud.

Fashion is a spirited satire on the folly of newly rich Americans who in the 1840's regarded everything French as wonderful and everything American as commonplace. It owes a considerable debt to Sheridan, but Mrs. Mowatt's knowledge of New York society enabled her to endow her characters with a genuine American flavor.—B. H.

Fastnachtsspiel ("carnival play"). The earliest form of German secular drama, originating in the pre-Lenten carnival (*Fastnacht*) of the late middle ages. Although the high point of this form was reached in the fifteenth and sixteenth centuries, its roots extend far back into the spring and fertility rites of pre-Christian Europe. Unlike the modern drama, which attempts to create a reality of its own, the Fastnachtsspiel was an integral part of the revelry: Rather than disengage the audience from its bacchanalian festivity, the play tended to bring the public into the dramatic activity through form, structure, content, and mode of performance.

The plays, which were performed by members of the community as they wandered about town in the course of the celebration, began and ended completely within the context of the carnival. Groups of revelers established themselves at a convenient tavern, house, or other public place and announced the beginning of the play; at the conclusion, the players returned to the crowd from which they had emerged, and proceeded to the next place of performance, leaving the revelers to carry on their carousing. The humorous content of the plays and their relatively short length (average: 300 lines) helped keep them within this framework.

The material of the plays themselves was not exotic but derived from the everyday world of the players and spectators. Thus, the plots often involved courtroom scenes, which create a natural audience situation. Characters were often type-caricatures of familiar individuals, such as the peasant, whose stupidity was legendary among the city dwellers. The plots were rarely new and generally consisted of traditional material. In most cases, however, the core of the humor was an overt but intellectual sexuality; the hallmark of earlier plays had been a rather blatant obscenity, which was suppressed by later moralizing tendencies.

The plays assumed two forms. The older Fastnachtsspiel, the sequential play (*Rheihenspiel*), formerly known as the *Revuespiel*, consisted of a series of characters delivering the same humorous monologue. A typical plot involved several women proclaiming their desire for one man, who in turn would choose the last. The later development of the play, known as the *Handlungsspiel*, or simply "plot-

ANNA CORA MOWATT (MUSEUM OF THE CITY OF NEW YORK)

play," resembled more the type of drama to which present-day audiences are accustomed. It featured a plot, with one or more central characters. The texts were rhymed couplets in a four-beat line known as *Knittelvers*.

The center of Fastnachtsspiel writing was Nuremberg, with Hans Rosenplüt and Hans Folz (c. 1450–1515) representing the earlier workers in the form. The play reached its high point with the work of HANS SACHS in the sixteenth century. Sachs's plays diverged somewhat from the more compilatory earlier works and exhibited a distinct moralizing tone.

The form died out with Jacob Ayrer (c. 1540–1605) in the sixteenth century. It was suppressed in Protestant areas with the disappearance of the pre-Lenten carnival, and in Catholic areas the SCHULDRAMA (Latin "school drama") took on some of its functions. The texts of about 150 Fastnachtsspiele exist today.—B. M. M.

Father, The (Fadren, 1887). A play by August STRINDBERG. An army captain finds himself locked in a struggle to the death with his wife, Laura, over the education of their only child, Bertha. Her future is the only afterlife the captain believes in, but his religious convictions are challenged by female piety and superstition of many kinds. Laura causes him to doubt his paternity, and this doubt deepens. The captain is a scientist as well as a military man, and Laura combats him in that quarter as well by intercepting his correspondence and circulating rumors about his sanity. Indeed, the captain does become increasingly distraught until, after some stormy scenes, he is coaxed into a straitjacket by his old governess and dies of a stroke.

Laura has murdered him by the power of her will.

She is not vicious, Strindberg would probably say; just predatory according to the instincts of her kind. She is the stronger in the battle of the sexes, and her victory adumbrates the approaching matriarchy that Strindberg anticipated.

The captain is fundamentally somewhat neurasthenic. With this in mind, Strindberg buttresses his character with literary and mythic identifications. He shares Agamemnon's *hybris,* Othello's suspicion, Hercules' subjugation by woman (the Asian queen Omphale), Hamlet's Oedipal impasse, and Lear's suffering at the hands of woman. Strindberg even puts Shylock's best speech into his mouth. Thus, in a manifold way, he elevates the captain to tragic status.

The Father may be "red in tooth and claw," but Zola, in writing a generally laudatory Preface to the play's French edition, could not accept it as fully naturalistic. It may be described, perhaps, as a modern tragedy that has not fully divested itself of melodramatic trappings. Nevertheless, *The Father* is one of Strindberg's best-known plays.

The text may be found in *The Plays of Strindberg,* Vol. 1 (1964), translated by Michael Meyer.—R. B. V.

Faust (Part I, pub. 1808; **Part II,** pub. 1832). A tragedy by Johann Wolfgang von GOETHE. In *Faust* Goethe develops the character of the legendary Faust as the old scholar who yearns to comprehend not so much all knowledge as all experience. In the "Prologue in Heaven," God, at Mephistopheles' challenge, gives the latter permission to test the integrity of Faust. Faust then strikes his bargain with the devil: If Mephistopheles can grant Faust one moment of complete contentment, a moment that he might wish to last an eternity, Faust will give his soul over to the devil. In *Part I* Mephistopheles rejuvenates Faust and presents him with the world of desire and passion. Faust falls in love with and seduces the young Marguerite. She bears him a child but panics and drowns it; the last scene of *Part I* is set in the dungeon where, awaiting execution for her crime, she refuses to flee with Faust and puts her trust in God.

Having failed to discover in the "small world" of personal feeling and experience a moment so wonderful that he wishes it would last an eternity, Faust enters, in *Part II,* the "great world" of history, politics, and culture. In this part, Goethe takes the opportunity to develop many of his ideas on mythology, culture, art, statesmanship, war, courtly life, economics, natural science, and religion. And although here Faust tastes every form of intellectual and worldly power, he again fails to discover his wonderful moment, much to Mephistopheles' discouragement. Finally, once again an old man, Faust takes interest in a project to reclaim the land from the sea, a project that will bring no personal gain but that will bring good to countless numbers of people. In this socially constructive, disinterested undertaking, Faust, much to his surprise, finds profound happiness, a moment he could wish would last forever. But Mephistopheles' victory is only apparent; Faust's soul is rescued by a choir of angels who speak the motto: *Wer immer strebend sich bemüht, / Den können wir erlösen* ("He who exerts himself in constant striving, / Him we can save"). Mephistopheles has lost the wager, not with Faust, but with God.

Femmes savantes, Les (The Learned Ladies, 1672). A comedy by MOLIÈRE. The household of Chrysale, a Parisian bourgeois, is divided into two groups. On the one hand, his wife, Philaminte, his sister Bélise, and his daughter Armande have all fallen in love with literature, science, and philosophy and will have nothing to do with the life of the senses, including marriage. On the other hand, his younger daughter Henriette, his brother Ariste, and Clitandre, a former suitor of Armande who is now in love with Henriette, remain faithful to a normal bourgeois life. Philaminte is ready to sacrifice Henriette to her need for "intellect" and wants her to marry the ridiculous poet Trissotin. Gradually, Trissotin turns out to be a grasping and brutal hypocrite. Through trickery, Ariste unmasks him, and Henriette can now marry Clitandre.

Les Femmes savantes is outstanding for the psychological complexity of the characters—Philaminte's formidable strength, Chrysale's weakness and love of homely comforts, Bélise's repressed hysteria, Armande's regrets and frustration, Trissotin's hateful duplicity—as well as for the scenes in which the philosophical and literary delirium of the "learned" is given free rein.

This play has been translated by Joachim Neugroschel under the title *The Learned Ladies* (1966). —Ja. G.

Ferreira, António. See PORTUGAL.

Feydeau, Georges [Léon Jules Marie] (1862–1921). French playwright. Feydeau's parents were Lodzia Slewska, a Polish lady, and Ernest Feydeau, maliciously described in the Goncourt Brothers' *Journal* as "a stockbroker who is crazy about Egypt and goes about everywhere with a plaster cast of Egyptian [statuary] under one arm." The elder Feydeau was also a novelist (his best-known book was the fleetingly sensational *Fanny,* 1858), playwright, and author of an archeological study, *History of Funeral Customs and Graves of Ancient Peoples* (1862). Young Feydeau was acquainted with his father's literary friends, who included Flaubert, Gautier, Baudelaire, and Sainte-Beuve. Yet his work is singularly "unliterary." Perhaps he overheard, and reacted with distaste to, salon conversation on such topics as the dependence of ideas on form. However, he did acquire from his father a lasting interest in the stock market.

He was educated by a private tutor at his home in Paris, and later went on to the Lycée Saint-Louis. He wrote plays during his childhood, he claimed, as an escape from doing his homework. His first produced comedy, *Par la Fenêtre* ("Out the Window," 1881), was written when he was eighteen. Four productions and seven years later he had his first hit, *Tailleur pour dames (Ladies' Tailor),* written while he was in the army. Yet another seven disappointing receptions elapsed before his thirteenth and fourteenth plays, *Monsieur chasse!* ("The Gentleman's in Pursuit!") and *Champignol malgre lui* ("Champignol in Spite of Himself"), were mounted within three weeks of each other in 1892 at the Palais-Royal and the Théâtre des Nouveautés, respectively; each ran for more than a thousand performances. Success followed success; in 1894 alone four of his farces opened, among them *Un Fil à la patte* (the untranslatable title means that the hero is tied to his mistress like a dog, with a string attached to one of his paws) and *L'Hôtel du Libre Echange* (*Hotel Paradisco*), while *Le Système Ribadier* ("The Ribadier System," 1892) and two earlier works were still being given.

But Feydeau, who lived well and gambled passionately with stocks, was always in debt. Instead of making his fortune, his plays continually rescued him from penury. In 1903 he was forced to sell most of his extensive collection of impressionist paintings. This was at a time when Feydeau and his friend Georges COURTELINE had supplanted Victorien Sardou in popular esteem in the Parisian theater; when his style was being imitated and his lines freely plagiarized by numberless other dramatists; and when his scripts were being translated and staged in half-a-dozen other countries. He continued to write actively. In the twenty years from 1896 to 1916 he produced as many plays. Then he stopped. Five years later he died of a cerebral hemorrhage.

Feydeau was himself an accomplished actor and a skillful director. His scenes exploit the stage and its trappings relentlessly, whether they are set in the reception hall of a chateau, a drawing room, a modest apartment house, a restaurant, out of doors, or, most often, in a bedroom. Beds are Feydeau's most versatile property. They serve for sleeping in, pretending to sleep in, hiding in and under, bouncing on, and as an unreliable platform to declaim from. Strangers of opposite sexes frequently find themselves lying side by side in a Feydeau bed at a moment when one or the other's spouse is coming up the stairs or knocking at the door. In *La Puce à l'oreille* (*A Flea in Her Ear,* 1907) Feydeau even makes use of a Murphy bed, which comes out of a wall and disgorges new characters into the room, to everyone's embarrassment.

The plots, impossible to summarize, borrow from sources as ancient as Plautus and generally depend on cases of mistaken identity. Two characteristics that distinguish a Feydeau farce from those of his predecessors—Sardou, Labiche, Beaumarchais, and Molière—are, first, the richness of the complications as each situation intensifies from trouble through danger to panic (Feydeau constructs his action with geometrical progression and efficiency); and second, the unsparing quality of his mockery. He went well beyond the conventional "good taste" of his time in assailing marriage, physical deformities and disfigurements, parenthood, and the military: in *Occupe-toi d'Amélie* (*Keep an Eye on Amélie,* 1908) a father pimps for his daughter and a general for his monarch. Like Labiche, Feydeau has no respect for any people or any institutions; and his work, like Molière's, is especially brutal toward social climbers and pretenders.

The wildly improbable happenings in a Feydeau play are somehow made to seem plausible in context, perhaps because the author deliberately functioned as a realist:

> Each of us in life gets mixed up in farcical situations without necessarily losing our individuality in the process . . . I set about looking for my characters in living reality, determined to preserve their personalities intact. After a comic explosion, I would hurl them into burlesque situations.

Some fifteen of Feydeau's farces are cyclically revived by the Comédie-Française; at least two are in the repertory at any given time. The company performs Feydeau's works with heightened, almost cartoon-like characterization, at a dizzy pace, and with acrobatic prowess; yet the lines are spoken lovingly, with measured effect. This combination of contrasting styles in movement and speech has yet to be mastered by other companies, especially outside France. As a result, the bulk of Feydeau's writing, which constitutes the finest farce of the modern theater, is foreign to British and American audiences. When done in English, which is seldom, the plays tend to lack the *jeu d'esprit* of the French productions.

There is almost no published autobiographical or biographical material on Feydeau, and criticism consists almost entirely of reviews of the individual productions. *Théâtre complet de Georges Feydeau* (1948–1956) in ten volumes reprints the thirty-nine plays, which are introduced by the playwright Marcel Achard. Achard's anecdotal Introduction, translated by Mary Douglas Dirks, appears in *Let's Get a Divorce! and Other Plays* (1958), edited by Eric Bentley. *L'Esprit de Georges Feydeau* (1927), edited by Léon Treich, is a book of reminiscences. English translations include: two versions of *Occupe-toi d'Amélie*—Noel Coward's *Look After Lulu* (1959) and Brainerd Duffield's *Keep an Eye on Amélie!* (in *Let's Get a Divorce! and Other Plays,* see above); *L'Hôtel du libre echange,* adapted by Peter Glenville as *Hotel Paradiso* (1957); *Going to Pot* (*On purge Bébé*), translated by Norman R. Shapiro, together with Shapiro's essay on "Suffering and Punishment in the Theater of Georges Feydeau" in the *Tulane Drama Review* (Autumn, 1960); and a number of dated, unpublished translations of individual plays (available in the Promptbooks and Typescripts section of the Drama Research Division, Lincoln Center Library for the Performing Arts, New York.)
—A. C. B.

Field, Nathan (1587–1620). English actor and playwright. The son of a well-known Puritan minister, Field attended St. Paul's Grammar School. While a student there he was pressed into service as an actor with the Children of the Chapel, probably against the wishes of his theater-hating father. Field soon rose to prominence as the most talented of child actors and came under the tutelage of Ben Jonson. Jonson's *Bartholomew Fair* (1614) contains an allusion to Field and Richard Burbage as the best actors of their day. As an adult Field joined Shakespeare's company, the King's Men, and soon was sharing leading roles with Burbage. Among his great parts was the title role in George Chapman's *Bussy D'Ambois* (c. 1604).

Field is the author of *A Woman Is a Weathercock* (c. 1609) and *Amends for Ladies* (1611), two studious imitations of Jonsonian humour comedy that only occasionally come to life. He also collaborated on a few plays with John Fletcher and with Philip Massinger. Of these, the most worthy of note are *The Fatal Dowry* (produced between 1616 and 1619), with Massinger, and *Four Plays in One* (1616), with Fletcher.—E. Q.

Fielding, Henry (1707–1754). English novelist,

journalist, and comic playwright. Fielding came of a landowning West County family. He was educated at Eton and by the time he was twenty had written a comedy in the Restoration manner, *Love in Several Masques* (1728), which ran only four nights. After a brief enrollment at the University of Leyden, Fielding was back in London by 1729 to take up playwriting in earnest. Over the next eight years he established a remarkable record of productivity, turning out some twenty-five plays.

It was soon evident that Fielding's bent was for dramatic satire, and he had no difficulty in finding material to his purposes in the contemporary scene. Fielding's sympathies at the time lay with the group of men, the so-called Patriots, who were leading the opposition to Sir Robert Walpole and his Whig administration. His satire became increasingly political and increasingly pointed. King George II, Queen Caroline, Walpole, and other prominent figures were introduced in his plays under the thinnest of disguises and submitted to the sharpest ridicule. It was only a matter of time before the authorities struck back. In June 1737, the Theatrical Licensing Act was passed, and Fielding was effectively throttled. Only Drury Lane and Covent Garden theaters were permitted to remain open and, with a more rigid censorship of plays, political satire was driven from the stage. Fielding then turned to the law and was admitted to the bar in 1740.

Fielding's satiric response to Samuel Richardson's novel *Pamela* (1740), the short but deadly parody entitled *Shamela*, appeared in 1746. With the publication of *Joseph Andrews* the following year his career as a novelist was under way. Since Fielding is chiefly remembered as a novelist and journalist, the latter part of his career has received most attention. There is no denying that his achievement as a novelist far outweighs his dramatic accomplishments; yet in the history of eighteenth-century comedy Fielding the playwright is an important, indeed almost a major, figure.

Of his plays, the one most often noticed is *The Tragedy of Tragedies; or, The Life and Death of Tom Thumb the Great* (1731), an elaboration of his earlier *Tom Thumb* of the previous year. Laid at the court of a decidedly unromantic King Arthur, it is an uproarious parody of the heroic drama associated with John Dryden, Nathaniel Lee, and John Banks. Although Fielding was carrying on the satirical tradition established by the duke of Buckingham's *The Rehearsal* (1671), he had already made sport of the theatrical fare and had done so with quite as much wit in his earlier *The Author's Farce* (1730). In *The Covent Garden Tragedy* (1732), continuing this kind of satire on drama, he burlesqued Ambrose Philips' *The Distrest Mother* (1712), which was taken as an example of Augustan tragedy. But the plays that most deserve attention are, in addition to *The Author's Farce, The Welsh Opera* (1731), *Don Quixote in England* (1734), *Pasquin* (1736), and *The Historical Register For the Year 1736* (1737). All of these are of the irregular sort of drama in which Fielding excelled. Satiric, realistic, topical, they reveal why George Bernard Shaw, with an enthusiasm not wholly groundless, referred to Fielding as "the greatest practising dramatist, with the single exception of Shake-

spear, produced by England between the Middle Ages and the nineteenth century."

Fielding's plays can be found in Vols. VIII to XII of the *Complete Works* (reprinted in 1967), edited by William Ernest Henley and others. The detailed study by Frederick Homes Dudden, *Henry Fielding: His Life, Works, and Times* (2 vols., 1952), contains discussions of all the plays. In the Regents Restoration Drama Series there are separate editions, with excellent introductory commentaries, of *The Author's Farce, The Historical Register,* and *The Grub-Street Opera* (a revision of *The Welsh Opera*). —R. Q.

Figlia di Iorio, La (The Daughter of Iorio, 1904). A pastoral tragedy by Gabriele D'ANNUNZIO. Set among the shepherds and peasants of the mountains of the Abruzzi, the tragedy recounts the story of a morally lost woman, Mila di Codro, whom the shepherd Aligi saves from the fury of a band of reapers who have been excited by the sun and by wine. Aligi welcomes her to his house, tracing the sign of the cross on the threshold, which no one dares tread upon. Subsequently, an unforeseen and pure love develops between Mila and Aligi, who abandons his newly wedded and still untouched wife to take refuge in the mountains with Mila. They live in chaste cohabitation, meditating on the possibility of making a pilgrimage to the pope in Rome to request an annulment of Aligi's marriage. One day, however, Lazaro, Aligi's father, surprises them. Burning with desire for Mila, he assaults her. Aligi intervenes, killing his father with an ax. Mila flees, and Aligi is about to submit to the mortal punishment reserved for parricides. While Aligi awaits execution, already stupefied by drugs that a compassionate person has given him, Mila reappears and confesses that she killed Lazaro and that she had bewitched Aligi. Aligi himself becomes convinced that he was a victim of witchcraft and curses Mila, who goes smilingly to the purifying stake.

La Figlia di Iorio belongs to the cultivated tradition of the Italian pastoral drama. Although mannered and fastidiously written, it is sustained by powerful dramatic vigor and by a sensuous and imaginative language that gives vividness to the forceful protagonists and to their exalted passions.—L. L.

Figueiredo, Guilherme (1915–   ). Brazilian playwright and journalist. Son and grandson of soldiers, Guilherme Figueiredo was born in Campinas, in the state of São Paulo. His father led an eventful career as a liberal conspirator against the Vargas regime. Several relatives on his mother's side were writers. So it was that Figueiredo entered the Colégio Militar, in whose journal he wrote poems. Soon he abandoned the uniform and matriculated in a course of law, which he completed in 1936. He then divided his time between journalism, law, and the editing of programs for radio and television. Since 1964 Figueiredo has lived outside of Brazil as cultural attaché.

His first play for the stage, *Lady Godiva,* was performed in 1948. Soon after came *Greve geral* ("General Strike," 1949), based on *Lysistrata* of Aristophanes, and *Um deus dormiu là em casa* ("A God Slept There at Home," 1949), making use of the classical figures Amphytryon and Jupiter. It is about Alcmene, a sophisticated woman who does not believe in the gods. This play won the prize of the Brazilian Society of Drama Critics and the prize of the Brazilian Academy of Letters.

At the same time Figueiredo was publishing novels and traveling through several European countries, where his plays have often been performed. One of them is *A rapôsa e as uvas* ("The She-Fox and the Grapes," 1952), which has as its focal point an episode in the life of Aesop. It was a prize winner in Brazil, was performed for three consecutive years in Buenos Aires, and took first place in the Festival of Dance and Music in Moscow (1957). Other successful plays are *D. Juan* (1950), *Os fantasmas* ("The Ghosts," 1959), *Tragédia para rir* ("Tragedy for Laughter," 1962), and *O asilado* ("The One in Asylum," 1962).

There is no translated edition of Figueiredo's plays.—J. P.

film. See SCREENPLAY.

Filumena Marturano (1946). A comedy by Eduardo DE FILIPPO. The protagonist, Filumena, after having lived for some time in a house of prostitution, is rescued from it by the rich Domenico Soriano. Enamored of her, he keeps her by his side, first as mistress, then as a humble and devoted housekeeper. One day, when Domenico is about to marry a young woman, Filumena becomes ill and appears to be at the point of death. She calls upon Domenico to marry her *in articulo mortis,* which he consents to do as an act of compassion, certain that shortly thereafter she will die. They are scarcely married, however, when Filumena arises from bed, cured. Her illness was a ruse that she had thought up to force Domenico to marry her and thus give his name to the three children she has supported by daily robbing him. It was for this reason, it turns out, that she had patiently put up with her status. Domenico becomes indignant and tells her that her ruse has been useless because a marriage contracted under false pretenses is obviously invalid. Filumena then reveals that one of the three children is his. Finally, after Domenico has attempted in vain to force her to tell him which one it is, he consents to give his name, as well as his paternal love, to all three.

Written almost entirely in a very beautiful Neapolitan dialect, the comedy is among the most powerful expressions of the profoundly human and popularly based art of De Filippo. The protagonist has an animal attachment to the values of the family. Since her profound sense of justice is not bounded by the formality of law, she passes over it without scruple in order to attain a justice that is more humane. She is among the greatest female characters in the entire history of the Italian stage.—L. L.

Finland. The history of Finnish literature covers thousands of years of folk poetry and some four centuries of written literature. Before settling down in Finland (after A.D. 100) and forming a nation, the Finns wandered westward from the river Ob together with other tribes speaking Finno-Ugric languages. The earliest forms of primitive drama were shamanistic rituals; the shaman also had a role to play in the arctic rituals celebrating the killing of a bear or an elk. These rites date back to the period from 3000 to 2500 B.C. and resemble satyr plays in their combination of crudely comic and obscene elements. Closer

to us in time (about 1000 B.C. to A.D. 100) and geography are the proto-Finnic wedding and funeral rituals, with their rich poetry of lamentation. The folk poems recorded in these areas, south and east of the Gulf of Finland, also include the medieval rite of Sämpsä Pellervoinen, a strange mixture of Christian and pagan influences. Sämpsä is a god of fertility worshiped in Dionysian spring festivals. In Finland itself there are remnants of some processional theater forms, partly Catholic, partly pagan in origin. These and other rituals did not, however, lead to any tradition of national drama or theater.

Under Swedish rule (about 1155–1809) Finland was made a part of Scandinavia and Western Europe. The Renaissance court of Juhana Vaasa, duke of Finland from 1556 to 1563, favored theatrical performances and school plays. A modest flowering period followed the founding of the first university, in Turku; under its jurisdiction (and in a few schools, such as in Viipuri) there were plays given from 1640 to 1674. Connected with academic festivities, they were patronized by Count Pietari Brahe, the governor general, and by the professors. The plays were in Latin, Swedish, or Finnish; only three scripts are preserved, all in Swedish. They show the strong influence of medieval and Renaissance traditions in drama by being didactic and boisterous, solemn and coarsely comic, and by mixing the worlds of antiquity and seventeenth-century Finland. *Surge* ("Get Up," 1647) and *Bele-Snack* ("Wooing Talk," 1649) by Jacob Chronander include stories of industrious and lazy students, dryly academic debates, fighting scenes full of action, and elements of social criticism. Both are loose in structure; both can be connected with the Lutheran school plays based on the parable of the prodigal son. *Genesis Aetherea* (1659) by Erik Kolmodin is a Christmas play. In 1650 a Finnish play, now lost, was performed; it was probably a translation by Eerik Justander of the Swedish *Filius Prodigus* by Samuel P. Brask. After Brahe had left Finland, the group of eager student actors was dispersed and the drama tradition suppressed by the Finnish version of Puritanism. There was no popular theater tradition and the drama performed in the courts of noblemen was short-lived; the Humanists were alone. The prologue was followed by an interval of a century full of wars.

Then, traveling companies and amateur spectacles appeared; as in the United States, companies from abroad preceded the creation of native drama. They came from Sweden (since 1761) and from St. Petersburg and the Baltic countries, especially during the early decades of Russian rule (1809–1917). The languages spoken on the stage were Swedish, German, Russian, and, rarely, French; Finnish was the language of the uncultivated majority of people. The companies usually traveled through the southernmost cities of the country, creating habits of theatergoing, introducing playwrights like Molière, Shakespeare, Schiller, and August von Kotzebue, and building or encouraging the Finns to build several theaters. After the 1820's it was customary to have a foreign company in Helsinki, the new capital of the country, during the winter season, for two to six months. All this contributed to the beginnings of native drama.

Two early exercises by Jaakko Juteini, published in 1817, were followed by *Silmänkääntäjä* ("Trickster," written 1834), the first play in Finnish fit for the stage and played by amateurs in 1846. Its author, Pietari (Pekka) Hannikainen, was also the first to develop the idea of a national, Finnish-speaking theater. Similar plans were cherished in the 1840's by Agathon Meurman and Zachris Topelius (1818–1898), a theater critic, poet, playwright, novelist, and national figure; they had a Swedish or bilingual stage in mind. A farce with a youthful charm about it by J. L. Runeberg (1804–1877), the national poet, was produced in 1846 and others followed. In 1850 there were as many as twenty-five original plays written in Swedish, of which fifteen had been produced.

Amateur activities had been lively in many cities and towns. They culminated in the first performance of *Kung Carls jakt* ("King Carl Goes Hunting," 1852), an opera by Topelius and Fredrik Pacius. Topelius continued with *Regina von Emmeritz* (1854), a play also based on Finnish history, while Runeberg wrote the comedy *Kan ej* ("Cannot," 1862) and *Kungarne på Salamis* ("The Kings of Salamis," 1863), a Hellenistic tragedy. An established classic in the genre of historical plays is *Daniel Hjort* (1862) by J. J. Wecksell (1838–1907). It deals with a conflict between loyalty to the king and a wish to promote the freedom of the common people; there are echoes from *Hamlet*.

The Swedish stage in Helsinki was dominated by managers and actors imported from Sweden up to the year 1916; native plays were staged every now and then. The need for a national theater was urgent among the Finnish-speaking population, who were experiencing a great cultural awakening around the middle of the nineteenth century. The *Kalevala* (1835, enlarged edition 1849) was a collection of epic poems constructed by Elias Lönnrot from folk poetry; it revealed cultural riches where nothing was thought to exist. Its tragic elements were studied by Fredrik Cygnaeus, a scholar and playwright, and they inspired Aleksis Kivi (pseudonym of Alexis Stenvall) to write his tragedy *Kullervo* (completed in 1864, but not produced until 1885).

Aleksis Kivi (1834–1872) was a rare combination of originality and full consciousness of his task as a writer in the European tradition. Living without a regular income and without the support of a reading or theatergoing public, he was capable of laying the cornerstones of Finnish drama and the novel. He read Cervantes, Shakespeare, and Ludvig Holberg; his works blend idealistic and realistic elements, literary influences and a deep insight into the Finnish character. His style and rhythm are thoroughly individual. *Kullervo* is a revenge play with a secondary theme of incest; its language is both archaistic and wildly expressive. *Nummisuutarit* (*The Country Cobblers*, also translated as *The Heath Cobblers*, pub. 1864) is Kivi's dramatic masterpiece: full of vitality and good humor with a rich orchestration of the materials. The hero, Esko, a simple-minded, obstinate, and amiable boy, has the misfortune of arriving at the wedding of the girl he thought he was to marry; there is no more demanding or gratifying role for a comic actor in Finnish drama. *Kihlaus* (*Betrothal*, pub. 1866) is a one-act comedy of merit; both of these plays are constantly revived. *Karkurit* ("The Refugees," pub. 1867), a full-length romantic play, is influenced by *Romeo and Juliet*. The rest of Kivi's

plays show glimpses of greatness. His masterful novel *Seitsemän veljestä* (*Seven Brothers*, pub. 1870) belongs to the stage, too: there are numerous adaptations.

Kivi's biblical and lyric playlet *Lea* (pub. and prod. 1869) marks the beginning of professional theater in Finnish. Dr. Kaarlo Bergbom (1843–1906), a scholar in drama and the author of two romantic tragedies, directed the performance. In 1872 he founded The Finnish Theatre (1902–1962, The National Theatre; since 1962 The Finnish National Theatre). Bergbom had eighty-nine plays to start with, either Finnish originals or translations. His company was supported by national enthusiasm: it was a task of honor to prove the Finnish language fit for the stage. Gradually, he gathered together a group of dramatists and translators and advised them. The most talented pupil in Bergbom's school was Minna Canth (1844–1897), a female Ibsen. From folk plays she graduated to realistic dramas of social commitment, with emancipation as a recurrent theme. *Työmiehen vaimo* ("The Laborer's Wife," 1885) and *Koven onnen lapsia* ("Children of Misfortune," 1888) are aggressive indignation plays, while *Papin perhe* ("The Parson's Family," 1891), *Sylvi* (1893), and *Anna Liisa* (1895) show better balance and a tendency toward reconciliation. Canth was a woman of quick intelligence and warm sympathies; she followed closely the contemporary European discussion on literary and social ideas and gave a truthful picture of the conflicts between the generations, classes, and sexes.

Robert Kiljander (1848–1924) and Gustaf von Numers (1848–1913) are remembered for their comic treatment of small-town or country societies, Teuvo Pakkala (1862–1925) for his play about loggers, while Paavo Cajander (1846–1913) was the first to translate the entire Shakespearean canon into Finnish. K. A. Tavaststjerna was a realist writing in Swedish (*Uramon torppa*, 1892).

Bergbom laid the foundations for the program policies of most Finnish theaters: native and foreign classics are constantly revived, in addition to new plays. On the average, every second play produced is Finnish. A traveling company (1887–1897) was followed by new repertory companies founded in Helsinki (1899, 1901), Viipuri (1899), Tampere (1901, 1904), Turku (1916), and elsewhere, until the network of entirely or partly professional companies covered most parts of the country. In 1968 there were thirty-two theaters, among them four Swedish, subsidized from municipal and government funds, for a population of 4.5 million.

After 1900 a new generation of writers entered the stage. Its spokesman was Eino Leino (1878–1926), a man with the range and prolificness of a genius: newspaperman, translator of Dante's *Divina Commedia*, theater critic, playwright, first and foremost a poet. Influenced by Nietzsche, Leino demanded and wrote "holy dramas," with beauty, poetic atmosphere, and stylized action. His heroes, often placed against a background of Finnish history (*Lalli*, 1907; *Maunu Tavast*, 1908; *Simo Hurtta*, 1921; *Tuomas piispa*, pub. 1909) or ancient Greece (*Alkibiades*, 1910), are destroyed by their hubris. Leino also combined contemporary subjects with his experiments with form.

As a rule, Finnish playwrights rarely specialized in drama alone. Neo-Romanticism or symbolism influenced not only Leino but also Arvid Järnefelt (1861–1932), Larin-Kyösti (pseudonym of Karl Gustaf Larson, 1873–1948), Johannes Linnankoski (pseudonym of Johan Viktor Peltonen, 1869–1913), and Mikael Lybeck (1864–1925), all established writers of prose or poetry. Järnefelt, a Tolstoyan novelist, blended his ideology with symbolistic overtones in his plays (*Kuolema*, "Death," 1903; *Titus,* 1910). Larin-Kyösti, a poet, wrote the dream play *Ad astra* (pub. 1906), and Linnankoski created ambitious closet dramas, such as *Ikuinen taistelu* ("Eternal Fight," 1910). Lybeck, a remarkable novelist in Swedish, turned from stage symbolism in *Ödlan* ("Lizard," 1908) to intimate psychological analysis in *Bror och syster* ("Brother and Sister," 1915).

Aside from these experiments there was Maiju Lassila (pseudonym of Algot Tietäväinen-Untola, 1868–1918), with his outspoken, partly sunny, partly satirical folk comedies and their repeated character types (*Kun lesket lempivät,* "When the Widows Make Love," 1911; *Mimmi Paavaliina,* 1916). Politically, Lassila was an exponent of the second social and ideological movement promoting the theater in Finland: the awakening of the working class.

Maria Jotuni (1880–1943) started by writing impressionistic short stories of country life; as a playwright, she was influenced by Ibsen and Chekhov. Her classic comedy *Miehen kylkiluu* ("Man's Rib," 1914) has a stratified structure, with the theme of love treated on several social levels. *Kultainen vasikka* ("The Golden Calf," 1918) is a harsh satire on wartime speculators and *Tohvelisankarin rouva* ("Mrs. Henpecker," 1924) is a grotesque erotic carrousel with the characters chasing one another. Jotuni, an avowed antisentimentalist, showed in her last plays an inclination toward more imaginative flights of fancy combined with firm moral standpoints. She was also an aphorist; her dialogue is crisp and tight. Never neglected, her plays had a revival of interest in the 1960's following the posthumous publication of two works. One of these was the unfinished, yet editable, comedy *Amerikan morsian* ("The Bride from America," 1966).

Finland declared her independence in 1917. In the boom of the 1920's poetry and new experimental productions in the theater were more conspicuous than native drama. Runar Schildt (1888–1925) wrote three plays in which the atmosphere is charged with approaching death that cannot be averted by the self-sacrificing female characters. *Galgmannen* ("Gallows' Man," 1923) is a taut one-act play and *Den stora rollen* ("The Great Role," 1923) uses the recent Finnish civil war (1918) as the background for a private tragedy.

Expressionism had an impact on production techniques and on a few plays. Lauri Haarla (1890–1944) made an effort to apply this style to motives from Finnish folk poetry and history in *Lemmin poika* (1923) and *Velisurmaajat* ("The Fratricides," 1926). His eagerness to proclaim, in a rather vague manner, and his restless search for an adequate, archaistic language resulted in a specific variety of "storm and stress" plays. *Juudas* (1927), a historical

drama closer to realism, is Haarla's most sober achievement. Hagar Olsson (1893–   ) treated contemporary themes along the lines of German psycho- and socio-expressionism in *Hjärtats pantomim* ("The Pantomime of the Heart," 1928) and *S.O.S.* (1929). Her *Lumisota* ("Snow-balling," written 1939) is an antifascist family drama, and *Kärlekens död* ("The Death of Love," 1952) is a fairy tale still marked by expressionism. There is also a touch of expressionism in the early plays of Arvi Kivimaa (1904–   ), since 1950 the general manager of the Finnish National Theatre.

Instead of plays of the "living newspaper" type, the 1930's produced journalists writing fairly conventional, realistic descriptions of present-day life, mostly in the light vein. Kersti Bergroth (1886–   ), with her idyllic *Anu ja Mikko* (1932), and Artturi Leinonen (1888–1963) deal with life in the countryside, while Yrjö Soini (1896–   ) has written a series of successful farce comedies, and Serp (pseudonym of Seere Salminen, 1894–   ) has shown her sense of historical milieus. Erkki Kivijärvi (1882–1942) was a critic, theater manager, and playwright. There is more substance in the plays of Valentin (pen name of Ensio Rislakki, 1896–   ), originally a typical representative of the 1930's. *Kunnioittaen* ("Sincerely Yours," 1952) and *Musta Saara* ("Black Saara," 1957), a play about missionaries in Africa, deserve mention. Ilmari Turja (1901–   ) succeeded in creating comic figures of wide dimensions in his *Särkelä itte* (1944). Turja's *Päämajassa* ("In the Headquarters," 1966) is a partly critical documentary play about Field Marshal Mannerheim, commander of the Finnish army in the latest wars. Mika Waltari (1908–   ), a widely translated writer of historical novels, has also created picaresque comedies for the stage.

Estonian-born Juhani Tervapää (pseudonym of Hella Wuolijoki, 1886–1954) wrote a cycle of five plays on the changing fates of a farmhouse, Niskavuori (1936–1953: "The Women of Niskavuori," "The Bread of Niskavuori," and so forth). Built around the monumental figure of the old proprietress, these dramas reveal a series of conflicts between the old farming culture and the new social ideas. Wuolijoki, easily the most important playwright from the thirties, had clear visions, an alert eye for the dramatic possibilities immanent in everyday life, a sense of the theater, and a talent for characterization. Her comedy *Juurakon Hulda* (1937) shows her sympathy for a self-educated girl and for a socially active way of living. While in Finland (1940–1941), Bertolt Brecht collaborated with Hella Wuolijoki on *Herr Puntila und sein Knecht Matti* ("Mr. Puntila and His Man, Matti," 1948). Toivo Pekkanen (1902–1957), a fine novelist and social thinker, based his play *Sisarukset* ("Sister and Brother," 1933) on the tension between love and class consciousness. He developed antirealistic ideas in *Demoni* (1943), a study of the creative efforts of an actor, and in *Täyttyneiden toiveiden maa* ("The Country of Fulfilled Hopes," 1956), an allegorical play.

The economically depressed 1930's and six years of war were followed by social reforms and an Anglo-American, and partly French, orientation in cultural life. A whole generation was missing, especially among dramatists. There was no immediate new start and several new dramatists did not go on composing plays.

Sirkka Selja's (1920–   ) *Eurooppalainen* ("A European," 1947) was an expression of the current feeling that the time was out of joint. Juha Manner-korpi (1915–   ), a lonely moralist, has written monologue plays with a grotesquely tragicomic atmosphere (*Avain,* "The Key"; pub. 1955) and a suggestive, psychological puzzle play (*Pirunnyrkki,* pub. 1952). There are grotesque and absurd elements also in the works of V. V. Järner (1910–   ), who made his debut in 1950 and was one of the dramatists who shared the first government drama prize in 1967 for his ironic *Självständighetsfesten* ("Independence Day Party"). Rabbe Enckell (1903–   ), a mod-ernist poet, has written a series of closet dramas in verse located in ancient Greece.

The most prolific playwright (over sixty radio, television, and stage plays) of these years is Walentin Chorell (1912–   ), the only internationally known Finnish postwar dramatist. He shares Eugene O'Neill's interest in the downtrodden and their miserable pipe dreams; he tends to emphasize the importance of childhood experiences. His range ex-tends from serious probings of character to farce. *Madame* (1952) is a tragicomic portrait of an aging prima donna; *Systrarna* (*The Sisters,* 1955), a study of a life of fantasy shared by two girls; and *Kattorna* ("The Cats," 1961), a third example of Chorell's in-sight into female psychology, this time projected onto a group of characters. A tense young man about to be deceived by life, a recurrent figure, is the hero in *Gräset* ("Grass," 1958), where realism and theat-ricalism are employed in good balance to treat the theme of incest. Chorell's limitation lies in the trans-parency of his dramatic psychology; in his latest plays he has shown a surer control over individual scenes than over the structure as a whole.

Gräset won the play competition of Tampere, where the scripts were judged after production; this contest was one of the measures taken to encourage native dramatists. A prize for the best Scandinavian play was given to *Ennen pitkääperjantaita* ("Before Good Friday," 1955) by Jussi Talvi (1920–   ), a play about a soldier sentenced to death for coward-ice. The fate of refugees from Karelia inspired Kyllikki Mäntylä (1907–   ) to write *Opri* (1953) and other plays with local color and warm humor. A potential dramatist without a single original play to his credit is Väinö Linna (1920–   ), whose re-markable war novel *Tuntematou sohlas* (*The Un-known Soldier,* 1954) has been adapted and per-formed in the open-air theater of Tampere, with its nearly unique rotating auditorium. The play has run for two months every summer since 1961. Linna has a clearly dramatic sense of situation and full com-mand over dialogue; no wonder that two parts of his next novel, *Täällä Pohjantähden alla* ("Here Under the North Star," 1959–1962), a trilogy dealing with recent social history, have also been adapted for the stage and screen.

An experimental line of development in postwar playwriting goes through the three plays of Paavo Haavikko (1931–   ), a leading poet of the 1950's and 1960's. His *Münchhausen* (1958) is a witty and

lyrical description of Catherine the Great's court. *Nuket* ("The Dolls," 1960), about Nikolai Gogol's writing *Dead Souls,* shows development in drama-turgy in its clearly shaped situations; Haavikko's concern for a writer's problems gives interesting re-sults. *Agricola ja kettu* ("Agricola and the Fox," 1968) deals, in a skeptical vein, with Mikael Agric-ola, the sixteenth-century Lutheran reformer and father of Finnish literature, and with his involvement in the dilemma of the power politics between West and East, Sweden and Russia.

Another renowned poet to turn to playwriting is Eeva-Liisa Manner (1921–   ). She rejected the highly poetic, ethereal atmosphere of her *Eros ja Psykhe* (1959), a play in free verse, in favor of an Edward Albee type of analysis of a group of modern intellectuals in *Uuden vuoden yö* ("New Year's Eve," 1965). The endeavor resulted in an intimate and realistic chamber play with sting and striking power. Manner's next plays are more open to criti-cism. Lauri Kokkonen (1918–   ), exclusively a dramatist, began with realistic, sympathetic analyses of everyday people, then abandoned realism in his *Viimeiset kiusaukset* ("The Last Temptations," 1960), in which the past of a well-known religious leader is searched by means of a boldly visual and poetic technique. With the help of theatricalistic machinery, Paavo Rintala (1930–   ), in his *Kunnianosoitus Johann Sebastian Bachille* (*Tribute to Johann Sebastian Bach,* 1963), follows the effect of Bach's music on posterity, instead of writing a purely biographical play.

Veijo Meri (1928–   ) moves closer to the real-istic wing of the epic theater. He has a world of his own, slightly absurd, yet full of grim realities; his scenes move swiftly through different milieus. In *Sotamies Jokisen vihkiloma* (*Private Jokinen's Mar-riage Leave,* 1965) Meri, an expert in military life, sends a Chaplinesque little man home from the front in search of a bride. *Uhkapeli* ("A Game of Chance," 1968) is set in Germany during World War I and the tone is picaresque.

Within the school of more orthodox realism there is a fine talent in Lauri Leskinen (1918–   ). His second play, *Kunniakuja* ("Line in Honor of the De-ceased," 1966), is a quietly Chekhovian, sympa-thetic, and mature tragicomedy in which a primary school teacher weighs his life and the lot of his gen-eration on the day of his retirement. Eila Pennanen (1916–   ) and Eeva Joenpelto (1921–   ) are two experienced novelists, each with one play so far. Pennanen places a group of Finnish "hippies" in the yard of a philistine family in *Aurinkomatka* ("A Sun Tour," 1967), while Joenpelto reflects recent histori-cal events in the fates of two brothers in *Liian suuria asioita* ("Too Great Matters," 1968). *Ruusubaletti* ("Ballet of Roses," 1967) by Anu Kaipainen (1933–   ) is a satirical description of small-town life mixed with fantastic elements. Heimo Susi (1930–   ) dissects young intellectuals in his comitragedy *Elämisen tekniikka* ("The Technique of Living," 1967); all of his characters commit forgeries, in one way or another. These five plays are prize-winning products of the 1960's.

Kyllikki Kallas (1917–   ) has written a sharp analysis of the political scene (*Der Herr Parteisekre-*

tär, "Secretary of the Party," 1958). Leena Härmä (1914–   ) and Inkeri Kilpinen (1926–   ) are authors of widely successful farce comedies. Reino Lahtinen (1918–   ) has an eye on the dramatics of everyday life (*Arvottomat, The Worthless,* 1959, and *Ketunpesä,* "Fox Hole," 1964). Jouni Apajalahti (1920–   ) has dealt with youth in *Kenen on vastuu?* ("Who Is Responsible?" 1964). Juhani Peltonen (1941–   ) is a surrealist playwright of promise (*Päivän Sankari,* "Hero for the Day," 1968; television plays).

The youngest generation in the theater has been influenced by Brecht and is interested in political cabaret and documentary plays. *Lapualaisooppera* (1966) by Arvo Salo (1932–   ) had a strong impact in its aggressive disavowal of the ideals behind a fascist movement in the 1930's. Lars Huldén (1926–   ) and Bengt Ahlfors (1937–   ) are writers of cabaret plays.

In nineteenth-century Finland even philosophers and party politicians took an interest in promoting the theater and native drama. One of the results was that the stage has always been taken as a cultural institution worthy of support from public funds. Though this (or any other) form of art has not retained its specifically national character or value, an appreciative attitude has prevailed, combined with a willingness to respect the freedom of artistic expression.

At the turn of the century the theater was a center of a lively, mainly literary, discussion. Since the break-through of mass communication media, drama has lost ground somewhat, yet it is far from being a peripheral phenomenon in present-day Finland. Radio and television have not only exploited dramatists but also fostered them, for the good of the stage. They have also won for Finnish playwrights limited international audiences in Germany and England, always a difficult problem in a country behind a language barrier.

Though Finland is a country with a lively theater tradition, native drama has not been as consistently important as poetry or the novel. No Finnish Strindberg or Ibsen has entered the international stage. Yet the best dramatists have not only reflected European modes of thought and dramatic formulas but have also added to these impulses their own creative work, their skill, and their vision. They have spoken to their audiences, a *sine qua non* in all drama. More specifically, there seems to be a modest flowering period in Finnish drama since the late 1950's. In the decade of the 1960's several schools of playwriting have been in existence simultaneously.

There is no general history of Finnish literature or drama available in English. *Suomen kirjallisuus 1917–1967* (1967) by Kai Laitinen covers all literature of those fifty years; it includes many fresh standpoints and connections with social history. It is published in German (*Neue Finnische Litteratur*); Swedish and English translations will appear. —T. T.

Firebugs, The (Biedermann und die Brandstifter, 1958). A learning play without a lesson by Max FRISCH. Gottlieb Biedermann, implies Frisch, is Everyman, Babbitt, the man, like all men, who does not learn from experience. An average businessman of the bourgeois mold, Biedermann is a millionaire in the hair lotion business, but his hair lotion is as useless as urine to bathe one's bald pate with. His closest employee invented the formula, but he has been dismissed and will eventually kill himself. Biedermann, therefore, has no moral foundation.

He happens to know well the manner in which arsonists operate, how they insinuate themselves into a house and burn it to the ground the next day. Precisely while Biedermann is reading an account of the latest case of arson, an arsonist, pretending not to be one, virtually forces his way into Biedermann's house. He is cordial, gentle, and unobtrusive, but manages to take over Biedermann's attic all the same. Then a second arsonist is furtively brought in and barrels of gasoline are lugged up to the attic and stored. As Biedermann is feebly about to show he will not stand for such a thing and is about to call the police, the police arrive to announce the suicide of his fired inventor-employee. The arsonists are well established by now and Biedermann tries to make the best of a bad situation, to make friends with them. By his doing so, perhaps they will leave him be. But no. They are now so secure that they openly announce to him that they will burn down his house. Biedermann believes that they must be joking. At dinner they hear a fire engine go by. Biedermann remarks that it is fortunate that it is not his house on fire. The arsonists reveal that they always plan a false alarm on the outskirts of town prior to setting a blaze and that they are also planning several other blazes in the vicinity, with the gasworks as their ultimate objective. Before returning to their attic, they ask Biedermann for a box of matches, which, in utter defeat, he gives them, thus assuring himself of his own destruction.

In an epilogue Biedermann and his wife are seen in hell, burned to a crisp. Yet even with their monumental experience behind them, they have still failed to learn anything; indeed, they cannot believe that they are anywhere but in heaven. Biedermann, to the last, is naïvely ignorant of his own guilt.

One of the most incisive plays of our time, *The Firebugs* is an allegory depicting the rise of the totalitarian state. The pattern of action used by the arsonists is that of all internal revolutionaries. But it is the bourgeoisie—the passive, dull-witted, naïve, helpless, unresisting men who crumble as a result of their own internal guilt—that Frisch is most intent upon criticizing. As drama the play is tremendously effective. Its multilevel staging technique is highly theatrical, and the use of the Greek-like chorus of firemen, who always surround the action, often comment and warn, but cannot come until called, is a unique and impressive contribution to the contemporary theater.

The Firebugs is translated by Mordecai Gorelik (1959). The play is also discussed critically in the volume by George Wellwarth, *The Theater of Protest and Paradox* (1964), and in another by Ulrich Weisstein, *Max Frisch* (1968).—C. R. M.

Fisherman's Revenge, The (Ta yü sha chia). A Chinese play of anonymous authorship. Best known as *The Fisherman's Revenge,* the play is also known by several other titles, among them *The Lucky Pearl* and *A Fisherman Kills a Family.* The play constitutes a tradition in itself, extending through at least three centuries. Early versions differ widely from that now current, which owes its form largely to changes instituted by a series of major actors during the nineteenth and twentieth centuries, most notably, Mei Lanfang.

The play's story derives from the conflict between peasants and landowners after the Liangshan Revolt was crushed early in the twelfth century. It relates the ruthless treatment of an old fisherman, Hsiao En, by a grasping landlord and a constabulary subservient to him. The fisherman, his age notwithstanding, knocks down the policemen and in the end invades their master's house, killing him and all his family. Such a story has, naturally, been favorably received in the official judgment of the communists. But the play has long been popular chiefly because of its comic verve and lyric charm rather than its political propaganda. In reality, the play is anything but crudely didactic. Rather, it is excellent popular comic theater for entertainment in almost any time or place and has been successfully produced by Mei Lan-fang on his tours of Europe. America, and Japan.

The play's leading figure is the embodiment of one of the best-known comic types, a soft-spoken old man who pretends to be weak and harmless but when pressed beyond endurance easily defeats a gang of loudmouthed and ferocious braggarts. Moreover, this old man has a daughter who merely transposes the same comic spirit from masculine to feminine. At first apparently timid and bent on restraining what she knows to be her father's hidden fury, in the end she joins him with a courage equal to his own. Her reversal of mood (for she complies fully with Aristotle's view of this dramatic formula) occurs literally in midstream, on a boat. The episode supplied the climax of the play as performed by Mei Lan-fang. Rowing toward the house of the landlord, the two reach the main current, when the daughter, suddenly aware of the bloody task ahead, is smitten with a fit of terror. For a few moments she cries aloud to return. Then, abruptly, she reverts to her rightful role as true daughter to her heroic father, pledging him her fullest efforts on their expedition. The scene gives admirable occasion for comic miming.

The lyric aspect of the play is closely associated with its hero's occupation, fishing. Several songs are sung in praise of this allegedly gentle art and of the singular beauty of the scenery along the river and its shores. Humor is, accordingly, extracted not only from the contrast between Hsiao En's boldness of heart and mildness of speech but between his extreme courage and his love for an idyllic lyricism devoted to the quieter beauties of nature. This theme is not uncommon among Chinese comedies.

There are three translations in English of *The Fisherman's Revenge:* one, with critical commentary by Ma Yen-hsiang, is by Yang Hsien-yi and Gladys Yang (1956); another, by L. C. Arlington and Harold Acton, is in *Famous Chinese Plays* (1937; reprinted 1963); and, possibly the most artful of the three, by Yao Hsin-nung in *The Tien Hsia Monthly*, Vol. I (1935).—H. W. W.

Fitch, Clyde (1865–1909). American playwright. Fitch, the first American playwright to gain wide recognition abroad, was born in Elmira, New York. On graduating from Amherst College in 1886, he went to New York to make a career of writing. His first success was *Beau Brummell* (1890), a romantic comedy written for actor Richard Mansfield. In

CLYDE FITCH (WALTER HAMPDEN MEMORIAL LIBRARY AT THE PLAYERS, NEW YORK)

nineteen years, Fitch wrote thirty-three original plays and twenty-two adaptations of novels or foreign plays, many of which were tailored for leading actors. He directed the actors in many of his own plays and in addition concerned himself directly with the scenery, costumes, and properties.

Fitch's plays were extremely popular in his day; in the 1900/01 season, he had four plays running concurrently in New York. In one of them, *Captain Jinks of the Horse Marines,* a light romantic comedy, young Ethel Barrymore became a star. Another play, *The Climbers,* a satire on greed for money and social position, is typical of his work in its mixture of sharp social comment with sentiment and melodrama.

Fitch frequently used as his dramatic focus a woman with a weakness: kleptomania in *The Girl and the Judge* (1901); jealousy in *The Girl with the Green Eyes* (1902); and inability to tell the truth in *The Truth* (1906), generally regarded as his best play.

Fitch's most ambitious play, *The City,* completed shortly before his death in 1909 and produced a few months later, is a realistic study of degeneration in a family which moves to the city from a small town, where its members had been respected leaders for generations.

Influenced by Ibsen, Fitch tried to write serious dramas dealing with contemporary social problems, but he lacked Ibsen's breadth and depth of comprehension and skill in dramatic construction. Fitch's plays are interesting today principally for their minor characters, often sharply etched satirical types Fitch had observed in New York society. The success of several of his plays abroad brought prestige to American playwriting.

The best sources are M. J. Moses and Virginia Gerson, *Clyde Fitch and His Letters* (1924) and the same authors' edition of his plays in four volumes (1915).—B. H.

Fitzmaurice, George (1877–1963). Irish playwright. Fitzmaurice was born in Listowel, County Kerry. While a young man he moved to Dublin where he obtained a civil service position and began his writing career. After a series of early successes he appears to have been plagued by illness. In any case he dropped from public sight and his plays failed to receive any professional productions. All this time he continued to write in lonely seclusion. At the time of his death in 1963, he was virtually unknown. Since then however, his reputation has developed to the point that he is now regarded as one of the leading Irish dramatists of the twentieth century.

The earliest and still the best known of Fitzmaurice's plays is *The Country Dressmaker* (1907), a realistic peasant comedy enlivened by its rich language and boisterous characters. *The Country Dressmaker* was followed by two distinguished one-act plays: *The Pie Dish* (1908), a tragicomic rendering of artistic creation in the face of death, and *The Dandy Dolls* (1908), a mysterious and darkly grotesque fantasy. One of Fitzmaurice's longer efforts is *The Moonlighter,* a nationalist play that presents the conflict between the country and the family in grimly effective terms.

Most of Fitzmaurice's later work consists of a series of one-act plays published over the years in *Dublin Magazine* and largely unacted. The best of these is *One Evening Gleam* (1949). A tragedy about the death of a blind man being attended by his mother, the play is a moving realization of the pathos of unfulfilled ideals. Other notable one-acters by Fitzmaurice include *The Green Stone* (1926), *There Are Tragedies and Tragedies* (1948) and *The Enchanted Land* (1957). These plays are representative of Fitzmaurice's unique blend of fantasy and realism.

The Plays of George Fitzmaurice is a projected edition of his works by the Dolmen Press, Dublin. Volume I was published in 1967.—E. Q.

Flemish drama. See BELGIUM; and DUTCH AND FLEMISH DRAMA.

Fletcher, John (1579–1625). English playwright. Fletcher was born at Rye in Sussex, the son of the vicar of Rye, who later became bishop of London. Nothing is known of Fletcher's schooling or his early life. In 1608 he began his famous collaboration with Francis BEAUMONT and his less easily defined but equally important collaboration with William Shakespeare. Upon Shakespeare's retirement, sometime about 1612, Fletcher succeeded him as chief dramatist of the King's Men, a position he occupied until his death. Besides Beaumont and Shakespeare, he had a number of collaborators during that period, chiefly Philip MASSINGER, who succeeded him as King's Men's chief playwright.

Two decades after Fletcher's death, in 1647, a folio collection of thirty-four plays attributed to Beaumont and Fletcher was published. A later edition in 1679 enlarged the collection to fifty-two plays. Beaumont, who retired from the stage in 1613, had nothing to do with the majority of these plays. A recent authoritative analysis by Cyrus Hoy estimates that fifteen of the plays were written by Fletcher alone; thirteen by Beaumont and Fletcher; nineteen by Fletcher and Massinger (some of these in collaboration with others as well); and the remaining plays by Fletcher in collaboration with others. Thus, Fletcher is involved as sole author or collaborator in fifty-one of the plays, Beaumont in only fourteen. Nevertheless, the dominant and distinctive tone of most of these plays was established in precisely those works that were written in collaboration with Beaumont. Thus, the spirit if not the letter of historical accuracy justifies the general designation "Beaumont and Fletcher."

The exact nature of the tone of the plays is easily explained. Since both writers were of a higher social status than the ordinary Elizabethan playwright (Beaumont the son of a judge, Fletcher of a bishop), they were ideally suited to take the drama in a direction toward which it was inevitably moving in the reign of the Stuarts. It was a direction away from the people and toward the court, a direction symbolized in the early years of the collaboration by the opening of the private Blackfriars theater within the precincts of London. The audience at the Blackfriars was largely aristocratic, with an acquired taste for masque-like romances and brittle satire. The depth and turbulence of tragedy on the Shakespearean scale held little appeal for them. The Beaumont-Fletcher response to this taste was the development of TRAGICOMEDY, a genre that allowed for serious treatment of serious themes without a tragic resolution. This does not mean that their dramas are trivial or escapist—only that their concerns are with the narrower aristocratic mode of life, a mode whose roots are less deep than those of the great tradition in which Shakespeare worked.

Of the many plays in the Beaumont-Fletcher canon, none is so representative of its best aspects as *Philaster* (c. 1610). The story centers on three characters: Philaster, a young prince deprived of the throne by a usurper; Arethusa, daughter of the usurper; and Bellario, Philaster's page. Philaster and Arethusa are secretly in love; Bellario serves as their go-between. When Arethusa is accused of having an affair with Bellario, Philaster believes the scandal. The consequent difficulties are not resolved until it is revealed at the end of the play that Bellario is a girl in disguise, in love with Philaster. Superficially, the play resembles Shakespeare's *Cymbeline* and *The Winter's Tale;* but whereas Shakespeare's plays exhibit a deep and abiding preoccupation with such themes as death and rebirth, suffering and reconciliation, and a celebration of the mystery of life, *Philaster* focuses, not without insight and penetration, on certain ideals of the Renaissance court tradition.

Beaumont and Fletcher also essayed the realm of pure tragedy, their most successful attempt being *The Maid's Tragedy* (c. 1611). This play deals with the frustrated love of Amintor and Aspatia: The king breaks their engagement and forces Amintor to wed Evadne. After the marriage Evadne reveals to Amintor that she is the king's mistress and has no intention of living as Amintor's wife. The results of this mismating are tragic for all concerned. Aspatia kills herself by falling on Amintor's sword; Evadne, in a fit of repentance, kills the king; subsequently, both she and Amintor commit suicide.

The weakness of the play lies in the absence of a significant central character. The tragic impact is thus diffused and weakened. Amintor, the logical candidate for the tragic hero's role, is never allowed to develop but is merely portrayed as the victim of one difficult situation after another. Nevertheless, the play contains some striking individual scenes and some fine poetry.

Another celebrated product of the Beaumont and Fletcher collaboration is *A King and No King* (c. 1611). It tells of King Arbaces, who discovers he is in love with his sister. He decides to commit suicide, but before he can do so, the "sister's" true identity is revealed, thus providing the necessary happy ending. The character of Arbaces is extraordinarily well done.

The best known of Fletcher's collaborations with Massinger is *Sir John Van Olden Barnavelt* (1619), a tragedy. Among the plays written solely by Fletcher are *Bonduca* (1613), a historical tragedy set in Roman Britain; *The Woman's Prize, or The Tamer Tamed* (c. 1611), a sequel to Shakespeare's *Taming of the Shrew*; *A Wife for a Month* (1624), a tragicomedy; *The Humorous Lieutenant* (1619), a skillful mixture of romance and satire; and *The Faithful Shepherdess* (c. 1608), described by its author as a "pastoral tragi-comedy." The play is a masque-like ordering of individual scenes rather than a developed narrative. It opens with the solemn song of the shepherdess Clorin, sung at the grave of her lover, followed by a dance of satyrs. The play's action centers on a sequence of love affairs among pairs of rustic lovers. This series of tableaus serves to highlight the conflict between lust and chastity and of the ultimate triumph of the ideal of chastity. The play represents an interesting attempt to realize the principles of tragicomedy. The Beaumont-Fletcher contribution to dramatic literature is difficult to assess. Long regarded as the chief representatives of the "decadence" alleged to have begun in English drama after the death of Shakespeare, they have come to be recognized as skilled practitioners of a narrow, conventionalized, highly ornate art form.

Listed below is the breakdown of the shares in the Beaumont and Fletcher canon as given by Cyrus Hoy (*Studies in Bibliography*, XV, 1962):

Beaumont alone:

The Knight of the Burning Pestle

Fletcher alone:

Bonduca
The Chances
The Island Princess
The Humorous Lieutenant
The Loyal Subject
The Mad Lover
Monsieur Thomas
The Pilgrim
Rule a Wife and Have a Wife
Valentinian
A Wife for a Month
Women Pleased
The Wild Goose Chase
The Woman's Prize
The Faithful Shepherdess

Fletcher and Massinger:

Sir John Van Olden Barnavelt
The Custom of the Country
The Double Marriage
The Elder Brother
The False One
The Little French Lawyer
The Lovers' Progress
The Prophetess
The Sea Voyage
The Spanish Curate
A Very Woman

Fletcher and Beaumont:

The Captain
Cupid's Revenge
The Maid's Tragedy
Philaster
The Woman Hater
The Coxcomb
A King and No King
The Noble Gentleman
The Scornful Lady

Fletcher, Beaumont, and Massinger:

Beggars' Bush
Love's Cure
Thierry and Theodoret

Fletcher, Beaumont, and Jonson:

Love's Pilgrimage

Fletcher, Massinger, Jonson, and Chapman:

Rollo, Duke of Normandy

Fletcher and Field:

Four Plays, or Moral Representations, In One

Fletcher, Field, and Massinger:

The Honest Man's Fortune
The Knight of Malta
The Queen of Corinth

Fletcher and Shirley:

The Night Walker

Fletcher and an unidentified reviser:

Wit Without Money

Fletcher and Rowley:

The Maid in the Mill

Fletcher and Middleton:

The Nice Valour

Fletcher, Massinger, Webster, and Ford:

The Fair Maid of the Inn

Fletcher and Shakespeare:

THE TWO NOBLE KINSMEN
HENRY VIII

The standard edition of the plays is *The Works of Beaumont and Fletcher* (1905–1912), edited by A. Glover and A. R. Waller, in ten volumes. The best critical study is Eugene Waith's *The Pattern of Tragicomedy in Beaumont and Fletcher* (1952). —E. Q.

Flies, The (Les Mouches, 1943). A play by Jean-Paul SARTRE. *The Flies* was first performed in 1943 under the direction of Charles Dullin at the Théâtre Sarah-Bernhardt. Sartre's new treatment of the fable of Orestes seemed to the public of 1943 to bear a strong relationship to the moral dilemma of the German occupation of France.

Some of the essential elements of Aeschylus' *Oresteia* are preserved in *The Flies.* Clytemnestra has married Aegisthus, who has usurped the throne and is tyrannizing the people, while Electra, daughter of Clytemnestra and legitimate heiress, is impoverished. Full of hate, Electra sits at the door of the palace and prays for fate to bring her brother, Orestes, home from exile. To these familiar elements Sartre adds the figure of an ironic Jupiter and a swarm of gigantic flies, evil-smelling, avenging spirits who subject the city of Argos to a mysterious plague.

Orestes returns to the plague-ridden city of his birth, in obedience, as he explains it, to a need to return home, to feel himself one with his own people. The relationship between Orestes and the people of Argos is a moving, dramatic situation in *The Flies,* and it is the source of much of the existentialist philosophy in the play. Orestes exercises his freedom when he defies the gods by killing his mother for the sake of justice and the people of Argos. He thus redeems the people of their existential guilt, but he must stand alone, alienated and guilty of the worst crime—matricide. For the existentialist philosopher, the people of Argos represent the old collective power that is enslaved and propagandized. By making his choice, Orestes exists and creates his self.

The Flies has been translated by Stuart Gilbert in *No Exit and Three Other Plays* (1955).—W. F.

Fonvizin, Denis [Ivanovich] (1745–1792). Russian playwright, pamphleteer, and polemicist. Fonvizin was born and educated in Moscow, first at the Latin School attached to Moscow University and then at the university itself, where he was strongly influenced by the writings of Denis Diderot, Charles de Montesquieu, Jean Jacques Rousseau, and Voltaire. He translated into Russian Voltaire's comedy *Alzire* as well as the works of the Danish fabulist Goldberg.

After the palace coup of 1762 that put Catherine the Great on the Russian throne, Fonvizin obtained a position as translator in the Department of Foreign Affairs and moved to St. Petersburg. In 1764 he was transferred to the Imperial Cabinet of Petitions. At this time his translations were known, but his own writings remained mostly unpublished because of their satirical twist, and they circulated only in manuscript form. Although Fonvizin was known to be the author of fables satirizing the regime, he remained unmolested because of the early liberalism and enlightenment of the new monarch, who herself professed to admire Voltaire and Montesquieu.

As a member of the Cabinet of Petitions, however, Fonvizin accompanied Catherine on an inspection tour of her empire in 1767, and he soon realized that

DENIS FONVIZIN (JOEY CARMICHAEL, *An Illustrated History of Russia,* REYNAL & CO., 1960)

her enlightenment was only superficial and that she had very little real interest in rectifying the inequities and abuses of serfdom. Fonvizin's own views on the subject and his feelings about the Russian landed gentry were expressed in his first comedy, *Brigadir* (*The Brigadier,* 1769), which he wrote after the inspection tour. Here he shows the ignorance, brutality, and primitive ways of the gentry, who either are filled with snobbish and stupid admiration for French culture, of which they understand only the outward manifestations, or else they denounce it as being effete and likely to restrain the good old Russian brutality. But, quite aside from its political and social overtones, *Brigadir* stands out among the contemporary plays as something more than a mere adaptation of a foreign comedy to a Russian setting with characters representing certain vices; instead, there are complex and confused, almost plausible people, each speaking his own colorful language. Thus, Fonvizin made a lively and original comedy out of what would have otherwise been a standard farce, based on a series of unexpected infatuations during a matchmaking in which everybody wants to marry everybody except the prospective bride and groom, who want nothing to do with each other. It was these new qualities that made *Brigadir* an immediate success, even with the empress.

In the introduction to the reform party's program entitled "The Indispensable Laws for a State," Fonvizin described the regime of Catherine the Great as one in which "every citizen must be either a victim or an oppressor." During this period Fonvizin was also working on his major comedy, THE MINOR, which was the most important Russian play up to that date; indeed, it was the first genuine Russian play and in many ways determined the further development of the Russian theater; its influence can be traced through Alexander Griboyedov and Nikolai Gogol all the way down to Anton Chekhov.

In 1782, following the dismissal from government service of members of the reform party, Fonvizin went into retirement and devoted himself entirely to polemical and satirical writings. The best known is the satirical essay *Vseobshchaya pridvornaya grammatika* ("A Comprehensive Grammar for the Courtier," written 1885), in which he advises those who aspire to careers at the imperial court and goes into a lengthy discussion of flattery and success. He also wrote an autobiography entitled *Chistoserdechnye priznaniya v delakh moikh i pomyshleniyakh* ("Sincere Confessions of My Actions and Thoughts"), only part of which is extant, and a comedy, *Vybory guvernera* ("The Governor's Election"), in 1791. None of the works written during this later period was published during his lifetime, although *Brigadir* and *The Minor* continued to be performed. —A. MacA.

Ford, John (1586– c. 1639). English playwright. Ford was a native of Devonshire. His early life remains a mystery, although he is probably the John Ford registered at Exeter College, Oxford, in 1601. The following year he entered Middle Temple, from which he was expelled in 1603. For the next fifteen years he seems to have been primarily concerned with practicing law, although he occasionally tried his hand at various literary activities. His playwriting career began in earnest about 1620 when he collaborated with Thomas Kekker and William Rowley on *The Witch of Edmonton,* a play written largely by Dekker. Ford remained active in the theater until his death.

Ford's earliest dramatic works were collaborative efforts. These include *The Spanish Gypsy* (1623), with Thomas Middleton; *Keep the Widow Waking* (1624), with Dekker, John Webster, and Rowley; and *The Sun's Darling* (1624), with Dekker. Throughout this apprenticeship period, Ford steadily developed the dramatic technique that was to distinguish his major works. The first of these is *The Lover's Melancholy* (1628). Based upon the insights and perceptions of Robert Burton's *Anatomy of Melancholy* (1621), the play is in effect a dramatized analysis of melancholy, that "commotion of the mind, o'ercharg'd / With fear and sorrow . . ." His analysis is worked into an elaborate and complex tale of romance and disguise reminiscent of the later plays of Shakespeare. Related to this play in tone, although here the resolution is tragic, is *Love's Sacrifice* (1632). The story concerns the passionate but chaste love between Bianca, wife of the duke of Pavin, and the duke's friend Fernando. Urged on by his jealous sister and his Machiavellian secretary, the duke surprises the lovers and kills his wife. Later repentant, he orders an elaborate funeral. When he opens the door of his wife's tomb, he discovers Fernando, who thereupon swallows poison and dies. The loss of his wife and friend leaves the duke devastated by remorse. He stabs himself and, as he dies, asks only that

all three bodies be buried together as symbols of love's sacrifice.

Though interesting, both *The Lover's Melancholy* and *Love's Sacrifice* are unsuccessful plays. Enriched by a consistent lyric beauty and by occasional moments of real dramatic power, they nevertheless lack a coherent dramatic design. In both plays Ford was unable to integrate the differing demands of poetry and drama. Far more successful in this effort are Ford's best-known plays, 'TIS PITY SHE'S A WHORE and *The Broken Heart* (1633). A story of frustrated love and revenge, *The Broken Heart* focuses on the figure of Orgilus, prevented from marrying his beloved Penthea by her brother, Ithocles. Ithocles himself, however, discovers the nature of true love when he becomes enamored of the princess Calantha and repents having interfered with his sister's desires. He is killed, however, by the enraged Orgilus, who, after confessing his crime to Calantha, kills himself. Calantha thereupon presides over an elaborate funeral for Ithocles that reaches its culmination in her own death. She dies declaring that "art / Can find no comfort in a broken heart." The play is remarkable for the classical simplicity and dignity of its language and thought.

Less well known than *The Broken Heart* is Ford's only surviving chronicle play, *Perkin Warbeck* (1634). Based upon the career of a fifteenth-century pretender to the throne, *Perkin Warbeck* is, in the words of T. S. Eliot, "one of the very best historical plays . . . in the whole of Elizabethan and Jacobean drama." The play's distinction lies in the character of Perkin himself, who is presented as a sincere, inherently noble, and dignified figure. Perkin's imposture is depicted as a grand illusion that serves as a measure of his heroic stature. The play successfully enlists the audience's sympathy for this view of the hero without altering the historical facts.

The last of the great Elizabethan dramatists, Ford made a unique contribution to the rich tradition of dramatic literature he inherited. Lacking the fierce intensity and complex sensibility of his Jacobean contemporaries he nevertheless brought to the drama a deep and abiding interest in human nature quickened and illuminated by a pervasive compassion.

The standard edition of the plays is *The Works of John Ford* (1895), edited by W. Gifford and A. Dyce, in three volumes. T. S. Eliot's estimate is included in his *Essays on Elizabethan Drama* (1956). The best full-length treatment is Clifford Leech's *John Ford and the Drama of His Time* (1957).—E. Q.

Forest, The (Les, 1871). A comedy in five acts by Alexander OSTROVSKY. A rich, middle-aged, tyrannical widow keeps on her estate a poor twenty-year-old girl—her distant cousin Aksyusha—and a school dropout—the young man Bulanov—who is conveniently supposed to be Aksyusha's fiancé but on whom the widow has designs. Aksyusha loves Peter, the son of a greedy peasant who is buying up the old woman's forest bit by bit and cheating her in the process. Peter's father will not allow his son to marry Aksyusha unless she is given 1,000 rubles for her dowry. Thus, caught between the greedy peasant and the hypocritical rich widow, Aksyusha and Peter are in a desperate position until the appearance of the old woman's nephew, Neschaslivtsev, an itinerant provincial actor, drunkard, brawler, and liar. He finally saves the situation by using his acting talent to make the peasant return the money he has cheated the widow out of, by collecting from his aunt his own 1,000-ruble share of the family fortunes, and, at the last moment, by giving it to Aksyusha as her dowry to enable her to marry Peter.

This play was an immediate and tremendous success. Although it is built around Ostrovsky's eternal theme of the simple and tender aspirations of young people crushed by the artificial and hypocritical values of their elders, this play is interpreted by Soviet critics as the clash of three social classes: the rich widow, representing the gentry; the greedy peasant, the forerunner of the kulak; and the rough diamond of the itinerant actor, the proletarian intelligentsia.—A. MACA.

Forssell, Lars (1928–). Swedish poet and playwright. A Stockholmer by birth and present preference, Forssell was educated at Augustana College, Illinois, and the Swedish university Uppsala. With the publication of five volumes of poetry during the 1950's, Forssell made a name for himself as one of Sweden's leading poets, but his bent for the drama was clearly indicated in his use of personae in his poetry, his part in the composition of little revues, and a sensitive book on Charlie Chaplin.

Forssell made his debut in the theater with *Kröningen* (*The Coronation*, 1956), a retelling of the Alcestis story, in which Admetus wallows in his self-pity to the extinction of any vestigial nobility. The best known and most successful of the three charades published under the title *Prototyper* (*Prototypes*, 1961) is *Charlie MacDeath*, in which ventriloquist and dummy change places and the play takes the form of an absurd dialogue between self and soul. With *Charlie MacDeath* as curtain raiser, *Mary Lou* (1962) gave Forssell his first resounding success in the theater. Ingrid Thulin played the title role of "Axis Sally" from Joliet, Illinois, a fascinating study of loneliness, neurosis, and betrayal.

In the period piece *Söndagspromenaden* ("Sunday Promenade," 1963), which, in its comedy, is occasionally reminiscent of Thornton Wilder's *The Matchmaker*, Forssell is chiefly concerned with a flamboyant merchant who has cut himself off from love by retreat into a world of elaborate, synthetic rituals. Adding to his menagerie of eccentric heroes, Forssell then turned to the chronicle play in *Galenpannan* ("The Fool," 1964), essentially a portrait of Gustav IV of Sweden in exile, with flashbacks to the years preceding his deposition in 1809.

In a number of screenplays, of which the best known is probably *Dockan* (*The Doll*) and in his translations of Molière and Georges Schéhadé, Forssell indicates a continued commitment to the theater. His dramatic invention is considerable, and his compassion for sad, lonely, slightly crazed heroes is inexhaustible.

For *The Coronation,* see *Players Magazine* (November 1963), pp. 41–56. See also Harry G. Carlson, "Lars Forssell—Poet in the Theatre," in *Scandinavian Studies* (February 1965), pp. 30–57. —R. B. V.

Fourberies de Scapin, Les (The Cheats of Scapin, 1671). A comedy in prose by MOLIÈRE. In an imaginary Naples, the valet Scapin helps two young men trick their fathers in order to get money from them and make them consent to their marrying girls of their own choice. The charm of *Scapin* lies in its theatricalism and in the farcical rebounds due to Scapin's very Italian virtuosity when in conflict with the two tyrannical and obstinate old men.—Ja. G.

France: *middle ages and Renaissance.* The origins of French medieval drama lie not in the forms of ancient theater, but in the Mass. Though the middle ages possessed an awareness of such authors as Terence and Plautus, the term "drama" was early separated from the concept of a story acted out upon a stage, and "comedy" and "tragedy" were used simply to distinguish between works that ended happily and unhappily. At the same time, the Mass, with its music and vestments, its enactment before the faithful of a symbolic, yet real, story, provided the middle ages with ample means to recapture the sense of a dramatic spectacle.

The introduction of tropes may be considered the initial step in that long development that leads from the Mass to medieval drama. Probably first used in France, the trope was a poem, sometimes in dialogue, appended to different parts of the liturgy to serve as both embellishment and commentary. For example, one trope, preserved in a Saint Gall manuscript of the tenth century, was sung before the Introit of the Mass on Easter morning. By the eleventh century the same trope, the *Visitatio sepulcri,* had been transferred to the end of the Mass and was sung just before the *Te Deum.* The general intent of medieval art and architecture to make visible to the people the teachings of the Church may be sufficient to explain this transfer. Stage directions in the Saint

ENGRAVING OF A MEDIEVAL OUTDOOR MULTIPLE STAGE (NEW YORK PUBLIC LIBRARY)

Gall manuscript make clear that the singers were now specifically to take the roles of the Marys and the angels. As a result of this shift in position, the trope no longer retained its intimate relationship with the Introit but became the conclusion, a dramatic conclusion, to the morning's meditation. In this way, medieval drama was born.

To the *Visitatio sepulcri* were added an apostle scene with Peter and John running to the empty tomb, Christ appearing to Mary Magdalene, the spice merchant selling his wares to the Marys, and Roman soldiers. Similarly, the *Officium Pastorum* grew around a trope that questions the shepherds who have come to see the Child, just as, in the Saint Gall trope, the Marys had been questioned at the sepulcher. The *Officium Pastorum* was merged with the Magi play performed at Epiphany and included Herod's anger as well as the Massacre of the Innocents. These additions are not all of the same nature. Christ's being and role were synonymous, whereas Herod was expected to rage, the merchant to haggle, and the apostles in some manuscripts to run a race to see who would arrive first at the tomb. In short, Christ and the Marys gave religious depth to the scene but the other characters gave real life. This distinction escaped no one. Between the twelfth and the sixteenth century, poets developed their material by accentuating now the sacred, now the profane elements at their command. The dramatic versus entertaining quality of the plays depends largely on the proportions that are accorded to each.

Once the dramatization of the Christmas and Easter stories had acquired a recognizable form, it was not difficult to transform parables, Old Testament accounts, and events from hagiographical legends into similar spectacles. The success of such attempts is testified to both by the ten dramas on varied religious subjects in the Fleury Play Book and by the *Raising of Lazarus, Daniel,* and *Iconia Sancti Nicolai* by Hilarius (twelfth century). An analysis of these Latin plays of the twelfth century points to continued separation of liturgy and drama. Although the *Daniel* is specifically related to Christmas, the manuscript states that its closing song may be either the *Te Deum* or the *Magnificat,* depending on whether the work is performed at matins or vespers. Plays were thus considered more and more independent of the liturgical context from which they had sprung. Secondly, for two of his plays, Hilarius introduced refrains in the vernacular among the Latin stanzas. Perhaps they were introduced to emphasize the lyric qualities of the texts; perhaps it was being realized that mere visual representation of religious subjects could not suffice to communicate fully their message. As long as the plays remained in Latin, the content was lost to the people. Other developments in medieval drama suggest that the second possibility is the more likely.

The *Sponsus* ("The Bridegroom," written c. 1100), an anonymous dramatization in Latin of the parable of the Wise and Foolish Virgins, is the earliest extant text in which extensive use of the vernacular can be found. Nearly half of the play's lines are in French. The test is preceded by one of the Easter tropes and followed by the *Ordo Prophetarum,* a parade of prophets, each of whom announces the coming of Christ. All these elements relate the work to very early manifestations of medieval drama. Because the Latin text contains a complete story, many have assumed that the French verses were added later to aid the audience in following the action. This is an hypothesis that cannot be proved conclusively. It is possible to demonstrate that the *Sponsus,* despite its extreme shortness and pronounced dependence on the liturgy, is a highly successful drama.

Ecclesia opens the play by announcing the coming of Christ and warning the Virgins to be watchful. The Foolish Virgins ask the Wise for oil. They have slept too long and have no more. They are sent to the merchants, who cannot help them. Christ appears and repulses the Foolish Virgins, who are led to hell by demons. Within 105 lines a warning has been given, impending disaster realized, hope kindled and crushed. Nothing detracts from the play's message; everything contributes to its tension and tragedy.

Another great play of this early period is the *Jeu d'Adam* ("The Play of Adam," also called the *Mystère d'Adam,* c. 1140–1174). It was written virtually throughout in French. In addition, it was performed outside the church and, unlike the *Sponsus,* was meant to be acted, not sung. The play is a trilogy composed of the story of Adam and Eve, the slaying of Abel, and the familiar *Ordo Prophetarum.* Its enactment of the fall is the most interesting part, since it combines with a purely didactic aim a delightful touch of realism that reveals the poet's consciousness of his audience and desire to engage them.

Long speeches and monologues appear only with the couple's realization of their sin. Prior to this moment, the play is composed of confrontations in which the dramatic tempo of warning (God's insistence on obedience), hope (Adam's refusal to be tempted), and despair is only slightly expanded to include Satan's temptation of Eve. At the same time, each confrontation is rich in terms familiar to the experience of the public. Eve is tempted by the devil, a character versed in feminine psychology. Adam is taunted by Eve, a wife who knows how to get what she wants. Throughout, the poet maintains a skillful balance between the real and the symbolic, between the homely and the universal within the same dramatic economy of the *Sponsus.* Indeed, the play is so much richer than its Latin predecessors that one critic has hypothesized a vernacular tradition as a source for the *Jeu d'Adam.* Given that no vernacular drama earlier than the *Jeu* survives, such a hypothesis cannot be substantiated.

Jeu de Saint Nicolas ("The Play of Saint Nicholas," written c. 1200) by Jean Bodel (1165?–1210) highlights the continued popularity of the miracle play and the theme of Saint Nicholas, already found in the Fleury Latin plays. The work, especially when compared to the *Jeu d'Adam,* shows that the two aims of educating and entertaining medieval audiences were not necessarily bound to the concept of a dramatic action.

This is a very long play. Its story takes place in diverse places, all of which were probably indicated to the audience at the outset, and the characters moved from one part of the stage to another to designate a change of scene. (Simultaneous décor was used in France into the seventeenth century.) Bodel's *Jeu* is about the miraculous restoration of a stolen treasure, but within this plot we are treated as well to long tavern scenes and a battle sequence between Christians and Saracens. The characters are nearly all extremely human and vivid, perhaps too much so. The triumph of Saint Nicholas emerges not from a tight-knit drama but from a sprawling mixture of the serious and the amusing.

It is Bodel's drama rather than the *Jeu d'Adam* that points ahead. The anonymous *Courtois d'Arras,* in dramatizing the story of the Prodigal Son, so lingers over the boy's wayward life in an inn that the play can properly be considered a comedy rather than a serious piece of didacticism. The famous *Miracle de Théophile* ("Miracle of Theophile," written 1261) by Rutebeuf (?–c. 1285) depicts an angered ecclesiastic who makes a pact with the devil only to repent and be saved from his pact by the Virgin. Here the dramatic qualities of the story are passed over in favor of an outburst of lyricism, for Rutebeuf was primarily a poet. Psychology and motivation interest him little; rather Théophile's laments before and after his pact and his prayer to the Virgin constitute the *Miracle*'s finest passages.

It should come as no surprise then that in his *Jeu de la fauillée* ("Play of the Canopy," written in 1276 or 1277) Adam le Bossu (1235?–?1285) executed a witty, rambling comedy about himself and friends, which is related to serious medieval drama only insofar as the characters discuss a traditional practice of the women of Arras at Pentecost and leave at the close of the play to visit the shrine of Notre Dame, exposed under a canopy of leaves (a *feuillée*). Little surprise, too, that the several anonymous *Miracles de Notre Dame* ("Miracles of Our Lady," written c. 1339–1382) build a miraculous appearance of the Virgin to a sinner around material as diverse as the *chansons de geste,* hagiology, and popular legends or contain plots with the most rudimentary psychology and interminable lyric passages of lament, thanksgiving, entreaty, and repentance.

A formal rupture between the edifying and the entertaining elements of this theater came with the fourteenth century, when it was deemed necessary to enliven the heavy sermonizing with purely comic sequences (whence the word "farce," since these lapses were used to stuff—*farcir*—the general plot with amusement). By the fifteenth century each element had undergone further development, as the anonymous *Actes des Apôtres* ("Acts of the Apostles," written 1452–1478) or the *Mistère du Vieil Testament* ("Mystery of the Old Testament," collated c. 1450) show. Interminable works requiring days to perform, they conveyed their messages through allegory, scholastic debate, and lyric lament, accompanied by farcical scenes of unabashed license, even vulgarity. Comedy in the middle ages, it should be noted, never rises above the level of farce. While the quality of the anonymous *Maître Pierre Pathelin* (written before 1470) is exceptional, its plot—the study of dupers duped—is not.

It is this theater of sermons and farce that the sixteenth century, the Renaissance, inherited. This century also inherited the discontent of those many men who formed the world of Humanism. Humanism is a difficult term to deal with; it encompasses a broad spectrum of ideas, not all mutually inclusive and not all held by those generally considered Humanists. Many were deeply religious, even mystical, souls

who decried the emphasis placed by scholastic teaching on logic. They sought inspiration in the mystical literature of antiquity, Italy, and the Low Countries. Some went far in their criticism of the Catholic Church and sought to attack the attitudes or practices with which they disagreed by reexamining the original biblical texts and their scholastic commentaries. Others were scholars, devoted to the editing and dissemination of classical texts. Whatever their precise aim, the Humanists soon discovered that they could not pursue their aims without perfecting their knowledge of Greek. In this context of study and reform, a gradual transformation of French drama took place.

Of course, one did not need to be a militant reformer to deplore the licentious and irreverent liberties of the farces. The decision of the Parlement de Paris in 1548 to ban the performance of all *mystères* with a religious subject can be interpreted as a reaction of the more pious Catholics to the burlesque quality of medieval drama. On the other hand, those Humanists who had read and translated Greek tragedy to improve their comprehension of the language must have soon recognized the differences between classical and medieval drama. The Humanists were proud, sometimes angry, men, eager to distinguish themselves from their opponents. As they emphasized the simple piety of the primitive Church in order to bring out the abuses of the Church of their day, so they contrasted the gravity and dignity of classical literature to the formless, popular dramas of the middle ages. Scholars such as François Tissard (1450?–?1500) and George Buchanan (1506–1582) translated Greek tragedy into Latin. In 1537 Lazare de Baïf (1496?–1547) published his translation into French of Sophocles' *Electra.* During the following decade Jacques Amyot, Guillaume Bochetel, and Thomas Sébillet did likewise. Original dramas by the Humanists are fewer but appear as early as 1514. These works raise the question as to how deep was their grasp of classical tragedy and to what degree the Humanists broke with medieval practices.

The ban of 1548 hardly destroyed medieval theater n France. It was especially popular in the provinces throughout the sixteenth century, but as time wore on the Protestants found fault, not only with the excesses of the farces, but with the representation of God on the stage and the extensive use of the lives of those saints to which Protestants were particularly hostile. Certain Catholics feared that these plays would create an interest in the public to read the Bible. Thus, abandoned by the Humanists and found wanting by both the reformists and counterreformists, medieval drama could not survive forever. At the same time, it was the one indigenous tradition of France.

All the early surviving neo-Latin dramas in France, including Buchanan's *Jephthes sive votum* ("Jephthah or the Vow") and *Baptistes* ("John the Baptist"), both written between 1539 and 1544, emphasize the importance of France's medieval tradition. *Theoandrothanatos* ("The Death of the Man-God," pub. 1514) and *Theocrisis* ("The Last Judgment," pub. 1514) by Gian-Francesco Conti, called Stoa (1484–1557), are both divided into five acts with choruses. *Christus Xylonicus* ("Christ Crucified," pub. 1529) by Nicholas Barthélémy (1478–c. 1540) has choruses and classical rhetorical patterns for its verse. These plays are classical in form and style only. Despite the division into acts, despite the Senecan rhetoric employed for the speeches and the choruses, Stoa and Barthélémy produced passion plays whose content has nothing to do with the theater of antiquity.

Buchanan's *Jephthes,* written when the Humanist was in Bordeaux, is inspired by a passage from the Bible yet changes the account in several ways. In Judges xi: 30–40, Jephthah vows in return for victory in battle to sacrifice the first person who comes to him when he reaches home. He is greeted by his daughter, who agrees to die if she may first spend two months in prayer. To fill his five acts Buchanan added the characters of Jephthah's wife and the high priest. The wife bemoans the unhappy lot of her family and pleads with Jephthah to spare their child. Patterned after Hecuba, the wife testifies to Buchanan's excellent knowledge of Greek. The role of the high priest is to engage Jephthah in a long debate over vows, a debate that recalls standard medieval practices and links the play to a long-standing use of the theater for propaganda. (Jephthah's views are close to those of many reformers of the day.) If we attempt to understand from the Prologue, spoken by an angel, whether Buchanan sees tragedy as divine punishment meted out for sinful acts or a blind force that strikes man at the peak of good fortune, we find only conflicting and inconclusive statements. In structure, tone, and style, however, the work vividly mirrors classical tragedy, especially the plays of Seneca. The Prologue announces what is to happen. The chorus comments on each "act" (they are not so called) with Senecan commonplaces on the uncertainty of fortune; the mother foresees disaster in an allegorical dream; and the death of Jephthah's daughter is related by a messenger in the final scene.

If *Jephthes* possesses many traits to distinguish it from medieval drama, the play is without the love plot, extensive interest in human psychology, and strict adherence to the unities so characteristic of Racine's classical drama to come. Indeed, with its long passages of lament and its debate scene, *Jephthes* in many ways looks back, not ahead. This situation may be explained in part by the fact that early Humanists were not aware of Aristotle's *Poetics.* They derived their definition of tragedy from medieval commentators such as the Roman grammarian Aelius Donatus (fourth century), who differentiated between comedy and tragedy in these terms: "In comedy the circumstances of the men are middling, the pressures of perils small, the outcome of the actions joyful, whereas in tragedy all things are the opposite, the characters exalted, the tenor great, the outcome calamitous." This definition, plus a reading of Euripides, Sophocles, and especially Seneca, whose language and texts were most accessible to the Humanists, might serve to stimulate changes in form but it did not exclude lament from the stage. Lament is so common in both classical and medieval drama that its absence from Humanist tragedy would be truly remarkable. As a result, when Étienne Jodelle (1532–1573) responded to poet Joachim du Bellay's plea in the book *Deffence et illustration de la langue françoyse* ("The Defense and Illustration of the French Language," 1549) that comedy and tragedy be returned to their former dignity, he wrote a play nearly devoid of action and psychology but fully

tragic, given the characters' station, the impending doom, and the final catastrophe.

Jodelle's *Cléopâtre captive* ("Cleopatra Captured," 1552), the first tragedy written in French in France, has only 1615 lines, few characters, and a chorus. Acts I and IV are in alexandrines, the remainder in decasyllabic verse. Like *Jephthes,* the play begins with a speech (spoken by Anthony's ghost) predicting disaster: Cleopatra will die before the day is out. Act V describes her death. The intervening acts are little more than the preparation for that event. The Senecan form is replete with a dream, confidantes, and sententia. A modicum of characterization appears in Cleopatra's pride, which, in addition to her desire to rejoin Anthony, determines immediately her intent to die. Octavius does not wish to be undone in his effort to bring Cleopatra to Rome as a captive, but their wills do not really clash, and the plot contains no attempt to dramatize Cleopatra's situation. Acts II, III, and IV are rendered possible by Cleopatra's postponement of her suicide, not by any hesitation. By referring at the end of the first act to the inconstancy of fortune, the chorus prepares the audience for the usual tragic spectacle Donatus defined. That Jodelle has the chorus refer after Act II to human pride which excites the wrath of the gods, yet is content merely to present Cleopatra's flaw rather than make it gradually become the source of her fate, shows (as does *Jephthes*) how unconscious these dramatists were of the idea that tragedy is a dramatization of a being's fault. *Cléopâtre captive* remains in the tradition of Donatus and Buchanan. Jodelle's other tragedy, *Didon se sacrifiant* ("Dido's Suicide," written 1560?), while more skillfully executed, does not depart substantially from the techniques of the first.

In the years following 1552, Humanists still continued to translate the classical texts, but gradually they produced a number of original dramas, the most important of which are *César* (pub. 1561) by Jacques Grévin (1538–1570); *Aman* (prod. 1561; pub. 1566) by André de Rivaudeau (1540?–1580); the David and Saul trilogy entitled *Tragédies saintes* ("Sacred Tragedies," pub. 1563) by Louis Des Masures (1515–1574); and *Saül le furieux* ("Saul's Madness," pub. 1572, but probably composed before 1563) by Jean de La Taille (1540?–1608).

The group offers some surprises. None has to do with love. The playwrights are all Protestants. In every case save Grévin's the choice of material for a tragedy depended in some measure on the possibility of adapting that material to include a commentary on contemporary events. *Aman*'s reference to the afflictions of the Jews, victims of tyrannical, idolatrous princes, or Des Masures' insistence upon the rewards awaiting those who suffer yet put their faith in God had a specific meaning in a time of increased hostility between Protestants and Catholics. By the same token, we see that a desire to propagandize and edify had not disappeared from the world of French drama.

These same titles also name men of history or of the Bible who have fallen from power. From this fact alone we can appreciate the degree to which Donatus' conception of tragedy continued to guide French dramatists. Still, all these plays are not alike. Des Masures' trilogy ends happily. It uses simultaneous décor and innumerable characters (even Satan), whereas the works of Rivaudeau, La Taille, and Grévin resemble in tone as well as form the tragedies of Jodelle. Des Masures' technique recalls the tragedy *Abraham sacrifiant* ("Abraham's Sacrifice," pub. 1550) by Théodore de Bèze (1519–1605). The play is written in French, but since it was acted and printed in Switzerland, it does not qualify as the first French classical tragedy. The play contains a chorus, however, and echoes of Euripides' *Iphigenia at Aulis.* It also uses simultaneous décor and the figure of Satan, ends happily, and alludes to the Protestant cause. Bèze's preface to the play makes clear that the poet's intent is religious. He so deprecates the literary efforts of the more worldly Humanists that we need not be astonished by the marked influence of medieval religious drama on *Abraham sacrifiant.* Rivaudeau, La Taille, and Grévin were Humanists as well as Protestants. They all knew of Aristotle, whose fortunes began to soar with the publication in 1561 of *Poetices libri septem* ("Seven Books of the Poetics") by Jules-César Scaliger (1484–1558).

From their exposure to the principles of the *Poetics,* these playwrights gleaned diverse observations recorded in prefaces which accompany their dramas. Rivaudeau accentuates the need for a unity of time but little else. Grévin explains that he composed his chorus of soldiers because it was against the principle of verisimilitude to have the choruses sing. La Taille alone among these Humanists provides an extensive discussion of dramatic technique. His *De l'Art de la tragédie* ("On the Art of Tragedy") was written later than *Saül,* probably for the 1572 edition of this tragedy. La Taille insists that the plot should be well constructed according to the unities of time and place. It should be devoid of allegorical figures and theological arguments and its hero must not be too wicked or too virtuous. He specifically states that Abraham's sacrifice and the death of Goliath are not subjects for tragedy—a patent criticism of those plays to which Bèze and Des Masures had given the title of *tragédie.* However, as La Taille's choice of subject shows, these remarks were aimed more at discrediting the persistent medieval influence on tragedy than at reorienting Humanist drama along lines other than those prescribed by Donatus and put into practice by Jodelle.

Scaliger's remarks on tragedy are similarly brief and fragmentary. He mentions the six constituent parts of a tragedy as given by Aristotle and defines peripetia. Catharsis is commented upon, but rather negatively, since Scaliger does not consider that all subjects produce such "purgation." Indeed, while he reproduces in Greek Aristotle's definition of tragedy, he adds his own: "A tragedy is the imitation of the adversity of a distinguished man; it employs the form of action, presents a disastrous denouement, and is expressed in impressive metrical language." Donatus or Jodelle would hardly have objected to such a definition. As a result, while the discovery of Aristotle heightened those differences that existed between medieval and classical forms, it contributed relatively little at this time to the formulation of the French classical drama to come. Even Robert GARNIER, the most talented of French dramatists of the period, did not effect any significant changes in the concept of tragedy held by his predecessors. His

tragicomedy *Bradamante* (pub. 1582), which firmly establishes the genre, is his most significant technical innovation. This interest in a hybrid form heralds the salient traits of French drama at the close of the sixteenth century.

Bèze and Des Masures demonstrate the vigor of the medieval theater in midcentury. As time wore on, it was felt all the more as the century tired of the Humanists' gravity and erudition and returned to earlier practices. The necessity of the unities was questioned. Playwrights brought violence from the wings onto the stage. The lines dividing comedy and tragedy were blurred. After all, Scaliger himself recognized that some ancient tragedies ended well and that many comedies brought misfortune to its characters. It also became increasingly difficult to distinguish between Humanist tragedy and serious medieval drama. Numerous works entitled *tragédie* were little more than mystery plays. Humanist tragedy did not die, however. Antoine de Montchrestien (1575–1621) wrote Senecan tragedies decades after Garnier's *Bradamante,* but the sixteenth century eventually bequeathed to the succeeding period a variety of dramatic practices almost as great as the spectrum of styles it embraced within its hundred years.

The drama of the sixteenth century does not mark a pinnacle in the history of world drama. Its value is largely historical. The works of Jodelle and Garnier are essential steps in a line of artistic activity that leads to the remarkable achievements of Corneille and Racine. *Jephthes* and *Cléopâtre captive* emphasize the sincere effort of French Humanists to recapture in the modern age that dignity of classical letters they found wanting in the theater they inherited from the middle ages. That these men were not able to cast off all vestiges of medieval drama testifies to the deep roots of this tradition in so-called Renaissance France. At the same time, the Humanists did offer new subjects, new forms, and a sympathetic attitude toward the more studied works of antiquity. For the most part young men when they composed their works, they displayed more erudition than knowledge of the theater; their understanding of the subtler qualities of classical drama and dramatic practices appears limited. Seneca's form and Aristotle's remarks were imitated as unfeelingly as were the styles of Vergil and Homer by practitioners of the epic during the Renaissance. Even the most regular plays demonstrate little awareness of most of the dramatic consequences resulting from a use of the unities. We can hardly expect Humanist tragedy to have won popular favor.

The development of comedy parallels closely that of Humanist tragedy. In the comic sphere, too, the sixteenth century inherited a formless and vulgar genre: the farce. Far from possessing a logical concatenation of events leading to a denouement, the farce usually brought together characters rendered either as abstractions (the husband, the wife, the servant) or as allegorical personifications (le Monde, "the World," *Venez-tost,* "Come-Quickly," *Gens-nouveaux,* "New People") who interacted merely to create continuous amusement.

By the middle of the sixteenth century, however, Humanist activity had made available the works and forms of classical comedy through *Le Grand Terence en françois, prose et rime* ("The Great Terence in

FRONTISPIECE FROM THE 1493 FRENCH EDITION OF TERENCE'S *Comedies en latin* (ILLUSTRATION BY ROBERT HAINARD FROM *Promenades Aux Oiseaux,* EDITIONS CLAIREFONTAINE ET LA GUILDE DU LIVRE, LAUSANNE)

French, Both Prose and Verse") in particular and a translation of Plautus' *Amphitryon.* In 1567 Antoine de Baïf translated Plautus' *Miles Gloriosus* as *Le Brave,* and in 1573 he adapted Terence's *Eunuchus.* As a consequence, for some time critics concluded that Humanist comedy was the product of an amalgam of medieval farce and Latin comedy. Jodelle's *Eugène* (1552) and poet and Humanist Jacques Peletier's *Art poétique* ("Art of Poetry," 1555) certainly substantiated such a view. Jodelle, describing the intrigues of a dissolute abbot who becomes the rival in love of a soldier and takes another man's wife, created a "new" drama only in that its form adhered to classical models. *Eugène* begins with a Prologue, contains five acts, and ends with a command to applaud. Peletier's discussion of comedy treated of the same formal elements and the acceptable characters for comedy, the characters of Róman comedy.

At the turn of the twentieth century, the critic Pierre Toldo proved that further developments in Humanist comedy derived as much, if not more, from Italian comedy. Again, the basis for imitation was an accumulation of translations. In 1543 Charles Estienne translated the anonymous *Ingannati* and two years later Jacques Bourgeois translated

Lodovico Ariosto's *Suppositi.* La Taille translated in 1573 another play by Ariosto under the title of *Le Négromant* ("The Necromancer"). Moreover, in 1548 and 1555 Italian plays were presented before the court, which throughout the remainder of the century proved more open to comedy (and especially Italian comedy) than to tragedy.

Grévin's *Les Esbahis* ("The Astonished," pub. 1561); La Taille's *Les Corrivaux* ("The Rivals," pub. nineteenth century); *La Reconnue* ("A Daughter Recovered," pub. 1578) by Rémy Belleau (1528–1577); *Les Contens* ("The Contented," pub. 1584) by Odet de Turnèbe (1552–1581); and *Les Neapolitaines* ("The Women of Naples," pub. 1584) by François d'Amboise (1550–1620) are among the major comedies composed in France using Italian models. The most productive writer of comedies during this period, Pierre de Larivey (1540/41–1619), merely transposed into French settings and situations a long series of Italian works.

Itself derived from Latin comedy, Italian light drama nevertheless updated its sources or created new characters and plots. The *sensex* ("old man") of Latin comedy evolves into Pantalone and the Dottore. The Pedant is an entirely new creation. Marvelous resemblances, enchantments, the disappearance of children, and their sudden recognition all receive in Italian drama noticeable amplification before passing to France.

The parallel development of comedy and tragedy became complete when by 1600 these elements of plot were mixed with material from the pastoral or even tragedy, and when the Humanist emphasis on classical form gave way to experimentation with the old and the new. This lapse of interest in rules and form should not efface the significance of the Humanists' innovations. The masterpieces of Molière and Racine forcefully attest to the importance of those advances accomplished in the sixteenth century.

General studies on medieval and Renaissance drama in France are few; however, Grace Frank's *The Medieval French Drama* (1954) provides in reliable, readable form the essential information on its subject. O. B. Hardison's *Christian Rite and Christian Drama in the Middle Ages* (1965) attempts a provocative revision of earlier theories on the relationship between rite and drama. Erich Auerbach offers an interesting discussion of the *Jeu d'Adam* in his *Mimesis* (1953). Buchanan's tragedies were translated into English in 1870 by Alexander Gibb. An illuminating study on the tragicomedy is H. C. Lancaster's *The French Tragi-Comedy, Its Origins and Development from 1552 to 1628* (1907).—D. S., Jr.

classical (seventeenth-century) drama. "Classical," in the narrow sense of the term, is generally used to describe the French writers who reached literary maturity between 1660 and 1700 and who, in their works, sought simplicity of form, clarity of expression, and verisimilitude and were interested chiefly in psychological and moral action. The means used to achieve these goals were a certain number of rules drawn from antiquity (Aristotle and Horace) but essentially justified by good sense or reason. Yet while it is true that the major works of French classicism were thus produced during the first forty years of Louis XIV's personal reign (1643–1715), it is also true that the classical spirit was born and had, in part, been formulated in an earlier period of very rich theatrical production. Moreover, not only is it generally agreed that the golden age of the French stage began around 1630, at the time of the doctrinary debates between the partisans of a "regular" theater and those of freedom in the theater, but also that the great works produced at the time of Louis XIV's glory had a lasting influence, which was sovereign during the first decades of the eighteenth century.

The so-called classical production, in the broad sense of the term, may be divided into four periods. The first is characterized by a whole generation of writers, born between 1595 and 1610, who held sway in the theater from around 1630 until the Fronde (a rising of the aristocracy and the Parliament against Mazarin and Anne of Austria, 1649–1653). The most important of them was Pierre Corneille. The second period, which began directly after the Fronde and ended before the beginning of Jean Racine's career (1664), was characterized less by the advent of a new generation than by a revival in the theater in the realm of comedy, on the one hand, and by a development in the direction of a new *préciosité,* on the other. These were the years of Pierre Corneille's second resumption of dramatic activity, Molière's return to Paris (1658), and the first great triumphs of Thomas Corneille, Pierre's brother, and of Philippe Quinault. The third period may be called that of high classicism and began after 1660. It was dominated by the Corneille brothers, but above all, by Racine and Molière. Finally, the end of Louis XIV's reign, the Regency, and the reign of Louis XV (1715–1774) were dominated, on the one hand, by writers of tragedy such as Jean Galbert de Campistron, Prosper Jolyot de Crébillon, and, from 1718 on, Voltaire and, on the other, by a large group of comic writers, all more or less haunted by the shade of Molière but also wishing to renew the art of comedy.

The proliferation of playwrights that began around 1630 was in part favored by new theatrical and social conditions. Although since 1548 secular theater had been very alive in Paris, it was not until 1629 that the troupe of clowns and tragedians known as "the King's Players" became definitively established, as the first permanent professional company, at the Hôtel de Bourgogne. At the same time, a second troupe, directed by the actor Montdory, appeared in Paris and in 1634 also became permanent when it set up in the enclosed tennis court of the Marais district. From 1643 to 1645 a third troupe, directed by Madeleine Béjart and including Molière, tried to become established but finally failed. Nevertheless, the two large permanent French companies (for there was also an Italian troupe) stimulated the writers' interest in the theater. The theaters themselves, however, in comparison with those of other countries, were very poorly equipped. Former *jeux de paumes* (enclosed tennis courts), rectangular in shape, with a gallery around three sides, above a pit with no chairs, formed an amphitheater at one end and a stage at the other. The theater of the Hôtel de Bourgogne was about 100 feet long (including a 40-foot depth of stage) and about 55 feet wide. The visibility was bad for most of the audience, and it became customary to take seats on the stage itself at a very high price.

Despite such discomforts, the theater, which had been scorned at the time of Henri IV, was from then on a stable institution with eminent patrons. Cardinal Richelieu, himself a playwright, was the patron of the Marais theater, granted pensions to (and controlled) a certain number of writers, and organized police protection, making it respectable to attend the theater. In addition, a new audience came into being. Previously all male and violent, comprised of students, artisans, and riotous soldiers, the audience, particularly in the loges and galleries, grew to include members of the new polite society, noble or bourgeois, male and female, schooled by a reading of Italian and Spanish literature as well as Honoré d'Urfé's pastoral *L'Astrée.*

The influence of the psychological analyses and subtleties of this pastoral novel, published from 1607 to 1619 and continued by Balthazar Baro in 1627, was complemented by that of the dramatic pastoral, a genre inspired by the works of the Italians Torquato Tasso and Battista Guarini and represented in France primarily by Racan's *Bergeries* ("Pastorals," pub. 1625). Lyricism, the analysis of delicately shaded feelings, and a type of realism were already taking precedence over purely ROMANESQUE conventions and fantasy. Added to the new audience's interest in psychological subtlety and depth was a desire for simplification, order, decorum, and intelligibility. As early as 1621 Théophile de Viau's tragedy *Pyrame et Thisbé* showed the way toward the unification of the drama around a single and fatal conflict between love and a hostile destiny. Performed again in 1634, and despite scoffing provoked by some excessively baroque metaphors, the play continued in its renown throughout the seventeenth century. The new audience, which included the "learned" (theoreticians, critics, academicians), was of course still avid for dramas portraying strong emotions, but its newborn "civility" demanded an impression of unity and propriety that opened the way to early classicism, as a reaction against the extreme irregularity, violence, fantasy, and actual incoherence of the drama of the 1620's. However, a strong popular taste for the freedom of form of the old theater persisted, which explains why, even when the rules officially triumphed, "irregular" plays were to continue to be performed.

From 1628 to 1631 a doctrinal quarrel arose that clearly characterizes the turning point in the development of the classical spirit in the theater. The year 1628 may be considered the high point of "irregular" theater. On the one hand, it was then that the fifth and last volume of Alexandre Hardy's *Théâtre* was published—an incomplete edition of his works, comprised of six hundred plays of all genres and of extremely free form; on the other hand, it was then that the second version of Jean de Schélandre's *Tyr et Sidon* was published, with a Preface by François Ogier. The play itself, a reworking of the subject of a 1608 tragedy, is a tragicomedy that unfolds in the space of two days, with a great number of characters, places, and adventures and a final marriage replacing the death of the heroine in the first version. A comparison of the two versions shows how in just a few years a taste had developed for the most extravagant forms and, in particular, for tragicomedy—that is, for very lively plays in which the action, comprised of numerous bloody and glorious adventures, had its share of comic or lowly elements and led to a happy ending. But more important still was the Preface by Ogier, a vigorous manifesto of the "free" theater that had been in fashion during the 1620's: In the name of faithfulness to reality and most particularly in the name of the pleasure drama should give, Ogier affirmed the freedom to mix genres—to mix the tragic substance with comic details—and in the name of the relativity of customs, he rejected the authority of the ancients—their rules and their unities. However, two years later, in 1630, the classical avant-garde asserted itself: Jean Chapelain, in his *Lettre sur la règle des 24 heures* ("Letter on the 24-hour Rule") and then in his *Discours de la poésie représentative* ("Discourse on Representative Poetry"), in the name of the same faithfulness to life—called verisimilitude—became the champion of rules, not because of the authority of Aristotle, but because of the good sense and practice of the great ancient writers.

The next year, in 1631, Jean MAIRET presented *Sylvanire,* a "regular" pastoral, and prefaced his play with a defense of the rules in a kind of manifesto of the "new theater" as opposed to the disorderly recent past. In the following years, even though there was still a larger production of irregular plays, the regular theater gained ground and a series of tragedies respectful of the rules made their appearance. At that time the rules were essentially those of unity of action, unity of time (the action was supposed to last twenty-four to thirty-six hours), and unity of place. The latter must be understood in a broad sense: The action had to unfold within the boundaries of one city or one forest, but several "rooms" were permitted. The rooms were compartments built side by side on the stage, some of which had curtains that opened or closed according to the shifts in the action. In the course of the seventeenth century the unities of time and place were to become increasingly rigid. However, behind the pedantry of the discussions they provoked and the misinterpretation of certain of Aristotle's and Horace's remarks about them, they were, nonetheless, as early as the 1630's, the sign of an effort to increase the dramatic credibility by giving the action a fixed locality similar to the spectator's and a time as close as possible to the spectator's actual lived time. Moreover, the comic elements were considerably reduced and sometimes altogether absent in the tragedies. Finally, there was a notable search for "propriety." The playwrights did their best to avoid too much physical violence and blood onstage. It is probable, for example, that Massinisse, in Mairet's *Sophonisbe* (1634), stabs himself after the curtain has fallen on Sophonisbe's room. And while the first edition of Georges de Scudéry's *La Mort de César* ("The Death of Caesar," 1636) would seem to indicate that Caesar's murder is viewed by the spectator, in the second edition (1637) the spectacle is eliminated and there is a marginal indication that the "compartment" representing the Senate "closes so that the stage not be steeped in blood, against the rules."

The first French classical tragedies came in rapid succession: in 1634 Jean Rotrou's *Hercule mourant* ("Hercules Dying") and Mairet's *Sophonisbe;* during the 1634/35 season Pierre Corneille's *Médée;* in 1635 Scudéry's *La Mort de César;* and in 1636 *Mari-*

ane, by François TRISTAN L'HERMITE, and Pierre du Ryer's *Lucrèce.* Before Corneille's tragicomedy *Le Cid* (1637), the regular tragedies *Sophonisbe* and *Mariane* had the greatest public success. *Sophonisbe,* which was performed just a few months after *Hercule mourant,* is considered the first French classical tragedy, not only because it conforms to the unities, but also, and above all, because of the conception of the action it represents: rich in peripeties, it is nonetheless organized around one peril (the Roman political threat that weighs on Sophonisbe and all her actions) inextricably linked to a swift psychological crisis (the apolitical love of Sophonisbe and Massinisse) in a conflict of simple interests that, within a few hours, hastens the protagonists to their deaths.

Despite striking differences, these first classical tragedies belong to a common dramatic universe. Not only the sensuality and laments of the characters, but the choice of resolutely ancient subject matter strongly recall the Humanistic Renaissance tragedy. References to the wheel of fortune as a symbol of fate (in Mairet, Scudéry, and Tristan), the taste for maxims and moral aphorisms similar to Seneca's (although limited, very characteristic of Corneille, for example), the use of premonitory dreams, even of magic (in Corneille's *Médée*), and certain philosophical or erudite debates (the origin of dreams and the four humours in *Mariane* and epicurianism as opposed to stoicism in *La Mort de César*) are also reminiscent of Humanism and the interests of previous decades. The chief originality of these plays consists in the fact that they keep some of tragicomedy's effects of violence, shock, and surprise, while at the same time they tone down and boil down those effects into one psychological crisis. Of course, the pathos springs more often from the victimization of the characters, from their distress, which leads them to a kind of madness, than from their inner conflicts. But while they indulge in sensual and almost lunatic passions, they consider the consequences of such self-abandon a necessary evil and find their glory in the recognition of that necessity. The murders and suicides committed at the denouement are thus, above all, pitiable, but they do not lack grandeur. *La Mort de César* ends with the apotheosis of the dictator; Médée flies off in a chariot drawn by dragons; and by their double suicide, Sophonisbe and Massinisse escape the Romans and make their love triumph.

As tragedy was re-created, so—in a parallel way—was comedy, which soon took precedence over farce. While farce did not disappear, it happened that the great clowns of the Hôtel de Bourgogne died one after the other during the 1630's; the last one, Guillot-Gorju, retired in 1641; and the public's new taste encouraged the development of a literary and decorous comedy either drawn from Latin models or patterned after the Italian or French pastoral. As early as 1629 *Mélite* by Pierre CORNEILLE initiated this genre. Indeed, up until *Le Cid,* and excepting *Médée,* a tragedy, and *Clitandre* (1632), a tragicomedy, the young Corneille was, above all, a writer of comedies. In addition to *Mélite,* he had five of them performed at the Marais theater. During those same years Mairet, Du Ryer, Scudéry, and Rotrou also made their contributions to the new genre. All of very different inspiration, the comedies of the 1630's were clearly a first attempt at developing a comic genre

FRONTISPIECE FROM THE 1664 EDITION OF PIERRE
CORNEILLE'S *Works* (NEW YORK PUBLIC LIBRARY)

This, for the most part, was because the "doctrines"
were concerned with serious theater, giving comedy
far greater freedom. The most striking comic work of
that period, altogether exceptional in its fantasy, is
still Corneille's *L'Illusion comique* ("The Comic Illusion," 1636). It is made up of evocations of distant
events in the turbulent life of a young lover—visions provoked by a magician.

A writer who was able to judge skillfully the taste
of both the popular and educated public, Corneille
came into the forefront and eclipsed his contemporaries in January 1637 with LE CID, performed at the
Marais theater. This first masterpiece of the French
classical school is, above all, a tragicomedy because
of the number of rebounds in the action and a nonbloody end that indicates the possibility of happiness
in the near future. Moreover, the play satisfied the
new demands of the educated public for coherence
and concentration. Also, *Le Cid* presented the public, not only with characters who were both lyrical
and active, but also with a portrait of "beautiful
souls" devoted to an exalting and dynamic ethic and
blessed with the psychological grace that was the
ideal of the nobility at the time of Louis XIII:
"generosity." Finally, the form of the play corresponded to the unities as they were understood at that
time, and, at least in the eyes of the public, the
proprieties were respected: Duels and battles take
place offstage.

The *"Le Cid* dispute," which made the play a success, is one of the high points of interest in the history
of French classicism. One must forget professional
jealousies, such as that of Mairet, who attacked the
play, stating that it had been quite simply plagiarized
from the Spanish original, as well as the clumsy and
brutal irascibility of Corneille himself. Behind the
inevitable and ridiculous pedantry of the learned,
one finds a real effort on their part to clarify certain
rules. And it is also obvious from the debate that despite a common tendency toward clarity, simplicity,
verisimilitude, and propriety, there were then two
conflicting concepts of classicism: one, a living classicism, sought by the public, for whom pleasure and
emotion were the goals of such works and justified
the rules that procured them; and the other, the
classicism of the theoreticians, who, in the name of
reason and sometimes of Aristotelian authority, denied that any pleasure outside the rules could be of
good quality.

After Scudéry, in his *Observations sur Le Cid*
("Commentaries on *The Cid,*" April 1637), had accused the play of lacking in verisimilitude and in the
proprieties, Richelieu, with the reticent approval of
Corneille, submitted the play to the French Academy
(founded in 1635) for a decision. In December 1637
Jean Chapelain, on the part of the institution, drew
up *Les Sentiments de l'académie sur Le Cid* ("The
French Academy's Opinions on *The Cid*"), in which
Le Cid, despite its unquestionable merits, is accused
of "irregularity" and of being based on a bad subject. At the same time, the academy more rigorously
defined certain rules: Verisimilitude is clearly separated from the true, and propriety must prevail over
truth. The two rules—of verisimilitude and propriety—are the key to the aesthetic of the learned.
They acknowledged the fact that theater should procure "reasonable contentment," but only on condi-

that was sustained, but quite different from the conventional pastoral and tragicomedy, and pleasing,
but with a preference for the charms of good form
rather than the laughter-at-any-price of farce. Moreover, even while the love stories were drawn from the
pastoral or the action recalled the dangers of death,
violence, and crimes of tragicomedy, many of these
comedies tended to take place in a contemporary
French setting. In addition, there was an occasional
interest in characterization. Even though the young
leads in Corneille often seem interchangeable, in
their love scenes and key feelings (love, jealousy,
chagrin) they show themselves to have specific personalities, being more or less bold, playful, melancholy, or proud, with numerous variations. Other
characters appeared that were highly individualized
because of a vice, a flaw, an obsession, or particular
habits. In 1637 *Les Visionnaires* ("The Visionaries")
of Jean DESMARETS DE SAINT-SORLIN was performed.
This comedy sacrifices plot to a gallery of portraits
and mixes together eight characters who are all
gently mad—the kind of fashionable madness "for
which one is not put away" (Desmarets, Preface of
1640)—and who have a certain literary or social
snobbishness typical of the period.

Although the comic genre during those years was
still a second-rate and badly defined art, the few
works performed were impressive in their variety.

tion that there be no shocking departure from customs, either in the sense of the normal habits of the characters onstage or in the sense of morality (Chimène's shamelessness in agreeing to talk with Rodrigue in her rooms). Some of the reproaches are similar to modern conceptions of realism: How, for example, was it possible for Rodrigue to enter Chimène's rooms without encountering even one servant? Moreover, as a result of the praiseworthy effort of respecting the unity of time, the many events lacked verisimilitude, and the unity of place, in the broad sense, caused "confusion in the minds of the spectators." This dispute, which Richelieu put a stop to when it degenerated into personal attacks and vulgar parodies, shows that the French Academy and the learned really wanted to orient serious theater toward tragedy. They wanted a form of tragedy in which the unities could be respected with no effort at all and which would be characterized by a yielding to good sense and perhaps a moral conformity quite different from the exalting and individualistic impulses of the tragicomedy of Corneille.

The consequences of both *Le Cid*'s success and the dispute were several and sometimes contradictory. Officially, the learned and the regular spirit triumphed, and Corneille, his pride wounded, left the theater until 1640. On the other hand, *Le Cid* continued to be a great public success. The essayist Guez de Balzac, a rigorous stylist, wrote to Scudéry in August 1637, apropos of the play: "Having satisfied a whole Kingdom is greater than having written a play according to the rules . . . Knowing the art of pleasing is worth less than knowing how to please without art." Moreover, *Le Cid's* success, in spite of the French Academy, for some time encouraged writers to return to tragicomedy, and since some of them respected the rules, the distinction between tragicomedy and tragedy gradually became blurred. Paradoxically, on the other hand, tragedies remained irregular.

Although Corneille was silent for three years, without, however, losing the patronage of Richelieu, he compensated for it between 1640 and the end of 1643 with performances of four tragedies: HORACE, CINNA, POLYEUCTE, and *La Mort de Pompée* ("Pompey's Death"). While public taste was still hesitating between rules and freedom, Corneille, with *Horace,* opted in favor of regular tragedy. Moreover, he revived the tradition that went back to Mairet's *Sophonisbe* and Scudéry's *La Mort de César:* that of tragedy based on a subject borrowed from Roman history. These four tragedies are regular and respectful of the unities if one accepts certain improbabilities, like the king's visit to a private citizen in *Horace* or, in the same play, a very broad interpretation of unity of action. Although borrowed from Roman history and no longer from Spanish legend, as *Le Cid* was, the subjects of these tragedies enabled Corneille to write plays in much the same spirit: Forced by circumstances and by the choice of certain values (family honor, patriotism, religious faith, political duty) into becoming mortal enemies, the heroes and heroines end by trying to outdo one another in generosity and, through greatness of soul, to admire one another in their struggle to the death, in order sometimes to achieve a higher reconciliation than the revenge or victory they were seeking.

In 1644, with RODOGUNE, a new conception of characters and their relationships was created. In this tragedy, as in those that were to follow it until 1652, alongside the "generous" characters there are "monsters," or at least Machiavellian characters, whose magnanimity is perverted and leads them to commit the foulest deeds. However, the horror or indignation they provoke in the spectator is still "Cornelian"; that is to say, their behavior and their calculations, whether they succeed or fail, are sometimes so extreme, so inhuman, that they necessarily provoke the feeling that Corneille considered equal if not superior to the Aristotelian feelings of terror and pity: admiration. After a rather bad flop in 1652, Corneille left the stage for seven years and devoted himself to a translation of *The Imitation of Christ.*

Corneille's tragedies of the 1640's make up a group of truly classical works in their regularity of form, the concentration of the action on one inevitable crisis, the characters' constant analyses of the motives that cause them to act, the fact that each analysis both explains and leads to a new act, and, with the exception of Christian conversions, an action based solely on human decisions. However, the great popularity of tragedy during the forties was not only due to Corneille. Besides his tragicomedies and comedies, Du Ryer had at least five tragedies performed from 1640 to 1650 and Tristan at least three. Yet, among the numerous writers who, while remaining faithful to other genres, tried to go along with the fashion for regular tragedy, the best, apart from Corneille, was unquestionably Jean ROTROU. While he constantly wrote tragicomedies and comedies, Rotrou had, between 1646 and 1648, his three last tragedies performed, which were among the best of the period: SAINT GENEST, *Venceslas,* and *Cosroès.* More than Corneille, Rotrou remained attached to the illusions and the workings of chance of the former tragicomedy, as well as to the themes of the passivity or weakness of the hero faced with forces —political or superhuman—that transcend him. But like Corneille, Rotrou believed in finely drawn characters and a rigor of action even within the great variety of peripeties.

During the 1640's comedy, although still an inferior genre, was becoming more clearly formulated and acquiring a dignity that later led to its being termed "high comedy." On the one hand, it was generally written in alexandrines, was comprised of five acts, and although the unities were not always respected, tended toward tighter action and an intelligible chain of peripeties. Moreover, it began systematically to be drawn from two recent foreign sources: the sixteenth-century Italian *commedia erudita* and the Spanish *comedia.*

The Italian commedia offered extremely adventurous plots, similar to those of tragicomedy, and was peopled with conventional characters. After having written adaptations of Plautus' comedies, Rotrou contributed the best comedy inspired by Italy, *La Sœur* ("The Sister," 1645/46). Typical of the genre, the play is based on the confusion created by mistaken identities due to the kidnapping of the characters by Turkish pirates. Certain comedies of this type are occasionally enlivened by actual buffoons as characters: crafty valets, pedants, parasites, braggarts. But the interest lies largely in the skillful mechanism by which, from reversal to reversal and from discovery to discovery, the characters' fates change several times in a few hours until the happy ending is inevitably brought about by, at last, an unexpected return or the establishment of real identities.

To all appearances equally romanesque, the "Spanish" comedies proved to be richer and more exalting. They made less use of the mystery created by the kidnapping and substitution of children and kept more rigorously to the torments and heroic deeds of young, extremely passionate lovers in a Spain that, as in *Le Cid,* is violent and very touchy where honor is concerned. Blood often flows, and the characters duel or fight bulls, while comic relief is offered by gluttonous and cowardly valets drawn from the Spanish *graciosos* ("fools").

Initiated by Antoine de Metel d'Ouville, an imitator of Lope de Vega and Calderón, and satisfying the public's taste for exoticism, on the one hand, and passionate gallantry, on the other, this type of comedy moved in a very particular direction with the works of Pierre SCARRON and the acting of Jodelet of the Marais theater, who was probably the greatest French comic actor before Molière. As early as 1643, *Jodelet ou le maître valet* ("Jodelet or the Mastervalet") balances the violence of Spanish comedy (a girl seduced, murder, a duel) and its heroic style with a very special humor called "burlesque": Because of the needs of the plot, the gracioso Jodelet is obliged to pass himself off as his master, Don Juan; but being vulgar, cowardly, and gluttonous, Jodelet manages to be no more than a grotesque parody of the noble lover. Analogous contrasts are found in Scarron's *Jodelet duelliste* ("Jodelet the Fencer," 1645). In his *Don Japhet d'Arménie* ("Don Japheth of Armenia," 1647, performed again in 1651) the serious love story is almost eclipsed by the presence of Don Japhet—the fool of Emperor Charles V—who believes that he is descended from Noah, whose language is a constant hyperbolic parody of the heroic style, and who is humiliated in every way possible.

The critics of the high classical period scorned the burlesque spirit in theater, as well as in poetry and the novel, and saw nothing in it but the baseness of parody. Moreover, the brutal juxtaposition of touching or passionate adventures, expressed in seriously heroic language, and the most farcical humor, combined with a frenzied verbal imagination, was contrary to the classical spirit of unity of style. Nevertheless, burlesque brought frank laughter back to comedy and at the same time passed judgment on a certain extravagance of heroic theater.

The most unified and least extravagant—that is, the most classical—Spanish-type comedy of the 1640's was Pierre Corneille's *Le Menteur (The Liar,* 1643). Without violence, the action, located in Paris, is comprised of the vicissitudes of love that are typical of the genre, provoked by the fantastic lies of the hero—lies that are not burlesque buffooneries but true products of the imagination of a poet who is more charming than ridiculous and finally, as was Corneille's intention, admirable because of his very flaws.

The works of this period are characterized, not only by a tendency toward simplification, concentration, and the presentation of vigorous characters, but also by a taste for heroism, extreme and surprising acts, and transformations due to the moral effort of the characters or to illusions—all of which relate the works of this first period of French classicism to baroque art.

The Fronde considerably slowed down theatrical activity in Paris, perhaps because, during the uprising, life itself had become a tragicomedy. Moreover, the generation of 1630 seemed to be fading out: Rotrou died in 1650; Corneille, disappointed by his failure early in 1652, left the stage; Tristan limited his production to one pastoral and a comedy and died in 1655; Du Ryer, reduced to penury, devoted himself almost entirely to translating and died in 1658; and Mairet had retired from the theater in 1640 to go into diplomacy.

Meanwhile, tragedy itself fell into disfavor, due, according to some, to the incoherencies and defeat of the Fronde, during which the illusory aspect of the great political and moral ideals—which had been the subject matter of tragedy—gradually became evident. All that remained was the amusement procured by high comedy, which reached the height of fashion between 1650 and 1656: Scarron continued in his career, oscillating between burlesque and works in the vein of tragicomedy; Philippe QUINAULT was launched in 1653; and Thomas CORNEILLE, after his first comedy in 1649, had seven Spanish-type plays performed by 1656, the most renowned of which is *Le Geôlier de soi-même* ("His Own Jailer," 1655).

The taste for complex love stories, skillfully linked together, which ensured the success of high comedy, opened the way in 1656 for a new type of tragedy (sometimes called tragicomedy when it had a happy ending) based on gallantry, in the sense of amorous attention or pursuit. Actually, this period was characterized by the success of the great French *précieux* novels (concerned with the refinement of manners and language, the idealization of love, and the freedom of women), in which the heroic adventures of historical characters—who guaranteed the credibility of the anecdote—are inextricably linked to, or motivated by, the obligation of seeking perfection in love, according to the précieux imperatives. The heroes of this new préciosité, glorious kings and princes, borrowed from ancient history and hence worthy of the tragic genre, make world history conform to virtues or ambitions that are no longer political but gallant. The year 1656 marks the beginning of a new wave of tragedy, drawn from the new novels. Opening at the Marais theater in 1656, Thomas Corneille's *Timocrate* was more successful than any other play in the seventeenth century, lasting for about eighty successive performances, at a time when even twenty-five to thirty performances meant a triumph. Besides, it is probable that at the same moment the play was also performed at the Hôtel de Bourgogne.

Like *Le Cid,* this is a work that happened to be in perfect harmony with the public's taste at the time. (It should be noted that while popular audiences were still sovereign in the pit, the educated public, comprised of the learned, the précieuses, and members of literary salons and coteries, then determined the fate of most of the works and, on the whole, imposed its judgment on the rest of the spectators.) To begin with, as far as form is concerned, the unities and the proprieties were strictly observed: and the linking of scenes—a difficult technique that had made slow progress and the goal of which was never to leave the stage empty—was assured. Thus, the formal requirements were satisfied. As for substance, the play offered the pleasure of attending the performance of an episode from a fashionable pseudohistorical novel (La Calprenède's *Cléopâtre*). The action, full of reversals and misunderstandings, is based on the dual identity of a prince in love with an enemy queen. This type of dilemma is tragic to a certain degree, for it confronts the hero with a hundred problems of conscience. But it is also terribly artificial.

The fashion for plays with complicated and anguished love stories, in which historical characters disguise themselves, change identity, and juggle with high political interests, in order to satisfy the précieux code of perfect love, marks the end of the 1650's. Typical of the genre are Thomas Corneille's *Bérénice* (1657) and *Darius* (1659) and Philippe Quinault's *Amalasonte* (1657), *Le Feint Alcibiade* ("The False Alcibiades," 1658), and *La Mort de Cyrus* ("Cyrus' Death," 1658). These works of regular form, with plots that are complex but unified by the dialectics of love, show to a certain degree a return to the former theater of adventure: the old tragicomedy is mixed with Cornelian heroism, here deflected toward gallant love. Nevertheless, together with high comedy, they represent an important stage in the history of French classicism—the end result or, as it were, the formulation, in exaggerated form, of the desire for formal and psychological subtlety that had been evident since the 1630's.

While Thomas Corneille and Philippe Quinault were dominating the theater, in 1659 Pierre Corneille ended his silence and returned to the stage with the tragedy *Œdipe*, in which, on the one hand, the hero puts out his eyes with a very Cornelian challenge ("to take our revenge upon heaven, let us scorn its light"), but in which the very complex plot is centered around a dynastic marriage and includes a discussion of the obligation of Thésée, or Theseus, who has become the fashionable perfect lover.

This second period of French classical theater was characterized, not only by the triumph of gallantry, the adventures implied by it, and its oversubtle points of conscience, but also by a renewal of the doctrinary debates on the theater and by a new and searching examination of the meaning of the classical rules. Pierre Corneille played a foremost role in this debate with the publication, in 1660, of his works, accompanied by *examens* ("analyses") and three long "Discourses" on the art of theater. In the perspective of history these texts by Corneille may be considered an answer to the Abbé d'Aubignac's *Pratique du théâtre* (*The Whole Art of the Stage*), begun around 1640 and published in 1657. The two writers have several traits in common: Both were playwrights of the same generation (D'Aubignac was born in 1604 and had his tragedies performed during the 1640's); in their critical methods both make use of Aristotle but base their theories on the actual practice of dramaturgy —Corneille thinking mostly of his own works; both affirm that theater is not only morally useful but also a source of pleasure; and both believed in the need for a doctrine—that is, for rules and precepts drawn from Aristotle and from, above all, the great master-

works of the past, old and recent. The idea that the rules are necessary because they are based on reason and experience is the keystone of the French classical doctrines; but the conclusions drawn from that initial principle were greatly divergent.

For Corneille the unity of time was necessary but could extend to some thirty hours; for D'Aubignac, although twelve hours was acceptable, his ideal was to make the duration of the action coincide with that of the performance. For Corneille the action had to unfold in only one décor, but a décor that was not clearly defined, so that, without shocking the spectator, scenes might be performed that in reality were located in several different places in the same city; for D'Aubignac the action had to be situated in one set of rooms, and one only. A more important divergence is that which divided the two writers on the use of verisimilitude and historical truth. For Corneille that which is true (in other words, that which is affirmed by history or myth) was necessary; even if some particular grandiose or monstrous act was not probable, the authority of history led the spectator to believe in it, and the emotion provoked by it was all the stronger; on the other hand, the playwright had the right to transform details in order to reinforce the central truth. For D'Aubignac verisimilitude (in other words, submission to that which was acceptable to the delicate minds of the moderns) came before anything else, and thus imaginary subjects were often preferable, for the writer could comply integrally with the conventions of his day without being guilty of falsifying history. Both critics were also divided on the concept of action and on the structure of plays. For Corneille action was based on the unity of peril: The peripeties, the episodes, and even the subplots are all reactions, decisions, or acts directly provoked by some one peril, illustrate that peril, and transform it. For D'Aubignac tragic action was based on the portrayal of illustrious misfortunes; not that he was returning to the tragedy-lament of the Renaissance, but he limited the action to a swift play of the passions. That is why he wanted a simple and continuous plot, with a minimum of secondary incidents, and one that portrayed the action "at its very last moment"—that is, "as near to catastrophe as possible."

Thus, in 1660 Corneille confirmed the aesthetics of early classicism—its broad interpretation of the rules and its taste for extraordinary truths and for, above all, the dynamism of heroes. For his part, D'Aubignac, who admired Corneille more for the passions he portrayed than for the unified complexity of his characters' great deeds, paved the way for the swift tragedy of passion, "filled with little content," which was to be, in theory at least, the ideal of Racinian theater.

During the years that preceded Louis XIV's majority, a theatrical event took place in Paris that completely changed the direction taken by comedy: this event was the establishment of a third troupe, directed by Jean Baptiste Poquelin, called Molière. Well known and patronized in the provinces, the troupe, after thirteen years of peregrinations, set up in the Théâtre du Petit Bourbon. Far more spacious than the Hôtel de Bourgogne or the Marais theater, it was used mostly for performances of the Royal Ballet. When Molière took it over, he had to share it with an Italian company. At first only a minor event, Molière's presence in Paris came to the forefront of theatrical life with the performance in 1659 of his one-act farce LES PRÉCIEUSES RIDICULES.

Although no longer very original, high comedy in five acts and in verse was still, at that time, the only decorous and fashionable comic genre. Molière himself tried his hand at it, patterning himself after the Italians. However, the innovation that Molière brought to Paris, and which immediately divided the public into admirers and vilifiers, was the revival of a genre that had been dead in Paris since the retirement of Guillot-Gorju in 1641 and that, besides, had been scorned even before by the "delicate" audiences of the 1630's—farce, which was then called "little comedy" and which the provinces had continued to esteem. At a time when Paris was laughing either at the *commedia dell'arte* of the Italian company or the burlesque moments in high comedy, Molière brought back to the Paris stage one-act entertainments that were performed at the end of the show. To the themes and devices of the old French farce (cuckoldry, slapstick, and gratuitous verbal fantasy), he added a way of acting, a rhythm, and a sense of directing borrowed from his Italian colleagues. From the very beginning, Molière provoked laughter by returning to an elementary form of comedy that, at the same time, he transformed. The extraordinary success of *Les Précieuses* in December 1659 was due, not only to this new type of humor, but, above all, to the very subject of the play, which surprised the public. Not only had the conventional themes of farce been replaced by contemporary satire, but the lowest genre was drawing its substance from the most exquisite contemporary fashions and customs—a very bold innovation. Secondly, the farce was no longer concentrated on various adventures but on a trick played on some character; hence the genre gained in unity. Finally, *Les Précieuses* shifted the angle of the illusion, the very subject of comedy: it dealt with errors due, not to outer circumstances, as in the past, but rather to a natural blindness of the characters. Although Mascarille is a valet disguised as a précieux marquis, the objective of that crude masquerade is to show the blindness of Cathos and Magdelon. Thanks to the simplicity of the farce and to the inner fixed quality of the characters, the art of comedy was moving in the direction of so-called character comedy.

In 1662 Molière presented L'ECOLE DES FEMMES, a comedy in five acts and in verse that immediately provoked a great dispute and marks the definitive turning point of the art of comedy. Related to high comedy in its length, general form, and its romanesque denouement, the play is nevertheless based on farce, and the very simple plot is reminiscent of the farces dealing with cuckoldry. The work was savagely attacked, largely because of professional jealousy but also for moral and aesthetic reasons: On both levels it was considered a degradation of high comedy.

In two short plays of 1663, *La Critique de l'école des femmes* (*The Critique of the School for Wives*) and *L'Impromptu de Versailles* (*The Versailles Impromptu*), Molière answered his adversaries and drew up a theory of comedy as he understood it. To begin with, to the extent that it was a portrait of contemporary manners, the genre of comedy was placed above tragedy and its heroic extravagances. To the learned who reproached him with having been false to the rules, Molière answered that, on the one hand, the only objective of the rules was to give pleasure and that, on the other hand, he had respected the essence of them by making the behavior of his protagonist coherent and by contriving that all the episodes have one effect only: Each of the protagonist's acts, which are meant to make him triumph, turn, on the contrary, against him and punish him. To the précieuses and the prudes who reproached him with "filth," he showed that the somewhat strong expressions were justified by the character. Finally, he made clear that the art of comedy as a whole is based on an observation of the general follies of mankind and that verisimilitude consists, not in logic applied from the outside, but in references to what is true or possible in actual reality.

Molière's works are obviously richer and more varied than this outlined theory. Indeed, his intense theatricalism makes his plays more than a simple portrayal of customs and characters. Nevertheless, 1662 marks the victory of comedy with a simple action, based on the conflicts of the inner forces that constitute man, over comedy with romanesque plots.

During the 1660's and the beginning of the 1670's theater was particularly active and highly promoted. There were then three professional French troupes in Paris: those of the Hôtel de Bourgogne and the Marais, and Molière's. Since the Petit Bourbon was destroyed in order to enlarge the Louvre, Molière's company in 1660 took over the Théâtre du Palais-Royal, which was still a fairly uncomfortable theater but at least had the advantage of a tiered pit.

Writers and actors, despite the strong hostility of the pious (Jansenists, preachers, and members of the Compagnie du Saint Sacrement), enjoyed eminent patronage and pensions, which Louis XIV finally institutionalized. The king himself was directly interested in artistic activities and extended his personal patronage to Molière's troupe in 1665. This was the period of the great royal festivals at the Louvre, Saint-Germain, and especially Versailles, which in 1664 had begun to be enlarged and embellished. During these festivals the theatrical companies, and Molière's in particular, were invited to perform old and new plays. The king's taste was more or less sincerely copied by his court; and in turn, the town (that is, the Parisian public) generally went along with their views. Fortunately, young Louis XIV's taste was varied and ran to comedy, tragedy, and "machine plays." And like its king, the public wanted to laugh, cry, or be amazed by the magnificence of great spectacles.

The period of high classicism was relatively short: Molière died in 1673; Pierre Corneille stopped producing altogether in 1674; and Racine's career extended only from 1664 to 1677, with a short comeback between 1689 and 1691. Among the second-rate writers, Quinault forsook tragedy around 1670 for the writing of opera librettos, and Thomas Corneille fell into disfavor around 1680. Moreover, the production of that period was rather scant compared to the period of 1630–1650. It also seemed less varied, since the genres were better defined. Tragedy and comedy held sway, although tragicomedy, sometimes called "heroic comedy," was not completely dead; in addition, the taste for great spectacles made for the development of a new kind of theater, with tragic or comic subjects, but meant to amaze and enchant through the use of machines and music. Almost all the writers contributed tragedy-ballets, comedy-ballets, and machine plays.

In spite of Molière's preference and the proliferation of comedy, tragedy remained the higher genre, and in spite of the great success of secondary writers, Pierre Corneille was considered the unquestionable master of it until Racine's first triumph in 1667. When Corneille returned to the stage in 1659, his *Œdipe* was a success, perhaps because of its romanesque coloring, and in 1662 the success of *Sertorius* made it preferable for Corneille to live in Paris once again. There he was the center of a whole clique of admirers, writers, and fashionable people. But despite that support, the tragedies that followed, performed at the Hôtel de Bourgogne or at the Palais-Royal, were coldly received. Corneille then, in 1667, went into retirement yet again, interrupted in 1670 by *Tite et Bérénice,* which obviously he wrote to compete with Racine, who was then known to be writing BÉRÉNICE. The typically Cornelian denouement of *Tite et Bérénice* gave the play its success; and that same year Corneille had a triumph with *Psyché* (performed by Molière in the Tuileries theater)—a tragedy-ballet written in collaboration with Molière and Quinault. Two last plays in 1672 and 1674 seem to have interested the public but provoked no great enthusiasm. Thus, during those years, Pierre Corneille was a case of the great aging writer, considered the genius of the stage, and from whom a lot was expected, but who was often disappointing, while at the same time being deeply admired. His last works, on the whole, appeared complicated. Although the action is very tight, Corneille based it on a situation that was generally political, rather than on the passion or fate of one character. Several characters act and react to one another as a result of the situation, and the tragedy is thus made up of conflicts due to uncertainties and hesitations within which the characters—heroic, of course, but ambiguous—struggle. Such characters seek to affirm themselves, as in the tragedies of the 1640's, but self-affirmation is no longer a simple, difficult act; it becomes a tortuous quest, sometimes involving compromise, and one that often leads to defeat. Thus, Corneille's last tragedies gain in psychological and dramatic value what they lose in optimistic grandeur.

Compared with such original and profound works, the many tragedies of Thomas Corneille appear more as products of the times. He imitated his contemporaries, imitated himself, and to a degree satisfied every taste; he never completely eliminated the romanesque elements that still occasionally pleased the public, and he sought out subjects centered around political or historical situations, in the manner of his brother. It must be said, to his credit, that he realized that romanesque tragedy had to make way for the tragedy of passion—that is, a genre in which the simple violence of love prevailed over the subtlety of analyses and précieux acts. As early as 1661, with *Camma,* he anticipated the murderous and frenzied lovers of Racine's theater, and the play was a triumph. Much later, in 1672, with *Ariane,* Thomas Corneille wrote a very simple and very moving tragedy on despair in love. In 1678, before he fell into disfavor, he produced a tragedy with a modern subject, *Le Comte d'Essex* ("The Earl of Essex").

Before he veered off into opera, Philippe Quinault achieved glory with a few love tragedies. He too kept many romanesque effects but mostly sought to move the audience by the tenderness of his characters and their all-powerful love, to which they sacrifice all other interests. Such love, even if often expressed in an insipid manner, is fatal and becomes the touching justification for the relinquishment of heroic values.

Despite its unquestionable merits, the love tragedy in the manner of Thomas Corneille or Philippe Quinault seems very pale in comparison with the works of Jean RACINE, a former student at the Jansenist school of Port-Royal. After having had three plays refused and having been tempted by an ecclesiastical career, Racine, an ambitious young man of twenty-five, got his start in the theater in 1664, helped by Molière, with *La Thébaïde* (*The Theban Brothers*), a tragedy in the style of Rotrou and Pierre Corneille. It was a failure. However, in 1665 *Alexandre* (*Alexander the Great*), a gallant tragedy in the style of the period, was a success at the Palais-Royal and then at the Hôtel de Bourgogne, which Racine chose as his theater, betraying and forsaking Molière. His real triumph came in 1667, when he became a playwright of the first rank with ANDROMAQUE and achieved renown because of its originality, its success, and the dispute it provoked. Sensitive to the novelty of a work that threatened to dethrone the old master, the Corneille clique immediately attacked the play by minimizing it and accusing Racine of having written no more than a banal gallant tragedy in which lovers taken from fashionable novels were disguised as Greek heroes. Of course, as in the romanesque tragedies and then in the gallant tragedies of the 1660's, love is the motivating force of the play. But *Andromaque* is far superior to the fashion to which it is related. It is concerned, not with characters who act according to or against the literary code of love, but, couched in the vocabulary of the period, with brutal and elementary conflicts. Thus, in 1667 Racine did for tragedy what Molière had done for comedy in 1662: The very techniques of great tragedy or great comedy were shown to be the ideal methods for really bringing to light primitive forces, whether loathsome or laughable. The miracle—that is, the unique quality—of French high classicism was the discovery of that meeting point between the perfect rationalism of form that had been slowly developed over the decades and the fundamental irrationalism of human nature. That is why, if theater is essentially tension, this was great theater. Not only did Racine and Molière use tensions in the conflicts they staged, but their works themselves are tensions of the most extreme types—dazzling lights that pierced the depths of darkness.

With Racine, darkness takes the form of both psychology and fate. And the two are linked: the mechanism of love is irreversible; every cry, every gesture, is irretrievable. Thanks to Racine, fate was reintroduced into tragedy in an internal form: love is a curse on the soul that leads infallibly to murder, madness, or suicide. In all of Racine's works that feeling of fate is reinforced by the very structure of the plays. The extreme simplicity of form leaves only one road open for the characters to take, without the possibilities and hopes for evasion implied by complex plots. Moreover, Racine applied the Abbé d'Aubignac's rule: "Begin the play as near to catastrophe as possible"—that is, at a point when the characters are already prisoners of a whole past life of decisions and acts that condemn them to fall, with no appeal possible.

From 1667 to 1677 Racine had seven tragedies performed—enough to make him the equal of Corneille. This entire period was characterized by rivalries, plots, and disputes. The last attack was aimed at PHÈDRE, to which Racine's enemies contrasted Pradon's *Phèdre,* being performed at the same time. After that particularly vicious dispute, Racine left the theater and did not return to it until 1689, at the request of Mme. de Maintenon, with *Esther* and then in 1691 with ATHALIE, both biblical tragedies.

In spite of the striking differences between Pierre Corneille, the gallant writers, and Jean Racine, a new climate was generally apparent in the tragedy of the period. The heroes, of course, still had the grandeur characteristic of the genre, but they no longer dominated the inner forces that made them act. While in Corneille they became uncertain, troubled by contradictory impulses and passions, and prouder than they were self-controlled, in Racine they were destined for crimes and suffering over which they had no power. In other words, the tragedy in French high classicism is that of the loss of confidence in self-control and in inner freedom—the tragedy of the imperfection of human nature, its weaknesses, and, in the long run, the curse that hangs over it. And on the whole, it satisfied a public that wanted, above all, to be moved and to weep.

That same public wanted to laugh as well, and here Molière was the chief provider. The comedy he offered was extremely varied in its external aspects. Sometimes, with its slapstick, its cudgeling, and its verbal delirium, it remained very similar to farce. Sometimes, for the royal entertainments, the comedy became gallant and heroic, peopled by princely characters and situated in a romanesque universe. More often, it was concerned with characters clearly taken from contemporary reality, whether provincial, Parisian bourgeois, or aristocratic. Finally, every one of the genres had the possibility of including songs and ballets.

The unity of Molière's works lies at a deeper level, in his conception of the very substance of comedy: the presentation of characters who, out of blind egotism or stupidity, deny reality and seek to impose their false visions of themselves and of the world or who, through egotistic, altruistic, or poetic calculation, consciously invent illusions in order to take in the others. Since the creative impulse of both types of characters is extremely vigorous, all the humor comes from the way they contrive to frustrate each other's plans as well as those of the "reasonable" characters, who try to open their eyes or unmask them.

Molière's career itself could not have been more turbulent, for Louis XIV's protection was not enough to secure him from his enemies. The attack launched against him at the time of *L'École des femmes* was renewed even more virulently in 1664, when it became known that he had written TARTUFFE, a play about a pious hypocrite, which was thus prohibited until 1669. However, in spite of his enemies, Molière had brought farce back to the stage and the comedy of character and of manners into fashion. Clearly, although their output was copious, Molière's contemporaries and rivals remained far beneath him to the extent that they broke away less than he from the former styles of comedy or else merely imitated him. Noteworthy, nevertheless, were the works of Donneau de Visé and those of the actor Hauteroche. Even Jean Racine, with *Les Plaideurs (The Litigants,* 1668), achieved no more than a rather dull satire on judiciary customs, though the play did offer a few amusing silhouettes and showed a certain sense of farce.

Besides tragedy, with its single and imprecise décor, and comedy, which was generally confined to a salon or some bourgeois house, the production of the period offered many works, tragic and comic, that compensated for the very human and simplified aspect of the two major genres by the use of machines. As early as 1650 Corneille's *Andromède* had dazzled audiences with its changing décors, flying chariots, heavenly apparitions, and many representations of mythological gods. Louis XIV's taste for the sumptuous encouraged the development of that genre of entertainment, exemplified by the gigantic spectacles in 1664 at Versailles, Molière's *Amphitryon* (1668), and Corneille, Molière, and Quinault's *Psyché* (1671). Akin to opera, the ballet entertainments and machine plays enjoyed a great freedom from the rules: Fantasy was allowed and styles were mixed. Actually, they meant an escape into an artificial world where everything was at once possible and false, far from the cruel realities presented by actual tragedy and comedy.

During the 1670's the rules and principles that had been set forth since 1630 became definitively established. After Chapelain and the Abbé d'Aubignac, the doctrine was picked up, most particularly in Racine's prefaces and in the works of Father René Rapin and Nicholas Boileau (*Art poétique,* 1674). It corresponded at that time to the taste of the public, and the great writers generally and naturally conformed to it. But because of its formalism, it soon was to contribute to the creation of works without either originality or content.

After Molière's death in 1673, the French theater went through a difficult period. The Théâtre du Palais-Royal was given over to Lully and opera; Molière's troupe joined up with the Marais company. In 1680 the Comédie Française was founded when that new troupe merged with the Hôtel de Bourgogne company. There was thus in Paris only one French professional company, which was more and more strictly controlled by the king. Under pressure from the pious, who gained increasing influence as a result of the king's renewed involvement in religion, and from Mme. de Maintenon, Louis XIV's wife, all types of regulations were applied to drama, culminating in censorship in 1702. Meanwhile, in 1697, the Italian troupe was driven out. Indeed, there was only one encouraging event: In 1689 a new theater of Italian design was built for the Comédie Française.

With Racine's retirement in 1677, writers of tragedy, such as Jean Galbert de CAMPISTRON, became prisoners of their models, of a doctrine that was too formalistic, and of a new tendency toward the insipid, in the manner of Quinault. Actually, the most authentic tragedy late in the century was one of two biblical plays by Racine, *Athalie,* written as part of a movement attempting to reconcile theater and religion. Then, at the end of Louis XIV's reign, an original writer came to the fore: Prosper Jolyot de CRÉBILLON, who went back to the romanesque tradition but, in the name of Aristotelian terror, oriented tragedy toward frenzied madness and horror, in contempt of the proprieties.

Under the Regency (1715–1721) a new writer of tragedy came to the stage who considered himself— and was considered by most of his contemporaries —the successor to Corneille and Racine: VOLTAIRE. From the performance of *Œdipe* in 1718 until his death in 1778 he had some twenty tragedies performed, all classical in form and all moving, tender, or heroic. Yet, despite undeniable moments of passion and strong, living characters—in ZAÏRE most especially—his plays served as vehicles for philosophical ideas, particularly the idea of religious tolerance. Performed for the most part with great success, they nevertheless pointed to the end of high classical tragedy.

Among the many successors of Molière, the most noteworthy were Jean-François REGNARD, whose originality consisted in exaggerating the drollery of language and acts, sometimes with great brutality,

ENGRAVING OF A SCENE FROM REGNARD'S *Le Joueur* (NEW YORK PUBLIC LIBRARY)

ENGRAVING OF A SCENE FROM DESTOUCHES'S *Les Glorieux* (NEW YORK PUBLIC LIBRARY)

and Florent DANCOURT, who emphasized the new manners and customs. However, the best comedy of all, which was a study both of character and of the customs at the end of Louis XIV's reign, was TURCARET. This comedy, by Alain-René LESAGE, is based entirely on the quest for money. As a reaction to the cynicism found in these works, which was very far from the spirit of Molière, the playwrights of the 1730's and 1750's—typified by DESTOUCHES— while going back to Molière's general pattern, put great emphasis on virtue, thus shifting comedy's center of interest. Gradually, comedy became moralistic or tearful, since its objective was not so much to provoke laughter as a reaction to the characters' flaws but rather to make the audience cry over virtuous characters, who always ended by converting the villains, in a general atmosphere of touching sentimentality. In other words, despite a respect for classical form, comedy was moving toward *drame bourgeois.*

The most original writer at the beginning of Louis XV's reign was Pierre de MARIVAUX, who was interested less in characters than in the very detailed analysis of the surprises, hesitations, bad faith, and joy created by the early stages of love. He had little admiration for Molière and jeered at tragedy. His theater, related to classicism in its formal rigor and psychological interest, is almost unique in the history of the French theater.

By the end of the seventeenth century the unities began to be criticized. Tragedy, most particularly, was attacked because of its fixed nature. In 1721 Antoine Houdar de La Motte, in order to renew the genre, called for "multiplicity" and the use of prose. Finally, around 1760, Denis DIDEROT and Pierre Caron de BEAUMARCHAIS rejected classical tragedy as outmoded and extolled a serious genre that would be a mirror of life, with its sorrows and joys, in which modern characters would be involved in contemporary family or professional situations and which would serve to demonstrate the difficult but grandiose practice of domestic and bourgeois virtues. Thus, the borderline between the genres was to disappear and a new genre of theater was born: DRAME BOURGEOIS. In practice, the works themselves were mediocre, the best of them still being *Le Philosophe sans le savoir* (*The Duel,* 1765) by Michel Jean SEDAINE.

The history of classicism in the theater is generally

thought to stop at that date. In fact, plays of classical structure continued to be written during and after the revolution. And in 1943 Jean Cocteau amused himself by writing a classical tragedy in the manner of Quinault: *Renaud et Armide*. As for the classical spirit, it survived in writers concerned with a tight, economical style and psychological truth. Nevertheless, the rigors of the classical doctrine were discredited after the 1760's, opening the way to the freedom of Romantic theater and to the varied forms of modern drama.

The monumental work by Henry C. Lancaster, *A History of French Dramatic Literature in the Seventeenth Century*, 9 vols. (1952), followed by *Sunset, a History of Parisian Drama in the Last Years of Louis XIV, 1701–1715* (1945) and by *French Tragedy in the Time of Louis XV and Voltaire, 1715–1774* (2 vols., 1950), gives detailed information on almost all the dramatists and their works during the period of French classicism. For a less scholarly study, chiefly concerned with Molière, Corneille, and Racine, see Martin Turnell, *The Classical Moment* (1947). P. J. Yarrow, in *The Seventeenth Century, 1600–1715* (1967), studies the theater in detail and situates it in the context of the literature of the period.—Ja. G.

pre-Romantic (late eighteenth-century) drama. The drama of the second half of the eighteenth century in France, like that of the nineteenth century generally, is germinal in character. Although the majority of plays written and performed were cast in traditional molds and were timid pieces, imitative of the few striking or unique models each movement produced, these models stand out because of their departures from the conventional forms, because of the risks their authors took in writing them. They paved the way for the myriad disruptive and creative experiments (Romanticism, realism, naturalism, symbolism, avant-gardism) of the nineteenth and twentieth centuries. In 1750 it was customary for young aspiring playwrights to compose docile stereotyped tragedies of five acts in verse on classical themes in the manner of Racine, or comedies satirizing social types in the style of Molière. The few plays that survive and possess literary merit show initiative and individuality, however feeble.

Voltaire was still writing for the stage in 1760 when Denis DIDEROT saw his first play, *Le Père de famille* ("Father of a Family"), produced. Published in 1758, this work and *Le Fils naturel* ("The Illegitimate Son," written 1757, performed 1772) are the first examples of the DRAME BOURGEOIS. The plays themselves are sentimental, declamatory, and melodramatic, but Diderot's theory, expressed in *Entretiens sur "Le Fils naturel": Dorval et moi* (*Conversations on "The Natural Son,"* 1757), *Discours sur la poésie dramatique* (1758), and other essays, acted as the springboard for the mid-nineteenth-century social plays of Émile Augier and Alexandre Dumas fils. Influenced by the *comédies larmoyantes,* or "sad comedies," of Nivelle de La Chaussée (1692–1754) and by such English attempts at middle-class tragedy as George Lillo's *The London Merchant* (1731) and Edward Moore's *The Gamester* (1753), Diderot intensified the break with classical tradition by advocating the abandonment of classical tragedy and comedy in favor of social dramas of middle-class characters. Moral conclusions were to be drawn from

pathetic situations for the spectator's benefit. A better example of drame bourgeois than Diderot's plays, because less pretentious and even humorous, was *Le Philosophe sans le savoir* (*The Duel,* 1765). This play by Michel Jean SEDAINE about a family problem in a middle-class home is concluded on a note of bourgeois civic virtue.

In the same year a poor play, but one nevertheless indicative of a new interest in France in Shakespeare and English history, *Le Siège de Calais* by Pierre Laurent Buirette de Belloy (1727–1775), mingled a conventional style with grotesque details. Jean François Ducis (1733–1816) adapted, from poor existing translations, several of Shakespeare's more popular tragedies, and his script was used for the first production of *Hamlet* (1769) in France. The French Revolution produced one playwright who appealed to the growing revolutionary fervor, Marie Joseph Chénier (1764–1811). His *Charles IX, ou la Saint-Barthélemy* (1789) combined dramatic tension with poetic language and disguised contemporary events. Although the revolution, in closing the theaters and then reopening them to all comers, put an end to the monopoly of the Comédie Française and the Opéra in 1791, it did not cause a great hiatus in the life of the popular theater, as did the closing of the theaters in London in 1642. Nearly forty new theaters emerged in Paris, but Napoleon's classical taste suppressed experimentation and true originality in the better playwrights of the First Empire (1804–1814) and stifled all but imitative and second-rate dramatic talent. Népomucene Lemercier (1771–1840), the most promising playwright at this time, tried unsuccessfully to establish historical romance in his *Pinto* (1800), characterized by fancy, humor, and wit, and *Christophe Colomb,* which caused a riot at its première in 1809 because Lemercier dared to discard the classical unities and use familiar language in the dialogue.

But only one playwright was destined to stand out in the chaos of tears, piety, blood, and dullness that characterizes most of the later eighteenth century. Pierre Augustin Caron de BEAUMARCHAIS wrote the two best comedies of the century, though the production of both encountered great difficulties and delays. *The Barber of Seville* began as a light opera but was finally produced as a brilliant comedy in 1775, after a delay of three years. Beaumarchais meanwhile founded the Société des Auteurs in order to attack

DRAWING OF A SCENE FROM BEAUMARCHAIS'S *The Barber of Seville* (RONDEL COLLECTION, BIBLIOTHÈQUE DE L'ARSENAL, PARIS)

the actors' traditional system of payment to authors and other privileges. Nevertheless, the second comedy, THE MARRIAGE OF FIGARO, was performed in 1784 after a similar delay of three years. Both are swift, gay comedies of intrigue centered on Figaro, the barber and valet of Count Almaviva, and they are the sources of the famous operas *The Barber of Seville* (1816) by Rossini and *The Marriage of Figaro* (1786) by Mozart. In the first the count wins Rosine with the clever barber's help. In the second, the count tries to seduce Figaro's fiancée, Suzanne. The social satire directed at the aristocracy, although it brought Beaumarchais a brief imprisonment, was applauded by this same class, which was dazzled, attracted, even a bit resentful, but apparently blind to the political significance of the satire. Ironically, this play in its own way anticipated the spirit of the revolution, from which the aristocracy was to suffer. Beaumarchais's characterization, dialogue, and spirit were original. Figaro and several other characters are uniquely individualized. But in overall technique Beaumarchais was strictly traditional, taking over the comedy of intrigue from his predecessors Pierre Carlet de Chamblain de Marivaux (1688–1763) and Molière, and ultimately from Plautus and Latin comedy.

After the revolution the many new theaters attracted the semiliterate, even the illiterate, masses. Consequently, the stage was dominated by several popular forms of theatrical entertainment, including operetta, or *opéra comique; vaudeville* (light, satirical songs originally sung at the theaters of the Paris fairs with new words rhymed to old popular airs; later, light, seriocomic plays incorporating such songs); and MÉLODRAME. This last genre flourished in the popular theaters of the Paris boulevards and, in the successful hands of Guilbert de PIXÉRÉCOURT, provided a foundation for the new dramas of the Romantic school that thrived from about 1829 to 1843. Charles Nodier, a leader of the Romantic movement, claimed that "romantic drama is nothing but melodrama ennobled by verse." The heyday of the mélodrame corresponded more or less to the period of Pixérécourt's active career, 1797 to 1835, and the stereotyped plots, characters, and situations were crystallized during this period. In its arbitrary blend of the comic and the tragic and its dependence upon unconventional, versatile, and emotional acting, mélodrame prepared theatergoers for the techniques used by the later Romantic writers. Several famous Romantic actors got their start in the second-class, popular theaters along the Boulevard du Crime (so named from its serving the interests of the writers and actors of these lurid tales of mystery and terror). Early in the nineteenth century Pixérécourt's more popular pieces found their way to London and America, often in unacknowledged adaptations, and thus helped to spawn innumerable melodramas, soap operas, and westerns of radio, film, and television.

Romantic (early nineteenth-century) drama. Meanwhile, the Comédie Française continued to offer a fast-depleting audience of aged and pedantic spectators a cold, unappetizing fare of tragedies and tasteless comedies. A change was needed and it came with the full tide of Romanticism, in the form of a manifesto, *Le Préface de Cromwell* (1827) by Victor HUGO. Influenced in part by the Paris performances

A DRAWING OF THE PREMIÈRE OF VICTOR HUGO'S *Hernani*

by English actors in 1822 of plays by Shakespeare, Hugo demanded a new kind of drama, particularly historical plays vitalized by scenery and costumes to give local color, unhampered by the classical unities and freely combining the tragic and the comic (the sublime and the grotesque) with an intensified, ennobled action. Popular appeal centered on the romantic hero, a Byronic individualist, lonely and introspective, inspired by pure love for an idealized and elusive heroine or some lofty ideal, such as personal or family honor. Hugo's plays, with the possible exception of RUY BLAS, have little appeal today, for he was much more a poet than a dramatist. His characters are essentially unreal, and he relied heavily upon the trappings of melodrama. His *Hernani* (1830) signaled the victory of the Romantic movement in the theater, when the Romanticists defeated the neoclassicists in a noisy fracas at the première. The movement came virtually to an end in 1843 when his *Les Burgraves* ("The Governors") failed. While Hugo was the acknowledged leader of Romanticism, Alexandre DUMAS père was a more inventive and gifted dramatist. The first of the Romantics to have a play produced, Dumas's *Henri III et sa cour* ("Henry III and His Court") was performed early in 1829. His other pieces were drawn from history, legend, and his own novels. His best plays are *Antony* (1831), a tragedy of adulterous passion and a skillful study of the unconventional lover-hero, and the wonderfully inventive melodrama *La Tour de Nesle* (*The Tower of Nesle,* 1832). Alfred de VIGNY helped to popularize Shakespeare by doing the most imaginative and faithful translation of *Othello* yet attempted in France. *Othello, ou le more de Venise* ("Othello, The Moor of Venice") was performed in the summer of 1829. His only outstanding original play, *Chatterton* (1835), is an attempt at bourgeois tragedy, showing the misery of the poet at the hands of society. Vigny focuses upon the destiny of the central character rather than those staples of Romanticism, intrigue and local color.

The most original talent of the Romantics, however, was that of Alfred de MUSSET, whose plays, because they were not written to be staged, were unhampered by contemporary theatrical conventions. The fact that many of them were not performed until years after they were written reduced their influence on the acted drama of the day. They are either poetic fantasies reminiscent of Shakespeare or light, clever enactments of popular proverbs. Although many of these have a unique delicacy and fanciful charm, the best play of the period, LORENZACCIO, is a penetrating psychological study of a would-be idealist hopelessly depraved by a life of crime. Like many of Musset's plays, it externalizes conflicting forces and tensions within the author, the struggle between the stable idealist and the dissolute cynic.

Fifteen years after its inception, Romanticism in France was officially dead. In 1838 the appearance of the greatest actress of her day, Éliza Félix Rachel (1821–1858), as Camille in a revival of Corneille's *Horace,* and her subsequent re-creation of a variety of classical roles, especially Racine's Phèdre, hastened the demise of Romantic drama and seemed to promise a classical revival in the French theater. In 1843 the neoclassic drama *Lucrèce* by François Ponsard (1814–1867) was applauded, while Hugo's *Les Burgraves* failed, marking the close of a tempestuous, flamboyant period. And yet, ironically, what is perhaps the best (certainly it is the most popular) of all Romantic plays, CYRANO DE BERGERAC, by Edmond ROSTAND, was produced in 1897, fifty-four years after the close of the period. In its delightful and harmonious blend of comedy and pathos, the dashing virility and touching humanity of Cyrano himself, the tenderness of its idealized love, the swashbuckling bravado of its action, its wit, and the imaginative *brio* of its language, *Cyrano* surpasses all that the Romantic playwrights sought to achieve in the first half of the century.

realistic (mid-nineteenth-century) drama. The demand for a robust, living theater from the late 1830's on was satisfied, however, not by a classical revival, but by the beautifully constructed and vivacious, but artificial, plays of Eugène SCRIBE and his immediate successor, Victorien Sardou. These plays established a genre known as the WELL-MADE PLAY. At a time when the drama had become lofty, insipid, and formless, Scribe concocted bourgeois comedies of common sense that, in their own way, helped to restore some of the compact dramatic form that had characterized the best neoclassical plays. Besides entertaining the prosperous middle class, his more serious plays—*Le Mariage d'argent* ("Marriage for Money," 1827), *Bertrand et Raton, ou l'art de conspirer* (*A School for Politicians,* 1833), *La Calomnie* ("Slander," 1840), and *Le Verre d'eau, ou les effets et les causes* (*The Glass of Water,* 1840)—usually offer a modicum of moral thesis or satire, for Scribe followed Molière's precept, inherited from Horace's *Ars Poetica,* that the theater should both please and instruct. His formula for making a moral thesis amusing attracted Augier and the younger Dumas to the technique of the well-made play. After the revolution of 1848 they led the theater in the direction of a more serious social drama and wrote *pièces à thèse* ("thesis" or "problem plays") that depended heavily upon the well-made play. Indeed, whereas the precise classical

forms of tragedy and comedy and their various components were being disseminated among the variety of genres, the well-made play continued to shape and control many of these genres, from the artificial historical romances of the declining Romantic school, through the bourgeois comedies of Scribe and his followers, to the farcical plays (*Un Chapeau de paille d'Italie, An Italian Straw Hat;* 1851) of Eugène LABICHE, the light operas (*La Vie parisienne,* "Parisian Life"; 1866) and musical burlesques (*La Belle Hélène,* "Beautiful Helen"; 1864) of Henri Meilhac (1831–1897) and Ludovic Halévy (1834–1908), with music by Jacques Offenbach, and those highly developed bedroom farces *Le Monde où l'on s'ennui* ("The Status Seekers," 1881) of Edouard Pailleron (1834–1899) and *La Dame de. Chez Maxime* ("The Lady from Maxime's," 1899) of Georges FEYDEAU.

The moral and social corruptions of the Second Empire (1852–1870) claimed the attention of Émile AUGIER and Alexandre DUMAS fils. Diderot's eighteenth-century conception of social drama, sidetracked by Romanticism, now was realized in about fifteen major plays apiece that the two playwrights produced in the course of careers lasting more than thirty years. Augier, who had contributed verse plays to the short-lived classical reaction against Romanticism in the 1840's, soon began to produce satirical thesis plays in prose that, in their penetrating studies of character, laud the virtues of the bourgeoisie and damn the greed, hypocrisy, and cynicism of the era of Napoleon III. His most outstanding play compares the moral values of the old aristocracy with those of the new wealthy bourgeoisie; *Le Gendre de M. Poirier* (*Monsieur Poirier's Son-in-Law,* written in collaboration with Jules Sandeau, performed 1854) analyzes sympathetically the class struggle as it affects marriage, and favors the virtues of the older class (honor, devotion, respect, love) over the stupid pride, selfishness, and vulgarity of the newer.

Dumas's plays possess emotional power, but he was more didactic than Augier and employed *raisonneurs* (obvious mouthpieces for his own views), which give much of his work an artificial and self-conscious sermonizing quality. His work is further marred by a rigidity of attitude toward social evils and a distortion of them stemming from his own unhappy and rebellious childhood. Even so, the more outstanding plays—*Le Demi-monde* (1855), *Les Idées de Mme Aubray* ("Mrs. Aubray's Ideas," 1867), *La Femme de Claude* (*The Wife of Claude,* 1873), and *Denise* (1881)—influenced later naturalistic experimenters and prepared Dumas's audience, through an intense discussion of social and ethical problems, for the cataclysmic breaks with convention still to come with the avant-garde theater of revolt.

Of the many playwrights to perpetuate the tradition of the well-made play, Victorien SARDOU most resembled Scribe in technique and in the quantity and quality of his plays. The discriminating reader can list three or four merits of Sardou, or possibly excuses for him, but he is altogether a more facile, shallower playwright than his master. Unfortunately, his most popular plays were wretchedly adapted in English. Late in his career, however, Sardou did create some impressive acting roles for the incomparable Sarah Bernhardt, notably *Fédora* (1882), *Théo-*

dora (1884), and *La Tosca* (1887). Then too, Sardou contributed a Gallic zest and tang to some of his characters, like Suzanne in the early and ever-popular *Les Pattes de mouche* (*A Scrap of Paper*, 1860), and to his farce *Divorçons* (*Let's Get a Divorce!*, 1880). And, magician-like, he could draw gorgeous historical pageants and spectacles out of a theater wardrobe and prop box (*Patrie!* "Fatherland"; 1869). But in the last analysis, Sardou, who attempted every genre, from thesis drama to comédie-vaudeville, from historical romance to farce, reduced all subjects he treated to a commonplace, trivial level, and in spite of great theatrical gifts, he failed to breathe life into most of his characters.

naturalistic (late nineteenth-century) drama. The first period of realism, dominated by the well-made play, had about run its course, although Scribean dramaturgy has continued to the present day in comedies of manners, social plays, and farces in France, England, and America. Another revolution in the arts, marking the beginnings of the modern, or avant-garde, drama, was at hand. The formation of two experimental theaters, the Théâtre Libre (1887–1896) by André Antoine (1858–1943) and the Théâtre d'Art (1890–1893) by Paul Fort (1872–1960), gave impetus to two new movements, naturalism (see REALISM AND NATURALISM) and anti-naturalism (or symbolism), respectively. But the first seeds of naturalism had already been sown in the theater by way of the novel. While the new realism was evolving in the novels of Zola, Balzac, Flaubert, and the Goncourts, Émile ZOLA dramatized his novel *Thérèse Raquin* (1867). Performed in 1873, it was the first naturalistic drama in France and prepared the way for the plays of Henry Becque, its Preface serving as a manifesto for the new naturalistic revolution in the theater. Zola called for the scientific study of heredity and environment. The stage was to become a laboratory where human behavior could be clinically dissected, especially that of the lower middle class. His views reflected the growing importance of the positivistic philosophy of Auguste Comte and the environmental determinism of the historian Hippolyte Taine.

Repelled by the corruption and immorality in Parisian life, and a determined opponent of the well-made play, Henry BECQUE fought for years to get his two great naturalistic plays accepted by leading theaters. THE VULTURES was ultimately performed in 1882 and *La Parisienne* (*Woman of Paris*) in 1885. Uncompromisingly photographic and dispassionately condemnatory, these plays, with little action and no conventional structure, caused an uproar. They possessed a feature demanded by Zola (though Becque in fact disagreed with many of Zola's precepts): They were *tranches de vie* ("slices of life"), recreating on the stage situations drawn from sordid reality. *La Parisienne* was also the first of the *comédies rosses* ("cynical comedies") that were popular in the closing years of the century.

At the Théâtre Libre Antoine produced several of these cynical comedies, including *La Sérénade* (1887) by Jean Jullien (1854–1919) and *Les Inséparables* (1889) by Georges Ancey (1860–1926). Antoine also sought out experimental works, not necessarily naturalistic, by then little-known French playwrights, such as Georges de Porto-Riche (1849–

1930), François de Curel (1854–1929), Henri Lavedan (1859–1940), Eugène Brieux, and Georges Courteline. And he enriched and broadened the narrowly self-contained cultural milieu of France by staging controversial works by the great European dramatists Henrik Ibsen, August Strindberg, Gerhardt Hauptmann, Giovanni Verga, and Leo Tolstoy.

Porto-Riche's *Amoureuse* (*A Loving Wife*, 1891), written shortly after Antoine produced his *La Chance de Françoise* (*Françoise' Luck*, 1888), established a precedent for penetrating plays treating the psychology of love and marriage and was followed in this category by *Amants* ("Lovers," 1895) by Maurice Donnay (1859–1945). Curel's *Les Fossiles* (*The Fossils*), staged at the Théâtre Libre in 1892, studies the predicament of a noble family living in a world no longer aristocratic. Lavedan, who had had some brief dialogues performed by Antoine in 1888, was destined to have some dozen plays of contemporary manners produced in Paris between 1891 and 1914, of which *Le Prince d'Aurec* (1892) is one of the more penetrating in its portrait of an aristocratic snob. *Boubouroche*, a witty but brutal farce about a gullible cuckold by Georges COURTELINE, was produced at the Théâtre Libre in 1893.

Of all the playwrights to graduate from Antoine's experimental theater, Eugène BRIEUX was the most significant and also the most naturalistic. Dedicated to a theater aimed at the cure of social evils, he concentrated too narrowly on immediate problems of politics, divorce, birth control, social disease, and gambling, thereby courting the possibility of oblivion. Nevertheless, he created a few viable plays with plausible characters and moving situations. His greatest play, *La Robe rouge* (*The Red Robe*, 1900), universalizes injustice and human degradation stemming from the temptation of men to misuse authority. Later works, like *Les Avariés* (*Damaged Goods*, 1905) which exposes the ravages of venereal disease, aroused timely controversy in England and America but remain ineffective as drama.

symbolist and avant-garde (late nineteenth-century) drama. Meanwhile, the objective imitation of reality was being challenged by Fort's Théâtre d'Art, which developed a new kind of artistic truth deriving from the symbolistic poetry and theories of Stéphane Mallarmé. Fort used nonobjective scenery and poetic effects to create a mood and an inner reality to be discerned through the outward ritual. In 1893 Aurélien Marie Lugné-Poë (1869–1940) succeeded Fort with the Théâtre de l'Oeuvre, which became the temple of the avant-garde. Here the commercial drama of the boulevards was opposed by the SYMBOLISM of *Pelléas et Mélisande* (1893) by Maurice MAETERLINCK and the crude, nihilistic farce *Ubu Roi* (*King Ubu*, 1896) by Alfred Jarry. These very different works opened, respectively, the two main roads over which the plays of the twentieth century would travel: the literary plays of such dramatists as Paul Claudel, Jean Giraudoux, Jean-Paul Sartre, and Jean Anouilh, and the so-called antitheater of Samuel Beckett, Arthur Adamov, Jean Genet, and Eugène Ionesco. Other early plays of Maeterlinck, like *L'Intruse* (*The Intruder*), *Les Aveugles* (*The Blind*), both performed 1891, and *L'Intérieur* (*Home*, 1895), exemplify his theory of "static" or mystical "inner" drama, depicting, through states of feeling rather than physical action, man's fear of the hidden forces of destiny. Maeterlinck's belief that marionettes (actors "spiritualized by distance") could express the silent language of the soul better than speaking actors anticipates, indirectly at least, the use of masks and "distanced" characters in the plays of Genet, Eugene O'Neill, and Bertolt Brecht.

Edith Melcher, *Stage Realism in France Between Diderot and Antoine* (1928), traces advancements in realistic staging and production (advocated by Denis Diderot) from the mélodrames of Pixérécourt to the plays of Zola. J. B. Ratermanis and W. R. Irwin, *The Comic Style of Beaumarchais* (1961), analyze in detail the comic techniques of *The Barber of Seville* and *The Marriage of Figaro*. Alexander Lacey, *Pixérécourt and the French Romantic Drama* (1928), describes in detail the technique of the mélodrame and traces the influence of this technique on the principal plays of Victor Hugo, Alexandre Dumas père, and Alfred de Vigny. F. Rahill, *The World of Melodrama* (1967), discusses, in the context of their times, the most memorable and influential French, English, and American melodramas of the eighteenth and nineteenth centuries. S. S. Stanton, ed., "Introduction to the Well-Made Play," in *Camille and Other Plays* (1957), analyzes the dramatic technique of several playwrights—Eugène Scribe, Victorien Sardou, Émile Augier, and Alexandre Dumas fils—who wrote well-made plays in the realistic tradition. B. H. Clark, *Contemporary French Dramatists* (1915), discusses the chief plays of the outstanding naturalistic and realistic playwrights. F. W. Chandler, *The Contemporary Drama of France* (1921), has a systematic arrangement of playwrights by genres: "Precursors of the Moderns," "Masters of Stagecraft," "Naturalism and the Free Theatre," "Ironic Realists," "Moralists," "Poets and Romancers," "Makers of Mirth," "Reformers," and so forth, that offsets rather brief, general summaries of most of the important plays. H. A. Smith, *Main Currents of Modern French Drama* (1925), thoroughly discusses the chief movements, playwrights, and plays of the nineteenth and early twentieth centuries. S. A. Waxman, *Antoine and the Théâtre Libre* (1924, reprinted 1964), discusses the naturalistic drama generally, the Théâtre Libre, and the contribution of its founder, André Antoine. An appendix lists by author and year of performance the plays produced at the Théâtre Libre. J. Chiari, *The Contemporary French Theatre* (1958), analyzes the "flight from naturalism," principally in the twentieth century, but takes Edmond Rostand as his point of departure. A. Symons, *The Symbolist Movement in Literature* (rev. ed., 1958), contrasts the shortcomings of Émile Zola's naturalistic style with the merits of Maurice Maeterlinck's mystical style.—S. S. S.

twentieth century. The theater lives or dies depending upon the support of a community. It is a spectacle mounted with the hope of attracting and holding a public that has to be renewed every evening. The thought of a man as expressed in a literary text and the physical appearance of men on the stage form the substance of what is called theater, provided there is a paying audience in front of the stage, assembled in order to watch and hear the unfolding of some dramatic action. Theoretical writing on the theater is abundant in France. There are contributions from actor-directors (Louis Jouvet, Jean-Louis Barrault), philosophers (Henri Gouhier, Gabriel Marcel), theater administrators (Pierre-Aimé Touchard), playwrights (Henry de Montherlant), and theater critics (Robert Kemp, Pierre Brisson). Each writer, in his own particular approach to the theater, has tried to explain the fundamental mystery of the art: the experience of communion, rather than mere communication, that has to take place between the man acting a given character on the stage and the spectator following the action and listening to the speeches.

If the plays of the modern French theater do not fulfill the laws of classical tragedy or classical comedy, the most successful among them do create and sustain an atmosphere of tragedy and an atmosphere of comedy. The fundamental divergence between the two genres of tragedy and comedy still exists in forms that only superficially give the impression of mingling or confusing the genres. In such plays as *Break of Noon* by Paul Claudel, *Queen After Death* by Montherlant, *The Flies* by Jean-Paul Sartre, and even such experimental plays as *The Bald Soprano* by Eugène Ionesco, *Endgame* by Samuel Beckett, and THE CAR CEMETERY by Fernando ARRABAL, a tension is created by the drama. It is a Dionysian tension in the sense that the spectator can easily feel his own fate merged with the fate of the character he is watching.

One of the oldest centers of the French theater is the Comédie Française, which has been playing almost uninterruptedly for three hundred years. By its very nature as a state-subsidized theater, it is a kind of museum of French dramatic art. The members of this company are distrustful of vogues, and yet in recent years they have performed such new plays as Ionesco's HUNGER AND THIRST and Jean Genet's *The Screens*. The function of the Comédie Française, far from being that of discovering the new significant plays, is rather that of protecting the past, of constantly reviving and enlivening it. The privilege of its actors is that of playing a variety of different roles over a number of years and thus achieving a smoothness and harmony of ensemble that is almost impossible to accomplish in the usual kind of theatrical company.

On April 8, 1959, André Malraux, as minister of state for cultural affairs, announced a program to revitalize the French national theaters. The second theater, now called the Théâtre de France or simply the Odéon, was entrusted to Barrault and his company, who opened in October 1959 with a production of Claudel's *Tête d'or* (never before performed in Paris), followed by productions of Jean Anouilh's *Le Petit Molière* ("Young Molière," 1959) and Ionesco's *Rhinocéros*. Another government-subsidized theater, the Théâtre National Populaire (T.N.P.), was given over to the direction of Jean Vilar.

The art of certain directors and the particular kind of training to which they submit their actors account, to a large degree, for the evolution of the French theater in the twentieth century. Jacques Copeau was the most prominent of these men. Of almost equal importance were the four directors whose major contributions were made between the two wars and who are known collectively as the Cartel: Charles Dullin,

Louis Jouvet, Gaston Baty, and Georges Pitoëff. The type of play they chose to direct helped to form the French literary taste. These directors were quick to perceive and utilize the influences that were being felt in all domains of literature, such as the growing importance of Freud, Proust, and Pirandello.

The life of the French theater during the past three generations has been sustained largely through the labor and creative imagination of a series of these directors. Each director's name designates a style and a particular theory of theatrical production. Called either *metteur-en-scène* ("director") or *animateur* ("animator"—a more laudatory title), he unites all that is seen and heard on the stage.

André Antoine (1858–1943) was the first of the distinguished line of directors. His Théâtre Libre, founded in 1887, operated for only nine seasons, but this period was long enough to establish his revolution and create a standard for the type of realistic production which is the basis of the modern French theater. Antoine instituted greater naturalness in speech and action and an extreme realism in his care for details and use of real objects on the stage.

Only one director in Paris successfully opposed the theories of Antoine. Aurélien François Lugné-Poë (1869–1940), in his effort to introduce symbolist theories and to create a theater of dreams and poetry, represented an antidote to Antoine's realism. Lugné-Poë wanted to found a theater of ideas that was the antithesis of the "slice of life" theory of Antoine. In his Théâtre de l'Oeuvre, Lugné-Poë introduced to Paris such playwrights as Gabriele D'Annunzio, Henrik Ibsen, August Strindberg, Hugo von Hofmannsthal, George Bernard Shaw, and Paul Claudel.

Even more important than Lugné-Poë, however, was director Jacques Copeau (1897–1949). His activities, theories, and ideals formed the most significant single contribution to the modern French theater. He was first a literary man, who, with André Gide and Jean Schlumberger, founded the literary magazine *La Nouvelle Revue française* in 1908 and served as the editor until 1913. This was the year in which he opened his theater Le Vieux Colombier. It soon closed because of the war, but after the war it reopened and continued until 1924. As successor to Antoine, Copeau dominated the French theater for a quarter of a century. The artistic importance of Le Vieux Colombier far outdistanced its brief material success.

Copeau was primarily a discoverer, an experimentalist who learned how to reveal, in the movements and voices of the performers he trained, the beauty of dramatic poetry. He was a religious man who at one time became interested in the work of the Catholic playwright Henri Ghéon and in the possibility of establishing a new religious theater in France. Copeau believed that the spirit of celebration should animate the drama: the public should gather in a theater as it does on the annually recurring feast days of the liturgical calendar.

At the beginning of his career, when he was a literary critic, Copeau denounced the technique of the "well-made play" used by Edmond Rostand, Eugène Brieux, and Henry Bernstein at the very moment of their greatest successes. Later, the financial failure of Le Vieux Colombier was due largely to Copeau's unwillingness to flatter bad public taste and compro-

mise the ideals of his art. His work was continued by the four directors of the Cartel, who revealed similar traits of devotion, industry, and imagination.

Charles Dullin (1885–1949), a member of the Cartel, had his first intensive training as an actor in the company of Le Vieux Colombier. In 1921 he founded L'Atelier, an avant-garde theater in Montmartre, which continued until 1938. Basing his productions on the assumption that realism is not a natural part of the theater, Dullin emphasized the mysterious, poetic, and fantastic qualities of the literary text. He was the discoverer and trainer of actors—Jean-Louis Barrault, among others—and he was responsible for the first productions of such playwrights as Armand SALACROU, Marcel Archard, Anouilh, and Sartre.

Another member of the Cartel who was an actor as well as a director was Georges Pitoëff (1886–1939), a Russian who presented to the Paris public an exceptional number of plays between 1919 and 1939. More than the other members of the Cartel, Pitoëff was influenced by the Russian director Constantin Stanislavsky (1863–1938), who fused the best elements of Antoine and Lugné-Poë. Pitoëff's repertory showed a marked predilection for foreign playwrights, such as Chekhov, Shaw, Ibsen, and Shakespeare, but he also directed the original productions of Jean Cocteau's *Orphée* in 1926, Gide's *Oedipe* in 1932, and Anouilh's *Le voyageur sans bagage* (*The Traveler Without Luggage*) in 1937.

Only one Cartel director was not an actor: Gaston Baty (1885–1952). Of the four directors, Baty's theory of art led him furthest away from Copeau. Baty was obsessively fearful of the literary aspects of the theater, and he opposed the domination of the text of the play over the production. He tried to reduce the importance of the text, of what he called *Sire, le mot* ("My Lord, the word"). He claimed that there extends a zone of silence beyond the text, an atmosphere that is the function of the director to express. He added to the bare power of the word the supplementary powers of acting, miming, forms, colors, lighting, voices, noises, and silences.

If Baty is remembered as the opponent of the "word" in the theater, Louis Jouvet (1887–1951) stands as its principal defender, as the director who created essentially a verbal theater in which the text is given first place. The outstanding trait of Jouvet's art was the study he made of each play and the close collaboration he established with the various playwrights he served: Jules Romains, Bernard Zimmer, Stève Passeur, Marcel Achard, and especially Jean Giraudoux. Between 1928, when Giraudoux's *Siegfried* was first performed, and Giraudoux's death in 1944, Jouvet was the perfect collaborator. Because of Jouvet's brilliant direction, the public was able to follow the subtle, complex, ornate thought of Giraudoux. Jouvet defined the function of the director as that of rediscovering the author's state of mind. In his posthumous writings on the theater, *Témoignages sur le théâtre* (pub. 1952), Jouvet analyzes the attraction of the stage, of the spell that it can cast over men.

The apprenticeship of director Jean-Louis Barrault (1910–) was carried out in Dullin's company. Indefatigable, clear-minded, and articulate, Barrault became a famous screen and stage actor in the 1930's. In 1946, with his wife, Madeleine

Renaud, he founded his own company at the Théâtre Marigny on the Champs-Élysées. Barrault was a dominating personality in the French theater during the forties and the early years of the fifties; energetic and imaginative, he was almost fanatical in his devotion to the theater. All of his major productions have been both castigated and praised: Gide's *Le Procès*, an adaptation of Franz Kafka's *The Trial; L'Etat de siège* (*State of Siege*, 1948) by Camus, one of Barrault's distinct failures; *Malatesta* (1946) by Montherlant; *Break of Noon* by Claudel; and *The Screens* by Genet.

A contemporary of Barrault was Jean Vilar (1910–   ), who directed an out-of-doors theater in Avignon for several summers. In 1951 Vilar was appointed director of the Théâtre National Populaire, a government-subsidized theater inaugurated in 1920 in order to bring productions of major plays to large audiences. The bareness and austerity of a Vilar production are reminiscent of the style of Dullin and Pitoëff.

The type of play these directors produced changed greatly after the First World War. The drama of adultery and the well-made play, so popular before the First World War, were slow to die, but a few new plays began attracting attention: *Martine* (1921), for example, by Jean-Jacques Bernard and *Le Paquebot Tenacity* (*The Steamer Tenacity*, 1920) by Charles VILDRAC. Jules Romains' *Knock* (*Dr. Knock*), with Louis Jouvet in the title rote, was a resounding success in 1923 largely because it was so far removed from the already worn-out theme of adultery in the bourgeois class.

During the 1930's and 1940's, when such professional playwrights as Henri René LENORMAND (*La vie est un songe, Time Is a Dream,* 1919) and Salacrou (*L'Inconnue d'Arras, The Unknown Woman from Arras,* 1935) were providing new plays with great regularity, a number of highly competent, esteemed writers, especially poets and novelists, became known as playwrights and brought the prestige of literary creation to the theater. These writers included Paul Claudel, Jean Cocteau, Jean Giraudoux, Henry de Montherlant, André Gide, François Mauriac, Jean-Paul Sartre, Albert Camus, and Julien Green. These novelists and poets wrote their plays in a new kind of strong, lyrical language that had not been heard for a long time in contemporary plays. They brought a seriousness to their work, and they focused on political and religious themes. Sartre's *Les Mains sales* (*Dirty Hands,* 1948), for example, *Dialogues des Carmélites* (*The Carmelites,* 1949) by Georges Bernanos, and *Bacchus* (1951) by Cocteau emphasized themes that had been absent for a long time from the French theater. These writers chose for their plays ambitious and well-tested subjects. They favored classical themes from mythology and thus renewed the Greek tradition of Jean Racine's tragedies. Because of Racine, these subjects are better known to contemporary audiences in France than in other countries. In *The Infernal Machine* Cocteau dramatizes the story of Oedipus; Giraudoux's *Tiger at the Gates* is about Hector and the theme of war; Anouilh's *Antigone* is the playwright's interpretation of the Sophocles tragedy; and in his play *The Flies* Sartre presents the story of Orestes and the problem of man's freedom.

The art of Jean GIRAUDOUX is an assimilation of traits that have been persistent throughout French literature. The preciosity of his images is constantly offset by the conciseness and bareness of his expression. His themes of grandeur are counteracted by the simplicity of his tone. He considers all the gravest of human problems: the conflicts between the practical life of the city and the abstract laws of justice, between love and the cruel passing of time, between the purity of man's idealism and the necessity to be committed to an idea, party, or nation.

For Giraudoux tragedy is the persistence of human sacrifice. There is always a duality present in tragedy: religious belief and the shedding of blood. Giraudoux perpetuated a celebrated precept of Aristotle when he claimed that tragedy, by its symbolic reenactment of blood sacrifice, satisfies collectively the instinctive need of the public to commit crimes. Giraudoux never believed that his age measured up to Athens of the fifth century B.C., Elizabethan England, or France under Louis XIV, and hence a twentieth-century tragedian could not aspire to the formal solemnity of a Sophocles or a Racine.

For fifteen years, particularly between 1930 and 1940, the texts of Giraudoux's plays and their productions by Jouvet enchanted Paris. His characters were chosen to illustrate contemporary problems: Siegtried (*Siegfried*), for example, exemplifies the often repeated conflict between Germany and France, and Hector (TIGER AT THE GATES) poses the problems of the veteran soldier who is willing to accept dishonor if war can be avoided. This "journalist of the theater," as Giraudoux called himself, had to adapt his talents to the receptivity and intelligence of his public. His audience more easily accepted tragic dilemmas when they were presented with irony and literary wit. A kind of philosophical wisdom emerges from Giraudoux's plays, a sense of balance that is to be found in the joining of individual happiness with the individual's responsibility toward mankind, as in THE MADWOMAN OF CHAILLOT.

When Giraudoux's contemporary Jean COCTEAU began writing for the theater at the end of the First World War, the important dramatists were Eugène Brieux, François de Curel, Georges de Porto-Riche, Henry Bataille, and a few others who today are totally neglected. Claudel had been writing for twenty years, but his plays were still unknown. Giraudoux was not to produce his first play until ten years later. In 1917, the year of Cocteau's *Parade*, Dadaism was the new artistic movement. The Ballets Russes of Diaghielev was in fashion, and its lavishness, spectacular beauty, and perfection of a synthesis of all the arts dominated the theater in Paris.

Cocteau's first three works for the stage came from his intimate knowledge of the Ballets Russes and from his desire to simplify dramatic art form and restore it to its more primitive form of pure theater. *Parade* was a pantomime that, divested of the richness of the ballet, was more affiliated with what the French call *le music-hall*, and even with the circus, the fair, and the out-of-door theater. In *Le Boeuf sur le toit* ("The Ox on the Roof," 1920) and *Les Mariés de la Tour Eiffel* (*The Eiffel Tower Wedding Party*, 1921) Cocteau incorporated this basic concept of theater and at the same time moved in the direction of a literary theater. Cocteau's Preface to the latter is a manifesto calling for the revival of the poetic theater in France. He alludes to a special kind of "poetic" language for the stage—not poetry in a technical sense—that would reveal the hidden meaning of objects. Each of the major experimentalists of the twentieth century—Cocteau, Giraudoux, Beckett, Genet, Henri Pichette, and Georges Shehadé—has tried to create a poetic language along these lines by means of which the world would appear new and virginal. This is a tenet of SURREALISM. The theater, by rehabilitating the commonplace word and situation, by "poetizing" them, has sought to give a new meaning to daily life, to see its form in a new perspective.

Greek mythology is the basis of Cocteau's first original full-length play: ORPHÉE. It is a play of condensed richness with a surrealistic enactment of the most tender and profound myth of mankind: the descent of a living man into the realm of death and his return from there. Cocteau conceives of death as a magical substitution for life, as a passage through a mirror. The swift, mathematical progression of the action is sufficient in itself to create the illusion of the supernatural.

Cocteau's THE INFERNAL MACHINE has become a classic in the modern French theater. In this play Cocteau focuses on the machinations and the ingeniousness of the gods in destroying man. Against the machine of the gods, in its perpetration of woe and death, there is no defense. Dramatic art is an illusion and a travesty. Very few modern playwrights, except Pirandello, García Lorca, and Cocteau, have emphasized this doctrine. The central problem for Oedipus in *The Infernal Machine* is how he can know his destiny. This search and this eternal questioning have never been better illustrated than in the myth of Oedipus, which Cocteau here refurbishes with his own uncanny sense of situation, enigma, timing, and characterization.

Like Cocteau, Henry de MONTHERLANT was not exclusively a playwright. QUEEN AFTER DEATH was the first play written during the years that Montherlant devoted to the theater, between 1942 (when Jean-Louis Vaudoyer, director of the Comédie-Française, asked him to adapt an early Spanish play) and 1954 (when *Port-Royal* was first performed at the Comédie-Française). *Fils de personne* (*No Man's Son*, 1943) would be classified by the French as a *drame bourgeois*. It appears in strong contrast with the baroque historical play *Queen After Death*. Montherlant has stated that he wanted to write a play of inner psychological action, of total simplicity in plot and language.

The title of Montherlant's play *La Ville dont le prince est un enfant* ("The City Whose Prince Is a Child," 1952) is taken from a verse in the book of Ecclesiastes. The playwright classifies this play with two others—*Le Maître de Santiago* (*The Master of Santiago*, 1947) and *Port-Royal*—as his Catholic plays. He calls all three *autos sacramentales* ("sacramental acts"). *La Ville* is at least a key, if not the principal key, to all the writings of Montherlant. The crisis of this drama, which concerns the paternity of a priest as being the source of a grave spiritual peril, is reached and resolved within the strict confines of a Parisian boys' school. The text is Montherlant's purest in structure and most human in feeling and pathos.

For PORT-ROYAL Montherlant chose an austere subject from the history of Jansenism. The time is a day in August 1664 when the nuns of Port-Royal refuse to sign the Formulaire that was issued by the pope condemning Jansenism. Montherlant's bare but powerful and varied style is admirably suited to the characters and the dramatic situation of *Port-Royal*. The melodramatic action, reduced to its barest simplicity, exists as a pretext for that inner psychological action that Montherlant has always claimed uniquely interests him. What in English-speaking countries would be called the plot of this play is a series of moments of the soul, which the playwright has successfully projected with a maximum of truthfulness and intensity.

While Giraudoux and Montherlant came to the theater from the novel, and Claudel from poetry, Jean ANOUILH has written only for the theater. Since World War II, no single playwright in France has occupied the exceptional place held by Giraudoux during the thirties. The one possible successor, however, is Anouilh, who has written twenty-one full-length plays during a span of twenty-six years. On the occasion of each new play by Anouilh, the skillfulness of its construction and dramaturgy are readily apparent.

Anouilh's view of the world and of human existence has not altered through the years. He has Antigone say: "I refuse life." The central figure in an Anouilh play is the one who says "no," who contradicts life: Creon's niece in *Antigone;* Thérèse in *La Sauvage* (*Restless Heart*, 1934); Jeanne d'Arc in THE LARK; and Eurydice in *Eurydice* (*Legend of Lovers*, 1941). Anouilh reveals and studies with an implacable perseverance a deep incompatibility between his heroes and the world. His protagonists live in terms of an absolute that the world will not permit. Good and evil are clearly defined and tragically separated by Anouilh. His female characters are all fundamentally the same heroine whose purity of being and purpose are contaminated. Even if the heroine is wholly innocent, she cannot live because of what others say about her. Anouilh focuses his dramatic action on the cruel difference between what an act is for his character and what it is for those around her, for those who observe and judge her and consistently refuse to believe in her innocence. The individual is fatally compromised by his world, his family, society, and friends. In several of his plays, *Pauvre Bitos* (*Poor Bitos*, 1956), for example, and *L'Invitation au château* (*Ring Round the Moon*, 1947), Anouilh accords an almost mystical power to money, which represents a form of compromise.

By 1959 Anouilh had written and produced more than twenty plays. The constancy of theme in these plays gives his work the appearance and the forcefulness of an ideology. He is perpetually opposing two types of attitudes, best illustrated by Antigone and Creon in ANTIGONE. Antigone consistently refuses any kind of happiness that will be marred by compromise or impurity. Her purity of intention reveals the ugliness of the world. "All would have gone smoothly if it hadn't been for Antigone," one of the characters remarks. Creon, on the other hand, is the pragmatic politician who is willing to make compromises in his effort to maintain order.

The story of Antigone is one of the three or four classical tragic situations. The victim is not responsi-

A SCENE FROM JEAN ANOUILH'S *Poor Bitos* (FRENCH CULTURAL SERVICES)

ble for the tragedy that befalls her, and this is upsetting to the moral judgment of the spectators. Anouilh's treatment omits any intervention of the gods, and there is a total absence of any religious interpretation of the protagonist's fate. This means that Anouilh's understanding of tragedy is as far removed from Sophocles' as it is from Claudel's. Antigone's fate, in Anouilh's version, is known from the start. At the beginning of the dramatic action, she is fully aware of her fate and of the futility of opposing it. In this sense, Anouilh's understanding of tragedy appears in opposition to the Sartrean, or existentialist, concept of tragedy, which is based upon a belief in the individual's freedom to choose.

At one moment in the play, when Antigone defines the kind of being she is, she defines at the same time the leading traits of Anouilh's characters and, indeed, an austere psychological trait visible in much of contemporary French literature. Antigone claims that she is one of those who ask questions up to the very end. There is no facile human answer, however, to the questions asked by the characters of Anouilh or, for that matter, by the characters of Julien Green,

François Mauriac, and Georges Bernanos. In their novels as well as their plays, their characters have in common the fact that they are placed in exceptional situations, in great tests of moral experience, where they are mercilessly revealed and exhibited. The moral struggle the characters carry on within themselves reveals the corruption of the world around them. Anouilh's *Antigone* underscored with as much vigor and precision as Sartre's *The Flies* the new French consciousness, in the early 1940's, of the concepts of freedom and responsibility.

Like Giraudoux, Cocteau, Montherlant, and Anouilh, Julien Green (1900–   ) also uses the genre of tragedy. When Green's first play was announced for March 1953, something of the same curiosity was aroused in Paris that had been felt at the première of Mauriac's ASMODÉE. Green's SOUTH is one of the few successful attempts in recent years at creating the pure tone of tragedy. The unity of the play is built on the action of a man discovering his real nature. *South* begins as an elaborate social tableau with a good deal of military and political discussion. Gradually two figures emerge: Regina, who

JULIEN GREEN (FRENCH CULTURAL SERVICES)

is in love with Ian, and Ian, who treats her with some degree of cruelty as his own hopeless love for Eric propels him toward catastrophe. For Ian, love is forbidden in that irremediable way that the French associate with the tragedies of Racine.

While the tradition of tragedy has continued in the twentieth-century French theater, the Christian tradition has been carried on only in the plays of Paul CLAUDEL. Except for the dramas of Claudel, there have been few successful plays in the twentieth century in which the religious sentiment or the religious conflict dominates. The plays of Gabriel Marcel and Henri Ghéon have not projected conflicts of faith and religious destiny as dramatically as certain isolated plays by authors not as Catholic-minded as they are: *South* by Green, for example, and *Port-Royal* by Montherlant. The plays of Mauriac are not as successful as his novels, but he is concerned in both with the case of the Christian pharisee. The final work of Georges Bernanos, *Dialogues des Carmélites,* seems to be an authentic masterpiece in the Christian tradition.

But aside from the work of Claudel, there is an absence in the contemporary theater of religious plays that are edifying and dramatically moving. Apologetics, when used in a play, inevitably formulate a thesis, and a thesis inevitably transforms a play into a demonstration. But in the case of Claudel, who defines the law of the Christian as a principle of contradiction and who believes that the demands of the world and of religion force man to live in a permanent state of mobilization, we have a playwright who is able to create a viable, modern religious drama.

The first version of Claudel's first play, *Tête d'or,* was written in 1889. It is his only non-Christian play. (Not until Christmas, 1890, four years after his conversion, did Claudel make his formal return to the Church.) *Tête d'or* is the drama of an adventurer who attempts to elevate himself by the sole means of his own strength and intelligence. Behind the obvious impulse in *Tête d'or* to take possession of the earth is the problem of love, which was to become the principal theme in Claudel's later plays.

After the study of man in himself, with his conqueror's power (*Tête d'or*), Claudel chose for the object of his contemplation the arrangement of the city. *La Ville* (*The City,* 1931), Claudel's second play, written in 1890 and considerably revised in 1897, is about the meaning of the city and the organization of men.

In THE TIDINGS BROUGHT TO MARY Claudel stresses the mystical paradox of human relationships. Out of a familiar plot centering on two sisters, one good and one bad, Claudel created a lofty poetic drama. The good sister, Violaine, is the type of mystic who represents for Claudel an analogue with the poet. The other sister, Mara, has a passion for the material things of the earth: the farm of Combernon and an inheritance. The miracle, which takes place in the third act, is accomplished in a liturgical manner on the stage, and it leads to the play's Epilogue, in which Claudel defines love as man's gift of himself, the power to give of himself what he does not know. The sorrow of human love comes from its desire for complete possession, but the soul cannot possess anything or anyone. Love has nothing to do with justice. These are the words spoken by Violaine in her renunciation scene of the second act.

The première of Claudel's BREAK OF NOON took place in December 1948 at the Théâtre Marigny, forty-two years after the play was written. One sentence in the text describes the emerging of the soul from the body as if it were a sword, half unsheathed. The play is the drama of this apparition, the desire for absolute possession—both carnal and spiritual. The drama of physical love for the characters Mesa and Ysé in *Break of Noon* is the anguish of knowing that their love can never be complete on earth because of previous marriage vows, sacredly indissoluble. Beyond their temporal and earthly love, there is the hope of a mystical and complete union for them after death. The play is more awesome than the others of Claudel, and despite its melodramatic ending, it is the barest and the closest to pure tragedy of Claudel's plays. In this dramatization of human freedom and responsibility, Claudel does not introduce any supernatural intervention. In *Break of Noon* the subject of eternity is never absent from the complex psychological problems, but it is always enmeshed in the complications of immediate life. The symbol of the power of the sky prevents the familiar action of violence, sensuality, adultery, and coquetry from appearing trivial in *Break of Noon*. The force above the lives of the characters is either solar (*partage de midi*) or astral (*partage de minuit*), moving the characters beyond their earthly world to a consummation in another world.

Claudel's greatest play, THE SATIN SLIPPER, is one of the most complicated plays ever written and yet one of the simplest. The three principal characters form one of the most familiar relationships in the history of the theater: an aged husband, a young wife, and a lover. Behind the personal relationships of these three characters, Claudel develops a historical drama about Renaissance Spain.

While Claudel is concerned with religious concepts, many of his contemporaries are preoccupied with metaphysical problems. Some of their plays are the most striking that have been written during the past twenty years, in terms of structure, brevity, intensity, and pessimism. Such plays as Sartre's *No Exit,* Genet's *The Maids,* Ionesco's *The Chairs,* and Beckett's *Waiting for Godot* reflect aspects of modern philosophy and art: existentialism, surrealism, and the writings of Franz Kafka and James Joyce. In them, the drama of ideas dominates the drama of characters. This type of play, with its background in mythology, religion, and philosophy, is not entertainment in the usual sense of diversion, escape, and relaxation. Each one presents an ordeal, a drama on the condition of life. Anxiety, which the existentialists have defined as inherent in existence itself, pervades and forms the action in these particular plays.

One of the main exponents of this "theater of ideas" was André Gide (1869–1951), who, for the subject matter of his three plays *Saül* (1896), *Le Roi Candaule* (*King Candaules,* 1900), and *Œdipe,* turned to the Bible and Greek mythology and hence followed the tradition of the French classical theater. But the modern spirit and Gide's own sensitivity and understanding of personal morality are everywhere present in these plays. In his treatment of the three heroes—Saul, Candaule, and Oedipus—Gide shows little respect for them. He seems to be observing them critically and at times uses them as fools of a *sotie* rather than as characters of a drama.

Gide's ideology is present throughout his *Œdipe.* It is a dryer, more intellectualized treatment of the Greek story than Cocteau's *The Infernal Machine.* All of Gide's characters move far away from their traditional roles and assume a modern stance in dealing with a modern problem. Gide's plays are among the hardest of the modern dramas to perform, the hardest to project. They have tempted four of the best directors—Copeau, Lugné-Poë, Pitoëff, and Vilar —but they have not yet been produced in such a way as to bring out to the fullest their subtleties of argument, their high dramatic moments, their sardonic touches, and their lyricism.

Like Gide, Jean-Paul SARTRE is concerned with metaphysical problems. Without being a professional dramatist in the sense that Anouilh is, Sartre has used theatrical forms with considerable ease and naturalness. Traditionally, the theater in France is looked upon as a domain that the leader of a new movement is anxious to capture and utilize. This was true for Voltaire in the eighteenth century, for Hugo in the nineteenth, and is true for Sartre in the twentieth. Sartre presents certain philosophical problems, such as man's solitude, freedom, and responsibility, with greater clarity in his plays than in the other literary genres he employs. His dramas contain not only a variety of ideas, but psychological subtleties and dramatic insights expressed by poetic metaphors. So substantial is the intellectual nourishment in a Sartre play that we forget what it lacks.

His new treatment of the fable of Orestes in THE FLIES seemed to the public of 1943 to bear a close relationship to the moral dilemma experienced during the German occupation. The moving, dramatic relationship between Orestes and the people of Argos is also the source of much of the existentialist philosophy in the play. Orestes exercises his freedom by making a choice; at the end of the play he takes on the fear and the guilt of his people, and he experiences alienation.

All of Sartre's plays are dominated by the existential view of man; man is called upon, during the unfolding of his existence, to create the very meaning of that existence. Man's dream is to become placidly immobile, like a stone. This is his cowardice, his desire to play the social comedy of conformity, to appear before other men as one of them. Sartre dramatizes this idea in NO EXIT when one of the characters describes the six mirrors in her bedroom where she used to enjoy seeing herself as other people saw her.

One of the goals of literature for Sartre, defined in his elaborate theory of literature as commitment (*engagement*), is to reveal the petrification of man when, as a coward, he becomes fixed in a social pose. The plays of Sartre have the dynamics of existentialist exercises. In them he exposes the alibis we make in our daily lives and denigrates the system of routines that governs so many historical events. The fear of standing alone that forces men to adopt these routines is exemplified in Sartre's work by the fear in the people of Argos (*The Flies*), the static quality of hell (*No Exit*), and the goal of security in the bourgeois world (*Les Mains sales*).

Sartre's interest in existential philosophy and his use of various literary forms is paralleled by his con-

ANDRÉ GIDE (FRENCH CULTURAL SERVICES)

temporary Albert CAMUS. During his early years in Algiers, Camus developed a passion for the theater. His first two plays, *Le Malentendu* (*The Misunderstanding*) and *Caligula,* were performed during the German occupation in 1944, when Camus was editor of the clandestine newspaper *Combat.* His last two plays, *L'État de siège* (*State of Siege,* 1948) and *Les Justes* (*The Just Assassins,* 1950), were not as successful as the first two. Today Camus's high position in French letters is due not to his plays but to his role as polemicist and chronicler. The plays represent, in the unfolding of his thought, a moment of tragic lucidity. They are quite literally the spectacle of his thought as it tried to comprehend that other spectacle of contemporary society lost in its political machinations.

When it was first performed, CALIGULA stimulated interest and reflection and revived the fresh memories of the occupation. Today it resembles a philosophical drama. The play is not a dramatic conflict, because we do not see the moral crisis in the character of Caligula. Instead, we witness a comment on an elaborate spectacle that is the result of a moral crisis.

Since the productions of the philosophical plays of Sartre and Camus in the 1940's, a great change has taken place in the French theater. The new French playwrights are those interested in writing a poetic kind of play, lyric in tone but not written in verse. These new writers include Jacques AUDIBERTI, Henri Pichette, and Georges Shehadé. Among the works of these new writers the metaphysical farces of Michel de GHELDERODE reveal a diabolical and mystical dualism between good and evil in the tradition of Baudelaire. Another group of playwrights, more philosophical in intention, includes Arthur Adamov (of Russian origin), Ionesco (of Rumanian origin), Beckett (of Irish origin), Arrabal (of Spanish origin), and Genet. These dramatists have in common a scorn for the traditional form of the "well-made play" that flourished in France for almost one hundred years. During the 1940's the very marked commercial successes of Sartre, Anouilh, and Montherlant threw into disrepute the older fixed formulas of the thesis play and the adultery play of Henry Bernstein and Henri Becque. With the successes of Artaud, Beckett, Ionesco, and others in the 1950's, the Bernstein play became outdated, and it was replaced by the new, experimental theater.

A leading exponent of this new theater was Antonin ARTAUD. The most cherished dream of Artaud was to found a new kind of theater in France that would be, not an artistic spectacle, but a communion between spectators and actors. As in primitive societies, it would be a theater of magic, a mass participation in which the entire culture would find its vitality and its truest expression. Artaud saw the beginnings of this theater in the critical writings of Stéphane Mallarmé, in the plays of Maurice Maeterlinck, and in the example and writings of Alfred Jarry. Artaud found an instance of it in Guillaume Apollinaire's THE BREASTS OF TIRESIAS, which he contrasted with the popular plays of the day by Bernstein and François de Curel. The most successful plays of recent years, those of Sartre and Anouilh, are closer to the traditional form of the French play than to the experimentations of Apollinaire or Jarry.

The second goal of the theater, Artaud claimed, is

GUILLAUME APOLLINAIRE (FRENCH CULTURAL SERVICES)

to communicate delirium whereby the spectators will experience trances and inspiration. A true play, according to Artaud's concept, will disturb the spectator's tranquility of mind and his senses, and it will liberate his subconscious. Aristotle had emphasized the ethical power of the theater; Artaud intended to release its mediumistic force. The method he proposed is to associate the theater with danger and cruelty, as he tried in LES CENCI. Language will become an incantation. Here Artaud draws upon the poetic theory of Mallarmé and Arthur Rimbaud.

The principal tenet of Artaud's book *Le Théâtre et son double* (*The Theater and Its Double,* pub. 1938) states that reform in the modern theater must begin with the production itself, with the *mise en scène.* The real objective of the theater is the translation of life into its immense universal form, the form that will extract from life images from which the audience can derive pleasure. This is what Artaud means by the word "double." The theater is not a direct copy of reality; it is another kind of dangerous reality where the principles of life are always just disappearing beyond the spectator's field of vision. Artaud wanted to see stage gesticulations elevated to the rank of exorcisms. In keeping with the principal tenets of surrealism and his own THEATER OF CRUELTY, he claimed that art is a real experience that goes far beyond human understanding and attempts to reach a metaphysical truth. The artist is always a man inspired who reveals a new aspect of the world. The best surrealist playwright, with whom Artaud established the Théâtre Alfred Jarry in 1927, was Roger Vitrac, who was criticized, along with Artaud, by André Breton and the other surrealists for this commercial theatrical enterprise. In 1924 Artaud himself directed Vitrac's *Victor, ou les enfants au pouvoir,* a play written in the surrealist and antiplay tradition.

While Artaud was the major proponent of the theater of cruelty, Samuel Beckett was concerned with another type of experimental drama: the theater of the absurd. During the years following the liberation of France, Beckett wrote in French three novels and two plays. In 1953 Roger Blin produced Beckett's first play, Waiting for Godot, at the Théâtre de Babylone. The plan of the play is simple to relate. Two tramps are waiting by a tree for the arrival of M. Godot. They quarrel, make up, contemplate suicide, try to sleep, eat a carrot. Two other characters appear, a master and a slave, who perform a grotesque scene in the middle of the play. A young boy arrives to say that M. Godot will not come today, but that he will come tomorrow. The play is a development of the title, *Waiting for Godot.*

The unity of place, the particular site on the edge of a forest that the two tramps cannot leave, recalls Sartre's use of the unity of place in his second play, *No Exit,* where hell is in the guise of a living room that the three characters cannot leave. In *Godot* the two tramps in their seemingly improvised dialogue arouse laughter in the audience, despite their alienation from the social norm and the total pessimism of their philosophy. To trace the ancestry of this situation would be to present a list of those European and American writers who, during the past century, have written strong indictments against our civilization and especially its industrialization. *Godot* and the novels of Samuel Beckett are among the leading works of revolt in our age, along with the novels and plays of Jean Genet and the essays and manifestoes of Antonin Artaud. Preceding these works in France are *Une saison en enfer* (pub. 1873) by Rimbaud and the entire writings of Le Comte de Lautréamont. Such an anthology of revolt would include pages of Louis-Ferdinand Céline, D. H. Lawrence, and Henry Miller, as well as Kafka and Pirandello. No one work of the writers in this list, however, has so immediately affected its public as *Waiting for Godot.*

The second Beckett play, Endgame, was finished in July 1956 and published in February 1957. The first production, again by Roger Blin, was performed in the Studio des Champs-Élysées in May 1957. The title of the play is a term used in chess to designate the third and final part of the game. This term was perhaps chosen for its indeterminateness, for its capacity to designate the end of many things, the end of life itself. The approach to "the end" is indeed the principal theme of all of Beckett's writings, including Happy Days. Whereas *Godot* is concerned with the theme of waiting, *Endgame* is on the subject of leaving. We have the impression of watching the end of something, possibly the end of the human race.

The drama that Beckett presents to the audience, although it is not understood by his stage characters, is the lack of meaning that the spectacle of life provides. In the dialogue between the two tramps of *Godot* and between Hamm and Clov, the two key characters in *Endgame,* there is an inverted kind of

desperate intellectualism. In the space of a very few years, Beckett has gained the stature of an international figure because his indictment against civilization is thoroughly simple and lucid.

Another rebel dramatist who is interested in exposing the faults of civilization is Jean Genet. The first production of Genet's The Maids was directed by Jouvet at the Athénée in 1947. The life of the two maids in this play has been so reduced by serving their mistress, by the silence imposed upon them, that the only way they feel they can exist independently and assert their repressed hatred of their mistress and of their servile position is by committing a crime; but the planned murder of their mistress turns against them. Solange and Claire—the victims —become the executioners and annihilate themselves as their game becomes too real. This is an example of Artaud's theater of cruelty. It is the revelation of a moral distress able to turn human beings into sufferers.

The action of Genet's second play, Deathwatch, takes place in a prison cell, where a very precise and powerful hierarchy of sexual seductiveness exists among three young men. Yeux-Verts, the murderer of a girl, is the *maudit* ("accursed"), but without the romantic halo of rebel and apostle. With a prestige based upon the power of evil, he is able to dominate a second prisoner, who in his turn dominates a third prisoner, a mere thief.

Genet's subject matter is that which is condemned by society, and, as an authentic playwright, he gives it an infernal order in *The Maids, Deathwatch, Le Balcon (The Balcony,* 1956), *Les Nègres (The Blacks,* 1958), and The Screens. Such a character as Yeux-Verts is the beneficiary of a perverted kind of grace and power. In Genet's conception, maids and criminals belong to the order of evil; they represent an absolute of disorder that is the opposite of the order of society.

In a new edition of *The Maids (Les Bonnes et l'atelier d'Alberto Giacometti,* pub. 1958), Genet published an important letter about his play and his opinion of the theater in general. He is repelled by the clichés and formulas of the Western theater, and he claims that our Western plays are masquerades and not ceremonies. What transpires on the stage is always childish. Genet wrote *The Maids* through vanity, he says, because he was asked to by a famous actor. He was depressed by his knowledge that it would be performed in accord with the conventions of the modern theater, where everything is visible on the stage, where the actions of men and not of the gods are depicted. In becoming a diversion, an entertainment, the modern theater has adulterated the significance of theater. Genet suggests that what is needed is a clandestine theater, which the "faithful" would attend in secret.

Roger Blin's production of *Les Nègres* attempted to represent this kind of theater. If during the performance one thinks of African ceremonies, black masses, and certain esoteric-erotic *boîtes-de-nuit* ("night clubs") in Paris, one is constantly pulled back to the specific play of Jean Genet, to the poet's creation, which transcends all the histrionic types it evokes. In the original performance, Blin created the dramatic ambiguity that is the central situation of the play; namely, the conflicting relationships between actors and public on the stage and the public in the audience. Blin did not neglect a more subtle relationship existing between the desire of the actors to amuse themselves as they act and their desire to amuse the audience at the same time. Blin himself, as *metteur-en-scène*, was the master of ceremonies, the master of the strange liturgy that unfolded with alternating spasms of humiliation and fury.

Arthur ADAMOV is a contemporary of Beckett and Genet and a practitioner of experimental theater. In Adamov's first play, *La Parodie* ("The Parody," 1950), the subject of man's solitude, the impossibility of communication between men, is demonstrated as blatantly as possible. This first play was a sign of rebellion for Adamov, who had been strongly influenced by Artaud's *Le Théâtre et son double* and disgusted with the so-called psychological plays of his day.

For his second play, *L'Invasion* (*The Invasion*), performed in 1950 and directed by Jean Vilar, Adamov believed he was inventing a new stratagem in the theater by having a character heard by another but not having him say what he meant to say. Later Adamov discovered that this kind of dialogue distinguishes the plays of Anton Chekhov!

With these two plays, and also with his third, *La Grande et la Petite Manoeuvre* ("The Big and the Small Maneuver," 1950), it was clear that Adamov was dramatizing the ideas of a deeply pessimistic philosophy concerning the uselessness of man trying to oppose the forces destined to crush him. In Adamov's drama an action is accomplished only to be defeated, a passion is experienced only to be denied. Everything fatally results in failure.

PROFESSOR TARANNE is a play about fantasies of a very cruel order, and it is one of the most successful theatrical projections of Adamov's world. The protagonist (a university professor accused of appearing naked on a beach) is completely confined within the tragedy of his existence. A long series of affirmations on the part of Taranne are immediately turned against him and act negatively on his case. Every word he uses exposes him in the wrong way and ends by annihilating him.

Like Adamov, Eugène IONESCO was also influenced by the theories of Artaud. At the performance of an Ionesco play, there is considerable laughter in the audience: it is man laughing at his own emptiness, his own intimate triviality. This kind of laughter had been exploited by the surrealists and by those close to surrealism, such as Alfred Jarry in *Ubu Roi* and Cocteau in *Les Mariés de la Tour Eiffel*.

The text of THE BALD SOPRANO is an example of the burlesque inventiveness of Ionesco, of the verbal fantasies he can create, but the laughter the text generates covers up a rather serious worry of man, a malaise. It is a text made up of commonplaces that are skillfully reconstructed. We laugh because of the persistent disparity between the words as they are said and the behavior of the characters speaking the words.

Victimes du devoir (*Victims of Duty*, 1952) is the most complex of the early plays of Ionesco, the profoundest perhaps, and the one with which the playwright himself has expressed the most satisfaction. The subject of the play is mythological and even oneiric in its relationship to primitive mystery: the son is projected in the dual role of slayer of his father and redeemer. Under the power of the maternal force in the household, both father and son attempt to justify their existences, but the will to destruction is dominant.

Within the text of the play itself, Ionesco makes a profession of faith about the theater and at the same time initiates a violent attack against the traditional psychological theater. One of the characters says:

> The theater today is still a prisoner of old forms. It has not moved beyond the psychology of a Paul Bourget. It does not correspond to the cultural status of our age. There is no correspondence between it and the spiritual manifestations of our time.

The creation of a new theater is associated in Ionesco's mind with the coexistence of contradictory principles: tragedy and farce, the poetic and the prosaic, fantasy and realism, the familiar and the unusual. In RHINOCEROS Ionesco shows an average man, Bérenger, growing into the stature of a protagonist because he is not influenced by words and speeches. At the end of the play, after having observed a clinical study of conformity and contamination, Bérenger is totally alone. This solitude of man is at the center of all of Ionesco's plays, and it is always manifested in the same way with the same admixture of irony, burlesque, and humor.

In the tradition of Ionesco, Roland DUBILLARD uses the techniques of silence and the repetition of banalities and platitudes in his play *La Maison d'os* ("The House of Bones," 1963) to create a poetic form of drama. Similar in style to Ionesco and Dubillard is Boris VIAN, who strongly attacks the bourgeois world.

While the humor in Ionesco's plays makes people laugh, the first play by Georges SHEHADÉ made the audience angry. In 1951, when Shehadé's *Monsieur Bob'le* was performed, a hostile press did all it could to close the theater. They looked upon it as a return to the escapism of the 1930's. A few poets, such as André Breton and René Char, came to the defense of Shehadé, and two drama critics, Thierry Maulnier and Jacques Lemarchand, spoke in his favor. The action of the play gravitates around the lovable, mysterious Monsieur Bob'le. The story of this man's departure from his village, his absence, and his death has the simplicity of a village myth. He is a sage or a poet who gives life to a small village and who dies far away from it.

The poetic qualities of Shehadé's plays are reminiscent of Giraudoux. When *Monsieur Bob'le* was first performed, some of the theatergoers remembered the poetic eruption of Giraudoux's *Siegfried* in 1928. Georges Shehadé, a Syrian, has joined the ranks of the few French poets of modern times who have written for the stage: Claudel, Apollinaire, Audiberti, and Jules Supervielle. With the vision of a seer, Shehadé established communication between worlds that are usually closed off from one another: between life and death, old age and the past.

With the poetic theater of Georges Shehadé, and to some extent with the two plays of Henri PICHETTE, *Les Epiphanies* (1947) and *Nucléa* (1952, written in alexandrines), dramatic writing moved farther away from the "bourgeois theater" than it had with the experimental plays of Beckett, Ionesco, and Adamov. The nonpoetic theater has had a long history and seems deeply entrenched. It speaks of what is immediately apprehended: a scene of adultery, an event from history, a problem in psychology. The efforts of Shehadé and Pichette, of Audiberti and Supervielle, are perhaps the first steps in an important revindication of poetic drama. The racial tensions created by the French colonial system are revealed in the poetic plays of Aimé CÉSAIRE of Martinique and Yacine KATEB of Algeria. The fight for racial justice and freedom is evoked by both these writers by means of an incantatory, poetical rhythm that pulsates with the awakening feelings of freedom and dignity of colonized men in both Algeria and the Congo. Throughout the history of the theater, the suffering of man, his pathos, has been inextricably bound up with lyricism. The most noble way man has devised for the translation of his suffering is the theater: the art of narrating, miming, dancing, and acting.

During the first fifty years of the century, the major French writers were primarily concerned with man's moral adventure. They were keenly aware of what André Malraux called "man's fate" (*la condition humaine*) as it was related to the moral issues of their day. This topic concerned such different but equally important writers as Gide, Malraux, Bernanos, Camus, and Sartre. By 1950, however, this focus seemed to change with the first plays of Ionesco, Beckett, Adamov, Genet, and later with Robert PINGET, who treats themes that are similar to those found in Beckett's metaphysical farces. In the style of their writing and in the themes of their work, these new playwrights were defiant of the usual moral issues. Instead, they imposed a new vision of man's experience by avoiding any rationalization about it. By comparison with the theater of the two preceding decades, the new plays of the 1950's were characterized by an absence of moral problems and moral interrogations.

Unquestionably, the new art of the theater was a symptom of something more important than art itself, of a change that had taken place in man's own opinion of himself. Traditionally, in keeping with the humanistic ideals of the Renaissance, man had looked upon himself as the measure of all things, as that being for whom the universe was created, but today he appears in the theater of the absurd as a mere element without clarity of measurement or importance.

Thus far in the twentieth century, the French theater has produced two important generations. The first flourished in the 1930's, with such playwrights as Giraudoux and Cocteau, and the second in the 1950's. This latter type of theater has continued into the 1960's under the designation of theater of the absurd. Between these two generations, in the war years and the second half of the 1940's, the existentialist theater, with the plays of Sartre and Camus and the work of the independent playwrights such as Montherlant and Anouilh, was predominant. The structure of those plays written and produced in the forties was more traditional than experimental. Not until the early 1950's, with the first plays of Ionesco, Beckett, and Genet, was there a marked change in the mode of composition and the manner of theatrical production that could be termed avant-garde.

No permanent meaning can be attached to avant-garde or its contemporary equivalent *absurde* save that of "revolt." It is revolt usually against a moral or literary tradition. In recent years "the beat generation" in America and "the angry young men" in England have unquestionably had their effect on the theater. The new theatrical art of Edward Albee and Le Roi Jones in America and Harold Pinter in England is not without parallels in the new Paris plays. The prevalent trait in these plays that caused them to be called "experimental" by most critics and theatergoers is the effort of the playwright to awaken the spectator to a sense of the unusual, to the *insolite* that is everywhere around us in the most familiar objects and habits of living. The theater should reveal to us things we look at without seeing and should arouse in us emotions we ordinarily refuse to admit.

No program or school unites the new playwrights of the 1950's and 1960's. Each has developed his own discipline, which is a form of anarchy, a dramaturgy that will not resemble the well-made play, the thesis play, nor the more classical play of psychological analysis. The new type of drama does not easily lend itself to analysis, and it avoids a narration. It is a theater characterized by a deliberate renunciation of psychological discourse.

François BILLETDOUX, in his two short plays *Tchin-Tchin* (1959) and *Va donc chez Torpe* (*Chez Torpe*, 1961), dramatizes the impossibility of communication between people and the nature of love, life, and death with ironic detachment. The one-act or short play, which by its limitations emphasizes a lack of motion or development, has been widely used by the new dramatists in France. This genre includes such works as *La Dernière bande* (*Krapp's Last Tape*, 1958) by Beckett; *Oraison* (*Orison*, 1958) by Arrabal; *La Leçon* (*The Lesson*, 1950) by Ionesco; and *Professor Taranne* by Adamov. As the significance of the contemporary play turns from psychology to metaphysics, from an analysis of predictable action to a questioning of reality and first principles, a fundamental pessimism about man has become more evident.

The plays appear difficult because they do not correspond to our traditional concept of the theater. UBU ROI, in the presurrealist days, was an attack on the conventions and habits of the theatergoing public, and Alfred JARRY, when questioned about his mystifications, used to reply that comprehensible matters would only dull the minds of the spectators, that what was absurd (Jarry was the first to use this now overused word) would train the faculties and memory of the audience.

The new theater has stressed the presence of objects in the play's dramaturgy. In *Orphée* in the middle of the 1920's, Cocteau used in a magical way a horse, a window, and a mirror. An almost bare tree in *Waiting for Godot* attracts considerable attention in Beckett's play, while a telephone and a dress in *The Maids* are constant preoccupations in Genet's play. Ionesco, more than any other playwright, has utilized objects: the corpse that grows in size in *Amédée* (1953), the coffee cups in *Victimes du devoir*, and a bicycle in *Le Piéton de l'air* (*A Stroll in the Air*, 1963).

In this last-named play, the character Bérenger speaks quite directly about literature and the art of the theater. He claims that literature has never had the tension or the power of life. He recapitulates a thought associated with the dramatic theories of Artaud when he insists that in order to equal life literature will have to be a thousand times more cruel and more terrifying. With Jarry, Apollinaire, and Artaud, Ionesco is one of our contemporary writers who has reflected deeply on the state of the theater today and its meaning.

Beckett's tramp (*clochard*) is a choreographic representation of the "outsider," the everyman of the avant-garde theater. He is the type of amnesiac who has lost contact with the past. Alienation is the fundamental theme of the new plays, and the spectacle of this alienation that we watch on the stage is fully calculated to turn the spectator's vision inward, to force him to examine the human condition. The characters of Jean VAUTHIER, Arrabal, Genet, and Beckett are, in this sense, our own consciences that have reached a superior degree of sincerity. In these dramas the playwright is more concerned with depicting the condition of man's fate than in demonstrating the tragedy of any one, individual hero.

More than any other art, the theater is a social art and offers to the men and women of a given generation their own portrait. The new playwrights are concerned with man's freedom of spirit, and in order to make their public feel the necessity for this freedom, they show us in their plays the various forms of serfdom in which man habitually lives. We are bound like slaves to slogans, ideologies, verbal mannerisms, and manners. The method of this writing is an exposure on the stage of our anguish. By seeing our own obsessions on the stage, we are probably liberated from them for at least the time it takes to perform the play. This theory of the purification of our passions was the mission of the theater for Aristotle.

In each of his plays Ionesco dramatizes an obsession and leads the public to laughter over it. In *Le Nouveau locataire* (*The New Tenant*, 1957) furniture is accumulated on the stage until there is no space left for the protagonist. This could be man's mania for collecting things, the material encumbrances that stifle our lives. The old man in THE CHAIRS incarnates man's dream of greatness and the vanity of this dream.

Antitheater is clearly the opposite of a theater of ideology or a theater of engagement such as Sartre has written. The new theater is a means of exposing the vanity of many of the habits that fill our lives. Even if the tone of many of the new plays is scoffing or mocking, concealed behind it is a deep anguish. Despite their farcical elements, the seriousness, and sometimes the religious seriousness, of the new plays cannot be doubted. Beckett's *Godot* is reminiscent of the medieval debate between the body and the soul, between the intellect and the nonrational in man. The typical hero of the Arrabal plays is the little man, comparable to Beckett's tramps and reminiscent of Chaplin and the solitary heroes of Kafka. The parable in Ionesco's *Rhinocéros* is on the sacred individuality of man. The hero, Bérenger, refuses to comply with the collective mania, the standardization of his world. He is compelled to engage in an experience of solitude.

On several occasions, in articles and reviews, Ionesco has spoken of a feeling of human anguish he has been aware of since childhood and which he believes comes not only from his life but also from the lives of all men. It is a sense of isolation, of being encircled by a void where one is incapable of communicating with others. The kind of banal conversation in his plays for which he has become famous is precisely the dramatization of man's inability to communicate. His plays often give the impression of being autopsies of our unacknowledged, invisible manias. Ionesco has often said that when he begins to write a play he has no specific intention or plan, but he has in his mind at that moment multiple semiconscious or ill-articulated plans. He places himself among those artists who are hostile to all forms of "truth" or "ideology," which, by their very nature, seem destined to become forces of oppression. Ionesco has referred to two forces of oppression that he considers the most dangerous for the artist: the sclerosis of the bourgeois mentality and the tyranny of political power.

The new French playwrights of the 1950's and 1960's, such as Marguerite DURAS and Armand GATTI, have not formed a cohesive movement or school. Each one remains a solitary figure, almost fanatically independent. There has been no program uniting them save a determination to create a new kind of theater. Each of the new plays gives a startling effect of a separate work, of being a play without antecedents in which all movement, action, and character development have been arrested. In Beckett's *Endgame* the two principal characters move in opposite directions, Hamm toward death and Clov toward life, but one impulse cancels out the other, and finally no progress is made in the bare room that contains the two men.

The antidramas of Ionesco in the early 1950's and the films of Alain Resnais in the 1960's show us man in situations where his intelligence is unable to cope with his anguish, where he feels surrounded and besieged by an inhuman element. He lives quite literally the drama of the absurd, which is at the same time a drama of mystery and one of solitude, where he is conscious of the presence of familiar things that have no meaning for him.

In the space of a very few years, dramatic works that are strange, paradoxical, even subversive have been adopted by an important segment of the theatergoing public in Paris, and the adoption of these plays in translation has been widespread in other countries. For five uninterrupted years the director-actor Nicolas Bataille maintained his production of Ionesco's The Bald Soprano and *La Leçon* at the Théâtre de la Huchette. No such success accompanied the early experimental plays of Jean Cocteau in the 1920's. As the experimental plays of the 1950's established themselves with some degree of permanence, the once popular melodramatic play in Paris, called the *théâtre de boulevard,* gradually disappeared. The wit and sentimentality associated with that form of theater belonged to the 1930's and has no connection with the present decade.

The experimental theater of the 1950's and 1960's would not have developed without the help, and often disinterested help, of some gifted and courageous directors: Roger Planchon, Roger Blin, Jean-Marie

Serreau, Georges Vitaly, and André Reybaz, among others. For ten years at least, and longer in some cases, the plays of Adamov, Beckett, Vauthier, Genet, and Ionesco were produced for small, limited audiences in Paris.

The difference between the mise en scène of Copeau in the earlier period, for whom the text was uppermost, and the mise en scène of Artaud, with his technical innovations, is still reflected today in the direction of Jean Vilar. Vilar deprecates the domination of the metteur-en-scène and gives first place to the author's text, while Roger Planchon, in his effort to find a conjunction between a dramatic text and the general preoccupation of the moment when it is performed, often directs a production that seems in contradiction to the text.

There is great diversity today in the new productions of such directors as Blin, Barrault, Vilar, Antoine Bourseiller, and Jacques Poliéri. At times the production seems to be designed to shock the audience, to awaken it from its lethargy, while at other times it seems to be an attempt to stimulate the thinking of the audience and to make a place for the theater in the general life, even the political life, of the city.

Jean-Louis Barrault, more than any other director today, has maintained the tradition of the Cartel. His art depends very much on violent, stylized gestures, a huge space on the stage, and a complicated set. For Barrault a theatrical production is a celebration where he is free to incorporate music, films, and pantomime to achieve the effects he wants. The text is often recited as an incantation that is supported by plastic movement. He runs the risk, however, of succumbing to an overrichness of style and even a confusion of styles. He was responsible for productions of plays by three of the new playwrights: Shehadé (*La Soirée des proverbes*, "Evening of Proverbs," 1954), Vauthier (*Le Personnage combattant*, "The Fighting Personage," 1956), and Ionesco (*Rhinoceros*, 1960).

Antoine Bourseiller, another experimental director, has acknowledged his debt to the film director Alain Resnais. Bourseiller has profited from surrealism, expressionism, and Brecht's theater in his effects of shock and aggressiveness. There is something of Artaud's violence in Bourseiller's productions, such as the early Claudel plays and Brecht's *Dans la Jungle des villes* (*In the Jungle of the Cities*).

A mise en scène is, for Bourseiller, something to be seen, something decorative, but for director Jacques Poliéri it is something like a musical score, an organization of vocal parts and gestures where he will use abstract painting and concrete music. His productions of the work of Jean Tardieu illustrate a balanced relationship among voice, gesture, image, and movement. It is hard for Poliéri to find texts suitable for his kind of production.

Jean Vilar has always granted first place to the text and has always opposed the concept of a spectacle for the sake of a spectacle. He uses a minimum of technical devices and properties. He has rejected the idea of a stage framed by the proscenium and has, instead, used the full width of the proscenium and suggested stage scenery by the use of lighting. Vilar produces his plays for the general public, and he wants to influence their thinking about political and social prob-lems of the day. Stylistically, he owes almost everything to Copeau.

Vilar's contemporary Roger Planchon has produced several plays in Lyon and Villeurbanne. In Paris he was responsible for the production of three Adamov plays: *Professor Taranne* (1953), *Le Sens de la marche* ("The Meaning of the March," 1953), and *Paolo Paoli* (1957). Planchon often emphasizes the social behavior of the characters rather than their psychological involvements. This was true of his production of Molière's *George Dandin*, where Dandin was presented not only as a cuckold but as a rich peasant who was tricked because he was a peasant.

Beckett found in Roger Blin an admirable metteur-en-scène who understood the subtlety and asceticism of the texts, and entrusted to him the production of all his plays with the exception of *Comédie*, which was put on by Serreau. Genet also has given most of his plays to Blin, who has brought out in these productions the incantatory, magical, histrionic effects of the texts.

Ionesco worried so much about the interpretation of his plays that he used a large number of directors: Nicolas Bataille, Sylvain Dhomme, Maurice Jacquemont, Serreau, Poliéri, and Barrault. The stage designer Jacques Noël did almost all the sets.

From 1953 on, the new Paris stage directors were influenced by the Berliner Ensemble and the Brechtian type of very exact, rigorous productions that were based upon an effect of distance to be maintained between audience and stage and between an actor and the character he incarnates. But such theatrical elements were already in the productions of Charles Dullin and were visible, before the direct influence of Brecht, in the mise en scène of Blin, Serreau, and Bataille.

In the mid-1960's the art of the French theater reached an important point in its development. It had two major outlets in Paris: the state-subsidized theaters where, for the first time, a few of the new plays were produced, but where there was always the danger of the dogmatic imposition of theory and style, and the small, privately owned theaters where there was much more chance for experimentation, especially the kinds of experimentation associated with Artaud, surrealism, and the avant-garde theater of the 1950's. There the danger was always the use of the futile type of shock effect on the audience and obscurity of meaning. The two types of French theater, the more standard and the more experimental, were able, at the most fertile moments, to profit from one another as well as from foreign plays and productions.

For a study of a prominent aspect of modern French drama, see Martin Esslin, *Theatre of the Absurd* (1961). Wallace Fowlie's *A Guide to Contemporary French Literature* (1962) and *Dionysus in Paris* (1960) are surveys of twentieth-century French drama. David Grossvogel focuses on four playwrights in *Four Playwrights and a Postscript: Brecht, Ionesco, Beckett, Genet* (1962) and on the modern theater in *The Self-Conscious Stage in Modern French Drama* (1958). Jacques Guicharnaud makes a critical survey of twentieth-century French drama in *Modern French Fiction* (1961) and *Modern French Theatre from Giraudoux to Beckett* (1961). Leonard

C. Pronko's *Avant Garde* (1964) is an enlightening and interesting study of the avant-garde playwrights. Harold Hobson's *The French Theatre of Today* (1953) is a survey, and George E. Wellwarth's *Theater of Protest and Paradox* (1964) focuses on certain aspects of contemporary drama. Henri Peyre's critical anthology *Contemporary French Literature* (1964) provides a basis for studying the trends of the modern French writers. Joseph Chiari's *The Contemporary French Theatre, The Flight from Naturalism* (1959) provides a general study of the subject, while more specific studies can be found in Thomas Bishop's *Pirandello and the French Theater* (1960) and Roger Shattuck's *The Banquet Years* (1958). Also of great interest is Lionel Abel's *Metatheatre: A New View of Dramatic Form* (1963), which studies the avant-garde playwrights.—W. F.

Francesca da Rimini (1853). A tragedy by George Henry BOKER. Written in three weeks in 1853, *Francesca da Rimini* was only a mild success when it was first produced in 1855 at the Broadway Theatre in New York.

The play is set in medieval Italy, where a marriage of state has been arranged between Francesca, daughter of Guido da Polenta of Ravenna, and Lanciotto, the hunchback son of Malatesta da Verrucho of Rimini. Lanciotto sends his brother, Paolo, to Ravenna for Francesca, who mistakes him for Lanciotto and falls in love with him. She discovers her mistake, but does not learn of Lanciotto's deformity until she reaches Rimini. The marriage takes place, but Lanciotto, sensing that his bride does not love him, goes off to war. Paolo and Francesca yield to their love, and Pepe, the court fool, learns their secret. He steals Paolo's dagger and goes to Lanciotto with the lie that he was sent by Paolo to kill him. Lanciotto murders the guilty lovers, as honor demands, and then kills himself out of love for Paolo.

Francesca da Rimini has a single, well-unified plot. The principal characters are interesting and well realized: Lanciotto, whose ugly exterior conceals a noble and sensitive spirit; Francesca, proud and passionate; Paolo, young, handsome, and charming; and Pepe, seeking revenge for the insults he has suffered from the brothers. The blank verse is effectively used to express both passion and wit.—B. H.

Fredro, Count Aleksander (1793–1876). Polish playwright, the greatest writer of comedies in the Polish language. After a period of distinguished service in the Napoleonic wars, Fredro left Paris, where his military fortunes had taken him after the disastrous campaign against Russia, and returned to his native Galicia in Austrian Poland. There he divided his time between playwriting and living the life of a country squire. His major work began appearing from the early 1820's. In 1821 he staged *Pan Geldhab* ("Mr. Moneybags"), a comedy about a social climber in some ways reminiscent of Molière's *Le Bourgeois gentilhomme;* in 1822, *Mąż i żona* ("Husband and Wife"), a skillfully executed comedy of extramarital intrigue with only four speaking parts; in 1825, the excellent farce *Damy i huzary* (*Ladies and Hussars*) about the invasion of an all-male officers' retreat by a group of very determined women; in 1832, the comedy *Pan Jowialski* ("Mr. Joviality"), a satirical probe of the conditions of upper gentry life

ALEKSANDER FREDRO (CAF, WARSAW; POLISH EMBASSY)

in that part of Poland claimed by Austria in the Partitions; in 1833, the delightful comedy *Śluby panieńskie* (*Maidens' Vows*) about two girls' vows not to marry and a young man's triumph over them. Anti-Romantic, to some extent, the play also reminds one of Marivaux and Musset in its treatment of love. In 1834 Fredro produced the comedy generally recognized as his masterpiece, *Zemsta* ("The Vengeance"), about a feud between two old-world Polish squires and their eventual reconciliation through the love and marriage of their children. A year later it was followed by *Dożywocie* ("The Life Annuity"), a clever Molièresque comedy about a usurer and his trials and tribulations trying to keep control of the life annuity of a young hellion.

In 1835, and again in 1842, Fredro found himself savagely attacked by young Romantics of revolutionary political inclinations for his presumed political conservatism and indifference to the cause of Polish national liberation and regeneration. The attacks were without justification but so embittered Fredro that he ceased writing for the public until about 1851 or 1852, when he resumed writing, producing some dozen new plays before his death. Most of these later plays are in prose (unlike the comedies of the "pre-silence" period); with few exceptions they are satirical and set in Galicia under Austrian rule. They began to be staged for the first time in 1877, a year after Fredro died, and continue to be performed from time to time on Polish stages, although none seems to have won any permanent place in the Polish repertory. For many years Fredro's later plays were dismissed as significantly inferior to those done in the period from 1821 to 1835. It is true that none of them compares to such masterworks as *Damy i huzary, Śluby panień- skie,* and *Zemsta,* but they have attracted more favor- able attention in recent times. While such comedies of the later period as *Wielki człowiek do małych in- teresów* ("A Great Man for Small Affairs") and *Świecka zgasła* ("The Candle Has Gone Out") have little possibility of rivaling Fredro's major works in the affection of the Polish theatergoing public (for whom a Fredro performance is always something of an occasion), they are respectable plays that can stand on their own merits.—H. B. S.

Freytag, Gustav. See GERMANY: *nineteenth cen- tury.*

Friel, Brian (1929–   ). Irish playwright. A native of Northern Ireland, Friel began his career as a schoolteacher. At present, he devotes his full energy to writing, residing most of the time in a remote sec- tion of County Donegal. His first play, *The Enemy Within* (1960), is based on the life of St. Columba (543–615), one of Ireland's early Christian scholar- saints. His best work thus far, *Philadelphia, Here I Come* (1964), deals with the private emotions of a young Irishman about to emigrate to America. The young man's private self is represented by a second character who is invisible to everyone but the audi- ence. This theatrical device serves to reinforce the play's theme of the impossibility of communication, particularly with one's self. Friel's latest play is *The Loves of Cass McGuire* (1966). It focuses on an in- domitable seventy-year-old woman, living in an old- age home, whose capacity for life is never diminished by rejection or defeat. *Lovers* (1967) consists of two contemporary one-act plays. The first of these, *Win- ners,* focuses on two spirited young lovers on the last day of their lives. The companion piece, *Losers,* deals with a pair of middle-aged lovers farcically at- tempting to outwit a puritanical parent. Friel's other plays include *The Doubtful Paradise* (1961) and *The Blind Mice* (1961).—E. Q.

Frisch, Max [Rudolf] (1911–   ). Swiss play- wright, novelist, journalist, and architect. Frisch, al- though generally considered a Swiss, possesses as varied an ancestry as his plays are international and unpredictable. In the autobiographical sections of his published diaries he remarks that not even his family name is Swiss; rather it was brought south by his pa- ternal grandfather from the environs of Austria. His mother had served as a nursery governess in tsarist Russia, and his father was an architect, who, because he lacked a formal education in his field, desired to see his sons become academicians. Nonetheless, Max and his brother had the prerogative to choose their individual ways. His brother chose to become a chemist.

Frisch claims that he read little as a youth (he was more interested in soccer) but that he was especially fond of two novels—*Uncle Tom's Cabin* and *Don Quixote.* It was a production of Schiller's *Die Räuber* (*The Robbers*), albeit a bad one, that first aroused his interest in the theater. He claims to have been totally amazed the first time he saw a play that was not an established classic, a play about contemporary situa- tions and played in contemporary dress. It made him realize for the first time that plays were still capable of being written.

With this realization to impel him onward, he wrote his first play, *Stahl* ("Steel," never published or produced), at the age of sixteen. Not long after having it rejected by Max Reinhardt, he discovered a complete set of Ibsen's plays, which influenced the writing of his next two or three efforts. Eventually, however, he retired to the university as the inevitable recourse. As a student of Germanic studies he was lonely, rash in judgment, uncertain, and wound up in a love affair about which the girl knew nothing. When Frisch was twenty-two, his father died and he was forced to make his own way in the world. This necessity led him into journalism, as a result of which he traveled widely. This series of adventures was the impetus for, in his own words, "an all-too-early novel," which nonetheless won him the Swiss Schil- ler Stipend in 1943 but which made him realize the danger of writing for public consumption before one has anything to say. At the age of twenty-five he re- turned to school, to study architecture. A year later Frisch destroyed all his unpublished writings and secretly determined never to write again. This re- solve lasted for two years, for in 1939 he began a diary that was to be published in 1940, the year he received his diploma in architecture.

His next literary ventures were novels, one pub- lished in 1943 and one the following year. Time for such literary efforts arose from having set up his own architectural establishment. In 1954 he wrote per- haps his most successful novel, *Stiller,* which con- cerns a sculptor who assumes a double personality in order to escape others' opinions of him.

His activity as a playwright began again in 1944, when his romance *Santa Cruz* (1946) was written. It is a Strindbergian kind of dream play in which time and space are freely handled. Frisch calls this first produced play, *Nun singen sie wieder* ("Now They Sing Again," 1945), an attempt at a requiem for those slaughtered in the Nazi holocaust. Its implicit burden is that those who died did so in vain and that nothing at all was learned from the experience. The play is close in spirit to Thornton Wilder's *Our Town.* One of Frisch's most famous plays is *Die chi- nesische Mauer* (*The Chinese Wall,* 1946), a farce centered upon man's inability to learn and the danger of total annihilation. It is a play of great freedom of form and with anachronistic juxtaposition of charac- ters. *Als der Krieg zu Ende war* (*When the War Was Over,* 1949), an epic drama set in Russian-occupied Berlin, is fraught with despair and defeatist ideas. *Graf Öderland* ("Count Öderland," 1951) deals even more violently with despair as well as with an existential absurdity. Crime is presented as an in- tellectual choice, although the end result is the hero's self-destruction. DON JUAN OR THE LOVE OF GEOME- TRY shows the great lover as one more interested in mathematics than in amorous adventures, for love lacks the precision of geometry. He finally marries, but without love, seduced but never seducing. THE FIREBUGS deals with the stupidity of man in averting obvious destruction.

Most typical of Frisch's work is his constant at- tempt to deal with current problems of vital political import and, more universally, with man's helpless- ness, or perhaps stupidity, when faced with the ques- tion of his own survival. Frisch's cynicism and paci- fism depend ultimately on the power inherent in irony. In form his plays are generally experimental, at times in a Strindbergian psychological sense, at other times in a Brechtian structural sense. Frisch has written some of the most vital and theatrical plays of the last few decades and has furthered the theater's role as a significant force in contemporary society.

There is only one book devoted completely to Frisch, by Ulrich Weisstein, *Max Frisch* (1968). Essays dealing with him are by George Wellwarth, "Friedrich Dürrenmatt and Max Frisch: Two Views of the Drama," *Tulane Drama Review* (March 1962), and "Max Frisch," in the same writer's *The Theater of Protest and Paradox* (1964). Frisch is also discussed in a book by H. F. Garten, *Modern German Drama* (1959). Two other essays are by Peter Seidmann, "Modern Swiss Drama: Frisch and Dürrenmatt," *Books Abroad,* Vol. 34 (1960), and by Theodore Ziolkowski, "Max Frisch: Moralist without a Moral," *Yale French Studies,* No. 29 (1962). —C. R. M.

Frogs (Batrachoi, 405 B.C.). A comedy by ARISTOPHANES. Athenian drama is dead, and the patron god of the theater, Dionysus, decides he will have to go to the Underworld and bring back Euripides to revive theatrical art. Dressing himself in the costume of Herakles (who has made the expedition once before to bring back Cerberus) and taking his faithful retainer Xanthias as porter, Dionysus sets out, not too bravely. After some farcical incidents of mistaken identity, caused by his disguise and the still-fresh memory of Herakles' misbehavior on the previous occasion, Dionysus arrives at the plains of Elysium in time to act as arbitrator in a conflict between Euripides and Aeschylus, both of whom are claiming the Underworld throne of poetry. After a long and bitter contest Dionysus decides that Aeschylus is, after all, the better poet. He returns to Athens with him.

Frogs was a great success when first produced and achieved the special honor of being given a repeat performance. Its popularity was due, not to the classic comic scenes during Dionysus' journey, but to the serious advice that Aristophanes, through the Chorus, offers to the citizens of Athens. The city had experienced an antidemocratic coup (411 B.C.) followed by a countercoup that sent many citizens into exile. Meanwhile, the war with Sparta was going badly, and a vital sea battle the year before the play's production had been won only at the cost of including many slaves and noncitizens in the fleet. Aristophanes urges the Athenians to give amnesty to the exiles and bind up the wounds of the revolution. On a larger perspective, the whole of the second half of the play, too often regarded as a purely literary debate between rival schools of aesthetics, should be seen as an expression of a conflict that affected all the values

and traditions of Athenian life. In this conflict, Euripides represents a new order, which leveled social classes and viewed moral issues in relativist terms, while Aeschylus stands for the traditions and attitudes of the age of Marathon and Salamis (490–480 B.C.), when Athens was entering the era of her greatest power and prestige. This use of the playwrights to represent certain political values is consistent with the position of artists in Athenian society— bearers of the national image and perpetuators of the ancestral values—a point on which Aeschylus and Euripides agree, though they agree on nothing else. By reincarnating Aeschylus, Dionysus is hoping to regenerate Athens.

A few months after the production of *Frogs* Athens lost a decisive battle, her food supplies were cut off, and the war was over. The attempt to bring back to life the spirit of Marathon was a failure.

Translations of the play are listed under Aristophanes.—K. C.

Full Moon in March, A (1935). A one-act verse play by William Butler YEATS. Based upon a Celtic legend about "an ancient Irish Queen" and her beheaded lover, with parallels to the tale of Salomé, *A Full Moon in March* is in the style of Yeats's modified Japanese *noh* drama and expresses a ritualistic variation of the theme of "heroic wantoness" with which the poet was preoccupied in his later years. It is one of his "Plays for Dancers," with two Attendants who serve as a chorus and accompany the speeches and movements of the two characters, the cruel Queen and the Swineherd poet, with drum and flute and zither. The cold and chaste Queen, with "crown of gold," is confronted by the Swineherd, who has "rolled among the dung of swine" and now comes to win her as his wife by singing of her great beauty and predicting that after a desecrating night of love she will beget his child in the dung. She feels insulted and orders that he be beheaded, but before he is taken away he foretells that a drop of blood from his severed head will enter her womb and get her with child. After he is beheaded, the play reaches its climax in the Queen's dance of adoration with the severed head, which she finally kisses in a symbolic gesture of her fated "desecration and the lover's night." In Yeats's lunar interpretation of human destiny, *A Vision* (1925), the full moon represents the phase of greatest subjectivity and "unity of being"; and March for him is "the month of victims and saviors." Thus, like a sacrificed and resurrected god, the prophetic Swineherd fulfills his destiny and is ritualistically united with the impregnated and beatified Queen—"crown of gold" mingled with "dung of swine," the consummation of sacred and profane love. Yeats wrote another version of this play in *The King of the Great Clock Tower* (1934).—D. K.

G

Galileo (Leben das Galilei).   A play by Bertolt BRECHT. Written 1938/39, a second, American, version was written between 1945 and 1947 in collaboration with Charles Laughton. In the latter, two of the original fifteen scenes have been cut and rhyming verses introduce each scene.

Galileo is a badly paid lecturer at the University of Padua, which belongs to the Republic of Venice, and he has to give time-consuming private lessons to increase his income. He lives with his daughter Virginia, his housekeeper Mrs. Sarti, and her little son Andrea. His student, Ludovico Marsili, who has just returned from Holland, tells him about the invention of the telescope. Galileo unscrupulously copies it and presents it as his own invention to the senators of the republic. The telescope also enables him to establish the truth of Copernicus' hypothesis that the earth revolves around the sun and is only one star among others. Asked where God is in this new world, Galileo answers: "Within ourselves. Or— nowhere." To find more time for research, Galileo accepts the invitation of the grand duke of Florence to become his court mathematician. Galileo's friends warn him against exchanging the freedom of Venice for the financial security of Florence. For Galileo, however, it is equally important to have time for experiments and to have money "to fill his belly." He soon discovers that reason cannot, as he had thought, overcome religious dogma. When he proves that the earth is not the center of the universe, the chief astronomer of the Papal College has to admit that Galileo's findings are correct, but the Inquisition forbids the publication of these facts.

For eight years Galileo keeps silent. Ludovico wants to marry his daughter but only under the condition that her father does not take up the "forbidden studies" again. That is exactly what Galileo does, however, and although the new pope is a mathematician and a friend of the sciences, the power of the Inquisition proves to be stronger. Galileo is arrested and brought to Rome. He is shown the instruments of torture and abjures his teachings. When his pupils hear the news, Andrea cries: "Unhappy the land that breeds no hero." Galileo replies: "Unhappy is the land that needs a hero." Until his death Galileo lives in a country house as a prisoner of the Inquisition.

A SCENE FROM BERTOLT BRECHT'S *Galileo* (FRENCH CULTURAL SERVICES)

He is allowed to write his "Discorsi," but the finished pages are locked away. One day his former pupil Andrea Sarti visits him before he leaves for Holland. When they are alone for a moment, Galileo hands him a secretly made copy of the completed "Discorsi." Andrea, who had shown disgust for Galileo's cowardice, now admires him: "The fear of death is human. But science is not concerned with our weaknesses." Galileo discards this excuse: "As a scientist I had an almost unique opportunity. In my day astronomy emerged into the market place. I have betrayed my profession." Galileo has not used science to change the world and to serve mankind, but rather to serve the authorities. "I surrendered my knowledge to the powers that be, to use it, no, not to use it, abuse it, as it suits their ends." Andrea succeeds in smuggling the manuscript out of the country.

Galileo, regarded by many critics as somewhat autobiographical, is a good example for tracing Brecht's influence on modern playwrights. Robert Bolt considers his *A Man for All Seasons* to be a Brechtian play, which led to a big controversy between him and the British drama critic Kenneth Tynan, reprinted in Tynan's book *Left of Right* (1967). Like *Mother Courage* and *Galileo,* it is a historical play set in the Renaissance. John Osborne's *Luther* has been viewed, by Henry Popkin among others, in this tradition, and Heinar Kipphardt's *Oppenheimer* deals with the same basic problem as Brecht's *Galileo:* the role of the scientist in modern society. In France, Arthur Adamov is considered a Brechtian playwright. He himself said in 1962 that "Brecht and the Algerian war became the inducing factors for my development." Under the influence of Brecht, Adamov began to write more historical and socially concerned plays. He even rewrote Brecht's *Die Tage der Commune* ("The Days of the Commune"), which deals with the Paris uprising of 1871.

Aufbau einer Rolle—Galilei (1958) contains text, photographs, and Brecht's account of the collaboration with Laughton. Ernst Schumacher, the Marxist critic, in his *Drama und Geschichte* (1965) (excerpts of which have appeared in *The Drama Review,* T 38, 1968) regards *Galileo* as a demonstration of Brecht's later notion of a "dialectical theater."—H. R.

Galsworthy, John (1867–1933). English novelist and playwright. Galsworthy was educated at Oxford and qualified for the law, but he preferred travel to active legal practice. His legal training, however, can be seen in certain elements of his plays that smacked of the courtroom—debate evenly balanced on both sides, scrupulous attention to the demands of justice and fair play, and behavior limited by a code of sportsmanlike conduct as strictly confined as the etiquette of the law court (to which it must be added that some of his characters are, so to speak, guilty of contempt of court). He first won attention as a novelist and was one of those men of letters who were induced to write plays for the Royal Court Theatre when John E. Vedrenne and Harley Granville-Barker were running it. In 1906 Galsworthy published his novel *The Man of Property,* which was the first volume of his trilogy *The Forsyte Saga,* and his first play, *The Silver Box,* was presented at the Royal Court. This conventionally realistic "well-made play" made its social point by contrasting the two kinds of justice meted out to two drunken ne'er-do-wells—a poor man who steals a silver cigarette box and goes to prison and a rich man who capriciously steals a woman's purse and settles the matter privately. Galsworthy was hailed as a fine dramatist, but his play of the following year was a disappointment. *Joy,* unlike most of his plays, does not touch upon social issues. In interpreting an adolescent's discovery of the world, it is more like Galsworthy's fiction. *Strife* (1909), one of his most admired plays, vividly presents the struggle between two diehard leaders of capital and labor, both of whom are destroyed by the costly strike that they unnecessarily prolong. The protagonist of JUSTICE is a victim of circumstances, hounded by the law and ruined by prison life. *The Pigeon* (1912) balanced the scale by showing a philanthropist victimized by the unfortunates whom he tries to help. *The Eldest Son* (1912) brings to mind the themes and techniques of *The Silver Box,* for here again two kinds of justice are shown: A young heir has gotten a girl into trouble, and so has an employee on his estate, but only the employee is compelled to do right by his girl and marry her. As usual, the issues are fully argued out, and the private inclination of the individuals concerned is made to seem secondary. Duty is all. *The Fugitive* (1913) is a more personal play, recalling some of the characters and events of *The Forsyte Saga:* A clergyman's daughter, bored to death by an unhappy marriage, leaves her husband, tries to earn her own way, lives with an impoverished artist, tries to become a prostitute, and finally kills herself. *The Mob* (1914) is a strident antiwar, antipatriotic play about a principled politician who pays with his life for his principles. *The Foundations* (1917), a comic conjecture about social upheavals following the war, was a departure from Galsworthy's usual themes and style.

The Skin Game (1920) did, however, mark an alteration in Galsworthy's career in the theater. It ran for nearly a year and made him, for the first time, a commercially successful dramatist. Curiously, it offers the same themes he had used earlier—a conflict between two families, the genteel Hillcrists and the *nouveaux riches* Hornblowers, over a plot of land that the Hornblowers want to use for commercial purposes, thereby ruining the Hillcrists' view. Each side has some justification, but each is morally compromised before the play is over. While *The Skin Game* is no better than *Strife* or *The Silver Box,* it gave a considerable boost to Galsworthy's fortunes. *Loyalties* (1922), another commercial success, is about a wealthy Jew and an officer who are at odds over a sum of money that the officer is charged with stealing from the Jew; as the conflict develops, it becomes no longer merely personal but pits the honor of a gentleman against the honor of a Jew. *Old English* (1924) is, for once, not a play about issues, but an affectionate portrait of an octogenarian business tycoon facing a variety of crises. *Escape* (1926) was novel in its design, but it offered some familiar ingredients—a victim of circumstances and a conflict between fair play and the demands of the law. In a series of brief episodes, an escaped convict encounters a number of individuals who must decide whether to turn him in or to help a likable underdog fighting against great odds.

In 1932 Galsworthy won the Nobel Prize for literature. He wrote twenty-one full-length plays and seven short plays; most of them combined the realistic "well-made" form, shrewd theatrical sense, and social protest that stemmed not so much from any coherent social philosophy as from a sportsmanlike desire to see fair play for the underdog.

The standard biography is H. V. Marrot's *The Life and Letters of John Galsworthy* (1935). John Russell Taylor's *The Rise and Fall of the Well-Made Play* (1967) provides a contemporary analysis of the plays. —H. P.

Game of Love, The (Liebelei, 1895). A play by Arthur SCHNITZLER. *The Game of Love,* like most of Schnitzler's plays, takes place in the Vienna of his time. It concerns Christine, a young, gentle, and sensitive girl of the middle class, who makes the mistake of taking her lover seriously. She falls in love with a dashing young Viennese gentleman, Fritz, who is already engaged in an amorous affair with a married woman. The woman's husband challenges him to a duel, Fritz is killed, and Christine, believing in his love for her, yet realizing too late that it was mere illusion on her part and that she was only a pastime, commits suicide.

The Game of Love, though sentimental on the surface, is at its base a solid and bitter indictment of society, of its superficial and delusory orientation. A play about morals, there is no moralizing. Schnitzler's dissection of social and sexual mores of imperial Vienna at the turn of the century is graceful yet always directed at his desired end. He shows in Christine's violent, passionate, but always human revolt against convention (the acceptance of the rules of the game) the end of an age. Her act tears a rent so wide in the curtain of bourgeois respectability that it can never again be mended. Perhaps this has made this work one of Schnitzler's most popular and resilient plays.

The most recent translation of the play is by Carl R. Mueller, in *Masterpieces of the Modern Central European Theater* (1967), edited by Robert Corrigan.—C. R. M.

Gammer Gurton's Needle (c. 1560). A farce probably written by William Stevenson (1521–1575). The attribution of the play to Stevenson, a fellow at Christ's College, Cambridge, where the play was first produced, is now generally accepted. The plot, such as it is, concerns the series of mishaps and misunderstandings arising from Gammer Gurton's needle, lost while she was sewing the pants of her servant, Hodge. Thanks to the marvelous capacity for mischief-making of Diccon, a Bedlam beggar, the simple loss becomes magnified into a *cause célèbre* within the little English village. Charges and countercharges fill the air, all of them generated by Diccon's pranks. In the end everything is resolved when Diccon slaps Hodge on the seat of his pants. Hodge's screams leave little doubt as to the location of the lost needle.

Like *Ralph Roister Doister,* the other early English regular comedy, the play manages to blend the formal framework of classical comedy with the substance of native English humor. In this respect, *Gammer Gurton's Needle* is even more successful in its manipulation of contrasting elements. The result is a play of undiminished vitality. See ENGLAND: *Tudor drama.*—E. Q.

FEDERICO GARCÍA LORCA (NEW YORK PUBLIC LIBRARY)

García Lorca, Federico (1898–1936). Spanish poet and playwright. García Lorca is the best-known Spanish poet of the twentieth century and the most widely translated Spanish dramatist of the age; his dramatic works are constantly in production all over the Western world. These facts owe something to Lorca's tragic death at the hands of the Falangists; they also derive from the oddly symbolic way in which Lorca's intensely personal work reflects the death of liberty and the creative imagination in Spain, coinciding with the death of the Spanish Republic after three years of civil war (1936–1939).

Lorca was born on June 5, 1898, the son of a wealthy farmer, in Fuentevaqueros (the province of Granada), Spain. Before he was eight, he had built a miniature theater and had improvised plays in which the servants and members of the family were all made to participate. The family moved to the city of Granada when at sixteen he took up studies in philosophy, letters, and law at the provincial university. He had been writing poetry for some time and in 1918 he printed a small edition of his first book, *Impresiones y paisajes (Impressions and Landscapes),* a series of impressionistic prose pieces that were the fruit of a tour through Spain. The following year Lorca arrived in Madrid with a manuscript of poems and enrolled in the Residencia de Estudiantes, a liberal, English-style college.

On March 22, 1920, Lorca's first play, *El maleficio de la mariposa (The Butterfly's Evil Spell),* was produced in Madrid, where within a year his first book of poems (*Libro de poemas*) was also published. Due in part to his lifelong habit of reading to friends new poems and plays from manuscript—a habit which satisfied him more than publication—many of his works appeared much later than the actual date of composition. *Canciones* (*Songs*), his second book of poems, was not published until 1927, and *Romancero gitano* (*Book of Gypsy Ballads*) did not appear in print until 1928, although many individual poems in these volumes go back to the early twenties and before. *Mariana Pineda,* his play about a nineteenth-century historical figure who was sacrificed in the cause of liberty, was produced in 1927 in Madrid and Barcelona. By the end of 1928, Lorca had become a widely celebrated poet and dramatist.

But troubled by personal problems, Lorca went to New York City in June 1929, having completed a new play, *Amor de Don Perlimplín con Belisa en su jardín* (*The Love of Don Perlimplín and Belisa in the Garden,* 1931), some months earlier. Though it lasted only a little over a year, his North American stay, including a visit to Cuba to give readings and lectures, was unusually fruitful. It gave birth to his remarkable book of semisurrealist poems, *Poeta en Nueva York* (*Poet in New York*), published posthumously in 1940, and the comedy THE SHOEMAKER'S PRODIGIOUS WIFE, a play actually begun a few years earlier in Spain. There were also other plays and verses written during this trip: some completed later and produced in Spain, others left unfinished, and still others finished but lost or published posthumously.

The last seven years of Lorca's life were his most productive. Impelled by his new experiences abroad and by his appointment as director of the government-sponsored traveling theater La Barraca, he wrote in rapid succession the three great folk plays by which he is most often represented in theater around the world: BLOOD WEDDING, YERMA, and THE HOUSE OF BERNARDA ALBA. Other full-length dramatic works include *Así que pasen cinco años* (*When Five Years Pass,* written 1930–1931), *En el retablillo de Don Cristóbal* (*The Frame of Don Cristóbal,* 1935), and *Doña Rosita la soltera, o el lenguaje de las flores* (*Doña Rosita the Spinster, or the Language of the Flowers,* 1935). Lorca published the magnificently moving elegy *Llanto por Ignacio Sánchez Mejías* (*The Lament for the Death of a Bullfighter*) in 1935, and in the last year of his life he was planning new plays; he may even have completed two of these—*Los sueños de mi prima Aurelia* ("The Dreams of My Cousin Aurelia") and *El público* ("The Audience"). Lorca also had two new collections of poems, *El Divan del Tamarit* (*The Divan at the Tamarit*), published after his death, and *Sonetos del amor oscuro* ("Sonnets of Dark Love"), now presumably lost. In the early summer of 1936 Lorca was preparing for a trip to Mexico to produce several of his plays, just as he had done in 1933 when he went to Buenos Aires to direct *Mariana Pineda, The Shoemaker's Prodigious Wife,* and *Blood Wedding.* But this time, in a quick change of mind, he went back for a visit to his home in Granada. Two days later, on July 18, the civil war broke out, and on August 19, 1936, Lorca was captured, taken out by a Falangist firing squad, and executed in an open field in Viznar, near Granada.

Lorca's folk plays reflect the kind of society in which a woman may be made to enact a dominant role, that is, a preromantic or matriarchal society where her action is functional and not sentimental. In Spain, the maternal and matriarchal ideals that have survived until recently gave rise to a literature of Mariolatry, feminine martyrdom, the ethical norms of the *dueña,* and a castigated Don Juanism. Lorca, in his folk plays, seems to be saying that the society that for centuries had sustained such ideals has by now completely devitalized them. What remains is an anachronistic virtue that propels its representatives to inevitable defeat, since its value can no longer be fulfilled. The refuges into which all his female protagonists escape are fatally predetermined by the enormity of their basic but insatiable needs. And so Lorca's heroines endlessly perpetuate desire in an eroticism which, like Yerma's, ends in a metaphysical suicide, or, like that of Bernarda's daughters, surges up briefly only to be snuffed out within the walls of a white house—their prison and tomb. The denouement in play after play leaves the audience with the same paralyzed circumstance of defeat; there is no resolution that reveals a multilevel tragic insight. This prevents Lorca's plays from rising out of pathos into real tragedy, although the same may be said of Chekhov's or Strindberg's plays, and for similar reasons. A tragedy that validates personal integrity evidently fails in the modern world, where it cannot be resolved in terms of social acknowledgment, since society invariably degrades by nullifying the virtue of personal integrity.

But it must be recognized that Lorca, perhaps uniquely among the modern poets, succeeded in writing serious plays that have been popular successes on the stage. He used his knowledge of the poetic art as much as his lifelong activity in the theater to create these plays. Lorca's imaginative extension of poetic imagery into the structure of his drama emphasizes his sharply defined quest for a personal expression —an expression that begins to merge with the anonymity of folk art in such plays as *Blood Wedding, Amor de Don Perlimplín,* and *Doña Rosita la soltera.* Lorca could work unusual verbal and scenic devices into the marrow of his drama. And even after wandering in his surrealist period through difficult, unresolved material, he returned to the source of his genius and, from his poetic experiments, distilled dramatic possibilities for the great plays that followed almost immediately. In these ways and by transmuting widely connotative emotions from the folk ballad to drama, he approached a resolution to the often-posed problem of the period—how to integrate the mutually antagonistic effects of poetry and drama in the theater. When Lorca did best, as in *Yerma* and *The House of Bernarda Alba,* he showed, probably better than W. B. Yeats or T. S. Eliot, the only other poet-playwrights of the age, that a courageous poet working on his own terms in the theater can command the respect of international audiences.

For a biography and criticism see Arturo Barea's *Lorca, the Poet and his People* (1949), Manuel Durán, ed., *Lorca—A Collection of Critical Essays* (1962), Edwin Honig's *García Lorca* (1963), and Robert Lema's *The Theatre of García Lorca* (1963). For translations see J. Graham-Lujan and R. L. O'Connell's *Five Plays* (*Comedies and Tragicomedies*) (1963) and their translations in *Three Tragedies* (1947).—E. H.

Garnier, Robert (1545?–1590). French tragic playwright. Garnier, the most talented of French sixteenth-century writers of tragedy, was born at La Ferté-Bernard. We are uncertain not only about his birth date but about nearly all aspects of his young life. A poem Garnier wrote in 1564, entitled *Chant royal,* intimates that he became familiar rather early with the Pléiade school of French poetry, but it is not yet possible to state whether he knew these poets personally or indirectly. In 1564 he traveled to Toulouse to study law. There he composed his first tragedy, *Porcie,* which was published in Paris, where Garnier lived between 1566 and 1569. The play was printed with sonnets by Pierre de Ronsard, Rémy Belleau, and Jean-Antoine di Baïf—a clear sign that by this period Garnier was well known to the leading poets of his day. In 1569 he bought a court post at Le Mans, which he held for seventeen years. The poems composed at this time show a firm Catholic and royalist stance. For this reason, while the difficulties of maintaining order in so troubled a time can explain why Garnier by 1583 was seeking to change posts, it is surprising to learn that he eventually participated in the Catholic League against his king. His actions are best explained by the desperation many Frenchmen felt as the religious wars progressed. Indeed, Garnier is said to have died of "chagrin," pursued by debts and grief.

Garnier composed one tragicomedy, *Bradamante* (1582), and seven tragedies, *Porcie* (1567), *Hippolyte* (1573), *Cornélie* (1574), *Marc Antoine* (1578), *La Troade* ("The Destruction of Troy," 1579), *Antigone* (1580), and *Les Juifves* ("The Jewish Women," 1583). Historical allusions within the plays belie the chronological spread indicated by the dates of publication. All save *Les Juifves,* which appears to have been written after 1582, Garnier composed between 1564 and 1574. While the list of titles shows material derived from Roman history, Greek legend, and the Bible, Garnier approached his sources in a uniform manner. He related them to contemporary events and drew his moral. *Porcie* preaches pardon and reconciliation in a time of civil war. *Cornélie* portrays in Garnier's words "a great republic torn by the ambitious discord of its citizens." The entire action of *Les Juifves* depicts the suffering of a people that has turned away from its God. Even *Bradamante,* which is taken from an episode in Lodovico Ariosto's *Orlando furioso,* begins its now serious, now comic plot with Charlemagne's decision to rebuild his domain, ravaged by the Saracens.

The form and content of Garnier's tragedies derive from traditional French Humanist theory and are modeled on Seneca in particular. They are in five acts, with a chorus, sententia, and stichomythia. They portray rulers, crushed by fate, who lament their misfortune in an elevated style. Were his plays only this, however, they would have little to recommend them over innumerable others written between 1550 and 1600. In truth, Garnier possessed a definite dramatic sense and a particularly lyric voice. The numerous scenes of confrontation and lament indicate to what degree Garnier sought particular effects within the familiar tale of the reversal of fortune. As characters argue, suspense grows; when disaster strikes, Garnier knew as no other writer of his time how to transform the realization of doom into a poignant, moving scene.

Unfortunately, at present there are no studies on Garnier in English and no English editions of his plays.—D. S., Jr.

Garrett, [João Batista de] Almeida (1799–1854). Portuguese novelist, poet, and playwright. The life of Garrett is linked to the political events in Portugal during the era in which absolutists and liberals disputed for power. He was born in Oporto and studied law at the University of Coimbra. From the time that he arrived there in 1816 he distinguished himself in politics by his liberal ideas, in society by his painstaking elegance, and in literature by writing neoclassic tragedies and poetry. Immediately after finishing his studies, Garrett was accused of writing an immoral poem: *O retrato de Venus* (*The Portrait of Venus,* pub. 1821). He gave a brilliant defense in his own behalf in the court of justice, thus becoming well known in public circles. A series of military uprisings by the conservatives obliged Garrett to seek asylum in England and France, where he wrote patriotic poems on the Portuguese playwright Luís de Camões and on a medieval Portuguese theme. Gradually, he adopted the Romantic aesthetic. Upon his return to Portugal with the victory of the liberals, with whom he served as a common soldier, Garrett was commissioned by the government to draw up a plan for the reorganization of Portuguese theatrical activity. He established the National Conservatory for the fostering of actors and writers and promoted the construction of a theater, the present-day Maria

ALMEIDA GARRETT (CASA DE PORTUGAL, NEW YORK)

II Theatre, in Lisbon. Of unstable character, Garrett frequently turned against his own liberal friends and had a very irregular amorous life also.

His principal plays are *Um auto de Gil Vicente* ("An Act by Gil Vicente," 1838), *D. Felipa de Vilhena* ("Dona Felipa of Bilhena," 1840), *O alfageme de Santarém* ("The Armorer from Santarém," 1842), and the *obra-prima* of modern Portuguese theater, *Frei Luís de Sousa* ("Friar Luiz of Sousa," 1843). This prose drama in three acts deals with an historical event from the time of the Spanish occupation, to which Garrett added scenes from his imagination. The structure is classical, just as is the elegant language, but the sentiments of patriotism and brotherly love are dealt with in accordance with the Romantic vision of the author. The action accrues little by little the elements of the final tragedy and ends with a synthesis in which fatherland and religion are glorified, in spite of the adverse destiny of the family of Manuel de Sousa Coutinho, whose head becomes a priest, changing his name to Friar Luís de Sousa.

Besides having been the initiator of Romanticism in Portugal, a renovator of the drama, and a politician and diplomat, Garrett was an energetic journalist who dealt with the most diverse topics of national interest.

The plays of Garrett have not been translated into English.—J. P.

Gascoigne, George (1542?–1577). English playwright and poet. Educated at Trinity College, Cambridge, and Gray's Inn, Gascoigne began his career as a courtier and court entertainer. In the latter capacity he assisted in the preparations for two lavish theatrical pageants (at Kenilworth and Woodstock) presented before Elizabeth in 1575.

Gascoigne is best known for his nondramatic works: *The Steel Glass* (1576), one of the earliest formal verse satires in English; *The Adventures Passed by Master F. J.* (1573), the first English novel; and "Certain Notes of Instruction" (1578), the earliest English treatise on prosody. His dramatic work is also distinguished for its pioneering qualities. In 1566 he wrote, in collaboration with Francis Kinwelmershe (fl. 1566–?1580), *Jocasta*, a tragedy in blank verse. Translated from an Italian version of Euripides' *Phoenician Women*, *Jocasta* is the earliest English play based upon Greek drama. In the same year Gascoigne also produced his *Supposes,* a translation of Ariosto's *I suppositi* and the earliest extant prose comedy in English. A comedy of intrigue, *Supposes* is a fast-moving, skillfully plotted farce. It attained considerable popularity and underwent a number of transformations on the Elizabethan stage, the best known of which is as the source of the subplot (Bianca and her suitors) of Shakespeare's *The Taming of the Shrew*. Gascoigne is also the author of *The Glass of Government* (c. 1575), a "tragicall comedie." Probably designed only as a closet drama, this early example of tragicomedy is yet another instance of Gascoigne's literary pioneering.

The standard edition of Gascoigne's works is *The Works of George Gascoigne* (1907–1910), edited by J. W. Cunliffe in two volumes. The best biography is C. T. Prouty's *George Gascoigne: Elizabethan Courtier, Soldier and Poet* (1942).—E. Q.

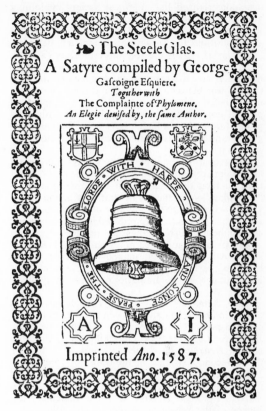

TITLE PAGE FROM GEORGE GASCOIGNE'S *The Steel Glass* 1587 (NEW YORK PUBLIC LIBRARY)

Gas Trilogy, The (Die Gas Trilogie, 1917–1920). A trilogy by Georg KAISER, which traces in a loose, expansive manner the history of a family which attempts to cope with the social and economic problems of a modern technological society.

Die Koralle (The Coral, 1917) shows the attempts of Billionaire to rid himself of the memories of his wretched childhood. He realizes that his driving ambition for power and wealth was actually a desire to break with his past and to "wash away" the hardships he had endured. However, despite his wealth he finds himself alone and unhappy when his children reject him. He then sees another way to erase his past. By assuming the identity of his secretary—his physical double—whose childhood was a happy one, he hopes to rid himself of his "ghosts." However, since he had to commit murder for this new identity, he must suffer the death penalty.

In *Gas I* (1918) the Billionaire's son rejects the capitalist system of his father and tries to raise his workers up to the level of the "new man." He does this first by socializing his own gas-producing factory with the intention of creating an industrial utopia. This fails, however, for the workers hope to see their share in the profits increase even though the gas is used as an implement of war. They assume all the evil characteristics of the typical capitalist. The son then tries to lead the workers to a complete rejection of this industrialized but unethical society by joining him in a pastoral utopian community. This attempt is likewise rejected by them. Thus he finds his dreams and aspirations for his workers completely defeated.

In *Gas II* (1920) the full force of Kaiser's pessimism is felt. The great-grandchild of the original Billionaire is now a worker in the gas factory during a time of war between the Blues and the Yellows. He urges his fellow workers to join him in a campaign of patient, nonviolent endurance. They reject him and proceed to produce a highly poisonous, fatal gas. The great-grandson despairs and blows up the factory and all with it.

In the history of drama Kaiser's plays represent a high point in abstraction, in a "derealization" of action. In fact, they have been called *Denkspiele*—"idea plays"—for the slight dramatic action is obviously secondary to the playing out of the dialectical arguments. Characters are reduced to nameless types; environmental surroundings are replaced by a few symbols; language is compressed to a "telegram style." All these radical maneuvers are devices to bring to the foreground the speculative conflict of ideas rather than the dramatic conflict of individuals. —C. A. M.

Gatti, Armand (1924–   ). French playwright. Gatti's intention has always been to write politically oriented plays. The concentration camp is the background for *L'Enfant Rat* ("The Child Rat," pub. 1960) and *La Deuxième Existence du camp de Tatenberg* ("The Second Existence of the Camp of Tatenberg," 1962). The failure of a strike, in which Gatti's own father participated, is the subject of *La Vie imaginaire de l'éboueur Auguste G.* ("The Imaginary Existence of the Scavenger Augustus G.," 1962). Performed in 1959 in the Théâtre Récamier, *Le Crapaud-buffle* ("The Toad-Buffalo") is a series of sketches that allude to French and international politics. In the style of the American author John Dos Passos or the new French novelist Claude Simon, Gatti is indifferent to the order of time and space. He directed one of his own plays at the Théâtre National Populaire: *Chant public pour deux chaises électriques* ("Public Song for Two Electric Chairs," 1966). The subject of the play is the suffering, between 1920 and 1926, and the execution of the two Italian anarchists Sacco and Vanzetti in the Boston penitentiary.—W. F.

Gay, John (1685–1732). English poet and playwright. Gay was born in Barnstable, Devonshire, where he attended the local grammar school. When about seventeen he was apprenticed to a London silk mercer. Some five years later he became secretary to poet and playwright Aaron Hill, whom he had known in Barnstable. From then on Gay managed to maintain himself through wealthy patronage, Lord Burlington and the duke and duchess of Queensbury being his chief benefactors. *Wine*, the first of Gay's poems, appeared in 1708, and his first dramatic composition, *The Mohocks*, never acted, was published in 1712. Gay, by this time a well-known personality among London wits and writers, now associated himself with the famous Tory group that included Jonathan Swift, Alexander Pope, and Dr. John Arbuthnot. In the years that followed, a succession of poems and dramatic pieces came steadily from his pen, and as a result of the phenomenal success of THE BEGGAR'S OPERA, Gay achieved widespread fame. He was

buried in Westminster Abbey with the pomp associated with a peer of the realm.

As a dramatist, Gay is now remembered almost exclusively for *The Beggar's Opera*, the revival of which in the 1920's and again in the 1960's has helped further to focus attention on this single work. Yet Gay fathered, in all, twelve plays, of which nine reached the stage sooner or later. They include five comedies, a farce (*The Rehearsal at Goatham*, pub. 1754; never staged), two ballad operas (*The Beggar's Opera* and *Polly*, the latter pub. 1729 but not acted until 1777), a tragedy (*The Captives*, 1724), a "pastoral tragedy" (*Dione*, pub. 1720; never staged), an opera (*Achilles*, 1733), and an "English Pastoral Opera" (*Acis and Galatea*, 1731; music by Handel). Many of these are of mainly historical interest, but three of the comedies—*The Mohocks, The What D'Ye Call It* (1715), and *Three Hours After Marriage* (1717; in collaboration with Pope and Arbuthnot) —are as amusing inventions as are to be found anywhere.

If *The Beggar's Opera* reveals Gay at the height of his powers as an ironist, the three comedies display the earlier phases of his ironic imagination. It delights Gay to show his characters putting on disguises; are not most of us playing roles? The realistic, antiromantic commentary on human behavior is further enforced by the topical allusions, the amusing people who appear (fashionable bullies, country yokels, provincial justices, all engaged in being themselves to the top of their bent), and the indelicate language and the equally indelicate situations. *The Beggar's Opera* has in addition charm, and it is by virtue of this very charm that it proves a masterpiece of ambiguity.

The most accessible collection of Gay's dramatic works is *The Plays of John Gay* (2 vols., 1923). William H. Irving's *John Gay, Favorite of the Wits* (1940) gives an accurate factual account of his career. The most recent comprehensive critical treatment is that of Patricia Meyer Spacks in her *John Gay* (1965).—R. Q.

Gelber, Jack [Allen] (1932–   ). American playwright. Jack Gelber is one of the most influential playwrights produced by the Off-Broadway theater in the 1950's and 1960's. Born and raised in Chicago, he graduated from the University of Illinois with a B.S. in journalism. With his first play, *The Connection* (1959), Gelber achieved notoriety both for himself and for The Living Theatre, the company that presented it. Although the relentlessly naturalistic production by Judith Malina and Julian Beck shocked and alienated many members of the audience, the author and company became known as explorers of new subjects and styles. The film version of *The Connection*, directed by Shirley Clarke, captures much of the style and power of that first production. Gelber has continued to present his plays Off-Broadway, though none has had the success he achieved with the first. He has also published a novel, *On Ice* (1964).

Gelber's interests lie less with the sordid, shocking subjects he uses than with the possibilities of contrasting the real with the theatrical, truth with fiction, in many ways reminiscent of Luigi Pirandello's dramatic experiments. The slight story of *The Connection* presents a group of addicts who wait for their supplier and their varying responses to the heroin

JACK GELBER (WIDE WORLD PHOTOS)

after they take it. The story is presented by a producer and an author who say they have brought together real addicts and jazz musicians to improvise on a prepared outline. However, the junkies ignore the plan and succeed in drawing the author into their reality. In *The Apple* (1961) the stage is at once a stage and a coffee shop being treated as a stage. The actors retain their real names and attempt to improvise a play or a ritual, but they are interrupted by a drunk, who turns out to be a former screen actor. Through the confusion, an image emerges of life as chaotic and absurd, pervaded by frustration and violence. *Square in the Eye* (1965) has a straightforward plot about a schoolteacher who wants to be a painter but finds himself hemmed in by family and friends. Films and tape recordings play a major part in the production; the hero often addresses the audience; while some scenes are realistic, others are grotesquely stylized, and in the second half of the play the scenes are in reverse chronological order.

All of Gelber's plays are published by Grove Press. —M. L.

Gélinas, Gratien (1909–   ). French-Canadian director, playwright, and actor. First an actor, it was by coincidence that Gélinas became an author. On the radio he created a famous character, Fridolin, and started writing revues in 1938. In 1948 he wrote his first play, *Tit-Coq* ("Lil' Cock"), which met with considerable success. Presented in New York a few years later, however, the play was a failure, and Gélinas returned to Montreal, where he opened a theater. Since then, he has combined the occupations of director of a theater, playwright, and actor.

Gélinas' work presents a satiric view of French Canada. Written in a popular language, often padded with slang and English words, his plays favor and defend the ordinary, common people. It is *populiste*

theater, in traditional form, and is not without melodrama. In *Bousille et les justes* ("Bousille and the Just Ones," 1960), Gélinas presents Bousille, who is treated as a poor cousin because of his limited intelligence. When one of the family is on trial after being implicated in a tavern brawl, Bousille is called upon as a witness. Despite the advice his family gives him, his testimony is very different from what they had hoped for. As he sees things, he might compromise the apparent respectability of the family. Torn between what he thinks is true and his loyalty to the clan, he hangs himself. In this melodrama, Gélinas is defending someone rejected by society. Even more than the subject matter, it is Gélinas' way of presenting the characters that makes this play appealing.

Gélinas' *Tit-Coq* is considered the first milestone in the French-Canadian theater. The play is the story of a young French-Canadian soldier in World War II who has fallen in love with the sister of a regiment comrade, leaves for Europe, and, when he returns, finds the girl married. The intrigue is not very original and the tone is often melodramatic, but the play has a free-flowing quality and a typical French-Canadian joy. The populiste style that Gélinas developed, realistic and melodramatic, has scarcely any imitators.—J. B.

género chico. See SPANISH AMERICA.

Genet, Jean (1909–   ). French novelist and playwright. Most men succeed in playing some kind of role in society. By feeling thus integrated into a social group, they justify their existence. Jean Genet is concerned in his plays and novels with the type of man who is alienated from society, who accepts a role outside of the social structure, although he can discover no justification for his role. Sartre, in his critical work on Genet, *Saint Genet comédien et martyr* (pub. 1952), finds in the writings of Genet ex-

JEAN GENET (FRENCH CULTURAL SERVICES)

amples of a gratuitous and absurd existence. Genet's maids (in THE MAIDS) and criminals (in DEATH-WATCH) have to play at being normal, integrated characters. The maids play at being their mistress and the criminals form a hierarchical society in their cell. But Genet's characters in *Le Balcon* (*The Balcony*, 1956) and *Les Nègres* (*The Blacks*, 1958), as well as in the first two plays, know what they are doing. They know that they are counterfeiting society, and that the actions they invent will not justify their existence. We are always watching two simultaneous actions in the plays of Genet: the inverted actions of the characters playing at being something they are not and the fatal drama of alienation.

The two maids in *The Maids* and the two prisoners in *Deathwatch* are pairs of beings who are concurrently drawn to and repelled by one another and who dream of committing a murder. One play ends with a suicide and the other with a murder. Genet calls the relationship of such couples the eternal marriage between the criminal and the saint. Maids and criminals represent an absolute of disorder that is the opposite of the order of society. This dramatization of conflicting orders imparts a sense of ambiguity to Genet's work. While he seems to advocate the revolt of a *maudit* ("accursed") against society, in reality he is opposed to such destruction. But Genet does not protest against exclusion from society, neither his own exclusion nor that of the characters he calls maids (*The Maids*), criminals (*Deathwatch*), Negroes (*Les Nègres*), and Arabs (THE SCREENS).

For critical studies of Genet's work, consult the following: Eleanor Clark, "The World of Jean Genet," *Partisan Review*, XVI (April 1949); Wallace Fowlie, "The Case of Jean Genet," *Commonweal*, LXXIII (1960) and "New Plays of Ionesco and Genet," *Tulane Drama Review*, V (September 1960); Thomas B. Markus, "Jean Genet: The Theatre of the Perverse," *Educational Theatre Journal*, XIV (1962); and Jean-Paul Sartre's *Saint Genet, Actor and Martyr* (1963), translated by Bernard Frechtman. —W. F.

Genroku. The era in Japanese history known as "the Genroku," a term much used in histories of Japanese drama, roughly corresponds to the use of the word Elizabethan in histories of English drama. In both cases the period of time referred to by these designations differs distinctly according to whether the discussion is of cultural history or of political history. In political history the Genroku marks the years 1688 to 1703, a part of the reign of Emperor Higashiyama and of the shogunate (military governorship) of Tokugawa Tsunayoshi; culturally, it is generally taken to signify the eras of Empo and Kyoho as well, extending from 1673 to 1735.

One of the most dynamic periods for all Japanese arts, and for theatrical activity in particular, the Genroku era witnessed the rise of many of Japan's great artists: illustrious actors, notably Ichikawa Danjuro I; Japan's most famous playwright, Chikamatsu Monzaemon; outstanding musicians, such as Takemoto Gidayu; the artists Moronobu and Ogata Korin; and great poets, especially Basho, master of the *haiku*. This accelerated activity on many sides proved in every respect stimulating to dramatic art, synthetic as it is by its very nature. The theaters, both the unique doll theater and the *kabuki* with its

live actors, responded wholeheartedly. Power was passing from the hands of a feudal aristocracy and from a court closely bound in fetters of obsolete ceremony to the moneyed class thriving in the large cities. Like the Elizabethan age again, this was a time of peace and growing material prosperity. The Elizabethan culture was relatively more intellectual, the Japanese more aesthetic. Japan may have known periods of more refined taste, but none of such fecundity in the arts. The drama of the age can be only partially understood if the social, political, and economic factors are overlooked.

See Sir George Sansom, *Japan, A Short Cultural History* (1936), and Earle Ernst, *The Kabuki Theatre* (1956).—H. W. W.

Georgian comedy. See ENGLAND: *eighteenth century*.

Germany. In an effort to provide a comprehensive picture of the development of German drama, this article is concerned with all drama written for persons predominantly German in their language background. Thus it includes some Latin Jesuit drama and some drama in exile, although these are more fully covered in separate articles.

middle ages. Beginnings of dramatic dialogue in German territory have been found in the expanded liturgical responsories in Latin of two ninth-century monks at St. Gallen Monastery in Switzerland: Notker Balbulus ("Notker the Stammerer") and Tutilo. These tropes parallel the preliminaries to drama of virtually all areas affected by the Judeo-Christian tradition. Charlemagne imposed this tradition upon the Germanic tribes and hoped for a liter-

SCENE FROM HROTSVITHA'S *Calimachus* (RONDEL COLLECTION, BIBLIOTHÈQUE DE L'ARSENAL, PARIS)

ary expression of it in (Old High) German. There was some immediate response in the epic form, but the German drama emerged slowly from the liturgy over a period of centuries.

Latin was also the language of the first German dramas in the Greco-Roman tradition. These were the six Christian moral comedies written polemically by the tenth-century nun HROTSVITHA of Gandersheim to eliminate from the Church readings the six frivolous comedies of the pagan Terence. Hrotsvitha's Latin was inelegant, but she copied the technique of Terence quite well and courageously faced problematical situations of life. These plays, intended for reading only, were : *Abraham,* in which a hermit rescues his niece from a brothel; *Calimachus,* a love-death play whose hero is resurrected by prayer, converts to Christianity, and regrets his passion; *Gallicanus I* and *II* treat the conflict between Emperor Constantine and Julian the Apostate; *Paphnutius* and *Sapientia,* both dealing with the consolations of higher learning; and *Dulcitius,* a grotesque farce exposing the follies of a lecherous young husband guarding the virtue of saintly virgins. Hrotsvitha's work stands alone. The Greco-Roman tradition was submerged in medieval times by the Christian tradition and pagan Nordic influences until it emerged again virtually *de novo* in the fifteenth century under the spur of the Renaissance and of Humanism.

The medieval phase of German drama was nonliterary. Religious education and popular desire for amusement were its driving forces. Expanding liturgical tropes led gradually to Latin miracle, morality, and passion plays; soon German translations were provided (for reading purposes only); then German lines crept into the Latin text; finally, texts became entirely German. As the Church moved some of its festive rituals, such as the Transubstantiation (1264) and Corpus Christi (1316) out of the church building into the streets, the plays also moved out and nonclerical volunteers took the roles. The artisan players and directors added down-to-earth broad comedy touches and local color. We do not know the authors and we identify the plays by the towns performing them. The earliest plays in Latin seem to have been the Tegernsee "Antichrist" (*Ludus de antichristo*), presumed to be of the ninth century, and two Benediktbeuren plays, both titled "Passion Play," in the thirteenth century. The earliest in German were probably the Vorau *Isaak und Rebecca* and the Regensburg *Prophetenspiel* ("Prophet Play"), both from the end of the twelfth century. Other German-language dramas of this type, first performed in the fourteenth and fifteenth centuries, were those of Alsfeld, Augsburg, Eger, Erlau, Frankfurt, Heidelberg, Kloster Himmelgarten, Künzelsau, Lucerne, Oberammergau, Redentin, Tirol, Trier, Vienna, and Wolfenbüttel. Approaching literary quality were the Eisenach *Spiel von den fünf klugen und den fünf törichten Jungfrauen* ("Play of the Wise and Foolish Virgins," 1322); *Mirakelspiel von der Hl. Dorothea* ("Miracle Play of St. Dorothea," c. 1350) in Kremsmünster; and the well-known *Spiel von Frau Jutten* ("Play of Frau Jutta") written by the priest Dietrich Schernberg in Mühlhausen (1480) and combining the problems of a female pope and making deals with the devil. In the German-speaking area special attention was given to Easter plays (depicting angels and women at Christ's tomb), beginning with the thirteenth-century play of Muri (Switzerland) and gradually building up into full passion plays. See OSTERSPIEL.

The emphasis on Easter is usually explained by Church desires to supplant the persistently popular pagan rites of spring. The battle between winter and spring was a favorite theme of medieval German epics and ballads and frequently took the form of a dramatic dialogue (as in, for example, the poems of Walther von der Vogelweide). Other pagan themes received similar treatment in dialogic poetry and doggerel, including the sordid and ribald ballads peddled by "jugglers" and street-singers. Public presentation of such repertory items, initially limited to court festivals, gradually invaded the marketplace. The biggest presentation day was Shrove Tuesday, carnival time. For this occasion the butcher-mummers (*Schembartläufer*) put on their pagan cultic pageantry and dances. And for this occasion also, partly to compete with the butcher-mummers by putting on a more moral display, the first peculiarly German drama was developed: the Shrovetide or carnival play. See FASTNACHTSSPIEL.

The Fastnachtsspiele dealt with everyday situations, including family scenes, peasant settings, courtroom trials. They began with processions introducing the characters and ended with a plea to enjoy the subsequent carnival dancing. The plays were usually in one act of about four hundred irregular four-beat verse lines (*Knittelvers*) spoken in declamatory fashion by three to six type-characters. Changes of scene were announced rather than presented. The dominant theme was the exposure of human folly, especially follies of the lower classes, by the good, moral burghers. These plays seem to date from as early as the fourteenth century, but the authors of the early plays, probably wandering scholars, clergy, and players, remain unknown. Among the early, anonymous Fastnachtsspiele are the *Spiel von Rumpold und Maret* ("Play of Rumpold and Maret"), perhaps of the best literary quality; *Neidhart,* a popular farce of two thousand verses extravagantly portraying the capers of the legendary peasant minstrel and prankster Neidhart of Reuenthal; and the serious, secular, and popular *Tellspiel* ("Play of William Tell"), performed in Uri, Switzerland, in 1511. These writers carried the plays to various towns in southern Germany and Switzerland, although the real center for the development of the Fastnachtsspiel was Nuremberg. From this Bavarian city came the four known authors of Fastnachtsspiele. The first, Hans Rosenplüt, to whom about a dozen such plays are ascribed, wrote in the middle of the fifteenth century, gave bold Nurembergian moral and political advice, but achieved no literary distinction. Hans Folz (c. 1450–1515), born in Worms, settled in Nuremberg and there produced eight (according to some, seventeen) Fastnachtsspiele of strong realistic and satirical content and a modicum of artistic quality. *König Salomon und Markolf* ("King Solomon and Markolf") and *Ein hübsch Vastnachtspil* ("A Pretty Carnival Play") were among his best. He also introduced imaginative innovations in the art of the mastersong (*Meistergesang*) that developed at this time.

The acknowledged master of the Fastnachtsspiel

was another mastersinger, Hans SACHS. As he himself put it, he "Was a shoe-/maker and poet, too." A dedicated craftsman, steeped in tradition (popular and cultured) but tolerant of new ideas (Reformation, Humanism), benevolent and good-humored but intolerant of malice and folly, he produced sixty-one tragedies and sixty-four comedies, treating traditional themes (*Judith, Alcestis, Siegfried*) in what he considered to be the classical literary form. These 125 plays were against sin, earnestly educative, and quite dull. He is remembered rather for his eighty-five Fastnachtsspiele, in which he concentrated on simple human foibles, deceptions, and delusions and specialized in gross nonsense—with drastic dramatic and comic effect. In *Das Kälberbrüten* (*The Calf-Hatching*) a farmer is shown sitting on a basket full of cheeses hoping to hatch out a calf to replace the one he had lost. In *Der fahrende Schüler im Paradeis* (*The Travelling Scholar*) a priest is disguised as a devil to escape a returning suspicious husband. In *Der schwanger' Bauer* (*The Pregnant Farmer*) the miser Kargas is declared to be pregnant and is "cured" in bed on the stage. In *Das heiss Eisen* (*The Hot Iron*) a husband carries a hot iron (with the aid of wooden holders) and thereby forces his wife into a penitential confession of her infidelities. The slightly crude, choppy, four-foot verse lines of Hans Sachs with their oversimplified bold woodcut-like imagery —the Knittelvers—have come to be recognized as something nonclassical and distinctly German.

The fourth Nuremberger, Jacob Ayrer (1540–1605), continued, in the main, the tradition of the Fastnachtsspiel. Like Hans Sachs, he also wrote tragedies and comedies that had little success. Altogether, he wrote sixty-nine plays, of which thirty-six are lumped together as "carnival or farce plays." A transitional figure, Ayrer moved toward farce, copying some of the ribaldry of the Elizabethan drama (then beginning to reach Germany), and introduced the figure of the jester in its popular, clownish form with the name Hans Wurst ("Jack Sausage"). Performed little, Ayer's plays received more attention when they were published posthumously in 1618. He is remembered chiefly as a transitional figure in the trend from the Fastnachtsspiel to the baroque and for his innovation of explicit stage directions.

Reformation and late sixteenth century. Classical Latin drama was revived in Germany in the fifteenth and sixteenth centuries through the influences of the Renaissance and the scholarly Humanists. Terence and Seneca were rediscovered and became part of the curriculum of the University of Heidelberg in 1450. Learned dialogues in Latin were written as intellectual and linguistic exercises and then were performed at university occasions. Johannes Tröster, a Viennese imperial secretary, produced such a dialogue between the unhappy lover Philostratus and his friend Eudion in 1456. The Heidelberg scholar Jacob Wimpheling (1450–1528) included a Latin comedy, *Stilpho,* with a dialogic attack on Church benefices in his promotional lecture at Heidelberg in 1480 (pub. 1494).

More seriously dramatic in purpose and achievement were the two Latin dramas of Johannes Reuchlin (1455–1522) in Heidelberg. *Sergius* (1496), a Humanistic dialogue, attacks a hypercritical monk. *Scaenica Progymnasmata* ("Dramatized School

Lessons") also known as *Henno* (1497) combines folkloristic characters of the Fastnachtsspiel with the action of the well-known French farce of *Maître Pathelin* (the peasant lad who cheats everyone by bleating like a lamb) to produce an almost live comedy. Actions are reported rather than portrayed, lines are declaimed rather than acted, the emphasis is pedagogical. While the play has the length of a Fastnachtsspiel, it has the form of classical drama— five acts, each with two scenes, and a chorus at the end.

The union of the Fastnachtsspiel and the classical form in Latin was continued and sharpened by two Hollanders who were active in Germany. Georg Macropedius (1475–1558), calling himself the pupil of Reuchlin and using Terence as a model, wrote twelve Latin plays distinguished by realistic detail taken from daily Dutch life. Knuyt van Sluyterhoven (1462–1510) adds Renaissance glitter in his one small comedy, *Scorletta* (1490), which introduces court festival pageantry in the Germanic drama. Such festive Renaissance displays, couched in Latin verse modeled after Horace and Ovid, were developed especially by the Würzburger Konrad Celtes (1459–1508). Brought to Vienna by the emperor Maximilian, he edited the plays of Hrotsvitha in 1494 and glamorized the Austrian court in his *Ludus Dianae* (*Play of Diana*, 1501), a festive display in the Italian style with music and ballet. A further Latin extravaganza by Celtes, *Rhapsodia de laudibus et victoria Maximiliani de Boemanis* ("Rhapsody of the Glories and the Victory of Maximilian of the Bohemians," 1504) virtually constituted the first Baroque opera, a genre that soon established itself in Vienna and lives today in the Viennese operetta. Additional efforts in this vein, with the addition of Christian allegorical figures, were contributed by Jakob Locher (1471–1528) in Freiburg, Sebastian Brant (1457–1521) in Strassburg, Hans Sachs in Nuremberg, and Helius Eobanus Hessus (1488–1540) in Erfurt. The strongest dramatic talent in the Latin play was displayed by the Tübingen professor Nicodemus Frischlin (1547–1590), whose satirical classicism—modeled on Aristophanes—was so sharp that he was arrested and jailed. He died attempting to escape. His *Julius redivivus* ("Julius Revived," written between 1572 and 1584) called on the Germans to reform and rise up against their western and southern neighbors. His *Priscianus vapulans* ("Priscianus Afflicted," 1571) attacked his stuffy university colleagues. He was strongest in the portrayal of dissolute characters. His *Dido* (1581), based on Vergil, was an unsuccessful attempt at strict classicism.

Latin school dramas (see SCHULDRAMA), written for study and performance in schools only, reached wider circles than the noninstitutional classical Latin plays and in general created more excitement because they were deeply involved in the religious controversies attending the Reformation. The ground breakers here too were the Dutch. Gnaphaeus (pen name of Willem de Volder, 1493–1568) dealt with the prodigal son in his *Acolastus* (1529), as did Macropedius in *Asotus* (1510). The latter also revived the Everyman play in his *Hecastus* (1538). The significant German names in the Latin school drama were Sixtus Birk (1501–1554) in Augsburg (*Judith,*

1536; *Susanna,* 1538); Naogeorgus (pen name of Thomas Kirchmeyer, 1511–1578) in Thuringia (*Pammachius,* the pope as the anti-Christ, 1538; *Mercator,* 1540; *Incendia,* 1541; *Haman,* 1543; *Jeremiah,* 1551; *Judas,* 1552), and the previously mentioned Nicodemus Frischlin.

A discernible shift from the learned and didactic drama toward spectacular and professional theater began toward the end of the sixteenth century. Tangible influences in this direction were the English players and, to a lesser extent, the Italian players of the *commedia dell'arte*. Both stressed the farcical and the grotesque. The English players, roving professionals, had considerable success, first performing crude versions of the crudest plays of George Peele, Robert Greene, Christopher Marlowe, and Thomas Kyd, later adding inaccurate versions of Shakespeare's plays. These were performed in English for a time, then were translated and performed in German. Jacob Ayrer, as noted, initiated some of the ribaldry but did not succeed in his avowed efforts to write new drama in their style. A somewhat more successful imitator was Duke Heinrich Julius of Braunschweig (1564–1613). He brought English players to his court, maintained a theater, and wrote ten plays for it. They were crude efforts, senseless and bloody tragedies and Fastnachtsspiele in bombastic, baroque prose, all written in the years 1593–1594. The duke's ribaldry appears to derive more from the commedia dell'arte than from Elizabethan drama, but his clown—Johann Bouset—is avowedly an Englishman. The duke found an emulator in Landgrave Moritz von Hessen (1572–1632), who also brought in English players, maintained a stage, and wrote German and Latin plays—but none of his texts has been preserved.

In opposing the Reformation, Humanism, and the mundane levity of the English players, the Counter Reformation—led by pragmatic Jesuits—made extensive use of the drama. The Jesuit drama found an effective formula in using physical and material means to dramatize its strictly Catholic spiritual message. This formula was its chief innovation and decisively affected German drama throughout the Baroque period. Technically, the Jesuits followed the traditions of the medieval mystery plays, the later Fastnachtsspiel, and the Latin school drama, and they wrote in Latin. But they added lavish displays and intellectual debate both to overwhelm and persuade their audiences in the schools and in the marketplaces. Topically, they stressed biblical subjects and legends of saints and martyrs, but they also used classical, historical, and contemporary subjects when these suited their purpose: to show the vanity of material endeavor, the cataclysmic fall of great men, the glory of God and the hereafter. Plays of this type became more numerous in the second half of the sixteenth century and reached a peak early in the seventeenth century. Most of the self-effacing authors are unknown. Some outstanding leaders emerged, however, and have been identified.

The greatest probably was Jakob Bidermann (1578–1638), born in Swabia but working chiefly as professor of rhetoric in Munich. His plays followed discernibly the patterns of Plautus and Terence and were famous for their burlesque confrontations between angels and devils. Nicolaus Avancini (1612–

1686), probably the most extravagant Jesuit playwright, was an Italian by birth, but the official darling of the court in Vienna. His twenty-seven plays, written and produced between 1655 and 1675, were scenarios for enormous theatrical festival displays involving all the available arts and artists. Their titles imply their scope, for example, *Pietas victrix sive Flavius Constantinus Magnus de Maxentio Tyranno victor* ("Piety Victorious, or Flavius Constantine the Great, Victor over Maxentius the Tyrant," 1659). Further development in this direction led to the purely theatrical Baroque festival spectacles. (See JESUIT DRAMA).

seventeenth century. The main lines of German Baroque classical drama were laid down by Martin OPITZ from Silesia. A convinced Humanist schooled in Heidelberg and Holland, Opitz simply advocated the application of classical aesthetics to plays in the vernacular German, not Latin, and contributed some reasonably good models of his own. His treatise *Buch von der deutschen Poeterey* ("Book of German Poetics," written 1624) was based on Aristotle and on the work of two well-established, more recent critics, the Italian-born Frenchman Julius Caesar Scaliger (1484–1558) and the Hollander Daniel Heinsius (1580–1655). Opitz strove for eloquence and elegance. He stressed the use of verse, lofty and ornate language (German!), regular meter, and pure rhymes and established the alexandrine verse form as the standard German equivalent of ancient classical dramatic verse. Among the modest models he contributed were German translations of Seneca's *Trojan Women* (1625), Sophocles' *Antigone* (1636), Ottavio Rinuccini's libretto of *Dafne* (in the musical setting by Heinrich Schütz this became the first German opera, 1627), and Giuseppe Salvadori's light opera *Judith* (1635). Although his creative gifts were minor, his aesthetic criticism set the style for classicist Baroque drama in Germany for the next hundred years.

The man who produced what Opitz wanted in the drama—and a good bit more—was his fellow Silesian Andreas GRYPHIUS. Learning from Joost van Vondel in Holland, Pierre Corneille in France, and the opera and commedia dell'arte in Italy, Gryphius first produced German translations of Vondel's *Gibeonites* (1652; German title *Rache Gabaon*) and the Latin *Felicitas* (1653) by the Jesuit Causinus. These stressed human suffering, lamentation, martyrdom, and the death wish, and in this vein he then wrote a series of mournful tragedies: *Leo Arminius* (1646), based on the Jesuit play by Joseph Simeons (pen name of Emmanuel Lobb); *Catharina von Georgien, oder Bewehrete Beständigkeit* ("Catharina of Georgia, or Constancy Stands the Test," 1647), which had better characterization and use of suspense than the first play; *Carolus Stuardus, oder ermordete Majestät* ("Charles Stuart, or Majesty Murdered," 1649), dealing with the shocked reaction to the decapitation of Charles I of England; and *Der sterbende Aemilius Paulus Papirianus* ("Aemilius Paulus Papirianus Perishing," 1659), in which classical reserve was abandoned and torture and murder were displayed on stage. More original and more enduring in the theater were Gryphius' *Cardenio und Celinde* (1647), a tragedy with only one murder and a miraculous transformation of the repentant sinners,

FRONTISPIECE OF ANDREAS GRYPHIUS' *Tragedies, Odes, Sonnets,* 1663 (RONDEL COLLECTION, BIBLIOTHÈQUE DE L'ARSENAL, PARIS)

which was, incidentally, the first German "bourgeois tragedy"; the double play *Das verliebte Gespenst— Die geliebte Dornrose* ("The Infatuated Ghost— The Beloved Bramble Rose," 1660), performed by alternating the acts of the two plays—the first is a formal social comedy, the second a rustic carnival play with good characterization and action; *Absurda Comica, oder Herr Peter Squentz* ("The Absurda Comica, or Master Peter Squentz," written 1648, pub. 1657), a farcical literary satire based—probably indirectly—on the journeymen comedy in Shakespeare's *A Midsummer Night's Dream;* and *Horribilicribrifax, oder Wählende Liebhaber* ("Horribilicribrifax, or Choosing Lovers," 1663), a farcical satire ridiculing the *précieuses* of high society, in the extravagant form of seven pairs of lovers. Gryphius is generally considered the best of the German Baroque dramatists.

The neoclassical restraints that informed the work of Opitz and Gryphius played no part in the rest of the German Baroque period. Other dramatists of the period went all out for action, blood, thunder, and melodrama. August Adolf von Haugwitz (1645–1706) wrote *Maria Stuarda* ("Mary Stuart") and *Der betörte, doch wieder bekehrte Soliman* ("Deluded but Then Converted Soliman"), which were but weak and dandyish imitations of Gryphius. Daniel Caspar

Lohenstein (1635–1683) of Silesia fashioned six bloody tragedies between 1650 and 1680 in which he developed morbid character portrayal and outdid the exaggerations of Giovanni Battista Marini, Luis de Gongora, and John Lyly. Johann Christian Hallmann (c. 1640–1704) wrote German Jesuit dramas full of glamor, bucolic sentimentality, and religious fervor. The development and popularity of Baroque opera rapidly displaced the spoken Baroque drama toward the end of the seventeenth century.

A new direction was shown, while the Baroque was still dominant, by Christian WEISE. This schoolteacher from Zittau, Saxony, represented the opposite of Lohenstein. He was coolly rational, down-to-earth, deliberately bourgeois, and cheerfully optimistic, that is, a phenomenon of the dawning era of the Enlightenment and a direct forerunner of Gotthold Ephraim Lessing. Between 1670 and 1702 he wrote fifty-five plays for school use. These were biblical and historical plays and light comedies, virtually all with large casts (to accommodate many students) and with a gently but firmly developed Protestant moral. He wrote in clear prose, strove for verisimilitude with realistic details, and stressed the power of the intellect. His tragedies were polite and weak (*Der Markgraf von Ancre,* "Margrave of Ancre, 1679; *Der Fall des Marschall Biron,* "The Fall of Marshal Biron," 1683; and *Masaniello,* 1688). His comedies were sprightly, gently satirical, and stressed stage action and gestures. Among them may be mentioned *Die verfolgten Lateiner* ("The Persecuted Latin Scholars," 1690); *Komödie von der bösen Catharine* ("The Comedy of Nasty Catherine," 1702), a drastically realistic treatment of Shakepeare's *Taming of the Shrew; Der bäuerische Macchiavellus* ("The Rustic Machiavelli," 1679), with the message that everybody is a Machiavelli; *Tobias und die Schwalbe* ("Tobias and the Swallow," 1682). These comedies have been called intellectualized commedias dell'arte. Not all of Weise's plays were published and the productions did not go beyond the unprofessional school theaters.

eighteenth century. The drama of the Enlightenment in the eighteenth century did not at first follow the lead given by Weise. The Enlightenment as a whole developed rather slowly in the disjointed German-language territory, which was exhausted physically and bewildered intellectually and culturally by the ravages of the Thirty Years' War. The primacy of mind over matter, as taught by Descartes in France, was not at all self-evident to the Germans; Leibnitz accepted it but gave it a secondary importance and remained at bottom a philosopher of the Baroque; the interpreters of Descartes in Germany, Christian Thomasius and Christian Wolff, simplified and trivialized the ideas of the Enlightenment virtually to the degree represented by Voltaire's Dr. Pangloss ("All is for the best in the best of all possible worlds") in *Candide.* It has also been argued that systematic logic, which declares all problems to be soluble, destroys the very conflicts that constitute drama. Whatever the reasons may have been, the fact is there was not one noteworthy drama written in German territory in the thirty years following Weise's death in 1702. When the drama reappeared it was in the dress of the French classicism of Corneille, Racine, Molière, and their followers. In search of theatrical elegance and glamor, the Baroque period had already produced many German translations of Jesuit Latin plays and foreign dramas, especially those of the French classicists. Leipzig had become a German center for the emulation of French culture. When the East Prussian rationalistic critic Johann Christoph GOTTSCHED, a student of Christian Wolff, came to Leipzig in 1723, he was able to establish himself very quickly as dictator of German letters in the French style for his generation. The university gave him a professorship. His *Versuch einer critischen Dichtkunst vor die Deutschen* ("Attempt at a Critical Poetics for Germans," 1730) set down the rules in the tradition of Aristotle, Horace, Scaliger, Opitz, and Boileau. His chief models were Corneille, Racine, Destouches, and their Danish disciple, Ludwig Holberg, who for Gottsched represented reasonableness, natural moral order, clarity, and dignity. He demanded close observance of the unities of time, place, and action and avoidance of all esoteric or extreme language, characters, and action—particularly the ribaldry of the clown figure—and totally rejected the use of miraculous events, ghosts, and the *deus ex machina*. His prime targets were Lohenstein, the opera, and Shakespeare.

Since he found no German models, Gottsched sought translations of the classical dramas, that is, new translations that followed his rules. Together with several friends and his wife he had eight "regular tragedies" available for production by 1723, among them his own highly rationalistic translation of Racine's *Iphigénie*. Between 1740 and 1745 he published these and some fifteen additional plays, some of which were "original German" dramas, in six volumes, called *Deutsche Schaubühne, nach den Regeln der alten Griechen und Römer eingerichtet* ("The German Stage, Arranged According to the Rules of the Ancient Greeks and Romans"). His own major original contribution, *Der sterbende Cato* ("Dying Cato," written 1730), was performed repeatedly in several cities and had ten printings, although he himself admitted that everything good in the play came from Émile Deschamps and Joseph Addison (three acts from Deschamps, one from Addison, one by Gottsched). His other original tragedies, such as *Agis* and *Die Parisische Bluthochzeit* ("The Blood Wedding of Paris"), were unsuccessful. He was very successful, however, in adapting the pastoral comedy to his rules and managed the light touch of the rococo so well in his *Atalanta* (1741) that it became the model for a spate of shepherd comedies.

The success of *Der sterbende Cato* and Gottsched's reforms in the drama and the theater was due also to his discovering a fine theater troupe in Leipzig. Johannes Neuber and his ultimately more famous wife, Caroline, had already established their well-trained and disciplined troupe along lines designed to attract the more cultured segment of Leipzig audiences and to make the acting profession acceptable to respectable society. They had already formally banished the clown from their stage (not for aesthetic reasons, but to discredit their chief competitor in Leipzig, the famous clown Müller) and worked closely for over ten years with Gottsched until their ambitions and fame led them to other cities. Patriotic Germanic critics, inspired by the massive demolition

of Gottsched by the Swiss critics Johann Jacob Bodmer and Johann Jacob Breitinger and by his more enlightened successor Lessing, have belittled Gottsched's contribution. But Gottsched was significantly responsible for the revival of literary drama in Germany. He raised the literary sights in many areas, contributed some sharper logic and clarity to the use of the German language, revived the concept of form, helped to enlarge the repertoire, furthered the acceptance of the professional theater, and stimulated those who came after him both affirmatively, as we shall see, and negatively by the very vigor of his intolerance as a critic.

Within Gottsched's orbit was, first but not foremost, his wife, Luise Adelgunde Viktoria Gottsched (1713–1762). Her comedies were somewhat independent adaptations with enough sentimental human touches to make them reasonable German equivalents of the French *comédie larmoyante* ("tearful comedy") of Destouches and La Chaussée. Her *Die Pietisterey im Fischbeinrocke* ("Pietism in Whalebone Skirts," 1736) was based on *La Femme Docteur*, a satire on the Jansenites by the Jesuit Guillaume Hyacinthe Bougeant; her *Die ungleiche Heirat* ("Misalliance," 1741) was an adaptation of Molière's *Georges Dandin*. Her plays were more favorably received than her husband's.

The most gifted dramatist among Gottsched's followers was a Saxon, Johann Elias Schlegel (1719–1749), whose relative effectiveness may have been due to his unwitting disloyalty to his master's canon. He was avowedly committed to the Enlightenment, to his master's rules and models, to mind over matter, to high principles over emotions (his adaptation of Euripides' *Iphigenia in Tauris*, entitled in 1739 *Die Geschwister in Taurien*, "Brother and Sister in Tauris," and in 1742 renamed *Orest und Pylades*, displayed rather modern Greeks who criticized the wisdom and justice of the gods in terms of the Enlightenment). But he smuggled in a good bit of emotional language and action, presented some genuine human suffering, and generally created moving characters and plot. Schlegel's endings followed the gracious lines of Corneille, but his dialogue was more that of Racine, as in his adaptation of Euripides' and Seneca's *Hecuba*, later entitled *Die Troianerinnen* ("The Trojan Women," 1747). He was even more venturesome in his patriotic and original *Hermann* (1743), dealing with the virtuous triumph of the Cheruskian Teutons over Rome in A.D. 9; in his original *Canut* (1746), about the virtuous triumph of the Danish king over the Mephistophelian Ulfo; and in his outright character comedies, *Der geschäftige Müssiggänger* ("The Busy Idler," 1741); *Der Triumph der guten Frauen* ("The Triumph of the Good Women," 1746), a comédie larmoyante; *Der Geheimnisvolle* ("The Secret-Monger," 1747); and *Die stumme Schönheit* ("The Speechless Beauty," 1748), a rococo comedy in verse, considered his most lively play. He also showed an appreciation of Shakespeare in his (generally ignored) critical writings, pointing out that Shakespeare was occasionally more true to Aristotle than were the French. The critical consensus is that Schlegel was the best dramatist among the Gottsched group and that he died too soon (at the age of thirty).

The most popular Gottsched collaborator was the

master's colleague at the University of Leipzig, Christian Fürchtegott Gellert (1715–1769), a man of genuine graciousness, kindness, enlightenment, and a gifted rococo stylist. While Gellert's fame rests chiefly on his rhymed fables and *Geistliche Oden und Lieder* ("Spiritual Odes and Songs," 1757–1759) and on his personal benevolence, his comedies also deserve recognition as original and charming German *comédies larmoyantes*. His habilitation monograph, *Pro comoedia commovente* (1751), presented his program: His "serious" comedies were to enlighten by smiling at folly and weeping over both rewarded and unrewarded virtue; he wanted no satire, no loud laughter, but kindly sentiment and humane citizenship; he was dedicated to the ideals of what some have called "the bourgeois enlightenment." His literary hero was Samuel Richardson. Gellert's program had not yet been applied in his first comedy, *Die Betschwester* ("The Prayeress," 1745), a sharp satire on religious hypocrisy, but was in evidence in *Das Los in der Lotterie* ("The Lottery Ticket," 1746), in which true virtue takes the prize; *Die kranke Frau* ("The Sick Woman," 1746); and *Die zärtlichen Schwestern* ("The Affectionate Sisters," 1747), in which the mercenary lover is exposed. Some of his characters and situations afforded genuine glimpses of the Saxon middle class of the time.

Gellert's pupil Baron Johann Friedrich von Cronegk (1731–1758) tried his hand at classical tragedy and mingled Baroque melancholy with the reasonableness of the Enlightenment, producing two lyrical, pathos-filled plays: *Codrus,* about a noble suicide, written in language showing the influence of Edward Young and awarded Friedrich Nicolai's prize for the best German tragedy in 1757; and the unfinished *Olint und Sophronia,* based on episodes of Tasso's *Gerusalemme liberata* and intended to outshine Corneille's *Polyeucte* in the vein of a Jesuit martyr play. Cronegk died at twenty-seven and is remembered mostly because Lessing gave him some critical recognition in his important critical work *Hamburgische Dramaturgie* (*Hamburg Dramaturgy*).

Johann Christian Krüger (1722–1750), though less closely allied with Gottsched and Gellert than was Cronegk, produced work more to their taste. He was one of the earliest resident dramatists in Germany, working with the Hamburg troupe of Schönemann. His model was Pierre de Marivaux, whose *L'Héritier de village* he translated into Hamburg dialect. His playful rococo touch and command of effective theater made successes of his original comedies: *Die Geistlichen auf dem Lande* ("The Ministers in the Country," 1743), *Der blinde Ehemann* ("The Blind Husband," 1747), and *Die Candidaten* ("The Candidates," 1747), a really ambitious social satire.

The most short-lived of Gottsched's satellites was the farthest from his orbit. Joachim Wilhelm von Brawe (1738–1758) used the classical rules in writing two tragedies, but in content, characterization, and emotional emphasis, his models were Shakespeare and Lessing. His entry for Nicolai's prize in 1756, *Der Freigeist* ("The Free Thinker"), a tragedy in classical form, took its theme from Lessing's comedy with the same title and won second prize. His *Brutus* (1757), a drama of father-and-son conflict,

had Shakespearean touches in the characterization and in the use of iambic pentameter (the earliest known use of this meter in German drama).

The acknowledged culmination of the German drama of the Enlightenment was Gotthold Ephraim LESSING, a Saxon of broad and great spirit, who absorbed all the stimuli of his age, sifted them in his critical writings, sublimated them in the first classic classical German drama, *Nathan der Weise* (*Nathan the Wise*) and opened the door wide for further developments. At bottom he was a bookish man, an omnivorous critical reader—as a child he even wanted his portrait painted amid a pile of books—and hence more a critic than a poet or dramatic genius. However, he possessed a good portion of the newly developing cultural skepticism—not quite that of Jean Jacques Rousseau, but clearly that of Voltaire, with whom he would have gotten on well if he had been a bit more discreet with one of Voltaire's confidential manuscripts—and took himself with a large grain of salt, having some doubts about the Enlightenment, about the inevitability of the triumph of virtue, about the supposed diabolical nature of the emotions, about the possession of the absolute truth by anyone other than God, and even about the value of book learning. Lessing's early models were Plautus (he translated *Trinummus* and *The Prison-*

SCENE FROM GOTTHOLD EPHRAIM LESSING'S *Minna von Barnhelm* (NEW YORK PUBLIC LIBRARY)

ers), Terence, and, particularly, Molière, whom he emulated in several early comedies in prose: *Der junge Gelehrte* (*The Young Scholar*, 1748), about the follies of the bookworm; *Der Misogyne* (*The Misogynist*, 1748); and *Die alte Jungfer* (*The Old Maid*, 1749). His skepticism took on a more serious intellectual and psychological tone in the ideological prose "comedies" *Der Freigeist* (*The Free Thinker*, 1749) and *Die Juden* (*The Jews*, 1749), both of which advocated respect for differing views and beliefs. In the 1750's Lessing began to work on a *Faust* (only some scenes and random comments on the play have been preserved), in which, anticipating Goethe, he deeply sympathized with the great intellectual rebel and (contrary to the tradition) planned to have the heavenly hosts win his soul back from the forces of hell. Lessing was evidently not averse to bringing spirits on the stage even in an enlightened era, for, as he pointed out in his critical writings, if the spirits are effectively presented—as for example in Shakespeare—the audience will willingly suspend disbelief and share the feelings of the characters who see these spirits.

Feelings, emotions—especially fear—were for Lessing the essential ingredients of high drama. This, as he made plain in his *Briefe, die neueste Literatur betreffend* ("Letters Concerning the Most Recent Literature," pub. 1759–1764) and in his *Hamburgische Dramaturgie* (*Hamburg Dramaturgy*, pub. 1767–1769), was the lesson he learned from his studies of Shakespeare and Aristotle. He insisted that Aristotle's "phobos" signified, not *terreur* (as the French classicists thought), not theatrical fright and shock—which are unexpected, sudden, brief, and shallow—but deep human fear fully experienced by an audience sharing the destiny of the characters onstage. Mere declarations of fear from the stage and mere portrayals of terrible events could not produce catharsis, Lessing contended. All-black or all-white characters prevented audience identification. The characters had to be rounded, "mixed" human characters, for only then could audiences identify with and be deeply affected by their struggles—in comedy as well as in tragedy.

It was on these grounds that Lessing disliked Corneille, ridiculed the already faded polite art of Gottsched and his followers, and produced his four most significant plays. *Miss Sara Sampson* (1755) was essentially a wordy sentimental tragedy, but its prose portrayal of the fair middle-class maiden done to death by a wastrel lover, a jealous mistress, and a foolish father brought enough human passion into play to produce feelings of destiny, pity, and tragedy. It was a bourgeois tragedy, Sophoclean in its directness and irony, taking its form from Aristotle and not from Shakespeare or the French classicists, and taking its setting somewhat from Samuel Richardson's novel *Clarissa* and George Lillo's tragedy *The London Merchant, or, George Barnwell*. Lessing's prose high comedy, *Minna von Barnhelm, oder das Soldatenglück* (*Minna von Barnhelm, or the Soldier's Fortune*, 1767), was a fine mixture of serious characterization, strong emotions and convictions, the gaiety of Marivaux, and the commedia dell'arte (including a deus ex machina). It was his most German play and was stimulated by his military experiences in the Seven Years' War, in which Saxony and Prussia were

on opposite sides. In the vigorous action of the play, the serious and potentially tragic sense of honor of the Prussian Major von Tellheim was overcome by the love of his high-spirited and enterprising Saxon sweetheart, Minna (the name in German means "the loving woman"). Thus love conquered all and even reconciled the Prussian and the Saxon.

Emilia Galotti (1772) was conceived as a model for the application of the principles Lessing set down in his *Hamburgische Dramaturgie*, that is, Aristotelian form with German content. The result was a "well-made" prose bourgeois tragedy with mixed characters, emotional actions that arouse fear and pity, general observance of the unities, irony, suspense, surprise, and a sense of destiny. The German content was disguised by setting the play in Italy, but the social implications for Germany were understood by the intellectual audiences who saw or read the play: There must be something wrong with a society whose aristocratic and cultured leaders are lecherous seducers who sell their citizens to the armies of other nations and engage opportunistic courtiers (Marinelli, the courtier-villain, is a caricature of Machiavelli) to cater to their whims and murder their rivals.

NATHAN THE WISE was the breakthrough to genuine German classicism in that it was a harmonious marriage of Aristotelian poetic and dramatic form with significant modern and humanly universal (not necessarily patriotically German) content. Lessing, an idealistic Freemason and frequently embroiled in theological and religious controversy, wrote the play expressly to argue his conviction that human decency existed in all lands, among all peoples, and took precedence over religious dogma and national or political differences. He modified one of Boccaccio's Crusades stories in the *Decameron*—the famous parable of the three rings (the three chief religions) that are all of divine origin—by making Sultan Saladin, the adopted daughter of the Jew Nathan, and a deeply Christian Knight Templar discover they all belong to the same family. The deep-seated and tragically dangerous conflicts of convictions and emotions are exposed, talked out, and eliminated by the profoundly humane Nathan, who patiently searches for the true facts. In the central figure Lessing achieved an extraordinary synthesis: the combination of an enlightened Jewish philosopher (his model was in part his friend Moses Mendelssohn) and the Sophoclean Oedipus in Colonus. Though the text is somewhat discursive, its language is both lucid and poetic, and its iambic pentameter is so appropriate that it became the standard meter for German classicism.

The admixture of emotional elements in Lessing and in German classicism reflected a further contemporary development. This was the twin extravaganza called *Empfindsamkeit* ("sentimentalism") and *Sturm und Drang* ("Storm and Stress"). Lessing provided the name Empfindsamkeit when he suggested its use in the translation of Sterne's *Sentimental Journey*. But both developments were more visceral, more theatrically baroque, and more intensely Shakespearean than anything in Lessing. Empfindsamkeit, advocated by the Swiss critics Bodmer and Breitinger and emphasizing pictorialization and astonishment, was not noted for its drama. Yet two of its followers made dramatic contributions. Saxony-born Friedrich Gottlieb Klopstock (1724–1803) added an element of religious and patriotic eloquence in his undramatic lyrical plays (*Der Tod Adams,* "The Death of Adam," 1757; *Die Hermannsschlacht,* "Hermann's Battle," 1769; *Hermann und die Fürsten,* "Hermann and the Princes," 1784; *Hermanns Tod,* "Hermann's Death," 1787). And Christoph Martin Wieland (Wurtemberg, 1733–1813) supplied both eloquence and elegance in his rococoprose translations of twenty-two Shakespearean dramas (1762–1766), which led to a new Shakespeare cult in Germany.

At this time the social and ideological ferments that produced political revolutions in America, France, and (abortively) England were also stirring in German lands. The same social discontents were present in Germany and Austria, the same slogans were advocated—but here there was only a brief intellectual and literary explosion, Sturm und Drang, extending roughly from 1760 to 1785. It was prolific in turbulent dramas and hence was appropriately named after a play, Klinger's *Der Wirrwarr* ("The Hurly-Burly," 1776), renamed *Sturm und Drang* at the suggestion of the odd Swiss genius Christoph Kaufmann. The writers took cues from the Baroque, from the neo-mysticism of the Pietists, of Bodmer and Breitinger and Klopstock, of Edward Young, of James Macpherson's *Ossian,* of the East Prussian "prophet" Johann Georg Hamann (1730–1788), from the anticultural skepticism of Jean Jacques Rousseau, and from the great inexplicable geniuses: Homer, Christopher Marlowe, and Shakespeare. The dramatic heroes of the Sturm und Drang were titanic supermen and rebels, from Prometheus and Satan through Faust, from Helen of Troy to the figure of the unwed mother who murders her child. While the plays stressed emotion, imagination, exclamation, and suspense, they also dealt with social problems in strong, pungent, realistic language and settings. The writers either went off their heads or switched to more conventional topics and classical forms. In spite of some tendencies shared with later Romanticism, Sturm und Drang was essentially a nonescapist, free-form, irrational, hyperthyroid prelude to German classicism. It was precisely that for Goethe and Schiller.

Hamann's visionary and aphoristic axioms (*e.g.,* "Poesy is the mother tongue of the human race") began to appear in 1759 under the title *Sokratische Denkwürdigkeiten* ("Socratic Memorabilia"). His more lucid and explicit student and fellow East Prussian Johann Gottfried Herder (1744–1803), came to the University of Strassburg on a visit in 1770, found a group of like-minded spirits there, including young Goethe, and became the catalyst for what was quickly recognized as a new "movement." The young self-styled "geniuses," revolting against the now stale rigidities of the bourgeois enlightenment, sought new inspiration in all areas they considered "natural," "naïve," "original," and "primitive," such as the folk song, the folk epic, legends, sagas, the art of primitive peoples, and—rather inconsistently—Gothic art and Shakespearean drama. The cult of Shakespeare spread beyond the Strassburg group. Even before Herder, Heinrich Wilhelm von Gerstenberg (Schleswig, 1737–1823) wrote essays describing Shakespeare as the total

natural genius, ridiculed the sweetness of Wieland's translations, and in 1767 tried to out-Shakespeare Shakespeare in his tragedy *Ugolino,* a savage prose portrayal in five acts of the death by starvation of a titanic Renaissance man and his three sons. Lessing and Herder agreed that the play made some Shakespearean noises but lacked the true essentials of action, character, and poetic language.

The greatest Shakespeare fanatic of the Strassburg group (he arrived there after Herder had left) was Jakob Michael Reinhold Lenz (Livonia, 1751–1792). His critical treatise, *Anmerkungen übers Theater* ("Notes on the Theater," 1774), not only considered Shakespeare the total natural genius who created a universe equal to that made by God, but also implied that equal achievements would be attained by any genius who could shed his critical inhibitions and let his imagination go as freely as did the English bard. Lenz considered Goethe such a genius and went to such extremes in emulating him that he made himself socially impossible. His ecstasies and frustrations ended in insanity. In the four brief years of his productive activity, however, he contributed sprightly prose translations of five comedies of Plautus and two very original, boldly unconventional, and quite effective serious social comedies: *Der Hofmeister oder Vorteile der Privaterziehung* ("The Family Tutor or the Advantages of Private Education," 1773), a tragicomedy of the little man driven by his servile social status to become a titanic fool; and *Die Soldaten* ("The Soldiers," 1775), a tragicomedy of the little man who becomes a soldier to avenge the seduction of his fiancée by the playboy officers. These comedies had action, frequent scene changes, pungent characterization, and strong language and today appear almost modern in their social criticism and human compassion. They were quite independent of Shakespeare, as were the lesser dramas of Lenz, *Der neue Menoza* ("The New Menoza," 1774); *Pandämonium Germanicum* (1775), a literary satire; *Freunde machen den Philosophen* ("Friends Make the Philosopher," 1776); and *Der Engländer* ("The Englishman," probably written in 1774).

Friedrich Maximilian Klinger (1752–1831) became a Sturm und Drang dramatist through friendship with his neighbor in Frankfurt, Goethe. He was a passionate moralist, a man of action and discipline who rejected his own early dramatic extravaganzas, wrote two classical plays, and ultimately made a military career, ending as a general in the Russian army. Goethe's experiment in Shakespearean drama, *Götz von Berlichingen,* inspired Klinger to make a similar effort, the tragedy *Otto* (1774), a baroque theatrical concoction of horror and intrigue with passages strongly reminiscent of *Hamlet.* His plays were glorified orgies of passions and, being sensational theater, enjoyed considerable theatrical success. His tragedy *Die Zwillinge* ("The Twins"), on the Cain and Abel theme and ending in slaughter, won the Schröder contest in 1775. *Das leidende Weib* ("The Suffering Woman," 1775), also a tragedy, equated passion with the life force. Heroic love was worshipped in *Die neue Arria* ("The New Arria," 1776); the hero both in battle and in love was glorified in *Simsone Grisaldo* (1776). At this point Klinger was appointed resident dramatist for the Seyler troupe and whipped up the wild fantasy *Der Wirrwarr* (later renamed *Sturm und Drang*), which resolved all the European social malaise in revolutionary America in Shakespearean prose (including a love scene adapted from *Romeo and Juliet*). His next play, *Stilpo und seine Kinder* ("Stilpo and His Children," pub. 1780), was an unsuccessful historical tragedy. In 1780 he began to move in a new direction with a charming, gay comedy, *Der Derwisch* ("The Dervish"). His two classical plays, *Medea in Korinth* ("Medea in Corinth," 1787) and *Medea auf dem Kaukasus* ("Medea in the Caucasus," 1790), displayed a good command of controlled form and free verse. At the same time his profound involvement with Sturm und Drang was shown in his ambitious novel of a titan: *Fausts Leben, Taten und Höllenfahrt* ("Faust's Life, Deeds and Descent into Hell," 1791).

The lesser dramatists of Sturm und Drang included Friedrich "Maler" ("the painter") Müller (Kreuznach, 1749–1825) with his two dramatic idylls, *Die Schafschur* ("The Sheep-Shearing," 1775) and *Das Nusskernen* ("The Nut-Cracking," 1776), his five-act tragedy *Golo und Genoveva* (1776), and the unfinished sprawling epic drama *Fausts Leben, dramatisiert* ("Faust's Life, Dramatized," written 1778, pub. 1850); Müller's friend Baron Otto von Gemmingen (1755–1836) with his bourgeois drama *Der teutsche Hausvater* ("The German *Paterfamilias*," 1780); the Lessing disciple Johann Anton Leisewitz (Hannover, 1752–1806) with his relatively restrained Cain and Abel tragedy, *Julius von Tarent* ("Julius of Tarento," 1776), his only play; and Heinrich Leopold Wagner (Strassburg, 1747–1779) with his prose translation of *Macbeth* (1777), his six-act tragedy of intrigue, *Die Reue nach der Tat* ("Repentance After the Deed," 1775), his two satires, *Prometheus, Deukalion und seine Kritiker* ("Prometheus, Deucalion and His Critics," 1775) and *Voltaire am Abend seiner Apotheose* ("Voltaire in the Evening of His Apotheosis," 1778), and his six-act prose tragedy, *Die Kindermörderin* ("The Murderess of Her Child," 1776), a naturalistic bourgeois tragedy, parts of which Goethe considered stolen from his plans for *Faust*.

The acknowledged poetic master of Sturm und Drang, as well as of German classicism and—as a yardstick at least—of German Romanticism, was Johann Wolfgang von GOETHE. His creative power produced works of world-wide renown in virtually every style of his time and in every literary genre. His dramas were poetically significant even when they were lacking in dramatic power. As a student in Leipzig he easily surpassed Gottsched and Gellert with the charming rococo pastoral comedy in alexandrines *Die Laune des Verliebten* ("The Moody Lover," 1767, pub. in English as *The Lover's Wayward Humor*), in which he already used one of his favorite themes: feminine wile and wisdom as a cure of masculine ills. Mephistophelean characters and social criticism began to appear in his second drama, *Die Mitschuldigen* ("The Accomplices," 1769, pub. in English as *The Fellow-Culprits*), a serious comedy in alexandrines. In 1770 Goethe went to the University of Strassburg in a general search for vitality and freedom. Personal experiences now entered into all his writings, which he called "fragments of a great confession." His reading and discussion of Shake-speare with his friends led to two appreciative essays and the rambling but powerful prose tragic history play GÖTZ VON BERLICHINGEN. It was an ebullient panoramic portrayal, with innumerable scene changes, of an idealistic robber baron who became a titan of justice, a Robin Hood, a righter of the wrongs committed by the degenerate selfish nobility, but who was destroyed by his own trusting goodness. The central dramatic conflict was that of *Hamlet:* the creative idealist versus his own conscience and a world full of selfish and destructive villains. The characters were genuine and colorful, the action picturesque and variegated, the conflict strong and moving, the language robust and rich.

While working on *Götz,* Goethe discovered the dramatic possibilities of schizophrenia, wrote the prison scene of the child-murderess, Marguerite, and began to build his *Faust* around it, using prose, free verse, and *Knittelvers* (the four-beat rhymed doggerel he learned from Hans Sachs). This Faust fragment of 1775 was found by Erich Schmidt and published in 1887 as *Urfaust* ("The Proto-Faust"). During the same period, in 1774, Goethe expressed his traumatic experiences in Wetzlar (his futile love for the betrothed of another man) in his universally acclaimed epistolary novel, *Die Leiden des jungen Werthers,* (*The Sorrows of Young Werther*). A first-person confession cast in a narrative frame, *Die Leiden des jungen Werthers* has the quality of a dramatic monologue of the sensitive bourgeois artist disintegrating into madness and suicide under the pressures of uncontrollable passion and personal and social frustration. At this time Goethe also started to work on two further dramas of revolutionary heroes, *Egmont* and *Prometheus* (unfinished).

His association with the court in Weimar (from 1775) as companion to the young duke of Sachsen-Weimar led Goethe to impose increasing restraints on his mode of life and work. The Sturm und Drang genius now sought classical balance. He adopted Lessing's *Emilia Galotti* as his new dramatic model, producing two Sturm und Drang plays, bourgeois tragedies in prose, in Lessing's "well-made play" form. The first, *Clavigo* (1774), is a fusion of a Beaumarchais story and Goethe's personal experience, in which a successful writer abandons his sweetheart because of his career and is killed by the girl's avenging brother. The second, *Stella* (1776), is about Fernando, a Don Juan who leaves wife and child to live with Stella, leaves her to return home, and is finally confronted by the two unhappy women. The first version of *Stella* ends with a revolutionary solution, a *ménage à trois,* and the revised version with Fernando's suicide. In both plays the emphasis on mood and character analysis smothers the action. Nonetheless, both plays proved to be effective in the theater.

Goethe also tried his hand at dramatic satires, skits for social occasions, festival plays, and light opera librettos (SINGSPIELE), particularly during the Sturm und Drang period and the first years in Weimar. Though they were intended for light entertainment and have no major dramatic significance, Goethe fondly revised some of them, and some found significant composers: *Bastien et Bastienne* (Mozart); *Erwin und Elmire* (Beethoven), and *Claudine von Villa Bella* (Beethoven). A lyrical-operatic quality also dominated the final major Goethe drama that can with any justification be assigned to Sturm und Drang: EGMONT. Here, the thematic material, which in Goethe's first version was social and revolutionary, was changed to concentrate on the central revolutionary hero. He is portrayed as a handsome titan of idealism, a noble political criminal, too gracious to survive in a world controlled by the ruthless realist, Count Alba. The bourgeois tragedy of his beloved, Clara, was made sweetly touching rather than dramatic. Goethe's prose developed a lyrical quality, his stage directions called for incidental instrumental music (contributed later by Beethoven), and Clara sang a romantic love song. The play had elements of the Baroque, Shakespeare, Lessing, Sturm und Drang, and even Romanticism, all elegantly blended. 1782 happened also to be the year of Goethe's elevation to the nobility. On the basis of *Egmont* alone he had earned his title.

The play was reviewed favorably, though its lack of dramatic intensity was noted by Friedrich SCHILLER, who by this time was also modifying his early Sturm und Drang leanings and who—despite occasional jealousies on both sides—was soon to become Goethe's close friend and collaborator in classicism (see below). The review subtly revealed the central differences between the two men's work: Schiller was a moralist; he admired significant action; he had learned that freedom of conscience was a product of conflict; he believed deeply that true freedom could, in principle, conquer destiny but could not conquer God; he had a stronger Baroque background and a better sense of the theater than Goethe; he was more of a romantic thinker and dreamer. He described these differences most fully in his oft-quoted essay *Über naive und sentimentalische Dichtung* ("On Naïve and Nostalgic Poesy," 1795, pub. in English as *Concerning Naïve and Sentimental Poetry*).

Schiller's dramatic and theatrical orientation stemmed initially from the Baroque court theater in Ludwigsburg, where he saw mostly opera. His growing revolt against the rigid and militaristic Karl-School and its tyrant owner, Duke Karl Eugen, led him and his friends to the study and discussion of Lessing, Klopstock, and the dramas of Sturm und Drang. Through Professor J. F. Abel he came to study Shakespeare in the Wieland translation. He wrote his first major play, THE ROBBERS, secretly, giving it the motto *In tyrannos* and smuggling it out to Mannheim, where it was published anonymously. He played truant from school to attend the play's sensational première in Mannheim in 1782. *The Robbers* combines the themes of the noble criminal and the rival brothers in a ribald and eventful prose portrayal of evil and the search for freedom. Against the indirectly described background of a corrupt feudal society and a stagnant, bookish "ink-smearing era," Schiller places a gallery of rogues dominated by two rival criminals of titanic Sturm und Drang dimensions. Karl von Moor, the rebellious titan of justice and freedom, is driven by circumstance to lead his band in robbery, arson, and murder—but in the end repents and turns himself over to justice. Franz von Moor, the rebellious titan of vengeful immoralism, freely chooses to steal his brother's birthright, his honor, and his betrothed, falsifies letters, imprisons his father—and in the end does away with himself.

Schiller soon fled from school to Mannheim where he could get support from the theater director Wolfgang Dalberg and the publisher Schwan. His second play, *Die Verschwörung des Fiesko in Genua* (*The Conspiracy of Fiesko in Genoa,* 1783), was not well received. In it, Schiller again explored the problems of freedom and the human heart, but now in a historical setting and in restrained prose. The injustices committed by the profligate Duke Gianetto Doria, especially his seduction of the bourgeois Verrina's daughter, are left unpunished by the benevolent but aged despot Andrea Doria. This leads to a conspiracy that seeks to establish a republic. The conspirators choose as their leader the influential, handsome, and clever duke of Fiesco. When the dedicated bourgeois republicans discover that Fiesco is at bottom interested only in his personal success and power, Verrina assassinates him. The play is overcontrived and smothered by complex intrigues.

Almost simultaneously, Schiller moved more fully into the track laid by Lessing and produced the very successful prose bourgeois tragedy *Kabale und Liebe* ("Intrigue and Love," pub. in English as *Cabal and Love,* 1784). He minced no words here, took his material from a German newspaper story and from his personal experiences with court intrigue, and delivered a blistering portrayal of tragedy wrought by corrupt aristocratic exploitation. His plot was tight and swift: A feudal governor, von Walther, wants to further his and his son's careers by marrying him to the mistress of his powerful duke; the son, an idealist in love with a musician's daughter, refuses; the girl and her father refuse an attempt by the governor to buy them off; by intrigue and force the musician is arrested, his daughter is driven to write a compromising letter, the son is cast into confusion, and both daughter and son are driven to suicide; the duke's mistress, nobly transformed by the horrors committed because of her, leaves for England, and von Walther is left with nothing but contrition and remorse. Despite occasional melodramatic extravagances, the play is still on the boards today.

In an address in 1784, later revised and entitled *Die Schaubühne als moralische Anstalt betrachter* ("The Stage Considered as a Moral Institution"), Schiller expressed his discontent with a merely therapeutic catharsis; he asked for intellectual and moral edification as the ultimate product of drama. Nor was he content with the mere illumination of the human condition but asked for leadership in showing the way to a life of brotherhood, beauty, dignity, and sublimity. These were to become central ideas for German classicism and, in more esoteric form, for German Romanticism. In later essays he developed these ideas more fully.

Thus oriented, Schiller moved spontaneously toward classical form in 1784. His Sturm und Drang attempt at a tragic history play in prose of Don Carlos was recast in Shakespearean blank verse and appeared in 1787 as DON CARLOS, INFANTE OF SPAIN. Schiller tried here to concentrate his moral passion in a restrained "dramatic poem" and wrote five long acts of resonant dramatic verse without adequate central unity. The weak Hamlet-figure of Don Carlos cannot cope with the cry for freedom from the Netherlands and the loss of his beloved to his tyrant father, Philip II. His equally idealistic but more mature friend, the marquis of Posa (invented by Schiller), tries to find a way through the maze of court intrigues, wins the king's confidence with his frankness ("Sire, give us freedom of thought!"), but overestimates the maturity of Carlos, has bad luck with intercepted letters, and vainly sacrifices his life. Philip, feeling betrayed by all, grows hard and cold, dispatches the ruthless Alba to the Netherlands, and turns Carlos over to the Inquisition. Schiller took considerable liberties with history and showed what he wanted: the tragic defeat of idealism by intrigue. But his Sturm und Drang theme and characters were overshadowed by the Lear-like classical tragedy of King Philip.

Schiller's development toward classicism continued in 1788 with translations of *Iphigenia in Aulis* and scenes of *The Phoenician Women* by Euripides. His association with Goethe completed the development. Try as he would, however, he never fully achieved the German classical ideal postulated by the art critic and historian Johann Joachim Winckelmann: "Noble simplicity and quiet grandeur." Even Schiller's most objective and restrained efforts, including his purely historical writings, were infused with the complexities of conflict and the disharmony of the real and the ideal. This dramatic and romantic bent even prevailed in the classical ballads he wrote in friendly competition with Goethe. His monumental historical trilogy, WALLENSTEIN, begins with the turbulent *Wallenstein's Camp,* written chiefly in Knittelvers. The opportunistic mercenary army is shown ready to follow Wallenstein wherever he would lead them. The second play, *The Piccolomini,* in five acts and iambic pentameter, presents the shifting loyalties of Wallenstein's officers. They are all plotters, intriguers, and opportunists, except for the fiery young idealist Max Piccolomini, who has fallen in love with Wallenstein's daughter and in classical Sturm und Drang language denounces his own father's duplicity toward Wallenstein. The final five-act blank verse tragedy, *Wallenstein's Death,* reveals the general's central hybris: he dreams of giving peace to all of Europe by seizing all the power and making himself emperor. This motivates all his maneuvers with the Vienna court, his treasonous negotiations with the Swedes, and his plan to use his daughter for a politically profitable marriage instead of letting her marry Max. Now nemesis comes swiftly: Compromising letters are intercepted, the officers defect to Octavio Piccolomini and the emperor, Max seeks and finds death in combat against the Swedes, and Wallenstein is assassinated. The classical principles were substantially observed in this essentially German tragedy in Aristotelean structure and Shakespearean verse. Even nobility and grandeur were achieved. But simplicity and quiet were not much in evidence.

Two characteristic products of Schiller's classicism in the year 1800 were his translation of *Macbeth,* which imposed his moralizing rhetoric upon Shakespeare, and his five-act blank verse tragical history, *Mary Stuart,* which was perhaps his most perfect classical play. Schiller boldly—and contrary to history—had Mary and Queen Elizabeth confront each other at Fotheringhay and mercilessly lash out at each other. He pits the warm and loving human being against the power-seeking intriguer and re-

solves both characters tragically: Mary loses her life and Elizabeth loses her friends. The action is kept relatively simple, the characters are developed in depth, the verse dialogue is poetic, emotionally based, but restrained and relatively free of pathos. An indelible contrast is achieved by having Mary realize her fault—too much love—and accept her fate, while Elizabeth never quite realizes her fault—too much power, too little love. Mary's religious acceptance and resignation give the play a Baroque-Romantic touch. The play was acclaimed and is still performed in many countries today.

Esoteric Romantic and theatrical elements were more in evidence in two major works completed in 1801: a classical blank-verse adaptation of Carlo Gozzi's Chinese fairy tale, *Turandot,* and the five-act blank verse tragedy *Die Jungfrau von Orleans* (*The Maid of Orleans*), which Schiller himself called "a romantic tragedy." He portrayed Joan's strength and success as a product of her love of God and her assigned mission and her weakness as her humanity: She falters and loses her powers when she falls humanly in love with the handsome British Lord Lionel (Schiller's invention). After a profound internal struggle, she tears this love out of her heart, regains her powers, and goes on to victory. Schiller has her die in battle, surrounded by the now unified French military, falling on her personal flag, and then buried under flags. A lyrical, bucolic Prologue, occasional lyrical passages, and incidental music show how close Schiller was here to Baroque and Romantic opera.

Nonetheless, Schiller's true objective was a classical universal idealism and not a romantic never-never-land. His final dramatic efforts made this clear. *Die Braut von Messina oder die feindlichen Brüder, Trauerspiel mit Chören* (*The Bride of Messina or the Inimical Brothers, A Tragic Play with Choruses,* 1803) was a determined virtuoso effort to achieve universality by using the forms of a Greek ritual play. As Schiller pointed out in his Prefatory Essay, *Über den Gebrauch des Chors in der Tragödie* (*Concerning the Use of the Chorus in Tragedy*), he chose a setting that afforded a sense of objective remoteness, where Greek, Moorish, and Christian traditions mingled, and provided further poetic "ideal distance" with a dramatically divided chorus. Tetrameter was used for the choral passages, pentameter for dialogue. There were four scene changes but no act divisions. The Sturm und Drang theme of rival brothers (Don Cesar and Don Manuel) is given only remote social overtones; passion for power motivates the rivalry but disappears when both brothers fall passionately in love only to reappear when they find themselves in love with the same woman. Don Cesar kills Don Manuel, then discovers the woman is their sister, concealed by the fearsome mother because of an oracular dream. In spontaneous remorse and atonement, Don Cesar kills himself. The elements of inscrutable fate, only partly embodied in the characters, impressed the now romantically inclined audience greatly and stimulated a spate of romantic "fate plays" in which all events were mysteriously foreordained.

Schiller's last completed play, *Wilhelm Tell* (1804), took the form of a classical-Romantic dramatic idyll. Hewing closer to historical facts than did the Uri folk play of 1511, Schiller made Tell a goodhearted peasant dreamer rather than a convinced or deliberate republican leader. As Tell responds humanly in the opening idyllic scenes to aid a fisherman in distress, so he responds personally to the undeserved ordeal of having to shoot the apple from his son's head. His outraged retaliatory assassination of the district governor ironically makes him a revolutionary hero. The play was given panoramic breadth, song interludes, and a generally hearty tone—in blank verse—that glorified family, home, community, and fatherland. It was what in German territory is called a SCHAUSPIEL, a serious festive play with a happy ending. A similar hearty and lyrical tone also pervaded Schiller's blank verse translation of Jean Racine's *Phaedra,* performed in Weimar early in 1805, a few months before his death.

Goethe's classical plays were more poetic and less dramatic than those of Schiller. *Iphigenie auf Tauris* (*Iphigenia in Tauris,* 1788) and *Torquato Tasso* (1789), initially written in poetic prose, were presented recast in blank verse. The first became the acknowledged poetic and dramatic realization of Winckelmann's classical ideal of uncomplicated natural sublimity as well as a monument to Goethe's regard for his benevolent friend Charlotte von Stein. It was a festive Schauspiel, in five balanced acts, with five three-dimensional characters, in a single temple grove setting, the action taking place on a single day. Iphigenia, endowed with saintly humanity and wisdom born of suffering, forced to serve in exile from Greece in a barbaric land that slaughters all visiting strangers, has succeeded in getting King Thoas to abolish human sacrifice. Two Greek strangers then appear, plotting, as the result of the ambiguous oracle of Apollo, to steal the statue of Diana. The danger of renewed human sacrifice because of the strangers and the discovery that the Greeks are her brother, Orestes, and his friend Pylades, fill Iphigenia with joy and fear. The ancient curse upon her family is upon them again. Resolved to do only what is humane and just, she stands up to manifest destiny and therapeutically talks out the madness that has infected Orestes (the "furies" of his guilty conscience). He now realizes that the oracle's request means that he should bring his own sister, not Apollo's sister Diana, back to Greece. Iphigenia tells all to Thoas and appeals to him in the name of humanity, and he lets them go, thus removing the last trace of the family curse. The sovereign wisdom of Iphigenia was underlined by Goethe by having her speak several odes that Euripides would have given to a chorus.

TORQUATO TASSO, on the other hand, has a tragic end. The Renaissance poet is portrayed as a man of glorious fantasy and enlightening words but unable to function in the courtly world of decisive action. Here the saintly woman, Leonora d'Este, whom he cannot possess, merely drives him deeper into despair; the rational logic of Antonio merely inflames his jealousy and distrust; the advances of Leonore Sanvitale both flatter and bewilder him; and the gaiety and graciousness of Duke Alfonso nauseate him. His writing is his only therapy, but he keeps sinking deeper into misery and despair. Here the play ends—and scholars are still debating what the indeterminate ending means. Goethe called this play, too, a Schauspiel. The form was slightly less strict than in *Iphigenia,* the blank verse a bit more intense and earthy, the unities a bit less observed.

Goethe's third classical play, *Die natürliche Tochter* ("The Illegitimate Daughter," written 1799), was an attempt to combine universality with current events, that is, to give a poetic and philosophical commentary on revolution, particularly the French Revolution, by showing what happened to an innocent and fine girl in a chaotic political world. The treatment is highly abstract; the only character with a name and a personality is the title heroine, Eugenia, all others being generalized allegorical types, such as King, Old Duke, Young Duke. The political action is not shown; the "action" consists almost wholly of Eugenia's varying spoken reactions to her role as a pawn in an inscrutable, chaotic game of chess. She finally resigns from the feudal, feuding world and marries Magistrate. Goethe called it a "Tragical Play," but it is more accurately a classical morality play. The plan to make a trilogy of it was abandoned.

Minor dramas of Goethe's classical period were the prose satires of the French Revolution, *Der Grosskophta* ("The Grand Cophta," 1790, revised 1791); *Der Bürgergeneral* ("The Citizen General," 1793); and *Die Aufgeregten* ("The Agitated People," 1794). From 1791 to 1817 Goethe also served as director of the Weimar Theater, imposing rather rigid classical formalism but performing Schiller, a few other domestic and numerous foreign authors. His ideas on theater were set down in *Regeln für Schauspieler* ("Rules for Actors," 1794), in the novel *Wilhelm Meister,* and in occasional minor critical writings.

His monumental superdrama, FAUST, consisting of two long five-act dramatic poems, straddled and transcended all the epochs of Goethe's long and active life. Goethe called it a "tragedy," for Marguerite dies young and Faust, too, at long last meets his end. But their immortal souls are ultimately shown moving toward heaven, as forecast in the "Prologue in Heaven"; hence, the overall form of the play, its frame, is that of a medieval mystery ending in apotheosis. The Prologue is preceded by a "Prelude on Stage," in which the director requests a *theatrum mundi* that "in the narrow house of boards traverses all the circle of creation." What happens between the Prologue and the apotheosis, then, is the life of man on earth between heaven and hell, good and evil, idealism and materialism, creation and destruction, the rival forces or "souls" that Faust felt in his breast. The Sturm und Drang rebel is shown running the gamut of human endeavor, driven by lust for life, by thirst for knowledge and sensation, by inescapable guilt, through baroque and romantic escapades of magical hocus-pocus, rejuvenation, love, politics, pursuit of classical beauty (Helen), reclamation of land, creation of the synthetic homunculus—amid comments on innumerable phenomena of the last two thousand years—until "Care" and blindness end his life. He is "a good man, groping in the dark," and exemplifies the saw: "Man errs as long as he strives." Yet, as long as Faust strives, Mephistopheles cannot win his soul, the nihilistic devil is cheated of his prey, the angels drive off the devils in the end, for the grace of God can be won by those "who eternally strive." Productions of this elaborate fantasy were slow in coming, for the technical problems and the costs are prohibitive. But the modern stage produces it quite regularly.

Classicism relegated comedy to a minor status. It was practiced for purposes of entertainment by Goethe and not at all by Schiller (his translations of two minor French comedies and his adaptation of Gozzi's *Turandot* lacked humor). Yet comedy survived on the theatrical level and four "satellites" of the classicists were performed on German-speaking stages everywhere more regularly than their literary superiors. Christian Felix Weisse (1726–1804), a friend and follower of Lessing, produced voluminously in prose, alexandrines, and blank verse. Among his comedies were *Amalia* (1765; applauded by Lessing) and a series of operettas (Singspiele), notably his sensationally successful adaptation of Coffey's *The Devil to Pay* (*Der Teufel ist los*, 1752). His less successful tragedies included *Richard III* (1759; rejected by Lessing) and *Jean Calas* (1775; modeled after Goethe's *Götz*).

Friedrich Ludwig Schröder (1744–1816), an actor and director in Hamburg and a follower of Lessing, wrote well-constructed comedies of good citizenship: *Der beste Mann* ("The Best Man," 1772), an adaptation of Fletcher's *Rule a Wife and Have a Wife; Der Fähnrich* ("The Sergeant," 1782); and *Das Porträt der Mutter oder die Privatkomödie* ("Mother's Portrait or the Private Comedy," 1786). August Wilhelm IFFLAND, an actor in Gotha and Mannheim and director in Berlin who knew both Goethe and Schiller, wrote somewhat more serious bourgeois comedies (Schauspiele), which were neatly contrived to get sentimental responses: *Verbrechen aus Ehrsucht* ("Crime for Glory," 1784, pub. in English as *Crime from Ambition*); *Die Jäger* ("The Hunters," 1785; pub. in English as *The Foresters*); *Die Hagestolzen* ("The Old Bachelors," 1793); and *Der Spieler* ("The Gambler," 1799).

The most successful of the classical satellite playwrights was August von KOTZEBUE, who flooded the stages with over two hundred sentimental comedies and who was assassinated for supposed reactionary and pro-Russian activities. The best known of his plays were *Menschenhass und Reue* (*Misanthropy and Repentance*, 1789); *Die beiden Klingsberg* ("The Two Klingsbergs," 1801, pub. in English as *Father and Son*), *Die deutschen Kleinstädter* ("German Small-Town Folk," 1803); and *Pagenstreiche* ("Pages' Pranks," 1804).

At the level of the popular comedy, the contribution of Austria now achieved special significance (see AUSTRIA). In Hapsburg territory the Roman heritage was dominant at all levels of society from the very beginning. The area also was a busy fairground for the peoples and cultures of Central Europe and the Middle East since the time of the Crusades, a kind of *theatrum mundi*, a playground or showcase of the world. Its center, Vienna, became receptive to all sorts of theater featuring gaiety and pomp and circumstance, particularly the commedia dell'arte and the opera. The city became the embodiment of the philosophy of *carpe diem* with an underlying tone of melancholy that seemed to say, "Make the most of this theater today, for tomorrow we die."

As already discussed, Austria contributed indigenous drama steadily in the medieval period, brought Konrad Celtes to Vienna with Renaissance festival plays, and had its outstanding lavish representative for the Jesuit play in Nicolaus Avancini. In Salzburg the non-Jesuit Simon Rettenpacher (1634–1706) wrote Latin school dramas. In the Baroque period drama was secondary to opera, but by the end of the seventeenth century the always active commedia dell'arte began to take on a middle-class Austrian coloration, as the clown, "Jack Sausage," took charge of the theater, directing his extempores more to the townsfolk and wheedling his way into "higher" society. Some of the actors transformed their own specialized clown figures into independent colloquial characters and hence were credited with the creation of new drama on a "respectable" bourgeois level. Such men were Josef Anton Stranizky (1676–1726; called the Salzburg "Head-and-Cabbage Chopper"), Gottfried Prehauser (1699–1769; "Jack Sausage"), and Johann Josef Felix von Kurz (1715–1785; "Bernardon"). Kurz, following the example set by Carlo Gozzi in Italy, also injected magic and mysterious events in his adaptations (as, for example, in *Die Zaubertrommel,* "The Magic Drum," 1755). The result was unique in German-speaking territory: a tradition of magical, baroque, colloquial comedy that was popular, that is, acclaimed by all social classes and not merely by an elite.

This tradition made it very difficult for classicistic or classical dramas to penetrate Austria, though they were encouraged by the court in Vienna. A French classical theater troupe survived for a while in the Burgtheater. General Cornelius Ayrenhoff (1733–1819), a Gottschedian, bored everyone but King Frederick II and Emperor Joseph II with tragedies in alexandrine verse (*Aurelius,* 1766; *Hermann und Thusnelda,* 1768; *Antiope,* 1772). Baron Tobias von Gebler (1726–1786) produced a classical fate play, *Adelheid von Sigmar* (1774). Gebler and the actor Joseph Sonnenfels agitated for classical reforms and in 1770 the latter became stage censor. Improvisation was then officially forbidden. In 1774 Joseph II made the Burgtheater the National Theater. Shakespeare and the Sturm und Drang dramatists, especially Schiller, were considered improper and subversive. Schröder was brought in to direct the Burgtheater in 1780 and began to broaden the repertory. A dramatist devoted to the ancient Greek drama and to the classical Schiller finally appeared in Heinrich Joseph von Collin (1771–1811), but his pseudo-Greek plays were narrowly moralistic (*Regulus,* 1801; *Coriolanus,* 1802; *Polyxenia,* 1803). It was well into the nineteenth century before literary classicism and Romanticism fully arrived in Austria in the plays of Franz Grillparzer.

While classicism languished, Baroque farce and comedy continued to flourish in Austria. They approached literary quality in form, without losing their popular and folkloristic content, in the well-made semipoetic magical comedies of Philipp Hafner (1735–1761)—in, for example, his *Megära, die förchterliche Hexe* ("Megara, the Terrible Witch," 1758) and *Der Furchtsame* ("The Timid Man," 1764)—and Emanuel Schikaneder (1751–1812), the librettist for Wolfgang Amadeus Mozart's *Zauberflöte* (*The Magic Flute,* 1791). This tradition later produced two outstanding playwrights, Ferdinand Raimund and Johann Nestroy, and is still in evidence today.

nineteenth century. The German literary drama, in the wake of the classicists, moved on in the direction already noticeable in the later works of Goethe and Schiller: Romanticism. The chief pilot of the new course, the highly sophisticated Friedrich Schlegel, boldly extended the idealistic horizons recognized by classicism and set a new goal: the total transformation of the world by poets into poetry, into a harmonious "thing of beauty and a joy forever." For this end absolute freedom of the arts and in the arts was essential—a view partly seen in Sturm und Drang and rejected in classicism. The floodgates of fantasy were opened wide, every variety of theme and form was encouraged, all the torments of life were shown ending in harmony or (in "open" endings) the promise of harmony. In this view, destiny was conquerable and tragedy avoidable. Thus the early absolute Romanticists had no actual tragedy, only comedy and Schauspiel.

The purest example of this was Berlin-born Ludwig Tieck, whose intended "tragedies" were unconvincing theatrical chillers based on contrived accidents and mystifications. He later admitted he had substituted ghostly elements for human elements. *Der Abschied* ("The Farewell," 1792) and *Karl von Berneck* (1795) were outright fate tragedies (see Schicksalstragödie) suggesting that resolution of conflict through love would come after death. *Leben und Tod der heiligen Genoveva* ("The Life and Death of Saint Genevieve," 1799) was a moody lyrical mixture of legend, folk tale, and fantasy that replaced all action with musical poetry. Tieck's *Kaiser Octavian* ("Emperor Octavianus," 1804), based on chapbook accounts, resolved the events of a legendary life into a virtuoso exhibition of every variety of verse and fairy-tale enchantment. The same techniques, however, were highly effective in his fairy-tale comedies: *Der gestiefelte Kater* ("Puss in Boots," 1797), a brilliant abandonment of dramatic rules, with a virtuoso use of the play-within-a-play and interaction between audience and play; *Ritter Blaubart* ("Sir Bluebeard," 1796), a satire; *Prinz Zerbino oder die Reise nach dem guten Geschmack* ("Prince Zerbino or the Journey in Search of Good Taste," 1798); *Die verkehrte Welt* ("The Upside-down World," 1798), a literary satire, directed chiefly against Kotzebue, which led to a short war of stage satires between Kotzebue and the Romanticists Clemens Brentano and A. W. Schlegel; and *Fortunat* (1816), an unsatirical and almost realistic dramatization of the man with the magical purse and hat. Tieck also translated (1811) medieval English dramas, edited (1817) German dramas of the sixteenth and seventeenth centuries, wrote (1801) a Fastnachtsspiel in the style of Hans Sachs, edited large sections of the A. W. Schlegel–Dorothea Tieck–Wolf Baudissin translation of Shakespeare, and brought about the belated discovery of Heinrich von Kleist through editions of Kleist's unpublished manuscripts (1821) and collected works (1826).

In the wake of Tieck's fate plays came theatrically successful efforts in this genre by several playwrights, among whom were Zacharias Werner, *Der 24. Februar* ("The Twenty-Fourth of February," 1810; see below); Adolf Müllner (1774–1829), *Der neunund-*

zwanzigste Februar ("The Twenty-Ninth of February," 1812) and *Die Schuld* ("Guilt," 1813); Baron Ernst von Houwald (1771–1845), *Die Freistatt* ("The Sanctuary"), *Die Heimkehr* ("The Homecoming"), *Das Bild* ("The Image"), *Der Leuchtturm* ("The Lighthouse"), *Fluch und Segen* ("Curse and Blessing"), all between 1818 and 1821; and Franz Grillparzer, *Die Ahnfrau* (1817; see below).

Except for the dramas of Kleist, the most significant contributions to the drama made by the early Romanticists were their translations of Shakespeare, Calderón, and Lope de Vega. Here they provided great drama in good poetic German, even when the original did not exemplify their Romantic convictions. The degree to which they romanticized the originals was small. The key to this special skill presumably was in the personalities of the translators, but a share must be attributed to the Romantic desire to use any and all varieties of style. This was noticeable even when original dramas were written on new subjects modeled after foreign styles. Thus August Wilhelm Schlegel (1767–1845), translator of seventeen plays by Shakespeare and five by Calderón, wrote a Grecophile drama, *Ion* (1803), which was more Greek than German, and his brother Friedrich Schlegel (1772–1829) produced a Romantic Spanish drama, *Alarcos* (1802), which was more Spanish than German.

Later writers of Romantic drama were more personal and individualistic. Clemens Brentano (1778–1842) presented a world of his own in *Die Gründung Prags* ("The Founding of Prague," 1815), the Libussa story romanticized; and *Ponce de Leon* (1804), an overclever portrait of the author as a playboy, later reformed by love. His close collaborator and friend Achim von Arnim (1781–1831) freely transplanted the miraculous Baroque world of Gryphius' *Cardenio und Celinde* to the present in *Halle und Jerusalem* (1811). Joseph von Eichendorff (1788–1857), a great lyricist and also a translator of Calderón, satirized every variety of stuffiness in every variety of verse in his dramatic folk tale *Krieg den Philistern!* ("War to the Philistines!" written 1822), and showed a charming escape from unpleasant reality into the world of folk song in *Die Freier* ("The Suitors," 1833), a comedy of disguise resembling Calderón's *Phantom Lady*, but vastly more complex. August von Platen (1796–1835) was a stricter formalist and an even sharper satirist. His *Der gläserne Pantoffel* ("The Glass Slipper," 1823), a combination of *Snow White* and *Cinderella*, was spiked with wit; *Der Schatz des Rhampsenit* ("The Treasure of Rhampsenit," 1824) was a fairly strict commedia dell'arte. His Renaissance comedy *Treue um Treue* ("Loyalty for Loyalty," 1821) sang the praises of the happy world of fables. Ironically, Platen also helped to liquidate Romantic drama when he turned Romantic satire against contrived Romantic products. In the technique of Aristophanes he demolished fate plays with a dramatic lampoon, *Die verhängnisvolle Gabel* ("The Fateful Fork," 1826), and ridiculed claptrap imitations of Shakespeare and Calderón with *Der romantische Ödipus*, ("The Romantic Oedipus," 1829), especially directed against Immermann (see below).

Three dramatists worthy of the name stood out during (and after) the Romantic period and also stood apart from it. Their precise status is still controversial. Zacharias WERNER, supported by Goethe, an avid reader of drama and student of theory from Aristotle through Schiller, developed a highly successful theatrical formula that was not fully convincing dramaturgically. Based on Calderón (*The Devotion of the Cross*) and the German Baroque tradition, this formula showed the salvation of all manner of men and women, an overcoming of tragedy through religious faith and resignation from mundane ambition as well as through the love of and for God with the aid of an intermediary. The formula was not to teach any particular Church dogma, but was to create a sustaining poetic myth. It was applied in a well-made technique, with baroque pomp, rich characters, and romantically ecstatic language. In this vein, between 1803 and 1810, Werner wrote: *Attila; Wanda; Kunegonde; Die Söhne des Tals* ("The Sons of the Valley"); a drama in two parts entitled *Die Templer auf Cypern* ("The Templars on Cyprus") and *Die Kreuzesbrüder* ("The Brothers of the Cross"); *Das Kreuz an der Ostsee* ("The Cross on the Baltic"); *Luther oder die Weihe der Kraft* ("Luther or the Consecration of Power"); and *Der vierundzwanzigste Februar* ("The Twenty-Fourth of February"), a fate play. His search for salvation induced him to convert to Catholicism in 1810. He was later ordained as a priest and wrote no more plays.

Heinrich von KLEIST, the difficult Prussian rejected by Goethe because he portrayed "confusion of emotions," performed hardly at all in his lifetime and mostly with failure. A tragic suicide at age thirty-four, he gained recognition only after his death. The modern world has greater understanding than Kleist's own time for his intense personal sincerity and the pathological complexes of his characters.

Kleist wanted to outstrip Goethe and Schiller. The means he chose was absolute tragedy based on human pathology and the pathology of a world out of joint. When his efforts found no recognition, he grew despondent. His language was sincere and musical, but also crotchety and forced. Yet he produced one strong tragedy, several effective Schauspiele, and one outstanding comedy. *Die Familie Schroffenstein* (*The Feud of the Schroffensteins*, 1803) was an intense tragic treatment of a family feud and a Romeo and Juliet problem based on human blindness; it has no Romantic resolution, only destruction and resignation. His second play, *Robert Guiskard*, was burned in discontent and only partially restored. In PENTHESILEA Kleist achieved poignant tragedy: The Amazon queen must conquer Achilles in battle to possess him; he conquers her, acts as if she conquered him—for he is now in love with her—they confess their love, then she discovers the truth and in a frenzy of frustration has her dogs tear him to pieces and dies herself in a state of ecstasy. The form is strictly classical (one act in blank verse) but with occasional flamboyant imagery: a unique classical-Romantic love tragedy.

Das Kätchen von Heilbronn oder die Feuerprobe (*Cathy of Heilbronn, or The Trial by Fire*, written 1808, performed 1810) was an ambitious medieval romantic fantasy with knights, witches, angels, and a secret court. The supernaturally protected Cinderella-heroine turns out to be the emperor's illegitimate daughter and marries her Prince Charming. Prose and all sorts of verse alternate. This was Kleist's only stage success in his lifetime. *Die Hermannsschlacht* (*The Battle of Hermann,* written 1809, pub. 1811), a bloody, sadistic portrayal of the Cheruskian slaughter of Varus and his Roman legions in A.D. 8, was actually a disguised patriotic appeal to the Germans to cast off the French yoke. Napoleon's victories over Prussia dashed Kleist's hopes and he withheld the play. The irregular classical form here was incongruous and grotesque. On the other hand, the same Prussian patriotism enabled Kleist to produce another classical-Romantic classic, the Schauspiel PRINZ FRIEDRICH VON HOMBURG. Dealing freely with historical events of 1675, with fully credible fantastication, the play portrays the romantic dreamer-hero winning the battle of Fehrbellin through insubordination. Imprisoned for this, the heroic prince expects to be executed and—given free choice by his master, the duke elector of Prussia—freely chooses execution as his morally deserved sentence. At the execution, when his blindfold is removed, he is awarded the hand of his beloved Princess Natalie (a dream come true) and hailed as a national hero: The humane duke has pardoned him. Thus both the prince and the duke achieve a deeper sense of responsibility. The blank verse here is poetic, lucid, terse, and semirealistic. The action is based on character: The resolution of the potential tragedy comes through realistic responsible judgment.

Kleist also produced one weak and one strong classical-Romantic comedy. His highly original adaptation of Molière's *Amphitryon* (pub. 1807) was too tense to be really amusing. He did add a new note to the theme: the frustration of Jupiter at his essential failure to take Amphitryon's place in Alcmene's affections. She can only love him when he is completely Amphitryon, never when he is himself. The strong comedy, a repertory item today, was THE BROKEN JUG. This one-act piece in blank verse is classical in structure and realistic in substance. It was freely invented as a literary interpretation of a French painting. Kleist used a rustic Dutch village setting. Charges are brought before the village judge, Adam, that a lecherous attack has been made upon the robust maiden Eve by a young yokel, resulting in one broken jug. Adam, the actual culprit, is shown suffering the tortures of a comical Oedipus as he investigates the case and seeks to escape his own prosecution. His exposure, self-exposure, and flight are hilarious. The incongruity of Kleist's classical blank verse spoken by simple townsfolk adds to the comedy. Kleist is as realistic here as in his realistic short stories.

The third controversial figure was the Austrian Franz GRILLPARZER. His versatility, sensitivity, and cultural heterodoxy made him an enigma to friends and critics alike. Beyond cavil was his dedication to high poetic and theatrical quality. He was steeped in Austrian tradition, enamored of Calderón and Lope de Vega, receptive to Romantic motifs and forms, and ideologically a classical meliorist like Goethe and Schiller.

The essential tragic conflict between human aspiration and the world around us became central to Grillparzer. He dealt with it in concrete poetic and psychological forms, never abstractly or metaphysically, in varying moods of regret, resentment, resignation, horror, dismay, and even classical acceptance.

Blanca von Kastilien ("Blanca of Castile," 1809) was a dramatic exercise in imitation of Schiller's *Don Carlos. Die Ahnfrau* (*The Ancestress,* 1817), his greatest stage success, was a balladesque, folkloristic fate play. In *Sappho* (1818) he achieved a gentle classical tragedy, in subtle poetic blank verse, with a Romantic resignation: the Greek poetess—here a noble blend of Goethe's Iphigenia, Thoas, and Tasso—cannot win the love of the charming younger man Phaon and, realizing that her kingdom is not of this world, casts herself into the sea. The expansive classical trilogy *Das goldene Vliess* (*The Golden Fleece,* 1821), made up of *Der Gastfreund* (*The House Guest*), *Die Argonauten* (*The Argonauts*), and *Medea,* using very few Romantic trappings (dreams, omens, premonitions), portrays the epic events and the human aspirations and inadequacies that destroyed Phryxus, Absyrtus, Kreusa, and the children of Jason and Medea. The tragic flaw here lies not in moral error but in visceral, neurotic, and cultural limitations, especially in both Medea and Jason.

The Baroque conviction of the vanity of human endeavor was embellished with classical ethical moderation in Grillparzer's tragical history play *König Ottokars Glück und Ende* (*King Ottokar, His Rise and Fall,* 1825). Without Romantic trappings, in reserved blank verse, Grillparzer here showed how the ambitious Bohemian king had to yield to the humane and just "Emperor who never dies," Rudolf I, the first Hapsburg emperor. *Ein treuer Diener seines Herrn* (*A Faithful Servant of His Master,* 1828), a less tragical history play, portrays the ordeal of the old martyred Bancbanus, who survives the ruination of his young wife by the tyrant Duke Otto, withstands all the temptations of the unlimited power given him by Otto, and even ethically reforms his lord and master, all without the slightest thought or act of disloyalty. *Des Meeres und der Liebe Wellen* ("The Waves of Love and the Sea," pub. in English as *Hero and Leander,* 1831) again combines a classical theme in classical form with a Romantic ending: Leander's love conquers the Hellespont and the vows of the priestess Hero, but not the dedicated opposition of the high priest, who finally puts out the light that guides Leander. But love and the sea unite the lovers forever in death: He drowns and she drowns herself. The mood here is one of rueful acceptance. Rejection of ambition, on the other hand, is the message of *Der Traum, ein Leben* (*The Dream Is Life,* 1834), in which Calderón's *Life Is a Dream* is inverted in a dramatic fairy tale with a dream play within the play. Rustan, tempted by his slave Zanga, wants to forsake his rustic life and his beloved Mirza to seek a greater fortune. Entranced by a dervish, he then experiences in a dream onstage his rise and fall in an adventurous grand career—and wakes up cured of his excessive ambition. The verse line here is Calderón's rhymed tetrameter. In the comedy *Weh dem, der lügt!* ("Beware of Telling a Lie!" 1838, pub. in English as *Thou Shalt Not Lie!*), good-natured acceptance is the mood. A rustic classical play, Bishop Gregory of Chalons issues the title warning in permitting his enterprising kitchen-helper Leon to attempt the rescue of Gregory's unjustly imprisoned nephew; the illegal rescue is carried out gaily by open declaration of

criminal intent, which nobody believes; Gregory accepts the tainted success with the words: "This weed, I see, cannot be rooted out, / With luck perhaps, the wheat will yet outgrow it."

This subtle comedy was rejected by the farce-minded Viennese public and the embittered Grillparzer released no further plays. The three dramas published after the self-styled "old grouch" died (1872) were among his very finest. *Ein Bruderzwist im Hause Habsburg* ("A Falling Out of Brothers in the House of Hapsburg," pub. in English as *Family Strife in Hapsburg*) is a historical meditation, in blank verse dialogue, a drama of inaction. Indeed, inaction is exalted here as the epitome of wise statesmanship, for the sensitive tragic hero, Rudolf II, sees the inevitable approach of the Thirty Years' War and is forced to see that any positive action will only hasten its arrival. In this central figure Grillparzer not only produced a detailed portrait of a complex old recluse but also a self-portrait and a resigned vision of the inability of the Austro-Hungarian monarchy to survive in the harsh modern world. *Libussa* (unlike Brentano's treatment in "The Founding of Prague") portrays poetically and philosophically the vain attempt of a matriarchal, sensitive, and humane sibyl to manage the world of men. She loves man, represented by the pragmatic enterprising Primislaus, descends to earth, and marries him, even experiments with a communal-communistic social order, but cannot make the harsh decisions the material world requires. Her self-willed death, in which she leaves the world and Prague to Primislaus, is accompanied by her prophecy that someday beauty, harmony, love, and truth will return to earth. *Die Jüdin von Toledo* (*The Jewess of Toledo*), suggested by several Lope de Vega plays, tersely treats in effective classical form King Alfonso's conflict between love and duty. Repelled by the harsh demands of his position and the cold formality of his queen, the sensitive king seeks warmth and joy in the arms of the fascinating vivacious Jewess—and neglects pressing affairs of state, including war against the Moors. The grandees and the queen, finding the king unresponsive to appeals, assassinate the Jewess. The king's vital personal impulses and rebellion die with her, he resumes his duties, and goes off to war. The harsh ending with a political murder reiterates Grillparzer's basic discontent with a world that has no place for sensitive, warm human beings.

Grillparzer's more successful competitors in Austria were of two kinds. The one group followed the lead of Hafner and Kotzebue with humdrum comedies of manners spiced with a bit of magic and literary satire. The leaders were Joseph Alois Gleich (1772–1841), Karl Meisl (1775–1853), and Adolf Bäuerle (1786–1859). They produced not one memorable play and are remembered only as shopkeepers who continued the tradition and made possible the emergence of the second group: the masters of the *Zauberposse,* the "hocus-pocus farce," Ferdinand RAIMUND and Johann Nepomuk NESTROY. Both were experienced and accomplished actors.

Raimund became the master of gracious and morally uplifting fantastication in the vein of *The Magic Flute* with *Der Barometermacher auf der Zauberinsel* ("The Barometer-Maker on the Magic Island," 1823); *Der Diamant des Zauberkönigs*

("The Diamond of the King of Magic," 1824); *Das Mädchen aus der Feenwelt, oder der Bauer als Millionär* ("The Girl from Fairyland, or the Farmer as a Millionaire," 1826); *Der Alpenkönig und der Menschenfeind* ("The Alpine King and the Misanthrope," 1828); and *Der Verschwender* ("The Wastrel," 1834). In all of these, Christian humility conquers every conceivable Baroque monster, but the forces of good and evil are so subtly and symbolically portrayed that the audience recognizes them as genuine realistic human drives. Consequently, in spite of the obligatory Viennese incidental music and songs, these are not musical comedies but dramas that engage the audience.

Nestroy became the master of the fantastic spoof, a virtuoso of ecstatic ridicule, in such Zauberpossen as: *Die Verbannung aus dem Zauberreich oder Dreissig Jahre aus dem Leben eines Lumpen* ("Banishment from the Magic Kingdom or Thirty Years of the Life of a Bum," 1828); *Der konfuse Zauberer oder Treue und Flattergeist* ("The Confused Magician or Loyalty and Whimsy," 1832); *Der böse Geist Lumpazivagabundus oder das liederliche Kleeblatt* ("The Evil Spirit Lumpazivagabundus or The Untidy Trio," 1833); and *Der Zauberer Sulphurelektrimagnetikophosphoratus und die Fee Walburgiblocksbergiseptemtrionalis* ("The Magician S. and the Fairy W.," 1834). These musical farces all expose romantic human follies and explore, with occasionally choleric humor, the possibility of a deterioration of the entire cosmos: The magicians and gods themselves have lost control. This would be "theater of the absurd" except for the underlying Viennese attitude that says, "The situation is hopeless, but not serious." Nestroy also contributed highly successful satirical social comedies (*Zu ebener Erde und im ersten Stock oder die Launen des Glücks*, "Downstairs and One Flight Up or The Vagaries of Fortune," 1835; *Das Mädl aus der Vorstadt oder Ehrlich währt am längsten*, "The Girl from the Suburbs or Honesty Wins in the End," 1841; *Einen Jux will er sich machen*, "One Last Fling," 1842, on which Thornton Wilder based his *Matchmaker*; and *Freiheit in Krähwinkel, Freedom Comes to Krähwinkel*, 1848, a political satire of a small town) and brilliant theatrical lampoons, namely of Friedrich Hebbel's *Judith* in *Judith und Holofernes* (1849) and of Richard Wagner's *Tannhäuser* (1857) and *Lohengrin* (1859). Nestroy's true comic genius may never be recognized outside German-speaking territory because his local color, his use of local dialect, his puns and plays on words virtually defy translation.

The steady march toward everyday realism, already noted in the Austrian drama, was even more marked in Germany proper. On the most popular level the successes of Kotzebue were matched by those of Ernst Raupach (1784–1852), who is best remembered for his notorious sixteen-part theatrical tour de force *Geschichte und Schicksal der Hohenstaufen* ("History and Destiny of the Hohenstaufen Family," nearly all parts performed from 1830 to 1837). Raupach exploited romantic historical nostalgia while using realistic stage technique.

Intellectually more ambitious efforts at historical veracity and stage realism were made by Karl Lebrecht Immermann (1796–1840), who served as theater director in Magdeburg and Düsseldorf. As a playwright Immermann was barely more than a facile imitator, a role that he shared with the contemporaries he portrayed in his novel *Die Epigonen* ("The Epigones," 1836). His best historical play, *Andreas Hofer, der Sandwirt von Passeyer* ("Andreas Hofer, Master of the Sands of Passeyer," 1833); his stark tragedy *Cardenio und Celinde* (1826); his mythical fantasy *Merlin* (1832); and his historical trilogy *Alexis* (1832) all are sincere but emotionally flat. His heroes are martyrs rather than men of action.

Christian Dietrich GRABBE, the son of a prison guard in Detmold, Westphalia, was seemingly the polar opposite of Immermann. He was an uncontrolled chaotic genius whose brief life abounded in failures. With the pathos of Sturm und Drang, as a disciple of Schiller and Lenz, he lashed out at a universe he considered out of joint and worthy of destruction, and became one of the earliest playwrights of nihilism. His heroes are supermen: *Barbarossa* (1829), *Don Juan und Faust* (1829), *Napoleon* (1831), *Hannibal* (1834), and *Die Hermannsschlacht* ("The Battle of Hermann," 1838). The devil is the tragic hero of Grabbe's fantastic comedy *Scherz, Satire, Ironie und tiefere Bedeutung* ("Spoof, Satire, Irony, and Profounder Significance," 1822). Grabbe freely departed from traditional forms: His *Napoleon* and *Die Hermannsschlacht* are episodic "station plays" with many features of the "epic theater," later defined by Bertolt Brecht and Erwin Piscator. His historical realism is pungent and direct, though selective and episodic, and hence more dynamic than that of Immermann. Yet both men shared a realistic bent.

A greater and even more short-lived genius was Georg BÜCHNER, the intellectually gifted son of well-established parents in Hessen. Successful as a student of physics, mathematics, and medicine, he was outraged by the German police state of the 1830's, became a revolutionary activist, fled to Strasbourg, and died of typhus in Zurich. His disillusioned liberalism expressed itself in drama as a terse and dynamic materialistic nihilism. He rejected the possibility of ideological victories and considered man, whether big or small, to be the pitiable victim of historical and social circumstance. His big man, Danton of DANTON'S DEATH, is so depressed by the depravities of the French Revolution and human nature that he virtually seeks death at the hands of Robespierre. His little man, Woyzeck in WOYZECK, is pitilessly crushed by sickness, poverty, exploitation, lust, infidelity; he murders his unfaithful wife and drowns himself; his world is a cold machine driven by destructive material forces. The episodic station play, or balladesque, structure of the piece derives from Lenz, whom Büchner memorialized in a novella. *Woyzeck* is often considered the earliest play of harsh modern realism, of expressionism and of drama of the absurd. It is usually performed today in English in the Eric Bentley translation and in the opera version composed by Alban Berg (*Wozzeck*, 1925). In *Leonce und Lena* (*Leonce and Lena*, published in cut version in 1839, full text in 1850), Büchner also contributed a juicy bittersweet comedy, a fairty-tale spoof in which pure love just barely bridges the nihilistic abyss of social and cosmic disorder. Grotesque satirical scenes of corruption in high places alternate with scenes of romantic bucolic charm. The paradox that the solution is a fairy tale is both Romantic and modern.

Grabbe and Büchner were isolated harbingers of later developments. The main line of realism in the German drama was represented by the more openly political liberals Heinrich Laube and Karl Gutzkow. They believed in ideological and political solutions, applied George Wilhelm Friedrich Hegel's historical triad (thesis, antithesis, synthesis) to dramatic structure, and pressed their belief in progress—together with Immermann, Ludwig Börne, and Heinrich Heine—in a loosely organized movement called Young Germany. Their realism was sociological and melioristic (they admired Schiller and Eugène Scribe) and stressed effective dramaturgical technique. Laube directed the Vienna Burgtheater and the Leipzig Stadttheater, and founded the Vienna Stadttheater. Gutzkow served as dramaturgical director at the Dresden Hoftheater. Their dramas were well-made, idealistic, successful, and a bit dull.

Heinrich Laube (1806–1884) had modest successes with the comedies *Rokoko* (1842), *Gottsched und Gellert* (1845), and *Die Karlsschüler* ("The Students of Karl School," 1846, featuring young Schiller as a character), and with the *Trauerspiele* ("sad plays") *Monaldeschi* (1845) and *Struensee* (1847). Karl Gutzkow (1811–1878) had good reception for his comedies *Der Königsleutnant* ("The Royal Lieutenant-General," 1852, featuring young Goethe as a character); *Zopf und Schwert* ("Queue and Sword," 1844, featuring the liberalism of King Frederick William I of Prussia); and *Das Urbild des Tartuffe* ("The Model for Tartuffe," 1847, featuring Molière and his friends). Gutzkow's *Trauerspiele* *Uriel Acosta* (1846), concerning the problem of the converted Jew, and his *Wullenweber* (1848), about the last hero of the Hanseatic League, were also well received.

The natural culmination of historical, political, and dramaturgical realism was a magnificent mediocrity named Gustav Freytag (1816–1895). He was a good professional journalist from Silesia, a faithfully reporting sociological novelist, a great popularizer of German history in his voluminous pseudohistorical accounts, and a monumental trivializer of dramatic criticism and dramaturgy in his three-volume *Die Technik des Dramas* ("The Technique of the Drama," 1863), the standard German dramaturgic reference work until World War I. This book, a detailed manual of play construction, provided the ultimate German definition of the well-made play: Aristotle, Lessing, Goethe, Schiller, Laube, and Freytag, rolled into a slick package to satisfy totally the moral and patriotic bourgeoisie of the age of Otto von Bismarck. It lacked appreciation of the dynamic and demonic human forces, as did all but one of Freytag's dramas. Only in *Die Journalisten* ("The Journalists," 1852), a political comedy, did Freytag succeed in creating vital tensions with problematical characters modeled after those of his favorite writer, Charles Dickens. In the figure of Schmock he created the stereotype of the Grub Street hack who can write in any style.

Realistic, well-made plays without literary significance were also supplied in considerable quantity by Charlotte Birch-Pfeiffer (1800–1868; *e.g., Die Grille,* "The Cricket," 1856), Friedrich Halm (1806–

1871; *e.g., Griseldis,* 1835, *Der Sohn der Wildnis,* "Son of the Wilderness," 1842, and *Der Fechter von Ravenna,* "The Swordsman of Ravenna," 1857), Adolf von Wilbrandt (1837–1911; *e.g., Der Meister von Palmyra,* "The Master of Palmyra," 1889, and *König Teja,* "Teja the King," 1908), Roderich Benedix (1811–1873; *e.g., Die Hochzeitsreise,* "The Honeymoon," 1849), and Ernst von Wildenbruch (1845–1909; *Christoph Marlow,* 1884, and *Heinrich und Heinrichs Geschlecht,* "Henry and the House of Henry," 1896).

The final stage of nineteenth-century German realistic drama was characterized by a return to poetic, philosophical, and nonrational elements. New emphases on emotional forces in the individual, in society, and in regional landscape paved the way for the scientific skepticism of Henrik Ibsen, August Strindberg, and their German counterparts Gerhart Hauptmann and Frank Wedekind. The cerebral-philosophical Hegelian approach of Friedrich HEBBEL, supported by the experiences of poverty in a barren landscape, led him to produce dramas depicting realistically a tragic cosmic dichotomy. In his view tragedy is universally inevitable because God has produced a polarized world. Great individuals are doomed to conflict with others or with society precisely because they are individuals and are great. Immaculate moral conduct cannot restore the broken harmony. Hebbel's hope is that mankind will move forward slightly with each destructive cataclysm. Accordingly, his dramas deal preferably with great turning points in history. His characters tend to be idealogues rather than people. The conflicts are harsh and unsentimental, resulting in tragedy without tears. His comedies were all failures. His tragedies, however, became a modest part of standard German and Austrian repertory.

In *Judith* (1839) the Jewish heroine cannot kill the enemy of her people, Holofernes, until he rapes her. The act of murder then destroys her, too, for she loves the man she killed and also cannot face the possibility of bearing her public enemy's child. In *Genoveva* (1843) the saintly heroine is cast out by her unbelieving husband because of Golo's uncontrolled passion for her. In *Maria Magdalena* (1844), the foolish bourgeois heroine, Clara, destroys herself and her suitors through fear and respect for her sternly moral father. The title characters of *Herodes und Mariamne* (1850) destroy each other through possessiveness, distrust, and vindictiveness. The title heroine of *Agnes Bernauer* (1855) is demolished innocently by her angelic beauty, which gets in the way of the dynastic purposes of her princely lover's father and his political advisers. As in the philosophy of Hegel, the interests of the state are paramount.

Gyges und sein Ring (*Gyges and His Ring,* 1856) is to many critics Hebbel's most poetically and humanly successful tragedy, perhaps because its departure from daily reality, its legendary theme, permits greater suspension of disbelief. Powerful King Kandaules, possessor of a most beautiful queen, seeks appreciation of his possession from his friend Gyges, a highly cultured Greek. He persuades Gyges to use his magical ring of invisibility and be an unseen witness in his bedroom. Queen Rhodope finds out, makes Gyges kill Kandaules, marries Gyges, and then kills herself. Legend in full dress is the substance of Hebbel's last completed play, the trilogy *Die Nibelungen* ("The Nibelungs," 1862), made up of *Der gehörnte Siegfried* ("Horn-skinned Siegfried"), a one-act prelude; *Siegfrieds Tod* ("The Death of Siegfried"), a five-act classical tragedy; and *Kriemhilds Rache* ("Kriemhild's Revenge"), a five-act classical tragedy. Hebbel here imposes his formula on the expansive German folk epic: The forceful and vengeful pagans destroy each other, and Christian humility becomes the new synthesis. The relatively good success of this work on the stage was probably due to its spectacular and patriotic subject matter, which was also used at that time by other authors, most notably by Richard Wagner in his "music drama," the cycle *Der Ring des Nibelungen.*

Hebbel's philosophical drama was categorically opposed by the realistic novelist Otto Ludwig (Thuringia, 1813–1865). Ludwig stressed emotional, poetic, and aesthetic factors and made numerous efforts in a spate of mostly unfinished dramas to break the enslavement of the German drama by theory and contrivance and to create physically real and genuine plays. He succeeded chiefly in replacing abstract contrivance with concrete contrivance. His plays, dealing with social problems, are gracious and well-made, pleasant but not moving. His Judeophile panorama play, *Die Makkabäer* ("The Maccabees," 1853), probably owed its success to the brilliant direction of Heinrich Laube. His best effort, *Der Erbförster* ("The Hereditary Forester," 1850) was acclaimed, not for its fate-play contrivances, but for the realism of its earthy characterizations and its rustic environment, that is, its "regionalism," or *Heimatkunst.* See also Otto LUDWIG.

The first true dramatist of regionalism, however, was the Viennese actor and journalist Ludwig Anzengruber (1839–1889). His problem plays, though burdened with occasional tendentious pathos and theatrical melodrama, are solidly based in realistic delineation of environment and character. His first success, *Der Pfarrer von Kirchfeld* ("The Priest of Kirchfeld," 1870), about liberalism versus dogmatism in a village of the Austrian Tyrol, has been compared with Henrik Ibsen's *Brand* and *An Enemy of the People.* His *Der Meineidbauer* ("The Farmer Forsworn," 1871), concerning greed and insanity among feuding farmers, is considered a powerful tragedy. *Das vierte Gebot* (*The Fourth Commandment,* 1878) is as depressing an exposé of moral decay in Vienna as any advocate of naturalistic portrayal could ask for. Even more convincing and popular with his comedies, Anzengruber took the earthy characters of the "magical farce" tradition, the crotchety originals of Raimund and Nestroy, and put them into realistic environments with real material problems. *Die Kreuzelschreiber* ("The X-Markers," 1872) uses the Lysistrata situation of wives on strike in depicting a political battle between ecclesiastical and peasant interests. *Der G'wissenswurm* ("The Worm of Conscience," 1874) deals humorously with the vain attempts of greedy people to fleece a farmer of his property by exploiting his guilty conscience. *Der Doppelselbstmord* ("The Double Suicide," 1875) gaily transplants the Romeo and Juliet problem to a Tyrolean village and ends it happily.

The period of realism ended—not as paradoxically as it may seem—with the realistically motivated master of artifice and theatrical contrivance, Richard WAGNER. George Bernard Shaw (in *The Perfect Wagnerite*) was not alone in interpreting Wagner as an eminently practical materialistic socialist. Some have gone so far as to look upon all of Wagner's librettos as realistic exploitations in Romantic trappings of the great Germanic legends for the sole purpose of material success. Whatever may be the quality of Wagner's literary contribution—it is, at best, controversial—his advancement of theatrical expression is unquestioned. In his search for the *Gesamtkunstwerk,* the "total work of art," he gave the theater not only a new house of magic in Bayreuth but a big push in the direction of the spectacular. No doubt the troupes of the duke of Meiningen contributed more to realistic theater. But Gordon Craig, Adolphe Appia, Max Reinhardt, indeed most of the theatrical developments of the twentieth century are most deeply indebted to Richard Wagner.

The European crisis of scientific skepticism discernible in such realists as Büchner, Grabbe, Grillparzer, Hebbel, and Anzengruber began to dominate drama in Germany and Austria at almost the same time as it did elsewhere. Henrik Ibsen was performed in German on German stages from 1872 on, most of his premières being in Germany. The beginning of the new naturalistic drama is usually dated 1889 from the opening of Otto Brahm's theater, Freie Bühne ("Free Stage"), in Berlin with Ibsen's *Ghosts.* A few weeks later the same stage was in an uproar over its first German naturalistic play: Gerhart Hauptmann's *Vor Sonnenaufgang* (*Before Dawn,* also translated as *Before Sunrise*). The positivistic theoretical background for the naturalistic approach had been derived from Auguste Comte and Hippolyte Taine, exemplified by Émile Zola, and programmed for Germany in the essays of the brothers Heinrich (1855–1906) and Julius (1859–1930) Hart and the essayistic poetry and prose of Arno Holz (1863–1929) and his friend Johannes Schlaf (1862–1919). Holz and Schlaf gave the extreme formulation: "Art tends to reconstitute nature; it becomes nature according to the materials and the way they are handled." With this technological method they produced an extreme model drama, *Die Familie Selicke* ("The Selicke Family," 1890), a gray, detailed, depressing, sordid, unedited slice of the life of pitiable victims of heredity and environment.

Gerhart HAUPTMANN had much more to offer than this photographic and phonographic copy technique. Even in his most naturalistic plays he has depth of character, poetic command of language—whether in local dialect or in "High German"—and a profound human compassion, all of which lift his work above the level of technique and invite comparison with Goethe, whom Hauptmann deeply admired. In fact, in his humanism, variety of intellectual and artistic interests, variety of genres and styles, and personal involvement in his writings, Hauptmann emulated Goethe. He even claimed he possessed the polar dualism of Faust in that he had "double vision," an eye to see simultaneously both immediate reality and the metaphysical. In any case his writings quite consistently combine surface realism with otherworldly mysticism. About half of his voluminous writings consists of forty-five dramas, most of them well received and about ten of them still repertory pieces today. Those produced before World War I are generally considered his best. He was a tired man in his seventies when the pressures of National Socialism pushed him into formal patriotic support of the regime—for which he was roundly condemned in most literary circles. All in all, he was not a National or any other kind of socialist, but a humane dramatic national and social seismograph. He was in line with Goethe, Büchner, and Ibsen rather than with Richard Wagner or Friedrich Nietzsche.

BEFORE DAWN deals with the deterioration of a peasant family when coal is found on its land. An idealistic but stupid reformer appears and sets off a chain reaction. The ugliness of alcoholism, sheer animal sexuality, and rigid moralism are shown indelibly and in detail. *Das Friedensfest* (*The Reconciliation*, 1890), based on actual events in the home of Frank Wedekind, is an ironic and depressing display of family neuroses that result from a misalliance. *Einsame Menschen* (*Lonely Lives,* 1891) combines the theme of the vain struggle of the reformer-scientist with his family with the theme of the inability of the misunderstood husband to choose between his inadequate wife and an understanding modern woman. THE WEAVERS is a tragedy with a group hero, a "station play" in five scenes in Silesian dialect, detailing the futile revolt of the impoverished and diseased weavers against their employers. The play has been called the first socialistic drama but is actually a cry of pity for all victims, including bystanders. In the same year Hauptmann also successfully explored the comic vein of naturalism. *Kollege Crampton* (*Professor Crampton,* 1892) is a humorous yet kindly portrait of an art professor whose limited gifts in a competitive academic environment make a drunkard and faker out of him. *Der Biberpelz* (*The Beaver Coat,* 1893), one of the greatest of German comedies, shows in grim and humorous detail how an enterprising washwoman, "unsinkable" Mother Wolff, achieves financial progress and "respectability" for herself and her family by a series of thefts. In her animal cunning she is as unaware of her immorality as are her provincial neighbors. Her society is too involved in personal gain, bureaucratic rigmarole, and political prejudices to catch a bold thief. Her society deserves her and she "stoops to conquer."

The same year witnessed the emergence of the romantic, poetic side of Hauptmann. *Hanneles Himmelfahrt* (*The Assumption of Hannele,* 1893) projects the death of a mistreated poor girl in a profound switch from naturalistic treatment into the girl's hallucinatory or "dream" visions. In the visions, sordid reality is transformed into heavenly bliss with the nurse as an angelic mother and the teacher as Christ. Naturalism again dominates in the historical tragedy *Florian Geyer* (pub. 1896), which portrays in six broad panoramic scenes (a prelude and five acts) the historical evidence that Florian Geyer and not Götz von Berlichingen (as in Goethe) was the actual overly trusting hero of the Peasants' Revolt in the sixteenth century. Later productions of this play succeeded in doing justice to the documentary detail of this spectacle, but it failed in Berlin in 1896.

This failure, the collapse of his first marriage, and a growing skepticism toward naturalism led Hauptmann to a second romantic effort in the same year.

Die versunkene Glocke (*The Sunken Bell*) depicts in blank verse the failure of an artist, the bell-maker Heinrich, to overcome domestic responsibilities, Christian morality, bourgeois conventions and to escape into the creative elfin world of Silesian fairy tales and the water-nymph Rautendelein. His superbell is sabotaged by sprites and burghers, falls to the bottom of a lake, where his drowned wife rings it dolefully. The play had considerable success and led to the composition of the opera *La campana sommersa* (1927) by Ottorino Respighi. The destructive power of woman engaged Hauptmann further in *Elga* (1896); in *Fuhrmann Henschel* (*Drayman Henschel,* 1898), a pungent naturalistic portrayal of the demolition of a sensitive man by an animalistic woman; in *Michael Kramer* (1900), where the woman is incidental to all the forces of reality that destroy the artistically gifted but ugly and maladjusted son of a righteous and only modestly gifted artistic father, who in the process experiences God's suffering in the death of Christ; *Der rote Hahn* (*Arson,* 1901), in which Mother Wolff of *Der Biberpelz* outsmarts herself, commits arson, and comes to a grievous end; *Gabriel Schillings Flucht* (*Gabriel Schilling's Flight,* 1906), about the suicide of a sensitive painter to escape the women he cannot live with; *Kaiser Karls Geisel* ("Charlemagne's Hostage," 1907), in which it takes a man of this stature to resist a nymphomaniac; and *Vor Sonnenuntergang* (*Before Sunset,* 1932), a realistic but lukewarm "Lear" tragedy, in which a melancholy old widower is rejuvenated by love for a young girl and is destroyed by the battle with her and his family.

The misery and ruination of woman by man, treated in some of Hauptmann's early plays, is dominant in *Rose Bernd* (1903), a naturalistic tragedy of a vigorous but naïve farm girl who loves a married man, runs afoul of blackmail, kills her child, and becomes insane; in *Griselda* (1909), a dramatized legend in twelve scenes, in which Griselda suffers physical violence, social prejudice, rejection by her jealous husband during pregnancy and childbirth, becomes a washwoman in her own house, but wins back her husband by infinite love and by teaching him to love her less; and in *Dorothea Angermann* (1925), a realistic tragedy of the woman who is forced to marry a man with whom she has had an affair, is forced into prostitution by him, and ends by taking poison.

Preoccupation with the battle of the sexes did not limit Hauptmann's range of vision or literary vocabulary. The following selection of further plays makes this clear: *Schluck und Jau* (1899), a gay dream spoof taken from the *Arabian Nights* in which two gracious drunkards are duped into playing the roles of a lord and lady and are taught humility; *Der arme Heinrich* ("Poor Henry," 1902), a dramatized legend in verse of Hartmann von der Aue's medieval epic of the leper saved by the willingness of a pure maid to die for him; THE RATS, a tragicomedy of the woman who becomes a mother by "buying" a child, interlarded with a debate on modern drama; *Und Pippa tanzt* ("And Pippa Dances," pub. 1906), a romantic symbolic fairy tale of a beautiful fragile maiden made invisible by the clumsy attentions of German glass blowers but remaining visible to idealists who are physically blind; *Der Bogen des Odysseus* ("The Bow of Odysseus," 1912), a classical verse drama with Freudian analysis and a successful hero—Odysseus regains his family and home; *Der weisse Heiland* (*The White Saviour,* 1917), a fantasy in Calderonian tetrameter, showing noble King Montezuma of the Aztecs deceived by his beliefs and by Fernando Cortez and enduring the sufferings of a maligned Christ; *Indipohdi* (pub. 1920), a fantasy based on Shakespeare's *The Tempest,* but with Prospero's own son Ormann as his adversary and with Prospero drowning his "book of Magic" by suicide, by returning to the nonexistence praised in the Indian legend of the hero Indipohdi; *Hamlet in Wittenberg* (1935), a gay portrait of the engaging, roguish, and activist young prince—in his adaptation of Shakespeare's *Hamlet* of 1928 Hauptmann made him into a man of bold action; and finally the classical tetralogy of the Atrides, an adaptation of the *Oresteia* of Aeschylus: *Iphigenie in Delphi* (1941), *Iphigenie auf Aulis* (1944), *Agamemnons Tod* ("Agamemnon's Death," 1948), and *Elektra* (1948). Here destiny—probably including German destiny—is viewed as an inevitable descent into nonexistence, a pathological and philosophical tendency toward self-destruction, a will to end all by self-sacrifice. Hauptmann the social reformer thus ended even more skeptically than he began.

Among the lesser playwrights of naturalism only a handful made mentionable contributions. Hermann Sudermann (East Prussia, 1857–1928) had more stage successes than Hauptmann but was systematically demolished after 1900 when the critics exposed his indebtedness to Iffland and Kotzebue, his emphasis on sensational effects, and his lack of sociological substance and social conscience. Yet some of his social problem plays still stand as models of the well-made realistic play: *Die Ehre* ("Honor," 1889) shows bourgeois sense of honor to be materialistic and elastic; *Heimat* ("Home," 1893) concerns a girl who makes mistakes, leaves home and becomes a famous singer, visits home and finds her family still unable to accept her free artist's way of life, which destroys her father; *Johannes* ("John the Baptist," 1898) is a serious historical drama of religious and social change; *Es lebe das Leben!* ("Here's to Life!" 1902) is about the well-considered acceptance of error and its consequences as an inevitable part of life; *Das Blumenboot* ("The Flower Float," 1905) is a pungent exposé of the mess that morally "free" living can produce; and *Die Raschoffs* ("The Raschoffs," 1919) is about a father who sacrifices his life to extricate his son from a scandal and enable him to carry on the family business. Sudermann also became a successful novelist. He reflected his era more accurately than Hauptmann, perhaps because he was less above it.

Other naturalistic playwrights had isolated achievements. In the field of social satire Max Dreyer (1862–1946) is remembered only for his *Der Probekandidat* ("The Teacher on Trial," 1900) in which social pressures make a young advocate of Darwinism lose his job but win true love and the admiration of his students; Otto Ernst (1862–1926) only for *Flachsmann als Erzieher* ("Flachsmann as an Educator," 1901), in which a modern teacher stands his ground successfully; and Otto Erich Hartleben (1864–1905) only for *Rosenmontag* ("Rose Monday," 1900), in which Prussian social pressures destroy a young officer and his lower-class fiancée. In the field of regionalism or drama of local dialect Max Halbe (1865–1944) is remembered for *Jugend* (*Youth,* 1893), about young love destroyed by perverse morality and brutality but, despite its somber theme, embellished by lyrical local color; Fritz Stavenhagen (1876–1906) for *Mudder Mews* ("Mother Mews," 1903), a peasant tragedy in low German dialect; Emil Rosenow (1871–1904) for *Die im Schatten leben* ("Dwellers in the Shadows," 1912), dealing with the struggles of Rhenish miners; and Ludwig Thoma (1867–1921) for his Bavarian satirical comedies, notably *Die Lokalbahn* ("The Branch Line," 1902), about the political inadequacies of timid small-towners and timid liberals, and *Moral* ("Morality," 1908), which shows how a prostitute gets protection by having the top citizens in her little black book.

In Austria the regional realistic drama of Anzengruber was followed by psychological and mystical regional analyses by the Tyrolean physician Karl Schönherr (1867–1943), who achieved strong theatrical effects in *Erde* ("Earth," 1907), in which love of life and the soil keeps a farmer alive; *Glaube und Heimat* (*Faith and Home,* 1910), depicting the tragic conflict between attachment to home and religious belief during the Counter Reformation and resolved in favor of faith; and *Der Weibsteufel* ("The She-Devil," 1915), a tragedy with only three roles, including a portrayal of the predatory female.

Naturalistic writers in all genres tended to present total unedited sensual detail of physical objects and beings in the belief that the mysterious life force, the secret of life, would be revealed in these details. Some practitioners, especially the more sophisticated ones in large cities, noticed that certain details stood out because they had more color or more meaning. They also detected that color and meaning might be imparted by some extrinsic factor like illumination, perspective, or contrastive juxtaposition. This aesthetic realization, coupled with the prevailing skepticism of modern life, led to the notion that truth like beauty was in the eyes of the beholder, that there was only a thin line—if any—between illusion and reality, and that the subjective impression was the decisive factor. This notion, when applied in an artistic style, led to the editing out of irrelevant detail and to concentration on the glittering points that suggested a meaningful impression, the style commonly called impressionism. In content it featured mood and atmosphere, the ambiguity of dreams, a lot of melancholy with brief moments of sweetness and light, the latter called "living hours" by Arthur Schnitzler.

The development of impressionism in the German drama can be seen in the Gerhart Hauptmann of *Hanneles Himmelfahrt, Die versunkene Glocke,* and *Michael Kramer,* in the mood pictures of Hartleben's *Rosenmontag,* in the stylistic change of Arno Holz from the unselective detail of *Die Familie Selicke* to the suggestive laconic jargon of *Traumulus* ("Dream Boy," 1905) and the sensory purple patches of *Sonnenfinsternis* ("Eclipse of the Sun," 1908). The most natural locale for impressionism in the drama was Vienna at the turn of the century, the Vienna of Sigmund Freud. Gay and melancholy "old" Vienna, steeped in theater, music, and opera, uncomfortably aware that its splendor was dying, that it was a theatrum mundi of make-believe, brought forth a group of sensitive writers dedicated to rejuvenate Vienna and hopefully calling themselves Young Vienna. They tried nobly to bridge the gap between aristocratic popular tradition and modern skepticism. World War I ended their dream. The outstanding impressionists among them were Hermann Bahr, the leader of Young Vienna, and Arthur Schnitzler, their theatrical genius.

Hermann Bahr (1863–1934), renowned as a critic of naturalism, as an advocate of impressionism, and as one of the heralds of expressionism (in 1914), was also a good satirical comedy writer. Two of his plays are still on the boards: *Der Meister* ("The Master," 1903), in which a coldly reasoning doctor makes a mess of his life and ends wondering whether he is a master of life or merely its comical puppet, and *Das Konzert* (*The Concert,* 1910), a hilarious situation comedy exposing the follies of "emancipated" liberals and artists who try to appear young by continually having affairs.

Arthur Schnitzler, like Karl Schönherr and Anton Chekhov a practicing physician, was equally successful as a brilliant and strong stylist in short stories and drama. Well remembered among his plays are *Anatol* (1893), presenting seven affairs of an aristocratic escapist Vienna playboy; The Game of Love, dramatizing the tragic consequences of seeking romantic love in a world full of playboys and marriages of convenience; The Green Cockatoo, about Paris playboys in 1789 who play at revolution—and it comes; La Ronde, the now famous, elegant, and clinical presentation of the sex game with interchanging partners; *Der Schleier der Beatrice* ("The Veil of Beatrice," 1900), about Renaissance lust for life at the end of an era; *Der einsame Weg* (*The Lonely Way,* 1903), giving the lonely retrospections of men and women at the end of the road of life; *Der junge Medardus* ("Young Medardus," 1910), an adaptation of a strange tale of self-deception contained in E. T. A. Hoffmann's story *Die Elixire des Teufels* ("The Elixirs of the Devil"); and *Professor Bernhardi* (1912), depicting anti-Semitism in many guises among the doctors in Vienna. Schnitzler was at his best in short stories and in short plays, such as the little scenes of *Anatol, La Ronde,* and the collection of one-act plays called *Lebendige Stunden* (*Living Hours,* 1902). Schnitzler's most outright warning against "modern" gamesmanship was cast in the form of an ingenious farce, a virtuoso theatrum mundi: *Zum grossen Wurstl* ("The Great Punch and Judy Show," 1910), in which a hand-puppet play, a marionette play, and a legitimate stage play seen by an onstage audience are all exposed as fakes and the spectators are asked whether they themselves are any more genuine.

Other impressionists of sorts were Alexander Lernet-Holenia (1897–   ), with his long series of slick plays about the dying Austrian monarchy;

A SCENE FROM ARTHUR SCHNITZLER'S *Anatol* (THEATRE COLLECTION, NEW YORK PUBLIC LIBRARY AT LINCOLN CENTER)

Stefan Zweig (1881–1942), with his minor successes, notably *Tersites* ("Thersites," 1907), *Der verwandelte Komödiant* ("The Changed Comedian," 1913), *Jeremias* (*Jeremiah*, 1917), an anti-World War I play; and Jakob Wassermann (1873–1934), with *Lukardis* (1908). Impressionistic tendencies were also present in Thomas Mann's only play, *Fiorenza* (1907), about the undramatic struggle between Savonarola and the dying Lorenzo de Medici for the preservation of the beauties of Florence, and in the early short plays of Hugo von Hofmannsthal.

These two writers (Thomas Mann was not at all a dramatist) were moving in a new direction, however, which might be called "liberal traditionalism" and which has been labeled neo-Romanticism. In the broadest terms they and their collaborators opposed the melancholy determinism and superficial glitter of both naturalism and impressionism. In spite of their modern skepticism, they hewed to the old Romantic line that man can be free, that he is capable of changing his environment and transforming himself, and that beauty is not only attainable but is itself both truth and salvation. These views could lead to radical activism and did: from Sören Kierkegaard and Friedrich Nietzsche through expressionist, existentialist, and absurdist drama. More conservatively pursued, these views could lead to a classical-Romantic dynamic balance and moderate progression, that is, the line of German idealism seen by many in Goethe's *Faust*. The importance of Hugo von HOFMANNSTHAL as a dramatist of this tradition in the twentieth century has been recognized and is still being debated. His success, like Goethe's, was more literary than theatrical. The longevity of his dramas on the stage is due in part to the popularity of his librettos for the operas of Richard Strauss. These librettos, like his dramas, show in a variety of elegantly handled styles that only extremists like Electra and Oedipus cannot be saved. All reasonable seekers of life, no matter how complex or peculiar, can find or make the adjustments necessary to overcome their rigidities or tragedies and live a new life. Hofmannsthal implies in his drama what is explicit in his essays: Old Austria, too, and old Europe with its classical tradition need not die but can adjust to the new and live a new life.

This vitalism is present, though very subdued, in Hofmannsthal's early and rather florid lyrical plays, such as *Gestern* ("Yesterday," written 1891); *Der Tor und der Tod* (*Death and the Fool*, written 1893), in which an aesthete achieves vitality only when confronted by death; *Alkestis* (written 1893), an adaptation of the tragedy by Euripides in which the zestful and tipsy Heracles wrests Alcestis out of the hands of death; *Der Kaiser und die Hexe* (*The Emperor and the Witch*, written 1897), in which the rock-ribbed Emperor Porphyrogenitus breaks the spell of his sexual bewitchment; and *Das kleine Welttheater* (*The Little Theater of the World*, written 1897), showing the inadequate existence of a variety of characters engrossed in their youthful dreams and unable to enter the mainstream of life.

Vital *élan* is more firmly and less exotically portrayed in Hofmannsthal's two Casanova treatments, *Der Abenteurer und die Sängerin* ("The Playboy and the Singer," written 1899) and *Christinas Heimreise* (*Christina's Journey Home*, 1908), in both of which

the seducer is a catalyst who unwittingly helps the seduced woman to find aesthetic and domestic contentment. The same is true for the plays seeking to reinterpret Greek myths: *Elektra* (1903), a Freudian study of the destruction wrought by guilt, vengeance, and perversion of love; *Ödipus und die Sphinx* ("Oedipus and the Sphinx," 1905), a semi-Freudian view of Oedipus as a vital superman, the Sphinx as the punishment for fear of life, and Jocasta as the natural zestful mate for Oedipus; and *König Ödipus* ("Oedipus the King," written 1906, performed 1911), a slightly adapted translation of Sophocles, as terse and unromantic as the original, with Oedipus still a superman, even in blindness and contrition.

As World War I approached and the possibility of a cultural holocaust loomed ever larger, Hofmannsthal sought to reach the broadest popular levels with his liberal-traditional message. Among his many efforts were his opera librettos—he hoped that the addition of music to drama would provide a further emotional and intellectual factor—his further translations and adaptations of plays by great Europeans, and his revival of the medieval English morality play *Everyman*, published in 1911 as *Jedermann*. The latter, deftly rewritten to suggest medieval simplicity, modern cynicism, and the universal moral answer to materialism, became a stage fixture when Max Reinhardt produced it in 1920 for the opening of the Salzburg Festivals. The festivals themselves were in part the result of Hofmannsthal's agitations for the preservation of Western culture.

Four major achievements in the 1920's complete Hofmannsthal's dramatic opus. *Der Schwierige* (*The Difficult Man*, 1921), a Molièrish character comedy, defends more than exposes the aristocratic and fussy man of principle whose neatly contrived bachelor's life of inaction is subtly demolished by a beautiful and clever woman. It has been well received as one of the rare effective high comedies in the German language. Its companion piece in the Molière vein, *Der Unbestechliche* ("The Incorruptible Man," written 1925), is a charming comedy with a lighter touch, casting a family butler in the role of the true aristocrat who is also the true man of action and who rescues his entire household from its seemingly rigid entanglements. *Das Salzburger grosse Welttheater* (*The Salzburg Great Theater of the World*, 1922) is a greatly enlarged adaptation of Calderón de la Barca's *El gran teatro del mundo*, a medieval mystery play amplified by Baroque theatricalism and deftly orchestrated with modern problems of ethics, aesthetics, religion, materialism, capitalism, and Bolshevism. The beggar, a "have-not" and potential Bolshevik, has an epiphany at the climax of the play and saves the order of the world by *not* striking the first blow of revolution. The play employs semipopular blank verse colored with Austrian dialect and uses motifs of the commedia dell'arte, the Austrian Baroque, and the magical farce. Though not doctrinaire in its Catholicism or its political conservatism, the play's human and political message made it even more popular after World War II than after World War I. Calderón also supplied the vehicle for Hofmannsthal's last play, *Der Turm* (*The Tower*, pub. 1925, rev. 1927, prod. 1928, and successfully revived in 1947). *Der Turm* is an elaborate reinterpretation of *La vida es sueño* embodying Hofmannsthal's final and rather pessimistic views on the fate of Europe. Though strictly adhering to its seventeenth-century setting, it suggests that beauty, truth, kindness, and justice are "the stuff that dreams are made on," that fathers and sons will fall out, and that violence will reign. The implied forecast of World War II in the version of 1925, which ended in the hope that a new and uncorrupted "King of the Children" might prevail, is sharpened in the version of 1927, which ends with power in the hands of Oliver, the man of violence.

A spate of lesser neo-Romantic drama flooded the German-speaking stages with temporary successes extending into the era of National Socialism. The playwrights and a few titles are remembered chiefly as evidence of the popularity of the romantic fashion at this time. Richard Beer-Hofmann (1866–1945) combined melodic lyricism and deeply religious feeling in *Der Graf von Charolais* ("Count Charolais," 1904) and in his biblical fantasy cycle, *Die Historie vom König David* ("The Historical Play of King David," 1918 ff.). Herbert Eulenberg (1876–1949) resolved the dramatic problems of his self-centered heroes in dream fantasies, for example, in *Ritter Blaubart* ("Sir Bluebeard," 1905). Wilhelm von Scholz (1874–   ) tried to revive medieval mysticism, as in *Der Jude von Konstanz* ("The Jew of Constance," 1905). Emil Gött (1864–1908) followed Nietzsche and wrote Dionysian mysteries, notably *Edelwild* ("The Noble Beast," pub. 1911). Ernst Bacmeister (1874–   ) advocated Buddhistic contemplation in, for example, *Der indische Kaiser* ("The Emperor of India," 1944). Carl Hauptmann (1858–1921), brother of Gerhart, tried to outdo his brother in mysticism with, among others, *Die armseligen Besenbinder* ("The Indigent Broom-Makers," 1913). Anton Wildgans (Vienna, 1881–1932) sentimentalized reality in *Armut* ("Poverty," 1914) and *Dies irae* (1918). Ernst Hardt (1876–1946) gloried in purple patches, especially in *Tantris der Narr* (*Tantris the Jester,* 1907), about the return of Tristram in disguise. Eduard Stucken (1865–1936) produced wordy verse fairy tales in his endless cycle of dramas on the Holy Grail (1902–1916). Ludwig Fulda (1862–1939), best known as a translator of Molière, also wrote dramatized fairy tales, among them *Der Talisman* ("The Talisman," 1892), about the emperor's new clothes. Karl Gustav Vollmöller (1878–1948) wrote numerous lyrical plays in imitation of Hofmannsthal with his collaborator, Leo Greiner (1876–1926), but is remembered only for his pantomime, *Das Mirakel* (*The Miracle,* 1912).

The conservative tendencies that stimulated neo-Romanticism also tempted a few playwrights to revive the ethical and aesthetic standards of German classicism. On rather simplistic patriotic grounds this was first done by Ernst von Wildenbruch (1845–1909) with historical dramas in the vein of Schiller. His *Die Karolinger* ("The Carolingians," 1882), *Die Quitzows* ("The Quitzow Family," 1888), and *Die Rabensteinerin* ("The Lady of Rabenstein," 1904) exploited the Teutonic past with the chauvinistic pathos to be expected of an author who was a Prussian nobleman. His attempts to compete in classical form with the social drama of naturalism, *Die Haubenlerche* ("The Hooded Lark," 1890) and *Meis-*

ter Balzer ("Master Gamecock," 1892), were failures. A genuine and intellectually respectable effort to establish what he called neoclassicism was made by Paul Ernst (1866–1933), whose book of essays, *Der Weg zur Form* ("The Road to Form," 1906), and twenty-three highly idealistic dramas, such as *Demetrios* (1903), *Canossa* (1907), *Brunhild* (1909), *Preussengeist* ("Prussian Spirit," 1915), and *York* (1917), developed a considerable and tenacious following. A small coterie of critics and scholars still worships him today. Though he criticized Hebbel's dramas for excessive emphasis on ideas, Ernst's work was found to have the same weakness. His Rhenish contemporary Wilhelm Schmidtbonn (1876–1952) shared Ernst's views and was a better stage practitioner, but his classical-Romantic legend plays lacked idealistic and poetic substance. Among them were *Mutter Landstrasse* ("Mother Highway," 1901), a modernization of the prodigal son theme; *Der Graf von Gleichen* ("Count von Gleichen," 1908), a tragic treatment of the war returnee with both a new wife and an old wife; *Der Zorn des Achilles* ("The Anger of Achilles," 1909); *Der verlorene Sohn* (The Prodigal Son," 1912); and two German war plays, *Der Geschlagene* ("The Vanquished," 1920), in which a blind airman is rehabilitated by his wife's pure love, and *Die Fahrt nach Orplid* ("The Journey to Orplid," 1922), in which German *emigrés* seek a new land and penance through work.

The virtual simultaneity of the different directions taken by Hauptmann, Schnitzler, Hofmannsthal, and Ernst just before the turn of the century betokened both profusion and confusion. Yet the picture, to be complete, must include still another direction, that of Frank WEDEKIND. Variously referred to as an absolute naturalist, an animalist, a bohemian, and a forerunner of expressionism, Wedekind somehow jumped the gap between skeptical social determinism and ecstatic statement of belief. In this he paralleled the path taken by his favorite model, August Strindberg, and was in the dramatic lineage of Lenz, Grabbe, and Büchner. Born to the stage (his parents were stage folk, traveling in California at his birth, and such admirers of American liberty that they named their son Benjamin Franklin), an accomplished professional actor, a pioneer of the German cabaret, Wedekind created for himself the role of adventurer and clown, lived it in its comic and tragic fluctuations, and fashioned his plays around it. In this role he could flout the "unnatural" behavior of his era, lay its sensual and sexual flesh bare with his sarcastic whip (the whip borrowed from Nietzsche, the woman-hater, and written into the role of the animal tamer in *Erdgeist*), show off the superiority of "the genuine animal, the wild beautiful animal" over the domesticized weaklings of naturalism, and—ironically—also expose the tragic consequences of playing the adventurer and clown. He became a master of uncommunicative (not absurdist) dialogue and dramatic caricature.

Wedekind's grotesque stage and speech imagery is fully developed in his first play, SPRING'S AWAKENING, vehemently debated in public but not performed until 1906. Here the sordid tragedy of adolescents uninformed about sex is overshadowed by a surrealistic symbolical ending in which a "masked gentleman," transparently personifying lust for life, prevents a further suicide. *Erdgeist* (*Earth Spirit*, pub. 1893, performed 1898) is Wedekind's most famous play. In a series of balladesque scenes introduced by an animal trainer with a whip, Wedekind shows the beautiful animal, the metaphorical "snake" Lulu, whose bold and subtle animal cunning, oblivious of bourgeois morality and other environmental pressures, enables her to live a free life, satisfy her natural appetites and desires, and sleep the sleep of the innocent. The social "lions" and "bears" whom she ensnares cannot cope with her or with their environmental bonds and—quite to her displeasure—destroy each other and themselves. In a sequel, *Die Büchse der Pandora* (*Pandora's Box*, 1903), Wedekind then shows the stages of Lulu's decline and fall at the hands of a society that does not know what to do with her. She is gradually reduced to the life of a prostitute and is killed by a sex maniac. Her destruction is shared by her lesbian friend, Countess Geschwitz, whom Wedekind considered the most tragic of all his characters because she bore the curse of being unnatural. Wedekind later combined both plays into one, entitled *Lulu*, on which Alban Berg based his opera *Lulu* (1937).

Further successes of Wedekind were *Der Marquis von Keith* (1901), about the rise and fall of a brilliant impostor, cripple, and confidence man, who has Lulu's lust for life and enjoys hoodwinking the hypocrites of bourgeois morality; *König Nicolo oder So ist das Leben* (*King Nicolo or, Such Is Life*, 1902), a balladesque vindication of a deposed king who becomes first a tailor, then an actor of kings' roles, and ends with some satisfaction as the jester of the new king; *Hidalla* (1905), originally titled *Karl Hetmann, der Zwergriese* ("Karl Hetmann, the Dwarf Giant"), about the rise and fall of a social reformer, the leader of an international society for the breeding of lovers of life, who commits suicide when, as a final indignity, he is offered a job as a clown; *Der Kammersänger* (*The Tenor*, 1900), a one-act sketch, often performed in cabarets, showing the egotistical business-as-usual character of the supposedly heroic Wagnerian tenor; *Tod und Teufel* (*Death and Devil*, 1906), three scenes exposing the daughters of joy as the daughters of misery, ending in the suicide of the procurer; *Schloss Wetterstein* (*Castle Wetterstein*, 1910), an exposé of the tragic skeletons in a family closet with the lover of life, Effie, ending in suicide; and *Franziska, Ein modernes Mysterium* ("Franciska, a Modern Mystery," 1912), in which a lover of life, in this case a girl of the middle class, explores all sorts of unconventional adventures—including getting married as a man—and then settles down in a conventional marriage.

twentieth century. Expressionism in the German drama (see EXPRESSIONISM) was to a large extent the product of emotional reactions before and during World War I. If the holocaust was a punishment visited on man by God, it called for deep reflection, renewed declaration of faith, and more consistent action in line with faith. If it was a product of man alone, it called for a new type of man, a man of heroic love of man, of compassion, of noble action, of justice. In either case new programs, couched in a new and intensified language of love and faith, were required. Not skepticism, nor scientific analysis, nor laborious researches to modify heredity and environment would serve the need. This, it was felt, was a time for crusades and revolutions. Hence, expressionism stimulated a hymnic ritualistic drama of shouted slogans, stammered confessions, and generally ecstatic explosions of language. Its characters lost their individuality and tended to be types, masks, personifications, abstractions of ideas and forces; accordingly, they were named "the father," "the son," "first banker," "second banker," and so on. The conflicts tended to be melodramatic: the good versus the bad, or most usually the compassionate new man, the messianic (not specifically Nietzschean) superman versus the inhuman or subhuman opposition. Dramatic plots tended to disappear, the action became a series of episodes of the progress of the hero, a station drama.

Expressionistic playwrights took as their models the medieval morality plays, the ecstatic plays of the Baroque, some Romantic dramas, Grabbe, Büchner, Strindberg, and Wedekind. The earliest representative expressionist play to be recognized as such by spokesmen of the new direction (Franz Pfemfert, Herwarth Walden, Ludwig Rubiner, and Kasimir Edschmid in Berlin, Hermann Bahr and Karl Kraus in Vienna, René Schickele in Zurich) was *Der Bettler* (*The Beggar*, written 1911) by Reinhard Johannes Sorge (1892–1916), a hymnic ritual featuring the beggar-poet as a high priest impelled by compassion to relieve his sick parents through mercy killing. The close association of expressionism with the visual arts is indicated by the dramas of the Austrian expressionistic painter Oskar Kokoschka (1886–   ), who wrote *Mörder, Hoffnung der Frauen* (*Murderer, Hope of Women*, 1907), *Der brennende Dornbusch* (*The Burning Bush*, 1910), and *Orpheus und Eurydike* (1918), and those of the North German sculptor Ernst Barlach (1870–1938), who wrote *Der tote Tag* ("The Dead Day," 1910), *Der arme Vetter* ("The Poor Relation," 1918), *Die echten Sedemunds* ("The Genuine Sedemunds," 1920), *Die Sündflut* ("The Flood," 1924), *Der Findling* ("The Foundling," 1922), *Der blaue Boll* ("The Blue Boll," 1926), and *Die gute Zeit* ("Good Times," 1929). Barlach, a devout believer in renascence, has had a renascence himself in recent years. A genuine seeker for godliness in worldly affairs, he portrayed man in the form of the *bas relief* imbedded in a cosmic matrix of evil spells and rare divine blessings.

The most extreme form of expressionistic drama was displayed in the unsuccessful dramas of the lyricist August Stramm (1874–1915), such as *Erwachen* ("Awakening"), *Kräfte* ("Forces"), and *Geschehen* ("Happening"). All written in 1914 and 1915, his plays were pantomimes accompanied by isolated words. Among the most effective dramatists of expressionism were the following: Fritz von Unruh (1885–   ), the son of a Prussian general; a pacifist, he attacked the authoritarian state and its bureaucracy in *Offiziere* ("Officers," 1911), *Louis Ferdinand Prinz von Preussen* ("Louis Ferdinand Prince of Prussia," 1913), *Ein Geschlecht* ("A Family," 1917), *Platz* ("Square," 1920), and *Bonaparte* (1927); Walter Hasenclever (1890–1940), whose pacifism and support of the younger generation are apparent in *Der Sohn* (*The Son*, 1914), *Antigone* (1917, adapted from Sophocles), and *Die Menschen* (*Humanity*, 1919); Ernst TOLLER, a visionary and poetic communist, in *Die Wandlung* (*Transfiguration*, 1919), *Masse Mensch* (*Man and the Masses*, 1919), *Die Maschinenstürmer* (*The Machine-Wreckers*, 1922), *Der deutsche Hinkemann* (*Brokenbrow*, 1926), *Hoppla, wir leben!* ("Yippee, We're Alive!," pub. in English as *Hoppla!*, 1927), *Feuer aus den Kesseln* ("Bank the Fires," 1930), and *Pastor Hall* (1939), about the ordeal of Pastor Martin Niemöller in Nazi Germany; Carl STERNHEIM, a cold and deliberate exhibitionist and demolition expert who pilloried the materialistic and status-seeking citizenry in twenty thematically interrelated satirical comedies, among them A PAIR OF DRAWERS, an exposé of the business of lechery, *Der Snob* (*The Snob*, 1912), dealing with how to become a tycoon, *Bürger Schippel* (*Citizen Schippel*, 1912), about how a low-brow can become a middlebrow, *1913* (1915), in which the children of a tycoon become lowbrows, *Tabula rasa* (1916), in which a skillful socialist becomes a capitalist, and *Fossil* (1922), on how capitalists become fossils; and Georg KAISER, the most prolific, versatile, and effective of all the expressionists. An apostle of the flesh like Wedekind, Kaiser portrays the lust for life of the misbegotten and is the prophet par excellence of the "new man," the super-martyr and supersavior. His comic-tragic plays range from neo-Romanticism to neorealism. Among them might be mentioned *Rektor Kleist* (written 1905, performed 1918); *Die jüdische Witwe* (*The Jewish Widow*, written 1911), about Judith and Holofernes; *König Hahnreih* (*King Cuckold*, written 1913, performed 1919) about King Mark of Cornwall as a misbegotten lover of life; THE BURGHERS OF CALAIS, in which the supermartyr is the one of seven martyrs whose suicide saves not only the town but also the six potential martyrs; *Von Morgens bis Mitternachts* (*From Morn to Midnight*, pub. 1916), in which a little bank teller with lust for life is frustrated and crucified on the day he tries to break with his humdrum existence; the sequence of three plays—*Die Koralle* (*The Coral*, 1917), *Gas I* (1918), and *Gas II* (1920)—in which the idealistic search for universal and absolute happiness is blocked by the security neuroses of the machine age and the machines produce nothing but increasingly destructive explosions (see THE GAS TRILOGY); *Hölle, Weg, Erde* ("Hell, Road, Earth," 1919), about the utopian dream as a potential reality; *Der gerettete Alkibiades* (*Alcibiades Saved*, 1920), in which man's noble determination to acquire both a beautiful body and a brilliant mind is defended; *Nebeneinander* ("Side by Side," 1923), illustrating that helpful bystanders only get hurt; *Zweimal Oliver* ("Oliver Twice," 1926), showing the folly of trying to turn illusion into reality; two strong and idealistic plays condemning dictatorial power and militarism—*Der Soldat Tanaka* (*Soldier Tanaka*, 1940) and *Das Floss der Medusa* (*Medusa's Raft*, 1948); and finally a classical trilogy: *Amphitryon, Bellerophon, Pygmalion* (1945).

Further contributions to expressionist drama were made by Paul Kornfeld (1889–1942), notably in his *Die Verführung* ("The Seduction," 1918) and *Himmel und Hölle* ("Heaven and Hell," 1920), two dramas creating ranting and raving as a style; Franz Werfel (Prague, 1890–1945), a dramatist of somewhat turgid operatic and religious fervor who wrote, among others, *Die Troerinnen* (*The Trojan Women,*

1915), *Spiegelmensch* (*Mirror Man,* 1920), *Juarez und Maximilian* (1924), *Das Reich Gottes in Böhmen* ("The Kingdom of God in Bohemia," 1930), and *Jakobowsky und der Oberst* (*Jacobowsky and the Colonel,* 1943); Hanns Johst (1890–   ), a pied piper who changed his tune from trumpet calls for the messiahs of freedom and humanity—as in *Der Einsame* ("The Lonely Man," 1917) and *Der König* ("The King," 1920)—to trumpet calls for messiahs of National Socialism—as in *Thomas Paine* (1927) and *Schlageter* (1932), which earned him top rank in the Hitler regime; Hans Henny Jahnn (1894–1959), a virtuoso contriver of dramatic devices that produce theatrical shock in expressionistic and surrealistic terms, as in *Pastor Ephraim Magnus* (1919), *Medea* (1925), and *Armut, Reichtum, Mensch und Tier* ("Poverty, Wealth, Man and Animal," 1948); Alfred Mombert (1872–1942), a wholly mystical visionary advocating a superman from outer space in three plays: *Äon der Welt-Gesuchte* ("Äon the One Sought by the World"), *Äon zwischen den Frauen* ("Äon Betwixt the Women"), and *Äon vor Syrakus* ("Äon at the Gates of Syracuse"), all written between 1907 and 1911; the Austrian Arnolt Bronnen (1895–1960), a theatrical expressionist with traces of neorealism, as in *Vatermord* (*Patricide,* 1922), *Anarchie in Sillian* ("Anarchy in Sillian," 1924), and *Ostpolzug* ("East Polar Expedition," 1926), an ingenious monodrama contrasting in alternate scenes an ancient Alexander who fails with a modern Alexander who succeeds; and Franz Theodor Csokor (1885–   ), the "grand old man" of Vienna today, an ethical idealist and accomplished formalist moving from expressionism in *Die rote Strasse* ("The Red Road," originally called *Die Wollust der Kreatur,* "The Lust of the Creature," 1921), which portrays a He and a She unable to control the drives within them and the, symbolically speaking, drives of the world around them, to symbolical neorealism in *Gesellschaft der Menschenrechte* ("The Society for Human Rights," 1929), a historical portrayal of the tragedy of Georg Büchner, and *Dritter November 1918* ("The Third of November, 1918," 1937), showing the collapse of the Austro-Hungarian army under the pressures of provincialism, patriotism, and racism. Csokor's countryman, the great journalist and social critic Karl Kraus (1874–1936), also wrote several expressionistic plays. His one great play, *Die letzen Tage der Menschheit* ("Mankind's Last Days," pub. 1915–1919), the most forceful and inclusive of all antiwar plays, is also the most unstageable because of its enormous length and high production cost. Social criticism in expressionistic form also characterized the thirty plays (written between 1915 and 1955) of Hans José Rehflisch (1891–1960).

Isolated successes were scored with such expressionistic plays as *Seeschlacht* ("Sea Battle," 1917) and *Scapa Flow* (1919) by Reinhard Goering (1887–1936); *Hans im Schnakenloch* ("Hans in the Mosquito Patch," 1915) by the Alsatian René Schickele (1883–1941); *Der Kreidekreis* (*The Chalk Circle,* 1925) by Klabund (pen name of Alfred Henschke, 1890–1928); *Der Patriot* (1927) by Alfred Neumann (1895–1952); and *Revolte im Erziehungshaus* ("Revolt in the House for Education," 1928), in praise of a radical student revolt, by the Austrian Peter Martin Lampel (1894–   ). A revival of expressionism in both form and content took place in West Germany after World War II, most notably in the genre of the *Hörspiel*, or "radio play." *Draussen vor der Tür* (*The Man Outside*, 1947), an expressionistic radio play by Wolfgang Borchert that became a stage success, is a vitriolic and imaginative series of scenes depicting the rejections suffered by a soldier returning home. In broad terms the influences of expressionism continued to color German-language drama inside and outside Germany from World War I on and are still in evidence in current drama.

The emergence from expressionism of a theatrical dramatist of the dimensions of Bertolt Brecht has overshadowed the developments in drama of the last fifty years, that is, from the end of World War I to the present. Yet it would not be accurate to call this period "the age of Brecht," for there were considerable areas of development in the drama that he did not lead or control. The period is broadly and clearly characterized by a desire for hard-nosed, pragmatic realism, for a new look at the facts of life, for rejection of visionary dreams and slogans, for recognition of the dynamics of everyday living, and for the control of these dynamics and their consequences in the interest of attainable goals. The literary style of this realism was functional, streamlined, unsentimental, ironic, and at the same time often infused with a subtle religious element, a belief in the positive value and divine origin of reality. It was commonly labeled *Magischer Realismus* ("magical realism"), or *Die neue Sachlichkeit* ("the new matter-of-factness"). Since this neorealism stressed pragmatic solutions instead of irreconcilable conflicts, it is surprising that it produced drama at all.

The standard dramatic products of neorealism are represented by the entertaining comedies of Curt Goetz (1888–1960), for example, *Hokuspokus* (1927) and *Dr. med. Hiob Prätorius* (1929), both plays-within-plays; of Rolf Lauckner (1887–1954), with his *Der Hakim weiss es* ("The Hakim Knows," 1923), a satire of cowardice in a small town; and of Bruno Frank (1887–1954), with his *Sturm im Wasserglass* (*Tempest in a Teapot*, 1930); by the realistic and regionalistic miracle and morality plays of Max Mell (1882–   ), an Austrian follower of Hofmannsthal who wrote *Das Apostelspiel* (*Apostle Play*, 1923) and *Das Nachfolge Christi Spiel* (*Imitatio Christi*, 1927); of the Bavarian Richard Billinger (1893–1965), with his *Rauhnacht* (*Hallowe'en*, 1931), *Die Hexe von Passau* (*The Witch of Passau*, 1935), and *Der Gigant* ("The Giant," 1937); of Ernst Wiechert (1887–1947), an anti-Nazi who decided to stay in Hitler's Germany, spent time in a concentration camp, and was considered the outstanding writer of "the inner emigration" for his, among others, *Der verlorene Sohn* ("The Prodigal Son," 1934) and *Das Spiel vom deutschen Bettelmann* ("The Play of the German Beggar," 1935), treating Job as a German; by the problem plays of Friedrich Wolf (1888–1953), a communist propagandist who emigrated to Russia in 1933 and who wrote *Der arme Konrad* ("Poor Conrad," 1925), *Zyankali* ("Potassium Cyanide," 1929), *Matrosen von Cattaro* (*Sailors of Cattaro*, 1930), *Professor Mamlock* (1935), about persecution of Jews under Nazism, and *Das trojanische Pferd* ("The Trojan Horse," 1942); of Günther Weisenborn (1902–

), anti-militarist and survivor of the concentration camp who wrote *U-Boot S4* (1929), *Die Mutter* ("The Mother," 1932), adapted from Maxim Gorki's novel and written in collaboration with Bertolt Brecht, and *Die Illegalen* ("Those Outside the Law," 1946), a portrayal of the German anti-Nazi resistance; and of Leonhard Frank (1882–1961), an expressionistic pacifist novelist who dramatized his novel *Karl und Anna* under the same title (1929).

The stronger dramatists of neorealism were few. As previously noted, Georg Kaiser took this direction in his last several plays. The outstanding and successful master of dramatic realism, a social realist who depended on folklore for his sources, was and is Carl Zuckmayer (1896–   ). His vitalism and lust for life came less from his expressionistic beginnings than from his inherited Rhenish-Dionysian background. His characters stand on firm ground, are earthy and robust, and battle with visceral vigor and peasant cunning for justice, freedom, and worldly pleasure. They are aware of the hereditary and environmental influences that make up human nature but also have a conscious will to change. Hence there is a human lift in both his comedies and his tragedies: *Der fröhliche Weinberg* (*The Merry Vineyard*, 1925), in which the right decisions emerge from inborn feelings of right and wrong; *Schinderhannes* ("Jack the Ripper," 1927), a balladesque portrait of the real and legendary, gay and tragic Robin Hood of the Rheinland; *Katharina Knie* (1929), portraying the painful but deliberate decision of the circus artist to keep the show going while sacrificing love and security; *Der Hauptmann von Köpenick* (*The Captain of Köpenick*, 1930), a satiric comedy based on a real case history and on German folklore, in which an unemployed ex-convict hoodwinks the Prussian military by wearing a borrowed uniform; *Der Schelm von Bergen* ("The Rogue of Bergen," 1934), a serious comedy of a young executioner who, instead of taking lives, cures a queen of her childlessness and is elevated to the nobility; *Des Teufels General* (*The Devil's General*, 1946), written chiefly on Zuckmayer's farm in exile in Barnard, Vermont, about the gradual and horrible realization of a passionate flyer that he has blindly served the devil, Hitler; *Barbara Blomberg* (1949), about the sufferings and sacrifices of the illegitimate mother of a king; *Der Gesang im Feuerofen* ("The Song in the Fiery Oven," 1950), in which French anti-Nazi resistance fighters condemn one of their number as a traitor; *Ulla Winblad* (1953), a balladesque biography of the Dionysian composer Carl Michael Bellman and his unfaithful beloved; *Das kalte Licht* (*The Cold Light*, 1955), the moral confusions of the cold scientist who becomes a communist spy—the story of Klaus Fuchs; *Die Uhr schlägt eins* ("The Clock Strikes One," 1961), a depressing spectacle of the moral confusions of young and old in the "economic miracle" days of post-World War II West Germany; and *Leben des Horace A. W. Tabor* ("The Life of Horace A. W. Tabor," 1964), the portrait of a gay American tycoon.

A significant effort along more intellectual lines was made by the Austrian Ferdinand Bruckner (pen name of Theodor Tagger, 1891–1958). A theater professional, Bruckner founded the Renaissance Theater in Berlin in 1923, directed it until 1927, then fled from Nazism to the United States. His brand of realism is somber and foreboding, his conflicts arise like those of Strindberg and Wedekind from visceral depths, from power drives and their frustrations and perversions. His plots often stop cold while a crisp and dialectical dialogue argues the problem, and his conclusions are depressing admonitions. Like George Bernard Shaw and Bert Brecht he aims to shock, to displease, and to educate, but he is not obtrusively didactic or dogmatic. His *Krankheit der Jugend* ("Disease of Youth," 1926), is an intimate and morbid study of hope, anxiety, and perversion in the lodgings of university students. *Die Verbrecher* (*The Criminals,* 1928), is a Dostoyevskian analysis of the causes of criminality so depressing that Brecht's *Threepenny Opera,* produced in the same year, seems optimistic by comparison. This play uses a three-level stage for simultaneous effects. *Elisabeth von England* (1930) uses a stage-within-a-stage in analyzing the power drives of a schizoid queen and her messianic adversary. *Timon, Tragödie vom überflüssigen Menschen* ("Timon, the Tragedy of the Superfluous Man," 1932) is a surrealistic revision of Shakespeare's *Timon of Athens* portraying the tragic weakness of the cultured intellectual when faced with a power-seeker, in this case Alcibiades; in retrospect, the play reflects prophetically the weakness of the Weimar Republic and the man with the umbrella at Munich, as well as the coming victory of the strong man of Munich. *Die Rassen* (*The Races,* 1933) exposes not only Nazi anti-Semitism but also the lack of moral fiber in its opponents. *Simon Bolivar* (1945, premièred in New York) is an episodic panorama portraying Bolivar's idealistic struggle against the principle of dictatorship, his acceptance of it under tragic and painful realistic pressures, and his return to idealism and freedom—after victory.

In Austria a serious and substantial realist, Fritz Hochwälder (1911–   ), rooted in the popular theater tradition but seeking answers to modern questions, explored the ethical and religious problems of justice in a series of important plays. Their very modest stage successes were probably due to Viennese dissatisfaction with the author's liberalism and earnest morality. *Das heilige Experiment* ("The Holy Experiment," 1947) is a realistic historical depiction of Paraguay's Jesuit theocracy in the eighteenth century; the conflict of secular versus ecclesiastical authority is resolved in favor of the former on grounds of *Realpolitik,* but justice is clearly on the side of the idealistic padres and the realistic Indians. *Meier Helmbrecht* (1948) is a dramatization of the thirteenth-century Bavarian satire depicting a peasant Don Quixote who imitates the madcap escapades of knighthood no longer in flower. *Der öffentliche Ankläger* (*The Public Prosecutor,* 1949) analyzes justice and injustice under Robespierre. *Donadieu* (1953) treats guilt among the Huguenots in seventeenth-century France and finds a solution in a "dona Dieu," a "gift to God." *Die Herberge, Dramatische Legende* ("The Inn, A Dramatic Legend," 1957) presents the simple pragmatic morality of Ukrainian peasants: Business-as-usual leads to robbery, the investigation brings out a series of interrelated crimes that are happily and ethically resolved, then everybody returns to business-as-usual. *Donnerstag, Modernes Mysterienspiel* ("Thursday, a Modern Mystery

Play," 1959) is a piece of satirical-philosophical make-believe in the vein of Raimund and Nestroy using every variety of electronic gimmickry and science fiction in a battle for the soul of the great architect Pomfrit; the forces of evil try to make a robot out of him and he has already had himself declared dead in the desire to become a pure scientist, but three days of effort by the forces of good bring him to a comical epiphany during his last rites, and he drinks the wine of life and love and starts life anew on Thursday morning with a devout prayer. Hochwälder's most recent play, *Der Befehl* ("The Order" or "The Command," 1967) is most interesting, since it was broadcast internationally on television and deals with the Anne Frank case in a psychological-documentary manner.

The preeminence of the Bavarian genius Bertolt BRECHT among the neorealistic playwrights, if it can be explained at all, is probably due to three factors: He developed a grasp of theatrical and dramatic themes and forms that extended over the whole expanse of both Western and Eastern traditions; he had a profound gift of language, that is, the ability to find words and word images to serve for every variety of poetic and prose expression; and, finally, he had a dramatic sense of reality that enabled him to move with the force and speed of a triphammer from illusion to reality, from fantasy to substance, from past to present, from vision to concrete message. His justly famous *Verfremdungseffekt* ("alienation effect"), which he developed in collaboration with his erstwhile Berlin stage director, Erwin Piscator, is only the most tangible of the many devices he found for bringing his audience up sharply to face immediate reality. His actors were coached to be prepared and to prepare the audience for this jump. Yet he was not opposed to verisimilitude or to audience empathy with sympathetic or unsympathetic stage characters. He deliberately used illusion and disillusionment to sharpen the impact of reality and impress it indelibly through the incremental repetition that led to the Piscator-Brecht label of "epic drama." His messages were unmistakably colored by his communistic convictions, yet even his most doctrinaire propaganda pieces did not satisfy the party-liners but gave broader realistic images that illuminated significant areas of modern life. His drama, though avowedly non-Aristotelian and didactically asserting the solubility of all human problems, though persistently denouncing man as evil and stupid, nevertheless created a galaxy of interesting and sympathetic characters—little men and little women—whose destinies earn our human concern.

The Brechtian opus is very extensive. Among its major contributions are the following: *Baal* (1923) displays the orgiastic and orgasmic career of an angry and cynical young vitalist in choppy, expressionistic, uncommunicative dialogue; he is an animal god joyfully devouring a world he despises. Brecht's basically moral rage at the modern jungle is further vented expressionistically but with increasing social realism in *Trommeln in der Nacht* (*Drums in the Night,* 1922), the portrait of a soldier returned from war who is content to live as a pig, and *Im Dickicht der Städte* (*In the Jungle of the Cities,* 1923), depicting the senseless mutual destruction of two greedy businessmen. At this point Brecht becomes a Marxist and becomes more deliberately didactic. In *Mann ist Mann* (*A Man's a Man*, 1926), he transparently demonstrates that a man can be transformed at will, in this case into a bestial soldier; the alienation devices, such as the "Songs" and other comments addressed to the audience, begin here. THE THREEPENNY OPERA then establishes his fame; using the story line of John Gay's *The Beggar's Opera* (1728) and his now fully developed bag of alienation tricks—stage placards, coarse philosophical songs à la François Villon with ostensibly harsh music supplied by Kurt Weill, playing to the audience, deliberately shocking language and scenes, even a *deus ex machina* on horseback— Brecht transforms the whole into a cynical and hilarious indictment of the idealistic genteel tradition; sweet charity is itself exposed as a racket; everyone is gaily immoral and corrupt; hence it is fitting that the model of all corruption, the supercriminal Mac-Heath, is pardoned at the end. *Aufstieg und Fall der Stadt Mahagonny* (*Rise and Fall of the City of Mahagonny*, 1930), tries—less effectively—to demonstrate a similar message in the locale of an American boom town. When Nazism swept over Germany, Brecht went to Denmark and later to the United States.

Die heilige Johanna der Schlachthöfe (*St. Joan of the Stockyards*, 1934) is a demonstration of the inability of a well-meaning Salvation Army lass to cope with the bulls and tycoons of Chicago; it is also a parody of German classicism with take-offs on Goethe, Hölderlin, and Schiller's *Die Jungfrau von Orleans*. Of the many short didactic plays demonstrating communist philosophy, which he wrote in the years of exile, the most interesting perhaps is the radio play *Das Verhör des Lukullus* (*The Trial of Lucullus*, 1938), a poetically refreshing skit whose title hero poignantly concludes that he will be remembered only for his cherry trees. Brecht's anti-Nazi plays are not politically doctrinaire and show genuine compassion for Hitler's victims. *Der aufhaltsame Aufstieg des Arturo Ui* (*The Resistible Rise of Arturo Ui*, 1941) demonstrates the moral weakness of the bourgeois Germans and the ballyhoo tactics through which Hitler came to power. THE PRIVATE LIFE OF THE MASTER RACE displays the human tragedies and the political stupidities and bestialities that, as Brecht expected, would wreck the Nazi machine. *Schweyk im Zweiten Weltkrieg* (*Schweik in World War II*, written 1944/45, prod. 1959) showed Jaroslav Hasek's dog-loving little man triumphing over Hitler in the snows of Stalingrad.

Five further plays show Brecht at his best with strong central characters, broadly human conflicts, and a hard but compassionate realism. MOTHER COURAGE epically and dramatically portrays the dogged but futile struggle of a little woman to get her family through the Thirty Years' War; the story is taken from one of the seventeenth-century tales of Hans Jakob Christoffel von Grimmelshausen; the shrewd but—in Brecht's opinion—foolish woman can only make a living by selling wares to the soldiers from her cart. This exposes her and her children to the war's devastation; she loses her children and finally her horse, and is left at the end pulling her cart by hand. GALILEO treats the scientist's dilemma: Should he stand by his discoveries and be a victim of the Inquisition, or should he recant and stay alive? He re-

cants, is arrested nevertheless, secretly writes up his researches, condemns himself for being afraid of the torture chamber, but his students smuggle his papers out and his work survives. THE GOOD WOMAN OF SETZUAN uses a Chinese parable to treat the dilemma of generosity versus survival; the helpless gods seek a "good" woman and find her in a prostitute, Shen-te; but she cannot survive the greed and meanness of the world around unless she assumes the role of a hard and flinty man, Shui-ta; the dilemma is not resolved and Brecht has the woman ask the audience for a solution. In THE CAUCASIAN CHALK CIRCLE Brecht combines the contest of two women for a child with the contest between common folk and the social order, between justice and the law; justice and the common folk win out, and the efficient and responsible foster mother, the maid Gruscha, gets the child. Similarly, in *Herr Puntila und sein Knecht* (*Master Puntila and His Servant*, 1940), the handyman of the people is morally and pragmatically superior to his master; Brecht's comedy here is sharp and cutting but has the farcical touches of the commedia dell'arte. Brecht's final years were spent in making adaptations and directing productions for the Theater am Schiffbauerdamm in East Berlin. Pragmatic and independent to the end, he put his money in Swiss banks and gave his publishing rights to a West German firm, Suhrkamp. See also Ödön von HORVATH.

German drama under National Socialism was politically controlled to serve the state. It stressed the Teutonic superman, the political and military hero, and the athletic paganism of "blood and soil." Its most prominent dramatist was Hanns Johst (see above). Isolated, politically assured successes were scored by Erwin Guido Kolbenbeyer (1878–1962) with *Gregor und Heinrich* (1930), in which Henry IV wins a Germanic victory over Pope Gregory; by Friedrich Bethge (1891–   ) with *Marsch der Veteranen* ("The March of the Veterans," 1935), in which Russian veterans of 1815 find a *Führer* and the patriotic dead rise and march again; by Eberhard Wolfgang Möller (1906–   ) with *Panamaskandal* ("The Panama Scandal," 1936), in which corruption riddles a democracy; by Richard Euringer (1891–1953) with *Deutsche Passion* ("German Passion Play," 1936), in which the unknown soldier has a vision of a new Christ, a new salvation, and he fights against the forces of evil—corrupt intellectuals and capitalists—with the aid of the underprivileged to build a new and happy empire; and by Kurt Heynicke (1891–   ) with *Der Weg ins Reich* ("The Road to Empire," 1938), in which a militant loyalist defeats a traitor and unifies the people for reconstruction. The two last-mentioned plays were samples of a possible new genre advocated by the authorities, *Thingspiel* or "thing play" (from the name of the ancient German tribal court, Thing), presenting courtroom debates with choruses of the people, and delivering judgments of what was good or bad. The German drama written outside Germany proper easily outranked the native product in the years 1933 to 1945.

Since 1945 the leadership in German-language drama has been in the hands of two Swiss, Max FRISCH and Friedrich DÜRRENMATT. Their plays have had a world-wide reception although they were plainly addressed to the Germans, the Austrians, and the Swiss (see SWITZERLAND). Both schooled themselves on Brecht and share his didactic tendencies, though not his politics. Both are skeptical intellectuals, cultured Europeans, gifted with poetic vision and language, but deeply pessimistic—or at least agnostic—about man's chances of survival. What feelings of hope they have are expressed more in their admiration of Thornton Wilder than in their plays. Frisch is the more serious and distressed of the two, Dürrenmatt the more comic and the more skillful stage manipulator. Both are surrealists in the sense that they contrast everyday reality with a serious or comical metaphysical reality. Frisch's best are *Die chinesische Mauer* (*The Chinese Wall*, 1946), a pessimistic theatrum mundi; *Don Juan oder Die Liebe zur Geometrie* (*Don Juan or The Love for Geometry*, 1953), showing Don Juan as the victim of women; *Biedermann und die Brandstifter* (*The Firebugs*, 1958), with Mr. Everyman as the master of indecision who cannot believe the naked truth (arsonists move into his home, declare they will burn him out, and do so); *Andorra* (1961), in which Andri, the illegitimate son of a cowardly father, is adopted and made to think he is a Jew, is accepted as one, is persecuted as a Jew, accepts himself as one, and dies as a Jew; and *Biographie: Ein Spiel* ("Biography: A Play," 1968), a play-within-a-play, in which a professor and his wife get a chance to relive their lives, he makes very minor changes, and she walks out. Dürrenmatt's best are *Es steht geschrieben* (*Thus It Is Written*, 1947), an absurd comedy of absurd Baptist proceedings; *Ein Engel kommt nach Babylon* (*An Angel Comes to Babylon*, 1953), an absurd theatrum mundi full of whimsical byplay showing that beggars are the best people, though some are not of this world—the angel—and some are fakes—Nebuchadnezzar in disguise; *Der Besuch der alten Dame. Eine tragische Komödie* (*The Visit*, 1956), a surrealistic tragedy of the fallen girl who marries a millionaire, systematically ruins her home town to force it to kill her seducer, and then richly rewards the now completely immoral town; and *Die Physiker* (*The Physicists*, pub. 1962), an international tragedy transformed into a madhouse comedy; the physicists all act insane to get each other's secrets, are all committed to a madhouse, expose each other, but all their secrets are copied and are in the hands of the politically controlled woman who runs the madhouse. Dürrenmatt continues this theme in *Der Meteor* ("The Meteor," 1965), in which a Nobel prize-winner wishes to abdicate from a mad and materialistic world; however, this world will not let him rest in peace.

In addition to continued production by older playwrights mentioned above, the German-speaking stage since 1945 has witnessed a fair number of isolated successes by playwrights who do not appear to be of first rank. They are mentioned here to show trends and to give tentative judgments, which will surely be revised in the light of their further efforts. Since the era under consideration is dominated by political tensions, it is natural that these tensions affect the substance and form of drama and its reception. This time the war does not lead to a revival of realism in the West, but to savage absurdism, expressionistic nihilism, and "black" humor. Goethe's *Faust* is now reinterpreted as a document of deprivation. The insane asylum becomes a favorite locale and the world outside seems—as it was to Ezra Pound—even worse. In spite of this despondency, the didactic tendency continues to prevail, morality plays abound, suggesting that some viable ethic can still be found. Thus there are some gropings in drama for a way of life better than that of discredited previous regimes. Leopold Ahlsen (1927–   ) has a *Philemon und Baukis* (1956), showing a replica of the ancient couple operating in modern Greece among partisans and Nazis and choosing death as the way out, and *Sie werden sterben, Sire* ("You Will Die, Sire," 1963), an unwitting parallel to Eugène Ionesco's *The King Is Dead,* but treating Louis XI as a real man in history, dying in absolute isolation and frustration. Tankred Dorst (1925–   ) offers *Die Kurve* ("The Curve," 1960), an absurdist farce showing the neatly amoral racket operated by two brothers who profit from the car victims of a road curve; *Freiheit für Clemens* ("Freedom for Clemens," 1960), an absurdist farce similar to Samuel Beckett's *Endgame* and describing the steps necessary to live in "freedom" in an empty jail; and *Grosse Schmährede an der Stadtmauer* ("Grand Denunciation at the Town Wall," 1961), an absurdist drama showing surrealistically the frustrations of a woman trying to get her husband back from the army, which, like all the other authorities (here the situation is reminiscent of Franz Kafka), is behind a wall. The dichotomy of the nursery tale and modern reality is presented somewhat nostalgically in the plays of Richard Hey (1926–   ): *Thymian und Drachentod* ("Wild Thyme and Dragon Death," 1955), presenting idealism versus capitulation; *Der Fisch mit dem goldenen Dolch* ("The Fish with the Golden Dagger," 1958), presenting involvement versus escapism; and *Weh dem, der nicht lügt* ("Woe to Him Who Cannot Tell a Lie," 1962), admonishing man not to be a machine. Wolfgang Hildesheimer (1916–   ) provides such grotesque absurdist satires as *Die Eroberung der Prinzessin Turandot* ("The Conquest of Princess Turandot," 1955), in which only permanent switches of identity can make life livable; *Die Uhren* ("The Clocks," 1959), in which a man and wife are reduced to figures in a clock; and *Landschaft mit Figuren* ("Landscape with Figures," 1959), a love triangle and its artistic creators reduced to marionettes dancing the dance of death for a glazier who forever installs purple windows. Rolf HOCHHUTH has had theatrical successes with two surrealistic documentary plays, *Der Stellvertreter* (*The Deputy,* 1963), in which Pope Pius XII is held responsible for the political death of many Jews under Hitler, and *Soldaten: Nekrolog auf Genf* (*Soldiers: An Obituary of Geneva,* 1967), concerning the responsibility for the war in Vietnam. Peter WEISS had sensational successes with *Die Verfolgung und Ermordung des Jean Paul Marats dargestellt durch die Schauspielgruppe des Hospizes zu Charenton unter Anleitung des Herrn de Sade* (*The Persecution and Assassination of Jean Paul Marat Portrayed by the Acting Company of the Asylum at Charenton under the Direction of M. de Sade,* known in English simply as *Marat/Sade,* 1964), an orgiastic absurdist ritual play in a house of horrors, showing men and women, great and small, reduced by circumstance to the mechanical operations of itching, scratching, bath-

A SCENE FROM PETER WEISS'S *Marat/Sade*, AT THE
1966 RUHR FESTIVAL IN RECKLINGHAUSEN (GERMAN
INFORMATION CENTER)

ing, dancing, role playing, and murdering; and with
Die Ermittlung (*The Investigation*, 1965), a documentary showing the greatness and the guilt of Winston Churchill.

Other lesser successes in Germany were Günter
Grass's (1927–   ) *Die bösen Köche* (*The Wicked
Cooks*, 1961), a transparent caricature of present-day
political leaders as absurd cooks making a mess of
the world, and *Die Plebejer proben den Aufstand*
(*The Plebeians Rehearse the Uprising*, 1966), a sardonic portrayal of Brecht working with his East Berlin theater troupe; Manfred Hausmann's (1898–
) *Der Fischbecker Wandteppich* ("The Fisch-
beck Tapestry," 1955), based on the popular legend
of Helmburgis saved by divine intervention and here
modernized by showing the theater rehearsal of a
play based on a tapestry depicting the legend; Bernt
von Heiseler's (1907–   ) *Das Haller Spiel von der
Passion* ("The Passion Play of Schwäbisch Hall,"
1954), giving the biblical story of Christ in medieval
manner but with modern psychology and modern
emphasis on the paradox that all participants consider themselves innocent; Siegfried Lenz's (1926–
) *Zeit der Schuldlosen* ("The Time of the In-
nocent," 1961), an expressionistic modern morality
play demonstrating that innocence is indifference or
self-deception, that everyone must atone for collective as well as personal guilt; Otto zur Nedden's
(1902–   ) *Das Testament des Friedens* ("The
Testament of Peace," 1951), a realistic and semipoetic portrayal of Alfred Nobel's self-deception,
remorse, and testament for peace, and *T. E. Lawrence* (1954), a classical morality play with a prologue, an epilogue, and a flashback portrayal of Lawrence's journey through hell on earth, his resignation
and apotheosis, with a chorus representing world-
wide public opinion; Dieter Wellershoff's (1926–
) *Anni Nabels Boxschau* ("Annie Nabel's Box-
ing Show," 1962), the dance of death of a fading
champion as the main attraction of a side-show world
in which two ravens personify death; Karl Wittlinger's (1922–   ) *Kennen Sie die Milchstrasse?*
(*Do You Know the Milky Way?*, 1956), a surrealistic
comedy in which a daredevil driver of "flying
saucers," who lost his identity during the war, sur-

vives by hallucinating that he has come here from outer space—at the end the psychiatrist, with whom he
reviews his case in a hospital for the insane, joins him
in leaving this world for the Milky Way; Hans
Helmut Kirst's (1914–   ) *Aufstand der Soldaten*
(*The Soldiers' Revolt*, 1966), a documentary of the
officers' ill-fated revolt against Hitler; Martin
Walser's (1927–   ) *Der schwarze Schwan* ("The
Black Swan," 1966) and *Die Zimmerschlacht* ("The
Room-Battle," 1968), two absurdist efforts to seek
new lives by playing games; and Felix Lützkendorf's
(1906–   ) *Dallas, der 22. November* ("Dallas,
November 22nd," 1968), a documentary on the
assassination of President John F. Kennedy. The
Austrian and Swiss play productions since 1945 dis-
play qualities and patterns quite similar to those of
Germany.

Drama in East Germany has had very little reception in the world outside the Iron Curtain and has
been extensively ignored by the critics. Officially required to serve the state, it must be realistic and optimistic and in general meet the specifications of Socialist Realism (See RUSSIA: *twentieth century*). The
leaders in this vein have been two elderly men,
Friedrich Wolf (see above) and Johannes R. Becher
(1891–1958), primarily a poet, both of the German
expressionist generation. Recent relaxations of official restrictions have resulted in cautious experiments with freer forms and ideas. Considerable successes were scored most recently in West Germany
and Great Britain by Heinar KIPPHARDT, now living
in the West and considered Western, with two semi-
documentary plays, *Joel Brand, Die Geschichte eines
Geschäfts* ("Joel Brand, the History of a Business
Deal," 1963) and *In der Sache J. Robert Oppenheimer* (*In the Matter of J. Robert Oppenheimer*,
1964). Among the other East German playwrights
who are beginning to attract wider attention are
Peter Hacks (1928–   ), originally from West
Germany, who went to the East to study with Brecht
and is one of the few East Germans continuing in the
direction taken by Brecht; Harold Hauser (1912–
     ), Jochen Koeppel (1930–   ), the team of
Heiner Müller (1929–   ) and Inge Müller (1925–
     ), Erwin Strittmatter (1912–   ), and Hedda
Zinner (1907–   ).

There is as yet no complete history of the German
drama in English. The reader of German, of course,
has a wide choice ranging from the relatively brief
Geschichte des deutschen Dramas (1963) by Otto
Mann, to the compendious *Das europäische Drama*
(3 vols., 1956–1958) by Paul Fechter. The general
reader can get historical and other background information from *An Outline History of German
Literature* (1966) by Werner P. Freiderich (who also
lists English translations) and from Jethroe Bithell's
Germany. A Companion to German Studies (1932).
Available histories include A. A. Waterhouse, *A
Short History of German Literature* (1947); Ernst
Rose, *A History of German Literature* (1960); and
John George Robertson, *A History of German Liter-
ature* (4th rev. ed., 1962). For some periods of the
drama we find individual treatments, such as Robert
R. Heitner, *German Tragedy in the Age of the En-
lightenment* (1963), and Hugh F. Garten, *Modern
German Drama* (1959). Most of the individual au-
thors have been treated in periodical articles and

books too numerous to mention here. Introductory and critical material can also be found in school textbook editions of individual works and in such broad analyses as John Gassner's *Masters of the Drama* (1940) and Allardyce Nicoll's *World Drama from Aeschylus to Anouilh* (1950).—H. L.

Ghana. See AFRICA: *Ghana.*

Ghelderode, Michel de (1898–1962). Belgian playwright. This Belgian writer became the principal playwright for the Théâtre Populaire Flamand, where his play *Barabbas* was produced in 1928. He became known in France in 1947 when director André Reybaz produced two of his plays: *Hop! Signor* (first produced in Belgium in 1935) and *Fastes d'enfer* (*Chronicles of Hell*). In most of his plays Ghelderode incorporates elements of magic: ghosts, masked figures, tombs, and diabolical fits. Lucifer's influence pervades these texts, and Ghelderode often engages in macabre or priapic wit. Barroom jokes about sex and beer in profane language vie with mystical passages. In the minute directions he gives for the stage presentations of his plays, he insists on their plastic quality. Instead of analyzing his characters, Ghelderode would rather dramatize their behavior and antics.

Many of Ghelderode's more than thirty plays have never been performed. They were written during the period between the two wars, but a few were first performed after 1945. Ghelderode uses many traditions of the Flemish theater: the improvised stage of the fair, vaudeville, and the marionette show. Pervading his work is an atmosphere of medieval Christianity: a sense of the supernatural and a deep-seated fear of the

MICHEL DE GHELDERODE (BELGIAN INFORMATION SERVICE)

physical aspect of death. Ghelderode's universe is as menacing, mocking, and tragic as the universe of those painters who inspired him: Pieter Brueghel especially, but also Hieronymus Bosch, Diego Velásquez, and James Ensor.

Truculence, coarseness, and verbosity characterize the art of Ghelderode. His plays inspired by medieval tradition (*Escurial,* 1948, and *Fastes d'enfer*) and his biblical dramas, such as *Barabbas,* have been produced more often than the others. The story of Christ's passion in *Barabbas* is told by the rabble and the criminals. Barabbas himself, the robber who is released in Christ's place, longs to avenge the death of Christ, but he is killed by the priests just as he begins to consider himself a follower of Christ. In speaking of this play, Ghelderode called it the dramatization of man's desire for purity. The motif in the text is the terrifying obsession over Christ's death, as in *Entretiens d'Ostende* (*The Ostend Interviews,* 1956).

For critical studies of Ghelderode's work, consult the following: Lionel Abel, "Our Man in the Sixteenth Century: Michel de Ghelderode," *Tulane Drama Review,* VIII (1963); Samuel Draper, "An Interview with Michel de Ghelderode," *Tulane Drama Review,* VIII (1963), "Discovery of Ghelderode," *Commonweal,* LXXIII (1960), and "Michel de Ghelderode: A Personal Statement," *Tulane Drama Review,* VIII (1963); George Hauger, "The Plays of Ghelderode," *Tulane Drama Review,* IV (1959); and Micheline Herz, "Tragedy, Poetry and the Burlesque in Ghelderode's Theatre," *Yale French Studies,* No. 29 (1962).—W. F.

Ghosh, Girish Chandra. See PAKISTAN: *Bengali drama.*

Ghosts (Gengangere, 1882). A play by Henrik IBSEN. *Ghosts* was written in five months in Rome and Sorrento. First played in Chicago, in Norwegian, its progress across the major new stages of Germany, France, and England largely charts the advent of modernism in the theater.

Mrs. Alving, though an intellectually emancipated woman, has dedicated herself to the suppression of a truth, namely the profligacy of her late husband, Captain Alving; but the past cannot so easily be erased. Her son, Oswald, recently returned from Paris, bears the heritage of syphilis from his father and gives the appearance of being a replica, a ghost, of his father in sexual waywardness. Oswald's proposed union with Regina, the maid, would be incestuous, since it is revealed that her father is not Engstrand, the carpenter, as it first appears, but Captain Alving. A newly built orphanage, which Mrs. Alving has financed as a memorial to her husband, burns to the ground as a result of Engstrand's machinations, and this conflagration coincides symbolically with Oswald's "burning" within. When paresis attacks Oswald at the end of the play, the audience is left to wonder whether Mrs. Alving will administer morphine to her son as she has promised to do.

Ghosts created a furor wherever it was first played because it dealt openly with taboos. But it is less about hereditary venereal disease, incest, and euthanasia than it is about the dead conventions, the "ghosts," that weigh down a society seeking vitality. Action in the old sense is minimal; development of plot is in the form of a series of revelations contrived somewhat after the fashion of the Scribean "well-made play." Mrs. Alving, as the chief bearer of the gathering truth that she has not had the courage of her liberal convictions, emerges as the protagonist of *Ghosts,* one of the most important plays of Ibsen's realistic period.

The text may be found in *Ibsen,* Vol. V (1961), edited by J. W. McFarlane. *Ghosts* (1965), edited by Henry Popkin, contains critical essays by George Bernard Shaw, Francis Fergusson, Eric Bentley, and others.—R. B. V.

Ghost Sonata, The (Spöksonaten, 1908). Also translated (unhappily) as **The Spook Sonata.** Expressionist fantasy by August STRINDBERG. A mysterious manipulator, Jacob Hummel, confined to a wheelchair, engages the services of a young man, simply called the Student, to direct his attentions toward Hummel's bastard daughter, the Hyacinth Girl, with intent to marry. He then introduces the Student to the strange society where the Hyacinth Girl lives: her mother, the Mummy; a grotesque who cackles in her closet; the Mummy's present husband, the Colonel; and a number of others. Hummel systematically penetrates the affluence of the household and the multiple deceptions practiced by the Colonel. Nothing is what it seems to be. Eventually the unveiler is unveiled; the death screen is produced and Hummel himself, a vampire character with a criminal past, dies behind it at the end of the second scene.

The third and last scene, in the inner sanctum of the house, is largely devoted to the fate of the Girl and the Student. She succumbs, a victim of the cruel, bloodsucking society about her; he survives to proclaim that the world is a charnel house and that the only hope is an afterlife, rendered graphic by the final tableau, Arnold Böcklin's romantic canvas "The Isle of the Dead."

The Ghost Sonata is a gallery of grotesques, with an unmistakable Gothic heritage from E. T. A. Hoffmann. It is also a sonata after a fashion. Opus No. 3 of the so-called chamber plays, its chief musical model is presumably the second movement of Beethoven's *Geistertrio,* Opus 70, No. 1, in D Major. Like all of Strindberg's chamber plays, *The Ghost Sonata*'s chief theme is the disparity between appearance and reality, the one bright and clear, the other corrupt and sordid. The French man of the theater Antonin Artaud elaborated on its surrealistic elements and saw in it an important precursor to his own "theater of cruelty." *The Ghost Sonata* also anticipates the "theater of the absurd."

The text may be found in *The Plays of Strindberg,* Vol. 1 (1964), translated by Michael Meyer. See also *Tulane Drama Review,* Vol. VIII (Winter 1963), pp. 50–57.—R. B. V.

Giacosa, Giuseppe (1847–1906). Italian playwright. Giacosa was born near Turin of a bourgeois family. He studied law but in 1872 abandoned it for the theater, where he already had excellent successes with one-act "proverbs," that is, plays intended to illustrate the proverbs of their titles, in the manner of De Musset. In 1888 he became director of the Accademia dei Filodrammatici of Milan, and in 1891 he went to the United States with Sarah Bernhardt for the American première of his *Signora di Challant* (*The Lady of Challant*).

GIUSEPPE GIACOSA (ITALIAN CULTURAL INSTITUTE)

Giacosa's first successes were cast in a popular form of the time: stylized dramas in verse set in the middle ages. These dramas include *Una Partita a scacchi* ("A Game of Chess," 1873) and *Il Trionfo d'amore* ("The Triumph of Love," 1875). He also wrote some comedies set in an equally stylized eighteenth-century environment, one of which is *Il Marito amante della moglie* ("The Husband Who Is His Wife's Lover," 1876). After 1880, under the influence of the realistic French theater, Giacosa sharply altered his course, writing a series of plays in prose in a bourgeois setting. These include *Tristi amori* (*Unhappy Love,* 1887), *I Diritti dell'anima* (*The Rights of the Soul,* 1894), and *Come le foglie* (*Like Falling Leaves,* 1900). Using the characters and situations common to all European realistic theater, Giacosa was able to illuminate them with his excellent writing—at once justly proportioned and spare—and an authentic bitterness of tone. —L. L.

Gide, André. See OEDIPE.

gigaku. From Korea in the seventh century A.D. there arrived in Japan the *gigaku* dance, which possessed strong dramatic features. It is said to have been imported by a monk who assumed the Japanese name Mimashi. A record exists of his performance in 612. The dance called for an ensemble of three instruments: a flute, hand drum, and cymbals. A considerable number of remarkable gigaku masks are still in existence; the finest are preserved at Nara, but admirable specimens are in the United States, notably in the Boston Museum of Fine Arts. These masks are very large but most delicately and skillfully molded. Many are of animals. The dance rituals or dance dramas in which they were used were presumably mythological stories with impersonation and miming. There is no evidence that gigaku had literary significance.—H. W. W.

Gilbert, Sir **William S**[chwenck] (1836–1911). British playwright and librettist, inevitably linked with Sir **Arthur [Seymour] Sullivan** (1842–1900), for whose music Gilbert wrote the libretti. It is often forgotten that Gilbert was a dramatist in his own right and wrote many plays before his collaboration with Sullivan began. Gilbert's path to the theater was as circuitous as some of the logic in his operatic lyrics. After preliminary study at Boulogne, he attended Great Ealing School and later went to Kings College, Cambridge, and the University of London, graduating in 1857. Gilbert then spent four miserable years as an assistant clerk in the Education Department of the Privy Council Office, playing practical jokes on his fellow employees to relieve the monotony of his work. He resigned at once when he inherited four hundred pounds from an aunt. He next studied for the bar at Clement's Inn and practiced four years. Most of his time, however, was spent writing for the various journals of the day, particularly for *Fun*. It was for this periodical that Gilbert wrote the famous *Bab Ballads,* as well as dramatic criticism, art criticism, and stories; and it was through his journalism that he met the other famous writers, critics, and dramatists of the time, including the playwright Thomas W. Robertson.

Robertson, who by this time was a success, encouraged Gilbert in his writing for the stage. Gilbert had written a number of plays when he was at Great Ealing and had followed the theater while working at the Privy Council Office. Robertson, however, provided the necessary extra incentive, allowing Gilbert to watch rehearsals of his plays and giving him practical advice. After *Dulcamara* (1866), Gilbert's first produced play, came a series of various types of dramas: more burlesques like *Dulcamara;* dramatic sketches; comedies; verse fantasies and romances, notably *The Palace of Truth* (1870), *The Princess* (1870), and *Pygmalion and Galatea* (1871); and "serious" plays such as *Sweethearts* (1874), *Dan'l Druce* (1876), *Blacksmith* (1876), and *Engaged* (1877).

Gilbert met Sullivan in 1870, and their collaboration on the Savoy Operas began in 1871, with *Thespis*. The team's first success was *Trial by Jury* (1875). In 1876 Richard D'Oyly Carte formed a company to produce their works. *The Sorcerer* (1877) was followed by *H. M. S. Pinafore* (1878), their first big success. Next came the première of *The Pirates of Penzance* (1879) and *Patience* (1881). In that year the Savoy Theatre was built for the D'Oyly Carte company—hence the name "Savoyards," which came to refer to the company as well as to the Gilbert and Sullivan following. In quick succession came *Iolanthe* (1882), *Princess Ida* (1884), *The Mikado* (1885), *Ruddigore* (1887), *The Yeomen of the Guard* (1888), and *The Gondoliers* (1889). During the latter's run a quarrel between Gilbert and Sullivan

brought twenty years of collaboration to a temporary halt. Though later reconciled, their work never reached its earlier standard, as *Utopia Limited* (1893) showed. Their last collaborative effort was *The Grand Duke* (1896).

A master of intricate verse patterns, a connoisseur of words, and a pungent commentator on the contemporary scene, Gilbert provided Sullivan with libretti that wittily satirized London society, British customs, and popular attitudes. Though his plots were sometimes borrowed from the French and Italians, the product was purely English, a fact that may explain the Continent's indifference to the works. Rousing choruses and clever "patter" songs were outstanding features. Though some people label the works operettas, they have little in common with Parisian and Viennese models, and the creators usually preferred to call them "comic operas."

Sullivan, whose real interest was, ironically, serious music, which he composed with varying degrees of success, achieved fame for his comic opera scores rather than for his more earnest efforts. He was able to complement Gilbert's texts, supporting and intensifying characterization and comedy. Avoiding the boulevard gaiety of Offenbach and the lilt of Strauss, he created a style distinct and memorable. Parodic traces of Bizet, Verdi, Wagner, Gounod, and Rossini are all detectable in Sullivan's scores.

It is also ironic, in the light of Gilbert's almost compulsive desire to be a "legitimate" playwright, that, like Sullivan, his reputation today rests principally on the comic operas. However, his "serious" plays deserve close attention, for they contain the same Gilbertian wit, satire, and techniques found in the Savoy pieces. In these plays, of which *Engaged* is typical, we find Gilbert exposing the Victorian world of philistinism and hypocrisy with his verbal wit, topsy-turvy humor, and satiric genius. The unperceptive observer might be misled by the surface humor of the plays, and particularly Gilbert's evident delight at playing with language, but the underlying purpose—exposure of folly and corruption—always comes through. Perhaps the key to Gilbert's method is the inexorable logic with which he proceeds to carry out each idea to its obvious conclusion, so that all the Victorian (and human) vices and faults—greed, cheating, lying, smugness, complacency, prudery—become accepted ways of behavior in the world created by the playwright. This method was not to be seen again until the appearance of Oscar Wilde's comedies, which reflect Gilbert's stylistic brilliance and some of his techniques. Later on, of course, George Bernard Shaw's plays were to carry on even more vigorously Gilbert's battle against the evils fostered by Victorian philistinism.

A satisfactory biographical study of Gilbert and Sullivan is Isaac Goldberg's *The Story of Gilbert and Sullivan* (1928). For a good survey, *Martyn Green's Treasury of Gilbert and Sullivan* (1961), edited by Martyn Green, provides insights into the textual difficulties and problems of performance in their works. The thoughtful, scholarly *Gilbert: His Life and Strife* (1957) offers Hesketh Pearson's urbane interpretation of the partnership. See also Pearson's *Gilbert and Sullivan, A Biography* (1935). Audrey Williamson studies the continuing values and the pe-

A SCENE FROM GILBERT AND SULLIVAN'S *H.M.S. Pinafore* (ANTA COLLECTION, WALTER HAMPDEN MEMORIAL LIBRARY AT THE PLAYERS, NEW YORK)

riod aspects of the works in *Gilbert and Sullivan Opera, a New Assessment* (1953). Books about Gilbert include Sidney Dark and Rowland Grey's *W. S. Gilbert: His Life and Letters* (1923) and Edith A. Browne's *W. S. Gilbert* (1907).

Gioconda, La (1898). A tragedy by Gabriele D'ANNUNZIO. The plot of *La Gioconda* revolves around the love of Lucio Settala, a sculptor, for his model, Gioconda Dianti, who has gradually become the inspiring muse for his art. Torn between the old affection and duties that tie him to his wife, Silvia, and the passion that drives him to Gioconda, Lucio attempts to kill himself in a moment of desperation. Through Silvia's devoted care he regains his calmness and comes to feel that he now can do without Gioconda. But his creative spark seems to be extinguished, and when Gioconda writes telling him to await her in his studio, the emotion he feels is such that he realizes that only she can make him find again a full life of artistic creation. Silvia, aware of the danger that Gioconda's love incurs, faces Gioconda in Lucio's studio and, in a last attempt to wrest her husband away from her rival, tells Gioconda that Lucio is no longer interested in her. Infuriated, Gioconda tries to turn over a statue of Lucio's that she had inspired. Silvia tries to save it, crushing both her hands in the process. Not even this sacrifice,

however, can hold Lucio back, and he now affirms his right to fulfillment as beyond any existing moral conventions, beyond the values of good and bad: he has the right to follow Gioconda because in her he finds the ideal of beauty that animates his art. The play, written with refined D'Annunzian verbosity and not without dramatic effectiveness, is basically only a specious theorization of the right to individual pleasure, in the name of a proclaimed priority of art over life, and in the name of a contemptuous, aristocratic conception of the egotistical freedom of the superman-artist.—L. L.

Giraudoux, [Hippolyte] Jean (1882–1944). French novelist, essayist, diplomat, and playwright. Giraudoux was born in the small town of Bellac to a lower-middle-class family. After receiving his degree from the Lycée Lakanal in Paris, he traveled extensively in Europe. In 1910 he returned to France to work in the Ministry of Foreign Affairs, and when war broke out, he served with distinction. Having been successful with his short stories and novels, he agreed to director Louis Jouvet's request that Giraudoux transform his novel *Siegfried et le Limousin* (1922) into a play. The result, *Siegfried* (1928), was a resounding success, and it initiated Giraudoux's career as a playwright. His works for the theater include *Judith* (1932), *Intermezzo* (1933),

TIGER AT THE GATES, *Electre* (1937), *Ondine* (1939), and THE MADWOMAN OF CHAILLOT.

Each age produces the tragedies it deserves, and Giraudoux's are adapted to the style and the limitations of the twentieth century. Like Jean Racine, whom Giraudoux greatly admired, he chose for his heroes and heroines celebrated figures of mythology and the Bible, figures like Judith, Electra, and Helen, who slumber in books when they are not fulfilling their destinies in works the poets have devised to keep them alive. Giraudoux called one of his plays *Amphitryon 38* (1929) to indicate the large number of versions of the same story that antedated his own.

Giraudoux calls the art of the theater prophecy or divination. It reveals to men the most surprising and the most simple truths that are never fully realized, such as the inevitability of life and death, the meaning of happiness and catastrophe, the fact that life is both reality and fantasy. He always emphasized the importance of the text in theatrical production, and this was faithfully followed by Louis Jouvet. Both men defended the literary theater at the expense of the more spectacular kind of production in which the text was sacrificed to the *mise en scène*.

For critical studies of the work of Giraudoux, see the following: Eugene H. Falk, "Theme and Motif in *La Guerre de Troie n'aura pas lieu*," *Tulane Drama Review*, III (May 1959); Wallace Fowlie, "Giraudoux' Approach to Tragedy," *Tulane Drama Review*, III (May 1959); Donald Inskip, *Jean Giraudoux, The Making of a Dramatist* (1958); Laurent Lesage, *Jean Giraudoux His Life and Works* (1959); and Georges May, "Jean Giraudoux: Diplomacy and Dramaturgy," *Yale French Studies*, No. 5 (Spring 1950).—W. F.

Gitagovinda ("The Song of the Divine Herdsman," twelfth century A.D.). A long, semidramatic poem by Jayadeva. The poem belongs to dramatic literature as much by virtue of the extensive dramatic activity that it has inspired as in its own right. This powerful, eclectic work possesses features of narrative, dialogue, and lyrical verse; as for its content, it is a major classic in Indian erotic literature and a leading document in the cult of Krishna, one of the greatest of the Hindu deities. Some scholars discover the very origins of Indian drama in the rituals associated with Krishna worship, despite the fact that in the classics of the Sanskrit theater the god Siva is generally regarded as the chief inspirer and patron of both dance and drama. In any case, countless plays have from early times been associated with the Vishnu-Krishna worship.

The main theme of the *Gitagovinda* is the love story of the youthful Krishna and his bride, Radha. These two figures, together with Krishna's foster mother, Yashodhara, have long been among the most familiar and beloved on the Indian popular stage. Moreover, Indians have experienced small difficulty in transposing semidramatic poems, such as that by Jayadeva as well as works by other poets of the Krishna cult, such as Candidasa and Vidyapati, into actual performances. When transferred to the stage, the *Gitagovinda* and the group of poems resembling it are treated with much license and the derivative versions are seldom printed or regarded as of literary value. This is not because they lack such value but because the original poems possess it more fully. Re-

lations of Indian drama and literature to the popular stage do not resemble those in any other country. All qualifications notwithstanding, works such as the *Gitagovinda* are widely recognized as possessing an important place in the history of the drama.

The *Gitagovinda* has been freely translated by Sir William Jones (1894). A verse arrangement in English can be found in *Poems* (1880) by Sir Edwin Arnold. For a discussion of the work, see *The Sanskrit Drama* (1924) by A. B. Keith.—H. W. W.

Gladiator, The (1831). A tragedy by Robert Montgomery BIRD. Written for Edwin Forrest, who first played it at the Park Theatre in New York, *The Gladiator* was one of the most popular tragedies of the nineteenth-century American stage. Its theme of revolt against oppression was first equated by audiences with the American Revolution; in 1846 Walt Whitman said it was "as full of 'Abolitionism' as an egg is of meat."

Under the leadership of two Thracians, Spartacus and his brother Pharsarius, the gladiatorial slaves rebel against their Roman masters and win a great victory. After rescuing his wife and child, Spartacus wants to seek reinforcements in Sicily. Pharsarius, however, intoxicated with dreams of glory, leads most of the rebel army in a futile attack on Rome. Unable to embark for Sicily, hemmed in by superior forces, his wife and child murdered, Spartacus rushes upon the foe and dies after superhuman feats of strength and courage.

Spartacus is a kind of noble savage whose integrity and humanity are contrasted with the lack of principle and the cruelty of the decadent Romans. The revolt of the gladiators and Spartacus' heroic death are powerful scenes.—B. H.

Glass Menagerie, The (1944). A play by Tennessee WILLIAMS. First produced in Chicago on December 26, 1944, the play opened in New York on March 31, 1945, and ran for more than a year; it received the Drama Critics Circle Award. Based on a Williams short story, "Portrait of a Girl in Glass," and first dramatized in an unproduced screenplay, *The Gentleman Caller,* it is, in the playwright's words, a "memory play," a label intended not to emphasize the obvious autobiographical elements in it but to indicate the structure and the mood of the piece. No more than an anecdote, the play tells the story of the night Tom Wingfield, at his mother's insistence, brought a young man home to dinner, only to have her discover that he was engaged and thus ineligible as a possible suitor for Tom's sister Laura. The substance of the play is in the vitality (often comic) of Amanda, the mother, and the almost pathological shyness of the slightly crippled Laura, who uses her glass menagerie as an escape from the world. The defeat implicit in the play's action is tempered by the fact that the events are remembered by the play's narrator, Tom, and are thus softened by his memory —and by Williams' use of music, lighting, and suggestive sets. The printed play calls for a screen device that projects slides showing pictures or phrases that are comments on the action, but Eddie Dowling, who produced, co-directed, and played Tom in the first production, discarded the device, a practice that is usually followed when the play is staged.—G. W.

God of Vengeance (Got fun Nekome, 1907). A tragedy by Sholem ASCH. "Uncle" Yankel Chapchovich, proprietor of a brothel below the apartment in which he lives, hopes partially to redeem his sinfulness but above all to sanctify his home for his daughter, Rivkele, by installing in her room an expensive parchment Torah scroll. Deluded that she is ignorant of the business downstairs, he seeks a respectable and learned bridegroom for her and has visions of their establishing a virtuous Jewish household. Rivkele, however, is passionately fond of Manke, one of Uncle's prostitutes. Fearful that marriage will break up their secret relationship, both run off to another brothel. Yankel is crushed by the discovery, but Sore, his wife, rallies her strength and succeeds in getting her daughter back the next day. She even manages to have a marriage broker bring the father of a prospective bridegroom to discuss an alliance. Uncle, however, having learned that his daughter is no longer chaste, denounces her bitterly before the astonished strangers, shouting "Down to the whore house! Downstairs!"

God of Vengeance is an indictment of the moral schizophrenia of a society that deludes itself that it can maintain true morality in its personal relationships while thriving on human exploitation and on the laws of the marketplace. The symbol as well as the victim of that delusion is Yankel Chapchovich. From the opening moment, his tragic downfall is inevitable as life proceeds to exact the price of violating one's fellow man.

Despite the harshness of the life he depicts here, Asch is no naturalist. He is a firm believer in a universe where justice is fulfilled as well as in man's yearning for goodness, however roughhewn he may be. Yankel, despite his occupation, has in his self-deception remained essentially untouched by his evil. It is his very refusal to compromise with virtue and accept mere respectability that both reveals his crude nobility and leads to his downfall. There is a touching and tragic simplicity in his passionate indignation with God, whose refusal of Yankel's efforts at atonement make Him guilty, in Yankel's eyes, of being a God of vengeance who lacks humane compassion.

God of Vengeance is included in *The Dybbuk and Other Great Yiddish Plays* (1966), translated and edited by Joseph C. Landis.—J. C. L.

Goethe, Johann Wolfgang von (1749–1832). Poet, court administrator, one of Germany's greatest writers, and with Schiller, leader of German classicism. Born into the family of a well-to-do Frankfurt merchant, Goethe enjoyed a comfortable upbringing. His earliest exposure to the drama was through a Count Thoranc, quartered in the Goethe home during the French occupation of the city. Thoranc, the French commandant, saw to it that the boy received a more than adequate introduction to the French theater in town. As a spectator at local Punch and Judy shows, the young Goethe also witnessed presentation of some of the material that later provided the background for his *Faust*. Beginning his studies in Leipzig, the "little Paris" of Germany, Goethe wrote plays in the rococo idiom, such as *Die Laune des Verliebten* (*The Lover's Wayward Humor*, 1767), before proceeding to Strassburg, where he completed his formal education with a law degree in 1771. After a five-month clerkship in Wetzlar in 1772, the personal side of which he transformed into

JOHANN WOLFGANG VON GOETHE (WALTER HAMPDEN MEMORIAL LIBRARY AT THE PLAYERS, NEW YORK)

his extremely popular novel *Die Leiden des jungen Werther* (*The Sorrows of Young Werther*, 1774), he returned to Frankfurt to establish a legal practice. His activities were scarcely confined to the profession, however, and his house became a meeting place for young artistic rebels of the STURM UND DRANG ("storm and stress") movement. His *Rede zum Shakespeares-Tag* ("Memorial on Shakespeare's Birthday," written 1771), a manifesto of the Sturm und Drang, was, in fact, breathlessly delivered to these friends at his home. In the fall of 1775 his career reached a turning point when he accepted an invitation from Karl August, the young duke of Saxe-Weimar, to become a court minister in Weimar, the seat of the little duchy. Goethe remained there basically for the remainder of his life. His activities encompassed, not only amateur and, later, court theater directing and acting, but administration of finances, mining, and the military establishment of the duchy. Goethe also carried on extensive scientific research, particularly in botany and anatomy. His friendship with Friedrich Schiller is the high point of German classicism, but Goethe remained to his death the Renaissance man of the period, an Olympian figure in German culture.

Any discussion of Goethe's activity as a dramatist must be viewed against the background of his individual development from the Sturm und Drang idea of the poet as a reincarnation of God, through the court-oriented classical writer, to the almost mystical, aged poet who found the infinite in every heartbeat of the finite. Through all of these phases one factor predominates: the internalization of the dramatic to a focal point on the individual in his organic evolution to the highest plane, within the framework of a universal whole.

Despite the basic honesty of Götz, hero of GÖTZ VON BERLICHINGEN, one of Goethe's earliest heroic creations, the old knight nonetheless bows to the forces of decay about him. The drama, already written by the time Goethe reached Strassburg, is representative of the Sturm und Drang phase of the poet's life (see GERMANY: *eighteenth century*). Some of the heroes of Goethe's early poetry, such as Mohammed and Prometheus, come closer to exemplifying the creator reborn in the poetic spirit, but Götz is nonetheless a titanic, though doomed, figure. In a historical play written later in the Weimar period, EGMONT, this greatness is shown to have more of a demonic, potentially destructive character than that shown in *Götz*. In *Iphigenia auf Tauris* (1788) the traditional "family curse" has given way to an ethic that recognizes the limitations of human life and at the same time gives these limitations a greater value through assumption of responsibility: Thus Orestes comes to recognize his own humanity and the value of trust between human beings, a prime condition for the peaceful continuation of the social and natural order. If the ethos of German classicism was the individual-humane, it was achieved not through moral greatness, as with Schiller, but through unceasing personal development.

For Goethe, the traditional concept of tragedy did not exist. His *Rede zum Shakespeares-Tag* lavishes praise on the creator obeying an inner law, and *Götz* must be construed as a tragedy in the sense that the hero is forced by his "demon" to go to his doom. Late in his life, Goethe commented once more on Shakespeare, in an essay called *Shakespeare und kein Ende* ("Shakespeare Without End," 1813–1816). To the mature Goethe, where tragedy had once lain in the chasm between obligation and fulfillment, he now saw it lying between obligation and the wish to fulfill. Thus, in FAUST, a play labeled a tragedy, Faust appears to have lost his wager with the devil. But Mephistopheles, entirely a part of the human being rather than an independent force, has in fact lost his wager with the Lord; for Faust, never realizing that life itself was the infinite—albeit cyclical—strove without end in an attempt to find it. That Faust admits defeat by accepting a moment that he would have last forever is not the crux of the matter: For by his striving through a vast range of human experience, he has in fact been "saved," and thus ascends to the heaven where "everything capable of perishing is but a parable," a parable of life itself. See also TORQUATO TASSO.

Goethe is not so much recognized for dramatic innovation as for complete mastery of preexisting forms. In *Faust,* for instance, almost every type of diction makes an appearance: prose, *Knittelvers* (four-foot verse lines), classical hexameter, blank verse, free forms; rhythmic and metric changes are never without meaning in the dramatic context, and thus the language itself takes on a symbolic significance.

Many works have, of course, been written on Goethe in English. For those readers with less background, Henry Hatfield's *Goethe* presents an adequate, if slightly one-sided, view of the poet. Those with some knowledge of German letters and the period covered by the poet's life span will find much of interest in the English translation of Erich Friedenthal's *Goethe. His Life and Times.*—B. M. M.

Gogol, Nikolai [**Vasilevich**] (1809–1852). Russian novelist, short-story writer, and playwright. Gogol, famous for his novel *Dead Souls* and such short stories as "The Overcoat," "The Diary of a Madman," and "The Nose," also wrote some comedies, including THE INSPECTOR GENERAL, a masterpiece that made him the rightful successor to the theatrical tradition of realistic comedies of Denis Fonvizin and Alexander Griboyedov.

Gogol's role in the Russian theater was also important because of his determined denunciation of the cheap melodrama that had invaded the Russian stage and his explicit rejection of sensationalism. ("Only mediocrities," he wrote, "desperately grab at the unusual . . . murder, fire, wild passion . . . .") In his comedies, therefore, Gogol used as inspiration unsensational, everyday occurrences, revealing by highly stylized characterization the ridiculous elements in ordinary life—vulgarity, stupidity, corruption, hypocrisy, and so forth. It was probably because of his dislike for contrived, inane vaudeville and the satirical element in his own writing that Vissarion Belinsky, the leading Russian literary authority, classified Gogol as a "critical realist," a term still accepted by all Soviet and most Russian émigré critics.

Gogol's second important comedy, *Zhenitba* (*The Marriage,* 1842; better translated as "Matchmaking"), written in 1833, is a brilliant farce about a bride-to-be, a matchmaker, and a group of grotesque matrimonial candidates who voice their arguments

NIKOLAI GOGOL (JOEY CARMICHAEL, *An Illustrated History of Russia,* REYNAL & CO., 1960)

for and against marriage in the most idiosyncratic and unexpected terms. Gogol, who never married, hints at his own feelings at the end of the play by making his shy protagonist, Podkolesin (meaning "under the wheel"), jump out of the window when he is finally chosen over all the other candidates.

Gogol's other dramatic sketches—*Utro delovogo cheloveka* (*An Official's Morning*, 1842), *Tiazhba* (*A Lawsuit*, 1842), and *Lakeiskaia* (*The Servants' Hall*, 1842)—are amusing grotesqueries that inspired Anton Chekhov's early one-act plays, and they are closer to the modern "theater of the absurd" than to any variety of realism. His *Igroki* (*The Gamblers*, 1842) is an extravagant farce about a gang of card-sharps.

Finally, in his dramatic sketch *Teatralnyi razezd posle predstavleniya novoi komedii* ("Leaving the Theater After the Performance of a New Comedy," 1842) Gogol offers the playwright's explanation and justification of the "critical" (that is, satirical) elements in his play by having his character, the author of a play, answer various remarks that he overhears people make as they leave the theater after a performance of his play. Gogol's view may be summed up as follows: the regime itself is great, but some of its human tools are wicked freaks and it is at them that the public is invited to laugh. This is the traditional Russian attitude, which still prevails to this day: don't touch those who are in power, attack only their expendable subordinates.

An informative study of Gogol is Janko Lavrin's *Nikolai Gogol, 1802–1852: A Centenary Survey* (1951), and a highly unorthodox but brilliant appraisal is given in Vladimir Nabokov's *Nikolai Gogol* (1944).—A. MACA.

Golden Boy (1937). A tragedy by Clifford ODETS. On the day before his twenty-first birthday, Joe Bonaparte gives up his youthful dream of becoming a violinist and starts out on a vastly different way of life—a career in prizefighting. Economic and social pressures have forced him to this choice. For one thing, boxing pays much better than music; for another, by doing well in the ring he can somehow make up for the taunts he received in childhood because of his curious name and squinting eyes. The change in his plans, which is accompanied by a change in manner, is disappointing to his father, an Italian immigrant with a great love of music, and to his brother, a labor organizer. Nor is it altogether easy for Joe. Not until he breaks the bones of his hand in a fight, thus putting an end to the possibility of his going back to the violin, does he begin to use his full strength in the ring. Meanwhile he has found solace in the love of Lorna Moon, the mistress of his manager, and has been introduced to high life by Eddie Fuseli, a gangster. As his successes in the ring continue, his arrogance builds to such a peak that sportswriters detest him and even the experienced Lorna is shocked by the change. The savagery of his profession has poisoned his character, and he rebuffs every warm gesture made toward him. When disaster comes, it is enough to destroy him. In an important fight he delivers so powerful a blow that, although it is not a foul hit, it kills his opponent. Shattered by what he has done, Joe drives off into the night with Lorna. They crash into a tree, and both are killed.

Despite the all-too-evident "well-madeness" of its structure, *Golden Boy* is an impressive American social tragedy. Like most of the memorable plays of the 1930's, it has for its theme the familiar biblical quotation, "What shall it profit a man if he gain the whole world and lose his own soul?" The audience is to understand that had Joe renounced his material wealth, gained at the cost of the spiritual values symbolized by music, he might have had a happy life. Yet it is in Odets' employment of music—specifically, the art of the violinist—as a symbol that the play reveals its greatest weakness, for very slight indeed is the probability that a man who can master the violin will be capable of mastery in the boxing ring.—M. G.

Goldfaden, Abraham (1840–1908). Russian-born Yiddish playwright. Goldfaden (originally Goldenfodim) was born in Starokonstantinov, Volyn, in the Ukraine, on July 12, 1840. He received a secular as well as a traditional religious education in Hebrew and studied Russian and German. While a student at the government rabbinical seminary in Zhitomir, he had his first taste of the stage—he directed his fellow students in an amateur theatrical. During the decade following his graduation in 1866, he tried his hand, unsuccessfully, at teaching and business. He also made a brief attempt to study medicine in Munich. Finally, he determined to devote himself entirely to literature, having acquired a small reputation with his two books of songs and sketches. Hoping to establish a Yiddish theater (then nonexistent), he wrote lyrics and music for two popular entertainers of the day, rehearsed them in a "plot," with dialogue to be improvised in the manner of the *commedia dell'arte*, and in early October 1876 presented the two-act "nonsensical mish-mash" (as he later described it) in Shimon Mark's refreshment garden in Jassy, Rumania. This event is usually regarded as the birth of the modern professional Yiddish theater. The performance was a great success and Goldfaden continued to write and to enlarge his company. Soon there were other popular dramatists (Joseph Lateiner, "Professor" Isaac Hurvitch) writing for the new companies that sprang up. During the years that followed, Goldfaden wrote some of his most popular musical plays for the company with which he toured the Jewish Pale of Settlement in Russia: *Shmendrik* (1877), *Brayndele Cossak* (1878), *Di Kishef-Makharin* ("The Sorceress," 1879), and *Di Beyde Kuni Lemel* ("The Two Kuni Lemels," 1880). With the closing of the Yiddish theaters in Russia in 1883, Goldfaden went to Warsaw, where he was very successful with his historical plays *Shulamith* (1881) and *Bar Kokhba* (1883). In 1887 he emigrated to New York, but he was coldly received by the American producers, who feared his competition, and intrigue finally forced him out of the theater. He left New York in 1889 and during the years that followed, Goldfaden lived in London, Paris, and Lemberg. In great need, he returned to New York (1903), where his brothers lived, "to die among his kin." In 1906 he wrote his last play, *Ben Ami*, inspired by George Eliot's *Daniel Deronda*. Produced shortly before his death, the play was a failure, and Goldfaden died on January 9, 1908, disheartened as well as impoverished.

The inscription on Goldfaden's tombstone reads, "Poet, Playwright, and Founder of the Yiddish Theater." He was indeed all of these and more. Of the approximately sixty musical plays that he wrote, for many of which he provided both lyrics and music, a surprising number have remained in the repertoire of the Yiddish theater, expressing, as they do, the suffering, the hopes, and the nationalist moods of the Jewish masses of his day. If he was often crude and naïve, it was in part because he was the first professional dramatist of the modern Yiddish theater, with no dramatic tradition on which to draw. In addition, his audience was also unfamiliar with the theater and demanded entertainment rather than art. And, finally, he had no actors for whom to write. It is to Goldfaden's credit that he set his sights above entertainment alone and that he succeeded not only in creating a substantial number of charming plays but also in training and teaching both audience and performers. In doing so, he helped make possible a modern Yiddish drama as well as a professional theater to stage it.—J. C. L.

Goldoni, Carlo (1707–1792). Italian playwright. In 1747 Goldoni abandoned the law, for which he had trained, and settled in his native Venice as "company poet," that is, the writer-in-residence for the Teatro Sant'Angelo, directed by Girolamo Medebach. In 1748 he achieved his first real success with *La Vedova scaltra* ("The Crafty Widow"), in which he gives a precise indication of the dramatic reform he intended to effect. On the one hand, he rejected the literary mannerism of the theater in verse and, on the other, the vulgarity and tastelessness into which the *commedia dell'arte* had fallen. (See ITALY: *commedia dell'arte and Goldonian reform*.) Instead, he developed a realistic theater in prose, which mirrored the life, the manners, and the problems of Ital-

CARLO GOLDONI (ITALIAN CULTURAL INSTITUTE)

ian society, particularly Venetian society. This reform continued to develop both during Goldoni's six years at Sant'Angelo and afterward when he moved to the Teatro San Luca to work for the Vendramin brothers, Francesco and Antonio.

In 1750 Goldoni upheld his promise to give the public sixteen new comedies in one season. Among them were *Il Padre di famiglia* ("Father of the Family," which was subsequently imitated by Diderot in *Le Père de famille*), *La Famiglia dell'antiquario* ("The Antiquarian's Family"), and *Il Teatro comico* ("The Comic Theater"). Among the most significant of the plays that followed are *Il Feudatario* ("The Vassal," 1752); LA LOCANDIERA; *Il Campiello* ("The Little Piazza," 1756); *I Rusteghi (The Boors,* 1760); *La Trilogia della villeggiatura* ("Trilogy on Holidays in the Country," 1761); and LE BARUFFE CHIOZZOTTE.

Although Goldoni's reform was greatly popular among the general public, it provoked the hostility of the supporters of the traditional theater, who were led first by Abate Chiari, and then by Carlo GOZZI. After fifteen years of uninterrupted and fervid activity, Goldoni grew tired of the fight. He accepted an invitation in 1762 to go to Paris to write for the Comédie Italienne, where he remained until his death. There he wrote in Italian *Il Ventaglio (The Fan,* 1764), and in French *Le Bourru bienfaisant* ("The Kindly Grouch," 1771). He also produced three lively volumes of reminiscences, *Mémoires* (1787).

Of Goldoni's 212 dramatic productions, a certain nucleus is of fundamental importance to the history of the European theater. Some in Italian, some in Venetian dialect, the plays of this nucleus reflect, with poetic, refined realism and great technical mastery, the daily life and problems of Venetian society, which, in advance of the rest of Europe, had by the eighteenth century attained a bourgeois consciousness, mentality, and morality. More than a mere reformer of a very meager Italian theater, Goldoni is —earlier than Denis Diderot in France, and more than Ephraim Lessing in Germany or George Lillo in England—the founder and theorist of the modern bourgeois theater. Indeed, in many of his works he employed the masks of the commedia dell'arte, but he did so only to meet the public's demands and always in a realistic way. The traditional Harlequins and Pantalones, immersed in the realistic world of Goldoni, quickly lose every vestige of distortion and caricature; they are freed from their old ways and assume the solid outlines of real personalities typical of the people, particularly the Venetian bourgeoisie. —L. L.

Goldsmith, Oliver (1730?–1774). Irish-born English essayist, poet, novelist, and comic playwright. Goldsmith, Anglo-Irish on both sides of his family, grew up in Lissoy, Westmeath, where his father, a clergyman of the Established Church, served the Anglican parish. He received the A.B. degree from Trinity College, Dublin, in 1750, and thereafter studied medicine at the University of Edinburgh and at one or more Continental universities. After making his way across Europe—he was by this time penniless—Goldsmith arrived in London early in 1756, and in a year's time had become a Grub Street, or hack, writer. By 1760, when his enjoyable series

OLIVER GOLDSMITH (WALTER HAMPDEN MEMORIAL
LIBRARY AT THE PLAYERS, NEW YORK)

of essays known as the "Chinese Letters"—reprinted later as *The Citizen of the World*—was appearing in one of the newspapers of the time, Goldsmith was firmly established as a professional writer. The publication of his poem *The Traveller* at the close of 1764 made him one of the best known of living men of letters. Two years later came the novel *The Vicar of Wakefield* and then the production of his first comedy, *The Good Natur'd Man* (1768). Goldsmith's reputation as a poet was placed beyond all doubt by *The Deserted Village* (1770). By summer of the following year Goldsmith had begun work on a second comedy, as yet nameless. The trials and tribulations he endured before persuading playwright George Colman the elder to accept this new play for production were manifold; but SHE STOOPS TO CONQUER—so entitled at the last minute—finally opened, and to Colman's surprise and Goldsmith's gratification was accorded an enthusiastic reception. Goldsmith's sudden death brought to a regrettably premature close the career of one who, on the basis of only two plays, has taken his place among England's notable comic dramatists.

Although Goldsmith did not turn to the drama until he had already proved himself as essayist, poet, and novelist, he had from the first exhibited the liveliest interest in the theater and had frequently expressed his views about the contemporary status of the drama in England. There are, for instance, several amusing pieces in his "Chinese Letters" describing what awaited anyone paying a visit to one of the

London playhouses. He considered the English theater a national institution of great importance, but he deplored the poor taste shown by the public and the undue importance given to the actor-managers of the period. Goldsmith had always been a foe of sentimentalism in literature, and in his well-known *Essay on the Theatre,* appearing in one of the magazines shortly before the production of *She Stoops to Conquer,* had made a comparison between sentimental comedy, which he derided, and what he called "laughing comedy," which, instead of causing us to shed tears of commiseration, makes us laugh at our own absurdities and follies. *The Good Natur'd Man* is, as a matter of fact, an ironic maneuver against the sentimental comedy in that parts of it, especially the ending, have by design been given some of the characteristics of sentimentalism. Thus the hero is made to experience a gratifying reformation, but from foolish benevolism to common sense. *The Good Natur'd Man* is often amusing and much of it is clever, but it suffers from an overly complicated plot line. Goldsmith triumphs rather in *She Stoops to Conquer,* which breathes a kind of good nature reminiscent of George Farquhar's plays. It unfolds so easily and so charmingly that one can easily be beguiled into overlooking the fact that it is, after all, making a comic statement. The action abounds in errors, deceits, and discoveries, but all lead to the hero's discovery of the real Anne Hardcastle and of his own true self. Comic distance is preserved at all times.

The definitive edition of the plays is found in Vol. V of the *Collected Works* (1966), edited by Arthur Friedman. The most recent full-length biographical treatment is by Ralph M. Wardle in *Oliver Goldsmith* (1957), to be recommended for its accuracy and its avoidance of the legendary material that has attached itself to Goldsmith's name. A recent critical work is *Oliver Goldsmith: A Georgian Study* (1967), by Ricardo Quintana.—R. Q.

Golem, The (pub. 1921). A dramatic poem in eight scenes by H. LEIVICK. *The Golem,* written in Yiddish (1917–1920), was first performed in Hebrew translation by the Habimah in Moscow in December 1925. It was performed in Polish translation in January and again in June 1928. It was given its first Yiddish performance by the Vilna Troupe in Lodz, Poland, in August 1930. The acting script, prepared by Leivick himself, is an abbreviated version of the printed text.

When the Jews of sixteenth-century Prague are threatened by a plot to accuse them of using Christian blood for baking Passover matzos, Rabbi Arye Levi, known as the Maharal, creates a clay man, a golem with magical powers, in order to frustrate the plot. Golem resists the life that is about to be thrust upon him, and his spirit predicts dire consequences. Despite the warning and his own doubts, the Maharal bestows life on Golem, determined to make of him not only a defender of the Jews of Prague but a redeemer of the world, a messiah of the fist in a time of fists. When the messiah of peace, Messiah ben David, comes to Prague accompanied by the prophet Elijah, the Maharal drives them off; their time has not yet come. He sends Golem via underground paths to fetch the two bottles of blood hidden beneath the synagogue by Thaddeus the priest to be used as evidence against the Jews. In a surrealistic, symbolic scene, Golem meets two fellow redeemers, the Messiah ben David and Jesus, all three outcasts from the world that crucifies its redeemers. Golem saves the Jews of Prague. In the course of his existence as a living thing, however, his humanity has grown. No longer merely a thing of clay, he has learned to fear, to love, to hate, to yearn for his own redemption—and to destroy. In the last scene, Golem holds the Maharal prisoner after attacking a crowd of Jews with his ax. The Maharal realizes the error of his bold dream and takes the only course open to him: he destroys Golem.

The play is based on a legend that the Maharal, rabbi of Prague during the late sixteenth century, created a golem to save the Jewish community from a blood accusation, but Leivick transforms this legend into a philosophical drama of man's suffering and of his yearning for redemption. The melodrama of intrigue and rescue has been muted. Even the conflict between the two antagonists, the Maharal and Thaddeus, is suppressed as plot gives way to lyrical and philosophical verse expressing the fears, hatreds, anguish, yearning, and loneliness of men, of victims and victimizers. The Maharal's boldness in planning, not only to save the Jews but to liberate the world by force, and his humbled discovery that force does not liberate man from the human condition; the hatred of Thaddeus, the true antagonist in his repudiation of Christian love and charity; the fear set loose by the underground evils that tyrannize over man; the sorrow of the redeemer, who is always crucified by the world he comes to save; the pathos of the golem's slow humanization and discovery of the inevitability of human suffering; the mad anguish of the eternal victim—all these are powerfully expressed in verse that is typical of Leivick in its utter simplicity of language unadorned by metaphor, verse whose dignity at times, in its very simplicity, approaches grandeur.

The Golem is included in *The Dybbuk and Other Great Yiddish Plays* (1966), translated and edited by Joseph C. Landis.—J. C. L.

Gómez de Avellaneda, Gertrudis (1814–1873). Cuban poetess and playwright. Born in Cuba, she emigrated to Spain in 1836, but her poetry bears the seal of her birthplace, and she had taken part in Cuban theatrical productions. Her tempestuous and tragic personal life did not influence her dramas, which are remarkable for the solidity of technique and moderation of dialogue.

Her first major play is *Munio Alfonso* (1844), a historical tragedy set in twelfth-century Spain. Although the exaggerated code of honor is typically Romantic, the interest lies in the inner conflict of the characters. Outstanding among her many other works are *Saúl* ("Saul," 1846), *La hija de las flores* ("The Child of the Flowers," 1852), and *Baltasar* (*Belshazzar*, 1858). *Saúl* is a biblical tragedy that anticipated her greatest success, *Baltasar*, whose careful structure, psychological insight, and lack of posturing are strikingly un-Romantic. In *La hija de las flores*, Gómez de Avellaneda's greatest popular success, the author skillfully handled a plot that is almost a résumé of Golden Age comic practices and created a series of charmingly unbelievable characters. Like her more serious works, it is delightfully anachronistic in its avoidance of heavy-handed Romanticism.

Belshazzar (1914) is W. E. Burbank's translation. The standard introduction to Gómez de Avellaneda is Edwin B. Williams' *The Life and Dramatic Works of Gertrudis Gómez de Avellaneda* (1924).—F. D.

Good Woman of Setzuan, The (Der gute Mensch von Sezuan, 1943). A parable play by Bertolt BRECHT made up of ten scenes, short interludes, a verse epilogue, and six songs. Written between 1939 and 1941, the play was not performed until 1943 in Switzerland. A prologue shows the descent of three gods to earth. To justify their own existence and that of this world, they have to find at least one really good human being. But the only good person they can discover is the prostitute Shen Te. She offers them her place for the night, and when the gods leave in the morning, they reward her with some money.

Shen Te uses it to set herself up in a small tobacco shop. But her kindness makes her the victim of all kinds of parasites. To protect herself, she has to invent a ruthless male cousin, Shui Ta. Disguised as the cousin, Shen Te betrays the poor to the police and plans a marriage with a rich barber. Resuming her real identity, she falls in love with Yang Sun, a penniless aviator. They plan to get married, but Shui Ta soon realizes that the aviator is interested in Shen Te's money. He refuses to sell the shop, and as a result Yang Sun does not go through with the wedding ceremony.

Shen Te finds out that she is pregnant, and she is about to lose her shop, when the barber gives her a blank check, hoping to marry her later. Shen Te decides to call upon her cousin for a last time so that she can defend her child. Shui Ta opens a tobacco factory. By exploiting the workers he is able to earn a fortune, and Yang Sun soon becomes foreman, ruthlessly suppressing the laborers. The neighbors are distressed by the disappearance of the good Shen Te, and Shui Ta is suspected of having murdered her. He is arrested and brought to trial. The three gods appear as the judges. Shui Ta finally reveals that he is Shen Te, and that this mask was necessary to enable her to survive: "To be good and yet to live/was a thunderbolt:/it has torn me in two/ . . . to be good to others/and myself at the same time/I could not do it." The gods refuse to acknowledge the dilemma, they refuse to change the world and its laws. Convincing themselves that they have after all found a good person, they return to heaven on a pink cloud. Shen Te despairs and pleads for help. Since the gods have obviously failed to find a solution to the problems of this world, the audience is asked in an epilogue to think of a way out. For this much is certain: The world as it now is has to be changed, and the play has to be brought to a happy ending.

The Good Woman of Setzuan is one of a number of plays influenced by the Chinese theater, but as Brecht pointed out: "The province of Setzuan in this parable, which stood for all places where men are exploited by men, is no longer such a place." In short, Brecht is not talking about a province in China but about a capitalistic society, where man is perverted by the system and where the poor are no better than their masters. Torn between morality and necessity, love and need, men can exist only with a split personality.

For a discussion of the play in a wider perspective,

see Ronald Gray, *Brecht* (1961), p. 76 ff., and "Materialien zu Brechts Der gute Mensch von Sezuan," Edition Suhrkamp, 1968.—H. R.

Gorboduc or Ferrex and Porrex (1561). A tragedy by Thomas Norton (1532–1584) and Thomas Sackville (1536–1608). Celebrated as the first English tragedy in blank verse, this play was written and performed by the law students of the Inner Temple, one of the Elizabethan Inns of Court. Its successful reception initiated a vogue of Senecan drama in English that continued throughout the sixteenth century. The plot deals with the disastrous consequences of the decision of Gorboduc, the aging king of Britain, to divide his kingdom between his two sons, Ferrex and Porrex. Once the division takes place, the two brothers, incited by evil counselors and their own ambition and mistrust, engage in civil war. The result of the conflict is that Porrex slays his older brother, Ferrex. In retaliation Porrex is then slain by his mother, Queen Videna. The death of Porrex unleashes anarchy in the kingdom: the common people revolt, slaying both Gorboduc and Videna and leaving the gored nation prey to the ambitions of Fergus, a ruthless nobleman. On this ominous note the play concludes.

Aside from its historical significance (see ENGLAND: *Tudor drama*), the play is notable for its skillful modulation of the blank verse form and for the grim intensity of its dramatic impact.—E. Q.

Gordin, Jacob (1853–1909). Russian-born Yiddish playwright. Gordin was born on May 1, 1853, in Mirgorod, Poltava Region, in the Ukraine. He received a traditional religious education as well as secular instruction under private tutors and studied Russian and German as well as Hebrew. At seventeen he joined a Ukrainian separatist movement and began to study Ukrainian. Two years later he married, went into business, and failed. He tried his hand, unsuccessfully, at several occupations, working as a farmer, longshoreman, itinerant actor, schoolteacher, and journalist. In 1881, Gordin organized the Spiritual Biblical Brotherhood, dedicated to religious reform and based on the humane ethical principles of the Bible. The brotherhood was widely attacked and had little success. He emigrated to America and landed in New York on July 31, 1891, accompanied by his wife and eight children. (He was to have six more.) He turned from Russian to Yiddish, began to contribute to the socialist weekly *Di Arbeiter Tseitung* and shortly thereafter wrote his first play, *Siberia,* which opened on November 13, 1891. Though he apparently never considered it worth publishing, it nevertheless opened a new chapter in the history of the Yiddish theater in America by attracting a new audience, the intellectuals, who had hitherto left the tawdry Yiddish stage to the working masses. A second play two months later further enhanced his reputation, especially among the actors. When a number of top-flight artists, headed by Jacob P. Adler, combined to form a company in 1892, they invited Gordin to serve as company dramatist. Thereafter, he remained with the Yiddish theater, and at his death he had written between seventy and eighty plays.

Most of Gordin's plays were of little value and were never published. Often they were merely translations from German, Russian, French, or English, given new titles to suggest Jewish themes. On occasion, however, though still indebted to foreign sources for subject and idea, he transmuted the borrowed material into a new and ultimately original play. In this category are such works as *Der Yidisher Kenig Lir* ("The Jewish King Lear," 1892), *Mirele Efros* (1898), *Got, Mentsh, un Tayvl* ("God, Man, and Devil," 1900), *Sappho* (1900), *Kreuzer Sonata* (1902), and *Elisha ben Abuya* (1906). Despite the didacticism that was characteristic of the problem plays he wrote, Gordin was successful in airing the fears and hopes of his audience and in probing the problems of a Jewish world in upheaval and transition, not only geographic but also social, moral, and religious. His best plays became a permanent part of the repertoire of the Yiddish theater and his influence effected a major reform of the American Yiddish stage. The stilted, declamatory style and dramatic posing of the actors, the pompous and pretentious Germanized Yiddish, and the tawdry and melodramatic trifles of the popular play manufacturers were in Gordin's dramas replaced by probability of plot, by realistic Yiddish dialogue suited to the character, and by the demand for naturalistic acting techniques to project credible human beings. His plays dominated the New York Yiddish stage from 1895 to 1908. The competition for the continuing stream of hundreds of thousands of new immigrants, however, made producers increasingly wary of serious drama, to which the new audience did not respond, and Gordin's last years were years of growing neglect. So embittered did he become that his last words before his death were "Finita la commedia" ("The comedy is finished").

Melech Epstein's *Profiles of Eleven* (1965) contains a biography of Gordin. David S. Lifson's *The Yiddish Theatre in America* (1965) and Sol Liptzin's *The Flowering of Yiddish Literature* (1963) contain discussions of Gordin's work as a dramatist.—J. C. L.

Gorky, Maxim. Pen name of **Alexei Maximovich Peshkov** (1868–1936). Russian novelist, essayist, short-story writer, poet, and playwright. Gorky, meaning "The Bitter One," lost his father when he was five, his mother soon afterward, and was brought up by his maternal grandfather. In his relations with his grandson, this former Volga barge-hauler proved very handy with the knout. Within three years—when Gorky had reached the age of eight—the old man decided that he had given the youngster a sufficient foretaste of brutality and that it was time for him to go out into the world and fend for himself.

So young Gorky tasted more brutality, as a bootmaker's apprentice, a domestic servant, a dishwasher on Volga steamers, and a messenger for an icon painter, to mention a few, for beating was common practice among masters dealing with their employees, especially those who were young and helpless. Gorky saw the inside of police stations and flophouses, rubbed elbows with derelicts of all sorts, and he wrote about what he saw. He wrote with authority and a feeling of urgency, and his tone was very different from that used by the many literary, drawing-room champions of the underdog whom he often loathed almost as much as he did the oppressors of the poor.

MAXIM GORKY (TASS FROM SOVFOTO)

At the turn of the century Gorky was in a unique position, and his fame and popularity were much greater than the depth of his vision or his writing talent warranted. His stories and novels about tramps, unemployed workers, wife-beaters, and heartless landlords made him one of the three best-selling living Russian writers (the other two were Anton Chekhov and Leonid Andreyev). And when Gorky got into trouble with the authorities because of the rather grandiloquent rebellious message in his two blank-verse poems—"The Song of the Falcon" and "The Stormy Petrel"—it gave him the romantic halo of a revolutionary hero.

THE LOWER DEPTHS, Gorky's best-known play, reflects his personal experience of squalor, his longing for a better life, and the influence of the books he had read—Tolstoy, whom he admired, Dostoyevsky, whom he loathed—and of the political views of Lenin, with whom he had a precarious relationship. And, of course, in his playwriting technique he was influenced by Chekhov's way of conveying the atmosphere of stagnation and drifting and of making his characters indulge in continuous, ineffective talk. Unlike Chekhov, however, Gorky put his point of view directly into the mouths of his characters.

Gorky's popularity continued after the Soviets came to power, because his work was viewed as an exposé of tsarist ills. He came to be considered a sort of founding father of Soviet literature, and he was also credited with inventing the literary theory of Socialist Realism.

Gorky's personal attitude toward the revolution was, to say the least, ambiguous. He never seemed satisfied with the new order, lived abroad for many years, and when he returned to the Soviet Union in 1929, spent much of his time trying, with varying success, to save other writers who, because of their refusal to conform to his "socialist realism," were threatened with physical eradication. Thus, although Gorky really remained a prerevolutionary revolutionary writer, he was ushered into the Soviet literary pantheon and groomed to fit the Soviet mythology.

Since 1902, when he wrote *The Lower Depths,* Gorky has been considered an expert on the seamy side of life. As the only practicing writer of genuine proletarian stock, he was acclaimed as the natural mouthpiece of the oppressed. The more than fifteen plays he wrote, however, seem very dated, even by Soviet standards, for they do not transcend the particular political situations on which they focus. Of these plays, only *Yegor Bulychov i drugiye* (*Yegor Bulychov and the Others,* 1931) and, to some extent, *Vassa Zheleznova* (1935) are more than period pieces, possibly because Gorky managed to smuggle some human warmth into the portrayals of Yegor and Vassa, two representatives of the doomed "enemy classes."

Among the recent books on Gorky are Dan Levin's *Stormy Petrel: The Life and Work of Maxim Gorky* (1965) and Richard Hare's *Maxim Gorky, Romantic Realist and Conservative Revolutionary* (1962).—A. MACA.

Gottsched, Johann Christoph (1700–1766). Rationalist critic and teacher, whose poetics exercised great influence on German drama of the mid-eighteenth century. Born in Königsberg, Gottsched took up theological and philosophical studies at the university there, leaving abruptly in 1724, when his size attracted the glances of Prussian army recruiters. Taking up residence in Leipzig, then a leading cultural center, he adroitly established himself as a leading critical oracle. In 1730 he was made professor of logic and rhetoric at the university, and four years later obtained the professorship in logic and metaphysics. At this point he was in a position to achieve what few had previously attempted in Germany: an amalgamation of the theoretical-academic with the practical-theatrical. For an understanding of Gottsched's significance in the Age of Reason, it must be appreciated that he did not merely spring up overnight and announce his arrival as the new messiah of German poetics. His path to academic and literary authority lay through his activity in the *Teutsch-übende Gesellschaft* (literally, the "German-practicing Society"), a middle-class organization founded to avail members of self-education, particularly in the use of their native language. Two years after joining, Gottsched became the "senior" of the group and thus established himself as an authoritative teacher.

Gottsched was entirely a child of his age, the German Enlightenment. Among the doctrines espoused by this era were several basic ideas: Nature was correct, and what was correct was natural. Man was infinitely perfectible: A consequence of this was a strong educational impulse. A third belief was in rationality as the key to human progress and perfection. To Gottsched, it was thus clear that good taste subscribed to reason and sought to imitate nature. On this basis he sought to codify aesthetic rules and transform the stage into a morally oriented instrument of education. Having established himself as an authority, Gottsched found his practical prophetess in Caroline Neuber, wife of the principal of a troupe of actors. Through her work he was able to translate his theory into stage reality. The core of his theories was that all good poetry imitates nature and that since everything was perfectible, aesthetic pleasure becomes inseparable from moral purpose. Art can be learned according to rules. Accordingly, he set down the *Versuch einer critischen Dichtkunst vor die Deutschen* ("Attempt at a Critical Poetics for Germans") in 1730.

Gottsched saw the paradigm of dramatic perfection in the French drama of Racine and Corneille and exhorted his followers to adhere strictly to the usage of these works as models for the new German drama. Thus a great deal of his *Deutsche Schaubühne, nach den Regeln der alten Griechen und Römer eingerichtet* ("The German Stage, Arranged According to the Rules of the Ancient Greeks and Romans," 6 vols., pub. 1740–1745), a compilation of plays, is composed largely of translations of French drama. Gottsched deplored the English drama for its "unnatural and apparent rulelessness," and thus found himself embroiled in a controversy with proponents of English drama. Gottsched himself wrote few dramas, but his *Der sterbende Cato* ("The Dying Cato," 1732), modeled after both French and English versions of the same material, was intended to serve as an example to his followers.

Gottsched's wife also took an active hand in his affairs and, in fact, collaborated with him on model comedies that were intended to reform and purify the form. The resultant plays, patterned after the works of Ludwig Holberg and Molière, set the tone for

"comedy according to rules," and the figure of Hanswurst, the German Harlequin, was banished from the stage.

Although it has been frequently stylish to deprecate Gottsched, his immediate influence on German drama cannot be debated. For a period of twenty-five years under his authority, the "drama according to rules," slavishly retaining the classical unities, dispensing with the comic person and subplot, was the order of the day on the German stage. German opera, long opposed by Gottsched, temporarily left the boards in 1740; Hanswurst never really returned at all. Gottsched's rules, full of contradictions and a naïve trust in reason, appear laughable today. Nonetheless, his comedy paved the way directly for Lessing's great contributions, and in general, he was a major voice of his age, one to be reckoned with, either pro or con, in the second half of the eighteenth century.—B. M. M.

Götz von Berlichingen (1773). A play by Johann Wolfgang von GOETHE, loosely based on the life of Götz von Berlichingen (1480–1562), a German knight. In Goethe's treatment, Götz becomes a typical *Sturm und Drang* hero, a powerful individual personality, unwaveringly committed to his own straightforward conception of justice but in the end not able to escape the subtle maneuverings of his political adversaries. Formally, Goethe wished to emulate Shakespeare, in opposition to the prevailing neoclassicism, and the play is written in powerful, rough-and-ready prose, with short, pithy scenes and constant changes of setting between them.

The play's reception in its day was sensational. It became a standard repertory piece for German-speaking stages. Sir Walter Scott translated it into English. A spate of dramas of knights followed it. Jean Paul Sartre used it for his *Le Diable et le Bon Dieu* (1951). A new American translation is in preparation.

Gozzi, Carlo (1720–1806). Italian writer and playwright. Of a noble but impoverished Venetian family, Gozzi precociously dedicated himself to letters. In 1747 he helped to found the Accademia dei Granelleschi, which had as its objective the defense of the Italian literary language against any introduction of popular or realistic elements. A vehement enemy of all innovation, in politics as well as art, Gozzi indulged in lengthy polemics against reformist writers and literary currents of the time. A large part of his vast and multifaceted literary production arose out of these diatribes. Particularly long and fiery was his polemic against Carlo GOLDONI, whose conceptions of the function of art contradicted his, and whom he accused of negligence and of an arid adherence to the reality of the most meaningless daily events. In opposition to the bourgeois and realistic theater of Goldoni, Gozzi set up the theater of the fabulous. Freely constructed along the lines of the *commedia dell'arte,* Gozzi's drama was open to every exotic fantasy and his language and action were spontaneous. He wrote ten *fiabe* (fairy tales) between 1761 and 1765, among which the following stand out: *L'Amore delle tre melarance* (*The Love for Three Oranges,* 1761), *Re cervo* (*The King Stag,* 1762), TURANDOT—which is perhaps his best work—and *L'Augellin belverde* ("The Beautiful Green Bird," 1765). The ostentatious liberty of form evident in

CARLO GOZZI (ITALIAN CULTURAL INSTITUTE)

these fiabe—written partly in Italian and partly in Venetian dialect, partly in verse and partly in prose, and also in part left open for free improvisation by masked actors—fails to produce a unified result. They remain as testimony to a lively wit but one devoid of spiritual and psychological insight, one staled by constant negation of the new currents in contemporary morality and culture.—L. L.

Grabbe, Christian Dietrich (1801–1836). German playwright. Born in Detmold, the son of a prison warden, Grabbe had a brief but stormy life that was filled with failures, disappointments, and escape through alcoholism. He died of incurable tuberculosis at the age of thirty-five.

The tragic paradox of Grabbe's life and work lies perhaps in the historical circumstances with which he was determined to contend. His genius, which he defined as "hunger"—hunger or passion for a titanic, for a superreal personification of life and its forces—compelled him to cope with historical circumstances that would no longer permit any convincing notion of the titanic or the heroic. The extreme polarity of his personal psychology and dramatic ambitions—on the one hand, his desire to revitalize the notion of the heroic but, on the other hand, his cynical inability to believe in or to realize this goal personally or artistically—provides the fundamental problematic of this sorely tormented man.

Unfortunately, Grabbe could not see history in the same light as Goethe or the Romantics did. His contemporaries entertained the very positive and rather consoling notion that all individuation, whether historical or natural, was a marvelous manifestation of the existence of the Divine. Grabbe denied history any transcendence or divine immanence and consequently denied the presence of any ethical or metaphysical idea that would redeem the empirical from itself and its senselessness. Drama, as a representa-

tion of this absolute contingency, became the tragic reflection of this historical consciousness.

Grabbe's heroes, in the face of the onslaught of history, are not permitted sanctuary in the world of ideas. The metaphysical dimension of experience, which was the sustaining power of the classical heroes, is denied Grabbe's heroes and they are left to be confronted and overwhelmed by the blind furies of history. Only in a passive acceptance of the historical condition does the Grabbe hero find tragic dignity. In the play *Scherz, Satire, Ironie und tiefere Bedeutung* (*Jest, Satire, Irony and Deeper Meaning,* 1822), in which the hero is, in grotesque-humorous fashion, the devil, the "deeper meaning" is that the historical forces at play in nature and society are completely absurd.

In Grabbe's historical drama *Napoleon und die hundert Tage* (*Napoleon and the Hundred Days,* 1831) the hero is the victim of historical forces. In *Die Hermannsschlacht* (*The Battle of Hermann,* 1838) Hermann is deserted by his people. This potential hero with a powerful will and a vision of greatness is destroyed by the almost demonic, irrational forces of history as represented by his people, for they remain incapable of grasping the greatness of the "hero." See HANNIBAL.

If the apprehension of reality is so sharply radicalized by the outright rejection of the classical-idealistic notion of a preestablished harmony, such an extreme speculative change must perforce effect a similarly extreme formal change. A dramatic vision must give way to an epic vision attended by a concern with minute detail and mass scenes of dynamic

CHRISTIAN DIETRICH GRABBE (GERMAN INFORMATION CENTER)

monumentality. Logical development of plot must be supplanted by the station play, a seemingly haphazard arrangement of dramatic moments ordered more for their dynamic emotional impact than sequential consequence. The former emphasis on dramatic causality must be redirected to a dramatic collage, in which each event has a curious independence from the preceding and forthcoming action and yet is mysteriously closely woven into the fabric of the plot. Finally, the protagonists, instead of commanding and propelling the action, must appear as marionettes, grotesque and frightening in their helplessness.

If Grabbe's dramas as works of art are mediocre and of little aesthetic value, their structural and stylistic techniques have made important contributions to the genesis of modern epic drama.

Scherz, Satire, Ironie und tiefere Bedeutung was translated by Maurice Edwards as *Jest, Satire, Irony and Deeper Meaning* in 1966.—C. A. M.

Grand Guignol. A brief horror play about rape, ghosts, murder, and the like, designed to shock and titillate the audience. Performed at the Parisian cabaret called Théâtre du Grand Guignol, the plays were very popular in Paris during the 1890's and 1900's and appeared in England in a somewhat modified form at the turn of the century.

Guignol was originally the name of a marionette in a kind of Punch and Judy show, dating from the end of the eighteenth century. The general cruelheartedness of that puppet show and of Guignol in particular provide the namesake for the Grand Guignol theater.

Granville-Barker, Harley (1877–1946). English playwright, actor, director, critic, perhaps more closely identified with the Edwardian renascence of English drama than any other man of the theater (with the exception of Shaw). Often regarded as a disciple of Shaw, he deserves recognition in his own right, not only as an actor and director, but as one of the "new" dramatists who attempted to bring to English audiences in the late nineteenth and early twentieth centuries plays that had content as well as structure. As might be expected, Granville-Barker was connected with the theater from an early age. Born in London in 1877, he made his first public appearance in a play at the age of thirteen and soon began touring with various companies, making his first London appearance in May 1892 in a musical at the Comedy Theatre. His rise was predictably rapid, for Granville-Barker was serious, intelligent, and ambitious, and by 1899 he was acting in Mrs. Patrick Campbell's company and in William Poel's Elizabethan Stage Society and becoming acquainted with many important figures in the theatrical world, including Gilbert Murray, William Archer, and, of course, George Bernard Shaw.

Granville-Barker's ambition naturally led him into other areas of the theater, and he was soon active as playwright and director as well as actor. It was as director that he perhaps best realized his hopes for the new drama, for it was his work in that capacity with both the Stage Society and the Court Theatre (1904–1907, with J. E. Vedrenne) that enabled him not only to bring back older plays that deserved to be done but also to encourage contemporary playwrights and to provide audiences with the new drama of ideas. Among the productions at the Court were two of his own plays, *Prunella* (with L. Houseman, 1906) and *The Voysey Inheritance* (1905). "No one," wrote Desmond MacCarthy in his account of the Court Theatre, "can help being struck by the number and variety of these plays; no other modern managers have given so many memorable performances in so short a time." The other important area in which Granville-Barker made an impression as director was that of Shakespearean revivals, the most important evidence of this influence being his famous and illuminating *Prefaces to Shakespeare* (1927–1947).

Granville-Barker was twice married, the first time in 1906 to Lillah McCarthy, herself a famous actress and a very good friend of Shaw's, the second in 1918 to Helen Huntington, a poet. His last years were spent in less publicized positions connected with the theater. He did some lecturing in many countries, including America, spent some twelve years as chairman of the council of the British Drama League, and from 1937 to 1939 was director of the British Institute of the University of Paris.

The significant dramas of Granville-Barker—*The Marrying of Ann Leete* (1901), *The Voysey Inheritance* (1905), *Waste* (1907), and *The Madras House* (1910)—reflect his own interest in the drama of ideas, in theater that is concerned with meaningful commentary rather than superficial entertainment. Although Granville-Barker's place in the movement is that of follower rather than leader, he deserves an honored place in the ranks of the playwrights of the Edwardian period. In his treatment of such problems as the double standard, class distinction and prejudice, the new woman, and other difficulties arising mainly from conventional mores and behavior of the middle classes, Granville-Barker brought to the Edwardian theater the same questioning attitude and probing curiosity as Shaw. The difference between the two is seen in their techniques and styles; Barker, less flamboyant and rhetorical, more "realistic," even naturalistic, depended far more than did Shaw on understatement and restraint for dramatic effect. In this way he felt that he could better succeed in accomplishing in his plays what Desmond MacCarthy described as Granville-Barker's main purpose: "to see human emotions in relation to a moral or social order."

For a good introduction to Granville-Barker, see C. B. Purdom, *Harley Granville-Barker* (1956). See also Desmond MacCarthy, *The Court Theatre* (1907) and Gerald Weales, "The Edwardian Theater and the Shadow of Shaw," *Edwardians and Late Victorians,* English Institute Essays, Richard Ellmann, ed. (1960). Granville-Barker's own writings, particularly his *Prefaces to Shakespeare* (1927–1947) and his *The Exemplary Theatre* (1922), should also be consulted.—M. T.

Grass, Günter. See GERMANY: *twentieth century.*

Great Divide, The (1906). A drama by William Vaughn Moody. Under the title *The Sabine Woman, The Great Divide* was first produced in Chicago and a few months later in New York. It had a long run in New York, followed by an extensive tour, and in 1909 it was produced in London.

Act I of the play takes place in a cabin in the Southwest where Ruth Jordan, a born and bred New

Englander, is visiting. She has refused to marry a man she has known from childhood because he seems to her "finished." Left alone by her hosts and attacked by three desperadoes, she offers herself to the least repulsive of them, Stephen Ghent, if he will save her from the others. Stephen buys off one and shoots the second. Act II finds Stephen and Ruth married and settled in the Cordilleras, where Stephen, in love with Ruth, is industriously working a silver mine. Ruth, however, tortured by a conscience that tells her she has been "bought," finally leaves her husband. Act III is set in her brother's home in New England, where she has borne Stephen's son and is profoundly unhappy. Stephen arrives and makes her see that he has changed, that she really loves him, and that their love is good.

The first act is melodramatic, some of the dialogue is inappropriately literary, and the resolution is reached through discussion. Nevertheless, *The Great Divide* is a significant expression of the fundamental conflict in American life between inhibiting puritanism and the free spirit.—B. H.

Great God Brown, The (1926). An expressionist drama by Eugene O'NEILL. *The Great God Brown* follows the inner torment of artist Dion Anthony, whose extreme sensitivity in a materialistic world makes a neurotic and a drunkard of him. Dion, the man of imagination, is contrasted with his friend and rival Billy Brown, an uncreative, complacent man who employs the gifted Dion as an architect and takes credit for the latter's designs. In no other play did O'Neill symbolize the theme of the artist in a materialistic, unsympathetic society so intensively. The symbols are, in fact, schematized to such an extent that credibility of character and situation often suffers. Splitting his characters into sharply contrasted personalities, O'Neill even resorted to the use of masks to represent the antinomies of the artistic and the pragmatically bourgeois temperament. At one point the masks are interchanged—Brown taking the dying Dion's mask—for the purpose of dramatizing the seemingly placid bourgeois personality's envy and attempted incorporation of the artist. But despite believing that in stealing Dion's mask he has gained the power to create, Brown has actually, in O'Neill's words, possessed himself only of "that creative power made self-destructive by complete frustration"—a provocative idea for which O'Neill unfortunately found an incredibly melodramatic plot rather than a simple objective correlative.—J. G.

Greece: classical period. The origins of Greek drama have been the subject of great controversy since ancient times. Aristotle's statement that both tragedy and comedy grew out of improvisation, the former of the dithyramb (hymn to Dionysus), the latter of phallic songs, has been interpreted in every conceivable way as well as denied outright; and even the one point on which practically all are agreed, that the drama originated somehow in the cult of Dionysus, has recently been vigorously opposed. Other theories of ritual origin, such as the cult of the heroes or of a year-spirit, have been successfully refuted, but are still held by some. To the ancients the inventor of tragedy was Thespis of Icaria in Attica, who is said to have added a prologue and a set speech to a dithyrambic chorus. These were spoken by a costumed actor, so that a choral performance was transformed into a mimetic, or dramatic, one. Whether or not drama originated in the Dionysian cult, it was performed exclusively at the Dionysian festivals (the City, or Great, Dionysia, the Rural Dionysia, the Lenaea). Thespis appears to have presented his plays first at the country festivals, but in 535 B.C., the date that marks the official beginning of the dramatic contests, he gave a performance at the Great Dionysia in Athens.

The dramatic festivals were supervised entirely by the Athenian government. When a dramatist had completed a work, he submitted it to the appropriate magistrate for approval. Official state approval appears seldom, if ever, to have involved political censorship, the standard being artistic and dramatic quality. Once approved, a play would find support from the city, which paid the actors. Originally, there was only one actor. Aeschylus is supposed to have added the second, and Sophocles a third. All were male, and no matter how many characters, or of what sex, were represented, the limit was strictly observed, with a very few exceptions, though silent supernumeraries were freely granted. The all-important chorus (originally twelve in number, but raised by Sophocles to fifteen) was trained by the poet himself, though the producer was generally some gentleman of means who had agreed to sustain the expenses of the whole play except for the salary of the actors. This benefactor was known as *choregus*. If the play won a prize, it went officially to the choregus, who was then entitled to erect a monument, usually a tablet, in honor of his effort. Considering the expense involved in the elaborate costumes, masks, and high buskin boots—not to mention the feast that he was expected to provide for all the players after the performance—this honor was perhaps only his due. The function of the choregus was regarded as a highly honorable and special service to the official state religion. Fortunately, ancient sources have also preserved the name of the actual author of the victorious play. At the most important of the festivals, the City Dionysia, each of the three tragic competitors who were admitted produced three tragedies, and often a satyr play. We have no conclusive evidence about the time or circumstances of comic presentations, except that they formed part of both the City Dionysia and the Lenaea.

The earliest theaters probably consisted of no more than the concave slope of a hill rising above a level area, or orchestra, where the chorus danced and sang. There may have been seats, perhaps temporary, but the raised stage may not have appeared until the great age of drama had passed. On the other hand, some kind of setting is clearly implied by the earliest extant plays, and the invention of painted scenery is attributed by Aristotle to Sophocles. Although the stage setting might represent anything, the façade of a palace or temple was in very frequent use, with three doors, the central one conventionally reserved for the principal characters. Normally the scene did not change, but there were exceptions, as in the *Eumenides* of Aeschylus and in Sophocles' *Ajax*. (According to the testimony of an Oxyrhynchus papyrus [2257, 1], the *Aitnaiai* [*Women of Aetna*] of Aeschylus may have had five changes.) At either side of the orchestra and near the stage, whether raised or level, was an entranceway (*parodos*). Because the theater in

Athens faced south, with the town and harbor at the audience's right and the open country to its left, the convention arose that characters (or the chorus) entering from the right were supposed to have come either from the town or by sea, and those entering from the left from a long distance and by land. Later, when permanent stone structures were built around three sides of the long, narrow stage, the same conventions applied to the two side entrances as well as to the three doors at the rear. Various kinds of stage machinery existed, the most important being the *mechané* ("machine") and the *eccyclema*. The former was a device for making gods appear in the sky or fly through it, the latter presumably a platform on wheels that could be rolled out of one of the doors to reveal an interior scene. Other machinery included devices for suspending actors on wires, imitating thunder, or bringing ghosts up from underground. Since all performances were out of doors in broad daylight, there was of course no stage lighting, and darkness, as at the beginning of the *Agamemnon,* simply had to be imagined.

Such stylization and lack of illusion in the theater is paralleled by the language, form, and substance of Greek drama itself. Though comedy, except when parodying tragedy, used everyday speech, the language of tragedy early became a lofty, austere, quite artificial poetry, appropriate to the heroic grandeur of its subject matter. Though the dialect is essentially Attic, it admits words and forms from epic, and also from Doric, which was felt to possess a special solemnity. Particularly in Aeschylus and the earlier works of Sophocles there is an abundance of resonant compound words, bizarre expressions, and recklessly proliferating imagery that combine to produce an elevation comparable to little else in any literature. In his later works, Sophocles writes in a less exuberant, more subtle style, but the tone is still high and remote from common speech. Euripides, however, moved in the direction of a more naturalistic idiom, introducing little homelinesses that so reduced the grand, tragic reverberations that Aristophanes tirelessly accused him of ruining the art. Indeed, tragedy did virtually die after Euripides, partly because of ever-increasing naturalism, but also because of the decline of Athenian greatness and the rise of political and philosophic rationalism.

Unlike tragic language, with its gradual changes, the form of Attic tragedy showed a remarkable conservatism. Although, so far as is known, Greek drama made no use of any fixed symbolism such as the emblems of the Elizabethan stage, it adhered throughout to an extremely rigid exterior shape. A tragedy regularly begins with a prologue in iambic verse, spoken by a single actor, or sometimes in dialogue with another. (Two extant plays of Aeschylus, *The Persians* and *The Suppliant Maidens,* have no prologue.) There follows the entrance of the chorus into the orchestra (*parodos*), often chanting in anapestic rhythm (the meter of exits and entrances), sometimes singing in lyrical verse. Then comes a series of scenes in dialogue in which the action develops (*epeisodia*), divided from each other by lyrics sung by the chorus (*stasima*). Frequently a lyric lament, with a meter almost exclusively its own, occurs at some high point of dramatic action, where an actor on the stage sings or speaks antiphonally with

the chorus in the orchestra. A long speech by a messenger, relating events offstage, is a regular feature, for little real action is shown on the stage. Finally, there is the *exodos* ("denouement"), which is everything after the chorus' last song. The play as a rule closes with an anapestic tag as the choristers march out of the orchestra. Though any actor may sing in a lyrical part, the only speaking part in the chorus is, normally, that of the leader (*coryphaeus*). Very rarely the chorus will leave the stage temporarily, as in the *Ajax* of Sophocles, or the *Helen* of Euripides.

This virtually unchanging, traditional form indicates an early connection with ritual, and indeed, throughout its history tragedy itself remained a ritual, in the sense of a reenactment. With three or four exceptions, the subjects of tragedy were drawn from the traditional mythology and heroic legends; even the exceptions, whose subjects are historical, as, for example, *The Persians,* which celebrates the battle of Salamis, are less exceptional than they might seem, for until the end of the fifth century history and mythology were not very carefully distinguished in the Greek mind. It would be a mistake, however, to regard tragedy's reenactments of old stories as merely that. The earliest extant plays are already sophisticated works of art, and a poet was at liberty to treat a myth in any way he chose, provided the main outlines remained recognizable. Often a story, such as that of Orestes or Philoctetes, was used by all three great tragedians with vast differences in style, emphasis, and interpretation. Thus Aeschylus' Orestes is a good man driven unwillingly into crime; for Sophocles he is a stainless redeemer; and for Euripides he is a neurotic weakling. Yet, though outright propagandist plays were occasionally written, the myth was more than a mere peg on which the poet could hang his own ideas. The myth embodied an archetypal story, and the poet's effort was to express the meaning inherent in the archetype as he saw it. In the later fifth century, when the official religion was fading before the enlightenment, myth began to lose its archetypal function in Greek thought, so that in a number of Euripides' plays the myth is more the vehicle than the source of the dramatic message. Yet in some of his later works Euripides returned to the older feeling about myth, once more finding it meaningful in itself, though in new perspectives. The traditional legends ceased to be the subjects of tragedy only with Agathon (c. 447–c. 400 B.C.), who, probably in the early fourth century, produced a play called *Antheus,* in which the plot and characters were all the poet's own invention. But the age of tragedy had passed.

Of equal importance as myth to the life of Greek tragedy was the chorus. To modern taste the choral passages may seem intrusive or irrelevant, but the Greeks often referred to dramatic performances simply as "choruses," and when a play was accepted for production, the choregus was said "to get a chorus." Aeschylus is said to have curtailed its role, but all his plays, except the *Prometheus Bound,* have long choral lyrics of great power and beauty. Their relevance is never in doubt, for the Aeschylean lyric carries implicitly the wholeness of the action, which the scenes can dramatize only part by part. The lyrics of Sophocles are much shorter and not always so easy to relate to the action. Though a few, like the famous "Ode on Man" in the *Antigone,* form independent poems in themselves, most of them are meditations on the emotions roused in the preceding scene, holding them in a kind of suspension in anticipation of the next phase of action. Euripides was singularly gifted in the lyric, though unlike his two predecessors he did not write his own music. But often his odes have only the most tenuous—sometimes, in fact, undetectable—connection with the play. Once more, it remained for Agathon to give up all attempt at relevance and let his chorus simply sing interludes, a practice condemned by Aristotle and certainly symptomatic of the decline of tragedy.

Of the drama before Aeschylus little is known. Nothing survives of Thespis except four dubiously reported titles, and Choerilus is scarcely more than a name. Ancient sources provide a fair amount of information, however, about Phrynichus (c. 540– c. 470 B.C.), son of Polyphrasmon. He won his first tragic victory sometime between 511 and 508 B.C., and the titles of eight of his plays are preserved: *Alcestis,* said to have influenced Euripides; *Aigyptioi* (*Egyptians*) and *Danaides* (*Daughters of Danaus*), titles also of two lost plays of Aeschylus; *Antaeus; Tantalus;* the *Pleuroniai* (*Women of Pleuron*), which treated the story of Meleager; the *Phoinissai* (*Phoenician Women,* 476 B.C.), written in celebration of the battle of Salamis, with Themistocles as choregus; and, most famous of all, the *Miletou Halosis* (*Sack of Miletus,* 493 or 492 B.C.). Miletus, an Athenian colony, was destroyed by the Persians in 494, and Herodotus tells us that the Athenians were so upset by Phrynichus' play that, instead of rewarding him, they fined him a thousand drachmas. Once more, Themistocles was the archon who granted the poet a chorus, and there may be reason to believe that he deliberately used this play as propaganda in support of his vigorous anti-Persian policy. Very sparse fragments of Phrynichus' work survive, and none of them offers any idea of the delicate lyricism for which he was admired by Aristophanes.

One other pre-Aeschylean poet deserves mention, Pratinas of Phlius (c. 540–470 B.C.), to whom was attributed the invention of the satyr play. More likely he developed it into a genuine art form and got it introduced into the tragic contests. He also wrote tragedies, but his heart lay in the satyr play, and if the fifteen-odd lines that survive from one of them are typical, his work must have been lively indeed. Pratinas took great pride in his achievement. In the fragment mentioned, what seems to be a punning and uncomplimentary reference to Phrynichus suggests that he regarded his own manly Dorian art as standing in direct opposition to the refined sweetness of Phrynichan tragedy.

All too little is known of the satyr play, though one complete work by Euripides, the CYCLOPS (based on Book X of the *Odyssey*), and half of another by Sophocles, the *Ichneutai* (*The Trackers,* based on the "Homeric" *Hymn to Hermes*), have come down to us. The main features were the chorus of satyrs and the burlesquing of a myth, sometimes, but not always, connected with the tragic performance preceding it. The language was that of tragedy, but the spirit was comic and Dionysian, admitting farce and obscenity as freely as Old Comedy did.

SATYR PLAY WITH DIONYSUS, ACTORS, CHORUS, POET, AND FLUTE PLAYER (VASE IN MUSEO NAZIONALE, NAPLES. COURTESY OF ALINARI–ART REFERENCE BUREAU)

AESCHYLUS, son of Euphorion of Eleusis, lived during the whole period of Athens' rise to greatness, from the fall of the Pisistratid tyranny and the establishment of the democracy, through the Persian wars, in which he fought, to the beginning of the age of Pericles. The enterprise, optimism, and heroic energy of the Athenians of those two generations are reflected in the broad, cosmic scope of Aeschylus' dramas and the towering magnificence of his language. Only seven of his plays survive, roughly a tenth of his work, but we can be sure from the fragments of the others and from the portrait of him in Aristophanes' *Frogs* that these seven are representative and that Aeschylus' style was the grand style par excellence. Aeschylus also excelled in the aspect of tragedy that Aristotle calls "spectacle." In the anonymous *Life of Aeschylus* of the Medicean manuscript, we read that Aeschylus "exalted tragedy with the most noble emotions, adorned his settings, and astounded the eyes of the spectators with their brilliance—with paintings and stage-devices, altars and tombs, trumpets, ghosts, Furies." He also seems to have greatly elaborated the costumes of the actors, in accordance with the kings, heroes, and gods whom they presented. The addition of a second actor enabled him to produce conflict, and hence real drama, as distinct from the work of his predecessors, which must have been little more than quasi-epic narrative, interrupted by lyric responses. Conflict was essential to Aeschylus, not merely as the basis of drama, but as the basis of life itself and the world, which he saw as evolving through the tug or clash of opposing forces, eventually to achieve equilibrium perhaps, but an equilibrium that might yet again be upset by some bold act reaching beyond the *status quo*. The conflict could appear in any form, between Greeks and barbarians, between members of one family, between generations of the gods themselves; it might appear as a conflict of irreconcilable motives, or in the moral ambiguity of a deed. It has even been persuasively shown that the work of Aeschylus can be read as a conflict of the sexes, with the male representing intellect and innovation, which destroys one thing as it creates another, and the female representing passive love and acceptance, which preserves but is static and bound. Seldom, if ever, is the conflict simply between good and evil, for Aeschylus regularly moves toward reconciliation, and pure good and evil, by their nature, will not be reconciled. Rather the goods and evils inherent in the conflict are mingled in an equivocal moral tapestry fully as complex as the images that express them.

The nearest exception to this statement is Aeschylus' earliest extant play, THE PERSIANS. Xerxes' attack on Greece was certainly regarded by Aeschylus as an act of *hybris,* or highhanded violence and pride, and his defeat at Salamis was certainly a good for Greece. But the scene is the Persian court, and the action consists wholly of the arrival of the crushing news, climaxed by the return of the humbled king himself, lamenting antiphonally with the Chorus of Elders. Though the battle is narrated, all is presented through the eyes of the Persians, the king's mother, and the ghost of his father, Darius, whose apparition serves to recall the real greatness of Persia, in which to an extent Xerxes also shares. The moral is clear enough, but so too is the tragic disruption of the world that, in Aeschylus' drama, attends any bold, adventurous act. *The Persians* is the only play in the whole tragic corpus that clearly and explicitly follows the Herodotean hybris-punishment formula, sometimes mistakenly supposed to be the key to all Greek tragedy. Aeschylus has used it but hardly for its own sake; rather as a means of presenting the dangerousness of action and its relation to the totality of things —or, as he would probably say, Zeus.

The Persians is not part of a connected trilogy, which was the form favored by Aeschylus and perhaps invented by him. His other extant plays are all trilogic, the earliest of them being the SEVEN AGAINST THEBES. It is the last play of a trilogy, the other two being the *Laius* and the *Oedipus,* both lost; the satyr play was the *Sphinx.* The *Seven Against Thebes* dramatizes the quarrel between the two sons of Oedipus for the throne of Thebes, ending in their mutual slaughter under the curse placed on them by their father. It is sometimes said that in this play Aeschylus gives us our first example of a true tragic hero in the person of Eteocles, the regnant brother who stands in defense of his city against Polyneices, who is trying to storm it. There is some truth in this, but it should be remembered that Eteocles, though previously sane and steadfast, just before he enters the fatal conflict bursts

out in a maniacal denunciation of his brother and, after devoting the whole race of Laius "to the stream of Hell," dashes into the fight, not out of heroic patriotism at all, but out of hate amounting to insanity. Aeschylus was ambivalent about heroes and saw heroic action as having ambivalent motivation and results; for though Thebes is saved, the royal family is extinguished, and the play closes (once the spurious ending is removed) in lament. Whether the original ending offered any assuagement or resolution is unknown.

THE SUPPLIANT MAIDENS, long thought to be the earliest play but now dated in the late 460's, is the first in the so-called *Danaid,* or Argive, trilogy. It relates the flight of the fifty daughters of Danaus to Argos, to avoid marriage with their cousins, the sons of Aegyptus. The two lost plays dramatize the enforced marriage, the massacre of the husbands by their brides at the direction of their father, and the trial of Hypermnestra, who alone disobeyed and spared her husband. Apparently she was defended by Aphrodite herself, who, in a beautiful fragment, speaks of herself as the principle that brings earth and heaven into fruitful union. Here, in the cosmic terms of divinity, Aeschylus has attained reconciliation after a conflict that has led to rape and murder. *The Suppliant Maidens,* though dramaturgically stiff, contains some of Aeschylus' finest poetry, chiefly in the long hymnic odes of the chorus, who constitute the real protagonist.

The ORESTEIA, usually considered Aeschylus' masterpiece, and the only complete trilogy preserved, is the story of the murder of Agamemnon on his return from Troy by his wife, Clytemnestra; of her death at the hands of Orestes, her son; and of Orestes' trial and acquittal before the court of the Areopagus in Athens. Clytemnestra's crime is only one in a series of horrors that have haunted the house of Atreus since Thyestes, Atreus' brother, put a curse on it after being tricked into eating his own children. No adequate description can be given of this magnificent study of self-renewing crime, guilt, and suffering and the eventual dissolution of the curse through the intervention of Athena. The principle, familiar from earlier works, that he who acts must suffer is balanced here by the theme of wisdom-through-suffering as the action slowly moves toward the reestablishment of order. Great emphasis is laid on Zeus as the god of justice who presides over this process of blow and counterblow, mysteriously working out his will through the crimes of those who must learn. As the poet says, "The grace of the gods [on their holy thrones] comes somehow through violence." In the *Oresteia* we can really see how a trilogy worked and why, perhaps, Aeschylus adopted it. The evolution of justice needs time, more time than could be represented in a single play, and a family curse affects generations before it can be exorcised. But the progress is there. After all the caliginous gloom in which seven-eighths of the trilogy takes place, the trial scene with its final release in the bright Athenian air, with the goddess herself presiding, points to an ultimate optimism in Aeschylus' work. It is significant too that the salvation of Orestes is achieved in Athens. In the Persian wars Athens had been the savior of Greece and, as a democracy, could be the redeemer of the individual. But the *Oresteia* is remarkable not only for its moral, theological, and political themes. With the possible exception of Eteocles, Aeschylus had hitherto paid little attention to character, finding the essence of tragedy in the tragic act and consequent suffering. But in Clytemnestra he created one of the greatest characters ever conceived. She completely dominates the first play, though it is called the *Agamemnon.* She is a living portrait of a powerful-minded woman whose will to slay her husband has grown out of an understandable hatred of him for his sacrifice of their daughter, Iphigenia, and also out of her own involvement with her paramour, Aegisthus. She reappears briefly, but with all the same vigor, in the *Choephori* (*Libation Bearers*), when she is slain by Orestes, and her ghost rises near the beginning of the *Eumenides* ("Furies"). The other characters, though convincing enough, pale before this daemonic, yet somehow appealing, criminal. Finally, the poetry of the *Oresteia,* particularly of the *Agamemnon,* is perhaps its crowning splendor.

The date of the Prometheus trilogy is unknown, but it is probably very late. All that remains is the first play, Prometheus Bound, in which Prometheus by order of Zeus is chained to a crag in requital for his theft of fire. The fact that the protagonist is immobile throughout makes this play perhaps more of a dramatic poem than a drama. Yet Aeschylus has managed to provide spectacle enough: the arrival of the chorus in a winged chariot, of Oceanus on a "four-footed bird," and of Hermes through the air, not to mention the apparition of Io costumed, at least partially, as a heifer. These gave the audience visible wonders comparable to the lofty rhetoric of the hero. Indeed, in the final scene, Prometheus having refused to tell the secret by which Zeus's rule will be assured, the crag is split by lightning, and everything, including the chorus, sinks into the abyss. Once more, we see the ambiguous effect of a heroic act: the gift of fire saved mankind from extinction and gave rise to all the arts and crafts, but it has also disrupted the world of the gods. How harmony was restored is a matter of guesswork. In the *Prometheus Lyomenos* (*Prometheus Unbound*) Heracles releases the hero. The third play, *Prometheus Pyrphoros* (*Prometheus the Fire-Carrier*), may have centered around the establishment of the torch races at Athens in honor of Prometheus.

Aeschylus won the dramatic prize thirteen times and was greatly honored during his life. He produced plays not only at Athens but also at the court of Hieron of Syracuse around 470. He returned to Sicily later, for reasons unknown, and died there at Gela, where his tomb became an international shrine. The Athenians passed a decree that anyone who wished to revive a play by Aeschylus would automatically get a chorus.

Sophocles, son of Sophilus, is generally regarded as the poet who brought tragedy to its perfection. Like all the art of the high classical age, that of Sophocles is marked by symmetry, control, and a deceptive simplicity. These qualities, combined with what we hear of his serene temperament and social grace, have sometimes led to a picture of him as a man rather apart from the stormy events and intellectual revolution of the fifth century. Yet Sophocles held high political and military offices and was fully in touch with the intellectual milieu of his time. Both

the decline of religion, as a result of the so-called Sophistic movement, and the growing imperialism and bureaucracy of Periclean Athens had their effect on him. Though he reacted less violently than Euripides did, he certainly did not share Aeschylus' optimistic faith either in the gods or in Athens, both of which grew steadily more remote and alien to the individual. For this reason, doubtless, Sophocles abandoned the trilogy in favor of the single play as a form better suited to the study of the individual soul in isolation. His protagonists are heroes, but unlike those of Aeschylus, they are moral archetypes as well as carefully characterized human beings. For Aeschylus, crime ineluctably brought suffering; for Sophocles, suffering followed just as ineluctably on high moral action. With the exception of Ajax, his heroes bring about their own suffering or death through a guiltless action or adherence to principle. Aristotle's theory of the "tragic flaw," though often applied to Sophocles, simply will not apply, at least to the 7 plays surviving out of the 123 that he wrote.

The Ajax still shows some strong Aeschylean influence, both in the rich language and in tragic structure. The hero, offended that the prize of Achilles' arms has been given to Odysseus rather than to himself, resolves to murder all the Greek leaders but goes mad and kills a herd of animals instead. When he recovers, he decides that suicide is the only means of restoring his integrity, and he falls on his sword. A debate arises as to whether the would-be assassin should be buried or cast out to the dogs, but Odysseus, here represented as a sane and generous man, prevails in favor of an honorable burial. The use of crime as a tragic motivation recalls Aeschylus; but in fact Ajax committed no crime, and his only regret is that he failed to do so. There is no suffering-learning process; Ajax suffers, but he does not learn, and the real moral question is that raised in the debate over burial, namely the evaluation of a man who does not fit into society but towers over it with grand, though dangerous, stature. The question is characteristically Sophoclean. By the end of the play, the balance seems to have tipped in favor of Ajax.

The Antigone deals even more clearly with the question. After the two sons of Oedipus have slain each other, their uncle Creon orders, as king, that Polyneices shall not receive burial because he had attacked his own city. Antigone, his sister, buries him anyway and is sentenced to death. Creon rejects all pleas on her behalf, even that of his son Haemon, who is betrothed to her, and she is immured alive. The prophet Teiresias warns Creon that the gods are angry at his inversion of the natural treatment of living and dead, and Creon agrees to release Antigone and bury Polyneices. But Antigone has already hanged herself in the tomb, and Haemon and his mother both commit suicide.

Many have seen in Creon a righteous but stubborn ruler who upholds law even at the expense of family ties, and since Hegel's famous critique of the play it has been customary to regard it as a conflict of antinomic rights. Certainly the sharply antithetical style prompts criticism of the sort. But the divine omens make it clear that Creon's original edict was a violation of nature and that Antigone was quite right to disobey it. Thus the whole question of the legality of law arises; more pointedly, the poet raises the question of how the morally responsible individual must behave in the face of social institutions that do not support, but rather deny, individual responsibility and that conflict with human nature itself. The *Antigone* is one of the earliest and most poignant reflections of that alienation of the individual from existing conventions, which was beginning to be a burning issue among the so-called Sophistic thinkers and was to lead, by the end of the century, to serious disruption of Athenian society. The character of Antigone has been much disputed, but few would deny her high-spirited heroism. Probably the best description of her is her own, "a holy transgressor."

No date can be given for the TRACHINIAI, but stylistic and structural features favor the middle thirties. After a long absence, Heracles sends word to his wife, Deianira, and son, Hyllus, whom he has left in Trachis, that he will soon return from the triumphant conquest of Oechalia. Meanwhile he has sent on a group of captive women, among whom is Princess Iole, for whose possession he had attacked the city. The gentle Deianira, thinking it a love charm that will recover her husband's affection, sends him the fatal "shirt of Nessus," which destroys him. She stabs herself, and Heracles, after forcing Hyllus to marry Iole, orders his own funeral pyre on the top of Mount Oeta.

Sophocles may well have been the first to represent Deianira's deed as innocent of evil intention; her name means "husband-killer," and probably the common tradition was that she acted out of jealous revenge. There is no trace of this in Sophocles' play. The *Trachiniai* certainly is one of Sophocles' darkest and saddest works, ending as it does with a powerful denunciation of the heartlessness of the gods. Deianira, with her tremulous delicacy and sympathy for all, including Iole, is a masterpiece of womanly portraiture, shown as utterly destroyed. The ghastly fate of Heracles, though he is drawn rather unsympathetically, and the grotesque, forced marriage of Hyllus create a picture of a world totally "out of joint," where true knowledge comes too late and true love cannot prevail. Whereas the heroic stature of Ajax and Antigone gave them a kind of tragic victory in death, Deianira is heroic only in her steadfast, patient devotion, and her death has in it no trace of victory. Like its two predecessors, the play has been called a diptych and accused of falling into two halves. But the poetry is a miracle of unifying, interlacing images, especially of night, day, bestiality, and disease. The *Trachiniai* has sometimes been thought to show the influence of Euripides' *Alcestis,* but the case can be argued either way.

The OEDIPUS TYRANNUS is ordinarily dated around 429, for no better reason than that it begins with a plague and that Athens suffered a plague in that year. In the drama, the plague has broken out in Thebes because the murder of the former king, Laius, has gone unpunished and uninvestigated. The people beseech Oedipus, now king and husband of the widowed queen Jocasta, to help them. Oedipus promises to seek out the murderer and pronounces a solemn curse upon him. Through a series of indescribably complex and masterly scenes Oedipus pursues the search, only to find out, not only that he himself had unwittingly killed Laius in self-defense in a fight on the road to Delphi, but also that he is the son of Laius

and Jocasta. The queen hangs herself, and Oedipus strikes out his eyes.

It has often been noted that this plot is unlikely to the point of absurdity; yet Sophocles made of it what is usually considered the greatest of Greek tragedies. Perhaps the *Oedipus* could be looked upon as a remote ancestor of the "theater of the absurd," for both involve an inscrutable world and a search for the self. But Sophocles' play is heroic in that Oedipus is a man of tremendous stature and force of will. Gentle and benignant toward his people, yet capable of fierce anger when he feels attacked, he conducts the search with a relentless single-mindedness that grows only the more relentless as the evidence begins to indicate that he himself is guilty. The play moves with characteristically Sophoclean speed, yet the truth emerges bit by bit, with exquisite timing, up to the shattering close. Though all the characters are convincing, the play belongs to Oedipus, heroically isolated in his moral quest. Less lyrical than any other play by Sophocles, the poetic force of the *Oedipus* derives more from double meanings and ironic wordplay than from exploitation of key imagery (though the recurrent theme of sight-blindness is prominent).

The ELECTRA, of unknown date but certainly in Sophocles' mature period, has the same plot as the *Choephori* of Aeschylus: the revenge of Orestes on Aegisthus and his own mother for their murder of his father. Sophocles, however, focuses strictly on Electra and her suffering while she awaits the coming of her brother, who appears only in the Prologue and near the end of the play, to commit the actual murder. Critics have been puzzled by Sophocles' treatment of the matricide, for no indication is given of its aftermath, Orestes' pursuit by the Furies, and his trial in Athens, which, however, may be Aeschylus' invention. Sophocles follows the earlier version as told in Homer and Hesiod, in which Orestes' act is regarded as an act of necessary justice with no aftermath. Why Sophocles did so is clear: he wanted to concentrate on the isolated Electra, whose steady devotion to her father and refusal to bow before the tyranny of Clytemnestra and Aegisthus create a protagonist of typically Sophoclean heroic fiber. For sheer passionate outpourings her eloquence is unmatched, whether it be of hate to her mother, lamentation over the supposed burial urn of her brother, or joy when she is united with him in what is probably the greatest "recognition scene" in Greek drama. The *Electra,* like the *Oedipus,* is very tightly knit, an example of Sophocles' most economical dramaturgy.

The PHILOCTETES recounts how the Greeks before Troy tried to recover the services of Philoctetes, whom they had marooned on Lemnos ten years earlier because of a festering and offensive snakebite on his foot. It has now been prophesied that they cannot take Troy without him and his famous bow of Heracles. Odysseus and Neoptolemus are sent to get him back by intrigue, since the embittered hero would never come willingly. He is tricked into giving his bow to Neoptolemus, but the young man suddenly repents, tells the truth, and returns the bow. In the impasse that follows, the deified Heracles appears *ex machina* and orders Philoctetes to go to Troy, promising him healing for his wound and great glory.

A SCENE FROM SOPHOCLES' *Electra* (GREEK NATIONAL TOURIST OFFICE)

Philoctetes yields, and the play closes with his singularly beautiful farewell to the island.

The intrigue scenes, with their subtle and ironic interweaving of truth and falsehood, are done with great skill, and the character of Neoptolemus is very appealing. Philoctetes himself is the most isolated of all Sophoclean heroes, both morally and physically. To underscore that fact Sophocles, in an early use of scenic symbolism, has turned Lemnos into a desert island, which it was not. But the real force of the drama lies in the heroic dilemma: if a hero, out of justifiable resentment, rejects society and retires from it, he forfeits his heroism; if he yields to an unjust society, he forfeits his integrity. Sophocles has gotten Philoctetes between the horns by letting him find in Neoptolemus one man, at least, who cannot bear to maintain a lie.

The OEDIPUS AT COLONUS was not produced until 401, five years after Sophocles' death, doubtless because of the desperate conditions before and after the fall of Athens in 404. The blind Oedipus, now old and in exile, arrives with his daughter Antigone at a sacred grove of the Eumenides in Colonus, a suburb of Athens and Sophocles' own birthplace. An oracle has said that his body would bring blessing and victory to the land where it was buried, and Oedipus, who has developed second sight, realizes that this grove is the place. Although frightened of him at first because of his pollution, the Athenians, led by Theseus, take him in and protect him, despite attempts by the Theban Creon, who also knows the oracle, to get his body for Thebes. The war between Polyneices and Eteocles is imminent, and the former enters to ask his father's blessing. But Oedipus curses both his sons for allowing his exile, and Polyneices goes to his doom. At last, thunder is heard and Oedipus, recognizing that the time has come, enters the grove with Theseus, where he is mysteriously translated in a place that must remain a secret.

Though it does not have the tight dramatic economy of the *Oedipus Tyrannus* or the *Electra,* the *Oedipus at Colonus* is in some ways Sophocles' greatest work, his final testament of the heroic spirit. Through "time, suffering, and inner nobility," Oedipus has learned acceptance; but he has also achieved a kind of daemonic knowledge and power, which, while hinted at throughout, reveals itself magnificently in the moment when, blind though he is, he leads the way into the grove. The play is a mystery play, with the metaphysical import necessarily left obscure. It is also a play in celebration of Athens as protector of the suppliant and the individual, and the famous "Ode on Athens" is surely the poet's most beautiful lyric. It is almost as if, in his last years and within months of the city's fall, Sophocles were trying to re-create the Athens of Aeschylus' *Eumenides.*

Though never revered quite as Aeschylus was, Sophocles was more successful, winning more prizes than his two great rivals together. The polished elegance of his language marks, perhaps, the high point in the development of literary Attic Greek. The fact that six out of the seven extant plays involve oracles that are fulfilled, combined with certain apparently deeply reverent odes, has given Sophocles a reputation for an almost simplistic piety. But the great master of irony was doing more than instilling little moral lessons. He was searching for the validation of the individual in a world growing ever less responsive, and finding it in his own created version of self-isolating moral heroism.

EURIPIDES, son of Mnesarchus (or Mnesarchides), provides the greatest possible contrast with Sophocles, both in his temperament and in his work. Where Sophocles was genial and enjoyed good company, Euripides was rather a recluse with a reputation for moroseness, writing his tragedies in a cave in Salamis. Where the work of Sophocles shows a high degree of unity and consistency throughout, both in theme and texture, Euripides is probably the most diverse and experimental Greek poet known to us. Angular, almost jerky in construction, his dramas abound in the unexpected and in contradictions, both in character and attitude, which often make them very difficult to comprehend. If for Sophocles the world was paradoxical and the gods remote, for Euripides the world was chaos and the gods, if existent, inclined to malignity. The result is a chaotic, nervous, and constantly varying dramaturgy, in which little or nothing is ever completely resolved, though the *Iphigenia among the Taurians* and the *Helen* may be exceptions. Euripides could not find order in the heroic individual, for he saw humanity as driven by raw passions amid an irrational fall of chance events. It was fashionable for the comic poets to represent him as an atheist; rather he seems intensely religious, but uncertain about what. Some modern critics have made him into a detached, ironical rationalist, mockingly reenacting the traditional myths in a way designed to show their absurdity to those keen enough to catch his hidden meanings. But the theory is too esoteric and quite at odds with the unmistakable passionate involvement of the poet. Euripides has been better called an "irrationalist." Certainly he was deeply influenced by the Sophistic enlightenment, as is clear from the kind of rhetorical arguments used in his famous "debate scenes." But the Sophists used rhetoric and reason as a tool to sway what they elsewhere demonstrated to be an utterly irrational, self-oriented psyche. If man in Sophocles is alienated from society, in Euripides he is alienated from himself as well, so that if the often-applied word "psychologist" is appropriate to him, it is in this sense, and not in a comparative sense, that Sophocles had no knowledge of psychology. Of the nineteen plays that survive out of ninety-two, only seven can be dated with certainty, but the probable order of the others can be conjectured on stylistic grounds, specifically metrical tendencies in the iambic trimeter line and also in lyric meters.

The ALCESTIS was produced in lieu of a satyr play. The old heroic legend of the wife who was willing to die for her husband, when he had the choice, was dramatized by Euripides entirely from the point of view of the husband, Admetus, whose callow self-regard gradually yields to a humane realization of what he has done. A converse change takes place in the generous Alcestis, for though she is brought back from the dead by the mighty Heracles and returned to Admetus, her veiled and voiceless figure at the end gives the impression that she will have little to say to him again. The irony is typically Euripidean. Despite its speciously happy ending and the somewhat comic scene of Heracles drunk, the *Alcestis* is a genuine tragedy and one of the most subtle of the poet's works.

The MEDEA is perhaps the best example of Euripides' interest in criminal pathology. Deserted by Jason in favor of the Corinthian princess Creusa, Medea slays her own two sons by Jason in revenge

and sends a poisoned robe to Creusa, who is consumed by it. She then flies off in a dragon chariot to Athens, there to find refuge. The fine characterization, especially in the confrontation between the frigid Jason and the blazing Medea and in the scene in which she struggles with herself over the murder of the children, has made this play a stage favorite. Medea's flight to Athens, usually the refuge of the oppressed rather than of criminals, is a bit mystifying. It was part of the tradition, yet Euripides could have left it out. But there was another tradition that it was the Corinthians, not Medea, who slew the children in revenge for the destruction of Creusa. In this version the refuge in Athens is more understandable. As it stands, in sending this bloodthirsty sorceress to Athens, which is described in a beautiful ode as the home of Harmony and the Muses (824 ff.), Euripides perhaps wished to hint at that mingling of high-mindedness and dangerous passion that characterized the city, and eventually destroyed it.

THE CHILDREN OF HERACLES and the ANDROMACHE may well be grouped. Both were written in the early years of the Peloponnesian War, and both are highly anti-Spartan. In the first, Eurystheus, who had persecuted Heracles all his life, is now persecuting Heracles' children. Under the care of Iolaus, the now-aged nephew of Heracles, they take refuge in Athens. Eurystheus attacks Athens but is defeated, captured, and handed over to Alcmena, Heracles' mother, who has him executed in spite of the intercession of the Athenians. This play is scarcely Euripides at his best. Perhaps the two most interesting things in it are the momentary rejuvenation of Iolaus, a favorite theme of Euripides, and Eurystheus' prophecy that his dead body (like that of Oedipus) will always be a protection to Athens but hostile to all descendants of Heracles—that is, Spartans. The *Andromache* is perhaps even more explicit. The heroine, now concubine of Neoptolemus, is persecuted in his absence by his wife, Hermione, and her father, Menelaus. They are about to kill her but are prevented by Peleus, Neoptolemus' grandfather, again suddenly rejuvenated. Orestes appears and, having persuaded Hermione to marry him, murders Neoptolemus. The play closes with an epiphany of the goddess Thetis, who gives orders for Neoptolemus' burial and prophesies immortality for Peleus. Hermione, Menelaus, and Orestes all represent Sparta in blackest terms. But though the chauvinism is jejune, Andromache is finely characterized and there is some good poetry in the play.

The HIPPOLYTUS has had more influence than any other drama of Euripides except, perhaps, the *Medea* and the *Iphigenia among the Taurians*. Phaedra, married to Theseus, is in love to the point of sickness with her stepson, Hippolytus, but tries to keep it to herself. Concerned for her, her old nurse plays the bawd and informs Hippolytus. He, characterized as a pure and celibate devotee of Artemis, bursts out in a violent denunciation of Phaedra and all women but decently promises that he will not tell Theseus, who is absent. In a mingling of shame and revenge, Phaedra hangs herself, but leaves a tablet for Theseus alleging that Hippolytus has raped her. On his return, Theseus reads the tablet and denounces Hippolytus, who denies the charge but keeps his promise not to tell the real truth. His father sends him into exile and prays to Poseidon to destroy him. As Hippolytus is driving his chariot along the shore, a great bull rises from the sea, and the terrified horses drag the young man to death. He is brought onstage still breathing, when Artemis appears ex machina and reveals the truth. Father and son are reconciled in one of the most moving finales in all drama, as Artemis slowly fades away before being polluted by the sight of death.

In point of sheer character-drawing the *Hippolytus* may be Euripides' greatest work. Hippolytus' almost priestly purity verges on sanctimonious prudery, but it is real, as is his courage and magnanimity. In the Prologue Aphrodite explains that because of his refusal of all sex she is going to destroy him, and psychologically minded critics have seen in the bull a symbol of suppressed sexual drives bursting out. There may be some truth in this, for Aphrodite works strictly through the characters and not by any direct interference. More likely, Euripides intended to show the destructiveness of all passion, whether for purity or for sex. Phaedra is even more complex. Despite the viciousness of her revenge, she wins great sympathy, and the interplay between the lyricism of her delirious desire and her efforts at controlled reasoning makes her the earliest example in Western drama of the conflict between honor and love. The poetry of the *Hippolytus* is matchless.

The HECUBA is really two tragedies with little to do with each other. The first is the tragedy of Hecuba's daughter, Polyxena, who was sacrificed after the fall of Troy on the tomb of Achilles. The other is the tragedy of Hecuba's son, Polydorus, who had been entrusted to King Polymestor of Thrace for safekeeping but was murdered by him. Hecuba blinds Polymestor and is then transformed into a mad dog. In its disunity of plot (as in its theme), the *Hecuba* anticipates *The Trojan Women*. It is simply an antiwar play, demonstrating how in war the innocent are either slain or transformed into beasts. The figure of the virgin martyr is a recurrent one in Euripides.

THE SUPPLIANT WOMEN, usually dated around 421, has now been placed with great probability in 424. It recounts the proud old legend of how the Athenians, led by Theseus, recovered the bodies of the "seven against Thebes," to whom the Thebans had refused burial, and how they interred the bodies at Eleusis. It is a strange play, in that it celebrates in its first half the gallantry of the Athenian action, while in the second half the mood turns somber and yields to an antiwar tone. No play of Euripides has occasioned more dispute and confusion than this one. Attempts have been made to connect it with the battle of Delium (423 B.C.), where the victorious Thebans refused burial to the Athenian dead, but the new date precludes that. Since the Argive king Adrastus, sole survivor of the seven, is made to swear an oath of alliance with Athens, it has been thought that some hope of an alliance with Argos was in the air. But that hope was always in the air, not to materialize until 420. Probably no specific event was involved. From the artistic point of view *The Suppliant Women* presents a rather extreme example of Euripides' contradictory way of seeing everything in two ways at once. Again there is a scene of martyrdom, as Evadne leaps into the pyre of her husband, but its dramatic point is not very clear. The drama remains one of Euripides' moving, but mysterious, creations.

The HERACLES probably belongs also to the late 420's. In it Euripides returns to the theme of irrational evil. Heracles returns from Hades just in time to rescue his family from the usurping tyrant Lycus, only to go suddenly mad and slay them all himself. On his recovery he contemplates suicide but is prevented by Theseus, who leads him to Athens to be purified of his crime.

This powerful play contains a foretaste of the *Bacchants*. In the first five hundred lines, before the arrival of Heracles, keen tension builds up as Lycus tries to force Amphitryon, Megara, and the children from their refuge at an altar. At the threat to burn them out, Megara persuades them to yield to a better death, which is about to be carried out, when Heracles comes and kills Lycus. As he leads the children into the house, there is terrible irony in his tender remarks about parental love. The goddess Lyssa ("Madness") enters in person, a rare kind of personification in Greek tragedy (Power and Violence in Aeschylus' *Prometheus Bound* being the nearest analogues); strangely enough, she declares her reluctance to afflict Heracles with insanity but says that she is forced to it by Hera. It is as if irrational evil were protesting against its own existence and attributing it to hostility in the very scheme of things represented by the gods; there are other remarks in the play about the cruelty and moral delinquency of the gods. The description of the massacre is particularly horrifying in its details. There is some abatement when Theseus, who, as always, represents Athens as the savior of the helpless, persuades Heracles to live, but the tragedy is only half resolved. The structure of the play is tight and firm and the ode celebrating the twelve labors of Heracles a masterly tour de force.

The ELECTRA differs remarkably from either of its predecessors. In it the heroine is married, in name only, to a peasant; she masochistically forces herself to menial tasks that she would gladly spare her. Orestes, anything but heroic, has to be needled and stung by his spiteful sister into joining the murder plot. When he does kill Aegisthus it is at a sacrifice, and he cleaves his spine from behind with a meat chopper. Clytemnestra is tricked into visiting Electra by the false news that she has had a son. The queen is characterized as aging, weary, and half-repentant, and certainly wins more sympathy than her daughter. She is murdered, whereupon Orestes and Electra burst out in hysterical remorse and lamentation. The Dioscuri appear, condemn the deed, but blame it on Apollo for directing Orestes to it; they command Electra to marry Pylades, and Orestes to go to Athens for trial and acquittal, as in Aeschylus' play. Whether Euripides' play preceded or followed Sophocles' is unknown, though the latter is more likely; in any case, it completely reverses Sophocles' version and seems to answer, even parody, it. Some critics have thought that Euripides, shocked at Sophocles' presentation of the avengers as heroic and guiltless, presented them as mean, spiteful neurotics whose nervous breakdown at the end is the natural consequence of their warped souls. As a study in criminal psychology, the *Electra* rivals the *Medea* but has little of its brilliance.

THE TROJAN WOMEN has essentially no plot. Written almost certainly in reaction to Athens' atrocious massacre of the Melians, it stands as the antiwar play of all time. Its scenes are a series of laments, as one Trojan princess after another is led away to a life of slavery. Hecuba, the image of shattered magnificence, dominates the play, bidding her daughters farewell with an unparalleled eloquence of sorrow. The eloquence turns to a different sort, however, when Helen is brought out to be handed over to Menelaus. Hecuba begs Menelaus to kill her, which is indeed his intention. Helen defends herself with arguments drawn from the Sophistic schools, and, as a trial-debate arises, Hecuba replies with similar ones. But it is clear by the end that Menelaus will do nothing to Helen, who has blunted his purpose by her sheer beauty. The whole scene forms a striking foil to the others, with their outpourings of grief. Perhaps the most moving one of all comes when Hector's little son, dashed to death from the walls of Troy, is buried by Hecuba in the hollow of his father's shield. The final scene is the burning of the city.

The IPHIGENIA AMONG THE TAURIANS is probably the first and certainly the most popular of three plays, including the *Ion* and the *Helen,* all written around the same time and variously termed "romances," "melodramas," or "tragicomedies." They come in striking contrast to everything Euripides had written before and reveal a poet concerned with noble, rather than destructive, passions, and with the idea of salvation. The *Iphigenia* presents an Orestes who, only partially absolved of his matricide, is still pursued by Furies. To obtain release from them, he must bring the sacred statue of Artemis from the land of the Taurians to Attica. Iphigenia, thought to have been sacrificed at Aulis but miraculously saved, is now priestess at the Taurian shrine and herself in charge of sacrificing all Greeks to the goddess. She is about to sacrifice her brother, but they recognize each other in a scene whose skill Aristotle justly admired, and they escape with the statue by means of an elaborate intrigue. Their pursuit by the Taurian king is stopped by Athena ex machina.

The theme of self-sacrifice is strong throughout, and the speech of Orestes explaining why he, not Pylades, should die at the altar exhibits a magnanimity that is rare in Euripides' male characters, though often present in the female. The characters have little depth but are firmly drawn, and some of Iphigenia's speeches convey a direct, vocal tone somewhat foreign to the formal rhetoric of tragedy. The lyrics, sung by the Chorus of captive Greek women, are particularly splendid, with their sea imagery and poignant expression of the longing for Greece.

The HELEN has a plot so similar to that of the *Iphigenia* that it has been thought a parody of it. The story that Paris abducted only a phantom Helen, while the real one was transported to Egypt, was known in various forms to older poets, and Herodotus has a variant on it. Throughout the ten years of the Trojan War and for eight more after it Helen has been in Egypt, under great pressure from King Theoclymenus to marry him. Like the king of the Taurians, he too kills Greeks. Menelaus, who at the fall of Troy had recovered the phantom and has been wandering all over the sea with it, finally arrives shipwrecked. Husband and wife recognize each other and plan their escape. By some ingenious chicanery they induce Theoclymenus to lend them a ship, and

they return to Greece. Pursuit is stopped by the Dioscuri. The most interesting part of the play is the scene with the king's sister, Theonoe, who has prophetic and clairvoyant powers. She is always able to tell her brother when a Greek lands in Egypt, and the problem is to win her over and persuade her not to report Menelaus' presence. The theme of self-sacrifice appears as, at risk of her own life, she agrees to keep silent, but she too is saved by the Dioscuri.

The *Helen* has been labeled everything from deeply moving drama to farce; certainly its tone is uneven, and the character of the blustering, helpless Menelaus verges sharply toward the comic. But Helen's laments, the solemn other-worldliness of Theonoe, and above all the constantly recurrent motifs of truth and seeming, reality and mere name, point to a serious intention on the poet's part, however lightly he chose to handle it.

The ION is by far the most subtle of the three "romances." The Athenian queen Creusa had been violated as a girl by Apollo and bore in secret a son whom she exposed and thinks dead. Years later, married to Xuthus but childless by him, she comes with her husband to Delphi to consult the oracle about the possibility of offspring and there meets Ion, her son, who had been rescued by Apollo and brought up as a temple servant. The oracle tells Xuthus that the first person he meets as he leaves the temple will be his son, presumably by some illicit affair, and this turns out to be Ion. Creusa, in fury that Xuthus and not she should have a child, tries to poison Ion, but the plot is discovered, and Creusa, condemned to death, takes refuge at Apollo's altar. Ion, on the verge of dragging her from it, is stopped by the Delphic priestess who reared him and is given the cradle in which she found him, together with tokens whereby he may find out who his parents are. The recognition follows, but Ion, still dubious as to whether he is really Apollo's son or not, starts to question the oracle. Athena appears, explains all, and prophesies Ion's future greatness as the founder of the Ionian people. Xuthus, though he will have legitimate children by Creusa, is never to learn the truth about Ion.

The *Ion* is often deemed an attack on Apollo and the gods in general, but such a view is hardly consistent with the ending, when Creusa, bitter enough against the god formerly, accepts and praises him in her joy at recovering her son. Rather it is a drama of the quest for identity, not only for Ion but also for Creusa, who in some ways is Euripides' greatest female character. The slim thread of hope that had sustained her through years of secret agony is at last fulfilled, and she finds herself a whole woman. Ion is awakened from his charming but callow innocence into self-knowledgeable manhood. Throughout, the delicate irony constantly points to the latent, long-withheld truth, which, when it finally emerges, brings with it a kind of real purity for the two principal characters. Indeed, purity, its violation and inviolability, might be said to be the main theme. Though there are touches of the comic, especially in Xuthus, the *Ion* is tensely tragic in tone, and there are few scenes to equal the recognition, in which Creusa, held captive by Ion's followers, names the tokens in the cradle without seeing them and convinces her would-be murderer that he is her son.

THE PHOENICIAN WOMEN resumes the theme of the

A SCENE FROM EURIPIDES' *Ion* (ITALIAN STATE TOURIST OFFICE)

horror of war, this time making use of the legend of the seven against Thebes. Polyneices, with his army at the gates, enters Thebes under truce to parley with his brother, Eteocles. Jocasta does her best to reconcile her sons, but Eteocles will hear of no compromise. In the battle that follows they kill each other and Jocasta slays herself. Meanwhile, Menoecius, son of Creon, immolates himself as a result of a prophecy that only thus can Thebes defeat the Argives. Creon assumes the throne, refuses burial to Polyneices, and sends the aged Oedipus, together with Antigone, into exile.

The Phoenician Women was admired in antiquity for its striking spectacle and many fine sentiments, but certain parts of it even then were thought spurious, and the ending, as we have it, is full of inconsistencies that no scholar has been able to unravel. As in the case of certain other plays in which theatricalism is paramount, the probability of actors' tamperings is high. Though there are some powerful scenes, the play has too much in it and lacks dramatic unity.

The ORESTES is marred by similar theatrical excesses but is better unified. The theme is madness, and the treatment of character recalls Euripides'

early studies of gross and irrational passions. Shortly after the murder of Clytemnestra, Orestes, now maddened by the Furies, has been condemned to death by the Argives and is confined in the palace with Electra. Later he is joined by his friend Pylades, who is determined to share his fate. Their only hope is that Menelaus, who is on his way to Argos with Helen and their daughter, Hermione, will be able to reverse the judgment. Menelaus promises to try but in effect does not, nor is he much concerned. Orestes' madness now seems to spread to Electra and Pylades, and the three contrive to force Menelaus to save them by killing Helen and keeping Hermione hostage; if he does not capitulate, they will kill Hermione and burn the palace. Orestes attempts to kill Helen, but she is miraculously taken up into heaven. Hermione, however, is trapped, and presently Orestes appears with her on the roof, holding a dagger to her throat, as Menelaus enters. The bargaining is inconclusive, Orestes calls for fire, and Menelaus tries to beat in the doors. Apollo appears, explains Helen's apotheosis, orders marriages between Orestes and Hermione, Pylades and Electra, and enjoins upon all the worship of the goddess Peace.

Euripides' purpose in this medley is at best obscure. All the characters, except Hermione, are, or become, repellent. Yet Helen is deified, and the others are changed, "in the twinkling of an eye," by Apollo. As a study of infectious insanity the *Orestes* has some truth, but the dramaturgy lacks control and the melodrama goes too far.

The BACCHANTS is generally considered Euripides' greatest work. The last year or so of his life was spent at the court of King Archelaus, and the poet may have been influenced by the wild Dionysiac rituals that prevailed in northern Greece; at any rate he found in them the supreme expression of both the lyrical vitality and the irrationality of life that he had always felt.

Dionysus arrives at Thebes leading a troupe of bacchant women. His mother's sisters have denied that he was born of Zeus, and he has driven them and all the other Theban women in Bacchic frenzy to go out on the mountain slopes clad in fawnskins and carrying thyrsi. Even old Cadmus and Teiresias join the cult, but young King Pentheus, son of Agave, violently rejects it and orders the women arrested. He puts Dionysus, whom he takes to be merely the cult leader, in a dungeon, but the god walks free and the whole palace is shaken to the ground. Pentheus is still unconvinced, but, hearing by report how the maenads on the mountains are performing miraculous deeds, he conceives a desire to see them himself. Here follows an eerie scene in which Pentheus is brought hypnotically under Dionysus' spell and, in spite of himself, becomes a maenad. Dressed as a woman, he is led by Dionysus to where his mother, Agave, and the others are. He climbs a tree to spy on them but is discovered and torn to pieces. Agave enters carrying his head, under the delusion that it is a lion's. When Agave recovers her senses, Dionysus appears in his divine shape and in cold, relentless words declares his divinity and orders Agave and Cadmus into exile.

The *Bacchants* is a singularly forceful and terrifying expression of the ambiguity of the Dionysiac religion, with its mystical transports, miraculous accesses of strength and fertility, life-giving force, and death-dealing madness. Dionysus is, in a, way, life itself. In at least one of his aspects he is a god who dies and is resurrected, hence a type of the life-death cycle in nature, and the *sparagmos,* or "rending," of Pentheus clearly echoes the death-by-rending of Dionysus in that aspect. The puritanical young king would suppress the cult as immoral, but the cult is the cult of nature itself; it is amoral, and Pentheus is part of it willy-nilly. The end is violent enough, but if the maenads can rend Pentheus (as well as herds of cattle), they can also suckle fawns, draw milk from the earth and honey from their thyrsi, and gird their fawnskins with live serpents. All the power of nature itself runs through them like an electric current and discharges itself in lyric after lyric rhapsodically praising "the noisy god," the liberator of body and spirit, whose way ultimately transcends all the words of the wise and restraints of the prudent, being in itself the true prudence.

The IPHIGENIA AT AULIS seems to have been left unfinished when Euripides died and was produced by his son along with the *Bacchants.* There are two prologues, one a regular monologue in iambics, the other a dialogue in lyric anapests. Though both may be by Euripides, they do not fit very well together, and it is not clear which was to come first. The end of the play is manifestly a forgery, probably quite a late one, and there seem to be numerous actors' interpolations throughout. The plot tells how Iphigenia is lured to Aulis by Agamemnon on the pretext of marrying her to Achilles but in reality to sacrifice her to Artemis, who in anger is keeping the Greek fleet wind-bound. There are many sudden changes of mind. For example, Agamemnon, forced to concur in the slaughter, tries secretly to warn Clytemnestra not to bring Iphigenia, but Menelaus intercepts the letter. He bitterly rebukes Agamemnon but then suddenly softens and bids him save the girl. Achilles, who had known nothing of the plot, is furious and ready to fight the whole Greek army in Iphigenia's defense but presently gives up in a curiously unheroic way. Iphigenia herself begs pathetically for her life but suddenly decides that she will be a willing martyr for the sake of Greece. It is probable, but not certain, that she was saved by Artemis, who substituted a deer on the altar. In tone, diction, and prosody, the second *Iphigenia* has strong affinities with comedy. Agamemnon and Menelaus quarrel in a very everyday, household manner. Achilles is a paper hero, and the scene between him and Clytemnestra is distinctly funny. Iphigenia is appealing throughout, but the sudden wave of patriotism that overcomes her fear of death seems less in keeping with character than with the other self-reversals that occur in the play. Given the text as we have it, it is hard to know what Euripides intended, but it is likely that he was writing tongue in cheek.

The RHESUS, of unknown date, dramatizes the tenth book of the *Iliad,* in which Diomedes and Odysseus, on a night raid, capture and kill the Trojan spy Dolon and then murder the Thracian king Rhesus, an ally of Troy, in his sleep. Even in antiquity it was doubted that this play was genuine Euripides, though a *Rhesus* was listed under his name. Modern critics are divided on the question. It is a well-constructed drama and moves more rapidly than most of Euripides' plays, but it is strangely lacking in depth, either of character or of total meaning. The language is certainly that of Euripides, as are some tricks of style and rhythm, and the lack of elevation and sparkle could be paralleled in other, lesser plays. On balance, it seems better to consider it genuine, though it is possible that it is an early effort of the poet's son, Euripides the younger, written under his father's strong influence.

Euripides, though popular with the younger intellectual groups, was not very successful during his life; he took only four prizes. After his death his reputation became enormous and far overshadowed that of his two rivals. His plays were translated and imitated by the early Roman tragedians, and the number of his surviving fragments, whether by quotation or on papyrus, is much greater than any other tragedian's. He had great importance for the development of comedy too. Certain of his plays, especially the three romances, are clear forerunners of New Comedy, in that they, like it, are built around a long-lost person, an intrigue, and the idea of Fortune almost personified into a goddess, as indeed she was soon to be in Hellenistic times. His interest in etiology also foreshadows that of the Hellenistic writers; many of his plays go out of their way to explain the origin of a cult or custom, or even a name. In this respect he recalls Aeschylus, for whom such origins formed part of the structure of his world; but for Euripides it is more a matter of decorative detail. He has been criticized for the stiffness of his "playbill" prologues, which are usually rather detached from the plays, and for the excessive use of the deus ex machina. Yet these devices do not arise from poverty of invention; they frame the play between past and future, the prologue regularly narrating antecedent action and the god prophesying what is to come. Such a consciousness of past and future events contrasts strongly with Sophocles, whose significant action all takes place within the play. But again, it recalls Aeschylus' exploitation of long periods of time, and the tripartite division of prologue-play-epilogue faintly suggests the trilogy.

As to Euripides' feelings about Athens, it is hard to generalize, though there is a tradition that he left it in his old age out of despair at his unpopularity. He wrote splendid passages in the city's praise and some equally critical ones. But that is perhaps only symptomatic of a mind so given to ambivalence about everything. Euripides always seems to see things in two ways at once, and this double perspective lies at the base of his apparent inconsistencies, self-reversals, even perversities. But it is the token of his art in all its penetration and variety.

The origins of Greek comedy are as obscure as those of tragedy. The name, derived from *kōmos* ("revel"), points to certain fertility rites in which bands of revelers, costumed as animals, marched or danced in procession hurling taunts and obscenities at each other and at those they met. But many other elements, both popular and literary, went into the making of Old Comedy as we know it. The Greeks attributed its creation to a certain Chionides, who won the prize at the first official contest at Athens in 486, or to Magnes, who won in 472 and a number of other times. But these are mere names, as is Susarion, another early comic writer. Moreover, it is not entirely clear to what extent Attic comedy was affected by certain Dorian forms, such as the Megarian farce,

the *phlyakes* (or tragic burlesque, of south Italy), or the Sicilian mime.

The first fully identifiable figure in the history of comedy is Epicharmus, whose long life probably extended from the middle of the sixth to well into the fifth century B.C. Born in Cos, he lived in Syracuse and wrote travesties of myths as well as the more famous comedies of manners, whose stock characters —cook, braggart, courtesan, and so forth—became the dramatic stereotypes of New Comedy. No complete play survives, but the many quotations indicate an art that was more philosophic than hilarious. Indeed, Epicharmus' works were called dramas, not comedies, and his interest in philosophy may have extended to his having written seriously on the subject. But there is abundant wit also and pithy aphorisms for which he was much admired in antiquity. His plays seem ordinarily to have had no chorus, but certain of the thirty-seven titles that have come down to us, as, for example, the *Choreutai* (*Dancers*), suggest that some, at least, did. Epicharmus was held in high esteem by Plato, whose own art, with its mingling of philosophy and humor, may owe something to the great master of Sicilian comedy.

Attic Old Comedy is a wholly different form, strictly the product of, and coexistent with, the political and intellectual vitality of Athenian fifth-century democracy. Aristotle's statement that it originated in phallic songs is doubtless true, but by the mid-fifth century it had become an unparalleled farrago of fantasy, parody, lyricism, obscenity, satire, and pure nonsense. It had also achieved an exterior form almost as strict as that of tragedy. The prologue, often quite elaborate, outlines the situation or dilemma to be solved and proposes, by way of solution, a fantasy whose logic lies in its absurd illogic. The chorus then enter, sometimes in support of the scheme, but more often in opposition to it. The choristers are often, but not always, costumed as animals. After their parodos the all-important *agōn* ("contest") begins, in which the hero overcomes all opposition by whatever means. The action is now interrupted by the *parabasis* ("stepping forward"), in which the chorus, partially abandoning their dramatic role, step forward and address the audience in the name of the poet. When complete, a parabasis has seven parts, two being lyrical, the rest spoken lines comprising everything from the airiest whimsy to sharp personal invective or a direct bid for the prize. The action is resumed in a series of short scenes, separated by choral songs, as the hero's scheme works itself out, each triumph being greater and more absurd than the last. Sometimes there is a second, shorter parabasis. The finale is regularly a celebratory feast, often a marriage feast, though the marriage is more certain to be consummated than consecrated. Such is the form as we know it from Aristophanes, his *Birds* being the perfect example, though he often varied the form, especially in his later plays. Costumes were grotesquely padded, and the male characters wore the large leather phallus, though whether the choristers ever did is uncertain.

Cratinus (c. 484–c. 419) was the senior member of the Old Comic triad formulated by Hellenistic scholars, Eupolis and Aristophanes being the other two. His dates are very uncertain, but it is clear that he was old and in retirement when Aristophanes was first exhibiting (*Knights*, 531 f.). The latter's remark (*Peace*, 700 f.) that Cratinus was dead by 422 is almost certainly not to be taken seriously, but he could not have lived much after that. Only fragments survive, but in sufficient numbers to show that his style was grand and torrential, his invective unsparing. We know the titles of twenty-eight plays on a wide range of subjects, including mythological travesty and literary and especially political satire. His favorite target was Pericles and, with him, Aspasia, whom he attacked repeatedly, especially in the *Nemesis*, the *Chirones* ("The Wise Centaurs"), and the *Dionysalexandros* (430 B.C.).

Like all Old Comic poets, Cratinus took the conservative view in social and political matters and praised the golden past, a practice that was probably simply a convention of the form. In the *Knights* Aristophanes taunted him with decrepitude and drunkenness, describing him as a lyre with its pegs fallen out and strings all slack. The old man was roused and in 423 he produced the *Pytine* (*The Wine Flask*), in which he staged himself as an old rake who had deserted his true wife, Comedy, for a harlot named Methe ("Inebriety"). In a speech of defense he claims that the juice of Dionysus is the true source of good comedy, and that teetotalers are worthless writers. His play defeated Aristophanes' *Clouds*. It is the only known comedy in which the main figure is explicitly the poet himself. Cratinus is sometimes thought to be the inventor of the Old Comic form and the first to introduce political, in contrast to personal, satire. Though sometimes criticized for poor structure, his plays enjoyed a great reputation among the ancient critics, especially for creativity and obscenity, in which latter, as one late writer tells us, he far exceeded Aristophanes.

Eupolis (c. 445–410 B.C.), the principal rival of Aristophanes, may also have been his collaborator for a time in his early years, but to what extent, if at all, is not known. Ancient sources give the number of his plays variously as fourteen or seventeen, most of whose titles are known. Nothing is known of his life, for there is no support for the one anecdote about him, that Alcibiades drowned him in the sea for having attacked him in the *Baptai* (*The Bathers*, c. 416 B.C.?). The fragments suggest that he dealt less in fantasy than did either of his rivals and concentrated more on personal, social, and political invective. Besides Alcibiades, he attacked the demagogue Hyperbolus (the *Maricas*, "The Catamite," 421 B.C.), pederasty (the *Philoi*, "The Friends"), profligacy (the *Kolakes*, *The Flatterers*, 421 B.C.), evasion of military service (the *Astrateutoi*, *The Slackers*), and Athenian imperialism in general (the *Poleis*, *The Cities*, 422 B.C.?). One play, the *Demoi* ("Villages," 415 B.C.), of which considerable papyrus fragments have been found, can be reconstructed with a degree of certainty. Various great Athenians of the past rise from the dead and restore the city to moral and political dignity. Beyond this, little is known of the work of Eupolis except that he was admired for his polished wit and satirical dexterity. He is said to have won the prize seven times.

ARISTOPHANES, son of Philippus, wrote forty-four comedies, of which four were condemned as spurious by the ancient critics. The eleven that are extant present a fair picture of the range and development of his extraordinary art. His themes are those of Old Comedy in general: politics, war, education, and literature. The principal victims of his satire are the demagogue Cleon, Euripides, and Socrates. It is a mistake, however, to regard satire as the essence of Aristophanes' comedy; the essence lies in the fantasy by which the hero, distracted by some social or political evil, sets about a cure. The fantasy as a rule stands the world on its head, and within its limitless contours all the frustrated drives of humanity, especially those for food, sex, and physical comfort, are satisfied. To what extent Aristophanes was really the serious reformer that he often gaily claims to be has been much disputed, but it seems likely that his structures of magnificent nonsense, with their lyrical abandon and highhearted dismissal of all moral barriers, were built more for their own sake than for any ulterior purpose of improvement. His politics are similarly in doubt, so that he has been labeled everything from an extreme democrat to an extreme oligarch. But Old Comedy was by convention conservative, always deriding the new in favor of the old; yet it could breathe only the air of the democracy, which permitted such indispensable features as complete freedom of speech and utter licentiousness. It was bound to no political commitment, least of all to any kind of consistency, and though Aristophanes' hatred of Cleon seems to have been real enough, it has more of a personal than a civic ring. Rather the goal, especially in the early plays, seems to be the redemption of the individual in a world that, under the pressures of war and empire, was growing steadily more alien.

Like the tragic poets, Aristophanes saw the erosion of human values in late fifth-century Athens, but the comic answer was to take the lost, helpless individual and set him, by fantasy, trickery, and miracle, in triumph over everything. This transformation of the world comes about through a kind of acting out of metaphor and a brilliant manipulation of language. For though the diction of Old Comedy is that of daily speech, the style is abundantly figured and, despite ever-present obscenities, the Roman rhetorician Quintilian could describe it as "grand, elegant, and charming." In the later plays the key is lower pitched, as Old Comedy yielded to New.

Aristophanes began his career at an early age with the *Daitales* (*Banqueters*, 427), a play on the old and new forms of education, and *Babylonioi* (*Babylonians*, 426), an attack on Cleon, who arraigned the young poet before the Council but seems not to have obtained a conviction. For reasons that are not clear, Aristophanes produced these plays under someone else's name, a practice that he continued occasionally throughout his life.

The ACHARNIANS is the earliest play extant. Its hero, Dicaeopolis, unable to persuade the Assembly to make peace with Sparta, makes a private treaty for himself and his family. It is easily done, for in Greek the words for "truce" and "libation" are the same, and Dicaeopolis, equipped with a jar of thirty-year-old "peace," proceeds to celebrate the Rural Dionysia and set up an open market for trade with all the states with which Athens is at war. But he is attacked by the Chorus of charcoal burners from Acharnae, a village in Attica that had suffered severely at the hands of the invading Spartans. His speech of defense is a parodic montage of a speech in the lost *Telephus* of Euripides, and to deliver it effectively he goes to Euripides' house and borrows some tragic rags for costume. The rags also represent Sophistic rhetoric, by the tricky force of which Dicaeopolis overcomes not only the Chorus but also General Lamachus, a real person here rather unfairly represented as a braggart and warmonger. The open market now runs smoothly, with Dicaeopolis profiteering with shameless skill and obtaining contraband commodities in great quantities. At the end he wins a drinking match and goes off to a feast with two harlots, while Lamachus, who has fallen into a ditch while on guard duty, laments and groans.

One of the most complex, witty, and beautiful of the comedies, the *Acharnians* is sometimes read too seriously as a document. Though the wish for peace is genuine, the political comments are too absurd and inconsistent to frame any doctrine. Rather the power of the play lies in its poetry, in the caricature of Euripides, in such scenes as that in which an informer is crated up for delivery in Boeotia upside-down, and above all in the hero himself and the unscrupulous ingenuity with which he transcends reality.

The KNIGHTS is an exceptionally savage attack on Cleon, who is represented as a Paphlagonian slave of Demos ("the people"), very skillful at flattering his master and getting his two fellow slaves into trouble. The other two learn from an oracle that the Paphlagonian can be overcome only by someone viler than he, and this turns out to be a vulgar sausage seller. The Chorus of young aristocrats of the cavalry, called Knights, abet the sausage seller's efforts to outdo the Paphlagonian in bribing, gorging, and flattering Demos. In the end, the sausage seller wins and, suddenly turned miracle-worker, restores the doddering Demos to the youthful prime of Marathon days.

Eupolis claimed to have helped Aristophanes in writing this play, which has similarities to Eupolis' *Demoi.* Certainly the extreme bitterness and close political focus are rare for Aristophanes, who usually wrote with a lighter touch, so that one may fairly infer Eupolidean influence at least. Like the *Acharnians,* the *Knights* won first prize. Cleon made no attempt at reprisal, nor was his popularity damaged, for he was elected general the next year.

The CLOUDS dramatizes the efforts of Strepsiades, a peasant, to extricate himself from debts incurred by his son Pheidippides, who takes after his aristocratic mother and keeps race horses. The father goes to Socrates' school to learn the "unjust logic," namely the Sophistic kind of rhetoric by which one could win any case or argument, however lame. But Strepsiades has no talent and he persuades his son to go. Pheidippides has great aptitude, but instead of talking his way out of debt, he beats up his father and then proceeds to prove, by the unjust logic, that he was right to do so. Strepsiades burns down the school.

Though one of the most famous of all satires on pseudo intellectualism, the *Clouds* presents serious problems. The wholesale misrepresentation of Socrates as a professor of the new education has been found hard to explain. The Chorus of cloud nymphs, a complex symbol representing the atheism, materialism, specious rhetoric, and airy nonsense that the poet attributes to Sophistic teaching, change character toward the end and become a group of moralizing goddesses of retribution. The hero repents his folly instead of triumphing in it, and the ending is the precise opposite of the usual celebration. The answer to these anomalies probably lies in the fact that the extant version of the play is a revision of an earlier one, which failed badly in 423. Aristophanes was greatly chagrined and set about rewriting it but gave up before finishing, so that the text as it stands cannot represent his final intention.

The WASPS similarly treats an educational theme and the difference between the old and new generations. Old Philocleon ("Cleon-lover") is passionately addicted to jury duty at three obols a day and has never acquitted anyone. His son, Bdelycleon ("Cleon-hater"), tries to keep him at home, but with no success until, in a long debate, he convinces him that a juryman is not an all-powerful magistrate and that he and his fellow jurors (costumed as wasps) are the dupes of Cleon's regime. Philocleon, convinced but unable to forego litigation, sets up a court at home and tries the watchdog for stealing cheese. Having been tricked into an acquittal, he feels that his career is ruined and allows his son to introduce him into high society at a banquet. But he gets drunk, insults everybody, steals the flute girl, and makes off with her homeward, punching people all the way. It is clear that he will be back in court next morning, but in a different role.

Like the *Clouds,* the *Wasps* treats the conflict between law and human nature and the incorrigibility of the latter. Philocleon is one of Aristophanes' greatest creations, a symbol of Athenian love of litigation, but also of the indomitable spirit of the old men who fought at Marathon. The theme of rejuvenation, frequent in Old Comedy, is well illustrated in Philocleon, who seems to grow younger scene by scene, until at last he assures the flute girl that he will marry her as soon as he becomes of age and can be released from his son's guardianship. Subtle images of circularity throughout the text reflect the vicious circle of the plot, while certain scenes, especially the trial of the dog, stand out unforgettably and make the *Wasps* the most hilarious of the comedies.

The PEACE was written, perhaps rather hurriedly, in celebration of the Peace of Nicias, which ended the first phase of the Peloponnesian War. Trygaeus, a farmer, flies to heaven on a giant beetle to demand the restoration of the goddess Peace to the earth. He finds that she has been buried in a deep pit, but with the help of the Chorus of farmers, he hauls her up with a block and tackle, together with her two attendants representing Harvest and Sacred Embassies. He walks back down through the air with the two attendants, one of whom he presents to the Council, while he marries the other (Harvest). The play ends with a feast. A rather slight work, the *Peace* nonetheless has great poetic charm, vivid in its imagery as in the joyful sweep of its total rhythm. It is also laced with passages of indescribably ingenious ribaldry, appropriate to a fertility rite upon the release from war.

The BIRDS is generally accounted Aristophanes'

masterpiece, though there is little agreement as to what it is about. Disgusted with Athens, Peithetaerus ("Persuasive") and Euelpides ("Hopeful") go in quest of a better city and seek the advice of Tereus, formerly king of Athens, but now transformed into a Hoopoe. He is of little help, but Peithetaerus has the idea of organizing the birds and building a city in the air, which will cut off the sacrificial smoke from the gods and starve them into submission. Convinced by Peithetaerus that they are the oldest and only true gods, the birds set to work. The city is built, the gods capitulate, and the now-winged Peithetaerus finds himself master of no less than the universe, with Basileia ("Princess," or "Empire") for a wife.

Every kind of allegorical interpretation has been put upon this supreme fantasy. But the *Birds,* unlike all the earlier plays, is laid outside of Athens, which implies a different, less intimate perspective. Insofar as there is satire, Athens as a whole is satirized, and the play owes much of its power to its wistful irony: in order to escape the misery of living in an imperial city, the hero builds a city so imperial as to depose the gods themselves. Thucydides attributes to Pericles a remark to the effect that once one has an empire one must retain it, even if unwillingly, and the *Birds* seems to reflect such a necessity. At the same time it presents Aristophanes' boldest extension of the dream of individual autonomy. Of all comic heroes, Peithetaerus is the most quick, unscrupling, and eloquent rogue, and he grows only more confident and masterful as his dizzying achievements multiply in his conquest of the boundless. But it is all done with words, the pure lubricity of speech. Metaphor, pun, folk saying all become the facts of Peithetaerus' Cloudcuckooland, and every problem is overcome by a deft twist of language that would put the wiliest Sophist to shame. Words are the structure of a new transcendent reality, which, however, is only the old reality, for Basileia has all the attributes of Athena, including thunderbolts, and of Athens, such as navy yards and finance commissioners. For sheer comic poetry, the *Birds* is unequaled, though it also contains passages of simply lyrical import. Personal satire and obscenity are scarce, nonsense and wordplay rampant; but throughout this beautiful text runs a strain of melancholy, which was to culminate in the *Frogs.* The poet seemed to be realizing for the first time that Athens was destroying herself.

The LYSISTRATA was produced during the short-lived oligarchic revolution that followed the Sicilian disaster, and doubtless for that reason it markedly avoids overt political allusion. The theme is peace, and in order to attain it Lysistrata persuades the women of Greece to refuse intercourse with their husbands until they end the war. The original plan was for them to parade before the men, beautifully adorned but unattainable, but it is carried out only in the scene in which Myrrhine performs a striptease in front of her husband and then runs away. The women's main action is to seize the Acropolis, whence the men try to drive them with fire and threats. But the women hold out despite the difficulties they themselves are having with their own desires, and the men are forced to negotiate. Lysistrata presents them with *Diallagé* ("Reconciliation"), probably in the form of a naked woman, and they surrender. The play ends with alternate choruses of Athenians and Spartans singing hymns of joy, as the men recover their wives.

The extreme and explicit treatment of the theme of sex, for which the *Lysistrata* is famous, should not obscure the fact that it is a play about marriage; images of domesticity, such as babies and wool baskets, abound. Moreover, though everywhere bawdry meets the ear, as priapism meets the eye, the poetry is wrought with peculiar delicacy and care, so that it seems a misnomer to call the *Lysistrata* obscene. Its charm is too winning and its heroine, a

A SCENE FROM ARISTOPHANES' *Lysistrata* (GREEK NATIONAL TOURIST OFFICE)

finely drawn character, too high-minded and well-purposed for such a dismissal. The fundamental absurdity is in Aristophanes' best self-contradictory manner: What is the meaning of denying sex to men who, as the complaint is, are always away fighting anyway? But as usual, the absurdity works, and the mingling of gaiety and seriousness, of rabid sex and the vision of peace-love-home, makes this one of the most beautiful of the plays.

The THESMOPHORIAZUSAE is a full-length satire on Euripides, based on his supposed misogyny. It is learned that the women are planning to condemn him to death at the Thesmophoria, a feast of Demeter from which men are strictly excluded. After failing to persuade the effeminate tragic poet Agathon to disguise himself and go to speak in his defense, Euripides disguises his kinsman Mnesilochus instead. Mnesilochus' defense consists of enumerating all the female misdeeds that Euripides has failed to mention. He is exposed, arrested, and tied to a post under guard, and the rest of the play is devoted to Euripides' efforts, barely successful finally, to release him. Euripides' method is revealing: He acts out scenes from his own plays, with Mnesilochus picking up the cues, in the hope that the Scythian guard will believe that they really are the characters whom they are acting. After a series of these fine but ineffectual travesties, Euripides gives up and distracts the guard's attention with a dancing girl while he and Mnesilochus escape. The point seems to be that Euripidean tragedy lacks the power to convince, but the play is all so lighthearted that it might be considered simply parody for its own sake. It has been plausibly observed that Euripides must have felt highly complimented by such a meticulous and extended concern with his work.

The FROGS is Aristophanes' last real Old Comedy, written on the eve of Athens' collapse. Since both Sophocles and Euripides had died in the preceding year, Dionysus, god of the theater, sets out for Hades to bring Euripides back, lest drama die. Disguised, or partly so, as Heracles, of whom he asks directions, he descends, meets Charon, and rows across the Styx to the singing of frogs. These frogs, though the play is named for them, are not the main Chorus, which consist of spirits of the initiates into the Eleusinian Mysteries. After some buffoonery, a great noise is heard: Aeschylus and Euripides are fighting over the throne of tragedy; Sophocles is too gentlemanly to compete. They agree to a contest, with Dionysus as judge, the winner to be brought back to life. The long competition has five parts, in which the tragedians criticize each other's moral outlooks as poets, their prologues, lyrics, the "weightiness" of their individual verses, and their practical value as advisers to the city. Though Euripides delivers some good thrusts, he is doomed to be defeated from the first, and the heroic Aeschylus is escorted back to Athens, over the solemn roll of dactylic hexameters, to revive the golden age.

The real gravity of the *Frogs* is only partly concealed by the comic surface. The death of the two younger tragedians really did mean the death of tragedy, without which Old Comedy too could not live. But tragedy, as Athens' chief cultural expression in the fifth century, here stands for Athenian culture itself, the very spirit of the city, which, as everyone knew, was about to fall. Aeschylus is recalled to save not only tragedy but Athens, as is explicitly stated (line 1501). The Chorus of initiates too lend solemnity, for despite the decline of religion the Athenians continued to regard the Mysteries with great awe. The great contest itself is a unique mixture of quite serious moral questioning, half-serious literary criticism, and inspired parody. The details are numerous and complicated, but the mere mention, toward the end, of the name of Alcibiades, who had materially helped to bring his city to her knees, could not have raised any very comic emotions. When Aeschylus is chosen, Euripides protests, but Dionysus retorts with a couple of Euripides' own lines, one of which, "Who knows if life be death and death be life?" aptly points the ambiguity about both which was first expressed when the initiates called the living "the upper dead." The *Frogs* is a comedy, but it is even more a lament, a kind of comic tragedy. It received first prize and the unique honor of a second performance.

The ECCLESIAZUSAE is less of an Old Comedy than a forerunner of the intermediate forms of the early and middle fourth century. Praxagora ("Assembly-maker") and her friends, in garments borrowed from their sleeping husbands, go to the Assembly and vote themselves into power. They set up a bizarre form of communistic government, in parody of the theories of communism that were current in the schools of philosophy, later to appear in Plato's *Republic*. Plato was to propose community of females; Praxagora establishes community of males, with a special provision that a man may enjoy a young woman only after he has gratified any old woman who wants him. This law leads to the play's funniest scene, in which a young man attempts to visit a young harlot but is nearly torn in pieces by three old hags. The finale is the usual feast. Poorly constructed and heavily loaded with coarse obscenity, the *Ecclesiazusae* lacks either movement or climax, except, perhaps, for the seventy-two-syllable word for "hash" with which it closes.

The PLUTUS is not an Old Comedy at all, but an early example of Middle Comedy. A good man, Chremylus, meets the blind god of wealth, Plutus, and restores his eyesight so that he may give his benefits to those who deserve them, instead of at random. He is opposed by Penia ("Poverty") in a lively debate, but he triumphs. Wealth is now distributed justly, and in order to get it everyone becomes good, with the result that the gods themselves are forced to surrender to Plutus, now supreme deity, and join in the feast at which he presides.

The *Plutus* is a moral allegory, for the most part lacking in Aristophanes' boisterousness and totally lacking in lyricism; indeed, the Chorus, which had played only a small role in the *Ecclesiazusae,* have all but disappeared. But there is no lack of wit and humor of the less riotous kind, which was to become the characteristic tone of later comedy.

It has been observed by the critic Gilbert Murray that the warhorse, Old Comedy, died under Aristophanes and that he was forced to adapt himself. Literary history has recognized him as one of the creators of later comedy, as well as the master of the old. But his heart lay in the fifth century, in the furious outpouring of energy that Athens, even in the midst of her political decline, was able to produce and inspire. Aristophanes may be admired for, but not identified with, the two last extant plays and two lost ones, which distinctly foreshadow New Comedy. But he left no heir to the shameless cheer and exuberant poetry of the Old Comic form, which died with the fall of Athens. Of his life we know nothing except that he raised a family, probably had an estate in Aegina, and certainly was bald. We may be sure that he hated Cleon, on whose grave he danced with uproariously godless joy, but the satiric parodies of Euripides indicate affection and spiritual affinity rather than, as is often naïvely assumed, real disapproval. As for Socrates, whose judicial murder in 401 B.C. is sometimes laid at Aristophanes' door because of his portrayal of Socrates in the *Clouds* twenty-two years earlier, we have finer evidence in the *Symposium* of Plato, in which Socrates' greatest pupil represents the comedian and the philosopher as intimate friends. Plato could scarcely have done this had there been any connection between the *Clouds* and the tragedy of 401. Nor could Plato's epitaph of Aristophanes, whether or not genuine, ever have been even attributed to him, had there been enmity:

> The Graces, seeking an appropriate shrine,
> Found it in the soul of Aristophanes.

Grace, the grace of imagination and the grace of language, was the soul of Aristophanes, as Plato was almost the last in antiquity to see.

Late ancient critics recognized a transitional phase between Old and New Comedy. Though the names of some fifty poets of the so-called Middle Comedy are known, the fragmentary remains provide only slight evidence for the nature of their work. The parabasis, missing also in the *Lysistrata, Ecclesiazusae,* and *Plutus* of Aristophanes, was abandoned. The choral song became merely a scene-breaker, and the themes were generally narrowed. Personal invective died hard, but political matters were no longer of such compelling concern as to provoke satire on the grand scale. Mythological burlesque, mild social satire, and travesties of philosophers are the principal subjects, though the interest in lost and rediscovered babies and in romantic love foretells the enthronement of New Comedy. Aristophanes had anticipated the form in the lost *Cocalus* and probably in the *Aeolosikon,* and it seems probable that the influence of the philosophical Epicharmus (c. 550–460 B.C.) was making itself felt in the age of Plato. Comedy had ceased to be a rite and a riot and was becoming more of a gentle ironic contemplation.

By the death of Alexander the Great (323 B.C.), New Comedy was a fully developed form and one that was to persist as a model for centuries to come. With a very few exceptions, such as an occasional mythological burlesque, the plots are all nearly alike. The theme is romantic love, and the action consists of surmounting obstacles to the marriage, or marriages (there may be two, or even three, pairs of lovers). The obstacles may be lack of money or parental opposition, or the heroine may be supposedly a slave or of low rank, in which case the regular solution is a revelation, by tokens, that she is really wellborn and free. Intrigue bulks large in the development of the action, which now falls regularly into five acts, with choral interludes unconnected with the plot and designated as a rule simply by the stage direction "chorus." The prologue is of the playbill type, frequently spoken by a personified abstraction, such as Misapprehension. The language is simple, meant to reflect everyday middle-class speech, and only two or three meters are used, in contrast with the wide variety in Old Comedy. Obscenity, together with lyricism and personal allusion, has all but vanished. The New Comic poets themselves recognized their debt to Euripides, who by then was very popular, and the similarity between his "tragicomedies" and the new form is evident, with intrigue, long-lost persons, and Fortune lying at the heart of both.

The characters are an elaborate series of stereotypes, developed probably from those of Epicharmus: old man, young man, old woman, young woman, soldier, cook, parasite, courtesan, slave. But most of these could be divided into subtypes: the old man might be benign or ill-tempered or a miser; the young man might come from the country or the city; the courtesan might or might not have a heart of gold. The subtypes were numerous (there were fourteen kinds of young woman), but they were limited, distinct, and fixed. Character-drawing, therefore, labored under austere restrictions, but character, except with Menander, was not the main concern. Rather the poets strove to devise new variations in the plot, new intrigues, new combinations of the stock figures. As with all Hellenistic art, the aims were to achieve polish, sophistication, and charm, while reflecting ordinary life with a carefully simulated realism within highly artificial limits. It was a philosophic kind of comedy, abounding in aphoristic lines, and it grew more and more serious, until the Romans adopted it and Plautus restored the *vis comica.*

Out of the many New Comic poets, of whom some seventy names are known, the Alexandrian scholars selected a canonical triad consisting of Diphilus, Philemon, and Menander. Philemon (c. 361–262 B.C.) of Syracuse wrote ninety-seven comedies, of which only fragments survive. He was granted Athenian citizenship and, though later opinion did not agree, he was often preferred to Menander in his own time. Diphilus (c. 360–?280 B.C.) of Sinope also worked in Athens with great success, producing about one hundred plays, some of which seem to have been on mythological subjects. Only fragments remain, but they reveal a poet of no little vigor and imagination.

MENANDER, son of Diopeithes, was a native of Athens. His philosophic tendencies were nurtured, no doubt, by his friendship with Theophrastus, under whom he may have studied, Epicurus, and Demetrius of Phaleron, while his interest in comedy was stimulated by Alexis, the most distinguished poet of Middle Comedy. He gained only eight prizes with more than one hundred plays, but after his death his fame was immense. The gnomic single lines of this great master of aphorism were made into collections, which until recently were approximately all that was known of his work, save for Roman imitations and scattered fragments. In the late nineteenth and early twentieth centuries a series of papyri was found containing substantial portions of four plays, and smaller ones of many others, identifiable but beyond certain reconstruction. More recently a complete play was found, the *Dyskolos,* and extensive fragments of various others.

Menandrian comedy, though humorous and once in a while slightly boisterous, is essentially a delicate reflection of, and upon, the life of middle-class people. Unlike Philemon and Diphilus, he took no interest in mythological burlesque but concentrated on character and sentiment. Though he kept the stock masks, he drew them with a subtlety and human concern that make them truly three-dimensional. The influence of Euripides is great, both in characterization and in the use of the theater as a philosophic medium. No doubt this subtlety and loftiness account for his relative unpopularity in his lifetime, as well as for the fact that Plautus made little use of him, while Terence made much. His was the comedy of cultivated people, and the refinement of his taste and outlook is reflected in the sensitivity and poignancy of his lines.

The DYSKOLOS has a relatively simple plot for a New Comedy. Sostratus, a wealthy young man, falls in love with the daughter of Cnemon, a poor misanthropic farmer with a vicious temper. Cnemon has also a wife and stepson, Gorgias, who, however, refuse to live with him. Sostratus tries to ask for the girl's hand but is violently driven off. He strikes up a friendship with Gorgias, who suggests that he join in tilling the fields side by side with himself and thus perhaps gain the old man's ear. The plan fails, but an accident turns the tide. Cnemon's maid has dropped a pitcher into the well and Cnemon, in trying to recover it, falls in. He is rescued by Gorgias, whom he had always mistreated; touched and still frightened, he is converted to the realization of human interdependence and grants Sostratus his daughter. Sostratus gives Gorgias his sister, and the play ends with a feast. Cnemon, though not badly injured, goes to bed, but the slaves, after teasing him for a while and rousing some of his former temper, half persuade, half drag him to join the party.

It is something of a structural weakness that the solution of the plot depends upon an accident rather than upon some kind of plan. Yet in the Hellenistic age Fortune (*Tyche*) was personified as a goddess and regarded as a powerful force in human life, and there is much about Fortune in the *Dyskolos.* The final scene with Cnemon also seems gratuitous and only half motivated, but perhaps Menander did not want to let this excellent character merely fade away without some further display of his amusing explosiveness. The play has many charms, especially the characters. The two young men, with their fine moral speeches, are drawn with a loving smile at the high-mindedness of youth. The cook, the slaves, and Sostratus' mother, who is somewhat manic about visiting shrines, all have their differentiating, humanizing touches. Even the girl, though onstage only a minute or two, manages to convey a kind of tremulous charm. But Cnemon is the masterpiece and the real central character. His conversion speech is genuinely moving, conveying, as it does, no little of Menander's own attitude. But even before his conversion, one feels a certain sympathy for his misanthropy as at least an understandable, if unlovely, judgment on the world. He is on balance lovable, even if he is in the habit of thrashing everybody, in-

cluding his daughter, and greeting his visitors by throwing rocks at them. The *Dyskolos* won Menander his first victory.

The *Samia* (*The Girl from Samos*), of uncertain date but probably early (310?), was very famous in antiquity. Only some 340 lines were known until recently, but a new, as yet unpublished papyrus with another 300 lines will hopefully clear up many difficulties. The plot is only partially clear. Demeas, a wealthy man of middle age, is married to Chrysis, a woman from Samos, but informally, since it was forbidden by Athenian law to marry a foreigner. During Demeas' absence on a business trip (a regular necessity for older men of New Comedy), Chrysis has a baby by him, while his adoptive son, Moschion, has one by the daughter of their neighbor, the penniless Niceratus. The plot is obscure from this point on, but certainly Chrysis, in order to protect Niceratus' daughter and Moschion, takes their child and is caught suckling it by Demeas, who instantly concludes that Moschion, whom he genuinely loves, has seduced Chrysis, whom he adores. He drives Chrysis from the house, though he gives her servants and money, and bids her turn whore. It is not clear what happened to Chrysis' baby; often it is assumed that hers had died, which is why she was so ready to take the younger girl's, but others say that there were two babies in the house, between which Demeas could not distinguish. But there is no doubt that Moschion and his beloved were married and that Demeas was reconciled with Chrysis, who may have turned out (fortuitously) to be an Athenian and therefore legally marriageable.

Certainly Chrysis is a wonder of feminine appeal, even from the little that we see of her. Though he abuses her unjustly, Demeas maintains logic and magnanimity in his rage and disappointment, and when his rage is gone, he manages skillfully to calm the maddened Niceratus, who wants to kill practically everybody. Demeas is a wonderful variant on the older man aggrieved. The minor characters, what we see of them, are also touched off with equal deftness, especially Parmeno the slave, who, having run away from a flogging, returns, reviews the evidence, finds himself (rightly) innocent, and then asks why he ran away. The answer, a quiet parody of Socratic morality, is simple: Being flogged is simply impolite.

The *Perikeiromene* (*The Girl with Her Hair Cut Short,* c. 305?), was also very famous. Only some four hundred lines are preserved, including some of the Prologue, which followed the first act. A young man, Moschion, suddenly finds himself embraced and kissed by a young woman, Glycera. He does not know, though she does, that they are brother and sister, there having been the usual confusion of New Comic babies. The young woman's lover, Polemon, a soldier, catches her in the act and shears off her hair. A long series of misunderstandings follows, during which Polemon undergoes deep anguish at his treatment of Glycera, but eventually all is restored to balanced love and understanding.

The most remarkable character is Polemon, whose name and mask should designate him as a *miles gloriosus.* He is far from that, but rather a sincere lover who, in a moment of intense and, so far as he knew, justified jealousy, committed an act of minor, but regrettable, violence. It was thought by some in antiquity, and it seems more than likely, that the Glycera of the *Perikeiromene* was Menander's own devoted mistress of that name. Their love was famous, and the epistolographer Alciphron composed an imaginary letter from her to him in which she mentions "the play you put me in." Certainly the name is rare in extant New Comedy, appearing only in this play and in a fragment ascribed, whether or not rightly, to one other. It is tempting to think that the *Perikeiromene* reflects some quarrel between the poet and his mistress (hopefully without the hair shearing), written perhaps as a humorous, affectionate atonement.

The *Epitrepontes* (*Arbitrators*), of uncertain date but clearly belonging to the poet's most mature period, was regarded by Quintilian and other ancient writers as a particular masterpiece. A little less than seven hundred lines are preserved, including the vivid arbitration scene from which the play takes its name. In the darkness of a night festival Charisius had raped Pamphila and given her a ring. A few months later, without knowing each other, they marry and live happily, until Pamphila has a baby, somewhat too soon. She manages to conceal the fact and expose the infant with tokens, including the ring, but the slave Onesimus tells Charisius, not out of malice but the inability to keep a secret. Charisius goes to live at a friend's house, where he carouses with friends and a harp girl, Abrotonon. Pamphila's father, Smicrines, hears of it and tries to take back Pamphila and the dowry, but Pamphila will not agree. Meanwhile, the baby has been found by a shepherd and given to a charcoal burner, but without the tokens. The charcoal burner wants the tokens so that the child may discover his identity, but the shepherd, who intends to sell them, refuses to give them. In accordance with Greek custom in minor disputes, they refer the matter to the first passer-by for arbitration; Smicrines, who is passing, decides that the tokens go with the baby. After a series of complications and intrigues, in which Onesimus and Abrotonon are chiefly instrumental, the truth is revealed. Husband and wife are reunited, Smicrines subsides, and Abrotonon and Onesimus are given their liberty.

The *Epitrepontes* is the complete New Comedy. All the regular themes appear: the lost baby, the tokens, the misapprehension, the intrigue (here designed with peculiar ingenuity), and the role of Chance, or Fortune. The plot is arranged with extreme skill. But its real beauty lies, as usual with Menander, in the characters. Pamphila's scenes are too fragmentary to give a full impression, but her loyal and forgiving nature is clear. Charisius is more complex. Too much in love with his wife either to divorce her or to live with her when he feels betrayed, he turns to riotous living; but, as we learn from Abrotonon, he consoles himself with wine, not with women. His hot-headedness is handsomely balanced by the integrity of his contrition, and though he seldom speaks a kind word to Onesimus, he sets him free. The latter is certainly the most interesting and amusing slave in extant New Comedy, and Smicrines, though sharp-tongued and rather miserly, has justice and affection at heart. Abrotonon is a really rare creation, for though the benevolent harlot keeps appearing throughout the history of drama, she is usually tinged with a sentimentality that Menander's harp girl totally lacks. Gay, clever, and quite content with her profession, she devises an intrigue, at some risk to herself, for the sole purpose of making sure that what emerges is the real truth. In no play does Menander display more fully his own humanity and his basic belief in that of others.

The kings of tragedy stand amid the universe, with all its gods and mysteries. The trampled poor, or underprivileged, of uncomprehending modern societies stand in a nowhere that is seldom comic or tragic, though often slaughterous. Greek New Comedy is the mirror of the middle class; it provided a form that was to prove inexhaustibly productive for the understanding of the majority of lives. Repetitious in form, expectable in its necessary happy conclusion, it represents a shape consonant with an odd mingling of rigid sexual morality and the need for love and fertility. Gilbert Murray once observed that, to the Greeks, "a baby without a marriage was a much more hopeful situation than a marriage without a baby." Somehow, even in its last bourgeois phase, comedy remained a celebration of fertility, though the sophistication of its form turned the focus less toward the result than toward the problems of the participants. The greatness of Menander lies, perhaps, primarily in his sympathetic understanding of the creators of human continuity, who, though they may start in violence or misunderstanding, end in better wisdom and find their better selves. If the Old Comic feeling for the fire and rumpus of procreation is gone, in New Comedy the elegant, self-giving grace of the lovers is enshrined in a framework of humane tenderness, which, though sometimes mechanically employed, has always remained at the service of the *virtuosi* of the theater.

Recommended books on the general subject of Greek drama are: E. R. Dodds, *The Greeks and the Irrational* (1951, 3rd printing 1959); Gerald F. Else, *The Origin and Early Form of Greek Tragedy* (1965, reprinted 1967); John Jones, *On Aristotle and Greek Tragedy* (1962); H. D. F. Kitto, *Greek Tragedy* (1939, 3rd ed. 1961, reprinted 1966) and *Form and Meaning in Drama* (1957); Albin Lesky, *Greek Tragedy* (1965), translated by H. A. Frankfort; Katherine Lever, *The Art of Greek Comedy* (1956); Gilbert Norwood, *Greek Tragedy* (1920, 4th ed. 1948, reprinted 1960) and *Greek Comedy* (1931, reprinted 1963); Sir Arthur Pickard-Cambridge, *Dithyramb, Tragedy and Comedy* (2nd ed. 1962, reprinted 1966), *The Dramatic Festivals of Athens* (2nd ed. 1968), and *The Theatre of Dionysus in Athens* (1946).

On Aeschylus: John H. Finley, Jr., *Pindar and Aeschylus* (1955); Gilbert Murray, *Aeschylus, the Creator of Tragedy* (1940, reprinted 1962).

On Sophocles: G. M. Kirkwood, *A Study of Sophoclean Drama* (1958); Bernard M. W. Knox, *The Heroic Temper* (1964) and *Oedipus at Thebes* (1957); Cedric H. Whitman, *Sophocles* (1951).

On Euripides: D. J. Conacher, *Euripidean Drama* (1967); G. M. A. Grube, *The Drama of Euripides* (reprinted, with minor corrections, 1961); Gilbert Murray, *Euripides and His Age* (1913, revised 1965, with new introduction by Kitto and revised bibliography).

On Aristophanes: Victor Ehrenberg, *The People of Aristophanes* (1951, 3rd ed. 1962); Gilbert Murray, *Aristophanes* (1933, reprinted 1964); Cedric H. Whitman, *Aristophanes and the Comic Hero* (1964).

On New Comedy: A. W. Gomme, *Essays in Greek History and Literature* (1937, reprinted 1967); T. B. L. Webster, *Studies in Menander* (1950, 2nd ed. 1960).

For translations, see the individual playwrights. —C. H. W.

modern period. Modern Greek drama reflects the influences of its own ancient and Byzantine heritage; of European drama, many of whose playwrights were translated and produced even before the Greek War of Independence; of the linguistic struggle of those who wrote in *katharevousa* (purist Greek) versus those who wrote in the demotic (vernacular Greek); and of the influence of the several foreign invaders who occupied their shores.

The beginnings of modern Greek drama first assume importance in Crete during the closing years of the sixteenth century, when that island was under Venetian occupation. Eight dramas written in the Cretan dialect between 1600 and 1669 have come down to us: three tragedies, three comedies, one pastoral drama, and one religious drama. Like their Italian models, the Cretan plays are generally divided into acts and scenes with *intermedia* ("interludes") between the acts that have no connection whatever with the play. In language, subject matter, and poetic imagery, however, these dramas are indigenous to Cretan soil.

Erophile (written c. 1600; pub. posthumously in 1637) was written by Georgios Hortatsis, born in the latter part of the sixteenth century. Best known of the three Cretan tragedies, *Erophile* is a five-act play in Cretan dialect, written in the fifteen-syllable Byzantine line known as political verse, in perfect rhymes with Latin characters, and modeled after *Orbecche* by Giovanni Battista Giraldi (1504–1573). The action in *Erophile* takes place in the Memphis of ancient Egypt and concerns the love and martyrdom of the secretly married heroine, Princess Erophile, whose husband is murdered by her father the king. The incidents of the four intermedia are drawn from *Jerusalem Delivered* (1575) by Tasso. After the fall of Crete to the Turks in 1669, *Erophile* made its way to the Ionian Islands, especially to Zante, where Cretans found refuge. *Erophile* was revived in 1934 and again in 1961. *O Basileus Rodolinos* ("King Rodolinos," pub. 1647), the second of the Cretan tragedies, is a verse tragedy of revenge by Ioannes Andrew Troilos. Also set in Memphis of ancient Egypt, *Rodolinos* deals with the tragic dilemma of its hero, Trotilos, king of Persia, caught between friendship and love, and ends in the suicide of all the principal characters. "King Rodolinos" was revived in 1962. The third Cretan tragedy, the anonymous *Zenonas* ("Zeno"), was written in Candia just before the fall of Crete. Written in political rhymed verse, "Zeno" is an imitation of a blood-and-horror tragedy written in Latin verse by an English Jesuit, Joseph Simeons, or Simon, and printed in Rome in 1648. The characters are mythological personalities who discourse on how to bring an end to the reign (474–491) of the Isaurian emperor Zeno to assure the succession to Anastasius I.

The three Cretan comedies, *Katzourbos*, *Stathis*, and *Fortounatos*, show the influence of the Italian *commedia erudita* and *commedia dell'arte* and the New Comedy of Menander. The subject is similar in all three: the romance of two young people is blocked by a dissolute old man who turns out to be the father of one of the lovers, abducted as a child years before. *Katzourbos*, the most significant and oldest of the three comedies, written sometime between 1595 and 1600, was found in Corfu and published in Greece for the first time in 1964. The author is not mentioned, but scholars have established this to be the work of Hortatsis because of the play's great similarity to *Erophile* in language and expression. *Katzourbos* is a simple comedy with social overtones manifested in the intermingling of classes and in the romance of the two servants, who are the central characters in the play. Although the form of *Katzourbos* reflects the Italian influence, its lively idiomatic language and poetry and the realistic action of the richly comical situations are native to Crete. *Katzourbos* has four intermedia, three of which are taken from Tasso's *Jerusalem Delivered* and one from a part of Ovid's *Metamorphoses*.

Stathis, a comedy in political rhymed verse written sometime between 1620 and 1645 during the Venetian occupation by Pholas, or Papholas, is a realistic gallery of comic portraits of the various occupations and professions that made up Cretan bourgeois society of the time. There are two unconnected intermedia, one on anti-Turkish themes and the other on the Trojan War. A finer play than *Stathis*, both in its lyricism and its dramatic structure, is *Fortounatos* by Markos Antonios Foscolos of Candia, written in 1669 and produced in Athens for the first time in 1962. Set in Kastro, Crete, the play is in five acts and is written in Latin characters. Its four intermedia treat of the Judgment of Paris. The play concerns the rich doctor Louras, who is in love with Petronella, a young girl who loves and is loved by Fortounatos. Later it is discovered that Fortounatos, abducted by pirates when very young, is the son of Louras. Louras, overjoyed at recovering his son, renounces his passion for Petronella and consents to her marriage with his newly found son. The language in *Fortounatos* recalls the pornographic wordplay of Aristophanes and Rabelais.

The anonymous *Gyparis*, also from Crete, is a pastoral tragicomedy in five acts, written in the spoken Greek with Italian characters. Composed in the third or fourth decade of the seventeenth century, it was inspired by *Callisto*, a bucolic comedy by the sixteenth-century Italian poet Luigi Groto. *Gyparis* is written in rhymed political verse and has no intermedia. More poetic than dramatic, it reveals the influence of its Italian prototypes and the classical pastoral romances of Theocritus, Heliodorus, Longus, and Tatius, but it is set on Mount Ida, its characters are Cretan boys and girls, and it depicts the contemporary bucolic life of Crete. This Aristophanic comedy of the sexes concerns the love of two shepherds for two shepherdesses who reject them.

Finest of all the plays of the Cretan theater is *I Thysia tou Avraam* ("The Sacrifice of Abraham") by Vincenzo Kornaros (d. 1677), author of the demotic epic poem *Erotokritos*. First printed in Venice in 1635, *I Thysia tou Avraam* is structurally modeled on Luigi Groto's *Lo Isach* (pub. 1586), but its poetry and humanity surpass that of the Italian play. It consists of 1,154 lines written in political rhymed meter with no scene and act division. The plot follows the biblical story but the Greek author has humanized God, and Kornaros depicts Abraham, not as a Hebrew patriarch, but as a distraught father torn between his desire to obey God and his fatherly love for Isaac. Kornaros has added two maidservants for Sarah and two for Abraham, all of whom reveal a sense of humanity in their appeals to Abraham when they are admitted into the secret of the proposed sacrifice. While the dramatic structure of *I Thysia tou Avraam* is somewhat loose, there is dramatic tension in the conflict between the parents and in the attitude of the servants who, like the ancient Greek chorus, voice the opinion of the people. *I Thysia tou Avraam* has been translated into all the major European languages, and since 1928 it has been revived often in Athens and in the provinces.

After the fall of Crete to the Turks in 1669, modern Greek theater continued to develop in the Ionian Islands, especially in Zante, where Cretans migrated and which came to be identified with the unique genre known as the *omilia*. The word *omilia*, which means "speech," signified a popular theater in the vernacular. In the main the omilies constituted a record of Venetian reminiscences. Influenced by the Italian commedia dell'arte, the omilies were performed in public places by actors and singers who altered existing lyrics and improvised others. All the omilies were spoken in political-verse couplets, mostly written by unknown folk artists. Outstanding among the omilies that have come down to us are the anonymous *I Kephalonitai* ("The Cephalonians"), a satire on the Cephalonian workers; *I Yanniotai* ("The People of Yanina"), a satire written by Ioannis Kantounis (1731–1817), a doctor and a successful translator of the dramas of Metastasio; and *I Moraitai* ("The People of Morea," 1789), written by Savoias Soumerlis.

While the omilies were performed in the open public places of Zante, other theatrical pieces, written in the katharevousa, were performed indoors for conservative aristocratic circles, and between the two theatrical activity was intense. The outdoor vernacular folkloric art of the omilies contrasted with the "learned" art of the purists mainly in the language. Later, the two forms were fused into the social drama that ultimately developed and was used to satirize the bourgeoisie.

Demetrios Ghouzelis (1774–1843), a talented writer of comedy, also wrote omilies. *Hassis* (meaning "loser"), written in 1795 in perfectly rhymed political verse, portrays Hassis, a typical Zantean and a genuine comic type reminiscent of the characters in the New Comedy. Unity of scene and act is lacking, but the idiomatic Zantean dialect and its beautiful lyrical passages with its Italian expressions realistically reflect the age of Ghouzelis. *Hassis* was revived in 1964.

A unique phenomenon that developed naturally from the omilies was the *theatro skion* ("theater of shadows"), or Karaghiozis, as it is commonly known —a synthesis of cartoon, music, and painting. The theater of shadows is an open-air marionette theater with the figure of Karaghiozis (*kara,* meaning "black," *ghoex,* meaning "eye," hence "the man with the black eyes") cut in profile and manipulated behind a screen so as to move from one side to the other. According to the well-known Greek critic K. Demaras, Karaghiozis was known in Greece before the revolution (c. 1820); other Karaghiozis critics state that this type of theater was introduced in Greece by John Vrahalis in 1860, when the first theater of shadows was seen in Athens. This genre was adapted to Greek culture by Demetrios Mimaros (1865–1902), considered the founder of the Greek Karaghiozis. It is generally agreed that Karaghiozis came to Greece via the Near East, the Arab countries, and the Turks who occupied the Mediterranean area. Contrary to this tradition, Antoine Papoulias (1871–1948), known under the name of Mollas and identified with the Athenian and worldly Karaghiozis, rejects absolutely the tradition that attributes an Oriental origin to the theater of shadows. He affirms that Karaghiozis is Greek, even Athenian. Mollas, renowned for his Athenian Karaghiozis theater, which he directed for forty-five years, made his own shadow figures, wrote his own plays, and voiced the lines of all the characters. Mollas has published about thirty-seven of his Karaghiozis comedies.

The Greek Karaghiozis, expressing comic elements in rowdy, Aristophanic manner, became a symbol of protest for all who desired freedom. Introduced with a song and a quintet of wind instruments, Karaghiozis, who has a many-faceted personality, is actually a counterpart of the commedia dell'arte and the punchinello. Ugly, humpbacked, with a hooked nose, Karaghiozis is a wise and goodhearted jack-of-all-trades who satirizes himself, ridicules heroic persons and deeds, and concentrates chiefly on the struggle for independence and the aspirations of the Greek people. Karaghiozis is always penniless and hungry and gains his daily bread by treachery, thieving, and robbing the dead; despite his vices, however, his antiheroic suffering reveals that good prevails over evil in the end. A variety of elements go into the Karaghiozis plays: the demotic songs and legends, Alexander the Great, and the heroes of the Greek War of Independence. More recently the Karaghiozis plays are concerned with the political and social happenings of the day. All Karaghiozis plays seem to have one end in view: to reveal and release the creative abilities of the Greek people. There are twelve theaters in Athens where performances of Karaghiozis are still given today. Although the Karaghiozis plays have been handed down orally from one shadow-show player to another through the years, there are approximately three hundred extant plays of the theater of shadows, but no scholarly effort has been made to compile and evaluate all of them.

In the eighteenth and nineteenth centuries, significant advances in the Greek theater were made outside of Greece, especially through the *Filike Etaireia* (Society of Friends), an organization of prominent Greeks of the diaspora who supported Greek independence. In the Greek-populated Danubian provinces of Valachia and Moldavia, especially in Odessa and Bucharest, dramatists used their own history as a revolutionary arm for the liberation of Greece from the Turks. The plays they wrote during this time manifest the democratic ideals of the French Revolution, but they are written in the conservative, archaic katharevousa spoken in the *phanar,* the chief Greek quarter in Constantinople under the Turks.

Probably the greatest dramatist of historical plays of this period is Ioannes Zambelios (1782–1856), disciple of Alfieri. Many of Zambelios' plays, written in the simple purist Greek, continued to be played in Greece until 1912. They are written in political unrhymed verse and, dominated by patriotism, they immortalize the national heroism. His best-known play is *Timoleon,* inspired by Alfieri's play of the same title. Published in Vienna in 1818 and produced in Bucharest the same year, *Timoleon* depicts the Greek statesman and general (c. 411–c. 337 B.C.) who brought about his brother's death to save the democratic form of government in Corinth.

Also worthy of mention is Iakovos Rizos Neroulos (1778–1850), whose play *Korakistika* ("Jargon of the Crows," 1813) satirizes the conflict between the Atticist theoreticians, who wanted to create a new language for the Greeks, and the moderate purists. Among other plays by Neroulos is *Aspasia* (1813), presented in Odessa in 1819 and regarded as the first tragedy in modern Greek after the disappearance of the Cretan theater. In *O Efimeridofovos* ("He Who Fears the Newspapers," 1837), a comedy in five acts and regarded as one of the most interesting comedies of modern Greek theater, Neroulos denounces the abuses and doings of certain Athenian journalists.

After the Greek War of Independence (1821–1829) there was considerable dramatic activity all over Greece. During the first fifty years in the life of the newly liberated people, fifteen theatrical companies were formed and made tours in the interior of Greece and even abroad. Dramatists turned more and more to history to stabilize their young nation and their democratic way of life. Also, an increasing number of European authors were produced in translation.

The two most important dramatists of this period are Alexandros Soutsos (1803–1863) and his brother Panayiotis (1806–1868). Alexandros Soutsos wrote a number of comedies satirizing the mores of the time. Best known of these is *O Prothypourgos* ("The Prime Minister," 1843), one of the finest comedies of the modern Greek theater and still timely in its daring charge against the unscrupulous minister. His brother Panayiotis Soutsos is identified with the romantic school of Greece. His two best verse tragedies are *Georgios Karaiskakis* (pub. 1842), depicting the Greek soldier who was mortally wounded in the Greek War of Independence, and *O Odiporos* ("The Wayfarer"), a patriotic romantic tragedy in five acts, written in 1825 and produced in 1831 in Nauplion and later with unusual success in Athens.

Worthy of mention too is Mihail Hourmouzes (1801–1882), a satirist who wrote a number of plays ridiculing the customs of the period from 1830 to 1860. Chief among these works are *Leprentis* and *O Tychodioktis* ("The Adventurer"), both written in 1835 and highlighting and interpreting the true sentiments of the Greek people toward the Bavarians in the court of Otho, first Greek king after the War of Independence. In *O Ipallilos* ("The Civil Servant") and *Malakof* (1865) Hourmouzes satirizes the *phanarioti* of Constantinople.

Antonios Matessis (1794–1875), an ardent demot-

icist, is noted for his play *Vassilikos,* written in 1829 and produced in his native island of Zante by amateurs in 1832, when the British governed the Ionian Islands. It is a social drama in five acts written in the demotic Zantean idiom and patterned after *Louisa Miller* by Schiller. The story goes back to 1712 when Zante was still occupied by Venice, and in its lively folklore and racy demotic and ideological content, it portrays the customs of Zante of that epoch. *Vassilikos* has enjoyed many excellent productions during the last forty years.

During the reign (1832–1862) of Otho, dramatists, motivated by the victory of the Greek War of Independence and seeking to liberate those Greek areas still under Turkish domination, wrote and produced plays even more daringly related to national patriotism, their democratic heritage, and their demotic idiom, which they sought to establish as a recognized language. *I Babylonia* ("The Tower of Babel"), written by Demetrios Vyzantios (1790–1840) in 1836, was the first postrevolutionary comedy produced in Athens. A folk comedy, *I Babylonia* is a Molièresque satire on the rivalries of the diverse theoreticians who championed the different dialects spoken in Greece. The play was produced a number of times in Paris and enjoyed recognition in a series of performances given at the *Ethniko Theatro* (National Theater) in 1932 and was revived again in 1947. Vyzantios wrote a number of other satiric comedies, but none reached the stature of *I Babylonia.*

Alexandros Rizos Rangavis (1809–1892), an aristocrat who wrote in the katharevousa, tapped all periods in Greek history though he preferred the Byzantine period. He is most successful, however, in his comedy *Tou Koutrouli O Gamos* ("The Wedding of Koutroulis," pub. 1845 and translated into German in 1857). According to the author, he wrote this comedy to apply the Aristophanic manner to contemporary mores and matters.

After the fall of Otho on October 29, 1862, there was a new spurt of dramatic activity in the Greek theater. The excavations of 1867 brought to light the Odeum of Herodes Atticus, and Sophocles' *Antigone* was presented there the same year. In 1869 the Boukouras Theater was built, and there contemporary historical tragedies written in the pompous and stilted style of the katharevousa were presented. In 1900 King George I founded the National Theater where translations of foreign masterpieces and the classics, as well as original plays, were produced for the next seven years.

The playwrights of the period that followed sought to open new dramatic perspectives in the modern Greek theater. One of the most successful of these dramatists is Spiridon Vassiliadis (1845–1874), an anti-Shakespearean dramatist who affirmed that Greek genius is antithetical to the Shakespearean genius. Vassiliadis is noted for several plays, but his most successful drama is *Galatea* (pub. 1873; produced in Hungary in 1878), a romantic drama of Pygmalion with an original twist. Based on a folk song, it is a prose romance in five acts written in purist Greek but relieved by sensitive lyrics. Demetrios Vernardakis (1843–1907), one of the pioneers who tried to create a repertory of national dramaturgy and one of the chief representatives of nineteenth-century Greek neoclassicism, used Byzantine sources for his dramatic plots. His masterpiece, *Maria Doxapatri* (written in 1858; prod. 1865; revived in 1963), taken from the famous "Chronicle of Moreas," is a five-act verse drama written in iambic twelve-syllable lines alternating with prose and depicting an episode of the Frankish occupation of the thirteenth century. Vernardakis' *Fausta*, based on the history of Constantine the Great, was first played in Athens in 1893 in two theaters simultaneously. Written in the katharevousa, it was inspired by the *Hippolytus* of Euripides. In the *Kypselidai* (pub. 1860), modeled after the German *Der König Periander* (1823) by Immerman, Vernardakis returns to the mythical times of Periander to depict his misfortunes. In *Merope* (pub. 1866), he frees himself from all influences and writes a compassionate drama which, despite the stiltedness of the katharevousa, surpasses both Voltaire's and Alfieri's plays of the same title. Anghelos Vlahos (1838–1920) is important as a transitional figure, coming between the reign of the katharevousa and the ascendancy of the demotic. He is best remembered for his successful political satire *I Kori tou Pantopolou* ("The Grocer's Daughter," written in 1865), which was produced more than thirty times during the first year.

In reaction to archaic tragedy and the katharevousa, three new genres in the demotic language emerged during the second half of the nineteenth century: the *comedyllion,* a purely Greek vaudeville form usually written against the background of the Aegean Islands and its simple people; the dramatic idyll, with drama and song depicting life in the mountain areas; and an outgrowth of both the comedyllion and the dramatic idyll, the *Hellenike Epitheorisis,* or Greek revue, an open-air spectacle satirizing the enemy or the antidemocratic acts of the day. A creator of the Greek comedyllion and the dramatic idyll is Demetrios Koromilas (1850–1898), an aristocrat who wrote more than fifty pieces from 1872 to 1892. His most important and still very popular comedyllion is *I Tychi Tis Maroulas* ("Maroula's Fate," pub. 1889), with songs arranged by Demetrios Kokkos (1856–1891), adapted from his own one-act comedy *I Petra tou Skandalou* ("The Scandalous Pebble"). In *I Tychi Tis Maroulas,* the main character is a sewing maid in a wealthy Athenian household, and Koromilas depicts the mores of the time. Koromilas' best dramatic idyll is *O Agapitikos tis Voscopoulas* ("The Shepherdess' Sweetheart," 1889). Inspired by a demotic song with its subject derived from the life of the mountaineers, it was revived in 1955 and is still in the repertory of Greek theatrical companies. Demetrios Kokkos also wrote comedyllions, many of which are still popular today. Two of his best known are *I Lyra tou Gerou Nikola* ("The Lyre of Father Nicholas," 1891) and *O Kapetan Giakoumis* ("Captain Giakoumis," pub. 1892), a fine three-act satire, which was produced posthumously in 1894.

In the new Hellenike Epitheorisis genre, the first revue, entitled *Ligo Ap' Ola* ("A Little of Everything," 1894), was written by Mikios Lambros (1844–1902). This was followed by four revues written by other writers, and then the genre was forgotten until 1907 when it reappeared with the popularity that it continues to enjoy to the present. One outstanding writer of revues worthy of mention is Paul Nord (1901–   ), some of whose revues are regarded as classics of political satire. Among these are *Mesa Oloi* ("All In," 1929), *Exo Oloi* ("All Out," 1930), *Kati Trechi* ("Happenings," 1931), *Allo Prama* ("Out of This World," 1934), and *Idiotikon Nekrotomeion* ("Private Morgue"), which Nord himself staged in Saratoga Springs, New York, in 1960. Nord, who lives in New York, continues to write in the same genre, either in Greek, as in *O Chrysos Aeonas* ("Golden Age," 1939), or in English, as in *God Strikes Back* (1943) and *Haven in the Dark,* first produced in 1949 and revived in 1953. Greek revues are now produced by special companies and created by teams rather than individuals. The most popular of these teams are Alekos Sakellarios (1913–   ) and Hristos Yannakopoulos (1904–1963), whose countless revues are enjoyed for their light and sophisticated charm. Outstanding among their successful joint efforts are *I Dexia, I Aristera, Kai O Kyr. Pantelis* ("The Right, the Left, and Mr. Pantelis") and *I Germanoi Xanaerchontai* ("The Germans Come Back"), produced in 1946.

A direct outgrowth of the comedyllion, the dramatic idyll, and the revue is the light satiric comedy, one of the most popular forms in modern Greek theater today. One of the earliest exponents of this type of play was Bobby Anninos (1852–1934), who raised satiric comedy to the level of a character play in *I Niki tou Leonida* ("The Conquest of Leonidas"), his best-known bourgeois comedy, and *Ziteitai Yperetis* ("Wanted a Servant," pub. 1891). Other early practitioners of the genre include Timos Moraitinos (1875–1952) and Paul Demetriou Palaiologus (1885–   ). A more recent practitioner of this genre is Panayiotis Georgiou Kayias (1901–   ), who has had fifteen of his works produced. Among his greatest successes are *Topiko Paragonta* ("Local Factor," 1945), an Aristophanic comedy that satirizes political compromising, and *Timoni Ston Erota* ("A Check on Love"), written and produced in 1939 and revived in New York in 1958. Nikos Georgiou Katiforis (1903–   ) writes comedy with satiric overtones. In *To Meraki tou Archonta* ("The Longing of a Nobleman," 1939), which he characterizes as a comedy of mores, he satirizes the speculator of the provinces. Demetrios Ioannou Ioannopoulos (1904–   ) won three drama awards for his excellent use of the comic technique. Best known of his comedies is *Mia tou Klephti* ("Chances of a Thief"), which enjoyed a successful run in 1941. Demetrios Ioannou Psathas (1907–   ) wrote his first play, *Stravoxylo* ("A Blundering Fellow"), in collaboration with Georgios Roussos (1910–   ) in 1940 and saw it produced the same year. His *O Eaftoulis Mou* ("Little Me," 1941), to single out one of a dozen successful comedies, was revived annually from 1957 to 1961. His *Hartopaichtis* ("The Card Player") had seven hundred successive performances. Georgios Roussos, who wrote his first play in collaboration with Psathas, is noted for a number of his own comedies. Best of these is *O Protovousianos* ("The Man from the Capital," 1940), satirizing a son educated in Athens who returns to his native island to "civilize" the islanders. *I Sopherina* ("Sopherina"), produced in 1955 under the title *To Proto Psema* ("The First

Lie"), was revived in 1961. In this play Roussos dramatizes the theme that one lie drags behind it a thousand others. Roussos also wrote *Mando Mavrogenous* (1959), a historical play about one of the greatest heroines of the Greek revolution. Nikos Tsekouras (1911–   ) wrote a well-constructed folkloric satire of upper-middle-class society in *An Doulepsis Tha Phas* ("If You Work You Eat," 1945). Another comedy, regarded by critics as Tsekouras' best work, is *O Monosantalos* ("The One-Sandaled Man"), produced in 1945 and revived in 1955, the theme of which is human communication in the Greek villages. Nikos Tsiforos (1911–   ) wrote a successful comedy of fantasy in *I Pinakothiki Ton Ilithion* ("Fools' Gallery," 1944), which presents as a game the significance people give to material interests. Alekos Sakellarios and Hristos Yannakopoulos, already mentioned for their popular revues, have also written numerous light comedies. *Thanassakis, O Politevomenos* ("Thanassakis, Politician"), a satire produced in 1953, was awarded the Xenopoulos prize for the best play of the year. One of their most popular comedies is *O Phanouris Kai to Soi Tou* ("Phanouris and His Tribe"), first played in 1957 and revived in 1961. This play concerns a brother who is obliged to provide a dowry for his sister. *Allimono Stous Neous* ("Pity the Young," 1961) concerns an old man who sells his soul to the devil to discover whether it is preferable to be old and rich or young and penniless.

Although comedy continues to flourish abundantly, a significant number of Greek dramatists have sought to emulate the "theater of ideas"—the social, psychological, and philosophical drama of the Continental and American theaters. These writers have been influenced by the naturalist plays of Hauptmann and Zola, the social drama of Ibsen and Chekhov, as well as the symbolic plays of Maeterlinck. More recently they have been influenced by the plays of Eugene O'Neill, Arthur Miller, and Tennessee Williams, all of whose works have been translated into the demotic Greek. The plays of Beckett, Ionesco, Brecht, Anouilh, Genet, and others identified with the "theater of the absurd" have also been translated and produced. In their efforts to reinterpret their democratic heritage in terms of the contemporary world and their own individual and national problems, some Greek dramatists have looked to their Byzantine history for sources, while others have turned to their native folklore to reinterpret the mores of the common people in terms of the modern world.

Costis Palamas (1859–1943), one of the greatest poets of Greece, who advanced the cause of the demotic speech and led in the movement to make Ibsen known to the Greek people, wrote one drama, *Trisevgene*, in 1903, which was not produced until 1915. *Trisevgene* is more lyrical than dramatic, but the poet has succeeded in giving his heroine "a conscience that bursts out now and then and a soul that manifests itself in lengthening flashes."

Yannis Kambyssis (1872–1901), influenced by European authors, was concerned with the foibles of Athenian society at the end of the nineteenth century. *I Farsa tis Zoes* ("The Farce of Life," 1893) depicts the vices and faults that crush a family. *I Kurdai* ("The Kurds," pub. 1897; produced posthumously in 1903), symbolizes all those who use the power of their wealth to exploit the people. In *Miss Anna Cooksley* (pub. 1897 with *I Kurdai*), Kambyssis satirizes the excitement over the victories of the first Olympic contests of 1896/97 and the people's frenzy that followed the defeat in Pharsala and Domoko. In his last works, *To Dachtilidi tis Manas* ("The Mother's Ring," 1908) and *Anatoli* ("The East," pub. 1901), he manifests a tendency opposed to naturalism.

Pavlos Nirvanas (1866–1937), inspired by symbolism and greatly influenced by Western philosophy, wrote plays that were marked by a profound pessimism regarding man's struggle with his fate. *O Architecton Marthas* ("The Architect Marthas," 1907), influenced by Ibsen, reverses the Norwegian's theme of *The Wild Duck* and portrays a protagonist who destroys himself and his wife because he believes that life is more pleasant when you hide disagreeable truths.

Georgios Xenopoulos (1867–1951), who headed the National Theater for a score of years, is credited with orienting the modern Greek theater toward realism and the social drama. Influenced largely by Ibsen and the Russian theater, he turned to his own Zantean folklore for the native types and the mores he knew so well, and he presented these in an atmosphere of urban naturalism and in the demotic idiom as spoken in Athens. By his own statement, he is a democratic socialist. His first play, *Psychopateras* ("Foster Father," 1895), is a psychological study exposing the chicaneries of an exploiting uncle enjoying the purest of reputations; *O Tritos* ("The Third One," 1895) is a tragedy of passion; *Komodia tou Thanatou* ("Comedy of Death," 1897) is a three-act satire on human mourning. In *To Mystiko tis Kontessas Valerainas* ("The Secret of Contessa Valairaina," 1904; revived in 1918, 1953, 1962, 1964), he dramatizes the futility of the heroine's suicide. *Photiny Sandry* (1908), a dramatization of his own novel *Kokkinos Vrahos* (*The Red Rock*), presents the love of an Anglo-Zantean girl for her unworthy cousin. In *Stella Violanty* (pub. 1903; prod. 1909), a sentimental play based on the author's novel *Eros Estavromenos* (*Love Crucified*), the conflict between the daughter and the father is meant to symbolize the conflict between the bourgeoisie and the aristocracy. Xenopoulos' *O Peirasmos* ("Temptation," 1910), a four-act folkloric play revived in 1936 and 1961, presents a middle-class home in which the chambermaid throws the men of the house into confusion without actually provoking it herself. *Monakrivi* ("An Only Child," 1912) is a psychological drama of an only child who is suddenly confronted with an older sister by her father's first marriage; *Heruvim* ("Cherubim," 1911), a comedy, deals with a bourgeois Athenian family in which the eldest daughter loses her fiancé to her conniving younger sister. Xenopoulos seeks to restore the reputation of his Zakinthean compatriots in *To Phiori tou Levanti* ("The Flower of the Levant," 1914; revived in 1961), a folkloric comedy in three acts; in *Psychosabbato* ("All Souls' Day," 1911), which the dramatist regards as a tragedy, an intermedia brings about the confession and subsequent death of the murderess. Xenopoulos portrays a picture of student life of the time in *Phoititas* ("The Students," 1919; revived in

1936 and 1960); in *Anthropino* ("The Humane," 1922), a psychological drama, he depicts the plight of a man who learns that he has cancer; and Xenopoulos contrasts the bourgeoisie with the dying aristocracy in *O Popolaros* ("The Bourgeoisie," pub. 1913 as a story), a folkloric Zantean comedy revived in 1959. In all the forty plays by Xenopoulos, there is an optimistic philosophy, a democratic point of view, and a steady moving from the sentimental toward the tragic.

Theodoros Synadinos (1880–1959), a master of lively situation, wrote all of twenty-five plays in various genres, most of which satirize middle- and upper-middle-class family life, but he preferred to be identified with the theater of ideas. His most famous play is *Karaghiozis* (1924), a naturalist tragedy about an illegitimate child that embraces the psychology of a whole neighborhood. According to the dramatist, *Karaghiozis* symbolizes "a biological truth, the antithesis of the existing natural and social laws of daily life." In *Maikynas* (1926) the patron who exploits artists is satirized. Synadinos, who was one of the eminent directors of ancient drama in the National Theater, also adapted Kornaros' demotic epic poem *Erotokritos* for the stage in 1930.

Pantelis Horn (1881–1941) wrote some symbolic dramas but is more closely identified with Athenian folklore. Best known among his plays are *Petroharides* (1908), a symbolic drama that depicts the economic decline of an old klepht, and *Fintanaki* ("Young Plant," 1921; revived in 1933), a naturalist play depicting life in a lower-middle-class courtyard. *Fintanaki* is regarded by critics not only as Horn's most important work but also, because of its theatrical types and sense of humanity, as the most significant folklore drama to date. *Flantro* (1935), another folklore drama, is actually a pathological study of a fiery, aristocratic, twice-married widow.

In the bourgeois drama of Spyros Melas (1882–1966), we find a varied ideology that sometimes vacillates from one extreme to the other. Influenced largely by German naturalism and the naturalism of Zola, this talented and versatile dramatist gave his plays a deeper social meaning and at times a symbolic cast. In *O Ghios tou Iskiou* ("The Son of the Shadow," 1908), his first play, Melas presented a Nietzschean protagonist who commits a series of destructive acts in order to win the girl he loves. In *To Halasmeno Spiti* ("The Ruined House," 1909), Melas presents a socially deranged middle-class family headed by a drunken and depraved father; Melas symbolizes the conflict between two brothers in the title of *To Aspro Kai to Mavro* ("The White and the Black," 1924): white represents the idealist, black the new man of ideas. An adopted son saves a girl from giving herself to a man to cover up for her father's deficit in *Mia Nychta Mia Zoe* ("One Night, One Life," 1924). Melas turns to historical drama in *Judas* (1934; revived in 1959) and portrays his protagonist as a revolutionary leader who joins Jesus to help in the liberation of Judea. Unfortunately, the splendid, original purpose of the author to create sympathy for Judas as a revolutionary hero lacks conviction after his betrayal of Christ. The first act of the play, translated into English by Rae Dalven, was published in *Athene* (Summer 1945). *O Babbas Ekpaidevetai* ("Father Gets Educated," 1935),

Melas' finest satirical work and his greatest box-office success, is characterized by the author as a comedy of mores. Aristophanic in spirit, it has been translated into several European languages and is still regularly performed in Greece, most recently in 1962; it was even turned into an operetta. Melas turned again to a historical personage in *Papaphlessas* (1937; revived in 1940, 1962), which dramatizes the story of a friar who became a revolutionary hero during the National Insurrection of 1821. Other historical dramas by Melas are *O Basileus kai O Skylos* ("The King and the Dog," 1953), a study of the philosopher Diogenes, nicknamed "the dog," and his evolution toward cynicism from the time of his capture by pirates until his meeting with Alexander the Great, and *Rhegas Velestinlis* (1962), better known as "Rhigas Ferraios," a portrait of the hero of the Greek rebellion of 1821. Despite Melas' aspirations to give universal scope to his themes, and despite the liveliness of his dialogue and the dexterity of his dramatic structure in many of his plays, his work is in the main an expression of topical life in Greece.

In the field of drama, Nikos Kazantzakis (1885–1957), eminent novelist and poet, is known for his primeval tragedies of historical and biblical personages who epitomize his own ascetic preoccupation with the problems of evil. *O Protomastoras* ("The Master Builder," pub. 1910) is a tragedy of character influenced by Ibsen. Probably his most famous tragedies of despair are *Ioulianos O Paravatis* ("Julian the Apostate," pub. 1945; produced posthumously in 1959 and revived in 1962) and *Constantinos Palaiologos,* a saga of the last emperor of Constantinople, regarded by critics as the peak of tragic poetry in modern Greek theater. It was turned into an opera by Manolis Kalomiris (1883–   ), who used orthodox anthems of the Greek Mass. The novel *O Christos Xanastavronetai* (*Christ Recrucified,* 1956), screened as *He Who Must Die,* was adapted for the stage by Notis Pergialis and Gerassimos Stavros; *Kapetan Mihalis* ("Captain Mihalis"), a novel about one of the heroes of the Cretan liberation, was translated into English as *Freedom or Death* and was adapted for the stage in 1959 by Gerassimos Stavros and Kostas Kotzias. Among other plays by Kazantzakis are *Melissa* (pub. 1939; prod. 1962), a tragedy regarded by some critics as Kazantzakis' masterpiece; *Kapodistrias,* a tragedy produced in 1946; and *Sodoma kai Gomora* ("Sodom and Gomorrah"), translated into English by Kimon Friar and entitled *Burn Me to Ashes,* which received a brief and unsuccessful Off-Broadway production in New York in 1963.

Anghelos Sikelianos (1884–1951) re-creates with poetic fervor the beauty of classical and Byzantine Greece. By turning to this period, Sikelianos re-affirms his own philosophy of freedom and his contemporary social and intellectual beliefs, which he resolves metaphysically. In *Dithyrambos tou Rodou* ("Dithyramb of the Rose," 1933), he used the Orphic mysteries to represent unity and love. Unfortunately, though fascinating as poetry, the play is weak as tragedy. In *O Christos stin Romei* ("Christ in Rome," pub. 1946), a static "religious mystery" set in the period of Nero, Sikelianos presents both the chorus and the actors as one entity who express their thoughts in rhythmical melodies. In *Daedalos,* Sikelianos symbolizes modern man trapped in his own mechanistic cleverness by dramatizing the inventor of the Cretan labyrinth caught in its intricate passages. *Asklepios* is a poetic and philosophic drama set in the sanctuary of the god of healing at Epidaurus. *Sibylla* ("The Sibyl"), written in 1941 but not produced until 1962, is the incarnation of mythical Greece.

Vasilis Rotas (1889–), director of the People's Theater from 1929 to 1937 and translator of the ancient writers, Aristophanes in particular, as well as Shakespeare, Schiller, and Hauptmann, has written comedies, historical dramas, and tragedies, but he is best known for his historical verse drama. In *Na Zei to Messolonghi* ("Long Live Messalonghi," 1928), a one-act play, Rotas deals with the exodus of Messalonghi; in *Rhegas Velestinlis* (1936), which Rotas calls a poetic tragedy, he realistically presents the revolutionary poet and visionary prophet. In an effort to revive the classical spirit of tragedy, Rotas wrote *Ellinika Neiata* ("Hellenic Youth," pub. 1946), a play based on the resistance movement of World War II and written in thirteen-syllable verse with some prose scenes. Also written in thirteen-syllable lines is *Kolokotronis* (1955), in which a narrator introduces and interprets with objective historical perspective the realistic scenes that follow.

Demetrios Bogris (1890–1964), dramatist and film writer, examines events of provincial life with poetic intuition and a sentimental tone. The tragedy *Arravoniasmata* ("Betrothals," 1925) won the Kotopouli and Averof awards, and *I Stringla* ("The Female Dragon," 1928) won the Kotopouli medal. *Phouskothalasses* ("Heavy Seas," 1937) is a folklore satire of an island captain, nurtured on the mores of the island life, who learns to adjust to the ways of Athens.

Demetrios Alexandrou Photiades (1898–), who translated the Greek classics, also devoted himself to historical drama. His two finest plays are *Makriyannis* (1946), a hymn to the heroic figure of General Makriyannis, an uneducated soldier who wrote his memoirs in a melodic folk idiom, and *Theodora* (written and produced in 1945), a satiric comedy denouncing the absolutism of royalty. In collaboration with Gerassimos Stavros he wrote *Karaiskakis* (1957), a historical drama about the leader in the War of Greek Independence.

Manolis Georgiou Skouloudis (1901–), translator of Shakespeare and founder, with the actress Marika Kotopouli, Spyros Melas, and Mitsou Myrat, of the Free Stage, is also a music and drama critic. He adapted Dostoevski's novel *O Ilithios* (*The Idiot*) for the stage in 1947, but it was not produced until 1957. His dramatic comedy *Stavrodromi* ("Crossroads") was produced in 1938 with music composed by the author and revived in 1952. Probably his best-known play is *Lambros and Maria* (1939), written in eleven-syllable lines and based on Demetrios Solomos' poem of the same name. Among other plays by Skouloudis is *I Tragodia tou Lordou Byron* ("The Tragedy of Lord Byron"), produced in 1952 and revived in 1955, which begins during the adolescence of the poet and ends at Messolonghi, where Byron died. In *Ypothesis Dreyfuss* ("The Dreyfus Case," 1960) Skouloudis dramatizes the latest revelations on this famous trial.

Dionysios Alexandrou Romas (1906–)

turned to the folklore of Zante for his background. In *Zakinthini Serenata* ("Zakinthian Serenade," 1938; revived in 1958), a verse drama written in the Zantean vernacular larded with Italian expressions, the author exploits the customs of Zante amid carnival songs, scenes full of local color, and well-developed native types. *Zakinthini Serenata* won the Prize of the Twelve in 1958. Other plays by Romas are *Treis Kosmoi* ("Three Worlds," 1934; revived in 1951), a historical play set in the Zante of 1820, and *Zambelaki* (1957).

Georgios Mihail Theotokas (1906–), a highly literary dramatist, gets his inspiration from Byzantine tradition, folk songs, and tales, which he often treats with humor, as in *Oneiro tou Dodekamerou* ("Dream of the Twelve Days," pub. 1944; broadcast on the radio in 1954). *Oneiro tou Dodekamerou* is a playful fantasy inspired by a Byzantine legend that states that between Christmas Day and the Epiphany on January 6 evil spirits come out. *To Paichnidi tis Trellas kai tis Phronimadas* ("The Play of Madness and Wisdom," written in 1947; prod. 1955 and revived in 1965) is based on the demotic song of "Mavrianos and His Sister." *Alcibiades* (written in 1957; prod. 1959) depicts the hero as a great politician and a famous military chief who dared to entertain thoughts of Greek unity, instead of the young, spoiled dandy we often imagine Alcibiades to be. According to the author, Alcibiades goes far beyond his own possibilities and the time limit set to him. *Katsantonis*, depicting a hero of the Greek War of Independence, was produced in 1952.

Anghelos Demetriou Terzakis (1907–), who concentrates on Byzantine and biblical figures, writes with a lofty sense and seeks to project eternal problems of conscience. In *Aftokrator Mihail* ("The Emperor Michael," 1936) religious mysticism stresses the poetic rather than the dramatic. *Gamilio Embatirio* ("Bridal March," 1937) is a bourgeois drama, and *O Stavros kai to Spathi* ("The Cross and the Sword," 1939) is a poetic play. In *Theofano*, a tragedy written in 1946, broadcast over the radio in 1954, and finally staged in 1956, Terzakis has written a psychological drama of Empress Theofano that is regarded by critics as the best of Terzakis' dramatic works and one of the most beautiful Greek plays written in the past twenty years.

Pantelis Georgiou Prevelakis (1909–), a translator of classic tragedy, has been influenced by the ideology of Kazantzakis. *To Iero Sphayie* ("The Holy Slaughter") and *Ta Cheria Tou Zontanou Theou* ("The Hands of the Living God") were written in 1952; the latter was produced in 1957. In *Lazarus* (1954), Prevelakis wrote original choral odes and used the legend to examine the attitudes of an early Christian toward the new religion, which he dramatized according to the classical concepts of tragedy.

A concerted effort has been made in the twentieth century to bring ancient drama to the people. The first important attempt to create a renaissance of Attic tragedy occurred in Delphi in 1927. Here the poet and dramatist Anghelos Sikelianos and his American wife, Eva Palmer, attempted to establish a university on the site of the Amphictyonic Council (an ancient congress of confederate states) as a means of synthesizing the demotic spirit with the ancient arts. They produced *Prometheus Bound* (1927) and *The Sup-*

pliants (1930) by Aeschylus, both translated into the demotic by the poet Yannis Gryparis and directed by Eva Sikelianos. As a result of this pioneering effort, the government subsidized the Ethniko Theatre (National Theater), and on March 19, 1932, two plays symbolically connected were presented: one ancient Greek play, *Agamemnon* by Aeschylus, and *To Theio Oneiro* ("The Divine Dream") by Gregorios Xenopoulos. A drama school of the National Theater was started soon after. Since then the National Theater gives summer festivals of classical plays at Epidaurus and Dodone in Epirus and in the autumn at the Herodes Attikes in Athens and at Piraeus. Foreign plays in translation and original Greek plays are produced at the National Theater throughout the year.

In the last twenty-five years enormous advances have been made in the Greek theater. In 1942 Karolos Errikou Koun (1908–   ) opened his Art Theater, where he has been directing ancient comedy, foreign plays in translation, and original Greek plays. In 1959, a group of young writers influenced by Ionesco, Beckett, Brecht, and the theater of the absurd formed a company of their own named Twelfth Curtain, the title of which refers to the legislation that forbids a company to give more than eleven performances a week. This group presents plays of young, untried playwrights on Mondays, when theaters in Greece are normally closed. In 1960, three new playhouses were opened: the New Theater, the Elsa Vergli Theater, and the Dionyssia Theater. Since then seven new theaters have been built in Athens and Thessaloniki. The latest report states that there are twenty-three theater companies in production today. A large number of plays in all genres have been produced in the last seven years.

Several dramatists who had been personally involved in World War II wrote successful plays about the Nazi occupation. Chief among these is *Bloc C* ("Block C," 1945), the only drama of the eminent novelist Elias Mihail Venezis (1904–   ). Sotiris Patatzis (1916–   ) wrote *Epistrophe apo to Buchenwald* ("Return from Buchenwald"), his first theatrical work. Formerly a translator, after his first play was produced in 1948, Patatzis devoted himself exclusively to the theater. Some of his other successes are *O Kalos Stratiotis Schweik* ("The Good Soldier Schweik," 1956), based on Jaroslav Hašek's novel with an original adaptation; *I Chrysi Phylaki* ("The Golden Prison," 1958), a comedy; and *Don Camillo* (1959), a dramatic adaptation of Guareschi's novel in which the author takes a stand against all extremism.

Kostas Kotzias (1921–   ), who translated Garcia Lorca's *Blood Wedding,* dramatized the foreign occupation and the Greek resistance during World War II in his drama *To Xypnima* ("The Awakening," 1946). Kotzias treated other themes in *Anapoda enas Kosmos* ("A World Inside Out," 1952), a satirical comedy, and *To Pnevma tis Panayiotas* ("The Spirit of Panayiotis," 1954). In 1957 Kotzias was awarded the People's Athenian Prize.

Since World War II Greek dramatists are making even greater efforts to reinterpret Greek life and their history in terms of the contemporary world. Worthy of mention in this group is Alexandros Matsas (1910–   ), who reinterprets classical tragedy in keeping with the psychology of modern audiences. In his verse drama *Clytemnestra* (1956) he offers a poignant defense of his heroine. Another postwar playwright is Georgios Thanou Tzavellas (1916–   ), who has written several plays with an original twist. In the spiritual fantasy *To Paramythi Enos Phengariou* ("Tale of a Moon," 1946), each of the three acts represents the moon: the first quarter in the first act symbolizes desire, the full moon in the second act

SCENE FROM ALEXANDROS MATSAS' *Clytemnestra* (ROYAL CONSULATE GENERAL OF GREECE)

represents culmination, and the last quarter in the third act signifies disillusionment. The midcentury dramatist Alexis Solomos (1918–   ) satirizes all those who persist in adhering to their family traditions in order to appear worthy of their relatives in *O Teleftaios Asprokorakas* ("The Last White Crow"), written in 1943 and produced the following year. Notis Pergialis (1920–   ) depicts a young girl who falls in love with a co-villager and is seduced by him in his *Nyphiatiko Tragoudi* ("Wedding Song," 1949). In *To Koritsi Me To Kordellaki* ("The Girl with the Ribbon"), written in 1953 and produced the following year, Pergialis depicts a group of unemployed who have become ragpickers and set up stalls in uncultivated fields where they spend their poverty-stricken days in dreams. In *Antigone tis Katochis* ("Antigone of the Occupation," written in 1960), the action takes place during the German occupation. Iakovos Stephanos Kambanellis (1922–   ) is noted for several unusual plays that enjoyed successful runs. Chief among these is *Avli ton Thavmaton* ("The Courtyard of Miracles"), a poignant drama produced in Athens in 1957 and in London in 1961. In *I Gorilla kai I Ortensia* ("The Gorilla and the Hydrangea") the eminent professor Mr. Williams is a gorilla and his chauffeur the only human being. In *Ilikia tis Nychtas* ("Age of Night," 1959), a son, stifled by the bourgeois feelings of his family, finds that suicide is his only way out. Alexis Parnis' *Nisi tis Aphroditis* ("Isle of Aphrodite") was produced first in the Soviet Union in 1960 and ran there for 5,732 performances; it was published in *Theatro* (Vol. 2, March 1962) and was produced in Athens in 1963; it even had a brief Off-Broadway production in New York in 1967. Margarita Lymberacki wrote *Allo Alexandro* ("The Other Alexander"), which was produced in France in 1957 and published in Athens in 1964. Loula Anagnostaki, also a film writer, wrote a trilogy of three one-act plays touching on the absurd, which Karolos Koun has undertaken to produce: *Dianykterefsi* ("Spending the Night"), *Poli* ("The City"), published in *Theatro* in 1965, and *Parelasi* ("Parade").

As one views the whole output of plays, it can be said that modern Greek theater is making an enormous contribution through its many festivals of ancient drama translated into the demotic that hundreds of thousands of people from all parts of the world see every year. The countless foreign playwrights from all countries translated into the demotic each year and the abundance of original Greek plays produced manifest the determination of the Greek people to reach the high level of excellence of its own dramatic heritage that saw the birth of drama. There is room for greater utilization of this heritage, and a still closer alignment to world drama and the contemporary world is needed for a more universal interpretation of the Greeks' own individual and national problems.

Non-English sources of information about the modern Greek theater include Mitsou Liyizou, *To Neoellinike Theatro plai sto Pankosmio Theatro* (1958), an analysis of leading plays and productions of the nineteenth and twentieth centuries in Greece, and M. Valsa, *Le Théâtre grec moderne de 1453–1900* (1960), a comprehensive survey of modern

Greek theater. For material in English, the reader might consult *The Modern Greek Theater* (1957), an official publication of the International Theater Institute, translated by Lucille Vassardaki, and *World Theater*, a quarterly review published by the International Theater Institute.—R. D.

Green, Julien. See SOUTH.

Green, Paul E[liot] (1894–   ). American playwright. A native of Lillington, North Carolina, Green has found most of the material for his writing in his home state and the South. A graduate of the state university, he has taught both playwriting and philosophy there, and he helped establish the Carolina Playmakers, a writing and producing organization connected with the university. In the late 1920's and early 1930's Green produced a number of critically esteemed plays on Broadway and spent a brief time at screenwriting, but since about 1935, he has devoted himself almost exclusively to the creation of what he calls "symphonic dramas."

In 1939 Green published a collection of his plays under the title *Out of the South: The Life of a People in Dramatic Form*. The titles and subtitles of the individual plays underline his concern with regional folk material. For example, *The House of Connelly* (1931) is labeled "A drama of the old South and the new" and deals with the last, shabby-genteel remnants of a once-powerful plantation family. *In Abraham's Bosom* (1927) is called "The tragedy of a Negro educator" and traces the doomed effort to establish a school for Negroes. Even *Johnny Johnson* (1936), Green's antiwar play set largely in France and New York in which he employs some sophisticated theatrical techniques (as well as music by Kurt Weill), has as its hero a shy farm boy whose Southern ways become the mark of his goodness. The one-act play *Hymn to the Rising Sun* (1936), "A tragedy of man's waste," is a picture of the chain gang "somewhere in the South." In style, these plays vary from well-made realism to playful fantasy, but all share a deep social concern and a yearning on the author's part to attain a poetic eloquence.

The Lost Colony (1937) was Green's first historical pageant. It was written to commemorate the 350th anniversary of Raleigh's colony at Roanoke, Virginia, and was designed for performance in an open-air amphitheater. Green created a form that provided a blend of history, social commentary, music, spectacle, and heightened speech. He has called such works "symphonic dramas." *The Highland Call* (1939) deals with the Scots settlement in the Cape Fear Valley of North Carolina; *The Common Glory* (1947) dramatizes the role of Jefferson and the state of Virginia in the early Federal period; *Faith of Our Fathers* (1950) is focused on Washington's career; *The Founders* (1957) is the story of the Jamestown Colony; and the subjects of *The Confederacy* (1958) and *Stephen Foster* (1959) are identified in their titles. All of these were designed for specific theaters and occasions, and most have been produced annually since their premières.

There is no standard edition of Green's plays. A full discussion of his works appears in Agatha Adams' *Paul Green of Chapel Hill* (1951).—M. L.

Green Cockatoo, The (Der grüne Kakadu, 1899). A play in one act by Arthur SCHNITZLER. *The*

Green Cockatoo takes place in a sordid Paris tavern in 1789, on the night of the storming of the Bastille. Various actors from local theaters are performing impromptu scenes of crime for the debased delectation of the slumming Parisian aristocracy. One actor, whom they believe to be pursued, tells of pickpockets at work outside; another relates how he set fire to a house; a third tells how he came upon a murder. The host of the tavern derides the noble guests as rogues and pigs and says he hopes they are next in line for extinction by the citizens. No one knows whether he is acting for the gentry's delight or if he is serious. Henri, a good-natured actor, reveals to the shuddering guests how he has just murdered a nobleman who was his wife's lover. The host of the tavern knows this affair to be a true fact; what he does not know is whether Henri is acting or telling the truth. As it happens, Henri is only acting, but not for long. For he soon learns the truth, and when that same nobleman enters the tavern, Henri stabs him to death. Havoc breaks loose and is further amplified by the stormers of the Bastille rushing in, causing the frightened gentry to flee for their lives.

The Green Cockatoo is one of Schnitzler's most skillful and effective pieces, particularly because of the tension generated through the fluctuating uncertainty between reality and illusion and the fact that in the end illusion, true or otherwise, bursts out into bloody reality.

The only translation of this play presently in print is the one by Ethel van der Veer, in *Thirty Famous One-Act Plays,* edited by Bennett Cerf and Van H. Cartmell.—C. R. M.

Greene, Robert (1558–1592). English playwright, poet, and pamphleteer. Born in Norwich, Greene was educated at Cambridge (B.A. 1578; M.A. 1583) and at Oxford (M.A. 1588). Between 1578 and 1583, he toured Italy, engaging, according to his autobiographical repentance pamphlets, in debauchery and loose living but at the same time absorbing the new developments of the Italian literary renaissance. Upon his return to England he married and began to write his euphuistic prose romances such as *Mamillia* (1583); *Pandosto* (1588), the source of Shakespeare's *The Winter's Tale;* and *Menaphon* (1589), which contained a preface by Greene's friend Thomas Nashe. These were followed by his famous cony-catching pamphlets, popular exposés of the activities and techniques of the London underworld.

At the same time that these pamphlets appeared, Greene, apparently working at a furious pace, was writing both plays and his so-called repentance pamphlets. The latter—*Greene's Mourning Garment* (1590), *Greene's Never Too Late* (1590), *Greene's Farewell to Folly* (1591), and *Greene's Groats-worth of Wit* (1592)—are autobiographical accounts (although in all probability exaggerated ones) of his dissolute life. They are particularly interesting to students of the theater for their frequent disparaging allusions to the professional actors of London. Easily the most famous of these allusions is the reference in *Greene's Groats-worth of Wit* to "an upstart crow, beautified with our feathers" who imagines himself "the only Shake-scene in a country." This remark is the earliest known reference to Shakespeare as an actor and playwright. *Greene's Groats-*

worth of Wit was written as Greene was dying, a fact that has led a number of scholars to suggest that it was actually written by Greene's editor, Henry Chettle.

Although many plays have been attributed to Greene, either in whole or in part, only five are unquestionably his. These are *Alphonsus, King of Aragon* (c. 1587), an imitation or, more probably, a burlesque of Christopher Marlowe's *Tamburlaine; A Looking Glass for London and England* (c. 1590), written in collaboration with Thomas Lodge; *Friar Bacon and Friar Bungay* (c. 1590), a charming romantic comedy based on English folklore; *Orlando Furioso* (c. 1591), an adaptation of Ariosto's epic; and *James IV of Scotland* (c. 1591), despite its title a purely fictional, romantic comedy.

As a playwright, Greene's talents lay in the area of romantic comedy explored in *Friar Bacon* and *James IV*. These two plays reveal a charm and invention that continue to provide pleasure. They are particularly creditable for their heroines, Margaret in *Friar Bacon* and Dorothea in *James IV,* two not unworthy prototypes of the heroines in Shakespeare's romantic comedies. Both plays are also interesting as early examples of the use of the double plot. As the innovator of this technique of dramatic construction, Greene made an incalculable contribution to Elizabethan drama.

The standard edition of Greene's works is *The Plays and Poems of Robert Greene* (1905), edited by J. Churton Collins, in two volumes.—E. Q.

Green Fields (Grine Felder, 1919). A comedy by Peretz HIRSHBEIN. Levi-Yitskhok, a wandering young rabbinical student, comes to the farm of Dovid-Noyakh, who welcomes him eagerly and persuades him to remain as a tutor for his young son Avrom-Yankev and the children of Elkone, a neighboring farmer. Dovid-Noyakh's daughter, Tsine, falls in love with Levi-Yitskhok, who reciprocates her love and decides to take Tsine as his wife.

A tender and fragile play, *Green Fields* is one of Hirshbein's folk comedies. In it he portrays the simple piety and human decency of the Jewish farmer, who, because his isolation often prevented him from providing even the rudiments of an education for his children, was somewhat disdainfully regarded as an ignoramus and a boor by his town brethren. Hirshbein's farmers are neither boors nor oafs. Rooted in the soil of a bountiful nature, they glow with the warmth of a summer sun. They are Hirshbein's vindication, even exaltation, of one variety of the Jewish common man, who, with his respect for learning, piety, and decency, no matter how small his own education, is the perennial hero of Yiddish literature. Levi-Yitskhok's decision to marry a farmer's daughter is only in part the result of his love for Tsine. Levi-Yitskhok, the town-bred scholar, has also learned the value of these rural folk and has come to respect their basic humanity and piety. Tsine, Hirshbein's most winning heroine, grows under the impetus of love from a hoydenish, barefoot country girl to a sedate young woman, prepared to play her role as a Jewish matron and scholar's wife.

The importance of plot is minimal. The play depends for its effectiveness on the charming simplicity of its characters, the gentleness of its mood, and the warmth and good will of its atmosphere. Hirshbein's touch is sure, and he never crosses the line that divides sentiment from sentimentality. The result is an idyllic rendering of a world in which inner peace is matched by the tranquility of a way of life and the benevolence of nature.

Joseph C. Landis has translated *Green Fields* in *The Dybbuk and Other Great Yiddish Plays* (1966). —J. C. L.

Gregory, Lady **Isabella Augusta** (1852–1932). Irish playwright. A native of Galway, Lady Gregory was the wife of Sir William Gregory, the owner of a large estate at Coole in western Ireland. After the death of her husband in 1892, she developed a strong interest in Irish literature and history. In 1898 she met William Butler Yeats, and together they helped to found in 1902 the Irish National Theatre Society, which became the nucleus of the Abbey Theatre Company. Acting as a director until her retirement in 1928, Lady Gregory played an indispensable role in the development of the Abbey, both writing successful plays and working tirelessly on the complex, tedious administrative and financial problems that always threatened to engulf the theater. Probably her finest moment in the administrative capacity was her leadership of the Abbey Company on tour in America in 1911/12. As recorded in her memoir *Our Irish Theatre* (1914), that tempestuous tour of major American cities was greeted with rioting and demonstrations by Irish-American nationalists and finally the technical arrest (for their own protection) of the actors. Through it all Lady Gregory displayed an unyielding commitment to the integrity and value of the plays that were presented. See IRELAND.

Lady Gregory's dramatic work includes two of the best one-act plays in the English language: *Spreading the News* (1904) and *The Rising of the Moon* (1907). *Spreading the News* concerns what Lady Gregory called "the Irishman's incorrigible genius for mythmaking." Put less elegantly, the play deals with the hilarious repercussions resulting from half-understood gossip as it sweeps through a small town in Galway, a town whose chief business is the "minding of one another's business."

Less funny but theatrically more effective is *The Rising of the Moon*. Set on a darkened quayside, the play deals with the encounter of an Irish policeman and a fugitive political prisoner. Among her many other successful one-act plays are *The Workhouse Ward* (1908), a humorous picture of two friendly enemies confined in a poorhouse, and *The Gaol Gate* (1906), a tragedy with a strong nationalist tone.

Lady Gregory's rich imagination is evident in her "wonder plays," dramatized fairy tales subtly underscored with ironic humor. Among the most successful of these are *The Dragon* (1919), *The Travelling Man* (1910), and *Aristotle's Bellows* (1921). Somewhat more ambitious are her folk-history plays, which she divided into tragedies—*Grania* (1906), *Kincora* (1909), and *Dervorgilla* (1907)—and tragicomedies—*The Canavans* (1906), *The White Cockade* (1905), and *The Deliverer* (1911). Among the tragedies the most impressive is *Dervorgilla,* the story of the legendary queen of Ireland who was responsible for first bringing the English to Ireland. The best of the tragicomedies is *The White Cockade,* a sharply satiric portrait of James II, the English king

who, leading Irish forces, was defeated at the battle of the Boyne (1690). Less successful dramatically but more striking politically is *The Deliverer,* an allegory on the fate of the Irish hero Charles Stewart Parnell.

Lady Gregory also assisted William Butler YEATS in writing many of his plays. Her help consisted largely in rendering with accuracy and ease the Irish peasant dialect. Among the plays on which she worked with Yeats are *The Pot of Broth* (1902), *Cathleen ni Houlihan* (1902), and *On Baile's Strand* (1904). In his turn, Yeats assisted Lady Gregory in the writing of some of her plays, notably on *The Rising of the Moon.*

The distinguishing characteristic of Lady Gregory's work is the distinctive folk dialect of western Ireland in which she cast all of her plays. That dialect influenced many later playwrights, as did her innovations in one-act comedies and folk histories. The artistry of these plays, together with the enormous personal influence she wielded on such men of genius as Yeats and John Millington Synge, testifies to Lady Gregory's central importance in the development of modern drama in English.

Lady Gregory's *Collected Plays* (1962) has been issued by the Dolmen Press, Dublin. A full-length study of her life and work is Elizabeth Coxhead's *Lady Gregory* (1961). Her collaboration with Yeats is analyzed in Daniel Murphy's "Yeats and Lady Gregory," *Modern Drama,* VII (1964), 322–328. —E. Q.

Greville, Fulke. 1st Baron **Brooke** (1554–1628). English playwright, poet, and biographer. A native of Warwickshire, Greville was educated at Cambridge. He held a number of prominent positions in the courts of Elizabeth and James I, including that of chancellor of the exchequer (1614–1621). He is best known as the author of a sonnet sequence, *Caelica* (1580–1600), and a biography of Sir Philip Sidney, *Life of the Renowned Sir Philip Sidney* (1610–1612). He is also the author of two extant dramas, *Alaham* (c. 1601) and *Mustapha* (written between c. 1603 and 1608). They are both closet dramas, designed for the study, not the stage; both, however, closely modeled on Seneca, have a solemnity and power that command respect. They are designed to exhibit political morals: *Alaham* dramatizes the danger to the state of a weak ruler; *Mustapha,* the danger of a willful tyrant. Beyond these themes, however, is a brooding and eloquently voiced picture of the human dilemma reflected in the famous passage from *Mustapha:*

Oh wearisome Condition of Humanity!
Borne under one Law, to another bound:
Vainely begot, and yet forbidden vanity,
Created sicke, commanded to be sound:
What meaneth Nature by these diverse Lawes?

The standard edition of Greville's work is *The Poems and Dramas of Fulke Greville* (1959), edited by Geoffrey Bullough, in two volumes.—E. Q.

Griboyedov, Alexander [**Sergeyevich**] (1795–1829). Russian playwright. Griboyedov was born and brought up in Moscow. During the Napoleonic invasion of 1812, he interrupted his studies at the Moscow University to join the army, where he served until 1816, when he was discharged and entered government service in the Department of Foreign Affairs. His duties left him enough leisure to lead the gay life of a high-society dandy and to write several comedies. His first effort, *Molodye suprugi* ("The Newlyweds," 1815), was a one-act comedy written in alexandrines. Then, in collaboration with I. Katenin, he wrote a three-act comedy in prose, "The Student," in 1817, in which he satirized Russian sentimentalists. In 1817 Griboyedov, together with A. A. Shakhovskoi and N. I. Khmelnitsky, wrote *Svoya semya* ("One's Own Family"), a comedy in verse that gave a foretaste of the high quality of WOE FROM WIT. This high quality was even more evident in *Pritvornaya nevernost* ("Pretended Infidelity"), written in 1818 in collaboration with A. Gendre.

In 1818 Griboyedov fought a duel over the famous ballerina Istomina, had the little finger of his left hand shot off, and was sent to Persia to serve as secretary of the Russian legation. He distinguished himself there by his diplomatic work and by the speed with which he mastered the Persian language. In 1821 he was transferred to Tiflis, in Georgia, as diplomatic secretary to the Russian proconsul. It was in Tiflis that he started working on his masterpiece, WOE FROM WIT, which he finished in Moscow between 1823 and 1824 while on an extended leave. *Woe from Wit* is a brilliant comedy in which the topical themes of the day are expressed in a vernacular so powerful that phrases from the play are still part of the Russian language.

During that time he became involved with various members of the abortive Decembrist movement and in 1826 he was arrested. Since none of the charges against him could be proved, however, he was released and sent back to his post in the Caucasus just as Russo-Persian hostilities broke out. In 1827 Persia sued for peace and it was Griboyedov who conducted the negotiations for Russia and who drafted the Turkmanchai peace treaty (1828). He earned for this work a triumphant reception in St. Petersburg, an audience with the tsar, and, despite his vehement protestations, the post of Russian minister to Teheran. His reluctance to accept this post proved fully justified. Barely three weeks after he had taken up his duties in that capital, the Russian legation was stormed by a mob of Persians exasperated by the harsh terms the Russians had imposed on their country; later Griboyedov's mutilated body was identified only by the missing little finger of his left hand. —A. MACA.

Grieg, [Johan] Nordahl [Brun] (1902–1943). Norwegian poet, novelist, and playwright. Grieg's early seafaring experiences led him to write the volume of poetry *Rundt Kap det Gode Håb* (*Round the Cape of Good Hope,* 1922) and an important first novel, *Skibet går videre* (*The Ship Sails On,* 1924). After studying at Oxford (1923–1924), he published a study of such British poets as Keats, Byron, Brooke, and Owen in *De unge døde* (*The Young Dead,* 1932). Grieg worked as a war correspondent in China (1927), translated Jack London into Norwegian while he lived in Russia (1932–1935), and visited Spain during its civil war. His Marxism was individual enough not to be dissident with the strong patriotism that came to manifest itself in his poetry. In 1940 he was instrumental in smuggling Norway's gold re-

serves to England, where the Norwegian government in exile was located. While accompanying as observer a bombing mission over Berlin, Grieg was shot down on December 2, 1943.

Grieg's first play, *En ung mands kjærlighet* ("A Young Man's Love," 1927), while conventional in structure, immediately asserts what was to become a major theme in his work, the place of violence and brutality in society. Dialectic is developed and form rendered more supple in *Barabbas* (1927), a biblical paraphrase of events in the Chinese civil war. Grieg's next two plays deal with profiteering and exploitation, namely *Atlanterhavet* ("The Atlantic," 1932) and *Vår ære og vår makt* (*Our Power and Our Glory,* 1935). The latter contains especially fine studies of Norwegian seamen exploited by callous shipping interests during World War I. *Men imorgen—* ("But Tomorrow—," 1936) directs its indignation at the developing arms industry. *Nederlaget* (*Defeat,* 1937), in its masterfully diversified canvas of the Paris Commune of 1871, argues that freedom has to be fought for and guarded vigilantly at any and all times. Not unexpectedly, the play came to attract the admiration of Bertolt Brecht, and it is without much question Grieg's most significant play. Some unused film scenarios remain, including one of the life of Grieg's distant relation, the composer Edvard Grieg.

Grieg's social passion and his knowledge of Russian dramaturgy and film art made him one of the most important Norwegian playwrights between the wars. His plays almost invariably gave rise to extensive controversy.

Defeat has been published in a separate volume (1944) and is also in *Scandinavian Plays of the 20th Century,* second series (1944). See also Graham Greene, "Nordahl Grieg: A Personal Note," in *Norseman,* Vol. II (1944), and Olav Rytter, "Nordahl Grieg," in *Norseman,* Vol. II (1944). —R. B. V.

Grillparzer, Franz (1791–1872). Austrian poet and playwright. Grillparzer was born into a familial structure that affected him the length of his long life. Psychological investigations have revealed that the entire Grillparzer family tended toward severe mental illness. The effect of so ill a family on so impressionable a child as Franz Grillparzer is illuminated in the story of his life as recorded in his voluminous diaries and letters. He shared virtually every illness from which his family suffered: hypochondria, paranoia, schizophrenia, melancholia, and suicidal tendencies.

As a child, Grillparzer never found the love and approbation he needed. His mother was sickly most of her life and therefore unavailable a great deal of the time; his father, a lawyer, was a near recluse and a misanthrope. He was strict to the extreme, had little sense of humor, and was an excessive moralist. When Grillparzer sought praise from his father for his early attempts at poetry (which culminate in the poetic lyricism of HERO AND LEANDER), his father rejected his advances and severely criticized his work; he regarded poets and poetry as suspect and would fly into tirades over a figure of speech or any ornamentation of a poetic nature. Such things, to him, were reprehensible and degenerate. But it was the father's total withdrawal that most affected the young Franz and caused his life to be beset by psychopathic symptoms.

FRANZ GRILLPARZER (*Goetheundseine Welt* BY
HANS WAHL, INSEL VERLAG)

For much of his life Grillparzer was a public servant in state employ, a position he thoroughly detested yet maintained while he continued his dramatic writing. His total dramatic output of nearly a dozen completed works constitutes virtually the foundation of high drama in Austria. Born in Vienna, he absorbed various indigenous elements of the popular Viennese theater, in addition to elements of the so-called fate drama, a form of drama in which fate is seen as a willful and malicious force that plots the destruction of man. Yet he tended to make these elements thoroughly his own, only to have their influence fade rapidly after his initial play meant for public distribution, *Die Ahnfrau* (*The Ancestress,* 1817).

An extremely sensitive man, Grillparzer finally withdrew in 1856 from public life when he ran into difficulty with imperial Viennese censorship. The remainder of his works were written out of compulsion rather than desire, for self-therapy rather than for public acclaim.

Even in his earliest works, however, Grillparzer was wont to mirror his unhappiness and dissatisfactions. In his youth he drew open dramatic portraits of his troubled relationship with his father. But it was not until several years after his father's death, when Grillparzer was seventeen, that the poet began to express his torments in his plays, from *Die Ahnfrau* through *Die Jüdin von Toledo* (*The Jewess of Toledo,* conceived and written between 1816 and the mid-1850's; prod. 1873). It is the story of a young king who hides behind duty to conceal from himself and his subjects his incapacity for heterosexual love, a factor that played no small part in Grillparzer's own life.

Grillparzer's need to expiate was always at odds with his intense desire for withdrawal. This tends in almost every instance—from *Die Ahnfrau* through his last play written for public performance, *Weh dem, der lügt!* (*Thou Shalt Not Lie!,* 1838)—to manifest itself in ingenious and devious ways. He never states his aberrations or conflicts blatantly in these plays but conceals them, often to the point of placing his personal problems in various of his female characters, as, for example, in his Medea in the trilogy *Das goldene Vliess* (*The Golden Fleece,* 1821) and SAPPHO.

Among the problems Grillparzer mirrors are his search for a father figure, his fear of women, and his homosexual tendencies. Two of his three later "private" plays—*Ein Bruderzwist im Habsburg* (*Family Strife in Hapsburg,* completed in 1850; prod. 1872) and *Die Jüdin von Toledo*—are harsh, bitter, and uncompromising self-portraits. *Ein Bruderzwist im Habsburg* is a portrait of Grillparzer as Rudolf II of Austria, for in that character is seen Grillparzer's melancholy, his paranoia, his homoerotic tendencies, and his hypochondria. The play deals with Rudolf's inability to be a strong and decisive ruler of the Austro-Hungarian Empire. These plays he intended to have destroyed at his death. Fortunately, they were preserved and constitute the most mature expression of his art.

The essence of Grillparzer is to be found in his personal confessions, rather than in his social commentary on the state, statecraft, monarchy, and civilization itself. To be sure, these criticisms are there, but the plays are far more: Grillparzer's knowledge of his problems, including his fear of them, infuses his plays with a psychological profundity and truthfulness perhaps worthy of Freud himself.

Studies of Grillparzer in English are rare, and those that exist are for the most part blindly unaware of the psychological nature of his plays and the importance of a biographical approach in regard to the full understanding of them. Only one study in English, therefore, is cited. It is by Douglas Yates, *Franz Grillparzer, A Critical Biography* (1953). Though this work covers roughly only the first half of Grillparzer's life and is weak in what little psychological approach it does take, it is still the best there is in English. As for the works of Grillparzer in English translation, all the plays have appeared between 1938 and 1953. The translations are acceptable though scarcely felicitous.—C. R. M.

Gryphius, Andreas. Latinized name of **Andreas Greif** (1616–1664). Outstanding Silesian dramatist and poet of the German Baroque era. Gryphius left his native Glogau in 1638 and remained abroad, chiefly in Holland, for the next twelve years. A learned man, he knew seven languages and was greatly influenced by Shakespeare, Seneca, Hooft, and Vondel. Although he wrote dramatic works in several genres, Gryphius is noted today chiefly for his tragedies and comedies.

The tragedies followed the precepts of Martin OPITZ closely, dealing, with one notable exception, with kings and other highborn nobles. The exception is *Cardenio und Celinde* (1647), a tragedy of members of the lower nobility. Owing to the rules of the form, this play was tantamount to a middle-class tragedy. Unlike most of his other tragic dramas, it

ANDREAS GRYPHIUS (GERMAN INFORMATION CENTER)

did not deal with a martyr figure. However, the thematic material and moral message of all Gryphius' plays were the same: Tragedy is the transitoriness of all earthly existence. It underlies the praise of belief, joys of Christianity, and worldly vanity, which, presented in the plays as thesis against thesis, argument against argument, in fact dictated their composition. The characters have little life. Charles Stuart, whose execution shook up Europe severely, is presented in *Charles Stuart, oder Ermordete Majestät* ("Carolus Stuardus, or Majesty Murdered," 1649) as the idealized epitome of the Christian martyr. The characters about him are clearly placed into "good" and "bad" groups, and show no development in the course of the play. The crime against the crown is clearly the crime against God. The play itself is merely an exchange of speeches, sometimes delivered in lengthy alexandrine monologues, sometimes in stychometric fashion. The general impression is one of a book-drama rather than a stage production.

In his comedies, Gryphius adheres to the dictum that comedy portray only the lower classes on the stage. He is innovative, however, in *Die geliebte Dornrose* ("The Beloved Dornrose," 1660), which is written almost entirely in Silesian dialect, thus pro-viding a degree of realism then new on the German stage. *Absurda Comica, oder Herr Peter Squentz* ("The Absurda Comica, or Master Peter Squenz," written 1648; pub. 1657), a version of the "Pyramus and Thisbe" scene of *A Midsummer Night's Dream,* at times approaches the slapstick of farces; but the plays on words, the personification through the adroit misuse of high style, and displays of false erudition, coupled with the constant falling out of the dramatic framework, leave little doubt concerning the comic artistry of the author.

Gryphius' tragedies are no longer part of the everyday life of the German stage, but *Die geliebte Dornrose* was produced successfully as late as 1954. The author's more lasting contributions are in the firm establishment of the five-act division, increased use of the chorus (even if in a moralizing role), and the use of dialect as the major language of a play.
—B. M. M.

Guarini, Giovan Battista. See IL PASTOR FIDO.

Guinea, The Republic of. See AFRICA: *Guinea, The Republic of.*

Güntekin, Reşat Nuri (1889–1956). Turkish novelist, short-story writer, and playwright. Güntekin, born in Istanbul, was appointed general inspector at the ministry of education and cultural attaché in Paris; he also served as deputy in the Turkish National Assembly. Güntekin's literary career began as a short-story writer and drama critic in 1917–1918. With the publication of his novel *Çalıkuşu* (*The Autobiography of a Turkish Girl*) in installments in the newspaper *Vakit* in 1922, Güntekin earned great fame. Almost all of Güntekin's novels are realistic and also romantic and are about the people and social problems of Anatolia. He is the most widely read novelist in Turkey.

Güntekin made a play out of his novel *Yaprak Dökümü* ("The Fall of the Leaves," 1943), which set the pattern for many plays by other playwrights about the decay of the Turkish upper classes after World War I. The social consciousness of Güntekin's novels and the humor of his short stories are reflected in his plays. They are usually hilarious social satires, such as *Hülleci* ("The Hired Husband," 1935); or sentimental dramas about family life, such as *Taş Parçası* ("A Piece of Stone," 1923) and *Eski Şarkı* ("The Old Song," 1951).

With his enormous output of novels, short stories, and plays, as well as other writings, the work of Güntekin has been a rich source for other dramatists.
—N. O.

H

Hagoromo (The Robe of Feathers), 14th century. A Japanese *noh* play by Zeami MOTOKIYO. *Hagoromo* is one of the most lyrical and frequently presented of the noh plays. In this brief, one-act play, a fisherman sees a wonderful and bright robe of feathers suspended from a tree standing beside the famous beach at Mio. Instinctively, he seizes it, only to be startled by the apparition of a maiden who claims it as hers. She is one of the thirty minor deities of the moon and has for some unspecified cause descended to earth. Although at first the fisherman declines to return the mysterious garment, the maiden's grief at her forlorn and wingless condition moves him to pity. He returns it on condition that she perform for him one of the famous dances known to be given at the moon palace. This she does, assuring him that her blessing will fall upon him and upon all the courteous land of Japan. At the play's conclusion, she is imagined to ascend to her home in the moon.

Zeami's poetry in this play shines with unearthly beauty. Especially celebrated are the lines sung by the chorus as the spirit performs her ceremonial dance and ascends to the moon. The lines evoke the calm of a night in spring, with splendor of the sea, sky, and mountain under the rays of the full moon. —H. W. W.

Hairy Ape, The (1922). An expressionistic drama by Eugene O'NEILL. *The Hairy Ape* tells the story of a steamship's superstoker, Yank, who discovers his shortcomings from a chance meeting with one of the passengers, cultured and wealthy Mildred. He has hitherto considered himself as the Atlas of the world, but stung by Mildred's revulsion at his greasy appearance, he throws up his job and goes forth to find a place where he can belong, as well as to avenge himself on those who have destroyed his self-confidence by their superiority. But Yank finds he cannot belong, cannot even avenge himself on the rich. Seeking the companionship of a gorilla in the zoo, he discovers he has no place in the brute world either as the beast crushes him to death.

Beneath the surface of this story is a larger, metaphysical, and not readily transparent meaning more clearly defined by O'Neill himself in a published interview (*New York Herald Tribune,* November 16, 1924). Yank, it was plain, is not merely a stoker based upon O'Neill's memory of a rough and powerful stoker whose acquaintance he had made in a waterfront dive, but an intellectual concept of man's alienation in an indifferent universe. He was a symbol, as O'Neill put it, of man "who has lost his old harmony which he used to have as animal and has not yet acquired in a spiritual way." Yank, with his narrow spirit and limited intelligence, O'Neill went on to explain, is incapable of achieving any really developed humanity, even though no longer content with his previous animal-like status. He strikes out but blindly and in vain against a reality he cannot affect or comprehend. The power of the play succeeded in fascinating its audiences even though they saw, as O'Neill had reason to complain, only the baffled stoker, not the symbol.—J. G.

Halpern, Leivick. See H. LEIVICK.

Hamlet (c. 1600–1601). A tragedy by William SHAKESPEARE. The Stationers' Register entry (July 26, 1602) indicating that the play was "lately acted" by the Lord Chamberlain's Men is the earliest allusion to a performance of *The Tragedy of Hamlet, Prince of Denmark.* It was first published in 1603 in a quarto edition. The First Quarto is a "bad quarto." The Second Quarto, an authoritative text based primarily on Shakespeare's manuscript, appeared the following year. The First Folio (1623) contains a slightly different, but also authoritative, text derived from an acting version.

The Hamlet story is rooted in ancient Scandinavian and Celtic legend, first put into written form by Saxo Grammaticus in his *Historia Danica* (c. 1200). In 1576 a French version appeared in the fifth volume of François de Belleforest's *Histoires tragiques* (translated into English in 1608). An English dramatic version, attributed to Thomas Kyd, was written in the 1580's. Literary allusions and dramatic records between 1589 and 1596 indicate that this lost play—called by scholars *Ur-Hamlet*—was well known to Londoners. It was *Ur-Hamlet* that served as Shakespeare's immediate source. What appears to be a version of *Ur-Hamlet* has survived in the early seventeenth-century German play *Der Bestrafte Bruder-mord (Fratricide Punished).*

Shakespeare's version relates how Prince Hamlet learns from the ghost of his lately deceased father, King Hamlet, that the king's own brother, Claudius —the current ruler of Denmark—foully murdered him. The ghost calls upon Hamlet to revenge his murder, but without bringing harm upon Gertrude, Hamlet's mother, who is now the wife of Claudius. In the course of carrying out the ghost's charge, Hamlet —feigning madness and seeking further confirmation of that charge—begins a cat-and-mouse game with Claudius. Taking advantage of the visit of a troupe of actors, Hamlet presents his "mousetrap" play. Claudius, deeply disturbed, abruptly leaves the performance. The king decides to send Hamlet to England in the company of Rosencrantz and Guildenstern, friends of the prince previously summoned to help uncover the reason for Hamlet's strange behavior. But first, in another attempt to penetrate this

JOHN PHILIP KEMBLE AS HAMLET (NEW YORK PUBLIC
LIBRARY)

concerned themselves with a study of the protagonist and his delay in answering the revenge call. During the Romantic era, particularly, these studies tended to divorce the character Hamlet from the play.

Hamlet is basically a revenge tragedy written at a time when there appears to have been a demand for such works on the Elizabethan stage. The play, moreover, is a revision of the popular *Ur-Hamlet*, owned by Shakespeare's company. Shakespeare had to retain the stock situations and basic characterizations of *Ur-Hamlet* since they had become familiar to his audiences. Yet his own artistry was such that he transmuted the baser Kydian melodramatic tragedy of blood into something more golden. That something—as scholars recognize on the basis of the available evidence—was in his masterful development of Hamlet from a mere avenger to a highly complex character. The prince is perhaps the most multifaceted character in literature. Ophelia describes him as "The courtier's, soldier's, scholar's, eye, tongue, sword; / Th' expectancy and rose of the fair state, / The glass of fashion and the mould of form, / The observ'd of all observers."

Hamlet so closely resembles a human being that critics and audiences may tend to forget he is a literary creation confined to the boundaries of a five-act play. Dramaturgical elements aid this forgetfulness. The role is the longest in Shakespeare. Hamlet is alone more than any other character in a Shakespearean play, and he speaks more soliloquies—soliloquies that are far more introspective than those found in earlier plays. Thus, *Hamlet* provides ample raw materials for the countless theories attempting to explain why the prince delays his revenge. Yet the plot never makes this completely clear.

Certain elements of the story help show why the issue is clouded. *Hamlet* has its roots in the primitive Germanic blood-revenge ethos but is presented in a Christian Renaissance setting before an Elizabethan audience for whom private blood revenge was illegal. Secondly, Claudius—Hamlet's shrewd antagonist—is a lawful ruler; hence, killing him without evidence is regicide. And who will accept the testimony of a ghost? Hamlet, therefore, is caught in a practical dilemma foisted on him by plot structure.

The plot, moreover, has two minor story lines: the political situation between Denmark and Norway and the Polonius family story. As the predominating imagery of disease suggests, all three story lines focus on unwholesome elements within and without the kingdom. Consideration of what lies behind such unwholesomeness is as important as is an analysis of Hamlet's character. Questions are raised in the play about the results of unchecked emotion, about the relationship between appearance and reality, and about the *why* behind the destruction of innocent human beings.

An outstanding edition of *Hamlet* is the New Cambridge Edition (2nd ed., 1936), edited by J. Dover Wilson.—W. G.

behavior, Polonius, Claudius' aged and garrulous counselor, arranges to eavesdrop at a meeting between Hamlet and his mother. Polonius is accidentally slain, providing an excuse for shipping Hamlet abroad with a secret order for his death. Polonius' daughter, Ophelia, in love with Hamlet but rejected by him in his revenge quest, goes mad under the combined stress of Hamlet's rejection, the loss of her father, and separation from her brother, Laertes, who had gone to Paris. Laertes returns in anger over the murder and secret burial of his father. Meanwhile, through a pirate attack on his ship, Hamlet escapes and returns to Denmark. Having learned of Hamlet's role in the death of his father and further inflamed over Ophelia's madness (the girl subsequently drowns), Laertes agrees to aid Claudius in doing away with the prince during a fencing match. The plot succeeds, but not before Laertes is stabbed with the same poisoned rapier he used on Hamlet, nor before Gertrude accidentally drinks the poisoned wine intended also for Hamlet. Before he expires, the prince kills Claudius. Of the central characters, only Horatio, Hamlet's loyal friend, remains alive to tell the true story. No longer is something "rotten in the state of Denmark." Fortinbras, the Norwegian prince, will now rule the purged kingdom.

Hamlet—the first of Shakespeare's great tragedies—has been subjected to more commentaries than any other dramatic work. Most analyses have

Hamsun, Knut (1859–1952). Norwegian novelist, poet, and playwright. Hamsun's early life of vagabondage led him twice to the United States, where he worked variously as farm hand and streetcar conductor. His novel *Markens grøde* (*The Growth of the Soil*, 1917), that impressive panegyric to simple virtue and the good earth, won him the

KNUT HAMSUN (NORWEGIAN INFORMATION SERVICE)

Nobel Prize in 1920 but tended to obscure his gift for probing the irrational and its "feverish progeny," evident in such early novels as *Sult* (*Hunger,* 1890) and *Mysterier* (*Mysteries,* 1892), and the complications of free eroticism, in *Pan* (1894) and *Victoria* (1898). Hamsun is in the tradition, not so much of Ibsen, but of Nietzsche and Strindberg. His intellectual elitism led him to espouse the Nazi cause in World War II, but though he was heavily fined as a collaborator, his literary reputation survives unimpaired.

Hamsun professed indifference to the theater, yet he wrote six plays that have had some life outside Scandinavia, chiefly in Russia and Germany. The trilogy *Ved rigets port* (*At the Gate of the Kingdom,* 1895), *Livets spil* (*Game of Life,* 1896), and *Aftenrøde* (*Red of Evening,* 1898) portray three stages in the life of Ivar Kareno, a Nietzschean zealot who is ravaged in succession by love and then by old age. *Munken Vendt* (*Vendt the Monk,* written 1902) is a broadly conceived verse drama, somewhat reminiscent of Ibsen's *Peer Gynt.* It had to wait until 1926 for production, in Heidelberg, with Heinrich George in the title role. Somewhat less interesting is *Dronning Tamara* (*Tamara the Queen,* 1903), a historical play with an Eastern setting. A modern comedy, *Livet i vold* (*In the Grip of Life,* 1910), was staged by the Moscow Art Theater as early as 1911 and produced by Max Reinhardt in 1914 in Germany under the title *Vom Teufel geholt.*

Hamsun's eminence still rests on his fiction, but his plays are not totally negligible. In general, what he lacks in structure he makes up for in character and dialogue.

See Harald Beyer, *A History of Norwegian Literature* (1956), translated by Einar Haugen; and James McFarlane, *Ibsen and the Temper of Norwegian Literature* (1960).—R. B. V.

hanamichi. In Japanese *kabuki* theater, a raised platform or bridgeway extending from a point close to, but not at the left-hand extremity of, the stage, as viewed from the audience, to a curtained doorway in the rear of the auditorium. The *hanamichi* is an acting area, used in many ways traditionally established.

Its derivation has occasioned much inconclusive controversy. It obviously bears some resemblance to the HASHIGAKARI of the *noh* stage. Yet there are striking dissimilarities. The hashigakari does not extend through the main part of the auditorium but leads from the rear left of the square noh stage to a dressing room on one side of the total structure. The term hashigakari used in respect to the kabuki stage designates an area on the stage itself where the audience at one time deposited flowers, although more recent practice favors the hanamichi for this purpose. Many forms of theater in Japan include long avenues of approach to the stage. This was true of the traditional *dengaku* and *kanjin* as well as of the noh; a parallel is also found in the traditional wrestler's ring.

Whatever the hanamichi's derivation, it is certain that it is used with much theatrical effectiveness and greatly assists in drawing the audience psychologically into the players' world. The best seats in the theater are held to be those nearest the hanamichi. Flowers are thrown over favored actors; in earlier times theater addicts pinched the legs of villains making their exits. The curtain in the rear is often rattled when an actor is about to enter, thus turning all eyes in this direction.

Several actors in the play may enter on the hanamichi but only leading actors use it for their exits. On it they frequently dance or strike dramatic poses; they may speak from it to themselves, directly to the audience, or to other characters on the stage. It is also used for processions and ceremonies and is bordered by lights which may be raised or dimmed. Action on it may be directly integrated with a scene on the main stage, or one scene may be enacted on the hanamichi while another, imagined as taking place in some distant location, may be performed on the main stage. A trap door is generally located on it, of use especially for representations of the supernatural. There are stated positions along the hanamichi where traditional actions may be performed. In the earlier kabuki theaters there was even a supplementary hanamichi running parallel to the larger structure but leading through the right-hand section of the auditorium.

The hanamichi has proved one of the most brilliant and useful inventions in Japanese theater architecture. Although no attempt has been made to duplicate it in, or to transport its many functions to the stages of the West, it has indirectly exercised a perceptible influence on twentieth-century Western stage design, especially where groping exists toward an architecture realizing an increasingly intimate relation between actor and audience.

For good drawings of the hanamichi stage and further discussion, see Earle Ernst, *The Kabuki Theatre* (1956), and Kawatake Shigetoshi, *Kabuki: Japanese Drama* (1958).—H. W. W.

Hankin, St. John [Emile Clavering] (1860–1909). English playwright. St. John Hankin was one of the writers who benefited most from the Edwardian dramatic renascence, particularly from the impact of the drama of ideas, the noncommercial theater that emphasized art and substance rather than mere amusement and entertainment. Born in 1860 in Southampton, he attended Oxford, where he did especially well in the classics, and after his graduation in 1890 went to London to take up a career in journalism. He later spent a year in India, but malaria

SCENE FROM A KABUKI PLAY SHOWING THE *Hanamichi* (JAPAN NATIONAL TOURIST ORGANIZATION)

forced him to return to London, where he resumed his journalistic career, contributing articles to the English magazine *Punch* and doing the dramatic criticism for the London *Times*. His active years as playwright were in the first decade of the twentieth century, and he was fortunate in having both the Stage Society and the Court Theatre available to do his plays, for it is doubtful that any commercial company would have been interested in producing his type of drama. He suffered from ill health much of the time and in 1907 developed neurasthenia, from which he never recovered. He committed suicide by drowning himself in the River Ithon in 1909.

Hankin is usually linked with Harley Granville-Barker and George Bernard Shaw as the major figures in the development of the new drama in the 1890's and the early years of the twentieth century. His major works—*The Return of the Prodigal* (1905), *The Charity That Began at Home* (1906), *The Cassilis Engagement* (1907), and *The Last of the De Mullins* (1908)—reflect the themes and concerns of the drama of the period, particularly such matters as caste, snobbery, and sex and the new woman. *The Return of the Prodigal*, for instance, demonstrates Hankin's ironic view of family life, for he portrays a son "blackmailing" his father into supporting him in idleness the rest of his days. In *The Cassilis Engagement* Hankin treats of the difficulties that arise when

a young man considers marrying out of his class, and *The Last of the De Mullins* takes up the problem of the Shavian and Ibsenite "new woman."

In these plays, Hankin's gift for comedy is evident, as is his insight into the foibles and absurdities of human nature. What is perhaps his greatest weakness is, paradoxically, also his strongest artistic quality: his ability to let the characters speak for themselves, his complete detachment from every one of them. It is this detachment, however, that detracts from whatever forceful thematic impact Hankin might have liked his plays to have. Whether he would have gone in any other direction had he lived longer will, of course, never be known. The plays that he did write, however, demonstrate that he deserves special mention in any history of the Edwardian dramatic renascence. His concern with both manner and matter, form and content, and his ability to portray as well as to analyze character, mainly through dialogue, attest his right to be ranked among the leading playwrights of the movement.

A good introduction is John Drinkwater's comments in *The Dramatic Works of St. John Hankin* (3 vols., 1912). See also Desmond MacCarthy, *The Court Theatre* (1907); J. W. Cunliffe, *Modern English Playwrights* (1927); Montrose Moses, *Representative British Dramas* (rev. ed., 1931); and Gerald Weales, *Edwardian Plays* (1962).—M. T.

Hannibal (1835). A tragedy by Christian Dietrich GRABBE. In this five-act play, the source of which is Plutarch's *Lives,* the playwright depicts the confrontation of a highly gifted, extraordinary individual with the masses upon whom he must to some extent rely. Hannibal is forced to capitulate before the strength of the insensitive masses. His goals remain unrealized and he perishes through no fault of his own but because of the overwhelming power of circumstances.

There is a strong autobiographical element in this drama, for Grabbe too blamed the circumstances of his life for his failures. The play remains a highly pessimistic, sharply satirical statement of this belief. —C. A. M.

Happy Days (Oh! Les Beaux Jours, 1963). A play by Samuel BECKETT. *Happy Days,* Beckett's third major play, was first performed in English in New York in September 1961, and later it was produced in Paris in French in October 1963 at the Théâtre de France. In the first act Winnie is half buried in a mound of sand. She has in front of her as she faces the audience a large handbag and a few objects she uses: a mirror, a toothbrush, a lipstick, a nail file, and an old Browning revolver. In the second act she has sunk down farther in the sand and only her head is free. She continues her monologue and speaks from time to time to her husband, Willie, who most of the time sleeps behind the sand pile.

The scene is a desert with implacable sunlight in which almost all traces of life have disappeared. Winnie's memory is not too faithful, and she confuses the chronological order of things in her effort to recall the past. She can will herself to go to sleep and to wake up, but she fears the terrible silence that will settle over everything if she stops speaking. This silence threatens her at every moment. The drama of the end of the play is the same as that of Beckett's *En Attendant Godot (Waiting for Godot,* 1953) and *Fin de Partie (Endgame,* 1957). There is no ending for these plays. The waiting for Godot will continue, the supposition that all is about to end is repeated in *Fin de Partie,* and Winnie can say nothing more but feels she has to continue speaking.

Happy Days was translated by Beckett in 1961. —W. F.

Harrigan, Edward (1844–1911). American actor, manager, and playwright. Harrigan, born on New York's lower East Side, entered the theater in 1867 as a singer and banjo player in San Francisco variety houses. He wrote comedy sketches and topical songs for himself and a succession of partners, the last of whom was Tony Hart (1855–1891), singer, dancer, and female impersonator. From 1876 to 1884 Harrigan and Hart presented variety programs that included Harrigan's short plays. In 1884 the partnership was dissolved, but Harrigan continued to act alone until 1909.

In *Old Lavender* (1877), his first long play, Harrigan played a bank cashier, a genial drunk who takes the blame for others' misdeeds. Very popular was the series of plays begun with *The Mulligan Guard Ball* in 1879, which featured Irish Dan Mulligan, played by Harrigan, in conflict with German Gustave Lochmuller. Other typical plays are *Squatter Sovereignty* (1882), set in the shantytown near the East River and presenting a comic conflict between squatters and

legal owners; *Cordelia's Aspirations* (1883), in which Cordelia Mulligan persuades Dan to sell their little house and move to a Fifth Avenue mansion, where the life of high society is too much for them; and *Dan's Tribulations* (1884), in which the Mulligans, overwhelmed by debts, are saved by their son Tom.

Harrigan had little interest in plot; his plays are put together with the casualness characteristic of musical comedy. Many of them end in a comic free-for-all fight. Some of the dialogue is reminiscent of minstrel routines, but his characters are readily recognizable city types carefully imitated from life and acted with surface realism. His work is a link in a line that leads from Benjamin Baker's *A Glance at New York* (1849) to Elmer Rice's *Street Scene* (1929). —B. H.

Harsha, Sri (590?–647). King of northern India who ruled from 606 to 647. Harsha achieved fame as a prince successful in war, as a patron of the arts in time of peace, and as a notable playwright. Under his patronage was the court poet Bana, who proudly celebrated his master's achievements. Harsha was devoted, not only to the arts, but to religion. In the early part of his reign he supported Hinduism; in the latter part, Buddhism. His play *Nagananda* bears witness to his zeal for the latter faith. It is true that of recent years scholars have viewed with some skepticism his claims to the three plays long attached to his name. The designations may conceivably be honorific. But he appears to have been in so many ways an unusually gifted man that the ascriptions will presumably outlast the not-unreasonable doubts. It is certain that the plays represent the taste and philosophy of King Harsha's court.

The earliest of the three is *Priyadarsika,* a court comedy closely modeled on Kalidasa's *Malavika and Agnimitra.* There are some interesting features, notably a play-within-the-play. The story relates the king's ardent pursuit of a girl apparently of humble birth whom the queen naturally views as a rival. When the girl's true status as a princess is discovered, the king receives her as a new queen and the old queen graciously accepts the changed situation.

Several parts of the play are clumsily handled. To all appearances its author set himself the task of writing another play on the same general theme in which the chief blemishes of his early work would be removed and positive improvements made, hence *Ratnavali,* a work that became one of the most applauded in the class of court comedy. As in *Priyadarsika,* the *vidusaka,* or clown, guides the intrigue. In a well-conceived episode the heroine, disguised as the queen, attempts to commit suicide. As the king rushes to prevent her, the queen herself suddenly appears. This intrigue has much of the flavor of baroque light opera in the West. Another well-handled incident worth noting is the betrayal of lovers' secrets through the speech of a parrot. *Ratnavali* is a graceful, lively play of no great pretension but considerable adroitness and charm.

Nagananda is a much more unusual production. The hero, Prince Jimutavahana, is conceived as a *bodhisattva,* or mortal who has achieved immortality, and hence, despite the convention that denied the dramatist the right to represent death upon the stage, could be presented as dying before the eyes of the audience. The play offers a disquisition on love in Buddhistic terms. From its first moments indications are given of the hero's saintliness. Acts I to III seem in general a conventional courtly love story with gentle hints or overtones occasioned by the peculiar character of the hero. Abruptly, but not inartfully, the action turns to an incident of religious sacrifice. The divine hawk, Garuda, exacts a daily tribute from the *naga* ("snake") kingdom, of a tender young naga, whom he consumes. Prince Jimutavahana meets the young snake-man destined to be eaten. Assuming the snake disguise, the prince takes the place of the proposed victim. He is killed but by divine intervention of the Gauri is brought to life and the bloodthirsty Garuda converted from his brutality to new and humane practices.

Nagananda is an able work and, in its Buddhistic inspiration, quite unlike most Sanskrit plays. The chief dramatic activity fostered by Buddhism took place under other auspices, notably in the traditional drama of Tibet and the conservative theater of southern India, where Tamil was the native tongue.

Ratnavali has been translated, and considerably modernized, by P. Lal in *Great Sanskrit Plays* (1964). *Nagananda,* as translated by Palmer Boyd, appears in *Six Sanskrit Plays* (1964), edited by H. W. Wells. Thoughtful descriptions of Harsha's works appear in *The Sanskrit Drama* (1964) by A. B. Keith. Valuable comments are also found in *History of Hindu Drama* (1957) by M. M. Ghosh; in *Drama in Sanskrit Literature* (1947) by R. V. Jagirdar; and in *Sanskrit Drama: Its Origins and Decline* (1960) by Indu Shekhar.—H. W. W.

Hart, Moss (1904–1961). American playwright. Born and raised in New York City, Hart rarely ventured beyond the metropolitan area. As a young man, he quickly tired of the business life his family encouraged; he wanted to enter the theater. His experience as an entertainer on the "Borscht Circuit" (resorts in the Catskill Mountains) revealed his skills as a creator of comedy. Though he had not distinguished himself with his first attempts at playwriting, he persuaded George S. KAUFMAN, already a successful playwright, to collaborate on the script which was to become *Once in a Lifetime.* Success followed success, and until his death, Hart was active as a playwright, librettist, and director.

Kaufman and Hart, in a collaboration that stimulated the best work of both men, wrote three classics of American comedy. *Once in a Lifetime* (1930) satirizes the confusions in Hollywood during the transition to the "talkies." *You Can't Take It with You* (1936) presents the uninhibited Sycamore family, oblivious to the concerns of wage earning and the problems of the Depression as they happily follow their urges to express themselves in writing, dancing, printing, painting, firecracker manufacturing, or any other activity that strikes their fancy. Confrontations with the "sensible" world of tax collectors, police, and so forth, always end in a victory for the Sycamores. The wild farce *The Man Who Came to Dinner* (1939), suggested by the career of Alexander Woollcott, presents in detail the havoc created by the stay in a conservative Ohio household of Sheridan Whiteside, a selfish, bad-tempered, but inexhaustibly witty, radio personality. *Merrily We Roll Along* (1934), *I'd Rather Be Right* (1937), and *George Washington Slept Here* (1940) are other works in

which the collaborators took a skeptical look at American society.

Lady in the Dark (1941), with a score by Kurt Weill, was one of Hart's most important works written without Kaufman's collaboration. Hart deals with the psychoanalysis of a woman executive and cleverly uses fantasy and music to reveal her fears and desires. *Winged Victory* (1943), a tribute to the Air Force, and *Light Up the Sky* (1948), a comedy about the pre-Broadway tryout of a new play, are other important works. In his autobiography, *Act One* (1959), Hart describes his life up to the moment of the successful opening of *Once in a Lifetime.* As a director, he is best known for the original production of the musical comedy *My Fair Lady* (1956).

There is no standard edition of Hart's plays. Critical comments can be found in the major studies of modern American drama.—M. L.

hashigakari. In Japanese *noh* theater, the passageway for the principal entrances and exits. The *hashigakari* extends from the left side of the stage farthest removed from the center of the auditorium at a backward diagonal to a curtained doorway dividing it from the so-called mirror room. In this room an actor presently to make his entrance remains seated for a short time, reflecting on his role and examining his costume, mask, or make-up.

The passageway has a low railing. Beside it at equal intervals are three small pines. The actors as a rule proceed along it slowly. It is rarely used as a fully developed acting area on which the actors speak and enter completely into their parts. Instead it is conceived of as providing a visible prelude to the action that follows. The entrance music, however, is generally raised to a considerable volume and the actor may engage in impressive dance or mime. It is in obvious ways related to the HANAMICHI of the later *kabuki* theater, but precisely in what manner, historical research has been unable conclusively to discover. Aesthetically, the principles of the hashigakari and the hanamichi differ widely. The noh actor enters, as it were, from a great distance and from a point as far removed from the bulk of the audience as the overall plan of the noh theater building admits. Hence the figure gains in dignity, mystery, and grandeur, qualities much more valued in the noh than in the kabuki. The actor on the kabuki's hanamichi, on the contrary, passes within the closest possible proximity to the audience, who may pelt him with flowers or chide him with abuse, as they see fit. The hashigakari is a passageway to the sublime; the hanamichi, a device to make the theater itself essentially a social institution.

For the fullest description of the function of the hashigakari and noh theater design in general, see P. G. O'Neill, *Early Noh Drama* (1958), and A. C. Scott, *The Kabuki Theatre* (1955).—H. W. W.

Hashr, Agha. See PAKISTAN: *Urdu drama.*

Hauptmann, Gerhart (1862–1946). German playwright and writer of fiction. Born in Obersalzbrunn in Silesia, the son of an innkeeper, Hauptmann had to struggle for a number of years before he discovered his dramatic talents. After a rather undistinguished performance in high school, he took up an apprenticeship in agriculture from 1880 to 1882. He then studied sculpture briefly at the art institute in Breslau. In spite of some interest in the theater dur-

GERHART HAUPTMANN (WALTER HAMPDEN MEMO-
RIAL LIBRARY AT THE PLAYERS, NEW YORK)

ing this period, the young Hauptmann devoted his energies mainly to his sculptural studies, for which purpose he journeyed to Rome in 1883. Luckily he soon realized his lack of talent and in 1884 went to Berlin to take up a new course of studies at the university. It was here that he came under the influence of the Hart brothers, whose periodical *Kritische Waffengänge* ("Critical Positions") had formally launched the naturalist movement in Germany in 1882. At this time other theoreticians, who had taken their inspiration from Zola's scientific realism, had considerable effect on Hauptmann's aesthetic orientation. William Bolsche published his naturalist poetic *Die naturawissentschaftlichen Grundlagen der Poesie* ("The Scientific Bases of Poetry," 1887) significantly just two years before Hauptmann's first naturalist drama. The playwright also thought highly of the theoretical writings of Arno Holz and Johannes Schlaf. In fact, he contributed articles to the periodical *Freie Bühne für modernes Leben* ("Free Theater for Modern Times"), which was edited by Holz. After the successful performance of his first major drama, BEFORE DAWN, it was only natural to regard Hauptmann as the focal point of the naturalist movement in Germany.

Nevertheless, in spite of the play's obvious adherence to the tenets of naturalism—painstaking attention to detail (*Sekundenstil*), the thematic brutality, the shocking nature of the persons and circumstances —there was sufficient indication that this so-called naturalist work had gone beyond the aesthetic formulas of the naturalist creed. Hauptmann had indeed begun to create his own dramatic formula, which was to emerge, not so much from any rigid aesthetic

code, but from his profound human compassion for the sufferings of the unfortunate. This is apparent in the characterization of the socialist agitator and idealist Alfred Loth, the protagonist of *Before Dawn*. Apparently deeply dedicated to humanitarian ideals, Loth is determined to bring a message of hope to the wretched coal miners and dares to preach moral reform to the spiritually and physically dissipated *nouveaux riches*. However, Loth compromises his ideals. Herein lies the unique Hauptmann dialectic, which is manifested in many of his heroes, for example, Vockerat in *Einsame Menschen* (*Lonely Lives*, 1891). Because of a fundamental weakness of will and lack of faith, Hauptmann's heroes capitulate before the apparent imponderables of biological and environmental forces: Alfred Loth before the irreversible laws of heredity, Vockerat before the intimidations of his family. In THE WEAVERS, Hauptmann created, not an individual hero, but a collective hero, sorely tried by hostile social and economic conditions. This collective hero is also unsuccessful in its revolt against its oppressors because it lacks sufficient strength of purpose and unity of action. On the other hand, *Der Biberpelz* (*The Beaver Coat*, 1893), one of the best German comedies, offers a fascinating account of Mother Wolf, who is capable of surviving because she does not suffer her poverty in passivity but maintains herself by resorting to all sorts of trickery and cunning.

One can observe this same thematic arrangement in most of Hauptmann's dramas. The protagonists of *Fuhrmann Henschel* (*Drayman Henschel*, 1898), *Rose Bernd* (1903), and *Florian Geyer* (pub. 1896) tragically succumb to the hardships imposed upon them by their environments. In the dramas *Hanneles Himmelfahrt* (*The Assumption of Hannele,* 1893) and *Die versunkene Glocke* (*The Sunken Bell,* 1896), one sees the unhappy attempt by the protagonists to escape from their bleak environment to the realm of visions and fantasy. In these two plays, the aesthetic consequences of Hauptmann's dualism become apparent. Because of the emphasis on the subjective rather than the objective sphere of experience, these dramas are more symbolist than naturalist in nature. *Und Pippa tanzt* ("And Pippa Dances," pub. 1906) is a further example of Hauptmann's symbolist drama and another compelling instance of his dialectical vision. Pippa, the personification of ephemeral beauty, is surrounded by creatures who destroy her in their admiration of, and desire for, her delicate beauty.

In spite of the various sources of, and influences on, Hauptmann's later dramas—Greek tragedy, medieval epics, Shakespeare, *Fastnachtsspiele* ("carnival plays")—in such diverse plays as *Der Bogen des Odysseus* ("The Bow of Odysseus," pub. 1914), *Der weisse Heiland* (*The White Saviour,* pub. 1920), *Indipohdi* (pub. 1920), and the *Die Atriden Tetralogie* (the tetralogy of the Atrides, prod. 1941–1948), the fundamental interest of this playwright remains the compassionate observation of man in his suffering. See also THE RATS.

During his life Gerhart Hauptmann was much honored for his literary endeavors. Already in 1896 Erich Schmidt had recommended him for the Schiller Prize, although it was ultimately denied him by Wilhelm II. In 1905 he received an honorary doctorate from Oxford, and in 1912 was awarded the Nobel Prize for literature. In spite of some critical questioning of the rank and quality of his work, Hauptmann enjoyed until his death in 1946 universal respect for his literary accomplishments and for his personal stature as a humanitarian. Thomas Mann immortalized Hauptmann's compelling personality in the figure of Mynheer Peepercorn (*The Magic Mountain*). Mann wrote in *Die Entstehung des Doktor Faustus* (*The Story of a Novel: The Genesis of Dr. Faustus*) that he believed this character study to be a fitting expression of his admiration for the *immer ergreifenden, tief gewinnenden, zu Liebe und Ehrfurcht anhaltenden Erlebnis seiner Persönlichkeit* ("for Hauptmann's human qualities which always inspired profound respect and love"). Gerhart Hauptmann died after having had to witness as an octogenarian the horrible sufferings and atrocities of World War II.

A collection of English versions of Hauptmann's works is *The Dramatic Works* (1912 ff.) edited by L. Lewisohn. Critical studies include *Gerhart Hauptmann* (1954) by H. F. Garten; *Modern Continental Writers* (pp. 268–298) (1931) by Frank W. Chandler; *A History of Modern Drama* (pp. 78–85) (1947) by Barrett Clark and George Freedley; and *Masters of the Drama* (pp. 446–466) (1945) by John Gassner.—C. A. M.

Havel, Václav (1936–   ). Czech playwright. Born in Prague, Havel worked in a chemical laboratory while studying at high school in Prague. He attended Technical College from 1955 to 1957 and then completed his military duty. From 1959 he worked in the Divadlo ABC (Theater ABC) as a scene shifter for one year and then moved to the Divadlo Na zábradlí (Theater on the Balustrade), where he did the same work and later became an electrician, secretary, manuscript reader for the director, and then at last literary manager in 1961. While working, he studied dramaturgy at the Academy of Visual Arts in Prague from 1962 to 1967. Since 1956 he has published a number of articles on the theater.

After his first play, *Autostop* (1961), written in collaboration with Ivan Vyskočil, Havel became well known with the production of his play *Zahradní slavnost* ("The Garden Party," 1963), which was translated into many languages and performed abroad. In this play Havel created the Czech penchant for the contemporary "drama of the absurd." It is a sharp satire directed against the various mechanistic relations of both public and private life that make human life inhuman. According to Havel, the middle-class mentality provides fertile ground for such relations. In a very impressive way Havel succeeded in expressing these various monstrous social mechanisms.

In his second play, *Vyrozuměni* (*The Memorandum*, 1965), Havel develops this theme further by showing people who succumb to an absurd mechanical system—here the absurd language Ptydepe—to forward their careers.—F. Č.

Hay Fever (1925). A comedy by Noel COWARD. Judith Bliss, an aging former actress, her husband David, their daughter Sorel, and their son Simon have each invited a guest for the weekend without telling the other members of the family. Each guest seems inappropriately chosen: Judith has invited a prize fighter; her husband, a half-witted flapper; her daughter, a middle-aged diplomat; her son, an actress older than himself. All the guests are put off by the eccentricities of the Bliss household, and they infuriate Judith by failing to throw themselves with proper spirit into her favorite game of acting out adverbs. The Blisses perform bits of Judith's old plays, and, increasingly, the guests are left to one another. At last, after an appalling breakfast (punctuated by a guest's celebrated remark, "This haddock's disgusting"), the guests, without a word of farewell, tiptoe out during a family quarrel.

Coward asserted in his autobiography *Present Indicative* (1937) that the Bliss family was based on the American actress Laurette Taylor, her husband, Hartley Manners, and their two children. In 1964 *Hay Fever* became the first play by a living Englishman (and the third by any living author) to join the repertory of the new National Theatre in London. The dramatist himself directed this revival, in which Dame Edith Evans played Judith Bliss.—H. P.

Heartbreak House (written 1913–16; prod. 1921). A play by George Bernard SHAW. The action unfolds in Heartbreak House, in a room designed to resemble the interior of an old-fashioned ship. Eccentric Captain Shotover, aged eighty-eight, a retired seafaring man who specialized in inventing destructive devices, speaks to Ellie Dunn of his two daughters, Lady Ariadne Utterword and Hesione Hushabye, whom he does not particularly like. Strong-minded Hesione fears that Ellie is being driven into a marriage for money with Boss Mangan by her selfish father, Mazzini Dunn, an idealistic crusader for lost causes and a totally unsuccessful businessman. Ellie, however, has fallen in love with a mysterious adventurer she recently met; to her utmost shock and disillusion, he proves to be none other than Hesione's own philandering husband, Hector Hushabye. Thus, when commonplace Mangan turns up, Ellie is more determined than ever to go through with her marriage to him.

Mangan admits to having deliberately ruined Ellie's father for business reasons and wants no gratitude, but she still wants to marry him. The captain advises Ellie to think of her soul. She says her soul can't flourish properly without money, but finally decides that she wants to marry *him,* the captain! In his shrewd analysis of the others, he says his daughters' generation wastes its time on romance and sentiment and snobbery; Ellie's contemporaries have revolted in favor of money, comfort, and hard common sense. This is not to say that the captain approves of Ellie's choice of husband. The truth is not fixed or constructed. Neither hypocrisy nor capitalism can bring about the reform so needed by Heartbreak House, by Europe.

That evening everyone seems moved to profound, even prophetic, comment. Hesione says, "We are useless, dangerous and ought to be abolished," but Lady Utterword insists that all England needs is more horses and stables. Mangan confesses that he has no actual money—only credit and power, which have brought him a cabinet post in the government. Ellie then breaks their engagement, announcing that she will become the bride of Shotover. Shotover predicts shipwreck for England, symbolically suggesting that the uniting of the vigor of youth with the farsightedness of enlightened age could lead to the forcible supplanting of the established order with practical yet spiritual renewal. Just then an air raid starts. Defying the rules, Hector turns on the lights in the house, but only Mangan and a burglar, who flee to a gravel pit for safety, are killed. The raid passes, and all the survivors, exhilarated by the experience, eagerly look forward to the next.

In describing *Heartbreak House* in the play's subtitle as "A Fantasia in the Russian Manner on English Themes," Shaw himself invited comparison with Chekhov. But no play could be further from the rueful, becalmed Chekhovian world in which quietly despairing souls struggle wistfully to communicate their vague yearnings in trailing fragments of talk. From start to finish, *Heartbreak House* crackles with furious infighting and head-on clashes in which no one ever fails to hit the nail precisely on the head. Though by no means as obvious as in a Restoration comedy, the unusual names surely evoke symbolic undertones. Does "Shotover" suggest some desired mark fatally overshot? Do Hector and Hesione Hushabye lull themselves into dreamland with their frivolous romancing? Is Lady Utterword convinced that her sharply expressed opinion will settle any issue? Even more cryptic are the given names of Hesione, Ariadne, and Hector, which bear only the most conjectural resemblance to their mythological namesakes. Hesione's name recalls the less aggressive femininity of the Hesione of mythology, whose husband, Telamon, is the sort of hero that Hector Hushabye ought to have been. Ariadne's name would suggest at least the whole maze of British bourgeois morality and middle-upper-class hypocrisy. Hector may perhaps be seen as the archetype of the hero disguised as a fool, whose sleeping heroism is awakened in time of crisis. With bomber planes overhead, Hector recklessly acts to invoke the calamity he hopes will be a scourge. In fact, in the play only the guilty and cowardly are killed as a result of the air raid. The possibility of destruction brings home to them the real force of Don Juan's declaration in *Man and Superman* that "it is not death that matters but the fear of death. It is not killing and dying that degrades us, but base living, and accepting the wages and profits of degradation." Shotover speaks the play's last important lines: "The judgment has come. Courage will not save you; but it will show that your souls are still live."

The very fact that Shaw's vision in *Heartbreak House* is a complex one that eludes easy analysis is indicative of the play's ultimate worth. Like *Major Barbara*, it is exploratory rather than definitive. In the play's symbolic overtones, emotional reverberations, and allusive associations, the work is indeed characteristic of the work of Chekhov and the late plays of Ibsen. In *Heartbreak House*, Shaw has somehow combined the drily rational with an almost poetic complexity.

An indispensable work in understanding Shaw's "Fantasia" is Frederick P. W. McDowell's "Technique, Symbol, and Theme in *Heartbreak House*," *PMLA*, 68 (1953). He uses William Irvine's *The Universe of G.B.S.* (1949) in defining the symbolism of the play's characters but deals much more understandingly with the play's themes and structure. Eric Bentley in his *Bernard Shaw: A Reconsideration*

(1947) chooses to disregard the surface inconsistencies of the play and to apprehend it as a vital and unique organism.—D. J. L.

Hebbel, Friedrich (1813–1863). German dramatist and poet, whose theory of tragedy represented a complete change from the optimistic classical ideal. Born in Holstein into the family of a Mason, Hebbel was able to study on his own and succeeded in enrolling in the University of Heidelberg, where he took up history and literature. Returning to Hamburg in 1839, he embarked on his career as a playwright with *Judith* (1839), which was a success in Berlin. Although his early promise gained him a travel stipend from the Danish crown, the remainder of his dramas did not achieve the popularity of his first effort, and some, in fact, were not produced in his lifetime.

Hebbel's philosphy has a decided Hegelian cast, although the author claimed to have arrived at his formulations himself and, in fact, found that Hegel's ideas affirmed his own. Tragedy to Hebbel was not in the death of a protagonist but inextricably tied to life itself. Drama was the highest form of expression and was only possible in regard to a problem situation arising in conjunction with a decisive historical transformation. Thus he selected as settings for his plays epochs such as the era of the birth of Christ (*Herodes und Mariamne*). Hebbel's characters are measured according to whether they change. The dramatic theory behind this concept of tragedy is that the attempt on the part of the individual to assert himself against the historical process of the social order results in his destruction. The moral question of freedom of choice is no longer relevant. The existential guilt of the individual can, however, be atoned for if he succeeds in submerging himself again into the "world organism." But the matter of good and evil is no longer of prime importance. The larger view of Hebbel's socially bound individual, however, is not necessarily pessimistic. The entire system func-

FRIEDRICH HEBBEL (GERMAN INFORMATION CENTER)

tions dialectically: The thesis of society reacts with the antithesis of the individual disturbing the process, and the synthetic result raises humanity another step toward a higher plane of existence. Thus an optimistic, progressive world history replaces fate as a force greater than the individual.

The dialectic process may not always be obvious in Hebbel's plays, but it is there, if not explicitly, in the plots, implicitly in the background of the drama, or in the characters and their consciousness of themselves. The sin of Agnes Bernauer, heroine of the play of the same name (1855), is merely that she is exceptionally beautiful. This "flaw," however, stands in the way of the normal political operation of the state. Marriage, an integral part of her individualism, is out of the question, since Albrecht, the man she loves, is a prince, and she a commoner. Both her demise at Albrecht's hands and the subsequent continuity of the state are necessary to Hebbel's tragedy.

In *Herodes und Mariamne* (1850), the conflict is presented between Herodes' all-possessive will and the untouchable inner freedom of his wife, Mariamne. On two occasions, as Herodes departs for a journey, he leaves orders that Mariamne be killed in the event that he does not return. Hearing of these orders, Mariamne pretends to be guilty after Herodes' second return, in order to prove her innocence to him through her death. Nonetheless, she dies. As opposed to Schiller, whose morally oriented philosophy proclaimed the inner freedom of the individual, Hebbel does not allow his characters a way out. While his theory represented something radically new for German drama, he was a playwright largely without influence in the age of German realism.—B. M. M.

Hecuba (Hekabe, c. 425 B.C.). A tragedy by EURIPIDES. *Hecuba* is one of Euripides' most admired plays, but its disunity has often been criticized. In the first half, Hecuba, the captive queen of Troy, learns that the Greek conquerors have voted to sacrifice her daughter Polyxena to please the ghost of Achilles. Her appeal to Odysseus, whose life she once saved, is useless, and she is left to mourn her daughter. In the second half of the play the interest shifts to Hecuba's vengeance on discovering that her young son Polydorus has been murdered for profit by Polymestor, the Thracian king into whose keeping he had been entrusted. The queen and other captive Trojan women lure the treacherous king to their tent with the promise of more gold, kill his two young sons, and blind him.

These two main actions in the play are externally linked. Polydorus' death is announced in the Prologue by his ghost and he is referred to several times in the first half. A smooth transition between the parts is achieved when Polydorus' body is found by Hecuba's attendants while they are fetching water for Polyxena's funeral rites. The real dramatic unity, however, is in Hecuba herself. She represents the two aspects of war often almost inseparable in Euripides: suffering sorrow and vengeful hatred, with all the degradation they bring. And since Hecuba is never a mere *mater dolorosa*, not even in her unsuccessful appeal on Polyxena's behalf, the change in her from sorrow to vengeance is not entirely unexpected. Some of her reflections—about the gods, the law, inherited mobility—have been condemned as irrelevant philosophizing by the poet, but why should a queen not think? Furthermore, although her thoughts are of the fifth century, they are in character, and are only the usual Euripidean anachronism.

The other characters are sensitively drawn: the noble Polyxena, willing to die and unwilling to beg for her life; the sophistical, diplomatic, unfeeling Odysseus; Agamemnon, weak, not unkind, but cautious; even Talthybius, the herald, who tells of the impression Polyxena made upon the army at her death.

The odes of the Chorus of fellow captives are relevant throughout and beautiful. One unusual feature is that their entrance song is in effect a messenger's speech that describes how the decision to sacrifice Polyxena was taken. And it is not a god but Polymestor, blinded, and his children killed, who foretells at the end that Agamemnon and Cassandra will die and that Hecuba will become a hound of hell.

Translations of the play are listed under Euripides.
—G. M. A. G.

Hedda Gabler (1891). A play by Henrik IBSEN. Hedda has recently been married to the scholar George Tesman, but, as the title indicates, it is no real marriage. She cannot escape a strong identification with her father and the heritage of his military caste, nor can she adjust to routine, middle-class life. Procreation is repugnant to her as well, but somehow she wants to "mold a human destiny." Her misguided efforts are turned upon a former suitor, an imaginative but delicately balanced scholar, Eilert Løvborg. Instead of molding a destiny she is an accomplice in his death. Her destructiveness extends to the burning of his new manuscript, a major piece of work that would threaten Tesman's chances of a pro-

A SCENE FROM HENRIK IBSEN'S *Hedda Gabler* (NORWEGIAN INFORMATION SERVICE)

fessorship. The crime becomes—in the language of the play—a metaphoric infanticide, accompanied shortly after by Hedda's revulsion when she discovers that she is pregnant. Trapped by Judge Brack, who controls the overextended finances of the Tesmans, knows about Hedda's criminal complicity, and presses for a *menage à trois,* Hedda commits suicide. At end of the play Tesman and Thea Elvsted, the woman in Løvborg's life, reconstruct the burned manuscript from notes and presumably also piece a future together.

Hedda Gabler ranks very high among Ibsen's plays, partly for its social portrayal of the emergent "new woman" who has not yet developed any capacity except for "boring herself to death" (all drive and no direction), partly for its psychological portrayal of twisted sexuality and near demonism (Ibsen himself applied the term), and partly for an unusual amplitude that is novelistic but does not lose control over dramatic moment and development.

The text may be found in *Ibsen,* Vol. VII (1966), edited by J. W. McFarlane. See also George Bernard Shaw's *The Quintessence of Ibsenism* (1913). Else Høst's *Hedda Gabler* (1958), in Norwegian, is the most comprehensive critical study.—R. B. V.

Hegge Plays, The. See N-TOWN PLAYS.

Heiberg, Gunnar Edvard Rode (1857–1929). Norwegian poet, essayist, and playwright. Born in Oslo, Heiberg was early associated with the writer Hans Jæger (1854–1910), the leader of Oslo bohemia. His poetry belongs chiefly to this period, for example "A Soirée Dansante," influenced by Byron and Kierkegaard, and "Genesis of Man" (both 1878). Heiberg's essay collections, written in the later years, range from *Pariserbreve* (*Paris Letters,* 1900), treating the Dreyfus affair, to *Ibsen og Bjørnson på scenen* (*Ibsen and Bjørnson on the Stage,* 1918). But he was chiefly known for his plays written from 1883 to 1913. In their interaction of idea and dramatic form, they constitute the major link between Ibsen and Helge Krog.

Tante Ulrikke ("Aunt Ulrikke," 1883) has to do with emergent socialism; *Kong Midas* ("King Midas," 1890) satirizes the kind of political idealism exemplified in the plays of Bjørnstjerne Bjørnson. *Balkonen* ("The Balcony," 1894) and *Kjærlighetens tragedie* (*The Tragedy of Love,* 1904) are both studies of eroticism, the latter dealing with a favorite Norwegian subject, namely the conflict between love and career. A number of Heiberg's plays are chiefly political in nature, such as *Hans Majestæt* ("His Majesty," 1896), which directs an attack upon Swedish monarchy, and *Jeg vil værge mit land* ("I Will Defend My Country," 1912), which deplores Norway's concessions upon its separation from Sweden in 1905. *Paradesengen* ("The Catafalque," 1913) is a sharply executed satire on the unseemly scramble of the heirs upon the death of a great man to whose greatness they cannot aspire.

Heiberg is a satirist and humanist of considerable force. Wit and urbanity chiefly characterize his drama, and it is the drama that takes precedence over his other writing.

The Tragedy of Love is in *Chief Contemporary Dramatists,* second series (1921), edited by T. H. Dickinson. See also Harald Beyer, *A History of Norwegian Literature* (1956), translated by Einar Haugen, pp. 254–257.—R. B. V.

Heiberg, Johan Ludvig (1791–1860). Danish critic, playwright, and man of the theater. Heiberg made his literary debut with the publication of *Marionetteater* (*Marionette Theater,* 1813), containing, among other things, a Don Juan play admired by Kierkegaard in his treatise *Enten/Eller* (*Either/Or,* 1843). He concluded his doctoral studies in 1817 with a dissertation on the Spanish dramatist Pedro Calderón and then proceeded to Paris to visit his father, a writer in political exile. Heiberg founded the weekly *Copenhagen Flying Mail* in 1827 and was for many years attached to the Royal Theatre in Copenhagen, from 1849 to 1856 as its director.

Having encountered vaudeville while in Paris, Heiberg introduced it into Denmark and wrote a number of this kind of musical comedy between 1825 and 1836—some specifically for his distinguished wife, the actress Johanne Luise. He often had to defend the integrity of the form against the attacks of its denigrators. Among Heiberg's best are *Aprilnarrene* ("April Fools," 1826), a gentle comedy about amatory intrigue at the Bitter Almond School for Girls; *Recensenten og dyret* ("The Critic and the Beast," 1826), a not-so-gentle satire on irresponsible reviewers of plays; *De uadskillelige* ("The Inseparable," 1827), which pokes fun at prolonged engagements; and *Nej* ("No," 1836), a triangular comedy of courtship.

Commissioned in 1828 to write a play for the wedding of Crown Prince Frederik, Heiberg wrote *Elverhøj* ("Elf Hill"), a fantastic comedy of errors built around the figure of one of Denmark's great cultural heroes, Christian IV. The play, supplied with the folk melodies of Friedrich Kuhlau, has become the national festival drama of Denmark.

JOHAN LUDVIG HEIBERG (DANISH INFORMATION OF-
FICE)

In *Nye digte* ("New Poems," 1841) Heiberg published the so-called apocalyptic comedy *En sjæl efter døden* ("A Soul After Death"), which tells of the search of an apparently honorable Copenhagen citizen for a suitable afterlife. Rejected by Saint Peter at the gates of heaven and by Aristophanes at the entrance to the Elysian Fields, the protagonist ends up in the nether regions, happy with the futile job of replenishing the bottomless vessel of the Danaïdes.

In his time Heiberg was very influential in establishing norms of taste in both drama and criticism. His experiments with the materials and techniques of comedy did much to determine the direction of the theater in Denmark.

See P. M. Mitchell, *A History of Danish Literature* (1958), pp. 135–142.—R. B. V.

Heijermans, Herman (1864–1924). Dutch playwright, novelist, and journalist. Heijermans was born in Rotterdam of Jewish parents. His father, Herman Heijermans Sr., was a reporter and editor for the *Nieuwe Rotterdamsche Courant,* and his journalistic talents were an important influence on his son. The formal education of Heijermans Jr. came to an end with his graduation from secondary school. In spite of his early interest in writing, he went into banking and then into business for himself. Initial success gave way to disaster, and only the intervention of his father saved him from bankruptcy. He began his literary career as a journalist in Amsterdam, and made his pseudonym, Samuel Falkland Jr., famous through a series of newspaper sketches or

HERMAN HEIJERMANS (NETHERLANDS INFORMATION SERVICE)

Falklandjes, producing some eight hundred of them in twenty-one years.

His first play, *Dora Kremer* (1893), is a study of middle-class marriage in Dutch rural society and reveals the influence of Henrik Ibsen's *A Doll's House* (1879). Although it was a good first attempt, it showed some of the weaknesses of the beginner, and Heijermans smarted under its critical reception. He took his revenge on the critics with his next play, *Ahasverus* (1893), hiding his identity behind the Russian-sounding pseudonym of Ivan Jelakowitch, which was appropriate for the play. This one-act study of a Jewish family trapped in the violence of the Russian pogroms was a highly effective play, and the critics greeted the work of the unknown young Russian with joyous enthusiasm. Within a month André Antoine produced it at the Théâtre Libre in Paris, and Heijermans revealed that he himself was the young Russian genius. He mocked the critics by printing their praises of *Ahasverus* side by side with their criticisms of *Dora Kremer.*

It was with *Ghetto* (1898) that Heijermans really established his position in the Dutch theater. Less than a year after its première in Amsterdam, a revised version appeared on the stage in London and New York. Revealing himself as a born dramatist, Heijermans combined a critical view of the society of his day with a warm and realistic picture of life in the old Jewish section of Amsterdam. Having attacked narrow-minded and intolerant orthodoxy among the Jews in *Ghetto,* Heijermans went on to indict the conservatism of middle-class morality among the Christians in *Het Zevende Gebod* ("The Seventh Commandment," 1899). Both plays examine middle-class marriage against the background of the conflict between the generations.

Heijermans was unusually skillful in the creation of one-act plays, such as *Saltimbank* (pub. 1904), in which he portrays the disintegration of a marriage against the bohemian background of a traveling circus. In *Het Kind* ("The Child," 1903) Heijermans expresses his deep love for children through the tragedy of a child born blind. He presents the lighter side of parenthood in *Het Kamerschut* ("The Screen," 1903), a one-act farce. His interest in socialism led him to write a number of one-act plays in behalf of the working class. Thus, the political message is rather obvious in such plays as *Puntje* ("The Dot," 1898), *Het Antwoord* ("The Answer," pub. 1898), and *Nummer Tachtig* ("Number Eighty," pub. 1898), as well as *De Machien* ("The Machine," pub. 1899), *Een Mei* ("May Day," 1900), and *Feest* ("Jubilee," 1908). Heijermans' most famous one-act play is *In de Jonge Jan* ("At the Jonge Jan," 1903), which he wrote for the actor Henri de Vries, who almost made a profession out of acting all the roles in this mystery drama. De Vries took the play to New York in 1906, where it appeared as *A Case of Arson.*

Heijermans' efforts in advancing the cause of the workers also resulted in several longer plays, of which the most important is *Op Hoop van Zegen* (*The Good Hope,* 1900). This four-act drama of the sea portrays the life of the Dutch fishermen and their exploitation by the shipowners. It is a highly successful fusion of the ideas and characters of the men who go out in ships and the women who wait for their return. It is the greatest and most famous of all his plays, and it gave him an international reputation. The popularity of the play in the Netherlands played a role in the passage of the Ships Act in 1909, which was designed to protect sailors on commercial vessels. In *Ora et Labora* ("Pray and Work," 1902) Heijermans attempted to present a similar picture of the Frisian peasants in their struggle to wrest a living from the soil. *Het Pantser* ("The Suit of Armor," 1901) expresses Heijermans' antimilitarist feelings in a drama based on the father-son conflict. *Bloeimaand* ("Maytime," 1904) is a "play of the city" that is set in a home for the aged and shows what becomes of a poor old worker who has spent his life in honest toil. *Glück auf!* ("Good Luck!" 1911) is an attempt to portray the exploitation of the miners by the mine owners in the manner of *Op Hoop van Zegen*, but it is less successful.

He was able to portray the middle class with the same skill and mastery that went into his working-class dramas. *Schakels* (*Links, 1903*) is a drama of a successful self-made man who has given his children everything but becomes the victim of their plot to prevent his remarriage. This dramatic interpretation of the conflict between generations became one of Heijermans' most popular plays. *De Opgaande Zon* (*The Rising Sun,* 1908) is a combination of a moving study of a middle-class businessman haunted by the specter of bankruptcy and an effective portrait of a father-daughter relationship. *Beschuit met Muisjes* (*Blessed Event,* 1910) presents a dramatic caricature of middle-class fortune hunters.

Although Heijermans won his reputation in the drama of realism, he had imagination and a love of fantasy. His *Uitkomst* (*The Way Out,* 1907), for example, is one of his most striking plays. Like Gerhart Hauptmann's *Hanneles Himmelfahrt* (1893), with which it has often been compared, it is a fantasy of the world as revealed through the delirium of a dying child. There is a romantic side to Heijermans' art, and his willingness to soar on the wings of fancy is the most prominent trait setting him off from the naturalists. It is evident in *Dageraad* (*Dawn,* 1918), which probes the position of the artist in society and expresses the hope that the machine will someday create a utopian society for mankind. *De Wijze Kater* (*The Wise Tomcat,* 1918), "a malicious fairytale," is a satirical critique of society in which a tomcat is the hero. Among his other comedies are *Robert, Bertram & Comp.* (1914), *De Groote Vlucht* (*The Great Flight,* 1908), and *De Vliegende Hollander of De Groote Weddenschap* (*The Flying Dutchman or The Big Bet,* 1920).

His pantheistic philosophy appears in *Allerzielen* (*All Souls, 1904*), whose heroine, the mother of an illegitimate child, is also a symbolic figure, representing the people. *De Schoone Slaapster* (*Sleeping Beauty,* 1909) is a socialist allegory on man and society in which Sleeping Beauty represents the people. *Eva Bonheur* (1916) is a remarkable comedy that depends on character rather than situation for its humor and that also contains Heijermans' deepest philosophical beliefs. It appeared in New York in 1925 as *The Devil to Pay*. His last play, *Van Ouds "De Morgenster"* (*The Good Old "Morning Star,"* 1923), is not the equal of his earlier dramas.

Heijermans is the most important Dutch dramatist of modern times, and the only dramatist since Joost van den Vondel who has enjoyed recognition outside his own country. He has done more than any other playwright in the Netherlands to revive the Dutch drama.

For a brief account of the Dutch drama in the second half of the nineteenth century and a biographical and critical study of Heijermans, see Seymour L. Flaxman, *Herman Heijermans and His Dramas* (1954).—S. L. F.

Heir in His Old Age, An (Lao sheng erh). A Chinese play by Wu Han ch'en. *An Heir in His Old Age* ranks with the foremost plays of the Yüan dynasty (1280–1368). It has enjoyed considerable popularity in China and in the West has attracted more attention than given to all but a half-dozen works of similar origin. It may roughly be described as a bourgeois tragicomedy, somewhat like George Lillo's famous work of the eighteenth century, *George Barnwell,* save that it has the customary Chinese happy ending.

The central figure, an old man named Lew, learns the true use of riches, turning at last away from greed in money-getting to a just and genial view of the value of wealth. His experience further demonstrates the supreme worth of family piety and cohesion. The leading moral is expressed in the sentence: "Honor the graves of your ancestors and in one or two years you shall become rich."

A shallow young man marries into a family thinking that since its head is old and without a son he will inherit the estate through the old man's daughter. He is deceived. The old man has a second, or subordinate, wife, who finally presents him with an heir. The daughter, who is truly loyal, knows of this woman's pregnancy and of the hatred in which the expectant mother is held both by the jealous first wife and the dishonorable son-in-law. Out of loyalty to her father she sends the woman into hiding, where she and her son can live in peace and safety. In the last act the secret is revealed.

Meanwhile the father has repented of his avaricious ways, chiefly through association with his beguiling nephew. This young man, who belongs legitimately to the old family, is decidedly more pious and faithful than the calculating son-in-law. The nephew combines the character types of aspiring young scholar and prodigal son. Although at first harshly repudiated by his miserly uncle, in the chief scene of the play he performs pious offices at the ancestral graves, while daughter and son-in-law are negligent and arrive late for the ceremony.

The old man and his first wife are deeply moved on witnessing the nephew's pious act and completely reverse their views of the two young men. In the end the first wife is even more hostile to the son-in-law than is her husband and even more partial than he to the reformed nephew, who inherits the estate. The play provides an educational object lesson. Everyone, even the villain, learns to think more justly of life. The antagonist is not actually punished; indeed, he has committed no heinous crime, though he has followed mistaken notions of true value.

In these events is seen a touch of Hogarthian ethics, notably in the contrast between the prudent and imprudent young men. But the Englishman suffers in the comparison, for the wisdom urged by the Chinese dramatist is not the importance of acquiring wealth but, on the contrary, the wise use and disposition of it and above all the proper family devotion toward ancestors and toward the living members of the clan. Hogarth erects his altar to the god of wealth, Wu Han ch'en to devotion to the family and its traditions. The Chinese play is emphatically middle-class drama, not court drama, yet expresses ideals deemed vital in all branches of Chinese society. The scene in the graveyard ranks among the most striking in Chinese dramatic literature.

This is the first play to have been translated directly from the Chinese into English. It was rendered by the pioneer scholar J. F. Davis (1817). The style is vigorous. Two years later it was translated into French by A. Bruguière de Sorsun.—H. W. W.

Helen (Helene, 412 B.C.). A tragicomedy by EURIPIDES. *Helen* is, like *Ion* and *Iphigenia among the Taurians,* a tragicomedy, but the comic element is cruder and more obvious. The impossible nature of the miracle upon which the story is based is more frequently impressed on us than it is in the other two plays, and its consequences are funny. It was not Helen, it turns out, who was carried off to Troy by Paris but a phantom fashioned of a cloud by Hera, who had not forgiven Paris for once awarding a beauty prize to another goddess. The real Helen was wafted by Hermes to Egypt, where old King Proteus would keep her safe (and chaste) for her husband, Menelaus. Proteus has died, however, and the new king, his son Theoclymenus, wanting to marry Helen himself, kills all Greeks who have the misfortune to land in Egypt. A threadbare Menelaus arrives, shipwrecked after seven years of wandering in a vain attempt to get home to Sparta from the Trojan War. He is happily reunited with his wife and they enlist the aid of Theoclymenus' sister, the prophetess Theonoe, in escaping. Helen concocts an elaborate ruse involving a mock funeral and, being Helen, easily deceives the belligerent but gullible Theoclymenus. She and Menelaus sail away to Sparta.

The first part of the play, in which Helen expresses her longing for home and husband, has the seriousness of tragedy. So have the choral odes throughout. Comedy enters with Menelaus. Bravura rather than bravery is his characteristic and he is bombastic and impractical when they plan their escape. Theonoe tells them that their fate is being debated by the gods and the decision is left to Theonoe herself. This is not antireligious propaganda but the irreverence of comedy.

The play was produced soon after the disastrous Athenian defeat in Sicily, and it is tempting to read into the play Euripides' feelings about war, particularly in the Demeter ode. Commentators also have sought deep significance in the antithesis of illusion and reality and error and truth, which is only to be expected in a play about the wraith and the real Helen. However that may be, *Helen* is undoubtedly a tragicomedy with most of the emphasis on comedy.

Translations of the play are listed under Euripides. —G. M. A. G.

Hellman, Lillian (1905–   ). American playwright. Until her sixteenth year, Lillian Hellman spent about half of each year in New Orleans, where she was born, and the other half in New York, for her father's business interests involved such shuttling. Miss Hellman completed her education in New York, including some study at New York University and Columbia, but her knowledge of the South is reflected in many of her works. She worked as a publisher's reader, book reviewer, and theater publicist. In 1925 she married Arthur Kober, and they were divorced in 1931. She was encouraged to write plays by her friend Dashiell Hammett, who selected a Scottish court case as the type of story she might try. The result was *The Children's Hour* (1934), which immediately established its author as a serious playwright.

A careful craftsman, Miss Hellman works and reworks her scripts until they are tightly constructed and polished. Her subjects usually involve a taut situation in which she explores an aspect of evil. In *The Children's Hour* a malicious child's suggestion that her teachers are lesbians begins a chain of destruction. In *Watch on the Rhine* (1941) and *The Searching Wind* (1944) her characters are caught in the struggle against fascism. In *The Lark* (1955), an adaption of Jean Anouilh's play about Joan of Arc, Miss Hellman deals with the uneven balance between good and evil.

Her most fascinating plays, *The Little Foxes* (1939) and *Another Part of the Forest* (1946), are about the rapacious Hubbard family. In the first, Regina Hubbard Giddens destroys her husband and drives away her daughter as she achieves a financial victory over her brothers. In the second, Miss Hellman looks back to the Hubbards' youth, observing how their values developed under their greedy father and helpless mother. Though aimed at condemning a materialistic ethic, these two plays are most forceful in their character studies.

Other works by Miss Hellman include *The Autumn Garden* (1951), a quiet, Chekhovian play in which a group of middle-aged vacationers come to realize that they are no longer able to change; the book for a musical version (1956) of Voltaire's *Candide,* with music by Leonard Bernstein and lyrics by Richard Wilbur; and *Toys in the Attic* (1960), the account of a young man's painful escape from the possessive love of his sister. Her only attempt at light comedy, *My Mother, My Father and Me* (1963), was not financially successful but marked a distinctive shift in her interests.

There is no standard edition of Miss Hellman's work. Critical discussions can be found in the major studies of modern American drama.—M. L.

Henry IV. See ENRICO IV.

Henry IV, Part One (c. 1596). A chronicle play by William SHAKESPEARE. *The First Part of Henry the Fourth* was initially published in 1598 in two quarto editions. Only an eight-page fragment survives of the earlier edition (designated Qo). The First Quarto, which was set up from Qo, contains the complete text and is considered the authoritative version of the play. Five subsequent quarto editions (1599, 1604, 1608, 1613, and 1622) were printed before the appearance of the 1623 First Folio. The 1613 Fifth Quarto served as the copy text for the Folio version.

Although the first recorded performance of *1 Henry IV* took place in 1600, there is general agreement that it was first acted late in 1596 or early in 1597. It has been popular ever since.

The main sources for the historical material in the play are Raphael Holinshed's *Chronicles of England,*

THE
HISTORY OF
HENRIE THE
FOVRTH;

With the battell at Shrewsburie,
betweene the King and Lord
Henry Percy, furnamed
Henrie Hotfpur of
the North.

With the humorous conceits of Sir
Iohn Falftalffe.

AT LONDON,
Printed by P. S. for *Andrew Wife*, dwelling
in Paules Churchyard, at the figne of
the Angell. 1598.

TITLE PAGE OF THE FIRST QUARTO (1598) OF SHAKE-
SPEARE'S *Henry IV, Part One*

Scotland, and Ireland (2nd ed. 1587) and Samuel Daniel's *The First Fowre Bookes of the Civile Wars betweene the Two Houses of Lancaster and Yorke* (1595). The account of Hal as a wild prince derives primarily from the anonymous play *The Famous Victories of Henry the Fifth* (written and prod. c. 1586–1594). The character Sir John Oldcastle, molded from a historical personage, appears in this play, and he was carried into *1 Henry IV* as the roguish fat knight. Evidence exists that Oldcastle's descendants—the Brooke family headed by the powerful William, Lord Cobham—objected to the portrayal and protested the use of the Oldcastle name. Shakespeare altered it to Falstaff, after the historical Sir John Fastolfe, a knight previously depicted as cowardly in *1 Henry VI*.

The play opens showing England beset with troubles on her frontiers, so that King Henry IV has been prevented from carrying out his pilgrimage to the Holy Land in expiation of the murder of Richard II. The Welshman Owen Glendower has defeated an English army under Edmund Mortimer, earl of March, and has taken Mortimer prisoner. In the north the king's forces under Henry Percy, known as Hotspur, have turned back the Scots led by the earl of Douglas. At home, King Henry is disturbed by the roistering life his son, Prince Hal, is leading. When Hotspur arrives at court, the king demands that the young nobleman turn over his Scottish prisoners—which he had previously refused to do. Again Hotspur refuses the king's request unless Henry will

ransom Mortimer, Hotspur's brother-in-law. Henry will not accede to this because he has learned that Mortimer has married Glendower's daughter and allied himself with the Welsh chieftain. The king delivers an ultimatum concerning the prisoners and departs, leaving Hotspur in a rage. His uncle, the earl of Worcester, and his father, the earl of Northumberland, calm Hotspur by telling him that they are fomenting a rebellion against the king aided by the forces of Glendower, Mortimer, Douglas, and the archbishop of York. The bulk of the play is taken up with the Percy rebellion, which is partially brought to a head at the battle of Shrewsbury, where a large portion of the rebel forces is defeated and where Hotspur is killed by Prince Hal.

Interwoven with the historical material are the adventures of the madcap Prince Hal and his roistering companions, chief among them Sir John Falstaff. These adventures commence with the famous episode of the robbery at Gadshill and continue with scenes of revelry in the Boar's Head Tavern in Eastcheap. Finally, in an interview between Hal and his father, in which King Henry inveighs against the prince's unseemly conduct, Hal vows to reform. His conduct proves exemplary in the campaign against the Percys, and at Shrewsbury he performs one valorous deed after another.

There is scholarly consensus that *1 Henry IV* is Shakespeare's finest chronicle play. In its masterly blend of comedy and history, it makes cogent comments on the nature of power, on the dangers of civil war, and on the need for stability in the kingdom among the lower as well as the ruling classes. It does this not through didactic moralizing but through exciting adventure, spectacular battle scenes, a brief and tender love scene, and hilarious comedy. Structurally, the serious and comic plots are interwoven in such a way that they parallel, contrast, and comment on one another, not only in their story lines, but in their character delineation.

The main characters are developed as complex individuals, each possessing a blend of attractive and negative traits. Hal appears both a wastrel and a noble prince; Hotspur a proud, hot-tempered individual and a chivalric knight; Falstaff a fat rogue and a lover of life. The contrasts are linked to the thematic lines of the play through portraitures of varying attitudes toward the concept of honor. Thus Prince Hal in his dalliance is contrasted with Hotspur, who in his appetite for battle appears to be "the theme of honor's tongue." At the same time Falstaff —for whom "honor" is a word, "a mere scutcheon"—becomes the polar opposite of Hotspur. Within these complex relationships, Hal finally emerges as a true, valorous prince for whom honor is a way of life. The play, on one level, deals with his learning of his chivalric responsibilities—the historical Hal was indeed a wild prince—and has been likened to the biblical Prodigal Son story. In this respect Falstaff has been linked with the Vice of the morality plays, a character who thrived by ensnaring youths.

Falstaff, Shakespeare's greatest comic creation, is, however, more complicated in his origin, containing within him elements of the *miles gloriosus* (the braggart warrior of Latin comedy), the classical parasite, and the court fool. In spite of all his negative traits

—this white-haired "tun of flesh" is a liar, cheat, thief, and rogue—Falstaff endears himself to audiences with his rapier wit and shrewd commentary.

For many theatergoers the Falstaff scenes are the center of the play. However, as the title indicates, it is the reign of Henry IV that is being presented. Several passages in the play consciously hark back to *Richard II*, reminding the viewers of the bishop of Carlisle's prophecy about future troubles in the land and recalling that Henry's claim to the crown was questionable. An Elizabethan audience, unsure of who would succeed their queen, would have been particularly alert to the political overtones of the play and to the observations about disorder filtering down to the lower classes in the absence of strong, responsible leadership.

An outstanding edition of *1 Henry IV* is the New Arden Edition (reprinted 1961), edited by A. R. Humphreys.—W. G.

Henry IV, Part Two (c. 1597). A chronicle play by William SHAKESPEARE. *The Second Part of Henry the Fourth* was first published in the quarto of 1600. Two issues of this quarto appeared. The first (known as Qa) omitted, apparently by accident, Act III, scene 1, necessitating its reissue (Qb) with the missing scene. The exact relationship between the quarto— the sole printed version before the publication of the First Folio of 1623—and the Folio text has not been definitively determined. The quarto text is considered the authoritative one. However, copy for the Folio version is thought to come either from a transcript of the playhouse prompt-book or from a collation of the quarto with some manuscript version. The primary sources for the play are Raphael Holinshed's *Chronicles of England, Scotland, and Ireland* (2nd ed. 1587) and the anonymous play *The Famous Victories of Henry the Fifth* (written and prod. c. 1586–1594). The quarto title page notes that *2 Henry IV* had been publicly acted "sundry times" by the Lord Chamberlain's Men.

The play continues the story of the Percy rebellion developed in *1 Henry IV*. It opens after the battle of Shrewsbury, with the earl of Northumberland— who never participated in the battle because of supposed illness—awaiting news of its outcome. Rumor brings him favorable tidings, but soon he learns the truth: His son Hotspur has been killed by Prince Hal; Worcester and Douglas have been taken prisoner; and a royal army has been dispatched against him. Northumberland considers joining forces with the archbishop of York, who has gathered several noblemen around him in rebellion against Henry on the grounds that the king is a usurper. Northumberland's wife and daughter-in-law dissuade him from joining with the archbishop, and he flees to Scotland. The rebels meet the king's army at Gaultree Forest, where a royal emissary, the earl of Westmoreland, brings them a peace bid. A parley is held, and Prince John, the king's general, promises to redress the grievances of the rebels upon the dispersal of their army. No sooner is this done than John seizes the rebel leaders and orders them executed. In London King Henry, who is ill, receives news of the end of the rebellion and of the defeat of Northumberland, who had finally taken to the field. (Henry had already learned of the death of Glendower, his Welsh adversary.) The king takes a sudden turn for the worse and

THE

Second part of Henrie

the fourth, continuing to his death,
and coronation of Henrie
the fift.

With the humours of sir Iohn Fal
staffe, and swaggering
Pistoll.

As it hath been sundrie times publikely
acted by the right honourable, the Lord
Chamberlaine his seruants.

Written by William Shakespeare.

LONDON
Printed by V .S. for Andrew Wise, and
William Aspley.
1600.

TITLE PAGE OF THE FIRST QUARTO (1600) OF SHAKE-
SPEARE'S *Henry IV, Part Two*

it confined to a chamber, where Prince Hal finds him asleep. Hal, it is thought, has slipped back to his roistering days. However, in a deathbed scene with the king, made all the more poignant by a misunderstanding over Hal's removal of the crown from the king's pillow, Hal and his father are reconciled, and the king gives his son important advice on the art of government. The play closes with the coronation of Hal as Henry V.

Interwoven with the historical material are further adventures of Falstaff. As in *1 Henry IV*, he is shown as a tavern-haunter, but he is also depicted as Captain Jack Falstaff. Thus, on his way to join the campaign against the rebels, he appears in Gloucestershire to recruit men for his company. It is in this country setting, at the home of his old acquaintance Justice Shallow, that Falstaff receives word of the death of the king. He hastens to London to his beloved Hal, only to be publicly rejected by the newly crowned monarch.

It has long been debated in scholarship whether Shakespeare had originally intended to write two plays on the reign of Henry IV, whether because of sheer bulk of material he was forced to split one chronicle play into two parts, or whether Part Two was an unplanned sequel as a result of the popularity of Part One (stemming primarily from the role of Falstaff). Whatever the answer, *1* and *2 Henry IV* were written fairly close in time to one another and

form a tightly knit unit. They have been likened to
one long ten-act play. Yet each is distinct in tone, and
each is complete as a dramatic entity.

Although in Part Two Falstaff appears in eight out
of sixteen scenes—as opposed to six out of fourteen
in Part One—and although the same alternation of
historical and comical scenes is used in both parts, *2
Henry IV* is a darker play. Sickness and disease pervade it not only in the action, in which a land infected with rebellion is depicted, but in the imagery
and in the characters—where age and infirmity are
stressed in the portrayals of the king, Northumberland, Shallow, even Falstaff. Shakespeare has broadened the scope of Part Two, presenting not only the
city and court life of Part One but also English country life. And all appear in a debased manner. In
Gloucestershire Shallow's bribe-taking and the
"draft-dodging" of the recruits for Falstaff's company reflect the activities of the roistering tavern-
haunting London cronies of Falstaff. In Part Two
they are made more condemnatory by the appearance of new low-life characters: the blustering Pistol
and the prostitute Doll Tearsheet.

But out of sickness comes health. The wild prince
Hal continues his education in the responsibilities of
kingship. In *2 Henry IV* he learns the lesson of civic
responsibility, demonstrated through the prominence
of the lord chief justice and Hal's submission to his
wisdom. Shakespeare underlines the educational
process by keeping Hal, except for one scene, physically separated from Falstaff—who appears a more
debased character in Part Two than in Part One—
and by having Hal utterly reject the fat knight in the
final scene (an act that has provoked great controversy among critics). Thus, by the conclusion of Part
Two Hal has learned what it means to wear the
crown. Furthermore, he can don it in a land purged
of its illness: The rebels are gone; Henry IV, tainted
by his usurpation of Richard II's throne, is dead; and
the tavern-haunters are imprisoned. In the last play
of the tetralogy, *Henry V*, Hal will be seen as an ideal
monarch.

An outstanding edition of *2 Henry IV* is the New
Arden Edition (1966), edited by A. R. Humphreys.
—W. G.

Henry V (1599).   A chronicle play by William
SHAKESPEARE. *The Life of King Henry the Fifth* was
initially printed in 1600 in a quarto edition. The
First Quarto, a "bad quarto," was reprinted in 1602
and in 1619, with a 1608 date on its title page. The
First Folio version (1623) stands as the authoritative
one. The primary sources for the play are Raphael
Holinshed's *Chronicles of England, Scotland, and
Ireland* (2nd ed. 1587), Edward Hall's *The Union of
the Two Noble and Illustre Families of Lancaster and
York* (1548), and the anonymous play *The Famous
Victories of Henry the Fifth* (written and prod. c.
1586–1594). The First Quarto title page notes that
Henry V had been publicly acted "sundry times" by
the Lord Chamberlain's Men; the first recorded performance, however, took place at court on January 7,
1605.

The play deals with the claim of Henry V of England to the throne of France through lineal descent
from Edward III, Henry's great-grandfather. When
King Charles VI refuses to surrender his crown,
Henry, who has scrupulously ascertained the justice

MACREADY AS HENRY V

of his claim, invades France. He first besieges
Harfleur, which surrenders when no relief troops are
sent. Henry continues his advance; with his men
weakened and greatly outnumbered, he faces the
overconfident French army at Agincourt and re-
soundingly defeats it. A peace treaty is drawn up,
which foremost among its terms gives to Henry in
marriage Princess Katherine, whom he had already
successfully been wooing. King Charles further
agrees to name Henry heir to his throne.

Henry V centers on Henry as "the mirror of all
Christian kings." As the capstone play of both historical tetralogies, it presents a portrait of an ideal
king. Shakespeare carefully keeps the "star of England" free of blemishes. In the first scene it is established that the madcap Prince Hal of the *Henry IV*
plays went through a miraculous transformation
upon his ascension to the throne, "Leaving his body
as a paradise/To envelope and contain celestial spirits." In all his actions, Henry reveals that he has
learned well his lessons of the *Henry IV* plays, appearing in *Henry V* as a just, merciful, chivalric, and
democratic ruler, as his scenes with the common soldiers illustrate. To keep the portrait untarnished,
Shakespeare isolates him from his former roistering
companions. Thus Falstaff, whose reappearance was

promised in the Epilogue to *2 Henry IV*, has been banished from the play and relegated to a touching offstage death scene described by Hostess Quickly.

Henry V is a military play and concerns itself with the problems of a monarch in time of war. It further shows a united British nation, as epitomized by the Welsh, Scots, and Irish officers who are part of the invading English army.

Critics have been sharply divided over both the merits of the play and Shakespeare's interpretation of Henry. Some believe the portrait too pat; others that Shakespeare is critical of the Lancastrian monarch, depicting him as a pragmatist seeking to fob off responsibility for unpleasant decisions. Criticism of the structure of *Henry V* has centered on the use of prologues, the long, rhetorical passages, and the overly patriotic tone. It is indeed conceivable that by the time Shakespeare wrote *Henry V*—his ninth chronicle play—he had not only become jaded with English history but was trapped by the overall thematic design of the two tetralogies. (*King John* stands outside this group.) Moreover, by 1599 Shakespeare was writing his "joyous comedies" and was beginning his great tragedies, having penned *Julius Caesar* the same year as *Henry V*.

An outstanding edition of *Henry V* is the New Arden Edition (1954), edited by J. H. Walter.—W. G.

Henry VI, Parts One, Two, and Three (1590–1592). A trilogy by William SHAKESPEARE. Shakespeare's dramatization of the War of the Roses is primarily based upon the accounts of the Tudor historians Edward Halle and Raphael Holinshed. By modern standards, neither was a model of historical objectivity or impartiality. Thus, in his account of the diabolism of Joan of Arc in Part One and the villainy of Richard III in Part Three, Shakespeare is accurately reflecting the attitudes of his sources.

Part One moves alternatively from the battlefields of France to the palaces of England, where quarreling factions of English nobles sap the strength of the nation. With the death of Henry V the throne is occupied by his young son, while the wise duke of Gloucester acts as lord protector until Henry VI comes of age. Gloucester's enemy, Cardinal Beaufort, has instigated a quarrel that results in a street conflict between their followers. At the same time, the earl of Somerset, of the house of Lancaster, quarrels with Richard Plantagenet, the aspiring duke of York. This dispute is the seed that will blossom into the War of the Roses. In the meantime, the war in France is a see-saw affair. The French forces are led by Joan of Arc, here pictured as a sorceress with demonic powers. Aligned against her are the English troops led by the noble and valiant Lord Talbot. As the war nears its end, Talbot is killed in battle, and Joan, finally captured by the English, is burned at the stake as a witch. Peace is concluded between France and England, and Henry is persuaded by the earl of Suffolk to marry a French noblewoman, Margaret of Anjou.

In Part Two the earl of Suffolk's plan to have the young and timid Henry marry Margaret has succeeded. Now Suffolk and the new queen are the *de facto* rulers of England, since Henry is easily dominated by his strong-minded wife. Suffolk oversteps himself, however, when he arranges the death of the duke of Gloucester. He is banished from England

and while on the high seas is killed by pirates. The troubled kingdom is now beset by a peasants' revolt led by Jack Cade, who claims to be the true heir to the crown. Cade is eventually killed and the rebellion put down. But a new pretender to the throne has appeared in the person of Richard, duke of York. York traces his lineage back to the third son of Edward III, while the Lancastrian line goes back to John of Gaunt, Edward III's fourth son. Over this point the English aristocracy splits into two armed camps. The Yorkist forces defeat the king's army in their first encounter, and the War of the Roses has begun.

Part Three picks up the story where Part Two ended. After his initial defeat, Henry agrees to name the duke of York as his heir, but Queen Margaret, enraged by her husband's disinheriting of her son, continues the fight. York is defeated and killed by the fierce queen. Two of York's sons, Edward and the humpbacked Richard, together with the earl of Warwick vow to carry on. This time the Yorkists are victorious, and Edward is proclaimed king. Warwick goes to France to arrange the marriage of Edward to the sister-in-law of the king of France. In the meantime, however, Edward has met and married Lady Elizabeth Grey. Furious at this development, Warwick joins forces with Queen Margaret and, aided by the king of France, returns to England to renew the battle. He captures Edward and reinstates Henry as king. Edward escapes, however, and after gathering a force of men, assisted by his brother Richard, defeats Warwick and then the queen. Her young son is butchered before her eyes, she is exiled, and her husband, the hapless Henry VI, is murdered in the Tower of London by the fiend-like Richard, whose subsequent career is to be chronicled in Shakespeare's *Richard III*.

These three plays represent Shakespeare's earliest sustained effort as a dramatist. They reveal many of the problems of the beginner: diffuseness, overly declamatory verse, and a certain inability to weave the intractable material of historical fact into a coherent dramatic design. For all their flaws, however, the plays also demonstrate on a small scale some of Shakespeare's great virtues: his capacity for characterization, the flexibility of his poetry as a vehicle of spoken verse, and his ability to shape a variety of disparate events in order to reflect the significant aspects of a controlling theme, in this case the impersonal, inexorable cyclicality of history.

A recommended edition of the *Henry VI* trilogy is the New Arden Edition (1957–1964), in three volumes, edited by A. S. Cairncross.—E. Q.

Henry VIII (1613). A chronicle play by William SHAKESPEARE. Shakespeare may not have been the sole author of *Henry VIII*. Many scholars have supported the conjecture that this drama, like *The Two Noble Kinsmen,* is a result of a collaboration between Shakespeare and John Fletcher. Divided authorship, among other things, helps to account for the difficulties of the play—its lack of linear development or central focus.

Henry VIII covers the years 1510 to 1533. The court of Henry is dominated by the figure of Cardinal Wolsey, master of political intrigue. Wolsey's machinations enable him to bring about the downfall of the duke of Buckingham, his old enemy. However, he makes a fatal error when he tries to arrange a divorce between Henry and his queen, Katherine of Aragon. Wolsey's ultimate goal is to bring about a marriage between Henry and the heiress to the French throne and, thereby, to consolidate his powers. Henry, however, has other plans. He has fallen in love with the queen's lady-in-waiting, Ann Boleyn. Politically ambitious herself, Ann manipulates the downfall of Wolsey, thus clearing the way for Henry's divorce and remarriage to her. Shortly after the marriage, Ann gives birth to a girl. At the baby's christening, Archbishop Cranmer, a trusted and trustworthy cleric whom Henry has defended from court intrigues, prophesies of the glory that the child shall bring to England. Shakespeare's audience would be well aware of the accuracy of the prediction, since the child is of course the future Queen Elizabeth I.

Despite its apparently loose organization, *Henry VIII* is unified by the theme of the providential design of history. The triumphs and defeats of great men are here seen as part of a larger pattern in which the forces of history exhibit themselves as the expression of divine will.

A recommended edition of *King Henry VIII* is the New Arden Edition (1957), edited by R. A. Foakes. —E. Q.

Henshaw, James. See AFRICA: *Nigeria*.

Heracles or The Madness of Heracles (Herakles or Herakles Mainomenos, 422–416 B.C.). A tragedy by EURIPIDES. *Heracles* is one of several of Euripides' plays that have considerable power even though they flout every Aristotelian canon of unity. In Heracles' absence in Hades, from which no mere man has ever returned, his children, his wife, Megara, and his old father, Amphitryon, have taken refuge at the altar of Zeus from Lycus, who has usurped the Theban rule. Gradually losing all hope of Heracles' return, they surrender and are allowed to prepare for a decent death. Suddenly Heracles appears, saves them, and kills Lycus. The first part of the play, which has shown Heracles as a loving husband and kind father and celebrated his greatness, ends with an ode of triumph.

Now, suddenly, Iris and Madness appear to announce that Hera has decreed that Heracles shall go mad and murder his children and his wife. They enter the house and the horrible slaughter is described by a messenger in a masterly speech. Heracles slowly recovers his sanity. On learning what he has done he wants to kill himself, but his friend Theseus arrives and persuades him that his very greatness requires him to bear his new burdens. Unafraid of the pollution a murderer's presence may bring, he offers Heracles refuge in Athens.

Where is the dramatic unity? The very appearance of Iris and Madness seems to underline the idea that Madness comes from outside, not from the man himself or his past history. Perhaps Euripides is dramatizing the very old Greek feeling that superhuman greatness is dangerous, even though it be achieved without incurring guilt. Perhaps he is also saying that peace must be made by humans and is not to be expected from the warring forces of heaven, a feeling not infrequent in his plays. If so, we must take the gods, the fatherhood of Zeus, the miracles, and the epiphanies at their face value. If we do not, *Heracles*

loses all meaning, and a good deal of its power as well.

Translations of the play are listed under Euripides. —G. M. A. G.

Herne, James A. (1839–1901). American actor and playwright. Herne, whose name was originally Aherne, was born in Cohoes, New York, made his stage debut in 1859, and soon became a leading character actor in the new realistic style of the day. In 1874, he began to adapt novels to the stage and in 1879 collaborated with David BELASCO on three plays, of which *Hearts of Oak* had a lasting success. In 1878, Herne married Katharine Corcoran, an excellent actress who, as his leading lady and adviser, exercised a strong influence on his later writing.

Herne's early work was influenced by Dickens, his later work by Tolstoy, Ibsen, and Zola. *Margaret Fleming* (1890), which deals with the problem of a husband's infidelity, was a landmark in the development of American realistic drama. *The Reverend Griffith Davenport* (1899), which survives only in part, deals with the Civil War in terms of the conflict between freedom and slavery and between federal law and states' rights. Even *Shore Acres* (1892), basically a sentimental melodrama about life on the Maine coast, uses the techniques of realism. Herne's realism, however, has more in common with that of William Dean Howells than with Ibsen's or Zola's; a typically American idealism pervades his work. —B. H.

Hero and Leander (Des Meeres und der Liebe Wellen, 1831). A tragedy in verse by Franz GRILLPARZER. Hero is about to pledge her life as a virgin priestess of Aphrodite in the temple of Sestos. In so doing she voluntarily renounces society, marriage,

and love. As she is about to take her vows, she sees Leander, a shy youth from Abydos, across the Hellespont. She realizes then that woman's happiness lies in love for a man. Leander, too, falls passionately in love with Hero. The following night Leander swims across the Hellespont and climbs the tower in which Hero lives. Hero gives him refuge so that the weary swimmer may rest. Leander protests his love, and there ensues one of the most splendid love scenes in all of German drama. He asks her to place a lamp in her tower window facing the sea at night so that on later occasions it will aid him in swimming the Hellespont in the dark. Hero's uncle, the high priest, learns of Leander's intrusion and the next night, when Hero has fallen asleep, manages to have the lamp positioned in such a way that the wind will extinguish it. Leander again swims the Hellespont, but with no light to guide him he is dashed onto the rocks, and the next day his body is washed ashore. Hero, now a woman as a result of her love, dies of grief beside her dead Leander.

Hero and Leander is one of the most lovely plays in all of German-speaking drama. Its gentleness, its imagery, its splendid verse, but most importantly the simple yet very profoundly human characteristics of its chief figures make it the well-deserved classic it has become on the modern German stage.

There are two translations of *Hero and Leander,* the first by Henry Harmon Stevens (1938), the second by Arthur Burkhard (1962). Both are in verse and fairly successful.—C. R. M.

heroic play. A special development of tragedy, featuring protagonists of vast stature whose great potentialities are stressed more than their limitations and who are sometimes shown triumphant in the end. Exalted ideals of love, honor, and valor provide the chief themes. Most heroic plays in the early part of the English Restoration period were in rhyming pentameter couplets, and the term is sometimes confined to these plays. It may be extended, however, to cover plays in blank verse that have similar characters and themes. Heroic plays draw mainly upon the traditions of epic and romance (see EN-GLAND: *Restoration drama*).—E. W.

He Who Gets Slapped (Tot, kto poluchaet po shchechiny, 1916). A drama in four acts by Leonid ANDREYEV. This play is the story of HE, a refugee from the intellectual world who tries desperately to become an ordinary, nameless individual. In his former life he was a famous man who had written a book far above the heads of ordinary people; his ideas were stolen by another author who, by popularizing them, immediately became famous. To escape his world, HE joins a circus as a clown. His act consists of being a "great man" who is slapped in the face but who is so divorced from the real world that he smiles blissfully, taking the slaps for applause. The circus is run by Papa Briquet, a simple and kind man, and his wife, Zinida, a lion-tamer, who is unhappily in love with Bezano, a handsome young equestrian. The star of the circus is Consuela, an uneducated, beautiful young horseback rider, supposedly the daughter of Count Mancini, who, in order to obtain money for his own pleasures, arranges for a rich baron to marry Consuela.

The action of the play, which is almost static in the first three acts, takes place offstage, and tension is gradually built up through the increasing desperation of Zinida and Bezano. Like HE, Bezano is in love with Consuela, and so when HE realizes that his own efforts to prevent Consuela from marrying the baron are futile, he asks Bezano to take her, or even to kill her, rather than to let the baron lay a hand on her. When that fails too, HE poisons her as well as himself, whereupon the baron, in despair over his love for Consuela, shoots himself.

He Who Gets Slapped, the most successful play Andreyev wrote and one of his last, expresses, according to Soviet critics, his "morbid obsession with metaphysics." Actually, the idea tormenting the author is quite down to earth: namely, the difficulties of an artist and intellectual in communicating with ordinary people and the need for a writer to remain in touch with the world of feeling. Andreyev makes the point that vulgarization is not the answer to the ivory tower nor sensuality to cold and uncommunicative reasoning. What an artist needs, Andreyev seems to be saying, is to find new ways of expressing what he has to say, so that he may convey his esoteric view to others. HE tries to establish real contact with the world by joining the circus and becoming "he who gets slapped," that is, by placing himself in a humiliating position and coming down to the level of those with whom he is trying to communicate.

The other circus performers are simple people who are able to talk directly to their audience, thus implying the Dostoyevskian idea that reason must be bypassed to reach feelings directly. The circus manager constantly repeats that education spoils performers. When his wife is unhappy and takes unnecessary risks with her lions, he blames it on her books.

HE, while rejecting the intellect that cannot communicate with the masses, decides to deliver his complex message in the language of simple emotions. Through his act, HE conveys directly the ridiculous and lonely predicament of an intellectual wrapped in esoteric glory. He exposes his superiority as phony. The act is a success, but HE has still not achieved true simplicity. More than any of the other characters, Consuela is the embodiment of real simplicity. She, who is so silly, vulgar, and ignorant, is a goddess, the Venus whom HE worships once he has given up the complex, lofty gods of his former world. She understands nothing about the world of men around her. To her, art comes completely naturally, while the others must work at it.

At the end when HE is dying, he feels he has succeeded in turning his back on the false, stifling little world of intellect and reason and has entered the world of feeling and emotion, where he has joined in the deadly combat between spiritual and earthly love, between the true worship of beauty and the carnal lusts of the world. Andreyev seems to suggest in this play that the refined artist must not give up his refinement but instead must devise an emotional language with which to reach the crowd.

Leonid Andreyev's *He Who Gets Slapped* is translated by Andrew R. MacAndrew in *20th Century Russian Drama* (1963).—A. MacA.

Heywood, John (c. 1497–c. 1580). English playwright and poet. Heywood was employed as a musician at the courts of Henry VIII, Edward VI,

JOHN HEYWOOD (THEATRE COLLECTION, NEW YORK
PUBLIC LIBRARY AT LINCOLN CENTER)

and Queen Mary. He married the niece of Sir Thomas More and became one of the disciples of his distinguished uncle. At the accession of Elizabeth (1558) he lost favor at court and was eventually forced to leave England because of his adherence to Catholicism. He died at Louvain sometime after 1578. His son Jasper (1535–1598) became a Jesuit and achieved some literary distinction as the chief translator of the plays of Seneca into English. The distinguished literary tradition of the Heywood family was continued by the poet's grandson, John Donne.

Heywood's best-known nondramatic work is *The Spider and the Fly* (1556), a long allegorical poem attacking Protestantism. His dramatic reputation rests largely upon his achievement as a writer of the INTERLUDE, an early sixteenth-century playlet that was an important precursor of Elizabethan drama. The best of Heywood's interludes are *The Play of the Weather; The Four P's; The Pardoner and the Friar;* and *John John, Tyb and Sir John,* all of uncertain date. As products of the medieval tradition, these plays are striking for their nonmoralistic quality. *The Play of the Weather,* although an allegory, departs from the medieval mode in avoiding a Christian or even a didactic formula. The other three are realistic comedies with a structure resembling that of the medieval *debat* (a narrative form in which two characters debate). All three contain some anticlerical

satire, but the dominant quality of the plays is more farcical than satiric. *The Four P's* concerns a contest among a peddler, a palmer, a pothecary, and a pardoner to see who can tell the biggest lie. Of more dramatic value is *John John, Tyb and Sir John,* a spirited farce about a henpecked cuckold.

Heywood's interludes are dramatically even more primitive than the morality plays out of which they developed. Nevertheless, they represent a significant milestone in the secularization of the English drama, which resulted in the great achievements of the age of Shakespeare. In addition, the playlets themselves have a comic verve and high-spiritedness that underlie the best Elizabethan comedies.

Heywood's works have been edited by Burton Milligan in *John Heywood's Works and Miscellaneous Short Poems* (1956). Robert Bolwell's *The Life and Work of John Heywood* (1921) provides a full-length study of the dramatist.—E. Q.

Heywood, Thomas (c. 1574–1641). English playwright. The date and place of Heywood's birth are not known. He is probably the son of a clergyman who resided in the county of Lincolnshire. Educated at Cambridge, Heywood left without taking a degree and by 1596 was working in London as a writer and actor, the latter until 1619. At the same time he was busy turning out the almost two hundred plays in which he claimed he had a hand "or at least a main finger." Heywood was also responsible for a long series of nondramatic works, including translations, prose pamphlets, and long poems.

The vast majority of Heywood's plays are not extant, but the twenty-odd that do survive give us a good taste of his quality. His plays are the product of a facile pen: simple, straightforward, and good-humored. Designed for a popular audience, they express popular tastes. At their very best, such as in *A Woman Killed with Kindness* (1603), his masterpiece, they combine genuine emotion and firm characterization. At their worst they are sentimental and burdened with stock characters. In the latter category falls *If You Know Not Me, You Know Nobody* (1605), a two-part play based on the early life of Queen Elizabeth. More representative of Heywood's history plays is *Edward IV*. Again a two-part play, it focuses on that favorite Elizabethan heroine, Jane Shore.

A more ambitious entry into pseudohistorical drama is Heywood's Ages quintet: *The Golden Age* (c. 1611), *The Silver Age* (c. 1612), *The Brazen Age* (c. 1613), and the two-part *The Iron Age* (c. 1613). These five plays dramatize the major legends of classical mythology from the opposition of Saturn and Titan to the fall of Troy and the murder of Agamemnon. Another classical drama is his *Rape of Lucrece* (1607), an interesting combination of high tragedy and low comedy.

Among Heywood's numerous other plays, two that stand out are *The English Traveller* (c. 1627) and *The Fair Maid of the West* (produced between 1610 and 1630). *The English Traveller,* like *A Woman Killed with Kindness,* deals with an erring wife, who in this case is false to her lover as well as her husband. *The Fair Maid of the West* is a two-part play of which the first is far superior to the second. It tells of the adventures of Bess Bridges, a tavern maid who rises to become captain of a ship that she uses to rescue her wounded lover, Captain Spencer. The story has an ample assortment of the staples of popular entertainment: disguises, mistaken identities, and a much-beleaguered but pure-hearted heroine. Despite its swashbuckling extravagances, it has a fresh and direct charm that remains untarnished.

Heywood's last years were crowded with activity. During the 1630's he produced a large number of pamphlets and other nondramatic works. From 1631 to 1639 he wrote an annual pageant given on the Lord Mayor's Day in London, all the while continuing his professional dramatic activity. Among the plays written during this period were the tragicomedies *A Maidenhead Well Lost* (c. 1634) and *A Challenge for Beauty* (1634/35?), two plays representing Heywood's attempt to appeal to a more courtly audience.

Heywood's work is so varied, uneven, and, in cases of disputed authorship, unknown, that it is impossible to categorize it. His unflagging energy and ingenuity are beyond question. In fecundity of imagination, popular appeal, and rich humanity he bears comparison, as Charles Lamb pointed out, with Shakespeare. But it goes without saying that his work lacks the poetic genius, not to mention the breadth and intensity, of his great contemporary.

Heywood's works have been edited by R. H. Shepherd in the six-volume *Dramatic Works* (1874). A detailed critical study is given in F. S. Boas' *Thomas Heywood* (1950).—E. Q.

Hippolytus (Hippolytos, 428 B.C.). A tragedy by EURIPIDES. *Hippolytus* is one of the great tragedies of Euripides. Once we realize that Hippolytus, not his stepmother, Phaedra, is the chief character, we see that the structure of the play is well-nigh perfect. The two epiphanies, of Aphrodite at the beginning and of Artemis at the end, put the human drama into universal context as a struggle between two powerful forces in human life.

The introductory monologue shows Aphrodite, the goddess of sexual passion, in all her dangerous power, especially dangerous to those who deny her, as Hippolytus does. Phaedra's guilty infatuation for her stepson is only an instrument of vengeance for the ruthless goddess, although Phaedra dies of it. And when, immediately after the monologue, Hippolytus addresses a beautiful little prayer to Artemis and insults Aphrodite, we know that he is doomed.

We see Phaedra in a state of near collapse from fighting her guilty passion, which she has so far kept secret; she is starving herself to death. The lengthy scene in which she finally confesses her feelings to the Nurse (and the Chorus) is one of the finest in Euripides. Betrayed by the Nurse to Hippolytus, who replies with a violently tactless attack upon all womankind, Phaedra fully realizes that only death can save her from dishonor. At the same time she determines to punish Hippolytus for his coldness. She hangs herself, but with a letter in her hand accusing Hippolytus of raping her. When her husband, Theseus, returns from a journey, he believes her calumny against his son. In his rage, Theseus pronounces a curse that brings about Hippolytus' mortal injury in a chariot crash. He learns the truth only in time to win the young man's forgiveness as he dies.

Phaedra is beautifully drawn. Before a fifth-century Greek audience all Euripides' skill was probably required to evoke any sympathy for Phaedra at all. Modern commentators sympathize with her too much. Some of them say that their interest flags after Phaedra's death, or (even worse) that the tragedian's own interest flagged and that he composed the rest of the play "somewhat mechanically." One can but be aghast at such a lack of understanding and imagination. The Greek audience would certainly regard Phaedra's letter as a vicious kind of revenge, and it should at least cool down our sympathy for her.

Hippolytus is a fascinating character, drawn with all Euripides' skill. It is not because he is a virgin that he infuriates Aphrodite but because he makes a cult of virginity and cuts himself off from the source of human life. He is incredibly complacent and, confronted with Phaedra's accusation in the crucial scene with Theseus, his defense consists largely of a catalogue of his own virtues. Yet there is much to admire in him: there is beauty in his worship of Artemis, and when he addresses her his language becomes fresh and lovely. But to his father his language is precious, artificial, and therefore rhetorical. This is in character; it is not merely Euripides' rhetoric.

The epiphany of Artemis at the end balances that of Aphrodite at the beginning. And we note that there is no peace or reconciliation in heaven: Artemis plots vengeance on Aphrodite, while Hippolytus forgives his father and clears him of bloodguilt—his most affecting gesture. And if he is somewhat complacent even here, who would not forgive him?

The messenger's description of Hippolytus' fall from his chariot is excellent. The choral odes are relevant to the action throughout. If anyone worries that Theseus should have used a second wish to cancel the first, we may answer that a curse could not be recalled, unless perhaps it was done at once. The miracle of the bull from the sea that frightened Hippolytus' horses should be taken at face value. These are trivia that would not worry the Greek audiences in the theater, only scholars in their studies.

Translations of the play are listed under Euripides. —G. M. A. G.

Hirshbein, Peretz (1880–1948). Russian-born Yiddish playwright, novelist, and travel writer. Hirshbein was born on November 17, 1880, in a water mill near a small town in the province of Grodno, Russia. He received a traditional religious education but in his early youth became acquainted with secular works in Hebrew and in Yiddish. In the hours after his religious studies, he began to read widely in both languages and to study Russian. When he was twenty, Hirshbein settled in Vilna as a tutor in Hebrew. There the poverty of the Jewish masses, especially the shock of being accosted by a very young Jewish streetwalker, turned him from the lyric Hebrew verse he had been writing to realistic drama. After his first few plays in Hebrew (which he later translated into Yiddish), all of Hirshbein's plays were written in Yiddish. In 1908 he moved to Odessa, where he soon became the central figure in the organization of a theatrical company (shortly thereafter known as the Hirshbein Troupe) whose purpose was to raise the artistic level of the Yiddish theater. A pioneering group in the Yiddish art theater movement, the Hirshbein Troupe was well received during the two years of its existence. During the years that followed, Hirshbein lived in various European countries and finally settled in the United States in 1914, where he became a regular contributor to the newly founded Yiddish daily *The Day*. The bulk of his ensuing work was published in its columns. From his earliest years, Hirshbein had loved to travel, and he published half a dozen books on his world-wide travels. These experiences also provided him with the material for his three novels and two published volumes of memoirs.

Of the more than fifty works of varying length that Hirshbein wrote for the stage, the best are his plays of the Jewish countryside: *Di Puste Kretchme* (*The Idle Inn*, 1912), *A Farvorfn Vinkl* ("*A Remote Corner*," 1913), *Dem Shmid's Tekhter* ("*The Blacksmith's Daughters*," 1915), and GREEN FIELDS. In the last three, his idyllic folk comedies, the Jewish farmer is portrayed not as an object of disdain for his lack of education, as he had been so often before, but as a man whose very simplicity is an expression of his piety and decency. The world Hirshbein creates is a world of quiet charm and gentle, kindly humor, a world of decent folk and bountiful nature. Character and atmosphere take precedence over the minimal plot, which deals with little more than the fulfillment of innocent love between naïve lads and lasses, and the dialogue has the natural power of their simplicity.

Hirshbein's second major contribution to Yiddish drama was his impact on the art theater movement, of which the Hirshbein Troupe was only the first of several with which Hirshbein was associated. As Jacob Gordin had earlier begun a new era in the Yiddish theater by writing serious plays that avoided the tawdry devices of the entertainment stage, so Hirshbein helped begin a new chapter some twenty years later, when his plays (and some of the veterans of the old Hirshbein Troupe) helped launch Maurice Schwartz's Yiddish Art Theater on a twenty-year career. The financial as well as artistic success of Hirshbein's plays made viable a sophisticated Yiddish theater capable of presenting the work of the Yiddish dramatists of the 1920's and 1930's.

Discussions of Hirshbein's literary career can be found in Joseph C. Landis, translator and editor, *The Dybbuk and Other Great Yiddish Plays* (1966); Sol Liptzin, *The Flowering of Yiddish Literature* (1963); and Charles A. Madison, *Yiddish Literature: Its Scope and Major Writers* (1968).—J. C. L.

history play. See CHRONICLE PLAY.

Hochhuth, Rolf (1931–). German playwright and editor. Hochhuth belongs to a generation of German writers who were too young to prevent the catastrophe of World War II yet old enough to experience its devastating results. As a dramatist, he sees his task as rewriting history and enlightening audiences so that history will not be able to repeat itself. He did research on his first play, *Der Stellvertreter* (*The Deputy*, 1963), for five years while working as an editor for a German publishing firm. When the documentary epic—playing time estimated to be five and a half hours—was produced in abridged form by Erwin Piscator on February 20, 1963, it caused an international controversy. Hochhuth's drama (five acts written in blank verse) is a forceful protest accusing Pope Pius XII of political absti-

ROLF HOCHHUTH (GERMAN INFORMATION CENTER)

nence and intrigue. Hochhuth believes that individual guilt always has collective implications. For instance, the pope fears the lonely void within himself through which he would have had to pass if he had protested against the Nazis. He will not combat his anxiety, and because of this, he commits himself and the Church to a course both politically and morally reprehensible. The alternative to such a crime and its consequent guilt is revealed by the young priest Riccardo, who first acknowledges his participation and then refuses further complicity. Collective guilt entails self-deception, which Riccardo cannot bear. With a sense of belonging to the institution, Riccardo acts by speaking directly against the Church's role in World War II. The pope turns his back on his role of Church leader, and the euphemistic terms in which he speaks become the sign of his irresponsibility.

Hochhuth's attacks on the pope have been interpreted by various critics as a German's attempt to balance the account of history. However, Hochhuth never shies from exploring German crimes. His novella *Die Berliner Antigone* ("The Berlin Antigone," 1965) is an explicit condemnation of the Germans' political atrocities. As in his dramas, the action takes place in 1943 and deals with a young German woman who is placed on trial by a Nazi court for hiding the dead body of her traitor brother, which the state had designated for scientific experiments. As a political writer, Hochhuth protests and abhors the sacrifice of personal integrity to inhuman institutions and their arbitrary laws. In his most recent play, *Soldaten: Nekrolog auf Genf* (*Soldiers: An Obituary of Geneva*, 1967), he has again touched upon a taboo, which has caused an uproar in England. Against the wishes of Sir Laurence Olivier and Peter Brook, the board of governors of the National Theatre refused to grant Hochhuth's play a permit to be performed. The dispute centered on the play's leading figure, Sir Winston Churchill, whom Hochhuth takes to task for his decision to level the city of Dresden on February 13, 1945. Hochhuth uses Churchill in this drama as he did the pope in *Der Stellvertreter:* He is a chief representative of his time, a maker of history, who has lost contact with people and therefore with his own sense of humanity. Churchill is opposed by the bishop of Chillister, Dr. Bell, who demands the cessation of saturation bombing. Churchill cannot defend his position rationally, for he is a romantic with a mission and unaware of the evil in his actions. However, Churchill's personality is not the main issue of the drama. Hochhuth is directly concerned with saturation bombing in general, and his play takes the form of an argument for some type of international agreement to protect civilians in time of war. Hochhuth's self-imposed task as documentary dramatist is to probe history and make it speak for the present. He is a moralist in the German tradition of Lessing and Schiller, but he has moved beyond Germany to consider the world as his proper congregation.

The Storm over "The Deputy" (1964), edited by Eric Bentley, contains essays and articles about Hochhuth's drama.—J. D. Z.

Hochwälder, Fritz. See SWITZERLAND.

Hofmannsthal, Hugo von (1874–1929). Austrian poet, playwright, short-story writer, and essayist. Hofmannsthal's entire life and outlook were almost inextricably bound up with the city of his birth, Vienna, which was at the time the world capital of art, music, and theater. While he studied romance philology at the University of Vienna, poems, short stories, novellas, essays, reviews, and short lyrical dramas, all of high quality, flowed from this young man's pen. In 1901 he married and for the remainder of his life lived outside of Vienna, in Rodaun, where he died in 1929.

His first play was written at the age of sixteen, before he had completed his secondary education. By the age of seventeen his lyric poetry had captivated his contemporaries with its profundity, beauty, and formal perfection. The first decade of his literary life, from 1890 to 1899, was almost wholly devoted to the short lyric. When Hofmannsthal took up writing in the dramatic form, he in fact called his one-act plays *lyrische Dramen* ("lyrical plays"). They are little more than lyric poems in dramatic form, yet their verse is of tremendous distinction and subtlety. As all of his works, they are intensely personal, focusing on the relation of the poet to life. His approach to drama was always through his poetic sensibility.

Hofmannsthal's vast and deep knowledge stirred him to revive plays from other times, thus bypassing the influence of Friedrich Hebbel and Henrik Ibsen. From the Greeks he borrowed *Alcestis, Electra,* and the Oedipus myth; from the Elizabethans, Thomas Otway's *Venice Preserved* (*Das gerettete Venedig,* written 1905); from the Spanish, Calderón's *Life Is a Dream,* which became the basis for his full-length play *Der Turm* (*The Tower,* written 1925; second version 1927); and from the early English drama, the morality play *Everyman* (JEDERMANN). In each instance, however, Hofmannsthal did more than merely translate; rather he transformed, reshaped, revivified, made something new of a past master-

HUGO VON HOFMANNSTHAL (EDITIONS ALBERT MORANCÉ, PARIS)

work. In this endeavor his debt to the Austrian director and producer Max Reinhardt is inestimable, for Reinhardt, too, was devoted to the ideal of bringing new and meaningful life to the classics of the past.

Under the influence of Maurice Maeterlinck and other leading symbolists, the early lyrical dramas are pervaded with a sense of loneliness, futility, and pessimism. In true Maeterlinck fashion, Hofmannsthal's stage is a place of misty atmosphere, labyrinthian passageways, pools, forests, towers, fountains, and grottoes. The plays depict the attempts of a poet seeking a means of communication in a world that is not only mysterious, but cruel, inexplicable, and distant. Yet Hofmannsthal's vision is not despairing, for he still sees life as fascinating in its vast richness of experience. Although the poet renders himself an observer, detached, disillusioned, and tired, there is inherent in the plays a realization that this attitude is destructive and self-defeating. The poet's attempt to capture reality despite his aloofness often leads to tragic inner conflicts, as in his first lyrical plays, *Der Tor und der Tod* (*Death and the Fool,* written 1893) and *Der Tod des Tizian* (*The Death of Titian,* written 1892).

One of the major problems with Hofmannsthal's most poetic, "private" plays is finding a point of compromise between the private vision and the exigencies of the physical stage. It is this refusal to compromise fully that led Hofmannsthal into the use of SYMBOLISM; for logical, rational language, the language of everyday communication, was suspect as being unable to convey the mysterious beauty and wonder of the universe. Thus, all human utterance and communication are called into question. The literary and physical symbol, however, gave greater and deeper meaning to his art.

One of Hofmannsthal's most successful ventures in

the theater was his collaboration with the composer Richard Strauss. Out of this union came a series of operatic librettos that are brilliant in conception, poetic sensibility, dramatic relevance, and total aptness for the operatic stage. Hofmannsthal's first operatic success was based on his play ELECTRA, for which Strauss composed the score. The rest of his works for the operatic stage were written specifically for Strauss: *Der Rosenkavalier* (*The Cavalier of the Rose,* written 1911), *Ariadne auf Naxos* (*Ariadne on Naxos,* written 1912), *Die Frau ohne Schatten* (*The Woman Without a Shadow,* 1919), and *Arabella* (1933). The most famous and successful of these collaborations remains *Der Rosenkavalier,* an opera of Mozartian grace and utterly Viennese atmosphere and charm in the age of Maria Theresa of Austria.

Aside from his operatic collaborations, Hofmannsthal is perhaps best known for his *Jedermann,* a very free adaptation of the English *Everyman,* from which he borrowed scarcely one hundred lines. It is a thoroughly modern piece in its viewpoint and application. A vast outdoor pageant, *Jedermann* combines music, dance, drama, and moral precept; it is about the exaggerated respect of man for monetary value in a materialistic society.

Hofmannsthal has often been deemed an esthete and decadent. Since his death, however, and particularly since the end of World War II, his reputation as a writer in virtually all forms has grown to an extraordinary extent. His aim was to rejuvenate the great tradition of European drama and to restore to it the individual and collective conscience of a people. Seemingly old-fashioned and decidedly literary, Hofmannsthal's plays are nonetheless vitally theatrical and are excellent examples of poetic drama.

An excellent and most informative biography of Hofmannsthal is that by Hanns Hammelmann, *Hugo von Hofmannsthal* (1957). In addition, the Bollingen Foundation has published Hofmannsthal's *Selected Writings of Hugo von Hofmannsthal* (3 vols., 1952–1963). The translations are by various hands, and the volumes edited by Michael Hamburger.—C. R. M.

Holberg, Ludvig (1684–1754). Danish-Norwegian historian, satirist, and playwright. Holberg was born in Bergen, Norway, the last of twelve children. He first visited Copenhagen in 1702 and took a theology degree there in 1704. He traveled extensively in England (1706–1708), where he supported himself with language lessons and the flute, and in France and Italy (1714–1716). The first trip led to an intense interest in Swift and the literary journalism of Addison and Steele; the second to a preoccupation with *commedia dell'arte* and Molière, as well as with the latest trends of skeptical rationalism.

In 1711 Holberg published his first book, *Introduktion til de europæiske rigers historie* ("Introduction to the History of the Kingdoms of Europe"), and in 1714 he was appointed to the first of a series of professorships in Copenhagen, though it was not until 1730 that he obtained a chair in his chosen field of history.

Holberg first made a name for himself in a literary way with the immensely popular *Peder Paars* (1719 –1720), a lengthy mock-epic poem satirizing various aspects of Danish society. In September 1722 the first Danish theater was opened on Little Green

LUDVIG HOLBERG (DANISH INFORMATION OFFICE)

Street (Lille Grønnegade, now Ny Adelgade), and between that date and its closing in 1728 Holberg wrote some twenty-eight comedies, fifteen of them in as many months. Holberg concluded this period by issuing his collected plays, *Den danske skueplads* ("The Danish Stage," 1731), and then turned to the writing of history: city history, Danish history, church history, the history of the Jews. Among his chief works in the 1740's were *Niels Klims underjordiske rejse* (*The Subterranean Journey of Niels Klim,* 1741), a utopian travelogue written in Latin and showing the influence of Swift's *Gulliver's Travels;* and a quantity of *Moralske tanker* ("Moral Thoughts," 1744) and *Epistler* (*Epistles,* 1748–1754), in which he emulates Montaigne, Addison, and Steele, with a strong assertion of his own originality. Holberg accepted a barony in 1747 and the following year became connected with the newly opened Danish National Theater, for which he wrote six plays that display intelligence but a diminution of the zest that characterized his earlier work for the stage.

Much of Holberg's production can be classified as a "comedy of character," even when situation is rather more fundamental to it than an imbalance of humours, as in Jonson and Molière. Surely the best known of his comedies is *Jeppe på bjerget* (*Jeppe of the Hill,* 1722), in which the besotted peasant hero is duped into thinking he is a baron, somewhat like Christopher Sly in the framing story of *The Taming of the Shrew,* though Holberg's source is not Shakespeare's play but a tale in Jacob Bidermann's *Utopia* (1640). Scolded, belabored, cuckolded by his wife, Nille, Jeppe awakens a measure of sympathy, but his tyrannies as baron make it necessary for the play to impose some chastisement—which may or may not shake him out of his drinking ways. The situation is similar in *Den politiske kandestøber* (*The Political Tinker,* 1722), in which the politick-would-be Herman von Bremen has his day as mayor and is driven to distraction by the multitudinous and complex chores of the office. When the joke is revealed to him, he confesses the error of his former presumption. In both plays an essentially conservative, antidemocratic view of society is transcended by acute comment on frequently encountered human foibles.

Essentially himself a schoolmaster, Holberg gives elaborate and recurrent attention to pedantry in all its forms, a pedantry that has to be exposed and disposed of to ensure social peace and harmony. The Erasmus Montanus of the play of that name (written 1723; prod. 1742) is really the pretentious student Rasmus Berg, who has Latinized his speech along with his name and made of himself a total caricature of learning, even when it happens—as it sometimes does—to be sound learning. He is conscripted by a trick, which Holberg probably learned from George Farquhar's *The Recruiting Officer,* and the experience carries with it a measure of chastisement. *Jean de France* (1722) reveals what happens to the young Dane when too much of Paris rubs off on him. A collusion between his fiancée, Elsebet, who has fallen in love with someone else, and her servants disguised as Parisians forces the affected chap out of his folly—and out of the country. The play's mixture of Danish and French—admittedly abused French—must have made it a perfect vehicle for the company of Little Green Street, which had French origins.

It is not to Holberg's discredit that he plundered Plautus so thoroughly. He usually builds on his models. *Diderich Menschenskræk (Diderich the Terrible,* 1724) may portray a fairly stereotyped braggart soldier, but *Jakob von Tyboe* (1724), with its conflict between the *miles gloriosus* of the title and Magister Stygotius for the hand of Lucilia, creates a symmetry and cross reference of vanity. The braggart soldier is also, in his florid manners and battle-infiltrated speech, a pedant. Another kind of pedantry, unless it is simply nervous habit, is talking too much. To show his appreciation of the man of few words, Holberg portrayed the opposite in *Mester Gert Westphaler (The Talkative Barber,* 1722), in which the title character loses in love because he is unable to curb the insane flow of words. Gert may be viewed as a literary forerunner of Figaro, but he is far less interesting, and the play has been only infrequently performed.

Den vægelsindede (The Weathercock, 1723) for several reasons occupies a special place in the Holberg canon: It was very likely the first of his plays; it was considerably revised between 1723 and 1731, and therefore reveals a good deal about Holberg's dramatic development; it is the only one of his plays with a woman as protagonist; and its study of fickle temperament seems to reflect something deep-seated in Holberg's own character, and perhaps for this reason the play is one of the most deeply "humoured" in its central character portrait. On the other hand the play's Lucretia has its literary models, in part the Célimène of Molière's *Misanthrope* but even more the male protagonist of Philippe Destouches's *L'Irrésolu.*

One of the most modern and durable of Holberg's plays is *Den stundesløse (The Fussy Man,* 1726), in which the protagonist, Vielgeschrey, organizes and multiplies the trivialities of his life (*à la* Parkinson)

into "much ado about nothing." The intrigue is set in motion when he attempts to marry off his daughter, against her will, to a bookkeeper who will lend a hand in Vielgeschrey's burgeoning affairs. Another dominant humour in Holberg's day, which might be literally translated as "rank sickness," is the theme of two plays, *Don Ranudo de Colibras* (written 1723; prod. 1752) and *Den honnette ambition* ("Honest Ambition," written 1724; prod. 1743). In both cases, an unsuccessful attempt is made to marry off a daughter into nobility, thus thwarting true love. Any possible tragedy in the hungry, threadbare nobility of Don Ranudo and his wife is undercut by the comic business of the play and by its very title (Ranudo read backward is "O du nar(r)"—"Oh you fool"). *Den honnette ambition* is Holberg's attempt at a *Bourgeois Gentilhomme,* but by no means so successful.

Even more of Holberg's comedy places situation over character. Indeed, the characters tend to be stereotypes moving according to the demands of the intrigue. It is often a recognizable family: the young lovers Leander and Leonora; the parents Jeronimus and Magdalone; Leonard, the friend, neighbor, or father-in-law-to-be; Henrik and Pernille, the clever servants; Arv or Troels, the dimwit; and Jesper Oldfux, the itinerant trickster. The resemblance to commedia dell'arte is striking. If there is no doctor, it was because medicine was sufficiently advanced in Denmark even then (Holberg says), so that the doctor was not a figure for mirth. The commedia factota Harlequin and Columbine even make an appearance in *De usynlige* (literally, "The Invisible Ones"; *The Masked Ladies,* written 1726; prod. 1747), perhaps under the stimulus of Holberg's encounter with Riccoboni and the Italian theater troupe on his 1725–1726 visit to Paris, about the time this play was written. Henrik and Pernille, Danish versions of the same, have a play of their own (*Henrik og Pernille,* 1724), which Holberg considered his most perfect in matters of construction. It involves a transposition of roles much like that in Marivaux's *Le Jeu de l'amour et du hazard (The Game of Love and of Chance,* 1730), six years later, but in general Marivaux is more sentimental than Holberg, more of a precursor of Romanticism. Henrik and Pernille appear also, along with most of the Holberg comic family, in *Mascarade (Masquerade,* 1724), though not quite in the same character. Furthermore, *Mascarade* has a greater amplitude. In general, when Holberg could build his action into a social ritual the play gained thereby, as the Danish composer Carl Nielsen may have realized when he made an opera of *Mascarade.*

Indeed one can speak of a group of plays based on special social occasions. In *Julestue (The Christmas Party,* 1724) yuletide mummery is cheerfully presented as a cover for cuckoldry. In *Barselstuen* ("The Confinement," 1723) the theme of dubious paternity is combined with the ritual of visiting the confined —a parade of provincial ladies. There is also in Holberg the ritual taking of the waters, with all its possibilities of intrigue, in *Kilderejsen (The Healing Spring,* 1724); and a pair of plays whose strategies of trickery are set at the time of year when notes come due and mortgages are to be paid off, namely *Den 11 juni* ("The Eleventh of June," 1723) and *Den pantsatte bondedreng (The Peasant in Pawn,* 1726).

Anyone as much involved in theater as Holberg was bound to reflect on the nature of theater itself. The plays that do so form an interesting category transcending parody. *Ulysses von Ithacia* ("Ulysses of Ithaca," 1724), as the title suggests, makes sport of a particularly bombastic and involved kind of German theater then current in Denmark. But this drastic conflation of *The Iliad, The Odyssey,* and *The Aeneid* has its originality. Holberg gives Odysseus a witty, ironic servant named Kilian (a kind of Sancho), cuckolds Odysseus sixteen times, and, as Claes Hoogland has observed (*Den satiriske Holberg,* 1963), breaks the dramatic illusion over and over in a very nearly Brechtian style. *Melampe* (1724), on the other hand, is a parody of all the neat balances and stylizations of classical French tragedy. The protagonist, a lap dog, is cleanly cleft in twain to satisfy the two possessive ladies who contest ownership. Still other plays extend Holberg's commentary on theater and authorship. *Hexeri eller blind alarm* ("Witchcraft, or False Alarm," written 1724; prod. 1742) plays ironically with the theater as a kind of black magic, viewed with suspicion by the populace; *Det lykkelige skibbrud* ("The Fortunate Shipwreck," written 1724; prod. 1754) is an evaluation of the social efficacy of satire (it is constructive, not destructive); and *Den danske comoedies ligbegængelse* ("Last Rites for Danish Comedy," 1727) not only deals with a perennial subject, the death of theater, but parades Holberg's major comic characters across the stage in honor of the dead. It was by no means Holberg's last play, but it marked the end of his prime.

Holberg was the beginning of drama, not merely for Denmark, but for all of Scandinavia. He took the plots and conventions of comedy wherever he found them, but at his best he made them very Danish and quite his own. He had an ear sensitive to idiosyncrasies of speech, an eye wary to human posturing, and a feeling for Danish character and the Danish scene. He is a Goldoni with more satiric guts and moral fiber, a playwright of infinite jest and zest.

Fifteen plays are available in English, in the following: *Comedies by Holberg* (1935), edited by Oscar James Campbell; *Four Plays by Holberg* (1946), edited by Campbell; *Seven One-Act Plays* (1950), edited by H. Alexander; and *Three Comedies* (1957), edited by R. Spink. For criticism consult Oscar James Campbell, *The Comedies of Holberg* (1914).—R. B. V.

Horace (1640). A tragedy by Pierre CORNEILLE. At the time of the war between Rome and Alba Longa, the young Horace, Rome's champion, kills all three Curiatii, the champions of Alba Longa. When his sister Camille, the fiancée of one of the Curiatii, curses Rome after his victory, the young Horace, enraged, kills her. Defended by his father, he is acquitted by the king of Rome. The action of *Horace* is based on Horace and his father's absolute and passionate patriotism, which crushes the values of the other characters one after another.

This play has been translated into English blank verse by Lacy Lockert in *Chief Plays,* 2nd ed. (1957). —Ja. G.

Horváth, Ödön [Edmund Josef] von (1901–1938). Hungarian-born German playwright, novelist, poet. In 1938, a Paris evening newspaper reported that a sudden afternoon storm had uprooted a chestnut tree on the Champs-Élysées, which fell upon a thirty-seven-year-old German writer, killing him instantaneously. This anonymous writer was Ödön von Horváth, who at that time and until recently had fallen into oblivion. At present he is being "rediscovered" in Germany, and audiences as well as critics are somewhat taken by the playwright's remarkable career and plays.

After spending most of his youth in Hungary— his father was a career diplomat—Horváth studied at the University of Munich and was asked at that time to produce a pantomime, *Buch der Tänze* ("Book of the Dances," 1922) for one of Siegfried Kallenberg's musical scores. Strangely enough, Horváth had never shown an interest in writing. After this, he never stopped writing and became one of the most successful dramatists of his day. His early works, *Revolte auf Cote 3018,* later entitled *Die Bergbahn* ("The Mountain Railway," 1927), a folk play about the revolt of construction workers, and *Sladek der schwarze Reichswehrmann* ("Sladek, the Black Imperial Soldier," 1929), a historical drama about inflation, reveal Horváth's concern with German tradition, social change, and political movements. Horváth was one of the first German writers to take an openly strong position against Hitler and the wave of fascism threatening Germany. In his two best dramas, *Italienische Nacht* ("Italian Night," 1930) and *Geschichten aus dem Wienerwald* ("Stories from the Viennese Woods," 1931), he portrays the gradual annihilation of a humane folk tradition by the new fascist forces, and he makes use of parody and irony to criticize the Nazis. *Italienische Nacht* is based on his own experience in Murnau (southern Germany), where a traditional festival turned into a brawl between Social Democrats and National Socialists. In the play, the Nazis make fools of themselves, while the Social Democrats are pathetic creatures because of the split in their ranks. In the end, order is restored to the sleepy little town, but Horvath leaves us with a question: What type of order? This same question is asked in *Geschichten aus dem Wienerwald,* which is a bourgeois tragedy with a Mary Magdalene format. Marianne, a young woman from a respectable lower-middle-class family, infuriates her father by running off with a ne'er-do-well, who in turn abandons her. She gives birth to a baby boy, deposits the child with relatives in the country, and prostitutes herself in order to make a living. After an encounter with her father, a reconciliation is effected. However, it is too late. Marianne's child dies, and with it dies an entire tradition of humanity.

Almost all of Horvath's plays have folk elements running through them. This is the case with *Kasimir und Karoline* ("Kasimir and Caroline," 1932), which portrays simple people at a loss to cope with the economic depression and disintegration of values. After writing this play and after the Nazi takeover of power, Horvath's life was constantly in danger. He finished *Glaube Liebe Hoffnung* ("Faith, Love, Hope," 1933), a satire about the injustices done to small lawbreakers, and *Die Unbekannte aus der Seine* ("The Stranger from the Seine," 1933), a comedy of errors, and then traveled from city to city in middle Europe seeking a place of refuge. While in Vienna during 1935, he overcame a creative crisis and wrote his last four outstanding plays: *Don Juan kommt aus dem Krieg* ("Don Juan Returns from War"), *Figaro lässt sich scheiden* ("Figaro Gets a Divorce"), *Der jüngste Tag* ("The Day of Judgment"), and *Pompei*. These dramas show Horvath to be a great humorist with a keen sense of man's foibles. He was a master of dialogue and structured his plays in epic fashion to expose the struggles of small people—struggles that have universal significance. His plays blend local color with political events and evoke a nostalgic picture of man lost in the chaos of his times. Horvath himself never lost his orientation, but his times were most unkind to him. —J. D. Z.

House of Bernarda Alba, The (La casa de Bernarda Alba, written 1936, first prod. Buenos Aires 1945). A folk tragedy by Federico GARCÍA LORCA, this play is part of a trilogy that includes BLOOD WEDDING and YERMA. This play, subtitled "A drama about women in the villages of Spain," was not produced in Spain until nine years after Lorca's death. It is written entirely in prose, and the realistic intention apparent in the subtitle is confirmed in a brief prefatory author's note: "These three acts are intended to be a documentary photograph." No male character appears in the play. Bernarda, a fiercely indomitable widow with five marriageable daughters, is the chief character. All her daughters are in love with Pepe el Romano, whose presence and fatal attractiveness is felt throughout the play. The action takes place indoors, where the whiteness of the walls and the arched doorways, the bland atmosphere of enclosure with the dim sound of bells tolling outside, suggest the interior of a nunnery or a hospital. Whiteness is a major motif in the play; besides the physical interior and the embroidered linen that preoccupy the daughters, there is the tragic whiteness of virginity—the note on which the play ends. Even the name Alba, meaning *dawn* or *daylight* in Spanish, also means *white,* as in Latin.

A harsh, wealthy woman, Bernarda has just buried her husband and dismissed the mourners; she vows to shut out all future visitors and to keep her daughters in mourning for eight years while sealed in the house she has inherited from her father. Amid stories of erotic adventures and the townspeople's cruel victimization of the townswomen involved, the first act delineates the muted hysteria of sexual frustration. Poncia, Bernarda's much-needed confidante and house servant, who apparently was once the mistress of Bernarda's husband, is the butt of Bernarda's contemptuous attacks on the poor. Adela, the youngest daughter, hears that Angustia, the eldest sister, having inherited all her father's money, will soon be engaged to Pepe. Adela flies into a rage, and the act closes with the wild entrance of Maria Josefa, Bernarda's eighty-year-old mother, who is kept a prisoner in her room. Maria Josefa shouts, "I don't want to watch these old maids, dying to get married, grinding their hearts to dust."

The sense of impending violence darkens the second act as the conflict among the sisters grows. Bernarda, who has chosen to ignore it, since recognition of it would offend her pride and put her honor in doubt, is forced finally to act when Pepe is reported to be seducing Adela. Although Bernarda's rifle shot misses its mark, Martirio, a jealous sister, lying, reports Pepe's death to Adela, who consequently hangs herself. Bernarda can at last take the situation in hand, exclaiming triumphantly, "My

A SCENE FROM FEDERICO GARCÍA LORCA'S *The House of Bernarda Alba* (FRENCH CULTURAL SERVICES)

daughter died a virgin. Carry her to her bed and dress her as though she were a virgin. Say nothing about this to anyone . . . . At dawn, let it be known so that the bells may be rung twice." Far from being consumed by the tragedy, Bernarda rises to consume it. A force of repression, she survives behind various masks: family pride; inverted, traditional honor; and religious piety. Bernarda perpetuates the principle of sterility notable in Lorca's late drama and thus symbolizes Spain itself, in its little jail of localism and narrow intolerance, bent on its own self-destruction.

This play has been translated by J. Graham-Lujan and R. L. O'Connell in *Three Tragedies* (1947). —E. H.

Howard, Bronson (1842–1908). American playwright. Howard, the first American to make playwriting his sole profession, was born in Detroit, Michigan. His first successful play, *Saratoga*, a farce about fashionable people in that resort, was produced in New York in 1870. Altogether Howard was the author of twenty-one plays, the success of which made a fortune for him. By his example, his founding of the American Dramatists Club in 1891, and his leadership in securing better copyright protection for the dramatist, he advanced playwriting as a profession in America.

One of Howard's most popular plays, *Shenandoah* (1888), is a sentimental drama with farcical elements in which the Civil War complicates the romances of four pairs of lovers. More characteristic of Howard's work are *The Banker's Daughter* (1878), the drama of a woman who marries a man she does not love to save her father from financial ruin; *Young Mrs. Winthrop* (1882), in which the demands of business and of social life nearly destroy a marriage; *The Henrietta* (1887), a satire on the passion for speculating in the stock market; and *Aristocracy* (1892), in which a California millionaire conquers New York society by way of London.

Howard was an excellent craftsman, keenly aware of the requirements of actors and audiences. Like the

BRONSON HOWARD (NEW YORK PUBLIC LIBRARY)

fiction of William Dean Howells and Henry James, Howard's plays widened the canvas of American social drama to include the businessman and Americans abroad.—B. H.

Howard, Sidney Coe (1891–1939). American playwright. Howard was born in Oakland, California, to John L. Howard, a successful businessman, and Helen Coe Howard, a professional organist and pianist. Both parents encouraged their children to share their own great interest in literature and music, and Howard early turned his attention to poetry. He graduated from the University of California at Berkeley in 1915 and went on to Harvard to study playwriting with George Pierce Baker. Early in World War I, he served with the American Ambulance Corps, and after the United States entered the war, he was commissioned captain in the aviation branch of the army. After the war, Howard worked as a reporter for *The New Republic* and other magazines, but he never stopped writing plays. His poetic melodrama *Swords* (1921) was unsuccessful, but in 1924 *They Knew What They Wanted* won the Pulitzer Prize and established Howard as a leading dramatist. Howard was killed in his garage when a tractor he was starting pinned him to the wall, crushing his chest.

In most of his plays, Howard deals with problems of marriage and family strife; though the plots are frequently melodramatic, the author's firm social theses add dimension to the domestic themes. In *They Knew What They Wanted* the protagonist is a middle-aged Italian immigrant winegrower who attracts a bride from San Francisco by sending her a picture of his handsome foreman; though the girl succumbs to the sexual charms of the younger man and becomes pregnant by him, she chooses to accept the security and love of her husband. The play explicitly rejects the stereotyped evaluations of the fallen woman, the cuckold, and the corrupt seducer. In *The Silver Cord* (1926) Howard dramatizes the damaging effects on her two sons of a possessive mother's love, a startling subject for its time. In *Lucky Sam McCarver* (1927), *Ned McCobb's Daughter* (1927), and a dramatization of Sinclair Lewis' *Dodsworth* (1934), family frictions and marital failures take place in a context of abrasive business dealings and destructive materialistic ethics. Two of Howard's major plays do not follow this social-domestic formula: *The Late Christopher Bean* (1932), a wry comedy about art fashions and New England toughness, and *Yellow Jack* (1934), a vivid portrayal of the conquest of yellow fever.

There is no standard edition of Howard's plays. Critical comments can be found in the major studies of modern American drama.—M. L.

Hoyt, Charles [Hale] (1860–1900). American playwright of farces and satirical comedies. Hoyt's travels throughout the United States, his legal training, and successful career in journalism enabled him to develop quickly his satirical talents as social critic and popular humorist. A column in the *Boston Post* entitled "All Sorts" contained prototypes of characters that later appeared in his plays. When at the age of twenty Hoyt became the *Post's* drama critic, he entered the theater world where, almost immediately, he won fame and fortune by boisterously but genially deriding daily life in a series of seventeen satires depicting the contemporary scene. By 1891, Hoyt was successful enough not only to produce a new play every season, as well as to keep several companies on tour, but also to operate his own theater, The Madison Square, in New York. Here Hoyt's *A Trip to Chinatown* (1891) achieved the longest run (657 performances) of any nineteenth-century American play. In 1896, Hoyt added politics to his schedule by being elected to the New Hampshire legislature. After his second wife died at an early age, as had his first, Hoyt went into a state of depression that resulted in hospitalization in an asylum just before his death.

Unlike the satirical sketches of New York's immigrant life by Edward Harrigan, Hoyt's plays encompassed various areas of the United States for their settings, thereby scrutinizing a wide range of American personalities and professions. But whether satirizing city types, rural figures, Western aboriginals, or people of his own profession, Hoyt never forgot that they were all part of the American public, which he aimed to entertain and, incidentally, to enlighten. He hoped that by laughing at their daily lives, both the exploiters and the exploited would recognize themselves and each other and, as a consequence, would better meet the challenge of a changing age. In fast-paced farces, some incorporating songs and extraneous entertainments, Hoyt satirically observed hotel management in *A Bunch of Keys* (1883), sporting crazes in *A Rag Baby* (1884), urban domestic life in *A Tin Soldier* (1885), railroads in *A Hole in the Ground* (1887), superstition in *A Brass Monkey* (1888), rural life in *A Midnight Bell* (1889), Washington politics in *A Texas Steer* (1890), temperance in *A Temperance Town* (1893), small-town militia in *A Milk White Flag* (1894), baseball in *A Runaway Colt* (1895), American manners in *A Black Sheep* (1896), woman suffrage in *A Contented Woman* (1897), café society in *A Stranger in New York* (1898), and big business in *A Dog in the Manger* (1899). Hoyt's best-known work, *A Trip to Chinatown*, containing three songs of enduring popularity—"The Bowery," "After the Ball," and "Reuben, Reuben, I've Been Thinking"—is still produced in universities and summer stock companies. Hoyt's harmless sort of satire of American life paved the way for other playwrights who brought to fruition a particular brand of satiric farce that first found favor in the sketches of Edward Harrigan and Tony Hart and that seems to have come to an end with George S. Kaufman and Moss Hart.

Five Plays (1941) by Charles Hoyt, edited by Douglass L. Hunt, contains *A Bunch of Keys, A Midnight Bell, A Temperance Town, A Milk White Flag,* and *A Trip to Chinatown.* "The Satire of Charles Hoyt: A Critical Study" (1964), Nancy Foell Swortzell's doctoral dissertation for Yale University, is an evaluation of Hoyt's contribution to satiric comedy in American drama.—N. F. S.

Hrotsvitha. Also **Hrosvitha** or **Roswitha** (c. 935– c. 1001). German poet, dramatist, and historian. Hrotsvitha was a nun at Gandersheim, a Benedictine canoness monastery under the patronage of the court and an important cultural center administered by abbesses of noble rank. Documentary evidence about her life being scant, she is known mainly through her works, which consist of six short plays (*Paphnutius,*

Sapientia, Gallicanus, Dulcitius, Calimachus, and *Abraham*), eight religious poems, an historical account of the deeds of Otto I, and a history of the foundation of the Gandersheim monastery. Evidence strongly suggests that all of these were written between 955 and the close of the century.

As a teacher Hrotsvitha had access to the plays of Terence, which were popular reading in the monasteries of her day. In the prefaces to her plays she says:

> There are many, and we cannot entirely acquit ourselves of the charge, who, attracted by the polished elegance of the pagan writers prefer their works to the holy scriptures. There are others . . . who make an exception in favor of the works of Terence, and, fascinated by the charm and the manner, risk being corrupted by the wickedness of the matter.

So in writing her plays she says, "I have not hesitated to imitate in my writings a poet whose works are so widely read, my object is to glorify . . . Christian virgins in the self-same form of composition." Thus she writes in the manner but not the matter of Terence.

The keynote of her dramas is to insist on adherence to chastity as opposed to passion. In so doing she is giving expression to the ideas of contemporary Christian teaching, which saw in passion, not the inborn force that can be applied to good or evil purpose, but simply a tendency in human nature that manifests a lack of self-restraint. The nun does not disparage marriage, nor does she inculcate a doctrine of celibacy. She simply espouses self-control. This is the prevailing motif of the plays. She is not hampered by narrowness of thought nor pettiness of spirit. In the dramas we find a variety of surroundings and come in contact with a wide range of personalities. The transition from heathendom to Christianity supplies mental and moral conflicts.

Hrotsvitha, like all early playwrights, used available sources for her plots, namely, *Acta Sanctorum,* the *Aprocryphal Gospels,* and the Christian legends of Greece. Since the plays are founded on well-known legends, the facts are followed very closely. But as Christopher St. John indicates, Hrotsvitha develops dramatic characters who are often merely indicated in the legends. Three of the plays, *Gallicanus, Dulcitius,* and *Sapientia,* deal with the conflict between infant Christianity and paganism, with martyrdoms under the emperors Hadrian, Diocletian, and Julian the Apostate.

In *Calimachus, Abraham,* and *Paphnutius,* Hrotsvitha deals with the conflict between the flesh and the spirit and the long penance that must follow for those who have been converted and wish to atone for their crime against God's laws.

The material in all six plays is presented in a variety of moods—tragic, comic, heroic, romantic, and didactic. In *Gallicanus, Part I,* a woman's strategy results in the winning of a battle, the conversion of the would-be suitor, and his subsequent vow of celibacy. *Part II* recounts his exile and martyrdom under Julian the Apostate. John and Paul, who befriend him, also suffer death under the same tyrant and are thereby instrumental in converting their executioners.

In *Dulcitius,* the supernatural elements confound

Dulcitius to his ridicule, and Sisinnius to his terror, when the virginity of the three maidens, Agape, Chionia, and Irena, is preserved contrary to the merciless orders of Diocletian.

In *Calimachus* the illicit and unwelcome love for Drusiana leads Calimachus to the brink of hell, when the intervention of John the Apostle restores him to life and grace.

In *Abraham* the prayerful monk Abraham turns his niece Mary from a life of sin to one of penance and solitude.

The Thais legend lives again in *Paphnutius*. At the exhortation of this saintly hermit, the courtesan Thais renounces unlawful worldly pleasures for eternal joys.

In *Sapientia* the three Greek virgins Faith, Hope, and Charity, through the sustaining strength and wisdom of their mother, Sapientia, endure a cruel and prolonged martyrdom at the hands of the emperor Hadrian.

In a historical survey, it is recognized that Hrotsvitha is especially important as the main link between classical and medieval drama. Her Christian themes and sentiments are enlivened by wit, humor, and theatricality.

An excellent introduction to the playwright and her contribution to the history and development of the theater is *The Plays of Roswitha*, translated by Christopher St. John with an Introduction by Cardinal Gasquet and a Critical Preface by the translator. Further information about Hrotsvitha, her life, her times, and her place in literary history is documented by Konrad Algermissen in a series of articles in the German publication *Unsere Diözese,* and later included in a history of the Diocese of Hildesheim. —M. M. B.

Hughes, Thomas. See THE MISFORTUNES OF ARTHUR.

Hugo, Victor [Marie] (1802–1885). French poet, playwright, novelist, and politician. The acknowledged leader of French Romanticism, Victor Hugo is a titanic figure in the literary and political life of nineteenth-century France. His life may be divided roughly into five periods. The first (1819–1827) marked his development as poet and novelist. Early academic experiments in classical verse gradually gave way to a warmer, more personal, and exotic tone; his Catholic and royalist ideals were slowly eclipsed by those of collective humanitarianism. He published *Odes et poésies diverses* in 1822 and two novels of romantic fantasy, *Han d'Islande* in 1823 and *Bug-Jargal* in 1826.

His second period, that of his greatest contribution to the drama, was launched in 1827 with the publication of the elaborate and controversial Preface to the unstageable verse drama *Cromwell*. As the credo of French Romanticism, however, the Preface championed a free and outspoken style of dramatic poetry that would embrace both tragedy and comedy (the sublime and the grotesque), after the manner of Shakespeare, and would eliminate the traditional device of the caesura and encourage the smoother, more supple rhythms resulting from the use of enjambment. When his second verse drama, *Marion de Lorme* (written 1829), was refused performance until 1831 because of Charles X's restrictions on the freedom of speech (one of the characters in the play was

VICTOR HUGO (WALTER HAMPDEN MEMORIAL LIBRARY AT THE PLAYERS, NEW YORK)

Louis XIII), Hugo retorted with his most famous play, *Hernani* (1830), the première of which caused a riot, putting the embattled principles of the *Cromwell* Preface into practice (albeit artificially) for the first time.

Indeed, February 25, 1830, is the most important date in the history of the nineteenth-century European theater. Ready to condemn the new play were the defenders of literary decorum and, to praise it, the champions of the new freedom. For *Hernani* was, in the words of John Gassner, not only a play, but a cause. And Hugo won it on that memorable night when his romantic outlaw hero rebelled in eloquent poetry against society.

Betrothed to her uncle, a duke, Doña Sol loves and is loved by the wellborn outlaw Hernani, but also by the king of Spain. Hernani's father has been killed in a feud with the royal family, and Hernani seeks revenge. In a series of melodramatic scenes, each of these men assists or saves one of his rivals in a demonstration of supreme honor. When the king becomes emperor of Europe, he rights the injustice done Hernani's family by giving him Doña Sol in marriage. But after the wedding, the jealous duke, who had refused earlier to betray Hernani, a guest in his castle, exacts vengeance. Hernani had pledged his life to the duke in gratitude for his generosity and had given the duke his horn, requesting that he blow it when he needed Hernani. The duke now sounds the horn and demands Hernani's life. Pleading futilely for more time, the lovers drink poison and die. The duke stabs himself.

Le Roi s' amuse (*The King Amuses Himself*), from which Giuseppe Verdi adapted his opera *Rigoletto,* followed in 1832. (Publication the year before of his novel *The Hunchback of Notre Dame* helped to seat Hugo in the Académie Française in 1841.) Beginning a lifelong intimacy with the beautiful but untalented actress Juliette Drouet, Hugo was inspired to write roles for her. Three mediocre plays in prose, *Lucrèce Borgia* (1833), *Marie Tudor* (1835), and *Angelo Tyran de Padoue* (1835), were followed in 1838 by the poetic drama RUY BLAS. This second period of Hugo's life ended somewhat ignominiously with the failure of the theatrical extravaganza *Les Burgraves* ("The Governors") in 1843.

The years 1843 to 1851 encompass his third—the political—period, one of increasing disillusionment with the right-wing Louis Napoleon. Forced into exile by the *coup d'état* of December 1851, Hugo lived the fourth period of his life on the Channel Islands, returning to Paris in 1870 after the fall of the Second Empire. During this period he wrote his most famous work, the novel *Les Misérables* (1862).

Seeing himself increasingly as a sage endowed with the genius to inspire mankind to liberate itself from the tyranny of society, Hugo wrote, during his last period (1870–1885), many volumes of prose and verse, including the drama *Torquemada* (1882) and a collection of short plays, *Le Théâtre en liberté*, posthumously published in 1886.

Hugo's historical dramas have been called irregular, pseudoclassical tragedies in lyric couplets. Despite his fondness for the banal trappings of *mélodrame*—outlaw heroes, wistful heroines, traitors and assassins, poisons and secret passageways—he could exalt in passionate verse his lyrical themes of the suffering and joy of love, honor, and patriotic pride. Perhaps his most distinguishing trait as a playwright is his conception of life as a series of paradoxes and antitheses of moral character. He employs disguises to heighten the contrast between reality and appearance and arranges characters in startling contrasts. Sometimes he is attracted by ambivalent forces within a single character. Yet his characters are always unreal. He sees their propensities for good or evil, their embodiment of the tragic or the comic, the sublime or the grotesque, the ideal or the real, in theatrical and lyrical—rather than truly dramatic—terms. The plays remain, in the last analysis, little more than acted poems.

The most recent English version of *Hernani* is Linda Asher's in *The Romantic Influence* (1963), Vol. II of *Laurel Masterpieces of Continental Drama*, edited by Norris Houghton. *The King Amuses Himself* and *Ruy Blas*, in translations by F. L. Slous and Camilla Crosland, respectively, are reprinted in *Three Plays by Victor Hugo* (1964), edited by H. A. Gaubert. The authoritative biography is André Maurois's *Olympio: The Life of Victor Hugo* (1956), translated by Gerard Hopkins. Elliott M. Grant's *The Career of Victor Hugo* (1945) is a reliable and readable critical study.—S. S. S.

Hungary. Hungarian drama began, as did Hungarian literature, with the oral tradition of the Magyar people prior to their entrance into the Carpathian basin in A.D. 896. Drama became a major force only with Romanticism; yet Hungarian theatrical traditions are rooted in the nomadic, pagan heritage. Myths of national origin have preserved such dramatic vestiges as sequences of first-person narratives by several personages. Early recorded literature is predominantly in Latin. The second surviving vernacular piece, a lament of Mary from about 1300, indicates dramatic conception. Similarly, theatrical imagination manifests itself in illustrations of Márk Kálti's so-called *Képes Krónika* ("Pictorial Chronicle," middle of the fourteenth century). Latin remained important: as the language of parliamentary debate, it was not replaced by Hungarian until 1844, and the political status of the national tongue is due, in part, to pioneers of Hungarian theater during the 1790's, in whose wake Hungarian drama came of age.

The seven warlike tribes that united under Magyar rule did not easily mold into a settled, European, Christian nation; that process lasted well into the thirteenth century. Nor were prophetic and magic rites of the *táltos* ("shaman") on the one hand and mimetic verse chronicles of the wandering *regös* ("jongleur") on the other entirely suppressed even then. Pre-Christian incantations and oral traditions are incorporated in the *Chronica* of Sebestyén Tinódi Lantos (d. 1556) and are still recognizable in folk songs and ballads recorded in the eighteenth through the twentieth century; they also appear in the first Hungarian dramatic efforts.

Liturgical drama does not directly bring a truly national bloom of drama, but in some countries it becomes the root of vernacular religious drama with a national character. This was not so in Hungary, although there is evidence of considerable religious theatrical activity. In the wake of familiar liturgical dramas (for example, *Tractus stellae*, c. 1090) followed a performance of the Passion by students at Bártfa in the middle of the fifteenth century; the latter is attested to by a surviving cast list. An adaptation of *Dulcitius*, entitled *Három körösztyén leán* ("Three Christian Maidens," pub. 1518), came close on the heels of the first printing in 1501 of the plays of the German nun Hrotsvitha. The adaptation set a precedent followed by Hungarian translators of plays ever since: the plot is set in a local, rather than a Roman, milieu and populated by native characters. The introductory didascalia suggest an appeal beyond the cloister's walls, possibly a performance for the villagers.

The first flowering of Hungarian drama, however, derived its impetus from the Reformation. This is natural, for since the defeat at the hand of the Turkish forces in the 1526 battle of Mohács, the central part of the country was under the Ottoman Empire, its northwestern third under Hapsburg rule, and its most thriving portion Protestant-dominated Transylvania. Mihály Sztáray's (d. 1575) disputation play *Az igaz papság tiköre* ("Mirror of True Priesthood," pub. 1559) has forceful dialogue and action, along with folksy, earthy imagery, rendering it eloquent and stageworthy. The play's irreverent, satirical attack on the clerical hierarchy and trappings of the Church certainly appealed to the simple people. In contrast, György Válaszuti's *Debreceni Disputa* ("Dispute at Debrecen," pub. 1570) concerns the more remote theological issues between Calvinists and Unitarians—although an attempt is made to portray the protagonists in their home, in order to dramatically enrich the ridicule of theory through parallel character development.

Of the same vintage is the anonymous and secular

Balassi Menyhárt árultatásáról való komédia ("Comedy of Melchior Balassi's Treachery," pub. 1569), a political piece, the theatrical effectiveness of which has been proved by modern production. The ruthless oligarch Balassi is cleverly and violently lampooned by means, among others, of an elaborate confession scene. *Magyar Elektra* ("Hungarian Electra," pub. 1558), an adaptation of Sophocles' *Electra,* by Péter Bornemissza (1535–1584) is as worthy a product of the Humanistic endeavor to produce tragedy as is *Balassi* in the comic vein. Another early adaptation followed the pastoral pattern; it is the only surviving play of the eminent lyric poet Bálint Balassi (1554–1594). Its printed version, known as *Szép magyar comoedia* ("Beautiful Hungarian Comedy," pub. 1589), is incomplete; an entire draft was recently discovered under the title *Credulus és Julia* ("Credulus and Julia").

There is no evidence that these early plays were produced, although introductory remarks and stage directions attest to such intentions. Proof of theatrical entertainment of a more varied nature exists, however, in royal records and in court diaries. We know of appearances of Italian and other foreign actors beginning with the reign of King Matthias Corvinus (1458–1490). *Ioculatores* ("jongleurs") frequently performed at both popular and court festivities, and though they were regularly rewarded, at times even with land grants, contemptuous references often link them with the pagan *regösök.* Gradually, their place was taken by students, who added the formal tradition of school drama to the festivities. This genre flourished in the generally invigorating Counter Reformation but rose to no great heights. An early example, known to have been performed, is Lőrinc Szegedi's *Theophania* (pub. 1575), a four-act treatment of the childhood of Cain and Abel, in which a prefiguration of doom occurs: Cain hides when God appears and calls him.

Under the tripartite political condition, which lasted for about a century and a half, it was only natural that the first initiator of Hungarian professional theater be a Transylvanian Protestant. In 1696 Unitarian György Felvinczi (d. 1716) abandoned his family and went to Vienna for the emperor's permission to form, and tour with, a company of actors. The permit, and with it freedom from taxation, was granted. Regrettably, no record of the troupe remains, although tradition points to a house in Kolozsvár (now: Cluj, Rumania), where they allegedly performed. Felvinczi also authored *Comico-Tragoedia* (2nd ed. 1693), the most significant vernacular school drama of the century, and a Protestant one. It concerns Pluto's complaint against Jupiter's imposition of too narrow territorial limits for hell and the former's attempt to keep men out of heaven and steer them into hell. The play and its likely performance was probably influenced by the famous Baroque opera *Il pomo d'oro* (text by Sbarra, music by Cesti), for Felvinczi was apparently connected with its Viennese production.

Hungarian Baroque drama, then, was primarily school drama, and its major contribution was a strengthening of national consciousness through cultivation of the language, utilization of Hungarian forefathers as heroes, and historical plots with covert reference to current politics. There were, of course,

other forces at work: Writers of the Enlightenment and of the vogue of sensibility aided the transition to Romanticism, bringing about the birth of a professional national theater.

The struggle for national existence through national institutions resulted in direct confrontations with Austrian efforts at domination during the 1790's. The nation rejected the reforms of Joseph II and strove for a Hungarian ruler who would restore the national constitution. Attempts to create Hungarian cultural institutions took on political meaning. The Martinovics conspiracy, brutally crushed in 1795, involved and affected the vanguard of the Hungarian Enlightenment, who were concerned that the nation keep in step with European trends, that it shape its historical fate, that it refine and cultivate its national language.

The issue of the national language was a particularly burning one. From the dawn of nationhood Hungarian had been the people's tongue, and after the fifteenth century it became the language of literature as well. But the language of government had been Latin, and Hapsburg domination after 1700 led to the increased use of German. Rather than accept the oppressor's tongue, the Hungarian nobility was determined to retain Latin as the language of parliament. Recognizing the importance and the cohesive power of a national tongue, champions of the Enlightenment renewed their efforts to raise the standards of spoken and written Hungarian and to win pulpits and tribunals for is practice. They launched the Language Renewal, aimed at enrichment of the vocabulary and the development of a systematic grammar. Efforts to initiate journals, create a national academy, and form a national acting company were simultaneous. The latter received additional impetus with the establishment of a German theater in Pest, in 1784. Thus the cause of drama and theater became a patriotic one, part of the Language Renewal and of the national reassertion of independence.

In the feverish effort to increase literary output and to supply drama for a national acting company, translations of foreign masters carried no less weight than new plays. The former would open windows to the West, while the latter focused on the Hungarian past. A Molière translation is on record as of 1769; Ádám Teleki put Corneille's *Le Cid* into Hungarian in 1773; Antal Zechenter turned to Racine and Voltaire; János Endrödy edited a four-volume drama collection (pub. 1792–1793) containing adaptations from the French, the German, and the Italian, along with one original play; and Ferenc Kazinczy (1759–1831), the guiding light of the Enlightenment by virtue of his correspondence with all Hungarian men of letters, became the first adapter of Shakespeare.

Hungarian plays in the French manner are found among the school dramas of Jesuits, Franciscans, Paulines, and Piarists. Productions followed European Baroque theater traditions: witness several eighteenth-century programs indicating frequent changes of scenery and employment of elaborate machinery as well as participation by nobles, burghers, and the military. Protestant school plays pointed more in the direction of popular comedy, with techniques reminiscent of the *commedia dell'arte.* Thus, the Lutheran *Cyrus* (pub. 1698) treats a troupe of itinerant gypsy musicians. A century later the comic spirit had caught on, and the Pauline interlude *Kocsonya Mihály házassága* ("The Marriage of Michael Jelly," pub. 1765) is an excellent exemplar of the unbridled secular comedies of plebeian spirit that emerged from the school drama; it exposes the backward Hungarian gentry to ridicule.

The best school dramatists joined with the Enlightenment to create the National Acting Company. Amateur attempts culminated in a performance of Voltaire's *Mahomet* at Pest in 1784, when Austrian authorities helped establish a German theater in the capital. Kazinczy insisted that the time was ripe for Hungarian theatrical productions to coincide with the next session of the National Assembly to be held in Pest-Buda, as the capital was then called. To that end he translated *Hamlet*, secured financial backing, and had a cast recruited among university students and other young citizens.

László Kelemen (1762–1814), who had gone to a Piarist school and had some legal training, emerged as a leader of the National Acting Company. Officially formed on September 21, 1790, this spirited troupe was beset with many complex problems. Its members aspired to be actors, although none had been trained; furthermore, to be labeled "actress" amounted to public dishonor. They had no theater and no funds for rent or salaries. They had to show local authorities cause why they should be permitted to use city-owned buildings for public performance. Finally, they had to compete for an audience with the established and well-financed German theater. Nevertheless, their dream became reality. Since time was short, the small and inexperienced group's plans to open with Kazinczy's *Hamlet* adaptation were abandoned. Instead, a less demanding, but politically more expedient piece, Kristóf Simai's *Igazházi, egy kegyes jó atya* ("Truehouse, A Pious Good Father"), was readied for production. It was given on October 25, 1790, in Buda (the Danube's western bank) and two days later in Pest (the east bank). The authorities' denial of access to any building usable as a theater halted the activity of the Kelemen troupe for about a year and a half. But no regulation could halt the work of playwrights.

The first major figure of the Hungarian Enlightenment, György Bessenyei (1747–1811), was a member of the Imperial Guard in Vienna, where his political, cultural, and dramatic efforts germinated under French influence. He embraced Jacobin ideals, proposed the establishment of the Hungarian Learned Society, and wrote a series of historical dramas (*Hunyadi László tragédiája, Ágis tragédiája,* and *Buda tragédiája,* pub. 1772–1773). Later he turned to comedy and was most successful with his last, satirical effort, *A filozófus* ("The Philosopher," pub. 1777), in which progressive ideas are supported by effective plotting and remarkable characterization. Parmenio, the young philosopher, is sharply contrasted with gallant society and wins a mate worthy of his sentimental values. The play's most memorable figure is Pontyi, the petty nobleman who is satirized with some nostalgia and emerges as a complex, and at times likable, character.

András Dugonics (1740–1818), a Piarist monk, turned playwright when his sentimental novel *Etelka*

was dramatized by another author and successfully staged in 1792. Dugonics first wrote a sequel to that play, then turned to historical drama. His four plays were published in 1794, after having been performed by the Kelemen company. His best play, *Bátori Mária* ("Mary Bátori," 1793), abounds in sentiment but leaves potentially effective aspects of the story unexploited. Paternal opposition to love and marriage, ensuing court intrigues, and a confrontation between the heroine and the groom's father are among the wasted theatrical opportunities.

Many other writers supported the company with their pen, including József Kármán, author of the best Hungarian sentimental novel, who wrote its by-laws. Among important adaptations, those of Shakespeare came to prominence: *King Lear* was transferred into pre-Christian Magyar history as *Szabolcs vezér,* and *Richard III* became *Tongor, vagy Komárom állapottya a 8-ik században* ("The State of Komárom in the Eighth Century"). In addition to Simai, who wrote and adapted several plays, János Illei excelled among school dramatists with a full-blooded version of Molière's *Le bourgeois gentilhomme* as *Tornyos Péter.*

After May 1792 the Kelemen troupe resumed production on a regular basis. For about four years they played twice a week, alternately performing in a number of small theaters. In addition to Hungarian plays, some by Bessenyei and Dugonics, their repertory included Goethe, Voltaire, Lessing, and Shakespeare.

Thus, foundations of a national drama and national theater were laid, although playwrights were handicapped by inexperience and by expected adherence to foreign "regular" or neoclassic examples of the Gottsched variety. The great rococo lyric poet Mihály Csokonai Vitéz (1773–1805) attempted rebellion within that very framework. But *A Méla Tempefői* ("The Melancholy Tempefői," subtitled "Crazy Is He Who Turns Poet in Hungary," pub. 1795), in which he dramatized the dilemma of the poet who strives for refinement and beauty amidst the enmity and scorn of barbarian nobles, is unfinished and overburdened with soliloquies. Three other plays, presumably written for student performances and not for literary acclaim, bear marks of the improvisational tradition of the commedia dell'arte. *Az özvegy Karnyóné s az két szeleburdiak* ("The Widow Karnyó and the Two Coxcombs," 1799) especially shows Csokonai clever in plotting and at ease in constructing robust comic dialogue.

Károly Kisfaludy (1788–1830) won both popular and critical acclaim by combining patriotic sentiment with effective dramaturgy (modeled on Kotzebue) and memorable characters in *A kérök* ("The Suitors," 1817) and *Stibor vajda* ("Voivoda Stibor," 1818). He reached greatest refinement of both plot construction and versification with *Iréne* (1821), in which the sacrificial marriage of a Byzantine maiden to the sultan turns out to have been in vain.

To this day, *Bánk bán* ("Governor Bánk") by József Katona (1791–1830) is thought to be Hungary's most significant national tragedy. While a law student, Katona tried acting, adapted a dozen German plays and novels, and wrote three original history plays before he entered *Bánk* in a competition in 1814. It did not attract the jury's notice, but after thorough re-writing the play was accepted for production by a traveling group in 1819, only to have the performance canceled by the censor. *Bánk bán* was published the next year, but the author gave up all hope of performance, returned to law practice, and never wrote another play.

The plot of *Bánk bán*—based on thirteenth-century history previously dramatized by Philip Massinger, Hans Sachs, and Franz Grillparzer—focuses on a confrontation between Hungarian nobles allied with the people, and German oppressors. It was ideally suited to the national issues of the day: the hated yoke of foreign domination and the destitution of serfs. In the absence of King Endre II, who is ruled by his German queen, Gertrudis, Bánk acts as governor, invested with all royal power. In that capacity he is caught between his sympathy for the nobles' protests against German intrigues and the discovery that the complaining nobles are plotting to murder the queen. While seeking a peaceful end to strife, Bánk learns of an attempt at seducing his wife, Melinda, encouraged by Queen Gertrudis. Further moved by the sorry lot of the serfs as reported by old Tiborc, Bánk confronts Gertrudis, who makes an attempt on his life. He disarms and kills her, thus becoming in effect the arm of the conspiracy he tried to quell. Uncertain whether his motives were primarily patriotic or just selfish and whether his act was justified, Bánk is dishonored and reduced to despair upon the news of Melinda's brutal murder and the king's return. Although the hero's spiritual downfall is not the result of an unbroken chain of necessary acts, the play succeeds through its intense emotions, carried by elevated diction.

The next important dramatist was the leading Romantic poet Mihály Vörösmarty (1800–1855). He was one of three poets who undertook the Hungarian rendition of the Shakespeare canon—though never completed, the project enriched the repertory with excellent translations—and was active in the struggle for the National Theater, which opened in 1837 with his one-act *Árpád ébredése* ("Árpád's Awakening"). The mood of his best play, *Csongor és Tünde* ("Csongor and Tünde," 1831), is one of disillusioned romanticism. This fairy-tale drama of philosophical profundity is based on a sixteenth-century romance and concerns two pairs of lovers in pursuit of heavenly and earthly love, respectively. Its moral wisdom is presented by means of three travelers, the Merchant, Prince, and Scholar, whom Csongor (the chief hero and advocate of heavenly love) twice encounters at the crossroads. At first, all three feel certain of being on the path to fulfillment. But by the second meeting the Merchant's ships have perished, the Prince's armies beaten, and the Scholar driven mad by doubt. The noble aims of human struggle have come to naught, yet the lovers have learned the necessity of compromise between dreams and reality. *Vérnász* ("Blood Wedding," 1831) was one of Vörösmarty's most popular plays. Although the play's total effect is melodramatic, the conflict is broadly structured, the psychological motivations are convincing, and social problems are stated unobtrusively yet effectively. His recently revived *Czillei és a Hunyadiak* ("Czillei and the Hunyadis," 1844) was intended as the first part of a historical trilogy.

The excellent overall mood notwithstanding, the plot is carried by history rather than by the dramatis personae.

The rise of realistic drama was slow, its initiators neither numerous, prolific, nor of major impact. Pioneers before the ill-fated 1848 War of Independence included Baron József Eötvös (1813–1871), the novelist and statesman, with a political comedy, *Éljen az egyenlöség!* ("Long Live Equality!" 1844); László Teleki (1811–1861) with *A kegyenc* ("The Favorite," 1841), a portrayal of moral decay in public life; Ignác Nagy (1810–1854), with a series of social comedies, especially *Tisztujitás* ("County Elections," 1843); Zsigmond Czakó (1820–1847); and Károly Hugó (1804–1871) with social and historical tragedies of middle-class orientation. After the defeat, the nation was under tyrannical oppression and in a state of shock that was reflected in the drama. Two men formed the transition: Károly Obernyik (1815–1855), who switched from social plays with pointed messages to family dramas of moral and psychological conflict (although the theme of his *Brankovics György* ["George Brankovich," 1855] is clearly political), and Ede Szigligeti (1814–1878). The latter began with mediocre history plays, but in 1848 wrote the rather remarkable *II Rákóczi Ferenc fogsága* ("The Captivity of Ferenc Rákóczi II") and his best comedy, *Liliomfi* (the leader of a troupe of strolling players). Posterity remembers him primarily as an able manager of the National Theater and initiator of the genre *népszinmü* ("folk drama"). Originally a play on a folk hero, utilizing Hungarian dance, music, and folklore—as exemplified by Szigligeti's first effort of the kind, *A szökött katona* ("The Deserter," 1843)—*népszinmü* became toward the end of the century a fashionable cult about a romanticized, unreal people, garnished with slick music. For this degeneration Szigligeti's imitators were primarily to blame.

The next great figure in the history of Hungarian drama is renowned for a single work, *Az ember tragédiája* (*The Tragedy of Man,* written 1861), although in addition to this work and philosophical poems Imre Madách (1823–1864) wrote numerous other plays: *Commodus* (written 1839), *Mária királynö* ("Queen Mary," written 1855), *Mózes* ("Moses," written 1861), *A civilizátor* ("The Civilizer," written 1859), and *Férfi és nö* ("Man and Woman," written 1840–1845). They deal primarily with the conflict of the individual and community and with the struggle between man and woman. The theatrical feasibility of Madách's masterpiece, *Az ember tragédiája*, was not acknowledged until Ede Paulay, then manager of the National Theater, premièred it in 1883.

This most significant and most debated Hungarian drama probes the relation of existence to essence, the worth of human endeavor and of life in view of the gap between what exists and what ought to exist. Since the play's hero is the first man created, responses to questions raised in the play decide the fate of mankind literally rather than allegorically. The opening scenes (creation and the fall of Lucifer, the fall and expulsion from Eden, and outside Eden)—which, along with the final one (Adam confronts the Lord), form a framework—establish the three central characters, Adam, Eve, and Lucifer. The next eleven scenes form a dream sequence, a historical progression in which Adam, accompanied by Eve and guided by Lucifer, searches for the answer to a question uttered only in retrospect: "And shall those who come after me progress . . . ?"

Adam dreams history. Egypt, Greece, Rome, Byzantium, Kepler's Prague, Paris 1789, and nineteenth-century London are his stations in the past. Then he ventures into the future: a utopian phalanstery of Orwellian tone, outer space, and a new ice age—a dream more real than its frame, which is myth. He is an active participant in each scene, be it a historical person in the past or a visitor in the future; he is never a passive onlooker. Adam comes to history from the outside, while Eve is a child of each age. Yet both remain recognizable to each other and to the spectator; character traits displayed before the dream reappear and develop.

Madách's preoccupation with Hegelian dialectics is manifest in theme and structure. The battle and union of good and evil is a central issue, and successive scenes, as well as ideas, form dialectic triads. Lucifer, the spirit of negation, intensifies affirmation and provokes creation. He inspires the doubts that drive Adam on despite repeated failure. Because the negative side of each historic epoch is very vivid, a majority of critics concluded that Madách had written a pessimistic work, and he has been condemned on religious and on political grounds. Yet *Az ember tragédiája*'s conclusion is positive. In outer space Adam discovers that "the struggle of itself is Man's real aim"; and in the closing scene he receives the Lord's confirmation: "Strive on, strive on, and trust."

Madách was only an island in the torrent of cheap folk dramas and operettas of *fin de siècle* Hungary. But there was another trend, one that was to grow into the mainstream. Two playwrights, who appealed on a more sober level to the belatedly rising middle class, stood out. Mór Jókai (1825–1904), the prolific novelist, turned a handsome profit writing "well-made plays" with historic themes and patriotic sentiment. More importantly, the excellent craftsman Gergely Csiky (1842–1891) followed French examples: First he wrote neoromantic drama and, later, "thesis plays." His *pièces à thèse* paved the way for a flowering of Hungarian bourgeois drama, which reached its peak after World War I. Among more than twenty plays, Csiky's *Proletárok* ("Parasites," 1880), a critical treatment of the false patriotism of the gentry, and *Cifra nyomorúság* ("Fancy Misery," 1881), an often-imitated, excellent rendering of lower-middle-class milieu, may be pointed out as the best.

Csiky's activity was followed by a period of vacuum during which the first privately owned Hungarian theater, the Vigszinház (Gay Theater), was established in 1896. In due course, many other private theatrical enterprises came into existence, but the Vigszinház remained the only surviving institution and continued to challenge the National Theater, to rival it in nurturing playwrights and actors, as well as in the quality of its productions. In its early days, however, it did little to break the monotonous fare of contemporary English comedies, French dramas, jaded operettas, and dated history plays.

The vacuum ended when the popular novelist and short-story writer Sándor Bródy (1863–1924)

turned his talent to playwriting. He made his debut with a dramatization of his novel *Hófehérke* ("Snow White," 1901), a showpiece of beautiful theatrical prose. In successive plays Bródy treated character conflicts in a social context with great force and made theatrical use of the Budapest idiom. He steered the native drama toward European naturalism. *A dada* ("The Nurse," 1902) and *A tanitónö* ("The Schoolmistress," 1908) show his mature handling of theme and technique especially well. The heroine of the former is a peasant girl who will not accept dishonor but maintains her dignity in death. Although influenced by, and aimed at, success, *A tanitónö* still bespeaks Bródy's compassion and fine craftsmanship. It treats love as it crosses class boundaries and interferes with a strong vocational commitment. Aware that such a conflict was not palatable to the public, the dramatist provided two endings—one with a compromise and the other without. Despite increasing attention to the box office, Bródy's realism, character portrayal, and excellent stage diction made his plays a lasting influence.

In 1904 Sándor Hevesi formed the Thália Society to revitalize Hungarian drama in the manner of little theaters across Europe; the society's only discovery, Menyhért Lengyel (1880–   ), dramatized social issues and ardent passions. One of his plays, *Tájfun* (*Typhoon,* 1909), which deals with the moral weakness of a Japanese scientist, achieved international fame; another play became the basis of Béla Bartók's *Miraculous Mandarin.*

Representative of the metropolitan spirit of Budapest, Jenö Heltai (1871–1957) progressed from cabaret skits to neoromantic dramas, the best of which, *A néma levente* (*The Silent Knight,* 1936), has been a success abroad and at home. Dezsö Szomory (1869–1944) cultivated the Budapest dialect in a highly stylized way in history plays remembered for their broad scope and for a unique tonal quality of their diction.

Two very different playwrights dominated the domestic stage and enjoyed international reputation well into the 1930's. Ferenc Herczeg (1863–1954), a gentleman writer of the middle class, glorified the fallen gentry and gilded the feudal past in elegant, clever plays, but his characterization was superficial, and he avoided pressing human problems by turning to distant, unreal historical conflicts of Orient and Occident, as in *Bizánc* ("Byzantium," 1904), his best play.

Ferenc Molnár (1878–1952), on the other hand, is indubitably the most internationally known and most controversial figure of twentieth-century Hungarian drama. Although his well-drawn characters are of an unmistakable "pesti" ("Budapester") mold, his work, more successful abroad than at home, has been pejoratively labeled "export drama." Only recently has Molnár been rediscovered in Hungary, but his true achievement has yet to be internationally acknowledged. His urbanity and exquisite craftsmanship have been used to prove his so-called shallowness. Few have observed that Molnár's vast knowledge of the surface enabled him to expose the undercurrent without directly dealing with it. No matter how naïve and fairy-tale-like his famous *Liliom* (1909) appears, it offers a penetrating vision of violence and love in the human soul and of the

FERENC MOLNÁR (NEW YORK PUBLIC LIBRARY)

social milieu's impact upon the soul. Nor is Molnár's frequent use of theater people and theatrical situations accidental; it affords opportunities to comment as profoundly on the fragile distinction between reality and illusion as does Pirandello in his works of a graver disposition.

Each of the three playlets that make up Molnár's *Szinház* (*Theater*, 1921) is a *coup de théâtre* in itself, *Prelude to King Lear* being the most effective because it deals with the effect of the role of Lear upon the actor and his pursuer. But *A testör* (*The Guardsman*, 1910) probably best demonstrates the connection between surface and essence in Molnár's work. It concerns an actor who, in order to test his wife's fidelity, attempts to seduce her in the disguise of a Russian officer of the guard. A frivolous anecdote, the play nevertheless touches on the dilemma of a man who, not loved for what he thinks he is, needs to masquerade as what he believes his wife wants. Since the disguise is his test not only as a man but as an actor as well, it calls into question his worth on those two counts as well as the motives in choosing acting as a career. Further tension is created when the wife's expected betrayal of her husband with his masquerading self is replaced by the Actor's self-revelation, voided of meaning by the wife's pretense of pretense.

Zsigmond Móricz (1879–1942), the great novelist of sweeping narrative power and eruptive populist style, whose total dramatic output falls between the wars, is perhaps the best prose writer Hungary ever produced. His first play, *Sári biró* ("Mayor Sadie," 1910), is rooted in the fin de siècle vogue of folk drama, but its characters are more real, and the germ of social conflict is present. His best-known piece, *Uri muri* ("Gentlemen on a Spree," 1928), is a superb indictment of the vanishing feudal order, and mingles awesome and grotesque elements of moral bankruptcy with breathtaking suspense.

Among noteworthy dramatists of the post-World War II period, Gyula Háy (1900–   ) made his first attempts on the stage in the 1930's. After an apprenticeship as a scene designer while a political exile in Germany, Háy had his first play, *Isten, császár, paraszt* ("God, Emperor, Peasant," 1932), produced

at Max Reinhardt's theater. A historical drama focusing on the Hussites, it is also relevant to the Weimar Republic and shows the influence of German expressionism. Another prewar play, *Tiszazug* ("Tisza Nook," 1946) depicts the oppressive atmosphere of Horthy's Hungary. After the war, Háy wrote Stalinist thesis plays of declining quality and popularity. Having had a change of heart during the years 1953 to 1956, he was imprisoned from 1957 to 1960 and then was given amnesty. His plays are still produced in the West, for example, his *A ló* ("The Horse," 1964), an Aristophanic comedy about Caligula.

Tibor Déry (1894–   ), an accomplished communist novelist and short-story writer in the tradition of critical realism, started to write plays only after World War II. In *Tükör* ("Mirror," 1946) and *Itthon* ("At Home," 1947) he tried, unsuccessfully, to greet the advent of the social order he fought and suffered exile for. His dramas stand no comparison with his other work, except for the one-act satire *A talpsimogató* ("The Bootlicker," 1953), in which he cleverly assails the personality cult.

László Németh (1901–   ), a philosopher and man of letters with a doctorate in medicine, is the foremost Hungarian writer of prose alive. He began in the populist tradition, and his early essays and novels made a great stir in the thirties. His first play, *Villamfénynél* ("In a Flash of Lightning," 1938), was written on a dare, and its production by the National Theater was a surprise. In it, as in his subsequent social dramas, he measured his own growth as an intellectual along with the relationship of intellectuals to social action in general and found the account wanting. In historical plays Németh likewise scrutinized the consequences of interaction (or lack of it) between great men and the masses. After the war, none of his plays was produced until *Galilei*, written in 1953, was performed a few days before the Hungarian Revolt in October 1956. That première was repeatedly postponed, since the analogy between Galileo, who strove to be a "good Catholic" but was prevented from this by the Church itself, and the nationally inclined communists was considered dangerous. Party critics still condemn the play as "erroneous" and harmful on ideological grounds. A production of *Széchenyi* (1946) was banned after four sold-out performances in May 1957 to avoid embarrassing comparisons between the post-1848 oppression, which drove the play's hero to insanity and suicide, and the current domestic atmosphere. More recently, in *A két Bólyai* ("The Two Bólyais," 1961), Németh treated the abyss separating father and son, a pair of eminent nineteenth-century mathematicians. In *Utazás* ("The Journey," 1962) he attempted to formulate a political compromise under the impact of a recent journey to the Soviet Union. Professor Karádi, a middle-of-the-road scholar, returns from Moscow. Each character expects his report to reinforce impressions he already has: Communists want to hear enthusiastic praise; reactionaries, complete scorn. By offering both favorable and critical comment, Professor Karádi alienates everybody.

Hungary's preeminent living poet, Gyula Illyés (1902–   ), also began his career as a populist. Compared to his momentous poetry and monumental prose, his first play, *Lélekbuvár* ("Soul-diver,"

1948), was a disappointment. An unsophisticated satire of Freudian psychology, it was not redeemed by its construction and sparkling wit. An inspired filmscript, *Két férfi* ("Two Men," 1950), dealing with heroes of the 1848 War of Independence, followed; then Illyés turned his attention to the past and present fate of the poor peasantry from which he sprung. *Ozorai példa* ("The Example of Ozora," 1952) powerfully dramatizes the principle that patriotism depends on a sense of ownership in one's country. This idea coincided with the communist stand on land reform, but not with the one on collectivization. *Fáklyaláng* ("Torchflame," 1953) pits Kossuth and Görgey—traditionally regarded as hero and traitor of 1848–1849—against each other as representatives of an unyielding stance for the people and for independence and of politically and militarily realistic compromise, respectively; this noble battle of aspirations echoed into the post-Stalin climate of Hungary. In *Ozorai példa* Illyés employed robust physical action in exterior settings and with large crowds, whereas most of the primarily cerebral conflict of *Fáklyaláng* unfolds in the confines of a single room. In his next powerful history play, *Dózsa* (1956), Illyés restated the crucial political function of the Hungarian peasantry through a spirited poetic examination of the ill-fated peasant rebellion of 1514 and its leader, György Dózsa. He successfully blends both the sentiments and the techniques of his previous two dramas. Since 1956 Illyés has written more plays, one of which, an adaptation of László Teleki's previously cited play *A kegyenc* ("The Favorite," 1841), was produced in April 1968. Events and personalities of the declining Roman Empire, as treated in this piece, lead to the conclusion, according to a communist critic, that the sole refuge from overwhelming tyranny is found in love; when that fails, no hope is left. Another critic, admitting the profundity of the philosophy and the effectiveness of the dramaturgy, warns against facile application of any conclusions to current conditions.

The quality of some of the current dramatists must be appraised against a political background, unfortunately. Among more or less talented apologists of the ever-changing party line, Lajos Mesterházi (1916–   ) has made successful attempts at theatrical experimentation in *Pesti emberek* ("People of Budapest," 1958) and *Tizenegyedik parancsolat* ("Eleventh Commandment," 1960). More consistent probing characterized the dramatic work of Imre Sarkadi (1921–1961) until his premature death by suicide. His *Oszlopos Simeon* ("Simeon Stylite," 1967) created a great stir with the sympathetic portrayal of a nonconformist. Miklós Hubay (1918–   ) has achieved some success in music drama and one-act plays. He provided the libretto for Emil Petrovic's opera *C'est la guerre* (1962); in cooperation with the poet István Vas and the composer György Ránki, he created the only successful Hungarian musical, *Egy szerelem három éjszakája* ("Three Nights of a Love," prod. 1966; filmed 1967). Most recently he completed a cycle of one-act plays, *Néró játszik* ("Nero Playing," 1968), a satirical treatment of tyranny's seven aspects. A most successful dramatic

work by Ferenc Karinthy (1921–   ) is a bill of one-act plays, *Négykezes* ("Four-Handed Piece," 1966). Each of the two plays is for two actors. The first one, entitled "Steinway Grand," might be described as black comedy. The Seller, an elderly widow, advertises a piano for sale. The Buyer answers the advertisement with a dizzying succession of phone calls by pretended customers, driving the lady to distraction. This study in varied kinds of loneliness contrasts with "Cheese and Eggs," its companion piece. This play tells of a more traditional chance encounter of two desperate people, although the outcome of their relationship is left in doubt. Although better known as a writer of short stories and novels, István Örkény (1912–   ) has written and adapted half-a-dozen plays. His latest, *Tóték* ("The Tót Family," 1966) has enjoyed some popularity in Hungary and opened in the fall of 1968 in Paris. This grotesque tragicomedy concerns the visit of a major whose warbred idiosyncracies deprive his family of sleep and self-respect; he is then suitably rewarded. The latest bright star to appear on the horizon of Hungarian drama is László Gyurkó, whose *Szerelmem, Elektra* ("Electra, My Love," 1968) is concerned with the questions: Is there an absolute morality? Can a demand for justice be a virtue in one situation and a vice in another?

Rooted in a relatively short but respectable historical tradition, and recovering from a post-World War II temporary lull, Hungarian drama of the 1960's shows considerable promise.

A discussion of Hungarian drama may be found in Klaniczay, Tibor, *et al., History of Hungarian Literature* (Budapest, 1964). Other books on Hungarian drama have not been translated into English. —R. K. S.

Hunger and Thirst (La Soif et la faim, 1966). A play by Eugène IONESCO. When the Comédie-Française presented *Hunger and Thirst* in 1966, it entrusted the direction of the play to the avant-garde director J. M. Serreau and the sets to Jacques Noël, who had done the stage designs for almost all of Ionesco's plays.

The leading character, Jean, is an incarnation of Bérenger, who had previously appeared in *Tueur sans gages* (*The Killer*, 1958), *Rhinocéros* (1960), and *Le Piéton de l'air* (*A Stroll in the Air*, 1963). In the first act Jean is stifling in the peacefulness and regularity of his home with his wife and daughter. He leaves this familiar comfort to seek something beyond the bread and water of stable affection. In the second act he is seen in a high, arid place where he is waiting for the young woman he loves, but she does not come. The third act is a kind of monastery-prison where Jean has asked to live with a strange group of monks who carry on a didactic investigation of Jean's feelings and desires.

The play resembles a quest that at times seems the search for happiness and at other times the renunciation of happiness. The gratification of the thirst and hunger for joy, life, and love is always represented as a disappointment.—W. F.

Hung Shen. See THE PALACE OF ETERNAL YOUTH.

Ibsen, Henrik [Johan] (1828–1906). Norwegian poet and playwright. Ibsen's early years in his native village of Skien were blighted by his father's bankruptcy, and at the age of fifteen he was sent to Grimstad to fend for himself as a druggist's apprentice. Toward the end of those six years he wrote his first two plays, *Cataline* (written 1849), an academic effort, and *Kjæmpehøien* (*The Warrior's Barrow*), a one-acter modeled after the Danish plays of Adam Oehlenschläger, which became, in 1850, his first staged play. That year Ibsen moved to Christiania (now Oslo), but after an unsuccessful effort to advance his academic career he went to Bergen in 1851 to assume a post at the national theater newly founded by Ole Bull. Under the influence of national romanticism, he wrote a number of plays based on Norwegian myth and history, of which the more memorable are *Fru Inger til Østråt* (*Lady Inger of Østråt*, 1855) and *Gildet på Solhaug* (*The Feast at Solhaug*, 1856), the latter his first genuine stage success. From 1857 to 1862 Ibsen was director of the Norske Theater in Christiania, where, in spite of his well-intentioned efforts to create an indigenous theater art, he met with predominant failure. Marriage to Suzannah Thoresen in 1858 brought him a much-needed stability, reflected somewhat in the plays that followed.

Kjærlighedens komedie (*Love's Comedy*, written 1862; prod. 1873), though in verse, was Ibsen's first attempt at contemporary social criticism, and its reflections on marriage awakened public indignation. The success of *Kongsemnerne* (*The Pretenders*, 1864), a historical play probing the subject of national responsibility, brought a resumption of confidence, and Ibsen was on the way. From 1864 to 1891 he lived abroad, chiefly in Italy and Germany, with only infrequent trips home. A stipendium took him abroad, but his displeasure with Norway's failure to support Denmark's war with Germany in 1864 prolonged his absence and gave rise to the two great verse plays that followed, namely *Brand* (written 1866; prod. 1885) and PEER GYNT, which, like two sides of a coin, deal with inflexible idealism and wayward irresponsibility.

From this point onward Ibsen's life was his work. With *De unges forbund* (*The League of Youth*, 1869) he for the first time treated contemporary subject matter in realistic format, but it was not until *Samfundets støtter* (*The Pillars of Society*, 1877) that he began to write what is called the PROBLEM PLAY, which established the pattern for the social drama of our day. On a return visit to Norway in 1874, Ibsen had been disturbed by the direction of conservative politics, and the result was a swing to the left and an

HENRIK IBSEN (WALTER HAMPDEN MEMORIAL LIBRARY AT THE PLAYERS, NEW YORK)

espousal of the new social militancy of the Danish critic Georg Brandes, who had a considerable influence on the development of his dramatic writing, as on almost everything literary in Scandinavia. Using exclusively prose now, set in the format of the WELL-MADE PLAY (his theater experience had exposed him intimately to Scribe), Ibsen proceeded, in Brandes' phrase, to create a debate around the great problems.

There has been a considerable tendency to see those problems in a limited way. In A DOLL'S HOUSE, Ibsen was not so much the suffragist that Strindberg thought him (always fulminating) as a man arguing for a maximum of individual realization in a given social context. Likewise, GHOSTS is not just a play about hereditary syphilis and euthanasia, though both ideas play a part. Its real import is an insistence that human vitality must not be suppressed by the opinions of a conventional society. Certainly in the progress of the play through Germany, France, and England it could well be said that the modern spirit had asserted itself on the stages of Europe. It is to the credit of the United States that this controversial play was first produced in Chicago.

By now Ibsen was receiving honors and awards from all quarters, yet the fact did not keep him from questioning the role of the artist in society, in his later, almost confessional, plays. At the same time there seems to have been a feeling that realism was not enough, exemplified in the psychological symbolism of *Rosmersholm* (1887) and the mysticism of *Fruen fra havet* (*The Lady from the Sea,* 1889). Apart from passing platonic infatuations with younger women, Ibsen threw all his energies into the drama, and even those infatuations enhanced the gallery of female roles in his plays. Everything went into his art, and the result was monumental.

Ibsen's major work—from *Brand* to *Når vi døde vågner* (*When We Dead Awaken,* 1899)—may be said to begin and end with an avalanche, and in both plays the theme is man versus mission. Brand is a fanatic who sacrifices his wife and his son for his ministry. When he dies in a landslide, which may or may not be divine retribution, a voice speaks to him: God is love. While the play may deplore the absence of *caritas,* as we tend to think today, Brand carries with him much of the intensity of Kierkegaard, his model, and Ibsen could say that "Brand was himself in his best moments." The sculptor Rubek, of *Når vi døde vågner,* who has similarly made life second to mission, dies by avalanche in an ecstatic attempt to capture what he has denied himself.

In the plays framed by these two, the theme is generally a search for self in a context of conflicting social demands. As often as not, the search is marked by failure and self-inflicted death. Whether these suicides are tragic in the old, elevated fashion is debatable; on the other hand, there is no question that the tragic sense was implicit in all that Ibsen did, along with the realization that there are no easy formulas to proper human action. Peer Gynt is poetic and picaresque, and his search for experience makes of him a Faust of the Norwegian mountains (and an American capitalist as well), but the absence of direction and the lack of genuine identity make him a desperately errant figure with tragic overtones. The real truth of human action must lie somewhere between the extremes of Brand and Peer Gynt.

The realistic plays from 1879 to 1899 form an interesting concatenation; each furthers a continuing investigation of man's role in society. Nora, of *A Doll's House,* who has been kept a pampered child bride by her fatuous husband, Helmer, nevertheless has moral fiber and emancipates herself from his bondage. An alternate ending, in which she has second thoughts and returns, only confirms the original drift and intention. Nora must, at least metaphorically, find herself. A woman who could not act so boldly, one intellectually but not emotionally and practically liberated, is Mrs. Alving of *Ghosts.* Had she not stayed by her dissolute husband and put the mask of respectability on his doings, she might have avoided the chain reaction of tragedy that led to her son's collapse with paresis. All the smug hopes and the graven images of society are concentrated in the word "ghosts." The play's inexorable unraveling has its parallel with Greek tragedy, as is suggested by the somewhat limiting but apt observation that "fate has

been replaced by a staphylococcus in the blood stream."

But the individual cannot act without some knowledge of society, and this is Dr. Stockmann's tragedy —or comedy—in *En folkefiende* (*An Enemy of the People,* 1883). Dr. Stockmann possesses an absolute and undeniable truth, that the spa is polluted, but the community will not accept a truth that denies them, even temporarily, their livelihood. Dr. Stockmann is ostracized and stripped of his privileges as a doctor, but is he a tragic figure on that account? Arthur Miller thought so, in his adaptation that makes the most of a parallel with corruption in New York City politics. In fact, however, Stockmann is something of a *Strudelkopf,* as Ibsen later admitted. No scientific truth has any validity apart from human truth, and the presiding irony of the play is that Dr. Stockmann never realizes it.

Pursuing this relativistic philosophy, Ibsen wrote THE WILD DUCK, which demonstrates the consequences of Brand's kind of fanaticism. Gregers Werle's passion to make everyone see the truth and see it whole brings on one of the most pathetic of tragedies, the suicide of a teen-age girl. People can stand only so much truth, and a measure of illusion is necessary to make life tolerable. The chilly, inflexible Ibsen was becoming humanized.

Apparently, the well-known author Rebecca West took her name out of admiration for the character so named in *Rosmersholm,* but it is difficult to see why. Whatever the intensity and independence of Rebecca's passions, she willfully brought about the death of Beata Rosmer, for love of Beata's husband. Her guilt grows in her and it is only a matter of time before she and Rosmer resort, not to marriage, but to double suicide. Folk symbolism (the white horse of the millrace, where the suicides are staged) makes its appearance and marks a new direction in Ibsen's dramaturgy. Furthermore, this is the last of the plays with any political content.

Symbolism evolved into something approaching mysticism, and with it came a looser form, in *Fruen fra havet,* in which Ellida is landlocked in a loveless marriage to Dr. Wangel but mentally bound to the sea and the seaman she once jilted. When she is given absolute freedom of choice to join the returned seaman, she decides in favor of her husband. HEDDA GABLER is also, in large part, a play about marriage. Hedda is trapped in a marriage of convenience with the scholar George Tesman and is infatuated with a kind of Dionysian ideal in the person of the writer Eilert Løvberg. The problem is that Hedda is destructive, to the extent that she is compounded of energy, ordinariness, and a trace of demonism. She inevitably brings about Eilert's death and her own. She is not ready for emancipation, or for any kind of creative act for that matter. *Hedda Gabler* looks like a regression to psychological realism, but in fact its perfect fusion of the real and symbolic makes it a play of unusual amplitude, perhaps Ibsen's finest.

Ibsen's last four plays, including *Når vi døde vågner,* all have to do with guilt, introspection, and faltering powers in the professional man. They ask "Was it worth it, the sublimation of self and all that?" but they are not nearly so personal as most of Strindberg's plays. THE MASTER BUILDER is, in its phallic symbolism, the most specifically sexual in its study of an encounter between age and youth. *Lille Eyolf* (*Little Eyolf,* 1894), a strange blend of realism and folklore, makes the undersexed partner and the oversexed partner share the guilt of what they conceive to be the fruits of their sin and look for absolution in good works. *John Gabriel Borkman* (1896) is a kind of Nietzschean case history, a study of a man who sacrificed love for power and thereby moves inexorably toward death. Somewhat the same could be said of *Når vi døde vågner,* except that there the power is that of high artistry and on that account more justifiable.

Ibsen's great influence on almost the whole of modern drama after him has been, for better or worse, a matter of form. Ibsen built his plays around the climax, interwove exposition with action so artfully that audiences did not know they were being briefed, and taught several generations of playwrights to come how to endow people, events, and things with symbolic value at exactly the right dramatic moment. At best, he made of the "well-made play" a compact, classical vehicle; at worst his patness became a formula that found its way into virtually every book on playwriting. The quintessence of Ibsen's heritage is that he fathered the modern problem play.

The standard edition in English is that being edited by J. W. McFarlane, *Ibsen* (1960–). The revised Halvdan Koht biography, *Henrik Ibsen* (to be published in English translation) is still the best life of Ibsen, but the well-known Ibsen translator Michael Meyer has issued the first volume of a new biography, *Henrik Ibsen* (1967). For Ibsen's technique, the best critical studies are: J. R. Northam, *Ibsen's Dramatic Method* (1953), and P. F. D. Tennant, *Ibsen's Dramatic Technique* (1948). In the realm of ideas, the following are important: H. J. Weigand, *The Modern Ibsen* (1925); M. C. Bradbrook, *Ibsen the Norwegian* (1946); B. W. Downs, *Ibsen: The Intellectual Background* (1946); and Maurice Valency, *The Flower and the Castle* (1963).—R. B. V.

Iceland. Drama was late coming to Iceland, partly because the dispersion of population made for few stages on which to play, and partly because Iceland's dependency on Denmark until home rule was obtained in 1918 in a measure postponed the emergence of indigenous talent. The romantic folk play *Utilegumennirnir* ("The Outlawed Men," 1862), by Matthías Jochumsson (1835–1920), found an audience, it is true, in barns, schools, and private homes and established itself in tne hearts of the people. But in the long run the theater is more than "two boards and a passion"; it took the initiative of the economist and playwright Indriði Einarsson (1851–1939) to bring into being the Reykjavík Dramatic Society in 1897 and indirectly the National Theater in 1950, which opened, appropriately enough, with his own *Nýjársnóttin* ("New Year's Night," 1871), like *Utilegumennirnir,* a manifestation of national romanticism.

Three Icelandic playwrights got their start in Copenhagen and as a consequence wrote in both Danish and Icelandic, namely Jóhann Sigurjónsson (1880–1919), Gunnar Gunnarsson (1889–), and Guðmundur Kamban (1888–1945). Sigurjónsson went to Copenhagen to study veterinary science but soon turned to the theater. Of his five plays, the two that have done most to establish his classical position in Icelandic literary history are *Bjœrg-Ejvind og hans hustru* (*Eyvind of the Hills,* 1911), another story of outlawry, which the Swedish director Victor Sjöström filmed and starred in as early as 1917; and *Galdra-Loftur* (Danish title, *Ønsket; The Wish,* 1914), which, in its handling of a witchcraft plot, owes something to Goethe's *Faust,* to Nietzsche, and to *Anne Pedersdotter* (prod. in Copenhagen in 1909), by the Norwegian playwright Hans Wiers-Jenssen.

Gunnarsson's reputation chiefly attaches to his novels, but Kamban is remembered for *Hadda-Padda* (1914) and *Vi mordere* ("We Murderers," 1920). The latter is, in its infelicitous fashion, a problem comedy set in New York City, and chiefly suggests to a modern reader that the Icelander was having some difficulty extending the range of his subject matter in a plausible way.

Halldór Kiljan Laxness (1902–) is surely the most cosmopolitan and urbane of Icelandic writers, having lived in Paris, tried a monastery on for size, traveled widely, and made the *pro forma* pilgrimage to Hollywood and to Upton Sinclair. He is, however, only secondarily a playwright and is best when he is dealing with the Icelandic scene, whether ancient or modern. In his adaptation of *Íslands-klukkan* (*The Bell of Iceland,* novel 1943, play 1950) he converts the seventeenth-century farmer Jón Hreggviðsson, condemned to death for murdering the Danish king's hangman, into a symbol of Iceland's indomitable spirit; in *Silfurtunglið* (*The Silver Moon,* 1954) he attacks (as did a good many others) the presence of American air bases in Iceland. Halldór Laxness was awarded the Nobel Prize in 1955, but chiefly in recognition of his accomplishments in fiction.

Icelandic drama is at its best, so far, in exploring the country's own history and folklore. Since 1940 one play may be said to stand out in each category. *Bishop Jón Arason,* by Tryggvi Sveinbjörnsson (1891–), is significant, not merely because it won the National Theater's playwriting contest of 1950, but because it is the latest and best of a series of dramatizations of the life of this sixteenth-century Icelandic patriot, the last Catholic bishop and a passionate advocate of home rule. It is a straightforward chronicle play built on the skeleton of militant conflict, the church versus the state, or, more correctly, home rule versus the autocratic rule of a remote foreign power, Denmark. The play had only commemorative appositeness, since Iceland had attained its complete freedom from Denmark in 1944.

Probably the best of the folk fantasies is the poetic *Gullna Hliðið* (*Golden Gate,* 1941), by Davið Stefánsson (1895–). It deals with the translation into heaven of the wayward peasant soul of one Jón Jonsson, who has jeopardized his chances for salvation by a weakness for brandy, women, and his neighbor's sheep. "Talk like a Christian, Jón dear," his wife admonishes; to which Jón replies: "I'll talk just as I please—like every other Icelander." There is no better summation of the independent Icelandic spirit.

In matters of dramatic form, however, Icelandic theater still tends to be conservative and conventional. Its chief originality might be said to lie in manipulating the convergence of the old and the new, frequently the living past and the dead present. A good farcical example is *Kjarnorka og kvenhylli* (*Atoms and Madams,* 1955), by Agnar Thorðarson (1917–   ), which brings together an American swindler prospecting for uranium, a member of the Icelandic parliament, and a very funny rustic. The social criticism of the play, while not of a delicate order, gives an excellent picture of the climate of opinion in Iceland and the direction of its drama.

Icelandic drama is fairly extensively treated in a volume in the series of literary histories sponsored by the American-Scandinavian Foundation: *A History of Icelandic Literature* (1957), edited by Stefán Einarsson. Some of the more recent plays have appeared in the Foundation's *Scandinavian Plays of the 20th Century* series. Iceland is particularly well represented in *Fire and Ice: Three Icelandic Plays* (1967), translated and edited by Einar Haugen.—R. B. V.

Iceman Cometh, The (1946). A play by Eugene O'NEILL. Though overlong, *The Iceman Cometh* is an impressive study of human frailty and self-deception. In Harry Hope's waterfront saloon, life's exiles and failures lead a besotted and befuddled existence and subsist on hopes of recovering their lost status. Most of them are reasonably happy until their drinking companion, the flashy traveling salesman Hickey, shows up for one of his periodic drinking bouts. Instead of joining in the expected revels, however, he is bent upon making them face the truth about themselves—that they no longer have anything to hope for. Accepting his challenge at last, that they leave the saloon and proceed to accomplish the restitution of reputation and position with which they have long deluded themselves, they sally forth, only to return, one by one, frightened and dispirited. Nothing feels right anymore, and even the liquor in the saloon has lost its savor and has no effect on them. Contentment returns to them only after Hickey's revelation that he has murdered his long-suffering wife to free her from the misery of loving him, although he has also hated her for her infinite trust and forbearance.

They derive comfort from the conviction that Hickey, who has given himself up to the police, is stark mad and relapse into their comforting illusions. The liquor begins to work on them again, and all is well so far as they know or care. Only Larry, the disenchanted radical, has grasped Hickey's meaning when Hickey called for the abandonment of illusions as the only way of attaining peace. The death of illusion is the end of life—death, "the Iceman," being the sole possible release. For, as Larry has said earlier about men's dependence on false hopes, "the lie of a pipe dream is what gives life to the whole misbegotten mad lot of us, drunk or sober." Larry, in fact, performs one act of kindness at once; he persuades a miserable youth, who has betrayed his anarchist mother to the police, to put an end to his inner torment by committing suicide. Rich in detail, complex in contrivance yet seemingly natural, naturalistic in speech and situation yet also somewhat symbolic and grotesque, *The Iceman Cometh* looms large in the O'Neill canon. Even its prolixity has redeeming qualities; Hickey's confessional speech, which lasts some

fifteen minutes on the stage, constitutes gripping theater. Its defects are repetitiveness, some of which can be reduced without injury to the play, and some banality of expression.—J. G.

Iffland, August Wilhelm (1759–1814). German actor, director, and writer of very popular sentimental plays at the end of the eighteenth century. Although today regarded as a minor literary figure at best, Iffland was one of the foremost theatrical people of his day, an actor and director of exceptional talent and a dramatist whose work was enjoyed by an extremely broad segment of the public. Iffland's entire career was devoted to the theater. Moving from the Court Theater in Gotha, through Mannheim, where he met and acquired a distaste for Schiller, he rose to direct the National Theater in Berlin (1796) and ended his career as general director of the Royal Playhouse in the same city. His successes as a dramatist were achieved in oversentimental and moralizing melodramas. He created characters with which the middle-class audience could easily identify, as opposed to the distance established by the declamatory heroes of classical drama. His major vehicle was the "family play," in which virtue was always rewarded, vice was always punished, and the entire affair was bathed in extraordinary amounts of tears. At least one of his more than thirty plays, *Die Jäger* ("The Hunters," 1785; pub. in English as *The Foresters*), was still being produced with success at the end of the nineteenth century and exerted a great influence on *Der Erbföster* ("The Hereditary Forester") of a later dramatist, Otto Ludwig.—B. M. M.

Ile. See EUGENE O'NEILL.

Importance of Being Earnest, The (1895). A comedy by Oscar WILDE. First produced at the St. James's Theatre, and a great success, *The Importance of Being Earnest* is acknowledged by both critics and the public to be Wilde's best play. Often described as "brilliant" and "flawless," the play does have just claim to be considered as one of the outstanding comedies of the nineteenth century and perhaps, as is often said, the finest comedy since the Restoration. It is best regarded as pure farce, for Wilde was certainly not concerned with plot or content in this story of the vicissitudes of two couples (John Worthing and Gwendolen Fairfax, Algernon Moncrieff and Cecily Cardew) making their way toward inevitable unions. To talk of theme in connection with the play is also to bring forward what would seem to be gratuitous, although there is more justification for doing so than many critics would seem to grant. Ultimately, it is style and manner conveyed through witty dialogue and a mock-serious tone that distinguish the piece.

It is this mock-seriousness that contributes most to the "serious" aspect of the play, for there is no doubt that in putting forward his own kind of topsy-turvy logic (with considerable debt to W. S. Gilbert) Wilde is making some pointed satiric comments on various customs and institutions highly regarded by his Victorian contemporaries, including the church, politics, marriage, and moral earnestness in general. In addition, in parodying the popular dramatic genres of his own time, especially the "well-made play" and sentimental comedy, Wilde indicates his own recognition of the failure of his fellow playwrights not only to expose but even to acknowledge the hypocrisy and self-deception of their age.

The success of the play, however, rests largely on its stylistic brilliance, evident chiefly in the epigrammatic and aphoristic quality of the lines and in the impressive literate nature of the verbal wit. "The limitation, the very condition of any art is style," Wilde has Vivian say in his essay "The Decay of Lying" (1889), and as a dramatist Wilde illustrates this maxim. What is most appealing in *The Importance of Being Earnest* is the playwright's superb portrayal of an artificial world that transcends the real and yet retains both credibility and meaning through the sheer force of Wilde's own ideas and words. Examples to illustrate this last point pervade the play. Lady Bracknell, for instance, is sure that a man who desires to get married should know "either everything or nothing" and does not approve of anything that "tampers with natural ignorance." She is also certain that "to be born, or at any rate bred, in a hand-bag, whether it had handles or not, seems . . . to display a contempt for the ordinary decencies of family life that remind one of the worst excesses of the French Revolution." Algernon is sure that divorces are made in heaven. When Cecily insists that when she sees a spade she calls a spade a spade, Gwendolen, in the best Wildean manner, retorts that she is glad to say that she has never seen a spade. "It is obvious," she concludes, "that our social spheres have been widely different." Perhaps the key to the fullest appreciation of this most successful of Wilde's plays lies in seeing his great gift of making clear the inseparability of art and life, style and substance. Unlike John Worthing, Wilde would not have regarded it a terrible thing "to find out suddenly that all his life he had been speaking nothing but the truth."—M. T.

India. Indian drama encompasses a field of the widest scope. In geographical terms it embraces the larger part of the Asian subcontinent; in temporal terms it extends from an indefinite but unquestionably considerable time before the birth of Christ up to the present. It is examined here under three subheadings: Sanskrit drama, which flourished from the beginning of recorded activity to approximately A.D. 1000; folk drama, which can be studied properly only in the field, though its roots are often in a remote past; dance drama, similarly spaced in time but including work on all levels of Indian society. India has also been the chief inspirer of a provincial school of drama that has flourished in Tibet for an unspecified number of centuries (see TIBET). For the more recent literary drama in India, see Rabindranath TAGORE.

Sanskrit drama. The classical drama of India is, with few exceptions, written in the Sanskrit language, the speech brought into India by Aryan invaders during the second millennium B.C. The origins of Indian drama are, of course, matters of conjecture. References to plays and actors are found in the epics, the *Mahabharata* and the *Ramayana,* and in some of the most ancient Sanskrit texts. The nature of the entertainments so mentioned can only be conjectured. Dancing, miming, and singing presumably surpassed the verbal elements in importance. There were two major types of play: the *nataka,* plays of mythological or historical content, and the *prakarana,* plays with invented stories and less exalted characters.

The dating of the earliest extant plays or fragments of plays, such as the works ascribed to Bhasa (see TRIVANDRUM PLAYS) and Asvaghosa, is subject to doubt. Recent scholars incline to believe them older than was formerly supposed. It is probable that some either belong to a period considerably before the Christian era or are revisions of such ancient works. This early dramatic activity apparently existed from one end of India to the other. Broadly speaking, Sanskrit drama as known today extended throughout the first millennium A.D. of the Western calendar. A few pieces may be earlier; others, of much diminished interest, are of even later origin. The most highly praised dramatist is KALIDASA. Among his chief successors are Sri HARSHA, BHAVABHUTI, Visakhadatta (see MUDRARAKSASA), Murari, Bhattanarayana, and Rajasekhara. The remarkable THE LITTLE CLAY CART, of uncertain date, is ascribed to King Sudraka, an ascription almost certainly erroneous.

Linguistically, the composition of these plays is complex, owing in part to the linguistic development of the country. Most of them are court dramas, representing the thought and habits of a ruling class and an aristocracy of learning. The playwrights were as a rule in the employ of princes and were themselves endowed with considerable classical learning, acquainted with the Vedas, the epics, and the philosophical literature. The dignity of the audience and the training of the dramatists favored a distinctly classical idiom. Meanwhile, Sanskrit, in various debased forms, was spoken by persons of only moderate education and to some extent adulterated by the native languages of the Indian provinces. These less dignified forms of speech are known as Prakrits. A play almost invariably employed both Sanskrit and Prakrits, the former used by gods, princes, Brahmans, and high officials, the latter by women, servants, and persons of lower rank. The style of the plays was further refined by the use of both verse and prose. The more elevated passages are in verse. The verse passages, frequently lyrical in form, tend to be those addressed with most emphasis to the audience. An extremely large number of meters are employed. Prose is used in the more colloquial parts, in easy exchange of speeches, in passages dispensing information to the audience, especially those implementing the plot. The aim of any scene is to cultivate a certain mood, or *rasa.* It is clear that this aim is achieved primarily through the verse passages, which set the emotional mood desired. Prakrits is employed in the verse passages but is less common in them than the Sanskrit. Thus, in that most eminent yet representative play, Kalidasa's *Shakuntala,* a large proportion of both the verse and the Sanskrit is contained in the lyrical stanzas entoned by the hero, King Dushyanta.

Sanskrit drama, of which some seven hundred plays exist, is distinguished, among much else, for that form of sophistication that accompanies aesthetic self-consciousness. Several important manuals of critical literature exist, among which the NATYASASTRA, ascribed to Bharata, is the most impressive and probably the most thorough and exhaustive examination of the principles of drama in existence. It is typical of this field that neither the identity of the author nor his period is really ascertainable. Conjectures have ranged over several centuries, although at present general opinion places the author in about

A SCENE FROM KALIDASA'S *Shakuntala* (COURTESY BALWANT GARGI)

the first century A.D. The form in which his work has come down to us, however, is generally thought to derive from approximately the eighth century. Bharata himself is traditionally held to have ascended to heaven, where he oversees the daily production of plays acted by *apsaras,* or celestial spirits, for the pleasure of the gods. He is held virtually the lord and god of drama, his counsel and his rules regarded as wholly binding. No sentence of a play is to be written—nor movement to be performed—without reference to this supreme authority.

Drama is conceived in the *Natyasastra* as the apex or confluence of all the arts and thus as aesthetic activity brought to its fullest and highest flowering. Bharata's work contains a general theory of aesthetics: The end of art is to induce serenity by the strategy of depicting life in its actual emotional excitement and at the same time of holding this picture at a distance that removes all unpleasant experience of tension and stress. In other words, art gives pleasure that is itself so serene as to be a step toward the ultimate peace of the mystic's meditation. It should be exercised in the service of religion. It is intrinsically neither moral nor intellectual but spiritual. Hence life's grosser aspects are not to be openly represented.

Bharata writes at length on all the arts, describing in the greatest detail countless conventions of the stage, defining gesture, dance, décor, and the rules for playwriting, theater architecture and equipment, poetic composition, and, indeed, for the entire gamut of theatrical production. The book avoids a narrow-

ing or confining tyranny of opinion by describing many types of plays, all legitimate, though some possessing much greater dignity than others.

From the earliest times in India dance and drama have been in the closest relationship. This condition is well exemplified by the highly extensive use of symbolical gestures and finger movements prescribed for dancers and actors alike. Most of the dancing has been dramatic and much of the drama choreographic. The *Natyasastra* gives elaborate directions in these regards. The dance impinges on mime and both on even the most literary forms of drama. Scenes and episodes of the plays are greatly affected by this condition. Thus, such incidents as a girl attacked by a bee became commonplaces on the stage. Two bee pantomimes appear in Kalidasa's *Shakuntala.*

Bharata describes drama as the fifth Veda, a sacred art that appeals to all classes of mankind, both literate and illiterate, whereas the more exalted Vedas are reserved only for scholars and persons of formal education. Drama is founded upon nine major rasas, or sentiments: The erotic, the comic, the pathetic, the furious, the heroic, the terrible, the hateful, the marvelous, and, finally, the peaceful. From these are derived nine *bhavas,* or stable sentiments, manifest in drama as love, laughter, pathos, anger, energy, fear, disgust, wonder, and quietude. Psychological distinctions are multiplied with much ingenuity and with at least a hint of scholastic pedantry. Bharata enumerates determinants or inducements to the different bhavas. He names, for example, thirty-two "unstable sentiments." Each character in a drama has a dominant rasa, though he may appear in its many variants. Each play also has its dominant sentiment, such as the erotic or the pathetic. The system, however, by no means prescribes a static performance. The playwright is instructed to conjugate his leading sentiment through as many derivative parts as possible. His success depends on turning the mood about through the greatest possible number of angles, thus creating something of the condition known in Western music as theme and variation.

In fact, this general doctrine of drama is closer to the West's theories of music and musical experience than to its theories of the stage. Each act of a Sanskrit play may be viewed as a movement in a sonata or similar Western musical form. No such aim as catharsis, instruction, or revelation is proposed. The highway of the Sanskrit drama is designed to lead through pleasure to serenity and ultimately to peace. The word rasa itself suggests the pleasure of taste or smell. The enjoyer is to relish a particular flavor that leaves him overjoyed and entranced. Plays, whether serious or amusing, are thus aimed to lead us by differing means to a single end: the ultimate consummation of the aesthetic experience. This is also a metaphysical experience inasmuch as the mood transcends the senses and in itself negates action. Sensuous experience and intellectual stimulus serve only as means to achieve this ideal end. This system of aesthetics is basically attractive to modern thinking, although much of the argument and manner of Bharata's treatise, with its tireless proliferation of detail, is likely to seem pedantic to the impatient Western reader.

The *Natyasastra* deals in much detail with plot construction, with conventions for the ceremonial opening of the play and the conclusion, and with the introductory episode and conclusion appropriate for each act. (See SUTRADHARA; VIDUSAKA; VISKAMBHAKA.) Scores of types of plays, from monologues to ten-act dramas, are defined. No less elaborate is the treatment of meters. It would almost seem that nothing that a Sanskrit dramatist is known to have done remains undefined and unclassified. Despite all this elaborate statement, the dramatist is left comparatively free, for he has a vast range of possibilities from which to choose. Playwriting became in time repetitious and decadent but more from a failure in imagination than from binding "laws" imposed by Bharata. The *Natyasastra* is less a book of laws for the drama than a comprehensive dramatic dictionary. Likewise, a typical book on Sanskrit dramatics compiled in the 13th century or later, Sagaranandin's *Natakalaksanaratnakosa*, is frankly a dictionary, defining theatrical terms, 3,205 in number. Its aim is less to direct the playwright than to assist him in naming his tools and in encouraging him with a conspectus of the vast province in which he may move. No more sophisticated or self-conscious dramatic tradition than the Indian is thinkable. From the most general ideas to the most minute particulars, Sanskrit criticism is virtually inexhaustible.

A. B. Keith's *The Sanskrit Drama* (1924) has maintained its position as the standard work on this subject, although it has been superseded in several special fields of inquiry. Of much value is Indu Shekhar's *Sanskrit Drama: Its Origins and Decline* (1960). Also useful is R. V. Jagirdar's *Drama in Sanskrit Literature* (1947), and a detailed study by M. M. Ghose, *History of Hindu Drama* (1951). Still of value is *Le théâtre indien* (1890) by S. Levi. For a study of Sanskrit drama from the standpoint of comparative literature, see *The Classical Drama of India* (1963) by Henry W. Wells. Source books for the study of Indian dramatic theory and technique are *Natyasastra*, ascribed to Bharata, translated by M. M. Ghose in 1951; *Natakalaksanaratnakosa*, by Sagaranandin, translated by Myles Dillon, Murray Fowler, and V. Raghavan (1960); also *The Dance of Siva* (1948) by A. K. Coomaraswamy. For studies of the Indian theater today, see *Theatres in the East* (1956) by Faubion Bowers, and *Theatre in India* (1962) by Balwant Gargi. For translations of major plays, see *Six Sanskrit Plays* (1964), selected by Henry W. Wells.

folk drama. India has long possessed probably the most remarkable tradition of folk drama. By this is meant a popular theater with some claim to poetic excellence, distinguished from superficial entertainment and from any school of drama cultivated by formally educated or literate groups. Such plays, whether given in villages or in cities, are intended for the majority of the population, removed from the direction either of a social aristocracy or an intellectual elite. Princes or scholars may attend and enjoy the performances but the impulse springs from the people. Where productions have no literary merit, they cannot properly be regarded as drama; where they have aristocratic or intellectual refinement, they cannot be of the folk. Many popular entertainments in India are, to be sure, of little or no literary substance, being comprised primarily of dance, spectacle, or song with words of no poetic worth. They are better described as folk vaudeville than as folk drama. Yet a large number of shows intended for the populace possess every qualification to be accepted as folk drama. Their authors and actors may or may not be professionals. Where families have for generations been dedicated to their art, Western distinctions between professional and amateur have small relevance. Folk drama in India is more spontaneous than commercial.

Only an extremely small proportion of such plays has found its way into print and scarcely any have been translated. They incline toward freedom, anonymity, and improvisation, with strongly drawn character types. No two productions of the same play, given year after year and often century after century, are identical, yet no radical deviation is allowed. The work seems the more vital for being never twice the same. As a rule there is no known author, or rather, there are two authors in harmonious collaboration: tradition and the dedicated actor. These plays have of late attracted a considerable number of theater scholars and are being eagerly studied, since a fear exists that the traditional forms, having long seemed immortal, will shortly disappear before the advance of the new media of film and television.

The almost unique character and importance of the folk drama derives from Indian social and cultural conditions, decidedly unlike those in China or elsewhere in Asia. For centuries the Indian elite viewed the Sanskrit drama with reverence, studying

A SCENE FROM *Ramayana* (COURTESY BALWANT GARGI)

it as pure literature, while the vitality of the acting tradition that created it had for the most part vanished. After A.D. 1000 no memorable plays in Sanskrit were written and the skills for producing the Sanskrit classics had been lost or forgotten. Accordingly, for centuries India possessed no important theater of the upper or learned classes, a condition of the utmost importance in a society built severely upon caste lines. Yet the people remained very much devoted to the performing arts, not only to music and dance, pantomime, and puppetry, but to various forms of unmistakably dramatic art as well. Although the main stem of the illustrious Sanskrit drama had fallen, various features of it were disseminated throughout the very different folk drama. These popular plays employed the legends and myths that had been used with far different effect in the court theaters that had witnessed the works of Kalidasa, Harsha, and Bhavabhuti. They borrowed their stories and even parts of their dialogue from famous poems and plays, such as the *Ramayana* and GITA-

GOVINDA, freely translating or paraphrasing the Sanskrit into the local languages. Thus a vast and highly animated theatrical activity persisted on a new level. In the twentieth century scholars and theater producers seeking to recover the style of the Sanskrit stage glean much information from examination of both Indian folk plays and dances.

This folk drama has never been entirely subliterary or known only through oral tradition. Thus the plays of such a popular and recent producer as Shri Krishan Pahlwana, poet, playwright, and actor, are published in crude pamphlets distributed even in villages where the humblest forms of folk drama are seen. Although such plays are entirely without the overall forms of the classical or sophisticated theater, they possess forms of their own, which would no doubt be shocking to the sensibilities of the ancient masters. Frequently the plays employ a chorus. Yet almost all preserve the convention of the *sutradhara,* or narrator, who introduces the play and, as his name suggests, holds the thread of its narrative in his hand.

The style of acting in these plays, a synthesis of mime and speech, the imaginative costumes, and the traditional and mythological subject matter relate them to the poetic drama of India's classical age.

The popular stage in India has also long been devoted to propaganda plays. Such works carried considerable weight in the long and bitter agitation for freedom from British rule. Typical of these are works by Dinabandhu Mitra, whose *Neel Darpana* (1872), a Bengali play dealing with plantation life, was given in widely separated parts of northern India. Of similar purpose were spirited plays by D. L. Roy, especially *Mewar Patan* (1908), *Shah Jehan* (1909), and *Chandragupta* (1911). Equally notable were propaganda plays given in the Hindu theaters in and about Bombay, commencing in 1945 under the direction of Prithvi Raj.

It is true that many popular Indian plays delight their audiences with lavish spectacle that tends to dwarf what literary value they may possess. Such are the extremely popular works recently presented by the Rajamanickam Company of Madras. These plays have a strong religious impulse. Similar gaudy productions of mythological dramas have been presented by S. V. Shasranamam in the Tamil language. New plays based on old themes and possessing some inherited merit as poetic literature are especially popular in southern India. In the province of Andhra a long verse play, *Krishna Rayabaram,* has won much applause; in Mysore a pageant drama, *Kurukshetra,* using episodes from the *Mahabharata,* has enjoyed a similar success. A group known as Chakyr actors in Kerala still presents versions, modified in only secondary respects, of Sanskrit plays by Bhasa and Harsha. Thus plays originally produced in the courts of princes are at present given in humble settings before popular audiences in the guise of folk drama.

How eclectic have been the influences on popular dramatic performances is seen in the instance of the most famous Indian drama festival of the nineteenth century. Wajid Ali Shah, Nawab of Oudh, gave lavish patronage to traditional celebrations of the cults of Krishna and Rama. He employed a French attendant at his court to supply much of the music and choreography. Yet he also made earnest experiments in introducing onto his nineteenth-century stage classical and highly aesthetic concepts from early periods of native Indian culture. He gave stage presentations of ancient *ragas,* or musical modes, as illustrated in Rajput paintings, a style developed in northern India in the 16th century. The performers enacted the emotions, or *bhavas,* to accompany the music and in a manner described by the theorists as harmonious with the paintings. These comprehensive studies in color, sound, and word were remarkably artful. Many thousands assembled to witness these gigantic outdoor semireligious festivals. In such great outdoor performances the audience would be charged no stated admission, but a contribution, as at a religious ceremony, was frequently taken up. Devout members of the audience might even contribute their jewels to the honor of the god whose cult worship was being observed. Thus Indian folk drama often flourished as a poetic creation midway between religion and entertainment.

The most comprehensive study of Indian folk drama is *Folk Theatre of India* (1966) by Balwant Gargi. The book contains many excellent illustrations. Also of much value are *Hindi Folk Drama* (1956) by Suresh Awasthi and *Drama in Rural India* (1964) by J. C. Mathur.

dance drama. As in the case of its folk drama, India has produced a unique dance drama that has only recently come to the attention of scholars in the Western world, where the philosophy of dance differs materially from the Indian. In Western dance the story does not greatly matter, though it gives the dance a firmer body and cohesion than it might otherwise possess. In Indian dance, however, the story or myth is of immense importance. The dancers are in the service of their theme, which is often religious and so much more compelling on this account. Their dance is still a form of worship and to subordinate its subject matter would be to betray its heart. Since it presents a sanctified narrative, the Indian dance can never be abstract. The plot of a play by Kalidasa matters much less than the plot of a play by Shakespeare, but the story in a dance drama designed by Uday Shankar is much more important than the story in a ballet designed by Diaghilev.

The death in A.D. 1000 of Sanskrit drama as a live, performing art was undoubtedly a factor in the rise of both folk and dance drama. For centuries the ancient Sanskrit plays had virtually disappeared from the stage, surviving only as poetry or literature. The deep love of Indians for performing arts was meanwhile gratified in the two sources—the folk and dance drama—that became perhaps all the more prolific because the most powerful of the earlier sources of inspiration were sealed. The dance divided, not always rigidly, into folk dancing and temple dancing. Where the distinction is to be made, the major difference lies in the tendency of the more popular form to be correspondingly more dramatic.

Indian dance perfected beyond any other a precise and complex language of symbolism, a parallel to the amazingly precise rules for Sanskrit rhetoric. The human figure as a whole was enlisted in this art, hands and fingers most clearly of all. The dance became a sign language, a form of silent speech. This might seem an esoteric discourse to persons foreign to the tradition, but the majority in an Indian audience at any time grasped the dancer's gesture as clearly as the poet's word. The dancer spoke. Moreover a musical symbolism of *ragas,* or modes, and a rigorous color symbolism added to the force and clarity of the meaning.

Still a third consideration assisted the dance to approximate poetry and hence the spoken drama. Indian dances as a rule narrated events related in an epic or a narrative poem known to the spectators from their childhood. In some instances, especially in folk and village presentations, a reciter actually told the story while the dancers performed it in their own medium. Thus the dancers' movements were all the closer to inducing dramatic understanding, not only because a sign gesture was known as equivalent to a known word, but because the entire story was known. The characters in drama, poem, and dance were the same. The ratio between spoken drama and dance drama was virtually one-to-one. Moreover, the stories used in the Sanskrit plays merely passed on to the popular play festivals and village dances.

UDAY SHANKAR AS THE GOD SIVA AND AMALA SHANKAR AS THE GODDESS PARVATI (COURTESY BALWANT GARGI)

Given these conditions, India produced and still produces the world's most spontaneous dramatic dances. The dance is the supreme art of India, as literature was of Shakespeare's England, music of Bach's Germany, and painting of Raphael's Italy. It is hardly too much to say that Indians are born dancers. Siva, lord of the dance, is also supreme as patron of all Indian arts, the god most commonly invoked in the prayer, or *nandi*, traditionally spoken at the commencement of each Sanskrit play. For these reasons, no consideration of Indian drama can afford to overlook the dance as drama nor regard it as materially beneath the spoken play in essentially dramatic qualities.

It is, obviously, difficult to document the history of the dance, though several manuals on Indian classical dancing, especially Bharata's *Natyasastra,* exist and the sculptural record of the dance is more comprehensive in India than in any other land. Sculptures from the ninth century A.D. at the Chidambaram temple in southern India represent 108 dance poses described by Bharata. "Bharata Natyam" has been termed the most ancient and well-preserved classical dance in the world. Its dance episodes are traditionally interspersed with songs, all producing a narrative and dramatic effect. It is much alive in the twentieth century. Balasaraswathi of Madras has been the

chief exponent of this school. Rukmini Devi, pupil of Meenakashi Sundaram Pillai, is also of Madras and eminent in the even more dramatic Kathakali dance forms of southern India as well as in the Bharata Natyam. In northern India the Kathak maintains great distinction in dramatic forms. It was brought to the world's attention early in the twentieth century by Kalkaprasad Maharaj and in more recent times has been most brilliantly represented by Damayanti Joshi. Raslila, the celebrated dancer from Manipur, excels in dramatic dances dedicated to the cult of Krishna.

Most famous of all twentieth-century Indian dancers and teachers of the dance is Uday Shankar, born in 1900. As a young man he studied in Europe, dancing with Pavlova in *Radha Krishna.* The subjects of many of the chief dances by his company show their affinity with leading themes and characters of the Indian stage for a period of some two thousand years. He has created brilliantly dramatic dances on the Krishna legend and on the story of the *Ramayana.* Shankar made profound studies in Indian dramatic music. Nothing that was Indian, it seemed, escaped him. In the same performance he boldly combined elements from racy folk dances and from the more decorous and classical temple dances. Problems of the dramatic dance were approached from the opposite angle by Rabindranath Tagore, poet and playwright, who studied dance forms and inspired and encouraged dancers. He composed several dance dramas; one of his happiest and most typical creations is *Chitrangada,* based on *Chitra,* a play he had written in his early years.

India, which once discovered the soul of drama in dramatic poetry, has sustained an insight into the mysteries of drama only in the drama of the dance, where unparalleled forms have been achieved. Solo dancers of as great genius and even as great dramatic genius as those of India have long flourished in China, Korea, and Japan, but the dramatic dance with an ensemble of characters has been most brilliantly achieved in India.

The chief source for knowledge of the art dance of ancient India is the *Natyasastra,* ascribed to Bharata, of which there is a partial translation by M. M. Ghose (1951). A valuable study and interpretation of this dance tradition is given by A. K. Coomaraswamy, *The Dance of Siva* (1948). The social background of the Indian dance is examined in *The Other Mind: A Study of Dance and Life in South India* (1953) by Beryl De Zoete. A similar study is contributed by Louis Frédéric in *La Danse sacrée de l'Inde* (1956). For the present state of dancing in India, see *Dance in India* (1953) by Faubion Bowers. —H. W. W.

Indonesia. Since drama has played an essential role in Indonesian religious and social life from the earliest periods, plays cannot be understood apart from the milieu in which they developed and even today are performed. Also, unlike modern Western drama in which the spoken word is the most important element, drama in Indonesia is a composite art form incorporating prose dialogue, rhythmic narrative, songs, music, and movement patterns. As a consequence, drama tends toward stylization and reflects the practical requirements made by music, dance, puppet manipulation, and songs in performance. Drama has evolved in Indonesia primarily in three areas: Java (the eastern and central parts of the island of Java where Javanese is spoken), Sunda (the western part of the island of Java where Sundanese is spoken), and the island of Bali.

Java. The most important and most influential dramatic form in Indonesia is that which evolved out of performances in Java of *wajang kulit* (wajang means "puppet" and kulit means "leather," hence, by inference, "shadow plays by leather puppets"). Whether shadow theater originated in Java or was brought from China or India in the remote past is not certain, and its origin is not of great importance, for in its mature form wajang kulit drama owes little to outside influences. It is a unique Javanese creation unlike any other drama in the world.

Wajang kulit plays are performed by a single *dalang* ("puppeteer"), who speaks the dialogue of all characters, narrates between scenes, sings mood songs to establish the proper atmosphere, cues the accompanying *gamelan* ("musical ensemble"), and manipulates flat leather puppets before a light so as to cast stylized shadows on a white screen. The cast of any given play will require the use of fifty to sixty standard puppets out of a set of several hundred. The audience sits on both sides of the screen, so that some

PUPPETEER MOVING THE HAND OF AN OGRE KING IN A *wajang kulit* PLAY BASED ON EVENTS FROM THE *Mahabharata* (JAMES R. BRANDON, *Theatre in Southeast Asia,* HARVARD UNIVERSITY PRESS, COPYRIGHT © 1967 BY THE PRESIDENT AND FELLOWS OF HARVARD COLLEGE)

spectators see a shadow drama and some see a puppet drama. Traditionally, a play begins at eight thirty in the evening and continues, without interruption, for eight or nine hours until the gray of predawn appears in the sky. The dalang is assisted by musicians, a female singer, and an assistant who hands him puppets. The accompanying gamelan orchestra is tuned in the five-toned, or *slendro,* scale and consists of twelve or more mellow-sounding tuned sets of bronze gongs, bowls, and bars; several drums beat with the fingers; a wooden xylophone; a two-stringed fiddle; and a zither. Music underscores almost every moment of performance, and even to people not familiar with Asian music gamelan is extremely beautiful.

The earliest accounts of wajang kulit are contained in epics written at Hindu-Javanese courts in east Java in the eleventh century. The description of audiences weeping as they are caught up in the spell of shadow play performances shows that wajang kulit was already a sophisticated dramatic form. Two other theatrical forms competed for court favor at this time: *wajang beber* ("paper-scroll play") and *wajang topeng* ("masked dance play"). Characters from Hindu epics (mainly the *Ramayana* and the *Mahabharata*) were incorporated into Javanese mythology, and in their "Javanized" form they became central figures for the plays of wajang kulit. When most of Java was converted to Islam (c. fifteenth and sixteenth centuries), the dramatic content of wajang kulit was already so firmly rooted in Hindu-Javanese culture that only a few, largely inconsequential Islamic elements found their way into traditional wajang kulit plays. Refinements in performance technique and puppet carving and painting occurred continuously from the seventeenth to the twentieth century, and, while the same original cast of mythological characters remained largely unaltered through the centuries, new plays placing these heroes in new situations were constantly being composed and performed. Wajang kulit is the most widely performed type of play in Java (five thousand or more dalang perform today), and is a highly revered expression of traditional Javanese culture.

The wajang kulit repertory is composed of four cycles of plays known collectively as *purwa* (literally, "original") plays. The first, or "animistic," cycle contains about half-a-dozen plays that dramatize animistic legends, particularly those concerning the creation of plants and animals. In the second cycle, another half-dozen plays depict the victory of Ardjuna Sasra Bau over the ogre king Rawana (in one of Rawana's former lives). The third cycle, of eighteen plays, dramatizes Prince Rama's banishment from the Kingdom of Ayodya, the kidnapping of Rama's wife, Sinta, by King Rawana, and Rama's eventual rescue of her in a long and arduous battle during which King Rawana is slain. Plays of these first three cycles are few in number and are only occasionally performed. The heart of the wajang kulit repertory is, and has been for ten centuries, the fourth cycle—the Pandawa cycle. There are at least 150 Pandawa cycle plays, and performances of these dramas account for perhaps 95 percent of the shadow play productions in Java.

The nuclear conflict dramatized in plays of the Pandawa cycle concerns the struggle for control of the "jeweled kingdom" of Astina between the five virtuous Pandawa brothers (Judistira, Bima, Ardjuna, Nakula, and Sadewa) and their cousins and enemies, the ninety-nine Kurawa brothers led by the eldest, King Durjudana. This basic story comes from Indian and Javanese versions of the *Mahabharata* epic. About fifty plays in the Pandawa cycle are based on events taken directly from the epics and are called *pokok,* or "trunk," plays. *Bima Bungkus* ("The Birth of Bima"), *Parta Krama* ("The Wedding of Ardjuna and Sumbadra"), and *Bale Segala-gala* ("The Exile of the Pandawas"), for example, dramatize well-known events in the Javanese and Indian epics. Events in the epic are followed quite closely in *Karna Tanding* (*The Death of Karna*), one of the twelve plays dramatizing The Great War (*Bratajuda*), which concludes the epic and in which many Kurawas, Pandawas, and their allies are slain.

The largest number of Pandawa plays, however—more than one hundred—do not dramatize the epics but are instead either elaborations of minor events slightly touched upon in the epics or completely new creations. The bulk of these plays shows the Pandawas during their Golden Age (following their banishment from Astina and before the slaughter of The Great War) when they sported at the palace of Amarta, which was, for a few short years, the envy of the world. Young, exuberant, supremely confident, the Pandawas are pictured as the brilliant heroes of a seemingly endless series of chivalric exploits. They are the favorites of the gods, and they bring to Amarta as their brides scores of the most beautiful maidens in Java. They slay ogre kings and at every turn best their envious Kurawa cousins. When the gods are in danger, it is to the Pandawas that they turn for help. The plays are lofty in sentiment and aristocratic in mien (except for comic scenes) and are composed of royal audiences, romantic episodes, abductions, battles, and meetings with seers. The mythological cast of characters—gods, nobility (and their clown-servants), ogres, and holy seers—excludes merchants and peasants. Plays about common life, like the "domestic" plays of Japanese *bunraku* puppet drama, did not develop in wajang kulit.

Owing little or nothing to epic sources, these new plays about the Pandawas, set mostly during the Golden Age, are known as *tjarangan* (literally, "branch") plays. Branch plays may have been composed as early as the tenth century; by the seventeenth century they exhibited a unique dramatic structure in which the old epic-derived, two-sided conflict between Pandawas and Kurawas was largely replaced by a three-sided struggle among Pandawas, Kurawas, and an ogre kingdom. The ogre kingdom was not Javanese (as both Pandawas and Kurawas were) but a foreign or "overseas" (*sabrangan*) kingdom. One of the key ogre figures of these newer plays came to be the puppet Tjakil (literally, "Fang," because of his protruding tusks). As a lieutenant of the ogre king, Tjakil is dispatched to Java to fulfill a mission for his king, and, after meeting Ardjuna (or one of his sons) in the forest, he is slain with his own dagger. The battle in which he is killed is called the flower battle (*perang kembang*), and of all of the six to eight battle scenes in a play, this one is the most beautiful, the most elaborate, and the most demanding of the dalang's skills. Tjakil, created in 1630, is not mentioned in any epic nor in Javanese mythology. He is entirely a theatrical creation whose function is simply to appear in the same scenes in play after play. We can imagine that as the dalang created more and more plays for their Pandawa heroes, it proved difficult to invent new situations within the already fixed patterns of Pandawa-Kurawa relationships. It must have been easier to invent a whole new cast of antagonists headed by the ogre Tjakil, thus bringing about a radical reorientation of the drama.

The trend in both trunk and branch plays was toward ever greater Javanization of the wajang world. This is a complex matter, but a few examples illustrate this tendency: Drupadi's marriage to the five Pandawas, repugnant to the Javanese, was changed so that she was married only to Judistira; the Great Mountain of the gods, Mahameru, became associated in the popular mind with Java's highest mountain; the ancient Javanese earth deity, Ismaja, materialized in wajang as the god-clown-servant Semar, who serves and advises his Pandawa masters and who is even more powerful than the god Guru (Shiva); the traditional placement of rooms in a Javanese palace was precisely reflected in the arrangement of the first four fixed scenes of the classic wajang play; even dress, speech, and manners of the puppet figures followed Javanese court customs.

In general, it can be said that the Pandawas represent the "good" side in wajang drama, while the Kurawas are, at the least, "less good," and the ogres are the "bad" side. By and large, the Pandawas are refined and virtuous, and they are favored by the gods and eventually defeat the Kurawas; the Kurawas, in crucial moments, are motivated by greed, lust, and chicanery; and the crude, stupid ogres are driven by their need to satisfy their baser instincts. Yet one of the most characteristic features of the world view presented in wajang is that both admirable and undesirable traits reside side by side in most characters.

The god Kresna assists the Pandawas, yet he lies to and tricks the Kurawas constantly. Ardjuna, third of the Pandawas, "shining warrior," and perhaps the chief wajang hero (he and his sons Abimanju and

PUPPETS REPRESENTING KARNA AND ARDJUNA FIGHTING WITH DRAWN DAGGERS (JAMES R. BRANDON, *Theatre in Southeast Asia,* HARVARD UNIVERSITY PRESS, COPYRIGHT © 1967 BY THE PRESIDENT AND FELLOWS OF HARVARD COLLEGE)

Irawan are central figures in forty plays), is modest, graceful, the beau ideal of women, and invincible in battle, yet he is utterly incapable of human sympathy. Bima, the second Pandawa brother, is the strongest of all wajang warriors, implacable once his mind is made up, and "pillar of the kingdom," yet he is half-ogre, blunt, and so proud he will not even bow before the gods. Durjudana, eldest of the Kurawas and king of Astina, is himself a powerful, just, and generous ruler, though he is the Pandawas' chief opponent. The enormous ogre Kumbakarna, from the Rama cycle, is admired for his loyalty. Judistira, eldest of the Pandawas, so pure in spirit that "his blood flows white," is helpless in dealing with practical matters and must rely upon his more active brothers and allies to protect him. In short, the hundreds of wajang plays present a complex view of the world rich in ethical and moral subtleties.

These plays, grouped loosely according to theme and subject matter, are performed on special occasions (never in public theaters or with public ticket sales) with a sponsor selecting a play that suits the occasion. One major type of play, *Wahju Purba Sedjati* (*The Reincarnation of Rama*), for example, which depicts the receipt of a gift from the gods, would be requested when the host has asked, in the form of a prayer, some favor of the gods, has received his request, and now wishes to repay the gods. This production is called a *kaul,* or "thanksgiving" performance. (Similar performances are seen in Thailand and Cambodia.) Such a play is philosophic in tone, and battle scenes are less important here than in other kinds of plays. Marriage plays are another type, performed for wedding celebrations and, occasionally, for Moslem circumcision celebrations. There are dozens of famous wedding plays, of which *Irawan Rabi* (*Irawan's Wedding*) is one of the most admired. They tend to be light in tone and filled with the joking of the clowns. A typical plot will have a princess abducted, either by the lover-hero or his rival, followed by numerous complications, and concluding with the lovers happily united. Time and again the Kurawas have their hearts set on a bride only to have one of the Pandawas spirit her away. Another group of plays concerning affairs of state and the fate of kingdoms is serious in tone and contains lengthy battle scenes. They are suitable for performance on public holidays and are often produced at the palaces in Jogjakarta and Surakarta. *Karna Tanding* and the other plays of The Great War are of this type.

Wajang kulit's close ties with Javanese religious beliefs are manifested in many ways. As assurance of a fruitful harvest, at rice-planting time a village may sponsor a play from the animistic cycle about the Goddess of Rice, Dewi Sri. Another play, *Purwakala* or *Murwakala* ("The Birth of Kala"), combines animistic and Hindu-derived religious elements and is performed specifically as an animistic exorcism to protect children born under certain magically inauspicious circumstances from being devoured by the voracious god Kala. In the play, the god Guru descends to earth with Semar and other gods and invents gamelan music and wajang kulit. He does this for religious reasons; in the play the character of the god Guru speaks a prayer that will ward off the dangerous Kala. Today, when a dalang speaks the words of this prayer, it is as if the dalang were a priest pronouncing the blessing of the highest god. All who hear this prayer are believed to be safe from harm. According to some interpretations, one reason a shadow play lasts till dawn is that the audience would face great danger from evil spirits if they returned home at night, but by dawn the malignant spirits have retired and man is more secure. A dalang is required to speak several prayers before a performance, and offerings to the spirits are made by the host. Such magically powerful plays as *Purwakala* may be performed only by the oldest and wisest dalang, for an error in performance is believed to cause all manner of misfortune. For the same reason the tragic plays of the *Bratajuda*, in which so many of the kings and princes of Java's mythological age meet their death, were rarely performed before World War II. Prayers and fairly expensive offerings must be made when the puppet figure of the god Guru, ruler of the kingdom of the gods, is carved out of water-buffalo leather and again when the figure is painted and covered with precious gold leaf.

It is possible to interpret wajang drama in a variety of ways. The plays can be viewed as vehicles for royal propaganda, for a striking feature of them is the extravagant and constant praise of Javanese kings and the mythological Javanese kingdoms of Astina, Amarta, and Dwarawati. The Pandawa cycle dramatizes the descent of Javanese kingship through twelve generations, from the god Wisnu to Ardjuna's grandson, Parikesit. Parikesit, in turn, in another cycle of plays dramatized in *wajang madya* ("middle plays"), is shown to be the father of Jadajana, considered in Javanese dynastic histories the first historical king of Java. Other forms of the shadow play dramatize succeeding generations of Javanese kings down to the reigning ruler of Surakarta in the 1920's, thus popularizing through the shadow play the notion that Javanese kingship has continued unbroken from the age of mythology to the present. Wajang kulit plays specifically dramatize Wisnu's reincarnations—first as Ardjuna Sasra Bau, then as Rama, and finally as Kresna and Ardjuna—thus demonstrating that by the incarnation of the god's powers in succeeding generations the right of Javanese kingship has been legitimately passed on. (This concept is purely Javanese; there is no hint in India of any such linkage between the *Ramayana* and the *Mahabharata*.)

Interpreting wajang drama on a symbolic level, the screen may represent heaven, the stage earth, the puppets man, and the dalang God bringing man to life. Or, the first part of the play may be said to show man's youth when he acts unthinkingly; the second part of the play shows man in middle age striving to conquer external evils (represented by Tjakil and his ogre companions); while the final part of the play shows man in maturity, having reached an ultimate, spiritual harmony after defeating his enemies. In another interpretation the puppets and their actions on stage are viewed only as an external manifestation of the inner conflict that rages in every man's spirit, with the Pandawas standing for parts of a single personality—Bima is pure will, Ardjuna introspection, Judistira selflessness, and so on. Mysticism plays an important role in Javanese religious experience, and the number of possible symbolic interpretations of wajang drama is virtually endless. But most members

of a shadow play audience view a performance in more concrete terms, and their appreciation of wajang drama does not depend upon such abstract interpretations.

The most comprehensive compilation of standard plays in wajang kulit's mythological repertory contains 177 titles, of which 147 are from the Pandawa cycle. But this is only a partial list. It is difficult to say how many wajang plays there are, for few are preserved in fully written form. The shadow play began in the oral tradition and remains largely within that tradition today. (The few complete wajang texts that have been published in recent decades are intended mainly for the reading public.) What has existed in the past are brief scenarios, from which a dalang takes his basic plot. Every wajang play is divided into three parts, named after the three modes of gamelan music played in them. In theory, each part is supposed to last for three hours. Within each part certain standard scenes occur with great regularity. Part One (*patet nem*) is the most fully structured, almost always containing in this order the following: first audience scene, in which the king discusses a problem with his ministers and orders his army dispatched; inner palace scene, in which the king relates to his wife (or wives) what has occurred and then meditates; outer audience scene, in which the king's army is ordered to march; forest-clearing battle, in which the marching army clears a path through the forest; foreign audience scene, similar to the first but set in a second kingdom (often an overseas, ogre kingdom); the concluding opening-skirmish scene, in which armies of the two kingdoms meet and one is put to flight without loss of life.

Part Two (*patet sanga*) opens with a description of earthquakes and floods that are ravaging the earth, the consequence of the universe being disturbed by the effects of the meditation of the major Pandawa hero in the play (often Ardjuna). This description is immediately followed by a long scene of jokes and buffoonery by Semar, Gareng, and Petruk, the three clown-servants of the hero. The hero makes his first entrance in a hermitage scene, where, accompanied by the clowns, he receives advice from a holy seer. The flower battle follows. The number and types of scenes included in Part Three (*patet manjura*) are determined by the requirements of the plot, but as the play reaches its climax, several scenes normally occur: battle of Part Three, in which the rival king's plans are foiled by the hero or his allies; great battle scene, in which the rival king, hearing the news of his army's defeat, leads his forces into battle himself and is decisively defeated (and often killed); final audience scene, in which the victorious king and his allies celebrate their victory.

This is the classic or "textbook" structure of a play which every student dalang learns. Branch plays tend to fit within its pattern to a remarkable degree; trunk plays, however, do not include the flower battle nor, usually, an ogre kingdom. It will be noted that only the beginning of the plot and its resolution are covered in these dozen standard scenes; that is, these scenes reveal the structure of the typical play, not its content. The raveling and unraveling of the plot occur in about an equal number of additional, unspecified scenes.

A common characteristic of literature in the oral

tradition everywhere in the world is the use of set epithets (Homer's "rosy-fingered dawn," for example). In wajang many such epithets occur but their complete range has not yet been studied. The most important of these have, within the past few decades, been written down and published in textbooks for student dalang. Major kingdoms and the attributes of chief wajang figures are described in set phrases. There are standard dialogue sequences, incorporating formula phrases for greeting a king, ordering the troops to march, and challenging warriors to battle. There is a set scene in which a son pledges fealty to his father the king. Fixed terms are appropriate for speaking to a king, a god, and a servant.

There is also an elaborately worked-out system of matching certain instrumental melodies, songs, and puppet movements to certain scenes, characters, and actions in a play. A major textbook lists how and where 120 instrumental melodies and thirty-five to forty songs should be used. For example, in the first audience scene the instrumental melody named "Kabor" is suitable if the kingdom is Astina, but the melody "Kawit" if the kingdom is Amarta, and "Krawitan" if the kingdom is Dwarawati. The dalang must sing the song "Ada-ada Budalan Mataraman" when the troops are ordered to march in the outer audience scene, but he must use the song "Ada-ada Astakuswala Sanga" at the particular moment in the flower battle when the hero draws his bow. These musical selections are not appropriate for any other occasion in a play. In other cases the dalang may choose between several possible musical selections (one of five instrumental melodies, for example, for the marching army's exit).

A dalang also learns thirty to forty model battle scenes (ogre versus refined warrior, female versus god, monkey versus muscular warrior, etc.) that contain the over one hundred standard biting, kicking, striking, and throwing movements. There are several basic types of puppet figures. Each moves and fights in a different way: arms of a small figure hang loosely, muscular figures absorb blows while small figures avoid them, ogres roll on the ground and throw rocks, monkeys bite, and so on. Elaborate battle scenes are improvised around these models for performance. Furthermore, the pitch of music within each part of the play rises, and the dalang, in delivering narration or dialogue, matches his voice to this pitch. Similarly, each character has a traditional voice pitch (Bima is very low; Kresna is high), which the dalang must scrupulously follow.

Since dialogue, narration, songs, music, and puppet movements are not indicated in a scenario, a complete play normally exists only in oral form, that is, in performance when the dalang fills out the skeleton of the plot by drawing upon his knowledge of these various traditional dramatic patterns. It might be thought that with so many standardized parts wajang plays would tend to lack individuality, but the opposite is true, for the system actually allows for great variation. In a long wajang play many situations are not covered by tradition; textbooks present only traditional usage, not laws, and a good dalang will not hesitate to break tradition if it seems best to do so. Since no two dalang are alike, no two plays will ever be alike—individual variations occur in structure, plot, interpretation of character, and in the

host of spontaneous details that comprise a performance.

During wajang kulit's long history, a dozen other cycles of shadow plays came into being that closely copied both its dramatic form and techniques of performance. Different periods of Javanese history were dramatized, and for each new cycle of plays a different set of puppet characters was created. Some of these newer shadow plays are: *wajang madya* (previously mentioned); *wajang gedog*, about the legendary Javanese hero Prince Pandji, who is known as Inao in Thai, Cambodian, and Burmese drama; *wajang klitik*, about Damarwulan of the Madjapahit era (c. 1300–1500) and portrayed by flat wooden shadow puppets; *wajang Menak*, about the Islamic hero Amir Hamzah; *wajang Djawa*, about Prince Diponegoro and his revolt against the Dutch in the Java war of 1825–1830; *wajang Pantja Sila*, a modern form in which the five Pandawas symbolize the five principles, the Pantja Sila, of Indonesian national ideology; and *wajang suluh*, about contemporary events as they are portrayed by realistic puppets. None of these forms has ever become very popular, and performances are rarely given.

Wajang orang or *wajang wong*, literally "human wajang," is a dance drama in which the traditional Pandawa and Rama plays taken from wajang kulit shadow drama are performed by actor-dancers in the style of classic Javanese court dance. This form of dance drama originated in the Surakarta court between the eighteenth and nineteenth centuries, although classic dance was widely performed at court much earlier. Plays are shortened to three or four hours; most narration and mood songs are cut in order to emphasize dramatic action. Full-length performances are no longer seen at court, but commercial troupes (first established in the late nineteenth century) regularly perform in about thirty major cities.

Wajang golek, literally "doll-puppet wajang," has been for several hundred years an important medium for performing Islamic stories centering on the exploits of Amir Hamzah. The play cycle is the same as the shadow play cycle performed in wajang Menak. The structure of wajang golek closely follows that of wajang kulit: performances last nine hours, gamelan accompanies performance, and basic performance techniques are similar to wajang kulit. A screen, however, is not used in wajang golek; therefore, the figures of the doll-puppets are seen in a three-dimensional view. Several dozen dalang perform wajang golek west and south of Jogjakarta.

In addition to traditional wajang kulit and its derivative dramatic forms, there are two forms of popular drama that reflect twentieth-century interests: *ketoprak* (from *ketok* and *keprak*, onomatopoetic words for the sounds of rice pounding) and *ludruk* (developed from a folk dance play called *ludruk besutan*). Both are spoken dramas in which music and dance are only incidental elements. Most ketoprak plays dramatize events in Javanese history and Islamic stories. Plays tend to be melodramatic and romantic in style; nationalist themes are important. In spite of the fact that ludruk performers are all men, ludruk plays are the most modern and realistic of any in the professional theater in Java today. Ludruk plays focus on contemporary life in Java's large

A BATTLE POSE FROM A JAVANESE *wajang orang* (EMBASSY OF INDONESIA; JAMES R. BRANDON, *Theatre in Southeast Asia*, HARVARD UNIVERSITY PRESS, COPYRIGHT ©1967 BY THE PRESIDENT AND FELLOWS OF HARVARD COLLEGE)

cities, especially dramatizing class conflicts arising from marriage between partners from different social strata. There are perhaps 120 professional ketoprak troupes and 30 professional ludruk troupes in Java.

Sunda. The area of west Java where Sundanese is spoken has two major dramatic forms: wajang golek and *sandiwara*. Wajang golek in Sunda represents a combination of doll-puppet performance techniques and the Javanese wajang kulit repertory. The Pandawa cycle makes up the bulk of plays performed, but somewhat more Rama-cycle plays are performed in Sunda than in Java's wajang kulit, and several Sundanese legends are also dramatized. A Sundanese gamelan ensemble accompanies the performance, playing Sundanese melodies. The language of performance is Sundanese, except for some of the traditional songs that are still sung in the original old Javanese lyrics of the twelfth and thirteenth centuries. In general, the religious and social functions and the artistic prestige of wajang golek in Sunda parallel those of wajang kulit in Java.

Sandiwara ("drama" or "play") companies are popular, commercial troupes that perform not only wajang orang dance dramas about the Pandawas (in Sundanese language and with Sundanese dance and gamelan music) but also plays of Indonesian history, Islamic plays, and some modern dramas as well. Adaptations of Western plays and of current foreign motion pictures are commonly staged; *Hamlet*, for example, is a perennial favorite with some troupes and is revived every few years. Some forty professional sandiwara troupes are active at present.

Bali. The drama of Bali is inseparably wedded to dance, music, and religious ceremony. It is possible, however, to single out for special consideration here several forms of Balinese performing arts in which the dramatic element is of major importance. Balinese wajang kulit is one such dramatic form, and it developed either concurrently with Javanese wajang kulit in prehistoric times or came from Java at a later period. In any case, between the eleventh and sixteenth centuries Bali was ruled by Javanese princes, and a great influx of Javanese cultural and artistic traditions left a lasting imprint on the arts of Bali. Javanese epic poems were written on palm leaves, recopied periodically, and preserved in Bali until the present day, while almost every copy on the island of Java has been destroyed. Our knowledge of ancient Javanese literature is based on what is preserved in Bali. Some of these writings in wajang play form represent the oldest written evidence we have of play scenarios in Indonesia. The repertory of Balinese wajang kulit includes the standard Pandawa plays, Rama plays (which are very popular), and several local Balinese legends. The fact that Balinese shadow puppets are less refined in their carving, cruder in outline, and more realistic than the Javanese puppets of today leads most experts to believe that the Balinese puppets represent the older style of puppet used in Java prior to Islamic contact. Balinese performance is accompanied by four xylophones (*gender*), which form a gamelan group that is small compared to the large ensembles used in Java. Nine-hour performances are known, but four to five hours is more usual. On some occasions performance is during the daytime. No screen is used and the dalang performs with naked torso, for he functions as a Brahman priest and conducts the performance as a religious rite rather than as audience entertainment.

The *barong* dance drama is better known as the "trance dance" to visitors of Bali. Its nickname derives from the climax of the play in which performers press sharp daggers against their chests and roll on the ground in a frenzied trance. They are caught between two powerful forces—the evil magic of the witch Rangda, who tries to drive the daggers into their bodies, and the beneficent powers of the lion, the Barong, who attempts to shield them from Rangda's demonic spell. The barong play, like the drama *Tjalonarang* ("Tjalonarang the Witch"), dramatizes the central thesis of Balinese religion: that good and evil spirits exist which constantly struggle for dominance, and when malevolent spirits become too powerful, man must perform religious acts to restore to the village a proper balance between good and evil. A performance of the barong play is one such religious act and makes the sponsoring village safe for a time. The cast of characters is drawn from various sources —Rangda may be purely Balinese or derived from

BRAHMAN PRIEST ENTERS FROM THE TEMPLE TO END A *barong* PERFORMANCE (JAMES R. BRANDON, *Theatre in Southeast Asia*, HARVARD UNIVERSITY PRESS, COPYRIGHT © 1967 BY THE PRESIDENT AND FELLOWS OF HARVARD COLLEGE)

the Hindu goddess Durga; the Barong (especially its outer lion form) seems certain to have originated in China; two figures (Kunti and Sadewa) are contained in the *Mahabharata* epic; a monkey figure in the forest probably derives from the *Ramayana* epic; and Shiva is from the Hindu pantheon of gods. Yet, irrespective of their origins, these characters have been localized, adapted, and made a part of a purely Balinese cosmology. The process of localizing borrowed dramatic figures, noted in Javanese wajang kulit and evident here, is a widespread phenomenon in the drama of Southeast Asia that belies any superficial description of the drama as merely dramatizations of foreign stories.

Balinese wajang wong is a counterpart of Javanese wajang orang. It is a dance drama in which most characters wear masks and in which recitation of poetic passages constitutes a major element of performance. Plays of the Rama cycle make up the bulk of this repertory, while plays of the Pandawa cycle are done in a similar style in a play form called *wajang purwa* (literally, "original plays").

Plays based on the Pandji stories are dramatized in *ardja*, a type of operetta. Ardja troupes are professional (while barong and wajang wong troupes are folk troupes), and they perform wherever hired. Attractive girls often play the role of Pandji and other refined heroes. This custom is probably borrowed from professional Javanese wajang orang troupes, whose most attractive actresses play Ardjuna and his

sons. A play is alternately sung and danced, and the emphasis is on romantic byplay, joking by the clowns, and fast action. While Pandji plays form the core of the repertory, the Pandawa and Rama cycles and even Javanese historical legends and Chinese love tales are performed occasionally.

Translations of three Javanese wajang kulit plays as well as a general description of performance techniques appear in *On Thrones of Gold: Three Javanese Shadow Plays* (1969), edited by James R. Brandon. The origins and meaning of Javanese drama are examined in fascinating detail in W. H. Rassers' *Panji, The Culture Hero: A Structural Study of Religion in Java* (1959); a general description and analysis of plays is found in James R. Brandon's *Theatre in Southeast Asia* (1967). The relation of wajang drama to Indonesian culture is examined from a Western point of view in Benedict Anderson's *Mythology and the Tolerance of the Javanese* (1965) and by an eminent patron of Javanese arts, the late Mangkunagoro VII of Surakarta, in *On the Wayang Kulit (Purwa) and Its Symbolic and Mystical Elements* (1957), translated by Claire Holt. R. L. Mellema's *Wayang Puppets: Carving, Colouring, and Symbolism* (1954), translated by Mantle Hood, describes puppets and their iconography.

Two important books describe gamelan music and its use in Indonesian drama: Jaap Kunst's *Music in Java: Its History, Its Theory, and Its Technique* (2nd ed., 1949) 2 vols., translated by Emile van Loo, and

Mantle Hood's *The Nuclear Theme As Determinant of Patet in Javanese Music* (1954).

Miguel Covarrubias' *Island of Bali* (1950) gives a superb picture of the place of the performing arts in Balinese society, and Beryl de Zoete and Walter Spies's *Dance and Drama in Bali* (1938) is an encyclopedic and fascinating description of the scores of theater forms found on Bali.—J. R. B.

Infernal Machine, The (La Machine infernale, 1934). A tragedy by Jean COCTEAU. Cocteau's original treatment of the Oedipus theme in *The Infernal Machine* focuses on the machinations and ingeniousness of the gods of Olympus in destroying man. Against the machine of the gods, in its perpetration of woe and death, there is no defense. Oedipus is a prototype and the most famous searcher for truth behind the lies and illusions of life.

The Infernal Machine was produced by Louis Jouvet in 1934. The original settings, designed by Christian Bérard, were used in the revival in 1954. The first act, specifically inspired by *Hamlet,* transpires on the ramparts of Thebes, where some soldiers are anxiously awaiting the nightly return of the ghost of the assassinated king. The second act is set in the countryside where young Oedipus, who has just killed his father, meets the Sphinx. The third act is the marriage night of Jocasta and Oedipus. In the fourth act, Cocteau adheres closely to the Sophoclean model: Oedipus learns of his crimes and puts out his eyes; Jocasta hangs herself; and the daughter Antigone goes with her father into exile.

The pure inventions of Cocteau remain the strongest elements of *The Infernal Machine*: his concept of the Sphinx as a young girl who is weary of killing and in love with Oedipus; the marriage night of Jocasta and Oedipus where the bed of incest appears almost in the form of a funeral pyre; and the reappearance of Jocasta in the last act where, invisible to all except Oedipus, she leads him to his destiny.

The Infernal Machine has been translated by Carl Wildman (1936).—W. F.

Ingannati, Gli ("The Deceived Ones," 1531). An anonymous Italian comedy. Written "in only three days," as the Prologue asserts, the play is the work of a group of academicians, the Intronati of Siena. Their intention in writing the play was to ask their ladies' pardon for another play, which had been presented earlier on the night of Epiphany, in which each one had pretended to burn up all the souvenirs of his own lady. The protagonist is Lelia, who, to regain the love of Flaminio, dresses as a man and enters his service. Flaminio is enamored of Isabella and employs Lelia as his messenger of love. Isabella, however, falls in love with Lelia, believing her to be a man. At last the sudden appearance of Fabrizio, twin brother of Lelia, brings the action to its natural conclusion: the marriage of Fabrizio and Isabella, on the one hand, and that of Flaminio and the loyal Lelia, on the other. These marriages take place after a series of comic misunderstandings. Also contributing to the humor of the comedy are two old men, Gherardo and Virginio; the colorful world of the servants; and characters drawn from contemporary life, such as the Spanish soldier and the pedant.

A SCENE FROM JEAN COCTEAU'S *The Infernal Machine* (FRENCH CULTURAL SERVICES)

The play is very rich in ideas and situations and is written in a lively realistic prose. From *Gli Ingannati* comes a long series of translations, imitations, and rewritings, directly or indirectly indebted to it. Some of them are *Gli Scambi* by B. Bulgarini, *Gli Inganni* by N. Secchi, *Les Abusés* by C. Estienne, *Los Engañados* by Lope de Rueda, *Laelia,* performed in Latin at Cambridge, and *Twelfth Night* by Shakespeare.—L. L.

Inge, William (1913–). American playwright. Inge was born in Independence, Kansas, to Luther C. and Maude Sarah Inge. His mother's family included a number of people in the theater, and the boy decided early to be an actor. He majored in drama at the University of Kansas and both before and after graduation worked with stock companies and traveling shows. He went on to get an M.A. at George Peabody Teachers College, taught in high schools for a few years, and then at Stephens College in Missouri. In 1943 he left Stephens to become drama critic for the St. Louis *Star Times,* and the experience convinced him that he could succeed as a playwright. An interview with Tennessee Williams following the successful Chicago opening of Williams' *The Glass Menagerie* (1944) acted as the final stimulus, and since then Inge has devoted himself to playwriting.

Come Back, Little Sheba (1950) was the second of Inge's plays to be produced, and it brought him immediate fame. Dealing with a near-tragic crisis in the lives of an alcoholic struggling to regain some dignity and his slatternly, pathetic wife, the play displays Inge's skill in building a tightly constructed drama around a simple situation and fully realized characters. *Picnic* (1953) deals with the effect a virile vagabond has on a group of women in a small Kansas

WILLIAM INGE (WIDE WORLD PHOTOS)

town. *Bus Stop* (1955), concerned with a group of people temporarily stranded in a small café, and *The Dark at the Top of the Stairs* (1957), a somber picture of a family haunted by prejudices, regrets, and unfocused fears, also profit from Inge's knowledge of small-town life and his ability to give form to the deep, though unsensational, yearnings and guilts of simple people. In all these plays, and in his film script for *Splendor in the Grass* (1961), Inge demonstrated his control of well-made realistic drama. In more recent works—*A Loss of Roses* (1960), *Natural Affection* (1963), and *Where's Daddy?* (1966)—he has tried to deal with more sensational subjects but has failed to attain the fusion of observations and sound plot structure that gave strength to his earlier work.

There is no standard edition of Inge's work. A full discussion can be found in R. B. Shuman's *William Inge* (1965).—M. L.

Inspector General, The (Revizor, 1836). A comedy in five acts by Nikolai GOGOL. Although the censors first rejected *The Inspector General,* Tsar Nicholas I liked this comedy so much that he overruled them and the play was produced at the Alexandrinsky Theater in St. Petersburg a few months after it was written.

In the play the officials of a small provincial town are warned by reports that an inspector general is coming to their town incognito to check up on them. In their panic they are convinced that Khlestakov, a petty clerk from St. Petersburg who is staying at the local inn after having lost all his money in a card game, is the dreaded inspector in disguise. To stop him from reporting the corruption and bribery rampant in their local government and from listening to the complaints of the townspeople, the officials wine and dine Khlestakov. At first surprised, he soon recovers and takes advantage of the situation. He asks each official for a loan. Having proposed to the mayor's daughter and collected more loans from the merchants, Khlestakov then leaves town just before he is exposed by the postmaster, who opens a letter Khlestakov has written to a friend explaining the whole situation. The play ends with the mayor and all the officials bewailing their mistake when they learn about the arrival of the real inspector general.

Probably no single play has had as great an influence on the theater of a country as *The Inspector General* had on the Russian theater. There were such violent protests from the civil servants, however, that even after the play had been approved by the censors, some cuts had to be made in future performances. Some people, however, went on insisting that it was still a calumny against the regime, while others proclaimed it as a truthful and lively picture of the national scene, a useful exposure of existing evils, and a great piece of "critical realism," as characterized by the social-minded critic Vissarion Belinsky. Indeed, the impact of the play was so strong that Gogol, an extremely insecure man, became frightened and lamely tried to explain what he had had in mind when he wrote the play. When reproached with the fact that there were only villains and freaks in the play and not one noble hero, Gogol replied that his hero was laughter and that the real inspector general, who arrives after Khlestakov is exposed, represents divine justice and therefore his play must be considered deeply religious. He announced publicly that he was unconditionally loyal to the regime, which he considered established by God, and that he was only criticizing the unworthy individuals who had infiltrated the administration and were now abusing their power.

Whatever Gogol's real intentions were, *The Inspector General* has been variously interpreted by critics, stage directors, and actors. Some, for instance, see in Khlestakov an arrogant, calculating imposter, while others see just an empty-headed, happy-go-lucky man who takes advantage of the cupidity and stupidity of others. Still others see in him a picture of a nonentity automatically filling the position of power conferred upon him. There have also been endless arguments about whether this is an accurate picture of Russia in the 1830's or a whimsical caricature. Soviet critics interpret the play as the castigation of the tsarist regime and apply to it Belinsky's term "critical realism" (as opposed to the Socialist Realism of the authors who praise the "good" Soviet regime under which they write).

Today, however, such arguments seem pointless. The tsarist regime is dead, but the ideas raised in *The Inspector General* are still very much alive everywhere, perhaps especially under the rule of the Soviet superbureaucrats. *The Inspector General* is really a much greater play with much vaster implications than even many of its admirers have suggested, although the adjective "realistic" hardly applies to this play.

The Inspector General has been translated by Andrew R. MacAndrew in *19th Century Russian Drama* (1963).—A. MACA.

interlude. Court drama of a comic nature, called the interlude in England, the *intermezzo* in Italy, the *entremés* in Spain, and the *entremets* in France. The interlude is considered a transitional form between the English miracle and morality plays of the middle ages and fully developed Elizabethan drama. During the Tudor reign, interludes written by John Heywood (c. 1497–c. 1580) were performed by the Players of the King's Interludes. They are brief skits, or dialogues, designed to entertain royalty between courses of a long banquet. During the same time, didactic interludes, written in Latin and with an edifying moral, were given in English public schools.

In early Spanish theater (fifteenth century), the entremés was played between the acts of a long play. They are short, comic pieces, often ending in music and dance. The entremés later developed into a one-act play, the most famous of which were written by Cervantes and Luis Quiñones de Benevente.

In the Italian court of the fifteenth century, intermezzi were performed as short accompaniments to the popular pastoral plays, with the actors often costumed as shepherds and shepherdesses. At first simple pieces, they became more complex as additional actors and elaborate scenery were added. In its most developed form, the intermezzo is a MASQUE.

intermezzo. See INTERLUDE.

In the Shadow of the Glen (1903). A one-act play by John Millington SYNGE. Based upon an incident Synge heard from an old storyteller in Aran, *In the Shadow of the Glen* parallels the folk tale common in many countries about a jealous old husband who pretends death in the hope of trapping his faithless young wife. In Synge's play, Nora, the central char-

acter, is an imaginative young woman who has become hopelessly frustrated by her loveless marriage to an ill-tempered old farmer, Dan Burke. While Dan is stretched out under a sheet in a mock wake, Nora, who up to this point has been unfaithful in spirit, not body, is confronted by two men who commiserate with the "widow" and offer to take Dan's place. One is Michael Dara, a timid and nervous neighbor whom she rejects because he will probably turn sour like Dan; the other is the strange young Tramp who wanders in out of the rain full of poetic talk about the freedom and beauty of life on the road, and she is obviously attracted to him. But before any attachments can develop, in a typical Synge scene combining broad farce and sharp irony, the "dead" Dan sneezes under the sheet and jumps out in a rage, threatens Nora with a stick and orders her out of the house. Whereupon she condemns Dan to his mean and black life and goes off with the Tramp to her perilous freedom.—D. K.

In the Zone. See S.S. GLENCAIRN.

Ion (421–408 B.C.). A tragicomedy by EURIPIDES. Long before the play begins, Creusa, a daughter of the Athenian king Erechtheus, has abandoned her infant son by Apollo. Unknown to her, the god has arranged for his son's rescue, and the boy, Ion, has grown to young manhood as an attendant in Apollo's temple at Delphi. Creusa is now married to Xuthus, who has come with her to inquire of Apollo's oracle how they may have children. Xuthus is told to accept the next man he meets as his son—and he meets Ion. Creusa, assuming that Ion must be an illegitimate son who will now supplant any that she may bear her husband, tries to poison him. She is about to be punished with death when the old priestess proves with certain tokens that Creusa is Ion's mother. Xuthus, still imagining that the boy is *his* son, intends to make him his heir. Athena greets the youth as ruler of Athens, through his mother's blood, and ancestor-to-be of the Ionians.

Euripides, as always, shows great skill in setting the emotional tone of the play at the beginning. That tone is the lighthearted one of tragicomedy. We feel pity for Creusa, certainly, but no fear of anyone, not even the gods. Hermes' monologue, quite unemotional, tells us that all will be well. A charming monody follows as Ion sweeps the temple and shoos the birds away. Then the Chorus of Athenian women sing an equally graceful song as they dart here and there admiring the decorations of the temple. This is a uniquely lighthearted beginning—and that lightheartedness seems to continue through the play except for the scenes with Creusa, who longs for the child she has lost and feels betrayed by Apollo. She is genuinely tragic until the recognition scene.

Such irony as there is seems unusually gentle for Euripides. It is hard to be very much stirred even by the attempted poisoning when the only victim is a dove, and the messenger spends more time describing the tapestries than the poisoning, which we know will not succeed. Xuthus' false recognition of his son is at least in part comic, and while Xuthus should have a genuine grievance against Apollo for deceiving him, he will never know it. Besides, Xuthus' part is very small, and he is deliberately kept away after meeting his supposed son.

Many critics have taken the playwright's attacks

on Apollo very seriously indeed. But the main accusation is that he has deserted the boy, which he has not. That Ion is shocked by the god's conduct seems intended only to characterize the boy's youth and naïveté. When Athena appears, because, she says, Apollo might be embarrassed, the irony is still gentle. In a real tragedy, Apollo would not be so squeamish.

Ion has also been taken as a serious play celebrating the glory of Athens. There are indeed many references to Athens, but most of them are to the Athenians' complacency and their feeling of superiority to foreigners like Xuthus. There may well be some irony here, as when Athena declares that Dorus and Achaeus, eponymous ancestors of all Dorians (who included the Spartans) and Achaeans, will be the sons of Creusa and Xuthus.

Translations of the play are listed under Euripides. —G. M. A. G.

Ionesco, Eugène (1912–). Rumanian-born French playwright. At a performance of an Ionesco play, there is considerable laughter in the audience. The source of the laughter is as old as the theater itself. It is man laughing at his own emptiness, his own triviality. Ionesco's first two plays, THE BALD SOPRANO and *La Leçon* (*The Lesson*, 1950), are filled with a ludicrous babbling and chattering. Language seems unable to adapt itself to the sentiments and the truths that man is attempting to express.

In *Amédée ou comment s'en débarrasser* (*Amédée*, 1953) the bitterness between husband and wife is very marked. Love is over between them, and in its place a feeling of guilt grows. They feel the presence of a corpse in the apartment—obviously the corpse of their love. It begins growing until it fills the apartment and threatens to break through the walls.

In his early experimentations with playwriting and the production of his plays, Ionesco discovered that the essence of the theater for him was in the exaggeration of its effects. Rather than trying to conceal the

EUGÈNE IONESCO (FRENCH CULTURAL SERVICES)

various artificialities and conventions of a performance, he believed that they should go as far as possible in grotesqueness and caricature. Ionesco recalls theories of Artaud when he advocates a theater of violence, in which the psychological study of characters will be replaced by metaphysical themes. He deliberately calls his plays "comic dramas" or "tragic farces," because the elements of the comic and tragic are not fused. For Ionesco they coexist, and each stands as a criticism of the other.

At the source of all the plays of Ionesco is a personal obsession, a philosophical anguish over the fate of man, which is to be an isolated spirit condemned to die while the heavy and opaque material world that surrounds and assails him remains. Derision is his principal means of projecting this anguish. He derides family and social relationships and the theater itself, with its long-established forms of didactically expounding truisms and supposedly revealing reality on the stage. Ionesco believes that his personal obsessions are shared by all. When he is most personal in his writings, he is then reaching the community of men. The action of most of the plays takes place within a family. This is not so much to demonstrate certain social characteristics as to show the encirclement to which man is condemned. Water surrounds the home of the old couple in THE CHAIRS; the new tenant has just enough space to sit down in an armchair (*Le Nouveau Locataire, The New Tenant*, 1957); Amédée and his wife are cut off from the outside world. This confinement is for Ionesco the modern figuration of hell. See also HUNGER AND THIRST and RHINOCEROS.

For critical studies on the work of Ionesco, consult the following: Richard N. Coe, *Eugène Ionesco* (1961); J. S. Doubrousky, "Ionesco and the Comic of Absurdity," *Yale French Studies*, No. 23 (1959); Wallace Fowlie, "New Plays of Ionesco and Genet, *Tulane Drama Review*, V (September 1960); C. J. Greshoff, "A Note on Ionesco," *Yale French Studies*, No. 15 (1961); Jacques Guicharnaud, "A World Out of Control: Eugène Ionesco," *American Society of Legion of Honor Magazine*, XXXI (1960); Eugène Ionesco, "Notes on My Theatre," translated by Leonard Pronko, *Tulane Drama Review*, VII (1963); and Rosette C. Lamont, "The Hero in Spite of Himself," *Yale French Studies*, No. 29 (1962).—W. F.

Iphigenia among the Taurians (Iphigeneia he en Taurois, 414–412 B.C.). A tragicomedy by EURIPIDES. Miraculously and secretly saved by Artemis from sacrifice at Aulis (see IPHIGENIA AT AULIS), Iphigenia is the goddess's priestess in the land of the barbaric Taurians, where she must officiate at the sacrifice of any Greek stranger. Her brother, Orestes, whom she has not seen since childhood, comes to this land with his faithful friend Pylades because Apollo tells him that he will be freed of his fits of madness if he steals the statue of Artemis. In a long scene, which is both ingenious and touching, brother and sister recognize one another. Their escape, complicated at first by the mutual loyalty of Orestes and Pylades, is finally effected through an elaborate ruse engineered by Iphigenia. Thoas, the Taurian king, is deceived, and the three Greeks sail away in Orestes' ship.

Thus, the play ends happily. There are no violent passions, bloody deeds, or bitter debates. On the other hand, we are not assured at the outset (as in

Ion) that all will be well. The whole play has something of the atmosphere of a good thriller. The situation is serious, and no scenes are definitely comic. The characterization, though not in depth, is more than adequate.

The Chorus of Greek attendants of the priestess express their longing for Greece in beautiful lyrics, a longing Iphigenia shares in spite of her experience at Aulis. The dialogue between the two friends as to which of them shall live, if only one may, is genuine and affecting, and so is Iphigenia's eagerness for news of her family. After the recognition scene, which Aristotle praised for its naturalness, the tone lightens.

The miracle at Aulis is "outside the play"; once the situation is accepted its impossibility is not forced on our attention (as it is in *Helen*). The epiphany of Athena does not change the course of events; in fact, Euripides invents a last-minute storm to motivate her appearance. She does save the Chorus and we are grateful to her, in this kind of play.

Iphigenia among the Taurians is not high tragedy, nor was it meant to be. It is, however, a very good and enjoyable tragicomedy.

Translations of the play are listed under Euripides.
—G. M. A. G.

Iphigenia at Aulis (Iphigeneia he en Aulidi, 406/ 05 B.C.). A tragedy by Euripides. Euripides may have left this play unfinished. It was, like *Bacchants,* produced after his death. There are two parallel first scenes, and the finale, after Iphigenia's last lyrics, is certainly not genuine; yet the main body of the play is undoubtedly by Euripides. The Greeks have been told by the high priest Calchas that their fleet will not have favorable winds to sail for Troy from Aulis unless Agamemnon sacrifices his daughter Iphigenia. He reluctantly agrees, under pressure from the other leaders, especially his brother, Menelaus. Iphigenia arrives with her mother, Clytemnestra, lured by a false promise of marriage to Achilles. They learn of the deception and Achilles, annoyed that he has been involved without his permission, promises to prevent the sacrifice. The pleas of mother and daughter cannot dissuade Agamemnon from his determination.

A SCENE FROM EURIPIDES' *Iphigenia* (COURTESY OF BRUCKMANN-ART REFERENCE BUREAU)

When Achilles is threatened by the entire army for defending Iphigenia, she offers herself freely and is led away to the sacrifice. In the spurious ending, a messenger reports that the goddess Artemis has wafted Iphigenia away and substituted a deer on the altar.

As in other of Euripides' plays, one difficulty is the change of tone halfway through. At first Euripides indulges his tendency to humanize (or should one say debunk?) the legendary heroes. The vacillating Agamemnon and his brother, the hypocritical Menelaus, give a most unflattering account of themselves and each other. Achilles is very young, complacent, and inexperienced when he gives Clytemnestra promises of help that he cannot possibly fulfill. The only genuinely affecting episode is Iphigenia's gay and joyful greeting of her father.

But when the impending sacrifice becomes known to all and members of the royal household face each other, the whole tone lifts. In her plea to save her daughter, Clytemnestra rises to her full tragic and dangerous height. Iphigenia's plea, though self-centered, is beautifully pathetic, as is her following lamentation. Agamemnon's reply is dignified and convincing. Achilles, in realizing his helplessness against the whole army, has matured. The change in him is paralleled by a greater change in Iphigenia, who now tells Clytemnestra and Achilles that she is willing to die to save Greece. Her last lyrics are excellent.

Aristotle condemned Iphigenia's conversion as unmotivated. We need not agree with him; we may feel that she was swayed by her father's earnest words and even more by the beautiful young hero's willingness to defend her to the death.

How Euripides would have ended his play we cannot tell. The present text miraculously saves Iphigenia, thus making the whole play a not very convincing tragicomedy.

Translations of the play are listed under Euripides.
—G. M. A. G.

Iran. See Persia.

Ireland. Ireland has been the cradle of some of the greatest names in the English theater. Dramatists such as George Farquhar, Richard Steele, Richard Sheridan, Oliver Goldsmith, Oscar Wilde, and Bernard Shaw and actors such as Charles Macklin, Spranger Barry, Thomas Sheridan, Eliza O'Neill, Peg Woffington, and Barry Sullivan were all Irish by birth. Despite this unequaled array of dramatic talent, Irish drama—plays written either in English or Gaelic, on Irish subjects by Irish playwrights, and performed by Irish actors—was almost completely undistinguished until 1900. One of the reasons for this phenomenon lay simply in the irresistible lure of the London theater for any Irishman with real dramatic talent. The financial, intellectual, and prestigious superiority of a London to a Dublin career was such that the choice of the latter would have demanded a heroic self-sacrifice. Such a choice would have been foolhardy as well, since the theatrical tastes and traditions of the two cities were virtually identical. The result, at least among audiences in Dublin, was, in theater-scholar W. J. Lawrence's words, that ". . . Dublin never showed any particular partiality for mirroring of its own life, and to chance upon an Irish-produced play or opera with the scene laid at home comes upon the investigator like thunder from a clear sky." From the seventeenth to the twentieth century Ireland was a cultural as well as political colony of England. The Irish supported a lively and popular theatrical tradition in the provinces as well as in Dublin, but that tradition was indisputably English.

The first Irish playhouse was the Werburg Street Theatre in Dublin, established in 1637. To this theater flocked a number of professional English players and one distinguished English playwright, James SHIRLEY. Shirley's contributions to the Irish theater included one play that ranks as the earliest extant "Irish" play: *St. Patrick for Ireland* (1639), a tragicomedy based upon the legends surrounding the conversion of Ireland to Christianity by St. Patrick. A contemporary of Shirley's was Henry Burnell (fl. 1635–1645), the first native-born Irish playwright of the new theater. Burnell's *Landgartha* (1639), a historical romance, now lost, achieved considerable popularity.

In 1642 Dublin theater, along with its English counterparts, was suppressed by order of the Puritan-controlled Parliament. Drama returned to Ireland in 1662 with the opening of the Smock Alley Theatre in Dublin. Its repertory consisted primarily of English plays, notably Shakespeare's, although it also featured contributions from such a prominent representative of the English ascendancy as Katherine Philips (1631–1664), the English poet known as "the Matchless Orinda." Her translation of Corneille's *La Mort de Pompée* was one of the Smock Alley's early successes.

The Irish stage also produced a number of imitations of the comedy of manners developing in England at this time (See ENGLAND: *Restoration drama*). Richard Head's *Hic et ubique or The Humours of Dublin* (1663) and William Phillips' *St. Stephen's Green or The Generous Lovers* (1700) reflect (and dissect) Dublin society in much the way that the Irish-educated William Congreve was exposing the foibles and follies of London life.

In the early eighteenth century, the most notable dramatist regularly writing plays for the Irish theater was Charles Shadwell (d. 1726), the son of Dryden's old enemy, poet laureate Thomas Shadwell. The best of Shadwell's contributions are *Irish Hospitality* (1717), a comedy, and *Rotherick O'Connor or The Distressed Princess* (1719), a pseudohistorical verse tragedy based on the twelfth-century invasion of Ireland by the Normans.

The success of *Rotherick O'Connor* led to a few other attempts to dramatize Irish history. William Phillips' *Hibernia Freed* (1722) deals with the Danish invasion of Ireland. Robert Ashton's *The Battle of Aughrim* (1727) is a heroic tragedy based upon the final defeat of James II and the Irish forces in 1691, and Francis Dobbs's *The Irish Chief or Patriot King* (1773), like *Hibernia Freed,* is set in the period of the Danish occupation. Among the other Irish-oriented plays of the period were Thomas Sheridan's one-acter *Captain O'Blunder or The Brave Irishman* (1738), Charles Coffey's *The Beggar's Wedding* (1728), a Dublin variation on John Gay's *Beggar's Opera,* and Charles Macklin's *The True Born Irishman* (1762), a comedy about an Irishman whose wife apes English manners. By the middle of the eigh-

teenth century, flourishing and popular theaters had been established in the provinces as well as in Dublin. Touring companies soon found lively, appreciative, and profitable audiences in such cities as Cork, Waterford, Derry, and Belfast. The pervasive theatrical activity provided a firm soil for the development of the two greatest dramatists of the period, Oliver GOLDSMITH and Richard Brinsley SHERIDAN, as well as a host of less gifted but distinctively talented playwrights, including Arthur Murphy, Hugh Kelly (1739–1777), John O'Keeffe (1747–1833), Kane O'Hara (1714–1782), and W. C. Oulton (1770–1820). With the exception of O'Hara all of these playwrights eventually emigrated to England, where they did their most important work. Nevertheless, O'Keeffe, O'Hara, and Oulton made early attempts to deal specifically with Irish material. O'Keeffe, later praised by Hazlitt as "the English Molière," was a native Dubliner and began his career as an actor in the Smock Alley. Before moving to England, he wrote a number of plays for Irish audiences, among which are *Colin's Welcome* (1770), a pastoral; *Tony Lumpkin in Town* (1778), an Irish adaptation of Goldsmith's *She Stoops to Conquer*; and *The Comical Duel* (1775), a farce.

O'Hara, who remained a resident of Ireland all his life, is remembered chiefly as the author of *Midas* (1761), the most popular comic opera of its day. Oulton, who emigrated at an early age, nevertheless produced a number of successful Dublin plays while still in his teens. The best of these were *The Haunted Castle* (1784) and *The Madhouse* (1785).

Despite the superficially Irish characteristics of these plays, their tone, style, and substance were essentially English. The only attempt to establish a native Irish drama was that made by the actor Robert Owenson (1744–1812). In 1784 Owenson inaugurated a "national theater" in Dublin designed to emphasize Irish plays by Irish playwrights. The enterprise proved to be short-lived. Owenson was forced to close his theater in 1786 when a rival company was given an exclusive patent to plays performed in Dublin.

Irish drama in the nineteenth century is completely devoid of distinction. What little "native" drama there was represented an attempt to capitalize on the stereotyped "stage Irishman" who had grown to be one of the comic characters of the English and American theaters. The actor-playwright Tyrone Power (1797–1841) found the character a particularly successful formula in such farces as *O'Flannigan and the Fairies* (n.d.) and *Paddy Carey, the Boy of Cloghern* (n.d.). Even more successful in this mixture of sentiment and slapstick was Dublin-born Dion BOUCICAULT, whose *Colleen Bawn* (1860), *Arrah Na Pogue* (1864), and *The Shaughraun* (1874) fixed the image of the stage Irishman.

Thus Irish dramatic genius could not be nurtured in native soil until the end of the nineteenth century when Irishmen began to awaken to the long-neglected legacy of Gaelic culture, and the London stage was no longer regarded as a mecca by thoughtful and talented men. The history of indigenous Irish drama of any import begins in 1899. In that year William Butler YEATS and Lady Augusta GREGORY, together with Edward MARTYN and George MOORE, formed the Irish Literary Theatre, a society devoted to the fostering of a native, poetic drama. Their aspirations were expressed in a fund-raising letter sent to a small number of wealthy friends:

> We hope to find in Ireland an uncorrupted and imaginative audience trained to listen by its passion for oratory, and believe that our desire to bring upon the stage the deeper thoughts and emotions of Ireland will ensure a tolerant welcome and that freedom to experiment without which no new movement in art or literature can succeed.

For its first production the society rented a hall where, on May 8, 1899, it presented two plays: Edward Martyn's *The Heather Field* and Yeats's *The Countess Cathleen*. The latter was violently attacked by a sizable minority of the press and public for being both anti-Catholic and anti-Irish. The production, however, was generally a success, and it marked the beginning of Yeats's dreams of realizing a poetic theater. "The theater," as Yeats stated, "began in ritual and it cannot come to greatness again without recalling words to their ancient sovereignty."

The Irish Literary Theatre existed for three years. During that time it employed only professional English actors. When it was reorganized as the Irish National Theatre Society in 1902, it featured an all-Irish acting company headed by William (1872–1947) and Frank (1870–1931) Fay. The first performance of the new company was given on April 2, 1902. The plays performed on this occasion were *Deirdre* by A.E. (George Russell) and *Cathleen Ni Houlihan* by Yeats. The success of the plays brought the company into prominence. In 1903 they gave two special performances in London and won the enthusiastic support of leading London critics. Present at one of these performances was Miss A. E. F. Horniman (1860–1937), a devoted patroness of repertory theater. Impressed by the plays and the performances, she offered to build a theater in Dublin to house the company. The following year the playhouse, known as the Abbey Theatre for its location in Abbey Street, was leased to the company. On opening night, December 27, 1904, four short plays were presented: Yeats's *Cathleen Ni Houlihan* and *On Baile's Strand*; *Spreading the News* by Lady Gregory; and *In the Shadow of the Glen* by John Millington SYNGE. In the history of the theater it is difficult to conceive of a more auspicious opening night's program.

Despite the quality of the plays and the excellence of the acting company, the Abbey was viewed with suspicion and distrust by the average Dubliner. Its leading figures—Yeats, Lady Gregory, Synge, Miss Horniman—were Anglo-Irish Protestants, and the plays, although rooted in the soil and speech of Ireland, were more concerned with revealing dramatic truth than portraying the political struggle for Irish independence. The distrust erupted into a full-scale riot over the production in 1907 of Synge's *The Playboy of the Western World*. Attacked as "a libel on the Irish race," the play evoked a storm of rioting in the theater that had to be quelled by the police. Yeats and Lady Gregory, however, refused to yield to public pressure, and the play ran for a full week despite the rioting at each performance.

In the meantime the Abbey had begun to attract a number of exciting new dramatists—Padraic COLUM, George FITZMAURICE, T. C. MURRAY, Lennox ROBINSON, and others—who, under the influence of Synge and Lady Gregory, were reproducing with fidelity and skill the rhythm and cadences of Irish peasant speech. Their plays, such as Colum's *The Fiddler's House* (1907), Murray's *Birthright* (1910), Robinson's *The Clancy Name* (1908), and Fitzmaurice's *The Country Dressmaker* (1907), were distinguished attempts to articulate the long-suppressed Irish tragic experience. Their excellence has been overshadowed by the genius of Synge, whose *Playboy* and *Riders to the Sea* (1904) are plays of a stature and significance that far exceed the narrow boundaries of national drama.

The most popular of the new playwrights was William Boyle (1853–1923). His plays were all written for the Abbey Theatre, although he withdrew them for a time following the production of Synge's *Playboy of the Western World*, which Boyle considered a libel against the Irish peasantry. Boyle is best known for his own satirical comedies of rural Irish life. His plays were among the most popular of those presented in the early years of the Abbey Theatre. Among the best of these are *The Building Fund* (1905), based upon the ancient comic motif of the "trickster tricked"; and *The Mineral Workers* (1906), the account of a returning Irish-American's attempt to rouse his former countrymen to the spirit of American enterprise. Other plays include *The Eloquent Dempsey* (1906), the first Abbey play to depict small-town Irish life; and *Family Failing* (1912).

In 1909 the Abbey experienced new difficulties when it attempted to produce George Bernard Shaw's *The Showing-up of Blanco Posnet*. The play had been banned in England for its alleged blasphemy, and the Abbey production was interfered with by the English authorities in Ireland. Yeats and Lady Gregory, however, refused to be intimidated by the English governors as they had earlier refused to submit to the Irish public. The play was performed, thus adding the illustrious name of Shaw to the list of those Irish dramatists who have had a first production of one of their plays in the Abbey.

The battle-scarred history of the Abbey entered a new phase during 1911/12 when the company undertook an extended tour in England and the United States. In England the players met with unprecedented success, but in America the production of *Playboy* ignited in Irish-American organizations a new series of violent protests that culminated in the technical arrest (for their own protection) of the players by the local authorities in Philadelphia during the performance there. Despite these obstacles, the tour was a financial success and enabled the company to achieve a measure of economic stability for the few years following.

World War I and the period immediately following of the Black-and-Tan Wars (1919–1921), during which the Irish fought for and won their independence, was an inauspicious time for Irish drama. Men's minds and hearts were intensely involved in political and social questions; drama and the other arts suffered as a result. This lack of public interest in the arts continued during the period of "the troubles" (1921–1923), when the newly established Irish

Free State was torn asunder by civil war. The Abbey barely managed to remain open during these years. It lost some of its finest performers, and there were few plays comparable to the great works of the Abbey's first decade, although there were some fine contributions from St. John ERVINE, Seumas O'KELLY, and Lord DUNSANY.

In 1923, however, a new dramatist appeared who singlehandedly revived the faltering hopes of the Abbey group. This playwright, the product of a Dublin slum, was Sean O'CASEY. Using vivid, vital language in a blend of comedy and tragedy, O'Casey brought to life the inhabitants of those slums. His plays—*The Shadow of a Gunman* (1923), *Juno and the Paycock* (1924), and *The Plough and the Stars* (1926)—made the Abbey the focus of international attention. The production of *The Plough and the Stars,* a drama about the Easter-week insurrection of 1916, provoked new storms of protest and riots at the Abbey. Outraged Irish nationalists objected violently to O'Casey's scathing portrayal of the emptiness of patriotic ideals. Once again the directors refused to capitulate to public pressure. Striding on the stage after an early performance of the play, lordly and majestic as always, Yeats contemptuously addressed the noisy and abusive audience: "You have disgraced yourselves again. Is this to be an ever-recurring celebration of the arrival of Irish genius . . . . From such a scene in this theater went forth the fame of Synge. Equally the fame of O'Casey is born here tonight. This is his apotheosis." Yeats proved to be correct. O'Casey achieved international fame, all of which made even more astounding the next development in the history of the Abbey. In 1928 O'Casey, by this time recognized as Ireland's greatest living dramatist, submitted his new play, *The Silver Tassie,* to the Abbey board of directors: Yeats, Lady Gregory, Lennox Robinson, and Walter Starkie. All but Starkie advised that the play be rejected as unworthy of production by the Abbey, with the result that O'Casey severed relations with the Dublin theater. To many observers the loss of O'Casey marked the beginning of a decline in the fortunes of the Abbey that has continued to the present day.

The year 1928 proved to be significant in the development of Irish drama for another reason. In that year the Dublin Gate Theatre was founded by Hilton Edwards (1903–   ) and Michael McLiammoir (1899–   ). As an experimental repertory theater, the Dublin Gate has been devoted to the production of highly stylized experimental drama by European, American, and Irish playwrights and to the revival of Shakespeare and the Greek classics. One of its notable early productions was the presentation of THE OLD LADY SAYS "NO," a play by Denis JOHNSTON that had been rejected by the Abbey. Johnston's play marked the first successful expressionist drama written by an Irish playwright, and it introduced a modern, European tone to the nationalist character of Irish drama. Johnston's next play, *The Moon in the Yellow River* (1931), was produced at the Abbey, as were the early plays of the most significant Irish dramatist of the thirties, Paul Vincent CARROLL. Carroll's plays, the finest of which are *Shadow and Substance* (1937) and *The White Steed* (1939), all deal either peripherally or centrally with one of the most complicated, intense problems of Irish life—the

function and status of the Catholic clergy. Along with Carroll and Johnston, the most significant work of the period was done by Lennox Robinson. Robinson's *Church Street* (1934) represented the highest achievement of a dramatic career that worked in a variety of styles with distinction and skill for more than forty years. Other noteworthy productions of the period included Mary Manning's *Youth's the Season* (1931), a witty and provocative portrait of the lost generation, Irish-style, and Teresa Deevy's *Katie Roche* (1936), a fine blend of poetry and realism. Mention should also be made of the dramatic contributions of the earl of Longford (1902–1961) and his wife, Lady Christine Longford (1900–   ). In addition to the financial and practical assistance they offered, first to the Gate Theatre group and later to their own Longford Productions, Lord and Lady Longford were themselves able and accomplished dramatists. The best known of Lord Longford's dramas is *Yahoo* (1933), a study of Swift, that perennial subject of Irish drama. Lady Longford is celebrated for her perceptive comedy *Mr. Jiggins of Jigginstown* (1933), her Irish history plays, notably *The Earl of Straw* (1944), and her satirical comedy *The Hill of Quirke* (1953).

Also active at this time was still another school of Irish drama, located in Belfast and known as The Ulster Literary Theatre. Founded in 1904, this theater has tried to be to the Orangemen, the predominantly Protestant northern Irish, what the Abbey has been to their southern compatriots. The Ulster's most famous playwrights are Rutherford MAYNE, the author of a distinguished group of plays about the peasant of northern Ireland, and George SHIELS, who has written many popular comedies for the Abbey as well as for the Ulster Theatre. The Ulster Literary Theatre was succeeded by the Group Theatre, an organization that has produced three of Ireland's best contemporary playwrights: Sam Thompson (1916–1965), Joseph Tomelty (1911–   ), and Brian FRIEL. Thompson is best known for his *Over the Bridge* (1960), a searching, realistic study of anti-Catholic bigotry in the Belfast shipyards. Tomelty, who is perhaps better known as a fine character actor in motion pictures, has produced a number of excellent dramas including *The End House* (1944), a poignant picture of life in a Belfast slum, and *All Souls' Night* (1948), a tragedy reminiscent in setting and tone of Synge's *Riders to the Sea.* Another of Tomelty's plays is *Is the Priest at Home?* (1954), an objective, unromantic, and nonpolemical view of the role of the priest in Irish life. Friel, who has been represented on the London and Broadway stages by three productions, *Philadelphia, Here I Come* (1964), *The Loves of Cass McGuire* (1966), and *Lovers* (1968), is currently the best known and most promising of today's Irish dramatists. His work is marked by inventive and imaginative use of expressionist techniques.

An interesting offshoot of the Ulster Theatre has been the Lyric Players' Theatre in Belfast. Since its inception in 1951, this group has been dedicated to the presentation of Yeats's plays—particularly his plays for dancers—which were designed for a highly specialized and limited audience. Another center of verse drama has been the Lyric Theatre in Dublin under the influence and direction of Austin

A SCENE FROM BRIAN FRIEL'S *Philadelphia, Here I Come* (IRISH TOURIST BOARD)

Clarke (1896–   ). Clarke, now widely regarded as Ireland's greatest living poet, is the author of numerous plays in verse, including *Sister Eucharia* (1939), an intense religious drama; *Black Fast* (1941), a light farce; and *The Moment Next to Nothing* (1953), a sensitive evocation of the world of Celtic folklore. Another mainstay of the Lyric Theatre has been Donagh MacDonagh (1912–   ), whose best-known play is *Happy as Larry* (1941). A richly comic, verbal feast, *Happy as Larry* is steeped in the language and songs of the Dublin pubs. Other successful verse plays by MacDonagh are *Step-in-the-Hollow* (1957), a lively farce about a rakish old judge, and *Lady Spider* (1953), a dramatic rendering of the Deirdre legend.

Since World War II the Irish theater in general, and the Abbey in particular, has been seriously wounded by its old enemies: emigration, censorship, financial instability, internecine quarrels, and public opposition or indifference. Against such formidable obstacles the continuing vitality of the Irish drama is a source of wonder. Although the period has not produced anyone of the stature of Synge, Yeats, or O'Casey, it has nurtured some exceptionally talented dramatists who deserve to be better known. Their relative obscurity is, as Robert Hogan points out in *After the Irish Renaissance* (1967), more the result of the economics of the modern theater than of any inadequacy on their part. The best known of the post-

war playwrights is Brendan BEHAN, whose passion for publicity and prodigious drinking has tended to obscure the sober, critical fact that *The Quare Fellow* (1954) and *The Hostage* (1956) are two of the best modern plays in English.

Behan's plays represented a departure from the realistic tradition that has dominated modern Irish drama. To some extent that tradition has proven too rigid and unyielding. Many Irish dramatists of the forties and fifties, particularly those writing for the Abbey, have lacked the venturesome, experimental spirit of Yeats and O'Casey. Nevertheless, even within the narrow confines of the realistic tradition, there have been a number of first-rate plays, among which are *Home Is the Hero* (1952) by Walter Macken and *Design for a Headstone* (1950) by Seamus Byrne. The latter play, a controversial prison drama containing some antireligious remarks, touched off an abortive riot, faintly reminiscent of those that attended the première of *Playboy* and *The Plough and the Stars*.

More interesting, however, are those departures from realism represented in the work of men like Bryan MacMahon (1909–   ). A well-known novelist, MacMahon has utilized the wide-ranging perspective and episodic structure of the picaresque novel in his *The Honey Spike* (1961), a lyrical, tragicomic rendering of the life of modern Ireland.

One major source of the theatrical vitality in Dublin is the Dublin Theatre Festival, the presentation of new plays and revived classics which has now become an annual event. Among the excellent plays that have had premières during the festivals are *Stephen D* (1962), Hugh Leonard's adaptation of Joyce's *A Portrait of the Artist as a Young Man; The Ice Goddess* (1964), a symbolic drama by James Douglas; and Friel's *Philadelphia, Here I Come.*

Two other major contributors to contemporary Irish drama are John B. Keane (1928–   ) and Michael Molloy (1917–   ). Both men have produced a substantial body of dramatic work, most of which has strong roots in the Irish soil. Keane's work is distinguished by its bold theatricality in an age more attuned to irony and undertone. His *Sive* (1959), one of the most popular of recent Irish plays, is an intensely savage representation of rural Irish life. His *Many Young Men of Twenty* (1964) is a moving musical drama focusing with passion and perception on the continuing Irish problem of emigration. His *The Man from Clare* (1962) deals with the attempt of a professional football player to achieve a more stable set of values than his life as a sports figure has allowed him.

Even more intensely involved in the life of rural Ireland is Michael Molloy, whose plays focus with unsentimental compassion on the rapidly disappearing traditions and values of rural Ireland. Representative of his dramatic work is *The Visiting House* (1946), which focuses on the activities of the old country meeting houses celebrated for their songs, stories, and lively talk and which have now all but vanished from modern Ireland. A better-known play of Molloy's is *The King of Friday's Men* (1948). Set in eighteenth-century rural Ireland, the play represents an attempt to recapture the spirit and the tragic limitations of an earlier time. Like Keane's *Many Young Men of Twenty,* Molloy's *Wood of the Whispering* (1953) touches on the inability of the traditional way of life to sustain and nurture a new generation, who continue in large numbers to seek economic, social, and personal fulfillment outside of Ireland.

The divorce from older traditions marks a particularly ironic note in the development of the Irish theater. The drama that at the beginning of the century was created to foster and celebrate ancient traditions now appears to be the chronicle of the dissolution of that heritage. However, it should be noted that the most successful production of the Abbey in 1968 was a revival of Boucicault's *The Shaughraun,* the prototype of the dramatic tradition the Abbey was created to supplant. This suggests that the traditions are not dead, rather that their vitality takes on a much more complex form than we have previously imagined.

There are several excellent anthologies of modern Irish drama: *Irish Renaissance* and *Plays of Changing Ireland* (1936), both edited by Curtis Canfield; *The Genius of the Irish Theater* (1960), edited by Sylvan Barnet, Morton Berman, and William Burto; and *Seven Irish Plays 1946–1964* (1967), edited by Robert Hogan. The best historical treatments of the early period are La Tourette Stockwell's *Dublin Theaters and Theater Customs* (1939); G. C. Duggan's *The Stage Irishman* (1937); and William Smith Clark's *The Early Irish Stage from the Beginnings to 1720* (1955) and *The Irish Stage in the Country Towns* (1966). For the modern period the best his-

tories are Lady Gregory's *Our Irish Theatre* (1914), Peter Kavanagh's *The Story of the Abbey Theatre* (1950), Una Ellis-Fermor's *The Irish Dramatic Movement* (2nd ed., 1954), and Robert Hogan's *After the Irish Renaissance* (1967).—E. Q.

irony. In drama the term is usually taken to refer to a situation in which characters anticipate exactly the opposite of what occurs or in which they suggest the outcome but not in the sense in which they intend it. The classic expression of the first type is Sophocles' *Oedipus Rex,* and the term Sophoclean irony is often used to denote the phenomenon. An example of the latter is Othello's lighthearted remark to Desdemona before his suspicions have been inflamed by Iago:

Excellent wretch! Perdition catch my soul—
But I do love thee; and when I love thee not,
Chaos is come again.

The term irony is used in reference to comedy to characterize a particular comic tone that leans toward satire but which is generally less strident and severe in its presentation of human foibles. Irony in this sense is an important aspect of plays such as Shakespeare's *As You Like It,* Goldsmith's *She Stoops to Conquer,* and Giraudoux's *The Madwoman of Chaillot.*

Israel. A close observation of the dramatic scene of modern Israel, with regard to original plays, reveals two important facts: First, in the twenty years since the establishment of the state of Israel in 1948, about one hundred original plays have been produced by the various ensembles of the professional theater. Considering the fact that playwriting is a fairly new medium for the Israeli writer, this number is remarkable. Second, Israeli theater is of a highly international character; its translated repertoire encompasses nearly all of dramatic literature. But the relation between the number of original Israeli plays and the total number of theater productions reveals that only about one out of every six or seven plays produced is an original play. It becomes clear that in spite of the rich and excellent repertoire of the Israeli theater (Israeli "hits" include works by Shakespeare, George Bernard Shaw, Eugène Ionesco, Bertolt Brecht), its chief problem remains the lack of original plays. There is a continuous search for the Israeli dramatist who can measure up to the international models with which he has to compete in the theater.

Israeli drama is as unique and complicated a topic as the modern State of Israel. Its uniqueness lies first of all in the eclectic nature and inherent diversity of Israel's culture. Politically, the State of Israel has been a reality since the declaration of its independence in May 1948, yet its culture dates back thousands of years to the origins of the Bible. Culturally, Israel really never ceased; it was the culture of a homeless people living among many nations, writing in its original Hebrew tongue as well as in many foreign tongues, always influenced by the cultures in which it lived, yet distinctly autonomous, nonassimilating. Hebrew was always the language of prayer and sacred studies, and the revival of the Jewish center in Israel, or what was then called Palestine, was infused with the renaissance of the Hebrew culture and language.

During the Russian Revolution, a group of pioneering and enthusiastic young Jewish actors was accepted by the Moscow Art Theatre and they formed the Habimah, the first professional Hebrew theater in history. One of its memorable productions was the folkloric play *The Dybbuk* (1922), directed by the gifted Armenian director Eugene B. Vakhtangov. Written initially in Yiddish by S. Ansky, it was translated into Hebrew by the great master and poet of the Hebrew language Chaim N. Bialik (1873–1934). Though there is not an abundance of Hebrew drama before the creation of the Habimah, there are some Hebrew plays which date from the sixteenth century, such as the first Hebrew comedy, *Tsachut Bdichuta D'kidushin* ("A Comedy of Betrothed"), attributed to Yehuda Somo, known by his Italian name Leone Ebreo di Somi (1527–1592). Some scholars even maintain that certain books of the Bible, for example, the Song of Songs or the Book of Job, were written in a marked dramatic form and therefore should be considered drama. There are some Hebrew dramas from the seventeenth century, among them the historical play *Yesod Olam* ("The Foundation of the World") by Moshe Zacut (1630–1697), and *Asirei Hatikvah* ("The Prisoners of Hope"), a morality play by Joseph Pensa de la Vega (1650–1703). The most noteworthy dramas of the eighteenth century are the biblical drama *Ma'ase Shimshon* ("The Story of Samson," 1724) and the allegorical plays *Migdal Oz* ("The Mighty Tower," 1727) and *La-Yesharim Tehillah* ("Praise to the Righteous," 1738), all written by the mystic and moralist poet Moshe H. Luzzatto (1707–1746). These works, however, though conceived in dramatic form, were apparently not written for the stage. Thus, there were only a few Hebrew dramas from earlier times of which a modern Hebrew theater could avail itself. It soon became quite evident that the non-Jewish dramatists throughout the ages had been the ones to resort to the dramatic Jewish history, the Bible, and other Jewish writings as a source for dramatic compositions. In its search for a "Jewish repertoire," the Hebrew theater thus wisely turned to these sources—ranging from Pedro Calderón de la Barca's *Absalom's Locks* (in its Habimah production entitled *Keter David*, "King David's Crown") to André Obey's *Noah* (1931) or Christopher Fry's *A Sleep of Prisoners* (1951). This is, of course, not to say that among the Hebrew dramas of the past or the preindependence days there were no plays that could be adapted, or perhaps modernized, for the use of the contemporary Israeli theater. Indeed, it has been continually suggested that the dramatic works of two master poets of the earlier part of the twentieth century would lend themselves perfectly to this purpose. The poetical plays by Matityahu Shoham, such as *Tsor V'Yerushalayim* ("Tyre and Jerusalem," 1933), one of the high points in modern Hebrew literature, and the allegorical dramas by Ya'acov Kahan could not only be revitalized but would add a dimension to the contemporary Hebrew theater.

Then, of course, there are the works of the Yiddish writers who created a wealth of dramatic material even before the professional Yiddish theater was founded through the efforts of Abraham Goldfaden (1840–1908) in the last quarter of the nineteenth century. Some of these plays were translated into Hebrew by their own authors, who intuitively saw the coming of a renaissance of Hebrew language and culture. These works, dealing primarily with Jewish life in Eastern European communities, were the second group of plays to be reclaimed by the Israeli theater. To complete the picture of Jewish repertoire we should add the works of Jewish dramatists like H. Leivik, Sholem Asch, Richard Beer-Hoffman, and many others who lived and wrote outside of Israel. Although they did not use the Hebrew language, they presented themes of Jewish significance. (See YIDDISH DRAMA.) With these three supply lines and the international dramatic reservoir began the realization of a modern Hebrew theater as a cultural institution of the ancient Jewish homeland. It soon became evident, however, that one thing was missing, namely, a contemporary drama.

By 1930, two years after the Habimah had settled permanently in the country, Palestine could boast of having three professional theaters with an enthusiastic audience. However, although there were many accomplished writers of prose and poetry, there were very few dramatists. Among the latter is Nathan Bistritsky-Agmon (1896–   ), who wrote two historical plays that were produced by the Habimah: *Blayil Zeh* ("On This Night," 1934), depicting the days of the destruction of the Second Temple, and *Yerushalayim Ve'Romi* ("Jerusalem and Rome," 1939), about the controversial character of Josephus Flavius. Aharon Ashman (1896–   ) continued in the Romantic tradition by using biblical and historical themes in his first play, *Michal Bat Shaul* ("Michal, the Daughter of King Saul," 1941), a play with passions and intrigues. Two years later, however, Ashman wrote another play, *Ha'adana Hazot* ("This Soil," 1943), in which he dealt with the pioneering days of an Israeli settlement. In itself, the play, being extremely contrived in its dialogue, situation, and characters, may not have had great dramatic merit, but it certainly was a turning point in Israeli drama. It proved beyond any doubt that both the theater and the audience were waiting for a dramatist to immortalize the heroism of Israel's pioneering times, notwithstanding how romantically and idealistically it was treated. This total identification between stage and spectator was very successful, and the Habimah not only had a "hit" in its repertory but also a play that since its initial performance has had numerous revivals. In 1945 another play on the theme of the rebuilding of Israel was produced by the Habimah—Asher Beilin's *Banim Ligvulam* ("The Return of the Children to Their Land"). The colorful life of the many ethnic groups in Israel, a subject that was often used in the revival of the Israeli arts, was portrayed by Yehoshua Bar-Yoseph in *B'simta'ot Yerushalayim* ("In the Alleys of Jerusalem," 1941). Since 1941 Bar-Yoseph, a prolific Israeli novelist and short-story writer, has become a regular contributor to the Israeli drama. Many of his plays deal in an impressionist manner with Jerusalem before and after the War of Independence.

To understand the drastic change in Israeli drama since 1948, we must understand the social and political scene of the times. The fate of Israel was at stake during the decade of the forties. There were threats of a Nazi invasion and a fight with the British mandatorial power over free immigration to Palestine and free settlement in the country. The younger generation of Israelis was fostered and mobilized during that time in underground camps, waiting for the hour to strike. A new life had developed among the mobilized units of the Palmach, later to become the commando units of the defense forces of Israel. Sitting around the campfires after a long day of training, stories and legends, jokes and songs were created. A new slang developed that was not understood by the older generation. It was definitely the birth of a new generation, which, among other things, carried on a social, political, and cultural revolution. In this quiet, slowly spreading cultural rebellion, no blood was spilled and no books burned. New, young writers soon became the spokesmen for this new generation. Among these writers are two important ones who later became the *prima mobile* of the new Israeli drama: Yig'al Mossenson and Moshe Shamir. In addition to this new dramatic talent, changes in the theater were needed to bring it into line with the rapidly changing literary developments. Two significant events should be mentioned. The first of these was the creation in October 1944 of the Chamber Theatre (Kameri), founded by young actors from the Habimah. The Kameri ensemble was dedicated, at least in its formative years, to the promotion of original Israeli plays. As an ensemble of young actors, the Kameri group could present a more genuine portrayal of the younger generation—the new heroes of the Israeli drama—than the older actors, who not only had received their training in foreign countries but were still speaking with foreign accents and playing in a more theatrical, outdated style. Second, the Habimah started a new policy, admitting young actors. These developments have called forth a variety of changes in the theatrical scene of Israel, manifested in its repertoire, directing, acting style, scene design, and make-up.

The first two plays to reflect these changes were Mossenson's *B'arvot Hanegev* ("In the Wastes of the Negev," 1949) and Shamir's *Hoo Halach Basadot* ("He Walked in the Fields," 1949). Moshe SHAMIR, whose play was a dramatization of his novel of the same name, created, perhaps unknowingly, the first modern Israeli drama in which the real hero is the group, the young generation and its experience. Shamir's objective naturalism, lacking any serious examination of issues and having only a sketchy character delineation, soon became the prototype used by many Israeli playwrights who wanted merely the effects of verisimilitude. The tremendous success of *Hoo Halach Basadot* in the Chamber Theatre production resulted from Shamir's realism; the characters were known and recognized by all—but hitherto unseen on the stage. The dialogue, a mixture of standard Hebrew and the contemporary slang, was strikingly new and authentic. The play is characterized by honesty and simplicity, a youthful naïveté, and a straightforward approach. The play by Yig'al MOSSENSON was of a different kind, a more conventional war drama with a besieged kibbutz as its focal point. Although Mossenson's characters were stock types of the kibbutz and the times, he presented a heroic drama to a generation that cared little for depth or psychological probing, that was still smelling of battle's blood and covered with the dust of the Negev. Like Shamir's play, *B'arvot Hanegev* was

peppered with the slang of the period, a language soon to become obsolete with the next generation. In the following year, 1950, Nathan SHACHAM, who at the time promised to become one of the major dramatists of Israel, had his play *Hem Yagee-oo Machar* ("They Will Arrive at Dawn") produced at the Chamber Theatre. As a dramatization of an earlier short story about a military situation, this play continued the realistic trend that characterized the earlier Israeli plays, although Shacham always exhibited a more critical realism than did the other playwrights. With a great deal more dialogue than action, the play holds the interest of the audience through its tense situation. The main characters are intrinsically believable, involved not only in the action, but also in the meaning of the action. The language they use is realistic but heightened, cleansed of most of the slang so dominant in the earlier plays.

Also in 1950 one of the most powerful, poetic plays of modern Israel was produced. Written by one of the established novelists of the old guard, Chayim Hazaz, the play, entitled *B'ketz Hayamim* ("At the End of Days," 1950), deals with the medieval figure of the self-proclaimed messiah Shabetai Zvi, a subject used by many other dramatists. Hazaz, however, did not intend to romanticize this exotic figure. He emphasized Shabetai Zvi's prophetic vision, anticipating the catastrophe approaching the Jewish people. Symbolically, Hazaz represented the two fundamental approaches to the future of Jewish life in the diaspora: the total negation and the so-called realistic approach, the need for adjustment. Thus, it is a modern play of ideas, bearing strong analogies to the Jewish holocaust in Europe and the future of Jewish life outside of Israel. In this respect, Hazaz was unusual for, contrary to what might be expected, there are only a few plays (as well as novels) by Israeli writers on the subject of the destruction of European Jewry in World War II. Among them is Chanoch Bartov's dramatization of his own novel *Shesh Knafayim L'echad* ("To Each One Six Wings," 1955), which in its stage version was a tragic melodrama, and Ben-Tsiyon Tomer's *Yaldei Hatsel* ("The Children of Shadow," 1963), a play in which people are haunted by the hellish past and try to escape it in their desire to become like born Israelis.

There were scores of plays depicting local scenes and local issues that were written in the conventional mode of realism, a genre that the Israeli dramatists seemed to have discovered at the time that it was rejected by most playwrights throughout the world. Shacham took a critical look at Israeli society in his next play, *Cheshbon Chadash* ("A New Account," 1954); Aharon MEGED poked fun at false patriotism in *I Like Mike* (1951) and sketched the mishaps of a kibbutz farmer in the big city in his next play. Mossenson wrote *Kazablan* (1954), a psuedo detective story with a strong central character, a Jew from Morocco, who serves as the author's *raissoneur* in denouncing prejudice and discrimination. In *Eldorado* (1955) Mossenson depicted a slum area of Jaffa, its colorful characters, and its saucy language. Indeed, many playwrights have since used this ethnic color and folklore. In his episodic play *Yamim Shell Zahav* ("Golden Days," 1965) Shlomo Shva depicts with humor and nostalgia a panorama of characters from the early days of Tel-Aviv. Like Shva's play,

Ya'acov Bar-Nathan's *Hashchuna* ("The Neighborhood," 1965) is also in the mainstream of Israeli drama. In Bar-Nathan's play the young drift away from their homes—symbolized by a house in which two families live together, one of Oriental origin (Sephardic) and the other of Western (Ashkenazic). This subject, in fact, has been treated by many Israeli dramatists before, including Bar-Nathan, who has written a number of full-length plays as well as one-acters. *Hashchuna* contains at least one fully developed, colorful, and sympathetic central character. The entire play, although weak in structure and contrived in its conflict, emanates warmth and honesty.

Israeli drama was, and to some extent still is, dominated by this close personal attachment to the characters and their environment and the authentic, impressionist reproduction on stage of its dialects, customs, dress, and so forth, often treated with good humor. This is not to say that Israeli drama lacks ideas. On the contrary, the preoccupation of the Israeli playwright with theme as the predominant dramatic value often makes the play seem contrived. The characters are often nothing more than mere mouthpieces for the author's "message."

There has been a lack of good comedy in Israel for a long time. It is remarkable that the same Jews who could laugh at themselves in the ghettos of European towns and give birth to a Sholem Aleichem could now be devoid of a sense of humor. It was only with the arrival of Ephraim KISHON, a brilliant and prolific humorist who immigrated from Hungary in 1949, that this gap started to close. It was his unique wit, a skillful use of traditional comic technique, and the inventions of colorful native characters that caused not only his own plays to be performed in so many theaters throughout the world but often paved the way for other Israeli playwrights. Yet there is still no native Israeli tradition of comedy.

In the mid-1950's biblical and historical plays appeared in Israeli theaters. The young Israeli dramatists had been carefully avoiding this material for a long time, because two major problems had to be solved first: a fresh and modern interpretation was needed and a proper language, which would not be archaic and yet would still be removed from the pedestrian, had to be created. These difficulties have been masterfully overcome in two significant plays: *Achzar Mikol Hamelech* ("Cruelest of All, the King," 1953) by Nissim ALONI and *Milchemet Bnei Or* ("The Battle of the Children of Light," 1956) by M. Shamir. Aloni portrayed the rebellious Jeroboam Ben Nebat at a critical moment for the kingdom of Judea. Ben Nebat is torn between his desire for the woman he loved in his youth, now the queen of Judea, Rehaboam's wife, and his mother's thirst for power, her dreams of her son becoming king of Israel, and her hatred for the queen. Although the biblical characters on stage speak in an elevated Hebrew, it is still a modern play with tragic overtones. Aloni not only transcends conventions but with consummate skill weaves the play's fabric, rich with passions and ambiguities. In *Milchemet Bnei Or* Shamir's choice of events, concerning the biblical conflicts between Alexander Janeus and the Zealots, and his marked allusions to contemporary issues turned the play into a political statement by a modern, socially minded dramatist. His modified Mish-

naic, a postbiblical Hebrew dialect, was highly convincing and helped to disperse the fears of using the ancient tongue. The 1960's show a marked change in the Israeli playwrights' attitude toward utilizing the Bible or Jewish history as possible sources for his dramatic vision. Meged paraphrased in modern language the first chapters of the Book of Genesis, and in his play *Ha'ona Haboeret* ("The Busy Season," 1967) he used names of characters from, as well as the form of, the Book of Job. Shamir also used historical material in *Halaila L'ish* ("Tonight I'll Belong to a Man," 1963), a play based on one of the five scrolls, the Story of Ruth. Two other noteworthy plays in this trend are Yehudah Amichai's *Masah L'Ninveh* ("A Voyage to Ninve," 1964), a modern rendering by an Israeli poet of the biblical character of Jonah, and Benjamin Galai's *Sippur Uria* ("The Story of Uria," 1967), a play about Uria the Hittite, Bathsheba's husband, treated in a most vital, unconventional manner. It is Galai's first play to be produced, although he has written a number of very modern, sophisticated, and intriguing plays. It is interesting to note that the greatest success in Israel after *The Dybbuk*, which has been performed by the Habimah over a thousand times throughout the world, is the biblical comedy *Shlomo Hamelech V'Shalmai Hassandlar* ("King Solomon and Shalmai the Cobbler"), based on an ancient legend. This comedy, written in German by a Jewish writer from Germany, Sami Gruniman, and brilliantly translated into Hebrew with rhymes and ingeniously witty inventions by Israel's poet and dramatist Nathan Alterman, was first produced in 1944. Twenty years later it was revived as a colorful musical. The play is the story of King Solomon's changing parts with Shalmai the cobbler and the mistaken identities and entanglements that followed.

One other paradox to note about the Israeli drama is its scarcity of poetic works. It is a paradox because of the nature of the Hebrew renaissance. The revival of the Hebrew language in the last generations drew primarily on biblical and postbiblical sources, because there were no other periods in which the language was a living language, spoken daily. This style always sounded flowery and heightened, removed from everyday life, and therefore served well the poets and romanticists. Yet the need to create a pedestrian language for communication was not only one of the basic needs of modern Hebrew but a prerequisite for the development of any form of realistic prose—novel and drama alike. This accounts for the fact that the majority of Hebrew drama prior to the establishment of the State of Israel was written in verse or some sort of high-flown poetic prose. Thus, the young Israeli dramatists of the 1940's were intoxicated by the new avenues of expression opened to them and, perhaps subconsciously, rejected the ornamented Hebrew of olden times. It was, therefore, a major victory for the Israeli theater when one of Israel's greatest poets, Nathan ALTERMAN, joined the world of the drama with his *Kineret, Kineret . . .* (1961) and a year later with one of the best dramatic achievements of Israel, *Pundak Haroochot* ("The Inn of Ghosts"). This play, a personal, expressionist statement of a poet made in theatrical terms, momentarily lifted Israeli drama from its pedestrian and prosaic plane. These experiments were later enhanced by Amichai's "A Voyage to Ninve" (1964), a symbolic play-poem interwoven with satiric allusions to modern life in Israel. The play was a significant contribution to the creation of a modern Israeli poetic-drama.

In the late 1960's a new group of young dramatists appeared. Among them is Nafthali Ne'eman, whose first play, *Marko* (1967), is an honest and angry attack on the Israeli establishment. Israel Eliraz, although he won a playwriting contest and a number of his plays were published, did not have any of his plays produced until 1968—*Rachok Min Hayam, Rachok Min Hakayitz* ("Far from the Sea, Far from the Summer")—when it was given an experimental production. *Mored Vamelech* ("Rebel and King," 1968), a biblical drama depicting the conflicts between King David and his rebellious son Absalom, as expressed by two different points of view, is another play by Eliraz, produced by the Haifa Municipal Theatre. Another young Israeli playwright, hitherto known as a fine talented actor, Nafthali Yavin, directed his own first play, initially written in Hebrew and then translated into English by the author himself, for a production in London. The play, *Regaim Yekarim* (*Precious Moments,* 1968), which has six episodes and moves on a variety of levels from realism to surrealism, is written from a director's angle and shows Yavin's aspirations as a director-playwright.

There are no books in English, or in Hebrew, for that matter, which could serve as a reference for Israeli drama.—Z. R.

Italy: *middle ages.* The origins of Italian dramatic literature go back to the thirteenth century, when writers—especially poets—abandoned the use of Latin and turned to the languages actually spoken by the people; by distillation from the various regional dialects they produced the Italian language, which first appeared in the writings of Sicily and the areas of Tuscany and Umbria and which in the course of the fourteenth century became the national literary language.

Some of the forms that early drama took were inherited from the medieval Latin theater. Because of the unified culture created in Europe by the Catholic Church during the middle ages, the history of dramatic literature in Italy is similar to that of both France and the German-speaking lands. In Italy, as elsewhere, beginning in the tenth century, it is possible to document the existence of a "liturgical drama" used as a theatrical interval inserted in the ordinary of the Mass at Easter (*Officium Sepulchri*). The most ancient extant manuscript containing such an interval, and dating from the tenth century, is preserved in the Benedictine Abbey of San Gallo in Switzerland. But it is probable that even earlier, at Rome, during the eighth or ninth century, the following brief exchange of remarks took place with a minimum of *mise en scène* between a priest and two clerks: Priest: "Quem queritis?" Clerks: "Jesum Nazarenum." Priest: "Non est hic." Clerks: "Alleluja!" (Whom do ye seek? Jesus of Nazareth. He is not here. Hallelujah!) Liturgical drama, then, developed when the potential drama in the text was sensed and put into dialogue form, and its scope was widened to include other episodes in the life of Christ

and other religious festivals (for example, Nativity, Epiphany).

This type of drama might better be called the "dramatic office," thereby underscoring its complete subordination to the liturgy. The history of the dramatic office, fairly rich in textual evidence, also illustrates various aspects of the change from the Latin used in the liturgy to the vernacular, as well as the introduction of rhyme and accentuation in place of Latin quantitative metrics. Above all, it reveals the gradual movement of dramatic action away from the altar, an example being a twelfth-century *Passion* at the Abbey of Montecassino, which probably took place in various parts of the church. A twelfth-century Paduan version of the *Officium de Peregrino,* concerning the apparition on the way to Emmaus, concluded with the scattering of sweets from the roof of the church, which were grabbed up in a colorful contest among the people below.

The comic and secular theater also began, in a certain sense, in the shadow of the Church, the central force and source of order in all medieval life. But whereas the sacred theater arose with the help of the liturgy, the secular theater developed out of a parody of it. In the eighth century at Rome the Libertates Decembris (the ancient Roman Saturnalis) reappeared. At these festivities, which occurred between Christmas and the New Year, the people and the lower clergy took unaccustomed liberties and carried on a parody of the religious ceremony that culminated in the jesting consecration of a bishop—the Pope of Fools. The secular and carnival spirit of the

AN ENGRAVING OF ITALIAN TROUBADOURS (NEW YORK PUBLIC LIBRARY)

Libertates Decembris was not slow to influence liturgical drama as well, forcing it away from the altar and enriching it with comic and profane elements. In the twelfth and thirteenth centuries orgiastic excesses and violently satirical elements were introduced. Although Pope Innocent III prohibited the celebration of the Libertates Decembris in 1207, it continued to be celebrated in various parts of northern Italy.

From this tradition of popular entertainment there branched out the literary works of the Italian troubadours and jongleurs, including the first manifestations of drama in the Italian vernacular that may be documented on a textual basis. These entertainers were poets, mimes, and dancers who circulated from piazza to piazza and from court to court displaying their repertoire of monologues and songs on themes of love or, more rarely, on politics and current events. The earliest known European troubadours, whose activities centered in the courts of southern France, had used the Provençal language, which they developed to a high degree of literary refinement. Because of its literary value, the poets and jongleurs of northern and central Italy at first also employed Provençal, until the poetic flowering in Sicily and in Tuscany and Umbria compelled the use of the Italian dialects, which Dante referred to collectively as the *lingua del sì*.

During the eleventh and twelfth centuries, the troubadour's monologue gave rise to the *contrasto,* a clearly dramatic form very probably intended for theatrical presentation, consisting of a dialogue between a knight and a lady. In a contrasto by the Provençal poet Rambaldo of Vaqueiras (twelfth–thirteenth centuries), the knight speaks Provençal and the lady replies in the dialect of Genoa. The contrasto (dated between 1230 and 1250) by the Sicilian Cielo d'Alcamo is the first dramatic document in any Italian dialect and proves the extraordinary expressiveness and musicality of the vernacular. The secular contrasto was short-lived, exhausting itself at the same time as the Sicilian School (thirteenth century), a group of poets associated with the court of Emperor Frederick II at Palermo, who were among the first to use Italian as a literary language. The contrasto form, however, was soon used again by the Umbrian and Tuscan authors of the religious *laudi.*

In the course of the thirteenth century there was a vast production of mystical poems called laudi, or "lauds." The appearance of these poems in the vernacular is related to a vast popular movement of great idealistic and mystical force that profoundly shook religious sentiment in central Italy between 1259 and 1260. It reached its peak at Perugia in Umbria, where the preaching of Renato Fasiani provoked a wild outburst of fanaticism in the form of public self-flagellation. In this climate of religious fervor the laudi flowered as the authentic expression of lay confraternities, such as "The Disciplined Ones" and "The Flagellants." The authors of the laudi were monks and clerics, who participated actively in the popular reawakening. First among them is the Umbrian JACOPONE DA TODI, a Franciscan and an enemy of Boniface VIII. His very beautiful laudi, the first great monument of Italian literature, express the religious concerns of the middle ages—the irreconcilable tension between flesh and spirit, be-

JACOPONE DA TODI (ITALIAN CULTURAL INSTITUTE)

tween heaven and earth. The literary expression of this tension took the form of the contrasto, but the dialogue between the lover and his lady was replaced by a dialectic encounter between Soul and Body, Friar and Devil, and so on. Obviously intended for a rudimentary mise en scène, the laudi quickly assumed a more complex dramatic form. For example, in Jacopone's famous *Pianto della Madonna* ("Complaint of the Madonna"), the dialogue form of the contrasto develops into a completely dramatic structure with several speakers and various situations. The original center of the dramatic laudi was Perugia, whence it spread to all of central Italy in the thirteenth and fourteenth centuries. In addition to the collected laudi of Jacopone and Ugo Panziera da Prato (c. 1330), there are also important anonymous collections extant, written in Perugia, Orvieto, and L'Aquila.

The evolution of the laudi into a fully dramatic form was almost instantaneous. More complex, however, was the passage from the austere and solemn simplicity of the dramatic laudi to the theatrical complexity of the so-called *sacra rappresentazione* ("sacred play"). The latter became widespread in Tuscany and in Rome in the second half of the fifteenth century. As the lauda spread from Umbria throughout the Abruzzi, Tuscany, and Rome, it lost its primitive character. Its typically austere line gave way to the hendecasyllabic line of what Dante called the *dolce stil novo* ("sweet new style") of the thirteenth-century lyrical, poetic movement of Tuscany. The laudi were thus enriched with ingredients of the romance and enhanced by a refinement of language, choreographic and theatrical elements, and the use of primitive theatrical equipment. Ultimately, even its name was changed: to sacred "festivity" or "play," that is, sacra rappresentazione, or, as in English, "mystery play."

The chief center of these plays was wealthy Florence, where the spectacles took on particularly rich and gorgeous characteristics. In spite of its poetic and dramatic surface, the sacra lacked force largely through the loss of the ardor that is so characteristic of the laudi. This was true even in the hands of such capable poets as Feo Belcari (1410–1484), the author of the *Rappresentazione e festa d'Abraam e Isaac* ("Play and Festival of Abraham and Isaac," 1449), and Castellano de' Castellani (1461–1519), author of various texts prized by his contemporaries. The best of the works is the anonymous, early sixteenth-century *Rappresentazione di Santa Uliva* ("Play of Saint Uliva"), in which deep religious feeling is ingenuously and delicately expressed. *Santa Uliva* is an exception, however, and in the course of the sixteenth century the sacra rappresentazione wore itself out in an empty display of theatrics devoid of moral and idealistic content.

The principal problem of the history of the Italian theater may perhaps be expressed thus: Why did the medieval theater, so free in form and realistic in content, not continue its evolution? By enlarging its scope to include secular materials, it might have given rise to a national, popular theater, as was the case in Elizabethan England, for example. Instead, the medieval theater became extinct, leaving the way clear for a dramatic theory based, not on divergent principles, but on downright contradictory ones. The causes for this sharp change of course are not to be found in the theater itself but in the social and political conditions of fifteenth- and sixteenth-century Italy. Unlike other European nations, Italy had neither unity nor national independence. The Italian people had only one cultural factor in common— religion—and it is from this religion that the laudi flowered. When the intense religious spirit of the middle ages was dissolved by the secular, aristocratic interests of the Renaissance, no commonly held national sentiment arose to replace it. Further, proximity to the center of Christianity—Rome—generally served to hinder popular reform movements. The Church frequently joined feudal powers in repressing polemical and satirical expression of discontent with the social and political order and condemned naïvely mystical outbursts against its own weaknesses. Thus, the Italian people resorted to the anonymous and crude displays produced by impoverished roving entertainers and wandering players. On improvised stages in piazzas and marketplaces, comedy, employing masked actors, slowly evolved. Likewise, the sacred theater not infrequently took up the function of the circus games of the Roman Empire, which were intended to amuse the common folk; it became a purely formal, empty expression of a religiosity devoid of real meaning. Moreover, the scholarly pursuits of the Humanists had begun to create a gap, which persists today, between the cultured elite and the people. The opulent ducal and seignorial courts and the papal court provided many oases of culture throughout the country. But court tastes became increasingly specialized and

refined, orienting literary and artistic productions toward their own ends. In England and France the postmedieval theater retained in whole or in part its national character (thanks to the equilibrium among social classes attained in England after the War of the Roses and guaranteed in France by the absolute monarchy itself). In Italy, however, the postmedieval theater arose as the expression of a narrow elite, thus creating a split between the cultured and the popular theaters.

Renaissance (c. 1350–1600). The Renaissance theater developed out of love and admiration for the classics, which had been rediscovered and reevaluated by the Humanists, and out of a renewed taste for the life of this world. The new theater was preceded by many experiments in performing the plays of Plautus, Terence, and Seneca in Latin and by even earlier attempts to imitate their style. The famous and bloody Latin tragedy *Eccerinis* by Albertino Mussato (1261–1329), written in verse along Senecan lines, goes back to the beginning of the fourteenth century. The Renaissance theater was truly launched with the *Paulus* written in 1390 by the Humanist Pier Paolo Vergerio (1370–1444), a young student of logic at the University of Bologna.

To begin with tragedy, it should be noted that Humanistic tragedy was not a phenomenon limited to Italy, but in Italy it first appeared and the principles that were to constitute its foundations were developed there. In 1513 Giangiorgio Trissino (1478–1550) wrote *Sofonisba* in imitation of Euripides; in 1514 or 1515 Giovanni Rucellai (1475–1525) imitated Sophocles with his *Rosmunda*. Both works, however, were intended more for reading than for presentation. Giovambattista Giraldi Cinthio (1504–1573) was both theorist and writer of regular tragedy, that is, tragedy along classical lines. He wrote *Intorno al comporre delle commedie e delle tragedie* ("Concerning the Writing of Comedies and Tragedies," 1543), thus becoming the first to enunciate the principles of unity of action and time. Another theorist, Julius Caesar Scaliger (Latinized name of Giulio Cesare Scaligero, 1484–1558), in his posthumous *Poetices libri septem* ("The Seven Books of the Poetics," 1561), added to it the unity of place. Cinthio's tragedies, among which are *Orbecche* (1541), *Didone*, and *Cleopatra* (the last two published posthumously in 1583), and certain tragicomedies manifest not only a rigorous adherence to the Aristotelian unities, but also that taste for the horrible and monstrous that Italian writers of tragedy often display. *Il Re Torrismondo* (1587) by Torquato TASSO is closely akin to Cinthio's works, not only in its rigid neoclassicism, but also in its taste for horror. Arising, then, from an arid imitation of the classics, this movement often exalts an austere Roman, or "romanic," grandeur that is far removed from, and unsuitable to, the spirit of its age. Even *Orazia* (1546) by Pietro ARETINO is not exempt from this judgment, although Benedetto Croce labeled it the most beautiful tragedy of sixteenth-century Italy. Its several well-delineated characters do not compensate for the artificiality of construction imposed by the traditional form, which was so alien to the free and unrestrained spirit of its author.

Renaissance Italian playwrights, unlike Racine and Corneille in France, were incapable of establishing a viable neoclassical tragic theater. What is more, adoption of the classical tragic form prevented the development of some other form of tragedy that might have employed tragic themes more congenial to the taste of the time—themes which, indeed, existed in the imaginations of the authors and were successfully elaborated in narrative form. It is significant that the collections of Italian *novelle* (such as Cinthio's *Hecatommithi,* from which Shakespeare drew the plot of *Othello*) inspired English dramaturgy. The free dramatic form of Elizabethan tragedy, untrammeled by Aristotelian prejudices, easily absorbed nonclassical themes.

The pastoral drama (*favola pastorale*), which drew its subjects from classical bucolic and mythological poetry and its early form from the classical eclogue and the contemporary sacred play, was more congenial than tragedy to the dramatic endowments of Italians. In it, melancholy and sentiment replaced the austere climate of tragedy, a subtle sensuousness supplanted intense passion. In the first pastoral drama, *Favola d'Orfeo* (*Orpheus,* 1480) by Angelo Poliziano (1454–1494), the structure of the sacred drama is quite evident despite the secular material. Whereas two centuries before, the lauda had assumed the dramatic form of the secular *contrasto* of love, Poliziano's highly secular material—exalting an unrestrained epicureanism and totally lacking in moral bias—was cast in the form of sacred drama. It is, however, exactly because of the adherence to the form of sacred drama and the use of a content so ostentatiously at variance with it that the *Favola d'Orfeo* stands as a forerunner to the fully developed pastoral drama with its contradiction between classical format and nonclassical feeling toward nature. The *Favola d'Orfeo* also serves as a forewarning of the pastoral drama's purely rhetorical love for the rustic and simple life of shepherds and shepherdesses. This love was inspired neither by contemplation of nature nor by dislike of the artificiality of city life, but rather by the admiration of learned courtiers for the eclogues and idyls of the classics. The pastoral drama appears in a classical format—in five acts and in verse. The plays charm us with their evocation of a mythical golden age, when shepherds and nymphs played at being in love in an idealized climate among well-manicured woods and brooks.

A SCENE FROM TORQUATO TASSO'S *Aminta*

The pastoral drama was popular in Italy and in Europe during the sixteenth century. Among the innumerable unoriginal plays in this form, two are important: Torquato Tasso's AMINTA and IL PASTOR FIDO by Giovanni Battista Guarini (1538–1612). *Aminta* is the masterpiece of the genre, not because of its dramatic impetus, but because of the exquisite musicality of its verse. *Il Pastor Fido* won for Guarini wide popularity. Its complicated and confusing plot constitutes a kind of treatise on the casuistry of love.

The secular spirit of the Renaissance—cynical, irreverent, comical to the point of ruthlessness—found adequate expression in the literary comedy that flourished throughout the sixteenth century, particularly during its first half. Italian comedy was preceded by the exhumation for performance at the end of the fifteenth century of the classical Latin comedy, as well as by a proliferation of imitative works in Latin displaying overwhelmingly obscene comedy. The literary comedy took as its models the New Comedy of Menander and the plays of Terence and Plautus (twelve comedies of the latter were rediscovered in the course of the fifteenth century). These models provided Italian comedy with characteristic plot situations—misunderstandings, character exchanges, confusions, final recognitions, and tricks played by youthful lovers on lecherous old men. (See ROMAN COMEDY.) Nevertheless, comedy reflected contemporary reality more than did tragedy, and an attempt was made to liberate it from excessive subordination to classical models. Although comedy flourished for only a few decades, there was in it a discernible evolution toward greater realism. For example, the conventional setting of action in a mythical Rome or Athens was replaced with local settings; characters were imbued with contemporary traits; verse was abandoned in favor of a more realistic prose; and the prose itself sometimes bordered on or actually was dialect.

Ludovico ARIOSTO inaugurated Renaissance comedy in 1508 with *Cassaria* ("The Strong Box"). Still tied to classical models, he used a hendecasyllabic line rhymed in *sdruccioli* (triple rhyme, the last accent falling on the antepenultimate syllable); the sole merit of this line was that it imitated the movement of Latin iambic trimeter. By 1513, with CALANDRIA by Bernardo Dovizi da Bibbiena (1470–1520), prose was decisively adopted and contemporary life strongly reflected. Niccolò MACHIAVELLI perfected the art of comedy in two plays: LA MANDRAGOLA and *La Clizia* (1525; Clizia, the titular heroine, never appears onstage). In both plays, contemporary action and characters are molded into classical form without any distortion. Realistic characters and situations and a total independence from classical models characterize the best comedies of Pietro Aretino. The Venetian Andrea Calmo (1510–1571) stands out among writers who used dialect. Giovan Giorgio Alione (c. 1460–c. 1521) of Piedmont wrote rough, vivacious farces, dispensing entirely with classical influences. Like Machiavelli, on the other hand, is the Paduan Angelo BEOLCO, called "il Ruzzante," who achieved a perfect blending of his material with the classic form. With the use of dialect brought to extreme perfection, he poetically transforms popular realism into works of skillful craftsmanship and learning. Others who created at least one successful comedy are: Donato Giannotti (1492–1573); Anton Francesco Grazzini, called "il Lasca" (1503–1584); Annibal Caro (1507–1566); and Giovan Maria Cecchi (1518–1587). Also to be mentioned are two anonymous works: GLI INGANNATI, written in 1531 by a group from the Accademici Intronati of Siena, and LA VENEXIANA, written sometime during the first half of the century.

Literary comedy during the first half of the sixteenth century seems to provide cynical laughter at the decadence of Italian Renaissance civilization. The second half of the century, dominated by the spirit of the Council of Trent with all its repercussions, ushers in a new spiritual climate, one that calls for more solid ethical and civic principles. It is a significant fact that Italian Renaissance comedy concludes with the isolated masterpiece of the philosopher Giordano Bruno (1548?–1600), IL CANDELAIO. Its plot, based on a terrible jest, is narrated with a despairing morality that stands in dramatic contrast to the cynical amorality of the first half of the century. Equally significant is the fact that the fertile and fluent Neapolitan Giovan Battista Della Porta (1535–1615) was popular during the two centuries that his life bridged. The author of numerous comedies liberated from all classical imitation, Della Porta found a rather different public from that attached to the courts. His works, although written with witty good humor and with a baroque taste for the unexpected, have a certain narrowness of scope and tone quite alien to the interests of the Renaissance and thus at times foreshadow the climate of the bourgeois theater.

seventeenth century. The crisis of the Renaissance imposed a profound reevaluation upon the world of Italian letters. The new century emerged —under pressure from political events, particularly the religious schism and the subsequent Counter Reformation—divested of those excesses of life and of that profligacy that both letters and the arts had exploited in the preceding century. An Ariosto or an Aretino would have been unthinkable in the seventeenth century, and even Machiavelli survived only at the cost of a painstaking adaptation, on the part of Catholic thinkers, of his thought to the new Catholic morality. The courts were replaced by the academies and the *camerate* (private scholarly clubs) as centers of culture in which the physical sciences were cultivated alongside letters.

Literary comedy became completely decadent in the works of Giacinto Andrea Cicognini (1606–1651), where love for adventurous intrigue replaces a taste for words and the study of character. The realistic equilibrium of the writers of the sixteenth century is here frequently upset by lachrymose sentimentality and gratuitous comic triviality.

Pastoral plays (see PASTORAL DRAMA) proliferated, though they were no more than dramatized madrigals repeating the formulas inherited from the sixteenth century. Guarini's *Il Pastor Fido* was followed by sterile productions such as *Filli di Sciro (Phyllis of Scyros,* 1605) by Guidobaldo Bonarelli (1563–1608), which was distinguished solely by the poet's great ability as a versifier. Michelangelo Buonarroti the Younger (1568–1646), with his *La Fiera* ("The Fair," 1619) and, particularly, *La Tancia* (1611), was

the only man to strike a note of freshness and poetic simplicity. Historically, the real significance of pastoral drama is that it was dressed in music and thus gave life to the *melodramma,* or "musical drama."

The musical drama had its origins in the experiments of the sixteenth century. Sometimes these experiments were practical, that is, intended for public performance and popular use; sometimes they were mainly theoretical, as in the works privately performed and debated by the Camerata dei Bardi in Florence. It was these latter experiments that led directly to musical drama, or opera, since the polyphony of the practical experiments was unsuited to dramatic expression. From the literary point of view, the genre of musical drama must be considered as the realization of the musical vocation that the pastoral drama had manifested from the beginnings of its history. Its authors had always cultivated the sound of the syllables and emphasized the singable qualities of the verse, something that we recognize in the madrigal as well. The history of musical drama, however, is of predominant interest to music rather than drama. Ottavio Rinuccini, Alessandro Striggio, and others prepared texts for the music of Jacopo Peri and Claudio Monteverdi, employing the traditional subjects of Orpheus, Daphne, and so on, but these texts have no particular importance in the history of dramatic literature.

Seventeenth-century Italian tragedy is negligible, particularly if measured against Elizabethan or neoclassical French tragedy. Unlike comedy, tragedy remained rigorously faithful to the Aristotelian unities, to the use of verse and the five-act structure, and to the restriction of the characters to the number essential to the plot. Generally, this tragedy was intended for reading—a fact that was the cause and the consequence of its eminently cultivated and bookish quality. Its initiator was Federigo Della Valle (c. 1560–1628) of Piedmont, who lived obscurely at the court of Savoy in Turin. Della Valle's works, written between 1590 and 1627, were completely unknown to his contemporaries. His first tragedy, *Reina di Scozia* ("Queen of Scots," written 1590), was neither published nor produced. His *Judit* and *Ester,* written shortly after 1600, were also passed over in his day. These tragedies, which have been reevaluated in our own time, possess an unusual dramatic inspiration and a happy blending of matter and form. Della Valle had a poetic talent capable of expressing tragic sentiments and human grandeur with a theatrical force entirely new to the Italian tragic stage. His work was followed by *L'Adamo* (1613) of Giovan Battista Andreini (1579–1654); *Solimano* (1619) by Prospero Bonarelli (1582 or 1588–1659); and *Aristodemo* (1657) by Carlo de' Dottori (1618–1680). In the last a taste for horror is ennobled by a dramatic force and power of expression. But these works are rare, and hardly noteworthy, exceptions to the sterile, tedious, and unoriginal output of seventeenth-century tragedy.

Nevertheless, it was during this century that great contributions were made, not only to the Italian stage but to the European stage in general. The musical drama, or opera, which began to develop during the seventeenth century, assumed mature national and popular stature in the following centuries. It was, in fact, the most original contribution of the modern

Italian theater to European culture. The development of the art of scene painting and stage decoration as well as development of stage machinery took place in this century. These Italian accomplishments were to dominate the technical aspects of the theater up to present times. Finally, it was during this period that the incomparable theatrical artistry that lies at the base of the phenomenon of the improvised comedy of the *commedia dell'arte* developed and spread throughout Europe. Without literature and without dramatic poetry, but nevertheless very rich in theater, the seventeenth century was to see its labors bear fruit in the following centuries. Indeed, it was from the refinement of improvised comedy that the theater of the new bourgeois society arose during the eighteenth century. But before we examine the commedia dell'arte and its maturation into valid literary forms, we must point out how, in the latter part of the seventeenth century, the split between the cultural elite and the people became aggravated.

The literati and the poets had adopted an essentially literary language, one that had little in common with everyday speech. The political fragmentation of Italy, however, retarded the adoption of a common language and instead favored the use of dialect. Dialects were favored also by the fact that the various regions of Italy often had more contact with foreign countries than among themselves and were, therefore, subject to different linguistic influences. Thus Piedmont formed a part of the duchy of Savoy, which also included French areas; Venice gravitated to the states bordering the Adriatic Sea, and its dialect—employed even in the diplomatic documents and spoken all along the coast that is now Yugoslavia—manifested all the dignity and vigor of a distinct language; Naples and Sicily, completely isolated from northern Italy by the Papal States, were culturally and politically tied to Spain. In reaction to this disunity and lack of common language, writers adopted "the language of Dante and Petrarch," which alone was considered worthy of being used in literature and in art. Thus was established a serious critical prejudice, which endured throughout the nineteenth century and beyond, against all literary efforts in dialect. Dramatic literature in particular suffered, for dramatic literature, more than any other literary form, is grounded in language as it is actually spoken. The literati used and brought to perfection a "Tuscan language," which was in part artificially created; popular writers, on the other hand, used the spoken language for their theater but lacked, obviously, the culture that would give the language an ordered, literary quality. During the whole of the sixteenth and seventeenth centuries, various isolated authors sought to bridge this gap. The Milanese Carlo Maria Maggi (1630–1699) was the author of conventional tragedies in verse, musical dramas, and sacred dramas, but also of five comedies, part in Italian and part in Milanese dialect, in which he consciously attempted to reproduce actual Milanese life. Also to be noted is the Piedmontese Carlo G. B. Tana (1649–1713), who wrote a comedy in Tuscan and Piedmontese dialect. But Maggi and Tana were exceptions in an atmosphere otherwise restricted by aesthetic preconceptions that forced most writers to adopt the literary language and to employ the accepted forms of pastoral drama and tragedy.

commedia dell'arte and Goldonian reform. Unlike the literary comedy recited by groups of dilettanti, courtiers, and literati during the Renaissance, COMMEDIA DELL'ARTE is a theater of professional actors who follow the theatrical trade and obviously descend from the wandering players and jongleurs of the middle ages. The *commedia dell'arte,* which first appeared early in the sixteenth century, was improvised comedy, for the actors did not follow a precise literary text but instead an outline or scenario that briefly listed successive scenes, substance of dialogues between characters, and various incidents. From these suggestions the actors "improvised" their dialogue. This does not mean that the comedians of the arte created nightly new repartee and new *lazzi* (theatrical "gags"), for these were the fruit of long custom and of exceptional harmony among members of the various companies. The text and the spectacle, however, remained open forms that could be quickly modified by actual events or a bright idea. The comedians of the arte evolved an exquisite theatrical convention based, on the one hand, on their eclectic virtuosity as actors, mimes, singers, musicians, and acrobats and, on the other, on the invention of masks, which, along with costumes, became visual representations of contemporary character types. Among the stock symbolic figures of the commedia dell'arte may be mentioned the buffoons, or *zanni* (Harlequin, Brighella); the merchant (Pantalone); the evil Spanish soldier (Matamoros, Captain Spavento); the youthful lovers from good family (Lelio, Isabella); the learned graduate of the University of Bologna (Doctor Balanzone).

Companies of comedians of the arte traveled throughout Europe, beginning with the final decades of the sixteenth century, taking along their scenarios. The decidedly secondary nature of the literary component of the commedia dell'arte rendered its exportation very easy, and these comedians left a deep imprint on all European theater. The scenarios, which the comedians drew with extreme liberty from the classic and modern repertory, from collections of tales, and from the Spanish and French theater, have little literary or poetic value. They are filled with improbabilities, superficialities, and vulgarities. Thus, collections of scenarios have an exclusively technical and documentary interest. The same may be said of the lists or manuals of lazzi ("gags" of every type used by comedians in search of ideas) and collections of *tirate* (searching, philosophical monologues), *soliloqui* ("soliloquies"), *uscite* ("witty retorts"), *maledizioni* ("curses" upon a prodigal son or unfaithful lover), *rodomontate* ("blustering rants"), *dichiarazioni amorose* ("declarations of love"). At a certain point the repartee, the lazzi, and the situations became repetitious, as the very existence of manuals proves. The arte nevertheless mirrored a genuine and fresh popular culture and, through the masks worn by the actors, distinguished and stylized types and characters that were fundamental to contemporary Italian society.

The commedia dell'arte did not give rise, then, to a dramatic literature but became itself the material for dramatic literature. As performances degenerated into routine spectacles full of incongruities, nonsense, and meaningless vulgarities, the masks lost contact with the social types from which they had

SKETCH SHOWING STOCK FIGURES OF *commedia dell'arte*—BRIGHELLA, GIANGURGOLO, DOCTOR,
HARLEQUIN, PIERROT, AND THE SPANISH CAPTAIN   (NEW YORK PUBLIC LIBRARY)

sprung. The modern Italian theater was born when the commedia was completely renovated and when it began once again to take its inspiration from contemporary life rather than from manuals and ancient tradition. This renovation, known as Goldonian reform, was effected by the Venetian Carlo GOLDONI, who worked at Venice between 1747 and 1762, and then in Paris. That the reforms took place at Venice is no accident, for Venice had a more solidly developed bourgeois society than any other city of Europe. In Venice—which was politically isolated from the rest of the Italian peninsula—the mercantile bourgeoisie was the dominant class. The city had attained that hegemony of which only the German cities of the ancient Hanseatic League were able to boast. Throughout the seventeenth and well into the eighteenth century, this bourgeoisie was content with the rough vulgarity of the commedia dell'arte, but their gradual cultural refinement helped to create a climate favorable to reform. The bourgeois Goldoni became the interpreter of the latent dissatisfaction, among the more enlightened of the bourgeoisie, with the outworn dramatic form. He felt the need for a dramaturgy that reflected the customs, ideals, and problems of his society, one which fused artistic integrity of performance with the didactic aims of denouncing excesses and condemning vice. His intention was to castigate with laughter and to teach by amusing.

The reform took place gradually. At first Goldoni limited himself to writing the dialogue for scenes in which everyday, contemporary characters, as opposed to stock figures, appeared. The masks, which were so dear to the public, remained on some of the characters, as did the lazzi and the improvised speeches, all of which provided a kind of abstract counterpoint of buffoonery within the body of the comedy. As time went on, Goldoni brought the masks back to their original function of representing servants, landlords, soldiers, and the like, and forced

even these stock figures to follow a precise written text. The use of lazzi as an end in itself was dropped, so that the masked characters, even though they retained their fantastic costumes, came to play a part both in language and function in a completely recognizable reality. Finally, when there was no longer any justification for the simultaneous presence on stage of realistic and masked characters, Goldoni divested the Pantalones and the Harlequins of their costumes and masks and turned them into entirely realistic characters having names and surnames. Pantalone is a perfect example of this development. The old commedia dell'arte scenarios view him through the eyes of the rabble, above which he has himself only just risen. He is the old miser who is ready to defend even with his teeth the money he has earned. He attempts to seduce female servants; he is despised by elegant youths and made a fool of by male servants. In Goldoni's hands, Pantalone undergoes a change—the same evolution that the bourgeois mercantile class had lived through. In the playwright's early plays, the character remains, if not exactly sordid and libidinous, then at best an old blockhead; very quickly, however, he becomes the embodiment of enlightened bourgeois good sense, as far removed from the ignorant vulgarity of the rabble as from the decadence of the nobility. He becomes, in short, the excellent father of a family.

The twenty-five or thirty comedies that make up the principal corpus of Goldoni's work constitute a complete picture of bourgeois life in its most typical incidents. Plot developments have only casual points in common with traditional resolutions. They adhere to reality, are credible and logical. The plays are written partly in Tuscan and partly in Venetian dialect, depending on which is more natural for the characters to speak. Thus, Goldoni's plays realized the ideals of European playwrights (from Denis Diderot to G. E. Lessing to George Lillo) who had reacted against neoclassical formalism and who had been only slightly successful in bringing it into being. Goldonian comedy had a large frame of reference, which included not only the bourgeoisie but also embraced with sincere interest the feelings of the common folk. It displayed great theatrical mastery, poetic realism, and a courageous originality in moral affirmation. And while the commedia dell'arte died in Goldoni's reform, its content and art were revitalized in his work. These attributes make Goldonian comedy one of the most exalted pages of European theater history in the eighteenth century.

eighteenth century comedy, tragedy, and opera. Goldonian reform did not have worthy successors. Social conditions favorable to a concretely bourgeois dramaturgy were lacking outside of Venice, while Venice itself declined, becoming provincial and poorer than in the past. Moreover, the reform had fierce adversaries in Venice, first among whom was the abbé Pietro Chiari (1711–1785), the author of extravagant, exotic comedies. He was followed by Count Carlo Gozzi, an adherent of the old social order dominated by the nobility. In his theatrical *fiabe* ("fairy tales") Gozzi preached the free reign of fantasy, which he mixed with farce. In contrast to Goldoni's spare realism, Gozzi's texts were a mixture of verse, prose, song, and dance, and his masked and realistic characters were blended in picturesque disorder.

At Venice the struggle between the old and the new theater was at its most extreme. In Italy as a whole, the theater merely continued along lines begun in the previous century. Traditional comedy followed its banal road, only to a moderate degree setting aside Spanish influences for the more mature examples provided by eighteenth-century French comedy. This process did not provide results worthy of notice even in the works of the best Tuscans, Giovan Battista Fagiuoli (1660–1742) and Jacopo Angelo Nelli (1673–1767). Some influence of Goldoni may be found in the works of Francesco Albergati Capacelli (1728–1804), but the preponderant influence on Capacelli was that of the exaggerated, sentimental

comedy of France during that period, the *comédie larmoyante,* or "tearful comedy." It would therefore seem that the Goldonian reform was premature, at least on a national scale.

The French influence was dominant in the realm of tragedy. The writers of theoretical works on the subject looked to the France of Racine and Voltaire. First among them was Ludovico Antonio Muratori (1672–1750), who, in his treatise *Della perfetta poesia italiana* ("Concerning the Ideal Italian Poetry," 1706), outlined the ideal components of tragedy: Racine's profound psychology within the rigorous forms of ancient tragedy. Pier Jacopo Martelli (1665–1727) attempted an outright imitation of the French alexandrine by employing a line uniting two seven-syllable fragments, which, under the name of the "martelliano," enjoyed a reputation that was as extraordinary as it was fleeting. Even the Jesuits, who, during the preceding century had evolved their own sacred theater in Latin and Italian for didactic ends, turned to France.

One work stands out in the otherwise desolate panorama of the first half of the century: *Merope* (1713) by the cultivated Venetian man of letters Scipione di Maffei (1676–1755). After reviving for production several Italian tragedies from the past, Maffei wrote the play as a challenge to the alleged superiority of the French drama. Composed in verse, in five acts, in accordance with classical rules, *Merope* had an immediate and enthusiastic success: it passed through many editions and was translated throughout Europe. Nevertheless, however superior it was to the works of contemporary tragedians— because of the exquisite ease of the verse and felicitous characterization—it remains a lightweight tragedy, confirming once again the fundamental ineptitude of Italian writers in the tragic genre.

Aspirations toward a more authentic tragic theater, expressed during the first years of the eighteenth century by Muratori and others, were at last fulfilled in the second half of the century with the work of Vittorio ALFIERI. In nineteen tragedies written be-

A SCENE FROM CARLO GOLDONI'S *I Rusteghi* (FRENCH CULTURAL SERVICES)

tween 1775 and 1789 on themes drawn from biblical, Roman, and Renaissance history, Alfieri fused in a rigorously classical form a psychological insight worthy of his French models. In the history of the Italian tragic stage, Alfieri is at once isolated and irreplaceable. His isolation derives, not from a desire to imitate the ancients, as with other Italian tragedians, but from the fact that he found classical form most congenial to his urge toward powerful expression. Indeed, in ancient Rome, in its civil and moral greatness, and in the tyranny of the passions in Greek and Roman heroes, Alfieri did not, like his predecessors, discern an occasion for rhetoric; rather he saw a concrete and positive ideal of life, which stood in contrast to the inane mediocrity and servile flabbiness of his own time. Alfieri is irreplaceable because, in the adoption of a rigorously classical form, he gave dramatic expression to that tragic sense of impotence that he felt when confronting a world that appeared to him divided between slaves and tyrants. Within this form Alfieri's characteristic frenzy—the full strength of his feelings—seems compressed, constrained, and imprisoned by the five acts and the three unities. The result is a sharp and constricted verse that is extraordinarily concise and stinging. Precisely because of the sharp reduction to bare essentials, Alfieri's tragedies lend themselves to reading rather than to presentation. In fact, their life on the boards continued only as long as certain great romantic actors used them as exhibition pieces and the Italians' fight for independence during the nineteenth century gave relevance to the longing of Alfieri's heroes for liberty. Even with Alfieri, therefore, the Italian tragic theater continued to be only half a theater—a theater for readers. And, if the tragedians who preceded Alfieri were essentially literati, those who followed him were essentially lyricists. Their works do not live because of their theatrical qualities; they live—insofar as they live—because of their lyric passages and poetic brilliance, and because of the intimately autobiographical details that are often found in them. Such plays—those by minor tragedians such as Alessandro Verri (1741–1816), Ippolito Pindemonte (1753–1828), and Vincenzo Monti (1754–1828), as well as those by Alfieri— are to be recommended more for reading than for presentation.

Along with the bourgeois comedy of Goldoni, eighteenth-century Italy's most original contribution to the European theater was her musical drama. Its practitioners also aspired to create a tragic theater, but they were unsuccessful. For the overwhelming clash of passions of tragedy, they substituted the encounter of sentiments; rather than a harsh, regular verse, they preferred an easy and varied line employed chiefly for the sake of its musicality; heroic dimensions in character and action gave way to a sensuousness and delicacy that replaced the baroque taste of the seventeenth century with a style fluctuating between the Arcadian and the rococo. The chief center for the production of *melodramma* was the court at Vienna, where the two most important representatives of the genre, Apostolo Zeno (1668–1750) and Pietro Trapassi, known as METASTASIO, occupied, one after the other, the position of court poet. Metastasio, who wrote one literary tragedy and twenty-seven musical dramas between 1723 and 1782, entertained the conviction that he was giving to Italy a true tragic theater. In reality, however, although his facile ease as a versifier, his virtuosity in the use of words, and his sincere but conventional morality produced a dramatic form of extraordinary refinement and indubitable theatricality, he lacked tragic power. His work found its natural complement in the music composed for it by the innumerable maestros of the age, from Galuppi to Vivaldi and Mozart. Soon, however, in musical drama, or opera, as it came to be called, music came to prevail over the text, and the latter became a mere "libretto," often lacking completely in literary importance. In the century following, and in particular in Verdian opera, the text lost all autonomy. Its function as a prop to an essentially musical narration constrained it to employ summary, if sometimes robust, plots and psychology. Its characters became sharply one-dimensional, its plots self-evident. And as far as poetic expression is concerned, the lines were disordered and compressed to the point that the ugliness of many librettos became proverbial. Only toward the end of the century was the libretto brought back to a level of full literary dignity by Arrigo Boïto (with his librettos for Verdi's *Otello* and *Falstaff* and for his own *Mefistofele*) and by Luigi Illica and Giuseppe Giacosa, with their librettos for Puccini. Even these three, however, were unable to alter the total subordination of the libretto to the requirements of the music.

nineteenth century. Nineteenth-century Italy was dominated by the Risorgimento—the fight for unity and national independence that the Italian people conducted against Austria, the Bourbons, and the Papal States. The struggle was viewed with a certain passivity by the Italian lower classes, who possessed neither linguistic nor cultural unity and who were divided by centuries of profound separatism. The only true national unity, which went back to the fourteenth century, was that of aesthetic attainment and refined art. The only classes that saw a need for a unified state, therefore, were the depositaries of that culture—the bourgeoisie in the north and the more enlightened of the nobles in the south, where, because of the backwardness of economic and social conditions, no bourgeoisie had ever existed. Nationalistic demands were reflected in literature and on the stage, but, lacking any solid support from the people, these demands were but a rehashing of the motif of unity inherited from tradition. No difference, either formal or substantial, may be found between the "Canzone all'Italia" ("Song to Italy") of Petrarch in 1345 and the "Ode all'Italia" ("Ode to Italy") of Giacomo Leopardi in 1818, unless it be the rhetorical excitement that the urgency of the fight dictated to the latter. Literature inspired by the Risorgimento expressed only the superficial and romantic motifs of patriotism and exaltation of liberty. Attempts to produce a more acute and realistic examination of the situation in Italy (attempts which flowered in realism) made progress only with difficulty. In the nineteenth century, the only cultural achievement that was truly national and popular in scope was the operas of Verdi, Mascagni, and Puccini. These works brought together and reflected the cultural and idealistic contributions of the Italian nation in all its complexity. This achievement was possible perhaps because music expresses feelings rather than ideas. Elsewhere, as in the theater, where ideas found their expression in words, the language was that of an elite literary tradition, and the greater part of the nation felt itself excluded.

Italian tragedy in verse was only vaguely and superficially influenced by Shakespeare, Schiller, and Goethe and was unable to free itself from its eminently literary disposition to ape the classics. Some typical examples are the works of Ugo Foscolo (1778–1828): *Tieste* (*Thyestes*, 1798), *Aiace* (*Ajax*, 1811), and *Ricciarda* (1813); and those of Alessandro Manzoni (1785–1873): *Il Conte di Carmagnola* (*The Count of Carmagnola*, 1820), and *Adelchi* (1822). These works are notable for their lyric moments and their oratorical enthusiasm for patriotism and liberty. The choruses from *Adelchi* are a part of the most exalted Italian lyricism of the nineteenth century. Unfortunately, these compositions are essentially literary, lyrical, and formalistic. They are frankly bookish rather than theatrical.

Other tragedians, however, gave greater thought to the stage itself—among them Silvio Pellico (1789–1854), whose *Francesca da Rimini* enjoyed great success in 1815, and Giovan Battista Niccolini (1782–1861), whose *Arnaldo da Brescia* ("Arnold of Brescia," 1843) expressed well the robust versifier's sincere patriotism and unrestrained romantic feeling. The success of these works, based as it was on their appeal to emotions stirred by current events and on a rough simplicity of character and situation, is the same as the success enjoyed by the similarly motivated and constructed works of the operatic stage. Lacking as they do, however, the music of Verdi, they do not have real aesthetic force.

In the second half of the century tragedy in verse became unworkable in the plays of Pietro Cossa (1830–1881). Cossa tried to create a kind of realistic tragedy in verse. Two plays stand out from his abundant production: *Plauto e il suo secolo* ("Plautus and His Century," 1873) and *Nerone* ("Nero," 1871), in which the emperor is shown, not as a genius of evil, but as a mediocre actor. His works show that it was impossible for the classical dramatic form to survive in the realistic climate that was then developing.

More acceptable and coherent, in a certain sense, was the vast movement toward setting tragedy in the middle ages. This mannered movement became very much the mode of the late nineteenth century, but its popularity actually goes back to Pellico's *Francesca da Rimini*. A group of journeymen versifiers took part in it, among whom Leopoldo Marenco (1831–1899) and Giuseppe GIACOSA stand out. The plays of this genre are more acceptable and coherent than other nineteenth-century tragedy, because their authors openly avoid reality and take refuge in a fabulous world. Their literary quality, their use of verse, and their artificial and archaic language are therefore justifiable. It is among writers in this genre that we find the only writer of tragedy with literary and theatrical force in the late nineteenth and early twentieth centuries: Gabriele D'ANNUNZIO. He countered the vulgar romanticism of Giacosa and Marenco chiefly through his literary and poetic mastery; he found an affinity between the stylized middle ages and the sensuous and sensual components of his own poetic world. The medieval tragedies of D'Annunzio—for example, *Francesca da Rimini* (1901), *La Fiaccola sotto il moggio* (*The Light Under the Bushel*, 1905), and *La Parisina* (1912)—always retain something of the character of literary exercises. His dramatic masterpiece, however, LA FIGLIA DI IORIO, is set among the shepherds of the Abruzzi and is called a "pastoral tragedy." This name in past times signified for Italians the failure of, or the deviation from, tragedy. Even in this case, in spite of the excellence of the play, the impossibility of writing tragedy on themes devoid of concrete reality is confirmed.

Comedy and prose drama in the nineteenth century came increasingly under the French influence. Some comedies were tardy imitations of Molière; others displayed a vulgar sentimentalism inspired by the *comédie larmoyante* of La Chausée. Dramas of adventure exhibited empty theatricality; and sentimental, melodramatic feuilletons showed their derivations from René Pixerécourt, and Jules Lemaître. There were short dramas, which, in the style of De Musset, took their titles and themes from proverbs, and so-called thesis plays, dealing with social and moral problems, which followed in the footsteps of Alexandre Dumas fils, Émile Augier, and others. In general, then, the Italian theater of the nineteenth century was imitative of the French, and only rare and isolated voices expressed authentic and original ideas. It was not until the end of the century, with the flowering of naturalism, that independence and originality of thought developed.

As for the Italian tradition of comedy, Goldoni found no followers in the nineteenth century. Rewritings and adaptations of his work abounded, but there was no utilization of his realistic method. Several men who tried to give attention to the life of their own times stand out from the plethora of wearisome rewriters. The Roman count Giovanni Giraud (1776–1834) found inspiration for at least two comedies in the niggardly and backward Rome of the popes: *L'Ajo nell'imbarazzo* ("The Embarrassed Tutor," 1807) and *Il Galantuomo per transazione* ("Gentleman by Arrangement," 1833). In these works Giraud manifests an acute psychological penetration and satirical ability. Another realist, Francesco Augusto Bon (1788–1858), of Trieste, is the author of the isolated *Trilogia di Ludro* ("Trilogy of Ludro," written 1832–1837), inspired by Goldoni and Beaumarchais. Around the figure of his adventurous protagonist he created a vivid and detailed ambience reflective of contemporary life.

In the second half of the century, however, the determining influence was the French "thesis play" of Alexandre Dumas fils, Émile Augier, and Edouard Pailleron. Such plays were at first grossly imitated by the Italians—at times with ridiculous results—but they nevertheless enjoyed success with the unsophisticated Italian public. Among the successes might be mentioned *La Morte civile* (*The Outlaw*, 1861) by Paolo Giacometti (1816–1882), in which the theme of divorce is discussed with powerful but rhetorical theatricality, and certain dramas by Paolo Ferrari (1822–1889), the author of charming historical comedies on the lives of Goldoni and Giuseppe Parini. Ferrari's thesis plays are atypical in that they reaffirm, rather than criticize, certain formalities and hypocrisies of society. His *Il Duello* ("The Duel,"

1868), for example, far from condemning the duel, argues the need for it; in *Due dame* ("Two Ladies," 1877) he reasserts the upper-class prejudice against marriages with women of the lower classes, however noble in spirit and richly endowed with virtue they are.

As time went on, the thesis theater matured. That it did not attain true originality is to be attributed to the fact that its premises are those of the great European movement of naturalism. It attained a unique critical spirit, however, and, particularly with the generation of writers born between 1840 and 1870, it developed into a dramaturgy that appeared concretely and typically Italian. This development took place in both language and theme. The language adhered more closely to reality than did the scrubbed-up Italian of literary tradition, and the arid and disordered language employed in the translations from the French (the notorious "Italiese") was avoided. The themes had their roots deep in the problems of contemporary Italian life. At the foundation of this new dramatic literature lay a civil and moral preoccupation, which looked upon the theater as an indispensable tool for social criticism that could teach, satirize, and denounce. In a certain sense one might say that Goldoni's only authentic followers in the Italian theater were the writers of the naturalistic school. There was, however, a fundamental difference. The Venetian bourgeoisie, which was both public and protagonist in Goldoni's theater, was a social class in positive upward movement. The milieu of naturalistic plays, however, was restricted to the atmosphere of the narrower and more repressed Victorian and French bourgeoisie. While Goldoni was substantially in accord with the society in which he lived, these writers viewed their surroundings with a profoundly critical, bitter, and distressed attitude, and the literature to which they gave rise was prevailingly denunciatory.

The naturalistic theater had its center in northern Italy—Giuseppe Giacosa (whose later works were naturalistic) was from Turin and Girolamo Rovetta (1851–1910), Marco PRAGA, and Carlo BERTOLAZZI from Milan—where society was rather more solidified than in the south. In their works, almost all of which have a bourgeois setting, the world appears closed within its own conventions, hypocrisies, and egotism. Its many moral shortcomings are hidden beneath a patina of clamorous optimism. The naturalistic theater cannot claim the high poetic force of Goldoni's work. Often it is limited by preoccupation with its thesis, by the urgency of its denunciations, and by its insistent and violent sarcasm. This criticism, however, holds true for a large part of European naturalism. At least some of the works of the writers we have mentioned are worthy enough to appear in a representative anthology of the naturalistic theater: Praga's *La Moglie ideale* ("The Ideal Wife," 1890) and *Il bell' Apollo* ("Handsome Apollo," 1893); Bertolazzi's *El nost Milano* ("Our Milan," 1893) and *L'Egoista* ("The Egoist," 1900); and Giacosa's *Come le foglie* (*Like Falling Leaves*, 1900).

The naturalistic theater could not flourish except in northern Italy—the southern parts having not yet emerged from an essentially feudal state. At Naples flourished a popular theater of considerable vivacity and color, derived from the commedia dell'arte. In Sicily existed the curious phenomenon of the *teatro dei pupi* (a popular theater of marionettes), which borrowed materials from Renaissance poems of chivalry or from the "matter of France," the medieval legends dealing with the adventures of Roland and the other paladins of Charlemagne. But everywhere in the south conditions for a modern bourgeois theater were lacking. The sole southern writer of interest to this discussion is the Neapolitan Achille Torelli (1841–1922), whose best work, *I Mariti* ("Husbands," 1867), deals with the superiority of the serious and hard-working bourgeoisie over the lazy and decadent nobility. The Sicilian Giovanni VERGA, a very great storyteller, merits special mention. Although he dealt with realistic themes solidly inspired by the Sicilian life of his time, he employed in his theatrical works a mannered and literary language that has none of that vivacity and force so characteristic of the language of his stories. His plays include *Cavalleria rusticana* (literally, "rustic chivalry," 1884), *La Lupa* ("The Wolf," 1896), and *Dal tuo al mio* ("From Yours to Mine," 1903). In the last, the contrast between nobility and bourgeoisie is once again presented. In all of these plays there is apparent the unbridgeable gap between, on the one hand, realist themes, settings, characters, and action and, on the other, an artificial and conventional language. The plays are, therefore, rather more suggestive and powerful in translation than in the original Italian. See also Roberto BRACCO.

twentieth century. The naturalistic school died out in the years between the turn of the century and World War I, perhaps because its adherents realized the impossibility of being heard. Shaken by the problems that arose from unification, Italian society was also faced with the difficult task of creating the moral and cultural unity that lay beyond political unity. ("Italy has been created," D'Azeglio had said in the nineteenth century, "now it is necessary to create Italians.") Italian society had moved into that phase of its history that was to conclude with a fascist dictatorship. Bound up in a blind and class-conscious conservatism, Italy refused to confront the age-old problems of its society—hunger, ignorance, civil and economic backwardness. Instead, it abandoned itself to a nationalistic exaltation of self that was as tenacious as it was unrealistic. That literature that had courageously adopted naturalism was the first victim of this situation. It is significant that two authors—D'Annunzio and Verga—who up until this time had been united by a realistic attitude underwent sudden changes. The former abandoned his realistic approach and struck out along the road to decadent romanticism or what we may call "Dannunzianism"; the latter was more consistent and practically stopped writing. Thus, if Giacosa was applauded by the bourgeois public of the time, it was because of the sentimental distortions that deprived his works of much of their bitterness. Bertolazzi, far too explicitly bitter to be easily sweetened, never had success in his lifetime.

A final appendage of this critical and realistic school is the "theater of the grotesque." Its most typical and successful author is Luigi Chiarelli (1884–1947), who, in fact, inaugurated the genre with his comedy LA MASCHERA E IL VOLTO and enjoyed a certain following in the years immediately after World War I. The principal achievement of this theater lay in representing social conditions full of contradictions and inadequacies and then in underlining the comic and grotesque aspects of these contradictions. Bitterness thus relaxed into laughter and irony, denunciation was transformed into a complacent and satisfied wink. The contradiction that was denounced became rose-colored within the grotesque and studied paradox. All of the reactions against naturalism in Italy were of a regressive nature; they did not propose, that is, to raise the social involvement of naturalism to the level of poetic perfection achieved by Ibsen and Chekhov. All that they wanted was merely to take away from it its bitterness and its critical force.

Even the plays of Luigi PIRANDELLO—a brilliant exception among these apostles of diluted naturalism whose work was unique during the first forty years of this century—had a markedly evasive quality in this respect; for they translated the real problems present in contemporary life into philosophical, and sometimes metaphysical terms. Sometimes the paradoxes of the theater of the grotesque are to be found at the base of his work; sometimes there is a posture of disdain for reality, of exaltation of the creative fantasy of the poet and of the "truer" reality of the stage itself; sometimes the possibility of concrete epistemology is called into doubt, in a world in which substance and appearance appear to be merely flaccid and uncertain ideas. It is significant, for example, that the theme of the veteran, treated by Somerset Maugham, Sean O'Casey, William Faulkner, and many others (the theme, that is, of the man who, on returning from the war, is no longer capable of taking his place in a world transformed by crisis), is given in Pirandello's theater an entirely interior and philosophical treatment, as in the action of ENRICO IV. A Sicilian by birth but middle-European by education, Pirandello found that the dialogue between himself and Italian life was always difficult and rich with misunderstanding. The Italian public discovered him only after he had been consecrated abroad. Critical opinion was largely hostile to him and often insisted stubbornly on its preference for Pirandello as a storyteller or for the "minor" Pirandello of the rough Sicilian sketches written before 1917. The truth is that Pirandello fits better into the general European picture than into the specifically Italian picture. The despairing solitude, the bitter uncertainty, the existential anxiety, all of which are basic to the humane and poetic meaning of his plays, have nothing to do with the Italian stage between the two wars, with its emptiness and superficiality. The Italian stage was not nourished by contact with the best foreign works, for the Fascist government had banned them, chauvinistically preferring Italian productions. For the most part the stage was filled with escapist literature (the so-called literature of white telephones) or with little, sentimental dramas, written without any spirit of originality in servile imitation of the light and sentimental comedies of the boulevards. It was not Pirandello, then, who became a part of the life of the Italian theater. Rather, it was "pirandellism"—the banal imitation of his dramatic paradoxes, such as his *Gioco delle parti* (*The Rules of the Game*, 1934) or *Come tu mi vuoi* (*As You Desire Me*, 1931). These imitations were reduced to dialectic games or to more or less witty syllogisms. Because Pirandello was

both too exalted for the escapist and superficial official Italy of Fascism and too indirect and disengaged to offer any opposition to it on a real civil and political plane, he remained a much more isolated and anomalous phenomenon in the Italian theater than is generally believed. Only in the 1960's, when the Fascist period, and the period of reaction to Fascism as well, had passed, did Pirandello come to his rightful position.

Other isolated phenomena of the period between the two wars were the futurist theater of Filippo Tommaso Marinetti (1876–1944), an eccentric and ingenious attempt to pass beyond realism; the eminently literary and lyric theater of Pier Luigi Maria ROSSO DI SAN SECONDO, which expresses a sincere anguish with life in imaginative and baroque language; and, most important of all, the bitter and pessimistic theater of Ugo BETTI, which gives disquieting expression to a collective sense of guilt and warns of an impending crumbling of values. To these cases we may add certain manifestations of the unofficial theater, which, because it was written in dialect and in forms not consecrated by literary tradition, has always been given slight consideration and at times has been neglected as minor theater. In particular, we may mention the plays of Ettore Petrolini (1886–1935), who, as *chansonnier* and actor, was an unusual figure. Gifted with a spontaneous and spirited sarcastic force, his plays ridicule certain aspects of the life of the time, carrying their more absurd sides to the point of paroxysm and thereby creating in the idiocy of the most typical characters a paradoxical category of the spirit. This scattering of isolated playwrights continues in the period following World War II, and even today the problem of a dramaturgy with precisely Italian characteristics appears to be rather far from any reasonable solution.

The most important development in the postwar period was the birth of subsidized public theaters. First among them was the Piccolo Teatro di Milano, which was founded in 1947 by Paolo Grassi and Giorgio Strehler. These theaters assumed the difficult task of cultural updating that was so necessary after twenty years of Fascist isolation. They also undertook to rebuild the intellectually open and lively public that had been estranged from the theater by the insipid dramatic repertory of the interwar period. For the moment, this necessary cultural updating delayed the possibility of developing a new Italian dramaturgy. As a logical reaction to the cultural autarchy of the Fascist period, Italian stages were dominated for ten years by the works of French, English, and American writers. Although imitators and followers of the influences that came from abroad were not wanting, their works did nothing but provide greater evidence of the backwardness of Italian theatrical culture. The ideals of anti-Fascism and the Resistance, the problems of the democratic Italy born of the crises of war and the liberation found expression in fiction and above all in the cinema, not in the theater. In the cinema, the neorealistic school of Vittorio De Sica and Roberto Rossellini represented the most important contribution of Italian art to European culture after the war. Both the cinema and fiction, by their example, have made still more evident the want of reality in the literary language that continues to be used in the drama.

Only two tendencies, both of which failed, can be isolated in the Italian theater of the past twenty years. The first, a dramaturgy of Catholic inspiration, proposed to discuss the many social and moral problems of the new Italy in the light of the Catholic faith. Typical of this tendency and of this failure is the theater of Diego Fabbri (1911–   ), a writer of undoubted talent. His plays begin with a courageous statement of the problem he has chosen to treat, but then he invariably turns to a hasty and sticky acquiescence to dogma and to a call for a vague sentiment of love and Christian fraternity. His most significant works are *Il Seduttore* ("The Seducer," 1951), *Processo a Gesu* ("The Trial of Jesus," 1955), and *Veglia d'armi* ("Armed Watch," 1956). They were written in the final phase of the papacy of Pius XII, in a period that was not favorable to free discussion among Catholics. Fabbri himself was so conditioned to this period that he was forced to change the end of *Il Seduttore,* removing the protagonist's suicide.

The second tendency is a dramaturgy of vaguely Marxist inspiration, the most representative authors of which are Dario Fo (1926–   ) and Franco Parenti (1921–   ), who together wrote two works in a free cabaret form—*Il Dito nell'occhio* ("A Finger in One's Eye," 1953) and *I Sani da legare* (Sane Bodies to Bind Up," 1954)—and Luigi Squarzina (1922–   ), whose *Romagnola* (*Woman of the Romagna,* 1959) is the best dramatic work inspired by the war period and the Resistance. This dramaturgy failed for two reasons: the first is its scattered and casual nature unsustained by clarity of idealistic vision; the second is found in Italian society —in the existence of censorial prejudices against attempts at political satire and satire of morals. Only in the past years, since the abolition of preventive censorship in 1962, has the force of Dario Fo's very personal comedies been felt. His *Settimo: ruba un po' meno* ("Seventh: Thou Shalt Steal a Little Less," 1964) and *La Colpa é sempre del diavolo* ("It's Always the Devil's Fault," 1965) are genial and forceful pastiches in which the traditional and eclectic art of the Italian actor is put to use.

The most authentic and accomplished voice in contemporary Italian dramaturgy is found in the dialectal Neapolitan theater, and specifically in the work of Eduardo DE FILIPPO. The Neapolitan popular theater of the nineteenth and twentieth centuries developed without loss of continuity from the commedia dell'arte. It was favored by the centuries-old isolation of southern Italy (that is to say, the Kingdom of the Two Sicilies, of which Naples was capital) from the rest of Italy and Europe in general. This theater had created its own characters, first among them being Pulcinella, an expression of the sentimental and cunning, capricious and poetic mind of the Neapolitan people. It had elaborated rough and colorful materials for its scenarios and its lazzi. Its plots, freely gathered and manipulated, came from fiction, from the Spanish theater of the seventeenth century, and from French *mélodrame* in prose of the nineteenth century. Everything was fused into a theatrical style based above all on the art of the actor— on his gifts of improvisation, his eclecticism, and his exceptional ability to communicate. During the nineteenth century this material had at times assumed regular literary form, although stress was still placed on performance rather than literary values. Among the more fortunate and more characteristic writers, we may cite Pasquale Altavilla (1806–1872), Antonio Petito (1822–1876), and above all Eduardo Scarpetta (1853–1925), the creator of a kind of realistic mask—Don Felice Sciosciammocca—which may be considered a bourgeois reworking of the old Pulcinella. The maturation of this lively material into a regular literature continued in the twentieth century with the work of Salvatore Di Giacomo (1860–1934) and Raffaele Viviani (1888–1950), but it found its fulfillment in the comedies and dramas of De Filippo. Those gleams of poetry and art —pleasing but scattered and disorganized—that are found in the works of his predecessors are transformed by him into a mature conception of art and life. He fulfills for the popular Neapolitan theater a function that is exactly analogous to that fulfilled by Goldoni for the popular Venetian theater. This function consists of gathering together those simple and sincere expressions of life that have been produced during centuries of evolution but that have been crystallized into forms that are no longer representative of reality. De Filippo brings these aspects of life together in a regular literary form, one in which ancient tradition, ancient situations, character types, and themes are related to contemporary conditions. His best works are a group of comedies, naturally in dialect, written during the 1950's. They were inspired by the difficulties of Neapolitan life during the war and afterward, during the return to normality. Because of the dramatic force and psychological penetration of De Filippo's work, because of its wealth of invention and beauty of language, and, finally, because of the realistic moral posture, it can be compared to the neorealistic cinema. It is, in fact, the only work of the contemporary Italian theater that may be defined as realistic in the full sense of the word.

It is important to take note of the following fact concerning the two greatest dramatic writers in Italy born during the nineteenth and twentieth centuries, Luigi Pirandello and Eduardo De Filippo. The first belongs properly to the high road evolved by the European theater. The other follows the vein of a geographically circumscribed dialect. This situation is symbolic of Italy's history, which passed from a regional to a European phase without first passing through a national phase. To achieve a sound national drama, written in a language that is solidly based on the daily usage of the whole of Italian society, remains the most urgent and sensitive problem of the Italian theater. But such a language does not now exist and to create it is obviously above the powers of writers. It must await the solutions of the traditional problems of the country since its unification—problems concerning Italy's living conditions and its moral and cultural life, which are too diversified from class to class and from region to region. It must, in short, await the attainment of genuine national unity. Until that time, the Italian theater will be able only to struggle within the old vicissitudes and limitations that have conditioned its history. A useful overview of Italian drama is Joseph Spencer Kennard, *The Italian Theatre* (2 vols., 1932). A more specialized study is A. Nagler, *Theater Festivals of the Medici 1539–1637* (1964). The modern period is examined in two books by Lander McClintock: *The Contemporary Drama in Italy* (1920) and *The Age of Pirandello* (1951).—L. L.

Ivanov (1887). A drama in four acts by Anton CHEKHOV. In his first full-length play Chekhov portrays the sad and ineffectual life of Ivanov, a ruined landowner who is in debt. He is married to a converted Jewess, Anna, who had to break with her rich family to marry him and who is still desperately in love with him after years of dull drudgery. But he has become tired of her, just as he has become tired of life itself. Living among insipid mediocrities, Ivanov, once a thinking man, now has only one preoccupation—to find ways of meeting his most pressing debts by borrowing money wherever he can. Aside from this concern, the only interest he has is Sasha, the young daughter of a neighboring landowner to whom he owes a considerable sum. He realizes he appeals to Sasha's romantic imagination, and this pleases him. He begins to resent violently his marriage, and in a sudden fit of anger he rejects his dying wife (rather dramatically he calls her "Jewess," but is at once terribly ashamed of himself). After she is dead and he is about to marry Sasha, however, he realizes the futility of trying to make a new life for himself, especially as there is no real love between him and Sasha. So he shoots himself. Throughout the play, indignant comments on the stupidity and shallow selfishness of Ivanov's life are supplied by the frank, outspoken, and hard-working Dr. Lvov, who has been in love with Anna all his life.

The fact that Chekhov had originally thought of calling his leading character Ivan Ivanovich Ivanov —the equivalent of John Smith—is taken by many critics as proof that the protagonist is a *lishnii chelovek,* the "superfluous man" invented by Ivan Turgenev, one who, in late-nineteenth-century Russia, is a supernumerary as a result of the agrarian reforms and the changing conditions of life. It is, indeed, very likely that Chekhov himself considered an idle life such as Ivanov's an outmoded and doomed existence, especially since he himself had an extremely busy life. Chekhov was fully aware of the preciousness of time and the absurdity of idleness. It would seem that Chekhov was concerned with portraying not only a typical, doomed landowner of a certain period but also a man who lives a misguided life, as so many men do. (Today it would be called a noncommitted or alienated life.) And when such a person finally realizes the vacuum in which he lives, Chekhov suggests, his logical impulse may be to put an end to his pointless existence.

Ivanov has been translated by Ronald Hingley in *The Oxford Chekhov* (1964).—A. MACA.

Ivory Coast. See AFRICA: *Ivory Coast.*

Izumo, Takeda (1691–1756). The most celebrated Japanese playwright to follow in the footsteps of Chikamatsu, who led the revival of Japanese drama at the close of the seventeenth century. Izumo worked for the doll theater at Osaka but is best known for his contributions to the *kabuki* stage. Showing a less flamboyant imagination than that exhibited by Chikamatsu, his plays for puppets required less revision when transplanted to the kabuki than did those of his master. To Izumo are assigned two of the most popular pieces in the kabuki repertory, SUGAWARA DENJU TENARAI KOGAMI and CHUSHINGURA, the latter presenting the tragic story of "the forty-seven *ronin.*"—H. W. W.

J

Jacobean drama. See ENGLAND: *Jacobean drama.*

Jacopone da Todi. Born **Jacopo di' Benedetti** (c. 1230–1306). Italian poet and playwright. Jacopone was born of a noble Umbrian family. After doing severe penance for ten years, beginning in 1268, he donned the robes of the Friars Minor of Saint Francis. In 1298 he was among those who declared that the election of Pope Boniface VIII (after Celestine V had renounced the papal throne) was illegal. Excommunicated and thrown into prison, Jacopone was absolved and freed in 1303, when Benedict XI succeeded Boniface VIII.

Jacopone wrote mystic songs in Latin (today there is a tendency to attribute to him the very beautiful *Stabat Mater*). He composed in the vernacular a hundred *laudi* (mystical poems in a rudimentary dramatic form), of which eighty-eight are attributed to him with certainty. They deal with episodes from the lives of Christ, the Virgin, and the saints, as well as with other edifying themes. They are written in a rough and vigorous language and are very simple and powerful in form. Jacopone's laudi are the greatest poetic expression in Italian literature—just coming into being at the time—of the medieval religious concern with the irreconcilable warfare between body and spirit. Important among them are the so-called dramatic laudi, generally limited to a dialogue between two interlocutors, in accordance with the medieval form of the *contrasto,* or amorous debate. Sometimes, however, Jacopone's laudi are developed into a more complete dramatic structure, as is the case of *Pianto della Madonna* ("Complaint of the Madonna," Lauda XCIII). In it speakers and situations are multiplied. Even though there is controversy concerning how many laudi were actually intended for presentation, the precise theatrical directions contained in other contemporary laudi prove that at least some of them were intended for performance.—L. L.

James, Henry (1843–1916). American novelist, short-story writer, and playwright. This great American novelist was devoted to the theater all his life, both as a playgoer and a dramatist. His popular success in the theater, however, was posthumous: After his death, other writers dramatized his novels and made their compromises between the precious drama of his fiction and the more earthbound demands of the box office. Their efforts and the intrinsically dramatic nature of his fiction turned James into a substantial theatrical figure at last and led others back to his plays.

Following three trivial playlets, *Pyramus and Thisbe* (pub. 1869), *Still Waters* (pub. 1871), and *A Change of Heart* (pub. 1872), minor comedies of love and courtship written for publication, James began in earnest to write for the stage, working first in the tradition of Victorien Sardou and the "well-made play." In 1882 he dramatized *Daisy Miller,* his popular novelette of three years before, coarsening the original story by supplying a melodramatic villain, a happy ending, and a spectacular triumph for American innocence over European depravity; the play was published the next year but never staged in the author's lifetime. James's technique was similar when he responded to the invitation of the actor-manager Edward Compton to dramatize his novel *The American* in 1891. Again, melodrama intervenes, motives are coarsened, and happy endings prevail: the haughty French family rejects its prospective American son-in-law only for reasons of money, not snobbery; the French daughter marries her American, instead of entering a convent. To give Compton full satisfaction, James wrote a revised fourth act that permitted the heroine's brother (shot dead in the novel) to recover from wounds received in a duel. In London in 1891 the play had a mixed reception and a short run. The new fourth act was inserted when Compton took it on the road in the following year.

Vowing that *The Tragic Muse* (1890), in which an actress is a leading character, would be his last long novel, James embarked upon new plays. He began with *Tenants* (written 1890), about a woman of the demimonde who struggles to win a place in society for her illegitimate son, and *Disengaged* (written 1891 or 1892), a frivolous comedy based on his relatively serious story "The Solution." In 1891 in London, Augustin Daly rehearsed the latter play but, following a quarrel with James, did not perform it publicly. Two more unproduced plays were possibly written in 1891. *The Album,* which blends melodrama and farce in dramatizing a dispute over an inheritance, and *The Reprobate,* whose title character is an innocent recluse of thirty, confined by his family after an escapade at twenty. Except for the more solemn *Tenants,* these plays exhibit an engaging frivolity that never appears in James's fiction. All four were published under the title *Theatricals* (1894–1895).

By the time these two volumes came out, James had written (in 1893) his most serious play, *Guy Domville,* which presents the dilemma of the last descendant of a noble British family, a young man torn between his responsibility to his family line and his vocation in the Roman Catholic priesthood. It is surely an allegory of a conflict that James keenly felt, the conflict between the attractions of the world and the vocation of the artist. It is also a serious, conscientious play that attempts, but fails, to transfer to the stage the Jamesian drama of awakening consciousness, done to perfection in such novels as *The Ambassadors.* Its opening night in London, January 5, 1895, was a disaster, and a traumatic experience for James. He stayed away from the performance and so did not know of the play's hostile reception. At the end of the performance, in response to calls for the author, he was brought onstage by the actor-manager George Alexander and greeted with boos, hoots, and hisses. He returned home to confide to his journals that he had abandoned the stage forever. Thereafter, his fiction was more than ever dramatic in form, and he more frequently resorted to dramatic metaphors to describe his technique—but he did not abandon the stage for more than a few months. Later in 1895, he wrote the one-act play *Summersoft,* which later became the novelette *Covering End* (1898), and then a full-length play, *The High Bid.* The subject—the successful efforts of a delightful American widow to save a beautiful estate from a rapacious capitalist—is typical of James and is presented with considerable verve. Staged by the Forbes-Robertsons in London in 1907, *The High Bid* was the best received of James's plays, and it was warmly welcomed when it was revived in London in 1967. By 1907, the impact of Ibsen and Shaw had apparently made the London stage ready for James's return.

In 1908 James turned his short story "Owen Wingrave" into a one-act play, *The Saloon,* a drama of the pacifist heir of an ancient military family. For once, one of James's adaptations proved equal to the original. Curiously, *The Saloon* shares its main themes with both *Guy Domville* and *The High Bid* —its preoccupation with the fate of a great estate and with the conflict between tradition and innovation.

James began *The Other House* as a play, published it as a novel in 1896, and turned it back into a play in 1908 and 1909. Ibsen's influence is visible in this drama of a strong-willed woman, cast in the mold of Ibsen's Rebecca West, who commits murder in a vain effort to win the man she loves. Although it has never been performed, it is probably the most actable of James's plays. It was followed by *The Outcry,* written in 1909, converted into a novel, and staged only after the author's death. In this play an American millionaire bids for a painting owned by an irascible English peer and thereby creates a public "outcry" against the loss of a national treasure—but here the conflict between tradition and innovation has worn thin.

Plays adapted by others from James's novels include *Berkeley Square* (1928), by John Balderston and J. C. Squire, from *The Sense of the Past; The Heiress* (1947), by Ruth and Augustus Goetz, from *Washington Square*; and *The Innocents* (1950), by William Archibald, from *The Turn of the Screw.* James's own uneven but frequently distinguished dramatic *oeuvre* is collected in *The Complete Plays* (1949) of Henry James, edited by Leon Edel. His discerning essays on the theater comprise *The Scenic Art* (1948), edited by Alan Wade.—H. P.

Japan. Few people have been as devoted to the dramatic arts as have the Japanese for approximately a thousand years. They have also shown a notable predilection for establishing well-defined schools of the theater. Hence the history of Japanese drama is based on the record of these traditional types of plays. The clarity of the record is occasioned by the self-contained character of Japanese civilization and the comparatively small area of the islands. It also results from a marked disposition to systematic thinking in aesthetic matters. In these respects Japanese drama strikingly contrasts with the Chinese and Indian. The chief types of Japanese plays, examined elsewhere in this book under separate headings, are the ancient and ritualistic NOH, the venerable KOWAKA, the melodramatic KABUKI, the farcical KYOGEN, and the highly inspired puppet theater—the BUNRAKU. Traditional dance forms, BUGAKU and GIGAKU, went into the making of the noh, as did DENGAKU, a popular type of entertainment that flourished as early as the eleventh century. Finally, there is SEWAMONO, a school of dramatic realism that developed in the seventeenth century and depicted the life of the middle classes. For aspects of Japanese acting, see ARAGOTO; MIE; MICHIYUKI; SHITE; and WAKI. The Japanese have been as inventive and resourceful in architecture as in drama. Hence the design of their playhouses has attracted special attention in the West in recent years. See also HANAMICHI; HASHIGAKARI.

Good general surveys may be found in Faubion Bowers' *Japanese Theatre* (1952) and Frank A. Lombard's *An Outline History of Japanese Drama* (1966).—H. W. W.

Jarry, Alfred (1873–1907). French novelist and playwright. Jarry called himself a Breton—he was born in Laval, a town fairly close to Brittany—and as an adolescent he became a spectacular *potache,* a student representing a mixture of goodness and wickedness. In 1891 he went to Paris at the age of seventeen to complete his studies at the Lycée Henri IV. He participated in the literary gatherings at the office of the magazine *Le Mercure de France* and attended some of the Tuesday evenings at Stéphane Mallarmé's apartment.

Like the painter Paul Cézanne and the poet Arthur Rimbaud, Jarry vigorously opposed the taste and the artistic successes of his period. Between the end of the nineteenth and the middle of the twentieth century, Jarry's legend continued to grow. The writer Jarry is now confused with his character Ubu Roi.

Largely because of his play UBU ROI, the generation of writers in France who knew him personally looked upon him as a leader, or at least a key figure. In the novel *Les Faux-Monnayeurs* of André Gide, Jarry appears as a character who bears his own name. Apollinaire, André Salmon, Max Jacob, and their disciples were influenced by Jarry. The surrealists in the 1920's and 1930's looked upon him as one of them, and his example was often evoked by André Breton, Antonin Artaud, and Jean Cocteau. In 1949 the Collège de 'Pataphysique was founded in his honor.

Before he died, at the age of thirty-four, Jarry had added two further works on the subject of Ubu in which he continued his farce about human stupidity and the cruelty of despots. For Jarry humor was a form of wisdom, a way in which he was able to bear his suffering from alcoholism, loneliness, and poverty. Humor is both the mockery and the alleviation of pain.

For a critique on Jarry's work, see Roger Shattuck, *The Banquet Years* (1958), and Ruth B. York,

"Ubu Revisited: The Reprise of 1922," *French Review*, XXXV (1962).—W. F.

Java. See INDONESIA: *Java*.

Jayadeva. See GITAGOVINDA.

Jedermann (Everyman, 1911). A one-act morality play in verse by Hugo von HOFMANNSTHAL. The plot of *Jedermann* is based on the English morality play titled EVERYMAN. Everyman lives a thoroughly materialistic life. He knows neither pity nor mercy; he is cruel and indifferent and ignores his mother's attempts to rescue him from a life of debauchery, luxury, and licentiousness. At a gorgeous banquet, Everyman is met by Death, who lays a cold hand upon the libertine's heart. All of Everyman's false friends desert him, including his beloved Mammon. After Everyman suffers terrible agonies, only Faith and Good Deeds, a poor, maimed creature, remain to help him regain his soul and assist him past the Devil to his final journey.

In striving to achieve a simplicity and honesty in this play, Hofmannsthal drew much of his language and imagery from another great writer of moralities, Hans Sachs (1494–1576). The result is a rich piousness that is at once natural, exalted, and deeply moving.

Jedermann is produced yearly for the Salzburg Festival on the great square in front of the baroque cathedral. Max Reinhardt's production for the first Salzburg Festival (1920) has remained intact. The proceedings transpire on a wooden platform constructed over the steps of the cathedral, and virtually all of the old part of the city of Salzburg takes part. Death's call to Everyman from the fortress high above the city echoes through various towers and finally bellows hollowly from the great maw of the church. All the bells of Salzburg resound at the end, until the air is filled with the deafening jubilation of redemption. This immensely theatrical experience provides the contemporary spectator with a vivid understanding of the effect the dramas of the middle ages must have exerted on the masses who attended.

In the course of the years two translations into English of this play have appeared, both of which are currently out of print. The first bears the title *The Play of Everyman*, translated by G. Sterling and R. Ordynski (1917). The other (1936) maintains the title of the original German version, *Jedermann*; the translator is anonymous. In addition, some very fine things are said about the play and its production in an article by Alfred Schwarz, "The Allegorical Theatre of Hugo von Hofmannsthal," *Tulane Drama Review* (March 1960).—C. R. M.

Jefferson, Joseph. See RIP VAN WINKLE.

Jellicoe, [Patricia] Ann (1927–). English playwright, director. Ann Jellicoe, born in Middlesbrough, Yorkshire, first gained wide attention as the author of *The Sport of My Mad Mother* (1956), which won third prize in the London *Observer* Play Competition in 1956 and was later produced at the Royal Court Theatre. It was not the work of a theatrical beginner, since Miss Jellicoe had trained at the Central School of Speech and Drama and had worked as an actress and director, besides founding the open-stage Cockpit Theatre in 1951. But the play was a total departure from existing theatrical practice —a rhapsodic evocation of adolescent group behavior, showing the rituals of an East End gang led by a demonic mother-figure identified with the goddess Kali. The play bypasses plot and individual character and aims to arouse visceral emotions by means of violent group actions and the use of words strictly for their rhythmic and sound values. It handles gang speech much as Jerome Robbins handled gang movement in the musical *West Side Story*.

The same feeling for adolescent speech rhythms animates her best-known play, *The Knack* (1961), and *The Rising Generation* (1967), a feminist pageant for a cast of hundreds commissioned in the 1950's by the Girl Guides Association. Miss Jellicoe's subsequent play, *Shelley* (1965), is an uncharacteristic essay in documentary melodrama.—I. W.

Jesuit drama. From the very beginning of their educational activities, the Jesuits included drama in their curriculum. Such practices were not new in themselves, since school dramatics had become generally accepted as part of the educational system of the Humanists. There, however, the use of drama was dictated primarily by the realization that performances of Latin plays could serve as an ideal tool, not only for the teaching of that classical tongue, but also for what we today would call "personality development." The Jesuits, on the other hand, at once recognized the theater as a dynamic force that might be used for much broader and, in terms of the order's missionary program, more significant ends. The awareness that here was a powerful weapon for the implementation of counterreformatory propaganda was responsible for the development as well as for most features of that unique phenomenon, the Jesuit school theater.

From its foundation in 1540 to its temporary suppression in 1773, the order carried on a vast theatrical program. During nearly two and a half centuries, Jesuit priests and their students devoted a large portion of their time and energy to work in every conceivable area related to the stage. Since one of the characteristics of all Jesuit undertakings was their rigidly disciplined uniformity, it is possible to point out typical features of the Jesuit school theater, regardless of national or local differences. Although these, at times, did influence certain details, they were never permitted to interfere with the basic principles that guided the order's educational and missionary institutions.

The Jesuit school theater was a propaganda theater. As a matter of fact, it may be said to have been the first theater consciously used for propagandistic ends. These were naturally more conspicuous during the first decades of the order's existence, when new ground had to be won, chiefly by reaching huge audiences and impressing them with the spiritual message of Roman Catholicism. At that time, therefore, the theatrical form used was frequently, although by no means exclusively, the open-air pageant, which could assume considerable proportions. One such spectacle, to name an outstanding instance given in Munich in 1574, lasted two days and employed 1,000 players, among them 185 actors.

Such mass performances, however, favored in Germany and Austria, where Protestantism had registered ominous gains, were exceptional even there, and they soon disappeared almost entirely. Around 1600, the Jesuit school theater retired into the college building, using for its productions the *Aula*, or Festival Hall. Obtaining security and power in those countries where the Counter Reformation had proved victorious, the Jesuit fathers were now in a position to organize their theater with that mixture of determination and flexibility that contributed not only to their success but just as much to the antagonism, and even hatred, they so frequently aroused. During what may be called the Jesuit school theater's golden age, the seventeenth century, regular stages were installed in most colleges, equipped with all technical achievements available at the time. Some institutions possessed even two theaters, one for the major productions, another for the numerous dramatic exercises on a smaller scale that occurred throughout the year. Usually the main event, carefully prepared for months, took place at the end of the school year, coincident with the distribution of prizes. However, in some more important colleges, especially those situated in larger cities, several major productions might be presented during one academic year, sometimes on festival occasions related to political events or local holidays.

Just as the actors appearing in the plays were students, the playwrights were, without exception, Jesuit priests. Certain ranks among the teachers were under the obligation to provide the dramatic material, whether this consisted of full-length plays or merely of short dialogues for classroom use. All Jesuit plays were to be written in Latin; at least the exclusive use of this language was stipulated in the *Ratio Studiorum,* the body of rules governing the order's educational methods. This particular rule, however, was not always followed; short scenes and, in exceptional instances, even entire plays in the vernacular were tolerated. Besides, the native language proved indispensable in comic interludes, which soon became standard features of many Jesuit dramas.

One of the principles adopted by Jesuit colleges was to avoid the revival of plays previously performed at another school. Although exceptions are known, this policy was largely followed, with the result that most Jesuit plays were "originals." Yet this term has to be taken with a grain of salt. Jesuit playwriting was based on imitation and convention rather than on creativeness and originality. While some of the order's dramatists deservedly attained fame as truly creative writers, the majority composed their pieces following a rather rigid and uninspired formula derived either from other Jesuit dramas or from the numerous Jesuit manuals on playwriting. It is not surprising, therefore, to learn that the hundreds of plays written each year were cut to one and the same pattern. On the other hand, Jesuit playwrights had no literary ambitions but considered themselves merely dutiful providers of the required dramatic fare. There is ample proof that thoughts of fame or posterity never entered their devout minds, an attitude that also explains why so few Jesuit dramas have survived and why still fewer have ever been printed. The text of a play was regarded merely as the score to be used for a theatrical performance but never as an end in itself.

Many Jesuit dramas did survive in fragmentary form, namely in the so-called *Periochi,* that is, synopses distributed among the spectators in order to enable those unfamiliar with the Latin language to follow the action. It is questionable, however, whether such aids were really necessary, since on the Jesuit stage the spoken word was relatively unimportant, modestly taking its place alongside the other production elements that frequently overshadowed the dialogue. A Jesuit performance was to be an irresistible appeal to senses and emotions rather than to intellect and reason. The spectator was to be virtually hypnotized by a concerted attack of all known theatrical devices until he surrendered his entire being to the drama's spiritual message. This appeal to the senses, a tendency the Jesuit theater shared with the other arts of the Baroque period, may explain the extraordinary and well-documented effect its productions had even on largely illiterate seventeenth-century audiences. For the reasons just indicated, the Jesuit theater also served as an ideal weapon in the order's missionary activity among non-European peoples where, as for instance among the Indians of South America, its suggestive power was used with striking results.

Form and content of all Jesuit dramas were determined by their ultimate educational and religious aims. In the order's constitution, these were clearly defined as follows: "The object of this Society is to labor not only for the salvation and perfection of our own souls, by the help of God's Grace, but also, by the same help devote ourselves zealously to the salvation and perfection of our neighbors." Consequently, the tendency of every play was to exalt the blessings of a devout life and to inspire the audience with the Christian virtues of humility and piety. The subjects, chosen accordingly, demonstrated the instability and vanity of fame and fortune and urged constant watchfulness against the ever-present seductions of the world. The ending exemplified the play's message by showing either the hero's conversion rewarded by salvation and heavenly bliss or his stubborn refusal to listen to the word of God punished by eternal damnation in hell. The variety of subjects used to illustrate what may be called the dominant theme of all Jesuit plays, namely the persuasive antithesis World-God, is, in view of their never-changing pattern, truly astounding. The Bible provided useful material, as did legends and stories related to saints and martyrs. Favorite topics were the lives of enemies and protectors of the Church or of historical characters whose fates could furnish object lessons for the order's missionary activity. It has been correctly stated that the Jesuits used virtually all significant themes of world drama, many of them for the first time. Their uncanny flair for theatrical values no doubt proved stimulating for contemporary as well as later playwrights.

Closely related to the Jesuits' principle to convey their message through an appeal to the senses rather than by relying on the spoken word was their continuous use of allegorical figures. Personifications of ideas, attitudes, desires, were a familiar sight on Jesuit stages, as were representations of ghosts, angels, devils, and the spirits of the dead. Such figures were used in the frequent dream scenes, in episodes showing magicians and sorcerers at work, in frightening images of hell, or in dazzling visions of heaven. In some instances a chorus of allegorical characters was employed to comment upon the play's meaning.

Not only allegorical figures but other characters as

well were often seen in another standard feature of
Jesuit dramaturgy, the interludes. What the play's action showed in terms of human beings, these interludes explained mostly in terms of allegory. A device
such as this again facilitated the spectators' comprehension of a drama acted in a language that most of
them could not understand.

Another device, used for a similar purpose, was
the *Scena Muta,* that is, the "mute scene," or "dumb
show," where allegorical characters pointed out in
pantomime the play's meaning either by predicting
events that were to follow or by summing up the significance of what had just occurred on the stage.

The obviously didactic character of the Jesuit
school theater, however, was never allowed to become obtrusive. On the contrary, with admirable
skill the Jesuits succeeded in presenting their message
in the most enticing manner, shrewdly disguising it
under the colorful cloak of splendid entertainment.
To achieve this aim, they never hesitated to use for
their own purposes all existing dramatic and theatrical forms. Without exaggerating in the least, one can
state that there was not a single theatrical genre that
could not, at some time or place, be seen in a Jesuit
theater. A list would have to include not merely tragedy, comedy, pantomime, pastoral play, and farce
but also opera and ballet. One must never forget, on
the other hand, that even these last-mentioned types,
which we usually associate with the not exactly religious court spectacles of the Baroque age, were admitted to Jesuit schools only as long as they could be
made to serve the order's never-changing aim. This
was further emphasized by the practice of printing, at
the end of every synopsis and at the bottom of every
program, the letters O.A.M.D.G., an abbreviation of
the motto *Omnia Ad Majorem Dei Gloriam,* "All to
the Greater Glory of God."

We can well understand the necessity of stressing
this lofty purpose when we hear of what was no doubt
one of the most baffling disguises a religious message
has ever assumed: the ballet. While theatrical dancing was developed especially at the order's Paris College, it was encouraged in other Jesuit schools too.
Naturally, the fathers hastened to point out, not only
in theoretical writings on the art of the dance but also
through the choice of suitable subjects, that here too
the basic aim of their theater was firmly upheld. Consequently, we must not be astonished to find on Jesuit
stages dancing saints and martyrs, emperors and generals, not to mention a host of allegorical figures who
had also been seized by this outburst of a religiously
inspired balletomania.

In order to stage such a variety of theatrical forms,
elaborate scenic effects were required, and the Jesuit
priests provided them generously. The familiar
equipment of the Baroque theater, with its trap doors
and flying machines, its lightning and thunder, was at
once taken over by the Jesuit colleges. Numerous
changes of scenery, one of the chief attractions of the
contemporary operatic stage, contributed greatly to
the popularity of the school performances, as did
spectacular costumes and lovely music. It is symptomatic of the significance assumed by the Jesuit theater in its time that distinguished composers like
Orlando di Lasso (1530?–1594) and Johann Caspar
Kerll (1625–1692) wrote original scores for some of
its productions.

Although the order's achievements in dramatic literature were slight, its school theater nevertheless
had considerable influence on European drama.
Many distinguished playwrights were pupils of Jesuit
colleges where they first came into contact with the
stage. In France, Molière, Pierre and Thomas Corneille, Lesage, Diderot, and Voltaire were educated
by the Jesuits. Voltaire, who can hardly be credited
with much sympathy for the order's ideals, even
stated in his later years that the plays produced at the
Paris College had been by far the best part of the
education he received there. The Jesuit school theater in Spain profoundly influenced the work of Calderón de la Barca, whose religious dramas show
numerous analogies with the methods and techniques
of Jesuit plays. In Holland, the celebrated Joost van
den Vondel, and in Germany, Andreas Gryphius, the
country's first significant tragic author, both testified to the positive achievement of the Jesuit school
theater. In Austria, one of the order's strongholds,
Jesuit influence was to a great extent responsible for
numerous characteristics of the popular stage, particularly for the development of the Viennese fairy-
tale plays. One of these may be assured of immortality: the libretto of Mozart's opera *The Magic Flute*
(1791).

Many Jesuit priests dealt with theatrical subjects in
books whose circulation was by no means restricted
to members of the order. Jesuit manuals on dramatic
theory and playwriting, far too numerous to be mentioned, were widely read and used. The first comprehensive history and theory of the dance ever written,
Des Ballets anciens et modernes, published in Paris
in 1682, was by a French Jesuit, P. Claude François
Menestrier.

In view of the scope and variety of the Jesuits' contribution to the arts of the stage, it is hard to understand why this momentous and colorful chapter in
theatrical history has been so sadly neglected by most
historians. Its study is not only indispensable for a
full comprehension of the Baroque theater, of which
it formed an essential part, but also, because of the
conscious use it made of the sensual aspects of the
stage, for any exploration of the aesthetic foundations of dramatic art. Moreover, in the Jesuit school
theater, the attempt was made for the first time to use
the stage, not as the Humanists had used it, mainly
for the sake of teaching Latin, but as a formative influence on the student's entire personality.

For further information about Jesuit drama, see
W. H. McCabe, *An Introduction to the Early Jesuit
Theatre* (1929), and E. Boysse, *Le Théâtre de Jesuites*
(1887). For a list of Jesuit plays see "Plays" in *Bib-
liography of the English Province of the Society of
Jesus 1773–1953* (1957).—H. S.

**Jeu de l'amour et du hasard, Le (The Game of
Love and Chance,** 1730). A comedy in prose by
Pierre de MARIVAUX. Without knowing one another,
Silvia and Dorante are destined for each other by
their families. They decide, without each other's
knowledge, to pass themselves off as servants—she
as her maid Lisette, he as his own valet—in order to
observe one another. The false valet falls in love at
first sight with the false Lisette. The real Lisette and
the valet Arlequin, disguised as his master, Dorante,
also immediately lose their hearts to each other. The
whole subject of the play consists in the progress of

A SCENE FROM PIERRE DE MARIVAUX'S *Le Jeu de l'amour et du hasard* (FRENCH CULTURAL SERVICES)

love within the characters in spite of themselves and in the way it helps Dorante overcome the irrelevant social obstacle that keeps him from Silvia, whom he still believes is a servant. Silvia, who finally discovers Dorante's true identity, reveals her own to him. The play ends with a double marriage.

Le Jeu de l'amour et du hasard is an extremely rigorous and swift comedy, in which the psychological action progresses without interruption. The humor stems largely from the fact that the spectator, through the very language of the characters, continually discovers the strength of feeling that the characters themselves are unaware of or wish to ignore. This play is translated into English by·Richard Aldington in *French Comedies of the Eighteenth Century* (1923).—Ja. G.

jig. In drama a brief skit that features songs and dances. A popular entertainment in the Elizabethan theater, the jig generally followed a performance of a regular play. Usually satirical and ribald, jigs were a great favorite with the audience and gave rise to the sternest invective of Puritan opponents to the stage. The favorite theme of the jigs seems to have been marital infidelity. The best example of the genre is *Mr. Attowel's Jig* (pub. 1595). A standard study and collection of jigs is C. R. Baskerville's *The Elizabethan Jig* (1927).

Johnston, Denis [W.] (1901–). Irish playwright. A native Dubliner, Johnston studied at Christ's College, Cambridge, and entered the profession of law upon graduation. While practicing law, he became interested in the theater and began writing plays. His earliest and best-known play, THE OLD LADY SAYS "NO," was submitted to the Abbey Theatre in 1929. The play was rejected by Lady Gregory, the theater's director, but the Abbey partially subsi-

dized its production at the rival Peacock Theatre. While continuing his legal career, Johnston became more and more involved with the theater and from 1931 to 1936 he was a director at the Gate Theatre in Dublin. Throughout the next decade he was a program director with the BBC, and since 1961 he has been head of the Theater Department at Smith College. His autobiography, *Nine Rivers from Jordan,* was published in 1953.

After *The Old Lady Says "No,"* Johnston's best work is *The Moon in the Yellow River,* produced at the Abbey Theatre in 1931. A brilliant ideological drama, *The Moon in the Yellow River* depicts the Ireland of the twenties, a nation nurtured on violence and rebellion from which reason and order seemed to have disappeared. In its deft interweaving of low comedy and moving tragedy, the play recalls O'Casey at his best.

Of Johnston's other plays, *The Dreaming Dust* (1930) is a provocative and unusual dramatic rendering of the life of Jonathan Swift in terms suggestive of a medieval morality play. His *The Scythe and the Sword* (1958), like O'Casey's *The Plough and the Stars,* takes place during the Easter-week uprising in 1916. Although its title is modeled on O'Casey's play, *The Scythe and the Sword* bears little resemblance to *The Plough and the Stars.* Johnston's play, an antiromantic account of the revolt, presents the rebels and the British with the objectivity of a good historian. Among Johnston's other plays are *Blind Man's Buff* (1936), a free translation of Ernst Töller's *Die Blinde Göttin; A Fourth for Bridge* (1942); and *Strange Occurrence in Ireland's Eve* (1956), a drama based upon a nineteenth-century murder trial.

Johnston's work covers a wide range of styles and subjects. The chief virtues that sustain all of his plays are his intelligence and objectivity, which enable him to avoid much of the sentimental emotionalism that is often prevalent in Irish drama.

Six of Johnston's plays have been published under the title *The Old Lady Says "No" and Other Plays* (1960).—E. Q.

Jones, Henry Arthur (1851–1929). English playwright and critic. After Shaw, Jones was perhaps the most influential English dramatist of the last two decades of the nineteenth century. His path to the theater was as indirect as William S. Gilbert's, another contemporary. The son of a tenant farmer, Jones attended the local school until he was twelve, then began working for his uncle in the drapery business. He was later employed as a commercial traveler and spent the years from 1869 to 1879 in the London, Exeter, and Bradford districts. His interests lay in other directions, however, and he spent much of his time during this period reading, writing, and keeping up with his main interest, the theater. One of the results of this period was a three-volume novel, the plot of which was to form the basis of *The Silver King* (1882), a successful melodrama written in collaboration with Henry Herman. Although his first play to be performed was the one-act *It's Only Round the Corner* (1878), it was *The Silver King* that gave him the financial independence that enabled him to devote all his effort to the drama.

HENRY ARTHUR JONES (WALTER HAMPDEN MEMORIAL LIBRARY AT THE PLAYERS, NEW YORK)

From this time on, Jones was to write prolifically, producing not only drama but critical works in which he stated those principles on which his own plays were based. His dramas may be categorized as melodramas (*The Silver King*, 1882, and *The Middleman*, 1889); serious problem plays (*Saints and Sinners*, 1884; *The Masqueraders*, 1894; *The Triumph of the Philistines*, 1895; and *Michael and His Lost Angel*, 1896); and, especially during his later years, comedies of manners (*The Liars*, 1897, and *Dolly Reforming Herself*, 1908). The first group provided him with means and experience; the last demonstrates his dramaturgical skill; the middle group reveals those qualities that connect Jones to Ibsen and the other significant "thesis" playwrights of the period. Jones was particularly insistent that drama be more than mere entertainment; that the dramatist should be free to portray "all aspects of human life, all passions, all opinions"; and, above all, that the dramatist should fight for largeness and breadth of view, against the cramping and deadening influence of "pessimistic realism." One of his central convictions was that there is a great difference between mere "realism" and truth.

Although he did not wholly succeed in getting beyond surface realism to the truth, he deserves recognition as a dramatist whose plays have a great many qualities that more than compensate for their obvious flaws, flaws that may be attributed as much to his time as to Jones himself. These redeeming qualities are the sincerity of his concern with certain problems, the willingness and courage to treat various heretofore unexplored themes, and the veracity of his insight into human nature, if not into specific characters. While Jones's plays may not impress with their brilliance or profundity, they are the work of a playwright who is thoroughly familiar with his craft and is able to present a solid piece of theatrical fare.

Jones's most important criticism may be found in the various prefaces to his plays and in *The Renascence of the English Drama* (1895); *The Foundations of a National Drama* (1913); and *The Theatre of Ideas* (1915). See also D. A. Jones, *Life and Letters of Henry Arthur Jones* (1930); Clayton Hamilton, ed., *Representative Plays of H. A. Jones* (4 vols., 1926); Richard A. Cordell, *Henry Arthur Jones and the Modern Drama* (1932), one of the most satisfactory studies of Jones.—M. T.

Jonson, Ben[jamin] (1572–1637). English playwright and poet. After graduation from Westminster School, where he was a scholarship student, Jonson entered the trade of his stepfather, a bricklayer. Shortly thereafter he left England to serve as a soldier in the Netherlands, returning to England in 1592. In the ensuing years he joined one of London's professional acting companies, first as an actor and later as a dramatist. He was arrested in 1597 for his performance in, and part-authorship of, *The Isle of Dogs* (1596), a topical satire so scandalous that it resulted in the temporary closing of the London theaters. The following year Jonson was again imprisoned, this time for killing a fellow actor, Gabriel Spencer, in a duel. During his prison term, Jonson was converted to Catholicism, which he abjured twelve years later. By 1601 Jonson had become well enough known as a playwright to appear as a central figure in the so-called WAR OF THE THEATERS, and when James I acceded to the English throne in 1603,

BEN JONSON (THEATRE COLLECTION, NEW YORK PUB-
LIC LIBRARY AT LINCOLN CENTER)

Jonson immediately won favor and became the chief author of court masques. Two years later, however, he found himself in prison again, as one of the authors of *Eastward Ho!*, a satire that offended the king. In 1612/13 he traveled on the Continent as companion to Walter Raleigh's mischievous son, Wat. In 1616 he oversaw the printing and publication of his collected works in a handsome folio edition. This achievement was notable not only in itself but because it provided the impetus for another folio publication seven years later—the First Folio of Shakespeare—to which Jonson contributed two commendatory poems.

In the meantime, Jonson continued supplying plays and masques for court entertainments, many of the latter in conjunction with Inigo Jones (1573–1652), the brilliant architect and scenic designer.

Jonson included among his friends and patrons some of the leading nobles of England, among whom he was honored as the unofficial poet laureate. His quick wit, deep learning, and imperious manner qualified him for still another role—that of literary dictator. From his relatively early days at the Mermaid Tavern and subsequently at numerous other inns and taverns, he was acknowledged as the supreme arbiter of literary taste, particularly among those younger poets who were proud to be numbered among the "sons of Ben." Some of his magisterial and controversial critical comments were recorded by William Drummond, a Scottish poet whom Jonson visited in 1618. Others are included in his own commonplace book *Timber* (pub. post. 1640). Jonson died on August 6, 1637, and was buried in Westminster Abbey. His tombstone bears the famous inscription "O rare Ben Jonson."

The dramatic genre most intimately associated with Jonson's name is the "comedy of humours." The term *humour* is derived from the psychological and physiological principles of Jonson's day. The humours were the four liquids that, corresponding to

the four elements, controlled the human body. Ideally, these four liquids—blood, black bile, yellow bile, and phlegm—existed in harmony, thus producing perfect physical and mental health. Whenever one of the humours became dominant, however, there was a corresponding imbalance in the temperament of the individual. Jonson's "humour" comedies focused on individuals who were controlled by one humour. The earliest examples of this genre are his *Every Man In his Humour* (1598) and *Every Man Out of his Humour* (1599). These two plays are little more than exercises in invective, as are two others, *Cynthia's Revels* (1600) and *The Poetaster* (1601), his contributions to the war of the theaters. Inconsequential as these early works were, they proved to be seeds out of which his mature comedies developed.

In VOLPONE, EPICENE, and THE ALCHEMIST, three of the greatest plays of English drama, humour figures are prominently featured. Jonson makes no attempt to represent human character realistically. Rather, his characters exist merely as embodiments of one dominating humour. His art, as T. S. Eliot has pointed out (*Essays on Elizabethan Drama*, 1956), is the art of caricature. The result is a peculiar clarity of focus that leaves readers and audience with a sense of observing events through a magnifying glass. Thus, *Volpone* is not merely a play about greed; it is a play saturated with that element, seen in every conceivable aspect from every conceivable perspective. It is in fact a morality play, deriving its essence—despite its Italian setting and its overt resemblance to classical Roman comedy—from the native English medieval tradition. Its characters are allegorical, its purpose rigorously moral and didactic. So too in *The Alchemist*, where human greed is compounded with credulity and hypocrisy. Nevertheless, the allegorical-moral structure in these two plays never overshadows the spirited exuberance of the comic plot nor the vitality and paradoxical charm of the characters. *Epicene* exhibits these latter characteristics even more prominently.

Of Jonson's other comedies, those most deserving of mention are BARTHOLOMEW FAIR, *The Devil Is an Ass* (1616), and *The Staple of News* (1626). *Bartholomew Fair* is a furiously paced farce vividly recreating a seventeenth-century London fair. *The Devil Is an Ass* is another sharply satirical picture of human cupidity reminiscent of *Volpone* and *The Alchemist*. The plot concerns the visit to London of a devil who, after experiencing the folly and vice of the city, concludes that "hell is / A grammar school . . . ." compared to London. *The Staple of News* is a satire on the newly emerging news industry, which Jonson sees as symptomatic of the impulse to gossip and of the appetite for slander.

Jonson wrote two tragedies, *Sejanus* (1603) and *Catiline* (1611). Both plays are best described as "tragic satires," the tragic equivalents of the picture of human nature presented in *Volpone* and *The Alchemist*. *Sejanus* is a naked presentation of an all-consuming lust for power; *Catiline*, an analysis of political intrigue.

One other dramatic genre with which Jonson is associated and in which he had no peer is the MASQUE. In collaboration with Inigo Jones, he produced a number of lyrical and sumptuous spectacles. Earlier, masques had little literary value, being essentially pantomimes. Jonson brought to these visual entertainments his own severely disciplined lyrical gifts. He also created the antimasque, a comic parody of the main plot of the masque. His best-known masques are *Hymenaei* (1606), *The Masque of Beauty* (1608), *The Hue and Cry after Cupid* (1608), *The Masque of Queens* (1609), and *The Gipsies Metamorphosed* (1621). He also wrote a fragmentary pastoral drama, *The Sad Shepherd* (pub. post. 1640). (See PASTORAL DRAMA.)

Long overshadowed by his great contemporary, Jonson has only comparatively recently been given his due as a dramatist. He has been disparaged, not only for not being Shakespeare, but for not appreciating him. (As a matter of fact, the evidence is clear that Jonson was a friend and admirer of the man whom, as he said, he honored "this side idolatry.") He has been pictured as an unimaginative neoclassicist, encumbered by his own erudition and incapable of passion or warmth. Fortunately, however, these charges have not been made of late; Jonson has come to be considered on his own terms, not as a Shakespeare *manqué* but as a great comic dramatist, a caricaturist whose only equal in English literature is Charles Dickens.

The standard edition of Jonson is *The Works of Ben Jonson* (1925–1952), edited by C. H. Herford and Percy Simpson in ten volumes. The second volume of this edition also contains the standard biography of the author. An excellent popular biography is Marchette Chute's *Ben Jonson of Westminster* (1953). A good collection of critical articles appears in *Ben Jonson* (1963), edited by Jonas Barish. —E. Q.

jōruri. The word *jōruri* as applied to the Japanese theater has two meanings, each naturally associated with the other. First, it may mean a chanter, or narrator, in either the puppet theater or the *kabuki*; second, it refers by extension to the doll theater as a type in itself (see BUNRAKU). The more extended meaning is easily explained by the great importance of the chanter in puppet drama. Not only does he speak for all the doll characters who are seen on the stage, but he also serves in the role of chorus, expounding the meaning of the action, clarifying the story, and describing its physical setting. The jōruri performance is in its essence an illustrated recitation.

The Japanese theater for live actors is often and naturally enough described as above all a theater of spectacle. Westerners are generally familiar with the brilliant theater prints depicting it. The costumes dazzle the eye; the settings for the kabuki are highly elaborate. It will be recalled that even the chaste design for the *noh* plays appeals conspicuously to the viewer. In actual performance the speaking and singing voices may at first fail to fall graciously on Western ears. But for beauty and force, as well as for amazing virtuosity, few performances equal those by the jōruri chanters for the now almost extinct puppet stage. The range of the voice, its astonishing flexibility, and the powerful rhythm and finely studied interrelation between jōruri and his accompanist, the samisen player, mark one of the triumphs of the Japanese stage.—H. W. W.

Julius Caesar (1599). A tragedy by William SHAKESPEARE. Thomas Platter, a Swiss traveler in London in 1599, attended a production of *Julius Caesar* on September 21. This is its earliest recorded performance. *The Tragedy of Julius Caesar* was first printed in 1623 in the First Folio. Its source is Plutarch's *Lives of the Noble Grecians and Romans*, as translated into English (1579, 1595) by Sir Thomas North from a French translation (1559) by Jacques Amyot.

Combining material from the lives of Julius Caesar, Marcus Brutus, and Marcus Antonius, Shakespeare developed a plot revolving around the assassination of Caesar. Afraid that Caesar desires to become king of Rome, thereby changing the state from a republic to a monarchy, the patrician Brutus —an idealist and a Stoic—persuades himself to join a conspiracy to assassinate Caesar. He does not realize that the motives of the conspirators, headed by the jealous malcontent Cassius, are anything but honorable. The plot succeeds. Antony, Caesar's loyal follower, requests permission of the conspirators to speak to the populace at the funeral. Against the advice of Cassius, Brutus grants the request. Antony succeeds in turning the crowd against the conspirators, and Brutus and Cassius flee. Antony joins with Octavius—Caesar's great-nephew—and Lepidus in forming a triumvirate to rule Rome and avenge Caesar's death. In Sardis, Brutus and Cassius meet. After a bitter quarrel, the two reconcile their differences and plan their military strategy. Although Cassius offers sound objections, Brutus decides they will march on Antony and Octavius at Philippi. In the ensuing battle Cassius, mistakenly believing that his forces are overcome, takes his life. Brutus, upon the defeat of his army, runs on his sword. Antony and Octavius pay final homage to the noble Brutus.

A powerful play to see, with absorbing characterizations of the four male leads, *Julius Caesar* is disturbing to analyze because of its ambiguous focus. Is it a character study primarily? If so, who is emphasized—Caesar, who does not appear after the beginning of the third act, or Brutus? If Brutus (portrayed as an idealist who fails as a pragmatist), why is the play named after Caesar? Or is it a play about politics? Although Caesar dies, his spirit dominates the second half; and in the end the chaos engendered by the toppling of lawful central authority has given way to peace.

Shakespeare in 1599 was fresh from writing a cycle of English chronicle plays in which the idea of history as a teacher for the cause of political stability had come to take the center of interest. It is conceivable that the ambiguity of focus in *Julius Caesar* may be attributed to the hold history still had on Shakespeare while he was turning his attention to a type of tragedy he had not earlier attempted—one in which probing the nature of man would receive primary emphasis. In the tragedies immediately following, Shakespeare learned how to subordinate events to character study, and he successfully kept his protagonists in sharp focus.

An outstanding edition of *Julius Caesar* is the New Arden Edition (1955), edited by T. S. Dorsch. —W. G.

Juno and the Paycock (1924). A tragicomedy by Sean O'CASEY. The action of *Juno and the Paycock* centers on the Boyle family, caught in the cross fire of the civil war in Dublin in 1922 when Irishmen were killing Irishmen: those who supported the newly formed Free State government against the Irish Republican Army, which rejected the partition of the country. But it is their own folly as well as the brutality of the war that destroys the Boyles. Although they are dispossessed by the mismanagement of an expected inheritance, the whole family is living on borrowed time as well as money. Juno sees through the antic poses and defections of her husband, "Captain" Jack, yet she herself succumbs to his insensitive views when she says that Mrs. Tancred may have deserved to lose her diehard son in the war. It is not long before she discovers that her own son Johnny has been slain for having betrayed his IRA friend, Hughie Tancred. Her daughter Mary is seduced by the lawyer Bentham, who mismanaged the inheritance papers. And of course, it is Jack Boyle's general betrayal of the family, his cowardice, vanity, and drunkenness that hastens the whole tragedy of the disintegrating Boyles.

There is in this play, as in others by O'Casey, a strategic balance of tragic and comic elements. In ironic contrast to Juno's essentially heroic stance, we have the grotesque antiheroism of "Captain" Jack, the strutting "paycock." He and his crony, Joxer Daly, are drawn in the tradition of the archetypal braggart-warrior and parasite-slave. Together they insulate themselves from the world of terrible realities—responsibility and the danger of death—by living in an illusory world of absurd fantasies and drunken bravado. O'Casey satirizes them unsparingly for the shiftless rascals that they are, yet because he sees in their guile the amusement of a universal frailty, he often laughs with, as well as at, them. "Captain" Jack Boyle may lack the girth of Captain Jack Falstaff, but he has the same flamboyant humor and glorious mendacity, the ingenious sense of self-indulgence and self-preservation. —D. K.

Justice (1910). A play, subtitled *A Tragedy,* by John GALSWORTHY. Falder, a clerk who is a weakling but not at all a criminal type, steals money from his employer so that he can run off with a married woman who is cruelly mistreated by her husband. At his trial the extenuating circumstances are amply presented, and Falder's attorney argues that imprisonment will destroy him; nevertheless, he is found guilty and sent to prison. The crusty but kindly managing clerk under whom he worked tries to visit him but is sent away because Falder is in solitary confinement. A moving but wordless scene shows Falder pacing his cell and then beating frantically on the door. Out of prison and much the worse for his imprisonment, he is offered a job by his former employer on the condition that he stop seeing the woman for whose sake he committed the original theft. Before the issue can be decided, a police officer interrupts, seeking Falder for failing to report to the police. Rather than go back to prison, Falder jumps out of a window and kills himself. Galsworthy's intention was to present the case for the thief who steals out of weakness of character and also to effect reforms in the prisons. Winston Churchill, who was then home secretary, saw the play and was moved to initiate the necessary prison reforms. This play's specific social function as a piece of reformist and realistic drama has dated its appeal.—H. P.

K

kabuki. From the mid-seventeenth century to the mid-twentieth the *kabuki* has been the most popular form of theatrical entertainment in Japan and remains the most typical of the theatrical arts in that country. It is an eclectic form, as its name, commonly taken to mean skill in song and dance, implies, inheriting features from most of the earlier forms developed in a country singularly prolific in theatrical activity. The word appears originally to have signified "eccentric." But the heresy of yesterday soon became orthodoxy.

Kabuki is unusual in its extremely large stage, its passion for the spectacular, and its violent inclination to popular melodrama. Its literary value is distinctly less than that of such earlier forms as the *noh,* the puppet theater, or the *kowaka,* but as elaborate spectacle it stands without a rival. Moreover, it has achieved an amazing technical virtuosity. This is the more conspicuous because of the singularly stylized nature of its acting and of much of its *décor.*

A survey of this eclectic art form shows that many of its stories, scenes, dances, and much of its music derive from the aristocratic noh plays, some from the more popular Japanese puppet theater, now commonly called *bunraku,* while in a few instances the plays are more or less original. All, however, are imbued with Japanese tradition. It is possible even in the modern productions of kabuki to trace elements derived from the earliest-known popular theatrical

life in Japan, extending for at least a thousand years. The form as now understood, however, emerged at the close of the seventeenth century, though popular entertainments bearing the same name were given at the beginning of the century by the woman singer and dancer O'Kuni. During the seventeenth century several groups, such as "the Women's Kabuki" and "the Young Men's Kabuki," flourished briefly, to be extinguished, primarily on moral grounds, by a censorious officialdom.

The rise of the kabuki properly so called is attributed to drastic social, political, and economic developments of the GENROKU period, technically bounded by the years 1688 to 1703 but, as more liberally understood, extending from 1673 to 1735. This period saw the emergence of a new mercantile class, a new town life, and a strongly secular, materialistic outlook favoring flamboyant taste in all the arts. Something of the severe discipline of the aristocratic noh united with powerful elements in folk art largely of a peasant origin to create a radically new theatrical form. One of the most paradoxical theaters in the world was the result—a theater both passionately disciplined and shamelessly sensational. Its popularity in Japan is now certainly on the wane. Production costs are extremely high. The old formulas for acting and the moral values they express are growing outmoded and would seem altogether remote were it not for the superb skill that the practi-

SCENE FROM A KABUKI PLAY (CONSULATE GENERAL OF JAPAN, NEW YORK)

tioners of the art still command. It is a theater of unrivaled virtuosity, melodrama in apotheosis.

The form of the stage itself is unique, reflecting the strong genius of Japanese architecture and the communal spirit of the native theater. The kabuki stage as it stands today is by no means the type used in the first few brilliant decades of kabuki drama. Its stage, however, has always been large, yet the theater has always been intimate. The Kabuki-za, in Tokyo, the most celebrated of the nineteenth-century theaters, has a proscenium about ninety feet wide and twenty-one feet high while the depth of the auditorium is only sixty feet. The stage is comparatively shallow, being about thirty-five feet. From the left side of the stage, but not directly against the auditorium's left wall, there extends through the depth of the entire auditorium a runway, the HANAMICHI, five feet wide. This is an acting area of much importance. Leading characters make their entrances and exits along it, frequently taking much time in the process. It serves also for ceremonial processions. Minor characters as a rule use exits and entrances on the main stage. In the center of this is a revolving platform, first introduced in 1757, well before any such platform was employed in Europe. At least two trap doors are available on kabuki stages, one in the center of the revolving stage, the other approximately a third of the way from the front of the stage along the hanamichi. These prove especially useful where supernatural episodes are introduced.

The modern kabuki theater uses several curtains, the most important being the main curtain between stage and auditorium. This does not rise and fall but pulls from the sides. The combination of proscenium and curtain, unquestionably borrowed from the West, is relatively young in kabuki history. In earlier years the main stage projected into the audience; curtains were used only in the rear; a secondary and narrower hanamichi extended along the right side of the auditorium parallel to the main hanamichi. Seating in the modern kabuki theater is largely in the European manner. Auditorium and balcony have that useful object of furniture, the chair, seldom if ever seen in ancient Japan. The older theaters used an arrangement fully compatible with the social customs of Japanese life and theatergoing. The Western custom whereby persons go to the theater two by two or even individually was little known in earlier times. The people came in larger, often family groups. With these practices in view, boxes extended from three sides of the auditorium's rectangle in a manner somewhat similar to the eighteenth-century Western opera houses, except that the seating was on the usual Japanese mats. The auditorium floor was divided into small enclosures, each accommodating six or seven persons. These enclosures were separated by extremely narrow partitions that have been described by Western commentators as "cat-runs." The spectators could look about them only with some craning of the neck. Nevertheless, the audience was well placed to enjoy the activity on the hanamichi. The action had the effect of enveloping the audience. The theater was both an aesthetic delight and a social institution ideally fit to serve the Japanese regard both for family life and for social parties where the geisha, or woman of pleasure, was conspicuous. Like the Chinese theater, the older kabuki theater provided entertainment for an entire day; indeed, the show began in the midmorning and was likely to last till after midnight. The earliest theaters, similar to the Elizabethan, were roofed only insofar as the main stage and balcony were concerned, leaving most of the auditorium open. For many years, however, the theaters have been entirely enclosed. In recent years electric lighting has been used, though at times not in the most artful manner. Until very recent years there has been absolutely no dimming of the house lights. The Japanese early developed an exquisite art of colored lanterns that contributed much to the beauty of the theaters from the seventeenth to the nineteenth century.

The kabuki is a dance and musical theater. Its flooring is of highly polished wood and wooden construction throughout is favorable for acoustics. The musicians have stated places for particular plays or types of play but are almost always visible and wear a rich, traditional costume, virtually a uniform. Their most familiar position is onstage to the extreme left. In the more ceremonial plays or dance dramas they may occupy the entire back section. A narrator, who is also a chanter, known as JŌRURI, sits, together with his accompanist, who plays the samisen, on a small revolving stage to the right. The movable feature of this stage provides a relief for this exacting part, at least two chanters serving the same function by alternation. This feature is, quite logically, even more conspicuous in the puppet theaters than in the kabuki, and therefore the usage is especially prominent in the kabuki plays derived from the puppet theaters. There is, finally, an offstage ensemble to produce what, for want of a better term, may be called sound effects.

The theater architecture provides the result that the Japanese audience so clearly desires, an intimate relation between audience and performer. The audience, especially in earlier years, participated actively in the day's entertainment. The spectators commonly exclaimed their approval or disapproval of the actors and the actors digressed to address the audience. Sometimes the play itself was halted while an announcement was made from the stage, especially if a new honor had recently been conferred upon an actor. Such an interruption was termed a *kojo*. The spectators made themselves thoroughly at home. Assembled for many hours, they brought their own food and came and went, as occasion called, to the neighboring teahouses. In short, the kabuki theater was a thriving social center as well as a home for many kinds of artistic activity.

Although the performance in the kabuki has always been highly eclectic, to the Japanese at least no uncomfortable inconsistency is felt. In a given play there are passages of naturalism, followed by passages, as a rule more extended, of extreme stylization. Some scenes or extended episodes are pure miming. Some productions are dramatic dances in which words are merely a frail accompaniment to the dance or, perhaps, no words are used at all. Serious and farcical scenes jostle each other. Occasionally, although today with decreasing frequency, a very long play is presented over a series of days. By far the more usual practice is to give many short plays in one day's program or, what is still more common, to present favorite scenes from plays of considerable length. Inasmuch as the majority in the audience are inveterate theatergoers, the enveloping action in the case of a famous scene will be well known and in need of no explanation whatsoever. Program notes would be out of the question. There is actually more form in the theatrical year than in the theatrical day. By tradition, at least, certain plays or types of play are always produced in the New Year season or at other stated times. Cheerful plays are deemed appropriate to the spring, plays with ghosts for the winter season, when the audience may shiver from terror and cold alike. Theatergoing thus becomes a ritual. Yet, like other rituals, it depends on the society that creates it and in time wears thin as social change inevitably arises.

Kabuki is to an extraordinary degree a stage spectacle. Its actors are not only dancers but acrobats. Its costumes are lavish, its stage sets flamboyant. The music and sound effects, though highly developed, are clearly secondary to the appeal made to the eye. It is a theater for lovers of the pictorial who may well be, when seen from another point of view, thoroughly illiterate. The manner in which a word is pronounced, or mouthed, intoned, shouted, or sung is considerably more important than the word itself; indeed, to the informed the word becomes almost superfluous.

The playwrights, if such they may be called, possessed an uncanny sense for the theatrical but a truly subversive view of dramatic literature. They subjected plays that preceded and inspired them, such as those for the noh and the puppet theaters, to the peculiar violence required by their own standards. At first the repertory was composed almost entirely by the actors themselves. By the beginning of the eighteenth century, however, the high professionalism that everywhere appears in the craft of the traditional kabuki overtook the playwriting and not only a profession but a systematic procedure was created. Each company had its own master playwright under whom a small but well-defined hierarchy of lesser playwrights served. It became customary for the leader to compose only the more important scenes, which were arranged to occur at certain stated places in a full-length drama. By far the greater number of the favorite plays on the kabuki stage derive from the seventeenth and eighteenth centuries. A few are of the nineteenth century, while virtually nothing derives from the twentieth, although minor changes are continually made even in the most sacred kabuki classics. In these respects the kabuki as a classical theater active today is surpassed in its conservatism only by the noh. Unfortunately for the kabuki, the noh is a great poetic theater that, at least as poetry, declines to grow old, whereas the kabuki, founded more on spectacle than on poetry, declines with the passage of time.

Although formalism in the kabuki is anything but pedantic, certain types of plays are readily discerned. There are, first of all, the plays dealing with the epic, heroic, and feudal periods in Japanese history, celebrating the moral code of the samurai and animated with scenes of fighting and general violence. The most famous of these deal with the stories of the Soga brothers, the feuds between the Heike or Taira and the Genji or Minamoto clans. These are the most colorful of the plays. To splendid costumes are added gorgeous armor and all the appurtenances of feudal ceremony. Japanese audiences were long thrilled by legends springing from an age that in Western chronology would be called medieval. The sense of honor and of moral values generally pertaining to this age lingered long and lustily in Japan. Pieces of this nature in particular evoked a style of acting termed ARAGOTO, established and perfected by the most celebrated of all Japanese actors, Ichikawa Danjuro I (1660–1704). The contortion of poses and gestures in this style may well suggest caricature to a Westerner but by the Japanese are understood in complete seriousness. A superior play in this category is *Kanjincho,* derived from the noh play ATAKA.

Another highly important type of play is termed SEWAMONO, or "common-people's play." This was chiefly inspired by the naturalistic tragedies of the best known of Japanese playwrights, CHIKAMATSU, who wrote primarily for the puppets. Such plays are rich in pathos. THE LOVE SUICIDES AT AMIJIMA affords a good example. When they are well acted, the audience weeps profusely.

Many plays that do not deal with the older epic materials nevertheless are inspired by the code of loyalty and honor derived from the earlier period. Such are the plays concerning the famous forty-seven *ronin,* who avenged their lord. CHUSHINGURA, first produced in 1748 and written by Takeda IZUMO in collaboration with Namiki Senryu and Miyoshi Shoraku, ranks among the best known on this theme. Another famous play, not feudal in its setting but similar in its morality, is SUGUAWARA. The play is seldom given in full, but the section known as *Tarakoya* is well known and stands among the most famous of kabuki masterpieces.

Some of the best kabuki plays are farces derived from one of the oldest and most popular branches of Japanese drama, oddly associated with the religious noh, namely the *kyogen,* which as early as the fourteenth century served for comic relief. Since in such cases an example is more helpful than a definition, *Migawari Zazen* (1911), adapted by Okamoto Shiko, may be instanced as typical. A husband tells his wife that he is going to a Buddhist ceremony where the worshipper, in his meditation, holds a cloak over his shoulders. Substituting his servant, he goes off to an assignation. Discovering the trick, his wife takes the servant's place. The husband returns, thoroughly drunk, boasting of his amorous exploits, as he supposes, to the servant. At the height of his drunken merriment, his wife, emerging from under the cloak, confronts him with his deed and drives him offstage.

The dance dramas may be either serious or comic. *Kagamijishi,* by Fukuchi Ochi, first staged in 1893, is nevertheless based on a theme venerable in Japanese mythology. It is in two parts. Part I presents a dance by a maiden seized by the spirit of a lion. Part II, performed by the same dancer, presents the lion himself in all his prowess and ferocity. This is as serious a dance ceremony as kabuki is capable of providing. *Takatoki* (1885), on the contrary, is a bizarre but essentially humorous dance play concerning a cruel lord who takes revenge on the killing of his pet dog by killing a young man. In the midst of his rejoicing he is suddenly attacked by a pack of long-nosed goblins who, in the course of a wild revel, completely humble his pride.

These instances give some conception of the extraordinary variety within the kabuki program. The last major kabuki playwright was Kawatake MOKUAMI. In the present century there have been eminent kabuki actors but no notable dramatists. Among the last great actors have been Ichikawa Danjuro IX (1838–1905), Nakamura Utaemon V (1865–1940), Matsumoto Koshiro (1838–1905), Onoye Kikugoro VI (1885—1949), and Ichimura Uzaemon XV (1874–1945).

As seen from the foregoing, acting became in Japan the tradition of certain celebrated families. As in China, actors were trained from early childhood, as a rule reaching the peak of their profession only in their later years. They have at all times been regarded as a class by themselves, in earlier periods treated harshly or at least with social condescension, though of late much emancipated. Plays and the profession itself have been repeatedly attacked by severe government pressure. Nevertheless, the great actors have always been idolized by the theatergoing public. Each family has its crest, or *mon,* worn on its stage costumes. Again, as in China, the greatest actors in Japan have often been those specializing in feminine roles (see ONNAGATA). Not until the present generation has a woman appeared on the true kabuki stage, now over three centuries old. Among the conventions in acting technique developed with particular success have been the MICHIYUKI, or imaginary journey, accomplished by proceeding about the stage with much miming, and the MIE, or pose, struck by a male actor to produce the effect of climax or extreme emphasis. To the skeptical this appears the performing artist's ultimate expression of egoism. The usage often accentuates the pictorial aspect of the kabuki; its chief moments have, in fact, been termed by the Japanese themselves "stage pictures." This further accords with the enthusiasm of Japanese artists throughout the kabuki's golden age for depicting its extravagant poses and costumes. Almost all these depictions are to be interpreted in a favorable or flattering sense, although in the case of the ambiguous work of SHARAKU, it is possible that caricature is intended.

A large literature exists on the kabuki. The most thoughtful criticism in English is by Earle Ernst, *The Kabuki Theatre* (1956). A lively description may be found in *Japanese Theatre* (1952) by Faubion Bowers. For a scholarly and most reliable analysis of kabuki technique, see A. C. Scott, *The Kabuki Theatre of Japan* (1955). Valuable especially for its appendix, with generous explanation of the terms in this field, is *The Kabuki Handbook* (1956) by Aubrey S. Halford and Giovanni M. Halford. Consult also *Kabuki: Japanese Drama* (1958) by Kawatake Shigetoshi.

Kabuki plays, as previously observed, are of dubious literary value. Few were published in Japan until quite recent times and only a handful have been translated. See, however, A. C. Scott, *Kanjincho* (1953), the original play by Namiki Gohei III, and by the same translator, *Genyadana* (1953), the original work by Joko Segawa. See also Earle Ernst, *Three Japanese Plays from the Traditional Theatre* (1959), and *Six Kabuki Plays* (1963), translated by Donald Richie and Miyoko Watanabe.—H. W. W.

Kaiser, Georg (1878–1945). German playwright. Georg Kaiser, who has been called the classi-

cist of German expressionist drama, was born in Magdeburg in 1878, the son of an insurance salesman. His early interest in literature and the theater led him to read intensively Plato, Shakespeare, Goethe, Kleist, Büchner, Ibsen, and contemporary literary figures, such as Arno Holz, some of whose poems he always carried with him, Gerhart Hauptmann, whose classic comedy *Der Biberpelz* (*The Beaver Coat,* 1893) he adapted in his own play *Die melkende Kuh* (*The Milking Cow,* 1903), and Nietzsche, whose superman concept of a higher order of man capable of redeeming the fragmented man of modern technological society through his superior power of intellect and sacrifice contributed much to Kaiser's own notion of the "new man."

In 1903 Kaiser severed connections with the literary circle of the German poet Stefan George because of very significant differences in aesthetic intent. Kaiser's statement, *Ein Werk ist kein Werk für sich* ("A work of art does not exist in and for itself") shows his decisive rejection of the art for art's sake theory. Art does not stand sovereign in the human condition oblivious to everything but its own inner aesthetic laws and intentions. Instead it must have a vital commitment to *der gekonnte Mensch,* "the man made manifest." The essential purpose of art is therefore didactic. The aim of dramatic art is to depict the extraordinary intellectual, moral, and spiritual efforts of the new man and to record his arrival at the state of perfection.

In a programmatic essay entitled "Der kommende Mensch oder Dichtung und Energie" ("The New Man or Poetry and Energy," 1922) Kaiser goes to great lengths to describe his understanding of the new man. He is not the man of the technological age fragmented through specialization. Instead, he is the man of infinite potential and inherent universality—*Der Mensch ist das All* ("Man is the Omni-"). In a curious combination of idealistic and vitalistic thinking Kaiser proceeds to state that *durch den Menschen dringt die Idee zur Darstellung,* that is, through the activity of self-realization man becomes the personification of the idea, the moral principle that governs the preestablished harmony of the universe. *Dichtung proklaimiert die Synthese—Mensch.* It is the function of literature to proclaim this synthesis of the moral and natural order in the human order of the new man.

Many critics have claimed that it is difficult, if not impossible, to deduce a universal notional formula for Kaiser's dramas. However, much might be gained in viewing his plays as exercises in the definition of *der gekonnte Mensch,* or "the new man." Kaiser's plays have been called *Denkspiele*—"idea plays"—for the slight dramatic action is obviously secondary to the playing out of dialectical arguments. The playwright apparently felt the necessity for a speculative conflict of ideas rather than a dramatic conflict of individuals for the presentation of his "man made manifest." It is not the personal psychology of the hero that determines the nature of the dramatic situation but the content, vigor, and validity of his ideas. Thus, in *Von Morgens bis Mitternachts* (*From Morn to Midnight,* written 1912, pub. 1916) the idea of the clerk's fascination with a newly awakened desire for physical gratification and for money is tested for validity against the background of society. This litmus test reveals the deception and untruth of the idea. The protagonist can only atone for his false idea, his lack of wisdom, by complete sacrifice. His *Ecce homo* death not only redeems the hero from his sins but also manifests to society the inherent falsity of its values and the need for change.

THE BURGHERS OF CALAIS manifests another dimension of the new man. Eustache dares to reject the traditional political tactics of aggression and bravely embraces the humanitarian cause of pacifism. His death represents the full commitment of the enlightened private man to the political welfare of the people. Its significance lies in the determination of the hero to prevent the false idea of defense and destruction from winning out over the new idea of preservation of life and peace.

In the trilogy *Gas* (1916–1919) we find an excellent example of the confrontation of two notions of man: the fragmented man of the technological age and the total man of an idealistically envisioned utopia. The playing out of this argument results in perhaps Kaiser's most pessimistic statement, for everything is destroyed in the heated struggle between the forces for progress on the one hand and the forces for peace on the other. See THE GAS TRILOGY.

However, in Kaiser's *Kolportage* (*Colportage*, written 1923–1924) we note a more optimistic view of the unlimited potential of man. The individual is apparently capable of crossing the arbitrary lines of social position and economic status to play any role and to succeed in any activity. This demonstration of human flexibility apparently reaffirms Kaiser's belief in the universality of the new man.

For his dramatic vision, Georg Kaiser suffered bitter persecution during the thirties. His name was removed from the Prussian Academy of Arts; his books were burned on May 10, 1933; he barely escaped with his life to Amsterdam in June 1938. This was the beginning of his exile and the last period of literary activity, which included plans for a philosophical work, lyrical and epic compositions, and an anthology of German literature. He died in 1945 while in the process of writing the novel *Ard*.

From Morn to Midnight, translated by Ashley Dukes, can be found in *Twenty Best European Plays on the American Stage* (1957), edited by John Gassner. *Coral* is in the anthology edited by T. H. Dickinson entitled *Continental Plays*, Vol. II (1935). *Gas I* and *Gas II* are in the collection *Twenty-five Modern Plays* (1953), S. M. Tucker, ed.

Critical studies include Robert Kauf's *Faith and Despair in Georg Kaiser's Works* (1955); Brian J. Kenworthy's *Georg Kaiser* (1957); and H. F. Garten's "Georg Kaiser and the Expressionist Movement," in *Drama*, 37 (1955).—C. A. M.

Kalidasa (373?–?415). Most celebrated of Indian dramatists and poets. Kalidasa has largely evaded his biographers. None of the many attempts to locate his place of birth or activity or the years in which he lived has remained unchallenged. Conjectures range from those of scholars who place him in the ninth century A.D. to those of others who prefer the second century B.C. The fourth century A.D. has had the most advocates but the most recent tendency has been to push Kalidasa's dates backward in time, along with those of other masters of the Sanskrit stage. A tradition of much antiquity associates him

with Kashmir but more recent scholars locate him in the kingdom of Chandragupta II, in central India, probably in the court at Ujjain, giving the probable dates as A.D. 373–415. These, thus far, seem the most plausible conclusions.

Although little is known of Kalidasa's life, more is known of him as a writer than of most early Sanskrit dramatists. His authorship of several poems especially rich in amorous sentiment, nature imagery, and religious enthusiasm, such as his *Cloud Messenger*, is no less assured than his authorship of his plays. Three plays have come down to us: a courtly comedy, *Malavika and Agnimitra*; a highly heroic, mythological drama, *Vikrama and Urvashi*; and his masterpiece, SHAKUNTALA, which sometimes bears the title *The Recovered Ring*.

Kalidasa's plays are similar in their choice of erotic themes treated with much idealism. In *Malavika and Agnimitra* the spirit is primarily that of pleasure-loving court life; there is more gaiety and humor than passion. The clown, or VIDUSAKA, a clever intriguer, guides the plot. The play was written for a spring festival. *Vikrama and Urvashi* is much more highly pitched. The story concerns the marriage of the hero to a celestial nymph and his wars in heaven. Act IV contains some celebrated nature poetry; the hero seeks news of his lost love from beasts, birds, and plants. *Shakuntala* also relates the story of a heroine lost and found but with a better story, more discernment in the psychology, and a richer and still more poetic symbolism.

Kalidasa is almost unanimously granted the highest place in Sanskrit drama. This is not only because of his remarkable gifts as a dramatic poet but because he so well exhibits the special qualities gratifying to Indian taste and minutely described in Indian dramatic criticism. Fortunately, these values are in general acceptable, or at least intelligible, to the civilized world as a whole. Hindu aesthetics constitute a rarefaction of the aesthetic, a pinnacle of imaginative idealism. Its ideas are elaborately defined in the chief Sanskrit work on the subject, the NATYASASTRA, attributed to Bharata. Whether this critic flourished before or after the great dramatist is unknown. In any case, the two speak to one purpose. The end of art is conceived by both as a state or mood of blissful detachment, a way station on the road to religious enlightenment. The theater is conceived as the apex of the arts, where the lines of all arts converge. Kalidasa's plays best exemplify the standards and practices laid down by the preceptors for his art. No vulgar, odious, or hateful deed is presented on his stage. The plot is allowed to illustrate the malignancy of fate but not of men. Suffering must not be depicted as occasioned by either moral or psychological defects. Hero, heroine, and their associates belong to a superior order of human beings or may even be incarnations of deities. Distortions of comedy are admitted for pleasing relaxation, standing in humorous and revealing opposition to the extreme idealism of the leading characters, a salt to ensure the absence of insipidity or sentimentality. The playwright cares less for the play's action than for the moods evoked. Each act has its particular mood. Each play belongs to its particular type of mood. These principles are nowhere more fully exemplified than in *Shakuntala*.

The conception of the stage as synthesis of the arts

is well exhibited even in Kalidasa's least impressive play, *Malavika and Agnimitra*, in which singing, dancing, and miming are deftly harmonized. But in *Shakuntala* the synthetic principle is employed to more serious ends and with much greater art. Provisions for miming and for various levels of elocution are astonishingly artful. It is one of the most joyous works ever produced for the stage.

Whether or not, then, Kalidasa followed such Sanskrit treatises on dramatic theory and technique as we now possess, it is widely accepted that he embodied in *Shakuntala* the finest potentialities of Indian aesthetic theory and procedure. To an extraordinary degree he was in harmony with the culture in which he flourished. Thus his work provided a model for the drama of his age, repeatedly to be imitated by his followers or, more cordially speaking, to inspire them. Yet brilliant as many of the later Sanskrit plays are, such as those by Bhavabhuti or Harsha, none equals or in any intimate sense resembles Kalidasa's work. The true measure of his peculiar genius is that while he certainly conformed to innumerable "laws" of his own tradition, he nevertheless achieved work of high originality. Possessing a sovereign command of nuance, he has neither a really close follower nor predecessor. He worked in silk and gold while others labored to the same ends with less precious materials. His masterpiece reveals the Indian drama in its most suave and consummate form. His plays have proved to be classical in the same sense as Shakespeare's, being both widely imitated and essentially inimitable.

For an able account of Kalidasa's work, see *Kalidasa, His Art and Thought* (1962) by Trimbak Govind Mainkar. A sensitive appraisal is found in *Kalidasa et l'art poétique* (1917) by Hari Chand. *Shakuntala* was first translated by Sir William Jones in 1790. The most widely approved translation into English is that by Arthur W. Ryder (1959). An attractive rendering made by A. Hjalmar Edgren in 1894 appears, somewhat revised, in *Six Sanskrit Plays* (1964, edited by H. W. Wells. *Vikrama and Urvashi* is translated in *Select Specimens of the Drama of the Hindus* (1871) by H. H. Wilson. The best rendering, however, is by Aurobindo Ghosh (1911); this is somewhat free but of an exceptionally high poetic quality. *Malavika and Agnimitra* is best translated by Arthur W. Ryder (1915). An earlier rendering, thoroughly competent, is by C. H. Tawney (1891). *The Cloud Messenger* is well rendered into English by Franklin and Eleanor Edgerton (1964). *Ritusamhara, or The Pageant of the Seasons* has been translated by R. S. Pandit (1947).—H. W. W.

K'ang Chin-chih. See LI K'UEI CARRIES THORNS.

Kanjincho. See ATAKA.

Kao Tse-ch'eng. See ROMANCE OF THE LUTE.

Karaghiozis. See GREECE: *modern period*.

Karvaš, Peter (1920–   ). Slovakian playwright and writer. Born in Banská Bystrica, Karvaš began his career as a writer for radio during World War II. He took part in the Slovakian national uprising; after the liberation of Czechoslovakia in 1945, he graduated from the philosophy faculty of J. A. Komenský University in Bratislava in 1947. He then worked as a literary manager of the Czechoslovak broadcasting division of the Slovak National Theater. From 1949 to 1951 he worked in the diplomatic service and then became chief of the theater section of the government's cultural department in Bratislava, the editor of the magazine *Kultúrný život* (Cultural Life), and the secretary of the Federation of Slovakian Writers. In the early 1960's he became a lecturer at the Academy of Visual Arts in Bratislava.

Karvaš is the most important Slovakian dramatist since World War II. He is part of Slovakia's communist intelligentsia who fought against fascism in World War II and who, after the liberation of the Republic, helped establish the communist government of Czechoslovakia. He uses the stage as a political platform, because he believes that the theater should take an active part in forming the society. In his plays he expresses the important experiences of his youth—the uprising, war, concentration camps—and the problems of postwar society. He deals with political realities and often portrays an intellectual as the hero of his plays.

In his early dramas, *Meteor* (1945), *Návrat do života* ("Coming Back to Life," 1946), and *Bašta* ("The Fort," 1948), Karvaš used allegories to express universal, eternal problems. In his later plays, *Srdce plné radosti* ("The Heart Full of Pleasure," 1953) and *Pacient stotrinásť* ("The Patient 113," 1955), he used realism, in accordance with the current trend of socialist drama. He combined both these styles, allegory and realism, in his most successful drama, *Polnocná omsa* ("The Midnight Mass," 1959), in which he analyzed Slovakian society at the end of World War II. In this play Karvaš celebrated the heroism that was displayed during the Slovakian national uprising and he condemned the role played by the bourgeoisie in modern Slovakian history. In *Antigona a tí druhí* ("Antigone and the Others," 1962), in which he portrayed the lives of prisoners in a Nazi concentration camp, Karvaš tried, from the socialist point of view, to answer the questions that concerned Sophocles in his *Antigone*. In his play Karvaš champions the fight of the progressive people for human dignity and freedom. In *Jazva* ("The Scar," 1963) Karvaš recalled political errors made during the years of the personality cult.

Karvaš also wrote satirical comedies: *Spolok piatich P* ("Five P's Society," 1946), *Hanibal pred bránami* ("Hannibal Before the Gates," 1947), *Ľudia z našej ulice* ("People Living in Our Street," 1950), *Diplomati* (1958), and *Zmrtvýchv-stanie deduška Kolomana* ("Grandad Koloman's Return to Life from Death," 1960). His most important work in this genre is the tragicomedy *Veľká parochňa* ("Great Wig," 1964). In this satire about the mutual persecution between bald and hairy people, Karvaš ridicules those systems in which the egotistical interest of the individual or group is passed off as an important interest of the whole society.

Karvaš, who worked for many years as a theater critic and theorist, comes out in his plays mainly as a socialist thinker. His every play is an intellectual construction. His plays have attractive themes, clear conflicts, and a precise construction. Karvaš' dialogue is a witty, rational, often ironical, disputation. Karvaš' plays are written to appeal to the intellect of the theatergoer. He reached a maximum of emotional effects in his drama *Polnočná omša*, which was performed in many Czech and foreign theaters.

Karvaš is also a successful author of satirical stories and novels.—F. C.

Kateb, Yacine (1929–). Algerian-born French playwright. A strong poetic realism characterizes Kateb's play *Le Cadavre encerclé* ("The Encircled Corpse"). It was performed in Brussels in 1958 under the direction of Jean-Marie Serreau. During the Algerian War there were a few almost clandestine performances in Paris in 1959 at the Théâtre Lutèce. The background of the play is the revolt against colonial oppression, but the power of the play is in the explosive quality of its language, in the spirit of SUR-REALISM. In the liberation of language the playwright seeks to express national liberation. The play is about a colonized man dying and being reborn in the cycle formed by his desperate search for freedom and for a reason to live. He was killed and he tells the story of the massacred Algerians who lie in the streets with him.—W. F.

Kaufman, George S[imon] (1889–1961). American playwright. A native of Pittsburgh, Kaufman found his way to the theater by an indirect route. After two years of law school, he tried the world of business but found that he was more successful as a stenographer than as a salesman. He began submitting items for F. P. Adams' humor column in the New York *Evening Mail* and soon acquired a following. After a brief try at running a column of his own, Kaufman moved on to the New York *Times*, first as a theater reporter, later as drama editor, a job he retained for many years after he became a success-ful playwright. In 1918 his first play (*Someone in the House*, in collaboration with Larry Evans and Walter Percival) was produced, and until his death he remained one of the most influential figures in the American theater, not only as a writer but also as a director and "play doctor."

Kaufman's collaborators were varied, and with each he developed a different style. With Marc CON-NELLY, he wrote a series of satires often leavened with fantasy. *Dulcy* (1921) mocks a pompous, platitudinous woman originally created for F. P. Adams' column. In *Beggar on Horseback* (1924) a sensitive composer imagines, in vivid, expressionist style, what his life will be like if he marries a businessman's daughter. (See EXPRESSIONISM.) *Merton of the Movies* (1922) set the pattern for satires on Hollywood. A very different collaborator was the novelist Edna Ferber, with whom Kaufman wrote more realistic, though no less theatrical, plays. *The Royal Family* (1927) examines the flamboyant life of a family of actors; *Dinner at Eight* (1932) probes into the lives of a varied group of people invited to a party given by a provincial social climber; and *Stage Door* (1936) presents the tragicomic experiences of a group of young actresses living in a shabby boardinghouse. With Morrie Ryskind, Kaufman wrote the book for *Of Thee I Sing* (1932), a musical about the grotesqueries of American politics. He also collaborated with Ring Lardner, Alexander Woollcott, Katharine Dayton, Nunnally Johnson, Lueen MacGrath, Howard Teichmann, and Abe Burrows. Only one play, *The Butter and Egg Man* (1925), a light comedy about a naïve young man in the city, bears Kaufman's name as sole author.

By far Kaufman's most important collaborator was Moss Hart, who first worked with him on *Once in a Lifetime* (1930), another Hollywood satire. Their most distinguished works, *You Can't Take It With You* (1936) and *The Man Who Came to Dinner* (1939), reveal Kaufman and Hart as the best satirists in American drama. (See MOSS HART.)

There is no standard edition of Kaufman's work. Critical comments appear in the major studies of modern American drama.—M. L.

Kenya. See AFRICA: *Kenya*.

Killigrew, Thomas (1612–1683). English dramatist and theater manager. Killigrew, born in London, the fourth son of Sir Robert Killigrew, became a page to Charles I. His importance for the English theater, though not so great as that of William DAVENANT, was of the same nature. Like Davenant, he wrote plays before the civil war that anticipate the themes of Restoration drama. He became a favorite of Charles II, who made him groom of the bedchamber and gave him the patent for the King's Company, one of the two theatrical troupes licensed by the king in 1660. Killigrew took for his actors a group of older men, some of whom had acted before the closing of the theaters. He was a less successful manager than Davenant, however, and the company had such financial difficulties that in 1682 it was obliged to merge with the other company.

The Prisoners (1635) and *Claracilla* (1636) are heroic and intensely romantic tragicomedies, while his comedy *The Parson's Wedding* (1641) is witty and bawdy. Unlike Davenant, Killigrew did not continue to write in the Restoration period.

GEORGE S. KAUFMAN (WIDE WORLD PHOTOS)

The only available edition of Killigrew's drama is a reprint (1966) of an early edition: *Comedies and Tragedies. Written by Thomas Killigrew*. The standard biography is Alfred Harbage's *Thomas Killigrew, Cavalier Dramatist 1612–83* (1935).
—E. W.

King John (c. 1596–1597). A chronicle play by William SHAKESPEARE. *King John* is based upon an earlier drama, the anonymous *Troublesome Reign of John, King of England*, which Shakespeare considerably revised and condensed, probably around 1596 or 1597.

The story deals with the latter part of John's reign. Despite the dubious legitimacy of his claim to the throne, John, aided by his mother, Eleanor of Aquitaine, is determined to maintain royal power. His claim is disputed by King Philip of France, who supports the claim of John's young nephew, Prince Arthur. Enlisting on his side the spirited bastard Philip Faulconbridge, John invades France and captures Arthur, dispatching him to England to be killed. John's treatment of Arthur convinces the English lords of his tyranny, and they join forces with the French. John's troops, led by the courageous Faulconbridge, succeed in staving off the French attack. The English nobles desert the French forces, but John's victory is a hollow one. Poisoned by a monk, he dies in an agony of fear and contrition.

The key figure in *King John* is not John but Faulconbridge, who represents the spirit of the English nation. Without illusions and self-critical, the bastard is nonetheless committed to the unity and well-being of the nation. His loyalty to John, an altogether unworthy king, is directed to John's symbolic, not personal, value. As such, he gives expression to the governing theme of the play—the preservation of the commonwealth.

A recommended edition of *King John* is the New

MRS. BARRY AS CONSTANCE IN SHAKESPEARE'S
King John

Arden Edition (1954), edited by E. A. J. Honigman.
—E. Q.

King Lear (c. 1605). A tragedy by William SHAKESPEARE. The earliest recorded production of *King Lear* is that of a court performance on December 26, 1606. *The Tragedy of King Lear* was first printed in 1608 in a quarto edition known as the "Pied Bull" Quarto. The Second Quarto, although imprinted 1608 on the title page, was published in 1619. Both the Second Quarto and the 1623 First Folio text are based on the First Quarto. The First Quarto, however, is corrupt in many respects, and the relationship between it and the Folio text—which most scholars regard the superior version—is still a matter of vigorous bibliographical debate.

The Lear story first appeared in Geoffrey of Monmouth's *Historia Regum Britanniae* (c. 1137). Shakespeare developed his version of the story primarily from accounts in Raphael Holinshed's *Chronicles of England, Scotland, and Ireland* (2nd ed., 1587), Edmund Spenser's *The Faerie Queen* (1590, II, x), John Higgins' 1574 edition of *A Mirror for Magistrates*, and from the anonymous play *The True Chronicle History of King Leir and His Three Daughters . . .* (written c. 1590; prod. c. 1590–1594; pub. 1605). The subplot of Gloucester and his sons derives from Sir Philip Sidney's *Arcadia* (pub. 1590). The tragic tone of Shakespeare's play comes more from this source than from the Lear legend.

The main plot recounts what happens to the aged King Lear as he implements his decision to divide his kingdom among his three daughters. He egoistically declares that he will distribute his territory according to the degree that each daughter describes her love for him. Goneril and Regan, the two oldest—respectively married to the dukes of Albany and Cornwall—speak with overwhelming flattery, whereas the youngest and favorite, Cordelia, replies simply that she loves him as befits her filial obligation. Enraged, Lear disinherits her and banishes her from his presence. The king of France, willing to marry the dowerless Cordelia, leaves for home with her. In the ensuing scenes Goneril and Regan reveal their baseness when they maltreat the old man, finally turning him out on a stormy night when all three meet at Gloucester's castle. On the heath, Lear goes mad. Warned by Gloucester of a plot on the king's life, the earl of Kent—who has returned to Lear's service in disguise after having been banished for interceding for Cordelia—takes the king to Dover, where Cordelia and a French army have landed to right the wrongs done to Lear. The king is restored to sanity. He and Cordelia are taken captive by the opposing British army. As a result of a secret execution order, issued by Edmund and countermanded too late, Cordelia is hanged. Lear dies with her body in his arms.

In the subplot, Edmund, the bastard son of the earl of Gloucester, conspires against his brother, Edgar, causing the latter to flee his home. For protection Edgar assumes the disguise of a mad beggar. Edmund, diabolically opportunistic, betrays his father's loyalty to Lear to the duke of Cornwall (now Lear's enemy) and is taken into the duke's service. When Cornwall is killed by a servant after the cruel blinding of Gloucester, Edmund becomes Regan's lover. He also engages in an illicit romance with

Goneril. Meanwhile, Edgar, in his wanderings, has come upon his father. After a reconciliation with his son, Gloucester dies peacefully. Edmund's treachery is uncovered, and Goneril's adultery revealed. Goneril, jealous of her sister's involvement with Edmund, poisons Regan and then stabs herself. Edmund is killed in a chivalric duel with the disguised Edgar. Upon learning his opponent's identity, Edmund dies, realizing "The wheel is come full circle."

Although the debased conduct that pervades the play may in plot summary imply a work resembling Grand Guignol melodrama, *King Lear* is the most profound of Shakespeare's plays. The unnatural behavior of parent to child, child to parent, brother to brother, and man to man—which culminates in the vicious onstage blinding of Gloucester—is part of a carefully conceived plan by which Shakespeare probes the very essence of man. To do this, he first chooses a story with a pagan British setting—one outside the pale of Christian tradition. To it he joins a subplot in which the deeds of the characters mirror those in the main plot, thus placing in a universal context, and giving more verisimilitude to, the conduct patterns he depicts.

The play revolves around two subjects: filial ingratitude and, secondarily, the political instability unleashed when a monarch dismembers his kingdom. The topics are united through their concern with order in the family and order in the state. To these is added order in the individual, as emotion—particularly anger—initially rules Lear. The principal characters fall into two basic groups: Lear, Cordelia, Edgar, and Gloucester represent the good; Goneril, Regan, Edmund, and Cornwall, the evil. Such a clear-cut division has led some critics to see the play as a sublime morality play. These characters, however, are far from simple abstractions; each is portrayed as a complicated human being. The structure of the play aids the morality interpretation, for although the climax occurs in Act I with a long falling action for the rest of the play, Acts I and II present a series of unnatural deeds, which culminate in the world of storm in Act III. Both plot lines are organically intertwined in this act. The final two acts show the defeat of the forces of evil, with love and harmony on the ascendant.

Growth is an important pattern in the play. From nothing, a trifling whim of an egotistical old man, grow all sorts of frightful complications. A comparable growth of evil—again rooted in human personality—is developed in the subplot. Against this growth the two patriarchal figures go through a reducing process. The physical and material stripping of Lear and Gloucester is linked to the flaws within them: they lack insight into themselves and the world around them. For Lear, this stripping culminates in his seminakedness and madness in the heath scene. For Gloucester, it is the loss of his eyes. But out of their physical and mental darkness comes spiritual light. And ultimately the evil characters are defeated, not by supernatural intervention, but by the excesses that they themselves commit, excesses that, as the imagery underscores, place them on a level lower than the bestial.

King Lear portrays the chaos that results from unnatural conduct in the individual, the family, and the state and that brings death to the innocent. Its overtones are cosmic; its philosophical ideas complex. The thematic content is so firmly enmeshed in an interlocking pattern of dramatic structure, characterization, choric commentary (in the role of the Fool), symbolism, and imagery that *King Lear* remains one of the most difficult plays to produce in the entire Shakespearean canon.

An outstanding edition of *King Lear* is the New Arden Edition (reprinted 1957), edited by Kenneth Muir.—W. G.

Kingsley, Sidney (1906–   ). American playwright. A native of New York City, Kingsley has drawn much of his inspiration from the life of the metropolis. As a student at Cornell University, his major interest was drama, and he began writing plays and winning prizes for them while he was an undergraduate. Soon after graduation, he approached producers with a play about doctors and hospital life called *Crisis*. Accepted by the new Group Theatre and retitled *Men in White* (1933), it became the first major production of the Group and established that company's reputation for tough, realistic drama. Except for service in the U.S. Army during World War II, Kingsley's life has been entirely bound up with the theater, as a writer, director, and producer.

Sidney Kingsley has provided the American theater with its most distinguished examples of naturalism. *Dead End* (1935), set on and around an East River pier and dealing with the corrupting effects of poverty and slum life, has never been surpassed in its vivid evocation of a specific locale meticulously reconstructed on the stage. Norman Bel Geddes' magnificent settings were a major factor in the play's success, but even more precedent-shattering were the slum boys, the Dead End Kids, with their free-flowing profanity and their amorality. *Men in White*, with its hospital setting, and *Detective Story* (1949), with its vividly re-created police station, make fewer demands on designer and actors, but, like *Dead End*, these plays are more successful in their creation of atmosphere than in their somewhat melodramatic plots. Even with Kingsley's adaptation of Arthur Koestler's novel *Darkness at Noon* (1951), a play with far more subtle characterization than Kingsley developed in his other plays, his finest achievement was the creation of the prison atmosphere and the painfulness of a brutal interrogation.

In *Lunatics and Lovers* (1954) and *Night Life* (1962), both dealing with the Manhattan world of night clubs, Times Square denizens, and petty gangsterism, Kingsley was unable to fuse the naturalistic details with a dynamic story, and both plays were failures. *The Patriots* (1942), about the struggle to establish a democracy in postrevolutionary America, was greeted enthusiastically when it appeared in the dark days of the Second World War, but now it appears obvious in its patriotic appeals and mechanical in its structure.

There is no standard edition of Kingsley's work. Critical comments appear in the major studies of modern American drama.—M. L.

Kipphardt, Heinar (1922–   ). German playwright, essayist, and doctor. Though not well known in America, Kipphardt is considered by many critics to be among the best of Germany's contemporary dramatists. He began his career while studying medicine in East Berlin. From 1950 to 1959 he worked at the Charité Hospital and at the same time became the chief dramaturgist at the Deutsches Theater. It was during this period that his first plays were produced: *Shakespeare dringend gesucht* ("Shakespeare Urgently Sought," 1952), a satire, and *Der Aufstieg des Alois Piontek* ("The Rise of Alois Piontek," 1956), a farce. Due to various pressures, Kipphardt decided to move to West Germany in 1959, where *Die Stühle des Herrn Smil* ("The Chairs of Mr. Smil," 1961), a parody of East German bureaucracy, was performed in Wuppertal. Shortly after this, he followed with his three most important plays, which have given him the reputation of being Germany's leading documentary dramatist: *Der Hund des Generals* ("The General's Dog," 1962), *In der Sache J. Robert Oppenheimer* (*In the Matter of J. Robert Oppenheimer*, 1964), and *Joel Brand: Geschichte eines Geschäfts* ("Joel Brand: The History of a Deal," 1965).

Schooled in the Brechtian tradition, Kipphardt works with sparse language and hypotactic structures to reconsider the evidence of disputed political cases. In *Der Hund des Generals,* he places a German officer on trial for sending an entire regiment of soldiers to their deaths because one of them had accidentally killed his pet dog. Though graphically portrayed, the general's inhumanity is not the main point of the drama. Kipphardt is more concerned with the fact that this general (among others) is today a free, respected, rich man in West Germany. The past, according to Kipphardt, has been buried all too quickly, and guilt is only felt by those who are willing to accept the truth. In *In der Sache J. Robert Oppenheimer,* the question of German guilt gives way to universal guilt and responsibility. Here Kipphardt uses the recordings of the Atomic Energy Commission's Investigation Committee to show that Oppenheimer unwittingly sacrificed the good of humanity to the interests of an irresponsible state. Oppenheimer eventually repents his past activities and refuses to be further employed as a tool of the American government. Kipphardt's antipathy for devious and corrupt political institutions is also demonstrated in *Joel Brand* where the Eichmann proposition to exchange 1,000,000 Jews for 10,000 trucks is undermined by the intrigues of petty governmental bureaucrats. In laying bare the hypocritical position of the Americans and English in this documentary drama, Kipphardt does not apologize for the Germans. He bluntly questions the basis of political action and examines the position of minority groups caught in a power struggle between larger nations. In doing so, Kipphardt, who moved from East to West, has slowly come to challenge the claims of the "democratic" West, and in his latest comedy, *Die Nacht, in der Chef geschlachtet wurde* ("The Night the Boss Was Slaughtered," 1967), he sees the Western technologically advanced society in terms of a nightmare.—J. D. Z.

Kishon, Ephraim (1924–). Hungarian-born Israeli humorist, journalist, and playwright. Kishon was born in Budapest in 1924 and studied history of art at the Art Academy and Budapest University. After escaping from World War II German and Russian camps, he immigrated in 1949 to Israel, where he soon replaced his native Hungarian with Hebrew.

Since 1952 Kishon has run a daily satirical column in the Israeli newspaper in *Ma'ariv.* He has published to date about fifteen books—satires, novels, and plays. He won critical acclaim with his latest books —*Look Back, Mrs. Lot; Noah's Ark, Tourist Class;* and *The Seasick Whale*—and his film *Sallah* (1964), which he both wrote and directed.

He has written about eight comedies that have been produced by Israel's professional theaters (often under his direction) as well as numerous farcical one-acters, light sketches, and radio plays. His plays have been acclaimed in many theaters outside of Israel and some of them have been broadcast and televised in foreign countries.

Kishon's work first appeared on the stage in 1951 when his comedy *Shmo Holech L'fanav* ("His Friend at Court"), a satirical play about bureaucracy and favor, was produced by the Habimah. It was followed in 1956 with an allegorical satire on racial discrimination, *Sachor Al Gabei Lavan* ("Black on White"), also produced by the Habimah. A light comedy-farce about marriage and parenthood, *Haketubah* ("The Marriage License," 1958) was one of the longest-running productions and has since been revived a number of times. His latest play, *Totsi Et Hashteker, Hamayim Rotchim* ("Pull Out the Plug, the Water Is Boiling," 1965), is a satire on modern art and ignorance.

The most important element in Kishon's comedies is his highly inventive situations, often bordering on the incredible. His characters, however, while representing a variety of local types that are familiar to the Israeli audience, usually lack any delineation. All but one of his plays are written in a realistic style, depicting everyday life in pedestrian language and perked up with an abundance of "Kishonian" wisecracks. —Z. R.

Kivi, Aleksis. See FINLAND.

Kiyotsugo, Kwanami. See SOTOBA KOMACHI.

Klabund. See GERMANY: *twentieth century.*

Kleist, [Bernd Wilhelm] Heinrich von (1777– 1811). German playwright, officer, and journalist. Like numerous other problematic writers of his time, Kleist never received the recognition he desired. It is only in the twentieth century that he has been accorded a rank among the greats of German drama, and even now some critics still tend to agree with Goethe, who was suspicious of the "sick" element in his works. On the surface, a biographical account of Kleist's career would seem to indicate that he was a "sick" poet. After being educated in a military academy (many of his ancestors were generals), Kleist served in the Prussian army until he could no longer tolerate the discipline and sterility. He then enrolled at the university in Frankfurt an der Oder but had to leave in 1800 because he had taxed his nerves. The following year he underwent his "Kant crisis." An intensive study of either Kant or Fichte unsettled his mind when he realized the impossibility of determining absolutes. About this time, Kleist became engaged to Wilhelmine von Zenge, who broke the tie in 1802 when Kleist insisted that she live with him as his common-law wife in the Swiss woods. Aside from Wilhelmine, he formed a close and somewhat strange attachment to his half sister Ulrike, with whom he traveled a great deal. From 1803 until his death in 1811, Kleist concentrated mainly on his writing

HEINRICH VON KLEIST (GERMAN INFORMATION
CENTER)

the ten years that Kleist wrote dramas, he was concerned with this problem of self-knowledge and self-mastery. The highly stylized and inflammatory verse of his plays reflects Kleist's own life struggle. Primarily influenced by Shakespeare, Kleist also borrowed elements from Greek tragedy and historical documents to give epic breadth to his dramas. In *Die Familie Schroffenstein* (*The Feud of the Schroffensteins,* 1803), Kleist takes the Romeo and Juliet motif, adds a Gothic setting, and plays upon mistaken identities to increase the pathos of two families unwittingly bent on destroying their own children. In the final analysis, the play is very similar to one of Shakespeare's first plays, *Titus Andronicus*—the quality of true passions is sacrificed for horror effects. This is also the case in *Die Hermansschlacht* (*The Battle of Hermann,* written 1809, pub. 1811), in which Kleist meant to draw a parallel between the occupied Germany in Roman times and the occupied Germany of his own time in order to foster German patriotism. In this historical drama, the German princes unite under Arminius, prince of the Cherusci, and drive out the Romans, using all possible means at their disposal. In another play, PENTHESILEA, a magnificent psychological drama that stresses cruelty and eroticism, Kleist displayed how a misunderstanding of an outer situation can distort one's already disturbed inner feelings. Hence, Penthesilea, queen of the Amazons, dismembers Achilles and drinks his blood because she has mistaken his gesture of love for one of treachery.

In almost all of Kleist's plays, the world is about to fall apart, and only a noble and supreme effort on the part of the protagonists can prevent tragedy. In *Das Kätchen von Heilbronn oder die Feuerprobe* (*Cathy from Heilbronn, or The Trial by Fire,* written 1808, perf. 1810), the knight Wetter vom Strahl at first disdains the love of Kätchen because he cannot see a dream in the right light. Only after he almost causes Kätchen's death does he recognize that his former fiancée is a witch and consent to marry Kätchen instead. It is also at this point that the averted tragedy blossoms into a romantic fairy tale, for Kätchen is the long-lost princess of Swabia. Tragedy is also avoided in Kleist's other romantic drama, PRINZ FRIEDRICH VON HOMBURG, when the prince realizes that the elector is correct in sentencing him to death for disobeying orders in a battle. It is due to this realization that the elector pardons him and grants him the Princess Natalia's hand in marriage.

Kleist did not deal with the theme of misunderstanding and deception only in a romantic and tragic fashion, but also wrote two comedies that depend on deceiving and deceit for their humor. In his brilliant adaptation of Molière's *Amphitryon* (1807), Kleist portrays an Alkmene pure in heart even though Jupiter makes love to her in the guise of her husband, Amphitryon. Because of her great love for her husband, she is never really blinded by her passions as are Jupiter and Amphitryon. In THE BROKEN JUG, the eccentric judge Adam eventually convicts himself in a comic effort to dupe his neighbors and the district inspector into believing that he did not attempt to seduce a village maiden. In all of Kleist's plays, comic and tragic, one has the impression of a serious artist at work, who is determined to comprehend the secrets of the universe. In many respects Kleist is like

(aside from his dramas he wrote some excellent novellas) while holding various jobs, such as a civil servant and a journalist. In 1808 he founded a literary monthly, called *Phöbus* with Adam Müller, and in 1810 he began a political magazine, *Berliner Abendblätter.* After this periodical was censored and forced to close, Kleist was desperate for some means of financial support and security. During November 1811, he formed a suicide pact with a friend, Henriette Vogel, who was dying from an incurable cancer. On November 21, he shot her on the shore of the Wannsee in Berlin and then took his own life.

This brief description of Kleist's life might seem to bear out Goethe's opinion of him. Yet it would be an injustice to Kleist to label the grotesque and surrealistic elements in his works as projections of a sick mind. Kleist was an intense, sensitive individual with a keen mind. He was not afraid to probe the inner recesses of the human psyche in an attempt to solve ontological problems of cognition and creativity. In fact, it was probably because Kleist had the courage to move ahead of his times in such endeavors that he was compelled to submit to feelings of alienation and despair.

Kleist himself was aware of the dangers inherent in his philosophical experiments and strove to overcome his more pessimistic moods. In his important essay "Über das Marionettentheater" ("On the Marionette Theater," 1810), he emphasized that only self-awareness leads to knowledge of the outside world. Without a full understanding of his inner drives and needs, man will never comprehend the macrocosmos. As in a puppet show, an individual is governed first by his own inner principles, and like the puppet, the individual must master his own mechanism before he can function in the world. In the hero of his unfinished drama *Robert Guiskard* (written 1808). In this fragment the Norman duke Guiscard is on the verge of conquering Byzantium when the plague infects him and his army. As panic gradually breaks out in his camp, Guiscard majestically tries to maintain order. Kleist, too, saw infection and corrosion all around him, but he failed to maintain control over himself and the situation in which he was lodged.

Critical works in English dealing with Kleist as a dramatist include John C. Blankenagel, *The Dramas of Heinrich von Kleist* (1931), which contains close analyses of the plays; E. L. Stahl, *Heinrich von Kleist's Dramas* (1948); and John Geary, *Heinrich von Kleist: A Study in Tragedy and Anxiety* (1968). The reader might also wish to consult Walter Silz, *Heinrich von Kleist* (1961), a good compendium of essays that contribute to an understanding of Kleist's work.—J. D. Z.

Klicpera, Václav Kliment (1792–1859). Czech novelist and playwright. After working as an apprentice to a dressmaker and then to a butcher, Klicpera became a student in Prague at the Academic Lyceum in 1808. From 1813 to 1819 he studied philosophy at the Charles University and then taught that subject in Hradec Králové until 1846. In that year he moved back to Prague and became a professor and then the headmaster at the Academic Lyceum, where he stayed until 1853.

Klicpera began writing plays at the end of the Napoleonic wars, when the Czech countries were under Austrian subjugation. Oppressed by the reactionary feudal lords, the frightened Czech petite bourgeoisie collaborated with the Austrians, while the Czech intelligentsia retreated from public life. As a playwright, Klicpera championed the struggle of the national liberation movement by contributing plays of quality.

Klicpera's early dramas reveal the influence of chivalrous plays. In one of his first plays, *Blaník* (1816), he combined the form of chivalrous plays with the subject matter of contemporary national events. His deviation from this form was marked by his farce *Hadrián z Římsu* ("Hadrián of Rímsy," pub. 1822), in which he parodied chivalrous plays. The hero of this play is a rather sickly, stupid knight, the antithesis of the ideal feudal hero. This play reflects Klicpera's comic, satiric talent.

At the same time, Klicpera concentrated mainly on writing comedies about contemporary life, which, up to his time, had had rather little success. Because he was educated by an enlightened generation and not limited by narrow political interests nor bound by the bourgeois tactics that later constricted the Romantics, Klicpera was able to portray in his comedies the absurd actions of the dull, small-town philistines. In the comedies *Divotvorný klobouk* ("A Magic Hat," pub. 1820), *Rohovín Čtverrohý* (pub. 1825), *Lhář a jeho rod* ("The Liar and his Clan," pub. 1820), *Veselohra na mostě* ("Comedy on a Bridge," pub. 1828), *Každý něco pro vlast* ("Everyone's Duty for the Country," pub. 1829), and *Ptáčník* ("Bird-keeper," pub. 1862), Klicpera satirized these provincials who held the power in the towns of that time and who were governed by excessive passions rather than reason. In opposition to these reactionaries Klicpera favored the students and artists of the

younger generation. His ideal was a harmonious combination of keen intellect and noble qualities and interests.

Klicpera's work is the best expression of Czech drama during the transitional period between classicism and Romanticism. His interest centered around the personalities of "people full of passion," characters who were drawn from life but, according to the principles of classical aesthetics, were slightly ennobled. He constructed complicated plots in accordance with the model of Roman comedy. Klicpera's classical education is also revealed in his artful dialogue in which the playful stylization of language is permeated with foreign words and citations and literary allusions. Through his dramatic talent, Klicpera follows two traditions: the Italian *commedia dell'arte* and the popular Czech Baroque drama.

For reasons of national prestige, the Czech intelligentsia asked Klicpera to write poetic drama. In response Klicpera wrote *Soběslav, kníže selské* ("Soběslav, the Peasant Prince," pub. 1826), *Eliška Přemyslovna* (pub. 1862), *Izraelitka* ("The Jewish Woman," pub. 1847), and many others. Although these poetic dramas were not successful, they prepared the ground for the Romantic dramatists of the next generation. Strong Romantic tendencies are expressed in Klicpera's dramatic fairy tales, such as *Jan za chrta dán* ("John Given for a Greyhound," pub. 1829).

As a short-story writer, novelist, playwright, and amateur actor and director, Klicpera took an active part in stirring up the awakening spirit of Czech nationalism. For the Czech intelligentsia of the first half of the nineteenth century, Klicpera stood for the attempts made to reach a higher level of Czech culture. —F. Č.

Knights (**Hippēs**, 424 B.C.). A comedy by ARISTOPHANES. Demos, a personification of the Athenian public, is under the spell of his Paphlagonian slave, a personification of the powerful politician Cleon, Aristophanes' enemy. Two other slaves of Demos, Nicias and Demosthenes (in real life, two Athenian generals), decide to oust the Paphlagonian by using his own tactics against him. With assistance from the Chorus of Cleon-hating knights, they find an extravagant vagabond from the gutter, a sausage seller, who is even cruder than the Paphlagonian. By adroit manipulation of the Paphlagonian's own techniques of flattery and abuse, the two slaves manage to turn Demos against his former favorite and to assure him of a better life in the future, in accordance with oracles promising a new golden age and a new Athens.

Knights is almost entirely devoted to an exhaustive and ingeniously orchestrated contest of mudslinging. Buried beneath the pile of abuse, however, is a serious portrait of the psychology of the Athenian public —eternally gullible, pathetically optimistic in adversity, and (according to Aristophanes, at least) in need of moral and spiritual regeneration.

Translations of the play are listed under Aristophanes.—K. C.

Kokoschka, Oskar. See AUSTRIA; EXPRESSIONISM.

Koralle, Die. See THE GAS TRILOGY.

Korea. The beginnings of Korean theater and drama can be found in the rituals and ceremonies, the dances and songs of the prehistoric tribal ancestors offering their sacrifices to the nature gods they worshipped. Korean drama evolved from the divine image and human fantasy, from physical movement and creative spirit, which, indeed, seem to be the sources of drama in other parts of the world as well. The path may have varied, but the result is much the same.

In view of this, one must take a glance at Korean traditions, according to which the history of dance and music in Korea commences with the reign of the first legendary king, Dan-Gun, in 2333 B.C. Dan-Gun, the legend goes, established the first civilization on the peninsula. He worshipped Hanŭnim, lord of heaven, and celebrated the gods of the earth with dancing and music. But it was not exclusively a royal privilege to regale the gods with singing and dancing. The people, too, celebrated their religious festivals with wine, song, dance, and music.

Although Koreans have practiced primitive forms of dramatic art since the earliest days, detailed accounts of theatrical presentations in the histories are to be found only from the time of the Three Kingdoms—Silla (57 B.C.–A.D. 935), Goguryŏ 37 B.C.–A.D. 668), Bĕgzĕ (18 B.C.–A.D. 660)—onwards. The records of the kingdom of Silla, in particular, furnish most of the information, for the masque plays were highly developed there.

The masque plays of Silla may be divided into three groups—the *Gŏm-Mu* ("Sword Dance"), the *Hyang-Ag O-gi* ("Five Styles"), and the *Czŏyong* dance. In addition to the masque plays, there was the *Gi-Ag* masque dance drama with religious significance to Buddhist believers. The latter was transformed by secular influences after the Goryŏ period into the *Bongsan-Talchum* ("Bongsan Masque Dance") and *Yangjoo-Sandĕ-Nori* ("Yangjoo Sandĕ Play"). The transformation of the Buddhist religious dance into the secular masque play should remind us that in medieval Europe the religious miracle play tended to become transformed into secular romantic drama of adventure, just as the morality play gradually lost its didactic purpose and became a form intended for sheer entertainment.

The *Narye,* another masque play from the early period of the Goryŏ dynasty (935–1392), was traditionally performed on the last night of the year. It served a dual purpose: to exorcise all the evil spirits of the passing year, for which purpose the performers wore horrifying masks, and to welcome in the new year. This masque play originated in China, where it was supposedly performed during the period of the Chou dynasty (1122–249 B.C.). It is not known, however, when it reached Korea.

The Narye developed into another masque play, called the *Sandĕ,* about the middle period of the Goryŏ dynasty. About the time of the Yi dynasty (1392–1910), the Sande underwent another transformation, developing into the characteristic Korean masque play known as the *Sandĕ-Dogam,* which was a combination of all masque plays thus far known. This play began with a religious service, then went on to criticize the corrupt priests and the *yangban* ("nobility"), and at the end showed the mortality of man and made supplication for the dead. The religious service was a kind of prologue intended to ensure the safety of the participants in the performance. The following part, criticism of the corruption among

MASK OF A SORCERESS (COURTESY DR. JOHN KARDOSS)

priests, was not so much an attack on Buddhism itself as it was an assault upon those corrupt priests who disobeyed the commandments and caused a great deal of trouble for the royalty and for the whole nation. For this reason, the play was popular with both pro-Buddhists and anti-Buddhists. When considering criticism of the nobility, it ought to be remembered that the audiences of the masque plays were mostly common people who enjoyed finding fault with the privileged classes, which grabbed all the positions of wealth and rank even though they may have lacked character or intelligence. Because of this last feature, the plays achieved great popularity with the majority of the people.

The masque plays were presented on temporary raised stages or in the open fields or on hillsides. There were no sets or curtain. The scenes were separated by brief intermissions. On the left side of the stage was a box of clothes where the masks and costumes were changed.

The chief characteristic of the players was their masks. Altogether, twenty-eight masks were used in the play, and also a puppet. The masks owed their being without question to the religious ceremonies from which the plays were derived. A six-piece band, consisting of harps, flutes, and drums, was usually employed; the music generally rendered for accompaniment was the dance tunes known as *Semaczitaryŏng.* The performances, illuminated by the flickering light of bonfires, usually lasted throughout the night.

Apart from the Sande play, there were two other

kinds of masque plays—*O-Gwangdĕ* ("Five Buffoonery Plays") and its offshoot, *Yayu* ("Outdoor Play").

Another form of ancient dramatic expression in Korea is the puppet play, still being performed today. Perhaps the oldest popular manifestation of drama, the puppet play probably originated in India, whence it was transferred to China. In China it was modified and from there it reached Korea and, later, Japan. Despite changes it went through in the new countries, and however independently it flourished later, there remained an underlying uniformity in aim, style, and execution.

In Korea, there are two types of puppet play, the *Ggogdu-Gagsi,* or *Bag Czŏm-Zi,* and the *Mansŏg-Zung.* The puppets, most of them made of wood, are usually one to three feet high, painted and dressed in traditional guise. They are manipulated with strings. In the Ggogdu-Gagsi, there are thirteen puppets in human form and three in animal form. The play is interlaced with Buddhist sentiments and the main plot is humorous. Like the masque play, it criticizes the nobility, government officials, and corrupt priests and has a domestic drama woven into the story.

The birthday of Buddha on the eighth day of the fourth month by the lunar calendar served as an occasion for the second type of puppet play, the Mansŏg-Zung. As in the Ggogdu-Gagsi, the puppeteers pulled the strings from a hidden position to the accompaniment of music, but unlike the Ggogdu-Gagsi, this was a silent play. The Mansŏg-Zung was

A *Bag Czŏm-Zi* PUPPET (COURTESY DR. JOHN KARDOSS)

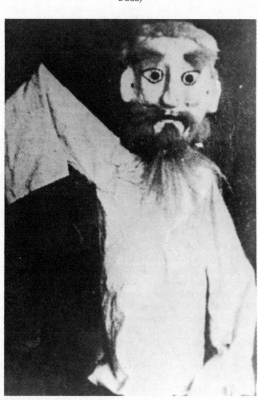

performed by five puppets—a human-like puppet called the Mansŏg-Zung, a deer, a horned deer, a carp, and a dragon.

In the early period of the Yi dynasty, novels of a highly evolved form were introduced into Korea from China. As the time passed and their popularity grew, they were bound to exercise a great deal of influence upon Korean narrative literature, and many of them were dramatized. The most outstanding work from what is called "the golden age of the classical novel" came sometime during the reigns of the twenty-first king of the Yi dynasty, Yŏng-jo (1725–1776), and the twenty-second ruler, Jong-jo (1777–1800). This was *The Story of Chun-hyang (Chun-hyang-jun)*. Written in Korean, instead of the traditional Chinese, by an anonymous author, it has been the most popular of all similar works up to our own time. It lent itself well to treatment by Korean librettists and composers for stage adaptations.

The political history of nineteenth-century Korea is, in effect, the reaction of Koreans to pressures from modern nations. In the history of the Korean theater and drama a new chapter commenced with the Gugŭg, or "Old Play," also known as "Classical Play."

The Korean musical drama in its classical form was born in the nineteenth century through the genius of Sin Che-Ho (1812–1884). It was Sin who gave musicodramatic expression to such perennial Korean stories as *Chun-hyang, Sim-chŏng,* and *Jŏgbyŏg.* The innovations Sin introduced were sweeping. All those who were engaged in creative activity in the sphere of musical drama were his disciples. The *Gwangdĕ* group of singers has had these dramatic songs on their programs since the composer wrote them. In their dramatic interpretation they use gestures, movements, facial expressions, but they have no theater and no scenery on their temporary stages.

A milestone in the history of the Korean drama and theater was reached with the opening of the first national theater, the Wŏngag-Sa, on July 26, 1908, in Seoul. This important cultural institution started under the direction of novelist-playwright Yi In-Jig (1861–1916). Modern drama came four months after the opening, when Yi dramatized his own novel, *The Silver World (Un Segĕ),* and presented it on November 15, 1908. The author named the stage version of his novel *The New Drama of the Silver World,* and it was the first "new [modern] drama" presented in Korea.

Yi In-Jig spent ten years, from 1884 to 1894, as a political exile in Japan, where he saw the "political dramas" of Sudo Sadanori (1866–1909) and Kawakami Otojiro (1864–1911) currently popular in the Japanese Shimpa theater. Yi must also have read the popular romances, at that time being published serially in newspapers of large circulation such as the *Miyako Shimbun.* Yi's political convictions for much-needed reforms in his own country were certainly reinforced by the far-reaching and rapid social and economic changes taking place in Japan, while the literature of Restoration Japan made a lasting impression on the novelist and playwright.

Yi's first play, *The Silver World,* was written not so much to entertain as to instruct. It was a dramatic means of conveying the political ideals of the progressive reform group with which the author was associated. The story deals with a boy, Ok-nam, and his sister, Ok-sun, who leave Korea for five years to study in America. They live in a hotel there and deliver lengthy speeches to each other about the advantages of civilization and the need for sociopolitical reforms at home.

Yi's second play, *The Plum in the Snow,* was presented at the Wŏngag-Sa in 1909. It is an adaptation of Suehiro Tetsujo's novel (1885) of the same name and is constructed in fifteen episodes, a form not uncommon in the Chinese-influenced traditional Korean literature. As with his first work, the didactic element dominated Yi's new play.

A drama group called the Hyŏblyul Sa was touring the country about this time, presenting masque plays, semilegendary tales, and classical music until 1914.

In 1911 Yim Sŏng-Gu (1887–1921) and his actor colleagues organized a drama group called Hyŏgsin-Dan (Reform Society). They presented plays first at the Ŏsŏng-Zwa and later in the Dansŏng-Sa theaters. Their first production was *Heavenly Punishment for the Unfilial,* a straight translation from the Japanese Shimpa play. Some other plays included *The Law of Laws, The Murder of the Sworn Brother,* and *The Pistol-Robber.* This dramatic genre was known as the *Sinpa Yŏn-gŭg,* or "New Style Play." The Hyŏgsin-Dan group disbanded in the spring of 1920.

In 1912 Bag Sŭng-Pil built a new playhouse, the Gwangmu-Dĕ, where a diversified program, including the Old Plays, was presented.

Yun Bĕg-Nam (1888–1954), a playwright who had studied the new drama in Japan, organized the Munsu-Sŏng drama group in March 1912. Their first production was *The Cuckoo,* an adaptation of a Japanese drama, at the Wŏngag-Sa Theater. This was followed by other plays of the Shimpa theater, including *Deep Sorrow Dream* and *My Sin. Deep Sorrow Dream,* one of the most popular plays of the time, was an adaptation of Ozaki Koyo's *The Golden Demon* (1897). The Munsu-Sŏng group experimented also with the production of original plays, including *The Youth* by Cho Il-Chĕ in cooperation with Lee Ha-Mong.

Yuil-Dan (Only Society), a dramatic group founded by Yi Gi-Se which staged plays in the Yŏnhŭng-Sa Theater, joined forces with the Munsu-Sŏng under the name of Yesong-Zwa (Art-Star Seats). They presented *Double Jade Tears,* a Korean play adapted from a Korean novel of anonymous authorship; a dramatization of Tolstoy's *Resurrection;* and other plays, but they soon disbanded.

Many other small, enthusiastic dramatic groups existed for a while during this period: Yi Gi-Se's Munye-Dan (Literary Society); Kim Do-San's Singŭg-Zwa (New Play Seats); and Kim So-Rang's Czwisŏng-Zwa (Gathered Star Seats). None of these dramatic ventures lasted long; the most enduring was the Czwisŏng-Zwa, which disbanded in 1929.

When studying in Tokyo, Korean students organized the Dramatic Art Association and toured all over Korea during their school vacations. Their repertory consisted of *The Death of Kim Yong-Il,* a sentimental three-act melodrama by Cho Myŏng-Hi; *The Last Handshake,* whose story is somewhat similar to Ibsen's *A Doll's House,* by Hong Nan-Pa; and *The Glittering Gate* by Lord Dunsany, translated by Kim Su-San. The leaders of this group were producers Hong Hĕ-Sŏng and Kim Su-San, authors Zo Po-Sŏg, Ma Hĕ-Sŏng, and Yu Czun-Sŏb. In spite of its comparatively short existence, this group exercised considerable influence on the new movement in Korea and compelled the commercial theaters to improve the standards of their productions.

Hyon Chul (1891–1965), a graduate of the Actors' Studio affiliated with the Tokyo Academy of Arts, returned to Korea in 1920 and founded the Academy of Arts, which in three years developed into the Actors' Studio in Korea. This studio presented two trial productions—Ibsen's *A Doll's House* and Chekhov's *The Bear* and *The Proposal.* Hyon Chul, an erudite and versatile man, translated *Hamlet* from Japanese into Korean.

Yun Bĕg-Nam, who failed with the Munsu-Song group earlier in 1922, founded the Minzung-Gugdan (Popular Drama Society), and presented his own plays, *The Eternal Wife* and *Fate.* Also in 1922 the Yesul-Hyŏphoe (Art Association) was organized by another veteran producer, Yi Gi-Se, offering *The Tears of Hope.* Neither of these producers had much more success than before, and after touring the country, both companies disbanded. Apparently a man of faith and courage, Yun Bĕg-Nam founded a new group, the Manpa-Hoe (Ten Thousand Waves Society). Engaging most of the noted actors of the time, Yun presented Victor Hugo's *Louis the Sixteenth* and a dramatization of his novel *Les Misérables,* as well as other plays, but his brave enterprise was again short-lived.

A higher artistic standard was attained by the dramatic organization called Towŏl-Hoe (Earth and Moon Society). It was founded in 1922 by producer Bag Sŭng-Hŭi, critic Kim Gi-Jin, artist Kim Bŏg-Jin, and two journalists, Yi Sŏ-Gu and Kim Ul-Han. In 1923 they presented Bag Sŭng-Hŭi's original play, *Kilsik.* Their repertory included works of Tolstoy, Shaw, Chekhov, and others. The artistic standard of the Towŏl-Hoe productions created a sensation at the time. With the impact of modern Western drama, the Korean theater was gradually outgrowing the New Style Plays and the Towŏl-Hoe's contribution can be considered vital to the new development.

In the spring of 1924 the Towŏl-Hoe group, still under the leadership of Bag Sŭng-Hŭi, was reshuffled and from that time on they tended to compromise with commercialism. They staged popular plays of the New Style, and from 1925 they revived such perennial favorites as *Chun-hyang-jun, Sim-chong-jun, Chang-hwa-hong-nyun-jun,* and Lee Kwang-Soo's *Pitiless.* Owing to their gradually declining reputation, they changed their name in 1932 to Tĕyang (Sun).

In an effort to oust the Japanese Sinpa theater, which became dominant after the days of the Reform Theatrical Society, the Towŏl-Hoe group tried to revolutionize dramatic form and technique without diminishing the play's literary value. In other words the Towŏl-Hoe pioneered the way for the Sin-Gug, or "New Drama," period of the 1930's.

The Heart of One's Native Soil by Hong No-Zag was presented in 1929 by a dramatic group, the Sanyuhwa-Hoe (Mountain Flowers Society). Two more drama groups were formed during the same year, but their existence was ephemeral. The Czwisŏng-Zwa, however, lasted through thirteen epoch-making years, most of the time touring the peninsula.

Hong Ně-Sŏng, an actor who had won his reputation in Tokyo at the Tsukiji Little Theater, returned to Seoul in 1929 and began to organize the Sinhŭng-Gŭgzang (Newly Risen Theater). His first production was a Korean version of a Chinese play in November 1930.

The Koreana Artista Proleta Federation (Federation of Korean Proletarian Art, or KAPF), a Marxist group founded in 1925, extended its activities in 1930 from literature to the performing arts and painting.

That year the dramatic section planned to stage a revolutionary play, *Hammer,* in Fengian. The police and the censor raised obstacles, forcing them to abandon this first play. However, rehearsals of another play, *The General Strike in Fengian,* commenced. Authorities interfered again, whereupon the leaders of the KAPF reorganized the dramatic section as an independent unit. Not long afterwards, in a number of districts, Marxist drama groups grew apace. Japanese authorities, suspecting that the activities of these drama groups promoted less the arts of the theater than the ideas of Marxism, imprisoned the whole group of active KAPF members in July 1930.

KAPF effected a swift reorganization. In Seoul a professional drama group, the Seoul-Yen-Pol-Kikjen (Seoul Blue Shirts), was formed in 1931. The new group planned to stage such plays as *The Miners* by Lou Marten, *The Thief* by Upton Sinclair, and dramas by Japanese comrades of the Proletarian Theatrical Society of Japan (such as Murayama's *All Along the Line,* Susaki's *Wheelbarrow,* and Fujimori's *What Made Her Do That?*). But again, the police and the censor prevented the performance.

In 1931 two new Marxist groups were organized in Seoul—the Megaphone and the New Construction Theatrical Group. The first managed to put on a production immediately, the second prepared a number of plays by Korean authors. The Megaphone group broke away from the Marxist setup and formed an independent organization for progressive elements. They toured the provinces.

At the same time that the Marxists were forming drama groups, the Drama-Cinema Club was founded by actor Hong Hě-Sŏng (1893–1957) and playwright Yu Chi-Jin (1905–   ) in June 1931. They organized the first exhibition of drama and cinema in Korea. The following month they established the Society for Research in Dramatic Art in cooperation with students of foreign literature. In order to promote the art and craft of acting, they trained actors in the Academy of Dramatic Arts. In November they founded the Shilhŏm-Mudě (Experimental Stage).

At about this time schools were presenting dramas, and the two leading Korean newspapers, the *Donga Il-bo* and *Chosun Il-bo,* organized annual literary contests to provide the incentive for new dramatists. *The Country Teacher* by Yi Gwang-Ně, *The Clay Wall* by Han Tě-Dong, and *The Floating People* by Kim Sung-U were staged as a result of these contests.

From May 1932 onward the Experimental Stage presented a number of plays by European playwrights. Naturally, they staged Korean plays as well, mostly those of Yu Chi-Jin, the first of them being *The Earthen Hut,* presented on February 9, 1933. In

a manner reminiscent of Ibsen, the author created a small, self-contained family whose peace and security are suddenly shattered by an outsider, the postmaster who tells the family about a parcel for them at the post office. This sets things into motion until the final tragedy. The story is about a poor Korean peasant family living in their earthen hut, which one of the leading characters, Myŏng-Sŏ, calls a "grave." All their hopes are centered around a son who has been in Japan for seven years. The two-act play ends in the post office, where the family makes the tragic discovery that a package that has arrived for them contains the ashes of their son, killed in Japan for having taken an active part in the Korean freedom movement.

Some other early plays of Yu Chi-Jin are *The Clay House* and *The Scene of a Village Where the Willow Tree Stands.* Both have themes that serve to expose the social injustices of the time. *The Cow* is a rural comedy about this bovine animal who plays a life-or-death role in the lives of the farmers whose values center around it. *The Waiting Wife* is an adaptation from an historical novel.

The Experimental Stage group continued with their cultural mission until March 1938, when pressure from Japanese authorities forced them to abandon their work.

Some years later the Society for Research in Dramatic Art was reorganized under the name of Gŭgyŏn Zwa (Drama Research Seats). Members of this group endeavored to apply the art of Western drama to the new plays written by Korean playwrights. There were two other influential groups— the Nangman-Zwa (Romantic Seats) and the Chungang Mudě (Central Stage).

Well-known novelists, such as Yi Mu-Yŏng, Sŏng-Yŏng, Chě Man-Sig, and Kim Yŏng-Su, all had a keen appreciation of dramatic values and attempted to apply their talents to the service of the Korean stage. Yi Mu-Yong held up a mirror to society's unmade-up face in his satirical plays *The Daydreamers* and *Recuperation Without Payment; I Wish I Were a Christian* and *The Feast Day* were written by Chě Man-Sig; Sŏng-Yŏng penned *The Mountain People* and *The New Chairman of the Board,* while *The Fault* came from Kim Yŏng-Su during the same period.

Approximately one hundred commercial and experimental drama groups traveled all over the peninsula presenting a varied range of programs from the New Style Plays, New Dramas, and plays which were a combination of Sinpa and Singŭg. This era may be termed the golden period in Korean dramatic history, lasting until the 1940's, which, in turn, proved to be the dark age of the nation's cultural life.

The control of Japan over Korea became stricter with the outbreak of the Sino-Japanese War, and by the end of 1940 this led to the foundation of the Chosun Theater Association, sponsored indirectly by the government. In July 1942 it was reformed into the Chosun Cultural Theater Association, with which only sixteen drama groups were affiliated with the approval of the government. Through this officially sponsored organization the government supervised the activities of member groups by holding annual dramatic contests.

The successor of the Drama Research Seats was a

newly organized drama group, the Hyŏndě Gŭgzang, or the Modern Theater, managed by Yu Chi-Jin, dramatist and producer, Ham Dě-Hun, critic and novelist, and Chu Yoňg-Sŏb, producer. Other groups, such as the Gŭgdan Gohyŏb (Gohyŏb Dramatic Society), and the Gŭgdan Arang (Arang Dramatic Society), had association with the playwrights Bag Yŏng-Ho, Yim Sŏn-Gyu, Kim Tě Jin, and Sŏng-Yŏng and producer An Yŏng-Il. These three drama groups, together with other dramatic organizations, took part in the annual contests arranged at the Citizens' Hall in Seoul, while the regular performances were usually presented at the playhouses.

In spite of an atmosphere of political and cultural oppression, Korean playwrights managed somehow to create several notable plays: *The Amur River* of Yu Chi-Jin, *The Village of Camellia* by Yim Sŏn-Gyu, and *Genghis Khan* by Kim Tě-Jin.

When World War II ended, confusion, disorder, and intricacy entangled not only Korean political affairs but extended also to the world of the theater. Rightists and leftists spent much time and energy engaged in ideological discussions. Nevertheless, during the political struggle there were such plays born as *The Fatherland* and *The Self-Beating Drum* by Yu Chi-Jin, *His Excellency Yi Chung Sěng* and *The Wedding Day* by O Yŏng-Jin, *Brain Surgery* by Chin U-Chon, *The Cosmos* and *The Playground* by Kim Chin-Su, and *The Artery* by Kim Yŏng-Su. Most of these dramas reflected the hope of a long-suffering nation, just liberated from a colonial tyranny, for a brighter life in a better world.

The central government sponsored a national theater in April 1950 and set up a committee to maintain and control the former Citizens' Hall, which became the largest theater in Seoul—the National Theater. Yu Chi-Jin and his colleague Sŏ Hang-Sŏg established a drama company to present plays there. Korea was the first Asian country to establish and maintain a national theater.

In 1950 the nationalists formed a new organization, the Singŭg Hyophoe, or the Council of New Drama, which developed into the Shinhyop Theatrical Group of young dramatists. In April of the same year the National Theater offered its first production, *Wŏn Sul-Lang* by Yu Chi-Jin. The second première was that of Tsao Yu's modern Chinese drama *A Thunder Storm.* The quality of both presentations stood the test of critics and audiences alike as far as play, direction, and histrionics were concerned.

The Korean War, which broke out on June 25 of the same year, dealt a sudden and crippling blow to dramatic activities. During the armed conflict playwrights, directors, and actors fled to Taegu. The Shinhyop drama group staged a series of performances for the military. They also presented their shows to the public in Taegu and Pusan. As there were no movies, the dramatic performances offered the only escape to the people from the tragic realities of a war-torn country.

Yet in spite of these catastrophic circumstances, a few Korean playwrights were able to raise the voice of humanitarianism against the man-made inferno —Yu Chi-Jin in *I Will Be a Human, Too,* Kim Chin-Sui in *Out of the Waste,* Kim Yŏng-Su in *Seoul Under the Reds,* and Han No-Dan in *War and Flowers.*

The Shinhyop group, exclusive drama company of the National Theater, while still in refuge at the Moonhwa Theater in Taegu, presented in 1953 *A Field Flower* by Yun Běg-Nam. When in June 1957 the National Theater returned to Seoul, the Shinhyop group was the only drama company in Korea whose productions approached American or European standards.

The student drama movement that started in 1959 was a new trend with far-reaching impact on the contemporary theater of Korea. It began on the campuses of Seoul National, Korea, and Yŏnsei universities and resulted in the formation of the Experimental Theater Group.

The Korean Research Institute for Dramatic Art has a stimulating effect on theater arts in the country, especially by encouraging and advising potential dramatists. Since its inauguration in April 1962, the leading playwrights of Korea have associated themselves with the Drama Center, which is equipped with all the facilities to serve as the headquarters of the Korean drama movement.

Yu Chi-Jin was appointed director of the Drama Center, of which the first production was Shakespeare's *Hamlet.* Some other presentations of the Drama Center include Eugene O'Neill's *Long Day's Journey into Night,* Dubose Heyward and George Gershwin's *Porgy and Bess,* and Yu Chi-Jin's *The Han Flows.*

The vitality of Korean creative artists' spirit was shown by the emergence of a new generation of dramatists who wrote their plays during and after the war. Noteworthy contributions to Korean dramatic literature from these new playwrights include *The Dream City* by Choe Pom-Sog, *The Engine Which Lives on Flower Petals* by Im Hi-Jě, *The Ignored Ones* by O Sang-Wŏn, *Free Marriage* by Ha Yu-Sang, *The Well* by Kim Hong-Gŏn, *The Eclipse of Life* by Gang Mun-Su, and *The Family* by Yi Yŏng-Chan.

An examination of modern Korean authors' playwriting style and technique is now in order. According to Seoul drama critic Lim Young-Woong, Korean drama can be classified into three categories. In the first category are those plays that are written in the traditional method. *I Will Be a Human, Too* by Yu Chi-Jin is one of the representative works in this class. It deals with a composer who lives in North Korea before the outbreak of the Korean War. He has agonizing doubts about the communist society where man's freedom is denied and in desperation decides to go to Seoul to find liberty. The well-constructed play's theme is the revolt of an individual against forced regimentation of man's body and soul by the Marxists.

Han Ro-Dan's *Interchange,* another play in this category, is a domestic tragedy set in a seaside villa. Its story delineates the power of destiny, affecting the lives of the play's characters by the interchange of the Oedipus and Electra complexes. Also noteworthy is *Tropical Fish* by Cha Bŏm-Sŏg, a tragedy about race relations that starts to unfold when a family's eldest son returns from his studies in the United States with his Negro fiancée, whom he is determined to marry.

In the second category are plays that are composed in a new style or that imitate modern Western drama forms. According to Lim Young-Woong, the style of these plays is in marked contrast with the dramas of the previous category.

Oh Yŏng-Jin is considered one of Korea's most representative playwrights and one who always produces excellent works, though not frequently. His drama *A Woman Diver Goes Ashore* is about a woman who gets involved to the point of insanity in the confusion, intrigue, and wrangling that develops over the issue of how the inheritance bequeathed by a millionaire ought to be divided. The play expresses the author's contempt toward people who are obsessed by materialistic desires and bitterly criticizes modern society, which seems to destroy the purity of human nature.

Another representative work of this category is Lee Gun-Sam's *Lion's Share, Sir*. The author is one of the few Korean playwrights who has a flair for comedy. Lee has a talent to make the audience not only laugh but also think. The hero and narrator of *Lion's Share, Sir* is a simple clerk who, when realizing that it is difficult if not impossible to succeed in life with sensible words and deeds, changes his attitude and becomes successful but, alas, unhappy.

An avant-garde dramatist is young Kim Eui-Kyung. In his drama *Deeper Are the Roots* (originally entitled *Song of Reeds*), Kim portrays the distressing early life of a prostitute. To quote Lim Young-Woong, "the play is unique in that it expresses the writer's own protests against reality by means of bringing forth persons whom he conceives into the society which he conceives without fixing any specific society and time." This play stirred immediate interest in epic drama in the literary and theatrical circles of Korea.

In the third category of Korean drama—adaptations of other works—belongs *The Martyred* by Kim Ki-Pal. It is an adaptation from a best-selling novel with the same title by Richard E. Kim. The original story, which deals with the problem of God being pursued amid the circumstances of war, is developed on stage by means of a magic lantern, films, and captions. Kim Eui-Kyung's second full-length play, *Kiwi*, is based on a short story by Lee On-Yŏng. It is about the pathetic life of a discharged air force pilot. During his younger years, the hero of the play lived in despair and defeat. Illustrating his ordeal, the author attempts to show the tragic image of modern man.

Since 1960 the Korean theater seems to be in a process of fermentation. Conflicting ideas and opinions, rampant criticism between the older and the younger members of the Drama Center regarding all kinds of artistic, literary, directorial, and financial problems prompted the younger artists to leave the Center. Those who left founded in January 1963 the Minjung Theatrical Group. Their first production, *The Egg* by Felicien Marceau, was successful. With the help of the Asia Foundation they also staged such plays as Sacha Guitry's *Villa for Sale* and *The Bald Soprano* by Eugène Ionesco. The program policy of the Minjung group has been to present Western dramas in opposition to the traditionalism of Korean plays.

The Sanha group, another dramatic association of young artists, was founded in the summer of 1963. Their productions included *Unwanted Men* by Im Hi-Jĕ and *A House with a Blue Roof* by Cha Bŏu-Sŏg.

Members of the three dramatic groups, the Minjung, the Sanha, and the Experimental Theater have been largely college graduates, exerting a considerable influence on the development of the modern Korean drama.

One consequence of the Korean War is that it brought the Korean theater in closer contact with that of America and Europe. The plays of such playwrights as Eugene O'Neill, Thornton Wilder, Tennessee Williams, Arthur Miller, William Inge, Erskine Caldwell, Edward Albee, Samuel Beckett, John Osborne, Jean Paul Sartre, Jean Anouilh. Eugène Ionesco, and others have been translated, presented, and discussed. Naturally, the works of these dramatists have had a direct influence on Korean playwrights.

A remarkable phenomenon of recent years is the maturing of Korean playgoers. Mere amusement-seekers have been replaced by intellectuals and students. Cheap though effective melodramas are no longer the staple fare on Korean stages. Trite and slipshod productions are no longer run, for the simple reason that "trained" audiences demonstrated their dislike by being conspicuously absent.

In trying to indicate how much Korea has become an organic part of the world theater, it should be noted that in January 1964 the manager of the National Theater, Yoon Kil-Koo, the director Lee Hae-Rang, and a number of college professors came together to discuss, plan, and organize the celebrations in Korea commemorating the fourth centennial of Shakespeare's birth. They talked with representatives of Seoul dramatic groups about producing some of Shakespeare's plays in cooperation with the National Theater as part of the festive occasion. This was the first time in the history of the Korean theater that six different drama groups joined forces for a common purpose. The month-long presentation of Shakespeare's plays aimed not only to celebrate one of the greatest dramatic poets of mankind but also at arousing interest in the dramatic art in Korea.

The current trend in Korea toward imitating Western dramatic style may be considered as temporary experimentation at random, a quest of the dramatists of a long-oppressed nation for cultural identity. There are some among the Korean playwrights who are trying to assimilate their ancient heritage and to develop at the same time closer ties with the modern Western drama forms. It is possible that with the advent of a creative genius in this field the blending of East and West may lead to an excitingly new dramatic experience.

There are no full-length books published in English on Korean theater or drama. The only survey printed in the United States is a brief one: *An Outline History of Korean Drama* (1966) by John Kardoss. A chapter is devoted to Korean theater and drama in George Freedley and John A. Reeves's *A History of the Theatre* (1941). Bernard Sobel's *The New Theatre Handbook and Digest of Plays* (1948) gives a short account of Korean drama, though some of his information has been superseded. Encyclopedic in scope are the *Unesco Korean Survey* (1960) and *Korea, Its Land, People, and Culture of All Ages* (1963), both treating the development of Korean theater and drama, each using a different system of

Romanization. Informative articles on Korean drama have appeared in the *Korea Journal*, Vol. 4, No. 6 (June 1964), namely, "History of Korean Drama" by Lee Doo-Hyun and "Young Artists Revive Drama Art" by Lee Gun-Sam. S. Honda recorded "The Revolutionary Theatre Movement of the Korean People" in *International Theater*, No. 1 (1934). A special Romanization system was employed by Zŏng In-Sŏb in his concise study, *Korean Drama* (1955).—J. K.

Kornaros, Vincenzo. See GREECE: *modern period*.

Koromilas, Demetrios. See GREECE: *modern period*.

Kotzebue, August von (1761–1819). Extremely prolific German dramatist, writer of sentimental comedies, one of the most popular playwrights of his age. Kotzebue was born in Weimar in 1761, the son of a court official. Preparing for an administrative career at the universities of Jena and Duisberg, he established himself as a lawyer in Jena in 1780. During his studies, however, he had already taken a serious interest in the theater, and the duality of playwright and civil servant marked his life to its end at the hands of a political assassin. After 1783, Kotzebue assumed various government posts in East Prussia. Following a playwriting interlude in Vienna and Weimar (1797–1799), he combined both careers in Petersburg as both court councilor and theater director. He remained in Russian services until his assassination as a suspected Russian spy.

Kotzebue was unquestionably one of the most prolific and successful dramatists in German literary history. He wrote over two hundred plays, which were successes in Germany and abroad when played in translation. For example, of the 4,156 performances produced at Weimar under Goethe's directorship, over six hundred were plays of Kotzebue. Although his work is today not taken seriously by literary historians, one of his works, *Die beiden Klingsberg* ("The Two Klingsbergs," 1801; pub. in English as *Father and Son*), played more than 170 performances as late as 1951. In addition to attracting large numbers to the theater, Kotzebue's plays were avidly read at home by a remarkably broad section of the public.

Although Kotzebue wrote some tragedies, occasional prose, and dabbled in political polemic (*Der weibliche Jakobinerklub, The Female Jacobin Club*, 1790), his idiom was the sentimental comedy. The subjects of his plays were manifold and tended toward the exotic. All, however, revolved about a central point: the excitation of strong emotion. In this respect, Kotzebue contributed little to the development of German drama. Dispensing with the use of the stage as a pulpit, he capitalized on the middle-class expectations and attitudes that made Goethe's *Werther* one of the prose best-sellers of the era. Despite the unimportance generally meted out to Kotzebue by literary historians, his drama is well-deserving of further study for deeper insight into the popular culture of the eighteenth century.—B. M. M.

kowaka. One of the most extraordinary of Japanese dramatic forms, the *kowaka* has only recently come to the attention of Western scholars as living theater. So far as reported, it exists today as performing art only in the small village of Oe, in Kyushu, the southernmost island in Japan, where the form was es-

tablished after being transplanted from the great center of aristocratic art, Kyoto. Originating as dance drama at an unspecified time, it was destined to lose its general popularity in Japan by the end of the seventeenth century, lingering on only in remote provinces. The kowaka is essentially a compromise between dance and mere recitation, from the usual point of view less than the former and rather more than the latter. In short, it is a ceremonial performance of an epic story. An art form can scarcely be imagined with greater dignity and decorum. It may be regarded as a less gifted or versatile cousin of the much better known *noh* plays. The kowaka itself developed from a form both literary and choreographic, the *kusemai*. Its name derives from the family of performers who, it is conjectured, first formulated its laws in the fifteenth century. From preceding forms it borrowed much, yet modified virtually all to serve its own purposes.

The stage was a square approximately twenty by twenty and elevated to at least a modest height above the audience. To this extent it much resembled the noh stage. Until the present century the production at Oe was given on a temple porch. Now a raised platform, with thatched roof, is used. There are three actors, dressed much like minor noblemen of the early Edo period but wearing insignia emblematic of their function as celebrants of patriotic sentiments, family and art traditions, and dramatic rituals. The principal player sings all the solos and recites some of the narrative passages. His assistants recite as chorus and chant the remaining narrative sections. When moving about the stage, all three use artificial steps and gestures and when stationary assume rigidly prescribed poses. Action is slow and solemn. There are solos performed entirely by the leader, vocal ensembles, and passages of recitative and even of common speech. The drum sounds continually but with varied rhythm. The assistants move very little; the leader executes several patterns about the stage, frequently stamping his feet with rhythmic beats.

The chief aim of the performance is to confer deeper meaning, passion, and dignity to the text. There is little that can be called miming. Whatever is done on the stage is by visual and vocal means designed to create the mood proper for the appreciation of epic narratives and epic poetry. The kowaka sets the key to this receptivity as no lecture, musical number, nor ordinary reading could be expected to do. What is seen, and even more, what is heard, is imposing and impressive. All serves the text, which in itself may be described as a species of poetic prose. Its style and function have suggested the Western heroic ballad as well as the Western epics.

For many years the kowaka texts have been printed with some frequency. There are approximately fifty librettos, ranking with the finest of Japanese imaginative or poetic literature. By far the greater number deal with the familiar stories of Japan's feudal period, the adventures and misadventures of the Heike and the Genji clans and of the Soga brothers. Two are in praise of Hideyoshi, the great war lord of the sixteenth century; one relates a Chinese tale of supernatural adventures; the other, a tale of adventures more recognizable as belonging to our mortal world. The last has been likened to the wanderings of Ulysses. The temper of both text and performance is truly aristocratic. Although given today only by rice growers in a village as remote as possible from the centers of political and intellectual life in Japan, this is in no sense folk art. The audience is small and miscellaneous. The plays are presented perhaps more to satisfy a few persons spiritually and unselfishly devoted to them who enjoy their efforts in presentation than to entertain or impress those who come to see and hear. A number of children are said to stand and stare at them with amazement. Recently the peasants performed their favorite plays simply to acknowledge with gratitude the visit of an inquiring scholar. The plays nonetheless have high value both intrinsically as art and historically as documentation of theater history. As already implied, their texts have great beauty. But the performers no longer hold a place in Japanese life as a whole. One of the most truly aristocratic forms of art known in the world today lingers precariously in the care of a handful of reverent farmers.

Texts have recently been published in Japan and examined in a fair amount of scholarly writing. The music and dance have also been scrutinized, usually on the basis of early descriptions. Much of this study concerns the relations among the kowaka, the noh, and the older forms to which both are allied. There is only one thorough description in English, the admirable volume by James T. Araki, *The Ballad-Drama of Medieval Japan* (1964). This contains translations of two plays, *Atsumori* and *Izumi's Fortress*. The rendering of the former is of much literary merit and justifies a statement that the kowaka play is in this instance hardly inferior to the famous noh play by Zeami Motokiyo on the same theme. Much that is implied in the noh is made explicit in the kowaka. At least to the Western reader the kowaka text is almost certain to appear the less mannered form, possibly less lyric but closer to the epic style.—H. W. W.

Krasiński, Zygmunt (1812–1859). Polish poet and playwright. One of the major talents of Polish émigré literature, Krasiński was the son of a Polish general who fought with Napoleon and later entered Russian service. Krasiński was so sensitive on the matter of his father's "treason" that he published practically all of his works anonymously and for that reason came to be known as the "anonymous poet" of Polish Romanticism.

Although the author of a considerable body of poetry and prose, some of particular interest in charting the development of Polish Romantic messianism in the émigré period, Krasiński is now remembered only for his two major dramatic works, *Irydion* (begun 1832, pub. 1836, first staged 1908) and *Nieboska Komedia* (*The Undivine Comedy*, pub. 1833, first staged 1902). The first, set in the ancient Rome of the Emperor Heliogabalus, may be read as an indictment of the immorality of the use of treacherous means to achieve just and noble ends (as, for example, the independence of Poland). Irydion, the titular character, is a young Greek patriot who swears vengeance on Rome for its conquest of Greece. He makes a pact with the devil as the price of fulfillment of his most ardent wish in life, but when he is given the chance long after his death to behold the ruins of Rome, he no longer feels the hatred and thirst for vengeance that so consumed him earlier.

Staged far more often than *Irydion,* and a better

ZYGMUNT KRASIŃSKI (CAF, WARSAW; POLISH EMBASSY)

work, *Nieboska Komedia* is one of the few masterpieces of Polish Romanticism to attract attention abroad. It has been translated into several languages including Arabic and has been performed on a number of stages in Western and Eastern Europe, including the Soviet Union. Reflecting Krasiński's historical and philosophical inquiries and particularly the teachings of Hegel, *Nieboska Komedia* explores the nature of social and political revolution in his own era and expresses the belief that the solution of the conflicts rests with an acceptance of Christ and a return to true Christian brotherhood and love. An important secondary aspect of the play is the poet's renunciation of Romantic poetic posturing and illusions.—H. B. S.

Krechinsky's Wedding (Svadba Krechinskogo). A comedy in three acts, the first play in a trilogy by Alexander SUKHOVO-KOBYLIN. The other plays in the trilogy are **The Case (Delo),** a drama in five acts, and **Tarelkin's Death (Smert Tarelkina),** a comedy in three acts. The first play in this trilogy was written between 1852 and 1854 and produced in 1855. The second was written in 1857 but was banned by the censor and not produced until 1881, under the new title of *Otzhitoe vremya* ("Bygone Times"). The third was written between 1857 and 1869 and was also banned until 1900, when a censored version first appeared; the full version was not produced until 1917.

Krechinsky's Wedding is the story of a bold attempt by a ruthless gambler and dissolute adventurer, Krechinsky, to settle his affairs by marrying Lidochka, the daughter of the rich, provincial, hardworking landowner Muromsky. In order to convince the father that he is a solid landowner himself,

Krechinsky, who does not even have the money to pay for a wedding reception, borrows a diamond brooch from Lidochka and uses it as security to raise a considerable sum of money. At the last moment, however, he manages to hand to the moneylender a worthless replica instead of the jewel. Krechinsky, a *déclassé* gentleman, is not a vulgar thief; he intends to return the brooch to Lidochka at once and then to redeem the worthless replica from the moneylender with the dowry he expects to receive. His plan, however, collapses when Nelkin, Lidochka's virtuous admirer, tells Muromsky that Krechinsky has stolen his daughter's diamond brooch and pawned it to obtain the sum needed to deceive the father. Krechinsky then produces the real brooch and returns it to Lidochka, who says she lent it to him to show to a friend. The honest Nelkin is confounded and the wedding plans proceed. At the last moment, however, the moneylender, who discovers the substitution, arrives on the scene and Krechinsky is arrested, despite Lidochka's noble gesture of giving the real diamond to the moneylender.

Despite the rather banal intrigue, this is a first-rate comedy with a highly original cast of characters. The ending does not really clear up anything, since it leaves the heroine in despair and the "positive hero" Nelkin miserable. There are a variety of interpretations of the play, including, of course, the accepted Soviet one that Krechinsky represents the "decaying aristocracy" and his acolyte Raspluyev, the ragged, smalltime crook whom Krechinsky uses as his messenger and whom he mistreats, represents the corrupt bourgeoisie. According to this Soviet interpretation, the pathetic portrayal of Muromsky shows the author's misplaced sympathy for a capitalist landowner, even if he is a hard-working one.

The Case is in part a sequel to *Krechinsky's Wedding*, although Krechinsky appears only as the author of a letter warning old Muromsky of a blackmail plot being hatched against him and advising him that the only way to escape the justice officials is to pay them off. Krechinsky's letter, a discourse on graft, is the key to the whole play. There are three kinds of graft, he explains: innocuous agrarian graft, collected in kind; graft on profit, collected on business operations, inheritances, and so forth, which is also not too bad; and, worst of all, graft on crime—"trap graft," "usually collected until the victim is bled white." In *The Case* trumped-up charges are brought against Lidochka: she is accused first of being Krechinsky's accomplice in deceiving the moneylender and then of infanticide on the grounds that she must have been Krechinsky's mistress, must have had a child by him, and therefore must have done away with the child. Muromsky indignantly rejects these charges and, by irritating an "all-powerful" personage, spells his own doom. When he finally submits and pays every penny he has to save his daughter, the money is pocketed by the officials, except for a small sum that is used as evidence of his attempt to corrupt a civil servant. Muromsky explodes into a helpless, indignant tirade and dies of a stroke, as his loyal friend Nelkin vows to expose the murderous legal government machine. As to the grafters, the bigger fish, Varravin, manages to deprive his shifty subordinate, Tarelkin, of his due share of the spoils.

It is this last "injustice" to the smaller crook that is the subject of the last comedy in the trilogy, *Tarelkin's Death*. Here, Tarelkin, in an attempt to get back his "rightful" share of the loot, steals Varravin's correspondence in order to blackmail him and force him to pay off. Tarelkin stages his own death and changes his identity, but Varravin discovers the fraud and, with the assistance of Raspluyev, who has fittingly become a police officer in the meantime, Varravin builds an absurd case against Tarelkin (accusing him of being a vampire). He uses torture and depositions by false witnesses. In the end Tarelkin capitulates, returns the compromising papers to his former superior, and is allowed to vanish. Thus, the bigger fish, that is, the greater evil, again triumphs.

There is no doubt that the last two plays of this trilogy present a sinister picture of prerevolutionary Russia's soulless bureaucracy, but it is also a much more general comment on the corruption engendered by power. It is hardly surprising that it took Sukhovo-Kobylin twenty and thirty years, respectively, to see *The Case* and *Tarelkin's Death* staged in Russia. This fact also accounts for the slowness with which he was acknowledged as one of the greatest Russian playwrights.

Krechinsky's Wedding has been translated by Robert Magidoff (1961).—A. MAcA.

(1961).—A. MAcA.

Krog, Helge (1889–1962). Norwegian critic and playwright. The product of a radical home atmosphere, Krog early attached himself to socialist causes. After taking a degree in economics, he became a literary critic well before he attempted playwriting. Krog's essays show him to be a prose stylist and polemicist of nearly Shavian proportions. A political refugee in Sweden during World War II, Krog edited several collections of Norwegian belles-lettres and waged his own personal war against National Socialism. An important *Festschrift* appeared in 1949, on the occasion of Krog's sixtieth birthday.

Krog's early drama is clearly in the Ibsenesque tradition of the "problem play." *Det store vi* ("The Great We," 1919) exposes oppressive conditions among garment workers and the corrupt involvement of the daily press; *Jarlshus* ("The House of Jarl," 1923) deals with the problems of collective bargaining. The ensuing plays largely concern themselves with portraits of women in society and the emergence of a healthy eroticism. Sonja, of *Konkylien* ("The Conch Shell" 1929), is a protowoman in search of satisfaction. The play is not Arthur Schnitzler's *La Ronde* in slow motion, however, because cynicism is absent. Revolt is compounded in Cecilie, the heroine of *Underveis* (*On the Way*, 1931), who is a doctor, a communist, and about to be the unwed mother of a child—by a Jewish fellow traveler. Somewhat more plausible is the pattern of revolt in *Oppbrudd* (*Break-Up*, 1936), in which Vibeke, an architect, frees herself from the complicated, jaded triangle formed with her lawyer-husband, Ketil, and writer-lover, Kåre, in order to strike out on her own. Characteristically, in Krog's *Don Juan* (1930), written as a joint summer *jeu d'esprit* with the well-known novelist Sigurd Hoel, the protagonist is a sexually unenterprising manager of a pasteboard factory who is in flight from an assortment of aggressive women.

With both passion and irony, Krog advanced the emancipation of women in society. Though he did little to break away from the Ibsenesque mold, he developed an interesting rhythm of lyricism and logic that gives unusual thrust to his dialogue. Krog may very well be the best of Norway's twentieth-century playwrights.

See *Break-Up and Two Other Plays* (*On the Way; On Life's Sunny Side*) (1939); and Sverre Arestad, "Helge Krog and the Problem Play," in *Scandinavian Studies*, Vol. 37 (1965), pp. 332–51.—R. B. V.

Kuan Han-ch'ing (fl. 1275–1300). Chinese playwright, generally acknowledged to be the most popular dramatist of the Yüan dynasty (1280–1368). More of Kuan Han-ch'ing's plays are extant and have remained in the standard repertory than is the case with any of his contemporaries. Dates of his birth and death are unknown but it is evident that he was at the height of his powers in the last quarter of the thirteenth century. He lived and worked in Cambulac, the capital of the conquering Mongols in North China. There he became a leader in an association of scholars and writers known as "the Yu-ching Book Society." Titles of more than sixty of his plays are known; eighteen of them have survived. Among the best are SNOW IN MIDSUMMER, *The Butterfly Dream, Lord Kuan Goes to the Feast,* and *The Death of the Winged-Tiger General.* He is said to have had exceptional talents in many fields, such as music, dancing, and acrobatics. In his early years he composed songs and poems with remarkable facility. Later his theatrical work, actually more representative of the Yüan school of dramatizing than conspicuously above it, was recognized as the outstanding dramatic achievement of his times. (See CHINA.)

For translations of eight plays see Yang Hsien-yi and Gladys Yang, *Selected Plays of Kuan Han-ch'ing* (1958). The translation is conscientious but pedestrian, indicating the general intention of the playwrighting but giving little or nothing of its style or flavor. There is a more critical discussion in Liu Wu-chi's *An Introduction to Chinese Literature* (1966). —H. W. W.

Kurşunlu, Nazĭm (1911–   ). Turkish playwright. Kurşunlu has worked as an engineer for the Turkish government and currently he works in the capacity of engineer for the Ankara State Theater. As a writer, Kurşunlu first wrote short stories and then plays for radio. Since 1951 he has written nine plays for the stage. Kurşunlu's play *Fatih* ("The Conqueror," 1953) was performed at the Municipal Theater of Istanbul to commemorate the five hundredth anniversary of the conquest of Istanbul.

Kurşunlu's plays are about man's exploitation of man, the unfavorable position of Turkish women in society, and man's basic loneliness. Kurşunlu believes in the educational mission of the theater in society and scoffs at theater for mere entertainment. His plays are good theater, however, and are never didactic.—N. O.

Kwanami Kiyotsugo. See SOTOBA KOMACHI.

Kyd, Thomas (1558–1594). English playwright. Kyd was born in London and attended the Merchant Taylors' School. From there he apparently became a scrivener before taking up playwriting. He was a close friend of Christopher Marlowe and allegedly shared the latter's unorthodox religious views. In 1593 he and Marlowe were arrested on charges of atheism. Shortly after their release Marlowe was killed in a tavern brawl and Kyd died a year later, disgraced and impoverished.

Of Kyd's extant work only two plays, *The Spanish Tragedy* (c. 1588) and *Cornelia* (c. 1593), are definitely known to be his. Among those that have been attributed to him are *Soliman and Perseda* (c. 1589), a tragedy; the so-called *Ur-Hamlet* (c. 1588), the source of Shakespeare's tragedy; and ARDEN OF FEVERSHAM. Kyd is probably also the author of The First Part of Hieronimo (c. 1586), sometimes known as *The Spanish Comedy.* This play, the only extant version of which is a corrupt, pirated text published in 1605, was apparently designed as part one of *The Spanish Tragedy.*

Kyd's reputation rests solely on *The Spanish Tragedy,* one of the most popular and influential of Elizabethan plays. Here the theme of vengeance is introduced into Elizabethan drama, making this play the first of the long line of revenge tragedies popular throughout the period. In dramatizing the story of old Hieronimo's grief, madness, and ultimate revenge for the murder of his son, Kyd borrowed heavily from the traditions and conventions of Senecan tragedy. However, he avoided the static, declamatory mode of his classical model by crowding his scenes with theatrically effective, visually sensational incidents including a climactic play-within-a-play. Much of the language is stilted and too rhetorical, but the great virtue of the play is its plot, artfully constructed to evoke intense excitement in its audience. That it succeeded in this purpose is attested by the fact that it remained among the most popular plays for thirty years.

The standard edition of Kyd's plays is *The Works of Thomas Kyd* (1901), edited by F. S. Boas. An excellent account of *The Spanish Tragedy* is given in Fredson Bowers' *Elizabethan Revenge Tragedy* (1940).—E. Q.

kyogen. Traditional farces of Japanese drama. *Kyogen* is one of the most substantial and closely contained forms of broad comedy, or farce, that is anywhere to be found. Although no definitive statements can be made concerning its origins and no well-established professional companies dedicated to its continuance exist today, it is known that its roots extend into the earliest periods of Japanese history, and considerable vitality still remains in it as living theater. Kyogen presents a longer and more continuous tradition than does the *commedia dell'arte* in the West. Few art forms better deserve to be called popular, since it unquestionably arose among a peasantry and became the leading comic fare of an entire nation peculiarly devoted to theatrical entertainment.

In modern Japanese the word *kyogen* simply means "play" in the sense of a theatrical performance, but it is said originally to have signified "mad words." The plays are extremely brief, always with considerable miming and a fair amount of brisk dialogue set to a rhythmic pattern, so that the general impression is of a comic dance accompanied by words. In terms of usages in theaters of the East in general and of Japan in particular, these one-act plays are notably unpretentious. They make little use of musical accompaniment or of masks. In spite of the refined school of professional acting that developed around their performance, the plays preserve the strongest evidence of their amateur origin among the folk because of their racy and earthy idiom. It has been conjectured that in some past so remote as to be thoroughly obscure the plays had their birth in comic religious observances. This, however, remains more or less irrelevant conjecture. The truth is that, insofar as they are known today, their continuous spoofing, though outwardly altogether innocent and mirth-provoking and in no sense didactic, presents a humorous parody of life and even of art, maintaining a confirmed secular point of view. Many subject gods and devils to ridicule. But ridicule, not satire, is uppermost. The kyogen's comment on life is imaginative and poetic, neither intellectual nor moral. The ridicule is comprehensive and consistently unformulated. The strict formal elements are those peculiar to the species itself, as types of characters, situations, and humorous attitudes.

The kyogen's ancestors, then, were village entertainments, such as comic dances and contests in word and action. Though all evidence points to a rigorously established tradition as early as the fourteenth century, the kyogen are not known to have been committed to writing until the seventeenth century. At present several hundred have been printed and manuscripts as yet uncollected remain in private hands. A systematic study, promising rich rewards, has only just begun. Such study must of necessity be critical and psychological, for little or nothing can be ascertained as to authorship. As in all folk art, anonymity is of the essence.

Virtually all kyogen contain passages of violent slapstick comedy. It is the law of their being that a good proportion of their comedy shall be physical. But prominent as the physical element unquestionably is, they possess much more substance than this, inasmuch as human folly and pretension in almost all instances provide the implicit theme. In other words, a few inferior plays may offer nothing more than slapstick, after the fashion of the more childish Punch and Judy shows, but kyogen are as a class childlike, not childish. A clever young servant, named Taro, is their champion. Vanity, greed, boastfulness, timidity, and all the more familiar human weaknesses are exposed. No class or type escapes. There is no real hero, as there is no villain. Hence the art is purer than in another Japanese theatrical form, the *kabuki*. All men are seen as fallible, the most fallible being those possessed of the most power, notably the feudal lords and the gods themselves. Like everyone else, Taro comes to grief, but unlike most people in real life or even on the stage, he rises above his misfortunes, bouncing back and forth between triumph and defeat, laughter and tears, with mercurial speed. Such farces are a glad song celebrating the resilience of the soul. Insofar as the kyogen possess a thesis, it is that laughter is lord of all and in the end dominates both the stage, which represents art, and the audience, which in this instance with unusual justice represents the whole people. The laughter of the kyogen, which began in the village, ascends to comprehend general mankind.

It would misrepresent a truly great art to point to individual masterpieces. So brief are these lyrical plays that even when they are in their own terms

aesthetically perfect and spiritually profound, to use Emily Dickinson's phrase, "their unpretension stuns." Their value lies in their collective worth, not in outstanding instances, much as their history is contained in their overall effectiveness and not in the fame attached to prominent authors. In this sense their power to generalize appears philosophical. It is impossible to date any play with assurance, since their origins reach beyond the margins of history.

The most remarkable feature of the kyogen's history is its relation, at once paradoxical and logical, with the chief serious and poetic form of Japanese drama, the NOH. The aristocratic noh plays, which arose in the fourteenth century, exist entirely within the province of history. Precisely how they formed their inviolable marriage with the popular kyogen is unknown, but at the earliest date that has been established for the noh the two are seen united. Doubtless kyogen were occasionally performed on programs without the noh, but evidence is that the greater number of productions were in conjunction with those religious works. Moreover, many kyogen—and at least passages in almost all the plays—parody the noh. This odd *entente cordiale* between the two was apparently established on the pragmatic ground that each flourished the better in conjunction with the other. The high seriousness of the one could be fully realized and sustained only with refreshing relief from the other; the hilarious mood as an outlook upon life proved convincing only at times and when placed side by side with its opposite, much as negative and affirmative aid in defining each other. It will be recalled that the Greeks had reached somewhat similar conclusions, but the Greek genius for mathematical thought notwithstanding, the more aesthetic Japanese arrived at the more rigid formulas. A program of noh, generally consisting of five serious plays, was lightened by the introduction of two, three, or four kyogen. Modern scholars discover a rationale for such an arrangement, yet in practice we find the composite program hard to achieve. In present-day Japan farces at least derived from kyogen are as often seen on the kabuki stage as incorporated in revivals of the noh. Unfortunately, it seems hard to find a place for them in modern professional production, even though their subtlety calls for the extreme precision of professional clowning. At present they show a tendency to return to their own innocence as entertainment on a folk or amateur basis.

Kyogen have also of late, critical remarks to the contrary, possessed considerable attraction to readers. That poetry is older than literature cannot be denied, though unhappily may too easily be forgotten. Modern poetry, with so difficult a style that repeated readings are obligatory, tempts the learned to forget that poetry has enjoyed many of its greatest triumphs with no readers at all. Persons of even moderately developed poetic or theatrical imagination evidently have found kyogen distinctly attractive as literature. Small difficulty need be experienced in imagining the conventional actions implied by the texts. Speeches and gestures are inveterately rhythmical. The realm of implication and nuance that is by definition that of poetry seldom exists so clearly as in the kyogen texts. Zeami Motokiyo and the great masters of the noh were thus unquestionably inspired in welcoming the marriage of the two seemingly disparate forms. It is further of some interest and even of importance for the kyogen that, a familiar Japanese proclivity to the contrary, more sexuality appears in the noh than in the farces, as evidenced in the unique feature of the kyogen, the mischievous servant who is its most conspicuous character. Man, said the Elizabethans, is a poor, bisected vegetable, a zoological mandrake—a conclusion that Japanese theatrical history strongly substantiates.

The kyogen are briefly discussed in almost all general histories of Japanese drama or literature but no thoroughgoing analysis as yet exists. The first printed collection, with 203 plays, was made by Toraaki Okura in 1638. The best Japanese text is still *Kyogen Zenshu* (3 vols., 1903), edited by Nariyuki Koda. Also useful are *Kyogen-Ki* (2 vols., 1917) with 200 plays, edited by Hachiro Nomura, and *Kyogen Shushei, or Cyclopaedia of Kyogen* (1931), edited by Kaizo Nonomura and Tsunejiro Ando. Three collections of translations into English merit attention. The most attractive is *The Ink-smeared Lady and Other Kyogen* (rev. ed., 1960) by Shio Sakanishi. See also *Ten Kyogen in English* (1907), translated by Arthur Lindsay Sadler, and *Japanese Plays: Nō—Kyogen —Kabuki* (1934), translated by Harukichi Shimoi. —H. W. W.

L

Labiche, Eugène (1815–1888). French author
of vaudevilles, farces, and comedies. Labiche, who
became the scourge and also the favorite playwright
of the French bourgeoisie, was born fifteen days before the Battle of Waterloo into a Parisian family of
bons bourgeois. He was a model son and student, not
brilliant at his schoolwork—he attended the Lycée
Condorcet and the Collège Bourbon—but fortified
by a prodigious memory that enabled him to learn
the examination manual of the *baccalauréat* by heart.
At his father's instigation, he compliantly took a law
degree (1834), and then a culture-seeking trip to
Sicily (1835) by way of Switzerland and Italy. On his
return he went unexpectedly into casual journalism.
In 1839 he published at his own expense his first and
only novel, and some months later withdrew it permanently from circulation.

Labiche's early career as a playwright dates from
1841 to 1850, during which time he wrote *Monsieur
de Coyllon* (1841) and a succession of short farces, vaudevilles (comedies with songs), pochades
(sketches), and fantasies, most of them in collaboration and staged at the Théâtre du Palais-Royal. His
first success, *Un Jeune Homme presse* (*Young Man in
a Hurry,* 1848), was soon eclipsed by *Un Chapeau de*

EUGÈNE LABICHE (FRENCH CULTURAL SERVICES)

paille d'Italie (*An Italian Straw Hat,* 1851), one of
the nineteenth century's truly durable farces. Thence-
forth, he proved to be the most prolific dramatist
since Scribe, turning out on his own initiative or to
order over 160 brief and long scripts. His plentiful
royalties paid for an estate at La Sologne, some
eighty miles south of Paris, to which Labiche and his
family moved. There he lived like a gentleman
farmer, cultivating wheat and breeding livestock and
returning to Paris only at intervals to supervise rehearsals of his plays. This rural setting provided him
with backgrounds and character types which he introduced into many of his subsequent plays. In the
late 1860's he became mayor of the local village.
During these years he received two awards from the
Légion d'honneur. The Comédie Française commissioned a work from him in 1864; he responded with a
full-length comedy, *Moi* ("Myself," 1864). In 1880
he was elected to the Académie Française.

Long before his death in 1888 Labiche was generally acknowledged to be the leading comic dramatist
of his time in France, indeed, in the world. Today his
reputation rests on such works as *La Poudre aux
yeux* (*Dust in Your Eyes,* 1861), *Célimare* (1863), *La
Cagnotte* (*Pots of Money,* 1864), *Le Grammaire*
(*Grammar,* 1867), *Les Trente Millions de Gladiator*
(*Gladiator's 30 Millions,* 1875), *Le Prix Martin* (*The
Martin Prize,* 1876), *Un Chapeau de paille d'Italie,*
and the perennial *Le Voyage de Monsieur Perrichon*
(*Monsieur Perrichon's Journey,* 1860). The last has
become a favorite classroom text for good reasons
and also for such dubious reasons as the one given
below in an English edition, which says that *Perrichon*

> presents abundant advantages for the acquir-
> ing of a vocabulary, as it places the reader al-
> ternately in a railroad station, in a country
> inn, in Perrichon's home [in Paris] . . . and
> makes him familiar with words needed by
> travelers.

Several of Labiche's plays do have multiple settings
and are like comic-epic adventures. Even his pot-
boilers, which stay closer to the narrow circumscrip-
tions of the "well-made play," have no infusions of
the sentimentality characteristic of his contemporaries.

Labiche goes to almost any length for a laugh. He
once wrote:

> A play is a thousand-legged creature which
> must keep going. If it slows up, the public
> yawns; if it stops, the public hisses.

To this end, he gets humorous dividends from such reliable techniques as repeating motifs or identification lines and filling his work with bustle and chases: in *Un Chapeau de paille d'Italie* a procession of wedding guests careers from one location to the next through five breathless acts. He also makes thorough use of props, rarely displaying one that will not critically change the plot later, e.g., a letter in a hatband in *Célimare;* the paste tiara in *La Cagnotte;* even an unseen elephant in *Les Trente Millions de Gladiator.*

Labiche's characters are dropped or lured into baffling situations. They are unworldly and psychologically shallow, though each has his vivid quirks. The older men constitute the principal (and sometimes secondary) sources of character humor. Merchants, small farmers, and local professionals, they were instantly recognizable to the audience because they were the audience. Labiche ridicules their worries about preserving a respectable front, raising dowries for their daughters, and ruthlessly seeking prestige. The pompous Champboursey in *La Cagnotte* will never let the community forget its debt to him for supplying its only fire pump. Major Mathieu in *Perrichon* revels in his grotesque militancy, taking offense at any imagined affront.

Labiche's women and younger men are negligible characterizations: sighing damsels; stock, stout maiden ladies and wives who believe themselves to be irresistible; and youths who are indistinguishable from one another. Even Fadinard, the hero of *Un Chapeau de paille d'Italie,* is a bland booby.

During his lifetime Labiche's more acidulous plays failed to win the public. *La Chasse aux corbeaux* ("The Vulture Hunt," 1853) depicts financiers and speculators as vultures and compares in theme and bitterness with Henry Becque's *Les Corbeaux,* staged at the Comédie Française six years before Labiche died. This work of Labiche, like his popular ones, may undergo new evaluations in France and elsewhere. Labiche is regarded now as a great entertainer who also transformed the old songs-and-smiles vaudeville play into an instrument of satire.

Eugène Labiche: sa vie, son oeuvre (1945) by Philippe Soupault is the only biography of Labiche, but a good, critical one. *Théâtre complet d'Eugène Labiche* (1886), in ten volumes, contains fifty-seven plays that Labiche thought worth preserving, nearly all written with collaborators. The Preface by Émile Augier, an important dramatist in his own right, has been translated by Mary Douglas Dirks in the *Tulane Drama Review* (Winter 1959). English versions of the plays include: *Célimare,* translated by Lynn and Theodore Hoffman, and *A Trip Abroad (Perrichon),* translated by R. H. Ward, both in *Let's Get a Divorce! and Other Plays* (1958), edited by Eric Bentley (Bentley's book also includes a related essay, "The Psychology of Farce," written by himself); *Pots of Money (La Cagnotte),* translated by Albert Bermel in *Genius of the French Theater* (1961), edited by Albert Bermel; *Grammar* (1915), translated by Barrett H. Clark; *The Man Who Set Fire to a Lady,* translated by Fred Partridge, in the *Tulane Drama Review* (Winter 1959); *90° in the Shade* (1962) and *Dust in Your Eyes* (1962), both translated by Emanuel Wax; and *An Italian Straw Hat,* translated by Lynn and Theodore Hoffman, in *The Modern Theater,* Vol. III (1955), edited by Eric Bentley.—A. C. B.

Lagerkvist, Pär (1891–   ). Swedish poet, novelist, and playwright. Born of pietistic parents in Småland, educated at the Swedish university Uppsala and in Paris, Lagerkvist has lived most of his life as a near-recluse in Sweden. Between 1912 and 1918 he largely established the expressionist direction of Swedish modernism, in the essay *Ordkonst och bildkonst (Word Art and Picture Art,* 1913), in which he advocates an espousal of primitivism and the "taut, architectonic style" of the cubist painters; in *Modern teater (Modern Theatre,* 1918), a manifesto advocating an intense fusion of theatricality and inner vision; and in *Ångest (Anguish,* 1916), a collection of poetry that picks up the cry of the Norwegian painter Edvard Munch and sets the tone for the harsh, restless era ahead. Lagerkvist was elected to the Swedish Academy in 1940 and honored with the Nobel Prize in 1951. Outside of Sweden he is chiefly known for such novels as *Dvärgen (The Dwarf,* 1944), in which the attendant of a Renaissance court assumes the symbolic role of the evil in all men; *Barabbas* (1949), a quasi-biblical novel later turned into a play; and *The Sibyl* (1956), in which Lagerkvist experiments with the convergence of a Greek and a Judaic myth. The closest Lagerkvist comes to autobiography is in the early work *Gäst hos verkligheten (Guest of Reality,* 1925), a sensitive study of childhood.

Lagerkvist's early short plays, *Den svåra stunden* ("The Difficult Hour," 1918), a triptych, and *Himlens hemlighet* ("Heaven's Secret," 1919), represent a fusion of the taut cubist style and expressionism. This fusion somewhat resembles the plays of the Austrian Oskar Kokoschka and anticipates the "theater of the absurd." His later plays range from political allegory, *Mannen utan själ* ("The Man Without a Soul," 1936) and *Seger i mörkret* ("Victory in the Dark," 1939), to oratorio, *Låt människan leva* ("Let Man Live," 1949), where the martyrs of history unite their voices. *Han som fick leva om sitt liv* ("He Who Got to Live His Life Over Again," 1928) couches a

PÄR LAGERKVIST (SWEDISH INFORMATION SERVICE)

determinism of character in a lyric passion and thus very well exemplifies the partial fusion of the new and the old in Lagerkvist. In *Midsommardröm i fattighuset* ("Midsummer Night's Dream in the Poor House," 1941) Lagerkvist emerges momentarily from the dark night of his soul, but in *Den vises sten* ("The Philosopher's Stone," 1947), he is back there again, posing the rigorous question of whether the pursuit of scientific truth justifies any and all means.

In spite of its compelling intensities, the drama of Lagerkvist has proved a little too abstract and austere for popular consumption, and he is chiefly known for his novels. Nevertheless, Lagerkvist has had a strong impact on the Scandinavian theater scene.

See *The Eternal Smile and Other Stories* (1954), edited by R. B. Vowles; *Modern Theatre: Seven Plays and an Essay* (1966), edited by T. Buckman; and A. Gustafson, *A History of Swedish Literature* (1961), pp. 392–407.—R. B. V.

Land of Heart's Desire, The (1894).   A verse play by W. B. YEATS. First performed in London as a curtain-raiser to Bernard Shaw's *Arms and the Man* in 1894, this one-act verse play is a fantasy written in the early romantic style of Yeats's Celtic Twilight period. The heroine, Mary Bruin, a newly married peasant girl, has become disillusioned with the plodding world of reality and tries to escape by reading a wonder book of Celtic legends about the ancient heroes and the Sidhe (pronounced Shee), the Faery Folk who represent the free and wild imagination as they sing and dance upon the wind in Tir na nOg, the land of eternal youth, which for Mary now is "The Land of Heart's Desire." According to the legends, the Sidhe often tempt and abduct mortals by sending a Faery Child to lure them away to the faery world. The unhappy Mary cries out to the spirits to save her:

Come, faeries, take me out of this dull house!
Let me have all the freedom I have lost . . .
For I would ride with you upon the wind,
Run on the top of the dishevelled tide,
And dance upon the mountains like a flame.

When presently a Faery Child appears and beckons to her, Mary's husband and his parents and the priest warn her that it is an evil spirit. But Mary succumbs to the enchantment of the singing and dancing Faery Child and goes with it at the end to be liberated in death. In later years Yeats was embarrassed by the immense popularity of this charmingly naïve play, especially with amateur theatrical groups, and he called it "a vague sentimental trifle." Nevertheless, it introduces a theme to which he was to return often in his poems and plays, the conflict between mundane reality and the unfettered imagination.—D. K.

Langer, František (1888–1965).   Czech novelist and playwright. Born in Prague, Langer studied medicine at the Charles University and graduated in 1914. At the Russian front during World War I, Langer was first an Austrian soldier, and then later he joined the Czech army in Russia. After returning home through Siberia and Japan in 1920, he became an officer of the health service and, at the same time, pursued a literary career and worked as an organizer of the cultural life by participating in the PEN Club. From 1930 to 1935 Langer was literary manager and, until 1938, artistic adviser for the City Theater at Vinohrady in Prague. When the Germans occupied the Czech territory, Langer went to France and then England to escape political and racial persecution. As an émigré, he was appointed chief of the health service of the Czech army abroad, and as a writer, he participated in the struggle against Hitler. In 1945 he returned to Czechoslovakia and in 1947 was awarded the title of The National Artist.

On the eve of World War I Langer wrote his first plays, *Noc* ("The Night," pub. 1922) and *Svatý Václav* ("Saint Wenceslas," pub. 1912), in an accomplished, neoclassical style. In this same period, in collaboration with J. Hašek and others, Langer wrote satires, such as *Pogrom na kresťany v Jeruzalémě* ("Violence to Christians in Jerusalem," date unknown), that were produced by members of an eccentric group called the Party of Moderate Progress Within the Pale of the Law. Langer also wrote the scenario for Jaroslav Weinberger's pantomime *Evelinin únos* ("Abduction of Evelina," 1915).

Milióny ("The Millions," 1915), Langer's first attempt to write realistic drama, was set in the milieu of an international plutocracy. Through the plot, Langer portrays tragedy and conveys his criticism of modern capitalists.

After Langer's return from the army, where he had written plays for a Siberian theater group made up of Czechoslovak legions, he created several very popular comedies about the contemporary life of the Prague common people and bourgeoisie: *Velbloud uchem jehly* (*The Camel Through the Needle's Eye*, pub. 1923), *Obrácení Ferdyše Pištory* ("Conversion of Ferdyš Pištora," pub. 1929), and *Manželství s r.o.* ("Limited Liability Marriage," pub. 1934). The main characters of these comedies belong to the *lumpen proletariat,* people getting into petty conflicts with the law. Charmed by their life energy, humor, uncultivated intelligence, and sense of honor, Langer infused his portrait of these people with a touch of irony. In these works Langer developed a comic situation according to the structure of classical comedy. Using his knowledge of the speech pattern of this social group, Langer created dialogue that sharply characterized his people. He presented petty conflicts between the lumpen proletariat and the bourgeoisie, which he tried to harmonize. Another of these works is Langer's *Grandhotel Nevada* (pub. 1927), set in a world of American millionaires. Two poor Czech immigrants find good fortune in this milieu because of their own wit and cleverness. This category of social comedy also includes Langer's dramatization (1930) of Charles Dickens' novel *Pickwick Papers.*

Langer's fame abroad was a result of his experimental dramas. In *Periférie* (*The Outskirts,* pub. 1925) he tried to solve the problem of crime and punishment. The protagonist is Franci, a young man on the periphery of society, who, although desiring punishment for his involuntary murder of a man, cannot persuade anyone of his guilt. To free himself from his suffering and to ensure his punishment, he acts on the advice of an obscure "lawyer of the poor" and murders his girl friend with her help. The pursuit of justice is the leading motif of *Periférie* as well as Langer's other dramas. The solution in *Periférie* was widely criticized, so Langer wrote another ending in which Franci is forgiven by a court for the involuntary murder of a man. This drama, composed in a cinematic style with many acts, has all the features of

Langer's art and is also influenced by the expressionist dramatic structure.

In the utopian play *Andělé mezi námi* ("The Angels Among Us," pub. 1931) Langer is concerned with the problem of euthanasia. Dr. Mise, an angel sent to earth in order to shorten the lives of seriously ill people, is sentenced to death by human judges. In *Dvaasedmdesátka* ("The Seventy-second One," pub. 1937), in which he uses the structure of a play-within-a-play, Langer fought against miscarriages of justice. In the period of fascist danger Langer wrote *Jízdní hlídka* ("The Mounted Patrol," pub. 1935), in which he celebrated human courage and solidarity and presented a true picture of the part played by the Czechoslovak army in Russia after the October Revolution. Langer pays homage to the theater and life in his optimistic comedy *Jiskra v popelu— Pocta Shakespearovi* ("A Spark in Ashes—Honor to Shakespeare," pub. 1948). His last play, *Bronzová rapsodie* ("The Bronze Rhapsody," written in 1952; pub. 1962), has never been performed.

In addition to writing plays, Langer also wrote stories and novels. His puppet plays for children were also very successful. His works still appear today on the Czech stage, in translations abroad, and on radio, television, and the movie screen.—F. Č.

Lark, The (L'Alouette, 1953). A play by Jean ANOUILH. *The Lark* was first performed in 1953 at the Théâtre Montparnasse Gaston-Baty. When the curtain goes up, Jeanne d'Arc is in the presence of her judges. The Englishman Warwick and Cauchon are in a hurry to conclude the affair. As the questions continue, the episodes of Jeanne's life become the play: her childhood, her departure from home, her visits to Baudricourt, the recognition of the king at Chinon, her departure for Orléans. Anouilh, avoiding the burning at the stake, ends his play with Jeanne's preparation for the coronation of her king at Reims.

Certain characteristics of Jeanne seem to come from other Anouilh heroines, from Thérèse of *La Sauvage* (*Restless Heart,* 1934) and from Eurydice and Antigone. As in his other works, there is the same grouping in this play of traditional characters around the central character: the narrow-minded and coarse father of Jeanne; the rascally mother who gives her daughter the advice of a procuress; the queen; and Agnès Sorel, the king's mistress. The pattern of caricature, always visible to some extent in Anouilh's plays, is perhaps more swiftly, more dexterously applied in *The Lark* than in the others. The art at times recalls that of the Parisian *chansonniers* in its popular medley of pathos, wit, and vulgarity.

The Lark has been translated by Christopher Fry (1955).—W. F.

Latin America. See BRAZIL; PUERTO RICO; and SPANISH AMERICA.

Lawler, Ray (1922–   ). Australian playwright and actor. Lawler, with his upbringing in a working-class suburb of Melbourne, was the first Australian playwright who dealt effectively with the modern idiom of that country. His long experience as an actor and playwright may in part explain the technical competence of his only international success, *The Summer of the Seventeenth Doll* (1955). This drama, working through the characters of Australian barmaids, sheep shearers, and cane cutters in

RAY LAWLER (AUSTRALIAN NEWS AND INFORMATION BUREAU)

the northern tropics, is successfully generalized into an examination of the difficulties of losing one's youth with dignity. In Lawler's next play, *The Piccadilly Bushman* (1959), he attempts to explore the nature of the Australian identity. Although not a dramatic innovator, Lawler nevertheless influenced his contemporary playwrights by his use of ordinary Australian speech in a colorful and unstilted manner. See AUSTRALIA.—A. W. and H. V. D. P.

Lee, Nathaniel (1648?–1692). English tragic dramatist. Lee, the son of a clergyman, was educated at Charterhouse and Trinity College, Cambridge. Little is known of his early life, but by 1672 he was a bit player in the Duke's Company in London. When he had no success in this capacity, he turned to playwriting and in 1674 completed *Nero*, a tragedy which he dedicated to the earl of Rochester. Though *Nero* was not a great success when it was produced in 1674, *Sophonisba* (1675) won fame for Lee the next year. He became a friend of John Dryden, with whom he collaborated on *Oedipus* (1678) and *The Duke of Guise* (1682), and like Dryden, he was for some years under contract to the King's Company to write plays for them. After enjoying great popularity, Lee suffered a number of reverses. Two of his plays (*The Massacre of Paris* and *Lucius Junius Brutus*) were suppressed because of their Whiggish political implications, and others were coolly received. In 1684 Lee was committed to Bedlam for insanity, and though he was released four years later, his career was ruined.

Lee wrote one licentious comedy, *The Princess of Cleve* (1681), but he made his name with tragedies. Of the twelve he wrote (including his two collaborations) the best are *Sophonisba*, THE RIVAL QUEENS, and *Theodosius* (1680), all three distinguished by the emotional entanglements and the passionate confrontations in which Lee specialized (see ENGLAND: *Restoration drama*). He took the heroic characters of these plays in part from ancient history and in part from romances in which these figures had been idealized. His themes, as this combination suggests, were the "love and valor" that Dryden had spoken of as the proper subjects of the heroic play.

The standard modern edition of *The Works of Nathaniel Lee* (1954) is that of Thomas B. Stroup and Arthur L. Cooke. For biography see Roswell G. Ham's *Otway and Lee: Biography from a Baroque Age* (1931).—E. W.

Leivick, H. Pen name of **Leivick Halpern** (1888–1962). Russian-born Yiddish poet, playwright, and essayist. Leivick was born in Ihumin, White Russia, where he received a traditional religious education. In his early teens, however, he came into contact with Hebrew secular literature and turned away from formal religion. About 1905 he became active in the illegal Jewish revolutionary movement, the Bund, and at the same time began writing Yiddish verse. In 1906 he was arrested for his revolutionary activity and spent two years in a Minsk jail awaiting trial. At the trial he refused legal counsel and boldly proclaimed his revolutionary hopes. He was sentenced to four years at hard labor and exile to Siberia thereafter. While in prison Leivick wrote his first dramatic poem, *Di Keytn fun Meshiakh* ("The Chains of Messiah," pub. 1939). At the end of March 1912, he began the long march to Siberia. During the nine-month winter of 1912/13, he wrote poetry and a drama, *Dort Vu di Frayhayt* ("There, Where Freedom," pub. 1952). Money sent him by comrades who had emigrated to the United States enabled Leivick to buy a horse and sleigh and begin a two-thousand-mile journey to the nearest railroad. Several months later, during the summer of 1913, he arrived in New York.

He earned his living as a paper hanger and continued to write poetry after work. His first two books of verse contained the record of his suffering, loneliness, and personal visions. The publication of the dramatic poem THE GOLEM in 1921 brought him into the first rank of Yiddish poets. Hoping to improve his economic situation, he turned to the drama and during the next decade wrote seven realistic plays in prose and on social themes, but none was very successful. In 1932 he was stricken with tuberculosis and spent four years recuperating in sanatoriums. Illness did not, however, interfere with his productivity, and by the time the Yiddish cultural world was celebrating his fiftieth birthday (1938), Leivick had attained a position of preeminence as its spokesman. A special fund was raised by his admirers to finance the publication of his collected poetry, which appeared in two volumes in 1940.

The horrors of Hitlerism reawakened the profound note of pain at the irrational in man, an echo of the pessimism that had characterized so much of his early work. His visit to the D. P. camps in Europe produced a volume of essays, *Mit der Sharis Hapleyte* ("With the Survivors," 1947) and the mystical dramatic poem *Di Khasene in Fernvald* ("The Wedding in Fernwald," 1949). The problem of human suffering, which had been at the center of Leivick's creativity, received its last dramatic ex-

pression in the dramatic poem *In di Teg fun Iyev* ("In the Days of Job," 1953). His last works were a volume of poetry, *A Blat oyf an Eppleboym* ("A Leaf on an Apple Tree," 1955) and a volume of recollections of his years in prison, *Oyf Tsarisher Katerge* ("At Tsarist Hard Labor," 1959). He suffered a stroke in September 1958 and lay paralyzed and speechless until his death on December 23, 1962. The years of his last illness were, ironically, years of honors heaped upon him for his achievement as the greatest living Yiddish dramatist and poet—perhaps the greatest poetic voice in the language.

In Leivick's twenty-one plays in prose and verse, in his ten volumes of poetry, and in the prose volumes of essays and memoirs there is one dominant concern—human suffering. His work is the record of a lifelong struggle with the moral dilemmas posed by the problem of the pain that man must endure. He was the voice of man's outcry against anguish and indignity and the voice of man's constant yearning and unending need for redemption. "Man is always; redemption lasts a while." Although he was known in his earlier years as the poet of doom, the very ordeals of his own life seemed to deepen his faith in man, and he emerged during his middle years as the poet of redemption. His profound intellectuality and sometimes mystical visions and flights of symbolism are clothed in language of utmost simplicity and power. He was, as one critic justly remarked, "the majesty of Yiddish literature."

Joseph C. Landis, translator and editor, *The Dybbuk and Other Great Yiddish Plays* (1966); Sol Liptzin, *The Flowering of Yiddish Literature* (1963); and Charles A. Madison, *Yiddish Literature: Its Scope and Major Writers* (1968) contain substantial discussions of Leivick's work.—J. C. L.

Lena, La (1528). A comedy in verse by Lodovico ARIOSTO. The plot revolves around a bawd named Lena, who is the wife of Pacifico and the paramour of the elderly Fazio. Lena intrigues to fulfill the love of the youth Flavio for Licinia, Fazio's daughter. Flavio hides in a barrel, which is the object of a dispute between Pacifico and one of his creditors. Fazio proposes that the barrel be carried to his house, there to be protected as surety to the litigants. Flavio thus reaches Licinia (who never appears on the stage). The plot is concluded by the marriage of the two young people. The play's marginal episodes are inspired by various Latin comedies and the barrel episode by a novella in Boccaccio's *Decameron*.

La Lena is one of the first comedies in the Italian language and is considered Ariosto's best contribution to the stage. Although written in imitation of Plautus and Terence and in a verse form that attempts to reproduce the rhythm of Latin iambic trimeter, the play manifests a precise attention to contemporary life. It takes place in Ferrara and is rich in observations of the manners and customs of that city.—L. L.

Lenormand, Henri René (1882–1951). French novelist, poet, and playwright. Lenormand received a degree in English from the Sorbonne in Paris. His works—plays, short stories, and prose poems—were practically unknown for a long time. Recognition came fairly late, but when it did come, his dramas were produced all over the world.

For several years during the twenties the plays of

Lenormand were admired as efforts to restore and rehabilitate the French theater. His work reflects many influences: Maurice Maeterlinck, for example, with the theme of the unknown elements of human destiny; Edgar Allan Poe, with the theme of the mysteriousness and strangeness of human life; Luigi Pirandello, with the belief that the personality is not unified and coherent; and Freud, who was perhaps the strongest influence on Lenormand, especially on the last plays. *Le Simoun* ("The Simoon," 1920) and *Le Temps est un songe* (*Time Is a Dream,* 1919) are good examples of the metaphysical type of play for which Lenormand was famous in the 1920's and in which the conflict is always between a man as he appears in his ordinary life and the desires he conceals that make of him a being foreign to himself.

For a critical study of Lenormand, see Kenneth S. White, *The Development of Lenormand's Principles and Purposes as a Dramatist* (1958).—W. F.

Lesage, Alain René (1668–1747). French novelist and playwright. Born in Brittany and orphaned at the age of fourteen, Alain René Lesage was reduced to penury by his guardian, went to Paris in 1692 to seek his fortune, and as a livelihood devoted himself to translating from the Spanish. Thus, under the influence of Spanish literature, he wrote picaresque novels that were situated in Spain but portrayed and satirized French customs (*Le Diable boiteux,* 1707; *Gil Blas de Santillane,* 1715–1735). His dramatic career was extremely difficult. Not until 1707 did he have some success, and a few years later he fell out with the Comédie Française and found himself reduced to writing, in collaboration, innumerable farces for the fair theaters. He most especially detested the actors of the Comédie Française; and ironically, two of his sons became precisely that, one of them being the famous actor Montménil.

Of Lesage's plays one may single out his first success, a one-act comedy, *Crispin rival de son maître* ("Crispin, His Master's Rival," 1707), whose incisive and cynical tone is more original than its subject matter (a crafty valet passes himself off as his master in order to obtain a dowry), and above all, TURCARET, a five-act comedy in which the motive of all the action is money.

Lesage actually was a one-play dramatist, *Turcaret* being characteristic of the comic spirit at the end of Louis XIV's reign: a joyous theatricalism that served as a vehicle for sharp and cynical social satire. —Ja. G.

Lessing, Gotthold Ephraim (1729–1781). German dramatist, critic, scholar, theologian, and theoretician, who represents the high point of the German Enlightenment and the beginning of the modern era in German drama. Born in Kamenz, Saxony, in 1729, Lessing studied in Leipzig, where he was acquainted with Gottsched's collaborator, Caroline Neuber. Unlike most of his contemporaries, he was able to support himself solely with his pen. He was, in fact, one of the first writers in modern Germany who lived without the comforts of a sinecure position or a guaranteed income. This fact is of great importance in assessing the new, middle-class orientation of drama, in whose vanguard Lessing found himself, for the rising middle classes were now economically able to support literature and criticism directed toward themselves, rather than toward a

GOTTHOLD EPHRAIM LESSING (GERMAN INFORMATION CENTER)

courtly audience. Lessing was at times a private secretary and became the ducal librarian in Wolfenbüttel in 1770. But the balance of his career was taken up with literature, particularly drama, philosophy, scholarship, religion, aesthetics, and seemingly endless polemics. In all endeavors Lessing demonstrated a remarkable combination of Enlightenment rationality and intuitive insight into the fundamental currents of his time.

Lessing's dramatic activities can be divided into the journalistic-critical and the writing of plays. In 1748, at the age of nineteen, he journeyed to Berlin to work for the *Vossische Zeitung,* a periodical. Two years later he published his *Beiträge zur Geschichte und Aufnahme des deutsches Theaters* ("Contributions to the History and Reception of the German Theater"). Following his taking of a master's degree in 1752, he began work on *Briefe, die neueste Literatur betreffend* ("Letters Concerning the Most Recent Literature," pub. 1759–1764). In this series, which dealt with many and varied literary topics, he violently attacked Gottsched's autocratic position on the drama (Letter No. 17). His chief objections were to Gottsched's slavish adherence to French models for German drama and to the use of idealized characters implicit in Gottsched's attitudes. Lessing found his own ideal in the English drama, particularly Shakespeare's, and he became a strong advocate of this cause. Many of Lessing's ideas were propounded in his important critical work *Hamburgische Dramaturgie* (*Hamburg Dramaturgy*), which he edited from 1767 to 1769. This publication combined theoretical comments with criticism of the latest plays.

Perhaps the best examples of Lessing's goals and contributions, however, are found in his major plays themselves: *Miss Sara Sampson* (1755), *Minna von Barnhelm, oder das Soldatenglück* (*Minna von Barn-*

helm, or, the Soldier's Fortune, 1767), *Emilia Galotti* (1772), and *Nathan der Weise* (1779). The first-named, heavily indebted to Lillo's *The London Merchant* of 1731, represents a break with tradition, yet without the disruption of the Aristotelian unities. This family tragedy, in which unity of time and place are carefully observed, represents a divergence from the ideals characterizing Enlightenment tragedy in Germany: Virtue and vice are not presented as unconditional opposites—as the father is brought to understand in the course of the drama—but passions, the true subject matter of the play, are presented as potentially destructive to the social order. For the first time in German drama, a middle-class family situation is given the dignity of tragedy. This represents both a recognition of the growth and tastes of the new middle-class public and a guidepost on the road to a new intermediate form, the SCHAUSPIEL.

With the creation of *Minna von Barnhelm* Lessing initiated a new era in German comedy. After Gottsched successfully closed the German stage to the clown character, Hanswurst, it remained only for a break to be made with the stereotype characters of the comic form. The principals of *Minna* suffer, not from one-sidedness and folly, nor from the machinations of malicious servants, but from their own individuality. The play is a comedy in that the audience —and the protagonists—know that love will triumph. It is serious in that the conflicts between the pride of the ex-officer and the love of his Saxon lady friend drive the all-too-human characters to extremes. Further realistic background was provided by the recently ended Seven Years' War.

Lessing's last major play, NATHAN THE WISE, is a philosophical dramatic poem, uniting classical form with the Enlightenment ethic of tolerance. Despite the great potential the play holds for the bizarre, exotic, and even *Sturm und Drang*, Lessing created a very human hero with a very human solution to the problems of prejudice. Retaining the unity of time, Lessing put the final form of the play into iambic pentameter. This verse form had already made its appearance in German drama, but Lessing's *Nathan* conclusively established it as the poetic matrix of the classical drama, particularly for the work of Schiller.

It is difficult to outline Lessing's significance for the modern era in just a few lines: He was not merely a dramatist but a man of many and varied intellectual interests; in the true Enlightenment sense, a true turning point in German literary and intellectual history. For further study, H. B. Garland's book, *Lessing, The Founder of Modern German Literature,* is recommended.—B. M. M.

Libation Bearers. See ORESTEIA: *Choephori.*

Liberia. See AFRICA: *Liberia.*

Life Is a Dream (La vida es sueño, 1635). A metaphysical "problem play" by Pedro CALDERÓN DE LA BARCA. In *Life Is a Dream* Prince Segismundo has been imprisoned in a wasteland tower since infancy by his father, Basilio, king of Poland; the king wishes in this way to forestall the prophecy, made at the prince's birth, that Segismundo would usurp the throne and become a tyrant. The main action begins with Basilio, now an old man, suggesting that the throne be given to a nephew, Astolfo, duke of Moscow. But some uneasiness causes the king to decide first to test the prophecy. Segismundo is brought un-

conscious from the tower into the glittering royal palace, where he wakens and is treated as a royal prince. The abrupt change and a sense of the injustice that has deprived him of his station in life for so long enrage him. He throws a servant out of the window, tries to assault two ladies, makes a murderous attack on his keeper, fights with his cousin, and threatens his father's life. These actions convince Basilio that the prophecy was correct, and Segismundo is put to sleep again and returned to his tower. Awaking there, Segismundo concludes that what occurred was only a dream. But news of his existence spreads through the kingdom, where there is opposition to the succession of Astolfo. Consequently, a party of the people's rebellion appeal to Segismundo, who becomes their leader. He defeats his father's forces and is acclaimed king. Instead of avenging himself, Segismundo forgives his father, restores peace and harmony to the kingdom, and acts in all ways as a model prince. Having learned a hard lesson from the nature of his experience, he is able to exert his own free will to counteract the auguries of fate.

Life Is a Dream has been translated by Roy Campbell in *The Classic Theatre,* Vol. III: *Six Spanish Plays* (1959), edited by Eric Bentley.—E. H.

Light That Shines in Darkness, The (I svet vo tme svetit, 1912). The play has also been translated as *And Light Shines in Darkness.* An autobiographical drama in five acts by Leo TOLSTOY. Written between 1880 and 1900, the play was published in 1911. The theme of this autobiographical play is, like that of Tolstoy's dramatized legend *Peter Khlebnik,* a wealthy man's sudden realization that his life is wrong and that he must refuse to participate in the unjust organization of society and live instead like a true Christian. But whereas Peter is a legendary character who lived in Syria in the third century A.D. and had himself sold as a slave to give the proceeds to the poor, the central protagonist of *The Light That Shines in Darkness* is a nineteenth-century Russian landowner very much like Tolstoy. Just like Tolstoy, Nikolai Sarnytsev decides to give his land to the peasants but is persuaded not to. Instead, he simply transfers all his possessions to his wife's name to avoid actively participating in the system of exploitation. Everything the protagonist does seems doomed to failure: his wife and children do not understand him; his disciples either suffer in vain and perish or renounce their faith; and his Christianity is denounced by the clergy. Indeed, he himself recognizes the uselessness of his renunciation, but deep down he feels that he is doing the right thing.

As many Soviet critics point out, this autobiographical play shows better than anything else the bankruptcy of Tolstoy's own philosophy of nonresistance to evil. It may be objected, however, that Tolstoy simply had the disadvantage of too great a perspicacity: he could see that violent remedies (which were later used) would not improve matters. —A. MACA.

Li K'uei Carries Thorns (Li K'uei fu ching). A Chinese play by K'ang Chin-chih (fl. 1280). *Li K'uei Carries Thorns* is treasured as one of the happiest examples of romantic comedy as developed during the Yüan dynasty (1280–1368). As often in the Chinese theater, the play is extraordinarily advanced in artifice, convention, and stylization, yet contains an undercurrent of pertinent criticism of both social and political life. Its universal appeal is analogous to that of the British Robin Hood stories and ballads. More specifically, or historically speaking, it reflects conditions of life under the Yüan dynasfy, when Chinese loyal to their native institutions and with thinly veiled opposition to the Mongol conquerors expressed their plight and their longings in factitious forms. The legend utilized as plot for this play is part of the long Yüan novel *The Men of the Marches*.

In the play a company of noble bandits, bent on stealing from the rich to give to the poor, live on a lofty mountaintop. Their leader decrees a three-day holiday, an extraordinary weekend, when his followers may leave their mountain citadel to enjoy themselves in lowly villages. Li K'uei, a black-faced, clownish, but also a fabulously lusty member of the clan, visits a wineshop, where he discovers an instance of signal injustice that he at once takes upon himself to correct. Two boastful cowards have run away with the innkeeper's hardly reluctant daughter. Li K'uei promises to recapture her regardless of all obstacles, placing his own head in forfeit if he should fail to do so in the time allotted for the holiday. Though he succeeds in the task, it takes longer than the allotted time and consequently his head is due to fall. In view of his undoubtedly good intentions, however, he is pardoned for mere tardiness. One explanation for this tardiness is that he is habitually drunk and on the holiday is more than usually so. This, too, is overlooked by his leader. All is forgiven in the case of so generous-hearted, though imprudent, a humorist. The play is itself an amusing conjunction of political idealism and Taoist insouciance. It is anything but sober, yet no one can expect sobriety of a work that stands somewhere midway between high comedy or social satire and low comedy or heart-easing farce.

The broad characterizations are excellent. These include the roles of the half-blind innkeeper, his half-chaste daughter, the braggarts disguised as heroes, the noble bandits themselves, and, of course, the clown who gives the play its name. The title signifies Li K'uei's enforced penance, bitter fruit of his carefree attitude toward the sublime laws of banditry. Among its abundant merits the play contains some excellent nature poetry and some sophisticated and truly beautiful lyric passages.

Broad as the humor at times may be, like all the most typical art of China's chief periods, it is rich in nuances, which confront a translator with singularly difficult tasks. A hand for this work has, however, been found. The American scholar James Crump renders the play with equal bravado and fidelity to its highly conscious style and lyrical sentiment. His translation first appeared in *Occasional Papers*, no. 1, the University of Michigan (1962); this rendering is included in *Anthology of Chinese Literature* (1965), edited by Cyril Birch.—H. W. W.

Lillo, George (1693?–1739). English tragic playwright. Lillo, presumably of Flemish and English descent, was born in London, the son of a jeweler, and was taught his father's trade. His first appearance as a dramatist was in 1730, with the presentation of a ballad opera, *Silvia, or The Country Burial*, in imitation of the style of *The Beggar's Opera* by John Gay. It was not well received, but the following year his prose tragedy *The London Merchant, or The History of George Barnwell* proved one of the great theatrical successes of the time and was universally admired at home and influential abroad. Before his death Lillo composed five other dramatic pieces: two blank-verse tragedies, an adaptation of Shakespeare's *Pericles*, a historical verse drama, and a masque. He left unfinished an adaptation of *Arden of Feversham*, an anonymous sixteenth-century play.

Lillo's originality lies in his choice of material. *The London Merchant* is a bourgeois tragedy, while *Fatal Curiosity* (1736) concerns the humblest of characters. He has sometimes been classed among the sentimental dramatists of the century, and while it is true that the latter scenes of *The London Merchant*, for instance, are marked by a high degree of emotionalism, it is to be observed that Lillo's moralism is far removed from good-natured benevolism. Lillo was a pious dissenter who looked upon the tragic play as an opportunity to show and to enforce emotionally the consequence of sinfulness.

There is no modern edition of Lillo's collected works and as yet no modern critical biography. *The London Merchant* and *Fatal Curiosity* have been reprinted frequently. The best modern editions of these two plays are those edited by William H. McBurney (*The London Merchant*, 1965; *Fatal Curiosity*, 1966). McBurney supplies good biographical and critical summaries.—R. Q.

Lincoln Plays, The. See N-TOWN PLAYS.

List of Assets, A (*Spisok blagodeyanii*, 1931). A play in eight scenes by Yuri OLESHA. In *A List of Assets* Lola Goncharova, a Shakespearean actress, performs before an audience of workers the scene in which Hamlet scornfully explains to Guildenstern that a human being is not a musical instrument, that he cannot be played upon to produce the desirable sounds. During a question-and-answer period following this reading, a worker asks Lola why she chose *Hamlet* rather than some topical Soviet play. She answers that the topical Soviet plays are "sketchy, false, unimaginative, heavy-handed, and obvious" and that "doing them impairs one's acting ability." Lola, who tries to be fair to the new Soviet regime, keeps a diary in which she scrupulously enters all the advantages and disadvantages resulting from the revolution, listing these items either as deficits or assets. The lack of concern of Soviet audiences for Hamlet's subtle soul-searching is, in her opinion, a deficit, a point against the regime.

When, however, she goes on a tour to Paris, where she hopes to find the old interest in Shakespeare, she discovers that cultural values have also been debased in the West, although in a different way and for different reasons. There, Monsieur Margaret, a greedy and uncouth capitalist music hall manager, reacts rather unexpectedly to Lola's offer to perform the same scene from *Hamlet* in his establishment. He decides that Lola should begin her act by playing some sad little tune on her recorder and then swallow the recorder and play a cheerful melody from the other end of her anatomy. The public, he explains, likes to be sent home on a cheerful note.

After various experiences, Lola's carefully drawn-up balance sheet between the two worlds tips in favor of the new. In the end she prefers to join a communist street demonstration in Paris than to attend a ball to which she is invited by Russian émigrés. Thus, her choice is made. And when a bullet is fired by the police at the communist leader, she shields him with her body. Dying, she repents her Hamlet-like hesitations and asks the comrades to wrap her in a Red banner. But at that moment new police reinforcements arrive, and, unfurling their banners and rushing to meet the enemy, the demonstrators leave Lola's corpse lying uncovered and forgotten in the street.

Like Olesha, Lola is caught between two worlds and feels allegiance to both. Her dilemma is like Hamlet's. Has the new world killed the old, as her feelings tell her it has? And if so, should she oppose it, go over to the other side, become an émigré? The squalor, stupidity, stuffiness, and dogmatic stiffness of the Soviet Union offended her. She was impatient to leave for the old world, because she herself was born during the old order of things. But once there, she is disillusioned. The parallel failure of both worlds to understand Shakespeare's subtle plea for the acceptance of man's complexity is the crux of Olesha's thought, and, although the old world's failure is presented in more grotesque colors, the spurning of Shakespeare by the emancipated workers affects Lola more, because it was her mission to bring culture to them.

Yuri Olesha's *A List of Assets,* translated by Andrew R. MacAndrew, appears in *Envy and Other Works,* (1967).—A. MACA.

Little Clay Cart, The (Mrcchakatika, c. A.D. 150?). Sanskrit play of unknown authorship, sometimes named "The Toy Cart." *The Little Clay Cart* is the best known example of the type of play designated by Indian critics as the *prakarana.* This type presents an action derived neither from mythology nor history but from the dramatist's own invention. It is closer to the Western conception of comedy than to the Sanskrit mythological play; characters and scenes are more naturalistically conceived than in plays deemed by Indian tradition more serious, religious, or spiritual. This by no means signifies a wide divergence between the distinct types of drama. In their basic aesthetic principles and elaborate stage conventions all major forms of Sanskrit drama are substantially alike. Nevertheless, in its own country *The Little Clay Cart* has never remotely won the acclaim bestowed on works by Kalidasa, Bhavabhuti, Harsha, and other playwrights. It does not even conform strictly to the orthodox rules for a prakarana. In contrast with the more typical Indian works, the action and figures appear less exalted and more explicitly human. Especially the minor characters are readily imagined as encountered on a city street. There is considerable satire and even some propaganda in behalf of the lower classes. Idealism there is indeed, as in the portraiture of the generous, sensitive hero and of the high-minded courtesan or *hetaera.* By no standards is this a greater play than the works of Kalidasa, Bhavabhuti, or other of their countrymen, but it is unquestionably closer to Shakespearean comedy, to Plautus, or even to Molière than other Indian works.

Its authorship is unknown, though the Prologue declares it to have been written by a king named Sudraka, whose virtues are extolled in such hyperbole that even in as highly rhetorical a literature as Sanskrit the description can hardly be taken at its face value. Whoever the author may have been, he was

A SCENE FROM *The Little Clay Cart* (COURTESY OF BALWANT GARGI)

clearly a genius and a consummate master of his craft. No conclusive evidence exists to determine the play's date of composition within so much as a matter of centuries. Internal evidence points, however, to a mature period in Indian dramatic development. Approximately A.D. 150 has been suggested by one scholar. The verse passages are especially well developed, suggesting a comparatively late date; sheer theatrical adroitness is extreme.

These problems of dating and authorship are intimately related to a play in the Bhasa canon (see TRIVANDRUM PLAYS), *Charudatta in Poverty.* This work parallels closely, frequently line for line, Acts I to IV of *The Little Clay Cart,* which itself extends to ten acts. The comparative sketchiness of *Charudatta in Poverty* suggests that it was an earlier work of which we possess only the first section. The cause for its unmistakably truncated form lies apparently in the political complexion of a secondary plot, which gave occasion for censorship. The most plausible explanation is that the first part of the popular *Charudatta in Poverty* was saved for the stage and the second part, now missing, contained short versions of most of the scenes known today only through *The Little Clay Cart. Charudatta in Poverty,* itself a brilliant piece for acting, is even less brilliant in this respect than *The Little Clay Cart* and incomparably less significant as a dramatic poem. It is not wholly impossible that the two versions originated within four or five years of each other or, for that matter, within four or five centuries. Such is the almost unique obscurity of the chronology of the Sanskrit stage. For this frustrating condition, the long-lived continuity in Indian thought must largely account.

As in several other Sanskrit plays, the plot of *The Little Clay Cart* is built with much ingenuity about a few stage properties, in this instance jewels at one time deposited in a toy cart, a plaything of the hero's young son. There is considerable highly imaginative burlesque: Brahman ritual is parodied in a scene of housebreaking; a pompous judge is ridiculed; a prince is depicted as a half-wit and an absurd pretender to learning; a well-meaning clown is shown as the cause of the hero's misfortunes. There are several scenes of pure miming, a few highly choreographic episodes, much symbolism, and many passages of rare poetic excellence.

In Western opinion the play is commonly thought of as a classic in stylized action. It was the first play to be given in the progressive Neighborhood Playhouse in New York, which opened its doors December 5, 1924. Subsequently it has received frequent productions in different parts of the world.

The English translation most faithful to the spirit of the original is that by Revilo P. Oliver in *Six Sanskrit Plays* (1964), edited by Henry W. Wells. There is a good English rendering by Arthur W. Ryder (1905). See also C. K. Bhat, *Preface to Mrcchakatika* (1953), and C. B. Pandey, *Sudraka* (1958).—H. W. W.

Little Orphan of the Family of Tchao, The (Chao Li jang fei). A Chinese play of the Yüan dynasty (1280–1368), attributed to Chi Chun-hsiang. *The Little Orphan of the Family of Tchao* is important in its own right and by virtue of its unique history. It was the first Chinese play to be translated into a Western language, the first to beget imitations on the Western stage, and even exerted an influence on the

theater in Japan, where it inspired scenes of several well-known dramas, including Chikamatsu's romantic masterpiece, *The Battles of Coxinga,* and Takeda Izumo's almost equally famous work, *History of the Transmission of the Art of Calligraphy by Sugawara.* Although it concludes conventionally enough with justice meted out to the few who survive the disasters of its own narrative, it maintains a tragic tone to a remarkable degree. More deeply serious and lofty in spirit than most Chinese plays, it has attracted readers in societies whose drama has admitted more elements of pure tragedy than are generally current on the volatile Chinese stage. Its theme is clan and family loyalty, willingness to sacrifice self to the point of death, and the bestowal of complete devotion on the overlord and his heirs. This dedication to an absolute ruler has on the whole proved more representative of other lands than of China, where, in the minds of his subjects, the emperor has assumed more the position of the Son of Heaven with the force of a philosophical conception than that of an absolute personal monarch with total political power.

The convoluted plot cannot be related here in detail; the barest outlines sufficiently indicate its general character. The orphan, or heir to leadership in his clan, is an infant pursued by inveterate enemies. A loyal follower substitutes his own newborn infant so that the villain, a second Herod, fails in his design to eradicate the race of his foes. On reaching maturity, the child, with his defenders beside him, comes into his rights at last, executing vengeance on the hereditary foe. The scene throughout is of a clan feud. The mother of the sacred child is no less heroic than the hero. The plot is contrived so that one impressive scene follows another, piling Pelion upon Ossa. Even in the major drama of the West few plays maintain a purer dignity of diction or intensity of emotion. The scenes are more spontaneous than in most analogous works in either Japan or the West.

This thirteenth-century Chinese play has a curious and important history in the annals of eighteenth-century drama in the West. It was first rendered in French in an abridged form by the French Jesuit J. Prémare and included in a general history of China edited and published in Paris by Du Halde in 1735. Two English renderings (1736 and 1741) of Du Halde's book contained two anonymous versions of Prémare's translation. In 1762 a slightly different version was produced by Bishop Thomas Percy, editor of the most famous collection of Scottish ballads. The play's political implications pleased the French at the height of the Bourbon regime, shortly before its world-startling fall. The work further provided a basis for Voltaire's *L'Orphelin de la Chine* (1755), often celebrated as the first serious play to be presented on the French stage in over a century without baroque costume and showing a compromise with historical *décor.* Prémare's version omitted all the lyrical passages, in Chinese eyes the very heart of the play. The occasion for stately dialogue in an Augustan manner attracted the enterprising minds of eighteenth-century admirers. In England a sentimental melodrama was derived from it by a minor playwright, William Hatchett: *The Chinese Orphan: an Historical Tragedy, Alter'd from a Specimen of Chinese Tragedy in Du Halde's History of China, Interspers'd with Songs.* Here the original was twice "alter'd." The songs were purely English but at least the British exhibited an intuition for the Chinese lyrical stage not up to this time evidenced by the more conservative French. The Chinese play was finally, without abridgment, translated into French by the eminent scholar Stanislas Julien and published in London in 1834. This was reissued in Paris in 1869. The curious fact remains that more attention was given in the West to this impressive play in the eighteenth century than at any later period.—H. W. W.

liturgical drama. See ENGLAND: *middle ages.*

Living Corpse, The (Zhivoi trup, 1911). A drama in six acts by Leo TOLSTOY. In this play, perhaps the best-constructed drama he ever wrote, Tolstoy's theme is the inadequacy of official justice. The play, written in 1899, was inspired by the trial of a married couple, Nikolai and Katerina Gimer: In order to free his wife and enable her to marry a man whose religious beliefs forbade him to marry a divorced woman, Gimer faked suicide. Later, when the hoax was discovered, both the Gimers were tried for fraud and Katerina and her new husband for bigamy. In Tolstoy's play, the first husband, a weak and charming drunkard, is faced with the dilemma of either seeing all three of the accused sentenced to deportation to Siberia for willfully conspiring to commit the crime of bigamy or, if acquitted, having the second marriage annulled and being forced to resume the first, unhappy union. Although the first husband seems like a weakling, when he realizes how cruel and senseless official justice is, he rises to the occasion by killing himself, in order to make a bona fide widow out of his former wife.

Out of consideration for Katerina, whom Tolstoy had met, he requested that this play not be published until after her death.

Today *The Living Corpse* is often produced in the Soviet Union, where the absurdity of "bourgeois justice" under the tsarist regime is emphasized. —A. MACA.

Livings, Henry (1929–   ). English playwright. Livings, born in Prestwich, Lancashire, is one of the few of England's new-wave playwrights who have succeeded in making audiences laugh. His first play, characteristic of what was to follow, was *Stop It Whoever You Are* (1961), a farce set in a public lavatory. Some of the quality of his humor can be deduced from the titles of his other plays: *The Quick and the Dead Quick* (1961), about Villon; *Big Soft Nellie* (1961); *Nil Carborundum* (1962), about the R.A.F.; *Eh?* (1964); and *The Little Mrs. Foster Show* (1967), about emergent Africa.

With the exception of the melodrama *Kelly's Eye* (1963), Livings has specialized in farce, but of a very personal type. His plays are episodically constructed on the assumption that audiences have an attention span of no more than ten minutes. They usually show one of the underdogs of technological society throwing a spanner in the works—like the hero of *Big Soft Nellie,* who sabotages a radio repair shop, or Valentine Brose in *Eh?,* a teen-age night watchman who is left disastrously in charge of a monster marine boiler.

Livings' aggressive regionalism, his crude jokes, and his disruptive attitude toward class have caused him to be labeled a working-class playwright. In fact, he came from a middle-class home.

In performance, Livings' plays are apt to go into a decline after seeming wildly funny to begin with. But there is no doubt of his dazzling comic flair or of the fact that he has brought a signally unfunny tract of the modern world into comic focus.—I. W.

Locandiera, La (The Mistress of the Inn, 1753). A comedy by Carlo GOLDONI. The protagonist is Mirandolina, the proprietor of an inn in Florence where a group of people customarily gathers: the im-

SCENE FROM CARLO GOLDONI'S *La Locandiera*

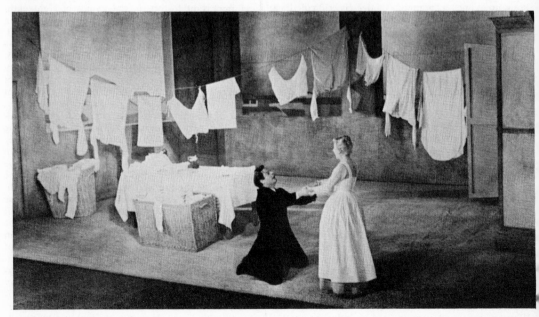

poverished marquis of Forlipopoli; a newly named count, Albafiorita; and the chevalier Ripafratta, a capricious hater of women. In a short time even the chevalier is enslaved by the fresh grace of Mirandolina, who pretends to approve of his misogyny and subsequently causes him to propose marriage to her. Caught between the bold attentions of the first two men and the declarations of the converted misogynist, Mirandolina maneuvers with astuteness and sagacity to avoid compromising herself, on the one hand, and losing her three best customers, on the other. When she does resolve to marry, she chooses youthful Fabrizio, the serious and loyal servant, who can help her run the inn.

Written with great theatrical mastery and with a happy delineation of characters, *La Locandiera* stands in opposition to the enlightened morality of the pretentious Pamelas of the theater of the time.

For its solution is based upon concrete and bourgeois good sense. The play exalts the practical wisdom of the middle class (Mirandolina), which, in its difficult navigation between the decadent and pretentious nobility (the marquis) and the rich bourgeois snob who expects to be ennobled (the count), does not fail to discover the way that is most in keeping with its own condition.—L. L.

Long Voyage Home, The. See S.S. GLENCAIRN.

Lorca, Federico García. See Federico GARCÍA LORCA.

Lorenzaccio (pub. 1834). A historical prose tragedy by Alfred de MUSSET. Published in 1834, this drama of Renaissance Italy was not performed until 1896, when Sarah Bernhardt played the central character, Lorenzo de Medici. According to the custom of the time, she had the play drastically cut and rearranged so as to focus, erroneously, upon Lorenzo's

A SCENE FROM ALFRED DE MUSSET'S *Lorenzaccio* (FRENCH CULTURAL SERVICES)

triumphant assassination of the evil duke of Florence. This conventional adaptation fulfilled the requirements of a stage still dominated by the "well-made play" but sacrificed Musset's intentions: to reveal, in the futility and sinister consequences of Lorenzo's deed, the corruption and decadence of an enslaved Florence. But the 1951/52 Avignon production of the Théâtre Nationale Populaire, with Gérard Philipe as Lorenzo, showed twentieth-century audiences what a masterpiece Musset had written.

The play unfolds the licentious activities of Alessandro de Medici, duke of Florence, who is aided by his cousin and seeming accomplice, Lorenzaccio ("Lorenzo the monstrous"). The duke's behavior is opposed by the Strozzi family: the idealistic Filippo, his honest but impetuous sons, and his virtuous daughter, who is treacherously murdered for resisting the advances of a libertine. Her death climaxes the Medici-Strozzi feud. To save his country from ruin, Lorenzo has participated in evil in order to destroy it (he assassinates Alessandro at the end of Act IV). But the once-idealistic Lorenzo has partially corrupted himself. His is the tragedy of lost innocence. Besides assisting the duke in the seduction of various women, including his own aunt, he also knowingly hastens his mother's death with his debauchery. In the last act Lorenzo is murdered by order of the depraved Council of Eight, and the new ruler swears to avenge the death of Alessandro.

Musset's main source is the *Storia Fiorentina* (written about 1543) of Benedetto Varchi (1502–1565), although he may have taken a few suggestions from George Sand's unpublished play *Une Conspiration de 1537* (written about 1833). In any case, *Lorenzaccio* is distinguished by a freedom of treatment characteristic of Musset, who was not writing it for the stage. It is, nevertheless, a credit to his innate sense of drama that the play can be performed successfully.

The play's appeal is partly psychological, partly structural and stylistic. Unlike most Romantic plays, *Lorenzaccio* creates its own suspense without the stereotyped situations and devices of melodrama, and the reader's attention is held by the overall structural unity. Like Shakespeare, Musset presents, in his first two scenes, a microcosm of the drama. In the first, the callous ruffian Alessandro is contrasted with Lorenzo, who has a more reflective nature. The decadent atmosphere of Florence is wonderfully evoked in the second scene, which, together with the fifth, reveals Musset's effective handling of crowds. But it is the psychological complexity of Lorenzo's character that most reminds one of Shakespeare's ambiguous and enigmatic characters. Several of the play's interpreters have noted the similarity between Lorenzo and Hamlet. In the partially unresolved ambiguity of his personality, Lorenzo also seems modern. He has even been likened to the existential heroes of Jean Paul Sartre's plays.

R. C. Bruce's excellent acting version (shorter than the original) is in *The Modern Theatre,* Vol. VI (1960), edited by Eric Bentley. R. Grimsley's "The Character of Lorenzaccio," in *French Studies,* XI (January 1957), is an enlightening psychological study. A more general treatment can be found in A. Tilley's *Three French Dramatists* (1933).—S. S. S.

Love for Love (1695). A comedy by William CONGREVE. This play was first performed in April by Betterton's Company, which was seceding from the United Company and reopening with this play. Congreve's complicated plot has mainly to do with the ultimately successful efforts of Valentine, a spendthrift, to win the hand of Angelica and to keep his inheritance in spite of his father's attempt to make him sign it away to his sailor brother Ben. Other strands of the plot relate to the designs of Scandal on the wife of the old astrologer, Foresight, and of Tattle on Foresight's daughter, Prue, who is intended for Ben.

The comedy was most successful in its own day and has continued to be so, owing to the repartee and the array of amusing characters, including the witty lovers, Tattle the fop, the superstitious old Foresight, his young wife and her worldly sister Mrs. Frail, Miss Prue the awkward country girl, and the rough-and-ready sailor Ben.

Emmett L. Avery has edited this play with introduction and notes for the Regents Restoration Drama Series. It will also be found in the Mermaid Dramabook *William Congreve, Complete Plays* (1961), and in *The Complete Plays of William Congreve* (1967), Herbert Davis, ed.—E. W.

Love's Labour's Lost (c. 1593). A comedy by William SHAKESPEARE. *Love's Labour's Lost* is generally believed to have been written especially for private performance at some courtier's house in late 1593. The earliest extant text is the quarto of 1598, which furnished the copy for the 1623 First Folio. No specific sources for the plot are known. Incidents in the play, however, resemble historical events occurring in France during the sixteenth century, and the main characters bear names similar to those of contemporary French nobility. Veiled topical allusions to certain Elizabethan courtiers and literary figures have been detected.

The plot revolves around the attempt of Ferdinand, king of Navarre, to turn his court into a Platonic-style academy for three years. During this period Ferdinand and three courtiers—Longaville, Dumain, and Berowne—vow to abstain from any association with women. The foolishness of their oaths is quickly revealed when the princess of France, accompanied by three sprightly ladies-in-waiting, arrives on a diplomatic matter. The earnest wooing that ensues is halted upon news of the death of the princess's father. Although the ladies must leave Navarre immediately, they promise to accept their suitors as husbands after a twelve-month waiting period. In the minor plot Don Armado, a comical Spanish nobleman, woos the country lass Jaquenetta.

Love's Labour's Lost is reminiscent in its tone and diction of the artificial courtly comedies of John Lyly. The ornate language, the wordplays, the combats of wit, and the probable satire on Sir Walter Raleigh's scientific discussion groups (Shakespeare's "School of Night") are the stuff for courtly audiences. The only play of its type among the comedies, it shows Shakespeare's flexibility in his early experiments to find the form of comedy most suited to express his views on mankind. Despite flaws in plot structure and superficiality in characterization, a clear-cut theme emerges: the debunking of those who believe learning can be divorced from life.

DRAWING OF A SCENE FROM WILLIAM CONGREVE'S *Love for Love* (WALTER HAMPDEN MEMORIAL LIBRARY AT THE PLAYERS, NEW YORK)

An outstanding edition of *Love's Labour's Lost* is the New Arden Edition (5th ed., 1956), edited by Richard David.—W. G.

Love Suicides at Amijima, The (Shinju ten no Amijima, 1721). A Japanese play, generally considered the finest among the so-called domestic tragedies, by Japan's most celebrated playwright, CHIKAMATSU MONZAEMON. This play, first performed in the puppet theater at Osaka, represents the dramatist's work at its fullest maturity. It is a reworking of *The Love Suicides at Umeda* (1706) by one of Chikamatsu's competitors, Ki-no Kaion. Moreover, it follows the path of Chikamatsu's own first great popular success in his realistic manner, the much simpler and briefer *The Love Suicides at Sonesaki* (1703). The theme of the double suicide of lovers became a cliché in Japanese drama and even stimulated the practice in real life, so that the subject was censored for a time.

As in a large proportion of plays in the realistic, or SEWAMONO, style, the story concerns the fatal infatuation of a weak-willed hero who sacrifices his wife and family to love for a courtesan, whom he proposes to liberate from the house of pleasure where she is bound. The episodes are brilliantly naturalistic, the dialogue is fully convincing, the stage business brilliant and shrewdly adjusted to the puppet theater. The most admired act is the last, where in a stage journey, or MICHIYUKI, the two death-devoted lovers make their way to an isolated spot in the countryside to perform their final, ceremonious death scene, trusting that they will be united in the mystic para-

dise provided by the sect of Amidha Buddhism. In this scene, as in like scenes in other plays, the heroine is presented as more courageous and determined than the man. The last tears are rung from the highly susceptible audience. The play was much revised and frequently performed on the *kabuki* stage by live actors.—H. W. W.

Lower Depths, The (Na dne, 1902). A drama in four acts by MAXIM GORKY. A group of derelicts live in a dark, dank flophouse run by a brute called Kostylev. His wife, Vasilissa, is in love with the thief Vaska Pepel, one of the flophouse dwellers. She wants Vaska to kill her husband so that they can be together openly. But when Vaska does kill Kostylev, it is to save Vasilissa's younger sister Natasha, who is constantly mistreated by the couple. Among the other human wrecks in the flophouse are a former actor, now an alcoholic; Klesh, an unemployed locksmith; his dying wife; the Baron, a man ruined by gambling and women; an illiterate Tartar; Nastia, a prostitute; and Satin, who, unlike the others, tries to face the truth of what he has become. Into their midst comes Luka, an old hobo who invents reasons for the others to hope for something better or encourages the lies some of them are already telling themselves.

The play is built up to its climax by two devices —first, the rising hopes of the derelicts, encouraged by Luka, and second, the mounting violence of the villains, which bursts out in the beating of Natasha by her jealous sister and brother-in-law. The outcome of the explosion of pent-up anger spells the doom of Vaska Pepel, Natasha, and Vasilissa. Without forethought, Vaska kills Kostylev while trying to protect Natasha; the locksmith's wife dies; the Tartar is incapacitated by an accident; and Luka leaves, going south in search of a new religion. Those who remain spend much of the last act discussing Luka, his lies, and their hopes. Satin explains that Luka lied out of compassion because it was the only way he could help them. "Some people need lies," Satin says, but he himself wants to face the truth and be the master of his fate. He goes on to deliver a sermon on the purpose of life through a parable about a carpenter who advances his trade by twenty years. But then the Actor hangs himself and Satin, on hearing this, says: "Ah, he's spoiled our song, the fool!" For the audience, lulled into quiet hope after the earlier brutality, this cruel acceptance of the hopeless situation is a bitter ending.

Soviet scholars, in a 1960 edition of *The Lower Depths*, dwell at length on the industrial stagnation at the turn of the century, on the unemployment that filled the flophouses, on the rottenness of the tsarist regime that mass-produced human derelicts. But, whatever he thought, Gorky makes no comment on what hurled his cast of characters into the lower depths. The rottenness and inefficiency of the tsarist regime may well have been responsible for the unemployment in 1901, but the Baron, the Actor, and Satin are hardly its victims: they have all degenerated from personal causes.

Luka belongs to a long line of "wisdom-carriers" in Russian literature; he is a simple man who speaks a simple language but whose wisdom shines through every word and dispenses peace and comfort. Nevertheless, Luka does not necessarily speak for Gorky, who later (perhaps under pressure) expressed some second thoughts about the success of his characterization; some critics believe that Satin gives the rebuttal to Luka's philosophy of soothing lies. Gorky does not seem to reject Luka, however, but rather to present Satin's view as the next step, as an elaboration of Luka's ideas.

Although Gorky does not appear to see an answer for his flophouse derelicts, he does have one, albeit a rather vague one, for mankind at large: "A man who is his own master," Satin says, "who doesn't scrounge on anyone else—what would he need lies for? Lies are the religion of slaves and of their masters—and the god of the free man is truth." Man must live by the truth. He *is* the truth. He is born "to see things get better." "Everyone thinks he's living just for himself, but in truth he's here to make the world better," one character says. This rather woolly profession of faith in eventual improvement is the only assertion about the future in the play and it hardly seems sufficient to support the Soviet interpretation of it as a harbinger of the revolution, filled with "social content."

The Lower Depths has been translated by Andrew R. MacAndrew in *20th Century Russian Drama* (1963).—A. MACA.

Lucifer and the Lord (Le Diable et le Bon Dieu, also translated as **The Devil and the Good Lord,** 1951). A play by Jean Paul SARTRE. During the first half of *Lucifer and the Lord,* the protagonist, Goetz, is constantly deriding God. During the second half, he expresses religious aspiration, but this desire is impeded by men who do not reward holiness and by God who does not exist. Sartre's philosophy in this play redefines man's fate as something absurd.

The steady flow of language, filling four hours in performance, has all tones and modes: impiety, mockery, atheistic existentialism, the nothingness of man, the emptiness of heaven, the power of evil and its persistent logic, the impotence of the good and its ridiculousness. The play, an assembly of characters and arguments, is, in a sense, a vast, elaborately staged demonstration of Sartre's atheism. At the end, Goetz accepts a limited human morality. The conclusion for man would seem to be social, but the play is confusing in its philosophical implications as well as in its structural organization. The strongest part of the text is in the opening tableaus where Goetz appears as the incarnation of evil, as powerful as Lucifer and as convincing as Mephistopheles.

This play has been translated by Kitty Black under the title *The Devil and the Good Lord* (1960). —W. F.

Ludus Coventriae. See N-TOWN PLAYS.

Ludwig, Otto (1813–1865). German playwright and writer of fiction. Born in Thuringia, Ludwig spent a dismal, rather uneventful youth. After a brief interest in the study of music he turned his attention to the theater and began his intense devotion to the demands of serious drama.

Ludwig was never able, however, to achieve the success in his dramatic undertakings that was commensurate with his painstaking efforts and his bold ambitions, among the latter that he could compete with the forbidding stature of Friedrich Hebbel. In spite of quite a few youthful attempts, he was able to complete only two dramas of some stature: *Der Erbförster* (*The Hereditary Forester,* 1850), which Ludwig considered to be the sequel to Hebbel's *Maria Magdelena,* and *Die Makkabäer* (*The Maccabees,* 1854), in which Ludwig dared to treat the same complex historical-mythical material that had aroused the interest of Franz Grillparzer and Hebbel. Although both dramas were considered noteworthy for their psychological and scenic realism, they were flawed by Ludwig's basic inability as a dramatist to develop a sufficiently consequential and effective presentation of the thematic material.

If Ludwig's creative contributions to the German stage remain of minor significance, his theoretical contributions, that is, his reflections on the laws and techniques of the drama, which he published in the *Shakespeare Studien* (*Shakespeare Studies,* 1871), merit considerable attention. It is in fact true that Ludwig's critical powers seemed to have far outstripped his dramatic abilities. Unfortunately, he sought the correct way to serious drama by means of theory and lost the direction to creative drama. There is a further ironic note to Ludwig's literary activity in that he never recognized that his unique and considerable talent lay in the writing of fiction and not drama.

The Hereditary Forester and *Between Heaven and Hell* can be found in the anthology *The German Classics* (1913–1914), edited by K. Francke and W. G. Howard.—C. A. M.

Lyly, John (1554?–1606). English playwright and prose stylist. Lyly was the grandson of William Lyly, whose Latin grammar was the standard text used in English schools for three hundred years.

John's birth date is unknown, but he was probably born about 1554 in Canterbury, where his father held a minor position in the local cathedral. He attended Magdalen College, Oxford, receiving his B.A. in 1573 and his M.A. in 1575. He moved to London, where in 1578 he published *Euphues, the Anatomy of Wit*, a prose narrative distinguished by the highly ornate, elaborate style that has come to be known as euphuism. *Euphues* was an immediate and spectacular success and won its author a place in the service of the earl of Oxford, to whom Lyly dedicated his sequel, *Euphues and his England* (1580). Under the earl's auspices Lyly wrote two plays presented at court during the Christmas revels of 1583/84: these were *Campaspe* and *Sapho and Phao*. By 1588 his association with Oxford had ended, and he spent the remainder of his life in futile supplication for the post of master of the revels, a title that Queen Elizabeth promised to him but never delivered. During these years Lyly joined the horde of hangers-on at Elizabeth's court, precariously existing in a series of positions more honorific than remunerative. He died in 1606, the prize of courtly preferment eluding him to the end.

There are eight plays in the Lyly canon. The earliest of these is *Campaspe*, the story of Alexander the Great's unsuccessful wooing of his captive, Campaspe. His second play, *Sapho and Phao*, is little more than a dramatized debate between the opposing principles of love and chastity and concludes with an elaborate compliment to Elizabeth. The essentially medieval technique of the allegorized debate is further elaborated in Lyly's next two plays, *Endymion* (1588) and *Midas* (1589/90). All of these plays are dominated by a ruling figure whose virtues or vices serve to highlight Lyly's repeated theme—the nature of kingship and the embodiment of that abstraction in Elizabeth.

A somewhat different concern is evident in *Galathea* (c. 1588), a pastoral set in the English countryside. Here the moral allegorical aspect of the work is subordinated in an intricate artistic design. Lyly's other plays include *Love's Metamorphosis* (c. 1590); *The Woman in the Moon* (c. 1590), his only verse play; and *Mother Bombie* (c. 1590), a comedy of intrigue and the most atypical of Lyly's plays.

Lyly's chief distinction as a dramatist has traditionally been thought to be derived from his influence on later playwrights, notably Shakespeare. Quite apart from this positive influence, however, Lyly's work is distinguished in itself. Although its elaborate artificiality and formal elegance have not found favor with modern audiences, it is precisely these qualities, coupled with his intelligence and wit, that recommend his work as the product of the half-medieval Elizabethan sensibility.

The standard edition of *The Complete Works of John Lyly* (1902) is edited by R. W. Bond. An excellent, sensitive critical study is G. K. Hunter's *John Lyly* (1962).—E. Q.

Lyndsay, Sir David. See ANE PLEASANT SATYRE OF THE THRIE ESTAITIS.

Lysistrata (Lysistratē, 411 B.C.). A comedy by ARISTOPHANES. The women of Athens, exasperated and frustrated by the long-drawn-out war between Athens and Sparta, join with women from the other states of Greece to bring the war to an end. Led by the Athenian Lysistrata ("Disbander of Armies"), they finally resolve to refuse to sleep with their men until peace has been declared. The plan is put into effect, the older women seize the Acropolis, and the men are refused admission. The effects of this strategy on both sides soon become painfully apparent, but in spite of attempts by the less iron-willed of the women to go back on the agreement, the females turn out to be the stronger sex. The men capitulate, negotiations begin, and a normal life, both peaceful and sexual, is resumed.

Apart from the straightforward and explicit phallic imagery, the overriding tone of *Lysistrata* is one of desperation. Over and over again there are references to the "madness" that has engulfed Greece. This madness is seen as coming from the exclusively male domination of public life, so that it is left to women to bring sanity and common sense back into the conduct of affairs. The weapon they use—the erotic principle—is the age-old one by which women overpower men, and the comedy consistently plays on the idea that women are now on top—in politics as well as in bed. This idea is presented as posing a grave threat to Greek male self-esteem, and much of the action is devoted to restoring the proper balance of power. In the last scene, strikingly similar to the ending of Aeschylus' *Eumenides*, the ominous Chorus of old women who have captured the Acropolis are transformed from a band of "furies" into kindly givers of joy and plenty. Coincidentally with the composition of *Lysistrata*, the political life of Athens was reaching a point at which an antidemocratic coup was becoming possible, such was the chaos and pessimism aroused by the war. The coup did take place a few weeks after the performance of *Lysistrata*. But despite the coup and the play, the war went on.

Translations of the play are listed under Aristophanes.—K. C.

M

Macbeth (c. 1606). A tragedy by William SHAKE-SPEARE. Dr. Simon Forman, in his *Bocke of Plaies,* gives an account of his attendance at a performance of *The Tragedy of Macbeth* at the Globe in April 1611. This is the earliest record of production for the play. Evidence exists suggesting that it was acted at Hampton Court on August 7, 1606, during the visit of King Christian IV of Denmark to King James, and that it may have been especially written for a royal performance. Passages complimentary to King James have long been detected in the play, and its shortness may stem from James's known dislike for long plays. The text was first published in the 1623 First Folio. The Hecate scenes in III, v, and IV, i, are regarded as non-Shakespearean additions, with their songs interpolated from Thomas Middleton's *The Witch* (c. 1612). The principal source of *Macbeth* is Raphael Holinshed's *Chronicles of England, Scotland, and Ireland* (2nd ed. 1587).

The story deals with the ambition of Macbeth, thane of Glamis, to become king of Scotland. Macbeth is first seen as a valorous warrior who with Banquo, his co-general, has succeeded in turning back a Norwegian invasion and quelling a rebellion against King Duncan, his kinsman. On the way to join Duncan, the two generals encounter three witches, who state that Macbeth will become thane of Cawdor and then king and that Banquo will be a begetter of kings. Confirmation that Macbeth has been made thane of Cawdor soon arrives and touches off thoughts within him that he may achieve the crown also. Lady Macbeth, informed by letter of what had transpired, resolves that her husband indeed shall be king. When she learns that Duncan will spend the night at their castle, she determines that he must be murdered. Abetted by his wife, Macbeth stabs the king, framing Duncan's two grooms for the crime and killing them before they can be questioned. Fearing for their own lives, the king's two sons flee—Malcolm, the heir to the throne, to England and Donalbain to Ireland. Their flight brings suspicion on them, and thus Macbeth is proclaimed king. Fear of Banquo and of the prophecy that he would be "father to a line of kings" now seizes Macbeth, and he arranges to have Banquo and his son, Fleance, murdered. The scheme only partially succeeds, for Fleance escapes. Distraught over the news and haunted by the appearance of Banquo's ghost at a banquet, Macbeth seeks out the witches to learn more of his destiny. They warn Macbeth, in equivocating statements, against Macduff, the thane of Fife, tell him that he need fear no man of woman born, and state that he is safe until Birnam Wood advances to Dunsinane Hill. They also reaffirm that Banquo's descendants will rule Scotland. When Macbeth learns Macduff has fled to England, he orders his castle seized and his family killed. Macduff joins Malcolm, who has raised an army to topple Macbeth. Lady Macbeth, meanwhile, has gone mad with guilt, as the famous sleep-walking scene reveals, and she dies haunted by her role in Duncan's murder. The invading army, camouflaged by boughs from Birnam Wood, marches on Macbeth at Dunsinane Castle. In the battle Macduff and Macbeth meet on the field, and Macduff, who "was from his mother's womb untimely ripp'd," slays Macbeth. Malcolm is hailed as the new king.

Macbeth differs from the other great tragedies in that its protagonist is basically a good person, a valiant nobleman who, fired by ambition, consciously performs an evil deed and ultimately destroys himself through fear. He is married to a strong-willed woman who becomes a victim of her guilty conscience. The play is more than a character study of these two individuals, however. Shakespeare uses them to probe the nature of evil and the consequences of evil acts. In doing so, he abandons his usual multiple-plot structure. From the opening brief scene in which the witches speak against a background of thunder and lightning, the supernatural and natural worlds are firmly joined to the political and personal worlds of Scotland and Macbeth to show that evil—an unnatural force—cannot be self-contained. As Lady Macbeth's doctor says, "Unnatural deeds/Do breed unnatural troubles." And Macbeth's crime is an unnatural one. In killing Duncan Macbeth has committed regicide, murdered a kinsman, and violated the host-guest relationship. Thus, his crime becomes a violation of order and harmony. Shakespeare underscores the significance of the deed by establishing a reversal-of-values theme immediately in the first scene with the line "Fair is foul, and foul is fair." The physical setting (night dominates the play) and recurring images of blood, death, darkness, disease, and sleeplessness further comment on the thematic lines. The synthesis of plot, character, theme, and language makes *Macbeth* one of Shakespeare's most artistic and powerful plays.

An outstanding edition of *Macbeth* is the New Arden Edition (9th ed., 1962), edited by Kenneth Muir.—W. G.

Macedonia. See YUGOSLAVIA.

Machiavelli, Niccolò (1469–1527). Italian political theorist and playwright. Born of a noble Florentine family, Machiavelli entered the civil service of Florence in 1498, becoming a member of various diplomatic legations to foreign and Italian courts. In 1512, with the return of the Medici family to power,

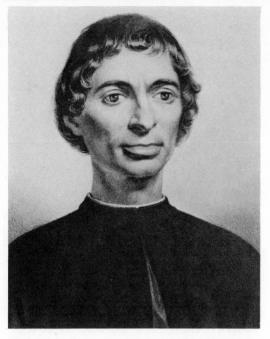

NICCOLÒ MACHIAVELLI (ITALIAN CULTURAL INSTITUTE)

he was forced to leave public life. Retiring to a nearby farm, he began to write about history and politics, his principal works being *Discorsi sopra la prima deca di Tito Livio* ("Discourses upon the First Decade of Titus Livy," 1512–1517); *Il Principe* (*The Prince,* 1513); and *Istorie Fiorentine* ("History of Florence," 1520–1526).

Machiavelli was already writing for the theater in 1504 when, according to the testimony of a relative, "he composed, in imitation of *Clouds* and other comedies of Aristophanes, a discussion in the form of comedy . . . and he entitled it *Le Maschera* ["The Maskers"]." Unfortunately, this play is lost. He then translated Terence's *Andria.* Inspired by various short stories of Boccaccio, he wrote in 1520 La MANDRAGOLA, the first great comic masterpiece in the Italian language. In 1525, perhaps having been commissioned by a rich Florentine, he wrote *Clizia,* using as his inspiration Plautus' *Casina.* In it, Machiavelli relates the story of the senile love of Nicomaco for the young and beautiful Clizia, and in this story it seems that he humorously outlines his own love for the beautiful actress Barbara Salutati. This supposition is confirmed by the name "Nicomaco," which appears to be compounded from the first syllables of the author's first and last names. *Clizia,* like *La Mandragola,* whose perfection and novelty it does not possess, is constructed along classical lines with five acts and observance of the classical unities. It is a form that accords with that posture of skepticism and detached amorality from which Machiavelli views his age.—L. L.

Ma Chih-yuan. See THE SORROWS OF HAN.

MacKaye, Percy (1875–1956). American playwright and poet. MacKaye, son of producer-playwright Steele MacKaye, was born in New York

City and grew up in the theater. Before he entered Harvard, he wrote plays and choral songs for his father's projected pageant-drama *Columbus.* After graduating from Harvard in 1897, he studied abroad and taught for four years in New York. His *Jeanne d'Arc,* a tragedy in blank verse, was produced in 1906. In addition he published poetry, essays, and a biography. His *Epoch; the Life of Steele MacKaye* was published in 1927. In 1942 he received the Shelley Memorial Prize for poetry and in 1948 the Academy of American Poets Fellowship. In 1949 his tetralogy *The Mystery of Hamlet, King of Denmark,* using characters in Shakespeare's play, was produced by the Pasadena Playhouse. Altogether, MacKaye had twenty-five plays produced on Broadway.

MacKaye's best serious play, *The Scarecrow* (1909), is a historical fantasy. His best comedy, *Anti-Matrimony* (1910), satirizes young people "emancipated" by the plays of Ibsen and Shaw. *This Fine-Pretty World* (1923) is a dialect folk-comedy of the Kentucky Mountains. Typical of his masques are *Caliban by the Yellow Sands,* in which Prospero regenerates his brutish slave, and *St. Louis* (1914), which dramatizes that city's history. A fondness for historical and folk materials, fantasy, and large-scale dramatic spectacles characterizes MacKaye's work.

The best source is Thomas H. Dickinson's *Playwrights of the New American Theatre* (1925). —B. H.

Madam Cassia (Ch'i Shuang Hui). A Chinese play, of uncertain date and authorship, but probably deriving from the Ming dynasty (1368–1644). *Madam Cassia* has enjoyed much popularity in its own country and has been translated into English twice. Representing the Chinese theater in its ripest stage of development, it realizes perhaps more fully than any Chinese play save *The West Chamber* the sophisticated Chinese sense of humor that produces the flower of high comedy. The spirit of this type of comedy is that of neither fantasy nor burlesque, satire nor tragedy, yet shares elements with all these. The play's story duplicates the plots of many earlier and more sober works where the torment and distress of a prisoner are gruesomely depicted and family devotion leads to heroic actions. These serious plays, such as *Snow in Midsummer,* are in no sense caricatured or lampooned. The mood is neither bitter nor pathetic. There is nothing here of the acidity found in *opéra bouffe.* The psychological basis of the playwriting is instead that of such prevailingly serious comedy as Molière's *Le Misanthrope.* Yet the temper is lighter and even more suave and urbane than that of Molière's masterpiece. The clue is the dramatist's amused presentation of characters who think of themselves more flatteringly than they are regarded by the playwright, by the audience, or even by other persons on the stage. For the greater comfort of their egos they have created an imaginary world that a discerning spectator will recognize as spurious or factitious. These are not illusions of sheer madness, such as attracted the great Scandinavian playwrights, Ibsen and Strindberg, but normal illusions of the normal man or woman, begetting follies, not vices, inducing smiles instead of anger.

The characters in the play are thoroughly conventional in Chinese playwriting, as are the incidents in the story. There is a timid wife, a bookish scholar, an august statesman, a cruel jailer, a slightly senile father, and an unmitigated villain. The tensions creating the plot involve relations between the members of a family and their in-laws. Long-separated members of the family are fortuitously united at the play's end. A brief scene occurs containing an intervention of a supernatural being. All this remains wholly familiar on the Chinese stage.

So, too, is the element of high comedy but here this reaches even for the Chinese drama a rare degree of refinement. The young scholar is more fatuous, conceited, and timorous than ever. His wife represents the Chinese conception of the illogical feminine paradox of modesty and boldness, frailty and strength, more conspicuously than ever. The old man is both more heroic and more farcical than ever. The very worst indignities and pains he suffers nobly, yet at last, when relieved from his most acute suffering, he becomes ridiculous. It appears that the prime values in Chinese life, such as sound scholarship and reverence for age, are themselves taken with a grain of salt. Hence the vigor and violence of popular melodrama are lightened by a finely civilized sense of humor.

With extraordinary sensitivity to its comic values the play has been translated by Yao Hsin-nung in *The T'ien Hsia Monthly*, Vol. I, 1935. It is competently rendered by A. C. Arlington and Harold Acton in *Famous Chinese Plays* (1963), first published in Peking in 1937.—H. W. W.

Madhusudan, Michael. See PAKISTAN: *Bengali drama.*

Madness of Heracles, The. See HERACLES.

Madwoman of Chaillot, The (La Folle de Chaillot, 1945). A play by Jean GIRAUDOUX. The tragic heroes and heroines created by Giraudoux are those who willfully separate themselves from mankind, who reject the order of the world and even the order of humanity. This principle of rejection is evident in the social satire *The Madwoman of Chaillot,* first performed in December 1945, soon after the playwright's death. The Madwoman, who represents the impoverished, hardworking people of Paris, leads a crusade against the financiers. The world in this play is evenly divided between the good and the wicked. It is an oversimplified, Manichean kind of world, but it reveals Giraudoux's social philosophy, his horror of usurpers and the vulgarity they spread in their act of usurpation. The corrupt world of finance that gathers at the Café Francis on the Place de l'Alma forms a kind of mafia organized to exploit the masses. In the play, however, the prevailing spirit in France of an awakening sensibility and responsibility, exemplified in the characters of Pierre and the Madwoman, is able to offset the spirit of greed.

The Madwoman of Chaillot has been translated by Maurice Valency in *Four Plays* (1958).—W. F.

Maeterlinck, Maurice (1862–1949). Belgian-born French playwright, essayist, and poet. Maeterlinck is remembered for his theory of "static," or mystical, "inner" drama and his early inspirational plays: simply constructed symbolical, pessimistic fantasies with medieval, romantic suggestiveness depicting man's spiritual loneliness and helpless fear of the occult forces of destiny. Maeterlinck's phenomenal debut in the European theater faded after he received the Nobel Prize for literature in 1911, and

MAURICE MAETERLINCK (BELGIAN INFORMATION SERVICE)

at his death he was virtually forgotten, for he had tried in vain to create great tragedy out of atmosphere alone. In believing that marionettes (or actors "spiritualized by distance") could express the silent language of the soul better than actors who spoke words, he was really bypassing life itself. Nevertheless, for a time August Strindberg, in his revolt against naturalism, worshipped and imitated Maeterlinck; the Moscow Art Theater produced three of his plays; his emphasis on "interior," repetitive, or unspoken dialogue—the inner drama of the emotions rather than outward, realistic action—influenced expressionist writers and playwrights as different as Leonid Andreyev, Anton Chekhov, and John Millington Synge; and he prepared the way for the tortured psychological dramas of Luigi Pirandello and Eugene O'Neill. Maeterlinck published more than twenty books and essays on literature, philosophy, and entomology, but his theory of static drama is mainly to be found in a chapter, "Le Tragique Quotidien," of *Le Trésor des humbles* (*The Treasure of the Humble,* 1896). His main point is that in drama, which should suggest the forces behind life, states of feeling should supplant physical action. (See SYMBOLISM.) Yet even his best stasis plays, *L'Intruse* and *L'Intérieur,* contain an element of conflict, and Maeterlinck told the American critic Barrett Clark that his theory of static drama was "worth what most literary theories are worth . . . almost nothing."

Born and educated in Ghent, Maeterlinck entered the circle of Parisian symbolists in 1886 but did not settle permanently in France until 1896, by which time he had formed with the talented singer and actress Georgette Leblanc a liaison that lasted until 1918. Most of the plays he wrote from 1896 to 1910 were vehicles for her acting. These plays and those that followed until his death (he married the actress

Renée Dahon in 1919) show an increasing conventionality and dependence upon the action of realistic events. The last plays also reveal a naïve, often sentimental and false philosophical optimism. During World War II he was forced to leave Europe and lived in New York City.

Maeterlinck's best work encompasses the period from 1889 to 1895. The poems in his first published work, *Serres chaudes* ("Hot Houses," 1889) echo Arthur Rimbaud's *Les Illuminations* in their hallucinatory disassociation of ideas. The wild mélange of blood, lust, tears, and terror that makes up the prose tragedy *La Princesse Maleine* (printed on a hand press in 1890; not performed) is morbidly Elizabethan, in the manner of John Webster and Cyril Tourneur. The extravagant praise given it by the drama critic Octave Mirbeau won Maeterlinck a prematurely high reputation. Nevertheless, the beginnings of the author's distinctive style are evident: shadowy, marionette-like characters, hysterical dialogue full of mystical suggestion and ominous pauses, action through mood pictures rather than logical or sequential pattern, and a fluid musical style composed of interior rhythms, assonance, and sonorous repetitions. The short masterpieces *L'Intruse* (*The Intruder*) and *Les Aveugles* (*The Blind,* both performed 1891) are mood studies of fear resulting from the mysterious intrusion of death in a gathering of individuals—death felt as a malignant, unseen force. In the same year the trifling *Les Sept Princesses* (*The Seven Princesses*) was published but not performed. *Pelléas et Mélisande,* Maeterlinck's most famous play, was performed in 1893, and, after many difficulties, Claude Debussy's opera version had a somewhat stormy première in 1902 because of its eerie, dreamlike atmosphere and amoral subject matter. But the play, reminiscent of the medieval tale of Paolo and Francesca and the Arthurian romance of Tristan and Isolde, is artistically conceived and poses a delicate question: should a naïve girl, tricked into an unhappy marriage, remain faithful if she finds her true lover? Should the social or the natural law be upheld? Maeterlinck offers no didactic answer, for the play creates a mood of poetic mystery. It has been called his most despairing play, but the compelling force is love, not death, as in the other early plays. Moreover, the play has several scenes of beauty and power, and the characters are more firmly conceived than usual. Maeterlinck's early period comes to a close with a grim trilogy of "little plays for marionettes," published in 1894: *Alladine et Palomides* (not performed), *L'Intérieur* (translated in England as *Home,* performed in Paris, 1895), and *La Mort de Tintagiles* (*The Death of Tintagiles,* performed 1906 or before). The first of these the author called a "decoction of Pelléas," and it enacts the same sadistic punishment of a young girl and her lover by a jealous older man. In *L'Intérieur,* one of Maeterlinck's two or three best plays, and exhibiting better than any the characteristics of static theater, we observe moving beyond a window the vaguely sketched figures of a happy family about to be informed of the drowning of a loved one. We casually overhear two strangers in a garden ready to break the news to the helpless victims of fate inside. Action is absent, but a feeling of ominous suspense persists. Destiny overwhelms happiness everywhere. In *La Mort de Tinta-*

giles, however, the puppet-like characters are offset by one vigorous individual. Although a boy king is murdered behind a huge immovable iron door by his evil grandmother, presented as an unseen impersonal force of destruction, the boy's sister, clawing at the door, suggests that the victims of fate are no longer passive. This play represents the turning point in Maeterlinck's pessimistic view.

In 1896 Maeterlinck began to write for Mlle. Leblanc more positive and optimistic plays. In *Aglavaine et Sélysette* (1896) a woman of determined character and mind steals the mismatched husband of Sélysette, a passive, fairy-tale heroine, who commits suicide. The play apparently signifies that man can adapt himself to the unaccountable workings of fate through strength of will, intelligence, and self-knowledge. In 1902 Mlle. Leblanc made a sensational appearance in *Monna Vanna,* directed by the famous Aurélien Marie Lugné-Poë, who had also produced *Pelléas.* The initial situation of a woman sacrificing her honor for her people suggests the biblical tale of Judith and Holofernes, but Monna Vanna comes to love her would-be seducer and abandons her husband. Mlle. Leblanc again triumphed in *Joyzelle* (1903), a pseudo-Freudian allegory of love that failed in Paris but was played to packed houses throughout Europe. Joyzelle, as the embodiment of pure and all-embracing love, forgives infidelity, resists jealousy, and even threatens to commit murder to justify her love for her beloved. As an adaptation of Shakespeare's *The Tempest,* the play is a rather silly parody. But Joyzelle herself is a more affirmative dream maiden than the heroines of Maeterlinck's earlier plays. *L'Oiseau bleu* (*The Bluebird,* performed Moscow, 1907; Paris, 1911) is Maeterlinck's most optimistic play. A fairy tale with allegorical significance, it is now played as a fantasy for children. (See CHILDREN'S DRAMA.) But it was very popular for more than three decades, when man's myopic quest for the elusive bluebird of happiness and love seemed more easily capable of fulfillment, and when the author's central theme that happiness is to be found at home seemed less trite than it does today.

After 1910 Maeterlinck wrote fourteen more plays, all showing a depletion of literary power. Among these are *Les Fiancailles* (*The Betrothal,* performed New York, 1918), *La Puissance des Morts* (*The Power of the Dead,* originally a film scenario, pub. 1926), and *La Princesse Isabelle* (written for Mme. Maeterlinck and performed in Paris, 1935).

Most of the plays and more important essays have been translated. *The Intruder* is in J. Gassner, *A Treasury of the Theatre* (1935). "The Tragical in Daily Life" and the "Preface" to the plays are in B. H. Clark, *Chief European Theories of the Drama* (1918, rev. ed. 1965). The most recent biography in English is W. D. Halls, *Maurice Maeterlinck: A Study of his Life and Thought* (1960). J. G. Huneker has a witty and perceptive section on Maeterlinck in *Iconoclasts* (1905). See Gassner's essay in *A Treasury of the Theatre* and E. Bentley's *The Playwright as Thinker* (1946) for good contemporary critical judgments.—S. S. S.

Maids, The (**Les Bonnes**, 1947). A tragedy by Jean GENET. In speaking of his first play, *The Maids,* Genet said it is "a tragedy of the confidants." The two confidants in this work are two maids who de-

votedly serve their mistress. Their life has been so reduced by this service and the silence imposed upon
them that the only way they feel they can exist independently and assert their own identity is by committing a crime. But the planned murder of their mistress turns against them, as Claire, pretending to be
madame, commits suicide by drinking the poison
intended for her mistress, and Solange imagines confessing as her murderer.

Genet found the subject matter for *The Maids* in
the accounts of the notorious crimes of the Papin
sisters. In the play each of the maids plays the part of
madame. At the beginning, Claire is pretending to be
madame and insults Solange, and we soon realize
that this game of pretense is played every evening.
The revolt of the maids against the order of the bourgeois world takes place only in their minds. By their
repetitive antics they almost reach the state of
schizophrenia, but it is clear that they wish to be enslaved, that they have no desire to change their state
of subservience.

The first production of *The Maids* was directed by
Louis Jouvet at the Athénée in 1947. More human
and more intense was the second production, seven
years later, at the Théâtre de la Huchette by Tania
Balachova. In this second production, the focus
shifted from the struggle between madame and the
two maids who want to assassinate her to the struggle
between the maids themselves.

The Maids has been translated by Bernard Frechtman (1954).—W. F.

Maid's Tragedy, The. See John FLETCHER.

Mairet, Jean (1604–1686). French playwright.
For a long time Jean Mairet's biography was partially obscure. He himself, wanting to appear precocious, tried to make everyone believe he was born in
1610. Born, in fact, in 1604 at Besançon, he went to
Paris to finish his studies, found high patronage
there, and became a friend of the poet Théophile de
Viau. He began his career in the theater in 1625 and
by 1634 was in the first rank of Parisian dramatists.
But eclipsed by Pierre Corneille, after having played
a rather dishonorable role in the dispute over *Le Cid*
(1637), Mairet left the stage in 1640. Europe at the
time was torn by the Thirty Years' War, and Mairet
was entrusted with several diplomatic missions in the
realm of Franco-Spanish relations. Then, under the
patronage of the king of Spain, he incurred suspicion
in France and was exiled in 1653 but pardoned in
1659, after the Peace of the Pyrenees. He then retired
to Besançon, where he lived peacefully.

Mairet's first plays were pastoral tragicomedies. In
1626 *Sylvie* was a huge success. In 1630, with *Silvanire*, he introduced classical rules into tragicomedy. In 1634, with *Sophonisbe*, he contributed
one of the first "regular" French classical tragedies.
After the *Le Cid* dispute, in which the theoreticians
championed verisimilitude and propriety in drama,
Mairet went back to a freer technique, rejecting the
unity of time as well as proprieties and mixing farce
with tragedy in plays like *Roland furieux* ("Orlando
Crazed," 1638) and *Athénais* (1638), whose action
takes nine days to unfold. His last tragicomedy,
Sidonie (1640), was a complete failure. In addition to
his tragedies and tragicomedies, Mairet wrote one
vigorous comedy: *Les Galanteries du Duc d'Ossone*
("The Duke of Ossone's Gallantries," 1632).

A SCENE FROM JEAN GENET'S *The Maids* (FRENCH
CULTURAL SERVICES)

Mairet has an important place in the history of
French classical theater. *Sylvie,* although of free
form, *Les Galanteries,* and *Sophonisbe* are still
among the best works of the time. They are lively and
peopled with coherent, true characters, imbued with
sensuality; *Sophonisbe,* moreover, shows a true sense
of the tragic in the portrait of two lovers inexorably
crushed by a political force to which they refuse to
yield. After 1634, *Sophonisbe* provoked a wave of
regular tragedies with simple and swift action and
throughout the seventeenth century remained a
model. Mairet's paradox was that he both initiated
French classicism, with his Preface to *Silvanire* and
with *Sophonisbe,* and repudiated his own principles,
returning to an outmoded technique.

For an analysis of *Sophonisbe,* see Jacques
Guicharnaud, "Beware of Happiness: Mairet's
Sophonisbe," *Yale French Studies,* No. 38 (1967).
—Ja. G.

Major Barbara (1905). A play by George Bernard SHAW. Lady Britomart Undershaft informs her
three children, Barbara, Sarah, and Stephen, that
their father, Andrew Undershaft, an immensely
wealthy munitions maker whom they have not seen
for twenty years, will visit them in a few moments.
When Undershaft arrives, he tells Barbara, who is a
major in the Salvation Army, that making guns is his
religion, that power is what counts whether it is used
to do good or evil. He agrees to come to her Salvation Army shelter and let her try to convert him, if
she will reciprocate and let him try to convert her at
his factory.

At the shelter, two habitual loafers discuss their
trick of confessing nonexistent sins in order to get a
free meal from the shelter. They are contrasted with
Peter Shirley, a jobless, middle-aged painter who still
has his pride, and Bill Walker, a lower-class ruffian
who is defiant enough to punch one of the Salvation

Army lasses in the eye. Undershaft arrives accompanied by Adolphus Cusins, a young professor of Greek who has joined the army for the sole purpose of marrying Barbara. Pleased by Cusins' lack of scruples, Undershaft admits that he is equally unscrupulous and intends to buy the army. Undershaft offers Barbara a large contribution. She refuses his "blood money" but is utterly demoralized when Mrs. Baines, the army commissioner, not only accepts money from Horace Bodger, the whisky king, but rejoices in Undershaft's offer to match the amount.

The next day, Andrew Undershaft tells his wife that traditionally the Undershaft firm has been left to a foundling rather than a descendant. He will not leave it to Stephen, who, he says, must become a politician or a journalist, since he is not intelligent enough to make good at a more difficult profession. At the munitions establishment, Undershaft's family and Cusins are amazed to see how clean and healthful it appears and how well the workers are cared for. Undershaft points out that there is only one sin in his religion: poverty. Only when men are rich and powerful can they be of any use to other men. Undershaft offers Cusins the manager's job when he learns, in a parody of Shakespearean recognition, that technically Cusins is a foundling, since his parents were never married according to English law. Cusins accepts. Barbara finally sees the truth in what her father has said. Meekness and humility are not the answer; one must fight the world with the weapons of the world.

In *Major Barbara* Shaw was attempting a synthesis of the two "undershafts," the two driving pistons of civilization, Barbara and Andrew, ideals and power, through Cusins, the self-confessed "collector of religions." It is Andrew Undershaft, rather than Cusins, however, who runs away with the play. He is one of Shaw's most remarkable supermen, who uses his vast power to create an ideal community for his workers. Presumably, enough such enlightened tycoons could reform the world, but history unfortunately reveals few, if any, men of Undershaft's caliber in his position. Yet, despite the unresolved, almost discursive verbosity of the third act, the play has been most successfully revived, and in 1941 was made with Shaw's cooperation into a classic British film.

Alick West's *George Bernard Shaw: A Good Man Fallen Among Fabians* (1950) concludes that the central weakness in Shaw's work lies in its un-Marxian failure to inspire the proletariat with a vision of their collective strength. As West explores this position in his chapter on *Major Barbara,* he often forgets his ideological stand and provides excellent dramatic criticism. Joseph Frank in *"Major Barbara: Shaw's Divine Comedy," PMLA,* LXXI (1956), suggests the universal implications of the play by seeing Act II as a Dantean Inferno and Purgatorio, with Act III as the promise of a Paradiso.—D. J. L.

Malade imaginaire, Le (The Imaginary Invalid, 1673). A comedy in prose, with music and dance, by MOLIÈRE. Argan, thinking that he is very ill, stuffs himself with medicine and surrounds himself with doctors and apothecaries. For his own well-being, he wants his daughter Angélique to marry a grotesque young doctor, Thomas Diafoirus, although she is in love with Cléante. Thanks to the maid Toinette's guile, however, he discovers his daughter's affection

ENGRAVING OF A SCENE FROM MOLIÈRE'S *Le Malade imaginaire* (THEATRE COLLECTION, NEW YORK PUBLIC LIBRARY AT LINCOLN CENTER)

for Cléante and allows her to marry him, while he is made his own doctor in an extremely farcical ceremonial ballet. A satirical caricature on the practice of medicine, *Le Malade imaginaire* is, above all, the portrait of a ridiculous egotist who lives in a world of illusion.

This play has been translated by John Wood in *The Misanthrope and Other Plays* (1959).—Ja. G.

Malagasy Republic. See AFRICA: *Malagasy Republic.*

Malawi. See AFRICA: *Malawi.*

Malcontent, The (1603). A tragicomic satire by John MARSTON. The play itself is preceded by an Induction that warns the audience against any attempt to discover hidden meanings in the work. According to the title page of the first edition of the play (1604), the Induction was written, not by Marston, but by John Webster.

The plot of the play centers on the activities of the deposed duke of Genoa, Giovanni Altofronto. Banished from Genoa by the usurper Pietro, Altofronto has returned to court disguised as Malevole, a cynical, malcontent jester. From this peripheral position he is able both to observe and manipulate the actions of his enemies. Thus, he is privy to the intrigue centering around Mendoza, a villainous cohort of Pietro. A Machiavellian *manqué,* Mendoza is continually weaving diabolical plots of murder in an effort to have himself established duke. His efforts are consistently frustrated by Malevole, who, however, leads him to believe that his wishes are being carried out. The play ends happily with a victory over villainy and the restoration of Malevole-Altofronto to his title.

The most striking characteristic of the play is its successful synthesis of widely divergent strains. It is both serious and comic, naïvely sentimental and radically satiric. What emerges is a sense of the median perspective of tragicomedy, a balance notably absent in Marston's more darkly satiric work. —E. Q.

Mali Republic. See AFRICA: *Mali Republic.*

Man and Superman (1905). A play by George Bernard SHAW. The play opens in the study of Roebuck Ramsden, an opinionated gentleman who still considers his Gladstonian liberalism "advanced." Sensitive young Octavius (Tavy) Robinson enters, in mourning for his late benefactor Mr. Whitefield, who, according to Ramsden, had hoped his daughter, Ann, would marry Tavy. Deeply in love with Ann, Tavy can scarcely believe this stroke of good fortune. His closest friend, Jack Tanner, detested by Ramsden for his outrageous liberalism, arrives to protest bitterly at having been named, along with Ramsden, coguardian for Ann Whitefield, whom Jack on the basis of lifelong acquaintance describes as utterly unscrupulous. Jack accuses Ann of scheming to marry Tavy, but it is clear to the audience, if not to him, that Jack himself is her real aim.

Acts II and IV are devoted to an exposition of how Ann, an embodiment of the Life-Force, manages to use all the other characters, including Jack himself, to win him as her spouse. "In the grip of the Life-Force," Jack goes down fighting, or at least talking, as he reluctantly admits that he loves Ann and really wants to marry her.

The third act is an extravaganza presentation of the play's theme. Since it is completely detachable from the play, it has almost always been omitted in production and has been successfully staged as a theatrical performance by itself. In Spain, home of Jack's legendary ancestor, Don Juan, Jack falls in with some whimsical bandits led by a romantic Jew called Mendoza. When all retire for the night, there follows an extraordinary dream sequence—the famous "Don Juan in Hell" scene—a long but profoundly interesting conversation in which Don Juan (Jack), Dona Ana (Ann), her father, the Commandant (Roebuck Ramsden), and the Devil (Mendoza) discuss the meaning of heaven and hell, love and marriage, and good and evil. Bored in hell, where he has only the same satisfactions he knew on earth, Don Juan dedicates himself to the Life-Force, which, operating through women, traps men into marriage. But all such unions tend ultimately toward producing a truly superior being ("creative evolution"). Knowing that her highest mission is to help create this superman, Dona Ana decides to follow Don Juan to heaven.

The struggle between Ann and Jack is an archetypal one. That Ann is the mother goddess seems clear enough. What Jack represents is more difficult to define. Jack at one point explains to Octavius that "Of all human struggles there is none so treacherous and remorseless as the struggle between the artist man and the mother woman." In his Preface Shaw observes that in such a struggle "the clash is sometimes tragic." *Man and Superman* remains a comedy because Jack—except in the "Don Juan in Hell Interlude"—submits to Ann's purpose and for the time at least fulfills a social responsibility rather than an individual ambition. If Jack were a genius, he would be able to ignore or assimilate Ann in his

greater drive; if he were Everyman, he would probably be assimilated in Ann's drive with little struggle. Shaw writes that "men of genius" are those selected by Nature to carry on the work of building up an intellectual consciousness of Nature's own instinctive purpose. Jack resists Woman and Nature until, as Shaw notes, "his resistance gathers her energy to a climax at which she dares to throw away her customary exploitations of the conventional affectionate and dutiful poses, and claims him by natural right for a purpose that far transcends their mortal personal purposes." That Jack has intelligence enough to know what it is to be a genius seems certain, at any rate, and through his struggles he provides the dramatic situation in which the conflict of man and woman can be given expression and out of which the superman may emerge.

Most critics probably would agree with St. John Ervine that *Man and Superman* is one of the greatest English comedies of the nineteenth century. That greatness rests in the characters and in the rhythm of their speech. We recognize Ann and Jack's basic situation, but their poise, their almost uncanny articulateness, and in many cases their acute self-evaluation make them more than human. At times the play seems like a huge chess game, but though the basic movements of the pieces are prescribed, they are capable of infinite variations and permutations. As Jack and Ann are moved by the Life-Force, they talk so incessantly, so wittily, so brilliantly about why they are moving or why they are not moving there that the physical movement itself seems unimportant except as a reflection of the tactical action of the mover.

Arthur H. Nethercot has devoted Chapters V and VI of his very useful *Men and Supermen* (1954) to a careful analysis of the Shavian male and female and of their conflicting purposes. D. MacCarthy's *Shaw* (1951), although no more than a collection of theatrical reviews, remains perhaps the best critical study of Shaw. His reviews of *Man and Superman* are memorable both for their dramatic awareness and philosophic depth.—D. J. L.

Mandragola, La (The Mandrake, 1520). A comedy by Niccolò MACHIAVELLI. Callimaco, enamored of the beautiful and virtuous Lucrezia, arranges to have himself introduced to her husband, the aged Nicia, as a doctor capable of curing her of what Nicia believes to be her sterility. Callimaco suggests as a remedy the mandrake potion, which, however, will have a fatal effect on the first man to lie with her afterward. To avoid dying, Nicia accepts Callimaco's suggestion to seize a passer-by by night and shut him up in a room with Lucrezia. Callimaco involves Fra Timoteo, Lucrezia's confessor, so that the friar, with his authority as a man of the Church, may overcome the scruples of the lady. When night comes, Callimaco naturally arranges to be the assaulted passerby. Thus, he is brought to the nuptial bed of Lucrezia who, overcome by the ardent passion of the young man, agrees to continue their affair.

La Mandragola, the first great comedy in the Italian language, is a perfect example of fusion between material rich in realistic situations, yet drawn from classical Latin models. Written in prose language of extraordinary realistic force and with characters who are masterfully delineated—especially the sordid

Fra Timoteo and the stumbling, stupid Nicia—the play is typical of Machiavelli's cynical and amoral pragmatism.—L. L.

Man of Mode, The (1676). A comedy by Sir George ETHEREGE. *The Man of Mode, or Sir Fopling Flutter* was first performed early in the year at the Dorset Garden Theatre.

Dorimant, whose character is modeled on the earl of Rochester, discards one mistress, Mrs. Loveit, has an affair with Bellinda, and eventually contracts marriage with the witty heiress Harriet. Much more important than the plot are the repartee and the comic view of polite society. The most amusing character is the affected would-be "man of mode" Sir Fopling Flutter. The brilliance of dialogue is surpassed only by that in Congreve's plays.

The Man of Mode has been edited by W. B. Carnochan with introduction and notes for the Regents Restoration Drama Series (1966).—E. W.

Marivaux, Pierre [Carlet de Chamblain] de (1688–1763). French playwright, novelist, and essayist. Born in Paris, Pierre de Marivaux spent his childhood and adolescence in the provinces, where his father held positions in various mints. In 1706 he wrote his first play. In 1710 he went to Paris, where he was made welcome by such fashionable writers as Fontenelle and La Motte, and began to frequent the literary and philosophical salons. Having lost all his money in 1720 with the failure of John Law's Mississippi scheme, he devoted himself entirely to literature as a livelihood. In addition to his plays, Marivaux's works include several novels, two of which are masterpieces: *La Vie de Marianne* (1731–1741) and *Le Paysan parvenu* (1735–1736). Starting in 1722, he wrote journals patterned after Joseph Addison's *Spectator,* and in 1742 he was elected to the Académie Française over Voltaire. His popularity declined toward the end of his life.

Marivaux had his plays performed, with varying success, by the Comédie Française and by the Italian players (who were driven out of Paris in 1697 but returned in 1716). The technique of the Italians, and particularly of the actress Silvia Benozzi, had considerable influence on his style. Indeed, the swift pace of Marivaux's dialogue corresponds to the vivaciousness of their acting. With the exception of one play in verse and one mediocre tragedy, Marivaux's dramatic works consist entirely of comedies of one, three, or five acts in prose. Some of them, such as *Les Petits Hommes* ("The Little Men," 1727) or *La Nouvelle Colonie* ("The New Colony," 1729), deal, in allegorical form, with philosophical—which at the time meant social—problems. But the subject of most (that is, about twenty) of his plays is the discovery and the effects of love. The most famous of these plays are *Arlequin poli par l'amour* ("Harlequin Refined by Love," 1720); *La Seconde Surprise de l'amour* ("The Second Surprise of Love," 1727); LE JEU DE L'AMOUR ET DU HASARD; *Les Fausses Confidences, 1737*); and *L'Epreuve* ("The Test," 1740).

"Marivaudage" is the term used to describe the very special spirit that pervades Marivaux's comedies. Pleasant young people fall in love with each other at first sight, but modesty, pride, and sometimes fear, bad faith, or ignorance keep them at first from acknowledging the feeling to themselves and

PIERRE DE MARIVAUX (FRENCH CULTURAL SERVICES)

then from declaring it to others. Nevertheless, the strength of their love, often encouraged by skillful servants, impels them to speak, and all the humor of the comedy is created by the multiple levels of their language, which is at once a mask, a weapon, and, ironically, a trap. Although mocked by Voltaire and other philosophes for too much subtlety, Marivaux's love comedies have been among the most popular with French audiences during the mid-twentieth century.

For detailed information on Marivaux and his plays, see Edward J. H. Greene, *Marivaux* (1965). In Kenneth N. McKee's *The Theatre of Marivaux* (1958), synopses are given of all the plays, with a few commentaries.—Ja. G.

Marlowe, Christopher (1564–1593). English playwright and poet. The son of a shoemaker, Marlowe attended the King's School in Canterbury and in 1581 went on to Corpus Christi College, Cambridge, on a scholarship established by Matthew Parker, archbishop of Canterbury. As a Parker scholar, Marlowe was required to study for the clergy, and the fact that he retained his scholarship for the full six-year period, taking his B.A. in 1584 and his M.A. in 1587, would indicate that the university authorities never ceased to regard him as a proper candidate for holy orders. Sometime after completing the requirements for the M.A. degree but before it was actually granted, Marlowe left the university for what appears to have been some kind of government service abroad, arousing suspicion that he had been converted to Roman Catholicism. That these suspicions were without foundation is made evident by an extant letter from the Queen's Privy Council to the Cambridge authorities praising Marlowe for his good service to his country and requesting that he be granted his degree.

From Cambridge, Marlowe went to London where he associated with such other Cambridge and Oxford graduates as Robert Greene, Thomas Nashe, and George Peele, who were engaged in writing for the burgeoning theater companies. Along with a few others, they are sometimes called the University Wits. Marlowe seems also to have made the friendship of Sir Walter Raleigh and a group of intellectuals associated with him, as well as of Thomas Walsingham, a cousin of Sir Francis Walsingham, who was Queen Elizabeth's secretary of state and chief of her secret service. We know little of Marlowe's relation with the theater companies, but it does not seem to have been a very active one, for his dramatic output was small. All of his plays were written in a period of about six years (1587–1593), as well as his narrative poem *Hero and Leander*, which he left unfinished at the time of his death and which was completed by George CHAPMAN. For a short time in 1591 Marlowe shared a room with the dramatist Thomas KYD, who was later to accuse him of atheism.

In 1589, along with the poet Thomas Watson, Marlowe was involved in a street brawl that resulted in the murder of William Bradley, the son of a London innkeeper. Marlowe was obliged to spend two weeks in Newgate prison before being pardoned by the queen. There were other difficulties with the law, culminating in a charge of atheism that was lodged against him in May 1593, largely on the testimony of Thomas Kyd. Before his trial could occur, however, Marlowe was murdered on May 30 by Ingram Frizer at a tavern in Deptford where the two men, along with Nicholas Skeres and Robert Poley, two rather unsavory characters, had been spending the day. We shall probably never know all the details of the affair, but Frizer was acquitted by the court for having acted in self-defense.

While at Cambridge, Marlowe translated the *Amores* of Ovid and the *Pharsalia* of Lucan, and it is possible that his career as a dramatist began at the university as well. *Dido Queen of Carthage*, almost certainly Marlowe's earliest play, was printed in 1594 with the statement that it had been performed by the Children of the Chapel Royal and with the names of Christopher Marlowe and Thomas Nashe as co-authors on its title page. It is now generally believed that Nashe had little to do with the play in the form in which it has come down to us, but it has been conjectured that he may have collaborated on an earlier version while the two were fellow students at Cambridge. *Dido* is based closely upon Virgil's *Aeneid*, with large sections being directly translated from the source. Aeneas is treated as a creature of destiny, the heroic instrument chosen by the gods to be the founder of Rome. Dido's love for him is part of the divine plan. In her death there is a suggestion of the human loss that must accompany the hero's steady march to greatness, an idea that Marlowe was to develop further in later plays.

In the summer and autumn of 1587 Marlowe wrote the two parts of *Tamburlaine*, which established his reputation as a dramatist. *Tamburlaine*'s influence was to dominate the English stage for at least a decade, giving rise to imitations that never succeeded in capturing the exoticism and the epic sweep of Marlowe's play. Based on the life of Tamburlaine, or Timur Khan (1336–1405), the Mongolian conqueror who had defeated the Turks at Ankara in 1402 and who thus unwittingly became the savior of Christian Europe, *Tamburlaine, Part I* was a heroic celebration of the victorious superman who rose by virtue of his own merits and in spite of the opposition of gods and men. Marlowe traces Tamburlaine's progress to supreme master of the Eastern world but at the same time suggests the human cost of the hero's triumphs—the cruel destruction of all who stood in his way, culminating in the slaughter of the innocent virgins of Damascus. The dominant tone of the play, however, is one of heroic eulogy. Marlowe seems to counter the basic Tudor doctrines of order and degree in a divinely controlled universe. His hero is the master of his own destiny, who succeeds by his own strength and will and who establishes his right to kingship by his own human power.

Most of the material for *Part II* is fictional, Marlowe having almost exhausted his historical sources in writing *Part I*. It is in *Part II* that the sense of loss begins to appear more markedly. Tamburlaine, incapable of defeat by any human force, must at last be defeated by death. The recognition that even the greatest of men must die qualifies the play's celebration of the heroic superman and adds to it a sense of futility and waste. This sense is supported by the subplot of Olympia's suicide, by Tamburlaine's killing of his own son, and by the death of Zenocrate, the ideal of earthly beauty whom the hero has worshipped but whom he cannot preserve.

None of Marlowe's remaining plays can be dated with certainty. *The Jew of Malta* and *The Massacre at Paris* are both concerned with the use of self-centered cunning to manipulate worldly affairs and other men. Both plays must have been written between 1588 and 1592, probably close to one another in time, and both have come down to us in very unsatisfactory texts. *The Jew of Malta*, which was not printed until 1633, shows signs of revision by another writer, possibly Thomas Heywood; *The Massacre at Paris* was printed in an undated octavo, so corrupt that it can give only the barest suggestion of the play that Marlowe actually wrote. An expanded version of one scene, known as the "Collier leaf" and now in the Folger Library, Washington, D.C., is almost certainly in Marlowe's own handwriting and gives some indication of what a perfect text of the play might resemble. Both plays are important in establishing the "Machiavel," the scheming villain who gloats over his own trickery, as a conventional stage stereotype.

The Jew of Malta traces the injuries done to Barabas the Jew, the revenge he visits upon his Christian enemies, and his final destruction by the excesses of his own villainy. Although he is somewhat of a superman in the initial scenes, he is a ludicrous and ignominious villain at the end. The play is so marked by grotesque comedy that critics have never been able to decide whether it was intended as a comedy or tragedy. One thing that can be said about it is that it depicts the defeat of self-interested policy and that if Barabas is evil, he is revealed as no more villainous than the Christians and Turks who oppose him. *The Massacre of Paris* is based upon the French civil wars that took place only a few years before the play was written. The central character is the historical figure

The Tragicall History
of the Life and Death
of Doctor FAVSTVS.

With new additions.

Written by Ch. Marlot,

TITLE PAGE OF THE 1628 EDITION
OF CHRISTOPHER MARLOWE'S
Doctor Faustus

the duke of Guise, another Machiavellian villain, who becomes more powerful as he perpetuates one political evil after another—including the St. Bartholomew's Day Massacre of 1572, which takes up much of the play—only to fall at the end like Barabas, revealed as a cuckold and a fool. On the basis of the text that we have, it is difficult to draw critical conclusions.

Marlowe's greatest achievements are *Edward II* and *Doctor Faustus,* both written in his final years. Most recent scholars are inclined to believe that *Faustus* was Marlowe's final play, possibly left unfinished at his death, for parts of the play as it has come down to us in the two unsatisfactory texts of 1604 and 1616 are the work of a collaborator, possibly Samuel ROWLEY. *Edward II* is preserved in a good text printed in 1594. Both plays are tragedies; *Edward II* is based on Raphael Holinshed's *Chronicles of England, Scotland and Ireland* (1587), and *Faustus* on an English translation, published in 1592, of the German *Historia von D. Johann Fausten,* published in Frankfurt in 1587 and describing the career of the semimythical German magician who had sold his soul to the devil. Although it is full of comic episodes, the German work is essentially a warning to sinners.

In *Edward II* the English history play is made a vehicle for tragedy. The personal decline and suffering of a man who is also a king are cast within a political context, and upon the model of this play William Shakespeare was to build in his own tragedy *Richard II.* Marlowe's play is carefully constructed to

reveal two parallel tragedies, that of Edward, who falls through his own weakness and his inability to exercise the royal power he has inherited, and that of Mortimer, who steadily declines in moral stature as he rises in political power, only to be struck down and destroyed when he has reached the top of Fortune's wheel. Marlowe holds these two situations in relation to one another. Edward, as he declines in power, acquires to some extent a new humility and self-understanding through suffering, thus gaining some audience sympathy; Mortimer, rising as Edward falls, is alienated from the audience as it witnesses the slow erosion of his humanity. *Edward II* differs from the great body of Elizabethan history plays, Shakespeare's in particular, because it does not mention the divine right of kings or the king's responsibility to God. A king's power in *Edward II* rests only upon his own ability to maintain it in spite of opposition. When he cannot assert his power, he loses all of the attributes of royalty. But at the same time, to exercise power to the limit, as Mortimer does, is to destroy oneself. The play is terribly pessimistic in its view both of the human condition and of the nature of political power.

Doctor Faustus is the only one of Marlowe's plays that has a specifically Christian setting and deals with theological issues, but the precise meaning of the play has been a subject of considerable debate. Some have seen it as a perfectly orthodox view of damnation in Christian terms, while others have seen it as a protest against Christianity's harsh limitation upon the normal aspirations of mankind. Whichever position is taken, it must be admitted that the play portrays the damnation of a human soul with greater tragic power than it had ever before been portrayed in drama, evoking terror, pity, and a sense of human loss that are the ingredients of tragedy.

The play's contrary values are clear: the belief in submitting to divine will versus the belief in man's own power to control nature. All we can say with certainty is that Marlowe's hero does not make the Christian choice and pays highly for his refusal to accept the deity. Although the damnation of Faustus is portrayed in conventional theological terms, to many readers the author seems to be celebrating his hero's tragic but heroic defiance. *Doctor Faustus* is a play that has had no real imitators in English drama; it is a unique achievement that must rank among the tragic masterpieces of all time.

Marlowe, perhaps more than any of his contemporary University Wits, may be said to have ushered in the great age of Elizabethan drama, pointing the various directions that others were to follow. His *Dido* is the first love tragedy in English; his *Tamburlaine* established a tradition of heroic drama that was to have many successors, culminating probably in Shakespeare's *Henry V;* his *Jew of Malta* helped to establish a stock character who continued to appear in various forms until the closing of the theaters; his *Edward II* not only brought the history play to maturity but also, with *Doctor Faustus,* marked the true beginning of English tragedy. Shakespeare, who was also born in 1564, had by 1593 written nothing comparable. Although Shakespeare was of a different mind and temperament from Marlowe, and the influence of Marlowe upon him has often been exaggerated, there can be no doubt that in many matters he followed the lead that Marlowe had established. Marlowe developed a distinctive kind of blank verse—sometimes called "the mighty line"—which helped establish blank verse as the basic poetic tool of English drama. He contributed to a store of poetic diction that was to be drawn on by dramatic poets —including most notably the early Shakespeare— for the next half-century.

Standard editions of Marlowe's works include the six-volume *The Works and Life of Christopher Marlowe* (1930–1933), edited by R. H. Case; *The Works of Christopher Marlowe* (1910), edited by C. F. Tucker Brooke; and *The Complete Plays of Christopher Marlowe* (1963), edited by Irving Ribner. The standard biography is John Bakeless, *The Tragicall History of Christopher Marlowe* (1942) in two volumes. Important critical studies include D. M. Bevington, *From Mankind to Marlowe* (1962); D. W. Cole, *Suffering and Evil in the Plays of Marlowe* (1962); U. M. Ellis-Fermor, *Christopher Marlowe* (1926); P. H. Kocher, *Christopher Marlowe: A Study of His Thought, Learning and Character* (1946); Harry Levin, *The Overreacher: A Study of Christopher Marlowe* (1952); J. B. Steane, *Marlowe: A Critical Study* (1964); and F. P. Wilson, *Marlowe and the Early Shakespeare* (1954).—I. R.

Marqués, René (1919–   ). Puerto Rican playwright, short-story writer, essayist, novelist, and film writer. Born and raised in Puerto Rico, Marqués received a degree in agronomy and worked for two years with the Department of Agriculture. Having become interested in literature, he went to Spain in 1946 to study at the University of Madrid. After returning to Puerto Rico, Marqués founded a little theater group in his native city of Arecibo. In 1948 he received a Rockefeller grant to study playwriting in New York and returned to San Juan in 1950 to write educational materials, including films, for the government. In 1951 Marqués helped found the Experimental Theater of the Ateneo in San Juan and was its director for three years. Having received a Guggenheim grant, he spent 1957 in New York writing his first novel, *La víspera del hombre* ("The Eve of Man," 1959).

Marqués' insular and agrarian background helps to explain in part his unyielding love of the land, a theme that appears frequently in his writings. His drama *La carreta* (*The Ox Cart,* 1953), for example, pleads for a return to the "land which gives life" as opposed to the false values of mechanized society, which can only degrade and destroy an individual and rob him of his dignity as a human being. *Los soles truncos* ("The Truncated Suns," 1958) is concerned with the increasingly difficult and perhaps ultimately impossible task of trying to preserve all that is beautiful and good in Puerto Rico's Spanish heritage from the onslaught of "foreign" contemporary values and ways of life.

Another theme that recurs in many of Marqués' works is that of political independence for his homeland. As a staunch believer in liberty on both personal and national levels, Marqués is an avowed exponent of political sovereignty for Puerto Rico. His writings were the first in Puerto Rico to make use of the revolutionary activities of the Nationalist movement as thematic material for stories and plays. Rarely, however, is this material used exclusively for propagandistic purposes. Almost always it is subordinated to the literary and artistic ends of the work itself. An exception to this is his one play in English, *Palm Sunday* (written 1949). It deals in a straightforward, realistic way with the armed suppression of a Nationalist demonstration in Ponce ordered by the American chief of police, and its effect on his Puerto Rican wife and their teen-aged son, who willingly sacrifices himself for the cause of independence. The characters are two-dimensional and not as well drawn as those in the later plays, and the action is melodramatic at times. However, in such plays as *La muerte no entrará en palacio* ("Death Shall Not Enter the Palace," written in 1956 but still unproduced) and *Un niño azul para esa sombra* ("A Blue Boy for That Shadow," 1960) Nationalist ideas and activities are skillfully combined with the most modern techniques of writing and staging to be used up until their appearance in Puerto Rican theater. *La casa sin reloj* ("The House Without a Clock," 1961) makes use of the Nationalist theme in a more humorous context, while the historical drama *Mariana o el alba* ("Mariana or the Dawn," 1965) couches the twentieth-century cry for independence from the United States in terms of an actual nineteenth-century abortive revolt against Spanish domination in Puerto Rico.

Also of basic importance in Marqués' theater is the theme of guilt. In a broad sense his plays can be taken as dramatic metaphors for what he sees as a national guilt complex and a desire for self-destruction on the part of his fellow countrymen, a desire stemming from their frustrating and ambiguous position in a political and spiritual no man's land between two cultures. This metaphor is perhaps most obviously developed in *El apartamiento* ("The Apartment," 1964), in which it is projected in the style of "theater of the absurd." This treatment is most fitting for what Marqués considers to be his island's absurd position in the world today.

Most of Marqués' plays have appeared in their original Spanish in separate editions or anthologies published in Puerto Rico and Mexico. His one play in English, *Palm Sunday,* has been mimeographed but not published.

Frank Dauster's "The Theater of René Marqués," *Symposium* (Spring 1964), skillfully analyzes and interprets several of Marqués' plays and gives particular emphasis to the themes of guilt and self-destruction that underlie much of Marqués' work. Charles R. Pilditch's *A Study of the Literary Works of René Marqués from 1948 to 1962* (1966), a doctoral dissertation, is an analysis of Marqués' theater, short stories, and novel. Pilditch has also translated *La carreta* (*The Ox Cart,* 1969).—C. R. P.

Marriage à la Mode (1672?).   A comedy by John DRYDEN. *Marriage à la Mode* was first acted by the King's Company either late in 1671 or early in 1672 at the Lincoln's Inn Fields Theatre. Of the two plots in the play, one is heroic, dealing with the love of Leonidas for Palmyra, the daughter of the usurping king of Sicily. At the end, discovering that he is the rightful prince, Leonidas wins the throne and Palmyra. Contrasted with the lofty ideals of the protagonists in this plot is the cynical and libertine behavior of the two couples in the comic plot. Rhodophil and Doralice are bored with each other after two years of marriage and begin affairs with

Melantha and Palamede, who are engaged to be married. After several complications the men make a pact "not to invade each other's property."

The comedy of the second plot is heightened by witty and licentious repartee and forms a satiric commentary on Restoration society. The character of Melantha, the affected social climber who lards her conversation with French phrases, contributes a great deal toward making this an unusually amusing play.

Alan S. Downer is editing this play with introduction and notes for the Regents Restoration Drama Series. It is available in the Mermaid Dramabook *John Dryden. Three Plays* (1957), George Saintsbury, ed.—E. W.

Marriage of Figaro, The (Le Mariage de Figaro, ou la folle journée, 1784). A comedy by Pierre Augustin Caron de BEAUMARCHAIS. Written in 1778, the play was not performed until 1784. Considerable irony accompanies the favorable reception given this play, which, with the help of Mozart's opera version, was to become the most popular French comedy of the eighteenth century. Conceived in an atmosphere of political freedom, during Beaumarchais's involvement in shipping arms to the American colonists in 1776, it was finished by 1778, three years after the success of his *Le Barbier de Seville* (*The Barber of Seville,* 1775). Thus, the *Marriage,* even more than its predecessor, became the center of political controversy, as Louis XVI sensed the play's threat to the old regime. Finally allowed to be performed six years later, it was applauded most by the aristocratic class, whose fall it perhaps unintentionally portended. Napoleon is said to have called it "the Revolution already in action," and there is no doubt that it helped to hasten the disintegration of the conventions of the old order. But this was the result, not of any deliberate revolutionary purpose on Beaumarchais's part, nor of any conscious artistic objective, but rather of his delight in his own allusive and irrepressible wit.

Figaro successfully defends his fiancée, Suzanne, from Count Almaviva's lustful designs, forces the count to forego the barbaric rite of enjoying the bride of his vassal on her wedding night, and obtains his approval of the wedding. The comic imbroglio involves, on the one hand, the count's frequent attempts to seduce Suzanne, and, on the other, Figaro's plans, aided by the countess, the count's page Chérubin, and Suzanne, to fool the count into thinking his wife is unfaithful and to expose his amorous advances. The deftly ingenious plot culminates in the count unwittingly making love to his own wife disguised as Suzanne, which triggers Figaro's jealousy and elicits his famous fifth-act soliloquy containing the lines, "Because you are a great lord you think you are a great genius. Nobility, wealth, honors, emoluments—it all makes a man so proud! What have you done to earn so many advantages?"

Figaro, Count Almaviva, and Countess Rosine continue to be dramatically consistent in this sequel to *Le Barbier de Seville.* But Suzanne and Chérubin are newly and happily conceived, especially the latter, who is a delightfully impertinent servant who mocks his master. In the eighteenth century, when Beaumarchais was the most polished composer of dramatic dialogue, the art of conversation hinged on diverse interests lucidly presented yet fused into a common situation. And the sustained excellence of Beaumarchais's dialogue has rarely been equaled, even by Molière. Possibly the heterogeneous language of the play is the one true herald of social revolution. Its idiomatic simplicity marks the subtle differences in speech between nobles, professional people, servants, and others of differing degrees of education.

Despite Figaro's being taken, by 1850, as the prototype of emancipated modern man, Professor Jacques Barzun has pointed out that the play's theme seems to concern the nature of love rather than social upheaval. Indeed, Figaro is much more than a mere prototype of anything; he is the descendant of a long comic tradition, that of the picaro, and also incorporates much of the dramatist's own individual, outspoken, and adventuresome personality.

The best English version is by Jacques Barzun in Robert Lowell and Jacques Barzun's *Phaedra and Figaro* (1961).—S. S. S.

Marston, John (1576–1634). English playwright. Marston, the son of a lawyer, was educated at Brasenose College, Oxford. Upon graduation in 1592 he attended the law school at Middle Temple but abandoned the pursuit of a legal career after the death of his father. His earliest published works were *The Metamorphosis of Pygmalion's Image* (1598) and *The Scourge of Villainy* (1598), two collections of searing, often scurrilous verse satires modeled on Juvenal.

Turning his satiric talents to the stage in 1599, he began to write plays for the newly formed Children of Paul's company. In collaboration with Thomas Dekker he produced *Satiromastix* (1601) and thereby precipitated the so-called WAR OF THE THEATERS, the famous theatrical quarrel between Marston and Ben Jonson. Marston's contributions to the war included his *Jack Drum's Entertainment* (1600), in which Brabant Senior is a satirical portrait of Jonson, and *What You Will* (1601), in which he ridiculed Jonson as Lampatho Doria, the hypocritical satirist. Jonson retorted in a series of plays, notably *The Poetaster* (1601), which portrayed Marston as Crispinus, a posturing poet with a pretentious vocabulary. Apparently the quarrel escalated into something more than a verbal duel. William Drummond reports that Jonson said "he had many quarrels with Marston, beat him and took his pistol from him, wrote his *Poetaster* upon him; the beginnings of them were, that Marston represented him on the stage." During this time Marston also wrote *Antonio and Mellida* (1600) and its sequel, *Antonio's Revenge* (1601), two bloody melodramas.

By 1603 the war with Jonson had been settled amicably. In 1604 Marston dedicated his best play, *The Malcontent,* to his former enemy and collaborated with him and George Chapman on a comedy, *Eastward Ho* (1605). THE MALCONTENT was one of the first plays Marston wrote for the Children of the Queen's Revels, the acting company with which he was to be associated until 1608, when he quit the stage. His dramatic career ended in that year when he was imprisoned on an unknown charge. Shortly thereafter he entered the church. An unfinished play, *The Insatiate Countess,* was later completed by William Barkstead (fl. 1607–1630). In 1616 Marston secured the living at Christchurch, Hampshire, which he retained until 1631.

Marston's is an extraordinary, although radically uneven, dramatic achievement. He contributed to the Jacobean drama an unparalleled intensity and an unvarnished honesty. Refusing to overlook the self-deception and hypocrisy that for him lay close to the heart of man's motives, Marston was one of the main contributors to the macabre and malevolent spirit that dominated the drama of the first decade of the seventeenth century.

In *The Malcontent* Marston ruthlessly satirizes the decadence and self-serving that characterized Renaissance court life. In *Antonio and Mellida* and its sequel, *Antonio's Revenge,* he charts the path of its youthful hero from innocence to the responsibilities of mature action in a darkened world.

The Dutch Courtesan (1605), a comedy whose thought and language are indebted to Montaigne, focuses on the need both to affirm and control men's natural, specifically sexual, impulses.

The Fawn (1606) and *Sophonisba* (c. 1605–1606) reveal the increasing compulsion with which Marston returns to the idea of sex as the source of evil. Finally, however, his disgust with his subject reached a pitch of intensity that undermined the dramatic structure. Thus, his plays frequently lapse into mere displays of invective. But Marston, for all his faults, was a writer with a powerful vision. Unable to articulate that vision in a finally realized dramatic form, he nevertheless brought to birth dramatic values that were adopted by greater dramatists, such as John Webster and Shakespeare.

The standard edition of Marston's plays is *The Plays of John Marston* (1939), edited by H. Harvey Wood. His poetry is available in *The Poems of John Marston* (1961), edited by Arnold Davenport. Anthony Caputi's *John Marston Satirist* (1961) provides a full critical treatment of the author.—E. Q.

Martyn, Edward (1859–1923). Irish novelist and playwright. Martyn was born in County Galway and educated at Christ Church, Oxford, which he left without taking a degree. His first published work was a satirical novel, *Morgante the Lesser* (1890). Some time after, he became interested in the drama and in 1899 formed, with William Butler Yeats, Lady Gregory, and George Moore, the Irish Literary Theatre, the nucleus from which developed the Abbey Theatre (see IRELAND). In 1901 he founded the Palestrina Choir, a musical society devoted to liturgical reform. The following year he quarreled with Yeats over the direction in which the Irish Literary Theatre was developing and abandoned both the theater and playwriting for the next decade. He returned to the theater in 1912 when he began writing plays for the Independent Theatre Company, an organization devoted to bringing contemporary drama of Europe to the Irish public.

Martyn has been called "the Irish Ibsen." Like his younger contemporary James Joyce, he was a devoted student of the Norwegian playwright and an ardent publicist of Ibsenism. The Ibsenite influence is evident in his first play, *The Tale of a Town* (1899), a satirical comedy exposing the impotence and divisiveness of political life in rural Ireland. Before its first production, the play was revised by George Moore and presented in 1900 under the title *The Bending of the Bough. The Heather Field* (1899) was

the first of Martyn's plays to be produced and is probably his finest work. It tells the story of Cardan Tyrrell, obsessed with the romantic dream of reclaiming a heather field submerged under water. Venturing everything—his wealth, his family, and finally his sanity—Tyrrell is defeated by the shattering of his dream. He emerges from defeat, however, with undiminished nobility of spirit. The theme of uncompromising idealism is developed even further in Martyn's next play, *Maeve* (1900). This play portrays a girl whose vision of a Celtic fairyland becomes so real as to absorb, and finally claim, her life. *Maeve* had a special significance for its original audience, who saw it as an allegory of the Irish people, hypnotized by a romantic past and laboring under the tyranny of the present. These two works mark Martyn's major achievement in the theater. His later plays were less ambitious and less worthy of note. The best of them is *The Dream Physician* (1914), a satirical comedy.

Martyn's contribution to the Irish theater rests primarily on his roles as a founder and the principal financial supporter of the Irish Literary Theatre. Nevertheless he has also earned a secure if minor place as a dramatist on the basis of *The Heather Field* and *Maeve.*—E. Q.

Mary Stuart (Maria Stuart, 1800). A tragedy by Friedrich von SCHILLER. *Mary Stuart,* in five acts and blank verse, is written in Schiller's classical vein. It treats the conflict between Elizabeth I and Mary Queen of Scots while the latter is in England awaiting execution for her crimes. In Schiller's version, though Elizabeth wants Mary out of the way, she is unable to make the final decision commanding her death and, in the end, contrives to make it seem as though a hasty official is responsible for Mary's execution. The play is impressive for its array of finely contrasted characters, particularly Mary, warm and loving, and Elizabeth, intriguing and power-seeking. The theme of freeing the soul through suffering is explored in Mary's tragic acceptance of her fate and her consequent moral ascension.

Maschera e il volto, La (The Mask and the Face, 1916). A comedy by Luigi Chiarelli (1884–1947). Paolo Grazia discovers that his wife, Sabina, has been unfaithful to him. His impulse is to pardon her, but because he had once publicly declared to his friends that a man who has been deceived has no recourse but to kill his wife, he forces Sabina to disappear forever, thus avoiding dishonor and ridicule. Paolo is then arrested and tried for the murder of his wife but is absolved, largely through the passionate defense of his wife's lover. Sabina then returns to Paolo to live penitently with him, but now he too must flee with her, this time to avoid being arrested for having simulated a crime.

Chiarelli's comedy discusses the paradoxical conventions that rule society, a world in which life assumes a mask that is ultimately universally accepted and tolerated as if it were the true face of reality. To this new reality human feelings, as well as the rationale of social life itself, are sacrificed. *La Maschere e il volto* inaugurated a genre that in Italy enjoyed a wide, if temporary, vogue—the "grotesque." In a certain sense, it thus prepared the climate for the much more profound paradoxes of Pirandello.—L. L.

masque. A form of private theatrical entertainment that flourished in Renaissance Italy and that was avidly adopted by the aristocracy of France and England in the sixteenth and seventeenth centuries. Although the origins are to some extent obscure, the masque is clearly a sophistication of seasonal folk customs dating back to pre-Christian times. In contrast to the rowdyism of the carnival and the high jinks of English mummery, the masque developed into an artistic medium. It often combined poetry, music, the dance, elegant costumes, and elaborate stage machinery with an allegorical or mythological theme providing unity to the entire performance. Characterized by spectacular machinery, such as castles and ships mounted on wheels, the masque nevertheless eventually became a genre of literary distinction in the hands of Ben Jonson. The English masque reached the height of its development in the court of James I with the collaboration of Jonson and Inigo Jones, the celebrated stage designer and architect. The masque, despite its limitations as an artistic vehicle, has influenced the development of the opera, the ballet, and the modern stage.

Paradoxically, the court masque, the sophisticated entertainment of Renaissance celebrities and royal courts throughout Europe, is even more primitive in its origins than the modern drama. It is an outgrowth of agricultural festivals and fertility rites that go back to the dawn of Western civilization. Primitive peoples almost universally celebrate the arrival of spring, the harvest time, and the winter solstice with some ritualistic dance. In addition to celebrating critical periods in the cycle of the year, primitive religions celebrate rites of passage in the life of the individual, such as puberty, betrothal, marriage, and death. The court masque, as a direct descendant of these ancient traditions, was performed on days related to seasonal festivals, such as May Day and the Twelfth Night of Christmas, and at banquets celebrating royal betrothals and weddings.

The essence of the masque has always been the arrival of a group of disguised and costumed individuals at a banquet or other private festival to perform a dance or to offer a gift to the guest of honor. Henry VIII (1509–1547), who wanted the English court to share in the lavish entertainments and social customs of Renaissance Italy, introduced a form of the masque to England on the Twelfth Night of 1512. According to Edward Hall, "On the daie of the Epiphanie at night, the kyng with ix. other wer disguised, after the maner of Italie, called a maske, a thyng not seen afore in Englande . . . ." When King Henry and his masquers asked ladies of the court to dance, some of them refused, apparently scandalized. The first English masque appears to have been an import of a notorious social custom fashionable in Modena and Ferrara and not the theatrical entertainment associated with Florence and Lorenzo de' Medici. The ladies who refused to dance with the king's masquers were probably aware that the custom called for licentious wit and gallantry.

It is not at all surprising that the masque, whether in the form of a dubious social custom or in the form of genteel entertainment, should have originated in Italy, for Italy was the *axis mundi* of the world of art, fashion, and pageantry during the Renaissance and the home of ancient folk festivals like the January Kalends and the Saturnalia. In May and during the carnival season preceding Lent, Italian cities swarmed with citizens disguised as royalty and courtiers. These revels, particularly in Florence, became crude parodies or degenerations of the traditional seasonal folk customs. Lorenzo de' Medici, with the help of artists and poets, adopted these crude displays to the needs of sophisticated and polite society. Lorenzo believed that each entertainment should have a definite theme and should be accompanied by songs explaining the meaning of various costumes and the symbolism of the performance.

The history of the masque can be said to have begun with efforts of the fifteenth-century Italian artist Cecca, who invented fanciful devices for the processions and parades on St. John's Day and other public festivals of Florence. In addition to improving these pageants, Cecca supervised the arrangements for private celebrations sponsored by guilds or by gentlemen in their own homes. The evolution of the banquet and its attendant entertainment throughout the fifteenth century is crucial to the development of the masque proper. Contemporary diarists, in their colorful descriptions of court banquets, depict the gradual development of these entertainments from the simple and traditional morris dance to elaborate performances requiring the creative efforts of poets, painters, musicians, dancers, and choreographers.

In 1473 Cardinal Pietro Riario, a nephew of the pope, held an elaborate banquet in the carnival season at Rome. After dinner the guests were treated to a theatrical entertainment, which included a mock battle between Christians and Turks, the conversion of a captured troop of Turks, who expressed their devotion to Christ, the pope, and Cardinal Riario in song, and finally a triumph through the city of Rome. At another banquet in the same year honoring Leonora of Aragon, Riario's guests were entertained by dancers in the guise of eight famous pairs of lovers from classical antiquity.

The most celebrated social event of the age, the marriage of Lucrezia Borgia to Alfonso, eldest son of Duke Ercole of Ferrara, inspired a banquet given by the pope featuring masked dancing as entertainment, with Caesar Borgia himself taking part, and an allegorical representation of the alliance between Rome and Ferrara. Not to be outdone by the pope, Duke Ercole arranged nightly entertainments when the couple arrived in Ferrara, one of which included a dance of savages for a beautiful woman. The wild men were interrupted by the appearance of the god of love, accompanied by musicians. When the god set the maiden free, the guests discovered a large globe that split in half and began to give forth strains of music. Finally, twelve Swiss, armed and dressed in their national colors, executed a sword dance.

In addition to formal banquet entertainment, Duke Ercole took part in another form of masquerading that had developed in his native city, the crashing of supper parties during carnival time to dance with the guests, the very custom that Henry VIII attempted to introduce to his court on the Twelfth Night of 1512.

The opposition to the masque on the part of the ladies of Henry VIII's court vanished almost overnight. The Tudor masque, however, apparently remained a fig-leafed version of the Continental custom. The king and his fellow masquers only pretended to be uninvited gate-crashers. This simple form of masquerading lasted at least until 1532, when

Henry entertained the French king at Calais in much the same manner as he had his own court two decades before. Gradually, however, uniform masquing costumes were to disappear, and the masque itself was to specialize in elaborate settings, rehearsed dances, and its characteristic dramatic representation.

Elizabeth (1558–1603), despite her efforts at fiscal responsibility, enjoyed lavish and expensive court entertainments as much as had her father. Early in her reign there were productions of masques representing various trades and professions, such as fishermen, sailors, farm girls, and the like—a form of entertainment closely resembling the first production of Lorenzo de' Medici, which had been a masque of sweetmeat vendors. A regular feature of the Elizabethan masque was a spoken introduction given by a "presenter." The development of dramatic masques is due partially to the expansion of the role of the presenter and partially to the absorption of characteristics of court plays, interludes, and debates.

The English queen's progresses through the provinces occasioned shows and festivities that contributed to the development of the court masque. In August 1578, for example, at Norwich "there was an excellent princely maske brought before hir after supper, by Mayster Goldingham, in the Privie Chamber; it was of gods and goddesses, both strangely and richly apparelled," according to a contemporary account. This entertainment included a procession of Roman deities, torchbearers, and musicians. The deities, in turn, made complimentary speeches to Elizabeth and offered her a gift. Thomas Churchyard was among the poets who wrote for the occasion.

At Shrovetide of 1594 some gentlemen of Gray's Inn presented the masque *Proteus and the Adamantine Rock* at Elizabeth's court. According to Enid Welsford, this performance was a landmark in the development of the English masque, since it illustrates, for the first time, the norm of the masque developed by Ben Jonson and his fellows. "Later masques were more elaborate," Miss Welsford suggests, "but with the exception of the antimasque all the elements are here: the introductory song and dialogue, the entry of the masquers, the masque dances, the revels, the final song and dialogue recalling the masquers to the scene and concluding the performance, and finally the motiving of the whole by a slight story and dramatic action." In *Proteus* the introductory speeches unify the performance. The masquers appear in a machine, dance by themselves and then with the guests, and, finally, exit in their machine.

Up to this point the English masque had developed in a haphazard manner. The term was applied to practices as varied as disguised gentlemen asking ladies to dance at a court banquet and the presentation of gifts to the monarch during a trip through the countryside. Related, as it was, to pan-European folk customs, to mummery, and to public, religious, and private pageants in France and Italy, the nebulous form of the English court masque took shape in the hands of Ben Jonson during the reign of James I (1603–1625). With Jonson in charge, the court masque became a unified theatrical performance, with poet, architect, and musician working in harmony.

Under the patronage of two successive Stuart queens, Anne of Denmark (wife of James I) and Henrietta Maria of France (wife of Charles I), the English court rivaled Florence and Paris as centers of elaborate entertainment. Ultimately, however, their munificence was to prove a mixed blessing, since it led to an emphasis on elaborate stage machinery and grandiose visual effects that destroyed the dramatic unity of the Jonsonian masque. When Jonson lost his position as chief masque writer to the court because of the enmity of his rival and colleague, Inigo Jones, the English masque began to decline as a serious form of art.

In 1603 Ben Jonson began his career as poet of the revels when he wrote *Satyr* to entertain Sir Robert Spenser's royal guests, Queen Anne and Prince Henry. *Satyr* is a charming pastoral that features Queen Mab and the appealing fairy lore associated with Shakespeare's *A Midsummer Night's Dream*. Despite this early success, Jonson did not write a masque for the court until the Twelfth Night of 1605, a date doubly significant because it also marks the beginning of the collaboration between Jonson and Inigo Jones.

Inigo Jones had traveled to Italy where he was influenced by the architecture of Andrea Palladio and the stage devices of Sebastiano Serlio, a pupil of Baldassare Peruzzi. He returned to England glowing with enthusiasm for neoclassical architecture and staging. To Jones, therefore, the masque was primarily a vehicle for spectacular display. To Jonson, however, the masque was essentially a dramatic poem based upon sound classical scholarship. Jonson emphasized dramatic unity and scholarly accuracy in regard to mythological elements. The quarrel that developed between these self-confident and irascible artists seems to have been inevitable. At the time of their first collaboration, the Twelfth Night of 1605, Jonson, the most prominent man of letters of his age, was clearly the senior partner.

Since Queen Anne let it be known that she and her fellow masquers wished to appear disguised as Africans, Ben Jonson had to account for the sudden appearance of a bevy of black women at the English court. Jonson's poetic justification for their appearance was that the daughters of the river Niger, in despair because they had learned that nymphs living in other parts of the world were more beautiful than they, had been traveling, in obedience to a vision, in search of a cure for their blackness. For the *Masque of Blackness* Jones eliminated the system of dispersing scenic elements throughout the hall by concentrating his scenery on a raised stage viewed in perspective. Upon the stage he devised an artificial sea and a pageant upon which the masquers along with mermen and sea monsters were revealed when the curtain was drawn. According to Enid Welsford, the *Masque of Blackness* was indebted to the Florentine tournament of 1579, which celebrated the wedding of Francesco de' Medici to Bianca Cappello.

The *Masque of Queens Celebrated from the House of Fame,* written by Jonson and staged by Jones for the Twelfth Night of 1609, was a turning point in the development of the masque. A product of their fifth collaboration, this masque—in which the queen herself was to appear—included for the first time an ANTIMASQUE that functioned as a integral part of the performance. The antimasque (variant forms of the term include anticmasque and antemasque) as conceived by Jonson was a grotesque or comic foil to the serious dramatic action that followed. Although it provided contrast, Jonson insisted that the antimasque remain strictly relevant to the entire performance. In the *Masque of Queens,* for instance, the principal action involves Perseus, representing heroic virtue, descending to describe the masquers, twelve great queens of antiquity; the antimasque, by way of contrast, features eleven witches, representing vices, summoned into hell by Hecate.

From 1609 to 1617 Jonson produced a number of masques that maintained the norm established by the *Masque of Queens.* During this time, however, masques written by rival poets like Samuel Daniel and Thomas Campion in collaboration with Inigo Jones reveal tendencies that ultimately undermined the masque as a vehicle of dramatic art. These tendencies include the subservience of literary content to spectacle and the introduction of antimasques unrelated to the theme. Though modern commentators on the masque regret the waning of Jonson's influence, the contemporary audience clearly preferred Inigo Jones's stagecraft and his submission to French and Italian influences. Even Jonson himself eventually gave way before popular demand for multiple grotesque dances in his *Vision of Delight,* which was presented to the court in 1617.

In a recent study Stephen Orgel concludes that *Neptune's Triumph for the Returne of Albion* (1624) is the most successful of the masques that Jonson wrote during the reign of James I. The antimasque of *Neptune's Triumph* is provided by a comical cook and it is organically related to the main masque prepared by a poet. The rivalry between the cook and the poet as expressed in the metaphorical dishes they serve the court is a witty and complex affair and a brilliant critique of the masque as an art form.

Jacobean masques by Thomas Middleton, a poet who had his hand in the preparation of many pageants and public revels of his day, often merely celebrated symbolically the holiday that occasioned them or in general portrayed the succession of night and day or the seasons of the year. Middleton, as well, adapted the masque to the requirements of the theater and therefore contributed to the increasing vagueness of the term masque itself. The term was loosely used also to describe any sort of play or entertainment performed privately. Milton's *Comus,* though described as a masque by its author, is not properly a masque in the traditional sense.

According to Enid Welsford, however, entertainments and masque-like plays, such as James Shirley's *Honoria and Mammon* and Milton's *Comus* as well as a few old-fashioned masques such as Thomas Nabbes's *The Spring's Glory,* remained generally true "to the style of the earlier English Renaissance, at a time when the court masque was being developed in a very different direction and was absorbing the worst characteristics of foreign revels."

With the accession of Charles I (1625–1649) and Henrietta Maria, the masque became even more significant as a form of social festivity. The king himself, unlike the aloof James I, often played the role of chief masquer. With Jonson in eclipse, Inigo Jones became the dominant hand in the preparation of court masques. The taste of the queen and the court combined with the dominance of Jones over collaborators like Aurelian Townshend and William Davenant to produce masques that were merely excuses for ingenious scene changes and a variety of unrelated dances. Ironically, as the royal entertainments grew more chaotic artistically, the nation itself was heading for the chaos of the Puritan revolution.

For the Twelfth Night, 1638, Inigo Jones and William Davenant prepared a masque to be presented by the king at Whitehall: *Britannia Triumphans.* One of the forces over which Britain was apparently to triumph is Puritanism. In this masque an allegorical character, Action, complains of men

> such as impute
> A tyrannous intent to heavenly powers,
> And that their tyranny alone did point
> At men, as if the fawn and kid were made
> To frisk and caper out their time, and it
> Were sin in us to dance.

The storm that was brewing had its effect even on the court, however, for Lady Carnarvon refused to take part in a masque if it were to take place on Sunday. The last masque performed before the outbreak of the Puritan revolution, *Salmacida Spolia* (1640), includes a violent storm scene in which Fury "invoked evil spirits to bring discord throughout England."

The history of the masque comes to an abrupt halt with the outbreak of the revolution. With the monarchy overthrown, the social conditions that supported court entertainments disappeared, and the few masques performed thereafter were anachronistic. Enid Welsford speculates that the decline of the masque during the reign of Charles I cannot be attributed to the influence of Inigo Jones alone but may be related to "a general failure of inspiration in the nation as a whole." In any event, what had been a golden world of imaginatively realized and relevant ideals in the Jacobean age gave way to courtly compliments, extravagance, and pomposity as the spirit of the dance itself vanished from the Caroline masque.

Source materials for the study of English court festivals are available in J. Nichols' *The Progresses, and Public Processions, of Queen Elizabeth,* four vols. (1788–1821) and his *The Progresses, Processions, and Magnificent Festivities of King James I,* four vols. (1828). Modern scholarly studies of the masque include M. Sullivan's *Court Masques of James I* (1913), J. R. Allardyce Nicoll's *Stuart Masques and the Renaissance Stage* (1937), and Stephen Orgel's *The Jonsonian Masque* (1964). The most comprehensive treatment of the subject is Enid Welsford's *The Court Masque: A Study in the Relationship between Poetry and the Revels* (1927).—J. F. L.

Massinger, Philip (1583–1640). English playwright. Massinger was born near Wilton, the famous estate of the earl of Pembroke, in whose service Massinger's father was employed. The dramatist was educated at St. Alban Hall, Oxford, which he left at the time of his father's death in 1606. Massinger may have entered the theater as an actor, but by 1613 he had already begun his career as a playwright. Most of the plays written in the early phase of his career were collaborations, chiefly with John FLETCHER. The extent of the Massinger-Fletcher collaboration is not known, but it is estimated that Massinger had a hand, either as collaborator or reviser, in at least nineteen of the plays that are listed as part of the Beaumont and Fletcher canon. With the death of Fletcher in 1625, Massinger succeeded him as the chief playwright of the King's Men. A prolific and successful playwright, he continued in that post until his death in 1640. His energy and imagination are reflected in the almost sixty plays of which he was the sole or part author.

Among the plays produced during Massinger's early period as a collaborator are *The Fatal Dowry* (1616–1619), written with the actor-dramatist Nathan Field, and *The Virgin Martyr* (1620), written with Thomas Dekker. The latter is based on the early Christian legend of St. Dorothea and reflects Massinger's interest, evident in other plays as well, in Catholicism.

Massinger's collaboration with Fletcher spanned the years from 1616 to Fletcher's death in 1625. Written during this period was *Sir John Van Olden Barnavelt* (1619), a tragedy, the chief interest in which lies in the fact that the playhouse manuscript, containing the notes of the prompter and the censor, is extant. Other products of the Fletcher-Massinger collaboration include *The Custom of the Country* (1619–1622), a romance; *The Bloody Brother or Rollo Duke of Normandy* (c. 1616), a tragedy; and *The False One* (c. 1620), a historical drama based on the romance of Caesar and Cleopatra.

Of the plays written solely by Massinger, the best known is A NEW WAY TO PAY OLD DEBTS, one of the most popular comedies in the history of the English theater. A less well known but equally deserving effort is his THE CITY MADAM, a comedy of manners that ranks with the best examples of that genre produced during the Restoration.

One distinction that marks some of Massinger's other work is his penchant for writing plays topically related to important political problems and personages of his day. In this category is *Believe As You List* (1637), a play not licensed or published in its own day because of "dangerous matter" relating to contemporary political developments in Portugal. Another political play is *The Bondman* (1623), dedicated to the earl of Pembroke and containing a sharp satire of the earl's enemy, the powerful duke of Buckingham. *A New Way to Pay Old Debts* also gibes at the Buckingham faction; the character of Sir Giles Overreach is based on Sir Giles Mompesson, a follower of the duke.

Other plays of Massinger include the tragedies *The Roman Actor* (c. 1627), which he regarded as his best work, and *The Duke of Milan* (1621/22), chiefly notable as an imitation of Shakespeare's *Othello*. Also worthy of mention are *The Maid of Honor* (c. 1621), a romantic drama, and *A Very Woman* (rev. 1634), a romantic comedy.

In general Massinger's plays lack the passion and the great poetry of the best Elizabethan drama. He is too often content to work within his age's standardized conceptions of character and action. His considerable talents as a dramatic craftsman offset, but do not entirely compensate for, these drawbacks. His finest work is in his comedies of manners in which he anticipates the best of the Restoration dramatists.

Massinger's plays are available in *The Plays of Philip Massinger* (1813), edited by William Gifford. A biographical and critical study is provided in T. A. Dunn's *Philip Massinger* (1957).—E. Q.

Master Builder, The (Bygmester Solness, 1892). A play by Henrik IBSEN. Halvard Solness, a builder of considerable prestige, is at that point in life when his sexual powers are diminishing and his professional assurance is faltering. The result is petty tyranny and easy infatuation with the women around him, except, of course, for his abject, invalid wife, Aline. Solness is galvanized by the sudden appearance of Hilde Wangel, half troll and half refugee from finishing school. She reminds him of a kiss and a pact (the nature of which is intended to be ambiguous) made ten years earlier, when he was at the height of his reputation. In fulfillment, Solness mounts the tower of the building he has recently completed, a striking symbol of phallic wishful thinking, and in applying the dedicatory wreath he falls to his death, while Hilde, below, "hears harps in the air."

The play has been frequently read as a *drame à clef* with Solness variously identified as playwright Bjørnstjerne Bjørnson, Bismarck, Gladstone, or Ibsen himself. However, it is far more relevant to view *The Master Builder* simply as a realistic play that transcends itself by means of mythic and psychological symbolism.

The text may be found in *Ibsen*, Vol. VII (1966), edited by J. W. McFarlane.—R. B. V.

Matesses, Antonios. See GREECE: *modern period*.

Maugham, W[illiam] Somerset (1874–1965).

W. SOMERSET MAUGHAM (WALTER HAMPDEN MEMORIAL LIBRARY AT THE PLAYERS, NEW YORK)

English playwright and novelist. Born January 25, 1874, in Paris, Maugham was trained as a physician before becoming a writer. His first play to reach the stage, the one-act *Marriages Are Made in Heaven* (1902), was directed by Max Reinhardt in Berlin and acted in German under the title *Schiffbrühig*. His first full-length play, the drama *A Man of Honour* (1904), had a cool reception. It dealt with a man who marries below his social station; Maugham kept returning to this sort of misalliance, whether sanctified by marriage or not, in such plays as *Smith* and *For Services Rendered* and in his best-known novel, *Of Human Bondage* (1915). *Lady Frederick* (1907) began the series of artificial, epigrammatic comedies which made his name; it was famous for the scene in which the irresistible charmer of middle age who gives her name to the play shows herself as she looks without artificial aid in order to discourage a youthful suitor. In 1908 Maugham set a record by having four successes running at once in the West End of London—*Lady Frederick* and three plays that opened in that year, *Mrs. Dot, Jack Straw,* and *The Explorer.* His comedies, including *Smith* (1909), *The Land of Promise* (1914, a modern variation on *The Taming of the Shrew*), and *Caroline* (1916), continued to appear regularly and to succeed.

His fame rests mainly on his later comedies. The first of them to win lasting admiration was *Our Betters,* which opened in New York in 1917 and then ran for eighteen months in London beginning in 1923. In this comedy, title-hunting American heiresses are vigorously exposed, and one of them is virtually caught *in flagrante delicto* with another titled heiress' gigolo; this experience is enough to send one young and eligible heiress back to America in search of true love. What is unusual about this play is its cynicism and ruthlessness in showing people who sell their emotions and their bodies for money and titles. *Home and Beauty* (1919) is equally cynical but much lighter in tone. It presents "a dear little thing" who rejects both her husbands (a war hero who was presumed dead and another war hero who thought he was marrying a widow) in favor of a civilian with black-market connections. Maugham's most admired comedy, THE CIRCLE, got a mixed reception when it opened in London in 1921; perhaps its satirical treatment of two cuckolded husbands (father and son) was a bit too much for London to bear. *The Constant Wife* (New York, 1926; London, 1927) also dealt light-handedly with adultery. Constance, the wife of the title, proclaims: "I may be unfaithful, but I am constant. I always think that's my most endearing quality." A model of wifely virtue, she covers up for her husband when another angry husband justly accuses him of adultery; she does not herself take a lover until she is economically independent of her husband. In this play, as in *Our Betters* and *Home and Beauty,* we are reminded that love and money are not unrelated. *The Breadwinner* (1930), about the conflict of the generations, was the last of Maugham's successful comedies.

Maugham's serious plays, which were much liked in their own time, command less attention now. They include *Caesar's Wife* (1919), about a husband, his faithful wife, and the man she loves; *East of Suez* (1922), a wildly improbable melodrama in which a decent Englishman has the bad judgment to marry an amoral Eurasian; *The Letter* (1927), a more probable melodrama about an unfaithful wife who has murdered her lover; *The Sacred Flame* (New York, 1928; London, 1929), a sentimental problem play vindicating euthanasia and, in special circumstances, a wife who takes a lover; *For Services Rendered* (1932), more of a social play than Maugham was used to writing, exhibiting the tragic effects of the war and other misfortunes upon a middle-class family in Kent; and *Sheppey* (1933), about a barber who wins a fortune in the Irish sweepstakes and resolves to follow Christ by sharing his wealth with the poor. The unfavorable reception of *Sheppey* induced Maugham to announce that he would no longer write for the stage, although he was later co-author with Guy Bolton of *Theatre* (1941), adapted from Maugham's 1937 novel of the same name.

Theatrical Companion to Maugham (1955), by Raymond Mander and Joe Mitchenson, gives details of productions.—H. P.

Mauriac, François. See ASMODÉE.

Mayakovsky, Vladimir [**Vladimirovich**] (1893–1930). Russian poet and playwright. Mayakovsky was a revolutionary before the revolution, both as a poet and political activist. He was expelled from school for following the Social Democrats (a Marxist group) and later was briefly imprisoned for agitating for the Bolshevik faction of that party. In writing, he joined the most radical literary movement, the futurist school, which was out "to emancipate words from their meaning," to discard all the classics, and so on.

Actually, Mayakovsky wrote some magnificent poetry and it is very fortunate that he spent much more time and energy on shocking the settled and

VLADIMIR MAYAKOVSKY (NEW YORK PUBLIC LIBRARY)

staid than on eradicating meaning from his verse. Although the years preceding World War I were quite unsettled and filled with all sorts of artistic eccentricity and wild behavior, this huge, violent man managed to shock Moscow with his poems and rowdiness. He welcomed the revolution, called upon all artists to take their work into the street and become integrated in the revolutionary stream, and thus wasted much of his talent writing rhyming slogans and edifying little poems for children and illiterates.

But Lenin's tastes in art were quite conservative, and soon an almost Victorian prudishness silenced the cocky avant-garde artists with their left-wing theories and practices. Mayakovsky made the painful discovery that the connection between the Bolshevik revolution and the revolution in the arts was purely verbal in nature. The "dictatorship of the proletariat" could coexist perfectly with the petit bourgeois in art, in which were included all the great classics. In fact, Lenin viewed such traditional art as much more useful to the "building of a communist society" than wild experiments and innovations. Mayakovsky protested, fulminated, went off on trips abroad as often as possible (until the authorities refused to issue an exit visa to him), and finally, for reasons that are quite debatable to this day (unhappy love, disappointment, boredom), shot himself.

For some strange reason Mayakovsky's reputation as the great revolutionary literary genius survived in the Soviet Union throughout the darkest days of Stalinism, and in 1935 he even received Stalin's official sanction as "the most talented poet of our Soviet era." It is difficult to account for this anointment of a man who had attacked Soviet bureaucracy much more violently than many who had been officially obliterated, who had indulged in a very experimental, unorthodox style at a time when nineteenth-century conformism was *de rigueur* in Soviet letters, and who had put the regime in a rather awkward position by blowing his brains out, thus implying at least the possibility of disappointment in the Soviet government. Perhaps, however, it was his death that saved him from persecution and official obliteration, because a dead man is so much more malleable than a live one. The pundits were able to assert that Mayakovsky had expressed faith in communism itself and in the real Soviet people who, in official parlance, were "struggling" to bring about communism, despite the parasites who, with time, were to be steamed out in the "bathhouse." And it is true that on this point Mayakovsky really does sound quite sincere.

Mayakovsky's contribution to the state (except for a few satirical sketches) were *Misteriya buff* (*Mystery-Bouffe*), *Klop* (*The Bedbug*, 1928), and THE BATHHOUSE. *Misteriya buff*, staged by Vsevolod Meyerhold in 1918 on the first anniversary of the revolution, was one of those mass spectacles in vogue during that period, a vast panoramic pageant representing the triumph of the "dirty" (the proletarians) over the "clean" (the exploiting classes), comprising such diverse exploiters as the Abyssian Negus, fat Russian merchants, and German army officers. The struggle is shown in a pseudobiblical style interspersed with irreverent quips and ends with the "salvation of the dirty" as they gain a promised land

where bread grows everywhere. When *Misteriya buff* was restaged in 1921, Mayakovsky brought the text up to date by introducing some topical characters, such as Georges Clemenceau and Lloyd George, among the "clean" oppressors.

In *Klop* a man (called Prisypkin) from the transitory Soviet society of 1928 is preserved in a frozen state for fifty years and then he is brought back to life with a bedbug that has been accidentally frozen along with him. To the communists of 1978, this man, a former worker and a well-known versifier who became corrupted during the "temporary ideological retreat" of the New Economic Policy, looks somewhat like his companion the bug—a curious creature from the bleak past whom they label *bourgeoisius vulgaris*. Both man and insect are treated with humane, if rather disgusted, interest and exhibited as curiosities. But despite his unattractiveness, this repulsive relic from the past lets out a stirring howl of loneliness in his new-world cage, so stirring, indeed, that some have felt that the author was identifying himself with Prisypkin, the man who has lost his party card—that is, his soul—and who is unable to find a place for himself in the millennium for which he once worked. A similar time trick was used in Mayakovsky's most accomplished play, *The Bathhouse*.

Useful information on Mayakovsky can be found in Vera Alexandrova's *A History of Soviet Literature, 1917–1964* (1964) and in Patricia Blake's Introduction to *The Bedbug and Selected Poetry* (1960) by Vladimir Mayakovski.—A. MᴀCᴀ.

Mayne, Rutherford. Real name **Samuel J. Waddell** (1878–   ). Irish playwright and actor. Mayne abandoned his early profession of engineering for a career of acting and playwriting. He was one of the founders of the Ulster Theatre, Northern Ireland's equivalent of Dublin's Abbey Theatre. His earliest plays, *The Turn of the Road* (1906), *The Drone* (1908), and *The Troth* (1908), are set in Northern Ireland and deal with the bleak struggle for existence in that land. His finest one-act play, *Red Turf* (1911), is, in its gravity and simplicity, reminiscent of Synge's tragedies. Another of Mayne's better plays is *Bridge Head* (1934), which dramatizes the attempt of the Free State Land Commission to redistribute landholdings in Northern Ireland. The play records the commission's efforts to bring about change among recalcitrant and unyielding rural citizens. His plays faithfully reproduce the atmosphere and dialect of rural Northern Ireland.—E. Q.

Mayor of Zalamea, The (El alcalde de Zalamea, 1640–1644). A historical play by Pedro CALDERÓN DE LA BARCA. This play is based on an actual incident in the campaign of Philip II to annex the Portuguese throne, left vacant by the sudden death of King Sebastian in 1578. As the play begins, a regiment has just arrived in the town of Zalamea. Pedro Crespo, a rich farmer, is preparing quarters in his home for the captain Don Álvaro. When Álvaro arrives, he manages to burst in on Crespo's daughter Isabel, who has moved to an upstairs room out of the way of the troops. Don Lope de Figueroa, the field commander, arrives in time to stop the quarrel between Crespo and the captain. Since he cannot have Isabel, the captain contrives to abduct her after Don Lope leaves the house with Crespo's son Juan, now the commander's orderly. When Crespo interferes, Álvaro has him bound to a tree in the forest and then rapes Isabel. Pursuing Don Álvaro, Juan wounds him and he secretly returns to town to treat the wound. Isabel, meanwhile, releases Crespo and both return to Zalamea; there Crespo learns that he has been selected mayor of the town. At once he orders the arrest of Don Álvaro and his accomplices but privately offers the captain all his wealth and estate if Álvaro will marry Isabel and repair the insult. When Álvaro refuses, Crespo has him jailed. Don Lope returns to punish the mayor for imprisoning a nobleman, but Crespo refuses to release the captain. There is a show of force between troops and peasants when the king arrives. The king hears Crespo's well-conceived defense, is shown the captain already garroted in his cell, and concludes the play by honoring the peasant with the permanent mayoralty of Zalamea. Crespo's personal cause, stated early in the play—"My life and property I render/to the King; but honor is/the heritage of my soul,/and my soul belongs to God alone"—has been thoroughly vindicated.

The Mayor of Zalamea, translated by Edwin Honig, is included in *Calderón: Four Plays* (1961). —E. H.

Measure for Measure (1604). A comedy by William SHAKESPEARE. *Measure for Measure* was acted at court on December 26, 1604, its earliest known performance. The text was published initially in the 1623 First Folio. Various literary and historical works serve as the source. Principal among these are a tale from Giraldi Cinthio's *Hecatommithi* (1565), later dramatized by Cinthio under the title *Epitia* (1583); and George Whetstone's version of Cinthio's tale, a two-part play called *The Right Excellent and Famous Historye of Promos and Cassandra* (1578), which Whetstone reworked into a prose tale for his *Heptameron of Civil Discourses* (1582). Recent scholarship has found parallels—regarded as deliberate—between Shakespeare's portrait of Duke Vincentio and the life and writings of King James I.

The play is set in Vienna, where Duke Vincentio, aware that he has been lax in enforcing his laws and desirous of testing the governing abilities of Lord Angelo, supposedly departs from the city and leaves Angelo to rule as his deputy. The duke assumes the disguise of a friar in order to move among his people unrecognized and to observe how Angelo will rule. To end the licentiousness rampant in Vienna, Angelo immediately orders the razing of the brothels and, invoking a long-dormant law against lechery, arrests and sentences to death the young Claudio for making his betrothed Juliet pregnant. Claudio's sister, Isabella, entering her novitiate in a strict religious order, is summoned from her nunnery to sue for her brother's life. Her pleas for mercy awaken a passion for the maiden in the coldhearted Angelo, and, in a second interview, Angelo agrees to free Claudio if Isabella will surrender to him. She refuses, and visits Claudio to tell him of Angelo's shameful proposal. Claudio, to Isabella's surprise, begs his sister to go through with the bargain and save his life. Shocked at his request, Isabella wishes him death. At this point, the disguised duke, who has overheard the interview between brother and sister, launches a plan whereby Claudio will be freed yet Isabella's chastity remain unsullied. The duke proposes that Isabella arrange the required assignation with Angelo, but that a substitute will be provided—one Mariana, to whom Angelo had once been betrothed and who still loves him. The "bed trick" works, and, in a long denouement, Angelo's villainy is revealed and a series of happy reconciliations made.

The play centers on sex, ranging from the licentiousness of the brothel to the extreme chastity of the nunnery. Sex is used neither to titillate the audience nor primarily for comic effects. Instead, it serves to probe the basis for a healthy state as manifested in the relationship between law and morality and to probe human conduct under emotional stress. The issues are serious, the tone—as in the other comedies of the period 1601–04—dark. Yet the play is a comedy in the classical sense of the word. By the end, each of the principal characters has become educated and has learned that moderation—one of the seventeenth-century meanings of "measure"—is the best course for the health of society.

Structurally, *Measure for Measure* is a mixture of elements: tragedy in the first half, with Angelo in his temptation emerging as a potential tragic protagonist; and a comedy of intrigue in the latter. The sharp division in structure, the machinations of the omnipresent duke, and the use of the bed trick have in varying degrees alienated audiences and critics over the centuries. Modern critics, who have been subjecting the play to closer scrutiny than it received in earlier periods, have produced markedly diverse interpretations. Some see it as religious allegory, some as a "problem play," and some as satire. An outstanding edition of *Measure for Measure* is the New Arden Edition (1965), edited by J. W. Lever. —W. G.

meddah. Turkish storyteller. Literally, *meddah* means panegyrist or eulogist in Arabic, but gradually the word began to be used for a storyteller who used mimicry, appropriate gestures, and voice modulation to transcribe comic scenes from life, without any special idea of eulogy. In the form of dialogue, meddahs imitated the voices and dialects of the numerous characters involved. They could also imitate various sounds such as gurgling, munching, and vomiting. Some meddahs could recite five hundred different stories from memory, but very few of these stories are extant. Meddahs used mainly two props, a cudgel and a handkerchief wrapped around their necks.

The Turks probably borrowed this art from the Arabs, although the origin is traced to China. Meddahs were popular even in the early days of the Ottoman Empire and flourished in the courts of the sultans of the seventeenth and eighteenth centuries. At the beginning of the nineteenth century meddahs were often the owners of coffeehouses in which they performed. Sultan Abdülhamit (1876–1909) heavily censored the stories and no political satire was allowed. In the second half of the nineteenth century adaptations were made from the works of European authors. Toward the middle of the twentieth century this lively art form disappeared.

Metin And's *A History of Theatre and Popular Entertainment,* published in Ankara in 1963, and *The Turkish Theater* by Nicholas N. Martinovitch (1933) both have sections on the meddah.—N. O.

Medea (Medeia, 431 B.C.). A tragedy by EURIPIDES. Some years before the beginning of the play the

Eastern princess Medea betrayed her father and nation in order to save with her witchcraft the life of the Greek adventurer Jason and to win him the golden fleece. Jason brought her home to Greece as his wife, but he now wishes to divorce her, a barbarian, in order to marry the daughter of Creon, king of Corinth. Creon, afraid of Medea's sorcery, exiles her and her two sons by Jason but grants her one day's respite to seek a haven. Aegeus, king of Athens, happens by at this opportune moment and promises to welcome her at Athens if she will help him with her arts to have the children he lacks. Medea now plots revenge on Jason. She induces him to let her send their sons to his new bride with gifts—a crown and a robe—so that they may plead to be spared exile. The gifts, poisoned, destroy both the bride and her father. Completing her vengeance on Jason by murdering their two children, Medea flies away to Athens in a chariot drawn by dragons.

Medea is no mere victim of jealousy and circumstance. Her wild, passionate nature is given free rein in her first scene with Jason and repeatedly before the Chorus. However, she can and does control it: in her first speech to the Chorus, on the woes of womankind, to secure their sympathy and silence; in her scene with King Creon, who grants her a day's delay before exile; with Aegeus, who promises her a refuge in Athens; and in her second scene with Jason, in which he allows her to send the children to take the robe to his bride. Medea loves the children whom she will murder to punish Jason; indeed, we witness a violent struggle in her between maternal love and the desire for vengeance. But it is then, in any event, too late to save the children.

Her vengeance is well chosen, for Jason is vulnerable only in his love for his children; in all other respects he is complacent, insensitive, cold, calculating, and unfeeling. If we, and the Chorus, feel sympathy for him in the end, it is only because Medea has forfeited all the sympathy that was abundantly hers at first.

The Chorus' odes and comments are thoroughly relevant to the action throughout, and through them Euripides manipulates the feelings of his audience in a masterly fashion. No question arises as to the unity of the plot. The messenger's speech describing the death of the princess and Creon is one of the greatest, most vivid in ancient tragedy. The theme of children is very skillfully kept before the audience throughout.

Aristotle notes two flaws in the structure of the play: the coincidence of Aegeus' arrival and the appearance of the chariot of Helios, which gives Medea a supernatural means of escape. The coincidence must be admitted, but Aegeus does link up in other ways with other elements in the play, and the divine chariot makes possible the last essential confrontation between Jason and Medea. In any event, ancient audiences were less sensitive on either count than was Aristotle or ourselves.

Translations of the play are listed under Euripides. —G. M. A. G.

medieval drama. Recent scholarship has demonstrated that the origins and development of medieval drama are more complex and obscure than had hitherto been assumed. The traditional view of that development had operated on the assumption that medieval drama "evolved" from the liturgical services of the church. The beginnings of that evolution were usually traced back to the *Quem queritis* trope, thought to be an elaboration of the Easter mass inserted in the regular service some time during the tenth century. From this seed developed the popular drama of the middle ages—the mysteries, miracles and moralities performed in the vernacular throughout Europe.

In opposition to this view O. B. Hardison and others have argued that liturgical services—far from being primitive seeds of later drama—were themselves complex, evolving dramatic structures. Thus the liturgical and vernacular dramas are seen as two separate developments interrelated in their origins and exerting reciprocal influences, not as a simple evolution from the sacred to the secular or from the simple to the complex. What emerges from this view is the realization that the great achievement of the vernacular drama in the middle ages was sustained and structured by the ritual of the Christian church.

For a discussion of the development of medieval drama see the relevant sections of the national entries, especially ENGLAND: *middle ages;* FRANCE: *middle ages and Renaissance;* ITALY: *middle ages;* GERMANY: *middle ages.*

The two most important discussions of medieval drama are Karl Young's *Drama of the Medieval Church* (1933) and O. B. Hardison's *Christian Rite and Christian Drama in the Middle Ages* (1965). —E. Q.

Meged, Aharon (1920–   ). Polish-born Israeli novelist, essayist, and playwright. Meged was born in Poland in 1920 and in 1926 immigrated to Israel, where, after completing his studies, he became a member of Kibbutz Sdot-Yam (1938–1950). For over ten years he has been the editor of "Masah," the literary section of one of the Israeli dailies. Many of Meged's novels and short stories have appeared in print, and some critics have emphasized the influence of Kafka on his work.

His first play, *I Like Mike* (1951), a comedy about false patriotism, was followed by *Chedva Va'ani* ("Chedva and I," 1954), a comedy depicting the adventures of a former kibbutz farmer in the big city. The same year he scored a major success with his musical comedy *5–5.* In 1958 the Habimah produced his *Chana Senesh,* a play based on documentary material and his own personal knowledge of this legendary young woman, once a member of Meged's kibbutz, who in 1942 was sent by the Allies to her homeland, Hungary, where she was caught and executed. In the 1960's Meged has written two major dramatic works: *Breishit* ("Genesis," 1962) and *Ha'onah Haboeret* ("The Busy Season," 1967). Produced by the Habimah, both plays are significant in the development of Israeli drama: the first one for its modern interpretation of a biblical account and the latter as a modern morality play concerning the present relations between Israel and Germany and using the biblical story of Job as its model. This use of biblical material by a young, modern Israeli dramatist has proved most rewarding.

Other plays by Meged include *Incubator Al Haselah* ("Incubator on the Rock," 1950) and

Baderech L'Eilat ("On the Road to Eilat," 1952). He has also written numerous one-acters and radio plays.—Z. R.

Mei Lan-fang (1894–1961). The leading actor, director, and scholar in the Chinese theatrical world of the twentieth century. Like almost all actors in China for centuries, Mei Lan-fang came of a theatrical family and lived intensely within the world of the theater. His grandfather was a celebrated impersonator of female roles. When his father's career in the same field was cut short by early death, the boy was brought up by an uncle who excelled as a musician in the theater. He began his training as soon as he was able to walk and master his limbs, first appearing in public at a famous Peking theater, the Kuang-ho Lou, or Palace of Extensive Knowledge, at the age of ten. Although as a youth he ardently followed many avocations—training his flock of passenger pigeons; collecting, playing, and even making musical instruments; and painting pictures—the classical Chinese style of acting, with dance, song, and mime as constituent features, always commanded his chief efforts. He appeared in roles of many different descriptions but took female parts in by far the greatest number of his performances.

His career was one of unquestioned leadership and extraordinary enterprise. He even experimented with a modern style on one occasion, acting the part of a working girl wearing modern dress and sitting before a symbol of industrial progress, a Singer sewing machine. His chief ideal was the preservation of traditional Chinese styles of acting, especially the refined *K'in-chu.* But he admitted compromise and wel-

MEI LAN-FANG (CHINESE INFORMATION SERVICE)

comed a degree of eclecticism where these were consonant with artistic excellence. In a period when China labored in the throes of violent social and political change, he worked with considerable success to maintain the standards of taste and the vitality of imagination that for centuries had been the grounds of China's cultural greatness.

His fame rapidly became international. He performed in Japan in 1919 and 1924, in the United States in 1930, and in Russia in 1935. A visit to England proved a disappointment, since no arrangement was made there for a stage performance. During his tour of the United States, he acted in New York, Chicago, San Francisco, and Los Angeles. He was received with great enthusiasm, winning special praise for his dramatic monologue, *A Nun Craves Worldly Vanities,* and his performance in the Chinese play paralleling the story of Judith and Holifernes, *The Killing of the Tiger-General.* In Russia he appeared in both Moscow and Leningrad, where he was particularly commended for his remarkable sword dancing and for his brilliant acting in the old play of revolutionary tendency, *The Fisherman's Revenge.*

During the Sino-Japanese War, he displayed dignified but ardent patriotism. He grew a beard as signal of his defiance of the invaders, thus declaring his refusal to act, as he had done for many triumphant seasons, in feminine parts.

In the latter years of his active life he appeared in several films, including *The White Snake, The Drunken Beauty, The Emperor's Farewell to His Favorite,* and *The Sword of the Universe.* Although he was the last great female impersonator on the Chinese stage, he favored the introduction of women into the acting profession and in this, as in countless other ways, helped to effect innovations and vitalizing changes.

Widely as he was acclaimed outside his own country, it was there that he reached an eminence such as no actor, perhaps, in recent times has anywhere achieved. During years of the greatest trial and distress, he saved the best in the Chinese theatrical arts and almost singlehandedly rescued what could possibly be salvaged in a period of revolution and profound unrest.

The best general study of the man and his work is A. C. Scott's *Mei Lan-fang* (1959). The most adequate appreciation of his art and style is contained in Stark Young's *Immortal Shadows* (1948).—H. W. W.

Melas, Spyros. See GREECE: *modern period.*

mélodrame. Now used to designate sensational plays abounding in terrifying incidents, artificially motivated characters, overstated pathos, or tension arbitrarily provoked by chance, *mélodrame* originated in France in the 1760's and spread to Germany a few years later. By around 1780 it had absorbed the dramatic pattern and the connotations it has held in the theater ever since.

In France Jean Jacques Rousseau used music in his one-act monologue *Pygmalion* (1770) to express the emotions of a character or situation as the actor first pantomimed them and then conveyed them in words. Here was the germ of the later meaning of the term: a play depending on emotional situations rather than plausible motivation and development of character. In Germany a Bohemian, Georg Benda, transformed Greek plays into the operas *Ariadne auf Naxos* (1774) and *Medea* (1775) with orchestral accompaniment for spoken passages. These also were called mélodrames and exemplify mélodrame as musicians understand it. Mozart and Beethoven wrote passages of this kind. Friedrich Schiller's *The Robbers* (1781) set the precedent for character types, setting, and atmosphere for most mélodrames for the next hundred years: the long-suffering heroine in captivity, the falsely accused hero, the cold-blooded villain in the usurped castle with dungeons and trap doors. Thus, two countries contributed to a popular dramatic form that has pervaded theatrical entertainment in the Western world.

Other formative influences on the development of mélodrame in France were the Parisian pantomimes and *ambigus* (mélanges of tragedy, comedy, parody, song, and dance) performed in the last years of the eighteenth century, the *opéras-comiques* of Michel Jean Sedaine, the sentimental plays of Louis Sébastien Mercier, and the popular, sensational, but shallow dramas of the German playwright August Friedrich Kotzebue (1761–1819).

From 1797 to 1835 the Boulevard du Temple (home of second-class theaters in Paris) was the stronghold of mélodrame. Here were performed the luridly sentimental plays of Guilbert de Pixérécourt and his disciple Joseph Bouchardy, whence it was nicknamed the Boulevard du Crime. Especially during the Second Empire, the dramatization of morbid tales of mystery and terror, with music between passages of dialogue, helped to crystallize the conventions of mélodrame, which strongly influenced Alexandre Dumas père, Victor Hugo, and other dramatists of the Romantic period. The new genre accustomed the public to plays blending comedy and tragedy; it also called for a new, vigorous style of acting and helped instill in Romantic leaders a love of Shakespeare, Schiller, and Sir Walter Scott.

French mélodrame crossed the English Channel in 1802, when *A Tale of Mystery*, a free adaptation by Thomas Holcroft of Pixérécourt's *Coelina, ou l'Enfant du Mystère* (1800), was performed at Covent Garden, London. But, as was customary at this time, the original author was not credited. Thus began nearly a century of pervasive French influence on British dramatic art.

The most complete work on mélodrame in France, England, and the United States is F. Rahill's *The World of Melodrama* (1967).—S. S. S.

Menaechmi (The Twin Menaechmi). A comedy by PLAUTUS. Neither the date of the production nor the author of the Greek play on which *Menaechmi* is based is known. *Menaechmi* portrays the laughable confusions that arise when Menaechmus of Syracuse, searching for his long-lost twin brother, arrives with his slave, Messenio, in Epidamnus, the home of his brother. The brother's cook, parasite, mistress, wife, and father-in-law all mistake him for Menaechmus of Epidamnus. The resultant bewilderment of Menaechmus of Epidamnus is more plausible than the failure of Menaechmus of Syracuse to realize the truth. The minor characters are well drawn and the intricacies of the plot are handled with unusual skill.

Menaechmi, Plautus' most successful comedy of errors, provided a model for many later plays, among them Giovanni Giorgio Trissino's *I Simillimi* (1547), Hans Sachs's *Monechmo* (1548), Agnolo Firenzuola's *I Lucidi* (1549), Jean de Rotrou's *Les Ménechmes* (1636), Jean François Regnard's *Les Ménechmes* (1705), and Carlo Goldoni's *I Due Gemelli Veneziani* (1748). The most famous adaptation, Shakespeare's *The Comedy of Errors* (written c. 1590–1593), has even more complications with the addition of twin servants (inspired by Plautus' *Amphitryon*), but is usually considered inferior to the Roman original. *The Boys from Syracuse* (1938), a Rodgers and Hart musical comedy adapted from Shakespeare by George Abbott, is Plautine in its emphasis on song and dance and its many farcical situations.—G. E. D.

Menander (c. 342–c. 292 B.C.). Greek comic playwright. The son of Diopeithes, an upper-class Athenian, Menander lived through a period when Athens was governed by the victorious armies of the Macedonian Empire, and Alexander the Great was penetrating to the frontiers of India. Menander, said to have been a pupil of Theophrastus, the teacher and author of a book called *Character Types*, was a friend of Demetrius of Phaleron, military governor of Athens from 317 until 307 B.C.

In 321 Menander produced his first play, *Orge* (*Anger*), at the Lenaia Festival, and won first prize. In 316 he again won first prize, with DYSKOLOS, at the same festival, and the next year won a victory at the Dionysia with a play the name of which has been lost. Only two other plays can be dated: *Imbrioi* (*Imbrians*, 301) and *Heniochos* (*Charioteer*, possibly 312). In all, he is said to have written 108 plays and won first prize eight times. After 307, when Demetrius was exiled, Menander was in some political trouble because of his connection with the Macedonian commander. But influential friends saved him, and he continued to write and produce plays until his death in 292 B.C., when he drowned while swimming in the Piraeus.

Little is known about Menander's life, except some gossip to the effect that he squinted, that he was a friend and apprentice of Alexis, a playwright of Middle Comedy, and that his methods of composition were considered eccentric. One story, for example, is told by Plutarch ("On the Glory of Athens") about a friend who met Menander a few days before the festival of the Dionysia and remarked on the fact that his play was not finished. "Yes it is," said Menander. "I've done the plot, now all I have to do is write the lines."

Much of the mystery surrounding his life is due to the nature of the drama he wrote—nonpolitical, domestic comedies, dealing with everyday situations of romantic love, long-lost children, marriage, and family squabbles, typical of the New Comedy, of which Menander was the foremost writer. This kind of play left no room for autobiographical detail, nor did it reflect specific public issues of the day.

In another sense, however, Menander's plays are extremely topical. They reflect perfectly the mood of Greek life in his time—and in many times to come. After his death, Menander was by far the most popular comic playwright of the ancient world, as the long list of his imitators proves; they range from Plautus, Shakespeare, and Molière to television situation comedy.

In Menander are found most of the stock charac-

RELIEF OF MENANDER AND THREE MASKS (THE ART MUSEUM, PRINCETON UNIVERSITY)

ters and situations of conventional light comedy—the old father, the young lovers, the clever servant, the whore with the heart of gold, children lost and found, marriage as a state of perpetual warfare. This is not to say that Menander was an innovator. In fact, many of his themes appear in the plays of Aristophanes, and even in Greek tragedy. The child who discovers his parents through a talisman left with him at birth can be tragic (Sophocles' *Oedipus*), melodramatic (Euripides' *Ion*), or purely comic (Oscar Wilde's *The Importance of Being Earnest*). Although Menander dispensed with mythical elements, which can be found even in Aristophanes, many of his plots have a folktale quality, and his debt to Euripides, especially, is immense.

Out of respect for the tastes of his audience, Menander also dispensed with the frank bawdiness, the personal references, and the choral fantasies of Old Comedy. Instead, he dramatized the hopes and fears of the small man, the middle-class merchant or farmer. For "fate" he substituted "luck"; for a cosmic world view, resigned acceptance of the ironies and mixed blessings of life.

Only one of Menander's comedies, *Dyskolos,* has survived intact. Remaining fragments of the others show that his style was conversational, easygoing, economical. He expressed in succinct phrases the private philosophy of an entire society, and a selection of quotations from his works was compiled by scholars, teachers, and librarians in later centuries. Among the famous lines:

Whom the gods love, die young.

Conscience makes every man a coward.

Every accident has a meaning.

In marriage, there are no known survivors.

Among the fragments of Menander's work that have survived are large sections of four plays: *Perikeiromene* (*The Girl with Her Hair Cut Short*), *Samia* (*The Girl from Samos*), *Epitrepontes* (*Arbitrators*), and *Heros* (*Hero*). (See GREECE: *the classical period.*) The complexity of their plots and the large gaps in the text make synopsis impossible, but there are certain common factors. Each play involves a child, sometimes twins, who has been exposed at birth and, as an adult, is unaware of his true parents. At the end of the play, families are reunited. Along the way, a brother may have mistakenly tried to make love to his sister, a slave turned out to be freeborn, or a husband falsely accused his wife of adultery (when all along he was the man with whom she slept). In such plays social comment is restricted to the fun poked at stock characters, such as the hanger-on or the spendthrift youth. But there is continuous social commentary in the dominating interest of all the characters and in the power this interest has over all other events. That interest is money, and it is the power of money that has replaced the power of destiny. Menander, consciously or unconsciously, recognizes this fact, and for this reason his plays have had especial powers of self-regeneration in all succeeding materialistic ages.

For a comprehensive review of the existing fragments, as well as a discussion of the influences on Menander and the influence he, in turn, exercised on others, see *Studies in Menander* (2nd ed. 1960) by T. B. L. Webster. A convenient translation of *Dyskolos* and some of the other remains can be found in *Menander—Plays* (1967), translated by Philip Vellacott.—K. C.

Merchant of Venice, The (c. 1596). A comedy by William SHAKESPEARE. The Heyes Quarto of 1600 (the First Quarto), the first published text of *The Merchant of Venice*, furnished the copy for the 1623 First Folio. According to the quarto title page, the work had been acted "divers times" by the Lord Chamberlain's Men. Two tales, cleverly synthesized, serve as primary sources for the plot. From Ser

TITLE PAGE OF THE FIRST QUARTO (1600) OF SHAKE-SPEARE'S *The Merchant of Venice*

The moſt excellent
Hiſtorie of the *Merchant of Venice*.

VVith the extreame crueltie of *Shylocke* the Iewe towards the ſayd Merchant, in cutting a iuſt pound of his fleſh : and the obtayning of *Portia* by the choyſe of three cheſts.

As it hath beene diuers times acted by the Lord Chamberlaine his Seruants.

Written by William Shakeſpeare.

AT LONDON,
Printed by *I. R.* for Thomas Heyes, and are to be ſold in Paules Church-yard, at the ſigne of the Greene Dragon.
1 6 0 0.

Giovanni Fiorentino's *Il Pecorone* (1558) comes the pound-of-flesh story; the story of the caskets derives from a tale in the *Gesta Romanorum* (translated into English in 1577, revised 1595). The play also shows influences from Christopher Marlowe's *The Jew of Malta* (c. 1590). Tenuous attempts have been made to link Shakespeare's play with an actual event of the day—the hanging for high treason in 1594 of Dr. Roderigo López, a converted Portuguese Jew serving as personal physician to the queen.

The plot revolves around a bond made between Antonio, the merchant of the title, and Shylock, a Jewish usurer, so that Antonio may finance his young friend Bassanio in an expedition to Belmont to woo the wealthy and beautiful Portia. In order to win the lady, Bassanio, on arriving in Belmont, must undergo the test of the three caskets. He selects the correct one, and Portia, already in love with him, consents to be his wife. Meanwhile, report comes to Antonio that his ships have been wrecked. Shylock demands payment for his loan, calling for the prearranged penalty of a pound of flesh. Bassanio, upon receiving the news, returns to Venice. Portia follows in male disguise, leaving her estate in care of Bassanio's friend Lorenzo. Lorenzo and his wife, Jessica—Shylock's daughter—having eloped, are new arrivals in Belmont. Shylock presses his claim in court. Posing as a lawyer, Portia, through deft legal argument, saves Antonio. The play closes in Belmont with all confusions set aright.

By genre, *The Merchant of Venice* is a romantic comedy. It is concerned with love, mirroring and anatomizing various facets of that emotion. Shylock is the comic butt, the antilove figure. The very settings underscore the themes, for Venice is depicted as a harsh, morally bankrupt city, whereas Belmont—where Shylock never sets foot—becomes the epitome of beauty and harmony, symbolized by the moonlit night and music of the too-easily-dismissed last act. The main characters are complexly constructed, especially Shylock, who has been endowed with some highly positive traits that lift him far above a typical stage villain. Although *The Merchant of Venice* shows a great advance over the earlier comedies in its integration of plot, characters, setting, and poetry, it is diffuse in tone and focus.

Stage and political history have also had their clouding effect in interpreting the play. Commencing in the mid-eighteenth century actors, fascinated by the complexities of Shylock, began a still-current tradition of playing him as a serious, sometimes tragic, character. The play has become centered around Shylock, although the usurer appears in but five of the twenty scenes. It has been further wrenched out of focus as a result of the periodic waves of anti-Semitism that have swept over Europe, culminating in the Nazi persecutions. Today, the play has social overtones almost certainly never intended by Shakespeare.

An outstanding edition of *The Merchant of Venice* is the New Arden Edition (1955), edited by John Russell Brown.—W. G.

Merry Wives of Windsor, The (1597). A comedy by William SHAKESPEARE. Stage tradition has it that *The Merry Wives of Windsor* was written especially at the command of, and performed before, Queen Elizabeth. The First Quarto title page confirms the

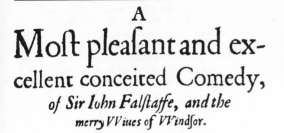

A
Moſt pleaſant and ex-
cellent conceited Comedy,
of Sir Iohn Falſtaffe, and the
merry VViues of VVindſor.

VVith the ſwaggering vaine of An-
cient *Piſtoll,* and Corporall *Nym.*

Written by W. SHAKESPEARE.

Printed for *Arthur Johnſon,* 1619.

TITLE PAGE OF THE SECOND QUARTO (1619) OF
SHAKESPEARE'S *The Merry Wives of Windsor*

royal performance. Recent scholarship has adduced evidence to fix the date of that occasion as April 23, 1597, St. George's Day, in conjunction with ceremonials of the Order of the Garter. Direct allusions to the Garter in Act V, scene v, indirect textual references, and the Windsor setting combine to link the composition of the play with the Order of the Garter. The First Quarto (1602), the first published text, is regarded a "bad quarto." The First Folio version (1623) stands as the authoritative one. No direct source for the plot has been found. Analogues exist suggesting that the play has its origins in Italian Renaissance novellas, but it probably is a direct reworking of a lost Italianate comedy.

The main plot shows Sir John Falstaff, an impoverished, old, stout lecher, attempting to replenish his purse by wooing simultaneously Mistress Page and Mistress Ford, the wives of two of Windsor's wealthy citizens. The ladies quickly discover his plan and engage in some farcical intrigues to discommode and discredit Falstaff. They are unwittingly aided in their tricks by the passionately jealous husband of Mistress Ford. In the subplot, carefully integrated with the Falstaff story, the young Mistress Anne Page successfully carries on a romance with the handsome Fenton against parental wishes and against the importunings of two foolish rivals—the country gull Master Slender and the French physician Dr. Caius.

This rollicking farce with its village setting is Shakespeare's sole play depicting contemporary English life. It bears several marks of hasty composition, among them the appearance of Falstaff and his cronies from the *Henry IV* and *Henry V* plays. The best, and now generally accepted, explanation for the peculiarities of text, character, setting, and Order of the Garter allusions is that the comedy was written on short notice in response to the queen's request and in honor of Shakespeare's patron, George Carey, Lord Hunsdon, who had become lord chamberlain in April 1597 and who was elected to the Order of the Garter that same month. The Falstaffian elements in the play represent an unsuccessful attempt, through lack of time, to borrow materials from the history plays for integration into an Italianate source play. The perennial popularity of *The Merry Wives of Windsor* demonstrates that theatergoers have not been particularly disturbed by the dramaturgical weaknesses of the play and have enjoyed the antics of Falstaff—here portrayed as a duper duped—and the colorful village inhabitants.

An outstanding edition of *The Merry Wives of Windsor* is the Signet Classic Shakespeare (1965), edited by William Green.—W. G.

Messager, Charles.   See Charles VILDRAC.

Metastasio, Pietro.   Born **Pietro Trapassi** (1698–1782). Italian poet and playwright. The son of a Roman merchant, Metastasio displayed a precocious poetic talent, which interested G. V. Gravina, man of letters of the Arcadian Academy of Rome. Gravina

PIETRO METASTASIO (NEW YORK PUBLIC LIBRARY)

changed Trapassi's name to the Hellenic-sounding Metastasio. Educated in the academic climate of the Neapolitan Arcadia, Metastasio, after an instructive trip through Italy, met enthusiastic success in 1724 with his drama for music, DIDONE ABBANDONATA. In 1729 he succeeded Apostolo Zeno as court poet at the imperial court in Vienna. He remained in Vienna until his death, where he enjoyed an uncontested glory and continued to write innumerable poems, songs, madrigals, idylls, and occasional verse, as well as twenty-seven dramas for music. Notable among the latter are *Catone in Utica* ("Cato in Utica," 1728), *Semiramide* (1729), *L'Olimpiade* (*The Olympiad,* 1733), *La Clemenza di Tito* (*The Clemency of Titus,* 1734), and *Attilio Regolo* ("Prince Attilio," written 1740, first produced 1750). These and other librettos were set to music by almost every composer of the eighteenth century.

Metastasio's theatrical success can be attributed to the exceptional ease of his poetic style and to the exquisite coquetry with which he develops the casuistry of love, so dear to the Arcadian and rococo taste of the age. These very gifts, however, prevented him from attaining the austere tone of classic tragedy to which he aspired. His characters are not animated by passionate feeling. Instead, they are polite bearers of fanciful baroque conceits and of yearning Arcadian ideals. The dramatic conflicts that lie at the base of his dramas have the flavor of witty and refined dialectic. The neatness of the *mise en scène* and the musical verse provide a suitable frame for the qualities and sentiments of his art.—L. L.

Mexico. See SPANISH AMERICA.

michiyuki. One of the most effective and typical conventions of the traditional Japanese stage, seen in all its types of drama, the *michiyuki,* or simulated stage journey, has received special attention from theater scholars. Its basic conception is simple. Any number of actors—although two is the most usual number—move at a more or less regular pace about the stage, describing their travels as they go. As the usage developed, it proved to be the occasion of some of the most striking dance, mime, music, and lyric poetry found in the Japanese theater.

In the *noh* plays the michiyuki customarily takes the form of a lyric prologue, starting the play on its course. The convention helps to establish the principal place and scene. The figures move from a place of no special consequence to the location where the main action will be performed. The poetry as a rule abounds in symbolic language or even in play upon words, inasmuch as the place names are chosen for their indirect reference to the play's central theme. The conclusion of the passage gains special importance, since most noh plays are in some sense a celebration of place, the temple or landscape in which the central action occurs having much significance. The main action takes place at the end of the journey.

In the puppet plays and hence in the later *kabuki* theater, on the contrary, the michiyuki often takes place in the last act. Thus in the celebrated "domestic tragedy" by Chikamatsu, *The Love Suicides at Amijima,* the two lovers proceed with many shifts in their emotions to the scene of their ritualistic death. The michiyuki may be performed either on the main stage or on the *hanamichi* ("corridor"). The

michiyuki typifies the effectiveness of a stylized or unrealistic manner of production.—H. W. W.

Mickiewicz, Adam (1798–1855). Polish playwright and poet, the major figure of nineteenth-century Polish émigré literature. Mickiewicz studied at Wilno University and taught at Kowno (1819–1823). Shortly thereafter he was arrested for allegedly anti-Russian political activity and in 1824 was exiled to Russia. He left Russia in 1829 and in 1831 returned to Poland too late to join the unsuccessful Polish uprising against Russia. In Paris he lived with his family in precarious financial condition until he was given the chair of Latin literature at Lausanne in 1839. In 1840 he was appointed professor of Slavonic literature at the Collège de France, but was forced to leave the post four years later. In 1848 he organized a Polish legion in Italy to join the campaign against Austria and made a fruitless attempt to secure the pope's backing. He died in Turkey while trying to organize Polish forces to fight against the Russians in the Crimean War.

Mickiewicz's first book of poetry, titled simply *The Poetry of Adam Mickiewicz, Volume I* (1822), is a landmark in Polish literary history, marking the beginning of the era of Polish Romanticism. Included in his second volume of poetry (1823), was his drama *Forefathers' Eve, Parts II* and *IV.* This drama was based on the pagan ancestor-worship rites of the Belorussian peasantry, whose customs the poet knew well from his childhood in Lithuania. Against the mysterious background of the celebration of the rites of the forefathers in a deserted graveyard at night, *Part II* deals with the appearance of various spirits during the folk celebration; *Part IV* is little more than a Wertherian tale of unrequited love ending in suicide. In both parts, the folk element is little more than a frame for the presentation of conventional Romantic themes and characters.

Forefathers' Eve, Part III, Mickiewicz's major dramatic work, was added by the poet almost a decade after the appearance of *Parts II* and *IV.* The subject is the poet's imprisonment (1823) and later exile (1824–1829) to Russia. Sensitive to the fact that he did not participate in the insurrection of 1830, Mickiewicz wished to dramatize his own earlier experiences to show that he too had suffered for his country. The central character of the play is the young poet Gustaw who, under the impress of the events he lives through, undergoes a mystical experience from which he emerges as a national bard, a *wieszcz,* the voice of the ideals and aspirations of his nation. Of the nine scenes of *Forefathers' Eve, Part III,* eight have nothing to do with *Parts II* and *IV;* the folkloric elements appear only in scene 9, added as no more than a mechanical link with the earlier published parts of the work. Polish émigrés living in the West (mostly in Paris) after 1831 had no permanent stage, and *Forefathers' Eve,* like other émigré Polish plays, was never staged in the lifetime of its author, although it constitutes his most significant contribution to Polish drama.

Mickiewicz wrote two other dramatic works—mainly for financial reasons—both originally in French and both on Polish historical subjects. These were *Les Confédérés de Bar* and the unfinished *Jacques Jasinski, ou Les Deux Polognes.* Among Mickiewicz's least impressive works, they were writ-

ten in 1837, never staged in France, and published for the first time—in fragments only—in 1867.
—H. B. S.

Middle Comedy. Term used to describe Greek comedy from about 400 B.C. to about 320 B.C. Middle Comedy, to judge by the few extant examples, departs from OLD COMEDY by moving away from the strong political and personal satire that marks the latter genre, by having a less episodic structure, and by toning down the obscenity that marks Old Comedy. Middle Comedy also all but eliminated the chorus from the plot of the play. Two examples of Middle Comedy are Aristophanes' *Plutus* and *Ecclesiazusae*. (See NEW COMEDY.)

Middleton, Thomas (1570?–1627). English playwright and poet. Although very little is known about Middleton's life, he appears to have been born in London and to have been the Thomas Middleton who entered Queen's College, Oxford, in 1598. His literary career began with a group of poems: *The Wisdom of Solomon Paraphrased* (1597), a paraphrase and expansion of material from the Apocrypha; *Micro-Cynicon* (1599), an attempt at formal satire in the manner of Juvenal and Persius; and *The Ghost of Lucrece* (1600), a tragic complaint in the manner of *A Mirror for Magistrates*, the great collection of tragic tales in verse begun by William Baldwin in 1559 and constantly re-edited and augmented throughout the sixteenth and seventeenth centuries. In 1604 he published two pamphlets, *The Ant and the Nightingale* and *The Black Book*, each devoted to satirical treatment of social evils, a subject that was to be his concern as a dramatist as well. He seems to have begun to write for the stage around 1602, providing plays (now lost) for Philip Henslowe, and then for the Children of St. Paul's. Sometime before 1604

THOMAS MIDDLETON (NEW YORK PUBLIC LIBRARY)

he married Maria Marbeck, the sister of Thomas Marbeck, an actor and musician associated with the Lord Admiral's Men, which would suggest that Middleton had some connection with that acting company.

Between 1602 and 1608 Middleton wrote satirical comedies for children's companies. When these companies began to decline, he wrote for adult professional troupes, often in collaboration with other dramatists. Around 1613 he began to write municipal pageants for the city of London, an enterprise in which he continued to be engaged for the rest of his career. On September 6, 1620, he was appointed chronologer of the city of London, a post that had few duties but that provided him with a livelihood. Following the performance of his political satire *A Game at Chess* by the King's Men in 1624, which offended the Spanish ambassador, Middleton seems to have had some difficulties with the authorities, and there is some possibility that he may have been imprisoned. He appears to have spent his entire life in London, and he was buried in the parish church at Newington on July 4, 1627. His widow some months later received a gift of twenty nobles from the city of London.

The canon of Middleton's plays is extremely difficult to establish, and until we know exactly what he wrote, it may be impossible to estimate his achievement. The chronology of his plays is virtually impossible to determine and has accordingly been a subject for much scholarly argument. He had both the vices and the virtues of the professional playwright: much that he wrote is trivial and unimportant, but he shows at times a flair for the theatrically effective that is not equaled by many of his contemporaries. A handful of his plays must rank among the great achievements of the Elizabethan and Jacobean eras.

The comedies that Middleton wrote for the Children of St. Paul's cannot be dated exactly, but all had been entered in the Stationers' Register by 1608. The earliest were *The Family of Love*, in which Middleton held up to scorn a dissenting religious sect, and *The Phoenix*, in which a prince wanders in disguise among his people observing their vices and attacking them in lengthy speeches. The play *Blurt, Master Constable* probably belongs also to this period. Nowhere did Middleton excoriate the foibles of society more ruthlessly than in a remarkable group of four plays, all of which were entered in the Stationers' Register in 1607 and 1608: *Your Five Gallants, Michaelmas Term, A Trick to Catch the Old One,* and *A Mad World, My Masters.* In these plays greed is the worst of all sins, and the rising merchant classes of London are held up to scathing ridicule. His city comedies have sometimes been called amoral works because they contain only characters who are vicious and contemptible. But Middleton's point of view is that of the satirist who cannot really ridicule and castigate vice without moral standards by which he judges the manners of his age. Also among Middleton's great achievements in comedy is *A Chaste Maid in Cheapside*, performed by Lady Elizabeth's Men sometime between 1611 and 1615. The christening scene of this play is one of the finest moments in Jacobean comedy.

Of Middleton's collaboration with other dramatists we know relatively little. Between 1604 and 1608 he appears to have worked with Thomas Dekker, with whom he wrote the two parts of *The Honest Whore* and *The Roaring Girl.* After 1612 he worked closely with William Rowley, a comic hack writer capable of little independent work of value but whose talents joined felicitously with those of Middleton. Between 1613 and 1618 they seem to have been engaged in work on tragicomedies, which included *A Fair Quarrel, The Old Law,* and probably *The Spanish Gypsy.* Other of Middleton's tragicomedies include *The Witch* and *More Dissemblers Besides Women.*

It has sometimes been argued that *The Revenger's Tragedy,* published anonymously in 1607 and usually attributed to Cyril Tourneur, is in fact Middleton's work. The evidence for this is not very great, and if it were true, it would mean that Middleton had begun to write tragedy at a time when he seems to have been entirely occupied with his city comedies. The three tragedies that we are sure that he wrote are all of uncertain date, but none could be earlier than 1616. These include *The Mayor of Quinborough, or Hengist, King of Kent,* a powerful story of sex and murder in Celtic Britain; *The Changeling,* written in collaboration with William Rowley; and *Women Beware Women,* which adds the theme of incest to murder and adultery.

As a writer of tragedy, Middleton is remarkable for the penetrating psychological realism of his character portraiture and for his ability to create a sense of utter depravity in the world his characters inhabit. In THE CHANGELING the dramatic focus is upon Beatrice Joanna, a seemingly virtuous girl who slowly but inevitably becomes aware of her own inner corruption as she draws closer and closer to De Flores, the dog-faced character she had once detested and whom she had employed to rid her of an unwelcome suitor. The comic subplot of this play, in which two courtiers pretend to be madmen in order to seduce the wife of a madhouse keeper, has usually been attributed to Rowley, and critics have sometimes censured Middleton for permitting this seemingly absurd matter to destroy his play. Many recent commentators have argued, however, that the subplot is in fact closely related thematically to the main plot, providing a grotesque comic commentary upon it. *Women Beware Women* ends with a grotesque wedding masque in which all of the corrupt characters of the play, who have lived by moral equivocation, destroy one another. This final scene has also been sometimes called an absurdity that mars the play, but as a symbolic vision of the total dissolution of a hopelessly corrupt world it is extremely effective.

There has been a tendency to regard Middleton as a kind of hack dramatist who was capable of writing a few scenes of intense psychological realism but whose plays are without unity of theme or consistency of point of view. Of him, T. S. Eliot, for instance, has written: "He has no point of view, is neither sentimental nor cynical; he is neither resigned, nor disillusioned, nor romantic; he has no message. He is merely the name which associates six or seven great plays." That there is great diversity in Middleton's work, with his best plays standing far apart from his worst, is obvious, but his greatest work, both in comedy and tragedy, reveals a dark and pessimistic vision of human corruption that is as moral an attitude as it is distinctive.

The Works of Thomas Middleton (1885–1886), edited by A. H. Bullen in eight volumes, remains the standard edition of Middleton's plays. There is an excellent edition of *The Changeling* by N. W. Bawcutt in The Revels Plays series (1958). Critical studies include R. H. Barker, *Thomas Middleton* (1958); W. D. Dunkel, *The Dramatic Technique of Middleton in his Comedies of London Life* (1925); and Samuel Schoenbaum, *Middleton's Tragedies: A Critical Study* (1955).—I. R.

Midsummer Night's Dream, A (c. 1594–1595). A comedy by William SHAKESPEARE. Most scholars believe that *A Midsummer Night's Dream* was written to celebrate the wedding of some nobleman. The text was first published in the Fisher Quarto of 1600 (the First Quarto). The First Folio (1623) basically follows this copy. The plot, containing four closely interwoven action lines, is Shakespeare's own invention. Its raw materials derive from several literary sources and from folklore. Topical allusions to Elizabethan court intrigue and to King James VI of Scotland have been detected in the play.

The approaching wedding of Theseus, duke of Athens, and Hippolyta, queen of the Amazons, serves as the unifying action of the plot. The main story line deals with the matching and mismatching

TITLE PAGE OF THE FIRST QUARTO (1600) OF SHAKE-SPEARE'S *A Midsummer Night's Dream* (NEW YORK PUBLIC LIBRARY)

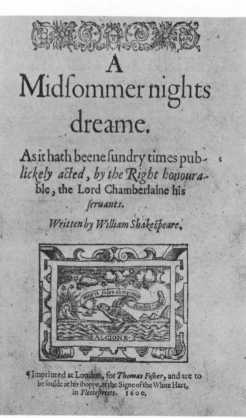

of two young Athenian couples. Defiance of parental authority and Athenian law and supernatural meddling by Oberon, king of the fairies, and his attendant Puck impel the action forward. Most of the play is set in the woods near Athens, to which Oberon and his queen, Titania, have come to be present at the wedding of Theseus and Hippolyta. Also to be present are a group of artisans who are preparing a Pyramus and Thisby play for the occasion. By the end, every Jack has his Jill, and Bottom and his actor-companions have successfully presented their play.

No plot summary can capture the mood of this romantic comedy. The magical world of the moonlit forest, where the diminutive fairies hold forth, contrasts markedly with the world of reality and reason, epitomized by the Athenian court. The poetry, the nature imagery, the music—ranging from the delicate songs of the fairies to the hunting horns of Theseus—give the play a quality hitherto unseen in Shakespeare's work. It is a play about love, about rational and irrational reactions to this emotion. The title gives insight into the thematic lines, for although the play is set around May Day, midsummer night festivals suggest enchantments and a time for giving free reign to passions. Furthermore, in the dream world reality and reason give way to fantasy. The handling of the multiple plot lines is virtuostic; even the Pyramus and Thisby interlude comments dually on the foolishness of irrational love and on the crudity of amateur theatrical performances often played before Queen Elizabeth on her progresses. Through plot and through characters who range in station from the fairy king to Bottom the Weaver— one of the great roles of comedy—Shakespeare masterfully shows, in Puck's words, "what fools these mortals be."

An outstanding edition of *A Midsummer Night's Dream* is the Signet Classic Shakespeare (1963), edited by Wolfgang Clemen.—W. G.

mie. On the Japanese *kabuki* stage, a spectacular, highly stylized acting device. The *mie* may be described as a pose struck by an important actor in a male role to underscore a climactic moment in a kabuki play. The actor's body remains motionless while extreme emotion is expressed by the face, head, and eyes. With a skill difficult to acquire even with long practice, the actor crosses his eyes, giving an extraordinary effect of staring in a manner suggesting compulsive madness. Although the mie may be presented on any part of the acting area, it is used with much frequency on the *hanamichi*, or passageway, leading from the main stage to the rear of the auditorium. At the same time the orchestra performs with special violence. As a rule the audience breaks into exclamations of delight.

Although the pose is supposed to constitute a part of the action, it has the inevitable tendency of focusing attention on the actor as an actor, gaining for him the total attention of the audience. When the actor's public is already familiar with him and favorably disposed, the device has the effect of opening a path to hero-worship. Egoism, which is never far removed from displays of presentational art, discovers by this means an ideal field in which to disport itself. The mie reached its height of popularity in the eighteenth century, when the large numbers of women in the typical kabuki audience gained an opportunity to worship their theatrical idols. Nevertheless, in its essence, the convention belongs to the universal language of melodrama. It is probably the most piquant manner yet found for the actor to win applause.

The *onnagata*, or female impersonators, do not perform the full mie, since doing so would too much deface their feminine charm. They do not so violently distort face or body. But in a limited degree they participate in this meretricious usage.

One of the happier consequences of the mie is the extremely large number of striking theater prints that it has begotten. The pose, often held for a considerable time, naturally attracted the eye of many artists, as, for example, SHARAKU, who seems to have taken the practice somewhat less than seriously.—H. W. W.

Miles Gloriosus (The Braggart Warrior, 205 B.C.?). A comedy by PLAUTUS, based on the Greek comedy *Alazon,* of unknown authorship. *Miles Gloriosus* contains two delightful deceptions, both engineered by the clever slave Palaestrio against Pyrgopolynices, the boastful soldier, whose lust and stupidity motivate the greater part of the action. The first trick, involving a secret passage between two houses and a pretended twin sister, is one version of a famous story that has appeared in numerous forms throughout the Near East and Europe. In the second trick, a cunning courtesan poses as the wife of an aged man next door and pretends to fall in love with the soldier.

Many modern scholars have believed that Plautus combined in one comedy the plots of two Greek originals, with possibly a scene taken from a third play. The arguments for such a theory are not convincing, inasmuch as the success of the second deception provides for the escape of the girl of the first trick with her lover. Most of the scenes are Plautine farce at its best. Pyrgopolynices is the most amusing of the many braggart warriors in Roman comedy and the model for many similar characters in later comedy, such as Nicholas Udall's *Ralph Roister Doister* (c. 1553), Shakespeare's Falstaff and Pistol, Ben Jonson's Captain Bobadill in *Every Man in His Humour* (1598), and Pierre Corneille's Captain Matamore in *L'Illusion comique* (1636). Other dramatists influenced by *Miles Gloriosus* include Pietro Aretino, Lodovico Dolce, Jean Antoine de Baïf, Giovanni Maria Cecchi, John Lyly, Beaumont and Fletcher, Paul Scarron, Antoine Mareschal, Cyrano de Bergerac, Ludvig Holberg, Carlo Goldoni, Jean François Cailhava, Jakob Michael Reinhold Lenz, George Bernard Shaw, and Bertolt Brecht.

Daniel C. Boughner, *The Braggart in Renaissance Comedy* (1954), discusses the influence of *Miles* on Italian, Spanish, and French comedy and on English comedy before Shakespeare. John Arthur Hanson, "The Glorious Military," in T. A. Dorey and Donald R. Dudley, *Roman Drama* (1965), examines the role of the braggart warrior in Shakespeare, Beaumont and Fletcher, Holberg, Shaw, and Brecht.—G. E. D.

Miller, Arthur (1915–   ). American playwright. Miller was born in New York into the family of a prosperous manufacturer who was hit hard by the Great Depression of 1929. After graduating from high school in 1932, Miller took a job in an automobile parts warehouse. In 1934 he entered the University of Michigan, where he won Hopwood Awards for two undergraduate plays and the Theatre Guild

ARTHUR MILLER (WIDE WORLD PHOTOS)

National Award for another play. Following graduation, he took various jobs but principally applied himself to writing radio plays. In 1944 he went to army camps to collect background material for a war film and set down his observations in a book published in that year, *Situation Normal.* 1944 was also the year of his first Broadway play, *The Man Who Had All the Luck,* which was unfavorably reviewed and closed after four performances. In this play the protagonist feels guilty because he has had good luck all his life; after vainly waiting for retribution, he sets out to create his own misfortune. The play provides an early instance of Miller's preoccupation with guilt. In his novel *Focus,* published the following year, a man of vaguely anti-Semitic leanings is taken to be Jewish when he wears glasses; like characters in future Miller plays, he, too, is accused.

Miller's first popular success in the theater came in 1947, when *All My Sons* ran for nearly a year and won the Drama Critics Circle Award for the best American play of the season. Its leading character, Joe Keller, is a manufacturer who has sold defective material to the air force and thereby caused some plane crashes. His partner went to prison, and he himself feels no guilt. But now, in the present time, these old issues are raised again when Joe Keller's surviving son proposes to marry his dead brother's fiancée, the daughter of the man who went to prison and suffered unjustly for Keller's neglect. The younger Keller confronts his father with his responsibility, reveals that his brother, a pilot in the war, sought death because of his father's guilt, and threatens to tell the authorities everything. Acknowledging that all the young men who fought in the war were his sons, Keller passes judgment upon himself and com-

mits suicide. In its form, and especially in its exposition of the impact of past events upon the present, *All My Sons* recalls the works of Ibsen and contains particular echoes of Ibsen's *Pillars of Society.* While it is a suitably representative play on the war years, one index to the play's limitation is the comparatively small interest in reviving it, in contrast with the numerous revivals of such plays as *Death of a Salesman, The Crucible,* and *A View from the Bridge. All My Sons,* incidentally, began Miller's long association with Elia Kazan, who directed it, and Arthur Kennedy, who played the younger Keller.

Miller's next play, DEATH OF A SALESMAN, opened early in 1949, directed by Kazan with a cast that included Lee J. Cobb as the salesman and Arthur Kennedy as his older son. It won the Drama Critics Circle Award and the Pulitzer Prize and was extremely popular.

At the end of 1950, Miller's version of Ibsen's *An Enemy of the People* opened and ran for only thirty-six performances. Miller made the drama seem more immediate, but he simplified the protagonist as well as the play, making Dr. Stockmann more heroic and coherent than Ibsen's "muddleheaded" character, thus turning *An Enemy of the People* into a "thesis play," more like *All My Sons* than like the original Ibsen work.

THE CRUCIBLE, a play about the Salem witch trials (with obvious parallels in Senator Joseph McCarthy's political "witch-hunting"), opened early in 1953, directed by Jed Harris, with Arthur Kennedy in the leading role of John Proctor. It had only 197 performances on Broadway, but it won attention around the world and later had a longer run Off-Broadway. Miller's political views were again aired when, in 1956, he testified before the House Committee on Un-American Activities that he had allied himself with some Communist and Popular Front causes, but he denied ever having been a member of the Communist Party. He refused to give any information about others and consequently was cited for contempt of the committee. On being found guilty, he appealed the conviction and was vindicated by the United States Court of Appeals.

A Memory of Two Mondays and *A View from the Bridge,* a pair of one-act plays, opened on Broadway in the fall of 1955. The length of the run was only 148 performances, but *A View from the Bridge,* in its expanded, prose form, has enjoyed a long life on the stage both at home and abroad. (As originally published, this play had many passages in verse, not of high poetic quality. Miller seems to have acknowledged his error in judgment when he lengthened and rewrote it entirely in prose for his *Collected Plays,* 1957.) The briefer curtain raiser, *A Memory of Two Mondays,* gives us two glimpses, in its two scenes, of life in an automobile parts warehouse as seen through the eyes of a young man who leaves at the end to go to college. Miller's aim is to evoke concern for those who are left behind, the friendly, pitiful fellow workers, all inexorably trapped in the warehouse. The dramatist has understandably spoken of his love for this play.

A View from the Bridge is intended as a sort of Greek tragedy; its characters are Sicilian Americans (Sicily was once a Greek colony), and one of them acts as a chorus. It is the tragedy of Eddie Carbone, a longshoreman who refuses to acknowledge his excessive interest in his niece. Like others in his neighborhood, he and his family shelter illegal immigrants from Italy. When one of them shows a romantic interest in his niece, Carbone betrays him and another illegal immigrant to the immigration authorities. The other immigrant kills him, but Carbone has, in effect, sought death at his hands. The immediate, contemporary issue of the play is informing; obviously, Eddie Carbone, who broke the community's law of silence regarding the illegal immigrants, was comparable to those men who had gone before investigating committees as "friendly witnesses," naming members and former members of the Communist Party. Technically, they were obeying the law, but they were guilty of betrayal. Miller was consistent with the values of this play when he refused to name names before a congressional committee in the following year.

An equally important matter in the play is Eddie Carbone's attachment to his niece, which drives him to betrayal. He persuades himself that the young immigrant is a homosexual and an opportunist, bent on finding an American wife so that he can stay in the United States. Carbone's guilty preference for his young niece over his plain but estimable wife has its parallel in John Proctor's romance with young Abigail in *The Crucible* and in Quentin's attachment to Maggie in *After the Fall*. It has been suggested that all these relationships reflect Miller's connection with Marilyn Monroe, whom he married in 1956; they were divorced in 1961. During their marriage, Miller wrote no plays, but he did write the script for a film that starred Miss Monroe, *The Misfits*. It is, in a sense, a cowboy film, showing the lives of men who capture wild mustangs—for dog food.

After his third marriage, to Ingeborg Morath, a photographer, in 1962, Miller returned to playwriting. By 1964, he had two plays ready for the Lincoln Center Repertory Theater—*After the Fall*, which opened in January, directed by Elia Kazan with a cast headed by Jason Robards, Jr., and *Incident at Vichy*, which opened in December, directed by Harold Clurman. *After the Fall* is an extremely subjective, apparently semiautobiographical play about a lawyer named Quentin who survives family rivalries as a child and his family's loss of its prosperity as an adolescent. He becomes involved in left-wing politics; one of his friends is ruined by his allegiance to Communism, but another becomes a "friendly witness" before a congressional committee. (The latter character was assumed to represent Kazan, with whom Miller had recently reconciled his differences.) He becomes infatuated with a popular singer named Maggie, divorces his first wife, and marries her. Thereafter, all his time is taken up with Maggie's career, her infidelities, and her demands on him. (Maggie is taken to be a portrait, very likely an unfair one, of Marilyn Monroe.) At last, he breaks off this relationship and marries a serene lady of German or Austrian origin (no doubt corresponding to Ingeborg Morath). The incidents are interesting enough, but the play is marred by Miller's concern with making a case for Quentin, exonerating him of any responsibility for his political associations and for Maggie's suicide. Miller's familiar theme of guilt and passing judgment is present, and yet Quentin's

defense is to turn the accusations against everyone else: everyone has wronged him. In its form, *After the Fall*, alone among Miller's plays, recalls the subjectivity and the semiexpressionism of *Death of a Salesman*.

Incident at Vichy, a long one-act play, takes place during the war in unoccupied France. Some Jews and suspected Jews are herded together to be exported to a concentration camp. An Austrian nobleman gives up his pass to save a Jewish psychoanalyst, whose need to survive he takes to be greater than his own.

By this time Miller had become closely attached to the Lincoln Center Repertory Theater. He withdrew from it in the last days of 1964 when his associates, Robert Whitehead and Elia Kazan, resigned. His next play was produced on Broadway; it was another long one-acter, *The Price*, opening early in 1968, produced by Whitehead and directed by Ulu Grosbard, with Pat Hingle and Arthur Kennedy (making his fourth appearance in one of Miller's plays) in the leading roles. *The Price* might almost be the sequel to the family story at the beginning of *After the Fall*. Two brothers meet after a long separation to decide what to do with their family's old, abandoned furniture. Long before, when the family lost its fortune, one son went to college while the other dropped out to help support his parents. One became a wealthy surgeon and the other a policeman. Now, in the present, the policeman agrees to a low price for the furniture offered by a charming and witty old furniture dealer. The surgeon observes that, once again, his brother has been misled by a persuasive old man, as he was years ago by their father: his sacrifices were unnecessary because the family would have survived without his help. Thus, the play seems to defend the surgeon against any responsibility for his brother's unfulfilled life. On the other hand, Miller has expressed surprise at this emphasis, noting that the policeman has a much happier family life and so is better off. *The Price* is a good example of a typical Ibsenish play, presenting issues of guilt and responsibility, cast in an Ibsenish form, but for once omitting any wider social reference. It has the liveliest character Miller ever created, the old furniture dealer.

A collection of stories, *I Don't Need You Any More*, appeared in 1967. The two most useful books on Miller are probably *Arthur Miller: The Burning Glass* (1965), by Sheila Huftel, and *Arthur Miller* (1967), by Leonard Moss.—H. P.

Milton, John (1608–1674). English poet and publicist. Milton, the greatest of English nondramatic poets, wrote three dramatic works, *Arcades*, *Comus*, and *Samson Agonistes*. The first two belong to his youth. On receiving his M.A. at Cambridge in July 1632, Milton retired to his father's house in Hammersmith and entered upon a course of private study that lasted until his Italian tour (1638–1639). *Arcades* (1629?–?1633) was a graceful miniature masque presented in honor of the illustrious dowager countess of Derby by young members of her family at her Harefield estate. The invitation to devise this courtly compliment probably came from Henry Lawes, a well-known musician, who commissioned, produced, and acted in the far more elaborate "Mask Presented At Ludlow-Castle" on September 29, 1634. The occasion was the inauguration of the countess's son-in-law, the earl of Bridgewater, as lord

JOHN MILTON (WALTER HAMPDEN MEMORIAL LI-
BRARY AT THE PLAYERS, NEW YORK)

president of Wales. The text—with some important passages not in the acting version—was printed by Lawes in 1637/38, with Milton's consent but without his name, and was included in his *Poems* of 1645. The illogical but convenient title *Comus* first came into use with eighteenth-century adaptations for the stage.

The MASQUE, a favorite form of entertainment at court and in noble houses, had been especially and seriously developed by Ben Jonson. The essential core of formal compliment was embedded in an allegorical and often mythological libretto and was lavishly embellished with spectacle, dance, and song. The young Milton, while fulfilling normal requirements, gave exceptional dramatic, ethical, and religious weight to plot, dialogue, and theme; his courtly and pastoral art and his exalted ardor created verse of radiant beauty.

The plot combines the archetypal idea of a quest (the earl's children journeying to Ludlow through a dark and dangerous wood) with the likewise old theme of sensual enchantment, here transferred from Circe to her imagined son, Comus, a lord of misrule. The parts of the three travelers were acted by Lady Alice Egerton (aged fifteen) and her younger brothers. Henry Lawes was the Attendant Spirit, who is virtually a guardian angel, though his powers are limited. In the central debate between the enchanter and the captive lady, Comus, in verse of remarkable visual and tactual immediacy, argues for man's free use of nature's prodigal bounties, including sexual license. The lady replies first on the level of reason;

then, with "sacred vehemence," she rises to the young poet's conception of chastity, which is not mere abstinence but the Christian-Platonic love of the Good (as he was to say in the personal passage in *An Apology for Smectymnuus*, 1642). When Comus and his crew escape from the brothers and the Attendant Spirit, the unconquered but still immobilized lady is freed from the spell by Sabrina, the goddess of the nearby Severn River, who seems to represent divine grace. The victory of good over evil ends in courtly, festive, and religious joy. Although the masque largely preserves a "pagan" decorum, hints of Christian meaning—and a Miltonic purity of tone—begin with the opening lines: "Before the starry threshold of Jove's court / My mansion is"; and the full theme is distilled in the Epilogue: "Or if Virtue feeble were, / Heav'n itself would stoop to her."

It is a long way from the lyrical idealism of *Comus* to the massive and complex treatment of temptation, sin, and recovery in *Samson Agonistes*. The drama was published, with *Paradise Regained*, in 1671, and it has commonly been regarded as Milton's last poetic work, at any rate as of the period 1660–1670. Although a few modern scholars have pushed composition back into the 1640's, one may still hold the traditional view. The Restoration had nullified Milton's twenty years of strenuous effort on behalf of the Puritan Revolution and, thinking of that heroic past, the blind poet could feel the lot of God's champion now "Eyeless in Gaza at the mill with slaves" (though the drama is kept wholly impersonal); he could also affirm his much-tried but invincible faith in God's providence and in the regenerative strength of the individual soul.

As a Renaissance humanist, with no thought of stage performance, Milton naturally followed the Greek pattern, and *Samson* is the one English drama of that kind that ranks with its ancient models. Because of his lifelong saturation in them, and his own artistic and religious temper, his work has affinities with the tragedies of all three of the Greek writers, particularly with *Prometheus Bound* and *Oedipus at Colonus*; and he was aware of modern Italian drama. The very consciously European poet always worked in, and re-created, established genres, and *Samson* is at once traditional and uniquely original. In diction, syntax, and the rhythms of both blank and irregular verse there is a new, sinewy, semicolloquial expressiveness.

The protagonist is raised far above the brawny Hercules of the book of Judges, and, until the reported catastrophe, the action is psychological. At first Samson's consciousness of his guilt is almost submerged in self-centered bemoaning of his grievous fate; but he moves steadily (with one heavy relapse) toward selfless penitence and then to a humbler, surer faith in his renewed acceptance as God's champion. The agents of this process of salvation are the chorus and the individual interlocutors, Samson's father Manoa, Dalila, and the Philistine giant Harapha, because, ironically, all these interviews have an effect upon Samson contrary to what the visitors anticipated. Ironic ambiguity works also in countless details, from the title and the first line to the end. As the drama proceeds, Samson is more and more isolated, even from his sympathizers, who see only outward things, not his inward suffering and victory. While it has been said that a Christian tragedy is a contradiction in terms, *Samson* is a tragedy and is in effect Christian: the working out of God's purposes may include what, from the human standpoint, seems mysterious pain and tragic waste. Not the least remarkable thing about this strong and subtle drama is that Milton suggests the operation of grace without ever touching a specifically Christian idea, without violating Hebraic decorum; for Samson there is no promise of heaven.

The standard edition of Milton's complete works is that of the Columbia University Press (20 vols., 1931–1940). Among countless annotated editions of the complete poems are those of M. Y. Hughes (1957) and D. Bush (1965). Manuscript and early printed texts of *Arcades* and *Comus* are reproduced in H. F. Fletcher's facsimile edition (Vol. I, 1943). There are small biographies by J. H. Hanford (1939) and D. Bush (1964), a massive one by W. R. Parker (2 vols., 1968). Four essays, on *Arcades, Comus,* and *Samson,* are reprinted in *Milton: Modern Essays in Criticism,* A. Barker, ed. (1965). Among essays on *Comus* are those of A. S. P. Woodhouse (*University of Toronto Quarterly,* 11, 1941/42, and 19, 1949/50) and R. Tuve (*Images & Themes in Five Poems by Milton,* 1957). Three studies of *Samson* are: W. R. Parker, *Milton's Debt to Greek Tragedy in Samson Agonistes* (1937); Arnold Stein, *Heroic Knowledge* (1957); and a reprint of J. H. Hanford's essay in his *John Milton: Poet and Humanist* (1966); see also Barker, above.—D. B.

mime. A performance in which the story is conveyed through body movements rather than words. (See PANTOMIME.) In Greek and Roman drama, however, mime is a short, improvised, dramatic farce. Classical mimes were restricted to one scene and were frequently used as interludes in the performances of regular plays. Their popularity was doubtless heightened by the fact that women were allowed to perform in them.

Often indecent and produced without masks, the mime reached Rome not later than 211 B.C. and became a literary form in the late Republic. The chief writers were Decimus Laberius (c. 115–43 B.C.), and his contemporary Publilius Syrus. Of their works we have only titles and fragments, including several hundred lines of *sententiae,* or proverbial sayings, excerpted at a later date from the mimes of Publilius. In the Roman Empire the mime supplanted tragedy and comedy as the most popular form of dramatic entertainment.—G. E. D.

Ming Huang (685–762). The famous Chinese emperor whose reign (713–756) marked the most brilliant years of the T'ang dynasty (618–906). Ming Huang is traditionally regarded as archpatron of Chinese drama and founder of it in the classical form still preserved to us. No surviving plays, however, can properly be assigned to his reign. It is presumed that the entertainments in his court were largely musical, choreographic, mimetic, or recitative and that the dramatic form as now generally understood was not perfected in China until some five centuries thereafter. Nevertheless, this emperor undoubtedly established lavish official patronage for all the performing arts. Despite its cultural distinction, his reign ended in political debacle. He was driven from

his capital, forced to renounce his great extravagance, and ultimately to resign his throne. For a further account of his place in dramatic history, see CHINA; PEAR GARDEN.—H. W. W.

Minna von Barnhelm. See GERMANY: *eighteenth century;* Gotthold Ephraim LESSING.

Minor, The (*Nedorosl,* 1782). A comedy in five acts by Denis FONVIZIN. *The Minor* is generally considered the first major original Russian comedy, despite its plot, which at first glance may seem to be a traditional comedy situation. Sofia, the orphaned ward of greedy landowners, suddenly turns out to be the heiress of a rich and wise uncle. Thus, from a downtrodden dependent, she is instantaneously transformed into an alluring match for her guardians' spoiled, moronic son, Mitrofan the minor, and for the minor's maternal uncle, whose only interest in life is raising pigs and to whom a rich bride is just a means of acquiring more pigs. The minor's adoring mother, Mrs. Prostakov, a wicked matriarch and absolute ruler of the estate, who beats her husband and has her servants whipped at her slightest whim, pushes her pig-loving brother aside, determined to wed her former ward to her good-for-nothing son. Her plans, however, come to nothing: it so happens that the young officer who arrives to investigate the abuse of serfs by landowners is Sofia's secret lover. Then the wise and rich uncle appears in person to bestow his niece's hand on her beloved and to tell the wicked landowners what he thinks of them.

Despite the moralizing tirades by the "positive characters" and their long-winded definitions of virtue and social justice, the play is full of life and is highly amusing. At the same time it presents a vivid picture of the grim mores prevalent among the landed gentry in the Russia of Catherine the Great. What is also striking is that, even more than in his earlier and lesser comedy *Brigadir* (*The Brigadier,* 1769), Fonvizin succeeds in imparting a strange realism to his caricature characters. The sixteen-year-old oaf feels that the rudiments of learning that by law every young gentleman was supposed to acquire and that his three preposterous tutors were trying to pass onto him were much too complicated. Instead, he keeps pleading, "I don't want to study, I want to marry," and this rhyming Russian phrase has remained a Russian saying to this day. His doting mother, the otherwise fierce Mrs. Prostakov, warmly sympathizes with him: why, she wonders, should a young gentleman clutter his mind with such things as geography when a person in his position can just hail a cab and give the coachman the address where he wishes to be driven. Thanks to Fonvizin's colorful language, many such bits of dialogue have remained part of the Russian language.

In many ways *The Minor* is a prototype of what is often referred to as "Russian realistic theater"; its influence is obvious in the plays of Alexander Griboyedov and Nikolai Gogol and is even recognizable in those of Alexander Sukhovo-Kobylin, Ivan Turgenev, Anton Chekhov, and others.

The Minor, translated by F. D. Reeve, appears in *An Anthology of Russian Plays,* Vol. I (1961). —A. MACA.

miracle play. See SAINT'S PLAY.

Misanthrope, Le (1666). A comedy by MOLIÈRE. Alceste, who has pretensions to sincerity, who will

ENGRAVING OF A SCENE FROM MOLIÈRE'S *Le Misan-thrope* (FRENCH CULTURAL SERVICES)

not agree to share friendship or love, and who loathes the customs of his time, has, nevertheless, a pleasant opportunist, Philinte, for a friend and is in love with the flirtatious Célimène. He tries to make Célimène reject her other suitors and devote herself entirely to him. When it is finally discovered that, in spite of her love for Alceste, she treats all her admirers in the same manner, her friends forsake her. Alceste then suggests that he marry her and take her far away from Paris. Since she hesitates, he renounces her and decides to leave Paris alone. *Le Misanthrope* is a comedy about the absolute incompatibility of two very different natures—one exclusive, the other gregarious and eager for compliments—and presents the portrait of an egotistic, self-satisfied society.

This play has been translated in English verse by Richard Wilbur (1954), reprinted in *The Classic Theater* (1961), Vol. IV, Eric Bentley, ed.—Ja. G.

Misfortunes of Arthur, The (1588). An academic tragedy by Thomas Hughes (fl. 1587), presented before Queen Elizabeth in her palace at Greenwich on February 28, 1588. The play was produced by Hughes and a group of his fellow law students at Gray's Inn, among whom was Francis Bacon. Although devoid of literary merit, the play is notable as an interesting attempt to adapt Senecan drama to an English mold. The story is derived from legendary English history—the reign of King Arthur. The rest of the play, however, is pure Seneca, including the presence of a ghost, a messenger to report events offstage, and a tragic chorus commenting on the action. The Senecan motif is completed by the frequent appearance of translated lines from the Roman dramatist, which are woven into the play.—E. Q.

Miss Julie (Fröken Julie, 1889). A one-act tragedy by August STRINDBERG. Strindberg called *Miss Julie* the first naturalistic play in Scandinavia, and his

epoch-making Preface not only offers a useful summary of the naturalist's theory of character but anticipates the doctrines of expressionist theater. This important play, more or less a *quart d'heure* written with an eye on director André Antoine's Théâtre Libre, has found a place in international repertoire and has also been adapted to film (Alf Sjöberg, 1951), dance (Birgit Cullberg, 1950), and opera (Ned Rorem, 1966).

The play focuses upon a sexual encounter between Miss Julie, neurasthenic and of noble family, and the footman Jean, a vulgar aspirant to a better way of life. Their rendezvous, which happens at the witching moment of midsummer, is brief, violent, and premature because, as some say, "the classes are not yet ripe for fusion." Two-thirds of the play is a *post coitum* impasse filled with bickering and stridency relieved by patches of introspection. Eventually, Jean's rising line is halted by the return of the Count, Julie's father, and Jean snaps back to servility. Julie's downward line rises; she recovers a measure of dignity and moves offstage, like a sleepwalker, to her death by suicide. Interestingly enough, she must still be in the mesmerizing power of Jean to accomplish this. A sunrise (which Strindberg later deplored) and

TITLE PAGE FROM THE 1673 EDITION OF JEAN RACINE'S *Mithridate* (NEW YORK PUBLIC LIBRARY)

MITHRIDATE,

TRAGEDIE.

PAR MR RACINE.

A PARIS,

Chez CLAVDE BARBIN, au Palais, fur le fecond Perron de la Sainte Chapelle.

M. DC. LXXIII.

AVEC PRIVILEGE DV ROY.

A SCENE FROM AUGUST STRINDBERG'S *Miss Julie* (FRENCH CULTURAL SERVICES)

a fragment of biblical quotation impart a ritual tone to the ending.

In *Miss Julie* Strindberg transcends a projection of his own divided class sensibility, at least partially a source of the play, and anticipates for better or worse the themes of D. H. Lawrence's *Lady Chatterley's Lover* and Tennessee Williams' *A Streetcar Named Desire* (which critic Eric Bentley described as a rewrite of *Miss Julie*). But the play is more psychological and ritualistic than sociological. It moves toward the stylized impersonations of Jean Genet's *The Maids*, as critic Evert Sprinchorn has pointed out, and the control of its jagged emotional course elevates it above naturalism.

The text may be found in *Miss Julie, An Authoritative Text Edition with Critical Material* (1965), edited by Henry Popkin. See also Evert Sprinchorn, "Julie's End," in *Essays on Strindberg* (Stockholm, 1966), pp. 19–27.—R. B. V.

Mithridate (1673). A tragedy by Jean RACINE. In 64 B.C. Pharnace, a traitor and ally of the Romans, and his brother Xipharès vie for the heart of Monime, fiancée of Mithridate, their father, whom they believe to be dead. Mithridate reappears and has Pharnace arrested. When he learns from Pharnace that Monime loves Xipharès, he decides to have both of them killed. But Pharnace escapes and stirs up the people against his father, who, when trapped, stabs himself. Xipharès runs to his aid, and the old dying king unites Xipharès and Monime. In the political scenes of the play Mithridate has all the heroic grandeur of Pierre Corneille's heroes; but he is portrayed chiefly as an old man, the victim of a degrading passion from which he can be freed only by death.

This play has been translated into English verse by Samuel Solomon in *Complete Plays* (1967). —Ja. G.

Mitra, Deenabandhu. See PAKISTAN: *Bengali drama.*

modern dramatic criticism. Modern dramatic criticism, as T. S. Eliot said of the modern era in general, draws its style and much of its substance from Romantic sources: from Leigh Hunt and especially William Hazlitt, both Englishmen. Their writing was the first to reveal the capacities of dramatic criticism as an art in itself, particularly when it was in response to fine acting. Without an Edmund Kean, there would have been no Hazlitt.

It is also quite probable that Hazlitt would not have achieved his place in criticism if Leigh Hunt (1784–1859) had not prepared the way. Hunt was the first critic of quality to report on all the theater events of importance in his day. From 1805 to 1807, he was critic for the *News* and from 1808 to 1813 for the *Examiner,* where Hazlitt followed him. Hunt also passes on to modern criticism the tradition of the critic-playwright, a tradition that culminates in George Bernard Shaw. Hunt's plays, unlike Shaw's, are rarely heard of (*A Legend of Florence*, 1840, is no exception), but his criticism is still valuable. The best of it is collected in *Dramatic Essays by Leigh Hunt* (1894), edited by William Archer.

Hunt focused on the Romantic concern for imagination, harmony, and naturalness in acting. In comedy, for instance, he preferred cordialness to the artificial show and grace of earlier acting conventions. His other concerns are clear in his remarks about an actor named Mr. Pope:

> The best character he performs is Othello, because he performs it in a mask: for when an actor's face is not exactly seen, an audience is content to supply by its own imagination the want of expression, just as in reading a book we figure to ourselves the countenance of the persons interested. But when we are presented with the real countenance, we are disappointed if our imagination is not assisted in its turn; the picture presented to our eyes should animate the picture presented to our mind; if either of them differ, or if the former is less lively than the latter, a sensation of discord is produced, and destroys the effect of nature, which is always harmonious. [*Dramatic Essays by Leigh Hunt*]

The greatest contribution of William Hazlitt (1778–1830) was to bring the exercise of dramatic criticism to the status of an independent art, in terms of originality of thought and felicity of execution. He had superb actors for subject matter: besides Edmund Kean, there were Mrs. Siddons, Mrs. O'Neill, and the Kembles (John Phillip and Charles). He appreciated an actor like Kean, whose electricity could virtually shock his imagination. A Mrs. O'Neill, he said, could elicit only praise, and that was far less interesting to him.

Besides style and imagination, Hazlitt also had the advantage of a point of view, a general outlook against which he could measure individual performances. This—his ideal theater—is best described in his *Characters of Shakespeare's Plays* (1817), a work that participates in the Shakespeare revival begun by Samuel Coleridge at the turn of the century. His best criticism is collected in *A View of the English Stage* (1818) and is drawn from the reviews he did for the *Morning Chronicle* and the *Examiner* from 1813 to 1818.

A friend of Keats, Hazlitt shared with the poet a spirit of geniality that is both generosity of spirit and genius of intellect. As seen in *Hazlitt on Theatre* (1895), edited by William Archer, underlying Hazlitt's criticism is the belief that "the stage is an arduous profession, requiring so many essential excellences and accidental advantages, that though it is an honour and a happiness to succeed in it, it is only a misfortune, and not a disgrace, to fail in it." As for genius, Hazlitt's style of response to a play was one of "brief oracles and broken revelations." A contemporary wrote that "he never wrote willingly, except on what was great in itself, or, forming a part of his own past, was great to him." His genius required genius to ignite it.

Kean was Hazlitt's favorite actor and Hazlitt thought his best performances were the murder scene in *Macbeth* and the third act of *Othello*. His remarks about *Othello* are lapidary: "Mr. Kean's *Othello* is his best character, and the highest effort of genius on the stage. We say this without any exception or reserve. Yet we wish it was better than it is."

A fuller view of Hazlitt's approach is seen in his review of Kean's *Richard III:*

> Mr. Kean's manner of acting this part has one peculiar advantage; it is entirely his own, without any traces of imitation of any other actor. He stands upon his own ground, and he stands firm upon it. Almost every scene had the stamp and freshness of nature. The excellences and defects of his performance were in general the same as those which he discovered in Shylock; though, as the character of Richard is the most difficult, so we think he displayed most power in it. It is possible to form a higher conception of this character (we do not mean from seeing other actors, but from reading Shakespeare) than that given by this very admirable tragedian; but we cannot imagine any character represented with greater distinctness and precision, more perfectly *articulated* in every part. Perhaps, indeed, there is too much of this; for we sometimes thought he failed, even from an exuberance of talent, and dissipated the impression of the character by the variety of his resources. To be perfect, it should have a little more solidity, depth, sustained, and impassioned feeling, with somewhat less brilliancy, with fewer glancing points, pointed transitions, and pantomimic evolutions. [*Hazlitt on Theatre*]

The exposure to genius had its dangers for the critic:

> The knowledge we acquire of various kinds of excellence, as successive opportunities present themselves, leads us to require a combination of them which we never find realized in any individual, and all the consolation for the disappointment of our fastidious expectations is in a sort of fond and doting retrospect of the past. [*Hazlitt on Theatre*]

Hazlitt's attitude toward actors and acting was loving, genuine, almost philosophical:

> They are the only honest hypocrites. Their life is a voluntary dream; a studied madness. The height of their ambition is to be *beside themselves.* . . . We see ourselves at second hand in them; they show us all that we are, all that we wish to be, and all that we dread to be. [*Hazlitt on Theatre*]

Unfortunately, his high regard for acting and his championship of the stage against its puritanical enemies led him to a positive moral enthusiasm that, even in the most generous contemporary view, must appear naïve:

> We will hazard a conjecture that the acting of *The Beggar's Opera* a certain number of nights every year since it was first brought out has done more towards putting down the practice of highway robbery, than all the gibbets that ever were erected. [*Hazlitt on Theatre*]

George Henry Lewes (1817–1878) was the son of the actor who created the part of Fagin in Sheridan's *The Rivals* and was the common-law husband of the novelist George Eliot. Until 1856 Lewes wrote plays, mostly comedies and farces (*Wanted, a She-Wolf* and *Buckstone's Adventures with a Polish Princess,* to name only two) under the entertaining pseudonym Slingsby Lawrence. His best criticism is found in the volume *On Actors and the Art of Acting* (1875).

Out of this highly colored background emerged

another most perceptive critic of acting. For among the many other things Lewes was, he was also a biologist and psychologist, and his criticism shows a scientific reflectiveness and classical detachment that are far removed from Hazlitt's "brief oracles and broken revelations" but quite proper to a contemporary of Darwin.

Lewes is rarely a phrasemaker but frequently a cosmologist of acting relationships, with a fine capacity for locating and defining:

> . . . to personate a character, there are three fundamental requisite conditions, which I will call—1. *Conceptual Intelligence;* 2. *Representative Intelligence;* 3. *Physical Advantages.* The first condition is requisite to *understand* the character; the last two are requisite in different degrees to *represent* the character. . . . I proceed to apply [these principles] to Macready; and first say that, inasmuch as he possesses in an unusual degree the three requisites laid down, he must be classed among the *great* actors. His conceptual intelligence everyone will acknowledge. . . . But I do not go along with those who exalt his intellect into greatness. I am not aware of any manifestation of greatness he has given. His conception always betrays care and thought, and never betrays foolishness. On the other hand, I never received any light from him to clear up an obscurity; my knowledge of Shakespeare is little increased by his performances. I cannot point to any one single trace of illumination —such as Edmund Kean used to flash out. . . . The intelligence most shown by Macready is that which I have named representative intelligence, and which he possesses in a remarkable degree. Certain peculiarities and defects prevent his representing the high, heroic, passionate characters; but nothing can prevent his representation of some others; and connecting this representative intelligence with his physical advantages, we see how he can execute what he conceives, and thus become an actor. [Cited in *Dramatic Essays by John Forster and George Henry Lewes* (1896), edited by William Archer.]

Firm in the belief that "the failures of distinguished artists are always fruitful in suggestion," Lewes noted how the great Romantic ideal of "the natural" (meaning the organic) was gradually corrupting into artificiality, into a convention of "the natural," into "the natural" meaning realism. Speaking of Charles Albert Fechter's Othello, he extracts the principle that caused its failure:

> . . . The confusion between realism and vulgarism works like a poison. It is not consistent with the nature of tragedy to obtrude the details of daily life. All that lounging on tables and lolling against chairs, which help to convey a sense of reality in the *drame,* are as unnatural in tragedy as it would be to place the "Sleeping Fawn" of Phidias on a comfortable feather-bed. When Fechter takes out his doorkey to let himself into his house, and, on coming back, relocks the door and pockets the key, the *intention* is doubtless to give an air of reality; the *effect* is to make us forget the "noble Moor," and to think of a sepoy. [*On Actors and the Art of Acting*]

Lewes' distinction between the organic and the artificial led him to attack the conventional, as opposed to original, actor:

> . . . Within the limits which are assigned by nature to every artist, the success of the personation will depend upon the vividness of the actor's sympathy, and his honest reliance on the truth of his own individual expression, in preference to the conventional expressions which may be accepted on the stage. This is the great actor, the creative artist. The conventional artist is one who either because he does not feel the vivid sympathy, or cannot express what he feels, or has not sufficient energy of self-reliance to trust frankly to his own expressions, cannot *be* the part, but tries to *act* it, and thus is necessarily driven to adopt those conventional means of expression with which the traditions of the stage abound. [*On Actors and the Art of Acting*]

In the absence of what Lewes regarded as true acting genius like Kean's, he could only lament the subordination of dramatic art to theatrical effect:

> It is the incalculable advantage of the actor that he stands in the suffused light of emotion kindled by the author, and is rewarded, as the bearer of glad tidings is rewarded, though he has had nothing to do with the facts he narrates. [*On Actors and the Art of Acting*]

If Lewes brought a balanced, if occasionally bitter, voice to bear against the actor-manager system that led to theatrical effect rather than dramatic art, George Bernard Shaw (1856–1950) usually enjoyed fighting the tradition with its own weapons. The famous work he did for *The Saturday Review* from 1895 to 1898 is collected in *Our Theatre in the Nineties* (1932), and a good selection from that is found in *Shaw's Dramatic Criticism* (1959), edited by John F. Matthews.

Shaw's success as a reviewer lay not only in his own highly quotable theatricality and his cunning choice of targets but also in the fact that the pressure behind Shaw the critic was Shaw the dramatist. Before he began dramatic criticism and while he was writing music criticism (from 1888 to 1894, under the pseudonym Corni di Bassetto), Shaw had finished *Widowers' Houses* (begun in 1885; prod. 1892), *The Philanderer* (written 1893; prod. 1905), *Mrs. Warren's Profession* (written 1893; prod. 1902), and *Arms and the Man* (1894). Shaw says about the dramatist-critic:

> Those of our critics who, either as original dramatists or adapters or translators, have superintended the production of plays with paternal anxiety, are never guilty of the wittily disguised indifference of clever critics who have never seen a drama through from its first beginnings behind the scenes. . . . On the whole there is only as much validity in the theory that a critic should not be a dramatist, as in the theory that a judge should not be a lawyer nor a general a soldier. You cannot have qualifications without experience; and you cannot have experience without personal interest and bias. That may not be an ideal arrangement; but it is the way the world is built;

and we must make the best of it. [*Shaw's Dramatic Criticism*]

Concerning Shaw's favorite targets, the first thing to note is that they were not small: the profession of acting, popular plays, and, with special, slightly perverse enthusiasm, Shakespeare. Shaw's frequently negative criticisms of actors of the stature of Henry Irving, Barry Sullivan, Mrs. Patrick Campbell, and Sarah Bernhardt often arose from a sense of danger about the notion of professionalism itself, in acting and other fields:

I have . . . friends who are law-mad—who believe that lawyers are wise, judges high-minded and impartial, juries infallible, and codes on the brink of perfection. The military-mad and the clergy-mad stalk at large throughout the kingdom. Men believe in the professions as they believe in ghosts, because they want to believe in them. Fact-blindness —the most common sort of blindness—and the resolute lying of respectable men, keep up the illusion. No mortal, however hard-headed, can feel very safe in his attempts to sift the gold of fact and efficiency out of the huge rubbish heap of professionalism. [*Shaw's Dramatic Criticism*]

On the simply practical (and biased) level of a dramatist looking for actors for his play, Shaw adds:

Nothing is more appalling to the dramatic author than the discovery that professional actors of ten years' standing have acquired nothing but a habit of brazening out their own incompetence. . . . At the end of a lifetime so spent, the "actor" will no doubt be a genuine expert at railway travelling, at taking lodgings, and at cajoling and bullying landladies; but a decent amateur of two years' standing, and of the true irrepressible sort, will beat him hopelessly at his art. [*Shaw's Dramatic Criticism*]

Shaw's famous accusation of "Sardoodledom" for the vehicle plays favored by the commercially successful actor of his day is a crystallization of the following kind of playgoing experience, a result of seeing Sardou's *Fédora:*

Up to this day week I had preserved my innocence as a playgoer sufficiently never to have seen Fedora. Of course I was not altogether new to it, since I had seen Diplomacy Dora, and Theodora, and La Toscadora, and other machine dolls from the same firm. And yet the thing took me aback. To see that curtain go up again and again only to disclose a bewildering confusion of everything that has no business in a play, was an experience for which nothing could quite prepare me. The postal arrangements, the telegraphic arrangements, the police arrangements, the names and addresses, the hours and seasons, the tables of consanguinity, the railway and shipping time-tables, the arrivals and departures, the whole welter of Bradshaw and Baedeker, Court Guide and Post Office Directory, whirling around one incredible little stage murder and finally vanishing in a gulp of impossible stage poison, made up an entertainment too Bedlamite for any man with settled wits to preconceive. [*Shaw's Dramatic Criticism*]

Shaw attacked the Sardou type of play for its irrelevance to the point of immorality. His designation and denigration of Shakespeare as "our national theatrical Minotaur" was, however, an attack not so much against Shakespeare as against the Shakespeareans who trapped and destroyed themselves artistically by the rites of imitation they paid their idol:

Those who desire to rejoice in Shakespear must confine themselves (as they generally do) to reading his own plays. Read those which have been written since he overwhelmed English dramatic poetry with his impossible example, and you will wish that he had never been born. [*Shaw's Dramatic Criticism*]

It was particularly galling to Shaw that Shakespeare should absorb the energies of talented actors who, he felt, should devote themselves to the best plays of contemporary relevance. He speaks of Ellen Terry's attempts "to extract a precarious sustenance for her reputation from Shakespear," and adds:

When I think of the originality and modernity of the talent she revealed twenty years ago, and of its remorseless waste ever since in "supporting" an actor who prefers The Iron Chest to Ibsen, my regard for Sir Henry Irving cannot blind me to the fact that it would have been better for us twenty-five years ago to have tied him up in a sack with every existing copy of the works of Shakespear, and dropped him into the crater of the nearest volcano. [*Shaw's Dramatic Criticism*]

Shaw's championship of Ibsen (*The Quintessence of Ibsenism* appeared in 1891) is based on his belief that Ibsen's "cold passion of the North" is

that essentially human passion which embodies itself in objective purposes and interests, and in attachments which again embody themselves in objective purposes and interests on behalf of others—that fruitful, contained, governed, instinctively utilized passion which makes nations and individuals great, as distinguished from the explosive, hysterical, wasteful passion which makes nothing but a scene. [*Shaw's Dramatic Criticism*]

Any final analysis of Shaw must concede that he himself made more than a scene. He raised the dramatic critic into something more than a "connoisseur of virtuosity." In moving from the actor's manner to the dramatist's matter, he was the first to prescribe and embody a social function for the critic, a function that the modern critic abandons at the cost of his relevance to contemporary life.

Max Beerbohm (1872–1956) was Shaw's successor on *The Saturday Review,* writing there from 1898 to 1910. "The incomparable Max" was a caricaturist and literary man, the author of the delightful novel *Zuleika Dobson* (1911) as well as minor plays. His best criticism is in the volume *Around Theatres* (1930).

Beerbohm did his best to correct what he considered the imbalances of his predecessor, beginning with Shaw's own plays. Of *Man and Superman,* he said, "Never has he thought more clearly or more wrongly." But Beerbohm's vision was generous with regard to Shaw, especially Shaw in the theater as opposed to Shaw on the printed page. He went so far as to belittle his own imagination in his praise of *Major Barbara:*

> . . . to deny that he is a dramatist merely because he chooses, for the most part, to get drama out of contrasted types of character and thought, without action, and without appeal to the emotions, seems to me both unjust and absurd. His technique is peculiar because his purpose is peculiar. But it is not the less technique. There! I have climbed down. Gracefully enough to escape being ridiculous? [*Around Theatres*]

Beerbohm could never, however, revise his estimate of Ibsen as an unlovable self-hater. Beerbohm's critical equipment was much more responsive to charm than venerability. His favorite actors were French and he often berated the English actor for his painfully comfortable domesticity. Amid the "hob, fender, and fire-irons" theater of his day, Beerbohm's eye was happy to find and praise the early work of Gordon Craig.

Although Beerbohm found writing difficult, he thought of himself chiefly as a writer and "a lover of words . . . where no words are is a void for me." His familiarity with theater was a "matter of circumstance rather than choice," but he was nonetheless a willing provider of much amiability and insight:

> Shakespeare had his shortcomings. Love of him does not blind me to his limitations and his faults of excess. But, after all, the man is dead, and I do not wish to emulate that captious and rancorous spirit—inflamed, as it often seemed to me, by an almost personal animosity—in which my predecessor persecuted him beyond the grave. *Nil de mortuis nisi bonum,* say I: else, what is to become of the classics? In that they were directed against one who could not defend himself, I regarded Mr. Shaw's attacks as cowardly; in that Mr. Shaw was a dramatist himself, I regarded them as suspect. Yet would I have heartily approved of them, had I imagined that they would induce managers not to revive certain of Shakespeare's plays quite so frequently. But I have just said that defamation of the dead will tend to destroy the classics. And so it may, if it be used discreetly. And if it do, so much the better for Shakespeare. When a play has become a classic in drama, it ceases to be a play. It may become a classic in literature without any detriment to itself, but, when it becomes also, like "Hamlet" or "Romeo and Juliet" or "Macbeth," a classic in drama, all, if I may be allowed to say so, is up with it. [*Around Theatres*]

James Agate (1877–1947) held a major critical post probably longer than any other English dramatic critic. His tenure at the *Sunday Times* lasted from 1923 until his death. He edited the important anthology *The English Dramatic Critics* (1932). His series of eight *Ego* volumes—diaries and reflections—ran from 1932 until 1947 and attest to a rather charming, self-acknowledged egotism.

Neither an aesthete nor an intellectual, Agate possessed an enthusiasm for great acting that grew out of a sense of connoisseurship. One has the uneasy sense with Agate that acting genius has really become "temperament," a kind of spirited good breeding that he was liable to find as readily in harness horses as actors. He appreciated animalism in actors and believed it was never surpassed by those following Irving and Bernhardt. He was generally unfriendly to the modern movement in art and drama and berated Shaw for trying to turn theater into philosophy and O'Casey for "writing not badly but politically." He admitted that he would be content if drama had terminated with Ibsen.

While Agate has been described as a "philistine with the conscience and equipment of an intellectual," he was really a critic of execution rather than conception; native wit was his strong point. Tyrone Guthrie's 1946 production of *Hamlet* with Robert Helpmann gave it some typical exercise: "Was Mr. Helpmann thinking along Shakespeare's lines? No, he was reciting them." About Guthrie, Agate remarked:

> . . . this has proved to be one of the most exciting theatrical events for many a long day. Exciting even if the event turned out to be a disappointment for the favourite's supporters. How so? Because, in racing parlance, the Lord Hamlet after a good start fell away in the middle, came again and lost by a short head to Production, whose clever jockey rode the race throughout in the way he had obviously planned. [Cited in *James Agate: An Anthology* (1961), edited by Herbert Van Thal.]

In the last *Ego* volume, Agate's self-obituary states that "his shop-window was superb, and perfectly concealed the meagerness of the academic stock within," and that "his enemies will miss him."

Turning to America, George Jean Nathan (1882–1958) is the first critic of any influence, if not stature. Nathan began writing for the New York *Herald* in 1905 and from 1914 to 1924 co-edited the magazine *The Smart Set* with H. L. Mencken. Much as Shaw in England, Nathan espoused the modern drama of ideas in a theater dominated by the tastes of producer and playwright David Belasco, "the gooroo of greasepaint," as Nathan called him. Nathan introduced important foreign dramatists like Ibsen, Strindberg, Shaw, and O'Casey, and he was among the first to recognize and champion O'Neill and Saroyan.

But Nathan was not uncritical of O'Neill's work, especially what he considered disasters of experimentation like *Dynamo* and *Days Without End*. However, his efforts to bring the public to an understanding of O'Neill seem to fall in the category of public relations rather than criticism:

> The real O'Neill is no more like the public's generally accepted view of him than the real George Washington or Gaby Delys was in turn like the pictures of them. While it is true that he reads everything bearing on the nature of whatever play he happens to be working on, his chief reading pleasure, indulged in at least once a day even when he is working hardest, consists in detective and mystery novels (he averages no less than six or seven a week), in the hardly psychopathic stories of Damon Runyon, whose slang is a source of supreme

enjoyment to him, and in the sports pages of any and every newspaper he can lay his hands on. So far as conversation goes, he would rather talk about prize-fighters and prize-fighting than about ten herd of Freuds and Strindbergs. He likes nothing better than . . . to have retailed to him, since he hardly ever goes to the theatre, the latest low jokes of the musical show clowns. He would trade in fifteen Shakespearean actors any day for one Jimmy Durante and he would supplement the fifteen with ten head of Ibsen actresses for one Bobby Clark. [*Encyclopedia of Theatre* (1940)]

Reading Nathan today gives one a sense of clever journalism and *épater le bourgeois*. His worship of *Kultur* seems more a matter of saying than having. Of all O'Neill's plays (by 1940), he preferred *Strange Interlude* and *Moon of the Caribees*. However, he was basically a playwright's critic. He maintained that it was impossible to know anything about acting and took steps to prove it by disliking Chaplin. During the 1930's he delighted in referring to the propaganda playwrights of the left as the "Little Red Writing Hoods."

Nathan's summation of American playwriting is easily self-condemning: "American playwriting by and large enjoys all the attributes of a violin, save only its melodiousness. The necessary guts are there, but the bow lacks the gift of evoking poetic song from them."

Eric Bentley's remarks about drama critics as a class seem to apply to Nathan with special force:

Whatever a man's estimate of the total intelligence of drama critics, high or low, he cannot fail to notice that—except for a Young or a Clurman—they know far less about acting and directing than about literature. Which is another funny thing about this remarkable class of men. They know something of literature though they are anti-literary; they are pro-theatrical but know little of acting. [*The Dramatic Event* (1954)]

Dramatic criticism in America reaches its high-point with the *New Republic* critics: Stark Young, Eric Bentley, and Robert Brustein. Stark Young (1881–1963) was the critic for the *New Republic* from 1921 to 1947 and of *The New York Times* for the 1924/25 season. He translated Chekhov's *The Sea Gull* (1939) and wrote valuable book-length essays on theater: *The Flower in Drama* (1923), *Glamour* (1925), and *The Theatre* (1927). His best criticism is found in the volume *Immortal Shadows* (1948).

Young's two greatest contributions were to think in terms of the "art of theatre" (thereby giving respectability to theatricality) and to be the best critic of acting since Hazlitt.

. . . In the art of the theatre precisely as in the other arts, say music, painting, poetry, the reality must be restated in terms of the art concerned before there is any art at all. It must have the charm of presence and absence, as Pascal said of portraits. An element must be there which was not there before. It must be incredibly translated into something else; it must be the same and not the same, like the moon in water, by a certain nameless difference born anew. [*Immortal Shadows*]

Like Hazlitt, Young often approached the criticism of acting with a thorough knowledge of character conception as well as execution. He says of Shaw's Caesar:

This Caesar is original because of the purity and strength of his organism, its freedom from characteristics and actions not its own. He appears to illustrate qualities that we label as generosity, cynicism, clemency, poetic idealism, practical shrewdness; but as qualities these are only instances of the inevitable functioning of his nature, and we may resent them as much as we like so long as we recognize them for their natural rightness. They are forms of biological intelligence. It is to secure this end that Shaw has arranged Caesar's speeches and actions in a sequence so baffling. One minute Caesar is what we call elevated, poetic, generous, the next he is what we call hard, civil, prosaic. You sit and watch this man and wonder what to think of him; just as you thought him good and great he is something else, just as you said he was a lover, a poet, you find him a cynic and a politician and the next moment an orator.

The purpose of this method is to keep you from sticking sweet labels over Caesar and making him a goody hero in your own evasive style. [*Immortal Shadows*]

Young appreciated what he called "generosity" and "spiritual audacity" in acting, and Duse was the exemplar of it for him:

Duse does not exemplify the art of acting so much as she illustrates the fundamentals of all art. All art, obviously, is concerned with the expression of life. To this purpose the artist is the first means, and after the artist the medium, color, words, sound, whatever it may be, that he works in. Duse's art illustrates first of all the principle in art of the necessity of the artist's own greatness, his sensitivity and power in feeling, in idea, in soul, in the education and fine culture of all these. Her art illustrates the necessity for a fierce and subtle and exact connection between the artist's meaning and his expression of it. It illustrates the universal problem of rhythm in art, of line, emphasis, mood, all rhythm. It illustrates supremely the nature of the poetic as it applies not only to poetry but to every art. And it illustrates the nature of realism in general, especially of that best Italian realism which, as it occurs most of all in sculpture, is so capable of rendering by means of only actual or possible external details the inmost idea. [*Immortal Shadows*]

Young could be quite expressive too about the absence of generosity:

. . . Mme. Sorel is the most delightful example I have ever known of empty competence. I have never seen so much expression which expressed nothing. Nothing gets through that perfect enameled skin. The heart within that handsome bosom beats with the pulse of the Rue de la Paix. I enjoy this Sorel performance, for a change now and again, because it is so divinely callous. It rests us from the sting of life. It is such pure theatre without any content to carry from life except the burden of the chic; it relieves all throes of immortality because it has no soul. It is as near to pure substance or material, sheer sight, sound and texture, as the human agent in art can attain. [*Immortal Shadows*]

Nothing elicits so much from Young's capacities as a critic of technique as Shakespearean verse-speaking. He writes of a performance of *Macbeth:*

In speaking the lines of such long passages as that of Macbeth's about sleep . . . we must discover a method that will convey the effect of the mind's being opened so that we see its contents, which may all be present in one flash. To read the passage with breaks in it, as if these reflections arose as one bit of thought after another, is only to make the character sound rambling or irrelevant to the dramatic moment and truth, and the dramatist more or less talky or false. [*Immortal Shadows*]

Young's review of John Barrymore's Hamlet, which he generally liked, is even more detailed and instructive, especially for the actor:

Mr. Barrymore's important technical limitations at this stage of his achievement seem to me to be two. The first concerns the verse. The "resistant flexibility," to use an old phrase, that is the soul of fine reading, he has not yet completely acquired. Much of his reading is excellent; but now and again in his effort to keep the verse true to its inner meaning and to the spiritual naturalness that underlies it— and because, too, of a lack of concentration on his projection at times—Mr. Barrymore seems to be afraid to admit the line for what it is, verse. Sometimes he allows the phrases to fall apart in such a way that the essential musical pattern of the verse—which is a portion of the idea itself—is lost. In the line—to take an example—

Why, she would hang on him,

he put a heavy stress on the word "hang" and almost let the "him" disappear; a useless naturalism, for the same effect of sense emphasis can be secured and yet the verse pattern of the lines preserved, by sustaining the nasals in "on" and "him" with no more actual stress on them than Mr. Barrymore used. [*Immortal Shadows*]

If Young was sensitive to the musical and evocative capacities of poetry in drama, he was also clear about its limitations, as the following comparison reveals:

For intuitive perception, grace of rather more minor understanding, and lyric dispersion, *Richard II* is grouped among Shakespeare's lyric dramas. But Marlowe's play of *Edward II* is miles beyond it as drama. For my part I contend that the march of a bold and inevitable theme surpasses a figure of subtle complexities with regard to character. And I contend that firm lines in the dramatic pattern say more, ultimately, than dainty or passionately cerebral variations in psychology, two thirds of which sometimes in Shakespeare may consist of pure literary ornament. [*Immortal Shadows*]

Young's insights into what made for viable dramatic literature applied to more than the past. With his preference for things Mediterranean rather than Nordic, he felt more at home with Pirandello and Lorca than with Ibsen. His insight into O'Neill's problems as a dramatist seem to reach to the writer's roots:

The other aspect of his gift is that for making myths. There can be no doubt that one of the things that has carried him furthest into people's memories is the capacity that his themes possess for effective recounting. In numbers of his plays the theme or central idea sounds infinitely suggestive and fruitful as one recounts it to others or as a newspaper story hands it on; and upon it the imagination builds and weaves onward to dazzling possibilities and infectious meanings. Whereas the play seen in the theatre is not half so good as we thought it might be; and what we have projected for it promised more than what has been created or accomplished. The play of *The Hairy Ape*, for instance, is only fair; it is effective and for one seeing may come off well enough. But the fable is capital—this Man with the Hoe, reduced to beast, returning to the beast's cage, finding no place even there; a few lines say it, and the theme of it remains unforgettable. [*Immortal Shadows*]

Young was also a keen critic of that modern phenomenon, the intrusive director. Lee Strasberg's direction of Sir James Barrie's *A Kiss for Cinderella* brings about untypically stern comments:

. . . The whole course of the production's movement and meaning lacks any great joy or whimsey, which are Barrie's way of covering up and exploiting both the sentiment and the pathos—especially the sentiment, which sometimes, I am afraid, is almost arrant. It might seem to Mr. Strasberg that there is something intellectual in thus muffing the moon and happy sugar in Barrie's writing. We have had plenty of these examples of intellectualism, where the director or the producer or both knew only too well the follies of his author and how to set all that straight. Intellectual though it assumes to be, this attitude is about on a par with the commercial geniuses reducing pork to chicken liver, or changing the flavor of something long eaten with pleasure into what is now to be enjoyed with approval. But there is nothing intrinsically intellectual about all that; it is really a subtle form of the obtuse. Nothing is less functional . . . than the right brain in the wrong skull. There are times when we are well sick of these people in the offing who know better what the author meant than the author himself knew. The sum of all which is to say that it is hard for second-rate people to let anything alone, and equally hard for first-rate people to listen to their inferior's proposals toward greater perfection. . . . To obscure the essential nature of a thing in art is a stupid resolution, false and flat. . . . There is nothing very distinguished in these improving confusions and these misleading aspirations—they are mostly the result of greedy encroachments. . . .

The right kind of directing for Barrie is to try for some, as it were, innocent stream of playing, in which stream the coy details, the jests, antitheses and dear obvious oddities can take their place easily and in a spirit more or less natural to the whole. Once you have established a current and plane for such writing, everything might bob in and out as it should. [*Immortal Shadows*]

For further discussion and appreciation of Stark Young, see Eric Bentley's essay "The China in the Bull Shop" in his *In Search of Theatre.*

The second of the *New Republic* critics is Eric Bentley, a professor of dramatic literature at Columbia University. Bentley wrote reviews for this magazine and others from 1952 to 1956. Selections from his criticism are available in *The Dramatic Event* (1954), *What Is Theatre?* (1956; reprinted 1968), and *In Search of Theatre* (1959). Bentley's biography *Bernard Shaw* (1948) is a standard source and he has been a prolific translator and advocate of Bertolt Brecht's drama in the United States: Also a brilliant theorist, his *The Playwright as Thinker* (1946) and *The Life of the Drama* (1967) are major reassessments of drama and theater.

While Bentley acknowledges and practices the truth that the primary experience for the critic is contact with the live actor, his special contribution to criticism is his sensitivity to the political, social, and intellectual character of his age and his ability to pick out a drama's confusions and pretensions about the modern world. The task of the critic in this state of affairs is, in a sense, to sin bravely:

> That we are tentative and skeptical in our philosophy is not to say that we have to be cagey and non-committal in discussion: that is the road, not to truth and joy, but to evasion and respectability. The critic is uncompromising, not because he regards himself as infallible, nor even because he feels very sure of himself, but because it is his job to be so. It is true, he enjoys this job; he enjoys a fight; his writing embodies his zest for living. Yet he doesn't enjoy all of the job. The constant infliction of pain is a burden to him, the price he has to pay for the right to practice his profession. For the journalist-critic, the only alternative to a sharp tongue is a mealy mouth. [*The Dramatic Event*]

As both a journalist and an intellectual with portfolio, Bentley cautions against false intellectuality, or what he calls "Bright Ideas":

> Ours is the age of substitutes: instead of language, we have jargon; instead of principles, slogans; and, instead of genuine ideas, Bright Ideas. Bright Ideas win elections, and a cluster of them constituted a "theory" which justified the slaughter of six million Jews. A Bright Idea is an invalid idea which has more appeal to the semi-literate mind than a valid one; a phenomenon of some importance in a culture whose diagnostic is semi-literacy. It is a thought which can't bear thinking about; but which is all the more influential on that account; it surprises or reassures, it flatters or inflames; if it cannot earn the simple epithet "true" it frequently receives the more characteristic modern eulogy of "intriguing" or at least "interesting." At the very worst it is praised as "cute." The modern person, engaged in that search for meaning in life which formerly was known as the religious and philosophic quest, marries one Bright Idea after another, divorce being as

frequent in the ideal as in the real world. "I can't *tell* you what this book will do for you," a Los Angeles lady once sighed into my ear, "it's so semantic!" She had a Bright Idea.
> . . . Can't a man improve his plays by filling them with Improving Ideas? Can't he make them profounder by referring to profound subjects? . . . Ideology is a great temptation. You imagine that all you need to do is to refer to "schizophrenia" and you are exempt from the onerous duty of *creating* a schizoid character. You imagine that all you need to do is refer to religion many, many times and you have dramatized faith. [*The Dramatic Event*]

Bentley is informative and cautionary about another phenomenon, not peculiar to the theatrical occasion alone—the programmed response:

> If our admiration remains abstract, and we do not enjoy ourselves, it is, as much as anything, because the actors assume a manner that tells us what attitude we are to take. Explicitly in the program and Mr. Power's introductory speech, implicitly in the style of the performance, we are told how to respond. A modern phenomenon! Our concert programs tell us that the symphony we are about to hear will "carry us away," lest otherwise we fail to be carried away; and the result is we do fail to be carried away; because we are thinking *about* being carried away. When a performance tells us what our response should be it thereby prevents us from having that response. [*The Dramatic Event*]

Bentley's sense of dramatic history affords him insights into the causes of the current dearth of drama, as he shows in the course of reviewing the dancer Martha Graham:

> In the nineteenth century, drama became too exclusively dramatic—that is, too exclusive of epic and lyric. In the twentieth century the movies reminded us of the value of the epic element in dramatic entertainment, and the best movies were Mr. Chaplin's. The lyrical element was also farmed out to another medium—not the movies but opera and ballet. Of the poets who essayed drama, even the greatest were less dramatic in their plays than in their poems. It was an inspired idea of Martha Graham's to exploit the dramatic quality of non-dramatic modern verse as she does in *Letter to the World*. [*The Dramatic Event*]

Bentley's enthusiasm for the new rarely overcomes his distrust of the unauthentic. Writing in the early 1950's of the Off-Broadway movement, he is forced to say:

> Our conception followed the model of the Provincetown Playhouse in its early days: a theatre of young people coming forward with something of their own to offer. Today, the Greenwhich Village theatre offers plays by established authors in productions that are barely competent, let alone interesting. The few new plays they have put on have not (with an exception or so) whetted the appetite for more. It's not just that they aren't works of genius, which they don't have to be, but that

they have no real identity. True, the homoerotic element is rather insistent; yet such a
recurrent theme doesn't give an intellectual
identity to a generation, even to the extent
that, say, proletarianism did in the thirties. An
epidemic is not a movement. [*The Dramatic
Event*]

It was the good fortune of Robert Brustein, the
third and current *New Republic* critic, to be writing
at a time when Off-Broadway and Off-Off-Broadway
began to fulfill their promise, even to the extent of
providing productions of homoerotic genius, such as
Genet. But before turning to Brustein, chronology
demands a return to England, where another young
critic, Kenneth Tynan, was glorying in the dramatic
renaissance ushered in by the "angry" movement in
the late 1950's.

Kenneth Tynan (1927–   ) was drama critic for
the *Observer* from 1954 to 1963 and for *The New
Yorker* from 1958 to 1960. In 1963 he became the
literary manager of England's National Theatre. His
two volumes of collected criticism are *He That Plays
the King* (1950) and *Curtains* (1961). A recent volume, *Tynan Right and Left* (1967), contains drama
and film criticism and random essays.

Early in his career, Tynan espoused frank theatricalism and found a model of it in the work of
Anouilh. That 1956 watershed of English drama,
Look Back in Anger by John Osborne, however,
converted him and many others to the drama of social purpose. His generally left-wing views and his
aesthetic sense have achieved a happy marriage:

What I look for in our new drama is the sort of
play that is not ashamed to assimilate and acknowledge the bourgeois tradition, which includes a multiplicity of styles (*vide* Ibsen), not
all of them despicable. Otherwise, the drift of
writers towards television and the cinema will
rise to a flood, since dialogue composed in
snippets soldered together by dissolves and
background music will always be easier to
write than dialogue orchestrated into the
longer cadences of set-pieces and acts. Nothing
is more crucially stupid than to dismiss the
artistic achievements of a social class because
one deplores its historical record. [*Curtains*]

Tynan is a critic of sprightliness and erudition as
well as commitment, as his commentary "Notes on a
Dead Language" indicates:

When the London theatre takes to its bed, the
habit of criticism is to scourge the invalid; the
sick-room resounds with bullying cries of
"Who are the new English playwrights?" A
more acute inquiry might be: "Who were the
old ones?" For the brute fact is that no Englishman since the third decade of the seventeenth century has written an acknowledged
dramatic masterpiece. Note that I say "acknowledged"; I might make claims for Otway
or Dryden, you for Pinero or Maugham, but in
the general censure we should be outvoted.
The truth would out: that the legend of English
drama springs partly from Shakespeare, our
luminous accident, and mostly from an Irish
conspiracy to make us ashamed of our weakness. English drama is a procession of glittering Irishmen: Farquhar, Goldsmith, Sheridan,
Shaw, Wilde, Synge, and O'Casey are there;

and even Congreve slips in on a quibble, since
his Irish upbringing served to correct the fault
of his English birth. We should not mourn that
there are no great English playwrights; we
should marvel that there are any English playwrights at all. [*Curtains*]

A former actor himself, Tynan is a sharp critic of
acting; he knows what went wrong and where to lay
the blame. He says of Paul Scofield's 1955 Hamlet:

Mr. Scofield's outline is impeccable. What is
surprising is the crude brushwork with which
he fills it in. Vocally and physically he is one
long tremendous sulk; a roaring boy is at large,
and not (as when he played the part before) a
scholar gipsy. The new Mr. Scofield protests
much too much. The note struck on "Vengeance!" is thrice repeated, with diminishing
returns; too many speeches are mechanically
gabbled; and the actor's face is a mask devoid
of pathos. To hold our attention he will hit
wrong notes or leap up the scale halfway
through a line, but the grip seems artificial, as if
he had decided that what could not be coaxed
into life had better be shouted to death. Potentially, Mr. Scofield is still Sir Laurence Olivier's natural heir, but in the technique of realistic acting he is badly out of practice. We have
fed him on rhetoric and starved him of life,
and if he fails to move us, it is as much our
theatre's fault as his. [*Curtains*]

Tynan's recent work with the National Theatre has
been a major reason for the success of that institution. The move was unusual for a critic, but it did not
go long unimitated. The effort to bring critical intelligence to the theater by working from within is what
prompted Robert Brustein (1927–   ) to accept in
1966 the deanship of the Yale School of Drama.
Brustein has been writing for the *New Republic* since
1959. His book *Seasons of Discontent* (1965) covers
American theater from 1959 to 1965. His *The Theatre of Revolt* (1964) is an important study of modern
drama and existentialism.

Brustein's special force in criticism comes from
the fact that he is as much a critic of audiences as of
actors and plays. In his essay "Why I Write," he explains that the critic

establishes his claim to serious criticism when
discussing a genuine work of art, bringing his
whole experience and expertise into the service of analysis, illumination, and interpretation. And this is why I bite with such obvious
relish into the occasional masterpieces that
come my way; and why, lacking these, I often
choose to belabor you with extra-critical lectures on the dismal state of our culture, our
theatre, and our national spirit. For if the
critic is the humble servant of genuine art, he
is the implacable enemy of pseudo art, waging
war on all the conditions which produce it, including the writer's cynicism, the producer's
greed, the actor's ambition, and the spectator's
spiritual emptiness. [*Seasons of Discontent*]

Painfully sensitive to the manipulations of the cultural hipster, Brustein is careful to sift the meretricious from the genuine in the culturally exploded
avant-garde. Of Edward Albee's *The Zoo Story*, he
says:

. . . I am depressed by the uses to which this talent has been put. In its implicit assumption that the psychotic, the criminal, and the invert are closer to God than anyone else, *The Zoo Story* embodies the same kind of sexual-religious claptrap we are accustomed to from Allen Ginsberg. The tendency of Beat writers to invest the French Rebel tradition (de Sade—Rimbaud—Jean Genet) with a pseudoreligious flavor seems to me quite similar to the tendency of Broadway playwrights to identify romantic love with God; and although such ideas may endear these writers to the Luce publications, they signify a general flabbiness in American feeling and thought. [*Seasons of Discontent*]

The search for a living audience was sometimes successful, and Brustein was happy to point out the genuine contributions of a group like the Living Theatre:

. . . Endowed with a spirit of joyous anarchy, [it] is constantly breaking the hallowed theatrical contract, constantly destroying the barriers between life and art. The company's talents, I suspect, are not shaped for more literary works of drama; and while there are a number of suitable European works, few American plays can be presented profitably in such an irreverent manner. But The Living Theatre is creating an atmosphere in which such works will surely be written. In its unique understanding that there can be no living theatre without a living audience, this group is paving the road toward real advance. [*Seasons of Discontent*]

The intense revival in theater since those words were written in 1959 is some indication of the value in criticism of lending support to the new and authentic and thereby advancing the day when the critic can find more than "the occasional masterpiece" coming his way.—G. R.

Mokuami, Kawatake (1816–1893). Japanese playwright. As author of some fifty *kabuki* plays during a career that virtually spanned the nineteenth century, Mokuami is regarded as one of the leading Japanese dramatists and is often called the last important playwright for the kabuki stage. For the form of his plays he looked back toward the earlier and more classical years of the kabuki, but in content his work shows him to be something of a radical. To the type of "domestic play" as composed by his chief predecessor, Chikamatsu Monzaemon, and generally known as SEWAMONO, he added new elements of melodramatic violence and sensationalism. Typical of this development is his popular *Izayoi Seishin* (written 1859). He delighted especially in plays dealing with thieves and outlaws, such as the famous *Aoto Zōshi Hana no Nishikie* (*Benten the Thief,* 1862). His gangsters have been described as supermen, heroes only in an ironic sense of the word. He also indulged in horrors descending from a supernatural world of vampires and ghosts.—H. W. W.

Molière. Pen name of **Jean Baptiste Poquelin** (1622–1673). French playwright, actor, and director. Born in Paris, the son of an upholsterer in the service of the king, Jean Baptiste Poquelin studied the humanities at the Jesuit Collège de Clermont and then, around 1640, went into law. However, the idea

MOLIÈRE (WALTER HAMPDEN MEMORIAL LIBRARY AT THE PLAYERS, NEW YORK)

of a bourgeois law career was forsaken around 1642, when he encountered a group of actors directed by the Béjart family. In 1643 he signed a contract with Madeleine Béjart, founding a company called the Illustre Théâtre, and the following year adopted the name Molière. The Illustre Théâtre experienced great difficulties: in 1645 Molière was imprisoned for debt, and at the end of the year the troupe was forced to leave Paris. From 1645 to 1658 Molière and his friends toured the provinces, especially the southwest, Languedoc, and the Rhone valley. During those years, with the support of the nobility, Molière gained experience in the theater and made a name for himself in the provinces as an actor and a writer of farces and comedies. Moreover, he became director of the troupe, which he enlarged by acquiring the best actors of other road companies. Molière and his company arrived in Paris in the fall of 1658. On October 24, in the guard room of the old Louvre, he performed for Louis XIV Pierre Corneille's tragedy *Nicomède* and a farce of his own that is now lost, *Le Docteur amoureux* ("The Amorous Doctor"). Amused by the farce, Louis XIV granted Molière and his troupe the right to remain in Paris, where at the time there were only three professional companies: those of the Hôtel de Bourgogne and the Marais district, and one Italian troupe. Molière took over the Théâtre du Petit Bourbon, which he shared with the Italians (directed by Tiberio Fiorelli, called Scaramouche), who kept the best days of the week (Tuesday, Friday, and Sunday) for themselves. When the Petit Bourbon was destroyed to make way for the facade of the Louvre, Molière, after three idle months, was authorized to take over the Théâtre du

Palais-Royal, which he was again obliged to share with Scaramouche, but this time Molière kept the best days of the week for himself. Scaramouche and the *commedia dell'arte* had a profound influence on Molière as an actor.

Molière's life was marked by domestic misfortunes (a not very successful marriage in 1662 to Armande Béjart and the death of his children in infancy) and a serious lung ailment that was to be the cause of his death in 1673. But his life was primarily a constant struggle for success and to provide for the needs of his troupe. With the triumph in 1659 of LES PRÉCIEUSES RIDICULES, he incurred the hostility of much of the fashionable public. In 1662 L'ÉCOLE DES FEMMES caused a scandal and provoked violent attacks on his aesthetics, his ethics, and even his private life. The prudes and the learned considered him a morally dangerous writer and a degrading actor. In 1664 he presented before the king a three-act version (or the first of three acts) of TARTUFFE, a comedy about religious hypocrisy. Louis XIV was entertained but preferred that the play, against which the pious had raised a strong protest, not be performed in public. In 1665 DOM JUAN OU LE FESTIN DE PIERRE was interpreted by the pious as a monstrous profession of atheism, some of them demanding that Molière be burned; and that same year Racine forsook him and had his plays performed at the Hôtel de Bourgogne, later taking with him one of Molière's great actresses, Mlle. du Parc. In 1667 a second version of *Tartuffe* was prohibited, and it was not until 1669 that a third version was authorized.

Nevertheless, Molière enjoyed the favor of the pit, the enlightened public, and the king himself. Amused by *Le Docteur amoureux,* Louis XIV was even more beguiled by *Les Fâcheux* (*The Impertinents,* 1661), which he saw at Vaux-le-Vicomte. A short time after, the king had the play performed again, with an extra scene inspired by him, at Fontainebleau. From that time on, Molière was entrusted with the theatrical pleasures of the king. Indeed, in 1665 his troupe became "The King's Company." Almost every year Molière and his company were called upon to present a new comedy at Versailles or wherever the court then happened to be. The 1664 *Tartuffe* in three acts, for example, was performed during a seven-day festival in May at Versailles. And there Molière presented another new comedy, two comedies that had already been performed, as well as ballets, parades, and other entertainments.

However, for political and religious reasons, royal favor was not steadfast, and in 1672 Louis XIV withdrew it from Molière and granted it to Jean Baptiste Lully. Disappointed, exhausted, and very ill, Molière had convulsions at the end of the fourth performance of LE MALADE IMAGINAIRE, on February 17, 1673, and died the same night. Although the pious wanted him to be refused a Christian burial, he was buried normally on February 21, but at night, so as to "avoid scandal."

After having written numerous farces in the provinces, only two of which remain—both of doubtful origin—Molière launched into fashionable high comedy with *L'Etourdi* (*The Blunderer,* performed in Lyons in 1655 and again in Paris in 1659) and *Le Dépit amoureux* (*The Amorous Quarrel,* performed in Béziers in 1656 and again in Paris in 1659). The latter, in particular, conformed to fashion: the substitution of one child for another, a girl playing the part of a man, imbroglios, a parallelism between masters and servants in love quarrels, and so forth. The Parisian public favorably greeted these comedies, which, given the genre and their high literary standards, were in line with the taste of the period. Nevertheless, Molière's first great success was due to a one-act farce, *Les Précieuses ridicules,* which was actually a reaction against the excesses of fashion. With *Sganarelle ou Le Cocu imaginaire* ("Sganarelle or the Imaginary Cuckold," 1660), Molière remained faithful to the spirit of farce. In 1661 he suffered defeat with a great heroic comedy, *Dom Garcie de Navarre* ("Don Garcia of Navarre") but had new success with a three-act comedy that was both farcical and literary, *L'Ecole des maris* (*The School for Husbands*), and with *Les Fâcheux,* the first of his court entertainments. After *L'Ecole des femmes* and the dispute that followed, which was of prime importance in the history of French classical theater, Molière in 1664 wrote a comedy-ballet, *Le Mariage forcé* ("The Compulsory Marriage") for the king, then *La Princesse d'Elide* ("The Princess of Elis"), and the first *Tartuffe*. During the five years of the "*Tartuffe* affair" he wrote *Dom Juan, L'Amour médecin* (*Love's the Best Doctor,* 1665), LE MISANTHROPE, *Le Médecin malgré lui* (*The Physician in Spite of Himself,* 1666), several court entertainments in 1666/67, *Amphitryon* (1668), *George Dandin* (1668), and L'AVARE. After *Tartuffe* was authorized, he provided the court with farces like *Monsieur de Pourceaugnac* (1669) and a great comedy-ballet with heroic characters, its subject suggested by the king, *Les Amants magnifiques* ("The Magnificent Lovers," 1670). Also in 1670 LE BOURGEOIS GENTILHOMME was presented. In 1671 Molière collaborated with Pierre Corneille and Philippe Quinault on *Psyché,* a tragicomedy-ballet, and staged the play in the "machine" theater of the Tuileries. That same year he returned to pure farce with LES FOURBERIES DE SCAPIN; 1672 was the year of LES FEMMES SAVANTES; and 1673 that of *Le Malade imaginaire*.

Molière's originality consisted in moving away from romanesque comedy toward farce and making great theater of it. Instead of using the rebounds of a complicated plot as the center of interest, Molière started off with certain fixed masks and made them into human types by adding to them characteristics observed in contemporary life. This genre, called "character comedy," presents a spectacle of inner forces embodied in individualized characters who seek to dominate or to protect themselves with a persistence that provokes laughter through its extreme results but that is similar to the fatality of passion in Racine. Molière's protagonists are thus absolute egotists who invent values—generally illusory, hence the humor—to satisfy their appetites. Dupes of themselves or calculating creatures, such characters are prisoners of their own natures. Molière's enemies, in fact, could not bear the pessimism represented by his comic spirit, for he implied that every human impulse can be reduced to an illusion that masks a tyrannical egotism, and hence the values or interests that are considered most sacred may become objects of derision.

Since comedy by definition must have a happy

ending and more precisely a uniting of lovers, Molière's comedies—with a few exceptions (*George Dandin, Le Misanthrope*)—end with the vanishing of the obstacle to the marriage of a likable young couple. But the devices through which this is generally brought about merely point up the invincible strength of the power of illusion or deception. The ROMANESQUE endings of *L'Ecole des femmes* and *L'Avare* or the royal intervention in the fifth act of *Tartuffe* show that the denouement cannot come from the protagonists' conversions. And the denouements of *Le Bourgeois Gentilhomme* and *Le Malade imaginaire* are possible only because the protagonist is made to sink altogether into his madness, not because he is cured. Only theatrical illusion can give an image of happiness, for the real illusions of human nature are dead ends. This is doubtless the ultimate meaning of *Les Fourberies de Scapin,* in which the happiness of two couples is ensured by a rogue, who in fact is a kind of stage director of life.

Ramon Fernandez, in *La Vie de Molière,* translated by Wilson Follet under the title *Molière, The Man Seen Through the Plays* (1958), analyzes Molière's personality and temperament. For a biography with summaries of the plays, see Wyndham D. B. Lewis, *Molière: The Comic Mask* (1959). In *Molière, A New Criticism* (1962), Will G. Moore studies the works in themselves.—J. G.

Molnár, Ferenc. See HUNGARY.

Montherlant, Henry de (1896–   ). French novelist, essayist, and playwright. Montherlant was born in Paris, the son of an old, aristocratic French family. As a soldier in World War I, he was seriously wounded. After the war, the novels he wrote about the sports in which he participated, such as football and bullfighting, were extremely successful.

HENRY DE MONTHERLANT (FRENCH CULTURAL SERVICES)

Montherlant's eight plays, written and produced between 1942 and 1954, received extensive critical attention and some degree of popularity. He announced his formal farewell to the theater and gave, in 1956, what he called the definitive edition of his *Théâtre* in the Pleiade series, but he has since written two more plays.

Despite the baroque richness of QUEEN AFTER DEATH, Montherlant's first play, despite the abundance of moralistic and aphoristic speech, there is an underlying asceticism evident in the carefully constructed scenes and the deliberate focus on a few characters and a few problems. *Fils de personne* (*No Man's Son,* 1943), written in Grasse in 1943, has a skeletal quality that is also part of the play that is its continuation: *Demain il fera jour* (*Tomorrow the Dawn,* written 1948, prod. 1949).

Malatesta was not performed until the end of 1950, but it was written in Grasse in 1943/44. Malatesta and Alvaro (in *Le Maître de Santiago, The Master of Santiago,* 1947) have similar traits—nobility, aloofness, cruelty, and violence. From Portugal (Ferrante in *Queen After Death*), France (Carrion in *Fils de personne*), Spain (Alvaro), and Italy (Malatesta) Montherlant has created a dominant character who is ambiguous in his nobility and cruelty, his Christianity and paganism, and his seductiveness and fearfulness.

The title of the play *La Ville dont le prince est un enfant* ("The City Whose Prince Is a Child," 1952) is taken from a verse in the book of Ecclesiastes that condemns a country whose prince is a child. The work, first published in book form in 1951, has as its setting a Parisian boys' school directed by a religious order. The paternity of the priest, whom so many call "Father," is a source of great personal suffering and grave spiritual peril for Abbé de Pradts. See also PORT-ROYAL.

For a critical evaluation of Montherlant's work, see John Cruickshank, *Montherlant* (1964); David L. Gobert, "Structural Identity of *La Reine Morte* and *Le Maître de Santiago,*" *French Review* (October 1964); and P. J. Norrish, "Montherlant's Conception of the Tragic Hero," *Yale French Studies* (1960) and "Montherlant as a Moralist," *Australian Journal of French Studies* (Sept.-Dec. 1964).—W. F.

Month in the Country, A (Mesyats v derevne). A comedy in five acts by Ivan TURGENEV. Written in 1850, the play was approved by the censors five years later, after considerable revisions had been made. It was not published until 1869 and the first production was in 1872.

A Month in the Country describes the disruption of life in the country estate of the rich landowner Islaev after he hires a university student as a tutor for his son. Both Islaev's wife, Natalia, who is loved by Rakitin, a weak and ineffectual friend of the family, and her ward, the innocent seventeen-year-old Vera, fall in love with the gay and pleasant young tutor. Once Natalia discovers that Vera is her rival, she tries to marry her off to an elderly neighbor. Natalia soon finds out, however, that it is not Vera that the tutor loves but herself, although he is too intimidated by her to declare his love. The emotional situation reaches such a pitch that Natalia's husband, who assumes that the trouble is caused by Rakitin's love for Natalia, asks Rakitin, as a friend, to leave. Finally, the tutor decides that he must leave too and the play ends with Vera vowing to marry the neighbor in order to leave the house also.

Many contemporary critics found a resemblance between *A Month in the Country* and Honoré de Balzac's *Stepmother* and Augustin Scribe's *The Ladies' Battle*. The fact is, however, that Turgenev's play is free of the melodramatic elements of these French plays, and Turgenev's emphasis on the inner emotions of the characters rather than on outward, physical happenings makes his play a completely original work. Almost the entire "action" takes place in the minds of the various characters and Turgenev succeeds in creating suspense by producing in every member of the cast unexpected, albeit well-motivated, emotional changes and twists. This quality makes *A Month in the Country* a direct precursor of Anton Chekhov's major plays and it also raised new problems for actors by demanding of them much more subtle acting methods.

A Month in the Country, translated by Andrew R. MacAndrew, appears in *19th Century Russian Drama* (1963).—A. MACA.

Moody, William Vaughn (1869–1910). American poet and playwright. Moody was born in Spencer, Indiana. His parents died when he was young, and he supported himself by teaching before he entered Harvard in 1889. From 1895 to 1903 he taught English at the University of Chicago, where he edited Milton's poems and, with Robert Morss Lovett, compiled *A First View of English and American Literature* (1902). Moody's bent, however, was toward the writing of lyric poetry and drama, and as soon as he could afford to do so he gave up teaching.

The first of a projected trilogy of poetic dramas, *Masque of Judgment*, was published in 1900; the second, *The Firebringer*, in 1904; and the third, *The Death of Eve*, was left unfinished. None of these plays was produced. Moody wanted to treat contemporary life in poetic drama, but he yielded to the taste of the time in two prose dramas of American life, THE GREAT DIVIDE and THE FAITH HEALER.

Moody's trilogy, in Miltonic blank verse, interspersed with lyrics in varying meters, is concerned with man's relation to God, with the problems of free will, and of evil in a world of God's creation. In *The Masque of Judgment*, the Serpent triumphs over God, because God has failed to make the highest use of the will with which He has endowed man. *The Firebringer* dramatizes the story of Prometheus to depict man's revolt against the tyranny of God. In *The Death of Eve*, God and man were to have been reconciled through Eve, who is both the mother of Cain and a foreshadowing of Mary, mother of Jesus.

The same themes appear in Moody's dramas of American life. *The Great Divide* presents the conflict between the American East and West in terms of the battle between inhibiting puritanism and man's free spirit. The conflict between earthly and spiritual love is dramatized in *The Faith Healer*.

Moody's plays are few but noteworthy. They show a rapidly increasing command of dramatic technique, unusual intellectual power, and rare philosophical depth. If Moody had not died so young, he might have become a dramatist of the first order.

The best sources are David Dodds Henry's *William Vaughn Moody* (1934) and Moody's *Poems and Plays* (2 vols., 1912).—B. H.

Moon of the Caribbees, The. See S.S. GLENCAIRN.

Moore, George (1852–1933). Irish novelist, playwright, and critic. The son of a member of Parliament, Moore was born at Moore Hall in County Mayo. He developed an interest in art that took him to Paris as a young man. There he made the acquaintance of the French impressionists and such literary figures as Zola and Mallarmé. Returning to England, Moore pursued a literary career as a novelist. At the outbreak of the Boer War he went back to Ireland, where in 1899 he helped to found, with William Butler Yeats, Lady Gregory, and Edward Martyn, the Irish Literary Theatre (see IRELAND). Moore remained in Ireland for the next decade, during which time he maintained a lively interest in the new theater and wrote two plays for it. In 1911 he returned to England, where he completed his autobiography, *Hail and Farewell* (1911–1913), in which he delightfully but maliciously excoriated his Irish associates at the Abbey. He continued his literary output unabated until his death at the age of eighty-one.

Best known as a novelist, Moore is also the author of several plays. The earliest of these is *The Strike at Arlingford* (1894), written in England. His first work written for the Irish theater was *The Bending of the Bough* (1900), a refashioned version of his friend Edward Martyn's *A Tale of a Town*. This play was followed by *Diarmuid and Grania* (1901), written in collaboration with Yeats. The play was unsuccessful, the authors quarreled, and Moore stopped writing for the young theater. Later in his career he wrote a number of plays, notably *Esther Waters* (1911), a dramatization of his own novel.

Moore's achievement as a dramatist is negligible, but his role as propagandist and publicist for the new Irish theater in the critical, early stages of its development entitles him to a place of honor in its history. —E. Q.

morality play. A medieval religious play in the vernacular in which the forces of good and evil act upon a protagonist who represents mankind. In the morality play, the forces of good and evil are personified in the figures of allegorical characters who are named for the moral quality they represent, such as Mercy, Shame, Beauty, and so on. The central conflict, the salvation or damnation of man's soul, was, before the advent of Calvinism, usually resolved in favor of salvation. The most famous example of a morality play is EVERYMAN. See also ENGLAND: *middle ages*.

Moravia. See CZECHOSLOVAKIA: *Bohemia and Moravia*.

Mortimer, John [Clifford] (1923–). English playwright. Mortimer, the barrister son of a barrister father, was born in Hampstead, London, and began his literary career as a novelist. He arrived in the theater with the stage production in 1958 of his radio duologue *The Dock Brief*, which formed half of a double bill with his family comedy *What Shall We Tell Caroline?* This was followed by three full-length plays, all presented by the West End: *The Wrong Side of the Park* (1960); *Two Stars for Comfort* (1962); and *The Judge* (1967). Besides several other one-acters, Mortimer also adapted Georges Feydeau's *La Puce à l'oreille* for the National Theatre's hugely successful production of *A Flea in Her Ear* (1965).

"Comedy," Mortimer once wrote in an introduction to *The Dock Brief*, "is, to my mind, the only thing worth writing in this despairing age, providing it is comedy on the side of the lonely, the neglected and unsuccessful." He justified this principle most completely in *The Dock Brief* and its companion radio piece, *I Spy* (1957), two studies of the underside of the law. In his full-length plays the loneliness is apt to appear rather calculated and the compassion a bit glib. The first two plays deal with the miseries of middle-class marriage and the third with a guilt-ridden old judge who returns to his home town to atone for a boyhood crime. The strength of Mortimer's plays lies mainly in their decoration: elegant, witty dialogue and as sharp an eye as any in the theater for the manners, morals, and pleasures of modern Britain.—I. W.

Mossenson, Yig'al (1917–). Israeli novelist and playwright. Mossenson appeared on the literary scene of Israel in the mid-1940's with two significant books: a collection of short stories entitled *Aforim Kasak* ("Grey as a Sack," 1944) and the novel *Mi Amar Shehoo Shachor* ("Who Said He Is Black?" 1946). Because of their realistic technique, a style new to the Israeli of the late forties, and the choice of a contemporary subject, both books elicited an electrifying response from critics and readers alike. In fact, it was soon evident that these two characteristics were Mossenson's strengths—and perhaps limitations—in the dramatic vision of the plays that followed.

In 1948, while serving as an education officer in the Israeli Defense Army on the southern front, he wrote his first important play, *B'arvot Hanegev* ("In the Wastes of the Negev," 1949). Because it mirrored the events of those heroic days, the play was a great success. Mossenson capitalized on a contemporary subject in *Kazablan* (1954), a play concerning one of the most painful internal issues of modern Israel— the relations and prejudices between Oriental and Western Jews. In 1966/67 *Kazablan* was transformed by Mossenson into a successful musical that was hailed as the Israeli *West Side Story*. His next play, *Eldorado* (1955), was another example of the limitations of the "shocking" naturalist approach. In fact, Mossenson followed the classic example initiated by the Moscow Art Theatre (exemplified by its production of Maxim Gorky's *The Lower Depths*, 1902) and took his actors to the scene of the action, the slums of Jaffa, where they observed the "real" characters and listened to their "real" speech. His next play, *Zrok Oto Laklavim* ("Throw Him to the Dogs," 1958), was another dramatization of an issue much discussed in Israel at that time: malpractices by reporters and newspapers concerning public exposure of individuals and threats of blackmail. For almost ten years Mossenson was away from the theatrical scene of Israel, living in the United States. Since his return to Israel in 1965, only one play of his has been produced: *Evev B'fith Avenue* ("An Evening on Fifth Avenue," 1965) by the Haifa Municipal Theatre. His other plays include *Tamar Eishet Er* ("Tamar, Er's Wife," 1947), a biblical play about Judah and his sons; *Im Yesh Tsedek* ("If There Is Justice," 1951), a play about a famous court-martial in Israel; *Adam Bli Shem* ("A Man Without a Name," 1953); *Cambises* (1955); and Hashabat Hash'chora ("The Black Sabbath," 1959).—Z. R.

Mostellaria (The Haunted House, c. 200–194 B.C.). A comedy by PLAUTUS, based on the Greek *Phasma* (*The Ghost*), possibly by Theognetus. *Mostellaria*, one of Plautus' best plays of deception, describes the love affair of a young man, Philolaches, with his sweetheart during his father's absence abroad, and the attempt of his slave, Tranio, to keep the father from the house when the latter returns unexpectedly. Tranio concocts a series of falsehoods about the coming of a ghost, the sale of the house, and the purchase of the house next door. The slave's impudence as his lies are discovered one by one is especially delightful. In addition to the element of the supernatural, the comedy has a dressing scene and banquet on the stage, an amusing episode of drunkenness, and several well-portrayed characters, notably the moneylender Misargyrides ("Hatesilverson"), an ancient Shylock.

Later comedies influenced by *Mostellaria* include Girolamo Berrardo's *Mostellaria* (1501), Ercole Bentivoglio's *I Fantasmi* (1545), Shakespeare's *The Taming of the Shrew* (c. 1593), Ben Jonson's *The Alchemist* (1610), Thomas Heywood's *The English Traveller* (1633), Antoine Jacob Montfleury's *Le Comedien Poète* (1674), Jean François Regnard's *Le Retour Imprévu* (1700), Joseph Addison's *The Drummer* (1716), Henry Fielding's *The Intriguing Chambermaid* (1733), and Ludvig Holberg's *A Ghost in the House or Abracadabra* (1752).—G. E. D.

Mother Courage and Her Children (Mutter Courage und ihre Kinder, 1941). A chronicle play of the Thirty Years' War by Bertolt BRECHT, in twelve

A SCENE FROM BERTOLT BRECHT'S *Mother Courage* AT THE 1966 RUHR FESTIVAL IN RECKLINGHAUSEN. LOTTE LENYA (RIGHT) PLAYED THE TITLE ROLE. (GERMAN INFORMATION CENTER)

scenes, including nine songs. The play was written in 1939 and first produced in 1941 in Switzerland. The main character is Anna Fierling, a mother of three illegitimate children by three different fathers. With her traveling canteen wagon she follows the Swedish and imperial armies selling her goods to the soldiers.

Mother Courage lives by the war but does not realize that the war also lives by her. First her son Eilif is recruited as a soldier. While she follows the Swedish army through Poland her business prospers and the brave Eilif is decorated for requisitioning a herd of cattle. Then her honest son, Swiss Cheese, becomes paymaster in a Swedish regiment. He is the first to die: When the camp is conquered by the Catholic army, he hides the regimental cashbox and is shot. Courage could have saved him by a bribe, but she haggles about the price until it is too late.

Mother Courage keeps following the war, which covers wider and wider territory. A field chaplain has joined her and helps out where he can. When the Catholic general Tilly is killed, Mother Courage fears that the war might end, but her optimism prevails, and she sends her daughter Kattrin to the city to buy fresh supplies. Kattrin comes back disfigured by soldiers. At that point, also worried about the disappearance of Eilif, Mother Courage curses the war. But shortly afterward, she worries again about another possible end of the fighting; a lasting peace would ruin her business. The chaplain consequently calls her "a hyena of the battlefield." He leaves her and his place is taken by a cook, an old acquaintance of Mother Courage. Eilif is executed for stealing cat-

tle from a farmer. The deed, so heroic during the war, is a crime in peacetime. But the war goes on.

During the winter the cook also leaves Mother Courage, because she refuses to abandon Kattrin and start a new life with him. Ironically, Kattrin is killed a few months later by Imperial soldiers. She has overheard a plan to surprise the city of Halle during the night and awakens the townspeople by beating a drum. Mother Courage, who had been away shopping, finds her dead. All alone now, she is still determined to get her cut. She harnesses herself to the wagon and follows the departing army.

Brecht took the main character of the play from two baroque novels by the seventeenth-century writer Hans Jacob Christoffel von Grimmelshausen. *Mother Courage* has been acclaimed as Brecht's masterpiece and the prime example of his "epic theater." As with *The Threepenny Opera,* however, many critics, for example Martin Esslin, see its success as due to a misunderstanding of Brecht's intentions. In Brecht's view, Mother Courage is a villainous character who fails to learn her lesson and remains governed by commercial instincts. The audience should be made to feel the need for action to end all wars. Realizing that the public was instead deeply moved by the human suffering of this woman, Brecht reworked his play in order to place greater emphasis upon her guilt. He did not want her to be mistaken for a Niobe figure. As Martin Esslin reports (*Brecht, The Man and his Work,* 1960), Brecht's own Berlin production was a triumph, but the East German critic Max Shroeder had this to say: "Mother Courage is a humanist saint from the tribe of Niobe and the *mater dolorosa,* who defends the life to which she has given birth with her bared teeth and claws."

Mother Courage has been produced in Germany more than any other play by Brecht, and possibly its influence on contemporary theater was increased by the movie made in 1960. A *Modellbuch* of Brecht's production has been published as well as a collection of source materials (Edition Suhrkamp, 1966). Translations of some of Brecht's notes, a number of essays, and a bibliography appear in Volkmar Sander's 1964 edition of the play. An excellent article by Roland Barthes can be found in the Brecht issue of *The Drama Review,* T 37 (1967).—H. R.

motion picture drama. See SCREENPLAY.

Motokiyo, Zeami. Called **Zeami** or **Seami** (1363–1443). Japanese playwright, the most celebrated of *noh* playwrights and master of poetic drama. Zeami was the son of Kan-ami Kiyotsugo (1333–1384), who was himself eminent in dramatic art (see SOTOBA KOMACHI). Father and son each directed his own theatrical troupe. There were many companies of players at the time, divided into distinct schools, each with its own style. Performances were before audiences of many different kinds—before the emperor himself, on the estates of great lords, in the courts of Buddhist shrines, and even in the villages. Kan-ami is known to have much improved and elevated all aspects of production, notably musical, choreographic, and poetic features.

Biographical information on the father is fragmentary and on the son only a little more extensive. They were evidently men of great initiative and imagination, contending, often without marked success, for princely favors. Much of what is known of Kan-ami derives from the critical and biographical writings of Zeami. Only a few plays by Kan-ami survive and almost all of these exist in versions presumably much altered by later revisers. In the instance of Zeami we are more fortunate. His plays were undoubtedly altered both before and after they were first committed to writing, but not as drastically as in his father's case. Moreover, we possess nearly a hundred of Zeami's plays, constituting almost half the number that survive in the repertory of noh companies today. In addition, we have Zeami's essays and memoirs, which fill a substantial volume.

Zeami's prose affords us our most valuable information on theory and practice in the early, formative period of Japanese drama. The essays are unsystematic but nonetheless revealing. They show a practical man of the theater, always eager to experiment with new forms. Zeami was at once playwright, musical composer, director, actor, and dancer. He was also a man of religious and philosophical insight, versed in theories of the various cults of Buddhism, notably the Zen and—which often came much to the same thing—in current aesthetic theory. Modern critics have searched for words or phrases to express Zeami's leading aesthetic conception succinctly, but however powerful this may still seem to us, the intellectual formulation of his ideal proves uncomfortably elusive. His highest ideal for art in general, and for the noh plays in particular, he expressed in the word *yūgen,* signifying serene meditation on beauty comprised in elegance of form and instilled with religious peace.

Completely clear from his prose writings, at least, is a dedication to art which he, his comrades, and his family experienced. Zeami himself submitted to personal indignity at the hands of his patrons in order to further his craft. For his father as a teacher, he felt the highest veneration. His essays were not intended for publication but as secret instruction for his promising son, Motomasa. This gifted youth, after successfully writing and performing in several plays, died prematurely. Thus bereaved, Zeami knew of no one worthy of receiving his "secret" writings. His words regarding this misfortune reveal something of his character as artist, as thinker, and as man:

> The innermost secrets of our art, from the time when I received the teachings of my late father until the time of my son Motomasa in this my old age, had one and all been handed on, and I, Zeami, awaited only the last great event of my life, when, all unforeseen, the early death of Motomasa brought our line to an end and the whole company to its ruin. His son is still a boy and, with none to receive this double bequest of our art [i.e., the teachings of Kan-ami and Zeami himself] it only obsesses this old man beyond all bearing and stands between him and his great release. If a worthy man existed, I would entrust to him at least my part of the bequest, even if he were a stranger—but no such person is to be found in our art.

How much justice there may have been in this gloomy view cannot be ascertained, but it is at least certain that the texts of many of Zeami's own plays have survived, that the noh play, which rests on the foundation laid down by his labors, is still honored as one of the finest forms of lyric drama, and that

Zeami's own speculative writings have, presumably with only minor textual corruption, remained to enlighten times far distant from his own. See the following plays, described in this book: Aoi-no-ue; Atsumori; and Takasago.

For the best account of Zeami and his school, see P. G. O'Neill, *Early Noh Drama* (1958), and by the same author, *A Guide to Noh* (1954). Also see, with special note of the Introduction, *The Nō Plays of Japan* (1921; new ed., 1950), translated by Arthur Waley.—H. W. W.

Mourning Becomes Electra (1931). A play in three parts by Eugene O'Neill. Turning to the Orestean theme treated by Aeschylus and his successors, O'Neill localized it in New England immediately after the conclusion of the Civil War (instead of the Trojan War) in 1865 and translated and paralleled it in terms of the American environment of that period. The scion of a wealthy mercantile family, General Ezra Mannon, the Agamemnon of *Mourning Becomes Electra,* returns from the Civil War to learn that his alienated wife, Christine (the Clytemnestra of O'Neill's treatment), has been unfaithful to him with the seafaring Adam Brant (O'Neill's Aegisthus), from a rival branch of the family. He is poisoned by her when he seeks a reconciliation. In the second part of O'Neill's trilogy, as in the *Libation Bearers* of Aeschylus and the *Electra*s of Sophocles and Euripides, the Electra character, whom O'Neill calls Lavinia, and her brother Orin (Orestes) avenge their father's death by killing their mother's lover, Adam, whereupon the mother commits suicide. In the third part of the trilogy, the burden of guilt rests heavily on the son, although unlike Orestes, he has not directly murdered his mother. Orin is virtually mad and so dependent upon his sister Lavinia that he won't allow her to marry anyone. The action ends with a rather melodramatic frenzy in which O'Neill's Electra drives Orestes to suicide, following which she is so overwhelmed with remorse that she renounces all possibilities of happiness, shutting herself up forever with her conscience in the mansion of the ill-fated Mannons.

The power of the play immediately communicated itself on the stage in 1931. But there was more to the play than the transcription of Greek matter into American terms. O'Neill, it is true, did not differ from the Greek tragedians in concerning himself with fate and the working out of the family curse in the story of a New England Brahmin family. But it was his intention to go much further and translate fate into modern terms, an enterprise already started by the late nineteenth-century naturalists who found an equivalent for the Greek idea of fate in their rudimentary scientific concepts of determinism by heredity and environment. Locating the determinism in the human psyche, O'Neill adopted the Freudian emphasis upon the sexual instinct, especially the much-publicized Oedipus complex.

The language of the play, rather too prosaic for tragedy, and the heavy emphasis on incestuous feelings elicited unfavorable comment, at first mostly in England and later in American literary circles, the most considered being perhaps theater historian Allardyce Nicoll's conclusion: "This is rather a magnificently presented case study than a powerful tragic drama."—J. G.

Mowatt, Anna Cora. See FASHION.

Mrcchakatika. See THE LITTLE CLAY CART.

Much Ado About Nothing (c. 1598–1599). A comedy by William SHAKESPEARE. The quarto of 1600—the first published text of the play—notes on the title page that *Much Ado About Nothing* had been publicly acted "sundry times" by the Lord Chamberlain's Men. The First Folio (1623) basically reprints the quarto text. A story from Matteo Bandello's *Novelle* (1554) furnishes the plot source, with added details from Lodovico Ariosto's *Orlando Furioso* (1516, translated into English 1591).

The main plot relates how Claudio, a young Florentine lord, rejects his bride, Hero, at the altar because he has been duped into believing that she had acted unchastely. The machinations of the self-labeled villain Don John and his follower Borachio in faking Hero's wedding eve assignation are revealed through the hilarious apprehension and interrogation of Borachio by the constable Dogberry and the Watch. In the underplot Beatrice and Benedick, in love-game comedy tradition, carry on a war of wit until they ultimately succumb to one another.

TITLE PAGE OF THE FIRST QUARTO (1600) OF SHAKESPEARE'S *Much Ado About Nothing*

Much adoe about Nothing.

As it hath been sundrie times publikely acted by the right honourable, the Lord Chamberlaine his seruants.

Written by William Shakespeare.

LONDON
Printed by V.S. for Andrew Wise, and William Aspley.
1600.

This romantic comedy has been regarded by critics as a brilliant but unbalanced work. The Hero-Claudio story of the main plot pales beside the wit combats between the high-spirited, sharp-tongued Beatrice and the confirmed bachelor Benedick—characters introduced into the source tale by Shakespeare. Dogberry and the other low-comedy characters, also Shakespeare's invention, further turn interest from the main characters. As the title implies, their plight is not to be taken seriously anyway. The "nothing" of the title puns on the word "noting," a homonym at the time, suggesting a primary theme of Shakespeare's: the ability to discern through observation the difference between appearance and reality. The play abounds in notings that lead to false conclusions. Dramatically, these suggest that Shakespeare placed Beatrice and Benedick into his plot to contrast the undiscriminating, conventionally romantic approach to love of Hero and Claudio with the more reasoned, intellectual probings of the emotion by Beatrice and Benedick.

Prose, the medium of their wit duels, predominates in the play. The use of prose for witty dialogue among aristocratic characters is an important new element in Shakespearean drama, one that many critics consider influential in the later development of high comedy.

An outstanding edition of *Much Ado About Nothing* is the New Cambridge Edition (1923), edited by Arthur Quiller-Couch and J. Dover Wilson.—W. G.

Mudraraksasa ("The Signet Ring of Rakshasa," c. 875). A Sanskrit play by Visakhadatta. The dramatist's only surviving play, *Mudraraksasa* is one of the masterpieces of the Sanskrit stage. Most of the memorable works in this literature belong to one of two forms specified by Indian critical theory, the heroic or the erotic. This play belongs to neither and is even less idealistic than the masterful romantic drama *The Little Clay Cart*. It bears witness to the scope of Sanskrit drama, from whose fertile fields so many works are irretrievably lost.

Visakhadatta was a prince, son of Maharaja Bhaskardatta. His birthplace is presumed to be Pataliputra, the modern Patna, in northeast India. His play was written about 875. It is thus one of the latest of the important dramas in Sanskrit. The playwright is commonly described by historians of drama as a radical. At the time of his writing, two types of stories enjoyed special popularity on the stage: quarrels between queens who are rivals in the king's affection and conflicts between epic heroes, which reflected morals and manners increasingly foreign to contemporary Indian life. The romantic species of play successfully cultivated by King Harsha, who reigned from 606 to 647, was growing increasingly effete. With studious deliberation Visakhadatta cultivated a style unpopular in his own times but from a critical point of view much in demand—a new realism. In the introductory passage he explains that a drama should reflect realities of life and the dramatist should construct his plot as a statesman lays out a carefully planned intrigue. He promises a play proceeding from the clear and cool intellect, not from the warm but vaguely conceived moods of the popular playwrights of his own times. Much of his play proceeds, in fact, as though no Indian criticism or drama before him had existed. His pages abound in aphorisms but are sparse in the lyrical passages that Kalidasa and his chief followers had cultivated so successfully. *Mudraraksasa* is aggressively masculine. Only one figure is a woman and she is of secondary importance.

The antithesis of most Sanskrit drama, this is an intellectual problem play worked out with the rigidity of a profoundly calculated game of chess. Its problem, with a difference easily described, is one familiar to writers of the age of Shakespeare, namely, the rivalry of lion and fox. In literature associated in the West with the influence of Machiavelli, the legend was customarily of the victory of the wily fox over the noble but insufficiently cunning lion. In the Sanskrit play the point of view is subtler. It is based on the thesis that each requires the other; to be fully effective, the hero needs the strategist and the strategist the hero. It is of considerable interest that in Visakhadatta's drama the more active agent is the wily strategist, not the nobler but quieter man from whom the play derives its name. In the beginning the two men are rivals and inveterate enemies. By devious means the clever fox compels the noble lion to renounce a cause to which he has given almost fanatical devotion and to join forces with him in support of a new regime. The fox is Chanakya, a Brahman and minister of the new king. The lion is Rakshasa, known as an extremely able general and statesman, celebrated for unqualified loyalty, wholly dependable once he is committed to a cause. Chanakya leads him to renounce his long devotion to the Nanda dynasty and so to join in the service of the new monarch, averting a civil war.

The plot is effected by undermining the loyalty of Rakshasa's corruptible followers and discrediting his secret service system. The securing of Rakshasa's seal ring is one means to this end. At least in this respect Visakhadatta remains faithful to conventions in Sanskrit drama, for the use of such a property as key to a dramatic action was at least as old as Kalidasa's *Shakuntala*. But the really crucial device in undermining Rakshasa's idealism lies in invoking his very idealism itself. His loyalty is primarily personal. He is long faithful to a monarch who has been defeated and slain. In the long course of intrigue and counterintrigue Rakshasa has committed himself to a relatively humble friend, a tradesman of exemplary character. Chanakya so maneuvers affairs that for Rakshasa to remain obstinate he must allow his friend and his friend's wife and children to be led to torture and death. Having promised protection for his friend, he yields and all intrigue is ended.

The play, then, moves with mathematical precision. Its exceptional qualities have been highly praised, especially by Western scholars. A. B. Keith, a most indefatigable, but rarely sympathetic, English historian of Sanskrit literature, states the case with much emphasis. Westerners easily grasp much of the play's meaning. In the meditative Rakshasa may be seen something of Hamlet; in the conspiring Chanakya, much of the subtle Iago. But the Indian outlook even here is by no means typical of Western thought. There is nothing sardonic in Visakhadatta's view. He is himself both realist and idealist. Both his major figures are looked upon with favor; the moral lies in their reconciliation. Visakhadatta is less sinister or sardonic than Machiavelli. He commends an intrigue where the goal is sound and favors an idealism that in the end compromises with the reality of a changing scene. The more this unusual play has been examined by recent critics, the higher its reputation has become.

For an able discussion of *Mudraraksasa,* see A. B. Keith, *Sanskrit Drama* (1924). The best translation into English appears in *Great Sanskrit Plays* (1964) by P. Lal. For a competent version following the original with fidelity, see *Mudraraksasa* (1923), translated by K. H. Poona. The play also appears in *Select Specimens of the Theatre of the Hindus* (1871) by H. H. Wilson.—H. W. W.

Munk, Kaj. Born **Kaj Petersen** (1898–1944). Danish pastor, prosist, and playwright. Kaj Munk, born on the island of Lolland, was orphaned early in life and brought up by a small-landowning family by the name of Munk, whose name he acquired. After taking a degree in theology in 1924, Munk assumed the pastorate of Vedersø, a small congregation on Jutland, where he remained the rest of his life. Though he displayed sympathies with fascism in the 1930's, he emerged as one of the leading fighters for freedom during World War II, chiefly from the pulpit. Munk was murdered by the Gestapo on January 5, 1944.

Munk's first play, *En idealist* (*Herod the King,* written 1924; prod. 1928), is an episodic study of obsessive evil, somewhat resembling Albert Camus's play *Caligula.* A failure in 1928, it met with resounding success on the Copenhagen stage in 1938. Other studies of the superman followed: *I brændingen* (*In*

KAJ MUNK (DANISH INFORMATION OFFICE)

the Breakers, 1929), in which the pillar of agnosticism was probably modeled after the Danish critic Georg Brandes; *Cant* (1931), about Henry VIII's relationship with Ann Boleyn; *De udvalgte* (*The Elect,* 1933), a play about King David; and *Sejren* (*The Victory,* 1936), a drama based on Mussolini and the Abyssinian campaign. Munk's modernization in 1935 of Shakespeare's *Hamlet* reveals his admiration for Elizabethan dramaturgy and his antidemocratic politics.

The miracle play *Ordet* (*The Word,* written 1925; prod. 1932) bulks very large in Munk's production. It explores the possibility of faith in a modern rural society against a background of religious faction. *Kærlighed* (*The Greatest of These,* written 1926; prod. 1934) probes the conscience of a country pastor of faltering faith and wayward emotion.

Munk's change of political view is clearly demonstrated in his anti-Nazi play *Han sidder ved smeltediglen* (*He Sits at the Melting Pot,* 1938), and the treatment of a fourteenth-century patriot in *Niels Ebbesen* (1942) was so transparent an appeal for resistance to the German occupation that it was suppressed. From this time on until the end of the war, all of Munk's plays were on the proscribed list.

Today Munk is more admired than played. He was a hasty, impetuous writer, and the result is unevenness. But he was capable of producing intensity and highly dramatic moments, especially in a virtuoso role like that of Herod.

The fullest collection in English is *Five Plays by Kaj Munk* (1953), edited and translated by R. P. Keigwin. Critical treatment may be found in P. M. Mitchell's *A History of Danish Literature* (1958), pp. 258–262.—R. B. V.

Murder in the Cathedral (1935). A verse play by T. S. ELIOT. Commissioned for the Canterbury Festival of 1935, the play is based on the struggle between Henry II of England and his archbishop of Canterbury, Thomas Becket. Historians believe that Henry chose his friend and chancellor as archbishop with the idea that in Becket he would have an ally in his attempt to diminish the sway of ecclesiastical law. Becket became, however, a great defender of the church, and the ensuing struggle between the two men resulted in Becket's flight to France, where he remained for seven years, and his assassination upon his return in 1170.

The play begins with a chorus of women awaiting Becket's return from France. They hope that nothing will occur to dispel the peace of their lives, but three priests express an active interest in politics. Becket enters to counsel patience and is beset at once with four tempters. They tempt Becket first with his past pleasures shared with the king; second, with the political authority he had had as Henry's ally; third, with a new alliance, which would include the barons, directed against the king; and finally, the dangerous temptation to seek martyrdom for reasons of pride. The first act closes with the archbishop's rejection of the tempters and is followed by an Interlude in which Becket delivers his Christmas sermon on martyrdom and the martyr's necessary subjection to God.

In the second act, four knights accuse the archbishop of political insubordination to the king. The priests try to protect Becket from a second visit by the knights, but Becket refuses protection and is

slain. The knights then address the audience in a modern prose, defending their act. The first knight introduces the others, the second pleads their disinterestedness, the third complains of Becket's disloyalty to the king and excessive loyalty to the church, and the fourth ingeniously argues that Becket provoked the assassination and demands "a verdict of Suicide while of Unsound Mind." The priests and the chorus conclude by celebrating Becket's martyrdom.

Murder in the Cathedral was filmed, and the text of the film, by T. S. Eliot and George Hoellering, was published in 1952. In this text, the knights' defense is cut to one speech because as originally written, the four speeches had proved too amusing to audiences. Eliot himself spoke the lines of the fourth tempter in the film.

The text of *Murder in the Cathedral* is in *The Complete Poems and Plays* (1952) of T. S. Eliot. A useful annotated edition has been edited by Nevill Coghill (1965).—H. P.

Murray, Thomas C. (1873–1959). Irish playwright. Born in Cork, Murray was one of eleven children. He began his career as a schoolteacher while writing in his spare time. His first published play, *Birthright,* was produced at the Abbey Theatre in 1910. Set in rural Ireland, *Birthright* is a stark domestic tragedy of two brothers stirred to violent hatred of one another by an aging parent. Another realistic tragedy is *Maurice Harte* (1912), an intensive study of a young man driven to insanity by the conflicting demands of his parents, who insist upon his becoming a priest, and the claims of his own conscience. In its simplicity and directness the play probes the soul of the Irish-Catholic countryfolk, struggling with devotion but tragically limited values to overcome the bleakness and poverty of their life. In his later career Murray never duplicated the achievement of these two early plays, although *Autumn Fire* (1924), a domestic tragedy, approaches them in intensity of feeling. Among his other plays are *Aftermath* (1922), *The Pipe in the Fields* (1927), *Michaelmas Eve* (1932), and *Illumination* (1939).

Murray's gifts as a dramatist rest in his ability to suggest the profound emotional roots of simple, uneducated people. His realistic tragedies provide compassionate portraits of Irish peasant life.—E. Q.

Musahipzade, Celâl (1868–1959). Turkish playwright. Musahipzade was born and raised in Istanbul. His grandfather, a composer, was a gentleman-in-waiting in the court of Sultan Selim III (1789–1807). From his old relatives Musahipzade learned the customs, diction, and manners of the courts as well as those of the common people of the early nineteenth century. Musahipzade was mainly interested in the Turkish traditional theater, in which he acted. From 1912 to 1934 he wrote nearly twenty plays, most of them satires on the old Turkish customs and manners. While lampooning the false values of the past, he had the present in mind, and in every play there is at least one character who serves as the mouthpiece for the author.

In *Bir Kavuk Devrildi* ("A Turban Falls," 1930) Musahipzade satirizes the ignorant, overambitious, and sexually perverted rulers who exploited the people and snubbed artists and artisans. *Mum Söndü* ("The Candle Is Out," 1931), written during the period when Atatürk was establishing secularism in

Turkey, ridicules the hypocrisies of sectarian sheiks who exploited their disciples for their own prosperity and sexual indulgence. These two plays, along with three or four other comedies, are the most popular of Musahipzade's plays, and they have been revived frequently.

Musahipzade's satirical plays, although amorphous in their construction, dominated the Turkish theater along with the comedies and adaptations of Ibnürrefik Ahmet Nuri (1874–1935) for about a quarter-century. No playwright has surpassed Musahipzade in capturing with authenticity the language, manners, and the general spirit of the Ottoman Empire. Inspired by the traditional theater, folklore, and history of Turkey, his output has served as source material for linguists, sociologists, and historians as well as other dramatists. Musahipzade is perhaps the most native of Turkish playwrights. —N. O.

musical comedy. A play in which music, lyrics, and possibly dances are interwoven with the plot. Clearly, a play with background music or a few songs and dances, as in Shakespeare's *A Midsummer Night's Dream* or John Osborne's *The Entertainer* (1957), is not a musical comedy. Music has been added to heighten atmosphere, relieve tension, or create diversion, but the play itself is the most important thing. In musical comedy, however, removal of the musical element would definitely damage the fabric of the drama.

The term musical comedy is widely and loosely used. Although it implies a humorous entertainment, many—such as *South Pacific* (1949) and *The Most Happy Fella* (1956)—combine humor with serious themes. Some musicals cannot be called musical comedies at all, and in these cases musical play would be the better term. *Lost in the Stars* (1949) with text by Maxwell Anderson and music by Kurt Weill is best described as a musical play. Based on *Cry the Beloved Country*, Alan Paton's novel of South African racial problems, the work was labeled "musical tragedy" by its creators. A good working distinction between musical comedy and musical play is that in the former the emphasis is on the musical aspects even though the story may be important, integral, and interesting, while in the latter the story and music are more nearly equal in importance.

A problem arises, however, in trying to classify specific works. How does one label works like *West Side Story* (1957), *Show Boat* (1927), *Porgy and Bess* (1935), and *The Threepenny Opera* (1928)? In *West Side Story,* Arthur Laurents' book retells the Romeo and Juliet legend in a New York slum setting. Leonard Bernstein's dynamic score and Stephen Sondheim's brilliant lyrics create the impression that the story is being told in music rather than in dialogue. Thus, the work upsets the customary balance between plot and music in the musical's play, where dialogue does not become submerged. It is clearly not a musical comedy either, though it has been so-called. Although satire and vital humor abound, the moments of laughter and exhilaration merely serve to heighten ironically the impact of the tragic finale. Some critics feel that, despite the popular flavor of many of the songs, the music has operatic dimensions and the story an urgent intensity that make this work almost a popular or folk opera.

Porgy and Bess, with a libretto by DuBose Heyward and Ira Gershwin and music by George Gershwin, was first regarded as a musical comedy or musical play. Today it enjoys the dignity of being bracketed with opera in several standard references. It has been suggested that *Porgy and Bess* can be given both "operatic" and "musical comedy" productions, depending on whether the emphasis is on singing or acting. This indicates that production values may have some bearing on a work's ultimate classification.

The Threepenny Opera, like *Mahagonny* (1928/29), a collaboration between playwright-librettist Bertolt Brecht and composer Kurt Weill, takes its subject matter and its spirit from the ballad opera. Brecht includes songs to interrupt plot and maintain interest, to weaken suspense and inhibit empathy, and to emphasize and teach. Weill's remarkable score, echoing with the strident sounds of the 1920's in Germany, is haunting but has more of the cabaret than the opera about it, even though Brecht called the work "epic opera." The music was intended to reinforce and develop the themes that are projected through cutting satire, acidly wild humor, and a deliberate coarseness. Because of the influence of phonograph records, however, *The Threepenny Opera's* music is now better known than its plot, and it is common to hear the play referred to as a musical comedy. Recent revivals of *Mahagonny,* unlike *The Threepenny Opera,* which is now done even by amateur groups, have been performed by opera companies.

Thanks to the richly melodic score of Jerome Kern and the sentimental book and lyrics of Oscar Hammerstein II, *Show Boat,* based on Edna Ferber's novel of the same name, is occasionally designated an operetta. Despite the overtones of operetta in its scoring, the subject matter—melodramatic and concerned with miscegenation—and its treatment are more consonant with the traditions of the American musical.

Musical comedies slowly came into existence in England and the United States in the last half of the nineteenth century, but America has been the most active parent. An exploration of the foundations of musical comedy and its recent history will help show its relation to the OPERETTA and to other forms of musical theater that have rather vague boundaries. It can also provide a survey of some of the better known works and their creators.

A variety of nineteenth-century entertainments influenced musical comedy, either directly or indirectly. An important theater form, which some commentators claim was the direct ancestor of musical comedy, is burlesque. The passage of time and Minsky's often crude showmanship turned burlesque into the amalgam of nudity and off-color humor that survives today. But at the time of John Poole's London burlesque *Hamlet* in 1828, the form was pure parody, usually of well-known dramas, though novels, poems, and personalities were also burlesqued. As entertainment, burlesque rapidly became popular, and improvements were continually made. In *La Mosquita* (1838), the Viennese dancer Fanny Elssler was lampooned. Dance had become a part of burlesque. In 1869, the arrival in the United States from England of Lydia Thompson and her "British

Blondes," who performed "gross and vulgar dances" [according to the distinguished drama critic Richard Grant White] in flesh-colored tights as embellishment to their parodic fare, helped create interest in the female form at the expense of the dramatic form.

Other types of entertainment, popular in England and America, that influenced the development of musical comedy are the pantomime, the extravaganza, and the spectacle, all of which have aspects that survive today in musicals. The musical comedy seems to have evolved from these forms, although operetta and comic opera have also left their marks. Pantomime, which is still played in England during the Christmas season, had harlequinade in the nineteenth century, but paradoxically most of the performance today depends upon dialogue, dance, music, songs, and astonishing scenic effects. The extravaganza, an offshoot of burlesque, also offered songs and dance, usually with scantily clad ladies in the chorus line. *Evangeline* (1874), an insane parody of Longfellow's poem of the same name, was a popular example of this type, played, as one critic of the time noted, with "ludicrous extravagance." The extravaganza was New York's answer to Paris, perhaps because the operettas of Offenbach were found at first to be too sophisticated for American audiences. Edward Harrigan and Tony Hart, with their Mulligan Guards shows, and Joe Weber and Lew Fields were leading actors in the form.

The most often cited ancestor of modern musical comedy, however, is the famed spectacle *The Black Crook* (1866). This concoction of music, elaborate fairyland scenery, beautiful ballet girls in tights, specialty acts, and a plot remotely related to the Faust legend, ran for sixteen months in New York City and made over a million dollars, something of a record for those times. That the visual and musical elements completely overshadowed the plot did not seem to bother audiences. This was to become the rule in musical comedy.

In 1879, Nate Salsbury's *The Brook* appeared on Broadway. It was the first musical show described as a "musical comedy," and it was thoroughly American in its locales and characters. Even though operetta continued to draw a large public in this period, the musicals with American themes that followed *The Brook* began to win an audience. Partly chauvinistic, partly a reaction against the Graustarkian world of operetta, they offered audiences the same escapism, optimism, and romantic sentiment found in Strauss and his disciples, but this gradually changed in favor of more realistic situations.

A London impresario, George Edwardes, gave impetus to a special variety of musical, the "girl" show. Among them are *The Nautch Girl* (1891), *The Shop Girl* (1894), *A Country Girl* (1894), *The Circus Girl* (1896), *A Runaway Girl* (1898), and *The Quaker Girl* (1910). These were vehicles tailored to the talents and designed to expose the charms of attractive young female stars. The team that usually created this form of entertainment was James Tanner (book), Adrian Ross and Percy Greenbank (lyrics), and Ivan Caryll and Lionel Monckton (music). New York audiences responded so well to the London invention that they soon had native versions such as *The Casino Girl* (1900) and *The Knickerbocker Girl* (1900).

London's *Floradora* (1899), written by Owen Hall, gave the world the Floradora Girls (a distinctive female chorus group that had many imitators) and a hit song: "Tell Me Pretty Maiden." It also possessed a complicated plot of singular inanity, featuring a wealthy, social-climbing American who tyrannizes his employees in a perfume factory on the Philippine island of Floradora. Despite the customary emphasis on pretty girls and comedy, the plot indicated a topical interest among Englishmen in Americans in the Orient, not surprising since the United States had just acquired the Philippines from Spain, a sign of potential imperialism that disturbed the British.

Far more pertinent as social comment was George Ade's satirical treatment of American occupation in a remote part of the world in *The Sultan of Sulu* (1902), with music by Alfred Wathall. Ade, with affectionate humor and real insight, showed his fellow Americans trying to inflict their culture and values on the happily ignorant natives of Sulu. What is most unusual, considering the generally low level of wit and character portrayal in early musical comedy, is that Ade's book and lyrics alternate charm with satiric bite. Many of his observations on Americans abroad seem quite modern. Among this humorist's other musicals are *The Night of the Fourth* (1900), *Peggy from Paris* (1903), *The Sho-Gun* (1904), *The Fair Co-ed* (1909), and *The Old Town* (1910). His comedy *The College Widow* (1904) became the musical *Leave It to Jane* in 1917.

By the turn of the century, the musical comedy was firmly entrenched in New York theater life. In the 1900/01 season, no less than thirty shows with music were staged; some were operettas—native, English, French, and German—and some were merely elaborate musical spectacles. At the same time, more and more musical comedies with local scenes and characters were appearing—works like *The Liberty Belles* (1901), *The New Yorker* (1902), and *The Belle of Broadway* (1902). Some curiosities of the era were *Broadway to Tokyo* (1900), a "spectacular fantasy"; *Little Red Riding Hood* (1900), an "extravaganza"; *Aunt Hannah* (1900), a "musical farce"; and *The Rogers Brothers in Central Park* (1900), featuring the popular team of Gus and Max Rogers in a "vaudeville farce with music." The duo of Joe Weber and Lew Fields appeared in the same year in a "musical extravaganza," *Fiddle-dee-dee*. David Montgomery and Fred Stone, another successful partnership, triumphed in a musical version of *The Wizard of Oz* (1903), adapted by the author himself, L. Frank Baum.

Not until the emergence of George M. Cohan at the opening of the new century, however, was the formula for musical comedy, especially in America, perfected. In Cohan's day a star or a group of well-known players were the customary starting point for a musical comedy, rather than a best-selling novel or a popular play as in recent practice. Any plot, no matter how ridiculous or banal, would do, as long as it could be embellished with choruses, comic sketches, romantic songs, specialty acts, and large-scale production numbers, usually at the end of each act. Good was always rewarded and evil punished. The boy got the girl, and occasionally the villain had to marry a most unattractive female comic.

Today Cohan's work seems naïve and elemental in

the extreme—as, unfortunately, does much American drama of the period—but he brought to the situations and dialogue a distinctly American flavor. Swiftly paced and exuberant, his musicals were noted for lively tunes and spirited dances. As author, lyricist, composer, director, and performer, Cohan enjoyed a tremendous following, which waned only after World War I, when tastes changed. His musicals include *Little Johnny Jones* (1904), *Forty-five Minutes from Broadway* (1906), *Fifty Miles from Boston* (1908), *The Yankee Prince* (1908), *The Man Who Owns Broadway* (1909), and *Hello, Broadway* (1914). He also wrote nonmusical comedies.

Some of the most enduring music in the genre was composed by Jerome Kern, who had among his collaborators Otto Harbach, Oscar Hammerstein II, Guy Bolton, and P. G. Wodehouse. Contemporary Americans in comic situations were the usual subjects of his shows, which include *Oh Boy!* (1917) and *Leave It to Jane* (1917), both with college-town settings; *Sally* (1920), set in the milieu of Long Island society; and *Show Boat*, with its Mississippi River setting. The locale of *The Cat and the Fiddle* (1931) was Brussels. In this work, Kern and his librettist Harbach produced a novelty: a musical comedy that concentrated on the story, avoiding big choruses and production numbers. *Music in the Air* (1932), with its Bavarian scene and operetta sentiment was perhaps a harbinger of *The Sound of Music*, since Hammerstein wrote both librettos. *Roberta* (1933) was a fashion show set to music, an enjoyable diversion during the Depression.

Although variety and vaudeville, along with music hall in England, were being displaced by motion pictures, artists with comic or acrobatic skills could still find a niche in those survivals of the extravaganzas and spectacles known as "revues." Revues, loosely connected sequences of sketches, songs, and production numbers, appeared in a number of editions, the most successful of which were the *Ziegfeld Follies; J. J. Shubert's The Passing Show;* George White's *Scandals,* with music by Gershwin; and Irving Berlin's *Music Box Revue.* Appetite for this type of show waned in the late 1940's, although the genre was briefly revived with Leonard Sillman's *New Faces* in 1952, 1956, and 1968. The revue format is still popular in England, where *Living for Pleasure* (1958), with music by Richard Addinsell; *One Over the Eight* (1961); and *Six of One* (1963) were typical popular successes.

In the twenties and thirties, although American musicals stressed native themes and people—as was also the case in England—many of the stories were insubstantial, often ridiculous love plots liberally laced with comedy. Composer Vincent Youmans is remembered in this period for *No, No, Nanette* (1925) and *Hit the Deck* (1927). The gifted George Gershwin, with his brother Ira as lyricist and Guy Bolton as a frequent collaborator on the book, created *Lady Be Good* (1924), *Oh Kay!* (1926), and *Girl Crazy* (1930). In contrast is Gershwin's *Of Thee I Sing* (1931), with a biting book by Morrie Ryskind and George S. Kaufman. It won a Pulitzer Prize in 1932 for avoiding the formula clichés and providing a sharp, amusing satire on American politics.

Attitudes were changing in the 1920's. The rustic innocence that had made possible long New York runs for pre-World War I dramas like the almost infantile *Mrs. Wiggs of the Cabbage Patch, Rebecca of Sunnybrook Farm,* and *Daddy Long Legs* was fading. At the same time, the really good shows became more interesting, more significant, less trivial, although the mass of musical comedies remained true cliché.

The long career of composer Richard Rodgers is coincident with the period of change, and, not surprisingly, he and his collaborators are responsible for a number of the most important innovations. *Dearest Enemy* (1925), with a book by Herbert Fields and lyrics by Lorenz Hart (1895–1943), dealt with the American Revolution so effectively that drama critic Percy Hammond called it a "baby grand opera." The same team produced *Peggy-Ann* (1926), which delved into dream psychology years before Moss Hart and Kurt Weill concocted *Lady in the Dark* (1941). *A Connecticut Yankee* (1927), loosely based on Mark Twain's novel, offered some songs that became favorites, such as "Thou Swell" and "My Heart Stood Still." *On Your Toes* (1936), a ballet story with book by Rodgers, Hart, and George Abbott, included the famous "Slaughter on Tenth Avenue" sequence, mixing dancers with gangsters. *Pal Joey* (1940) was unsuccessful until a 1952 revival, by which time author John O'Hara's title character, a heel who lives off wealthy women, was more acceptable. And, of course, the music was a great deal more familiar by then as well. The uncompromising subject matter was projected with vitality, color, and wit.

When Rodgers took Oscar Hammerstein II as his collaborator after Hart's death in 1943, a new era in musical comedy was forecast by many drama critics. The duo was to set new patterns and standards for America and England, the latter country's musicals having previously been too insular to survive in the new world. The opening of *Oklahoma!* (1943) signaled to reviewers the appearance of a fresh inspiration. Based on Lynn Riggs's *Green Grow the Lilacs* (1931), a local color drama with melodramatic overtones, Hammerstein's book celebrates American neighborliness and life and adventure on the frontier. Unlike almost all musicals before, the plot of *Oklahoma!* was paramount, but the music was not subordinated. Rather, it grew naturally out of character and situation, as did the dances of Agnes De Mille, reinforcing the story melodically and atmospherically. But even outside the framework of the story, semiorganic songs like "Everything's Up to Date in Kansas City" and "I Cain't Say No" achieved independent popularity. Curiously, disaster was predicted for *Oklahoma!* during out-of-town tryouts because it was too different from the established pattern. A death climaxed the action; there were no scantily clad chorines. The rest is history. It ran for five years and nine months on Broadway, 2,248 performances in all. It was on the road for over ten years. Companies have performed it in the major capitals of the world. It was one of the longest runs at London's Drury Lane, and it is frequently revived in stock and by amateur groups.

Next came *Carousel* (1945), based on Ferenc Molnár's *Liliom* (1909) but with a New England setting. Other profitable ventures were *South Pacific* (1949), based on James Michener's *Tales of the South*

Pacific; *The King and I* (1951), adapted from Margaret Landon's *Anna and the King of Siam* (and premiered in Munich only in 1966 and Vienna in 1967, owing to Rodgers' long-time ban on German productions); *Flower-Drum Song* (1958), taken from C. Y. Lee's novel of San Francisco's Chinatown and dubbed by critic Kenneth Tynan "the world of woozy song"; and *The Sound of Music* (1959), suggested by a film, *Die Trapp Familie*. The motion picture version of the musical broke all previous cinema profit records shortly after its release, perhaps proving that the public's taste is not that of the critics, many of whom found the music too reminiscent of former triumphs, the story too much reduced to a formula, and the approach far too sentimental.

After the passing of Hammerstein, Rodgers did his thirty-eighth show, *No Strings* (1962), by himself. A tale of interracial love that glossed over some of the more unpleasant realities, the show was unusual in that Rodgers orchestrated his score as the title indicates, without stringed instruments. Instead of the traditional pit orchestra, he had his musicians behind the scenes, allowing some of them to appear on stage as part of the production.

Kurt Weill (1900–1950), brought to America in 1935 by theater impresario Max Reinhardt, joined playwright Paul Green to indict war-lovers in *Johnny Johnson* (1936) for the Group Theatre. It retained a European flavor in its music, but the pacifist appeal was thoroughly American in its story. With *Knickerbocker Holiday* (1938), set to text and lyrics by Maxwell Anderson, Weill began to fashion his own American idiom. The nostalgia of "September Song" is a result, the love song of an aging Peter Stuyvesant courting a reluctant young lady. Among his other works are the psychoanalytical *Lady in the Dark* (1941), with its colorful Freudian dream sequences; *One Touch of Venus* (1943), a light fantasy by Ogden Nash and S. J. Perelman involving a statue of Venus come to life in modern New York City, with dances by Agnes De Mille that enrich and advance the plot; and *Lost in the Stars* (1949).

Rising tides of protest against social injustice caused by the Depression and despotic events in Europe prior to World War II encouraged outspoken dramas on the subject. But the musical theater was generally content to escape from reality or to sentimentalize. Marc Blitzstein's *The Cradle Will Rock* (1938), thoroughly in the Brecht-Weill tradition, dealt with strife between capital and labor, but the initial performance was halted.

Even as protean a talent as Leonard Bernstein began his Broadway career with two harmlessly lively salutes to New York: *On the Town* (1944), with book and lyrics by Betty Comden and Adolph Green; and *Wonderful Town* (1953), with Comden and Green doing lyrics and J. Fields and J. Chodorov adapting the book from *My Sister Eileen* by Ruth McKenney. But sharper works were yet to come. In 1956 *Candide* appeared, with a text by Lillian Hellman. Although it was a failure then, recordings have since ensured its popularity, at least as a score. *West Side Story*, previously discussed, grappled vividly with the problems of growing up in the New York slums.

Composers like Cole Porter and Irving Berlin worked well within the 1920's formula of love plots,

brightened with comedy. Porter's *Kiss Me, Kate* (1948), thanks partly to a book by Sam and Bella Spewak that gives *The Taming of the Shrew* a modern backstage framework and partly to Porter's brilliant combination of clever lyrics and vital tunes, has a parodic flavor of operetta about it that explains its great popularity in the German-language theater, where few American musicals have found a public.

Annie Get Your Gun (1946), with book by Herbert and Dorothy Fields, was one of Irving Berlin's most skillful attempts to integrate music with story, although many of his formula shows have found an eager public. An unusual and timely wedding of music and satirical story was *Finian's Rainbow* (1947), with book by E. Y. Harburg and Fred Saidy and music by Burton Lane. The authors attacked a variety of subjects—racial discrimination, socialism, greed, the poll tax, and human pretension. Lane so effectively created tunes that reinforced the lyrics that almost all his musical numbers became popular successes.

The team of Alan Jay Lerner (book and lyrics) and Frederick Loewe (music) produced an effective show in *Brigadoon* (1947), which nostalgically contrasted an ancient, mythical Scottish village with modern New York. It received the first Best Play Award to be given a musical comedy by the Drama Critics Circle. *Paint Your Wagon* (1951) successfully caught the spirit of the California Gold Rush. On the other hand, *Camelot* (1960), suggested by T. H. White's book *The Once and Future King*, seemed clumsily adapted, especially since the climactic scene—the rescue of Guinevere—was not staged. *My Fair Lady* (1956) was their most brilliant collaboration, wisely leaning heavily on its source, Bernard Shaw's *Pygmalion*. In Europe, where it has been enthusiastically received, critics explain its appeal in terms of the strength of Shaw's book and the operetta quality of much of the music.

Frank Loesser is an interesting composer who has not been afraid to try a variety of subjects. *Guys and Dolls* (1950) cleverly used Damon Runyon stories and types, in a book by Jo Swerling and Abe Burrows, the latter a comic craftsman also praised as a "play doctor." *The Most Happy Fella* (1956), based on Sidney Howard's *They Knew What They Wanted* (1924), was completely Loesser's work, and it verges on the operatic. Unfortunately, it was neither musical nor folk opera, but somewhere in between. *How To Succeed in Business Without Really Trying* (1961) was notable for several things: its long title; its host of collaborators in production; its source, a loose collection of merry maxims for office mayhem; and its success, despite the above drawbacks, as an entertaining parody of executive skullduggery.

It is not easy to speculate on the staying power of recent musicals. No matter how appealing the music, production memories fade and topical stories rapidly date. Perhaps Jule Styne's *Gypsy* (1959) and Jerry Bock's *Fiorello* (1959) will survive as period pieces. Of Meredith Willson's work, which includes *The Music Man* (1957), distinguished by some amusing lyrics and catchy tunes, and *The Unsinkable Molly Brown* (1960), it may be said that sentimental nostalgia and celebration of homey values have been *leitmotifs*. Of Jerry Herman's *Hello, Dolly!* (1964) and *Mame* (1966), it may be said that his sources, Thornton Wilder's *The Matchmaker* (1955) and Patrick Dennis' farcical novel *Auntie Mame,* are far superior to the books that have been fashioned from them, books that provide a story line from which most of the real humor and charm seems to have been excised to make room for the musical numbers.

English insularity and American isolation up to World War II helped keep the more uniquely native products at home, but in the postwar years popularity on Broadway of major musicals was often their passport to a West End opening. Despite brashness and brassy orchestration, traits that British critics occasionally objected to, a number of American musicals have been well received, especially the musicals of Rodgers and Hammerstein. Over the years the exchange has hardly been balanced even by Noel Coward plays with music. The conventionality and dainty, tinkling quality of many English musicals did not commend them to American tastes. After the advent of *Oklahoma!,* however, a more vigorous type of British musical started to emerge.

Best known of the new English composers is Lionel Bart, whose *Oliver!* (1960), his own adaptation of Charles Dickens' *Oliver Twist,* had an extended run in both London and New York. Frenzied stage activity, vigorous dances, wistfully raucous music, and Sean Kenny's deliberately rough-textured animated settings made the sordid evils of nineteenth-century London slums seem colorful, charming, in short anything but what they were. With *Blitz!* (1962), Bart's partnership with scene designer Kenny was, visually at least, more rewarding. Remarkably realistic effects of the bombing and fires in blitzed London evoked memories of past horrors with techniques that producers of the spectaculars of the last century would have envied. Bart's score pursued another course, supporting a folksy nostalgia for times of trial and detailing a Cockney *Abie's Irish Rose* plot. *Maggie May* (1964), the tale of a star-crossed prostitute and her docker lover, profited from Alun Owen's earthy, vital book, a realistic vignette of Liverpool life, and a vigorous, thrusting score. Once again the scenic devices of Sean Kenny were integral.

The Boyfriend (1954), a nostalgic parody on 1920's musicals, is considered a sort of classic, but its creator, Sandy Wilson, had little success with a sequel and several self-indulgent, minor musicals. Only *Valmouth* (1958), a brilliantly witty and marvelously melodic adaptation of Ronald Firbank's odd Catholic characters did Wilson much credit. Even though the book, lyrics, and music are all Wilson's, the subject matter was understandably limited in appeal, so the work has failed to command the attention it deserves.

Every London season brings forth, in addition to the crop of revues, operetta revivals, American musicals, and new British originals, some polite adaptations of literary classics. *Vanity Fair* appeared in 1962; others were, from *The Pickwick Papers, Pickwick* (1963); from *Kipps, Half a Sixpence* (1963); from *The Relapse, Virtue in Danger* (1963); from *Rape Upon Rape, Lock Up Your Daughters* (1959); and from *The Barretts of Wimpole Street, Robert and Elizabeth* (1964). But a new kind of musical emerged from Joan Littlewood's now-defunct Theatre Royal, Stratford East. It was *"Oh What a Lovely War"* (1963), a painfully moving tract against war,

conceived as a circus, constructed of sketches based on actual events in World War I, and studded ironically with sentimental songs. The entire cast, prodded and directed by Miss Littlewood, helped devise the show.

Although the musical comedy is obviously a popular form, it has seldom been respected by serious critics of the drama except as relaxation, and then usually only when the wit is challenging and the elements skillfully integrated. Even popular reviewers like Walter Kerr and Tom Prideaux have complained that the form has become formulaic, that the novelty of *Oklahoma!* has worn off, and that new ideas and "gimmicks" are needed. Kerr even recommended subordinating the plot again to the music and dance, noting that musical comedy books are seldom more than "drama at half-mast."

Since so many American musicals are based on other works—an original plot is a rarity—the stress on plot is understandable. With mounting production costs, however, the managements do not take chances, and the adaptations are often the product of a virtual committee of collaborators, each seeking to mix in the elements intended to delight audiences: handsome settings, colorful costumes, lilting love songs, flashy dance routines, show-stopping comedy, exciting stars, and pervasive sentimentality. With the resultant distortion of the novel or play, it seems odd that anyone should be greatly concerned about the primacy of plot. By the mid-sixties, even the music of most shows began to be prefabricated, as if it had been borrowed from various other shows. When Broadway productions began to cost half a million dollars (*Camelot*) or even $700,000 (*Funny Girl*), the development of musical comedy into anything more than a popular entertainment became decidedly problematic.

Dates, casts, and plot summaries are neatly presented in David Ewan's *The Complete Book of the American Musical Theatre* (revised, 1959). His survey, *The Story of America's Musical Theatre* (1961), is a useful if rather brief account of the course of musical drama in the United States, while Cecil M. Smith offers additional detail and insights in *Musical Comedy in America* (1950).—G. L.

Musset, [Louis Charles] Alfred de (1810–1857). French playwright, poet, and novelist. Musset was the most gifted of the French Romantic playwrights, and his plays alone, of all those written during the first half of the nineteenth century, are still staged today in France. He was first influenced by the literary founders of the French Romantic movement—a group known as the Cénacle, which gathered at the home of Victor Hugo. A brilliant student at the Lycée Henri IV in Paris, Musset turned to literature after briefly trying his hand at medicine, law, and painting. He soon became an elegant Parisian dandy and embarked on a life of dissipation. His first literary efforts were poems, published in 1830. They were fashionably romantic, unorthodox in form, and flippant in tone. He formally broke with the Romantics in 1830/31, however, and praised the French classical writers.

In December 1830 Musset's career as a playwright began at the Odéon with a slight one-act play in prose, *La Nuit vénitienne* (*A Venetian Night*). The failure of this play turned him against the stage until

1847, but he continued to write numerous plays that were intended to be read. Most of these plays, after revision, were given belated or posthumous performances. His first major collection of plays, playlets, and poems, many of them dramatizing selected proverbs, was published in 1833/34 in two volumes as *Un Spectacle dans un fauteuil* ("Armchair Theater"). Memorable among these are his first *proverbe dramatique, La Coupe et les lèvres (The Cup and the Lip,* not performed), the verse comedy *A Quoi rêvent les jeunes filles (Of What Young Maidens Dream,* not performed), and the prose plays *André del Sarto* (written 1833, prod. 1848), *Fantasio* (written 1833, prod. 1866, adapted 1873 for Jacques Offenbach's opera of that name), and *Les Caprices de Marianne* (translated as *The Follies of Marianne* and *Marianne,* written 1833, prod. 1851).

Musset's stormy love affair with the writer George Sand lasted almost two years and caused him much suffering, but it occasioned some of his finest lyrical poems and plays. *Fantasio* was written early in their affair. The historical prose tragedy LORENZACCIO was followed by *On ne badine pas avec l'amour* (translated as *No Trifling with Love* and *Camille and Perdican,* written 1834, prod. 1861), which blended tragedy and comedy. The comic element was more pronounced in *La Quenouille de Barberine* ("Barberine's Distaff," written 1835, later revised as *Barberine), Le Chandelier (The Candlestick,* written 1835), and *Il ne faut qu'une porte soit ouverte ou fermée (A Door Must Be Kept Open or Shut,* written 1845). The last three were performed in 1848.

Although less lively than the others, his last plays were of delicate comic invention and were inspired partly by a successful performance in 1847 of *Un Caprice (A Diversion,* written 1837) at the Comèdie Française, and partly by the 1848 productions of earlier plays. Some of these last plays are *Louison* and *On ne Saurait penser à tout* (the latter translated as *You Can't Think of Everything* and also *Journey to Gotha;* both written and prod. 1849), *Carmosine* (written 1850, prod. 1865), and *Bettine* (written and performed 1851). In 1852 Musset was elected to the Académie Française. A short, unpublished play in verse, *La Rêve d'Auguste (The Dream of Augustus),*

which he wrote in 1853, won him the post of librarian at the ministry of education. His last play was a failure: the one-act prose comedy *L'Âne et le Ruisseau (The Ass and the Brook,* written 1855).

Despite his voluntary break with the Romantics, Musset is nevertheless considered one of them because of his unstable temperament and the subjective, fanciful quality of his work. His plays are in no sense "well made," and they lack the local color, grandiloquent speeches in verse, and melodramatic effects of Victor Hugo's dramas or those of the elder Alexandre Dumas. But they appeal to twentieth-century readers and audiences because, although characters and settings are vaguely sketched and scenes deftly shifted, Musset filters the inner drama of the characters through a kind of delicate fantasy reminiscent of Shakespeare. His central theme is often the inspirational or redemptive power of love. And almost every play dramatizes the conflicting forces in Musset's own nature, embodied in one or more characters: on the one hand, the ardent idealist or stable man or woman of feeling and, on the other, the cynical, dissolute, or promiscuous lover.

Unlike most playwrights, Musset wrote for his own pleasure; he felt the need to externalize his tensions without having to conform to contemporary theatrical conventions. His natural gift for dialogue and situation helped him to effect a kind of catharsis in which his personal conflicts were purged and at least partially resolved.

The standard English edition is *The Complete Writings of Alfred de Musset* in ten volumes (1905, revised 1908). But a superior version of *Fantasio,* translated by Jacques Barzun, is included in *The Modern Theatre,* Vol. 2, (1955), edited by Eric Bentley. In 1962 Peter Meyer published his translations, together with an informative essay on Musset the playwright, as *Alfred de Musset: Seven Plays.* The most recent biography is C. F. Haldane's *Alfred: The Passionate Life of Alfred de Musset* (1961). For a careful analysis of the plays, see A. Tilley's *Three French Dramatists: Racine, Marivaux, Musset* (1933).—S. S. S.

mystery play. See SCRIPTURAL PLAY.

N

Nagananda. See Sri Harsha.

Namık Kemal (1840–1888). Turkish poet, journalist, novelist, critic, playwright, and patriot. Namık Kemal was born in Tekirdağ, Turkey. The Turkish poet and playwright Ibrahim Şinasi introduced him to Western ways of thinking and in 1865 left him the editorship of the newspaper *Tasvir-i Efkâr*. As a member of a secret society fighting oppression, Namık Kemal had to flee to Europe in 1867 but returned to Istanbul in 1870. At the first performance of his first play, *Vatan yahut Silistre* ("The Fatherland or Silistria"), in 1873 government officials, intellectuals, and students were gathered. The patriotic theme of the play kindled the imagination of the audience, among whom were military students. They demonstrated during and after the performance, shouting "Long live Namık Kemal!" Sultan Abdülaziz, seeing Namık Kemal as a potential leader of a revolution, had him arrested and deported to a dungeon in Cyprus, where he continued writing plays. After Abdülaziz was dethroned in 1876, Namık Kemal returned to Istanbul and worked on the new constitution. A few months later Abdülhamit II ascended the throne and Namık Kemal was banished to the island of Midilli, where two years later he was appointed provincial governor. Namık Kemal died as governor of the island of Sakız.

Namık Kemal saw the theater as a school of education and propounded his ideas in his newspaper articles. *Vatan yahut Silistre* is an impassioned play in prose, glorifying the Turkish army and singing the virtues of bravery and dying for the fatherland. The plot is tied together by a romantic love story. Although Namık Kemal was a champion of simplified Turkish, free of Arabic and Persian rules of grammar, his characters in this play, unlike those of Şinasi, all speak alike in a bookish style. *Akif Bey* (1874) is a melodrama of love and intrigue sprinkled with incongruous speeches by the title character, a naval officer, glorifying the nation and the navy. *Gülnihal* (1875) is about an insanely jealous and tyrannical governor. Namık Kemal, although a staunch advocate of Western ideals in art, science, and administration, was a strong nationalist and wanted to preserve what was good in his country. *Celâlettin Harzemşah* (1876) was written in praise of Islam. With *Zavallı Çocuk* ("The Miserable Child," 1874), Namık Kemal came out against fathers who exploit their own children. For Namık Kemal, all art was a vehicle for the education and betterment of the people, and he tirelessly advocated the ideals of freedom and patriotism in his poems and patriotism and social justice in his plays, articles, and letters.

Namık Kemal was the most stentorian voice during the *Tanzimat,* or reform, period, during and after which his influence was far and deep. His plays have served as models for generations.—N. O.

Nathan the Wise (Nathan der Weise, 1779). A play by Gotthold Ephraim Lessing. *Nathan the Wise* is set in Jerusalem during the Third Crusade. Nathan, a wealthy Jewish trader of the city, is a benevolent man called "the Wise." When a young German knight, captured by the Saracens, saves the life of Nathan's adopted daughter, Recha, Nathan wishes to thank him, but the Christian knight scorns the Jew. Nathan's impassioned plea for tolerance, however, makes an impression on the knight. Shortly thereafter, the Mohammedan Saladin, great leader of the Saracens, summons Nathan and asks him which is the true religion, Christian, Mohammedan, or Jewish. Nathan gives him as answer the parable of the ring: Throughout many generations of a family, a ring, supposedly of magic power, has passed from favorite son to favorite son. One father, however, has three sons whom he loves equally; he therefore has two replicas of the ring made and gives a ring to each. The original ring can thus never be identified, but, since the father's love impartially bestowed a ring on each son, the value or virtue of each ring is the same. Meanwhile, through a series of strange complications, it is revealed that Recha is actually the sister of the German knight, who himself is the nephew of Saladin. The ties of blood and gratitude that bind these characters thus symbolize the essential unity of the three religions. The play is essentially a philosophical dramatic poem and the character of Nathan exemplifies the ethic of tolerance that pervaded the Enlightenment. Though banned during the Nazi regime, the play is again in the German repertory.

naturalism. See REALISM AND NATURALISM.

Natyasastra. A treatise on drama ascribed to the sage Bharata. The *Natyasastra* is the chief treatise on Indian dramatic theory and practice of the classical period. It accompanied and guided the course of all the performing arts, with Sanskrit drama at their head. It must be acknowledged as one of the world's most remarkable treatises, not only on drama itself, but on general aesthetics. No conclusive statements can be made regarding the identification of the author or the date of his work. Bharata may well be an assumed name.

The book exists in two forms, a longer and a shorter, with no wholly convincing evidence as to which should be regarded as the older or more authentic. At present the preferred view is that the treatise has been many times revised; that it originated at least as early as 100 B.C.; and that it reached the forms in which it is now extant at approximately A.D. 800. It early came to be regarded as the supreme textbook for Sanskrit playwrights and an authentic statement for all aesthetic theory. Groups or sects who distrusted the theatrical arts—such as, on various occasions, the Buddhists—looked on the work with disapproval. But where actors, dancers, and musicians were to flourish, Indian thought conceded that this book was their prime authority and aid.

Such statements must be further explicated. With this treatise in view, Indians termed all actors and dancers *bharatas*. As a class the bharatas suffered at times from social deprivation. It is suggested by I. Shekhar that many actors and dancers were non-Aryans and therefore stood under suspicion from the conquerors who had invaded India from the north (2000–1200 B.C.). It is further suggested that the author was a Tamil and hence from southern India. The book itself contains a highly imaginative apology for the arts, couched in allegorical and mythological terms, claiming them and their patrons to be of divine origin. It is presumed that by this means the author hoped to combat opposition to his philosophy of the arts. It is also possible that the obscurity in which he now rests indicates some personal defeat, though it is certain that as the years passed ancient India gave him almost servile praise and in substance accepted his claim that his own book, along with dramatic performances themselves, constituted "the fifth Veda," or, in other words, the last of the great sacred texts. The kernel of the book's argument is that dramatic art is basically a form of religious experience, enlightenment, and inspiration. The contentment and bliss that is the aesthetic experience is described as portal to the ultimate and impalpable bliss of religious peace, meditation, and nirvana.

The metaphysics is subtly argued. The doctrine of *rasa* provides for certain permanent states, implicit in the human soul, that are stirred and gratified by a corresponding number of *bhavas*, produced through the sensuous stimulants of the art works. Inasmuch as the stage is the sum and confluence of all the arts, the treatise deals with all arts. It considers the nature of color, musical sound, gesture, dance, meters, and poetry, as well as the features peculiar to theatrical technique. The *Natyasastra* lends support to the view that drama proper derives from the dance and in its maturity is wedded to an even more potent art, poetry. The book seems both retrospective and prophetic. It records the ancient system of Indian dance, the *bharatanatyam*, and, through its description of drama as a subdivision of *kavya* ("poetry"), foreshadows the time, commencing approximately with the tenth century A.D., when "dramas" in India were more often to be read in recitation than produced as theater.

According to modern views the book is prolix. It lists and describes large numbers of musical instruments, many types of theaters, giving exact proportions, and specifies many rituals deemed necessary for artistic perfection. When writing specifically of the theater, Bharata seemingly directs each gesture and movement of the actor: he instructs the playwright on every conceivable aspect of his art—how to begin, continue, and conclude each scene and play; what moods are to be evoked, with the aid of what music from the stage and costumes for the actors;

what dialects are to be employed; when and how to use verse and prose; if verse, what meters to use; what types of plays are permissible; what characters are proper to each type of play. The indefatigable proliferation of detail too easily discourages modern readers, who might otherwise gain much enlightenment from the keen philosophical thought on which the entire treatise is based. The *Natyasastra* is, obviously, of the highest value for students of Indian aesthetics in general and of Sanskrit drama in particular.

Some conception of its importance in Indian eyes may be judged from the popular view that Bharata, whose very name was given to the practitioners of the performing arts, was translated into heaven, where he directs daily performances in which the *apsaras,* or heavenly spirits, are the performers and the gods themselves the audience. Although several treatises on virtually the same subject followed that by Bharata, none gained equal fame. Prominent among the authors of these later works on dramatics, poetics, and aesthetics are Mammata, Visvanatha, Panditaraja Jagannatha, and Abinavagupta. See INDIA.

There is an illuminating discussion of the *Natyasastra* by P. V. Kane in *History of Sanskrit Poetics* (1923) and an equally valuable study in *The Indian Theatre* (1954) by Chandra Bhan Gupta. Discerning commentary may also be found in *The Number of Rasas* (1940) by V. Raghavan and in *Mudra* (1960) by E. D. Saunders. There is a brief but able analysis in *Sanskrit Drama: Its Origins and Decline* (1960) by I. Shekhar. The work presents almost unique difficulties to both its translators and interpreters, partly because of the great number of its technical terms. A scholarly rendering has been achieved by M. M. Ghosh (1951).—H. W. W.

Naughton, Bill [William John] (1910–). English playwright. Naughton, the most popular English exponent of regional domestic comedy to appear in the 1960's, was born in County Mayo, Ireland. In his childhood the family moved to Bolton in the north of England, where his father worked as a coal miner. On leaving school, Naughton was successively a weaver, a bleacher, a laborer, a coal-heaver, and a long-distance truck driver. During World War II he moved to London and began to establish himself as a writer, partly with semi-autobiographical books and partly with magazine stories, one of which introduced into the English vocabulary the word "spiv," a flashily dressed black marketeer. Naughton also wrote a series of radio plays, upon which most of his stage comedies are based. The first play was *All in Good Time* (1963), a portrait of wedding-night rituals in Bolton, Lancashire. This was followed in the same year by *Alfie,* a character study of a compulsive Cockney lecher, and by another Bolton family comedy, *Spring and Port Wine* (1965). There have also been provincial productions of two other Lancashire pieces: *June Evening* (1965) and *Annie and Fanny* (1967).

Naughton's Bolton is an old-fashioned and sometimes sentimentally conceived place. But there is no question of Naughton's integrity and warmth or of his ability to show family life as being hell on earth, but finally to persuade the reader to join in his celebration of the domestic virtues.—I. W.

Nazım Hikmet [**Ran**] (1902–1963). Turkish poet and playwright. Nazım Hikmet was born in Salonica, Greece, and studied sociology and economics at the University of Moscow. After returning to Turkey in 1928, he wrote plays, film scenarios, poems, and articles for newspapers and magazines. In 1938 Nazım Hikmet was sentenced to twenty-eight years and four months in prison for alleged revolutionary activities. Upon his release from prison by a special amnesty in 1950, he escaped from Turkey and spent the rest of his life mainly in Sofia, Moscow, and Warsaw, where he became a Polish citizen.

Primarily a poet, Nazım Hikmet was greatly influenced by Vladimir Mayakovsky, whose style he adapted for Turkish poetry. His poems, generally, are in declamatory free verse, alliterative in style, and use the speech patterns of the common people. With his direct, unadorned style and socially conscious themes, he influenced especially the so-called new poets in the late 1930's. After a long ban on Nazım Hikmet's works, there has been a revival of his poems and plays in Turkey since 1960. The plays are mostly Marxist in their themes. *Kafatası* ("The Skull," 1932) is an anticapitalist play in which money is shown as a destroyer of individual freedoms and talents. In *Bir Ölü Evi* ("A Dead Man's House," 1932) property left by a dead man brings out the pettiness and greed in all the inheritors. Ferhat's love for Şirin in *Ferhat and Şirin* (written 1945; prod. 1948) transforms itself into love for society.

Nazım Hikmet's plays have been produced in France as well as in Russia and other socialist countries.—N. O.

Néricault, Philippe. See DESTOUCHES.

Nesin, Aziz (1915–   ). Turkish humorist, columnist, and playwright. Nesin was born in Istanbul of parents of poor peasant stock. His mother and four brothers and sisters died when Nesin was a child, and he was sent to a military school. After becoming an officer, Nesin wrote articles for newspapers under his father's name, Aziz Nesin. (Nesin's own first name was Nusret.) Nesin has continued to use his father's first name to this day. He left the army in 1944 and started to work for the leftist newspaper *Tan*. In 1945 a mob devastated the plant where the newspaper was published, and Nesin lost his job. Because no papers would accept his writings, he wrote editorials, interviews, novels, and short stories under dozens of different pseudonyms and published a humor magazine. (Nesin believes he has written more than two thousand humorous short stories.) Nesin spent five and a half years in prison for his writings, sixteen months of his term, he claims, for an article he did not write.

Nesin's first two plays are basically serious in tone, in which well-drawn, three-dimensional characters are placed side by side with symbolical characters. Their themes are the dignity of work and the importance of an uncompromising devotion to a life mission. *Biraz Gelir Misiniz? (Will You Come Here, Please?* 1962) was produced in several countries in Europe as well as in Turkey. *Bir Şey Yap Met (Do Something, Met,* 1964) was produced in California, several theaters in Europe, and an amateur theater in Turkey. His two humorous and witty plays are in the spirit of his short stories and owe much to the traditional Turkish theater. In 1968 Nesin won a prize for writing the best three modern *Karagöz* (shadow play) pieces.—N. O.

Nestroy, Johann [**Nepomuk**] (1801–1862). Austrian actor and playwright. Nestroy was one of eight children, only three of whom lived past infancy. He was a gifted child, with sharp senses and a keen understanding. Nestroy's original intention was to follow his father's profession of the law, which in fact he began to study. But he was also interested in the theater and took part in student productions and in other amateur theatricals. When his father's luck waned, Johann was forced to give up his expensive law studies.

From his early years Nestroy had demonstrated considerable talent in music. At thirteen he gave his first piano concert, and later he became a singer. In 1822 he was contracted by the Vienna Opera at the Kärntnertor Theater and made his debut in that year as Sarastro in Mozart's *The Magic Flute,* with great success. From this time on, the theater became foremost in his life. After his first contract in Vienna, he engaged himself with the Deutsches Theater in Amsterdam, then on to Brünn, Graz, Pressburg, Limburg, and finally back to Vienna and the Theater an der Wien.

A number of factors caused Nestroy to develop into a fully mature writer. First of all, he rapidly changed roles from singer to actor, chiefly of comic parts. When Nestroy grew dissatisfied with his highly conventional roles, roles that failed to express himself as actor and person, he began to write parts for himself. He first appeared in one of his own plays, *Der Zettelträger Papp* ("Papp, the Bill Distributor"), in 1827. Another formative event concerned his trouble with Viennese censorship. The police were eventually forced to deny him further freedom to improvise. Nestroy was not about to accept this suppression and retaliated by calling upon his sharp satiric wit as a poet and playwright. Thus, Nestroy was prepared at the death of his highly successful predecessor, Ferdinand Raimund, to carry on the tradition of the Viennese folk play.

In contrast, however, to Raimund's folk plays, with their good humor and ethic of poetic justice, Nestroy's plays at their best are satiric and caustic. Among his better-known works of this type are *Der böse Geist Lumpazivagabundus* ("The Evil Spirit Lumpazivagabundus," 1833), *Das Mädel aus der Vorstadt* ("The Girl from the Suburbs," 1841), and *Judith und Holofernes* ("Judith and Holofernes," 1849). They are socially oriented and often severely caustic. Raimund's world of fairies and spirits gives way to a realistic picture of Viennese life.

Nestroy seemed less concerned with a finished literary product than did Raimund. Consequently, he turned back to the early Viennese folk play. Less gifted poetically than Raimund, Nestroy was more inclined toward farce than toward Raimund's gentle fairy-tale charm. Yet there is vitality and joy in the baroque exuberance of Nestroy's use of Viennese dialect, one of the chief sources of his wit. It is this integral use of dialect and play on words that virtually precludes the successful translation of his works into other languages. At best they must be adapted, as, for example, was his *Einen Jux will er sich*

ENGRAVING OF JOHN VANDENHOFF AS SIR GILES OVERREACH IN PHILIP MASSINGER'S *A New Way to Pay Old Debts* (THEATRE COLLECTION, THE NEW YORK PUBLIC LIBRARY AT LINCOLN CENTER)

machen ("He Wants To Have a Fling," 1842), which became the basis of Thornton Wilder's *The Matchmaker.*

No complete books have been written about Nestroy in English, nor is there anything but short mention of him in most conventional histories of the drama. Only a few of his plays have been translated into English: *Freiheit in Krähwinkel* (*Freedom Comes to Krähwinkel*), *Tulane Drama Review* (1961); and *Three Comedies* (1967) which includes *Liebesgeschichten und Heiratssachen* (*Love Affairs and Wedding Bells*), *Der Talisman* (*The Talisman*), and *Der Zerrissene* (*A Man Full of Nothing*).

Netherlands. See DUTCH AND FLEMISH DRAMA.

New Comedy. Name given to Greek comedy that began to appear in the second half of the fourth century B.C. and that was subsequently adopted by Roman comic writers. New Comedy is distinguished by a coherent, well-constructed plot set against a background of contemporary life. Its characters are drawn from easily recognizable types: the young wastrel, the recalcitrant father, the courtesan, the parasite, the wily slave, and the braggart warrior. The action of the play usually focuses on a love affair between two young people that is opposed by members of the older generation, usually the father. The complication is resolved by a discovery (see ANAGNORISIS) that results in the assertion of the marriageability of one of the lovers.

Greek New Comedy is represented by the one complete play and various fragments of Menander.

Its Roman equivalent is found in the plays of Plautus and Terence.

New Way to Pay Old Debts, A (c. 1625). A comedy by Philip MASSINGER. Loosely based on Thomas Middleton's comedy *A Trick to Catch the Old One* (1608), Massinger's play centers on Sir Giles Overreach, a miserly knight. In his greed Sir Giles tries to control the destinies of his daughter and his nephew. He is thwarted in both of these attempts by the young people in league with the benevolent Lady Allworth. They successfully combine to dupe Sir Giles and to reduce him to a raging madman.

The play is an artfully constructed comedy of intrigue. The character of Sir Giles is based upon that of Sir Giles Mompesson, a notorious scoundrel who in 1621 fled England in order to avoid trial for extortion. The play has had an extraordinary popularity on the English stage. From the eighteenth century to the present time it has rivaled Shakespeare's comedies in the number of rivivals it has undergone and in the great actors who have been attracted to the role of Sir Giles. (See ENGLAND: *Caroline drama.*)

An account of the play's history is given in R. H. Ball's *The Amazing Career of Sir Giles Overreach* (1939).—E. Q.

Nigeria. See AFRICA: *Nigeria.*

Niger Republic. See AFRICA: *Niger Republic.*

Nobumitsu, Kwanze Kojiro. See ATAKA.

No Exit (Huis Clos, 1944). A play by Jean Paul SARTRE. *No Exit* was first performed at the Vieux-Colombier in May 1944 just before the liberation of Paris. Three characters, a man and two women, find themselves in hell, which for them is a living room with Second Empire furniture. Each of the characters needs the other two in order to create some illusion

A SCENE FROM JEAN PAUL SARTRE'S *No Exit* (FRENCH CULTURAL SERVICES)

about himself. Since existence, for Sartre, is the ability to create one's future, the opposite of existence is hell, where man has no power to create his future. Garcin's sin has been cowardice, and in hell he tries to use the two women, who are locked up forever with him in the same room under the same strong light, as mirrors in which he will see a complacent and reassuring picture of himself.

This play, an example of expert craftsmanship organized so that the audience learns very slowly the facts concerning the three characters, is Sartre's indictment of the social comedy and the false role that each man plays in it. The most famous utterance in the play, made by Garcin when he says that hell is everyone else, is, in the briefest form possible, Sartre's definition of man's fundamental sin. When the picture a man has of himself is provided by those who see him, by the distorted image of himself that they give back to him, then man has rejected what the philosopher has called reality.

No Exit has been translated by Stuart Gilbert in *No Exit and Three Other Plays* (1955).—W. F.

noh, also spelled **nō.** The name of the most important form of Japanese drama. The word *noh* is often rendered by English scholars as "accomplishment" in the sense of perfection of skill, and thus a noh play might be thought of as "a highly accomplished play." "Art play" might render the thought

equally well. Whatever is said of the Japanese word, however, there is no ambiguity about the form itself, which is singularly self-contained.

The noh play, which took its present form in the fourteenth century, presents a perfected harmony of dance, poetry, music, mime, and acting. Its roots are obscure, but it is clear that several branches of the Japanese performing arts entered into its creation. Among these earlier forms was GIGAKU, a form of entertainment brought from Korea as early as A.D. 612, which made use of music, dance, masking, and miming and was often of a satirical nature, but was part, nevertheless, of religious festivals. It introduced the still popular "lion dance." More refined were narrative and courtly dances known as BUGAKU. Japanese drama took considerable steps forward in its technique through SARUGAKU performers, who, playing before popular audiences, introduced new comic elements. Some of the founders of the noh school were trained in sarugaku, a branch of which—known as the DENGAKU—developed an increasingly popular style, enlivened with much acrobatics. No matter how popular or satirical these plays were, they were for the most part performed under religious auspices. The special devotion of the Japanese people to the theater may be traced to these early episodes in their cultural history, the noh plays following directly on their train.

SCENE FROM A NOH PLAY (CONSULATE GENERAL OF JAPAN, NEW YORK)

The noh are best regarded as scenes from the ceremonious life of the Japanese feudal aristocracy. They arose as a theater for a select class and are so today, although an intellectual elite now takes the place of an aristocracy. In the middle period of their history they appear to have enjoyed a larger audience than at their beginning or at the present time, but this, it seems, was acquired chiefly through condescending invitations from the superior class, who occasionally turned an about-face and actually banned attendance by the populace. It was a learned theater but certainly not a dry one. The plays were produced at seasons of festival. By tradition, they were given in series, as a rule five noh plays proper whose serious scenes were interspersed with farces of a distinctly racy, popular character known as KYOGEN. The styles and the formula for the entire productions were intricate and immutable. Under the guidance of two men, who together wrote nearly half the noh plays in the repertory today—Kan-ami (1333–1384) and his son Zeami MOTOKIYO—the noh form was completely realized. Few, if any, art forms have been so persistent. It is true that virtually no such plays of importance have been written since 1600. All the plays now in the repertory of the noh troupes were composed well before that. But the style of performance began as a ritual and has so continued. Translated into terms of English literary chronology, one might say that the actual period of playwriting commenced with the age of Chaucer and terminated with that of Shakespeare. It has been estimated that only a fraction of the noh plays written have ever been performed. There are today about 240 in repertory, some of which are given very rarely.

The plays themselves are divided into types, each having its traditional place in the program for a single day. Thus the first to be performed is likely to be a *waki* play, one of high seriousness, often devoted to the praises of a god and adorned with a solemn dance. Second comes an *asura* play, the name of which implies that a warrior hero of the epic period in Japanese history is its central figure. Third comes a "female-wig" noh, in which the actor, who is a man, impersonates a woman, often a madwoman or one in tragic circumstances. Fourth comes a play in which somewhat greater choice of subject matter is allowed, though the marked tendency is toward plays of emotional violence and sensationalism, especially those with ghosts and haunting spirits. If the central figure in this type is from the living world, this is known as a *genzai-mono* play. Fifth and last are *kiri* noh plays, where dancing, often of a warlike nature, is especially conspicuous and where the final episode turns toward solemn and grateful recognition of the occasion of the entire festival, which is presumed to have an auspicious character.

All major features of the noh plays, such as the characters, the style of acting, the masks, and the design of the stage, are strictly prescribed. Each type of play has a special music proper to it and to it alone. The prescriptions are almost interminable; only the barest outlines can be traced here.

With scarcely an exception, the plays are either in one or two parts. Most of the important and more ceremonious plays are in two parts; in Part I the leading character, or SHITE, appears in a humble, human disguise; in Part II, as the god or hero whom he really is, though if a hero, almost without exception as his ghost. God or hero, he appears in the second part as a supernatural being. As ghost he endures his penance for a violent action performed in mortal life. Hence he is essentially more "real" as ghost than as the humble human whom he pretends to be in Part I. In this second manifestation he is himself in another world, recalling and, according to the austere Buddhistic doctrine, repenting a worldly deed. Most of the plays are strictly religious in thought. Of these, by far the greater number are inspired by Buddhism, the remainder by the national religion, Shinto, which inculcates patriotism.

The noh's extraordinary appeal to aesthetic sensibility, together with the Zen tea ceremony of a later date, may be, without exaggeration, described as an expression of a cult of aestheticism. In his impressive treatise on the art of the noh, Zeami gives two goals for the essential achievements of the noh. The first and primary goal is a mood of quietness, meditation, and gratification known as *yūgen*. The term has, naturally, been ground for much subsequent discussion, and many have suspected, not only that there is no equivalent to the Japanese word in other languages, but also that the quality of the experience itself is not to be found in its purity in other cultures. The word "beauty" approaches Zeami's thought but fails to fulfill all its demands, partly because the Japanese, having made, with the help of their peculiar interpretation of Buddhism, a religion of beauty, enjoy an experience at once secular and sacred. It is certainly not erotic, whereas in the West a popular conception of beauty has become associated with physiological beauty, or the attraction of the human form. The word "elegance" is occasionally used as a translation of the Japanese term but the notion of a serene and aristocratic beauty is inadequate to comprehend the Japanese ideal, which signifies much more than that. It is at least clear that the noh induces a mood of spiritual gravity and serenity, the very opposite of the violent emotions to which its scenes allude. The play provides a therapy or spiritual discipline leading to a resolution of emotion and entrance into a state at once blessed with pleasure and with peace.

The second goal of the noh is more readily discerned in some of the plays than in others. This is most nearly suggested in English by the word "sublimity," and it adds to the Japanese conception of yūgen a sensation of grandeur, exaltation, or ecstasy. This becomes most apparent in the plays that as a rule begin and end a noh cycle, where worship of a deity stands at the heart of the performance.

The plays are performed on a type of stage peculiar to itself, although many of its features are clearly related to other traditional Japanese theaters older or younger, such as those for the *kowaka* or the *kabuki*. Briefly, the stage is a square, nineteen feet, five inches, raised two feet, seven inches above the floor of the auditorium, into which it projects on three sides. To the rear is a panel on which an aged pine tree is painted. To the left extends a bridgeway, the HASHIGAKARI, leading to a curtained doorway, the entrance and exit for the principal characters. The stage is covered with a roof supported by four corner pillars fifteen feet high. Three small trees are stationed at regular intervals along the bridgeway. In a shallow backstage entirely visible to the audience are seated four musicians, from left to right players of the horizontal drum, the large hand drum, the small hand drum, and the flute. The corner of the stage adjoining the front of the bridgeway is known as the station for the shite, or principal actor. Beside the pillar diagonally opposite is the station for the secondary actor, or waki. The juncture between the rear of the bridgeway and the back of the stage is known as the kyogen's seat. This man serves as stage attendant and may speak informally, giving what may be described as program notes between the two parts of the play. The actors and musicians may introduce such nuances as their development of technique allows but in all their major activity are strictly bound to the conventions of the form. The playwright has a large number of traditional dances from which to choose. The ceremony proceeds to formula, from its prelude to its obligatory conclusion. The manner is stylized to the highest possible degree. The shite is masked; so are his immediate followers, if there are any such persons. Other actors have mask-like make-up. Costumes are lavish and symbolical. In two-part plays, that of the shite is, of course, changed during the brief interval. This interval, as already observed, is filled by a recitation on the part of the kyogen, a person of secondary importance who relates in comparatively simple language the story of the play and may, in a few passing words, moralize upon it. This role is always considered impromptu; the kyogen's words are not included in the text, which is by long usage printed in a small and exquisitely decorated volume.

The play's style itself is refined and precious almost to the degree of being cryptic. Verse is used in the more elevated and lyrical passages, where spiritual and emotional qualities are at their height. Prose serves for the simpler speeches. The play is often introduced by a brief exchange of words between minor characters; this section commonly includes an imaginary journey (see MICHIYUKI), where symbolic scenery is described as the actors move slowly and gravely about the stage (protesting all the while that they are in the utmost haste). They then arrive at the scene where the chief confrontation is to occur. The notion of confrontation is useful here, for at most the plays rarely contain what in Western terms would be called an action; there is only the remembrance of an action. The mind confronts reality. The shite's entrance is delayed and rendered as solemn and imposing as possible. Much of the dialogue is quoted from classical poetry, about half from Japanese literature and half from Chinese. Many phrases are repeated. A chorus, seated to the right of the stage, sings, speaks for or as the leading actor, moralizes, and narrates. It commonly sings as the shite mimes the imagined action. Often it completes a sentence commenced by the shite, or the shite concludes a phrase commenced by the chorus. Two or more characters often speak in unison. Thus the text is treated more in the manner of an oratorio than in that of a Western play. In the category of either the learned poem or the lyric drama the noh plays can nowhere be surpassed.

Almost all the stories are taken from well-known sources in religious or secular literature, notably from Buddhist or Shinto texts, the saga of the Heike, the tale of Genji, and from any among the more widely known Chinese myths and legends. Noh dramatists, like those of ancient Greece, employed traditional materials, adjusted to the rigid conventions of the theatrical form. The Japanese conventions are even more intricate than the Greek.

Elsewhere in this volume are brief descriptions of some of the more famous plays, each typical of a particular type of noh. For a waki, or congratulatory piece, see TAKASAGO; for an asura play, see ATSUMORI; for a female-wig play, see HAGOROMO; for a madwoman play, see SOTOBA KOMACHI; for a onryomono or "revengeful ghost" play, see AOI-NO-UE; for a "living persons play," see ATAKA.

There is an extensive literature on the noh and many attempts at translation. For a general description, see *Nō: the Classical Drama of Japan,* by Donald Keene (1966). The most informative book on the sources of the form is *Early Noh Drama* (1958) by P. G. O'Neill. The best translations and general commentaries in English are in *Japanese Noh Drama* under the general editorship of the Special Noh Committee, Japanese Classics Translation Committee, Nippon Gakujutsu Shinkokai, the chairman of the Classics Translation Committee being Sanki Ichikawa, Tokyo (3 vols., 1955–1960). The first volume (1960) has been republished through UNESCO. An admirable translation of Zeami's *Birds of Sorrow* was made by Meredith Weatherby and Bruce Rogers (1947). See also *The Noh Plays of Japan* (1920), with translations, often abridged, by Arthur Waley; *The Old Pine Tree and Other Noh Plays* (1962), translated by Makoto Ueda; and *Japanese Noh Plays* (1932), translated with an introduction by Beatrice Lane Suzuki. Discerning criticism of the plays is contained in *Noh or Accomplishment* (1919), by Ernest F. Fenollosa and Ezra Pound. The most notable plays written in the West and influenced by the noh are the brief lyrical dramas by William Butler Yeats, which are discussed in *W. B. Yeats and Japan* by Shotaro Oshima (1965).—H. W. W.

Nord, Paul. See GREECE: *modern period.*

Norway. Until Norway began in the nineteenth century to establish its own national identity, separate from that of Denmark, its drama was very sparse indeed. One can say, of course, that there are assertive dramatic elements in the medieval *Edda,* in which some of the poems are in dialogue form, and in the tense encounters of the sagas, but real theater was a long time arriving. The earliest recorded performance of a play is in 1562, of *Adams fald* ("The Fall of Adam"), given in the cathedral churchyard of Bergen. In all probability the play was adapted from a European model by Wittenberg-educated Absalon Pederssøn Beyer (1528–1575).

It was also in Bergen that Ludvig Holberg was born, and the sea mentality of Bergen may have given him the all-important lust for travel and the concomitant exposure to Continental drama that molded him into a playwright. His acquaintance with Norwegian character—solid citizenry, peasant idiosyncrasy, and some pedantic aberrances—also contributes to make him something of a Norwegian playwright (Norwegians claim him), though his career is chiefly associated with Denmark, and Copenhagen in particular. For that matter, Norwegian literary life was a long time dissociating itself from that of Denmark, and long after the dissolution of the political bond in

1814 the consanguinity continued. Ibsen, for example, was generally first played and first published in Copenhagen.

Action and reaction were particularly interesting in the late eighteenth century, when the Norwegian Literary Society was founded in Copenhagen in 1772 in opposition to its Klopstock-oriented Danish counterpart and to the drama of Johannes Ewald. At that time Trondheim-born Niels Krog Bredal (1733–1778) was director of the Royal Theater in Copenhagen, and *Zarine* (1772), the French classical play by Johan Nordahl Brun (1745–1816), won a place in the limelight. But the chief Norwegian play that survives from this period is a sprightly parody of all the worst excesses of French classicism (represented in *Zarine* and its model *Zaïre*), namely *Kierlighed uden strømper* ("Love Without Stockings," 1772), by Johan Herman Wessel (1742–1785). It continues to delight audiences today, with or without the music by Scalabrini.

Incipient Norwegian nationalism had its dramatic beginning in the stormy life of Henrik Wergeland (1806–1845), who quickly dismissed Danish Romanticism as "sofa literature" and turned a part of his talent to the theater. While he considered his many farces "his bastard children," he obviously thought more highly of the tragedy *Sinclars død* ("Sinclair's Death," 1828) and of *Campbellerne* ("The Campbells," 1838), the first performance of which was a *cause célèbre* in Wergeland's pitched battle with the Danophiles. Bjørnstjerne BJØRNSON was soon to pick up the gauntlet of nationalism and to make better drama of it. Bjørnson was vigilant on many fronts. He began as a drama critic, was a vital force in the Bergen Theater (1857–1859), and was later director of the Christiania Theater (1865–1867). Bjørnson, now totally eclipsed by Ibsen, his contemporary, wrote a sizable body of plays: first, such chronicle plays as the trilogy *Sigurd Slembe* (1862); modern problem plays, best exemplified by *En fallit* (*A Bankruptcy*, 1875) and *Redaktøren* (*The Editor*, 1875); and a later pair of plays *Over ævne I* and *II* (*Beyond Our Power*, written 1883 and 1895 respectively; both prod. 1899), which even in their title suggest how the vigor of Bjørnson's inquiry was transcending its earlier limitations.

All the while the Norwegian language was splitting itself socially, politically—and literarily—into *landsmål*, which subsequently came to be known as *nynorsk*, paradoxically enough a synthetic language of provincial origin; and *riksmål*, later *bokmål*, closer to Danish. The result was separate literatures and separate theaters to produce those literatures. The Norwegian of Ibsen and Bjørnson is bokmål, but the Norwegian of a modern like Tarjei Vesaas, for example, is nynorsk.

But transcending all the schisms of Norwegian cultural life, though by no means oblivious of them, is the brooding, dominating figure of Henrik IBSEN. Ibsen ranged through most of the possibilities of the drama, from the chronicle play to lyrical pilgrimage to social dilemma to symbolic quest beset by doubt. Yet the focus is always upon a maximum of personal self-realization without damage to the harmony (not the structure) of society.

Ibsen cultivated the larger ambiguities and did so quite consciously, even when his sense of form was not loose enough and sometimes constricted him. His two dramatic poems, *Brand* (1885) and PEER GYNT, are magnificent studies of human rigidity and human flaccidity respectively. In realistic plays like *En folkefiende* (*An Enemy of the People*, 1883) and THE WILD DUCK we are confronted with a truth that is inflexible and therefore inevitably of tragic consequence. In HEDDA GABLER, the greatest of the realistic plays, Ibsen charts the tragedy that emerges from misguided romantic beliefs and a randomness of energy. In the later plays there is a gathering symbolism and mysticism, as well as a stretching of the WELL-MADE PLAY format. Some of the earlier plays were too well-made; Ibsen was sometimes too classical for his own good—and for the good of imitative playwrights to come. But in his incessant probing of ideas and in his attempt to couch the dialectic within reasonable limits, he explored all the resources of the realistic theater and moved a bit beyond.

The characteristic gesture of expressionism is the shriek, the Viennese critic Hermann Bahr once observed, with his eye upon a well-known painting by the Norwegian Edvard Munch. Certainly the undulant torment and psychopathic coloration of Munch's canvases are distinguishing landmarks of expressionism, but in spite of Munch's relations with playwrights, Strindberg among them, Norwegian drama displays no counterpart to the Swedish playwright, with the possible exception of the plays of Knut HAMSUN. There is no shriek, and not even the mordant innuendoes of satiric expressionism; there is instead the steady clarion voice of social protest raised again and again, by and large in a context of reasonable rationalism. In short, Ibsen cast a very long shadow.

The Ibsen heritage may be seen as a curve that descends through the sophisticated liberalism of Gunnar HEIBERG to the intellectual radicalism of Helge KROG and the candid communism of Nordahl GRIEG. Even before World War I the worker movement in Norway was of more radical character than in Sweden and Denmark. Class disparities were widened by the war, and the appearance of a syndicalist named Erling Falk in the early 1920's did much to establish the major stream of Norwegian literature. Sigurd Hoel (1890–1960) dramatizes his relationship with Falk in the play *Mot muren* ("Against the Wall," 1930), and Falk is the original for Karsten Trane, the social reformer of Krog's *Underveis* (*On the Way*, 1931).

Krog was a scrappy, irascible journalist and drama critic who became the best of Norway's twentieth-century playwrights. His finest plays deal with woman's emergent role in a new society. It is difficult to say why the assertion of individuality in Norwegian literature should be so often embodied in the female, not merely in her desire for some kind of professional fulfillment, but in her eroticism; but it is clear enough that the Noras and Rebecca Wests and Hilda Wangels of Ibsen found their successors in both Heiberg and Krog, with slight differences according to the context of the times. Perhaps the finest example is the architect-wife Vibeke, of Krog's *Oppbrudd* (*Break-Up*, 1936), who tires of the unbending personality of her lawyer-husband, Ketil, and the self-preoccupations of her lover, the writer

Kåre. "Nothing is true!" she exclaims in disgust; "everything is almost true!" And, coolly defiant toward such aimless relativism, she walks out in search of her new and undivided self. A shattered bust of Dante marks the end of idealized love, and erotic love is found wanting too, the "love for love's sake" of Heiberg.

The career of Nordahl Grieg, cut short by World War II, found its greatest successes in poetry, but his search for a new dramatic format for social statement led to a few noteworthy plays. Two motives dictated *Vår ære og vår makt* (*Our Power and Our Glory*, 1935): a desire on the part of Grieg to channel his newly discovered communistic zeal into an attack on capitalistic war profiteering; and a feeling that he should rehabilitate the ordinary seaman, ever since his first novel had been taken as an insult rather than an attempt to reform working conditions. The play is a broad satiric attack on Norwegian shipping merchants of World War I, in oversimplified characters like the hypocrite Detlef and the coldly cynical Freddy—flat, implausible characters, because Grieg did not know this level of society. His masterpiece is the ordinary seaman Vingrisen, the raw, earthy, courageous spirit of the people, immediately plausible and quite wonderful. The broad contrasts of the play can best be understood in cinematic terms. On his Moscow visit of 1932–1934, Grieg had been much impressed by the films of Eisenstein and the staging of Meyerhold, "whose form of expression had all the intensity of a tiger's spring." Ideology created oversimplification in most of Grieg's plays, but the intensity and diversity of *Nederlaget* (*Defeat*, 1937), a play about the Paris Commune of 1871, made it one of the most memorable in the Norwegian repertory.

Since World War II dramatic fare has been very thin indeed. Occasionally, plays from Tore ØRJASÆTER, Sigurd Christiansen (1891–1947), and Tarjei VESAAS have stirred up a measure of interest, but few new playwrights have appeared on the scene. It was not until 1966 that two plays seized upon the imagination of Norwegian audiences and presaged some hope for the future. *Gitrene* ("The Cages," 1966), by Finn Carling (1925–   ), takes place in a zoo setting and operates intricately on three levels —animal, human, and biblical. *Fugleelskerne* ("The Birdlovers," 1966), by Jens Bjørneboe (1920–   ), makes German tourism today (or any day) vibrate with memories of their earlier occupying habits. This somewhat Brechtian play, with music by Hans Dieter Hosalla, indicates that Bjørneboe is not just a middle-aged author of sensational novels and that Norwegian drama may be on the verge of a revival in keeping with the excellence of its stagecraft.

Norwegian drama is intermittently but fairly extensively treated in *A History of Norwegian Literature* (1956), a volume in the series of literary histories sponsored by the American-Scandinavian Foundation edited by Harald Beyer and Einar Haugen. Some of the more recent plays have appeared in the Foundation's *Scandinavian Plays of the 20th Century* series.—R. B. V.

Norwid, Cyprian Kamil (1821–1883). Polish poet, playwright, and prose writer. Norwid was one of the major talents of nineteenth-century Polish émigré literature. In his own time, he had little fame and less recognition; he died in a Paris poorhouse for Polish emigrants in poverty and obscurity. Since his "rediscovery" in the period of Young Poland (Młoda Polska) he has become the object of considerable study in Poland and now holds a truly preeminent position in the history of Polish literature.

Although thought of primarily as a gifted and original albeit difficult poet, Norwid produced a number of interesting prose works and several plays, which began appearing on Polish stages for the first time only twenty-five years after his death. The dramatic works fall into two main categories: plays based on ancient and medieval legends and history (principally Polish), such as *Wanda* (1847), a drama in six scenes; *Krakus* (1847), a tragedy; *Zwolon* (1848/49), a "monologue"; and the "historical tragedy" *Kleopatra i cezar* ("Caesar and Cleopatra," 1870–1878); and plays with contemporary settings devoted principally to romantic heroes and heroines and the conflicts born of romantic love, such as the one-act comedy *Noc tysiączna i druga* ("The Thousand and Second Night," 1850); the "dramatic fantasy" *Za kulisami* ("Behind the Curtains," 1866–1869), which is built around the device of the play-within-a-play and was known in a shorter, earlier version as *Tyrtej* ("Tyrtius," 1861–1863); *Aktor* ("The Actor," 1864); *Pierścień wielkiej damy* ("The Ring of a Great Lady," 1872), designated a tragedy; and the comedy *Miłość czysta w kąpieli morskich* ("Pure Love by the Sea"), written about the same time as *Pierścień wielkiej damy*.

The renewed interest in Norwid's literary work and in his original ideas on literature and art (he was also an accomplished sculptor and painter) has led to revivals of several of his plays in post-World War II Polish theaters. Although the objects of much curiosity, Norwid's plays are at times intriguing but difficult and require a certain initiation on the part of readers and audiences. In their form (all but *Noc tysiączna i druga* and *Za kulisami* were written in verse), their blending of legend, myth, fantasy, and symbol and the occasional obscurity resulting from the author's theory of the artistic significance of "silence," their appeal becomes often elusive and finally beyond the reach of most spectators. They do not readily lend themselves—in a truly satisfactory manner—to scenic realization, a difficulty compounded by the imperfect condition in which several of the texts of the works have come down to us. In this latter respect the most imperfect, ironically, is the one with potentially the greatest appeal, *Za kulisami*.

In the realm of drama, Norwid saw himself as an innovator. *Pierścień wielkiej damy* contains a prose introduction in which he states that the play represents the attempt to create a new form of tragedy, free of the murders and bloodletting of classical tragedy and therefore "white" tragedy, in his own terminology. In drama as in poetry, Norwid's views were opposed to the traditional and conventional as he endeavored to find new techniques of expression and the constant expansion of the horizons of art. But his virtual isolation from the literary community of the Polish emigration denied him any decisive impact on Polish writing and aesthetic theory in his own time.—H. B. S.

N-Town Plays, the (1468). A Corpus Christi cycle of forty-two scriptural plays of unknown authorship. The text (running to over 11,000 lines of verse) is found in the Hegge Manuscript, named after the early seventeenth-century owner, Robert Hegge; the manuscript is preserved in the British Museum. The N-Town Plays are so called because the introductory Proclamation contemplates performance "in N. town," the abbreviation N. apparently indicating the name (whatever it might be) of the next town at which the plays would be performed. From this and other evidence it appears that the cycle was a touring one, unconnected with any particular town. The N-Town Cycle is also sometimes called *Ludus Coventriae*, since this title is used in a seventeenth-century note written on the flyleaf of the Hegge Manuscript. But the N-Town Plays are not the Coventry Cycle, for the two extant plays of that cycle are entirely different from their correspondents in N-Town. The title may be simply an error, or, as K. S. Block suggests, the term *Ludus Coventriae* may have been used here in the generic sense of "a play of the type performed at Coventry." Another title for N-Town is *The Play Called Corpus Christi*, since this phrase, written in a sixteenth-century hand, stands at the head of the first page of the Hegge Manuscript. The term is evidently a generic one for a cycle of scriptural plays arising through association of such cycles with the Feast of Corpus Christi. Still another (though little-used) title is *The Hegge Plays*, on the analogy of the term generally used for the manuscript. Hardin Craig and other scholars believe that N-Town is an adaptation of the cycle of scriptural plays known to have been performed at Lincoln. This theory is attractive, but the supporting argument, although persuasive, is not conclusive; and in any case, even if the theory were accepted, one might not speak of N-Town as the lost Lincoln Cycle, since by definition that cycle would have had to differ greatly from the N-Town Cycle as we have it, the text of the Hegge Manuscript being a compilation from various sources.

N-Town differs radically from Chester, York, and Wakefield in that its production did not employ pageant wagons proceeding successively from stop to stop within a particular town but scaffolds situated about the perimeter of a round *platea*, or Place, constructed or found in the open country. The cycle was a touring one, and it was acted apparently not by the gildsmen of a particular town but by professional players. There is evidence that at least two days were required for production. The Cornish *Ordinalia*, a Place-and-scaffold cycle slightly shorter than N-Town, was performed on three successive days.

The N-Town Cycle consists of the following plays (elements absent from the Wakefield, Chester, and York cycles are starred):

From Old Testament narratives:
  (1)   Creation of the Angels, Fall of Lucifer
  (2)   Creation of the World, Fall of Man
  (3)   Cain and Abel
  (4)   Noah and the Flood, *Death of Cain
  (5)   Abraham and Isaac
  (6)   Moses (Burning Bush, Ten Commandments).
From narratives of the Nativity:
  (7)   Prophets
  (8)   * Conception of the Virgin

  (9)   * Presentation of the Virgin
  (10) * Betrothal of the Virgin
  (11) * Parliament of Heaven; Annunciation
  (12) Joseph's Suspicions about Mary
  (13) Visit to Elizabeth
  (14) * Trial of Joseph and Mary
  (15) Birth of Christ
  (16) Adoration of the Shepherds
  (17) Adoration of the Magi
  (18) Purification of the Virgin
  (19) Slaughter of the Innocents, Death of Herod
  (20) Christ and the Doctors.
From narratives of the Public Ministry:
  (21) Baptism
  (22) Temptation
  (23) Woman Taken in Adultery
  (24) Raising of Lazarus
  (25) Council of the Jews
  (26) Entry into Jerusalem.
From narratives of the Passion:
  (27) Last Supper, Conspiracy of the Jews with Judas
  (28) Betrayal
  (29) Prologue of Doctors and Contemplatio; Herod
  (30) Trial before Caiaphas, Peter's Denial, Death of Judas, First Trial before Pilate, Trial before Herod
  (31) Dream of Pilate's Wife
  (32) Second Trial before Pilate, Condemnation, Scourging, Procession to Calvary, Crucifixion
  (33) Descent into Hell of Anima Christi (first part of Harrowing of Hell)
  (34) Joseph of Arimathea, Longinus, Descent from the Cross, Burial.
From narratives of the Resurrection and Doomsday:
  (35) Guarding of the Sepulcher, Harrowing of Hell, Resurrection, *Appearance to the Virgin, Compact of Pilate and the Soldiers
  (36) Marys at the Sepulcher
  (37) Appearance to Mary Magdalen
  (38) Pilgrims to Emmaus, Doubting Thomas
  (39) Ascension, Choice of Matthias
  (40) Pentecost
  (41) Assumption of the Virgin
  (42) Last Judgment.

N-Town begins with a Proclamation of some five hundred lines in which the contents of the cycle are described to a prospective audience. This description, spoken by two "flag-bearers," does not, however, agree precisely with the cycle as we have it. N-Town is distinguished from the other three English scriptural cycles not only by its staging but also by a preoccupation with the life of the Virgin, a special concern for expounding theological doctrine through such choral characters as Contemplatio, Demon, Death, John the Baptist, and Doctors, and a greater seriousness of tone—there being neither a comic dispute between Noah and his Wife nor a comic scene for the Shepherds.

The N-Town Cycle has been edited as *Ludus Coventriae* by K. S. Block, Early English Text Society, Ext. Ser., No. CXX (1922). For critical studies, see Hardin Craig, "The Hegge Plays," *English Religious Drama of the Middle Ages* (1955). For a discussion of staging techniques, *The Medieval Theatre in the Round* (1957) should be consulted.—R. H.

O

O'Casey, Sean (1880–1964). Irish playwright. Born on March 30, 1880, of Protestant parents in predominantly Roman Catholic Dublin, O'Casey was christened John Casey, the last of thirteen children, eight of whom had died of infant diseases. A weak and sickly child, he contracted a chronic eye disease, trachoma with an ulcerated cornea, and as a result he had to struggle throughout his life against the threat of blindness. His poor eyesight made it difficult for him to attend school regularly, and with the help of his sister he taught himself to read and write by the time he was thirteen. He had already developed an enthusiasm for drama from an older brother, and the two boys often acted in amateur theatricals, performing scenes from the works of Shakespeare and Dion Boucicault. As a young man O'Casey's interests shifted temporarily from drama to an involvement in the cause of Ireland's freedom. He joined the secret Irish Republican Brotherhood; he learned the Irish language and taught it to workers in the Drumcondra Branch of the Gaelic League; he learned to play the bagpipes and became a founder-member of the St. Laurence O'Toole Pipers' Band; and he Gaelicized his name to Sean O'Cathasaigh. By the time he was thirty, however, he felt that Irish nationalism was too bourgeois and political, not vitally concerned enough with the economic and human needs of the people, and he put all his faith and energy into the Irish labor movement, then under the leadership of the dynamic Jim Larkin. During these years O'Casey had the proper credentials to be a member of Larkin's new union for unskilled workers, for he had worked at such odd jobs as stock clerk, railway laborer, pick-and-shovel navvy, hod carrier, and janitor. He began to write articles for the union newspaper and served directly under Larkin as secretary of the union's Irish Citizen Army during the turbulent 1913 general strike and lockout.

O'Casey's first published works were *Songs of the Wren* (1918), a collection of satiric ballads; *The Sacrifice of Thomas Ashe* (1918), a pamphlet about one of labor's martyrs in the 1916 Easter Rising; and a historical booklet, *The Story of the Irish Citizen Army* (1919). During the next few years he returned to the drama, and though the ABBEY THEATRE rejected three of his early playscripts, he persisted until THE SHADOW OF A GUNMAN was finally accepted and produced successfully in 1923. At this time he changed his surname from O'Cathasaigh to O'Casey and went on to write his other two antiheroic tragicomedies, JUNO AND THE PAYCOCK and THE PLOUGH AND THE STARS. The latter work provoked the famous riots in the Abbey Theatre, causing W. B. Yeats to shout down the protesting audience with the words, "You have disgraced yourselves again. Is this to be an ever-recurring celebration of the arrival of Irish Genius . . . ?" This stormy celebration of O'Casey's genius led to his alienation from his homeland, for he was now the target of abuse from overzealous nationalist and religious groups that accused him of desecrating Irish idealism and virtue, and he was treated with scorn by the Dublin literati, as well as by some of the Abbey actors, who were embarrassed by his intense working-class loyalties. It was therefore in sadness and anger that he left Dublin in 1926 to spend his remaining years in England in self-exile. The following year he married Eileen Reynolds Carey, a young Irish-born actress who was playing the lead in the London production of *The Plough and the Stars* when he met her.

The major crisis of O'Casey's career occurred in 1928 when the Abbey Theatre directors, under the leadership of the ailing Yeats, rejected his new, expressionist play, THE SILVER TASSIE, even though his three previous plays had saved the theater from artis-

SEAN O'CASEY (IRISH TOURIST BOARD)

tic and financial ruin. His alienation from Ireland was now complete, and thereafter he was often a playwright without a theater. Theater managers were reluctant to take risks with his dramatic innovations and forthright views, and as a result most of his subsequent plays were published before they were performed. Throughout the 1930's he had to support his family by writing reviews, essays, and sketches of his early life in Dublin. These latter efforts finally led to the publication of *I Knock at the Door* (1939), the first part of his monumental six-volume autobiography. He settled in Devon, living first in the village of Totnes, then in Torquay, where he died of a heart attack on September 18, 1964.

An antiheroic view of life, alternately tragic and comic, provides the unifying theme and mood in O'Casey's early works. His first three plays, *The Gunman, Juno,* and *The Plough,* deal with the historical events of the Irish War of Independence (1916–1922); but since he approaches this material as a pacifist more concerned with immediate human values than with nationalistic slogans, his main characters are not the patriotic heroes engaged in the fighting but the earthy tenement dwellers of the Dublin slums. And it is mostly the women who dominate the action: the mothers and wives and sweethearts, who realize there can be no victory in war for them if they lose their men and homes. The men, as they had done for centuries, abandon their families and go off to sacrifice themselves for a greater love, Kathleen ni Houlihan. When Johnny Boyle, whose hip is crippled in the Easter Rising and who loses an arm fighting with the IRA in the civil war, boasts that he would do it all again because "a principle's a principle," his mother, Juno, speaks for women everywhere when she replies: "Ah, you lost your best principle, me boy, when you lost your arm; them's the only sort o' principles that's any good to a workin' man."

Because the world of O'Casey's plays is so chaotic and tragic, his characters often resort to ironic and comic defenses in order to survive. Frustrated in their daily struggle for life's bare necessities, they can find a sense of liberation, even glory, only in the voluble and extravagant language O'Casey gives them. They are profligate with vivid words and phrases in a world in which they can be profligate with little else. While there is a sharp tone of outrage in his Daumier-like portraits of life in the slums of a war-torn city, O'Casey's plays do not follow the documentary patterns of naturalism—of Gerhart Hauptmann's *The Weavers* or John Galsworthy's *Strife*—for low comedy is not one of the handmaidens of naturalism. The structure of his plays is loose and flexible; the development of the action is contrapuntal, not dialectical. He works with an ensemble of contrasting characters rather than concentrating on a central figure. When the consequences of poverty and war become most crucial, he resorts to ironic counterpoint by introducing a music-hall turn, a randy ballad, or a mock battle presided over by his rude mechanicals. In the midst of antiheroic laughter there can be no total catastrophe. It is the comic resilience of his characters that saves the plays from pessimism and despair. Where there is suffering and death, no happy endings are possible, but where there is also a tenacious comic spirit, life goes on.

Having achieved so much in his early plays,

O'Casey thereafter refused to take the easy path by repeating past successes, and in his subsequent works he moved ahead in new directions. In his middle phase he used antirealistic techniques for a series of prophetic morality plays (see WITHIN THE GATES); and in his late phase he wove together elements of comedy and fantasy in an attempt to celebrate his affirmation of the vital life force (see COCK-A-DOODLE DANDY; PURPLE DUST; RED ROSES FOR ME). He was always original and daring in his search for new dramatic forms; at times he overreached himself and it was on those occasions that he became melodramatic and overly didactic. He called himself a communist and sometimes used mouthpiece characters to preach a version of the brotherhood of man in which the Star of Bethlehem and the Red Star became part of one great dream. In the latter years of his life he dedicated all his efforts as a man and artist to the quest for that dream; yet in the final reckoning his dramatic genius was fulfilled in his unique and many-sided assertion of the comic spirit.

The standard edition of O'Casey's plays is *The Collected Plays* (1949) in four volumes. His autobiography has been published in six volumes: *I Knock at the Door* (1939), *Pictures in the Hallway* (1942), *Drums Under the Window* (1946), *Inishfallen Fare Thee Well* (1949), *Rose and Crown* (1952), and *Sunset and Evening Star* (1954). Biographical and critical studies include *Sean O'Casey: The Man and His Work* (1960) by David Krause; *The Experiments of Sean O'Casey* (1960) by Robert Hogan; *Sean O'Casey, The Man Behind the Plays* (1963) by Saros Cowasjee; and *Sean O'Casey, The Man I Knew* (1965) by Gabriel Fallon.—D. K.

Odets, Clifford (1906–1963). American playwright and film writer. Clifford Odets was born in

CLIFFORD ODETS (WIDE WORLD PHOTOS)

Philadelphia but grew up in New York, to which his family moved in 1908. An amateur director and actor in his student days, Odets began to act professionally after graduating from high school. In 1928 he joined the acting company of the Theatre Guild, which at the time was enjoying its greatest prestige as a producer of distinguished new plays by European and American writers. Under the financial protection and encouragement of the Guild, the young company that was to call itself the Group Theatre made its first steps toward organization in 1930, with Harold Clurman, Lee Strasberg, and Cheryl Crawford as its directors, and Odets was among the actors invited to join it. In this congenial atmosphere Odets began to write plays, and the Group, always in need of playable, socially conscious scripts, was pleased to find in its own ranks a dramatist of very evident talent.

From 1935 to 1940 the Group produced seven plays by Odets. The first of his works to be staged, *Waiting for Lefty,* was, however, presented independently of the Group on January 5, 1935, off Broadway but with Group actors. The opening performance of this play revealed Odets as an outstanding spokesman for the perplexed young people of the Depression years—so much so that at the end the audience rose in the theater to join with the dramatic characters, militant members of a labor union, in a cry of "Strike!" So popular was the play that it was presented, not only by the Group for a run, but, according to Odets, in 104 cities in 1935 alone. Before bringing the play to Broadway in the spring of 1935, with a companion piece on Nazi Germany, *Till the Day I Die,* the Group staged Odets' AWAKE AND SING! With the success (critical if not financial) of this play, Odets was recognized as the most promising new dramatist of the decade. In this period of his first productions Odets joined the Communist party (late in 1934, only to leave it in the spring of 1935) and received much attention in leftist quarters, but his popularity extended far beyond them. Although the production of *Paradise Lost,* late in 1935, was a failure, GOLDEN BOY, presented two years later, was the most successful production in the Group's history. Meanwhile Odets, after much internal debate, had gone to Hollywood to write films. Of his last two plays for the Group, *Rocket to the Moon,* produced in 1938, received mixed notices, as did most Group plays, and *Night Music,* produced in 1940, was a flat failure.

In the twenty-three years of life remaining to him after the collapse of the Group Theatre, Odets offered only four plays: *Clash by Night* (1941), *The Big Knife* (1949), *The Country Girl* (1950), and *The Flowering Peach* (1954). While none of these is without interest, only *The Country Girl,* which Odets by his own admission wrote as a potboiler, was a box-office success. As a screenwriter for more than twenty-five years, Odets supplied Hollywood with a number of successful scripts, of which the most memorable is the first: *The General Died at Dawn* (1936). In 1963 he began to write a series of plays for television but had completed only two by the time of his death.

The plays of Odets are marked by a strong social sympathy that tended, no matter the political fashion of the year, to divide humanity into two classes: the exploiters and the exploited. Although this social view is especially evident in the early plays, it is never absent from Odets' work. Both *Waiting for Lefty* and *Awake and Sing!* are determinedly Marxist plays intended to demonstrate the thesis that only in the solidarity of the workers, who have put the profit motive behind them, will the world become joyous. *Waiting for Lefty* is an amplification of the form of drama known as "agitprop" (for "agitational propaganda"), developed by Russian workers' troupes and introduced to America in the 1920's by the communist journalist Michael Gold. In such plays, short, expressionistic scenes reveal the well-organized heads of industry, finance, the military, or other sorts of established orders as the class enemies of the unorganized, demoralized poor, whom they use unconscionably for their own ends. To the poor appears a leader, usually young, who brings them together into a monolithic mass ready to fight their exploiters. A sophisticated variant of the form, *Waiting for Lefty* presents a struggle between the corrupt leaders of a union of taxi drivers and the honest rank and file who want a representative union and are considering a strike. Scenes of their meeting alternate with scenes of their private lives, which show why they became drivers and why they are in need of higher wages. When their leader, Lefty, is reported dead with a bullet wound in his head, they heed another young leader, Agate, and call for a strike. *Awake and Sing!* is a heavily plotted, "well-made" play, quite unlike *Lefty* in structure, but it too ends with the emergence of a leader who clearly intends to bring members of the working class together and take them on to new glories in a world where avarice will not exist. Somewhat similarly, *Paradise Lost,* produced only ten months later, concludes with its middle-class, middle-aged protagonist, who has lost his home in a business failure, experiencing a sort of apocalyptic vision of the good life to be enjoyed soon by all men in a peaceful, fearless, and presumably classless society.

In his last three Group Theatre plays Odets began to reveal a capacity for growth as a dramatist at the same time that he began to show hints of the rigidity of social thought that eventually was to stifle his talent altogether. Joe Bonaparte in *Golden Boy,* Cleo Singer in *Rocket to the Moon,* and Steve Takis in *Night Music* are very young protagonists who, reasonably enough, do not set themselves up as leaders of the lower classes and yet are sympathetic. Odets presents them in the round, with a deeper probing into the life of the mind than he had previously managed. Even so, the messages of the three plays are awkwardly delivered. For the sake of his antimaterialistic theme Odets allows Bonaparte to be equally talented in music and boxing, two sharply different fields, and builds the play out of the events that follow his renunciation of the more spiritual, but less remunerative, of the two, without a thought to the unlikelihood that anyone should have such a choice. *Rocket to the Moon* and *Night Music* are no less perplexing in their strongly worded references to financial worries at a time when the national economy was, however slowly, beginning at last to strengthen.

Of his four plays produced after the Group Theatre came to an end, only in *The Flowering Peach,* the story of the biblical Noah told in the idiom of the middle-class Jews of New York, did Odets suggest that he had found it possible to make peace with the materialism of the world around him. This comes through the decision of Noah to make his home after the flood with Shem, his materialistic son, for the comforts Shem can provide. An appealing play, it nevertheless is weak in the second of its two acts, as though the playwright had lost his energy while writing. He followed this work with film and television scripts at intervals over the next ten years, most of which have no lasting value.

Uneven though Odets' plays may be, their strengths outweigh their weaknesses. If too topical to be revived on the stage, they continue to reward readers. Against the obvious, contrived method of construction, of which only *Waiting for Lefty* is free, may be placed the strong characters and the dialogue designed brilliantly in the idiom of the city. Against the futile Marxist propagandizing may be placed the genuine sympathy for the young and friendless and the victims of intolerance. When allowance is made for their excesses, the best of the Group Theatre plays offer arresting scenes of a hard-pressed and anxious, yet optimistic, society, such as America remained throughout the Depression years.

Six of Odets' plays have appeared in one volume, *Six Plays* (1939). These are *Waiting for Lefty, Awake and Sing, Till the Day I Die, Paradise Lost, Golden Boy,* and *Rocket to the Moon.* Published in separate volumes are *Night Music* (1940), *Clash by Night* (1942), *The Big Knife* (1949), and *The Country Girl* (1951). No satisfactory biography of Odets has yet appeared. An intimate portrait of him in association with the Group Theatre may be found in Harold Clurman's *The Fervent Years* (1945). A critical study, "Clifford Odets and the Found Generation" by Malcolm Goldstein, may be found in *American Drama and Its Critics* (1965), edited by Alan S. Downer.—M. G.

Oedipe (1931). A play by André Gide (1869–1951). *Oedipe* was performed at Avignon in 1949 in a new production directed by Jean Vilar. After Gide's death in 1951, Vilar revived his production for Jean-Louis Barrault's Théâtre Marigny in Paris. In this production, Oedipus, played by Vilar, was recognizable as the predestined tragic hero, but he was also the champion of the gratuitous act, which for Gide implies a strange and dangerous affirmation of one's liberty. Gide's Oedipus is more impertinent than the Greek model, and the drama incorporates elements of parody. Dramatically speaking, the scenes of Oedipus' revolt against God are more interesting than those of his final submission to fate. The text is concerned with the conflict that Gide studied most assiduously throughout his long career: the conflict between a religious disquietude that denies that life has sufficient meaning unless it appeals to something supernatural and a humanistic acceptance, without any aspiration toward the divine, of the condition of man in the universe.—W. F.

Oedipus at Colonus (Oidipous epi Kolonoi, 402 B.C). A tragedy by SOPHOCLES. The scene is the village of Colonus, just outside Athens. Oedipus, old and blind, exiled from Thebes by his sons and Creon, has come to Colonus accompanied by his daughter Antigone after long wanderings. He takes refuge in a grove, only to be ordered off by a villager, who tells him it is sacred to the Eumenides. Oedipus recognizes the fulfillment of a prophecy of Apollo that he would find rest in such a place and refuses to move; the villager goes to report to Theseus, the king. The Chorus, old men of Colonus, react with horror when they discover Oedipus' identity, but he proclaims his innocence. Ismene, Oedipus' other daughter, arrives with news that Oedipus' sons are at war for his throne. A prophecy from Delphi has promised victory to the city which shelters Oedipus' body, and Ismene warns her father that Creon, on behalf of Eteocles, will come to take him home. But Oedipus,

A SCENE FROM SOPHOCLES' *Oedipus at Colonus* (GREEK NATIONAL TOURIST OFFICE)

with a curse on his sons, chooses to die in Athens. Ismene is sent off to offer sacrifice on his behalf to the Eumenides. When Theseus arrives, Oedipus asks for protection and explains the gift of victory he brings. Theseus makes him a citizen. After the famous ode on the glories of Athens, Creon arrives with a bodyguard and tries to persuade Oedipus to return. A contemptuous refusal provokes him to angry insults and violence; he has already seized Ismene and sent her off under guard, and he now has Antigone dragged away. He is about to seize Oedipus himself when Theseus arrives. Creon pleads his case; among his arguments is the prospect of the pollution that Oedipus' unholy crimes will bring on Athens, and this provokes Oedipus to defend his past once again with a claim that he acted in ignorance. Theseus decides for Oedipus, arrests Creon, and goes off to rescue the girls. When he returns with them he speaks of a mysterious suppliant who asks for an interview with Oedipus. When Oedipus realizes that it is his son Polyneices, he refuses to see him, but Antigone prevails on him to do so. Polyneices begs for Oedipus' presence and support in the coming attack on Thebes; his answer is a terrifying accusation ending with a frightful curse—a prophecy that he will kill and be killed by his brother. Antigone begs Polyneices to give up his plans for attack, but he goes his destined way to his death. Now the thunder and lightning announce that Oedipus' end is near. He sends for Theseus and with sure-footed speed the blind man leads the way to the place of his death, where, one day, Athens' enemies will be defeated. A messenger describes his last moments: After Oedipus' farewell to his daughters the voice of the gods themselves was heard summoning him. Then, accompanied by Theseus alone, Oedipus moved off to his miraculous disappearance; how he died no man can tell. The play ends with the daughters' lamentations for their father and Antigone's announcement that she will return to Thebes to fulfill her promise to Polyneices that she would see to his burial.

Oedipus at Colonus is a religious mystery play which presents the transformation of Oedipus from human being to what the Greeks called *heros,* one who, through great deeds and suffering in life, acquired after death power for good and evil over the living. We are shown the stages of his metamorphosis —from the humble acquiescence of the opening scene, through the increasing sureness of his decisions and pronouncements, to the unearthly authority of his curse on Polyneices, and finally of his progress to the place of his death. There is no doubt that Sophocles had the earlier play, *Oedipus Tyrannus,* in mind; the action in the later play is the fulfillment of an obscure prophecy made by Oedipus the king about his future—that he was reserved for some strange and dreadful end. There are also many parallels of situation and of language. In *Oedipus at Colonus* Sophocles presents the final justification and reward of a man whose heroic action and intelligence served in the earlier play as the great example of the precarious instability of all human achievement.

See R. C. Jebb, *Oedipus at Colonus* (1900), and T. G. Rosenmeyer, "The Wrath of Oedipus," in *Phoenix,* Vol. VI (1952), pp. 92–112.—B. M. W. K.

Oedipus Tyrannus (Oidipous Tyrannos, Oedipus the King, 430?–?425 B.C.). A tragedy by SOPHO-CLES. The scene is the palace of Oedipus, king of Thebes. Plague is raging in the city. Oedipus promises the priest and a crowd of citizens that he will do all he can to end the plague. He expects news from Creon, sent to consult the Delphic oracle. Creon delivers Apollo's command to find the murderer of Laius and purify the city by his death or banishment, and Oedipus undertakes to do so. He pronounces a curse on the murderer, cutting him off from all human contact. Tiresias, sent for by Oedipus, refuses to reveal what he knows about Laius' murder but later, angered by Oedipus' furious reaction, accuses the king himself of the deed and, in veiled terms, hints at his incest. Oedipus denounces the prophet as an agent of Creon in a conspiracy against the throne. Creon arrives to defend himself, but Oedipus, in spite of the pleas of the Chorus, condemns him to exile. Jocasta wins a reprieve for Creon and then inquires what so angered her husband. Once informed, she tells him that prophets are not infallible; her proof is the prophecy made to Laius that he would be killed by his own (and her) son. But the son was left to die on the mountains and Laius was killed at a place where three roads meet. This detail strikes terror into Oedipus, who now reveals that he once killed a man at such a crossroads; question and answer establish that it was the same place and that the descriptions of the two men concerned coincide. Oedipus' one hope now rests on the fact that all accounts of the murder spoke of several assailants, whereas Oedipus was alone; there was one survivor of Laius' party and Oedipus orders this eyewitness sent for at once. Jocasta reluctantly agrees but reaffirms her disbelief in prophecy, human or divine. The Chorus, appalled by her blasphemy, exalt the divine laws and condemn human pride, calling on Zeus to fulfill the oracles: If they prove false, "divine order is dead and gone."

A shepherd from Corinth brings news: Polybus, Oedipus' supposed father, is dead and Corinth calls Oedipus back to be its king. For Jocasta this is the final proof that oracles are false, for Oedipus was to kill his father. Oedipus exultantly agrees, but he will not go back to Corinth: His mother is still alive. The messenger frees him of his last remaining fear by telling him that he is not the son of Polybus of Corinth; he himself brought Oedipus as a child from the mountains and gave him to the childless royal pair. He got the child from another shepherd, one of Laius' men. Jocasta has now realized the truth, and when Oedipus, determined to solve the mystery of his birth, asks her to find this man, she makes a desperate attempt to stop the inquiry. But Oedipus *will* know the truth and Jocasta rushes offstage with a despairing farewell. Oedipus, however, is at his high point of confidence in his destiny. He proclaims himself the son of chance, who brought him to this eminence and will not desert him now. For a brief moment the Chorus share his hopes. The next scene, the crossexamination of the shepherd of Laius, is a masterpiece of theatrical economy and precision. Oedipus confronts the two shepherds, one an eager, the other a reluctant, witness. Finally with a threat of torture, he forces out of the shepherd of Laius the dreadful truth, which he has begun to suspect—that he is the son and murderer of Laius, the son and husband of Jocasta. "O generations of mankind," sing the

Chorus after he rushes into the palace, "I add up the total of your life and find it equal to nothing." A messenger tells how Oedipus found Jocasta hanged and put out his own eyes. When he appears he seems to be the living proof of the Chorus' despairing summation.

In the last scene a strange transformation takes place. In his attitudes to the Chorus and to Creon, who now rules in Thebes, Oedipus begins to show an increasing confidence and self-assertion. His justification of his self-inflicted blindness and the repeated demands he makes on Creon recall the imperious temper of the Oedipus of the opening scenes; in fact, Creon's last speech is a forceful reminder to him that he is no longer king. This resurgence of aggressive vitality in a hero who has suffered the most catastrophic reversal of fortune in all Greek tragedy suggests that, far from being equal to nothing, as the Chorus state, man can endure and even win a personal victory over the worst that life can do to him.

See R. C. Jebb, *Oedipus Tyrannus* (1893); J. T. Sheppard, *The Oedipus Tyrannus of Sophocles* (1920); Bernard M. W. Knox, *Oedipus at Thebes* (2nd ed., corrected, 1966).—B. M. W. K.

Oehlenschläger, Adam [**Gottlob**] (1779–1850). Danish poet and playwright. Oehlenschläger grew up at Frederiksberg Castle, where his father was steward. Attempts at acting and the study of law proved abortive, and he turned to literature. His famous sixteen-hour meeting with the Norwegian mineralogist and philosopher Henrik Steffens, fresh from Germany, marked the beginning of Danish Romanticism in 1802. After extended travel abroad, 1805–1809, Oehlenschläger was named professor of aesthetics in Copenhagen. Stormy literary debates followed, but by 1829 the Swedish poet Esaias Tegnér could crown him in Lund Cathedral the unchallenged laureate of all Scandinavia.

Oehlenschläger's first drama, *Sanct Hansaften-spil* ("A Play of Midsummer Night," 1803), an interesting fusion of lyricism, satire, and nature mysticism, presents a love story against a background of genre scenes in Copenhagen's Royal Deer Park. *Aladdin* (1805) not only introduced Shakespearean blank verse into Danish drama but also established itself as the high point of Danish Romanticism. Its rich episodic tapestry, based on *One Thousand and One Nights,* is a symbolic version of the victory of emotion over reason.

The tragedy *Hakon Jarl* (1807), like so much of Oehlenschläger's work, dips into Scandinavian mythology as source material. Itself owing much to Friedrich von Schiller's *Wallenstein* as a model, *Hakon Jarl* came to have an important influence on Strindberg. *Balder hin gode* ("Balder the Good," 1807), "a philosophical-poetical allegory of nature" (as Oehlenschläger described it), also owes something to Schiller, this time to *Die Braut von Messina* (*The Bride of Messina,* 1803). Written in Germany, these two plays by Oehlenschläger appeared in *Nordiske digte* (*Scandinavian Poems,* 1807).

Axel og Valborg ("Axel and Valborg," 1810), written in Paris and modeled on French classical tragedy, retells a story of ballad origin about conflict between love and duty. *Correggio* (1811), which Oehlenschläger wrote in German and subsequently translated into Danish, makes use of Giorgio Vasari's

ADAM OEHLENSCHLÄGER (DANISH INFORMATION OFFICE)

biography of the Italian painter in order to examine doubt and self-discovery in the mentality of the artist. Of the trilogy *Helge* (1814), only the third part, *Yrsa,* is couched in dramatic form, the rest being a poetic cycle leading up to it. The whole constitutes a powerful reworking of the Volsunga Saga.

Oehlenschläger's plays are not very stageworthy in modern terms, but *Aladdin* continues to be read, studied, and occasionally played on the radio.

No English translations are presently available, but critical treatment may be found in P. M. Mitchell, *A History of Danish Literature* (1958), pp. 105–115.—R. B. V.

Oflazoğlu, Turan (1932–). Turkish playwright. Oflazoğlu was born in a village in Adana, Turkey, and graduated from the philosophy and English philology departments of the University of Istanbul. Oflazoğlu's first play, *Keziban* (1964), was written and first produced at the University of Washington, where he studied drama.

Oflazoğlu's plays are either in part or wholly in poetry. He has treated the themes of ignorance, false values, and superstitions in Turkish villages, using well-drawn characters and subtle irony. His two long plays—*Deli İbrahim* ("Ibrahim the Mad," 1967) and *Sokrates' in Savunması* ("The Defense of Socrates," 1969)—are philosophical and thought-provoking. Oflazoğlu prefers the dramatic theater as opposed to the epic but freely borrows from the theatrical heritage of all times, including the convention of the Greek chorus.—N. O.

O'Kelly, Seumas (1881–1918). Irish playwright

and short-story writer. A native of Galway, O'Kelly began his career as a newspaper reporter. While still a young man, he suffered heart damage as a result of a severe illness and was thus forced to curtail his activities. He was active in the extreme home-rule movement, Sinn Fein, as editor of the organization's official paper, *Nationality*. He was killed in a riot in the offices of *Nationality* by British soldiers celebrating the armistice.

O'Kelly is the author of four plays, a large number of short stories, and one novel, *The Lady of Deerpark* (1917). His plays are *The Matchmakers* (1908), *The Shuiler's Child* (1909), *The Homecoming* (1912), and *The Bribe* (1913). The best of these works is *The Shuiler's Child,* a touching, occasionally sentimental tragedy. It portrays Moll Woods, a "shuiler," or vagabond, and her attempt to find a home for her child at the expense of her own happiness. Moll's tragic self-sacrifice is movingly realized in the play's final scene. O'Kelly's last play, *The Bribe,* is a sharp satire of Irish politics loosely modeled on Ibsen's *An Enemy of the People.*—E. Q.

Oktay Rifat [Horozcu] (1914–   ). Turkish poet and playwright. Oktay Rifat was born in Trabzon, Turkey, where his father was governor. He received a law degree from the University of Ankara and in 1937 was sent to Paris by the government to study for a doctorate in law, but the occupation of Paris in 1940 forced him to return to Turkey. Today, he is a practicing lawyer and, in the field of literature, is best known as a poet.

Oktay Rifat's first play, *Kadınlar Arasında* ("Among Women," 1948), describes the utter poverty of a family and their resistance, informed by class-consciousness, to authority. This kind of social criticism was unheard of in the Turkey of 1948, and the minister of education of the period had the play discontinued at the State Theater of Ankara after thirteen performances. The incident caused heated polemics in the press.

Not finding a suitable modern theatrical tradition in Turkey for his tastes when he started writing plays in 1948, Oktay Rifat experimented with form for many years. He borrowed from the traditional *Karagöz* (shadow theater) and the epic theater, but the plays that he wrote in these styles, although poetical, were dull and lacked dramatic action. *Çil Horoz* ("The Freckled Cock," 1964), however, is in a realistic style and dramatic form and is a highly moving account of life in a shantytown in Turkey. Oktay Rifat has expressed his intention to continue to write in this vein.—N. O.

Old Comedy. Term used to describe Greek comedy from its beginnings to about 400 B.C. Old Comedy is distinguished by extensive personal lampooning and a mixture of realism and myth. Its greatest practitioner was Aristophanes, who used the form as a political and social weapon while giving free vent to his extravagant and witty imagination.

Old Comedy exhibits the following structure:

1. prologue
2. parados—the entrance of the chorus
3. agon—a contest or debate
4. parabasis—a speech to the audience by the chorus on behalf of the author
5. further episodes punctuated by choral songs

The death of Old Comedy is traditionally fixed around 404 B.C., the date of the defeat of Athens in the Peloponnesian War. (See MIDDLE COMEDY; NEW COMEDY.)

Old Lady Says "No," The (1929). An expressionistic play by Denis JOHNSTON. The play centers around an actor who, having suffered a head injury while playing the role of the eighteenth-century Irish patriot Robert Emmet, now imagines that he is actually Emmet plunged into the midst of twentieth-century Ireland. The audience sees the succeeding events from the same hallucinatory perspective as the actor, a vantage point that produces a sharp and effective satire of postrevolutionary Irish life. Many lines in the play are studded with allusions and quotations from Irish literature and thus accentuate the disparity between the great ideal for which Emmet died and the contemporary reality. This device brings the play's satiric strain to its culmination in the final, passionate speech with its ironic parallels to the final words of the historical Emmet. The play's style of EXPRESSIONISM produces a kaleidoscopic effect in which music, poetry, and topical allusions are important elements.—E. Q.

Olesha, Yuri [Karlovich] (1899–1960). Russian novelist, short-story writer, and playwright. Olesha was born in Elisavetgrad, the son of an excise official from the impoverished landowner class. When he was three, his family moved to Odessa, where he lived until the middle 1920's and began to write poetry. Within a few years he ranked high among Odessa's surprising concentration of gifted writers that included Edward Bagritsky, Valentin Katayev, Isaak Babel, Ilya Ilf, and Evgeny Petrov, all of whom worked together later in Moscow on the magazine *Gudok* ("The Whistle").

Olesha, who hated the restrictions of the tsarist regime and placed great hopes in the revolution, welcomed the new regime jubilantly. At first, like many liberal intellectuals, he was eager to disregard and excuse as temporary aberrations the ugly and seamy sights he witnessed, especially the restrictions on freedom that were at least as strict as those under the tsar. But the years passed and, if anything, the straitjacket of the new order tightened. According to the official Soviet dogma, an artist was supposed to "offer a spontaneous reflection of reality," the "reality" being the "ideological superstructure on the economic base." Olesha, trying to reconcile himself to it, accepted the regime with his reason and proceeded to argue against his heart and his feelings.

This inner dialogue ran through his novel *Envy,* his short stories, film scripts, and plays (*Zagovor chuvstv—The Conspiracy of Feelings—*and A LIST OF ASSETS). In Olesha's dreamy world this conflict seems to be between the new impersonal materialism and all the personal human feelings, whether good or bad, noble or vulgar. Olesha saw the emotional revulsion against the soulless streamlining of life as a "conspiracy of feelings." The play by that name was based on *Envy,* a poem-like novel full of nostalgia for the discarded old world, in which the attitudes of the various characters toward the wholesale eradication of the unwanted but familiar and comfortable sentiments and their replacement by new, "goal-directed," rational relations range from open rebellion to enthusiastic endorsement. Although the book was at first hailed by Soviet critics, they soon had to revise their verdict because readers were identifying with the wrong characters, the "negative heroes" in Soviet parlance. As a result, Olesha's writings were soon virtually out of print. The play *Conspiracy of Feelings* was so efficiently removed from circulation that it is now impossible to find a complete text of it. Olesha's other play, *A List of Assets,* fared somewhat better: although it never received permission to be produced, some copies of it do at least exist.

When Olesha realized that any protest or resistance was futile, he simply stopped writing. For many years he was known to the younger generation of Soviet readers as the author of the novel-length fairy tale *Tri tolstiaka* ("Three Fat Men," adapted for ballet) and occasional newspaper articles. After Stalin's death, literary controls were somewhat loosened and many of Olesha's writings were circulated again, accompanied by "explanations" by Soviet critics. Physically, Olesha survived the worst purges and died in 1960 in his apartment in Peredelkino, the Soviet writers' village.

Some biographical and critical information on Olesha can be found in Andrew R. MacAndrew's introductory essay to *Envy and Other Works* (1967) by Yuri Olesha.—A. MacA.

O'Neill, Eugene [**Gladstone**] (1888–1953). American playwright. Eugene O'Neill was born in a hotel room in the very heart of New York's theatrical district. He was the son of the matinee idol and

EUGENE O'NEILL (F. RAY KEMP)

successful actor-manager James O'Neill, who amassed a fortune touring in a melodrama based on Alexandre Dumas's famous romantic novel *The Count of Monte Cristo*. His family was tragically disturbed (his mother suffered from drug addiction and his elder brother was a confirmed alcoholic) and O'Neill had an unstable childhood, touring the United States with his parents and receiving an irregular education in different private boarding schools. Encouraged by his irresponsible actor-brother James, he was inducted into the bohemian life of the theatrical world at a tender age. After a year at Princeton University, he was suspended in 1907 for a student prank. In 1909 he entered into a secret marriage, later dissolved. That same year he went prospecting for gold in Central America with a mining engineer, but having contracted malaria in the course of this fruitless expedition, he joined his father's company as an actor and assistant manager.

Growing restless again, he shipped to Buenos Aires and found employment there with American companies located in the area, until, unemployed, he joined a British vessel bound for New York. Here he promptly relapsed into a life of dissipation on the New York waterfront, frequenting a disreputable tavern, "Jimmy-the-Priest's," which he was to re-create in the milieu of two of his best-known plays, *Anna Christie* and *The Iceman Cometh*.

After joining his father's company again and playing a small part in *Monte Cristo,* and with several months of intemperate living intervening, he went to New London, Connecticut, and joined the staff of the local newspaper, the *New London Telegraph,* as a reporter. He had begun to publish humorous poetry in a column of that newspaper when his journalistic career was abruptly terminated by a blow O'Neill could only consider ironic fate. His health undermined by his profligate mode of life, he was hospitalized in 1912 with tuberculosis. A term of six months in a sanatorium, however, proved to be doubly beneficial: it arrested the disease and made an avid reader of O'Neill. He read widely during his convalescence, falling under the influence of the Greek tragic poets and Strindberg. He began to write plays in 1913, and in 1914 he enrolled in a course in playwriting given at Harvard University by the famous George Pierce Baker.

The next year he moved to Greenwich Village, the "Left Bank" of New York, and in 1916 joined an avant-garde group of writers and artists who had established an amateur theatrical company. Their first season in the summer of 1915 had been presented on an abandoned wharf in the artists' colony of Provincetown, on Cape Cod, Massachusetts, for which reason they came to call themselves the Provincetown Players. O'Neill began to write short plays for them and soon became their foremost playwright as well as one of their directors when they moved to a small theater in Greenwich Village. O'Neill and his associates, the critic Kenneth Mcgowan and the great American scenic artist Robert Edmond Jones, ran a second enterprise, the Greenwich Village Theatre, from 1923 to 1927. Both the Provincetown and the Greenwich Village ventures were among the most influential of groups in the seminal "little theater" movement, which gained momentum after 1912 and succeeded in modernizing the American theater in the 1920's.

Before turning to the plays it is helpful first to note that O'Neill attracted attention with two styles of theater rather than one, being equally adept in the styles of realism and expressionism, and with two radically disproportionate types of drama, since he was equally effective in one-act plays and in cyclopean dramas twice the normal length of modern plays. His search for expressive form, in his case a combination of private compulsions and public ambitions to incorporate modern concerns with life and art, led him to undertake numerous experiments with symbolic figures, masks, interior monologues, split personalities, choruses, scenic effects, rhythms, and schematizations. In O'Neill's work there is a veritable *summa* of the modern theater's aspirations as well as its more or less inevitable failures. In all his major work he traced the course of a modern dramatist in search of an aesthetic and spiritual center. It is not certain that he found it often, if ever, but the labor involved in the effort was usually impressive and sometimes notably rewarding. His plays embodied the ideas and conflicts of the first half of the twentieth century, assimilated its advances in dramatic art and theatrical technique, and expressed its uneasy aspirations toward tragic insights and dramatic vision. His impressiveness as a dramatist is ultimately, in fact, the result of his determined effort to trace a thread of meaning in the universe virtually emptied of meaning by a century of scientific and sociological thought. He did not, it is true, find any comforting assurances in the world, but he had the integrity to acknowledge his failure and the persistence to dramatize. O'Neill's experiments were not undertaken to suit the whims of a volatile trifler or the calculations of a theatrical opportunist. See EXPRESSIONISM; REALISM AND NATURALISM.

O'Neill started with short "slice of life" dramas dealing with the miseries, the delusions, and obsessions of men adrift in the world. With the appearance of a cycle of sea pieces, beginning with the Provincetown Players' production of *Bound East for Cardiff* in 1916, he became the undisputed master of the one-act play form in America. The sharply etched playlets *In the Zone* and *The Long Voyage Home* (1917) and *The Moon of the Caribbees* (1918), along with O'Neill's first Provincetown production, made up the remarkable quartet of one-acters subsequently produced under the collective title of S.S. GLENCAIRN. A number of independent pieces, such as *Ile* (1917), *The Rope* (1918), and *Where the Cross Is Made* (1918), also enhanced their young author's reputation by the end of World War I. *Ile* is especially representative of his early naturalistic-symbolic style with its mordant treatment of a New England sea captain's obsessive pride in his ability to hunt whales for their "ile" (oil), which drives his lonely wife mad. This little play exemplified O'Neill's taste for tragic irony, his characteristic concern with destructive obsessiveness that resembles the *hybris* of classic tragedy, and his fascination with the sea as a mystery and a seduction, and as a symbol of the malignity of fate.

The same interests soon appeared in a richer and more complicated context when O'Neill began to write his early full-length plays. He gave his sense of tragic irony full scope in the first of these, the satur-nine drama of fate and frustration BEYOND THE HORIZON, for which he won a Pulitzer Prize in 1920. In *Diff'rent* (1920) fate plays an ironic trick on a New England girl who breaks off her engagement because her seagoing fiancé is not chaste enough to satisfy her puritanical principles: having doomed herself to a life of lonely spinsterhood, she ultimately rebels against frustration by succumbing to a designing rascal many years younger than herself. In ANNA CHRISTIE, first produced under a different title in 1920 and successfully revived a year later, it is the attraction of the sea that is blamed for the combination of circumstances making a prostitute of the heroine. Whereas *Diff'rent* makes crude use of both the irony of fate and the theme of sexual repression attributed by O'Neill's generation to the rigors of New England puritanism, *Anna Christie* moves naturally and smoothly up to its climax, the rejection of Anna by a young Irishman on his discovering her sordid past. Only the ending of the play seems marred by vaguely promising a reunion between the lovers. Although O'Neill's dissatisfaction with it arose from a belief that he must write unalloyed tragedy to fulfill his vision of life and his destiny as a significant tragedian, he nevertheless had no reason to be ashamed of what he had accomplished in this pungent, affecting play, for which he won a second Pulitzer Prize.

In one way or another, the characters in these and other early works were entangled with circumstances which, if not tragic in any strict sense of the term, were destructive of happiness, and O'Neill was by no means a poor judge of his potentialities as a dramatist in believing that his forte was tragedy. He was least successful when the quality of the characters fell short of tragic elevation. *The Straw* (1921) deals with the love of two tubercular patients in a sanatorium, one of whom is cured after a few months and leaves behind him the girl, whose hopeless situation is alleviated only by the illusion that she will join him someday. In *The First Man* (1922) a scientist destroys his prospects of happiness by resenting the intrusion of a child into his married life; and in *Welded* (1924), a play written under the influence of Strindberg, husband and wife are consumed with resentment while drawn to each other so powerfully that they cannot live apart. But it was not long before O'Neill lifted himself out of the morass of petty and pathetic situations and attained tragic power in DESIRE UNDER THE ELMS.

Here is a naturalistic New England variation on a classical theme—the Phaedra-Hippolytus theme—involving the passion of Eben for his young stepmother, a passion relentlessly driven to its tragic conclusion. Suffering in this play is produced by strong passions and conflicts of will on the part of the determined characters, and if it ultimately lacks the elevation, it nevertheless possesses the strength of tragedy. If its stream of action is muddied by Freudian details of characterization in the portrayal of Eben, it nevertheless proceeds with mounting energy towards its destination, reflecting in its course the wind-swept landscape of the human soul. Nothing comparable to this work in power derived from a sense of tragic character and situation had been achieved by the American theater in the 150 years of its history.

A more complacent playwright than O'Neill would have been content with this achievement and endeavored to repeat it. Not so O'Neill, who did not give the American stage another naturalistic adaptation of classic matter until 1931 with *Mourning Becomes Electra.* The plays that followed *Desire Under the Elms* were *The Fountain,* unsuccessfully produced in December 1925 at the Greenwich Village Theatre, and *The Great God Brown,* presented at the same theater in the next year. They represent O'Neill's strivings to enrich the American drama with styles radically different from the naturalistic— namely, the romantic, the symbolist, and the expressionistic.

The effort started earlier, in fact, with the production of *The Emperor Jones* in 1920, and some several months later with *Gold,* an expanded version of the one-acter *Where the Cross Is Made.* The first production was decidedly auspicious, the second inauspicious; the first virtually introduced expressionism into the American theater, the second inaugurated O'Neill's ventures into symbolist-romantic drama with which he only succeeded more—and but moderately even then—with *Marco Millions* in 1928. In the contrived and awkwardly written melodrama *Gold,* a sea captain is driven mad by his lust for gold, contracted on a desert island when, crazed by thirst, he thought he found a treasure trove. Its successor in the romantic style, *The Fountain,* fared scarcely better with the overextended story of the legendary search of Ponce de León for the Fountain of Youth, which becomes obsessive until he finally realizes that "there is no gold but love."

It was not theory but a felt belief in the potentialities of nonnaturalistic drama that motivated O'Neill in the series of expressionistic experiments that started with the Provincetown Players' productions of *The Emperor Jones* and *The Hairy Ape* in 1920 and 1922 respectively and continued, with a variety of modifications, in *All God's Chillun Got Wings* in 1924, in *The Great God Brown* in 1926, in *Strange Interlude* and *Lazarus Laughed* in 1928, and as late as 1934 in *Days Without End,* a drama of a split personality played by two different actors. It was a personal pressure that dominated these plays and the statement of principles he set down for playwriting when he drafted the program note on Strindberg for the Provincetown Players' production of *Spook Sonata,* which he co-produced:

> . . . it is only by means of some form of "super-naturalism" that we may express in the theater what we comprehend intuitively of that self-defeating, self-obsession which is the discount we moderns have to pay for the loan of life. The old "naturalism"—or "realism" if you prefer . . . —no longer applies. It represents our Fathers' daring aspirations toward self-recognition by holding the family kodak up to ill-nature. But to us their old audacity is blague; we have taken too many snapshots of each other in every graceless position; we have endured too much from the banality of surfaces.

The first product of his reaching out for expressive form was THE EMPEROR JONES, which deals with the flight of a Caribbean Negro dictator from his aroused victims. Here O'Neill's success was dual: it was an original play—virtually a dramatic monologue without intermissions in which fantasy cut across reality and the subjectivity of the protagonist was converted into objective reality for the mesmerized audience.

The Emperor Jones was followed by an even more exciting and certainly more provocative expressionistic drama, THE HAIRY APE, which is somewhat baffling in meaning yet also richer and more complex in action and symbolization than *The Emperor Jones.* Here he succeeded in producing a powerful dramatic experience through the sheer vigor of the writing and the vibrancy of the action distributed in concise and visually arresting scenes. The fact, acknowledged by the playwright himself, that the public did not grasp the larger symbolic content did not greatly militate against the fascination and direct effect of the play.

O'Neill was less fortunate in a third expressionistic experiment, *All God's Chillun Got Wings,* involving the marriage of a tarnished white girl and a devoted Negro lover. Here a metaphysical conception of fate seems somewhat arbitrarily inserted into racial and psychological conflicts sufficiently immediate to make abstruseness a limitation rather than a valid extension of the drama. O'Neill dealt here with the subject of miscegenation and an ensuing Strindbergian duel of the sexes in the course of which the neurotically jealous Ella destroys her Negro husband's chances for a career and then, after going berserk and trying to kill him, lapses into a remorseless dependency upon his forgiveness and devotion. O'Neill dissolved the substance of this provocative drama by placing the burden of guilt on God and fate instead of on society. Once more, though, O'Neill's intensity of feeling and uncanny sense of theater came to the rescue of his dramatic reasoning.

The same talents saved his next expressionistic experiment, THE GREAT GOD BROWN, from total disaster, leaving him with a flawed and overworked drama that was nevertheless impressive enough to win respect for his earnestness and his theatrical imagination while disappointing sociological critics. Here too O'Neill hit upon a recognizable social fact, which may be defined as the defeat of the artist in a materialistic and unsympathetic society, and here too he concentrated on private psychology and metaphysical intimations rather than sociology. Here, however, far from veering from the logic of his argument, he pursued it so persistently that he pushed schematization to extremes of abstraction and weakened credibility and reality of character in the melodramatically snarled action of the drama. *The Great God Brown,* which exemplified so much of O'Neill's striving for personal expression that it became his favorite play, was its author's most "successful" failure not merely in practical but also in dramatic and poetic terms. *Marco Millions,* which followed it some two years later (1928), was pallid by comparison. O'Neill's animus against materialistic society led him to write a sardonic comedy on the career of Marco Polo, who turned rapidly into a philistine impervious to beauty and romance despite his travels in the wondrous East of Kubla Khan and the love of Princess Kukachin, the khan's granddaughter. The playwright proved to be too heavy-handed and repetitive, making his point long before the conclusion and overextending the play in performance with his quasi-poetic rhetoric and requirements of spectacle. A lighter touch and a swifter pace, as well as greater verbal and situational inventiveness, were needed to realize its potentialities as satiric comedy.

A return to his metaphysical vein in *Lazarus Laughed* (1928) led him into the blind alley of reiterative pseudophilosophy from which he emerged too rarely to make this huge and unwieldy drama much more than an enormous spectacle strung upon a slender thread of plot and, despite its abundant rhetoric, a subliterary ritualistic effusion. In any case, this work was more suitable for outdoor pageantry than for the ordinary stage. Its chief interest lies in the variety of theatrical means—masks, choruses, crowds, choreographic movement, and other visual effects—O'Neill's stage-struck imagination could muster in the service of an idea. O'Neill was aware of the possibility of pursuing substitutes for religion and dramatized the search for them throughout his career. In *Lazarus Laughed* he temporarily found, or thought he found, an ersatz religion consisting of a mystical denial of death. It provided a doctrine of salvation by affirmation that was vastly more rhetorical than substantial. In *Dynamo*, his next engagement with the problem of faith, which had an unsuccessful though (largely thanks to the scenic genius of Theatre Guild designer Lee Simonson) visually stunning production early in 1929, he dramatized the substitution of machine worship after his hero's renunciation of the puritanical faith of his fathers. While watching a dynamo in operation turning the energy of Connecticut rivers into electricity, O'Neill had been impressed with it as a veritable image of the new god of the scientific age and used it as the dominant symbol in *Dynamo*. Nevertheless, he could not resist his need to return to the subject of faith and the conflict with skepticism, which he described as the "big" subject behind all the little subjects of plays and novels whenever an author is not merely "scribbling around on the surface of things." He returned to the theme but with rather dreary results in *Days Without End*, which O'Neill's latter-day producing organization, the Theatre Guild, presented for a short Broadway run in 1934. This play is for the most part a lesson on the need to return to conventional religious faith (the divided hero, John Loving, who loses his skeptical, diabolical alter ego at the foot of the Cross, apparently appealed more strongly to the Irish than to Americans), even if it is doubtful that O'Neill himself ever regained such faith for more than a brief period.

O'Neill had started a return to modified realism and interest in character drama some half-dozen years earlier with STRANGE INTERLUDE, which became a great Theatre Guild success in the year 1928 and won him a third Pulitzer Prize in 1929. Instead of dealing with metaphysical content and struggles over faith, O'Neill concerned himself here with character dissection and inner conflict. Whatever means he adopted in this play, his schematizations and his recourse to the Elizabethan device of the "aside" on a scale never before attempted on the stage served the author's sole objective of portraying a modern woman in her roles of daughter, wife, lover, and mother. *Strange Interlude* impressed the majority of reviewers and playgoers as a weighty experiment

and, more than that, as a human document. What rigorous criticism was soon tempted to dismiss in that document as mere cliché overinsistently communicated was redeemed by effective confrontations of the chief characters and by the substantiality of Nina Leeds. And its augmented realism was sufficiently successful to direct its author back to the paths of realism he had followed rewardingly in the early sea and waterfront plays.

This was apparent in his MOURNING BECOMES ELECTRA trilogy, when he domesticated Greek legend and its various treatments by the Greek tragic poets. This was truly an enormous undertaking worthy of his ambition to treat significant themes and apply to them the insights and idiom of his own age. Although he employed formal elements in this work, such as a truncated chorus and masklike facial expressions, these did not undercut the fundamentally naturalistic character of the work but merely punctuated and magnified it. Some necessity of art and personal expression kept O'Neill moving back to realistic drama as the style of writing by which his reputation would stand or fall. In *Mourning Becomes Electra* it led him to yield to psychopathology and lapse into Gothic melodrama, for if the play derives much of its power and intensity from Freudian interpretations, the characters are deprived of tragic stature insofar as they become clinical cases. It also led him, two years later, to the pleasant alternative of producing the genial genre painting of *Ah, Wilderness!*, a family comedy set in a small Connecticut city at the beginning of the century. *Ah, Wilderness!* is nothing more —and nothing *less*—than a sunny and uncomplicated comedy of adolescence and peaceful middle age. For the author himself it was only a brief holiday from his most persistent memories, which were normally bleak, and from the contemporary world, about which he never felt particularly cheerful. That it represented only a vacation from a gloomy view of *la condition humaine* was to become evident in his last plays, first brought to the stage many years later while O'Neill was leading a life of mental and physical torment and, in the case of several of his plays, after his death in 1953.

More than a decade, which included World War II, elapsed between the middle and last periods of O'Neill's career, although he received the Nobel Prize in 1936. Illness hampered him and depression over the state of the world, which was veering rapidly toward a global war, immobilized him and kept him virtually bedridden at times. It was not a period to encourage optimism, and there was none forthcoming from O'Neill as he brooded on the past that prepared the way for the dreadful present while he worked on a tremendous cycle of plays tracing the tragic history of an American family from colonial times to his own, destroying some of his completed drafts and leaving other planned plays unwritten or unfinished.

Shortly after the conclusion of World War II, it became possible for him to entertain prospects for new productions, and to allow the publication of two new plays, *The Iceman Cometh*, written in 1939, and *A Moon for the Misbegotten*, completed in 1943. Both were to a degree memory plays, the first dealing with the period of his waterfront days at Jimmy-the-Priest's dive, the second with the broken life of his alcoholic brother James. But the mordancy of both plays derived not from memories (the autobiographical elements were thoroughly transformed) but from a strong and vivid sense of man's private and public failure, which the recently concluded holocaust and the growing materialism of the world only served to confirm. In an interview he gave to the press in September 1946, on the occasion of the Broadway opening of *The Iceman Cometh,* O'Neill held out little hope for man. He included in his indictment his own nation. His country had been given more resources than any other, but while moving ahead rapidly, it had not acquired any real roots because its main idea appeared to be "that everlasting game of trying to possess your own soul by the possession of something outside it."

THE ICEMAN COMETH proved to be one of O'Neill's most powerful as well as most pessimistic plays. Bearing considerable resemblance to Maxim Gorky's turn-of-the-century classic *The Lower Depths* (both plays are set in a cheap boardinghouse for the disreputable and the derelict, and both show man trying to subsist on illusory hopes), *The Iceman Cometh* nevertheless presents a radically different view, in its complete pessimism, from that entertained by the Russian author. O'Neill expressed no hope for man at all and therefore considered illusion to be the necessary anodyne and death a welcome release for bedeviled mankind.

The failure of O'Neill's next production, *A Moon for the Misbegotten,* which was withdrawn after its out-of-town tryout in February and March 1947, marked the end of its author's active participation in the theater. *The Iceman Cometh,* which opened in New York on September 2, 1946, was the last of O'Neill's plays to be seen on Broadway in his lifetime. During his final years O'Neill was stricken with an obscure degenerative disease that made writing and finally even locomotion extremely difficult, although his mind remained clear.

Three years after O'Neill's death, and a decade after *The Iceman Cometh* opened, his posthumous career on Broadway began brilliantly with the José Quintero production of *Long Day's Journey into Night,* which was awarded the Pulitzer Prize in 1957. In many respects a simple naturalistic family drama, without plot contrivances and "well-made" play intrigues, the play presents uncommonly moving revelations of character and human relations.

After *Long Day's Journey into Night,* the New York production of *A Moon for the Misbegotten,* which opened about half a year later (in May 1957), was bound to seem anticlimactic despite the services of the gifted British actress Wendy Hiller in the role of an oversized farm girl who tries to bestow her love on a guilt-laden alcoholic lacking all capacity to receive, let alone to return, it. Faulty in several respects, it was nevertheless another work of considerable compassion, here presented largely in terms of grotesque comedy. Also weak in some respects, *A Touch of the Poet* (which, although written in 1936, first opened on Broadway in 1958, about six months after its world première in Stockholm, Sweden) is chiefly noteworthy for giving us an inkling of what its author had in mind for the dramatic cycle he had planned under the title of *A Tale of Possessors Self-Dispossessed* and abandoned. This play, the sole

finished survivor of the project, dramatized the beginnings of the American family with which the cycle was to deal. Here the daughter of Con Melody, an Irish pretender to aristocratic status reduced to keeping a pub near Boston, resolves to marry the poetical scion of a wealthy Brahmin family despite parental interference. The full significance of the play could not be established without reference to the nonexistent cycle, but its self-sufficient qualities were considerable.

Another play, *More Stately Mansions,* which was apparently to be the fourth in his eleven-play cycle and was to follow *A Touch of the Poet,* was retrieved from the O'Neill papers in Yale University's O'Neill Collection and produced in Stockholm, in November 1962, in considerably shortened form by Dr. Karl Ragnar Gierow, the Royal Dramatic Theatre director who had staged productions of two other posthumous O'Neill works. The manuscript was revised for publication by Dr. Gierow and Donald Gallup, the curator of the O'Neill Collection at Yale. Since this version, released by the Yale University Press in 1964, was prepared from the Swedish acting script, it cannot be judged as an original O'Neill work; the original manuscript is more than twice as long as the published play. Whatever the favorable impression of the Swedish production, the published play may well strike a reader as decidedly scattered in effect. But it is plain that O'Neill wanted to indict the growth of materialism in the modern world. Con Melody's daughter Sara of *A Touch of the Poet* is here married to the young man, Simon Harford, she fancied. But her possessiveness and her rivalry with his equally possessive mother prove to be her undoing; the poet in him dies and he becomes a relentless materialist before breaking down mentally. O'Neill's old feeling for compulsive conflict is once more uppermost in this salvaged but inchoate drama.

There was one more posthumously published work of the final period that shows no decline or dispersion of O'Neill's power, the short two-character masterpiece *Hughie,* written in 1941 and published in 1959, the first of a projected series of one-act plays entitled *By Way of Orbit.* For the most part a monologue spoken by the "Broadway sport" Erie Smith to the night clerk of a shabby New York hotel in the late 1920's, *Hughie* is a tour de force that does not flag for a moment in revealing the emotional vacuity of the narrator and a deceased night clerk, Hughie, whom he used to fill with wonder at his inflated gambling exploits. Marvelously vivid and rhythmic dialogue that seems utterly authentic in its colloquialism and slang in this play recalls O'Neill's early achievements in the best sea pieces of the *S.S. Glencairn* series. *Hughie* was the last testament to O'Neill's prowess in naturalistic playwriting and to his lingering attachment, despite his success with oversized dramas, to the spare one-act play form with which he had first established his reputation as an authentic American playwright.

Nothing needs to be added perhaps to this brief chronicle of the efforts of the one American playwright whose place in the hierarchy of world dramatists seems more or less secure. His power is not often separable from his repetitiveness or even verbosity. His sense of theater was so strong that more often than not his best plays, when well structured, proved to be considerably more effective on stage than a literary reading of them could possibly suggest. His sense of drama was so rarely "posture," despite his not always trustworthy flair for theatricality, that much of his work seemed wrung from him rather than contrived or calculated. In it, a uniquely tormented spirit subsumed much of the twentieth century's dividedness and anguish, largely existential rather than topical. And while the penalty for his metaphysical brooding was often a quasi-philosophical windiness, the reward for his refusal to settle for small temporary gratifications was a dark impressiveness not easily to be dismissed by dwelling on verbal limitations.

The standard editions of O'Neill's works are *The Complete Plays of Eugene O'Neill* (1934–1935) in 12 volumes and *The Plays of Eugene O'Neill* (1946) in 3 volumes. The definitive biography is Arthur and Barbara Gelb's *O'Neill* (1962). Other biographical studies include Doris Alexander's *The Tempering of Eugene O'Neill* (1962) and Agnes Boulton's *Part of a Long Story* (1958). Full-length critical studies include Edwin Engel's *The Haunted Heroes of Eugene O'Neill* (1953) and John H. Raleigh's *The Plays of Eugene O'Neill* (1965). *O'Neill: A Collection of Critical Essays* (1964), edited by John Gassner, provides a wide-ranging selection of critical approaches to the plays.—J. G.

onnagata. In *kabuki* drama, a female impersonator. The *onnagata* has occupied a conspicuous place on the Japanese stage from the earliest recorded times. In 1629 the governmental shogunate issued a decree forbidding women on the stage because of the undesirable effects the women's kabuki (*onna kabuki*) had on social morals. As a result of this ban, male actors began to play female roles by using artificial, stylized female gestures. The art of the onnagata, which reached perfection during the eighteenth-century Genroku period, rests in the symbolic representation of the female roles.

The conventions for the onnagata were established by the first great female impersonator in the kabuki theater, Yoshizawa Ayame I (1673–1729). In his book of sayings, *Ayamegusa,* Yoshizawa advocates a complete mixing of professional and personal life for the onnagata, whereby the onnagata dresses and plays the part of a female, not only on the stage, but also in his private life. For many years this practice was followed, but today the onnagata leads a normal personal life, acting and dressing as a woman only when he appears on stage.

There are several well-established female roles that the onnagata perform, such as the faithful wife, the elegant courtesan, the young girl, and the old woman. In the dramas of chivalry even female warriors appeared, though these are less common on the Japanese than on the Chinese stage. The frail, slender, coy but amorous young woman is the most familiar part.

The onnagata's subtle conventions for femininity provide the degree of formality that sets the standard for the kabuki theater as a whole. In the kabuki theater, this stylization is considered more expressive than realism. This preference for stylization can be seen in the audience's aversion to modern actresses who have tried to perform female roles by imitating the style and gestures of the onnagata. The spectators of the kabuki theater prefer the male onnagata to the

Onnagata IN A SCENE FROM A KABUKI PLAY (JAPAN NATIONAL TOURIST ORGANIZATION)

female actresses because the viewers do not want the distinction between actor and character blurred, as it is when a female plays the part of a woman.

The recent, great Japanese female impersonators, Nakamura Tokizo and Nakamura Utaemon, are dead. But the kabuki theater is still active, and the onnagata, the stronghold on which this type of theater rests, continues to perform.

Probably the best description in English of the art of the onnagata is in *The Kabuki Theatre of Japan* (1955) by A. C. Scott. See also Faubion Bowers, *Japanese Theatre* (1952), and Earle Ernst, *The Kabuki Theatre* (1956).—H. W. W.

operetta. Combining music and drama has produced many felicitous results, but it has also given rise to a variety of names intended to describe them. Unfortunately for classifiers, dividing lines between genres are not clear and the names are not always mutually exclusive. The definitions in *Webster's New International Dictionary* (2nd ed.) for the closely related types, operetta and musical comedy, seem almost interchangeable:

operetta. A light, amusing, often farcical musical-dramatic work with an inconsequential plot, cheerful music, and spoken dialogue.

musical comedy. A type of theatrical performance, typically whimsical or picturesque, consisting of musical numbers and dialogue, with a slender plot.

Hence, the most effective way to define and discuss operetta is to show how and from what it has developed. Not only does this approach help clarify some other terms commonly associated with works that combine music and drama, but it also indicates the antecedents of musical comedy. See MUSICAL COMEDY.

The roots of operetta, which literally means "little opera" in Italian, can be traced to two works, one English, the other Italian. The first, *The Beggar's Opera* (1728), a ballad opera with a satiric text by John Gay and a score arranged from popular ballads by John Pepusch, was a direct reaction to Handelian and Italian opera, with their noble themes, exalted personages, and elaborate baroque music. Gay's work was an immediate success, not merely because it was novel, but also because it treated contemporary events and people with a wry, dry humor and found its subject matter not on Mount Olympus nor among history's elite but in London's underworld. The ballad opera, of which *The Beggar's Opera* is a prototype, with its simple, familiar music, appealed to the average theatergoer and became firmly established in England, paving the way for future developments in comic opera.

The second, Giovanni Pergolesi's *La Serva padrona* (*The Servant-Mistress*, 1733), marked the beginning of *opera buffa* (comic opera) in Italy. It was derived from the *intermezzo*, a comic sketch with music, popular in the sixteenth and seventeenth centuries and often played between the acts of serious operas to lighten the tension. Pergolesi's librettist, G. A. Federico, drew his characters from daily life, treating them with lively humor. Domenico Cimarosa, Giovanni Paisiello, and Gioacchino Rossini also composed works of this genre.

Paris first saw the Pergolesi-Federico work in 1752, performed by a traveling Italian troupe. As a strong contrast to the classical operas of Jean Philippe Rameau, the opera buffa was welcomed, especially by Jean Jacques Rousseau, who imitated the form in *Le Devin du village* (*The Village Soothsayer,* 1752).

Before that time, however, a new French form, the *opéra comique,* was developing. It was designed to evade the restrictions on opera performances that gave the Académie de Musique a virtual monopoly. Initially, it was a mixture of short sketches, topical songs, and parodies of well-known operas. Performed at the fairs of St. Laurent and St. Germain, these works proved so popular that in 1715 they came under the control of the Théâtre de l'Opéra-Comique. Actually, opéra comique was not always comic, as the name suggests. The works differed from conventional serious opera chiefly in having spoken dialogue rather than recitatives and music that was lighter and more melodic than the customary baroque elaboration. A distinctly comic offshoot of the opéra comique was the *opéra bouffe,* similar to the Italian opera buffa in manner and materials.

In 1848, with the emergence of the conductor-composer Hervé, whose real name was Florimond Ronger (1825–1892), opéra bouffe became *opérette,* though both names have been used to describe works of the latter genre. Hervé, somewhat in the manner of the Marquis de Sade at Charenton, helped lunatics confined in Paris' Bicêtre Hospital to forget their obsessions, at least temporarily, by allowing them to participate in short musical plays. So much were these admired that Hervé was made conductor of the Théâtre du Palais-Royal, a position that gave him the opportunity to compose and experiment. Eventually he earned fame as a composer of opérettes such as *Mam'zelle Nitouche* (1883), in which lively songs are linked to a plot by Henri Meilhac and Albert Mil-

DRAWING OF A SCENE FROM JOHN GAY'S *The Beggar's Opera* (THEATRE COLLECTION, NEW YORK PUBLIC LIBRARY AT LINCOLN CENTER)

laud. The story is typical of the genre: a convent school organist, Célestin, a seemingly pious young man, is actually a composer of operettas. His equal in sham piety is Denise, a student who longs for the worldly life of Paris. Hilarious but improbable plot complications include Denise stepping into the starring role of a new operetta on opening night, with no previous stage experience. Naturally, she is a tremendous success, thus firmly welding another theater cliché to the world of music.

It has long been the fashion to dismiss the plots of operetta as incredible, sentimental, romantic, nostalgic, or fantastic, but to do so is to slight the potential of the operetta librettist and the ability of the composer to sustain, develop, and enlarge the librettist's conception. Excellent examples of successful collaborations are the operettas created by playwrights Henri Meilhac (1831–1897) and Ludovic Halévy (1833–1908) with composer Jacques Offenbach. These men brought the genre to its peak as an instrument of telling satire during the Second Empire (1852–1870). Although the relative value of words and music in the lyric theater has often been debated, equal appreciation for the contributions of both sides seems to have greeted most of the products of this collaboration. With the passage of time, however, Offenbach's music has become more familiar, while the satirical content of Halévy's and Meilhac's librettos, at least in topical terms, has become more remote. Add to this development the custom of referring to works for the lyric theater by composer rather than by librettist, and it is small wonder that Meilhac and Halévy are now seldom mentioned in connection with Offenbach.

Nonetheless, they established patterns and standards for their successors, especially the Viennese. Plots always revolve around one or more love affairs, frequently complicated by misunderstandings, rivalries, prohibitions, and other barriers to Eros. Customarily the closing moments of operettas provide happy endings as predictable as they are untrue to life. Characters are stereotypes, and they appear in each plot in slightly altered guises. Such conventions, endlessly repeated, have led critics to attack playwrights for their lack of invention, saving their praise for the composers' music. Yet the very nature of the genre requires that the plot and characters be somewhat subservient to the demands of the musical theater. This does not mean that plots were customarily structured to fit previously composed music, though that of course has happened. In many cases, the initiative in establishing a collaboration was taken by a theater manager or by the composer, not by the librettist. Offenbach had a number of coworkers at various times. Meilhac and Halévy, both men of the theater, well understood the technical and formal demands of operetta. They knew Offenbach's special strengths; they realized Parisians expected lively dance numbers and were more interested in the stars and the music than in the story; they were aware that Offenbach had to balance the voices and that tenors, sopranos, baritones, and basses were traditionally associated with certain character types.

The achievement of these librettists is that, given such limitations, they were able to create formula plots that managed to make a pertinent satiric comment on contemporary life, even though their subject matter varied widely. Its range included myth—*La Belle Hélène* (1864); fairy tale—*Barbe-Bleu* (*Bluebeard*, 1866); romantic fantasy—*La Grande Duchesse de Gérolstein* (1867); exaggerated reality—*La Vie Parisienne* (*Parisian Life*, 1866); and period fiction—*La Périchole* (1868). Their characters, though typed, are something more than mere puppets. The collaborators understood the importance of relating music to action, although they were not as successful at this as the best writers and composers of the more recent and more realistic musical theater.

Although the material of Offenbach's writers seems now rather dated—what was once a sharp thrust into the ego is now a soft, sentimental pat—the frequent new productions in Austria, Germany, France, and England, where Offenbach's works remain popular, indicate that Meilhac, Halévy and Offenbach still offer some amusing insights into human character, despite the formulas. In fact, attempts in recent Sadler's Wells productions to modernize the operettas with up-to-date settings, costumes, and topical references have been most successful.

A summary of *Parisian Life,* which Offenbach himself labeled an opéra bouffe, displays the typical elements. Gardefeu and Bobinet are waiting at the Gare du l'Ouest for a young lady, Metella. When the train arrives, she snubs them. Gardefeu's former valet, Joseph, now working as a guide for the Grand Hotel, has come to meet the Swedish Baron Gondremarck and his wife. Gardefeu bribes Joseph to take them to his own house, to be disguised as a hotel annex, in hopes that he can court the beautiful baroness. Also among the arrivals on the train is a rich Brazilian who has come to spend his fortune on Parisian women.

At home, Gardefeu quickly enlists his shoemaker, Herr Frick, and a glovemaker, Gabrielle, in the plot. To deceive the baron and create the right hotel atmosphere, they will bring their servant friends. Bobinet proposes an elaborate bogus reception at his aristocratic aunt's temporarily vacant apartment. The baron has a letter of introduction to Metella, which he asks Gardefeu to deliver. Later she arrives. The phony hotel guests assemble, noisily clamoring for dinner, generally mocking the behavior of Second Empire society with their grotesque mannerisms.

The next evening, Bobinet's reception pleases the baron, who takes a fancy to a maid who is presented as the wife of the admiral of the Swiss navy. The baroness is being entertained elsewhere by Gardefeu. A champagne supper provides an atmosphere of joyous hilarity, capped by Offenbach's finale, "Tout tourne, tout danse."

Discovering the trick Gardefeu has played, the baron moves to the real hotel. He meets Metella for a private supper, but she tells him she is returning to her former lover, Gardefeu. She persuades him to give her heavily veiled friend—actually the baroness—supper instead. The baron, enraged, breaks into the rich Brazilian's dazzling party in the same restaurant to challenge Gardefeu to a duel. The host calms him, and the baron eventually has to agree that Gardefeu did provide good entertainment and that he has not behaved well toward his own wife. All are reconciled as the party increases in hilarity, infected by the spirited cancan.

In only twenty-five years, Offenbach wrote more than ninety operettas. But, with the fall of Napoleon III, his works went out of style. French audiences were less receptive to the ribaldry and needling satire of the plots, possibly because of the humiliating French defeat in the Franco-Prussian War and the growth of Republican sentiment. Offenbach was quickly replaced in popular favor by Charles Lecocq, who, with the help of various librettists, provided escapist fare, avoiding specific, critical comments on his times. His best-known works are *La Fille de Madame Angot* (*The Daughter of Madame Angot*, 1872), *Giroflé-Girofla* (1874), and *Le Petit Duc* (*The Little Duke*, 1878). The latter, a tears-and-smiles period piece, owed its book to Meilhac and Halévy, who were nothing if not able to move with the times.

Lecocq's successors include Robert Planquette, composer of *Les Cloches de Corneville* (*The Chimes of Normandy*, 1877), who also composed for the London stage; André Messager, who wrote *Véronique* (1898); and Reynaldo Hahn, who conceived *Ciboulette* (1923). Also among the more successful practictioners of the genre in France were Louis Varney, Claude Terrasse, Henri Christiné, and Maurice Yvain.

Spain, geographically and often culturally cut off from the rest of Europe, developed its own version of operetta, the *zarzuela,* which began as a play interspersed with songs and dances. The great Spanish dramatist Calderón wrote the first—*El Golfo de las Sirenas* (*The Gulf of the Sirens,* 1657). Initially, traditional music was used, as in the ballad opera, but in time the tunes were specially composed. Another form, the *tonadilla,* was similar to the Italian intermezzo. Both were temporarily obliterated when the Italian opera invaded Spain, but the zarzuela was revived in the mid-1830's. Audiences were often expected to participate by singing along and by chatting with the actors, which made it a truly popular form.

Resembling French operetta and having one to four acts, the zarzuela features Spanish types such as glamorous bullfighters, villainous bandits, beggars, and portly clergy. The stories are held together with generous doses of folk music and dance. Though generally light, they can be tragic. Among the better ones are Joaquin Gaztanbide's *El Valle de Andorra* (*The Valley of Andorra,* 1852), *Catalina* (1855), and *Los Magyares* (*The Magyars,* 1857) and Amadeo Vives' *Bohemios* (1920) and *Dona Francisquita* (1923).

It was in Vienna that the operetta reached its zenith, but its exact origins there are in dispute. Some commentators insist that because of Offenbach's popularity in the Austrian capital—and because of the high fees he demanded—a native and less expensive substitute had to be found. It is true that the emergence of Johann Strauss II, at the age of forty-five, as an operetta composer was due to pressure exerted on him by Maximilian Steiner, a Viennese manager, and by Strauss's wife, the singer Jetti Treffz, who were sure he could match the Parisian's success. He proved to be the man who could displace Offenbach, but that does not mean that the German-language operetta can simply be labeled an extension or a development of French models, strong as their influence may have been.

Operetta in German can trace its ancestry back to the *Singspiel,* a mid-eighteenth-century entertainment. Devised by Johann Hiller, it is derived from a German adaptation of *The Beggar's Opera* and hence related to the English ballad opera. The Singspiel combined dialogue with songs that often used well-loved folk tunes. At the same time, Italian opera buffa was also popular, attracting Gluck, Haydn, Dittersdorf, and Mozart to compose for the genre. Mozart's contribution to the Singspiel form includes *Der Schauspieldirektor* (*The Theatre Director,* 1786), which is charming but slight, and his *Die Entführung aus dem Serail* (*The Abduction from the Seraglio,* 1781), which continues to hold the stage.

From Singspiel the German comic opera of the nineteenth century developed, represented by such composers as Otto Nicolai and Albert Lortzing. Franz von Suppé made the transition from comic opera to operetta with such works as *Die Schöne Galatea* (*Beautiful Galatea,* 1865) and *Boccaccio* (1879), although the dividing line between the genres became somewhat blurred in the process.

It was Strauss, however, who came to dominate the Viennese operetta scene. Already in 1844 a successful dance-band conductor and composer, Strauss soon showed why he had earned the title of the "Waltz King." In his operettas, a rich mixture of romantic sentiment, lively humor, aristocratic glitter, and mistaken identities was plotted in such a way as to include inevitably an elaborate ballroom scene with an obligatory waltz. Strauss, not bound to any one playwright, had a number of collaborators and used the books that offered him the elements he needed. Critics were quick to note that he wrote light, lilting music for comic and character songs, using a more operatic mode for romantic numbers. His works, perhaps more than most operettas, explain the old aphorism: operetta requires singers who can act, not actors who can sing.

Among the more famous of his operettas are *Die Fledermaus* (*The Bat,* 1874), *Eine Nacht in Venedig* (*A Night in Venice,* 1883), *Der Zigeunerbaron* (*The Gypsy Baron,* 1885), and *Weiner Blut* (*Vienna Blood,* 1899).

Die Fledermaus, which is sometimes offered in English as *Rosalinda,* involves Viennese society in love intrigues, deceptions, mistaken identities, elaborate balls and parties, and in the less elegant side of life as well. If these ingredients bear a strong resemblance to those of Offenbach's *Parisian Life,* it is no mere coincidence. Strauss's librettists, Carl Haffner and Richard Genée, plundered a script, *Le Réveillon* (*The Midnight Supper*), by Meilhac and Halévy, for the burden of their plot, framing it with details lifted from R. Bendix's comedy *Das Gefängnis* (*The Prison*).

In detail, fortunately, the similarity to Offenbach's work is less obvious. Eisenstein, a wealthy man, is preparing to go to jail for a week for insulting a policeman. His friend, Dr. Falke, arrives to invite him to Prince Orlovsky's fabulous party, where all the ladies of the ballet will be present. Eisenstein agrees to delay jail until the morrow and goes off with

Falke, little suspecting this is part of a plot. Falke wants revenge. (On their way home from a masquerade, Eisenstein once left the alcohol- and sleep-befuddled Falke, dressed as a bat, alone in the woods. Walking home the next morning, Falke was ridiculed and as a result acquired the nickname of "Dr. Bat.")

Meanwhile, Eisenstein's pert maid, Adele, has also received an invitation to the party, which her dancer sister will also attend. To leave the house, she pretends she has a sick relative, but Eisenstein's beautiful wife, Rosalinda, is glad to be rid of her. She is entertaining an old love, the tenor Alfred. An intimate supper is interrupted by the prison governer, come for Eisenstein. Embarrassed, Rosalinda can only insist that Alfred is her husband and send him off to prison.

At the elaborate ball, Falke introduces the disguised Eisenstein to Adele, also in disguise. He is charmed by her, but later is even more impressed by a ravishing Hungarian countess—actually Rosalinda, who is aiding Falke's plot. She steals Eisenstein's watch so she can later reproach him for his philandering. Eisenstein and the prison governor strike up a friendship, neither aware of the other's true identity. Adele and her sister find themselves a center of attention. Finally, at the prison, all conflicts are resolved. Eisenstein's dallying with the countess is canceled by Rosalinda's flirting with the luckless Alfred.

Rivaling Strauss in output was Franz Lehár, whose most famous operetta is *Die Lustige Witwe* (*The Merry Widow*, 1905). His *Das Land des Lächelns* (*The Land of Smiles*, 1929), borrowed from an earlier stage work, *The Yellow Jacket*, has also continued to hold the European operetta stage despite its puerile notions of the marriage of East and West. Oscar Straus—no relation to Johann Strauss II—was more wise when he chose Shaw's *Arms and the Man* as the basis for his *Der Tapfere Soldat* (*The Chocolate Soldier*, 1908), in a version by Rudolf Bernauer and Leopold Jacobson.

Emmerich Kálmán, who frequently depended for his librettos on either the team of Leo Stein and Bela Jenbach or that of Julius Brammer and Alfred Grünwald, included in his generous collection of operettas a range of aristocratic titles, such as *Die Czardasfürstin* (*The Gypsy Princess*, 1915), *Die Gräfin Mariza* (*Countess Mariza*, 1924), *Die Zirkusprinzessin*, (*The Circus Princess*, 1926), *Die Herzogin von Chicago* (*The Duchess of Chicago*, 1928), and *Kaiserin Josephine* (*Empress Josephine*, 1936).

Other practitioners of the Viennese style—which also had its imitators in Berlin—were Karl Millöcker, with *Der Bettelstudent* (*The Beggar Student*, 1882); Karl Zeller, with *Der Vogelhändler* (*The Bird-Seller*, 1891); Richard Heuberger, with *Der Opernball* (*The Opera Ball*, 1898); and Leo Fall, with *Die Dollar Prinzessin* (*The Dollar Princess*, 1907).

Both overfamiliarity and lack of sophistication have made many of these works no longer viable on the American stage, although obvious nostalgia for former, perhaps better times—especially the days of the titled aristocracy—has helped them to survive in Europe. The tradition of state-subsidized repertory theaters has never allowed the genre to die out; and it has never had to depend on commercial re-

vivals, although these have generally been quite successful. In Munich, the Theater am Gärtnerplatz, and in Vienna, the Volksoper, both subventioned theaters, provide a nearly year-round program of French and German operetta, introducing now and then a comic opera or modern musical into the repertory. Operettas like *The Merry Widow* and *Die Fledermaus*, which have maintained their popularity in America, appear to survive because of their appealing and well-loved scores, not because of their plots. One of the last of the type to be written in German was Ralph Benatzky's *Im Weissen Rössl* (*White Horse Inn*, 1930), with a book by Hans Müller and Erik Charell and lyrics by Robert Gilbert. Viennese composer Robert Stolz still works in the genre.

While all of these works, which were so successful on the Continent, were also generally admired in England and America, it must not be thought there were no practitioners in English. England's break with serious opera, as noted, began with *The Beggar's Opera*, a ballad opera that encouraged a long succession of imitations. Many of these enjoyed great popularity, giving rise in time to the genre of comic opera. The works of William S. Gilbert and Sir Arthur Sullivan (see Sir William S. GILBERT) are the most impressive achievement, both because of their number and because of the skilled integration of book and score to provide a parody portrait of contemporary life far more witty and penetrating than anything of Offenbach. There are those who would classify *The Mikado* (1885) as an operetta, along with, say, Lehár's *The Land of Smiles*. Though convenient, this is also confusing, for the world of Gilbert and Sullivan has nothing in common with that of Lehár and Strauss.

From the burlesque, a popular form of entertainment in nineteenth-century London, musical comedy gradually developed. Musical comedy also borrowed from operetta and comic opera and gradually displaced them, although the two latter genres continued to have advocates well into the twentieth century. Noel Coward's *Bittersweet* (1929) was one of the last and best evocations of a dying world, a way of life that had been swept away by war and progress. Ivor Novello wrote, composed, and starred in a series of imitation Viennese operettas, depending on Christopher Hassall for his lyrics. These Ruritanian adventures, which Novello described variously as "musical romances" and "romantic plays with music," include *Glamorous Night* (1935), *The Dancing Years* (1939), and *King's Rhapsody* (1949).

The American musical stage saw its first production of the English ballad opera *Flora* in a Charleston, South Carolina, courtroom in 1735. The genre remained popular, and, in the absence of native inventiveness, other musical forms were imported from England, among them the burlesque and the extravaganza. In these forms are to be found the precursors of American musical comedy. During the second half of the nineteenth century, however, the operettas of Offenbach and Lecocq, of Franz von Suppé and Johann Strauss II, and the comic operas of Gilbert and Sullivan won great popularity. They were immediately imitated. Even the "March King," John Philip Souza, tried his hand, producing *El Capitan* (1896) and *Victory* (1915), among some dozen operettas. The influence of Viennese works was clear when artists like Reginald De Koven, Victor Herbert, Rudolf Friml, and Sigmund Romberg presented their efforts to the public. De Koven's *Robin Hood* (1890) is now chiefly remembered, if at all, for "Oh, Promise Me," a song much favored at weddings in the early decades of the new century.

Victor Herbert used various librettists, collaborating with Henry Blossom on three favorites: *Mlle. Modiste* (1905), *The Red Mill* (1906), and *Eileen* (1917). It is in Herbert's music, not in the books, that the strength of most of his operettas lies. *Eileen,* a story of the Irish Rebellion of 1798, had perhaps the most effective libretto. Herbert spent more time on this score than on any other, and its lack of success remained a permanent disappointment to him. Critics admired his scores, noting that they often verged on the operatic in conception, as in *Sweethearts* (1913). Other Herbert successes are *The Fortune Teller* (1898), *Babes in Toyland* (1903), and *Naughty Marietta* (1910).

Composer Rudolf Friml teamed with Otto Harbach to create *The Firefly* (1912), at the invitation of producer Arthur Hammerstein, when it became clear that Herbert would not write it as previously planned. Another collaboration at Hammerstein's behest was *Rose Marie* (1924), with composer Herbert Stothart and librettists Harbach and Oscar Hammerstein II, both of whom were to make contributions to the genre of musical comedy.

Sigmund Romberg, like his follow composers, worked with a number of librettists. *Maytime* (1917) linked him with Rida Young and Cyrus Wood; *Blossom Time* (1921) and *The Student Prince* (1924), with Dorothy Donnelly; *The Desert Song* (1926), with the ubiquitous Harbach and Hammerstein, assisted by Frank Mandel; and *The New Moon* (1928), with Hammerstein, Mandel, and Lawrence Schwab.

The increasing number of people involved in carpentering the plots is a sign of the growth of musical theater in America as a valuable commodity, packaged by a committee of entrepreneurs and artists. What is notable is that in such a climate men like Friml, Romberg, and Herbert were still able to project their musical talents onto an often banal book and give the material interest, charm, and even dignity.

In general it is not unfair to say that the business of writing dialogue and lyrics for operettas has not been the playwright's shining hour. The ingenuity with which current productions are staged in Europe suggests that these works have already won a permanent place in lyric theater as period pieces and for their scores. Yet it is for their music that they are most valued. The pen is mightier than the sword, but the conductor's baton may prove to be more powerful than either.

David Ewen, an informed, tireless anthologizer and commentator on operetta and musical comedy, offers in his *The Book of European Light Opera* (1962) pertinent information on production dates, casts, and plot summaries, as well as general remarks about the genre. *Kulturgeschichte der Operette* (1961), by Bernard Grun, is an interesting survey of the development of this form. Of Mark Lubbock's *The Complete Book of Light Opera* (1962), it may be said that it is far more inclusive than Ewen's book cited above, thanks in part to the fact that the American section has been provided by Ewen himself. Wilhelm Zentner has put together an excellent and compact guide in *Reclam's Opern- und Operettenführer* (1964), which can be especially useful to German-reading theater-lovers.—G. L.

Opitz, Martin (1597–1639). Silesian poet, critic, and court functionary, whose poetics set the definitive tone in German letters for the seventeenth century. Born in Bunzlau into a middle-class family, Opitz studied at Frankfort on the Oder, concluding his education with a journey to Holland and Jutland in 1621. Returning home, he assumed the position of a secondary-school teacher in Transylvania but from 1623 on lived in Liegnitz, holding various civil service posts. He eventually entered the diplomatic services and finally served as historiographer to the king of Poland in Danzig. His major contributions, however, were in poetry: In 1625 he was officially crowned laureate in Vienna.

Opitz' reputation today rests chiefly on his activities as a writer of sonnets and purifier and improver of the German language. His *Buch von der deutschen Poeterey* ("Book of German Poetics"), written in 1624, was one of the earliest modern German attempts to formulate poetic rules. Taking his models for rhetoric from classical antiquity, France, Italy, and Holland, the poet attempted to answer the need for improved verse technique. Although his work deals largely with poetry, its effects on the development of the drama were nonetheless considerable. Ignoring the "German" drama of Hans Sachs and Jakob Ayrer, and disclaiming English influences, Opitz formulated drama based on classical and

MARTIN OPITZ (GERMAN INFORMATION CENTER)

French patterns. He also reaffirmed the general artistic precept of the period, that art, in this case drama, served a moral purpose, providing a concrete, idealized example of behavior in fortune or misfortune. Comedy and tragedy were differentiated according to subject matter, a dichotomy that was to be enforced until the time of Lessing: Only kings and the most noble persons were worthy of tragedy. Only the royal will, violence, fires, incest, and similar topics were fit for presentation in the tragedy. Comedy, on the other hand, was obliged to portray figures of low birth and their activities, such as weddings, games, lies, and deception.

Opitz translated Seneca and *Antigone,* wrote several dramas of his own, by way of illustration, and translated the first German opera text, *Dafne,* in 1635. His efforts, important as they were to the contemporary seventeenth-century stage, nonetheless influenced German drama for some time to come. His attention to classical antiquity as a source of materials and values, as well as his disavowal of indigenous German drama, affected both tragedy and comedy until far into the eighteenth century. These restrictions also reaffirmed the notion that German drama is the property of the learned.—B. M. M.

Oresteia (458 B.C.). A tetralogy by AESCHYLUS. Aeschylus presented this group of plays—*Agamemnon, Choephori (Libation Bearers), Eumenides,* and the satyr play *Proteus*—at the tragic contest of the Great Dionysia, Athens, and won first prize. The first three are extant, and together constitute the only complete example of a dramatic form in which Aeschylus, unlike the later Greek tragedians, seems to have specialized: the connected tragic trilogy.

Agamemnon. It is the darkness before dawn, sometime in the tenth year of the Trojan War. On the roof of King Agamemnon's palace in Argos, a bored Watchman waits for the beacon signal which will announce the fall of Troy. He at last sees "the dark fire . . . night's day light"; with a cry of joy and a murmur of foreboding he leaves his post. Enter the Chorus of Argive elders. In a chant and song which form the longest and perhaps the finest choral passage in Greek tragedy (lines 40–257), they explore the moral background of the war: a confused tissue of rights and wrongs. Paris' theft of Helen was avenged on all Troy by Agamemnon's armada—but that armada could not sail without the king's sacrifice of his own daughter, Iphigenia. At the center of the great ode, a hymn within a song, stands a meditation on Zeus as the solution to perplexity, the imposer of the law "learning by suffering." In the following scene Queen Clytemnestra convinces the still bewildered old men that her relays of fire across the Aegean Sea have told the truth: Troy is annihilated. After another great song in which they balance the crime of Paris against the folly of Agamemnon's war (355–487), the Chorus see a herald arriving. His news is good and bad: Agamemnon is home, but only after losing much of his fleet in a mighty storm. In a third ode (681–781) the Chorus' imagination pictures with terrible vividness another partner in the Trojan crime, Helen, and, equally vividly, the contasting figures of Hybris and Justice. Now follows the

A SCENE FROM AESCHYLUS' *Oresteia* (GREEK NATIONAL TOURIST OFFICE)

"tapestry scene," beginning with King Agamemnon's entrance in a chariot, followed by his captive mistress, the inspired Cassandra, daughter of Priam. After Clytemnestra and Agamemnon have greeted each other in tense speeches, she tempts him to walk into his palace on purple tapestries: as a token of his superhuman glory, he must not touch the earth with the foot that has trampled on Troy. Agamemnon yields doubtfully and exits through the palace door. The Chorus are terrified, but they do not quite know why. The next scene only increases their muddled, paralyzed fear. Cassandra, prophesying in song and speech, envisions all the evil that has built up to this explosive point: not only the crimes of Troy, but the wickedness latent in Agamemnon's family—the Thyestean feast (in which Atreus, Agamemnon's father, had tricked his brother Thyestes into eating his own children's flesh) and Clytemnestra's adultery with Thyestes' surviving son, Aegisthus. At the same time Cassandra clearly describes the imminent murders of Agamemnon and of herself. Even when she has stripped off her prophetic robes and walked through the palace door, the Chorus remain uncomprehending—until the death scream of Agamemnon from within. Clytemnestra appears triumphant at the open door, standing over the bodies of Agamemnon and Cassandra. But her triumph gradually subsides in the following dialogue (partly sung) with the Chorus, in which the responsibility for these horrible events is debated. By the time her paramour, Aegisthus, enters, crowing over his vengeance, she is subdued. She even restrains him when, in the final turbulent lines of the play, he is about to set his bodyguard on the Chorus, who rebelliously invoke the name of Agamemnon's son, Orestes.

Choephori. The earlier part of the play's action is centered on Agamemnon's tomb mound. Orestes, returning from his long exile in Phocis with his friend Pylades, enters and offers a lock of his hair at the grave. The two young men stand aside at the approach of a dismal, black-clad Chorus of captive women accompanied by Orestes' sister, Electra. The women have been sent by Clytemnestra, in consequence of an ominous dream, to propitiate the dead king with tomb offerings, but they persuade Electra to pervert the ritual into a prayer for the return of Orestes as his father's avenger. As she pours her libations on the mound, Electra notices the hair and footprints of Orestes. Her intuition of the truth is confirmed when he steps out from his concealment and shows her a piece of tapestry that she wove for him as a child. Orestes explains how Apollo, with dreadful threats, has sent him home to avenge his father. Orestes, the Chorus, and Electra in turn lament Agamemnon in a grim operatic episode and seek to conjure strength from his grave. Finally Orestes outlines his murder plan. Alone, the Chorus sing of the wickedness of women in past time and of the near approach of Justice (585–691).

After this central ode, the door of the palace (which has probably been visible in the background from the start) becomes the focus of action. Orestes and Pylades enter, disguised as Phocian travelers, and announce to Clytemnestra that Orestes has died in exile. In reward for this service, Clytemnestra graciously welcomes them in. The Nurse, who looked after Orestes as an infant, is in tears at the news. She

has been sent to tell Aegisthus to come with his bodyguard, but the Chorus easily persuade the simple old woman to change the message: let him come alone. After a choral ode, Aegisthus arrives and passes into the palace; shortly afterward an offstage howl announces his death. Clytemnestra enters, to be confronted by Orestes. Encouraged by Pylades, who here speaks for the only time in the play (900–902), Orestes forces his mother—line by line, step by step—back into the door. The Chorus now sing an ode of joy, at the end of which the door is thrown open again, and Orestes is seen standing over the dead Clytemnestra and Aegisthus. On his orders, servants hold up a bloodstained relic, the great robe in which Agamemnon was murdered. But Orestes (unlike his mother in the corresponding tableau of *Agamemnon*) shows no sign of triumph, only anger, then sadness, and finally frenzy as he sees, in his mind's eye, the Furies of his mother's curse closing in on him. He rushes wildly from the stage to seek the help of Apollo at Delphi. The Chorus recoil from joy to grief: when will the storm of suffering end?

Eumenides. Before Apollo's calm temple at Delphi, the Prophetess solemnly prays to the gods of the locality before the day's ritual. She enters the sanctuary but a moment later crawls out again, terrified. In Apollo's own house she has seen a man dripping with blood and, sleeping by him, a black swarm of unspeakable female beings, the Furies. She calls on Apollo, who dismisses Orestes on a long series of wanderings which are to culminate at Athens. Now enters the piteous ghost of Clytemnestra, who rouses the sleeping chorus of Furies from the temple to hunt down her murderer. During their opening song the ghost disappears, and the Furies are next confronted by Apollo, who threatens them with his bow and rudely dismisses them from the sanctuary. The Furies leave in pursuit of Orestes.

At line 235 the temple in the background becomes a temple of Athena at Athens, probably on the Acropolis. An unknown length of time has passed. Orestes, his wanderings over, enters and clasps Athena's image, but he is followed closely by the Furies, who encircle him and sing a magic "binding song." At this crisis Athena herself enters (347), and, after courteously inquiring into the identity of the Furies and Orestes, announces that the issue between them can only be settled by a trial. She leaves to select a jury of Athenian citizens. After a song by the Furies (490–565) comes the great "trial scene." The Furies prosecute Orestes for matricide, Apollo defends him, and Athena presides over a court which she now formally establishes forever: the Athenian Areopagus. By direction of Athena, Orestes is acquitted on an even vote and leaves for Argos, vowing eternal friendship between his city and Athens.

Thus the human vendetta (which originated so far away, even before the beginning of the trilogy—in Troy, in the Thyestean feast) is ended in a court of law. But there remains a feud which threatens to split the universe. In the scene 778 ff. the Furies storm in song against the Olympian gods who have thus taken away their right to prosecute bloodguilt. With loud appeals to their mother, Night, they threaten to blight the land with their venom. Only slowly do Athena's calm speeches persuade them to remit their right and instead to accept an honored place in

Athens, worshipped as fertility goddesses in the rock-cleft under the Areopagus. A triumphant musical dialogue follows, sung by the Furies (who are now becoming the *Eumenides,* "Kindly Ones," of the play's title) and chanted by Athena. The blessings of fertility, justice, and civic peace are called down on Athens. Toward the end a great procession of Athenians forms up, and the Chorus are dressed in purple robes. In a final burst of song they are escorted, by the glare of torchlight, toward their new home in the Areopagus rock.

Proteus. The title and the few fragments of this lost satyr play, which rounded off the *Oresteia* as designed by Aeschylus, are enough to show that it concerned a rather absurd adventure of Agamemnon's brother, Menelaus, who was driven astray in the great storm described by the herald in *Agamemnon* (lines 617–633 in that play surely point forward to *Proteus*). The story was evidently taken, in outline, from Homer's *Odyssey.*

A spectator at the original performance of the *Oresteia* saw in one sense four dramas but, in another, a single super-drama, of a scale and complexity never surpassed in the ancient theater. The *Oresteia* trilogy (from here on the lost *Proteus* must be left out of account) is essentially a sustained vision of humanity's emergence out of moral and political chaos into a state where the opposing forces that govern life are recognized and controlled. In this vision plot and character, as understood by post-Aeschylean dramatists, are by no means the only significant elements. Aeschylus here fuses their effects with the effects of choral lyric, verbal, and physical imagery, emotional suspense, and visual shock into what can only be described as a total assault on his audience. A Greek story (found in the anonymous ancient *Life of Aeschylus*) that the first appearance of the Furies in the *Eumenides* caused children in the audience to faint and women to miscarry has been ridiculed by scholars. But even though it is probably an invention, it pungently summarizes an important aspect of the dramaturgy of the *Oresteia.*

Each of the three plays has its own character and atmosphere, in accordance with the progress of the vision. Nowhere is Aeschylus' endless versatility more impressively demonstrated than in this trilogy. *Agamemnon* has the compulsive, bewildering quality of nightmare, where everything can dissolve into everything else. The apparently simple imagery of the victorious light that flashes out of darkness in the Prologue is soon seen to be utterly ambiguous; according to the participant's viewpoint it means victory and disaster, joy and sorrow. The sexes and their relations are confused: Clytemnestra has a "man-thinking heart" (11); Aegisthus is a "woman" (1625); the center of Cassandra's prophecy—which no one present understands—is "Female slayer of male!" (1231). All parties claim that *dike* (one meaning of which is "justice") is on their side. No man is what he seems: smiling faces mask villainous thoughts (788–798, and the entire "tapestry scene"). There is only one constant meaning in this dream world: murder means murder. As Agamemnon killed Iphigenia, so he must die in turn. The drifting memories of the Chorus in the first three odes—of the chain of crimes that links defeated Troy

to victorious Argos—are not irrelevant to Agamemnon's death; nor are Cassandra's visions, of an ancient palace steeped in blood. All this guilt, personal and national, culminates in Clytemnestra's murder stroke.

In *Choephori* the issues and the individuals become more distinct, and the dramatic action is correspondingly faster. The rule that murder means murder persists, and Orestes, in the view of the Chorus and of Apollo's oracle (269 ff.), has simply to carry it out. Superficially, much of *Choephori* concerns the mechanics of his vengeance: how he is reunited with his sister after their long separation; the trickery by which he obtains access to the palace and to his wary victims; how he succeeds in committing the murders. The result is that this play as a whole (with the exception of the operatic tomb ritual in 306 ff.) is the nearest Aeschylus ever came to the drama of action, plot, and character, which, from Sophocles to Oscar Wilde, has passed as the norm. Although Aeschylus never learned to load and discharge a plot in Sophocles' manner, the final scenes of *Choephori* move, in their own way, as fast and as devastatingly as the ends of *Antigone* or *Oedipus the King.* Yet meanwhile, in and through the stage action, the moral vision of the entire trilogy continues to unfold. Aeschylus stresses that Electra and Orestes, though pressed by god and man to execute the retaliatory law, do so joylessly and in a very different spirit from that of their mother. The visual and moral contrast between the murder tableaus in *Agamemnon* and *Choephori* respectively should be observed, and so should Electra's words at lines 120–122 and 140–141. Further, the last two scenes suddenly give meaning to the confused theme of the relation between the sexes that has resounded through the *Oresteia* since the Watchman's opening speech. Orestes' act of vengeance for his father, authorized by the male Olympian Apollo, has brought him into flat opposition with the ancient earth goddesses, the Furies, who protect the rights of the female. The counter-murder has solved nothing. It has merely widened the circle of the family vendetta to embrace Heaven and Earth, Male and Female, Light and Dark.

As *Choephori* clarifies and polarizes much of the hitherto ambivalent imagery of the *Oresteia,* so the *Eumenides* makes concrete that imagery and brings it onto the stage. In the early scenes at Delphi, Apollo and the Furies are visibly paraded and confronted. Behind the former, offstage, loom Zeus and the new Olympians; behind the latter, Night and the Fates. Thereafter, at Athens, another ambiguity is given a concrete and definitive shape: *dike* now materializes in its specific meaning of a "trial at law." At the end of the *Eumenides,* when a balance has at last been struck between the opposing cosmic forces, the other nightmare ambiguities of the *Oresteia* are resolved. The frightful masks of the Furies will henceforth conceal nothing but good; the purple robes which they receive in exchange for their black are a visible sign of their kindness, contrasting with the earlier flashes of purple in the trilogy (the tapestries and the murder robe); and the torch flames of the final procession toward their new cavern sanctuary, quite unlike the "dark fire" seen by the Watchman long ago, signify a secure and ordered universe.

Like the last movement of Beethoven's *Ninth Symphony,* the last play of the *Oresteia* crashes through the conventions of its genre. The *Eumenides,* with its unearthly actors and chorus, its staccato episodes at Delphi, its unparalleled shift of scene to Athens, its celestial pettifoggery in the equally unparalleled "trial scene," its hymns of rage, its gorgeous, joyful finale, defies criticism as a "tragedy."

So, perhaps, does the *Oresteia* as a whole. At its psychological, political, and cosmic levels the trilogy is a progress through confused anarchy to the point where the irrational and rational elements in human life are isolated, recognized, and brought into effective harmony. Although it represents this progress by histrionic, musical, and (in the original performance) choreographic media, it is hardly "tragedy," even on Greek terms. Rather, in this terrifying masterpiece of his last years, Aeschylus passed through tragedy and out onto the other side: to a Divine Comedy of the stage.

Translations of the *Oresteia* are listed under Aeschylus. The most recent edition of the *Oresteia* with Introduction and commentary in English is by George Thomson (2 vols., 1966).—C. J. H.

Orestes (408 B.C.). A tragedy by EURIPIDES. In *Orestes* (as in *The Phoenician Women*) Euripides brings together persons whom the usual versions of the myth kept apart. A short time after the murder of Clytemnestra we find present in Argos, not merely her daughter Electra with her brother, Orestes, and his loyal friend Pylades, but also Helen and Menelaus and old Tyndareus, the father of Helen and Clytemnestra. Orestes, urged on by Electra, has killed their mother to avenge their father, whom she and her lover had murdered. Maddened by the Erinyes, he is tended by Electra, while the Argive assembly meets to determine the fate of the matricides. Brother and sister appeal for support to their uncle, Menelaus, who has just returned from the Trojan War, but he excuses himself, after Tyndareus has delivered a diatribe against the murderers. The assembly votes death to Electra and Orestes. In desperation they plot with Pylades to kill Helen and hold Hermione, her daughter by Menelaus, as hostage until they can escape. They carry out the plan, but instead of dying, Helen is deified, and Apollo appears to order Orestes to marry Hermione, not kill her. The god undertakes to reconcile the Argives to Orestes and, in time, to give him the throne.

The first, and longer, part of the play, up to the final violence, is dramatically very effective, with brilliant characterization. The mutual affection of the two outcasts is very touching and their jealousy of the prosperous house of Menelaus very natural. Orestes' fits of madness, his sense of guilt, his self-conscious, awkward defense before his grandfather, his reluctant, arrogant supplication of Menelaus, and his insistence on addressing the assembly himself, which does not help his case, are all excellently portrayed. So is the cautious, selfish, hypocritical Menelaus. The short confrontation between Helen and Electra is excellent theater.

The second part of the play does not reach the same high level, not because the sudden switch from utter despair to a strong drive for vengeance is abrupt, for this is natural, but because both the plot to kill Helen and hold Hermione as hostage and the execution of it are melodramatic in tone and feeling. Moreover, the long scene with the escaping Phrygian slave is unmotivated. The epiphany of Apollo is cold and lifeless. While dramatizing the situation with real people, Euripides seems to have allowed them to run away with the story, and he is unable to fit them back convincingly into the known legend that predicted their future.

Translations of the play are listed under Euripides.—G. M. A. G.

Orhan Kemal [**Mehmet Raşit Öğütçü**] (1914–). Turkish novelist, short-story writer, and playwright. When Orhan Kemal was in the eighth grade, his father, a lawyer, farmer, and politician, escaped to Syria and Lebanon under political pressure. Orhan Kemal had to leave school and work as a laborer. He joined his father in Syria and Lebanon for a year and returned to Turkey in 1932. Orhan Kemal never went back to school but became an avid reader. In his short stories, novels, and plays Orhan Kemal describes with sympathy and depth of understanding the multitude of people he has met. Today, Orhan Kemal earns his living primarily as a novelist and a scenarist for films.

Three of Orhan Kemal's plays have been produced. *Ispinozlar* ("The Chaffinches," 1964) was adapted for the stage from one of his novels. This play was slightly revised and produced again under the title of *Yalova Kaymakamı* ("The Governor of Yalova," 1967). *72. Koğuş* ("The Seventy-second Ward," 1967), produced by the Ankara Art Theater, was a great success.

All of Orhan Kemal's plays, as well as his short stories and novels, are declarations of faith in man. In *72. Koğuş,* no inmate of the jail loses his basic humanity, however low he may fall. Orhan Kemal argues that crime is caused not by man's nature, but by the chaos in society. This chaos, however, is not eternal. Orhan Kemal believes that man is bound to find happiness in a perfect order which is to come.—N. O.

Ørjasæter, Tore (1886–). Norwegian poet and playwright. Serious illness turned Ørjasæter from a natural inclination to farming, and he made his debut as a poet in 1908. Ørjasæter's first play, *Jo Gjende* (1917), concerning a nineteenth-century Norwegian reindeer hunter of that name, and *Anne på torp* ("Anna on the Farm," 1930) are both realistic studies of the individual's search for self in relation to soil and milieu. Ørjasæter, unlike most of his Norwegian compeers, then turned to forms of expressionism. His best-known play, *Christophoros* ("St. Christopher," 1947), depicts an artist's attempt to finish a portrait of Saint Christopher bearing the Christ child at the same time that he, the artist, is assuming his own family responsibilities. His negative, blocking self is embodied in a *Doppelgänger* of recognizable stamp. *Den lange bryllaupsreisa* ("The Long Honeymoon," 1949) is an episodic passion play in which the groom is forced to confess and atone for sins of omission and commission during the German occupation of Norway in World War II.

Ørjasæter's devotion to the Gudbrandsdal region of Norway is combined with a visionary search for truth somewhat after the manner of Strindberg.

See Harald Beyer, *A History of Norwegian Litera-*

ture (1956), translated by Einar Haugen, pp. 302–303.—R. B. V.

Orphan, The (1680). A tragedy in blank verse by Thomas OTWAY. *The Orphan, or The Unhappy Marriage* was first performed early in the year at the Dorset Garden Theatre by the Duke's Company. The twin brothers, Castalio and Polydore, are in love with Monimia, an orphan who has been brought up by their father. After Castalio has secretly married her, Polydore, who overhears what he supposes to be an assignation between the two, takes his brother's place in the dark. When the true situation is discovered, all three commit suicide.

What was long considered an emotionally gripping tragedy now seems contrived and too exclusively dependent on pathos.

Aline Taylor is editing this play with introduction and notes for the Regents Restoration Drama Series. —E. W.

Orphée (1926). A tragedy by Jean COCTEAU. Greek mythology is the basis of Cocteau's first original full-length play, *Orphée,* written in 1925, performed in 1926 by the Pitoëffs in the Théâtre des Arts, and later translated into English. According to the Prologue, the purely magical action of this tragedy occurs very high up in the air. Like a poem that reveals the mystery and the magic, the risks and the chances that occur with the discovery of the invisible, the movement in this play is cut off from all material and realistic strategies, and like some trapeze formation, it is enacted in a sphere other than the usual one. Yet we recognize familiar beings: a man, a woman, a horse, a window repairer.

At the beginning of the play, Orpheus is lured toward death by a horse whose messages come from the realm of the dead, and then he is more strongly attracted to it by the death of Eurydice. Cocteau conceives of death as a magical substitution for life, as a passage through a mirror. In his play the limits that separate life and death lose all hardness and precision. The swiftness of the action and the mathematical neatness with which it progresses are in themselves sufficient to create the illusion of the supernatural. Orpheus and Eurydice fulfill their destiny on time, because Cocteau, who has very little sense of the mystical, places his emphasis on the mechanical devices of the myth: conundrums, mirrors, and poison.

Orphée has been translated by Carl Wildman (1933). —W. F.

Orton, Joe (1933–1967). English playwright. Orton, born in Leicester, was one of the sharpest stylists of the English new wave and a playwright who outdid all his contemporaries in offending the traditional West End audience. In its callous gaiety, its "bad taste" humor, and in treating death as the biggest joke of all, Orton's work has an unrivaled claim to the black comic label.

Orton began his literary career as a radio dramatist with *The Ruffian on the Stair* (1964), which owed a good deal to Harold Pinter. He hit his true vein in *Entertaining Mr. Sloane* (1964), his first play to reach the stage and a winner of the London *Evening Standard* award for the best new play of the year. It deals with a young criminal who murders an old man and is blackmailed into sexual submission by a predatory pair of middle-aged siblings. The source of its comedy is the deliberate gulf between a brutally anarchic action and ostentatiously genteel dialogue. The same technique is used with even greater effect in *Loot* (1966), a satire on police corruption and the conventions of detective fiction.

Whether or not one accepts the assessment of Orton as a latter-day Oscar Wilde, he certainly ranks as a modern pioneer in the comedy of manners. The only influence Orton acknowledged is that of Voltaire, and he summed up in an interview his dramatic philosophy in the line, "People are profoundly bad, but irresistibly funny." He began his career as an unsuccessful repertory actor and once served a prison sentence for defacing library books. Orton left behind an unproduced play, *What the Butler Saw,* after being battered to death with a hammer by a male companion, an event fearsomely compatible with his own dramatic invention.—L. W.

Osborne, John [James] (1929–   ). English playwright. Osborne was born in London, the son of an asthmatic commercial artist of Welsh extraction and a Cockney barmaid. He had a sickly and unsettled childhood, and shortly after his failure to pass the grammar school entrance examination his father was taken into a sanitorium to die. This released a small sum of life insurance money, which sent Osborne to Belmost College, Devon. He hated public school life, however, and brought it to an end by striking the headmaster. After two years at home he took a job in trade journalism at the age of seventeen and began writing poetry and "very sad" short stories. In 1948 he secured a toe hold in the theater, first as a tutor to children in a touring play, and then as the company's assistant stage manager. Later he joined a traveling theatrical company run by the

JOHN OSBORNE (WIDE WORLD PHOTOS)

Canadian actor-playwright Anthony Creighton, with whom he wrote two plays: *Personal Enemy* (never produced), which, now suppressed by Osborne, is a study of communist witch-hunting in the Midwest; and *Epitaph for George Dillon* (1957). After the collapse of the company and the failure to find a market for the plays, Osborne went back into provincial repertory. He then returned to London and completed *Look Back in Anger*, which went the round of the West End managements before it was accepted by George Devine for the newly formed English Stage Company at the Royal Court Theatre.

The first performance of this play, on May 8, 1956, is commonly accepted as the beginning of a new age in the British theater. It also catapulted Osborne to a dominant position, which he has consolidated in his subsequent work. Since 1956 he has averaged a new production a year. THE ENTERTAINER, commissioned for Sir Laurence Olivier and written under great pressure, appeared in 1957; *George Dillon* followed in 1958, and the musical *The World of Paul Slickey* in 1959; then, in 1960, his only television play, *A Subject of Scandal and Concern*; *Luther* (1961); *Plays for England* (1962); *Inadmissible Evidence* (1964); *A Patriot for Me* (1965); and *A Bond Honoured* (1966), an adaptation of Lope de Vega's play *La Fianza Satisfecha*, commissioned by the National Theatre. In association with Tony Richardson (who directed *Look Back in Anger*), Osborne also founded Woodfall Films, for which he wrote the screenplays of *Tom Jones* (1964) and *The Charge of the Light Brigade* (1968).

Even setting aside his scathing journalism, Osborne's place in the English scene is more personal than that of any other playwright of the century. As the original "angry young man," he began, like others of his generation, as a voice in opposition; but he has remained in opposition, changing his targets and resisting allegiance to any group. On the strength of his early assaults on the British establishment (particularly the Royal Family and the Tory government) Osborne was mistaken for an apostle of social revolution. But as the list of targets grew to include Labour politicians, literary critics, and the left-wing sympathizers who had at first welcomed him, it became clear that his revolution was strictly a one-man affair. Since his writing is usually on the offensive and disdains conceptual argument, it is sometimes hard to see what Osborne approves of. But, taken as a whole, his plays are fired by a sense of negative patriotism, a disgust for the present quality of life in Britain counterbalanced by an affection for such things as the Edwardian music hall (as in *The Entertainer*) and the loyalties of nineteenth-century military life (as in *A Patriot for Me*).

Since his naturalistic beginnings in *Look Back in Anger* (which he later described as an old-fashioned play), Osborne has repeatedly set out to assimilate stricter forms. *Luther* is a chronicle play on the model of Bertolt Brecht's *Galileo*; *The World of Paul Slickey* is an attempt to revitalize the old British musical comedy into modern satire; *A Patriot for Me* is a romantic epic complete with gypsy violinists; *A Bond Honoured* is a modern exercise in the Jacobean revenge tradition. One might say that the more detached the form and historical the theme, the more intimate the content; alternatively that Osborne—

never at his strongest with plot construction—has explored these categories for technical reasons.

As an orthodox technician Osborne can be faulted. Inside heavyweight forms he tends to get muscle-bound, and it is always a relief when he breaks the mold and speaks out directly to the spectator. Technically Osborne's main achievement is still *Look Back in Anger:* the rediscovery of the tirade. It has often been objected that his plays are written for a single character and a company of invertebrate stooges, but this is to miss the point that dramatic conflict in Osborne takes place less between the play's characters than between the protagonist and the audience. His talent is that of a popular revivalist preacher. When Osborne first appeared he said that he wanted to give audiences "lessons in feeling," and not since George Bernard Shaw has there been any English dramatist whose voice fills a theater with such authority. But it is always the voice of a single character. The best known is Jimmy Porter, the working-class intellectual rebel in *Look Back in Anger*, and the first of the "anti-heroes." Porter's prevailing characteristics of excoriating wit and seething dissatisfaction recur in his successors: Archie Rice, the broken-down music-hall comedian in *The Entertainer*; Henry Maitland, the self-destructive legal philanderer in *Inadmissible Evidence*; and the chronically constipated scourge of the Vatican in *Luther*. What they, and other Osborne heroes, have in common is a calculated unattractiveness that puts them at immediate odds with the audience, and that the characters must overcome during the play. The criticism that Osborne makes things too easy for his protagonists is the reverse of the truth; he is actually at great pains to burden them with handicaps.

The range of Osborne's talent involves obvious formal difficulties. Nevertheless, he has retained pre-eminence among his generation partly through possessing an unsurpassed store of creative energy and partly for being the only English playwright capable of creating heroes of our time.

Osborne's plays are published in separate editions. A short critical book about Osborne (1968), by Ronald Hayman, is in the *Contemporary Playwrights* series.—I. W.

Osterspiel ("Easter play"). The oldest form of German religious drama, deriving from the Easter liturgy of the Mass in the middle ages. Dating from the ninth century, the Osterspiel originated in an extension of the Resurrection section of the Easter Mass. Originally depicting only the grave scene, the drama was enlarged to include humorous elements, such as the race of the Apostles to the empty grave, and was eventually freed from the Latin Gospel text. Through an enlargement of the story to include more of the life and death of Christ, the Easter play gave rise to the *Passionspiel* ("Passion play"). By the thirteenth century the original Latin text had given way completely to the German vernacular. The most well-known plays were those from Muri (Switzerland) and Innsbruck.—B. M. M.

Ostrovsky, Alexander [Nikolaevich] (1823–1886). Russian playwright. The most prolific of Russian playwrights, Ostrovsky is the author of more than eighty plays. Born in Moscow, the son of a minor civil servant, Ostrovsky failed to complete his

ALEXANDER OSTROVSKY (WIDE WORLD PHOTOS)

THE FOREST, provide a glimpse of Ostrovsky's contemporary bohemia—the world of provincial actors.

There can be no doubt that Ostrovsky has left a striking picture of the world he knew and that this picture is critical, stark, and sarcastic. But it is very doubtful that the widespread interpretation of his plays (particularly by Soviet critics) as outcries of a political radical and harbingers of the forthcoming revolution could be seriously maintained. Socially significant implications have even been read into his fairy-tale play *Snegurochka* ("The Snow Maiden," 1873), which Maxim Gorky, to express his approval, called "realistic."

Actually, if one can speak of a dominating theme in Ostrovsky, it could be described as the conflict between the ardent aspirations of a pure heart and the false values imposed by the environment, a conflict that has existed in every human society.—A. MACA.

Othello (1604). A tragedy by William SHAKESPEARE. A production at court on November 1, 1604, is the earliest record of presentation of *The Tragedy of Othello, the Moor of Venice*. The play was first printed in 1622 in a quarto edition. The interval between performance and quarto printing is the longest for any Shakespearean play. The exact relationship between the First Quarto, an authoritative text, and

TITLE PAGE OF THE FIRST QUARTO (1622) OF SHAKE-SPEARE'S *Othello*

THE
Tragœdy of Othello,
The Moore of Venice.

As it hath beene diuerſe times acted at the Globe, and at the Black-Friers, by his Maieſties Seruants.

Written by VVilliam Shakeſpeare.

LONDON,
Ｐ&d by *N. O.* for *Thomas Walkley,* and are to be ſold at his ſhop, at the Eagle and Child, in Brittans Burſſe.
1622.

law studies at the Moscow University and in 1843 went to work as a clerk, first at the Arbitration Court and then at the Commercial Tribunal. He remained an employee of the Ministry of Justice for eight years and during that time learned a great deal about the private affairs of members of various social classes; he put this knowledge to good use in his plays.

In 1850, after his first comedy, *Bankrot* ("The Bankrupt"), appeared in the magazine *Moskvityanin,* Ostrovsky left his job and devoted all his time to writing plays. At first the censors banned the production of *Bankrot* but later, due to the intervention of Prince V. F. Odoyevsky (who wrote: "Russia had three great tragedies [sic]—*The Minor, Woe from Wit,* and *The Inspector General.* Now, with *The Bankrupt,* it has four."), it was produced under the title *Svoi lyudi—sochtiomsya (It's a Family Affair —We'll Settle It Ourselves,* 1850). In this play, as in those that followed it, realistic characters are portrayed in the prosaic, mostly lower-class setting of Ostrovsky's Russia.

Among his better-known plays are *Ne v svoi sani ne sadis (Don't Ride a Sledge That Isn't Yours,* 1853), *Bednost ne porok (Poverty Is No Crime,* 1854), *Staryi drug luchshe novykh dvukh* ("One Old Friend Is Better Than Two New Ones," 1860), and THE THUNDERSTORM, which is generally considered his masterpiece. In these plays he depicted the sordid mores of the merchant class in which the uncouth heads of families—the patriarchs or, often, the matriarchs—bully and tyrannize all those around them, forcing on them values that are false and cruel.

Other plays, such as *Puchina* ("The Abyss," 1866) and *Bespridannitsa (The Poor Bride,* 1852), deal with the work of petty officials, while still others, such as the text in the First Folio of 1623—which has minor differences—has not been determined. The plot derives from a tale in Giraldi Cinthio's *Hecatommithi* (1565), a work that, since no English translation was available, Shakespeare read either in Italian or in the French translation of 1584. He changed the rambling, melodramatic narrative into a tight psychological drama.

The story opens in Venice, with Iago, a skilled combat officer, enraged that the Moor Othello has not promoted him to second in command. Instead, Cassio, an officer untried in battle, has received the post. Othello, meanwhile, has secretly married Desdemona, daughter of the Venetian senator Brabantio. Over her father's objections to the match, Othello—whom the Venetian council has appointed governor of Cyprus and has charged with repelling an impending Turkish attack—leaves for his new command accompanied by Desdemona, his officers, and Roderigo—a rejected suitor of Desdemona who becomes the dupe of Iago.

On Cyprus, which has been saved from the attack when a storm destroys the Turkish fleet, Iago—whose bitterness is compounded because he suspects that the Moor may have cuckolded him—skillfully employs every opportunity to "even with him, wife for wife" and convinces Othello that Desdemona is carrying on an adulterous relationship with Cassio. When Othello demands "ocular proof" of his wife's unfaithfulness, Iago, with the unwitting aid of his wife, Emilia, filches a handkerchief Desdemona dropped and piants it in Cassio's room. Othello later sees Cassio with the handkerchief, which was Othello's first gift to his wife. Now, completely consumed by jealousy, the Moor vows to kill Desdemona, leaving Cassio to Iago. In the concluding scenes, Desdemona, Roderigo, and Emilia are killed; Cassio is wounded; Iago is caught and his treachery revealed. Othello, at last aware of the perfidy to which he has fallen victim, stabs himself, declaring that he "lov'd not wisely, but too well."

Othello is unique among Shakespeare's great tragedies in that it centers on domestic issues; no kingdoms are imperiled, no rulers toppled. Instead, Shakespeare presents an intense study of jealousy in which the passions of love, lust, and hate—pushed to an extreme—precipitately hurl the characters to their doom. Othello is not a simple victim of jealousy. He—the noble general, the capable governor—is inexperienced in the ways of love. Othello's doubt about himself as a husband-lover, therefore, turns Iago's base insinuation into a fear within Othello that he is being cuckolded, that his good name will be sullied through violation of the marriage sacrament.

In developing his powerful character portrayals, Shakespeare depended on certain modes of conduct appreciated by the Elizabethans but no longer totally relevant for most contemporary audiences. At the time, even suspicion of cuckoldry was sufficient to permit a husband to take violent action against his wife. Thus, Othello strangles Desdemona in the belief that he is performing an act of justice. Furthermore, the loving, kindhearted Desdemona, in marrying in secret and without parental consent and in interfering in her husband's professional affairs, engages in actions that an Elizabethan audience would regard as improper for a noblewoman, thereby permitting suspicions about her to arise.

The ironies in the inability of the characters to penetrate surface conduct—manifested particularly in the way the epithet "honest" clings to Iago—are masterfully presented in the synthesis of color and animal imagery with characterization and plot development. White and black in the play are more than skin tones; they become linked with purity and evil. (Miscegenation is not an issue.) The animal imagery comments strikingly on the bestiality in Iago and its infestation of Othello. The use of double time —after the first act the events take place in about a day and a half, although the time span appears much greater—compresses the action so that Othello cannot think. He can only become passion's slave. Although in scope and grandeur the play ranks below the other great tragedies, *Othello* stands as one of Shakespeare's finest plays through its blending of dramaturgical elements, its concentration of plot, and its intense character portrayals.

An outstanding edition of *Othello* is the New Arden Edition (repr. 1962), edited by M. R. Ridley. —W. G.

Otway, Thomas (1652–1685). English dramatist. Otway was born in Sussex and educated at Westminster School and Christ Church, Oxford. After an unsuccessful try at acting in a play by Aphra Behn, he began writing for the stage. During his short life Otway wrote ten plays, the first of which, *Alcibiades* (1675), contained a part in which Elizabeth Barry made her name as an actress. She was the object of Otway's unrequited passion, and some of his letters to her were published after his death. Obliged to support himself by his pen, he secured the patronage of such nobles as Lord Buckhurst and the earl of Rochester, neither of whom supported him for long. Disappointed in love and tired of his dependence upon fickle patrons, Otway left London after the performance of his comedy *Friendship in Fashion* (1678) and for a time was in the army in Flanders. Despite the merit and success of some of the plays he wrote after his return, his financial difficulties gradually increased until, at the end of his life, he was in abject poverty.

His three most important plays are the tragedies *Don Carlos* (1676), THE ORPHAN, and VENICE PRESERVED, in all of which he demonstrated his ability to write moving scenes, somewhat influenced by Shakespeare and the Jacobean dramatists. Compared with the heroic plays of the preceding years, Otway's tragedies had a less formal style and more psychologically credible characters (see ENGLAND: *Restoration drama*). In her interpretations of the heroines of *The Orphan* and *Venice Preserved,* Mrs. Barry was highly successful in projecting the pathos that was Otway's most characteristic effect. Thomas Betterton was famous for his acting of the tormented heroes of these plays.

The best edition of Otway is *The Works of Thomas Otway* (1932), J. C. Ghosh, ed. The most interesting study of his plays is Aline M. Taylor's *Next To Shakespeare: Otway's Venice Preserv'd and The Orphan* (1950). For biography see Roswell G. Ham's *Otway and Lee: Biography from a Baroque Age* (1931).—E. W.

Our Town (1938). A tragedy by Thornton

WILDER. The play is performed on a stage that has no scenery other than two arched trellises for people who must have scenery of some kind. Minimal furniture is brought on stage when necessary, but the impression received by the audience is of a vast emptiness stretching from the edge of the proscenium to the back wall of the stage—if the stage has a proscenium and a back wall. This space represents a specific community, Grover's Corners, New Hampshire, but it also represents the entire universe, stretching out into infinity. The action begins in 1901 and ends in 1913 and includes flashbacks and glimpses into the future. Each of the three acts has a title of its own: "The Daily Life," "Love and Marriage," and "Death"; the last title is not told to the audience but is obvious from the action. During the course of the performance, the events are introduced by a benign character called the Stage Manager. He knows and comments upon the past, present, and future of the other characters' lives. The two principal families are named Gibbs and Webb. From their first appearance it is obvious that they are quite ordinary people, neither heroic nor downtrodden. All that distinguishes them from their neighbors is the fact that the heads of the two households are a doctor and a newspaper publisher and editor. The first act consists of a series of the simple events that make up daily living from early morning to bedtime. In the second act George Gibbs and Emily Webb, the older children of the two families, fall in love with one another and marry. At the beginning of the last act the audience learns that Emily has died in childbirth after nine years of marriage. Reluctant to join the dead without a last glance at life, she learns that she can return for another look but that she must be both participant and spectator and choose a particular moment to relive. She chooses her twelfth birthday, a day of no great significance to her. But a review of even this unimportant day is too much for her, because it makes her aware that she, in the way of all human beings except the saints and poets, failed to value life while she lived it, not recognizing that even its simplest events are experiences to be cherished. Sadly, she goes to her place among the dead. George, overwhelmed by grief, sinks to the stage at her feet.

The seemingly simple plot is a closely woven structure of characters and incidents. As the play proceeds, it becomes clear to the audience that Grover's Corners is the focal point of all creation and that the lives of George and Emily stand for the lives of all men and women everywhere. Held by some critics to be only an exercise in sentimentality, the play is much more. It is a completely honest, profoundly moving tragedy that reminds theatergoers of the inevitability of death while persuading them to make the most of their time. It has proved to be one of the most popular plays in American dramatic history. —M. G.

Özakman, Turgut (1930–   ). Turkish playwright. Özakman was born in Ankara and raised in Istanbul. His father held a variety of jobs, and Özakman had a taste of both opulence and poverty. Özakman practiced law for six months and studied drama for a year in Cologne. After returning to Turkey, Özakman worked for the government's press agency and the Ankara radio. Currently, Özakman is the vice president of the Radio and Television Corporation of Turkey.

His *Duvarların Ötesi* ("Beyond the Walls," 1958) and *Sarıpınar, 1914* (1968) won the critics' award as best plays of the season. Two of Özakman's plays have been made into films and one of his plays has been broadcast over the Cologne radio.

Özakman writes about the problems of city people. Although his plays are sociologically oriented, Özakman never preaches. The plays are noted for their good characterizations, dialogue, and suspense. —N. O.

P

Pair of Drawers, A (Die Hose, 1911). A bourgeois comedy by Carl STERNHEIM. This drama is one of a series of plays, *Aus dem bürgerlichen Heldenleben* (*The Heroic Life of the Bourgeoisie,* 1911–1922), in which the farcical and hypocritical nature of the bourgeois way of life is ludicrously demonstrated. The low comic event upon which the action is based is a woman's loss of her bloomers in full view of a royal procession. She attracts so much attention that her husband is besieged by people who want to rent his rooms. As a result, his finances improve measurably so that at the end of the play he can proudly declare to his wife that they are finally able to afford the much-desired child.

Der Snob (*The Snob,* 1914), a three-act comedy in prose, continues the history of the family by depicting the rise of the heir, Christian, to the position of general director and marriage with a countess. He too capitalizes on the "drawers affair" by suggesting that he is the product of his mother's liaison with a nobleman.

A second sequel, *1913* (1915), depicts the defeat of Christian in a competitive struggle with his oldest daughter, who has become far more unscrupulous than he or his father.

Sternheim continues the social criticism of Frank Wedekind and the early Strindberg but with the addition of the low comic element. He employs grotesque, almost absurd situations to reveal the brutality, the "money bags" mentality, the "get ahead at no cost" drive of the bourgeois nature; these characteristics are revealed as the essence of that nature. The ideals of the bourgeoisie are unmasked as naked hypocrisy. The characters are purposely not human but puppet-like. The language serves a dialectical purpose and hence is stripped of all rhetorical adornment. And yet the sharp, cynical irony of this form of criticism does not prevent Sternheim's characteristically expressionist demand for the "new man" from emerging.—C. A. M.

Pakistan. Pakistan emerged as an independent state in August 1947. Because it is divided into two halves—East Pakistan and West Pakistan, separated by a thousand miles of Indian territory—the government decided to have two national languages: Urdu, the common cultural language of West Pakistan, and Bengali, the only spoken and written language of East Pakistan. Both languages are flourishing in India. In preindependence days the centers of Urdu literature were Delhi and Lucknow in northern India and Hyderabad in Deccan, and the center of Bengali literature was Calcutta. With the partition of the subcontinent into India and Pakistan, Pakistan inherited the traditions of dramatic writings that had evolved in these areas and in such other Indian centers as Bombay.

These traditions have been remodeled and reshaped in independent India, but Pakistani dramatists have hardly drawn on later developments. They are more dependent on Western plays. Because there is no national or commercial theater and no theater company in Pakistan, playwrights write for literary periodicals, radio, university performances, or for the cinema. As a result, a typical Pakistani tradition of Urdu or Bengali drama has not as yet been evolved.

One major difficulty confronting Pakistani dramatists lies in the absence of a dramatic tradition in Muslim culture. Whereas Hindu playwrights find a long-standing cultural tradition of playwriting in their classics and in the tradition of folk plays based on Hindu myths, Muslim writers must fall back upon the new theatrical patterns evolved during British rule or on their knowledge of world dramatic literature. The only inspiration from their own culture comes in the form of Persian passion plays dealing with the martyrdom in A.D. 680 of Husain, grandson of Mohammed, at Karbala; and then, only Urdu drama has utilized this heritage.

Bengali drama. Before the advent of British rule in 1757 the only kind of plays performed in Bengal were Jatras. They were based on Hindu Puranas, old legendary tales, and consisted of songs and long perorations in verse. Modern Bengali drama in its form, manner of presentation, and characterization is the product of Western education, which brought about significant changes in the sensibility of the newly educated public and made them conscious of new creative traditions. It is therefore not surprising that a Russian called Herasim Lebedeff was the first writer to write and produce the first modern Bengali drama, *Chhadwaveshi* ("The Disguised"), on the first Western type of stage in 1795. This modern influence gave impetus to the nationalist sensibility of the newly educated writers, and they started to look at their own cultural heritage in a new way. Hindu writers translated Sanskrit dramas or wrote new ones as a means of rousing Hindu national sentiments or criticizing the abuses of their old society as seen from a modern point of view. *Avignana Shakuntalam* (1835), written by Nandakumar Ray on the basis of SHAKUNTALA by Kalidasa, was thus, appropriately enough, the second drama produced on a modern Calcutta stage.

With the translations of Sanskrit drama, attempts were made to synthesize the dramatic technique approved by Sanskrit poetics (see INDIA: *Sanskrit drama*) and the Western technique of a prologue and a five-act form. G. C. Gupta's *Keertivilash* (1852), a tragedy in imitation of Racine's *Phèdre*, and *Bhadrarjuna* (1852) by Taracharan Shikdar, a comedy dealing with a Hindu Puranic tale drawn from the *Mahabharata*, were the first original plays written and produced in this new form. The new critical consciousness was expressed in the first Bengali farce, entitled *Kuleen Kulasarvaswa* ("The Highest Caste as an End in Itself"), written by Ramnarayan Tarkaratna (1822–1886) in 1854. It deals with the evils of the Kaulinya system (the uppermost grade among the Brahmans) as seen in marriage arrangements and rituals. Shakespeare also inspired some dramatists, and Harachandra Ghosh translated *The Merchant of Venice* in 1852 and *Romeo and Juliet* in 1864.

Drama in the meantime had become an effective instrument for propaganda against British rule, for social reform, and for national-cum-mythical symbolizations in the Hindu community. These plays were first produced on private stages, but as the reformist and political sentiments grew, a public demand for a playhouse was created, and the first commercial theater was opened in 1872. Within a few years several professional theater companies were founded, and several theater houses were opened in Calcutta. Important playwrights such as Michael Madhusudan (1824–1873), Deenabandhu Mitra (1843–1887), Girish Chandra Ghosh (1844–1912), and D. L. Roy (1863–1913), and less important but significant dramatists such as Jotirindranath Tagore (1848–1925), Amritalal Basu (1853–1929), Upendranath Das (1862–1909), and Khirodprasad (1863–1927) made the period 1872–1912 the heyday of Bengali drama. Social satire, historical and patriotic plays, religious drama, melodrama, romances, and farces were popular. However, when films were introduced in the early 1920's dramatic output declined, with the notable exception of Rabindranath Tagore's plays. Today, the novel is the dominant literary form.

Because the form of Bengali drama was influenced by Western theaters, the open-air stage of the Jatras was discarded. The Western dramatic structure also supplanted the chronicle-type representation of the Jatras, in which action proceeded for an indefinite period and the dramatic performance took a whole night. Hence restrictions were imposed on the size and form of the drama, and the prologue and five-act form with scene divisions, as in Shakespeare's plays, was accepted. Madhusudan, well versed in Greek, Latin, French, and English drama and poetry, was the first prominent dramatist to write plays specifically for the stage and to free Bengali drama from the clutches of Sanskrit poetics—to "create characters," as he said, "who speak as nature suggests and not mouth mere poetry," and thus make the dialogue dramatically functional. He also introduced the Western concept of tragic conflict; this he did in his best play, *Krishnakumari* (1861). The tragic ending of *Krishnakumari* arouses pity and terror, whereas Gupta's *Keertivilash* follows the Sanskrit aesthetic and arouses pity and pathos. Comic and tragic elements were not mixed in the same play, but the two genres began to take their distinctive shapes. Madhusudan himself gave a convincing dramatic form to his comedies in *Ekei Ki Bale Sabhyata* ("Is This Civilization?" 1860) and *Buro Shaliker Ghare*

Ro ("The Old Fool's Fads," 1860), and Mitra and Roy followed suit. Thus there developed a definite tradition of tragedy, comedy, and social satire.

With the new social awareness, it became a common practice of writers to reinterpret history and mythology consciously in the light of social problems. English atrocities provided a common theme after Mitra had written his *Neeldarpan* ("The Indigo Planters," 1860), in which he gave a lurid picture of the tragic and brutal consequences of the exploitation of the Bengali rural public by British indigo planters and their administrative supporters. Though the characters of the upper class are stereotypes and the ending highly sentimental and almost unrealistic, the dialogue is lively, the story well knit, and the theme well explored. *Nabeen Tapaswini* ("The Young Saint," 1863), *Leelavati* (1867), and *Kamale Kamini* ("The Lotus Girl," 1873) also deal with social conflicts. Mitra exploited this theme successfully as well in farces and light satires, such as *Shadhovar Akadashi* (1866), *Biye Pagla Buro* ("The Old Madman," 1866), and *Jamai Barik* ("To Entertain the Son-in-Law," 1872). This tradition of reform through satire continued through the nineteenth century, and Pakistani writers have inherited that tradition.

Interpretation of history and myth had a political and religious bias. The theme of Hindu raj and Hindu independence was used by Jotirindranath Tagore, Ghosh, Khirodprasad, and various other writers. Tagore carried on the tradition of satiric and farcical plays that expose the flaws of Hindu social systems, but he succeeded more fully in writing plays from the perspective of Hindu history. His basic theme is the conflict between patriotism and love, in such plays as *Purubikram* ("The Heroism of Puru," 1874); *Sarojini* (1874), which deals with the conflict between a king's royal and parental duties; and *Asrumati* (1879). His best play is *Shapnamayee* (1882), which has better characterizations and greater organic unity.

Girish Chandra Ghosh's interpretation of Hindu myths is religious. In his later plays, such as *Jana* (1894), religious figures are conceived as ideal men. He also wrote domestic tragedies and dramas on mythical tales having pathetic endings. *Prafulla* (1889), his best tragedy, deals with the downfall of a middle-class Calcutta family. When the Swadeshi political movement started in the early twentieth century, Ghosh wrote historical plays such as *Sirajuddawla* (1909), *Mir Qasim* (1906), and *Chatrapati* (1907), in which there is emphasis on heroism, love of freedom, and the inevitability of tragedy as the result of an individual's shortcomings and treachery.

D. L. Roy carried on this tradition of interpreting history, in *Durgadas* (1906), *Noorjahan* (1907), *Mebarapatan* ("The Fall of Mebar," 1908), *Shahjahan* (1910), and *Chandragupta* (1911).

Rabindranath TAGORE wrote, not for the professional stage, but for the amateur stage. Though he wrote dramas that deal with human action and conflict and use the usual Western dramatic techniques, Tagore's unique and typical contribution is the creation of lyrical plays, which in his later life became song-and-dance dramas. In these, dramatic effect is carried mainly through songs and dances rather than through action and conflict. The most successful dramas in the first category are *Raja O Ranee* (The

King and the Queen, 1889) and *Visbarjan* (*Sacrifice,* 1890). The dramas of the second category have variety. At one extreme are purely symbolic plays using song, such as *Sharadotshav* ("Autumn Festival," 1908), *Phalguni* (*The Cycle of Spring,* 1914), *Vasanta* ("Spring," 1923), and *Shesh Varshan* ("The Last Drops of Rain," 1925). At the other extreme Tagore has written lyrical dramas in which human action symbolizes basic ideas. This type includes *Chitra* (pub. 1892) and *Malini* (pub. 1893), through *Raja* ("King," 1912) and *Achalayatan* ("The Immovable," 1912), to the more complex *Muktadhara* ("The Free Stream," 1924) and *Rakta Karavi* (*Red Oleanders,* 1924). His dance dramas are *Chitrangada* (based on his *Chitra,* 1936), *Chandalika* (1938), and *Shyama* (1939). Dance, according to Tagore, is the most refined form of symbolizing human sentiments and even action.

Stylistically, all of these dramatists indicate a definite evolution: they have all written in prose. Madhusudan wanted to write verse drama; hence he created Bengali blank verse. He used it in his epics and dramatic monologues, but he died before he could make it an effective dramatic instrument. Ghosh and Roy sometimes used free verse but they did not succeed in creating fruitful models of the style. It is Tagore who created a tradition of verse plays, but his emphasis on dance and song made that tradition ineffective. Since Madhusudan's first success with *Krishnakumari,* dramatic dialogue has been used functionally, although rhetoric and long perorations were used by Roy as late as 1912. Modern cinema, however, has made this type of acting ridiculous.

Pakistani dramatists have inherited the traditions created by Hindu writers. Muslim writers, however, could not create an independent dramatic tradition before 1947 because, for political reasons, educational opportunities were not open to them. The first Muslim playwright, Meer Mosharraf Hossain (1847–1912), wrote his first tragedy, *Vasantakumari* (pub. 1873), based on a love theme drawn from the Hindu past and patterned on Sanskrit poetics. His second play, *Jamidar-Darpan* ("A Mirror for Landlords," pub. 1873), deals with the cruelty of a Muslim landlord who tries to seduce a tenant's wife, kills her, and gets away with it. Muhammad Abdul Karim (1854–?), in his only drama, *Jagatmohini* (pub. 1875), and Qader Ali (dates not known), in *Mohinir Prempash* ("The Bonds of Love," pub. 1880), also took love themes from Hindu life.

Nazrul Islam (1889–   ), the well-known poet, took themes from folk tales and imitated Tagore's lyrical dramas. In 1930 he published *Jhilimili* ("The Window Screen"), containing four one-act plays: *Jhilimili,* about the tragic consequences of losing a beloved; *Setubandha* ("The Bridge"), dealing with unconquerable nature; *Shilpi* ("The Artist"), about an artist who must choose between domestic love and love for his art; and *Bhuter Bhoy* ("The Fear of Ghosts"), a political play. *Aleya* ("Illusion," 1931), his next lyrical play, which is known also as an opera, followed the pattern of Tagore's dance dramas. In 1948 his *Vidyapati,* dealing with the life and love of the famous poet of the title, was released on the screen, and in 1949 *Sapure* ("The Snake Charmer") was filmed.

The tradition of choosing historical themes for political ends especially inspired Muslim playwrights after the Khilafat movement (1920–1930) and the emergence of Turkey as an important power. Ebrahim Khan (1894–   ) was the first notable playwright to popularize such themes. His *Kamal Pasha* (1926) and *Anwar Pasha* (1926) became popular at once. The former deals with Kamal Pasha's rise to power and his bravery, love, patriotism, and ultimate victory. *Anwar Pasha* deals with Anwar's downfall and tragic end. With independence, acute social problems attracted Khan's attention, and he wrote *Kafela* ("The Caravan," pub. 1963), in which the conflict between the new and the old is shown. His other plays are *Jangi Begum* (pub. 1956) and a one-act social play, *Reem Parishodh* ("The Debt Cleared," 1955).

It is evident that the treatment of history in all the history plays that preceded and followed *Kamal Pasha* falls into two types. The intention of the dramatist is either to show the drama of history as history or to use history only to delineate human tragedy or comedy. *Kamal Pasha* belongs to the first category.

The plays of Shahadat Hossain (1893–1953) belong to the second category. He wrote three history plays, produced on radio: *Anarkali* (1945), *Masnader Moha* ("The Fascination for the Throne," 1946), and *Sarfaraz Khan* (1947). In *Masnader Moha,* his best play, Hossain chooses Shujauddin's entry into Murshidabad as the basic action and, through conversation with his second wife, reveals Shujauddin's relationship with his first wife and its consequences. The dialogue is full of life and poetic fervor, and the characters are competently drawn.

Akbaruddin (1896–   ) is more in line with Khan. His *Sindhu-Vijoy* ("Conquest of Sind," pub. 1946) deals with Muhammad Bib-Qasim's victory and downfall through treachery, and *Nadir Shah* (pub. 1953) depicts the title character from his rise to power until his murder. The emphasis is not on human problems but on the course of historic action. *Mujahid* ("A Religious Fighter," 1963), a three-act play, deals with the battle between the East India Company and Torab Ali, the landlord of Sandwip Island.

Raktakto Prantor ("The Blood-Stained Battlefield," 1962) by Munier Choudhury (1925–   ) was first produced by the students of the Engineering University of Dacca and deals with the tragic conflict between patriotism and love in the mind of the heroine, Zohra, in the context of the third battle of Panipat. The ending is more melodramatic than tragic, however. Choudhury has also translated George Bernard Shaw's *You Never Can Tell* and written a comedy, *Chithi* ("A Letter," pub. 1966), a successful light comedy dealing with student life in Dacca. He is more successful as a writer of comedy and satire than as a writer of tragedy.

Ashkar Ibni-Shaikh (1924–   ) has written two history plays: *Agnigiri* ("Volcano," 1957), produced by students at Dacca University, and *Raktapadma* ("The Red Lotus," pub. 1961). The former deals with the Fakir movement, which involved the struggle of the Bengalis to free the country from the brutal oppression of Warren Hastings through Devi Singh in the late eighteenth century. *Raktapadma* deals with the freedom movement of 1857. Though Ibni-Shaikh introduces love themes in both, the historical course of action is the most significant part of the dramatic action. He has also written various social plays, such as *Virodh* ("Conflict," pub. 1964), *Padakshep* ("Footsteps"), *Vidrohi Padma* ("The Rebellious Padma," 1957), and several other plays dealing with the changing social life in East Pakistan.

The plays *Sirajuddaula* (pub. 1965) and *Mahakavi Alaol* ("The Epic Poet Alaol," pub. 1966) by Sikander Abu Jafar (1918–   ) belong to the category of descriptive history plays. Two radio plays—*Aulad* ("Progeny," 1952) and *Natun Sakal* ("The New Morning," 1954)—and *Prativeshi* ("Neighbor," 1967), a television play, are plays on social themes, in which Jafar experimented with new techniques.

Along with history plays, social satires have become popular, especially those by Nurul Momen. He has a keen eye for plot construction and characterization, though occasionally he creates stereotypes and depends too much on the coincidence of events. *Rupantar* ("Transformation," pub. 1948) is a fine social comedy, the point of which is made through dialogue. *Nemesis* (1952), a serious play, creates character using the device of one person talking over the telephone. *Jadi Amon Hoto* ("If It Were Like This," 1957) is a five-act comedy dealing with an idealistic man, Fayez, who has chosen teaching as his profession but whose idealism is tested by his future wife. Some of the events in this play seem to be forced. *Alo-Chaya* ("Light and Darkness," pub. 1962) and *Naya Khandan* ("The New Aristocracy," pub. 1962) are comedies dealing with the conflict between the old moorings and prejudices and new attitudes and habits in the rapidly changing East Pakistani society.

A. N. M. Bazlur Rashid (1911–   ), Anandamohan Bagchi (1915–   ), Shaukat Osman (1919–   ), Syed Waliullah (1922–   ), Prasad Biswas (1922–   ), Shamsuzzaman (1927–   ), and Kalyan Mitra (1938–   ) are other good writers on social themes. Each one has written at least one notable play and each seems to have an ideal against which he can judge social behavior.

All the playwrights mentioned have written in prose. Poetic drama has been written by Syed Ali Ahsan (1920–   ) and Farrukh Ahmed (1918–   ) as literary exercises. Ali Ahsan's dramatic poems *Qurbani* ("Sacrifice"), *Zohra O Mashtari* ("Venus and Mercury"), and *Zulaikha* (all published in *Anek Akash,* 1959) were written in imitation of William Butler Yeats's *noh* plays. Farrukh Ahmed's *Naufel O Hatem* (pub. 1961) is, in spite of its being a literary exercise, a highly actable verse play which deals with the ultimate victory of the famous Hatem's self-sacrifice and his conquest over Naufel, leading him to the path of goodness.

The other literary venture is the use of folk tales. Jasimuddin (1902–   ) is the most successful poet to dramatize the mystical theme of the conflict between the charms of the world and the joy of the soul, as in *Padmapar* ("On the Other Bank of the Padma," pub. 1949); the tragedy of the snake-charmer girl Champa in *Veder Meye* (pub. 1951); and the story of love and fulfillment through suffering in the three-act play *Madhumala* (pub. 1956).

Pakistani drama has thus traveled a long way among Muslim writers. In social plays the emphasis has been on the problems of corruption, conflict between the old and the new in a rapidly changing society, and criticism and satire of the new society. History has also provided patriotic themes. With the tradition of Muslim drama only recently established, however, no great dramatist has yet emerged.

Books containing information on Bengali drama are *Western Influence in Bengali Literature* (1947) by Priyaranjan Sen, and *Bengali Literature* (1948) by Jyotish C. Ghosh.—S. A. A.

Urdu drama. Because the Urdu language is a mixture of Persian, Arabic, and the dialects prevalent in the Indo-Pakistan subcontinent at the time of the Muslim invasions (eighth century A.D.), its literature has its roots in the central Asian, the Persian, and the Indian traditions. The traditions of Indian drama—the courtly, or classical, and the popular—have contributed to Urdu drama, especially Kalidasa's *Shakuntala.* Translated into Urdu in 1801, it formed a part of the repertory of every theatrical company. The story of Shakuntala and King Dushyanta, who are separated and united again after many romantic adventures, has taken root in romances, music, dance, comedy, and pathetic tragedy.

Though classical drama declined in subsequent Hindu and Muslim periods, popular traditions prevailed through the activities of Natak Mandalies (popular dramatic groups), the Naqqals and Bhands (mummers and comedians), the Domnis (women actors), the Swangs (pageants and processions), the Kathakali (the dance drama of southern India), the Kathputtalis (puppets), and the Nautanki (popular stage).

Opera preceded the drama. It is believed that a Frenchman first thought of entertaining the last nawab of Oudh, Wajid Ali Shah (1827–1887), and erected a stage and presented an opera. Wajid Ali Shah himself composed some of the songs and dances of the operas that were staged in his time. It was at this time that Amanat (1816–1859) produced his *Inder Sabha* ("The Court of Inder," 1853), which took the entire country by storm. It deals with the love of a fairy for a mortal. She entices him to paradise, but angry gods hurl him down. She then wins the favor of the god Inder through her songs and is reunited with her lover. The songs, dances, gorgeous settings, elaborate costumes, and the fantasy of this drama were so appealing that it was translated into nearly all the languages of the subcontinent, and the India Office library has forty editions of it.

By the sixteenth century, when European traders started coming into the country, Urdu was understood everywhere. Portuguese missionaries of Calicut staged religious plays in Urdu, and the French and British had their theaters too. The Parsis (originally Zorastrians from Iran), a prosperous business community, pioneered the establishment of a commercial theater, which flourished from 1873 to 1935. Since Urdu was most widely understood, Urdu plays came to be written and staged.

Agha Hashr (1876–1935) is the most important, and the most versatile, dramatist of this period. He wrote historical plays (*Asir-i-Hirs,* "The Victim of Greed"), mythological plays (*Rustam O Sohrab* and

Sita Banbas), plays in Hindi (*Puran Bhagt*), and social plays (*Ankh Ka Nasha,* "Illusory Intoxication").
Like other dramatists, Hashr studied Shakespeare
and adapted many of his plays, such as *Sofaid Khoon*
from *King Lear* and *Khoon-i-Nahaq* from *Hamlet.*
His most popular play, which has been successfully
filmed, is *Yahudi Ki Larki* ("Daughter of the Jew").
It deals with the love of Marcus, son of the emperor
of Rome, for Rahil, daughter of Azra, the Jew. The
Jew and his daughter are to be burned alive, when it
is revealed that Rahil is really the daughter of Brutus,
the social and religious reformer who had condemned her to death. Azra had saved her in the great
fire of Rome, even though the Jew's baby had been
ordered burned to death by Brutus. The happy ending was brought in to please the audience of the day,
but the theme of political and religious oppression is
implicit. At that time new political consciousness was
rising in India, and the skillful handling of dramatic
tension and the use of irony made the play captivat-
ing. Hashr's social plays have a reformative purpose
and deal generally with virtuous wives bringing back
their errant husbands to the path of virtue through
their goodness and devotion. Social evils such as
drinking, gambling, and prostitution are exposed; in
the end virtue always wins and vice is condemned. In
spite of their contemporary messages, Hashr's plays
deal mostly with historical and mythological figures
and begin with a hymn or prayer. He relies on spectacle, melodrama, and rhetoric and his plays are
highly stylized. Hashr is one of the first playwrights
to have introduced prose, though it is interspersed
with verse. Whatever controversy there may be about
the suitability of Hashr's plays for our time, all are
agreed that in craftsmanship and dramatic competence no subsequent dramatist has been able to rival
him.

Imtiaz Ali Taj (1900–   ), influenced by Hashr,
is another important Urdu writer. His *Anarkali* (pub.
1922) is well on its way to becoming a classic. It deals
with the love of Prince Salim (who later came to be
known as Jehangir), son of the Mogul emperor
Akbar, for the slave girl Anarkali. According to the
legend, Anarkali was buried alive. Imtiaz Ali Taj has
chosen a historical theme, which requires all the
grandeur of the Mogul court, music, and dance, and
has made use of such devices as the confidante, intrigue, and counterintrigue. But the play owes its
greatness to his interpretation of the theme. The
tragedy is Akbar's as much as it is Salim's. The emperor Akbar, with his dreams of an empire, wins; the
father Akbar loses.

By the 1930's the cinema had ousted the theater as
a means of entertainment. The development of Urdu
prose and the growth of literary magazines and
journals led to the rise of the novel and, particularly,
the short story. There was no professional theater
and, therefore, hardly any drama. At the same time
there were those who had lived through the Hashr
period, and thus wished to keep drama alive. There
was also some demand for plays by the literary
magazines and by amateur theater groups, particularly in the colleges. Radio also required new plays.
Writers such as Dr. Ishtiaq Qureshi (1903–   ),
Shaukat Thanvi (1904–1963), and Ibrahim Jalees
(1924–   ) have written plays for these media.
However, the one essential prerequisite for good

drama—a living, professional theater—was missing.

The partition of the subcontinent caused another
setback to drama in Pakistan, since many actors and
playwrights were separated from one another. However, enthusiastic theater groups in Pindi, Lahore,
and Karachi are making valiant efforts to keep it
alive. Themes have also changed. Refugee problems,
nostalgia for a settled past, problems of a new life, the
Kashmir issue, and the demands of a rapidly changing cultural situation are engaging the attention of
contemporary dramatists.

Among those now writing plays is Agha Babar
(1945–   ), in Pindi. His *Bara Sahab* ("The Big
Boss," 1961) is an adaptation of Gogol's *Inspector
General,* with a Pakistani social and political context. *Cease Fire* (1958) is a political play dealing with
border forces on the Kashmir front.

In Lahore a host of young playwrights are writing
plays for the stage and for television. Ahmed Kamal
Rizvi (1930–   ) has compiled a bibliography of
Urdu drama, published two volumes of selected plays
under the title *Muntakhab Urdu Drama* (1960), and
has written and produced many plays. Recently he
produced *Aadhi Baat* ("Half-Said," 1968) by Bano
Qudsia, which ran successfully in Lahore and Karachi. It is a very fine portrayal of a retired headmaster, who looks nostalgically back at the "good
old British days" when he had run several schools.
Unable to manage the affairs of his family, his "circumstances" force him to take up another job.

In Karachi, Ali Ahmed is a veteran producer and
actor who has written and directed plays for the
avant-garde theater. All his plays have a sociopolitical theme. Nasir Shamshi (1920–   ) has written
one good play, *Tere Kooche se jub Hum Nikle*
("Thrown Out of Your Lane," 1948), which deals
with an aristocratic family in Delhi who must leave
their home and their beloved city because of the riots
that ravaged the subcontinent before and after partition. Khwajah Moinuddin (1925–   ) has written
on the same theme but in a different vein. His *Lal
Qile se Lalukhet Tak* ("From the Red Fort to
Lalukhet," 1958) also depicts the plight of the refugees in their journey from the Red Fort in Delhi to
their straw huts in Karachi. The incidents are fraught
with humor and pathos. In *Mirza Ghalib Bunder
Road Per* ("Ghalib on Bunder Road," 1962), a social
satire, he imagines the Urdu poet Ghalib (1796–
1862) visiting a street in Karachi. The poet is
amused and shocked by the changes he finds in
manners and customs and, particularly, in the Urdu
language. Moinuddin's sense of stagecraft and his all-
pervading sense of humor prevent the play from becoming merely topical. He was awarded the Pride of
Performance prize in 1966. Other plays by Moinuddin are *Zawal-i-Hyderabad* ("The Fall of Hyderabad," 1950), a sociopolitical play, and *Naya
Nishan Kashmir* ("Kashmir, the New Sign," 1952).

Ehver Enayatullah (1925–   ) is another competent dramatist. His latest play, *Razdam 'Apna* ("My
Confidante," 1966), is a comedy in which a wealthy
doctor and his wife, who spend their time evading
income tax, find that their daughter is engaged to an
income tax collector. *Aurat Aur Tash Ke Patte*
("Women and Cards," pub. 1965) is a satirical
comedy depicting the attitude of an upper-middle-

class family toward love and marriage. When the rivals, the poet and the artist, quarrel over the same girl the issue is decided by a pack of cards. The game is still in progress when the curtain falls. His best play is *Jab Tak Chamke Sona* ("Gold as Long as It Shines," 1961), which shows how a pillar of society is involved with a group of racketeers who adulterate medicines. In the end he ironically falls victim to his own medicine. Some topical references detract from the play, but each act is carefully built and the final exposure and crisis cleverly manipulated—something rare in Urdu drama.

Urdu drama has come a long way from Agha Hashr. The struggle for independence and the social, political, and economic problems demand realistic themes and realistic treatment, and the drama has come close to everyday life. The absence of a professional theater is a serious drawback because quite a number of dramatists lack knowledge of stagecraft, but during the 1960's more and more has been written in Urdu about Urdu drama and a greater number of plays have been produced. This augurs well for its future.

There have been no translations of Urdu plays into English. Rambabu Saxena's *History of Urdu Literature* (1940) contains a chapter on drama, and Muhammad Sadiq's *History of Urdu Literature* (1964) also has a very brief chapter on the subject.
—M. J.

Palace of Eternal Youth, The (Ch'ang sheng tien, written 1688). A Chinese play, by Hung Shen (1634–1704). *The Palace of Eternal Youth* is one of the major works in Chinese drama. Hung Shen lived at the beginning of the Ch'ing dynasty

(1644–1912), shortly after the Manchu conquest and the downfall of the Ming empire (1368–1644). He belonged to the old established literary class. His wife was a musician and woman of literary education, the granddaughter of a prime minister under the Ming. His own attitude toward the conquerors was less than cordial. His chief play contains political overtones that were interpreted as disloyal to the Manchu regime, with the result that he was expelled from the Imperial College and a large number of his associates were dismissed from their government posts. He left the court in an impoverished condition, returning to his home in the south. His biographers give a highly romantic account of his later life and of his death. They report that he led a lonely life in retirement by the shore of the West Lake, where his chief pleasures were wine and poetry. They further record that in 1704, on his way back from Nanking to the capital, when drinking wine on a boat, he fell into the river Wuhsing and was drowned.

The Palace of Eternal Youth, which Hung Shen wrote over a period of ten years and twice revised, is a long play in forty-nine scenes or lyric episodes. Its action, taken from one of the most famous episodes in Chinese history, depicts the splendor of the T'ang court under the Emperor Ming Huang (who reigned from 713 to 756), his downfall and abdication, the restitution of his dynasty, his love for his favorite concubine, Yang Kuei-fei, her death, and her entrance into the immortal world. She is depicted in the play as one of the moon goddesses, for a stated period condemned to a mortal life. After her execution and a purgatorial ordeal of suffering, her spirit rejoins the

SCENE FROM HUNG SHEN'S *The Palace of Eternal Youth* (CHINESE INFORMATION SERVICE)

goddesses of the moon in heaven and is there reunited with her worldly lover, Ming Huang, also at length purged of his weaknesses.

The writing is equally successful in the sung and spoken passages. Much of the play's poetry is indebted to one of the most celebrated of Chinese narrative poems, Po Chü-i's *The Everlasting Sorrow.* The story has also been memorably related in prose works by Chen Hung and Yueh Sheh. The heroine's supernatural proficiency in song and dance gives occasion for the large number of musical and dance scenes, which are artfully balanced by vigorous political episodes. The theme of purgation is admirably treated as an essential part of the story's development, both in the purgation of the emperor's devotion to luxury and in the gradations by which Yang's ghost rises from its initial misery to celestial beatitude. Long as it is, the play moves smoothly and rapidly. It surprisingly combines frank political realism with metaphysical idealism, Confucian ideals of state with Taoistic ideals of the soul, thus well earning its place among the world's major dramas.

Yang Hsien-yi and Gladys Yang in their translation (1955) of the play rise considerably above the pedestrian level of their usual workmanship to do some justice to this masterpiece. Their translation is accompanied by a brief account of the play and its history by Tu Pien-pu.—H. W. W.

Palamas, Costis. See GREECE: *modern period.*

pantomime. A theatrical entertainment in which the story is narrated through dance or other symbolic, physical gestures. In classical drama the term was reserved for a presentation in which a dancer or group of dancers enacted a story, which was sung by a chorus. The practice was revived in England and France during the neoclassical period. In England the term is still used for entertainment performed during the Christmas season.

parados. See GREECE: *classical period;* OLD COMEDY.

Parasite, The (Nakhlebnik, 1857). (Also published under the title *The Boarder,* but better translated as "The Free-Loader.") A comedy in two acts by Ivan TURGENEV. Written in 1847, it was first produced in 1857. A penniless gentleman, Kuzovkin, lives on the estate of a wealthy neighbor long after the neighbor's death. While his moody benefactor was alive, Kuzovkin had to act as a sort of court jester and at times had to put up with considerable humiliation. Now, after an absence of many years, the late landowner's daughter, Olga, who had left as a little girl, returns to her family home with her husband, Yeletsky. He is a young civil servant who is determined to make a brilliant career but is otherwise cold and unimaginative. At a dinner party, Kuzovkin is deliberately forced to drink by a neighbor who knows of his former humiliation and who demands that he sing and dance for them. Kuzovkin rebels and suddenly blurts out that he is Olga's real father. Later he tries to retract what he said but, under Olga's questioning, he admits that he told the truth. In the end, after painful hesitations, he accepts a sum of money from the young couple and leaves the region, loudly assuring everybody that he hadn't known what he was saying when he was drunk and that there is no truth in it whatsoever.

The total degradation that could befall a "gentleman" in the circle in which Turgenev moved in mid-nineteenth-century Russia is masterfully and subtly conveyed in this play, which was written so that a friend, the famous actor Shchepkin, could be cast in the main role. Unfortunately, as with so many Russian plays, critics and producers have overemphasized the social "message" by seeing in this universal, timeless study of human degradation merely a portrayal of Russia's prerevolutionary "superfluous" man.—A. MACA.

pastoral drama. Drama is but one of many genres in which pastoralism has been expressed. The pastoral mode is, most simply, the idealization of the rural setting and character. It implies that urban life is corruptive, that only in the pastoral scene can the most satisfying life, which is at once the simplest and noblest, be led.

The earliest pastoral poems, such as the *Idyls* of Theocritus (c. 270 B.C.), are rather realistic portraits of rustic life in Sicily. In time the setting changed to Arcadia and the description of life there became increasingly idealized, until what began as the most natural mode of literary expression came to be the most conventional and artificial. Even Vergil's *Eclogues* (37 B.C.) tend to present the urbanite's fanciful picture of rural life, an unreal but pleasant vision of shepherds and nymphs frolicking on the ever green countryside, singing about nature and the elements, duty and honor, friendship and love, and the only vexation being the pain of a love unrequited.

Though many of the early pastoral poems were in the form of narrative or monologue, others were written wholly in dialogue. Nevertheless, there was no real application of the pastoral mode to drama until the late sixteeenth century, when a vogue of pastoral drama swept Italy. Throughout Europe poets were turning to eclogues and pastoral romances, and in England the trend included a number of pastoral plays.

Italian pastoral drama developed naturally from the dialogue form of the eclogue, such as the pastorals of Petrarch and Boccaccio. Some of these *ecloghe rappresentative* were known to have been recited at festive occasions, but they were clearly designed as poems, not plays. It was not until the time of Agostino Beccari that a distinctive pastoral drama was written. His *Sacrifizio* (1554) combined the ideals, themes, and verse of pastoral poetry with the characterization and action of regular drama. But the plays generally accepted as the masterpieces of the form and the plays most influential in extending its vogue to England were the *Aminta* (1573) of Torquato Tasso and *Il Pastor Fido* (1590) of Battista Guarini. Both are set in Arcadia, concern the courtship of shepherds and nymphs, and end in marriage. Both also have a satyr character whose commentary and bawdy pranks provide welcome comic relief from the main plot. Subsequent pastoral drama in Italy tended to be highly imitative and the form's decline was far more rapid than its development.

In Spain no such drama developed. Juan Encina wrote a number of dramatic eclogués that may well be considered pastoral plays (as the *Egloga de tres pastores,* c. 1508), but more popular were pastoral romances in prose. These romances were modeled on the Italian work of Jacopo Sannazzaro, whose *Arcadia* (1489) was translated into Spanish in 1547.

Though not dramatic themselves, many of these pastoral romances served as source material for English romance and drama: Shakespeare's *Two Gentlemen of Verona* (1595), for example, is ultimately based on Jorge de Montemayor's pastoral romance *Diana Enamorada* (1542).

In England, however, both pastoral romance and pastoral drama flourished around the turn of the seventeenth century. A native pastoral tradition was combined with the Continental eclogue in such works as Edmund Spenser's twelve eclogues *Shepheardes Calendar* (1579). Spanish pastoral romance produced such English versions as Sir Philip Sidney's *Arcadia* (1581). But most influential was Italian pastoral drama itself, which most educated Englishmen of the day could have read in the original. The majority of English pastoral plays of the period can be classified as translations, imitations, or adaptations of the Italian.

Native pastoral elements can be found in royal entertainments performed for Queen Elizabeth (1558–1603) and in the plays of John Lyly and George Peele, all done before English versions of Italian pastoral plays were available. But English pastoral drama itself did not appear until after Tasso

and Guarini were known, and their influence can be found in virtually all the pastoral plays of the seventeenth century. The first English translation of *Aminta* was done by Abraham Fraunce in 1587. An anonymous translation of Guarini's play appeared in 1602. Both plays were to be translated a number of times in the following decades, and one such translation, Richard Fanshawe's *Il Pastor Fido* (1647), was especially well received.

Samuel Daniel, who had met Guarini in Italy, began a series of imitations with his *The Queen's Arcadia* (1605), subtitled "A Pastorall Tragecomedie." It was this play and others like it that led Ben Jonson (in *Volpone*) to complain of the number of English writers who were stealing from *Il Pastor Fido*. Jonson's protest did not prevent subsequent playwrights from leaning heavily upon Italian sources, as Daniel's in *Hymen's Triumph* (1614), Thomas Randolph's *Amyntas* (1634), and Joseph Rutter's *The Shepherd's Holiday* (pub. 1635), to mention but a few.

In his *The Faithful Shepherdess* (1608) John Fletcher set out to adapt the Italian Arcadian drama to the needs of the English stage. Though initially a failure, the play was revived successfully in 1633

A SCENE FROM WILLIAM SHAKESPEARE'S *As You Like It* (NEW YORK PUBLIC LIBRARY)

when the English audience was more familiar with pastoral conventions. It was perhaps because of this revival that Jonson began his own pastoral, *The Sad Shepherd* (pub. 1640). In it Jonson goes a step beyond Fletcher, attempting not merely to adapt the pastoral play for the English theater but to transform it entirely into a native genre. Thus, in an English forest setting, characters with English names, including Robin Hood and his merry men, speak in a rustic northern dialect. That Jonson completed barely half the play before his death is regrettable.

Pastoralism also became associated with the semi-dramatic form known as the court MASQUE. A combination of play, spectacle, and dance, the masque lent itself to pastoral treatment as early as Sidney's *Lady of May,* presented for Elizabeth in 1578. Shakespeare used a pastoral masque in *The Tempest* (1611) and an "antimasque," a dance of satyrs, in *The Winter's Tale* (1611). The most noteworthy contributions to this form, however, are Milton's *Arcades* (c. 1633) and *Comus* (1634).

Since pastoral drama flourished in an age we associate with the name of Shakespeare, some final comment on his use of the mode seems in order. In both *Two Gentlemen of Verona* and *The Winter's Tale* Shakespeare underplayed the pastoral elements in his sources. But in *As You Like It* (c. 1599–1600) he gave the pastoral mode his full attention, and the result was a play that has been called both a summation of pastoral ideals and an ultimate rejection of them. His source, Thomas Lodge's *Rosalynde* (pub. 1590), was replete with the conventions of pastoral romance. Shakespeare, himself a product of rustic environment and so aware of both the advantages and drawbacks of real country life, presented in his play both the ideal and the real, in startling juxtaposition. Thus, the shepherd Silvius courts the disdainful Phebe in the most artificial pastoral manner and thereby prompts Touchstone to recall his old rustic belle, Jane Smiles: "I remember the kissing of her batler and the cow's dugs that her pretty chopt hands had milked." Life in the Forest of Arden does indeed seem like the golden world to the banished duke who asks whether his exile is not more sweet "Than that of painted pomp? Are not these woods / More free from peril than the envious court?" But at the play's end he and his followers prepare to return to that court and forsake the pleasant dreams of Arden.

English pastoral drama did survive into the eighteenth century, with John Gay's *Dione* (written 1720), but its energy was clearly spent. Pastoralism had proven itself finally unsuited to the requirements of the drama, though it survived in other genres, most notably the lyric. Shakespeare's idea of it in *As You Like It* is sound: noble but alien, agreeable but remote, charming but irrelevant.

A good summary of the sources of English pastoral drama with descriptions of a dozen such English plays is Homer Smith's "Pastoral Influence in the English Drama," *PMLA*, XII (1897). Ashley Thorndike sees a strong tradition of native pastoralism in his "The Pastoral Element in the English Drama Before 1605," *Modern Language Notes,* XIV (1899). But the most thorough and best-known work on the subject is W. W. Greg's *Pastoral Poetry and Pastoral Drama* (1906).—R. E. L.

SCENE FROM BATTISTA GUARINI'S *Il Pastor Fido* (UNIONE TIPOGRAFICO—EDITRICE TORINESE)

Pastor Fido, Il (The Faithfull Shepherd, pub. 1590, prod. 1598). A pastoral tragicomedy in five acts by Battista Guarini (1538–1612). Set in Arcadia, the play narrates a complicated love story in which Amarilli, engaged to the youth Silvio, is in love with Mirtillo, who loves her with equal ardor but who is in turn loved by Corisca. The latter, moved by envy, connives to have Amarilli and Mirtillo surprised in a grotto. Amarilli—in accordance with the laws of Arcadia—is condemned to death; Mirtillo himself wishes to have the same fate. Suddenly, however, Montano, Silvio's father and a priest whose duty it is to condemn the two young people, discovers that Mirtillo also is his son. The oracle then announces opportunely that the gods do not want the sacrifice. Mirtillo and Amarilli marry, Silvio finds love with Dorinda, and Corisca promises to change her ways.

In blank verse that is interspersed with choruses and dance, Guarini's tragicomedy is, with its seven thousand lines, a kind of *summa* of the casuistry of love so much to the taste of the age. It heralds the Baroque period with its verbal virtuosity and complicated and prolix development of plot. Only occasionally effective through the resonant medium of the verse, *Il Pastor Fido* nevertheless enjoyed enthusiastic reception throughout the seventeenth century and was the inspiration, more or less directly, of the subsequent development of European pastoral drama.—L. L.

Peace (Eirēnē, 421 B.C.). A comedy by ARIS-

TOPHANES. Trygaeus, a typical farmer from the countryside of Attica, is convinced that Zeus intends to destroy Greece. He decides to fly up to heaven on the back of a giant dung beetle and question the father of the gods about his true intentions. When he reaches heaven he finds that Zeus and the other gods have abandoned mankind, buried Peace, and left the Greeks to the tender mercies of War and Turmoil. Trygaeus manages to give these two monsters the slip, and with the help of the Chorus of friendly farmers, he digs up Peace and brings her back to earth, along with the spirit of high summer and holiday time. In the carnival that follows, all war mongers and war profiteers are driven offstage and out of mind.

The comic fantasy of the first half of *Peace* is among the most inventive and well-aimed in all of Aristophanes' plays. The second half of the drama comes down to earth, in more ways than one, and the scenes become a series of "routines" built on contemporary caricatures.

Translations of the play are listed under Aristophanes.—K. C.

pear garden, the. Chinese actors are often called "children of the pear garden," in reference to the first academy for actors known to have been established in China. This was brought about by a decree of the Emperor Ming Huang (A.D. 713–756). The actors met, studied and performed in the pear garden of his court at Chang-an. Little is actually known of these events but the memory remains an indestructible legend of the Chinese theater. Chinese actors from the eighth century to the present have traditionally regarded the Emperor Ming Huang as a patron of their craft, to whom a form of daily worship should properly be paid. See CHINA.—H. W. W.

Peele, George (1557?–1596). English playwright. Born in London, Peele was the son of the chief administrator of Christ's Hospital, a combination orphanage, school, and charity hospital. In 1571 he entered Oxford, where he received two degrees. Returning to London in 1581, he married and embarked upon a career of playwriting. During his lifetime he had a reputation for riotous living, which, whether based on fact or not, became enlarged as a result of some popular jestbooks to which his name was attached. He died in 1596, a victim, according to Francis Meres's *Palladis Tamia* (1598), of venereal disease.

Peele's earliest work is *The Arraignment of Paris* (pub. 1584), an arcadian pastoral performed before Queen Elizabeth. Similar in style and subject to the court plays of John Lyly, *The Arraignment* is a delicate fantasy structured more like a medieval debate than a drama and interspersed with lovely songs. *The Battle of Alcazar* (c. 1588), a historical play based on a medley of unrelated events, represents Peele's exploitation of a genre popularized by Christopher Marlowe's *Tamburlaine*. His versatility is further reflected in *Edward I* (c. 1590), a chronicle play, and *David and Bethsabe* (1594), an unusual attempt to adapt the biblical story to the stage. Peele's most successful work is *The Old Wives' Tale* (c. 1593), a charming play-within-a-play that is a recasting of popular folklore. The play presents a potpourri of magic, errant knights, embattled princesses, and

benevolent ghosts, all sustained by the gentle, satiric strain and lively lyrics that pervade the action.

Peele's plays betray their medieval roots, being largely episodic and concerned primarily with crowding in as many incidents as possible. Thus, his work is marred by an almost total absence of dramatic structure. Nor does he show any distinctive talent in the portrayal of character. His virtues are those of a gifted fantasist and lyric poet, skilled in sustaining on a very limited scale the fragile art of Elizabethan romance.

An edition of Peele's works, two volumes of which have been published, is now being prepared under the general editorship of C. T. Prouty.—E. Q.

Peer Gynt (written 1867; prod. 1876). A dramatic poem by Henrik IBSEN. *Peer Gynt* was first produced with incidental music by Edvard Grieg, which in 1948 was "deromanticized" by the composer Harald Sæverud.

Peer, a picaresque hero of folk origin, from the Gudbrandsdal region of Norway, is part poet, part pariah. He lives his life out in a fusion of realism and fantasy in an effort to find himself. The King of the Trolls adjures Peer "To thyself be [not true, but] enough," and that dark blob of ectoplasm, the Great Boyg, urges him to "go round about," instead of following the straight and narrow. Basing his life on these dubious premises, Peer makes of himself a successful capitalist of American cut. His fantastic journey takes him through a number of Mediterranean escapades before he finally returns to his native Norway. Approaching the shores, Peer is visited on shipboard by a mysterious stranger (who may be Destiny, his other self, or even Kierkegaardian dread, as some say), and on land by an even more mysterious factotum of local folklore, namely the Buttonmolder, who wants to melt his dross-like character down to something more useful. Peer is saved through Solveig, the patient woman in his life. He is of some positive value in the mind of Solveig ("You've made my whole life beautiful"), just as he was once meaningful to his mother, Åse, as a poet-adventurer. And so, Peer gains a slight extension of his lease on life.

In comparative mythology Peer lies somewhere between the soaring, romantic aspiration of Faust and the haunted search for self of today's antihero. He transcends the national symbolism of a feckless Norway refusing to join Denmark in the fight with Germany over Schleswig-Holstein. Peer becomes, then, a romantic, folk precursor of existential man.

The text may be found in *Peer Gynt* (1964), edited and translated by Rolf Fjelde. See also Henri Logeman, *A Commentary on Henrik Ibsen's Peer Gynt* (1917), published in The Hague.—R. B. V.

Pena, [Luís Carlos] Martins (1815–1848). Brazilian comic playwright. Son of a judge and grandson of soldiers, Martins Pena was born in Rio de Janeiro, where he studied commerce. After finishing his studies he attended the Academy of Fine Arts, with courses in architecture, painting, and sculpture. At the same time he studied music and English, Italian, and French. Martins Pena made his debut as a playwright in 1838, with *O juiz de paz na roça* ("The Justice of the Peace in the Country"), and was to write nineteen more comedies and five dramas in the last ten years of his life. He could not dedicate himself exclusively to dramatic literature, because the principal Brazilian companies of his time preferred to stage foreign works or only those national dramas in the ultraromantic tradition. Economic difficulties obliged him to seek a more stable profession, and he proceeded to London, where he spent the last year of his life as a diplomat. He died in Lisbon, a victim of tuberculosis.

Although regarded, almost at once, as the creator of Brazilian comedy, Martins Pena received due consideration only after his death. His comedies form a gigantic panorama of Brazilian life, pointed with careful attention to its ridiculous aspects. The lively criticism rarely falls upon the aristocratic or the poor but upon the middle class's small problems of daily life. Martins Pena does, however, extend his range geographically to include both city and country. Although political and religious customs are ridiculed, neither the Church nor the state is actually attacked. Foreign characters, especially Frenchmen and Englishmen dedicated to business enterprise and Portuguese in all sectors of Brazilian life, are viewed in terms of their failure to adapt themselves to national sentiments and aspirations. However, such criticism does not go beyond what is picturesque in the situation. Altogether, the result is a picture of the urban bourgeoisie in formation, with the inevitable clashes between the older and the younger generations. Pena takes sides with the new against the old, the modern world against the ancient, the nationals against the aliens, and a practical morality against a traditional one. Among his comedies two three-act plays stand out: *O noviço* ("The Novice," 1845) and *As casadas solteiras* ("The Wedded Spinsters," 1845), and four one-act plays, *O Inglês maquinista* ("The English Engineer," 1845), *O Judas em Sábado de aleluia* ("The Judas on the Saturday of the Resurrection," 1844), *O diletante* ("The Dilettante," 1845), and *O caixeiro da taverna* ("The Counterman of the Tavern," 1846).

Because his dramas are not liberated from the dramatic conventions of Romanticism, they are now forgotten. Only his *Witiza or O Nero de Espanha* ("Nero of Spain," 1841) and a short play called *O segrêdo de estado* ("The State Secret," 1846) are performed today.

The plays of Martins Pena have not been translated into English.—J. P.

Penthesilea (1808). A tragedy by Heinrich von KLEIST. Though Kleist's drama follows the Aristotelian scheme, it is a difficult piece to produce because of the bombastic rhetoric, unwieldy action, and crude psychological manifestations. Kleist stated that the core of his very being was in the play—all the pain and, at the same time, the radiance of his soul. Here is a clue to the paradoxical action of the drama. Penthesilea eventually kills Achilles, whom she loves, because her love for him is too passionate. She becomes confused by Achilles' well-meaning gesture, and this confusion leads to her savage attack on him with dogs, elephants, and all the weapons of war imaginable. After killing him and drinking his blood, she is brought to her senses and is horrified by the cruelty of her passion. Penthesilea now repents her deed and coldly takes her own life. Kleist is not merely concerned with distorted passions in this play, but as in *Prinz Friedrich von Homburg,* he wants to determine the validity of absolutes. According to Amazon law, Penthesilea must marry the man she defeats in battle and kill him after the wedding. It is this law as well as her desire to break it that causes Penthesilea's confusion. Kleist was himself torn by the conflict between natural impulse and duty during the course of his life. Here twenty-four powerful scenes shape a tragic action that, as in other works by Kleist, finds its cathartic resolution only in suicide. —J. D. Z.

Peony Pavilion, The (Mou tan ting). A Chinese play by T'ang Hsien-tsu (1550–1617). This long drama in fifty-five scenes, or acts, ranks among the most celebrated works for the Chinese theater. In its chief features it complies with standards of the dramas of southern China written in the Ming dynasty (1368–1644). The scholar-playwright, who was himself a poet of considerable distinction, made, however, a number of innovations, especially in the parts for singing. His play is singularly romantic, abounding in sentiment, pathos, and the supernatural.

The story is of Li Niang, a girl who dreams that she meets her ideal lover in a garden. Failing to discover him in real life, she languishes and dies, being buried at her request beneath a plum tree. A young scholar, whose name signifies both willow and plum, on seeing her picture, falls in love. By divine grace Li Niang comes to life. After many vicissitudes, both political and personal, the two are united. The play fully gratified the Chinese love for pathos and for tales of miracle and magic. The style is highly dramatic but the story follows the general lines of Chinese fiction. The work displays its author's remarkable talents for characterization, theatrical effect, and, in some of its scenes, even for a sense of refined comedy. There is as yet no complete translation into English.—H. W. W.

Peretz, Yitskhok Leybush (1852–1915). Polish-born Yiddish short-story writer, poet, playwright, and essayist. Peretz was born in Zamosc, Lublin Region, Poland, on May 18, 1852. He received a traditional Jewish religious education, but while still a youth, feeling the stirrings of religious doubt, he turned to secular Hebrew literature. He also began to study Polish, German, and French, and he read widely in these languages. After a brief and unsuccessful business career, he went to Warsaw in 1875 to study law. After completing his studies, he returned to Zamosc, passed the bar examination, and began to practice law. All the while Peretz wrote verse in Hebrew and in Yiddish, publishing a joint volume of Hebrew verse with the father of his first wife in 1877. After a decade of highly successful law practice, he was accused of Polish separatist activity in 1888 and was forced to give up the law. He returned to Warsaw and accepted an invitation to join Jan Bloch's statistical survey of Jewish life in rural Poland. Shortly thereafter, in 1889, Peretz became a bookkeeper for the Gmine, the Jewish community organization of Warsaw, and later an official, a position he held the rest of his life. In 1890 he published his first collection of short stories in Yiddish, *Bakante Bilder* ("Familiar Pictures") and soon thereafter a volume of sketches based on his field study for Bloch.

Peretz was now fully committed to Yiddish literature and Jewish life, and he plunged into literary and educational activity, writing, editing, and teaching. In 1891 he began editing an annual, *Di Yidishe Bibliotek* ("The Yiddish Library"). In 1894, with the help of the Yiddish writer David Pinski, he began to issue *Yomtev Bleter* ("Holiday Leaves"), a periodical that was published irregularly for the Jewish holidays. The same year Peretz participated in a collective volume, *Literatur un Lebn* ("Literature and Life"), in which most of the contributions were his own. He continued to produce a prolific output of short stories and essays on Jewish life and letters, which appeared in various Yiddish periodicals. Above all, his powerful personality became a lodestone for Yiddish writers, especially the young men aspiring to a career in Yiddish literature who came to him for judgment of their work and for encouragement. His home at 1 Ceglana Street became a world-famous Yiddish literary address. By the end of the nineties, Peretz had become the revered leader of the renaissance in Yiddish, that brilliant, half-century efflorescence of Yiddish culture and creativity that was all but terminated by the Nazi holocaust.

From the mid-nineties on, Peretz produced his Hassidic stories and his folk tales, reasserting, now with irony, now with compassion, but always with terse precision, a faith in ordinary man and in traditional Jewish humane morality and joyous affirmation of life. During these years Peretz also became very interested in the Yiddish stage and began a continuing effort to improve the quality of the Yiddish theater. At the same time he concentrated his own creative work in the drama. Although he had published some one-act plays as early as the mid-nineties, his first full-length drama, the much revised *Di Goldene Keyt* ("The Golden Chain"), a play in verse, was published in 1907. In it Peretz attempted to portray the downfall of a dynasty of Hassidic rabbis through successive generations. The same year he published *Klezmer* ("Musicians"), a three-act play better known as *Vos in Fidele Shtekt* ("That Which Is in a Violin"), a drama about the fate of the artist, whose art redeems those who enjoy it yet who is himself doomed to suffer. In the fall of 1907 Peretz published a second verse play, "a dramatic poem in four acts," *Baynakht oyfn Altn Mark* ("In the Old Marketplace at Night"). A symbolic *dance macabre* with much in it that is mystical as well as mystifying, it projected a deeply pessimistic view of Jewish life in Poland. The last of his major plays, also a verse drama, *In Polish oyf der Keyt* ("Chained in the Synagogue Vestibule," pub. 1908), was an attempt to portray the stagnation in Jewish life that resulted from its adherence to ritual and dogma that bear little relevance to modern times.

Peretz died on April 3, 1915, worn out by his efforts on behalf of the multitudes of Jewish refugees from the war zones who streamed into Warsaw. He was found at his desk, an unfinished children's poem before him. In the years that followed, his stature grew. Almost every city, town, and hamlet where Jews lived named some institution or cultural organization after him, and on the anniversary of his death, thousands of school children, intellectuals, and writers made pilgrimages to the monument that was built in 1925 to embrace the graves of Peretz and his lifelong friends S. Ansky and Yankev Dinezon. On April 19, 1943, during the week of Passover, the week when Peretz had died twenty-eight years before, the Warsaw ghetto revolted. When the fight was over, no Jew was left alive in Warsaw and no Jewish edifice remained standing. But the Peretz monument in the Jewish cemetery remained unharmed. The symbolism would have appealed to Peretz.

During his lifetime Peretz became known as the father of modern Yiddish literature, as Mendele Mokher Sforim was called its grandfather and Sholem Aleichem the grandson in this triumvirate of founding fathers. Mendele and Sholem Aleichem were so honored because of their achievements as writers; Peretz' distinction derives not only from his writing but also from the charisma of his personality and the powerful role he played in leading and inspiring a whole generation of young writers. His achievement as a writer rests ultimately on his short stories more than it does on his verse or his drama; and dramatizations of his stories have been more frequently performed in Yiddish and in English than the plays themselves. In part, the theatrical difficulty of his plays derives from his inability to master a longer art form; in part, from his very approach to the drama. He thought that the theater "should portray only what man sees in his dreams," and he was contemptuous of the "fools" who needed to have things spelled out. Always attracted to the ecstatic and exalted moment, Peretz was impatient of the ordinary or the quotidian. His plays tend to be brilliant fragments pieced together. He filled them with symbolism but he left them without dramatic movement, more suitable to the theater of the mind than to the stage. Yet the very difficulties presented by their abstruseness and their lack of tight construction coupled with the grandeur of his bold attempts excited the imagination of his readers and prompted an occasional venturesome director to spend months in adaptation and rehearsal. Even in his comparative failures Peretz played his characteristic role as the most vital intellectual force in modern Yiddish literature.

The autobiographical *My Memoirs* (1964) is Peretz' own account of his youth. Maurice Samuel's *Prince of the Ghetto* (1948) is a narrative that combines biography, translations from Peretz' work, and critical commentary.—J. C. L.

Pericles (1606–1608). A romance by William SHAKESPEARE. *Pericles* was first printed in 1609 in a corrupt text, the title page of which ascribed it to Shakespeare. It was, however, omitted from the collected edition of Shakespeare's plays, the First Folio, edited by members of Shakespeare's company. This omission, together with the highly uneven quality of the writing, has led many scholars to conclude either that the text as we have it is a result of Shakespeare's collaboration with another, markedly inferior, dramatist or that it represents Shakespeare's incomplete revision of a play written by someone else. A third possibility is that this is a reported text, that is, one set from memory by the agent of a piratical printer. In any case, there is virtually unanimous agreement that this revision does not represent Shakespeare's completed conception of the entire play.

Pericles, prince of Tyre, is a suitor of the daughter of the king of Antioch, but in order to win her hand

THE LATE,

And much admired Play,

Called

Pericles, Prince of Tyre

With the true Relation of the whole Hiftoric, aduentures, and fortunes of the faid Prince:

As alfo,

The no leffe ftrange, and worthy accidents, in the Birth and Life, of his Daughter MARIANA.

As it hath been diuers and fundry times acted by his Maiefties Seruants, at the Globe on the Banck-fide.

By William Shakefpeare.

Imprinted at London for *Henry Goffon*, and are to be fold at the figne of the Sunne in Pater-nofter row, &c. 1 6 0 9.

TITLE PAGE OF THE FIRST QUARTO (1609) OF SHAKE-SPEARE'S *Pericles*

he must solve a riddle. Presented with the riddle, he discovers its hidden meaning: the king has been guilty of incest with his daughter. Fearful lest his knowledge of the secret will cause the king to wage war on Tyre, Pericles leaves his native land. While at sea, his ship is destroyed in a storm and he is washed ashore at Pentapolis. There at a tournament he wins the hand of Princess Thaisa. After his marriage to her he is summoned back to Tyre. Returning with his wife, he is again caught in a storm, during which Thaisa gives birth to a girl and apparently dies. Casting the body of his wife overboard in a casket, he heads for Tarsus, where he leaves the child in the custody of the king and queen of that land and proceeds to Tyre.

Fourteen years later the child, Marina, has grown to become a young lady of such beauty and accomplishment that she has provoked the jealousy of the queen of Tarsus. The queen orders Marina murdered, but before the deed can be accomplished Marina is captured by pirates, who in turn sell her to

a brothel keeper. But Marina's character is so pure and virtuous that the brothel customers cannot bring themselves to take advantage of her. She even captures the heart of the governor of the island, who rescues her from the brothel. Meanwhile, Pericles has returned to Tarsus for a reunion with his daughter. Hearing of her death, he is plunged into despair. On the return to Tyre his ship stops at the island on which Marina lives, and in a beautiful scene the two discover each other's identity. In a dream Pericles is told to go to the temple of Diana in Ephesus. There he discovers his long-lost wife, who had been miraculously preserved from death.

Pericles is the first of Shakespeare's romances, those last plays in which he attempted to reconcile the conflicting visions of comedy and tragedy and, consequently, to extend the range and significance of his art. As such, the play should be regarded as an early exploration of modes and themes that in *The Winter's Tale* and *The Tempest* were to be fully realized.

A recommended edition of *Pericles* is the New Arden Edition (1963), edited by F. W. Hoeniger. —E. Q.

Persia. Persian drama can conveniently be divided into two categories: traditional and modern. The traditional drama consists mainly of passion plays, which are called *ta'zia* ("consolation") or *shabih* ("simulated"). These are, in intent as well as in stage presentation, similar to the passion plays of medieval Europe. The traditional plays that were intended for mere amusement were generally of the farce type, appealing to the less subtle intellects, even though they were also performed at court to divert the king and the courtiers.

Except for the passion plays, drama has no significant place in Persian literary tradition and does not constitute a literary genre. This does not mean, however, that theatrical experience was or is confined to the tragedies of the ta'zia or the comic performances of farce. As early as the eleventh century, references can be found in Persian literature to marionette-type plays (*lo'bat-bāzi*), a version of which continues to this day. Such theatrical experiences, however, unlike the narration of folk epics, were not translated into a literary form and did not engage, until recently, the attention of Persian writers. They remained oral and folkloric. Passion plays, on the other hand, by adopting poetic diction and idiom achieved literary status. They differ from Persian narrative poetry only by being written in dialogue form. In diction, imagery, and meter they follow the trends and conventions of narrative elegies.

Writing about the passion play of traditional Persian drama, Louis Gray points out in Hasting's *Encyclopaedia of Religion and Ethics* (1908) that the "ta'zia is the most striking mystery-play of the entire Orient." Closely related to the beliefs of the Shiite sect of Islam, these plays focus on the events that led to the martyrdom of Husain, the beloved and deeply mourned leader of the Shiites.

To understand the themes of ta'zia, one should recall that after the death of Mohammed, the prophet of Islam, in A.D. 632, a controversy arose concerning his succession. The Shiites believe that Mohammed's sole legitimate heir was his cousin and son-in-law Ali, but that three caliphs in succession usurped the leadership of the Muslims before Ali assumed the caliphate. On the other hand, the Sunnites, the majority faction of the Muslims, respect the first three caliphs, as well as Ali, as legitimate successors to the Prophet.

After assuming the caliphate, Ali was soon defied by Muawiyah, the governor of Syria, who managed to establish a pro-Arab and anti-Shiite dynasty, despised by the Shiites and the Persians alike. The Shiites maintain that the spiritual leadership that resided in the House of Ali passed on from him to his eldest son, Hasan, and then to Husain, Hasan's younger brother. The Persian Shiites believe in a line of twelve spiritual leaders (imams) of the House of Ali, who are considered by definition sinless, infallible, and in possession of the true knowledge of the religion and the holy scripture.

Thus, the first three caliphs, as well as the House of Muawiyah, became the targets of mounting Shiite resentment and hatred. But none was so fiercely detested or abused as Muawiyah's son, Yazid, who was responsible for Husain's martyrdom, for none of the imams had been so greatly loved as Husain, whose suffering and death form the central theme of the most elaborate and profound mourning rites in the East.

The historical events behind the episodes of the ta'zia are the following: In 680, twenty years after the assassination of Ali, his son Husain set out with his family and a few followers toward Kufa, a city in lower Mesopotamia, in order to challenge the tyrannical rule of Yazid and wrest the caliphate from him. But on the plains of Karbala, north of Kufa, Husain was intercepted and easily overwhelmed by Yazid's army. Husain and almost all of his small group of supporters perished in the fight.

Soon a web of myths and legends—which also embodied some of the ancient legends of Persia and western Asia—was woven around the figure of Husain and the events of Karbala. The Shiites maintain that Husain marched to his martyrdom with full knowledge of what was going to happen. In submitting himself to the will of God, he was in fact sacrificing himself for the redemption of the people, washing away with his blood the sins of mankind. This explained Husain's refusal of the help offered him by a prince of the Jins ("genies") and by a group of angels. The legend of Husain has often been compared with the myths of Tammuz and Adonis. There is no doubt that the Shiite legends, as developed in western Persia and Mesopotamia, adopted a number of ancient beliefs, myths, and customs of the Middle East, cloaking them in Islamic robes.

The martyrdom of Husain took place on the tenth day of the month of Muharram, the first month of the Islamic lunar calendar. For the Shiites, this and the following month, Safar, are periods of mourning. The mourning rites (which include elaborate processions, various forms of self-mortification, chanting of the passions of Husain and his family, presentations of scenes from the events of Karbala, and the staging of passion plays) begin on the first of Muharram and end on the tenth, when the mourners are afflicted with a profound sense of grief and loss. But ta'zias are not confined to the months of mourning; they may be performed at other times of the year as an act of piety.

Ta'zias may be divided into two kinds: those dealing directly with the events of Karbala and those only indirectly referring to those events. The first category consists of a cycle of plays that represent the following events: the journey of Husain and his family from Medina; the capture and murder of his envoy Muslim, who had been sent ahead to muster support from the people of Kufa; the captivity and maltreatment of Husain's two small sons; the besieging of the party; the enemy's denial of water to the crusading family for more than three days of scorching heat; the exploits of Abbas, a valiant half-brother of Husain, who loses both hands while desperately trying to get some water from the Euphrates for the children of the holy family; the martyrdom of Husain's nephew Qasim, whose wedding with Husain's daughter turns into a mourning feast; the martyrdom of Husain's two young sons, Ali Akbar and Ali Asghar; the lamentations of Husain's sisters, mother, and wife over the cruel fate that is befalling them; the martyrdom of the seventy-two able-bodied men in Husain's camp; and, finally, amid the lamentations of his womenfolk, the martyrdom of Husain himself, whose head is cut off by the abominable Shemr, a shameless and brutal leader of Yazid's army. Scenes of the captivity of the remaining women who are carried off to Yazid in Damascus complete the cycle.

The scenes dealing with the martyrdom of Husain and his immediate relatives are the most popular of all the ta'zias, as well as the most moving. The involvement of women and small children, the sanctity of Husain's family and their blood ties with the Prophet, the contrast between the heartless, arrogant, and impious utterances of the enemy leaders, and the tender, pitiful tones of the holy family are all fully exploited dramatically to create that profound pathos that is at the center of the tragedy of Karbala. This pathos, in turn, engenders a catharsis, illustrated by the weeping and wailing of the spectators. A single tear shed in the memory of Husain and his family is said to be the equivalent of a lifetime of worship and prayer: it washes away one's sins and assures one a place in paradise.

In the plays of the second category, that is, those with a central theme other than the tragedy of Karbala, a way is generally found to refer to the martyrdom of Husain, sometimes providing the play with its only *raison d'être*. One play, for example, treats the conversion to Islam and Shiism of a European king and his people. When King Kania inquires about the extensive mourning of a foreign tribe that has come to inhabit his kingdom, he is told of Shiism and the martyrdom of Husain. As a Christian, he considers the claims of the mourners pretentious, but in a dream the angel Gabriel tells him of the truth of the mourners' claims, and he has a glimpse of Husain on the battlefield at Karbala with 1,950 wounds. The king is deeply moved, utters the confession formula, and wakes up a Muslim.

Some of the spectacles take the form of a play-within-a-play, such as the play that treats of Abraham's willingness to sacrifice his son Ishmael (not Isaac, as in the biblical version). When Gabriel appears to Hagar, Ishmael's mother, to alleviate her bewilderment and grief, he bids her to consider that her suffering is nothing compared with that to be endured by the holy family; to bring the matter home to her, he orders a group of angels to enact what is ordained to occur at Karbala. Another of these plays involves the great Muslim conqueror Tamerlane. Invading Syria, Tamerlane discovers that the governor of Damascus is of the House of Muawiyah, and so he spends his wrath upon the governor and later drives away his beautiful daughter, whom he had intended to marry. Agitated by this reminder of the catastrophe at Karbala, and unable to find sleep or peace, Tamerlane is advised by his vizier to seek comfort by attending a ta'zia. Tamerlane takes this advice and scenes from Karbala follow.

The reference to the holy family is occasionally more oblique in these "miracle plays" that have didactic or romantic themes. In *Āq-e vāledeyn* ("The Disobedient Son"), for example, the protagonist is ultimately rescued from the fires of hell by the intercession of Husain. In another play, concerned with Laila and Majnun, the famous lovers of Islamic literature, the only religious element consists in Majnun's seeking advice from the Ja'far-e Sadeq, the sixth imam.

In the course of time, a number of ta'zias have developed satirical scenes in which the enemies of the holy family are ridiculed and abused. They are presented in gaudy or ragged costume with a preponderance of red, the symbolic color of the antagonists. Some ta'zias, such as *Ebn-e moljam* ("The Ta'zia of Ibn Moljam"), are almost entirely given over to satire, of a generally farcical type. Occasionally, but rarely, a ta'zia may deal with some happy event, thus qualifying as comedy (for example, *'Arusi-ye dokhtar-e qoreysh,* "The Wedding of the Daughter of Qoraish"), but the general mood and purport of the ta'zia remain that of a passion play.

Ta'zias are written in verse and are anonymous. The quality of their poetry varies: at times the verses are eloquent, tender, and moving and can compete with the best of narrative or elegiac Persian poetry; more often, however, ta'zias are of uneven or inferior verse.

Ta'zias may be presented in public or private places, in the open air or under a roof or tent. Most often, they are performed in *tekyas,* town or village centers for religious activities. The plays are most appropriately staged on elevated terraces around which the spectators gather. To secure a good seat, people frequently arrive in the early morning, often equipped with a basket lunch. The well-to-do used to have their own loges in tekyas, to which they invited relatives and friends.

The stagecraft is simple and plain: scenery is almost absent and scene changes are indicated by the players moving from one corner of the stage to another or by a change of cast. Settings are indicated symbolically: a bucket of water, for instance, symbolizes the Euphrates; walking around the stage once or twice signifies travel; a horse or a camel laden with boxes or pots and pans represents the arrival of Husain at Karbala; a rimmed hat or a vest designates a European. The director of the play, who is also the prompter, stage manager, and occasionally a player, has no compunction about moving on and off the stage, helping players with their costumes or armor, or giving them necessary directions. The classical unities are not pertinent to Persian passion plays, and even the unity of action is often disregarded.

Women's roles are played by men generally dressed in long, black robes, black kerchiefs that come down to their hands, and veils that mask their mustaches and beards. Some players memorize their parts, but most read them from a manuscript. Music plays an important role: the players chant or sing their parts, and instrumental music is used to heighten the mood.

But none of these conventions—some of which would be considered imperfections on a realistic stage—robs the ta'zia of its profound effect. The events and the scenes are already well known to the spectators, and the grief-ridden atmosphere in which the plays are performed has already prepared them for the final catharsis. The melancholy music of the chanted parts and the moving imagery of the verses help to invoke a deep sense of loss. There is a good deal of repetition and occasionally there are protracted scenes, but a climactic moment is easily reached when the martyrdom or a reference to it finally occurs.

Apart from resident companies, there were and still are itinerant ta'zia troupes, and occasionally a ta'zia is performed by amateurs as an act of piety.

The historical development of the ta'zia is not quite clear. Its origins probably lie in the chanting of the passion of Husain, but it does not appear to have taken dramatic form until the period of the Safavid kings (1502–1736), who were ardent and devout Shiites. It was their zeal and militancy that made Shiism the official religion of Persia. No reference to ta'zias is made, however, prior to 1788, when W. Franklin, an official of the East India Company, mentioned two well-known ta'zia scenes: "the martyrdom of Qasim" and "the Frankish Ambassador."

Ta'zias had their greatest vogue under the Kajar kings (1786–1925), whose patronage of state-supported ta'zias stimulated the development of religious drama and the addition of new pieces to the repertoire. The State Tekya (*teya-ye dowlat*), the best known of its kind in the history of Persian theater, was built in Tehran on the eastern precincts of the Golestan Palace during the reign of Shah Naser-ed-Din (1848–1896). This building was an open circular theater, 60 meters in diameter, surrounded by a three-story circular gallery, which included loges for the royal family and the dignitaries. The State Tekya, which could seat up to 20,000 people, was covered by a dome-shaped scaffolding that could be covered by shades in order to protect the spectators from the glare of a hot summer sun. A huge chandelier hung from the middle of the scaffolding, and in the evenings, thousands of candles and oil lamps helped to light the spectacles.

The Constitutional Revolution of 1906 and the increasing impact of the West weakened the official support for the mourning rites; and with the accession of Reza Shah Pahlavi (1925–1941), founder of the present dynasty, efforts to reform and modernize the country, renamed Iran, led to the discouragement of the ta'zia, mourning processions, and other rites, particularly in their more extreme and morbid forms.

Today, ta'zias are seldom seen in the big cities, and when they are, they are by no means as elaborate and colorful as they used to be. But the tradition is far from extinct; the plays are still performed by resident or itinerant troupes in Persian towns and villages during the month of Muharram and occasionally at other times. The texts of the ta'zias have now been printed and reprinted, and cheap editions, often illustrated, are sold in popular bookshops and by book vendors.

The other category of traditional Persian drama, although not as important as the ta'zia, is the amusement play (formerly called *tamāshā,* "spectacle"). These plays consisted mainly of farce and buffoonery pieces (*baqqāl-bāzi*) for gay occasions. Laughter was often elicited at the expense of a dupe tricked by clever connivers, a helpless master bullied by an impudent servant or a Negro slave, a greedy old man exposed in his schemes to marry a pretty young woman, or a fake hero (*pahlavān kachal*) engaged in mock heroics or quixotic escapades. Such plays, however, were devoid of literary significance and were rarely written down. Important in these works were the improvisations of the actors, who made much of provincial accents and affected speech to amuse the audience. Satirical allusions enlivened some of these performances, and the clownish art of the comedian was similar to that of the court jester, whose comical words and deeds were primarily intended to generate laughter, frequently at the expense of some high-ranking official or courtier. A strain of this farcical tendency lives on in modern Persian comedies and is particularly noticeable in the pieces staged in popular playhouses. A more direct descendant of the farcical amusement plays, however, are the low comedies (*ru-howzi*) performed by entertainers at weddings and other happy occasions.

Note should also be taken of two popular practices, one of religious import, the other secular, which, although strictly speaking are outside the field of drama, have strong affinities with it and impart a sense of the drama.

The first is *shamāyel-gardāni* ("moving portraits around"). Here crowds gather around a narrator who shows them pictures drawn in oil on canvas, illustrating such religious episodes as the exploits of Ali, the punishments inflicted upon the infidel in hell, battles of Mohammed against the unbelievers, and scenes from the events of Karbala. Painted scenes are substituted here for the live theater of the ta'zia, while the narrator furnishes a running commentary that brings the painted figures to life.

The second practice is the performance of the storyteller (*naqqāl*), whose art of narrating episodes of the Persian folk epics borders on theatrical performance and has a long tradition behind it. Unlike the performers of the ta'zia, who lack acting abilities are not considerable and who rely largely on the music of their voices and the pious mood of their audience, the naqqāls are generally actors who dramatize their stories through expert mime, exuberant hand and body movements, and a wide range of vocal pitch and rhythm—all of which sustain the impact and excitement of the narrative. Their art, which is, in fact, dramatic monologue involving several characters, is still practiced in the teahouses, despite the invasion of modern mass-media entertainments.

Modern Persian drama owes its origins to Western influences. Though the plays are Persian in content and import, their forms and techniques are derived from European conventions. Western customs began to influence various spheres of life in the early years of the nineteenth century, when the enlightened Kajar prince Abbas Mirza sent a number of Persian students to study in Europe. A knowledge of Western drama was introduced to the Persian elite by these students, and translations of Western plays soon appeared. In 1869 Mirza Habib Isfahani's translation in verse of Molière's *Le Misanthrope* was published and at about the same time Molière's *Le Médecin malgré lui* was translated and adapted by Mohammed Hasan Khan E'temad al-Saltana.

Among the first plays translated into Persian were the satires of Mirza Fath'ali Akhund-zadeh (1812–1878), written in Azeri Turkish. Akhund-zadeh was born of Azerhaijani Persian parents in the Caucasus, lived mostly in a Persian cultural climate, and later took an interpreter's job in Tbilisi, where he wrote his plays. This reform-minded liberal directed his biting satire against the abuse of power by court and government officials, the corruption and hypocrisy of the clergy, and the superstition, ignorance, and sheepishness of the people. A number of these plays were translated into Persian in 1871 by Mirza Ja'far Qarachehdaghi, and two of them were published in the same year. These were enthusiastically received in Persia, where the people were awakening to the urgent need for social and political reform. In 1874 Mirza Ja'far published a collection of seven Persian translations of plays by Akhund-zadeh, including *Vazir-e khān-e lankarān* (*The Wazir of Lankaran,* pub. 1882), *Mollā ebrāhim khalil-e kimiyāgar* (*The Alchemist,* pub. 1886), and *Yusof-shāh-e sarrāj* (*Yúsuf shāh,* pub. 1895). These plays had considerable impact on Persian political thought; they served as a model for a series of satires written between about 1870 and 1925.

Among the most successful satirists of this period was Mirza Malkom Khan (1833–1908). Educated in Persia and France, he served for some time as a high-ranking official in the Persian government until, in 1871, he was exiled for his liberal views and his intrigues at court. He lived for a year in Istanbul, where he wrote a number of satirical plays and critical essays. His plays, resembling those of Akhund-zadeh, reveal his genuine dramatic talent, satirical wit, and flair for fluent dialogue. When the occasion required, he even showed himself a stylist well versed in classical Persian literature. Malkom Khan's plays and articles did much to prepare the ground for the Constitutional Revolution of 1906. One of his best plays is *Hokumat-e Zamān Khān* ("The Rule of Zaman Khan," pub. 1908), in which he exposes the corruption and tyranny of the Kajar rule.

The development of modern Persian drama may be traced through several phases. The first, beginning with the translation of Akhund-zadeh's plays and lasting until Reza Shah Pahlavi's coronation in 1925, was dominated by patriotic plays and plays of social and political intent. The latter were generally reformist in outlook and satirical in tone. The patriotic plays responded to rising nationalistic sentiment by glorifying the Persian past and presenting hopeful visions of the future. Among the playwrights of this period, Mirza Ahmad Mahmudi (1875–1931), who may be called the first modern Persian dramatist, and Mortezagholi Fekri (1868–1917) are outstanding. Mahmudi's *Ostād nowruz-e pina-duz* ("Master Nowruz, the Cobbler," pub. 1919), written in colloquial Persian, marks a break with the tradition of using polite speech in writing. In his satirical plays, such as *Hokkām-e jadid, hokkām-e qadim* ("Old and New Governors," pub. 1915), Fekri, a liberal politician, journalist, and playwright, was greatly influenced by Akhund-zadeh and Malkom Khan. Zabih Behruz' notable play *Jijak'ali shāh* ("King Jijak'ali," pub. 1923), a satirical burlesque on the Kajar courts in free verse, is in this tradition. Hasan Mogaddam's *Ja'far khān az farang āmadeh* ("Ja'far Khan Has Returned from Europe," 1922), on the other hand, is concerned with social mores and satirizes the snobbishness and affected speech of some Persian students who, returning from the West, exhibit outlandish behavior and invoke laughter because of their corrupted Persian speech. The verse dramas of Mirzadeh Eshqi (1893–1925), such as *Rastākhiz-e salātin-e Iran dar Kharābehā-ye madāyen* ("Resurrection of Persian Kings in the Ruins of Ctesiphon"), in which the writer invokes the ghosts of ancient kings and heroes to bewail the present state of their beloved country, are typical of the sentimentally patriotic plays of the period. In writing such plays, however naïve and theatrically limited, the playwright responded to the prevailing mood, which was partly defensive and partly idealistic.

The second phase of modern Persian drama began with the advent of Reza Shah in the postrevolutionary period. He embraced the cause of reform and began to modernize and rule the country with an iron hand. Satirical and reformist plays almost lost their raison d'être. The mood that dominated the early period of Reza Shah's reign prompted the writing of a number of patriotic and didactic dramas. *Arusi-e Ā-Hosein Āqā* ("Wedding of Hosein Āqā," pub. 1939) by Sayyed Ali Nasr (1893–1965) is typical of this breed. In it Nasr compares the old way of life with the new, in order to bring into focus the benefits of literacy and education, the fruits of independence and self-reliance, and the evils of dope addiction, superstition, and ignorance. The intent of this play may be gathered from a caption that follows the title: "This critical and social play has been written for the enlightenment of my less-developed compatriots." In *Māziyār* (pub. 1933) Sadeq Hedayat (1903–1951) shows the chivalrous stand of the Persian prince and warrior Maziyar against the Arabs who crucified him in 839. Continuing the trend of patriotic plays are Hedayat's *Parvin dokhtar-e sāsāni* ("Parvin, the Sassanian Maiden," pub. 1930), Aflatun Shahrokh's *Mādar-e vatan* ("Motherland," date unknown), and Abd al-Rahim Khalkhali's *Sargozasht-e Barmakiān* ("The Life Story of the Barmakids," pub. 1925), which dramatizes the tragic fate of the Barmakids, the famous Persian statesmen massacred by the Abbassid caliphs after long years of loyal and splendid service. An increasing number of European plays, particularly those by Molière and Shakespeare, were translated and staged.

The komedi-e Iran, an amateur theater company founded about 1918 and headed by Sayyed Ali Nasr, continued the good work of an earlier, similar company, the Teatr-e Melli (the National Theater), and did much to popularize drama and promote social and educational enlightenment.

The next phase of modern Persian drama was heralded by the abdication of Reza Shah Pahlavi in 1941 because of pressure from the Allied forces, who resented his independence and suspected his motives. The entry of Allied troops into Iran brought a period of political and economic upheaval and released many pent-up political grievances. Leftist groups sprang up, and the Persian Communist Party, with Soviet support, gained strength through the discontent of the people. A number of new theatrical companies of leftist persuasion arose. Satirical plays, both original and translated, directed not only at the nation's political regime but also at the very structure of the society, found a receptive audience. In this period the artists of the Persian theater experienced considerable freedom of expression, made remarkable progress in technique and stagecraft, and created an atmosphere in which a number of excellent performers thrived. Taking a stand against Soviet and leftist pressure, however, the Persian government was careful not to let the playhouse become the home of subversive propaganda; as a result, the lives of the politically biased theaters, notably those organized by the actor-director Abdolhoseyn Nushin, were relatively short.

The latest phase of Persian drama may be dated from 1953, when Mosaddeq's government fell and the power of the monarchy was consolidated. From this date, Persia adopted a clearly pro-Western attitude and began to exercise an increasingly tighter control over its internal affairs. Plays critical of the regime were discouraged, and a number of well-known actors involved in communist politics, including Nushin and Mohammed Kheyrkhah, were sentenced and left the stage. This naturally led to a period of decline in the Persian theater, but soon economic growth and political stability stimulated theatrical productions and plays were produced for their artistic merit, rather than for their political commentary.

In the 1950's the Iranian Broadcasting Service showed an increasing interest in drama. The radio plays were mainly romantic, moralizing, or farcical, and they often exhibited weak dramatic construction and unconvincing character development. For dramatic impact, the writers of these plays relied much more on external expressions of human emotions than on internal tensions derived from the unfolding of the action. A number of these playwrights continued the broad farcical tradition: their characters achieved humor through exaggerated attitudes, comical dialects, and affected speech. Whereas plays of ideas were rare, maudlin plays abounded. The Broadcasting Service did offer, however, valuable opportunities for actors and playwrights to exercise their talent. In recent years radio playwrights have managed to broaden the range of their subjects and improve their technique.

In the 1960's Persian drama received fresh impetus through the efforts of the Department of Fine Arts (now the Ministry of Arts and Culture), the availability of the television screen, and the economic upsurge of the country. The department founded several drama schools and encouraged and sponsored a fairly large number of one-act plays on television. It also supported the production of both traditional and modern drama on television and the stage, encouraged the writing and translating of plays, and recently supported revivals of traditional drama and dramatizations of folk epics and stories (notably *Amir Arsalan, Pahlavan Akbar mimirad,* "P. A. Dies," 1966).

The establishment of the state-supported National Television in Tehran in 1966, in addition to the Television-e Iran, has provided Persian drama with added possibilities, and the expansion of the Broadcasting Service has enhanced both the quality and the quantity of radio plays. The establishment of the yearly Festival of the Arts, inaugurated in 1967, under the auspices of Queen Farah Pahlavi has generated further interest and enthusiasm among artists and art lovers and will no doubt encourage the further development of Persian drama.

A new and exciting generation of gifted playwrights has come into the fore in Persia. With their plays, Persian drama may be said to have finally come into its own. Among the earliest playwrights of this group is Ali Nasirian, who explores folkloric themes in his plays, especially in *Bolbol-e Sargashteh* ("The Wandering Nightingale," 1959).

A brilliant Persian dramatist in the 1960's is Sa'edi, who writes under the pseudonym Gowhar-e Morad. His satirical commentary on human nature in *Aye Bi-kolah, Aye Ba-kolah* ("Ay Without Hat and Ay with Hat," 1968) shows deft psychological insight; he portrays the absurd side of human behavior within a very realistic plot framework. An earlier play by Sa'edi, *Chub-be-dasthā-ye Varazil* ("The Stick-Wielders of Varazil," 1965), is an allegory with social and political implications. It deals with the inhabitants of a village whose farms are threatened by wild boars. The hunters that the villagers hire to drive out and kill the boars prove to be an even more noxious enemy than the boars. Character delineation and dialogue are achieved with a sure hand and a natural sense of dramatic effect, while the tension of the situation is periodically relieved by humorous episodes or remarks.

The plays of Bahram Beyza'i are more poetic. In fact, some of his plays are like dramatized poems spoken by mythic characters. In *Pahlavān Akbar Mimirad* ("Champion Akbar Dies," 1966) Beyza'i deals with a champion wrestler who is challenged by a young upstart but is faced with a dilemma because of his promise to help his opponent's anguished mother. In a sense, this is a play about divided loyalties, but its tone is poetic rather than heroic. A sense of melancholy pervades the dialogue, and an unfathomable fate seems to hover over the heads of the characters.

Forsi's *Chub-e Zir-e Baghal* ("Crutches," pub. 1962) also has a champion as a chief character, but Forsi's aim and orientation are totally different from Beyzai's. Here the champion is an ancient hero who is resurrected only to expose the vanity of pretentions about past glories. The strong social and moral bias of this play, like others by Forsi, are explored through allusion and allegory.

The "theater of the absurd" has appeared in Persia in a remarkable play by Na'lbandian performed at the 1968 Art Festival of Shiraz. The dialogue has an absurd logic, combining bookish recitation with coarse slang and poetic diction. Despite its apparent absurdities, there develops a convincing theatrical logic that transports the audience to a world at once united to and divorced from earthly existence.

Persian writers and actors show considerable native talent and can combine the rich heritage of their literature and religious drama with the newer techniques learned from the Western theater to enrich an important national culture.

A. Chodzko's *Théâtre persan, choix de téaziés ou drames* (1878) is an anthology of five ta'zias in French translations and contains a useful Introduction. An Introduction and translation of thirty-seven ta'zias is found in L. S. Pelly's *The Miracle Plays of Hasan and Hussein* (1879). S. G. W. Benjamin's "The Tazieh, or Passion Plays of Persia," *Harper's Magazine,* LXXII (1886), contains a general description of the ta'zia. In *A Literary History of Persia IV* (1928) E. G. Browne treats both the ta'zia and the beginnings of modern Persian drama. Charles Virolleaud reviews the tragedy of Karbala and gives illustrative translations from the ta'zia of the passion of Husain in *Le Théâtre persan ou le drame de Kerbéla* (1950). A general introduction to the history and development of Persian theater from earliest times to the present, with a list and selection of Persian plays, is contained in A. Q. Jannati Ata'i's *Bonyād-e namayesh dar Iran* (1955). M. Rezvani's *Le théâtre et la danse en Iran* (1962) is a general description of Persian drama and its development and contains bibliographies. A concise introduction to the history of Persian theater is contained in Mehdi Forugh's "Nemāyesh," *Iranshahr,* I (1963).—E. Y.-S.

Persians, The (Persai, 472 B.C.). A tragedy by AESCHYLUS. This play was part of a tetralogy with which Aeschylus won first prize in the tragic contest at the Great Dionysia, Athens. The tetralogy comprised *Phineus, The Persians, Glaukos Potnieus* (*Glaucus of Potniae*), and the satyr play *Prometheus* (probably subtitled *Pyrkaeus,* "Fire-Kindler"), staged in that order. Little survives of the other three plays in the group, but there can have been only a slender connection, at most, between their mythological subjects and the historical subject of *The Persians.* On this occasion, Aeschylus evidently abandoned his usual practice of building an entire tetralogy around a single theme; *The Persians,* alone among his extant tragedies, can therefore be treated as a dramatic entity complete in itself, like a tragedy of Sophocles or Euripides.

The dramatic time is the year 480 B.C. The scene is set before an ancient building in the Persian city of Sousa; nearby is visible the tomb mound of Darius the Great, father of the reigning king, Xerxes. No actor appears until line 155. Before then the theater is dominated, and the mood set, by the Chorus of Persian Lords. In the earlier part of their chant and song they evoke the majesty of the Persian empire and the irresistible strength of the horde which Xerxes has led out of Asia against Greece. At line 107, however, there is an abrupt break in theme and rhythmic structure. The Chorus suddenly remember "the cunning deceit of God," and their song collapses into wailing over the thought of a defeated expedition and a depopulated land. The entrance of Queen Atossa (widow of Darius and mother of Xerxes), in great pomp, maintains this mixed mood of pride and terror: she has been alarmed by a dream foretelling disgrace to her son. Her questioning of the Chorus about this, and about the nature of the Greek enemy, is broken off by the arrival of a messenger. In a series of epic-like speeches he paints disaster: the Persian naval defeat at Salamis, and the terrible retreat of Xerxes and the bulk of the land force through northern Greece. Queen and messenger now withdraw.

After a song of lamentation by the Chorus, the queen reenters, and the center of action is transferred to the tomb of Darius. The queen's offerings and the Chorus' incantations conjure up his ghost, shining in the full regalia of the Persian king of kings. He brings no comfort to his appalled audience; the disaster has been caused by Xerxes' rashness and pride, which have moved the gods to fulfill certain ancient oracles, dooming Persia. These oracles entail, besides the naval disaster, a military defeat at Plataea, which is still to come.

As the ghost sinks back into the tomb, the queen finally retires, and the Chorus break into a song describing the glory of Darius' peaceful empire. Enter, by contrast, Xerxes, in tattered robes. From now to its end, the play is a sung antiphony between him and the Chorus. At its wild crescendo the Chorus tear their robes and hair at Xerxes' bidding and then, still mourning, escort him from the scene.

The Persians, earliest of Aeschylus' extant plays, is also the only surviving fifth-century tragedy on a historical theme. This latter fact has caused many critics to question whether it should count as a tragedy in any sense of the word. Some see it as a triumphal pageant celebrating the Greek victory over the barbarians, even arguing that the final scene is meant as open mockery of the defeated king. Others treat it as if it purported to be a faithful dramatization of the historical event, and are inevitably led to charge Aeschylus with distortion of the truth, since the play is easily shown to be unsatisfactory as a factual record.

A reading of *The Persians* in its totality will hardly support either view. Apart from the vivid account of the battle, there is little that pretends to historicity. Praise of the Greeks, or even of the poet's own city, Athens, is surprisingly rare. Not one Greek individual is mentioned by name. The emphasis lies, from end to end, not on Greek triumph but on Persian disaster. The grim march from pride to humiliation, from pomp to rags, is sustained both visually and in song, with only one interruption: the Darius scene, in which the detached, resplendent ghost expounds the causes of the downfall. The causes are not such as apply only to Persians; they are universal. The *hybris* of Xerxes has set in motion a latent divine envy of greatness. "But when a man is in a hurry [toward disaster], God too takes a hand" (line 742).

Contemporaries of the great Persian war saw history itself conforming to the terrifying moral patterns of Greek myth. Aeschylus operates with the recent event no more and no less freely than Sophocles operates with prehistoric legend in his *Oedipus the King.* In both plays the universe is a mantrap, but Aeschylus, after his manner, shows not merely one individual but a great empire caught in its jaws. The technical resources—visual and choral, rather than histrionic—available to him at this period were superbly adapted to such a vast theme. His hesitant use of his two actors and his failure to develop a complex plot do not seem to affect the claim of his *Persians* to rank as the earliest European *tragedy,* as well as the earliest European drama in any genre.

Translations of the play are listed under Aeschylus. The most recent full commentary in English is by H. D. Broadhead, *The Persae of Aeschylus* (1960).—C. J. H.

Peru. See SPANISH AMERICA.

Peshkov, Alexei Maximovich. See Maxim GORKY.

Phantom Lady, The (La dama duende, 1629). A "cape and sword" drama by Pedro CALDERÓN DE LA BARCA. This tangle of shadowy complications, mischievous deceptions, appearances turning into realities, matters of fact turning into clinkers and dust is Calderón's most charming cape-and-sword drama. The play is dominated by Doña Angela, a young widow immured in her brothers' house, who creates a mystery by means of a movable panel separating her rooms from those of the gallant house guest Don Manuel. Closely guarded at home, where in effect she is "wedlocked to a brace of brothers," Angela slips out of the house to see the shows at the palace grounds. There she is observed and pursued by her libertine brother Don Luis, who does not recognize her because she is veiled. On appealing for help to a stranger (Don Manuel), she is enabled to reach home safely while he intercepts Luis. As Manuel and Luis duel, the other brother, Don Juan, appears, recognizes Manuel as his friend and invited guest, and takes him home. Luis is frustrated at every turn, and the more he is frustrated the more prurient he becomes, turning from his sister to Beatriz, his brother's sweetheart, and back again, unwittingly, to his sister. His strong incestuous drive is masked by his rigid adherence to the strictures of the sixteenth-century honor code. It is this incestuous drive that Angela's lover, Manuel, must thwart.

Manuel and his superstitious servant Cosme (who regards Angela as a devil) are inducted into a mystery created by Angela, dressed as a phantom lady, whose purpose is to convert the rule of honor into a rule of love. She thus suggests the veiled and hidden priestess of the new rule, accompanied by her servants and Beatriz. Accordingly, Manuel is the initiate whose faith must be tested by various trials that will indicate his fitness to serve and, eventually, marry the lady. He proves himself worthy, as of course he must, since Angela, the principal agent, is a woman with a cause that he helplessly serves. Acting in the tradition of comedy, she shares her knowledge and purpose with female accomplices who help her to penetrate her isolation, go through doors and walls, and light up the darkness. At the play's end the irrational, in the double form of phantom lady and imagined devil, has been given its due. The incest threat flickering across the anxious face of honor has been put down; the rites of love have superseded the bleak honor formula with its disastrous homicidal consequences.

The Phantom Lady, translated by Edwin Honig, is included in *Calderón: Four Plays* (1961).—E. H.

Phèdre (1677). A tragedy by Jean RACINE. Phèdre, daughter of Minos and Pasiphae and a descendant of the sun, confesses to her nurse Œnone that she is dying of love for Hippolyte, her husband Thésée's son, and is weighted down with guilt. Since Thésée is believed dead, Œnone persuades Phèdre to declare her love to Hippolyte, which, with great shame, she does. When Thésée's return is proclaimed, Phèdre, in

ENGRAVING OF A SCENE FROM JEAN RACINE'S *Phèdre*
(NEW YORK PUBLIC LIBRARY)

a state of total confusion, allows Œnone to tell him that Hippolyte has tried to seduce her. Thésée curses his son and calls down upon him the rage of Neptune. Phèdre, consumed with remorse, goes to Thésée and begs mercy for Hippolyte but learns from her husband that the young man is in love with Princess Aricie. Phèdre then succumbs to jealousy. When Aricie suggests the truth to Thésée, Œnone commits suicide. Although Thésée wants to put a stop to the curse on Hippolyte, it is too late: A sea monster brings about his death. Phèdre, who has taken poison, dies onstage, confessing her crime to Thésée. In *Phèdre* all the characters are more or less guilty, but Phèdre's continual agony dominates the tragedy: Her moral conscience and her superhuman efforts of will are powerless against the fatality of passion, an inexorable curse that weighs upon her and her race.

This play has been translated into English verse by Kenneth Muir in *Five Plays* (1960).—Ja. G.

Philoctetes (**Philoktetes**, 409 B.C.). A tragedy by SOPHOCLES. The scene is a beach on the desert island of Lemnos, where Philoctetes, struck down by disease, was abandoned by his fellow Greeks on their way to lay siege to Troy. Now, ten years later, Odysseus has come to bring him to Troy, because of a prophecy that only Philoctetes with the bow and arrows of Heracles can take the city. With Odysseus is Neoptolemus, the young son of Achilles, whose role is to deceive Philoctetes and lure him aboard ship. Odysseus knows that he himself would be killed on sight. Neoptolemus is at first appalled at the idea of using deceit but finally yields to Odysseus' arguments. He wins Philoctetes' confidence with a false story of his quarrel with the Greek commanders and, when Philoctetes asks for passage home, feigns a reluctant consent. A sailor sent by Odysseus brings news that the Greeks have set out in pursuit of Philoctetes, who now urges Neoptolemus to set sail immediately. But he is suddenly struck down by his disease and gives Neoptolemus the bow to keep for him as he sinks into unconsciousness. The Chorus, Neoptolemus' crew, urge their captain to leave him and sail off with the invincible weapon. But Neoptolemus has been moved to pity by the misfortunes and nobility of Philoctetes and now realizes that the meaning of the prophecy is the rehabilitation and triumph of the crippled hero. Philoctetes' gratitude when he comes to and finds Neoptolemus still there heaps coals of fire on the young man's head; in a sudden partial return to his true nature Neoptolemus tells Philoctetes where he is going. Philoctetes refuses, even though he is promised a cure for his disease; his refusal is made adamant by the sudden appearance of Odysseus, who first proposes to take him by force (Neoptolemus still has the bow) but then contemptuously tells him he can stay on Lemnos—others, not least Odysseus himself, can use the weapons of Heracles. Philoctetes is left alone with the Chorus, but even the certain prospect of starvation will not make him accept their pleas to change his mind. He prefers death and retires to his cave. Unexpectedly, Neoptolemus, followed by a puzzled Odysseus, reappears; he intends to restore the bow. When Odysseus, his arguments exhausted, threatens force, Neoptolemus replies in kind. Odysseus withdraws and Neoptolemus returns the bow and now tries to persuade Philoctetes that for his own good and glory he must go to Troy. He fails and is asked to fulfill his promise to take Philoctetes home. This will mean that he must renounce his own martial ambitions, but now that he has abandoned Odyssean deceit for Achillean truthfulness, he must go all the way and keep his promise. The two men move off to the boat—but of course it cannot end this way; Troy did fall, and Philoctetes must go to Troy. The god Heracles appears to tell him so, and, with a farewell to his island, the hero leaves for health and glory.

Philoctetes is remarkable for its unequivocally "happy" ending: dramatic tension depends, not on whether Philoctetes will go to Troy or to his home (for to Troy he must go), but on the success or failure of the means used to bring him from the island. The three possible methods, deceit, force, and persuasion, are all tried in turn, but since deceit and force are used first, persuasion fails. The development of the complicated plot gives scope for what is perhaps the most fully rounded characterization in Sophoclean drama, that of Neoptolemus, whose return to his true nature after his dangerously swift adaptation to Odyssean trickery moves through subtle psychological gradations to the final act of noble self-sacrifice. The appearance of Heracles is the only *deus ex machina* in extant Sophoclean tragedy, but it is not, as some have thought, a mere mechanical solution of difficulties raised by the plot. The weapons of Heracles were given to Philoctetes for the capture of Troy, not for use against the birds and beasts of Lemnos. They brought Heracles labors and suffering (the same word in Greek), and also glory. Philoctetes' suffering is over; the labors and the glory await him at Troy.

See R. C. Jebb's *The Philoctetes* (1898).—B. M. W. K.

Phoenician Women, The (Phoinissai, c. 411–409 B.C.). A tragedy by EURIPIDES. This play is not one of Euripides' great tragedies, but it has been too harshly criticized. Thebes is under attack by the armies of seven Argive leaders. They are determined to restore to Polyneices, son of Oedipus, his share in the Theban rule, of which his brother, Eteocles, has deprived him. Jocasta, the mother of the warring brothers, tries vainly to reconcile them before the battle. The seer Teiresias warns the Theban king, Creon, that only the sacrifice of his son Menoeceus will save the city from destruction. Creon refuses to commit such an act, but the youth kills himself for the city. The Argives are repulsed, but Eteocles and Polyneices kill each other in single combat and Jocasta commits suicide. Blind Oedipus, whose curse has brought this fate on his sons, is exiled by Creon, who has succeeded to Eteocles' throne. Creon enforces Eteocles' decree that Polyneices must remain unburied, but the dead man's sister Antigone promises to defy this rule. The play ends as Oedipus, mourning his wife and sons, leaves Thebes forever.

We realize what liberties a dramatist could take with the legends when we find Oedipus still alive and at Thebes. More surprisingly, Jocasta is still living. It is she who speaks the monologue. There is almost more action and more *personae* than a Greek play can carry, but there are some very good scenes. Jocasta, both in the exhaustion of sorrow and then in a state of wild passion, is drawn with considerable skill. Eteocles, young, ruthless, and inexperienced; Polyneices, the justice of whose cause is emphasized throughout; Creon, the wise councillor and desperate father; and the noble Menoeceus—all are lifelike and convincing.

The Phoenician Women remains a display of theatrical virtuosity rather than a successful tragedy, but it is easy to understand its popularity in later antiquity.

Translations of the play are listed under Euripides. —G. M. A. G.

Phormio (161 B.C.). A comedy by TERENCE, based on *Epidikazomenos* (*The Lawsuit*) by the Greek playwright Apollodorus of Carystus. *Phormio,* structurally perhaps the best of Roman comedies, lacks the serious content of Terence's *Adelphoe* but is its equal in brilliance of dialogue and is rich in suspense and surprise, in irony and humor. The plot is unusually complicated and contains both deception and mistaken identity. Antipho, son of Demipho, falls in love with a poor but respectable girl, Phanium. Phormio, a helpful parasite and one of the cleverest scoundrels in ancient comedy, arranges a marriage by making the fictitious claim that Antipho is Phanium's nearest relative, and, according to law, must marry her. Phaedria, son of Chremes (Demipho's brother), is devoted to a music girl but has no money to purchase her. When the two fathers return from abroad, Antipho fears that he will be divorced from Phanium, and Phaedria is sure that he will not be allowed to have his sweetheart. Chremes has been living a double life, with a second wife and a daughter abroad; he wishes Antipho to marry his daughter and therefore urges Demipho to insist that Antipho get a divorce. Phormio discovers Chremes' secret and uses it to bring about a successful conclusion to Phaedria's love affair, and Antipho is able to keep his wife when Phanium proves to be Chremes' daughter.

The best-known adaptation of *Phormio* is Molière's *Les Fourberies de Scapin* (1671), which was imitated by Thomas Otway in *The Cheats of Scapin* (1677) and by Edward Ravenscroft in *Scaramouch a Philosopher* (1677). George Colman's *The Man of Business* (1774) was influenced by both *Phormio* and Plautus' *Trinummus.*—G. E. D.

Pichette, Henri (1923–   ). French poet and playwright. Under the direction of Georges Vitaly, *Les Epiphanies,* the first play of Henri Pichette, was produced in 1947. The accompaniment to the text, *musique concrète,* dismayed half of the public attending the performances. It was played on the smallest stage in Paris, Les Noctambules, the former theater for *chansonniers* in the Latin Quarter. The play, divided into five rather static parts, is about the life and death of a poet. Influenced by the techniques of SURREALISM, it is a complicated dramatic poem about a refusal of the world as it is. There is no dramatic action as such, but the strident and moving poetry of the text seemed to announce a new kind of poetic theater.

Director Gerard Philipe urged Pichette to continue writing for the theater. The result was *Nucléa* (1952), a play directed by Philipe at the Théâtre National Populaire with sets by Alexander Calder. *Nucléa* is written in alexandrines, which reduced the volubility of *Les Epiphanies.* The two parts of the play, *Les Infernales* and *Le Ciel humain,* seem to designate the conflict between love and hate or good and evil. Although *Nucléa* was a failure, a renaissance of poetic drama is still one of the hopes of those concerned with the French theater, and in the two plays of Pichette this hope was realized to a limited degree.

Each of the plays of Pichette is a long poem for several voices. It is a lamentation or song on the suffering of a generation. Although there is a verbal power in the texts, there is not enough sense of dramaturgy to assure them a permanent place in French drama.

For a critical study on Pichette, see Roger Shattuck, "A Poet's Progress: Henri Pichette," *French Review* (December 1958).—W. F.

Pinero, Arthur Wing (1855–1934). English playwright and critic. Pinero began his theatrical career at the age of nineteen, becoming an actor in the stock company of Mr. and Mrs. R. H. Wyndham and making his first appearance in the Theatre Royal in Edinburgh on June 22, 1874. His parents had expected him to follow the profession of his father, a solicitor, and Pinero had actually worked in his father's office and studied law for a time. Even while engaged in the reading, however, he had taken elocution classes in the evening at Birkbeck Institute, giving the role of Hamlet at his graduation, had done some amateur acting, and had attended theatrical performances whenever possible. When the theater at Edinburgh burned down in 1875, Pinero went to Liverpool, and from there to London, where he first worked for R. C. Carton at the Globe and then for Henry Irving at the Lyceum. It was Irving who encouraged Pinero to devote all of his time to writing for the stage, and his first efforts were curtain raisers. With the production of his first play, *£200 a Year,* on

ARTHUR WING PINERO (BRANDER MATTHEWS DRA-
MATIC MUSEUM, COLUMBIA UNIVERSITY)

October 6, 1877, at the Globe, Pinero's career as
dramatic author was launched, a career that was not
to end until he had written some fifty plays and had
been knighted in 1909 by Edward VII.

A prolific writer, Pinero wrote all types of plays.
His first real popularity came with the series of farces
that he wrote for the Court Theatre in the 1880's, the
best known of which is perhaps *Dandy Dick* (1887).
He was also successful as the author of Robertsonian
plays of sentiment, his *Trewlaney of the "Wells"*
(1898) being typical of this genre. His reputation,
however, remains firmly based on his "thesis" plays,
that is, plays that treat the problems raised by characters in conflict with their society, to which genre belong *The Profligate* (1889), his first success in this
type; *The Second Mrs. Tanqueray* (1893); *The Notorious Mrs. Ebbsmith* (1895); and *Mid-Channel*
(1909). These plays reveal the influences so greatly
evident in the drama of this period: the "cup and
saucer" realism of Thomas W. Robertson, the "well-
made" tradition of Eugène Scribe, and the special
concerns and problems of Henrik Ibsen and his followers. The influence of Robertson on Pinero was
especially important. "If you ever write a history of
our modern English drama," Pinero once said, "be
fair to Tom Robertson. If it hadn't been for Robertson, I should never have been able to do what I have
done . . . ." Certainly Pinero's attempt to portray
life in the most detailed manner on the stage reflects
the practice of Robertson; Tom Wrench, the hero of
Trelawney of the "Wells," whom Pinero modeled on
Robertson, says at one point in the play: "I strive to
make my people talk and behave like people . . . .
To fashion heroes out of actual, dull, every-day men
. . . and heroines from simple maidens in muslin
frocks."

While clearly successful in portraying this Robertsonian realism on the stage, and undoubtedly impressive in his craftsmanship and dramaturgical technique, Pinero failed to bring to his plays what one

critic has called "an abiding philosophy"; certainly
he has not demonstrated in them or through them a
philosophical attitude that goes much beyond what
might be called conventional respectability or morality. The basic problems in his plays are never satisfactorily discussed, analyzed, or resolved; instead,
they are presented and, somehow, unsatisfactorily
"solved." In spite of this verdict, however, his plays
still remain convincing pieces of evidence for the
growing maturity of the drama during his period.
They also attest Pinero's rightful place as a pioneer in
helping to prepare the way for the "new drama" that
followed.

A good introduction to Pinero's life and plays is
Wilbur D. Dunkel, *Sir Arthur Pinero, a Critical
Biography with Letters* (1941); see also Hamilton
Fyfe, *Arthur Wing Pinero, Playwright* (1902), and
Sir Arthur Pinero's Plays and Players (1930); and
Clayton Hamilton, *The Social Plays of Sir Arthur
Wing Pinero* (4 vols., 1917), which contains a general
introduction and a critical introduction to each play.
—M. T.

Pinget, Robert (1920–   ). French novelist
and playwright. When *Lettre morte* ("Dead Letter"),
was first performed at the Théâtre Récamier in 1960,
Krapp's Last Tape by Samuel Beckett was on the
same program. Pinget is not in any strict sense a disciple of Beckett, but there are similarities of texture
and atmosphere in the two works. Pinget belongs to
the group of "new novelists" published by the Editions de Minuit, and his play *Lettre morte* is based
upon his novel *Le Fiston* (1959). During the two acts
of *Lettre morte,* the protagonist waits for news of his
son, although he knows there will be no news. The
same problems are rehearsed in each scene and the
same conclusion is always reached. It concludes with
the impossibility of being or doing anything.

Pinget adapted his play *Ici ou ailleurs* ("Here or
Elsewhere," 1961) from his novel *Clope au dossier.*
The themes in this play are in *L'Hypothèse* ("The
Hypothesis," 1966) are also, to some degree, those of
Beckett: the implacable solitude of man trapped by
time and speech. A radio play by Pinget, *La Mani-
velle,* was translated by Beckett under the title *The
Old Tune* and performed in England and America. It
is a dialogue between two old men.—W. F.

Pinski, David (1872–1959). Russian-born Yiddish playwright and novelist. Pinski was born in
Mohilev, White Russia, where he received a traditional Jewish religious education as well as an introduction to secular literature. In 1891 he went to
Vienna to study medicine, but the loss of his father's
business in Moscow as a result of the expulsion of the
Jews from that city caused Pinski to leave his studies.
He settled in Warsaw, where he worked as a teacher,
began to write in Yiddish, and became a leading
member of the circle of writers clustering around the
Yiddish writer I. L. Peretz. In his concern for the
welfare of the Jewish masses of Poland, he joined the
Committee for Popular Education of the Jewish
workers' party of Poland, the Bund. In 1896 he
studied briefly at the University of Berlin. Three
years later he settled in New York and began to write
regularly for Yiddish periodicals while taking his
doctorate at Columbia. For the next half a century he
wrote plays, novels, and short stories and was deeply
involved in efforts to support Yiddish cultural insti-

tutions in the United States. A lifelong Socialist and Zionist, Pinski emigrated to Israel in 1949, shortly after the establishment of that state. The last years of his life he suffered from a paralyzing stroke. He died on August 11, 1959, a revered elder of Yiddish literature.

Pinski wrote over sixty plays touching on the major social and intellectual concerns of his day. He was the first Yiddish writer to portray the urban working class, in *Isaac Sheftel* (1899), his first full-length play. *Di Familye Tsvi* ("The Tsvi Family," 1904, titled in English *The Last Jew*) is a drama of ideas, depicting the decline of old-fashioned traditional Jewish life and the emergence of new and conflicting ideologies. Pinski's power as a social satirist is evident in *Der Oytser* (*The Treasure*), a fierce attack on money madness, which was written in 1906 and produced by the Theatre Guild in New York in 1920, in Ludwig Lewisohn's translation. Love and sex were the subjects of *Yankel der Shmid* ("Yankel the Blacksmith," 1906), *Gabri un di Froyen* ("Gabri and the Women," 1908), and *Dovid Hamelekh un zayne Vayber* (*King David and His Wives*, 1920).

Pinski's dramas, historical, realistic, symbolist, are concerned not only with the specific problems of Jewish life but with the problems of men; however, his interest in the ideas overshadows and sometimes overpowers the work and its characters, and his plays often tend to be too talky and tendentious. His importance is nevertheless substantial and derives as much from his boldness in introducing new subjects into Yiddish drama and fiction as it does from the notable quality of his best plays.

Pinski's *King David and His Wives* is contained in *The Dybbuk and Other Great Yiddish Plays* (1966), translated and edited by Joseph C. Landis. *The Treasure* (1915) was translated by Ludwig Lewisohn; *Ten Plays* (1919) and *Three Plays* (1918) were edited by Isaac Goldberg.—J. C. L.

Pinter, Harold (1930–   ). English playwright. Pinter's family were originally Portuguese Jews whose name was Anglicized from da Pinta when they arrived in England early in the twentieth century via eastern Europe. Pinter grew up in the East End of London and went to the local grammar school, where he acted and wrote poetry. On leaving, Pinter joined the Royal Academy of Dramatic Art, but finding the other students too sophisticated, he escaped by faking a nervous breakdown. When he was called up for National Service he stood two trials as a conscientious objector and was discharged with a double fine. After another spell of student life at the Central School of Speech and Drama, Pinter spent eighteen months touring Ireland in the company of the veteran actor-manager Anew McMaster and then returned to England, acting under the name of David Baron.

Meanwhile Pinter was still writing, but it was not until 1957 that he wrote plays. In that year three were produced: *The Room, The Dumb Waiter,* and *The Birthday Party.* They owed nothing to the plays he had acted in and everything to his poetry and his experimental novel *The Dwarfs* (never published as a novel, but staged in 1963). A tour in 1958 of *The Birthday Party* culminated in a disastrous six-night run in London after an almost unanimously abusive press reaction. Pinter next contributed sketches—

HAROLD PINTER

One to Another and *Pieces of Eight*—to a couple of revues at the end of the 1950's and wrote two radio plays—*A Slight Ache* (1959) and *A Night Out* (1960)—before securing his first West End success with THE CARETAKER in 1960. His next full-length play, *The Homecoming,* was produced by the Royal Shakespeare Company in 1965.

To discuss Pinter in relation only to the theater is to distort the picture. He has written radio plays; television plays, such as *Tea Party* (1965) and *The Basement* (1967); and screenplays for *The Pumpkin Eater* (1964), *Accident* (1965), and *The Quiller Memorandum* (1966). Pinter has also regularly produced stage versions of his own radio and television works, such as *A Slight Ache* (1961), *The Collection* (1962), and *The Lover* (1963), and adapted *The Caretaker* for film in 1962.

To have taken possession of so much territory— from avant-garde theater to the mass media—is evidence of Pinter's unusual position in the English scene. He began as an uncompromising minority author and created the taste by which he is appreciated. At first, audiences were baffled by plays in which characters are not obliged to explain their motives or biographies and perhaps never speak a word of truth. It is a direct result of his work that these facts are no longer considered indispensable. Pinter has also established that a play, like a poem, can develop from a *donnée.* In Pinter's case, the characteristic donnée is the invasion of a closed space by an alien force. Furthermore, a play has no duty to justify itself in terms other than its own, Pinter feels, and for this reason his attitude toward his own work has been that of an impersonal protector. "Of course," he said to director Peter Wood on one occasion, "we don't know what the author's intentions are here."

Early in his writing career Pinter admitted to three influences: Franz Kafka, American gangster films, and Samuel Beckett (see THEATER OF THE ABSURD). At that time his plays, more than those of any other playwright's, were responsible for the newly coined term "comedy of menace." This phrase certainly makes sense when applied to *The Birthday Party,* in which a pair of mysterious hoods arrive at a desolate seaside guest house and kidnap its one resident; or to *The Dumb Waiter,* in which a pair of killers idle the time away as they wait for their victim to arrive. But "menace" is hardly the word for *The Caretaker,* and still less for subsequent plays in which Pinter increasingly exchanged his derelict settings and down-and-out characters for environments of moneyed elegance.

Nevertheless, the basic character of Pinter's work has not changed. The main confrontation is still between the man in the room and the man who invades it, and their dialogue still represents an instinctive evasion of communication (not to be confused with the famous "failure of communication"). However, it is impossible to boil Pinter's kind of writing down to statements of content, partly because action proceeds, not from traditional conflicts of character, but from the donnée, and because Pinter's characters have no capacity for conceptual argument, no self-awareness, and no language of affection. What they do possess is a ferocious sense of territory. They do not respond to psychological analysis. But they present few problems if one views them as animals, jealously guarding their lairs. (The clearest instance of this is in *The Homecoming.*) One of Pinter's claims to originality is that he was led, as an artist, to this view of human life some years before the notion of "territorial imperative" became popular.

If a single factor is mainly responsible for Pinter's success, it is his dialogue. To his many imitators, Pinter's dialogue amounts simply to the contrast between Cockney and sudden, seemingly outlandish dictionary words, and his tone, to a calculated gulf between a threatening situation and the characters' dulled response to it. At his worst Pinter himself can turn out this sort of play automatically (notably *The Collection*) as self-canceling machines. But generally his dialogue establishes a network of internal echoes that place the drama in a world of its own. It is a world made up of bits and pieces—details of London's overnight bus services, random information about places the speakers have visited in the past— that accumulate to transform the real landscape into a primitive map full of uncharted regions and rumored monsters. The effect is musical; each scrap of new material is announced like a fresh theme and developed for its thematic possibilities. Pinter, in other words, evolved his own type of poetic drama at a time when the poetic drama movement was at its most unfashionable. But his work relates back, not to T. S. Eliot's West End comedies, but to the Eliot of *Sweeney Agonistes.*

Pinter's plays are available in separate editions. —I. W.

Pirandello, Luigi (1867–1936). Italian poet, essayist, novelist, short-story writer, and dramatist. "I am the son of Chaos," wrote Pirandello, "and not allegorically but literally, because I was born in a country spot [near Porto Empedocle in southern Sicily] called by the people around *Càvusu,* a dialectal corruption of the authentic Greek word *Xáos.*" He was the second child of a sulphur-mine owner. After some private schooling at home, Luigi Piran-

LUIGI PIRANDELLO (ITALIAN CULTURAL INSTITUTE)

dello attended schools in Agrigento and, later, Palermo; in due course, he went to the university in Palermo and in Rome. In 1888 he proceeded to the University of Bonn, where he obtained his *laurea* (doctoral degree) three years later, by which time he had also published two volumes of poetry. Although originally intended by his father for a business career, by 1893 he had settled in Rome as a professional writer. This was the year his first novel, *L'Esclusa* (*The Outcast*), was completed. In 1894 he was married to a girl he hardly knew. Like the marriage of his father before him, it was a marriage made to unite two families of sulphur merchants. The Pirandellos had three children (1895, 1897, 1899), one of whom, Fausto, was to become an eminent painter. In 1904 an economic disaster proved also a personal and mental one. A flood destroyed the mine, and the families of both Pirandello and his wife lost their fortunes. When the Signora received the news, she fainted, was stricken with paralysis of the legs, and could not move for six months afterwards. She was mentally disturbed for the rest of her life. Until 1919 Pirandello refused to place her in an institution: she lived in one after that till her death in 1959. Meanwhile Pirandello found it necessary to supplement the earnings of his literary and journalistic work with teaching at a girls' school, the Istituto Superiore di Magistero di Roma. By the time World War I broke out, he had won a fairly solid reputation as a writer of novels and short stories, but he had given up poetry, and had as yet done very little playwriting. The war years, however, produced RIGHT YOU ARE, which would eventually become one of his three most famous plays, as well as *Pensaci Giacomino* ("Think It Over, Giacomino!") and *Liolà* (both 1916) and other dramas. His first real triumph with the theater public came with *Come prima, meglio di prima* ("As Before, Only Better") in 1920 (of which there would eventually be two Hollywood movie versions, 1945,

1956). There followed the two plays that are probably both his most celebrated and his best: SIX CHARACTERS IN SEARCH OF AN AUTHOR and ENRICO IV.

It was the success of his plays in the twenties that made Pirandello known outside Italy. The director Charles Dullin did much to make him known in France. The director Max Reinhardt did much to make him known throughout central Europe. He himself became an almost familiar figure in Paris, Berlin, London, and even New York. These are the years of the public Pirandello. Mussolini and he exchanged compliments in the press. Pirandello's nationalism was well meant: he needed subsidies for his Teatro D'Arte (1925–1928).

The relationship of Pirandello and Mussolini has not yet been fully described in English. There were items about it in the Italian press at the time. Since then, it has generally been thought bad taste to refer back to it, and all mention of it has been carefully omitted from the ostensibly complete works (1956–1960). In a book of the Fascist period, however, Pirandello's bibliographer of then and now wrote:

> During the Ethiopian campaign, he gave to the country all the gold he had, including the medal of the Nobel prize, a gesture that aroused in Sweden the indignation of the hypocrites and the imbeciles. [*L'opera di Luigi Pirandello* (1939), by Manlio Lo Vecchio Musti]

An American sidelight was reported in *The New York Times*. Clifford Odets and John Howard Lawson visited Pirandello at the Waldorf (July 22, 1935) and remonstrated with him. The maestro's political position was indeed very far from that of the American left. On the one hand, he considered the annexation of Ethiopia legitimate—like the white takeover, as he explained, from the Indians in North America. On the other, he didn't think art should take in politics at all.

And the truth is that, except for a sporadic beating of the drum for Pirandello's plays and Mussolini's politics, Pirandello was an intensely private person. He held, with Henry James, that you either live or you write, and generally he saw himself as a writer:

> I very rarely go to the theatre. By ten, every evening, I am in bed. I get up in good time every morning and usually work till 12. After lunch, I get back to my table at 2:30, usually, and remain there until 5:30; but after the morning hours, I don't do any more writing, unless it is urgently necessary; rather, I read or study. In the evening, after supper, I enjoy conversation with my small family, read the headlines and article titles in some paper or other; then to bed. As you see, there is nothing worthy of special mention about my life: it is all inside, in my work, and in my thoughts which . . . are not cheerful. ["Lettera autobiografica," 1914, reprinted in the sixth and last volume of the *Collected Works* (1960)]

Although Pirandello joined the Fascist party in the autumn of 1924, and never left it, his later works find him more, rather than less, withdrawn from the world around him, and his colleague Corrado Alvaro found a positive rebuke to the Fascists in the text of Pirandello's famous instructions (reprinted in the sixth volume of his collected works) on the treatment of his corpse:

My Ultimate Wishes To Be Respected

I. Let my death pass by in silence. I beg both friends and enemies not to speak of it in the papers, not to give any indication of it. No announcements, no get-togethers.
II. Dead, let me not be clothed. Let me be placed, naked, in a sheet. No flowers on the bed, no lighted candle.
III. Cart of the lowest class, of the poor. Naked. Let no one accompany me, neither relatives nor friends. The cart, the horse, the driver, and basta.
IV. Burn me. And let my body, as soon as it is burned, be dispersed. Because I don't want anything, even ashes, to continue on after me. But if this is not allowed, let the urn be carried to Sicily and be walled up in one of the rough stones of the countryside of Girgenti [Agrigento] where I was born.

The point made by Alvaro is that this document cheated the Fascists out of their plan to give Pirandello a state funeral, with his body swathed in the black shirt of a party member. All quite true. But it does not seem possible that Pirandello intended this, as the document, it is now known, dates back to 1911.

Among the many untold tales of Pirandello's later life (for one can hardly take literally his claim that nothing ever happened to him) would be that of his love for the actress Marta Abba. The gossips of Rome, who are as likely as anyone to know, have it that Miss Abba never became his mistress. Alvaro says that Pirandello was even asked by Mussolini: "Why don't you sleep with her?" Which precipitated the maestro's only known protest against the Duce. "He is a vulgar man," was his comment. Certainly, Marta Abba's image hovers over the last plays; and the maestro made her an outright gift, in his will, of nine plays.

In the collected works of Pirandello we encounter nearly 400 pages of poetry; over 400 pages of full-dress critical essays; over 400 pages of fragments and shorter pieces; 7 novels; 232 short stories; and 44 plays (28 of them based on his own narrative work). Two groups of plays stand a little apart from those which have made Pirandello known in the world. They are, first, a group of plays written in dialect and by that token belonging to Sicilian folk tradition and, second, the symbolistic later plays, culminating in the posthumous and incomplete *I giganti della montagna* (*The Mountain Giants*). But the world has probably not been mistaken in giving most attention to the so-called philosophical plays written between 1917 and 1924, among which the agreed masterworks are *Right You Are, Six Characters,* and *Enrico IV*.

The main thrust of the philosophy in these three plays is to undermine the traditional antinomy of appearance and reality with the nihilistic paradox: Appearance *is* reality, there is not really anything more to life than meets the eye. From which an ethic is derived: Be content with what meets your eye, be tolerant of what meets other people's eyes, and don't ask more of life. A defeatist metaphysic thus joins hands with a sad belief in the few human realities that are left when God and an intelligible universe are torn away—such realities as compassion and family piety.

> I am so impressed [Pirandello says] with this sense of a changing life, so deeply distressed at my inability to seize upon anything that is certain, fixed, definite, true, that almost in despair I cling to the sentiments that are most elemental and basic in me. Without my father, without my wife, without my children that I intensely feel as flesh of my flesh, I should be lost in the world. [Cited in *Essays in Modern Italian Literature* (1950) by Arthur Livingston.]

In the long run, Pirandello's philosophy and ethics are less significant than his psychology—that is, his presentation of inner experience. If Ibsen has presented an image of modern man as neurotic, Pirandello tends to see him as verging upon psychosis, if not actually tumbling into it. Thus *Enrico IV* has the form of grandiose tragedy, but its hero shows many of the marks of schizophrenia. *Right You Are* is haunted by unbearable traumatic shocks: the shock of losing a loved one by death, the shock of having a loved one taken away by force, the shock for a young woman of being made love to with excessive intensity, the shock for a young woman of being embraced as a daughter by a woman who is not her mother. Schizophrenia represents an attempt to get around otherwise unbearable pain at any cost: the high cost in fantasy is what society laughs at as lunacy. And so the small-town society of *Right You Are* laughs at the doings of three disturbed people who have found strange ways of making love possible and thereby making life bearable.

What is *Six Characters in Search of an Author* really about? The title begins to answer the question. To begin with, this is a play about the creative process: Pirandello used to feel that his characters were persons who came and asked him to put them in his books. Secondly, the play is about form in art: The visited author can only accept his visitors if he can also create the structure into which they fit. For art has a structure, even if life does not. Or as Pirandello might have put it: Art *better* have a structure, *because* life does not. So the play becomes among other things an endless paradoxical debate about the difference between art and life, acting and being. Up to a point, then, it is a philosophical play, but if one looks further into the story of the six characters, one again runs headlong into schizophrenia. The Father is markedly schizophrenic and has acted with mad destructiveness against those who are nearest and dearest. Again, the Pirandellian plot centers on traumas, and this time the classically Freudian ones: a father seducing his own daughter, a son seeing his parents make love, a sibling murdering a sibling. But these are not miscellaneous items. Rather they are arranged in sequence to articulate the drama of a Father in search of an Author. This author may be taken to symbolize more things than one. For example: God, the Author of our being. Among other things, this play laments the "death of God." But probably the main force of the symbol is fatherhood in its down-to-earth sense. The last hundred years have seen the breakdown, or partial breakdown, of paternal authority in the family itself, and modern families often live out their lives in search of a Father. In Pirandello's play, even the Father is searching for a Father: This is his tragedy. And the tragedy turns toward farce when he finds—through what is after all the main action on stage—a father as inadequate as himself: the Director.

There has been a tendency among Italian critics of the 1960's to regard Pirandello primarily as a master of the short story. It is open to those who take this line to note that his plays are of uneven quality and that only a small group of them are masterpieces that can be placed beside the best of Ibsen, Strindberg, Chekhov, and Shaw. To this, however, it can be retorted that Shaw and Strindberg—if not Ibsen and Chekhov—were uneven writers too and that, in any case, it is no mean achievement to have written several plays that are among the greatest of the past hundred years. The English critic Martin Esslin represents a substantial body of contemporary opinion when he writes of Pirandello the dramatist in this vein:

> Among the creators of the modern theater, Luigi Pirandello stands in the very first rank, next to Ibsen, Strindberg, and Shaw. And even though his plays may be less frequently performed in the English-speaking world today than those of Shaw or Ibsen (Strindberg is neglected equally unjustly), his influence on the work of the dramatists of our own age is far stronger, far more active, than that of those two giants.
>
> For Pirandello, more than any other playwright, has been responsible for a revolution in man's attitude to the world, in its way as significant as the revolution caused by Einstein's discovery of the concept of relativity. Pirandello has transformed our whole concept of *reality* in human relations . . . [*The New York Times,* June 25, 1967]

In Italian, there is a compact (six volumes) edition of the collected works in the Classici Contemporanei Italiani series (1956–1960). The sixth volume includes an updated version of the standard bibliography by Manlio Lo Vecchio Musti, which had appeared in two earlier forms: two volumes, 1937 and 1940 respectively, and a single-volume edition, 1952. (The earliest version of the bibliography remains necessary because it alone acknowledges the existence of Fascism. As for the six-volume edition itself, it is highly serviceable but it is not absolutely complete. And scholarly suspicions are inevitably aroused by the omission of such a thing as Pirandello's homage to Mussolini in a famous lecture that pretends to be meticulously edited—"variant readings" and all).

In English, not only is there no collected edition, but many of the works of Pirandello have gone unpublished altogether; a number of others have stayed in print for only a year or two; some of the plays have appeared only in acting editions not sold in the bookshops. Listed here are all drama titles by Pirandello published in the United States up through 1968. This means that titles published in Great Britain only are omitted, as are American anthologies, magazines, and newspapers in which plays by Pirandello have appeared. For lengthier bibliographies issued in America, the reader is referred to *Naked Masks,* as cited below, Appendix II, and "Pirandello in England and the United States," A Chronological List of Criticism, by Antonio Illiano (*Bulletin of the New York Public Library*, February 1967).

Three Plays (1922), contains *Six Characters, Henry IV, Right You Are If You Think So; Each in His Own Way,* and *Two Other Plays* (1923), the two other plays being *The Pleasure of Honesty* and *Naked; The One Act Plays* (1928) has eleven titles; *As You Desire Me* (1931); *Tonight We Improvise* (1932); *Naked Masks: Five Plays* (1952), contains *Liolà, It is So!* (*If You Think So*), *Henry IV, Six Characters, Each in His Own Way; Right You Are* (1954); *The Mountain Giants and Other Plays* (1958); *The Rules of the Game, The Life I Gave You, Lazarus* (1959); *To Clothe the Naked and Two Other Plays* (1962), the two other plays being *The Rules of the Game* and *The Pleasure of Honesty;* and *One Act Plays* (1964), contains thirteen titles. In the 1960's, the Samuel French catalogue has been listing seven titles in separate acting editions. Since no date of publication is given, the often much earlier copyright dates are misleading. The titles are: *Diana and Tuda, The Wives' Friend, As You Desire Me, No One Knows How, Tonight We Improvise, To Find Oneself, When One Is Somebody.*—E. B.

Pixérécourt, [René Charles] Guilbert de (1773–1844). French playwright. Sometimes referred to as the "Corneille of melodrama," Pixérécourt wrote some 120 plays, alone or in collaboration, of which 59 were popular melodramas. For thirty-eight years he enjoyed an unrivaled popularity in the second-rate theaters in the section of Paris known as the Boulevard du Temple or "Boulevard du Crime." Born in Nancy, he led a somewhat tormented life. He wrote sixteen melodramas filled with the vagaries and hubbub of the Paris streets but could not get them performed. Finally, the Ambigu-Comique put on *Les Petits Auvergnats* ("The Children from Auvergne") in 1797.

His fame actually began with the performance of *Victor, ou l'enfant du forêt* ("Victor, Child of the Forest," 1798), in which a bandit chieftain who has abandoned his son helps him, through a deathbed confession of his past, to marry a respectable girl. From a dime novel by François Guillaume Ducray-Duminil, Pixérécourt took the virtuous ingenue of his best-known and probably most representative MÉLODRAME, *Coelina, ou l'enfant du mystère* ("Coelina, Child of Mystery," 1800). Coelina is driven from home on the day of her marriage to the model son of her guardian when a jealous suitor casts doubts on the legitimacy of her birth. Later, fleeing in disguise, the villain is captured after a spectacular battle with a fortuitously introduced band of pursuing archers. Coelina's reputation is cleared and she is reunited with her fiancé. Other memorable examples of Pixérécourt's art are *Le Pèlerin blanc* ("The White Pilgrim," 1801), which, adapted as *The Wandering Boys,* enjoyed 1,500 performances in the United States; *Tékéli* ("Tékéli, or The Siege of Mongatz," 1803), about a seventeenth-century patriot who hides in a barrel for nearly a whole act; and *Le Chien de Montargis* ("The Dog of Montargis," 1814), in which a blind boy, falsely condemned for murder, is saved from the scaffold by a dog who recognizes the murderer.

Pixérécourt used the popular novels, historical tales, and *boulevard* entertainments of his day as sources. His formula for melodrama was fixed by the time he wrote *Coelina.* His plots dramatized suffering innocence and outraged virtue in various forms and always included the same four stereotyped characters: pure heroine, manly hero, unregenerate villain, and a well-meaning, bumbling fool who interjected comic relief at appropriate intervals. Sometimes the heavy father was added. Pixérécourt undoubtedly owed a debt to the late-eighteenth-century *Harlequinades* of the boulevards and the more serious, sentimental pantomimes of Jean François [Arnould-] Mussot. But he said himself that he studied the plays of Louis Sébastien Mercier and wrote "in the genre of Sedaine" (Michel Jean Sedaine, author of many tearful *opéras-comiques*). He deprecated his very obvious impact on the romantic dramas of Alexandre Dumas père, Alfred de Vigny, and Victor Hugo. His *Dernières Réflexions de l'auteur sur la mélodrame* ("The Author's Last Thoughts on Melodrama," 1843) are included in the last volume of his *Théâtre choisi.* Many of his plays were acted in England in free adaptations by Thomas Holcroft, Isaac Pocock, and others. The performance of Holcroft's *A Tale of Mystery* in 1802, a free adaptation of *Coelina,* marked the official introduction of French melodrama to England.

The best discussion of Pixérécourt's work and its influence upon French, English, and American melodrama is F. Rahill's *The World of Melodrama* (1967). For the impact of Pixérécourt's technique upon French Romantic playwrights, the reader should consult A. Lacey's *Pixérécourt and the French Romantic Drama* (1928).—S. S. S.

Plain Dealer, The (1676). A comedy by William WYCHERLEY. *The Plain Dealer* was first performed late in the year at the Theatre Royal in Drury Lane by the King's Company.

The main plot concerns Manly, the misanthropic "plain dealer" who is disgusted with the insincerity and disloyalty of mankind. Manly returns from war to find that his fiancée, Olivia, to whom he entrusted a large sum of money, has secretly married his friend Vernish. Determining to have Olivia as an act of revenge, he employs his page as an intermediary. In reality the page is Fidelia, who has disguised herself in order to follow Manly. When Olivia falls in love with the page and makes an assignation, Manly manages to substitute himself and brings about Olivia's disgrace. At the end he is prepared to marry Fidelia, whose identity and loyalty have been revealed. The subplot presents the tricks by which Manly's lieutenant Freeman gets money from the wealthy and litigious Widow Blackacre.

The suggestion for the central character, but little else, comes from Molière's *Le Misanthrope.* The part of the plot concerning Fidelia is pure romance, and the satirically drawn characters owe much to Ben Jonson. The satire of legal forms and jargon in the Widow Blackacre scenes is high-spirited and funny, while that in the main plot sometimes becomes so bitter that it has tragic overtones (see ENGLAND: *Restoration drama*).

Leo Hughes has edited this play with introduction and notes for the Regents Restoration Drama Series (1967). It is also available in Barron's Educational Series, edited by T. Ehrsam (1966).—E. W.

Plautus [**Titus Maccius**] (c. 251–184 B.C.). Roman comic playwright. Plautus was born in Sarsina, Umbria, and went to Rome at an early age. Here he acted on the stage, possibly as a clown in the *fabula Atellana.* In evidence of this, some scholars think that Plautus received the name Maccius because he played the role of Maccus, the clown. There was a story in antiquity that Plautus made sufficient money in the theater to invest in business but lost all his wealth and began to compose comedies while working as a laborer in a mill, but the tale is doubted by modern scholars. His early connection with the theater, however, is believed to explain his later mastery of stagecraft and farcical effects.

More than one hundred comedies were ascribed to Plautus in antiquity, of which perhaps as many as forty-five were authentic. The Roman scholar Terentius Varro selected twenty-one as undoubtedly Plautine, since they had been accepted by all earlier literary critics, and he favored a number of others as also genuine on the basis of their style and humor. The extant plays, twenty plus the fragmentary *Vidularia* (*The Tale of a Traveling Bag*), are probably identical with the twenty-one on Varro's first list, the *fabulae Varronianae.* They are all *palliatae,* or "comedies in Greek dress," based on originals of Greek New Comedy. The titles of the twenty plays by Plautus, and the authors and names of the Greek originals, when known, are: AMPHITRYON, *Asinaria* (*The Comedy of Asses;* based on *Onagos* of Demophilus), AULULARIA (Menander?), *Bacchides* (*The Two Bacchises; Dis Exapaton* of Menander), CAPTIVI, *Casina* (*Clerumenoe* of Diphilus), *Cistellaria* (*The Casket Comedy; Synaristosae* of Menander), *Curculio, Epidicus,* MENAECHMI, *Mercator* (*The Merchant; Emporos* of Philemon), MILES GLORIOSUS (*Alazon,* author unknown), MOSTELLARIA (*Phasma,* possibly by Theognetus), *Persa* (*The Girl from Persa*), *Poenulus* (*The Carthaginian; Carchedonios,* possibly by Menander), *Pseudolus,* RUDENS (original by Diphilus), *Stichus* (*Adelphoe* of Menander, but not the *Adelphoe* used by Terence), *Trinummus* (*The Three-Penny Day; Thesauros* of Philemon), and *Truculentus.*

The surviving comedies seem all to date from the last twenty or twenty-five years of Plautus' life. *Stichus* was presented in 200 B.C. and *Pseudolus* in 191 B.C. Numerous criteria have been established to determine the chronology of the other plays, one of the most convincing being the steadily increasing use of song and dance. It seems possible, at least, to separate the plays into an early, middle, and late period; to the early period (before 200 B.C.) are assigned *Asinaria, Mercator, Miles Gloriosus, Cistellaria,* and perhaps *Poenulus;* to the middle period (200–192 B.C.) *Stichus, Aulularia, Curculio,* and probably *Captivi, Rudens,* and *Trinummus;* to the late period (191–184 B.C.) *Pseudolus, Bacchides, Casina,* and probably *Amphitryon, Persa,* and *Truculentus.*

Plautus' plots usually portray love affairs, with the comic confusions resulting from trickery or mistaken identity or a combination of the two. The main characters, inherited from Greek comedy, are fathers, sons, wives, courtesans, intriguing slaves, and braggart warriors. The plays, however, cover a wide range, from vulgar burlesque (*Casina*) and farce (*Menaechmi, Stichus*) to serious and refined comedy (*Captivi, Trinummus*), from plays emphasizing character (*Aulularia, Truculentus*) to rollicking deceptions (*Bacchides, Miles Gloriosus, Mostellaria, Pseudolus*), from a mythological parody (*Amphitryon*) to a romantic comedy (*Rudens*).

Plautus' primary purpose was to arouse the laughter of his spectators, and he expanded his plots by means of comic repetitions and digressions. His stock in trade included improbable situations, unexpected and laughable developments, ludicrous contrasts, humorous monologues by slaves and parasites, comic asides, and violation of the dramatic illusion by direct address to the audience, as in *Aulularia,* when Euclio asks the spectators to point out the person who has stolen his gold.

In his desire for farcical situations and in his interest in song and dance, Plautus was probably far more indebted to the earlier dramatic forms of Italy than to Greek New Comedy. Above all, he was a comic genius, equaled only by Aristophanes and Shakespeare. His comedies are thoroughly Roman, in spite of their Greek plots and settings; they contain many local allusions and references, as well as parodies of legal and military terminology. He is especially famous for his mastery of colloquial Latin.

His language is rich in phrases of alliteration and assonance, jokes (sometimes obscene, but always effective), puns, plays upon words, humorous terms of abuse and endearment, parody of epic themes, incongruous similes and comic exaggerations, and monstrous but meaningful name formations, the most striking of which occurs in *Persa:* Vaniloquidorus Virginesvendonides Nugiepiloquides Argentumextenebronides Tedigniloquides Nugides Palponides Quodsemelarripides Numquameripides. This has been brilliantly translated as "Blabberodorus Maidvendorovich Lightchatterson Cashscrewer0utstein Ibn Saidwhatyoudeserve MacTrifle McBlarney Whatonceyougetyourhandson Neverpartwithitski." In all these respects Plautus differs from his successor in comedy, the more subtle and restrained Terence, who lacks his range and versatility.

The comedies of Plautus were produced on the Roman stage after Terence's death, and minor additions and alterations may have been made to the text of the plays during this Plautine revival. They were still presented in the time of Cicero, who praised the actor Roscius as an interpreter of Plautus. The plays continued to be read and edited during the Roman Empire, but were apparently less popular in the middle ages than were the more sedate works of Terence.

From the beginning of the Renaissance, Plautus has had a decisive influence on modern comedy, being translated, adapted, and imitated by the outstanding dramatists of Western Europe, including Lodovico Ariosto, Shakespeare, Ben Jonson, and Molière. The popular musical comedy by Burt Shevelove, Larry Gelbart, and Stephen Sondheim, *A Funny Thing Happened on the Way to the Forum* (1962), combined elements from several Plautine plays, especially *Miles Gloriosus, Mostellaria,* and *Pseudolus.*

George E. Duckworth, *The Nature of Roman Comedy* (1952), discusses numerous aspects of the plays of Plautus, including presentation, stage conventions, plots, characters, thought and moral tone, the comic spirit, language and style, meter and song, originality, and later influence. In *Roman Laughter: The Comedy of Plautus* (1968), Erich Segal maintains that Plautus delighted his spectators on holiday by turning Roman standards and moral values topsy-turvy: sons oppose fathers, wives domineer over husbands, slaves deceive masters with impunity. Translations of all twenty comedies of Plautus are by Paul Nixon (5 vols., 1916–1938), and by George E. Duckworth and others in *The Complete Roman Drama* (2 vols., 1942). Selected translations are by Lionel Casson, *Six Plays of Plautus* (1963), and by E. F. Watling, *The Rope and Other Plays* (1964) and *The Pot of Gold and Other Plays* (1965). See also translations listed under ROMAN COMEDY.—G. E. D.

Playboy of the Western World, The (1907). A tragicomedy in three acts by John Millington SYNGE. Synge's masterpiece, *Playboy of the Western World*, is a satiric and ironic work in which the repressed peasant imagination transforms the whining Christy Mahon, a would-be parricide, into a conquering hero of the West of Ireland. When the trembling Christy staggers into Michael James's pub and gives his bloody account of how he murdered his tyrannical father with a loy (spade), the people of Mayo are immediately captivated by what they consider his great and courageous deed. Life in this remote village has been so stagnant and depressing for the publican and his daughter, Pegeen Mike, that they succumb to the excitement and hire Christy to work in the pub and also to protect Pegeen, because "Bravery's a treasure in a lonesome place, and a lad would kill his father,

I'm thinking, would face a foxy divil with a pitchpike on the flags of hell."

Thus the mythology of the heroic Christy is launched, and after he has been exalted and fought over by Pegeen and the crafty Widow Quin, even the incredulous Christy becomes a believer: "It's great luck and company I've won me in the end of time—two fine women fighting for the likes of me—till I'm thinking this night wasn't I a foolish fellow not to kill my father in the years gone by." In direct contrast to the presumed heroism of Christy, there is the pietistic cowardice of Shawn Keogh, Pegeen's timid fiancé who is afraid of life itself and invokes the name of Father Reilly and the Holy Saints at the slightest provocation. Confronted by the prospect of marriage to a frightened fool like Shawn, Pegeen is eager to choose Christy instead, for she rightly sees a poet as well as a hero in him: "I've heard all times it's the poets are your like, fine fiery fellows with great rages when the temper's roused."

At the moment of his triumph, however, when Christy has won all the games and sports and fulfilled the legend that the people of Mayo so desperately created, his somewhat less than mortally wounded father, Old Mahon, comes in with a bloody bandage round his head and claims his errant son. Suddenly Christy's myth explodes as he grabs another loy and tries to "kill" his father a second time, for now the reality of "a dirty deed" committed in their own back yard destroys the romance of "a gallous story" for the villagers, and Pegeen herself leads them in a cruel attempt to torture Christy. But he rises up in a

A SCENE FROM J. M. SYNGE'S *The Playboy of the Western World* (IRISH TOURIST BOARD)

final display of genuine courage and reinvokes his playboy legend: "Ten thousand blessings upon all that's here, for you've turned me a likely gaffer in the end of all, the way I'll go romancing through a romping lifetime from this hour to the dawning of the judgment day." For poor Pegeen, however, this comic-ironic reversal turns to tragedy as she cries out in her lonely grief at the end, "I've lost the only Playboy of the Western World."—D. K.

Pleasant Satyre of the Thrie Estaitis, Ane (1540). A dramatic satire by the Scottish poet Sir David Lyndsay (1490–c. 1554). Performed before King James V of Scotland and his chief advisers, this play is a remarkable example of forthright criticism of authority in an age when such criticism was often regarded as treason. The principal target of attack is the clerical hierarchy, although neither the king nor the Scottish parliament escapes unscathed. Cast in the form of a morality play, the satire deals with the efforts of a king, Rex Humanitas, to reform his kingdom and himself. Having purged himself of his dissolute acquaintances, he summons the three estates: Spirituality (the clergy), Temporality (the aristocracy), and Merchant (the middle class). All three are subjected to the criticism of John the Commonweal. Temporality and Merchant quickly acknowledge their faults and promise to make amends. Spirituality, however, remains obstinate, acknowledging no authority but the pope. This recalcitrance forces John to elaborate his complaints, emphasizing the greed and sensuality of the clergy. As the various abuses are enumerated, the other two estates declare their determination to put an end to the wanton irregularities of the clergy. The play ends with a sermon by Folly, who proceeds to satirize all men, the king included, as fools.

Interspersed within the play are a number of episodes designed to illustrate in broad comic scenes the abuses of the Church. The complete play—alterations and additions were made in 1552 and 1554—is very long, running to more than 4,600 lines. A much abbreviated version was successfully produced in 1948 at the Edinburgh Festival under the direction of Tyrone Guthrie.

A modern edition of the play has been edited by James Kinsley (1954). W. Muirson's *Sir David Lyndsay* (1938) contains an extended discussion of the play's background.—E. Q.

Plough and the Stars, The (1926). A play by Sean O'CASEY. For the action of *The Plough and the Stars* O'Casey goes back to the most important event in modern Irish history: the 1916 Easter Rising against the British. He concentrates on the poor people struggling and dying in the Dublin slums, in contrast to the soldiers fighting and dying in the streets. We are continually confronted in the play by a series of tragicomic ironies: while the men are at a street meeting outside a pub listening to speeches about the "sanctity of bloodshed," two of the women, Ginnie Gogan and Bessie Burgess, are inside the pub engaged in a hair-pulling brawl about respectability; when the city is bombarded and wounded men appear, the women rage at each other in a mock battle over the ownership of a pram to be used in looting the shops.

Throughout the play the central characters spend most of their time attacking each other in varying degrees of hilarity and bitterness—Nora Clitheroe and Bessie Burgess, Bessie and Ginnie Gogan, Peter Flynn and the Covey, the Covey and Fluther Good —but when the shooting starts they shrewdly join forces against a common enemy—the war. The heroes at the barricades are constantly deflated by episodes of profane farce, and in the end the anti-heroes of the tenements become heroic by comic and ironic proxy, especially Fluther and Bessie. Before he gets roaring drunk, Fluther, the "well-flavored" man, risks his life to bring the distraught Nora back safely from the fighting area. The sharp-tongued Bessie gives a bowl of milk to little Mollser, who is dying of tuberculosis, helps Nora into the house, then risks her life in the machine-gunned streets looking for a doctor. At the end it is Fluther again who dodges bullets to make arrangements for the burial of the two children, Mollser and Nora's premature baby, and it is Bessie who nurses the deranged Nora through three sleepless days and nights, only to be shot trying to protect her. These noncombatants are the chief sufferers and ironic heroes as the city goes up in flames.—D. K.

Plutus (Ploutos, 388 B.C.). A comedy by ARISTOPHANES. An Athenian citizen, Chremylus, following the instructions of the oracle of Apollo at Delphi, is trying to make friends with a blind old man he has met by chance. The old man reveals himself to be Plutus ("Wealth"), condemned by Zeus to live forever sightless. Chremylus wants to persuade him to be cured, for, no longer blind, Plutus will then associate only with good men instead of, as now, with good and bad alike. However, Plutus is afraid of Zeus, but Chremylus convinces him that Zeus is in reality powerless, since it is only for the sake of Plutus that men worship him. Plutus is cured, over the objections of Penia ("Poverty"), who claims that only poverty makes men work and become useful citizens. The effects of Plutus' cure are revolutionary. All wicked people are reduced to penury; Hermes, Zeus's messenger boy, is forced to apply for a new job; and the Priest of Zeus the Savior resigns and offers his services to Plutus instead. Plutus is installed on the Acropolis, in the treasury of the Parthenon, and the play ends with a mass celebration.

Plutus was by far the most popular of Aristophanes' plays (more manuscripts of it survive than of any other play by him). For wild fantasy the play substitutes moralizing allegory, and its plot faithfully works out the intellectual implications of the debate between Wealth and Poverty. Aristophanes was clearly responding to a new audience, with new expectations—a bourgeois public, interested not in political controversy but in private concerns of money, personal behavior, and security. The character of Carion, foreshadowed by Xanthias in *Frogs,* is the prototype for the "clever slave" of New Comedy, and the usurpation of Zeus by Plutus is a perfect image of the change in Athenian life between the fifth and the fourth centuries B.C.

Translations of the play are listed under Aristophanes.—K. C.

Poland. Until the late fifteenth and early sixteenth centuries Polish vernacular drama was rare. The Latin language was used almost exclusively for Polish mystery and morality plays and the secular dramas of Humanist authors. Polish vernacular literature in general developed significantly only after the middle of the sixteenth century.

The only vestige of the late medieval and early Renaissance mystery and passion pageant to find a place in the permanent repertoire of the Polish theater was Mikołaj z Wilkowiecka's *Historia o chwalebnym Zmartwychwstaniu Pańskim* (*History of the Lord's Glorious Resurrection*), dating probably from the 1570's and written originally in the vernacular. It was adapted for the modern stage by the foremost theatrical producer of twentieth-century Poland, Leon Schiller (1887–1954), and staged for the first time since the sixteenth century in 1923, in the Reduta Theater of Warsaw, a theater that had attracted attention from the time of its founding by Juliusz Osterwa in 1919 for its devotion to the cause of Symbolist drama.

The Renaissance of sixteenth-century Poland brought a knowledge of the classical Roman drama of Seneca, Plautus, and Terence. Poland, Christianized in the late tenth century, clung tenaciously to the rich tradition of the Latin language and Latin culture almost down to the eighteenth century and in fact has never utterly forsaken it. The masters of classical Roman tragedy (Seneca) and classical Roman comedy (Plautus, Terence) were read and enjoyed in Poland among the educated gentry, which represented a relatively sizable proportion of the population. Roman plays were staged not only where expected—in the schools and at the University of Krakow (founded in 1364)—but also at the court. To capture audiences in towns and villages where the number of people able to read Latin was considerably smaller, the classics of Roman drama were extensively translated into Polish in the late sixteenth and early seventeenth centuries. These translations, often of high quality, were followed soon by freer adaptations, which came to function collectively as the foundation of an original Polish dramatic culture. A number of adaptations were made but the one generally acknowledged as the best and also the most influential was Piotr Ciekliński's version of Plautus' *Trinummus* (*Potrójny* in Polish, pub. 1597).

Although an original Polish drama was not yet developed in sixteenth-century Poland, the Renaissance did produce one major work, the *Odprawa posłów greckich* (*Dismissal of the Grecian Envoys*), a Senecan-type rhetorical drama on a classical subject written by the greatest poet of the Polish Renaissance (and in fact the best poet in the language before Adam Mickiewicz in the nineteenth century), Jan Kochanowski (1530–1584). Staged at the court theater for the first time in 1578 on the occasion of the wedding of the vice-chancellor of the Polish crown, the *Odprawa posłów greckich* is generally regarded in Poland as the one masterpiece of old Polish drama. It was not, however, the only dramatic work of old Poland to find a lasting place in the repertoire. The first prominent writer in the vernacular Polish language, Mikołaj Rej (1505–1569), a Calvinist, exercised his talent in the dialogue, which was among the best-cultivated genres of Renaissance Polish literature. Rej's major dialogues—primitive attempts at playwriting at best—included the satirical and sociologically interesting *Rozmowa między panem, wójtem a plebanem* ("A Conversation Between a Lord, Bailiff, and Parish Priest"), *Kupiec*

("The Merchant"), and the biblical *Żywot Józefa* ("Life of Joseph"). The last attracted the attention in recent years of producer Kazimierz Dejmek and was, like Mikołaj z Wilkowiecka's *Historia*, adapted for the contemporary Polish stage. In its new dress it was presented on the boards of the National Theater (Teatr Narodowy) in Warsaw in 1958.

The emergence of Polish comedy also dates to the second half of the sixteenth century. Out of the comicorealistic *interludia* and *intermedia* of the Jesuit school drama and the mystery plays, and no less indebted to the dialogue tradition of Renaissance Poland, there evolved a primitive comic drama, in its early stages of development very much akin to the late fifteenth-century German Shrovetide plays (*Fastnachtsspiele*). Most of the plays, of which about twenty are now extant, were written by writers of burgher origin, for the most part former teachers and students in Cracow who were driven by economic need to take employment as Latin teachers, sextons, cantors, and assistants to parish priests in the vast network of parochial schools organized in Poland after the Council of Trent (1545–1563). These amateur burgher writers, who often wandered from town to town, mostly in southeast Poland, in the late sixteenth and early seventeenth centuries in an effort to improve their lot, came to be known as *rybałci* (*rybałts*), a term borrowed from the Italian *ribaldo* and used during that time in Poland as the name for a sort of wandering minstrel. Because of this the comedy of these burgher minstrels is generally known in Polish as the *komedia rybałtowska*. Some of the extant plays from the 1590's deal with the wartime adventures of Albertus, a village sexton sent off to the army as a recruit in place of his parish priest, for example, *Wyprawa plebańska* ("The Parish Priests' Expedition," pub. 1590) and *Albertus z wojny* ("Albertus Returns from War," pub. 1596). They are reminiscent to some extent of the slight comedies (the *Ruzzante* playlets) of the sixteenth-century Venetian writer Angelo Beolco (1502–1543), which could conceivably have become known in Poland through Italian *commedia dell'arte* troupes that traveled as far as Russia in the sixteenth and seventeenth centuries. The so-called Albertus plays gave rise in turn to a cycle of equally primitive comedies in which the hero is no longer Albertus, but the carousing, hard-drinking, brawling minister's son Matiasz. Two of the rybałt plays deal exclusively with the harsh conditions of contemporary, parochial, village school life and reflect the milieu generally in which the komedia rybałtowska arose. These are *Komedia rybałtowska nowa* ("The New Rybałt Comedy," pub. 1615) and *Szkolna mizeria* ("School Misery," pub. 1633).

Structurally more advanced works than the rybałt comedies were several early seventeenth-century comedies which emerged from the tradition of Shrovetide entertainments. The most outstanding examples of this type of drama were the anonymous *Mięsopust* ("Shrovetide," pub. 1622), *Dziewosłąb dworski* ("The Courtly Wooer," pub. 1620), *Marancya* (pub. 1620–1622), and *Z chłopa król* ("The Peasant Become King"), written between 1629 and 1633 (first printed in 1637) by Piotr Baryka, a writer probably of burgher origin of whom little is known. Undoubtedly the best of the rybałt and Shrovetide comedies, *Z chłopa król* is a play-within-a-play built around the ancient motif of the transformed peasant.

The komedia rybałtowska and Shrovetide comic traditions reached their apogee in the first three decades of the seventeenth century. When town life disintegrated in the political and military upheavals of seventeenth-century Poland, the rybałt culture—and with it its drama—vanished, a unique and curious phenomenon in the history of Polish culture for which Western analogues are not easy to find. Although a number of seventeenth-century texts have been lost, presumably the last comedy in the rybałt and Shrovetide traditions is an anonymous work dealing with runaway peasants, *Uciechy lepsze i pożyteczniejsze* ("The Best and Most Useful Pleasures," 1655).

The court continued in the seventeenth and eighteenth centuries to function as something of a permanent theater in Poland, in view of the fact that a national theater as such did not exist. Under King Władysław IV (1595–1648; of the Swedish house of Vasa) and his brother King Jan Kazimierz (1609–1672) theatrical performances constituted a major source of court entertainment. Commedia dell'arte groups visited Warsaw and performed at the court, as did companies of the so-called English comedians who visited Warsaw after Danzig on their tours through central and eastern Europe. An English company led by John Green visited Warsaw and performed at the court in 1611 and 1613 and presented a repertoire that included Kyd, Marlowe, Lily, and possibly also Shakespeare. It was also at the court, in 1662, in the time of Jan Kazimierz, that Corneille appeared for the first time on the Polish stage—in an able translation of *Le Cid* by the foremost Polish Baroque poet, Jan Andrzej Morsztyn (1613–1693).

Members of the House of Saxony, Augustus II (1697–1733) and Augustus III (1733–1763), ruled over Poland from the end of the seventeenth to the mid-eighteenth century. In the reign of August II, Italian opera, French ballet, and commedia dell'arte troupes performed regularly on visits from the seat of Saxon power, Dresden. Native Polish offerings, however, were few and what Polish theater existed at the time consisted mostly of foreign productions.

When a native Pole, Stanisław August Poniatowski, returned to the Polish throne in 1764 bringing the intellectual stagnation of the Saxon era to an end, a need was keenly felt for a national theater. This finally came into being on November 29, 1765. Its first Polish production was a mediocre comedy modeled on Molière's *Les Fâcheux, Natręci* ("The Intruders") by a minor playwright of the period, Józef Bielawski (1739–1809). Although the Jesuit priest Franciszek Bohomolec (1720–1784), editor of *Monitor,* one of the foremost journals of the age, provided the beginnings of a Polish repertoire through numerous translations and adaptations from foreign (mostly French) works, in particular Molière, Voltaire, and Goldoni, the stock of Polish plays at the time was not deemed sufficiently important to sustain a national Polish stage in its infancy, and foreign entrepreneurs and troupes gradually became predominant. Polish plays and players tended to be thrust into the background as the theater was dominated by French, Italian, and German playing companies and foreign managers. If the National Theater in Warsaw were ever to be truly national, a solid repertoire of Polish plays had to be created and the management of the theater wrested from foreign hands. This two-pronged regeneration of the Polish theater now became a principal concern of several prominent figures in Polish intellectual life and culture in the reign (1764–1795) of King Stanisław Poniatowski. Prince Adam Kazimierz Czartoryski, a cousin of the king and one of the most learned and respected men of his time, contributed substantially to the elaboration of a Polish repertoire through his adaptations of Destouches and Regnard, several original comedies, and theoretical writings on the drama. The Introduction to his comedy *Panna na wydaniu* ("A Marriageable Miss," 1771), an adaptation of David Garrick's *A Miss in her Teens, or A Medley of Lovers* (1747), became a sort of general handbook on dramatic practice, particularly as regards the technique by which foreign plays were to be adapted for presentation before Polish audiences. The "Letter about Dramaturgy" that accompanied the edition of his play *Kawa* ("Coffee," pub. 1779) was another manifestation of his serious interest in the theory of drama. It also reflected the influence of Diderot's *De la poésie dramatique.*

During the period that the National Theater was controlled by foreigners and its boards dominated almost entirely by Italian opera and French theatrical troupes, the stage of the Warsaw Military School, or Cadet Corps, which Czartoryski headed at the time, fulfilled the most useful function of a Polish stage pro tem. The nagging problem of a repertoire was solved for the time being by clever adaptations of seventeenth- and eighteenth-century French plays for the most part and dramatic works of more original character. By his own theoretical guidance and playwriting Czartoryski made a significant personal contribution to the success of the Polish stage. His efforts were buttressed by Bohomolec's translations and adaptations and by the comedies of such prominent writers of the age as Bishop Ignacy Krasicki (1735–1801), Stanisław Trembecki (1739–1812), Franciszek Karpiński (1741–1825), Józef Wybicki (1747–1822), Franciszek Kniaźnin (1750–1807) and Adam Narusiewicz (1733–1796). The special indigenous type of adapted foreign comedy practiced by Bohomolec and for which the ground rules were laid by Czartoryski gave especially fortunate results in the case of Franciszek Zabłocki (1754–1821), a prolific comedy writer and the most genuine comic talent of the age. Zabłocki's most successful satirical comedies *Fircyk w zalotach* ("The Dandy A-Wooing," 1781) and *Sarmatyzm* ("Sarmatianism," 1785) owe their plots to such relatively minor seventeenth-century French comedies as Romagnesi's *Le Petit-maître amoureux* and Hauteroche's *Les Nobles de province.* The distinguished man of letters and statesman Julian Ursyn Niemcewicz (1757–1841, who visited America as an aide to General Kościuszko) wrote the most original political comedy of the Stanislavian period, *Powrót posła* ("The Envoy's Return," 1791). It is set against the background of the so-called Four-Year Sejm from which emerged the celebrated Polish Constitution of May 3, 1791.

The foreign domination of Polish theatrical culture ended decisively when the direction of the National Theater came to rest in the hands of the first professional Polish "man of the theater"— Wojciech Bogusławski (1757–1829). With the exception only of two relatively brief pauses, between the years 1783 and 1814, Bogusławski pursued with a characteristic single-mindedness the task of consolidating the position of a national Polish stage by reversing the policy of favoritism to foreign theater and opera. Bogusławski expanded the Polish repertoire of the National Theater and, of no less consequence, encouraged an interest in, and a demand for, a Polish stage that was truly national. This dedication to the cause of Polish theatrical life was such, moreover, that he extended the life of the theater in Poland beyond Warsaw by founding theaters in Poznań, Kalisz, Danzig, Białystok, Wilno, and Lwów. It was also through Bogusławski's efforts that a first-rate Polish company of actors came into existence and the first Polish theater school was formed.

Of Bogusławski's own contribution to the enlargement of a Polish repertoire only the comic opera on folk themes *Cud mniemany, czyli Krakowiacy i Górale* ("The Imagined Miracle, or Cracovians and Mountaineers," 1794) has a permanent place in the Polish theater, though a reawakened interest in old Polish drama has brought about the revival of two other plays: *Henryk IV na łowach* ("Henry IV on Hunt, 1792), set in Sherwood Forest, and *Dowód wdzięczności narodu* ("Proof of the Nation's Gratitude," 1791), an enthusiastic response to the drafting of the Constitution of May 3, 1791. Bogusławski, quite fittingly, has himself become the subject of several plays in Poland in the twentieth century: *Aktor wieczny* ("The Eternal Actor," 1929) by Emil Zegadłowicz and *Król i aktor* ("King and Actor," 1952) by Roman Brandstaetter.

Until the time of the major Polish Romantics of the 1830's, the young Polish stage knew only one popular success after Bogusławski. This was the late neoclassical tragedy *Barbara Radziwiłłówna* (1817) by Alojzy Feliński (1771–1820), which deals with events in the life of the queen of the sixteenth-century Polish king Zygmunt August. Reminiscent in some respects of Racine's *Bérénice*, Feliński's polished verse tragedy has from the time of its Warsaw première been considered the highest achievement of Polish neoclassical drama. It was also the last triumph of classicist drama on the Polish stage. Five years after its production there appeared the first volume of poetry by the poet destined to become the major figure of Polish Romanticism and the most revered name, in fact, in the history of Polish literature, Adam Mickiewicz.

Prior to the ill-fated November Insurrection of 1830/31, Polish Romanticism gave every evidence of pursuing conventional European paths of development. The collapse of the insurrection and the Great Emigration to the West that resulted changed that and set Polish Romanticism on a quite different course. Henceforth the greatest achievements of Polish Romantic literature were made by émigré authors, whose ranks included the most outstanding Polish literary talents of the first half of the nineteenth century. Emigration itself, moreover, and the manifold problems of the Polish émigré community became the issues about which much of the literature revolved. The appearance of Mickiewicz's first book

ADAM MICKIEWICZ (NEW YORK PUBLIC LIBRARY)

of poetry in 1822, followed by a second in 1823, heralded the advent of Romanticism on the stage of Polish literature. Included in the second volume were Parts II and IV of *Forefathers' Eve,* a drama Mickiewicz intended as his contribution to the revitalization (and romanticization) of the drama in Poland. Inspired, as Romantics elsewhere, by folklore, medieval drama, Shakespeare, and Calderón, Mickiewicz saw his *Forefathers' Eve* (*Dziady*) as opening a new era in the history of Polish dramatic culture. This it was certainly not able to do, ill-designed as it was for performance on the stage. Part IV, for example, consists almost entirely of a lengthy monologue and hardly lends itself to staging. Part II is operatic (parts of the work were meant to be sung) and is also generally ill-suited for performance.

Forefathers' Eve, Part III, dealing with the poet's imprisonment and exile for allegedly anti-Russian political activity, appeared almost ten years later and fragments of *Forefathers' Eve, Part I,* were discovered even later. Together, the four parts make up Mickiewicz's chief contribution to Polish drama, although, like most émigré Polish plays, it was never performed during the lifetime of its author. See Adam MICKIEWICZ.

Polish émigré Romantic literature had three major talents besides Mickiewicz: Juliusz Słowacki, Zygmunt Krasiński, and Cyprian Kamil Norwid. All three were poets who also contributed to the development of the drama in Poland. To varying extents and for different reasons, not one of the three was fully known or appreciated in his time. Słowacki, a prolific poet and dramatist, long regarded himself a talent equal if not superior to Mickiewicz. But it was an opinion that few of his fellow émigrés were willing (or inclined) to share. Much of Słowacki's career was a kind of poetic contest with Mickiewicz, a polemic

A SCENE FROM JULIUSZ SŁOWACKI'S *Kordian* (CAF, WARSAW; POLISH EMBASSY)

to demonstrate, not only the superiority of his poetic gifts, but at times no less importantly, the superiority of his reasoning ideologically on the status and future of the Polish émigré community. (See Juliusz SŁOWACKI.) Krasiński is the only prominent playwright of the Great Emigration who came to enjoy something of an international reputation as a dramatist. He is remembered chiefly for two dramatic works: *Irydion* (pub. 1836) and *Nieboska komedia* (*The Undivine Comedy,* 1833). (See Zygmunt KRASIŃSKI.) Of the major émigré poets, Norwid was the least known and only really discovered in the late nineteenth and early twentieth century when he came to be recognized as one of the most original talents of nineteenth-century Polish literature. See Cyprian Kamil NORWID.

In the period extending roughly from 1831 to 1863 (i.e., from the collapse of the November Insurrection to the outbreak of the January Insurrection), when Polish dramatic creativity was dominated by émigré writers in the West, Polish domestic literature produced the greatest writer of comedies in the Polish language—Count Aleksander Fredro. Fredro and his work really represent something of a paradox. Although forms of comic drama in Poland began to be developed in the second half of the sixteenth century, progress was considerably retarded by the wars and internal upheavals of the seventeenth century. Comedy was revived and extensively cultivated in the second half of the eighteenth century, but produced no outstanding works. The Stanislavian period, however, may be seen as a time of growth and formation, for without the fertile field prepared in the eighteenth century, it is doubtful that a comic dramatist of Fredro's originality could have appeared as early as the first half of the nineteenth century. Fredro emerged then from the traditions of eighteenth-century Polish comedy and in several important respects remained faithful to the conventions of classical comedy. His talent, however, outstripped that of any of his predecessors. Generally speaking, the Romantic age was not favorable to the growth of comedy, particularly the sort of classical comic art Fredro sought to preserve in his own works. Yet through Fredro Polish comedy reached new heights in the time of Romanticism. Not only was the dramatist generally impervious to Romantic influences but he felt alienated with regard to Romanticism and satirized certain aspects of it in his comedies. He was, moreover, physically out of touch with the émigré center of Polish Romanticism. See Aleksander FREDRO.

Comedy after Fredro generally followed the road he paved. In the second half of the nineteenth century only two names stand out: Józef Bliziński (1827–1893) and Michał Bałucki (1837–1901). Bliziński wrote some twenty plays, of which only two—*Pan Damazy* ("Mr. Damazy," 1877) and *Rozbitki* ("The Wrecks," 1877)—are remembered. Though it is a lesser work, *Pan Damazy* won fame in Poland for the same reasons that Fredro's *Zemsta* ("The Vengeance," 1834) did: each play is for Polish audiences a gallery of familiar old Polish gentry types presented with their strengths and characteristic foibles free of any overt sentimentalism. In *Rozbitki*, a four-act play, Bliziński left the sunny world of Damazy in favor of the moral problems (as he saw them) of his own age. Although weakened structurally by a clumsy fourth act, the play has several well-drawn characters, particularly Dzieńdzierzynski, the petty bourgeois with aristocratic snobberies and pretensions.

Long regarded as the *parens* of nineteenth-century Polish bourgeois comedy, Bałucki is best known as the author of the comedies *Grube ryby* ("Big Shots," 1881) and *Klub kawalerów* ("The Bachelors' Club," 1890). These two plays, which have been performed on stages in the Slavic countries and Austria, are prose situation comedies in which middle-aged or older bachelors living in a smug routine and anxious to preserve their bachelorhood are outmaneuvered by woman's wiles and either forced to give in or made to look foolish. Both comedies clearly owe much to Fredro's *Damy i huzary* (*Ladies and Hussars*, 1825).

Concern with the moral, psychological, and social problems of the age and the impact on the Polish consciousness of the philosophy of positivism, which supplanted the ideas and aspirations of Romanticism after the collapse of the January Insurrection of 1863, informed the plays of several other dramatists in the time of Bliziński and Bałucki. In the social comedies *Pozytywni* ("The Positive Ones") and *Epidemia* ("Epidemic"), Józef Narzymski (1839–1872) dealt with the related themes of financial intrigue and speculation in a manner reminiscent of the contemporary French dramatist Émile Augier. Plays by Kazimierz Zalewski, particularly *Przed ślubem* ("Before the Wedding"), adhered to the same general patterns. The best social dramatist after Bliziński and Bałucki remained, however, the former actress in Antoine's Théâtre Libre in Paris, Gabriela Zapolska (1860–1921), a foremost representative of naturalism in Polish literature.

Although an able novelist and short-story writer and regarded as something of an *enfant terrible* in her day, Zapolska is remembered now principally for her dramatic works. Of these, one enjoys the reputation of a classic of the modern Polish theater—a three-act satirical comedy on bourgeois morality, *Moralność pani Dulskiej* ("The Morality of Mrs. Dulska," 1907). In addition to the latter, Zapolska's most popular plays, built for the most part about the themes of marital misunderstandings, conflicts, and infidelity, are *Żabusia* (1896), *Ich czworo* ("The Four of Them," 1912), and *Panna Maliczewska* ("Miss Maliczewska," 1912), the last about the hard life of a young actress—a subject Zapolska herself knew well. Following the example of the positivists, Zapolska also made contemporary Jewish life in Poland a field of inquiry in her short stories, novels.

GABRIELA ZAPOLSKA (CAF, WARSAW; POLISH EMBASSY)

and plays. While not often performed in Poland, her "Jewish" dramas *Małka Szwarcenkopf* (1897) and *Jojne Firułkes* (1899) are particularly interesting for their approach to the large Jewish community of Poland in her time.

Zapolska's naturalism and her involvement in contemporary social issues were a link with the literature of Young Poland (Młoda Polska), as the period of Polish neo-Romanticism and symbolism is known. Young Poland reached the peak of its development between approximately 1890 and the outbreak of World War I in 1914. All the arts—plastic, literary, and theatrical—flourished in this, one of the most brilliant periods in the history of Polish culture. The drama, once again, as in the age of the Romantics, the creative tool of poets, achieved a new magnitude, and the Polish theater, first in Cracow under Tadeusz Pawlikowski and later in Warsaw under Leon Schiller, enjoyed a distinction it had not known previously.

The life of the drama was now enriched by the principal ideologist of Young Poland, Stanisław Przybyszewski (1868–1927), whose works—for example, the four-act drama *Śnieg* (*Snow*, 1903)—have a pronounced erotic flavor; by the lyric poet Lucjan Rydel (1870–1918), whose rather charming folk fantasy *Zaczarowane koło* ("The Enchanted Wheel," 1899) enjoyed considerable popularity in its day and can still be seen occasionally on Polish stages; by Jan August Kisielewski (1876–1918), whose *W sieci* ("In the Net") and *Karykatury* ("Caricatures"), both produced in 1899, provide some insight into the social and moral climate of Cracow which was the center of Young Poland; and by

Tadeusz Rittner (1873–1921), whose traditionally structured *W małym domku* ("In a Little House," 1904), *Głupi Jakób* ("Silly Jack," 1910), and *Wilki w nocy* ("Wolves in the Night," 1916) present somewhat poeticized yet essentially realistic pictures of various aspects of bourgeois and gentry life in the author's native Galicia. Rittner's plays reveal none of the enthusiasm for myth, legend, folklore, and fantasy, or formal experimentation so characteristic, in the main, of the drama of Young Poland. Perhaps the most interesting of his plays is *Wilki w nocy,* a bitter satirical indictment of the contemporary court system. Well constructed, however conventional, the drama achieves an inescapable power through its masterful control of a complex structure based on paradox.

Like Przybyszewski, Rittner grew up in a part of Poland that fell to a German-speaking power (Austria) in the partitions of the late eighteenth century. He was forced to study German in school and in time felt completely at home in the language. Przybyszewski also began his literary career in German and later translated his own works into Polish. Rittner alternated German and Polish, later translating from one language into the other. Because of his use of German, like Przybyszewski, he acquired a reputation in German literary circles and his plays were staged in Vienna, Berlin, and other German-speaking cities.

A contemporary of Zapolska and Rittner, and generally grouped with them as the foremost representatives of naturalism in the Polish drama, Włodzimierz Perzyński (1878–1930) has long been highly regarded for his sharply ironic vignettes of the life of the wealthy bourgeoisie of Warsaw and the technical excellence of his comedies of manners. Although much of Perzyński's playwriting falls into the years of World War I and the 1920's, his best work premièred in the first decade of the century. These included, above all, *Lekkomyślna siostra* ("The Lightheaded Sister," 1904), *Szczęście Frania* ("Franio's Luck," 1909), and *Aszantka* (1906).

While social and psychological investigation was paramount in the realistic-naturalistic dramas of Zapolska, Rittner, and Perzyński, symbolism and the theatrical experimentation of the nineteenth-century Romantics dominated the dramatic writing of the outstanding playwright of Young Poland, the poet and painter Stanisław Wyspiański.

Although Young Poland absorbed much of the positivism that characterized the thinking of Warsaw intellectual and literary circles in the wake of the defeat of the January Insurrection of 1863, it had natural aesthetic affinities with Romanticism. This explains why the writers of Young Poland in the period 1890–1914 devoted so many of their works to a penetrating reassessment of the great figures and literary monuments of the Polish émigré Romanticism of the 1830's and 1840's. The most searching investigation of Romanticism and its hold on the Polish consciousness came in the works of Wyspiański, one of the truly commanding figures in the history of the twentieth-century Polish theater. See Stanisław WYSPIAŃSKI.

After World War I, when Poland regained its independence, Polish writers generally (although obviously not completely) turned away from an absorption in issues of immediate concern only to Poles

and attempted to locate themselves once again in the mainstream of contemporary European writing. This is reflected in the dramatic writing of the 1920's and 1930's, the so-called interwar period. Of the major writers of Young Poland who contributed to the development of the drama, only one—Żeromski—continued to supply plays to the stage of independent Poland. His earlier plays *Sułkowski* (1909) and *Róża* ("Rose," 1909) had dealt with the Napoleonic wars and the Russian Revolution of 1905, respectively. While interesting for their subjects and the psychological development of character, neither play is particularly well suited for the stage and both are better read. It should be pointed out, however, that *Róża* was once superbly produced in Warsaw by Leon Schiller in 1926, a memorable event in the history of the twentieth-century Polish stage. Since then the work has rarely been performed.

After World War I, Żeromski produced several dramatic works, of which the most important were *Ponad śnieg bielszym się stanę* ("I Shall Become Whiter Than the Snow," 1921) about the war the Poles fought with the Soviets in 1920/21; *Turoń* (1923), about the famous massacre of landowning gentry by the peasants in Galicia in 1846; and the "sad comedy" *Uciekła mi przepióreczka* ("My Little Quail Has Flown Away," 1924), the best and most often performed of the three, about the conflict between personal feelings and a sense of social duty. A sequel to this drama, *Powrót Przełęckiego* ("The Return of Przełęcki"), was written by Jerzy Zawieyski in 1937.

Żeromski's concern with national history and the sacrifices demanded by commitment to the cause of social progress were rooted in the literary traditions of the epoch of Young Poland. In this sense the later dramas of Żeromski belong more to the past than to the reality of post-World War I Polish life. The same may be said of other dramatists such as Karol Hubert Rostworowski (1877–1938), Ludwik Hieronim Morstin (1886–   ), and Emil Zegadłowicz (1888–1941) who continued the tradition of symbolist, neo-Romantic verse drama based on mythology, legend, ancient history, and classical antiquity.

A political conservative, Rostworowski produced several works—of only fleeting fame—of an ideological nature, such as *Zmartwychwstanie* ("Resurrection," 1923), in which Mickiewicz appears prominently, and *Miłosierdzie* ("Compassion," 1920), on the French Revolution. He attracted more favorable attention with *Judasz z Kariothu* ("Judas Iscariot," 1913), a new interpretation of the motives behind Judas' "betrayal" of Christ, and *Kaligula* ("Caligula," 1917), about the inability of the superior individual to withstand the pressures of his environment. In 1929, in the play *Niespodzianka* ("The Surprise"), which is based on a true incident, Rostworowski turned away from ancient history and legend to the reality of the misery of the lot of the peasantry in his own time. The modern tragedy had a favorable reception and the author was encouraged to expand it into a trilogy, the other two parts of which were *Przeprowadzka* ("The Removal," 1930) and *U mety* ("At the Goal," 1932), both dealing with the social problems of educated people of peasant origin.

A prolific and influential writer and translator (of Sophocles, Lope de Vega, Calderón, Goethe) Ludwik

Hieronim Morstin found the subjects for his many verse plays chiefly in classical and legendary history, only occasionally turning his attention to contemporary issues. The author also of several plays after World War II (their subjects drawn in the main from classical antiquity and early Polish history), Morstin scored his greatest theatrical triumph with the three-act drama about the trials of Xanthippa's marriage to Socrates, *Obrona Ksantypy* ("The Defense of Xanthippa," 1939), which premièred in Warsaw and was performed on foreign stages as well. After World War II he added two more plays on classical subjects (*Penelope* and *Cleopatra*) to form, with *Obrona Ksantypy*, his classical trilogy.

A poet, novelist, and dramatist and, after World War I, the founder of the Czartak group of poets, who encouraged a return to regional themes and subjects and the primitive art of the peasantry (an outgrowth in all probability of the great interest of Young Poland in the peasant), Zegadłowicz first came to the notice of the public as a dramatist with his verse plays built around folk motifs, such as *Łyżki i księżyc* ("Spoons and the Moon," 1924), *Lampka oliwna* ("The Oil Lamp" 1924), and *Głaz graniczny* ("The Border Stone," 1925). He also wrote a play about the eighteenth-century Polish theatrical personality Bogusławski, *Aktor wieczny* ("The Eternal Actor," 1929), and translations of Calderón's *Circe*, Gozzi's *Turandot*, Hasenclaver's *Antigone*, and the whole of Goethe's *Faust*. *Domek z kart* ("The Little House of Cards"), a political play attacking the regime on the eve of the war in 1939, was found among his papers after his death and was staged in 1953.

In the realm of Polish comedy during the interwar period, few names stand out. Włodzimierz Perzyński, whose best work was done in the early twentieth century, continued writing plays until his death in 1930. Of the nearly dozen works he produced during and after World War I, only one attracted any attention, the play *Uśmiech losu* ("Smile of Fate," 1926), about a socially uprooted intellectual in the postwar era. Although the play begins promisingly, it lapses into melodrama and makes a less favorable impression than his earlier comedies, such as *Lekkomyślna siostra, Szczęście Frania,* and *Aszantka.*

The conditions of intellectual life in Poland in the 1920's and 1930's were also the concern of another comedy writer, Bruno Winawer (1883–1944), who was very popular in his day. Although careless about the structure of his works, Winawer attracted attention as a dramatist because of his sensitivity to the mood of his time. He also was the first modern Polish dramatist to select his major characters from the world of science and scholarship and to develop his plots out of problems peculiar to that world. Of the many social comedies he wrote, two are worth mentioning: *Księga Hioba* (*The Book of Job*, 1921), which despite its biblical title deals with the hardships of an impoverished scientist, and *R. H. Inżynier* ("R. H. Engineer," 1923), the most durable of Winawer's plays, about a mathematician's quest for economic security that leads him to a mental home, where he simulates mental disorders in order to remain an inmate. An interesting aspect of the work is its reflection of the enthusiastic response in Poland at the time to the teachings of Freud and the methods of psychoanalysis.

There is a curious footnote to literary history connected with Winawer's *Księga Hioba*. The comedy was published the day of its first performance in Warsaw in May 1921. Winawer sent a copy to Joseph Conrad (whom he had never met but admired) together with a letter in Polish. Conrad so liked the play that he himself translated it into English; the translation was published by J. M. Dent & Sons Ltd. in London in 1931.

Contemporary scientific theories and interests, particularly Freudianism, were the main subjects of Winawer's contemporary Antoni Cwojdziński (real name Wojdan; born 1897). Active also as an actor and producer, Cwojdziński evoked considerable response at one time for such light, clever, "scientific" comedies (in the tradition of Winawer) as *Teoria Einsteina* ("The Theory of Einstein," 1934), *Freuda teoria snów* ("Freud's Theory of Dreams," 1937), and *Temperamenty* ("Temperaments," 1938), about the theories of Kretschmer. Since 1939, he has been living outside Poland. In his playwriting since World War II, it is obvious that he remains interested in the same subjects. In 1959 the highly regarded and influential Warsaw drama monthly *Dialog* (*Dialogue*) published his comedy *Einstein wśród chuliganów* ("Einstein Among the Hooligans") and in 1964 his play *Hipnoza* ("Hypnosis") appeared.

Several dramatists whose careers were launched before the outbreak of hostilities in 1939 form a link with Polish dramaturgy after World War II and the establishment of the Polish People's Republic. Jarosław Iwaszkiewicz (1894–   ), a novelist, short-story writer, poet, translator, and librettist for the operas of Szymanowski and one of the most prominent figures in contemporary Polish literature, enjoyed considerable popularity in the 1930's for two plays about the lives of distinguished nineteenth-century artists. The first (and best known), *Lato w Nohant* (*A Summer in Nohant*, 1936), is about the love affair between Chopin and George Sand; after World War II the play was performed on stages in Paris and Vienna by Polish troupes; the second play, *Maskarada* ("Masquerade," 1938), a less successful effort, has the great Russian poet Pushkin as its subject. In 1949, Iwaszkiewicz wrote a third play along similar lines, this time choosing as his subject the Balzac-Hańska relationship and titled *Wesele pana Balzaka* ("The Wedding of Monsieur Balzac"). Iwaszkiewicz's first post-World War II success was *Odbudowa Błędomierza* ("The Reconstruction of Błędomierz"), first produced at the Festival of Contemporary Polish Art in 1951. Owing much to Ibsen's *Pillars of Society*, the play deals with the inability of the mayor of a small city in central Poland in the year 1945 to escape the consequences of certain ethical and moral transgressions in his past.

One of the most respected names in the history of the twentieth-century Polish theater belongs to Jerzy Szaniawski (1886–   ), well known for his little philosophic tales about the adventures of a certain Professor Tutka. Szaniawski began his career as a dramatist in 1917 with his comedy *Murzyn* ("The Negro"). He soon associated himself with the avant-garde Reduta theater directed by Juliusz Osterwa. In cooperation with Osterwa, Szaniawski turned out an impressive number of comedies in the 1920's and 1930's, among them: *Papierowy kochanek* ("The

JERZY SZANIAWSKI (CAF, WARSAW; POLISH EMBASSY)

Paper Lover," 1920); *Ewa* ("Eve," 1921); *Lekko-duch* ("The Frivolous Fellow," 1923); *Ptak* ("The Bird," 1923); *Żeglarz* ("The Sailor," 1929); *Adwokat i róże* ("The Lawyer and the Roses," 1929); *Fortepian* ("The Piano," 1932); *Krysia* (1935); *Most* ("The Bridge," 1939); *Dziewczyna z lasu* ("The Girl from the Forest," 1939).

Generally speaking, Szaniawski's plays are distinguished by relatively simple but original plots, at times lacking in force and concerned for the most part with demonstrating not only the persistence of myth in human affairs but even the apparent necessity for myth. His characters often have a delicate, fragile quality and dialogue tends to be poeticized in a manner reminiscent of the style of Young Poland. A master of dramatic irony, Szaniawski carefully avoids the glaring and harsh, moving his figures instead through a world of half-shadows, dim light, and soft pale colors. Not long after the end of World War II, in 1946, Szaniawski wrote a play titled *Dwa teatry* ("Two Theaters"), which occasioned much comment in Poland. Built around the familiar device of the play-within-a-play, in this case two one-act playlets, Szaniawski's work bares the conflict between two mutually antagonistic currents in contemporary theater—the drama of realism, concerned with social, moral, and ethical problems (represented in the play by the "Little Mirror Theater"), and the poetic drama of fantasy and illusion (represented by the "Theater of Dreams").

Probably the most important link between interwar Polish drama and that of the period 1956–1966 has been the long-ignored avant-garde theater of Stanisław Ignacy Witkiewicz. Polish historians of the drama and critics believe, with some justification, that as a dramatist Witkiewicz was in advance of his time and for that reason exerted virtually no influence on Polish drama in his own day. Now, however, with the firm implantation of the Western theaters of the absurd and grotesque in the soil of Polish drama, Witkiewicz has definitely come into his own. See Stanisław Ignacy WITKIEWICZ.

Since the end of World War II and the establishment of a communist regime, Polish dramaturgy falls into three major periods and several distinct currents. The first period, extending roughly from 1945 to 1949, was characterized by the attempt of dramatists to come to grips with the impact of the war years and the new domestic social and political conditions. Aside from Szaniawski's *Dwa teatry*, the most outstanding play in this period was the political comedy *Święto Winkelrida* ("Winkelried's Day," written in 1944, published in 1946, staged in 1956) by Jerzy Zagórski (1907–   ) and Jerzy Andrzejewski (1909–   ), the author of the well-known novel *Ashes and Diamonds*. With their point of departure the Polish Romantic poet Juliusz Słowacki's declaration in *Kordian* that Poland was the "Winkelried of nations," Andrzejewski and Zagórski set out to demonstrate the incompatibility of past national myths with the new conditions in which Poland would find itself after the war. In a sense, the play initiated what has become perhaps the single most abiding issue in contemporary Polish literature—the struggle between the romantic values and ideals of the past and the neopositivism that seeks an end to romanticism in favor of realism and pragmatism. Szaniawski's *Dwa teatry* dealt with the same problem but in terms of dramatic tradition, contrasting a poetic theater of dreams and illusion with a realistic theater absorbed in "civic" issues.

The imposition of a system of literary controls similar to those in force at the time in the Soviet Union along with the attempts to transplant the doctrine of Socialist Realism to Poland between 1949 and 1956 resulted in a stifling of dramatic creativity. In this second period of postwar Polish dramaturgy, plays dealing with contemporary social, political, and economic issues had to conform to an accepted conventional pattern. This led either to schematism or the conscious desire to avoid contemporary issues or treat them in an oblique way under the cloak of history. The latter tendency became the more pronounced and at the least produced several good costume plays. Light comedies, sometimes farcical and occasionally pungently satirical within well-defined limits, were also produced in large number in this period.

Of dramatists most seriously concerned with contemporary social and political issues in the first decade and a half after the end of the war, the most interesting—and the best known—was Leon Kruczkowski (1900–1962). He began his career as a playwright in 1935 but earned fame only with his postwar plays. His first work to attract attention—and arouse controversy—was *Odwety* ("Retaliations," 1948), a searching analysis of contemporary Polish political conflicts in terms of a confrontation of two people involved in a common family drama. The following year, 1949, his drama *Niemcy* (*The Germans*) became an international success. The first Polish attempt to understand the phenomenon of Nazi Germany from the "internal" viewpoint of a German intellectual family whose idealistic philosophy fails at the decisive moment, the play has been translated into over a dozen languages and staged in theaters from Paris to Tokyo. Until Andrzejewski's novel *Ashes and Diamonds*, the plays of Sławomir Mrożek, and Jan Kott's study *Shakespeare Our Contemporary*, it was the postwar Polish book best known abroad. There followed two less successful plays: *Odwiedziny* ("The Visit," 1955), about postwar Polish village life, and *Juliusz i Ethel* ("Julius and Ethel," 1954), a tragedy about the Rosenberg spy trial in the United States. Kruczkowski scored new successes with the existentialist but anti-Sartre psychological drama *Pierwszy dzień wolności* ("The First Day of Freedom," 1959), about the behavior of Polish officers their first day after being released from a German prison camp, and the highly interesting but formally less successful *Śmierć gubernatora* ("The Governor's Death," 1961), the Polish entry at the Parisian Festival of the Theater of Nations in 1961. Exploring the mechanism of power and the responsibilities it entails, the play is an adaptation of a novel by the Russian *fin-de-siècle* author Leonid Andreev (1871–1919).

Since the "thaw" of October 1956, the principles of Socialist Realism have no longer been in force and there has been a greater freedom of growth in the arts. Polish dramatists have responded accordingly and in the decade 1956–1966 some notable results were achieved. Philosophical plays analyzing the nature of power and the relation of the individual to society and history, still cloaked occasionally in the garb of history, began coming to the fore. One of the earliest to receive favorable notice was *Klucz od przepaści* ("The Key to the Abyss," 1955), by Krzysztof Gruszczyński (1925–   ), dealing with the psychological and moral problems of the American pilot of the plane that dropped the first atomic bomb on Hiroshima. In 1956, Roman Brandstaetter also wrote a politically topical drama, *Milczenie* ("Silence"), which was produced the same year and well received. But the most important post-thaw plays of philosophical substance were *Ciemności kryją ziemię* ("Darkness Covers the Earth," 1957) and *Imiona władzy* ("The Names of Power," 1957), both by Jerzy Broszkiewicz (1922–   ). The first is a stage version of a novel by Jerzy Andrzejewski set in the time of the Spanish Inquisition; the second, a dramatic triptych consisting of three one-act plays, each with its own plot and all bound by the common theme of political morality and the mechanism of power as revealed in different periods of history. Broszkiewicz's talent has since expanded in other directions. In such plays as *Jonasz i Błazeń* ("Jonah and the Clown," 1958), *Głupiec i inni* ("The Fool and Others," 1959), and *Dziejowa rola Pigwy* ("The Historical Role of Pigva," 1960), he has shown an inclination toward satirical social comedy rich in irony; the plays *Bar wszystkich świętych* ("The Bar of All Saints," 1960) and *Dwie przygody Lemuela Gullivera* ("Two Adventures of Lemuel Gulliver," 1961) exhibit a concern for moral issues; in *Skandal w Hellbergu* ("A Scandal in Hellberg," 1961), he produced a political play about Germany. Throughout his productive career as a dramatist, initiated in 1952, Broszkiewicz has not been content to work with established forms but instead has engaged in considerable formal experimentation, which has es-

tablished him as one of contemporary Poland's foremost dramatic innovators.

The achievements of contemporary Polish drama to gain the greatest interest abroad, however, have been the works of young writers who have carried innovation and experimentation further than Broszkiewicz. The more obvious connections between the Polish avant-garde and the Western traditions of the absurd and the grotesque, as seen particularly in Ionesco, Beckett, and Pinter, are not difficult to discover. When contemporary Western drama and theater became truly accessible to the Poles after 1956, it was the focus of considerable attention and controversy. This led not only to attempts to develop a similar drama but, of no small significance, to the rediscovery of that Polish precursor of the tradition, Witkiewicz. Too long neglected, Witkiewicz's plays were at last dusted off, reprinted, and staged; a new literature of appreciation and analysis grew up about him. He was studied not only for his own merits but for his impact on other Polish dramatists. Notable among those he influenced is Witold Gombrowicz (1904–   ), who has been living in exile in Argentina since 1939 and who gained an international reputation when his pre-World War II novel *Ferdydurke* was translated into several foreign languages, including English. The highly talented satirist Konstanty Ildefons Gałczyński (1905–1953) also owes much to Witkiewicz, and to Gombrowicz as well. Perhaps the most popular poet among Polish youth in the postwar period, Gałczyński left a number of dramatic works, including *Babcia i wnuczek, czyli noc cudów* ("Granny and Grandson, or A Night of Miracles," written 1950, published 1954, staged 1955), a "two-act farce with prologue and intermedium"; *Noc mistrza Andrzeja* ("The Night of Master Andrew," written 1951, published 1956, never staged), a play about the influential nineteenth-century Polish mystagogue and messianist Andrzej Towiański; and *Orfeusz w piekle* ("Orpheus in Hell," written 1951, staged 1957), a libretto to Offenbach's comic opera. Of Gałczyński's extensive work for the theater, his most characteristic and appealing effort has been *Zielona Gęś* ("The Green Goose," pub. 1946–1950), a cycle of one-act satirical sketches and dramatized anecdotes. One of them, for example, is entitled *Siedmiu braci śpiących* ("Seven Sleeping Brothers," 1946) and presents seven brothers each of whom snores in turn, after which the curtain falls.

The line of development in twentieth-century Polish drama extending from Witkiewicz to Gombrowicz and Gałczyński has been continued emphatically in the works of Tadeusz Różewicz (1921–   ) and Sławomir Mrożek (1930–   ), contemporary Poland's most popular playwrights and the ones best known abroad. In Mrożek's major plays, *Policjanci* (*The Police*, 1958), *Indyk* ("The Turkey," 1960), *Striptease* (1961), *Na pełnym morzu* (*Out at Sea*, 1961) and *Tango* (1965), character abstractions, absurd situations, and grotesque contrivances at once obscure and illuminate a profound concern for the most relevant moral and philosophical issues of our time. Although Mrożek generally avoids a Polish setting, thereby achieving a greater universality of appeal and significance, his plays cannot be divorced entirely from the milieu in which they arose. The penetrating observations about the nature of police authority in *Policjanci* apply to totalitarianism in any form, society, and age, yet become especially meaningful if read against the background of social and political conditions in Poland in the late 1940's and 1950's. The moral questions posed in *Na pełnym morzu* and the examination of will and freedom in *Striptease,* while obviously possessed of a relevance that transcends national boundaries and a given historical age, also reflect the realities of life in Poland since World War II and the modifications of communist rule after 1956. In the two-act "melofarce" *Indyk* Mrożek adds his voice to the dialogue with Romantic mythology to which so much of contemporary Polish literature is committed. *Tango* is an inquiry into the ineffectuality of the intellectual idealist as ruler. It reflects in no small degree the intellectuals' struggle in contemporary Poland to influence and thereby transform the character of political authority. Although Mrożek uses techniques refined in the Western "theater of the absurd," the intellectual substance of his plays clearly extends beyond the Western dramatists' concern with the problems of alienation, conformism, and the limitations of language as an instrument of communication. In this light, Mrożek should not be thought of merely as an imitator of dramatic forms developed in the West and introduced into Poland only after 1956, but as an original and skilled dramatist in his own right.

More obviously indebted to Western absurd drama, in particular that of Ionesco and Beckett, Tadeusz Różewicz, after Mrożek the most admired young dramatist in Poland today, addresses himself to what he sees as the problem of the stultifying complaisance of a contemporary Poland bereft (through the force of history) of idealism. In his first major play, *Kartoteka* ("The Card-Index," 1960), a dramatic work undivided into acts and scenes and featuring a chorus of elders (bringing to mind Polish Romantic and neo-Romantic drama), Różewicz aims his satirical barbs at those conditions of Polish life after World War II that, in his judgment, bear the responsibility for the spiritual numbness of his own generation. If Mrożek sees man's predicament in his hopeless inability to break out of the confines of a world of his own choosing, Różewicz laments the spiritual bankruptcy of a way of life in which the poetry of idealism and even ordinary humanitarianism have little place and men flee from the responsibility of moral involvement. Różewicz's play *Świadkowie, albo nasza mała stabilizacja* ("The Witnesses, or Our Little Stabilization," 1962), still simpler in its structure than *Kartoteka,* is fundamentally concerned with the same issues: a husband and wife, numbed by the trivialities of a humdrum, monotonous existence, witness first the tormenting and then the bizarre murder of a cat—the details of which the husband relates mechanically, without any emotion whatsoever. The inane, pointless, Beckett-like dialogue of two men in a coffeehouse in the third part of the work only serves to strengthen the image of spiritual ossification from which the husband and wife of the second part of the play suffer.

Różewicz and Mrożek stand in the forefront of creative dramatic talents in contemporary Poland. Their growing international reputations should not obscure the merits, however, of other promising young playwrights who made their debuts in the late 1950's and 1960's: Tymoteusz Karpowicz (1921–   ), Miron Białoszewski (1922–   ), Zbigniew Herbert (1924–   ), Bohdan Drozdowski (1931–   ), and Stanisław Grochowiak (1934–   ). Of this group, only the poet Herbert is known in the West. A number of his poems have been included in three English-language anthologies of contemporary Polish writings and his major play, *Jaskinia filozofów* (*The Philosophers' Den,* 1956), was translated into English in 1958. The steady relation of political tensions between the countries of Western and Eastern Europe has led to a mutually enriching expansion of knowledge about their respective cultures, and Polish theater now enjoys a dissemination and esteem it has never before known. Its unique qualities, its degree of indebtedness to, and independence of, Western theater no less than the world it reflects are becoming better known in other countries with each passing year. Translations prepare the way for appreciations and these in turn for the serious studies that will permit, not only a meaningful investigation of the course Polish dramaturgy pursues after the Różewiczes and Mrożeks of the 1960's, but also the curiosity that will eventually bring more light on the past of one of Europe's most interesting theaters and dramatic literatures.

There is no history of Polish drama available in English at the present time. The reader would do best to consult the general history of Polish literature by Manfred Kridl, *A Survey of Polish Literature* (1954). On the Polish theater, see the English translation of the Polish scholar Edward Csato's survey published under the title *The Polish Theater* (1963). There is also a brief survey in English and French of twentieth-century Polish drama and theater in the Polish theater journal *Le Théâtre en Pologne,* Nos. 6–7 (1964), pp. 12–22. For an extensive bibliography of Polish plays in English translation, see Bolesław Taborski, "Polish Plays in English Translations," *The Polish Review,* Vol. IX, No. 3 (Summer 1964), pp. 63–101, and Vol. XII, No. 1 (Winter 1967), pp. 59–82. There is interesting material on the contemporary Polish stage in the *Tulane Drama Review*'s issue devoted to Eastern European theater: Vol. II, No. 3 (Spring 1967).—H. B. S.

Polyeucte (1643). A tragedy by Pierre CORNEILLE. In Armenia during the third century A.D., Polyeucte is converted to Christianity and breaks the idols in a pagan temple. His father-in-law, Félix, a Roman governor and cowardly politician, imprisons him. At the same time Polyeucte's wife, Pauline, meets up again with the man she had once loved, Sévère, a Roman hero. While Polyeucte renounces the world and aspires to martyrdom, Pauline turns away from Sévère and tries to make Polyeucte abjure his faith. However, Polyeucte's martyrdom converts Pauline and Félix and convinces Sévère to try to stop the persecution of the Christians. The play is remarkable for Polyeucte's mystical ascension and the progressive spiritual reconciliation of the characters.

This play has been translated into English blank verse by Lacy Lockert in *Chief Plays,* 2nd ed. (1957). —Ja. G.

Poquelin, Jean Baptiste. See MOLIÈRE.

Porter, Henry (d. 1599). English playwright. Porter was one of the band of indigent playwrights in the service of Philip Henslowe during the 1590's. In 1599 he engaged in a duel with another playwright, John Day, and was stabbed to death. His sole extant play is *The Two Angry Women of Abingdon* (pub. 1599). A realistic farce set in the English countryside, it employs the tried-and-true comic formula of two young lovers opposed by their quarreling parents. Its plot has been seen as a comic reversal of *Romeo and Juliet* and its farcical incidents as reminiscent of *The Merry Wives of Windsor.*—E. Q.

Port-Royal (1954). A play by Henry de MONTHERLANT. *Port-Royal* is Montherlant's eighth play. Its melodramatic action, reduced in this work to the barest simplicity, exists as a pretext for that inner psychological action that Montherlant has always claimed uniquely interests him. The plot is a series of moments of the soul, which the playwright has successfully projected with a maximum of truthfulness and intensity.

The play is taken from the history of Jansenism. The time is a day in August 1664 when the nuns of Port-Royal refuse to sign the Formulaire, a decree from the pope denouncing Jansenism. The crisis of the entire religious community is projected, especially in the inner struggle of two nuns. Soeur Françoise discovers in herself an unusual combative strength, an unqualified sharing in Jansenist intransigency. Soeur Angélique, a niece of "le Grand Arnauld," one of the spiritual directors of Port-Royal, undergoes a devastating experience of religious doubt.

Montherlant's bare but powerful style is admirably suited to the characters and the dramatic situation of *Port-Royal.* The inner, psychological action of the play is so devoid of exterior action that in his Preface Montherlant invokes the name of Racine and the Greek tragic writers.

An English translation of *Port-Royal* is included in *Port-Royal and Other Plays* (1967), edited by Richard Hayes.—W. F.

Portugal. The first evidence of theater in Portugal appears in a document of 1193, when King Sancho I gave a certain property to the brothers Bonamis and Acompaniado, actors in *arremedilhos* —a kind of comic imitation of persons and animals. The beneficiaries were perhaps troubadors or more possibly medieval players from Provençe. The players, Portuguese, Galician, Provençal, and Spanish, made a living by singing, dancing, and reciting poems, as well as by clowning and tumbling. They performed as much for the people at the market fairs as for the nobles in their castles. Sancho I, having been a poet as well as a king, honored the interpreters of his work, and the deed of donation is the first document to refer to the dramatic art in Portugal. What is debatable is whether the arremedilho was written or improvised, or was only a mime. Not a single literary text remains from the period 1193–1502, although there is evidence of the existence of theater at court and even among the people.

Portuguese theater began as written literature in 1502, when Gil VICENTE (see also SPAIN: *Renaissance*) performed the *Monólogo do vaqueiro* ("Monologue of the Cowboy") in the bedchamber of Queen Mary, who had just given birth to the future John III. Vicente was assisted by others of the court, including "Old Queen" Leonor, widow of John II,

who became the playwright's protector. Her husband, in spite of his high position, had been an actor in *Momos* ("mummeries"). According to John II's biographers, Garcia de Resende and Rui de Pina, some of the Momos were very simple. The count of Vimioso wrote one for only four actors, of which two spoke. His Momo appears in the *Cancioneiro Geral* ("General Book of Poetry," pub. 1516) by Resende. But other Momos used as many as two hundred dancers, and *Cavaleiro do cisne* ("Knight of the Swan") was presented with a fleet of ships in front of drapes painted to represent waves, the roar of artillery, trumpets, and drums—which gives some idea of the magnificence of the production. It is not known who would have written such impressive works, but the king himself took part. Data from the fifteenth century indicate that actors were sent by John II and Afonse V to perfect their art in Italy, but there is no reference to Portuguese playwrights. They certainly existed, for in the fifteenth-century courts, as in those of the two preceding centuries, to write and recite poetry and to attend plays were signs of good taste. Because of the lack of detailed evidence, especially of texts, historians prefer to designate Vicente as the initiator of drama.

Vicente was the official court playwright from 1502 to 1536, the year in which he wrote his last play and presumably died. Because the Portuguese kings of the time married Spanish princesses, he wrote in these two languages, at times mixing them in the same play. He also used the Sayaguese dialect (spoken in the area shared by León and Castile) as well as Latin—either liturgical or intentionally incorrect for comic effect—and a Negro patois of Portuguese. Vicente wrote pastoral and morality plays, comedies and farces, and plays based on romances of chivalry. They were always in accord with the classical *parresia* ("license"), which permitted him to attack the dissolute habits of the clergy and even to refer mockingly to important personages of his time. In spite of his criticism of the human element of the Church, from the village priests to the popes and cardinals (the latter portrayed allegorically), Vicente had deep religious faith. He was also a medievalist in not observing the Renaissance rules of dramatic structure. They were already well known in the Portugal of his time, having been disseminated by Sá de Miranda, a poet who had spent five years in Italy and Spain in contact with the most advanced writers. Thus, Vicente's theater constitutes an inventory of the Portuguese middle ages—in his world view, in the customs, character types, and social relations he portrayed, and even in the folklore he documented. More important, there are in Vicente's plays a lyricism and comic sense that were never equaled in Portuguese theater, including the work of his imitators.

The playwrights known as disciples of Vicente are those whose works are published in *Primeira parte dos autos e comédias Portuguêsas, feitas por Antônio Prestes e por Luís de Camões, e outros autores Portuguêses cujos nomes vão no princípio de suas obras* ("First Part of the *Autos* ["Acts"] and Comedies of Antônio Prestes and of Luís de Camões and Other Portuguese Authors, Whose Names Appear at the Beginning of Their Works"). The edition was organized and financed by Afonso Lopes in 1587. It is evident from the title that more was planned, but it never appeared as far as is known. Although one cannot call Luís de Camões a disciple of Vicente, the other writers are in many ways. The seven autos of Antônio Prestes (?–1587), a judicial functionary in Santarém, are almost all about judicial affairs, as, for example, *Auto do procurador* ("Act of the Attorney") and *Auto do dezembargador* ("Act of the Judge of the Appeals Court"). Other authors in Lopes' edition are Jorge Pinto (?–?1523), a noble, author of *Auto de Rodrigo Mendo;* Anrique Lopes (dates unknown), author of *Cena Policiana,* so similar to *Quem tem farelos?* ("Who Has the Chaff?" 1515) of Vicente; and Jerônimo Ribeiro (dates unknown), author of *Auto do físico* ("Act of the Physician"). These playwrights were rescued from oblivion in spite of the disappearance of the first edition of Alfonso Lopes' collection. We encounter the existing edition with the notation that the plays are "newly collected and amended." The Inquisition must have confiscated the previous edition and is certainly responsible for the changes, because in its Indices the plays of these and other authors are referred to as authorized to be published only after cuts and alterations. Even Vicente was not exempt from the zeal of the Inquisitors. Some of his disciples, however, remain to posterity as nothing more than a name or writer of a few works, such as Afonso Álvares (alive in 1531), servant of the Bishop of Évora, who used *Aurea Legenda Sanctorum* ("Golden Legends of Saints") of Archbishop Jacobus Voragine (1230–1298) as a source for his autos. Even so, the Index of 1624 required deletions in all of the plays. The only remaining autos are those about Saint James, Saint Anthony, and Saint Barbara. The last is conserved intact, as a forbidden work, by the devout people of the villages of Minho. Also a disciple of Vicente and inspired by Voragine was the blind Baltazar Dias, whose autos in verse about Saint Alexis and Saint Catherine were printed in 1537. His other autos, about the Nativity and the Passion, were condemned and destroyed by the Inquisitors. There is nothing surprising about that, because in 1534 the constitution of the diocese of Évora prohibited performances "even if they are of the passion for our lord Jesus Christ or of the resurrection or nativity."

Finally, Antônio Ribeiro Chiado (?–1591) deserves to be remembered. He was a Franciscan monk of Évora who left the priesthood and went to Lisbon to become author, actor, and libertine. He was as popular a figure as any of the time, who, in contrast with Vicente, was not a playwright of the court but rather of the public squares. There are four plays by Chiado, among which are *Auto das regateiras* ("Act of the Fishwives") and *Auto de Gonçalo Chambão.*

Luís de Camões (1525?–1580), the most famous writer in Portuguese, has many obscure points in his biography. It is not known whether he was born in Lisbon, Coimbra, or some other city. It is almost certain that he studied at the University of Coimbra, for it would have been difficult for him to acquire his unusually fine education in any other way. Camões lived at court as a poor noble of lower rank, having undergone punishments for love affairs or a dissolute life. He fought against the Moors at Ceuta, where he lost an eye, and was sent to India as a common soldier. While in Portugal and India, Camões wrote lyric poems and, in India and other parts of Asia, the

epic poem *Os Lusíadas* (*The Lusiads,* pub. 1572), masterpiece of the Portuguese people. His drama is limited to three works: *Anfitriões* ("Hosts," pub. 1587), *El Rei Seleuco* ("King Seleucus," pub. 1645), and *Filodemo* ("Philodemus"), performed in India (1555?) and published in 1587 with *Anfitriões.* Camões resembles Vicente in his comic techniques as well as in his use of anachronism. For example, in *Anfitriões,* based on Plautus' *Amphitryon,* Camões mixes the Jupiter-Alcmene fable with Lisbon life without fundamentally departing from his source. *El Rei Seleuco* is derived from an episode that appears in Justinus, Plutarch, and Petrarch, whose *Trionfi* appears to have been Camões' most used source. The Prologue, in prose, reveals servants preparing the room where an enactment of the episode will take place. In their conversation, however, there are references to real persons and to customs of the time. And finally, *Filodemo,* reminiscent of the *Comédia de Rubena* of Vicente, resembles Italian pastoral comedies, with its neo-Platonic hero and baroque literary style.

It can be said that there is a link between Vicente and Camões, but there are more disparities because of the time that separated them—a whole century, one of the most effervescent in the arts. Camões wrote poetry in the *medida velha* ("old meter"), but this does not make us think of him as a medieval poet, as was Vicente. His most occasional lyrics (his plays seem to have been occasional also) followed the medieval traditions, but one cannot point to any single poet as his master. Since there is no other dramatist of universal importance between the time that he and Vicente wrote, some critics try to overemphasize their similarities. But their relationship would be more comprehensible if we studied Camões as an author in the transitional period, between the significant Vicentine theatrical world and the "theater to be read" of the Portuguese Renaissance.

Going backward a bit, we see that while Vicente was still alive the poet Francisco de Sá de Miranda (1485?–1558) had introduced the Renaissance into Portuguese letters, after a stay of five years in Italy and one in Spain. In 1526 he wrote *Os estrangeiros* ("The Foreigners") and later *Os Vilhalpandos* (a family name), comedies published not until 1559 and 1560 respectively, dedicated to the Grand Inquisitor, Cardinal Henrique. The plays take place in Italy and all five acts are in prose. Both comedies remind one of Lodovico Ariosto, but, not having been performed for a long time, they are completely forgotten, except as the first works in the "new manner" for theater.

A disciple of Sá de Miranda, Antônio Ferreira (1528–1569) wrote *Tragédia de Dona Inês de Castro* (*The Tragedy of Lady Inês de Castro,* pub. 1587), one of the few theatrically effective texts of the Portuguese Renaissance. *Castro* (*A Castro,* as it is known) portrays the illicit love of the crown prince Pedro for Inês, which is completely contrary to national interests. The episode is from real life and had been used in historical chronicles and in literature by such authors as Fernão Lopes, Lopes de Ayala, Rui de Pina, and Camões. The first four acts show the uneasiness of Inês and her sons, the vacillations of King Afonso IV, and the fiery temperament of the crown prince. The comments of the chorus increase the tension, which reaches catastasis at the end of the fourth act, when the interests of state prevail over humane sentiments and the king orders the death of Inês. The final act, the only one that fails to observe the classical unities, because the place changes, presages the terrible vengeance Pedro will wreak on the killers of Inês. Ferreira also wrote two other comedies, in prose, *O Cioso* and *Bristo* (the names of their protagonists, pub. 1622). They are of obvious moralizing intention, but very gay through to the happy endings. There are a few characters who, in spite of their lack of integrity, are attractive because of their intelligence and their wit, with which they tell the crudest truths.

The last name worthy of note in the Renaissance, although he wrote theater to be read, is Jorge Ferreira de Vasconcelos (1515?–?1585), author of *Eufrósina* ("Euphrosyne," pub. 1555) and two other comedies in prose with five acts and classic themes.

In 1555 the Jesuit theater began to gain in importance. At the University of Évora as well as the colleges that it maintained at Lisbon, Coimbra, and Braga, the Society of Jesus produced theatrical works in Latin, based on biblical passages, in the classic manner. From 1555 until the end of the seventeenth century (when Inquisition censorship was more and more rigorous) the theater was estranged from national life. Because of the language, subject matter, and the literary style of Jesuit drama, almost nothing remained of the lay and everyday life currents, especially in the sixty years of Spanish domination (1580–1640). In the succession of tragicomedies, allegories, and dramas with music, which repeated, in general, the classic themes and constructions, there was an evident predominance of rhetoric virtuosity in place of artistic creation and magnificent sets in place of dramatic content. Father Luís da Cruz (?–1604), composer and writer, took as his subject the destruction of Jerusalem in the tragedy *Sedecias*, published in 1605 with five other tragedies in *Tragicae, comicae actiones* ("Tragic and Comic Acts"). Father Antônio de Sousa (dates unknown) wrote *Tragédia real do descobrimento e conquista do Oriente* ("The Real Tragedy of the Discovery and Conquest of the Orient," 1619) in honor of Philip III of Spain, who was also king of Portugal at the time. In this production, more than three hundred actors were accompanied by a large orchestra, and there was a ship thirty spans long with ten real cannons firing in salute to the king. A few characters wore "1,090 diamonds, 3,000 large pearls, 248 of the finest emeralds and 1,139 rubies" according to an eyewitness, quoted by the historian Teófilo Braga.

An exception to this dramatically sterile period was the farce *O fidalgo aprendiz* ("The Apprentice Nobleman," written 1646; pub. 1676) by Francisco Manuel de Melo (1608–1666). It was "the only dramatic work of value in the seventeenth century," said historian Joaquim Ferreira. Melo was a noble related to the Spanish royal family. He had studied with the Jesuits and frequented the court when not combating the Dutch and the Catalonian separatists. Imprisoned (it is not known why) in 1644, he finished writing his farce two years later. In 1662, as the result of a *coup d'état,* he was freed and became a diplomat. His highly eventful life, first in the service of Spain and later of independent Portugal, did not keep Melo from writing several works concerned with ethics and

politics, in a style partly baroque and partly classical. *O fidalgo aprendiz,* however, revived the traditional roundel of Vicente as well as the comic quality in the popular taste. Although he criticized the rural gentry, it cannot be said that he adopted a definite position in regard to social conditions, for everything seemed wrong to Melo. What comes across most strongly is the grace with which he knows how to use language and stagecraft to maneuver his characters. In some of its aspects, *O fidalgo aprendiz* has been cited as one of Molière's sources.

From the end of the seventeenth until the middle of the eighteenth century, Italian operas, in original or adapted form, invaded the Portuguese theater. In imitation of them, but written for puppets, was the work of Antônio José da SILVA, the greatest Baroque Portuguese playwright. His brief life, marked by constant threats from the Inquisition, ended at the hands of the hangman, and his role as a critic of his society did not have, naturally, any followers. Nevertheless, Silva's few works have more modern application than do the numerous texts and the extensive dramatic theories of the writers belonging to the academies, the Portuguese arcadians of the eighteenth century. Of these, Manuel Figueiredo (1725–1801), who is "almost all the arcadian theater," according to historians Antônio José Saraiva and Oscar Lopes, did not wait for anyone to point out his defects. He anticipated them and correctly called himself one who gives incentive. Of his thirteen volumes of plays, still remembered are *Viriato* (1757) and *Inês* (1774), tragedies about personalities of Portuguese history who have remained in the consciousness of the people. Other arcadian dramatists are Reis Quita (1728–1770), *Castro* (1781); and Cruz e Silva (1731–1799), *O falso heroísmo* ("False Heroism," written 1755).

João Batista de Almeida GARRETT, a neoclassicist, wrote tragedies with themes from antiquity so skillfully manipulated that the spectators, seeing Cato or Caesar onstage, understood perfectly that the young poet was referring to contemporary Portuguese politicians. Changing his aesthetic direction, Garrett came to be the initiator of Portuguese Romanticism and the reformer of the theater. He remained within the tradition of historical drama on national themes but always worked for an aesthetic perfection to which the Portuguese theater was entirely unaccustomed. Thus the impact of his *Frei Luís de Sousa* (*Friar Luiz of Sousa,* 1843), a unique event in the dramatic literature of his country. Unfortunately, neither Garrett himself nor those authors who tried to contribute to the reform would again achieve the great artistic heights of this play.

The nineteenth century turned instead to "thesis drama," which soon palled, and to *revistas,* musical pieces with light sketches dealing with customs, principally political, and topics of even a more particular moment. In the genre of thesis drama, most notable is Gomes de Amorim (1827–1891), whose adventurer's life was spent partly in the north of Brazil and whose confused protest against social injustices reflects socialist ideas of the last half of the nineteenth century. He is the author of, among others, *Ódio de raça* ("Race Hatred," 1854), *Aleijões sociais* ("Social Deformities," pub. 1870), and *O cedro vermelho* ("The Red Cedar," 1856). Ernesto Biester (1829–

1880) combined social crusading with sentimental overstatement and an abundance of exaggerated situations of no psychological validity, all crowned with a moralizing effort, in such dramas as *Caridade na sombra* ("Charity in the Shadows," 1858) and *Pobreza dourada* ("Gilded Poverty," 1864). Mendes Leal (1818–1886) was perhaps the most popular dramatist in this tradition. The most skillful imitator of French authors, he wrote *Homem de ouro* ("The Golden Man," 1855), *Pobreza envergonhada* ("Embarrassed Poverty," 1858), *Pedro* (1861), and others. At the turn of the century appeared Marcelino Mesquita (1856–1919) with his historic and socially critical dramas, declamatory and bombastic, but very popular. João da Câmara (1852–1908), tending toward symbolism, was aesthetically more refined than the majority of his contemporaries. He is the author of, among others, *Os velhos* ("The Old Ones," 1893), *A toutinegra real* ("The Royal Warbler," 1895), and *Meia-Noite* ("Midnight," 1900). In the same search for literary perfection werę Eduardo Schwalbach (1860–1946) and Júlio Dantas (1876–1962). Among the latter's works are a one-act play in verse, *A ceia dos Cardeais* ("The Cardinal's Supper," 1902), which is still popular today for the sonority of its rhymes and for its atmosphere, simultaneously rococo and *fin de siècle*. Its melancholy elegance contrasts markedly with the desperate pathos bordering on insanity of Raul Brandão (1867–1930), soldier and writer of fiction and memoirs. His work is about the abjectly poor, those trampled upon by life, and his literary expression is as passionate as that of the Russian masters whose spiritual descendant he is. The best of his plays are in a modest volume that he published in 1923, containing *O gêbo e a sombra* ("The Humpback and the Shadow") and *O diabo e a morte* ("The Devil and Death"). He became known for this genre with *Jesus Cristo em Lisboa* ("Jesus Christ in Lisbon," 1927), a play he wrote with the poet Teixeira de Pascoais (1877–1952), portraying Christ as living in a working-class district of the Portuguese capital.

It is only in the last few years that Brandão's dramas have drawn critical interest. This has happened partly because contemporary authors and critics are resolved to break the monotony of the last hundred years and to give a new direction to plays by stimulating the public to prefer the most daring—in any sense of the word. It is certainly true that the writers most in tune with prevailing standards still enjoy great popularity, but it is not in vain that others, well known for poetry or novels, try to contribute to an improvement in the dramatic literature, if only once or twice. There are numerous authors in this category, such as José Almada Negreiros (1893–   ), Joaquim Paço d'Arcos (1908–   ), an important novelist, and Miguel Torga (1907–   ), one of the great Portuguese poets and author of *Terra firme* ("Firm Earth") and *Mar* ("The Sea"), published in the book *Teatro* (1941). Another poet equally important, with more dramatic works to his credit, is José Régio (1901–   ), who writes intellectual plays with mystic tendencies, shown in his mystery play *Jacob e o anjo* ("Jacob and the Angel," 1941), *Benilde* (1947), *Dom Sebastião* (1949), and *A salvação do mundo* ("The World's Salvation," 1953). While this current refines and intellectualizes Portuguese theater, another, with more adherents, sticks to neorealism: Carlos Selvagem, *Entre giestas* ("Among the Bramblebushes") and *Ninho de águias* ("Eagles' Nest"); and Bernardo Santareno, *O lugre* ("The Lugger") and *A promessa* ("The Promise"). As neorealists they fit into the general trend of the regionalist novel of both Brazil and Portugal. Belonging in part to the two groups mentioned or else eclectic in their preferences are Ramada Curto, Alfredo Cortês, Luís Francisco Rebelo, João Pedro de Andrade, and Stau Monteiro.

There is no bibliographical material translated into English.—J. P.

Po Sein. See BURMA.

Posse ("farce"). General German name for pretensionless low comedy, featuring a central figure characterized by an exaggerated human frailty. Type characterization and slapstick comedy lent themselves easily to local farces, often performed in dialect. Forerunners of the form were the Dutch *Kluchten,* German *Fastnachtsspiele,* and the Italian *commedia dell'arte.* From the Italian comedy the Posse derived an improvisational nature. In the 1730's Johann Gottsched, the German critic, chased Harlequin's German cousin, Hanswurst, from the stage, virtually ending the performance of this form of comedy in Germany. The Austrian tradition, however, continued on well into the next century, with Ferdinand Raimund and Johann Nestroy creating full-length plays of literary pretension and satirical intent. In the nineteenth century the one-act Posse often served to close the theatrical evening.—B. M. M.

Power of Darkness, The (Vlast tmy, 1895). A drama in five acts by Leo TOLSTOY. Written in 1886, the play was banned in Russia until 1895. Describing the cruel and backward life of village peasants, *The Power of Darkness* is the story of Nikita, a young man with a weakness for women, who works for a rich and ailing peasant, Peter, and is the lover of Peter's wife, Anisia. Instigated by Matryona, Nikita's mother, Anisia poisons Peter after she has obtained his money. Once Nikita has taken over Peter's house and married his wife, he takes to drink, hires someone else to work the farm, and seduces his stepdaughter, Akulina. Miserable and embittered, Anisia makes plans to marry Akulina off, but first they have to get rid of Akulina's baby by Nikita. Determined to make Nikita share the guilt of murder, Anisia, with the help of her mother-in-law, forces her reluctant but trapped husband to kill the baby and bury it in the cellar. Unable to bear this burden of guilt, however, Nikita breaks down at Akulina's wedding feast and makes a public confession, to the great joy of his father, a God-fearing, inarticulate old man who has been struggling to put into words his pain over his son's gradual corruption.

This play shows the ignorance in which peasants, particularly peasant women, still lived a quarter of a century after the emancipation of the serfs, when legal slavery had been replaced by economic bondage and money had become the most important commodity to the peasant. Anisia and Matryona, according to Tolstoy's explicit intention, are victims of that state of affairs; "Matryona must not be portrayed as a villain," Tolstoy wrote. "She is an ordinary old woman who is trying to help her son . . . . She believes that everyone is prepared to commit an evil act, that life would be impossible without them and she refuses to avoid them." Most of the peasants just drift toward evil ("darkness") because of the very nature of the society in which they live; Tolstoy shows this drifting through the eyes of a child (Anyuta, Anisia's ten-year-old daughter) and through the inarticulate mutterings of Nikita's father, Akim. Inarticulateness, it should be noted, is a favorite symbol of many Russian writers for the truth grasped by the extrarational abilities of small children or "simple" people.

Like so many other works by Tolstoy, the plot of *The Power of Darkness* was based on an actual murder that took place in Tula Province in 1880 and produced such a great impression on the writer that he visited the accused in prison.

The stark realism of this play and the extraordinary richness of the dialogue ("I looted my notebooks to write it," Tolstoy wrote) has made it one of the regular items in the repertories of Russian groups ever since the censors lifted their ban in 1895.

The Power of Darkness, translated by Andrew R. MacAndrew, appears in *19th Century Russian Drama* (1963).—A. MacA.

Praga, Marco (1862–1929). Italian playwright. Praga was born in Milan of a bourgeois family. His father, Emilio, was a poet and man of letters. Marco Praga dedicated himself at a very early age to dramatic composition. He belonged to that group of writers who adhered to the principles of naturalism and whose aim it was to reveal the bourgeois world of that time in Milan. These writers submitted to analysis and merciless criticism the conventions, myths, and egoisms that were hiding below the surface of respectability of the financial and industrial middle class. Praga was one of the major writers of this group, largely because of his keen psychological and sociological probing, his accurate attack, and the earnestness of his moral and social commitment, besides his more personal and autonomous adherence to foreign models, particularly the French. Praga captured his first success with *Le vergini* (1889), which was followed by *La moglie ideale* ("The Ideal Wife," 1890), made successful by Eleonora Duse, *La Porta chiusa* (1913), and others, in which he takes aim at the conventional bourgeois morals of matrimony. Also important was his activity as a critic, attested by the ten volumes of *Cronache teatrali* ("Theatrical Criticism," 1919–1928) and his organizational activity, which culminated with the founding of the Societa degli Autori (Society of Authors). —L. L.

Précieuses ridicules, Les (The Precious Damsels, 1659). A one-act comedy in prose by MOLIÈRE. First performed as a farce, then cut down, rewritten, and called a comedy, *Les Précieuses ridicules* portrays two young girls from the provinces who have recently arrived in Paris and who read fashionable novels. After having refused two worthy young men, they are tricked by the young men's valets, who are disguised as lions of Parisian society. The play ends with cudgeling and the valets actually undressing. Building his play entirely around one nasty trick played on two foolish girls, Molière, in *Les Précieuses,* used the often brutal devices of farce to satirize not only contemporary customs but also the grotesque power of illusion inherent in all snobbery.

This play has been translated by Morris Bishop in *Eight Plays* (1957).—Ja. G.

Preston, Thomas. See CAMBISES.

Priestley, J. B. See ENGLAND: *post-Edwardian drama.*

Prinz Friedrich von Homburg (The Prince of Homburg, written 1811, pub. 1821). A romantic drama by Heinrich von KLEIST. Considered to be Kleist's finest drama, *Prinz Friedrich von Homburg* contains the major problem that concerned Kleist his entire life: Is self-mastery in reality self-denial? Warned not to be rash in combat by the elector of Brandenburg, the prince of Homburg dreams of heroic feats and of winning the princess Natalia's love. It is because of his dream and uncontrolled idealism that the prince does not heed the elector's commands and violates them in the battle of Fehrbellin. Though the Germans are triumphant, the elector has the prince imprisoned and sentences him to death for endangering the Prussian forces. When Natalia intercedes for him, the elector gives the prince the right to decide whether the death sentence is just. After struggling with himself, the prince concedes the validity of the sentence. It is at this point that the elector, made aware of the prince's dream experience, pardons him and allows him to marry Natalia. Whether this conclusion reveals a humanization of the state or a denial of the individual's natural rights is in many respects a mute point. Kleist's drama begins and ends like a romantic fairy tale. The prince dreams a dream that he can realize only by comprehending what his real powers are. After a battle both with himself and with outside forces, he takes a step forward into a realm that he will shape. Kleist's five-act drama written in a mannered blank verse interweaves military battle scenes with psychological struggles. The final conquest of the self ends the hero's quest to fulfill a dream of glory.—J. D. Z.

Private Life of the Master Race, The (Furcht und Elend des Dritten Reiches, written 1935–1938). A documentary play in twenty-four scenes by Bertolt BRECHT. The original title for this play—*Deutschland—ein Greuelmaerchen* ("Germany—an Atrocity Story")—recalls Heinrich Heine's "Deutschland ein Wintermaerchen" ("Germany, a Winter's Tale"), while the later one is modeled after Balzac's *Splendeur et misère des courtisanes.* Eric Bentley's English translation (1945) contains seventeen scenes, and Brecht describes it in his notes as a stage version for the United States. The scenes are linked by choruses, to be sung by German soldiers on the typical armored truck of the Nazi army. The noise of the rolling truck can also be heard during the scenes that show how terror will make the people join the "war waggon."

The Private Life of the Master Race (in Meshdunarodnaya Kniga's 1942 translation *Fear and Misery of the Third Reich*) is based on eye-witness accounts and newspaper reports. The scenes document the Nazi takeover in Germany between 1933 and 1938. They demonstrate how fear and misery affected the lives of every German in every surrounding: the worker, the bourgeois, and the intellectual—at home, in the streets, in a concentration camp, and on the job. Some of the scenes are very short, mere black-out skits, but they often contribute just as much to the overall picture as the longer sketches. Frederic

Ewen (*Bertolt Brecht,* 1967, pp. 321 ff.) describes the author's main concern: "Foremost in Brecht's mind was the capitulation of the intelligentsia in the face of the terror. They are the subjects of the most brilliant of the sketches, as well as the most terrifying."

The list of characters includes a judge who is willing to decide anything the authorities want him to decide, but he pleads: "I must know what they want. If one does not know that, there is no justice any longer." There is a high school teacher who worries that his young son might be an informer and who reacts to the terror in the same way: "I am ready to teach anything they want me to teach. But what do they want me to teach?" And there is the Jewish wife who leaves her "Aryan" husband, a prominent physician, before he can send her away. But she does not understand herself what is really happening: "What's come over them? What do they really want? What am I doing to them? I never mixed in politics."

Brecht's anti-Nazi documentary can be seen as anti-Brechtian. The style is naturalistic and proves that Brecht could write excellent conventional theater. The sudden return to theater of involvement and identification is certainly motivated by the desire for an immediate political impact. But while Brecht was writing these traditional scenes, he also worked on the theatrical foundations of his new theater. And this combination—as Reinhold Grimm suggests (*Bertolt Brecht,* 1962, p. 33)—might well have led to the final synthesis of the traditional and the new forms that produced Brecht's greatest works.—H. R.

problem play. A term used to describe plays that dramatize controversial social questions, especially those related to the emancipation of women, sexual mores, family relationships, and personal or business ethics. Problem plays began to be written in the nineteenth century when liberal thinkers questioned the validity of traditional institutions and conventional wisdom. Although the problem play reached artistic maturity in the critical realism of Henrik Ibsen, its characteristic features were developed by Alexandre Dumas fils, and they remain viable today (1968).

In order to enliven a theater taken up with the commonplace, the younger Dumas introduced sensational and controversial material to the stage. His *Demi-Monde* (1855) dramatizes the role courtesans were playing in society. *La Question d' argent* (1857) portrays the sharp and unscrupulous practices of a self-made businessman. In later plays, Dumas fils concerned himself with the problem of illegitimacy (*Le Fils naturel*) and the woman question (*Idées de Madame Aubray*). Like his conservative contemporary Émile Augier, he wrote didactic plays defending a thesis and appealed to the social conscience of his audience. The younger Dumas's conceptions of virtue and vice appear simplistic, however, particularly when compared to the moral world of Henrik Ibsen.

Although Ibsen's first tragedy, *Cataline* (1850), is sympathetic to the rebel who shook the pillars of Roman institutions, the Norwegian playwright devoted his apprenticeship years to historical and romantic drama before turning to the contemporary social issues of the problem play. *Love's Comedy,* completed in 1862, is an unromantic study of modern marriage and Ibsen's first experiment with the problem play. Four years later in a basically affirmative

play, *Brand,* Ibsen attacked timidity, hypocrisy, and rapacity. Its protagonist, a clergyman probably based on Søren Kierkegaard, is a larger-than-life figure, however, cast in the heroic mold. *The League of Youth,* begun in 1868, exposes the venality of contemporary small-town politics, a theme Ibsen later developed more fully in *An Enemy of the People,* his strongest indictment of profit-seeking respectability. In *The Pillars of Society,* a play about the corruption and cowardice underpinning a man of power and reputation, Ibsen drew his first portrait of a modern woman—one who can think for herself.

A Doll's House (1879), Ibsen's next play, is centrally concerned with the woman question. Inspired by the feminism of its time, *A Doll's House* details the plight of a woman overprotected by her father and husband to the extent that she is unable to comprehend the basic realities of life and society. In upholding the bourgeois ideal of a wife, the men in her life encourage her to be mindless, cheerful, and innocent. *Ghosts,* which followed in 1881, portrays the hopelessness of a woman driven by convention into a loveless marriage with a syphilitic and unfaithful man. The masterful *Hedda Gabler* (1891) dramatizes the destructiveness of an intelligent, forceful, and neurotic woman.

In *Rosmersholm* (1887) Ibsen successfully wove together a number of themes he had developed in earlier problem plays. The protagonist of this drama, Johannes Rosmer, a former clergyman converted to liberal ideals, is able to resist the conservative pressures of society when buttressed by the vigor and moral courage of his housekeeper, Rebecca West, an intelligent and emancipated woman. When Rosmer learns that Rebecca is in part responsible for his wife's suicide, he loses his self-assurance and is at the mercy of his shrewd brother-in-law, the conservative Rector Kroll. Both Rosmer and Rebecca, haunted by guilt and the past, are destroyed. *Rosmersholm,* with its psychological insight and symbolic suggestiveness, is not merely an exposition of social problems. Ironically, its success, as in the case of his other plays, arises from Ibsen's skill as a creator of character, not as an expositor of social problems.

With Ibsen's success, other playwrights followed his lead in exposing a variety of social problems on the stage. Bjørnstjerne Bjørnson explored the contradictions of the double standard of morality in *The Gauntlet,* which appeared four years after *A Doll's House.* Strindberg sharply attacked the liberated woman in problem plays like *The Father* (1887) and *Comrades* (1888). Other Scandinavian playwrights, such as Helen Wuolijoki and Hjalmar Bergström, came to the defense of women's emancipation and social justice. In Holland Herman Heijermans attacked authoritarian religion and problems related to industrialism. The revolutionary theater of the late nineteenth century, led by Gerhart Hauptmann in Germany, Eugène Brieux in France, and G. B. Shaw in England, continued along these lines, and the genre eventually spread to Moscow and New York.

Typical problem plays continued to be written well into the twentieth century. Shaw, John Galsworthy, St. John Ervine, Miles Malleson, Sidney Howard, and Lillian Hellman offered a variety of problem plays to English-speaking audiences, and the genre itself eventually became a neat formula. The avant-garde, however, was going in the direction of naturalism and expressionism. Naturalism replaced the "well-made" problem play with a "slice of life," and its zeal for reform with a gloomy pessimism. Expressionism broke away from the realistic settings and the illusionism of the problem play. Nevertheless, despite the often drastic technical innovations and an almost complete turnabout in artistic strategy, the stage of the naturalists and expressionists carried on the critical spirit of the problem play, a tendency further developed in the epic theater of Bertolt Brecht.

From this broader point of view, the problem play, as it was developed by Ibsen, has had a profound effect on the modern drama. The term problem play, however, is often used derogatorily to describe plays, such as those of Émile Augier, that do little more than argue a position or assert a moral or social truism. The problem play in this limited sense is known under a variety of names—the *théâtre utile,* the *pièce à thèse,* the *tendenz* drama, and the purpose or thesis play. The thesis play absorbed the workmanlike technique of Eugène Scribe and introduced the *raisonneur,* a character whose purpose was to act as the author's mouthpiece. Although Ibsen abandoned the *raisonneur* in his mature problem plays, he remained indebted to the technique of Scribe.

Ramsden Balmforth's *The Problem Play and Its Influence on Modern Thought and Life* (1928), the only book-length study of the problem play, is helpful in regard to minor playwrights, but it is poorly focused. A more substantial study, which places the problem play in the larger context of the modern theater of ideas, is Eric Bentley's *The Playwright as Thinker: A Study of Drama in Modern Times* (1946). John Gassner's "Shaw on Ibsen," in *Ideas in the Drama* (1964), discusses aspects of the problem play as well as Shaw's interpretations of Ibsen.—J. F. L.

Professor Taranne (Le Professeur Taranne, 1953). A play by Arthur ADAMOV. *Professor Taranne* was written in 1951 and first performed in Lyons in 1953 under the direction of Roger Planchon. This fourth play by Adamov is about a man unable to live up to his public role of university professor, which may be less a profession than a symbol of any source of gratification to the conscious ego, and therefore a key to Taranne's universal humanity. Taranne is accused of immorality (of exposing himself to young girls) and of intellectual plagiarism. Although his accusers come and go as if they were the ghosts of a dream, there is no vagueness in the dramatic construction or the characterizations.

In speaking of his own play, Adamov expressed surprise over the audience's approval of it, since the play is dominated by the absurd logic of dreams, and usually spectators only accept a play if they are able to recognize themselves in the character. Even in the structure of the dream, it is obvious that Adamov is denouncing the absurd and implacable confusion of the modern world. No remedy is offered for the various forms of evil his plays dramatize.

Professor Taranne has been translated by Albert Bermel in *Four Modern French Comedies* (1960). —W. F.

Prometheus Bound (Prometheus Desmotes, date uncertain). A tragedy by AESCHYLUS. No record of production survives. Circumstantial evidence, however, makes it certain that *Prometheus Bound* was designed to be followed in performance by *Prometheus Lyomenos* (*Prometheus Unbound*), and likely that there was a third tragedy in the sequence, *Prometheus Pyrphoros* (*Prometheus the Fire-Carrier*). The date of this (presumed) trilogy has been much debated, but certain technical features strongly suggest that it was written after the *Oresteia,* produced in 458 B.C. In that case, it is datable within two years, since Aeschylus died in 456/55.

The scene is a peak of the Caucasus range, imagined as lying on the edge of the world. Enter Power and Violence, agents of Zeus, dragging Prometheus. With them is Hephaestus, who reluctantly, at Power's brutal orders, shackles the prisoner to the rock. Left alone by his tormentors, Prometheus is approached by the Chorus of Nymphs, daughters of Ocean. To them he expounds the so-called crimes which have brought him to that place. He tells how, having helped Zeus to conquer the Titans in the war for the throne of heaven, he had offended him by opposing his subsequent plan to destroy mankind; instead, he (Prometheus) had given men Hope and Fire! The exposition is interrupted by a visit from a fellow Titan, Ocean, who ineffectually offers to mediate with Zeus, and by a short choral ode. In the next scene (lines 436 ff.) Prometheus enlarges on his benefits to men: he has put all the arts of civilization in their power. After another choral ode there enters (561) a fantastic creature, half-girl, half-cow—Io. (For her legend in general, see THE SUPPLIANT MAIDENS.) In *Prometheus* she is introduced as a living token of Zeus's cruelty to mortals. In a series of majestic speeches Prometheus describes her tormented wanderings, past and to come—a mighty clockwise arc from Greece, through Eurasia and Ethiopia, to the Nile Delta. As he nears the end of this prophecy, the character of his vision changes. He sees Io gently healed by Zeus and made the mother of a noble line that will culminate in Prometheus' own liberator, Heracles. Yet this brief insight into a kinder future is lost from the moment that Io bounds in madness from the stage (886). Prometheus then rages at the cruelty of her present sufferings. In the final scene Prometheus shouts aloud that he knows the secret of Zeus's destruction. At this the messenger-god Hermes comes hurrying from the sky, with the threat that unless Prometheus reveals the secret he will be buried alive and will emerge only to be tortured by Zeus's eagle. Prometheus remains obdurate, and the play ends in a cosmic storm, during which he and the Chorus, who choose to suffer with him, are swallowed by the rock.

The opening and closing scenes of *Prometheus Bound* are as lively as any in the extant corpus of Aeschylus and hardly inferior in dramatic quality to the best of Sophocles or Euripides. It is the intervening scenes that have invited severe criticism: the motionless hero, the parade of unearthly visitors, and the lengthy, apparently static, speeches. Against this it may be argued that the bulk of *Prometheus* is conceived as a "drama of ideas," in several possible senses of the phrase. To the brute force of Zeus the shackled Titan cannot respond with force, or even with movement. He can rely only on his mind, and above all on his knowledge of the fatal Secret: that Zeus will in time fall in love with another girl, Thetis, whose child is doomed to be mightier than its father. The Secret is a driving power in the play. There are mysterious hints about it in the earlier half of the play. But it is only the sight of Io—a horrific reminder of Zeus's lust—that moves Prometheus to speak more plainly and at last to shout as much of his knowledge as he dares into the sky. Aside from that central dramatic motif, the speeches of Prometheus traverse immense tracts of time and space, and the lack of physical movement is compensated for by movement of the mind. Even as he speaks (especially in the two exposition scenes near the beginning), he is being elevated by Aeschylus, before our eyes, from the status of petty comedian, which all earlier Greek stories had assigned him, to a Titanic spiritual status, which he has retained to this day in the Western imagination. Above all, perhaps, the twentieth-century reader is struck by the political ideas that are developed from one end of the play to the other. *Prometheus*, in one aspect, is a sophisticated study of totalitarianism, its methods and results. Although the dictatorship concerned happens to be that of the universe, the analogies to human political experience are, unhappily, obvious.

No fair estimate of *Prometheus Bound* as drama or as poetry is possible if one forgets that, as it stands, it is only a thesis—mythological, religious, political. An antithesis certainly followed in *Prometheus Lyomenos,* and perhaps a synthesis in *Prometheus Pyrphoros.* Enough fragments of *Lyomenos* remain for the bare outline of the plot to be reconstructed. Prometheus, now suffering agonies from the eagle, is visited by a Chorus of Titans, by his mother, Earth, and by Heracles. To Heracles he prophesies his journeys (balancing those of Io, and closing the circuit of the earth) westward through Europe and into North Africa. Heracles shoots the eagle, and Prometheus somehow is released, receiving a symbolic bond— in the shape of a garland—to replace the actual one. Of *Pyrphoros* there are only two insignificant fragments, but its title alone ("Fire-Carrier") is enough to quicken the imagination.

The most recent scholarly edition of *Prometheus Bound* in English is by George Thomson (1932). —C. J. H.

Puerto Rico. Puerto Rican drama in the sense that one in the Western world understands it dates from as recently as the second half of the nineteenth century. More specifically, it was not until the 1930's that modern theater and drama really began to develop on the island.

No specific documentation is available concerning any dramatic presentations in Puerto Rico throughout the entire sixteenth century or during the first four decades of the seventeenth century. By analogy, however, with the other Spanish American colonies, it is most probable that short allegorical plays based on the Bible and the sacraments and teachings of the Catholic church were performed on feast days in the courtyards of churches, convents, and monasteries and in the plazas of the principal towns. It is known, for example, that the religious orders of St. Francis and St. Dominic were skilled in performing dramatizations from Scripture and the catechism. (The Dominicans were in Puerto Rico from the second decade of the sixteenth century.)

The first definite reference to a dramatic presentation in Puerto Rico is found in a letter dated September 27, 1644, written by the newly appointed Bishop Damián López de Haro. He states that upon his arrival from Spain he was received not only with the usual religious ceremonies but also with dances, bullfights, and comedies. Unfortunately, just what these "comedies" were or how, where, and by whom they were performed is not mentioned.

Throughout the eighteenth century, drama in Puerto Rico consisted mainly of presentations of classical Spanish plays of the Golden Age (sixteenth and seventeenth centuries) performed during religious celebrations and in honor of royal or papal coronations or visiting dignitaries. It is known, for example, that four plays by Spanish writers were performed in May 1747 in honor of the recently crowned king of Spain, Ferdinand VI.

During the latter part of the eighteenth and early nineteenth centuries dramatic activity in Puerto Rico was kept to a minimum, primarily because of political upheavals in Spain at that time.

The printing press was not brought to Puerto Rico until 1806, and it was not until the 1820's that announcements or reviews of theatrical performances or other spectacles appeared in newspapers. In 1811 the first play apparently written in Puerto Rico was printed. All that has been found of it is an anonymous untitled fragment in verse of some sixteen pages. Judging by these, it appears that the action takes place in Puerto Rico between 1795 and 1805 and deals with a husband's adultery and bigamy during a prolonged separation from his wife, the latter's unexpected return, and her lodging in the other woman's home.

Throughout the rest of the nineteenth century, drama in Puerto Rico suffered under the same handicaps that prevailed in most of Latin America. Dramatic presentations consisted primarily of poor comedies and melodramas performed chiefly by visiting companies from Spain. Similar troupes from Cuba, Mexico, and Venezuela are also known to have performed in Puerto Rico. The acting reflected the excessive romanticism of the period, and the companies, built around one leading actor or actress, emphasized commercial rather than dramatic values. Several native companies were also formed over the years and carried dramatic and musical presentations to all parts of the island.

The two most important nineteenth-century Puerto Rican playwrights, who wrote historical dramas in the Spanish romantic tradition, were Alejandro Tapia y Rivera (1826–1882)—*Roberto D'Evreux,* 1848; *Bernardo de Palissy,* 1857; *Camoens,* 1868; and *Vasco Núñez de Balboa,* 1872 —and Salvador Brau (1842–1912)—*Héroe y mártir* ("Hero and Martyr," 1870); *La vuelta al hogar* ("The Return Home," 1877); and *Los horrores del triunfo* ("The Horrors of Triumph," 1887).

In the first third of the twentieth century there was very little theatrical activity in Puerto Rico because of the political, social, and economic changes occasioned by the Spanish-American War (1898). A few significant dramas, however, were written, such as *El grito de Lares* ("The Cry of Lares," 1914) by Luis Lloréns Torres (1878–1944); *El héroe galopante* ("The Galloping Hero," published in 1935 but written much earlier) by Nemesio Canales (1878–1923);

Un hombre de cuarenta años ("A Forty-Year-Old Man," 1929) by Antonio Coll y Vidal (1898–   ); and *Juan Ponce de León* (1932) by José Ramírez Santibáñez (1895–1950) and Carlos N. Carreras (1895–   ).

The first serious effort toward the establishment of a national theater and the development of modern drama took place when the Ateneo (Atheneum) of Puerto Rico sponsored a contest for native playwrights and produced the three winning plays in 1938. They were: *Esta noche juega el jóker* ("Tonight the Joker Is Wild") by Fernando Sierra Berdecía (1903–   ); *El clamor de los surcos* ("The Cry of the Furrows") by Manuel Méndez Ballester (1909–   ); and *El desmonte* ("The Clearing") by Gonzalo Arocho del Toro (dates unknown).

In 1940 playwright Emilio Belaval (1903–   ) formed a dramatic society called Areyto, the aims of which were to stage plays by Puerto Rican authors, to develop and modernize all aspects of theatrical production, and to cultivate an audience and awaken a feeling for a national theater. In its two years of existence Areyto produced four plays: Méndez Ballester's *Tiempo muerto* ("The Dead Season"); *Mi señoría* ("My Lordship") by Luis Rechani Agrait (1902–   ); *He vuelto a buscarla* ("I Look for Her Again") by Martha Lomar (1895–   ); and Sierra Berdecía's *La escuela del buen amor* ("The School of Good Love"). Although short-lived, Areyto was the parent troupe for many later experimental groups.

Areyto's director, Leopoldo Santiago Lavandero, himself a product of the Yale Drama School, did much to help establish modern techniques of acting, staging, and directing not only for Areyto but also in his later capacity as director of the theater at the University of Puerto Rico. However, no plays by Puerto Rican authors were presented at the University Theater between 1944 and 1956. For obvious political reasons, it was the university administration's policy to stress European and American culture and values in preference to things Puerto Rican. During this time, however, Lavandero did produce many works of world drama at the university, thus enabling those on both sides of the footlights to become familiar with the standard classic repertory as well as the latest trends in acting and writing from Europe and the United States.

In 1956 the Institute of Puerto Rican Culture, an official organ of the commonwealth government, which by now had realized the need for fostering native cultural values in all the arts, appointed the Advisory Theater Council to prepare a step-by-step program for the further development of the theater. One of the council's recommendations was an annual theater festival of Puerto Rican plays, which have been presented each year since the first in 1958. Some of the plays for the festivals have been revivals; some produced for the first time. Among the highlights of the various festivals have been *Vejigantes* (a title referring to a native folk festival, 1958) by Francisco Arriví (1915–   ); *Los soles truncos* ("The Truncated Suns," 1958, 1966), *Un niño azul para esa sombra* ("A Blue Boy for That Shadow," 1960), *La carreta* (*The Ox Cart*, 1961), *El apartamiento* ("The Apartment," 1964), and *Mariana o el alba* ("Mariana or the Dawn," 1965) by René MARQUÉS; Sierra

Berdecía's *Esta noche juega el jóker* (1959); Méndez Ballester's *Tiempo muerto* (1962) and *Bienvenido, don Goyito* ("Welcome, don Goyito," 1965, 1966); and Belaval's *La vida* ("Life," 1963).

While the plays presented from 1938 to 1941 dealt primarily with immediate social problems and conditions, those of the 1958 Theater Festival and subsequent festivals were more concerned with the basic and broader problem of the nature of Puerto Rico. Also, in the last ten years the emphasis in drama has been away from the earlier tendencies of realism and naturalism. The majority of the newer plays rely heavily on the most contemporary techniques of writing and staging, such as the creation of poetic moods through language, music, and lighting; the use of flashbacks and dream sequences; experimentation with time sequence; and a more psychological type of character development. These techniques are not used as tricks or props to cover dramatic weaknesses but as legitimate means for heightening dramatic expression.

After eleven highly successful theater festivals and the more recent inauguration of an annual festival of international drama—in Spanish—plus occasional independent productions of works in Spanish or English, it is obvious that drama in Puerto Rico has undergone a radical change and has grown considerably in the last thirty years. The most important advances have been the complete renovation of staging techniques, the development of a strong nucleus of serious personnel in all phases of dramatic activity, and the creation of an ever-expanding repertory of Puerto Rican plays. Everything indicates that these past successes will be continued and that year-round commercial theater will soon be a reality.

Each year since 1959 the Institute of Puerto Rican Culture has published an anthology containing the plays presented during the previous year's theater festival. Most of these plays have also appeared in separate editions and other anthologies but have not been published in English.

Frank Dauster's "Drama and Theater in Puerto Rico," *Modern Drama* (September 1963), discusses the development of Puerto Rican theater from 1938 to 1961.—C. R. P.

puppet theater. See BUNRAKU.

Purgatory (1939). A one-act verse play by William Butler YEATS. One of Yeats's last works, *Purgatory* is the tragedy of a family curse and the desperate need for expiation. Although it is not one of his *noh* plays, it shows the influence of that highly compressed and ritualistic form in its concentration on one intense situation with supernatural invocations and only two characters, an Old Man and his bastard son. Now a wandering peddler, the Old Man has brought his sixteen-year-old son to a ruined house in which, when the Old Man was sixteen, he had killed his drunken father with a knife that he still carries in his pocket. As they study the desolate house, he explains that his mother, an aristocratic lady of a great family, had polluted the family blood by marrying a groom in a training stable and that she died giving birth to him, the peddler. Thereafter, the dissolute groom wasted the family fortune, and one night when drunk he set fire to the great house and on that same night the peddler, then sixteen years old, killed him in a vain attempt to exorcise the curse. Now, on the night of his mother's wedding anniversary, the tormented Old Man has been driven back to relive the original crime, just as his mother's spirit is doomed to relive her transgression until it can be purged away. Suddenly the Old Man sees an image of his mother in the house and hears the hoofbeats as his father rides home drunk. But his vulgar son is aware of nothing, concerned only with trying to steal his father's bag of coins. They fight and the Old Man stabs the boy with "the same jack-knife," crying out to his mother's spirit that he killed the boy in another attempt to end the pollution. But once more he hears the terrible hoofbeats, and he cries out:

> O God,
> Release my mother's soul from its dream!
> Mankind can do no more. Appease
> The misery of the living and the remorse of
>   the dead.

Thus he offers an anguished prayer in the realization that he has failed again, that his mother's spirit is still condemned to suffer.—D. K.

Purple Dust (1940). A play by Sean O'CASEY. With this play O'Casey launches the comic fantasies of his late period. Mainly a satire of pastoral affectations, this work also ranges over a variety of human follies. The plot develops out of the addlebrained attempt of two "English" Englishmen, Basil Stoke and Cyril Poges, to resurrect a crumbling Tudor mansion in the little Irish village of Clune na Gerra. Wealthy financiers from London on a misguided lark in rural Ireland, they have illusions about the glories of the Elizabethan age and plan to live as dashing country squires amid the amiable Irish peasants. They are such monumental fools that their pastoral masquerade would have collapsed soon enough if left on their own, but the crafty peasants are eager to mock their absurd affectations and hasten their downfall. In the two ringleaders of the peasants, Jack O'Killigain and Philib O'Dempsey, O'Casey creates a pair of shrewd Celtic foils for the English buffoons. The two Irishmen are primitive playboys who provide a norm of genuine pastoral life. They steal the mistresses of the Englishmen, who are left with a heap of "purple dust" as the villagers go about cheerfully wrecking the mansion. Meanwhile, O'Dempsey, who is described as "a wandherin' king holdin' th' ages be th' hand," prophesies that in the near future the Irish will ride into the hills to seek their own version of the good life, in the manner of the legendary Finn MacCoole. And this sets up the fantastic resolution. After Stoke and Poges are comically defeated, the heavy rains forebode the coming of a retributive flood. The sky darkens, lightning flashes, and suddenly the fantastic Spirit of the rising river appears and announces that the Deluge has come, that only those "who have lifted their eyes unto the hills" will be saved. The flood waters break through as O'Killigain and O'Dempsey and their friends ride off to the liberating hills.—D. K.

Pushkin, Alexander [Sergeyevich] (1799–1837). Russian poet, novelist, short-story writer, and playwright. Pushkin may be said to have launched the "golden age" of Russian literature, a cultural upsurge comparable to the achievements of Athens

ALEXANDER PUSHKIN (NEW YORK PUBLIC LIBRARY)

under Pericles or Elizabethan England. Coming from a family that was precariously balanced on the lowest rung of the upper classes, Pushkin was educated in the supremely elegant Lycée of Tsarskoye Tselo, to which he was admitted through the intervention of influential friends of his uncle, Vasily Pushkin, a minor poet of the period. Whether because of his insecure background or because of his coarse, exotic features (his great-great-grandfather Hannibal had been brought from Africa by Peter the Great) that set him apart from others, it was the humanitarian and equalitarian element inherent in his solid classical education that left the deepest mark on Pushkin. He always displayed democratic and liberal sympathies in his writings, that is, as much as was possible in the face of tsarist censorship. Not only did Pushkin divert Russian writers from their insipid imitating of the French neoclassicists, but he also showed them what a powerful instrument of social protest literature could be in a country subjected to political tyranny. The regime, however, sensed an enemy in Pushkin and on various occasions he was the victim of persecution, overt or covert. Indeed, it was with a strange satisfaction that the authorities greeted the announcement of Pushkin's death in 1837. Pushkin was killed in a duel that appeared to be a deliberate provocation engineered by government security agents.

Although mainly a poet, Pushkin reached a highpoint in Russian drama as a playwright too with his BORIS GODUNOV, which may be described as an acclimatization of Shakespeare to the Russian stage. In his Introduction to this play, Pushkin pays his due to the great Elizabethan, "offering up on his altar the [French] classical unities" of time, space, and action and also "the fourth unity" of French tragedy that is never mentioned—that of style. For, instead of French alexandrine verse, Pushkin declared himself free to use blank verse, rhyme, and even "vile prose" when he felt it appropriate. In that way, he felt he could bring to life people and historical periods. In 1830 Pushkin wrote four little tragedies—*Skupoi rytzar* (*The Avaricious Knight*, 1852), supposedly based on William Shenstone's *The Covetous Knight*, which, however, could never be found among Shenstone's works; *Pir vo vremya chumy* (*The Feast During the Plague*), inspired by John Wilson's *The City of Plague*; *Motsart i Saleri* (*Mozart and Salieri*, 1832), based on the false rumor that Mozart had been poisoned by his less talented rival; and *Kamyenni gost'* (*The Stone Guest*, 1847), based on Lorenzo Da Ponte's *Don Giovanni* (the libretto of Mozart's opera)—and *Rusalka* (*The Water Nymph*, 1832), a short Russian folkloric drama.

Despite the high quality of Pushkin's drama, particularly *Boris Godunov*, his influence on the Russian theater (which developed along the Fonvizin-Griboyedov-Gogol comedy line) was minor, perhaps because his plays were originally banned by the censors and were not regularly performed until much later. (They are occasionally included in Soviet and Russian émigré repertoires.) There is no doubt, however, that their influence can be found in such plays as Mikhail Lermontov's *Maskarad* ("Masquerade," 1835) and Alexei Tolstoy's historical trilogy written in the 1860's.

A good biography is *Pushkin* by D. S. Mirsky (1963).—A. MACA.

Q

Queen After Death (La Reine Morte, 1942). A tragedy by Henry de MONTHERLANT. *Queen After Death* was the first play that Montherlant wrote. Whereas the usual play is built around the coherence of character, *Queen After Death* is built around the incoherence of Ferrante, a kind of philosopher-king experiencing the horror of his own philosophy. He turns against his son Pedro because of his love for his son as a child and because he cannot love the mediocre character Pedro has become.

The play is about the conflict between love and politics, between the demands of the heart and the demands of the state. As the aging king of Portugal, Ferrante plans the marriage of his son Don Pedro and the very young Infanta of Navarre. The love of Inès de Castro for Don Pedro is the obstacle to the state marriage. Ferrante learns of this love and of the secret marriage between Inès and Pedro. His anger falls on Inès, whom he orders killed. Throughout the play Ferrante denies love, denies its power and reality as persistently as Inès proclaims it. At the end of the play his irritability and senile illogicality, more than any reason of state, cause him to turn on Inès

A SCENE FROM HENRY DE MONTHERLANT'S
Queen After Death (FRENCH CULTURAL SERVICES)

and demand her death. Ferrante kills Inès, not only to end an impossible situation, but also through sadism and a hatred for life itself, which he knows is ending for him. As Ferrante dies, he pulls the page Dino del Moro against him because Dino reminds him of his son as a boy.

Queen After Death has been translated by Jonathan Griffin (1951).—W. F.

Querolus (The Complainer). A Roman comedy of the late Empire, of unknown authorship, possibly dating from the early fifth century A.D. *Querolus* is the only Roman comedy extant in addition to the twenty-six plays of Plautus and Terence. It is wrongly considered a reworking of Plautus' *Aulularia*, for although both comedies have a household god as a character and a pot of gold buried by Euclio, the two plots are otherwise entirely dissimilar.

In *Querolus* Mandrogerus and his accomplices steal the pot from Querolus, Euclio's son, and hurl it back when they discover that it contains ashes, not realizing that the gold is concealed beneath the ashes. The comedy contains much astrological, religious, philosophical, social, and legal satire and in both language and content is characteristic of the late period in which it was written.—G. E. D.

Quinault, Philippe (1635–1688). French playwright and poet. Born in Paris, the son of a baker, Philippe Quinault, first a valet, then a lawyer, married a rich woman in 1660. In 1670 he became a member of the Académie Française and in 1671 was named commissioner of audit.

Quinault began in the theater with comedies drawn first from the Italian *commedia erudita* (*L'Amant indiscret*, "The Indiscreet Lover"; 1655) and then from the Spanish *comedia* (*Le Fantôme amoureux*, "The Amorous Ghost"; 1656). The Spanish influence is evident in his best comedy, *La Mère coquette* ("The Flirtatious Mother," 1665). After the triumph of Thomas Corneille's *Timocrate* (1656), Quinault turned to ROMANESQUE tragedy with, among others, *Amalasonte* (1657), *La Feint Alcibiade* ("The False Alcibiades," 1658), *La Mort de Cyrus* ("The Death of Cyrus," 1658), *Agrippa* (1662), and *Astrate* (1665), which was the source of John Dryden's *The Spanish Fryar*. Sensitive to changes in taste, he imitated Racine's *Andromaque* (1667) with *Pausanias* in 1668, and with *Bellerophon* in 1670 he used a situation that anticipated that of Racine's *Phèdre* (1677). In 1671 he collaborated with Pierre Corneille and Molière on the tragicomedy-ballet *Psyché*.

From 1672 on, Quinault wrote numerous librettos for Jean Baptiste Lully's "lyrical tragedies" (*Alceste*, 1674; *Isis*, 1677; *Proserpine*, 1680; *Armide*, 1686), in which the subject matter of tragedy, instead of conforming to the rules of French classicism, became a pretext for fantastic and musical spectacles.

Mocked by the critic Nicolas Boileau for his characters' excessive tenderness, but appreciated by Louis XIV, very popular with the audiences of his day, and later considered by Voltaire as one of the best poets of the seventeenth century, Quinault, in fact, lacked originality. Nevertheless, he had a good sense of theater, and despite a strong tendency toward the insipid, he was sometimes capable of evoking the depths and fatality of passion.

For detailed information on Quinault and his plays, see Henry C. Lancaster, *A History of French Dramatic Literature in the Seventeenth Century,* 9 vols. (1952).—Ja. G.

R

Rabinowitz, Sholem. See SHOLEM-ALEICHEM.

Racine, Jean (1639–1699). French playwright and poet. Born in La Ferté-Milon, about fifty miles northeast of Paris, Jean Racine was an orphan at the age of four. Penniless, he was taken in by the nuns of Port-Royal, one of whom was his aunt, and was educated primarily at schools attached to Port-Royal, then a center of Jansenism. The teaching there was conspicuous for the high quality of the instructors, the logical rigor, the study of French, which took precedence over the dead languages, the importance given to Greek over Latin, and, from a moral point of view, an austerity with regard to the Jansenist doctrine. In 1658 Racine continued his studies at the Collège d'Harcourt in Paris. Although his teachers wanted him to become a lawyer, the young Racine spent his time with literary groups, met Jean de La Fontaine, and showed marked leanings toward poetry. In 1660 he published an ode on the marriage of Louis XIV, for which he received a bounty.

At that time two tragedies by him (which have since been lost) were refused—one by the Marais theater, the other by the Hôtel de Bourgogne. Disappointed, Racine moved to Uzès, in eastern Languedoc, where he remained from 1661 to 1663 with an uncle, a canon of the church, in hope of going into the priesthood. Since he did not obtain the benefice he sought, he again started dreaming of literary glory and began a third tragedy. Back in Paris, he wrote several poems, for which he received royal bounties, and offered his new tragedy to Molière, who had become a director of the first rank in 1662 with his own *L'École des femmes* (*The School for Wives*). Molière refused Racine's play but gave the young poet great encouragement. In 1664 Racine's fourth tragedy, *La Thébaïde* (*The Theban Brothers*), which had been written according to an outline by Molière, was performed by Molière to vie with another *Thébaïde* then being performed at the Hôtel de Bourgogne. It was a complete failure. The following year Racine broke with both Molière and his friends at Port-Royal. To begin with, while Molière was successfully performing Racine's new tragedy, *Alexandre* (*Alexander the Great*), Racine secretly handed it over to the Hôtel de Bourgogne, a betrayal that created a scandal in Paris. Secondly, he launched out into a violent controversy with the Jansenists, who, like many religious groups of the time, were hostile to the theater. In 1667 he caused his mistress, actress Thérèse du Parc, to leave Molière's troupe to join that of the Hôtel de Bourgogne. And that same year Racine began the series of seven tragedies that, from 1667 to 1677, made him the equal of the aged Pierre Corneille and the master of tragedy in the theater. After the death of Thérèse

du Parc, for whom he had written ANDROMAQUE, he fell in love with another actress, La Champmeslé, for whom he wrote BÉRÉNICE. By 1673 he had become a member of the French Academy.

Living in a society that hungered for intrigue, Racine, in spite of, or perhaps because of, his unscrupulous ambition, had in his favor the women, the youth, the court, the king's mistress, Mme. de Montespan, and writers such as La Fontaine and Nicolas Boileau. Against him were the followers of Corneille and the enemies of Mme. de Montespan. But Racine did not hesitate to have their plots brought to a halt by the intervention of the court. He did not succeed, however, in 1677, when the king authorized the performance of Nicolas Pradon's *Phèdre* at the same time as that of Racine's own PHÈDRE;

JEAN RACINE (FRENCH CULTURAL SERVICES)

and his play was at first nearly a failure due to the maneuvers of his enemies. Moreover, he was accused of having written very abusive verses against the noblemen in the opposing clique. This dispute is thought to have been the reason for his retirement from the theater in 1677. However, we know that in the meantime Racine had begun to make his peace with Port-Royal and was well on the way toward a religious conversion. Besides, in 1677 he married and was then appointed royal historiographer on condition that he forsake the theater. He nevertheless returned to it from 1689 to 1691, but this time with two biblical tragedies, written at the request of Mme. de Maintenon, Louis XIV's wife, to be performed at her school in Saint-Cyr. In 1698, father of seven children and author of a short history of Port-Royal, Racine fell from the king's favor, because of his faithfulness to the Jansenists, and died in 1699. He was buried at Port-Royal. The man who before his conversion had been passionate, jealous, and winning ended his life as an austere Christian and most especially interested in the education of his children.

With *La Thébaïde* in 1664 Racine not only picked up a subject that had been hackneyed since the Renaissance and lent itself to political digressions but handled it in an outmoded fashion—hence its failure, despite the farces that Molière presented at the same time in order to save it. With *Alexandre* in 1665 he mixed together the tenderness and heroism characteristic of the romanesque tragedy that was then fashionable—hence its success. But it was not until the seven masterpieces that followed that Racine's true originality was revealed. With *Andromaque* love was shown to be not romanesque gallantry but pure passion, in all its brutality and expressed in clear, simple, and harmonious language. Henceforth, on the same footing but opposed to Corneille, Racine in 1669, with BRITANNICUS, took a Roman subject in the manner of the old master, centered on a struggle for power, and in 1673 he contributed what, on the surface, was the most "Cornelian" of his tragedies, MITHRIDATE; but in both cases the political and moral tragedy is diverted toward the portrayal of a destructive passion, monstrous or degrading, and its inexorable mechanism. While all of Racine's tragedies are based on a simple vision—that of destruction through passion—they are greatly varied. In addition to the two variations on Corneille mentioned above, he wrote an exercise in nonbloody tragedy—*Bérénice*—with only three characters, in which simplicity is pushed to an extreme, as well as a tragedy with an Oriental and historically recent subject—BAJAZET. With *Iphigénie en Aulide* (1674), Racine intended to revive the noble pathos of Greek tragedy; and with *Phèdre* he combined the Greek notion of fate with the modern notion of the remorse and guilt of an individual doomed, in spite of himself, to evil. As for his biblical tragedies, they represent an attempt to reintroduce choruses into tragedy in the Greek manner but with a Judeo-Christian subject. While *Esther* (1689) is somewhat insipid, ATHALIE has all the violence of his tragedies of passion: Fatality is merely replaced by a formidable God's election or rejection of the protagonists, with no appeal possible. Racine's only comedy, *Les Plaideurs* (*The Litigants*, 1668), is amusing but far inferior to his tragedies.

Certain critics attribute Racine's originality to the fact that instead of merely using the conventions of the literature of his time, he drew upon his own experiences and torments. And in fact, many of the situations and much of the behavior of his characters do correspond closely to what we know of his life and nature. But taken in themselves, his tragedies mark the high point of French classical theater: the form is rigorous, the rules are effortlessly respected, and the action advances swiftly and simply, filling the few hours that directly precede the catastrophe. But above all, the impression of an inner, destructive fatality is strictly maintained by the language itself: every speech—indeed, every line—is an act that wounds or moves others or that involves the character more deeply in his fate. The characters have no time to think of anything but the deadly conflict within which they struggle, and they never indulge in the digressions or general commentaries that are found, for example, in Corneille. Great princes out of mythology or ancient history (with the exception of Bajazet), they speak a language that is both extremely simple and decorous; thus, a constant tension is created between the noble harmony and clarity of the surface and the infernal forces the language brilliantly exposes.

For a comprehensive study of Racine, see Alexander F. B. Clark, *Jean Racine* (1939). For modern studies of the dramatic techniques and formal aspects of Racine's works, see John C. Lapp, *Aspects of Racinian Tragedy* (1956), or Bernard Weinberg, *The Art of Jean Racine* (1963). Roland Barthes, in *Sur Racine*, translated by Richard Howard under the title *On Racine* (1964), applies, in three essays, the structuralist method to Racine's works.—Ja. G.

radio and television drama in Britain. The mass communications media have been and are still playing an important part in the development and diffusion of drama in Britain. By a combination of propitious circumstances, some good luck, and the strong personality and passionate convictions of a man of genius, John Reith (now Lord Reith), Britain was spared the commercialization of radio, and subsequently television. Reith, who was appointed general manager of the British Broadcasting Company soon after it was formed by the telecommunications industry in 1922, became convinced that the public interest would best be served if the new mass medium was run as a public service. By its very nature, radio was bound to grow into a monopoly in a small compact country like Britain where the number of medium and long wave lengths available were necessarily limited and complete freedom of the air therefore impossible. Reith therefore evolved the concept of a public corporation, financed by a small annual license fee to be paid by everyone operating a radio receiver and so constituted that it would remain independent of political and commercial pressures. Reith's enthusiasm and Scottish puritanical fervor succeeded in persuading the government of the day, and on January 1, 1927, the British Broadcasting Corporation (BBC) began its activity under a royal charter. Under this charter the crown appoints a board of governors whose main function is the appointment of an executive officer, the director general of the BBC. The position of this executive is analogous to that of the editor of a newspaper who is solely responsible for its contents and policy. The history of the subsequent decades has proved that Reith's concept is, at least in the moral climate of Great Britain, fully workable and effective. Throughout its history the BBC has remained completely free of government interference; it is, in the field of drama, unaffected even by the censorship exercised by the lord chamberlain in the theater. The BBC's independence and the spirit of public service with which its staff has become imbued have enabled it to exercise the function of a major patron of the arts, and especially of music and drama.

The first dramatic broadcasts in Britain go back to the time of the British Broadcasting Company. The first play to be broadcast at comparatively full length was *Twelfth Night* (May 28, 1923). On January 15, 1924, the first dramatic work specially written for radio, *Danger*, by the Welsh novelist and playwright Richard Hughes, was broadcast. Nigel Playfair was the director on this memorable occasion. Hughes had ingeniously devised a situation in which the absence of the visual element was immaterial: *Danger* takes place in a Welsh coal mine and opens at the moment when, owing to an accident, all lights have gone out and the three characters are trapped in total darkness. *Danger* was a very short play; it ran for barely fifteen minutes. The first full-length play specially written for radio was *The White Chateau* by Reginald Berkeley, first broadcast on Armistice Day, 1925. This had been preceded by the first radio adaptation of a novel, Kingsley's *Westward Ho!* (April 1925). These efforts were, however, still undertaken with primitive technical equipment. The introduction of a special drama control panel, which enabled the director to blend sounds from several studios containing orchestras, chorus, and different acoustic backgrounds for dialogue, finally enabled the pioneer directors of radio drama to make full use of the new medium. Lance Sieveking's *The First Kaleidoscope* (September 1928), a sound picture of Man's life based on passages from great poets and composers, was one of the most impressive and influential of these experiments. From 1924 to the end of 1928 British radio drama was under the direction of R. E. Jeffrey, who held the title of productions director. He was, on January 1, 1929, succeeded by Val Gielgud (born 1900, Sir John Gielgud's elder brother), who remained head of the radio drama department until April 1963 and must be regarded as the chief creator of British radio drama.

By 1930 the BBC's radio drama department was producing about two hundred dramatic broadcasts of all kinds per year. Radio had become a mass entertainment and the demands of the public were insatiable. The range of radio drama extended from masterly thrillers, such as Patrick Hamilton's *To the Public Danger*, to adaptations of novels and daring experimental drama, such as Tyrone Guthrie's *Squirrel's Cage* and *The Flowers Are Not for You to Pick*. Guthrie's works were avant-garde plays that made full use of the new medium's ability to take the listener inside the hero's mind where the free play of thoughts and emotions creates a new associative time sequence. Besides works specially written for radio, the new medium gave evidence of its power to act as a speedy and efficient instrument for the diffusion of plays written for the stage, from current West End successes to the great classics.

Radio drama's finest hour and the peak of its popularity, however, came in the war and immediate postwar years. On the long, dark winter evenings of the war years, when the whole country was plunged into almost total darkness because of the blackout against German air attacks and the lack of public transportation made it a hardship to leave home, radio drama brought entertainment and comfort to audiences larger than any drama had ever held in history. Much of this wartime radio drama was simply entertainment; much of it was designed to raise the morale of the embattled islanders in the hour when the country stood alone. Notable among these works is Clemence Dane's cycle of seven plays, *The Saviours* (1941), which evoked figures of legend and history from Merlin to the Unknown Soldier of the First World War to bring comfort and hope to British listeners.

It is remarkable that serious experimentation with new forms also flourished in the war years. Geoffrey Bridson's *The March of the '45* (first broadcast on February 28, 1936) had been the first radio play in verse. It was in this direction, the verse play with music, that the most fruitful work was done during the war, notable in Louis MacNeice's *Christopher Columbus* (October 12, 1942; with music specially composed by William Walton and with Laurence Olivier in the title role) and in Edward Sackville-West's *The Rescue,* a majestic treatment of Odysseus' return to Ithaca, with obvious political overtones (November 25 and 26, 1943; music by Benjamin Britten). The popularity and the mass audience for verse drama, which these memorable broadcasts created, undoubtedly contributed to the flowering of poetic drama in Britain in the subsequent decade, culminating in the late plays of T. S. Eliot and the work of Christopher Fry. Radio drama itself continued to produce fine achievements in this vein in the first years of the postwar period. Louis MacNeice, who was on the staff of the BBC, wrote a series of notable plays, among which *The Dark Tower* (January 21, 1946) is probably the finest. The opening of the BBC's Third Programme (September 29, 1946), a network specifically designed for programs of the very highest standards and artistic standards, gave a further impetus to the use of radio as an avant-garde medium. Laurie Lee's *The Voyage of Magellan* (October 1946) continued the trend toward the verse play, while Dylan Thomas' *Under Milk Wood* (January 25, 1954) combined ecstatic poetic diction with a sardonic yet loving description of human nature in its picture of Welsh small-town life. Henry Reed, another of Britain's finest poets, wrote much for radio at this period, for example, *The Streets of Pompeii* (1952) and *A Very Great Man Indeed* (1953), which was the opening play of the "Hilda Tablet Cycle," a satirical saga about the foibles of the English artistic establishment.

By the late fifties the atmosphere had changed; the vogue of verse drama in a neoromantic vein was over. The new postwar generation of playwrights was coming to the fore. They were the first to be reared in a world where the finest classical drama had been freely available to everyone in their homes on radio —and the importance of this fact for the amazing creative upsurge of the new wave of British drama cannot be overrated. Radio, and particularly the Third Programme, played an important part in the training and development of the new-wave dramatists. In Giles Copper (1918–1966) radio produced a writer who, although successful in the theater and in television as well, undoubtedly did his best work in the freer medium of radio drama. His plays, among which perhaps *Mathry Beacon* (1956), *The Disagreeable Oyster* (1957), and *Unman Wittering and Zigo* (1958) could be singled out, are radio classics. They are examples of bitterly sardonic and somewhat cruel black humor, dry, witty, concise, and profound. Nor should it be forgotten that it was for radio, and the BBC, that Samuel Beckett wrote his radio plays *All That Fall* (1957), *Embers* (1958), and *Words and Music* (1964). Donald McWhinnie, who directed these plays, also commissioned Harold Pinter to write for radio, and thereby helped him in the difficult period after the failure of his first stage ventures. *A Slight Ache* (1959), *A Night Out* (1960), and *The Dwarfs* (1960) were the fruits of this radio collaboration. John Arden's first dramatic work, *The Life of Man* (1956), was written for radio as an entry in a radio play competition organized by the BBC's Northern Region. Robert Bolt's famous stage success, *A Man for All Seasons,* started its career as a play on the BBC Home Service in July 1954. Alun Owen, Bill Naughton, Willis Hall, David Turner, James Forsyth, John Mortimer, Henry Livings, James Hanley, and many other playwrights made their impact on radio before they achieved recognition on the stage.

The BBC's experience with radio drama and, above all, the corporation's tradition as a public service also deeply affected the rise of television drama in Britain. The BBC's financial freedom enabled it to devote a great deal of attention and capital to technical innovation and experiment and so it was the BBC (November 2, 1936) that opened the first regular television service for the general public. Years of technical and artistic experimentation had preceded the start of daily television broadcasting. Indeed, the first play ever to be broadcast on television had been transmitted more than six years earlier, in July 1930, when Lance Sieveking directed Pirandello's short play *The Man with a Flower in His Mouth* from John Logie Baird's experimental studio in Long Acre. The experiment, under the auspices of Val Gielgud's radio drama department, proved a success; the transmission was picked up by technical enthusiasts as far away as Dublin and Lisbon who had built their own receivers according to Baird's ideas.

Therefore, when regular television broadcasting began in 1936, drama was able to form an integral part of the new service, although at that time drama consisted almost exclusively of adaptations of stage plays. With the outbreak of war in September 1939, Britain's television service had to close down, as its transmissions might have been used as radio beacons by enemy aircraft. It was reopened June 7, 1946, but it was only in the early fifties, after the televised coronation of Queen Elizabeth II, that television broke through as a mass medium in Britain. By this time television drama had come into its own, and an increasing number of young, talented dramatists began to write specifically for television. In 1955 the BBC's monopoly of television was broken with the inauguration of a second service, run by a second public body, the Independent Television Authority (ITA), empowered to license commercial television companies financed by advertising. To avoid the worst effects of sponsorship, however, the law under which these companies operate specifies that all program production and editorial control must be in the hands of the television company, while advertisers remain responsible solely for the commercials themselves, just as in a newspaper editorial control and advertising are strictly separated. This separation excludes any influence on the part of advertisers over the content and timing of any of the programs. The advertiser merely buys an advertising spot at a specified time and has no influence on what program will be broadcast before or after his announcement. Advertising, moreover, is strictly limited to a specified number of minutes in each hour and is confined by law to the "natural breaks" between programs, or parts of programs.

The major television companies, notably Granada, Associated Rediffusion, ATV, and ABC, developed strong and adventurous drama departments, which provided very healthy competition for the BBC. As a result of this rivalry, the output of drama—not merely serials and light entertainment but also a very large amount of serious and even avant-garde drama —has remained very high; and this programming includes a considerable proportion of first-rate dramatic writing. The audiences for television drama are enormous; on the average plays are seen by five to eight million viewers (10 to 16 percent of the total adult population of the British Isles), while the most popular dramatic series, such as Coronation Street (Granada) or Z-Cars (BBC), regularly attract between twelve and twenty million viewers. This mass audience is, of course, largely working-class. That the language of all British playwriting has in the fifties and sixties increasingly veered away from the previous middle-class idiom toward a more earthy vernacular is undoubtedly due largely to the influence of television. Most of the leading younger playwrights have written plays specially for television: John Osborne (*A Subject of Scandal and Concern*); John Arden (*Soldier, Soldier* and *Wet Fish*); Harold Pinter (*The Collection, The Lover, Night School,* and *The Tea Party*); John Mortimer (*Call Me a Liar, The Headwaiter,* and other plays); and Arnold Wesker (*Menace*). Another group of important dramatists must be regarded mainly as television playwrights, although some of them have subsequently written plays for the stage as well. Among these are, above all, Clive Exton (*No Fixed Abode, The Silk Purse, Where I Live, The Big Eat, The Trial of Doctor Fancy,* and others), a master of the intimate effects peculiar to television drama, whose range extends from lovingly observed realistic low-life to fantastic and satirical black comedy; and David Mercer (*Where the Difference Begins, A Suitable Case for Treatment*—which later achieved world fame as *Morgan!,* a movie with Vanessa Redgrave and David Warner—*For Tea on Sunday,* and *The Birth of a Private Man*). The list of names of important and promising television writers is very long. Apart from those already mentioned, the following certainly deserve inclusion: Alun Owen, master of the Liverpool idiom; John Hopkins, who inspired Z-Cars, the famous realistic series about tough and fallible policemen, but has also written serious drama of high quality; Leo Lehmann; Nigel Kneale, author of the much discussed Quatermass series; Colin Morris; Rhys Adrian; Dennis Potter; Henry Livings; Francis Durbridge, the acknowledged master of the suspense thriller serial on radio and television; Troy Kennedy Martin, advocate of a contrapuntal style in which the pictures tell the story *in contrast* to an unseen narrator; and each year brings new and talented young writers to the fore.

The quantity of dramatic material required by the two electronic mass media in Britain is enormous: the BBC's three radio networks broadcast about a thousand plays each year, not counting repeats and soap opera serials. More than half of these are newly written plays, the rest revivals, adaptations of novels, current stage plays, or classics. The three British television networks (BBC-1, BBC-2, and ITA) together broadcast about the same number of plays and dramatic series as radio (not counting imported American film material) each year; and as television uses fewer classics because they are felt to be above the heads of the mass audience, and fewer stage plays for reasons of length, the pressure for newly written material may be even greater in this field. The consequences of this state of affairs on the status, profitability, and technique of dramatic writing in general are clearly considerable. More young people of talent than ever before see drama; more young writers are tempted to become playwrights by the obvious demand and the considerable rewards offered. Quantity in itself does not yet guarantee quality. Nevertheless, the sheer volume of dramatic writing, however mediocre the average may be, tends to ensure a certain proportion of work of really high standard. Radio, as the minority medium, with the highly intellectual Third Programme allowing the most esoteric kind of experiment, acts as the laboratory for the more adventurous avant-garde; while television, with its vast mass audience, forces dramatists to use the idiom of the masses to deal with subjects that will appeal to the millions. The live theater clearly provides many ideas and a stream of trained directors and performers for the mass media, but, on the other hand, many healthy impulses from the mass media manifest themselves in the British theater of today and indeed are to some extent responsible for its present creativeness and vigor.

Among general works on the aesthetics of radio the following are the best: Lance Sieveking's *The Stuff of Radio* (1934); Donald McWhinnie's *The Art of Radio* (1959); and Armin P. Frank's *Das Hoerspiel* (1963). Useful collections of radio plays can be found in Clemence Dane's *The Saviours, Seven Plays on One Theme* (1942); Giles Cooper's *Six Plays for Radio* (1966); and the anthology *New Radio Drama* (1966). The history of radio drama is dealt with in Maurice Gorham's *Broadcasting and Television Since 1900* (1952) and Val Gielgud's *British Radio Drama 1922–1956* (1957). Notable television plays can be found in the following anthologies: *Six Granada Plays* (1960); Donald Wilson and Michael Barry's *The Television Playwright, Ten Plays for BBC Televison* (1960); and *New Granada Plays* (1961).—M. E.

radio and television drama in Europe. Radio and television drama, despite their great differences have many things in common. Both belong to the field of mass communication. Both utilize highly developed twentieth-century techniques to establish an outer and inner contact between the studio and the consumer in the privacy of his home.

Both share some of their characteristics with other media like the theater and the movies, while showing individual traits that cannot be found in any other field of artistic expression. Each has its peculiar possibilities as well as its own limitations. However, while radio drama is firmly established in the field of dramatic writing in Europe, original drama for television is still in the process of finding its own laws of form, style, and expression.

The essence of dramatic writing for radio is the fact that it works exclusively with acoustics—with the voices of living beings, with music, mainly as a means of underscoring, and with noises, like train whistles or ship sirens, which in the early years often drowned out the voices of the speakers but were later given deeper emotional meaning or symbolic value, as when the pulsation of a ship's boiler was used to represent a human heartbeat. Silence as an effect is limited to fractions of a second. Where nothing can be seen, the sound must go on. Changes in pitch, strength, and speed help the listener to build an image of the proceedings. Where there are no costumes, scenery, or props, the performance must take place in the imagination of the listener. Where no view is granted him, he must have vision in order to understand and enjoy the action. *Sprich damit ich dich sehe* ("Speak so that I can see you") is the title of a German book on radio plays.

It took the European writers of radio plays some time until they fully understood the basic principle that radio was a new medium. Gradually, they also learned to make substantial use of the freedom of space and time they enjoy; in plotting, writers can violate the laws of chronological order, move back and forth among present, past, and future. And the setting may switch within seconds from the inside of a house or an open landscape to the mind or heart of a person. There can be continual shifts from reality to the realm of fantasy and dream.

Danger by Richard Hughes (given its première performance on the BBC in London, January 1924) seems to have been the first original European radio play on the air. The device of setting the action in the dark of a coal mine was the initial attempt to eliminate the problem of the lack of visibility, which at that time was still considered something negative, by choosing a setting where no visibility was imaginable. Immediately thereafter, plays began to occupy a regular part of the radio programming of stations throughout England and Europe, especially in France, Germany, Italy, and the Scandinavian countries. However, time and experimentation were required and misconceptions needed correcting before the original play written especially for radio emerged as an independent literary work. Only then did the inherent limitations of radio become assets, the basis of a new art form. In the first phase, radio programmers concentrated on the use of existing literature, classical and modern, plays and stories. But the strength of the originals did not come across, potent lines proved ineffective, units sounded like fragments, colorful language faded into colorless description. Adaptations—some rather radical, others still adhering too closely to conventional theater—were the second step. The introduction of a speaker to comment on those events that were cut out of the original text, or the interpretation of the action by two voices, one questioning or accusing, the other answering or defending, were already steps on the road to an independent form of art.

Gradually, European radio writers succeeded in freeing themselves from the laws of the legitimate theater. The decisive break came when the scene was shifted from the outer world to the inner. The themes were chosen mostly from the problems of contemporary life: war and prosecution, conscience and guilt, the individual's responsibility and isolation, the emptiness of life and the decay of beliefs and morality, the bleak present and the black, hopeless future. The stress was no longer on action but on the human beings involved. Their intellectual struggles, their spiritual impulses, their psychological distress replaced the external occurrences.

Some radio writers analyze human tragedy in a sober mood; others are sarcastic and aggressive in their criticism of modern society. But whatever the tone, the typical European radio play of today deals with the thoughts, memories, hallucinations, and dreams of people outside the boundaries of time and space, speaking from the mental realm. Its true subject is analysis and confession.

The American radio play of the 1930's attracted writers of rank and reputation. Archibald MacLeish, Maxwell Anderson, John Mason Brown, William Saroyan, and Orson Welles made sophisticated comments on current events in their scripts. But a decline of the radio play in the United States set in after a few years and proved permanent. European radio, on the other hand, was and still is one of the decisive channels for young writers making their way as well as for established names. It is no overstatement to claim that it would be almost impossible to find an important writer on the European continent (with the exception of Russia) who has not contributed original works to the medium of radio. Authors like Dylan Thomas, Samuel Beckett, Jacques Audiberti, Eugène Ionesco, Bertolt Brecht, Pär Lagerkvist, Ingmar Bergman, Friedrich Dürrenmatt, and Max Frisch prove the point. Many of their plays for the legitimate stage originated as radio plays. Besides these internationally acclaimed literary figures, there is a large group of generally less widely celebrated authors who have written radio plays of the highest literary merits: The Belgians Charles Bertin and Felicien Marceau; the Czechoslovaks Jan Drda and Jan Rys, Ivan Klima and Jiri Horcicka, Ivo Fischer and Ludvik Azkenaza, Karel Cop and Milan Uhde; the Austrians Ilse Aichinger and Ingeborg Bachmann; the Germans Heinrich Boll, Wolfgang Borchert, Gunter Eich, Fred von Hoerschelmann, Peter Hirche, Marie Louise Kaschnitz, Siegfried Lenz, Martin Walser, and Wolfgang Weyrauch; the Danes Eric Soya, Cecil Bødker, Ingar Christensen, and Anders Bodelsen; the French Claude Aveline, Marguerite Duras, Daniel Boulanger, Robert Pinget, Jacques Constant, Jacques Perret, and Jean Giono; the Italians Vasco Patrolini, Alberto Perrini, Alberto Casella, and Gian Giagni; the Swede Erland Josephson; the Norwegian Tormod Skagestad; the Poles Zbigniew Herbert, Jerzy Lutowski, Wlodzimierz Odojewski, Kazimierz Strzalka, and Michael Tonecki; the Hungarians Julius Hay, Rezso Szirmai, Endre Veszi, and Sandor Marai; the Yugoslavs Djordje Lebovic, Aleksander Obrenovic, Mirko Bozic, Zora Dirnbach, and Miodrag Djurdjevic. One hastens to emphasize that this is a partial listing only, and quite a few authors who have made important contributions in the field of original radio plays could be added.

Every year, European writers of radio plays compete for one of the special citations given in this field. In Germany, the Prize of the War Blinded (Der Preis der Kriegsblinden), awarded annually, has among its judges those who lost their eyesight during the war and are thus considered the ideal arbiters for radio plays. And writers from all over the world compete for the Prix Italian, established in 1949.

In spite of the inroads made by television, which has lured millions of listeners all over Europe away from radio, the radio play is one of the reasons why a hard core of intelligent listeners with an understanding of art continue to spend their evenings tuned to radio rather than television. The masses looking for undemanding entertainment have, of course, switched allegiance, but established radio writers and an ever new crop of younger talent will undoubtedly keep a radio audience for years to come.

Paralleling precisely the development of the radio play, the American television drama started with a Golden Age. However, the decade of wealth was followed by dearth. There is now, in the late 1960's, an extreme paucity of original drama, and in the deluge of trivia the movies on television have changed their status from standby to star billing.

In Europe, original television drama has not yet reached the heights of its early American counterpart. It started later, developed much slower, and is still in its beginning stages.

The television writer does not enjoy the same degree of freedom as his counterpart on radio. While the combination of visual and auditory components grants him a large variety of expressive means, the rather small dimensions of the projection compel him to limit his choices. The film can show the world populated by people. Television drama can only show people surrounded by the world. In this respect, a close connection exists between legitimate theater and television performance, although the theater audience—even from a seat in the family circle of a very large house—has a view of the stage many times larger than the television screen can ever offer. The accent in television, therefore, is on the individual, on an intimate view of his body, his face, his eyes, his hands. The actor is stressed, not the environment. Exactly like the theatrical play, the television studio production cannot deal with unlimited range and scope, as the films can (as in, for example, mob scenes, towering sets), limitations that the radio play has overcome by appealing to the listener's imagination.

The categories of the television play are identical with those of the stage drama: tragedy, comedy, melodrama. But acting techniques on television have to develop away from those used on stage. It took the actors many years to learn how to perform without an audience, how to approach and impress the viewer who remains invisible and whose reactions cannot be recorded. Yet, in spite of this difference, the television performance is based on the experience of stage acting, while, at the same time, its production technique owes almost everything to the development of cinematography. The refinement of sound on television makes use of the achievements of radio and radio plays.

Many discussions have been devoted to the question: Can there be original television drama that avoids compromises with either stage or film, standing completely on its own feet? Some commentators believe that television is a medium with an immense future, that there may be a time when the most significant drama will come from television. They claim that once television's status as the principal leisure-time companion of people all over the civilized world is accepted, its offerings will as a matter of course no longer be limited to popular entertainment. For them it is not too important which medium serves as the basis of television drama. It is the style of the adaptation, the originality of the new form that counts. The literary model has to be translated into visually suitable terms. Whatever can be turned into images of physical reality is useful material.

Other experts are less encouraging. They think television drama can never be an original art form, for television is only a means of transmission, offering almost nothing that could be new in context or style, as every type of television presentation is basically derived from other media. And because there is nothing original in the teleplay, television dramas that were produced live in the studios some years ago have now given place to filmed screenplays. In the opinion of this group, no writer ever created a new drama for television; even the best offerings were simply skilled adaptations of stage plays or other scripts. One drama critic is supposed to have said: "I don't know how to criticize television drama, for it hasn't any form of its own."

It is this lack of original form that the television writers on the European continent are still attempting to overcome, in contrast to their American colleagues, who dived into the unknown and came up with amazing treasures at the beginning (Kraft TV Theater, Studio One, Playhouse 90, to name a few.) Their so-called anthology drama dealt with human conflict. The closest parallel to the United States is Great Britain, where Harold Pinter and many others conquered the unknown territory with a number of memorable works especially written for the new medium. But, even there, no style has developed that would lead to an independent art form.

On the European continent, the pioneers of original television drama are few and can be found mainly in France, Germany, and Italy. Exactly as in the early radio programs, the first stage was the adaptation of dramatic literature, which very often ended in failure. Gradually, the writers learned that there are quite a few basic differences between stage play and teleplay, one of them the fact that television drama needs almost incessant action. For that reason, too, many radio plays proved not to be adaptable for the television screen. In a second phase, the authors turned to the treasures of epic literature, which at least delivered them rich stories filled with action. The printed programs of RAI (Radio Television Italiane), one of them called "Da Sofocle a Pirandello," read like a roster of the big names in world literature: Plato, Seneca, Calderón, Lope de Vega, Euripides, Molière, Lessing, Ibsen, Shakespeare, Schiller, Tolstoy, Shaw, and important names of twentieth-century world literature. This list is representative for all European countries. Original teleplays on the Italian screen were, and are, exceptions, like *Scena dalla viteo di Cagliostro* ("Scenes from the Life of Cagliostro," 1963) by Tomaso Landolfi or *I grandi camaleonti* ("The Great Chameleon," 1964) by Frederico Zardi.

The situation in West Germany is very similar. After having dug deeply into the literary works of the past and the present, the stations are now experimenting with new materials. Writers have learned that teleplays need a substantial amount of action, that their characters must be surrounded by a real world and cannot live in the realm of imagination. Numerous pioneer attempts have produced occasional successes. The leading channels in Germany publish their annual programs in artfully designed booklets. What makes these German publications especially interesting is the fact that they contain a synopsis of the action, selections both from the reviews and from the apparently huge numbers of audience letters. Exactly like their Italian counterparts, these program books read like a Who's Who in world literature, and one has to turn many pages until one finds a title headed "Play originally written for television." *Seelenwanderung* ("Transmigration of Souls") by Karl Wittlinger would be an outstanding example. In the search for new styles, some German authors who base their scripts on well-known novels or stories have attempted to free themselves from the traditional dramatic dialogue by sticking to the original and having a speaker connect with summary information the selected chapters or paragraphs. This could lead to a special type of television story rather than television play.

In France, the experts are firmly convinced that television, while a means of communication, is capable of transforming itself into an artistic form. They claim that tragic grandeur, as well as genuine lyricism, can be expressed especially well on television, even though the main domain of television drama is its intimacy, the type that is called *Kammerspiel* ("intimate theater") all over Europe.

The leading voice in the development of French teleplays is L'École des Buttes-Chaumont under the guidance of André Frank. In its first decade, starting in 1956, the repertory was drawn essentially from the theater, but very early during that period the probing for original scripts was begun. The principles and experiments of this school have crossed national boundaries and influenced television programming in the German Federal Republic and in the Scandinavian countries as well.

The first French texts written expressly for television were mainly dramatizations of authentic documents (in the manner of Peter Weiss, Rolf Hochhuth, etc.). But, as early as 1957, *Bartleby, the Writer*, a teleplay by Jacques Armand, based on a story by Herman Melville, was produced. In 1960, came *La Grande Breteche* ("The Great Breteche"), a television drama freely adapted from Balzac and reaping the top European awards in this field. A number of original teleplays appeared in 1963: in the tragic realm, *Eaux dérobées* ("Secret Waters") by Roger Kahane; the historic *D'un Bourgeois de Calais* ("The Citizen of Calais") by H. Boudet; in intimate theater, *D'un Homme de vérité* ("A Truthful Man") by Y. A. Hubert; and in a series about men of character, an original text (1965) by Jean Gohault on the life of the German archaeologist Heinrich Schliemann. One year later, a dramatic poem, *Chaka,* by L. S. Senghor (with music and choreography), gave a cosmic dimension to African folklore, proving that dramatic poetry could be a privileged domain of television drama.

European television drama has no past, a very slim present, but a bright, almost unlimited future. At its best, its combination of verbal and visual elements can lead to a genuine portrayal of human nature instead of the customary action-packed superficial adventure tales, quality and taste instead of brutality and clichés. A commanding character must be there, surrounded by a small group of people representing contemporary life. Meaningful television drama is needed, recovering some of the magic that characterized its beginnings.

There are no books in English dealing specifically with European radio and television drama. The following books are concerned with the problems and characteristics of radio and television plays in general: *Radio and Television* (1951) by Robert B. Turnbull; "The Future of TV Drama," *Television Quarterly,* V, 3 (Summer 1966), 4–38; *Television: The Creative Experience* (1967), edited by William Bluem and Roger Manvell; *The Age of Television* (2nd ed., 1958) by Leo Bogart; and *Teleplay: An Introduction to Television Writing* (1966) by Coles Trapnell.—F. G. G.

radio and television drama in the United States. It is futile—perhaps even misleading—to discuss the contributions American radio and television have made to our dramatic heritage without some understanding of the history, economy, and unique capacities of each of the two media. Both are primarily reportorial rather than dramatic forms of communication. Radio was, and remains, essentially a reporter of sound—and the supreme sound it has conveyed is music. Television is the supreme reporter of news for the very simple reason that it adds an essential visual component to the aural report. In neither case does drama come first as a compelling, nor as an effective, form of expression. No dramatic presentation can ever rival radio's transmission of the Toscanini and New York Philharmonic concerts; no television drama can hope to match the emotional impact of John F. Kennedy's funeral in Washington.

Radio's birth was untidy. The industry was composed of manufacturers—RCA, Atwater Kent, Westinghouse, etc.—whose business was to build receiving sets for the home; but how could the sets be sold if the air were still? There had to be something for the buyer to hear. This meant broadcasting, and supplying a regular program schedule seven days a week was costly, far too costly for the manufacturers alone to shoulder. Other dollars had to be found to distribute the burden. It was soon demonstrable that broadcasting could spur the sale, not only of radios, but of other products—a pack of cigarettes, a cake of soap, or even an automobile. Advertisers soon began to clamor for time on the air. Local stations grew rich and, once combined into networks, grew richer; but the price to the public was the stamp of a salesman's mind on the dramatic content and intent of every program put on the air. Good will is the *sine qua non* in the salesman's manual—controversy is anathema. Offend a customer's prejudices or convictions on sex, politics, or religion, and the buyer will take his business to the store down the street. On the other hand, a vigorous theater thrives on controversy, and in precisely those areas of prejudice and conviction—sex, politics, and religion—that are taboo for the salesman. The unnatural wedding between the seller of new products and the seller of new ideas was for radio—and later for television—so massive an obstacle in the path of exciting creative expression that the wonder is that anything of quality or substance ever reached the public air.

During the middle 1920's, broadcast standards came close to producing nothing of quality or substance. The Democratic National Convention of 1924 stimulated a country-wide recognition of radio as a reportorial medium. The Radio Corporation of America (RCA), as a manufacturer, controlled a large share of the physical facilities of broadcasting through its subsidiary, the National Broadcasting Company (NBC). The advertisers and their agencies controlled the production of all programs—barring, of course, news, religion, classical music, and children's programs. It was not until the late 1920's, when William S. Paley took over control of the Columbia Broadcasting System (CBS), that RCA and NBC were forced to face a challenge. CBS had no industrial giant behind it—its survival depended solely upon the impact of its program schedule. Three decisions made by Paley profoundly affected the standards of radio broadcasting during the 1930's: First, he attacked the tastelessness of commercial messages by refusing to accept laxative advertising on the Columbia air. Second, he invited Edward Klauber of *The New York Times* to join the Columbia network and to assemble its news staff. Until that time, the standard of radio news reporting and commentary had been deplorably low. Klauber proved so successful that within a few years CBS had established a dominance in news reporting unchallenged by any broadcasting competitor for the next fifteen years. Finally, Paley attacked the standards of dramatic production on radio by establishing the Columbia Workshop. The avowed purpose of this series was to explore radio's capacity to create a dignified standard in dramatic production. The initial emphasis was directed toward the writers: Those who had shunned radio were to be wooed, those who worked anonymously within the fold were to be given a free hand and maximum recognition. It was the first series dedicated to the principle that radio was capable of making a genuine creative contribution to the dramatic arts. Thanks to the Workshop, many writers began to emerge from obscurity, among them Robert Anderson, Irwin Shaw, and Ranald MacDougall. It is not a long list, since the good days lasted too short a time. World War II and the advent of television smothered a start that was never given a decent chance to flourish.

Radio writers, despite an interlude of adulation, had little lasting effect on our dramatic heritage. Nevertheless, it would be quite unfair to assume no imaginative contributions were made during the era of radio's transcendence. Indeed, radio's most severe limitation—sound without sight—was very often turned into a substantial, perhaps irreplaceable, asset.

Because advertisers were wary of controversial themes, so prevalent in the 1930's, fantasy rather than social drama became one of the dramatic staples of radio. And fantasy succeeded, not because it represented a "safe" compromise with the advertiser, but because it fortuitously turned radio's gravest handicap, the lack of a sight component, into an invaluable asset. Norman Corwin's *My Client Curley,* on the Columbia Workshop, is a noteworthy example: A small-time theatrical agent, very much down on his luck, stumbles on a very ordinary boy on a very ordinary sidestreet, who is discovered talking to a caterpillar. The caterpillar has a unique ability—he can dance to the tune of "Yes, Sir, That's My Baby." Pure fantasy—even preposterous fantasy—for in no other medium could the existence of a dancing caterpillar have commanded credence. With admirable skill and sly persuasiveness, Corwin continued to build on this outrageous premise until the mutation of Curley into a butterfly spiraled into a crisis of world-shaking proportions. This was radio at its best.

Fantasy was far from limited to the faintly avant-garde standards of the Columbia Workshop. In the hands of various writers, it won wide acceptance as an effective adjunct of commercial broadcasting as well. The weekly situation comedy Fibber McGee and Molly, with its improbable closet, the dimensions of which seemed to rival those of Grand Central Station, is another noteworthy example. Fantasy also became an essential component of terror—the intrusion of the mystic, the malevolent, even the supernatural into our mundane lives—and in the hands of a craftsman like Arch Oboler, incarnate evil became as real as a grocery list, the poltergeist as earthy as Will Rogers.

The transition from fantasy to subjective terror was inevitable, the classic example being Lucille Fletcher's *Sorry, Wrong Number.* Here the essential ingredient was claustrophobia. The subtlety with which this terrifying isolation was achieved represented a high degree of imagination in balancing fantasy with reality.

Despite the many dramatic series that radio bred—The Lux Radio Theatre, The Theatre Guild of the Air, The Ford Theatre, etc.—a vast preponderance of dramatic writing was devoted to the domestic scene, in the main homespun and aggressively righteous. Among the soaps, dramatic stimulus was supplied by physical injury or personal disaster; humor and wit were in short supply.

The few exceptions warrant recognition. The Goldbergs was based on situations developing out of a perceptive observation of character. Gertrude Berg endowed her people with an admirable amount of ethnic integrity and a high standard of legitimate characterization. In Ethel and Albert, Peg Lynch dared to dispense with any semblance of plot, relying on flashes of homely comment on our domestic scene sufficiently penetrating to delight her particular audience. In Easy Aces, Goodman Ace concealed beneath a zany exterior barbs of acerbic wit, aimed not alone at the domestic scene but at the political and social as well.

Despite the low acclaim for radio's dramatic literacy, a selective audience could find a surprising amount of humor, wit, and comment sandwiched in between a vast amount of commercial banality.

The Mercury Theatre, under the direction of Orson Welles, was somewhat of a sport during the 1930's. Welles's peculiar temperament and imagination lent vivid color to many of the shows he produced. They also won an enthusiastic, if limited, allegiance from the audience. The degree of involvement he was able to stimulate reached its climax with his adaptation of H. G. Wells's *War of the Worlds.* The fact that it caused a near nationwide panic among listeners who believed that a real invasion from Mars was being reported can, in retrospect, be viewed with some amusement; but as evidence of the persuasiveness that radio could achieve, it must be accorded recognition.

The best of radio drama was imaginative, literate, and masterly in establishing atmosphere and mood. What it lacked was depth of thought and depth of passion. While it is possible to recall with nostalgia certain moments of dramatic imagination and lyric reach, not to mention a goodly supply of genuine wit, the hard fact remains that radio had time only to scratch the surface of its potential before television invaded the air. It is sad to record that, out of its twenty years of dominance, only one American writer made a lasting contribution to radio's dramatic heritage—Archibald MacLeish with his *The Fall of the City.* Even at this level, MacLeish's script lacked the robust lyricism and theatrical durability of Dylan Thomas' *Under Milk Wood* on the British Broadcasting Corporation (BBC). Some measure of radio as a dramatic medium is symbolized by the origin of these two major efforts—both were selected or commissioned from outside the medium; neither was the product of an indigenous imagination. The collective record is bleak. Radio drama as a whole created little more than a ripple.

History, war, and a vast amount of intramural wrangling over technical standards deferred for many years the advent of television in this country. In the fall of 1939 NBC was ready and eager to secure a federal license for commercial broadcasting. CBS was tooling up to meet the challenge. The bellwether, however, had been the BBC in London. The British were at that time the prime promoters of television —the United States had been laggard but was champing at the bit to be granted authorization to move ahead.

In August Hitler invaded Poland; on September 3 England declared war. Within a matter of hours the BBC transmitter in London was silenced—a silence that was unbroken for the next six years. Sorry a blow as this appeared at the time to the pioneers of American television, in retrospect it can be viewed only as a fortuitous boon. For a fleeting period during 1941 and 1942, American broadcasting went on the air for a minimal number of hours per week. Despite any theoretical value deriving from this interval, its essential contribution was an exposure of the gross inadequacies of the electronic equipment then in use. No creative person could long have endured the shortcomings of the cameras themselves—shortcomings that critically limited any flexibility of movement or refinement of mood. It was only the pressures of war that supplied the technical answers essential to any creative use of the medium. So much may be accredited on the plus side to the war years.

On the minus side was the eruption of a bitter, and ultimately futile, dispute between CBS and RCA. During the summer of 1940, CBS announced the development of the first system of color transmission on television. This was at once recognized as a critical threat to RCA, which, under the guidance of General David Sarnoff, had poured millions of dollars into the development of the medium. While the wrangling was acrimonious, often petty, it nonetheless succeeded in delaying the commercial advent of television for a full two years after the war had ended.

It was only the pressure of public demand, stimulated by the World Series of 1947, that convinced CBS that broadcasting in black-and-white had to take precedence over any eventual solution of the color dispute. It was in the early summer of 1948 that NBC presented the Texaco Star Theatre with Milton Berle; CBS countered with Toast of the Town, starring Ed Sullivan. No doubt remained that commercial broadcasting was about to move into high gear.

It might be assumed that those entrusted with the large-scale launching of television would have been drawn from the ranks of radio. However, a great percentage of the creative leaders in radio displayed little respect for television, since it offered them no economic return commensurate with what they had been earning in radio. The few with foresight who offered their services suffered almost universal and often humiliating defeat. Expert as they were in an aural atmosphere, they were at sea in the area of visual communications.

The pioneers in the early years of television were young men of theatrical background, imbued with a high regard for theatrical standards. They were responsive to new ideas and literate expression; they were impervious to the sponsor's cynicism, which rated the American IQ somewhere below the level of a fourteen-year-old. Above all, they embraced with enthusiasm the challenge that television offered of developing a new and individual standard of visual storytelling. Being young, they made grievous errors, took unwise risks, and pressed the technical capacities of the medium too far. In short, they were often outrageously daring, but that very recklessness bred an excitement that won the allegiance of the audience to whom they made appeal. It was a small and highly selective audience, a fact seldom appreciated by the innovators, and while it lasted, it encouraged a lively atmosphere in which young, creative minds were able to prosper and flourish.

NBC had been experimenting with dramatic production for ten years. CBS, as a matter of policy, had offered no substantial competitive response until the fall of 1948. By that time the outstanding series on NBC was The Philco Playhouse; in early November CBS launched Studio One. It was immediately apparent to the industry, the critics, and the viewing

public that the competition between these two series was destined to establish the standards by which the success of dramatic performance in television was to be measured. At this moment the so-called Golden Age began.

In crude terms the Golden Age was a testing time for the creative effectiveness of NBC, reflecting David Sarnoff's wisdom and ability as a manufacturer, pitted against CBS and its responsiveness to William S. Paley's vision and imagination as a broadcaster; but few, if any, of the creative people working in the field were even dimly aware of this struggle behind the scenes.

Since The Philco Playhouse and Studio One were the recognized contenders in dramatic programming, their divergent philosophies and achievements are relevant and revelatory. By the fall of 1948 The Philco Playhouse represented NBC's cumulative experience in dramatic production dating back to 1938. Although Studio One was new and had only the theatrical conviction its creative personnel had built up during the years of the war, it had two outstanding advantages: no commercial sponsor to qualify or dilute its dramatic judgment and total directorial authority over its technical personnel.

To appreciate fully the impact of Studio One, it is essential to recognize the basic principles that lay behind its productions:

In pursuit of a more effective mode of dramatic presentation, CBS chose to apply a Shakespearean structure of scene development to all adaptations of dramatic material, modern or classical; it defied long-accepted motion picture, as well as television, practices in the use of cameras and lights; it expanded the physical bounds of studio production; and it was dedicated to the concept that literate, even provocative or controversial ideas could be made acceptable to a mass audience, provided the method of storytelling was sufficiently exciting.

The opening program on Studio One was an adaptation of a somewhat ordinary psychological mystery story entitled *The Storm,* starring Margaret Sullavan. While her appearance stimulated a more-than-average interest in the program, there were other factors far more provocative to the industry as a whole.

No one close to the scene failed to recognize the challenge it offered to the technical standards that had been in force up to then in the industry—meaning, of course, NBC. The introduction of atmospheric lighting, of flexibility in camera action, and the combining of film and live segments were clearly in defiance of accepted practices. (The film sequences, aimed at affording a greater mobility in action, were self-evidently beyond the capacity of the medium at this time. The experiment was a failure.)

There was but one controversial element in the presentation of *The Storm.* The story's denouement offered no solution to the mystery that had been presented; the audience was left to supply its own conclusions, which aroused a flood of protest. *The Storm* would never have been allowed on the air had any agency or sponsor been in a position to control story selection.

The battle lines were drawn. NBC technicians accused CBS of crude camera performance and substandard lighting. The accusations were partially just, particularly in fringe areas of reception. On the other hand, dramatic impact was so far heightened that carping criticisms on technical grounds carried little or no weight. As Studio One moved on to produce Gian-Carlo Menotti's *The Medium,* Shakespeare's *Julius Caesar,* Paul Vincent Carroll's *Shadow and Substance,* and Ellen Glasgow's *The Shadowy Third,* The Philco Playhouse had no choice but to adopt a technical flexibility closer to that of CBS. Since Studio One was concentrating its major efforts on advancing techniques in visual storytelling, Philco soon began to direct its efforts to the stimulation of original writing for the emerging medium. In their own areas of concentration, each achieved noteworthy results.

CBS further explored the limits of the medium's live capacity by sinking the battleship *Bismarck* in a studio measuring 65 feet by 45 feet; in *The Last Voyage* it presented the open decks of two submarines in an arctic storm; in *Waterfront Boss* it presented pivotal action on a pier along the New York waterfront. On alternate weeks its schedule would include an intermingling of classic and semiclassic productions—Shakespeare's *Julius Caesar; Torrents of Spring* by Ivan Turgenev; *The Wings of the Dove* by Henry James; *Henry IV* by Luigi Pirandello—along with an array of popular and commercial productions ranging from Dashiel Hammett's *The Glass Key* to *June Moon* by Ring Lardner and George S. Kaufman and *The Shadowy Third* by Ellen Glasgow.

In rebuttal, The Philco Playhouse began to present a series of original television scripts, a substantial proportion of which won critical attention and acclaim. During a two- to three-year period The Philco Playhouse gave initial exposure to a wide roster of young writers, among them William Alan Aurthur, Gore Vidal, N. Richard Nash, Horton Foote, and Paddy Chayefsky. Chayefsky's *A Catered Affair* and *Marty* were outstanding symbols of the perceptive encouragement young writers were being given under Philco's sponsorship. *A Trip to Bountiful* by Horton Foote and *The Rainmaker* by N. Richard Nash were so well received that each was produced on Broadway. Over the same period of time only one writer for Studio One warrants attention: Michael Dyne. His *Pontius Pilate* was the forerunner of his success on Broadway, *Most Honourable Gentleman.*

While The Philco Playhouse was making its major contribution by engaging talented writers, Studio One was unearthing a number of directors of commensurate stature, such as Franklin Schaffner, Yul Brynner, and Ralph Nelson. Studio One indirectly stimulated directorial standards at CBS, which resulted in the discovery of Sidney Lumet, Robert Mulligan, John Frankenheimer, and many others.

As the Golden Age progressed, The Philco Playhouse forced NBC to expand its technical capacities to a point where CBS's advantage was substantially eliminated. At the same time, Studio One discovered a number of new writers of notable imagination and ability. Reginald Rose's *The Remarkable Incident at Carson Corners* and *Twelve Angry Men,* along with Rod Serling's *Buffalo Bill Is Dead* and *Patterns* (eventually produced by the Kraft Television Theater), rivaled in impact and effectiveness the output of The Philco Playhouse's creative pool. The stage

was set for a continuing competitive atmosphere that was ready at a sophisticated level to test the imaginative abilities of the two series. The opportunity was there, the audience was ready, but a fresh and exciting era was at that moment choked off by factors in no way related to creative ability.

While the high-level competition between Studio One and The Philco Playhouse held the spotlight in dramatic production, another competition was initiated by NBC and answered briefly by CBS. The realm was opera, and in this instance NBC won the contest hands down. Under the guidance of the late Samuel Chotzinoff, and with the direction of Kirk Browning, the NBC Opera series warrants acclaim at least on a par with, if not actually exceeding, any single production on either Studio One or The Philco Playhouse. As a series, it had substantially no competitor.

One incident establishes the stature this series attained: When the scheduling of Giacomo Puccini's *La Bohème* on NBC was matched against the Metropolitan Opera's production of the same opera, qualified critics found the NBC television production notably superior to that of the Metropolitan—musically as well as dramatically.

The attention accorded Studio One and The Philco Playhouse should not becloud the fact that other dramatic productions crowded the air during the late forties and early fifties. In the main, they were either weak contenders or half-hour offshoots from the major productions. Robert Montgomery Presents, plagued by constant agency supervision, was a lowercase competitor with the Playhouse. The Kraft Theater, the first commercial hour-long dramatic series on television, was consistently hampered by an inadequate budget, an unimaginative sponsor, and a hidebound directorial staff. It was not until the twilight years of its run that Fielder Cook was able to score a notable success with *Patterns,* or that George Roy Hill was given enough financial support to produce *A Night to Remember.* Each was admirable—but came too late. They were the dying gasps of an era that was soon to be silenced. Meanwhile, The Ford Theatre had a desultory and colorless season; Omnibus mounted a few fine productions, notably *Anne of a Thousand Days,* by Maxwell Anderson, along with a number of highly uneven presentations. The Theatre Guild of the Air had a few excellent shows to its credit but was constantly hampered by a tasteless and uninspired agency and an overcautious and pedestrian sponsor. Few of the many other hour-long series warrant consideration.

There was a somewhat better record in the half-hour field. It is evident, nonetheless, that each of these series reflected to some degree the standards established by the two major contenders. Suspense gave an opportunity to Robert Stevens to develop his own particular style in camera usage. Danger, under Yul Brynner and Sidney Lumet, demonstrated relatively adult standards in choice of script and a high degree of imagination in visual realization. Albert McCleery caused a brief stir with Cameo Theater, but its accent on repetitive use of close-ups became so monotonous that it soon exposed the superficiality of its basic concept.

The two series that added a decent amount of originality to professional writing standards were The

Goldbergs and Mr. Peepers. Each displayed an integrity in characterization that spiced the humor with constant evidences of literacy. However, The Goldbergs fell victim to the pressures of McCarthyism; Mr. Peepers was too subtle and low-key to survive against the blunderbuss attack of situation comedies emanating from the West Coast. They were, nonetheless, reputable expressions of the age in which they were produced.

The Golden Age lasted a pitifully short time, roughly from 1948 to 1952. A just measure of its creative contribution has been as much degraded by its overardent advocates as by its slick and superficial detractors. It is quite as indefensible to extol the achievements of those years as the ultimate in mature and expert production as it is to sneer at those programs because of the admitted crudity of their technical performance. *Hamlet* was far cruder in structure than John Dryden's forgotten tragedies. Indeed, every exuberant pioneer effort is essentially crude; perfection of form is the hallmark of an encroaching decadence.

The seal of death was placed on television's dramatic aspirations the day the first major production was moved from New York to Hollywood. A respect for slick technical production was at that moment accorded priority. Thought, imagination, and daring were relegated to the dustbin. This change of standard was grist to the mill for the advertising agencies and the sponsors they represented. With the salesman again in the saddle, it took a very short time to liquidate a taste for literacy.

The Philco Playhouse was soon badgered for living too close to the kitchen sink and reveling in Southern decadence. Studio One was attacked for being too controversial, overly literate, and reckless. Caution became the watchword in place of excitement. Small heed was paid to the disenchantment and waning allegiance of the audience that had supported dramatic programming on television in its earliest years.

The intermediate years from 1952 to 1960 were years of surrender, even though, ironically, some of television's finest achievements were registered during these years. But the gradual intrusion of corporate greed resulted in a notorious "wasteland."

It began, as has been said, with the first move to the West Coast. Every astute observer recognized the profound danger to all responsible programming in a surrender of theater standards to the slick precision of Hollywood. But for the advertiser and the advertising agency technical precision was the pot of gold at the end of the rainbow. Ideas had irritated them from the start—they had been uncomfortable in an atmosphere of probing intelligence. They embraced the chance for escape to a milieu where synthetic mediocrity held sway.

The trek to the West Coast was swift and decisive. Within a bare three years, production in New York dwindled to a trickle. Studio One joined the pilgrimage, but, robbed of purpose and taste, faded gracelessly from the scene. The Philco Playhouse did not even bother to move west. Its demise was swifter, but quite as graceless, as that of Studio One. The Kraft Theater, Robert Montgomery Presents, The Theatre Guild of the Air, even the NBC Opera series were all victims of the westward hegira. The air was overrun by horses and scalpels, by the FBI and tommy guns.

There was scarcely room for an idea to take root within the crowded hours.

For a time the momentum of the early years carried over in isolated and sporadic instances. Hallmark continued to produce one or two literate shows each year; CBS launched its Playhouse 90; special programs were intermittently offered. Nevertheless, the curve of imagination was consistently downward. The root of these evils is planted within the insanity of a marriage between industry and creativity. The two can never be compatible.

There were other contributing factors. Spiraling costs were pivotal. Star performers who accepted $1,000 to $1,250 a show in 1950 began to demand $50,000 and over in 1960. Series that were sold in 1949 for $8,000 to $10,000 per program soon were costing $150,000 and more. But while costs began to skyrocket, so did profits. By 1960 NBC and CBS, which had formerly defended their creative personnel against the advertisers and their agencies, became as acquisitive and rating-conscious as the agencies themselves—often more so.

Important as these contributory factors were, none was so decisive as the composition of the audience itself. In the early years the sum total of television viewers was absurdly small, measurable in thousands. As a group it was relatively literate, relatively sophisticated, and very largely urban. It would at best represent no more than 20 percent of the audience today. From 1949 to 1954, however, that 20 percent was the sole audience whose allegiance mattered. Every new viewer added to an audience of five million tends to impose some compromise with integrity. During the middle fifties, the size of the television audience began to grow by leaps and bounds, with the result that compromise gradually became an accepted way of life. Within a matter of four years, network television had little left to offer but a lusterless vacuity.

In the main, however, the record was spotty. Playhouse 90 mounted a few admirable shows, notably Rod Serling's *Requiem for a Heavyweight, The Miracle Worker* by William Gibson, and Robert Mulligan's production of *The Moon and Sixpence,* with Laurence Olivier and Jessica Tandy. These were perhaps the most imaginative and best-realized programs television had produced up to that time. Week by week, however, imagination and daring were replaced by sluggish conformity. Any number of daytime serials began to evidence a maturity of thought and a sophistication in themes notably superior to anything presented during the evening hours. When soap operas can claim a dominant position in dramatic production, broadcasting as a whole is at a dangerously low ebb.

The full measure of network surrender to commercial negativism was epitomized in the production of The Play of the Week. This series could not in its time have been produced by any one of the networks. It was a local New York program whose potential financial success was based on eventual syndication rights from other local stations around the country. For a brief year and a half the best of television was reborn. The series was theater-oriented; it was produced in the East; it was unencumbered by sponsor or agency interference.

Its goal was to illumine a script with as much, or

more, insight than it had received on Broadway. While its successes were numerically less than its failures, The Play of the Week established a standard of overall theatrical effectiveness that no single series in the Golden Age ever equaled. August Strindberg's *Miss Julie,* Eugene O'Neill's *The Iceman Cometh,* and Jean Paul Sartre's *No Exit* were representative of television's capacity to compete with and even to excel their original stage productions.

The history of the sixties has been erratic and confused. While a vast amount of time has been taken over by mundane, even infantile, programming— witness Batman, My Mother the Car, Petticoat Junction, and Star Trek—Fred Astaire and Danny Kaye have contributed both style and distinction within their particular genre of entertainment. While dramatic programming has been desultory, many literate and effective documentaries were being produced on each of the three networks. Despite these compensating efforts, the deterioration in basic standards was so marked that the chairman of the Federal Communications Commission was impelled to describe the networks' weekly schedule as a "wasteland."

Predictably, the networks' response was defensive. In the course of the ensuing argument, everything and everyone was held to blame. Outcries against agency and sponsor control were rebutted by accusations that the networks were exercising a stranglehold on nighttime scheduling; Hollywood was blamed—and, of course, the public. While each of these accusations carries a measure of truth, no one was able effectively to dismiss the fact that network standards in programming had aroused vocal outrage from all parts of the country. Many of the most valued segments of the public had begun totally to ignore television; they had found it unworthy of attention, barring a limited amount of selective tuning-in for news and sports. For the dramatic hours there were substantially no defenders.

The networks were peculiarly vulnerable. Headlines had been proclaiming their acquisitions of enterprises only remotely connected with the business of broadcasting—record companies, publishing houses, even the ownership, or part ownership, of professional golfers and a major league baseball club. Saddled with such a complex of industrial activities, administrative responsibility in creative broadcasting had, of necessity, to be delegated to lesser authorities. The general outcry was impossible entirely to ignore. Lavish, if somewhat sporadic, gestures were made to reaffirm the integrity of the networks' concern for their public responsibility.

Two incidents appear to have induced a hardnosed review of the complacent assumption that there was no longer any appreciable audience for quality in dramatic programming: CBS's *Death of a Salesman* (1966) was not only one of the finest dramatic productions television had offered, it won an audience approval large enough to command a second showing; *The Bridge over the River Kwai,* though representing a totally different type of production—a motion picture rerun—did, nonetheless, secure a volume of viewers far beyond the advance forecasts. While these two broadcasts have been somewhat arbitrarily selected, they yet bear witness to the fact that there is still an audience in this country that is hungry for quality in entertainment—and a very much larger audience than had been suspected.

Each of the three networks (the American Broadcasting Company having achieved formal status as a network in 1946) has recently announced program schedules that include a notable increase in quality fare. Valid evidence of this shift in perspective is supplied by ABC's marathon production, *Africa.* Never before has a network elected to devote four solid hours of prime commercial time, and at a cost of $2,000,000, to the presentation of an historical and cultural documentary. The ultimate success of this new emphasis is unpredictable, but the mere evidence of such an intention carries a whisper of hope. It might well be that television is on the threshold of a more rational balance between mass appeal and a selective public service.

It should be recognized, however, that a critical shortage of supply besets the best intentions the networks may espouse. In the early years the pioneers were spendthrift—they had the whole range of theater and literature to choose from—yet the law of diminishing returns had begun to operate well before the Golden Age began to fade. The entire Elizabethan period, including Shakespeare, Christopher Marlowe, Ben Jonson, Beaumont and Fletcher, John Ford, John Webster, Phillip Massinger—throw in even the University Wits, John Lyly, George Peele, and Thomas Kyd—produced *in toto* less than a hundred plays of substantial worth—and that bridged a span of forty years. The entire range of theater from Aeschylus to Albee would have difficulty supplying the networks with quality programming for more than a year. The Play of the Week, drawing on public domain as well as available modern writers, was beginning to scrape the bottom of the barrel after a little over eighteen months. Modern playwrights from every part of the world produce in a single year fewer works than one weekly series on television might absorb in ninety days.

This stern reality commands attention. Standards can improve—of that there is no question— but a qualitative demand that goes beyond any rational ability to satisfy that demand can only worsen, rather than better, the situation. All three networks are now investing very sizable sums in underwriting and stimulating a better flow of dramatic writing, but they cannot guarantee that every time a set is turned on another *Death of a Salesman* or *Bridge over the River Kwai* will come on the screen.

It yet remains true that a healthy, competitive atmosphere tends to breed an excitement that has its own particular theatrical appeal. A door to the unknown generates suspense and anticipation. Lethargy is bred when what lies on the other side of the door is the same old room and the same old faces. Television has had little of mystery to offer in a long time. For the networks there will not again be a Golden Age. There can, however, come a time when a decently literate and discriminating viewer may find something better than a "wasteland" to tune to in the evening hours.

There are no available copies of the great mass of radio and television scripts from the early years. The only existent scripts of Studio One are held by the author; it has proven next to impossible to find the scripts for The Philco Playhouse. Much of the material on television for this essay was taken from an unpublished history of the industry written by Worthington Miner between 1942 and 1943.

There are, however, several published books and articles that will interest the reader. *Your Career in TV and Radio* (1936), by George N. Gordon and Irving A. Falk, although commercially oriented to young people seeking employment in television, offers a concise and accurate report of the early days in radio. *How Sweet It Was* (1966), by Arthur Shulman and Roger Youman, reviews television production over a span of close to twenty years. Its appeal is nostalgic, and without any particular point or point of view. Fred W. Friendly's "The Great Sellout to Soap Opera," in *Life* magazine, March 17, 1967, supplies evidence of how and why network executives were forced to relinquish immediate responsibility for programming. The article is one-sided and, at times, naïve, but it does portray a valid picture of the situation. "Public Television: A 'National Resource,'" by Lester Markel, in *The New York Times* (June 5, 1967), clarifies the pros and cons for government support of educational television. It affords no answers; it supplies no conclusions. Radio scripts may be found in *Three Short Plays* (1961), by Archibald MacLeish, which includes *The Fall of the City;* and *13 by Corwin* (1942), by Norman Corwin, in which appears the script for *My Client Curley.*—W. M.

Raimund, Ferdinand (1790–1836). Austrian actor, manager, and playwright. Raimund was a turner's son who, after brief schooling, was apprenticed to a confectioner. He became active in theater at the age of eighteen, when he deserted his confectioner's apprenticeship and joined a small group of traveling actors. In 1814 he was engaged in midseason by the artistic director of the Theater an der Wien. During the next season he was engaged by the Leopoldstadt Theater, a suburban Viennese folk theater, where he achieved considerable success as a character actor of popular farces. He remained at the Leopoldstadt Theater as an actor from 1817 to 1830 and eventually became manager of that theater. After a bout with mental illness, he died by suicide in 1836.

Raimund's first attempts at playwriting were to revise various of the plays in which he acted. In 1823 he wrote and produced his first original play, *Der Barometermacher auf der Zauberinsel* ("The Barometer-maker on the Magic Isle"), a farce in the style of the old Viennese extravaganza. Some of his more delightful plays are *Das Mädchen aus der Feenwelt, oder der Bauer als Millionär* ("The Girl from the World of Fairies, or The Millionaire Farmer," 1826), which treats of the necessity to be satisfied with smaller means than what one would like; and *Der Alpenkönig und der Menschenfeind* ("The King of the Alps and the Misanthrope," 1828), in which a misanthrope's being is taken over by a mountain spirit, and the misanthrope is forced to observe the trouble that he, when in possession of his own being, causes.

One of Raimund's major contributions was to transform the popular Viennese fairy-tale play into something artistic and graceful, with characters of human substance and life. Even his fairy characters are rounded beings, because it is they who bear the

FERDINAND RAIMUND (NEW YORK PUBLIC LIBRARY)

play's message: order, morality, conservatism. His plays are dedicated to the principle of poetic justice, by which good wins out over evil and common sense over conceit.

Despite Raimund's genius in the realm of the popular folk play, he was more interested in the serious drama, as in his *Moisasurs Zauberfluch* ("Moisasur's Magical Curse," 1827). It is about a princess who is punished with old age while personally she remains young, and with having to weep diamonds instead of tears, for having destroyed the temple of a powerful magician and constructed in its place a temple to virtue. However, Raimund's serious dramas did not meet with the same success as his lighter plays.

Raimund's greatest strength lay in his ability to infuse his plays with a Molière-like melancholy. This, in conjunction with the interweaving of everyday reality with the supernatural, and his praise of simplicity and contentment in life, made him the most popular and respected of the Viennese folk dramatists of his day.

There have been no plays of Raimund translated into English, primarily because of the difficulty of capturing the Viennese dialect and the local humor. Nor is there any treatment of his plays in English. Only the briefest mention of him and his work is to be found in conventional histories of the theater. —C. R. M.

Ralph Roister Doister (written between 1550 and 1553). A comedy by Nicholas Udall (1505–1556). This play is celebrated as the first "regular" English comedy, that is, the first attempt to present a fully developed English comedy modeled after those of Plautus and Terence. The titular hero of the piece is a swaggering boaster, the direct descendant of the

Plautine *Miles Gloriosus.* Aided by his parasitic cohort, Matthew Merrygreek, this braggart warrior attempts to woo and win the fair widow Dame Christian Custance. The widow, however, is engaged to the absent Gawyn Goodluck and wants no part of the preposterous Roister Doister. Despite this rejection, Ralph is duped by the mischievous Merrygreek into intensifying his pursuit. Finally threatened with physical harm by the blusterer, the widow turns on him and proceeds to deliver a thrashing that brings Roister Doister to his knees. She and Gawyn are reunited and everyone, Roister Doister included, joins in the celebration that ends the play.

The play is written in doggerel verse and filled with bustling action and high spirits. Its classical characteristics—its five-act structure and its use of stock comic types—impose a disciplined pattern on the robust native humor. See ENGLAND: *Tudor drama.*—E. Q.

Rama's Later History (**Uttraramacarita,** eighth century). A play by the Sanskrit dramatist BHAVA-BHUTI. *Rama's Later History* is the masterpiece of this playwright and the most generally admired of the innumerable plays on the subject of Rama, so frequently treated throughout Southeast Asia. As court poet in the province of Vidarbha, Bhavabhuti was active during the latter part of the eighth century. The plot, chiefly drawn from the last book of the epic the *Ramayana,* depicts the separation of the hero, Rama, from the heroine, Sita. It ends with their reunion. Sita, half-goddess and half-woman, whose name signifies furrow and who is symbolically associated with fertility and the earth, is married to Rama, descended from the race of the Sun. Before the play opens she has been abducted by the ten-headed demon Ravana to his capital city of Lanka, in Ceylon. There she remains captive until Rama, leading an army comprised largely of monkeys, kills Ravana and rescues her. Inasmuch as the citizens of Rama's kingdom murmur at the prospect of an heir who may, as they suppose, have sprung from Ravana and not from their own king, Rama sends Sita into exile, though still loving her dearly. The innocent Sita is cared for by divine protectors. Shortly, she gives birth to two sons. Both husband and wife suffer grievously during their separation. Finally, on the occasion of the ceremony marking the coming of age of the two children the parents are again brought together. The happy resolution of the story is not to be found in the *Ramayana.* In its morality the play celebrates the supreme value of family affection and the power of children to dignify and vitalize marriage.

Bhavabhuti excels in developing the pathetic sentiment. The last episodes, however, contain much in the heroic mode. In the final act the device of a play-within-the-play is artfully employed. This drama is in substance the sequel of Bhavabhuti's earlier work, *The History of Rama;* it is, however, much the more powerful and poetic, indeed one of the most eloquent of all Sanskrit plays. It promptly achieved wide fame and thus lent encouragement to the vast accumulation of works in drama, puppetry, dance, and mime that have celebrated Rama's story from Bhavabhuti's time to the present day. Sanskrit drama ceased to be a live art form approximately a century after Bhavabhuti's death but much of both the learned and the folk arts of southern Asia have continued along its paths of thought and legend. Hence the play occupies an important place in the history of drama throughout one of the most populous and aesthetically creative sections of the world.

Helpful commentary on Bhavabhuti's masterpiece appears in R. V. Jagirdar's *Drama in Sanskrit Literature* (1957) and in M. M. Ghosh's *History of Hindu Drama* (1957). The play has been translated by C. H. Tawney (1847). It is edited by P. V. Kane with a translation by G. N. Joshi (1915). This rendering appears in *Six Sanskrit Plays* (1964), edited by H. W. Wells. A translation with commentary has been made by Shripad Krishna Belvalkar (1915). The translation by P. Lal in *Great Sanskrit Plays* (1964) is much abridged and fails to suggest the poetic language of the original.—H. W. W.

Randolph, Thomas (1605–1635). English playwright and poet. Randolph was born in Northamptonshire and educated at Trinity College, Cambridge. While still at school he developed a reputation as a poet and wit. A disciple of Ben Jonson, he became, upon graduation in 1628, a professional London playwright, possibly, as G. E. Bentley suggests, acting as the principal playwright for the children's company of the King's Revels at the Salisbury Court Theatre. He returned to Cambridge to receive his M.A. in 1631.

Randolph's extant works include *Amyntas, or The Impossible Dowry* (1630), a pastoral play modeled on Giovanni Guarini's *Il Pastor Fido; The Jealous Lovers* (1632), a Plautine farce; and *The Drinking Academy,* a Jonsonian humour comedy not printed in its own day but extant in a manuscript now at the Huntington Library. Randolph may also be the author of *The Careless Shepherdess,* a pastoral drama usually attributed to Thomas Goffe (c. 1591–1629).

The *Poetical and Dramatic Works of Thomas Randolph* (1875) was edited by W. C. Hazlitt in two volumes. The fullest study is G. C. Moore Smith's *Thomas Randolph* (1927).—E. Q.

Rappaport, Shloyme Zaynvl. See S. ANSKY.

Rats, The (Die Ratten, 1911). A tragicomedy by Gerhart HAUPTMANN. In this five-act tragicomedy Hauptmann uses the poverty-stricken areas of Berlin as the background for the plot. After the death of her own child, Mrs. John "buys" her servant's newborn infant as a substitute. When the maid decides she wants her child back, Mrs. John has her murdered. Rather than face a trial, she commits suicide; her end is related to the audience by the theology student. The title of the play points to a fundamental motive of Hauptmann's dramatic production: Just as the rats gnaw away at the roof and foundation of the house in which these characters live, so too moral depravity erodes the foundations of society.—C. A. M.

realism and naturalism. Realism and naturalism are modes of dramatic expression, interrelated but not identical. Although they are of major importance in the modern drama, their influence has ebbed during the past twenty years, as their authority has been contested by other forms and concepts. The terms cannot be rigorously defined, and there is a good deal of latitude in the meanings attached to them. For this reason, it is desirable to place their specific modern development in a larger historical perspective. The portrayal of familiar events in a style that corresponds to the experience of the spectators is almost as old as drama. Aristophanes begins *The Clouds* with a man and his son in their beds, and these are the opening lines: "Great Gods! Will these nights never end? Will daylight never come?" Aside from the mention of plural gods, the scene could take place in today's New York as well as in Athens in 423 B.C.

This common variety of realism is often an attribute of comedy, but it seems to appear also when drama breaks with its religious or ceremonial origins, as in the Greek theater at the time of Euripides and Aristophanes. There is a similar tendency in the late middle ages in Europe when aspects of ritual came out of the churches to be performed in street processions. The *Second Shepherds' Play,* part of the Towneley, or Wakefield, cycle in fourteenth-century England, is in part a rough farce about the stealing of a sheep, but it ends with the three shepherds approaching the divine Child in the manger:

> Hail, little tiny darling . . .
> Hail! put forth thy hand,
> I bring thee but a ball
> have and play thee with all . . .

These lines, written by an unknown author, spoken on a wagon platform six hundred years ago, translate religious ritual into familiar language and common experience. The mystery is still accepted with touching faith, but the process of secularization has begun. The drama, released from ritual, must either deal with "reality" in terms of current customs or invent new allegories drawn from secular sources—history, legend, riddles, or symbols of man's fate. Shakespeare and his contemporaries adopted the latter course, creating dramatic images that transcend the banalities of daily life in a poetic synthesis of human suffering and aspiration. Shakespeare is interpreted in many ways. It can be said that he embodies the spirit of his time, an age of spectacular social and intellectual advance, when the glory of the Renaissance began to fade and the shape of the modern world was barely discernible. But Shakespeare's vision is romantic: the nightmare landscape of *King Lear* is not a literal transcript of human behavior in Stratford or in the London playhouses.

The roots of realism and naturalism appear, not yet differentiated, in a play produced when Shakespeare was starting his London career. *Arden of Feversham,* often attributed to Thomas Kyd, is literal and journalistic, portraying the consequences of greed and lust in a middle-class family. An epilogue printed in the 1592 edition of the play explains that it is an accurate report of events in a town in Kent, where a man was "most wickedlye murdered by the meanese of his disloyall and wanton wyfe . . . wherein is shewed . . . the vnsatiable desire of filthie lust and the shamefull end of all murderers."

Arden of Feversham served as the model for a few other plays, such as the anonymous *Warning for Fair Women* in 1599 and *Yorkshire Tragedy* in 1608. But this somber view of family life is only a minor factor in the drama of the next century. Molière's mockery of the bourgeoisie followed the traditions of *commedia dell'arte.* Tragedy imitated the Greeks and Romans, or made an uneasy combination of classical and Shakespearean forms. Realism and naturalism are associated with the rise of the middle class and the crystallization of moral and economic problems in the life of the bourgeois family. The English stage gave the first sign of change in 1731, with the London production of George Lillo's *The London Merchant.* Enormously popular and repeatedly revived, the play shows the fate of a young clerk driven to crime by his love of a prostitute; it ends as he leaves his cell for the gallows. There is no question of Lillo's debt to *Arden of Feversham*; one of his successes was a revised version of the earlier play.

Lillo in turn influenced a greater dramatist, Gotthold Ephraim Lessing, whose *Miss Sara Sampson* (1755) is a German adaptation of *The London Merchant.* Lessing is the first critic to develop a modern theory of play construction. In his *Hamburg Dramaturgy* (1767–1769), he stresses motivation ("to define the passions of each character") and a system of causation ("events that are rooted in one another, that form a chain of cause and effect"). Lessing revitalized the theories of Aristotle. He insisted on unity of action but found more profound psychological unity in Shakespeare than in the stilted repetition of classic forms that were fashionable in his time. Lessing's thought is transitional, seeking to link the dramatic values of the past to a new recognition of social and psychological problems.

While Lessing grappled with aesthetic theory, a simpler doctrine of dramatic "realism" was promulgated in France. Denis Diderot, a leading editor of the *Encyclopédie* and philosopher of the Enlightenment, announced the advent of "serious drama" (*genre sérieux* or *drame bourgeois*), exemplified in his own play *Le Père de famille* (1758), which he described as a summary of family relationships: "fortune, birth, education, the duties of fathers toward their children, of the children toward their parents." Although *Le Père de famille* was a failure, Pierre Augustin Beaumarchais was so impressed by it that he wrote a play in the same style, *Eugénie,* and expressed amazement at the "uproarious clamor and adverse criticism it has aroused."

The genre sérieux was too dry and "reasonable" to stimulate the dramatic imagination. But Diderot and Beaumarchais were ahead of their time in holding that the bourgeois family was the key to the themes and forms that would become increasingly significant in the life and drama of modern man. The audiences of the later eighteenth century, and the society they represented, were not ready to abandon aristocratic or romantic themes. Lessing's theories led not to studies of contemporary German life but to the lyric excesses of the *Sturm und Drang* ("storm and stress") school. In Paris, Beaumarchais turned to exuberant farce and political satire in *The Barber of Seville* and *The Marriage of Figaro,* which encountered censorship and violent controversy. These works also played a part in stimulating the resentment against aristocracy that exploded in the French Revolution.

The social changes at the beginning of the nineteenth century did not bring a transformation of the drama, and the first signs of a new outlook occur in a country that had not experienced an industrial or political revolution. Conditions in Russia led writers to adopt a first principle of realism—truthful presentation of aspects of contemporary life. Provincial corruption was exposed with biting wit and irreverence in Nikolai Gogol's *The Inspector General* in 1836. A more subtle mood of frustration, foreshadowing Chekhov, characterizes Ivan Turgenev's *A Month in the Country* (written 1850). Beginning with his first play, *The Bankrupt*, in 1850, Alexander Ostrovsky offered a truthful picture of the family and business intrigues of Moscow merchants and their wives.

In Germany, Friedrich Hebbel's *Maria Magdalena* (1844) is a sudden departure from the cloudy poetry of Sturm und Drang. Clara, the protagonist of this play, is the daughter of a puritanical father who is deeply wounded when his son is accused falsely of theft. Economic difficulties cause the father to spend Clara's dowry. Her fiancé, having had sexual relations with her, refuses to go through with the marriage when he learns that her dowry is spent, and the family's reputation is hurt by her brother's arrest. Finding herself pregnant and fearing her father's wrath, Clara drowns herself. This tragedy of false morality and sordid motives may be selected as the starting point of a separate development of naturalism. The Russian plays of the mid-nineteenth century examine social customs and psychological weaknesses, but the viewpoint is ameliorative and humanistic. This is the general philosophy of realism, which nourishes the hope that men possess the reason and will to improve their condition, or at least recognize the need of improvement. Naturalism, on the other hand, tends to regard emotional instability, selfishness, and moral blindness as inherent in the nature of man. The dark mood of *Maria Magdalena* is naturalistic. Hebbel's emphasis on sex and money may be traced back to *Arden of Feversham,* but the earlier play is a factual report, adorned with smug moral aphorisms. Hebbel offers a social and psychological theory, showing a mortal conflict between natural impulses and social laws.

The state of the drama in the mid-nineteenth century encouraged neither creativity nor the development of new techniques and talents. In metropolitan centers, and especially in London and Paris, the theater had become a thriving institution. It was an age of brilliant stars and elaborate stage machinery. Shakespeare was acted constantly, and in France the beautiful rhetoric of Corneille and Racine was rendered with grace and power. In Paris, Eugène Scribe and Victorien Sardou were the acknowledged masters of the "well-made" play, a more or less standardized product in which the characters were stereotyped heroes or villains, suspense was maintained by familiar devices, and the end offered a neat solution with virtue rewarded and vice punished.

Alexandre Dumas fils wrote *La Dame aux camélias* in 1852. The play, which has become a symbol of tearful sentiment, was intended as a declaration of war against the artificial standards of the well-made play. Dumas based his story on the life of a well-known courtesan, Marie Duplessis, and his portrait of her was a rebuke to bourgeois hypocrisy. The play retained its popularity and served as a vehicle for many actresses, including Sarah Bernhardt, Eleonora Duse, Ethel Barrymore, and Eva Le Gallienne, and in the 1930's Greta Garbo gave a memorable performance as Camille on the screen. The emotional power of the part contradicts the author's "realistic" intention. Camille's discovery of true love at the moment of her death is an acceptance of society's values. She is better than the bourgeois women who

despise her. Dumas was a skillful dramatist, but the fullness of life eluded him. In his Preface to *A Prodigal Father* in 1868, Dumas asserted that the most indispensable quality of drama was logic, which "must be implacable from beginning to end." His words echo the narrow rationalism proclaimed by Diderot in the eighteenth century.

Dumas was still under the spell of the Enlightenment, but a new spirit of desperate inquiry and foreboding stirred in the culture of the 1870's. Five years after Dumas made his plea for reason, Émile Zola proclaimed in the Preface to his *Thérèse Raquin* that there is "no logic of fact, but a logic of sensation and sentiment." Zola appeals to science; he interprets Darwin's principle of natural selection as proof that life is a harsh struggle for survival. A more immediate influence on Zola was the work of Dr. Claude Bernard, who conducted experiments in the physiology of the nervous system. Zola called his theory naturalism, which, he said, deals "with the human problem studied in the framework of reality. We must cast aside fables of every sort . . . every nursery tale, historical trapping, and the usual conventional stupidities." Although Zola goes much further than his predecessors in formulating a theory of instincts and emotional compulsions, *Thérèse Raquin* does not justify his claim to have broken with the forms and illusions of the past. On the contrary, the story structure reminds us again of *Arden of Feversham*; it is the same tale of the wife and her lover who kill her husband. After they have drowned him, they are so overwhelmed by remorse that they take poison.

The production of *Thérèse Raquin* had no immediate effect on dramatic practice. It was not until 1887 that André Antoine was able to establish a small playhouse, the Théâtre Libre, dedicated to Zola's principles. Antoine had difficulties at first, but for the next seven years the little theater was the citadel of the avant-garde: the playhouse was known and respected throughout Europe. Although Antoine's methods of production were in accord with Zola's doctrine of naturalism, the influence of the Théâtre Libre was largely due to the rising fame of Henrik IBSEN. In the great plays of his middle period, from *A Doll's House* in 1880 to *Hedda Gabler* in 1891, the Norwegian playwright explored the inner lives of his characters, the purgatory concealed behind the trim façade of the middle-class home.

Since Ibsen is the father of modern realism, it is essential to stress the difference between his forms and concepts and the naturalistic mode. Ibsen's characters are not driven by irrational impulses. They try as best they can to exert their will and cope with their environment. If they fail, they fail consciously. Ibsen's plays take place in a more or less "typical" Norwegian middle-class home, in a limited time, at a moment of crisis. The history of the situation is told retrospectively in dialogue. This form is different from the expansive poetry of Shakespeare. In its concentrated examination of a crisis and its probing of motives and morals, Ibsen's realism breaks with the conventions of the well-made play.

Ibsen was influenced by Zola's theories, as is evidenced in the treatment of heredity in *Ghosts* (1881). Ibsen, however, could not accept heredity as a blind force. He portrays the tragedy of Mrs. Alving and her son as a social and psychological history, a series of decisions that make the characters responsible for their own fate. The taint of syphilis is unavoidable for the son, but it is the result of the father's actions. The gap between Zola's naturalism and Ibsen's realism is clear if we compare the murder in *Thérèse Raquin* to the long discussion between husband and wife in *A Doll's House*. The murder is an explosion of animal instincts. The last act of *A Doll's House* is an exercise in conscious will, an examination of causes and effects. In Zola, sex is primary. For Ibsen, however, the woman's impulse is not mainly sexual, and the tension lies in her effort to fulfill herself as a person. Hedda Gabler commits suicide because, as Ibsen said, "it is the want of an object in life that torments her."

A woman's suicide is also the climax of *Miss Julie,* written by August Strindberg in 1888. The Swedish dramatist was twenty-one years younger than Ibsen. Strindberg was critical of the older writer and possibly jealous of his fame, but the crucial difference between them arose from the antithetical principles of realism and naturalism. In *Miss Julie,* the daughter of a count gives herself to a virile servant in a moment of abandon; horrified by what she has done, she kills herself. Strindberg described the play in a letter to his publisher as "the Swedish drama's first naturalistic tragedy," and he wrote in his Preface: "I have depicted my characters as modern characters, living in an age of transition at least more breathlessly hysterical than the age that preceded it. Thus I have made them more vacillating, disjointed." He speaks of Julie as "the half-woman, the man-hater"; she is driven, he says, by "suppressed desires," clinging to "a Romantic inheritance now being put to flight by Naturalism." The last phrase is noteworthy because it exposes the subjective nature of naturalism and points to a psychological dilemma. Julie has no contact with reality, no way of satisfying her emotional needs. Strindberg offers no solution and apparently has none. Julie is doomed because she is "romantic"; she follows her impulses and destroys herself. She is lost because all the romantic values have been shattered, and there is nothing with which to replace them. Strindberg abandons Zola's belief that there is a "science" of heredity. Turning his back on the Enlightenment, Strindberg decides that "reality" is his enemy, and his characters become enmeshed in dreams and desires they cannot master.

Strindberg's pessimism strikes a modern note, and his career links nineteenth-century naturalism with later dramatic forms. His journey from the strife-torn family in *The Father* (1887) to the nightmare world of *The Ghost Sonata* (also called *The Spook Sonata*) is like a dress rehearsal for the parade of forms from expressionism to Dadaism, surrealism, Antonin Artaud's "theater of cruelty," and the cult of "the absurd."

Realism as it is commonly understood—an imitation of actions that are "true to life"—seems to have a simpler history than naturalism. But even the phrase "true to life," despite its superficial appeal to the popular imagination, cannot be subjected to critical scrutiny without revealing a great variety of interpretations. Dramatic realism does not accord with popular assumptions concerning man and nature but is instead a protest against current illusions

and beliefs, a rebellious revelation of "realities" that have not been recognized, accompanied in many cases by advocacy of reform or social reorganization. The quality of protest and concern with social issues has been present in the whole course of twentieth-century realism, but there are crucial differences in the way playwrights have projected their version of what is "true to life."

George Bernard Shaw, who began his career as an ardent disciple of Ibsen, had broader intellectual interests than Ibsen, less concern with the inner life of the family, and a passion for discussion, which is so brilliant and uninhibited that it often impedes the action. Yet Shaw believed that human beings can shape their own destiny; he wrote in 1902 that drama "is the presentation in parable of the conflict between man's will and environment."

At this same time, Anton Chekhov portrayed the frustration of the will; his characters are engaged in an inner struggle between "romantic" emotions and the dull necessities of daily living. The sound of the breaking chord in *The Cherry Orchard* (1904) is not an objective phenomenon; it is an ironic comment on lost illusions, the impotent heart, and what we have later learned to call alienation. Maxim Gorky turned to the dregs of society, finding in *The Lower Depths* that the roots of alienation (the defeat of human hopes or values) went deep into the dark misery of the slums.

These three masters, Shaw, Chekhov, and Gorky, established the rudiments of later realism. They shared, to some extent, a common belief in humanistic values, a rational hope that the spirit of man will eventually triumph. Yet reason does not altogether support this expectation, which involves elements of faith. Shaw, who can be regarded as the most polemical of the three, arrived at a Chekhovian sense of broken illusions in *Heartbreak House*. He shows people paralyzed—even words have lost their magic—as planes drone overhead and death rains from the skies.

Forms of drama, like all art forms, are protean. Realism has a general technique and viewpoint—an interior setting, an avoidance of scenic fantasies or poetic flights, a concentration on middle-class problems, an image of man as a social being, and an ultimate hope of progress toward a more moral and meaningful existence. The breadth and uncertainty of these ideas, especially in times of change and stress, account for the diversity of the realistic mode and the undesirability of attempting narrow definition. While realism arose as a rebellion against idealistic and romantic conventions, the modern movement is by no means free of ideas that are also found in the culture of the eighteenth and early nineteenth centuries. Shaw turned from the apocalyptic vision of *Heartbreak House* to the unbreakable spirit of *Saint Joan* (1923) and to the confused fantasy of *The Simpleton of the Unexpected Isles* (1935).

Mention must be made of the doctrine of Socialist Realism, formulated in the Soviet Union in the late twenties and still practiced in some socialist countries. The theory combines a demand for accurate imitation of actual situations with a simplified view of human responsibilities and "heroic" conduct.

It may be because reality is such an indeterminate thing, involving the consciousness of the artist as well as the materials of his art, that realism has often tended to turn into imaginative forms. Sean O'Casey, for example, followed his masterpieces of realism, such as *Juno and the Paycock* in 1925, with the cloudy symbolism of *Within the Gates* (1933) and the revolutionary lyricism of *Red Roses for Me* (1942). We find a similar tendency toward a break with realism in some of the later work of Clifford Odets, Lillian Hellman, and Arthur Miller, as well as in the English playwrights John Osborne, Arnold Wesker, and others. It would be wrong to suggest that any of these writers are immune to what may properly be called "romantic" bias.

The significance of realism is underestimated when it is treated schematically as an "objective" imitation of human actions. Naturalism is of minor interest if it is dismissed as a subordinate and more "photographic" kind of realism. The essence of realism lies in its concept of drama as a conflict of wills, in which men make conscious decisions and face the consequences of their actions. Naturalism substitutes the id, or instinct, for conscious will and holds that dramatic tension arises from desperate frustrations and the absurdity of the human condition.

Both movements arose as a revolt against traditional forms and themes, paralleling similar developments in painting, music, and other arts. The tendency of twentieth-century realism to turn to allegory or dreams has been noted. Naturalism has exerted an influence on such diverse forms as expressionism, the "epic theater" of Brecht, and the theater of the absurd. As early as 1896 Alfred Jarry's *Ubu Roi,* a progenitor of the cult of absurdity, caused riots in a Parisian theater. Ubu, the greedy brute who makes himself king of Poland, is a caricature of the Shakespearean hero, and the mockery of the romantic tradition is explicit in the ending when Ubu is in flight and his ship passes under the battlements of the castle of Elsinore.

Bertolt Brecht wrote his first play, *Baal,* under the influence of naturalism. Completed in 1918 when the author was twenty, *Baal* depicts a "natural man," fiercely immoral, pursuing his sensual instincts without respect for laws or conventions. Brecht never abandoned this image of the human spirit as being torn by conflicting impulses, but in his later plays he held that the nature of man is molded by the "real" conditions of his existence. Thus he sought to combine the psychological viewpoint of naturalism with the social concern and moral sensitivity of the great realists. Brecht spoke in 1939 of "the tortured and heroic, abused and ingenious, changeable and world-changing man of this great and ghastly century."

Brecht's epic form and the theater of the absurd are two divergent attempts to explore the soul and condition of man. Both have learned to draw on the great traditions of the drama. Some scholars have argued that Shakespeare is our contemporary in his recognition that the human situation is absurd, as in Lear's madness or the gravediggers' scene in *Hamlet.* This view overlooks the complexity of Shakespeare's thought and the vital differences between his age and ours. But there is no doubt that both Brechtian and absurdist drama have made use of Elizabethan modes of expression, as well as commedia dell'arte and Oriental theater.

Myths and heroic themes are also present in the drama of the twentieth century. There is an inspiring development of these themes from Yeats to Jean Anouilh, to cite only two outstanding examples.

Eugene O'NEILL never ceased to experiment with forms, and his restless genius was never satisfied. Beginning with realism in the sea plays, he utilized expressionism, embarked on romantic adventures, enlarged the possibilities of domestic drama, and created an American version of Greek tragedy. Then, in anguished solitude, he wrote feverishly and destroyed much that he had written. In his last years O'Neill returned to a more profound realism in one of his greatest plays, *Long Day's Journey into Night.*

The diversity of O'Neill's art may be a key to the problems of contemporary drama. The settings and themes of realism—the middle-class home, the frustrated or broken family—may have reached a dead end in Samuel Beckett's *Endgame* or in the even more devastating destruction of domestic values in Harold Pinter's *The Homecoming.* But the interaction and interpenetration of forms is a creative necessity that may lead to a new synthesis, a new flowering of the dramatic imagination.

John Gassner, *Directions in Modern Theatre and Drama* (1966), analyzes the evolution of dramatic forms during the past hundred years. The most complete anthology of the theories of dramatists and critics is *European Theories of the Drama,* edited by Barrett H. Clark (1947), and this edition contains a supplement on the American drama. Another valuable collection is *American Playwrights on Drama,* edited by Horst Frenz (1965). The development of the avant-garde drama from 1887 to 1930 is described in Anna Irene Miller's *The Independent Theatre in Europe* (1931). A detailed account of Ibsen's ideas and technique is provided in his notes, *From Ibsen's Workshop,* Vol. XII of *The Works of Henrik Ibsen,* edited by William Archer (1912). Shaw's view of dramatic realism may be studied in *Shaw on Theatre,* edited by E. J. West (1958). —J.H.L.

Reaney, James [Crerar] (1926–   ). Canadian poet and playwright. Reaney, who was born in the small town of Stratford in western Ontario, is the author of a group of plays published in 1962 under the title *The Killdeer and Other Plays.* In addition to the title work, this volume contains a brief masque for one performer; the libretto of an opera, *Night Blooming Cereus* (for which the Canadian composer John Beckwith composed music; 1960); and the play *The Sun and the Moon* (1965). Two other plays, *The Easter Egg* (1962) and *Colours in the Dark* (1967), are not included in this collection.

Reaney is the most arresting and original playwright Canada has produced. His genre is pastoral comedy, but his buoyant, wayward drama eludes categorization. The geographical context is small-town Ontario, but in these plays both landscape and character are strangely transfigured. The force of his drama springs from the patterns of imagery and the moods these generate. This is particularly true of *The Killdeer* (1960), Reaney's most ambitious play, in which themes are projected and conflicting characters defined through sets of images expressing such large antitheses as innocence and experience, eternity and time, fertility and death.

The tangled wealth of character and incident in

The Killdeer defies summary. Insofar as it is legitimate to isolate a single theme, the action concerns the quest for maturity or, more exactly, the movement from a vulnerable and imperfect innocence to experiential wisdom, first by Harry, the mother-ridden adolescent, and then by Eli, a youth who has retreated to infantilism under the impact of traumatic shock. A corollary theme, the initiation of the tender consciousness into the repellent mysteries of the fallen world, appears in *The Easter Egg* and less prominently in *The Sun and the Moon.*

The flaws in Reaney's work are those of a poet who turned relatively late in his career to drama. His dialogue is sometimes unstageworthy, his exposition clumsy, and the various levels—symbolic, fantastic, naturalistic—on which certain of his characters are conceived fail to coalesce and, as a result, their effectiveness on any level diminishes. Finally, although Reaney is adept at farce and scenes of poignant charm, he has shown little capacity to project strong emotion. This would not necessarily be a matter for criticism except that such plays as *The Killdeer* and *The Easter Egg,* in spite of their comic framework, revolve around acts of great violence and horror. The imaginative perspective, however, from which these pieces are written tends to deny the reality of these acts and hence to nullify the sympathetic response of the audience toward the characters who are menaced by them.

Nevertheless, amid the somewhat conventional output of most other English Canadian dramatists, Reaney's plays shine with a peculiar brilliance. Not the least of his achievements is to have made, in a variety of dramatic forms, imaginative sense out of one geographical area of Ontario.

Two articles that provide a sensitive assessment of Reaney's use of myth and symbol are A. Lee's "A Turn to the Stage: Reaney's Dramatic Verse Part I," *Canadian Literature,* XV (Winter 1963), and "A Turn to the Stage, Part II," *Canadian Literature,* XVI (Spring 1963).—M. T.

Red Roses for Me (1942). A play by Sean O'CASEY. *Red Roses for Me* is O'Casey's most autobiographical, most lyrical, most affirmative play. The action mirrors his own experiences in the 1913 General Strike in Dublin when, like his hero Ayamonn Breydon, he was a railroad laborer who played a leading role in the strike. Mrs. Breydon closely resembles his mother; the Protestant rector is modeled after the man who was the foster father and spiritual guide of his youth; and Sheila is very like the Catholic girl he loved at that time. In its symbolic theme and structure, however, the play moves beyond these personal parallels, for O'Casey now completes the vision of tragic martyrdom that he had begun in *The Silver Tassie* and *Within the Gates.* Ayamonn carries on the fight for a fuller life for Dublin's poor, and after we see the sufferings, comic quarrels, and aspirations of the people in the first two acts, the symbolic third act projects a dream vision of the ideal Ireland. Miraculously the dark city of Dublin is transformed into a green-and-rose-colored carousel of gay people singing and dancing on the banks of the Liffey. But soon the terrible reality of poverty breaks through the allegorical dream. The demand of a shilling increase in wages is rejected, the strike call goes out, and the mounted police charge into the ranks of the strikers. Ayamonn is killed in the clash, and when his body is taken to the church, Brennan o' the Moor, his dear friend, goes to the bier and softly sings the title song, a ballad written by Ayamonn about a Kathleen ni Houlihan of the Dublin slums who graciously offers her symbolic red roses of hope to her people.—D. K.

Regnard, Jean François (1655–1709). French playwright. Born into the rich Parisian bourgeoisie, Jean François Regnard at first led an extremely adventurous life, about which he wrote a number of tales. In 1678 he was captured by pirates in the Mediterranean and sold as a slave. After two years in Algiers and Constantinople, he was ransomed by France, traveled through Scandinavia and Poland, and in 1683 returned to Paris, where he bought himself an office in the treasury. Regnard lived as an epicurean, and at the Chateau de Grillon, which he dedicated to Bacchus, he died in 1709 from a dose of horse medicine that he took for indigestion.

From 1688 to 1696 Regnard, often in collaboration, wrote numerous farces for the Italian players and the fair theaters. From 1694 to 1708 his comedies, almost all in verse, were performed at the Comédie Française. The most renowned of them are *Le Joueur* ("The Gamester," 1696) and *Le Légataire universel (The Residuary Legatee,* 1708). Regnard based most of his comedies on the notion of deception for purposes of obtaining money or contriving a marriage. Sometimes he created a central character (a gambler, an absent-minded lover, a laughing misanthrope, or an old amorous invalid), continuing in the tradition of Molière. But above all, during the period of boredom at the end of Louis XIV's reign, he tried to provoke guffaws of laughter. In fast-moving plays, he succeeded by means of a very whimsical theatricalism, often violent effects, extravagant disguises, daring language, highly cynical comments and acts, and portraits of insolent servants who are greedy for money and drink.

For detailed information on Regnard and his plays, see Henry C. Lancaster, *A History of French Literature in the Seventeenth Century,* 9 vols. (1952). —Ja.G.

Relapse, The (1696). A comedy by Sir John VANBRUGH. *The Relapse, or Virtue in Danger* was first performed at the Theatre Royal in Drury Lane in November by Rich's Company. The play is a sequel to Colley Cibber's *Love's Last Shift,* in which the strayed husband Loveless is reunited with his wife, Amanda (see ENGLAND: *Restoration drama*). In Vanbrugh's play, Loveless falls from virtue with his wife's cousin Berinthia, while Amanda is being besieged by Worthy. Virtue triumphs in the latter case, however, and Worthy repents of his attempted seduction. In the subplot Young Fashion contrives to cheat his older brother, Lord Foppington, out of his intended bride, the naïve country heiress Miss Hoyden, daughter of Sir Tunbelly Clumsey.

Though the play is not tightly knit, it is continuously entertaining, since much of the dialogue is clever, the situations amusing, and the characters well drawn. Lord Foppington, a lineal descendant of Sir Fopling Flutter in Sir George Etherege's *The Man of Mode,* is outstanding and dominates many of the scenes. Feminine hypocrisy is satirized in the scene in which Loveless carries off the willing

Berinthia crying "very softly" (so as not to wake her maid), "Help! help! I'm ravished! ruined! undone!"

Curt Zimansky is editing this play with introduction and notes for the Regents Restoration Drama Series.—E.W.

Restoration drama. See ENGLAND: *Restoration drama.*

Revenger's Tragedy, The (pub. 1607). A tragedy usually attributed to Cyril TOURNEUR, although many scholars ascribe it to Thomas Middleton. The play was first published in 1607 without the author's name on the title page. It was first attributed to Tourneur in a catalogue of plays published almost fifty years later in 1656. However, the presence of certain characteristics reminiscent of Middleton, together with the growing estimation of him as a significant playwright, has led a number of scholars to credit the play to Middleton. The controversy over the authorship of the play has been a lively one, with most scholars still adhering to the view that the play belongs to Tourneur.

Whoever its author, *The Revenger's Tragedy* is one of the best plays of the Jacobean theater. Its power derives from its fierce, uncompromising, almost insanely intense vision of human evil. The action focuses on the revenger Vindice, who, in avenging the murder of his beloved, sets in motion a train of events in which horror is piled on horror. Murder, betrayal, cupidity, and lust vie for the center of the stage as the action hurtles toward its bloody climax. Many of the characters have descriptive allegorical names (Lussurioso, Ambitioso, and so forth), thus lending the action the superficial appearance of a morality play. In fact, however, the play is devoid of any moralizing or didactic views other than that of utter contempt for human nature. The play has also been described as a satire. If it is, it is one of the darkest satires in literary history. The final effect is, in T. S. Eliot's words, that of "an intense and unique and horrible vision of life" (*Essays on Elizabethan Dramatists,* 1956).—E. Q.

revenge tragedy. Drama that focuses on a character whose revenge is motivated by the murder of some member of his family. In classical drama the form is identified with Seneca, who employed the revenge theme in such plays as *Thyestes, Medea,* and *Agamemnon.* By the time the Elizabethan playwrights had popularized the genre, the revenge motif had undergone considerable alteration. Revenge had become a psychological and moral problem, condemned by church and state yet popularly condoned. Thus, playwrights were provided with a theme that combined sensational action with the opportunity for subtle and probing characterization. The most popular of the Elizabethan revenge plays was Thomas Kyd's *The Spanish Tragedy.* Kyd's play explored in a tentative fashion a feature that was to become the most prominent feature of the genre: the degenerative effects of revenge on the avenger, even when he is nominally the hero of the play. Thus, in such plays as Cyril Tourneur's *The Revenger's Tragedy* and George Chapman's *The Revenge of Bussy D'Ambois,* the avenging hero moves from a morally justifiable position to an untenable one as his desire for revenge overwhelms all other considerations. In treating this problem in *Hamlet,* Shakespeare refined the moral dilemma even further by having his hero

acutely aware of the conflict and resolving it in a context that enables us to see in it an aspect of man's fundamentally tragic destiny.

Rhesus (Rhesos, 455–441 B.C.). A tragedy by EURIPIDES. The authorship of *Rhesus* is in doubt, but it is considered by most scholars to be an early work of Euripides. It is essentially a dramatization of the Doloneia in the tenth book of Homer's *Iliad,* in which the Trojans send Dolon to spy on the Greeks, and Diomedes and Odysseus set out on the same night to spy on the Trojans. They meet and kill Dolon, then kill, with the help of Athena, the newly arrived Trojan ally Rhesus and drive his famous horses back to the Greek lines.

A series of exciting scenes follow one another, but there is no deep emotion, no tragic focus. The Athena who appears in the middle of the play belongs to epic rather than to tragedy. She directs and protects the two Greeks to such an extent that any sense of real danger to them is nullified.

The ironic treatment of Rhesus is very Euripidean. Everybody human and divine except Hector emphasizes his tremendous heroism, but his boastful complacency when he appears does not bear out this reputation. Only minor characters, such as the Thracian messenger, reach any emotional depth. Hector is well drawn. The Chorus, at times, and the Muse, mother of Rhesus, at the end, speak beautiful lyrics. More than any other extant Greek drama, *Rhesus* is "a slice of the Homeric banquet," and it obviously is the work of no mean dramatist.

Translations of the play are listed under Euripides. —G. M. A. G.

Rhinoceros (Le Rhinocéros, 1960). A play by Eugène IONESCO. In February 1960 director Jean Louis Barrault presented Ionesco's play *Rhinoceros* at the Théâtre de France. The parable of the work is fairly simple. The inhabitants of a small provincial town are transformed into rhinoceroses. The character Bérenger, a type of average man, grows into the stature of protagonist because he is not influenced by words and speeches. He struggles against the exaltation of friends and colleagues, against an overwhelming force that isolates him. At the end of the play, after having observed, without always fully understanding it, a clinical study of conformity and contamination, he is totally alone. This solitude of man is at the center of all of Ionesco's plays, and it is always manifested in the same way with the same admixture of irony, burlesque, and humor. For the first time in his career, Ionesco won the approbation of a large public quickly and easily with this play. In using allegory, he loses some of the theatrical purity he had reached in *Les Chaises* (*The Chairs,* 1952) and *La Leçon* (*The Lesson,* 1950) where no didactic element blurred the simple functioning of the infernal machine.

Rhinoceros has been translated by Derek Prouse in *Plays IV* (1960).—W. F.

Rice, Elmer. Born **Elmer Leopold Reizenstein** (1892–1967). American playwright. A native of New York City, Elmer Rice grew up among the shabby apartment houses and mean streets that play so great a role in his work. At eighteen, he went to work in a cousin's law office and began attending law school at night. He graduated with honors and passed his bar exams, but his interest in the theater had been growing and, unwilling to face a lifetime of office routine, he left his job to devote himself to playwriting. His first play produced, *On Trial* (1914), was a great success. During the productive half-century that followed, he also developed as a producer and director; a film writer; a novelist, notably of *A Voyage to Purilia* (1930) and *Imperial City* (1937); and a theater historian in *The Living Theatre* (1959). As head of the New York region of the Federal Theater Project, he helped to develop "the living newspaper." He was a founder of the Playwrights Company and an active worker in many professional and civic organizations. He presents a vivid account of his career in his autobiography, *Minority Report* (1963).

Rice was one of the first American playwrights to experiment with dramatic form, and in the best of his plays form and content are effectively blended. Many of his innovations were quickly adopted by dramatists and film makers. In his *On Trial* he developed a flashback technique and even helped to design the "jackknife" set, in which the courtroom walls moved in order to reveal scenes from the past that explained the defendant's confession. In a series of expressionistic, often grotesque episodes, *The Adding Machine* (1922) tells the story of Mr. Zero, a repressed, colorless bookkeeper driven to one moment of passion when he murders the employer who replaced him with a machine; after a few pleasant moments in the Elysian Fields following his execution, Mr. Zero is ejected from heaven, for there he also fails to master the machine. (See EXPRESSIONISM.) For *Street Scene* (1929) the stage is occupied by the façade of a shabby brownstone apartment house, and while the tenants go in and out, sit on the steps, or lean out their windows, gossiping, scolding, laughing, and quarreling, a husband discovers his wife's infidelity and murders her and her lover. In a lighter vein *Dream Girl* (1945) dramatizes the romantic fantasies of a quiet salesgirl, each fantasy developed in a different, witty style. Rice was also successful working with conventional structures; an example is *Counsellor-at-Law* (1931), a tightly developed melodrama about an attorney maliciously accused of unethical behavior.

There is no standard edition of Rice's work. Critical comments appear in the major studies on modern American drama.—M. L.

Richard II (c. 1595). A chronicle play by William SHAKESPEARE. *The Life and Death of King Richard the Second*, as the Folio title reads, first appeared in print in the First Quarto (1597). Four subsequent quarto editions (two in 1598, one in 1608, and one in 1615) were issued before the play was published in the 1623 First Folio and attest to the play's popularity. Scholars accept the First Quarto as the most authoritative version of the play; however, it lacks the deposition scene, which was first printed in the 1608 Fourth Quarto. Copy for the Folio version, it is generally believed, was derived from some combination of the Third and Fifth Quartos. The primary source for the play is Raphael Holinshed's *Chronicles of England, Scotland, and Ireland* (2nd ed. 1587) with some additional material from Samuel Daniel's *The First Fowre Bookes of the Civile Wars betweene the Two Houses of Lancaster and Yorke* (1595). A notation on the 1597 quarto title page indicates that

THE
Tragedie of King Richard the second.

As it hath beene publikely acted by the right Honourable the Lorde Chamberlaine his Seruants.

LONDON
Printed by Valentine Simmes for Andrew Wise, and are to be sold at his shop in Paules church yard at the signe of the Angel.
1597.

TITLE PAGE OF THE FIRST QUARTO (1597) OF SHAKESPEARE'S *Richard II*

the play had been publicly acted by the Lord Chamberlain's Men. However, its earliest recorded performance took place on February 7, 1601.

Historically, *Richard II* depicts events of the last two years of the monarch's life. It opens with Richard airing charges of treasonous conduct that his cousin Henry Bolingbroke, duke of Hereford, has brought against Thomas Mowbray, duke of Norfolk. Attempts to reconcile the two fail, and Richard, in chivalric tradition, orders a trial by combat. At the lists Richard, exercising kingly prerogative, dramatically stops the combat just as it is about to start and sentences both dukes to exile, Mowbray for life and Bolingbroke for ten years (later reduced to six). Richard then prepares to leave for Ireland to put down a rebellion. Before departing, the king pays a visit to Bolingbroke's father, the dying John of Gaunt, duke of Lancaster. Gaunt, in some of the play's most famous speeches, chides Richard for wasting the national treasury and for surrounding himself with false, flattering courtiers. As soon as the old man dies, Richard seizes Gaunt's estates and leaves for Ireland. A number of noblemen, appalled by Richard's treatment of the Bolingbroke family and upset by the incompetent way Richard has been ruling, break with the king and give their allegiance to Henry Bolingbroke, who has come from France with an army. Bolingbroke continues to gain support, so that when Richard returns from his Irish expedition he finds a full-scale rebellion in England. Unable to regain control, Richard is forced to abdicate in favor of Bolingbroke, who becomes Henry IV. Richard is confined in Pomfret Castle, where he is murdered by Sir Pierce of Exton, who believes he is acting in accordance with Henry's wishes. King Henry denies complicity in Exton's deed and banishes the nobleman. The play closes with Henry planning a pilgrimage to the Holy Land to expiate the murder.

On one level *Richard II* is a chronicle play stressing Tudor concepts of government, particularly the sanctity of the throne. On another, it is—as the First Quarto title page notes—a tragedy depicting the fall of a prince. Critics are in general agreement that it is around Richard as both king and man that the play revolves and that the political themes are secondary. Thus, for many scholars Richard II is Shakespeare's first fully developed tragic protagonist. Treating his historical sources freely where he thought necessary, Shakespeare has drawn a portrait of a weak king who makes bad decisions, who falls prey to intriguing courtiers, and who is temperamentally unfit to rule. Richard might have been more successful as an actor or poet than as a monarch. In the course of the play, however, he gains insight and dies with dignity.

Yet no matter how responsible Richard was for his downfall, he was a legitimate monarch. As the bishop of Carlisle states, "What subject can give sentence on his king? / And who sits here that is not Richard's subject?" Thus, Bolingbroke's actions in forcing the abdication cannot be justified, and the deposition of Richard—regarded by the Elizabethans as the act that led to the War of the Roses—becomes a deed that constantly haunts Henry IV and subsequent Lancastrian kings.

Richard II, which critics believe was influenced by Christopher Marlowe's *Edward II* (written c. 1591–1592), is the first play in Shakespeare's second historical tetralogy. It is not definitely known whether at the time of its composition Shakespeare had projected the remaining plays: the two parts of *Henry IV* and *Henry V*. *Richard II* does mark an advance over Shakespeare's earlier history plays, particularly in the interplay between Richard and Bolingbroke and in the manner in which the imagery is integrated with the action of the play.

An outstanding edition of *Richard II* is the New Arden Edition (1956), edited by Peter Ure.—W. G.

Richard III (c. 1592–1593). A chronicle play by William SHAKESPEARE. *The Tragedy of Richard the Third* first appeared in print in the First Quarto (1597). Five subsequent quarto editions (1598, 1602, 1605, 1612, and 1622) were issued before the play was published in the 1623 First Folio. Scholars believe that the Folio text—regarded as the superior version—was derived either from the Third Quarto alone or from some combination of the Third and Sixth Quartos collated with a playhouse manuscript. The First Quarto is considered a memorial reconstruction of the script made by members of Shakespeare's company for a 1597 provincial tour.

The main source for the play is Raphael Holinshed's *Chronicles of England, Scotland, and Ireland* (2nd ed. 1587). Holinshed based his account of Richard's career on earlier historical writings, primarily Edward Hall's *The Union of the Two Noble and Illustre Families of Lancaster and York* (1548), Polydore Vergil's *Anglica Historia* (1534), and Sir Thomas More's *History of King Richard the Third* (written c. 1513). The Clarence scenes come from *The Mirror for Magistrates* (1559).

The earliest allusion to performance of the play is the notation on the 1597 quarto title page that it had "been lately Acted by the Right honourable the Lord Chamberlaine his seruants"; but *Richard III* was probably first acted around 1594. Richard Burbage, the tragedian of Shakespeare's company, was famous for his portrayal of Richard.

The play deals with the ambition of Richard of York, duke of Gloucester, to ascend the English throne, no matter how "subtle, false, and treacherous" he has to be to gain it. In his path stand his two elder brothers, King Edward IV and George, duke of Clarence, and their children. Embarking on the first of his villainous intrigues, Richard succeeds in having Clarence imprisoned and subsequently murdered. King Edward, who has been ill, soon dies. His sons, Edward—heir to the throne—and Richard, are brought to London and lodged in the Tower. Richard of Gloucester, now lord protector, implies the bastardy of the princes, thereby discrediting their claim to the throne, and successfully maneuvers to have himself declared the next king. After his coronation he arranges to have the princes murdered and to have Clarence's children removed as contenders for the title. Seemingly secure, Richard is now threatened with an invasion by the earl of Richmond, Lancastrian heir to the throne who has been in exile in France. The armies meet at Bosworth Field, where Richard is killed by Richmond (who becomes Henry VII, first of the Tudor kings). Richmond states his intention to marry Princess Elizabeth, thereby uniting the houses of York and Lancaster and bringing to an end the civil war that had made "poor England weep in streams of blood."

Richard III, the longest of Shakespeare's chronicle plays, appears to have been the dramatist's first success. Popular in its own day, as contemporary allusions and the publication of six quartos before the appearance of the First Folio attest, the play has continued to attract the attention of audiences to the present time. However, for almost two hundred years playwright and poet Colley Cibber's version of 1700 all but drove Shakespeare's original from the stage.

It is probably the character of Richard—a villain protagonist—that accounts for the play's perennial popularity. Richard dominates the action; he appears in fourteen of the twenty-five scenes and impels the drama forward in the others. He delivers ten soliloquies, five in the first three scenes. In his famous opening soliloquy he immediately presents himself as a demimonster. But his personality is much more complex as he reveals himself to be a skillful wooer, a master strategist, a cynical Machiavellian schemer, and the possessor of a sardonic sense of humor. Scholars see behind Shakespeare's treatment of his character traces of the Vice character of medieval drama, with its admixture of frightful and comic traits.

There is scholarly consensus that *Richard III*, along with the three previously written *Henry VI* plays, forms one of Shakespeare's two consciously composed tetralogies dealing with English political history. The historical Richard, however, does not appear to have been as villainous an individual as Shakespeare's usurper king. Shakespeare gained his knowledge of Richard's reign from the writings of the Tudor historians, who, following the political doctrine of the age, depicted this Yorkist ruler as an enemy of their royal house. The Elizabethan audiences would have been aware that behind the brilliant dramatic portrayal of Richard stood historical-political commentary on lessons that could be learned from Richard's reign. The bloody power politics in the play, the operation of a nemesis cycle in which courtier after courtier in a position of influence goes to his death for engaging in corrupt acts of statecraft, the reflection of civil discord engendered by the War of the Roses—all would strike responsive chords in an audience mindful that their political tranquility was far from assured since Queen Elizabeth had not yet resolved the problem of who would succeed her as monarch.

An outstanding edition of *Richard III* is the New Cambridge Edition (1954), edited by J. Dover Wilson.—W. G.

Richardson, Jack [Carter] (1935–   ). American playwright. Jack Richardson is one of the most promising writers to develop Off-Broadway in the 1960's. Following his graduation from Columbia University with a degree in philosophy, he went on to graduate work at the University of Munich. However, his interest in writing soon replaced his academic concerns. His first two plays were well received Off-Broadway, but he has had less success with his Broadway productions. He has written a good deal of drama criticism, most notably for *Commentary* magazine. A novel, *The Prison Life of Harris Filmore* (1963), attracted little attention.

Richardson's plays are characterized by articulate discussion, a rarity in current theater. He suggests Bernard Shaw in his wit, though he is closer to Jean Giraudoux and Jean Anouilh in the abstractness of his subjects and in his tone of ironic disenchantment. *The Prodigal* (1960), his most satisfying work, is a reworking of the Orestes legend. The hero is pictured as a cynical, uncommitted young man attracted neither by heroism nor power. However, unable to discover a philosophy to sustain him or to resist tradition and social pressure, Orestes ends by accepting the role of avenger. *Gallows Humor* (1961) consists of two related short plays. In Part I a prostitute convinces a condemned murderer that a chaotic life is preferable to a logical, predictable one. In Part II the hangman finds he cannot escape his life of mechanical routine. *Lorenzo* (1963) is set in Italy during the Renaissance. A traveling acting company is caught up in a small war, and these representatives of timeless universal art are drawn into the destructive tumult of life. *Xmas in Las Vegas* (1965), about a compulsive gambler and his family, attempts to

present a tragicomic image of the human condition within the framework of a light comedy and is the least successful of his works.

The Prodigal (1960) and *Gallows Humor* (1961) are his only published plays.—M. L.

Riders to the Sea (1904). A tragedy by John Millington SYNGE. Classically ordered in its compressed one-act structure and elegiac tone, this lyrical tragedy, set on one of the Aran Islands, deals with the archetypal conflict between a brave old peasant woman and the inexorable sea. Maurya, who has already lost a husband and five sons to the sea, is helpless now to prevent her sixth and last son, Bartley, from going to his death on his way to the Galway horse fair on the mainland. The body of a man who turns out to be her fifth son, Michael, has been found as the play begins, and the two chorus-voiced daughters, Cathleen and Nora, identify the body from some dropped stitches in one of his socks. Maurya meanwhile has been unable to give Bartley her blessing as he departs because, in a prophetic vision of death, she has seen him riding to the sea on the red mare, and her son Michael behind him on the gray pony. The terrible vision is presently fulfilled for Maurya when she learns that Michael has been identified, and then some neighbors come in with the news that Bartley has been knocked into the sea by the gray pony and drowned. It is in her final moments that she, in preparation for the wake, assumes her full tragic stature with stoical strength. She is noble in defeat. Keening softly, she commemorates all her dead men in a series of mighty laments, and then she comes to terms with her tragedy through a heroic and ironic release from the terrible grief: "They're all gone now, and there isn't anything more the sea can do to me. . . . It's a great rest I'll have now, and great sleeping in the long nights after Samhain, if it's only a bit of wet flour we do have to eat, and maybe a fish that would be stinking."—D. K.

Right You Are (Cosi è se vi pare, 1917). A play by Luigi PIRANDELLO. Other titles used in English have been: *As You Like It*, *Right You Are (If You Think You Are)*, *Right You Are (If You Think So)*, and *It Is So (If You Think So)*. The play is a dramatization of the Pirandello short story "Signora Frola and Signor Ponza, her Son-in-Law" (1915), which begins:

> You see that, don't you? It's enough to drive everyone right out of their minds, not to be able to figure which of them is crazy, this Signora Frola or this Signor Ponza, her son-in-law.

Signora Frola and Signor Ponza are recent arrivals in an Italian city. What has attracted attention is that they have elected to live in different parts of town. While arranging for the mother-in-law to live in the downtown section, Ponza himself lives in a tenement on the outskirts with his wife. The latter never goes out, and the older lady is not allowed in but has to resort to sending up written messages in a basket from the courtyard below.

There is so much gossip and speculation that Signora Frola and Signor Ponza separately decide to end it all by explaining the situation to some of the town's leading citizens. The first act of the three-act comedy is given over to, first, a brief expository passage showing us the agitated family of a leading citizen; second, a scene in which Signora Frola gives a provisional explanation to this family and its neighbors; third, a scene in which Signor Ponza upsets her explanation by "revealing" (as it seems) that she is crazy; and fourth, a second visit from Signora Frola in which she rebuts Ponza and attributes his version to *his* mental abnormality.

Theatrically, this first act of *Right You Are* is one of Pirandello's triumphs. The audience is invariably convinced, first, by Signora Frola, then by Signor Ponza; when Signora Frola returns, she damages Ponza's story, though this time, as to her own, the audience is aware of the possibility of being fooled and is no longer sure what will turn out to be true.

The tricks continue—if not quite so scintillatingly—through the two remaining acts. In the second act the townsfolk decide that the source of the confusion has been in hearing Ponza and Frola separately. They therefore trap them into a confrontation. It seems to prove Ponza a raving lunatic. But no sooner has the audience reached this conclusion than Ponza reappears onstage to report that he has played mad in order to sustain the Signora's illusions.

In the third act, a character who so far had been only an onlooker—Lamberto Laudisi—drives the action to its final . . . anticlimax. He mischievously suggests that the answer must lie in bringing all three Ponza-Frolas together. And so the townsfolk arrange for the three-way confrontation of this famous finale. The third party is, of course, Signora Ponza. Two views of her identity have been presented. According to Signora Frola, she is her daughter and it is Ponza's illusion that she has been replaced by another, second wife. According to Signor Ponza, the lady is his second wife, and Signora Frola is under the illusion that she is his first wife, her daughter. What will the lady herself say? She says:

> I am Signora Frola's daughter, and I am Signor Ponza's second wife. And to myself I am no one . . . I am the one that each of you thinks I am.

Laudisi, being a Pirandellian philosopher, had expected nothing more conclusive. The play ends on his laughter and his parting thrust: "That, my dear friends, was the voice of truth!"

Philosophically, the French title seems to put the play in a nutshell: *Chacun sa vérité*—"to each his truth." On the other hand, one suggested English title—"Thinking Makes It So"—only indicates a common misunderstanding. Pirandello is not speaking of the effect of thought upon events, nor yet of the effect of imagination upon thoughts. He is giving up on the quest for objective truth and settling instead for subjective impressions. Our impressions are all we have, and your impressions are worthy of as much respect, or as little, as mine.

During the 1920's there was much discussion of Pirandello's philosophy as such. But it has not worn particularly well and with the passage of time even a play such as *Right You Are* is less interesting for its idea than for some of the historical and psychological connections of the idea. What keeps the play alive is not so much the figure of Laudisi as the Ponza-Frola story with its deeply pathological roots. The hidden, vital subject here, surely, is a trauma of deprivation.

According to Signora Frola, Ponza had his wife snatched from him because his passion for her was too tremendous to bear: so he concluded she had died and that he now had a second wife. According to Signor Ponza, Signora Frola had her daughter snatched from her by death: she couldn't bear it and so concluded that the second wife was the same as the first one. Such are the deep troubles of this family neurosis. The play trembles with them; and in that tremor is its life.

The fullest discussion of the play in English is Eric Bentley's Introduction to his translation (1954).

Rip Van Winkle (1865). A comedy by Joseph Jefferson (1829–1905) and Dion BOUCICAULT. *Rip Van Winkle* was first constructed by actor Joseph Jefferson from three earlier dramatizations of Washington Irving's story. Then, revised by Boucicault and acted by Jefferson, the play became one of the most popular comedies on the American stage from 1866 to 1905.

The story tells of Rip, illiterate, easygoing, bibulous but honest and warmhearted, who has mortgaged his land in a Catskill village to the villainous Derrick. Derrick attempts to swindle Rip by obtaining his signature on a bill of sale, pretending that it is an acknowledgment of a loan, but Rip is suspicious and puts the document in his pocket. Later, Rip comes back from hunting, drunk and with no game. His wife, Gretchen, is furious; she drives him out into a storm where Rip meets Hendrick Hudson and his ghostly crew, drinks with them, and falls asleep. Twenty years later Rip awakens, an old man. Nobody recognizes him in the village. Derrick has his land and his wife and is determined that Rip's daughter Meenie shall marry Derrick's nephew. Meenie recognizes her father, Rip produces the unsigned contract, and Derrick is foiled.

The construction is clumsy, the characters stereotyped, the dialogue undistinguished, but the play provides a role in which Jefferson could display his genius for combining the comic and the pathetic, and his virtuosity in representing the aging of Rip. —B.H.

Ritterdrama. A manifestation of the German Romantic movement, specifically the *Sturm und Drang* drama, in the late eighteenth century. The plays are written in prose, of irregular form. They take place in medieval times and illustrate the valor and independence of the knights against a background of pageantry. The plays' sentiments are passionate and patriotic.

Among the most well known playwrights of the Ritterdrama are Josef August von Törring (1753–1826) and Joseph Marius Babo (1756–1822). Eventually banned in Munich by reactionary forces, the popularity of the Ritterdrama continued in Austria.

ritual origins of drama. If the origin of the drama is destined, by the very nature of things, never to be known, the theory of the ritual origin of the drama seems doomed, by the nature of man, to be forever embroiled in controversy. Although more than three-quarters of a century has passed since the publication of the first volumes of James G. Frazer's *The Golden Bough* (1890) and more than fifty years since the appearance of Jane Harrison's *Themis* (1912), the two works that laid the foundation for the ritual theory of the drama, the theory is still being attacked as though it were fresh-minted, still perversely wrong, still insidiously persuasive, still persistently alive. Yet despite Gerald F. Else's cold and constrained scholarship in *The Origin and Early Form of Greek Tragedy* (1965) and Joseph Fontenrose's hot and less than academic fulminations in *The Ritual Theory of Myth* (1966), the two most recent criticisms of the ritual view, the theory appears to gain more and more adherents among students of literature and more credulity in its applications to disciplines that are considerably removed from literature—indeed, among virtually all fields of study, except, ironically enough, that of classical scholarship, from which the idea first came and which it has done so much to keep alive. Arthur W. Pickard-Cambridge did not, after all, in *Dithyramb Tragedy and Comedy* (1927) say the last word in refutation of the ritual theory.

Though the ritual view of the drama is scarcely new—Aristotle's notes for his *Poetics* contain a direct allusion to it (49a9) and his discussion of tragedy is suffused with it, while Nietzsche's *The Birth of Tragedy* is the culmination of the Romantic preoccupation with it—the modern form of the ritual view was given its shape and direction by the misnamed "Cambridge school." Inspired by an unwilling leader who himself had been influenced by the work of a friend, William Robertson Smith in *The Religion of the Semites* (1889), the Cambridge group in the space of a mere decade produced book after book devoted to demonstrating the relevance of the ritual view to the totality of ancient Greek culture, including the drama. The reluctant leader, Sir James George Frazer, alone shied away from the implications of his monumental and encompassing *Golden Bough* (final edition, 1915). In 1903 Jane Harrison published the *Prolegomena to the Study of Greek Religion;* in 1907 Gilbert Murray wrote *The Rise of the Greek Epic;* in 1912 Jane Harrison issued *Themis,* with an excursus by Gilbert Murray on the ritual forms underlying Greek tragedy; in 1912 F. M. Cornford put out *From Religion to Philosophy;* and in 1913 E. K. Chambers published *The Medieval Stage* (a book never mentioned in connection with the Cambridge school but clearly written under the influence of Frazer's work), while in that same year Freud wrote *Totem and Taboo.* The ritual view was now complete in its formulation; what remained were exemplifications and refinements, particularly from the study of the cultures of the ancient Near East. Classical scholarship, the history of religion, archaeology, anthropology, and psychology were molded into a single new tool of literary history and criticism.

From 1913 on, there has been an almost unending succession of works that have deepened and widened our understanding of the drama through the use of the myth and ritual approach to literature: F. M. Cornford, *The Origin of Attic Comedy* (1914); Jessie L. Weston, *From Ritual to Romance* (1920); Colin Still, *Shakespeare's Mystery Play* (1920); F. C. Prescott, *Poetry and Myth* (1927); S. H. Hooke, editor, *Myth and Ritual* (1933); Lord Raglan, *The Hero* (1937); George Thomson, *Aeschylus and Athens* (1941); Gertrude R. Levy, *The Gate of Horn* (1948); Joseph Campbell, *The Hero with a Thousand Faces* (1949); Francis Fergusson, *The Idea of a Theatre* (1949); Theodor Gaster, *Thespis* (1950); Herbert Weisinger, *Tragedy and the Paradox of the Fortunate Fall* (1953); Northrop Frye, *Anatomy of Criticism* (1957); C. L. Barber, *Shakespeare's Festive Comedy* (1959); Richmond Y. Hathorn, *Tragedy, Myth, and Mystery* (1962); and O. B. Hardison, Jr., *Christian Rite and Christian Drama in the Middle Ages* (1965).

The myth and ritual pattern of the ancient Near East, which is at least six thousand years old, centers in a divine god-king-hero who was killed annually and who was reborn in the person of his successor. In its later development, the king was not killed but went through an annual symbolic death and a symbolic rebirth or resurrection. Starting out as a magical rite designed to ensure the success of the crops in climates where the outcome of the struggle between water and drought meant literally the difference between life and death, the pattern was gradually transformed into a religious ritual, designed to promote man's salvation. It finally became an ethical conviction, freed of both its magical and religious ritual practices but still retaining in spiritualized and symbolic form its ancient appeal and emotional certitude. Because the pattern begins with the need to survive, it never loses its force, for it is concerned always with survival, whether physical or spiritual. So far as can be ascertained at present, the pattern had a double growth—one along the lines of the ancient civilizations of the Near East, the Sumerian, the Egyptian, the Babylonian, both south and north, the Palestinian, first with the Canaanites and then with the Hebrews, and thence into Christianity; the other along the lines of the island civilizations of the Aegean, from Crete to the mainland of Greece, thence to Rome, and once more into Christianity. The two streams of development flowed into each other and reinforced themselves at this crucial juncture.

Despite the differences between the religions of the ancient Near East, as, for example, between those of Egypt and Mesopotamia, and between that of the Hebrews and of the others, they nevertheless all possessed certain significant features of myth, that is, the "scenario" of ritual, and ritual, that is, the "staging" of myth, in common. These features, in their turn, stemmed from the common bond of ritual, characteristic in one form or another, of all together, though none possessed completely all the elements, which varied in some degree from religion to religion. In this single, idealized ritual scheme, the well-being of the community was secured by the regular performance of certain ritual actions in which the king or his equivalent took the leading role. Moreover, the king's importance for the community was incalculably increased by the almost universal conviction that the fortunes of the community or state and those of the king were inextricably intermingled; indeed, one may go so far as to say that on the well-being of the king depended the well-being of the community as a whole. On the basis of the evidence covering different peoples at different times, we know that in the ancient Near East there existed a pattern of thought and action that so strongly gripped the minds and emotions of those who believed in it that it was made the basis on which they could apprehend and accept the universe in which they lived. It made possible man's conviction that he could control that universe for his own purposes, and it placed in his hands the lever whereby he could exercise that control.

From an analysis of the extant seasonal rituals, particularly the new year festivals, and from the coronation, initiation, and personal rituals of the ancient Near East, it is possible to make a reconstructed model of the basic ritual form. Essentially, the pattern contains these basic elements: the indispensable role of the divine god-king-hero; the combat between the god and an opposing power; the suffering of the god; the death of the god; the resurrection of the god; the symbolic re-creation of the myth of creation; the sacred marriage; the triumphal procession; and the settling of destinies. It must be remembered, however, that the theme of the dying and rising of a god constitutes but one illustration, so to speak, of the greater cycle of birth, death, and rebirth. The many and various rites connected with birth, initiation, marriage, and death in the case of the individual, as well as the rites concerned with the planting, the harvesting, the new year celebrations, and the installation ceremonies of the king in the case of the community, all repeat, each in its own way, the deep-rooted and abiding cycle of death and rebirth. Not only do these rituals symbolize the passage from death to life and from one way of life to another, but they are the actual means of achieving the change-over; they mark the transition by which, through the processes of separation, regeneration, and the return on a higher level, both the individual and the community are assured their victory over the forces of chaos, which are thereby kept under control.

The purpose of these rituals is to bring about by enaction a just order of existence, in which god, nature, and man are placed in complete and final rapport with one another; they are both the defense against disorder and the guarantee of order. In the myth and ritual pattern, then, man has devised a mighty weapon by which he keeps at bay, and sometimes even seems to conquer, the hostile forces that endlessly threaten to overpower him.

In the early stages of the development of the myth and ritual pattern, however, the best that man could hope for was an uneasy truce between himself and chaos, because the cycle merely returned to its beginnings; the god-king-hero fought, was defeated, was resurrected, and was momentarily triumphant, thus ensuring the well-being of the community for the coming year, but it was inevitable that in the course of the year he would again be defeated and would again have to go through his annual agony. Thus, nothing new could be expected, nor was it anticipated, and year after year man could hope for no more than a temporary gain that he was sure would soon be turned into an inevitable loss. To achieve genuine faith, therefore, was an act of courage, the attainment of which was both difficult and infrequent. It is no wonder that one detects in the myth and ritual pattern of the ancient Near East before the Hebraic-Christian tradition took over too strong a reliance on the mere machinery of ritual, leading ultimately, not to faith, but to superstition, tinged as well with the melancholy notes of despair and pessimism.

The Hebraic-Christian tradition, in the very process of adapting the pattern, transformed it, for by virtue of its unique and tenacious insistence on the mercy and judgment of its transcendent god, it introduced a new and vital element to the pattern, that of the dialectical leap from out of the endless circle onto a different and higher stage of understanding. But the crucial moment in this transformation of the myth and ritual pattern comes when man, by himself, undertakes on his own to make the leap. To him remains the decision and his is the responsibility. The Hebraic-Christian tradition utilized the cycle of birth, life, death, and rebirth to conquer chaos and disorder, but it made its unique contribution to the pattern by giving man the possibility of defeating chaos and disorder by a single, supreme act of human will that could wipe them out at one stroke. In so doing, it preserved the potency of the pattern and retained its ancient appeal and, at the same time, ensured its continued use by supplying the one element it had hitherto lacked to give it its permanent role as the means whereby man is enabled to live in an indifferent universe: it showed that man can, by himself, transcend that universe.

This, then, is the myth and ritual pattern. What are its implications for tragedy? To start with, in the myth and ritual pattern is the seedbed of tragedy, the stuff out of which it was ultimately formed. Both the form and content of tragedy, its architecture as well as its ideology, closely parallel the form and content of the myth and ritual pattern. But having said that, one must also say that the myth and ritual pattern and tragedy are not the same. Both share the same shape and the same intent but they differ significantly in the manner of their creation and in the methods of achieving their purposes. The myth and ritual pattern is the group product of many and different minds groping on many and different levels over long and kaleidoscopic periods of time under a stimulus of motivations quite different from those that produce tragedy. The process of its creation is not anything like the formerly accepted communal origin of the ballad, for we know that myth in its form as the complement to ritual must have been devised by the priest-astrologer-magicians of the ancient world. The intent of the myth and ritual pattern is control, and its method that of mimetically reproducing the rhythm of birth, death, and birth again to gain that control. But imitation here means, not acting like the thing imitated while maintaining a distinct and different attitude and behavior toward the thing imitated, but rather the interpenetration of, and union with, the imitator, the thing imitated, and the imitation, all three being one and the same thing.

Tragedy, on the other hand, is a creation compounded of conscious craft and conviction. If we describe the myth and ritual pattern as the passage from ignorance to understanding through suffering mimetically and at first hand, then we must describe tragedy as the passage from ignorance to understanding through suffering symbolically and at a distance. To speak of symbolic meanings is already to have made the leap from myth to art. In the myth and ritual pattern, the dying-reborn god-king-hero, the worshippers for whom he suffers, and the action of his agony are identical; in tragedy, the tragic protagonist undergoes his suffering at an aesthetic distance and only vicariously in the minds of his audience. For that reason does Aristotle say that tragedy is an imitation of an action. One participates in a ritual but one is a spectator of a play.

Moreover, tragedy reconstitutes the myth and ritual pattern in terms of its own needs. Of the nine elements that make up the myth and ritual pattern, four are virtually eliminated from tragedy: namely, the actual death of the god, the symbolic re-creation of the myth of creation, the sacred marriage, and the triumphal procession; two elements, the indispensable role of the divine god-king-hero and the settling of destinies, are retained only by implication and play rather ambiguous roles in tragedy; while the remaining three—combat, suffering (with death subsumed), and resurrection—give tragedy its structure and substance.

One of the characteristics of the myth and ritual pattern is its adaptability, its ability to change shape while retaining its potency. We should therefore not be surprised to find the same process at work in tragedy. What is revealing, however, is the direction of change. We find, first, that the theme of the settling of destinies—which is the highest point in the myth and ritual pattern and the goal of the struggle, since without it the passion of the god would be in vain and chaos and disorder would be triumphant—this theme, so elaborately explicated in the ritual practices of the ancient Near East, is no more than implied in tragedy, just as the correspondence between the well-being of the king and the well-being of the community, again so detailed in ritual, is only shadowed forth in tragedy, as a condition to be aimed at but not to be achieved in reality.

Second, we discover that even greater emphasis is placed on the small moment of doubt in tragedy than on the myth and ritual pattern itself. In the rituals of the ancient Near East, at the point between the death of the god and his resurrection, all action is arrested as the participants fearfully and anxiously wait for the god to be revived. After the din of combat, this quiet moment of doubt and indecision is all the more awful, for there is no assurance that the god will be reborn: "For a small moment have I forsaken thee." "But," continues Isaiah, "with great mercies will I gather thee." It is no wonder that the small moment is followed in the pattern by creation, the sacred marriage, and the triumphal procession as the people's expression of joy that the death of the god has not been in vain and that for another year at least "the earth remaineth, seedtime and harvest, and cold and heat, and summer and winter, and day and night shall not cease."

Clearly spelling out the implications of the second change made by tragedy in the myth and ritual pattern is the third, the freedom of choice of the tragic protagonist and the responsibility for the consequences of making that choice. For in that small moment of doubt and indecision, when victory and defeat are poised in the balance, only the moral force of man wills him on in action to success. The tragic protagonist acts in the conviction that his action is right and he accepts the responsibility for that action; for him to do less than that means the loss of his stature as a moral, responsible agent. The tragic occurs when by the fall of a man of strong character we are made aware of something greater than man or even mankind; we seem to see a new and truer vision of the universe.

But that vision cannot be bought cheaply, by blind reliance on the mere machinery of the myth and ritual pattern and by fixing the fight. Only the deliberate moral choice of the tragic protagonist, confronted by two equal and opposite forces and fully aware of the consequences of his choice, can bring off the victory; and then only at the expense of pain and suffering: "He was despised, and rejected of men; a man of sorrows, and acquainted with grief." But suffering can be made bearable only when at the same time it is made part of a rational world order into which it fits and which has an understandable place for it.

Tragedy therefore occurs when the accepted order of things is fundamentally questioned only to be the more triumphantly reaffirmed. It cannot exist where there is no faith; conversely, it cannot exist where there is no doubt. It can exist only in an atmosphere of skeptical faith. The protagonist must be free to choose, and though he choose wrongly, yet the result of the wrong choice is our own escape and our enlightenment. Nothing less than this sacrifice will do, and only the symbolic sacrifice of one who is like us can make possible our atonement for the evil that is within us and for the sins that we are capable of committing. Nevertheless, in Western thought, if man is free to choose, in the end he must choose rightly. He is free to choose his salvation, but he is punished for his wrong choice. Man is free, but he is free within the limits set for him by his condition as a man. So great is the emphasis placed on freedom of choice in tragedy that the settling of destinies, which in the myth and ritual pattern is the tangible reward of victory, recedes more and more into the background, and the messianic vision implicit in the settling of destinies is personalized and humanized in tragedy in the form of heightened self-awareness as the end of the tragic agony. In short, the myth and ritual pattern pertains to religion which proceeds by assertion, tragedy to literature which proceeds by assessment.

To sum up, then, the structure of tragic form, as derived from the myth and ritual pattern, may be diagrammed in this way: The tragic protagonist, in whom is subsumed the well-being of the people and the welfare of the state, engages in conflict with a representation of darkness and evil. A temporary defeat is inflicted on the tragic protagonist, but after shame and suffering he emerges triumphant as the symbol of the victory of light and good over darkness and evil. His victory is sanctified by the covenant of the settling of destinies, which reaffirms the well-being of the people and the welfare of the state.

But in the course of the conflict there comes a point when the protagonist and the antagonist appear to merge into a single challenge against the order of god. The evil that the protagonist would not do, he does, and the good that he would, he does not. In this moment we are made aware that the real protagonist of tragedy is the order of god against which the tragic hero has rebelled. In this manner is the pride, the presumption that is in all of us by virtue of our mixed state as man, symbolized and revealed, and it is this *hybris* that is vicariously purged from us by the suffering of the tragic protagonist. He commits the foul deed that is potentially in us, he challenges the order of god, which we would but dare not do, he expiates our sin, and what we had hitherto felt we had been forced to accept we now believe of our free will—namely, that the order of god is just and good. Therefore is the tragic protagonist vouchsafed the vision of victory but not its attainment.—H. W.

Rival Queens, The (1677). A tragedy in blank verse by Nathaniel LEE. *The Rival Queens, or The Death of Alexander the Great* was first performed in March at the Theatre Royal in Drury Lane by the King's Company. Cassander leads a conspiracy against Alexander the Great. To further his plans Cassander encourages the rivalry between the tempestuous Roxana, Alexander's first wife, and Statira, his second wife, who has vowed to go into seclusion because Alexander has broken his promise and renewed relations with Roxana. Taunted by Roxana, however, Statira decides to see Alexander again, whereupon he banishes Roxana. To revenge herself, Roxana murders Statira; Alexander is poisoned by Cassander.

The violent confrontations of Statira and Roxana, grounded as they are in the understandable jealousy of the two women, are the most effective scenes in the play (see ENGLAND: *Restoration drama*). They were probably responsible for its long stage history.

P. F. Vernon is editing this play with introduction and notes for the Regents Restoration Drama Series. It is included in *Plays of the Restoration and Eighteenth Century* (1966), D. MacMillan and H. M. Jones, eds.—E. W.

Robbers, The (**Die Räuber,** 1782). A play by Friedrich von SCHILLER. *The Robbers* presents two rebels of STURM UND DRANG dimensions: Franz von Moor, rebellious titan of vengeful immorality who steals his brother's birthright, his honor, and his betrothed, and Karl von Moor, rebellious titan of justice and freedom who is driven by his brother's treachery to form a band of roaming robbers, most of whom are victims of social injustice. Franz ultimately commits suicide and Karl, recognizing that antisocial action is not justified, gives himself up to the authorities. Franz was modeled in part after Richard III and, in turn, became a model for Raskolnikov in Dostoyevski's *Crime and Punishment.* The play is still on the boards today in Germany, Austria, and the Soviet Union.

Robertson, Thomas William (1829–1871). English actor and playwright. T. W. Robertson came from a theatrical family and was associated with the theater all his life. He began acting at the age of five when he played the role of Hamish, Rob Roy's son, in the musical drama *Rob Roy; or, Auld Lang Syne.* After a period of formal schooling, Robertson joined his father, who in 1843 had assumed the management of the Lincoln Company, and helped in every conceivable way: prompting, painting scenery, acting in small parts, writing songs, and even adapting plays.

The disbanding of his father's company and Robertson's consequent move to London mark the real beginning of his eventual rise to fame. His first years there were neither remarkable nor auspicious; he had difficulty securing acting roles, and his early plays, both originals and adaptations, although containing some marks of his later interest in "realism," were largely typical of the period, following a pattern of intrigue and action and containing recognizable types. His first play produced in London was an original two-act comic drama, *A Night's Adventure; or,*

Highways and Byeways (1851). His first great success, however, did not come until 1864, when the famous comedian E. A. Sothern starred in Robertson's *David Garrick.* Robertson's fame was made secure with the production of *Society* in 1865, and this was followed by the plays for which he is still remembered today: *Ours* (1866), *Caste* (1867), *Play* (1868), and *M.P.* (1870).

Society not only made his name famous, but it also established a new school of realistic drama. *Caste,* a play which deals with the difficulties of marriage between persons of different social rank, is Robertson's best and most famous example of this new genre. *Caste* illustrates Robertson's concern with realism in terms of acting, setting, and theme, the first marked by his avoidance of caricature and his insistence on ensemble acting, the second by his insistence on realistic props and extensive use of "practicable" items, and the third by his willingness to treat serious, even controversial, subjects. The play also demonstrates how Robertson extended this concern to other phases of production, especially in the evocation of atmosphere—particularly that of working-class daily life—and in the creation of natural dialogue and natural actions. The scene in *Caste* in which Polly, the heroine's sister, and Sam, her boy friend, converse on one side of the stage, while Esther, the heroine, and George, her fiancé, converse on the other is a very early instance of an attempt to present simultaneous conversation, and, more important, shows Robertson's willingness to do whatever is necessary, no matter how unconventional, to achieve that genuine realism that goes beyond the mere introduction of realistic settings and props. His success in this direction prompted William Archer, the famous critic and champion of the "new drama," to ask whether Robertson were not the initiator of modern drama, and whether one answers affirmatively or negatively, the fact still remains that Robertson's contribution to nineteenth-century drama was indeed a significant one. He was not only one of the important pioneers of the new drama but also an influential playwright whose impact on both his own time and ours has not been fully recognized.

For an account of Robertson's life see *The Principal Dramatic Works of Thomas William Robertson. With a Memoir by His Son* (2 vols., 1889, Vol. II containing the memoir), and T. Edgar Pemberton, *The Life and Writings of T. W. Robertson* (1893). See also T. E. Pemberton, *Society and Caste* (1905); G. B. Shaw, "Robertson Redivivus," *Dramatic Opinions and Essays* (2 vols., 1906), II, 284–289; Sir Arthur Pinero, "The Theatre in the 'Seventies," in *The Eighteen-Seventies,* Harley Granville-Barker, ed. (1929), 135–163; and M. Savin, *Thomas William Robertson* (1950). Of special interest are the discussions by Shaw and Pinero of Robertson's contribution to naturalism on the stage and his other contributions to the new drama of the nineteenth century.—M. T.

Robinson, Lennox [**Esme Stuart**] (1886–1958). Irish playwright. The son of an Anglican clergyman, Robinson was a native of Cork. He embarked on a literary career early in life and at the age of twenty-two had his first play, *The Clancy Name,* produced by the Abbey Theatre. Shortly thereafter he was invited by William Butler Yeats to become one of the Abbey's directors. For the next fifty years Robinson devoted most of his time to the Abbey, serving as director and member of the board of directors while at the same time supplying the Abbey with some of its best and most popular plays. A frequent visitor to the United States, Robinson was also an able publicist for the Abbey, writing a history entitled *Ireland's Abbey Theatre* in 1961. (See IRELAND.)

Among Robinson's many plays, the best-known of the early dramas are *The Clancy Name* (1908), a powerful one-act tragedy depicting the stubborn pride of the Irish peasant; *The Cross Roads* (1909), the first full-length realistic peasant play written for the Abbey; and *Patriots* (1912), a scathing tragic satire of political life in Ireland. After his early success with tragic themes, Robinson turned to writing lighthearted comedies, notably *The Dreamers* (1915) and *The White-Headed Boy* (1916). He returned to serious drama in *The Big House* (1926). Set during the period of the "troubles" (1921–1923), *The Big House* recounts the tragic experience of the Irish aristocracy caught between divided loyalties. The variety of Robinson's achievement was evidenced in *Church Street* (1934), an expressionist drama. Written under the influence of Pirandello, the subject of the play is the writing of a play. The apprentice dramatist who is the hero is the source of the play's constant shifting between fantasy and reality. The play draws to a conclusion in a series of apparently unrelated episodes that suggest that the final reality is the illusion created by the dramatic imagination. He extended his range further in *Killycreggs in Twilight* (1937), dealing with the decline of the Anglo-Irish gentry, and in *Roly Poly* (1940), an adaptation of De Maupassant's short story "Boule de Suife." In 1948 he visited the United States. At Bowling Green University he produced a comedy, *The Lucky Finger,* one of his last plays.

Robinson's work is distinguished by his sure command of the technical aspects of playwriting. Whether dealing with the political and social life of his time or experimenting with subjective, expressionistic techniques, his plays have a finished structure that is the mark of a professional craftsman.

There is no collected edition of Robinson's works. Most of his plays have been published individually. A critical biography of the author has been written by Michael J. O'Neill (1964).—E. Q.

Rodogune (1645). A tragedy by Pierre COR-NEILLE. Cléopâtre, queen of Syria, believes that her glory lies in taking revenge on Rodogune, her former husband's second wife. She has already killed him and decides to give the throne to whichever of her two sons, Séleucus and Antiochus, will kill Rodogune. However, both are in love with the princess, who promises her hand to whichever of the two will kill his mother. Cléopâtre therefore kills Séleucus and then tries to poison Antiochus and Rodogune, but, discovered, she poisons herself. *Rodogune* is one of the most melodramatic of Corneille's tragedies but also one of the most powerful because of Cléopâtre's monstrosity, Rodogune's strength, and the tortured generosity of the two princes.

This play has been translated into English blank verse by Lacy Lockert in *Chief Plays* (2nd. ed., 1957).—Ja. G.

Rodrigues, Nélson (1912–). Brazilian journalist, novelist, and playwright. Of a family of artists and journalists, Nélson Rodrigues was born in Recife, in the state of Pernambuco, though his intellectual life now centers entirely in Rio de Janeiro. He was first a journalist and still practices as such. Using his own name or the pseudonym of Suzana Flag, he has published chronicles on the sensational police cases of each day and several novels to do with scandals and now maintains a sports chronicle in the Rio dailies.

His first important appearance in Brazilian theatrical life was in 1943, with the presentation of *Vestido de noiva* ("The Wedding Dress"), about a woman's guilt for having fallen in love with her sister's boy friend. He had already made himself known with *A Mulher sem pecado* ("The Woman Without Sin," 1941), a psychological drama of jealousy and adultery. In *Vestido de noiva,* however, Rodrigues delved into the subconscious mind of the guilt-ridden woman with an audacity and lyricism until then unknown in Brazilian theater. For that occasion the Polish director Z. Ziembinsky went to Brazil, and an avant-garde theatrical company—The Comedians —was organized, which was responsible for many of the greatest artistic successes between 1943 and 1953. The performance of *Vestido de noiva* shook the intelligentsia and the public at large also with its expressionist setting, adapted perfectly to the text. The stage was divided into three parts, one representing the present action, another the woman's hallucinations, and the third her memory. The next plays of Rodrigues, which state that man's sexual life is responsible for his destiny, continued the controversy

NÉLSON RODRIGUES (BRAZILIAN EMBASSY)

sparked by the first work, and the government often prohibited performances.

Following the model of the Greeks, Rodrigues uses a chorus and poetic language in various plays, changing his direction in the last few years to a more accentuated realism. The world of crime and sexual aberration, compounded by the factor of moral defect, is localized by him through protagonists from Rio de Janeiro, with its characteristic mode of speech perfectly re-created. No dramatist has succeeded in reproducing the spoken dialect of the small Rio middle class so well as Rodrigues, and no one has been as provocative in relation to his public. His theater is defiant in a direct manner, as if the author were hurling accusations at the spectators while at the same time doing penance for his own mistakes. However, the grandiose dimension collides at times with aesthetic balance, resulting in exaggerated brutality.

Other principal plays of Rodrigues are: *Anjo negro* ("Black Angel," pub. 1946), *Album de família* ("Family Album," 1945), *A falecida* ("The Deceased," 1953), *Bôca de ouro* ("Gold Teeth," 1960), *Bonitinha mas ordinária* ("Beautiful but Common," 1963), *A valsa no. 6* ("Waltz No. 6," 1959), *Beijo no asfalto* ("A Kiss in the Asphalt Street," 1961), and *Tôda a nudez será castigada* ("All Nudity Will Be Punished," 1967).

The plays of Rodrigues have not been translated into English.—J. P.

Romance of the Lute, The (P'i pa chi, 1704). A Chinese play by Kao Tse-ch'eng (fl. 14th century). *The Romance of the Lute,* sometimes rendered also as "The Lute Song," is the most celebrated of classical Chinese plays. The work belongs to the drama of south China, which reached greater refinement in both literature and music than the schools of the north. At the time of the play's first performance in 1704, Chinese taste in all forms of expression—drama, poetry, and art—was marked increasingly by romantic sensibility. The play admirably expressed the temper of such an age. Nevertheless, it was written with such an artful hand and such delicacy of feeling that its place is firmly established in Chinese literature, almost irrespective of cultural changes in succeeding generations.

The play erects a monument to virtue and to tears, its readers or spectators alternately fortified by pious or drenched in pathetic sentiment. The story is of a young man, recently married, who is urged by his father to visit the capital and compete in the public examinations. This the young man does, despite his mother's forebodings. At the capital he takes the examinations, is qualified for high posts, and unhappily married at the emperor's request to the daughter of a cabinet minister. The deserted first wife of the young man, left with his parents, sacrifices herself to them during the extreme poverty in which they find themselves. Finally, lute in hand, she sets out to find her lost husband. After misadventures designed fairly to dissolve the audience into tears, she finds herself in her husband's house. The second wife, who pities her condition, receives her kindly. At first the heroine has hard words for her husband, but in the end the two, or perhaps one should say, the three, are united. A happy ménage is established with two complacent wives and a still more bland husband.

The play has for nearly three centuries been admired throughout China and become the object of a number of widely divergent opinions abroad. Western critics especially averse to romantic sentiment write harshly of it. In George Freedley's *A History of the Theatre* (rev. ed. 1956) we read: "Like so many of the literary plays of the Ming period this was enormously long, twenty-four acts in fact. Its lugubrious story of filial piety is rather sickening to the western mind." Possibly with more seasoned judgment Herbert Giles in *A History of Chinese Literature* (1923) remarks: "It had caught on, and henceforth forms the ideal pastime of the cultured, reflective scholar, and of the laughter-loving masses of the people." An ambivalence almost peculiar to the Chinese imagination does, indeed, allow for both laughter and tears virtually in the same scene or moment. Humor, to some degree at least, holds the pathos of this play to a measure of restraint, while the pathos is far too strong to admit it into the ranks of pure comedy.

Like the majority of the most popular Chinese dramas, *The Romance of the Lute* has gone through many rewritings, enlargements, curtailments, and rearrangements. Its considerable length and peculiarly exotic flavor have apparently discouraged translations into Western languages, despite the play's high prestige in China. There is no complete translation into English. A free rendering into French with an entertaining Introduction was offered by M. Bazin in 1841.—H. W. W.

Roman comedy. Preliterary rudiments of comedy existed in ancient Italy at an early date, in the form of Fescennine verses, which were jesting, abusive, and probably obscene, and were associated with weddings and harvest festivals; performances by Etruscan dancers who came to Rome in 364 B.C.; and a more elaborate medley of song, dance, and dialogue, later called *satura* by the historian Livy. Other early dramatic forms were the FABULA ATELLANA, a type of farce with masks and stock characters, and the MIME, played without masks and with the female roles acted by women.

In the third century B.C. the Romans came into closer contact with the Greeks of southern Italy and Sicily, especially during the First Punic War (264–241 B.C.). They realized how inadequate their own cultural growth had been, and they became interested in Greek poetry and drama. Roman comedy actually began in 240 B.C., when a Greek writer, Livius Andronicus, came from Tarentum to Rome and adapted a Greek comedy into Latin for presentation at the *ludi Romani* ("Roman games"). Since the play dealt with Greek characters in their native dress and settings, it was known as a *fabula palliata,* or "comedy in Greek dress." All extant comedies of Republican Rome are of this type, being based on the plots and characters of the Greek NEW COMEDY. This style of comedy, written by Menander, Diphilus, Philemon, and others in the fourth and third centuries B.C., dealt with social problems and was far more cosmopolitan than either Middle Comedy or the still earlier Old Comedy, from which period only the plays of Aristophanes are extant. Of the New Comedy we have only one complete play (DYSKOLOS of Menander), plus several fragmentary plays (also by Menander), all discovered on papyri in the twentieth century. Unfortunately, no Greek original of a Roman comedy has survived.

The poets Naevius (c. 270–201 B.C.) and Ennius (239–169 B.C.) wrote both tragedies and comedies, but PLAUTUS, CAECILIUS, and TERENCE devoted themselves entirely to the palliata. Of Caecilius' work we have only titles and fragments, although one ancient critic, Volcacius Sedigitus, considered him superior to Plautus. More than one hundred comedies are said to have been written by Plautus, but only twenty (and fragments of a twenty-first, *Vidularia*) have survived. These twenty, plus the six composed by Terence, form the extant corpus of Roman comedy. A few titles and fragments remain from the other comic dramatists of the period: Trabea, Atilius, Aquilius, Luscius Lanuvinus, Licinius Imbrex, and Turpilius, who died in 103 B.C. and was the last of the writers of the palliata. (For the creation of a comedy with Roman and Italian characters and settings, see FABULA TOGATA.) In the time of Cicero (first century B.C.) comedies by Plautus, Terence, and Turpilius were still performed on the stage. During the Empire, from the first century A.D. on, the fabula Atellana and especially the mime were the popular forms of dramatic entertainment. One unique comedy, QUEROLUS, with superficial resemblances to Plautus' AULULARIA, survives from the fifth century A.D.

Comedies in the days of Plautus and Terence were regularly produced in connection with Roman religious festivals: the ludi Romani in September in honor of Jupiter; the *ludi plebeii* in October, also dedicated to Jupiter; the *ludi Apollinares* in July, first celebrated in 212 B.C.; and the *ludi Megalenses* in honor of the Great Mother, first celebrated in April 204 B.C. The temple of the goddess on the Palatine was dedicated in 191 B.C., and on this occasion Plautus' *Pseudolus* was first produced. Two of Terence's comedies, ADELPHOE and *Hecyra* (*The Mother-in-Law*), were presented in 160 B.C. at the funeral games for Lucius Aemilius Paulus.

Temporary stages of wood were constructed for each performance, since attempts to build permanent theaters at this time were opposed by the authorities, who looked upon theatrical productions as harmful to public morals. The first permanent stone theater was ordered built by Pompey and was erected in the Campus Martius in 55 B.C. In the earliest period of the Roman theater spectators may have stood during the performance or brought their own stools, but wooden stands were soon provided. The many references to seats in Plautus cannot, as formerly believed, be post-Plautine additions to the plays. The stage, long and narrow, represented a city street, usually in Athens (for one exception, see Plautus' RUDENS). The wooden background consisted of doors providing an entrance to one, two, or three houses. The length of the stage, believed to be as much as 180 feet, made the numerous soliloquies and asides more plausible than they are on the modern stage and also provided excellent opportunities for characters to eavesdrop. The stage exit to the left of the audience led to the harbor and country, that to the right to the center of the city and the forum.

The characters of the palliata apparently always wore masks, signifying character types, as was true of Greek New Comedy, although some have argued that masks were not introduced until after the death of Terence. Female roles were performed by men, and the comedies were produced by companies of five or six actors, with a doubling of the minor roles to provide sufficient performers for each play (for example, Plautus' *Rudens* with thirteen roles, Terence's EUNUCHUS with fourteen). The comedies were played without interruption; the division of each into five acts, as found in modern editions, was made at a much later date and has no meaning for the presentation of Roman comedy in the second century B.C. These verse plays were sometimes spoken in a six-foot iambic meter without music, and other times in more elaborate meters, being recited or sung to a flute accompaniment. (See CANTICUM; DIVERBIUM.)

The extant comedies of Plautus and Terence have been classified as those primarily portraying character and customs; comedies of error, with mistaken identity and later recognition; those in which the comic confusions result from a combination of mistaken identity and deliberate deception; and plays of trickery, in which the misunderstandings are created by the lies and impersonations of one or more characters, usually engineered by an intriguing slave (*servus*), one of the most important roles in Roman comedy. The other characters include the youthful lover (*adulescens*), unable to marry his sweetheart or fearful that he will lose her; the old man (*senex*), who as a parent is either harsh and unsympathetic or excessively lenient, as an aged lover is ridiculous and the object of trickery, and as a helpful friend often assists in the intrigue; various female roles: young girl, wife, courtesan, maid; and numerous professional types: slave dealer, merchant, doctor, moneylender, cook, and especially the braggart warrior—often a rival of the young lover and the object of both deception and ridicule—and the parasite, the "handy" man and professional jokester, always eager for a free meal.

Although the comedies of Plautus and Terence have in general the same themes and types of charac-

WALL PAINTING OF STOCK CHARACTERS, A SLAVE AND A PAIR OF LOVERS (CASA DI CASCA, POMPEII. COURTESY ALINARI-ART REFERENCE BUREAU)

ters, which are all based on Greek New Comedy, the effect of their plays is very different. Plautus, a master of comic effect, whose expert knowledge of stagecraft was equaled by his control of language, handles his originals with considerable freedom, stretching amusing characters to grotesque proportions. His plays are farcical and robust and are especially rich in jokes, puns, wordplay, and comic names, such as Thensaurochrysonicochrysides in CAPTIVI. He violates dramatic illusion by having characters address the audience, has many scenes of song and dance, and, in several plays, festal conclusions that almost justify the term "musical comedy." The ingredients of Plautine comedy are three: Greek New Comedy, the preliterary farces of Italy, and his own contributions as a comic genius, in which respect he is said to rank with Aristophanes and Shakespeare.

Terence is also an innovator in his treatment of the Greek originals but, unlike Plautus, strives for greater artistry and a more subtle portrayal of character. His humor is restrained but often delightful, in spite of the fact that he lacks the exuberance and extravagance of his predecessor, as well as his versatility. Terence's many technical innovations include the substitution of dialogue for monologue, the divorce of the prologue from the action of the comedy, a greater use of surprise, and a preference for the double plot in which two love affairs are skillfully interwoven.

The richness and variety in the twenty-six comedies of Plautus and Terence provided a storehouse of plots, characters, and amusing situations on which later comic dramatists were able to draw. In Renaissance Italy, plays of Plautus and Terence were produced on the stage, new comedies based on the ancient works were composed in Latin, and, most important of all, numerous comedies likewise indebted to the Roman models were presented in Italian. Lodovico Ariosto, Lodovico Dolce, and Giovanni Maria Cecchi, among others, set their plays in contemporary Italy, but basically they reproduced the plots, structure, stock characters, even the conventions, of the palliata. In France numerous versions of Plautus and Terence were made by Jean Antoine de Baïf, Pierre de Larivey, Jean de Rotrou, and Molière, who, although considered more Terentian in spirit, is often Plautine in his use of farcical situations and devices. The list of English dramatists indebted to the two Roman comic writers is long and distinguished; it includes Shakespeare, Ben Jonson, George Chapman, Beaumont and Fletcher, John Marston, Thomas Heywood, and, later, John Dryden, Thomas Shadwell, Charles Sedley, Thomas Cooke, Richard Steele, and Daniel Bellamy. In the eighteenth century the more subtle Terence was favored as a model over Plautus.

George E. Duckworth, *The Nature of Roman Comedy* (1952), discusses the various aspects of the Roman plays, including presentation, stage conventions, plots, characters, thought and moral tone, the comic spirit, language and style, meter and song, originality, and later influence. William Beare, *The Roman Stage* (3rd ed., 1965), gives the history of Roman drama, both comedy and tragedy, from Livius Andronicus to its decline in the Roman Empire, and devotes special attention to the nature of the Roman theater and the staging of the plays. All

twenty-six comedies of Plautus and Terence, plus the late *Querolus,* are translated in George E. Duckworth, ed., *The Complete Roman Drama* (2 vols., 1942). Translations of selected plays include Philip Whaley Harsh, ed., *Anthology of Roman Drama* (1960); George E. Duckworth, ed., *Roman Comedies: An Anthology* (1963); and *Roman Drama* (1965), translated by Frank O. Copley and Moses Hadas. See also translations listed under Plautus and Terence.—G. E. D.

romanesque. In French classical drama the term romanesque designates all that is inspired by or similar to the romances and novels from the works of Lodovico Ariosto (1474–1533) to the French novels of the seventeenth century. Since such works of fiction recount either surprising and extraordinary adventures, with mystery attached to the characters' identities, or exalted and complicated love stories involving perfect lovers, or both at once, the term romanesque is applied to plays in which such characteristics prevail. The role of chance in adventure, the characters' idealization of love, and often their awareness of playing a part according to the prescribed rules are also romanesque traits. The romanesque quality may permeate the plays, as is the case in numerous French tragedies after 1655, or may be merely a device that leads to the denouement, as in certain of Molière's comedies.—Ja. G.

Romeo and Juliet (c. 1595–1596). A tragedy by William SHAKESPEARE. First performed by Lord Hunsdon's Men (the name of Shakespeare's company between July 1596 and April 1597), *The Tragedy of Romeo and Juliet* was initially printed in 1597 in a quarto edition. The First Quarto, a "bad quarto," was followed in 1599 by the Second Quarto, the authoritative text of the play. Of the subsequent three quartos, the Third Quarto—a reprint of the Second Quarto—served as copy for the 1623 First Folio text. The play has as its source Arthur Brooke's long narrative poem *The Tragicall Historye of Romeus and Juliet* (1562).

In Verona, the story relates, live two prominent families—the Montagues and the Capulets—who bear an "ancient grudge" toward one another. Romeo, a Montague, goes to a ball given by the Capulets to see Rosaline, who has rejected him as a suitor. There he meets Juliet, Capulet's daughter, and the two fall in love. In spite of their family enmity, they hasten to a secret marriage. Tybalt, Juliet's hot-tempered kinsman, precipitates a public quarrel with the Montagues. Mercutio, Romeo's friend, incensed by Tybalt's tauntings and Romeo's mild-mannered responses to them, draws his sword upon Tybalt. In the ensuing scuffle, Mercutio is mortally wounded, and Romeo slays Tybalt. The prince of Verona banishes Romeo. Juliet's father, unaware of the true situation, decides that Juliet should be quickly married to Count Paris. To solve her predicament, Friar Laurence gives Juliet a death-simulating potion to be taken on her wedding eve. Romeo will be sent for to remove her from the family vault, and they will flee to Mantua. Through accident, the plans go awry. As a result, Romeo, believing Juliet dead, poisons himself in her tomb; and Juliet, on awakening, stabs herself. The play ends with the realization by the two families that their enmity was responsible for all the deaths.

THE
MOST EX-
cellent and lamentable
Tragedie, of Romeo
and *Iuliet*.

Newly corrected, augmented, and amended:

As it hath bene fundry times publiquely acted, by the right Honourable the Lord Chamberlaine his Seruants.

LONDON
Printed by Thomas Creede, for Cuthbert Burby, and are to be fold at his fhop neare the Exchange.
1599.

TITLE PAGE OF THE "GOOD QUARTO" (1599) OF SHAKESPEARE'S *Romeo and Juliet*

One of the most beloved of Shakespeare's works—as its long production record attests—this tragedy of love is unique among the tragedies. Although the actions of the protagonists and the strife between their families are to some degree responsible for the outcome, a malevolent fate dogs the "star-crossed lovers" from their first to last meeting. Hereafter, Shakespeare would emphasize that man himself is the cause of his undoing. The use of fate as the focal point of responsibility has disturbed some critics, as has the great admixture of comic and tragic scenes in the play. But none will deny the power of the portrayal of pure, innocent love nor the great lyrical beauty of the verse.

An outstanding edition of *Romeo and Juliet* is the New Cambridge Edition (1955), edited by G. I. Duthie and J. Dover Wilson.—W. G.

Romulus the Great (Romulus der Grosse, 1949, revised 1957). A historical comedy without historical basis by Friedrich DÜRRENMATT. The historical facts about Romulus, the last of the Roman emperors, have been changed by Dürrenmatt to suit his own

thematic designs. For example, the historical Romulus was a mere boy of fourteen at the end of the Roman Empire (476) and had ruled less than a single year. Dürrenmatt's Romulus is an old man who has reigned for twenty years. He has ruled simply by *not* ruling. Rather, upon becoming emperor he has retired to his country villa and raised chickens. The result is that the Germanic hordes, under Odoacer, are about to take advantage of Rome's consequent weakness and invade the empire.

Romulus has become emperor solely for this purpose. Over the past twenty years he has skillfully brought Rome to the verge of destruction, a destruction about to become a reality. He declares that he doubts the necessity of the Roman state; it has become an institution so powerful that it has killed, suppressed, and ravaged other peoples—until he, Romulus, came into the picture. Since Rome, says Romulus, has existed only because it has had a powerful emperor, it became his duty to become emperor, and then fail to rule. It was the only way to liquidate the imperium. His wife calls him Rome's betrayer. He retorts that he is Rome's judge; he is destroying it for its sins. He justifies his act by determining to give his own life in order to expiate his betrayal. Interestingly, Romulus is not a pure rationalist who feels self-satisfaction in his act; rather, he is a moralist of a puritanic bent who must justify the deed by his own martyrdom. It is Romulus' desire to change the course of fate; he wants Imperial Rome to fall to its enemies. Of course, he fails.

Romulus expects to be slaughtered on the spot by Odoacer, but the German leader is as much a rationalist-moralist as is Romulus and is equally civilized. Upon entering, Odoacer throws himself at Romulus' feet. It is learned that Odoacer's sole purpose in conquering Italy is to subject himself and his German hordes to Romulus' and Rome's rule, because his nephew, the barbaric Theodoric, will turn the German people into a conquest-mad horde if he gains leadership. Odoacer's only salvation is to subject himself and his people to Rome's greatness, a civilized rather than a barbaric world power, despite its manifest ruthlessness. In defeat Romulus can only accept what fate brings him. He is no longer a judge, and he cannot now be a martyr. He is an old, retired emperor, with Odoacer ruling in his place as a good and watchful emperor. They can only wait for fate to take its course: for Theodoric to rid the world of both of them and resume the barbaric march of history.

Death and power are, typically, Dürrenmatt's themes. Death and destruction are always present, here in the very course of history, looming like a passive but inevitable ogre over the scene of action. Man's acts are all futile in the face of death, though they may not seem so at the time. Death is the common denominator that levels all and renders all absurd. Romulus spends a lifetime working out a scheme of inaction that will result in the beneficial destruction of Rome in his lifetime, under his rule, or lack of rule. But it does not happen. He is driven to a kind of madness under the guise of reason (Dürrenmatt would call it madness because it is idealistic). And thus folly, the curse of idealism, informs this play to a great degree and makes a sardonic comment on man's state and being.

Romulus the Great is in *Four Plays* (1965), translated by Gerhard Nellhaus. It is critically discussed in a volume by George Wellwarth, *The Theater of Protest and Paradox* (1964).—C. R. M.

Ronde, La (Reigen, pub. 1903, prod. 1912). A play in ten scenes by Arthur SCHNITZLER. *La Ronde* met with considerable benighted censorship problems from the time it was first written (1896–1897). Possibly because Schnitzler felt the play was extremely susceptible to misinterpretation, he had it privately printed in 1900, in an edition of two hundred copies, for distribution to his friends. As copies were transferred from one person to another, it soon became a literary sensation. In 1903 Schnitzler permitted a regular publisher's edition to be printed, but it was summarily attacked as subversive and obscene. Papers refused to review it; a public reading in Vienna was curtailed by the police; Germany confiscated and banned the publication. When an unauthorized production was mounted in Budapest in 1912, it was offensively and tastelessly performed and consequently banned by the police. The play caused subsequent riots in Munich and Berlin, occasioned a trial, and was even discussed in the Austrian parliament. Finally, in 1921, it received its Viennese première, causing further demonstrations, including proto-Nazi protests that it was "Jewish filth."

La Ronde is a series of ten "dialogues," each between a man and a woman, each leading to sexual consummation. The ten participants bridge the entire range of society, from the Prostitute, to the Soldier, the Parlormaid, the Young Gentleman, the Young Wife, the Husband, the Sweet Young Thing, the Poet, the Actress, and the Count. Beginning with the Prostitute and the Soldier, each succeeding scene utilizes the person representative of the next highest class from the scene before. Thus, the second scene engages the Soldier and the Parlormaid. In the final scene the Count and the Prostitute, of the first scene, are brought together; the highest and the lowest are reduced to a common denominator.

Schnitzler's most famous play, *La Ronde* is more than a series of sexual encounters; it is a keen and incisive picture of its time fully and succinctly realized as drama of psychological-sociological criticism. The uniting thread of the dialogues is the deception involved in the supposed act of love. The guiding motive behind each couple's physical consummation is the ideal of love, but in the end only animal passion has been expended. The final coup is insensitivity and egocentric unconcern for the former lover. Systematically, perhaps even to the point of cruelty, Schnitzler lays bare the inadequacy of mere sexual love and demonstrates with extreme dramatic economy the emptiness of the life of his time.

The latest translation of Schnitzler's play is by Carl R. Mueller, in the anthology *Masterpieces of the Modern Central European Theater* (1967), edited by Robert Corrigan.—C. R. M.

Rope, The. See Eugene O'NEILL.

Rosso di San Secondo, Pier Luigi Maria (1887–1956). Italian writer and playwright. Rosso di San Secondo was born in Caltanisetta, Sicily, of a noble family and was educated in Rome. He traveled a great deal, particularly in northern Europe, and it was during his travels that he published some of his most successful narrative works. Rosso gained sudden fame with his play *Marionette che passione!*, a play about three people who confess to and conflict with each other in a restaurant and who are nothing more than puppets totally controlled by their almost insane passions. This play signaled Rosso's originality as an author and was followed by several novels, short stories, and plays. Among the latter are *La Madre* ("The Mother," 1918), *La Bella addormentata* (1919), *La Scala* ("The Stairway," 1925), and finally *Tre vestiti che ballano* ("Three Dresses Who Dance," 1927), which concludes the author's period of most intense and prolific activity. Rosso's theater was open to various influences, from Pirandello's "theater of ideas" to the "theater of the grotesque," from symbolism to expressionism. Its most personal characterisics are Rosso's style, both lyrical and eminently literary, and his tragic sense of everyday life. His most successful and significant texts illustrate humble events in a chronicler's style, but the characters who live through them appear in the writer's fantasy like tragic puppets, driven by invisible and uncontrollable forces, who drag themselves and stumble on the scene of life, unable to distinguish between will and necessity, between reality and illusion.—L. L.

Rostand, Edmond [Eugène Alexis] (1868–1918). French playwright and poet. Rostand's fame rests upon his reawakening and briefly perpetuating, at the height of the naturalistic period, the Romantic spirit, born some seventy years prior to the climax of his career and long believed dead. In characterization, craftsmanship, and style he also improved upon the typically Romantic dramas that influenced him. But only once, in CYRANO DE BERGERAC, was he able to create a genuinely dramatic play that sparkled with poetry and was unified by sound craftsmanship. From a fusion of character and situation he gave his

EDMOND ROSTAND (WALTER HAMPDEN MEMORIAL LIBRARY AT THE PLAYERS, NEW YORK)

central character at the same time a rare gusto and a touching sadness.

Born in Marseille of wealthy, cultured parents, Rostand was endowed with the poetic, idealistic, and flamboyant temperament of the southern Gascon. Before attracting attention in the theater, he studied law and literature in Paris, published a slim volume of poems (1890), married the poetess Rosemonde Gérard, and wrote two ineffectual plays, one of which, *Le Gant rouge* ("The Red Glove"), was unsuccessfully performed in 1890, and the other, *Les Deux Pierrots* ("The Two Pierrots"), was neither performed nor published. *Les Romanesques* (*The Romantics*) was successfully performed at the Comédie Française in 1894. A romantic, fanciful variation of the Romeo and Juliet theme, taking place "wherever you please, provided the costumes are pretty," it satirizes the romantic naïveté of the adolescent lovers Percinet and Sylvette. After wandering independently in search of love, they find it together at home, proving that happiness lies within one's self. Rostand's next play, *La Princesse lointaine* (*The Faraway Princess,* performed in 1895 by Sarah Bernhardt), is a more sophisticated and serious development of the theme of the elusive quest for love —for the unattainable ideal. An idealistic hero, the troubadour-poet Joffroy Rudel, is betrayed by his friend for the love of Melissinde, princess of Tripoli, but at last dies in her arms, believing that he possesses her in death. Here is the first of the ironic "grand gestures" of Rostand that reach their climax in the disparity between the grandiloquence of Cyrano's dying speech and his commonplace death. The unsuccessful *La Samaritaine* ("The Woman of Samaria," also performed by Sarah Bernhardt in 1897) depicts Christ's conversion of the woman at the well. The première of *Cyrano de Bergerac* in December 1897 brought unbounded relief to audiences weary of twenty years of sordid naturalistic dramas.

In 1899 ill health forced Rostand to retire at thirty-one to his country estate at Cambon in his native Basque region. There, in quiet seclusion with his wife and two sons, he completed *L'Aiglon* (*The Eaglet*), performed in Paris in 1900 with Sarah Bernhardt playing the weak eaglet, the duke of Reichstadt, Napoleon's son by his Austrian wife. The play dramatizes the duke's futile conflict between ambition and conscience and his demise after seeing in a vision the victims of his father's conquests on the Wagram battlefield. Less spontaneous than *Cyrano*, too deliberately constructed, with a theme too narrowly patriotic, the play was a disappointment after its predecessor, but it was nevertheless successful in France and other countries.

The idea of writing a symbolic play with actors in the roles of barnyard animals had been in Rostand's mind since he moved to the country. When his health permitted, he worked on *Chantecler* (1910), which, in contrast to his plays drawn from French history, reflected Rostand's observation of nature. Despite its lyric beauty, the play was not successful because the serious theme (the correspondence on several planes of the cock and the pheasant hen with man and woman) was dwarfed by the costuming—rooster feathers. It was judged too clever, too obscure, too long. The trifling *Le Bois sacré* ("The Sacred Wood"), a pantomime parody of the Greek gods, was also performed in 1910. At his death Rostand had almost completed *La Dernière Nuit de Don Juan* (*The Last Night of Don Juan,* not performed until 1921).

Although *Cyrano* is his only masterpiece, *L'Aiglon, Chantecler,* and *La Dernière Nuit de Don Juan* are not without certain merits of their own. All are characterized by wit, grace, satire, and lyrical beauty. All reveal the virtuosity, technical skill, and idealism of which Rostand is master. He is indebted to Victor Hugo for his rhythm and versification, but his characters are more consistent than Hugo's. *L'Aiglon* reminds one of De Musset in its Hamlet-like theme of an indecisive hero struggling between an ideal goal and a guilty conscience. It is a strange hybrid of naturalistic and Romantic tendencies in its emphasis on heredity and its pathetic evocation of a lost grandeur. Even though *Chantecler* has not been effective on the stage, it is a satirical, yet sympathetic and even profound, portrait of man and woman. Bitter wisdom characterizes *La Dernière Nuit de Don Juan,* not one of Rostand's best plays. A novel, interesting twist is given the old Spanish legend of the deceiver of women. The sentimental idealist who is unsure of his ideal is condemned. Because Don Juan has seduced women in vain pursuit of a nebulous ideal, he possesses none of them; he has created nothing in his life. In the two best plays, *Cyrano* and *Chantecler,* a defensively aggressive hero and one nourished by intoxicating illusions heroically triumph over the disenchanting realities of life. Rostand too transformed the ugly facts of his life—his illness and forced retirement—into victory.

Six of Rostand's plays have been translated. The Barrett Clark translation of *Les Romanesques* is in *The Genius of the French Theater* (1961), edited by A. Bermel, together with an introduction and two critical essays. There is no biography in English. G. Jean-Aubry's essay in *The Fortnightly Review* (January 1919) is good. G. K. Chesterton's *Five Types* (1911), Ludwig Lewisohn's *The Modern Drama* (1915), and H. A. Smith's *Main Currents of Modern French Drama* (1925) include interesting studies. —S. S. S.

Roswitha. See HROTSVITHA.

Rotrou, Jean de (1609–1650). French playwright. Born in Dreux, in southern Normandy, into a very old family of gentry, Jean Rotrou studied law in Paris. There he made friends with writers and the actors of the Hôtel de Bourgogne, for whom he began to provide plays: Around 1634 he had already written over thirty of them to order. But once under the patronage of eminent men, including Cardinal Richelieu himself, he was able to write more at his leisure. Named civil lieutenant of Dreux, Rotrou returned there to live in 1639. He died heroically, it would seem, in a plague that devastated Dreux in 1650.

Of Rotrou's very abundant works, some thirty plays of every genre have survived. He was particularly prolific until around 1640. While he began with a tragicomedy, his first success was a decorous comedy in accordance with the new taste of the period, *La Bague de l'oubli* ("The Ring of Oblivion," 1629), a comedy inspired by Lope de Vega, who was also the source of Rotrou's *Diana* (1632), a comedy of intrigue but of "regular" form. In the meantime he had transformed Plautus' *Menaechmi* into *Les Menechmes* (1631) and then based his *Les Sosies* (1637) on

Plautus' *Amphitryon* and his *Les Captifs* (1638) on Plautus' *Captivi*. In 1634 Rotrou's *Hercule mourant* ("Hercules Dying"), a regular tragedy following the tenets of French classicism, preceded Jean Mairet's *Sophonisbe* by a few months but did not have the same profound influence. Rotrou, on the one hand, remained faithful to ROMANESQUE or Spanish-type tragicomedy, writing seventeen of them, including *Laure persécutée* ("Laura Persecuted," 1637), which has been compared to the work of Shakespeare. On the other hand, he was drawn to Greek subject matter: *Antigone* (1637), *Iphigénie* (1640).

After 1640 his activity slowed down, but it was during this period that he wrote his best plays. The comedy *La Sœur* ("The Sister," 1645/46) is the finest example of five-act high comedy in verse inspired by the Italian Renaissance, for it is filled with the disguises, false identities, and kidnapping by pirates typical of the genre, all of which endanger the characters (here the main danger is incest) but lead to a happy ending, with the help of a crafty valet. From 1644 to 1648 Rotrou had his best tragedies performed, certain of which were first called tragicomedies: *Bélisaire* (1644), SAINT GENEST, and *Venceslas* (1647), all three based on Spanish plays, and finally, *Cosroès* (1648).

A contemporary and an admirer of Pierre Corneille, Rotrou was considered almost his equal in his best plays. Like Corneille, he chose for his tragedies the inner conflicts and surprising deeds that provoke heroic transcendency and the passionate exigency of self-affirmation, and he showed the grandeur of that attitude as well as the catastrophes it led to. Initiated in the French classical rules since 1632 by the learned and, in particular, by Jean Chapelain, Rotrou, while remaining very independent and attached to certain baroque forms and themes, was, with Pierre Corneille, the most vigorous representative of the first period of French classical theater.

For detailed information on Rotrou and his works, see Henry C. Lancaster, *A History of French Dramatic Literature of the Seventeenth Century*, 9 vols. (1952).—Ja. G.

Rowe, Nicholas (1674–1718). English tragic playwright. Rowe was a student of law, but upon his father's death in 1692 he became a man of independent means and chose to pursue his literary interests. He was well read and possessed an extensive knowledge of foreign literatures. To his wide acquaintance among the literary men of the period, Rowe was known not only as a dramatist but also for his edition of Shakespeare's plays (1709) and his later verse translation of the epic *Pharsalia* by the Roman poet Lucan (A.D. 39–65). Rowe's blank-verse tragedies, avowedly designed to communicate terror and, above all, pity, gave to pathetic tragedy, which had already appeared in the last decades of the seventeenth century, the form it retained throughout the eighteenth century. His earliest tragedy, *The Ambitious Stepmother* (1700), while not a failure, did not enjoy the success attending his second effort, *Tamerlane* (1701). In this play Rowe, an ardent Whig, gave to his central figure the political features of King William III, and a tradition grew up of acting the play annually in commemoration of the Glorious Revolution and of William's landing in England in 1688. *The Fair Penitent* (1703) is a far better work and is

remembered as the first of Rowe's three "she-tragedies," plays depicting unfortunate heroines. *The Biter* (1704) was his only venture into prose comedy, and was followed by two tragedies, *Ulysses* (1705) and *The Royal Convert* (1707), the latter fiercely Protestant in tone. His career as a dramatist closed with his best-known play, *Jane Shore* (1714), and the last of the she-tragedies, *Lady Jane Gray* (1715).

Rowe's verse is not often memorable, but it never offends and it "speaks" effectively. His plots are skillfully handled and clearly focused; occasionally they afford highly striking scenes. He suffers from a limited sensibility, which sees events as merely lamentable. Human experience at the extreme edge of endurance lies outside the grasp of Rowe's tragic imagination.

There is no modern collected edition of Rowe's works. The best biographical account and the best critical commentary are in *Three Plays*, *"Tamerlane," "The Fair Penitent," "Jane Shore"* (1929), edited by James R. Sutherland.—R. Q.

Rowley, Samuel (c. 1575–1624). English playwright and actor. Throughout most of his career Rowley was an actor with the Lord Admiral's Men, the chief rival of Shakespeare's company. He is the author of two biblical plays, *Joshua* and *Judas*, and a play about Richard III, none of which is extant. His only extant play is *When You See Me, You Know Me* (produced between 1603 and 1605), a chronicle play based on the reign of Henry VIII. In 1602 Rowley and William Bird revised Christopher Marlowe's *Dr. Faustus*, adding to the play a comic underplot. To Rowley has also been attributed the authorship of *The Taming of a Shrew*, the presumed source of Shakespeare's play.—E. Q.

Rowley, William (1585?–?1642). English actor and playwright. It has been suggested that Rowley was the brother of the actor-dramatist Samuel Rowley, but no evidence of such a relationship exists. Rowley spent most of his career as an actor with Prince Charles's Men, switching over to the King's Men in 1623, a few years before his death. As a playwright, he is chiefly known for his collaborations with Thomas Middleton. The best known of these are THE CHANGELING and *A Fair Quarrel* (1617), for which Rowley wrote the comic subplots, and *The Spanish Gypsy* (1623), although some doubt has been cast on Middleton and Rowley's authorship of this play. The best known of the plays ascribed solely to Rowley is *The Birth of Merlin* (c. 1608). First published in 1662 as "Written by William Shakespear and William Rowley," its inclusion in the Shakespeare apocrypha is the chief claim to fame of this otherwise undistinguished play.—E. Q.

Roy, D. L. See PAKISTAN: *Bengali drama*.

Rudens (The Rope). A comedy by PLAUTUS, probably produced in his middle period (200–192 B.C.), and based on a Greek play by Diphilus. *Rudens*, considered by many to be Plautus' masterpiece, is primarily a comedy of mistaken identity and recognition. It is unique among the extant plays of Roman comedy in that the setting is not the usual street scene and houses of Athens or some other Greek city, but a lonely stretch of seacoast near Cyrene in North Africa, with a cottage of the aged Daemones and a temple of Venus in the background. The action begins in the morning after a storm and a shipwreck. The survivors who straggle ashore include Palaestra, one of Plautus' most attractive maidens; Ampelisca, a slave girl; Labrax, a dealer in slaves; and Charmides, an old man and a friend of Labrax. A fisherman, Gripus, pulls a trunk ashore in his net, and trinkets found in the trunk enable Palaestra to prove that she is the long-lost daughter of Daemones. The play combines romance and comedy and has an unusually high religious and moral tone.

Modern adaptations include Lodovico Dolce's *Il Ruffiano* (1560) and Thomas Heywood's *The Captives* (1624).—G. E. D.

Rudkin, [James] David (1936–   ). English playwright. Rudkin was born in London, the son of a Nonconformist minister. With his first play, *Afore Night Come* (1962), he appeared as one of the first exponents of a type of ritual drama that has since haunted the English theater, and particularly the Royal Shakespeare Company, which first presented Rudkin's work. The play is set in a rural pocket of the Black Country, where a group of casual laborers are at work in a pear orchard. The naturalistic style (much strengthened by the local dialect) changes with the arrival of an outsider, a work-shy Irishman who is silently marked down as a sacrificial victim. Knives are sharpened, and in the climactic scene he is murdered and decapitated while a plane overhead sprays the orchard with insecticide. The drama draws at once on the ritual ecstasy of Greek legend, the tribal blood sacrifice in Frazerian anthropology, and such local traditions as the unsolved "witchcraft murder" that took place in the Midlands in 1945.

Since 1962 no play by Rudkin has appeared in the theater. His subsequent work, for the Western Theatre Ballet (*The Stone Dance,* 1963) and for television (*Children Playing,* 1967), remains preoccupied with the same themes of intrusion and mob frenzy.—I. W.

Rumania. Long isolated from Western Europe by the political domination of the Turks and the geographical position of the Slavs, Rumania did not develop a unified national culture until the nineteenth century. Prior to that time in the old principalities that now comprise Rumania—Moldavia, Wallachia, Transylvania, and Bessarabia—the Oriental influence was evident in the popular puppet plays derived from the Turkish *Karagöz.* Primitive dramatic structures were also a prominent part of religious pageants and festivals, which were a pervasive feature of Rumanian folk culture.

A potent factor in the Westernization of Rumania was the political and cultural power of France. Aligned with this influence was the newly awakened sense of national consciousness prompted by the emphasis of Rumanian scholars and intellectuals on the Latin heritage of the country.

One outgrowth of this developing consciousness was the formation of dramatic societies by two distinguished Rumanian scholars, Ian Eliade (1802–1869) and George Asachi (1788–1869). These societies formed the nucleus of the National Theatre, established in 1840. One of the first directors of the National Theatre was Vasile Alecsandri (1821–1890). A prolific writer, he provided the new theater with plays ranging from vaudeville pieces to dramas based upon national legends. His most successful play is *Iorgu de la Sadagura* (1844), a comedy focus-

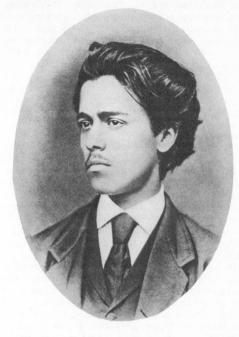

IOAN LUCA P. CARAGIALE (NEW YORK PUBLIC LIBRARY)

ing on the opposition of older people to the newly introduced Western customs. A contemporary of Alecsandri was Bogdan Hasdeu (1838–1907), whose *Dominita Rosada* (1868) represents the first successful historical tragedy in the Rumanian theater.

The pioneer activity of Alecsandri, Hasdeu, and others set the stage for the appearance of Rumania's greatest dramatist, Ioan Luca P. Caragiale (1853–1912). The son and grandson of actors, Caragiale's natural impulse to write for the stage was buttressed by his association with the group known as Junimea ("Youth"), a literary circle founded and led by the critic and theoretician Titu Maiorescu (1840–1919). Essentially conservative in its political and social attitudes, the Junimea provided Caragiale with a philosophical basis for his sharply satiric representation of middle-class aspirations of his day. Ironically, although Caragiale's satire was rooted in his conservatism, he is extolled today in communist Rumania simply as a critic of bourgeois society. Caragiale's greatest play is *O scrisoáre pierdutá* ("A Lost Letter," 1844), a searing satire of political and moral corruption in a provincial town. Equally striking in its indictment of moral hypocrisy is *O noápte fortunoása* ("A Stormy Night," 1878) and *De ale carnavalului* ("Carnival Scenes," 1885). Less successful were Caragiale's essays into serious psychological dramas, such as *Năpasta* ("False Witness," 1889), in which a wife drives her husband to his doom.

By the turn of the century the Rumanian theater was dominated by social and historical drama. An outstanding example of the former is *Manasse* (1900) by Ronetti Roman (1853–1908). A powerful and compelling story, *Manasse* deals with the assimilation of Jews into Rumanian society and the consequent dissolution of old traditions. Outstanding among historical plays of the period is a trilogy written by Barbu Delavrancea (1858–1918, real name Stefănéscu). Based upon the career of Stephen the Great, a fifteenth-century king of Moldavia, Delavrancea's trilogy—*Apus de soare* ("The Sunset"), *Viforul* ("The Storm"), and *Luceafărul* ("The Morning Star")—was first produced in 1900. Its purpose was to revive the faltering national spirit of the time. Another successful historical drama of the period was *Vláicu Vadă* ("Prince Vlaicu," 1902).

Noteworthy among the playwrights of the early twentieth century were Ion Slavici (1848–1925), who analyzed with compassion and skill the soul of the Rumanian peasant in such plays as *Moara cu Noroc* ("Mill of Good Fortune," 1908); Nicholas Iorga (1871–1940), who continued the tradition of historical drama in *Tudor Vladimirescu* (1922) and *Cleopatra* (1940); and Victor Eftima (1889–   ), who employed poetic fantasy and symbolism in such plays as *Story Without End* (1911) and *The Black Cock* (1913).

After the establishment of a communist regime following World War II, the Rumanian theater was dominated by Socialist Realism, which has been the hallmark of drama written in a communist state. With the liberalization of the ruling regime, however, Rumanian playwrights have begun to experiment with more imaginative and adventurous modes of dramatic expression. Two notable recent examples of this trend have been Ecsterina Aproiou's *I Am*

Not the Eiffel Tower (1964), which effectively employs modern cinematic technique, and Aurel Baranga's *Public Opinion* (1967), a Pirandello-like exploration into the nature of reality.

The best treatment of Rumanian drama is to be found in P. Hanes's *Histoire de la littérature roumane* (1934). A competent history in English is M. M. Coleman's "Rumanian Drama" in *A History of Modern Drama* (1947), edited by Barrett H. Clark and George Freedley.—E. Q.

R.U.R. : Rossum's Universal Robots (1921). A utopian drama by Karel ČAPEK. Celebrated for its use of robots on the stage, it was this play that introduced the word robot (from Czech *robota,* "toil" or "servitude") into the languages of the world. The play's title is in English in the original. The author described his work as a "collective drama," and the central symbol of the robot, which embodies the threat of modern technological civilization to dehumanize man, is conceived under the influence of contemporary German expressionist drama. In the play the robots, artificial men who closely resemble humans, seize power and wipe out mankind. But they are unable to reproduce until a biological miracle occurs: two of the younger robots fall in love. Thus, the author optimistically concludes that mankind will survive even the threat of his own technology to dehumanize or destroy him. See William E. Harkins' *Karel Čapek* (1962).—W. E. H.

Russia: *before 1780.* The seeds of the native theater in Russia, as in other lands, sprang from the universal

A SCENE FROM KAREL ČAPEK'S *R.U.R.* (THEATRE COLLECTION, NEW YORK PUBLIC LIBRARY AT LINCOLN CENTER)

human impulse to imitate and playact. Just as in the rest of the world, people mimed at pagan and Christian seasonal rites, and the itinerant *skomorokh* ("mummer," or "merryman") of ancient Russia was in many ways similar to the Greek faun or the Germanic *Spielman* ("mummer"). To the accompaniment of his native guitar (the *gusli*), the skomorokh sang his songs, performed with trained animals (mostly bears), and gave crude puppet shows. He traveled from village to village and was sometimes invited to give shows in the houses of rich boyars. Some rich princes and early tsars of Muscovy hired for their courts permanent troupes of skomorokhi, who thus became their private entertainers.

Because of Russia's geographical remoteness and her periods of political isolation, foreign influences on Russian cultural development in general, and on the theater in particular, were exerted by an irregular succession of waves from the more sophisticated West. Each of these waves eventually combined with the indigenous theatrical forms to produce a new, native art form. Then a new wave came to upset the balance again and superimpose new, alien forms on the existing amalgam.

An example of such early cultural imports was the Catholic morality play that reached Kiev via Poland in the sixteenth century. Although Russia had her own morality plays, they were very simple affairs, performed inside the churches in Church Slavonic, the language in which the services were conducted and which was easily understood by the worshippers. The Western morality plays, on the other hand, were much more elaborate and were performed outdoors in public squares, and usually in the vernacular rather than in Latin, since their real purpose was to elucidate the meaning of the sacred Latin texts. These imported plays eventually inspired such Russian playwrights as St. Dmitry of Rostov (d. 1709); his *Strast Khristova* ("Christ's Passion") and *Esfir i Akhashvir* ("Esther and Ahasuerus") became part of the repertory of itinerant actors for many decades and with time these works acquired more and more native Russian elements. Around the same time Polish puppet shows, considerably more sophisticated and more elaborate than the crude indigenous variety, reached Russia and radically changed that form of entertainment.

However, it was only under Tsar Alexei, who ruled from 1645 to 1676, that Russia made a deliberate effort "to catch up with the West" in the realm of the theater. Russian emissaries were sent to Germany to recruit actors, while the pastor of Moscow's German Lutheran Church, Johann Gregory, staged German religious plays in translation at the newly founded Imperial Theater in Moscow. The first of these plays was based on the story of Esther and called *Artakserksovo Deystvo* (*Artaxerxes Play*, 1672). The repertory of this first government-sponsored theater was made up of both the old plays that had been performed at the Kiev Theological Academy and the Western imports adapted to suit Russian audiences. At this time the Russian theater acquired a characteristic that has, to a greater or lesser extent, survived to this day. Since the theater was financed out of the treasury of the tsar, all those who worked in the theater were considered government employees and

therefore had to conform to the wishes of the monarch. Thus, the playwrights often stressed and stretched resemblances between the ruling tsar and some noble, heroic, biblical king.

Peter the Great, who reigned from 1682 to 1725, was determined to "Europeanize" Russia as rapidly as possible. He started by trying to eradicate Russia's Byzantine ways and he saw in the theater an efficient medium to achieve that goal. He imported wholesale from Germany a theatrical company headed by Johann Kunst. In 1702, in order to reach a larger audience, he moved the Imperial Theater from the palace grounds to Moscow's Red Square and later, in 1709, he established the St. Petersburg Imperial Theater in his new capital. Not only did this give Russian audiences an opportunity to see some of the latest Western plays (among others, adaptations of Pierre Corneille), but it also enabled Kunst and his successor Otto Furst to train native talent in foreign acting and playwriting styles.

Peter's overwhelming personality left a very deep imprint on the theater of his time. Both the foreign plays and the native imitations of them were tailored to the political needs of the moment (such as combating the influence of the clergy) and, of course, the tsar believed that the function of the theater was to justify and glorify his every action. When, for instance, Peter decided to replace his unattractive empress with a pretty German princess, a new version of *Esther* was staged in which the biblical king was depicted as selfless and noble in his decision to send away his unlovely wife and unite instead with a foreign paragon of beauty and virtue.

Under Empress Anna, who ruled ten years, from 1730 to 1740, the Russian theater remained under essentially German domination (a new company imported from Leipzig was to stay permanently in Russia); but the Italian influence began to be felt with the arrival of the *commedia dell'arte* and of the composer Francesco Araia, whose *Semiramis* and *Bellerophon* had sensational success with Russian audiences. At the same time Italian ballet was introduced into Russia by Antonio Fusano, who, however, was soon overshadowed by the Frenchman Jean Baptiste Landet when the French ballet was brought to Russia.

In the time of Anna's successor, Elizabeth, who ruled from 1741 to 1762, German influence in the theater was superseded by the French. Plays by Molière, Jean Racine, and Corneille were performed both in the national theater and the private theaters that had been authorized by the empress's decree of 1750. Inspired by the French classics, such Russian plays as the tragedy *Khorev* (1747), by Alexander Sumarokov (1718–1777), strictly followed the classical conventions of the unity of time, place, and action. And although these pseudoclassical dramas pleased the audiences, artistically the works were still quite alien and unassimilated. Pushkin later described them as misconceived, pompous, and sentimental. Sumarokov's "classical" version of *Hamlet*, expurgated of what were called its "vulgarities," is characteristic of the tragedies performed in this period.

On the other hand, a native development in Russian drama was introduced by Fyodor Volkov (1729–

1763), the son of a merchant, who, after a visit to St. Petersburg, became so interested in the theater that he returned to his home town of Yaroslavl and organized, together with his brother, a theatrical company. That company was so successful that its reputation reached Empress Elizabeth. She summoned Volkov and his group to the capital to perform at her court the old morality play called "The Repentant Sinner," in which angels and demons battle for the soul of man. The empress was greatly impressed by their production and she invited the Yaroslavl actors to stay in the capital "to study dramatic arts and to impart their knowledge to others," thereby creating a pool of Russian acting talent.

At one point Elizabeth was so obsessed with the desire to produce a truly national drama that she ordered a sort of "crash program" by mobilizing men who had made a name for themselves in other literary fields to take up playwriting. Among this group was the foremost Russian scientist and poet, Mikhail Lomonosov. He tried to write plays, but his carefully tailored tragedies turned out to be pretty dull.

In 1756 a new theater was established on Vassilevsky Island in the Neva, with Sumarokov as its director and with actors paid monthly salaries from the government treasury (with foreigners paid at much higher rates than Russians). The Vassilevsky Island theater staged many of Molière's comedies— *Tartuffe, École des maris,* and *Le Bourgeois Gentilhomme,* which was extremely successful with Russian audiences.

Catherine the Great acceded to the throne in 1762 and almost at once the theater was used to glorify the young empress: a drama festival was organized by Sumarokov and the Volkov brothers under the title of *Triumf Minervy* ("The Triumph of Minerva"). Soon Catherine became so interested in drama that she took to writing plays herself, or at least to gracing with her signature plays written by others. It was during her reign that the Bolshoi Theater was founded in 1779, and, like other imperial theaters, it was managed and controlled by the government. In some cases, however, the government licensed private theaters belonging to wealthy landowners. These theaters were much freer from central control and, when the owner was a man of taste and culture, often achieved exceptionally high standards (for example, the groups of Prince Yusopov and Count Sheremetiev). In these theaters, however, the actors were usually serfs whose positions were very precarious, as they could be traded or sold by their owners without their consent. Some actor-serfs, however, became very famous and earned their emancipation as a reward for their talents.

During the eighteenth century, a great many plays were staged in Russia, including tragedies by Racine and Corneille, comedies by Molière and Beaumarchais, and a number of works by Shakespeare, Goethe, Voltaire, and Carlo Goldoni. Gradually, under the influence of all these masterpieces, a stock of two or three hundred plays by Russians came into existence. Among these, the tragedies were rather crude imitations of their foreign prototypes; often, the settings of the foreign plays were merely moved to Russian locales. None of these imitations has survived, although at the time they had considerable

success with the Russian audiences, who were delighted to see scenes from their familiar Russian history and to hear the characters address each other by everyday Russian names. Indeed, some contemporaries, in their praise of Sumarokov's tragedies, went so far as to call him "the Russian Racine."

The imitators of Molière and Beaumarchais fared a bit better because their comedies, set in a humbler social environment, retained some genuinely native Russian folk features, which could be traced back to the skomorokhi, along with elements assimilated from earlier cultural imports from Poland and Germany. Nevertheless, even the comedies remained recognizably imitative and synthetic until in 1781 the exceptional talent of Denis Fonvizin succeeded in organically uniting all these disparate elements and producing a truly original Russian comedy—*The Minor.*

late eighteenth and nineteenth centuries. It was not until Fonvizin that the Russian theater really set out on its own original path and, developing in an atmosphere of rarefied freedom, it reached its high-water mark and attained European prominence at the turn of the twentieth century with the work of Anton Chekhov. Soon thereafter, however, the tsarist censorship was superseded by the more efficient Soviet controls, which gradually grew more and more stringent, and Russian drama, like the other forms of Russian art, suffocated from the lack of freedom.

Thus, the history of real Russian drama extends over only about 150 years, from the 1780's, when Catherine the Great was on the throne, until the 1930's, when the invention of Socialist Realism under Stalin silenced a highly talented generation of writers and playwrights by reducing them to mere deliverers of the party message.

Noteworthy is the fact that while the complete lack of freedom was finally to choke the Russian theater, it was just this scarcity of freedom that pushed it along its unique path of development and brought it in the nineteenth century to a position of prominence that paralleled the "golden age" of Russian literature. The explanation for this apparent paradox is quite obvious. In a society with restricted freedom of expression, art forms become the natural vehicles for voicing dissent. The Russian rulers, who were acutely aware from the start that the theater could be a platform for the dissemination of dangerous ideas, tried to forestall that danger by subsidizing the theater with government funds, thus turning playwrights, directors, and actors into civil servants of a kind. And, as could well have been expected, under a number of rulers, including Catherine the Great and Stalin, many plays were deliberately adapted or entirely rewritten to suit the purposes of those in power, or at least to flatter them, in order to guarantee the immunity of the author and the work. The trouble was that such efforts were doomed to failure, proved artistic flops, and were soon forgotten. It is doubtful, moreover, that the authorities ever derived any considerable advantage from these unconvincing tirades about the greatness of the tyrant, because convincingness is a function of artistry, which in turn depends on sincerity.

No tyranny other than total tyranny, however, can silence people who think and possess a talent for artistic expression. Such people will follow their urge to express their dissatisfaction with the existing regime and their longing for something better. In tsarist Russia this could not be done in public political statements or in openly nonconformist political or philosophical essays. Only those people talented enough to transmute their ideas into the literary forms of fiction or drama could afford to express themselves. They had to convey their feelings and ideas through the overall emotional impact left on the audience. Therefore, only by expressing independent and unorthodox ideas in an artistic manner did they have any chance of surviving censorship and reaching the public.

It is because of this situation that novelists and playwrights in Russia, perhaps more than anywhere else in the world, were engaged in politics and philosophy; these writers felt they were the only ones capable of circumventing the censorship of the state and the church. This situation also explains why a disproportionate amount of importance was given to Russian literary and drama critics, who were placed in the position of licensed political commentators and who often concentrated more on extracting and evaluating the social message than on judging the artistic merits of the work.

But even the special gifts that enabled the best Russian writers and playwrights to perform magnificently in the face of the tsarist censorship eventually proved helpless against the *active* Soviet controls. Under Soviet rule an author was expected to endorse the regime actively and to deliver whatever message was demanded of him: the greatness of the leader, the importance of collectivization and industrialization, the strengthening of the armed forces, the wickedness of the capitalist enemy, and so on. In fact, a writer had to deliver that message loudly enough to be heard by the innumerable vigilantes who were only too eager to denounce him for indifference or betrayal. And, of course, artistry is a delicate and brittle item that soon disintegrates under the threat of a club.

The comedies of Denis FONVIZIN, *Brigadir* (*The Brigadier,* 1769) and particularly THE MINOR, contain an artistically integrated ideological message that is found again and again in the mainstream of the Russian theater, because every Russian playwright worth his salt felt duty-bound to use his talent to express thoughts and feelings that could not be voiced otherwise. Moreover, Fonvizin demonstrated how much more effectively such a message could be conveyed by a play set in everyday surroundings familiar to the audience than in one set in the synthetic, outlandish locale borrowed from foreign tragedies that was so often used by his contemporaries. He also demonstrated how vivid, individualized, and colloquial the dialogue of a Russian comedy could be. Indeed, *The Minor* turned out to be such an entertaining and thought-provoking comedy that it remained an unmatched model and inspiration for Russian playwrights for almost half a century, until another man of exceptional talent, Alexander GRIBOYEDOV, a high civil servant like Fonvizin, produced his sparkling comedy WOE FROM WIT in 1824. This play achieved the excellence of and continued the tradition established in *The Minor.*

Besides the Fonvizin-Griboyedov school, in which plays were set in native middle-class or even humbler surroundings, the Russian theater also had a Romantic tradition, started by the greatest Russian poet, Alexander PUSHKIN, in whose Shakespearean BORIS GODUNOV and miniature tragedies (such as *Kamyenni gost, The Stone Guest,* 1830) legendary and historical characters move against an exalted background. But, because of censorship difficulties, Pushkin's plays were not staged in his lifetime and thus they did not exert the influence they might have. This fact is also true of *Maskarad* ("The Masquerade"), a Romantic drama written by Russia's other great poet, Mikhail Lermontov (1814–1841). This play, written in 1835, was not produced for almost thirty years. This censorship, however, did not completely destroy the Romantic tradition, and between 1865 and 1870 the poet Alexei Tolstoy (1817–1875) wrote in blank verse his historical trilogy *Smert Ivana Groznogo* (*The Death of Ivan the Terrible*), *Tsar Fyodor Ivanovich,* and *Tsar Boris,* three highly imaginative, well-constructed historical plays with lively, interesting characters.

For various reasons, in particular the censors' special nervousness about historical tragedies for fear that the ruling monarch might suspect or imagine some unpleasant parallel with the present, the Romantic dramatic impulses in Russia were for the most part transferred to opera and ballet. On the other hand, the down-to-earth school that followed the Fonvizin-Griboyedov tradition soon became enriched by Gogol's THE INSPECTOR GENERAL, which is probably the greatest Russian comedy.

Nikolai GOGOL, whose novel *Dead Souls* (1842) and short stories such as "The Overcoat" occupy a place in literature as important as *The Inspector General*'s in the theater, voiced explicitly his strong dislike of the flood of bad Russian plays and melodramas. Indeed, despite the great model provided by Fonvizin, many Russian playwrights either persisted in imitating unassimilated foreign plays or simply tried to cater to the mood of the moment. Vladislav Ozerov (1770–1816), for example, in his play *Dmitry Donskoi* (1812), emphasized the parallel between the Russian war effort against Napoleon and the struggle of the prince of Muscovy against the Mongols in the fourteenth century (a device also used by Soviet playwrights during World War II to whip up emotional feeling for Old Mother Russia). Denouncing such melodramas as "thoughtless and inane freaks," Gogol insisted that the playwright must look for and distill into a great play the ordinary events of life around him, instead of picking up all sorts of sensational elements in the hope that they will hold the interest of his audience. This advice, of course, may be described as the realistic method, although it is seriously debatable whether Gogol himself can be usefully classified as a realist, as he so often is. (See REALISM AND NATURALISM.)

Greatly influenced by Gogol's art and ideas, the famous novelist Ivan TURGENEV, on the other hand, can legitimately be described as a realist. His first notable attempt at playwriting was his drama THE PARASITE, written in 1847 at the request of the famous actor Shchepkin. Turgenev followed this up with some short comedies and finally produced his best-known play, A MONTH IN THE COUNTRY, a completely original contribution, a "break-through" in

A SCENE FROM IVAN TURGENEV'S *A Month in the Country* (THEATRE COLLECTION, NEW YORK PUBLIC LIBRARY AT LINCOLN CENTER)

playwriting, that could be described as a subtle, psychological comedy. An obvious forerunner of Chekhov's "inner-conflict" dramas, this play is a happy blend of native (Gogol) and foreign (Balzac's *La Marâtre*) influences. Because of censorship difficulties, however, it, like so many other Russian plays, had to wait twenty years to be performed.

Among the significant Russian comedies of the nineteenth century was *Smert Pazukhina (The Death of Pazukhin,* 1859), written by Mikhail Saltykov-Shchedrin (1826–1889), which was banned, after its first performance, for three decades. Like Saltykov-Shchedrin's famous novel *The Golovlevs,* this play deals with the greed and vulgarity of Russia's decaying gentry.

An important place in the history of the Russian national theater belongs to the tragedy *Gorkaya sudbina (A Hard Lot,* 1859) by Alexei Pisemsky (1820–1881), the author of the classic novel *One Thousand Souls* (1858). *Gorkaya sudbina,* the first Russian "peasant" tragedy, is about a proud peasant who murders the baby his wife has by their master, a weak, sickly, and kindly young landowner whom the wife loves. This forerunner of Leo Tolstoy's play *Power of Darkness* is full of "naturalistic" detail: for example, a peasant woman who is shocked by the scandal readily admits and casually dismisses her own "misbehavior" with her brother, which also resulted in a pregnancy. The play impressed the drama critics so much that in 1860 it shared the Uvarov Prize (awarded for the best play of the year) with Alexander Ostrovsky's famous *Thunderstorm.* This acclaim, however, did not prevent the Church

from having *Gorkaya sudbina* banned until 1862 because it was considered "in poor taste."

Alexander OSTROVSKY, the most prolific Russian playwright, wrote more than eighty plays. Most of them, such as THE FOREST, depict the grim mores of the Russian merchant class from which he originated. His work is the most voluminous individual contribution to the body of Russian theatrical material, and he raised a powerful voice of protest against prevailing abuses of power and the falsity of the generally accepted values. His most famous play, THE THUNDERSTORM, has been performed on almost all the stages of the world. On the Soviet stage, however, the suicide of the heroine, who is overcome by the stifling, stupid meanness surrounding her, was reinterpreted as an act of defiance and revolt by the oppressed to indicate that things will soon be changed by the approaching triumph of the proletariat. Such an interpretation shows Ostrovsky's importance: it apparently was considered important to claim that talented playwright as a member of the socialist camp.

Ostrovsky's contemporary Alexander SUKHOVO-KOBYLIN came from a higher social stratum. But, after traveling all over Europe and living like a dandy during his carefree youth, the rich young nobleman suffered a terrible blow. He was, probably unjustly, accused of murdering his French mistress, and he soon became directly acquainted with the corrupt, graft-taking, ruthless legal apparatus of mid-nineteenth-century Russia. Sukhovo-Kobylin transmuted this experience into his powerful trilogy KRECHINSKY'S WEDDING, in which he succeeds in convey-

ANTON CHEKHOV AND LEO TOLSTOY (NEW YORK PUB-
LIC LIBRARY)

ing, by almost expressionist devices, the nightmarish horror of a man caught in the claws of the law. Strangely enough, the three plays fared quite differently with the censors: the first was produced within almost a year of publication; the second had to wait twenty years; and the third, thirty to be performed.

One may wonder, however, in view of the impact of the exposé, what finally motivated the tsarist censors to authorize the performances of it at all.

Leo TOLSTOY, the great novelist and inveterate preacher, tried to use the stage as a platform for preaching, believing it would reach the underprivileged and uneducated more readily than prose fiction. His stark and realistic POWER OF DARKNESS, set among primitive peasants, caused a great stir among the audiences. In his next play, *Plody prosveshcheniya* (*The Fruits of Enlightenment,* 1891), Tolstoy showed that the emancipation of the serfs in 1861 was meaningless unless the peasants were given land at the same time and he challenged the right to own land of those who did not work it themselves. This drama was followed by THE LIVING CORPSE, a play based on an actual trial that gave Tolstoy an opportunity to attack the callousness with which justice was administered. THE LIGHT THAT SHINES IN DARKNESS is an autobiographical play conveying Tolstoy's personal dilemma—whether he had the right to renounce his wealth against the wishes of the members of his family. In his short plays, such as *Pervyi vinokur* (*The First Distiller,* 1866) and *Ot nei vse kachestva* ("Everything Stems from It," 1910), Tolstoy preached about the evil of idleness and indulgence as symbolized by alcohol.

Anton CHEKHOV, whose major plays represent the best work in Russian drama, started by writing one-act farces. These witty and amusing extravaganzas, however, were so strongly inspired by Gogol that this influence somewhat stifled at first their author's own original concept of theater. That concept developed only gradually, partly under the influence of Turgenev's psychological approach in *A Month in the Country* and partly as a result of Chekhov's collaboration with men like Vladimir Nemirovich-

A SCENE FROM ANTON CHEKHOV'S *The Cherry Orchard* (ANTA COLLECTION, WALTER HAMPDEN MEMORIAL LIBRARY AT THE PLAYERS, NEW YORK)

Danchenko (1858–1943) and Konstantin Stanislavsky (1863–1938), who were to produce and stage his plays. What Chekhov did, essentially, was to change the focus of his plays from the external events to the impact caused by these events on his characters. He accomplished this change by bringing out the inner, psychological reactions of the characters and by showing how the developments of the plot (usually quite simple) could wreak havoc with the secret aspirations, dreams, and ideas of various individuals. This sort of theater obviously posed new problems and created new demands upon the actors and the directors, which probably explains why the first productions of most of Chekhov's major plays were notorious flops. (*The Sea Gull,* for instance, was jeered and booed when first staged at the Alexandrinsky Theater in 1896.) For the vindication of his ideas on playwriting and for the further elucidation of those ideas, Chekhov was greatly indebted to the remarkable duo of Stanislavsky and Nemirovich-Danchenko, who headed the Moscow Art Theater at that time and were in open rebellion against the conventional, declamatory theatricality of the Russian stage at the turn of the century. These two men succeeded in solving the problem of staging Chekhov's plays, despite endless theorizing about the proper way of conveying realistically (that is, convincingly) the great variety of emotions in a Chekhovian play; despite heated arguments about the degree of emphasis on realistic, true-to-life details (rain, snow, mud, horses on the stage, as well as the strict historical accuracy of the setting), all of which were often unrelated to the development of the play and indeed risked distracting attention from its subtler points; and despite all the profound statements about the actor personally "experiencing" or "living through" the play. The new group certainly did succeed, for, two years after the original fiasco at the Alexandrinsky Theater, the production of THE SEA GULL by the Moscow Art Theater in 1898 was an overwhelming triumph. It was followed by the equally loud public acclaim of UNCLE VANYA, THE THREE SISTERS, and THE CHERRY ORCHARD. And it was also the Moscow Art Theater that redeemed, in 1904, the year of Chekhov's death, his earlier and less obviously "Chekhovian" tragedy IVANOV, which had had only a moderately warm reception in a conventional production in 1887.

Besides his tremendous contribution to the art of playwriting that goes far beyond the frontiers of Russia, Chekhov, on the threshold between two periods, is also a historical milestone: he is the last major Russian playwright who belongs entirely to the prerevolutionary regime of tsarist Russia.

twentieth century. Chekhov's associates survived him by many years, saw the arrival of the Soviet regime, and carried on with their work and theorizing in a new setting, completely different from anything they had known before. Stanislavsky, a former actor, and Nemirovich-Danchenko, once a playwright himself (his play *Tsena zhizni,* "The Worth of Life," won him the Griboyedov Prize in 1896 in a field that included Chekhov's *Sea Gull*), were the exponents of a true-to-life, realistic school, which sometimes went in for such a wealth of realistic trappings that it hid the symbolic meaning of certain details deliberately introduced by the author. Indeed, Chekhov, for one, had objected to this realistic zeal; but at the turn of the century almost every dramatic school took an extremist position.

In Russia perhaps the most articulate opposition to the realist school came from Nikolai Evreinov (1879–1953), who ridiculed all the efforts to bring realism to the theater, which he described as the most artificial and conventional art medium. According to Evreinov, there were two driving forces in art: the need for self-expression and the instinct for playacting and impersonation. It was the second need, according to him, that formed the basis for the theater. Therefore, Evreinov concluded, there was no need for the theater to imitate life. On the contrary, acting should be unmistakably conventional and deliberately stylized. The ideal to aim for, he declared, was to replace the actor by a perfect puppet. In the meantime, the most important quality an actor could have was complete control over his body; therefore, acting schools should devote their time to the athletic training of the actor rather than trying to teach him to understand his roles and "live" and "feel" them. Evreinov developed these antirealistic views in his books *Monodrama* (1909) and *The Theater for Ourselves* (1915) and illustrated his ideas by such pantomime-like plays as "The School of Stars" and "The Eternal Dancer." He also directed and produced in an avant-garde style symbolist plays by Fyodor Sologub (1863–1927), including *The Hostages of Life* (1913), *Nocturnal Dances,* and *The Little Demon.* Other directors, such as Alexander Tairov, followed Evreinov's concepts in staging Innokenty Annensky's symbolist play *Famira-Kifared* ("Thamira of the Cither," 1916). Evreinov's ideas also greatly influenced the most famous Soviet director of the 1920's and early 1930's, Vsevolod Meyerhold (1874–1937). A former pupil of Stanislavsky's, he switched his aesthetic allegiance and came to oppose the realistic theater, which he felt had reached a dead end. But, while sharing many of Evreinov's ideas, he did not follow his path of emigration from the Soviet Union but instead tried for many years to combine his loyalty to communist ideas with his experimentation with form—an attempt that ended tragically when he fell victim to his own aesthetic heterodoxy during the Stalin purges. Before the revolution, however, Meyerhold was one of those who wanted to replace the old stage, in which the actors were isolated, with great open-air pageants in which the public would be called upon to participate as in a religious ceremony. Such ideas were current then among left-wing intellectuals, who believed that all the old constraining forms—the schools with their rigid curricula, the conventional forms of literature, and, indeed, the state itself—would wither away and disappear.

It was amidst these hopes, discussions, and experimentations that the revolution came. Many people in the theater, as in other branches of art, saw in the revolution the long-awaited liberation and expected new forms of art freed from all restrictions to sprout in the new classless society. They waited hopefully for a few years, at first accounting for the delays by the necessities of the transition period but eventually becoming bewildered and distraught. Finally they

SCENE FROM *The Lower Depths* BY MAXIM GORKY (THEATRE COLLECTION, NEW YORK PUBLIC LIBRARY AT LINCOLN CENTER)

stopped waiting and even their bewilderment disappeared, for they were too busy just surviving as playwrights and as people.

The two important playwrights representing the two opposing trends of the transition period between the tsar and the Soviets were Maxim GORKY and Leonid ANDREYEV. Gorky, a true proletarian who, from its inception, was close to the revolutionary movement and to the future rulers of Russia, was above all interested in making the masses aware of the unfairness inherent in the tsarist regime. Gorky believed in stating his points explicitly and felt that realism such as Tolstoy's or Émile Zola's was the only suitable form for spreading his ideas. He regarded most of the experimentation that was going on under the name of symbolism, futurism, and imagism as an unconscious attempt to avoid the serious issues or, in some instances, as deliberate obscurantism. However, because he was a fair and decent man with a delicate sensitivity to talent, Gorky, already enjoying his own popularity, called the attention of literary circles to Leonid Andreyev, a talented young writer who was to become his rival in popularity during the last years of the old regime. But while Gorky's play THE LOWER DEPTHS was a tremendous success both before and after the revolution, and his *Yegor Bulychov i drugiye* (*Yegor Bulychov and the Others,* 1931) and *Vassa Zheleznovo* (1935) are still officially considered Soviet classics, Andreyev's plays were no longer performed after the change of government. He became an outspoken critic of the Soviet system and went into exile.

With obviously more affinity for playwrights like Maurice Maeterlinck and Knut Hamsun than for the realists of the Gorky variety, Andreyev, who never joined any particular school, became the legitimate target of every affiliated critic, even while his books were Russia's best sellers and his plays great box-office successes. The symbolists, for instance, dismissing his *Zhizn cheloveka* (*Life of Man,* 1906),

charged Andreyev with using symbolism inadequately to cope with a metaphysical problem over his head; the social-minded realists denounced him for misrepresenting the class struggle as a senseless twist of fate; and the Orthodox Church accused him of blasphemy. The only play of his that has often been performed abroad is HE WHO GETS SLAPPED. Only since Stalin's death are collections of Andreyev's plays and other writings being published in limited editions in the Soviet Union.

Gorky, on the other hand, thanks to his proletarian antecedents, his early political pronouncements, and above all his fidelity to the realistic school of writing of which Lenin approved, came to be considered a founding father and elder statesman of Soviet literature. Later he was even credited with the doubtful honor of inventing the set of rules that became known as Socialist Realism.

In the early years of the Soviet regime experimentation was still allowed and even encouraged under Lunarcharsky, the first commissar (minister) for cultural affairs. Along with the realistic art devoted to the praise of and the appeal for more revolutionary heroics, there mushroomed a multitude of experimental schools purportedly searching for a "new language to fit the new society." This temporary freedom enabled the brilliantly talented poet Vladimir MAYAKOVSKY to remain faithful to what he called the futurist school and to deliver his sincerely revolutionary message in an extremely unconventional language. Mayakovsky's futurist play *Misteriya buff* (*Mystery-Bouffe,* 1918) was actually based on a current, popular idea—the withering away of all barriers, namely, the obliteration of the boundaries of the stage and the gradual eradication of the difference between the actor and the audience. His *Klop* (*The Bedbug,* 1928) and THE BATHHOUSE, also highly experimental and produced by Meyerhold, were typical of those early years when extreme symbolism, expressionism, and experimentation were still considered proper modes for revolutionary left-wing art. A little later, however, Mayakovsky found himself under pressure to make himself "more understandable to the masses" (his style always irritated Lenin). Mayakovsky then spent as much time abroad as he was allowed and finally committed suicide. It may be noted that many exceptionally gifted playwrights who had welcomed the revolution had, in fact, a general outlook on life more akin to that of the "New Left" in the United States of the 1960's than to that of the grim sectarians of their time, who were quite scornful of aesthetic pursuits. Gradually, aesthetes were silenced or, if they tried to go on writing, their work became dull and valueless. Such was the case of, among others, Yuri OLESHA, author of the novel *Envy* and the plays *Zagovor chuvstv* (*The Conspiracy of Feelings,* date unknown) and A LIST OF ASSETS; Isaac Babel (1894–1942), author of the volume of stories *Red Cavalry* (1926), the Odessa short stories, and the plays *Zakat* ("Sunset") and *Maria;* and Mikhail BULGAKOV, author of *Dni Turbinikh* (*The Days of the Turbins,* 1926), many other plays, and several novels.

Under a regime in which everything had to be coordinated with the government's political goals, many plays were proclaimed as classics by the well-coordinated body of Soviet critics. Eventually, these works were also accepted as such in the West. This uncritical Western acceptance, probably due to the indiscriminate enthusiasm prevalent during the World War II alliance for everything Russian and Soviet, somehow lingered on after the war. For, obviously, these Soviet "classics" are at best skilled, made-to-order contrivances, each creating a lopsided, ephemeral little world with glaringly synthetic values, each eminently unconvincing because it was never emotionally accepted by the playwright himself. Among such Soviet "classics" are Vsevolod Ivanov's much-heralded *Bronepoyezd No. 14–69* (*Armored Train 1469,* 1922), Boris Lavrenyov's *Vragi* ("Enemies," 1929), Konstantin Trenyov's *Lyubov Yarovaya* (1926), and Nikolai Pogodin's *Aristokraty* (*The Aristocrats,* 1934). The last play, for instance, written under Stalin, was translated into English and performed in New York in the 1960's. Its theme is the educational role of the Soviet slave camps. It shows paternal *Cheka* (security police) overseers redeeming from their perdition whores, thieves, murderers, and even deviationists from the Stalinist party line and turning them into "useful builders of socialism."

Even since Stalin's death in 1953, the situation of the Soviet playwright has remained very constricted. Although he has been excused from the cumbersome requirements necessitated by the "personality cult" of Stalin, Socialist Realism is still the official set of rules, the party and the Lenin cult is still *de rigueur,* and the writer's themes are still likely to be "Lenin's great insight," "American neocolonialism," and the exposure of various un-Soviet activities. There is also still a considerable amount of persecution and a number of trials of literary figures who are too outspoken.

The result of these restrictions is the continued mediocrity of Soviet plays and the public's lack of interest in them. To satisfy the public demand for better plays, Soviet theaters have been staging probably more old Russian and foreign classics (real classics) than anywhere else in the world. Since, however, many ideas contained in the works of men like Tolstoy and Shakespeare fail to meet the requirements of the authorities, they have to be what is euphemistically described as "reinterpreted" and "modernized."

A special study of this process appears in a book entitled *Klassika na tsene* ("Staging of Classics"), published by the State Institute of Theater, Music, and Cinematography in Leningrad in 1964. *Klassika* describes various problems raised by a score of world-famous masterpieces and the way they should and should not be handled before being presented on a Soviet stage.

In *The Power of Darkness,* for instance, Tolstoy chose as the mouthpiece for his conscience the mumbling, inarticulate, deeply religious old peasant Akim. Such a character was hardly acceptable as a "positive hero" by Soviet stage directors and *Klassika* reviewed the various reinterpretations and modernizations of Akim's personality. At first, as a "bearer of outdated religious superstitions," Akim was turned into a puny, fussy, useless busybody who keeps superstitiously crossing himself at every pretext. Obviously, such an interpretation made a shambles of Tolstoy's views of sin and true Christian resistance to evil—views which, whether objectively correct or not, were inherent and true in the context of the world Tolstoy created in *The Power of Darkness.* Eventually, however, it was realized that Akim was much too important a wheel in the play simply to be made to turn in the opposite direction. The directors were denounced for "vulgar sociologism" (a phrase meaning the silly and too literal application of Marxist-Leninist dogma), and their successors restored Akim to his status of positive hero. They changed, however, this inarticulate, religious protester against sin into a firm, loud denouncer of the evils of capitalism who speaks up for the downtrodden masses and whose message includes a promise of justice in the approaching revolution. Thus, instead of directly and tactlessly ridiculing the very essence of Tolstoy's ideas, the later Soviet directors merely substituted an approved mysticism for Tolstoy's obsolete one.

It is obvious that as long as the worlds created by playwrights cannot be shown publicly without being "adapted" to certain officially sponsored world views (whatever their intrinsic merit), the Russian theater will have to remain in a state of suspension.

Among the very few comprehensive works in English on Russian drama are *History of the Russian Theater* (1951) by B. V. Varneke, *Russian Theater from the Empire to the Soviets* (1961) by Marc Slonim, and *A History of Soviet Literature, 1917–1964* (1964) by Vera Alexandrova.—A. MacA.

Ruy Blas (1838). A romantic tragedy in verse by Victor HUGO. Written in a single month, *Ruy Blas* is probably Victor Hugo's best play. He composed it to inaugurate the opening of the Théâtre de la Renaissance, which was given to him by the Duc d'Orléans for the performance of his plays. Although the play enjoyed only a partial success and was attacked in the press by the severe Gustave Planche for its

LITHOGRAPH OF A SCENE FROM VICTOR HUGO'S *Ruy Blas* (NEW YORK PUBLIC LIBRARY)

melodramatic qualities, it was successfully revived in 1872 at the Odéon with Sarah Bernhardt as the queen.

In the play the marquis Don Salluste tries unsuccessfully to dethrone the virtuous queen by having her take as a lover his supposed cousin "Don Caesar," who is really the commoner Ruy Blas. Pro-

moted to virtual ruler by the queen, whom he loves, "Don Caesar" suddenly finds himself in the marquis's power. He must either precipitate the queen's fall or lose her love by revealing his identity. To save her honor, he first kills the marquis, then (believing he has lost her) swallows poison.

This somewhat incredible plot and the impassioned poetry in parts of the play recall the assertion of the writer Charles Nodier (a leader of the Romantic movement) that "romantic drama is nothing but melodrama ennobled by verse." The play has undeniable merits: its arresting and faithful picture of the declining glory of seventeenth-century Spain, the eloquence of its poetic speeches in Acts I and III, and the contrasting farcical humor of the real Don Caesar in the fourth act. Yet the artificiality of its characters (who resemble the villain, the *homme fatal,* and the conventional romantic heroine of popular melodrama) and the strained quality of the love of a lackey and a queen ultimately relegate this play to the genre of *mélodrame.*

Camilla Crosland's translation is reprinted in *Three Plays by Victor Hugo* (1964), edited by H. A. Gaubert.—S. S. S.

Ruzzante, Il. See Angelo BEOLCO.

Rwanda. See AFRICA: *Rwanda.*

S

Sachs, Hans (1494–1576). Nuremberg cobbler, Meistersinger, and author of the best of the *Fastnachtsspiele* ("carnival plays"). The son of a tailor, Sachs was educated at the Nuremberg Latin school and took an apprenticeship in shoemaking. In his journeyman's wanderings, he traveled extensively throughout Germany and received instruction in the art of singing and the writing of Meistergesang. After his return to his home city in 1516, he took up the trade of cobbler and at the same time devoted himself to writing. Throughout his career, Sachs proved to be a prolific writer, turning out more than six thousand works of various sorts. He wrote over one hundred comedies and tragedies that have justifiably been forgotten today: They are little more than epic-didactic dialogues or sometimes chronicles in verse. During the Reformation he also put his talents to work on the side of Luther.

Sachs's most significant literary contribution was to the Fastnachtsspiel, to whose rawness he imparted a degree of Humanism, folksiness, and personal religion, coupled with the gentle humor pervading most of his work. His sources were mainly Boccaccio, Pauli's *Scherz und Ernst* ("Jocose and Serious") and *Eulenspiegel* ("Owl Glass"), but the middle-class moralizing tone he gave his creations was unique. At one period writing as many as ten to thirteen Fastnachtsspiele a year, the cobbler of Nuremberg was nonetheless capable of providing his plays with

HANS SACHS (GERMAN INFORMATION CENTER)

remarkable psychological depth and careful motivation, such as in the marriage farce *Das heiss Eisen* (*The Hot Iron*). Sachs's Germanness was later celebrated by Goethe, and Wagner immortalized him as the kindly guiding genius of his opera *Die Meistersinger von Nürnberg* (*The Meistersingers of Nuremberg*).—B. M. M.

Sá de Miranda, Francisco de. See PORTUGAL.

Saint Genest (1646). A tragedy by Jean ROTROU. In the course of a wedding at the court of Emperor Diocletian, the actor Genest performs a tragedy based on the martyrdom of Adrian. During the performance Genest identifies with the role he is playing, has a miraculous vision, and receives divine grace. Diocletian imprisons him and then has him put to death. *Saint Genest* is remarkable for the mystical metamorphosis of the hero, recalling that of Pierre Corneille's Polyeucte but situated in a far more miraculous world.—Ja. G.

Saint Joan (1923). A play by George Bernard SHAW. In the spring of 1429, Robert de Beaudricourt threatens his steward because the hens have not laid eggs recently, a lack the steward blames on a strange country maid. Summoned to De Beaudricourt's presence, the maid, Joan, is so blithely self-confident that he finally consents to her seeking out the uncrowned dauphin. The hens immediately start laying again.

In the castle at Chinon, the stately archbishop of Rheims, Gilles de Rais ("Bluebeard"), and the shabby, pathetic little dauphin decide to test Joan's powers by a trick in which Bluebeard pretends to be the dauphin. Joan nevertheless quickly picks out the real dauphin and, despite his chronic timidity, heartens him so that he gives her command of his army, which is waging war with England.

In the English camp, the earl of Warwick and the bishop of Beauvais agree that Joan is dangerous. Warwick whimsically coins the word "protestant" to describe Joan's way of dealing directly with God, without the aid of the Church, though he is much more concerned about her way of mediating directly between royalty and the people, without deference to the feudal nobility. Beauvais terms this tendency "nationalism." Coming to terms, Warwick says to Beauvais, "If you will burn the Protestant, I will burn the nationalist." Joan also has enemies in her own camp after the dauphin is triumphantly crowned king of France. Joan eloquently denounces her enemies, putting her trust in God, who, being alone Himself, can best understand her loneliness.

On May 30, 1431, the last day of Joan's trial as a heretic before an ecclesiastical court picked by the British, the inquisitor explains (in one of the best speeches in the play) the terrible consequences of

TRIAL SCENE FROM BERNARD SHAW'S *Saint Joan* (ANTA COLLECTION, WALTER HAMPDEN MEMORIAL LIBRARY AT THE PLAYERS, NEW YORK)

heresy, far worse than any amount of suffering by any one individual. Joan insists she will always obey God rather than the Church, though she fears the stake enough to momentarily distrust her "voices." As Joan is burned (offstage), the inquisitor regretfully declares that she was morally innocent, though technically guilty of heresy.

In June 1456, Charles VII, formerly the dauphin, dreams that Joan and all those involved in her rise and martyrdom appear in his bedchamber. A man from the distant future of 1920 announces that Joan has just been canonized a saint of the Church. All join in an almost poetic litany of praise for Joan, but when she offers to return to the world, all renounce her once again. Joan cries out, "O God that madest this beautiful earth, when will it be ready to receive Thy saints? How long, O Lord, how long?"

Though it was Shaw's wife who gave him the idea of writing a play about Joan of Arc, in retrospect she seems an inevitable subject. She was an unquestionably superior being, wise and magnanimous, yet warmly human. If not universally accepted as Shaw's greatest play, *Saint Joan* has certainly been one of his most popular. Some critics have deplored the dream epilogue as a needless spelling out of what any audience knows, but it plays so brilliantly that no production has ever omitted it. Historians, even Catholics, have objected that Shaw makes Joan's judges far more conscientious, fair-minded, and kindly than they actually were. But Shaw's thematic purpose was to make the trial a clash of irreconcilable goods rather than a melodrama of persecuted innocence.

It is this irreconcilable conflict that Eric Bentley focuses on in his comments on *Saint Joan* in *Bernard Shaw* (1947), underscoring the fact that Shaw does not wish to "defend" either side but merely to depict the clash. Louis Martz' "The Saint as Tragic Hero"

in *Tragic Themes in Western Literature* (1955), edited by Cleanth Brooks, explores the wider implications of that irreconcilability in *Saint Joan* and in T. S. Eliot's *Murder in the Cathedral*. Martz refers to the religious skepticism of the modern audience and all that this skepticism implies about the condition of tragedy in today's theater. H. Ludeke's "Some Remarks on Shaw's Historical Plays," *English Studies*, XXXVI (1955), offers a number of valuable insights on both Saint Joan and Caesar as superman types.—D. J. L.

saint's play. Also called **miracle play.** A medieval religious play in the vernacular, based upon the life of a saint or some miracle performed by a saint. The saint's play is non-scriptural and is therefore to be distinguished from the scriptural or mystery play (see SCRIPTURAL PLAY). The term "miracle play" is used by some authorities to include scriptural drama, by others in the restrictive sense defined above. Because of the resulting confusion, many prefer the restrictive term "saint's play." For a discussion of the substance of saint's plays, see ENGLAND: *middle ages.*

Salacrou, Armand (1899–   ). French playwright. Salacrou was born in Rouen and began his career as a journalist. His early plays, produced in the 1920's, caused great controversy.

His plays are varied in subject matter and theme, but they have a weakness that comes from the absence of a unified style. Several styles appear in a single play: romanticism, a very contemporary cynicism, sentimentality, fantasy, and satire. But despite this amalgam of tones and styles, there is a forcefulness and at times originality in such plays as *L'Inconnue d'Arras* (*The Unknown Woman from Arras*, 1935) and *Les Nuits de la colère* ("Nights of Anger," 1945). The manipulation of time and space and the use of burlesque or a circus atmosphere add to the surrealist and dreamlike quality of some of his plays. In *L'Inconnue d'Arras* Salacrou successfully uses such modern cinematic techniques as the flashback. The main character, having just committed suicide, relives his brief existence just as he is about to die, in the brief seconds between the act of suicide and its fulfillment. His fragmentary memories are unable to justify the determinism of his suicidal act.—W. F.

Samson Agonistes. See John MILTON.

Sánchez, Florencio (1875–1910). Uruguayan naturalist playwright. Born in Montevideo, Sánchez' life was that of a bohemian's amid economic pressures, until success as a dramatist brought relative stability. His own financial problems, his disenchantment with the Uruguayan political system, and his working-class background combined to produce a Socialist Party orientation that led to considerable difficulty for Sánchez during his journalistic career. He died in Italy while studying Italian drama.

Sánchez' works are all naturalistic, ranging from denunciations of the oppressive poverty of urban slums to portraits of the destruction of the old rural system under the impact of aggressive immigrants. He was sympathetic to the human values of the decaying way of life, as shown in *Barranca abajo* (*Down the Gully*, 1905), and he mistrusted the city, while recognizing that some harmonizing of the two was urgently needed. His longer works deal largely with this problem; *M'hijo el dotor* (*My Son the Lawyer*, 1904) attacks the corruption of morality in the metropolis, while *La Gringa* (*The Immigrant Girl*, 1904) presents a stubborn old farmer doomed to failure through his inability to comprehend change. Sánchez' dialogue is not polished and his solutions not always convincing, but his longer works contain an array of profoundly human characters. In several short works, such as *Canillita* (*The Newspaper Boy*, 1904), *El Desalojo* (*Evicted*, 1906), and *La Tigra* (*The Tigress*, 1907), Sánchez created a gallery of types bewildered and defeated by the city; in the best of these plays, the types are metamorphosed into human tragedies.

Representative Plays . . . (1961) has been translated by Willis Knapp Jones and includes the most important works. The best general study is Ruth Richardson's *Florencio Sánchez and the Argentine Theater* (1933); although some sections need updating in the light of recent investigations, it is an excellent introduction.—F. D.

Sanskrit drama. See INDIA: *Sanskrit drama*.

Sappho (1818). A tragedy in verse by Franz GRILLPARZER. On the surface the plot of *Sappho* is relatively simple and has often been interpreted as the story of an artist of high calling who renounces love for the sake of art. On a deeper level, it is a profound psychological study of a woman who finds herself unable to love a man whom in fact she greatly desires to love. At its core *Sappho* is a study in psychosexuality couched in deceptively romantic terms.

As the play opens, Sappho, a middle-aged woman, is triumphantly returning to her native island of Lesbos from Olympia, where she has won honor for her songs at the games. She brings with her Phaon, a youth much her junior, who fell at her feet in worship at the Olympic games. She gratefully listens to his veneration of her; yet he may well feel, not true love for her, but only deep admiration. Soon after his ar-

rival on Lesbos, Phaon falls truly in love with Melitta, a female slave of Sappho, of whom Sappho is extremely fond. Melitta looks upon Sappho, albeit unwittingly, as a substitute for her own lost father. Sappho becomes aware of the love between Melitta and Phaon and grows intensely jealous. The implications are that Sappho loves Melitta in an unnatural manner but at the same time, in an almost certainly sexually schizophrenic way, still wants to love Phaon. Yet she finds herself frustratingly incapable of such a love. She attempts to retrieve Melitta to herself and finally, in order to keep her from Phaon, sends her off to the island of Chios. Phaon follows Melitta to protect her. They are both captured, however, and returned to Lesbos. Phaon reproaches Sappho and reminds her of her position and greatness. Sappho, unable to face reality and the true nature of her sexuality, falls back on her crutch, her art. In so doing, she rationalizes her position and determines that her calling is so exalted that she must inevitably renounce earthly love. Once she is safe in her delusion, she plunges from high on a cliff into the ocean below, in exaltation and glory.

Sappho, for all its romantic trappings, is a deep and probing study of the sick mind of a universally acclaimed poetess. When seen in proper perspective, the play contains psychological tensions of tremendous power. Although these tensions are most skillfully hidden beneath the surface, they are perhaps all the more powerful for not being totally manifest.

There is an acceptable translation of *Sappho* by Arthur Burkhard (1953).—C. R. M.

Sardou, Victorien (1831–1908). French playwright. Next to his master, Eugène Scribe, Sardou was the most prolific and skillful writer of the WELL-MADE PLAY. Even more ingenious in constructing his plots than Scribe and more astounding in his creation of stage effects, Sardou was also shallower in his treatment of the subject matter. He was an entertainer, not a thinker. He wrote about eighty pieces for the theater, ranging from social satires to historical pageants, melodramas, opera librettos, and farces, because he wanted to please the public and make money. He adapted his themes to the changing taste of the times. He cared nothing about serious ideas as such, social or moral questions, theses, the satire of manners, the need for reform—in short, the theater as lecture hall, the theater of Émile Augier and Alexandre Dumas fils. A superb manipulator of tension, tears, terror, and laughter, he was elected to the Académie Francaise in 1878.

After abandoning medicine for the stage, he spent several heartbreaking years before reaching the heights of fame and prestige. Several trial flights resulted in his first real success—*Les Pattes de mouche* (*A Scrap of Paper*, 1860), a light comedy of intrigue centered on the mysterious contents of a love letter. Somewhat after the fashion of Augier's social comedies of manners, *La Famille Benoîton* ("The Benoîton Family," 1865) satirizes the money mania of France's Second Empire (1852–1870). His most ingenious historical spectacle is *Patrie* ("Fatherland," 1869). The international spy melodrama *Dora* (*Diplomacy*, 1877) became a model for Oscar Wilde's *An Ideal Husband* (1895). The risqué farce *Divorçons* (*Let's Get a Divorce!*, written in collaboration with Émile de Najac, performed 1880) was an immense international success. Toward the end of his career Sardou wrote spectacular melodramas for the great tragic actress Sarah Bernhardt. Solely as acting vehicles, *Fédora* (1882), *Théodora* (1884), and *La Tosca* (1887) were impressive, and as an opera by Puccini *La Tosca* (1900) can still move an audience. *Mme Sans-Gêne* (*Madame Devil-May-Care*, in collaboration with Émile Moreau, performed 1893) was composed for Gabrielle Réjane and has been played by many famous actresses in stage, screen, and television versions. This story of the spirited washerwoman who became the duchess of Danzig and, years later, on being asked to retire from court, presented Napoleon with his old unpaid laundry bill is partly historical.

The plays that best illustrate Sardou's wide range of genres and styles follow a general pattern. Sardou would read the first act of a play by Scribe, put it down, plot the rest of the play, and compare his result with that of the master. For Sardou play construction had to have the logic of a game of chess. He once explained that in plotting a play he always began with the *scène à faire* (the climactic, revelatory scene toward which the action has been building) and worked backward to the beginning. He built his plot out of some trivial or insignificant fact, incident, or secret that becomes tremendously exaggerated in importance (Clarisse's indiscreet note to Prosper in *Les Pattes de mouche*, the pretended divorce law in *Divorçons*, Napoleon's unpaid laundry bill in *Mme Sans-Gêne*). The action consists of withholding information from certain key characters while divulging it to others. Misunderstandings spring up and multiply.

Sometimes Sardou triumphed simply by allowing the stage effects to overwhelm the spectator. And yet he had that sense of the theater without which the greatest literary genius will fail as a playwright. He would adorn a historical drama with colorful pageantry, with crowds shouting their emotions in unison, with soldiers marching briskly to fife and drum, with a triangle plot of passionate love and political intrigue, with an emotional death scene. He was also a master harmonizer of incompatible genres within the same play (history, tragedy, comedy, melodrama).

A Scrap of Paper is in *Camille and Other Plays* (1957), edited by Stephen S. Stanton, which includes a bibliography of English translations of the plays and an introductory essay on Sardou and the well-made play. *Let's Get a Divorce and Other Plays* (1958), edited by Eric Bentley, contains, in addition to Sardou's play, an essay on the psychology of farce. The standard book on Sardou in English is Jerome A. Hart's *Sardou and the Sardou Plays* (1913).—S. S. S.

Saroyan, William (1908–). American playwright and novelist. William Saroyan was born in Fresno, California. His parents were Armenian immigrants, and the writer has frequently been drawn on the world of Armenian-American farmers for his subjects. The boy spent most of his childhood and youth in San Francisco. His formal education was fragmentary, but the public library became his school, and in his teens he decided to be a writer. In 1934 *Story* magazine published "The Daring Young Man on the Flying Trapeze," which brought Saroyan

recognition as an exuberant, unconventional writer. Extreme alternations between success and failure have made little change in Saroyan's prolific production of plays, short stories, novels, and autobiographical pieces.

Saroyan prides himself on writing swiftly and intuitively. At best, his plays have a vibrant spontaneity; at worst, a self-indulgent shapelessness. His essential theme is the triumph of childlike goodness over the corruptions of a materialistic society, a point of view that sometimes leads to saccharinity and sentimentality. His earliest plays best capture the freshness of his vision. *My Heart's in the Highlands* (1939) is a long one-act play about love and music overcoming poverty. In *The Beautiful People* (1941) Saroyan created a boy who embodies the playwright's sweetest ideals and a story made of wild flights of imagination. As an embryonic poet, the boy writes one-word books when he feels he has totally experienced the force of a word—for example, "tree"; or, eager to please his sister, who feeds mice, the boy spells out her name in flowers, as if the mice had done this in their gratitude.

With *The Time of Your Life* (1939) Saroyan achieved his highest distinction as a playwright. Set in a San Francisco waterfront saloon, the play presents a group of loosely connected stories in which some yearning character—ranging from a lovesick clerk to a pinball machine addict—experiences a chance to realize his dream. An idealistic, rich young man and a braggart of an old cowboy play the role of *deus ex machina* in resolving the central story of a prostitute and the young man who falls in love with her. A shadow of the war about to explode in Europe provides a more complex sense of evil than is apparent in most of Saroyan's work.

Other plays in which Saroyan achieves a vivid synthesis of optimism and unconventional dramaturgy are *Across the Board on Tomorrow Morning* (1942), *Hello, Out There* (1943), and *The Cave Dwellers* (1957). *My Name is Aram* (1940) is a collection of his most autobiographical stories. *The Human Comedy* (1943) is his most successful novel.

There is no standard edition of Saroyan's work. Critical comments appear in the major studies of modern American drama.—M. L.

Sartre, Jean Paul (1905–). French philosopher, novelist, essayist, and playwright. Born and educated in Paris, Sartre began his career as a teacher. He traveled extensively and studied philosophy in Germany. During the German occupation of France in World War II, Sartre was active in the underground Resistance movement. After the war, he was the leader of a group of intellectuals in Paris, and his extremely popular philosophy of existentialism strongly influenced the writers of that period. In 1964 Sartre was awarded the Nobel Prize for literature.

Sartre belongs to literature in his many roles as novelist, dramatist, essayist, and polemical writer. The characters of his plays seem separated from him and often appear more as arguments than as living human beings, but he places them in a world that is very much his own creation. Without being solely a professional dramatist, Sartre has used the theatrical form with considerable ease, naturalness, and spontaneity. As a dramatist, Sartre lacks some of those mysterious bonds that join the heroes of the stage

JEAN PAUL SARTRE (FRENCH CULTURAL SERVICES)

with their creators, and he lacks the full power of poetic expression by means of which spectators are able to follow the deepest dramas in the souls of dramatic heroes.

In each of his plays, Sartre emphasizes unusual and highly dramatic predicaments: a plague of flies in Argos (THE FLIES), a living room in hell (NO EXIT), and a torture chamber (*Morts sans sépulture, The Victors,* 1946). The analysis of the characters is limited to dramatizing the necessity they feel to adapt to the situation, to identify with and choose the situation. Whatever environment Sartre constructs for his characters, he is intent upon revealing the conflict that takes place between the sincerity of the character in his effort to choose his own life and the power of his conventional world as it seeks to trap and distort him.

If man's realization of freedom is the first stage in Sartrean morality, the use of his freedom—his commitment—is the second stage. Man, who before the realization and employment of his freedom is nothing and is comparable to the immobile things around him, becomes a "project." He becomes his own value. After killing Clytemnestra in *The Flies,* Orestes explains to his sister Electra that he has commited *his* act, that he will bear its responsibility, and that henceforth he will follow his own road.

In Sartre's last two plays, *Nékrassov* (1956) and *Les Séquestrés d'Altona* (*The Condemned of Altona,* 1959), he raises certain significant political issues. *Nékrassov* tries to demonstrate the difficulty of maintaining personal freedom in a society obsessed by the threat of communism. On one level, *Les Séquestrés d'Altona* is a parable on torture and the Algerian War. But there are also other themes and problems in Sartre's text that make it seem more metaphysical than political: the legitimate use of violence, the consequences of action, the relationship between an individual and society, between an individual and history. See also LUCIFER AND THE LORD.

For critical evaluations of the work of Sartre, con-

sult the following: Eric Bentley, "From Strindberg to Jean-Paul Sartre," *The Playwright as Thinker* (1955); Victor Brombert, "The Drama of Ensnarement," *Ideas in Drama* (1963), edited by John Gassner; Maurice W. Cranston, *Jean-Paul Sartre* (1962); Francis Fergusson, "Sartre as Playwright," *Partisan Review,* XVI (1949); M. Jarret-Kerr, "The Dramatic Philosophy of Sartre," *Tulane Drama Review,* I (June 1957); "The Theatre of Sartre," *Tulane Drama Review,* V (March 1961); and H. W. Wardman, "Sartre and the Theatre of Catharsis," *Essays in French Literature,* No. 1 (November 1964).—W. F.

sarugaku. This name, derived from the Japanese word for monkey, covers a large variety of popular entertainments that reached their height in Japan in the fourteenth century and did much to aid the birth of the first legitimate forms of the Japanese theater —the grave *noh* plays and the farcical *kyogen.*

Companies calling themselves *sarugaku* flourished as early as the eleventh century. Zeami Motokiyo, the founder in the fourteenth century of the noh drama as we know it, refers often to this form of entertainment in his extensive writings on the theatrical life of his time. The following, earlier description, translated from memoirs ascribed to a writer of no major importance, Fujiwara Akihira (991–1066) in his *A Record of the New Sarugaku,* is quoted by James T. Araki in his *Ballad-Drama of Medieval Japan* (1954):

The *sarugaku* which we saw tonight was of an excellence unmatched in any age. Especially amusing were the imprecators, the midget dance, the puppeteers, the T'ang tricks, the juggling with balls . . . the portrayal of a superintendent priest grabbing his skirt as he treads on ice, the flirtatious gesturing with a fan by a matron of Yamase, the tales recited by the biwa-playing monks . . . the Sage of Expansive Fortune searching for his priestly vestment and the Wondrous-Exalted Bhiksuni begging for swaddling clothes, the facial expression of the mimicker of an affairs director, the indiscreet whistling of the functionary who arrived on the job early, the image of the venerable elder in the dance of the auxiliary official, the love-struck look on the shrine-maiden, the "after you, sir" manners of the youths of the capital, the portrayal of an Easterner on his first visit to the capital, and, of course, the various emotive expressions of the rhythm men and the appearance and deportment of the "monks of great virtue." All these are forms of *sarugaku.*

Ample evidence survives to prove that an animated but largely amorphous theatrical life flourished in Japan at least three centuries before the birth of drama properly so called in that land, so long and passionately devoted to the presentational arts. The sarugaku was to all appearances the most vital as well as the most eclectic of all the earlier schools of entertainment.—H. W. W.

Satin Slipper, The (Le Soulier de satin, 1943). A poetic drama by Paul CLAUDEL. Between 1919 and 1924 Claudel's life was largely given over to the writing of *The Satin Slipper.* Repeating many of his earlier themes about the temporality of earthly desires, the power of the spirit, and the sense of ultimate salvation, this play marks a culmination in the poet's career, a *summa* that concludes a cycle begun twenty years earlier with *Partage de midi* (*Break of Noon,* written 1906). This play reveals the spiritual experience of Claudel's lifetime journey from revolt to acceptance.

The Prologue is a monologue spoken by a priest who is tied to the high mast of a ship that is sinking. In this scene, in which the priest prays for the salvation of his brother Rodrigue, Claudel is concerned with the role of the supernatural as it intervenes in the affairs of men. *The Satin Slipper* is a drama about the meaning of Providence.

The love story of Rodrigue and Prouhèze is at the heart of this play, and it unfolds against the background of the entire universe. The lovers are together in a spiritual sense but are separated by continents and oceans. This love is the drama of separation and incommunicability. In Claudel's conception of tragedy, the focus is not so much on the human destiny of the characters as on their eternal destiny. The dominant struggle of this play, prefigured in the Prologue where the dying priest speaks to eternity, is the clash between such a commonplace experience as human passion and the incomprehensible concept of eternity.

For Claudel love between man and woman is a drama of countless aspects whose setting is the universe. It is a quest leading across oceans and through deserts, the quest of a spiritual adventure carried out with purely human means, and, in *The Satin Slipper,* containing moments of burlesque, satire, and buffoonery.

The Satin Slipper (1931) has been translated by John O' Connor.—W. F.

satire.   The impulse to expose, condemn, correct, and annihilate institutions or people through ridicule is at least as old as the recorded history of man. The literary history of peoples as disparate as the Irish and the Arabs testifies to the prominence of satire from the earliest times. In ancient Greece the phallic songs that contained the seeds of Old Comedy also contained a large satiric element. The presence of satire in primitive literature, as R. C. Elliott has effectively argued, suggests that its function was magical: to serve to expel evil powers that threatened the community or to destroy a personal enemy through a kind of ritual word murder. In any case, the association of vilification and invective with humor seems to have been a later development.

The genus "satire" and the species "dramatic satire" are notoriously difficult to define. The term satire can be used to describe an intention or a tone or a specific type of literature. For our purposes satire will be defined as attack—attack raised to the level of art and employing the weapons of wit and humor. The humorous element may or may not be dominant.

In drama, the earliest noteworthy satirist is Aristophanes, whose plays, whatever other areas of the comic they embrace, are inherently satiric. The extant corpus of his work constitutes a comprehensive, if occasionally distorted, indictment of Athenian life in his time (fifth century B.C.). To an unerring eye for his fellow citizens' pretensions—whether intellectual (*Clouds*), litigious (*Wasps*), literary (*Frogs*), military (*Lysistrata*), or political (*Ecclesiazusae*)—he added an extravagant imagination, an extraordinary lyrical gift, and—the *sine qua non* of the satirist—a controlled but always discernible moral rage.

The Romans gave us the term satire (*satura*), which means "medley" or "potpourri" ("hash" in Northrop Frye's rendering). It apparently alluded to a type of vaudeville entertainment popular before the importation of Greek drama. The Romans also gave us the formal delineation of nondramatic satire, but no application of the mode to the theater. That phenomenon did not reemerge until the Renaissance.

A fine example of early Renaissance dramatic satire is Sir David Lyndsay's *Ane Pleasant Satyre of the Thrie Estaitis* (1540), consisting of eight interludes. It is an outspoken attack on the abuses of church and state in the Scotland of James V. In its indictment of social evils, *Ane Satyre* spares no one, including the king, before whom it was performed. Aside from the literary impressiveness of the play, the greatest distinction of *Ane Satyre* is that it should have been written, or in any case performed, at all. Political and religious satire on the existing establishments were all but totally suppressed in Renaissance Europe. Thus, on the Elizabethan stage satiric portraits of Puritans or Catholics were permitted, but no playwright dared abuse the Anglican Church without fear of reprisal. Political satire was even more closely watched by the authorities. In his first attempt at playwriting, Ben Jonson found himself imprisoned by the Privy Council for his role in the authorship of *The Isle of Dogs,* a lost play full of "very seditious and slanderous matter." Despite these restrictions, however, satire of a less specific nature flourished during the period.

The distinctive characteristics of Elizabethan satire were conditioned by the belief that the term originated in association with the satyr of Greek classical mythology. Thus, satire was thought to be a rough and irregular form, defined exclusively by its intention of reforming abuses through ridicule. Another development of the satyr-satire identification was the emergence of the half-savage, railing, malcontent-satirist as a central figure. Ben Jonson introduced the figure in *Every Man Out of His Humour;* John Marston magnified his importance in *The Malcontent;* and Shakespeare added scurrility to his characteristics when he created the character Thersites in *Troilus and Cressida.*

These and other plays of the period were particularly effective in their acidic portraits of human greed and lust. In fact, in the first decade of the seventeenth century satire was the dominant mode in English drama, and a sharp satiric strain became evident in tragedy as well as comedy. John Webster's *Duchess of Malfi* and *The White Devil,* Ben Jonson's *Sejanus, His Fall,* and Cyril Tourneur's *The Revenger's Tragedy* all betray a heavily ironic perspective that undercuts the heroic aspiration of their protagonists. This is also true of some of Shakespeare's plays, according to Oscar James Campbell, whose *Shakespeare's Satire* (1943) makes a particularly strong case for *Timon of Athens* and *Coriolanus* as the tragic equivalents of *Troilus and Cressida.*

In Molière, dramatic satire underwent a transformation that leaves it close to the comedy of manners, to the phrase "thoughtful laughter" that George Meredith, with Molière as his chief example, used to define comedy as distinct from satire. It is true that the plays of Molière are distinguished by a tolerance and flexibility not often associated with pure satire. Nevertheless, the satiric perspective is always present in Molière whenever a rigid universal view of reality is present. Thus the object of satire in *Tartuffe* is credulity as well as hypocrisy; in *Le Misanthrope*, the folly of social life as well as the intransigence of anti-social idealism.

Still, one must agree with the observation made in Rose Zimbardo's *William Wycherly: A Link in the Development of English Satire* (1965) that "Molière used satiric techniques in designing comedy while Wycherly used comic techniques in designing satire." It is clear that of all the Restoration comic writers Wycherly comes closest to being a pure satirist. In *The Plain Dealer* and *The Country Wife* he brought to the satiric mode the intensity of his Jacobean predecessors wedded to a more rigorously formal conception of the genre. But in the application of formal satire to drama, Wycherly had no successors. The great satiric achievement in the English drama of the eighteenth century is John Gay's *The Beggar's Opera,* but Gay's work is *sui generis.* The comedy of Oliver Goldsmith and Richard Sheridan, although sharply ironic in tone, lacks the sustained ferocity of true satire.

The type of satire represented by Wycherly and Gay was also considerably muted in the Continental drama of the eighteenth century. The best comedians —Ludvig Holberg in Denmark, Carlo Goldoni in Italy, and Beaumarchais in France—were solidly rooted in the Molière tradition. An exception is Beaumarchais's *The Marriage of Figaro.* The intensity of that play's satire on the French nobility was such that it served as one of the rallying cries of the French Revolution.

Toward the end of the eighteenth century dramatic comedy came under the influence of "the goddess of the woeful countenance—the sentimental Muse." Sentimental comedy, under the dominance of Romantic principles, lies at the other end of the spectrum from satire. Thus, social criticism tended to be transformed into a celebration of progress rather than into an attack on existing inequities. One exception was the drama of Russia, where Nikolai Gogol's *The Inspector General* provided particularly incisive social satire. In the same vein was Alexander Ostrosky's *We Shall Settle It Between Ourselves,* a biting portrayal of the acquisitiveness of the middle class, and Leo Tolstoy's *The Fruits of the Enlightenment,* an indictment of the aristocracy delivered with the author's characteristic moral fervor. In this connection should be noted the social, satirical strains evident in the complexly wrought dramatic structure of Anton Chekhov.

In nineteenth-century English drama—aside from the lighthearted satire of Oscar Wilde and W. S. Gilbert—the term must be applied, however inadequately, to the plays of George Bernard Shaw. Shaw vigorously denied that he was a satirist, and in a very fundamental sense he was correct. Insofar as he was an apostle of ideas, a visionary of human possibility, Shaw was much more interested in proposing than exposing. The attack was of secondary importance to him and it was frequently so qualified as to hardly deserve the term. However greater this fact renders Shaw as a comic dramatist, it denies him the title of satirist. Still, the earlier plays particularly— *Widowers' Houses, The Philanderer,* and *Arms and the Man*—are heavily satiric in intent.

One contribution to the decline of satire or its assimilation within the "comedy of ideas" has been the prevalence of dramatic realism. Satire requires an element of distortion and a clear moral norm in order to be most effective. As Northrop Frye puts it, "satire demands at least a token fantasy, a content which the reader recognizes as grotesque, and at least an implicit moral standard, the latter being essential in a militant attitude to experience." While the stage was dominated by realism, fantasy and distortion found scant acceptance, and satire flourished only in fiction and poetry. With the movement away from an exclusively realistic theater, pure satire, when it embraced a clear ethical standard, again emerged, as in the plays of Bertolt Brecht, Jules Romains' *Knock,* and W. H. Auden and Christopher Isherwood's *The Dog Beneath the Skin* and *Ascent of F6.*

The most recent development in the theater has been the employment of the satiric vision when even the possibility of a clear moral standard seems to have collapsed. In this category might be placed the plays of Jean Genet, Friedrich Dürrenmatt, and Harold Pinter and the extraordinary performances of the comedian Lenny Bruce. From this perspective, the object of satire becomes man's very existence, and the author's mockery and contempt are reserved, not for the characters and situations of his play, but for his confused and perplexed audience. With this development, satiric drama—however unfunny its present form—returns to its primitive roots as an expression of destructive impulses.

Among general studies of the subject are David Worcester's *The Art of Satire* (1940), Gilbert Highet's *The Anatomy of Satire* (1962), and R. C. Elliott's *The Power of Satire* (1960). An original and perceptive discussion is contained in Northrop Frye's *The Anatomy of Criticism* (1957).

Noteworthy specialized studies include Alvin Kernan's *The Cankered Muse: Satire of the English Renaissance* (1959), O. J. Campbell's *Shakespeare's Satire* (1943), and Rose Zimbardo's *William Wycherly: A Link in the Development of English Satire* (1965).—E. Q.

satura. Etruscan form of comedy, brought to Rome in 364 B.C. The saturae are related to the obscene Fescennine verses, commonly chanted at marriage ceremonies. These verses, with dance, song, and dialogue added, became the saturae. They most often depicted scenes of daily life. Performed as concluding pieces to the Roman tragic contests, they are thought to have been very popular with Roman audiences. The satura later became fused with such forms as the Atellan farce, which finally supplanted it.

satyr play. In the festivals at which Greek plays were presented, the tragic trilogies were followed by a satyr play. Satyr plays usually dealt with some popular myth, which would be distorted or burlesqued for the purpose of amusement. The chorus was dressed as satyrs—mythical figures in the service of Dionysus. The purpose of the satyr play was apparently to emphasize the values associated with Dionysus as opposed to those associated with tragedy.

Sayın, Hidayet (1929–   ).   Turkish playwright.

Sayın was born and raised in Aydın, Turkey. He entered the medical school of the University of Ankara and currently practices pediatrics in his native Aydın. Although his early plays were refused for production, both *Topuzlu* (1964) and *Pembe Kadın* ("The Woman Named Pinky," 1965) were great successes, the latter playing more than four hundred times in Istanbul.

Sayın's plays are crusades against ignorance, religious fanaticism, and hypocrisy. Keenly aware of the need for enlightenment of the masses in Turkey, Sayın has poured his firsthand experience, as well as his sense of the tragic and the comic, into his plays about the village. Sayın sees the theater as a place of entertainment as well as a place of education, a notion that has, probably, contributed to the artistic as well as box office success of his plays.—N. O.

Scarron, Paul (1610–1660). French playwright, novelist, and poet. Born in Paris, Paul Scarron, despite a taste for pleasure, at first chose the church as a career. In 1629 he was called the Abbé Scarron and from 1632 to 1640 was secretary to the bishop of Le Mans. In 1638 he began to suffer from the illness that was to paralyze his limbs, deform his body, and confine him to a chair for the rest of his life. Nevertheless, in 1652 he married Françoise d'Aubigné, the future Mme. de Maintenon and wife of Louis XIV. Scarron spent his last years in frightful pain but surrounded by many libertine friends who appreciated his sparkling wit.

In poetry Scarron introduced into France the burlesque genre. However, faced with the bad taste of certain contemporary poets, he renounced the burlesque and never finished his transposition of the *Aeneid, Virgile travesti* ("Vergil Disguised," 1648–1652). Indeed, his last satires are altogether devoid of burlesque. In addition to his poems, tales, and plays, Scarron wrote one very picturesque novel, *Le Roman comique* (1651–1657), about provincial life and theatrical road companies.

Scarron's career as a dramatist started in 1643, at the beginning of the fashion for high comedy drawn from the Spanish *comedia*. He first wrote two plays for the clown Jodelet: *Jodelet ou le valet maître* ("Jodelet or the Master-Valet," 1643) and *Les Trois Dorothées* ("The Three Dorothys," 1645), later called *Jodelet duelliste* ("Jodelet the Fencer"). These are actually heroic pieces in which all the humor lies in the gluttony, cowardice, and clumsy wiles of the *gracioso* ("fool") Jodelet. Around 1648 Scarron followed the same pattern with *L'Héritier ridicule* ("The Ridiculous Heir"), written for the actor Philipin. In his masterpiece, *Don Japhet d'Arménie* ("Don Japheth of Armenia," 1647; revived 1651), the gracioso is replaced by Charles V's fool, who is at the center of the play and is an exaggerated burlesque caricature of aristocratic and heroic pretensions. In his last plays, with the exception of *Le Marquis ridicule* ("The Ridiculous Marquis," 1655), dedicated to Fouquet, the comic element is relegated to the background and the ROMANESQUE spirit prevails. Together with Pierre Corneille's *Le Menteur* (*The Liar*, 1643), which is very different, Scarron's Spanish-type high comedies are the most imaginative of the genre.

For a general survey of Scarron's life and works, see Naomi F. Phelps, *The Queen's Invalid* (1951). —Ja. G.

scène à faire. See WELL-MADE PLAY.

Schauspiel. Nonspecifically, a German term used to designate any stage drama production. However, the word has come to refer to an intermediate type of drama, neither comedy nor tragedy. The Schauspiel usually embodies a happy ending by the solution of a dramatic conflict, but without the burlesque elements of comedy and without necessarily reaching the heights of the tragic. The Schauspiel owes its existence primarily to the middle-class origins and audience of the modern German drama. As playwrights moved away from the traditional limitation of tragedy to characters of noble circumstances, the designation of Schauspiel became more frequently employed, although not always without ambiguity. Schiller's *Die Räuber* (*The Robbers*), at first called *Tragödie* ("tragedy"), later was designated a Schauspiel. Some plays clearly fitting into the category are Lessing's *Nathan der Weise* (*Nathan the Wise*), Heinrich von Kleist's *Prinz von Homburg* (*The Prince of Homburg*), and Schiller's *Wilhelm Tell*.—B. M. M.

Schicksalstragödie ("fate tragedy"). Type of German tragedy, written in the first quarter of the nineteenth century, in which a sequence of events was fatalistically linked with particular places, objects, and days, producing a heightened emotional effect. Although the idea of fate was an important part of drama as early as the era of classical Greece, the exaggerated concept of a demonic, unconquerable, inhuman fate, as presented in the Schicksalstragödie, was created by only a handful of German writers. Fate imposed from without had been, of course, a time-honored theme in German drama. The German Romantic movement, however, brought to life the concept of a demonic destiny, and the combination of this idea with several dramatic motives made possible a tragic hero, who, although beyond all possible guilt, still suffers. The motives were generally the return home, murder of close relatives, a curse on the family, prophecy of evil, or incest. These were most often presented as serving fate through an ominous linking of events, often in connection with a weapon, such as a knife or ax.

The number of authors of Schicksalstragödie was small, as was the total output of the literature. The best known, Zacharias WERNER, wrote the prototype of the genre, *Der 24. Februar* ("The Twenty-fourth of February," 1810). The play is basically the well-known story of child-murdering parents. On the fateful date, the son returns home to his impoverished parents but chooses not to disclose his identity immediately. From that point on, the action drives straight to his murder by his parents, who take him for a rich stranger. Throughout the entire action attention is repeatedly directed to the dagger on the wall, the murder weapon. The analytic structure of the drama—a necessity for this type of play—also reveals a prior curse on the family.

Although there were several lesser-known fate dramatists, the form did not prove to be too popular and made, in general, less-than-lasting contributions to the German drama.—B. M. M.

Schiller, [Johann Christoph] Friedrich von (1759–1805). German dramatist, critic, poet, historian, and, with Goethe, a central figure of German classicism. Born in Swabia, the young Schiller grew up in the rococo atmosphere of Duke Karl Eugen's des-

FRIEDRICH VON SCHILLER (WALTER HAMPDEN
MEMORIAL LIBRARY AT THE PLAYERS, NEW YORK)

potic Württemberg. As a student in the duke's schools, he was trained in medicine but spent much of his time immersed in the works of writers such as Lessing, Rousseau, Seneca, and Shakespeare. Even before his graduation in 1780 and subsequent appointment as a regimental medical officer, Schiller had begun to write his first play, THE ROBBERS. The drama was a STURM UND DRANG-flavored affair, reflecting the author's strong disaffection for the tyranny about him. Although he subsequently moved to another idiom, the question of freedom is central to all of Schiller's works. The play was a great success when produced in Mannheim in 1780, and Schiller, seeing his opportunity, fled the duchy for a career in letters. His subsequent appointment as a playwright in Mannheim lasted only one year, 1784. The theater management asserted that it sought "something in the middle" in its drama, as exemplified by the works of August Wilhelm Iffland, and that the extravagances' of The Robbers and Schiller's next major play, Kabale und Liebe (Cabal and Love, 1784), were not to the taste of the public.

Schiller next turned to literary journalism, founding a magazine called the Rheinische Thalia ("Rheinland Thalia"), at the same time attempting unsuccessfully to establish himself in the court at Darmstadt. In 1785 he accepted an invitation from Gottfried Körner to come to Leipzig, where he took up the study of history, continued the Thalia, and worked on his next major play, DON CARLOS, INFANTE OF SPAIN.

With the rewriting of Don Carlos into verse in 1788, Schiller simultaneously broke with the rebellion of his youth and took a step toward German classicism by creating a relatively new type of play, the Ideendrama ("idea drama"). The play also established iambic pentameter as the verse form of the classical drama: It subdued and bound much of the potential Sturm und Drang prose inherent in the father-son conflict and raised the tone of the play. Don Carlos was potentially both a play of generational conflict and a history play. With the invention of the character of Marquis Posa, however, Schiller walked in the direction marked out by Lessing's Nathan der Weise. Posa's bid for freedom of thought (Gedankenfreiheit), rather than historical or familial elements, was made the pivotal point of the play. This type of freedom was not necessarily tied to anything political, regardless of Posa's role as a practiced intriguer. For Schiller, it pointed the way to classicism and led into the world of ideas.

The creation of Don Carlos marked the beginning of a ten-year lapse in dramatic activity for Schiller. Having already moved to Weimar in 1787, he married the following year and in 1789 became professor of history at Jena. He wrote his history of the Thirty Years' War and at the same time produced a series of aesthetic essays and studied the philosophy of Kant.

Schiller's theoretical discussions led to a dramatic theory based on his studies of Kant. The stumbling block to perfection, the impossibility of perceiving the "thing in itself," is overcome through spiritual, in Schiller's case aesthetic, freedom. Thus, the role of the artist is again that of the educator, but the education is not a series of black and white examples to be emulated or avoided: It is to show the moral growth of the individual pitted against the necessities of reality. Thus, Wallenstein, hero of the trilogy WALLENSTEIN, written in 1799, is largely a negative example. An archrealist, he nonetheless goes to his doom, since he sees only necessity governing human actions: When his calculations are upset by the unforeseen, regardless of his motives, he does not have the freedom to achieve the moral dignity thought necessary by Schiller to overcome the physical. Mary Stuart, on the other hand, heroine of the play by the same name (1800), does in fact achieve moral regeneration in the acceptance of her fate. It is significant, though, that her moral ascension comes only after protracted suffering.

Although Schiller's outlook on life and his aesthetic philosophies differed greatly from those of Goethe, the "working partnership" formed by the two in 1795 proved to be the keystone of German classicism: Unquestionably one of the ideals they had in common was a reverence for the classical Greek love of beauty and harmony in life. Their friendship was also characterized by mutual criticism and encouragement.

Schiller's classical ideals and their pagan forebears no longer have the same meaning to the world that they had at the close of the eighteenth century. The outer trappings of his dramas, the court, the Thirty Years' War, even the meaning of the history serving as their basis, no longer have the same emotional impact they had 160 years ago. Yet the basic human problems with which Schiller dealt—guilt, morality, the individual and society, power—have by no means become irrelevant. Indeed, Schiller's dramas, particularly Mary Stuart, are still produced and received warmly today. A more detailed discussion of

Schiller's aims and accomplishments is found in
Ernst Stahl's *The Plays of Schiller. Theory and
Practice.*—B. M. M.

Schlegel, A. W. See GERMANY: *nineteenth century.*

Schlegel, Friedrich. See GERMANY: *nineteenth
century.*

Schnitzler, Arthur (1862–1931). Austrian playwright, novelist, short-story writer, and physician.
Schnitzler utilized his medical background as well as
his literary talents to produce drama of major importance. His father was a well-known Jewish throat
specialist, who founded a leading medical journal of
the day. Schnitzler attended the excellent medical
school of the University of Vienna and graduated in
1885, having written his dissertation on the hypnotic
treatment of neurosis. While actively engaged in his
literary career, Schnitzler continued to review medical publications on such diverse topics as hysteria,
hypnosis, sexual pathology, and psychotherapy. As a
dramatist, his dissection of characters is as incisive
and scientifically lucid as if he were conducting a delicate surgical operation.

Although Schnitzler and his contemporary Sigmund Freud never met, despite the fact that they
corresponded and lived within walking distance of
each other, their scientific observations were carried
on simultaneously, and in many instances they arrived at like conclusions, as, for example, in regard
to depth psychology. Both Schnitzler and Freud frequently expressed profound regard for one another's
work.

Schnitzler's literary output is most often seen as a
reflection of an age, the fall of imperial Vienna,
typified by decadence and the pleasure-seeking instinct. Play after play, narrative after narrative disclose an atmosphere of sultry decline that verges on
disease. Yet Schnitzler wrote with charm and grace
and, more importantly, with great compassion when
faced with the tender, though often brutal frailty of
man.

Schnitzler's characters are bent on pleasure, on
squeezing from life its last drop of sensual enjoyment,
for fear that the angel of death, hovering above them,
may soon descend and destroy. The angel of death
appears in various forms. In THE GAME OF LOVE we
see him as the husband of Fritz's mistress; his appearance is austere and foreboding and judgmental.
In LA RONDE the angel of death is omnipresent in the
fear that tomorrow may never come, and the moment
is all that matters. Virtually the same is true of his
series of one-act plays under the title *Anatol* (1893):
the moment is all; time will not wait for man. Frenetic sex, as an escape from a crumbling society, is
the prevailing theme of most of his plays, as well as of
his narratives; there is little love. If much of Schnitzler's work seems precious and sentimental, it is so by
strict design, for he is mirroring his age. Below that
exterior, however, lurks cruelty, hardness, ruthlessness, skepticism, and despair.

Central to many of Schnitzler's works is a Pirandello-like vision of reality and illusion. Illusion, of
course, is the essence of his characters' escape; at
other times illusion is presented as manifestly that. In
the end, however, illusion turns itself into stark, cruel
reality. THE GREEN COCKATOO is a prime example of
this, for in that play what begins as play-acting indeed turns into reality of the most terrible and
bloody sort.

Schnitzler is also one of the earliest practitioners
of the stream-of-consciousness technique, as in his
novella *Leutnant Gustl* (*Lieutenant Gustl*, pub.
1901), and in parts of *Anatol*.

Schnitzler's keen and critical observation of man's
nature may well be the true inception on a wide scale
of psychological probing in modern drama and literature in general. Along with Freud, his insights are
still valid, because he viewed man not from a romantic, but from a humanistic and clinical point of view.

Only one full-length biography of Schnitzler has
appeared in English, by Sol Liptzin, *Arthur Schnitzler* (1932). Though scarcely comprehensive, having
been written so soon after Schnitzler's death, it is a
fairly good introduction to his life and work. A more
recent study is by Claude Hill, "The Stature of
Arthur Schnitzler," *Modern Drama*, Vol. IV (1961).
—C. R. M.

School for Scandal, The (1777). A comedy by
Richard Brinsley SHERIDAN. *The School for Scandal*
was put on at Drury Lane toward the close of Sheridan's first year as manager there. His first season had
proved a disappointing one and a new comedy by
him, it was hoped, might redeem matters. *The School
for Scandal* was instantly recognized as one of the
great comedies of manners that had been given to the
English stage. It has never lost its popularity, as
present-day revivals clearly prove.

The accepted formula for Georgian comedy called
for a pair of lovers, or better two pairs, about whom
the action could pivot. At the start the lovers would
find themselves unable to marry because of certain
obstacles, usually the objections of parents or guardians. Further complications would develop as the
loved ones and those opposing them schemed and
counterschemed to overcome or to uphold the obstacles. The denouement would resolve everything, and
would do so in the traditional manner of chance
events and sudden revelations and discoveries delivering heroes and heroines from their difficulties and
visiting punishment on all those guilty of villainous
behavior. And such is actually the formula that
Sheridan took over for his greatest comedy. But
being a master of stagecraft, he was able to bring a
new force to the old form.

Charles Surface and Maria, the first pair of lovers,
are being thwarted on many sides: by Sir Peter
Teazle, Maria's guardian, who disapproves of
Charles and believes him to be attracted to Lady
Teazle; by Lady Sneerwell, in love with Charles and
abetting Charles's brother, Joseph, in his advances to
Maria; and by a disagreeable lover of Maria's, the
poetaster Sir Benjamin Backbite, nephew of the
odious Crabtree. The other couple are Sir Peter
Teazle and his new wife, who constitute a brilliant
variant from the familiar dramatic formula. He is no
youth, while she is very young and, coming from a
country home, has had her head turned by city pleasures and fashionable follies. They are already at
odds with one another, to the distress of the fond and
bewildered Sir Peter. The link between these two
centers of action—Charles and Maria, Sir Peter and
Lady Teazle—is supplied by Joseph Surface, in
every way a contrast to his brother, Charles. Charles
is a prodigal and something of a rake, but he is frank,

PAINTING OF A SCENE FROM RICHARD SHERIDAN'S *The School for Scandal* (BRANDER MATTHEWS DRAMATIC MUSEUM, COLUMBIA UNIVERSITY)

honest, and generous. Joseph is a hypocrite, a back-biter, always professing the noblest sentiments, constantly delivering moral sentences. Joseph is on the point of corrupting Lady Teazle, while at the same time, under Lady Sneerwell's encouragement, he is playing for Maria's hand. And as a friend of Lady Sneerwell, Joseph directs the action of the play toward still another center of interest, the circle of scandalmongers who gather at Lady Sneerwell's: Lady Sneerwell herself, who puts about scandalous stories to discredit Charles in the eyes of Maria; Mrs. Candour; and Sir Benjamin Backbite and his uncle, Crabtree. The complications and the necessary untangling thereof occur along two lines. Sir Peter is enlightened, for it is Joseph, he finds, not Charles, who has been carrying on an intrigue, as yet innocent, with his wife. He learns the truth of the matter in the famous screen scene, which brought thunderous applause from the audience. Foolishly, Lady Teazle pays Joseph a visit. At Sir Peter's unexpected arrival she is forced to hide behind a screen in the room. Then, quite as unexpectedly, Charles turns up. The climax comes when Charles knocks over the screen and to his own and Sir Peter's astonishment reveals a fearful and already chastened Lady Teazle. The prospect is for the reconciliation of the Teazles; as Sir Peter puts it, "We may yet be the happiest couple in the county." The second line of resolution concerns Charles Surface, Maria, and Joseph Surface. It is learned that Sir Oliver Surface, the uncle and benefactor of Charles and Joseph, has just returned to England from a long absence in the East.

The question is whether Sir Oliver will listen to Charles's detractors and be taken in by Joseph's hypocrisy. But Sir Oliver is determined to find out the truth for himself and resorts to disguises to do so. He reveals his identity at the crucial moment, confounds Joseph, and rewards the good-natured Charles by removing the impediments to his union with Maria.

The habits of the town as here depicted make for a sustained manners comedy. The unfolding of the several plots—done with incomparable skill—holds our interest throughout every scene and confronts us with a sequence of situations of such dramatic effectiveness that any one would have been enough to ensure the play's success. Sheridan triumphs not as a creator of characters so much as a master of stagecraft. Everything about *The School for Scandal* has been fashioned with the stage in mind. The dramatis personae have been born with their make-up on. The spoken lines have been composed with a perfect ease of intonation. The high moments of the action, calling into service every device known to the trade, are theatrically foolproof. But in the end it is the spirit that the play diffuses that affects us most. We are drawn briefly into a world which, if by no means the best of all possible ones, is a place of comparative well-being for those who would choose to have it so.

The School for Scandal, together with a discussion of it, may be found in *Richard Brindsley Sheridan (Six Plays)* (1957), edited by Louis Kronenberger. —R. Q.

Schuldrama (Latin "school drama"). Latin, and

later German, drama written during the Renaissance and Reformation eras for use in German secondary schools. Accompanying the increase of Humanistic influences on German education in the fifteenth and sixteenth centuries, the form was developed for the environment of the secondary school, or gymnasium. It supplanted the medieval religious drama and was written for and produced by the students. The plays were pedagogically oriented, aimed at increasing facility in Latin, as well as inculcating a deeper interest in moral and Humanistic studies. Sources for the plays were the Bible, particularly the parables, and classical antiquity, the latter being exploited by a conscious imitation of the plays of Plautus and Terence. Not restricted to academic matters alone, the Latin school drama was also pressed into the service of the Reformation. At this time the transition was made to the German vernacular, using even such traditional verse forms as *Knittelvers*.

Although the audience and scope of the Latin school drama were limited, the form made some far-reaching contributions to German drama, particularly to that of the succeeding Baroque era: New materials created dramatic tension by concentration on a single heroic figure; length and cast size were reduced from the days-long, mass-cast productions of the Passion plays; classical antiquity was consciously utilized; division into acts was introduced. The most well known of the Latin school dramatists were Johannes Reuchlin, Gnaphaeus (pen name of Willem de Valder), and Georg Macropedius.—B. M. M.

Scotland.   The theater in Scotland has always had to grow on stony ground; it is not a native plant. Still, there were many signs in the fifteenth and sixteenth centuries that the individualism, humor, and imagination of the Scottish people, so well demonstrated in their ballads, was already finding a voice in the moralities and festival pageants that abounded. Scottish medieval drama reached its peak with the first performance, in 1540, of Scotland's one great play, ANE PLEASANT SATYRE OF THE THRIE ESTAITIS, by Sir David Lyndsay (1490–1555). Lyndsay's satire, with its bitingly realistic touches, was far in advance of any of the almost totally didactic English moralities of the time. But in the seventeenth century indigenous drama all but died out, and drama in the vernacular, on Scottish themes, acted by Scottish companies, was almost nonexistent in the urban centers until the 1920's. Religious prohibitions, civil strife, and perhaps geographical remoteness each played its part in blocking the rich Scottish poetic-satiric imagination.

It was not until 1736 that the first Scottish playhouse was opened, but it was promptly closed down under the licensing laws. By 1756 it was possible, but only with English players, to put on that remarkable work *Douglas,* by John Home (1722–1808), which was immortalized by the cry that greeted its first performance: "Whair's your Wullie Shakespeare now?" A romantic tragedy, it is about young Douglas, who is killed by the man whose life he has saved. Though the play is long, its action takes place within a twenty-four-hour period and is reminiscent of Racine in its tight plotting and intense, rational emotion. The language and atmosphere, too, mark the play as one of the memorable dramas of the eighteenth century. In spite of its classic form, the play is profoundly ro-

DOUGLAS:

A

TRAGEDY.

As it is ACTED at the

THEATRE-ROYAL

IN

COVENT-GARDEN.

Non ego fum vates, fed prifci confcius ævi.

EDINBURGH:

Printed for G. HAMILTON & J. BALFOUR, W. GRAY & W. PETER.
M,DCC,LVII.

[Price One Shilling Sixpence.]

TITLE PAGE OF THE 1757 EDITION OF JOHN HOME'S
Douglas

mantic in its attempt to preserve a semihistorical legend in blank verse and to present picturesque characters motivated by sentimental enthusiasms. Not the least remarkable aspect of the play's career is that it was produced at all, for in the early and middle eighteenth century actors in Scotland were ill paid, and their theaters were always in danger of being closed down under the licensing laws or burned down by religious enthusiasts.

In the nineteenth century theater came upon better days, at least in Edinburgh and Glasgow, as evidenced in the playbills issued by the Theatre Royals in these cities. But despite adaptations of Sir Walter Scott's *Rob Roy MacGregor* (1817) and *Guy Mannering* (1819) and other such plays that were calculated to rouse national pride, and despite the rise to eminence of some Scottish-born actors, theater remained a somewhat marginal business. Stock companies circulated and illustrious performers made periodic appearances, but most of the plays were English. The only really indigenous and original theatrical fare was pantomimes. Some of the dramatic collaborations of Robert Louis Stevenson and William Ernest Henley—*Deacon Brodie* (1880), *Beau Austin* (1890), and *Admiral Guinea* (1897)— were quite successful.

And, of course, there was Sir James M. Barrie, Scotland's first prominent modern dramatist who projected the Scot's pride and Scotland's atmosphere onto the international stage. Barrie originally wrote stories and novels about one of the strictest and narrowest religious sects in Scotland, the Auld Licht, on whose doctrines he was brought up. His first play, *The Little Minister* (1897), was tremendously successful in Scotland and England, although it is not a very good play when compared to his later work. But the new, strange use of psalm-singing and religious pride and prejudice as background to a love comedy struck exactly the right note for audiences. However, with the passing years, Barrie became increasingly an English dramatist. (See ENGLAND: *nineteenth century and the Edwardian period*.)

According to playwright James Bridie, John Brandane (pseudonym of Dr. John MacIntyre, 1869–1947) might well be called the father of modern Scottish drama. Brandane fought uncompromisingly for his ideal of a school of Scottish dramatists and actors who would derive sustenance from their native soil. In *The Glen Is Mine* (1923) he contributed to that movement its best Scottish comedy. It is a strongly constructed play alive with acute observation and humor. Its protagonist is Angus MacKinnon, a small farmer who saves his croft and the surrounding land from the attempts of the landlords and loaners to appropriate it and begin iron-mining operations. But there are no real villains. Old Colonel Murray is delighted that his son, the Captain, has been blocked in his efforts to mar the land and destroy the hunting. And the Captain himself is not cruel, just a bit stupid. It is the glen itself that seems to rise up through the simple farmer and proclaim its rightful owner. Brandane also wrote a number of other plays, some of which have been translated into Erse, Gaelic, and Norse. It was largely due to Brandane's influence that Bridie and others were encouraged to become playwrights in Scotland.

Scottish playwrights were also encouraged by the founding of the first professional theater, the Scottish Players Limited, during the period (1909–1914) when the repertory movement that followed the impact of Henrik Ibsen swept north from England. While the plays produced were still predominantly the works of Englishmen—George Bernard Shaw, Harley Granville-Barker, John Masefield, James Barrie, Arthur Pinero, and many others—Scottish dramas were also produced. *Campbell of Kilmohor* (1914) by John Ferguson (1873–1928), a one-act historical tragedy, remains the period's one native play that can be called truly effective.

This work, together with a few of the plays of Dr. Gordon Bottomley (1874–1948), was an early indication of the possibilities of a poetic treatment of Scottish history. Bottomley attempted to bring poetry to the stage in Scotland as William Butler Yeats had done in Ireland. Among Bottomley's suc-

cessful verse plays are *King Lear's Wife* (1915), *Britain's Daughters* (1922), *Gruach* (1921), and *Laodice and Danae* (1930). Bottomley was influenced by Masefield's theater at Oxford, the *noh* drama of Japan, and Yeats's *Four Plays for Dancers* in evolving his own concept of drama. But it was Scotland's fierce and tragic themes that were his greatest inspiration. *Gruach*, for example, is an exciting study of the first meeting between Macbeth and his future wife, a wildly passionate, ambitious girl who sweeps the bewildered young lord into an elopement on the eve of her promised wedding to a local nonentity.

The outbreak of World War I forced the Scottish Players Limited and the Glasgow Repertory Theatre to discontinue performances, but the tradition they had established was continued after the war by the Scottish National Players. This group of talented actors, devoted to native Scottish drama, was the first to produce in the years 1921 through 1936 the works of more than thirty Scottish dramatists, including, among others, Bridie, Brandane, Joe Corrie, Ferguson, Neil Gunn, and Robins Millar.

In January 1922, the Scottish National Theatre Society was formed. This group's objective was to support the Scottish National Players in their attempt to found a Scottish national theater along the lines of the Abbey Theatre in Dublin. It failed, apparently because of financial difficulties and the constant lure of London, which drew away many of the most promising Scottish actors, directors, and playwrights. Nevertheless, the Scottish National Players, though largely amateur, offered the public a wide selection of native drama. Six plays were commissioned each year. The average level of production was as high as that of Dublin's theater, though no play reached the heights of those by John Millington Synge or Sean O'Casey. Still, plays such as Brandane's *The Glen Is Mine* and *The Darkness* (1931) by Joe Corrie (1894–   ) had great distinction. Corrie supplied the modern Scottish dramatic movement with some of its most representative one-act plays, ranging through kitchen comedy, tragedy, and history. His *Red Roses* (1936), *A Plumber and a Man* (1937), and *Hewers of Coal* (1937) all have the qualities already ascribed to Brandane's work, but there is a solid concern with the workman combined with a poetic strain that is reminiscent of O'Casey.

In the late 1930's the effectiveness of the Scottish National Players waned. In its place a variety of "little theaters," repertory in nature, appeared. This movement encouraged local playwrights but produced hardly any players of stature or playmakers of first rank. It has been noted that places where the amateur movement is strongest are notoriously those that give the poorest support to professional theater. Unfortunately, there is a tendency toward competitive individualism that undermines the vision of a national theater.

Of the many playwrights developed by Scottish theatrical movements, only James BRIDIE has thus far succeeded in reaching beyond local appeal. The recurrent complaint about his dramas is that they have strong beginnings and weak final acts. Bridie always held that his plays were *sui generis* and that only God could write strong final acts. His distinguishing mark is a strong moral sense that is given delightful perspective through his wit. Even when he is deflating one of his self-satisfied, boastful characters, he does it with understanding laughter. Bridie, though facile, combined a knowledge of drama with a love of Scotland, resulting in plays that realize the dreams of Brandane and the Scottish National Players. It is significant in this respect that he took more joy in the Edinburgh Festival triumphs, *The Thrie Estaitis* in 1948 and the antique Scottish satire *The Gentle Shepherd* in 1949, than he did in the success of his own *The Golden Legend of Shults,* first produced at the Edinburgh Festival in 1948.

Today there are no more than seventeen places in the whole of Scotland where, for all or part of the year, the public is offered live entertainment. There is, of course, the annual Edinburgh Festival, which for three weeks uses every available and makeshift stage in that city, but it has had, so far, little effect on Scottish dramatic life. Almost all of Scotland's theatrical life is now concentrated in repertory companies, all recently formed. Among them, the repertories put on more than fifty productions a year, with a fair selection from the contemporary repertory and a small sprinkling of classics. Aside from the Edinburgh Festival, it is through them alone that Scottish audiences have had a chance to see anything of modern international drama. Since Bridie, there has been little Scottish drama worth noting, but what there is gets its showing in repertory.

There have been no published books on the general topic of Scottish drama.—D. J. L.

screenplay. A screenplay is a written version of a motion picture. It is a generic term for any transcription of a complete film, short or long, story, document, cartoon. There is no fixed form which is considered mandatory for a screenplay, but it must be sufficiently detailed to include whatever dialogue is used, with a description of action, movement, settings, backgrounds, transitions, and sounds. Variations in the style and arrangement of screenplays reflect the difficulty of translating sights and sounds into language. The only element in a motion picture that can be directly reproduced is the dialogue; the other elements require interpretation. The writer may place major emphasis on the color and texture of the cinematic events, or he may feel it is necessary to stress technical factors: camera angles, lighting and lenses, contrasting images and transitions, and use of sounds and music. Underlying these divergent approaches are problems concerning the relationship of cinema to other art forms, especially to literature and drama. The word "screenplay" implies that it is, at least in some respects, analogous to a stage play. A written drama is accepted as literature, and it is also the basis for theatrical presentation. A screenplay performs a similar service in the production of a film, but there are differences that are of such magnitude that they invalidate the comparison. The great length of time and elaborate organization needed for cinematic production are its most obvious characteristics and distinguish it from a stage play. There is a more fundamental distinction in the result: stage rehearsals lead to a creative event that is ephemeral in that it can be repeated on successive occasions and changed each time, and the same play may be interpreted in a different manner in other theatrical productions. The film, on the other hand, is a permanent record on a perforated ribbon of celluloid.

The screenplay has such an intimate bearing on the process of production that its aesthetic function cannot be considered without a brief examination of its role in commercial film-making. The starting point of a motion picture is something in writing, but it is only rarely that the project starts with a complete screenplay. The decision to make a film may be based on an idea or original story or on the selection of a novel, play, biography, or historical incident. In developing this material, the screenwriter cannot rely solely on his own creative impulse or judgment. He is not a free agent, because he is employed. The work is discussed in conferences with the producer, the director, and other persons involved in the business or technical aspects of the film. The writer's first task is to make a short synopsis, followed by a longer outline called a "treatment." There may be one or many drafts of the screenplay, and it may require the services of a number of writers. The considerations that govern this process are to a large extent economic and technical—cost of production, availability of performers, shooting schedules, and locations. When the director begins his work, he must adhere to the budget and fulfill each day's required number of scenes. But within these limits, he has a large measure of control and can modify the screenplay in response to the conditions of production, camera setups, temperaments of actors, unexpected lighting effects, and other contingencies. Further changes occur after shooting is completed in editing the strips of celluloid, introducing a musical score, combining images and sounds. When the final print of a film is made and duplicated for distribution, the screenplay seems to have faded or dissolved like a scene in a motion picture. But if the screenplay is published, it reappears, not in its earlier form, but as a finished work that has absorbed all the changes made during production. Having been subservient to all the necessities of production, the screenplay, freed at last from the shooting schedule and the cutting room, asserts a creative life of its own. If its creative identity is acknowledged, the fact must be faced that there is no satisfactory definition of the art of film. There is a great deal of theoretical discussion of cinema as a graphic art, as "painting with light," as a portrayal of "physical reality," or as a structure of sights and sounds. But these theories do not account for the storytelling function of the motion picture. The screenplay fulfills the narrative function; it relates film to drama and fiction, but it has an indeterminate place in the creative process. It can be regarded as a work of art, to be interpreted as a play is interpreted, or it can be relegated to secondary importance as little more than a stenographic record of the creator's manipulation of the camera and the microphone.

The role of the writer is one aspect of the problem, but it is not the sole issue. The view that the writer is the true creator and that the director should interpret the writer's vision is disproved by the history of cinema. Furthermore, this defense of the writer does not contribute much to our understanding of the screenplay, because many of the acknowledged masterpieces of cinematic art were written solely by the director. These examples tend to confirm the belief that film, like other arts, is the product of one person's unique inspiration. In the history of cinema, the director has been that person. Although his authority has seldom been absolute, he is habitually referred to as the film maker.

Dudley Nichols, who wrote *The Informer* and other outstanding American pictures, holds that the making of a film is

> a series of creations . . . a vast collaboration in which, if you have ever achieved a satisfactory film, you must accept a humble part. Yet the collaboration must always have a dominant will and personality if the work is to be good. Sometimes two people can work together with such sympathy and shared attitude that they can achieve a common style: and these two people must, I believe, be the writer and director.

Nichols has demonstrated the value of intimate cooperation in his work with director John Ford on *The Informer* in 1935 and *The Plough and the Stars* in 1936, and with Jean Renoir on *This Land Is Mine* in 1943. Every experienced screenwriter knows that the best results are obtained when there is a working relationship between writer and director. Experience proves, however, that the circumstances of production do not encourage such an understanding. A director is not inclined to share his authority with the writer or anyone else, and it is by no means certain that it would be desirable for him to do so.

The organization of Hollywood screenwriters, the Writers Guild of America West, founded in 1933 as the Screen Writers' Guild, has advanced screenwriters' economic interests and has had a constructive influence on film making. Leading writers are consulted not only concerning script problems but also in regard to the interpretation of their work. They have no control, however, over the way their material is used, changed, or discarded. Even the copyright is in the name of the corporation. The American screenwriter is more highly paid but has less creative authority than his counterpart in the film industries of other countries. This is due in part to the huge investment in American films and the business apparatus designed to safeguard the investment. The writer's place in the system of production has its origin in the early history of Hollywood. In the era of silent movies, scripts suggested situations and moods, but the director relied on his own craftsmanship and imagination, using the written material as a basis for improvisation. The introduction of dialogue made it imperative to follow the script closely and gave greater authority to the writer. At the same time, the technological difficulties of sound and the demands that speech imposed on actors increased the director's responsibilities. The modern development of film-making has tended to give added importance to all the creative personnel. This is evidenced in Hollywood in the abandonment of mass production methods and the growth of separate producing units, financed by banks or distributing companies. Outside of Hollywood, there has been a lively demand for artistic freedom in recent years. The demand has come from directors rather than from writers, as is seen in the rise of the "underground cinema" in the United States. The underground movement is not a cohesive group but instead represents many divergent trends. Its more striking successes, however, such as Andy

Warhol's films, Kenneth Anger's *Scorpio Rising* (1964), or Jack Smith's *Flaming Creatures* (1963), are directorial achievements, and their emphasis on spontaneity and improvisation gives less weight to the screenplay.

A more definitive assertion of the director's preeminence has come from Europe, especially in connection with the *nouvelle vague* ("new wave") in France. The theory of the *politique des auteurs*, proclaiming that directors are obligated as a matter of politics or policy to defend their position as the authors of their films, was announced more than a decade ago by a group associated with the French magazine *Cahiers du cinema*. Among them were Claude Chabrol, François Truffaut, André Bazin, Eric Rohmer, and Jacques Rivette. The *politique des auteurs* has played a part in securing international recognition for directors who are noted for their personal style, integrity, and dedication to the art of film. There are a growing number of these artist-directors in Europe, as well as in India and Japan. Their standing as the creators of works that bear their signature does not negate the value of the screenplay —and indeed may even enhance it since the screenplay is either written by the director or by writers who share his viewpoint.

There is far more extensive publication of screenplays in other countries than in the United States, and their appeal to readers seems to be in direct ratio to the film-maker's reputation. A volume of *Four Screen Plays* (pub. 1960) by the Swedish director Ingmar Bergman credits him with sole authorship. A book of Italian screenplays by director Michelangelo Antonioni (pub. 1963) includes the names of several writers who assisted in the preparation of the scenarios. Their contribution cannot be measured, but the title and Antonioni's Introduction leave no doubt that the energizing force and authority are his alone. Both these books are available in English translations, but no American director has been honored with a similar collection of his films.

It would be a mistake to conclude that the stronger position of the director reduces the writer to impotence. On the contrary, the growth of the art film has stimulated the interest of well-known authors who are attracted to cinema as an art form and are eager to work with directors whom they respect. Marguerite Duras, a prominent French novelist, collaborated with Alain Resnais on *Hiroshima mon Amour* (1959), and an equally important novelist, Alain Robbe-Grillet, worked with Resnais on *Last Year at Marienbad* (1961). More recently, Robbe-Grillet has undertaken the direction of a film.

These instances support the theory that the screenplay is an integral part of the creative process, but they do not throw much light on the relationship of the written film to the pattern of sight and sound. John Gassner defends "the screen play as literature" in his Introduction to *Twenty Best Film Plays* (pub. 1943). Gassner asserts that, "like any other vital form of writing, a screen play has its own construction and inner nature." Gassner felt that readers would be attracted to screenplays if a suitable form was devised that would dispense with technical details and at the same time preserve the essential quality of film experience, a literary equivalent of seeing and hearing.

But *Twenty Best Film Plays,* although invaluable as a collection of American films from the beginning of sound to the early forties, did not have a sufficiently wide appeal to justify the announced plan to publish a yearly anthology; the project was abandoned.

Among the few screenplays published in the United States, the selection is evidently affected by the author's reputation in other fields rather than by the cinematic value of the work. A volume of James Agee's films is to some extent an exception, since some of his writing for the screen is of unusual interest. But Agee's literary reputation and his standing as a film critic are factors in the publication of his screenplays, and it is fair to assume that there are similar considerations in regard to Tennessee Williams' *Baby Doll* (1956), Budd Schulberg's *A Face in the Crowd* (1957), Paddy Chayefsky's *The Goddess* (1958), and Arthur Miller's *The Misfits* (1961). Miller's work attempts to combine literary and cinematic elements. He calls it a "cinematic novel," observing that motion pictures "have willy-nilly created a particular way of seeing life, and their swift transitions, their sudden bringing together of disparate images . . . have infiltrated the novel and playwriting." Miller intends to give cinema "its full effect in language . . . . As a result of a purely functional attempt to make a film clear to others . . . there was gradually suggested a form of fiction itself, a mixed form if you will . . . ."

Miller's mixed form is closer to literature than to the sensations produced by the projection of a motion picture. He states the problem from a writer's point of view and thus emphasizes the inescapable difference between words on a page and the flow of images and sounds. Directors who comment on the problem tend to regard the tools that they use, the camera and the microphone, in somewhat the same way in which a sculptor regards the chisel and the stone, or a painter his brushes, easel, and canvas. Antonioni describes the screenplay as "provisional words which later will no longer have any use." He is guided, he says, by changes "suggested to me by the actual circumstances at time of shooting . . . . It is only when I press my eye against the camera and begin to move the actors that I get an exact idea of the scene." Antonioni concludes that "screen plays are on the way to becoming actually sheets of notes for those who, at the camera, will write the films themselves."

Antonioni's published screenplays are far more than suggestions and notes. They constitute an invaluable record of his concepts and purposes. The value of the screenplay as a guide to production depends on the way in which the film-maker works, the extent to which he imagines and shapes the materials of his art. Resnais is a director whose imagination is apparently stimulated by close collaboration with writers, and his screenplays are rich in psychological detail as well as technical notations. For example, *Muriel* (1963), written by Jean Cayrol and embodying ideas of past and present time, which appear in all of Resnais's films, is arranged so as to give an exact account of camera angles, cutting and transitions, the interaction of speech and image, and the time to the minute at which the action takes place. *Muriel* also contains studies of the characters and their personal

histories, descriptions of the city of Boulogne, past and present, and photographs to show the positions and movements of the people. Small pictures illustrate the camera angles noted in the text.

Whether this abundance of technical information is fascinating or confusing to a reader depends on the reader's taste and knowledge of film art. The publication of screenplays in many countries suggests that people can learn to enjoy the written film and to accept its form. Regardless of the public response, published film plays are desperately needed by scholars and cinema artists, whose work is impeded by the lack of essential materials. It is not always easy to obtain prints of films, and it requires a great deal of time to run a print repeatedly and analyze its elements. Manuscripts are stored in the vaults of motion picture studios, but scholars have no access to these records. Most of the films made during the past seventy years, including the acknowledged masterpieces that have changed the course of film development, are unpublished and therefore unavailable to anyone who does not have a print at his disposal. There is a fairly complete cinematic record of Charlie Chaplin's art, but there are no published texts; we are deprived of the opportunity to study the preparation and development of his work and the relationship between the design and the execution.

Confusion regarding the nature of cinema and its relationship to other arts is to some extent perpetuated by the dearth of available texts. The screenplay's status as literature can be disputed, but no one can deny that there is a vast backlog of screenplays, old and new, that should be published as a public service, an aid to research, and an essential historical record.

The following collections of screenplays are referred to in the text: John Gassner and Dudley Nichols, eds., *Twenty Best Film Plays* (1943) with two introductions, on "The Screen Play as Literature" by Gassner, and "The Writer and the Film" by Nichols; Gassner and Nichols, eds., *Best Film Plays of 1943–44* (1945); Gassner and Nichols, eds., *Best Film Plays of 1945* (1946). Gassner and Nichols have also edited *Great Film Plays* (1959). Collections of works by one author include James Agee, *Agee on Film: Five Film Scripts* (1964); Ingmar Bergman, *Four Screenplays,* translated by Lars Malmstrom and David Kushner (1960); Michelangelo Antonioni, *Screenplays,* translated by Louis Brigante (1963). Of special historical interest is Robert E. Sherwood, ed., *The Best Motion Pictures of 1922–23* (1923), containing brief summaries of sixteen films. There are several excellent anthologies of film criticism and theory, including various opinions concerning the relationship of cinema to fiction and drama: Lewis Jacobs, ed., *Introduction to the Art of the Movies* (1960); Richard Dyer MacCann, ed., *A Montage of Theories* (1966); Daniel Talbot, ed., *Film: An Anthology* (1966).—J. H. L.

Screens, The (Les Paravents, 1966). A play by Jean GENET. *The Screens* was first performed in West Berlin in 1961. The first Paris production did not take place until 1966, under the direction of Roger Blin at the Théâtre de France. The sets for this very long and complicated play are a series of screens on which objects and landscapes are painted. A character appears bearing his screen and therefore masked.

The Algerian War is the background of the play, composed of twenty-five tableaus, or scenes. One center of the play's action is formed by three wretched and impoverished Arabs: Saïd, his mother, and his wife, Leïla. Two prostitutes, Warda and Malika, form a second group. Those directly engaged in the war—the lieutenant, the sergeant, and the legionnaires—form still another center. But there are many other characters creating many subordinate actions, all of which are related in some way to the principal opposition Genet is interested in creating: that existing between the oppressors and the oppressed.

As the characters die or are killed, they mount to the highest level on the stage and continue to watch thoughtfully but without passion the activities of the living. Both French and Arabs are surprised that death is so simple. The revolt of the young Arab Saïd, a thief, murderer, arsonist, and traitor, is the incarnation of social negativity. He is outside the Arab village, the resistance movement, and even the newly established order. His refusal of any type of social power reaches far beyond the immediate revolt of the oppressed Algerian people. Corruption and self-betrayal are implicit within the revolutionary movement, within any reform, no matter what its nature. In order to prevent the oppressed from becoming like their former masters, one must radically refuse any compromise with the newly forming order. Saïd thus betrays his own race. By committing all possible sins, Saïd reaches his own sanctity in the full Genet tradition where the criminals and outcasts of society are like the saint because they rebel against society and assume the hatred of their culture by completely denying themselves.

The Screens has been translated by Bernard Frechtman (1962).—W. F.

Scribe, [Augustin] Eugène (1791–1861). French playwright and librettist. One of the most prolific of all playwrights, Scribe wrote and had successfully performed 374 works, including 216 *comédies-vaudevilles* (simple, seriocomic plays with satirical songs rhymed to old popular airs), 114 librettos for *opéras-comiques* and grand operas, and 35 full-length plays. In his plays he fused light satire of bourgeois foibles and an intricately precise plot structure, in which action, suspense, and *coups de théâtre* were more important than character development or psychology, in a formula that has become known since the mid-nineteenth century as the WELL-MADE PLAY. In many countries realistic drama, especially the problem or "thesis" play, owes a great debt to Scribe. In addition to being a superlative craftsman, he personified in his plays and in his personal life the solid values, tastes, and ideals of the French middle class. A lifelong resident of Paris, his success in the theater and his shrewd business sense made him a rich and respected man. He helped bring about a number of reforms in author-producer relations and theatrical management. Although he wrote his greatest successes during the heyday of the Romantic movement, Scribe made few concessions to it. Save in the operas and a few other works, he adhered to the classical tradition of satirical comedy from Plautus to Beaumarchais.

His first successful comédie-vaudeville was *L'Auberge, ou les Brigands sans le savoir* ("The Inn, or the Unwitting Bandits," 1812). Then followed in rapid succession (often several a year) successful performances of these light, entertaining plays, seasoned with witty songs and a dash of sober instruction: *Une Nuit de la Garde Nationale* ("A Night with the National Guard," 1815), *Le Solliciteur, ou l'Art d'obtenir des places* ("The Solicitor, or the Way to Succeed," 1817), *Le Charlatanisme* ("Charlatanism," 1825), *Le Mariage de Raison* ("The Arranged Marriage," 1826), *Malvina, ou le Mariage d'Inclination* ("Malvina, or the Impulsive Marriage," 1828), *La Famille Riquebourg, ou le Mariage mal assorti* ("The Riquebourg Family, or the Mismatched Marriage," 1831), and *La Frontière de Savoie* (*A Peculiar Position*, 1834), to name only a few of the most outstanding. The titles of some of these suggest their content: ridicule of speculation, unethical conduct or business methods, incompatible marriages. With the help of various collaborators, he improved this genre over the next fifty years and gradually expanded these sketches of contemporary manners into ambitious social comedies that became the true prototypes of the well-made play.

In 1827 the first of these ambitious plays, *Le Mariage d'Argent* ("Marriage for Money"), was performed at the Théâtre Français, which was to produce most of his long works. Despite the frequent charge that it is shallow or "materialistic," this serious comedy shows the misery that attends a mercenary marriage. (Even his early treatments of marriage warn of the dangers of marrying out of passion or impulse and stress social equality, parental sanction, and financial security as the bases of a sensible marriage.) *Bertrand et Raton, ou l'Art de Conspirer* (*A School for Politicians*, 1833) satirizes the revolution of 1830, attacks the stupidity of political conspiracy, and comically portrays the greed and vanity of the middle class. Various social evils were ridiculed in successive plays: political ambition in *L'Ambitieux* (*Ambition*, 1834); political fraud in *La Cameraderie, ou la Courte Echelle* ("Favoritism, or the Climb Up," 1837); slander in *La Calomnie* ("Slander," 1840); adultery in *Une Chaîne* ("An Entanglement," 1841); literary imposture in *Le Puff, ou mensonge et vérité* ("The Art of Puffing, or Lying and Truth," 1848). Though Scribe sacrificed historical accuracy to the mechanical intricacy of his plots, *Le Verre d'Eau, ou les Effets et les Causes* (*The Glass of Water*, 1840) cleverly illustrates his thesis, used more than once and taken from Voltaire, that overwhelming consequences follow from trivial causes. Here a spilled glass of water determines the fate of a nation, and, as in *Bertrand et Raton*, a shrewd, extremely clever statesman intrigues successfully for political power. It is one of Scribe's best-constructed plays and delights an audience even today. His only tragedy, *Adrienne Lecouvreur* (1849), written with Ernest Legouvé as a vehicle for the famous [Eliza Félix] Rachel, has attracted many famous actresses, but now seems a strained and melodramatic piece.

Even better constructed and more typical of the strengths and weaknesses of the well-made play than *Bertrand et Raton* or *Le Verre d'Eau* is *Bataille de dames* (written 1851, trans. as *The Ladies' Battle* and *The Queen's Gambit*), which may have served as a model for early plays of Henrik Ibsen, Bernard Shaw, and others. Legouvé again collaborated, although Scribe in effect took from his earlier play *La Frontière de Savoie* the clever decoy stratagem of two rival women hiding their lover from his enemy by disguising a gullible simpleton as the pursued man.

Although Scribe possessed tremendous talents, he is remembered today chiefly for his impact on modern drama rather than for his own plays, whose characters and situations seem for the most part shallow and artificial. Only Bertrand, Bolingbroke in *Le Verre d'Eau*, the countess in *Bataille de Dames,* and a few others stand out as interesting and plausible individuals. Nevertheless, to underrate Scribe or classify him as a mere hack writer (a charge often leveled against him during his life) is an error. "We are willing at last," wrote Eric Bentley in *What Is Theatre?* (1956), "to recognize the merit of that greatest non-genius of the drama, Eugène Scribe."

Bataille de Dames has been adapted by M. Valency as *The Queen's Gambit* (1956). *Le Verre d'Eau* has been adapted by D. Bodeen as *The Glass of Water* in *Camille and Other Plays* (1957), edited by Stephen Stanton, which also contains J. R. Planché's *A Peculiar Position,* a translation of *La Frontière de Savoie.* *Bertrand et Raton* was translated anonymously as *A School for Politicians* (1840). See the Introduction to *Camille and Other Plays* for a guide to available translations of the plays, commentary on Scribe's plays, and a study of the well-made play. The only book-length study in English is N. C. Arvin's *Eugène Scribe and the French Theatre: 1815–1860* (1924). Discussions of Scribe's technique and influence may be found in S. Stanton's articles: "Scribe's *Bertrand et Raton:* A Well-Made Play," *Tulane Drama Review,* II (November 1957); "Shaw's Debt to Scribe," *PMLA,* LXXVI (December 1961); and "Ibsen, Gilbert, and Scribe's *Bataille de Dames,*" *Educational Theatre Journal,* XVII (March 1965).—S. S. S.

scriptural play. Also called **mystery play.** A medieval religious play in the vernacular, based upon biblical history. Scriptural drama had its sources in the Old and New Testaments, the Apocrypha of both, and church liturgy. Although a few individual plays are extant, scriptural drama was typically organized into historical cycles encompassing the story of mankind from the creation to doomsday. These cycles were often known as Corpus Christi plays, for they were originally presented during the Feast of Corpus Christi. The plays were performed outdoors, a feature that distinguishes them from liturgical drama, which was performed in a church. Four full-length English cycles have survived: CHESTER PLAYS; YORK PLAYS; WAKEFIELD PLAYS; and N-TOWN PLAYS. See also ENGLAND: *middle ages;* SAINT'S PLAY; MORALITY PLAY.

Sea Gull, The (Chaika, 1896).   This play is more accurately translated as "The Gull." A "comedy" in four acts by Anton CHEKHOV. The young writer Treplev, whose work has not been published, writes a play in which he believes he has gone beyond the old, restraining conventions. The play, about the end of the world, is performed on Treplev's family estate before his mother, the aging, well-known actress Arkadina, and her lover, a famous writer named Trigorin. Nina Zarechnaya (from *za rekoi* meaning "beyond the river"), the daughter of an aristocratic landowner who lives beyond the lake, performs the

star role. Arkadina and Trigorin ridicule the young author's decadent affectations; Treplev feels annihilated. As a final blow, Nina, whom Treplev loves, falls desperately in love with Trigorin. At first Trigorin responds to her advances but he soon tires of her, thus inflicting on her a terrible wound. This situation is symbolically represented by Treplev's bringing in the body of a wantonly shot gull. The gull had lived on the lake between Treplev's family estate and that of Nina's parents.

After several years, Arkadina and Trigorin return to the estate. Treplev is now a reputed, albeit generally misunderstood, writer; Trigorin is still a celebrity, but obviously "no Tolstoy"; and Arkadina is an aging woman trying at any cost to hold on to her fickle lover and her fading glory. The illegitimate daughter of old Dr. Dorn (a bittersweet character who speaks the truth), Masha, who has always been in love with Treplev, looks on him with discreet devotion. Suddenly, Nina Zarechnaya appears on the scene. She is secretly staying in the vicinity, avoiding her family, with whom she has broken off, for she has become a lowly provincial actress. But, although she looks the picture of failure and defeat, she still believes in her art and still loves Trigorin. She declines Treplev's invitation to stay with him, but without her, Treplev now realizes, his art and his recognition are meaningless. When she departs into the night, he shoots himself.

When *The Sea Gull* was first produced at the Alexandrinsky Theater in 1896, it was a complete failure. Neither the director nor the actors understood Chekhov's art, in which nuances of intonation, seemingly insignificant details, and an apparent lack of responsiveness in the dialogue are actually the very means of conveying to the audience the development of the drama. So, despite the highly reputable cast, the "straight" interpretation destroyed the dramatic effect and *The Sea Gull* was literally laughed off the stage, eliciting from Chekhov the comment that he would never write a play again. Two years later, however, Vladimir Nemirovich-Danchenko, who admired the play, produced *The Sea Gull* at the Moscow Art Theater and this time it was received with unreserved enthusiasm. This striking reversal of fortunes is a good illustration of the problems presented by the new themes Chekhov brought to the theater and the way in which the directors and actors had to handle them.

The underlying theme of *The Sea Gull* is the loneliness and isolation of each character and his failure to achieve his dreams. What makes this theme subtle and difficult to bring to life, however, is the fact that each character feels his loneliness differently, that every individual's dreams and disappointments are unlike those of his neighbors, which he understands only by analogy with his own feelings. Thus, while Treplev's unhappy love for Nina is too much for him to bear and his relative literary success cannot compensate for it, Nina, who fails both in love and in her art, is still pushed to go on by a persistent hope. Similarly subtle insights are given into Masha's devotion to, and hopeless love for, Treplev, into Arkadina's acceptance of her compromised relations with the fickle Trigorin, and into Trigorin's recognition of his own mediocrity and his resigned acceptance of the position of a successful second-rater. Indeed, in *The*

Sea Gull Chekhov has used the theater as a short cut to create a world that would otherwise take a long novel to produce.

The text of *The Sea Gull* is included in *The Oxford Chekhov* (1964), translated by Ronald Hingley. —A. MACA.

Seami Motokiyo. See Zeami MOTOKIYO.

Secret Vengeance for Secret Insult (A secreto agravio, secreta venganza, 1635). An "honor" play by Pedro CALDERÓN DE LA BARCA. The classical honor predicament occurs in its starkest form in this play. Don Lope de Almeida, the Portuguese king's military commander, has married by proxy a Castilian lady, Doña Leonor. The king releases him from military obligations so that Lope may consummate his marriage. Leonor was formerly betrothed to a Spanish nobleman, Don Luis, believed killed in battle. As Lope is on his way to join Leonor, he meets Don Juan, an exiled friend now secretly returned from the Portuguese colony Goa. There, Juan says, his rash murder of the governor's son over a question of honor forced him to live in disgrace. Lope takes him under his protection as he joins Leonor, who meanwhile has also made a discovery: Don Luis is alive and has revealed himself. He is disguised as a traveling merchant, and is intent on regaining her love. In this involvement Sirena, Leonor's maid, acts as her confidante in the same way that Manrique (a valet) and Juan serve Lope.

An impetuous military man, Lope is unused to the niceties of courtship, the blandishments of marriage. His uneasiness immediately becomes a raging case of injured honor when Luis, invited to the house by Leonor in order to beg him to stop courting her, is discovered hiding there. Instead of killing the intruder, Lope follows his friend Juan's cautionary advice and dissembles his fears and jealousy; he even helps Luis to escape. "Secret insult most requires secret vengeance" is the principle leading to a delayed and complicated series of ruses before the husband can drown his wife's lover and then burn down the house where he has murdered her. The king approves the deed, which frees Lope to join the military campaign. But though he is perversely heroized for committing a double murder, Lope is left exhausted and ready "to end my life" on the battlefield, "if indeed misfortune ever ends."

Don Lope is evidently a victim of his own deeds dictated by the tyrannical laws of honor and the insult-vengeance complex, with its dehumanized rationale of an outmoded justice.

Secret Vengeance for Secret Insult, translated by Edwin Honig, is included in *Calderón: Four Plays* (1961).—E. H.

Sedaine, Michel Jean (1719–1797). French poet and playwright. The son of an architect, Sedaine first became a stonecutter, turning only in middle life to the drama by way of the *opéra-comique.* Fame first came in 1756 with *Le Diable à Quatre* ("The Hubbub"), and he was elected to the French Academy in 1786 for his *Richard Coeur de Lion* ("Richard the Lion-Hearted," 1784), which he wrote for the music of André Grétry. Among the many popular light operas to which he devoted more than thirty years of his life should be mentioned *Blaise le Savetier* ("Blaise the Shoemaker," 1759), *Rose et Colas* (1763), *Le Déserteur* ("The Deserter," 1769), and especially *On ne s'Avise Jamais de Tout* ("You Can't Think of Everything," 1761), which may have suggested *Le Barbier de Seville* (*The Barber of Seville,* 1775) to Beaumarchais. He played no role in the revolution, and his reputation as a dramatist rests entirely on his five-act *drame bourgeois Le Philosophe sans le savoir* (*The Duel,* 1765) and the one-act comedy *La Gageure Imprévue* ("The Unexpected Gambler," 1768). Both plays are still in the repertory of the Comédie Française. The title of the former is Sedaine's attempt to restore dignity to the word "philosopher" after seeing, in 1763, men of letters shamelessly ridiculed in Charles Palissot's *Les Philosophes* ("The Philosophers," 1760).

Once humorously referred to as "le meilleur ouvrage de Diderot," Sedaine possessed what his older contemporary lacked, the innate dramatic ability to realize Diderot's dramatic theories. Despite Beaumarchais's early efforts with the DRAME BOURGEOIS, Sedaine's *Le Philosophe sans le savoir* is usually considered the best example of this genre. In fact, closely conforming to the requirements (a simple plot, an imminent catastrophe resolved by a virtuous act, strong emotions, and silent tableaus) that Diderot was advocating in the *Discours sur la Poésie Dramatique* (*On Dramatic Poetry,* 1758), Sedaine's drama might almost be entitled *Le Père de Famille* (the title Diderot gave to the play he published with his essay). For the central character, an aristocrat, is a sort of *paterfamilias,* free of class prejudice and endowed with tolerance, reasonableness, and lofty principles. But the censors objected to Sedaine's making Vanderk père see the cruelty and barbarism of dueling and, Brutus-like, still stifle the voice of reason and send his son to fight, even while condemning the practice. The loss of dramatic intensity notwithstanding, they forced Sedaine to rewrite these scenes so that the father would try, unsuccessfully, to avoid the encounter with his son. In 1875 the Comédie Française presented the original version, which the discerning critic Francisque Sarcey found more forcefully dramatic than the watered-down version. It is perhaps of interest that George Sand, although admiring Sedaine's play, took the liberty, in her comedy *Le Mariage de Victorine* ("Victorine's Marriage," 1851), of bringing to a happy conclusion the unresolved romance of Vanderk fils and the appealing ingénue, an "amoureuse sans le savoir." The two pieces were often acted together at the Théâtre Français during Mme. Sand's last years.

There is no known English translation of the plays. *Le Philosophe sans le savoir* is included in *Four French Comedies of the Eighteenth Century* (1933), edited with informative critical introductions in English to each play by C. D. Zdanowicz.—S. S. S.

Sein, Kenneth. See BURMA.

Seneca, [Lucius Annaeus] the Younger (c. 4 B.C.– A.D. 65). Roman tragic playwright, essayist, and statesman. Seneca was the most distinguished member of a Hispano-Roman family which played a notable part in the literature and politics of the early Roman Empire. Born in Corduba, Spain, Seneca was brought to Rome as a child and there educated, primarily in oratory, for the legal and political career of a Roman gentleman. Even in adolescence, however, he was equally attracted by the more austere aspects of philosophy. His earliest works, probably composed

SENECA (STAATSBIBLIOTHEK [HANDKE], BERLIN)

in the thirties A.D., are lost; but by the time of his first extant publication (the prose essay *Consolation to Marcia,* written c. A.D. 40), he was clearly committed to a liberal form of Stoicism. This lifelong commitment to the moral grandeur of Stoicism and the magnificence of its vividly imagined cosmos constitutes one side of Seneca's experience which is important for any understanding of his writings, the tragedies no less than the prose works. Another side, just as important but standing in violent contrast to this Stoicism, is his political career, on the edge and for a time at the center of the Roman imperial court.

Shortly after A.D. 32 Seneca held the office of Quaestor and became a member of the Roman senate. In 39 he was already so famous as a speaker and writer that the maniacal but literary emperor Caligula, out of jealousy, momentarily contemplated Seneca's execution. It is probable that by this period Seneca's style, besides his philosophical creed, had reached the mature form seen in his extant prose and verse; nervous, staccato, alive with paradox, image, and epigram, it resembles little in earlier or later Latin literature. In 41 Seneca was abruptly exiled to Corsica by the emperor Claudius at the instance of Messalina (probably on political grounds, though adultery was the official charge). Here he lingered, his career apparently in ruins, until the palace revolution of 49 when Agrippina, succeeding Messalina as Claudius' wife, recalled Seneca to act as tutor in rhetoric to the young Nero. The functions of this post were not purely academic. From adviser and propagandist Seneca rose, after Nero's accession in 54, to chief minister in civil matters and became, as well, an immensely wealthy man. He witnessed the growing

horrors of the reign until, in 62, he fell from favor. For the next three years he lived in perilous semiretirement, which was ended by an exemplary Stoic suicide on imperial orders. Seneca's life as a whole presents rare paradoxes. The question which an enemy asked him in 58 remains unanswered by posterity: "What was the wisdom, and what were the philosophical teachings, by which you collected three hundred million sesterces in four years of Imperial friendship?" (Tacitus, *Annals,* XIII, 42).

Whatever Seneca's practice, however, it is certain that his imagination was shaped and colored by Stoicism. With the exception of the *Apocolocyntosis* (a savagely witty skit on the deification of Claudius, the authenticity of which is debated), the fifteen substantial prose works of his which survive from the period c. 40–65, despite their variety of titles, are all in fact discursive essays on the world and its problems in the light of Stoic moral philosophy. In modern times their repetitious and unfashionable moralization has brought them into disfavor, obscuring other features which are both interesting in themselves and of special importance for the student of Senecan tragedy: the brilliant pointed style, the almost morbid hypersensitivity to evil and its operation in human life, the tendency (natural for a Stoic) to envisage moral abstractions in vivid physical terms, and the extraordinary visual imagination displayed in certain descriptive passages. From the prose writings it is possible to picture the cosmic and religious backdrop against which both Seneca's imaginative life and his tragedies were enacted. In particular should be mentioned the *De Ira* ("Of Anger," composed in the years 41 and following; I.1, I.7–10, and III.4 outline Seneca's psychology of the passions—an important factor in the tragedies); the *Consolation to his Mother Helvia,* an unusually well-finished treatise composed early in the exile period; and two mature works from the period of his final semiretirement after 62, the *Naturales Quaestiones* (especially the majestic Preface to the First Book) and the *Epistulae Morales* ("Moral Letters" or rather "Essays"), which is the one Senecan work that has never entirely lost its popularity with the general reader.

The corpus of Senecan tragedy survives in medieval manuscripts, of which the earliest dates from c. 1100. It is important to note, since the fact is very often obscured in discussions of Senecan drama, that these manuscripts contain only the plain dramatic texts, without introductions, stage directions, or comment. Thus they supply no hint as to when the tragedies were written, or how, where, or even whether they were staged. The rest of surviving Latin literature does not offer any direct external evidence on such questions either. All statements made about the Senecan theater must therefore rest primarily on inference from the bare texts. On this admittedly unsatisfactory basis, the following conclusions at least seem reasonably likely. First, Senecan tragic verse, like nearly all Greco-Roman poetry, was designed to be heard, not read; practical experiment shows that it is as superbly suited to declamation aloud as the verse of Elizabethan or classical French tragedy. Second, the Senecan tragedies are not, however, declaimable aloud *by a single voice throughout,* as is often suggested. Such rapid interchanges as those in

Hercules Furens (lines 1293–1301) or *Medea* (lines 168–171) are quite unmanageable by a single speaker. At the least, therefore, we have to assume a production similar to that of a radio drama. Furthermore, we know that Neronian Rome possessed all the facilities for the staging of straight drama, both in public and private theaters, and that Nero himself was passionately interested in theatricals. Therefore, on the basis of this evidence, it seems quite likely that Seneca's tragedies were actually produced on the stage. The arguments which have been frequently adduced (though only since about 1800) to prove that these works could not be staged apply with equal force, or lack of it, to the tragedies of Aeschylus and Racine.

Ten plays are contained in the manuscripts under the name of Seneca. Of these, *Octavia* can hardly be Seneca's; most modern critics agree that it reads like the work of a close associate, composed shortly after the deaths of Seneca and Nero. A sensitive but technically amateurish piece, *Octavia* is chiefly interesting to the general reader as the only surviving Roman *fabula praetexta,* or historical drama. Among its characters are the emperor Nero; his first wife, Octavia; the ghost of his mother, Agrippina; and Seneca himself. Its subject, Nero's banishment of the young and defenseless Octavia in order that he might marry his mistress Poppaea, is one of the more frightful incidents of Nero's reign, but it is treated here with a moving, elegiac tenderness. *Hercules Oetaeus* is also not considered authentic by most critics. For most of its 1,996 lines—it is the longest of all ancient tragedies—it follows the subject matter of Sophocles' *Trachiniai*. *Hercules Oetaeus*, however, culminates uniquely in the apotheosis of Hercules (the patron-hero of the Stoics), his virtue purified and eternized in the funeral pyre on Mount Oeta. In style, structure, and ethos, *Hercules Oetaeus* is much nearer than *Octavia* to the unquestionably Senecan tragedies, and we cannot exclude the possibility that Seneca himself drafted the plot and even wrote certain passages. Its date of composition, if not actually before Seneca's death, cannot be set more than a few years later.

The titles of the remaining eight tragedies of the corpus, followed in parentheses by the Greek tragedies which they more or less resemble in narrative content, are *Hercules Furens* (Euripides, same title); *Troades* (Euripides, same title, with part of his *Hecuba* also); *Phoenissai* (Euripides, same title, with some resemblances to Sophocles' *Oedipus at Colonus*); *Medea* (Euripides, same title); *Phaedra* (Euripides' *Hippolytus*—not only the extant, but also the lost, earlier version); *Oedipus* (Sophocles' *Oedipus the King*); *Agamemnon* (Aeschylus, same title); *Thyestes* (tragedies of this title were composed by Sophocles, Euripides, and six other Greek tragedians, but none survives). The order given is that in which the plays appear in the oldest manuscript, but it would be unwise to assume that it represents the chronological order of composition. The later manuscripts give a different order and also different titles: *Thebais*, *Hippolytus*, and *Troas* for *Phoenissai*, *Phaedra*, and *Troades*, respectively. For the absolute or relative dating of the dramas there is in fact almost no reliable evidence. What there is suggests merely that Seneca was composing some tragedies in the early fifties A.D. and that *Hercules Furens* was completed before 54.

Phoenissai seems to be an unfinished sketch for one or more plays about Thebes at the time of the legendary war between Eteocles and Polyneices. In spite of the title, which implies a chorus of Phoenician women as in Euripides' play, there is no part or song for a chorus. All we have is three disconnected scenes for actors. Though the first of these scenes (a dialogue between the blinded, wandering Oedipus and Antigone) and the last (a debate between Jocasta, Polyneices, and Eteocles on the plain before Thebes) show impressive rhetorical power, it is difficult to judge such fragments as drama.

In the remaining seven complete tragedies, certain common external features are apparent. First, Seneca conforms to the Greek tragic convention by which no more than three, or on exceptional occasions four (*Oedipus*, Act II?; *Agamemnon*, Act V?) speaking parts are allowed together in one scene; this practice may be a further indication that he intended his tragedies for the actual stage. Second, for the first time in extant European tragedy five acts are the norm (on some analyses *Oedipus* and *Phaedra* have six, but they are the only possible exceptions). The rhythmic texture is rich and varied. As in Greek drama, the standard line for dialogue is the six-foot iambic line, here handled with less flexibility but greater sonority than by the Greek masters. Seneca's acts are separated by choral lyrics, often of considerable beauty and, in *Oedipus* and *Agamemnon*, of a metrical freedom and virtuosity unequaled in classical Latin song. The identities of the several choruses (for example, as Corinthian citizens in *Medea*) are not as strongly felt or sustained as in the Greek dramas; and while their songs are highly important to the total effect of the tragedies, their impact on the action is nil.

In short, so far as externals are concerned, Senecan tragedy continues in the Greek tragic convention with only slight modifications. But the same cannot be said of its contents. The plays are in hardly any sense translations from the Greek. Though their mythical material and to some extent even the outlines of their plots derive from the Greek theater, their wording, development, and atmosphere are Seneca's own. The world background against which they are played is as wide as Nero's empire; and the universe beyond it is a Stoic universe permeated by a Stoic providence. On both the macrocosmic and the microcosmic scale, Seneca's interest lies less in the clash between god and god or man and man than in the crucial battle between the Stoic absolutes of Passion and Reason; and he converts the Greek mythic themes accordingly. Thus, the vivid characterizations and the plots lucidly developed through the interaction of characters that are found in Euripides' and Sophocles' drama are absent from the work of Seneca. Instead, moral evil is the center: its emergence in a single human soul and its devastating impact on the outer world once it has obtained mastery. According to the Senecan and Stoic way of thinking (which can be richly documented from the prose works), *all* phenomena, psychological, moral, and physical, belong to the same order of being and are causally interrelated. Hence arise many of the features in Senecan drama which have been falsely criticized as mere rhetorical exaggeration: The growth and dominance of evil is, as we would put it, externalized not only in the actions and gestures of the human characters but also in the surrounding landscapes and even in the universe. (It is for Seneca, and should be for us, an open question, What sky is darkened in *Thyestes* when the father is deceived into eating his sons: Atreus'? Thyestes'? or God's?)

For the sake of brevity it is possible to divide the development of Senecan tragedy into three movements. First (in the Prologue, the equivalent of Act I), a god (as in *Hercules Furens*), a ghost (*Agamemnon, Thyestes*), or a major human character, usually in a monologue, evokes the heavy atmosphere out of which evil is about to burst; second (usually embodied in Act II), a human character meditates on a crime or passion, is dissuaded from it with reasoned arguments by an inferior, but finally succumbs; third (usually developed in Acts III through V), the catastrophic effects ensue. There are deviations from this pattern in *Hercules Furens* (where the second movement is lacking because the passion in Hercules is inspired from without by Juno); *Oedipus* (where again there is no second movement, since Oedipus' crime has been committed before the drama opens); and *Phaedra* (where the first movement evokes not the imminent evil but instead Hippolytus' glowing innocence). Yet the general development is common to all the seven complete tragedies; and it is a peculiarly Senecan development. As the Elizabethans and Racine instinctively saw, Seneca's form by no means precludes effective drama or moments of great drama. The scenes where Hippolytus confronts Phaedra face to face (*Phaedra*, lines 583–718) and where the tattered exile Thyestes finally accepts the scepter and diadem (*Thyestes*, lines 508–545)—fatal insignia, because the entire play is a fantasia on the Stoic theme that the only true kingship is the kingship of the mind—will stand comparison with any scene in ancient tragedy.

It is true that Seneca could not sustain such brilliance for long and that he too often lapsed into strange errors of taste. Nevertheless, he created a powerful and original form of drama which, in its interplay between the objective and the subjective, the psychological and the physical, remained unique until quite recent times. Its effect on European tragedy, from Mussato in the early fourteenth century until Racine in the seventeenth, is a different story, but an impressive one.

During the twentieth century the interests of the general reader of Seneca have been much neglected. There has been considerable research into technical problems such as textual criticism, but even this was scattered in obscure publications until 1966, when most of its results were presented in a critical edition of the Latin text by G. C. Giardina (*L. Annaei Senecae Tragoediae*). The standard English translation is that by F. J. Miller, *Seneca's Tragedies* (1917, with facing Latin text). This is very useful as a literal prose rendering of the sense but does not convey the poetic power. For some understanding of Senecan drama as poetry, the reader who does not know Latin may turn to Thomas Newton's *Seneca his Tenne Tragedies translated into English* (1581; reprinted with Introduction by T. S. Eliot in 1927 and 1966). The relatively few modern verse translations, of which the most recent is E. F. Watling's *Seneca:*

Four Tragedies and Octavia (1966), are more faithful to the sense but adopt an obsolete idiom and meter and thus obscure the vitality of the original. In the twentieth century Seneca has been poorly served by the literary critics also. The only full-length study of his tragedies is in French: L. Herrmann, *Le Théâtre de Sénèque* (1924). Essays in English include F. L. Lucas, *Seneca and Elizabethan Tragedy* (1922); E. F. Watling, Introduction to his *Four Tragedies;* and C. J. Herington, "Senecan Tragedy," *Arion,* V (1966), 422–471.—C. J. H.

Senegal. See AFRICA: *Senegal.*

sentimental comedy. See ENGLAND: *eighteenth century.*

Serbia. See YUGOSLAVIA.

Serjeant Musgrave's Dance (1959). A play by John ARDEN. The first production of *Serjeant Musgrave's Dance* was a financial failure and was withdrawn after about a week's run. Subsequently the play developed an underground reputation as a martyred modern classic and became a favorite for student productions throughout England. Set in a strikebound town in the north of England in the 1880's, the play shows the arrival of three soldiers, led by "Black Jack" Musgrave, whom the town officials welcome as a recruiting sergeant who will help them in breaking the strike. At a meeting in the town square Musgrave reveals his real purpose by hoisting up the skeleton of a local boy, for whose death in a colonial war Musgrave now intends to take revenge on the populace.

The issue, as always with Arden, is not clear cut, for Musgrave finally shows himself to be a religious maniac with whom one can no more take sides than with the corrupt mayor and mine owner. The relationship between fanatic idealism and human compromise is as ambiguous as it is in Henrik Ibsen's *Brand.* There is also a similar projection of a harsh winter landscape, a similar comment on a topical event (Britain's military engagement in Cyprus), and a similar magnetism in the central figure.—I. W.

Seven Against Thebes (**Hepta epi Thebas;** Latin, **Septem Contra Thebas;** 467 B.C.). A tragedy by AESCHYLUS. Aeschylus produced this play at the Great Dionysia in Athens as part of a tetralogy—*Laius, Oedipus, Seven Against Thebes,* and *Sphinx*—which gained first prize in the tragic contest. The other three plays are lost, except for small fragments, but it is clear that the tetralogy as a whole embraced a single theme: the fate of a legendary Theban dynasty through three generations, from the sin of Laius, through the sins of his son, Oedipus, to the quarrel between Oedipus' sons, Eteocles and Polyneices, which annihilated the male line. This grand design of the tetralogy as it was composed by Aeschylus must be borne in mind if one is to appreciate the full power of the surviving fragment, *Seven Against Thebes.* Here is the moment of disastrous detonation, but the fatal charge must have been gradually loaded in the lost *Laius* and *Oedipus.*

The scene throughout is the Acropolis of Thebes, the city's military and spiritual center. A silent, but surely significant, element in the drama is the group of images of the city gods, which is mentioned several times in the text. The reigning king, Eteocles, opens the play with a calm, majestic speech to his citizens, urging them to defend their country. Eteocles' exiled brother, Polyneices, who now claims the throne, has joined with Adrastus, king of Argos, to bring an Argive army against Thebes. A messenger arrives with news that the enemy is on the verge of attack: their seven captains (as yet unnamed) are drawing lots for their respective battle stations before the seven gates of the city. The following *parodos,* the entry of the Chorus of Theban Women, contrasts vividly, in its hysterical terror, with the atmosphere of masculine calm of the opening scene. Eteocles roughly orders the women to come away from the images of the city gods, to keep silent, and to leave the men to their practical task of defense. In the ensuing "shield scene," the messenger reappears and in seven speeches describes the enemy captains now advancing on each gate. To every speech except the last Eteocles replies with military coolness, detailing a Theban champion to oppose each captain. In the messenger's seventh speech, he names Polyneices as captain at the last remaining gate. Now, suddenly, it is Eteocles who is hysterical; for him the news means that the family curse has descended on him, and he blindly capitulates to it. In spite of the women's protests he shouts for his armor and leaves to fight his own brother. An ominous choral ode on the progress of the curse from Laius onward is followed by the messenger's announcement that the enemy as a whole has been defeated but that Eteocles and Polyneices died at each other's hands. Now follows a chorus of lamentation for both the brothers, breaking down into a lyric antiphony shortly after their bodies have been carried onto the stage (line 848). In the manuscripts part of this antiphony is assigned to the princes' sisters, Antigone and Ismene, and it is followed by a short spoken scene (1005–1078) in which Antigone defies the proclamation of a herald against burying the body of Polyneices. Several modern critics, however, have argued with considerable probability that these features belong to a post-Aeschylean revival of the play. If this view is justified, the original version by Aeschylus ends at line 1004 at the climax of the antiphonal lament, which was sung by the Chorus alone.

" 'I wrote a drama packed with War'—'And which was that?'—'The *Seven Against Thebes!*' " This, the earliest critical comment of any sort on the *Seven,* is put into Aeschylus' mouth by Aristophanes (*Frogs,* 1021); and so far as it goes it applies well to the tragedy's atmosphere from the Prologue to the last exit of Eteocles. No other ancient dramatic poetry, and perhaps no modern poetry either, presents with such concentrated power the situation of an entire community faced with total war. The fact that the community concerned is a Greek city-state, crammed within narrow walls outside which "the very air is mad with flickering spears" (line 155) merely increases the intensity. Yet the comment applies, at most, to the first two-thirds of the play, and even so concentrates on what may be called its ground-bass, the fate of the city. Moderns, at the other extreme, tend naturally to concentrate their criticism on the easily heard solo melody, the fate of Eteocles. Neither Aristophanes nor many moderns pay much attention to the third and last theme, which is first heard in this subtly orchestrated play at the moment when Eteocles capitulates to the curse at the end of the "shield scene," and dominates entirely after the appearance of the two corpses at line 848.

This is the impartial lament over *both* brothers, dead under circumstances of appalling pollution. Thus the finale transcends both the fate of the city and the fate of the individual hero, Eteocles, to culminate in the theme of the entire tragic trilogy: the operation of the dynastic curse, visually symbolized in the two bodies lying side by side on the stage.

As in all of Aeschylus' drama, so in *Seven Against Thebes*: the individual, the family, and the community form a continuum; we shall not do well to unpick the strands of Fate's rope, as Aeschylus conceives it. The many modern attempts to interpret the *Seven* as if it were Sophoclean or later tragedy are justified only by superficial similarities. Its opening is remarkably like that of Sophocles' *Oedipus the King,* and so is the general progress of Eteocles from the status of regal hero, devoted to the interests of his country, to the recognition of doom and consequent self-destruction. The end of the "shield scene" may even be compared to a moment in Shakespeare's tragedy *Macbeth*—when Macbeth, hearing that Birnam Wood is moving toward Dunsinane, calls for his armor. But the most that can properly be said is that in *Seven Against Thebes* Aeschylus came as near as he ever came (judging from the extant works) to the Sophoclean and Aristotelian tragic canon. To interpret the play entirely in accordance with that canon is to ignore two of its three major themes, and also to leave uncertain the answer to a crucial question: Where is the "tragic flaw," if any, which motivates the fate of Eteocles? The critics' answers to this have been so diverse that one can only conclude that the clue does not lie in the extant drama. Perhaps Aeschylus embodied it in one of the two lost dramas that preceded the *Seven;* or perhaps he did not look at life that way.

The most recent edition, with commentary, of *Seven Against Thebes* in English is that by T. G. Tucker (1908).—C. J. H.

sewamono. A species of Japanese *kabuki* drama specializing in scenes from middle-class life and marked by romantic pathos. *Sewamono* is a branch of the kabuki tree diametrically opposed to the quasi-historical plays of war, violence, and bombast acted in the ARAGOTO style. With their highly advanced naturalism, sewamono plays are set in contemporary rather than medieval times; indeed, use is made for their plots of events occurring a few weeks before the writing of the plays themselves. Their appeal has been especially strong to persons of the middle class similar to those whom they depict. The playwright's object has been to achieve the most intimate relation possible between himself and his audience. The basis for such work was established in the puppet theater by Chikamatsu Monzaemon in 1679 with a play *Yugiri Izaemen,* also known as *Kuruwa Bunsho.* A special type of sewamono, *kizewamono* (sometimes called in English "late" or "new" sewamono), developed in the nineteenth century. Such works deal with impoverished and wretched persons. The chief playwrights of the kizewamono are Tsuruya Namboku (1755–1892) and Kawatake MOKUAMI. See also KABUKI.—H. W. W.

Shacham, Nathan (1925–   ). Israeli novelist, essayist, and playwright. Shacham was born in Tel-Aviv and during the Israeli War of Independence he served in the commando units, Palmach. A member of Kibbutz Beit-Alfa, he divides his time between farming and writing. In fact, he became the major dramatist of Bimat Hakibbutz, the theater ensemble of the kibbutz movement in Israel. Shacham has also had a number of novels and short-story collections published.

His first play, *Hem Yagee-oo Machar* (*They Will Arrive at Dawn,* 1950), depicting an incident from the War of Independence and based on his own short story, scored a major success for Shacham and the Chamber Theater, which produced it, and it has since been performed in many countries. His next two plays, *Kra Lee Siomka* ("Call Me Siomka," 1951), a play concerning the days "after the war," and *Cheshbon Chadash* ("A New Account," 1953), satirically criticizing social and political changes in Israel, have made him one of the most promising playwrights of modern Israel. Unfortunately, however, this promise has not been fulfilled. Since 1953 Shacham has not written any significant play. —Z. R.

Shadow and Substance (1937). A drama by Paul Vincent CARROLL. The play deals with the effects of ignorance and bigotry in a small Irish village. Canon Thomas Sherritt, the pastor of a parish in rural Ireland, confronts two problems: an intense young girl, Brigid, who believes she has religious visions and a rebellious local schoolmaster who has surreptitiously written an anti-Catholic book. When the identity of the author is discovered, an angry mob attempts to stone him. The girl tries to prevent them and is herself killed by the mob. The efforts of the three major characters to define their conceptions of a religious life have been overwhelmed by the mindless violence of the mob. The canon's intellectualized vision of Catholicism and the schoolmaster's rebellious skepticism are both seen as self-indulgent posturing when contrasted to the impassioned simplicity of Brigid's belief. Her martyrdom defines the limitations and inadequacy of her elders' intellectualized formulations of life.—E. Q.

Shadow of a Gunman, The (1923). A tragicomedy by Sean O'CASEY. This play deals with illusions of heroism. The action occurs in Dublin in 1920, during the guerrilla warfare between the insurgent Irish Republican Army and the British forces, mainly the ruthless auxiliary troops known by their uniforms as the Black and Tans. Donal Davoren sees himself as a detached poet, uninvolved in the fighting, while his neighbors in the tenement house think he is hiding out as an IRA gunman "on the run." But he is actually a shadow of a poet as well as a "shadow of a gunman"—a shadow man who doesn't know who he is. Like Davoren, all the people in the house suffer from a variety of comic and tragic self-deceptions, and it is only the very droll peddler, Seumas Shields, Davoren's friend and comic foil, who understands that poetic and patriotic masquerades are equally absurd. In his own way, however, Shields is as ineffectual as Davoren, for he is a lazy, blustering, amiable coward who resorts to the efficacy of prayer or the comfort of his bed when trouble comes with a mysterious bag of bombs, left in the room by one of Shields's friends who is working for the IRA. Nevertheless, he is one of O'Casey's mock-heroic clowns, a wise fool who sees the great folly of fanaticism. Davoren allows the impressionable Minnie Powell to

fall in love with the romantic poet-gunman she thinks he is, and it is only after this deception leads to her tragic death that he sees himself and his shattered world with terrifying clarity.—D. K.

shadow theater. See ARAB DRAMA; GREECE: *modern period;* INDONESIA; TURKEY: *traditional theater.*

Shadwell, Thomas (1641?–1692). English dramatist. Shadwell was born in Norfolk, attended Caius College, Cambridge, and in 1658 went to study law at the Middle Temple, London. Shortly after the return of Charles II to the throne, Shadwell married an actress in the Duke's Company, the players for whom he was to write many of his works. Mrs. Shadwell appeared in her husband's first play, *The Sullen Lovers* (1668), based on Molière's *Les Fâcheux.* An attack in the Preface to *The Sullen Lovers* on John Dryden's theories of comedy (see ENGLAND: *Restoration drama*) began a quarrel that lasted for several years, in the course of which Dryden satirized Shadwell in *MacFlecknoe* as the epitome of dullness. However, Shadwell had a very considerable success and was made poet laureate in 1689 when Dryden was forced to give up the appointment.

Shadwell wrote many plays, of which several were adaptations of Shakespeare and Molière. In comedy, his forte, he was a staunch defender and follower of Ben Jonson and was not the dullard of Dryden's satire. A competent but never brilliant writer, the best of his plays, such as *Epsom Wells* (1672), *The Squire of Alsatia* (1688), and *Bury Fair* (1689), present an entertaining view of the life of the time. Some of the plays deal with particular segments of society, such as the underworld with its special cant (*The Squire of Alsatia*), or with institutions, such as the Royal Society (*The Virtuoso,* 1676) or the theater (*A True Widow,* 1678).

There is a lavish five-volume edition of *The Complete Works of Thomas Shadwell* (1927) by Montague Summers with a long and informative Introduction. For biography and criticism see Albert S. Borgman's *Thomas Shadwell, His Life and Comedies* (1928).—E. W.

Shaffer, [Levin] Peter (1926–   ). English playwright. Shaffer was born in London, the son of a real estate director. He is, in the commercial theater, one of the most accomplished English playwrights to have appeared since World War II. Like Robert Bolt, he works within the traditional limits of public taste and is a consummate manipulator of traditional forms.

Shaffer won overnight success with his first West End production, *Five Finger Exercise* (1958), a corrosive comedy of family warfare in which a standard Jewish situation (status-proud mother and philistine, breadwinning father) was skillfully universalized. This was followed by a neat double bill about sex war, *The Private Ear and The Public Eye* (1962), and Shaffer's most ambitious play to date, *The Royal Hunt of the Sun* (1964). One of the most popular productions in the repertory of the National Theatre, this romantic epic dramatizes the sixteenth-century Spanish conquest of Peru and explores the relationship between Pizarro and his royal captive, the Inca ruler Atahuallpa. The theatrical flamboyance of the play is overwhelming, though if one follows Shaffer's invitation to approach it as a metaphysical confrontation between the spokesmen of two religions, it

PETER SHAFFER (WIDE WORLD PHOTOS)

seems rather short of sinew. Since then Shaffer has provided the National Theatre with another hit, *Black Comedy* (1965), in which he drew on the conventions of the Chinese theater (miming darkness with the lights on) to show that standard boulevard farce can be revitalized by reversing the lighting values.—I. W.

Shakespeare, William (1564–1616). English poet and dramatist. Shakespeare was baptized in Holy Trinity Church, Stratford-upon-Avon, April 26, 1564, probably a few days after his birth, which is celebrated, with impartiality, upon the feast day of England's patron St. George, April 23. He died April 23, 1616, at fifty-two, and was buried in the Holy Trinity Chancel. If no records of his life survived, we could deduce from his writings, and from a study of the lives of his fellow playwrights, that he derived from a provincial middle-class family, did not proceed to a university, and was at one time a professional actor; but representative as it is in these respects, his life record is unique. The careers of most Elizabethan playwrights yield ample evidence of what is now called "alienation"—familial, social, temperamental—or at least of complete absorption into the life of the capital. Only he, so far as is known, was buried in the provincial church where he was baptized, bequeathed his children dwellings inherited from his parents, and remained attached in any practical way to the place, people, and system of values to which he was born. While his imagination ranged far, his affections remained close to home. Its intimation of this fact gives significance to the chronicle of the commonplace that must serve as his biography.

His father, John Shakespeare, son of a tenant farmer of Snitterfield, married Mary Arden of Wilmcote, daughter of the yeoman who owned their land. By 1552 John was established in Stratford as tanner of fine skins, glover, and dealer in wool and hides. The earliest experience of William, the eldest of four boys and two girls who grew up behind the shop, would have been of full family life, a home industry, and the bustle of a community that, though small by present-day standards, was a center of Warwickshire population and trade, surrounded by charming country. When he was four, his father, despite his probable illiteracy (normal enough in his generation), was given his turn as high bailiff, or mayor, by his fellow aldermen. Education for the sons of Stratford burgesses was provided free at the King's New School. After attendance from about six to sixteen, one's training in Latin language and literature was sufficient for university matriculation. Shakespeare's demonstrable acquaintance with Lyly's Latin grammar, the primary classics (especially Ovid), and the collections of Latin maxims, ancient and modern, dear to Renaissance teachers is most likely to have been acquired in this school, but it is doubtful whether he attended the full ten years. Ben Jonson said that he had small Latin and less Greek. Another contemporary reported that in youth he was a schoolmaster in the country. Perhaps the statements are not irreconcilable; in any case Shakespeare's breezy way with the classical heritage tends to support Jonson. By the time Shakespeare was thirteen, his father's prosperity had declined, and it is possible that he was set to work.

On November 27, 1582, a special license, such as would obviate delay, was issued for the marriage of the eighteen-year-old youth with Anne Hathaway of neighboring Shottery. Six months later, May 26,

WILLIAM SHAKESPEARE (FOLGER SHAKESPEARE LIBRARY)

1583, their child Susanna was baptized in Holy Trinity. On February 2, 1585, their twins Hamnet and Judith were similarly baptized. Hamnet died at eleven, and Susanna, after her marriage to the genteel Stratford physician John Hall, became Shakespeare's chief heir. Since Judith married late, Susanna's daughter Elizabeth was his sole grandchild at the time of his death. She died Lady Elizabeth Bernard in 1670, his last living descendant. The funeral monument of his wife, Anne, gives her age as sixty-seven in 1623, so that, if it is correct, she was eight years his senior. These are the sole known facts about the marriage. Scholars have grown weary of protesting that William's bequest of his "second-best bed" to Anne has no sinister metaphorical significance but was in fact a kindly provision.

With funds acquired as an actor and playwright in London, Shakespeare was able to restore family prosperity. In 1596 his father's earlier application for a coat of arms was granted. In 1597 he bought New Place, an imposing residence near the Guild Chapel and King's New School. His later investments in grain, land, land rents or "tithes," and in housing were all in Stratford or its vicinity except for one late purchase of a property in Blackfriars, London. He became increasingly involved in Stratford concerns and, by the time he ceased reserving London lodgings in 1612, was recognized as a leading citizen. More interesting, in view of the presumed philistinism of the place, his family was proud of his standing as a poet. Instead of the conventional allusions to virtue and piety we find tributes to his artistry upon the monument in the Stratford church, and this was installed prior to the issue of his collected works. This London memorial was brought out in 1623 by the stationers Isaac Jaggard and Edward Blount with the aid of Shakespeare's former fellow actors John Heminges and Henry Condell. These two, with Richard Burbage, had been the only ones except relatives and Warwickshire neighbors mentioned in Shakespeare's will. They stated in the dedication of the volume that their motive was not "self-profit or fame" but "only to keep the memory of so worthy a friend and fellow alive as was our Shakespeare."

As we turn to Shakespeare's professional career, we should recognize at the outset that there is nothing surprising about the appearance of a Warwickshire glover's son upon the London stage. Few of the actors and playwrights were London-born. Touring companies, recruited and active chiefly in the provinces, had played in Stratford in Shakespeare's childhood. He was twelve when the first London theaters were built and began to exercise their magnetic force. The coming of age of theatrical enterprise in the metropolis coincided precisely with the coming of age of Shakespeare. Although more information about his life as a whole would satisfy a natural curiosity, we really know as much as we need about his middle and later years. It is the period of his youth that urgently invites speculation. He was not necessarily domiciled in Stratford for the whole twenty years preceding the birth of his twin children. As a talented boy, he may have served, like Michael Drayton (also of Warwickshire), as a page in a manor house, or as a chorister in a chapel. He may have toured as an actor before marrying Anne Hathaway or supplied "interludes" to actors before becoming

one himself. He may even have begun his London career as aid of a chapel master in a "private" theater. The usual and quite reasonable assumption is that he joined in his twenties one of the companies that were gradually trading their itinerant existence for a more or less stable one in London. The records of these companies are so fragmentary that the absence of any mention of Shakespeare before 1592 has little significance. Robert Greene's allusion to him in that year as "an upstart crow, beautified with our feathers" was long taken to mean that he was a newcomer among the actors adapting to their use the plays of Greene and others, but this interpretation no longer prevails. In 1592 Shakespeare was twenty-eight, and there is an initial improbability that creative energies like his would remain so long in abeyance. He was evidently a successful playwright by 1590, when his *Henry VI* plays began to appear, and he may already have been acting and writing for several years.

Theatrical activity in London was ruinously interrupted by the plague from late 1592 to early 1594. During this period Shakespeare wrote and dedicated to the earl of Southampton *Venus and Adonis* (1593) and *Lucrece* (1594)—the first, of the Ovidian amatory type of narrative poems, like Christopher Marlowe's coeval *Hero and Leander,* and the second more nearly a moral exemplum, like Michael Drayton's coeval *Matilda.* Both are highly competent, and the first was sufficiently popular to give its author standing among nondramatic poets, who enjoyed somewhat more prestige than dramatic ones. In this period also were probably written at least some of the Sonnets, which Francis Meres in 1598 mentioned as circulating among his private friends and which were published in 1609. There was a rash of sonnet writing in the early 1590's, owing partly to the glamorous example of Sidney's *Astrophel and Stella.* Some of Shakespeare's seem little more than metrical exercises, while others (at least a few of them certainly written in later years) are the most poignant and perfect in the language. It is often assumed that Southampton, the dedicatee of the narrative poems, was his active patron, and even the "friend" mentioned in the Sonnets, but since we are concerned primarily with his dramatic career, we need not linger with this mare's nest of biographical theorizing. We should note, however, that he wrote narrative poetry, and played the dedicating game, only in this interval when there was no market for plays. He never veered again from theatrical professionalism, even to the extent of writing court masques and private entertainments. His persistence in focusing his energies upon writing for the popular stage distinguishes him from such contemporaries as Jonson, inveterate composer of masques and genteel shows, and even from Thomas Heywood and Thomas Dekker, who were miscellanists as well as playwrights.

In 1594 he became, with Richard Burbage, the rising stage "star," with Will Kempe, the successor of Richard Tarlton as leading stage comedian, and with other established actors, a sharing member of the Lord Chamberlain's Men, a professional troupe newly organized upon the cessation of the plague. For the remaining eighteen years of his activity in London, he acted and wrote exclusively for this company. When the company built its own theater, the

Globe on the Bankside, in 1599, he was one-tenth owner of the building; and when it acquired the lease of the roofed Blackfriars theater in 1608, he was again a sharer of the rental as well as other receipts. His final status as a gentleman of substance in Stratford derived from his income as actor, writer, and joint landlord of this company. Its primacy derived in turn from his association with it, at least in large measure. Its chief additional asset was the acting of Richard Burbage. The fact that it was designated as the King's Men in 1603, when all the London companies came under the sponsorship of members of the new royal family, is only one of the tokens of its remarkable success. It endured and retained the plays of Shakespeare in its repertory until the Puritan Parliament closed all the theaters in 1642.

Shakespeare's plays are the three HENRY VI plays, THE COMEDY OF ERRORS, RICHARD III, THE TAMING OF THE SHREW, TITUS ANDRONICUS, THE TWO GENTLEMEN OF VERONA, KING JOHN, A MIDSUMMER NIGHT'S DREAM, RICHARD II, LOVE'S LABOUR'S LOST, ROMEO AND JULIET, THE MERCHANT OF VENICE, HENRY IV, PART ONE, HENRY IV, PART TWO, AS YOU LIKE IT, HENRY V, JULIUS CAESAR, MUCH ADO ABOUT NOTHING, TWELFTH NIGHT, THE MERRY WIVES OF WINDSOR, HAMLET, TROILUS AND CRESSIDA, ALL'S WELL THAT ENDS WELL, MEASURE FOR MEASURE, OTHELLO, KING LEAR, MACBETH, TIMON OF ATHENS, PERICLES, ANTONY AND CLEOPATRA, CORIOLANUS, CYMBELINE, THE WINTER'S TALE, THE TEMPEST, HENRY VIII.

All the above thirty-seven plays except *Pericles* were printed in the first folio, *Mr. William Shakespears Comedies, Histories, & Tragedies,* in 1623, eighteen of them for the first time. The remaining nineteen, including *Pericles,* were first printed individually in quarto volumes between 1594 and 1622. Half a dozen of the quartos were "bad"—printed from copy botched up from memory, probably by venal hireling actors, so that printers might capitalize upon stage hits. These were replaced by texts released by Shakespeare's company and printed in "good" quartos and in the folio. In recent years we have been brought closer to Shakespeare the writer through bibliographical and textual rather than biographical research. Experts have been able to determine which of three major types of document provided printer's copy for each play: the author's draft, a scribal transcript of it, or either of the former converted into theatrical prompt-copy. By far the majority of the plays were originally printed from Shakespeare's own drafts; and certain interlineations and cancellations, as well as spellings peculiar to him, have been identified. The fruits of this effort are increasingly reliable modern editions and, occasionally, an exhilarating sense of watching the playwright at work. The reprints of most of the quartos and all those of the folio (1632, 1664, 1685) are now recognized as proferring only "derived" texts, that is, those without independent manuscript authority, although the fourth folio, with its accumulated misprints and conjectural emendations, was used as the basis of the first "modern" edition, that of Nicholas Rowe in 1709.

After centuries of discussion, formally initiated by Alexander Pope, who figures as the first "disintegrator" in his edition of 1725, about what parts of the Shakespearean plays Shakespeare did or did not write, there is now virtual agreement among scholars, if not among enterprising amateurs, that he wrote all parts of all thirty-seven with the following exceptions: perhaps some portions of the *Henry VI* plays (with those portions becoming fewer and harder to identify), perhaps the original draft of *Titus Andronicus,* certainly three brief passages in *Macbeth* (introducing non-Shakespearean songs and dances), probably the Prologue and several scenes (contributed by John Fletcher) of *Henry VIII,* and the first two acts of *Pericles* (unless these were printed from debased copy). Owing to Shakespeare's contemporary popularity, certain additional plays were printed under his name or initials, and of these, *Locrine* (1595), *Thomas Lord Cromwell* (1602), *The London Prodigal* (1605), *The Puritan* (1605), and *A Yorkshire Tragedy* (1608) were included in the third folio along with *Sir John Oldcastle* (1599) and *Pericles* (first printed as by Shakespeare in 1609). No one now regards any of these seven as Shakespeare's except *Pericles* and, conceivably, some part of *A Yorkshire Tragedy;* but this old "apocrypha" has been replaced by a new "apocrypha." A number of scholars and critics, with considerable justice, believe that he may have written the mob scenes in the manuscript *Book of Sir Thomas More* (mainly by Antony Munday and dating about 1595), the romantic love scenes in *Edward the Third* (printed anonymously in 1596), the madness scenes added to the 1602 edition of Thomas Kyd's *Spanish Tragedy,* and certain portions of THE TWO NOBLE KINSMEN, belatedly printed in 1634 as by Fletcher and Shakespeare.

In certain instances the received Shakespearean texts may not be those of the plays as originally written. This is probable in the case of *Titus Andronicus* and *Love's Labour's Lost* and not improbable in the case of *The Taming of the Shrew, The Two Gentlemen of Verona, King John,* and even *A Midsummer Night's Dream.* Normally, a practicing playwright would not revise his work after it had gone into production, especially in this era when the turnover in repertories was extremely rapid. However, the conditions of the years to which most of the above plays seem to belong were unusual. With the formation of the Lord Chamberlain's company after the plague years, there would have been considerable incentive for Shakespeare to refurbish some of his older work for its use. (To be sure, there has also been considerable speculation about whether he may have had anything to do with an earlier form in which *Hamlet* certainly existed and in which *The Merry Wives of Windsor* and *Pericles* may have existed.) At what time he began to write plays is a vital question. Involved is our assessment not only of his progress as an artist but of his total historical role. In 1590, when he was almost surely writing, English drama, paradoxically, was both very old and very new. There had been liturgical drama, miracle plays, moralities, and secular interludes since the tenth century and professional acting since the fifteenth. The grammar schools, universities, and inns of court had been experimenting with classical and Continental forms of drama for a generation, so that a process of cross-fertilization with the native stock is in evidence from about 1550 onward. Nevertheless, the "Elizabethan play" as we think of it was new in 1590. For instance we can point to no play wearing the destined livery of mingled blank verse and prose earlier than 1587, and the "epoch-making" *Tamburlaine* by Marlowe and *Spanish Tragedy* by Kyd are both usually dated in that year. Shakespeare's *Henry VI* plays and *The Comedy of Errors* suffer in comparison with his later works but do not read like those of a beginner. Of the group of writers credited with bringing English drama to its maturity—Lyly, Peele, Marlowe, Kyd, Lodge, Greene, and Nashe—only Lyly and Peele are represented by plays in print before 1590. Most of the others had been writing since 1587 but so also perhaps had Shakespeare. If so, he must be accorded a place among those always grouped as his "predecessors"—and must be viewed as a formulator as well as the perfecter of "Elizabethan drama."

Before distinguishing among the various kinds of plays in the canon, it would be well to consider the characteristics that all share in common. Until the mid-eighties popular English drama was invariably in rhyme, at first in stanzaic patterns and decasyllabic couplets, and then mainly in tumbling verse and "fourteeners," or ballad measure. (Examples of the latter appear like fossils in Shakespeare's *Comedy of Errors*, *Love's Labour's Lost*, and *Two Gentlemen of Verona*.) The greatest gift of the academic experimenters to the popular playwrights was emancipation from rhyme. Blank verse for serious drama and prose for comedy were introduced, and the two were combined in the typical popular play, with the occasional use of rhymed couplets for theatrical punctuation, moral emphasis, and lyrical effect. Shakespeare combines the three media in nearly all his plays, but in widely varying proportion. Thus, while 93 percent of *Julius Caesar* is in blank verse and only 6 percent in prose, *The Merry Wives of Windsor* is 87 percent prose and only 10 percent blank verse; and while *Love's Labour's Lost* is almost half in rhyme, a number of the plays contain scarcely any. In most of them rhyme is an occasional filigree, while prose in realistic and comic sections alternates with the predominant blank verse. Shakespeare's skill in passing from one medium to another keeps the discourse in key. The prose is colloquial and colorful except in a few grandiloquent passages that might have better been written in verse, and the verse is increasingly supple, metrically varied, and harmonious. Both are immensely projective, as dramatic speech must be, but succeed in preserving the rhythms of "natural" speech.

The form of the Elizabethan popular play did not ordinarily vary from type to type, and was, to use the terms of Polonius, usually "poem unlimited" rather than "scene individable" (unified). It was dangerously free. The medieval dramatizations of biblical narrative had proliferated rather than developed, and subsequent dramatizations of history, biography, and fiction followed a similar fashion of beading a varying number of episodes upon a chronological string. The secular interludes simply expanded in length with the increasing number of persons and events customarily represented. Neither classical example nor neoclassical precept was able to impose upon the English popular playwright, university trained or otherwise, a specified number of episodes (acts), a limited number of speakers (with the lower classes confined to comedy and the upper classes to tragedy), or the principle of unity in time, place, and action.

Without the guidance provided by an agreed-upon number of parts of a whole, with each part performing an agreed-upon function, a play by an inexperienced or untalented writer will be a formless sprawl. It is perhaps misleading to condemn such a play as "episodic," since the episode, one of the "doings," is the basic structural unit of all dramas. If the episodes, whether five or fifty, are poorly chosen and coordinated, the play is a formal failure. If the reverse is true, it is a success, however far the number of episodes may exceed the sacrosanct five. All we can say is that an increasing number of episodes increases the mathematical possibility of failure, and that freedom is a hard taskmaster.

All but one of the quarto, and a number of the folio, texts of Shakespeare's plays, and presumably his manuscripts, omitted any mention of acts and scenes. Each of his plays consists of simple or complex episodes presented in stretches of continuous action, each concluded by a cleared stage. The number varies from seven in *A Midsummer Night's Dream* to thirty-seven in *Antony and Cleopatra*, with an average number of nineteen to twenty. Obviously these are the structural units, whatever we call them, although editors customarily call them scenes and cluster them arbitrarily into five acts. That they are well chosen and coordinated is sufficiently indicated by the fact that we are so little conscious of their varying length and number. Since the history plays are crowded with events stretching over a considerable period of time, we might assume that they would contain on the average more "scenes" than the comedies and tragedies. Actually they contain fewer than the tragedies and not many more than the comedies. Even a person quite familiar with the plays would probably have to be told that the very short play *Macbeth* (2,113 lines) contains six more scenes than the very long play *Hamlet* (3,776 lines). The average Shakespearean play is about 2,700 lines long and would have been performed in about two and a half hours with few if any intervals. The *Henry VI* plays and one or two of the others might be called "episodic" in the pejorative sense, but the majority are well formed. The typical play is variegated in content and unpredictable in development, but it leaves us with a sense of a single entity rather than of a collection of parts. How the effect is achieved cannot be described in general terms. Each play solves in a different way a different structural problem.

The number of listed characters varies even more widely than the number of scenes, from fourteen each in *All's Well* and *Twelfth Night* to forty-seven in *Henry VI, Part Two*. The acting company, consisting of about ten principal players and about six each of hired players, boy learners, and available extras, could fill many roles, with doubling only in minor parts. The number of exacting feminine roles had to be restricted to two or three because of the small number of boys of the right age and experience to play them. Beyond observing the restrictions imposed by numbers, the playwright could proceed to create characters freely. Of course he wrote no parts for persons with three arms, but he did not have to tailor his characterizations to the personalities of members of his troupe: they *were* actors. If a Burbage could be tragical both as Hamlet and Othello, presumably a Kempe could be comical both as Launcelot Gobbo and Dogberry. The number of characters is immaterial so long as differentiation is sufficient to avoid confusion. The praise once accorded the "psychological consistency" of Shakespeare's characters was no doubt excessive, but the fact remains that they have its practical equivalent, individuality. That a play like *Henry IV, Part One* could present four principal characters as distinct in themselves and different from each other as the King, Prince Hal, Hotspur, and Falstaff is remarkable enough, but, with only a few dozen lines to speak, Mistress Quickly also comes alive. This is the Shakespearean bonus. The impact of characters like Richard III and Hamlet might be explained by sheer massiveness of presentation; each speaks over a thousand lines and is almost continuously onstage. But Shylock is as indelibly fixed in our minds although his role is only one-fourth the length of Richard's, one-fifth the length of Hamlet's, and he appears in only five of the nineteen scenes of *The Merchant of Venice*.

It goes without saying that each play meets its primary obligations of drama. By means of mimetic action and dialogue it tells an interesting story well. In only a few instances (conspicuously *Henry V* and *Pericles*) is there an interpolation of narrative parts. The plot complication is sufficient to sustain interest but escapes the hazard of a self-defeating density. Whether in a farcical intrigue like *The Merry Wives of Windsor* or a conflict between fell opposites like *Hamlet*, the story line remains clear; in the latter case the mere twists and turns of the plot and the excitement of the tale afford no small part of the fascination. In each play the situations provide constant stimulus to sentiment and passion, the characters are great responders, and the audience shares in their response. The emotional potential is high.

Shakespeare divided his efforts about equally among all four of the major categories of drama current in the great London arenas. The four are specified in the new patent his company when it became the King's Men in 1603: tragedies, comedies, histories, "pastoralls." A few years earlier Polonius had extolled the troupe visiting Elsinore as "the best in the world, either for tragedy, comedy, history, pastoral" and their permutations, "pastoral-comical," and so on; and a few years later, in his *Apology for Actors* (1612) Thomas Heywood reproduces the list: "tragedies, comedies, histories, pastorals." The "pastorals" of these inventories were not necessarily, or even commonly, plays about shepherds, shepherdesses, and woodland gods, but any in which lovers surmounted strange obstacles in winning through to union; they were dramatizations of the kind of material found in romantic fiction. The category is represented in Shakespeare in a wide spectrum of works, from the merry *Midsummer Night's Dream* to the grave *Winter's Tale*. Since all end happily, the editors of the folio made no distinction between the comedies and "pastorals," but modern criticism has inadvertently restored the fourth category to a limited extent by grouping *Pericles, Cymbeline, The Winter's Tale,* and *The Tempest* as Shakespeare's "romances." What distinguishes these late examples is their tragic potential. The prototype of the hero of *Pericles* is Job. In *Cymbeline* a king's virtuous daughter is rejected as in *King Lear*. In *The Winter's Tale* the jealousy of Leontes is as lethal as Othello's.

In *The Tempest* the brother of Prospero is as criminally treacherous as Claudius. Evil is a formidable presence even though it misses the final mark. In all four the shadow of sin and misfortune lying upon an older generation is dispersed by the bright innocence of a younger. All contain elements of the supernatural and the suggestion of perpetual redemption in the renewal of life through love. Except for *The Tempest,* which, along with *The Winter's Tale,* contains some of the loveliest passages in Shakespeare, these plays used to be somewhat disparaged, but criticism has now turned full cycle. The tendency may now be to take them too seriously, but they do indeed convey the impression that the poet knew he was having his last say and was unaggressively recording his personal faith. That his "philosophy of life" was essentially religious is generally conceded, but attempts to compress its expression into an orthodox Christian container or to dissolve it in the luminous myths of pagan pantheism work about equal injury on the plays. No doubt Shakespeare would have been astonished by the idea that either he or his plays might be taken as anything but Christian, but he was a secular writer, and somewhat ecumenical. Both legal restriction and artistic tact restrained him from being "theological" in his stage pieces.

All Shakespeare's comedies end in a reconciling marriage except *Love's Labour's Lost* (which evidently did likewise in its original form), and perhaps a Rosalind of *As You Like It* or a Viola of *Twelfth Night* has as just a claim to be viewed as a vernal maiden (a Persephone figure) as has a Perdita or Miranda. However, a spirit of jollity prevails in the earlier romantic plays; they are what Polonius would have classified as "pastoral-comical," and their easy charm and poetic appeal have tended to establish in our minds the Shakespearean norm in comedy. His comedies, in fact, are quite diverse in kind and include examples of all sorts in fashion except satirical treatment of London life. His most "classical" comedies, in the sense of having most in common with the plays of Plautus, Terence, and their Renaissance imitators, are *The Comedy of Errors, The Taming of the Shrew,* and *The Merry Wives of Windsor.* These are cleverly wrought and quite funny when staged, but the confusions attendant upon mistaken identity and intrigue in a middle-class milieu offered limited scope for imaginative and poetic powers. As examples of "pure comedy" the vow-breaking of *Love's Labour's Lost,* the Beatrice-Benedick courtship of *Much Ado About Nothing,* and the life-below-stairs scenes of *Twelfth Night* are generally preferred. Realistic fiction, usually originating in Italy, was dramatized in some of the comedies; and in the usury scenes of *The Merchant of Venice* and slander scenes of *Much Ado About Nothing* there is serious threat of disaster. The action is such as would now be called simply "dramatic." Such action is sufficiently dominant in *Measure for Measure* and *All's Well That Ends Well* that there has been an understandable reluctance to view these plays as comedies at all. The term "problem play" has been applied to them, and sometimes to *Troilus and Cressida,* which was called a "history" in the quarto and a "tragedy" in the folio edition. All are provocative, and *Measure for Measure* contains some of the most powerful scenes in Shakespeare, but modern readers have difficulty in coming to terms with them, perhaps because of their deceptive air of modernity. Their themes are modern enough, especially in the concern with the sanctions of sexual relationship, but their ethical assumptions are not. These are too permissive in one way and too strict in another for most twentieth-century tastes.

Samuel Johnson, whose Shakespearean criticism was written before the chronology of the plays was reasonably well established, astutely remarked that the dramatist made his mark in comedy early because he was a comic writer by nature. He was certainly endowed with a rich gift of native humor. It is as apt to appear in his histories and tragedies as elsewhere and is identical in its manifestations in his earliest plays and his latest. In what is perhaps the first of his extant works, *Henry VI, Part Two,* Jack Cade assures the butcher, the weaver, the sawyer, and sundry rebels that under his rule all will have seven halfpenny loaves for a penny and "the three-hooped pot shall have ten hoops."

> *All.* God save your majesty!
> *Cade.* I thank you, good people . . .

In what appears to have been Shakespeare's first experiment with romance, *The Two Gentlemen of Verona,* a dog has misbehaved in company and is sorrowfully reproved by the servant Launce, who has tried to set it an example in civil conduct: "When didst thou see me heave up my leg and make water against a gentlewoman's farthingale." In *Love's Labour's Lost* Costard shows a sympathetic understanding of why the curate Nathaniel has failed in his dramatic impersonation of Emperor Alexander the Great, although he is "a marvellous good neighbor, faith, and a very good bowler." This kind of thing is quite different from the vocational impudence and pun-mongering of the accredited jesters in the plays, which has worn less well than anything else in them. There is no attempting to define this native humor, except as endearing evidence of the seeing eye, the uncensorious heart, and delight in human absurdity. We think of imperturbable Bottom among the fairies, of the aged countryman Shallow musing over inevitable death and the market value of ewes, of Constable Dogberry and his wounded dignity, of the first gravedigger and his occupational pride. The glow never fades: in *The Tempest* the butler reproves his rebel guerrillas who have failed to hang on to their bottles of liquor—"There is not only disgrace and dishonor in that, but an infinite loss."

Falstaff, be it remembered, appears in a comedy only as a reprise, and there only in somewhat muted form. He lived and had his amplest being in the two parts of *Henry IV* where the throne of England is in hazard and armies are on the march. Mistress Quickly's comic-pathetic account of his death competes with a warrior king's battle oration at Agincourt as the most memorable passage in *Henry V.* The comic strain in these three histories contrasts with the tragic strain in those which preceded. Yet the individual plays within each group are nothing alike. *Richard III* and *Richard II* were both first published as "tragedies," and were written within a few years of each other, but the difference between them is spectacular, the first a brilliant rhetorical melodrama, the second a subtle poem on a strong man's rise and a weak

man's fall. The ten history plays are alike only in their subject matter, drawn in common from the English chronicles, and in their dual intent—to feed the sentiment of national solidarity at the same time that they entertain.

The CHRONICLE PLAY as a distinct genre appeared about the same time as the second edition of Holinshed's *Chronicles* in 1587 and may have owed something to the latter's popularity as well as to the spirit of national pride following the defeat of the Spanish Armada in 1588. Raphael Holinshed, following the lead of his predecessor Edward Hall, fostered the so-called Tudor myth—that the present ruling house had been heaven-ordained to bring peace and unity to England after the fifteenth-century wars between the houses of York and Lancaster. In the years when the history play flourished, 1590 to 1603, there was constant fear in England that civil war might return upon the death of the aging and childless Elizabeth. There is no question that Shakespeare's histories reflect the national solicitude—they are patriotic and committed to principles of order and legal succession —but they are not, as discussion sometimes makes them appear, overt political exempla. Their doctrine is only implied and does not include the idea that kings are good or bad in exact proportion to the legality of their claims. The idea that the right to rule may have something to do with the ability to rule is by no means excluded, and the one great hero among Shakespeare's kings, Henry V, is the son of a usurper.

Since only a few known history plays can be earlier than Shakespeare's first, and since Marlowe's *Edward II* is certainly not one of them, he can be said with some show of reason to have created the type as we think of it. *Richard II,* the *Henry IV* plays, and *Henry V* treat the events leading up to the Wars of the Roses, and the *Henry VI* plays and *Richard III,* although written sooner, treat the wars themselves. Together the eight plays dramatize English history from 1398, when Richard II began to invite his own doom, until 1485, when Richard III was defeated on Bosworth Field by Henry Tudor, and peace returned to England. *King John* is isolated from them in that it treats of thirteenth-century history, but its subject is much the same, the evils of misrule and rebellion. *Henry VIII* is isolated in a different way. It was written a decade after the other histories and has some of the qualities of a period piece as it pays homage to the son of the hero of Bosworth and father of Queen Elizabeth. A good many have learned their "history" from Shakespeare. His facts are as unreliable as his propagandistic sources, especially as regards the character of Richard III, and he has little to say of the influence of such things as wool staple in the shaping of political events, but he makes the past seem to live and never lets us forget that history is what happens to people.

It is the tragedies that first made Shakespeare a celebrity abroad as at home and that still have the widest currency. More has been written about four of them, *Hamlet, Othello, King Lear,* and *Macbeth,* than about the other thirty-three plays combined, although the latter have by no means languished in critical neglect. The most baffling mystery about the tragedies is why *Titus Andronicus,* performed as "new" and printed in 1594 should be so bad, while *Romeo and Juliet,* written no more than two years

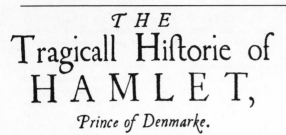

THE
Tragicall Hiſtorie of
HAMLET,

Prince of Denmarke.

By William Shakeſpeare.

Newly imprinted and enlarged to almoſt as much againe as it was, according to the true and perfeƈt Coppie.

AT LONDON,
Printed by I. R. for N. L. and are to be ſold at his ſhoppe vnder Saint Dunſtons Church in Fleetſtreet. 1604.

TITLE PAGE OF THE "GOOD QUARTO" (1604) OF
SHAKESPEARE'S *Hamlet*

later, should be so good. The best explanation of the defects of the former rests in the theory that it was an exercise in Senecan goriness originally written some years earlier in rivalry with Kyd's popular hit *The Spanish Tragedy* and was given a new verbal façade in 1594 when the Chamberlain's Men were assembling a repertory. For the merits of *Romeo and Juliet* the only explanation is that, in it, as in *A Midsummer Night's Dream* and *Richard II*, written about the same time, Shakespeare had reached his stride. It was not his first trial in handling tragic episode, even disregarding *Titus Andronicus*, since his earlier histories, as noted above, were all tragic in cast, but nothing like *Romeo and Juliet* had thus far appeared in the London theaters by himself or anyone else. It is an amazingly original play. Its lyrical treatment of young love and its sympathetic conversion of the lovers into sacrificial figures (although Christian suicides) had a strong and immediate impact upon playwrights as well as playgoers, as attested by imitations, some of them parodic.

In the four major tragedies, written between 1600 and 1606, the author's full powers as dramatist, poet, and responsive human being were deployed in prob-

ing the mystery of evil. In *Hamlet* it appears as a kind of malaise, fostered by undisciplined appetite, weakness, and folly, rather than as positive viciousness. Positive viciousness, a wanton relish of cruelty and destruction, appears in *Othello* in the diabolism of Iago, the snake in Eden preying upon innocence. In *Macbeth* evil is not similarly personified, even though the thane of Cawdor and his lady are the very emblems of murder and the witches appear as infernal acolytes. It is an insidious enemy mining in the soul. Here evil seems to create appetite, whereas in *Hamlet* appetite creates evil. In *King Lear* the invisible power threatens to take over the universe. In all four plays, and in the last particularly, appears the Shakespearean tendency to treat the resisting victims of evil as sacrificial figures. These powerful dramatic poems are spiritually bracing, partly because of the honesty of their confrontation of all that men have to fear, both in their universe and in themselves; partly because they so clearly espouse the good in the teeth of its mighty opposite; and partly because they contain the terrible within the beautiful.

Elizabethan tragedy is characterized by excess, and Shakespeare's tragedies, although they transcend their tradition in other respects, are far from restrained. They are great in spite of their containing some of the most primitive elements found in the author's entire works: devices lifted bodily from Senecan tragedy of revenge, a superfluity of corpses in the concluding scenes, samples (often miraculously effective) of medieval grotesquerie when clowning weds the ridiculous to the sublime. The Roman tragedies are far more chaste. *Julius Caesar* is perhaps of all his plays the most cleanly chiseled and, if the word may be used without reflecting upon Shakespeare's basic rationality, his most sane. *Coriolanus* is written with (in Coleridge's words) such "fine philosophical impartiality" that one has difficulty in finding in it anyone whom he prefers to anyone else. The appeal is intellectual as the advocates of aristocratic and of democratic government are tried, and both found wanting. *Antony and Cleopatra*, combining in what should be an impossible way the wrangles of aging lovers and the battles of rivals for the empery of the world, is the greatest *tour de force*, and the richest in human interest. Octavius becomes sole master of the Roman Empire as Antony deteriorates. The fate of this doting libertine and his tenacious mistress should seem sordid or absurd, but Antony's end is dignified by his selfless concern for the welfare of Cleopatra, and Cleopatra dies right royally. After losing command of everything else, this "pair so famous" gain command of our sympathies.

Also grouped with the tragedies by the editors of the folio are two plays on Greek history, or pseudo-history, *Troilus and Cressida* and *Timon of Athens*. The former presents such a deflated image of the ill-fated lovers and the Trojan War that critics have been unwilling to accept the treatment as tragic, even though Hector, the character most eligible as tragic hero, dies in its conclusion. The term "satirical tragedy" has been applied to it, and although the words may be self-contradictory, the play itself is somewhat so. If it is a "problem play," it is hard to decide whether the material or its treatment presents the problem. *Timon of Athens* also fails to satisfy as tragedy, partly because the theme of spoiled sentimentalist is a difficult one to dignify; one has no great sense of loss at the obsequies of a new-made cynic. *Timon* seems only provisionally completed and is the one play in the canon concerning which there is some doubt about its ever having been performed in its own day. The Elizabethans are reputed to have had less respect for the Greeks than for the Romans, but we can hardly attribute to this fact the greater tragic dignity of Shakespeare's Roman plays. Although they are as "historical" as the English ones—in fact Plutarch may have been a more reliable guide than Holinshed—they are not "histories," because their political interest is purely incidental. The focus is upon the fate of persons, not the fate of Rome.

Although dramatic poetry was not revered by the Elizabethans, it was appreciated; and Shakespeare was recognized as the leading dramatic poet. In 1592 he was commended by Henry Chettle as "excellent in the quality he professes" and for his "facetious [entertaining] grace in writing that approves [proves] his art." In 1598 he was said by Francis Meres to be "among the English . . . the most excellent in both kinds [tragedy and comedy] for the stage." He is called "soul of the age" in the great tribute by Ben Jonson in the 1623 folio:

> He was not of an age, but for all time!
> And all the Muses still were in their prime,
> When like Apollo he came forth to warm
> Our ears, or like a Mercury to charm.

In 1668 John Dryden called him "the man who of all modern, and perhaps ancient, poets had the largest and most comprehensive soul"; and in the Preface to his edition (1765) of the plays Samuel Johnson distinguishes him as "above all modern writers the poet of nature, the poet that holds up to his readers a faithful mirror of manners and of life"—thus affording "the stability of truth." In the early nineteenth century, Schlegel in Germany and Coleridge, Lamb, Hazlitt, and Keats in England refined upon these encomia; and ever since poets, dramatists, novelists, and critics in all nations have competed in singing Shakespeare's praise.

No modern critics of note have demurred from the judgment that Shakespeare stands first among dramatists, although George Bernard Shaw (a secret admirer) indulged in some amusing persiflage, and T. S. Eliot, at the time of his greatest devotion to Dante, deplored Shakespeare's "Stoicism." Leo Tolstoy rejected his work *in toto*, but at that time in his life when he was rejecting all literary "art" including his own. A position of eminence so high, and so long and securely held, must inevitably arouse in some quarters emotions of hostility. These have often taken the odd form of denial that Shakespeare wrote the Shakespearean plays—the only available alternative to denial that the plays exist. Much more usual is the tendency to view his work as a kind of Mount Everest—to be viewed at a respectful distance or scaled simply "because it is there." A reputation can be so formidable as to have a stultifying effect, inhibiting spontaneity of response. Perhaps the overawed modern reader would be more truly responsive to Shakespeare's merits if he permitted himself to be aware of Shakespeare's defects. The plays are not perfect. Every one contains at least some evidence of careless improvisation, and in quite a few this evi-

dence is far from slight. Heminge and Condell, in their folio address to the readers, said that "what he thought he uttered with such easiness that we have scarcely received from him a blot in his papers." Editors now know that they exaggerated—that he did "blot" and revise—but he never strove for ultimate polish in his manuscripts nor proofread his printed plays. Ben Jonson reproved the actors for fostering the worshipful legend that he never blotted a line by saying it were better he had "blotted a thousand"— and was himself reproved as envious. Actually "a thousand" is a very moderate estimate.

Nevertheless, our final judgment must be that his enormous prestige is justified. He wrote over a hundred thousand dramatic lines, with so many more than a thousand so "right"—with so many whole speeches and scenes so "right"—that improvement is unimaginable. His verbal distinction can be statistically demonstrated. Although his style is almost as monosyllabic as that of the King James version of the Bible, he brings into play a larger working vocabulary than any other English creative writer. His imagery is so abundant, varied, and functional that it has opened a career to a whole school of analysts. Nevertheless, his distinction as a poet does not ultimately reside in his possession of words, or his ear for the sound of their music. There have been twentieth-century writers with cerebral "speech-centers" as highly organized as Shakespeare's. Often, however, these miraculously articulate persons have little to say that anyone wishes to hear; the representative character of their experience of life and the width of their sympathies seem sometimes in inverse proportion to their powers of expression, so that they remain Shakespeares of the cradle. Ben Jonson and John Dryden perceived quite early that Shakespeare's distinction as maker with words had something to do with the dimensions of his soul. It is the wonder of the man that he was so *like* so many of his fellow men and that he could express what so many feel. His works, more abundantly than those of any other poet and dramatist, communicate among men. As we read we share the burden of our common fear that life may be a tale told by an idiot, and we share delight in the flowers of human experience that take the winds of March with beauty.

The quotations and line and scene counts in this article are from *The Pelican Shakespeare* (38 vols., 1956–1967), general editor, A. Harbage. The most fully annotated complete edition of the plays is *The Arden Shakespeare* (37 vols., 1899–1924), W. J. Craig and R. H. Case, general editors, which has been undergoing revision since 1951 under the general editorship of U. Ellis-Fermor, succeeded by H. F. Brooke and H. Jenkins. The standard scholarly analysis of facts about Shakespeare, printing biographical documents and contemporary allusions, is Sir Edmund Chambers, *William Shakespeare* (2 vols., 1930). The best current biographies are Marchette Chute, *Shakespeare of London* (1949), and Gerald Eades Bentley, *Shakespeare, A Biographical Handbook* (1961). The most comprehensive assembling of relevant facts and discussion is *The Reader's Encyclopedia of Shakespeare* (1966), O. J. Campbell and E. G. Quinn, editors. A compact and invaluable collection of the older landmarks of criticism is *Shakespeare Criticism* (1932), D. N. Smith, editor.

Anthologies of twentieth-century criticism are *Shakespeare, Modern Essays in Criticism* (rev. ed., 1967), L. Dean, editor; *Approaches to Shakespeare* (1964), N. Rabkin, editor; *Shakespeare: The Tragedies* (1964), A. Harbage, editor; *Shakespeare: The Histories* (1965), E. M. Waith, editor; *Shakespeare: The Comedies* (1965), K. Muir, editor.—A. H.

Shakespearean criticism. How simple it would be if we could say that Shakespearean criticism can be divided into the neoclassic, romantic, historical, and modern categories. Actually there are numerous schools of Shakespearean criticism, some of them obsolete (neoclassic), others of them old and venerable and continuing into the present (historical), and still others but recently evolved and still to run their course (existential). It is a tribute to the infinite variety of Shakespeare's art that he can be approached by about three dozen critical methods, of which only a few, besides those listed above, need be mentioned as representative of the variety: aesthetic, bibliographical, biographical, theatrical, metrical, psychological, eulogistic, linguistic, philosophical, "New," ethical, Hegelian, sociological, Marxist, and so on. One can even posit a clairvoyant school of criticism, which includes those critics who arrogate to themselves by some instinctive process the knowledge of precisely what Shakespeare meant and proudly divulge it to the world.

Properly speaking, all types of criticism are relevant, depending on what the reader is seeking. If we want to know whether Hamlet had an Oedipus complex, we consult the psychiatric or psychological critics. If we want to know about Shakespeare's language, we consult the linguistic critics. Although there is a vein of truth in Charles Knight's statement that "criticism as far as regards the very highest works of art, must always be a failure," it is still possible to get closer to a work by virtue of the knowledge, intellect, and sympathy of the critic. Since each new reader comes to Shakespeare with an open mind, hopefully, it may be of interest to him to know that neoclassic critics expected a play to follow the unities of time, place, and action and that they thought Shakespeare something of a barbarian for disobeying the rules.

If criticism fairly encompasses the relevant evidence, establishes sound dramatic principles, and does not distort aesthetics, it should be forever timely and interesting. The point is that the reader should be aware that there is more than one way to look at Shakespeare. The more a critic harps on his own method to the exclusion of others, the more wary a reader should be. Since the works of Shakespeare encompass so many kinds of criticism, the reader should be catholic enough to take what is most useful to his appreciation and understand as many points of view as possible.

Because the drama in Shakespeare's time was considered a popular form of entertainment, formal criticism as such did not then exist. It was not until John Dryden's *Essay of Dramatic Poesy* (1668) considered the possibility of following either the French, the Elizabethan, or the Classic schools that a formal critical evaluation of Shakespeare appeared.

Shakespeare's reputation had survived the Puritan period, but the dramatic principles of the Jacobean and Caroline periods had not. The theater was no longer "public" at a penny or more admission, but "private," at prices from one to four shillings. Entertainment was for the educated few rather than the semiliterate multitude. The presumably more correct critical principles imported by Thomas Rymer and others from France demanded that the pseudoclassic unities of time and place and action be adhered to, that decorum be maintained, that heroic love interests be introduced, and that "poetic justice," a concept derived by Thomas Rymer from Aristotle's punishment for the tragic flaw, be observed. Though Dryden censured Shakespeare for faults of language, especially his "blown puffy style," which the Elizabethan did not "distinguish . . . from true sublimity," he praised him for "the beauties of his thought remaining." Therefore, he says, "let not Shakespeare suffer for our sakes; 'tis our fault who succeeded him in an age more refined." Dryden, however, was impelled to refine the language, make clear the unintelligible, and "remove that heap of Rubbish under which many excellent thought lay wholly bury'd."

Rymer's *A Short View of Tragedy* (1693) castigated Shakespeare for writing *Othello* and *Julius Caesar* without regard for decorum and called the former the tragedy of the handkerchief. For his pains Rymer was labeled by George Saintsbury "the worst critic who ever lived." Charles Gildon's essay ("Some Reflections on Mr. Rymer's Short View of Tragedy and an Attempt at a Vindication of Shakespeare," 1694) attacked Rymer as others did after him. The new position was that Shakespeare had had to please his audience, all great men ignored rules, comedy and tragedy could be mixed, and Shakespeare's words did properly evoke passion and imagery without bombast.

Shakespeare's violation of rules was a constant theme. Joseph Addison, in *Spectator* 592 (1714), wrote that anyone would rather read Shakespeare "where there is not a single rule observed, than any production of a modern critic, where there is not one of them violated." Shakespeare was "a stumbling block to the whole tribe of these rigid critics." In other of the *Spectator* (number 230) and *Tattler* papers (numbers 8 and 71 by Sir Richard Steele) the moral value of Shakespeare was emphasized. The influence of these papers was wide; the ten thousand *Spectator* papers circulated three times a week, and a *Tattler* review was enough to fill a theater when it extolled a play, as playwright Colley Cibber remarked. Yet there was a dichotomy between the critics and the stage plays, as already noted. Addison himself wrote "regular" plays, and the public had little access to Shakespeare except for the four folios, extant quartos, and Nicholas Rowe's edition of 1709. Alexander Pope's edition did not appear until 1725. Only when thousands of individual plays were published in very cheap editions in the 1730's did the general public have much access to the plays.

John Dennis, in his *Essay on the Genius and Writing of Shakespeare* (1711), pondered how great Shakespeare would have been if he could have added to his great genius a knowledge of the ancients. Shakespeare made mistakes in history and committed anachronisms. He made the good suffer with the bad, he did not have time to revise, but was great nevertheless, Dennis asserted. Charles Gildon, after writing *An Essay on the Art, Rise, and Progress of the Stage in Greece, Rome, and England* (1710), which attacked Shakespeare for not adhering to the two-thousand-year-old tradition of the unities, also wrote *Remarks on the Plays of Shakespeare* (1710), the first separately printed book on Shakespeare. There is much interesting and contemporary-sounding criticism here. *Measure for Measure* is interpreted as a satire against reformers who forget that perfection is unattainable and overlook their own hypocrisy. But *Othello* deserves Rymer's criticism, Gildon insists, because a virtuous white woman would not marry a Negro, and a Negro should not be the hero of a play.

The early editors had much the same attitude as the early critics. Rowe, in his Preface to the first regularly edited edition of Shakespeare in 1709, properly noted that the mixture of comedy and tragedy was pleasing and that Shakespeare lived "under a kind of mere light of nature," making it unfair to "judge him by rules he knew nothing of." Rowe did not notice as Gildon did later (1710) that Shakespeare apparently did know and could follow rules, as he did in *The Comedy of Errors* and *The Tempest,* the first of which takes place in the light hours of one day and the second within about three hours.

Pope's Preface to his edition in 1725 extolled Shakespeare for his individualized characterization, but he rationalized his faults, which he attributed to Shakespeare's lack of "patronage from the better sort" and his desire to please an uncouth audience "for gain, not glory," as he had said earlier in his *Essay on Criticism* (1711). Shakespeare was "an original," drawing from nature and following "inspiration." Like "Gothic architecture," rather than modern, Pope concludes, Shakespeare has variety and inspires "greater reverence," though the means by which they are achieved are not regular.

Lewis Theobald's Preface (1733) also rationalized about the Elizabethan age but insisted that Shakespeare's "genius," the "blaze of imagination," "the richness and extent of his reading . . . the richness and the variety of his ideas," and "the mastery of his portraits" made him successful. Theobald echoed Pope's idea that to judge Shakespeare by Aristotle's rules would be "like trying a man by the laws of one country, who acted under those of another."

In the Preface to his Oxford edition (1744), Sir Thomas Hanmer followed his predecessors in apologizing for Shakespeare's faults, while praising his genius in comedy and tragedy. Like Pope, Hanmer relegated to the bottom of the page passages in the text he thought unworthy of Shakespeare.

The next editor, Rev. William Warburton, explained (1747) some of Shakespeare's supposed banalities as incrustations of "door-keepers and prompters" and editors, but it remained for Dr. Samuel Johnson's Preface to his edition in 1765 to remind the critics that the essence of drama is illusion and that those who can imagine that London is Egypt can "imagine much more." Therefore the unities need not be observed at all. Shakespeare excels in natural dialogue, his characters are "distinct," and the mixing of tragic and comic is true to life. Though in the end Johnson believed that Shakespeare's virtues overcame his vices, he did say that the poet "has likewise faults, and faults sufficient to obscure and overwhelm any other merit." Shake-speare is "more careful to please than to instruct," his moral purpose is not clear, he does not distribute poetic justice, and therefore fails "to make the world better," a fault "the barbarity of this age cannot extenuate." His plots are weak, he scants the ends of his plays, he commits anachronisms. Common people are frequently vulgar, ladies and gentlemen have little "delicacy," and his language is frequently pompous. A quibble "was to him the fatal Cleopatra for which he lost the world, and was content to lose it." Yet, Johnson says, "we fix our eyes upon his graces, and turn from his deformities, and endure in him what we should in another loathe and despise."

These early editors and their successors—frequently more scholarly than critical—set the tone for the century. One may call the period until 1766 "the age of rationalization." Shakespeare was deemed a product of an untutored age, but fortunately his wit, imagination, art, nature, and genius were sufficient to overcome all obstacles. By 1765 Dr. Johnson was able to say that Shakespeare had lived far beyond his period and had begun to assume the "dignity of an ancient." Later ages took up the analysis of his achievement.

Extended analyses of individual characters (the Romantic approach) were scarce in the first two hundred years of Shakespearean criticism. Thomas Rymer had attacked Othello for his unmilitary qualities, and Professor William Richardson of Glasgow University, in *Philosophical Analysis and Illustration of Some of Shakespeare's Remarkable Characters* (1774 and later editions), found Shakespeare's "genius . . . unlimited." In these and later *Essays* Richardson investigated various characters from a psychological and moral viewpoint and found them credible even when overpowered by a ruling passion or idiosyncracy. Hamlet, for example, chooses not to kill his uncle, because his desire for revenge and his "moral conduct" are for the moment in perfect balance.

Shortly after Richardson's analyses began to appear, Maurice Morgann wrote his influential *Essay on the Dramatic Character of Sir John Falstaff* (1777), maintaining that, contrary to the generally held belief, Falstaff was no coward, for there is no textual evidence to support that impression. Shakespeare permitted that impression to be assumed only for the sake of humor. Thomas Whately's incomplete and posthumously published *Remarks on Some of the Characters of Shakespeare* (1785) praised Shakespeare's naturalistic characters while noting their remarkable individuality. Macbeth and Richard III were subtly compared and contrasted.

The seventeenth and eighteenth centuries initiated most of the criticism that was to be developed in the succeeding centuries. Eulogy modified by neoclassic rationalism was the general theme, but in the notes of Peter Whalley (*Enquiry into the Learning of Shakespeare,* 1748), John Upton (*Critical Observations on Shakespeare,* 1746), and Zachary Grey (*Critical, Historical, and Explanatory Notes on Shakespeare,* 1754) Shakespeare's knowledge and reading are praised to such an extent that Dr. Johnson had to point out in 1765 that his "deep learning" is a mere myth, a proverbial or coincidental thought "as will happen to all who consider the same subjects." Dr. Richard Farmer, the Cambridge Shakespearean, two years later wrote the long *Essay on the Learning of Shakespeare* (1767), proving to the satisfaction of most of his contemporaries that though Shakespeare knew a little Latin, he read only English sources and used translations whenever available.

The collation of folios and quartos for correcting errors and improving the text was practiced to a greater or lesser extent by most of the early editors, but it was Edward Capell who made the first important steps in bibliographical, or textual, criticism with his edition of Shakespeare in ten volumes (1768). Not taste, conjecture, or imagination, but the best early text should be the criterion for editing Shakespeare. Capell abandoned dependence on the Fourth Folio (1685), used by his predecessors, collated all the folios and quartos he could find, distinguished the abridged, corrupted, pirated, and theatrical prompt texts, and in so doing practiced critical scholarship rather than pure criticism. George Steevens and Edmund Malone became his very able successors before the century ended.

Another aspect of Shakespearean studies developed in the eighteenth century was the critical examination of the sources of the poet's plots. The sources of twenty-two of Shakespeare's plays were collected and critically examined by Charlotte Lennox in her three-volume *Shakespeare Illustrated* (1753–1754). She found Shakespeare's additions frequently injudicious, citing as an example the unnecessary killing of Paris by Romeo.

Even the psychological study of Shakespeare's imagery was begun in the eighteenth century, by Walter Whiter, whose *Specimen of a Commentary on Shakespeare* (1794) was derived from John Locke's doctrine of the association of ideas. He analyzed image clusters as being a product of the operation and content of Shakespeare's unconscious mind. This approach was a natural outcome of the current interest of the philosophers Burke, Hume, Beattie, and others in the sublime and the imagination and what was internal rather than external to the author.

In the early part of the eighteenth century Voltaire, after a visit to England, came under the influence of Shakespeare. He praised his virtues but ranted about his faults to such an extent that Mrs. Elizabeth Montague's *Essay on the Genius and Writing of Shakespeare* (1769) was written with the express aim of attacking him and defending Shakespeare.

The Germans had a higher regard than the French for Shakespeare, anticipating the English in a Romantic appreciation of literature. In the context of Shakespeare, this kind of approach emphasizes the excellence of Shakespeare's natural genius rather than his anachronisms, disregard of the unities, and so forth. William Hazlitt's *Characters of Shakespeare's Plays* (1817) was written out of pique that Johnson and Richardson had not treated Shakespeare as well as had the Germans and that the Germans claimed a deeper appreciation of Shakespeare than did the English.

Samuel Taylor Coleridge imbibed the German influence when he studied at the University of Göttingen in 1798. A few years after his return to England he began in 1806 and continued through 1814 a series of lectures on Shakespeare and other subjects on the premise (1812) that "His [Shakespeare's] critics,

among us, during the whole of the last century, have neither understood nor appreciated him; for how could they appreciate what they could not understand." Coleridge pointed out that adherence to the unities caused absurdities; that Shakespeare followed the most important unity—of feeling or interest; that the puns and conceits were essential and worthwhile; that the opinions of Voltaire and others like him were "the judgment of monkeys . . . put into the mouths of people shaped like men"; that "Shakespeare's judgment was, if possible, still more wonderful than his genius"; that his characters were "genera intensely individualized"; that in Lear "old age is itself a character"; that Shakespearean criticism should be "reverential"; that "Shakespeare was the most universal genius that ever lived"; and so on.

Though much modern criticism has its origin in the eighteenth century, it is with Coleridge's attempt to understand rather than attack that modern Shakespearean criticism begins. There were, however, few critics in the nineteenth century who had Coleridge's insight. The writers who ventured to say something about Shakespeare were legion; those who are remembered today are comparatively few.

No better indication that Shakespeare had become literature rather than drama is found than Charles Lamb's emotional reaction to *King Lear, Hamlet, Richard III, Macbeth,* and *The Tempest.* He insisted in his essay "On the Tragedies of Shakespeare" (1812) that they were too great for the stage. Nor could Lamb tolerate *Othello.* When we read the play we see the "whiteness" of the Moor's mind, he said; when we see the play, Othello's blackness is intolerable. He concluded that "seeing is not believing . . . sight actually destroys faith." "The plays of Shakespeare are less calculated for performance on the stage than those of almost any other dramatist."

Dr. Johnson had noted that "in real life the vulgar is found close to the sublime and the merry and the sad usually accompany or succeed each other." Coleridge and the German critics found in comic scenes, not a playing down to the audience, but a higher purpose: juxtaposition for effectiveness. It remained for Thomas DeQuincey's famous essay "On the Knocking at the Gate in *Macbeth*" (1823) to insist that "feeling" rather than "understanding" is the essence of Shakespearean criticism and that our discovery of Shakespeare's design is a manifestation of his magnificent correctness. The porter scene, contrary to Coleridge's belief that it was not Shakespeare's, is a tour de force, according to DeQuincey. The knocking correctly turns the attention away from the murdered to the murderer. The tremendous contrast between what has just transpired and the porter scene brings us back to the existing world, where a reaction must take place.

Although Sir Walter Alexander Raleigh in 1907 attacked the Romantic critics for ranting about their feelings and for being inspired alike by the good and bad, they did realize that Shakespeare was an artist and that he wrote with his own laws. They could say, as Coleridge had pointed out, "I am proud that I was the first in time who publicly demonstrated to the full extent of the position, that the supposed irregularity and extravagance of Shakespeare were the mere dreams of a pedantry that arraigned the eagle because it had not the dimensions of the swan" ("Shakespeare's Judgment Equal to his Genius," 1818). In another analogy from nature, Walter Savage Landor, in his *Imaginary Conversations* (1824), tells us that "there is as great a difference between Shakespeare and Bacon as between an American forest and a London timber-yard": in the latter the lumber is cut, squared, and stacked; in the former, natural it is in all its glory, with the glades, mosses, shadows, birds, flowers—"everywhere multiformity, everywhere immensity."

Of the dozens of critics that fill out the nineteenth century we need mention only a few. Mrs. Anna Brownell Jameson wrote a very popular book, *Shakespeare's Heroines* (1832), in which she classified, sometimes with excessive adulation, the heroines according to temperament. Succeeding critics joined to extol Shakespeare's women. Thomas Carlyle, in his "Hero as Poet" lecture of May 12, 1840, declared that Shakespeare was superior to Bacon. Carlyle's often idolatrous criticism claimed that Shakespeare's art is not artifice; Shakespeare probably suffered as much as his characters and his sonnets reveal; his histories are a "national epic"; and that Englishmen from Paramatta to New York would also brag that Shakespeare is theirs.

Emerson, in his *Representative Men* (1850), introduces his remarks by saying that "great men are more distinguished by range and extent than originality." Shakespeare was much indebted to his sources but it is his poetry, philosophy, and "omnipresent humanity which coordinates all his faculties" that is more important than his dramatic power. "Originality is relative." Despite all the researches of the scholars, "Shakespeare is the only biographer of Shakespeare."

Correspondences between Bacon and Shakespeare by the aesthetic critics reveal that while some were seeking Shakespeare in his works alone others were digging into the archives of the past. Edmond Malone, Francis Douce, Nathan Drake, Joseph Hunter, Alexander Dyce, John Payne Collier, Stephan Fullom, James Orchard Halliwell-Phillipps, and other nineteenth-century critics were seeking Shakespeare's life outside his plays and sonnets. Their work had impact on the critics who welded life and work together and began to divide Shakespeare's life into periods of development and composition according to his ascertained or conjectured biographical influences.

The plays, if biographical inspiration could be read into them, were also said to reveal Shakespeare's personal feelings. From apprentice plays that smelled of the lamp, to the happiness of middle-life repose, to the despair of the tragedies, to the serenity of the romances, Shakespeare developed. Edward Dowden crystallized the method to be followed by George Brandes, Frank Harris, and many others. Hippolyte Adolphe Taine and his successors demonstrated that Shakespeare could not have been other than the product of all influences—social, political, economic, national, regional, climatic, as well as personal. However, others maintained that Shakespeare was too great an artist to permit personal feelings to color his work. Thomas Kenny (*Life and Genius of Shakespeare*, 1864) and David Masson (*Shakespeare's Personality*, 1865) agreed that Shakespeare had a singularly unobtrusive personality. It

remained for C. J. Sisson's important lecture on "The Mythical Sorrows of Shakespeare" (1934) to put a virtual end to extensive biographical criticism.

Meanwhile other critics were mining different areas. As early as 1678 the dramatist Edward Ravenscroft had doubted Shakespeare's authorship of *Titus Andronicus*. Pope was suspicious of *The Comedy of Errors* and parts of several other plays. Johnson was suspicious of *Richard II*, and Malone suspected *Henry VI*. After the mid-century F. G. Fleay and others in the New Shakspere Society (1873–1894) began to apply verse tests to the plays, resulting in the conclusion that almost all the plays contained the work of inferior collaborators. This criticism reached its apogee in the work of J. M. Robertson and J. Dover Wilson, whose keen senses disintegrated so many of the plays that E. K. Chambers rose to Shakespeare's defense in a British Academy lecture on "The Disintegration of Shakespeare" (1924), which insisted that Shakespeare was not always producing "at the top of his achievement," that the external evidence of Francis Meres, John Heminges, and Henry Condell (contemporaries of Shakespeare) must be accepted, that the verse tests are not wholly reliable and cannot produce a perfect curve of development, that vocabulary and diction tests are not definitive, and that therefore the disintegrationists are not to be trusted.

Many of the critics of the late Victorian period were eulogistic, pointing out Shakespeare's aesthetic and moral greatness as they saw it. Algernon Swinburne, in *A Study of Shakespeare* (1880), declared that the ear was better than numerical tests for analyzing Shakespeare's verse and that only Aeschylus was a greater dramatist.

Other critics were more concerned with Shakespeare's philosophy and structure. Denton J. Snider's *System of Shakespeare's Dramas* (1877, and later volumes on Shakespearean comedy, tragedy, and history) took a Hegelian ethical view. He noted how Shakespeare brought his characters along various threads of action, from chaos through mediation to harmony, by means of structurally well-developed plays. The plays begin with the destruction of institutions such as the state, society, and the family, and end with their restoration. The themes of the plays are seen through the institution, rather than the individual.

In the lectures and essays of A. C. Bradley (*Shakespearean Tragedy*, 1904) nineteenth-century criticism reached its height, created a plateau, and then heralded a reaction. Bradley's object was "to learn to appreciate the action and some of the personages with a somewhat greater truth and intensity." So incisive was this intensity that some professors still hold the book as their Bible of Shakespearean criticism. Bradley, like a twentieth-century Coleridge, examined the characters in *Hamlet, Othello, King Lear,* and *Macbeth* with a broad philosophical analysis and with almost total disregard for the plays as Elizabethan drama intended for a living stage.

Perceptive as Bradley's analysis was, other scholars were soon to emphasize historical rather than pure literary criticism. Dr. Robert Bridges (*On the Influence of the Audience*, 1906) on one level demonstrated that Shakespeare's dramaturgy was influenced by the expectation and the taste of his audience.

George Pierce Baker (*The Development of Shakespeare as a Dramatist*, 1907) likewise assumed audience influence, and Elmer Edgar Stoll in an essay on Shakespeare's "Ghosts" (1907) effectively introduced historical criticism in a reaction to Bradley that is still prevalent. Stoll said that to the Elizabethans ghosts were really not figments of the mind; they were personifications of Némesis, and Shakespeare's audience was medieval enough to be impressed. Wrongheaded criticism, said Stoll later (*From Shakespeare to Joyce*, 1944), stood in the way of understanding Shakespeare: ". . . in the process Shakespeare has become Maurice Morgann, or Coleridge, or Dowden, or Bradley." He disagreed with the "impressionist critics," saying that "a work of art does not [miraculously] change as the criticism changes" and the criterion of interpretation should be "the conscious or unconscious intention of the author."

Quite naturally there was controversy as to whose interpretation of Shakespeare's intention was the correct one. What seems psychologically improbable to us in the problem plays, as W. W. Lawrence (*Shakespeare's Problem Comedies*, 1931) says, was not so to the Elizabethans. An understanding of Elizabethan satiric conventions (Oscar J. Campbell, *Comicall Satyre*, 1938, and *Shakespeare's Satire*, 1943) and the medieval and contemporary dramatic heritage of the Elizabethans (W. Farnham, *The Medieval Heritage of Elizabethan Tragedy*, 1936; S. L. Bethell, *Shakespeare and the Popular Dramatic Tradition*, 1944; and L. L. Schücking, *Character Problems in Shakespeare's Plays*, 1919) proves that there is more than one key to Shakespeare's intent and that the poet was not a product of any precise aesthetic. Muriel C. Bradbrook (*Themes and Conventions in Elizabethan Tragedy*, 1935, and later studies) rightly says that Shakespeare made virtues out of both necessity and convenience. What he utilized from his past or present he made integral to his plays.

Lascelles Abercrombie's "A Plea for the Liberty of Interpreting Shakespeare" (1930) was interpreted by many as a license to extract any meaning for which they found a suitable reason. Abercrombie was merely crystallizing, however, a movement that was already under way. The reaction to Bradley's character criticism had led T. S. Eliot (*The Sacred Wood*, 1919) to seek "objective correlatives": objects and events as clues to emotion; Colin Still (*Shakespeare's Mystery Play*, 1921) and Henry W. Wells (*Poetic Imagery*, 1924) to emphasize symbols and "sunken images"; and Caroline Spurgeon ("Leading Motives in the Imagery of Shakespeare's Tragedies," 1930, and *Shakespeare's Imagery and What It Tells Us*, 1935) to develop the symbol, leading image, and image cluster approach. The word, the line, the theme, the image, the symbol—these became the basis of interpretation. F. C. Kolbe (*Shakespeare's Way*, 1924) simply counted, for example, that "counterfeit" or its equivalent is used 120 times in *Much Ado About Nothing*, confirming statistically an impression that the play concerns much ado about inaccurate *noting* of events, which leads the characters to draw false conclusions. Spurgeon enumerated the images of the same play and made deductions as to Shakespeare's own feelings about dogs, blushing,

and so forth. Others, like G. Wilson Knight in *The Wheel of Fire* (1930), for example, found the plays not composed so much of plot and character but rather of atmosphere and theme, a "burning core" such as music or tempest, without which the play is nothing.

The modern critical issue of whether there is a religious point of view in Shakespeare's plays stems also from Bradley. He asserted that the plays are secular. Starting with G. Wilson Knight, one school of critics has reacted against Bradley, perceiving the basis of Shakespearean tragedy in Christian terms. Paul N. Siegel (*Shakespearean· Tragedy and the Elizabethan Compromise*, 1957) insists that Shakespeare was obviously indebted to Christian Humanism, and M. D. H. Parker (*The Slave of Life*, 1955) concludes that Shakespeare was Roman Catholic in sympathy. In support of the Bradleyan conception of tragedy, D. G. James (*The Dream of Learning*, 1951) finds no guiding theory or philosophy in Shakespeare, nor any pervading Christian point of view. Sylvan Barnet's "Some Limitations of a Christian Approach to Shakespeare" (*English Literary History*, June 1955) objects to Tillyard, Knight, and others who have attempted to force Shakespeare into the pattern of Christian theology. But Knight later defended himself against those who said he had interpreted Shakespeare's plays as "pervasively" and "blatantly" Christian ("Shakespeare and Theology: A Private Protest," *Essays in Criticism*, January 1965). Roland M. Frye (*Shakespeare and Christian Doctrine*, 1963) denies that the plays can be used to show Shakespeare's religious views, but they do show that the poet was theologically literate and that he used his knowledge with dramatic effectiveness.

Hardin Craig (*The Enchanted Glass*, 1936), Knight (*The Olive and the Sword*, 1944), and many followers see Shakespeare developing plays that exhibit an intelligent world order and intellectual system in which each element in the universe—heaven, nature, and man; church, state, society, and family —has a fixed place. To disrupt the system or order is, in Shakespeare's terms, to invite chaos. Detractors of this theory say Shakespeare merely defends the *status quo*. A reaction to this finely ordered system is presently taking place (see *The Shakespeare Newsletter*, September 1968), because it is too pat and fails to include the effect of Machiavelli, church controversy, and so on. Whether or not the system is valid, it does establish a unifying theme in Shakespeare's eight chronicle plays, covering the period from *Richard II* to *Richard III*: Henry Bolingbroke had supplanted an anointed king and the crime was finally expiated by Richmond's defeat of the Machiavellian Richard III.

Psychological criticism has yet to run its course. Well over one hundred years ago Isaac Ray (*Contributions to Mental Pathology*, 1847) analyzed Shakespeare's tragic heroes from the point of view of madness, guilt consciousness, pseudosupernatural influence, and so forth. Freud went to greater depths. Discussing characters as realities rather than as fictional persons, he psychoanalyzed them to discover (*The Interpretation of Dreams*, 1900) in Hamlet and Lady Macbeth, for example, evidence of an Oedipus complex. Hamlet therefore cannot kill his uncle, and Lady Macbeth disintegrates because of her part in the murder of a man who resembled her father. Norman Holland (*Psychoanalysis and Shakespeare*, 1966) devotes an entire volume to discussing and analyzing the sometimes fantastic theories of these scholars.

There are other critical themes being developed. Shakespeare's pervading ethical sense is examined by John Vyvyan (*The Shakespearean Ethic*, 1961). He disagrees with Bradley's assertion that Shakespeare does not present his own feelings and uses the poet's concept of nobility, justice, and the hero and traitor to illustrate the point.

John Holloway's *Story of the Night: Studies in Shakespeare's Major Tragedies* (1961) was heralded as a potentially important book when it appeared because of its novel ideas on tragedy. He discusses tragedy from the point of myth and ritual and the hero's death as a scapegoat ritual.

From eccentric positions Shakespeare takes on new significance. Examining the poet as an existential thinker may offer new insights, but an authoritative study has yet to appear. David Horowitz's *Shakespeare: An Existential View* (1965) is one book on the subject. Jan Kott (*Shakespeare Our Contemporary*, 1964) presents the violence and passion of Shakespeare's world seen through the eyes of one who has experienced the horrors of war on the Eastern front. This book is especially significant because it has inspired such productions as the bloody *Henry VI* on the Royal Shakespeare Company stage (1964), an ultracontemporary *Hamlet* directed by Joseph Papp on the New York stage (1967), and controversial productions of *A Midsummer Night's Dream* in San Francisco, Pittsburgh, and New York (1966–1967), and in Stratford, Canada, and Stratford, Connecticut, in 1968.

All criticism should be addressed to those who wish to understand Shakespeare as a dramatist. The best criticism is that which clarifies the play to such an extent that it receives a better production on the stage and opens new vistas of clarity and understanding for the reader. Liberty of interpretation is possible; license should be understood for what it is. Eccentric criticism gives us insight into the critic; effective criticism gives us insight into Shakespeare and his plays.

There is as yet no complete history of Shakespearean criticism. Charles F. Johnson's *Shakespeare and His Critics* (1909) surveys the field up to its time but is naturally out of date. Augustus Ralli's *A History of Shakespearean Criticism* (2 vols., 1932) is the most thorough work on the subject, but it is not a history. It is a digest of the critical ideas contained in critical essays and books from the seventeenth century onward in England, the Continent, and the United States. It covers about 320 authors, whereas a full history could include about 500. In 1932 Herbert S. Robinson published *English Shakespearian Criticism in the Eighteenth Century*. The first fifty years of the twentieth century were evaluated by Kenneth Muir in "Fifty Years of Shakespearian Criticism: 1900–1950," in *Shakespeare Survey* (1951). The chapter "The Rage for Explication," in Louis Marder's *His Exits and His Entrances: The Story of Shakespeare Criticism* (1963), is a bird's-eye view of the highlights and vagaries of the critics and scholars to 1962. Arthur M. Eastman's *A Short History of Shakespeare Criticism* (1968) surveys the work of about fifty of the major critics. It, too, is a survey of criticism rather than a history of schools, movements, trends, and the like. For a continuing analysis of yearly criticism, see the annual volumes of *Shakespeare Survey* (1948 and continuing).—L. M.

Shakuntala (c. 400). The masterpiece of the Sanskrit dramatist KALIDASA and generally regarded as the finest of Sanskrit plays. Date and place of origin are conjectural but it is plausibly held that the play was written in approximately 400 at the court of Ujjain in central India. The work embodies the major features of Indian thought in many fields, notably aesthetic, psychological, religious, and philosophical. It complies, especially in Acts I to IV, with the Indian view of erotics, expressed, for example, in such a text as the *Kamasutra*, or "book of love." As the play advances, the mood becomes graver, Acts V to VII focusing largely on the ideal of the family, on the child as key to married life, and on family continuity through offspring.

Shakuntala conforms minutely to what are well known as the chief usages and principles of the Sanskrit stage as stated in the dramatic manuals, notably the NATYASASTRA, yet Kalidasa achieves a delicacy of expression unequaled elsewhere in Sanskrit drama. To describe its nuances would be impossible and to analyze its principles as drama or art would be for the most part to repeat a description of the *Natyasastra*, yet several features of the play are of unique interest.

The plot is a story familiar to folklore: a charm causes the lover temporarily to forget his beloved Shakuntala. The key to his oblivion is a magic spell embodied in a ring. The curse of forgetfulness is imposed by an irate sage to whom Shakuntala has denied hospitality, since for the moment the latter is absorbed in her own love thoughts. At the petition of her friends the sage mitigates this curse by declaring that when Shakuntala's husband, the king, to whom she has been secretly married, sees the ring he will recall their true relationship. By malignancy of fate Shakuntala loses the ring. It is later recovered from the maw of a fish, and no sooner has the king viewed it than his memory clears. Meanwhile Shakuntala, half-nymph to begin with, has been spirited away to the haven of a sacred retreat. Thither the king goes, after fighting in celestial wars in behalf of the gods. He not only meets his wife but their son as well, whom he has never seen. The family is happily united and the king blessed with an heir. The story of the private marriage, the curse of forgetfulness, and the magic ring is in large part duplicated, it may be recalled, in the Norse sagas used by Richard Wagner in his *Der Ring des Nibelungen*. Nowhere is the tale more effectively related than in Kalidasa's drama.

The Prologue is bound with unique gracefulness to the body of the play. Each act, as decreed in Indian dramatic theory, has its special mood. Shakuntala's reluctant departure from her foster father in Act IV, her repudiation by the forgetful king in Act V, his contrite mood in Act VI, and their joyous reunion in Act VII are presented with great effectiveness. The role of the clown, or *vidusaka*, is deftly handled, giving the desired contrasts to the king's nobility. Descriptive poetry accompanies the king's journey in his chariot, coursing in hunting expeditions over the earth or in celestial missions through the sky. Tender and generally admired is the picture of Shakuntala caring for her favorite plants and pet fawn. The play clearly is a cyclical myth, a pageant of nature and the seasons as well as of the vagaries of the human mind and heart.

Kalidasa handles his technical problems with complete mastery. Not only has the play a graceful Prologue; the individual acts have their equally skillful introductions. Playwriting in Sanskrit required a study in the interrelations of verse and prose, the verse used in stanzas each more or less sufficient to itself yet all embedded in prose and comprising a dramatic design. In this complex art Kalidasa became uniquely the master. Most of the stanzas are recited by the king. The prose is secondary but never dull, the verse heightened with rich color and warm feeling. To one who has true familiarity with the play, the prose is more or less assumed; it takes a backward place, like a continuo in Baroque music; the play's essence is in the verse; the stanzas may even be read in sequence without the prose, under which condition they roughly resemble a sonnet sequence or song cycle. Nowhere else is the formula for lyric drama so happily realized. The explanation lies, not only in the remarkably fruitful conventions of Sanskrit drama, but in Kalidasa's superior skill as poet. Several other Indian dramatists are also well known in the field of nondramatic poetry but none is so eminent as he. On turning to drama, he brought to its service his unsurpassed poetic art.

Translations of such an art are difficult. The early scenes to those unfamiliar or unsympathetic with the Indian system of erotics are especially likely to appear sentimental, affected, and meretricious. The sophisticated Indian outlook must not be confused with its opposite, bourgeois romantic sentimentality. Although the play was highly praised by Goethe shortly after its first translation by Sir William Jones in 1789, and has long been diligently studied in the West, it may be feared that no classic has more frequently been misunderstood.

The most widely read English translation of *Shakuntala* is that by Arthur W. Ryder, the latest edition of which was published in 1959. See also the translation by A. Hjalmar Edgren as revised in *Six Sanskrit Plays* (1964), edited by Henry W. Wells. —H. W. W.

Shamir, Moshe (1921–). Israeli novelist, essayist, and playwright. Shamir was born in the ancient cabalistic city of Zfat, Israel. As one of the foremost prose writers of modern Israel, Shamir has been awarded a number of prizes for his literary achievements and his novels have been translated and published abroad. His first novel, *He Walked in the Fields* (1946), portraying the young generation of Israel at the crucial period of its War of Independence, was dramatized by Shamir in collaboration with Joseph Millo, who directed the play at the Chamber Theatre (Kameri) in 1949. As the dramatization of a generation and its experience, this play was a turning point in Israeli drama. Its epic style is aided by a narrator who binds the various incidents and nostalgic flashbacks of the play into a coherent story.

In addition to being a prolific writer in both mediums, the novel and the drama, Shamir has also had more of his plays produced than has any other Israeli playwright. All his plays, sixteen to date, have been produced by the professional theaters. The majority of these plays deal with the contemporary scenes and problems of modern Israel; the others take their themes from Jewish history, with slight allusions to the present times. All but three are serious in tone, realistic in presentation, and constructed in the tradition of the "well-made play."

Beit Hillel ("The House of Hillel," 1950), a chamber play with a small cast of characters, is about pressures of life in a kibbutz and continues partially one of the themes of his first plays concerning the conflicts and pressures of marital life in a kibbutz. The comedy *Sof Ha'olam* ("The End of the World," 1954) depicts life in a settlement of new immigrants. He used historical material in *Milchemet Bnei or* ("The Battle of the Children of Light," 1956), a sequel to his best-known novel, *King of Flesh and Blood* (1954). *Halaila L'ish* ("Tonight I Will Belong to a Man," 1963) is a modern rendering of the biblical story of Ruth, and *Bayit B'matsav Tov* ("A House in Good Condition," 1962) is a comedy about contemporary family problems. It is only in his last play, *Hayoresh* ("The Inheritor," 1964), that some nonrealistic experiments can be seen.

His other plays include *Kilometer 56* (1949), *Leil Soofa* ("Stormy Night," 1954), *Gam Zo L'tova* ("Thanks for That," 1958), and *Agadot Lood* ("The Stories of Lyda," 1958).—Z. R.

Sharaku, Toshusai (fl. 1794–1795). Japanese artist. No theater has been more comprehensively documented by art than the *kabuki* theater of Japan, and no artist has equaled Toshusai Sharaku in giving such impressions to posterity. He worked in the medium of the colored block print, of which he was a master, though possibly in terms of technique and the most explicitly aesthetic standards several other Japanese artists surpassed him. It is his constant focus upon the stage and grasp of its subtler meanings that give him his preeminence as a theatrical illustrator. As an individual he remains a singular mystery. Though much is known of many of the contemporary Japanese painters and printmakers, only the meagerest information survives concerning Sharaku; indeed, his fame belongs much more to the twentieth century than to his own times. Dates of his birth and death are unknown. His entire work extends through a period of only eight months, in the season 1794/95, during which time he produced 136 pictures that have survived, all representing kabuki actors. The mystery deepens the more carefully the prints themselves are examined. Some art historians refer to them as caricatures; others apparently view them with no such suspicion. Those who see caricature quote a report that Sharaku had been a *noh* actor, had shifted to the vastly more popular kabuki, but failed to be at home in this vulgar world, which he viewed with thinly veiled disdain. Be this as it may, the kabuki style itself, with its exaggerated poses and gestures, fondness for tearing passions into tatters and for breaking forth in frantic violence or melting in deluges of tears, was by no means viewed favorably by all Japanese and especially not by those of aristocratic families. Much of the fascination of the Sharaku prints derives from their considerable objectivity. On examining them, one is convinced that this is almost certainly how the actors appeared.

Sharaku's pictures are considerably more convincing and spirited than the typical Japanese theater prints, where more attention is paid to the wardrobe than to psychological insight into the plays and their production.

The Japanese public as a whole evidently did not relish Sharaku's close-ups of their favorite performers. One is convinced today that whatever may have been his distortion of the true aspect of the stage, the stage was itself so contorted by melodrama that a caricaturist would have worked with hands tied behind his back before entering upon his task. Not even the most inspired caricaturist can succeed in painting the kettle black. It is improbable that the world will ever know just what Sharaku intended. Possibly he was a mad artist who failed to know this himself. But he remains a major illustrator of one of the most dynamic, though not most refined, of the world's acting styles.

For superior reproductions of Sharaku's pictures, see *Japanese Prints, Sharaku to Toyokuni, in the Collection of Louis V. Ledoux* (1950); also Laurence Binyon and J. J. O. Sexton, *Japanese Colour Prints* (1960), and James A. Michener, *Japanese Prints from the Early Masters* (1960).—H. W. W.

Shaw, [George] Bernard (1856–1950). Anglo-Irish novelist, publicist, critic, and dramatist. George Bernard Shaw—the George was first reduced to G. and later dropped—was born in Dublin, the third and youngest child of a bad marriage that had in it all the makings of a bad home: the father drunk, the mother undomestic. Yet the characteristic talent of the son unmistakably drew much from both parents: from his father a habit of making good jokes from

BERNARD SHAW (CONSULATE GENERAL OF IRELAND)

bad breaks, from his mother a habit of withdrawing from the chaos of everyday life into the joys of art. The Dublin schools, if we are to believe Shaw himself, contributed nothing except a conviction that schools are prisons. A university was never in prospect for him; he tried office work. A decisive "identity crisis" came at the age of twenty when he found the courage to leave Dublin for London, where his mother, separated now from his father, was living with his two sisters. There he wrote five novels: *Immaturity, The Irrational Knot* (1879), *Love Among the Artists* (1881), *Cashel Byron's Profession* (1882), and *An Unsocial Socialist* (1884). They had no success with the public (the first of them couldn't even find a publisher till the *Collected Shaw* was assembled decades later), and Shaw, who, once in London, soon put "honest work" behind him, relied on financial help from his mother and on a variety of journalistic labors: book reviewing for the *Pall Mall Gazette,* art criticism for *The World,* music criticism for *The Star.*

The 1880's were the period of his apprenticeship, not only as a writer of prose, but as a thinker in a number of fields, most notably politics. In 1882 he heard the land-reformer Henry George speak.

> Until I heard George that night I had been chiefly interested, as an atheist, in the conflict between science and religion. George switched me over to economics. I became very excited over his Progress and Poverty. . . . I brought the subject up at a meeting of [H. M.] Hyndman's Democratic Federation where I was told that no one was qualified to discuss the question until he had read Karl Marx. [Cited in *George Bernard Shaw, His Life and Personality* (1963) by Hesketh Pearson.]

(Hyndman was one of Marx's very few English followers.) By 1889, when one of the classics of British Socialism appeared under the title *Fabian Essays in Socialism,* the editor and most ample contributor (two long essays) was "G. Bernard Shaw." He was also the only contributor to discuss Marx: this is one historic point. Another, equally important, is that he mentions Marx chiefly in order to state an argument against the latter's labor theory of value. Shaw was much stimulated by the picture of industrial society given in the first volume of *Capital* but seems to have left most of Marx unread and the philosophical basis of Marxism undiscovered.

1890 arrived, and Shaw had still not completed a single play, but he and his friend the critic William Archer had begun one that would end up as Shaw's alone: *Widowers' Houses* (1892), which sets up on stage a model of the capitalist system and makes a comedy of it.

> . . . it deals with a burning social question [was Shaw's way of putting it in the Preface] and is deliberately intended to induce people to vote on the Progressive side at the next County Council election in London.

It received two special performances before an avant-garde audience. But by this time Shaw's dramatic genius could be held back no longer. A "new drama" was being preached and, if necessary, he would, as he put it, manufacture the evidence that it existed. From his pen flowed *The Philanderer* (written 1893; prod.

1905), *Mrs. Warren's Profession* (written 1893; prod. 1902), *Arms and the Man* (1894), *Candida* (1895), *You Never Can Tell* (1899). None of these established him as a success in the theater, so he made a special presentation of them to the reading public by writing out the stage directions in full narrative form instead of in the jargon of the green room. He also created on this occasion what would later be known as the Shavian Preface: an introductory essay usually dealing, not with the play as such, but with its subject. (This group of plays, plus *Widowers' Houses,* was divided into "pleasant" and "unpleasant" plays [1898], each section having its Preface. A similar Preface preceded the next collection of plays: *Three Plays for Puritans* [1901]—*The Devil's Disciple* [1897], CAESAR AND CLEOPATRA, and *Captain Brassbound's Conversion* [1900].)

Widowers' Houses, Shaw's first play, remains the only one that can be flatly described as "a socialist play." In the others, a broader human comedy is attempted, in which we see an interplay between free vitality on the one hand and the forces that would imprison it—institutions, conventions, habits, theories—on the other. This "free vitality" calls to mind a phrase that in fact had not yet entered history: *élan vital* (Henri Bergson). And *élan vital* is increasingly the heart of the Shavian matter.

"I had been chiefly interested, as an atheist, in the conflict between science and religion." Shaw's parents were Protestants, but far from devout. He was quickly on to the advanced—that is, antireligious—thought of the day. The first thing ever printed by Shaw was a letter to the Dublin press in which the young freethinker protested the appearance of the American evangelists Sankey and Moody in Ireland. That was in 1875. Seven years later he might "switch to economics," but he did not accept any form of socialism that was messianic, like Marxism, or evangelical, like the outlook of the British Labour movement. Fabian Socialism, which he not only accepted but helped to create, was austerely secular: that was both its glory and its limitation. The religious impulse of the Fabians had to turn elsewhere. Shaw's starting point was dual: it was no use fighting evolution, as many of the Christian churches were still doing, but Charles Darwin had not provided an adequate replacement for the religious outlook that he swept into the dustbin. Although Bergson's book *Creative Evolution* (1907) was not yet written, there existed a certain tradition of such thought in England, and Shaw found particularly cogent and attractive Samuel Butler, the author of *Evolution: Luck or Cunning?* (1887). Butler answered the query of this title with the word cunning. And such a purposive type of evolution seemed to Shaw to restore the lost sense of divinity in the world and, being "scientific," to be acceptable to all men of all backgrounds, thus laying the foundation of a universal religion, a new and true catholicism.

This idea was to be set forth most fully, *after* Bergson's book came out, in the Preface to *Back to Methuselah* (pub. 1921; prod. 1923), but it is immanent in the first Shaw play of the twentieth century, MAN AND SUPERMAN. In that play Shaw relates evolution to politics—his religion to his socialism. Politics (as Shaw sees things) is the realm of the short run in which institutions are made and unmade. But

these changes are not big enough to meet our social and political needs and, in any event, the human imagination craves something more awe-inspiring. Homo sapiens needs the faith that, in the long run, more is going on than mere change in social organization. Having lost the old sense of an eternal realm *"out* there" or *"up* there," he needs a sense, rooted in the modern feeling for history and development, of an eternal movement toward ever higher goals.

The French critic André Malraux has said that, if the mission of the nineteenth century was to get rid of the gods, the mission of the twentieth century is to replace them. A sense of "the death of God" and of the need for something that will serve "God's" purpose is felt in very many of Shaw's plays and underlies a group that was originally intended to be published as "Plays of Science and Religion": *Man and Superman, John Bull's Other Island* (1904), and MAJOR BARBARA.

It was in the first decade of this century that Bernard Shaw became a great public success. The fullest theatrical acceptance seems to have come in Central Europe, but his name became a byword throughout the civilized world. What established him most firmly in British theatrical history was the work of the Barker-Vedrenne management at the Court Theatre (1904–1907), in which enterprise Shaw's greatest debt was to his friend Harley Granville-Barker for his managing, his acting, and his directing.

Meanwhile, Shaw had worked out his own peculiar form of private life: married celibacy. As he confessed to one of his biographers, Frank Harris, he was a virgin till twenty-nine, had several affairs during his thirties, but at forty-three decided on lifelong companionship without family and without intercourse. His bride (1898) was Charlotte Payne-Townshend, an Irish heiress whom he had encountered among the Fabians. The plan worked, and the pair were together till Charlotte's death. The only publicly known cloud in the sky of this companionship was the passion Shaw conceived around the time of his mother's death (1912) for the actress Mrs. Patrick Campbell; and even Mrs. Campbell was probably never his mistress.

In the interim between the two world wars, Shaw had two subtle and by no means superficial relationships with women: he played a rather bossy, yet not unflirtatious, father to a young American actress named Molly Tompkins, and he played brother (actually calling himself Brother Bernard) to a Benedictine nun. Like his relationship with the actress Ellen Terry, these "liaisons" were mostly epistolary. But one should not underrate paper: Shaw certainly didn't. ". . . only on paper [he wrote in the volume of Shaw–Terry letters] has mankind ever yet achieved glory, beauty, truth, knowledge, virtue, and abiding love."

The First World War was a watershed for Western culture generally and for Bernard Shaw in particular. For one thing, what he wrote about the war aroused an animosity that is hard to credit at this distance in time. He was not a pacifist, but he took the war very seriously—that is, applied dispassionate critical intellect to it—and even he must have been surprised at the violence of the denunciations he met with. These polemics left their mark. But Shaw did not "live to regret" thoughts that stood up as sensible after those of his opponents had been exposed as irresponsible rhetoric. Rather, his writings after 1918 can be read as a warning against future world wars. Even *Back to Methuselah* is not a Bergsonian epic in the abstract, but a retort to the generation that made "the war":

> *Haslam*. Lubin and your father have both survived the war. But their sons were killed in it.

> *Savvy* (sobered). Yes. Jim's death killed mother.

> *Haslam*. . . . To me the awful thing about their political incompetence was that they had to kill their own sons. . . .

The classic Shavian presentation of the bankruptcy of that generation is HEARTBREAK HOUSE. It is also the first in a sequence of symbolistic plays—a new departure for an old playwright—all of which exist, one can say with hindsight, under the shadow of the atom bomb. Shaw was reaching out toward a kind of Aristophanic extravaganza that would provide a vivid tragicomic image of an impending man-made doomsday (*Too True To Be Good*, 1932; *The Simpleton of the Unexpected Isles*, 1935). Even when unaccompanied by apocalyptic imagery, a somewhat Aristophanic form is used to portray the life of modern politics (*The Apple Cart*, 1929; *On the Rocks*, 1933; *Geneva*, 1938).

The later plays are original, even "experimental," at times brilliantly so. Often, on the other hand, one is too aware that the aging author can no longer project the intensities that were once at his disposal. And *Geneva* is marked by a failure to imagine what Hitler is all about, which betokens an author from another century. Though *The Apple Cart* is a play of high merit throughout—and even a play written at the age of ninety has at least one superb scene in it (*Buoyant Billions*, 1947)—the only Shaw play written after 1920 that has constantly delighted his audiences is SAINT JOAN. This may be because of the subject. Yet not only is the treatment novel, the play contains some of Shaw's best dramatic writing and has proved a landmark in the history of chronicle plays.

Shaw's later life was, in general, the outwardly uneventful one of any writer: he wrote. But it should be said that he carefully created circumstances favorable to writing. His way of life was rural, though he liked to maintain an apartment in London as well. Mrs. Shaw died in 1943. Bernard Shaw outlived her longer than he wanted to. "Yes, I shall be glad to go home and get out of hell . . . . I want to die and I can't, I can't." But on Tuesday, October 31, 1950, he said: "I am going to die," and three days later he died.

As during the First World War, so also throughout his last three decades, Bernard Shaw came under attack on grounds of political turpitude. He always enjoyed taking the "wrong" side, and in this period he praised Mussolini and even Hitler. It usually escaped the notice of those who attacked him that he also said things like: "We ought to have declared war on Germany the moment Mr. Hitler's police stole Einstein's violin." In any case, Shaw's polemic in this period is mainly a defense of what would later be called "the East" against the "Free World." "If the experiment that Lenin made . . . fails [he said in a speech

broadcast in Russia in 1931], then civilization falls."

Estimates of Bernard Shaw have varied widely. In no department of his life and work has he not been spoken of with extreme admiration and extreme contempt. Enthusiasm for one Shaw is often accompanied with disdain for another or even all others. He can be considered a great music critic, for example, but a wretched political philosopher. (For a discussion of Shaw as a dramatic critic, see MODERN DRAMATIC CRITICISM.) One of his biographers wants him regarded as first and foremost a "personality," thus downgrading him as a critical mind, and even as a dramatist. Over the years there has been much tongue-clucking over Shaw the propagandist, and some have held that he was too much for Shaw the playwright. And so on. The plays would have made their way in the world more easily but for all the other kinds of interest that Shaw held for the public, which is a paradox when one considers that he originally exploited his other talents to promote his plays. Then again, an author's reputation has its natural ups and downs. If a writer makes a great impact in his youth or middle age, he may well have a hard time of it when he is old and for a while after his death. This happened to Shaw. Shaw was "old hat" during his last years and remained so during the fifties and early sixties when the "new thing" in world theater was Bertolt Brecht. But Brecht may now (1969) be due to become "old hat"; Shaw to be rediscovered. Gold for the new excavators: Shaw's deep concern at the "death of God" and his determination to "do something about it"; his equally deep concern with socialism and peace and his demonstration of the utter inadequacy of traditional liberalism to face the world around us; finally, his dramatic art, unequaled as it is in English since the seventeenth century. One could even add: his personality. For more is going to be found there too than was found in the past. It has often been stated that Shaw was not the clown GBS, but what he was has not yet been very fully explored. (See also CHILDREN'S DRAMA.)

Scholars must have recourse to British editions, as only in England has Shaw been properly published *in extenso*. The main item is the standard edition, *The Works of Bernard Shaw* (1930–1950), in thirty-six volumes. Also available is *The Prefaces* (1934) in one volume. Odhams Press of London has published *The Complete Plays of Bernard Shaw* in one volume (undated). The foregoing items may not legally be sold in the United States, but happily the same is not true for the Shaw volumes as reissued in paperback by Penguin Books: these are published in England but distributed throughout the world. It would seem that Penguin keeps about half the plays in print at most times. Shaw's American publisher, Dodd, Mead and Company, has always kept a good deal of Shaw in print, but rather higgledy-piggledy and in expensive, hardback volumes. Various Shaw titles have appeared in the United States under other imprints, notably half a dozen volumes of critical prose, published by Hill and Wang, Inc.

Even the thirty-six-volume English edition is far from containing the complete works, nor has all of Shaw yet been printed in any form. The collected letters have appeared only in part up to now (1969), and whether all scraps of Shaviana from the press, 1875–1950, will ever be collected is a question. No adequate Shaw bibliography exists, but the student who is seeking advice on what to read can find it in the bibliographies in various books on Shaw, such as Eric Bentley's *Bernard Shaw* (the most up-to-date edition of which was published by Methuen's, London, 1967). The thorough job that no one has done for Shaw publications has been done for Shaw productions in an essential work of Shaw scholarship: *Theatrical Companion to Shaw, A Pictorial Record of the First Performances of the Plays of George Bernard Shaw* (1955) by Raymond Mander and Joe Mitchenson.—E. B.

Shehadé, Georges (1910–). Syrian-born French poet and playwright. The poetic qualities of Shehadé's plays are reminiscent of the work of Jean Giraudoux. When Shehadé's *Monsieur Bob'le* was first performed in 1951, some of the theatergoers remembered the controversy over Giraudoux's *Siegfried* in 1928. Shehadé, a Lebanese whose poetry has been extolled by Max Jacob, Paul Eluard, and André Breton, joined the ranks of the few French poets of modern times who have written for the stage. He is sensitive to words, to their profound meanings and the power of their images. He is shrewd and wise in his creation of the innocent hero who is saint-like: Bob'le, in *Monsieur Bob'le;* Argengeorge, a kind of Parsifal in the midst of the aging, in his second play, *La Soirée des proverbes* ("Evening of Proverbs," 1954); and Vasco, in his third play, *Histoire de Vasco* ("Story of Vasco"), first performed in Zurich in 1956 under the direction of Jean-Louis Barrault.

With the vision of a seer, of the original kind of *vates* ("poet"), Georges Shehadé establishes communication between worlds that are usually closed off from one another: between life and death, old age and the past. In these plays, dramatic writing moves farther away from the "bourgeois theater" than it did in the experimental plays of Samuel Beckett, Eugène Ionesco, and Arthur Adamov. Shehadé's poetic drama is perhaps the most difficult kind of theater to reestablish in France. When a poet's language is used on the stage, the action of the play becomes the action of language. The pure verbal invention of the poet, as in the art of Shehadé, embellishes and stylizes the action. The efforts of Shehadé, Henri Pichette, Jacques Audiberti, and Jules Supervielle are perhaps the first steps in an important revindication of poetic drama.

The atmosphere of Shehadé's plays has been compared to that of Alain-Fournier's novel *Le Grand Meaulnes* (1913) where happiness is fragile and adolescent fervor is enchanted. But there is a deeper tone of cruelty in Shehadé's anguish and a deeper sense of tragedy in his irony than appear in Alain-Fournier's work. Shehadé does not create or re-create myths in his work, but he reveals worlds of imagination and memory that, although buried, can rise up again in the purity of a man's heart.—W. F.

Sheldon, Edward [**Brewster**] (1886–1946). American playwright. Sheldon was born into a wealthy family in Chicago and began writing plays even before he entered Harvard University, where he studied playwriting. He graduated from Harvard in 1907 and in 1908 his *Salvation Nell* was produced. In the next six years, eight of his plays were produced successfully. After 1921, handicapped by severe arthritis, he worked only with collaborators, and he ceased to write at all after 1930.

Salvation Nell is a sentimental drama in a realistic setting, while *The Nigger* (1909) is a realistic problem play about a Southern governor who discovers that he is a grandson of a Negro slave. Concerned with American business and politics, *The Boss* (1911) is perhaps the best of Sheldon's realistic plays. These plays were followed by two romantic melodramas, *The Princess Zim-Zim* (1911) and *Egypt* (1912). *The High Road* (1912) mixes politics and romance.

Sheldon's greatest success, *Romance* (1913), is set in New York in 1867 and concerns a young clergyman who falls in love with a glamorous opera singer. In *The Garden of Paradise* (1914), he dramatized Hans Christian Andersen's story *The Little Mermaid.* Sheldon collaborated with Sidney Howard on *Bewitched* (1924), a romantic fantasy, and with Charles MacArthur on *Lulu Belle* (1926), a realistic melodrama. Sheldon's last play, *Dishonored Lady* (1930), in collaboration with Margaret Ayer Barnes, was based on the Madeleine Smith murder case.

Sheldon's fifteen plays show considerable talent for the theater and some disposition to treat important social themes, but his early promise as a playwright was not realized; romance, fantasy, and melodrama characterize his later work.

The best source is Eric Wollencott Barnes' *The Man Who Lived Twice* (1956).—B. H.

Shelley, Percy Bysshe (1792–1822). English poet and playwright. Shelley was born in Sussex to a family of landed gentry. After an unspectacular attendance at Eton, he entered Oxford in 1810, only to be expelled almost immediately as the author of a pamphlet called *The Necessity of Atheism.* At the age of nineteen he eloped with his sister's schoolmate Harriet Westbrook, rescuing her (as he thought) from the tyranny of her parents and teachers. The next years were dedicated to various social causes in Eng-

PERCY BYSSHE SHELLEY (NEW YORK PUBLIC LIBRARY)

land, Ireland, and Wales and to self-education. By 1814, the growing estrangement between Shelley and Harriet ended in separation. At about the same time, Shelley became a member of the radical circle centered on William Godwin. He fell in love with Godwin's beautiful and intellectual daughter Mary and in 1814 eloped with her to Switzerland. Harriet's suicide in 1816 freed him to wed Mary, but the lord chancellor's refusal to grant him custody of his children by Harriet deepened his sense of the injustice in political institutions.

After 1818, he and Mary lived exclusively in Italy, where he sought a mild climate for a nervous condition that tormented him all his life, sanctuary from political persecution, and inspiration from the vestiges of the classical age. He wandered the length of the peninsula, living for a time in every major city, making few friends but studying literature in seven languages, recording his experiences in excellent letters to Thomas Love Peacock, and composing the works for which he is remembered. In 1822 he sailed up the coast to Leghorn in order to greet Leigh Hunt, newly arrived to organize a liberal journal with Byron. On the sail home, Shelley's boat was overwhelmed in a squall (there is evidence that she was rammed by a larger boat), and he drowned. His body, washed ashore at Viareggio, was cremated by Byron, Hunt, and Trelawney.

Shelley's dramatic production was conceived for two audiences: for the theatergoing public he wrote The Cenci and began Charles the First; for a more refined class of educated readers he composed the closet drama Prometheus Unbound. The latter occupied him for almost two years, from 1818 to 1820 (when it was published with several lyrics, including "Ode to the West Wind"). As it grew in his imagination from a single act in the Greek style to its ultimate four acts, it became increasingly symbolic, stressing the role of Asia (Prometheus' wife, who represents love) and of Demogorgon (the primal power of the universe). Having seen the French Revolution come to nought in the rise of Napoleon and the subsequent restoration of the Bourbons, Shelley argued in Prometheus Unbound that man's fiery spirit will not be freed by revolutions alone. Like an earthquake or volcano, Demogorgon bursts forth periodically to destroy; if from that destruction a new order is to rise, love and not hate must be joined to the spirit of rebellion. Because the symbolism and story line are obscure at points, the play has generated much conflicting interpretation and is more often read for its magnificently musical lyrics than for its philosophy.

As he was composing Prometheus Unbound, Shelley worked also on The Cenci, which he felt certain could be produced at Covent Garden. He had already chosen his leads (Eliza O'Neill and Edmund Kean) and had studied a large number of old plays to learn dramaturgy. Although his poetry is famous for its unworldly beauty, Shelley was always impressed with arts that mimicked nature—sculpture, painting, theater—and he seriously aimed for a career as playwright. His story, an actual event in the Italian Renaissance, concerns the conflict between a tyrannical father, Count Cenci, and his daughter Beatrice. With the connivance of the church, Cenci indulges

his maniacal compulsion to terrorize his family, climaxing his actions by sexually assaulting Beatrice. In retaliation, she has him murdered just as the Pope is about to intervene, and the messenger who arrives to summon Cenci to the papal court becomes instead the investigator of his death. Beatrice, her stepmother, her brother, and the hired assassins are convicted and go to their deaths with tragic acceptance. As a counterpoint to Prometheus Unbound, this play displays the consequences of repaying hate with hate. Like many successful contemporary plays, it is rich with echoes of Shakespeare and other Elizabethans, but despite the devotion that has resulted in numerous private and amateur productions (the first was given in England by the Shelley Society in 1886), it has never won a place in the standard repertory.

Shortly before his death, Shelley abandoned the few fragments of another play he had intended for production. Here his cue was from Shakespeare's Richard the Second, which dealt with events two centuries before its composition. Shelley went back a similar interval, to the Puritan Revolution, in which he saw parallels to his own time. Unable to call openly for a revolt against the prince regent, he tried to direct attention to what he hoped would be recognized as a precedent. But revolution alone was not enough; as he had pointed out in Prometheus Unbound, the real problem was to prevent the new ruler from becoming another tyrant. Had Shelley finished it, Charles the First would probably have analyzed both the king and Cromwell. His inability to do justice to both men within a dramatic framework may well have been his reason for abandoning it.

Shelley's other dramatic activities include translations of Euripides' satyr play The Cyclops, portions of Faust, and scenes from Calderón's Magico Prodigioso and Cisma de Inglaterra. He was much impressed with Goethe and Calderón, equating the latter with Shakespeare and learning German and Spanish primarily in order to read their works. The influence of both has been recognized in his original compositions. His lifelong homage to Milton is reflected in parts of what Mary published as "Fragments of an Unfinished Drama," parts of a masque in clear imitation of Comus. His desire to make political use of the theater underlies Oedipus Tyrannus; or, Swellfoot the Tyrant, a heavy-handed burlesque on George IV, and Hellas, a lyric drama inspired by the Greek declaration of independence from the Turks; modeled in general after the Persae of Aeschylus, this contains some of Shelley's best lyrics.

Undoubtedly, Shelley's dramas as dramas fall far behind his lyric accomplishment. Having had few opportunities to witness live performances, he possessed only a layman's appreciation of the playwright's craft. But in his capacity to create viable characters, dramatic suspense, well-constructed individual scenes, and a tragic atmosphere, he showed as much skill at the time of his early death as many greater dramatists did at the same age.

The standard edition of Shelley's verse (including his dramas) is The Poetical Works of Percy Bysshe Shelley (ed. Thomas Hutchinson, 1905), often reprinted but not edited to account for much modern scholarship. The standard life is Newman Ivey

White, *Shelley* (2 vols., 1940), supplemented by Kenneth Neill Cameron, *The Young Shelley* (1950), the first part of a projected life.—J. R.

Sheridan, Richard Brinsley (1751–1816). Irish-born English comic playwright. Sheridan's father, Thomas, had once been an actor and became a well-known elocution teacher in England; his mother, *née* Frances Chamberlaine, was the author, among other things, of the successful comedy *The Discovery* (1763). Thomas settled at Bath in 1771, and Richard, while passing the time at the famous spa, chivalrously offered his assistance to the beautiful Elizabeth Linley, the toast of Bath, in her plan to flee to the Continent to escape the unwanted attentions of an admirer. In 1772 Sheridan escorted her to France. Here Elizabeth's father caught up with her; she was returned to Bath; Sheridan fought two duels with the man who had precipitated these events; and in April 1773, her father no longer withholding his consent, Elizabeth and Richard were married.

Sheridan, only twenty-three, quickly found success in London. His first play to reach the stage was *The Rivals* (1775). Despite its later fame the play was not at first warmly received, but with revisions in the script and improvements in production it soon began to win favor. Sheridan followed it with a two-act farcical play, *St. Patrick's Day, or The Scheming Lieutenant* (1775), and before the year's end with a comic opera, *The Duenna,* both at Covent Garden. The last of these plays, which had an unusual run of seventy-five nights, proved the most popular. Meanwhile Drury Lane, under actor and manager David Gar-

RICHARD BRINSLEY SHERIDAN (WALTER HAMPDEN MEMORIAL LIBRARY AT THE PLAYERS, NEW YORK)

rick, was beginning to feel the stiff competition offered by the rival house, thanks to this newly discovered playwright. In 1776, when Garrick retired, Sheridan and several associates purchased Drury Lane, and the young dramatist became partly responsible for the management of the older of the two patent houses. In January of the following year he presented a revival of *The Rivals,* and a month later his adaptation of John Vanbrugh's comedy *The Relapse* (1696), renamed *A Trip to Scarborough.* But the great theatrical event of 1777, and the one that proved to be the high point of Sheridan's career as a dramatist, was the production of THE SCHOOL FOR SCANDAL. *The Critic,* his satire of drama reminiscent of the satire in *The Rehearsal* (1671) by George Buckingham and several of Henry Fielding's irregular plays, was produced in 1779. There are a few other pieces, minor in importance. The last of them, which does credit solely to his managerial shrewdness, is *Pizarro* (1799), which found great and long-continued favor with the public. It is best described as a patriotic melodrama and is as incredible in its way as the absurdities ridiculed in *The Critic.*

In 1780 Sheridan was elected to the House of Commons and began a distinguished political career lasting more than thirty years. Sheridan suffered financial losses, however, when it became necessary to rebuild Drury Lane in the 1790's and was ruined when the new structure was swept by fire in 1809. Then, in 1812, he was defeated when he stood for Parliament. Sheridan's last years were scarcely happy ones.

Throughout the 1760's and 1770's the English theater was plentifully supplied with new comedies of many varieties, but what is now generally thought of as High Georgian Comedy is the distinctive type of play associated with the two dramatic geniuses of the period, Oliver Goldsmith and Sheridan. Their "laughing comedies," avoiding pronounced sentimentalism, succeeded in creating an atmosphere of general good will and well-being. Without a trace of cynicism, they nevertheless affirmed the critical function of comedy by showing human nature and human society as sometimes ridiculous. Sheridan's sense of theater was unfailing, but fortunately his comic sense was just as strong. No one could unfold a comic plot more deftly or establish the occasion of time, place, and social ambience with such seeming lack of effort. His amusing characters, in all their humors of personality and speech, may be stage figures, but while the curtain is up they give the illusion of life. On at least two occasions, it must be said, Sheridan yielded to his showman's instinct: *A Trip to Scarborough* is a sadly watered-down affair, an unoffending corruption of a fine play, while *Pizarro* is spread-eagle patriotism. But in Sheridan's two great comedies, *The Rivals* and *The School for Scandal,* his comic intuition is in firm command, and also quite as triumphant in its way is *The Critic.*

The standard edition of the plays is *The Plays and Poems of Richard Brinsley Sheridan* (3 vols., 1928), edited by Raymond Crompton Rhodes. Good biographical studies are *Sheridan. From New and Original Material* (1909), by Walter S. Sichel, and *Harlequin Sheridan: The Man and the Legends* (1933), by Raymond Crompton Rhodes. There is a lively critical commentary by Louis Kronenberger in his

Richard Brinsley Sheridan (*Six Plays*) (1957).—R. Q.

Sherwood, Robert E[mmet] (1896–1955). American playwright and biographer. Robert Sherwood was born in New Rochelle, New York, to well-to-do parents who had a great interest in the arts, particularly the theater, and the boy was writing stories and plays before he had finished elementary school. At Harvard he was an editor of *The Lampoon,* and the Hasty Pudding Club produced his play *Barnum Was Right* (1917). His college work was cut short by the entry of the United States into World War I. Refused induction into the U. S. Army because of his height (6′7″), he enlisted in the Canadian Black Watch Regiment. Seriously wounded at Vimy Ridge and embittered by the war, Sherwood returned to America with a strong pacifist point of view that he never entirely abandoned. He worked for *Vanity Fair,* the old *Life* magazine, *Scribner's,* and the New York *Herald* until his play *The Road to Rome* was produced in 1927 and became a hit. His work in the theater did not cancel his interest in politics, and during World War II he wrote speeches for President Roosevelt and held an important position in the Office of War Information. *Roosevelt and Hopkins* (1948) is his account of the relations between the President and one of his most important advisers.

Sherwood's plays include polished light comedies and violent melodramas, but through all runs a concern about the relations between reason and power, man's civilized values, and his frequent descent into savagery. In *The Road to Rome* a witty Roman lady seduces Hannibal and convinces him that destroying Rome would be senseless. On the other hand, in *The Petrified Forest* (1935) the sensitive but uncommitted

ROBERT E. SHERWOOD (FROM *American Portraits* BY ENIT KAUFMAN, WITH BIOGRAPHICAL SKETCHES BY DOROTHY CANFIELD FISHER. COPYRIGHT © 1946 BY HOLT, RINEHART AND WINSTON, INC. REPRODUCED BY PERMISSION OF HOLT, RINEHART AND WINSTON, INC.)

intellectual is destroyed by the brutal gangster. The author intended this play to sound a warning about the rise of fascism. *Idiot's Delight* (1936) carried the warning further, though the medium was a polished high comedy; in an Italian hotel on the Swiss border, a wisecracking American and a svelte lady of the world he believes is an old sweetheart watch the outbreak of a world war brought on by the machinations of munitions manufacturers and the passionate nationalism of most men. In his next two plays Sherwood completely abandoned comedy. *Abe Lincoln in Illinois* (1938) is a study of the responsibilities of power in the face of inevitable war. In *There Shall Be No Night* (1940) Sherwood dramatizes the agonized decision of a Finnish intellectual to fight with his country's resistance forces and risk almost certain death.

Unlike Sherwood's political dramas, *Reunion in Vienna* (1931) is a tongue-in-cheek comedy of sexual maneuverings that suggests the point of view of such Continental playwrights as Ferenc Molnár and Arthur Schnitzler. Sherwood also worked on a number of films, the best of which is *Best Years of Our Lives* (1946), the story of returning war veterans and their adjustment to the postwar world. As with his best plays, this script combined his serious thought with his sense of the vividly theatrical.

There is no standard edition of Sherwood's work. A full discussion is in R. B. Shuman's *Robert E. Sherwood* (1964).—M. L.

She Stoops to Conquer (1773). A comedy by Oliver GOLDSMITH. *She Stoops to Conquer* opened at Covent Garden, though neither Drury Lane nor Covent Garden had shown much enthusiasm for the play. Only a few days before the opening performance the title, originally *The Mistakes of a Night,* was changed to the present one. That it was, to use Goldsmith's phrase, a "laughing comedy" the audience response left no doubt.

The basis of the comedy is the multitude of errors and deceptions making up the story. A marriage has been tentatively arranged between young Marlow and Kate Hardcastle by their respective fathers; neither has ever seen the other. Marlow, accompanied by his friend Hastings, is coming to pay a first visit to the Hardcastles, who live in the country in an old house that looks for all the world like an inn. Mr. Hardcastle awaits his visitor. But the puckish Tony Lumpkin, Mrs. Hardcastle's son by a first marriage, chances to meet Marlow and Hastings and directs them to what he describes as a neighboring inn but which is actually his parents' house. This, the first deception, produces a situation bordering on farce as the young men are received by the exquisitely courteous Mr. Hardcastle, whom they treat as an innkeeper. There are surprises in store for both Marlow and Hastings. Marlow learns that Kate is also at the inn and that he will shortly meet her—an event he dreads, because he can be at ease only with women of the lower class. Hastings discovers that his loved one, Constance Neville, is likewise here. The Marlow-Kate story runs its comic course: Marlow is nearly tongue-tied when he talks to Miss Hardcastle, but when she appears as a servant girl he makes vigorous advances. The Hastings-Constance situation is complicated by Mrs. Hardcastle, who it happens controls Constance's fortune and is determined to see the girl

A SCENE FROM OLIVER GOLDSMITH'S *She Stoops to Conquer* (ANTA COLLECTION, WALTER HAMPDEN MEMORIAL LIBRARY AT THE PLAYERS, NEW YORK)

married to Tony, on whom she dotes. Hastings, who now knows from Constance that they are all under the Hardcastles' roof, is forced to conceal from Mrs. Hardcastle the fact that he is Constance's lover. Ultimately both the Marlow-Kate and the Hastings-Constance affairs are happily concluded. Tony, with his own ideas about a wife, defeats his mother's scheme and delivers Constance and her fortune over to Hastings. Marlow makes a double discovery: he learns where he really is and who he really is. He is not a person either embarrassed or aggressive with the opposite sex but one glad to be his natural self with the charming Kate.

Consciously Goldsmith rejected comic wit in favor of what he considered to be a more natural kind of comedy, humorous by virtue of character and situation rather than wordplay. The result is what at first strikes us as the peculiar flatness of *She Stoops to Conquer*—as flat, it has been said, as the region of Ireland from which Goldsmith came. But the play endures. Its open hits at sentimentalism are token of the comic distance that the play establishes. We are looking at ourselves. The errors, deceptions, and discoveries that carry the story along point, whether we fully realize it or not, to the experiences we all pass through in coming to recognize where and what in reality we are.

She Stoops to Conquer is in Arthur Friedman's edition of *The Collected Works of Oliver Goldsmith* (Vol. V, 1966). The play is discussed at some length in *Oliver Goldsmith: A Georgian Study* (1967), by Ricardo Quintana.—R. Q.

Shiels, George (1885–1949). Irish playwright. Born in County Antrim, Shiels emigrated to Canada at an early age. While there, he sustained a crippling injury and was confined to a wheelchair until his death. Despite the dark circumstances that surrounded his life, his literary output consisted chiefly of a number of bright, well-constructed comedies that were among the most popular productions at the Abbey Theatre during the thirties and forties. The

best of these is *The New Gossoon* (1930), a witty and surprisingly sophisticated comedy set in the rural sections of Northern Ireland. The plot concerns a traditional subject of comedy: youth versus old age. The "new" gossoon, or boy, is a representative of the flaming youth of the twenties, brought to heel, not by the older generation who ineffectually oppose him, but by a young girl who combines the values of the new generation with the wisdom of the older one. Other notable comedies include *Paul Twyning* (1922) and *Professor Tim* (1925). The latter deals with the popular Irish theme of the emigrated relative who returns to his homeland. In this case the returning Irishman is not the great success his relatives imagined but a drunken failure. All is resolved happily, however, when the "drunkard" reveals himself as a success who has really been testing his relatives' fidelity.

Somewhat more serious are *The Rugged Path* (1940) and *The Summit* (1941), two plays that probe the Irish attitude toward law enforcement. The traditional Irish reluctance to turn informer is revealed as a source of anarchy and lawlessness. *The Rugged Path* is the longest-running play in the history of the Abbey Theatre.—E. Q.

Shirley, James (1596–1666). English playwright. A native of London, Shirley attended the Merchant Taylors' School and both Oxford and Cambridge. Upon graduation from Cambridge he secured a position as headmaster of the St. Alban's grammar school, which he lost in 1625 when he converted to Catholicism. Forced to seek a career as a playwright, he produced a large number of plays, of which thirty-one are extant, between 1625 and the closing of the theaters in 1642. From 1636 to 1640, he was living in Dublin and writing plays for the newly established Werburgh Street Theatre (See IRELAND). During the English civil war he fought on the royalist side. After the war he returned to London, taking up his old profession of teaching, at which he remained until his death.

One of the most striking features of Shirley's work is its uniform level of achievement. Whether writing comedies, tragedies, or masques, his craftsmanship is competent and his verse is elegant if uninspired. Among his best comedies are *The Witty Fair One* (1628), a lively comedy of manners, and *The Gamester* (1633), written, according to tradition, with the minor collaboration of Charles I. The best of his comedies is *The Lady of Pleasure* (1635). A satiric portrait of Caroline London, it tells of Lady Bornwell's desire to participate in the social pleasures of the capital city and of her subsequent disillusion. The play is artfully plotted and studded with bright, witty dialogue.

Among Shirley's best tragedies is *The Traitor* (1630), based upon the life of Lorenzo de' Medici. In the hero-villain of the play Shirley has drawn a striking portrait of resourceful and ruthless ambition. Another of his notable tragedies is *Love's Cruelty* (1631), a story of adultery and intrigue that has, for a Shirley play, an unusually strong emotional impact. His best tragedy is *The Cardinal* (1641), an uneven but powerful drama of murder and intrigue. The cardinal of the title is for most of the play an important but shadowy figure, manipulating the lives of the major characters from behind the scenes. In the last act, however, he emerges as an active villain who is ultimately hoist with his own petard. Reminiscent of John Webster's *The Duchess of Malfi*, the play exhibits boldly drawn characters who create genuine excitement. Written on the eve of the closing of the theaters, *The Cardinal* represents the last notable achievement of English Renaissance drama.

Shirley also wrote a number of masques, including *The Triumph of Peace,* an elaborate entertainment presented by the inns of court before the king and queen in 1634. Another of his masques, *The Triumph of Beauty* (1646), is chiefly notable as an imitation of the episode of Bottom the weaver and the "mechanicals" in Shakespeare's *A Midsummer Night's Dream.*

Shirley's achievement as a dramatist is a considerable one. Judged by standards other than the highest, he is an impressive figure. Even in the company of his great predecessors he has earned an honorable place in the second rank.

The standard edition of Shirley's works is *Dramatic Works and Poems of James Shirley* (1833), edited by W. Gifford and A. Dyce in six volumes. The dramatist's life and work are treated in A. H. Nason's *James Shirley: A Biographical and Critical Study* (1915).—E. Q.

shite. The leading figure in Japanese *noh* plays. The *shite,* a word meaning "performer," dominates by far the larger number of these lyric dramas that survive to the present day. Evidence indicates that during the period in which the form was taking its final shape, that is, the closing years of the fourteenth century, this was not always the case. In his commentary on stage practice and playwriting, Zeami Motokiyo, who brought noh drama to its perfection, strongly recommends this preeminent position for the shite. His statement shows that he was advancing a theory that had not hitherto been formulated.

The NOH play is a lyrico-dramatic introspection in which the true action takes place within the shite's soul. The presentation is thus as a rule highly sym-

bolic. The form especially favored by Zeami provides for a play in two parts, the first being largely an introduction, the second containing a spectacular scene with dance and mime, the poetry also rising to its chief lyric height. In the first part the shite commonly appears manifest in the disguise of some humble person, or, to speak more properly, reincarnated as this person. Only the discerning spectator, as the scene advances, suspects the true figure behind the apparition. After an interval, filled with an impromptu speech by an expositor called the *kyogen,* a minor figure hardly in the play properly so considered, the shite makes his second entrance, this time as a ghost. The play's theme concerns an action remembered and related objectively in the first part; in the second, presented subjectively. The ghost is, of course, that of the hero who recalls and repents some violent action committed long before in the world that men call reality and Buddhism regards as illusion. In plays without division into parts or changes of costume, at least a comparable revelation occurs.

Thus the entire play focuses upon the shite. He is talked about in Part I. His shadow dominates Part II. Only he and his followers, should he have them, wear masks. The play's chorus in particular reflects his thoughts and often sings in his behalf. Especially when the shite performs his chief dance, the chorus may be expected to take over by far the greater part of the spoken text. Thus the noh chorus is much more firmly woven into the noh play than, in analogous conditions, is the Greek chorus. The Japanese chorus is likely to speak for the shite, the Greek chorus either to speak to the hero or, much more frequently, to sing about him. All features of the brief noh plays strengthen the shite's role. This concentration on the single figure contributes importantly to the noh's lyric or subjective character. The noh play is its hero's lyric cry as he wanders, a homeless ghost, in quest of his salvation or entry into either the blissful Western Paradise of Amidha Buddhism or, enduring the austere and violent pang of annihilation, into nirvana.

For a sound analysis of the shite's role, see *The Noh Drama* (3 vols., 1954–1960), selected and translated by the Special Noh Committee, Japanese Classics Committee. Much of the early history of the shite may profitably be studied in P. G. O'Neill, *Early Noh Drama* (1958).—H. W. W.

Shoemaker's Holiday, The (1599). A comedy by Thomas DEKKER. In order to be near his beloved, Rose Oteley, Rowland Lacey, a young army colonel, disguises himself as an apprentice shoemaker and goes to the shop of shoemaker Simon Eyre to get a job. The vacancy in the shop has occurred from the impressment into service of the recently married Rafe Davenport, who is going to serve in the company commanded by Col. Lacey, who is now absent without leave. The shoemakers are a merry band but none merrier than the madcap Simon Eyre, who, for all his fun-loving disposition, is an extremely successful businessman. Simon is so successful in fact that he eventually becomes lord mayor of London. In the meantime, Rose Oteley has been wooed by Master Hammon, but she has rejected him in favor of Lacey despite her father's objections. Master Hammon then woos the wife of Rafe Davenport, who has been reported killed in action. Rafe returns to claim his wife, and Lacey and Rose elope, to the extreme discomfiture of their respective fathers. The play concludes with a feast given by Simon for all the members of "the gentle craft," and the highlight of the feast is reached with the arrival of the king himself, who comes to meet his celebrated and well-beloved lord mayor.

The word "holiday" well characterizes this comedy, with its boisterous high spirits and its ebullient energy. These are blended with scenes of quiet humor and romantic tenderness that are neither satiric nor sentimental. The result is a play whose simple charm commends itself even to the most jaded of viewers.
—E. Q.

Shoemaker's Prodigious Wife, The (La zapatera prodigiosa, 1930). A comedy by Federico GARCÍA LORCA. This comedy in two acts, which Lorca calls "a violent farce," contains typical folk elements as well as the tragicomic tone and poetic ebullience notable in all his plays, whether full-length tragedy or short puppet play. It is a pure Andalusian comedy, both ominous and lighthearted in spirit, in the tradition of Alarcon's *Three-Cornered Hat* (a work set to music by Lorca's piano teacher, Manuel de Falla).

In the Prologue an actor taking the part of the author mounts the stage to create the intimacy with the audience he desires, explaining half in jest what they may not expect from him—benevolence, fear, commercialism, vulgarity. Mocking the devices of conventional drama, Lorca insists not only on fantasy and imagination but also on earthy folk speech as well as poetry and spectacle. Self-conscious and somewhat overly demonstrative, the Prologue resembles in spirit the heroine herself. Impressed by her own beauty and youth, the shoemaker's wife feels tied down to her tired, colorless, old husband. After her outbursts and flirtations drive her husband out into the world, she turns the bootshop into a tavern in order to support herself. But suitors swarm in to drink and make advances, and this turbulence evokes the gossip of neighbors and an eventual scandal. Providentially, the husband returns, disguised as a traveling puppetmaster, to prove his wife's constancy. Only as they are being reunited and she happily consents to be a true wife does she triumph over the moral outrage of the neighborhood. This resolution anticipates the pathos of Lorca's three folk tragedies that followed.

The Shoemaker's Prodigious Wife, translated by J. Graham-Lujan and R. L. O'Connell, appears in *Five Plays (Comedies and Tragicomedies)* (1963).
—E. H.

Sholem Aleichem. Pen name of **Sholem Rabinowitz** (1859–1916). Russian-born Yiddish novelist and playwright. Sholem Aleichem was born in the small Ukrainian town of Pereyaslav. He received both a traditional Jewish and a secular Russian education. After his graduation from the Russian district school in 1876, he earned his living as a Russian tutor and then as a government rabbi from 1880 to 1883, when he married one of his students, Olga Loyev. He had, in 1879, begun sending contributions to the Hebrew press, most of which were rejected. In 1883 he turned to Yiddish and published his first story, "Two Stones," under the pseudonym "Sholem Aleichem" (the Yiddish equivalent of "hello," meaning "peace be with you"). Shortly thereafter, he

moved to Kiev, where he embarked on a business career as a stockbroker, while continuing to write for Yiddish periodicals. In 1888 he undertook the publication of a periodical, *Di Yidishe Folksbibliotek* ("The Yiddish People's Library"), and by his generous remuneration attracted some of the best Yiddish writers of his day. In 1890 he lost his money; thereafter, he traveled abroad, lived briefly in various cities, and unsuccessfully tried his hand again at business. All the while, he continued to write. His first full-length play, *Tsezeyt un Tseshpreyt* ("Scattered Far and Wide"), was written in 1903. Soon thereafter, Sholem Aleichem began a series of public readings from his works. The pogroms in Kiev and in other Russian cities in 1905 left him spiritually depressed and in a financially precarious situation. He left for America in the fall of 1906, hoping to establish himself on the New York Yiddish stage. Two of his plays premièred simultaneously on February 8, 1907, but Abraham Cahan's devastating review in the *Jewish Daily Forward* shattered these hopes and Sholem Aleichem returned to Europe. In July 1908, he contracted tuberculosis, which caused him almost continual suffering during the remaining years of his life; nevertheless, he traveled, gave readings, and produced an unbroken stream of stories, novels, and plays. He returned to America in 1914 and died in the Bronx, New York, on May 13, 1916. As the funeral cortege passed, thousands upon thousands of Jews lined the streets, paying homage to the best-loved Yiddish writer of his time.

Despite his failure on the stage during his lifetime, after his death Sholem Aleichem came into his own as the single richest mine of Yiddish dramatic mate-

SHOLEM ALEICHEM (YIVO INSTITUTE FOR JEWISH RESEARCH)

rial. His plays were produced with very great success, especially *Der Oytser* ("The Treasure," written 1908); *Shver tsu Sayn a Yid* (*It's Hard to Be a Jew*, written 1914); *Dos Groyse Gevins* ("Grand Prize," also known as *200,000*, written 1914); and *Tevye der Milkhiker* ("Tevye the Dairy Man," written 1915), his own dramatization of a portion of his novel of the same name. In addition, his fiction, so much of which is in monologue form, has provided inexhaustible material for dramatizations in English as well as in Yiddish. Of these the most spectacularly successful was the English-language musical *Fiddler on the Roof* (1964), adapted, with substantial alterations, from Sholem Aleichem's novel about Tevye.

Sholem Aleichem's achievement on the stage as well as in his fiction was his ability to convey, with humor and compassion, the experience of a generation and of a world in transition. He looked at the world through the eyes of the ordinary Jew, saw traditional eastern European Jewish life breaking up under the impact of industrialization, secular education, persecution, and emigration and reaffirmed the moral stature, courage, and integrity of his people. His compassion and understanding encompass his wrongdoers as well as his heroes and take the sting out of his satirical thrusts without diminishing their effectiveness. The phrase "laughter through tears" has become inseparably associated with Sholem Aleichem, and though it suggests a quality of sentimentality of which he is not often guilty, it also emphasizes the humor and the pathos that are native to his art. His knowledge of Jewish life was such that he created a greater gallery of memorable characters than any other Yiddish writer, and his linguistic ingenuity enabled him to tap the wells of folk idiom with spectacular stylistic success. So strong has been the appeal of Sholem Aleichem's art that he became a major figure in the Yiddish theater during the half-century after his death, and his international reputation continues to grow as translations increase, not only in the major European languages, but in Chinese and Japanese as well.

Though little of Sholem Aleichem's dramatic work is available in English, much of his fiction is. The only full-length biography is by Marie Waife-Goldberg, *My Father, Sholom Aleichem* (1968). *The Great Fair* (1955) is Sholem Aleichem's own memoir of his childhood.—J. C. L.

Sierra Leone. See AFRICA: *Sierra Leone*.

Silva, Antônio José da (1705–1739). Portuguese playwright. Although born in Rio de Janeiro, Brazil, Silva (nicknamed "The Jew") lived in Lisbon, Portugal, from the age of eight. His family was taken to Portugal by the Inquisition under suspicion of heretical practices. He himself was imprisoned while a student at the University of Coimbra (1726) and was obliged to publicly renounce Judaism. Again denounced in 1737 as a practicing Jew, he was imprisoned, tortured, garroted, and then burned at the stake.

Silva's favorite surrounding was the Bairro Alto of Lisbon, where a theater especially adapted for puppet shows stood. He wrote, then, a series of musical comedies, in imitation of Italian opera. In only four years of theatrical activity he wrote seven plays. Among the principal ones are *Vida do grande D. Quixote de la Mancha e do gordo Sancho Pança* ("The Life of the Great D. Quixote of la Mancha and of the Fat Sancho Panza," pub. 1733), *Anfitrião* ("Amphitryon," pub. 1735), *Guerras do alecrim e mangerona* ("Wars of Rosemary and Marjoram," pub. 1737), and *Variedades de Proteu* ("The Inconstancies of Proteus," 1738).

Silva's best comedy (he calls them "operas") is *Guerras do alecrim e mangerona*. Contrary to what the title leads one to suppose, there is no war in the play, but rather an ordinary dispute among adolescents, a kind of social playing that divides the gallant protagonists into two groups, each holding for its own symbol a variety of herb flower. A comedy of intrigue in the Spanish vein, it has the wit and sparkle of Lope de Vega's plays, adapted to the rococo mode. All the incidents revolve around the theme of love, with comic passages distributed principally among the servants and the elderly. Its diction is especially characteristic of the middle class in eighteenth-century Lisbon.

In the other comedies, Silva makes use of the classical tradition but adapts it to the taste of the lower class and seeks parallels with Portuguese life in order to make fun of socially exalted types.

The plays of Silva have not been translated into English.—J. P.

Silver Tassie, The (1928). A play by Sean O'CASEY. This is O'Casey's most ambitious and most impassioned antiwar play, a modern morality play. Harry Heegan, the Irish football hero who is about to go off to fight in France in the First World War, bestrides his Dublin world like a legendary hero who glories in the strength of his powerful limbs and uninhibited emotions. Like Synge's Christy Mahon, he is a conquering "playboy of the western world," victor in all games and fights. But where the comic movement of Christy's life goes from impotence to liberation and triumph, the tragic movement of Harry's life goes from liberation and triumph to impotence. In the first act Harry is on the heights from which he will soon fall when he is wounded in the war and abandoned by his friends and the girl he loves. The second act shifts to an allegorical transfiguration of no man's land in the war zone. This violent change in technique parallels the violent change in mood—from comic reality to tragic surreality. Partially influenced by the expressionist methods of Strindberg, Toller, and O'Neill, O'Casey introduces his now dehumanized soldiers as grotesque figures crouched on a chaotic battlefield, where a huge gun stands outside a ruined monastery near a broken stained-glass window of the Virgin. Amid the ruins the celebration of the Mass is heard, after which the soldiers intone their antiphonal speeches in the manner of the Plain Song of Gregorian chant, so that the rituals of faith are set against the terrible rituals of the war in a dissonant struggle between forces of good and evil. The last two acts move back to Dublin and a hospital ward where Harry, paralyzed from the waist down as a result of his wounds, is confined to a wheelchair. Since absolute war corrupts absolutely, Harry and his wounded friend are now ignored by everyone. In an ironic conclusion, with alternating realistic and allegorical modes, the martyred soldiers suffer for all mankind in a blood-and-wine ritual: red wine in the silver tassie, the now tarnished trophy of Harry's past victories.—D. K.

Şinasi, Ibrahim (1826–1871). Turkish journalist, poet, and playwright. Şinasi was born and raised in Istanbul. He studied finance in Paris and on his return to Turkey became a member of the council of education and published newspapers. He also established a printing house and published books cheaply for the education of the masses. Şinasi is generally considered the pioneer of *Tanzimat* literature, with which Western literary forms were introduced into Turkey. He advocated Western ideals in art, science, and administration in his articles, incorporated Western ideas into his poetry, translated French poetry of his day into Turkish, and wrote in 1859 *Şair Evlenmesi* ("A Poet's Marriage"), a play based on Western forms. It was published in installments in the newspaper *Tercüman-ı Ahval* in 1860 and marks the beginning of the modern theater in Turkey.

Şinasi upheld a new style in writing to eliminate or decrease the number of long and complex sentences, overornate expressions, and the Arabic and Persian rules of grammar that dominated the Turkish literature of his time. This movement to simplify Turkish language and literature has continued to the present day. Very much interested in language, Şinasi published a book of Turkish proverbs, but his notes on a dictionary of the Turkish language have been lost.

Şair Evlenmesi, a farce in one act, criticizes the old Turkish custom of arranged marriages. The Muslim priest in the play is not above accepting bribes, which is a warning to the audience that not all men wearing the religious turban are to be trusted. These were unexplored ideas for the literature of that day in Turkey. Mildly influenced by the French boulevard theater, the characters in Şinasi's play are exaggerated Turkish types, the humor is broad, and the plot develops quickly—all characteristics found in *Orta Oyunu*, the Turkish traditional theater. By utilizing the traditions of the Turkish people and having his characters speak in the natural idiom of the day, Şinasi pointed the way for other Turkish playwrights.

Şair Evlenmesi is not a great play, nor is Şinasi a good poet; furthermore, his output was scant. Yet because of his enormous influence on other writers, Şinasi is considered by many scholars to be the greatest figure of the Tanzimat period.—N. O.

Singspiel. The eighteenth-century German precursor to operetta. Singspiel was basically light drama with songs inserted into the dialogue. An intermediate form between opera and comedy, the Singspiel arose in the eighteenth-century *opera buffa,* stemming specifically from a Pergolesi opera of 1733. Performed by actors rather than singers, the Singspiel proved to be widely popular and achieved a rather antiaristocratic orientation. Goethe wrote texts to several Singspiele, the most important of which were *Erwin und Elmire* (1775) and *Claudine von Villa Bella* (1776), while the Austrian tradition produced Mozart's *Entführung aus dem Serail* (*The Abduction from the Seraglio,* 1782). Although the spoken word was of primary importance to the form, the Singspiel evolved directly into the operetta of the nineteenth century.—B. M. M.

Six Characters in Search of an Author (Sei personaggi in cerca d'autore, 1921). A tragicomedy by Luigi PIRANDELLO. A man has a wife and a male child. He also has a male secretary. Between the wife and the secretary there arises what the husband considers an understanding of a harmless sort. He wants to help them in some way, but whenever he speaks to them they exchange a significant look that seems to ask how they should receive what he says if they are not to annoy him. But this itself annoys him. He ends up firing the secretary. Then he sends the wife after him. In the wife's view, he fairly throws her into the secretary's arms; and the pair set up house together. The husband, however, does not lose interest in the wife. His continued interest, indeed, though he considers it "pure" (that is, asexual), is a source of embarrassment to the former secretary. When a daughter is born to the lovers, the husband is interested in her too—more, perhaps, even than he had been in the wife. And when she becomes a schoolgirl, he waits for school coming out, then seeks her out, and on at least one occasion gives her a present. The girl, of course, does not know who the strange gentleman is. At a certain point the secretary can bear the whole situation no longer, and he takes his family—there are three children by this time—to live somewhere else, out of the stepfather's reach. Subsequently the secretary dies. His family of four is now destitute; they have to sleep all in the same room. And at some point they return to the place where the husband lived. Here the mother gets employment as a kind of seamstress. But her employer's real interest is in employing the daughter, now in her late teens, as a prostitute. The dressmaker's shop is a front for a brothel. One day, the husband, a client of the establishment, presents himself and would have taken the girl in his arms had not the mother suddenly turned up to cry: "But it's my daughter!" After this encounter, the husband takes his wife back into his home along with his three stepchildren. At the time, he is living with his own son, now in his early twenties. This legitimate son is offended by the presence of the three bastards and wanders from room to room in his father's house, feeling displaced and desolate. The three bastards react to his hostility. The little girl, aged four, drowns herself in the fountain in the garden. The other child, a fourteen-year-old boy, witnesses the drowning, fails to offer any assistance, then shoots himself. The mother, who might have been keeping an eye on the young pair, was instead following her twenty-two-year-old son around the house, begging for forgiveness. He rushes out into the garden to escape her and there comes upon his stepbrother just at the moment the latter watches his sister die and kills himself. After this debacle, the older girl runs away from home. Left behind are father, mother, and son . . . .

Such is the story of the six characters who, in Pirandello's play, suddenly present themselves to a stage director, who is rehearsing another Pirandello play. They want (so they tell him) to be put in a play. The director agrees (end of Act I) to let them present their credentials. In Act II, they enact a key scene, and the actors try to copy it. In Act III, they proceed to the catastrophe in their story, after which the stage director decides against accepting their proposition.

As to what *Six Characters* is all about, opinions have been various, though not mutually exclusive, since this is a play that makes statements on several different planes. That one of its subjects is the difference (or lack of difference) between art and life is obvious. It is also clear that it presents a certain view of the creative process, its very starting point having been Pirandello's impression that he did not create characters at all but was visited by them. Beyond this, it seems to have been each critic for himself.

In what is perhaps the most detailed study of the play, at least in English ("Father's Day," a lecture separately published by the Istituto Italiano di Cultura, New York, 1968), Eric Bentley has stressed certain motifs previously overlooked or minimized. One is the quest for God—one meaning for the word "Author" in the title. Another is the quest for "father" in the modern family, where, as Strindberg had so dramatically acknowledged, the father's supremacy seems threatened. A paradox is that the father in Pirandello's play is himself in search of a father and tries to find him in the stage director. Bentley also finds this play related to *Enrico IV* in that both are, among other things, studies in the schizophrenic experience. A Freudian interpretation of some of these same points is offered in "A Psychoanalytic Study of Pirandello's *Six Characters in Search of an Author*," by Charles Kligerman (*Journal of the American Psychoanalytic Association,* October 1962).

Skin of Our Teeth, The (1942). A comedy by Thornton WILDER. The principal characters of the play are George and Maggie Antrobus; their servant, Sabina; and their children, Henry and Gladys. Although they appear to be a middle-class American family living in Excelsior, New Jersey, they are a group of persons who exist on several levels at once and collectively stand for all mankind. George and Maggie are Adam and Eve, Sabina is Lilith, and Henry is Cain. George represents man as intellectual, striving always to increase his knowledge, Maggie is the eternal mother and homemaker. Sabina is the sensual quality in man, and Henry is man as his own enemy. In addition, the characters frequently step out of their roles to speak as actors performing in a play titled *The Skin of Our Teeth.* Past and present are viewed simultaneously as the play moves forward. The family experiences such triumphs as the invention of the wheel and the alphabet and the discovery that the tomato is edible, and suffers through great calamities brought on by hostile nature and mankind's own evil surges. In the first act, which begins with Sabina dusting the furniture and worrying because her master is not yet home for dinner, the Ice Age descends upon New Jersey and the Antrobuses must burn the chairs of the theater to stay alive. The second act concludes with the coming of Noah's flood while the family is in Atlantic City to attend a convention of mammals. Fortunately, representatives of all species of mammals are present, along with representatives of all the other orders of living creatures, and off a pier a boat is anchored into which they can run when the sea rises. When the last act begins, the family is shown to have lived through a horrendous war in which, it soon appears, Henry was the enemy. Scattered during the fighting, the Antrobuses are reunited in Excelsior and will begin their civilization anew. Once they have made the start, the stage blacks out, and Sabina appears in her Act I costume to repeat her opening lines. Thus at the close the audience receives the author's suggestion that mankind, having lasted through so many disasters, will continue to endure, bravely facing and surviving its problems again and again through eternity.

Despite the complexity of its structure and the demands it makes upon the talents of actors and the resources of producers, *The Skin of Our Teeth* holds a place in the American repertory. As a presentation of the idea that for all mankind's absurdity, the human race is worth preserving at any cost, the play is intelligent but not pedantic, funny but not banal, and moving but not sentimental. The framing scenes of Sabina alone in the Antrobus home reveal that one of Wilder's sources is the smug domestic comedy of the nineteenth century. Another is slapstick of the silent Keystone films variety. Still another is James Joyce's difficult novel *Finnegans Wake.* But at no time does Wilder lose control of his materials or let the many identities of his characters sink into a muddle. All the disparate sources are kept in careful balance, and a lucid, original play results.—M. G.

slapstick. A type of comedy that depends for its humor upon ludicrous physical activity. Frequently, as a feature of farce, slapstick takes the form of one character's beating another. The recipients of physical maltreatment usually are unhappy servants (the Dromios in *The Comedy of Errors*), would-be seducers (Falstaff in *The Merry Wives of Windsor*), or braggart warriors (Pistol in *Henry V*).

Slovakia. See CZECHOSLOVAKIA: *Slovakia.*

Slovenia. See YUGOSLAVIA.

Słowacki, Juliusz (1809–1849). Polish poet and playwright, one of the leading figures of nineteenth-century Polish émigré literature. Słowacki began his career as a dramatist with *Mindowe* ("Mindaugas," written 1829), a dramatic work based on medieval Lithuanian history. It was a youthful exercise in Romantic drama, followed in 1830 by a similar Roman-

tic gesture, *Maria Stuart* (*Mary Stuart*, 1862). His talent ripened, however, in the Great Emigration that followed the unsuccessful Polish uprising against Russia in 1830/31. In 1832, doubtless in reaction to Adam Mickiewicz's poetic drama *Forefathers' Eve, Part III*, he produced *Kordian* (first staged in 1899), his first major play and a work many Polish critics regard as his supreme effort in the drama. Romantic in its loose structure, indifferent to the conventional unities, and owing something to Shakespeare (principally *Macbeth*), *Kordian* is a skillfully conceived refutation of the theses of *Forefathers' Eve, Part III*. In *Forefathers' Eve*, Mickiewicz hailed the imminent appearance of a poet-seer who would make his people's cause his own and lead the emigration and indeed the whole Polish nation back to the glory of a restored Poland. In *Kordian*, through the story of a doomed scheme to assassinate Tsar Nicholas I during a stay in Warsaw and the personal failure of Kordian to overcome the spiritual and psychological maladies of the Romantic age, Słowacki polemicizes with Mickiewicz on his belief in the effectiveness of the single individual, on the national mission of the mystic poet-seer, and on the ability of the emigration to realize its goal of return to a resurrected Poland.

After *Kordian*, which was designated "Part One" in a typical Romantic literary mystification with the promise (never fulfilled) of more to come, Słowacki temporarily left the arena of émigré politics and polemics and returned to more conventional Romantic themes in his next four plays. In 1834 he wrote *Balladyna* (pub. 1839, staged 1862), a drama based on folkloric motifs and very much indebted to Shakespeare's *Midsummer Night's Dream* and *Twelfth Night*, and *Mazeppa* (pub. 1840), about one of the heroes of Romantic lore from England to the Ukraine—Mazeppa. The latter was translated into Hungarian and first staged in Budapest in 1847; in 1851 it was staged for the first time in Poland. In 1835 Słowacki wrote the greater part of his unfinished realistic historical drama *Horsztyński*, which was based on events in the city of Wilno during the Kościuszko rebellion of 1794 and is rich in echoes of Shakespeare's *Hamlet*. A new play, *Lilla Weneda*, dealing with Slavic (and in particular Polish) prehistory, but alluding to political conflicts within Polish history of his own time, was published in 1840 and first staged in 1869. *Lilla Weneda* has long been regarded one of the poet's better efforts in the drama.

In 1843, under the influence of the teachings of the mystagogue Andrzej Towiański, who became so prominent a figure in the Polish émigré community of Paris in the early 1840's, Słowacki wrote in rapid succession three highly interesting and in some respects unusual plays reflecting Towiański's beliefs and not fully comprehensible without reference to mystico-prophetic ideas. Two of the plays, *Ksiądz Marek* ("Father Marek") and *Sen srebrny Salomei* ("The Silver Dream of Salomea"), are set in the time of the anti-Russian struggle of Polish patriots belonging to the so-called Confederacy of Bar (1768–1772), a conflict that ended in the first partition of Poland in 1772. The third work was a free-verse adaptation of Calderón's *El principe constante* (*Książe niezłomny*, in Polish), which Słowacki was attracted to at this time in his life because of its theme of the power of faith.

The interest in Polish history exhibited by Słowacki in *Mindowe, Mazeppa, Horsztyński, Kordian, Ksiądz Marek*, and *Sen srebrny Salomei* reappeared in his later plays *Zawisza Czarny* ("Zawisza the Black"), and *Samuel Zborowski*, both written in 1844/45.

The quantity of unfinished literary works and manuscripts discovered after Słowacki's death and published posthumously was truly voluminous. They included among others a play in French, *Beatrix Cenci, Złota czaszka* ("The Gold Vessel") and *Fantazy*. Of the three only the last, written probably in 1841 and first staged in 1867, merits serious attention. It is a well-executed satirical comedy, the only true comedy Słowacki ever wrote, aimed at exposing certain of the more ludicrous aspects of Romantic love and Romantic mythmaking.—H. B. S.

Snow in Midsummer (Tou Ngo vitan). A Chinese drama by KUAN HAN-CH'ING, the chief playwright of the Yüan dynasty (1280–1368). *Snow in Midsummer* is the most popular of all works in the large class of serious plays with an innocent and much persecuted woman as its chief character. Although its story lacks the world-wide appeal of such a folktale as that of the shrewd judge that constitutes the plot of *The Chalk Circle*, the Chinese play best known outside its own land, *Snow in Midsummer* admirably expresses values peculiarly prized in the East and intelligible elsewhere. It exhibits a remarkable fusion of theatrical brilliance and moral earnestness. The ethical bent of the Chinese mind gains the emphasis conferred by a sense of form and artfulness in utilizing the most of a given medium—in this instance, the stage.

As in many Chinese plays, the action covers a considerable period of time; here the span is thirteen years. The ample canvas gives space on which to draw the emphatic lines defining the Chinese sense of values, especially where the role of woman is concerned. The story illustrates the evils of enforced marriage and in particular the prejudice against second marriages. Character types familiar in Yüan drama are especially well drawn. The heroine, Tou Ngo, whose husband has died after three years of marriage, resists a grotesquely offensive lover only to find herself, as result of his later machinations, accused and condemned on the charge of murdering her father-in-law. Like so many women on the Chinese stage, Tou Ngo is led with a halter about her neck before a brutal judge. At the moment of her execution she makes three prophecies. She declares that if she is innocent her blood will rise and spatter the white banner floating overhead, that snow will fall in midsummer, and that three years of famine will blight the land. As the fatal ax descends, her blood miraculously rises to stain the banner crimson and at the same time the snow that was foretold commences to fall. For three years, as she has prophesied, famine devastates the province. She becomes a legend among the people.

The fourth and final act returns to the scene depicted in the beginning of Act I. Tou Ngo had been left in the care of an older woman by her father, the two women being widows. The father, himself a widower, is the conventional figure, the poor scholar who finds it all but impossible to make ends meet. In Act I he had left his daughter reluctantly but without choice, since he had to go to the capital to compete in the official examinations. Necessities of life keep him from his native province for thirteen years. Finally, having succeeded in his examinations and become an exalted judge, he is able to return to his old home. One night as he drowses over his official papers, his daughter's ghost enters the room. She explains to him the injustice done her at court and names the real criminal. The scene recalls the first act of *Hamlet,* but in Kuan Han-ch'ing's play the appearance of the ghost is the means by which the wicked at last will be punished and the name of the innocent Tou Ngo will be cleared. The ghost scene is strictly conventional, a device used in many other Chinese plays.

Although some of the minor and the grotesque characters are strikingly drawn, the play rises to high distinction only in Acts III and IV during the execution scene and the ghost scene. Each has great lyric and choreographic power. Each is, of course, enhanced by a supernaturalism made completely credible from the theatrical point of view. It is popular drama lifted to eminence as poetic drama. No one can doubt that *Snow in Midsummer* is a powerful work, a masterpiece in the pathetic mode.

There are innumerable collections in China containing this play and others derived more or less closely from it, but only one translation is available in English: Yuan Hsien-yi and Gladys Yang, *Select Plays of Kuan Han-ch'ing* (1958). English readers are indebted to these indefatigable translators for a large number of plays. Unfortunately, this translation is one of their more pedestrian efforts.—H. W. W.

Socialist Realism. See RUSSIA: *twentieth century.*

Sophocles (497/6 or 495/4 B.C.–406 B.C.). Greek tragic playwright. Sophocles' life span covers almost the whole century of Athens' rise to greatness and its fall. As a young man he took part in the celebration of the victory of Salamis (480), which launched Athens on the road to empire, and when he died the Athenian surrender to Sparta after a long, exhausting war was only two years away (404). In the great events of the fifth century he took his full part as an Athenian citizen, holding high office in peace as in war. He was treasurer of the Athenian naval league in 443/42 (a critical year in which the tribute lists were revised), was a general, with Pericles, in the war Athens fought to suppress the revolt of Samos (441–439), and was general again in 428 in a war against the Anaeans. It is probable, though not certain, that Sophocles was one of the Probouloi, the emergency committee appointed after the disaster in Sicily (412) to guide Athenian policy with a firm hand. He served often as ambassador, but, we are told, his love for Athens was so great that (unlike Agathon and Euripides) he refused invitations to live at the courts of foreign kings. Handsome (an important qualification in ancient Athens), wealthy (his father, Sophillus, owned many slaves and some kind of factory), and successful (he was never placed third in the tragic contest), Sophocles seems to have been universally popular, both as a dramatist and as a public figure. In the *Frogs* of Aristophanes, produced the year after Sophocles' death, Dionysus in Hades says of him, "He is good-tempered here, as he was there." His relations with Pericles were close and cordial; he himself reported Pericles' friendly remark that he was a better poet than he was a general. His friendship with

Herodotus is attested not only by the poem he wrote for the historian on his own fifty-fifth birthday (only the opening line is extant) but also by the frequent use of Herodotean material in the plays. Socrates (in Plato's *Republic*) speaks of hearing Sophocles in old age express his thankfulness for release from the passions of youth. And in 406, when news reached Athens of the death of Euripides in Macedonia, Sophocles showed his sorrow by bringing on his chorus at the *proagon* uncrowned and dressed in mourning.

Sophocles showed the same devotion to religious cult as to public duty. He was a priest of the healing deity Halon. In this capacity he received into his own house the god Asclepius (probably in the form of a sacred snake) when the cult was introduced to Athens from Epidaurus and the god's own shrine was not yet ready. After his death the Athenians made Sophocles himself a *heros* under the name Dexion ("Receiver"), and excavations on the west face of the Acropolis have uncovered a shrine containing inscriptions which honor Asclepius and Dexion.

Of his family life we know very little. He had a son Iophon, who became a tragic poet. There was also Ariston, a son by another woman. The story that Iophon, enraged by Sophocles' adoption of a son of Ariston, brought suit against his father for senile incompetence and that Sophocles won the case by recit-

SOPHOCLES (HEAD IN THE BRITISH MUSEUM. COURTESY R. B. FLEMING & CO. LTD.)

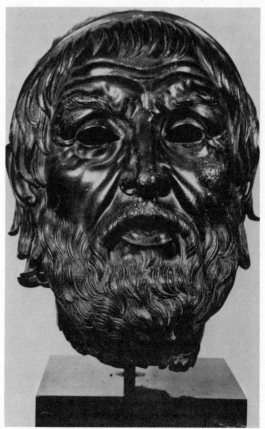

ing the choral ode in praise of Athens from his *Oedipus at Colonus* is a good story, but nothing more.

Sophocles' teacher in music—like all tragic poets, he composed the music as well as the words of the choral odes—was Lampros, and the model for his early dramatic style was, as he tells us himself, Aeschylus. Sophocles first competed at the Dionysia in 468 and was awarded first prize. The play was probably *Triptolemos,* and its fragments show marked Aeschylean influence. From this point on, Sophocles' dramatic production was consistently successful. For one who led such an active life in city affairs, it was also surprisingly voluminous; ancient accounts put the number of his plays at 123. Like Aeschylus, he performed in his own plays (taking the principal role in *Nausikaa,* for example). But early in his career he gave up acting, thus setting the precedent for Euripides, who seems never to have appeared onstage. Other Sophoclean innovations radically changed the nature of the tragic performance, giving it greater dramatic flexibility and intensity. He raised the number of the choral performers from twelve to fifteen. His reasons for doing so are not recorded but were probably explained in his prose work *On the Chorus,* which, unfortunately, has not survived. According to Aristotle, he also introduced "scene painting," and though the details are not known, this was clearly a move in the direction of more realistic presentation. The two most important of his innovations brought fundamental changes to the tragic art which Aeschylus had created. Sophocles introduced a third speaking actor, and he abandoned the Aeschylean practice of devoting the three tragic plays offered by the poet at the dramatic contest to a continuous story, presenting instead three separate plays which had no thematic connection.

The use of a third actor enabled Sophocles to increase significantly the number of speaking characters appearing in the play (Aeschylus has four in *The Persians* and three in *The Suppliant Maidens* as against six in Sophocles' OEDIPUS TYRANNUS and seven in his *Antigone*); it also made possible triangular scenes, which explored new and subtle dramatic relationships: for example, the confrontation of Lichas with his accuser before Deianira in TRACHINIAI, or the terrifying scene in *Oedipus Tyrannus* in which Jocasta, listening to Oedipus and the Theban messenger, suddenly realizes the hideous truth. The turning away from Aeschylean trilogic composition also worked toward greater dramatic economy and intensity, for the presentation of the myth in one play demanded skillful concentrated exposition in the prologue and swift plot development; the choral odes, though still a vital and integral element, had to yield space for dramatic action. But the Sophoclean single play was more than a mere technical innovation; it reflected an entirely new view of human action and suffering. In the Aeschylean trilogy the consequences of defiance of divine law are followed through one generation after another. The intricate pattern of human will and divine purpose interlocked covers long spans of time and presents each character in a context of family history; indeed, it has been said that Aeschylean tragedy deals, not with individuals, but with "houses," the house of Atreus, of Laius, of Danaus. The Sophoclean play narrows the dramatic focus to one solitary individual, in fact to one critical

moment in his life—his refusal to yield to time and circumstance. The past events which led up to the moment of decision are presented economically in a highly dramatic prologue (action and exposition inseparably combined); the future—the explanation, reconciliation, and release brought by the third Aeschylean play—is left blank. The action of the Sophoclean hero is thus isolated in time as he himself is isolated in human society (in PHILOCTETES, for example, the hero is marooned on a desert island); he makes his deliberate defiance absolutely alone, ignoring or more often rejecting, with scorn and anger, the warnings of his friends and the threats of his enemies. And the divine will, which in Aeschylean drama is finally made clear, finds expression in Sophoclean tragedy mainly through riddling prophecies, which even when finally fulfilled, as they always are, cast no light on heaven's purpose.

Yet the overall impression produced by the plays is not one of existential despair or proud exaltation of purely human courage. The greatness of the hero is by some mysterious alchemy identified with the gods, whose ordinances, as understood by others, he defies. Furthermore, the course of events vindicates the hero's action: AJAX ends with the hero's burial; ANTIGONE, with the burial of Polyneices and the punishment of Creon; ELECTRA, with the heroine's triumph over her oppressors; and in the last play of all, OEDIPUS AT COLONUS, the hero is summoned to his everlasting rest by the gods themselves. There is a mysterious justice at work in the Sophoclean universe that somehow makes possible human acceptance of a pattern of order which, harsh though it seems, exalts and justifies heroic action. But the working out of justice remains mysterious. "The gods conceal their designs," says a fragment of a lost Sophoclean play, "and you will not understand them no matter what lengths you go to in your search."

Of the seven plays which have survived intact, only one, *Philoctetes,* can be assigned an absolutely certain date: 409 B.C. There are good grounds for dating *Antigone* in 442, *Oedipus Tyrannus* 430–425, and *Oedipus at Colonus* close to 406, the year of Sophocles' death; it was first produced in 402. *Ajax* is generally thought to be earlier than *Antigone,* and *Electra* later than *Oedipus Tyrannus.* There is no agreement on the date of *Trachiniai;* some critics consider it very early, some close in date to *Oedipus Tyrannus.*

Recommended books about Sophocles are S. M. Adams, *Sophocles the Playwright* (1957); C. M. Bowra, *Sophoclean Tragedy* (1944, paperback 1965); Victor Ehrenberg, *Sophocles and Pericles* (1954); G. M. Kirkwood, *A Study of Sophoclean Drama* (1958); Bernard M. W. Knox, *The Heroic Temper* (1964); Albin Lesky, *Greek Tragedy* (1965); F. J. H. Letters, *The Life and Works of Sophocles* (1953); A. J. A. Waldock, *Sophocles the Dramatist* (1951, paperback 1966); T. B. L. Webster, *An Introduction to Sophocles* (1936); Cedric H. Whitman, *Sophocles, A Study in Heroic Humanism* (1951); and T. Woodward (ed.), *Sophocles, A Collection of Critical Essays* (1966).—B. M. W. K.

Sorrows of Han, The (Han Kung ch'iu). A Chinese play by Ma Chih-yuan (fl. 1250). *The Sorrows of Han* is one of the chief landmarks of Chinese drama. Although commonly associated with the important group of plays surviving from the Yüan dynasty (1280–1368), it belongs to a slightly earlier period and represents a relatively early stage in the development of Chinese drama as known to the modern world. Not quite "primitive" in the usual sense of the word in art history, it shows a less highly developed phase of playwrighting than that of the greater number of surviving Chinese plays. It is virtually a poetic monologue elaborated by occasional passages of dramatic action.

The Sorrows of Han is the standard stage representation of one of the most celebrated episodes in Chinese history, related countless times in verse and prose. It is the story of an unscrupulous minister, Mao Yen-shou, who persuades the emperor Han Yuan-ti that in recognition of his imperial dignity he should revive the institution of the royal harem, which had temporarily fallen into disuse. Accordingly, pictures of leading beauties throughout the empire are painted; the palace is to receive those ranking highest in pulchritude. Mao, however, falsifies the record, accepting bribes wherever possible in return for conferring the honor implicit in the imperial choice. The most beautiful woman in China in fact is Chao-chun, daughter of a poor family which refuses to offer the bribe. Mao thereupon defaces her picture, causing the emperor to take no interest in her. She is simply held in seclusion in the palace. Nevertheless, one day the emperor, on hearing her exquisite singing, demands to see her. Her presence at once proves to him his minister's treachery. The emperor falls in love with the lady, while the disloyal minister escapes to the kingdom of the Tartars, where he enters the service of the Great Khan.

Here he informs the khan of Chao-chun's unrivaled beauty. By treaty the khans had long agreed to keep peace on the Chinese border under the proviso that each year a girl be sent them from the emperor's court. The khan naturally demands Chao-chun and the emperor at first threatens to deny the tribute. Chao-chun herself, however, asks to be sent into exile on the ground that only so will the empire be saved from strife. Her lover bids her a sorrowful farewell as she starts on her long journey. Arriving at the riverbank that constitutes the frontier of the empire, she takes a cup of wine from the hands of the khan and, drinking in honor of her homeland and the emperor whom she loves, throws herself into the river. Although the stream flows through a desert, the grave where she is buried remains forever green. The magnanimous khan presently learns the story of the minister's deception, upon which he returns him a captive to the emperor's palace, where he receives the torment and death that he deserves. The emperor remains in inconsolable grief.

The play presents this story for the most part simply and directly. Scenes alternate between the imperial palace and the court of the khan. The focus, however, is on the emperor, the only character who sings. Chao-chun has few lines to speak and for the most part appears in mime. Much of the play is actually musical soliloquy by the emperor, his songs pitched in a long, drawn-out melancholy. He is not depicted as heroic in the Western understanding of this ideal. On the contrary, before his ministers he even appears weak and vacillating. Sorrow is the key to this distinctly lyrical play. There is really no an-

tagonist, though Mao is indeed a villain. The khan, sympathetically presented, hardly provides a foil to the emperor, unless self-esteem be regarded as foil to self-pity.

The final act contains the play's most memorable and significant passage, introducing a subjectivity and a note of typical Chinese sophistication in contrast to the uncommonly forthright style uppermost in the rest of the play. In a dream the emperor imagines his favorite returning to him as a ghost, only to see her snatched away by an intruding Tartar swordsman. On awaking he listens to the cries of a lonely goose flying over the night sky in the opposite direction from its regular migration, a familiar Chinese symbol for privation and misfortune. The passage develops along lyrical lines not far removed from Greek elegiac poetry.

The play was first translated into English, the lyrical passages generally omitted, by J. F. Davis in 1829. The play as translated by Donald Keene with its lyric passages restored is included in *Anthology of Chinese Literature* (1965), edited by Cyril Birch. Here, as is often the case, the title is given as "Autumn in the Palace of Han." Autumn, it should be noted, is traditionally a symbol for sorrow, the time when lonely geese cry among lowering clouds of evening.—H. W. W.

Sotoba Komachi (Komachi and the Gravestone, 14th century). A Japanese *noh* play in one act by Kwanami Kiyotsugo (1333–1384). Although by far the greater number of the important noh dramas show strong influence from Buddhistic sects, none is so impressive a witness to this relationship as *Sotoba Komachi,* long a favorite on the stage. The title signifies "Komachi on the Stupa," *stupa* being a monument of Buddha. An early version of the play is said to have been written by Kwanami Kiyotsugu (1334–1384), but this version is thought to have been substantially revised by his son Zeami Motokiyo to create the text that has come down to us. It was Zeami who did most to establish the form of the noh plays as they now exist. The assumed season for this somber piece is autumn. There is little or nothing that resembles a plot. A priest and his attendant have minor roles. Otherwise, only the leading figure, or *shite,* Ono-no-Komachi, appears. This woman had once been a celebrated courtesan. At the height of her youth and pride she rejected a courtly lover, Fukakusa-no-Shosho. Mocking him, she told him that if he came to her house at night a hundred times, on his last visit she would permit him to enter. Although he persisted in his visits, the last was fatal. A snowstorm was raging and he fell exhausted, to die on her threshold.

The play shows Komachi as a wretched old woman approaching her own hundredth year (obviously a symbolic parallel to her lover's final visit). The play's earlier lines comprise a theological debate with the priest. Tottering across the stage, Komachi is imagined to sit on a fallen stone that is actually a stupa. The priest accuses her of desecrating the image. She replies that there can be no desecration since all things are holy, including even such a ruined relic of life as herself. Quite the contrary, she holds, the ruined stupa and the ruined woman share much in common. After gaining the better of this religious controversy, she is suddenly attacked by madness, imagining that once again she is in the storm and the youthful lover whom she has rejected lies once more dead beside her. She mimes her emotions in a mad dance. Yet her agony augurs her expiation, and with the prospect of her salvation the play concludes. Its thesis is that in the aspect of cosmic vision good and evil, purity or indulgence, are one.

This is a grim, dark drama of remarkable force, moving to read and still more moving in performance.

For the best rendering in English, see *The Noh Drama,* selected and translated by the Special Noh Committee, Japanese Classics Translation Committee (Vol. III, 1960).—H. W. W.

South (Sud, 1953). A tragedy by Julien Green (1900–). In his dramaturgy, as in his novels, Julien Green easily passes from the real world to the surreal world. A supernaturally evil atmosphere surrounds many of the scenes, yet there is intense drama in the effort of the characters to resist their fate.

For the public at large, *South* was a perplexing play when it was first performed in March 1953. It is a remarkable composition and one of the few successful attempts in recent years to create the pure tone of tragedy in the ambiguities of the characters, the richness of their inner life, and the vigor, simplicity, and directness of the writing.

The action takes place on a South Carolina plantation on April 11, 1861, the day before the beginning of the Civil War. Lieutenant Ian Wiezowski is visiting the Broderick family, and their niece Regina is struggling against a strong attraction to Ian. Everyone in the family likes Ian except an old Negro servant who is blind and who plays a Tiresias part in trying to warn Mr. Broderick about the visitor. Ian meets the dinner guest Eric MacLure, a young planter and neighbor of the Brodericks, and forces Eric to speak of his love for Angelina, the young daughter of the Brodericks. Ian insults him, challenges him to a duel, and dies in the duel by offering himself to the bullets.

The play is a tragedy on the theme of homosexuality. Ian falls in love with Eric on meeting him but never confesses his love. His passion is doomed from the start, as irrevocably as Phèdre's for Hippolyte and Oedipus' for Jocasta. *South* begins as an elaborate social tableau with a good deal of military and political discussion. Gradually, however, two figures emerge: Regina, in love with Ian, and Ian, who treats her cruelly as his own passion for Eric forces him toward catastrophe.

South appears in an English translation in *Plays of the Year,* Vol. XII (1954/55).—W. F.

South Africa. See Africa: *South Africa.*

South America. See Brazil, Puerto Rico, and Spanish America.

Soutsos, Alexandros and **Panayiotis.** See Greece: *modern period.*

Soviet Union. See Russia.

Soya [-Jensen, Carl-Erik] (1896–). Danish novelist and playwright. Born in Copenhagen, the son of a professor of painting, Soya got his start in hack journalism, writing, among other things, detective stories under the names of Lillian D. Green and Martin Arrowhead. He made his theater debut with *Parasitterne* ("The Parasites," written 1926; prod. 1931), which deals realistically and somewhat luridly with murder by rat poison and bread knife. During the 1930's Soya produced almost a play a year, chiefly satiric fantasies. As a result of such activity he was twice interned by the Nazi occupation forces during World War II, and in 1945 he had to flee to Sweden. Chiefly a playwright, Soya is nevertheless best known abroad for two semiautobiographical novels, *Min farmors hus* (*My Grandmother's House,* 1943), which presents a fine picture of Copenhagen

A SCENE FROM JULIEN GREEN'S *South* (FRENCH CULTURAL SERVICES)

around the turn of the century, and *Sytten* (*Seventeen*, 1953), which busies itself exclusively and monotonously with adolescent sexual enterprise. In recent years Soya has been living in Ibiza, Spain.

Typical of Soya's satiric plays is *Det nye spil om enhver* ("The New Play of Everyman," 1938), in which the hero is brought before the highest court of judgment, guilty of egoism, tax evasion, philandering, and wistful thoughts of uxoricide, but is exonerated by a shift of the blame to science and religion, which have left him without moral principles to guide a heart essentially good. The irrespressible Soya has a way of turning up in his own plays, as, for example, Professor Spoya in *Min høje hat* ("My High Hat," 1939), in which he invades a dreary middle-class parlor to metamorphose the dissatisfied inhabitants into each his separate dream, the father into a pharaoh, the son into a young poet riding a prodigious Pegasus, the others into sadists, eroticists, and clowns. *Løve med korset* ("Corseting the Lion," 1950) is a vigorous antiwar satire, and *Petersen i dødsriget* ("Petersen in the Underworld," 1957) an amiable adaptation of the Orpheus myth.

In the 1940's Soya turned to a more philosophical drama, neorealism he called it, which took the shape of a tetralogy of problem plays dealing with the mysterious confluence of apparent law and accident in human existence. *Brudstykker af et monster* ("Pieces of a Pattern," 1940) is an interesting study of causality; *To tråde* ("Two Threads," 1943) juggles two separate plots that do not intersect until the end, and

then quite fortuitously; and the remaining two plays deal ironically with the notions of nemesis and poetic justice. All told, Soya is best in the format of the satiric play.

See *Contemporary Danish Plays* (1955), edited by Elias Bredsdorff, pp. 7–16 and 173–250. See also P. M. Mitchell, *A History of Danish Literature* (1958), pp. 264–267.—R. B. V.

Soyinka, Wole. See AFRICA: *Nigeria.*

Spain: *middle ages.* Drama is generally supposed to have arisen in Spain, as in the other Romance territories, from the paraliturgy of the medieval church. Only a few tropes, some liturgical dramas in Latin, and one in the vernacular exist to sustain the thesis that until well into the twelfth century the Spanish church drama developed according to the usual European pattern. There are no extant dramatic texts in Castilian Spanish for the 300-year period of 1150 to 1450; there are only some vague phrases in historical documents which may refer to some sort of dramatic activity. Although short liturgical plays in the vernacular appeared in the fifteenth century, no great Spanish cycles of miracle and mystery plays were written or performed. This phenomenon of "backwardness" is very important for the subsequent development of the Spanish theater of the Golden Age.

While dramatic activity in the central kingdoms was at a standstill, in the Catalan-speaking areas in the east of the Iberian Peninsula many liturgical dramas were composed. But these *misteris,* as they were called, were not full-fledged mystery plays either, and they seem to have had little influence on the Castilian-language drama.

The anonymous twelfth-century liturgical play usually referred to as the *Auto de los reyes magos* ("Act of the Magian Kings") is a polymetric fragment of 147 lines derived from French (probably Gascon) sources and related to the *Ordo Stellae,* the liturgical office for the Feast of Epiphany. The three kings, uncertain about the significance of the star, decide to offer their gifts to the Christ Child not as an act of homage but as a test of His claim to a divine nature: if he takes the gold, he must be king of the earth; if the myrrh, he must be a mortal man; if the frankincense, he must be king of heaven. The final scene, in which Christ presumably accepts all three gifts, is missing. The play is thematically quite advanced: the New Era heralded by Christ's Incarnation is associated with the rhyming words "charity" and "verity," while the rabbis, who still live in the Judaic world of the Old Testament, are not able to recognize the truth because they have no charity. The characters of the Magi are carefully differentiated by their varying degrees of skepticism and faith, and the contrast between them and the fourth king, Herod, is sharply drawn. The tradition of the *Ordo Stellae,* celebrating the doubting faith of the intellectual, lends itself to dramatic confrontations of this kind, and so to dialectic and dialogue. Unfortunately this tradition was not to prevail in Spain.

The only acceptable evidence of dramatic activity in Spanish during the period when texts are lacking is found in documents that are difficult to interpret. King Alfonso X, in his thirteenth-century code of laws, forbids laymen and priests to participate in *juegos de escarnio* (literally, "games of ridicule"), which may have been—no one knows for sure—

A SCENE FROM THE FOURTEENTH-CENTURY "REPRESENTATION" *Asumpcio de Madona Santa Maria* (AMPLIACIONES Y REPRODUCCIONES MAS)

dances, pantomimes, or the recital of coarse jongleuresque or goliardic diatribes. As a counterattraction, Alfonso's law specifically authorizes "representations" for Christmas, Epiphany, and Easter. From this encouragement of church drama, it cannot of course be inferred that this drama actually existed. The decrees of church councils, from Valladolid (1228) to Aranda (1473), contain similar prohibitions against the *juegos de escarnio* and similar encouragements of liturgical dramas. The medieval chronicles, on the other hand, describe *entremeses* ("interludes," originally between the courses of a banquet). In 1414 Enrique de Villena (1384–1434) produced such an entremés to celebrate the accession of Ferdinand of Antequera to the throne of Aragon. It was an allegorical pageant designed to capture the good will of the new prince. The record shows that this custom was followed on several ceremonial occasions in the fifteenth century. At the other end of the social scale unwritten folk or student drama may have existed. Some narrative poems, like the fifteenth-century *Vita Christi* of Fray Iñigo de Mendoza, seem to contain in written reproduction the relics of such performances. The *Auto del repelón* ("Act of Hair-pulling," pub. 1509), attributed until recently to Juan del Encina,

may be the end of a secular tradition of horseplay among the students of Salamanca University, but hypotheses of this sort remain very speculative.

The lacuna in dramatic texts ends with the *Representación del Nacimiento de Nuestro Señor* ("Representation of Our Lord's Birth"), written by Gómez Manrique (1412?–?1490) sometime between 1467 and 1481 for performance by nuns in the convent at Calabazanos. Loosely related to the *Officium Pastorum*, the liturgical service for Christmas Eve, it lacks the racy exchanges in the dialogue of the *Auto de los reyes magos*. The essence of the work is the adoration of Christ by the Virgin and the shepherds. The archangels Gabriel, Michael, and Raphael praise Mary and offer to serve her. An innovation is the allegorical presentation to the newborn Child of the instruments of his Passion. The play ends with a secular lullaby which has been rewritten as a religious hymn. Most critics consider Gómez Manrique's play even more primitive than the twelfth-century *Auto de los reyes magos*. Other poetic works by Gómez Manrique may conceivably have been playlets.

Renaissance. The most advanced dramatic text of the postmedieval period, generally referred to as *La Celestina*, is now known to have been published no earlier than 1500. It consists of an anonymous first act in prose that was discovered by a law student called Fernando de Rojas (d. 1541), who completed the text in two separate versions. The first version, in sixteen acts, he entitled *La comedia de Calisto y Melibea* ("The Comedy of Calisto and Melibea"); a few years later he expanded his work to a total of twenty-one acts and called it *La tragicomedia de Calisto y Melibea* ("The Tragicomedy of Calisto and Melibea"). The earliest readers of this closet drama, deciding that the old hag Celestina—a procuress, witch, and cosmetics vendor—was more interesting than the lovers, renamed the work in her honor. The play was supposedly written as a moral warning to those lovers who deify their ladies and ignore the treachery and avarice of the servants in whom they confide. But the work is full of subtle ambiguities; for instance, the lovers, whose sex play is boldly presented, confuse the didactic purpose of the work by capturing the reader's sympathy. The lack of understanding between the upper and lower classes of society causes much of the tension that leads to the final catastrophe. The servants kill Celestina and are executed for their crime; Calisto falls to his death from a ladder as he leaves Melibea's garden after an assignation with her; and Melibea commits suicide by flinging herself from a tower. The work was initially called a comedy because it followed in the tradition of the Latin elegiac and Humanistic comedies, but it is in fact a tragedy. It contributed themes rather than techniques to the developing Spanish drama.

Uncertainty about nomenclature, such as we have seen in connection with classifying *La Celestina* as comedy or tragicomedy, both plagued and emancipated Spanish drama from this time on. *La Celestina* spawned a number of unperformable prose dramas, culminating in Lope de Vega's *La Dorotea* (written 1632). But about the time *La Celestina* was being written and rewritten, plays were being composed to be produced in private houses. Juan del Encina (1469?–1529) called his works "eclogues," while his contemporary and rival Lucas Fernández (1474?–1542) exposed the tentative nature of playwriting at that time by using such dual terms as "farce or quasi-comedy" in his titles. Eventually the word *comedia* prevailed as a synonym in Spain for the catchall English word "play," thus indelibly imprinting even on serious drama or tragedy the characteristics of comic theory.

Juan del Encina is regarded with some justice as the "father of Spanish drama." He was also a considerable lyric poet and musician. In the 1490's he began

WOODCUT OF A SCENE FROM FERNANDO DE ROJAS' *La Celestina*

composing pairs of one-act plays for presentation at Christmas or Easter in the drawing room of the duke of Alba's palace near Salamanca. The first play of each pair is a sort of secular prologue to a typical liturgical drama in the *Officium Pastorum* tradition. As the term "eclogue" indicates, even plays not destined for performance on Christmas Eve are peopled with shepherds, distinguishable as such by costume, speech, or role, even when they are textually identified as hermits, biblical characters, or noblemen. The Christmas play must have attracted Encina because the real shepherds of the Salamanca region, with their amusing rustic dialect called *sayagués*, and the burgeoning fictional shepherds of the Renaissance pastoral could easily be fused with the shepherds of Bethlehem. As a result, the *Officium Pastorum* became, with fateful consequences, the prototype of the classical Spanish drama.

Encina, while never losing sight of this starting point, experimented continually, moving away eventually from the historical shepherds of the Nativity to fictional shepherds who were really courtiers in a rustic setting, and from two-part playlets to plays that, though only one act, ran to two thousand lines of verse. His fourteen eclogues all ring the changes on the power of love, whether Christian or profane, to transform its devotees from what they once were into something better. Encina discovered in the theater's magic of impersonation the magical power of transmutation that his dramatic poetry expressed. He metamorphosed his characters as he wrote about the process of metamorphosis. His great accomplishment along these lines was to secularize church drama by transferring it from the aegis of Christ to that of Venus. Encina's final, most daring innovations were the result of a visit to Italy, where the theater had reached heights unimaginable at that time in Spain. It was around 1513 in Rome that he wrote his masterpiece, the *Egloga de Plácida y Vitoriano* ("Eclogue of Plácida and Vitoriano"). Here, the first play of the customary pair is reduced to a simple prologue, a monologue spoken by a rustic shepherd. The rest is a kind of Pyramus and Thisbe action leading to the suicide of Plácida, who thinks herself spurned by her lover. Vitoriano is about to kill himself in despair, but before he does so, he recites a long liturgy in Latin and Spanish to Cupid, and he addresses a prayer to Venus. Responding, Venus induces Mercury, the god of metamorphoses, to resurrect Plácida. The tragic action is miraculously averted to produce a happy ending in accord with what Encina (and most of his Spanish successors) regarded as an immutable law of the theater.

Another versatile artist, Gil VICENTE, also wrote small plays for production at the great religious festivals. He was a Portuguese at the court at Lisbon. Some of his plays are in Spanish, some in Portuguese, and some in a mixture of both languages. Whereas Encina's experimentation was linear—almost systematic in its progression from liturgical drama to Italianate tragicomedy—Vicente's art was explorative, continually seeking new possibilities for dramatic expression without bringing any single line of development to its perfect form. Beginning like Encina with simple liturgical plays (still dominated by the shepherds of the *Officium Pastorum*), Vicente tried his hand at a variety of genres: works of devotion (sixteen *autos,* or "acts"), three comedies, ten tragicomedies, and twelve farces. A good example of the first genre is his *Auto da sibila Cassandra* ("Act of the Sibyl Cassandra," date unknown), in which the sibyl, foreseeing the birth of the Messiah, refuses to marry her suitor Solomon so that, by remaining a virgin, she can qualify to give birth to Christ. Her presumption is exposed when a curtain is drawn to reveal the divinely chosen virgin, Mary, and her Child. One of Vicente's farces, *Farsa do viuvo* ("Farce of the Widower," date unknown), opens with a widower being "consoled" by a henpecked neighbor who is in fact congratulating him on his emancipation from the bonds of matrimony. The widower is worried about his inability to rear his two fractious daughters. His problem is solved by the providential arrival of a prince, incognito, who falls in love with the older girl, while the prince's brother, coming in search of him, falls in love with the younger daughter. Perhaps Vicente's best play, the *Tragicomedia de Don Duardos* ("Tragicomedy of Don Duardos," date unknown), dramatizes a portion of a romance of chivalry. Highly lyrical, it evokes the romantic atmosphere of the popular fiction of the period. Prince Edward of England courts the Princess Flérida of Constantinople by the power of love alone. He discards his royal and knightly trappings to become, unrecognized, her gardener. With the coming of spring Flérida discovers the beauty and manliness of this simple, unadorned employee, who produces in a perfect rose the richest of treasures. She is of course not displeased to learn that he is really a prince.

The art of Encina and Vicente was hampered by its dependence on the unpromising model of the *Officium Pastorum* liturgical drama, with its absence of intellectual give-and-take and thus of any real possibility for dramatic tension. Unlike the sophisticated Magi from the *Ordo Stellae,* the Bethlehem shepherds, when Christ's birth is made known to them, make a simple act of faith without hesitation or doubt. In such an affirmation there is little room for the complexity derived from the interchange of thoughts and attitudes that is necessary for an advanced kind of drama. Although the liturgical tradition that they inherited denied to Encina and Vicente all possibility of exploiting the dialogic tension that is inherent in most drama, each playwright devised independently a solution that characterized Spanish drama in its Golden Age. They imposed on their works a pattern of ideological or poetic themes that was more or less autonomous of the dialogue. This superstructure served to endow their plays with a unity and a focus of interest that to some extent compensated for their dialectical poverty. Without this early discovery the dramatic art of Lope de Vega and Calderón would no doubt have been very different.

The early Spanish Humanist Bartolomé Torres Naharro (d. ?1524) lived in Italy, where he wrote dramas in Spanish that were produced in the houses of noblemen and church dignitaries. His plays reflect the much greater sophistication of the Italian private stage. His collected works, the *Propalladia* ("First Fruits of Pallas"), were published in Naples in 1517. In the Preamble he sketches a theory of drama in which, among other things, he fixes the number of acts at five, sets the number of characters between six

and twelve, and defines decorum. He discriminates between plays based on the observation of real life and plays written entirely from the imagination. The first category comprises realistic works like the [*Comedia*] *Tinellaria* ("Kitchen-Staff Comedy," date unknown), about the life of servants below stairs in a great house, and the *Soldadesca* ("Soldiering Comedy," date unknown), about the life of Spanish soldiers in Italy. His most remarkable play, the *Himenea* ("Hymeneal Comedy," date unknown), belongs to the group of imaginative dramas. Many scholars see *Himenea* as a forerunner of the Baroque comedy, the *comedia de capa y espada* ("comedy of cloak and sword"). The lady, her lover, and her brother (eager to preserve her "honor") suffer various setbacks in their triangular relationship, but these problems are eventually resolved. The servants, anticipating the later fools, or *graciosos,* act out contrapuntally their lower-class version of these amours. Torres Naharro's plays were complex and advanced compared to those written by his peninsular contemporaries, but it was only much later that his plays affected the development of Spanish drama.

Diego Sánchez de Badajoz (fl. 1525–1547) enriched the repertoire of religious one-act plays by writing both simple liturgical dramas, imaginatively embroidered with poetic conceits, and allegories with personified abstractions as characters. The kind of allegorical dramas developed by Sánchez de Badajoz, embryonic morality plays, must have enjoyed some popularity, for they are well represented in the *Códice de autos viejos* ("Codex of Ancient Acts"), an important collection of nearly one hundred primitive, anonymous religious dramas from the middle of the sixteenth century. The Valencian Juan de Timoneda (d. ?1583) rewrote some of the allegorical plays from this anthology in less rustic speech and form and so paved the way for the uniquely Spanish AUTO SACRAMENTAL, with its impressive formalism, seriousness, and erudition. The autos sacramentales were allegorical one-act plays related to the Eucharist and commissioned by municipalities as part of the celebration of Corpus Christi. José de Valdivielso (1560?–1638), Lope de Vega, and above all Calderón became the great masters of this special genre.

Another predominantly Spanish genre, the entremés, or "interlude," was cultivated by the great actor-playwright Lope de Rueda (1510?–1565). The entremés, no longer the medieval pageant described above, was now a one-act farce in prose designed to be played between the acts of a comedia. When Timoneda, who was also a bookseller and publisher, arranged Rueda's entremeses for publication, he called them by the Valencian name of *pasos* ("steps"). A typical example of the entremés is Rueda's *Las aceitunas* ("The Olives," date unknown), in which a farming family quarrels prematurely over their plans for spending the money they expect to realize on a grove of olive trees they have just planted. (Cervantes would later carry the entremés to great heights.) Rueda also wrote, usually in prose, Spanish plays of the pastoral type invented by Encina and adaptations of Italian urban comedies. Touring villages and cities, always in a theatrical environment, Rueda was the first truly professional man of the theater in Spain. He was much influenced by his professional rivals, the wandering troupes of the Italian *commedia dell'arte*.

In the last half of the sixteenth century a Humanistic theater arose in Seville. Although known to modern readers only as the author of a Humanist treatise, Juan de Mal Lara (1524–1571) was said—no doubt with exaggeration—to have composed a thousand tragedies, all of which have disappeared. Juan de la Cueva (1550–1610) has left fourteen comedies and tragedies that were published in 1588. In addition to plays on classical themes, he introduced some influential innovations in other plays, such as *La muerte del rey don Sancho y reto de Zamora* ("The Death of King Sancho and the Challenge of Zamora"); he was the first to adapt to the theater subjects taken from Spanish history and the first to make use of traditional ballads. Cueva's impact on later drama in other respects has been questioned, but there seems little doubt that the efforts of the Humanists created an environment in which the still primitive drama of Spain could be made more erudite by a dramatist like Lope de Vega, who, though aware of the liturgical and pastoral legacy coming to him from Encina, was also willing to contract a further debt to the theater of antiquity.

It was about this time—starting in 1565—that the first public theaters, called *corrales,* or "yards," and similar to the innyard theaters of London, were opened in Madrid. Conditions were ripe for the rise of dedicated professional companies. It is probable that Lope de Vega's first play, *Los hechos de Garcilaso de la Vega y moro Tarfe* ("The Deeds of Garcilaso de la Vega and the Moor Tarfe," written between 1579 and 1583), was designed for performance in a corral.

Golden Age. The *Siglo de Oro* (literally, "Golden Century") is in Spanish literary history an elastic term that is sometimes stretched to include the Renaissance but is used here to refer to the great period of Spanish drama in the seventeenth century that is often designated as the Baroque period. The writing of the period bears the imprint of the vigorous renewal of Catholic orthodoxy initiated by the Council of Trent (1545–1564). Indeed, the phrase "theological theater" has been applied to the whole of seventeenth-century drama, whether secular or religious. A powerful moral and dogmatic sense pervades it all, and a strictly Christian view of man's life as a pilgrimage in time—from and to eternity—underlies the poetic world of this drama. The key to its interpretation is the word *desengaño,* which, meaning literally "disillusionment," contains no pessimism but rather the sense of wonderment at the fact that to every man there comes a time when scales are removed from his eyes so that he can perceive his own condition and the world around him in terms of his eternal nature. The closest possible renderings of desengaño are "undeception," "illumination," or "revelation of ultimate truth." Before this moment of spiritual understanding the world appears to be an *engaño* ("deception"), an anarchical confusion, a maze in which man wanders with an imperfect perception of either its reality or its meaning. Comic plays tend to be set wholly in this world of engaño; serious works often begin in it, to emphasize man's

predicament, but the protagonist usually discovers its real nature before the play's end. While this view of man's fate pervades all Baroque literature, it is emphasized in the work of dramatists, like Calderón, who have a very strong moral purpose.

Two major attempts have been made to define the principles governing the dramaturgy of the Golden Age. First, there is that of A. G. Reichenberger, who points to the very important fact that all Spanish comedias follow a movement from "order disturbed" to "order restored." The order to which he refers may be moral, social, or political, but the homogeneity of the poet's world view implies a coherence among the various kinds of order. So, for example, moral disorder implies political disorder. Reichenberger's thesis has proved very helpful in the search for some understanding of the thrust of this drama. Another fruitful attempt to discern a pattern in classical Spanish dramaturgy was made by A. A. Parker, who sees it as a structure governed by five related principles: (1) the primacy of action over character; (2) the primacy of theme over action, with the consequent irrelevance of verisimilitude; (3) dramatic unity in the theme and not in the action; (4) the subordination of the theme to a moral purpose through the principle of poetic justice; and (5) the elucidation of the moral purpose by means of dramatic causality. The comedia is thus seen as essentially a vehicle for conveying a moral. Since the principle of poetic justice operates in it, it ought to follow that all comedias are indeed comedies, for a tragic hero is often punished in excess of his guilt. But Parker does not deny the existence of tragedy in the Spanish theater. His fourth principle compels least conviction when it is applied to tragic actions in many plays of the period.

Lope de VEGA laid the foundation stone of this "new comedy" on the pastoral drama of the sixteenth century. He modified the pastoral drama to permit it to absorb a much greater variety of material: Roman and Spanish history, classical mythology, tales from Italian *novellieri* and Spanish fiction writers, ballads, and so forth. Any plot or historical event might be adapted to his conception of drama. Since he was very prolific, he experimented until he devised the formula that, with few modifications, was accepted by all major playwrights of the century, with the possible exception of Cervantes. This formula is that of the comedia.

A Spanish play of this period consists of three acts, each of about one thousand lines of verse. Traditional Spanish meters and naturalized Italian meters are used with variations in a single play in deference to particular dramatic modes or poetic moods. Prose is reserved for letters and proclamations. The language of the comedia tends toward rhetorical embellishment and wordplay. Asides are often used, and two or three shifts of scene may occur within each act. Some stock characters regularly appear: a pair of lovers (the *galán* and his *dama),* a venerable old man, the king (in serious plays), and always at least one gracioso, or fool. The gracioso, a servant or other ignoble person, makes funny remarks and puns, but his main function is to criticize and debunk the action. In some plays, notably in Lope's later comedies and in those of Juan Ruiz de Alarcón and Agustín

Moreto, the fool manipulates the action by devising tricks to bring about a happy ending.

Lope describes his comedia form in his ironically ambiguous verse treatise *Arte nuevo de hacer comedias en este tiempo* ("New Art of Composing Plays at This Time," pub. 1609). A first reading suggests that he arrived at his formula empirically. To please the mass of playgoers, one must do certain things: mix tragedy and comedy; treat lightly the classical rules for unity; leave the denouement until the very end; and choose verse forms carefully. But there is a theory behind this practice. Lope claims paradoxically to be writing an art about how to achieve anti-art, which he calls nature. His plays, far from being works of art, are works of nature. Just as initially God created the world, so nature continually creates a varied landscape and Lope continually creates varied dramas. The only rule is that the landscape or the play should give pleasure to the beholder. The dramatist thus has total freedom to create as he wishes; he has an obligation to his public to ignore the legislation of Aristotle and Francesco Robortelli, because they aim at the creation of art (which is by definition anti-nature). Lope is not ashamed, as Cervantes' canon was (*Don Quixote,* Part I, Chapter 48) or as Nicholas Boileau would be (*L'Art poétique,* Chant III, lines 39–42), of the Spanish drama's occasional lapse into absurdity as a result of its wild independence of the unities of time and place. Lope

TITLE PAGE FROM A 1605 MADRID EDITION OF MI-
GUEL DE CERVANTES' *Don Quixote (The Northwest Passage,* Roald Amundsen, E. P. Dutton & Co., Inc.)

ends his treatise with a proud assertion that his manner of writing plays is the correct one for his time: "In short, I endorse what I have written, and I recognize that, although my plays would be better if written differently, they would not give as much pleasure; for sometimes what is unregulated gives for that very reason pleasure and delight."

Lope wrote hundreds of plays in accordance with this formula, although not all of them were equally successful. Spontaneity and improvisation produce hit-and-miss results. Where he is successful, it is because of the complexity of his poetic vision and his intuitive grasp of relationships inaccessible to reason or philosophy. *Fuenteovejuna* (written 1612), to take the best known of his plays, is about a revolution, but a revolution motivated less by hatred of the tyrant than by mutual love among the rebels. This great central theme is embroidered with closely connected subthemes based on musical harmony, political and military order, true and false courtesy, honor, social behavior in both its conventional and excessive manifestations, and perhaps a dozen more, all woven into the fabric of Renaissance pastoral bliss threatened by the ugly wild man symbolizing lust, who appears in so much medieval and Renaissance literature. The poetic unity of this complex dramatic structure confers artistic unity on the play. Viewed strictly as an action, *Fuenteovejuna* is loosely constructed. It is always necessary to perceive the primacy of the poetic structure of Lope's plays before one can grasp them as drama. It is, for example, tempting to misinterpret *Fuenteovejuna*—as was done during the Russian Revolution—as a play about a Marxian type of class struggle, but the reader who recognizes the poetic themes will not fall into such gross error.

Lope's dramas, then, are above all plays written by a facile but enormously talented lyric poet. His clear poetic vision protected the best of his work against the dangers implicit in his hasty, spontaneous method of composition. In the last twenty years of his life, however, Lope had second thoughts about his natural anti-art. Spiritual crises in his life forced him to recognize the need for restraining hedonism with discipline and order. The same crises impelled him to adopt an increasingly more responsible attitude toward his writing. As the playboy-cleric settled down to a single mistress, the writer began to supervise the publication of his works and the poet began to see the need to control his lyric flights in drama with a firm artistic organization. Some of the later works were evidently written as therapeutic exercises in self-control by a man whose life and writing were inseparable. They exhibit a much more disciplined craftsmanship, but no corresponding loss of poetic inventiveness. Although he acquired this sense of responsibility late in life, Lope transmitted it, along with his dramatic formula, to his contemporaries and successors.

The greatest of his immediate followers was the Mercedarian friar Gabriel Téllez (1571?–1648), who is known by the pseudonym Tirso de Molina. The pen name is probably composed of a pastoral first name in conjunction with the surname of Luis de Molina (1535–1600), the great Jesuit defender of the doctrine of free will. Indeed, Tirso's drama reflects both his fondness for the pastoral myth (with its implied sense of the superiority of rustic innocence to

TIRSO DE MOLINA (BIBLIOTECA NACIONAL DE MADRID)

urban corruption) and his strong theological interest in the casuistry of free will.

In *El burlador de Sevilla y convidado de piedra* ("The Deceiver of Seville and the Stone Guest," written before 1630) Tirso creates the great modern myth of DON JUAN. The protagonist seduces both shepherdesses and noble ladies of the court. He is dragged down to hell by God's agent, the statue of a man he has killed, not because he is a seducer, but because he takes the name of God in vain. His major error is excessive confidence in God's mercy; certain that he will have plenty of time to repent and be absolved of his sins, he is not prepared to die when his moment of death comes unexpectedly. A complementary play, *El condenado por desconfiado* ("Damned for Lack of Trust," written c. 1620), presents the saintly hermit Paulo, who has the presumption to ask God to reveal to him his fate in the afterlife. The devil, in the guise of an angel, replies that Paulo's fate will be identical with that of a certain Enrico, who turns out to be a swashbuckling gangster who commits all the crimes and sins in the book. In despair, Paulo himself turns to a life of crime so that he shall at least have had the thrills that precede damnation. Enrico, however, has one redeeming virtue: his love for his father. Through his father's intercession, Enrico repents at the time of his execution and is saved, while Paulo's despair of ever being pardoned by God causes him to be damned. These two works, with their emphasis on man's ability to choose his acts and, through these choices, control his fate in eternity, are good examples of the "theological theater" of the Baroque period. *El condenado* belongs to the genre of saints-and-bandits plays that includes such works as Cervantes' *El rufián dichoso* ("The Blessed Pimp," pub. 1615), Mira de Amescua's *El esclavo del demonio* ("The Devil's Slave," pub. 1612), and Calderón's *La*

devoción de la cruz (*Devotion to the Cross*, 1633). These playwrights shared a common assumption that the vital energy needed for sainthood can easily be perverted into criminality of the most horrendous kind and, similarly, that the greatest sinners make the best saints; lukewarm souls, on the other hand, are capable of neither depravity nor holiness.

In *El burlador* Tirso shows his strong political interests. Don Juan is not brought to justice, because of the special treatment accorded him by those members of his family who are the ministers of justice as well as privileged royal favorites. The condemnation of favoritism is a common theme in Tirso's drama and is especially important in the chronicle play *La prudencia en la mujer* ("Prudence in a Woman," written c. 1622). The prudence shown by the queen regent appears to be Machiavellian cunning, but it is really the astuteness inherent in the moral virtue of prudence. The Machiavellian "reason of state" is consistently denounced by the Golden Age dramatists, whose political ideal was the theocratic state.

Like Lope, Tirso also wrote pleasant comedies—such as *Marta la piadosa* ("Pious Martha," written 1615; rewritten 1618) and *El vergonzoso en palacio* ("A Bashful Man at Court," written 1611 to 1612)—in which his portrayal of feminine psychology is much admired by the critics. In fact, Tirso was quite misogynous, so that his title "Prudence in a Woman" is meant to be outrageously paradoxical.

Juan Ruiz de Alarcón (1581?–1639), who was born in Mexico, is usually considered to belong to the school of Lope despite his quite different dramaturgy. His comedies of manners—*La verdad sospechosa* ("Truth under Suspicion," written between 1618 and 1620) and *Las paredes oyen* ("Walls Have Ears," 1617)—are similar to the French classical comedies in their comfortable adjustment to Aristotelian "rules," their urbane pillorying of a man having a single peccadillo, and the presence of a valet who leads the plot with a sure hand and a clear mind to its denouement. In a sense French comedy has its origin in Alarcón's work, for it was Pierre Corneille who effectively launched French comedy when he adapted Alarcón's *La verdad sospechosa* to create *Le Menteur* (1642). Alarcón's production, unlike that of his fellow playwrights, was scant, a mere score of plays. They were not well received either by the public or the intelligentsia.

The Valencian Guillén de Castro (1569–1631) may be thought of as the inspirer of French classical tragedy. Valencia, a Spanish dramatic center second only to the capital, produced a group of classically minded playwrights, of whom Guillén de Castro is the best known. His *Las mocedades del Cid* ("The Cid's Youthful Exploits," pub. 1621), drawn from the rich materials of Spanish balladry, was the source of Corneille's *Le Cid* (1636). Luis Vélez de Guevara (1579–1644) also made a contribution to the French drama but in a later century. His *Reinar después de morir* ("Reigning after Death") inspired Henry de Montherlant's *La Reine morte* (1942). But these influences are just a few examples of the continuing inspiration of Spanish Golden Age drama on that of other countries.

All of these writers stamped their peculiar variations on Lope's pattern for the comedia, but none impressed on it as strong an artistic personality as

Pedro CALDERÓN DE LA BARCA, who was incomparably the greatest intellectual of the Spanish dramatists. He used the same polymetric three-act form, the same dramatis personae, and the same rhetoric, but with these raw materials he created a much more thoughtful, more carefully elaborated, more contrived drama. His drama corresponds very closely to the critic Lionel Abel's definition of metatheater: "pieces about life seen as already theatricalized." The two great themes of metatheater (the world is a stage and life is a dream) actually appear in the titles of two of Calderón's works: *El gran teatro del mundo* (*The Great Theater of the World,* 1633) and LIFE IS A DREAM. The analogy between human life and play acting is a commonplace rooted in classical antiquity and often adduced by Renaissance writers. For Sancho Panza, in *Don Quixote* (Part I, pub. 1605; Part II, pub. 1615) by Miguel de CERVANTES, the comparison is so hackneyed that he proposes instead an analogy between life and a game of chess. In *As You Like It* (c. 1600) Shakespeare gives Jaques his famous speech "All the world's a stage" to stress the multiplicity of parts played by each man. In Spain, however, each man is seen as an essence, a soul, capable of playing only one part from birth to death. Calderón uses this commonplace, not to decorate an idea, but to illustrate Christian sociology and theology. God assigns each man a role to play in his life on the great stage of the world but gives him no script to follow; God judges each improvisation as a performance in itself, without regard to the whole play. It is, therefore, pointless for an actor to prefer one part to another: the role of peasant or beggar is as challenging to him as the role of king or beauty. Man is wrong to complain about his station in life; it is his Christian duty always to strive to fulfill his role to the best of his ability, and all men are equally endowed with the ability to play the part assigned to them. The second theme—life is a dream—is based on the same Christian assumptions. Life is a dream only in the sense that each man dreams he is the character whose part he is playing: "all men dream the lives they lead," says Segismundo in *Life Is a Dream.* Reality exists beyond the grave in eternity. But the unreality of each man's life on earth is no excuse for irresponsible behavior. Life on earth is a rehearsal for eternity, a rehearsal so important that man's ultimate destiny depends on the quality of his performance. In *El gran teatro del mundo* the title of God's play is *Act Well, For God Is God;* in *Life Is a Dream* the refrain is the same maxim: "Act well, for God is God." The two themes are complementary.

Calderón's highly organized, deliberately artificial drama reflects a schematized, very precise understanding of man and his world. Thoroughly Catholic, rooted in both Augustinian and Thomistic thought, his drama is at all times serious and responsible. It constantly draws close to allegory, even in secular plays. In the genre of the auto sacramental, of which Calderón is the leading exponent, the secular themes are seen from a specifically religious—dogmatic and sacramental—point of view and hence are deliberately allegorized. In all his serious plays, however, he is concerned, in a theological sense, with man and his destiny. *Life Is a Dream* shows the process by which a natural man becomes a moral man; *El príncipe constante* ("The Steadfast Prince," 1629) pre-

sents a moral man in the process of becoming a saint; *El mágico prodigioso* ("The Prodigious Magician," 1637) demonstrates the triumph of free will and faith over the almost unlimited power of the devil.

This constant moral earnestness has seemed to some critics to be denied by two segments of Calderón's work. His numerous light comedies (comedias de capa y espada) do not deal with transcendental problems but instead with artificial situations in which young lovers battle against misunderstanding and deception until their true love is rewarded with marriage. But even in these frivolous plays—such as THE PHANTOM LADY and *Casa con dos puertas mala es de guardar* ("A Two-doored House Is Hard to Defend," c. 1629)—the deceptive world is precisely the same as that depicted in his metatheater. In all his plays the world of the senses is unreliable. If the comedias de capa y espada do not lead to tragedy or to moral transformation, it is because the lovers, still unmarried, are not fully committed by their acts; the world of the unmarried provides a second chance. These comedies are a kind of prelude to the serious plays.

The other segment of Calderón's work which is hard to reconcile with his posture as a responsible dramatist consists of the honor plays, in which he presents the world of married people, sacramentally and indissolubly united in a single flesh. For them there can be no second chance. In his *Arte nuevo* Lope had said that "honor cases are the best ones, because they move everyone so powerfully." Lope had written several plays in which conjugal honor is the principal motive, but Calderón's honor dramas are the masterpieces of this genre. In Calderón's typical honor play a husband kills his wife, whom he dearly loves, on the merest suspicion that she is unfaithful or has unfaithful thoughts. The fact that the husband is pardoned for his murder by the king—in his role as the supreme arbiter of justice—has led many critics to believe that Calderón condoned such barbaric acts of vengeance. But it is hardly likely that a man of Calderón's intellectual rigor and probity would regard the honor code as a secular morality, distinct from religious ethics. Instead, recent critics have viewed the honor plays as nothing more nor less than the exemplification of the error that the *lex talionis* ("law of retaliation") could induce, together with the social disruption that ensues from obeying it. In a play like DEVOTION TO THE CROSS, from the saints-and-bandits cycle, Calderón makes it clear that he regarded clemency as infinitely superior to the enforcement of the honor code. The difficulty with this interpretation of the honor plays as tragic illustrations of human error is that the traditional view of the king's role as the dispenser of poetic justice must be abandoned. In all other plays royal justice is impartial and strict; in the honor plays it appears to be perverse, because the king seems to condone a barbarous, cold-blooded murder committed on the basis of wrongly grounded suspicions. The matter is still under debate. The fact is that the honor plays are few in number: SECRET VENGEANCE FOR SECRET INSULT, *El médico de su honra* ("The Painter of his Dishonor," written between 1640 and 1644), and one or two more. They represent that scant part of Calderón's work that was devoted to tragedy. The honor plays are the tragedies of the Baroque, which insisted so much on the aesthetic value of *admiratio:* the audience's soul was to be purged not so much by pity and terror as by pity and amazement at the enormities of which men and nature are capable.

Calderón devoted the second half of his life to writing autos sacramentales for the city of Madrid and spectacles for presentation at the court. Among the latter are his mythological plays and operas. See also THE MAYOR OF ZALAMEA.

Francisco de Rojas Zorrilla (1607–1648), usually included in the school of Calderón, is renowned for his neo-Senecan tragedies. His most famous work, *Del rey abajo ninguno* ("No One Beneath the King," pub. 1650), though of doubtful attribution, is a beautiful play, set in a Baroque pastoral world in imitation of the complex poetry of Luis de Góngora (1561–1627). The hero, García del Castañar, is a nobleman living in the country in the disguise of a rich farmer because his father has been disgraced as a traitor. García's honor is assailed when a courtier attempts to seduce his wife. García has reason to believe—falsely, however—that the seducer is the king, and so he must restrain his desire to take vengeance on the inviolable person of the monarch. After the true identity of the courtier is revealed, García kills him, for he will permit an offense from "no one beneath the King." Here we have the elemental honor situation, but in this play the recasting in dramatic form of such Baroque lyric themes as buried treasure and the questing stranger gives it an unusual beauty and meaning.

Agustín Moreto (1618–1669) is the comic writer among the followers of Calderón. *El lindo don Diego* ("The Foppish Don Diego," pub. 1662) is a character study of an obnoxious but amusing fop whose arrival in Madrid threatens the happiness of two lovers. In *El desdén con el desdén* ("Disdain Turned Against Disdain," pub. 1654), Moreto presents a frigid blue-stocking who is converted into a willing lover after she discovers that she is as much disdained as she had previously disdained her suitors. Moreto, who lacked Calderón's sense of responsibility to art or society, secularized the Spanish drama to the point of irreverence. His art is clever but superficial. He is the precursor of the Versaillesque art of the eighteenth century.

eighteenth century. Although there was no lack of experimentation during the eighteenth century, Spanish drama, nevertheless, declined. It was not transformed by neoclassicism until the second half of the century, although the theorist of Spanish neoclassicism, Ignacio de Luzán (1702–1754), published the first edition of his poetics, *La poética,* as early as 1737. Even in the second half of the century the masses remained loyal to the dramatic art of the Golden Age. Vulgarized rewritings of plays by Lope and Calderón, done by hacks like Luciano Comella (1751–1812), were very popular. In his numerous short *sainetes* ("interludes," successors to the entremeses) Ramón de la Cruz (1731–1794) presented, almost without a plot, the manners of the lower classes of Madrid, reinforcing their sense of their own picturesqueness. The eighteenth-century sainete gave rise to several dramatic forms—subsumed under the label *género chico* ("short genre")—that still flourish today.

The comedia of the Golden Age developed into the tragicomedia when the subtle ironic interplay of tragic and comic elements was replaced by a more sharply defined polarity. Antonio de Zamora (1664–1728) and José de Cañizares (1676–1750) were chiefly responsible for this development, which ultimately led to the neoclassical separation of comedy and tragedy.

The late eighteenth-century playwrights tended to hark back to the pre-Lope theater of the Renaissance for their dramatic theory and practice. They studied and anthologized Renaissance drama; Leandro Fernández de Moratín (1760–1828), in his posthumously published *Orígenes del teatro español* ("Origins of the Spanish Theater"), did much to advance dramatic scholarship.

Moratín wrote five comedies after the fashion of Molière and Carlo Goldoni, strictly in accordance with the classical "rules," in order to ridicule some social vice and applaud the corresponding social virtue. His plays, of which the best known is *El sí de las niñas* ("The Maids' Consent," 1806), are the only ones from this period that enjoy some popularity today. In *El delincuente honrado* ("The Honorable Delinquent," 1774) Gaspar Melchor de Jovellanos (1744–1811) experimented with the sentimental comedy (*comédie larmoyante*) of Denis Diderot. While this play was relatively successful on the boards, it inspired no imitation. Jovellanos, the nearest person in Spain to an *encyclopédiste,* wrote the unsuccessful tragedy *Pelayo* (written 1769; prod. 1792). The most successful eighteenth-century trag-

GASPAR MELCHOR DE JOVELLANOS (AMPLIACIONES Y
REPRODUCCIONES MAS)

edy was *La Raquel* ("Rachel," 1778) by Vicente García de la Huerta (1734–1787). Although it was composed in accordance with neoclassical precepts, this tragedy harked back to the rhetoric and dramaturgy of Calderón. Its subject was a celebrated episode from medieval Spanish history. The story of how Rachel, the Jewish mistress of Alfonso VIII, was killed for reasons of state by some patriotic subjects had been frequently dramatized.

nineteenth century. The neoclassical movement was brought to an abrupt halt by the short-lived revolution of Spanish Romanticism. Over a period of some ten years, following 1835, Romantic playwrights held the Spanish stage with their melodramatic plots constructed partly by imitating French Romantic drama and partly by casting back to the themes and formulas of the Spanish Golden Age. The brief success of some of these plays was prolonged when they were transformed into Italian grand operas.

The first Romantic play to make an impression on the theatergoing public was *Don Alvaro o la fuerza del sino* ("Don Alvaro or the Force of Destiny," 1835, adapted by Giuseppe Verdi as *La forza del destino*), by Angel Saavedra, duke of Rivas (1791–1865). In this play Don Alvaro, the son of an Inca princess, having killed the father of his beloved Leonor, seeks death by service in the Spanish army. The persecuting force of destiny not only keeps him alive but leads him to kill Leonor's elder brother, Carlos. In anguish Don Alvaro enters a monastery, where, eventually, Leonor's younger brother finds him and also, in a suspiciously nearby hermitage, Leonor. A bloodbath finishes them all off and ends the drama. Other plays of this improbable kind were quickly written. Antonio García Gutiérrez (1813–1880) produced *El trovador* ("The Troubadour," Verdi's *Il trovatore*) in 1836. *Los amantes de Teruel* ("The Lovers of Teruel") by Juan Eugenio Hartzenbusch (1806–1880) was produced in the following year. The one Romantic play that has survived without benefit of music is *Don Juan Tenorio* (1844) by José Zorrilla (1817–1893). It presents an even more dissolute Don Juan than Tirso de Molina's original. Zorrilla's Don Juan is saved from hell, not because of his true love for Doña Inés (which might be theologically justifiable), but because she, like the Madonna, beseeches God to save the soul of her scoundrel of a lover. This play, with its massive apparatus of ghostly apparitions, is traditionally performed throughout the Spanish-speaking world to celebrate Halloween. In general, however, the Romantic hero, rebelling against society, hounded to his death by an inexorable and inexplicable fate, was unacceptable to the increasingly bourgeois society of Spanish theatergoers.

A counterrevolution, supporting middle-class values, soon set in with the production of 175 plays by Manuel Bretón de los Herreros (1796–1873). Bretón de los Herreros dabbled in all the theatrical genres, but he is best remembered for his sentimental comedies, such as *Muérete y verás* ("Die and You Will See," 1837). He creates an innocent dramatic world, void of great virtues and great vices. A greater sense of stagecraft is evident in the work of Manuel Tamayo y Baus (1829–1898), who was reared in a family of actors. His technical competence gave him a fleeting popularity. He is remembered today only for his prose play *Un drama nuevo* ("A New Drama," 1867), in which Yorick, an actor in Shakespeare's company, kills his wife's lover during the performance of a new Shakespearean play. Despite his Nobel prize, José de Echegaray (1832–1916) is only occasionally remembered, chiefly for plays like *El gran Galeoto* ("The Great Go-between," 1881— an allusion to the Paolo and Francesca episode in Dante's *Divine Comedy*). Toward the end of the nineteenth century, when thesis plays were all the rage, Benito Pérez Galdós (1843–1920), the great Spanish novelist, adapted some of his novels to the stage. In addition he wrote some original didactic Ibsenite plays, which were considered scandalous in their day. Although he was a more significant novelist than dramatist, he did introduce certain plots and themes that had never before appeared on the Spanish stage. Galdós made use of rudimentary symbolism to convey both his ideal of self-sacrifice and his rejection of all intolerance, especially that of the clergy. From the fictional world of his novels, he brought to the stage his readiness to engage in current controversies and his sense of the tragedy that exists in the life of the common man.

Finally, reference must be made to the género chico, or *teatro por horas* ("a show every hour"), that became very popular in the nineteenth century. The older sainete, now often accompanied by music, gave rise to one-act *zarzuelas* ("operettas"). The three-act zarzuela, which had been brought to perfection by Calderón, was also quite popular in the nineteenth century as an expanded presentation, after the fashion of Ramón de la Cruz, of contemporary life and customs.

twentieth century. The turn of the century wrought no significant change in the theatrical world of Madrid. The middle-class smugness of the theatergoing public was reflected in most of the works offered to them. Spain's abstention from World War I had the effect of prolonging its equivalent of the English Edwardian period until the declaration of the Spanish Republic in 1931. Indeed, the reactionary quality of social and political life under the Franco regime renewed the complacency of theatrical life even after the civil war of 1936–1939. Even today in the theaters of Madrid there is a preponderance of insignificant old-fashioned farces and popular flamenco entertainments calculated to reinforce the public's already firm belief in the superiority of traditional Spanish values. Largely insulated from European innovations, Spanish dramatists have been content on the whole to repeat tried-and-true formulas without experimenting with new ones.

The name that dominated the Spanish theater during the first half of the twentieth century was that of Jacinto BENAVENTE. In the tradition of the prolific Lope and Bretón de los Herreros, Benavente wrote some 170 plays; there was hardly a month when one or two of his works were not being performed in the capital. Aware that "the public cannot bear the idea that serious things may be treated seriously or that its frivolity may be the subject of jokes," he gave playgoers what they wanted: escape into a charming and insignificant dream world. By and large Benavente broke with the nineteenth-century thesis dramas, although in some of his best works, like *La malquerida* ("The Ill-loved One," 1913), he seems to assert a

Freudian interpretation of the incestuous relations between a peasant and his stepdaughter.

Gregorio Martínez Sierra (1881–1947), who wrote in collaboration with his wife, declared himself a disciple of Benavente. Martínez Sierra's masterpiece, *Canción de cuna* (*Cradle Song*, 1911), about the awakening of maternal instincts in a community of nuns, has become a favorite acting vehicle in the English-speaking world. By preference he dealt with the closed circles of convent or family life, but always from the comfortable assumption that men (and especially women) are good souls. His audiences were not at all displeased to learn from his plays that they were richly endowed with faith, hope, and charity. Eduardo Marquina (1879–1946) flattered Spanish patriotism with his modern chronicle plays in verse. The best known of these pageants, *En Flandes se ha puesto el sol* ("The Sun Has Set in Flanders," 1911), is designed to show that a precious and unique Spanish spirit still survives, even though the political empire founded on this ideal has been destroyed by the self-seeking materialism of the rest of Europe.

In a lighter vein Carlos Arniches (1866–1943) perpetuated the sainete with unusually sharp observation of the manners of lower-class Madrid and particularly its racy idiomatic speech. Serafin (1871–1938) and his brother Joaquín (1873–1944) Alvarez Quintero collaborated to compose a large number of sainetes (and comedies which are in effect expanded one-act sainetes) based on the picturesque customs of Andalusia.

In reaction to the theater of Benavente and other extollers of Spanish complacency, some distinguished poets and novelists tried their hand at writing for the experimental theater. The public, by absenting itself, ensured that their efforts were financially unrewarded, and the rigid censorship of recent years has made any performance of their works difficult or impossible. But Spanish lyric poets, who have produced poetry of a high order in this century, are accustomed to the disdain of the masses. Undaunted, they have pursued new forms in the drama that are interesting in their own right.

Antonio (1875–1939) and his brother Manuel (1874–1947) Machado joined forces to write a small number of plays, almost wholly in verse, based on historical or popular themes. To these stereotyped themes they brought a poetic vision that far excelled that of Marquina or the Quintero brothers. The Machados' plays, much less valuable than their lyric poetry, nevertheless exerted some influence on García Lorca's theater. Jacinto Grau (1877–1959), in *El señor de Pigmalión* ("Mr. Pygmalion," 1921), experimented in Spain with a theme associated with Luigi Pirandello and Karel Čapek: the creation of life from inanimate matter. Puppets representing types from Spanish folklore come to life to satirize all that the types stand for. Miguel de Unamuno (1864–1936), like Galdós, transposed his novels and short stories into dramatic form and also composed some original tragedies, including a *Fedra* ("Phaedra," 1911) and a *Medea* (1933). Through the mouths of his dramatic characters, Unamuno reiterated the ideas he had previously expressed in other literary forms. Insisting on the meaninglessness of literary genres, he boldly discarded stage conventions and allowed the unadorned dialogue of his passionate fictional creatures to carry his message. In a slightly precious style Azorín—the pen name of José Martínez Ruiz (1873–1966)—used drama, as he did his essays and novels, to present the past as an indestructible component of present-day life.

The most interesting experiments in drama were conducted by Ramón del Valle-Inclán (1866–1936). His *comedias bárbaras* ("barbaric plays," published in three volumes: 1907, 1908, 1922), written in prose, are set in a gloomy, imaginary version of his native province of Galicia, poeticized by its myths, superstitions, and folklore. The protagonist, a lustful hidalgo, is surrounded by his brawling sons in a life of extreme crudity. In the verse play *La marquesa Rosalinda* ("The Marchioness Rosalind," 1913) and the prose farce *La cabeza del dragón* ("The Dragon's Head," 1914) Valle-Inclán's lighthearted approach presaged the development of his special literary mode, the *esperpento* ("ugly person or thing"). In these plays, like *Los cuernos de don Friolera* ("Sir Trifle's Horns," 1921), Valle-Inclán systematically distorted reality in an attempt to express the tragic sense of Spanish life. Ramón Gómez de la Serna (1888–1963) attempted a similarly grotesque deformation of the world when he pointed to its pathos by means of a refined, almost surrealistic, comic technique. Best known for the novels he wrote and the genre he created (an aphorism based on poetic imagery, which he mysteriously called a *greguería*), he also wrote a few extremely original works for the theater that are almost forgotten today.

All of this experimentation bore fruit in the varied theater of Federico García Lorca. Primarily a lyric poet, Lorca had a practical interest in the theater—puppets and his traveling troupe of students—so that his dramas combine his lyric genius and his talent for theatrical innovation. "The theater," wrote Lorca, "is poetry in the process of becoming human."

Lorca's nine extant plays range from gay farces to stark tragedies. The text of his first play, *El maleficio de la mariposa* (*The Butterfly's Evil Spell*, 1920) has been lost, but a spectator has left a detailed description of it. The plot concerns the fascination that a butterfly holds for a cockroach. Lorca's next play, *Mariana Pereda*, was not produced until seven years later. The work is a lyrical meditation on the life of the Spanish Betsy Ross. (Mariana Pereda sewed a flag for some liberal revolutionaries at the beginning of the nineteenth century.) Poetic fantasy is still the predominant feature of Lorca's two farces, The Shoemaker's Prodigious Wife and *Amor de don Perlimplín con Belisa en su jardín* (*The Love of Don Perlimplín and Belisa in the Garden*, 1931), and also of his puppet play, *Retablillo de don Cristóbal* (*The Frame of Don Cristóbal*, written in 1931). In 1931 Lorca composed *Así que pasen cinco años* (*When Five Years Pass*), an expressionist drama that is by his own admission unperformable; it is concerned with the creation of time by means of dreams and with the interplay between the world of the dead and the world of the living. The last play produced in Lorca's lifetime, *Doña Rosita la soltera o el lenguaje de las flores* (*Doña Rosita the Spinster or the Language of the Flowers*, 1935), is a period drama about the tragic love of a middle-class girl in Granada between 1890 and 1910. The elaborate comparison of

A SCENE FROM FEDERICO GARCÍA LORCA'S *The Shoemaker's Prodigious Wife* (ANTA COLLECTION, WALTER HAMPDEN MEMORIAL LIBRARY AT THE PLAYERS, NEW YORK)

Doña Rosita's life to that of the flowers that her uncle grows in a hothouse provides the pervasive imagery of Lorca's most mature lyrical drama. All of these plays were to some degree experimental, enjoying no great popular success.

Lorca's fame as a dramatist rests on his successful trilogy of peasant tragedies. BLOOD WEDDING is the dramatic presentation, interspersed with lyric scenes, of a feud between two families that is suddenly exacerbated when a bride is abducted on her wedding day. In YERMA (the heroine's name, meaning "sterility") Lorca presents a wife whose intense maternal feeling drives her to kill her impotent and unsympathetic husband. Lorca's masterpiece, THE HOUSE OF BERNARDA ALBA, written in 1936, was not produced until 1945 (in Buenos Aires). Lorca called the play, which is almost entirely in prose, a "documentary photograph." All the characters are women who live confined in the grim house over which Bernarda, the mother, presides tyrannically. When one of Bernarda's daughters succeeds in meeting a young man, Bernarda kills her, triumphing in the knowledge that her daughter has died a virgin. In his peasant plays Lorca won public acclaim for a poetic and tragic drama that ran counter to the plays that were the box-office successes of the time.

Alejandro Casona—the pseudonym of Alejandro Rodríguez Alvarez (1903–1966)—also wrote some interesting plays during the Republican period, but they are a throwback for the most part to the wistful, wishful thinking of Benavente's drama.

Dramatists have had a hard time under the repressive censorship of Franco. Much of their effort has gone into disguising their message under a veil of ambiguities. It is not surprising, under these circumstances, that their message has been on the whole a social one. Antonio Buero Vallejo (1926–   )

despairs of change in Spanish life in his *Historia de una escalera* ("History of an Apartment-House Staircase," 1949) and *Hoy es fiesta* ("Today's a Holiday," 1956). In *En la ardiente oscuridad* ("In Burning Darkness," 1950) he experiments with symbolism; he presents a school for the blind whose inmates, falsely content and secure with their infirmity as a result of the director's constantly optimistic propaganda, finally have their spiritual eyes opened to their existential despair. Alfonso Sastre (1926–   ) also flirts with existentialism. In *Escuadra hacia la muerte* ("Patrol Toward Death," 1953) he depicts the irresponsibility of violence and the dignity of anguish.

Some representative Spanish plays may be read in the following anthologies: Seymour Resnick and Jeanne Pasmantier, eds., *An Anthology of Spanish Literature in English Translation* (1958); Eric Bentley, ed., *The Classic Theatre, III: Six Spanish Plays* (1960); Angel Flores, ed., *Spanish Drama* (1962); and Walter Starkie, ed., *Eight Spanish Plays of the Golden Age* (1964).

There is no historical survey in English of the Spanish theater, but a readable, short account in French is Charles V. Aubrun, *Histoire du théâtre espagnol* (1965). N. D. Shergold, *A History of the Spanish Stage* (1967), while concerned mainly with his original research into stagecraft, discusses incidentally a number of important plays. Richard B. Donovan, C.S.B., *The Liturgical Drama in Medieval Spain* (1958), deals with plays in Latin, but there is some discussion of vernacular plays and their problems. A. A. Parker, in his "Notes on the Religious Drama in Medieval Spain," *Modern Language Review*, XXX (1935), compares the development of the early theaters in Spain and England. The best introduction to *La Celestina* is contained in María Rosa Lida, *Two Spanish Masterpieces: The "Book of*

Good Love" and "The Celestina" (1961). The period
before Lope may be studied in the somewhat dated
J. P. Wickersham Crawford, *Spanish Drama Before
Lope de Vega* (3rd ed., 1967).

A. A. Parker's pamphlet *The Approach to the
Spanish Drama of the Golden Age* (1957) has been
reprinted in *Tulane Drama Review*, IV (1959); designed for the use of secondary school teachers in
England, it expounds in a very succinct, clear way
the author's brilliant insights into the nature of this
drama. A. G. Reichenberger, in "The Uniqueness of
the *Comedia*," *Hispanic Review*, XXVII (1959),
complements Parker's essay. Lionel Abel's *Metatheatre: A New View of Dramatic Form* (1963) is
concerned with serious drama that cannot be classified as tragedy; he illustrates his thesis by reference
to Calderón, and much that he has to say is of particular relevance to the Golden Age theater of Spain.
The peculiar genre of the entremés may be studied in
W. S. Jack's *The Early Entremés in Spain* (1923).

John A. Cook's *Neo-classic Drama in Spain: Theory and Practice* (1959) is a thorough survey of Spanish drama in the eighteenth century. Apart from E.
Allison Peers's somewhat discredited *History of the
Romantic Movement in Spain* (1940), scholars writing in English have understandably neglected Spanish drama of the nineteenth and twentieth centuries.
—B. W.

Spanish America. Although Spanish American
drama properly speaking does not begin until after
the Conquest of the New World, it is important to
recognize that in various areas there existed a tradition of drama that ranged from ritual song and dance
with some dramatic content, through piquant farce,
to the stylized official ritual form of the Incas and,
probably, the Aztecs. The latter form consisted of
epic narrative with chorus and drew its actors from
the higher social and religious strata. The existence
of this drama is corroborated by archaeological data
and by the testimony of the chroniclers of the Conquest, who almost invariably refer to such functions
in terms of the closest Spanish equivalents. This indigenous tradition did not die with the Conquest, but
was adapted by the missionary priests in their cate-
chizing.

Remnants of the original forms, sometimes in an
advanced stage of dramatic development, existed in
some areas of Spanish America until well into the
nineteenth century. The *Rabinal Achi* ("Warrior of
Rabinal") was first transcribed in Guatemala in 1859,
from a performance by the Indians of a remote village. The structure bears little resemblance to drama
in Spanish; the extensive use of song and dance,
ceremonial masks, long speeches of an epic nature,
and ritual sacrifice of the defeated warrior pose a
number of intriguing questions concerning its origin
and what type of dramatic form might have developed had the Conquest not truncated its development. It is clearly pre-Hispanic, and its performance
well into the nineteenth century speaks eloquently of
the strength of the native dramatic tradition. The
Nahuatl-Spanish *Güegüence,* a picaresque farce
whose title is a pun on the terms "venerable old
man" and "mouse," was discovered in Nicaragua in
1874 but probably dates from the late sixteenth or
very early seventeenth century; its structure is Indian, its humor Indian and Spanish.

The Conquest did not entirely obliterate indigenous forms even in the cities. Spanish drama was still
in a rudimentary form in the sixteenth century, and
the priests were quick to adapt it to missionary purposes. Simultaneously, they wrote catechistic works
directly in the native languages. The first plays presented in America in Spanish appear to have been a
series of Corpus Christi festivals in Mexico City in
1526, only five years after the definitive conquest of
the city. The actors of the missionary works were Indians, and they must have given a considerable native coloring to works that were not entirely removed
from their own tradition. The only preserved texts
are Mexican; typical is the *Adoración de los reyes*
("Adoration of the Wise Men," 1587?), a free
adaptation of a Valencian AUTO SACRAMENTAL. Though
this missionary theater declined toward the end of
the century, it subsisted in the folklore of northern
Mexico and the American Southwest until modern
times. A more learned, if less dramatic, form was the
exercises in rhetoric and declamation performed in
the schools; written by students, they were dialogues,
usually on sacred themes, in Latin, Spanish, or a mixture of both. Another type of ecclesiastical drama is
represented by the *Triunfo de los santos* ("Triumph
of the Saints," 1579), a historical work in the theological Humanist vein, with obvious influences of
Seneca and the Renaissance allegory.

At about this time profane theater appeared, although almost invariably in connection with a civic
or religious festival. Fernán González de Eslava
(1534–?1601) wrote a number of lost profane works
and twenty-four religious plays, primarily allegorical. They often reveal a considerable lyric delicacy,
and there are hints of an indigenous influence in several of the allegories. More lasting are his *entremeses*, brief comic one-acters of a popular and regional character, with a real sense of theater and
vivacious humor. The priest and Latinist Cristóbal
de Llerena (1540?–?1611) is the author of a picturesque farce satirizing the corruption and ineptitude of the Dominican civil authorities; it is an interesting combination of Renaissance learning and the
popular appeal typified by the fool of Spanish comedy. The first play by an author born in the New
World is also the work of a priest, Juan Pérez Ramírez (1545–?); his *Desposorio espiritual entre el
pastor Pedro y la iglesia Mexicana* ("Spiritual Wedding Between the Shepherd Peter and the Mexican
Church," 1574) is in the tradition of the Spanish pastoral eclogues.

By 1600 there were theaters of a sort in Lima and
Mexico City, and drama was rapidly becoming a part
of life in these cosmopolitan centers. The works were
drawn almost exclusively from the Spanish stage, and
the occasional original works by colonial playwrights
were only pallid reflections. A curious exception is
Juan Ruiz de Alarcón (1580?–1639); although born
in Mexico, his career in the theater was entirely
Spanish, and his works were staged in Mexico only
after his success in Spain. Alarcón is usually considered one of the major figures of the Spanish Golden
Age, although a substantial body of critical opinion
holds that he is also properly considered a Mexican.

The persistence of the allegorical religious tradition is visible in the brief *Auto del triunfo de la
Virgen* ("Auto of the Triumph of the Virgin," 1620)

by the Mexican priest Francisco Bramón. The simple design of the auto is relieved by the remarkably individualized characters. The overwhelming influence of Spanish playwright Pedro Calderón de la Barca stifled originality on the professional stage, with the exception of the Mexican Matías de Bocanegra (1612–1668) and the Peruvian Juan de Espinosa Medrano (1639?–1688). Bocanegra's work was lost until the recent discovery of his *Comedia de San Francisco de Borja* ("Comedy of St. Francis Borgia," 1640), in which an anguished meditation on the fragility of life relieves the stylized formalism of the play. Espinosa Medrano's *Amar su propia muerte* ("To Love One's Death") is indistinguishable from any other ornate imitation of Calderón, but in the *Auto sacramental del hijo pródigo* ("Sacramental Auto of the Prodigal Son"), written in Quechua, he achieved a simple realism and popular tone that are doubly impressive in contrast to the sumptuosity of the prevailing dramatic currents.

In the atmosphere of official and intellectual conformity, intolerance, and economic and political centralization in Spain and the renewed Inquisitorial zeal that characterizes the late seventeenth century, drama in Spanish was reduced to a mere formula, and the more or less inept imitators of Calderón attempted to conceal their lack of originality by creating purely external displays. It is startling to find coexisting with this decadence one of the most original artists and thinkers in Spanish America, the Mexican nun Sor Juana Inés de la Cruz. Although best known for her voracious intellectual thirst and her brilliant achievements in poetry, Sor Juana is also the best Spanish American dramatist of her time. *Amor es más laberinto* ("Love the Greater Labyrinth," date unknown), written in collaboration with Juan de Guevara, follows the complicated Baroque formula—extreme elaboration, a complicated plot with one or more subplots, and ornate versification—but *Los empeños de una casa* ("The Zeal of a House," date unknown) is a delightful filigree that both uses the formula and plays with it. This highly personal humor, so characteristic of Sor Juana, is at its best in her *Sainete segundo* ("Second Sainete," date unknown), remarkable for its open laughter at the world of seventeenth-century theater. Another facet of her multiple creative talent is the sacramental auto *El divino narciso* ("The Divine Narcissus," date unknown), a work of lovely lyric symbolism and quite probably the best of its kind written in America.

A minor contemporary of Sor Juana, the embittered Peruvian Juan del Valle y Caviedes (1645–?1697), is best known as a satirical poet. His three witty dramatic satires on love are of interest for their sardonic humor set within a courtly structure and for the ironic disillusion characteristic of much Peruvian poetry and drama.

In the first half of the eighteenth century the repressive censorship that hampered new ideological and cultural currents continued, although the descendants of the Spanish *comedia*—spectacles with elaborate trappings but little dramatic interest—were increasingly rivaled by French works. By the end of the century, the dominant star was French. Liberal authorities in Madrid had softened censorship to the point that French drama and even the works of the *encyclopédistes* circulated in printed form. Even the constant church-inspired polemics on the legitimacy and morals of the theater were unable to deter the lively interest, and permanent theater buildings were erected in nearly all sizable cities. This flourishing, however, was double-edged. The stages were almost bare of American plays; the programs were composed almost exclusively of Spanish plays of the Golden Age and the eighteenth century, especially plays by Calderón and Agustín Moreto. Ideological control had not loosened sufficiently to permit many French works to be staged, however much they may have influenced some Spanish authors. Despite considerable theatrical activity, there is little of interest in the theater establishment.

Perhaps the most successful commercial exponent of the decadent Baroque was the Mexican Eusebio Vela (1688–1737), actor, author, and impresario. In his three extant works he makes great use of spectacular trickery, such as storms, shipwrecks, and volcanos. The curious meeting of the clumsy melodrama of the decaying Spanish tradition and the incipient French influence is visible in the work of the Peruvian Pedro de Peralta Barnuevo (1664–1743). Although his best work is found in several brief satires, Peralta Barnuevo's *La Rodoguna* (1719?), a clumsy adaptation of Corneille's *Rodogune* (1644), and two short works based on incidents in Molière's *The Imaginary Invalid* (1673) and *The Learned Ladies* (1672) point the way to the neoclassical currents of the end of the century. Amid this ocean of conventional mediocrity, *El príncipe jardinero y fingido Cloridano* ("The Gardener Prince and Pretended Cloridano," 1733?), by the Cuban Santiago Pita (?–1755), is a lively and charming comic fantasy. Almost a compendium of Baroque dramatic procedures, and probably adapted from an Italian work by Giacinto Andrea Cicognini, *El príncipe jardinero* overcomes the artificialities of Baroque drama by its lyric tone and the sprightly activities of the traditional servant figures.

Despite such occasional pleasures, the real joy of the eighteenth century is found in the ubiquitous popular theater. The Peruvian Fray Francisco del Castillo (1716–1770) wrote conventional longer works, but his entremeses in the piquant traditional vein reflect the bohemian world he knew so well. An increasing regional consciousness is visible in such brief satirical pieces as *El charro* ("The Cowboy," date unknown) and *Los remendones* ("The Menders," date unknown) by the Mexican José Agustín de Castro (1730–1814). *El amor de la estanciera* ("The Love of the Ranch Girl") is a direct antecedent of the Argentine rural theater of a century later. Written between 1787 and 1792 and attributed to the Argentine Juan Bautista Maciel, its rural setting, dialectical speech, and animosity toward the city and immigrants are early manifestations of a social situation that was to explode in the theater and dominate the Río de la Plata stage for decades.

Certainly the most polemical of colonial dramas is *Ollantay*, a drama of rebellion and love among the Incas, whose manuscript in Quechua was discovered in 1837. Zealous partisans of the glories of Incan culture have gone so far as to affirm that *Ollantay* is an almost pure, authentic pre-Hispanic drama; others have seen it as a rewriting during colonial times of an ancient story well documented by early chroniclers.

The most reasonable theory is that *Ollantay* was written about 1780 to honor the rebellious chieftain José Gabriel Condorcanqui, and its author may well be one Father Valdez, a supporter of Condorcanqui. The play is certainly based on an ancient and widely known tale, but the division into scenes and acts, the changes of scene, the presence of characters straight out of a Golden Age comedia, the use of typical Spanish verse forms that did not exist in ancient Quechua, anachronisms, and a stage of linguistic evolution impossible in a work written prior to the Conquest are convincing evidence. Added proof that the play was written after the Conquest is the fact that it glorifies a commoner's revolt, while the Incan empire had a firmly authoritarian character, and open political eulogy of the ruling class pervaded its dramatic pageantry. Oddly, the furious debate about the work's supposed authenticity has obscured the fact that it is a drama of considerable aesthetic worth in a century not notable for such values.

The early years of the nineteenth century mark the definitive triumph of neoclassicism; the favorite authors were Joseph Addison, Vittorio Alfieri, and, among the Spanish, Moreto and Manuel José Quintana. Further, the political unrest that culminated in the War of Independence and the turbulence of the postrevolutionary period caused a severe decline in the theater. An important exception was Argentina, where the new government was quick to see the theater's propaganda possibilities; in 1817 it established the Society of Good Taste, with the double objective of elevating public taste with a steady diet of rational neoclassicism and using the theater as a political arm. The vast majority of the works presented were fleeting indeed, but *Tupac Amarú* (1821), a Rousseauan version of the rebellion of Condorcanqui by the Peruvian Luis Ambrosio Morante (1782–1836), is still of interest. In spite of Morante's neoclassical Jacobinism and rhetorical baggage, there is a real nucleus of dramatic power. The bulk of Spanish American neoclassical drama, however, suffered from political virulence or languid aesthetics; both contained a strong infusion of diluted Indianism, which is more often comic than dramatic for the reader of today. Upon occasion a faint glimmer of pre-Romanticism lightened the neoclassic pedestrianism. The artificiality of Spanish American neoclassical drama is underlined by contrast with the broad humor of *Las convulsiones* ("Convulsions," 1828), adapted by the Colombian Luis Vargas Tejada (1802–1829) from Albergati Capacelli's *Convulsioni;* while his five lifeless tragedies lie justly forgotten, *Las convulsiones* was recently produced with great success.

Romantic drama was profoundly influenced by Spanish and French playwrights; the stage was dominated by García Gutiérrez, the duke of Rivas, Victor Hugo, and Dumas père. The majority of playwrights were poets or novelists who wrote sporadically for the theater. Further, the special political and, in some cases, aesthetic conditions of the various regions conferred a local coloring on the general development, which proceeded from pseudoclassicism through Romantic melodrama to the critical portrayal of regional traits, known as *costumbrismo.* The civil turmoil and economic chaos that followed independence and the lack of a large potential audience with the means and inclination to attend theater made a stable drama impossible in all but a few large cities.

The works of the Mexican Ignacio Rodríguez Galván (1816–1842) could well serve as models of the Spanish American Romantic drama. The historical play *Muñoz, visitador de México* ("Muñoz, Inspector of Mexico," 1838) is based on the deeds of an infamous royal inspector; its violent action, abductions, murders, and tears are typical of the Romantic period, but they are also fairly close to historical fact. A far better dramatist was another Mexican, Fernando Calderón (1809–1845), most of whose work lies in the same line of heroic medieval drama. This furious Romanticism is totally lacking in his best play, the light satirical comedy *A ninguna de las tres* ("None of the Three," 1839?). Written as a sequel to Bretón de los Herreros' *Marcela o ¿a cuál de las tres?* (1831), *A ninguna de las tres* pokes delightful fun at the deficient education of women, affectation, romantic sentimentality, and the frivolous pursuit of the latest French styles. It is one of the finest works in the line of didactic neoclassicism.

The Cuban Gertrudis GÓMEZ DE AVELLANEDA is considerably less passionate in her dramas than in her flamboyant life. She avoided the truculent dialogue and rhetorical baggage of her contemporaries and suppressed the gratuitous violence and routine plot. Her works are historical, but she is concerned primarily with internal conflict, to the extent that *Baltasar* (*Belshazzar*, 1858), *Munio Alfonso* (1844), and others are virtually psychological studies. *La hija de las flores, o Todos están locos* ("The Child of the Flowers, or They Are All Mad," 1852) is a charming comedy that harks back to Lope de Vega's

GERTRUDIS GÓMEZ DE AVELLANEDA (UNION DE ESCRITORES Y ARTISTAS DE CUBA)

agile structure and avoids the heavy-handedness of much Romantic comedy.

Aside from the dramatists mentioned, Romantic theater was a routine copy of Spanish and French models, rarely of more than local significance. The exchange of medieval European locales for a pre-Conquest American setting, common to many dramatists, altered externals only, and special circumstances, such as the Rosas dictatorship in Argentina or the Polemic of 1842 in Chile, while of fundamental importance in other genres, produced little of lasting consequence in the drama. Meanwhile, virtually ignored by the cultivated classes, several nations were developing a vigorous and largely unwritten popular theater that was to flourish in the late nineteenth century, decay in the early twentieth, and live again in mid-century in the work of young playwrights seeking a native form in their countries' theatrical past.

Neoclassicism and Romanticism do not fall nicely into separate chronological periods. Fernando Calderón, obviously a Romantic, wrote his best play in the neoclassical tradition; the Mexican Manuel Eduardo de Gorostiza (1789–1851) was a neoclassicist to the end, decidedly didactic and almost totally lacking in any regional note, although he occasionally abandoned such conventions as the three unities. His best works are comic lessons of tolerance and common sense. Gorostiza's best-known play, *Contigo pan y cebolla* ("With You, Bread and Onions," 1830), uses his pet trick of a pretended intrigue to which some characters and, of course, the audience are privy to satirize the romantic dream of a poor but noble husband. Gorostiza's characters are often lacking in human individualism and he used the same tricks repeatedly, but his wit places him among the best comic playwrights in Spanish.

In Peru neoclassicism tended to lead directly into satirical costumbrismo, a frequent attitude in Peruvian drama from the early colonial period until today. Felipe Pardo y Aliaga (1806–1868) produced a series of implacably conservative comedies that reflect his aristocratic European leanings; they are still of interest because of the measured humor. Gayer, more enchanted with life is Manuel Ascensio Segura (1805–1871), who used the structure of the classical unities, the rules of versification, and the didacticism of a moral in a lighthearted fashion to ridicule absurdity. *El sargento Canuto* ("Sergeant Canuto," 1839) is a splendid *miles gloriosus* gone to seed; *Ña Catita* ("Missy Catita," 1856) is an acid portrait of an old procuress.

Costumbrismo is an outgrowth of Romantic interest in the picturesque, and as the nineteenth century drew to a close, this satire of social realities became the dominant mode. Its strength, however, is its own limitation; it is highly regional, relies on local color, and seldom transcends this localism. Even as skilled a comic author as the Chilean Daniel Barros Grez (1834–1904) tended to rely heavily on regional customs, dialect, and so forth, for his effects, although he overcame these limitations in his best work. His satires of provincial social-climbing and middle-class amorous frivolity include *Cada oveja con su pareja* ("Every Sheep with Its Mate," 1879), *El casi casamiento* ("The Almost Wedding," 1881), and *Como en Santiago* ("As in Santiago," 1875). From costumbrismo to overt realism is a relatively small step, although the persistence of Romanticism and the origins of costumbrismo make nineteenth-century realistic drama an amalgam of the two movements, particularly under the influence of the Spanish playwright Echegaray. Typical is the Mexican José Peón y Contreras (1843–1907), whose experience as a physician and analyst provided the raw material for his plays. He eliminated many of the Romantic excesses, but his plots are schematic and his characters individualized only in terms of their immediate problems. The violent subject matter and an Echegarayan weakness for verbal fireworks at climactic moments make his works only a foreshadowing of realistic drama, which is largely a phenomenon of the twentieth century.

In spite of political and cultural differences between nations within Spanish America, the development of drama is a process that shows strong similarities from one region to another. At the beginning of the twentieth century the stage was dominated by a rather unfortunate blend of realism, often of a social character, that echoed a moribund, decrepit Romanticism, regional costumbrismo, and the Spanish *género chico*—short plays, usually with music, that presented a sentimentalized vision of the life of Madrid's lower classes. The emphasis was different from one country to another, but the general panorama was the same, with the addition of a local variant of the género chico that became an important element in several areas, notably Argentina and Cuba. The next stage was a spurt of experimentation, usually in small private theaters, clubs, or even private homes. From place to place this movement showed a very different local coloring, but despite these variants, it was a coherent step in the process. The dates of the establishment of key experimental groups vary somewhat: Mexico, 1928; Argentina, 1930; Cuba, 1928. The process was delayed in some areas, and in a few it is still gestating, but it is the same process. Finally, about 1950, a third group appeared, those who are writing for the theater today. For purposes of convenience in handling such a substantial body of material, it is easiest and at the same time distorts least what is really a continuous process to divide the century at 1950.

The greatest achievement of realism and naturalism in Spanish American drama took place in the River Plate region of Argentina and Uruguay during the late nineteenth and early twentieth centuries. Its roots are in the rural gaucho tradition, and the glorification of the gaucho himself, the disdain for the city, and a strong anti-Italian tone spoke directly to a mass of people for whom the growing metropolis, the wealthy oligarchy, and the waves of recent immigrants had heightened the ancient quarrel between the capital and the provinces. Professional playwrights soon adapted this crude melodrama to the commercial stage, where its success continued unabated. In the hands of the Argentines Martiniano Leguizamón (1858–1935) and Nicolás Granada (1840–1915) the crude melodrama began to make the transition to social naturalism, a step that was consummated by the Uruguayan Florencio SÁNCHEZ, who also gave it a strong urban coloring.

Many of Sánchez' twenty extant works deal with problems of rural life; *M'hijo el dotor (My Son the*

Lawyer, 1904) shows the corruption of moral standards by life in the metropolis, and in *La Gringa* (*The Immigrant Girl,* 1904) the ancient rural system is destroyed by the austere customs of the new immigrants. The best of this rural cycle is *Barranca abajo* (*Down the Gully,* 1905), a moving laconic tragedy of the annihilation of an old gaucho by an alien way of life. In other works Sánchez focused on the degradation of the urban slum. Sánchez' theater is frankly social, influenced by Italian naturalism, André Antoine, and Ibsen's thesis plays, with a heavy dose of the philosophical socialism prevalent in Buenos Aires. His dramas are not literary and sometimes reflect an almost naïve belief in the possibility of harnessing the forces that were sundering his society, but in his best works, such as *La Tigra* (*The Tigress,* 1907) and *Barranca abajo,* he created vivid portraits of human beings suffering with dignity and compassion.

Other important figures include the Uruguayan Ernesto Herrera (1886–1917) and the Argentine Julio Sánchez Gardel (1879–1937). Although neither is of Sánchez' stature, both created works of interest in the same dramatic vein. River Plate drama became increasingly urban with the Argentines Roberto Payró (1867–1928) and Gregorio de Laferrère (1867–1913). By far the best technician of the group, Laferrère's forte lay in the satire of human foible; *Locos de verano* ("Summer Lunatics," 1905) is a joyous gallery of the ridiculous and *Las de Barranco* ("The Barranco Women," 1908) destroys the hypocrisy of a middle-class family on the edge of financial ruin.

A local variant of the género chico known as the *sainete orillero* achieved enormous popularity toward the end of the nineteenth century and maintained this hold on theater audiences until the 1930's. The plays were melodramatic versions of a basic formula that pictured the vices and deprivation of the metropolitan slums created in large part by immigration, industrialization, and the beginnings of the migration from the provinces. They were violent and full of posturing, but their simplistic vision of a difficult reality and their emphasis on music, notably the tango, made an immediate impact on the masses.

The dominance of this sainete form and the decay of the rural tradition produced an almost total vacuum in serious drama by 1930. The same year marks a decisive moment, the appearance of the so-called independent theater, whose origins lie in socialist and anarchist workers' clubs where it began as an indoctrinational technique. Although it arose as a direct consequence of the repressive Uriburu government in Argentina and the economic crisis of 1930 and has retained a strong social orientation, it soon transcended its immediate sources and became an important force in the drama, a position that it retains today. The independent theater is not, strictly speaking, an experimental movement in the usual sense, since many of its most important figures were and are simultaneously active in the commercial theater. The hallmark of the movement is its insistence on a professional attitude, its rejection of the box office and the star system, and its subordination of the individual to a team concept. Although the independent theater's chief contribution at this point was in production and

training, one playwright of importance was the Argentine Roberto Arlt (1900–1942). Deeply influenced by Luigi Pirandello, Arlt wrote eight works that demonstrate his preoccupation with the relations between reality and fiction, sanity and madness. *Saverio el cruel* ("Saverio the Cruel," 1936) oscillates between levels of psychological reality in a relentless portrait of human frailty and cruelty.

The most famous of Argentine dramatists is Samuel Eichelbaum (1894–   ); although not directly a product of the independent movement, he collaborated closely with it. Eichelbaum's great concern is with morality and ethics; his characters are trapped in spiritual dilemmas. *Un guapo del novecientos* ("A Tough Guy of the '90s," 1940) is the history of a *guapo,* an enforcer for a political boss; his loyalty leads him to kill his leader's adulterous wife, only to be faced with an insoluble problem— whether he, not being the injured party, had the moral right to kill. The ethical code in question may be narrow, but it is authentic and is authentically resolved. Eichelbaum's fascination with moral problems often leads him to ignore dramatic unity; some of his best works are weakened by unlikely time lapses, and decisive actions have a habit of taking place offstage. Despite these lapses, many of his works have genuine dramatic interest, and he is one of the most important Spanish American playwrights of his generation.

A totally different type of theater is found in the work of Conrado Nalé Roxlo (1898–   ), a Uruguayan whose plays, like those of Sánchez, were first presented in Buenos Aires. Isolated from the major currents of River Plate drama, Nalé Roxlo has written few plays, and these almost entirely from legendary or mythological sources. *La cola de la sirena* ("The Mermaid's Tale," 1941) is an uneven poetic version of the love of man for mermaid; in this, as in other works, Nalé Roxlo is best at creating a delicate atmosphere. In *Judith y las rosas* ("Judith and the Roses," 1956) he treats Holophernes and Judith with comic insight, but his best play is an enchanting poetic farce, *Una viuda difícil* ("A Difficult Widow," 1944). The qualities in Nalé Roxlo's dramas are the wit and delicacy that have made him a leading poet and humorist.

Although the Mexican movement followed a more orthodox course and produced nothing comparable to the independent theater, the results have in many ways been similar. An early effort known as the Group of Seven (1925) was largely unsuccessful, but in 1928 an informal group of young poets and painters established Ulysses Theater, which was soon metamorphosed into Orientation, which effected a radical change in the Mexican drama. Exotic and experimental, Ulysses was successful only while it had its amateur status; the first professional venture was a resounding failure. Formation of Orientation in 1932 with government funds as a training school for actors was the key support of the group, and although it disbanded after a few years, its members had both developed their own technical craft and helped form a generation of actors capable of handling the demanding roles of modern foreign drama. Just as the independent theater compensated, at least in part, for the tedium of commercial theater, graduates of Orientation and other experimental groups joined together as Theater of Mexico to keep drama alive during the nearly disastrous period of 1938 to 1942.

The nominal leader of the Ulysses-Orientation movement was Celestino Gorostiza (1904–1966), who, in a series of government positions, was extremely influential in stimulating theater. In the 1930's, influenced by French drama in his handling of dreams and the unconscious, he wrote a succession of avant-garde works; his longer works, written twenty years later, are realistic and satirical. Although Salvador Novo (1904–   ) has written almost all of his substantial body of dramatic works after 1950, his avant-gardism, close association with the Ulysses group, and his role as teacher of the recent generation place him in the pre-1950 movement. His mordant wit was applied to the hypocrisy of the wealthy class (*La culta dama,* "The Cultured Lady," 1951), the corruption of the press (*A ocho columnas,* "Eight Column Head," 1956), and the worlds of psychoanalysis and the theater (*Yocasta, o casi,* "Jocasta, or Nearly," 1962). Recently, he has deflated the heroic past in *La guerra de las gordas* ("The Fat Girls' War," 1963), a polished comedy of Aztec manners, and *Ha vuelto Ulises* ("Ulysses Has Returned," 1962). His finest play is *Cuauhtémoc* (1962), about the last Aztec emperor, in which Novo thoughtfully reassesses the past.

The most important member of Ulysses was Xavier Villaurrutia (1903–1950), creator of a lucid, intellectual theater. His work includes the provocative *Autos profanos* ("Profane Mysteries"), five one-act plays written between 1933 and 1937, and a series of witty dramas of the middle class, characterized by a style that brought him commercial success without his having to sacrifice his professional standards. Sophisticated without being slick, Villaurrutia dissected complex relationships. Some idea of what he might have accomplished had not the compromise in terms of form been necessary is found in *Invitación a la muerte* ("Invitation to Death"), written in 1940 and published in 1944, but first staged in 1947. *Invitación a la muerte* is a contemporary Mexican *Hamlet* in which the protagonist is obsessed with death and the anguish of existence. It is poetic theater at its best, a lucid nightmare from which its tormented protagonist can find no escape.

Contemporary and friend of the Ulysses-Orientation group but stubbornly independent, Rodolfo Usigli is widely regarded as Spanish America's finest dramatist. A sardonic moralist, he is akin to George Bernard Shaw in his critical vision of national error and private foolishness. His intransigence provoked critical enmity and public apathy until 1951, when his *El niño y la niebla* ("The Child and the Mist," written 1936) was an instant hit, more because of its sensational melodramatic theme than for any abrupt change in Usigli's work. *Jano es una muchacha* ("Janus Is a Girl," 1952) cemented Usigli's popularity in his own nation, despite its vigorous assault on the sexual hypocrisy that Usigli finds rampant in Mexican life. Two works stand out as examples of his highly personal vision of his nation and his technical capacity: *El gesticulador* (*The Gesticulator*) and *Corona de sombra* (*Crown of Shadows*). The former, written in 1937, was not performed until ten years later because of its supposed antirevolutionary character, although it is nothing of the sort. It is instead a

searching speculation on the Mexican's inability or unwillingness to perform as a human being without playing a role. *Corona de sombra,* written in 1943, was a failure at its first production in 1947, although it is now hailed as perhaps Usigli's best work. His skillful use of contrasting levels of time and his heterodox view of the fleeting empire of Carlota and Maximilian as a necessary step in Mexican history make it a provocative and moving drama which substantiates Usigli's high standing.

Chilean drama during most of the first half of the century was dominated by the realistic tradition that frequently included a social message. In the last quarter of the nineteenth century there was considerable activity in comic costumbrismo, and in the early twentieth century this activity focused on a realistic examination of national problems. The three leading dramatists of this period are Armando Moock (1894–1942), Antonio Acevedo Hernández (1886–1962), and Germán Luco Cruchaga (1894–1936). Moock, who early in life moved to Buenos Aires because of its greater economic rewards for the successful playwright, achieved a considerable reputation and success with sentimental comedies of middle-class life. His best work was his simple comedies of provincial purity, but in these and his urban plays, often in the style of the *boulevard* plays, sentimentality and simplistic psychology mark him as a moderately talented commercial success. Acevedo Hernández was a naturalist and an anarchist, and the influence of his masters Sánchez, Maxim Gorky, and Piotr Alekseyevich Kropotkin is visible in his aggressively obvious denunciations of urban misery and rural backwardness. The best work in this realistic vein is *La viuda de Apablaza* ("Apablaza's Widow," 1928) by Luco Cruchaga, whose antiquated technique and sentimental regionalism do not obscure the violent power of his rural Phaedra.

Despite the efforts of these and other dramatists to maintain the realistic tradition, Chilean drama found itself in an unstable state by 1930. The foundation in 1914 of the Society of Dramatic Authors and the creation of the first professional Chilean company in 1918 are symptomatic of the real effort to avoid disaster, but the financial crisis of 1929 to 1934 prevented any consolidation of their activities.

This precarious existence characterizes the Cuban theater as well; touring Spanish companies performed the works of the omnipresent Echegaray and Zorrilla, and in place of an organic national drama, cynical commercialism existed. Several experimental companies stimulated interest during the second decade of the twentieth century, but their economic failure, public apathy, and a singularly distressing political situation put an end to their activities. An additional factor was the *teatro bufo,* a Cuban version of the género chico, which was enormously popular until well into the 1930's. Despite this depressing prospect, several dramatists stubbornly wrote, even though their work was only occasionally performed. In his lengthy career José Antonio Ramos (1885–1946) shows influences ranging from Ibsen to Pirandello. His technical experimentation was sometimes incapable of containing his verbalism and social concerns, but in *Tembladera* ("The Quaking Land," 1917) he channeled his anger into a complex denunciation of exploitation of the land. Others such as

Gustavo Sánchez Galarraga (1893–1934), Ramón Sánchez Varona (1893–   ), and Luis A. Baralt (1892–   ) helped keep drama alive, if not flourishing, and in 1928 Baralt headed an experimental group known as The Cave, which in turn led to considerable activity beginning in 1941. This group, like the corresponding Chilean movement begun in the same year, and the Puerto Rican activity of 1938, did not produce new authors until about 1950.

By 1950 the experimental movement was firmly established in Argentina, Uruguay, Mexico, Chile, Cuba, and Puerto Rico. In all these nations it had begun to serve as a training ground for new dramatists, and in some it was as solidly based as the commercial theater. Broadly speaking, these new playwrights are open to all the currents of contemporary theater; Bertolt Brecht, Arthur Miller, Eugène Ionesco, Samuel Beckett, and others have left their mark. Conventional realism has all but disappeared; like his masters of the preceding generation, the new playwright is an experimentalist with forms. Noticeably absent is the rural setting; the new theater is urban and cosmopolitan in theme as well as in technique. All this, however, does not mean that it is a pallid imitation of foreign influences, for the young dramatist has an almost overriding concern: the meaning of being a Spanish American today. This means, obviously, a social theater, but not one of propaganda; the Spanish American dramatists are too concerned with the search for the meaning of their own and their nations' existence to be concerned with propagandizing.

The most significant and vital voices in the Argentine and Uruguayan drama today have sprung directly from the independent theaters, which continue to be an effective force. Uruguay was almost totally dependent on the Argentine stage for its sources until the break in relations in 1945 forced the development of a purely Uruguayan movement, which is closely related to the Argentine. Economic and political problems in both nations have given a marked coloration to recent drama, prolonging the original tone that characterized the independent movement at its beginning.

The simultaneous première by commercial and independent groups in 1949 of *El puente* ("The Bridge") by Carlos Gorostiza (1920–   ) is usually regarded as the beginning of the new theater in Buenos Aires. *El puente* was written with a complex structure in which the second and fourth acts duplicate the action of the first and third from a different point of view to contrast the life of differing social classes. In later works, Gorostiza has been preoccupied with metaphysical themes, particularly man's responsibility for evil (*El pan de la locura*, "The Bread of Madness," 1958). His most recent play, *Los prójimos* ("The Neighbors," 1966), pillories man's commitment to his own trifling concerns. Based on the Kitty Genovese murder in New York, which neighbors saw and ignored, *Los prójimos* contrasts the biblical flavor of its title (the normal word for a neighbor is quite different) with the self-centered aimlessness of modern civilization. Gorostiza is one of the few writers from the independent theater to use realism consistently.

The Argentine Agustín Cuzzani (1924–   ) possesses great imagination and a vivid sense of the the-ater; in each of his works he assails some aspect of society by using a highly personal idiom and employing lively theatrical effects that sometimes degenerate into trickery. *Una libra de carne* ("A Pound of Flesh," 1954) and *El centroforward murió al amanecer* ("The Center Forward Died at Dawn," 1955) show Cuzzani at his best: violently political, surprising, sometimes shocking, but always imaginative. Like Cuzzani, Andrés Lizárraga (1919–   ) regards the theater as a tool for social reform, a conviction shared by many contemporary dramatists. His most impressive work is the Brechtian *Trilogía sobre mayo* ("Trilogy About May"), particularly *Santa Juana de América* ("Saint Joan of America," 1960); his use of rapid scenes, flashbacks, and "alienation effect" are particularly successful in communicating the spare and violent epic feeling of his vision of the struggle for independence.

A number of other capable dramatists have appeared in recent years, among them Roberto Cossa (1934–   ) and Juan María Beccaglia (1927–   ), but the outstanding figure in Argentine theater today is Osvaldo Dragún (1929–   ), a highly versatile and socially oriented playwright. *Tupac Amarú* (1957) is a brilliant, tragic reconstruction of the rebellious Inca's revolt in 1781. Dragún's best later work reveals an absorption of technical principles drawn from other dramatists, primarily Brecht, in his effort to create total theater. *Y nos dijeron que éramos inmortales* ("And They Told Us We Were Immortal," 1962) is a cutting analysis of the moral malaise of Argentine youth in which Brecht's alienation effect is used to heighten, rather than dampen, the audience's emotional identification. In *Heroica de Buenos Aires* ("Eroica of Buenos Aires," 1966) he adapted Brecht's *Mother Courage* (1939) to his own place and time to express the anguish and alienation of his generation.

In spite of the nation's economic crisis, the Uruguayan independent movement has flourished, and the establishment of the National Drama Company in 1947 has had considerable impact. Among the dramatists of this period are Mario Benedetti (1920–   ) and Mauricio Rosencof (1928–   ); Carlos Maggi (1922–   ) is perhaps the most productive of this generation and most aware of the resources of the theater. His *La trastienda* ("The Back Room," 1958) moves from grotesque farce to total disaster, and this theme of inevitable frustration is best presented in a mixture of outrageous farce and black comedy in *La biblioteca* ("The Library," 1959).

Another of the Mexican theater's periodic crises led in 1947 to the establishment of a series of small theaters and experimental groups; at the same time the National Institute of Fine Arts organized a Department of Theater under the direction of Salvador Novo. These were the principal factors leading to the emergence of a restless and stimulating group of playwrights who rank with the best in Spanish America. The leading figure is Emilio Carballido (1925–   ), perhaps the most versatile technician of his generation in Spanish-language theater. His *Rosalba y los Llaveros* ("Rosalba and the Llavero Family," 1950), a joyous comedy of the impact on a narrow-minded provincial family of their enchanting and flighty city cousin, opened the way to a new treatment of the conflict between traditional customs and a new way of life, a line Carballido followed in *La danza que sueña la tortuga* ("The Dance the Tortoise Dreams," 1955). In later works he has created an objective picture of the crushing mediocrity of the petite bourgeoisie (*Felicidad*, "Happiness," 1955), experimented with the dramatic possibilities of the horror story (*La hebra de oro*, "The Golden Thread," 1956), and exalted the individual in brilliantly comic satires of modern life (*El relojero de Córdoba*, "The Watchmaker of Córdoba," 1960, and *El día que se soltaron los leones*, "The Day the Lions Got Loose," 1957). This desolate vision of the dehumanization of life underlies his latest play, *Yo también hablo de la rosa* ("I Also Speak of the Rose," 1966), and it lies at the heart of his best work, *Medusa* (written 1958), in which he utilizes the classical myth and the tragic structure to point out the spiritual death of our time.

Like Carballido, the Mexican Luisa Josefina Hernández (1928–   ) wrote first of the frustrations of provincial life, particularly for women in a society whose allegiance to equal rights was largely rhetorical. Her most recent works are Brechtian attacks on the status quo, evocations of the world of Maya myth (*Popol Vuh*, 1966), and dramatizations of the persecution of the Yaquis by the dictator Díaz (*La paz ficticia*, "The Fictitious Peace," 1960). Perhaps her best work to date is *Los huéspedes reales* ("The Royal Guests," 1957), a moving tragedy of a modern Electra.

Other Mexicans of the same generation include Sergio Magaña (1924–   ), Carlos Solórzano (1922–   ), and Elena Garro (1922–   ). Magaña writes little, but each of his works represents a different kind of technical challenge. Solórzano evolved from historical tragedy to *Las manos de Dios* ("The Hands of God," 1956), a bitter vision of good and evil in Mexico today, expressed through a total theater that makes use of chorus and dance; he also excels in the symbolic short play. Elena Garro has written only a group of short works, in the idiom of the "absurd," which reflect a conflict between illusion and reality that leads inevitably to the destruction of illusion. A number of other Mexican dramatists should be mentioned, among them Héctor Azar (1930–   ) and Jorge Ibargüengoitia (1928–   ).

The new Chilean movement was born in the universities; since 1941 the University of Chile, joined two years later by the Catholic University, has been very active in stimulating the drama. A clearly defined group of playwrights born between 1910 and 1920 was active as early as the late 1930's. The university programs and affiliated activities and in particular the formation of resident professional companies and the installation of well-equipped physical facilities at both universities in the mid-1950's have provided ample opportunities for these playwrights. The older group, born before 1920, numbers several authors of interest; Roberto Sarah (1918–   ) was most active from 1950 to 1952, and his best work, *Algún día* ("Some Day," 1950), dates from this period. Isidora Aguirre (1919–   ) was primarily a realist with social interests until she wrote *La pérgola de las flores* ("The Summer House," 1960), an internationally successful musical comedy.

The most important group in Chile today is that

born after 1920 and trained in the universities. Luis Alberto Heiremans (1928–1964) was successful in writing psychological and realistic drama, and he created the libretto for the first Chilean musical comedy, *Esta señorita Trini* ("This Miss Trini," 1958). His most significant work is in drama based on folklore, particularly *Versos de ciego* ("Blind Man's Poems," 1960), in which he used a structure patterned after the medieval Nativity plays. Egon Wolff (1926–   ) began as a realist, creating psychological studies and pessimistic visions of the middle class. In later works, such as *Los invasores* ("The Invaders," 1962), a sometimes startling fantasy of the silent invasion of a wealthy district by the poor, this apparent realism is used as a dramatic device to enhance the underlying unreality.

The Chilean Alejandro Sieveking (1934–   ) is particularly successful in writing psychological drama, although his greatest hit has been *Ánimas de día claro* ("Souls of a Clear Day," 1962), based on a popular superstition that those who die with some unfulfilled wish must remain on earth. Sergio Vodanovic (1927–   ) alternates between popular comedy and social satire; Fernando Josseau (1924–   ), after writing several dramas influenced by Jean Paul Sartre and Albert Camus, produced *El prestamista* ("The Moneylender," 1956), a demanding three-act monodrama that has received many awards. Two more authors of interest are Enrique Molleto (1923–   ), whose plays are tangential and horrifying glances of evil and guilt, and Jorge Díaz (1930–   ), who, profoundly influenced by the absurd, has disciplined his talent and lessened his reliance on purely theatrical shock values to a point where he promises to become a major figure.

Cuban drama in the years just prior to the fall of Batista was perilously close to nonexistence. Between 1941 and 1949, the establishment of several public and private organizations aimed at fomenting drama had given a strong impulse to theatrical development. Also, a substantial group of playwrights gave promise of creating a brilliant renaissance, which, however, was truncated. The best known of this group are Virgilio Piñera (1914–   ) and Carlos Felipe (1914–   ), both of whom have exercised great influence on the young, postrevolutionary theater. Piñera has a close affinity with some aspects of the absurd, but his best and most influential work has been in the use of mythic forms to explore Cuban reality: *Jesús* (1950) and *Electra Garrigó* (1948). Felipe has been deeply influenced by the psychoanalytical theater and his plays suffer from static moments and loquaciousness. A number of promising dramatists have apparently ceased writing for the theater; René Buch, Eduardo Manet, Roberto Bourbakis, Nora Badía, Ramón Ferreira, Matías Montes, and Fermín Borges all gave evidence of real promise. Rolando Ferrer (1925–   ) wrote several very impressive poetic dramas of frustration and repression, but of late he has produced only a few short propaganda works.

The advent of the Castro government produced considerable dramatic activity; the annual festival and contest in Latin America drama have provided opportunities for Cuban and other Spanish American dramatists. In Cuba there has appeared a new group of young playwrights whose work is among the best written recently in Spanish. Abelardo Estorino (1925–) achieved considerable reputation with *El robo del cochino* ("The Stolen Pig," 1961), a realistic study of family tensions in pre-Castro rural Cuba. In later plays he has cultivated new techniques, but his best work is still in the examination of the narrow egocentrism of provincial life. Manuel Reguera Samuell (1928–) is preoccupied with the disintegration of the family, both in the photographic realism of *Sara en el traspatio* ("Sara in the Back Yard," 1960) and in his more avant-garde efforts, such as *Recuerdos de Tulipa* ("Memories of Tulipa," 1962), a brilliant portrait of an aging dancer's affirmation of human dignity.

The Cubans Antón Arrufat (1935–) and José Triana (1933–) have been deeply influenced by contemporary currents. Arrufat's latest work has become increasingly myth-oriented in his search for underlying meaning in an apparently senseless world. His most important work to date is *El vivo al pollo* (1961), whose title comes from a proverb meaning that the dead are best forgotten, for the living have life to enjoy. The work is based on the teatro bufo, the popular theater of the late nineteenth century, and is a wildly comic parody on the fear of death. Triana, inspired by Piñera, has used the Medea myth to present his vision of daily life in a violent and irrational world in *Medea en el espejo* ("Medea in the Mirror," 1960), and has attempted to create a mythic framework out of folklore for the same theme in *La muerte del Ñeque* ("Death of the Ñeque," 1964). *La Noche de los asesinos* ("Night of the Assassins," 1965) takes Jean Genet's *The Maids* (1948) a step further in its complex vision of three adolescents playing out an interminable ritual of murder and guilt.

During much of the century, a few Peruvians struggled unsuccessfully to establish a viable drama. Recently, greater contact with world theater and the beginnings of some official assistance have stimulated new dramatists. Like most members of his generation in Peru, Sebastián Salazar Bondy (1924–1964) studied in Paris and his work bears the imprint of Camus. A versatile artist, he created amusing farces, but his most important plays are realistic visions of spiritual ruin in an uncomprehending world: *No hay isla feliz* ("There Is No Happy Island," 1954). As yet, the new stimulus has not produced other dramatists of his caliber.

PUERTO RICO is a rather special case, in that the roots of its drama today lie in a reassessment of its past and present, begun in 1930 by a group of historians concerned with the island's dual cultural patterns. By 1940 considerable dramatic activity had been generated in the form of a furiously nationalistic naturalism that focused almost entirely on socioeconomic patterns. The best dramatists have now abandoned this naturalism in favor of a symbolic expression of moral and psychological problems, almost always specifically related to the island's particular ethnic patterns and its ambiguous political condition. René MARQUÉS first achieved renown with his denunciation of the rootlessness of the mountain poor in *La carreta* (*The Ox Cart*, 1954). In his later works he presents a people trapped between an unacceptable reality and a hopeless dream of returning to a lost past: *Los soles truncos* ("The Truncated Suns," 1958) and *Un niño azul para esa sombra* ("A Blue

Child for That Shadow," 1960). In their complex structure and control of theatrics, they are among the best plays in Spanish America. Recently, Marqués has evolved a stylized expression of contemporary anguish. Francisco Arriví (1915–) broke with the obsessive insularism of the social concerns only to return to his island's reality in plays that study the solitude and alienation of those who reject their mixed ethnic heritage; his work includes the trilogy *Máscara puertorriqueña* ("Puerto Rican Mask," 1956–1959), which is psychologically sound and theatrically stimulating within a basically realistic approach. The most important younger dramatist is Luis Rafael Sánchez (1936–), who has yet to assimilate Marqués' influence and develop his own dramatic idiom.

In the other Spanish American nations, drama still consists largely of sporadic efforts by small amateur groups. Colombia's Enrique Buenaventura (1925–) has written interesting works in a Brechtian fashion, using historical and folkloric sources. A group of Venezuelans headed by Román Chalbaud (1924–) has achieved considerable notoriety through the political content and alleged obscenity of their works, but the least controversial, Isaac Chocrón (1932–), is by far the best Venezuelan dramatist today. *Mónica y el florentino* ("Monica and the Florentine," 1959) is a drama of the inability to communicate, a theme Chocrón used again in *El quinto infierno* ("The Fifth Inferno," 1961), about the hell of those who are unable to find love.

The best general study of pre-Conquest and colonial drama is José Juan Arrom's *Historia del teatro hispanoamericano. Epoca colonial* (1967), which traces both the persistence of the indigenous tradition and the influence of European currents in the developing Spanish American theater. A companion volume is Frank Dauster's *Historia del teatro hispanoamericano. Siglos XIX y XX* (1966), which emphasizes the period after 1928. Agustín del Saz's *Teatro hispanoamericano* (1964) is a two-volume survey covering the entire range of drama in Spanish America. The only book-length study in English is Willis Knapp Jones's *Behind Spanish American Footlights* (1966), a traditional approach stressing the nativist and autochthonous elements. —F. D.

Spook Sonata, The. See GHOST SONATA, THE.

Spring's Awakening (**Frühlingserwachen**, pub. 1891, perf. 1906). A play by Frank WEDEKIND. This drama depicts the tragedy of two teen-age lovers who are brought together by the awakening of a mutual physical and emotional attraction. Their natural uninhibited feelings are victimized by the inflexible moral code of bourgeois society. The girl dies as a result of an abortion attempt; the youth is held back from suicide in the cemetery by a masked man.

This play may be regarded as a collage of many aesthetic influences. Wedekind presents in *Spring's Awakening* one of his many dramatic variations on the sexual theme, a theme favored by the naturalists. Furthermore, he depicts with brutal realism the discrepancy between the natural needs of man and the rigid confines imposed upon him by society. Romantic and symbolist elements constitute an equally significant aspect of the dramatic presentation. The figure of the masked man in the final scene has been interpreted symbolically as a representation of the life force. Finally, the language and character structure point forward to the later expressionist techniques.—C. A. M.

S.S. Glencairn (1916–1918). A cycle of four one-act plays by Eugene O'NEILL. The setting of all the dramas is the tramp steamer *Glencairn* as it plies the ocean during World War I. Although the plays have several characters in common, their central incidents are unrelated. *Bound East for Cardiff* (1916) is an atmospheric drama of the death of a common sailor. In the more melodramatic *In the Zone*, the seamen, nervous in war-torn waters, grow suspicious of a reticent British sailor. Forcing open a mysterious box, they are embarrassed to discover the man's secret reason for going to sea. *The Long Voyage Home* (1917) concerns the attempts of a young Swedish seaman, long at sea, to return to his homeland. *The Moon of the Caribbees* (1918), another atmospheric piece, takes place when the ship puts in at a West Indian island. These plays have been presented as a cycle under the title *S.S. Glencairn.*—J. G.

Steele, Sir **Richard** (1672–1729). Irish-born English essayist and comic playwright. Steele, born in Dublin, received his early education at the Charterhouse, London, and proceeded in due course to Oxford. In 1692 he abandoned his studies to enlist in the army. As a young guardsman—eventually an ensign in the Coldstream Guards—Steele cut a dashing figure about town, fighting a duel and fathering an illegitimate child. He shortly repented of his misdeeds and composed a reforming tract, *The Christian Hero* (1701), to prove "that no principles but those of religion are sufficient to make a great man." His career as a dramatist began with the Drury Lane production of *The Funeral, or Grief à-la-Mode* (1701). Inoffensive in words and action yet lively and amusing, the play pleased London. His second venture, *The Lying Lover* (1703), adapted from Corneille's *Le Menteur*, sounded a new moral note. It had a run of only six nights. *The Tender Husband* (1705) was at first threatened with similar ill fortune but managed to survive. Steele's career now took a different course, and seventeen years elapsed before the appearance of his last play, THE CONSCIOUS LOVERS. In 1707 he had been appointed editor of *The London Gazette;* two years later, the first number of *The Tatler* appeared. This periodical was succeeded in 1711 by *The Spectator,* which in its original series ran to December 1712. Joseph Addison, a contributor to *The Tatler,* was Steele's close associate throughout the life of the later periodical.

A Whig from the first, Steele was increasingly motivated by extreme partisanship. He was elected to the House of Commons in 1713, only to be expelled the year following for his authorship of *The Crisis,* a political tract declared seditious by his opponents. However, later in 1714, after the coming of George I and the Whig triumph, Steele was made a governor of Drury Lane Theatre and knighted in 1715. But periodical literature still attracted him. *The Tatler* and *The Spectator* had contained some of the best dramatic criticism of the period, contributed both by Addison and Steele. The most notable of his later essay serials is *The Theatre* (1720), solely Steele's and much of it topical. Steele retired to Wales in 1724, where he spent his last years—unhappy ones —and where he died.

Besides the four produced plays by Steele there are two unfinished ones, *The School of Action* and *The Gentleman,* left in manuscript. It is a pity that Steele never completed these, for they would have displayed the side of his talent that we tend to play down when emphasizing the moral themes he introduced and the sentimental treatment he accorded them. The two fragments are inspired farce, much in the irregular manner of John Gay and Henry Fielding in their short pieces. The unfinished plays remind us that a rich vein of unencumbered comedy runs through Steele's plays. There is no difficulty in finding it in *The Funeral,* with its amusing portrayal of the undertaking business; and it is present in *The Tender Husband,* which contains situations of capital comedy quite different from the sentimental scene of reconcilation between Clerimont Senior and his wife in Act V. *The Lying Lover* is certainly not without its diverting moments, but the blank verse employed in the last act signifies the triumph of emotionalized morality. The most successful of the plays, *The Conscious Lovers,* is the one least likely to be found acceptable today, what with its sententiousness and the recognition scene at the end between father and long-lost daughter, with its passion "too strong for utterance."

Steele's four comedies and the two fragments are given in *Richard Steele* (1903), edited by George A. Aitken. The standard biography is *The Life of Richard Steele* (2 vols., 1889), by George A. Aitken. Interesting material bearing on Steele's life as a dramatist and a man of the theater is given by John C. Loftis in *Steele at Drury Lane* (1952). There is a discussion of Steele's plays by Frederick S. Boas in *Eighteenth-Century Drama* (1953). Calhoun Winton supplies a helpful introduction in his edition of *The Tender Husband* (1967).— R. Q.

Sternheim, Carl (1878–1942). German playwright. Carl Sternheim was born in Leipzig, the son of a banker. At a very early age Sternheim showed an active interest in the theater and at fifteen wrote his first play. In fact, his entire life was devoted to the study of literature and to the creation of highly controversial but nevertheless very successful satirical dramas. Indeed, Sternheim thought of himself as a modern Molière. However, because of the sharpness of his pen Sternheim is no doubt one of the most misunderstood and hence most unjustly criticized dramatists of the twentieth century. The reason for the misunderstanding of his dramas lies perhaps in the subtle dialectical thinking of his dramatic intention. As Wilhelm Emrich has pointed out, it is Sternheim's unique position in the drama of the twentieth century to have perceived and recorded the inevitable consequences of freedom for the individual in a modern technological society that harnesses the free individual to its needs and purposes, thereby making him unfree. In order to cure the individual of his illusion of freedom, Sternheim resorts to none of the well-known formulas of existentialism, nihilism, or Marxism. Instead of attempting to impose artificial thought structures on the order of things, Sternheim, in essence a realist, is dramatically intent upon recording and preserving the endless variety of human experience. In fact, it is the limitless potential for uniqueness and versatility that gives existence its ultimate philosophical justification, if it needs one. Sternheim does not lament the lack of a metaphysical dimension, for life needs none. Its meaning lies in the persistence of its creatures to establish their uniqueness and freedom in confrontation with their environment. This notion is in fact the theme of countless of his dramas: *Bürger Schippel* (*Citizen Schippel*, 1912), *Tabula Rasa* (1916), *Der Entfesselte Zeitgenosse* ("The Freed Contemporary," 1920).

If Sternheim's understanding of reality appears unique, his apprehension of the dramatic purpose and protagonist is also quite unusual. Traditionally, those figures who achieve an extraordinary position and psychology are given the designation of hero. This designation also applies to the heroes in a collection of his most significant plays entitled *Aus dem bürgerlichen Heldenleben* (*The Heroic Life of the Bourgeoisie*). But the heroes of Sternheim are not of the traditional cast—good, but not too good. They are, in fact, repulsive, malicious, cynical, morally degenerate creatures who nevertheless seem to win the approval of the author as exemplary representatives of vital principles in the order of things.

Theobold, the hero of A PAIR OF DRAWERS, is an unattractive, base man, greedy and unprincipled. However, he is the hero of the play, for he is, in comparison with the other male figures in the drama, the most decisive and determined, the most aware of himself in his limitations and ambitions. His cut-and-dried pragmatism gives him the vigor and power necessary to control his environment and ultimately to achieve his goal, which curiously enough is not all that base. Surprisingly, the reason for all his scheming does not lie in any ambition for extreme wealth but in the desire to provide for a child in modestly secure financial circumstances.

Theobold's son and heir, Christian, in the next play of the "Masken" series, *Der Snob* (*The Snob,* 1912), is also a hero, for he too masters all the masquerades of the society he wishes to rule. He comes to the task with only "courage," and he succeeds because he grasps fully the laws that govern this society. He not only realizes the necessity for understanding these social principles but also the need for the "re-creation" of his person according to these principles. In full possession of his "self" he can now proceed to gain complete possession of this society.

To be sure, there is much of the Nietzschean brand of heroism in Sternheim's character portrayals. However, there is something more, something unique to this playwright, and that is his dramatic intention—not to schematize his characters, not to bind them to a conceptual or psychological formula, but as he wrote ". . . to enjoy [their] uniqueness, to enjoy [them] without any prejudice of good, evil, beauty, ugliness."

Sternheim in fact had the same fear of standardization that his hero Christian has in the next play of the series, *1913* (1915). Christian, in an argument with his daughter Sofie, pleads for a change in the method of production: instead of mass production, something of "substance." Sofie answers that the method of production cannot abide two contradictory propositions; it must aim for simplicity, quantity and not quality. Christian asks in turn the foreboding question: What should happen if this method were to lead to war? In fact he proceeds to predict, "After us the collapse! We are ripe for it!" Such is Sternheim's prediction, interpolated here in a particular dramatic context, of the necessary outcome of the restriction of free definition of person or production. It can only conclude in catastrophe.

Carl Sternheim died in 1942 in Brussels, having lived long enough to see this thesis tragically materialize into a second world war.

The following are English translations of plays by Sternheim: *A Pair of Drawers,* in *Transition,* Nos. 6–9 (1927), and *The Snob,* translated by Eric Bentley in *From the Modern Repertoire* (1949), Eric Bentley, ed. For a critical study of his works see W. Drake, "Carl Sternheim" in *Contemporary European Writers* (1928), and Walter H. Sokel, *The Writer in Extremis* (1959), pp. 121–123. A significant article in German is Wilhelm Emrich, "Die Komödie Carl Sternheims" in the collection *Der deutsche Expressionismus* (1965).—C. A. M.

Stodola, Ivan (1888–   ). Slovakian playwright. Born in Liptovský Svätý Mikuláš, Stodola studied at the lyceums in Prešov and Kežmarok and then at medical schools in Budapest and Berlin. His university studies were interrupted by his military service. In 1913 he practiced medicine in his native town and during World War I he was active as a soldier on many fronts. After the war he took up the post of chief doctor in his native district, which he held from 1918 until 1934. From 1934 to 1938 he was the sanitary inspector for Slovakia and he lived in Bratislava. In World War II he participated in the Slovakian national uprising against the German army. After the war he lectured on social medicine at the J. A. Komenský University in Bratislava and since 1953 he has been living in Piestany.

Stodola, the greatest Slovakian dramatist of the interwar period, was not a professional writer. After writing some cabaret plays in 1925, he made his theatrical debut with his farce *Náš pán Minister* ("Our Minister," 1926). This work was followed by a series of satirical comedies—among them the most successful are *Čaj u pána senátora* ("Tea with the Senator," 1929) and *Jožko Púčik a jeho kariéra* ("Jožko Púčik and His Career," 1931).

Stodola worked successfully in the tradition of satirical comedy, the most successful genre of Slovakian drama. He sharply criticized the petite bourgeoisie who rose to power in the interwar period in Slovakia. Stodola did not attack their tendency to assimilate, as previous playwrights had done, because the danger of assimilation with Hungarians or Germans was no longer as great. Instead, he focused his criticism on the petite bourgeoisie's desire for property and power, their false humanism, their prejudices against their own origins, and their political careerism. Stodola tried to improve the morals of the Slovakian petite bourgeoisie. The heroes of his plays are little businessmen and petty intellectuals who want to gain as many advantages for themselves as possible under the new republican system.

Stodola's most successful play, *Jožko Púčik a jeho kariéra,* which was performed abroad, is a "satire about falsely understood humanism," according to the author. In this work he created the tragic, absurd hero Jožko Púčik, a poor and naïve clerk, whose living standard improved when he was called a criminal and several charitable associations took care of him. Stodola's comedies, written mostly in a traditional form, are sharp exaggerations of reality. He always creates just a few, sharply drawn characters who go through simple actions. He is a master of concise, concentrated, comic dialogue and uses various kinds of colloquial language.

During World War II, when the so-called Sloyenský štát was founded, Stodola satirized the reactionary rulers in such plays as *Ked jubilant pláce* ("When the Person Celebrating Jubilee Weeps," 1941), *Mravci a svrčkovia* ("Ants and Crickets," 1943), and *Komédia* ("Comedy," 1944). His play *Kde bolo— tam bolo* ("Where It Was—There It Was," 1947) was not successful and some of his later works were never performed.

Stodola was instrumental in developing Slovakian drama. In *Bačova zěna* ("Shepherd's Wife," 1928) he dramatized the complicated emotions of a country wife, and in *Básnik a smrť* ("Poet and Death," 1946) he wrote about the Slovakian national revolution. In his plays *Král Svätopluk* ("King Svätopluk," 1931), *Marína Havranová* (1941), and *Ján Pankrác* (1947) he successfully contributed to the tradition of Slovakian historical plays, which had not been particularly developed until Stodola's work. In *Král Svätopluk* Stodola portrays the last days of a great Moravian emperor who is full of inner conflicts. Using this text, Eugen Suchoň wrote an opera that was performed for the first time in 1960. Also, the film *Statočný zlodej* ("The Brave Thief") was based on Stodola's play *Jožko Púčik a jeho kariéra*. In addition to these works, Stodola has also written plays for children.—F. C.

Strange Interlude (1928). A play in nine acts by Eugene O'NEILL. In this portrayal of a modern woman, O'Neill shows Nina Leeds being driven by the strange life force in her blood stream to unconventional relationships and seeking multiple possession of men's lives before peace descends upon her at the end of the "strange interlude" of her premenopausal life history. With many details drawn from the mores of the "sophisticated" 1920's and contemporary, chiefly Freudian, psychology, *Strange Interlude* proved engrossing to its New York audiences throughout the greater part of its nine acts. Above all the characters stood Nina, the attractive daughter of a possessive university professor, who lost her athlete lover in World War I, regrets not having consummated her love with him, and seeks fulfillment in desperate promiscuity. Later, having married a man to whom she will not bear children after being warned by her mother that there is insanity in the family, she gives birth to a son by another man (the neurologist Darrell) but cannot bring herself to reveal the boy's true parentage. It takes a husband, a lover, a family friend, and an illegitimate son to fill her womanly life while at full tide.

In this play O'Neill was, if anything, too explicit in his spoken and especially unspoken dialogue—that is, the asides with which the author outlined the true thoughts and sentiments of the characters at the risk of redundancy. There could well be two strongly contradictory opinions about the recourse to asides and while British theater historian Allardyce Nicoll found O'Neill's use of them "tedious and fundamentally undramatic," others found much to applaud in this type of "interior monologue," which resembled James Joyce's stream-of-consciousness technique in *Ulysses*. *Strange Interlude* is too long and interest flags in the last two acts, but it commanded, as a dramatic novel and a character study, the interest of a large public grateful for an exacting and unconventional drama.—J. G.

Streetcar Named Desire, A (1947). A play by Tennessee WILLIAMS. First performed in New York on December 3, 1947, the play ran longer than any other Williams play and received both the Pulitzer Prize and the Drama Critics Circle Award. It tells the story of Blanche DuBois, whose first appearance "suggests a moth," a delicate, neurasthenic Southern woman, driven by her sexual hunger, her preoccupation with death, and her guilt over her husband's suicide. She seeks refuge with her married sister, Stella, in New Orleans, where she is destroyed. After being raped by Stanley Kowalski, the animal-like brother-in-law—an attack that she spends most of the play provoking—Blanche goes mad. Williams has said that the play's meaning "is the ravishment of the tender, the sensitive, the delicate, by the savage and brutal forces of modern society," and so it is often interpreted. It is, however, a more complicated moral fable than that, for Blanche is too subtle a character, too fascinating a combination of fragility and cruelty, of fantasy and mendacity, to fit so simple a reading. Her presence in the Kowalski household is a destructive one, and it is significant that the curtain comes down, not only on Blanche being led away, but on the sensual reconciliation of Stanley and Stella.—G. W.

Strindberg, [Johan] August (1849–1912). Swedish playwright, novelist, and polymath. Except for intermittent study at the Swedish university Uppsala (1867–1872), Strindberg's early life was chiefly associated with Stockholm, the city of his birth. He worked there as teacher, journalist, and librarian before he first found literary success with the *roman à clef Röda Rummet* (*The Red Room*, 1879). While his life thereafter was largely a literary one, he demonstrated his talents variously as painter, photographer, and amateur chemist—the latter chiefly in Paris in the 1890's during his so-called Inferno Period, charted in somewhat fictionalized form in his book *Inferno* (1897).

This period of psychological and spiritual turmoil effectively divides Strindberg's naturalism—the plays and autobiographical works of the 1880's— from his EXPRESSIONISM—the moralities, fantasies, and pilgrimage plays extending from *Till Damascus I* (*The Road to Damascus I*, 1898) to *Stora Landsvägen* (*The Great Highway*, 1909), a quasi-allegorical farewell to the world, which preceded his death by cancer by about three years. Mysticism and a strong identification with Beethoven informed the later years and gave them much of their character. A preoccupation with music in general had much to do with the idea behind the formation of Strindberg's Intimate Theater (1907–1910) and the so-called chamber plays, which were written with the Intimate Theater in mind.

Strindberg was not the misogynist he is often declared to be, but his relationships with women were complicated by the idiosyncrasies of his personality. He cherished domesticity but was married to three professional women: Siri von Essen, an aspiring actress of no great talent (1877–1891), Frida Uhl, an Austrian journalist (1893–1894), and Harriet Bosse, a Norwegian actress who went on to considerable success, frequently in Strindberg parts (1901–1904).

Since Strindberg was surely one of the most subjective of writers, these marriages provided background (and foreground) materials for much of his writing in both fiction and drama. The three ladies in question all found opportunity to tell their side of the story, so that Strindberg's marital life is elaborately chronicled.

Strindberg's stormy love affair with Sweden is another part of the story. Disaffection came in the early 1880's, partly as a result of a blasphemy trial over a flippant reference to the sacrament in the short-story collection *Giftas* (*Married*, 1884), but the late recognition of Strindberg's plays in Sweden was also a factor. Consequently, Strindberg spent much of his life from 1882 to 1897 in Switzerland, Germany, Austria, Denmark, and France. As it was to most literary Scandinavians of the times, a conquest of Paris was important to him, and he realized some success in the French capital from 1889 onward. At least five of his plays were staged in Paris and many of his articles were printed (he wrote extensively and passably well in French). After the Inferno Period (1894–1896) he returned to Sweden, where he wrote, in addition to the expressionist plays, a significant series of history plays that bear testimony to his reconciliation with Sweden and the general resurgence of interest in Swedish nationalism.

Strindberg's prickly, unsettling personality has always attracted much attention from psychologists, amateur and professional, most of whom have been equipped with elaborate theories but no knowledge of Swedish and therefore no access to a voluminous correspondence and the so-called *Ockulta dagboken* (*Occult Diary*, written 1896–1908; pub. 1963), of the later years. The last clinical word remains to be said, but the plays are ultimately more interesting read in their own right.

Strindberg made his theater debut with *I Rom* (*In Rome*, 1870), a short play about the artist's life in the Italian capital (with the Danish sculptor Thorwaldsen and himself as models). But his apprenticeship is best viewed in the historical drama *Mäster Olof* (1881), rewritten almost continuously from 1872 to 1877, in which he locates the dialectic of effective political action in Olaus Petri, Sweden's Luther; and *Komraterna* (*Comrades*, written 1886–1887; prod. 1905), a comedy of manners that curdles into acrimonious naturalism. His two great naturalistic tragedies followed: THE FATHER, the Agamemnon story retold; and MISS JULIE, in which sexual clash acquires ritual power without *The Father*'s literary and mythic identification. *Fordringsägare* (*Creditors*, 1889) fascinates in the triangular configuration of its plot (as does THE STRONGER) but loses power in its now antiquated scientific presumptions. A number of short plays followed, some of them tailored after French models. *Bandet* (*The Bond*, written 1892; prod. 1902), based on the dissolution of Strindberg's first marriage, terminates the naturalistic period. (See REALISM AND NATURALISM.)

The fragmentation of personality, so characteristic of Strindberg's expressionism, first appears in *Till Damascus*, a play with biblical overtones but at the same time a projection of the problems of Strindberg's second marriage. As afterthoughts occurred to him, the play accreted to a kind of trilogy, but only Part I, constructed somewhat fancifully after Kierke-

gaard's idea of repetition, fuses force and form. *Brott och brott* (*Crimes and Crimes*, 1899), based on the Kierkegaardian "either/or," the aesthetic versus the ethical, deals with the fall of man in a Parisian setting. Somewhat like it, *Påsk* (*Easter*, 1901) is a morality play. Its fascination is largely embodied in Eleonora, the girl of precarious mental balance, who is a fusion of Christ, Pippa, one of Strindberg's sisters, and Balzac's Seraphita.

From 1899 onward Strindberg wrote enough history plays (more than twenty) to make him the chief modern practitioner in the CHRONICLE PLAY form. Most of them, unfortunately for a universal audience, confine themselves to Swedish history, and some, like *Gustav Adolf* (1903), simply demand too much for the stage. *Kristina* (written 1901; prod. 1908), however, is a compelling character study in which the seventeenth-century queen and *demi-femme* displays all the incalculable wayward vivacity of the emergent new woman; and *Erik XIV* (1899) provides a Hamletesque portrait of indecision that has attracted notable productions from directors Eugene Vakhtangov (1921) and Jean Vilar (1960). Strindberg learned to fuse pageantry and the illusion of realistic improvisation to make a new kind of historical drama, perhaps best exemplified in the "still, sad music"—partially expressionist—of *Carl XII* (*Charles XII*, 1902), the Swedish king, as his reign dwindled to an end.

The influence of Maeterlinck is observable in Strindberg's ventures into the fairy-tale play *Svanevit* (*Swanwhite*, written 1901; prod. 1908) and the folk play *Kronbruden* (*The Crown Bride* or *The Bridal Crown*, written 1901; prod. 1906), which is particularly poignant in its lyrical treatment of a peasant Romeo and Juliet theme.

The full-blown expressionism that followed is chiefly represented by A DREAM PLAY, which did so much to free the stage from the shackles of time and place, and is also seen in the earlier THE DANCE OF DEATH. Using symbolism reminiscent of medieval allegory (the castle) and of alchemy (gold and transmutation), *A Dream Play* deals with the various miseries that beset mankind. THE GHOST SONATA, embodying the Hoffmannesque grotesque in quasimusical form, is an incremental revelation of the real horror of men behind the façades of affluence.

This is, as it happens, the chief and persistent theme of the later "chamber plays" (*The Ghost Sonata* is Opus No. 3 of some five). Most of them are really tone poems made of SYMBOLISM and an attenuated realism ranging from near stasis, in *Oväder* (*Storm Weather*, 1907), to bilious melodrama anticipating the absurd, in *Pelicanen* (*The Pelican*, 1907). These plays were conceived for the Intimate Theater, which was, after the Reinhardt pattern in Berlin, one of Strindberg's chief concerns during the later years. *Stora Landsvägen* fuses satire, allegory, literary allusiveness, and myth into a total metaphor of life, which, though only partially successful, constitutes Strindberg's farewell to the stage.

Always the romantic and the playwright's playwright, Strindberg left behind a body of drama that is far from flawless but usually provocative. His anguish anticipated the dilemma of modern man and his work was, as Thornton Wilder put it, the fountainhead of virtually all of modernism in the drama. If he was not actually the father of dramatic expressionism, he was certainly seminal to it and in turn to the "theater of the absurd." For Sean O'Casey he "shook down the living stars from heaven." Strindberg had his extravagancies: He was at all times an experimentalist, a distraught presence exploring the enigmas of the universe as well as those of dramatic form.

There is nothing like a definitive Strindberg in English, but the reader is referred to the translations of Elizabeth Sprigge, *Six Plays* (1955) and *Five Plays* (1960), and those of Michael Meyer, *The Plays of Strindberg,* Vol. I (1964). Miss Sprigge's *Strange Life of August Strindberg* (1949) remains the best biography in English, however brief. The only handbook is B. Mortensen and B. Downs, *Strindberg* (1949), and one of the best critical interpretations in broad aesthetic terms is Maurice Valency, *The Flower and the Castle* (1963). For bibliography and survey of scholarship, consult R. B. Vowles *et al., Modern Drama* (Winter 1962).—R. B. V.

Stronger, The (Den starkare, 1889). A one-act play by August STRINDBERG. Because the play is an encounter between Mrs. X and Miss Y, it gives the appearance of being both a psychological case history and a mathematical problem (Which of the two is the stronger?). The two women have been rivals in love. Mrs. X won the man, but as she talks compulsively she learns and we learn how much the influence of Miss Y is still involved. The plot is triangular, with the husband an absent member and Miss Y only partially present, for her role is all pantomime. The play is, therefore, something of a tour de force and a superb acting vehicle as either a dramatic monologue or an exercise in facial mime.

Originally, *The Stronger* seems to have been conceived as a *quart d'heure* for a traveling company, in which Strindberg's wife, Siri von Essen, could take either part, the silent one in countries where she did not know the language. It has proved to be one of the most durable plays in the one-act repertory, and its influence may be seen in Eugene O'Neill's *Before Breakfast* and in many another play involving a silent character.

The English text and an analysis are to be found in *The Plays of Strindberg,* Vol. I (1964), edited and translated by Michael Meyer.—R. B. V.

Sturm und Drang ("storm and stress"). A literary movement in late eighteenth-century Germany. In literary productions of the Sturm and Drang, emphasis was usually placed upon the energetic, demonic, Promethean quality of the individual in opposition to the rationalistic ideal of the Enlightenment and the formalism of French-influenced neoclassicism. The movement, which takes its name from the title of a play by Maximilian Klinger, was especially rich in drama and lyric poetry. Its other major figures were young Goethe, young Schiller, Reinhold Lenz, Heinrich Wagner, and Gottfried Bürger. In thought, the Sturm und Drang was strongly influenced by Edward Young, Rousseau, and Hamann. The representatives of the Sturm und Drang especially admired Shakespeare and James Macpherson's *Ossian,* and the effect of Johann Gottfried Herder's writings upon them can be seen in their frequent interest in folk material and the German past. For further discussion of the Sturm und Drang, see GERMANY: *eighteenth century.*

SIR JOHN SUCKLING (NEW YORK PUBLIC LIBRARY)

Suckling, Sir **John** (1609–1642). English poet and playwright. A native of Middlesex, Suckling attended Cambridge and the law school at Gray's Inn. His quick wit and good looks soon won him prominence at the court of Charles I. He traveled in Europe, serving in the Thirty Years' War under King Gustavus Adolphus. On his return to the English court, he became the most celebrated rake of his time, an incorrigible gambler, and a tireless lover. After the defeat of the royalist forces in the civil war, he escaped to France, where he died, according to one report, a suicide.

Suckling is better known as a lyric poet than as a dramatist, but in his own time his plays won him considerable fame within court circles. His most celebrated work was *Aglaura* (1637). Set in the royal court of the Persian emperor, the play was originally written as a tragedy, but the last act was later revised, allegedly at the request of the king, to provide a happy ending. The play's celebrity in its own day derived less from its intrinsic literary merit than from the sumptuous and expensive production acted before the king and queen during the Christmas revels of 1637/38.

Suckling's other work includes *The Goblins* (produced between 1638 and 1641), a comedy notable for its extensive borrowing from Shakespeare, particularly from *The Tempest.* Probably his best play is *Brennoralt* (produced between 1639 and 1641), a tragicomedy modeled on the Scottish opposition to King Charles and distinguished by its central character, a brooding, Byronic hero.

The standard edition of Suckling is *The Works of Sir John Suckling in Prose and Verse* (1910), edited by A. H. Thompson. An excellent account of Suckling's work is included in Alfred Harbage's *Cavalier Drama* (1936).—E. Q.

Sugawara Denju Tenarai Kogami (The House of Sugawara, written 1746). A play by Takeda IZUMO. Among the most popular Japanese dramas of pathos in the naturalistic, or SEWAMONO, style, *Sugawara* was written by one of Japan's major playwrights. The work was originally composed for the puppet theater in 1746 but has enjoyed its longest and greatest popularity in revised form on the *kabuki* stage, where it is performed by live actors. Here the work, which is of great length, is rarely seen in full; a section if it, *Tarakoya,* is well known. It exploits to the full certain actions familiar to the kabuki stage, such as a "head inspection" wherein an official meticulously examines the severed head of a person who has been executed to ascertain whether the head is or is not that of the condemned man. The plot of *Tarakoya,* borrowed from the traditional Chinese theater, depicts the heroism of a faithful retainer who sacrifices his own child to save the heir of his feudal lord. The most famous scene presents a schoolroom in which the pupils are gathered, the young prince present in disguise. The utmost pathos is extracted from this situation, especially in passages depicting the mother of the child who is slain by way of substitution. —H. W. W.

Sukhovo-Kobylin, Alexander [Vasilievich] (1817 –1903). Russian playwright. Unlike his prolific contemporary Alexander Ostrovsky, Sukhovo-Kobylin wrote only three plays—a trilogy made up of *Krechinsky's Wedding, The Case,* and *Tarelkin's Death* (for discussions of these plays see KRECHINSKY'S WEDDING). It may be argued, however, that by themselves these three plays make Sukhovo-Kobylin's contribution to Russian theater just as important and certainly more original than Ostrovsky's.

Sukhovo-Kobylin was obviously strongly influenced by Nikolai Gogol in his jaundiced outlook on life. But it was his personal experience of victimization by a merciless legal apparatus and its corrupt officials that communicated to his plays a fierce, sarcastic humor that is probably unique. In 1852 the battered body of Louise Simon-Demanche, Sukhovo-Kobylin's estranged French mistress, was found outside Moscow. Although her servants soon admitted their guilt, the police officials found it more profitable to disregard their confession and continue accusing the wealthy young aristocrat. For seven years Sukhovo-Kobylin was forced to pay off police officials to escape their harassments. When the charges against him were finally dropped for lack of sufficient evidence, it was still not the end of his troubles: his reputation in society was ruined. "Had it not been for the money and the connections I happened to have, I'd have wound up rotting in Siberia," Sukhovo-Kobylin wrote shortly before his death.

It was this firsthand experience with corruption and arbitrariness that prompted Sukhovo-Kobylin to write plays. Indeed, it was during his first arbitrary detention in 1852 that he started composing his first comedy, *Krechinsky's Wedding,* which he finished in 1854. This was followed by *The Case* (written 1856 to 1857) and *Tarelkin's Death* (written 1857 to 1869). During these years, he had to try and convince the censors, publishers, and actors that his plays could be performed; he cut out passages that might be considered objectionable and even changed titles. (Thus, *The Case* was renamed "Bygone Times" to convince the censors that the practices denounced in the play belonged to the past.)

Krechinsky's Wedding was produced about a year after it was written, but, despite all Sukhovo-Kobylin's efforts, it was about twenty years before *The Case* was produced and thirty years before *Tarelkin's Death* was staged, even in an adulterated form.—A. MACA.

Sullivan, Sir **Arthur [Seymour].** See Sir William S. GILBERT.

Sümer, Güner (1936–   ). Turkish playwright, actor, and director. Sümer was born near Ankara, where he completed his secondary education. While a student at the law school of the university, he became interested in the theater and joined amateur groups as a director and an actor. At this time he wrote, translated, and adapted plays for radio. In Paris, he worked as assistant to Jean Louis Barrault, Jean Vilar, and George Wilson. On returning to Turkey, he and others established the Ankara Art Theater, a theater dedicated to producing socially conscious plays. Currently, Sümer selects plays, acts, and directs at that theater. He has written two plays, adapted one, and translated several.

Sümer's plays deal with the lower classes of big cities. His materials are the sorrows, half-torn relationships, and unrequited loves of these people. Sümer attempts to shed light on social evils by presenting the problems of individuals. With Anton Chekhov as his model, Sümer finds subtleties and deep meanings in everyday conversation, with its pauses and seemingly insignificant utterances.—N. O.

Sunda. See INDONESIA: *Sunda.*

Suppliant Maidens, The (Hiketides; Latin, **Supplices;** date uncertain). A tragedy by AESCHYLUS. Before 1952 most reference works dated this play early in the career of Aeschylus, long before any other extant play. In that year, however, a papyrus was published which indicates that it was produced at Athens in 466 B.C. or later, perhaps 463—that is, in the last decade of Aeschylus' life. The same papyrus shows that Aeschylus won first prize in the tragic contest on that occasion, with the Danaid tetralogy containing *The Suppliant Maidens, Aigyptioi (Egyptians), Danaides,* and the satyr play *Amymone.*

In the tetralogy as a whole, Aeschylus was reinterpreting, for his own artistic purposes, a strange and almost barbarous myth. In outline, this told that Zeus once loved an Argive girl, Io, and that Hera, out of jealousy, turned her into a cow. Zeus adroitly turned himself into a bull, but Hera responded by sending a gadfly against Io and driving her in madness out of Greece through Asia. At last, arriving at the Nile Delta, Io found peace and glory: by his touch and breath alone (no sexual violence now), Zeus begot on her a son, Epaphus. From mother and son (the Isis and Apis of Egyptian cult) descended a line of gods and heroes. In its fifth generation, Aegyptus tried to force his fifty sons in marriage on the fifty daughters of his brother, Danaus. To escape this, Danaus and his daughters fled by sea to Argos, the home of their ancestress Io.

Danaus' daughters form the Chorus of Suppliant Maidens in this, the opening play of the tetralogy. The scene is the deserted Argive coast. The only visible object is a sacred mound with symbols of the Greek gods, at which the Chorus, after their opening song, take refuge on the orders of Danaus. Enter the Greek king, Pelasgus, at the head of his army. The Chorus, appealing to their common Argive ancestry, beg to be received as suppliants. This presents King Pelasgus with a terrible choice: if he refuses, he offends the gods; if he agrees, he brings war with the pursuing Egyptians upon his city. After much agony he agrees, and leaves with Danaus to influence the citizens of Argos to ratify his decision. A choral ode follows; then Danaus returns with news that the citizens have voted with the king. Very soon, however, he sights the Egyptian fleet from the top of the mound and hurries off for help. Here is the play's physical crisis, matching the earlier spiritual crisis, the debate with Pelasgus. In a wild flurry of song and dance the defenseless Chorus are assailed by an Egyptian herald, who tries to hustle them aboard the fleet. They are only just saved by the reappearance of the king. The herald is driven off, threatening war, and in a stately choral finale the girls withdraw toward their new home, Argos.

Such is the stage action, simple but spectacular. At least as important to the total impact of the play are the themes evoked in the magnificent series of choral odes; in fact, the proportion of choral lyric to dialogue is higher in *The Suppliant Maidens* than in any other Greek tragedy. In these songs Io and Zeus take on shapes hardly less vivid than those of the onstage actors, and their story constitutes a sort of super-plot. Its earlier phase, in which Io is loved against her will and tormented across the world, parallels the experience of the Chorus so far. Its gorgeous climax, in which Io is released from sorrow and gently made mother of a royal line, is appealed to as a guarantee for the future. At the same time a strange inconsistency develops in the Chorus' attitude: unlike Io, they hate marriage and the male on any terms whatever. In their exit song they hymn the virgin Artemis and reject Aphrodite, in spite of the warning hints of their handmaidens, who in this last scene form a supplementary chorus.

By the end of *The Suppliant Maidens*, in fact, a sort of sexual war has been declared. Very little is known about the lost play that immediately followed, *Aigyptioi*, but by the end of it the male cousins must somehow have enforced their claim to marriage. The few remains of the third play of the sequence, *Danaides*, suggest that after the horrific climax of the war on the human plane—the massacre of the male cousins, with one exception, in the bridal chamber—the gods were drawn into the struggle. The longest fragment reveals Aphrodite herself defending the primal union of Heaven and Earth, renewed each year in the spring rains: the source of life.

The Suppliant Maidens thus seems to have been no more than the opening lyric movement in a drama of cosmic proportions, the denouement of which is almost entirely lost. If it is appraised by conventional dramatic canons—even by those of the subsequent Greek theater—fault is all too easy to find. There are only three speaking parts—Danaus, Pelasgus, and the herald—and these are so distributed that only two actors are seen on the stage at any one time. Even so, the characters barely speak to each other, still less interact (in the manner of Sophocles' drama) to advance the plot. At the end of the play one hardly remembers them as individuals but rather as masked,

dreamlike figures moving on the border of the Chorus' experience: Father, Protector, Aggressor, uttering at the right times what is right for their mask. Here and there only—at the agony of Pelasgus' decision and in the angry confrontation between Pelasgus and the herald—are there signs of independent life.

Before 1952 critics generally explained these phenomena by assuming that *The Suppliant Maidens* was written extremely early in Aeschylus' life and represented tragedy at the primitive phase, when it was just emerging from its origins in pure choral lyric. Even now, when the play has been dated to Aeschylus' last years, there are some who hold that it is a reversion to the early phase. An alternative view is that the play was deliberately designed to reinterpret a weird yet powerful myth. The collective consciousness of the Chorus was to be all that mattered, to be what actors, heroine, and plot have been in subsequent drama. If that is correct, *The Suppliant Maidens* ranks as the boldest of all Aeschylus' theatrical experiments, besides being, as almost all critics have agreed that it is, the most moving lyrical poem in Greek.

Translations of the play are listed under Aeschylus. The most recent edition, with commentary, of *The Suppliant Maidens* is by T. G. Tucker (1889). Robert D. Murray's *The Motif of Io in Aeschylus' Suppliants* (1956) provides much helpful material. —C. J. H.

Suppliant Women, The (Hiketides, c. 424 B.C.). A tragedy by EURIPIDES. In this play the Chorus of mothers of the Argive leaders killed in a war with Thebes (see THE PHOENICIAN WOMEN) have come to Eleusis, together with the defeated Argive king, Adrastus, to beg Theseus, king of Athens, to compel the victorious Thebans to surrender the bodies of their sons for burial. Theseus refuses Adrastus' plea but grants that of the grieving mothers, especially when his own mother, Aithra, adds her plea to theirs. Defeating Thebes quickly in war, he brings back the Argive dead to Eleusis. The remainder of the play is a lament over the corpses, during which Evadne, the widow of Copaneus, flings herself onto his pyre. Athena directs the sons of the dead men to avenge their fathers by attacking Thebes as soon as they are grown.

The Chorus' odes are excellent and fully tied in with the action. There is a problem, though, in the Chorus' number: seven mothers but only five bodies; besides, the chorus of a tragedy customarily numbered fifteen. *The Suppliant Women* is a play to the glory of Athens. It is also a war play. Euripides, as often, emphasizes war's two aspects: sorrow and suffering, here represented by the mothers; and violence and vengeance, represented by the men, and here also by the sons, who are impatient for the time when they can avenge their fathers. It is also a political play. The debate of Theseus with the Argive herald over the virtues of democratic government strains the legendary framework to the breaking point by its anachronism, though it is vigorous enough and not entirely one-sided.

The spectacular is more prominent than is usual in a Euripidean play: the suppliants grouped around Aithra, at the beginning; the entrance of the young king with attendants and the Chorus in supplication at his feet; the bringing in of the bodies and later of the urns; and the sudden appearance of Evadne on a high rock and her leap onto the burning pyre of her husband.

There are textual problems. The messenger's description of the battle is confused and the language loose; Adrastus' funeral eulogies of the heroes contradict what was said before and are rather frigid. It may be Euripides' intention here to parody funeral speeches. Yet in spite of probable tampering with the text and some obvious imperfections, *The Suppliant Women* has many good qualities and is substantially the work of Euripides.

Translations of the play are listed under Euripides.
—G. M. A. G.

surrealism. Surrealism aimed to destroy the notion of literary categories and genres; it realigned writing on the broad bases of logical and analogical expression, the former to be considered journalistic and commercial, the latter poetic and liberating. The attack on formalism in the arts was part of a wider declaration of what André Breton called his "non-slavery to life," and a militant stand was taken against all procedures that tended to destroy the enigma of existence by submitting the unknown elements in man's words and actions to a rational understanding of them. *The First Manifesto* (1924) of Breton attacked the psychological novel directly and by implication similar approaches to the drama. But Breton conceded that dialogue as verbal communication was the most suitable channel for automatic writing. "It is to the dialogue that the forms of surrealist language are best adapted." In an effort "to restore dialogue to its absolute truth," Breton rejected the use of dialogue for polite conversation. Rather, it was to be a confrontation of two streams of spoken thought, not particularly relevant to each other nor having any inherent sequence but provok-

ANDRÉ BRETON (FRENCH CULTURAL SERVICES)

ing a spontaneous response. As a psychic release in which the speakers dispense with the forms of decorum, it was apt to reveal certain hostilities arising out of the intermittent interruptions of the verbal automatisms of the speakers. The first piece of writing acknowledged as "surrealist," *Les Champs magnétiques* (1919), a collaboration between André Breton and Philippe Soupault, was just such a form of dialogue: a juxtaposition of two soliloquies triggering each other. It was to be followed by a number of other attempts to structure drama on the basis of the dialogue.

Previously, Guillaume Apollinaire had stated in the Preface to his experimental play *The Breasts of Tiresias* (1918) that, whereas in the past theater had situated man in relation to society, it was time to relate the protagonist to a total universe and to view nature not in slices but in a snythesis of its facets and functions. In his burlesque fantasy he used the word surrealist for the first time, as he expressed his rebellion against the artist's imitative role in regard to nature. He identified surrealism with the power of invention in any field of human activity.

Since Apollinaire's preamble and Breton's manifesto, many currents and crosscurrents have intermingled in what has come to be called avant-garde theater. Of these conglomerate, unclassifiable writings in dramatic form, a very small number are truly surrealist, yet few are totally untouched by surrealism.

The most essential characteristics of surrealism in any form of the arts are the cult of the dream, the representation of the absurd, the erotic, and objective chance and the expression of the psychic experience of man through a form of writing that is "automatic" in the sense that it is uninhibited and as free as possible from the mental mechanism of criticism and censure. The progression of thought, the permeation of the author's sensibility into the reader's or viewer's awareness is to take effect through the use of free association and the explosive metaphor. Drama based on these premises would provoke direct, convulsive reaction—what Antonin Artaud, the theoretician of surrealist theater, called the THEATER OF CRUELTY.

But in classifying plays as surrealist, one must realize that the absurd, the erotic, and the dream are not the exclusive properties of the surrealists. The mere exercise of these states in scenario form does not constitute surrealist drama.

The absurd of the surrealists is not the caricature of life traits, which, since Seneca and Aristophanes, since the *commedia dell'arte* and Molière, and in recent times with Alfred Jarry and Eugène Ionesco, has created brutal farce out of the incongruities of human reality. For the surrealists, as Breton indicates, the absurd "is the conciliation of action with the dream," a level of existence verging on the sublime. It is not a corrective device, nor a superior mockery of the human condition. The absurd has to do with the capturing of a moment in objective chance when the natural laws of phenomena, of which we have no knowledge and over which we have no control, coincide with human intentions.

If love is dominant as a subject of surrealism, love drama is not necessarily surrealistic; for the surrealist, love is unsentimental, very physical, deemed sacred and sinless, unfrustrated, magnetic, and sparked by unexpected chance encounters. Unexplained and unaffected by social obligations or conventions, it is a totally free union. Plays dealing with the social and psychological problems of love do not fall into the surrealist orbit. For the surrealist, the analysis of love falls short of the actuality of love.

The dream is also something quite special in surrealism. It is not the antithesis of reality or an escape into fantasy; the surrealist writer introduces the spontaneous succession of events as they happen in the dream into the chronological course of events within the recognized measurements of time and space that we call reality, and he shows through his analogical vision the overflow of the natural banks of these relationships. Symbolist plays such as Maurice Maeterlinck's fairylands full of princesses or ghostly visitations, Villiers de L'Isle-Adam's *Axel* with its escapist, disoriented hero, and August Strindberg's *A Dream Play* (Artaud's production of this play caused his expulsion from the surrealist coterie) are the antithesis of surrealist drama. Their orientation is away from reality rather than an invasion of it, and the attitude of the poet-dramatist is one of withdrawal rather than of adventure. The symbolist creates a static state in the theater, turning personages into motionless *tableaux-vivants,* alienated from reality. The symbolist obliterates time, represents the unreal, empties space of the traces of human life, darkens the stage as a reflection of the process of abstraction and spiritualization of the human personality through his detachment from life. (See SYMBOLISM.) On the contrary, surrealist drama is a catalytic approach to time and an exploitation of the territory of the stage, an extension of it into the open air, a search for light and the unobstructed vision. Instead of stopping, time assumes a new flexibility and the drama focuses on temporal phenomena that are too slow or too rapid to be grasped by rational calculation. It is an onslaught on existence.

It was obvious from the first that the dynamism of surrealism in theory would be difficult to convey through the medium of the theater unless there first occurred a massive transformation of the structure and function of the theater. The dramatic works of the first generation of surrealists were blueprints for the new drama rather than finished works. There were about fifteen of these early works, dating from 1920 to 1940, and as a whole they were short, abortive attempts at playwriting that were performed only experimentally. Some of these are more Dadaist than surrealist, deriving from Jarry's and later Tristan Tzara's break with convention in the spirit of a rebellion against bourgeois morality; the surrealists, emulating the Cubists, were more concerned with the communication of vision than of action. Obviously, this tendency made them poor dramatists, and their plays were better suited to reading than performing. The legacy of Jarry's *Ubu Roi* can easily be distinguished from the purposes of surrealism. The subversiveness of the former is expressed in the absurdities of behavior and language, as in Tzara's *The Gas Heart* and even in Gertrude Stein's plays, with their hypnotic aberrations of language. The surrealist rebellion was not against abuses that can be corrected by legislation (as in socially oriented theater) nor against flaws in human nature that cannot be corrected at all (as in the "theater of the absurd"). The revolt was directed against the blunted eye and the parochial perspective, against patterns of group behavior that stunt personal verve and dull individual imagination. What is irrational in this instance is the author's way of demonstrating his protest against stereotyped, stunted perception, while he makes his audience aware of his built-in faith in the reversibility of the condition.

In *If You Please* (1920) Breton and Soupault mingle the mystery of the poetic sense of life with the speech of ordinary café and office conversation in which their nonconformist characters are engulfed. "The regions of the imaginative are vast," says one of the characters, but he does not demonstrate it. A dream-directed heroine, Valentine, believes in the primacy of desire; she has a surrealistic sense of the immediacy of time, of the magnetic power of words, and of their star-like illumination, but the characteristic revolver shot, emblematic of surrealism's rebellion, abruptly terminates her idyl and the unfinished play (the last act was intentionally never written).

Louis Aragon is often poetic, almost never dramatic, in the cataclysmic play *The Mirror-Wardrobe One Fine Evening* (1924). There are two forces in this play, but they do not come into conflict, because one is the colossal army, disciplined and confident in its task of making everyone "Red and perfectly content" (the words are for Aragon synonymous); on the other side are the ineffective dreamers whimpering that there is not enough elbowroom left even in dreams. The lover-dreamer cannot keep the tide diked up in an allegorical wardrobe; he will be overwhelmed, and the world must die before it can "become the world again." Many years later, in 1945, Robert Desnos, who spoke "surrealist" better than anyone else, finished the most substantial of the surrealist plays, *Place de l'Etoile* (begun in 1927). He creates, better than any of the other surrealist writers, the climate of the dream in its characteristic shaping of daily events, achieving it more through metaphors than through real plot. Among the dramatically presented metaphors are a five-cornered starfish that obsesses the hero and is multiplied in crescendo fashion as the play progresses and a fire that surrounds him but leaves him untouched, precipitating him from one love into another, that of Fabrice. A Nadja-like creature, Fabrice lives in dreams and waters the daily blossoms of the marvelous as an antidote to her abject condition as a prostitute. She is obsessed by the notion, characteristically surrealist, that love is free of sin and that whatever paradise there is she must find it here on earth. Ending his work on a less destructive note than the Breton-Soupault play, Desnos shows Fabrice in the last scene pressing for entrance into the room and the life of a new lover.

A number of these plays were collaborations, as Breton-Soupault: *Vous n'oublierez pas* (1922); Breton, Desnos, and Benjamin Péret: *Comme il fait beau* (1923); Breton and Aragon: *Le Trésor des Jésuites* (1929). The early plays of Roger Vitrac had the spontaneity of automatic dialogue in *The Mysteries of Love* (1927) and the combustible rebellion of childhood in *Victor ou les enfants au pouvoir* (1928), but Vitrac's representations of the absurd were brutal, as was the case in Jarry's *Ubu Roi,* and protest did not succeed in the poetic liberation of Vitrac's characters any more than in Jarry's.

Artaud's "theater," which was more theory than fact, preconized the power of words, freed the notion of theater from its dependence on plot and character, sought involvement of the audience in the play, and emphasized the communication of the metaphor through gesture and pantomime. If his point of departure is surrealism, his models are Jarry and the Balinese theater.

Jean Cocteau became generally identified with surrealism in the 1920's and 1930's because of his cult of the myth, his magical implementation of fantasy on the stage, as well as on the screen, in works such as the plays *The Eiffel Tower Wedding Party* (1921) and *Orphée* (1926) and the films *The Blood of a Poet* (1932) and *Beauty and the Beast* (1945). But Cocteau's wizardly calculated representation of the dream and the absurd, his ability to make the *insolite* tangible and alive reveal the tactics of a prestidigitator, which appear to be manipulation of nature rather than a deep occultation of reality. His alleged commercialization of surrealist techniques antagonized the surrealist coterie; he in turn proclaimed his independence, suggesting that one could be a legitimate heir of Picasso and Chirico without joining the surrealists. The fact is that despite the protests of both the surrealists and Cocteau, his film-poem *The Blood of a Poet* represents, better than *The Andalusian Dog* or *L'Age d'or* of Luis Buñuél and Salvador Dali, the mystical landscape of a psychic and multifaceted reality, revealed in a series of unexpectedly juxtaposed objects, of lights and shadows, of drawn personae communicating with live actors, of gaping wounds and symbols of chance, in cryptic images that convey the major emblems of surrealism on the screen with the luck of a beginner whose mistakes lead to discovery. What his theater lacks, in terms of surrealist theories, is the element of rebellion, while others who possess that power of attack falter before the techniques of stage and screen without which the insolite cannot come to life.

But surrealism, failing in the pure sense to create theater, helped with its iconoclastic views to break down many of the conventions of the conversational and philosophical drama that had turned theater into a dialectic and verbose form of literature. But demolishment of theater structure came later in France than in Germany. Some thirty years elapsed after the work of Apollinaire, Jarry, and the early efforts of the surrealists, during which time the plays of Henry de Montherlant, Jean Anouilh, Albert Camus, Jean Paul Sartre, and their counterparts in Western European countries and in America successfully prolonged the conventional theater of ideas.

But today's happenings, audience involvements, spontaneous dialogues, illogical sequences of plot, and the elimination of walls to produce direct actor-audience communication owe much of their acceptability as "theater" to the expansion of the term theater by the surrealists. However, the elements germane to surrealism are intermingled in today's living theater with several other traditions. On the one hand, the manner of *Ubu Roi,* which turns man into a puppet and then annihilates him, has not only survived but has proved seminal. Through the intermediary of the theater of violence of Artaud, it leads directly to the work of Jean Genet and Michel de Ghelderode. Before attributing any influences to surrealism, one must also acknowledge the freedom brought to the stage by the heirs of EXPRESSIONISM and the high prestige of Bertolt Brecht. On the other hand, the broad vein of modernism also includes, particularly in the presence of Samuel Beckett, the heritage of symbolism with its vacuum stage, nihilistic attitude, and simplicity of movement. In competition with these influences, the mark of surrealism (and the word is used more and more loosely, for every time the designator finds it hard to describe the unusual, he resorts to the word surrealist) is a matter of degree and spirit rather than a totality.

In the cosmopolitan theater of Paris in the third quarter of the twentieth century surrealism's clearest triumph can be discerned in the fact that many dramatists no longer feel the need to use the stage to discuss social and psychological problems; they are, instead, willing to assume the risk of throwing the stage open to the drama of self-identification and self-discovery, to the representation, rather than discussion, of states of liberty, to the demonstration with whatever means they have available, even if sometimes awkward, that man does not live by bread alone and that verbalization in the theater must provoke action rather than explain it.

Of the new dramatists, Henri Pichette reveals the clearest surrealist tendencies in *Les Epiphanies* (1947) and *Nucléa* (1952), with his large outdoor settings, big casts, and intuitive expressions, in the rebellion of lovers, and in the nonideological but nightmarish representation of war. His emphasis is on the poet and the lover as liberating forces in a world in chaos, their search for purity in the most unexpected environments, and in true surrealist fashion he tries to combine poetry and protest in a flow of metaphoric language that stops at times the tide of action, the better to project the eruptive force of his dream. The Spanish-born Fernando Arrabal's panoramas are emblematic of man's direct conflict and communication with the universe as envisaged by the surrealists, and his "theater of panic" is full of the kind of oneiric speech patterns explored in automatic writing. The Armenian-born French playwright Arthur Adamov, whose cultural background was equally German and French, vacillates between the influences of Kafka, Strindberg, and expressionism, on the one hand, and his close intimacy with the surrealists, in particular with Artaud. He demonstrates surrealism in the projection of metaphysical introspections and the incongruities of dreams in terms of the juxtaposition of monologues, such as can be detected in his early plays, *The Parody* (1950) and *The Invasion* (1950).

Because the Syrian-born Georges Shehadé, product of a broad Mediterranean culture, is poetic in his use of French, was an admirer of Paul Eluard, cultivates the illogical language of dreams, and searches for new myths, he has been likened to the surrealists, who in turn have protested against the association. The fact is that the escapist stage of Schéhadé, his cosmic wanderlust, and the transparence of his characters are better compared to the latter-day symbolism of Beckett. More surrealist in spirit is the Algerian Yacine Kateb, who is primarily a poet and whose basic subject is revolution, not as a potential but as a reality of the Algerian revolution, which he projects onto the stage, expressing the metamorphoses of the political state through the violations of the meaning of words themselves in *Le Cadavre encerclé* (1958).

Finally, among those who officially came into the orbit of the surrealist experience as disciples of André Breton, there is the West Indian Aimé Césaire. After writing surrealist poetry for many years in the wake of his meeting with Breton in Haiti in the 1940's, Césaire projected into his first play, *La Tragédie du roi Christophe* (1964), the images of black magic and metamorphosis by representing, in surrealist stylization, the theme of Negro liberation from slavery in Haiti. Another disciple, the Yugoslavborn Radova Ivsic, presents the surrealist concept of the magnetic power and proliferation of love, reminiscent of the marked belief in alchemy present in Breton's later works; in Ivsic's *Airia* (1960) the lovers seek identity in a repetition of the first line of Breton's *Nadja*: "Who am I?"; and actually, one of the characters clothes her total enigma in the name "!?" which is the only appellation that the author gives her. The intermingling of the human elements with those in nature is poetically evoked, although the dramatic structure remains very fluid.

The power of language in the late manifestations of surrealism, as in the earlier ones, is offered as a substitute for dramatic coherence and impact. Whereas surrealist effects are essentially dependent on the rapid, unexpected spark of recognition and revelation, the all-in-one-piece impact of a poem or a painting has so far proved inaccessible to the longer time span and larger space of the theater.

Antonin Artaud in his *The Theater and Its Double,* translated by Mary C. Richards (1958), describes his notions of the principles that should govern the theater of the future. Anna Balakian in *Surrealism: the Road to the Absolute* (1959) spells out some of the basic characteristics of surrealist language and form, as well as the principal concepts that motivate its philosophy. Michael Benedikt and George E. Wellwarth have brought together in an anthology of translations a number of surrealist plays never before collected, even in the original language: *Modern French Theater: the Avant-Garde, Dada, and Surrealism* (1964), which contains the largest number of primary materials accessible to the American in this area. Martin Esslin, in *The Theater of the Absurd* (1961), speaks very authoritatively about the lineage of plays that have created what is known as the theater of the absurd; not all of these plays are in the surrealist spirit, but acquaintance with them helps to see more clearly the different trends in the theater of the post-World War II era. Wallace Fowlie's *Dionysus in Paris* (1959) describes the plot and character of many plays of the French contemporary stage without attempting to classify them. André Fraigneau's *Cocteau on the Film* (1954) consists of a series of interviews with Cocteau in which the dramatist points out his techniques. J. H. Matthews' *An Introduction to Surrealism* (1965) does not deal with the theater specifically but it discusses the basic surrealist techniques and concepts. Robert Motherwell edited the best and most complete anthology of Dada writing that exists in any language: *The Dada Painters and Poets* (1951). Leonard C. Pronko's *Avant-Garde: the Experimental Theater of France* (1962) is the most up-to-date discussion of French dramatists, with some short résumés of plots. Henri Béhar's *Études sur le théâtre Dada et surrealiste* (1967) includes a play by Picasso and one by Erik Satie. —A. B.

sutradhara. Term for an important figure in Sanskrit drama. The *sutradhara* is director of the play, stage manager, speaker of the prologue, in general charge of the preliminary proceedings, and frequently an important actor in the play itself. His basic function is to lay down a bridge between the play and the audience, to speak to the spectators in behalf of both the playwright and his company. He gives the play its frame, so that, after careful and traditionally arranged proceedings, the whole drama is itself a play-within-a-play. He sets the key for all that follows. It is he who casts the magic spell.

The word itself has been subject of much discussion and controversy. The German scholar R. Pischel noted that the word *suta* signifies "string," or "cord," and hence assumed that the term suggested that the actors were puppets held in the hand of the sutradhara. From this inference he even derived the origin of Sanskrit drama from marionettes. Later scholars, such as I. Shekhar, differ from this view, which nevertheless has held currency for nearly half a century. It is now observed that the word possesses a wealth of connotations. The cord may be that of the architect or master carpenter, who oversees building operations. It is certain that the term signified the leading reciter of epic poetry. In the theater the sutradhara would thus be the leader who held the narrative in hand, not, literally speaking, as prompter, but as general manager. Although the origin of the term is still conjecture, as regards the drama and the stage its meaning is sufficiently clear.

Much is written about this traditional figure, both in the main treatise on Sanskrit drama, the *Natyasastra,* and in other sources. It is recommended that the performer of the role be a man of mixed caste, acquainted with all castes for the better serving of his managerial functions. He must be versed in languages, customs, manners, dress, architecture, mechanics, music, dancing, and literature. He must "hold the clue" for the play. He has full responsibility for the performance and especially for the comfort and contentment of the audience. In short, he is the general manager of the troupe.

The sutradhara, who is both an actor and the manager of the production, launches the performance on its course. All Sanskrit plays required elaborate ritual preparations, with music, dance, and prayer. The prayer, known as the *nandi,* was originally not composed by the dramatist; arrangement for it certainly lay within the province of the sutradhara. Later, as the literary texture of the performances bettered, the poet-dramatist became responsible for the prayer as well as for the play. After the prayer the sutradhara entered. Convention required him to address the audience, after remarking that the prayer and accompanying ceremonies were becoming tedious and should be terminated. He was then expected to announce the name and character of the play, to name its author, and to give some pertinent information about him. He might also be expected to give the time and place of the play's action. Rules for the introduction further provided that an important actress in the company, assumed to be his wife, should appear. This character commonly sang a song. The sutradhara would then be interrupted in his own discourse by a voice offstage; he would give some explanation of the unseen speaker and leave the stage as the speaker entered, repeating the words that he had spoken unseen.

The sutradhara's part is of decidedly different length in different plays. It may be either perfunctory or highly imaginative. In works ascribed to Bhasa, it is invariably brief, in certain cases almost identical from play to play. Brevity characterizes the introductory episode in *Charudatta in Poverty,* the truncated version ascribed to Bhasa of *The Little Clay Cart,* ascribed even more conjecturally to Sudraka. On the contrary, the role of the sutradhara in *The Little Clay Cart* itself is long, complex, and highly amusing, and was certainly composed by the playwright. Kalidasa's supremacy in Sanskrit drama is nowhere more in evidence than in the introductory passage of *Shakuntala,* where much is compressed into little. It concludes with a brilliant touch impossible to duplicate. The sutradhara observes that he and the audience have been captivated and entranced by his wife's singing much as the king, Dushyanta, is enthralled by the fascination of the chase of the deer which at that moment is imagined to leap across the stage. The sophisticated artistry of Sanskrit drama is nowhere more happily exhibited than in the variations played by the dramatists on the sutradhara's role.

This convention of the Sanskrit theater is ably examined in *The Indian Theater* (1954) by Chandra Bhan Gupta. The basis for theoretical study is the *Natyasastra,* ascribed to Bharata, translated by M. M. Ghosh (1951). For origins of the role, see Richard Pischel, *The Home of the Puppet Play* (1920). The role is thoughtfully analyzed by I. Shekhar in *Sanskrit Drama: Its Origins and Decline* (1960).—H. W. W.

Sweden. The mystery and the morality play did not exist in Sweden, so far as one can tell from surviving evidence. Indeed, the school drama based on biblical themes is very much secularized in the direction of gross comedy and incipient naturalism. True, the oldest preserved play, *Tobie Comedia* ("Comedy of Tobias," 1550), is religious, but not so Jacobus Petri Rondeletius' *Judas Redivivus* (1614) and Samuel Petri Brask's *Filius prodigus* ("Comedy of the Prodigal Son," 1645), which are unexpectedly profane considering their academic origins. Magnus Olai Asteropherus' *Thisbe* (1610) has a charm that makes it quite playable today, but Johannes Messenius' chronicles *Disa* (1611), *Svanvita* (1613), and *Blanckamäreta* (1614) establish a tradition of native historical drama without being very dramatic in themselves. Not surprisingly, Sweden's first acting company was comprised of Uppsala University students putting on, in the 1660's and 1670's, such tragedies as Anders Wollimhaus' *Dido* and Urban Hiärne's *Rosimunda* (1665). Hiärne (1641–1724), polymath, fellow of the English Royal Society, and moving spirit in this theater group, gave Sweden its first genuine tragedy, albeit one of Senecan limitations.

While Sweden enjoyed the presence of a French theater from 1699 to 1706, it was not until the en-

lightened reign of Gustaf III (1771–1792) that the foundation of the Royal Opera (1773) and the Royal Dramatic Theater (1787), and the king's deep-seated personal infatuation with theater, created a proper milieu for playwriting. The greatest triumph came with the collaboration between Gustaf III and Johan Henric Kellgren (1751–1795) in the opera *Gustav Vasa* (1786). The court poet Carl Gustaf af Leopold (1756–1829) contributed such tragedies as *Oden* (1790) and *Virginia* (1802), after the fashion of Voltaire, but the age saw as well an efflorescence of comedies, farces, and vaudevilles.

Interest in the drama, so largely and artificially stimulated by one man, declined with the assassination of Gustaf III in 1792; and it can scarcely be said that Swedish Romanticism did anything to sustain it. The fairy-tale play *Lycksalighetens ö* ("Isle of Blessedness," 1827), by P. D. A. Atterbom (1790–1855), and the novels *Amorina* (1821) and *Drottningens juvelsmycke* ("The Queen's Jewel," 1834), by C. J. L. Almquist (1793–1866), have, by virtue of adaptation, come into their own on the twentieth-century Swedish stage (*Lycksalighetens ö* as an opera by H. Rosenberg, 1945). *Drottningens juvelsmycke* may be viewed as a kind of bond between the rococo world of Gustaf III, which it treats, and Strindberg's chronicle play *Gustaf III* (written 1902; prod. 1916). At any rate, except for the adaptations that August Blanche (1811–1868) made of various foreign comedies, there was little drama until the advent of Strindberg.

August STRINDBERG, whatever his personal irresoluteness, never had much real doubt about his destiny as a playwright. He discovered himself in the writing of *Mäster Olof* (written 1872–1877; prod. 1881) and in so doing not only modernized the historical drama but became its most expansive practitioner since Schiller. Strindberg's interest in the new psychology of Ribot, Charcot, Mernheim, and Maudsley brought him briefly into the fold of naturalism in such plays as MISS JULIE, *Fordringsägare* (*Creditors,* 1889), and *Pariah* (1889). But there was a strong contending strain of pietism in Strindberg, and from the psychological and spiritual crisis known as his Inferno Period (1894–1896), Strindberg emerged with a new kind of drama—subjective, moral, mystical, and frequently oneiric in its shape and texture. The pilgrimage play *Till Damascus I* (*The Road to Damascus I,* 1898) is usually considered the beginning of EXPRESSIONISM, and A DREAM PLAY may be said to anticipate some aspects of surrealism and the "theater of the absurd." Strindberg always wanted to found his own theater and he was ultimately successful in doing so. His Intimate Theater (1907–1910) not only housed those later tone poems of his, which he chose to call "chamber plays" after the analogy with chamber music, but prompted a series of critical memoranda that touch upon almost every aspect of theater. Strindberg's restless mind moved everywhere, making him, as Eugene O'Neill put it, "the most modern of the moderns."

Pär LAGERKVIST saw the theater at a crossroads, the choice being between Strindberg's expressive drama and Ibsen's psychological realism. Undoubtedly he oversimplified, but in choosing the path of Strindberg in the manifesto-essay *Modern teater* (*Modern Theatre,* 1918) he established a pure Swedish tradition of anguish, dream, ecstasy, and fragmentation of character. Almost everything thereafter, through the fixed points of Strindberg and Lagerkvist, has been extrapolation. Lagerkvist himself has written more than twenty plays, among them such fantastic charades as *Den svåra stunden* (*The Difficult Hour,* 1918), an expressionist triptych of plays; such longer plays as *Bödeln* (*The Hangman,* 1934), actually the dramatization of a novel that studies the nature of violence in both a medieval and modern context; and *De vises sten* ("The Philosopher's Stone," 1947), which concerns itself with the scientist's role in society.

Because his dramas are usually more lyrical and portentous than theatrical, Lagerkvist has not been as frequently played on Scandinavian stages as has his near-contemporary, the rumpled, quizzical, quixotic Hjalmar BERGMAN. Lagerkvist has always been abstracted from the world; Bergman was very much a part of it, ranging from Swedish regionalism to cosmopolitan theater in a diversity of styles. *En skugga* ("A Shadow," 1918) is, like Lagerkvist's *Han som fick leva om sitt liv* ("He Who Got To Live His Life Over Again," 1928), an expressionist *Doppelgänger* play, but with a lighter touch, that of the "marionette" idea of Maeterlinck. Such regional novels as *Hans Nåds Testamente* (*The Baron's Will,* 1910) and *Markurells i Wadköping* (*Markurells of Wadköping,* 1919) were turned into stylish, viable vehicles for the comic stage (both 1930), and Bergman's kind of roistering, irreverent Swedish domestic comedy found its culmination in *Swedenhielms* (1925) before he burned himself out writing voluminously for stage, radio, and screen.

After random and fitful examples of good theater from Karl Ragnar Gierow (1904–   ) and Ragnar Josephson (1891–   ), poet and art historian respectively, and each, for a time, head of the Royal Theater, the Strindbergian tradition of anguish may be said to have resumed in a line of descent reaching from *Den dödsdömde* (*The Condemned,* 1947), by that desperately lost child of the World War II generation Stig DAGERMAN, to all the sensitively turned torments of the cinema of Ingmar Bergman (1918–   ). Of the newer playwrights, Werner ASPENSTRÖM harks back to the early Lagerkvist in his apocalyptic vignettes, and Lars FORSSELL to the comic spirit of Hjalmar Bergman. Both Aspenström and Forssell are poets first and playwrights next, but Forssell is making the fuller commitment to the stage, as is clear from his very ambitious *Kristina* (1968). In terms of sexual daring, a certain historicity, and the infusion of songs *à la* Brecht, the play certainly surpasses Strindberg's, but whether it is a better one remains to be seen. Among other modernists, Bertil Schütt (1909–   ) continues to make cheerful lunges in the direction of the absurd; Bengt Bratt (1937–   ) seeks a more plangent naturalism in the menaces of the teen-age underworld; and Sandro Key-Åberg (1922–   ) interrupts the writing of poetry from time to time to make satiric verbal "happenings" called *prator,* which are rather like extended Jules Pfeiffer dialogues, though less topical in subject matter.

The seasoned, older writers continue to work in dramatic forms. Vilhelm Moberg (1898–   ), chiefly known for his massive chronicle (four novels) of the Swedish emigration to the United States, has produced a dozen or more plays displaying more intensity than originality. Only Harry Martinson (1904–   ) has arrived at a kind of grandeur. His opera *Aniara* (1959), libretto by Erik Lindegren and music by Karl Birger Blomdahl, takes place in outer space and is known the world over as a harbinger of the desolations to come. His play about the Orient, *Tre knivar från Wei* ("Three Knives from Wei," 1964), is one of the major dramatic accomplishments to come out of Sweden in the past years.

Swedish drama is intermittently but fairly extensively treated in *A History of Swedish Literature* (1961), edited by Alrik Gustafson, a volume in the series of literary histories sponsored by the American-Scandinavian Foundation. Some of the more recent plays have appeared in the Foundation's *Scandinavian Plays of the 20th Century* series.—R. B. V.

Switzerland. Theatrical activity in Switzerland is as old as it is in the rest of Europe; Swiss drama, however, is a decidedly modern phenomenon, except for its important flowering in the middle ages. The Benedictine cloister of Saint Gall provided German-speaking drama its initial root in the Introit tropes written in dialogue form and in the most famous of all tropes, the Easter *Quem quaeritis,* discovered in a ninth-century manuscript. The extensive *Das Osterspiel von Muri* ("The Easter Play of Muri," earliest manuscript dates from the mid-thirteenth century), also of Swiss origin, is probably the earliest German-speaking religious drama. The 1300's produced further splendid examples of medieval drama, such as the *Play of Saint Gall,* dealing with the birth of Christ and the visit of the Magi. Toward the end of the middle ages even such events as the Ascension and the Last Judgment were staged. Among the most famous of all dramatic and theatrical events of the middle ages, as well as one of the most fully documented regarding its staging techniques, was the production of the *Easter Passion Play* (1583) in the wine market at Lucerne.

The Jesuit theater and drama played an essential part, too, beginning in the second half of the sixteenth century. Begun as a totally didactic enterprise presented as additional spiritual instruction for the lay students of the Jesuit colleges, the production of plays flowered into a highly elaborate theatrical operation. The Jesuit drama also gave impetus to drama in the cloisters, a tradition that today has passed over to the Swiss universities, where some of Switzerland's most ambitious theatrical activities occur, not only in the form of newly unearthed works of the past, but also in the form of premières and highly experimental undertakings.

Somewhat late in medieval times there developed in the German-speaking city of Oberwallis a highly creative peasant theater based on the forms of the early middle ages. This genre produced all manner of peasant sacred drama: allegories, violent Counter Reformation plays, and Shrovetide plays—but all in peasant guise.

Without a doubt Swiss theatrical activity has continued uninterrupted to the present. Following the Reformation and Counter Reformation, however, the production of native Swiss drama was not terribly distinguished when compared with the rest of

German-speaking Europe. Switzerland's principal contribution, especially in modern times, has been as a showplace for the drama of other nations. During the Second World War Zurich especially served as the leading producer of plays by Germans in exile from Hitler's domination.

It was at this time also that Switzerland began to rise to prominence as a major contributor to world drama, chiefly through the works of Fritz Hochwälder, Max Frisch, and Friedrich Dürrenmatt. Yet some quite interesting dramatic contributions were made before them, though few have achieved the recognition accorded Frisch and Dürrenmatt.

René Morax (1873–   ) wrote an epic drama entitled *König David* ("King David," 1921), with music by Arthur Honegger. Essentially, it is the life story of King David written from a historical point of view rather than from an idealized one; it tries to show David as a human reality rather than as a hero. He is seen both as God's servant and as one who also disobeyed. Each of the six scenes of this drama is built upon a musical structure and gives the impression of being a recollection in relief.

One of the most famous dramatic events was the 1918 Lucerne première of *L'Histoire du soldat* (*The Story of a Soldier*). The text was by Ferdinand Ramuz (1878–1947), the music by Igor Stravinsky, the decor by René Auberjonois, and the direction by Ernest Ansermet. The end result was an example of a perfect collaboration of the arts.

In line with Swiss tradition Paul Schöck (1882–   ) wrote *Tell* (1920) in brave despite of Schiller's famous *Wilhelm Tell*. *Tell* is based on the legendary events in the life of the fighter for Swiss freedom and independence. The play is perhaps provincial for the fact that it is written in Swiss dialect. One of its virtues, however, is its avoidance of the most famous incidents of Schiller's play, namely the scene of Tell's rescue of Baumgarten, the scene of the hat on the pole in the village square, the shooting of the apple from the head of Tell's son, the scene in the narrow pass, and the Parricida incident. In direct opposition to Schiller's many-scened play, Schöck's takes place wholly in the common room of an inn in Brunnen.

It was not until the time of the Second World War that Swiss drama began to move into international repute. Although born in Vienna, Fritz Hochwälder (1911–   ) may be considered a Swiss writer, for he fled Hitler's troops and settled in Switzerland, where he has lived and written ever since. He gained international recognition with his play *Das heilige Experiment* (*The Strong Are Lonely*, also known as *Faith Is Not Enough*, 1947). It deals with the tragic end of the Jesuit state in Paraguay in the eighteenth century, a true communist state that tried to hold itself aloof from material concerns in an attempt to establish the Kingdom of God on earth. Yet it had to give way to the greater interests of the Church. The play's chief conflict resides in the person of the Father Provincial, who must see and admit to himself the wrong he has lived in devising this state, and then must set about to destroy it. His illusions regarding the state are shattered, and he must reassess all he has lived and believed in the past. This theme—the conflict within the self and one's ultimate need to face one's errors and make them good in one way or another—is the basis of most of Hochwälder's dramas.

His second play, *Der Flüchtling* ("The Fugitive," 1945), concerns a border guard, his wife, and a fugitive. The fugitive comes upon the guard's wife, who feels morally obligated to help him flee Nazi Germany to neutral Switzerland. But her husband learns of this and is trapped in a dilemma: It is his military duty to turn the fugitive over to a horrible fate at the hands of the secret police. The guard, however, is a good man, yet he is able to turn off his human feelings at will when duty calls. He has orders. He is not responsible. In doing his duty he is only providing for his wife's safety and well-being. The regime is guilty of his dutiful acts, not himself. He decides to allow the fugitive to leave the house, and then he will shoot him in the back. But his wife in her simplicity and goodness is repulsed and locks herself in her room. The fugitive offers to try to cross the border without help, an act that would reconcile the guard and his wife. The guard agrees and offers the fugitive his hand, but the fugitive scorns the offer. At this moment the guard suddenly and overwhelmingly sees his entire past, looks deep into the abyss of his life, and finally understands why the fugitive cannot take his hand. With this transformation wrought inside him, the guard helps the fugitive escape, sending his wife along with the fugitive, and then shouts out his guilt to the approaching military, who promptly shoot him. *Der Flüchtling* is Hochwälder's view of the effect of the totalitarian state on the individual.

In *Esther* (1940) he wrote a close approximation of the biblical tale of Esther, with Haman the tyrant as the prototype of Hitler. The rise of Hitler is virtually the same as that of Haman, even to his tactics and devices, including the extermination of the Jews. Perhaps thinking wishfully in 1940, Hochwälder had his Haman be the victim of execution.

In *Donadieu* (1953) Hochwälder writes of the French Huguenot wars. Donadieu, a nobleman, discovers he has as a guest in his house the man who brutally murdered his wife some years before. Donadieu has lived in the constant desire for revenge, and now he has the man in his grasp. But there is one hindrance: the man bears the king's indulgence for the Huguenots their rights. But it is not for that alone that Donadieu forbears; he also comes to realize the emptiness of any revenge. Typical of Hochwälder's presentation of internal conflicts, Donadieu undergoes a moment of revelation and total spiritual and personal reorientation.

Along with Hochwälder are Max FRISCH and Friedrich DÜRRENMATT, who together constitute the most vital and vigorous development in postwar German-speaking drama. Both Frisch and Dürrenmatt are strongly influenced by the Brechtian technique, but it is never copied; rather, it is used as the basis for quite individual approaches. The most significant aspects of their work are their political concern and their deep involvement with the human condition, man's inhumanity to man, and the question of the survival of the species.

Frisch's *Nun singen sie wieder* ("Now They Sing Again," 1945) shows the painful fact of war and its effect on man. In the play the dead and the living come together in a plea for peace. In *Die chinesische*

Mauer (*The Chinese Wall,* 1946) Frisch deals with the miserable state into which man has plunged himself with his invention of the atomic bomb. In *Als der Krieg zu Ende war* (*When the War Was Over,* 1949) a woman falls in love with a Russian soldier after Berlin's surrender. But she still loves her husband, whom she has hidden from the occupation forces. Upon hearing of her husband's war crimes, however, she commits suicide. *Graf Öderland* ("Count Öderland," 1951) demonstrates the chaos of our age. A respectable man turns into a criminal, leads a terrorist movement, and tries to overturn the state's authority. As he is about to bring about his design, he returns authority to its proper sphere and, in his attempt to gain freedom from his aberration, kills himself. THE FIREBUGS demonstrates the stupidity of man for not nipping in the bud his capacity for self-destruction, which rises around him as a result of his own passivity and helplessness. In *Andorra* (1961) Frisch examines the problem of anti-Semitism. The small republic of Andorra is about to be overrun by a militaristic, anti-Semitic neighboring nation.

A far greater pessimist than Frisch, Dürrenmatt is given to exaggeration and the grotesque in his works in order to make his point. His chief concerns are the corruptive influence of power and death, which hovers over all that man does. His most famous international success, THE VISIT, reveals the evil of power and the absurd desire for revenge by an extremely rich woman on her former lover. She virtually owns industrial Europe and now is able to buy the life of the man who once wronged her. ROMULUS THE GREAT demonstrates the futility of trying to change the course of history. Romulus has tried to weaken Rome so that the Huns can overcome it and thus serve as punishment on Rome for her power, arrogance, and greed. *Die Ehe des Herrn Mississippi* (*The Marriage of Mr. Mississippi,* 1952) again deals with the idealist-moralist, in this instance with a number of them. Each tries to change the world, and each fails. *Frank V—Oper einer Privatbank* ("Frank V—Opera of a Private Bank," 1959) is a satirical comedy with music, in which a private bank goes broke only because it carries out its illegal activities with strong-arm tactics no longer in vogue, rather than with modern, sophisticated methods, such as merely concealing its illegalities under the cover of utter legality. *Die Physiker* (*The Physicists,* 1961) postulates the paradox that only through the suppression of scientific knowledge can mankind be saved. The play revolves around a famous physicist in a lunatic asylum, who realizes that if his knowledge and the results of his research are published the world, in its stupidity, would use them for its own destruction. Like all of Dürrenmatt's plays, this play, too, is highly pessimistic.

If one concern dominates modern Swiss drama since the Second World War, it is a vital interest in man's estate, his use of his potential, and the operation of his conscience as it relates to that estate of man. It would seem that the contemporary Swiss dramatist has taken upon himself the enormous task of showing the world where it is headed and what will happen unless it soon comes to its senses. In this regard modern Swiss drama is scarcely a stone's throw from the moralistic drama of the middle ages and the

didactic theater of the Jesuits. (For Switzerland's place in German-language drama, see GERMANY.)

Unfortunately, there is no single study in English on Swiss drama. The reader may, however, find individual essays about its playwrights in various modern treatments of contemporary playwrights. Hochwälder, Frisch, and Dürrenmatt are briefly considered in H. F. Garten's *Modern German Drama* (1959). The same three writers are given individual chapters in George Wellwarth's excellent *The Theater of Protest and Paradox* (1964). In addition there are three perceptive articles in various issues of the *Tulane Drama Review:* Melvin W. Askew's "Dürrenmatt's *The Visit of the Old Lady"* (June 1961); Adolf Klarmann's "Friedrich Dürrenmatt and the Tragic Sense of Comedy" (May 1960); and Gordon Rogoff's "Mr. Dürrenmatt Buys New Shoes" (October 1958). Also in *Tulane Drama Review* is George Wellwarth's "Friedrich Dürrenmatt and Max Frisch: Two Views of the Drama" (March 1962).—C. R. M.

symbolism. Symbolist drama is essentially the body of drama created by the poets of the symbolist movement and by followers who sought to apply the techniques and values of symbolist poetry to the theater. The term is not to be confused with "symbolic drama," for all dramatic representation is symbolic, just as all imaginative literary expression is inherently metaphorical. Often, however, such terms as "neo-Romantic," "impressionist," or "idealist" drama have been used as equivalents of symbolist drama. As a current and style, symbolist drama is basically French in origin, but in its development it came to include drama in virtually all of the principal Western countries. Its historical limits are approximately 1870 to 1920, coinciding with the chronological limits of symbolist poetry. Symbolist drama includes, but also goes well beyond, the plays written by symbolist poets; indeed, many of the most striking and even the most typical symbolist plays were written by playwrights who were not strict or conscious adherents of any literary school or movement. The principal symbolist playwrights are Villiers de L'Isle-Adam, Maeterlinck, Hofmannsthal, Strindberg, Claudel, and Yeats. The principal precursors of the symbolist drama are Wagner, Banville, and Mallarmé.

Symbolist drama is in part a deliberate repudiation of the overwhelming preoccupation with representational reality in the nineteenth-century theater. The so-called well-made play relied on complex and suspenseful plots and on recognizable characters and events, drawn in close conformity to external life. The conventional theater purported to present an illusion or copy of experience, a mirror of the world of common day. The symbolists turned away from the canon of literal realism and the dependence of dramatic action on material circumstances and events. They set forth a freer, more imaginative conception of the drama, in keeping with a new awareness of the role of dream, reverie, and mystical experience in art. It is important to see this new conception, not simply as a reaction to a stale and outworn realism, but as a positive assertion of a new mode of art.

Symbolist drama sought to replace the description of external events by the depiction or revelation of inner life. Suggestiveness and mood-creation displaced anecdotal statement and linear narrative. Symbolist drama was generally indirect, evocative rather than referential, with little or no plot action. It often took the forms of lyric drama, in its attempt to fuse poetry and theatrical expression, and static drama, in its reduction of narrative. In keeping with the values of symbolist poetry, it sought to present the mystery of being, the presence of the infinite in the finite, not directly and literally, but through analogies and correspondences. Music as well as the visual arts was used for suggestive and evocative purposes, and a style of stage design evolved in keeping with the indirectness and subtlety of the plays. For many of the symbolist playwrights, the new style restored the drama to its religious and ceremonial function. Not only were words and images endowed with magical power, the theater itself became a temple in which both actor and audience participated in the celebration of a sacred rite.

Richard Wagner is clearly among the main precursors of symbolist drama. It should be noted, however, that the high praise lavished by the symbolists on Wagner was not often accompanied by a clear understanding of his aims and that, in spite of important similarities, much in Wagner's theory and practice is sharply opposed to the tenets and art of the symbolists. Despite his insistence on the mythical and ritualistic character of the music drama, Wagner reduced the role of poetry in the theater and subordinated the spoken drama to music. It was in large part through Baudelaire's essay of 1861, "Richard Wagner and Tannhäuser in Paris," that later symbolists came to know of Wagner's program. Wagner's "total art," or fusion of the separate arts into a new grandiose artwork, is presented by Baudelaire as an expression of the universal harmony of correspondences. Wagner's music, Baudelaire insisted, is marked by an idealized mysticism, an expression of dream and mystery through the invocation of legend, fantasy, and myth. For Baudelaire, Wagner's music is more poetry than drama, yet Wagner's use of the term *drame lyrique,* or "lyric drama," refers specifically to his own opera rather than to a mode of poetic drama. Wagner is of major importance in pointing to the rich possibilities inherent in the appropriation by playwrights of operatic techniques. The presence of legendary subjects and mythical themes, as well as the insistence on an emotional or spiritual principle of dramatic unity and on a complex interrelation of the arts in the theater, was taken over by such dramatists as Villiers de L'Isle-Adam, Strindberg, and Claudel, as well as by scene designers such as Adolphe Appia, Gordon Craig, and Robert Edmond Jones.

Concurrent with the operatic and Wagnerian current of symbolist drama was a poetic tradition adumbrated by the mid-nineteenth-century French poet Théodore de Banville and developed by the leading theoretician and poet of the symbolist movement, Stéphane Mallarmé. Banville was a minor playwright whose comedies, generally set in classical antiquity and in a mythological and pastoral milieu, achieved a moderate success at the Comédie Française. He condemned the crude spectacle of the Romantic drama and the dullness of the drama of contemporary life. He urged a restoration of the centrality of poetry in the theater, and a fusion of music, mime, and language so as to invest the stage with magical and evocative power. Opera for Banville was the enemy of poetry in the theater. Instead of a drama of striking melodramatic and visual effects, he argued for a detheatricalized stage in which language would be wedded to dream and fantasy without any necessary conformity to literal events. The new lyric drama, he insisted, would be akin to the choral sections of Racine's last plays, fusing song and ode with dramatic dialogue.

The early dramatic compositions of Mallarmé, as well as his later theoretical writings on the theater, clearly reflect the precept and example of Banville. Yet Mallarmé, both in thought and expression, was a far more complex and powerful writer than Banville, with an unusual command of the resources of language and poetic structure. His great poems "Hérodiade" and "The Afternoon of a Faun" were begun as stage plays and point to a conception of drama revealing inner, spiritual experience. The complexity of his language is in keeping with his injunction: "Depict, not the object, but the effect which it produces"—hence the role of indirection, suggestion, and mood-creation in both his poetry and dramatic theory. "The theatre," he insisted, "is in essence Superior"; that is, it transcends the limits of purely material existence and exists on the ultimate plane of pure idea. Thus, ideally, the theater should express not acts or events but states of spiritual being reflecting the magic and mystery of the universe. In this sense, drama is the projection of dream and imaginative vision beyond any time or circumstance. It is a ceremonial rite, revealing the spirituality and wonder of the cosmos. *Hamlet* was for Mallarmé the ideal drama in its opposition of dream and destiny as the embodiment of the tragedy of the human condition, a drama of the mind without any necessary dependence on physical event.

Mallarmé's vision of a new theater is set forth in extreme terms in his critical essays. He poses the basic problem for symbolist drama: to what extent can a play embody symbolist values and satisfy the demands of stage presentation? Mallarmé's emphasis on mystery and spirituality issues ultimately in a theater of silence, but for his followers, language and silence intersect as part of a dramatic design.

Villiers de L'Isle-Adam (1838–1889), a contemporary and close friend of Mallarmé, held similar literary and philosophical ideals. He is clearly one of the leading symbolist playwrights and the first who was endowed with genuine dramatic talent. His early plays, *Elën* (1865) and *Morgane* (1866), are in the tradition of the Romantic melodrama of Victor Hugo or the elder Alexandre Dumas. Villiers gained a modest degree of recognition for his play of 1870, *The Revolt,* whose heroine anticipates Ibsen's Nora of *A Doll's House* in protesting against the vulgarity and mediocrity of her marriage. None of these early plays could be considered symbolist dramas, although Villiers' exaltation of the realm of the ideal and the grandeur of a life beyond life, to be realized through dream and ecstasy, point toward the new dramatic style. By far Villiers' greatest contribution to the drama was his play *Axel,* begun in the early 1870's under the full force of Wagner's example and reworked for a period of almost twenty years. The play was almost complete at the time of Villiers' death in 1889 and was published soon afterward. Its performance in 1894 was clearly a major event in the history of symbolist drama.

Axel is a loose, sprawling, and discursive play, apparently not meant to be performed exactly as it was written, yet by no means outside the scope of theatrical presentation. The long monologues and dialogues, expounding a mystical vision of man's place in the universe, enclose events of bold and stirring action replete with violence and melodrama. Yet the underlying doctrines and the implications of the action are thoroughly symbolist, repudiating the claims of material existence and concrete experience, even while the dramatic style is markedly akin to the Romanticism of Villiers' youthful compositions. The hero of the play, Axel, leads a life of self-imposed solitude and exile in his castle in the Black Forest, devoting himself to the teachings of the magus and seer Maître Janus and to the quest for spiritual perfection. Axel spurns the appeal of his worldly and materialistic cousin Kaspar to enter into "real life" and forces a duel on the officious Kaspar in which the latter is killed. In the climax of the play, he discovers the beautiful Sara, a mistress of occult knowledge, who has come to the castle seeking a vanished treasure. Axel falls in love with her, and when she reveals the treasure to him, he spurns it; their existence is already so full in their rapturous love that to continue living would be a sacrilege. "Live?" Axel exclaims, "our servants will do that for us." As Easter dawn approaches, Axel and Sara consummate their love in a double suicide, a love death unmistakably drawn after that of Tristan and Isolde. On his deathbed Villiers declared that he hoped to revise the conclusion of his play so as to provide a resolution more in keeping with Christian orthodoxy, wherein the liberation and transcendence of the self would be accomplished through faith in Christ. Mystical, occultist, and theosophical rites and beliefs move hand in hand with traditional Catholicism in Villiers' thought and art. His importance for the younger generation of symbolists was enormous. Late in life, W. B. Yeats, who attended the première of *Axel* in Paris, remarked: "It did not move me because I thought it a great masterpiece, but because it seemed part of a religious rite, the ceremony perhaps of some secret Order wherein my generation had been initiated." For Maeterlinck, Yeats, and a host of other followers, Villiers pointed the way to a theater of mystery and dream, of supernaturalism and wonder. Unlike most subsequent symbolist dramas, *Axel* is distinctly Wagnerian and operatic in both structure and style. Later symbolist playwrights were to respond to a more restricted, essentially literary conception of the stage, even while totally accepting the esoteric and transcendental idealism of Villiers' art.

The most successful symbolist drama is the early work of Maurice Maeterlinck. His art effectively embodies in some degree both the dramatic theories of Mallarmé and the visionary mysticism of Villiers de L'Isle-Adam. In Paris in 1886 the young Belgian became a disciple of Villiers, unreservedly accepting Villiers' searching critique of the conventional drama of the day. It was Villiers, as Maeterlinck was later to declare in his memoirs, who directed him to a theater of suggestiveness and mystery, of magic and spirituality. Recent research has shown that this decisive development in Maeterlinck's career was prepared for by his discovery of the work of the medieval Flemish mystic Ruysbroeck the Admirable, whose writings he subsequently translated. From Ruysbroeck, Maeterlinck derived the conviction that "all that we see is not present *merely for its own sake*, and matter *exists only spiritually.*" From both medieval and contemporary mysticism, Maeterlinck adopted the view that only through correspondences and analogies can we grasp the mysteries of the universe. Language must necessarily be suggestive, allusive, obscure. In a programmatic essay of 1890, Maeterlinck insisted that the "mystical density" of the work of art had been destroyed by representational realism. He contended that the theater is in fact "the temple of dream," and the playwright must create, not a replica of material reality, but "a shadow, a reflection, a projection of symbolic forms," through carefully induced atmospheric suggestiveness. These qualities are visibly apparent in Maeterlinck's first plays, *The Princess Maleine* (pub. 1890), *The Seven Princesses* (pub. 1891), *The Intruder* (1891), *The Blind* (1891), and *Pelléas et Mélisande* (1893). Maeterlinck later declared that he wrote his early plays "in the style of Shakespeare for a theatre of marionettes." *The Princess Maleine* combines subtle mood-creation with an elaborate and highly melodramatic plot, depicting the helplessness of feminine innocence confronted by depravity and crime. The lurid and macabre action is retarded at every turn through studied repetitions of word or phrase and calculated atmospheric effects. In the shorter plays that followed, and most successfully in *The Intruder*, Maeterlinck used the interplay of speech and silence to express the collision of visible and invisible planes of reality. Remarkable in its economy and compression, *The Intruder*, originally entitled *The Approach*, sustains to the very end an aura of mystery and dread expectation, while death as a moving presence invades the scene. The playwright employs a number of devices to provide foreshadowing and suspense; the sudden silence of the birds, the diving of the fishes in the pond, the mysterious opening and closing of doors, the dimming of the lamp, all help to project a sense of eerie and dread anticipation. The performance of the play in Paris in May 1891 marks the beginning of a theatrically viable symbolist art. Subsequently, Maeterlinck's plays came to constitute an essential part of the repertoire of the Théâtre de l'Oeuvre, directed by Aurélien François Lugné-Poë.

In his early essays and plays, Maeterlinck elaborated a theory of static drama wholly in keeping with the symbolist emphasis on interior action. In an essay of 1896, "The Tragic in Daily Life," he declared that true drama is internal, rooted within the soul. Great drama, therefore, is essentially static drama. External action and dialogue, Maeterlinck contended, are superfluous, for the essence of the drama is inner action set forth through an inner dialogue or "dialogue of the second degree," intimated rather than openly expressed. Despite the presence in *Pelléas et Mélisande* of a violent and melodramatic plot, the climax of the love relationship is rendered, not in word or gesture, but in moments of silence representing the rapturous communion between two souls. Maeterlinck's play of illicit love and murderous revenge also marks the beginning of an exploitation of romantic melodrama that ultimately was to make his theater far more conventional than the symbolist drama of the early 1890's. *Pelléas et Mélisande* dramatized the perils of extending the techniques of mood-creation and suggestiveness to encompass the scope of a full-length play. Most of the successful symbolist plays are lyric dramas, brief, compressed moments of mystical intuition and revelation. Maeterlinck's longer plays point all too clearly to an inherent opposition between symbolist premises and the demands of sustained theatrical elaboration. Just as their precursor and mentor Edgar Allan Poe could argue that a long poem is a contradiction in terms, so in the symbolists' dramatic efforts the attempt to produce ample and complex theatrical works collided with the evocation of mystery and silence. Maeterlinck's alleged static drama represents an emphasis rather than an absolute. Even his most subtle and sensitive dramas of inner life depend to some degree on external plot action. In his best symbolist plays the narrative is not eliminated but rather distended to the point where it all but loses intrinsic importance. Movement is present, but only incidentally and without any terminal value. Maeterlinck's plays have seldom been performed in recent years, yet in retrospect, his early work constitutes a remarkably imaginative attempt to widen the boundaries of the theater. The measure of his success can be seen in the widespread assimilation of his innovations in the work of such diverse playwrights as Chekhov, Hauptmann, García Lorca, and Beckett, to name but a few. The studied repetitions and silences of Beckett's static drama *Waiting for Godot* are in part a reflection of Maeterlinck's symbolist style.

In Germany the nearest approximation to the symbolist drama is the lyric drama composed by Hugo von Hofmannsthal during the 1890's. Hofmannsthal is not, strictly speaking, a symbolist poet or playwright, yet like many of his contemporaries, such as Rainer Maria Rilke, who wrote several plays in the symbolist manner, Hofmannsthal responded warmly to the new demand for a theater of mystery and the supernatural. In an essay of 1896, "Poetry and Life," Hofmannsthal described the aim of poetry as the evocation of a soul-state through mood-creation. His concern with analogies and symbols as figurative revelations of the mystery of the universe is derived as much from German Romanticism as from the French symbolists and issues for the Viennese playwright in a highly personal mysticism, at once Neoplatonic and archetypal. His early plays, such as *Yesterday, Death and the Fool,* and *The Little World-Theatre,* are striking examples of static drama, perhaps closer in their interior action to lyric poetry than to drama, yet representing an effort markedly akin to that of Maeterlinck to invest the stage with mystery and spirituality, revealed through the intensity of inner life. Early in his career Hofmannsthal translated some of Maeterlinck's one-act plays and was consciously influenced by the Belgian writer. Hofmannsthal's essay of 1901, "The Letter of Lord Chandos," at the end of a decade of symbolist endeavor, points directly to the danger that a symbolist drama, founded on a thoroughgoing mysticism, must end as a drama of silence. It is no surprise to find

Hofmannsthal subsequently turning sharply away from lyric drama to a more traditional dramatic structure marked by full and rounded characterization and plot action. Nevertheless, his lyric drama of the 1890's represents a significant effort to create a modern poetic theater.

While Hofmannsthal's early compositions are essentially poetic, restricted in movement, and dependent almost wholly on the poet's imaginative use of language, the symbolist plays of Strindberg and Claudel are largely operatic, marked by large and sweeping movement and by a bold and complex interrelation of the arts. Neither Strindberg nor Claudel can be strictly considered a symbolist playwright, yet both of them drew copiously on symbolist techniques. Their plays offer striking examples of the assimilation of symbolist elements in modern drama, freely combined with other dramatic styles. August Strindberg's preoccupation with suggestiveness, mystery, and occult correspondences reflected his close and extensive study of the Swedish mystic Emanuel Swedenborg, from whom the French symbolists had derived many of their leading ideas. During his residence in Paris in the 1890's, Strindberg came into contact with many of the French occultists, some of whom wrote dramas emulating Wagner's use of legendary or mythical subjects within a complex musical structure. Strindberg himself came to see Wagner as "a great poet . . . whose music is the only proper accompaniment to his words." In such dramas as Strindberg's *A Dream Play* (1902) and his trilogy *To Damascus* (1897–1904), the cosmic plane of action, long monologues, and alternation of verse and prose in strident rhythms all contribute to an operatic style in the Wagnerian manner. Maeterlinck's theory and technique also played an important part in stimulating Strindberg's experimentation, particularly in *Easter, Swanwhite,* and such "chamber plays" as *The Ghost Sonata.* The Swedish playwright greatly admired Maeterlinck's one-act plays, especially for their revelation of hidden cosmic forces in everyday life through an inner dialogue parallel to the spoken dialogue. The dramatic exploitation of silence in Strindberg's later plays is markedly akin to that of Maeterlinck, as in the lyrical love scenes in Part III of *To Damascus* or in Eleanora's supernatural vision in *Easter.* In exploring his private mysticism, Strindberg had earlier anticipated many of Maeterlinck's discoveries. The Belgian playwright was not so much a model for Strindberg as an incitement to continued expression of his own occultism in a drama replete with suggestiveness, mystery, and supernatural fantasy.

Paul Claudel began as a member of the circle of Mallarmé, and despite his highly personal and individualistic development as a playwright, he never wholly abandoned the symbolist premises of his youth. The notion of drama as a mysterious revelation of the hidden wonder of the universe, the correspondence between visible and invisible planes of reality, the suggestive and magical power of language, all enter forcibly into Claudel's artistic vision. His first major play, *Tête d'or* (1890), is plainly in the tradition of the loose and sprawling drama of cosmic quest, exemplified by the work of Wagner and Villiers de L'Isle-Adam. While Claudel came to be increasingly critical of Wagner, he recognized the

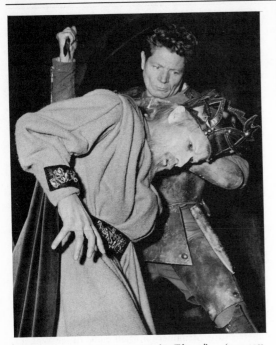

SCENE FROM PAUL CLAUDEL'S *Tête d'or* (FRENCH
CULTURAL SERVICES)

role of the composer in helping to liberate the theater
from the confines of realistic representation through
a drama of broad symbolic and mythic force. Like
earlier symbolists, Claudel saw the theater as a temple and dramatic performance as a collective ritual
akin to the drama of ancient Greece or the medieval
liturgical drama. In some of his plays, he experimented with the formal stylization of the Japanese
noh drama, which he admired for its sense of mystery
and ceremony. Almost from the beginning of his career as a playwright, Claudel was overtly preoccupied with Catholic doctrine and preachment and with
the great drama of salvation and damnation in
human experience, yet his turbulent incantatory style
is also part of a ceaseless effort to enlarge the scope of
drama through the exploitation of all of its imaginative resources. In this enterprise the techniques of
symbolist drama are an important element of Claudel's art.

W. B. YEATS is unquestionably the most important
writer in English who participated in the heritage of
symbolism. From Swedenborg and William Blake as
well as from Mallarmé, Villiers de L'Isle-Adam, and
Maeterlinck, he derived the view of poetry as a revelation of the invisible in a complex figurative language. Yeats's drama, like his poetry, reflects his
effort to wed the aristocratic and highly conceptual-
ized art of the symbolists to the legendary and mystical traditions of the Irish folk. Many of his early
plays are dramatizations of Irish history, legend, or
popular superstition, exploring the shadowy land between the material and the supernatural with a suggestiveness and mood-creation often reminiscent of
Maeterlinck. Yeats's most symbolist early play, *The
Shadowy Waters* (1900), is markedly close to *Axel* in
its celebration of the refusal to reduce life and love to

mundane reality. Forgael and Dectora, like Axel and
Sara, die and enter into a life beyond life. Yeats described *The Shadowy Waters* as an attempt "to create
for a few people who love symbol, a play that will be
more a ritual than a play, and leave upon the mind an
impression like that of tapestry where the forms only
half-reveal themselves amid the shadowy folds." Yet,
in the course of his career, he moved from a drama of
brooding introspection and mysticism to a somewhat
more objective presentation of the conflict of dream
and reality.

Yeats's boldest experimentation in the theater
came in 1916 with his conception of the plays for
dancers, drawn after his image of the Japanese noh
drama. Yeats had never seen a noh play and his
knowledge of the form was most imperfect, but he
seized on it as a way of combining "verse, ritual,
music and dance in association with action," in a
manner clearly akin to the symbolist ideal of a complex interrelation of the arts. Yeats proudly asserted
the claims of a deliberately "unpopular theatre" directed solely to kindred spirits, to "an audience like a
secret society." In *At the Hawk's Well* (1916) and in
the plays for dancers that followed, he created a
drama of subtlety and indirection, in a language of
taut, intense lyricism, with a minimal dependence on
anecdotal narrative. The plays for dancers are a significant extension of the symbolist ideal of static
drama, animated by the personal mythology that the
Irish poet subsequently embodied in *A Vision*. As
John Gassner has pointed out, Yeats was writing
symbolist drama at a time when the symbolist movement had largely receded in Western Europe. His
plays for dancers are a unique contribution to the
modern drama, but they are the work of a writer who
had turned sharply away from the contemporary impulses of the theater and they have had very little
effect on subsequent developments in the drama.
Nevertheless, Yeats's late experiments are plays of
considerable theatrical effectiveness if performed
with imaginative sympathy; they represent a challenging enlargement of the art of drama in our time.

Yeats is perhaps the last major symbolist playwright of any consequence. To be sure, some poets in
the symbolist tradition, such as Paul Valéry and Wallace Stevens, wrote plays and theorized about the
drama in a manner closely in accord with the thought
and expression of their symbolist predecessors, but
their plays are primarily extensions of their poetry:
dramatic poetry rather than poetic drama. By the
middle years of the twentieth century, the symbolist
drama had become simply one of the many stylistic
resources available to the modern playwright, and in
this assimilated form, it has entered freely into the
mixed styles of the modern theater. In retrospect,
while most of the symbolists were unable to reconcile
the values of symbolist expression and the demands
of stage presentation, it was chiefly in the one-act
play, as in the work of Maeterlinck, Hofmannsthal,
and Yeats, that a degree of integration of literary and
theatrical elements was achieved. The central problem for the symbolist playwright was the assimilation
of lyricism within a dramatic action. Excessive lyricism was an all-too-common weakness of the symbolist drama, yet mistiness and suggestiveness, as Anton
Chekhov proved, are not per se undramatic. Unquestionably, the symbolist preoccupation with the invis-

ible and occult made visible representation difficult, and perhaps the symbolist ideal was impossible for any dramatist to attain; yet, at their best, the symbolist playwrights lent immediacy and vividness to figurative representations of spiritual reality. Their art, despite its grandiose promise and limited fulfillment, remains in permanent readiness as a vital source of the imaginative transformation of the theater in our time.

Relatively little has been written in English on the symbolist drama. The best general essays may be found in Martin Lamm, *Modern Drama* (1952); John Gassner, *Directions in Modern Theatre and Drama* (1965); and Anna Balakian, *The Symbolist Movement* (1967). The history of symbolist drama in France is described in illuminating detail by Jacques Robichez in *Le Symbolisme au théâtre* (1957). For background discussion, see Haskell M. Block, *Mallarmé and the Symbolist Drama* (1963), and A. W. Raitt, *Villiers de L'Isle-Adam et le mouvement symboliste* (1965). Useful studies in English of symbolist playwrights are May Daniels, *The French Drama of the Unspoken* (1953), and Leonard E. Nathan, *The Tragic Drama of William Butler Yeats* (1965). Information on the early stage performances of symbolist plays in France may be found in Gertrude R. Jasper, *Adventure in the Theatre* (1947).—H. M. B.

Synadinos, Theodoros. See GREECE: *modern period.*

Synge, John Millington (1871–1909). Irish playwright. Born in Rathfarnham, a suburb of Dublin, on April 16, 1871, of an Anglo-Irish Protestant family, Synge (pronounced "Sing") was raised in the rigors of his mother's evangelical Christianity. His father, a Dublin barrister, died a year after Synge's birth, and the boy eventually found his mother's Calvinistic view of life so oppressive that he renounced Christianity when he was sixteen. A delicate and sickly child, he was educated by tutors at home and in private schools in Dublin and Bray. As a youth he developed an intense interest in nature, especially the study of birds, and he improved his health by taking long tramping trips through the nearby Dublin and Wicklow mountains. In 1888 he entered Trinity College, Dublin, and four years later he took a degree in languages, winning prizes in Gaelic and Hebrew. He loved music, took up the violin, and became so skilled at it that for a while he played in concert groups. Shortly after leaving Trinity, he spent four years traveling in Germany and Italy, settling in Paris, where he wrote poems and studied French, Italian, and Gaelic at the Sorbonne.

It was in Paris in December 1896 that Synge had his famous meeting with W. B. Yeats, and Yeats gave him the following advice: "Give up Paris, you will never create anything by reading Racine, and Arthur Symons will always be a better critic of French literature. Go to the Aran Islands. Live there as if you were one of the people themselves; express a life that has never found expression." Within two years Synge gradually abandoned his hope for a literary career in Paris and took Yeats's prophetic advice, spending each summer from 1898 to 1902 on the Aran Islands, about thirty miles from Galway off the west coast of Ireland, living among the peasants and beginning to collect the material that was soon to provide the themes and poetic idioms for his plays. With his

JOHN MILLINGTON SYNGE (CONSULATE GENERAL OF IRELAND)

notebook and violin he rapidly became a familiar and trusted figure among the islanders. Meanwhile, a fortunate coincidence of events hastened his permanent return to Ireland and the launching of his career as a playwright. In 1899 Yeats and Lady Gregory, with the help of Edward Martyn and George Moore, founded the Irish Literary Theatre, a group dedicated to the writing and performing of plays on Irish themes, in Dublin; in 1902, with further help from actors Frank and Willy Fay, it became the Irish National Theatre Society; and in 1904 it was finally set up in its own building as the Abbey Theatre. Synge was invited to join the new movement in 1902, and during the next seven and final years of his short life he wrote the six plays that established his reputation as the first great playwright of the Abbey. See IRELAND.

Two of his plays, RIDERS TO THE SEA and DEIRDRE OF THE SORROWS—the latter unfinished and published posthumously—are lyrical tragedies in a classical style, and the respective heroines, Maurya, a brave old peasant woman, and Deirdre, a passionate young queen, confront their tragic conditions with noble and stoical control. The four remaining plays, IN THE SHADOW OF THE GLEN, THE WELL OF THE SAINTS, THE PLAYBOY OF THE WESTERN WORLD, and THE TINKER'S WEDDING, might be described as dark comedies or even tragicomedies, for their farcical and irreverent humor is often accompanied by a contrasting mood of frustration or defeat that leads to mock-heroic resolutions for many of the characters —peasants and tramps and tinkers. Young Nora in *In the Shadow of the Glen* rebels against a loveless marriage and abandons her "dead" old husband, but there is no bright future for her as she leaves for the open road and damp ditches with the romantic tramp. In a satiric parable on human frailty, *The Well of the Saints,* the religious miracle that temporarily restores the sight of the blind Martin and Mary Doul only serves to expose their vanities and fantasies, as well as the cruelties of the villagers who torment them. The whining and self-pitying Christy Mahon is an unlikely candidate for heroism in *The Playboy of the Western World* until the repressed people of a Mayo village exalt his boastful deed of parricide and transform him into a triumphant playboy, only to turn on him when he tries to "kill" his father again in their own back yard. Even the earthy and exuberant *The Tinker's Wedding* is colored by comic ironies and defeats as the tinker girl Sarah loses her chance for a proper Christian marriage, mainly due to the shrewd irresponsibility of the tinker's randy old mother. Behind Synge's tinkers and tramps lies the mischievous and mock-heroic "shaughraun" or vagabond of Dion Boucicault's Irish plays, *The Colleen Bawn* (1860), *Arrah-na-Pogue* (1864), *The Shaughraun* (1874), sentimental but richly comic works that Synge admired for their sly and uniquely Irish humor.

Synge's characters aspire to a wild life of fantasy and freedom, and when this quest is limited or denied them in the world of reality, they invariably achieve it in the life of the imagination through the powerful and poetic Irish idiom they speak. Their passionate and overleaping rhetoric provides a vicarious gratification of their impossible dreams, and therefore the very language Synge creates for them must be considered as an organic aspect of his tragicomic and tragic themes. In his Preface to *The Playboy,* Synge insisted that the vitality of modern drama depends upon a rich language that grows spontaneously out of the living reality of a folk imagination, "the rich joy found only in what is superb and wild in reality. In a

good play, every speech should be as fully flavored as an apple or a nut." Like Yeats, he was reacting against the naturalism of Zola and Ibsen, and he objected to didacticism in the theater: "The drama, like the symphony, does not teach or prove anything." Ironically, however, Irish audiences nervously assumed he was trying to tell them something they did not want to know about the tragicomic realities of repression and puritanism in Irish life, and Synge was usually regarded with suspicion in his native land. In 1907 the audiences at the Abbey Theatre rioted for a week against *The Playboy* because they felt Synge had libeled the national character with his comic-ironic treatment of parricide and his shocking use of an indelicate word like "shift" (petticoat) in the dialogue. Perhaps it was a measure of Synge's artistic success that he had offended the right people by refusing to view his countrymen through a haze of sentimental idealism.

After a prolonged illness, on March 24, 1909, Synge died at the age of thirty-eight from a malignancy, Hodgkin's disease, or lymphatic sarcoma.

Standard editions of Synge's plays include *The Complete Works of J. M. Synge* (1935); *The Collected Works of J. M. Synge,* which is divided into *Poems* (1962), Robin Skelton, ed.; *Prose* (1966), Alan Price, ed.; and *Plays* (in preparation), Ann Saddlemyer, ed. See also in these editions the travel journals, which provide many sources for the plays, namely *The Aran Islands* (first pub. 1907) and *In Wicklow, West Kerry, and Connemara* (first pub. 1911). Biographical and critical studies include D. H. Greene and E. M. Stephens, *J. M. Synge, 1871–1909* (1959); Una Ellis-Fermor, *The Irish Dramatic Movement* (1939); Alan Price, *Synge and Anglo-Irish Drama* (1961).—D. K.

Syria. See ARAB DRAMA.

T

Tagore, Rabindranath (1861–1941). Indian author, poet, and philosopher. Born in Calcutta of a prominent Bengali family, Tagore became a figure of international importance in drama as well as in numerous other fields of literature. As playwright he possessed much inventiveness and a considerable knowledge of many aspects of theater in the West, yet he conceived himself, with much justice, as drawing his chief inspiration from two stems of Indian theater that were the most familiar to him: the classical drama in the Sanskrit tongue and the native Bengali folk drama, with its popular appeal, its eclecticism in the conjunction of realism and fantasy, and its fondness for dance, pantomime, and song. It is generally conceded that all his writings, not only in the field of drama but equally in pure poetry and expository prose, are materially more effective in Bengali than in translation. Although he spent considerable periods of his life abroad, residing in England and traveling in Europe and the United States, in China and Japan, leaving a strong imprint on the countries that he visited, his image of himself was essentially Indian and his aesthetically important works were written first in his native language. In some cases, however, he made his own translations into English, which he wrote with more fluency than inspiration. He was essentially an Indian with a desire to speak first to his own country and second to speak of it to the world. From radical movements in Western drama at the beginning of the twentieth century he derived much, especially from the newly revived Irish theater, but to the West he gave more than he received.

He is author of approximately fifty plays, some existing only in his own language. These plays are in a great variety of forms, sometimes to Western eyes appearing artless or primarily experimental. The English reader must at times be wary of judging his work through the veil of its too readily dated English style. Tagore himself was both an actor and director, completely sovereign in his own theatrical world. His plays have won great popularity in India both on the professional and amateur stage. Some were first presented in Calcutta, others at his own school and estate, Santiniketan ("the home of peace"), or at the internationally attended Visva-Bharati University. It is said by the dramatist and producer Balwant Gargi that "he invoked the spirit of Jatra ["folk opera"] which had been driven out of Calcutta by the professional stage." His works, which contain much song, mime, and dance, are singularly impersonal and have at times a mysticism that the unsympathetic have found vague. Many plays are in verse and even in verse of a strongly lyrical spirit. They are designed to be played on a stage largely bare, although the prop-

RABINDRANATH TAGORE (PRESS INFORMATION BUREAU, GOVERNMENT OF INDIA, NEW DELHI)

erties frequently have strong symbolic value. The language of the plays is often highly figurative and metaphorical. Tagore's leanings toward pure poetry are offset by passages or entire plays with colloquial speech and naturalistic action. Although he was content in no single style, his restlessness by no means signifies that he was not in some instances strikingly successful and successful even with the use of a great variety of modes.

The Post Office, one of his most widely popular plays, is in the pathetic mode. *The King of the Dark Chamber* and *Rakta Karavi* (*Red Oleanders*, 1924) contain strong elements of allegory. *Vis barjan* (*Sacrifice*, 1890), like several others, is a symbolic work, a freshly created myth, with nonviolence as its impassioned theme. Other plays, such as *Nature's Revenge*, following a pronounced trend in Sanskrit dramatic poetry, abound in nature imagery. In Tagore, however, this practice often draws the play away from the dramatic toward pure poetry or toward declamation, whereas in Kalidasa, whom Tagore recognized as his master, the theatrical element prevails even in the most opulent descriptive passages.

A writer of astonishing scope and versatility, Tagore was endowed with comic and satirical vigor, as witnessed in such pieces, less known outside India, as the realistic *Last Cause*, and *The Bachelor's Club*. In his later years he grew increasingly devoted to dance drama, typical of Indian tradition. Of this aspect of his art *Chitrangada* (1936) affords a favorable example. The work is based on his earlier play *Chitra* (pub. 1892). Other of his noteworthy dance dramas are *Shyama* (1939), with a romantic plot based on a Buddhist legend, and *Tasher Desh (The Kingdom of Cards)*, a satire on the Indian caste system.

Persuaded of a need for propaganda and instruction and keenly sensitive to many of the pressures of modern life and thought, Tagore was above all faithful at heart to Asian dramatic traditions and to the moral and spiritual values that he prized in Indian civilization. His plays show him convinced, with Bharata, the philosopher of the Sanskrit stage, that the theater should utilize the collective force of all the arts, with poetry, no doubt, at their head, but music, dance, pantomime, and spectacle also prominent factors. In India Tagore's reputation has always been high and has been gathering rather than losing force since his death in 1941. Although he may have left the world no dramatic masterpiece, his dramas will long provide a rich mine for inspection by all progressive and adventurous servants of dramatic art.

Critical literature on Tagore is extensive. Especially noteworthy are *The Philosophy of Rabindranath Tagore* (1961) by Sir Sarvepalli Radhakrishnan; *Tagore, a Master Spirit* (1963) by K. Chandrasekharan; and *Rabindranath Tagore—A Centennial Volume* (1861–1961), issued by the Sakitya Academy. A standard biography is *Tagore—Poet and Dramatist* (1948) by Edward Thompson. Valuable criticism may be found in *The Lute and the Plough* (1963) by G. Khanoikar, translated by Thomas Gay. Also useful is *Rabindranath Tagore* (1939) by Vincene Lesny.—H. W. W.

Takasago (Takasago Bay, 14th century). A Japanese *noh* play by Zeami MOTOKIYO. Takasago is commonly considered the best example of the important type of noh play the *kami-mai-mono,* or god-dance piece. This species of noh was used in introducing the series of dramas presented on single days of a festival. It is religious, solemn, and exceptionally ceremonious, also being of a congratulatory or affirmative spirit. *Takasago* adds to this a sentiment of patriotism and pride, celebrating, as it does, many aspects of Japan, such as the imperial house and the glories of Japanese landscape and poetry.

The play's legend concerns two aged pine trees, one beside the bay at Harima, the other at Sumiyoshi. These trees are personified in Part I as an old farmer and his wife; the scene is laid at Harima. In Part II, which is set at Sumiyoshi, the farmer has vanished, while in his place the leading actor, or *shite,* appears as the god of the pine, the chief deity of an important temple. The pines have been praised in poetry, even in poems by an emperor. Each pine is taken furthermore as symbolic of one of the two great imperial collections of Japanese poetry, the older *Manyoshu* and the younger *Kokinshu.* As in many noh plays, there is little real action but much moving poetry. An intricate network of symbols is woven. One understands that the venerable evergreens signify at once the stability of the empire itself and the immortality of the great poetry that the empire patronizes and supports. The play achieves a mood of sublimity and peace, an elegance and serenity expressed in the chief word employed in noh criticism, *yūgen.*

For the best exposition and rendering into English, see *The Noh Drama,* selected and translated by the Special Noh Committee, Japanese Classics Translation Committee (Vol. I, 1956).—H. W. W.

Taming of the Shrew, The (c. 1592–1593). A comedy by William SHAKESPEARE. The June 1594 record of performance of the play "the tamynge of A shrowe" is now considered by most scholars to refer to Shakespeare's *the Shrew.* The problem of identification arises because in May 1594 the anonymous *The Taming of a Shrew* was entered in the Stationers' Register and published later that year. Great scholarly debate has raged over the relationship between the two plays. The current consensus is that *the Shrew* is the prior play and that *a Shrew* is a "bad quarto," its text memorially reconstructed. *The Shrew* did not get into print until the publication of the First Folio (1623).

The source for the Induction—the Christopher Sly story—can ultimately be traced to "The Sleeper Awakes" tale from *The Arabian Nights.* The taming plot, also an old tale, is now regarded as based on the mid-sixteenth-century ballad "A Merry Jest of a Shrewd and Curst Wife . . . ." The Bianca subplot comes from George Gascoigne's play *Supposes* (1566). The three strands have been woven together through a play-within-a-play construction.

The drunken tinker Christopher Sly is found asleep outside a country alehouse and is taken to a lord's house. As a jest, Sly is convinced on awakening that he is a nobleman who has been mentally ill for fifteen years. To entertain him, a group of players present a comedy. This story disappears from the play in Act I. The main plot shows the wealthy young Petruchio, come from Verona to Padua on a wife-hunting expedition, wooing the young, beautiful, but shrewish Katharina. Against their knockabout adventures, during which Kate is tamed to obedience much as an animal is trained, Shakespeare presents the idealized love story of Bianca, Katharina's younger sister, and Lucentio.

This early and very popular comedy has primarily been played as broad farce. Despite realistic delineations of Sly, Petruchio, and Kate, character probing is minimal. The poetry is not distinguished. Running beneath the rough-and-tumble, however, are cogent comments on personality and marriage. As recent scholarship has shown, a basic unity underlies the three plot lines: an examination of the nature of identity. From the physical identity-switching, manifest in the Induction and Bianca plots, the play moves to a presentation of personality alteration, resulting in a harmonious relationship between husband and wife.

An outstanding edition of *The Taming of the Shrew* is the New Cambridge Edition (1928), edited by Arthur Quiller-Couch and J. Dover Wilson. —W. G.

Taner, Haldun (1916–   ).   Turkish playwright and short-story writer. Taner was born and raised in Istanbul. Subsequently, he studied economics in Heidelberg and theater arts in Vienna. Currently, Taner is a lecturer in theater history and dramaturgy at various Turkish universities. In addition to writing articles in the Istanbul daily *Tercüman,* for which he was the leading political columnist for two years, Taner has written short stories, which have been translated into twelve languages, including English, and have been represented in major anthologies abroad. Taner's first play, *Günün Adamı* ("Man of the Day"), was written in 1950, but the governor of Istanbul banned its performance in 1952 for fear that it might offend the government. In 1965 another play by Taner, *Eşeğin Gölgesi* ("The Shadow of the Donkey"), was charged by the public prosecutor with instigating strife between classes, and it was banned temporarily. Many of Taner's plays have been very popular with the public, however, *Gözlerimi Kaparım Vazifemi Yaparım* ("I Close My Eyes, and Do My Duty," 1964) was performed 600 times and *Keşanlı Ali Destanı* (*The Ballad of Ali of Keshan,* 1964) was performed 560 times in Turkey, as well as in Germany and England. In 1962 Taner introduced to Turkey the political cabaret theater and in 1967 established a cabaret theater to give regular performances.

Political satire and polemics are dominant in most of Taner's plays. His aim is to shock and arouse audiences while amusing them. Aware of the comic and satirical tradition, from Greek farces to Bertolt Brecht, Taner synthesized this heritage with the popular Turkish theater of *Orta Oyunu, Karagöz,* and *Meddah* to create for himself the most suitable dramatic form. Taner's plays utilize much of the verbal tricks and witticisms of the popular Turkish theater as well as those of Turkish folk tales. He has also borrowed effectively from the visual stylistic elements in Orta Oyunu and Karagöz.

Taner is the first Turkish dramatist to have synthesized Brecht's "epic theater" with native Turkish drama. His aim is to establish a new folk drama in Turkey that is native in form and progressive in social satire. Taner has widely influenced contemporary Turkish dramatists.—N. O.

Tanzania.   See AFRICA: *Tanzania.*

Tardieu, Jean (1903–   ). French poet and playwright. The sixteen sketches published in Tardieu's first volume (*Théâtre de chambre,* 1955) and the six in the second volume (*Théâtre II: poèmes à jouer,* 1960) are stylistic exercises for the stage, written in a style and language close to surrealism. They are farces, parodies, and poems that resemble the fantasy and anguish of dreams.

Like the playwright Jean Vauthier, Tardieu bases his dramatic action on rhythm and music. The sound of a word precedes its meaning. Words and gestures are reduced to a minimum, because, according to Tardieu, the loftiest expression of language is silence. In *Les Amants du métro* ("The Lovers in the Metro,"

1960) we read: "I am nothing, you are nothing, there is no one." In *La Sonate et les trois messieurs* ("The Sonata and the Three Gentlemen," 1955) each character is an instrument and recites the words in accordance with the rhythm that is to be created: largo, andante, finale. In *Une Voix sans personne* ("A Disembodied Voice," 1960) there is no actor on the stage; there are simply lights that play on objects. In producing this play, director Jacques Poliéri used *musique concrète* and projected paintings of Viéra da Silva.

For a critical study of Tardieu's work, see Robert Champigny, "Satire and Poetry in Two Plays of Jean Tardieu," *The American Society of the Legion of Honor Magazine,* No. 2 (1964).—W. F.

Tartuffe (1669).   A comedy by MOLIÈRE. First performed for Louis XIV in 1664, the play offended the pious and was banned, as was the second version produced in 1667. In 1669 the third version of the play was authorized. Orgon, a Parisian bourgeois, forces his family to accept the presence of the pious Tartuffe. Moreover, he wants Tartuffe to marry his daughter Mariane. But Tartuffe, who is in fact a sensual parasite, is attracted to Elmire, Orgon's wife. When Orgon finally realizes that Tartuffe is trying to seduce his wife, he wants to drive him out. But Orgon has already made over the whole of his estate to Tartuffe and has entrusted him with compromising political papers. Tartuffe would have had Orgon turned out of his own house and arrested if the king had not discovered, just in time, that Tartuffe was a dangerous criminal. In the end it is he who is arrested.,

Tartuffe is based on the relationship between two men, one of whom is ready to sacrifice blindly his family to the religious ideal embodied by the other, that other being a hypocrite who tricks him and makes game of him. Thus, not only hypocrisy but an excess of sincere piety are made the objects of satire and comic effects.

This play has been translated by Robert W. Hartle in *Tartuffe* (1965).—Ja. G.

Tasso, Torquato (1544–1595).   Italian poet and playwright. The son of Bernardo Tasso, a well-known man of letters and diplomat in the service of various Italian courts, Tasso spent his youth at the court of Urbino and in 1565 entered into the service of the house of Este at Ferrara. Between 1560 and 1575 he wrote his masterpiece, the epic poem *Gerusalemme liberata* (*Jerusalem Delivered*). Scruples concerning the moral and religious orthodoxy of the poem at once beset him, and the enervating task of revision, which he began in the same year, brought forward clear indications of madness. In 1579 he was confined in Ferrara in the Hospital of Sant'Anna. After his release in 1586, Tasso embarked on disturbed wanderings from one Italian city to another until his death in the Monastery of Sant'Onofrio in Rome.

Tasso began his career as a dramatist in 1573 with a pastoral drama, AMINTA, which enjoyed wide popularity and which remains the masterpiece of this literary genre. Of minor importance are a complicated comedy in prose, unfinished and published posthumously as *Intrighi d'amore* ("The Intrigues of Love"), and the tragedy *Il Re Torrismondo* ("King Torrismondo"), written in 1587. Its inclination

TORQUATO TASSO (ITALIAN CULTURAL INSTITUTE)

toward horror foreshadows the tragic theater of the next century.—L. L.

Tchrimekundan. See TIBET.

Tecer, Ahmet Kutsi (1901–1967). Turkish poet, folklorist, and playwright. Tecer was born in Jerusalem. As an active member of many organizations, Tecer left his mark on the cultural life of Turkey. He is noted for his lyrical poetry based on Turkish folk poetry and his scholarly research on native folk music, dances, and theater. Tecer's most famous play, *Köşebaşı* (*The Neighborhood*, 1947), was produced in English at the University of Wisconsin in 1952, thus becoming the first Turkish play to be produced in an English-speaking country.

Tecer's plays, both in verse and prose, deal gently with social problems. His *Köşebaşı* is a rather loosely constructed play, but with its lyrical prose and colorful, unpretentious dialogue, it provided a much-needed contrast with a Turkish theater dominated at the time by chauvinistic plays written in singsong verse, pseudo-expressionist plays, and light drawing-room comedies. Although not intended as a modernization of the traditional Turkish theater, *Köşebaşı* nevertheless reminded audiences of the traditional Turkish form *Orta Oyunu* and helped inspire other playwrights to delve into their native drama. —N. O.

television. See RADIO AND TELEVISION DRAMA IN BRITAIN; RADIO AND TELEVISION DRAMA IN EUROPE; RADIO AND TELEVISION DRAMA IN THE UNITED STATES.

Tempest, The (1611). A romance by William SHAKESPEARE. No major source exists for *The Tempest,* although part of its material appears to have been derived from popular travel literature, from the *Essays* of Montaigne, and from certain features of Renaissance Italian comedy.

On an enchanted island live Prospero, a magician and the former duke of Milan; his daughter, Miranda; his servant, the spirit Ariel; and the half-monster Caliban, whom Prospero keeps as a slave. Twelve years earlier Prospero had been driven from Milan by the machinations of his brother, Antonio, acting in collaboration with Alonzo, king of Naples. As the play opens Antonio, Alonzo, and a number of courtiers and attendants are shipwrecked by a storm at sea. The storm has been raised by Prospero's magic. He now uses his powers to draw all those on board to different parts of the island. The first to come ashore is the king's young son, Ferdinand. Under the influence of the invisible spirit Ariel, he is brought to Prospero's house and he and Miranda fall in love at first sight. Meanwhile, the royal party has landed. Lamenting the apparent death of his son, the sorrowing King Alonzo falls asleep. While Alonzo sleeps, Antonio plots with Sebastian, the king's brother, to murder the monarch. Their plot is foiled, however, by the timely arrival of Ariel.

In still another part of the island the king's jester, Trinculo, and his drunken butler, Stephano, come ashore to encounter Caliban. The latter, wishing to be freed from the controls Prospero has imposed on him, suggests to the two the murder of Prospero. Their scheme, too, is easily wrecked by Ariel's intervention. In the interim the members of the royal party have been alternately terrified and bedazzled by the mysterious events they encounter on the island. At last, weary and contrite, they are brought before Prospero, who, substituting compassion for revenge, forgives the wrongdoers. Prospero then abjures his magic, gives his blessings to the young lovers, and prepares to resume his role as duke of Milan.

The source of countless allegorical interpretations ranging from the political to the biographical to the theological, *The Tempest* has always been regarded as among Shakespeare's most beautiful and accomplished, if also most mysterious, plays. Part of the mystery has developed from the knowledge that the play represents Shakespeare's last great effort, tempting many to read it as his "farewell to his art." But even more productive of mystery is the richly suggestive atmosphere within which the play is enveloped. It is this atmosphere that lends a special significance to the themes of art and nature, appearance and reality, immortality and death, on which *The Tempest* evocatively but elusively touches.

A recommended edition of *The Tempest* is the New Arden Edition (1963), edited by Frank Kermode.—E. Q.

Tennyson, Alfred, Lord (1809–1892). English poet and playwright. Born at Somersby in Lincolnshire, educated at home and at Louth Grammar School, Tennyson early devoted himself to poetry, writing his first verses at the age of five. His first two publications (*Poems by Two Brothers,* 1827, with his brother Charles, and *Poems, Chiefly Lyrical,* 1830) reflect the strong influence of the Romantic poets. From 1828 to 1831 Tennyson studied at Trinity College, Cambridge, where he became a friend of Arthur Henry Hallam, whose sudden death in 1833 he mourned in his elegiac poem *In Memoriam* (1850).

ALFRED TENNYSON (NEW YORK PUBLIC LIBRARY)

Although Tennyson's third volume of poetry (*Poems,* 1832) was unfavorably reviewed, his next volume (*Poems,* 1842) was highly praised. His other important publications include *The Princess* (1847), *Maud* (1855), and *Idylls of the King* (the first four books published in 1859 and the entire series in 1889). In 1850 Tennyson succeeded William Wordsworth as poet laureate. In 1884 he was elevated to the peerage, accepting it only "for the sake of literature."

Tennyson is regarded today as the chief poetic spokesman of the Victorian era. Such works as *Idylls of the King* and *In Memoriam* reveal the poet's concern with, and response to, the various forces and ideas that dominated the period. This same interest is found in his poetic dramas, especially in the three that form the "trilogy of English history"—*Queen Mary* (pub. 1875), *Harold* (pub. 1877, produced 1928), and *Becket* (pub. 1879, produced 1893). Tennyson's active interest in writing for the theater covered the period from the middle seventies to the early eighties, during which time he wrote, in addition to the three plays cited above, *The Falcon* (1879), *The Foresters* (1892), *The Cup* (1881), and *The Promise of May* (1882). These last four plays exhibit the typical weaknesses of much of the poetic drama of this period, especially the tendency toward sentimentalism and melodrama and the absence of dramatic action. The poetic dramas that compose the trilogy, however, are more successful dramatically. The titles of all three indicate Tennyson's stress on history: he centered these historical studies on a single individual whose character encompasses the ideas

and reflects the movements of his time. The results of this approach are predictably varied. On the one hand, Tennyson's constant concern with historical accuracy led to a looseness of structure, a constant introduction of events and characters that have only peripheral bearing on the main action, and a lack of any real dramatic conflict in certain scenes. In *Queen Mary,* for instance, this desire for authenticity accounts for the tremendous cast of characters, many of which could have been omitted, and the great number of scenes. In *Becket* it is responsible for the need that Tennyson felt to have Becket and his various antagonists constantly discuss complicated points of theology and make fine distinctions regarding the responsibility of church and state, all of which succeeds only in slowing down the pace of the play at crucial moments.

On the other hand, because Tennyson focused on a single individual, he was able to portray with accuracy and fullness both the time in which that character lived and the development of the character's complex personality as he faces opposing characters or attempts to work out his own problems. Unlike many of his contemporaries who tried to depict historical personages and succeeded only in portraying caricatures, Tennyson was particularly successful in having his main characters reveal all of their varied and contradictory traits. Theatrically, the result is quite satisfactory, for, in the tradition of tragedy, one is able to follow Becket or Queen Mary and see the extent to which each is responsible for bringing about his own downfall. In this respect particularly, *Becket* is probably Tennyson's best poetic drama. Thus, while he did not substantially change the course of English poetic drama, Tennyson did give to it at a crucial period both a poetic distinction and a literary emphasis that it sorely needed.

For information about Tennyson's life and works see George O. Marshall, *A Tennyson Handbook* (1964). The best biographical account is Sir Charles Tennyson, *Alfred Tennyson* (1949); the best critical introduction to many of the works is J. H. Buckley, *Tennyson: The Growth of a Poet* (1960). For discussions of Tennyson's strengths and weaknesses as a dramatist and his place in nineteenth-century drama, see Harley Granville-Barker, "Some Victorians Afield: The Poet as Dramatist," *Fortnightly Review,* CXXXI (1929), pp. 655–672, and Henry James, "Tennyson's Drama: *Queen Mary* and *Harold,*" *Views and Reviews* (1908).—M. T.

Terence [Publius Terentius Afer] (c. 195–159 B.C.). Roman comic playwright. Terence, born in Carthage and brought to Rome as a slave, was educated and manumitted by his master, the senator Terentius Lucanus. He soon gained the friendship of Publius Cornelius Scipio Aemilianus and became a member of the literary and philosophic group known as the Scipionic Circle, which included the Greek historian Polybius, the Greek philosopher Panaetius, and the Roman satirist Lucilius. He is said to have submitted his first comedy, *Andria,* to the older playwright Caecilius, at whose house it was read with great applause after a dinner party. This story is viewed with suspicion by some scholars, since Caecilius died in 168 B.C., two years before Terence's first production.

Terence composed six comedies, all produced by

TERENCE (BUST IN MUSEO NAZIONALE, NAPLES.
COURTESY ALINARI-ART REFERENCE BUREAU)

the actor and theater director Ambivius Turpio, and
all based on plays of Greek New Comedy no longer
extant. He died in Greece, where he was possibly trying to procure more comedies by his favorite playwright, Menander, for adaptation on the Roman
stage.

The generally accepted order of Terence's six plays
is: *Andria* (*The Woman of Andros*), from Menander's *Andria,* produced at the *ludi Megalenses* in 166
B.C.; *Hecyra* (*The Mother-in-Law*), based on *Hekyra*
of Apollodorus of Carystus, presented at the ludi
Megalenses in 165 B.C. (this was a failure, because
the audience was distracted by a rope-dancer in a
nearby side show); *Heautontimorumenos* (*The Self-
Tormentor*), from Menander's play of the same title,
produced at the ludi Megalenses in 163 B.C.;
EUNUCHUS, from Menander's *Eunuchus,* produced
with great success at the ludi Megalenses in 161 B.C.;
PHORMIO, from *Epidikazomenos* of Apollodorus of
Carystus, produced at the *ludi Romani* in 161 B.C.;
ADELPHOE, based on a second *Adelphoe* by Menander (not the one used by Plautus in his *Stichus*), produced at the funeral games for Aemilius Paulus in
160 B.C. On this occasion *Hecyra* was again presented
on the stage, and again without success, being unable
to compete with a gladiatorial show. Later that same
year, probably at the ludi Romani, *Hecyra* had its

third production, this time successful. The first two
failures of *Hecyra* cannot be blamed entirely upon
rope-dancers and gladiators; it is an unusual Roman
comedy, a serious play of married life. Although
Hecyra is described by one modern critic as "the
purest and most perfect example of classical high
comedy," it lacks both the humor and dramatic action found in the other five comedies.

Terence is a master of the conversational Latin of
the cultured society of his day. His humor is subtle
and he avoids the farcical situations and exaggerated
characterizations of his predecessor Plautus. Terence
seeks to arouse thoughtful laughter. He is also an important innovator in dramatic technique. Plautus had
accepted the normal conventions of ancient comedy,
although he ridiculed them, but Terence, seeking new
variations on old themes, had his characters themselves express dissatisfaction with several conventions, such as offstage births, conversations from the
stage with persons indoors, and the revelations of
secrets on stage. His treatment of the slave is likewise
unconventional. The *servus* is no longer the trickster;
he is a bungler, or he tries to keep his young master
from wrongdoing, or (as in *Hecyra*) he is pushed off
the stage and kept in ignorance of the truth. Terence
changed the nature of the prologue by using it to defend himself against charges of plagiarism and
CONTAMINATIO brought by an older playwright,
Luscius Lanuvinus. By omitting from the prologue
the usual plot summary, he was able to create surprise rather than anticipation. He was especially fond
of the double plot, in which two young men are involved in two closely interwoven and interdependent
love affairs. This dual structure appears in all his
comedies except *Hecyra*. Terence's departures from
normal comic technique are most apparent in his first
three comedies. The others, however, contain not
only a better integration of plot and character but
also more effective humor.

From the Renaissance on, the plays of Terence
were extremely influential on writers of modern
comedy, especially Molière and the English dramatists of the eighteenth century.

Gilbert Norwood, *The Art of Terence* (1923),
analyzes Terence's six comedies and evaluates and
criticizes the plots and characters of each play.
George E. Duckworth, *The Nature of Roman Comedy* (1952), discusses numerous aspects of the plays of
Terence, including presentation, stage conventions,
plots, characters, thought and moral tone, the comic
spirit, language and style, originality, and later influence. Translations of all six comedies of Terence are
by John Sargeaunt (2 vols., 1912), in George E.
Duckworth, ed., *The Complete Roman Drama*, Vol.
II (1942), and by Betty Radice, *The Brothers and
Other Plays* (1965) and *Phormio and Other Plays*
(1967). See also translations listed under ROMAN
COMEDY.—G. E. D.

Terson, Peter (1932–   ). English playwright.
Terson, the most outstanding regional dramatist to
emerge in England during the 1960's, was born in
Newcastle-on-Tyne, the son of a joiner. After two
false starts as a trainee draftsman and a schoolteacher of physical education, he found his feet as
resident dramatist at the Victoria Theatre in Stoke-
on-Trent, a theater with a defiantly regional policy
and a deep commitment to its local community. The

Victoria presented a series of plays by Terson: first *A Night to Make the Angels Weep* (1964), *All Honour Mr. Todd* (1965), *The Mighty Reservoy* (1966), *I'm in Charge of These Ruins* (1967), and *The Ballad of the Artificial Mash* (1967). Terson also collaborated with the company in preparing documentary-style musicals of local interest, like *The Knotty* (about the history of the North Staffordshire Railway).

Much of Terson's work is set in the Vale of Evesham, Worcestershire, and presents a conflict between rural tradition and the forces of change. The plays share a common geography: a stony hilltop and a fertile valley whose inhabitants envy or resent one another. There are also recurring character types who are shuffled into varying alliances. What remains constant is the sense that something is denying nature and that nature will take its revenge. A good example of this theme is *The Mighty Reservoy,* in which the reservoir keeper and a white-collar guest gaze down on a valley from the top of a mountain of water, which comes to represent their pent-up natural resources.

Terson's command of dialect, his comedy, and his powers as a poet received wider recognition when *The Mighty Reservoy* appeared in London in 1967. This was followed in the same year by *Zigger Zagger,* a bitterly uproarious football spectacular exposing the social pressures that turn teen-agers into fans who live only for the next match.—I. W.

theater of cruelty. In the theater of cruelty Antonin ARTAUD, director and philosopher of the theater, conceived a ceremonial theater of magic purgation that has had a profound influence on avant-garde writers and directors from Jean Louis Barrault to Peter Brook. In a number of manifestoes Artaud passionately rejected the fossilized psychological theater of words and proposed a theater inspired by the sacred ritual theater of the Orient.

Artaud first began to crystallize his ideas on theater in 1931 when he witnessed the Balinese dancers at the Colonial Exposition in Paris. He was above all impressed by the exotic atmosphere, the allegorical masks, and the stylized gestures of the actors. What he found in the Oriental theater was a primitive mentality that exposed the human soul and the conditions in which it lives in a drama of cruelty. Artaud longed to reinstate the theater's primordial dignity by magically exercising the dramatic power of reality in order to affect man's senses so that he might understand his desires and acts from a larger perspective.

In October 1932 Artaud published his first manifesto, entitled "Le Théâtre de la cruanté" ("The Theater of Cruelty"), in the *Nouvelle Revue Française.* There he schematically formulated his theories concerning a total theater. He wished to move men profoundly, not only through their cerebral awareness, but also through their organic sensibilities.

Aware of the insufficiencies of the literary and psychological theater that presented characterizations and dry imitations of life, Artaud proposed a theatrical experience that would give a magic revelation of human destiny. By means of theatrical ritual he hoped to raise the theater to the level of a religious ceremony in which man would be reconciled with "becoming," the metamorphosis of ideas into forms. This is what Artaud understood as "metaphysics in activity." If we accept Artaud's conception, that our

ANTONIN ARTAUD (MR. AND MRS. PIERRE MATISSE)

acts are ideas transposed into form and that our gestures reveal a conscious reality or a metaphysical plan, we can understand that there is no fundamental difference between our ideas and our acts.

Artaud wished to reinstate the multiplicity of meanings inherent in theatrical acts by creating a language of action and gesture that by its plastic and expansive nature could not be ossified by habitual intellectual rationalizations. Words become superfluous because the actor's gestures are capable of evoking our instinctual emotions, because art in a stylized form can reach every man on an inner level where his obsessions, his hopes, and even his criminal tendencies are dealt with truthfully, without regard for the morals of the period.

Artaud's conception of the theater is a functional one: to overwhelm the spectator in such a way that he cannot be left intact. By liberating man's instinctual preoccupations with crime and eroticism, Artaud hoped to achieve a therapeutic transformation in the spectator. In order to experience true feelings the spectator must participate emotionally in the dramatic action, which consists of an event, or a happening.

Artaud wished to create a sort of collective delirium and even a physical shock in order to reveal the fundamental cruelty that is at the basis of every dramatic action. The cruelty of which Artaud spoke was not one of bloody killings onstage but rather a cruelty of lucid determinism to which we are all necessarily submitted. This cruelty is the permanence of evil, of the devouring forces of love, eroticism, and death; it is the transfiguration of forms that are always on the verge of returning to nothingness or chaos. Both resurrection and death participate in a metaphysical discipline of constant motion— renewal and disintegration.

The theater of cruelty is essentially physical in its attempt to reach man through his senses in order to reveal the organic relationship among man, society, nature, and objects. Artaud wished to present violent images that would hypnotize and virtually inundate the spectator caught in the "movement of superior forces."

Such a radical conception of theater, of course, implies a new conception of the director's role and of staging techniques. For Artaud it was not a question of theatricality but rather a very serious attempt to awaken the consciousness of life in the audience. For him there was to be no separation between art and life.

To revitalize the theater, he gave priority to the *mise en scène,* the stage setting and action, rather than to the literary text of a play. Theatrical action must take on a concrete representation, language must become "poetry in space," and the words must express an emotion by sound. Gestures must have an autonomous meaning distinct from words. Thus, the literary text loses its supremacy and makes way for a total theatrical art. The theater must utilize the particular elements of staging that distinguish it from other artistic forms. For Artaud the material with which an artist works creates its own form. To deny the specific orientation of the art of the theater would destroy its autonomous function and make it more decorative than revealing. The visual plasticity of staging had to become communicative. The theater had to utilize all means of expression relevant to the stage: painting, dance, gestures, movements, objects, colors, sounds, lights. This concrete language would be transcribed in much the same way as the ancient hieroglyphs. Thus, each thought and emotion would have a spatial existence on the stage as precisely readable symbols and correspondences. Artaud did not wish to do away with the spoken word entirely, but he wished to reveal the physical and affective side of language by having words explode and expand into space as screams, controlled sounds, and intonations in order to form vibrant incantations.

Artaud's conception of the theater demanded, not only new techniques of presentation, but also a new conception of theatrical space and of the relationship between the actor and the public. Based on the spectator's participation and total envelopment, Artaud preferred a single unifying space for a better communication between the actors and the audience. However, he wished to have the spectators placed in the center with mobile seats that would permit them to follow all the action surrounding them. Thus, the dramatic action could occur successively or simultaneously and spread like fire from place to place. Artaud hoped to achieve a total environment by means of new sound devices, new musical instruments, and moving lightscapes. There was to be no *décor,* only giant mannequins and objects, ritual costumes, and hieroglyphic characters as the concretions of verbal expression. Even the actors are to be used as objects, much in the same way a painter uses his pigments or his canvas. As in the Balinese dances, every action is rigorously defined.

In his list of projected productions to be given by the society of the theater of cruelty, Artaud wished to adapt a play from "Shakespeare's time" that would correspond to the concerns of Artaud's time. In addition, he proposed plays concerning the relationship between eroticism and cruelty: "the history of Blue Beard" and a story by the Marquis de Sade. The violence of inevitable or historic forces—of fate—could be represented by the biblical "History of Rabbi Siméon" and "the capture of Jerusalem," which would show the "panic" of the masses and the upheaval of the "king, the temple, the populace and the events." Without following the literary texts very closely, the actors could attempt direct stage presentations of Elizabethan drama similar to Peter Brook and Charles Marowitz' recent interpretation of *Hamlet* (1963) in London. Even romantic melodramas and a poetic play by Léon Paul Fargue could be adapted to Artaud's theories, as well as a precise literary text such as Georg Büchner's *Woyzeck.*

In the second manifesto of the theater of cruelty, published in 1933, Artaud described the cosmic and universal themes that he hoped would reveal the passions and anxieties of modern times, especially "social upheavals" and racial conflicts. His theater would address itself to the "total man," not to thin psychological characters "deformed by religion" or civilization. His heroes would take on "mythic dimensions" and would be the size of "gods" and "monsters."

The first project of the theater of cruelty was to be "La Conquête du Mexique" ("The Conquest of Mexico"), a scenario partially outlined in his second manifesto, but never produced. Artaud wished to demonstrate visually the force of events and "the fatality of history" that manifest themselves in the person of Montezuma, who is torn between "inner struggles" and ancient, astrological myths. Artaud felt that the problems facing Montezuma—the brutality and bloodiness of war, "the question of race superiority" brought on by colonization, and the decline of the Aztec monarchy as well as those of Europe—were relevant to modern Europe of the 1930's. "La Conquête du Mexique" deals with the theme of "the moral disorder" and the "tyrannic anarchy" of the Christian conquerors as opposed to the peaceful and spiritual order of the Aztec nation. The fatality of historic events is felt in the consciousness of the pulsating masses, either in their panic or in their desperation. The "revolt of the people against destiny" becomes all the more real with the metaphysical and moral breakdown of a betrayed people.

It was not until 1935 that Artaud attempted to implement his theater. After having proclaimed "the anonymus society of the Theater of Cruelty," which never came into existence, and proposing a program that included *The Revenger's Tragedy* by Cyril Tourneur, *The Duchess of Malfi* and *The White Devil* by John Webster, and *Woyzeck* by Büchner, he finally realized one of his own texts, LES CENCI, adapted from Shelley and Stendhal. Aided by the young Jean Louis Barrault, Roger Blin, and Balthus, who designed the costumes and the sets, Artaud presented his rather unsuccessful play in the old music hall Les Folies-Wagram. Although the production was rather conventional in its textual form, Artaud did use light projectors, new sound devices, electronic instruments, loudspeakers, and mannequins.

Even if Artaud's theatrical theories were a failure, or were never realized, he did triumph in another sense. His search for a means of generating existential awareness inspired many avant-garde directors and playwrights, such as Peter Weiss, who incorporated sounds, mime, and "happenings" into his play *Marat / Sade.* Not only Weiss, but also Peter Brook, Jean Louis Barrault, and Roger Blin acknowledge the influence of Artaud's ideas on their work. The general and theoretical nature of Artaud's ideas have also affected such writers as Jean Genet, Arthur Adamov, Fernando Arrabal, and Romain Weingarten.

For a critical study of the theater of cruelty, see the following: Eric Sellin, *The Dramatic Concepts of Antonin Artaud* (1968); *Tulane Drama Review,* Vol. 8, No. 2 (Winter 1963); *Tulane Drama Review,* Vol. 9, No. 3 (Spring 1965); and George Wellwarth, *The Theater of Protest and Paradox* (1964).—E. C.

theater of the absurd.   The term applies to certain European and American dramatists in the 1950's and early 1960's who were not part of any self-proclaimed movement but who held in common a sense of metaphysical anguish at the absurdity of the human condition.

The playwright of the absurd views life existentially, but unlike Jean Paul Sartre and Albert Camus (who first used "absurd" to define the human situation in his essay *The Myth of Sisyphus,* 1942), he expresses the senselessness of the human condition by abandoning rational devices. The playwright's sense of being is his subject matter, and it is this projection of the author's inner world that determines the theater of the absurd's nonrealistic form and that essentially separates absurd drama from existential drama.

While the roots of ˙surd drama can be traced as far back as Euripides ˻nd Aristophanes, the theater of the absurd is very much a product of our own times. The late nineteenth-century French playwright and poet Alfred Jarry is often considered the father of absurd drama, although elements of absurdism appear in the plays of the early nineteenth-century German Georg Büchner. The antecedents of the theater of the absurd are numerous: ancient mimes, *commedia dell'arte,* futurism, surrealism, as well as the peripheral theater arts of fair, circus, music hall, and film. Writers such as Anton Chekhov, Luigi Pirandello, Franz Kafka, Bertolt Brecht, and Antonin Artaud, who raged against the planned utility ordered by the conspiracy of civilization, presage absurdist drama. Another important influence was the Second World War. With its bizarre atrocities and meaningless devastations, World War II was undoubtedly instrumental in orienting the minds of the dramatists toward a serious reevaluation of man's role, not only as a social animal, but also as the inhabitant of a universe whose meaning and structure were rapidly disintegrating.

The task of the absurdist is metaphysical, beyond the psychological, moral, or social limits established by traditional drama. The absurd theater does not expound any theses or debate any ideologies. It is a theater of situation as against a theater of events in sequence. The action in an absurd drama does not tell a story in the usual sense but instead presents a pattern of images designed to communicate the perplexity and anxiety that spring from the recognition that man is surrounded by an indecipherable cosmos.

There is no plot to speak of in an absurd play, nor any "real" characters in conflict; consequently, most absurd drama is not dramatic in the usual sense of the term. Although there is usually much physical activity, it is pseudo activity, which does not really constitute an action; a great deal of movement relates the idea that no matter how one busies himself, nothing actually happens in his existence. The language of the absurd is often in conflict with the immediate action and is reduced to meaningless patter to show the futility of communication. Absurdists delight in using technological jargon, cant, clichés, and even baby talk. Frequently, the audience is confronted with characters whose motives and actions remain largely incomprehensible and ridiculous. It is almost impossible to identify with such characters, and as a result the play is comic, in spite of the fact that its subject matter is serious.

Many plays of the theater of the absurd have a circular structure, ending exactly as they began; others progress by a growing intensification of the initial situation. Instead of being provided with an answer, the spectator must formulate questions that will unfold the meaning of the play: suspense consists primarily in the unfolding of the dramatic image.

However frivolous and irreverent it may appear, absurd drama represents a return to the original, religious function of the theater, presenting, like Greek tragedy and medieval mystery, man's peculiar dependence on fate. Of course, the absurdist does not deal with universally accepted metaphysical systems; rather, he sees himself in a vatic position in an age that does not even blink at God's obituary. In this drama there is no coherent, recognized version of the truth; there is instead one individual's intuition of the ultimate realities.

The play that first fully represented the theater of the absurd in its mid-century form is Eugène Ionesco's *The Bald Soprano,* written in 1948 but first performed in 1950. While the play was no success, the reception it received encouraged Ionesco and other playwrights to continue writing in the same vein. The action of *The Bald Soprano* consists of characters sitting and talking about what appears to be nonsense. Mr. and Mrs. Martin and Mr. and Mrs. Smith keep reassuring each other of the obvious (that is, the country is quieter than the city). Ionesco discovered that repeating common automatic phrases reveals the mechanical process of thoughtlessness; he was inspired to write the play because he happened to be studying English at the time and was struck by the ridiculousness of the expressions in the phrase book. His technique is that of exaggerating selected aspects of everyday reality in order to demonstrate its pointlessness. He claims, not wholly tongue-in-cheek, that the three biggest influences on his work have been Groucho, Harpo, and Chico Marx. What gives Ionesco's work its special quality is the way it teeters between the playful and the moral.

It wasn't until 1953, however, with the Paris production of Samuel Beckett's WAITING FOR GODOT, that the theater of the absurd first attracted worldwide attention. The play unexpectedly became a great popular success and was eventually translated into more than twenty languages. Beckett wrote *Godot* in the late 1940's and gave the manuscript to director Roger Blin, who for three years was turned down by every theater in Paris for the obvious reason that no producer would spend money on a play about two lost tramps, a play with no plot, no apparent sense, and, worst of all, no female role. *Godot* has since played all over the world and is probably always playing somewhere. *Waiting for Godot* explores a static situation; the subject is not Godot, but waiting. Godot quite simply represents the object of our waiting: a person, a thing, an event, or even death.

When Beckett is asked who or what Godot is, he replies that if he knew he would have said so in the play. And the appeal of the play comes largely from this uncertainty, for we are all awaiting something and have no assurance that it will ever come—or that it even exists.

Jean Genet is sometimes linked with the theater of the absurd, although his drama, a drama of revolt expressed in ceremonial terms in which death and sex play dominant roles, is closer to Artaud's "theater of cruelty." Yet there are strong resemblances in Genet's work to absurd drama: the abandonment of conventional motivation, the concentration on states of mind and basic human situations as opposed to the development of a narrative plot, the devaluation of language, and, most important, the blatant confrontation of the spectator with the harsh facts of an obscene world and his own isolation.

Although there are at least a dozen Continental playwrights who write in the absurdist style, two French-language dramatists deserve mention here: Spanish-born Fernando Arrabal and Russian-born Arthur Adamov. Arrabal's first play, *Picnic on the Battlefield*, shows a soldier isolated in the front line of battle. His parents, too simple to understand the horror of modern war, come to have a Sunday picnic with him. As the party happily proceeds, a machine-gun blast destroys the entire family. Arrabal acknowledges his deep admiration for Beckett, whose influence is clearly seen in most of his works.

Adamov's themes are the tyranny of parental love, and the innate cruelty of society's confusion. In one of his most popular plays, *Ping-Pong* (1954), he views life in terms of an endless, aimless contest at a pinball machine. The characters, by surrendering themselves to a pinball machine, illustrate explicitly the futility of human endeavor. *Ping-Pong* is a powerful image of the alienation of man through the worship of a false objective.

The only American playwright whose works have gained notoriety because of their affiliation with absurdism is Edward Albee, notably for two one-act plays, *The Zoo Story* and *The American Dream*. *The Zoo Story* was first produced in Berlin in 1959 (American producers, like French producers ten years earlier, were hostile to the new drama). The play deals with the enormous difficulty two human beings have in communicating with each other. Our social order, as Albee sees it, is designed to protect the individual from the unpleasant realities of the human condition. In *The American Dream* Albee takes the traditional elements of the American dream and shows them in the grotesquely distorted form they have assumed; the dream has become a nightmare—a fact that no one seems to recognize in the play except the octogenarian grandmother on the verge of death. Jack Gelber (*The Apple*, 1961), Arthur Kopit (*Oh, Dad, Poor Dad*, 1962), Kenneth Koch (*Bertha*, 1962), Jack Richardson (*Gallows*

Humor, 1961), and Arnold Weinstein (*Red Eye of Love,* 1961) have also been considered American absurdists.

In England two playwrights achieved notable popularity as absurdist writers—N. F. Simpson and Harold Pinter. Simpson, like Ionesco, favors the average middle-class home as a setting in which to expose a society that has become absurd because of its routine and meaningless tradition. In Simpson's *One Way Pendulum* (1961) a character comes in every morning after breakfast to finish the leftover breakfast food. Simpson's plays are perversions of logic: the impossible made possible, and vice versa.

Harold Pinter is today the major exponent of absurdism in England—or, for that matter, anywhere else. In his earlier works, Pinter's characters were humorously but chillingly menaced by mysterious outsiders. In *The Room* (1957), his first play, an elderly woman is told by her landlord that a mysterious stranger has been waiting for days to see her. The man, who is a Negro, calls her by another name, which she seems to recognize. The man is eventually beaten to death by the woman's husband, the woman goes blind, and the curtain falls before the audience has a chance to contemplate the seemingly unmotivated actions. Pinter's characters frequently engage in poetically ambiguous conversation and action, which, unless viewed through a poetic filter, lead to ambiguous interpretations. Pinter's later works border on the psychological, but they still retain his poetic aura of the absurd.

As a movement, the theater of the absurd seems to have died a quiet death. With the exception of Pinter (who is now labeled neo-absurd), most absurd dramatists have found it difficult to sustain their world view throughout a full-length play. Beckett's latest play, *Coming and Going,* is forty-odd lines long and takes less than two and a half minutes to play. Ionesco's plays are becoming more personal and allegorical, and Adamov has abandoned absurdist techniques in favor of Brecht's "epic theater."

Nevertheless, as a liberating force on conventional drama, the effects of the theater of the absurd are still being felt, and will undoubtedly continue to be for some time.

For more information and a critical study of the subject, consult the following: John Mason Brown, *Dramatis Personae* (1963); Robert Brustein, *The Theatre of Revolt* (1964); Martin Esslin, *The Theatre of the Absurd* (1961); John Gassner, *Directions in Modern Theatre and Drama* (1965); Jacques Guicharnaud, *Modern French Theatre from Giraudoux to Genet* (1967); Leonard C. Pronko, *Avant-Garde: The Experimental Theater in France* (1962); John R. Taylor, *Anger and After* (1963); George E. Wellwarth, *The Theater of Protest and Paradox* (1964); and Gerald Weales, *American Theatre Since World War II* (1969).—A. A. W. and S. G.

Thesmophoriazusae (Thesmophoriazousai, "Women Celebrating Thesmophoria," 411 B.C.). A comedy by ARISTOPHANES. Euripides, the playwright, is under indictment by the women of Athens, and his trial is to be held during the festival of the Thesmophoria, when no man may be present. The charge against him: slandering the whole female sex in his plays. Euripides persuades his kinsman Mnesilochus to dress up as a woman and attend the trial to plead in Euripides' defense. Mnesilochus, shaved, be-wigged, and wearing a dress borrowed from the effeminate playwright Agathon, goes to the trial but is discovered and held a prisoner by the women. Euripides, drawing on his own plots for inspiration, attempts a series of daring rescues, all in vain until he hits upon the idea of sending a flute girl to seduce the guard appointed to watch Mnesilochus. The tactic succeeds, and the women agree to a compromise truce between themselves and Euripides.

Thesmophoriazusae is one of the best-plotted of Aristophanes' plays, leaving the audience in suspense until the very last minute. The comedy is made up of fail-safe devices—a man disguised as a woman, a crazy courtroom, farcical escape attempts—and the only drawback for a modern audience is that so much of the humor depends on parodies of lost plays by Euripides.

Translations of the play are listed under Aristophanes.—K. C.

Thomas, Augustus (1857–1934). American playwright. Thomas, the author of over fifty full-length plays and many one-acts, was born in St. Louis and was largely self-educated. While revising and adapting plays for a New York theater, Thomas had his first success with *Alabama* (1891), which dealt in melodramatic terms with the reconciliation of North and South after the Civil War. Other local color melodramas that succeeded were *In Mizzoura* (1893) and *Arizona* (1899). Typical of his comedies are *The Earl of Pawtucket* (1903), about an English nobleman who represents himself as an American in order to pursue a charming American woman, and *Mrs. Leffingwell's Boots* (1905), which presents the farcical consequences of the actions of a young man who has been rendered irresponsible by a concussion.

Thomas attempted serious drama in *The Capitol* (1895), a study of the pressures of business and religion on national politics; *The Witching Hour* (1907), which deals with the responsibility of the possessor of hypnotic power; and *As a Man Thinks* (1911), which is concerned with mental healing and the double standard in sexual morality. His best play, *The Copperhead* (1918), dramatizes the story of a civilian patriot during the Civil War.

Thomas had a sharp eye for the American scene and for topical events and developments, which he used effectively in his plays. Most of his serious plays, however, are marred by melodrama in the handling of plot and by lack of depth in the treatment of human problems.

The best source is Augustus Thomas' *The Print of My Remembrance* (1922).—B. H.

Threepenny Opera, The (Die Dreigroschenoper, 1928). A ballad opera by Bertolt BRECHT with music by Kurt Weill. The work consists of a prologue and three acts, with nineteen songs. The Prologue consists of the famous "Ballad of Mack the Knife," dealing with the well-known criminal, also known as Mackie Messer or Macheath, who can never be caught at the scene of his crimes. He makes a mistake, however, when he secretly marries Polly, the daughter of the "king of the beggars," Jonathan Jeremiah Peachum. Peachum runs a business called "The Beggar's Friend" and supplies appropriate outfits to beggars and thieves. While Peachum explains to the audience the difficulties of running a business de-signed to soften people's hearts, Polly and Macheath celebrate their wedding in an empty stable in Soho. Stolen furniture provides the respectable bourgeois setting, and the distinguished guests are London's police chief, Tiger Brown, an old friend of Macheath, and Reverend Kimball. The Peachums are outraged by their daughter's marriage. They plan to get rid of the undesirable son-in-law by reporting him to the police. Macheath turns his "business" over to Polly and escapes, but he is nevertheless caught—betrayed by his favorite whore, Jenny, while paying his regular weekly visit to a brothel. In prison Macheath finds another old love, Tiger Brown's daughter Lucy. Disavowing Polly, he persuades Lucy to help him escape, only to be captured again when he visits his whores. This time he is really going to hang. His old friend Brown can do nothing for him, because Peachum has threatened to ruin the coronation procession of the young queen by a mass turn-out of disgusting-looking beggars. Macheath is standing on the scaffold when Peachum steps forward and announces that Macheath shall not be killed, because this is after all an opera and not real life. A mounted messenger arrives bringing Macheath not only the queen's pardon but also a title of nobility, a castle, and a pension. In real life, unfortunately, mounted messengers rarely arrive. The opera ends with a hymn asking mankind not to be too severe toward injustice.

The Threepenny Opera made Brecht world-famous, and even today it is mainly this work that makes his name familiar to a wide audience. The play is based on John Gay's *Beggar's Opera* (1728). Brecht kept the basic situation and a number of scenes from the Gay work, but otherwise his adaptation, including songs based on Villon, bears little resemblance to the original. While Gay's satire was rather general—aimed at the Italian operatic style of the day, at Prime Minister Walpole, at marriage—Brecht presents an analysis of bourgeois capitalism. Macheath's crime syndicate is presented as a mirror image of society; aside from their professional activities, Macheath and his fellow gangsters look and behave like respectable citizens, not highwaymen. Brecht and Weill, whose musical score is a mixture of classical, modern, and jazz elements, also tried to attack the traditional "culinary" opera, that is, an opera that the audience was likely to experience as nothing more than a tasty meal. As Reinhold Grimm (*Bertolt Brecht,* 1962) emphasizes, it is at exactly this point that Brecht first begins to establish a really systematic theory of a new theatrical form. Some critics (like Walter Weideli, *The Art of Bertolt Brecht,* 1963, and Ronald Gray, *Brecht,* 1961) claim that the success of *The Threepenny Opera* is due to the ambiguous nature of the story. Brecht himself realized that he had failed to expose the social conflicts of his times and that his play was easily misinterpreted as a cynical attack, not only on bourgeois morality, but on the lower classes as well. When the opera was adapted for the screen in 1930, Brecht tried to give the story a much stronger anticapitalistic overtone but was prevented from doing so by the film company. *Das Dreigroschenbuch* (1960) contains Brecht's account of that struggle (which involved a court decision), his proposed film script "Die Beule" ("The Boil"), his *Threepenny Novel* (1934), and, among other materials, a recording of two songs sung by the author himself. For a discussion of the importance of *The Threepenny Opera* for Brecht's theories and his epic style, see John Willett, *The Theatre of Bertolt Brecht* (1964). A short account of the struggle over the film script is given in Martin Esslin's *Brecht, The Man and His Work* (1959).—H. R.

Three Sisters, The (**Tri sestry**, 1901). A drama in four acts by Anton CHEKHOV. Three sisters, daughters of a general now dead, sit surrounded by officers in a provincial garrison town in the Russian Far North and repeat to each other that they will soon return to Moscow, which seems sunny and warm compared with their bleak home in the tundra, buried under snow most of the year. Like all the other ambitions of the sisters, this hope is never fulfilled. The eldest sister, Olga, an eternally exhausted schoolmarm, dreams of a happy, married life in Moscow but ends up as the harassed and overworked headmistress of the local school. The second sister, Masha, who as a young girl married Kulygin, imagining he was a brilliant and cultured man rather than a boring schoolteacher, falls in love with Vershinin, a colonel in the regiment stationed in town. She has an affair with him but it comes to an end when the regiment is moved to another garrison. The youngest sister, Irina, who dreams of true love and interesting, useful work, comes to hate the job she takes and finally agrees to marry a man she does not love, Baron Tuzenbach, who, however, is killed in a pointless duel. The brother of the three sisters, Andrei, who has ambitions of becoming a university professor in Moscow, ends by marrying a local girl, Natalia, who gradually takes over control of the entire household.

To convey the sterility and emptiness of these people's lives, Chekhov gives the play a curiously static quality. For, although some action occurs, it all takes place offstage. With every new act, we find these reasonably well educated members of Russia's middle class still sitting and talking, talking about their personal hopes that are never fulfilled, and never really listening to each other.

Chekhov apparently considered the army in peacetime (with which all the main characters are somehow connected) an excellent subject for the study of a futile existence, for none of its members really work. Chekhov presents the full range of frustrated types, from the childish young lieutenants who have managed to avoid coming to grips with life to the despairing old army doctor who becomes stupefied with vodka until he loses his sense of identity. In the middle are Vershinin and Tuzenbach, who remain comparatively sane with the aid of their visions of the future—Vershinin pictures better things to come in two hundred years and Tuzenbach hopes to leave the army and redeem himself through work. Curiously enough, Masha's husband, Kulygin, a fatuous, pedantic, and limited man, is the only character who refuses to base his life on some mythical future. He is perfectly happy among his colleagues, who mercilessly bore his wife, and he is gratified to receive a decoration for his services in public education. Instead of clinging to some hope like all the others, he keeps repeating that he is extremely satisfied with what he has, even with his marriage with Masha, who he knows has been unfaithful to him and whom he

refuses to blame. He is the only one to accept the present and thus find a certain happiness.

No other character succeeds in making this adjustment and at the end of the play the three sisters are still weeping, clinging together (instinctively clinging to their past), and looking to some brighter future.

There is, of course, Natalia, the sister-in-law, who does quite well in life. But then she is both a ridiculous person and an unmitigated villain and can hardly be considered Chekhov's idea of a person who has made a wise and desirable adjustment to life.

The image of migratory birds constantly appears in this play. Life, Chekhov seems to be suggesting, is like the flight of birds: people may concoct all sorts of theories about life, be happy or unhappy, live well or badly; they may just live or they may puzzle over every step, but the force in them that keeps them going through life is something much deeper and quite inexplicable, similar to the force that makes the birds gather at a certain date, soar upward, and fly off together, going unerringly southward through wind and storm to their inevitable destination.

At the end of the play Chekhov conveys a feeling of complete stagnation by showing that the three sisters still hope, although their dreams have been shattered and they have accepted compromises. Yet the play closes on a hopeful note. Leaving town, the regimental band strikes up a gay march, stirring a responsive chord in the sisters and filling them with a purely irrational hope. Of course, it is a blind hope, an expression of the force of life and not in any way an answer. In fact, in the final line, Olga cries out: "Ah, if only we knew, if only we could know!" This appeal carries with it the unspoken realization that we do not and cannot know.

The Three Sisters, translated by Andrew R. MacAndrew, appears in *20th Century Russian Drama* (1963).—A. MACA.

Thunderstorm, The (**Groza**, 1859). It has also been translated as *The Storm*. A drama in five acts by Alexander OSTROVSKY. Set in a small town on the Volga, *The Thunderstorm* depicts the harsh life of a lower-class merchant family dominated by a matriarch. She imposes her will not only on her unmarried daughter and her married son but also on her son's wife, Katerina, a sensitive and mystical young woman who dreams of freedom. During her husband's absence, Katerina briefly satisfied her yearnings with a young man, the nephew of a tyrannical rich merchant. But soon she is so overcome with guilt that she cannot prevent herself from confessing publicly and thus bringing disgrace upon herself and her lover. Unable to continue living under her mother-in-law's domination, Katerina finally commits suicide by jumping into the Volga during a violent thunderstorm.

This play, generally considered Ostrovsky's masterpiece, depicts, like almost all his other plays, the grim and absurd environment of the Russian lower-middle classes in the second half of the nineteenth century. Although it certainly implies Ostrovsky's disapproval of the prevailing state of affairs, it is hardly the "revolutionary" play that Soviet critics tried to make out of it, following the lead of the nineteenth-century critic Nikolai Dobrolyubov. Dobrolyubov claimed that not only was *The Thun-*

derstorm an indictment of the tsarist regime but also that Katerina's suicide was a gesture of revolt against the prevailing order and therefore the play offered a message of hope.

Actually, Ostrovsky develops here his favorite theme—the tragic crushing of a sensitive person by a society based on false values. Symbolically, at the end, the atmosphere becomes so saturated that it bursts out into a deadly electrical storm.

The Thunderstorm, translated by Andrew R. MacAndrew, appears in *19th Century Russian Drama* (1963).—A. MACA.

Tibet. Tibet has for at least ten centuries been the scene of theatrical and dramatic activity though few plays have been printed until recent times. The plays appear to have been inspired by various sects of Buddhism. Existing today chiefly in manuscripts, they have been examined by only a few scholars. Good evidence exists, however, that from Tibet dramatic as well as religious culture spread its influence widely over central Asia. The chief scholar thus far in the field, Jacques Bacot, discovered manuscripts in Outer Mongolia, which he edited with translation and commentary. His own work has subsequently been translated into English.

Tibetan plays owe much of their character to religious literature reaching their own country from India. Buddhist plays were performed as early as the ninth century. The story of the most impressive Tibetan play, *Tchrimekundan,* fancifully ascribed to the sixth Talelama, Tsongs-Dbyangsrgyamthso, who reigned in the sixteenth century, is the same legend used in the older Tamil play derived from southern India, ARICHANDRA. It relates the temptations and tribulations of a king who resigns his throne, his riches and his power, his wife, his children, and even his eyes to comply with requests by a series of envoys and mendicants. He even gives up the jewel that in itself bestows supreme power. In the end, his sight, his family, and his throne are restored to him with added blessings. He proves to be not only a just king but a true saint. The tempters and mendicants were all deities in disguise.

The script reads like an amorphous conjunction of a narrative and a play, but a play it unquestionably is. Productions of this and other Tibetan dramas have been witnessed in recent years by visitors to Lhasa, the capital of Tibet. The productions are presumably much like those of a distant past. The actors are monks playing in their monkish robes and carrying scripts for their parts in their hands, this emphasis on literacy being impressive in the eyes of the illiterate audience. Much ceremony attends the productions, so that what appears in writing as a comparatively brief work requires several days to perform. Music and dances enlarge the performance, and improvisation is freely admitted. The plays are given outdoors, in the precincts of the great monasteries. Many as are the shortcomings of Tibetan drama when viewed in comparison with the more highly developed drama of its neighbors, India and China, the plays obviously have poetic as well as histrionic merit and, moreover, are of much interest from the standpoint of the origins and history of the stage.

Jacques Bacot, the pioneer in modern studies of Tibetan art and literature, wrote an important study of the native drama that has been translated by A. I. Woolf as *Three Tibetan Mysteries* (1924). The book gives a vivid account of the productions as Bacot witnessed them. A discussion of the plays can be found in Henry W. Wells's *The Classical Drama of India* (1963). A general review of Tibetan theatrical history is given in an article, "Tibetan Drama," by Frederic Bischoff, in *Asian Drama* (1966), a collection of papers edited by Henry W. Wells as a University of South Dakota publication.—H. W. W.

Tidings Brought to Mary, The (L'Annonce faite à Marie, 1912). A poetic drama by Paul CLAUDEL. The first version of this play was called *La Jeune Fille Violaine* and was published in 1892; the definitive version for the stage was published in 1948. At intervals during a span of fifty-six years, Claudel returned to the text, worked on it, and revised it. He got the idea for the play and for Violaine's miracle from an old German folk tale of a woman who miraculously revived a dead child by feeding it from her breast.

The action revolves around the relationship between two sisters who are totally different in temperament and yet indissolubly joined. Violaine is the good sister who represents Christian charity. Mara (whose name in Hebrew means "bitter") is the jealous sister who, at the end of the play, murders Violaine. Mara's infant dies and is brought back to life by Violaine. In the final revision of the text, Claudel's interest fixed on Mara. Her violent, almost brutal faith in God serves the function of revealing the sanctity of Violaine.

The character in the Prologue, Pierre de Craon, who was not in the original *Jeune Fille Violaine,* appears as a "guest" who is in reality a delegate sent by God in order to reveal certain truths. He is a leper in the Prologue, and Violaine's kiss to the leper is the supreme act of charity that precipitates the play's action. Pierre loves Violaine but he is aware that all she represents for him—earthly love and worldly happiness—is denied him because he has leprosy. He must follow an indirect path to God by finding his role in life and doing his work on earth. The miracle of revivification in the third act, the death of Violaine and the continuing life of Mara, the vocation of Pierre de Craon to give his life to the building of cathedrals, the king's consecration at Reims, and the ending of a historical period (the middle ages), testify to the physical-spiritual cycle of birth, death, and rebirth.

Tidings Brought to Mary has been translated by Wallace Fowlie (1960).—W. F.

Tieck, [Johann] Ludwig (1773–1853). German playwright, novelist, poet, translator, and director. Though Tieck is remembered today primarily for his novels and fairy tales, his contribution to the development of German drama is manifold. His creative talents were recognized while he was still attending the gymnasium in Berlin, and he began experimenting with fate tragedies (see SHICKSALSTRAGÖDIE) as early as 1792 with *Der Abschied* ("The Farewell"), followed by *Karl von Berneck* in 1795. However, Tieck's stature as a dramatist depends more on his surrealistic satires, which endow new meaning to motifs and themes borrowed from fairy tales. His most important plays along these lines are *Ritter Blaubart* ("Bluebeard the Knight," 1796), *Der*

A SCENE FROM PAUL CLAUDEL'S *The Tidings Brought to Mary* (FRENCH CULTURAL SERVICES)

gestiefelte Kater (*Puss in Boots*, 1797), *Die verkehrte Welt* ("The Upside-down World," 1798), and *Prinz Zerbino, oder die Reise nach dem guten Geschmack* ("Prince Zerbino, or the Journey in Search of Good Taste," 1798). Of these works, *Der gestiefelte Kater* is Tieck's masterpiece and explains why he was considered to be one of the masters of romantic irony. On one level, the play deals with a talking cat who helps his master Gottlieb, a poor farmer, win a princess and a kingdom. On a more subtle level, the play satirizes the sentimental taste and conventions of the day. Tieck makes full use of the alienation technique by having the author interrupt his own play and discuss it with the audience and stagehands. By the end of the drama, the author ironically concludes that he has "failed" in his attempt to free the audience from its typical melodramatic expectations. Aside from the fairty-tale satires, Tieck also wrote brilliantly conceived, epical closet dramas such as *Leben und Tod der heiligen Genoveva* ("The Life and Death of Saint Genevieve," 1799), *Kaiser Octavianus* ("The Emperor Octavianus," 1801), and *Fortunat* ("Fortunatus," 1816), which are virtually unperformable because of their sprawling nature. However, because there is such an interesting and unusual mixture of

genres in these plays, they are still of importance today. In particular, Tieck's *Genoveva* is in essence a sublime tragic comedy, which renders a new interpretation of the villain Golo, who wants to seduce Genevieve. Tieck always questioned the worth of morals when the world itself was out of joint, and Golo seems to reflect more the chaotic society rather than an absolute principle of evil. The influence of Shakespeare is apparent here, and it was predominant throughout Tieck's life. In fact, Tieck more or less abandoned writing his own dramas in 1817 in order to complete the A. W. Schlegel translation of Shakespeare's complete works—still considered the best in German to this very day. In 1819, Tieck made Dresden his home, where he gave his famous dramatic readings. He also found time to edit Kleist's collected works, become director of the Hoftheater in 1825, and write his novellas. In 1840, he returned to his native Berlin to direct classical drama at the Royal Theater, a post he maintained until his death in 1853.

Ludwig Tieck, the German Romanticist (1933) by Edwin Zeydel is a biography that deals with Tieck's life and works. A critical analysis of his works can be found in *Tieck's Romantic Irony* (1932) by Alfred E.

LUDWIG TIECK (GERMAN INFORMATION CENTER)

Lasky, and his reception in the United States is dealt with in *Ludwig Tieck and America* (1954) by Percy C. Matenko.—J. D. Z.

Tien Han. See THE WHITE SNAKE.

Tiger at the Gates (La Guerre de Troie n'aura pas lieu, 1935). A tragedy by Jean GIRAUDOUX. Giraudoux's art and his conception of tragedy are fully exemplified in this play, which is a combination of wit and seriousness, of the spectacular and the threat of war. The Trojan soldiers, having returned from a victorious war, are determined to preserve peace. Andromache, wife of the leading Trojan soldier, Hector, declares to her sister Cassandra that the Trojan War will not take place, that Ulysses will be politely welcomed, and that Helen will be given back to him. Cassandra, who is a prophetess of calamity, contradicts her sister by maintaining that the Greek ambassador will be insulted, Helen will not be given back, and the war will take place.

According to Giraudoux, even if man overcame his warlike instincts, destiny itself demands war. The dramaturgy of *Tiger at the Gates* shows how destiny, which wants the war, uses Hector as a pawn to bring it about. Although war is hateful, it is eternal, because it comes from man's negligence or selfishness. The real tragedy is that man does not direct the world; he is not the master of history. Behind the legend of the Trojan War, Giraudoux seemed to be referring in 1935 to the coming of the Second World War.

Tiger at the Gates has been translated by Christopher Fry (1955).—W. F.

Timon of Athens (c. 1607–1608). A tragedy by William SHAKESPEARE. *Timon of Athens* was first published in the 1623 First Folio, occupying a position originally intended for *Troilus and Cressida.* Two accounts from Plutarch's *Lives of the Noble Grecians and Romans,* as translated into English (2nd ed., 1595) by Sir Thomas North from Jacques Amyot's French translation (1559), serve as Shakespeare's primary source: a digression in the "Life of Marcus Antonius," in which Antony is described as following "the life of *Timon Misanthropos* the Athenian"; and the "Life of Alcibiades." No early record of performance exists; indeed, there is little likelihood that *The Life of Timon of Athens* was acted during the Jacobean era.

The story tells how Timon, a wealthy Athenian nobleman, lavishly entertains his friends and freely bestows gifts upon them until he exhausts his fortune. Faced with bankruptcy and set upon by his creditors, Timon sends to his friends for financial assistance, but is denied at every turn. In a misanthropic rage, he invites his former companions to a mock banquet, drives them from his house, and then abandons Athens. Taking up his abode in the woods, he accidentally finds gold, which, as news of his find spreads, he freely gives to those who in various ways would harm the Athenians, but denies to his old flatterers. He also rejects a plea from the Athenian senators to save the city from an attack by Alcibiades, a young military leader who had been banished for pleading for the life of a friend who had killed a man. The play ends with peace made between Alcibiades and the senators and with a report of the death of Timon.

Scholarly consensus holds that *Timon of Athens* is an unfinished play. Although the plot line is coherent and shows careful construction and although powerful scenes and speeches are present, there are many loose ends. Furthermore, the tragedy is flawed in its integration of the Alcibiades plot with the main plot, is uneven in its poetry, and is flat in its characterization. Why a play written late in the dramatist's career should be so flawed is one of the enigmas of Shakespearean scholarship. Perhaps Shakespeare was experimenting with the tragic mode. Or perhaps he found that he had selected a subject and a protagonist he could not make dramatically effective. Whatever the reason, he abandoned attempts to polish the play.

An outstanding edition of *Timon of Athens* is the New Arden Edition (1963), edited by H. J. Oliver. —W. G.

Tinker's Wedding, The (1907). A play by John Millington SYNGE. This two-act comedy about the tinker and Christian ways of life is one of Synge's most artistic and most neglected works. Probably its comic anticlericalism accounts for the fact that in the sixty-odd years since it was written it has never been performed at Dublin's Abbey Theatre. The farcical plot revolves around a pattern of comic illusions and ironies. Sarah Casey and Michael Byrne have been living together for many years in the free tradition of the vagrant tinkers, but now she feels that her beauty will fade and she cannot face old age without the security and respectability of a proper Christian wedding. She drives a hard bargain with a mercenary priest who agrees to perform the wedding for a reduced fee plus a gallon can that the reluctant Michael is soldering. But the arrangement is doomed from the start, largely due to the merry mischief and wisdom of that "wicked heathen" Mary Byrne, Michael's hard-drinking and unashamedly pagan mother, who really dominates the play and is mistress of the improvised revels. Mary offers the weary priest a drink and entertains him with "wicked" songs; and she shrewdly warns Sarah that a woman needs more than a marriage vow to keep her man. Then she steals the gallon can and trades it for more liquor, the priest refuses to go through with the wedding and threatens to call the police, and the three tinkers gag and tie him in a sack. When they release him, he cries out a Latin curse as they run off to love and drink and fight another day. So Christian respectability and security are defeated by tinker wisdom and freedom.—D. K.

'Tis Pity She's a Whore (c. 1630). A tragedy by John FORD. Ford's best-known play, *'Tis Pity She's a Whore,* deals with the sensational theme of incestuous love. Overwhelmed by a consuming passion, Giovanni seduces his sister Annabella, who becomes pregnant and marries the villainous Soranzo to conceal her guilt. Soranzo discovers her secret and plans to kill Giovanni. The lovers anticipate him, however, in a moving scene that ends with Giovanni's killing Annabella. Half-crazed, Giovanni then attacks and kills Soranzo and is himself killed.

The play has a fierce emotional intensity unusual in Ford's plays. This is particularly reflected in the character of Giovanni, a passionate skeptic who questions with a mixture of ardor and bitterness the laws of society and religion. The eloquence of his skepticism has led critics to charge that Ford is justifying his behavior. What is more nearly the case is that the author is operating, not with a fixed moral perspective, but with the strong sense of compassion reflected in the play's title.—E. Q.

Titus Andronicus (c. 1590–1594). A tragedy by William SHAKESPEARE. *The Lamentable Tragedy of Titus Andronicus,* as the Folio title reads, was a popular play in its time. Its earliest recorded production, listed in Philip Henslowe's *Diary* under the name *Titus & Ondronicous,* took place on January 23, 1594. Later that year it was published in a quarto edition (the First Quarto). The two quarto editions that followed, in 1600 and 1611, basically reprinted the First Quarto. The Third Quarto served as the copy text—with slight alterations and the addition of a scene (III, ii)—for the 1623 First Folio. No definitive source for the play is known. There is, however, an eighteenth-century chapbook, *The History of Titus Andronicus,* that appears to be a version of an old tale that may have been Shakespeare's source. A drawing of a scene from the play, executed purportedly in 1595—the only extant contemporary illustration for a Shakespearean play—has been preserved in the Longleat Manuscript.

In the main plot, Titus Andronicus, victorious over the Goths, returns to Rome with Tamora, the Gothic queen, her three sons, and Aaron the Moor as captives. Titus assents to a religious sacrifice of Tamora's eldest son, thereby engendering the queen's hatred. Meanwhile, Rome is to choose a new emperor. Titus renounces his candidacy, supporting Saturninus over Bassianus, the latter's brother. Titus consents to a marriage between his daughter, Lavinia, and Saturninus, although she is in love with,

and betrothed to, Bassianus. The lovers flee. Saturninus, in anger, vows enmity to Titus and immediately weds Tamora. A series of violent and horrible deeds are perpetrated by the Tamora faction on Titus and his family. The Andronici finally avenge their wrongs, but not before practically all the principals in the feud are dead. Lucius, Titus' surviving son, becomes the new emperor of Rome. In the underplot, Tamora and Aaron engage in an illicit romance that results in the birth of a dark-skinned boy.

Although this earliest and most violent of Shakespeare's tragedies opens and closes on a political note, *Titus Andronicus* is basically a revenge tragedy in the fashion of Thomas Kyd. It owes much to classical influences, particularly to Seneca and Ovid. The play shows careful plot construction, but its characters tend to be flat and the verse is self-consciously ornate. Some scholars believe that the playwright George Peele collaborated in writing Act I. The play's importance today is as a harbinger of the later tragedies.

An outstanding edition of *Titus Andronicus* is the

TITLE PAGE OF THE UNIQUE COPY OF THE FIRST QUARTO (1594) OF SHAKESPEARE'S *Titus Andronicus* (FOLGER SHAKESPEARE LIBRARY)

THE
MOST LA
mentable Romaine
Tragedie of Titus Andronicus:

As it was Plaide by the Right Honourable the Earle of *Darbie,* Earle of *Pembrooke,* and Earle of *Suffex* their Seruants.

LONDON,
Printed by Iohn Danter, and are
to be sold by *Edward White* & *Thomas Millington,*
at the little North doore of Paules at the
signe of the Gunne.
1594.

New Arden Edition (1963), edited by J. C. Maxwell.
—W. G.

Togo.   See AFRICA: *Togo.*

Toller, Ernst (1893–1939).   German playwright
and writer of prose. Ernst Toller was born in Samot-
schin, the Prussian part of Poland, of Jewish parents.
Although very much a child of the twentieth century
in his intense political and social interests, Toller's
spiritual and intellectual roots lie principally in German classicism and Romanticism. The theme of all
his dramas is fundamentally religious and ethical in
nature. However, Toller defined the religious experience in a classical-Humanist sense—that of union
with one's fellow men in the personal love of individuals or in the suprapersonal love of a brotherhood
of men. Toller also came to recognize the necessity
for uncompromising ethical behavior in the political
order, and his dramas reflect this thought development on the problem of good and evil.

Toller's biography reveals clearly his firsthand experience with the harsh realities of political life and
the resulting moral problems. He was imprisoned for
five years because of his participation in the Soviet
republic in Bavaria in 1919. He suffered self-imposed
exile in 1933 after bitter disappointment with the
political trends in postwar Germany. He committed
suicide in 1939 in New York after becoming completely disillusioned with the political situation of the
thirties. The writings *I Was a German* (1934); his letters written in prison, *Looking Through the Bars*
(1936); and a tragedy, *Pastor Hall* (1939), about the
concentration camps of the Third Reich, all attest to
this state of despair.

If Toller sought to realize his political beliefs in his
activities as a revolutionary, he tried in his dramatic
activity to present the genesis of his thinking on the
nature of the political condition. In *Die Wandlung*
(*Transfiguration,* 1919) the hero Friedrich returns
from the war to reject his original faith in nationalism and to embrace the cause of international socialism. Friedrich cannot find sufficient justification for
the terrible expense in human destruction that had
been condoned for the national cause. In *Masse
Mensch* (*Man and the Masses,* 1919) Toller plays out
the personal conflict of a revolutionary who seeks to
realize the highest ideals of Humanist thinking but
seems forced to resort to the most barbaric of means
in order to do so. If the rhetoric of peace and
brotherhood is a sufficient instrument for change in
Die Wandlung, only the total act of love through self-
sacrifice is adequate in *Masse Mensch.* Sonja cannot
convince her comrades to relinquish their revolutionary tactics of violence and bloodshed with the
mere rhetoric of universal harmony and peace as
Friedrich does in his conversion of the masses from
nationalism to socialism. Instead, she must make the
complete personal sacrifice, first, in order to atone
for the guilt she incurred in a not fully conscious act
of acquiescence to the demands of the revolutionaries, but more significantly, in order to underline
the unconditional moral stipulation of her Humanist
vision.

In *Der deutsche Hinkemann* (*Brokenbrow,* 1923)
Toller attempts to realize the union of two human
beings in a love that, because of circumstances, must
transcend the physical sphere. The character alignment of the play is very similar to that of Büchner's

ERNST TOLLER (GERMAN INFORMATION CENTER)

Woyzeck. However, Toller concentrates more on the
inner movement and spiritual development of the
characters than does Büchner. It is Toller's intention
to demonstrate the possibility in the human relationship of rising above selfish gratification of the senses
to selfless love in the spirit. However, although
Hinkemann's belief in Grete ultimately fails, thereby
forcing her to commit suicide, Toller does not leave
the audience with the feeling that this tragedy was inevitable, but just unavoidable in this unhappy instance.

It is, however, in his next play, *Hoppla, wir leben!*
("Yippee, We're Alive!" 1927; pub. in English as
Hoppla!) that the full force of Toller's pessimism can
be felt. In this tragedy one is overwhelmed by the
playwright's despairing conviction of the impossibility of the resolution of human differences in a universal brotherhood of men.

Hence, in view of the dramatist's exclusive preoccupation with the political condition of man, it is
quite understandable that Toller has been considered
by some critics to be the political playwright par excellence. But then the designation "political" requires clear definition. Certainly the scope of "political" cannot be limited to the notions of ideology,
propaganda, and practical manipulation. In fact, we
saw Toller reject these instruments in both his personal and literary life. However, if the definition of
"political" were extended to what Paul Kornfeld
termed "metapolitical" to signify the total condition
of man in his idealistic struggle for realization of a
brotherhood of men, the designation "political"

would be agreeable to Toller and consistent with his life and works.

That Toller failed in his attempt to realize his "political" goals puts not only the man and his works but also the age in tragic parentheses.

A collection of the English translations of Toller's plays is *Seven Plays* (1934). A short biographical sketch can be found in Kurt Pinthus' "Life and Death of Ernst Toller" in *Books Abroad,* 14 (1941). Critical studies of his works include W. A. Willibrand, "Ernst Toller's Ideological Sképticism" in *German Quarterly,* 19 (1946), and H. F. Garten, *Modern German Drama* (1959).—C. A. M.

Tolstoy, Count Leo [**Lev Nikolaevich**] (1828–1910). Russian novelist, essayist, and playwright. Tolstoy became interested in the theater in 1855 when he returned to St. Petersburg from Sevastopol after the Crimean War. There are only extant fragments of his early comedies, which, like his other writings of that period, denounced the moral decay of Russia's idle rich both in the city and the country.

His first full-length comedy, *Zarazhennoe semeistvo* (*The Contaminated Family*), written between 1862 and 1864, reflects Tolstoy's feelings on the nihilism that was widespread in Russia after the abolition of serfdom. In Tolstoy's play, considered "undemocratic and unsuccessful" by Soviet critics, the author ridicules not only the young nihilist, a sort of radical utopian socialist who plainly denies all nonmaterial values, but also the pseudoliberal who pays lip service to the new ideas and the bluestocking suffragette who expostulates about free love. Indeed, simple wisdom comes from the mouth of an old nanny, and it is the old-fashioned, albeit tolerant, landowner who does the right thing without philosophizing.

It was in 1886, after his moral crisis, that Tolstoy focused on the theater as a means of educating the uneducated. He dramatized his fairy tale about a devil inventing a method of corrupting hard-working peasants: first by providing them with more wheat than they need and then by teaching them how to distill it into vodka. The moral of the story is that excess wealth corrupts—one of Tolstoy's obsessions in his later years. The success of this play, *Pervyi vinokur* (*The First Distiller*), prompted him to write two more moralizing plays that year: *Peter Khlebnik* and *Dramaticheskaia obrabotka legendy ob Aggee* ("Dramatic Adaptation of the Legend of King Aggei"), both of which show the corruption of wealth and of power and the salvation granted through renunciation, poverty, and humility.

Later that same year (1886) Tolstoy wrote in less than three weeks the first draft of his most famous play, THE POWER OF DARKNESS, a powerful "peasant" tragedy (its only predecessor is Alexei Pisemsky's *Gorkaya sudbina, Bitter Fate*).

Tolstoy's next play, *Plody prosveshcheniya* (*The Fruits of Enlightenment*), was completed in 1889 and was performed in Moscow in 1891. Here again Tolstoy shows his deep disappointment in the results of the "enlightened" reforms of 1861: the insufficiency of the merely formal emancipation of the peasants; the unchanged misery of their plight; and the continued moral and intellectual corruption of the parasitic upper classes, whose energies are wasted on silly games, puns, and such ridiculous pursuits as spiritualism. In the skillfully constructed plot, the clever,

quick-witted chambermaid Tanya contrives, by manipulating a seance, to make her reluctant master sell a piece of land to peasants. During the seance she also succeeds in deceiving a pompous professor who is there to explain these mysterious phenomena. *Plody prosveshcheniya* was written at the same time as Tolstoy's last major novel, *Resurrection* (between 1880 and 1890), and uses many of the same themes, as does his next play, THE LIVING CORPSE.

THE LIGHT THAT SHINES IN DARKNESS is Tolstoy's autobiographical play, on which he worked off and on from the 1880's through the 1900's without ever finishing the last scenes.

Tolstoy's last play, *Ot nei vse kachestva* ("Everythings Stems from It"), written shortly before his death in 1910, is, as he described it, "an attempt to teach the same lesson" as his early play *Pervyi vinokur* but "without using a devil." It was produced by amateurs in 1912 and in the Petersburg Rabochii Theater in 1913.

As a dramatist, Tolstoy's primary concern, as he admits, was with preaching and all his plays are, to some extent, morality plays. Because of the incomparable power of his thought and inventiveness, however, Tolstoy made a unique contribution to the Russian theater.

Among the numerous works on Tolstoy, Henri Troyat's *Tolstoy* (1967) is probably the most readable and Ernest J. Simmons' *Leo Tolstoy* (1946) is quite informative.—A. MacA.

Topol, Josef (1935–   ). Czech playwright. Born in Poříčí nad Sázavou, Topol graduated from high school and then worked as a reader for the director E. F. Burian at the Army Artistic Theater in Prague from 1953 to 1956. From 1954 to 1959 he studied in the drama department of the Academy of Visual Arts in Prague. After graduation he concentrated on a literary career; since 1965 he has collaborated closely with director O. Krejča at the Prague Divadlo za branou (Theater Behind the Gate).

His first play, *Půlnoční vítr* ("The Midnight's Wind," 1955; pub. 1956), is a verse tragedy strongly influenced by Shakespeare. By reworking the old Czech legend about the struggles between the tribes of Lučané and Czechs, Topol expressed his hatred of war and its destruction of life, love, and work. The attraction of this work is Topol's unconventional portrayal of heroism, his complex characters, and his plastic, poetic dialogue.

Topol's artistic individuality emerged in his play *Jejich den* ("Their Day," 1959), in which, as a spokesman for the young generation that had matured after the socialist revolution in Czechoslovakia, he criticizes the generation of their fathers. The heroes of this play are angry young men who honestly and painfully look for their place in the world and who often encounter various careerists of the older generation. The many acts of the play reveal a complex picture of the stormy struggles of the young.

In his most important work to date, *Konec masopustu* ("The End of Shrovetide," 1963), Topol dramatizes the preparations for, and course of, a traditional carnival in a small Czech town. The traditional masquerade is this time directed against the last private farmer, more for the sake of entertainment than from enmity. The joyful whirl of the masques, however, unexpectedly changes into a tragedy at the end. Topol's subtle dialogue containing several meanings and the combination of a number of stories and problems portrayed reveal the author's concern with eternal questions of life and death. At the same time the play may be considered a complicated, synthetic image of the revolutionary changes that occurred as socialism consolidated its position in Czechoslovakia. Topol showed that socialism grew stronger in the country in spite of the fact that the bearers of this new system were not ideal human beings but complicated, imperfect people. In Topol's view of mankind, people's acts often fall short of the goals they set, and reminders of death are always present. In *Konec masopustu* Topol combined the tradition of Czech realistic drama with the interwar avant-garde theater.

In *Kočka na kolejích* ("The Cat on the Rails," 1965) Topol presents the contradiction between an ideal and reality and resolves the discrepancy by having the young main characters commit suicide. This play is also a dialogue about the basic existential problems of man. Topol was inspired by the "theater of the absurd" when he wrote his one-act play *Slavík k večeři* ("Nightingale's Dinner Invitation," 1967). In this work all great values crumble under the oppressive power of the petite bourgeoisie. This theme is dramatized in the meeting between the poet, Nightingale, and a petit bourgeois family at the end of which the poet is liquidated in a crafty way.

Topol has also translated and adapted Anton Chekhov's *The Sea Gull* (1960) and Shakespeare's *Romeo and Juliet* (1963).—F. Č.

Torquato Tasso (1789). A play by Johann Wolfgang von GOETHE based on the tragically troubled life of the sixteenth-century Italian poet. Classical in form, like the earlier *Iphigenie auf Tauris, Tasso* is not as optimistic about the ultimate solution of all human conflicts. Basically, it treats the incompatibility of the poet's inner nature with life in the external world, a theme not unlike that of Goethe's early novel *The Sorrows of Young Werther*. Tasso is presented as a morbidly sensitive character driven to despair and near-madness by his distrust of his patron and friends. He is furiously jealous of his patron and passionately in love with Leonora d'Este, who, though the poet brings her happiness, can never marry him because he is a commoner. Tasso turns to his writing, but the ending of the play is inconclusive. The play is distinguished for its understanding of the neurotic temperament and for its wholesome affirmation that a good poet is by no means more important than a wise statesman. It is essentially a grappling with the poet's place in the scheme of things.

Tourneur, Cyril (1575–1626). English playwright. The details of Tourneur's early life remain a mystery. The date and place of his birth, his family, the schools he attended are all unknown. As an adult he appears to have been employed in the households of the high-ranking Vere and Cecil families. His literary activity began in 1600 with the publication of an obscure satire, *The Transformed Metamorphosis*. His career as a dramatist began a few years later, but was soon ended in 1613. After that date he was employed in the services of Sir Edward Cecil, whom he accompanied on a naval expedition against the Spaniards in 1625. The expedition was a failure, largely because of an epidemic that decimated the English forces. Among the stricken was Tourneur, who was put ashore at Kinsale, Ireland, where he died.

Tourneur is generally regarded as the author of two extant plays, *The Atheist's Tragedy* (c. 1611) and THE REVENGER'S TRAGEDY, although only the first is indisputably his. Many modern scholars argue that *The Revenger's Tragedy* is by Thomas Middleton. *The Atheist's Tragedy* is a less distinguished work than *The Revenger's Tragedy,* but it is an interesting example of the reaction to the religious skepticism that was becoming pronounced in the early years of the seventeenth century. D'Amville, the atheist of the title, is a thoroughgoing villain completely committed to a life of sensualism and Machiavellian intrigue. Aligned against him is his nephew Charlemont, a model of Christian virtue. D'Amville, in the best tradition of Elizabethan "Machiavels," outwits everyone throughout the course of the play only to be hoist with his own petard at the very end. The play has none of the furious dramatic energy that pervades *The Revenger's Tragedy*. It is, however, a competent achievement, enlivened by some good comic scenes and by the presence of an engaging villain.

Beyond its sensational and melodramatic tone lies a seriously constructed play based upon the conflict of two contrasting philosophical positions: D'Amville's naturalism and Charlemont's theism. Like Edmund in *King Lear,* D'Amville worships at the shrine of nature. His perception of the disparity between the law of nature and the law of morality leads him to dismiss the latter contemptuously, until the power of events overwhelms him in the name of a force greater than nature. In contrast, Charlemont's religious passivity strikes a new note for the role of "revenge" in Elizabethan tragedy, one which reflects a deep faith in divine providence.

Tourneur's stature as a dramatist has been complicated by the dispute over the authorship of *The Revenger's Tragedy*. The author of that play is an artist of narrow vision but chilling effectiveness. The author of *The Atheist's Tragedy* employs a broader, more consciously philosophical view of life, which, unfortunately, is never entirely realized in dramatic terms. If both plays are by Tourneur, they represent both his philosophical growth and, paradoxically, his artistic diminution.

The standard edition of Tourneur is *The Works of Cyril Tourneur* (1930), edited by Allardyce Nicoll. —E. Q.

Towneley Plays, The. See THE WAKEFIELD PLAYS.

Trachiniai (Women of Trachis, date unknown). A tragedy by SOPHOCLES. Deianira, the wife of Heracles, has been left behind in Trachis while Heracles, his twelve labors completed, serves his penance of exile for killing a member of the royal house of Oechalia. Without news of him for many months, she is disturbed by riddling oracles which said that after his labors he would find rest. Her son, Hyllus, reports that his father, back from exile, is leading an army against Oechalia and is sent off to find him. The Chorus, women of Trachis, try to comfort Deianira. A messenger announces that Lichas, Heracles' herald, has arrived with news of victory. Lichas leads on a train of women captured at Oechalia who are now slaves. One of them, more noble in appearance than the rest, arouses Deianira's curiosity and sympathy, but she will not answer questions.

Lichas, professing ignorance of her identity, tells Deianira that Heracles' motive for sacking Oechalia was revenge. But the messenger tells Deianira that Lichas is lying; in the marketplace Lichas said that Heracles' motive was love of the king's daughter, Iole, the girl Deianira questioned. Lichas is faced with his accuser and his lies are exposed; he tells the truth after Deianira assures him that she can face the situation if he will only tell her the truth. But when we next see her, she tells the Chorus that she cannot bear the situation she now has to face—two wives in the same house, one young, one growing old. So she has decided to use a magic charm to regain Heracles' love. It was given her by the centaur Nessus, who was killed by the arrows of Heracles, and it is made of his blood. She has smeared it on a robe she will give to Lichas, for Heracles to wear at the victory sacrifice, and she has shut it up in a box, for it is not to be exposed to sunlight before use. When we next see Deianira, she is in an agony of fear; the tuft of wool she used to smear the robe, thrown away in the courtyard, has disintegrated under the sun's rays. Hyllus returns and accuses her of killing his father; he tells how Heracles, in torment as the poison ate into his vitals, threw Lichas from the cliffs to his death. Now, in his death throes, Heracles is on his way home. Deianira rushes silently offstage; her nurse describes her suicide. When Heracles is brought on, screaming and writhing in pain, his first thought is to punish Deianira. Hyllus tells him of her suicide and also of the love charm. Heracles, at the mention of Nessus, remembers an oracle that said he could not be killed by the hand of any living creature. This is its fulfillment. He accepts his destiny: no lamentations now, but preparation for death. He is to be taken up to Mt. Oeta and placed on a funeral pyre, and Hyllus is to set it aflame. Hyllus refuses (the Greek audience knew, although it is not mentioned, that Philoctetes lit the pyre and was rewarded with the unerring bow and arrows), but Heracles' second demand, that Hyllus marry Iole, is reluctantly agreed to. Accusing the gods of ingratitude, Hyllus leads the way to the mountain. The play ends with the enigmatic words (whether spoken by Hyllus or the Chorus we do not know): "Nothing of this that is not Zeus."

Trachiniai is the most problematical of all the plays; there is wide disagreement about its date, structure, and meaning. The Prologue (more narrative than dramatic) and the erotic theme have been thought to indicate Euripidean influence and a late date. The structure of the play, with its two main characters who never meet and who each have a separate drama, has been labeled a "diptych." The same term has been applied, with less excuse, to *Ajax* and *Antigone.* It is true that none of these three plays has the clear dramatic unity of *Oedipus Tyrannus* and *Electra,* but in all three there are firm connections between the two supposed separate panels. Ajax's corpse, visible onstage, is the cause of the quarrels that follow his suicide; in death as in life he dominates the action. Antigone's suicide causes the death of Haemon and so of Eurydice; though absent, she brings down vengeance on Creon. Deianira's one thought and motive throughout is her love for Heracles; the spectacle of the hero's aggressive vitality, undiminished by his unspeakable pain, explains the devotion that drives her to such lengths to regain his

love. But the last scene also brings to its conclusion a pervasive theme of the play—the riddling oracles which express the will of Zeus and which, once understood, put an end to Heracles' lamentations and prepare him for his death.

The divine will is in *Trachiniai* more enigmatic and apparently more cruel than in any other Sophoclean play. No reference to Heracles' deification softens the harsh emptiness of the ending, "all dark and comfortless." The final words are as riddling as the oracles, and only the overall religious attitude of Sophoclean tragedy makes it possible to interpret them in a positive sense.

Recommended editions of the play are R. C. Jebb's *The Trachiniae* (1892), and J. C. Kamerbeek's *The Trachiniae* (1959).—B. M. W. K.

tragedy. In Western literature, the tragic sense of life that became the basis for tragedy as a dramatic form is first evident in Homer's *Iliad* (c. eighth century B.C.), which depicts man's nobility and heroism in the face of certain defeat and a world in which man's powers are limited or dominated by the gods. Herbert J. Muller, in *The Spirit of Tragedy* (1956), has described this sense of tragedy in which

> . . . injustice is not merely the fault of a particular society, but the age-old story of man's inhumanity to man; that we can never do everything about it that we might like to do, or ought to do; that at best there will always remain suffering beyond remedy, bringing us back to the painful mystery of man's being in a mysterious universe.

After tragedy, as a dramatic form, had developed out of ritual observance (see RITUAL ORIGINS OF DRAMA)—the term *tragoidia,* meaning "goat song,"

RELIEF OF A TRAGIC MASK (THE METROPOLITAN MUSEUM OF ART, ROGERS FUND, 1913)

probably refers to song and dance in honor of the fertility god Dionysus—ARISTOTLE composed his *Poetics,* which are analytic notes on the elements of tragedy and still the most influential treatise on the subject. His systematic examination, designed as a reply to Plato's disparagement of tragedy as a dangerous model for the citizens of his imagined republic, was later raised to the status of dogma by neoclassical Italian and French rhetoricians of the sixteenth and seventeenth centuries (though faulty translations may have accounted for this error of interpretation). These critics were to insist, for example, that tragedy observe the unities of time, place, and action—the "Weird Sisters" of neoclassicism—though Aristotle had merely stated that many tragedies contained unity of action and presented the action within the revolution of the sun. Of unity of place, there is no mention. In short, the *Poetics* was designed, not as a handbook of rules, but as an empirical analysis of dramatic form.

In the *Republic* (c. 385 B.C.), Plato attacked Homer's *Iliad* and the great tragedies of the past for their depiction of human weaknesses with which the audience might too readily identify. The result, Plato insisted, was moral debilitation. But in Aristotle's *Poetics,* poetry (a generic term that included tragedy) was conceived of as superior to history, which dealt with particulars, and as a beneficial cathartic of the debilitating emotions of pity and fear. The tragic hero, Aristotle suggested, was freed from the accidents of reality and was ideally fulfilled, so that the tragic action could provide its audience with an ordered, elevated response.

Between Aristotle and the Roman critic Horace (65–8 B.C.) there was a notable absence of tragic theory. The Romans, whose genius was more inclined to comedy than to tragedy, first became aware of the grandeur of Greek tragedy when Livius Andronicus, in 240 B.C., produced a Greek play in translation. Horace's *Ars poetica* (*Art of Poetry,* c. 9 B.C., the title given by the Roman rhetorician Quintilian to Horace's *Epistola ad Pisanos,* or *Epistle to the Pisos,* was designed as a set of principles governing poetry in its varied forms. Horace urged tragic poets to study Greek models—the principle of imitation, important in later neoclassicism—and specified the principle of decorum, that is, consistency in character types and appropriateness of speech to each character's station and rank. In accordance with Greek practice, comic scenes or characters were to be excluded from tragedy. As to the end of tragedy, Horace concludes that the poet wishes to teach or to please or to do both—an axiom central to neoclassicism.

In the middle ages, there existed neither tragedy as a dramatic form nor a body of critical theory. (The tragedies of the Roman dramatist Seneca were known but thought to be designed for recitation rather than stage performance.) The popular drama, consisting of miracle, mystery, and morality plays, occasionally contained tragic themes, but Christian doctrine, stressing redemption in a world presided over by a beneficent deity, limited the possibility of depicting man's defiance. It was not until the more secular Renaissance that plays dealt with tragic heroes.

Medieval tragedy, therefore, was conceived as a narrative in which the "wheel of fortune," ambigu-ously suggesting the workings of an arbitrary fate or the intervention of divine providence, was designed to discourage the coveting of worldly success and to strengthen faith in God. The fall of illustrious men, as depicted in these narratives, may be seen in such fourteenth-century works as Petrarch's *De viris illustribus* (*Concerning Illustrious Men*) and Boccaccio's *De casibus virorum illustrium* (*Concerning the Falls of Illustrious Men*) and in John Lydgate's *Fall of Princes* (written 1430–1438). The term "tragedy," which entered the English language in the late fourteenth century, was used by Chaucer in the Prologue to the "Monk's Tale" (one of the *Canterbury Tales*) to describe the medieval concept:

> Tragedie is to seyn a certeyn storie,
> As olde bookes maken us memorie,
> Of hym that stood in greet prosperitee,
> And is yfallen out of heigh degree
> Into myserie, and endeth wreccedly.

Medieval tragic narratives thus eliminated the "tragic action" and final exaltation of Greek tragedy by substituting the spectacle of the fall as a warning against covetousness and as a reminder of man's primal fall.

By 1498, the renaissance of classical learning in Italy resulted in a new and complete Latin translation by Giorgio Valla of Aristotle's *Poetics,* virtually unknown during the middle ages. The authority of Aristotle, long supreme in metaphysics and ethics, was now extended to tragedy; with Horace's *Art of Poetry,* the *Poetics* provided the basis for a neoclassical theory of tragedy that would profoundly influence practical criticism and stagecraft through the eighteenth century.

Of the many Italian commentaries on the *Poetics* in the sixteenth century, one of the most influential was the *Poetices libri septem* (*Poetics,* 1561) of Julius Caesar Scaliger (1484–1558). In his insistence that tragedy observe fidelity to reality, Scaliger objected to plays that moved "from Delphi to Athens, or from Athens to Delphi in a moment of time" or that depicted the Trojan War in two hours. Such a misconception as to the nature of dramatic time, as opposed to "real" time, was not derived from Aristotle but from Scaliger's own literal-mindedness. Nevertheless, Scaliger was celebrated as the formulator of the three unities, or *les unités scaligeriennes,* as they were called, despite the fact that he had merely insisted on verisimilitude.

A follower of Scaliger, Lodovico Castelvetro (1505–1571) was in fact the first of the Italian neoclassicists to formulate the three unities in his translation and commentary *Poetica d'Aristotle* (*Poetics of Aristotle,* 1570): The plot should consist of "one action of one person, or two actions, which by their interdependence can be counted one"—the unity of action; "the time of action ought not to exceed the limit of twelve hours"—the unity of time; "tragedy ought to have for subject an action which happened in a very limited extent of place"—the unity of place. This interpretation of Aristotle's *Poetics* (which Castelvetro had frequently mistranslated to prove his own points) provoked numerous disputes on the Continent.

The influence of the Italian commentators first

reached England in *An Apologie for Poetry* or *A Defence of Poesie* (written in the 1580's, slightly different texts appeared in 1595) by Sir Philip Sidney (1554–1586). A defense of poetry against Puritan attacks, the *Apologie* relies upon the Italian theorists in its comment on the first English tragedy, Thomas Sackville and Thomas Norton's *Gorboduc* (1562). Sidney finds this play

> . . . full of notable morality, which it doth most delightfully teach, and so obtain the very end of poesy; yet in truth it is very defective in the circumstances: For it is faulty both in place and time, the two necessary companions of all corporal actions. For the stage should always represent but one place, and the uttermost time presupposed in it should be, both by Aristotle's precept and common reason, but one day . . .

In addition, Sidney, who wrote his defense before the great age of Elizabethan tragedy, regarded the mixture of comedy and tragedy as a "mongrel."

Sidney's essay had a significant effect in the seventeenth century, for it not only publicized the ideas of Continental neoclassicism but also justified the importance of poetry against Puritan charges—derived from Plato—that it was morally dangerous. There is no evidence that Shakespeare had read it; if he had, he ignored its precepts, as did most of the important Elizabethan dramatists. Only Ben Jonson, an avowed classicist, attempted on occasion to follow Sidney's prescriptions for tragedy. Shakespeare, Marlowe, and others were inspired by the tensions of the age, between the older beliefs and the new skepticism, rather than by devotion to rigid rules. Though John Milton, a Puritan and classicist, had praised Shakespeare in his poem "L'Allegro" for his natural genius, he himself preferred classical precedent. Thus, in the Preface to his verse drama *Samson Agonistes* (1671), Milton indicated that he had composed a true tragedy:

> This is mentioned to vindicate Tragedy from the small esteem, or rather infamy, which in the account of many it undergoes at this day . . . happening through the poet's error of intermixing comic stuff with tragic sadness and gravity, or introducing trivial and vulgar persons . . .

In all matters, Milton states, the play follows the practices of Aeschylus, Sophocles, and Euripides, "the best rule to all who endeavour to write Tragedy."

But though such major writers as Jonson and Milton attempted to follow classical precedent, the ambivalence of John Dryden (1631–1700), "the father of English criticism," toward such widely venerated precepts as the unities, decorum of character and style, and the rigid separation of the comic and the tragic provided yet another impulse for the eventual rejection of neoclassical dogma. In *An Essay of Dramatic Poesy* (1668), Dryden weighed but did not insist on the validity of traditional neoclassical rules governing tragedy; indeed, he gives to Neander, the imaginary speaker in the dialogue, lines that reveal his own preferences: "If I would compare [Ben Jonson] with Shakespeare, I must acknowledge

him the more correct poet, but Shakespeare the greater wit. Shakespeare was the Homer, or father of our dramatic poets. . . . I admire [Jonson], but I love Shakespeare." In his attempt to combine the English tradition with Continental neoclassicism, Dryden continually reexamined the problem of such a blending. Convinced that tragedy was not a historically fixed form, he jotted a note down in a volume of criticism: "It is not enough that Aristotle has said so, for Aristotle drew his models of tragedy from Sophocles and Euripides; and, if he had seen ours, might have changed his mind."

In seventeenth-century France, resistance to authority manifested itself in much the same terms. In his Preface to Jean de Schélandre's play *Tyr et Sidon* (1628), François Ogier (d. 1670) appealed, as did Dryden, to the validity of contemporary genius rather than to classical precedent:

> . . . the Greeks wrote for Greece. . . . We shall imitate them much better if we allow something to the genius of our country and to the taste of our language than if we force ourselves to follow step by step both their style of invention and their poetic forms.

Later in the century, the critic Saint-Évremond (c. 1614–1703), in his essay *De la Tragédie ancienne et moderne* (*On Ancient and Modern Tragedy*, 1672), questioned the wisdom of slavishly following Aristotle's *Poetics* (one should say, rather, neoclassical interpretations of this work), since there was "nothing so perfect in it as to be the standing rules of all nations and all ages." He questioned, moreover, whether Aristotle was correct in assuming that catharsis morally strengthened an audience; Plato, he suggested, was perhaps right after all: Since Greek tragedies "wholly consisted in excessive emotions of fear and pity, was not this the direct way to make the theater a school of terror and of compassion, where people learnt to be affrighted at all dangers, and to abandon themselves to despair upon every misfortune?"

Despite such doubt cast upon orthodox neoclassical assumptions, major critics, convinced that "good sense and reason" were involved, rose periodically to their defense. (Ironically, "good sense and reason" were habitually invoked both by those defending and by those attacking neoclassical rules governing tragedy.) Nicolas Boileau (1636–1711), for example, in his widely read poem *Art poétique* (*The Art of Poetry*, 1674), modeled after Horace, deplored the prevailing practice of Spanish tragedians who ignored the unities:

> But we, that are by reason's rule confined,
> Will that with art the poem be designed,
> That unity of action, time, and place
> Keep the stage full, and all our labors grace.

And in England, Alexander Pope (1688–1744), in *An Essay on Criticism* (1711), proposed that the rules governing each genre were not "devised" but "discovered" in nature. The ancient writers had grasped the unchanging truths of nature and had formalized them as rules:

> Learn hence for ancient rules a just esteem;
> To copy nature is to copy them.

In the great "Preface to Shakespeare" (1765) by Dr. Samuel Johnson (1709–1784), traditional recourse to authority and to the rules received its severest blow. Though a neoclassicist himself (in his belief that art should deal with general truths and contribute to moral development), he saw no grave error in Shakespeare's mingling of the comic and the tragic: "That this is a practice contrary to the rules of criticism will be readily allowed but there is always an appeal open from criticism to nature." In short, nature consisted of such mingling, and Shakespeare's greatness was that he understood that "all pleasure consists in variety." Of the neoclassical unities, Dr. Johnson contended that insistence on the unities of time and place involved a confusion between art and life—"representation is mistaken for reality." Therefore, tragedy, an imaginative creation, relies upon the imaginative grasp by the audience of time and place: "The truth is, that the spectators are always in their senses, and know, from the first act to the last, that the stage is only a stage, and that the players are only players."

Such reaction to the rigidities and misconceptions underlying neoclassical doctrine found further support in the *Hamburgische Dramaturgie* (*Hamburg Dramaturgy*, 1769) of Gotthold Lessing (1729–1781), Germany's first major drama critic. He attacked the French models for tragedy approved by his countrymen and urged adoption of the less classical but more flexible English forms. Accepting the Aristotelian premise that unity of action, involving "change of circumstances, recognition, and suffering," was essential to tragedy, he demonstrated that Shakespeare was, in fact, true to the principle. Of the unities of time and place, the Greeks, Lessing stated, saw them as "mere consequences" of the unity of action ("the first dramatic law"), not rigid molds to which the action must be accommodated. The French dramatists had mistakenly attempted to adapt the tragic action to the requirements of the rules: "When they found, however, how impossible this was, they made a truce with the tyrannical rules against which they had not the courage to rebel."

As a dramatist, Lessing (following English models, such as George Lillo's *The London Merchant*, 1731), wrote middle-class tragedies, the most famous being *Miss Sara Sampson* (1755). Indeed, as the century progressed, dramatists, disenchanted with neoclassicism and its eternal rules, its legendary or historical heroes, and its austere, elevated verse, turned increasingly to bourgeois tragedy and argued for its validity, as did the French playwright Beaumarchais in his *Essai sur le genre dramatique sérieux* (*Essay on the Serious Drama*, 1767):

> The true heart-interest, real relationship is always between man and man, not between man and king. Thus, far from increasing my interest in the characters of tragedy, their exalted rank rather diminishes it. The nearer the suffering man is to my station in life, the greater is his claim upon my sympathy.

With the growing Romanticism of the eighteenth century, bourgeois tragedy became increasingly sentimental, manifesting a reluctance to accept the inevitability of the hero's destruction. Belief in the essential goodness of man assumed the possibility of change, the alleviation of suffering, and redemption through love. Hence, "poetic justice," by which the good prospered and the wicked suffered, became operative.

In the early nineteenth century, a major challenge to this attitude toward tragedy occurred in the philosophical criticism of Georg Wilhelm Hegel (1770–1831). In his posthumously published *Vorlesungen über die Aesthetik* (*The Philosophy of Fine Art*, literally *Lectures on Aesthetics*, 1835–1838), he contended that ordinary morality—as conceived of in the bourgeois tragedy of his day—was inadequate as a basis for tragedy; it was necessary to understand the source of tragedy, which was fundamentally "a conflict of ethical substance." In his theory, derived from his admiration for Sophocles' *Antigone*, partial good is claimed as an absolute, and suffering arises from the struggle between rival claims, both of which have only partial validity. In short, good struggles against good: In *Antigone*, both the title character—in her insistence that religious custom demands that her brother's body be buried—and Creon—in his insistence that rebellion against the state warrants no such honor—are convinced that their claims are absolute; Creon realizes, too late, that his is only partially valid. (Hegel admitted that many Greek tragedies did not fit this thesis; neither did Shakespeare's.)

Hegel's theory of tragedy is derived from his metaphysical principle that *Geist,* or "spirit," manifests itself in the universe as the rational process of thesis, antithesis, and synthesis. Tragedy reconciles the conflict of ethical claims ("thesis" and "antithesis") at the moment of tragic illumination (for the audience and Creon but not for Antigone, who dies in ignorance). Tragedy, then, expresses a stage in the dialectic of historical development.

Opposed to such metaphysics, Arthur Schopenhauer (1788–1860), in *Die Welt als Wille und Vorstellung* (*The World as Will and Idea*, 1819, revised in succeeding editions), a work little read until the end of the century, rejects the rational operation of Hegel's Geist and postulates the existence of blind energy, or "will," which is irrational. Tragedy gives its audience insight into the nature of will, which can produce man's most profound suffering: "At the moment of the tragic catastrophe, we become convinced more clearly than ever that life is a bad dream from which we have to awake." But tragedy produces not despair but pleasure, for "it raises us above the will" and provides "the knowledge that the world and life can afford us no true satisfaction, and are therefore not worth our attachment to them." In this, states Schopenhauer, "the tragic spirit consists; accordingly it leads to resignation."

England's great philosopher-critic Samuel Taylor Coleridge (1772–1834), in a lecture on Greek drama (1818), contended that the tragic poet, by idealizing his characters so that "the spiritual part of our natures" are given "a more decided preponderance over the animal cravings and impulses than is met in real life," transports us into the "mythologic world in order to raise the emotions, the fears, and hopes, which convince the inmost heart that their final cause is not to be discovered in the limits of mere mortal life" (the idea of transcendence, characteristic of Romantic criticism) and produces an awareness of those "struggles of inward free will with outward necessity, which form the true subject of the tragedian." Tragedy, Coleridge contends, "reconciles and solves" those struggles, a judgment suggesting a Hegelian view.

Of the great philosopher-critics of the century, one of the most brilliant and suggestive was Friedrich Nietzsche (1844–1900), whose work *Die Geburt der Tragödie* (*The Birth of Tragedy*, 1872), opposed the widely held notion that Greek tragedy exhibited the Apollonian qualities of classical art—namely, order, repose, and harmony. Instead, Nietzsche emphasized the Dionysian elements of wildness and orgy associated with primitive ritual and celebration from which the tragic form emerged. Thus, Greek tragedy, dominated by the spirit of Dionysus, was in its early development a manifestation of man's deeper, wilder self—elemental men liberated from the restraints of reason and social custom—but as it developed in the plays of Euripides, tragedy moved toward the Apollonian spirit of restraint, rationality, and order. True tragedy, he argued, was "a manifestation and illustration of Dionysian states, as the visible symbolization of music, as the dream-world of Dionysian ecstasy." Apollo, one might say, provides the mask, but Dionysus provides the inspiration, or as Nietzsche expresses it:

> . . . the Apollonian illusion is found to be what it really is—the assiduous veiling during the performance of tragedy of the intrinsically Dionysian effect. . . . Thus then the intricate relation of the Apollonian and the Dionysian in tragedy must really be symbolized by a fraternal union of the two deities: Dionysus speaks the language of Apollo; Apollo, however, finally speaks the language of Dionysus; and so the highest goal of tragedy and of art in general is attained.

At the beginning of the twentieth century, with the increasing interest in the psychology of the tragic hero—the legacy of the Romantic movement—the analyses of A. C. Bradley (1851–1935), in his *Shakespearean Tragedy* (1904) and *Lectures on Poetry* (1909), discussed the tragic hero's internal divisions, the inner psychological confusion. This is more significant, Bradley insisted, than Hegel's ethical analysis. Every tragedy, Bradley wrote in his *Lectures*, reveals "a self-division and self-waste of spirit," and "*any* spiritual conflict involving spiritual waste is tragic." Thus, the greatness of the tragic hero is revealed in defeat.

The reassertion of the Hegelian conception occurred with the work of Prosser Frye (1866–1934), whose *Romance and Tragedy* (1922) is primarily concerned with Greek rather than with later modern tragedy, with its interest in psychology. He sees the fall of the tragic hero as an affirmation of the moral order. Indeed, the central question that the tragic dramatist must address himself to is the existence of evil in an ordered universe. Like Hegel, Frye regards *Antigone* as exemplary tragedy, since the title character's direct opposition to the existing order results in disaster. It is, Frye asserts, the tragic dramatist's function to reveal the source of error and its consequences. Too often, in tragedy following the Greeks, interest centers on the sympathetic hero; but unqual-

ified sympathy, Frye insists, undercuts the sharp edge of the tragic experience, as in the case of Shakespeare's tragedies, which focus on the psychological chaos of the hero.

Despite Frye's Hegelian conception of tragedy, most writing on the subject has been dominated by the notion that tragedy celebrates man's capacity to endure suffering, an idea derived from the Romantics and central to "The Tragic Fallacy," in *The Modern Temper* (1929), by Joseph Wood Krutch (1893–). Thus, Krutch writes, "tragedy is not an expression of despair but the means by which [the great ages] saved themselves from it." Like religion, tragedy gives us "a rationality, a meaning, and a justification in the universe." The reason that tragedies— comparable to those in the past—are not written today is that man has lost his faith not only in the greatness of God but also in the greatness of man. Thus, so-called modern tragedy dwells on the miseries of modern life but fails to give its audience the exaltation of spirit characteristic of earlier tragedy.

The question whether the writing of tragedy is possible in the modern world has been under constant debate since Krutch's essay. With the production of Arthur Miller's *Death of a Salesman* (1949), the question was again raised, by Miller himself in his essay "Tragedy and the Common Man," published shortly after his play opened. Miller is convinced that "tragic feeling is evoked in us when we are in the presence of a character who is ready to lay down his life, if need be, to secure one thing—his sense of personal dignity." Tragedy, moreover, is "the consequence of a man's total compulsion to evaluate himself justly." As for the rank of the hero, that, says Miller, is "but a clinging to the outward forms of tragedy." The experience of exaltation is derived from the "thrust for freedom" exercised by the hero, no matter what his station in life; the enlightenment that tragedy produces reveals the "enemy of man's freedom." The common man may acquire the stature of a tragic hero by "his willingness to throw all he has into the contest, the battle to secure his rightful place in his world." Tragedy, then, is optimistic about the perfectibility of man. Curiously, Miller's essay applies little to *Death of a Salesman,* the hero of which, Willy Loman, seems too confused and ignorant of the larger forces of his society to acquire tragic proportions. Miller himself states in his essay that pathos— which is pessimistic—results "by virtue of the hero's witlessness, his insensitivity or the very air he gives off, incapable of grappling with a much superior force"—a judgment seemingly applicable to Willy Loman.

Some critics, in judging Miller's play and those by other modern playwrights, have preferred the term "low tragedy"—as opposed to "high tragedy"—to suggest a less exalted experience than may be found in Greek and Shakespearean tragedy. The division of terms suggests, moreover, that tragedy has undergone a decline. Such is the thesis of George Steiner (1929–) in *The Death of Tragedy* (1961), which designates the seventeenth century as "the point of no return" with respect to tragic form and experience. The "triumph of rationalism and secular metaphysics" and the decline of the "organic world view and its attendant context of mythological, symbolic and ritual reference" spelled out tragedy's end—an idea previously suggested by Krutch. With the rise of other literary forms, such as the novel, which provided the public with entertainment closer to their middle-class experiences and assumptions, and with the rise of Romanticism and its social and religious view of personal redemption, the possibility of genuine tragedy faded. Thus, "modern tragedy" cannot portray a world capable of the unique experience of tragedy. As Steiner states the final effect of great tragedy:

> Man is ennobled by the vengeful spite or injustice of the gods. It does not make him innocent, but it hallows him as if he had passed through flame. Hence there is in the final moments of great tragedy, whether Greek or Shakespearean or neo-classic, a fusion of grief and joy, of lament over the fall of man and of rejoicing in the resurrection of his spirit. No other poetic form achieves this mysterious effect; it makes of *Oedipus, King Lear,* and *Phedre* the noblest yet wrought by the mind.

Recommended on the subject of tragedy are *European Theories of the Drama* (rev. ed. by Henry Popkin, 1965), edited by Barrett H. Clark; and *Tragedy: Vision and Form* (1965), edited by Robert W. Corrigan.—K. B.

tragicomedy. The dictionary defines tragicomedy as "a play combining the qualities of a tragedy and a comedy," but the centuries have brought small agreement as to what these qualities are or how they are combined. As early as the fifth century B.C. there was a combination of the tragic and the comic in the Athenian tragic tetralogy, since the three tragedies were followed by a comic satyr play. Though the forms were quite different for classical tragedy and comedy, diverse comic notes sound within certain tragedies: puns with their inevitable comic resonance; comic characters like the nurse of *Choephori* (*Libation Bearers*) by Aeschylus and the messenger of *Bacchants* by Euripides; happy endings for eight extant tragedies of Euripides. In a famous passage at the end of Plato's *Symposium* Socrates insists to Agathon, the tragic poet, and Aristophanes, the comic poet, "that the genius of comedy was the same as that of tragedy, and that the writer of tragedy ought to be a writer of comedy also." However, Socrates did not say that the qualities of tragedy and of comedy should be combined in the *same* play, and they were not combined until the Renaissance, when playwrights often wrote both tragedy and comedy as well as a blend of the two.

The word *comoedotragoedia* is found in a fragment by the Greek comic dramatist Alcaeus, but there is no indication of its meaning in context. Centuries later, the Roman Plautus coined the word *tragicomoedia* in the Prologue to his *Amphitryon*. Disguised as the slave Sosia, the god Mercury first refers to the play as "comedy," then designates it as "tragedy," and proceeds to tease his audience:

> What? Are you frowning because I said that this would be a tragedy? I am a god, I will change it. If you wish, I will convert this tragedy into a comedy, without changing a line. Do you wish it or not? But I am being quite foolish. As if I didn't know, I who am a god. I know your feelings in this matter. I will bring about a mixture: let it be tragicomedy. For I

do not think it proper to make it wholly comedy, since there are kings and gods. What then? Since there is also a slave, it will be just as I said, a tragicomedy.

Plautus thus invented the word tragicomedy to describe his breach of decorum—mixing gods and slaves in the same play—and a god disguised as a slave mouths the neologism. The humorous tone mocks rigid genre terminology, and *Amphitryon* itself is a comedy bordering on farce.

Genre terminology tended to be loose from late classical to late medieval times; variations from classical tragedy and/or comedy were indicated by sporadic use of such labels as *tragicocomoedia, comoedotragoedia,* and *comoedia tragica.* Rarely did such designations imply a mixture of the serious and the laughable, and such mixture is peripheral in the most coherent Renaissance definition of tragicomedy, that of Giovanni Battista Guarini, in his *Compendium of Tragicomic Poetry* (1599):

> He who composes tragicomedy takes from tragedy its great persons but not its action, its verisimilar plot but not its true one, its movement of the feelings but not its disturbance of them, its pleasure but not its sadness, its danger but not its death; from comedy laughter that is not excessive, modest amusement, feigned difficulty, happy reversal, and above all the comic order.

Within the "comic order" characters might be threatened with danger and death, and yet they come to happy ends, as in several so-called tragedies of Euripides. Guarini also points to *Amphitryon* to justify both his use of the word tragicomedy and the comic order.

Similarly, John Fletcher explains in a preface to his play *The Faithful Shepherdess* (c. 1608): "A tragicomedy is not so called in respect of mirth and killing, but in respect it wants deaths, which is enough to make it no tragedy, yet brings some near it, which is enough to make it no comedy." Fletcher's "mirth" and Guarini's "modest amusement" are only incidental in Renaissance tragicomedy; central are danger, reversal, and happy ending. Thus, Renaissance tragicomedy resembles modern melodrama more than modern tragicomedy, with its reciprocal interaction of the serious and the laughable.

Self-styled tragicomedy flourished briefly but vigorously in Renaissance Italy, France, England, and Spain. In the conclusion to his *Tragicomedy: Its Origin and Development in Italy, France, and England* (1955), Marvin Herrick attempts to link this form to modern drama:

> The term tragicomedy gave some assurance to poets who were willing, some of them even anxious, to follow classical tradition, but at the same time were compelled to satisfy the modern demand for the freer form. The term is now antiquated, for traditional labels have lost their importance, but most of the significant modern dramas still occupy a middle ground between tragedy and comedy.

Herrick's words still suggest that, rather than combining tragic and comic qualities, most Renaissance tragicomedy lies in some neutral ground between these two poles. But many dramas were based on *common* ground where tragic and comic qualities blend.

Medieval drama in Latin and in the vernaculars introduced comedy into a serious plot, though this practice was not restricted to plays designated as tragicomedy. Polonius does not mention tragicomedy in his catalogue of dramatic genres; yet Shakespeare's tragedies contain comic elements, in a mixture that Sir Philip Sidney had already denigrated as "mongrel tragicomedy." In John Dryden's *Essay on Dramatic Poesie* (1668) his spokesman, Neander, praises "a scene of mirth, mixed with tragedy" as providing "relief," though Dryden himself later came to believe that "mirth and gravity destroy each other." Samuel Johnson's dictionary, of the eighteenth century, defines tragicomedy as "drama compounded of merry and serious events." Contrary to classical rules, Dr. Johnson praises Shakespeare's mixture:

> Shakespeare has united the powers of exciting laughter and sorrow not only in one mind, but in one composition. Almost all his plays are divided between serious and ludicrous characters, and in the successive evolution of the design, sometimes produce seriousness and sorrow, and sometimes levity and laughter. That this is a practice contrary to the rules of criticism will be readily allowed; but there is always an appeal open from criticism to nature.

Similarly, Voltaire and Christoph Martin Wieland praise Shakespeare in spite of his irregularities, by appealing to nature. In eighteenth-century criticism and Romantic writing, there was marked interest in tragicomedy as a combination of the qualities of tragedy and comedy, and such drama was distinguished from sentimental comedy, which was neither tragedy nor comedy. Using Shakespeare as their model, Romantic writers demanded a blend of the serious and the laughable in the same play. August Wilhelm Schlegel espoused "mixed drama, particularly tragicomedy," and Victor Hugo's 1827 Preface to *Cromwell* declares: "Shakespeare is the drama; and the drama . . . molds the grotesque and the sublime, the terrible and the absurd, tragedy and comedy." These antithetical pairs are approximate parallels, and they predict twentieth-century problems of critical terminology. Tragedy and comedy are of course the classical poles, and have preoccupied critics from Aristotle to the present. The grotesque and the absurd, in contrast, are areas of recent critical investigation, which often overlap tragicomedy.

Beginning with Romanticism, the word tragicomedy tended to describe a mode rather than a form, a texture rather than a structure. But the boundary line between form and tone is not always distinct. Thus, Wolfgang Kayser in his 1957 study of the grotesque designates it as a structure, and yet his analyses emphasize tone. Though the grotesque originates in the graphic arts, it comes to embrace dramatic tragicomedy. Kayser writes: "Beginning with the dramaturgic practice of the *Sturm und Drang* and the dramatic theory of Romanticism, tragicomedy and the grotesque are conceptually related, and the history of the

grotesque in the field of drama is largely one with that of tragicomedy." This history has been studied only in German drama (by Karl Guthke), which is richest in modern examples of a genre in which comic and tragic elements interact in the same play. In dramas of Georg Büchner, Heinrich von Kleist, Friedrich Hebbel, and Christian Dietrich Grabbe, comedy heightens the tragic impact.

The French critic François Sarcey, who reacted against Romanticism, urged separation of the comic and the tragic in *Essay on an Esthetic of Theater* (1876). He pointed out that comic relief was routine in melodrama, but melodrama was an inferior genre. With the advent of realism in the 1880's and its emphasis on unhappiness, comic effects were occasionally introduced for ironic counterpoint, as in *Ghosts* or *The Wild Duck* of Henrik Ibsen. George Bernard Shaw recognized that "Ibsen was the dramatic poet who firmly established tragicomedy as a much deeper and grimmer entertainment than tragedy."

Most modern playwrights have built upon Ibsen's foundation. Early in Strindberg's *The Dance of Death*, Kurt describes the captain: "He would be comic if he were not tragic, and there's a touch of greatness in his pettiness." The description may be extended to other Strindberg characters and to his other plays, such as *Comrades, The Creditors, There Are Crimes and Crimes,* or even *The Ghost Sonata*. And the description is applicable, too, to the so-called comedies of Chekhov, whose comic characters are unhappy; to O'Casey, whose characters reach catastrophe by way of comic Irish idiom; to the late plays of O'Neill, whose obsession with tragedy made room, finally, for comedy; to the poetic plays of Yeats and Eliot, who tried to blend tragic and comic; and to Gerhart Hauptmann and Frank Wedekind, heirs of the German tragicomic tradition that developed from Romantic irony. Pirandello, a more oblique heir of Romantic irony, made ironic reflection the basis of much of his drama. His playwriting career was preceded by a series of lectures, *L'Umorismo* ("Humorism," pub. 1908, expanded 1920). Early in this essay, Pirandello specifies: "The Italian word *umore* is not the English *humour*." Related to both the grotesque and the ironic, Pirandello's "humorism" implies an attitude of self-consciousness about suffering, a self-examination that is both painful and comic, an awareness of the opposite of every thing, thought, and emotion. For Pirandello, this feeling of contraries distinguishes humorism from comedy and irony.

A modern Polonius might list a catalogue of genres that bear on tragicomedy as the ironic, the humorous, the grotesque, and the absurd. In recent criticism, the term irony is widely used in English, grotesque in German, and humor in French and Italian, whereas the use of the word absurd is indiscriminate and international. Ironists and humorists are aware of contradictions in the world and in themselves; their writings reflect such contradictions, usually within a realistic framework. Playwrights of the grotesque and the absurd, on the other hand, evoke a sense of disorientation; their kind of tragicomedy spurns realism and often borders on fantasy. Ibsen, Strindberg, Chekhov, and Pirandello are the giants of the first group. Later in the twentieth century, Federico García Lorca revived an old Spanish tradition of tragicomedy, and Michel de Ghelderode a medieval Flemish tradition. Stemming from Strindberg's late work, German expressionists incorporate grotesque elements into plays that end catastrophically. Playwrights of the absurd portray man's disorientation in the universe. Samuel Beckett, Jean Genet, and Eugène Ionesco are the giants, but absurdism also haunts early Arthur Adamov, Fernando Arrabal, early Edward Albee, Wolfgang Hildesheimer, and Robert Pinget. The grotesque and the absurd may be roughly distinguished in that the former presents ridiculous distortion through sensuous means, and the latter conveys ridiculous disjunction through verbal means. Kayser's list of techniques of the grotesque is, however, also applicable to the absurd: "the fusion of realms which we know to be separated, the abolition of the law of statics, the loss of identity, the distortion of 'natural' size and shape, the suspension of the category of objects, the destruction of personality, and the fragmentation of historical order." It is when such techniques evoke laughter that the grotesque and the absurd are tragicomic or seriocomic, since seriousness is often taken to provide the tragic component of modern tragicomedy. Examples are the old couple in ashbins in Beckett's *Endgame,* the altar-dumbwaiter in Harold Pinter's *The Dumb Waiter,* a growing corpse in Ionesco's *Amédée,* and chickens as Roman emperors in Friedrich Dürrenmatt's *Romulus the Great.*

Of contemporary tragicomic playwrights, Ionesco and Dürrenmatt have espoused the tragicomic in theory as well as practice. Ionesco: "I have never understood the difference people make between the comic and the tragic. As the 'comic' is an intuitive perception of the absurd, it seems to me more hopeless than the 'tragic.' The 'comic' offers no escape . . . . The comic is tragic, and the tragedy of man is pure derision." Dürrenmatt: "But the tragic is still possible even if pure tragedy is not. We can achieve the tragic out of comedy. We can bring it forth as a frightening moment, as an abyss that opens suddenly." Whereas Ionesco finds tragedy and comedy interactive and interchangeable, Dürrenmatt finds that modern tragedy must be expressed comically.

One of our foremost drama critics, Eric Bentley, in his *Life of the Drama* (1964), divides modern tragicomedy into two kinds: tragedy transcended (as opposed to Renaissance "tragedy averted"), and comedy with an unhappy or indeterminate ending. He provides the following operational definition of the latter:

> Where romantic comedy says: these aggressions can be transcended, and realistic comedy says: these aggressions will be punished, tragicomedy of the school here under consideration says: these aggressions can neither be transcended nor brought to heel, they are human nature, they are life, they rule the world.

Critics always lag behind creators, and there has been little sustained analysis of modern tragicomedy. J. L. Styan's *Dark Comedy* (1962) is subtitled "The Development of Modern Comic Tragedy," but about a quarter of his book is devoted to background. Stressing tone rather than structure, Styan comments on plays that "mingle the laughter and the tears." He finds that tragicomedy rises from irony or

a comic-pathetic hero. Karl Guthke's *Modern Tragicomedy* (1966) is mistitled, since less than half the book deals with post-Romantic writing. Guthke does, however, suggest patterns of modern tragicomedy: tragic character in comic milieu; comic character in tragic milieu; linked plots, one tragic and the other comic; comic character whose actions lead to disaster for others; contrast of world of illusion with that of reality; irony of the course of events; and internal character dichotomy. Though such patterns are reductive, and they do not always fit the examples, Guthke does provide a springboard for analysis of how the qualities of tragedy and of comedy are combined in tragicomedy. In his list, structures yield to textures, generic distinctions to modal shadings.

Tragicomedy, combining qualities of tragedy and comedy, has been elusive of critical definition. But playwrights have used the word and the form with or without definition. Thus, Ionesco calls *The Chairs* a tragic farce, Beckett calls his English translation of *Waiting for Godot* a tragicomedy, and Dürrenmatt calls *The Visit* a tragic comedy, which he defines as a comedy that ends tragically. Contemporary dramatists tend to express their tragic vision with comic devices, creating tragicomedy that is funny without being foolish, serious without being solemn. *Pace* Aristotle, today's tragicomedy arouses fear and pity through laughter. See also COMEDY; TRAGEDY.—R. C.

Tristan L'Hermite, François (c. 1600–1655). French playwright and poet. After a roving and adventurous youth, Tristan L'Hermite was in the service of Gaston d'Orléans from 1627 to 1648, when he went over to the Duc de Guise. He began to publish his verse in 1627. In 1649 he became a member of the French Academy but remained aloof from literary circles throughout his life. He died in Paris in 1655, after having been the patron of the young playwright Philippe Quinault.

Perhaps the greatest poet of his day, Tristan was also one of the best dramatists. He began in 1636 at the Marais theater with a "regular" tragedy, *Mariane,* written according to the tenets of French classicism, which was almost as successful as Pierre Corneille's *Le Cid* (1637). After *Mariane,* the most important of his tragedies, all of which are rigorous and austere, are *La Mort de Sénèque* ("The Death of Seneca," 1644), *La Mort de Crispe* ("The Death of Crispus," 1645), and *Osman* (1646). Tristan also wrote one pastoral, one comedy (*Le Parasite,* 1653), and one curious philosophical and scientific tragicomedy (*La Folie du sage,* "The Wise Man's Madness"; 1642).—Ja. G.

Trivandrum plays (possibly 3rd century B.C.). Thirteen plays, reputedly written by the Sanskrit playwright Bhasa, first edited and published by Pandit Ganapati Shastri from manuscripts found in Trivandrum, a city in southern India. The Trivandrum plays constitute one of the most notable groups of plays in Indian dramatic literature. Although their authorship is open to question, the ascription to Bhasa is commonly accepted, largely from want of evidence to the contrary. Bhasa is mentioned with high praise by Kalidasa, the great Sanskrit dramatist, in his play *Malavika and Agnimitra,* and it is plausible that he refers to the author of the Trivandrum plays. Although their dating is even less subject to proof than their authorship, it is widely presumed that these plays constitute the oldest group of Indian plays known to us and may conceivably date from as early as the third century B.C. They are less mannered than the work of dramatists assumed to be of later periods in Indian history but show nevertheless that at the time of their writing a high development in theatrical art had already been attained.

The themes of the Trivandrum plays are predominantly epic. Seven plays deal with important episodes in the oldest of the great Sanskrit epics, the *Mahabharata*; these are *The Middle One, The Five Nights, The Embassy, Potsherd as an Envoy, Karna's Task, The Broken Thighs,* and *The Adventures of the Boy Krishna.* Two, *The Statue Play* and *The Consecration,* borrow their stories also from the no less celebrated epic the *Ramayana.* Two others, *The Minister's Vows* and the most celebrated drama of the collection, *The Vision of Vasavadatta,* derive from a group of semihistorical legends concerning Udayana, king of Vatsas. Finally are *Avimaraka,* a romantic play with a story of love triumphant over obstacles not unlike those depicted in *Romeo and Juliet,* and an unfinished or truncated play, *Charudatta in Poverty,* closely parallel to the longer and more brilliant drama THE LITTLE CLAY CART.

Most of the scholarship dealing with the questions of dating and authorship raises questions still so widely removed from definitive answers that prolonged comment on these views here is inappropriate. H. C. Woolner and Lakshman Sarup observe that discrepancies in manner and merit point to divided authorship. They cite the artfulness of the episode that gives its name to *The Statue Play* and the much less eloquent style of the concluding acts. On the basis of internal evidence only, R. V. Jagirdar is of the opinion that four plays, *The Vision of Vasavadatta, The Minister's Vows, The Five Nights,* and *The Statue Play,* are by one hand and that the other plays were composed by another playwright or possibly represent the work of several authors. A few plays, such as *Karna's Task* and *The Broken Thighs,* are exceptional for the strength of their verse passages. Others, such as *The Vision of Vasavadatta,* are in an almost curt style, abridged to what might conceivably be acting versions. *Charudatta in Poverty* further suggests this possibility, especially when contrasted with the much more poetic *The Little Clay Cart,* ascribed to Sudraka. The usual view is that *The Little Clay Cart* is the later and artistically more mature of the two works. According to this view, the politically oriented second part of *The Little Clay Cart,* now missing in the Bhasa play, may have been suppressed in the earlier play, giving it its truncated quality; these scenes might then have been revived and enlarged when the second play was written. *Charudatta in Poverty* would then be regarded as the first half of a play in two parts. Of this there seems some evidence even in the title of the Bhasa drama. The second half might have been designated "Charudatta Restored to Prosperity." R. V. Jagirdar more radically suggests that *Charudatta in Poverty* is actually derived from *The Little Clay Cart,* purified from political allusions in the longer play and designed for a simpler form of staging.

Although *Charudatta in Poverty* is a spirited and eminently theatrical work, it must inevitably be overshadowed, not only by *The Little Clay Cart,* but

by other plays in the collection ascribed to Bhasa. The scope of, and variety within, these plays is extraordinary. Five of those based on the *Mahabharata* are short pieces, each consisting merely of a single act. *The Consecration,* on the contrary, has seven acts. *Karna's Task* and *The Broken Thighs* are the richest in their verse passages and in poetic texture. They have also more than once been singled out as closer to the Western conception of tragedy than generally regarded as typical of Sanskrit drama. *The Middle One* is distinguished for its broad humor and, as Woolner and Sarup observe, for its fairy tale atmosphere. Still more gaiety and lightness of touch, at times approaching Western pastoral drama, inform *The Adventures of the Boy Krishna. The Vision of Vasavadatta,* as its title suggests, in some respects a dream play with metaphysical connotations, successfully combines love scenes of tender pathos with scenes of superingenious political intrigue. The blending of these features, which seems extraordinary to the Western reader, was widely cultivated and much admired by Sanskrit dramatists.

All the plays are written with vigor and their situations conceived with a true genius for the theater. Although as a rule their subject matter is epic, they show scant trace of the archaic or the primitive, and although they are on the whole of small philosophical content, *Karna's Task* consciously illustrates the main theme of the most impressive of Sanskrit religious texts, the *Bhagavadgita,* a section of the *Mahabharata:* "virtue is in the effort; fortune is fickle." To be sure, these dramas lack the extreme ripeness of the more courtly Sanskrit plays of later years and none has achieved the world acclaim of the masterpieces of Kalidasa, Sudraka, and Bhavabhuti. But together they constitute one of the most impressive of Asian dramatic anthologies.

For a close scrutiny of the Trivandrum plays, see *Bhasa-Studien* (1918) by Max Lindenau. All general studies of Sanskrit drama since these plays were discovered deal with them in detail. One of the most illuminating in this respect is *Sanskrit Drama: Its Origins and Decline* (1960) by Indu Shekhar. Also valuable are *History of Hindu Drama* (1957) by M. M. Ghosh; *Drama in Sanskrit Literature* (1957) by R. V. Jagirdar; and *The Sanskrit Drama* (1924) by A. B. Keith. The plays have been translated, with a critical introduction, as *Thirteen Trivandrum Plays Ascribed to Bhasa* (2 vols., 1930) by H. C. Woolner and Lakshman Sarup.—H. W. W.

Troilus and Cressida (c. 1601–1602). A play by William SHAKESPEARE. *Troilus and Cressida* was first published in 1609 in a quarto edition. During its printing, the original title page was canceled and a substitute page run containing changes in copy. At the same time, an epistle to the reader was added. The quarto text (prepared from some form of author's manuscript) and the 1623 First Folio text (compiled from the quarto and an autograph manuscript) differ in certain respects, but both texts are considered authoritative. Medieval accounts of the Troy story, primarily William Caxton's *Recuyell of the Historyes of Troye* (1475), furnish the source for Shakespeare's play. The earliest allusion to performance is found in an entry in the Stationers' Register dated February 7, 1603, which states in part that the play was acted by the Lord Chamberlain's Men.

The complexity of thought in *Troilus and Cressida,* the involved rhetorical constructions, and the long discourses—such as Ulysses' famous speech on order and chaos (I, iii)—have led to a theory that the play may originally have been performed before law students and barristers at the Inns of Court.

Though dealing with the Trojan War, the work takes its name from the love story of Troilus and Cressida, a tale not part of the original Greek legend. In this story, Troilus, youngest son of Priam, the Trojan king, falls in love with Cressida, who, although she reciprocates his feelings, has been somewhat standoffish. Finally the lovers are brought together for an assignation by Pandarus, Cressida's uncle. In the meantime, Cressida's father, the priest Calchas—who has gone over to the Greeks—arranges for his daughter to be exchanged for the Trojan general Antenor. Brought to the Greek camp, Cressida proves to be a wanton and winds up the mistress of Diomedes. Troilus manages to observe the pair; in rage and disillusionment he vows to kill Diomedes. They do meet on the battlefield, but neither overcomes the other.

Superimposed on the love story is the account of how the Greek army, after seven years of fighting,

THE FIRST-ISSUE TITLE PAGE (1609) OF SHAKE-SPEARE'S *Troilus and Cressida*

THE
Hiſtorie of Troylus
and Creſſeida.

As it was aded by the Kings Maieſties
ſeruants at the Globe.

Written by William Shakeſpeare.

LONDON
Imprinted by *G.Eld* for *R Bonian* and *H. Walley*, and
are to be ſold at the ſpred Eagle in Paules
Church-yeard, ouer againſt the
great North doore.
1609.

still has not taken Troy. Dissension among the Greek commanders and the sulking of the prideful Achilles lie at the root of their troubles. Schemes to return Achilles to combat fail. However, when the Trojan prince Hector kills Patroclus, Achilles' friend, the Greek general goes into the field seeking revenge. He and his troops come upon Hector unarmed and resting; ignominiously, they slay the Trojan hero.

The play is perhaps the most difficult to classify in the entire canon. Its Folio title is *The Tragedy of Troilus and Cressida;* on both the original and cancel title pages of the quarto it is termed a history; and the epistle added to the quarto refers to it as a comedy. Critics, recognizing that there is a bitter, sardonic quality to the writing, have theorized that Shakespeare may have been experimenting with a new dramatic form, influenced by the satirical drama of Ben Jonson. Thus, the labels "comical satire" and "tragical satire" have been suggested. Those who view the play as comedy see Shakespeare debunking the great military heroes—both Greek and Trojan—by showing them to be pride-swollen individuals or embracers of false codes of honor. These critics similarly see idealized love ridiculed, pointing for evidence to the Elizabethan view that Cressida was little more than a harlot and citing in the language the tremendous amount of bawdy dialogue and the use of rhetorical devices that give tonal effects opposite to that of blank verse. These critics see the inconclusive ending as further evidence that Shakespeare, in the tradition of satire, was interested primarily in exposing the weaknesses of mankind. Those for whom the tragic tone predominates draw upon the medieval chivalric and courtly love traditions reflected in the play and tend to view Troilus as a young idealist who sees love and honor in absolute terms. Although Troilus does not die, he is defeated by "the common curse of mankind, folly and ignorance." However one categorizes the play, its subject matter is war and love, or as the railing Thersites puts it, "Wars and lechery."

An outstanding edition of *Troilus and Cressida* is the New Cambridge Edition (1957), edited by Alice Walker.—W. G.

Trojan Women, The (Troades, 415 B.C.). A tragedy by EURIPIDES. *The Trojan Women* was performed shortly after the capture of the small island of Melos, where the Athenians killed all adult males and enslaved the rest, and not long before the great Athenian armada sailed away to Sicily, where it later met its doom. The topicality of a play on the horrors of war and treatment of prisoners was obvious and immediate.

Comparison with Euripides' *Hecuba* is unavoidable. The captive Trojan queen is the chief character in both plays, and both choruses consist of Trojan captives. The theme is very similar, but there are basic differences in plot and structure. The two aspects of war, suffering and vengeance, are dramatized separately in *Hecuba;* in *The Trojan Women* there is more emphasis on suffering, and the desire for vengeance is less obtrusive, except in Hecuba's debate with Helen.

The epiphany of the gods in *The Trojan Women* is unusual. In the monologue Poseidon is about to leave the city of Troy, which he had favored in the war, when Athena appears. Outraged by the victors' desecration of her temple, she wants Poseidon's help in destroying the Greek fleet on its way home, to which the sea god readily agrees. This terrible threat from the gods throws a shadow over the whole play. When opposing gods agree (rare as this is in Euripides), it is to bring destruction upon mortals!

The dramatic structure is unusual. The Chorus' beautiful odes on the fall of Troy provide the background of suffering. From this Hecuba emerges as the focus of individualized suffering. Of her calamities two main themes are elaborated in the persons of Cassandra and Andromache. Cassandra, in excited lyrics and then in more sober iambics, celebrates her "marriage" to Agamemnon as bringing vengeance for the Trojans. The sorrows of Andromache, the enslaved widow of Hector, culminate when her small son, Astyanax, is snatched from her to be hurled to death from the walls of Troy. The boy is buried by his grandmother in the last scene, one of pure sorrow. Then the fleet sails, and we know what awaits it.

This play, with so little action, might well, in the hands of an inferior poet, have made a monotonous tale of woe. The beauty of the poetry and the delicate skill of Euripides in dramatizing intense emotions make *The Trojan Women* one of the most powerful dramas on the subject of war in all literature.

Translations of the play are listed under Euripides.—G. M. A. G.

Tudor drama. See ENGLAND: *Tudor drama.*

Turandot (1762). A play by Carlo GOZZI, and described by him as "a tragicomical theatrical Chinese fairy tale." Turandot, a very beautiful Chinese princess, refuses to marry unless she finds a suitor able to solve three riddles she proposes. Her father, Emperor Altoum, consents to her request that whoever fails the test be beheaded. Struck by the extraordinary beauty of the princess, Calaf, a Tartar prince who has been deprived of power and is now wandering incognito, decides to attempt the test. He unravels the enigmas, but Turandot is still reluctant. Calaf then tells her that if she is able to discover his name, she need not marry him. Turandot discovers his identity by trickery, and Calaf, in despair, attempts suicide. But the princess, having now fallen in love with Calaf, stops him and accepts him as her husband.

Into the fantastic, exotic frame of this fairy tale—which is written partly in verse, partly in prose, partly in Italian, partly in dialect, and in part left open for improvisation by the actors—Gozzi brought the masks of the *commedia dell'arte,* as well as all the choreographic and picturesque elements common to his theater. In this play, moreover, he attempted a psychological study of the emotional development of Turandot. Inspired by certain French models (including Alain René Lesage's *La Princesse de Chine*), it is the best known of Gozzi's works. Its fame is partly derived from the German adaptation by Friedrich Schiller, upon which Giacomo Puccini's opera *Turandot* is based. Schiller liberated the light and suggestive material of the fairy tale, as well as its colorful eclecticism, from the ugly and contorted hodgepodge of Gozzi's verse.—L. L.

Turcaret (1709). A comedy in prose by Alain René LESAGE. An unscrupulous financier, Turcaret, woos a baroness who wheedles presents and money out of him so that she may shower them on a young chevalier. The chevalier, for his part, tricks the baroness with the help of Frontin, a valet and pimp. Turcaret turns out to be married, and his wife, who has been surreptitiously in Paris in the guise of a countess, suddenly appears. Finally, Turcaret will be arrested for his dishonest practices. And Frontin, who has deceived almost everyone, has made a fortune in a few hours.

Turcaret is a satire of a cynical society, completely corrupted by money, at the center of which is the both formidable and ridiculous figure of the financier, who deserves his downfall but who will be replaced by another worse than himself.—Ja. G.

Turgenev, Ivan [Sergeyevich] (1818–1883). Russian novelist and playwright. Turgenev came from a rich, landowning family. The estate actually belonged to his strong, eccentric mother, for his father, a handsome, impoverished nobleman, had married for money. Turgenev was brought up in an atmosphere of tyrannical matriarchy in which his mother openly enjoyed having her sons and servants whipped in her presence. A kind and liberal man from his earliest years, Turgenev was a great admirer of the West and spent much of his time abroad, partly to escape the persecution he suffered for his Westernizing ideas and partly to be close to his lifelong love, the Frenchwoman Madame Viardot, who thoroughly dominated him.

IVAN TURGENEV (NEW YORK PUBLIC LIBRARY)

Although it is his novels that make Turgenev a major figure in nineteenth-century Russian literature, his plays are also of great importance. Like his other writings, they reflect his preoccupation with the fate of the individual, in particular with the emotional state of the members of the landed gentry in the slowly changing Russian society of the time.

Turgenev was a liberal and a Westernizer. He spent much of his life traveling abroad and disapproved of Russia's absolutist regime, both in the government and the family. Too much emphasis, however, has been placed on the social significance of Turgenev's plays and on his psychological studies of the nineteenth-century Russian who no longer has a place in the emerging society—the *lishnii chelovek,* the "not-needed" or, as he is better known to Western critics, the "superfluous" man. It seems more likely, however, that Turgenev simply set his plays in surroundings that were most familiar to him and used as his characters the country squire, his family, neighbors, servants, free-loaders, toadies, and village serfs. What really interested him were people in their environment, whether that environment was changing or static, whether the people in question were well-integrated (with a sound economic basis) or "superfluous" (poor and idle, for whatever reason). It is Turgenev's uncanny gift of observation and his understanding of every character that make his plays stand out from the other plays of the period, whose "social context" is of purely documentary interest today.

Turgenev's main plays are: *Gde tonko tam i rvetsia* (*It Snaps Where It's Thin,* 1847); THE PARASITE: *Zavtrak s predvoditelem dvorianstva* (*A Lunch with the Marshal of Nobility,* 1848); and A MONTH IN THE COUNTRY.

Two well-known works in English on Turgenev are *Turgenev, a Life* (1954) by David Magarshack and *Turgenev, the Man, His Art, and His Age* (1926) by Avrahm Yarmolinsky.—A. MACA.

Turkey. Asia Minor, where the Turks settled after migrating from central Asia, has been the seat of many civilizations. It was the home, or a province, of the Hittites, Phrygians, Greeks, Assyrians, Lydians, Persians, Romans, Byzantines, and Arabs. Later Seljuk and Ottoman Turks occupied the area, assimilating these influences as well as retaining some of their shamanistic culture from central Asia. Thus, Asia Minor has been a bridge between East and West for many ages. Crude peasant plays, which have survived to this day through countless generations, have been traced to central Asia as well as to festivals in honor of Dionysus and to Egyptian and Greek Mysteries celebrated at Eleusis and elsewhere. Main themes in these plays are death and resurrection or the abduction of a girl and her return. Masks, goat- or sheepskins, and the phallus, carried in processions, are common features.

The greatest influence on modern Turkish drama has been Western civilization, which the Ottoman Turks embraced in the eighteenth and, especially, nineteenth centuries. Until the emergence of the legitimate modern Turkish theater in the middle of the nineteenth century, the main forms of entertainment in Turkey were *Karagöz, Orta Oyunu,* and MEDDAH, in which the present Turkish playwrights are taking an increasing interest.

traditional theater. Karagöz is a shadow theater, which probably came to Turkey from the Far East via India and Egypt. Its first evidence in Turkey was in the sixteenth century, although legend puts it in the fourteenth century, during the reign of Sultan Orhan. By the middle of the seventeenth century it became the most beloved of diversions. Its popularity and high intellectual level continued into the reign of Abdülaziz (1861–1876), who, although a generous patron of Karagöz, put heavy censorship on it, and its wit and satire gradually deteriorated.

The plays use puppets, which are made of thin leather and are placed between artificial light and a screen on which their brilliantly colored shadows are cast. When the puppets are lighted they appear to be transparent. All the characters' dialogue is spoken by the Karagöz master, who must also have a good singing voice because many of the characters sing. His aide hands him the puppets in their proper order and plays the tambourine. The two main characters are Karagöz (literally "black eye"), from which the theater takes its name, and Hacivat.

Each shadow play is usually in three parts— *Mukaddeme* (prologue or introduction), *Muhavere* (dialogue), and *Fasıl* (the main plot, which is a series of loosely connected scenes). In the prologue Hacivat recites a poem and sings a song (*gazel*) that is mystical in its philosophy: all life is controlled by the Master who is behind the screen; the figures do not move of their own free will. The Master, of course, is not only the puppet master but the Creator, and the figures represent all living things. The world is transient. This mysticism, in fact, helped the Karagöz theater to be accepted in its beginning by the political and religious establishments. Some Karagöz masters were gifted philosophers as well as satirists, poets, and musicians and appealed to the best minds of their period by pouring their knowledge into the plays.

The Muhavere is usually not connected with the main plot. The puppet master improvises on current topics and, depending upon the degree of liberalism allowed by the rulers, jokes about and imitates common people, members of the audience, high officials, grand viziers, or even the sultan himself. The dialogue in this section is between Karagöz and Hacivat. In the main plot appear the various types of characters with distinguishing costumes, manners, and dialects, some of whom deliberately act and speak like famous dignitaries of the day or make remarks about them. When in the reign of Abdülaziz a corrupt pasha, easily recognizable by the audience, was brought to the screen the sultan banned all political satire and enforced severe restrictions. (Although these rules were often clandestinely broken, the intellectual level of Karagöz gradually deteriorated.) In addition to human figures there are various animal figures— dragons, jinns, mermaids, and serpents—and objects—houses, shops, mountains, carriages, boats, merry-go-rounds, trees, ropes, and chamber pots—all of which add color as well as supernatural and realistic touches to the general merriment.

There are about forty different plots in the shadow plays, the main outlines and themes of which have been followed by the puppet masters with limitless variations, depending upon the capacity of the performer and the level of the audience.

Orta Oyunu has often been referred to as the Turkish *commedia dell'arte,* but its origin is not definitely known. It may have been the commedia dell'arte itself, Karagöz, the ancient Greek mime, or the plays and dances that the Turks brought with them from central Asia. What is indisputable is the great similarity between Karagöz and Orta Oyunu in regard to characters, comic elements, and atmosphere. One uses puppets and the other live actors. Orta Oyunu literally means "play in the middle." Like the theater in the round, it is acted in an open space surrounded by the audience. According to some scholars, Orta Oyunu means regimental play, since *orta* means janissary regiment. The stage scenery consists of only two screens, the taller one representing a house and the other a shop. After the prologue between Kavuklu and Pişekâr, who are the Karagöz and Hacivat of the shadow play, comes the main plot. The humor is broad, although sometimes witty, and is based on improvisation. The style of presentation is nonillusionistic, that is, intentionally unrealistic.

Metin And, in *A History of Theatre and Popular Entertainment in Turkey* (1963), discusses the comic devices in Karagöz and Orta Oyunu under seven headings: 1. Repetition of a gesture, a movement, or an episode that has earned a laugh. 2. Element of disguise by which characters evade detection by assuming the appearance of other persons, a corpse, a gravestone, a frog, or a donkey. Supernatural, illogical, and surrealistic happenings are also frequent. For example, in the play *Tahmisçiler* ("The Coffee Grinders") the donkey on which Hacivat and Karagöz are riding splits in half. They take the donkey to a man who supposedly is an expert on repairing split donkeys, but he puts the pieces together wrongly, with the hind legs sticking up in the air. 3. Contrast and incongruity, as when, for example, the woodcutter comes to perform a circumcision with an ax in *Sünnet* ("The Circumcision"). 4. Exaggeration. For example, in about every play Kavuklu, upon seeing Pişekâr motionless on the stage, faints, thinking he is the headstone of a grave. 5. Slapstick and horseplay, which often require difficult movements. 6. Rhythmic movements, as when, for example, Karagöz beats Hacivat in time to the meter of his lines. 7. Verbal humor and witticism, derived chiefly from the use of different dialects, exaggerated elegant diction, speech defects, and play upon words. Language is often used, not as a means of communication between characters, but as a source of confusion and laughter. Characters coin words with quasi-meaningless sounds, utter sayings out of their normal context, and recite poems maintaining the sound but discarding the sense. Vulgar and obscene allusions are plentiful, as they are in ancient Greek and Roman comedies and popular theaters of other lands.

The literary historian Georg Jacob classified major Karagöz characters (which would also apply to Orta Oyunu characters) into four groups: 1. Main characters: Hacivat, Karagöz, Tuzsuz Deli Bekir ("drunkard" and "bogeyman"), Altıkulaç Beberuhi ("six-fathom dwarf"), and Çelebi (the "gallant"). 2. Characters speaking in dialect: the Persian, the Arab, the Jew, the Armenian, the Greek, the European, the Laz, the Albanian, and the Zeybek ("swashbuckler" from western Anatolia). 3. Pathological characters: the stutterer, Tiryaki (the "opium addict"), the drunkard, the madman, and the dancing boy. 4.

Women (always played by men) and children (always played by men or boys).

There are hundreds of characters and they have easily recognizable characteristics. Of these, two—Hacivat (or Pişekâr) and Karagöz (or Kavuklu)—warrant special attention. Although they are two old cronies, their personalities markedly differ. Hacivat speaks in high-flown Turkish full of Arabic, Persian, and archaic words, is well-versed in Islamic culture and music, and is generally pedantic. Karagöz, on the other hand, has never been to school, speaks like ordinary folk, and makes fun of Hacivat's pretentiousness. Hacivat is well versed in the etiquette of the high circles of the empire and is not above kowtowing to the authorities and getting involved in shady deals. Karagöz, in contrast, is very natural and has no material worries other than earning his daily bread. Hacivat always lands a job, is the local headman, and is well respected, whereas Karagöz is usually jobless and ridiculed. Hacivat, perhaps, is the symbol of opportunism and corruption in high places, whereas Karagöz symbolizes the common people—patient, simple, good-natured, but prankish and quite aware of what is going on.

Plots in Karagöz and Orta Oyunu are episodic, with little intrigue and action. The stories are so loosely tied that episodes could change places or be eliminated, or new ones could be added according to the wish of the performers. Social satire is more obvious in some plays than in others. In *Tımarhane* ("The Lunatic Asylum") the condition of Turkish state hospitals is satirized. The Greek or Italian doctor is drawn as no saner than the patients. The message is that the doctor should be locked up as well as many other madmen who walk about free. In *Kayık* ("The Boat") the Arab is presented as a hypocrite who, as a Haci ("pilgrim"), seeks to exploit Karagöz' sentiment of piety by taking a boat ride without paying a penny. In lieu of money he utters prayers in guttural language that are actually camouflaged curses. Evliya Çelebi, a celebrated Turkish seventeenth-century traveler, gives an account of a shadow play which is alleged to have been a great success in his time and which clearly reflected the state of mind of the people, weary of constantly being dragged into inextricable and exhausting wars. Sabri Estat in his *Karagöz* writes thus about the shadow play:

> On the Karagöz screen we can see a very daring parody of those feverish days. A young recruit hangs his lantern, which he is weary of carrying, onto the tail of his officer's [Hacivat's] horse, which causes poor Hacivat to fall under his own panic-stricken mount. Taking advantage of the accident and the darkness, the recruits escape and run off in all directions. Hacivat calls to them in vain to help him. No one comes. He promises them each a sou to buy the arms needed for the new expedition, but without any more success. The recruits do not want to hear any more about it.

Perhaps the most famous Karagöz or Orta Oyunu play is *Kanlı Nigâr* ("The Bloody Nigâr"): Çelebi, the dandy, has swindled two prostitutes. They pull the man by force to their house, strip him naked, and throw him out into the street. The neighborhood people—including Karagöz and Hacivat—pity the man and try to retrieve his clothes but meet the same fate before there is a happy end.

Cevdet Kudret, in his book *Karagöz,* finds a great deal of similarity between Orta Oyunu and Karagöz and playwrights such as Adamov, Beckett, Genet, Ionesco, Pinter, Schéhadé, and Tardieu, who, he says, have been trying to absolve the theater of its nonhistrionic elements, set rules, and conventions and turn it into a free, self-sufficient, and independent art form. He continues:

In point of fact, *Karagöz* discards treatment of a given subject according to the rules of exposition, development and denouement, shuns away from logical relationships between happenings and concepts of time and place, and approaches the abstract; dream and reality are intermingled—fantastical, illogical and surrealistic happenings are presented without any explanation as if they are part of reality; worn-out clichés, songs and poems are distorted, words and names are coined and the language, freed from its logical bonds, is directed towards the "meaningless" and the "absurd," and, thus, language, which is supposed to be a means of communication among people, becomes an independent entity in itself. Each character, isolated in his own world, either does not understand or misunderstands others and reaches adverse results. All these are similarities between *Karagöz* and the contemporary theater movement known as "the theater of the absurd." By observing the tension created in dialogues between Karagöz and Hacivat based on non-communication, Turkish dramatists should have done earlier what Ionesco has done with his *Bald Singer. The Lesson* by the same author and the "Mektep" ("School") dialogue of *Karagöz* should be compared in this respect. Much could be learned from such a comparison.

More and more Turkish playwrights are doing just that and delving into their native sources for inspiration in their work. Although both Karagöz and Orta Oyunu are almost dead as art forms and are rarely performed today, their influence is increasing.

modern period. Turks founded the Ottoman Empire under Osman in 1299. It gradually expanded, so that in the sixteenth century the frontiers reached Vienna in Europe, the Caucasus and the Arabian Peninsula in Asia, and all the northern shores of Africa. Gradually the strong Oriental institutions on which the empire had been built grew old and corrupt, and the Ottoman Empire came to be known as "the Sick Man of Europe." In 1839 a fundamental constitutional change, known as the *Tanzimat,* occurred. Reforms were made in the methods of administration, finance, education, and judicial procedures. The nation began to look, not to the Orient, but to the West for ideas. This change in culture brought about a new Turkish drama based on Western ideals.

The first published play was *Şair Evlenmesi* ("A Poet's Marriage," pub. 1860) by Ibrahim ŞINASI. A one-act farce, it ridicules the custom of arranged marriages. This was a very advanced idea for the Turkey of that period. The play also reveals the corruption of some Muslim priests who did business by accepting bribes and suggests that people should not blindly follow the priests' teachings. The characters, more types than real persons, spoke in the vernacular of the day. With its broad humor and swift development of theme, the play is not altogether removed from Karagöz or Orta Oyunu. The form, diction, and the satirical content of the play set the pattern for other playwrights to follow. In dozens of later plays conventions, irrational beliefs, and contemporary follies were challenged and ridiculed for the enlightenment of the public. Ahmet Mithat Efendi (1844–1912) attacked polygamy in *Eyvah* ("Alas!" 1886), bigotry of Muslim priests in *Açık Baş* ("The Uncovered Head," 1875), and ancient superstitions in *Çengi* ("The Dancing Girl," 1885). Mehmet Rifat (1851–1907), in *Görenek* ("The Tradition," 1873), showed the tragicomical effect of following silly traditions, in this case, having to pay for an elaborate circumcision ceremony. Cenap Şahabettin (1870–1934), like Şinasi, tackled the theme of arranged marriages in *Körebe* ("The Blind Man's Bluff," 1914). There was bound to be a backlash of the Westernization movement, however, and this was revealed in plays such as Nuri's *Zamane Şıkları* ("Dandies of Our Time," 1874), which satirized Turks aping European ways and manners, and *Yamalar* ("Patches," 1919) by Hüseyin Suat (1868–1942), which criticized mixed marriages.

A very important play of the period—another style setter—was *Vatan yahut Silistre* ("The Fatherland or Silistria," 1873) by NAMIK KEMAL. At the time of writing, the Ottoman Empire was seized by a crisis. The strong nationalism of the play kindled the audience's imagination and they—among them military students—demonstrated in the streets, shouting "Long live Kemal!" This alarmed Sultan Abdülaziz, who saw Kemal as a potential leader of a revolution, and he banished him. The play seems rather bombastic in style today, but it was very popular at the time and caused many other authors to write plays with patriotic themes, rhetorical speeches, and lines that preached a message. Some plays sang the glories of the Ottoman Empire, others the glory of Islam, while some idealized the Turanian Turks. Among the better-known plays in this vein are Mehmet Rifat's *Ya Gazi ya Şehit* ("Either a Veteran or a Martyr," 1873) and Mehmet Sadettin's *Tuna yahut Zafer* ("The Danube or Victory," 1874). Sometimes Persian mythology was a source of heroic deeds, and inspired plays such as Ahmet Mithat Efendi's *Siyavuş* (1885) and *Gave* (1877) by Şemsettin Sami (1850–1904), in which the title character, a blacksmith, rallies the people against the tyrant king. In Namık Kemal's *Gülnihal* (1875) a tyrant governor has annihilated all his potential rivals. His two cousins are in love with each other, but the tyrant also loves the girl; besides, he is jealous of his cousin's popularity with the people. He intrigues to turn the two lovers against each other, succeeds for a while, but in the end love triumphs. Ahmet Mithat Efendi, who had also been exiled by the sultan, wrote *Ahz-i Sar yahut Avrupa'nın Eski Medeniyeti* ("The Taking of Revenge or The Old Civilization of Europe," 1875) after his return. The play is set in France and revolves around feudal oppressors.

Abdülhamit II, who ascended the throne in 1876,

proved even more intolerant than Abdülaziz and heavy censorship was put on plays. No serious Turkish drama was written or performed until the declaration of the Second Constitution in 1908. After that date old patriotic plays were revived and new ones written, such as Ahmet Cevat's *Yıldız'ın Sonu* ("The End of the Yıldız Palace," 1909), as well as historical plays depicting earlier eras. *Sultan Selim Salis* ("Sultan Selim the Third," 1910) by Salâh Cimcoz (1877–1947) and Celâl Esat (1875–   ) describes the reformist sultan's martyrdom in the hands of reactionary rebels. *İlhan* (1913) and *Turhan* (1916) by AB-DÜLHAK HÂMIT glorify in Arabic-filled verse the deeds of the Turanian Turks. *Sardanapal*, a verse play by the same author, is laid in Assyrian times and deals with the uprising against a despotic king. His *Liberte* ("Liberty," 1913), inspired by Corneille's *Cinna*, sings in impassioned and archaic language the author's belief in freedom.

Many plays in this period deal with love (requited or unrequited), intrigue, misunderstandings, self-sacrifice for love, conflict between love and duty, and the plight of women, especially slave girls in society. In Namık Kemal's *Zavallı Çocuk* ("The Miserable Child," 1874), the heroine is in love with her cousin. A rich pasha wants to marry her and is willing to pay her father's debts. Out of loyalty to her father she decides to sacrifice herself and marry him, but her health cannot take it. As she lies dying, her lover drinks poison. *Akif Bey* (1874), by the same author, is the story of a naval officer whose flighty wife convinces the authorities that her husband has died in action so that she can marry her lover. After the officer's return the two men fight a duel and they both die. The officer's father kills the woman. The play is melodramatic and is further marred by incongruous patriotic speeches. *Habibe yahut Semahat-i Aşk* ("Habibe or Generosity of Love," 1875) by Ebüzziya Tevfik (1849–1913) is an adaptation of Victor Hugo's *Angelo*. His *Eceli-Kaza* ("The Accidental Death," 1872) is a Romeo and Juliet story. Mustafa Efendi's *Leylâ and Mecnun* (1869) and *Tahir and Zühre* and *Arzu and Kamber* by Güllü Agop (1840–1902) are dramatizations of Turkish and Oriental folk legends. *Vuslat yahut Süreksiz Sevinç* ("Union or Transitory Joy," 1875) by Recaizade Mahmut Ekrem (1847–1913) is the unhappy story of the love between a slave girl and the son of the master of the house. *Afif Anjelik* ("Angelique, the Chaste," 1872) by the same author deals with an innocent and pure woman who is unjustly accused of infidelity by her husband. Mehmet Rifat's *Pakdamen* ("The Honest," 1875) is a similar story. Cemil's *Talihsiz Delikanlı yahut Fıraklı Köy Düğünü* ("The Unlucky Lad or the Sad Village Wedding," 1876) is set in a village, which was rare for plays of this period. A rich man tries to separate two lovers to marry the girl himself. She attempts suicide, but fails. On the wedding day the bridegroom is poisoned and his friends swear to avenge his death. Ahmet Mithat Efendi's *Hükm-i Dil* ("The Command of the Heart," 1875) is set in France and Spain and holds that nobility of heart is greater than nobility of birth. The daughter of a count is in love with the son of their gardener and they elope to America. *Sabr-ü Sebat* ("Patience and Endurance," 1875) by Abdülhak Hâmit is in prose. A young man

is in love with a slave girl, but his family wants to marry him to another girl. He is thrown out of the house. After a long journey with improbable events he finds his long-lost love. This play was rewritten in vernacular Turkish by Selâmi İzzet Sedes and revived in 1961 to the delight of the audiences. *Duhter-i Hindu* ("The Indian Girl," 1876) by the same author is a love triangle set in India and involves a British officer and his love for an Indian girl. *Nesteren* (1877), another play by the same author, is in verse, and tells of the love of a princess for a man who has killed her father. She has to make the choice between her honor and her love. A similar theme is treated in his two verse plays—*Eşber* (1880) and *Tezer* (1880). In *Eşber* the sister of the king of Kashmir has to choose between her love for Alexander the Great and her patriotic duty. In *Tezer*, a Spanish caliph must kill for political reasons the woman he loves. The meter and rhyme in both plays today sound forced and artificial. Abdülhak Hâmit's *Finten*, however, written in 1886 and published in 1917, is partly in prose and has some eloquent passages. This play was influenced by *Othello* and *Macbeth*. In *Şir* (1880) by Sami Paşazade Sezai (1859–1936), the title character, an Afghan prince, falls in love with the daughter of the king he defeated in India. He marries her, and an intrigue by the prince's sister who is against the marriage fails. Ali Necip Paşazade Ahmet Nuri, in his play *Sanki Aşk* ("So-Called Love," 1883), ridicules romantic love and those who waste their time living in a make-believe world, by quoting profusely from sentimental plays. The novelist Halit Ziya Uşaklıgil (1866–1945) wrote a play called *Kâbus* ("Nightmare," 1918), which is about a crisis in a family after twenty years of marriage.

Special mention must be given to Ahmet Vefik Pasha (1827–1891) and Âli Bey (1844–1899), whose adaptations from the plays of Molière are so successful that they read like original Turkish plays about the foibles of nineteenth-century Turks. Their dialogue is very natural and in the vernacular. Their plays have been revived. (Half a century later İbnürrefik Ahmet Nuri [1874–1935] followed in their footsteps and wrote successful adaptations of plays by Georges Feydeau, Henry Bernstein, Tristand Bernard, Eugène Marin Labiche, and others.) Âli Bey also wrote three successful original farces, of which *Geveze Berber* ("The Chattering Barber," 1873) has enjoyed popularity to this day. Another play of this period worth reviving is Şemsettin Sami's *Besa yahut Ahde Vefa* ("Truce or Loyalty to an Oath," 1876), which is about Albanian life and character and concerns a man working for a feudal lord.

Parallel to the legitimate theater in the late nineteenth century was *Tuluat Tiyatrosu* (theater of improvisation). Much of its technique was borrowed from the traditional theater, but instead of the stock figures of Orta Oyunu, characters were taken from everyday life. Later it developed its own stock characters. Plays were adapted from the West and acted on a platform stage, but mere skeletons of plots were used, filled in with improvisation by the actors. Local events and town gossip provided some of their inspiration. Before the curtain opened, the theater manager would gather his company and instruct each to dress according to a particular type and then would give them the plot outline. Refik Ahmet Sevengil describes a typical instruction by the theater manager:

> The Heroine appears from the side and sits on a bench by the sea; she is in love with the Hero, but the Villain also has his eyes on her. He enters and tries to kidnap her. The Old Man is a witness to the scene, and informs the Hero. There is a fight. Just as the Villain is going to kill the Old Man the Comic enters. Funny business. Curtain! The second act is a forest. The Heroine is alone, she cries and attempts suicide. The Comic enters and saves the girl. Now the stage belongs to the Comic; he knows what he is going to do. Curtain! Act III is canto.

Improvisational theater continued until around the middle of the twentieth century.

Since Atatürk founded the Republic in 1923, Turkish drama has flourished. Muhsin Ertuğrul, who headed the Municipal Theater in Istanbul and the State Theater in Ankara for many years, and Cüneyt Gökçer, who heads the latter theater now, have both encouraged native playwriting. So have private theaters, some of which have been producing Turkish plays almost exclusively. There has been official and unoffical censorship through the years, but especially since the revolution in 1960 there has been much easing up of the pressure on playwrights, and many political and social themes not allowed by the state before are being explored. Various forms and styles have been used. Some plays are in verse and others are experimental, in which, for example, the past and present meet on one plane. The most simple classification is according to themes, except in the case of plays based on Karagöz and Orta Oyunu, native history, and history of previous civilizations.

Prompted by a desire to have the revolutionary changes in Turkey more readily accepted by the public, playwrights such as MUSAHIPZADE CELÂL and Reşat Nuri GÜNTEKIN ridiculed the old social and religious customs and political practices. Güntekin's *Hülleci* ("The Hired Husband," 1935) springs from the Muslim law that forbade a man to remarry the same wife for the fourth time unless she had been divorced by another. To get around this law a *hülleci* was hired to marry and divorce the woman. In this play the hülleci—a burglar—and the woman fall in love and refuse to divorce. In *Mum Söndü* ("The Candle Is Out," 1931) by Musahipzade Celâl sectarian hypocrisy and intrigue are derided in the form of a farce. *Aynaroz Kadısı* ("Judge at Mount Athos," 1928) by the same author ridicules the corruption of the clergy. His *Kafes Arkasında* ("Behind the Lattice," 1928) lampoons the ancient practice of polygamy and the custom of Turkish women having to hide themselves from men. *Bir Kavuk Devrildi* ("A Turban Falls," 1930), Musahipzade's most popular comedy, shows how in Ottoman times nonentities managed to become prime ministers, protected sycophants, and belittled craftsmen, who emptied the coffers and carried the empire from one disaster to another. More recent playwrights have also satirized old customs and superstitions that still prevail. For example, Turan OFLAZOĞLU, in his one-act comedy in verse, *Allahın Dediği Olur* ("Whatever Happens Is

the Will of God"), depicts a poor, young man who is in love with the daughter of a rich landlord. Not consenting to the marriage, the father keeps repeating the title phrase. The boy gets the girl by persuading the old man with the latter's own superstitions.

The postrevolution period of changes (after 1923) brought about many problems of adjustment for the old. The conflict between generations inspired plays such as *Sağanak* ("Downpour," 1929) by Yakup Kadri Karaosmanoğlu (1888–   ) and *Pembe Evin Kaderi* ("The Fate of the Pink House," 1951) by Turgut ÖZAKMAN. In *Cengiz Han'ın Bisikleti* (*Genghis Khan's Bicycle*, 1959) by Refik ERDURAN, a newly rich ex-officer of the Ottoman Empire must make the hilarious transition from fierce warrior with four wives to European gentleman with just one. *Koca Bebek* ("The Big Doll," 1947) by Cevat Fehmi BAŞKUT describes the decline of a big mansion with the corresponding changes in manners. The loss of good manners is lamented.

The plight of the Turkish woman in society despite her so-called emancipation has been the concern of many a playwright. In *Mine* (1959) by Necati CUMALI, the title character has been forced by her parents to marry an elderly civil servant. She remains faithful to him to the end but is taunted endlessly by the men in the small town for her friendship with a young author. In a fit of anger she kills one of her taunters. *Sultan Gelin* ("The Bride Named Sultan," 1963) by Cahit ATAY reveals the life of the Anatolian woman who is bought and sold as property. Sultan is auctioned off to a rich man who buys her as a wife for his sickly son and a farmhand for his estate. Comic and tragic elements are skillfully balanced in this play. *Ana Hanım—Kız Hanım* ("The Mother and Daughter Named Hanım," 1964) by the same author is the story of an old peasant mother and her daughter. The old woman must work in the fields while her lazy husband sits by the fire. Her daughter has been married off to a cripple, who blames her for not bearing him a child. She consents to his bringing another "wife" to the house, but there is no offspring. Humiliated, he packs and goes off to the city, leaving the two women behind. (Polygamy is no longer legal in Turkey, but in the villages many men take on extra "wives" by religious ceremony.) *Kurban* ("The Sacrifice," 1967) by Güngör DILMEN is a poetical play with a Medea theme. The aging wife of a farmer resists her husband's attempts at polygamy and refuses to accept into her house the young new "bride." When the wedding party threatens to break into the house, she kills her own children. *Pembe Kadın* ("The Woman Named Pinky," 1965) by Hidayet SAYIN explores the ignorance and hopelessness of the Turkish peasant woman. Simmering with anger because her husband deserted her many years ago never to return, the title character does not consent to her beloved daughter's marriage to anyone and kills her. Nazım KURŞUNLU wrote two plays, *Çığ* ("Avalanche," 1953) and *Yatık Emine* ("Loose Emine," 1966), the latter of which is a dramatization of a short story by Refik Halit Karay, on the theme that the fate of the Anatolian peasant woman is written not by God but by men in His name. *Kadın Erkekleşince* ("When a Woman Becomes Man-Like," 1932) by Hüseyin Rahmi Gürpınar (1864–1943) deals

ADALET AĞAOĞLU (TURKISH TOURISM AND INFORMA-
TION OFFICE, NEW YORK)

with the new city woman who must often combine
the role of wife and mother with that of wage earner,
to the disastrous neglect of the family.

False values regarding sex, marriage, money, social status, virtue, honor, morality, and religion are
the themes of many plays, serious and comic. Adalet
AĞAOĞLU shows in *Evcilik Oyunu* ("Let's Play
House," 1964) how under the pressure of the environment in Turkey the most natural sexual outlets
for both men and women are barred from puberty
on, until the individuals are thrown into despair.
Allahın Unuttukları ("Those Whom God Has Forgotten") by Vedat Nedim Tör (1897–) explores
the sexual frustrations of the intellectual bachelor in
Anatolia. *Kahvede Şenlik Var* ("There Is Festivity in
the Coffeehouse," 1966) by Sabahattin Kudret AKSAL
is a satire on bourgeois marriages. *Sönen Kandiller*
("The Oil Lamps Are Extinguished," 1926) by Halit
Fahri Ozansoy (1891–) is the story in verse of a
poor youth who, having been brought up by a rich
family, falls secretly in love with the daughter of the
house, who also is attracted to him. But he loses her
to a rich man after an arranged marriage. In the
Freudian play *Hayalet* ("The Ghost," 1936) by the
same author a poor young man commits suicide in
front of the nuptial chamber of the woman he loves,
and his ghost haunts her until her libido sends her to
her own suicide. *Deli* ("The Lunatic," 1957) by Refik
Erduran is a battle of wits between a ruthlessly avaricious woman and her scientist brother, whom she has
had declared legally insane on the ground that he was
squandering his share of the family fortune on irrational research projects. The scientist makes full use
of the freedom granted him by his formal designation

of madman to wreck his sister's schemes of social and
financial climbing. The conclusion leaves the audience wondering which of the two is the lunatic. Melih
Vassaf's *Nuhun Gemisi* ("Noah's Ark," 1966) presents the topsy-turvy society in which an average
football player not only earns more than a good doctor or a jurist but is even more respected. Necati
Cumalı's *Masalar* ("The Tables," 1967) reveals the
scale of values in a bureaucratic system, where it is
not what you know but whom you know that counts.
Greed for money and the violence and unhappiness it
causes is the central theme in such plays as *Para*
("Money," 1942) by Necip Fazıl Kısakürek (1904–
  ), which pictures a ruthless financier; *Para İçin*
("For the Sake of Money," 1949) by Nahit Sırrı Örik
(1914–1960), which is about people who worship
money; and Vedat Nedim Tör's *Hep ve Hiç* ("All
and Nothing," 1950), which concerns a successful
businessman who loses personal happiness. Cahit
Atay's *Hamdi and Hamdi* (1964) deals with two men
by the same name, one rich and the other poor, who
exchange places and discover that money does not
bring happiness. In *Tahterevalli* ("The Seesaw,"
1959) by Çetin Altan (1926–) a family, coming
to fortune, becomes richer and richer but at the end
longs for the good old days. *Bir Ölü Evi* ("A Dead
Man's House," 1932) by NAZIM HİKMET shows how
inherited property brings out the pettiness and greed
in the persons concerned. Virtue is the theme of Refik
Erduran's *Bir Kilo Namus* ("One Pound of Virtue,"
1958). A cosmetics manufacturer, condemned by
everybody as a lecherous rake devoid of all virtue,
decides to flood the market with cosmetics containing a chemical that has a strongly dampening effect
on the sexual urge. Very soon his fellow citizens decide that they are not very enthusiastic about "virtue" after all, as the national economy and their lives
turn out to be much more "vice"-oriented than meets
the eye. False understanding of honor and glory is a
recurring theme in Atay's poetical prose plays. In the
one-act comedy-fantasy *Pusuda* ("In Ambush,"
1962) the tyrant landlord of a village wants to marry
the fiancée of an educated young man returning from
his studies in the big city. He plots to have the young
man killed by aid of an innocent and ignorant gardener, to whom he speaks of the honor and glory of
being a killer: it will lead to being feared and respected by every villager after his return from a jail
sentence, which the landlord promises to be short on
account of the influence he has. At the end of the
play, the landlord falls into his own trap. *Karaların
Memetleri* ("The Memets of the Village Karalar,"
1963) by the same playwright consists of three parts
that can be performed separately. Each part deals
with a different hero—all named Memet. In the first
playlet Memet dreams that a religious order persuades him to kill Ali, a neighbor, so that Ali can go
to Paradise. Waking up, Memet carries out the order
and is treated by the villagers, not as a murderer, but
as a venerable holy man. The second playlet deals
with one of the major problems in Anatolia—the
blood feud. Memet meets İlyas, who has returned
from jail a dying man, after having murdered
Memet's father. Memet realizes that it is more manly
to forgive than to kill. He spares İlyas but has to flee
the village because he knows he will be branded a
coward by everyone, including his mother and the

girl he loves and was going to marry. The third play-let depicts the mythmaking power of the Anatolian people. Memet—a kind of Robin Hood—has been made into a legendary figure. Taking advantage of an amnesty, he returns to give himself up, but his scraggly appearance causes incredulity in everyone. To live up to the expectations of the community, he grabs his gun and goes to the mountains, again to the delight of everyone, including the gendarmes. *Çatallı Köy* ("The Village Called Çatallı," 1966) by Ali YÜRÜK is a poignant dramatization of the futility of vendettas. Turan Oflazoğlu's one-act play *Keziban* (1964), translated by the author into English under the same title, is a character study of a woman who, having had two sons murdered by a rival tribe, raises her grandson as an instrument of revenge. He kid-naps the wife of one of the enemy but is killed. When Keziban finds out that the woman is with child by her grandson, she is relieved because she may yet have another instrument for her revenge. Hidayet Sayın's *Topuzlu* ("Man with the Mace," 1964) contrasts Topuzlu, a liberal-minded peasant, with one who is a religious fanatic. The whole village—except Topuzlu—looks upon the fanatic as a holy man and consults him instead of a doctor when sick. They also look upon him as the rain maker. When drought hits the area the fanatic conducts a ritual to make it rain. One day the holy man insists that it will not rain, but Topuzlu predicts correctly, thanks to his rheuma-tism, that it will rain. Thereupon Topuzlu is made a holy man in spite of himself—with comic and tragic results. Erduran's fantasy *Uçurtmanın Zinciri* ("Kite on a Chain," 1965) depicts an Anatolian peasant who happens to be a mathematical prodigy. He resents being tied down and yearns for wider horizons. Aided by the schoolteacher of the village, he moves to the big city and then to America, where he causes a sensation in scientific circles. He is eventually chosen to accompany an astronaut. His wife objects to his going on a tour around the moon when his cows and relatives are starving in their village. Fail-ing to dissuade him, she goes home. After a mishap the scientist–ex-peasant, hesitating between the earth and the moon, manages to land the capsule near his village. When the television cameras arrive, they find him embracing his cows.

Ennui and man's desire to escape from his sur-roundings have been themes felt deeply by many playwrights. In Sabahattin Kudret Aksal's *Evin Üstündeki Bulut* ("Cloud Over the House," 1948) we feel the silent storm in a house, the inhabitants of which all long for a different sort of life. *Tersine Dönen Şemsiye* ("The Umbrella Which Turned In-side Out," 1958) by the same playwright is a senti-mental comedy depicting a completely bored mar-ried man's little affair with a young adventuress. Güner SÜMER, in his sensitive Chekhovian play *Bozuk Düzen* ("Disorder," 1964), depicts the frustra-tions and island-like relationships between individ-ua_., as compared with the rottenness in the greater scheme of things, subtly revealed. *Çil Horoz* ("The Freckled Cock," 1964) by OKTAY RIFAT presents in a realistic style life in a crowded shack in a shanty-town, where even staying alive is difficult. A member of the shack—a young woman—dreams of marry-ing the man with whom she is in love and leaving the shantytown to have a home with "light, water and a

toilet." At the end she is stabbed to death by her sister's husband while trying to stop him from raping her. Nazım Kurşunlu's *Dumanlı'da Telâki Var* ("Junction at the Railway Station of Dumanlı," 1963) contrasts the loneliness at a faraway train sta-tion with the people's intense passions, loves, and hatreds uncovered in flashbacks. *Yalan* ("The Lie," 1960) by Orhan ASENA pictures the family of a girl who has committed suicide. They all lie in self-defense during the investigations, but the phantom of the girl takes them back to their past and the chaos of lies with which they all lived. *İnsansızlar* ("People Without Identity," 1962) by Yıldırım Keskin (1932–), set in an unspecified place and at an un-specified time, has only two characters, a man and a woman, who hide their identity from each other. Al-though they realize that knowing who the other one might be is unimportant, suspicion drives them into a torture of hell. *Mikadonun Çöpleri* (*The Mikado Game,* 1967) by Melih Cevdet ANDAY is another tour de force for two characters, a lonely man and a woman, who hold the interest of the audience for two hours while they philosophize about life.

Many plays deal with abnormal psychology. *Huzur Çıkmazı* ("The Blind Alley Called Peace," 1962) by Haldun TANER is a psychological study in which a doting, all-forgiving and overly optimistic man drives his wife to insanity, adultery, and at-tempted murder. Oktay Rifat's *Zabit Fatmanın Kuzusu* ("Officer Fatma's Lamb," 1966), set in 1900, is the story of a domineering mother who causes her son to be impotent. In Çetin Altan's *Çemberler* ("Hoops," 1957) we enter the subconscious minds of four neurotic members of a family and see their vain attempts to break the bonds (the hoops of the play's title) around them. *Mor Defter* ("The Purple Note-book," 1961) by the same playwright traces a psy-chopath's imagination, as recorded in a notebook. In *Gölgeler* ("Phantoms," 1946) by Ahmet Muhip Dranas (1909–) a neurasthenic man's illusions come to life, where only the logic of the dream pre-vails. Cevdet Kudret's *Rüya İçinde Rüya* ("Dream Within a Dream," 1939) concerns a man who is unable to tell real life, where his son by his first wife makes love to his young second wife, from a dream. Halit Fahri Ozansoy's *İki Yanda* ("On Two Sides," 1967) is a written study of incest. *Tersine Akan Nehir* ("The River that Flows Backward," 1929) by Cevdet Kudret centers around a man who can see the future yet is unable to alter the course of his life.

Of plays that deal with people unable to adapt to changed conditions is Nazım Hikmet's *Unutulan Adam* ("The Forgotten Man," 1934), which is the drama of a man who has sunk into oblivion. The theme of Sabahattin Kudret Aksal's *Şakacı* ("The Joker," 1950) is the dictum of the pre-Socratic phi-losopher Heraclitus that one cannot enter the same river twice. A father plays a joke on the family and they believe that he died in another town. As they "mourn," the father returns, but he is not wanted; the daughter has been engaged to a man opposed by the father, and the son has taken over the firm. The wife is siding with the children. The father has no solution but to go away or die. In Güner Sümer's *Yarın Cumartesi* ("Tomorrow Will Be Saturday," 1961) a man wrongly convicted of a crime is released from

A SCENE FROM ORHAN ASENA'S *Hurrem Sultan* (TURKISH TOURISM AND INFORMATION OFFICE, NEW YORK)

prison, but he cannot adjust himself to life. *Satılık Ev* ("House for Sale," 1961) by Ahmet Kutsi TECER presents a man who, after a year's amnesia, regains his memory but finds his surroundings even more intolerable than they were before.

Some plays have dealt with the maladjustment of the artist or the scientist in a philistine, jealousy-ridden, and materialistic world. In Necip Fazıl Kısakürek's *Bir Adam Yaratmak* ("To Create a Man," 1938) a writer is driven to insanity by his oppressive surroundings. *Yüz Karası* ("The Disgrace of the Family," 1939) by Cemal Nadir Güler (1902–1947) concerns a young man who wants to become an actor but is looked upon as a disgrace by his family with their bourgeois conventions. *Sahne Dışındaki Oyun* ("Play Offstage," 1953) by Refik Ahmet Sevengil (1905–) is a drama of theatrical people. Haldun Taner's *Ve Değirmen Dönerdi* ("And the Mill Was Turning," 1958) is about a painter's struggle to find his true self in a bourgeois environment. Erduran's *Karayar Köprüsü* ("Great Chasm Bridge," 1959) is the study of an architect struggling

against the masses. Behçet Necatigil, in *Kutularda Sinek* ("The Fly in the Box," written in 1967), describes the plight of an artist in the hands of unappreciative and narrow critics who try to categorize every artist in neat little boxes. Altan's *Yedinci Köpek* ("The Seventh Dog," 1964) portrays a doctor dedicated to prolonging human life. He ends up in jail by false accusations of the neighborhood, which resents him for staying aloof and not conforming.

In many plays idealistic heroes fight against social injustice and political corruption. *Dilsizlerin Dili* ("The Voice of the Voiceless," 1954) by Sevgi Sanlı (1926–), Turgut Özakman's *Güneşte On Kişi* ("Ten People Working on the Newspaper Sun," 1955), and Recep Bilginer's *Gazeteciden Dost* ("A Newspaperman for a Friend," 1962) all deal with idealistic journalists fighting corrupt businessmen and politicians.

Perhaps the greatest number of worthwhile plays are about poverty, the desperate struggle for survival, and moral degradation caused by economic conditions. Reşat Nuri Güntekin's *Yaprak Dökümü*

("The Fall of the Leaves," 1943) describes the shattering effect of poverty on a bourgeois family. In *Balıkesir Muhasebecisi* ("The Accountant from Balıkesir," 1953) by the same playwright we witness the desperate efforts of a family to maintain their dignity in the midst of poverty. Oktay Rifat's *Kadınlar Arasında* ("Among Women," 1948) presents the plight of the family of a rich Ottoman pasha gone to ruin, because of extravagances of previous generations. *Branda Bezi* ("Sailcloth," 1952) by Nazım Kurşunlu tells the never-to-be-fulfilled desire of a family to own a house. Sabahattin Kudret Aksal's *Bir Odada Üç Ayna* ("Three Mirrors in a Room," 1956) describes the never-ending fight with life of middle-class people. Turgut Özakman's *Ocak* ("Home and Hearth," 1962) pictures an automobile repairman's family that is on the verge of disintegration because of poverty and lack of security. Adalet Ağaoğlu's *Çatıdaki Çatlak* ("Crack in the Skeleton," 1965) shows the absurd effects of individual do-gooders in a society that has not provided the basic securities to its citizens. *İspinozlar* ("The Chaffinches," 1964) by ORHAN KEMAL points out that both rich and poor families feel insecure and unhappy in a discordant society. Vedat Nedim Tör's *İşsizler* ("The Unemployed," 1924) depicts a man who, finding himself out of work after World War I, asks the help of a rich friend who is a war profiteer. The friend callously reminds him of his sister and suggests he use her as a prostitute. Melih Vassaf's *Sam Rüzgârları* ("Blight Winds," 1956) tells the story of a woman who actually does sell her flesh to feed her family. In Cevat Fehmi Başkut's play *Paydos* ("Break," 1948) an idealistic schoolteacher who cannot make two ends meet is forced to become a grocer after his marriage. Hidayet Sayın's *Kördüğüm* ("Deadlock," 1965) depicts the hopeless struggle for happiness on the part of a family headed by a retired schoolteacher. *Nalınlar* ("Wooden Shoes," 1962), a delightful farce by Necati Cumalı, hints at the economic reasons of elopements and abductions in villages. *Susuz Yaz* ("Dry Summer," 1967) by the same playwright describes the strife caused in villages by conflicting opinions regarding ownership of land, water, and women. *Göç* ("Migration," 1963) by Cevat Fehmi Başkut shows in an exaggerated way how Istanbul, the refined old city, is flooded by heavy-footed Anatolian peasants who by their rough and mercenary attitude disrupt the life of middle-class families to the extent that the latter's only salvation is to leave the city to the peasants and seek a haven for themselves in Anatolia. Kemal Tözem (1900–   ), with his *Kaf Dağlılar* ("Those from Mount Kaf," 1958), lays bare the social and economic dangers of migration to the big cities. Yüksel Pazarkaya's *Beklenen Tren* ("The Expected Train," 1967) analyzes the reasons for the migration of Turkish workers to Europe and criticizes the general labor problem in that continent.

Individuals' exploitation of individuals, governments' exploitation of their people, nations' exploitation of nations, and other political topics have been themes increasingly used by Turkish playwrights, especially since the revolution of 1960. Many of these plays will probably pass into oblivion as mere propaganda, but others, because of their sound dramaturgy and good characterizations, may enjoy longevity. Among noteworthy plays in this vein the following

warrant discussion: Orhan Asena's *Fadik Kız* ("The Girl Called Fadik," 1967) depicts the life of a helpless peasant girl who is first "used" by a peasant man and later a city lawyer, until she is no longer wanted. When the peasant discovers her in a house of prostitution, he stabs her. In *Yolcu* ("The Traveler," written 1939) Nazım Hikmet tells of war profiteers collaborating with the invaders as the Turkish nation fights for its independence after World War I. Recep Bilginer's *İsyancılar* ("The Rebels," 1964) traces the life of a typical village in Anatolia where landless peasants are being browbeaten by government officials. When they finally rise, they are persecuted as rebels. *At Gözü* ("Horse's Eye," written 1968) by Sermet ÇAĞAN describes how the ruling classes in underdeveloped countries attempt to divide the people and keep them ignorant in order to keep the status quo. Refik Erduran's *Kartal Tekmesi* ("The Kick of the Eagle," 1966) involves two members of the secret police who frighten and "milk" an unscrupulous business tycoon by inventing an "underground group" that supposedly threatens his enterprises. The situation becomes more involved than they had anticipated, however, when just such a group surfaces. *Teneke* ("The Tin Can," 1965), by YAŞAR KEMAL, adapted from his novel of the same name, tells how idealistic civil servants who wish to effect reforms in their areas are hampered and sent off to other places by the central government under the pressure of all-powerful landlords. Melih Cevdet's *İçerdekiler* ("Those Inside," 1965) depicts a teacher in an unidentified country held without trial for 345 days for distributing a manifesto that spreads "harmful ideas." The play is a battle of wits between the teacher and the chief of police, who resorts to subtle psychological torture to make his victim "confess." Orhan Asena's *Sağırlar Söğüşmesi* ("Cursing Among the Deaf") pictures three types from contemporary Turkey: Citizen A, an intellectual who speaks up only when his own interests are at stake; Citizen B, a ruthless comprador; and Citizen C, an unenlightened worker who is caught in the middle of a struggle between rightist and leftist factions. In Güngör Dilmen's *Ayak Parmakları* ("The Toes," 1965) a government official, lying lazily in bed one morning, finds himself in a strange dialogue with his toes, which are protruding from the other end of the blanket. The toes, played stylistically by actors, sound suspiciously like the voice of the underprivileged. Refik Erduran's *Kelepçe* ("Handcuffs," 1967) portrays a young intellectual with leftist pretensions but with very little direct knowledge of "the people." He spends a few days handcuffed to a rough peasant. The experience teaches him a great deal about "the people"—and about himself. Nazım Hikmet's *Kafatası* ("The Skull," 1932), set against an international background, reveals the capitalist world. Sermet Çağan's *Savaş Oyunu* ("The War Game," 1964) brings out the parallel between wars and economic interests. In Erduran's verse play *Sahib* (written 1962) a white settler in an African region that is being gradually taken over by native rebels refuses to budge, buys off all the farms of fleeing neighbors, and becomes the sole owner of a valley. Forsaken by all adherents except his young daughter, he prepares to defend his stake in life against "those black devils" by force. What defeats him in the end, however, is the surfacing collection of devils inside himself. Güngör Dilmen's *Canlı Maymun Lokantası* (*Live Monkey Restaurant*, translated into English by the playwright, 1962) takes place in Hong Kong in a special restaurant where monkey brains are served as a delicacy to rich customers. Such a couple, the newly wed Jonathans, walk in. They are dismayed when the only available monkey in the cage runs away. After a bitter bargain, they settle for a Chinese poet's brains. The play implies that money can buy anything when the poor allow themselves, under stress, to be exploited. Refik Erduran's *Merdiven Konçertosu* ("Concerto for a Ladder," 1964) is a tragicomedy with dance and music that narrates the revolts, counterrevolts, and all kinds of intrigues in a Middle Eastern country.

Plays that deal with various aspects of local politics include Reşat Nuri Güntekin's *Tanrıdağ Ziyafeti* ("Feast at God-Mountain," 1957), which is an allegorical presentation of the transition period in Turkey from oligarchy to one man's dictatorship. Haldun Taner's *Günün Adamı* ("Man of the Day," written 1950; banned from production until 1960) is a satirical presentation in the person of a professor who sees, after going into politics, that the political mechanism and the scientific attitude are irreconcilable. In Erduran's *Son Baskı* ("Extra! Extra!" 1961) an ex-convict breaks into the owner's suite in the office building of a righteous newspaper and is horrified, edified, and greatly enriched by what he finds. Cevat Fehmi Başkut in *Hacıyatmaz* ("Mr. Stand Upright," 1960) satirizes opportunistic politicians who kowtow to rulers. The same playwright relates in *Sana Rey Veriyorum* ("I Am Voting for You," 1950) two types of corruption—election irregularities and the vices of mercenary-minded medical men. Hidayet Sayın's *Küçük Devler* ("Little Giants," 1967) satirizes charlatans in the medical field. *Ha Babam Sınıfı* ("Class," 1965) by Rifat Ilgaz (1911–) exposes in the form of a hilarious farce the lamentable conditions in a Turkish high school, which is true of many other institutions of learning in Turkey. *Devr-i Süleyman* ("The Times of Süleyman," 1968) by Aydın Engin is a satire on the political and social conditions in present-day Turkey. It was banned by the governor of Ankara before it opened. The play opened anyway with slight changes and a different title—*Devr-i Küheylân* ("The Times of the Purebred Arab Horse")—but this time the theater was shut down, only to be reopened and the play reinstated by a decree from the Court of Cassation, which upheld the constitution.

Plays about human nature and the dangers confronting man include Turgut Özakman's *Tufan* ("The Flood," 1957), which is an antiwar play and describes the world after World War III. In Refik Erduran's *Aman Avcı* ("Please Hunter!" 1962) the hero carries on research to find out whether the preservation of the human race is desirable. He decides in the negative, but his gardener makes him change his mind. *Biraz Gelir Misiniz?* (*Will You Come Here, Please?* 1962) by Aziz NESIN is an allegorical play about a dedicated flute maker who sells his instruments cheaply to those who appreciate them but defies a business tycoon who wants to buy them to make rails for a fence around his yard. He also defies Death, who summons him with the title phrase.

At the end his ideal, which is "deathless," is carried on by his apprentice. In *Bir Şey Yap Met* ("Do Something, Met," 1964), Nesin implies that only those who work have a right to live. Orhan Kemal's *Eskici Dükkânı* ("The Old Thrift Shop," 1968) is about a lame, old shoe repairman who tries to run his house as he reminisces about the old mansion of his grandfather, a feudal lord. His aim to find a rich man for his daughter and a rich girl for his son is frustrated when they both marry poor people. He throws his children out of his house, but when they return home, having contracted a deadly disease, he battles to save them by selling his shop. The whole neighborhood, forgetting old enmities, helps them. Sabahattin Kudret Aksal's *Kıral Üşümesi* ("The King Is Cold," written 1968) is a belief in, and a eulogy on, man. Yıldırım Keskin's *Uzaktakiler* (originally written in French and titled *Le Lointain*, "The Distance," 1961) is about the inseparability of man. Despite the hatred and boredom that people feel toward one another, they still cling together. *Soruşturma* ("Investigation," 1964) by the same author asserts that all men are evil and that evil reigns supreme.

Dozens of plays could be classified under those delineating character. Halit Fahri Ozansoy's *Baykuş* ("The Owl," 1916), a play written a few years before the establishment of the Republic, portrays a man who loses two sons in one night. Vedat Nedim Tör's *Üç Kişi Arasında* ("Among Three People," 1927) and *Siyah Beyaz* ("Black and White," 1952) are about pathologically jealous people. *Kör* ("The Blind One," 1928) by the same author is the drama of a blind man who commits suicide to set his wife free. *Ceza* ("The Punishment," 1942) by Sedat Simavi (1896–1953) tells of a woman with a past who sacrifices herself for the sake of her son. Necip Fazıl Kısakürek's *Nam-ı Diğer Parmaksız Salih* ("Alias Fingerless Salih," 1948) is the story of a notorious gambler who sacrifices himself to shield his son, also a gambler. Galip Güran's *Batak* ("Quagmire," 1953) is about the decadence of a woman drug addict. Mahmut Yesari's *Sürtük* ("The Lady of the Streets," 1956) describes the life of the title character and her environment. In Orhan Asena's *Kocaoğlan* ("The Big Boy," 1961) the title character is a moron whose sexual satisfaction is derived from identification with his companion. *Son Durak* ("Last Stop," 1956) by Muvaffak Garan (1911–) is the portrayal of a criminal lawyer who exploits justice for selfish aims. Haldun Taner's *Dışardakiler* ("Those Outside," 1958) depicts an aging politician who finds meaning in the present as he starts writing his memoires in an asylum. Çetin Altan's *Beybaba* ("The Old Man," 1960) is the study of a retired old man, who, because of his absolute honesty, is alienated from all the dishonest acquaintances around him. Necati Cumalı's *Derya Gülü* ("Rose of the Sea," 1963) is a triangle involving an old drunkard, his kept mistress, and the old man's young helper. Orhan Asena's *Korku* ("Fear," 1956) analyzes the psychotic fear of a leader deserted by an ungrateful public. Turgut Özakman's *Duvarların Ötesi* ("Beyond the Walls," 1958) is a suspense-filled story of four convicts who escape from prison and hold a girl as hostage. The play reveals the backgrounds of the well-drawn characters and criticizes society for creating criminals and then treacherously punishing them. Orhan Kemal's *72. Koguş* ("Seventy-second Ward," 1967), adapted from a story by the same author, presents with insight the economic backgrounds and pains and dreams of highly varied simple characters in a prison.

Turkish history and folk legends are the sources for many plays. Ahmet Kutsi Tecer's *Köroğlu* (1949) depicts the Turkish folk hero Köroğlu, a kind of Robin Hood, who is the champion of the oppressed. *Akın* ("The Raid," 1932) by Faruk Nafiz Çamlıbel (1898–   ), written in singsong verse, glorifies the deeds of the Turks who migrated from central Asia on account of a drought. In *Fatih* ("The Conqueror," 1953) Nazım Kurşunlu portrays the conqueror of Constantinople as a superman who built a brave new civilization on the ruins of the defunct Byzantium. *Genç Osman* ("Osman the Young," 1956) by Musahipzade Celâl and Mehmet Şükrü Erden (1890–   ) expounds the waste in the practice of fratricide carried out legally and for reasons of state in the Ottoman dynasty. Orhan Asena's *Hurrem Sultan* (1959) shows how Suleiman the Magnificent had his most capable son, Mustafa, killed after palace intrigues. The play depicts Suleiman's conflict with his son as well as with himself.

In 1711 Catherine, wife of Peter the Great, spent a night in the tent of the victorious Ottoman commander Baltacı Mehmet Pasha, after which he retreated to be beheaded for "treason." Haldun Taner's *Lutfen Dokunmayın* ("Please Do Not Touch!" 1961) presents three different versions of what happened in that tent, with the suggestion that historians cannot be very objective. Turan Oflazoğlu's *Deli İbrahim* ("Ibrahim the Mad," 1967) describes the escapades of a mad sultan who misruled the Ottoman Empire for many years. Orhan Asena's *Simavnalı Şeyh Bedrettin* ("Şeyh Bedrettin of Simavna," written 1968) is the tragic story of a man who is considered by some historians as the first Muslim socialist. Torn between allegiance to the state and service to the people, he chooses the latter. In *Tohum ve Toprak* ("The Seed and the Earth," 1962) Orhan Asena shows how Mahmut II owed his throne and life to Alemdar Mustafa Pasha but sacrificed him as ransom to the counterrevolutionaries to save his own neck. Halit Fahri Ozansoy's *Nedim* (1928) depicts the life and loves of the famous eighteenth-century poet, set in perhaps the most colorful and extravagant period in Turkish history. *Suavi Efendi* (1961) by İlhan Tarus (1907–   ) recounts the failure of the title character, a liberal newspaperman, who attempted to depose Abdülhamit II. Güngör Dilmen's *İttihat ve Terakki* ("Union and Progress," written 1968) traces the years 1908–1918, when the Young Turk Revolution led to the proclamation of the Second Constitution, deposing of Abdülhamit II, and the final disintegration of the Ottoman Empire in the course of World War I. Refik Erduran's *Direklerarasında* ("In Old Istanbul," 1965) is a musical comedy. During the turn of the century, when Istanbul was a hotbed of vices that nevertheless refused to allow Muslim women on its stages, a stage-struck Turkish girl decides to pretend to be Armenian. This ruse, while making her song-and-dance career in the theater possible, involves her with a number of unexpected customers, among them Armenian revolutionaries plotting against the notorious Red Sultan

(Abdülhamit II). (A nonmusical version of this play is being prepared.) In Necip Fazıl Kısakürek's melodrama *Sultan Abdülhamit* (1968), however, the title character is presented as a wise and tenderhearted statesman who reluctantly chose to rule his country with an iron fist in order to avert anarchy and hold the empire together. Kısakürek argues that the Turkish Empire, which once commanded a vast portion of the world, fell with the arrival of unbridled freedom and chaos in 1908. *Oğuzala* (1955) by Selâhattin BATU employs the Turkish Oğuz myth that pictures the Turks as having established a just and strong order in central Asia. Urun Han is the symbol of bloody imperialism, whereas Oğuz symbolizes Atatürk. *Kerem and Aslı* (1943) by the same playwright is a tragic love story based on Turkish legend. *Aşk ve Barış* ("Love and Peace," 1961) by Suat Taşer (1919–   ) is the dramatization of one of the Dede Korkut tales. Sevgi Sanlı's *Menevşe Yaprağından İncinen Kız* ("The Girl Hurt by the Leaf of the Violet," 1967), inspired by an old Turkish tale, pictures a woman who scorns all earthly and heavenly goods to search for Truth.

The heritage of other civilizations in Turkey as well as the history of other lands has inspired Turkish playwrights to present contemporary themes on historical backgrounds. Orhan Asena's *Gilgameş ya da Tanrılar ve İnsanlar* ("Gilgamesh or Gods and Men," 1954) is a dramatization of the Mesopotamian epic *Gilgamesh*. The author takes Gilgamesh as a prototype of Atatürk and portrays him as the champion of freedom and a man of dauntless courage. Selâhattin Batu's *İfigenia Tauris'te* ("Iphigenia in Tauris," 1942) treats the Greek legend differently from that of both Euripides and Goethe. He stresses the humanity of Thoas and the Taurians, and at the end of the play East and West do meet. Another play of Greek origin by the same author, *Güzel Helena* ("The Beautiful Helena," 1954), shows the East as a peace-loving region that becomes disenchanted with the West. Haldun Taner's *Eşeğin Gölgesi* ("The Shadow of the Donkey," 1965) is a parody of the story by Lucian, which the author has applied to modern Turkey. Güngör Dilmen's *Midasın Kulakları* (*The Ears of Midas,* 1959) is a poetical play, partly in verse. Midas, king of Phrygia, is made judge over a musical contest between the gods Pan and Apollo. He proclaims Pan as winner and is punished by Apollo, who gives him a pair of ass's ears. At this point the play veers from the ancient myth. Midas first hides his ears but gradually becomes enchanted with them, so much so that he wants to exhibit them in public proudly, thus nullifying the punishment of the god. *Midasın Altınları* ("The Gold of Midas) and *Kördüğüm* ("The Gordian Knot") are the other two plays of the trilogy by Dilmen. In all the plays King Midas is pictured as an obstinate, passionate man ever aspiring to a form of godhead, thus suggesting the limits of mortal man. *Akadın Yayı* ("Akad's Bow," written 1967), again by Güngör Dilmen, is based on a Canaanite myth. Daniel, the corrupt judge of Canaan, steals the extraordinary bow belonging to the huntress Anat and hands it over to Akad, his young son, with the idea that Akad may become master, not only of Canaan, but of the whole world. Akad, much to his father's chagrin, refuses to use the bow for belligerent purposes but is constantly obsessed with the fear that others after him may lay their hands on the weapon and lead the world to destruction. Turan Oflazoğlu's *Sokrates'in Savunması* ("The Defense of Socrates," 1969), a play partly in verse and chorus, depicts Socrates on the verge of winning his case before the court, at which point the demon inside him warns him that he is winning the case but losing immortality. Socrates deliberately maneuvers the court into sentencing him to death. In the dungeon he goes through a character transformation and becomes a more balanced person. Yüksel Pazarkaya's *Alaban Tanrısı* ("The God of Alaban," 1965) is set in Alaban, a country that existed in eastern Asia Minor. Her people are kept ignorant by the landlords who run the country with the aid of the gods. When a man dies, according to custom, all his earthly possessions are buried with him and later pass on to the landlords along with all his land. One day an enlightened stranger comes to this region and, appalled by what he sees, takes action to set it right. He is opposed, however, by the very people whom he is trying to help. Not only are the peasants unready for progress, but they are also resentful of a stranger's mingling in their affairs. They stone him to death. In *Rasputin* (1967), by Aziz Çalışlar, the title character uses religion to his material advantage while allowing no worldly pleasures to those around him. Refik Erduran's verse tragedy *Büyük Jüstinyen* ("Justinian the Great," 1960) is about Justinian, who, as an idealistic Byzantine emperor, is confronted with a revolt. He must either flee and abandon all hope of greatness or suppress the rebellion bloodily and forfeit his claim to be remembered as the benefactor of the people. His wife, a harlot turned empress, advises him to do the latter. Thereafter, he concentrates on earning "greatness" by grand feats of building, lawmaking, and military conquest, but there is an ironic twist at the end of the play. Güngör Dilmen's *Montezuma* (written 1963) is about the fall of the Aztec Empire. Montezuma's belief that with the return of Mexico's white god, Quetzalcoatl, a new age will begin precipitates the drama. Cortez is received as the reincarnation of the mythical god and the ensuing events lead to the destruction of the empire.

Anti-illusionist plays that draw much of their spirit and technique from Karagöz, Orta Oyunu, Meddah, and the epic theater of Brecht are readily accepted by Turkish audiences. Haldun Taner's *Keşanlı Ali Destanı* (*The Ballad of Ali of Keshan,* 1964) is the story of a man from a shantytown in Istanbul who was thrown into jail for a crime he did not commit but who becomes a hero for his alleged murder of a much-hated bully. He assumes the personality that his environment forces upon him and at the end he actually becomes a murderer. Although the story takes place in a shantytown, the play is a satire on the big city, with its political machines, bureaucracy, mass hysteria, sentimental love, and myths. The play is treated in the epic manner. A woman restroom attendant comments on the action of the play, and the music, composed by Yalçın Tura for an Occidental orchestra, is partially folklorist and partially cabaretist in style. Sermet Çağan's *Ayak Bacak Fabrikası* ("The Feet and Legs Factory," 1964) uses the "alienation" technique in conjunction with the traditional Turkish theater and assails big-power diplomacy and the imperialistic exploitation of underdeveloped

countries. *Sarıpınar 1914* (1968) by Turgut Özakman, adapted from notes about Anatolia by Reşat Nuri Güntekin and treated in the epic manner, is a satire on the corrupt rulers, civil servants, and journalists during the last days of the Ottoman Empire. The narrator continually and ironically reminds the audience that "This was all back in 1914." *Gözlerimi Kaparım Vazifemi Yaparım* ("I Close My Eyes and Do My Duty," 1964) by Haldun Taner is a panorama of the last fifty years of Turkey, as symbolized in the lives of two neighbors, a sycophant and a sincere little man. The play is presented in a format reminiscent of Karagöz. *Zilli Zarife* ("Zarife with the Bells," 1966) by the same author is again in the epic manner and tells the story of a madame in a house of prostitution. Yaşar Kemal's novel *Yer Demir Gök Bakır* ("The Earth Is Iron, the Sky Copper") was made into a play (1967) with epic elements by Nihad Asyalı. The chorus is repetitive, however, and the play is further marred by a distracting subplot. A one-act version under the title *Uzun Dere* ("The Long Stream," 1966) by Nihad Özer was more compact and effective, and its production won the first prize at theater festivals in France and Turkey. The spirit of Karagöz is present in both versions. The play shows how people in an absurd society, overcome by fear and hopelessness, create myths and holy men for themselves as the only means for their salvation. Oktay Rifat's *Oyun İçinde Oyun* ("Play Within a Play," 1949) is based on a classical Karagöz play and is about two Orta Oyunu actors deceived by their wives. Their lives are presented both on- and offstage. Halit Fahri Ozansoy's *Bir Dolaptır Dönüyor* ("And the Plot Goes On," written 1949) comprises Karagöz and folk-tale characters and is a satire on the post-atomic-war world. *Kanlı Nigâr* ("Bloody Nigâr," 1967) by Sadık Şendil (1913–   ) is a faithful adaptation on the modern stage of the Orta Oyunu play of the same name. The story is sprinkled with gags about present-day politicians and events. Aziz Nesin's *Düdükçülerle Fırçacıların Savaşı* ("War Between Whistle-Makers and Brush-Makers," written 1968) is a brilliant satire on war, lampooning diplomatic hypocrisy and the selfishness of military-industrial complexes in two fictitious countries. The play, vaguely reminiscent of Karel Čapek's *The Insect Comedy* and James Thurber's *The Last Flower,* abounds in the buffooneries and verbal wit of Orta Oyunu and is in its non-illusionistic style. Refik Erduran's *Ayı Masalı* ("Bear Story," 1963) has many Orta Oyunu elements and is based on the Turkish popular saying, "Until you have crossed the bridge, call a bear Uncle dear."

Plotless plays presenting hosts of characters in loose, episodic scenes, usually introduced by a narrator, are not alien to the general concept of Karagöz and Orta Oyunu. Ahmet Kutsi Tecer's *Köşebaşı* (*The Neighbourhood,* 1947) presents a slice of life in a neighborhood of Istanbul. Its setting of the coffeehouse where all activities meet, decrepit old houses, and a torn street with a fountain and a mosque in the background is typical of many neighborhoods in Turkey. The loose structure, the parade of colorful characters, and some of the humor in the dialogue are reminiscent of Karagöz. With its unpretentious poetry and charm, this play has been considered a landmark in Turkish drama. Haldun Taner's *Fazilet*

Eczanesi ("Virtue Pharmacy," 1960) takes place in a pharmacy along the Bosporus, where many characters, old and young, meet. *Mahallenin Romanı* ("The Story of the Neighborhood," 1955) by Rifat Can (pen name of Kemal Tözem) portrays a gossip-ridden small town. Oktay Rifat's *Birtakım İnsanlar* ("A Group of People," 1960) presents a number of passengers in a boat-landing station who reconstruct their lives and dreams. The Dumb Fellow at the end speaks up and sings his faith in man. A fine example of the "theater of the absurd" is *Bal Sineği* (*The Plumber*, 1965) by Aydın Arıt (1928–   ). A couple on their honeymoon are confronted in a hotel room by a strange plumber, who upsets their bourgeois comforts and threatens their lives.

It is difficult to predict in what direction Turkish drama will develop. It may continue to be the works of highly varied individual playwrights. Perhaps a new synthesis may be made from the diversity of forms, styles, and themes and a rich heritage in the theater, culminating in the birth of a new school of drama.

Metin And's *A History of Theatre and Popular Entertainment in Turkey*, published in 1963, is a major source book on Turkish drama. *The Turkish Theatre* (1933) by Nicholas N. Martinovitch is actually a book on Orta Oyunu, Meddah, and Karagöz. Professor Sabri Esat Siyavuşgil's *Karagöz, Its History, Its Characters, Its Mystic and Satiric Spirit* was published in Ankara in 1955.

Ahmet Kutsi Tecer's play *The Neighbourhood* was translated by Nüvit Özdoğru and published in Ankara in 1964. Talat S. Halman reviewed this play in *Books Abroad* (April 1966). Güngör Dilmen's play *The Ears of Midas* was translated by Caroline Graham and published in Ankara in 1966. Haldun Taner's play *The Ballad of Ali of Keshan* was translated by Nüvit Özdoğru and mimeographed in Istanbul in 1965.

Articles in English include Metin And's "Turkey's Musical Theatre," in *The Music Magazine* (February 1962); H. R. Battersby's "The Karagöz Show or The Miniature Theatres of Turkey," in *Islamic Review*, Vol. 43 (1955); Alessio Bombacı's "On Ancient Turkish Dramatic Performances," in *Aspects of Altaic Civilization, Ural Altaic Series*, Vol. 23 (1963); Orhan Burian and Perihan Çambel's "Theater in Turkey," in *The Players Magazine* (May 1952); Caroline Graham's "Albee to Bard in Ankara," in *The New York Times* (September 24, 1961); Kenneth MacGowan's "Theater à la Turkey," in *The Theatre Arts* (December 1958), and "Notes on the Turkish Theatre," in *Drama Survey* (Winter 1962); and David C. Stewart's "Recent Developments in the Theatre of Turkey," in *The Educational Theatre Journal* (October 1954). Metin And's *A History of Theatre and Popular Entertainment in Turkey* (1963) is a major source book on Turkish drama. His *Dances of Anatolian Turkey* (1959) describes many dances that are pantomimic.—N. O.

Twelfth Night; or, What You Will (c. 1600–1601). A comedy by William SHAKESPEARE. The earliest record of performance of *Twelfth Night* is that of February 2, 1602, as noted in the diary of John Manningham, a barrister of the Inner Temple. According to a recent theory, not entirely accepted, the first performance took place the previous year,

when Queen Elizabeth entertained Don Virginio Orsino, duke of Bracciano, at court on Twelfth Night —January 6, 1601. The comedy received its initial printing in the 1623 First Folio. Although details of the main plot may be found in various Continental Renaissance works, Shakespeare's immediate source appears to be the tale "Of Apolonius and Silla" in Barnabe Riche's *Farewell to Militarie Profession* (1581).

In Shakespeare's version Viola, separated by a shipwreck from her brother, arrives in Illyria, where, disguised as a boy, she enters the service of Duke Orsino. She falls in love with him. Orsino, lovesick for Countess Olivia, sends Viola (now named Cesario) to woo her for him. Olivia, in her turn, falls in love with the disguised emissary. The plot complications that follow are heightened by the arrival of Sebastian, Viola's supposedly drowned identical twin. The play ends with the pairing off of Viola and Orsino and Olivia and Sebastian. The subplot deals with a trick played on Malvolio, Olivia's spoilsport steward, by members of Olivia's household.

By scholarly consensus, this last of the romantic comedies is considered to be Shakespeare's masterpiece in the genre. Even opening and closing to music and song, the play is also his most musical. Although Shakespeare had employed the same situations, plot devices, character types, and thematic lines in his earlier comedies, they are handled in *Twelfth Night* with such skill that a completely fresh, delightful play emerges. As in the other romantic comedies, love is the unifying idea. Only now, stripped of wit combats and with other forms of positive love relationships carefully subordinated to that of male-female love, *Twelfth Night* clearly states that the essence of true love springs from unselfish giving. Viola, beautiful of spirit and body, becomes in her every action the spokesman of this concept. In contrast stand the two aristocratic, sentimental self-deceivers, Orsino and Olivia. The boisterous, drunken Sir Toby, the fatuous Sir Andrew, and the pompous Malvolio—low-comedy characters drawn from the Jonsonian "comedy of humours"—further mirror the theme. They, especially Malvolio, exhibit varying degrees of self-love. Commenting on the actions of all is Feste, the witty jester.

That the mood of the play is sunny—the dark clouds that appear are quickly dispelled—is suggested by the title. "Twelfth Night" may allude to the specific season or holiday when the play was first presented, or it may reflect the lighthearted gaiety associated with the season's revels—or, as the subtitle indicates, "what you will."

An outstanding edition of *Twelfth Night* is the New Cambridge Edition (2nd ed., 1949), edited by Arthur Quiller-Couch and J. Dover Wilson. —W. G.

Twin Menaechmi, The.   See MENAECHMI.

Two Gentlemen of Verona, The (c. 1592–1593). A comedy by William SHAKESPEARE. *The Two Gentlemen of Verona* was first published in the 1623 First Folio. Its date of composition, conjectural at best, can be determined only by its stylistic characteristics, which are similar to those of the other early comedies. Based on the Spanish prose romance *Diana Enamorada* (1542) by the Portuguese Jorge de Montemayor, Shakespeare's comedy may be a reworking of the lost English play *The History of Felix and Philiomena* (1585). No record of performance earlier than 1762 exists.

The gentlemen of the title are two firm friends who, as the play opens, are taking leave of one another. Valentine, seeking honor, is bound for Milan; Proteus, consumed with love for Julia, remains in Verona. Proteus' father, however, sends the young man after his friend. Although he vows constancy to Julia before departing, no sooner does Proteus arrive in Milan than he falls in love with the duke's daughter, already beloved by Valentine. Thus, a conflict between love and friendship is precipitated. Proteus successfully schemes against his friend, causing the duke to banish Valentine. Captured by outlaws in a forest near Mantua, Valentine becomes their leader. Meanwhile, Julia, pining for Proteus, comes to Milan disguised as a boy. Although she discovers his faithlessness, she enters his service. Silvia, threatened by her father with marriage to the wealthy Thurio, decides to join Valentine. All the characters meet in the forest, where, in an incredibly rapid series of reversals, all is set right.

In this, his first romantic comedy, Shakespeare draws upon conventional materials from the prose romance and Italian sixteenth-century comedy. The result is a play that is not particularly distinguished. Yet it does point toward the great romantic comedies, for most of the elements are present: wooing, dangers, the heroine disguised as a boy, a low-comedy character cast in an English mold, song ("Who is Silvia?"), and themes touching on reconciliation and forgiveness.

An outstanding edition of *The Two Gentlemen of Verona* is the New Cambridge Edition (rev. ed. 1955), edited by Arthur Quiller-Couch and J. Dover Wilson.—W. G.

Two Noble Kinsmen, The (1613). A romance by John FLETCHER and William SHAKESPEARE. Students of the play are generally agreed that Shakespeare is the author of most of Act I and Act V and that Fletcher is responsible for the major portion of the play. The plot is based upon Chaucer's *Knight's Tale*. It tells the story of Palamon and Arcite, close friends who fall in love with the same woman, the beautiful Emilia. After a series of adventures they engage in a duel. The winner is to receive the hand of Emilia; the loser is to be put to death. Arcite is victorious, but just as Palamon is to be executed the news arrives that Arcite has been thrown from his horse and mortally wounded. Arcite's dying words give Emilia to Palamon.

Judged by the standards of Fletcher's other work, the play is a creditable example of the type of romance popularized by Beaumont and Fletcher. Shakespeare's hand in the play, however, forces us to judge it by the standards of his great romances, *The Winter's Tale* and *The Tempest*. In the latter context *The Two Noble Kinsmen* emerges as a pleasant but slight diversion, substituting fluency for depth and sentimentality for emotion.

The Two Noble Kinsmen is in *The Complete Works of Shakespeare* (1940), edited by G. L. Kittridge.—E. Q.

Tyler, Royall (1757–1826). American playwright and lawyer. The author of THE CONTRAST, the first comedy by an American to be performed by professional actors, Tyler was born in Boston and studied at Harvard and at Yale. After serving in the Revolutionary War, he began practicing and teaching law in Vermont. Besides plays, he wrote a novel, humorous essays, and humorous verse.

Tyler's plays that have not survived are *May Day in Town; or, New York in an Uproar* (1787), a farce; and *The Georgia Spec, or, Land in the Moon* (1797), a satire on the land speculation that followed the scandalous Yazoo Purchase. His plays that have survived include *The Island of Barrataria* (pub. 1941), a satirical farce; and three "sacred dramas" in blank verse: *The Origin of the Feast of Purim, Joseph and His Brethren* (pub. 1941), and *The Judgement of Solomon* (pub. 1941). In *The Contrast*, Tyler drew a lively picture of New York society, setting a pattern for American comedy that persisted for over fifty years, and introduced one of the most popular themes of early American drama, the contrast between native honesty and foreign hypocrisy. Moreover, he created in the character of Jonathan one of the first in a long line of stage Yankees.—B. H.

Tyl, Josef Kajetán (1808–1856). Czech playwright. Born in Kutná Hora, Tyl attended school in Prague and Hradec Králové. He left high school ("gymnasium") before graduation and became active in itinerant theatrical companies at the turn of the 1820's and 1830's. While employed as clerk for the army in Prague from 1831 to 1842, Tyl also worked as a journalist, translator, writer, actor, and director in a movement to organize Czech society on the eve of the bourgeois democratic revolution. From 1834 to 1837 Tyl was the head of a Prague avant-garde theater group (Kajetnské divadlo), and in 1846 he accepted the post of literary manager of Czech productions at the Stavovské divadlo (Estates Theater) in Prague, where he remained as chief until 1851. Because of his liberal political activity in the unsuccessful revolution of 1848/49, Tyl was persecuted for the rest of his life. He spent his last years working as a director and actor in Czech itinerant theater companies.

Influenced by the work of Czech playwright Václav K. Klicpera, Tyl first tried to write poetic drama. In his excellent dramatic poem *Čestmír* (1835), Tyl dramatized the crises of modern man by creating a pessimistic malcontent who championed Romantic social ideas. The right of the protagonist to unrestricted development, however, was denied at the end of the play because Tyl, for practical reasons of nationalism, favored the interests of society over the free growth of the individual. At the same time Tyl wrote a play about a subject that was considered very important by the younger generation of playwrights that he led: contemporary Czech life. In his local farce called *Fidlovačka* (1834) Tyl depicted the struggles of the patriotic Prague lower middle classes against the haughty, Germanized bourgeoisie. "Where is my Home?", one of the songs from this play, became a part of the Czechoslovakian national anthem in 1918.

Tyl's period of greatest creativity extended from 1845 to 1851, when he wrote a number of dramas set in the middle-class milieu. His didactic purpose in these works was to inspire a moral improvement in the middle classes. This aim is most evident in his play *Prazská devečka a venkovský tovaryš aneb*

Paličova dcera ("Prague Maid and Country Journeyman or Incendiary's Daughter," 1847), a social drama in which Tyl depicted the dark side of the life of the peasants and the bourgeoisie. Other plays in which Tyl is also concerned with middle-class life include *Paní Marjánka, matka pluku* ("Mrs. Marjanka, Mother of the Regiment," 1845), *Pražský flamendr* ("The Prague Reveler," 1846), *Bankrotář a kramářka* ("A Bankrupt and a Stall Keeper," 1848), and *Chudý kejklíř* ("A Poor Juggler," 1848). The protagonists of these dramas are burghers who have been reduced to paupers and folk characters. In these works Tyl criticizes the modern ruthlessness of the bourgeoisie.

Tyl's poetic talent is revealed in his dramatic fairy tales, which he wrote after 1847 as a reaction to the fast social changes that were taking place. They are pictures of contemporary Czech life. In his best romantic fairy tale, *Strakonický dudák* ("The Bagpiper of Strakonice," 1847), Tyl depicts the importance of a native country for man's life. In this play Tyl also presents a precise image of the Czech national mentality. In the excellent dramatic fairy tale *Tvrdohlavá žena* ("A Stubborn Woman," 1849) Tyl sharply satirizes political reactionaries.

In the revolutionary years Tyl used the form of historical drama in order to elucidate, by historical analogy, contemporary political problems. These plays, written under the influence of Shakespeare and Schiller, were a result of Tyl's thorough study of his material. On the basis of a historical event in his native town, he depicted with sympathy a contemporary strike of the proletariat in *Kutnohorští havíři*

("The Miners of Kutná Hora," 1848). This play occupies a notable position in that European drama of the nineteenth century that endeavored to portray the proletariat. In 1848 the Czech theater in Prague produced Tyl's dramatic poem *Jan Hus,* in which Hus voices the national political ideals of 1848. Other historical dramas, such as *Krvavé křtiny aneb Drahomíra a její synové* ("The Bloody Christening or Drahomíra and Her Sons," 1849) and *Staré Město a Malá Strana* ("The Old Town and the Lesser Town," written 1851, pub. 1868), show Tyl's political radicalism.

Tyl's dramas are the greatest expression of the Romantic Czech drama of the thirties and forties. Because of his use of realistic details, Tyl's work forms a transition between Romanticism and realism in the Czech theater. As a European master of complex psychological characterization, Tyl is the predecessor of the realistic Russian playwright Alexander Ostrovskÿ. Tyl created several typical Czech stock characters that were later used in Czech drama and opera. His realistic characters were often set in romantic stories that were not original. A weakness in some of Tyl's texts is the conciliation of conflict.

Tyl's work is considered to form the basis of Czech national drama, and some of his plays are still performed today. Some have also been adapted for radio, television, and the film, while others were used as scripts for operas and puppet-theater productions. *Strakonický dudák* is Tyl's most popular play for foreign stages and has been performed in many countries.—F. Č.

U

Ubu Roi (King Ubu, 1896). A farce by Alfred JARRY. This play has reached the status of a myth in the history of the Western theater. Its première, December 11, 1896, was so turbulent an event that it has been compared to the première of Victor Hugo's *Hernani* in 1830. An excellent actor from the Comédie-Française played Ubu, and the production was directed by Aurélien F. Lugné-Poë.

Jarry ironically denounces all the vulgarity and absurdity in the world by creating a monstrous clown, Père Ubu, who has all the cowardice and cruelty to be found in society. Père Ubu, an ignominious and grotesque character, is nagged by his shrewish wife, Mère Ubu, into killing the king of Poland. In an uproarious parody of *Macbeth,* Père Ubu kills all the noblemen in the country with his "disembraining" machine. He commits countless massacres for a sausage and an umbrella (metaphors for his gluttony and bourgeois desire to take power). Père Ubu becomes an absurd, evil force in the universe, killing everyone for their money (or "phynances" as he calls it). The supernatural atmosphere, the affected mannerisms of speech, the mechanical gestures, and the use of masks are a few techniques that are used in the play that have influenced much of the avant-garde theater and the genre of SURREALISM.

Among the spectators were three men in particular who commented on the première: Arthur Symons, Stéphane Mallarmé, and William Butler Yeats. The furor started with the initial word of the play, an obscenity to which Jarry had added one letter. The language, more scatological than sexual, and the prodigious vitality of the text caused Yeats in his *Autobiography* to call Jarry the "Savage God." Ubu, in his scandalous behavior and coarse humor, is the hero-villain who recalls Rabelais's Panurge. A more contemporary name was invented by the critic Cyril Connolly in 1945 when he called Jarry "the Santa Claus of the Atomic Age."

Ubu Roi does not resemble a polemical work but is, instead, a youthful work, the *potache*'s ("student's") vision of the functioning of society. There is also a more specifically French strain in the creation of Ubu: the ferocious hatred of the French artist for the lumpish bourgeoisie.

Ubu Roi has been translated under the title *King Ubu* by Michael Benedikt and George E. Wellwarth in *Modern French Theatre* (1966).—W. F.

Uganda. See AFRICA: *Uganda.*

U Ku. See BURMA.

U Kyin U. See BURMA.

Uncle Tom's Cabin (1852). A drama in six acts

SCENE FROM GEORGE L. AIKEN'S *Uncle Tom's Cabin* (MUSEUM OF THE CITY OF NEW YORK)

by George L. Aiken (1830–1876). Aiken's first version of Harriet Beecher Stowe's novel *Uncle Tom's Cabin* was subtitled *Life Among the Lowly,* and the play ended with the death of little Eva. In response to popular demand, however, Aiken provided a sequel, *The Death of Uncle Tom.* Two weeks later the two plays were combined, and successfully performed under the title *Uncle Tom's Cabin.* Several versions of the play were staged simultaneously in New York, on tour in the North, and in England. In Aiken's and other versions, *Uncle Tom's Cabin* was the most popular play on the American stage in the decade before the Civil War. After the war, it enjoyed another wave of popularity, which reached a peak in 1900.

The first two acts of this play are primarily concerned with the slaves George and Eliza Harris and their attempt to escape to Canada. They gain their freedom, with the help of Yankee Phineas Fletcher, by successfully warding off Haley and his slave hunters. Uncle Tom, the slave who dominates the rest of the play, is sold for a plantation hand to Legree. On Legree's plantation, Tom is beaten to death because he had shown compassion for his fellow slaves.

The play is loosely constructed and its dialogue, taken almost verbatim from the novel, is undistinguished, but it is full of colorful incidents and vital characters. Like the novel, the play is imbued with Christian spirit and moral fervor, and it is both a powerful attack on Negro slavery and a parable of good and evil. It helped arouse America's conscience, and it brought into the theater for the first time thousands who had believed the stage offered only temptation to evil.—B. H.

Uncle Vanya (Dyadya Vanya, 1899). A drama in four acts by Anton CHEKHOV. The plot of *Uncle Vanya* is a streamlined version of Chekhov's earlier play *Leshii* (*The Wood Demon,* 1889), which was produced by a private theater but rejected by the Imperial Theater as "an excellent story written in the form of a play but not a play." Several years later, Chekhov rewrote the play, excluding several characters, combining others into one, and changing the final suicide into an attempted murder. A comparison of the two plots shows which details Chekhov considered expendable and which he thought essential to the play.

Ivan Voinitsky, the Uncle Vanya of the title, gives up his share of an inheritance to his sister, who marries a pompous and dull professor. After his sister's death, Voinitsky continues to run the estate with his sister's daughter, Sonia. They support the professor, who has retired and spends his time writing about art. When the professor brings his beautiful new wife Yelena to live on the estate, Vanya discovers that his brother-in-law is an inflated nonentity. Vanya also falls in love with Yelena, a passion shared by his neighbor Dr. Astrov (Dr. Khrushchev, the "wood demon" in the earlier play), a man who has a passion for saving forests and planting trees and who is loved unrequitedly by Sonia. But nothing comes of all these loves (at the end of the earlier version the doctor and Sonia wound up together). All Vanya's pent-up bitterness explodes when the professor, who is tired of life in the country, suggests that the estate be sold. Vanya seizes a gun, fires twice at his ungrateful brother-in-law, and misses. In the end, however, all is forgiven: the professor and his beautiful wife leave for the city while Uncle Vanya and his niece promise to keep sending him money and go on working hard to make their unhappiness bearable. They will rest, Sonia says, when they die, not before, because that is their fate.

A SCENE FROM ANTON CHEKHOV'S *Uncle Vanya* (THEATRE COLLECTION, NEW YORK PUBLIC LIBRARY AT LINCOLN CENTER)

This is a less standard ending than that of *The Wood Demon*, where Vanya shoots himself offstage. In this play, apparently, as in all his mature works, Chekhov was trying to convey the tragedy of the individual by as sober means as possible and this toned-down ending may indicate Chekhov's artistic development.

Uncle Vanya has been translated by David Magarshack and appears in *The Storm and Other Russian Plays* (1960).—A. MACA.

Union of Soviet Socialist Republics. See RUSSIA.

United States: to 1914. American drama, like the people who created it, had its beginnings in Europe and gradually developed a character of its own. Its first models were the lofty tragedies and extravagant comedies popular in England in the latter half of the eighteenth century. But the history of American drama is the story of the movement toward realism intertwined with the movement toward independence; the development of realism and the Americanization of American drama went hand in hand.

The first impetus given to American drama was the struggle for political independence. The Revolutionary War provided a major American subject and introduced a popular American theme: the love of liberty and the hatred of tyrants. Some writers expressed this theme in awkward blank verse tragedies; others lampooned one side or the other in broad and sometimes scurrilous farces. Although the war provided subject matter for the young American theater, the development of American drama was hindered by the audiences' assumption that the only good plays were written in Europe. In addition to this unfavorable attitude toward their work, American playwrights also suffered from the fact that the performance rights to their work were not protected by a copyright law until 1865. Until that year, no system of royalty payments existed; the playwright sold his play outright to a manager or to a star actor for a fixed sum or for the proceeds of the third performance.

In 1787 the first noteworthy American comedy to be produced by professional actors was *The Contrast* by Royall TYLER. Although the play is modeled in form and style on the comedies of English playwright Richard B. Sheridan, Tyler's theme is the superiority of Americans to foreigners, and in the character Jonathan the play presents the first important native type, the rural Yankee. *The Contrast* became the prototype of American comedy for over fifty years. A younger contemporary of Tyler's was William DUNLAP, who was the first major American playwright, active from 1789 to 1828. In his play *André* (1798), Dunlap imitates the European form of blank verse and the neoclassic style, but his subject matter in this play is completely American; high-minded patriotism in an episode from the American Revolution. James Nelson BARKER also wrote several plays on American subjects, the most interesting of which is *Superstition* (1824), a romantic tragedy about persecution for witchcraft in early New England.

Although native writers of tragedy tended to look abroad for subject matter, they often found typically American themes in the history of other countries: for example, three tragedies by Robert Montgomery BIRD, *Pelopidas* (1830), THE GLADIATOR, and *Oral-*

loosa (1832), all dealing with the subject of revolt against tyranny.

An important native character, the Indian as hero, a noble savage resisting to the death the cruelty and duplicity of the white invaders, appeared in John Augustus Stone's *Metamora* (1829), a melodrama with an unhappy ending. Melodrama was first imitated from European models and then adapted to native materials, quickly becoming extremely popular on the American stage. Other popular native types at this time were the rural Yankee, depicted in crude comedies and farces, and the prototype of his frontier counterpart, Nimrod Wildfire, portrayed in James K. Paulding's farce *The Lion of the West* (1831). Out of the new proletariat in the East came the prototype of the urban cousin to rural Jonathan and western Wildfire—Mose the Bowery Boy and volunteer fire fighter who appeared in Benjamin Baker's *A Glance at New York* (1848). Native character types provided opportunities for actors to perform in a more realistic style. An outstanding example is Rip in RIP VAN WINKLE, which writer Dion BOUCICAULT and actor Joseph Jefferson put together from Washington Irving's story to create Jefferson's most popular acting vehicle.

JOSEPH JEFFERSON AS RIP IN DION BOUCICAULT'S *Rip Van Winkle* (MUSEUM OF THE CITY OF NEW YORK)

Romantic drama in verse is best represented by N. P. Willis' *Tortesa the Usurer* (1839) and romantic tragedy by G. H. Boker's FRANCESCA DA RIMINI. In prose comedy, Sheridan's great influence continued unabated. Mrs. Anna Cora Mowatt's FASHION, the most successful native comedy on the nineteenth-century American stage, is much like *The Contrast* in form and theme.

Other native themes were dramatized in melodramas, the most significant of which are the numerous dramatizations of UNCLE TOM'S CABIN. In these plays, which began to appear as soon as Mrs. Harriet Beecher Stowe's novel was published in 1852, the Negro was for the first time treated seriously, though sentimentally and melodramatically. The Civil War gave rise to a number of romantic melodramas that exploited the sentiment and suspense generated by divided loyalties. *Shenandoah* (1888), by Bronson HOWARD, is a good example of this genre. *The Reverend Griffith Davenport,* by James A. HERNE, which deals with the war's basic issues, did not appear until 1899.

The frontiersman as a hero and a symbol of the strength and endurance that had been pushing the nation's boundaries westward appeared in Frank Murdoch's *Davy Crockett* (1872). The Far West provided colorful settings for romantic melodramas such as *Horizon* (1871) by Augustin DALY and *The Girl of the Golden West* (1905) by David BELASCO. The Eastern American replaced the European as a symbol of decadence, and the Westerner became the symbol of American strength and vitality. In THE GREAT DIVIDE (1906) William Vaughn Moody expresses this contrast in a dramatic conflict between puritanism and individual liberty. The changing character of American cities is reflected in Edward Harrigan's artless comedies of lower-class New York life, written between 1879 and 1903. The materialism of growing America was exposed in Bronson Howard's comedy drama about Wall Street speculation, *The Henrietta* (1887), ridiculed in Benjamin Woolf's *The Mighty Dollar* (1875), and satirized in several plays by Charles HOYT.

Although most of the increased realism in American drama after 1850 was superficial, a few plays attempted to treat seriously problems of contemporary American life. The first of these, James A. Herne's *Margaret Fleming* (1890), deals untheatrically with the moral question of a husband's infidelity. William Vaughn Moody, in *The Great Divide* and more skillfully in THE FAITH HEALER, dramatized a basic conflict in American life between puritanism and the urge to self-fulfillment. Edward SHELDON, Henry JAMES, Augustus THOMAS, and Clyde FITCH attempted realistic problem plays in the manner of Ibsen. Fitch's later plays are essentially comedies of manners, but they contain serious elements. A successful union of the comedy of manners and the realistic problem play was achieved by Rachel CROTHERS in *The Three of Us* (1906).

A few playwrights, like John Luther Long (1861–1927), Josephine Preston Peabody (1874–1922), and Percy MACKAYE, remained outside the movement of realism. MacKaye, however, often used native materials. He initiated the outdoor dramatic spectacle which Paul Green later adapted to subjects from American history. MacKaye's *The Scarecrow*

(1909) uses colonial New England as the setting for romantic fantasy, and his *This Fine Pretty World* (1923), a dialect comedy set in the mountains of Kentucky, is an attempt at American folk drama in the spirit of Irish playwrights J. M. Synge and Lady Gregory.

PLAYBILL OF *Uncle Tom's Cabin* AT THE NATIONAL THEATRE, NEW YORK, 1853 (THEATRE COLLECTION, HARVARD UNIVERSITY)

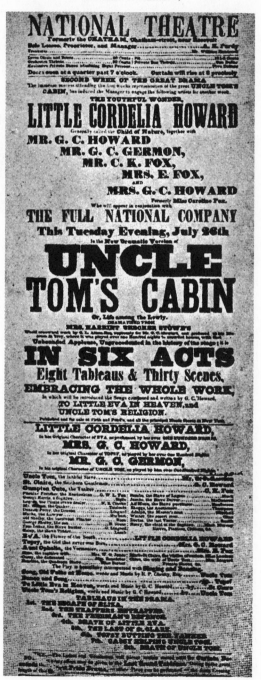

The plays of Long and Peabody, however, are exceptions to both the pervading Americanism and the prevailing realism of early twentieth-century American drama. In a century and a half American drama had changed from a style that sought to represent the ideal and the beautiful to a style that aimed to create an illusion of ordinary contemporary life. Americans were still influenced by European playwrights, particularly by the realistic writers, but the American playwrights made the techniques of Ibsen and Shaw their own, adapting them to native themes, settings, and characters. The best plays of Herne, Fitch, Moody, and Sheldon were received with respect abroad. All that was lacking for American drama to take its place on an equal footing with the drama of other Western countries was an American playwright of undeniable genius. The stage was set for the appearance of Eugene O'Neill.

The only comprehensive account of the early American drama is contained in Arthur Hobson Quinn's two volumes: *A History of the American Drama From the Beginning to the Civil War* (rev. ed., 1943) and *A History of the American Drama From the Civil War to the Present Day* (rev. ed., 1936). Brief accounts are to be found in Margaret Mayorga's *A Short History of the American Drama* (1932) and Walter J. Meserve's *An Outline History of American Drama* (1965). The principal collections of early American plays are Arthur Hobson Quinn's *Representative American Plays* (7th ed., 1957); M. J. Moses' *Representative Plays by American Dramatists* (3 vols.; 1918, 1920, 1925; A. G. Halline's *American Plays* (1935); and Richard Moody's *Dramas from the American Theatre 1762–1909* (1966).—B. H.

since 1914. Chief among American playwrights of the twentieth century is Eugene O'NEILL, whose long story is detailed elsewhere. Here we need only pay brief tribute to his contribution to American drama between his Provincetown days and the presentation of two parts (*A Touch of the Poet,* 1957, and *More Stately Mansions,* 1964) of his characteristically grandiose, and incomplete, eleven-play cycle *A Tale of Possessors Self-Dispossessed.* In a theater of social questions, O'Neill remained dedicated to exploring man's relationship, not primarily to his fellow man, but to God. In a business that worships success, he was often a magnificent failure; in one that basically fears novelty, he was, if anything, too insistent an innovator. He built a reputation in the twenties and sank from sight only to reappear in greater glory in the fifties. He remains America's most considerable dramatist so far.

O'Neill derided naturalism, distrusted "the banality of surfaces," and soon abandoned the conventional form of his first play, BEYOND THE HORIZON, for the expressionism of THE EMPEROR JONES and THE HAIRY APE and the symbolism of such plays as *Dynamo* (1929). Elemental passions raged in ANNA CHRISTIE and DESIRE UNDER THE ELMS, and O'Neill found in Strindberg (whom he thought the most modern of all moderns) the means to bring them vividly to view. THE GREAT GOD BROWN baffled audiences with its arty masks and most of the satire of *Marco Millions* (1928) eluded the public, but in MOURNING BECOMES ELECTRA O'Neill showed, fully realized, the intense power he had tested in *Lazarus Laughed* (1928) and in the multilevel, nine-act, stream-of-consciousness complexity of STRANGE INTERLUDE. *Mourning Becomes Electra* is a melodrama of malignant fate—in its theatricality it reminds us that O'Neill's father, James O'Neill, toured for years in *The Count of Monte Cristo*—but it amply demonstrates that if our current deterministic ideas of heredity and environment make true Greek tragedy impossible, a moving, modern psychological equivalent is attainable. O'Neill's somber theme, expressed continually in his work, he stated in his rather clumsy, greatly concerned, terribly earnest way as: "the death of an old God and the failure of science and materialism to give any satisfying new one for the surviving primitive religious instinct to find a meaning for life in, and to comfort its fears of death with."

O'Neill's variety is illustrated by the sunniness of his light comedy *Ah, Wilderness!* (1933) and the poignancy of one of his sincerest works ("He *had* to write it," his wife testified), *Long Day's Journey into Night,* a truly poetic "play of old sorrow," but his method remained single: emotion recollected without tranquility. ("I do not think you can write anything of value or understanding about the present.") His concern with social questions is evidenced in *All God's Chillun Got Wings* (1924), but he prefers to brood on the past, either very distant (*Lazarus Laughed* is set in the first century, *Marco Millions* in the thirteenth and fourteenth, *The Fountain* in the fifteenth and sixteenth) or somewhat distant (*A Touch of the Poet* is set in 1828, *Desire Under the Elms* in 1850, *Mourning Becomes Electra* in 1865–1866, and *Ah, Wilderness!* in 1906; *The Iceman Cometh* recalls his days at Jimmy the Priest's saloon in 1912). Even *Hughie,* a one-acter on his recurrent theme of man's alienation and dependence on "pipe dreams" written about 1941, is set in 1928; *A Moon for the Misbegotten,* written in 1943, is set twenty years earlier. Everything is left to steep in O'Neill's egocentric, romantic, brooding sensitivity. Everything is agonized first, set down later.

After the dismal failure of *Days Without End* (1934), O'Neill was silent for twelve years, but in 1946 THE ICEMAN COMETH, prolix but powerful, spoke once again of the illusions that make this bitter life endurable, though its full force was not to be felt until José Quintero's Circle in the Square revival in 1958. O'Neill declined in health after 1947 until he became, his doctor said, "a hull without a helm," but he has remained the Flying Dutchman of American drama, if not its pilot. The critics damned or ignored him, though he won several Pulitzer Prizes, but foreign appreciation impressed his countrymen. The Swedes built his reputation by awarding him the Nobel Prize (1936) and giving him posthumous premières (at The Royal Theatre, Stockholm) of *Long Day's Jour..ey into Night* (1955), *A Touch of the Poet* (1958), and *More Stately Mansions* (1962). At last the prophet gained honor in his own country.

From his early experimental one-act plays of the S. S. GLENCAIRN cycle (including *Bound East for Cardiff, In the Zone, The Long Voyage Home, The Moon of the Caribbees*) to the greatest expressions of his tragic spirit, O'Neill's dedication, scope, and achievement have remained as yet unequaled in American drama. Virginia Woolf said that the Elizabethans plunged into the sea of language and emerged dripping. O'Neill is sometimes waterlogged, but he rises from the sea like Proteus. There is grandeur if not grace in his ambitious work, and he is truly American in both his faults and his genius.

O'Neill was connected with George Pierce Baker's Workshop 47 at Harvard (1913) and its attempt to replace David Belasco and George M. Cohan with "adult dramatists." The Washington Square Players

(1915) in Greenwich Village led to the creation of The Theatre Guild (1918), which produced O'Neill on Broadway, while another group, the Provincetown Players, attracted O'Neill because of its high ideals and the talented men connected with it. After a year on a wharf on Cape Cod, the Provincetowners moved their insurgent stage to Greenwich Village in the winter of 1916/17 and there until the mid-twenties produced the experimental plays of O'Neill and the works of Edna St. Vincent Millay, Paul Green, Sherwood Anderson, Jasper Deeter, Kenneth Macgowan, and others.

After World War I the Theatre Guild made uptown successes of Ervine's *John Ferguson* (first produced in Dublin, 1915), *Beyond the Horizon,* Molnar's *Liliom* (1921), *Anna Christie,* Shaw's *Saint Joan* (1923), Anderson's *What Price Glory?* (1924), Howard's *They Knew What They Wanted* (1924), and even Shaw's massive *Back to Methuselah* (1923). Designer Robert Edmond Jones meanwhile showed at the Provincetown what he had learned from Max Reinhardt's productions in Europe. Gordon Craig's ideas reached Chicago with Maurice Browne and amateur and educational theater in the West with Sam Hume. Adolphe Appia's concept of space and design helped Lee Simonson, Joseph Urban, and Norman Bel Geddes to change not only professional but university experimental staging and by the use of wagon sets and projected scenery encouraged O'Neill and his successors to rely on lighting for mood effects and attempt greater freedom in dramaturgy. These foreign studies by Americans were bolstered by the impressive visits of great European directors (Jacques Copeau, Max Reinhardt) and troupes (the Abbey Players, the Moscow Art Theater). American artistic theater prospered. The Civic Repertory Theatre (Eva Le Gallienne) was formed in 1926, and in 1931 Harold Clurman, Cheryl Crawford, and Lee Strasberg brought Stanislavsky method to the aid of social agitation by founding an offshoot of the Theatre Guild, the Group Theatre. Playwrights Maxwell Anderson, George S. Kaufman, S. N. Behrman, Philip Barry, and Robert E. Sherwood came to the fore with varied gifts. The public was made socially conscious by Clifford ODETS in his AWAKE AND SING, even more in his *Waiting for Lefty* (1935), and by dramatic studies of the Scottsboro case (John Wexley's *They Shall Not Die,* 1934, and Langston Hughes's *Scottsboro Unlimited,* pub. 1932). At the same time society itself was put on trial in *The Case of Clyde Griffiths* (1926), Patrick Kearney's dramatization of Theodore Dreiser's great novel *An American Tragedy* (1925).

Expressionism's striking effects, introduced by Theatre Guild productions of Georg Kaiser, Karel Čapek, Ernst Toller, and Strindberg (as well as O'Neill), were commandeered for social protest. The public made Winchell Smith and Frank Bacon's character study *Lightnin'* (1918) and Anne Nichols' sentimental comedy *Abie's Irish Rose* (1922) the longest-running hits, but the leading playwrights were using the theater as a Shavian forum for ideas, or rather giving new meaning to Shaw's dictum: "All great Art and Literature is propaganda."

Elmer RICE used expressionism's stark settings, sparse dialogue, and two-dimensional characters for protesting satirically in *The Adding Machine* (1923)

and became even more forthright in *Street Scene* (1929) and *Judgment Day* (1934). Moss HART did better than Rice when freed by Freud; realism was expanded with the theme of psychoanalysis and the use of music added a new dimension in *Lady in the Dark* (1941). In the New Playwrights' Company John Howard Lawson (1895–) used expressionism for proletarian propaganda in *Roger Bloomer* (1923) and *Processional* (1925). George S. KAUFMAN and Marc CONNELLY used it in their comedy *Beggar on Horseback* (1924). This was a less heavy-handed work than Irwin Shaw's *Bury the Dead* (1936) or Marc Blitzstein's "opera" of decadent capitalism, *The Cradle Will Rock* (1937). Albert Maltz (1908–), fresh from the Yale Drama School, was typical of the period in the stridency of his collaborations with George Sklar (the political *Merry-Go-Round*, 1932, and the pacifist *Peace on Earth*, 1933) and his own *Black Pit* (1935) and *Private Hicks* (1936), about strikers. Even Mordecai Gorelik's dynamic realistic settings, symbolic of the whole action, spoke politically. The WPA (Works Progress Administration) operated an FTP (Federal Theatre Project) under Hallie Flanagan from 1936 to 1939 and produced more than twelve hundred plays, both classic revivals and such experimental "living newspaper" plays ("editor," Arthur Arent) as *Power* (1937) and ". . . *one third of a nation* . . ." (1938). At one time more than thirteen thousand were employed in the FTP's far-flung production units, and American theater reached out to a new public with exciting, contemporary, *agit-prop* attractions. The FTP, resembling the "flying squads" of Russia's Workers Theatre, was the first government-sponsored theater in the United States. The frank combination of theatricality and social conscience was echoed in Orson Welles's Mercury Theatre productions of Shakespeare's *Julius Caesar* (1937) and *Native Son* (1941) by Paul GREEN and even in Betty Comden-Adolph Green-Judy Holliday's "Revuers" skits and musical extravaganzas like Irving Berlin and Moss Hart's *As Thousands Cheer* (1933), Ryskind and Kaufman's *Of Thee I Sing* (1932), Kaufman and Hart's *I'd Rather Be Right* (1937), Kaufman and Dayton's *First Lady* (1935), Anderson's *Knickerbocker Holiday* (1938), and the shoestring success *Pins and Needles* (1936), by Arthur Arent, Marc Blitzstein, Harold Rome, and others. The stage was becoming a lecture platform, the theater a union hall.

Even the smash hit *Tobacco Road* (1933, adapted by Jack Kirkland and Erskine Caldwell from the latter's best-selling novel of 1932) was justified by social significance. But there were lighter, less brutal works: Rachel Crothers' clever *As Husbands Go* (1931); the urbane *Biography* (1932) and *No Time for Comedy* (1939) by S. N. BEHRMAN; George Kelly's *The Show Off* (1924) and deeper character study, *Craig's Wife* (1925); O'Neill's tender *Ah, Wilderness!* (1933); Ben Hecht and Charles MacArthur's breezy *The Front Page* (1928); Claire Booth's brightly bitchy *The Women* (1936); John L. Balderston's romantic *Berkeley Square* (1929); and Kaufman and Hart's zany *You Can't Take It With You* (1936) and *The Man Who Came to Dinner* (1939).

Robert SHERWOOD was symptomatic of the times. He wrote *The Road to Rome* (1927), debunking history; *The Queen's Husband* (1928), "a modest comedy" about a timid king; *Waterloo Bridge* (1930), a sentimental love story; and, he said, "some other knee-pants dramas nobody ever saw" before he arrived at the socially conscious melodrama *The Petrified Forest* (1935), the pacificist *Idiot's Delight* (1936), and the patriotic *Abe Lincoln in Illinois* (1938). But *Idiot's Delight* was shallow. Sherwood saw his limitations. "The trouble with me," he admitted, "is that I start off with a big message and end with nothing but good entertainment."

Yet in some ways Sherwood is more lasting than the deft, superficial portraits of the wealthy and the witless in the sophisticated comedies of manners by Philip BARRY—who began at the 47 Workshop with *You and I* (1923) and went on to the unconventional *Holiday* (1928), the mystical *Hotel Universe* (1930), the marriage play *The Animal Kingdom* (1932), and the drawing-room comedy of *The Philadelphia Story* (1939)—or the earlier Baker Workshop graduate Sidney HOWARD and his dated character studies like *The Silver Cord* (1926), *The Late Christopher Bean* (1932), and *Alien Corn* (1933). Today we are likely to remember not Paul Green's episodic *In Abraham's Bosom* (1926) or even Dorothy and Du Bose Heyward's superior *Porgy* (1927) but the charm of Marc Connelly's *The Green Pastures* (1930, based on Roark Bradford stories; we are apt to ignore the commitment of *Dead End* (1935) by Sidney KINGSLEY in favor of the excitement of *Detective Story* (1949).

Nonetheless, William SAROYAN would have done better had he had more purpose in writing about the poor than merely to amuse the rich. He refused the Pulitzer Prize for *The Time of Your Life* (1939) and repeated its fuzzy friendliness in *The Beautiful People* (1941).

Maxwell ANDERSON was long praised for his expansive, neo-Elizabethan verse dramas on historical subjects (*Elizabeth the Queen*, 1930; *Mary of Scotland*, 1933; *Joan of Lorraine*, 1947; *Anne of the Thousand Days*, 1948), but now it is clear that he needed what Galsworthy would call the "spire of meaning." There was evidence of such meaning in the social conscience of Anderson's very first play, *White Desert* (1923), a stark tragedy set in North Dakota. After the great popularity of his rather thin war play, *What Price Glory?* (1924)—written with Laurence Stallings (1894–1968)—Anderson grappled with the Sacco-Vanzetti case in *Gods of the Lightning* (written with Harold Hickerson, 1928) and again in his masterwork, *Winterset* (1935). It was in this verse tragedy and in *Lost in the Stars* (1948, a musical based on Alan Paton's novel *Cry, the Beloved Country*)—not in the vampire-cold reanimations of the Elizabethans—that he achieved theater poetry. Anderson's prose satire on Congress, *Both Your Houses* (1933), and satirical fantasy *High Tor* (1937) are both infinitely better than his highfalutin verse dramas insofar as the latter are written to impress, not express. American dramatists seem to require a few twigs of solid social fact to attach to before they can spin out of their poetic souls any fine artistic web. For every verse dramatist who succeeded here even occasionally, for every light-comedy writer of reliable skill, America had in the decade before the war a dozen social dramatists. In his article on American drama in the *Encyclopaedia Britannica*, John Gassner went so far as to assert that "in the writing of social drama Rice, Lawson, Kingsley, Odets, Hellman, and Miller were excelled only by the German playwright Bertolt Brecht." If, however, we are going to have to offer a name before the fifties to put beside that of Brecht, clearly the leading German dramatist of this century, it is probably that of Thornton WILDER. Wilder began with *The Trumpet Shall Sound* (1926) in one of the "little theaters" so important in the development of the American stage. He was a playwright even before his novel *The Bridge of San Luis Rey* catapulted him to fame (Pulitzer Prize, 1927). After some attractive one-acters, including the collection entitled *The Long Christmas Dinner* (pub. 1931), adaptations, and more novels, he returned to the drama in triumph with OUR TOWN, which has brought him more than half-a-million dollars in royalties and world-wide recognition. Now seemingly secure as an American classic, *Our Town* combines classic Chinese staging (the famous, obvious "no set") with simple everyday American life. Not the regional folk drama of the Carolina mountaineers such as we had in Lula Vollmer's *Sun-Up* or Hatcher Hughes's *Hell-Bent fer Heaven* or the Kentuckians of Percy MacKaye's *This Fine-Pretty World*—to mention only plays of 1923—*Our Town* is set in a larger world: "Grover's Corners; Sutton County; New Hampshire; United States of America . . . Continent of North America; Western Hemisphere; the Earth; the Solar System; the Universe; the Mind of God. . . ." Here is Gertrude Stein's observation on the generalizing tendency of Americans (in *The Geographical History of America,* 1936) with a vengeance! *Our Town* is a hymn of praise to ordinary American life written in

the notation of the heart. The unconventional devices intrude here even less than they do in the delightful though difficult comedy THE SKIN OF OUR TEETH, which was influenced by James Joyce. Wilder now has a project under way that involves fourteen short plays on the seven ages of man and the seven deadly sins, but nothing is likely to loom larger than the simple, sentimental grandeur of *Our Town.* "I came away from the theater," wrote Brooks Atkinson (influential drama critic for the *New York Times* from 1925 to 1960), "exalted by the bravery, kindliness, and goodness of American people. In the deepest sense of the word, *Our Town* is a religious play."

Those sterling qualities of the American people were about to be tried in the furnace of a second world war. The dramatists had dutifully warned the public of the impending danger, but once the war began, they seemed more equal to the task of fighting in it than of writing significantly about it. Broadway dimmed its lights and went to war, but chiefly with no more than Irving Berlin's revue *This Is the Army* (1942), benefits, and USO shows. American dramatists hardly noticed World War I; after it came the gay abandon of the Jazz Age. World War II impressed them largely by its melodrama. Comedy writers were slow to depict the war: it was not until 1948 that Thomas Heggen's novel *Mister Roberts* (1946) was adapted by Joshua Logan, and television writers are now producing World War II comedy. Satire was undistinguished, lacking the tough-mindedness of the John O'Hara-Richard Rodgers-Lorenz Hart musical *Pal Joey* (1940), for the plays of the period were often frivolous, catering to the tired businessman. Escapism demanded with Sabrina in Wilder's *The Skin of Our Teeth:* "Oh—why can't

SCENE FROM THORNTON WILDER'S *The Skin of Our Teeth* (MUSEUM OF THE CITY OF NEW YORK)

we have plays like we used to have, *Peg o' My Heart,* and *Smilin' Thru,* and *The Bat,* good entertainment with a message you can take home with you." The message of the multiple murders of Joseph Kesselring's *Arsenic and Old Lace* (1940) was not related to the mass murders of Hitlerism.

When wartime playwrights did offer a message, it was often as sloppy as that of Philip Barry's *Liberty Jones* (1941), the awkward allegory of a girl threatened by Three Shirts (Nazism, fascism, communism). Just before America entered the war Lillian HELL-MAN had tensely warned us about the Germans in *Watch on the Rhine* (1941), but she was really more at ease, not in the world of politics, but in the melodramatic world of *Another Part of the Forest* (1946), a return to the scene of her best work, *The Little Foxes* (1939), and *Autumn Garden* (1951).

Miss Hellman, especially in the reappraisal of prewar foreign policy in *The Searching Wind* (1944), rejected easy optimism, but more attuned to the public mood was Wilder's upbeat play "all about the troubles of the human race," *The Skin of Our Teeth* (1942). Dealing with two times at once (influenced by Joyce's *Finnegans Wake*), it so combined bafflement and vaudeville that the public hardly heard its popular message: the reaffirmation of the indomitable spirit of man. People turned instead to the pseudo seriousness of *Home of the Brave, All My Sons,* and *Oklahoma!*

Before Arthur Laurents wrote the book for the musical *West Side Story* (1957) he gave us *Home of the Brave* (1946), a trite play in which Coney examines the causes of his trouble (here sensitivity and anti-Semitism) to discover something he has not been facing up to. Also firmly rooted in cliché was Arthur Miller's *All My Sons* (1947), in which Joe Keller confronts those old favorites The Bitch Goddess (Success), The American Dream (Flawed), and Self-Interest versus Social Responsibility. Basically these plays were less serious and less sound than Jon Patrick [Goggan]'s sentimental *The Hasty Heart* (1945) and lively *The Tea-House of the August Moon* (1953), Mary Chase's whimsical *Harvey* (1944), Garson Kanin's farcical *Born Yesterday* (1946), and Howard Lindsay and Russel Crouse's warm *Life with Father* (1939) and topical *State of the Union* (1945).

While Broadway was worrying about an alcoholic's marriage in Odets' *The Country Girl* (1950), Off-Broadway there was a revival of interest. The Off-Broadway theater, which found new vigor in the fifties, had already made significant theatrical history. It dates back at least as far as the radical Progressive Stage Society (1905) and was given impetus in the twenties by the Provincetown Playhouse and in the thirites by the "little theater" movement and such dedicated groups as the Theatre of Action and the Cherry Lane Theatre. A renaissance after World War II led to increased activity and the founding of an Off-Broadway Theatre League. As the fifties wore on, soaring prices and the competition of movies and television began to kill off, not only dreary vanity productions, but even sincere experimental theater in New York. John Latouche and Jerome Moross in the Phoenix Theatre's 1954/55 season gave Off-Broadway a dazzling musical, *Golden Apple,* which eventually went uptown and has been revived as a classic. Musicals as different as Tom Jones and Har-

vey Schmidt's *The Fantasticks* (1960) and Brecht's *The Threepenny Opera* (New York, 1955) have run for years in Greenwich Village, but of new and exciting "straight" plays there have been too few, despite the efforts of Jerry Tallmer and other critics of the *Village Voice,* Ted Mann and José Quintero of the Greenwich Village theater Circle in the Square, teachers like Gene Frankel and Uta Hagen, producer-provocateurs like Judith Malina and Julian Beck (of the Living Theatre), Al Carmines and his pop colleagues at Judson Church, Ellen Stewart of La Mama (which first produced Jean-Claude van Itallie's mordant hit *America Hurrah* in 1966), and the late Joe Cino of the defunct Caffe Cino (which for eight years presented dramatists as different as the poetic Lanford Wilson and the prolific Tom Eyen). Uptown at Jan Hus auditorium or the new Phoenix, downtown at Theatre de Lys or the coffeeshops and cellars, there have been new plays and "way-out" happenings. Most recently interesting experiments have involved dance, mixed media and electro-media, space/time and drama/mime combinations, action theater and kinetic environments, and even *son et lumière* effects with strobe lights and din (described as acoustic space conditioning). The public has been generally baffled or (by the brutal Le Roi Jones, for example) incensed. The philistines have shuttered the Caffe Cino, forced La Mama to pose as an "experimental Theater Club" collecting "dues" instead of admission charges. Many little groups survive on "donations" and live in fear of licensing regulations in neighborhoods where tourists think them quaint but residents find them undesirable. It would be neither unjust nor surprising if all the bright, original spirits fled the experimental theater for the experimental cinema.

In the late forties and the fifties, Broadway itself had some excitement. Eric Bentley points out that the fad of Broadway's almost inevitable single set switched from the porch-and-surroundings (*All My Sons, Picnic*) to the "interior-and-exterior-combined." The drama also turned to both interior (psychological) and exterior (social) interests; and the sets actually reflected the desire to fuse symbolism and realism, past, present, and future. Americans attracted world-wide interest with expressionistic social melodrama (billed as "modern tragedy") in Miller's DEATH OF A SALESMAN and the more evocative, fragile power of Williams' THE GLASS MENAGERIE.

In *Death of a Salesman* Arthur MILLER wrote a moving Marxist tract on false American values and the failure of materialism. Tennessee Williams emerged as the most authentic poet of the theater since O'Neill in *The Glass Menagerie,* that early study of his favorite theme—how a callous world wounds, even mutilates the sensitive soul. Williams went on to develop his theme in the masterpiece A STREETCAR NAMED DESIRE, while Miller only managed to "soothe the bad conscience of a generation" (Bentley) with the well-crafted THE CRUCIBLE. A connection with ex-communist Elia Kazan gave to *The Crucible* added interest for some, as did Miller's marriage to Marilyn Monroe to *After the Fall* (1964), but longshoreman Eddie Carbone in Miller's *A View from the Bridge* (1955) is his greatest claim to interest in the documentation of guilt and recrimination.

Eddie, like Willy Loman in *Salesman,* is a "little man," and like all of Miller's protagonists distressingly inarticulate in moments of stress, but he has a certain Greek grandeur. Attention must be paid to such a playwright, even if *Incident at Vichy* (1965) and *The Price* (1968) deserve little.

But Tennessee WILLIAMS achieved sympathy as well as significance. By the mid-fifties Elmer Rice was able to write: "The recurrent themes of our plays are loneliness, rebellion against parental authority, incest-longings, emotional starvation, escape mechanisms, juvenile delinquency, crimes of violence, homosexuality, terror fantasies, sadism, and schizophrenia." Williams' characters, diseased and perverted, had conquered the stage. Williams established himself as an unequaled though uneven artist in his time, able to experiment and to learn from such diverse failures as *Battle of Angels* (1940), *Camino Real* (1953), *The Milk Train Doesn't Stop Here Any More* (1963), and *Slapstick Tragedy* (1966) as well as to create sensational successes. After a four-year wait for a full-length play, Williams recently wrote *The Seven Descents of Myrtle* (1968), proving his powers have not waned. "I can't handle people in ordinary situations," he admits, but it may be that the poster-sized art of the drama demands no such talent. Certainly he has many others.

Resembling at least in vividness the faded South of Williams is the bleak Midwest of William INGE. Author of *Picnic* (1953), *Bus Stop* (1955), and the fine *Come Back, Little Sheba* (1950), Inge long specialized in the plodding first act and a second act that exploded to leave the characters sadder but wiser. He far exceeded formula in his depth study of loneliness in a family, *Dark at the Top of the Stairs* (1957), establishing that "the overall pattern and texture of a play" are quintessential, not the plot "pay-off." Inge has gone on to *A Loss of Roses* (1960) and promises further achievement.

Many plays of the lively fifties were misjudged. George Axelrod's comedy *The Seven Year Itch* (1952) was more profound than many a more sober effort. Robert Anderson's evasive *Tea and Sympathy* (1953) was not the best first play on Broadway in the decade; that was probably Lorraine Hansberry's compassionate *A Raisin in the Sun* (1959). *The Connection* (1959) by Jack GELBER proved more ephemeral than Michael Gazzo's *A Hatful of Rain* (1955). Carson McCullers' *Member of the Wedding* (novel of 1946 dramatized in 1950) was far better than Archibald MacLeish's *J.B.* (1958), an allegorical play that was awarded the Pulitzer Prize and touted as a great work of the century. Very significant was *The Zoo Story* by Edward ALBEE, first presented at the Schiller Theater Werkstatt (Berlin, 1959) and then Off-Broadway at the Provincetown Playhouse (1960).

By 1964 Albee was a center of controversy, capable of eliciting diatribes like this from Tom F. Driver in *The Reporter:* "Four of Edward Albee's six bad plays are too short to fill an evening. Another is a dead adaptation of a famous story. The sixth is the most pretentious American play since *Mourning Becomes Electra."* WHO'S AFRAID OF VIRGINIA WOOLF was refused a Pulitzer Prize (Albee eventually received what he called that "honor in decline" for a lesser work) but *Virginia Woolf* makes up for boring

SCENE FROM TENNESSEE WILLIAMS' *A Streetcar Named Desire* (ANTA COLLECTION, WALTER HAMPDEN MEMORIAL LIBRARY AT THE PLAYERS, NEW YORK)

SCENE FROM EDWARD ALBEE'S *Who's Afraid of Virginia Woolf?* (MUSEUM OF THE CITY OF NEW YORK)

adaptations like *Malcolm* (1966) and even the basic fraud of *Tiny Alice* (1965). Mr. Albee is the current talent to watch. He has the earnestness of O'Neill with a little more articulateness; the Ibsenite craftsmanship of Hellman and Miller may be lacking— though *The Sandbox* (1961) is beautifully built— but the Strindbergian emotional intensity is there. With a little less reliance on Continental influences than O'Neill (who wanted to create "literature here") and a trifle less reliance on his own tensions than Williams (who says he uses art for therapy), Albee may surpass both in time, though the American drama still awaits the fiery revolt against the established theater which in Britain in the fifties brought aggressive and significant new writers to the stage.

Where is Broadway's renaissance? Too often blighted by boring old "stars" or instant "personalities," jaded audiences, ridiculous prices, avaricious unions, intellectual aenemia, and huge financial risks, Broadway is still merely "show biz." Television frequently displays the vitality of adolescence and the films are developing maturity, but on Broadway nobody wants a play, only a *hit.* Producers, who claim that though they may not know art they at least understand business, lose money more often than not. The critics have too much power, considering the nature of their task and their training. The playwright most often has not even the power to get his name on the marquee. Each season sees fewer good plays; in fact, each season sees fewer plays. (In 1927/28 there were 270 productions on Broadway.) In the twenties the strength of O'Neill's innovations and the very American smartness of sophisticated comedy lit "the great white way." In the thirties the Depression lent distinction to the voices of Hellman and Odets and others who, though not for all time, were for their age. America developed its deterministic tragedy, not humanistic but humanitarian. The forties started badly and the war produced no great play but in time there emerged such diverse talents as those of Saroyan and Wilder. Later Miller and Williams and Inge moved from bright promise to solid achievement. Most recently the sky has been lit by the fitful light of Albee and others. (See Jack RICHARDSON.)

Now, despite British imports, Broadway still offers some market for new American plays. A few dramatists are encouraged by such agencies as ANTA (American National Theatre and Academy) and IASTA (Institute for Advanced Studies in Theater Arts), but playwrights need audiences and the commercial theater's acid test. There are too few new plays seen in repertory companies like APA (Association of Producing Artists) or ACT (American Conservatory Theater) and almost none in struggling community theaters, commercial summer stock, or even subsidized city centers. Even ambitious new ventures like Lincoln Center cannot cope with new plays. Some new voices are heard in summer festivals, though these rely on Shakespeare chiefly. Off-Broadway and occasional campus productions offer the beginning playwright some hope.

The traditional American answer to everything has been money. Perhaps federal, state, and local subsidies may help the drama—if money can indeed be spared in the face of the urgent need for extensive and expensive repairs in the very fabric of American society. Perhaps the problems themselves will attract vigorous young voices to the mass communication outlet of the theater. If the ways of life that traditional drama has reflected, enlightened, and inspired can continue to exist, and if viable and encouraging theatrical conditions can be created, it is not to be thought that these United States, which have produced the passionate sincerity of Eugene O'Neill and the compassionate theater poetry of Tennessee Williams, will lack deserving talents ready to come forward to add luster to the long and varied tradition of American drama.

The annual lists of the Copyright Office (Washington, since 1870), the annual *Dramatic Index* (since 1910), and Blanche M. Baker's *Dramatic Bibliography* (1933, repr. 1967) are useful bibliographic tools. Arthur H. Quinn's *History of the American Drama from the Civil War to the Present Day* (rev. 1936) in two vols. must be supplemented by Glenn Hughes's *A History of the American Theatre, 1700–1950* (1951); John Gassner's *The Theatre in Our Times* (1954) and *Theatre at the Crossroads* (1960); Eric Bentley's *The Dramatic Event: An American Chronicle* (1954); Alan S. Downer's *Fifty Years of American Drama, 1900–1950* (1957) and *Recent American Drama* (1960); Joseph Wood Krutch's *The American Drama since 1918* (rev. 1957) and *"Modernism" in Modern Drama* (1953, repr. 1963); Barnard Hewitt's *Theatre, U.S.A., 1668–1957* (1959); and George Freedley and James Reeves's *History of the Theatre* (rev. 1968). Criticism is conveniently collected in Montrose J. Moses and John Mason Brown, *The American Theatre as Seen by Its Critics, 1752–1934* (1934), and Alan S. Downer, *American Drama and Its Critics* (1965), although students may wish to consult the drama criticism of Stark Young, George Jean Nathan, Brooks Atkinson, Mary McCarthy, Walter Kerr, John Simon, and others. Americans are well represented in anthologies by Toby Cole, *Playwrights on Playwriting* (1960) and *Directors on Directing* (with Helen Kritch Chinoy, rev. 1963), and Horst Frenz, *American Playwrights on Drama* (1965). Important studies include Helen Deutsch and Stella Hanau, *The Provincetown* (1931); Eleanor Flexner, *American Playwrights, 1918–1938* (1938); Burns Mantle, *Contemporary American Playwrights* (1938); John G. Hartman, *The Development of American Social Comedy* (1939); Clarence J. Whittler, *Some Social Trends in WPA Drama* (1939); Hallie Flanagan [Davis], *Arena: The Story of the Federal Theatre* (1940); Douglas Gilbert, *American Vaudeville* (1940); Cecil Smith, *Musical Comedy in America* (1950); Margo Jones, *Theatre-in-the-Round* (1951, repr. 1965); Harold Clurman, *The Fervent Years* (rev. 1957); Elmer Rice, *The Living Theatre* (1959); and Julia S. Price, The *Off-Broadway Theatre* (1962).

Significant collections of plays include Burns Mantle and Garrison P. Sherwood, eds., *The Best Plays of 1919–1920* to *1923–1924* (annually, 1920–1924); *The Best Plays of 1909–1919* (1933); the one-act plays in Barrett H. Clark and Kenyon Nicholson's *The American Scene* (1930), Margaret Mayorga's *One-Act Plays by American Authors* (1937), and Bennett Cerf and Van H. Cartmell's *Thirty Famous One-Act Plays* (1943); Frank Shay's *The Provincetown Plays* (1916) in three vols.; George Pierce Baker's four-volume *Plays of the 47 Workshop* [Harvard] (1918–1925); *The Theatre Guild Anthology* (1936); William Kozlenko's *The Best Short Plays of the Social Theatre* (1939); Pierre De Rohan's *Federal Theatre Plays* (1938) in two vols.; Vol. II of John Gassner's *A Treasury of the Theatre* (1951) and his *Library of Best American Plays* (1939–1961) in six vols.; Arthur H. Quinn's *Representative American Plays* (7th ed., 1953); Jack Gaver's *Critics' Choice: New York Drama Critics' Circle Prize Plays, 1933–1955* (1955); and Robert Warnock's *Representative Modern Plays: American* (1952). See also the collected works of Eugene O'Neill, Arthur Miller, Tennessee Williams, and others.—L. R. N. A.

University Wits. See ENGLAND: *Elizabethan drama.*

Unruh, Fritz von. See GERMANY: *twentieth century.*

U Pok Ni. See BURMA.

U Pon Nya. See BURMA.

Upper Volta. See AFRICA: *Upper Volta.*

Urdu drama. See PAKISTAN: *Urdu drama.*

Uruguay. See SPANISH AMERICA.

Usigli, Rodolfo (1905–   ). Mexican playwright. Although he has written poetry and a novel, Usigli's fame is due to his dramas. For many years his uncompromising insistence on artistic integrity and his caustic attacks on what he considered weaknesses of the Mexican character prevented popular or critical acceptance of his work and precluded his receiving any of the remunerative public or private posts that often are awarded to distinguished writers. Happily, this situation has changed, and he has served in the diplomatic corps for some time; presently he is ambassador to Norway.

Usigli's work reveals a spirit akin to George Bernard Shaw, and they were mutual admirers. His plays are often accompanied by long essays that develop the ideas of the plays themselves. They do not need this apparatus for success in the theater; Usigli is one of Mexico's finest technical innovators and an astute student of psychology. His greatest commercial successes have been psychopathological studies; their popularity has forced production and acceptance of his other works.

Among his many plays, a number of which are sharply critical of the middle class, his two most important are *Corona de sombra* (*Crown of Shadows,* 1947) and *El gesticulador* (1947; seen on American television as *The Gesticulator*). In *Corona de sombra* Usigli uses an ingenious split stage to contrast the empire of Maximilian at its height with a supposed return to sanity of his mad empress sixty years later. In addition to his skillful technique, Usigli presents a provocative and polemical vision of the role of the fleeting empire in Mexican history. *El gesticulador* is a realistic attack on the corruption of the ideals of the revolution of 1910; although denounced as antirevolutionary, it is now widely accepted as Usigli's best play and as a penetrating insight into the Mexican character.

Usigli's complete plays are now available in his *Teatro completo* (2 vols., 1963–1966). *Crown of Shadows* (1946) has been translated by William F. Stirling. There are no major lengthy critical studies; good introductions to two major aspects of his work are Eunice Gates's "Usigli as Seen in His Prefaces and Epilogues," *Hispania* (December 1954), and Vera Beck's "La fuerza motriz en la obra dramática de Rodolfo Usigli," *Rev. Iberoamericana* (September 1953).—F. D.

U Su Tha.   See BURMA.

V

Vanbrugh, Sir John (1664–1726). English comic dramatist and architect. Vanbrugh was the son of a London tradesman whose father had emigrated to England from the Netherlands. Little is known of his life before 1690, when he was arrested while traveling in France, then at war with England. Suspected of being a spy, he was imprisoned and, though not badly treated, was not released for eighteen months. After seeing Colley Cibber's *Love's Last Shift* in London in 1696, he wrote his sequel, THE RELAPSE, in six weeks, according to the Prologue. Thus began the first of his careers. Three years later he began his second by submitting a fashionable Palladian design for Castle Howard in Yorkshire. In 1705 he was entrusted with the design of the duke of Marlborough's stupendous Blenheim Palace. Among other buildings he designed was the Queen's Theatre in the Haymarket, of which he shared the management for a time with William Congreve. He was knighted by George I in 1714.

SIR JOHN VANBRUGH (BRANDER MATTHEWS DRAMATIC MUSEUM, COLUMBIA UNIVERSITY)

Of his several comedies the best are *The Relapse* and *The Provoked Wife* (1697), distinguished by witty dialogue and many farcical situations. Though these plays were not so licentious as some that had appeared, they earned Vanbrugh the wrath of Jeremy Collier (see ENGLAND: *Restoration drama*), against whom he defended himself with only moderate success. In his last years he stopped writing for the theater, but despite the smallness of his output, he remains one of the outstanding comic dramatists of the Restoration.

The best edition is Bonamy Dobrée's *The Complete Works of Sir John Vanbrugh* (1927–1928). For information about Vanbrugh's varied activities see Laurence Whistler, *Sir John Vanbrugh, Architect & Dramatist 1664–1726* (1939).—E. W.

Vauthier, Jean (1910–). French playwright. The verbal abundance and the vehement action and sentiment of Vauthier's plays are associated more with the dramatic art of Michel de Ghelderode and Jacques Audiberti than with the playwrights of the 1950's, yet Vauthier first attracted attention during the fifties. *Capitaine Bada* (1952) is, on the surface, the story of a clown-like struggle between the writer Bada and his wife, Alice. But it is in reality a struggle waged by Bada against his other self as it is caught in the rage and violence of the literature he is composing. In the first act Alice pursues Bada, who, after refusing to make love, finally gives in. In the second act, when the two are married, everything is reversed: Alice refuses to be loved. The third act shows the couple in their old age, and Bada, in the midst of his manuscripts, is tired of trying to put into poetry the various stages of the endless struggle between himself and his wife.

In 1956 at the Petit Marigny director Jean Louis Barrault put on Vauthier's *Le Personnage combattant* ("The Fighting Personage"), a drama for one character, played by Barrault. The text of the monologue, which filled the evening, is about the suffering of man and specifically the suffering of the writer as he faces his destiny. In a sense, the play is a recapitulation of *Capitaine Bada,* of the writer who has now become famous. He is sickened by his official success and struggles throughout the night to transform and redeem himself. Barrault played the part as if he were both a bull and a bullfighter.

In October 1965 Vauthier gave the continuation of *Capitaine Bada* in a play called *Badadesque,* where the marital struggle is resumed after death.

Vauthier has studded the texts of his plays with detailed directions that clearly indicate his conception of a play as a kind of musical concerto or dance organized in accordance with a visual and auditory rhythm. He writes, for example, that the role of Bada in the second act is that of an actor-dancer.—W. F.

Vega [Carpio], Lope [Félix] de (1562–1635). Spanish playwright, poet, and novelist. Lope de Vega (usually referred to by his first name) studied with the Jesuits in his native Madrid and at the nearby university at Alcalá de Henares. In 1583 he joined a two-month naval expedition to the Azores. On his return he fell in love with Elena Osorio, to the distress not so much of her husband as of her family, who vigorously opposed the affair. When in 1588 they denounced him to the authorities, he was arrested and sentenced to eight years of exile from the capital. He immediately broke the terms of his punishment by returning to Madrid to abduct and marry a gentlewoman, Isabel de Urbina. A few days after the marriage he enlisted in the Invincible Armada. Returning from the Armada disaster in 1589, he set up house with Isabel in Valencia in compliance with the terms of his exile. In 1595 his wife died. Pardoned by Elena's family, he returned to Madrid and developed another great passion—for an actor's wife, Micaela de Luján. He lived with her in Toledo and Seville, even after 1598, when he married Juana de Guardo, the daughter of a rich butcher. In 1610 Lope returned for good to Madrid with Micaela. When Juana died in 1613, Lope was already having another affair, with the actress Jerónima de Burgos. In an attempt to bring some order into his disorderly life, Lope had himself ordained a priest in 1614. By 1618, however, he had met Marta de Nevares, a businessman's wife. A cultivated woman who shared Lope's interest in the arts, she was to be the great love of his life. Their initial happiness, however, was an illusion, because even when Marta's husband died, in 1620, the lovers could not marry because of Lope's vow of celibacy.

LOPE DE VEGA (BIBLIOTHÈQUE NATIONALE, PARIS)

During this undisciplined life Lope wrote prolifically in all genres. His biographer Montalbán credits him with some 2,000 plays, but fewer than 500 survive. The disappearance of many is understandable in view of the chaotic way in which they were published. Booksellers and other interested persons edited and published them either in pamphlets (*sueltas*) containing a single play or in volumes entitled *Partes,* each containing a dozen plays. The texts, often taken from actors' or directors' manuscripts, tended not only to be incorrect but even to be attributed erroneously to Lope. In 1617 the ninth of the *Partes* appeared, for the first time under Lope's supervision. He continued to correct these editions until the twentieth *Parte* appeared in 1625, when, for some unknown reason, he abandoned the practice.

Lope wrote his numerous serious plays on religious, mythological, pastoral, historical, and fictional subjects; in addition he wrote many light comedies, *comedias de capa y espada* ("cloak-and-sword plays"), as well as *autos sacramentales* ("sacramental acts"). A certain number of his plays acquired great popularity and have been repeatedly published from the seventeenth century to the present. These few are naturally the best known of his works. The sheer quantity made Lope's *omnia opera* hard to handle and discuss critically. The greatest difficulty was the lack of a trustworthy chronology. A few authenticated and dated autograph manuscripts exist, and a few dates have been established on the basis of internal evidence. In 1940 the problem was largely solved by S. G. Morley and Courtney Bruerton, who published in that year *The Chronology of Lope de Vega's "Comedias,"* a monumental piece of scholarship. Suspecting that Lope varied the different poetic meters in a single play according to unconscious preferences at given moments of his life, Morley and Bruerton analyzed the verse structure of the dated plays and extrapolated their findings to the undated ones. They were able to assign each of the extant plays to a fairly narrow stretch of time. The subsequent discovery of dated autographs has confirmed the validity of their findings. As a result, research into Lope's drama can now proceed on a firmer footing.

Based on this metrical evidence, the composition of *El perro del hortelano* (*The Dog in the Manger*) is assigned to the short period between 1613 and 1615. In this good example of the comedy of manners, the comedia de capa y espada, a Neapolitan countess falls in love with her secretary, who is loved also by a maid in her household. Unable to demean herself by marrying beneath her station, the countess behaves like the proverbial dog in the manger, neither accepting him as her lover nor allowing the maid to have him. A deception engineered by the valet persuades everyone that the secretary is the long-lost son of a rich nobleman; the marriage is no longer blocked by social distinctions. In this work Lope has achieved more than a highly contrived happy ending. He has created a fiction in the "real life" of the stage and then converted this fiction into "real life." The deception may be the truth: the secretary may indeed be of noble blood, but the countess and her betrothed will never know for sure. What matters is that the alleged father of the secretary and the society of

Naples *believe* in the secretary's nobility. Truth has been created by the magic of the valet's art.

Lope's most famous plays deal with the efforts of the peasantry to right the wrongs inflicted on them by some perverse member of the nobility. Living in pastoral bliss, the peasants' idyllic world is shaken when their overlord casts lustful eyes on one or more of the young women of the village. When a village girl is raped (or threatened with rape), the honor of the village is ruined, but no machinery exists to remedy the dishonor. Whereas a hidalgo in these circumstances might kill his affronter with impunity, it is inconceivable that the peasants should lay hands on their overlord. Lope explores several solutions to the apparent impasse. In *Peribáñez* (written 1605–1608) the villainous comendador (who has an *encomienda,* or sacred "trust," to defend the interests of his villagers) attempts unsuccessfully to seduce the new bride of the peasant Peribáñez. To further his plan he has just raised Peribáñez to the status of a hidalgo in order to send him away from the village as the captain of a company of peasant soldiers. Peribáñez has been honored so that he may be dishonored. In *Fuenteovejuna* (written c. 1612) another rebellious comendador rapes several peasant women. In *El mejor alcalde el rey* ("The King's the Best Magistrate," written 1620–1623) a Galician baron kidnaps, imprisons, and violates the bride of the rustic hero on the eve of their wedding. In these three plays the steps taken by the villagers to remedy their dishonorable situation reveal a progression in Lope's thinking about the practice of justice. Peribáñez, relying on his new status as a gentleman, kills the overlord who tried to dishonor him and successfully claims immunity from legal penalties on the ground that they are equals in the sight of the law. The villagers of Fuenteovejuna, moved by their love for one another, kill the comendador in a rebellion. Sustained by their mutual love, they refuse under torture to reveal the name of the actual killer. Unable to execute a single murderer, the king perforce pardons the village and takes it under his immediate rule. The wronged hero of *El mejor alcalde el rey* appeals to the king for justice. The king, attentive to the needs of the lowest of his subjects, rides hundreds of miles to enforce the law in a spectacular way: he orders the baron to marry the girl he has wronged, forthwith has him beheaded, and marries the girl to her betrothed. This appeal to the source of all law, the king, would seem to be for Lope the ideal solution to the problem that concerned him.

Another play about rustics is quite different. *El villano en su rincón* ("The Peasant in His Nook," written 1611–1615) presents a countryman with the symbolic name of Juan Labrador ("John Farmer") who maintains a sturdy independence as "king" of his neck of the woods, a village near Paris. Rich and loyal to his sovereign, he nevertheless refuses to go to the city to see the king lest his innocence be corrupted by the life at court. His sterling qualities as the most perfect of subjects attract the interest of the king. Juan must learn the painful lesson that it is not enough to respect the king from afar; he must achieve an even greater perfection by loving the king as he serves his daily needs.

The play that has attracted the most critical attention in recent years is the tragedy *El caballero de Olmedo (The Knight from Olmedo,* probably written 1620–1625). Don Alonso, a fifteenth-century knight, falls in love at first sight with Doña Inés, who has been betrothed by her father to Don Rodrigo. When Alonso is making one of his regular trips from Inés' town of Medina to his own home town of Olmedo, he is treacherously murdered by the jealous and villainous Rodrigo. The play, based on several folk songs, is marvelously poetic. Alonso is repeatedly warned of his fate by symbolic dreams, by a peasant's singing of his death, and by the appearance of his own ghost. The tragedy lies in a transposition to dramatic form of the common poetic metaphor that to love is to die.

The secret of Lope's drama lies in its poetry. He was not, like Calderón, an intellectual, dedicated to ideas. Instead, Lope used all of the resources at his command to represent his peculiar poetic vision of the world in which he lived. To read his plays properly, one must be sensitive to the interplay of poetic themes. His best dramas are as dense as sonnets.

The best English translations, unfortunately in prose, are by Jill Booty in Lope de Vega, *Five Plays* (1961).

The standard biography, H. A. Rennert's *The Life of Lope de Vega* (1904), is much amplified and corrected in the Spanish edition: H. A. Rennert and Américo Castro, *Vida de Lope de Vega* (1919).

The best introduction to Lope criticism is R. D. F. Pring-Mill's excellent Introduction to Jill Booty's translations. B. W. Wardropper, "On the Fourth Centenary of Lope de Vega's Birth," *Drama Survey,* II (1962), reviews the present state of Lope studies. A. Zamora Vicente's *Lope de Vega* (1961), a useful popular handbook, is now available in English (1968). Further help in locating critical studies may be obtained from the commendable cooperative survey, edited by J. A. Parker and A. M. Fox, *Lope de Vega Studies (1937–1962): A Critical Survey and Annotated Bibliography* (1964).—B. W.

Venexiana, La (The Venexiana, first half of sixteenth century). An anonymous Italian comedy. The protagonist is Julio, a youth who, newly arrived in Venice, falls in love with a young married woman, Valeria. At the same time he inspires a violent passion in Angela, an elderly but vigorous widow who takes him to her house and after a night of love presents him with a golden chain. Julio subsequently obtains an interview with Valeria, but she, recognizing the golden chain of her rival, indignantly dismisses him. Julio starts to return to Angela, but Valeria repents and sends for him. Thus fought over by the two women, Julio finally cancels his rendezvous with Angela and goes instead to the house of the youthful Valeria, who, before taking him into her room, arranges with the maid that she not be disturbed by anyone, especially her husband.

Discovered by E. Lovarini in a Venetian codex and published in 1928, *La Venexiana* has been attributed to the learned and lettered Girolamo Fracastoro of Verona (1478–1553), but this attribution is far from proved. Written in five acts, the play employs the Italian language for Julio, Venetian dialect for the women, and Bergamesque dialect for a flunky in the service of Angela. It is therefore the work of some cultivated and lettered man. It stands apart from the literary and erudite comedy of its time,

Venice Preſerv'd,

O R,

A Plot Diſcover'd.

A

TRAGEDY.

As it is Acted at the

D V K E 'S T H E A T R

Written by *THOMAS OTWAY.*

L O N D O N,

Printed for *Joſ. Hindmarſh* at the Sign of the
Black Bull, over againſt the Royal
Exchange in *Cornbill.* 1682.

TITLE PAGE OF THE 1682 EDITION OF THOMAS OT-
WAY'S *Venice Preserved*

however, in its complete liberty of form, its substantial lack of intrigue, and its brusque and inconclusive
ending. The characters are marvelously delineated,
and the extremely vivacious dialogue is uncommonly
bold, even for the sixteenth century.—L. L.

Venezuela. See SPANISH AMERICA.

Venice Preserved (1682). A tragedy in blank
verse by Thomas OTWAY. *Venice Preserved, or A
Plot Discovered* was first performed early in the year
by the Duke's Company at the Dorset Garden Theatre.

Jaffeir, a brave Venetian, has incurred the wrath of
a senator, Priuli, by secretly marrying his daughter
Belvidera. Cruelly treated by his father-in-law, Jaffeir is the more easily persuaded by his friend Pierre
to believe that the government is corrupt and to enter
into a conspiracy against it. He is soon disillusioned,
however, when Renault, the leader of the conspiracy,
attempts to rape Belvidera. She induces Jaffeir to reveal the conspiracy to her and convinces him that it
is his duty to inform the Senate. This he does after
obtaining a promise that the lives of the conspirators
will be saved. When the promise is broken, Jaffeir is
overwhelmed with remorse, while Belvidera goes

mad. Forgiven by Pierre for having betrayed him,
Jaffeir kills his friend to save him from torture and
then kills himself. The notorious "Nicky Nacky"
scenes portray the courtesan Aquilina catering to the
masochistic wishes of a senator, Antonio.

In its day the success of the play was greatly
heightened by the relevance it seemed to have to the
"Popish Plot" of 1678, and by the satirical portrayal
of the earl of Shaftesbury in two characters, Renault
and Antonio. However, the extraordinary effectiveness of the play is due to Otway's rendering of the
opposed political philosophies and of the old theme
of love versus friendship in terms of the emotional
laceration of Jaffeir. A successful symbolic device is
Jaffeir's dagger—given to the conspirators as a
pledge of his loyalty, used by Renault to threaten
Belvidera, contemptuously tossed to Jaffeir by Pierre
when he is captured, and finally used by Jaffeir to kill
Pierre and himself. The emphasis upon the pathos of
the situations of Jaffeir and Belvidera is typical of
Otway (see ENGLAND: *Restoration drama*).

Malcolm Kelsall has edited this play with introduction and notes for the Regents Restoration Drama
Series (1969).—E. W.

Verga, Giovanni (1840–1922). Italian novelist
and playwright. Born in Catania, Sicily, into a family
of noble origins but liberal sentiments, Giovanni
Verga took active part in the struggle for national
unity. He lived in Milan from 1872 to 1893, returning to Sicily permanently after that. In Milan, he
spent the most intense and productive period of his
literary career, which had begun at an early age with

GIOVANNI VERGA (ITALIAN CULTURAL INSTITUTE)

novels and short stories of uneven quality. During the Milanese period he published his masterpieces, that is, his best-known novels, *I Malavoglia* (1881) and *Mastro Don Gesualdo* (1888), and his most famous collections of short stories, *Vita dei campi* (1880) and *Novelle rusticane* (1883). These works are distinguished by a powerful verism in their portrayal of the life of Sicilian peasants and fishermen.

Verga turned to the theater in 1884 with his play *Cavalleria rusticana,* based on one of his own novellas and brought to a clamorous triumph by Eleanora Duse. (Later, it formed the libretto for Mascagni's famous opera.) This was followed by seven other dramatic works of one or more acts, most distinguished of which are *La Lupa* (1896) and *Dal tuo al mio* ("From Yours to Mine," 1903). The first is constructed upon a bloody deed of passion and violence, the second illustrates the clash between the nobility and the bourgeois of Sicilian society. Verga's plays reveal an irremediable conflict between the concrete verism of events and characters and the artificiality of literary language, and this is why they do not approach the accomplishment of his novels.—L. L.

Vesaas, Tarjei (1897–   ). Norwegian novelist, playwright, and poet. Though Vesaas is chiefly associated with the Telemark region and writes in *nynorsk,* the self-consciously regional, second language of Norway, he has traveled widely in Europe. There are times when his fiction, for which he is best known, partakes of the international language of Franz Kafka and the French novelist Alain Robbe-Grillet.

Vesaas made his debut in the theater with *Prosten* ("The Pastor," 1925), a little idyll suffused with gentle humor, and *Guds bustader* ("God's Abodes," 1925), a drama of guilt and atonement. *Ultimatum* (1934), written in Strassbourg in 1932, on one of Vesaas' many stays abroad, concerns itself with the uneasy political situation in Europe. In *Bleikeplassen* ("The Bleaching Place," 1946), later turned into a novel, Vesaas uses a laundering establishment to deal expressionistically with the nature of human purity.

Vesaas' dramatic activity is chiefly linked with the nynorsk playhouse, Det Norske Teatret, and with the radio, on which many of his short stories have been presented in dramatized form. His lyricism and symbolic practice are frequently impressive.

See H. S. Næss, "Introduction," in *The Great Cycle* (1967).—R. B. V.

Vian, Boris (1920–1959). French poet, novelist, and playwright. In the middle 1960's Boris Vian became one of the favorite writers of the young generation. His work is varied: novels, poems, songs, 'pataphysic farces based on those of Alfred Jarry, and one important play, *Les Bâtisseurs d'empire; ou, le Schmürz* (*The Empire Builders*), first performed in the Théâtre Récamier at the end of 1959.

In the first act of this play, a husband and wife (who are the *bâtisseurs*) with their daughter and a maid occupy a two-room apartment. In the second act, trying to escape a mysterious noise, the mother and father go upstairs, where they occupy a single room, but the noise there is even more terrifying. In the third act, the father alone climbs up one more flight and closes himself within a small room under the rafters. There he dies as the noise grows even louder. A mysterious, mute character, Schmürz

(meaning "sufferer"), accompanies the father and dies a few minutes before he does. This ugly figure covered with bandages limps on a cane. Is he death, which the old man refuses to see? Is he the symbol of the old man's guilt or his innocence? The entire text of the play is a strong attack on the bourgeoisie and at times is close to the style and tone of Eugène Ionesco. The Schmürz is reminiscent of Ionesco's corpse in *Amédée.*—W. F.

Vicente, Gil (1465?–?1536). Portuguese actor and playwright. There exists little in the way of biographical data concerning Vicente, called the "founder of the Portuguese theater." The years of his birth and his death have been established by deductions. The basic doubt as to whether the playwright and the principal Portuguese goldsmith of the sixteenth century might have been the same person still prevails. Teófilo Braga, in *História do teatro Português* ("History of the Portuguese Theater," pub. 1870–1871), denies it, while the learned Braancamp Freire, in the most important biography on Vicente, has amplified research begun in 1917 that concludes in the affirmative. Contemporary critics still have not reached complete accord. Furthermore, it is not even known where the dramatist was born, although Lisbon, Santarém, or a city in the province of Beira

GIL VICENTE (CASA DE PORTUGAL, NEW YORK)

have been suggested. It is known for certain that he frequented the court of John II because his poetry was collected in the *Cancioneiro Geral* ("General Book of Poetry," pub. 1516) of Garcia de Resende. It is also a fact that his first play, *Monólogo do vaqueiro* ("Monologue of the Cowboy," 1502), was performed in the chambers of Queen Mary, wife of Manuel I, on the occasion of the birth of the future king John III. Present was the widow of John II, "Old Queen" Leonor, who from that moment on was to be the principal patron of the author. Vicente remained court dramatist until the day of his death, accompanying the royal family on trips across the territory of Portugal and writing his plays to celebrate births, royal marriages, and important religious events.

Having been accused of plagiarizing Spanish plays, Vicente wrote the farce *Inês Pereira* (1523) in order to prove his honesty. It is one of his most important works, written on the theme that was given to him: "I would rather have an ass that carries me than a horse that throws me." The play is about a poor girl who wants to marry a young boy, who is a poet, singer, and dancer. She despises an honest but ordinary rustic man. Through the aid of marriage brokers she is married, but the marriage is a disaster. When her husband dies, the girl marries the rustic, who she then cuckolds with a priest.

Vicente was harassed by the Inquisition because of his criticism of the clergy, which was inspired by the Humanist ideas of Erasmus. A profoundly Catholic writer nevertheless, Vicente wrote many moralities. *Auto da barca do inferno* ("Act of the Ship of Hell," 1517) is about persons of different social classes trying to gain admission into the boat going to heaven. *Auto da barca do purgatório* ("Act of the Ship of Purgatory," 1518) and *Auto da barca da glória* ("Act of the Ship of Glory," 1519) are also about souls trying to attain salvation. As in a court of justice, there is a prosecutor (the devil) and a judge (the angel of heaven). Vicente also wrote farces in which the clergy, the judiciary, and the nobility are ridiculed. *Clérigo da Beira* ("The Clergyman from Beira," 1529 or 1530) satirizes a priest who dedicates all his time to the hunt; *Juiz da Beira* ("The Judge from Beira," 1525 or 1526) pokes fun at a judge who does not understand the laws; and *Farsa dos almocreves* ("The Farce of the Muleteers," 1527) tells of a nobleman who must swindle others to pay his debts.

Vicente's plays remained within the medieval tradition, even though the Renaissance had been introduced into Portugal during the reign of John II. (See SPAIN: *Renaissance*.)

The plays of Vicente have not been translated into English.—J. P.

Victor; ou, les enfants au pouvoir ("Victor; or, The Children Take Power," 1928). A semisurrealist play by Roger VITRAC. *Victor,* Vitrac's second play, was produced by Antonin Artaud in 1928 in his Théâtre Alfred-Jarry. It was a failure and, like Jarry's *Ubu Roi* and Guillaume Apollinaire's *The Breasts of Tiresias,* shocked its audiences. In 1962, when *Victor* was revived at the Ambigu under the direction of Jean Anouilh, it was warmly received. The public, accustomed to the plays of Vitrac's admirer Eugène Ionesco, no longer felt a sense of shock.

Victor and Esther, aged nine and six, are giant children who combine cynicism and naïveté as they watch the stupidity and narrowness of their families. Victor's father is the lover of Esther's mother. The amorous intrigues, the endless quarreling, the pontificating of the families are not merely humorous; they are abject and the cause of Victor's death. Vitrac parodies in the play the themes of the typical bourgeois play and the values of the bourgeois mentality. There is a *boulevard,* or melodramatic aspect to the play, such as Georges Feydeau made famous, and aspects of almost tragic satire.

For a critical study of this play see Martin Esslin's *The Theatre of the Absurd* (1961) and Eric Sellin's *The Dramatic Concepts of Antonin Artaud* (1968). —W. F.

vidusaka. In Sanskrit drama, the figure of the clown. The *vidusaka* is one of the most persistent and fascinating figures maintained by stage conventions in India, seen from a time earlier than our own era until the conclusion of the classical dramatic tradition, more than a thousand years thereafter. A considerable literature exists on the subject, the most thorough study being *The Vidusaka* by C. K. Bhat.

The character appears in the earliest extant plays, notably the Trivandrum plays, ascribed to Bhasa, and the work of Asvaghosa, whose plays exist in fragmentary form. Although primarily a dramatic figure, he is also found in other literary forms. Invariably, he introduces a comic element into a work of some serious pretension. More specifically, he is the attendant on the hero; he may even be an attendant upon a god. In this capacity, declares the dramatist Bhasa, the humorous sage Narada gives pleasure to the austere Brahma. He is, so to speak, the king's jester. Similarly, Nandi is the humorous companion to the most dynamic of the Hindu gods, Siva, lord of drama and dance. Indian criticism itself distinguishes several types of vidusakas on the basis of whom they attend—god, king, minister, or merchant—and characteristics differ somewhat accordingly. In Sanskrit drama, where distinct types of comedy and tragedy are not acknowledged, humor and pathos are intermixed in all the major types of play. The vidusaka is the chief embodiment of the comic element.

Extensive speculation on the origin of the figure has led to no general agreement; he may derive from one or many sources. He has been associated with the fool in village festivals, with the licensed fool at court, and with motives ranging from the religious to the satirical or to a thirst for mere inebriated nonsense and fun.

His appearance is much more firmly established than his functions. He is dwarfish and deformed, lame and awkward, ugly and bald, and of an earthy complexion. He has staring red eyes and protruding teeth. He is frequently described as resembling a monkey. As a Brahman he wears a religious costume but the robe is disheveled. He carries a knotted staff, walks with difficulty, and much prefers to sit down. The kindly hero repeatedly offers him a seat. He employs the low-class speech, or Prakrits, in preference to the dignified Sanskrit of his heroic friend.

The character is by no means simple; he proves the more effectively absurd through representing a humorous conjunction of incongruities. Some of his aspects suggest satire on the priestly class but this element is never allowed to predominate. Ambiguity is of his essence. It is noteworthy that even his most gross blunders and absurdities are likely to be met with a straight face by his friend, the hero, as well as by all other persons in the play. It is understood that his wishes will be graciously acceded to and that any prophecy that he makes will invariably come true. No one doubts his word. Yet he is given to coarseness of expression, to gross error, and, above all, to extremes of gluttony and thirst. Friends continually ply him with wine and food. His taste runs especially to a sugary diet. His remarks are both inconsistent and incoherent. Occasionally he assumes the role of the chorus in Western plays, voicing the sentiment of the audience or giving the hero excellent advice. In courtly plays he is likely to be shrewd and, like the clown in Latin comedy, the deft manager of the intrigue. In plays pitched on a lower level, on the contrary, as *The Little Clay Cart,* his conduct may also propel the intrigue yet unwittingly lead the hero and heroine into their greatest difficulties. Whether by shrewdness or folly, he makes the play move forward.

He shows masculine vanity but small interest on his own behalf in sex, his function commonly being to aid the love desires of his friend and master with much unselfishness. He prefers jewels to sex and is regarded as in some sense pure in heart; as a priestly Brahman he possesses free entrance into the royal harem. Despite his greed and boastfulness, he is the hero's ever faithful friend, and the hero in return is warmly devoted to him.

The character changes with the centuries. In the early plays he enjoys relatively more dignity and respect. In later plays he degenerates into a common joker, losing his symbolic and virtually mythological significance. As Sanskrit drama itself became decrepit, the clown grew garrulous, vulgar, and tedious. Ever faithful, he did not outlast his royal master. He is one of the most engaging characters in world drama.

The most comprehensive study of the subject is *The Vidusaka* (1959) by C. K. Bhat. Highly valuable comment may also be found in two works by J. I. Parikh: *Sanskrit Comic Characters* (1952) and *The Vidusaka: Theory and Practice* (1953).—H. W. W.

Vigny, Comte Alfred [Victor] de (1797–1863). French poet, playwright, and novelist. The child of aristocratic parents who had suffered during the revolution, Vigny grew up in Paris among survivors of the old order. Thirteen years of monotonous army life from 1814 to 1827 deepened his nostalgia for the past and his pessimistic conviction that he was a victim of fate, lost between the echoes of glamorous wars. In 1825 he married a wealthy English girl, Lydia Bunbury, but the marriage was an uncongenial one, and his wife became a helpless invalid. When an English company of actors performed the works of Shakespeare in Paris in 1827, Vigny's interest in the theater was awakened and he became involved in the theater until about 1835. After his mother's death in 1837, Vigny broke his liaison with actress Marie Dorval and spent long periods on his estate in Charente, where he was engaged in the wine trade. Henceforth, he occasionally dabbled in the Parisian world of letters and politics. In 1845 he was admitted to the Académie Française after several rebuffs.

Three of his six plays, written between 1827 and 1835, were very faithful (if unintentionally academic) versions of Shakespeare, and they contained propaganda for a new vitality in the theater at a time when the Elizabethan's works were regarded by the establishment as barbaric and crude. Vigny's *Romeo et Juliette* (written 1828) was never performed; *Shylock* (adapted from *The Merchant of Venice* in 1830) was produced in 1905. Only *Othello, ou Le More de Venise* ("Othello, The Moor of Venice," 1829) was performed during Vigny's lifetime, and it was the second Romantic drama to be staged. It had sixteen performances and Vigny published with it a modest manifesto, "Lettre à Lord * * * sur la Soirée du 24 October, 1829," urging that pseudoclassical tragedy be replaced with a freer pattern.

In *La Maréchale d'Ancre* (1831), an unsuccessful historical melodrama, the plot links a double assassination (that of King Henri IV as the play opens and that of the minister Concini, Maréchal d'Ancre, as the curtain falls) with the villainous intrigues that for Vigny defined the reign of Louis XIII. The central character is the formidable *maréchale* herself, who is finally convicted for treason against the crown and sent to the stake. Borgia, her powerful husband's political rival, brings about her husband's ruin, and Borgia's jealous wife charges Borgia and the maréchale with adultery. A delicately profound one-act comedy of marital infidelity, *Quitte pour la peur* ("Fear Is the Best Teacher"), was successful in 1833 with Marie Dorval in the role of the erring but naïve duchess.

Vigny's dramatic masterpiece, however, was *Chatterton,* whose première at the Théâtre Français in February 1835 gave Mme. Dorval one of her best parts, that of Kitty Bell. The simple plot of a poet's tragic love for the sympathetic wife of an insensitive, crass businessman symbolizes for Vigny the hopeless plight of the artist in a materialistic society. When the lord mayor of London, representing British urban society, can employ the debt-ridden Chatterton in no better way than as a valet in his household, the curtain grimly and eloquently comes down on the suicide of the poet and the death of the despairing Kitty. The playwright's source was his own "Histoire de Kitty Bell," an account of the unhappy English poet Chatterton that forms one of the three stories about society's cruelty to poets that make up the volume *Stello* (1832). Like these tales, the drama depicts the injustice of a system in which everyone is supposed to contribute something useful and in which the poet, by his very nature, has no legitimate place. The purely romantic nature of the hero, whom Vigny called "more impassioned, purer, and more rare" than other men, and the classic simplicity of the plot have always interested readers. The play focuses upon the hero and his destiny rather than on local color or picturesque detail. In "Final Night's Work, 30 June, 1834," a prefatory essay to the published text, Vigny discusses at considerable length his conception of *Chatterton.*

The plays have not been translated into English. The latest biographical study is P. G. Castex' *Vigny, l'homme et l'oeuvre* (1952). E. Sakellaridès' *Alfred de Vigny, auteur dramatique* (1902) may be consulted on the plays. Of interest is R. C. Dale's article, "*Chatterton* Is the Essential Romantic Drama," in *L'Esprit créateur,* V (Fall 1965).—S. S. S.

Vildrac, Charles. Pen name of **Charles Messager**

(1882–   ). French poet, essayist, and playwright. Vildrac was a humanitarian playwright whose play *Le Paquebot Tenacity* (*The Steamer Tenacity,* 1920) achieved considerable success during the 1920's. His plays, notably *La Brouille* ("The Quarrel," 1930), reflect a faith and love of humanity. With his brother-in-law Georges Duhamel, Vildrac participated in an experiment in communal living at the Abbaye de Créteil, where he was attracted by the philosophy of unanimism. His texts are notable for the simplicity and spontaneity of their speech and for their pathos. —W. F.

Villiers de L'Isle-Adam. See SYMBOLISM.

Visakhadatta. See MUDRARAKSASA.

Visit, The (Der Besuch der alten Dame, 1956). A tragicomedy by Friedrich DÜRRENMATT. The scene of *The Visit* is the provincial town of Güllen in German-speaking Europe. It is a town on the verge of decay. The townsmen are generally unemployed and do little but dream of the time when Güllen was something more than now. Claire Zachanassian, now the richest woman in the world, is coming back to Güllen, her home town, for a visit. She is now a woman in her sixties and a multimillionairess since the death of her husband, the world's richest man. She owns virtually everything worth owning: oil companies, railways, broadcasting corporations, and the Hong Kong prostitution district. The townsmen see her as their only hope; they will ask her to invest money in their town. To accomplish this task they appoint Alfred Ill (Anton Schill in Maurice Valency's translation), with whom she once had a secret affair, to charm her into the bequest. He, too, is now an old man, married, with a family, and manager of the general store. Finally, Madame Zachanassian arrives with a highly unusual retinue in tow, which includes a butler, a black panther, two blinded eunuchs, and an empty coffin. In trying to win her over, Alfred takes her to the places where they once loved each other. But when he touches her hand, he finds it is no longer real, but of ivory. Claire is, in fact, a collection of many ivory artificial limbs. He succeeds, however, in having her promise to give millions to the town, though as yet he does not know her conditions. These terms are not revealed until she publicly proclaims at a banquet in her honor that she will give not only millions, but a billion—in exchange for the life of her former lover. It is revealed that Alfred had once bribed witnesses at a trial to deny the fact that Claire was carrying his child. These witnesses, it happens, are the two blind eunuchs in her entourage, whom she has traced down at great cost and brought to their present condition. Her motive: to bring justice to bear. As a result of the trial years ago, Claire was forced to leave Güllen and to become a prostitute in Hamburg. She now demands justice from the town through Alfred's life. The mayor indignantly rejects the offer, but almost at once things begin to happen.

Perhaps assuming that Claire will give Güllen the money—half to be divided among the inhabitants—without exacting the life of Alfred, the townspeople begin to buy luxurious items—on credit. Simultaneously, they gradually become aware of the terrible nature of Alfred's crime against Claire. In one of the most ironic and horrible scenes in modern drama, Alfred Ill is sentenced to death, with all the world's news media, including television and newsreels, covering the event. The murder then takes place on the spot as the townspeople close in slowly upon Alfred. When they draw away, he is dead—some say of a stroke, some say of joy, but none say that they were the instrument of his death. Claire Zachanassian deposits the body in the coffin she brought along and takes it to the mausoleum she has had erected for it on the isle of Capri. Upon leaving Güllen, she scornfully drops the check at the mayor's feet.

The staging of *The Visit* is exciting; sets fly in and out in full view of the spectator, and scenes shift with a rapidity that, as called for in the script, is breathtaking. Dürrenmatt utilizes elements from the Greek drama of antiquity in his chorus of townsmen, who serve by virtue of their formality to chill the blood. Essentially, the author's style is presentational. Townsmen become the trees of the grove and eavesdrop on Alfred and Claire's "love scenes." Yet, as Dürrenmatt says in the stage directions of the play, they are not men, but indeed trees. This is not a world of reality but an exaggerated world of the mind, yet one not terribly alien to our own.

Perhaps the most striking aspect of *The Visit* is the constant use of the grotesque in its fabric. This includes not merely the two ludicrous blind eunuchs who repeat everything twice but, more essentially, the characters' motives and the results of those motives. Rather than immediately reveal Claire's motive in coming to Güllen, Dürrenmatt serves it up horribly, and with consummate dramatic skill, at a banquet. Man is denatured and is made a grotesquerie by his deeds; he is corrupted by Claire's universal power. She in her turn has the power to do ultimate good but turns it, in characteristic Dürrenmatt fashion, into ultimate evil.

The Visit has been translated by Patrick Bowles (1962). An excellent article is to be found in the *Tulane Drama Review* by Melvin W. Askew, "Dürrenmatt's *The Visit of the Old Lady*" (June 1961). —C. R. M.

viskambhaka. In Sanskrit drama, a scene that serves as a prelude to any act of a full-length play. Explicit and extensive provisions for the *viskambhaka* were laid down in the chief manual for Sanskrit drama, the *Natyasastra,* and though it is by no means always used, it is employed frequently and to good effect. It is commonly seen when a considerable length of time has elapsed between two acts and the audience must be informed of intervening events. It also introduces actions that are shortly to follow or describes events inconvenient to represent on the stage. Battles and natural scenery are often depicted for the mind's eye in these poetic episodes. The characters participating in the dialogue are usually secondary or choral figures. Frequently they are spirits of an angelic nature, whose vision is presumed to be expansive and supernaturally keen. Kalidasa makes felicitous use of the convention in his *Shakuntala;* it is even more consistently employed, with great elegance, in Bhavabhuti's masterpiece, *Rama's Later History.* In many ways the viskambhaka prepares the mind for the major scene immediately to follow. If its characters are divine or of a higher caste, the scene is composed in Sanskrit; if of a lower class, in Prakrits. —H. W. W.

Vitrac, Roger (1899–1952). French playwright. The first play of Vitrac, *Les Mystères de l'amour* (*The Mysteries of Love*), a text strongly influenced by SURREALISM, was performed in June 1927 at the Théâtre Alfred-Jarry under the direction of Antonin Artaud. At the end of 1928, Artaud directed Vitrac's second play, VICTOR; OU, LES ENFANTS AU POUVOIR, which was given three performances. The attendant scandal in 1928 had completely disappeared when it was revived in 1962 by Jean Anouilh.

Despite the defects in the play, which Artaud pointed out in 1928, he praised *Victor* as being an expression of the disintegration of modern thought. Today the play clearly seems to be a forerunner of the "theater of the absurd" and especially an ancestor of the plays of Eugène Ionesco.—W. F.

Volpone, or the Fox (1605/06). A comedy by Ben JONSON. *Volpone* recounts the story of the gulling of a group of legacy hunters by a cagey old miser. Assisted by his servant, Mosca, Volpone, a wealthy Venetian, pretends to be dying in order to dupe a group of avaricious Venetians, each of whom desires to inherit Volpone's fortune. The would-be heirs are Voltore (vulture), Corbaccio (crow), and Corvino (raven), three birds of prey skillfully duped by the wily fox (Volpone) and the subtle gadfly (Mosca). No ordinary trickster, Volpone is also an extraordinary hedonist eager to gratify every sensual desire. The play owes a large debt to the medieval tradition. Its presentation is largely allegorical, offering a view of men transformed into animals by greed.

The play contains an analogous subplot of Sir Politic Would-be, an English traveler, whose passion for plots and stratagems marks him as a would-be Volpone. Eventually, the tricksters and dupes of both plots are uncovered and virtue (in the persons of the wife of Corvino and the son of Corbaccio) is rewarded.

Volpone has the impact of a morality play, but in the characters of Volpone and Mosca, it moves beyond the purely moral view. Both characters participate in the primitive, amoral, vital rhythm of comedy that has a more fundamental relation to the life of the play than any ethical formulation.—E. Q.

Voltaire. Pen name of **François Marie Arouet** (1694–1778). French philosophe, playwright, historian, novelist, and poet. Born in Paris into the rich bourgeoisie, François Marie Arouet studied at the Jesuit Collège de Clermont and at the same time moved in the libertine circles of Paris. As a very young man, he began to write verse, which led to his being exiled and then imprisoned in the Bastille. After he took the name Voltaire, he was exiled to England from 1726 to 1729 as the result of a dispute with a young nobleman. Indeed, Voltaire's entire life was taken up with the "philosophical struggle," to which he contributed innumerable tracts, poems, historical works, novels, letters, and so forth. At times close to the French court, at other times in danger because of his subversive works, he became Louis XV's historiographer in 1746 and a member of the French Academy. However, by 1750 he found it more advisable to take refuge with his friend Frederick the Great, with whom he quarreled in 1753. Unwelcome in Paris as well as in Berlin, Voltaire settled down in Ferney, near the Swiss border, and from there bombarded Europe with his philosophical writings, in which he attacked traditional religion and sought to have certain great judicial errors rectified. In 1778 he returned to Paris and was given a great ovation by the people, the French Academy, and the Comédie Française. That same year, after an incredibly active life and the production of a huge number of works, he died of overexcitement and fatigue.

All his life Voltaire had a passion for the theater. Not only did he like to appear onstage as an amateur, but most of all, he wrote over fifty plays, half of which are tragedies, eclipsing his immediate predecessors and his contemporaries, even Prosper Jolyot de Crébillon, from whom he borrowed certain subjects. He also wrote comedies, of varied styles and genres, from farce to personal satire, and including the genre that was to give rise to *drame bourgeois*—tearful comedy (*Nanine,* 1749). In his tragedies Voltaire proved to be far more faithful to the classical tradition. After *Œdipe* (1718), his most renowned tragedies are *Brutus* (1730), ZAÏRE, *Alzire* (1736), *Mérope* (1743), *Sémiramis* (1748), *L'Orphelin de la Chine* (*The Orphan of China,* 1755), *Tancrède* (1760), and *Irène* (1778).

Voltaire introduced a few innovations (subjects

VOLTAIRE (MUSÉE DU PETIT PALAIS, PARIS, PHOTO BULLOZ)

drawn from national history, exoticism, picturesque details, mob scenes, and ghosts) into tragedy, some of which were due to the influence of Shakespeare, whom Voltaire helped make known in France and whom he admired for his genius but detested for his strangeness and lack of taste. On the whole, however, Voltaire remained faithful to classical form. The novelty of his works lies most particularly in their orientation: Tragedy became "philosophical"; in other words, even if some of his tragedies are peopled by lively and convincing characters, the objective of the situations is to illustrate the effects, not of a tragic fate, but of ideological positions or prejudices— most often the damages wrought by fanaticism and religious intolerance. Those of his plays based on Roman history were revived most successfully during the French Revolution because of their republicanism. Nevertheless, while Voltaire lacked a sense of the tragic as such, he was highly skillful in constructing his plays, in his handling of alexandrines, and in creating powerful and spectacular effects.

For a survey of Voltaire's contributions in the field of tragedy, see Henry C. Lancaster, *French Tragedy in the Time of Louis XV and Voltaire, 1716–1774,* 2 vols. (1950).—Ja. G.

Vondel, Joost van den (1587–1679). Dutch playwright and poet. Vondel was born in Cologne, Germany, the son of Flemish parents who had emigrated from Antwerp. The family later settled in Amsterdam, whose glories Vondel celebrated in his poetry. Vondel played a role in public life, but his consuming passion was poetry. He began writing lyric poetry and then turned to satire. His greatest achievement lay in the drama, however, and in addition to a number of translations and adaptations, he produced more than twenty original dramas. Vondel

JOOST VAN DEN VONDEL (NETHERLANDS INFORMATION SERVICE)

was an unusual man who lived a long life and he wrote some of his best plays after he reached the age of sixty.

His didactic intentions are clear from the subtitle of *Het Pascha ofte de Verlossinge Israels wt Egypten, tragecomedischer wyse eenyeder tot leeringh opt tonneel gestelt* ("Passover, or the Deliverance of Israel from Egypt, Placed upon the Stage in a Tragicomic Manner for the Instruction of All," 1610). Vondel sees the Exodus as a foreshadowing of Jesus' deliverance of the faithful from their slavery to sin. This play reveals several characteristics of Vondel's dramatic work, such as the influence of both the Dutch dramatic tradition and the French neoclassical drama. It is a symbolic drama that also reflects the style of the emblem books of the seventeenth century. The symbolic and emblematic quality is also evident in *Hierusalem verwoest* ("Jerusalem Destroyed," pub. 1620), whose rhetorical and declamatory style shows the influence of Seneca. The play is filled with laments over the destruction of Jerusalem, which foreshadows the destruction of the world on Judgment Day.

Learning and scholarship were considered important attributes of a poet in Vondel's day, and his friendships with writers and scholars of the Humanist movement stimulated him to great activity as a man of letters. In the spirit of the period, he translated from the classics, turning Seneca's *Troades* into the Dutch verse drama *Amsteldamsche Hecuba* (pub. 1626), and his *Phaedra* into a Dutch *Hippolytus* (pub. 1628). That these translations are very important for an understanding of the development of his own dramatic technique is evident from his *Palamedes of Vermoorde Onnoselheit* ("Palamedes, or Murdered Innocence," pub. 1625). Using a Greek fable as his background, Vondel created a *drame à clef* in which he defends religious freedom in the great religious and political struggle that had resulted in Sir John von Oldenbarnevelt's death on false charges of treason.

Vondel wrote *Gysbreght van Aemstel* for the dedication of the new municipal theater in Amsterdam in 1637. He had studied Vergil's *Aeneid* before writing this play and drew upon the history of Amsterdam as a source of material. The drama symbolizes the decline of earthly grandeur, as against the enduring significance of such eternal values as humility and obedience to the commands of God. Here he combined three worlds: the world of classical antiquity, the Catholic world of the middle ages, and the world of his own day.

Vondel rejected the violence and inhumanity of Seneca's tragedies and their pagan spirit, retaining only their form and technique. He turned his attention from Seneca to Sophocles and translated *Elektra* (1639), which was important for the development of his dramatic work. Tacitus' *Annales* was the source for *Messalina,* a drama of adultery and murder that was not performed in Vondel's lifetime.

While *Maeghden* ("Virgins," pub. 1639) has many points in common with *Gysbreght van Aemstel,* it is filled with the spirit of Elektra. Thus, the heroine Ursula, like Elektra, is not defeated, but triumphs after her death and saves the city of Cologne for a glorious future. In its contrast between the Christian heroine and the barbarian hero Attila, it is a typically Baroque play. It also shows Vondel moving toward Catholicism.

Gebroeders ("Brothers," written 1639) is one of Vondel's biblical plays and is based on the story of God's punishment of Saul and his sons for violating an old treaty with the Gabaonites. Saul is killed, but the Gabaonites demand the sacrifice of seven of his male descendants. In this drama Vondel was under the influence of the idea of inexorable and merciless fate as he had found it expressed in Greek literature, but it is the belief in God and His rule that underlies the play.

The Bible also served as the source for his Joseph trilogy, *Joseph aan 't hof* ("Joseph at the Court," 1640), *Joseph in Dothan* (1640), and *Joseph in Egypten* (1640). *Joseph in Egypten* bears the influence of Seneca's *Phaedra*. It takes up the episode of Joseph and Potiphar's wife and explores the duality of good and evil. *Peter en Pauwels* ("Peter and Paul") was published in 1641, the year that is often suggested as the date of Vondel's conversion to Catholicism. It portrays the two worlds of Christianity and paganism, and the epic influence is strong in this static drama. *Maria Stuart of gemartelde Majesteit* ("Mary Stuart, or Martyred Majesty," pub. 1646) has many features in common with it, including its static quality.

With *Leeuwendalers* (pub. 1648), Vondel went off in a new direction, for this play is a comedy based on the peace that ended the Thirty Years' War. After *Maria Stuart* he turned from the passive suffering of the martyr-hero and the happy ending to a hero with a tragic flaw who comes to a tragic end. His *Salomon* (1648) shows how passion led to the tragic downfall of the great biblical hero. Vondel's outstanding tragedy is *Lucifer* (pub. 1654), a dramatic presentation of the revolt and fall of the angels. It is completely in the spirit of the Baroque, with great contrasts and violent conflicts. After only two performances the intervention of the clergy halted further presentations.

Jeptha of Offerbelofte ("Jephthah, or The Promised Sacrifice," pub. 1659) is a portrait of religious pride. Jephthah refuses to abandon what he considers his promise to God, in spite of the priest's willingness to absolve him of it. Vondel adheres to the unities, but his interpretation of Aristotle was influenced by the opinions of his Dutch and French contemporaries. He avoided the usual alexandrines and chose a form of verse that was influenced by the French poet Pierre de Ronsard. *Samson* (pub. 1660) is also a dramatic interpretation of a biblical story, but *Batavische Gebroeders* ("Batavian Brothers") and *Faëton,* both written in 1663, are drawn from classical sources, yet they are not without political allusions to their times. In 1660 Vondel translated Sophocles' *Oedipus Rex* and adapted Sophocles' *Trachiniae.* Vondel also came to admire Euripides and translated his *Iphigenia in Tauris.* He considered his *Phoenissae* to be the greatest of his works and turned it into Dutch as *Feniciaanse.* In 1661 Vondel wrote a defense of the stage, *Tooneelschilt of Pleitrede voor het Tooneelrecht* ("A Shield for the Stage, or A Defense of the Rights of the Stage").

Adam in Ballingschap ("Adam in Exile," pub. 1664) is Vondel's highest conception of the ideal man. *Noah of ondergang der eerste wereld* ("Noah, or The End of the First World," pub. 1667) forms the last part of the trilogy that includes *Lucifer* and *Adam.* Vondel's last original play, *Zungchin,* dates from the same year. It portrays a Jesuit missionary from Cologne, Adam Schall, who went to China. In spite of his firm attachment to the classical tradition, Vondel was a great poet with a powerful imagination. His Humanism enabled him to give balance to the Baroque.

For an account of Vondel's life and work, see A. J. Barnouw, *Vondel* (1925), and for a discussion of his work, including the results of the most recent scholarship, see W. A. P. Smit and P. Brachin, *Vondel (1587–1679)* (1964) in French. Vondel's *Lucifer* (1898), translated by Charles Leonard van Voppen, is the only one of his plays to be translated into English.—S. L. F.

Vultures, The (**Les Corbeaux,** 1882). French naturalistic play by Henry BECQUE. *The Vultures* is the prototype of the French naturalistic play, although it was preceded by Émile Zola's *Thérèse Raquin* (1873). Becque wrote the play in 1877, and he tried unsuccessfully for five years to get it produced. That it was performed at all is something of a miracle. Seven theaters refused it because it was not a "thesis" play of the type then in vogue, and its method of construction was not that of the "well-made play." It did, to be sure, present an unpleasant "slice of life," such as Zola was recommending, but it followed none of the latter's "scientific" precepts. Just as Becque was about to publish *The Vultures,* the retired director of the Comédie Française managed to get it accepted, but officials and antiquated methods of acting and staging prevented a fully successful production. Refusing to alter his text, Becque finally saw his play staged the way he had written it on September 14, 1882. Just as the première of Victor Hugo's *Hernani* in 1830 had been turned into a battle between the classicists and Romanticists, so that of *The Vultures* sparked a violent clash between conventionalists and naturalistic realists.

There is little action, but the emotional pattern of the play descends from lighthearted joy to hopeless futility. A happy family prepares for their youngest daughter's marriage to a neighbor's son. The gaiety is shattered as news of the sudden death of the girl's father concludes the first act. The dead man's aged business partner (a lecher and the shrewdest vulture) and the family lawyer move to despoil the grief-stricken and unsuspecting family. Because the daughter now lacks a dowry, her future mother-in-law (the most avaricious vulture) uses the fact that the girl has, in a weak moment, slept with her fiancé as a weapon with which to shame her and to prevent the marriage. The girl eventually loses her mind. While the lawyer cynically comments, "There is no such thing as love. Marriage is a business," another daughter, who refuses to become the old partner's mistress, agrees to marry him to save the family.

Becque had created what Balzac, Flaubert, the Goncourts, and Zola were unable to create: a masterpiece of realism that did not follow the conventions of the well-made play. The greatness of *The Vultures* consists of its presentation of reality without the author's comment or the use of a *raisonneur.* The initial exposition is cut to the minimum, and there is no *scène à faire* (reversal of action followed by a climactic scene) in the usual sense. The immoral characters condemn themselves by posing as virtuous people, but the audience penetrates the disguise. The good characters are plausibly differentiated, and the vultures are grotesquely ridiculed in the manner of Molière. Becque censures these evildoers with a final ironic touch: the worst vulture routs the last of his cohorts, saying to the daughter, "Child, since your father died, you've been surrounded by a lot of scoundrels." The only characterization that seems exaggerated in Becque's everyday world of common-place people and emotions is the daughter, whose mental illness results from a frustrated love affair with a man who has no speaking part and briefly appears onstage once.

The Vultures does not seem to have been performed in English, although at least two translations have been published. Freeman Tilden's *The Vultures* is included in *A Treasury of the Theatre* (1960), edited by John Gassner, whose discussion of the play, and those in H. A. Smith's *Main Currents of Modern French Drama* (1925), and S. M. Waxman's *Antoine and the Théâtre-Libre* (new ed., 1964), are helpful.
—S. S. S.

W

Waddell, Samuel J.   See Rutherford MAYNE.

Wagner,   [Wilhelm]   Richard   (1813–1883).
German poet, dramatist, director, conductor, composer, essayist. Born in Leipzig, Wagner lost his father, Friedrich, when he was six months old. Nine months later his mother married a family friend, Ludwig Geyer, whom some claim was Wagner's real father. Wagner wrote a play when he was fourteen, and by the time he was fifteen was writing orchestral music, having his first professional performance in 1830 in the Leipzig Theater. In the following year he entered the university to study music and in 1834 became conductor of the Bethmann troupe in Lauchstädt. *Die Feen* (*The Fairies*, finished in 1833), with a libretto based on Carlo Gozzi's *La donna serpente*, was his first complete text and score, although it was not produced until five years after his death.

In spite of early operatic successes like *Rienzi* (1842) and *Der fliegende Holländer* (*The Flying Dutchman*, 1843) and publication of essays, poems, and books, Wagner's extravagant tastes contributed to financial problems at various times throughout his life. In 1839 he fled Riga creditors, in 1840 spent twenty-one days in debtors' prison in Paris, and as late as 1864 hurriedly left Vienna pursued by creditors. His political writings and his participation in the Dresden uprising of 1849 also contributed to his difficulties.

Wagner's theories about art and music are important to an understanding of his work, especially the development of the music-drama. In *A Pilgrimage to Beethoven* (1841) Wagner explained Beethoven's influence on him. He felt that with Beethoven instrumental music had reached a pinnacle and could not be further developed. But refertilized by poetry, the symphony could become something more than it had been, perhaps something new. In Beethoven's symphonies, Wagner heard the instruments speak as "primal organs of creation and nature." In the human voice, he heard man's emotions. If these two were combined, they would soften, heighten, and unify each other. Perhaps in Beethoven's monumental *Ninth Symphony* Wagner had found this clue. Wagner saw the opera of his day, with its arias, duets, and choruses, as merely a patchwork of musical specialties, the plot being, if anything, only glue to hold it all together. It was designed to show off the beauty and skill, the talents and tricks of the leading singers, and thus demeaned both music and poetry.

Wagner developed his art theories in three major works. In *Die Kunst und Revolution* (*Art and Revolution*, 1849) he maintained that art is the pure expression of the community's joy in itself. Thus it should be accessible to all and should not have to support itself commercially. Using many comparisons to Attic Greece, Wagner made his Germany seem a nation of Babbitts, lacking the high ideals and artistic integrity of the ancient Athenians. He saw classic tragedy, with its music and dance, as a perfect art form and a public one as well, making viewers conscious of themselves and of their essence.

He expanded these ideas in *Das Kunstwerk der Zukunft* (*The Art-Work of the Future*, 1850). The new art should be a reunion with nature, a *Gesamtkunstwerk*, a united art work using all genres of art, not as ends in themselves, but as means to attain the universal folk aim: the representation of a perfected human nature. The whole man, Wagner theorized, was a combination of intellect (speech), heart or emotion (tone), and body (gesture). Thus, true art should unite the whole man by combining poetry, music, and dance. Poetry would be enhanced by music and dance because the emotion from the two latter arts would overflow into the words. The music-drama, Wagner thought, would be the most effective union of the arts. See SYMBOLISM.

Oper und Drama (*Opera and Drama*, 1851) further discussed his conception of the music-drama. Myth, not romance or history, is the appropriate source for poetic themes for such works, because myth is true for all time and its content is inexhaustible. The music-drama would have themes—later called *Leitmotivs* by Hans von Wolzogen—representing characters, objects, and concepts. These would emerge, intertwine, and alter each other symphonically. Though Wagner discussed problems of composition, he insisted the musician must be the servant of the poet. Ideally the composer and the poet would be, as with Wagner, united in the same person, a *Worttondichter*, or word-tone-poet.

Because Wagner envisioned music-drama as a union of the arts, it would have to be conceived with the visual aspects clearly in mind. This was easy for him, for as he created he saw the stage picture before him. In his scores, even acting cues are indicated. Wagner's influence on his productions is a direct result of his theories. He carefully selected his artists, when he had control, training them in the heroic realism he desired on stage and in the *Sprechsingen*, or musical declamation, required in his epic works.

His works fall into three periods: the experimental phase (1830–1842), with *Rienzi* its culmination; the romantic phase (1843–1848), which produced *Holländer*, *Tannhäuser* (1845), and *Lohengrin* (1850), among others; and the final phase (1854–1882), with the epic music-drama *Der Ring des Nibelungen* (1876) and *Parsifal* (1882). The *Ring* cycle, based on old Nordic legends, consists of a trilogy designed for a three-day performance (*Die Walküre,* 1870; *Siegfried,* 1876; and *Die Götterdämmerung,* 1876) preceded by a *Vorabend,* or a preliminary evening performance of the Prelude, *Das Rheingold* (1869). Wagner's early works were flirtations with various popular forms, but in his later works he tried to embody the theories he had put forth in his three books.

Just before he died of an attack of angina, Wagner conducted the last act of the last performance of *Parsifal* at Bayreuth, where he had built his *Festspielhaus.* His second wife, Cosima, the daughter of Franz Liszt, carried on the festivals at Bayreuth after his death until their son Siegfried was able to assume command. After World War II the festivals were discontinued until 1951, when Wieland and Wolfgang, Wagner's grandsons, took charge, astonishing audiences with remarkable modern interpretations of Wagner's works. Their uses of abstract forms and unusual lighting have influenced both opera and theater staging in Europe.

No librettist-composer of comparable stature has followed Wagner. Considering the chances he took, the enmities he aroused, the near-disasters he provoked, the disappointments he sustained, the remarkable fact of his achievement testifies to his unshakable belief in his mission and his gifts. The surge of approval that greeted him late in life found its match in a countersurge of anti-Wagnerism that spilled over into the twentieth century. But today a more rational, balanced appreciation is the rule.

The balanced criticism of Ernest Newman is widely regarded as nearly definitive. A standard evaluation is his *Wagner as Man and Artist* (1924), and his *Wagner Operas* (1949) provides valuable analytical insights and specific information that no student should overlook. An older source of details and judgments is Henry T. Finck's valuable *Wagner and His Works* (1904), in two volumes. Ludwig Marcuse's *Das denkwürdige Leben des Richard Wagner* (1963) is an effective union of new facts and interpretations about Wagner. *My Life* (1924), though the authorized biography, dictated by Wagner to his wife Cosima, suffers from his own myopia and desire for self-justification. Some critics insist that the amanuensis inserted corrections and changes of her own that worked even greater alterations on history. Texts of the operas are to be found in *The Authentic Librettos of the Wagner Operas* (1938). The extensive collection of essays, poetry, stories, plot outlines, and criticism is preserved in *Richard Wagner's Prose Works* (1892–1899), in eight volumes, edited with thought and skill by W. Ashton Ellis.—G. L.

Waiting for Godot (En attendant Godot, 1953). A play by Samuel BECKETT. In 1953 Roger Blin produced *Waiting for Godot* in the Théâtre de Babylone. It ran for four hundred performances and was continued at the Théâtre Hébertot. The action of the play is simple to relate. Two tramps are waiting by a sickly looking tree for the arrival of M. Godot. They quarrel, make up, contemplate suicide, try to sleep, eat a carrot, and gnaw on some chicken bones. Two other characters appear, a master and a slave, who perform a grotesque scene in the middle of the play. A young boy arrives to say that M. Godot will not come today, but that he will come tomorrow. The play is a development of the title, *Waiting for Godot.*

A SCENE FROM SAMUEL BECKETT'S *Waiting for Godot* (FRENCH CULTURAL SERVICES)

Godot does not come and the two tramps resume their vigil by the tree, which between the first and second day has sprouted a few leaves, the only symbol of a possible order in a thoroughly alienated world.

The purely comic aspect of the play involves traditional routines that come from the entire history of farce, from the Romans, the Italians, and the red-nosed clown of the modern circus. The language of the play is grave, intense, and concise. The long speech of the slave, a bravura passage that is seemingly meaningless, is reminiscent of the work of James Joyce. But the play, far from being a pastiche, has its own beauty and suggestiveness, and it embodies Beckett's comment on man's absurd hope and the absurd insignificance of man. (See THEATER OF THE ABSURD.) The despair, which is never defined as such but which pervades all the lack of action and gives to the play its metaphysical color, stems from the fact that the two tramps cannot not wait for Godot and the corollary fact that Godot cannot come.

Beckett himself has translated *Waiting for Godot* (1954).—W. F.

wajang (wayang). See INDONESIA.

Wakefield Plays, The (early fifteenth century). A Corpus Christi cycle of thirty-two scriptural plays of unknown authorship. The text (running to over 12,000 lines of verse) is found in the Towneley Manuscript, so called after the family that once owned it; the manuscript is preserved in the Huntington Library. Because of the name of the manuscript, Wakefield is also sometimes called the Towneley Cycle. Six of the plays are recognized as having been written by an author of genius, usually referred to as the Wakefield Master. Six other plays are essentially the same as their correspondents in the York Cycle. It seems likely that these and other similarities are due to direct borrowing (of Wakefield from York) rather than to collateral descent from a common (lost) original. Wakefield was produced on pageant wagons proceeding successively from stop to stop throughout the town; Martial Rose suggests that it may also have been produced on wagons grouped together about the perimeter of a Place, that is, a town square (see N-Town PLAYS). There is no indication of the length of time for production. Chester, a pageant Place wagon cycle slightly shorter than Wakefield, was produced during three successive days; York, a pageant wagon cycle slightly longer, during a single day.

The Wakefield Cycle consists of the following plays (elements absent from the York, Chester, and N-Town cycles are starred):

From Old Testament narratives:
(1) Fall of Lucifer, Creation of Adam and Eve (Fall of Man and Expulsion from Eden being lost from the manuscript)
(2) Cain and Abel
(3) Noah and His Wife, the Flood
(4) Abraham and Isaac
(5) * Jacob and Esau
(6) * Jacob's Wanderings
(8) Pharaoh, Moses, Exodus (misplaced in manuscript; York 11).
From narratives of the Nativity:
(7) Prophets (incomplete)
(9) Caesar Augustus
(10) Annunciation, Joseph's Suspicions about Mary
(11) Visit to Elizabeth
(12) First Shepherds' Play
(13) Second Shepherds' Play
(14) Adoration of the Magi
(15) Flight into Egypt
(16) Slaughter of the Innocents
(17) Purification of the Virgin
(18) Christ and the Doctors (York 20).
From narratives of the Public Ministry:
(19) Baptism
(31) Raising of Lazarus (misplaced in manuscript).
From narratives of the Passion:
(20) Conspiracy
(21) Buffeting (Trial before Caiaphas)
(22) Scourging (Trial before Pilate)
(32) Death of Judas (incomplete; misplaced in manuscript)
(23) Procession to Calvary (York 34), Crucifixion
(24) Talents (Casting of Lots).
From narratives of the Resurrection and Doomsday:
(25) Harrowing of Hell (York 37)
(26) Resurrection (York 38)
(27) Pilgrims to Emmaus
(28) Doubting Thomas
(29) Ascension
(30) Last Judgment (York 48).

Wakefield differs from the other three English scriptural cycles in omitting the Birth of Christ, Temptation, Woman Taken in Adultery, Entry into Jerusalem, Peter's Denial, First Trial before Pilate, Trial before Herod, and Pentecost. It is also unusual in having two Shepherds' plays (written perhaps for two different gilds). Wakefield is generally consid-

ered to be the best of the four English cycles from a literary point of view.

The Towneley Plays has been edited by G. England, Early English Text Society, Ext. Ser., No. LXXI (1897); *The Wakefield Pageants in the Towneley Cycle* (1958), edited by A. C. Cawley, contains the plays by the Wakefield Master: Nos. 2, 3, 12, 13, 16, 21. A modern translation that also contains a critical study is *The Wakefield Mystery Plays* (1962), edited by Martial Rose. Arnold Williams' *The Characterization of Pilate in the Towneley Plays* (1950) is a valuable critical study.—R. H.

waki. The word *waki* signifies the chief among the secondary characters in a Japanese *noh* play. He is clearly subordinate to the *shite*, or hero, and even stands on a lower plane than the shite's followers, such as the *tsure*, should these be present. Shite and tsure wear masks. The waki and his followers, or *waki-tsure*, do not. Only on rare occasions does the waki occupy a position analogous to that of the antagonist in Western drama. He is usually a relatively humble person whose role falls chiefly in the first half of the play. As a rule he enters quietly and before the shite, thus preparing for the shite's far more impressive entrance. Frequently he is a monk, traveling perhaps with his assistants. Often, too, his earnest prayers assist in bringing about the salvation of the shite's soul, which is, in spiritual terms, the goal toward which the entire drama moves. See NOH; SHITE. —H. W. W.

Wallenstein. A trilogy by Friedrich von SCHILLER, made up of *Wallensteins Lager* (*Wallenstein's Camp*, 1798), *Die Piccolomini* (*The Piccolomini*, 1799), and *Wallensteins Tod* (*Wallenstein's Death*, 1799). The trilogy is based upon the fall of the historic Bohemian general of the Thirty Years' War, Count Albrecht von Wallenstein (1583–1634). In Schiller's version, Wallenstein is tempted by the enormous strength he has built up as the principal general of Emperor Ferdinand II to entertain the idea of deserting the emperor and establishing his own political power. He never actually intends to commit treason, but the idea intrigues him, and he begins to correspond with the Swedish enemy. Jealous elements in the Viennese court discover this correspondence and use it to induce the emperor to outlaw Wallenstein. Wallenstein flees but is murdered by one of his generals. The play displays a new realism and fuller characterization compared with Schiller's earlier works.

Wang Shih-fu. See THE WEST CHAMBER.

war of the theaters. Term usually taken to apply to an apparent conflict among a group of Elizabethan playwrights. In 1599 the young satirist John Marston produced a play that contained a character modeled on Ben Jonson. In retaliation Jonson, in his next three plays, *Everyman Out of his Humour* (1599), *Cynthia's Revel* (1600), and *The Poetaster* (1600), lampooned both Marston and Thomas Dekker. Marston and Dekker retorted with a satiric portrait of Jonson in *Satiromastix* (1601). Students of the "war" have been led to speculate (usually on the basis of inconclusive information) on its significance. Some interpretations have suggested that the quarrel really reflects certain cultural and ethical differences of opinion about the nature of drama prevalent at the time. What does seem probable is that the quarrel was related to the competition between the companies of child actors who performed in small private theaters and the adult companies performing in the large public theaters. Shakespeare alludes to the competition in *Hamlet* (II, ii) where Rosencrantz explains the presence of the players at the court of Elsinore.

For a discussion of this dispute, see J. J. Enck, "The Peace of the Poetomachia," *PMLA*, 77 (1962).

Wasps (**Sphēkes,** 422 B.C.). A comedy by ARISTOPHANES. The central idea of this play is based on the passion for litigation and jury service that had seized the Athenian public. Philocleon and Bdelycleon ("I Love Cleon" and "I Hate Cleon") are father and son respectively, and the conflict arises from Philocleon's determination to attend the courts as juryman and Bdelycleon's equal determination to keep him at home. Philocleon, trapped in the house by his son, tries various means of escape—all futile. The friendly Chorus of wasps, embodiments of the Athenian juror, come to help him, but Bdelycleon manages to convert these violent and bitter old men to his calmer point of view. He shows them that the supposed benefits of jury service—power over men, flattery, bribes, and daily pay—are nothing when compared to the humiliation of being tricked out of fortunes by the politicians and clever young attorneys. At last Philocleon agrees to a compromise: he will hold court in his own home. His first case concerns the family dog, accused of stealing a cheese. By a trick, Philocleon is made to acquit the dog, and promptly faints from shock. His son then undertakes to make a socialite out of him, but the old man is a recalcitrant pupil and at his first party disgraces himself by getting drunk, breaking out into bawdy song, beating up the guests, running off with a flute girl, and punching everyone he meets in the street on the way home. Unrepentant, he leads the Chorus in a wild dance and retires indoors to enjoy his flute girl.

The conflict in *Wasps* is more subtly managed than in many of Aristophanes' comedies. The old man is both hero and villain—hero, in that he can get away with all kinds of forbidden acts, indulge his libido, and at the end be restored to youth; villain, in the Aristophanic sense, for his allegiance to Cleon, Aristophanes' political enemy, and his mindless acceptance of slogans and flattery. Bdelycleon is equally ambivalent. He is young, cool, clear-sighted, and is able to persuade the older generation that they have been misled and to open their eyes to the truth. At the same time he is affected, oversophisticated, and seems interested only in the latest fashion in pleasure. But whatever Aristophanes felt about the wasps, the juries, and Bdelycleon, it is clear that in Philocleon —recalcitrant, incorrigible, but eternally vigorous —we can see Aristophanes' own attitude toward the Athenians, the audience he loved and longed to redeem.

Translations of the play are listed under Aristophanes.—K. C.

Way of the World, The (1700). A comedy by William CONGREVE. This play was first performed early in the year at the Lincoln's Inn Fields Theatre by Betterton's Company. It is a comedy of manners that focuses on the courtship of Mirabell and Millamant. In order to conceal his suit to Millamant, Mirabell has paid court to her aunt, Lady Wishfort, who has discovered the truth and firmly opposes the marriage. Her opposition is cultivated by Mrs. Marwood, who is vainly in love with Mirabell, and by Mrs. Marwood's lover, Fainall, who is married to Lady Wishfort's daughter and wishes to control not only his wife's fortune but Millamant's as well. In the end his schemes fail, and Lady Wishfort agrees to the marriage of Mirabell with her niece.

The virtue of the play has little to do with this melodramatic plot and everything to do with the brilliance of the dialogue. Congreve makes fine distinctions between the genuine wit of Mirabell and Millamant, the pretensions to wit of Witwoud, the hearty crudity of his half-brother, Sir Wilfull Witwoud, and the affectations of Lady Wishfort. The tone is delicately balanced between urbane cynicism and hope that good nature may prevail (see ENGLAND: *Restoration drama*). *The Way of the World* is generally regarded as the best English COMEDY OF MANNERS.

This play has been edited with introduction and notes by Kathleen Lynch for the Regents Restoration Drama Series (1965) and will also be found in the Mermaid Dramabook *William Congreve. Complete Plays* (1961). For criticism see Paul and Miriam Mueschke, *A New View of Congreve's Way of the World* (1958).—E. W.

Weavers, The (**Die Weber,** 1892). A play by Gerhart HAUPTMANN. Considered the first socialist play in German literature, this drama presents a compelling account of the sufferings of the Silesian weavers and their unsuccessful revolt in 1844 against those who exploited them.

The detailed rendering of the historical circumstances gives the drama considerable epic coloration. The replacement of the individual hero by a collective one represented by the masses underscores the impossibility of effective dramatic action and contributes to the fundamental epic quality of the drama. —C. A. M.

Webster, John (1580?–?1634). English playwright. The major details of Webster's life remain a mystery. The earliest reference to him is a note in Philip Henslowe's diary in 1602. He began his playwriting career as a collaborator of Thomas Dekker. Among the plays produced by the pair were *Westward Ho* (1604) and *Northward Ho* (1605), two popular comedies written for the Children of St. Paul's company. The three extant plays written solely by Webster are THE WHITE DEVIL, THE DUCHESS OF MALFI, and *The Devil's Law Case* (1610–1623). The latter is a tragicomedy of intrigue, centering on the hero-villain Romelio, whose Machiavellian manipulations are given a peculiar dignity by the strength and resolve of his own character.

Webster also wrote a number of plays in collaboration with others: a sensational melodrama, *Keep the Widow Waking* (1624), with Dekker, John Ford, and William Rowley; *A Cure for a Cuckold* (c. 1624/25) with Rowley and John Heywood; and the tragedy *Appius and Virginia* (1607–1627), probably with Heywood. *Appius and Virginia*, set in classical Rome and reflecting the classical virtues of decorum and simplicity, lacks the impassioned illumination of Webster's great plays.

The time and place of Webster's death are unknown. He is presumed to have died by 1634, since a

DRAWING OF A SCENE FROM WILLIAM CONGREVE'S *The Way of the World* (WALTER HAMPDEN MEMORIAL LI-
BRARY AT THE PLAYERS, NEW YORK)

reference to him in that year uses the past tense. His personality remains equally mysterious, although the dark, brooding pessimism of his two masterpieces, *The Duchess of Malfi* and *The White Devil,* suggests at least one important aspect of the author's vision of life. Webster's morbidity has been denigrated by many who, echoing G. B. Shaw, dismiss him as a "Tussaud laureate," a minor explorer of the sensational and macabre. However, the cataclysms of the twentieth century have taught us that Webster's vision of life, while narrow and fragmented, penetrates to an area of human motive and experience that for all its darkness is not to be denied.

The standard edition of Webster's *Works* (1927) has been edited by F. L. Lucas in four volumes. Travis Bogard's *The Tragic Satire of John Webster* (1955) provides a good critical treatment of the author.—E. Q.

Wedekind, [Benjamin] Frank[lin] (1864–1918). German playwright. Frank Wedekind was born in Hannover, the son of a middle-aged doctor and a very young Hungarian actress. The colorful biographical notations of Wedekind's life—his politically radical father who rejected Bismarck and so admired the American form of democracy that he named his son Benjamin Franklin, his enthusiastic participation in circus life, his lively bohemian exis-

tence in Munich—pale before the intense, if not outrageous, activity this artist enjoyed in the world of drama. Wedekind peopled the stage with a wild world of adventurers, confidence men, artists, prostitutes, fools. Typical of this panorama is the play *Der Marquis von Keith* (*The Marquis of Keith,* 1901). Furthermore, Wedekind always intended the dramatic action to be bizarre and extreme, for he felt it his obligation to reveal bourgeois morality in its full absurdity and hypocrisy. Such is the intent of *Der Erdgeist* (*Earth Spirit,* pub. 1893, perf. 1898) and its sequel, *Die Büchse der Pandora* (*Pandora's Box,* 1903).

Wedekind's dramas were indeed exciting, controversial, and successful. He has been considered a respected exponent of naturalism, but he is perhaps more significant for his contributions to expressionism. In his thematic material, the operation of the sexual instinct and the exhibition of it in situations extremely shocking to the sensibilities of the philistine bourgeoisie, he did seem to adhere to the tenets of naturalism. If the naturalist wanted to present reality in all its ugliness and misery in order to achieve "accuracy in the appearance," Wedekind is realistic to an extreme, more radically realistic than all the naturalists. In his determination to present man as animal, he was uncompromising with his representa-

FRANK WEDEKIND (GERMAN INFORMATION CENTER)

tion of physical and psychical phenomena; so much so, that if he did not shock the naturalists, he certainly outdid them. The naturalist Max Halbe, for example, wrote a puberty play with the same thematic content as Wedekind's SPRING'S AWAKENING. But whereas Wedekind's drama created an outburst of furious discussion and bitter dissension, Halbe's play was exceedingly popular. The reason for the latter's favorable reception lay in the fact that the brutal contours of the explosive subject matter were softened by atmospheric color and by melodramatic emotional appeal. Wedekind's play resorted to no such dishonest devices. The brutality of an insensitive and inhuman society in its blind condemnation of a very human and moving experience was represented with the full force of its shattering truthfulness. Gerhart Hauptmann designated Wedekind's writings as *Darminhalte,* which might be roughly translated as "intestinal refuse."

Because of the extreme radicality of presentation, thematic as well as stylistic, Wedekind's dramatic intentions seem to transcend the limitations of naturalistic verisimilitude and to penetrate a far more fundamental sphere of reality. By unmitigated concentration on the thematic focal point, by omission of the relief of a panorama perspective, by compression of language to dynamically charged verbal structures, Wedekind's art appears to capture the essence of the human situation. *Das Zuständliche* (a term coined by Georg Kaiser), that is, "that which is circumstantial," that which is incidental and immaterial to the main point, has been intentionally eliminated from the dramatic complex. Hence we find a reluctance in Wedekind to use techniques of sociological, psychological, or historical development to further the action. Instead, we note the concentration on the

use of language in its typical patterns—the language of school children, businessmen, artists, prostitutes, etc. For language, accurately observed and recreated, constructs the fabric of a milieu both environmental and individual without distracting attention from the inner core of the dramatic experience to nonessential circumstances. The same emphasis on the power of the word, which the expressionists placed in their aesthetic thinking and writing, was already there in Wedekind's dramas.

Finally, the moral-didactic notion fundamental to all of Wedekind's plays, and always acting to filter the thematic presentation from any pornographic sludge, clearly distinguished his writings from the purely descriptive intentions of the naturalists. The same missionary impulse that invigorated the aesthetic creed of the expressionists is to be found in Wedekind's art.

Wedekind died in 1918 after having enjoyed an exciting life, not only in his literary activities, but also in his private affairs, for it is said that he practiced what he preached.

A collection of English versions of his plays is *Five Tragedies of Sex,* translated by F. Fawcett and S. Spender (1961). See Walter H. Sokel, *The Writer in Extremis* (1959); H. F. Garten, *Modern German Drama* (1959); and O. F. Theis, "Frank Wedekind" in *Poet Lore,* VII (1913) for critical discussions of his works.—C. A. M.

Weise, Christian (1642–1702). German educator and writer of some of the earliest pedagogically oriented dramas showing the influences of the German Enlightenment and the rise of the middle classes. Born in Zittau, Weise studied in Leipzig and, after two years as the secretary to a Halle nobleman, took up a career of teaching. Beginning as a private tutor, he soon became professor at the gymnasium in Weissenfels and in 1678 was made rector of the gymnasium in Zittau. His educational career provided both the purpose and casts of his plays: He regarded them solely as pedagogical instruments. Deliberately reacting against the courtly ethos and inflated language of the modish Silesian drama of the Baroque era, Weise sought to create his plays for and of the middle classes.

Due to the almost *ad hoc* setting of the performances, a three-day school festival at the close of the academic year, Weise's plays do little to commend themselves as works of art. The combination of Zittau audiences accustomed to five-hour productions and the pedagogical necessity of finding a role for every student obviated any economy in the plays and tended to fill them with much extraneous material. The tragedies, histories, and biblical plays, many written earlier in his career, are at best stories divided conveniently into acts.

Weise's comedies, on the other hand, are true precursors to the work of Lessing, almost a century later. These plays were subject to the same restrictions as the tragedies and histories, but the language and characterization truly reflected the reason-based middle-class ethos. Weise was one of the earliest German authors to portray the middle classes as reality. To the Enlightenment thinker, nature was equated with reason, and the everyday life around Weise was the nature that he sought to depict in his plays. A typical play was the *Liebes-Alliance* ("Alliance of Love," 1703), a marriage comedy in which two elderly people seeking marriage with someone younger find each other, leaving the "natural" union of the youngsters to take place by itself. Although the Baroque play also carried a moral message, it was invariably delivered in black and white, projecting an unrealizable, often supernatural example: Weise's comedy, on the other hand, sought to educate people by projecting them as they are.—B. M. M.

Weiss, Peter (1916–   ). German playwright, painter, film director, and journalist. Exiled by the Nazis in 1934, Weiss attempted to make a name for himself as a painter in London and Prague. Then in 1939 he migrated to Stockholm, Sweden, where he began to show more interest in writing novels and making films. His first success as a writer came with his autobiographical novels *Der Schatten des Körpers des Kutschers* ("The Shadow of the Body of the Coachman," 1960), *Abschied von den Eltern* ("Departure from the Parents," 1961), and *Fluchtpunkt* ("Point of Flight," 1962). It was not until the production of his unusual political satire *Die Verfolgung und Ermordung des Jean Paul Marats dargestellt durch die Schauspielgruppe des Hospizes zu Charenton unter Anleitung des Herrn de Sade* (*The Persecution and Assassination of Jean Paul Marat Portrayed by the Acting Company of the Asylum at Charenton under the Direction of Mr. de Sade,* known generally as *Marat/Sade,* 1964) that Weiss distinguished himself as a dramatist. Though the dialectics of the play have led numerous critics to label it ambiguous, the drama nevertheless does contain a bleak statement about the rigid cruelty of Restoration France and the insane quarrels of contemporary Europe as the madhouse Charenton. Weiss is fond of images that recall concentration camps, and the revolutionary playacting and debates of Marat, Sade, and the inmates are fruitless because the real power remains in the hands of the tyrannical keepers of the asylum, which is structured like a prison. It is against these philistine upholders of the *status quo* (and in a sense against the audience) that Weiss vents his anger. This is also the case in *Die Ermittlung* (*The Investigation,* 1965), which marks his first full documentary presentation of a historical situation with strong Marxist overtones. Here Weiss, who writes his plays in free verse, transforms a trial against the Auschwitz murderers into a prosecution of the present-day Germans, who deny knowing about the concentration camps and operate in a system that stimulates them to obliterate the past. By means of staging—the accused are anonymous and sometimes sit with the audience—Weiss confronts contemporary industrialists with charges of brutality and exploitation. Weiss wants to understand the roots of aggression and to check the violation of humanity.

One of Weiss's more recent works, performed by the Negro Ensemble Company in New York, is *Gesang vom lusitanischen Popanz* (*The Song of the Lusitanian Bogey,* 1967), an attack on the imperialistic rulers of Angola. Using music and documents, Weiss recalls the deplorable history of Portuguese exploitation in Angola before the native rebellion of March 15, 1961. He compares the situation in Angola to fascism in Germany and racism in South Africa and America. Though Weiss's *Song* is about depressing conditions, it strikes a note of hope in depicting the struggle for freedom of the natives. When bogeymen claim the right to fight for progress by suppressing and "civilizing" undeveloped peoples by force, Weiss calls upon these peoples to rebel against the imperialists. For Weiss, America represents the evil tide of colonialism today, and he takes the United States to task in his latest documentary drama entitled *Diskurs über die Vorgeschichte und den Verlauf des lang andauernden Befreiungskrieges in Viet Nam als Beispiel für die Notwendigkeit des bewaffneten Kampfes der Unterdrückten gegen ihre Unterdrücker sowie über die Versuche der Vereinigten Staaten von Amerika die Grundlagen der Revolution zu vernichten* ("Discourse on the Historical Background and the Course of the Continuous Struggle for Liberation in Viet Nam as an Example of the Necessity of Armed Warfare by the Oppressed against their Oppressors and Furthermore on the Attempts of the United States of America to Annihilate the Basic Principles of the Revolution," 1968). This title sums up both Weiss's political and dramatic development to date.—J. D. Z.

well-made play (*pièce bien faite*). The term given problem dramas, comedies of manners, or farces written since about 1825 in France, England, the United States, and some other countries, which combine certain specific features in a seemingly logical and plausible manner of construction. These features are (1) a plot based on a withheld secret that, revealed at the climax of the action, turns the tide in the hero's favor; (2) initial exposition that summarizes the story up to the raising of the curtain and slowly accelerating action and suspense sustained by such contrivances as precisely timed entrances and exits, letters which miscarry, mistaken identity, and *quiproquos* (in which two or more characters, by unwittingly misinterpreting a situation in different ways, become hopelessly entangled); (3) a series of ups and downs, or gambits, in a battle of wits between two adversaries, suspense being initiated by the planting of clues to imminent events and by the withholding of information from certain characters (this initiation of suspense is called the art of preparation); (4) a reversal in the action followed by a climactic, "obligatory" scene (termed the *scène à faire* by the critic Francisque Sarcey), representing, respectively, the nadir and the zenith of the hero's fortunes (the scène à faire is effected by the disclosing of the withheld secret); (5) a logical, credible denouement; and (6) a microcosmic repetition of the overall structural pattern in each act. Frequently, the hero experiences a conflict between love (with a pretty but naïve girl he wishes to marry) and duty (to an older and more worldly woman from whom he wishes to disengage himself without embarrassment). In the scène à faire some moral judgment is always implied, however trivial. That is, the characters are judged according to standards of right and wrong acceptable to the audience.

The true prototypes of the well-made play are the well-constructed but artificial plays of Eugène SCRIBE and his successor Victorien SARDOU, but the domestic dramas of Émile Augier and Alexandre Dumas fils fused the craftsmanship of these playwrights with their own serious social theses in a way that appealed to later dramatists, especially the writers of problem plays. The plays of Eugène Labiche, Georges Feydeau, and other French playwrights were strongly influenced by the pièce bien faite. In free translations these French plays were performed in England and America and satisfied the demand for a robust, living theater at a time when the drama, under the influence of the Romantic movement, had become lofty, insipid, and formless. Scribe had inherited from the eighteenth century the positivistic ideas that helped lay the foundations of naturalism, and his vitality and resourcefulness helped to restore some of the compact dramatic form that had characterized the best neoclassical plays. The plays of the nineteenth-century English dramatists Edward Bulwer-Lytton, Tom Taylor, and T. W. Robertson were successfully built on Scribean models. The young Henrik Ibsen directed some twenty plays of Scribe in Bergen, Norway, in the 1850's and incorporated their stagecraft into his own dramas.

Although Émile Zola attacked the well-made play in France (*Le Naturalisme au théâtre,* 1881) and Bernard Shaw tried to kill it in England (*Saturday Review,* London, May 27, 1895), both playwrights used its techniques for their own purposes. And it is very much alive today in both countries and in the United States.

For the survival of the genre in nineteenth- and twentieth-century British drama, the reader should consult John Russell Taylor's *The Rise and Fall of the Well-Made Play* (1967). Briefer discussions of the impact of the well-made play on modern drama are contained in Stephen S. Stanton's introduction to *Camille and Other Plays* (1957) and Evert Sprinchorn's introduction to *20th-Century Plays in Synopsis* (1965).—S. S. S.

Well of the Saints, The (1905). A play by John Millington SYNGE. For this satiric parable in three acts Synge used a theme from folklore to create a mordant comedy on the vanity of human wishes. It is the legend of a blind old couple, Martin and Mary Doul, happy beggars who enjoy their simple pleasures in a world of their own illusions in which they are attractive and the people around them are kindly. When a Saint arrives with miraculous powers that can cure blindness, Martin and Mary have their sight restored, and immediately a brutal reality crashes down upon them. Martin mistakes the beautiful but cruel young Molly Byrne for his hag of a wife, and as a vain old man he is savagely mocked by Molly and her fiancé, Timmy the Smith, as well as by all the sadistic villagers. When the Saint returns to tell the Douls they can retain their sight only if he gives them a second miracle treatment of holy water, the humiliated and bitter pair choose their protective illusions of blindness again. Although Synge's irony is aimed at the escapist Douls as well as the cynical villagers, blindness is more than an illusion or mere escape to Martin. When he is blind, his senses become heightened to the free and imaginative experience of nature and the physical world and he possesses the insight of a poet. At the end the Douls go off to the south in a dubious search for greater kindness and warmth, and though Timmy predicts they will probably be drowned in the floods, Martin has in his blindness chosen the act of poetic imagination as the greatest miracle.—D. K.

Werfel, Franz. See AUSTRIA; GERMANY: *twentieth century.*

Werner, [Friedrich Ludwig] Zacharias (1768–1823). German playwright and preacher. When Werner was born, his mother believed that she had given birth to a messiah. Though Werner himself never became as fanatic as his mother, he showed a strong tendency toward religious mysticism during the course of his life. After studying law at the University of Königsberg, he embarked on a career as civil servant in 1793. Later he moved to Warsaw, where his religious zeal was channeled into an interest in Freemasonry. His first drama, *Die Söhne des Tals* ("The Sons of the Valley," 1803), was divided into two parts, *Die Templer auf Cypern* ("The Templars on Cyprus") and *Die Kreuzbrüder* ("The Brothers of the Cross"), which concern the tragic defeat of the crusaders. After writing another drama similar in vein, *Das Kreuz an der Ostsee* ("The Cross on the Baltic Sea," 1806), Werner began to show more of an interest in Lutheranism and composed one of his best works, *Martin Luther, oder die Weihe der Kraft* ("Martin Luther, or The Consecration of Power," 1807), as a defense of the Protestant religion. The idea of destiny is predominant in the play. Luther, a priest, and Katharina von Bora, a nun, are drawn to one another by a force greater than both of them. Katharina sees in Luther a new messiah, while Luther sees in Katharina a guardian angel. In the end, they renounce the Catholic dogma for a new creed of faith and humanity. The question of fate haunted Werner, and he dealt with this theme (see SHICKSALSTRAGÖDIE) and mysticism in *Attila, König der Hunnen* ("Attila, King of the Huns," 1808), *Wanda, Königin der Sarmaten* ("Wanda, Queen of the Sarmatians," 1810), and *Kunegunde* ("Saint Conegonde," 1815). However, his greatest play about destiny—the drama for which he is remembered today—is *Der 24. Februar* ("The Twenty-fourth of February," 1810), which depicts a simple peasant family struggling against a curse that causes various members of the family to kill one another on February 24. Werner's tendency to stress violence and the mysterious unknown are evident in this tightly knit drama. Indeed, this is Werner's only well-made drama. Generally speaking, his plays are filled with bombastic language, weird moods, and amorphous religious notions. His last two dramas, written after he converted to Catholicism, are examples of Werner's uncontrolled genius. In *Die Weihe der Unkraft* ("The Consecration of Nonpower," 1814), he refutes the stand he had taken in *Martin Luther,* and in *Die Mutter der Makkabäer* ("The Mother of the Maccabeans," 1820), he indulges himself in religious ravings and horrors. Werner, who had been married three times, ended his career, not as a dramatist, but as a Catholic priest, a preacher of abstinence.—J. D. Z.

Wesker, Arnold (1932–   ). English playwright. Wesker, the strongest voice in postwar English social drama, was born in the East End of London. His parents, both tailor's machinists, were Russian and Hungarian Jews who had come to England in childhood to escape the pogroms. Since much of Wesker's work is autobiographical and since he is inclined to project private experience onto society at large, his biography is particularly relevant. He grew up in what he has described in a speech as "a *milieu* of young, militant Jewish Communists," and in a family atmosphere "where there was singing, discussion, comradeship, and a respect for learning and the arts. Because we were Communists it meant that we knew we were dependent on each other. It also meant that I was in contact with a very wild, poor, working-class-conscious set of school mates."

As a boy Wesker was a member of the Young Communist League and later of the Zionist Youth Movement. After leaving school and failing to get a scholarship to the Royal Academy of Dramatic Art, he took a series of manual jobs before being conscripted into the R.A.F., where he found himself "politically a marked man." On demobilization Wesker worked as a farm laborer and then in a series of hotels and restaurants, where he became a pastry cook and later a chef in a Paris restaurant.

By this time Wesker had written *The Kitchen* and *Chicken Soup With Barley*. *Chicken Soup* appeared in 1958, followed by *Roots* (1959) and *I'm Talking About Jerusalem* (1960). These three plays, known as *The Wesker Trilogy,* were restaged in London in 1960 at the Royal Court Theatre, where *The Kitchen* had appeared the year before. *Chips With Everything,* his only play to achieve a successful West End run, appeared in 1962.

In 1960 Wesker launched Centre 42, an organization with the double purpose of bringing the arts to a wider (in practice, working-class) audience and of placing the means of production within the control of the producing artists. The organization ran a series of festivals displaying local trades and gained a headquarters in North London, but despite the approval of the Labour government it has been crippled by lack of money. Wesker at one point resolved to stop writing for two years and devote all his energy to Centre 42, but before the time limit expired he returned to the theater with *The Four Seasons* (1965) and *Their Very Own and Golden City* (1966), which won the first Marzotto Drama Prize.

The connection between Wesker's life and work is undisguised. The *Trilogy* spans the years 1936 to 1959, following the political evolution of the Kahn family from ideological militancy in the East End to idealistic defeat in the Norfolk countryside. *Chips With Everything* shows the operation of the class system inside the R.A.F. And *Golden City,* whose architect hero wages a sixty-year campaign to build a group of cities owned by the inhabitants, is clearly related to Wesker's career as director of Centre 42.

Since he first started to write, Wesker has enlarged his approach to social drama to admit the psychological element, but the basic character of his work remains unchanged. Writing for him is a form of social action, and his main theme is human brotherhood. The assumption is that the playwright has a duty to help people enrich their lives and that he can reach their hearts by direct solicitation. Hostile critics have called him a preacher; it is a role that he is glad to accept. But he is not really a political thinker, for his socialism began instinctively and through people rather than books. The view of society that emerges from his plays is that of a big, quarreling family.

The least attractive side of Wesker's writing is a paternalism that can sometimes seem priggish, as in the party scene in *Chips,* when the lower-class conscripts are induced to renounce pop music for old English folk songs. The idea here, as elsewhere, is that culture is a means by which the underprivileged can escape the prison of numb subservience. Wesker's favorite metaphor for culture is "the bridge."

Among modern playwrights, Wesker stands alone in his directness of social purpose and total sincerity of statement. These are two-edged virtues, and they sometimes leave him vulnerable to charges of naïveté and of confusing the particular with the general. As a dramatist he is on stronger ground with robust naturalism than with the heightened language of *The Four Seasons* or the "flash-forward" technique of *Golden City.* Yet he remains one of the few English playwrights who can write convincingly about political idealists, and he has an unrivaled talent for translating the processes of ordinary work into theatrical life.

All of Wesker's plays are published in separate editions.—I. W.

West Chamber, The (Tsai tzu shu). A Chinese play by Wang Shih-fu, about whom little is known except that he flourished in the middle period of the Yüan dynasty (1280–1368). *The West Chamber* is based on a story by Yuan Chen (779–831), although the playwright treats his source material with the freedom customarily taken by Chinese dramatists. Like most of the chief Chinese dramas, it is written in a scholarly vernacular. The play has long enjoyed high favor and is still acted, though as a rule scenes are extracted for performance. Production of the entire work would take many hours.

Like many popular Chinese plays, *The West Chamber* has undergone an eventful history. The text is edited in a scholarly edition (1931) in two volumes by Hsu Hsiao T'ien as a play in fifteen acts. Some editions give sixteen acts, some many more. All the

SCENE FROM WANG SHIH-FU'S *The West Chamber*
(CHINESE INFORMATION SERVICE)

later acts were presumably added by later hands. Thoroughly different in spirit from the authentic play, they append only sensational melodrama to a restrained work and provide a speciously happy or moralistic ending whereby the Chinese passion for moralizing is gratified by a prosaic and elaborate distribution of poetic justice, with joy to the good and woe to the wicked. The shorter version, actually long in Western eyes, has been preferred by the more judicial critics.

With the exception of only two or three minor scenes, the action takes place within the walls of a Buddhist monastery, where distinguished guests are granted hospitality. A mother, conveying the body of her husband to his ancestral home in a distant province, is forced by political disturbances to seek refuge in the monastery. With her is her unmarried daughter, a son who is still a child, and a witty maidservant. To the same establishment comes the play's hero, the typical young man of Chinese high comedy. He is on his way to the official examinations at the capital. The conditions of the play present as inevitable the union of the daughter and the young man. Regarding her daughter as already plighted to the son of a deceased high minister of state, the mother does all in her power to prevent this union. While the dramatist is clearly opposed to the mother's severe and conventional attitude, he presents her with genial understanding. The hero and the heroine are viewed with both sympathy and amusement. As young lovers, they lack the confidence of inner conviction. In an early scene, when the girl is voluble, her lover is embarrassed and silent and both are frustrated. Conversely, when their love is gratified, she is silent while he is voluble. The balanced design complies not merely with the customary usage of the Chinese stage—only one actor sings in a given act—but with the psychological realities of the situation. Even more admired by actors as a rewarding role is the witty servant, whose point of view is close to that of the dramatist. She is presented, not only as the wisest figure in the play—wiser than either mother or aged abbot, the young scholar, or the young lady—but as a convincing and endearing figure in her own right. Two of her scenes show her, frail and small as she is, truly courageous and great-hearted. While the lovers meet in the warm privacy of their room, she stands first on one foot and then on the other in the chilly night outside the window to protect the privacy of the lovers. With utmost fortitude she later withstands a lashing with whip and tongue by the angry mother. Moreover, her wise words of reconciliation addressed to the mother alone guide the action to its rational and rightful conclusion.

This ending as given in the authentic and by far the best version is, nevertheless, itself more inspired than in keeping with the orthodox and conventional practices of the Chinese stage. It is, in fact, a bold and exquisite tour de force. Persuaded by the gentle words of the maidservant, the mother at last consents to the union. The hero is duty-bound to leave his love in order to complete his journey to the capital and compete in the official examinations. It is agreed that if he succeeds in this competition, he will win the girl as his wife. No spectator of the play can doubt that he does so. In the spurious additions this success is needlessly brought before the eyes of the audience, to-gether with the gratuitous disgrace and death of the hero's rival. In the vastly more artful version the profound happiness that the lovers have found is presented in skillful juxtaposition to their temporary parting.

The West Chamber is remarkable for its insight into the emotions and for its almost perfect theatrical style. Considered in its totality, it has the leisurely and careful development of psychological analysis found in fiction at its best joined with the sharpened focus of the stage. The sophisticated union of warm sentiment with the spirit of high comedy is eminently Chinese. The dramatist deals with problems existing throughout the civilized world but made especially acute by Chinese society. Religious ideas are viewed with a becoming reverence; special sympathy, however, is extended to the pair of lovers. Yet both are seen through the eyes of the true comic dramatist, too elegant to descend to farce and too refined to pour forth satire embittered by indignation or hate.

The West Chamber has been translated, with a keen sense of the overtones of high comedy, by S. I. Hsiung (1935). Another translation, from a superior text, is that of H. H. Hart (1936). There is a free and unacceptable rendering in German by Vincenz Hundhausen (1926), and a by no means satisfactory French translation in *L'Atsume Gusa* (1872–1880), by the eminent scholar Stanislas Julien. See also Tsiang Un-kien, *K'ouen K'iu, Le Théatre ancien chinois* (1932).—H. W. W.

Where the Cross Is Made. See Eugene O'NEILL.

White Devil, The (1611/12). A tragedy by John WEBSTER. *The White Devil* is based upon a sensational murder that occurred in Italy in the latter part of the sixteenth century. It tells the story of an adulterous affair between the duke of Bracciano and Vittoria Corombona. Aided by the villainous Flamineo, Vittoria's brother, the lovers arrange the murders of their respective spouses. Vittoria is arrested but is rescued by Bracciano, who flees with her to Padua. In the meantime, a revenge plot is hatched by Francisco, the brother of Bracciano's late wife, and his cohorts Lodovico and Gasparo. Disguised as Capuchin priests, the latter two arrange an elaborate and agonizing death for Bracciano, first poisoning and then strangling their victim. Now Flamineo, whose growth in villainy is measured by the senseless killing of his brother before the eyes of their mother, demands a reward from Vittoria. The two attempt to outmaneuver one another, but they too are quickly dispatched by Lodovico and Gasparo. The avengers are themselves immediately captured and imprisoned by Bracciano's son Giovanni.

A plot summary can do no justice to the play's brilliantly evocative sense of passion, pride, and, most tellingly, death; the death scenes in this play are among the greatest in all dramatic literature. The character of Vittoria, an unforgettable synthesis of grandeur and villainy, is matched by that of Flamineo, a Machiavellian villain, shrewd, courageous, and cynical, who is the catalytic agent of the drama. The result is a play of an intensity and penetration unsurpassed outside of Shakespeare.—E. Q.

White Snake, The (Pai-shih ch'uan). Title of several Chinese plays, each a different version of a favorite story in Chinese poetry, fiction, and play-

THE WHITE DIVEL,

OR,

The Tragedy of *Paulo Giordano Vrſini,* Duke of *Brachiano,*

With

The Life and Death of Vittoria Corombona the famous Venetian Curtizan.

Acted by the Queenes Maieſties Seruants..

Written by I o ʜ n Wᴇ ᴊ s ᴛ ᴇ ʀ.

Non inferiora ſecutus.

———————————

LONDON,
Printed by *N.O.* for *Thomas Archer,* and are to be ſold at his Shop in Popes head Pallace, neere the Royall Exchange. 1 6 1 2.

TITLE PAGE OF THE 1612 EDITION OF JOHN WEBSTER'S *The White Devil*

writing. Its latest rendering, that by the well-known dramatist Tien Han, has been among the works most often performed by the leading Chinese actor of the 20th century, Mei Lan-fang. It was given by this actor's company, not only in China, but in the United States, Russia, and Japan. An earlier version appeared during the Ming dynasty (1368–1644) under the title *Leifeng Pagoda.* During the same period the legend was included in a collection, *Stories Warn the World.* The main elements of the plot are present in a work of the Sung dynasty, *The Tale of the Three Pagodas in the West Lake.* The theme may be traced even farther back to the T'ang dynasty. In any event, it is certain that the story is very old and has great fascination, not only in China, but in other parts of the world as well. The legend is that of a snake-woman. According to the branch of the story considered here, her dual nature may or may not be explained, but she may at any time, difficult or impossible to foresee, when turned into a snake destroy her human lover. This is the tale related of the lamia of Corinth in Philostratus's *Life of Apollonius Tyana.* It has become familiar to English readers through John Keats's poem *Lamia.*

Tien Han's play depicts a romantic, vascillating, ineffectual but attractive young man, Hsu Hsien, who assists two women caught in a rain storm by giving them the shelter of his umbrella. One is Miss White (the white snake), the other Miss Green, her inseparable friend. Both are minor deities consigned for no explicit reason to a life among mankind. Miss White and Hsu fall in love, marry, and together manage an apothecary shop. One day a monk, Fa Ming, calls at their shop to warn Hsu that he lives in mortal danger through marriage to a snake-woman. As evidence, he tells Hsu that if on a certain feast day his wife drinks wine mixed with realgar her snake nature will appear. Hsu fails to take the warning seriously. Circumstances arise that cause him to do precisely what he should not. She drinks the fatal wine. Glancing by chance toward his wife's bed, he sees the apparition of the snake-woman, which frightens him so severely that he falls half-dead in a state of prostration. His wife, who loves him, as he also loves her, undertakes a heavenly journey, where she obtains the magic herb with which she revives him. He, however, is still disturbed. Seeking further advice, he goes to the monastery from which his religious adviser had previously come. Here he is advised to take monastic vows. His wife, hearing this, goes with Miss Green to the gates of the monastery, which she attempts to invade by force. Her violence fails, owing to her advanced state of pregnancy, but Hsu decides finally to leave the monastery. Their child is born. Shortly thereafter, the august abbot himself visits their home, carrying in his hand a magic alms bowl, with the aid of which he crushes Hsu and takes his wife captive. She is confined for three hundred years (presumably a Chinese expression for a long period of time) within an elaborate pagoda. At the end of this period Miss Green, who has been throughout the most vigorous and impetuous figure in the play, destroys the pagoda with the help of a celestial army and releases its prisoner. This relatively happy ending belongs to later versions of the story only. It is found, to be sure, in three versions dating from the reign of the Emperor Chien Lung (1736–1795), as well as in popular ballads. Yet the latest version bears undoubted witness to the optimistic spirit of the stage under communism. Before the communist ascendency in China by far the greater number of plays ended happily; since that event, all do.

The play offers the best example of both the supernatural and the mythological aspects of the Chinese stage. To the discerning members of the audience its symbolism signifies that great as man's good will, evils must inevitably beset him. It further signifies that the emotions associated with erotic desire may be succeeded in the individual life by growing awareness of spiritual and social values. The abbot with his alms bowl in hand is victorious. The play is a graceful homily. It is also a remarkably rewarding work for the theater, with many intensely dramatic scenes. Moreover, as produced by Mei Lan-fang it was brilliantly choreographic.

The White Snake has been translated into English, with an Introduction, by Yang Hsien-yi and Gladys Yang (1957).—H. W. W.

Whiting, John [**Robert**] (1918–1963). English playwright. Whiting, the most remarkable English playwright to emerge in the first postwar decade, was born in Salisbury, Wiltshire, the son of a solicitor.

First an actor, and then a minor author during the 1950's, he suffered four successive failures in the theater, and then abandoned the theater for films. After the 1956 "breakthrough" he was canonized as the progenitor and lost leader of the new English drama. However, Whiting was hardly more at home in the new age than in the old. In particular, he took exception to the new social drama, which in his view was childish and out of date. "The movement," Whiting once wrote for a magazine, "has a heart. . . . All the throbbing emotionalism proves it. We are asked to admire its virility. I am pleased to do so. It is that little tiny head which worries me."

Whiting would at any time have been an isolated figure in the theater. He was as indifferent to entertainment as he was to uplift and no more concerned with turning out a conventionally workmanlike product than with offering blueprints for the good life. He spoke of himself as "one of that disappearing species, a private individual." Whiting's first play, *Saint's Day* (1951), is concerned with precisely such a figure, a reclusive old poet who is tempted to attend a literary dinner in his honor. A plot synopsis does no justice to this strange piece, which, in its creation of action from imagery and its prevailing moods of graveyard comedy and routine violence, forecasts the drama that arrived at the end of the decade. Whiting's first play to reach the stage was *A Penny for a Song* (1951), a featherweight Napoleonic comedy somewhat reminiscent of the satirical novels of Thomas Love Peacock (1785–1866). Whiting's next piece, *Marching Song* (1954), is a study of political conscience set in a nameless European country. The play suggests the work of a British Ugo Betti and now

seems the most dated of his plays. After writing screenplays for some years (*Talk of the Devil*, 1956; *The Reason Why*, 1958; and *Young Cassidy*, 1960), Whiting was tempted back to the stage by director Peter Hall to write *The Devils* for the Royal Shakespeare Company's 1961 London season. Based on Aldous Huxley's *The Devils of Loudun*, this study of sexual and judicial hysteria among the clergy of seventeenth-century France at last enlisted the full range of Whiting's Jacobean sensibility. His other surviving plays are *No Why?* (1964), a one-acter about a small boy's suicide, an early piece suppressed by himself, *Conditions of Agreement* (1965), and *The Gate of Summer* (1956).

There is a collected edition of Whiting's first three plays, with an introduction by the author. *The Devils* is published in a separate text.—I. W.

Who's Afraid of Virginia Woolf? (1962). A play by Edward ALBEE. In the first act, "Fun and Games," we are introduced to a middle-aged history professor and his wife, George and Martha, who entertain a younger married couple, Nick and Honey, at their home after a faculty party. Nick is a biologist, engaged in experiments that may alter—and presumably improve—humanity. George and Martha quarrel and embarrass their guests. Martha, whose father is president of the college, nags George for his failures, and mysterious references are made to their son. In the second act, "Walpurgisnacht," painful incidents out of George's past are exposed, and it is revealed that Nick married Honey after her hysterical pregnancy. Honey gets very drunk, and Martha and Nick go off to make love. In the third act, "The Exorcism," they come back without hav-

A SCENE FROM HENRIK IBSEN'S *The Wild Duck* (NORWEGIAN INFORMATION SERVICE)

ing made love satisfactorily, and George announces the death of his and Martha's son, who has been purely imaginary, a myth that they have shared but which George has now exorcised.

At the heart of the play is the violent, quarrelsome relationship between George and Martha. "You can stand it!!" says Martha. "You married me for it!!" And, indeed, each married the other for it. For them, violence is a means of communication (recalling a theme of Albee's *The Zoo Story*), even a way of love. The shallow Nick is at first shocked, then angered, but he comes to appreciate the complexity of their lives.—H. P.

Wild Duck, The (Vildanden, 1885). A play by Henrik IBSEN. Gregers Werle, a man of gentle but firm monomania for what he considers to be the truth, returns to the village of his upbringing and forces his boyhood friend Hjalmar Ekdal, a would-be musician and inventor, to abandon his fuzzy illusions and face the facts. Werle progressively unveils the devastating truth that Ekdal's wife is really the left-over mistress of the elder Werle, that he was set up in marriage and the photography business to take care of the abandoned woman, Gina, and that his lovely daughter, Hedvig, is not his own. It is not difficult for Ekdal to make the connection between the elder Werle's faltering eyesight and Hedvig's defective vision. Hjalmar flies into a melodramatic pet and Hedvig, in reaction to her father's rejection of her, goes into the family's attic menagerie, presumably to kill the wild duck that has come to symbolize, in the metaphoric context of the play, an escape from reality. Instead, she kills herself. In the scene of infinite poignance that follows, Dr. Relling, a rummy doctor who is nonetheless Ibsen's mouthpiece, forcefully makes the point that only the "life-lie" makes most existences possible.

The play, a notable example of symbolic realism, attacks any rigid, narrow-minded interpretation of truth. Its concern with illusion versus reality puts it in the same family with Gorky's *Lower Depths* and O'Neill's *The Iceman Cometh.*

The best text and critical treatment are in *Ibsen,* Vol. VI (1960), edited by J. W. McFarlane. —R. B. V.

Wilde, Oscar [Fingal O'Flahertie Wills] (1854–1900). Irish-born English poet, playwright, novelist, and aesthete. Wilde's father was a distinguished surgeon and his mother a poet who wrote under the name Speranza. A precocious, brilliant child, Wilde enjoyed an excellent education, winning an exhibition scholarship at the age of fifteen to Trinity College, Dublin, where he won a gold medal for an essay on the Greek comic poets. In 1874 he matriculated at Magdalen College, Oxford, where he again displayed his brilliance and academic excellence, taking first honors in classics and winning the Newdigate Prize for verse with his poem "Ravenna." More important to Wilde himself, perhaps, was the influence of John Ruskin and Walter Pater, especially the latter's aesthetic preachments. Wilde called Pater's *Studies in the History of the Renaissance* (1873) "the golden book of spirit and sense, the holy writ of beauty."

After finishing his studies at Oxford, Wilde went to London and, calling himself "Professor of Aesthetics," proceeded to preach the gospel of "art for art's sake," to establish friendships with some of the lead-

OSCAR WILDE (WALTER HAMPDEN MEMORIAL LIBRARY AT THE PLAYERS, NEW YORK)

ing literary and artistic figures of the time and to gain a reputation for eccentricity and wit. His subsequent rise to fame or notoriety (depending upon one's view) as poet (*Poems,* 1881; *The Sphinx,* 1894); novelist (*The Picture of Dorian Gray,* 1891); dramatist; lecturer (he visited America in 1882); and critic (*Intentions,* 1891) and his eventual downfall and personal disgrace form one of the most famous and intriguing chapters in English literary history. Although he married Constance Lloyd in 1884, there were constant rumors of his homosexuality, and finally, angered by the accusations of the marquis of Queensberry, father of Lord Alfred Douglas, who had charged Wilde with sexual abnormalities, Wilde sued the marquis for libel. The suit backfired; Wilde's suit was dismissed, countercharges were filed, and in 1895 Wilde was found guilty of homosexual practices and sentenced to two years of hard labor. After his release from prison, during which time he composed the confessional *De Profundis,* he spent the rest of his life in France, rapidly declining in health and spirits, trying to continue writing. During this last period he wrote what is often regarded as his best poem, *The Ballad of Reading Gaol,* printed in 1898 under the pseudonym C.3.3., his prison number. He died in 1900, after a short illness, receiving the last rites of the Roman Catholic Church.

As a dramatist, Wilde is best known for the "trivial comedies for serious people," as he styled them, that he wrote in the 1890's—*Lady Windermere's Fan* (1892), *A Woman of No Importance* (1893), *An Ideal Husband* (1895), and THE IMPORTANCE OF BEING EARNEST—and the decadent, melodramatic *Salomé* (1893, in French). In the comedies, he demonstrated most clearly his gift of satire and his clever wit. Using the stock characters and conventional situations of the earlier Restoration and eighteenth-century comedies and the melodramatic "problem" plays of his own day, Wilde succeeded, mainly through verbal ingenuity and stylistic brilliance, in subtly but effectively revealing the shallowness and emptiness of English society. The best example of this genre is, of course, *The Importance of Being Earnest,* in which underneath the seemingly lightly tossed-off epigrams and witty, paradoxical statements is evident Wilde's perceptive analysis of Victorian hypocrisy, especially its willingness to close its eyes to unpleasant facts and events. *Salomé,* on the other hand, reveals the aesthetic and decadent Wilde, the side more evident in the poetry, which discloses his fascination with the bizarre, macabre, morbid aspects of life. It is, however, as the English wit and satirist of the comedies rather than the French decadent of *Salomé* that Wilde the dramatist is remembered.

A good introduction to Wilde's life and thought are Hesketh Pearson's *The Life of Oscar Wilde* (1946) and Arthur Ransome's *Oscar Wilde, A Critical Study* (1912). See also Rupert Hart-Davis, ed., *The Letters of Oscar Wilde* (1962); J. E. Agate, *Oscar Wilde and the Theatre* (1947); St. John Ervine, *Oscar Wilde* (1951); and Frank Harris, *Oscar Wilde; His Life and Confessions* (2 vols., 1920).—M. T.

Wilder, Thornton [Niven] (1897–   ). American playwright, novelist, essayist, and film writer. The son of a newspaperman who was to become American consul general in Hong Kong and Shanghai, Thornton Wilder was born in Madison, Wisconsin, and received his early schooling in that city,

THORNTON WILDER (WIDE WORLD PHOTOS)

in Hong Kong and Chefoo, and in Berkeley and Ojai, California. A writer of stories and plays from childhood, Wilder contributed frequently to the literary magazines of Oberlin and Yale, both of which he attended as an undergraduate. In 1926 he published his first novel, *The Cabala.* The same year saw the first presentation of a play by Wilder, when the American Laboratory Theatre in New York produced *The Trumpet Shall Sound,* an allegory about God's infinite capacity for forgiveness. In 1927 appeared his Pulitzer Prize-winning novel *The Bridge of San Luis Rey.* A collection of very short dramatic pieces, *The Angel That Troubled the Waters and Other Plays,* was published in 1928; most were written at Oberlin and Yale. Wilder followed this in 1930 with another novel, *The Woman of Andros,* a romantic adaptation of Terence's *Andria.* In the same year he became a member of the faculty of the University of Chicago. With intervals away for lecturing and writing, he continued at Chicago until 1938. During this period he translated André Obey's *Rape of Lucrece* for Katharine Cornell and Ibsen's *A Doll's House* for Ruth Gordon. The translations were produced in 1932 and 1937, respectively.

Although he had set most of his early work in the remote past or in distant locales, Wilder turned, after *The Woman of Andros,* to explorations of American life and attitudes. In 1931 he published *The Long Christmas Dinner and Other Plays in One Act,* a volume of six pieces, five of which take place in America. In 1935 appeared *Heaven's My Destination,* a novel of the Depression-stricken Midwest. After the failure (quite undeserved) of this novel, Wilder turned again to drama and created in OUR TOWN, first produced in 1938, one of the most enduring works of the American stage. For this play of a New Hampshire community at the beginning of the present century Wilder received his second Pulitzer Prize. Later in the year he offered another play, *The Merchant of Yonkers.* Set in the 1880's in Yonkers and New York City, it is an adaptation of the nineteenth-century Viennese comedy of Johann Nestroy, *Einen Jux will er sich machen,* which in turn is an adaptation of John Oxenford's English comedy, *A Day Well Spent.* A failure in 1938, the play achieved great success in Britain in 1954 and America in 1955, when, with slight revisions, it was presented as *The Matchmaker.* (In 1963 it appeared in musical adaptation as *Hello, Dolly!*) In 1942 came the production of THE SKIN OF OUR TEETH, a comedy bringing all creation into its compass but taking as its starting point a small town in New Jersey. For this controversial but successful play Wilder received his third Pulitzer Prize.

After the Second World War, Wilder continued to divide his effort almost equally between fiction and drama, and continued to receive honors. His first major postwar work, published in 1948, was *The Ides of March,* a novel of the last months of Caesar's life. At the Edinburgh festivals of 1954 and 1955, respectively, were presented *The Matchmaker* and *A Life in the Sun;* the latter, an adaptation of the *Alcestis* of Euripides, was not a success and was not transferred to America. Late in 1961 he announced a plan to write a double series of fourteen plays, seven on the deadly sins and seven on the ages of man. As *Plays for Bleecker Street* (the title indicating the location of the theater), three of the pieces were staged in

New York in 1962: *Someone from Assisi* (on lust), *Infancy,* and *Childhood.* Concerned lest encroaching age prevent his completing the series, Wilder determined to withdraw from social life until he had done so. The result of his withdrawal was unexpected: he turned from his plays and produced a novel of a murder and its sweeping metaphysical implications, titled *The Eighth Day* (1967).

Wilder's plays are distinguished by their originality and clarity of form and expression. All are variations on the theme of the marvels of the human adventure. The least vivid of them are, understandably, the apprentice works, which include *The Trumpet Shall Sound* and *The Angel That Troubled the Waters,* the latter being a volume of three-minute plays for three actors. These pieces, imbued with the humanistic spirit dominant in American universities during the early decades of the century, are overelegant in diction and overelaborate in setting. A sudden and welcome change in Wilder's manner is apparent in *The Long Christmas Dinner and Other Plays.* Three of the six one-act pieces, *Pullman Car Hiawatha, The Happy Journey to Trenton and Camden,* and the work that gives the volume its title, are vital antinaturalistic plays that point to the longer works to come. Written in simple, colloquial American speech and designed to be performed on a stage stripped bare of scenery, they are sketches of familiar American types, most of whom are revealed in situations stressing family relationships. Though all three plays touch on death, they are not pessimistic; rather, they offer an affirmation of all the varieties of experience that life brings to mankind. Introduced in these plays are elements that Wilder was to use in *Our Town* and *The Skin of Our Teeth:* movement back and forth in time, the "double vision" that sees the past at work in the shaping of the present, the omniscient stage manager, and interruptions of the action for sociological information and the wisdom of the great philosophers. These pieces should not, however, be taken for exercises leading to the longer plays but as works complete in themselves.

Each of Wilder's three Broadway successes, *Our Town, The Matchmaker,* and *The Skin of Our Teeth,* differs from the others in its presentational devices, though all have many elements in common. The celebration of human existence, which is the purpose of every Wilder work, takes the form in *Our Town* of the reminder that in his hurried trip through life the individual is likely to miss many of the wonders of ordinary, day-to-day events; in *The Matchmaker,* that every human being should make the effort to look for adventure; and in *The Skin of Our Teeth,* that man must never be discouraged from continuing in his existence or from the pursuit of intellectual development.

Despite the antinaturalistic devices of his plays— such as the lack of scenery or the unconventional use of it and the direct addresses to the audience by major characters—the situations that Wilder presents are candid views of human experience acted out by robust characters. Among the major plays, only *The Matchmaker* displays characters who consistently appear to be distortions of the norm of humanity. The essential truth-to-life of the plays, along with the theme of affirmation, is in large part responsible for their continuing popularity. But the same quali-

ties, it must be said, have caused Wilder to be taken by some critics as a sentimentalist who views mankind with unjustifiable optimism. Optimism is not smugness, however, and Wilder, far from expressing satisfaction with all of man's ways, calls for increased participation in life and an honest look at its sorrows as well as its delights.

Wilder's plays have been published in the following collections: *The Angel That Troubled the Waters and Other Plays* (1928), *The Long Christmas Dinner and Other Plays in One Act* (1931), and *Three Plays* (1957), which includes *Our Town, The Skin of Our Teeth,* and *The Matchmaker.* For a critical study, see Malcolm Goldstein, *The Art of Thornton Wilder* (1965).—M. G.

Williams, [Thomas Lanier] Tennessee (1911–). American playwright. Williams, who did not adopt the name Tennessee until late in the 1930's, was born Thomas Lanier on March 26, 1911, in Columbus, Mississippi, the son of a traveling shoe salesman. He grew up in St. Louis. He began attending the University of Missouri in 1929, and after an extended interruption while, among other things, he worked for a shoe company, he graduated from the University of Iowa in 1938. He had begun to write plays during those years and to have them produced locally. His first national recognition came in 1939 when he received a citation for a related group of one-act plays, *American Blues,* in a Group Theatre play contest. His first commercial production was *Battle of Angels* (1940), which closed in Boston after a losing struggle with censorship and its own inadequacies. He spent six months in 1943 as a contract writer for MGM, during which time he wrote an original script, *The Gentleman Caller,* which he eventually turned into a play, THE GLASS MENAGERIE,

TENNESSEE WILLIAMS (WIDE WORLD PHOTOS)

his first theatrical success. Since the New York opening of *Menagerie* (March 31, 1945), Williams has been accepted as one of the leading American playwrights. He has written steadily, averaging rather more than a play a year: *You Touched Me!* (1945), written with Donald Windham; A STREETCAR NAMED DESIRE (1947); *Summer and Smoke* (1948); *The Rose Tattoo* (1951); *Camino Real* (1953); *Cat on a Hot Tin Roof* (1955); *Orpheus Descending* (1957); *Suddenly Last Summer* (1958); *Sweet Bird of Youth* (1959); *Period of Adjustment* (1960); *The Night of the Iguana* (1961); *The Milk Train Doesn't Stop Here Anymore* (1963; revised 1964); *Slapstick Tragedy* (1966); *The Seven Descents of Myrtle* (1968). His greatest commercial and critical successes have been *The Glass Menagerie, A Streetcar Named Desire, Cat on a Hot Tin Roof,* and *The Night of the Iguana.* These plays not only had the longest runs, but they all received the Drama Critics Circle Award and two of them (*Streetcar* and *Cat*) were given the Pulitzer Prize. Williams has also published two volumes of short plays, three volumes of short stories, a novel, and a collection of poems. He has written extensively for the movies, adaptations of his own work, of which *A Streetcar Named Desire* (1951) and *Baby Doll* (1956), the latter based on two of his short plays, are the most important.

There is a thematic similarity in most of Williams' work. From the beginning of his career, he has been preoccupied with the man or woman who by virtue of being different can (in fact, must) stand outside and see the world clearly—which, for Williams, means to see the horror in it. Perhaps the best general description of the Williams outsider can be found in Alma's words in *The Eccentricities of a Nightingale,* a revision of *Summer and Smoke,* which was published in 1965 but has not played in New York: "My little company of the faded and frightened and difficult and odd and lonely." This company is presented satirically in the play, but then, Williams has always recognized that his outsiders (from Amanda in *The Glass Menagerie* to the heroine of *The Gnädiges Fräulein,* one of the two plays that make up *Slapstick Tragedy*) are—from one angle, at least—comic characters. This recognition in no way detracts from the courage or the pain of the characters, nor—from Williams' standpoint—the truth of their vision of the world. Since such characters are never at home in the world, since they are usually running to or from something, the label *fugitive kind,* which Williams used as the title for an early unpublished play and much later for the movie version of *Orpheus Descending* (1960), might best suit them. Within the fugitive kind, there are five general types: (1) The artist. Although the Williams canon has its share of painters, poets, and singers—most of them amateurs or failures—a Williams artist can be identified not by what he creates but by his temperament, his inclination. The best examples of the type are Blanche DuBois in *Streetcar,* who is only a schoolteacher who mentions names from the standard anthology but who thinks of herself as a person of special refinement, and Alma in *Summer and Smoke,* "The Nightingale of the Delta," who sings on the Fourth of July, teaches singing, and meets regularly with her bizarre literary society. (2) The insane. Disturbed would be a better word, but it would lose

the traditional connection between the poet and the madman. Most of the Williams heroines fall into this category, although the depth of their disturbances ranges from Catharine, in *Suddenly Last Summer,* who is shut in an institution, to Isabel in *Period of Adjustment,* whose nervous stomach keeps her on Pepto-Bismol. (3) The cripple. This would include those whose physical disturbances are partly mental —Laura, who exaggerates her limp in *The Glass Menagerie*—and those, like Big Daddy in *Cat on a Hot Tin Roof,* whose illness is a device to cover separateness. (4) The sexual specialist. From the virgins (Hannah in *The Night of the Iguana*) to those who need sex as a stimulant (Alexandra in *Sweet Bird of Youth*). (5) The foreigner. The wild Sicilians of *The Rose Tattoo* are the best example.

What is presumably shared by all of these types is a self-knowledge that separates them from the insider, the man who is protected, by insensitivity or by a strong identification with the dominant group and its conventions, from knowledge of himself and the terrors that surround him. In Williams' early work, particularly in the short stories, there is a kind of contempt for the insiders, but increasingly he has come to recognize that the terrors that menace his fugitive kind are on the trail of all mankind. His characters are under attack from other people (which provides the social criticism that shows up in some of the plays, as in *Orpheus Descending*), from themselves (the guilt that assails Brick in *Cat on a Hot Tin Roof*), and from the universe (the mortality that they all face in a universe that is empty at best, malevolent at worst). They try to escape usually by running (as in *Sweet Bird*) or accepting the momentary comfort of a necessarily transitory love (as in *Camino Real*). In recent years—in *The Night of the Iguana* and *The Milk Train Doesn't Stop Here Anymore*—Williams seemed to have begun to treat his old themes in terms of possible acceptance of life and death, but in *Slapstick Tragedy,* for all its broad comedy, he was back with the kind of desperation that has driven his heroines, at least since *A Streetcar Named Desire.*

As a playwright, Williams has wanted to tell his "real" truth about human beings, but he has not wanted to do so as a realist. He has made constant use of both literary and theatrical devices of a nonrealistic sort. They range from the subtle to the shockingly obvious, from organic machine to pure gimmick. In the Production Notes to *The Glass Menagerie,* he makes quite clear that he believes that poetic truth can best be depicted through a transformation that escapes the appearance of reality. Despite his aesthetic stand, he is enough in the tradition of the American theater to ask his characters to move and speak realistically when he wants them too. In *The Night of the Iguana,* for instance, there is character-defining action in the scene in Act II in which Maxine tempts Shannon with the rum-coco; in *Period of Adjustment,* there is character-revealing speech in Isabel's shift from the first to the third person as she tells her dream about serving a handsome doctor, which is, in fact, a standard movie plot. There is realism, then—a psychological soundness in the choice of gesture and word—at the heart of Williams' creation of character, but he goes out of his way to mask it. This can be seen in his frequent and conscious use of caricature, as in Flora and Bessie in

The Rose Tattoo, whom he describes as "two female clowns." Other antirealistic devices by which he transforms his characters are mythic identifications (particularly in *Orpheus Descending,* in which Val is both Orpheus and Christ) and the use of significant names (from A. Ratt in *Camino Real* to Val Xavier —pronounced Savior—in *Orpheus*). The mythic devices operate, not simply with the characters, but with the plots too, for in *Orpheus,* Williams hopes to make Val's death a kind of ritual that lifts the play from the realistic to the metaphorical. The references to Greek and Christian myth that sprinkle his plays serve as distancing devices, pushing the audience away from a strictly realistic reading. The verbal and visual symbols that flood the Williams plays have much the same use, although sometimes they can become ludicrous, as in *Summer and Smoke* with its plethora of symbolic indications of the body-soul split represented by John and Alma; sometimes, as with the roses of *The Rose Tattoo,* the surfeit of symbols is presumably intended as a joke. Caricature, myth, and symbol are literary devices, open to the playwright as to any worker in words, but Williams also makes use of every possible tool of the theater— sets, lights, props, sound—to emphasize that his plays are not realistic. Two examples of this are the bed in *Cat on a Hot Tin Roof,* "a functional part of the set," which, raked to become a playing area, is a continual reminder of the struggle between Brick and Maggie; and the mannequins in *The Rose Tattoo*— the bride and the widow—which are used not only to comment on Serafina's difficulties but on occasion to harass her—as in scene 5 in which they seem to be interfering with her attempt to get to Rosa's graduation.

Tennessee Williams is among the most important playwrights to emerge in America since World War II. He has made a consistent attempt to put the world as he sees it onstage in dramatic parables that will be both a pleasure and a shock to his audiences, an attempt that has brought attacks from those who imagined that his fables were realistic portraits. His sharp eye for nuance of speech and gesture has given the American theater a number of powerful and often funny characters. His attempt to impose nonrealistic plays on the essentially realistic American theater— even when it has failed—has been one of the major theatrical endeavors in the United States since 1945.

There is no collected edition of Williams' work; the plays are available in individual editions from New Directions, which also publishes his fiction and poetry. There are a number of critical and biographical works on Williams. Gerald Weales's *Tennessee Williams* (Pamphlets on American Writers, No. 53, University of Minnesota Press, 1965) is a simple introduction to both the themes and the dramatic technique of Williams. *Remember Me to Tom* (1963), by the playwright's mother, Edwina Dakin Williams (as told to Lucy Freeman), is of particular value for the Williams letters it contains.—G. W.

Winter's Tale, The (1611). A romance by William SHAKESPEARE. *The Winter's Tale* is based upon *Pandosto, or the Triumph of Time* (1588), a prose romance by Shakespeare's contemporary Robert Greene.

After a protracted visit with his boyhood friend King Leontes of Sicilia, Polixenes, king of Bohemia,

prepares to return home despite the pleas of his friend that he remain a while longer. He finally agrees to stay when to Leontes' efforts are added the graceful and eloquent entreaties of Leontes' beautiful wife, Hermione. Polixenes' reversal, however, triggers a fit of insane jealousy in Leontes, who quickly convinces himself that Polixenes and Hermione are cuckolding him. He orders one of his lords, Camillo, to murder Polixenes, but Camillo, certain that his master is deranged, warns Polixenes instead, and the two men escape to Bohemia.

Meanwhile, Hermione, the mother of a young son and now pregnant, is imprisoned by Leontes, to the horror and astonishment of everyone at court. While in prison she gives birth to a girl. Leontes, convinced that the child is not his, orders it to be taken to some remote place to be left to die. He then arranges a public trial of his queen, in the midst of which comes the news that the young prince, ill since his mother's imprisonment, has died. At the news Hermione falls into a deep swoon, which is followed shortly after by a report of her death to the now chastened king. In the meantime, the baby has been taken to Bohemia, where it is found by a kindly old shepherd.

Sixteen years later, the baby is now the beautiful shepherdess Perdita, who has won the love of Polixenes' son, Florizel. Polixenes strongly objects to the marriage of his son with a commoner and the two lovers go to Sicilia in order to escape his wrath. At the Sicilian court, Leontes, who has spent all this time in mourning and repentance, welcomes the two young lovers. The problem represented by the lowborn estate of Perdita is easily erased when the king and his daughter discover that a "statue" of Hermione they have been asked to admire turns out to be the queen herself, who has not died but has been in hiding all these years.

The subtitle of the source, "The Triumph of Time," might well be taken as the play's theme. Its dark and wintry opening gives way to the bright spring that characterizes the second half of the play. This seasonal movement provides the context in which time is seen as a benevolent force participating in life's natural processes. In giving expression and form to this fundamental experience, *The Winter's Tale* reflects a joyous, redemptive, and cyclical vision of the natural world and of man's place in it.

A recommended edition of *The Winter's Tale* is the Signet Classic Shakespeare (1963), edited by Frank Kermode.—E. Q.

Within the Gates (1933). A play by Sean O'CASEY. *Within the Gates,* from O'Casey's middle period, is a modern morality play set during the Great Depression of the early 1930's. O'Casey is here concerned with martyrdom, with the sacrifice of his heroine Jannice, the everywoman of his parable in Hyde Park. The park is a microcosm of the Depression world, and all the allegorical characters in it suffer from spiritual as well as economic depression; for O'Casey believes, with Shaw, that the failure of capitalism was in large measure the failure of Christianity. It is therefore a deeply religious work about damnation and salvation. The four stylized scenes, or tableaus, represent the cyclical pattern of life—a Spring Morning, a Summer Noon, an Autumn Evening, a Winter Night. The main action concerns the struggle of Jannice, a prostitute, to save herself from sin and fear, to identify herself with the life of freedom and joy as it is epitomized by the poetic Dreamer. The illegitimate daughter of a man who became a bishop and has now wandered into the park, she is confronted with alternative escapes through the Atheist and the Salvation Army; but the main struggle for her body and soul is fought out between the Dreamer and the Bishop. And while this struggle unfolds, O'Casey characteristically develops a series of comic subplots, low-level parodies of the salvation theme. An antic crowd of comic types streams through the park making soapbox speeches and arguing about the fate of man, the nature of God, and relativity. They speak in a ripe Cockney lingo, which indicates that they are close relations to O'Casey's Dublin clowns. The play is also richly scored for music and choreography, with many folk ballads and choral chants, and a number of seasonal and symbolic dances. After their final dance of tragic joy with the Dreamer, Jannice collapses, and at her dying request the humbled Bishop guides her hand in the sign of the cross. Like Jannice, the Bishop has gone through a spiritual crisis, and with a sense of universal guilt he cries out for God's mercy for everyone in the park.—D. K.

Witkiewicz, Stanisław Ignacy (1885–1939). Polish playwright. At the time he was doing his most original work—in the period 1918 to the mid-1920's—Witkiewicz was misunderstood, ridiculed, and dismissed as a mental case. His plays were performed almost exclusively in small, out-of-the-way experimental theaters with "entry prohibited to minors and soldiers." In 1939, shortly after the new division of Poland between Nazi Germany and the

Soviet Union, Witkiewicz committed suicide and it appeared that his theater was destined to die with him. But the popularity of the "theater of the absurd" in post-World War II Poland—particularly after 1956 when internal political conditions permitted greater access to contemporary Western culture—led to the "rediscovery" of Witkiewicz and his recognition as a highly original dramatist and a precursor of the type of drama for which playwrights such as Beckett and Ionesco were to gain international fame in the 1940's and 1950's.

Since then there have been a number of revivals of Witkiewicz's plays in Poland, particularly of *Pragmatysci* ("The Pragmatists," 1918), a five-act tragedy; *Oni* ("They," 1920), a "two-and-a-half-act" drama; *W małym dworku* ("On a Small Estate," 1921), a play in three acts; *Kurka wodna* ("The Water Hen," 1921), a three-act "spherical tragedy"; *Szewcy* ("The Tailors"), a "scientific" play with "songs" in three acts; and *Wariat i zakonnica* ("The Madman and the Nun," 1923), a "short play" in three acts and four curtains dedicated to "all the madmen of the world." The reawakened interest in Witkiewicz was fully confirmed by the publication in Poland in 1962 of a two-volume edition of his plays (the first of its kind).

A talented artist interested in problems of aesthetics, Witkiewicz first aroused attention for his vigorous espousal of the theory of "formism" or "pure form," to which he devoted his now-famous tract *Wstęp do teorii Czystej Formy w teatrze* ("Introduction to the Theory of Pure Form in the Theater," 1918) and about which several of his plays revolve, as, for example, *Oni.* Expounding a "catastrophic" world view shaped in part by the teachings of Spengler, Witkiewicz found playwriting the most productive vehicle for his talent and ideas and between 1918 and the late 1920's produced some thirty plays. His concern for man's loneliness, isolation from society, and "dehumanization" resulting from the ever increasing uniformity of contemporary civilization brings him thematically close to the leading practitioners of the theater of the absurd and have tended to obscure his roots in European expressionism and his affinities with surrealism, which reached its zenith when Witkiewicz's artistic powers were at their height. Fascinating for their surrealistic distortions and "deformations" no less than for their admixture of the absurd and fantastic, Witkiewicz's plays often suffer in their stageworthiness because of the author's use of them as vehicles for the dissemination of his ideas on pure form and their overly topical involvement in the scientific theories of the age. —H. B. S.

Woe from Wit (Gore ot uma; also translated as *Wit Works Woe* and *The Trouble with Reason).* A four-act comedy in verse by Alexander GRIBOYEDOV. Written in 1823/24, the play was banned until 1833, when production was authorized with substantial deletions. It was not performed in its entirety until 1869.

Upon his return to Moscow after three years of traveling abroad, the young gentleman Alexander Chatsky is horrified by what he finds at home. Sofia, the girl he had hoped to marry, is in love with her father's assistant, a sycophant named Molchalin ("the one who says nothing"). Her father, Famusov, a high civil servant who uses flattery and servility to further his career, is shocked by Chatsky's alien and unorthodox ideas about human dignity, education, and decency. At a reception given by Famusov, Chatsky meets a succession of smug nonentities, aggressively ignorant blimps, and vicious old countesses and princesses surrounded by their nincompoop husbands and empty-headed progeny. Even the intellectuals and liberals he meets are phony and exclusively preoccupied with externals. Chatsky reacts by delivering such violent tirades that the rumor quickly spreads that he is mad. To complete his disgust, he realizes that the servile Molchalin does not even return Sofia's love, since he is busy seducing the maid, who herself has an eye on the butler. The commotion that results from Chatsky's final explosive speech condemning society worries Famusov only insofar as "What will Princess Maria say about it all?" These are the closing words of the play.

This comedy, which, in Griboyedov's own words, contains "twenty-five fools and one sensible man," was hailed as a work of genius by the leading contemporary critic, Vissarion Belinsky. This opinion was shared by later authorities, such as the great novelist Ivan Goncharov, who wrote in 1871 that *Woe from Wit* was more important than any work of Alexander Pushkin's—a formidable statement for a Russian to make. Also, the twentieth-century poet Alexander Blok declared that this comedy is "unsurpassed in world literature."

Whatever these assessments may be worth, *Woe from Wit,* which is still frequently performed, is a brilliant comedy, written in sparkling, colloquial verse, that has left an indelible imprint on the Russian language. In 1894 a scholar calculated that sixty-one phrases and aphorisms from the play had been accepted as Russian proverbs. In this respect *Woe from Wit* surpasses even Denis Fonvizin's *The Minor,* which was certainly a great source of inspiration to Griboyedov.

The play has been translated as *The Trouble with Reason* by F. D. Reave in *An Anthology of Russian Plays,* Volume I (1961).—A. MacA.

Wood, [Gerald] Charles (1932–   ). English playwright. Wood, a specialist in the comedy and speech habits of closed communities, was born into a theatrical family in Guernsey. After leaving Birmingham College of Art, he passed through a variety of jobs, including that of solider. As an exponent of the military situation and its language, a rich idiom virtually unexplored in English drama, Wood arrived in the theater with *Cockade* (1963), a triple bill. He returned to the same material in *Don't Make Me Laugh* (1965) and tried with little success to extend his range of subject matter in *Meals on Wheels* (1965), a series of strident vaudeville sketches on the general theme of social repression. In *Fill the Stage with Happy Hours* (1966), Wood chose another closed community—that of the theater itself—for an unforgiving comedy of backstage life in a squalid provincial repertory company. Another army play, *Dingo,* was originally accepted by the National Theatre but shelved when it ran into censorship trouble. It was finally produced in 1967. *Dingo* is a horrendous farce about the Desert War, presented as an obscene swindle on the men who died.

Wood is a prolific writer. Besides his stage work he has written for radio, television, and films, notably

the screenplays for *The Knack* (1965), an adaptation of the play by Ann Jellicoe, and *How I Won the War* (1967).—I. W.

Woyzeck (written 1836, pub. 1879, perf. 1913). A tragedy by Georg BÜCHNER. There is no definitive version of this play because Büchner died before he could order the scenes and acts. However, the chronology of the play cannot be confused too much because Büchner based his work on an actual medical case. The true story involved the barber Johan Christian Woyzeck, who stabbed his mistress in a fit of jealousy and was sentenced to death in 1821. A controversy arose as to whether Woyzeck was insane, and this issue appealed to Büchner, who portrays his Woyzeck as a simple soldier, essentially goodhearted, who is driven to murder his wife. Woyzeck does not murder Marie out of jealousy, and this is where Büchner differs from historical fact. He shows subtle forces working on Woyzeck (environment, class, religion) that depress him and cause him to commit a crime he does not want to commit. Even Woyzeck's own death in a pond can be interpreted as caused by the hand of fate, since it is debatable whether he wanted to take his own life. Büchner shows the strong influence of Jakob Michael Reinhold Lenz in his use of autonomous scenes that build paratactically to an inevitable conclusion damning society. This conclusion is related to Lenz's social philosophy and that of the naturalists: Man is determined by his surroundings and social position. In showing Woyzeck victimized in this manner, Büchner called attention to the need for social reform and, at the same time, voiced his doubts as to whether this need would be fulfilled.—J. D. Z.

Wycherley, William (1640?–1716).   English comic dramatist. Wycherley was born in Shropshire of a distinguished family. When he was about fifteen he was sent to France, where he was introduced to some of the social and literary elite. Shortly before the restoration of Charles II, Wycherley returned to England and after a brief time at Queen's College, Oxford, went to study law in London at the Inner Temple. However, he soon drifted into the fashionable and literary circles of the court, where he became friendly with the duke of Buckingham, the earl of Rochester, and their group of "court wits." In 1679 he married a rich widow, the countess of Drogheda, who proved to be a most jealous wife. After her death in 1681 he was in serious financial difficulties for several years, until James II paid his debts and gave him a pension. In his later life he became a friend and admirer of the young Alexander Pope.

Like many of his friends, Wycherley wrote comparatively little. His four comedies are *Love in a Wood* (1671), *The Gentleman Dancing Master* (1672), THE COUNTRY WIFE, and THE PLAIN DEALER. The last two occupy unusually important places in the annals of Restoration drama (see ENGLAND: *Restoration drama*), for *The Country Wife* remains one of the funniest and best comedies of the period, and *The Plain Dealer* won for its author his reputation as one of the outstanding satirists of his age. In both plays he was considerably influenced by Molière.

The only complete edition is Montague Summers' four-volume *The Complete Works of William Wycherley* (1924). There is a popular biography by

Willard Connely, *Brawny Wycherley* (1930). A valuable critical study is Rose A. Zimbardo's *Wycherley's Drama: A Link in the Development of English Satire* (1965).—E. W.

Wyspiański, Stanisław (1869–1907). Polish poet, painter, and playwright. The son of a sculptor, Wyspiański studied at Cracow University and in the School of Art. He traveled abroad a great deal and was particularly attracted to Paris. In 1905 he became a professor of applied art.

Wyspiański's plays lend themselves to fairly easy categorization. The first group comprises dramas set in classical antiquity, dealing with Greek subjects: *Meleager* (written 1897), *Protesilas i Laodamia* ("Protesilas and Laodamia," written 1899), *Achilleis* ("Achilles," written 1903), and *Powrót Odyssa* (*The Return of Odysseus,* written 1907). The second group is made up of plays devoted to legendary and early Polish history: *Legendy I* ("Legends I," written 1893), *Legends II* ("Legends II," 1897), *Bolesław Śmiały* ("Bolesław the Bold," written 1903), and *Skałki* ("Crags," written 1906). In the third group belong modern tragedies dealing with contemporary Polish village life: *Klątwa* ("The Curse," written 1899), *Sędziowie* ("The Judge," written 1907). The last, and most impressive category, concerns the events and personalities of the unsuccessful Polish uprising against the Russians of November 1830, the Romantic movement, and the lingering effects of Romanticism on the Polish psyche: *Warszawianka* ("The Varsovienne," written 1898), *Lelewel* (written 1899), *Legion* (written 1900), *Wesele* ("The Wedding," written 1901), *Wyzwolenie* ("Liberation," written 1903), *Akropolis* ("Acropolis," written 1904), and *Noc listopadowa* ("November Night," written 1908).

Wyspiański's plays are characterized by an extensive use of myth and fantasy and the language of symbols; they are, with few exceptions, written in verse and pose a distinct challenge to the actor and producer. Yet they are among the most original plays in the history of the modern Polish stage. Affinities between the aesthetics of Young Poland (Młoda Polska, as the period of Polish neo-Romanticism and symbolism is known) and earlier Romanticism are particularly apparent in Wyspiański. Such plays as *Noc listopadowa* and *Wesele* demonstrate the Romantic preference for verse, disregard for the traditional unities, rapid changes of scene, fusion of the real and the supernatural with the introduction of mythological and folkloric characters who actually come to life as figures in the plays, and synthesis of drama, art, and music into a single theatrical entity. Ideologically, the plays carry a certain indictment of Romanticism for its inspiring but ultimately futile idealism, its fondness for magnificence of gesture and word, and its profound impracticality. In his searching analysis of the causes behind the collapse of the November Insurrection, Wyspiański credits the sincerity and the nobility of those principally involved but exposes the uprising as badly conceived and organized, ill-timed, and destined to failure.

In *Legion,* Wyspiański examines the role of the poet Mickiewicz in the mythology of Romanticism; in *Wesele,* about the nuptials of the Young Poland poet Lucjan Rydel and a peasant girl from a village near Cracow, he suggests that Romanticism can be a powerful force for evil—capable of stirring deep emotions, appealing to man's highest instincts, evoking responses it could not fully anticipate, and setting into motion deeds and events it not only could not control but was in fact terrified by.

Wyspiański's interest in the theater extended beyond playwriting. Rooted in the traditions of the Polish "monumental theater" (as the collective drama of the nineteenth-century émigré Romantics is usually known in Poland), Wyspiański saw a distinct challenge in formulating techniques for the staging of plays that were not written for the stage in the first place and had never been staged. Mickiewicz's *Forefathers' Eve,* to which so much of his own playwriting was indebted, received the focus of his attention. The elaborate program Wyspiański conceived for bringing this masterpiece of Polish Romantic drama to the stage was of profound impact on the development of theatrical experimentation in the interwar period; it has also been a *mise en scène* often employed in the staging of Mickiewicz's play cycle. Wyspiański's version, titled *Dziady, Sceny dramatyczne* (*Forefathers' Eve, Dramatic Scenes*) was first presented on stage October 31, 1901, in the Cracow Theater. Long attracted to Shakespeare's dramaturgy and the "theatricality" of his plays, Wyspiański also composed a brilliant and original reading of *Hamlet* to which he gave the title *The Tragical Historie of Hamlet* (1905).—H. B. S.

STANISŁAW WYSPIAŃSKI (CAF, WARSAW; POLISH EMBASSY)

Y

Yaşar Kemal [Gökçeli] (1922–   ). Turkish novelist, short-story writer, and playwright. Born and raised in a village near Adana, Yaşar Kemal, at the age of five, saw his father shot dead in a mosque. Yaşar Kemal worked as a farmhand, watchman, foreman, letter writer, employee at a gas company, and a shoemaker's apprentice while writing poems, and publishing them in various periodicals. He joined the Istanbul daily *Cumhuriyet* in 1951 and in 1967 established *Ant*, a weekly political magazine. Yaşar Kemal is also active in the leftist Turkish Labor Party. His most famous novel, *Ince Memed* (*Memed, My Hawk*), about the feudal elements in modern Turkey, has since its publication in 1955 been translated into twenty-three languages.

Yaşar Kemal has written only one play, *Teneke* ("The Tin Can," 1965), adapted from his novel of the same name. It is a brilliant political satire on vested interests, reactionaries who pay lip service to the great reformer Atatürk, and the pressures on idealistic civil servants. If Yaşar Kemal continues to write plays the caliber of *Teneke,* he could become as important a dramatist as he is a novelist.—N. O.

Yeats, William Butler (1865–1939). Irish poet and playwright. Born in Sandymount, a suburb of Dublin on the Liffey estuary, on June 13, 1865, the eldest son of upper-middle-class Protestant parents, W. B. Yeats spent the greater part of his first ten years in the west of Ireland at his beloved Sligo, his mother's ancestral home. His father, the distinguished painter and man of letters, John Butler Yeats, came from a family of clergymen but turned agnostic as a young man, whereas his son was destined to develop a strong interest in mysticism and the supernatural throughout his adult life. Partly educated by his brilliant father, Yeats had little formal education and was an indifferent student when he was in school; at the age of eleven he began five irregular years at the Godolphin School in Hammersmith when the family was living temporarily in London, followed by several years at the Erasmus Smith High School in Dublin when the Yeats family returned to Ireland in 1880. At eighteen he attended the Metropolitan School of Art in Dublin for a short time and there became a close friend of the young George Russell (A.E.), the poet, painter, and mystic. He had studied painting briefly because his father insisted that every young man should know about art; but he had already begun to write poems and plays, and by the time he was twenty he had published his first poems in a Dublin literary magazine and was determined to be a poet.

Yeats's early poetry was written in imitation of Shelley and Spenser and the pre-Raphaelites, but he also came under the influence of the Irish literary revival in the 1890's and soon became one of the leaders of that movement, turning to Irish themes and Celtic mythology for his poems and plays. It was during this period that he began to make plans for an Irish theater and wrote his nationalistic verse plays, *The Countess Cathleen* (1892) and THE LAND OF HEART'S DESIRE, and the prose drama CATHLEEN NI HOULIHAN. In 1899 Yeats and Lady Gregory, with the help of Edward Martyn and George Moore, founded the Irish Literary Theatre, a group dedicated to the writing and performing of plays on Irish themes in Dublin; and in May of that year the theater opened with a performance of *The Countess Cathleen.* With further help from the actors Frank and Willy Fay, the group became known in 1902 as the Irish National Theatre Society; and in 1904 it was finally established in its own building as the Abbey Theatre. Yeats remained, with Lady Gregory, an active manager and playwright of the Abbey until his death, and throughout his lifetime he encouraged and defended new playwrights and fought courageously for the arts against hostile pressure groups in Ireland.

When he was twenty-three Yeats met and fell hopelessly in love with Maud Gonne, a strikingly beautiful and talented young woman totally committed to the cause of Irish independence, who appropriately played the title role in his most nationalistic play, *Cathleen ni Houlihan.* For a short time Yeats was directly involved in the national movement, having joined the secret Irish Republican Brotherhood, although he sensed that a conflict might develop between his nationalist and creative impulses. The open break occurred in 1903 when Maud married a political activist, John MacBride, and the following year Yeats wrote *The King's Threshold,* a personal manifesto in the form of a heroic verse play about a legendary poet who sacrifices his life for the right of poets to occupy a primary position in society. Thereafter Yeats was to go his own way as poet and playwright, and when he wrote verse plays about Cuchulain and Deirdre he used the Celtic myths for private and artistic rather than nationalist purposes. His three outstanding tragedies, all written in the one-act, classical Greek form, are *On Baile's Strand* (1904), a poignant treatment of Cuchulain's inadvertent slaying of his own son, with a bold Shakespearean use of a Fool and Blind Man as a comic-ironic subplot; DEIRDRE, a noble characterization of the Irish Helen of Troy whose uncompromising love and death lead to the destruction of a kingdom, with its austerely heroic verse a striking contrast to John Millington Synge's more romantic dramatization of the tale in lyrical prose; and PURGATORY, a ritualistic

WILLIAM BUTLER YEATS (CONSULATE GENERAL OF IRELAND)

tragedy of a family curse in which an Old Man commits two murders in a vain attempt to purge the bloodguilt and liberate his dead mother's suffering spirit.

Yeats returned to the Cuchulain legend in four more plays, and two—AT THE HAWK'S WELL and *The Only Jealousy of Emer* (1919)—are of special importance in his career as a playwright. In 1916 he had discovered the fourteenth-century Japanese *noh* drama through a translation by Ernest Fenollosa and Ezra Pound, and he constructed his own version of this ritualistic form in these two plays, and in many subsequent works, calling them "Plays For Dancers." With his own modifications, he retained the Japanese concept of masks, dances, choruses, and formalized diction, the folding and unfolding of the symbolic cloth to the accompaniment of string and percussion instruments—but he grafted the whole ceremony onto Cuchulain and Christ legends and to various supernatural themes in later one-act verse plays such as *The Dreaming of the Bones* (1919), *Calvary* (1920), *The Cat and the Moon* (1926), *The Resurrection* (1931), *The King of the Great Clock Tower* (1934), A FULL MOON IN MARCH, and *The Death of Cuchulain* (1939).

In a further reaction against the conventional theater, Yeats intended these plays to be performed in a drawing room for no more than fifty enlightened people. When he founded his Irish Theatre he had originally called for a People's Theatre, but it soon became clear that what he had in mind was a theater for the "right" people, which would perform only plays that were "remote, spiritual, and ideal." He had at last fulfilled those early aims with his modified noh plays, which he triumphantly described in the following manner: "I have invented a form of drama, distinguished, indirect, and symbolic, and having no need of mob or Press to pay its way—an aristocratic form." But the visionary Yeats was probably far ahead of his time, for today this daring and esoteric drama remains a tempting but elusive challenge and has still to be interpreted and performed successfully, in exclusive drawing rooms or experimental theaters.

In 1917 Yeats married an Englishwoman, Georgie Hyde-Lees; from 1922 to 1928 he served as a senator in the Irish Free State; in 1923 he was awarded the Nobel Prize for literature. When he died on January 28, 1939, he was only moderately known as a playwright, but he was generally acknowledged to be one of the greatest English-language poets of the past hundred years.

Standard editions of the plays include *The Collected Plays* (1953), and *The Variorum Edition of the Plays* (1966), of special significance because it reproduces the constant revisions Yeats made in his plays. Biographical and critical studies include Joseph Hone, *W. B. Yeats, 1865–1939* (1943; rev. ed., 1963); Richard Ellmann, *Yeats, The Man and the Masks* (1949); Peter Ure, *Yeats the Playwright* (1963); and Helen Vendler, *Yeats's Vision and the Later Plays* (1963).—D. K.

Yerma (1934). A folk tragedy by Federico GARCÍA LORCA. This play is part of a trilogy that includes BLOOD WEDDING and THE HOUSE OF BERNARDA ALBA. *Yerma*, "a tragic poem in three acts and six scenes," is constructed on a more realistic and psychological base than *Blood Wedding*. The pervasive fatalism enveloping all the characters in *Blood Wedding* is here replaced by the carefully depicted struggle of one woman victimized by, perhaps victimizing herself in, frustrated motherhood. The curtain rises on Yerma's waking dream of a shepherd leading a child past her. The lights change to "the happy light of a spring morning" as she wakes. What follows is a scrupulous presentation of Yerma's predicament depicted by the alternation of opposite and complementary situations. First there is her husband, Juan—a dry, frugal farmer whose religion is work and who refuses to acknowledge her desire for a child. Then there is Maria, a pregnant peasant woman, whose condition excites Yerma's concern: "Don't walk about too much," Yerma advises, "and when you breathe, breathe as softly as if you had a rose between your teeth." And there is Victor, a robustly attractive shepherd who is drawn to Yerma, as she is to him, though neither admits it. Alternatives to Yerma's situation begin to emerge. The old pagan woman, hearing of Yerma's childlessness, denounces Juan's fatalism: ". . . there should be a God, even a very tiny one, to send lightning down on those men whose seed is rotten and who puddle up the happiness of the fields." Two young wives enter; when Yerma hears that one woman's child has been left alone, she anxiously inquires whether pigs are roaming about the house. This sends the young mother quickly home, while the other woman, with no interest in children, mocks Yerma's obsession. She would rather have a good time. Victor's reappearance elicits a short exchange of verses before Juan approaches, upon which Victor leaves and Yerma is sharply upbraided and sent home.

A lively washerwomen's song introduces the second act and deepens the sense of Yerma's dilemma. The women express different views of her situation; even Yerma's sisters-in-law, who join them, indicate a point of view by their silence. Yerma is still childless after five years of marriage. Juan, joined by his sisters at home, sets up a gloomy contrast to Yerma's uncontainable urgency. Although forbidden to leave the house, Yerma goes to see a conjurer at the end of the act.

In the third act Juan and his sisters find her there; his concern is not her predicament but that "people will begin to talk." For her part, Yerma has consistently refused all the alternatives: "I don't love him," she recognizes; "still he is my only salvation." Only the most extreme consequences may be expected now. A fertility dance in the form of a popular masque is held at night at a mountain shrine where childless women come to pray. There is a rising dramatic momentum in the erotic song and dance that follow. The pagan woman offers Yerma her own son as a virile male; Yerma refuses and is met by Juan. Their final confrontation makes it clear that he will never understand her. Realizing how destitute she is, she rises suddenly and chokes him to death. A chorus of women approaches. Relieved of her burden, Yerma's final cry is, "I'm going to rest without ever waking to see whether my blood has announced the coming of new blood. My body barren forever. What would you know? Don't come near me, because I have killed my child. I myself have killed my child!" Having killed Juan, she has also killed the life force within herself. According to her personal code, she is at last certain, with her husband dead, never to bear children.

Yerma, translated by J. Graham-Lujan and R. L. O'Connell, is included in *Five Plays (Comedies and Tragicomedies)* (1963).—E. H.

Yiddish drama. The drama among Jews derives from two main sources, both of which are secular celebrations that are only superficially related to religious observances: weddings and Purim celebrations of the downfall of Haman.

During the eleventh century, in France and Germany, masked dancers began to appear as part of the wedding entertainment. Later, speech was added —a monologue by a masked speaker. Gradually, the preparation and recitation of the monologue became a professional occupation by a *lets* ("jester"), later called *marshalik.* In Slavic countries this performer came to be called a *badkhn.* By the fifteenth century the profession of lets had become well established, often even hereditary, and by the seventeenth it had achieved a popularity that was undiminished until the twentieth century. The compositions of lets and badkhn produced an original repertoire of Yiddish theatrical material: bride and groom songs, riddles, parodies, and songs both comical and serious.

The major occasion for theatrical entertainment was, however, Purim, the most carefree holiday of the Jewish year. Purim celebrates the rescue of the Jews of Persia by beautiful Queen Esther and her uncle, Mordecai, and the downfall of their persecutor, Haman, the minister of King Ahasuerus. The biblical Book of Esther is read in the synagogue to mark the occasion, but solemnity is deliberately avoided, and the congregants greet every mention of Haman's name with derision, catcalls, and noisemakers. Among Italian Jews, Purim was celebrated by a masquerade in imitation of the Italian carnival. Later, the note of mockery that was part of the Purim spirit began to provide an outlet for satire as well as entertainment. Celebrations began to feature an en-

tertainer delivering witty improvisations and parodies. Frequently, this entertainer was a chorister turned bard or a wandering Yeshiva student (rabbinical seminarian), whose religious learning enabled him to contribute to the Purim spirit of mockery by his parodies of biblical passages, sermons, and deathbed confessions. During the fifteenth century the practice arose in Yeshivas of enlivening the Purim festivities by selecting a mock rabbi, called a Purim rabbi, to make pronouncements in the same spirit of parody, a practice that continued until late in the nineteenth century. By the sixteenth century, Purim plays in Yiddish with a Purim king as the central figure were already well established. Although the oldest extant manuscript of a Yiddish Purim play centering around King Ahasuerus dates from 1697, the text is certainly much older. Versions of an Ahasuerus play continued to be published into the nineteenth century.

The weeks in the spring before and after Purim had come to be a time for theatergoing, and the dramatic repertoire came to include other biblical subjects besides the Esther story: the sale of Joseph, the story of David and Goliath, the binding of Isaac, the exodus from Egypt, and the life and death of Moses. Despite the popularity of theatergoing among Jews, a professional theater was unable to gain a permanent foothold until the last quarter of the nineteenth century, and the very few Yiddish plays that were written had no hope of production.

The year 1876, when Abraham GOLDFADEN organized two professional entertainers into a "company" and presented his first musical "play," is usually designated as marking the birth of the modern Yiddish theater. The rapid growth of a professional Yiddish theater thereafter was not, of course, an isolated phenomenon. It was an aspect of the development of a modern secular Yiddish culture in Russia and Poland, in the neighboring lands of Hungary, Rumania, Czechoslovakia, and Germany, and, after the beginning of the great emigration from Eastern Europe during the 1880's, in France and England, in the countries of North and South America, as well as in Australia and South Africa.

The Jewish renaissance in Yiddish was a spectacular development in its achievement as well as in its brevity. Before 1875 there was only a single writer of large importance; by 1939 the Eastern European heartland of Yiddish was well on its way to almost total destruction, and in the countries of Western culture no generation after the immigrant took Yiddish for its daily use. In little more than half a century, Yiddish drama, like Yiddish literature as a whole, telescoped what other literatures took centuries to traverse and encompassed simultaneously literary movements and developments that elsewhere succeeded each other in half-century steps. With the sudden opening of the Eastern European *shtetl* ("small town") world, the influences of European literatures swept in and left their mark on youths who, in earlier generations, would have remained entirely within the enclave of traditional Jewish religious study; and the emigrating masses, often from a nearly medieval world, came into direct contact not only with foreign cultures but also with the harsher aspects of modern capitalist society.

These major social, economic, political, and geo-

S. ANSKY (YIVO INSTITUTE FOR JEWISH RESEARCH)

graphic changes and their psychological, moral, and intellectual concomitants provided the content of modern Yiddish drama as they did of modern Yiddish literature as a whole. Abraham Goldfaden's pioneering effort was immediately followed by a proliferation of Yiddish theaters in Eastern Europe and, after the prohibition of Yiddish stage productions by the Russian tsarist government in 1883, in America. Two major tendencies appeared in the commercial Yiddish theater: melodrama and musical mishmash concocted by the likes of Joseph Lateiner and "Professor" Isaac Hurvitch and serious drama by men of such differing talents as Jacob GORDIN, David PINSKI, Sholem ASCH, SHOLEM ALEICHEM, Yitskhok Leybush PERETZ, Peretz HIRSHBEIN, H. LEIVICK, and S. ANSKY.

A number of lesser figures both in America and in Eastern Europe also made significant contributions to the Yiddish drama. In America Zalmon Libin (pseudonym of Israel Zalmon Horowitz, 1872–1955) wrote realistic plays depicting the sad life of the Jewish working masses in the sweatshops of the New World. Leon Kobrin (1872–1946) depicted the conflicts that arose in the transition from the old way of life to the new. Ossip Dymov (pseudonym of Joseph Pearlman, 1878–1958) was best known for his comedy *Bronx Express* (1919). Fishel Bimko (1890–1965), the author of the very popular *Ganovim* ("Thieves," 1919), drew his earthy characters from the byways of life and involved them in dramatic conflicts of primitive passions. In Europe significant plays were written by a number of literary figures whose primary achievements were in forms other than the drama: Alter Katsizne (1855–1941),

whose varied literary output included a number of plays of sharp social satire; Dovid Bergelson (1884–1952), whose major achievements were in fiction; and the poets Moshe Kulbak (1896–194?) and Perets Markish (1895–1952).

The destruction in Europe and the gradual disappearance elsewhere of those generations whose native tongue was Yiddish struck most immediately at the Yiddish theater, which grew ever smaller as its audience diminished. As a result, recent years have seen a marked decline in Yiddish dramatic writing. Whatever the future of the Yiddish theater, however, the achievements of Yiddish drama during the half-century of ebullient creativity remain as a significant contribution to world theater.

Joseph C. Landis, translator and editor of *The Dybbuk and Other Great Yiddish Plays* (1966), a collection of five Yiddish plays in English translation, has included a sizable Introduction on Yiddish drama and theater and critical discussions of each of the five plays and playwrights included. David S. Lifson's *The Yiddish Theatre in America* (1965) is an informative history of the Yiddish commercial and art theaters in the United States. Sol Liptzin's *The Flowering of Yiddish Literature* (1963) and Charles A. Madison's *Yiddish Literature: Its Scope and Major Writers* (1968) contain extensive discussions of the major Yiddish dramatists.—J. C. L.

York Plays, The (late fourteenth century). A Corpus Christi cycle of forty-eight scriptural plays of unknown authorship. The text (running to over 13,000 lines of verse) is found in the Ashburnham Manuscript, preserved in the British Museum. Six plays are essentially the same as their correspondents in the Wakefield Cycle. It seems likely that these and other similarities are due to direct borrowing (of Wakefield from York) rather than to collateral descent from a common (lost) original. York (perhaps in an abbreviated version) was produced during one day on pageant wagons proceeding successively from stop to stop throughout the city.

The York Cycle consists of the following plays (elements absent from the Wakefield, Chester, and N-Town cycles are starred).

From Old Testament narratives:
    (1) Creation of the Angels, Fall of Lucifer
    (2) Creation to the Fifth Day
    (3) Creation of Adam and Eve
    (4) God's Prohibition
    (5) Fall of Man
    (6) Expulsion from Eden
    (7) Cain and Abel (incomplete)
    (8) Building of the Ark
    (9) Noah and His Wife, the Flood
    (10) Abraham and Isaac
    (11) Pharaoh, Moses, Exodus (Wakefield 8).
From narratives of the Nativity:
    (12) Annunciation, Visit to Elizabeth
    (13) Joseph's Suspicions about Mary
    (14) Birth of Christ
    (15) Adoration of the Shepherds
    (16) * Herod and His Son, Coming of the Magi
    (17) Herod's Plot, Adoration of the Magi
    (18) Flight into Egypt
    (41) Purification of the Virgin (misplaced in manuscript)
    (19) Slaughter of the Innocents
    (20) Christ and the Doctors (Wakefield 18).

From narratives of the Public Ministry:
- (21) Baptism
- (22) Temptation
- (23) * Transfiguration
- (24) Woman Taken in Adultery, Raising of Lazarus (both incomplete)
- (25) Entry into Jerusalem.

From narratives of the Passion:
- (26) Conspiracy of the Jews with Judas
- (27) Last Supper (incomplete)
- (28) Gethsemane (incomplete), Betrayal
- (29) Peter's Denial, Trial before Caiaphas
- (30) * Pilate and his Wife, Dream of Pilate's Wife, * Pilate's Beadle, First Trial before Pilate
- (31) Trial before Herod
- (32) Second Trial before Pilate, Remorse of Judas, * Purchase of the Field of Blood
- (33) Second Trial Continued, Condemnation (incomplete)
- (34) Procession to Calvary (Wakefield 23)
- (35) Crucifixion
- (36) Death and Burial.

From narratives of the Resurrection and Doomsday:
- (37) Harrowing of Hell (Wakefield 25)
- (38) Resurrection (Wakefield 26)
- (39) Appearance to Mary Magdalen
- (40) Pilgrims to Emmaus
- (42) Doubting Thomas
- (43) Ascension
- (44) Descent of the Holy Spirit (Pentecost)
- (45) Death of the Virgin
- (46) * Appearance of the Virgin to Thomas
- (47) Assumption of the Virgin
- (48) Last Judgment (Wakefield 30).

York does not omit any major narrative element found in the other three English scriptural cycles, except perhaps the Procession of the Prophets, which is narrated in a Doctor's prologue. It is the longest of the four cycles, but the relatively great number of plays is due to their being, in general, short and concerned with but a single episode. Thus, York treats in six plays (Nos. 2 through 7) what Chester treats in one (No. 2). York is distinguished by a number of powerful plays (chiefly in the Passion group) attributed to the so-called York Realist.

The text, *The York Plays* (1885), has been edited by Lucy Toulmin Smith. A modernized version, *The York Cycle of Mystery Plays* (1957), has been edited by J. S. Purvis. For critical studies, see Jesse Byers Reese, "Alliterative Verse in the York Cycle," *Studies in Philology*, XLVIII (1951), and J. W. Robinson, "The Art of the York Realist," *Modern Philology*, LX (1963).—R. H.

Yorkshire Tragedy, A (1606–1607). An anonymous English tragedy. The play is a good example of an Elizabethan domestic tragedy. It is based upon the life of Walter Calverley, who was executed for the murder of his children in 1605. The action largely concerns a nameless young man's dissolute life and the suffering it causes his family and friends. Recklessly engaging in every vice, he creates havoc for his wife and children and brings ruin on his younger brother, who had stood surety for his debts. The sudden realization of his own iniquity leaves him completely deranged, with the result that he kills two of his children and wounds his wife. He is finally apprehended and brought to prison.

A YORKSHIRE TRAGEDIE.

Not so New, as Lamentable and True.

Written by W. SHAKESPEARE.

Printed for T. P. 1619:

TITLE PAGE OF THE SECOND QUARTO (1619) OF THE ANONYMOUS *A Yorkshire Tragedy*, INCORRECTLY ASCRIBED HERE TO SHAKESPEARE

The play was first published in 1608 and on its title page attributed to "W. Shakespeare." Despite the attribution and the later inclusion of the play in the Third Folio (1664) of Shakespeare's plays, most critics see no trace of Shakespeare's hand in this crude, occasionally effective drama.—E. Q.

Yüan drama. The classical drama of the Yüan dynasty (1280–1368) has often been considered the chief dramatic literature that China has produced. Modern knowledge of earlier plays is still comparatively scant; the later plays tend to more romantic moods and solicitously cultivated sentiments than Western taste is willing generally to accept with enthusiasm. Recent scholarship has, however, to some extent modified the traditional Western view of the Yüan dynasty as being the only distinctly fruitful period for Chinese dramatic art. A few earlier plays are coming to light and many later plays are found considerably more deserving of attention than hitherto thought. Nevertheless, the sudden rise of a virile Yüan drama, practicable for the stage and distinctly viable as literature, has been amply confirmed. A bibliography has been compiled by William C. C. Hu, published in *Occasional Papers*, no. 1 (University of Michigan, 1962). Here 162 plays are listed.

Western translations and critical works as well as the chief Chinese play anthologies are included. For studies especially devoted to Yüan drama see Antoine Pierre Louis, *Théâtre chinois* (1838) and Rudolf von Gottschell, *Das Theater und Drama der Chineses* (1887). For a recent and authoritative description of this literature, consult *An Introduction to Chinese Literature* (1966) by Liu Wu-chi. —H. W. W.

yūgen. See NOH.

Yugoslavia. In order to make a just evaluation of the rich theatrical history of contemporary Yugoslavia, one must keep in mind the fact that Yugoslavia is a multinational state—primarily Slovene, Croatian, Serbian, and Macedonian—united as late as 1918 and transformed, by the constitution of 1945, into a federation composed of six republics. Since the ancient theatrical traditions of Yugoslav minorities have always developed in terms of geopolitical and linguistic multiplicity, the "theatrical map" of Yugoslavia does not have a single center of dramatic culture such as had developed in other European countries. One must also understand that, though the majority of native and foreign scholars date theatrical activity in Yugoslavia only from the official establishment of the so-called national theaters in the nineteenth century, there are far older documents and monuments that contradict this view.

The first testimony of early Croatian dramatic culture, which is fully credited by scholars, tells of the reception of Pope Alexander V in Zadar in 1117, when the clergy and crowds of people gave recitations of chants in their native language. Further, the almanac *Codex of Tkon* contains the text of two religious plays, dating at least as far back as 1492. These texts, usually considered to be the oldest preserved documents in Glagolitic script, are now almost universally regarded as either copies or free adaptations of an older manuscript.

The predecessors of the Croatian Renaissance theater are the monks Mavro Vetranović (1482–1576) and Nikola Nalješković (1510–1587). The first decidedly Renaissance play, *Robinja* ("The Slave"), on a wedding theme, was written about 1520 by Hanibal Lucić (1485–1553). The pastorals and comedies by Marin Držić (1508–1567), written and staged in Dubrovnik from 1547 to 1555, are, however, the culmination of the Croatian Renaissance. Držić's plays, in their original form and in various adaptations and translations, are still performed with great success in Yugoslavia and abroad, especially his comedy *Dundo Maroje* (*Uncle Maroje*), first staged in the palace of the rector in Dubrovnik in 1550.

The oldest Macedonian monument related to performing arts is a fresco in a church near Kumanovo, built between 1317 and 1318. It represents four comedians performing a grotesque dance from the episode of the mocking of Christ. Similar frescoes have been preserved in Slovenia: the dance macabre and scenes from a passion play (1490), and a portrait of a unicorn clown with bells (1520).

The first document testifying to the existence of Slovene writing dates from 972 to 1039. Records of public recitations of Jesuit students in Slovenia, Ljubljana, and Celovec are from 1599 to 1607. The first unambiguous records about a specific dramatic performance in Slovene date from 1657–1670, in Ljubljana, called *Igra o paradižu* ("The Play About Paradise").

The drama of the Baroque era shows clearly that the Slovene area was a transitional territory, culturally no less so than geographically. The Slovenes had a theater in the Jesuit school and saw luxurious Capuchin processions, visiting Italian opera singers and German comedians, and performances by Slovene students. A result of the cosmopolitan tolerance of the Baroque culture was the production of the longest extant dramatic text in the Slovene language, a Capuchin passion play that got its definite form sometime between 1721 and 1734. It was staged in Škofja Loka on Good Friday each year until 1765. This manuscript, by Father Romuald from Loka, has always attracted the close attention of scholars. The use of three languages makes it, in itself, a curiosity among similar European documents. Actors' parts, amounting to more than a thousand verses, are written in Slovene, the titles of individual scenes are in Latin, and the stage directions are in German.

Chronicles from the Baroque age indicate performances in Croatian in the Jesuit theater of Zagreb soon after 1644. A Latin school in Sremski Karlovci presented in 1736 the first secular play in the Serbian language, a "tragedocomedy." Its subject is the death of the last Serbian tsar, Uroš V, and the fall of the Serbian Empire. The piece was written by an author of Polish descent, Emanuilo Kozačinski, and was published in Budapest in 1798 in an adaptation by a former pupil of the Latin school.

The southern areas of Yugoslavia, under Turkish domination during this time, were restricted in their dramatic expression to folk song and dance. Similarly, with the expiration of Baroque culture in northern Yugoslavia, a permanent crisis occurred in the native theater. With the reforms of Joseph II, establishing German as the official language of Austrian provinces, national culture was reduced to a minimum or wholly crushed under Germanizing tendencies.

The nineteenth century was therefore a period of severe cultural crisis among Slovenes, Croats, and a large number of Serbs. Duke Metternich's intelligence system and the Theater Act (1850) of Alexander Bach succeeded almost completely in banning the Slovene tongue from the public stage. Productions during this time were a few modest bilingual performances, since even in Croatian and Serbian provinces visits of German theater groups were predominant. Only in the 1860's, with the fall of Minister Bach, could a political thawing be felt. As a result, several national theaters in Slavic provinces of the Austrian Empire were established.

Almost all nineteenth-century plays are testimonies to romantic partriotism, and only occasionally do some dramas illuminate this problematically. The national romanticism of southern Slavs, confined within the bureaucratic legislation of the Hapsburgian dynasty and autocratic laws of Turkish rulers, obviously had political roots. Because the Slavs were for a whole century pushed back into the position of national defense, dramatists could not help but convert the stage into a tribune of national

ideas if they wanted to fill their playhouses with enthusiastic audiences. Now that the problem of national identity has been solved and the fight against
foreign interests is no longer acute, only a few
nineteenth-century writers and a very limited number of plays are still relevant.

Of all nineteenth-century Serbian playwrights,
only plays by two writers are still performed: the satirical *Tvrdica ili Kir Janja* ("The Niggard or Kir
Janja," pub. 1837) and *Rodoljupci* ("The Patriots,"
pub. 1849) by Jovan Sterija Popović (1806–1856);
and two patriotic tragedies, *Maksim Crnojević* (pub.
1866) and *Pera Segedinac* (pub. 1881), by Laza
Kostić (1841–1910). Of the Croats, Dimitrije
Demeter (1811–1872) wrote the pseudohistorical
Teuta (pub. 1844) and August Šenoa (1838–1881)
the comedy *Ljubica* (pub. 1864). The Slovenes Fran
Levstik (1831–1887) and Josip Jurčič (1844–1881)
wrote jointly the tragedy *Tugomer* (pub. 1876),
which is still performed in a modern adaptation by
Bratko Kreft (pub. 1946).

Following the comic tradition of Popović was the
Serbian author Branislav Nušić (1864–1938), who
has had a permanent place in the repertory of Yugoslav theater since World War I. He is a clear-sighted
observer of human manners and vices, is deft in creating comic situations, and is a caricaturist delighted
in burlesquing social types. He is often justly compared to the Parisian boulevard playwrights, such as
Eugène Scribe and Georges Courteline.

Nušić's plays include *Sumnjivo lice* ("The Suspicious Person," pub. 1887), *Protekcija* ("The Privileged," pub. 1889), *Narodni poslanik* ("National
Delegate," pub. 1896), *Gospodja ministarka* ("The
Lady Minister," pub. 1929), *Dr.* (pub. 1936), and
Pokojnik ("The Deceased," pub. 1936). The essential
theme running through these comedies is power,
which is the title of his last, unfinished play (*Vlast,*
pub. 1938). Power at all costs is the main aspiration
of Nušić's characters, preferably in the indelicate
form of a sinecure granting the easy life. Basically
plays in the spirit of the nineteenth century, Nušić's
best comedies deserve to be classified as "comedies of
manners."

Ivan Cankar (1876–1918), the central figure of
the Slovene Modernist movement in literature, created his artistic opus in conditions that differed
greatly from those of Nušić. Nušić's carefree optimism had, in a considerable degree, its roots in an
intensified national consciousness, when Serbia was
becoming the predominant political power in a state
composed of many nations. Cankar was writing in
the midst of political and cultural struggle, when the
Hapsburgian monarchy was disintegrating and the
Austrian Slavs were fighting for national independence. Thus, his work is drenched both with melancholy and polemical vigor, and the ideological expression of his art is defined by the Viennese *fin de
siècle,* an anarchic protest in the form of a neoromantic Humanism.

Cankar wrote only six plays: *Jakob Ruda* (pub.
1900), *Za narodov blagor* ("For the Well-Being of
the People," pub. 1901), *Kralj na Betajnovi* ("The
King of Betajnovi," pub. 1902), *Pohujšanje v dolini
šentflorjanski* ("The Scandal in Saint Florian's Valley," pub. 1908), *Hlapci* ("The Knaves," pub.
1910), and *Lepa Vida* ("Beautiful Vida," pub. 1912).

Unlike Nušić, who remained in the channels of
romantic realism throughout the fifty years of his unrestrained dramatic output, Cankar, lyric by nature
and polemical in his attitude toward society, went
through all the metamorphoses of the European theater from 1900 to 1912. He ranged from an Ibsenite
criticism of social morals to a Maeterlinckian symbolism with its psychological subtleties. While satirizing the falsities of Slovene society, he could penetrate into the subconscious and treat sensual and
emotional complexities that could never be grasped
by a mere social satirist.

The plays of the Croatian author Miroslav Krleža
(1893–   ) are in some ways a continuation of
Cankar's work in their aggressive social criticism
and many-sidedness, manifested in the psychological
scope of Krleža's dramatic opus. His plays were created in three successive cycles, which are, in part,
interwoven. The first cycle, expressionist in tone,
treats in a polemic frenzy the moral restlessness that
afflicts man as a result of war and revolution. These
experimental plays are collected under the symbolic
title *Legende* ("Legends," pub. 1933), containing
Legenda ("The Legend," pub. 1913), *Maškerata*
("Masquerade," pub. 1913), *Kraljevi* ("Kings," pub.
1915), *Kristofor Kolumbo* (pub. 1917), *Michelangelo
Buonarotti* (pub. 1918), and *Adam i Eva* (pub. 1922).
In his second cyle, written in more concrete language
but with no less of a pessimistic spirit, Krleža dealt
with actual events of the war and their social impact
on Croatian peasants, soldiers, workers, and intellectuals. This group is in the form of a trilogy: *Golgota*
(written 1918–1920; prod. 1922), *U logoru,* originally called *Galizia* ("In the Camp," written and
prod. 1920), and *Vučjak* ("The Wolf Village," pub.
1923). In his third dramatic cycle Krleža abandoned
expressionism, at least in style, and retreated into the
sober order of Ibsenesque analytics. This retreat
from the visionary realm into the realm of psychology is artistically most potent in the trilogy *Gospoda
Glembajevi* ("The Glembays"), comprised of *Gospoda Glembajevi* (pub. 1928), *U agoniji* ("In
Agony," pub. 1928), and *Leda* (pub. 1930). Its theme
is the inevitable disintegration of a Zagreb middle-
class family from 1913 to 1925, approached with
merciless social criticism and deep insight into character.

The hallmark of Krleža's drama is protest, against
the provincial backwardness of public life, the gap
between the cultural potentials of Balkan peoples and
their civilization as it is, the greed of the *nouveau
riche,* the political undecidedness of the intelligentsia, and the Slavic brand of fatalism. His criticism of
the amoral autocracy of political activists is expressed in *Aretej* ("Aretheus," pub. 1959), subtitled
"Fantasy in Five Scenes." Critics have called this
play the most important dramatic work written and
staged in Yugoslavia since World War II.

The permanent position that Nušić, Cankar, and
Krleža have occupied in the Yugoslav theater for almost fifty years is not only a tribute to the depth of
their critical thinking and to the aesthetic interest of
their work but is also a sign of the Europeanization
of Serbian, Croatian, and Slovene drama. The effect
of the above-mentioned writers, who matured in the
period 1890–1920 and whose style ranged from
expressionism to symbolism, was felt most clearly in

the Croatian theater, with the appearance of Ivo Vojnović (1857–1929), Milan Begović (1876–1948), and Josip Kosor (1879–1961).

Though these dramatists experienced in their youth the atmosphere of the eclipsing Hapsburgs, they were not completely influenced by Middle European culture, that is, by Dostoevsky and Maeterlinck, Wedekind and Strindberg. Their work equally reflects a vigorous Mediterranean spirit (flourishing at the time of the Dalmatian renaissance), which they updated by introducing erotic themes, through obvious influences of D'Annunzio's hedonism and Freudian psychoanalysis.

Of the three, Vojnović is the link between the patriotic eloquence of the nineteenth century and the lyric sensualism of the fin de siècle. This is manifested in three artistically perfected dramas of pronounced Mediterranean flavor: *Ekvinokcij* ("Equinox," pub. 1895), *Dubrovačka trilogija* ("Dubrovnik Trilogy," pub. 1902), and *Gospodja sa suncokretom* ("Lady with a Parasol," pub. 1912). The impact of the first play is realistic, mainly because of the dialogue, but the action is governed by melodramatic surprises and the imagery has symbolic undertones. The second is a trilogy dealing with the death of the nobility of the Ragusine Republic when confronted with the growing strength of aggressive bourgeois tendencies during the Napoleonic Wars. It is a strong dramatic work, marked by a noble melancholy. The third play is a romance in a cosmopolitan milieu, and its dialogue abounds in symbolist imagery.

Begović, in his lyric poetry an ingenious verbalist with markedly erotic tones, operates in a wide variety of styles in his plays, ranging from symbolism to psychoanalytical introspection. His work always bears marks of an extraordinary technical skill, which he acquired while working in Hamburg (1908–1912) and Vienna (1912–1920). Of Begović's numerous plays, his trilogy *Tri drame* ("Three Dramas," pub. 1934)—including *Božji čovjek* ("God's Man," pub. and prod. 1924), *Pustolov pred vratima* ("Adventurer Before the Door," pub. and prod. 1926), and *Bez trećega* ("Without the Third," pub. and prod. 1931)—has been given a permanent place in modern Yugoslav theater. This modernistic trilogy bridges the author's poetic vision of erotic restlessness with his sober understanding of the subconscious.

Kosor's first play, *Požar strasti* ("The Fire of Passions," written 1910), about the peasant environment, is an early experiment in expressionism, mainly through its extremely sensual action. The play, performed in Germany and England about ten years earlier than it was in Yugoslavia (1922), won great recognition for Kosor, although it was not before the 1920's that he became popular in his own country. His other plays, either about the peasantry or big-city life, are *Pomirenje* ("Tranquility," pub. 1914), *Žena* ("Woman," pub. 1920), *Nepobjedive ladja* ("The Invincible Ship," pub. 1921), *U Café du Dome* ("In the Café du Dome," pub. 1922), *Rotonda* (pub. 1925), *Čovječanstvo* ("Mankind," pub. 1925), and *Njemak* ("The Dumb Man," pub. 1926).

Kosor's plays spring from the panerotism of the fin de siècle; yet there is a perceptible theme on the search for God. When these two themes conflict, the result sometimes borders on the absurd and some-

times on a satirical grotesquerie. Kosor had a titantic temperament that made it difficult for him as an artist to distinguish sufficiently between the material provided by life itself and its use in the context of dramatic art. Despite his occasional lack of artistic control, Kosor's work is always original in its imagery and dialogue.

The variety in the repertory of today's Yugoslav theater, which gained ground in the early 1950's, is an inevitable consequence of vigorous social dynamism in the new Yugoslavia. This dynamism is in part a reaction to the political and artistic suppression imposed by the Yugoslav regime between the two world wars and is in part a natural outcome of Yugoslavia's break with the Soviet Union in 1948. After the 1948 break, a great liberalization in all the arts took place. Contemporary authors, constantly confronted with foreign literary achievements, are going through incessant stylistic metamorphoses. The treatment of their subjects ranges from neorealistic reportage to surrealistic, ideological dramas. The new plays are intentionally abstract in argument and are influenced by such modes of thought as historic Marxism and existential dialectics.

Centers of theatrical activity are growing according to language units within the federation and beyond. Serbian drama has been developing mainly in Belgrade and Novi Sad, Croatian in Zagreb and Dubrovnik, Slovene in Ljubljana and Trieste (within the Slovene national minority in Italy), and Macedonian in Skopje and Bitola. There are also in each of the republics two or three professional theaters or experimental groups that forward Yugoslav theater either by the presentation of a daring choice of new and old plays or of outstanding artistic productions.

The pronounced pluralism in the dramatic activities of contemporary Yugoslavia is, at least after 1956, difficult to classify because the new styles are still evolving. Yet it is quite clear that the polemical temperament of Yugoslav audiences is again encouraging dramatists who have an unhidden zeal for social criticism.

Bibliographical information on the Yugoslav theater is virtually nonexistent, and even the plays that have been performed in English abroad have not been translated in published book form.—F. K. K.

Yukio, Mishima (1925–   ). Japanese playwright. One of Japan's most gifted living playwrights, Mishima Yukio was born in Tokyo. His dramatic work well exhibits a desire to be simultaneously of the East and West; often the form seems Japanese, the content European. He has written many full-length plays and ten unusual one-act plays, the latter strongly under the influence of the ancient tradition of *noh* drama. Such work he terms "modern noh." Invariably and ostentatiously, the scene is laid in the modern urban world, a highly mechanized society whose victims suffer the tribulations with which we are perhaps most familiar through French theater and fiction. Freudian psychology is also conspicuous. The persons depicted are highly neurotic. The plots, however, and even the titles are those of famous noh dramas.

Five of Yukio's works of this type have been ably rendered into English by Donald Keene in *Five Modern Noh Plays* (1957).—H. W. W.

Yürük, Ali (1940–   ). Turkish playwright.

Yürük was born and raised in a village in Anatolia. Currently, he is a student at the University of Istanbul and an actor with the Municipal Theater of Istanbul. Yürük's first and only produced play, *Çatallı Köy* ("The Village Called Çatallı," 1966), was written when he was twenty-two years old and produced in three different theaters. It is a play about vendettas, the abduction of women in villages, and the relationship between men and women in Anatolia. With its good characterizations and warm humor, this play has been recognized by many Turkish critics and laymen as one of the most moving plays about village life ever written.—N. O.

Z

Zaïre (1732). A tragedy by VOLTAIRE. Zaïre, of Christian origin, a captive of Sultan Orosmane, who wants to make her his wife, induces him to free a descendant of the Christian princes of Jerusalem, Lusignan, for whom the knight Nérestan has just brought the ransom. Once liberated, Lusignan discovers that both Zaïre and Nérestan are his children, and he makes Zaïre swear her fidelity to Christianity. Zaïre is torn between her love for Orosmane and her oath. Unaware of Zaïre's secret, Orosmane succumbs to jealousy, and when he learns that Zaïre and Nérestan plan to meet, he stabs her, not knowing that Nérestan is her brother. When he discovers the truth, he frees all the Christians and kills himself. The tragedy in *Zaïre* is dual: It is based not only on Orosmane's passion, both Racinian and inspired by Shakespeare's *Othello,* but on the grandiose religious intolerance of Lusignan.—Ja. G.

Zambia. See AFRICA: *Zambia.*

Zauberstück ("magic fantasy play"). A type of play, particularly popular in southern Germany and Austria, in which the dramatic action stems from the intervention of supernatural powers in human affairs. The Zauberstück was a mixture of the realistic and fantastic, often tied to a farce (*Zauberposse*) or opera (*Zauberoper*). The most well-known of the Zauberopern is Mozart's *Die Zauberflöte* (*The Magic Flute,* 1791). With roots in the low comedy burlesque of the seventeenth century, the form later aspired to literary heights in the stage creations of Raimund (*Alpenkönig und Menschenfeind* ("Mountain King and Misanthrope," 1828) and the social satire of Nestroy (*Lumpazivagabundus,* 1833).—B. M. M.

Zeami Motokiyo. See Zeami MOTOKIYO.

Zola, Émile [Édouard Charles Antoine] (1840–1902). French novelist, critic, and playwright. Al-

ENGRAVING OF A SCENE FROM VOLTAIRE'S *Zaïre* (BRITISH MUSEUM, PHOTO BULLOZ)

though Zola's literary reputation rests chiefly on the novels and critical essays that made him the leader of the naturalistic movement in the late nineteenth century, he wrote and saw performed and published, between 1865 and 1889, five naturalistic plays. He also had a hand in adapting for the stage eighteen of his novels and stories, all but one of which have been performed and eleven of which have been published. He published several volumes of reprints of his weekly articles that appeared in the Paris press from 1876 to 1881 on abolishing conventions of the stage and establishing the naturalistic drama, and he also wrote six opera librettos, which have been published.

The son of an Italian engineer and a French woman, Zola grew up in Aix-en-Provence, avidly reading Victor Hugo and Alfred de Musset and nourishing Romantic ideals. In 1858 he settled in Paris, completed his schooling, and worked briefly in a publishing firm. His first literary work, *Contes à Ninon* ("Stories for Ninon"), a mixture of the Romantic and the realistic, was published in Paris in 1864. In 1865 he wrote two plays: *La Laide* ("The Ugly Woman"), which, like three verse plays written in his teens, was never performed or published, and *Madeleine* (performed once by the Théâtre-Libre in 1889, but in the meantime transformed into the novel *Madeleine Férat*).

By 1867 he had turned against his earlier Romanticism and was increasingly championing a new kind of theater, fiction, and art, to be called naturalism, based upon the findings of positivist science, upon observable reality as advocated by Denis Diderot a century before, and upon the scientific study of heredity and environment. (SEE REALISM AND NATURALISM.) The stage must, in his view, become a laboratory where human behavior can be clinically dissected. Human truth—the pessimistic realization that human actions, desires, and goals are determined not by free will but by social forces beyond the control of any individual—must replace "art," with its artificialities and conventions. The "well-made play," the epitome of artificiality in the theater, must be destroyed. Every play must offer a *tranche de vie* ("slice of life"), revealing the impact of heredity and lower-middle-class environment on its victims in all its sordid, unsavory drabness. In 1873 Zola published his best play, *Thérèse Raquin*, its famous Preface serving as a manifesto for the new revolution in the theater. This Preface was to naturalism what Victor Hugo's *Préface de Cromwell* (1827) was to Romanticism forty-six years before. Zola's play was drawn from his novel (1867) of the same name.

In 1878 he published as *Théâtre* (Vol. I) four plays that had failed: *Madeleine* and *Thérèse Raquin* (domestic dramas of sexual passion), *Les Herétiers Rabourdin* ("The Rabourdin Heirs," prod. 1874; a satire of greed), and *Le Bouton de rose* ("The Rose-

bud," prod. 1878; a domestic farce). *Renée* (also a drama of sexual passion) was originally written in 1880 for Sarah Bernhardt, but failed in 1887, despite a run of thirty-eight performances.

Thérèse Raquin shows that one cannot escape one's past, that character is fate. A sensual woman plots with her lover to drown her sickly husband. A year later the lovers marry, but their passion has turned to guilt, fear, and hatred. The dead man's mother, learning the truth, is stricken with paralysis but gloatingly watches the guilty couple first try to kill each other, then commit suicide. Though the double suicide and the mother's unlikely recovery of her speech at the last moment seem melodramatic, and Zola has, contrary to all his preachments, constructed a rather crude well-made plot, *Thérèse Raquin* is a powerful drama. The characters are closely examined, and their disintegration at the end seems inevitable. This is not a detective story or a crime story as such, but a drama of fate with convincing characters, and it exemplifies fairly well Zola's conception of a naturalistic drama.

Zola was really not a dramatist, despite the discovery after his premature death of his grandiose plans for future plays. He will be remembered as a great novelist and critic, and, of course, as the founder of naturalism. He lacked the true gifts of the playwright. He mistakenly believed that art is synonymous with life. He never fully realized that the chaos of life must be transformed into art through form, that art is life treated, not conventionally, but by means of conventions, life seen through the artist's glass—sometimes darkly, sometimes not. Nevertheless, he did write one genuinely interesting specimen play, not without faults, to be sure. His other plays are negligible, except for his collaboration with William Busnach on the stage adaptation of the novel *L'Assommoir* (1877), which was the most popular of all his produced plays and had three hundred performances in 1879. Zola's genius for situations and characters and his naturalistic methods are largely displayed in his novels, but from the latter an effective drama was occasionally extracted.

Thérèse Raquin has been translated by Kathleen Boutall in *Seeds of Modern Drama* (1963; Vol. III of *Laurel Masterpieces of Continental Drama*), edited by N. Houghton. Zola's best essay on naturalism, "Le Naturalisme au théâtre" (1878), has been translated as "Naturalism on the Stage" for *Playwrights on Playwriting* (1961), edited by T. Cole. E. M. Grant's *Émile Zola* (1966) gives the facts of his life and discusses the major works. L. A. Carter's *Zola and the Theater* (1963) provides a detailed, scholarly treatment of this subject.—S. S. S.

Zuckmayer, Carl. See GERMANY: *twentieth century*.

Zweig, Stefan. See AUSTRIA.

APPENDIX

Basic Documents in Dramatic Theory

ARISTOTLE (384–322 B.C.)

Despite countless attempts to distort, disclaim, or idealize it out of existence, the *Poetics* of Aristotle remains the most celebrated critical analysis in the history of literature. It has brought to the language of criticism such complex and fundamental concepts as *imitation, catharsis,* and *hamartia* and has stirred endless commentary on the meaning of these and other terms. One major source of conflicting interpretations is the condition of the text itself. The *Poetics,* as it has come down to us, is not a finished treatise, but a compilation of notes written in elliptical, abbreviated style. Scholarship has come a long way toward eliminating or at least identifying problems of textual corruption. S. H. Butcher's translation, printed below, has been widely acclaimed for its sensitivity and good judgment in regard to these problems.

Poetics

I

I propose to treat of Poetry in itself and of its various kinds, noting the essential quality of each; to inquire into the structure of the plot as requisite to a good poem; into the number and nature of the parts of which a poem is composed; and similarly into whatever else falls within the same inquiry. Following, then, the order of nature, let us begin with the principles which come first.

Epic poetry and Tragedy, Comedy also and Dithyrambic poetry, and the music of the flute and of the lyre in most of their forms, are all in their general conception modes of imitation. They differ, however, from one another in three respects—the medium, the objects, the manner or mode of imitation, being in each case distinct.

For as there are persons who, by conscious art or mere habit, imitate and represent various objects through the medium of color and form, or again by the voice, so in the arts above mentioned, taken as a whole, the imitation is produced by rhythm, language, or "harmony," either singly or combined.

Thus in the music of the flute and of the lyre, "harmony" and rhythm alone are employed; also in other arts, such as that of the shepherd's pipe, which are essentially similar to these. In dancing, rhythm alone is used without "harmony," for even dancing imitates character, emotion, and action, by rhythmical movement.

There is another art which imitates by means of language alone, and that either in prose or verse—which verse, again, may either combine different meters or consist of but one kind—but this has hitherto been without a name. For there is no common term we could apply to the mimes of Sophron and Xenarchus and the Socratic dialogues on the one hand; and, on the other, to poetic imitations in iambic, elegiac, or any similar meter. People do, indeed, add the word "maker" or "poet" to the name of the meter, and speak of elegiac poets, or epic (that is, hexameter) poets, as if it were not the imitation that makes the poet, but the verse that entitles them all indiscriminately to the name. Even when a treatise on medicine or natural science is brought out in verse, the name of poet is by custom given to the author; and yet Homer and Empedocles have nothing in common but the meter, so that it would be right to call the one poet, the other physicist rather than poet. On the same principle, even if a writer in his poetic imitation were to combine all meters, as Chaeremon did in his *Centaur,* which is a medley composed of meters of all kinds, we should bring him too under the general term poet. So much then for these distinctions.

There are, again, some arts which employ all the means above mentioned—namely, rhythm, tune, and meter. Such are Dithyrambic and Nomic poetry, and also Tragedy and Comedy; but between them the difference is that in the first two cases these means are all employed in combination, in the latter, now one means is employed, now another.

Such, then, are the differences of the arts with respect to the medium of imitation.

II

Since the objects of imitation are men in action, and these men must be either of a higher or a lower type (for moral character mainly answers to these divisions, goodness and badness being the distinguishing marks of moral differences), it follows that we must represent men either as better than in real life, or as worse, or as they are. It is the same in painting. Polygnotus depicted men as nobler than they are, Pauson as less noble, Dionysius drew them true to life.

Now it is evident that each of the modes of imitation above mentioned will exhibit these differences, and become a distinct kind in imitating objects that are thus distinct. Such diversities may be found even in dancing, flute-playing, and lyre-playing. So again in language, whether prose or verse unaccompanied by music. Homer, for example, makes men better than they are; Cleophon as they are; Hegemon the Thasian, the inventor of parodies, and Nicochares, the author of the *Deiliad,* worse than they are. The same thing holds good of Dithyrambs and Nomes; here too one may portray different types, as Timotheus and Philoxenus differed in representing their Cyclopes. The same distinction marks off Tragedy from Comedy; for Comedy aims at representing men as worse, Tragedy as better than in actual life.

III

There is still a third difference—the manner in which each of these objects may be imitated. For the medium being the same, and the objects the same, the poet may imitate by narration—in which case he can either take another personality as Homer does, or speak in his own person, unchanged—or he may present all his characters as living and moving before us.

These, then, as we said at the beginning, are the three differences which distinguish artistic imitation—the medium, the objects, and the manner. So that, from one point of view, Sophocles is an imitator of the same kind as Homer—for both imitate higher types of character; from another point of view, of the same kind as Aristophanes—for both imitate persons acting and doing. Hence, some say, the name of "drama" is given to such poems, as representing action. For the same reason the Dorians claim the invention both of Tragedy and Comedy. The claim to Comedy is put forward by the Megarians—not only by those of Greece proper, who allege that it originated under their democracy, but also by the Megarians of Sicily, for the poet Epicharmus, who is much earlier than Chionides and Magnes, belonged to that country. Tragedy too is claimed by certain Dorians of the Peloponnese. In each case they appeal to the evidence of language. The outlying villages, they say, are by them called κῶμαι, by the Athenians δῆμοι: and they assume that Comedians were so named not from κωμάζειν, "to revel," but because they wandered from village to village (κατὰ κώμας), being excluded contemptuously from the city. They add also that the Dorian word for "doing" is δρᾶν, and the Athenian, πράττειν.

This may suffice as to the number and nature of the various modes of imitation.

IV

Poetry in general seems to have sprung from two causes, each of them lying deep in our nature. First, the instinct of imitation is implanted in man from childhood, one difference between him and other animals being that he is the most imitative of living creatures, and through imitation learns his earliest lessons; and no less universal is the pleasure felt in things imitated. We have evidence of this in the facts of experience. Objects which in themselves we view with pain, we delight to contemplate when reproduced with minute fidelity: such as the forms of the most ignoble animals and of dead bodies. The cause of this again is that to learn gives the liveliest pleasure, not only to philosophers but to men in general; whose capacity, however, of learning is more limited. Thus the reason why men enjoy seeing a likeness is that in contemplating it they find themselves learning or inferring, and saying perhaps, "Ah, that is he." For if you happen not to have seen the original, the pleasure will be due not to the imitation as such, but to the execution, the coloring, or some such other cause.

Imitation, then, is one instinct of our nature. Next, there is the instinct for "harmony" and rhythm, meters being manifestly sections of rhythm. Persons, therefore, starting with this natural gift developed by degrees their special aptitudes, till their rude improvisations gave birth to Poetry.

Poetry now diverged in two directions, according to the individual character of the writers. The graver spirits imitated noble actions, and the actions of good men. The more trivial sort imitated the actions of meaner persons, at first composing satires, as the former did hymns to the gods and the praises of famous men. A poem of the satirical kind cannot indeed be put down to any author earlier than Homer; though many such writers probably there were. But from Homer onward, instances can be cited—his own *Margites,* for example, and other similar compositions. The appropriate meter was also here introduced; hence the measure is still called the iambic or lampooning measure, being that in which people lampooned one another. Thus the older poets were distinguished as writers of heroic or of lampooning verse.

As, in the serious style, Homer is pre-eminent among poets, for he alone combined dramatic form with excellence of imitation, so he too first laid down the main lines of Comedy, by dramatizing the ludicrous instead of writing personal satire. His *Margites* bears the same relation to Comedy that the *Iliad* and *Odyssey* do to Tragedy. But when Tragedy and Comedy came to light, the two classes of poets still followed their natural bent: the lampooners became writers of Comedy, and the Epic poets were succeeded by Tragedians, since the drama was a larger and higher form of art.

Whether Tragedy has as yet perfected its proper types or not, and whether it is to be judged in itself, or in relation also to the audience—this raises another question. Be that as it may, Tragedy—as also Comedy—was at first mere improvisation. The one originated with the authors of the Dithyramb, the other with those of the phallic songs, which are still in use in many of our cities. Tragedy advanced by slow degrees; each new element that showed itself was in turn developed. Having passed through many changes, it found its natural form, and there it stopped.

Aeschylus first introduced a second actor; he diminished the importance of the Chorus, and assigned the leading part to the dialogue. Sophocles raised the number of actors to three, and added scene-painting. Moreover, it was not till late that the short plot was discarded for one of greater compass, and the grotesque diction of the earlier satyric form for the stately manner of Tragedy. The iambic measure then replaced the trochaic tetrameter, which was originally employed when the poetry was of the satyric order, and had greater affinities with dancing. Once dialogue had come in, Nature herself discovered the appropriate measure. For the iambic is, of all measures, the most colloquial: we see it in the fact that conversational speech runs into iambic lines more frequently than into any other kind of verse; rarely into hexameters, and only when we drop the colloquial intonation. The additions to the number of "episodes" or acts, and the other accessories of which tradition tells, must be taken as already described; for to discuss them in detail would, doubtless, be a large undertaking.

V

Comedy is, as we have said, an imitation of characters of a lower type—not, however, in the full sense of the word bad, the Ludicrous being merely a subdivision of the ugly. It consists in some defect or ugliness which is not painful or destructive. To take an obvious example, the comic mask is ugly and distorted, but does not imply pain.

The successive changes through which Tragedy passed, and the authors of these changes, are well known, whereas Comedy has had no history, because it was not at first treated seriously. It was late before the Archon granted a comic chorus to a poet; the performers were till then voluntary. Comedy had already taken definite shape when comic poets, distinctively so called, are heard of. Who furnished it with masks, or prologues, or increased the number of actors—these and other similar details remain unknown. As for the plot, it came originally from Sicily; but of Athenian writers Crates was the first who, abandoning the "iambic" or lampooning form, generalized his themes and plots.

Epic poetry agrees with Tragedy in so far as it is an imitation in verse of characters of a higher type. They differ, in that Epic poetry admits but one kind of meter, and is narrative in form. They differ, again, in their length: for Tragedy endeavors, as far as possible, to confine itself to a single revolution of the sun, or but slightly to exceed this limit; whereas the Epic action has no limits of time. This, then, is a second point of difference, though at first the same freedom was admitted in Tragedy as in Epic poetry.

Of their constituent parts some are common to both, some peculiar to Tragedy: whoever, therefore, knows what is good or bad Tragedy, knows also about Epic poetry. All the elements of an Epic poem are found in Tragedy, but the elements of a Tragedy are not all found in the Epic poem.

VI

Of the poetry which imitates in hexameter verse, and of Comedy, we will speak hereafter. Let us now discuss Tragedy, resuming its formal definition, as resulting from what has been already said.

Tragedy, then, is an imitation of an action that is serious, complete, and of a certain magnitude; in language embellished with each kind of artistic ornament, the several kinds being found in separate parts of the play; in the form of action, not of narrative; through pity and fear effecting the proper purgation of these emotions. By "language embellished," I mean language into which rhythm, "harmony," and song enter. By "the several kinds in separate parts," I mean that some parts are rendered through the medium of verse alone, others again with the aid of song.

Now as tragic imitation implies persons acting, it necessarily follows, in the first place, that Spectacular equipment will be a part of Tragedy. Next, Song and Diction, for these are the medium of imitation. By "Diction" I mean the mere metrical arrangement of the words: as for "Song," it is a term whose sense everyone understands.

Again, Tragedy is the imitation of an action; and an action implies personal agents, who necessarily possess certain distinctive qualities both of character and thought; for it is by these that we qualify actions themselves, and these—thought and character—are the two natural causes from which actions spring, and on actions again all success or failure depends. Hence, the Plot is the imitation of the action: for by plot I here mean the arrangement of the incidents. By Character I mean that in virtue of which we ascribe certain qualities to the agents. Thought is required wherever a statement is proved, or, it may be, a general truth enunciated. Every Tragedy, therefore, must have six parts, which parts determine its quality—namely, Plot, Character, Diction, Thought, Spectacle, Song. Two of the parts constitute the medium of imitation, one the manner, and three the objects of imitation. And these complete the list. These elements have been employed, we may say, by the poets to a man; in fact, every play contains Spectacular elements as well as Character, Plot, Diction, Song, and Thought.

But most important of all is the structure of the incidents. For Tragedy is an imitation, not of men, but of an action and of life, and life consists in action, and its end is a mode of action, not a quality. Now character determines men's qualities, but it is by their actions that they are happy or the reverse. Dramatic action, therefore, is not with a view to the representation of character: character comes in as subsidiary to the actions. Hence the incidents and the plot are the end of a tragedy; and the end is the chief thing of all. Again, without action there cannot be a tragedy; there may be without character. The tragedies of most of our modern poets fail in the rendering of character; and of poets in general this is often true. It is the same in painting; and here lies the difference between Zeuxis and Polygnotus. Polygnotus delineates character well: the style of Zeuxis is devoid of ethical quality. Again, if you string together a set of speeches expressive of character, and well finished in point of diction and thought, you will not produce the essential tragic effect nearly so well as with a play which, however deficient in these respects, yet has a plot and artistically constructed incidents. Besides which, the most powerful elements of emotional interest in Tragedy—Peripeteia or Reversal of the Situation, and Recognition scenes—are parts of the plot. A further proof is that novices in the art attain to finish of diction and precision of portraiture before they can construct the plot. It is the same with almost all the early poets.

The Plot, then, is the first principle, and, as it were, the soul of a tragedy: Character holds the second place. A similar fact is seen in painting. The most beautiful colors, laid on confusedly, will not give as much pleasure as the chalk outline of a portrait. Thus Tragedy is the imitation of an action, and of the agents mainly with a view to the action.

Third in order is Thought—that is, the faculty of saying what is possible and pertinent in given circumstances. In the case of oratory, this is the function of the political art and of the art of rhetoric: and so indeed the older poets make their characters speak the language of civic life; the poets of our time, the language of the rhetoricians. Character is that which reveals moral purpose, showing what kind of things a man chooses or avoids. Speeches, therefore, which do not make this manifest, or in which the speaker does not choose or avoid anything whatever, are not expressive of character. Thought, on the other hand, is found where something is proved to be or not to be, or a general maxim is enunciated.

Fourth among the elements enumerated comes Diction; by which I mean, as has been already said, the expression of the meaning in words; and its essence is the same both in verse and prose.

Of the remaining elements Song holds the chief place among the embellishments.

The Spectacle has, indeed, an emotional attraction of its own, but, of all the parts, it is the least artistic, and connected least with the art of poetry. For the power of Tragedy, we may be sure, is felt even apart from representation and actors. Besides, the production of spectacular effects depends more on the art of the stage machinist than on that of the poet.

VII

These principles being established, let us now discuss the proper structure of the Plot, since this is the first and most important thing in Tragedy.

Now, according to our definition, Tragedy is an imitation of an action that is complete, and whole, and of a certain magnitude; for there may be a whole that is wanting in magnitude. A whole is that which has a beginning, a middle, and an end. A beginning is that which does not itself follow anything by causal necessity, but after which something naturally is or comes to be. An end, on the contrary, is that which itself naturally follows some other thing, either by necessity, or as a rule, but has nothing following it. A middle is that which follows something as some other thing follows it. A well-constructed plot, therefore, must neither begin nor end at haphazard, but conform to these principles.

Again, a beautiful object, whether it be a living organism or any whole composed of parts, must not only have an orderly arrangement of parts, but must also be of a certain magnitude; for beauty depends on magnitude and order. Hence a very small animal organism cannot be beautiful; for the view of it is confused, the object being seen in an almost imperceptible moment of time. Nor, again, can one of vast size be beautiful; for as the eye cannot take it all in at once, the unity and sense of the whole is lost for the spectator; as for instance if there were one a thousand miles long. As, therefore, in the case of animate bodies and organisms a certain magnitude is necessary, and a magnitude which may be easily embraced in one view; so in the plot, a certain length is necessary, and a length which can be easily embraced by the memory. The limit of length in relation to dramatic competition and sensuous presentment is no part of artistic theory. For had it been the rule for a hundred tragedies to compete together, the performance would have been regulated by the water clock—as indeed we are told was formerly done. But the limit as fixed by the nature of the drama itself is this: the greater the length, the more beautiful will the piece be by reason of its size, provided that the whole be perspicuous. And to define the matter roughly, we may say that the proper magnitude is comprised within such limits that the sequence of events, according to the law of probability or necessity, will admit of a change from bad fortune to good, or from good fortune to bad.

VIII

Unity of plot does not, as some persons think, consist in the unity of the hero. For infinitely various are the incidents in one man's life which cannot be reduced to unity; and so, too, there are many actions of one man out of which we cannot make one action. Hence the error, as it appears, of all poets who have composed a *Heracleid,* a *Theseid,* or other poems of the kind. They imagine that as Heracles was one man, the story of Heracles must also be a unity. But Homer, as in all else he is of surpassing merit, here too—whether from art or natural genius—seems to have happily discerned the truth. In composing the *Odyssey* he did not include all the adventures of Odysseus—such as his wound on Parnassus, or his feigned madness at the mustering of the host—incidents between which there was no necessary or probable connection: but he made the *Odyssey,* and likewise the *Iliad,* to center round an action that in our sense of the word is one. As, therefore, in the other imitative arts, the imitation is one when the object imitated is one, so the plot, being an imitation of an action, must imitate one action and that a whole, the structural union of the parts being such that, if any one of them is displaced or removed, the whole will be disjointed and disturbed. For a thing whose presence or absence makes no visible difference is not an organic part of the whole.

IX

It is, moreover, evident from what has been said that it is not the function of the poet to relate what has happened, but what may happen—what is possible according to the law of probability or necessity. The poet and the historian differ not by writing in verse or in prose. The work of Herodotus might be put into verse, and it would still be a species of history, with meter no less than without it. The true difference is that one relates what has happened, the other what may happen. Poetry, therefore, is a more philosophical and a higher thing than history: for poetry trends to express the universal, history the particular. By the universal I mean how a person of a certain type will on occasion speak or act, according to the law of probability or necessity; and it is this universality at which poetry aims in the names she attaches to the personages. The particular is—for example—what Alcibiades did or suffered. In Comedy this is already apparent: for here the poet first constructs the plot on the lines of probability, and then inserts characteristic names—unlike the lampooners who write about particular individuals. But tragedians still keep to real names, the reason being that what is possible is credible: what has not happened we do not at once feel sure to be possible, but what has happened is manifestly possible: otherwise it would not have happened. Still there are even some tragedies in which there are only one or two well-known names, the rest being fictitious. In others, none are well known—as in Agathon's *Antheus,* where incidents and names alike are fictitious, and yet they give none the less pleasure. We must not, therefore, at all costs keep to the received legends, which are the usual subjects of Tragedy. Indeed, it would be absurd to attempt it; for even subjects that are known are known only to a few, and yet give pleasure to all. It clearly follows that the poet or "maker" should be the maker of plots rather than of verses, since he is a poet because he imitates, and what he imitates are actions. And even if he chances to take an historical subject, he is none the less a poet; for there is no reason why some events that have actually happened should not conform to the law of the probable and possible, and in virtue of that quality in them he is their poet or maker.

Of all plots and actions the epeisodic are the worst. I call a plot "epeisodic" in which the episodes or acts succeed one another without probable or necessary sequence. Bad poets compose such pieces by their own fault, good poets, to please the players; for, as they write show pieces for competition, they stretch the plot beyond its capacity and are often forced to break the natural continuity.

But again, Tragedy is an imitation not only of a complete action, but of events inspiring fear or pity. Such an effect is best produced when the events come on us by surprise; and the effect is heightened when, at the same time, they follow as cause and effect. The tragic wonder will then be greater than if they happened of themselves or by accident, for even coincidences are most striking when they have an air of design. We may instance the statue of Mitys at Argos, which fell upon his murderer while he was a spectator at a festival, and killed him. Such events seem not to be due to mere chance. Plots, therefore, constructed on these principles are necessarily the best.

X

Plots are either Simple or Complex, for the actions in real life, of which the plots are an imitation, obviously show a similar distinction. An action which is one and continuous in the sense above defined, I call Simple, when the change of fortune takes place without Reversal of the Situation and without Recognition.

A Complex action is one in which the change is accompanied by such Reversal, or by Recognition, or by both. These last should arise from the internal structure of the plot, so that what follows should be the necessary or probable result of the preceding ac-

tion. It makes all the difference whether any given event is a case of *propter hoc* or *post hoc.*

XI

Reversal of the Situation is a change by which the action veers round to its opposite, subject always to our rule of probability or necessity. Thus in the *Oedipus,* the messenger comes to cheer Oedipus and free him from his alarms about his mother, but by revealing who he is, he produces the opposite effect. Again in the *Lynceus,* Lynceus is being led away to his death, and Danaus goes with him, meaning to slay him; but the outcome of the preceding incidents is that Danaus is killed and Lynceus saved.

Recognition, as the name indicates, is a change from ignorance to knowledge, producing love or hate between the persons destined by the poet for good or bad fortune. The best form of recognition is coincident with a Reversal of the Situation, as in the *Oedipus.* There are indeed other forms. Even inanimate things of the most trivial kind may in a sense be objects of recognition. Again, we may recognize or discover whether a person has done a thing or not. But the recognition which is most intimately connected with the plot and action is, as we have said, the recognition of persons. This recognition, combined with Reversal, will produce either pity or fear; and actions producing these effects are those which, by our definition, Tragedy represents. Moreover, it is upon such situations that the issues of good or bad fortune will depend. Recognition, then, being between persons, it may happen that one person only is recognized by the other—when the latter is already known—or it may be necessary that the recognition should be on both sides. Thus Iphigenia is revealed to Orestes by the sending of the letter; but another act of recognition is required to make Orestes known to Iphigenia.

Two parts, then, of the Plot—Reversal of the Situation and Recognition—turn upon surprises. A third part is the Scene of Suffering. The Scene of Suffering is a destructive or painful action, such as death on the stage, bodily agony, wounds and the like.

XII

[The parts of Tragedy which must be treated as elements of the whole have been already mentioned. We now come to the quantitative parts—the separate parts into which Tragedy is divided—namely, Prologue, Episode, Exode, Choric song; this last being divided into Parode and Stasimon. These are common to all plays; peculiar to some are the songs of actors from the stage and the Commoi.

The Prologue is that entire part of a tragedy which precedes the Parode of the Chorus. The Episode is that entire part of a tragedy which is between complete choric songs. The Exode is that entire part of a tragedy which has no choric song after it. Of the Choric part the Parode is the first undivided utterance of the Chorus: the Stasimon is a Choric ode without anapests or trochaic tetrameters: the Commos is a joint lamentation of Chorus and actors. The parts of Tragedy which must be treated as elements of the whole have been already mentioned. The quantitative parts—the separate parts into which it is divided—are here enumerated.]

XIII

As the sequel to what has already been said, we must proceed to consider what the poet should aim at, and what he should avoid, in constructing his plots; and by what means the specific effect of Tragedy will be produced.

A perfect tragedy should, as we have seen, be arranged not on the simple but on the complex plan. It should, moreover, imitate actions which excite pity and fear, this being the distinctive mark of tragic imitation. It follows plainly, in the first place, that the change of fortune presented must not be the spectacle of a virtuous man brought from prosperity to adversity: for this moves neither pity nor fear; it merely shocks us. Nor, again, that of a bad man passing from adversity to prosperity, for nothing can be more alien to the spirit of Tragedy; it possesses no single tragic quality; it neither satisfies the moral sense nor calls forth pity or fear. Nor, again, should the downfall of the utter villain be exhibited. A plot of this kind would, doubtless, satisfy the moral sense, but it would inspire neither pity nor fear; for pity is aroused by unmerited misfortune, fear by the misfortune of a man like ourselves. Such an event, therefore, will be neither pitiful nor terrible. There remains, then, the character between these two extremes—that of a man who is not eminently good and just, yet whose misfortune is brought about not by vice or depravity, but by some error or frailty. He must be one who is highly renowned and prosperous—a personage like Oedipus, Thyestes, or other illustrious men of such families.

A well-constructed plot should, therefore, be single in its issue, rather than double as some maintain. The change of fortune should be not from bad to good, but, reversely, from good to bad. It should come about as the result not of vice, but of some great error or frailty, in a character either such as we have described, or better rather than worse. The practice of the stage bears out our view. At first the poets recounted any legend that came in their way. Now, the best tragedies are founded on the story of a few houses—on the fortunes of Alcmaeon, Oedipus, Orestes, Meleager, Thyestes, Telephus, and those others who have done or suffered something terrible. A tragedy, then, to be perfect according to the rules of art should be of this construction. Hence they are in error who censure Euripides just because he follows this principle in his plays, many of which end unhappily. It is, as we have said, the right ending. The best proof is that, on the stage and in dramatic competition, such plays, if well worked out, are the most tragic in effect; and Euripides, faulty though he may be in the general management of his subject, yet is felt to be the most tragic of the poets.

In the second rank comes the kind of tragedy which some place first. Like the *Odyssey*, it has a double thread of plot, and also an opposite catastrophe for the good and for the bad. It is accounted the best because of the weakness of the spectators; for the poet is guided in what he writes by the wishes of his audience. The pleasure, however, thence derived is not the true tragic pleasure. It is proper rather to Comedy, where those who, in the piece, are the deadliest enemies—like Orestes and Aegisthus—quit the stage as friends at the close, and no one slays or is slain.

XIV

Fear and pity may be aroused by spectacular means; but they may also result from the inner structure of the piece, which is the better way, and indicates a superior poet. For the plot ought to be so constructed that, even without the aid of the eye, he who hears the tale told will thrill with horror and melt to pity at what takes place. This is the impression we should receive from hearing the story of the *Oedipus*. But to produce this effect by the mere spectacle is a less artistic method, and dependent on extraneous aids. Those who employ spectacular means to create a sense not of the terrible but only of the monstrous, are strangers to the purpose of Tragedy; for we must not demand of Tragedy any and every kind of pleasure, but only that which is proper to it. And since the pleasure which the poet should afford is that which comes from pity and fear through imitation, it is evident that this quality must be impressed upon the incidents.

Let us then determine what are the circumstances which strike us as terrible or pitiful.

Actions capable of this effect must happen between persons who are either friends or enemies or indifferent to one another. If an enemy kills an enemy, there is nothing to excite pity either in the act or the intention—except so far as the suffering in itself is pitiful. So again with indifferent persons. But when the tragic incident occurs between those who are near or dear to one another—if, for example, a brother kills, or intends to kill, a brother, a son his father, a mother her son, a son his mother, or any other deed of the kind is done—these are the situations to be looked for by the poet. He may not indeed destroy the framework of the received legends—the fact for instance, that Clytemnestra was slain by Orestes and Eriphyle by Alcmaeon—but he ought to show invention of his own, and skillfully handle the traditional material. Let us explain more clearly what is meant by skillful handling.

The action may be done consciously and with knowledge of the persons, in the manner of the older poets. It is thus too that Euripides makes Medea slay her children. Or, again, the deed of horror may be done, but done in ignorance, and the tie of kinship or friendship be discovered afterwards. The *Oedipus* of Sophocles is an example. Here, indeed, the incident is outside the drama proper; but cases occur where it falls within the action of the play: one may cite the *Alcmaeon* of Astydamas, or Telegonus in the *Wounded Odysseus*. Again, there is a third case—<to be about to act with knowledge of the persons and then not to act. The fourth case is> when someone is about to do an irreparable deed through ignorance, and makes the discovery before it is done. These are the only possible ways. For the deed must either be done or not done—and that wittingly or unwittingly. But of all these ways, to be about to act knowing the persons, and then not to act, is the worst. It is shocking without being tragic, for no disaster follows. It is, therefore, never, or very rarely, found in poetry. One instance, however, is in the *Antigone,* where Haemon threatens to kill Creon.

The next and better way is that the deed should be perpetrated. Still better, that it should be perpetrated in ignorance, and the discovery made afterwards. There is then nothing to shock us, while the discovery produces a startling effect. The last case is the best, as when in the *Cresphontes* Merope is about to slay her son, but, recognizing who he is, spares his life. So in the *Iphigenia,* the sister recognizes the brother just in time. Again in the *Helle,* the son recognizes the mother when on the point of giving her up. This, then, is why a few families only, as has been already observed, furnish the subjects of tragedy. It was not art, but happy chance, that led the poets in search of subjects to impress the tragic quality upon their plots. They are compelled, therefore, to have recourse to those houses whose history contains moving incidents like these.

Enough has now been said concerning the structure of the incidents, and the right kind of plot.

XV

In respect of Character there are four things to be aimed at. First, and most important, it must be good. Now any speech or action that manifests moral purpose of any kind will be expressive of character: the character will be good if the purpose is good. This rule is relative to each class. Even a woman may be good, and also a slave; though the woman may be said to be an inferior being, and the slave quite worthless. The second thing to aim at is propriety. There is a type of manly valor; but valor in a woman, or unscrupulous cleverness, is inappropriate. Thirdly, character must be true to life: for this is a distinct thing from goodness and propriety, as here described. The fourth point is consistency, for though the subject of the imitation, who suggested the type, be inconsistent, still he must be consistently inconsistent. As an example of motiveless degradation of character we have Menelaus in the *Orestes;* of character indecorous and inappropriate, the lament of Odysseus in the *Scylla,* and the speech of Melanippe; of inconsistency, the *Iphigenia at Aulis*—for Iphigenia the suppliant in no way resembles her later self.

As in the structure of the plot, so too in the portraiture of character, the poet should always aim either at the necessary or the probable. Thus a person of a given character should speak or act in a given way, by the rule either of necessity or of probability, just as this event should follow that by necessary or probable sequence. It is therefore evident that the unraveling of the plot, no less than the complication, must arise out of the plot itself, it must not be brought about by the *Deus ex Machina*—as in the *Medea,* or in the Return of the Greeks in the *Iliad.* The *Deus ex Machina* should be employed only for events external to the drama—for antecedent or subsequent events, which lie beyond the range of human knowledge, and which require to be reported or foretold; for to the gods we ascribe the power of seeing all things. Within the action there must be nothing irrational. If the irrational cannot be excluded, it should be outside the scope of the tragedy. Such is the irrational element in the *Oedipus* of Sophocles.

Again, since Tragedy is an imitation of persons who are above the common level, the example of good portrait painters should be followed. They, while reproducing the distinctive form of the original, make a likeness which is true to life and yet more beautiful. So too the poet, in representing men who are irascible or indolent, or have other defects of character, should preserve the type and yet ennoble it. In this way Achilles is portrayed by Agathon and Homer.

These then are rules the poet should observe. Nor should he neglect those appeals to the senses, which, though not among the essentials, are the concomitants of poetry; for here too there is much room for error. But of this enough has been said in our published treatises.

XVI

What Recognition is has been already explained. We will now enumerate its kinds.

First, the least artistic form, which, from poverty of wit, is most commonly employed—recognition by signs. Of these some are congenital—such as "the spear which the earth-born race bear on their bodies," or the stars introduced by Carcinus in his *Thyestes.* Others are acquired after birth, and of these some are bodily marks, as scars; some external tokens, as necklaces, or the little ark in the *Tyro* by which the discovery is effected. Even these admit of more or less skillful treatment. Thus in the recognition of Odysseus by his scar, the discovery is made in one way by the nurse, in another by the swineherds. The use of tokens for the express purpose of proof— and, indeed, any formal proof with or without tokens—is a less artistic mode of recognition. A better kind is that which comes about by a turn of incident, as in the Bath Scene in the *Odyssey.*

Next come the recognitions invented at will by the poet, and on that account wanting in art. For example, Orestes in the *Iphigenia* reveals the fact that he is Orestes. She, indeed, makes herself known by the letter; but he, by speaking himself and saying what the poet, not what the plot, requires. This, therefore, is nearly allied to the fault above mentioned, for Orestes might as well have brought tokens with him. Another similar instance is the "voice of the shuttle" in the *Tereus* of Sophocles.

The third kind depends on memory when the sight of some object awakens a feeling: as in the *Cyprians* of Dicaeogenes, where the hero breaks into tears on seeing the picture; or again in the *Lay of Alcinous,* where Odysseus, hearing the minstrel play the lyre, recalls the past and weeps, and hence the recognition.

The fourth kind is by process of reasoning. Thus in the *Choëphori:* "Someone resembling me has come: no one resembles me but Orestes: therefore Orestes has come." Such too is the discovery made by Iphigenia in the play of Polyidus the Sophist. It was a natural reflection for Orestes to make, "So I too must die at the altar like my sister." So, again, in the *Tydeus* of Theodectes, the father says, "I came to find my son, and I lose my own life." So too in the *Phineidae:* the women, on seeing the place, inferred their fate—"Here we are doomed to die, for here we were cast forth." Again, there is a composite kind of recognition involving false inference on the part of one of the characters, as in the Odysseus Disguised as a Messenger. A said < that no one else was able to bend the bow; . . . hence B (the disguised Odysseus) imagined that A would> recognize the bow which, in fact, he had not seen; and to bring about a recognition by this means—the expectation that A would recognize the bow—is false inference.

But, of all recognitions, the best is that which arises from the incidents themselves, where the startling discovery is made by natural means. Such is that in the *Oedipus* of Sophocles, and in the *Iphigenia;* for it was natural that Iphigenia should wish to dispatch a letter. These recognitions alone dispense with the artificial aid of tokens or amulets. Next come the recognitions by process of reasoning.

XVII

In constructing the plot and working it out with the proper diction, the poet should place the scene, as far as possible, before his eyes. In this way, seeing everything with the utmost vividness, as if he were a spectator of the action, he will discover what is in keeping with it, and be most unlikely to overlook inconsistencies. The need of such a rule is shown by the fault found in Carcinus. Amphiaraus was on his way from the temple. This fact escaped the observation of one who did not see the situation. On the stage, however, the piece failed, the audience being offended at the oversight.

Again, the poet should work out his play, to the best of his power, with appropriate gestures; for those who feel emotion are most convincing through natural sympathy with the characters they represent; and one who is agitated storms, one who is angry rages, with the most lifelike reality. Hence poetry implies either a happy gift of nature or a strain of madness. In the one case a man can take the mold of any character; in the other, he is lifted out of his proper self.

As for the story, whether the poet takes it ready made or constructs it for himself, he should first sketch its general outline, and then fill in the episodes and amplify in detail. The general plan may be illustrated by the *Iphigenia.* A young girl is sacrificed; she disappears mysteriously from the eyes of those who sacrificed her; she is transported to another country, where the custom is to offer up all strangers to the goddess. To this ministry she is appointed. Sometime later her own brother chances to arrive. The fact that the oracle for some reason ordered him to go there, is outside the general plan of the play. The purpose, again, of his coming is outside the action proper. However, he comes, he is seized, and, when on the point of being sacrificed, reveals who he is. The mode of recognition may be either that of Euripides or of Polyidus, in whose play he exclaims very naturally: "So it was not my sister only, but I too, who was doomed to be sacrificed"; and by that remark he is saved.

After this, the names being once given, it remains to fill in the episodes. We must see that they are relevant to the action. In the case of Orestes, for example, there is the madness which led to his capture, and his deliverance by means of the purificatory rite. In the drama, the episodes are short, but it is these that give extension to Epic poetry. Thus the story of the *Odyssey* can be stated briefly. A certain man is absent from home for many years; he is jealously watched by Poseidon, and left desolate. Meanwhile his home is in a wretched plight—suitors are wasting his sub-stance and plotting against his son. At length, tempest-tossed, he himself arrives; he makes certain persons acquainted with him; he attacks the suitors with his own hand, and is himself preserved while he destroys them. This is the essence of the plot; the rest is episode.

XVIII

Every tragedy falls into two parts—Complication and Unraveling or Denouement. Incidents extraneous to the action are frequently combined with a portion of the action proper, to form the Complication; the rest is the Unraveling. By the Complication I mean all that extends from the beginning of the action to the part which marks the turning point to good or bad fortune. The Unraveling is that which extends from the beginning of the change to the end. Thus, in the *Lynceus* of Theodectes the Complication consists of the incidents presupposed in the drama, the seizure of the child, and then again * * <The Unraveling> extends from the accusation of murder to the end.

There are four kinds of Tragedy: the Complex, depending entirely on Reversal of the Situation and Recognition; the Pathetic (where the motive is passion)—such as the tragedies on Ajax and Ixion; the Ethical (where the motives are ethical)—such as the *Phthiotides* and the *Peleus.* The fourth kind is the Simple. <We here exclude the purely spectacular element>, exemplified by the *Phorcides,* the *Prometheus,* and scenes laid in Hades. The poet should endeavor, if possible, to combine all poetic elements; or, failing that, the greatest number and those the most important; the more so, in face of the caviling criticism of the day. For whereas there have hitherto been good poets, each in his own branch, the critics now expect one man to surpass all others in their several lines of excellence.

In speaking of a tragedy as the same or different, the best test to take is the plot. Identity exists where the Complication and Unraveling are the same. Many poets tie the knot well, but unravel it ill. Both arts, however, should always be mastered.

Again, the poet should remember what has been often said, and not make an Epic structure into a Tragedy—by an Epic structure I mean one with a multiplicity of plots—as if, for instance, you were to make a tragedy out of the entire story of the *Iliad.* In the Epic poem, owing to its length, each part assumes its proper magnitude. In the drama the result is far from answering to the poet's expectation. The proof is that the poets who have dramatized the whole story of the Fall of Troy, instead of selecting portions, like Euripides, or who have taken the whole tale of Niobe, and not a part of her story, like Aeschylus, either fail utterly or meet with poor success on the stage. Even Agathon has been known to fail from this one defect. In his Reversals of the Situation, however, he shows a marvelous skill in the effort to hit the popular taste—to produce a tragic effect that satisfies the moral sense. This effect is produced when the clever rogue, like Sisyphus, is outwitted, or the brave villain defeated. Such an event is probable in Agathon's sense of the word: "it is probable," he says, "that many things should happen contrary to probability."

The Chorus too should be regarded as one of the actors; it should be an integral part of the whole, and share in the action, in the manner not of Euripides but of Sophocles. As for the later poets, their choral songs pertain as little to the subject of the piece as to that of any other tragedy. They are, therefore, sung as mere interludes—a practice first begun by Agathon. Yet what difference is there between introducing such choral interludes and transferring a speech, or even a whole act, from one play to another?

XIX

It remains to speak of Diction and Thought, the other parts of Tragedy having been already discussed. Concerning Thought, we may assume what is said in the Rhetoric, to which inquiry the subject more strictly belongs. Under Thought is included every effect which has to be produced by speech, the subdivisions being—proof and refutation; the excitation of the feelings, such as pity, fear, anger, and the like; the suggestion of importance or its opposite. Now, it is evident that the dramatic incidents must be treated from the same points of view as the dramatic speeches, when the object is to evoke the sense of pity, fear, importance, or probability. The only difference is that the incidents should speak for themselves without verbal exposition; while the effects aimed at in speech should be produced by the speaker, and as a result of the speech. For what were the business of a speaker, if the Thought were revealed quite apart from what he says?

Next, as regards Diction. One branch of the inquiry treats of the Modes of Utterance. But this province of knowledge belongs to the art of Delivery and to the masters of that science. It includes, for instance—what is a command, a prayer, a statement, a threat, a question, an answer, and so forth. To know or not to know these things involves no serious censure upon the poet's art. For who can admit the fault imputed to Homer by Protagoras— that in the words, "Sing, goddess, of the wrath," he gives a command under the idea that he utters a prayer? For to tell someone to do a thing or not to do it is, he says, a command. We may, therefore, pass this over as an inquiry that belongs to another art, not to poetry.

XX

[Language in general includes the following parts: Letter, Syllable, Connecting word, Noun, Verb, Inflection or Case, Sentence or Phrase.

A Letter is an indivisible sound, yet not every such sound, but only one which can form part of a group of sounds. For even brutes utter indivisible sounds, none of which I call a letter. The sound I mean may be either a vowel, a semivowel, or a mute. A vowel is that which without impact of tongue or lip has an audible sound. A semivowel, that which with such impact has an audible sound, as S and R. A mute, that which with such impact has by itself no sound, but joined to a vowel sound becomes audible, as G and D. These are distinguished according to the form assumed by the mouth and the place where they are produced; according as they are aspirated or smooth, long or short; as they are acute, grave, or of an inter-

mediate tone; which inquiry belongs in detail to the writers on meter.

A Syllable is a nonsignificant sound, composed of a mute and a vowel: for GR without A is a syllable, as also with A—GRA. But the investigation of these differences belongs also to metrical science.

A Connecting word is a nonsignificant sound which neither causes nor hinders the union of many sounds into one significant sound; it may be placed at either end or in the middle of a sentence. Or, a nonsignificant sound which out of several sounds, each of them significant, is capable of forming one significant sound—as ἀμφί, περί, and the like. Or, a nonsignificant sound which marks the beginning, end, or division of a sentence; such, however, that it cannot correctly stand by itself at the beginning of a sentence —as μέν, ἤτοι, δέ.

A Noun is a composite significant sound, not marking time, of which no part is in itself significant: for in double or compound words we do not employ the separate parts as if each were in itself significant. Thus in Theodorus, "god-given," the δῶρον or "gift" is not in itself significant.

A Verb is a composite significant sound, marking time, in which, as in the noun, no part is in itself significant. For "man," or "white" does not express the idea of "when"; but "he walks," or "he has walked" does connote time, present or past.

Inflection belongs both to the noun and verb, and expresses either the relation "of," "to," or the like; or that of number, whether one or many, as "man" or "men"; or the modes or tones in actual delivery, e.g., a question or a command. "Did he go?" and "go" are verbal inflections of this kind.

A Sentence or Phrase is a composite significant sound, some at least of whose parts are in themselves significant; for not every such group of words consists of verbs and nouns—"the definition of man," for example—but it may dispense even with the verb. Still it will always have some significant part, as "in walking," or "Cleon son of Cleon." A sentence or phrase may form a unity in two ways—either as signifying one thing, or as consisting of several parts linked together. Thus the *Iliad* is one by the linking together of parts, the definition of man by the unity of the thing signified.]

XXI

Words are of two kinds, simple and double. By simple I mean those composed of nonsignificant elements, such as γῆ. By double or compound, those composed either of a significant and nonsignificant element (though within the whole word no element is significant), or of elements that are both significant. A word may likewise be triple, quadruple, or multiple in form, like so many Massilian expressions, e.g., "Hermo-caico-xanthus <who prayed to Father Zeus>."

Every word is either current, or strange, or metaphorical, or ornamental, or newly coined, or lengthened, or contracted, or altered.

By a current or proper word I mean one which is in general use among a people; by a strange word, one which is in use in another country. Plainly, therefore, the same word may be at once strange and current, but not in relation to the same people. The word σίγυννον, "lance," is to the Cyprians a current term but to us a strange one.

Metaphor is the application of an alien name by transference either from genus to species, or from species to genus, or from species to species, or by analogy, that is, proportion. Thus from genus to species, as: "There lies my ship"; for lying at anchor is a species of lying. From species to genus, as: "Verily ten thousand noble deeds hath Odysseus wrought"; for ten thousand is a species of large number, and is here used for a large number generally. From species to species, as: "With blade of bronze drew away the life," and "Cleft the water with the vessel of unyielding bronze." Here ἀρύσαι, "to draw away," is used for ταμεῖν, "to cleave," and ταμεῖν again for ἀρύσαι—each being a species of taking away. Analogy or proportion is when the second term is to the first as the fourth to the third. We may then use the fourth for the second, or the second for the fourth. Sometimes too we qualify the metaphor by adding the term to which the proper word is relative. Thus the cup is to Dionysus as the shield to Ares. The cup may, therefore, be called "the shield of Dionysus," and the shield "the cup of Ares." Or, again, as old age is to life, so is evening to day. Evening may therefore be called "the old age of the day," and old age, "the evening of life," or, in the phrase of Empedocles, "life's setting sun." For some of the terms of the proportion there is at times no word in existence; still the metaphor may be used. For instance, to scatter seed is called sowing: but the action of the sun in scattering his rays is nameless. Still this process bears to the sun the same relation as sowing to the seed. Hence the expression of the poet "sowing the god-created light." There is another way in which this kind of metaphor may be employed. We may apply an alien term, and then deny of that term one of its proper attributes; as if we were to call the shield, not "the cup of Ares," but "the wineless cup."

<An ornamental word . . .>

A newly coined word is one which has never been even in local use, but is adopted by the poet himself. Some such words there appear to be: as ἐρνύγες, "sprouters," for κέρατα, "horns," and ἀρητήρ, "supplicator," for ἱερεύς, "priest."

A word is lengthened when its own vowel is exchanged for a longer one, or when a syllable is inserted. A word is contracted when some part of it is removed. Instances of lengthening are— πόληος for πόλεως, and Πηληϊάδεω for Πηλείδου; of contraction—κρῖ, δῶ, and ὄψ, as in μία γίνεται ἀμφοτέρων ὄψ.

An altered word is one in which part of the ordinary form is left unchanged, and part is recast; as, in δεξιτερὸν κατὰ μαζόν, δεξιτερόν is for δεξιόν.

[Nouns in themselves are either masculine, feminine, or neuter. Masculine are such as end in ν, ρ, ς, or in some letter compounded with ς—these being two, ψ and ξ. Feminine, such as end in vowels that are always long, namely η and ω, and—of vowels that admit of lengthening—those in α. Thus the number of letters in which nouns masculine and feminine end is the same; for ψ and ξ are equivalent to endings in ς. No noun ends in a mute or a vowel short by nature. Three only end in ι,—μέλι, κόμμι, πέπερι: five end in υ. Neuter nouns end in these two latter vowels; also in ν and ς.]

XXII

The perfection of style is to be clear without being mean. The clearest style is that which uses only current or proper words; at the same time it is mean—witness the poetry of Cleophon and of Sthenelus. That diction, on the other hand, is lofty and raised above the commonplace which employs unusual words. By unusual, I mean strange (or rare) words, metaphorical, lengthened—anything, in short, that differs from the normal idiom. Yet a style wholly composed of such words is either a riddle or a jargon; a riddle, if it consists of metaphors; a jargon, if it consists of strange (or rare) words. For the essence of a riddle is to express true facts under impossible combinations. Now this cannot be done by any arrangement of ordinary words, but by the use of metaphor it can. Such is the riddle: "A man I saw who on another man had glued the bronze by aid of fire," and others of the same kind. A diction that is made up of strange (or rare) terms is a jargon. A certain infusion, therefore, of these elements is necessary to style; for the strange (or rare) word, the metaphorical, the ornamental, and the other kinds above mentioned, will raise it above the commonplace and mean, while the use of proper words will make it perspicuous. But nothing contributes more to produce a clearness of diction that is remote from commonness than the lengthening, contraction, and alteration of words. For by deviating in exceptional cases from the normal idiom, the language will gain distinction; while, at the same time, the partial conformity with usage will give perspicuity. The critics, therefore, are in error who censure these licenses of speech, and hold the author up to ridicule. Thus Eucleides the elder declared that it would be an easy matter to be a poet if you might lengthen syllables at will. He caricatured the practice in the very form of his diction, as in the verse:

$$\text{Ἐπιχάρην εἶδον Μαραθῶνάδε βαδίζοντα,}$$

or,

$$\text{οὐκ ἄν γ' ἐράμενος τὸν ἐκείνου ἐλλέβορον.}$$

To employ such license at all obtrusively is, no doubt, grotesque; but in any mode of poetic diction there must be moderation. Even metaphors, strange (or rare) words, or any similar forms of speech, would produce the like effect if used without propriety and with the express purpose of being ludicrous. How great a difference is made by the appropriate use of lengthening, may be seen in Epic poetry by the insertion of ordinary forms in the verse. So, again, if we take a strange (or rare) word, a metaphor, or any similar mode of expression, and replace it by the current or proper term, the truth of our observation will be manifest. For example, Aeschylus and Euripides each composed the same iambic line. But the alteration of a single word by Euripides, who employed the rarer term instead of the ordinary one, makes one verse appear beautiful and the other trivial. Aeschylus in his *Philoctetes* says:

$$\text{φαγέδαινα} <δ'> \text{ἥ μου σάρκας ἐσθίει ποδός.}$$

Euripides substitutes θοινᾶται "feasts on" for ἐσθίει "feeds on." Again, in the line,

νῦν δέ μ' ἐὼν ὀλίγος τε καὶ οὐτιδανὸς καὶ ἀεικής,

the difference will be felt if we substitute the common words,

νῦν δέ μ' ἐὼν μικρός τε καὶ ἀσθενικὸς καὶ ἀειδής.

Or if for the line,

δίφρον ἀεικέλιον καταθεὶς ὀλίγην τε τράπεζαν,

we read,

δίφρον μοχθηρὸν καταθεὶς μικράν τε τράπεζαν.

Or for ἠιόνες βοόωσιν, ἠιόνες κράζουσιν.

Again, Ariphrades ridiculed the tragedians for using phrases which no one would employ in ordinary speech: for example, δωμάτων ἄπο instead of ἀπὸ δωμάτων, σέθεν, ἐγὼ δέ νιν, 'Αχιλλέως πέρι instead of περὶ 'Αχιλλέως, and the like. It is precisely because such phrases are not part of the current idiom that they give distinction to the style. This, however, he failed to see.

It is a great matter to observe propriety in these several modes of expression, as also in compound words, strange (or rare) words, and so forth. But the greatest thing by far is to have a command of metaphor. This alone cannot be imparted by another; it is the mark of genius, for to make good metaphors implies an eye for resemblances.

Of the various kinds of words, the compound are best adapted to dithyrambs, rare words to heroic poetry, metaphors to iambic. In heroic poetry, indeed, all these varieties are serviceable. But in iambic verse, which reproduces, as far as may be, familiar speech, the most appropriate words are those which are found even in prose. These are—the current or proper, the metaphorical, the ornamental.

Concerning Tragedy and imitation by means of action this may suffice.

XXIII

As to that poetic imitation which is narrative in form and employs a single meter, the plot manifestly ought, as in a tragedy, to be constructed on dramatic principles. It should have for its subject a single action, whole and complete, with a beginning, a middle, and an end. It will thus resemble a living organism in all its unity, and produce the pleasure proper to it. It will differ in structure from historical compositions, which of necessity present, not a single action, but a single period, and all that happened within that period to one person or to many, little connected together as the events may be. For as the sea fight at Salamis and the battle with the Carthaginians in Sicily took place at the same time, but did not tend to any one result, so in the sequence of events one thing sometimes follows another, and yet no single result is thereby produced. Such is the practice, we may say, of most poets. Here again, then, as has been already

observed, the transcendent excellence of Homer is manifest. He never attempts to make the whole war of Troy the subject of his poem, though that war had a beginning and an end. It would have been too vast a theme, and not easily embraced in a single view. If, again, he had kept it within moderate limits, it must have been overcomplicated by the variety of the incidents. As it is, he detaches a single portion, and admits as episodes many events from the general story of the war—such as the Catalogue of the ships and others—thus diversifying the poem. All other poets take a single hero, a single period, or an action single, indeed, but with a multiplicity of parts. Thus did the author of the *Cypria* and of the *Little Iliad*. For this reason the *Iliad* and the *Odyssey* each furnish the subject of one tragedy, or, at most, of two; while the *Cypria* supplies materials for many, and the *Little Iliad* for eight—the Award of the Arms, the Philoctetes, the Neoptolemus, the Eurypylus, the Mendicant Odysseus, the Laconian Women, the Fall of Ilium, the Departure of the Fleet.

XXIV

Again, Epic poetry must have as many kinds as Tragedy: it must be simple, or complex, or "ethical," or "pathetic." The parts also, with the exception of Song and Spectacle, are the same; for it requires Reversals of the Situation, Recognitions, and Scenes of Suffering. Moreover, the thoughts and the diction must be artistic. In all these respects Homer is our earliest and sufficient model. Indeed, each of his poems has a twofold character. The *Iliad* is at once simple and "pathetic," and the *Odyssey* complex (for Recognition scenes run through it), and at the same time "ethical." Moreover, in diction and thought they are supreme.

Epic poetry differs from Tragedy in the scale on which it is constructed, and in its meter. As regards scale or length, we have already laid down an adequate limit: the beginning and the end must be capable of being brought within a single view. This condition will be satisfied by poems on a smaller scale than the old epics, and answering in length to the group of tragedies presented at a single sitting.

Epic poetry has, however, a great—a special—capacity for enlarging its dimensions, and we can see the reason. In Tragedy we cannot imitate several lines of actions carried on at one and the same time; we must confine ourselves to the action on the stage and the part taken by the players. But in Epic poetry, owing to the narrative form, many events simultaneously transacted can be presented; and these, if relevant to the subject, add mass and dignity to the poem. The Epic has here an advantage, and one that conduces to grandeur of effect, to diverting the mind of the hearer, and relieving the story with varying episodes. For sameness of incident soon produces satiety, and makes tragedies fail on the stage.

As for the meter, the heroic measure has proved its fitness by the test of experience. If a narrative poem in any other meter or in many meters were now composed, it would be found incongruous. For of all measures the heroic is the stateliest and the most massive; and hence it most readily admits rare words and metaphors, which is another point in which the narrative form of imitation stands alone. On the other hand, the iambic and the trochaic tetrameter are stirring measures, the latter being akin to dancing, the former expressive of action. Still more absurd would it be to mix together different meters, as was done by Chaeremon. Hence no one has ever composed a poem on a great scale in any other than heroic verse. Nature herself, as we have said, teaches the choice of the proper measure.

Homer, admirable in all respects, has the special merit of being the only poet who rightly appreciates the part he should take himself. The poet should speak as little as possible in his own person, for it is not this that makes him an imitator. Other poets appear themselves upon the scene throughout, and imitate but little and rarely. Homer, after a few prefatory words, at once brings in a man, or woman, or other personage, none of them wanting in characteristic qualities, but each with a character of his own.

The element of the wonderful is required in Tragedy. The irrational, on which the wonderful depends for its chief effects, has wider scope in Epic poetry, because there the person acting is not seen. Thus, the pursuit of Hector would be ludicrous if placed upon the stage—the Greeks standing still and not joining in the pursuit, and Achilles waving them back. But in the Epic poem the absurdity passes unnoticed. Now the wonderful is pleasing, as may be inferred from the fact that everyone tells a story with some addition of his own, knowing that his hearers like it. It is Homer who has chiefly taught other poets the art of telling lies skillfully. The secret of it lies in a fallacy. For, assuming that if one thing is or becomes, a second is or becomes, men imagine that, if the second is, the first likewise is or becomes. But this is a false inference. Hence, where the first thing is untrue, it is quite unnecessary, provided the second be true, to add that the first is or has become. For the mind, knowing the second to be true, falsely infers the truth of the first. There is an example of this in the Bath Scene of the *Odyssey.*

Accordingly, the poet should prefer probable impossibilities to improbable possibilities. The tragic plot must not be composed of irrational parts. Everything irrational should, if possible, be excluded; or, at all events, it should lie outside the action of the play (as, in the *Oedipus,* the hero's ignorance as to the manner of Laius' death); not within the drama— as, in the *Electra,* the messenger's account of the Pythian games; or, as in the *Mysians,* the man who has come from Tegea to Mysia and is still speechless. The plea that otherwise the plot would have been ruined is ridiculous; such a plot should not in the first instance be constructed. But once the irrational has been introduced and an air of likelihood imparted to it, we must accept it in spite of the absurdity. Take even the irrational incidents in the *Odyssey,* where Odysseus is left upon the shore of Ithaca. How intolerable even these might have been would be apparent if an inferior poet were to treat the subject. As it is, the absurdity is veiled by the poetic charm with which the poet invests it.

The diction should be elaborated in the pauses of the action, where there is no expression of character or thought. For, conversely, character and thought are merely obscured by a diction that is overbrilliant.

XXV

With respect to critical difficulties and their solutions, the number and nature of the sources from which they may be drawn may be thus exhibited.

The poet being an imitator, like a painter or any other artist, must of necessity imitate one of three objects—things as they were or are, things as they are said or thought to be, or things as they ought to be. The vehicle of expression is language—either current terms or, it may be, rare words or metaphors. There are also many modifications of language which we concede to the poets. Add to this that the standard of correctness is not the same in poetry and politics, any more than in poetry and any other art. Within the art of poetry itself there are two kinds of faults— those which touch its essence, and those which are accidental. If a poet has chosen to imitate something, <but has imitated it incorrectly> through want of capacity, the error is inherent in the poetry. But if the failure is due to a wrong choice—if he has represented a horse as throwing out both his off legs at once, or introduced technical inaccuracies in medicine, for example, or in any other art—the error is not essential to the poetry. These are the points of view from which we should consider and answer the objections raised by the critics.

First as to matters which concern the poet's own art. If he describes the impossible, he is guilty of an error; but the error may be justified, if the end of the art be thereby attained (the end being that already mentioned)—if, that is, the effect of this or any other part of the poem is thus rendered more striking. A case in point is the pursuit of Hector. If, however, the end might have been as well, or better, attained without violating the special rules of the poetic art, the error is not justified, for every kind of error should, if possible, be avoided.

Again, does the error touch the essentials of the poetic art, or some accident of it? For example, not to know that a hind has no horns is a less serious matter than to paint it inartistically.

Further, if it be objected that the description is not true to fact, the poet may perhaps reply—"But the objects are as they ought to be": just as Sophocles said that he drew men as they ought to be; Euripides, as they are. In this way the objection may be met. If, however, the representation be of neither kind, the poet may answer—"This is how men say the thing is." This applies to tales about the gods. It may well be that these stories are not higher than fact nor yet true to fact: they are, very possibly, what Xenophanes says of them. But anyhow, "this is what is said." Again, a description may be no better than the fact: still, it was the fact; as in the passage about the arms: "Upright upon their butt-ends stood the spears." This was the custom then, as it now is among the Illyrians.

Again, in examining whether what has been said or done by someone is poetically right or not, we must not look merely to the particular act or saying, and ask whether it is poetically good or bad. We must also consider by whom it is said or done, to whom, when, by what means, or for what end; whether, for instance, it be to secure a greater good, or avert a greater evil.

Other difficulties may be resolved by due regard to the usage of language. We may note a rare word, as in οὐρῆας μὲν πρῶτον, where the poet perhaps employs οὐρῆας not in the sense of mules, but of sentinels. So, again, of Dolon: "ill-favored indeed he was to look upon." It is not meant that his body was ill-shaped, but that his face was ugly; for the Cretans use the word εὐειδές, "well-favored," to denote a fair face. Again, ζωρότερον δὲ κέραιε, "mix the drink livelier," does not mean "mix it stronger" as for hard drinkers, but "mix it quicker."

Sometimes an expression is metaphorical, as "Now all gods and men were sleeping through the night"—while at the same time the poet says: "Often indeed as he turned his gaze to the Trojan plain, he marveled at the sound of flutes and pipes." "All" is here used metaphorically for "many," all being a species of many. So, in the verse "alone she hath no part . . . ," οἴη, "alone," is metaphorical; for the best known may be called the only one.

Again, the solution may depend upon accent or breathing. Thus Hippias of Thasos solved the difficulties in the lines δίδομεν (διδόμεν) δέ οἱ, and τὸ μὲν οὖ (οὐ) καταπύθεται ὄμβρῳ.

Or, again, the question may be solved by punctuation, as in Empedocles—"Of a sudden things became mortal that before had learned to be immortal, and things unmixed before mixed."

Or, again, by ambiguity of meaning—as παρώχηκεν δὲ πλέω νύξ, where the word πλέω is ambiguous.

Or by the usage of language. Thus any mixed drink is called οἶνος, "wine." Hence Ganymede is said "to pour the wine to Zeus," though the gods do not drink wine. So too workers in iron are called χαλκέας, or workers in bronze. This, however, may also be taken as a metaphor.

Again, when a word seems to involve some inconsistency of meaning, we should consider how many senses it may bear in the particular passage. For example: "there was stayed the spear of bronze"—we should ask in how many ways we may take "being checked there." The true mode of interpretation is the precise opposite of what Glaucon mentions. Critics, he says, jump at certain groundless conclusions; they pass adverse judgment and then proceed to reason on it; and, assuming that the poet has said whatever they happen to think, find fault if a thing is inconsistent with their own fancy. The question about Icarius has been treated in this fashion. The critics imagine he was a Lacedaemonian. They think it strange, therefore, that Telemachus should not have met him when he went to Lacedaemon. But the Cephallenian story may perhaps be the true one. They allege that Odysseus took a wife from among themselves, and that her father was Icadius, not Icarius. It is merely a mistake, then, that gives plausibility to the objection.

In general, the impossible must be justified by reference to artistic requirements, or to the higher reality, or to received opinion. With respect to the requirements of art, a probable impossibility is to be preferred to a thing improbable and yet possible. Again, it may be impossible that there should be men such as Zeuxis painted. "Yes," we say, "but the impossible is the higher thing; for the ideal type must surpass the reality." To justify the irrational, we

appeal to what is commonly said to be. In addition to which, we urge that the irrational sometimes does not violate reason; just as "it is probable that a thing may happen contrary to probability."

Things that sound contradictory should be examined by the same rules as in dialectical refutation—whether the same thing is meant, in the same relation, and in the same sense. We should therefore solve the question by reference to what the poet says himself, or to what is tacitly assumed by a person of intelligence.

The element of the irrational, and, similarly, depravity of character, are justly censured when there is no inner necessity for introducing them. Such is the irrational element in the introduction of Aegeus by Euripides and the badness of Menelaus in the *Orestes*.

Thus, there are five sources from which critical objections are drawn. Things are censured either as impossible, or irrational, or morally hurtful, or contradictory, or contrary to artistic correctness. The answers should be sought under the twelve heads above mentioned.

XXVI

The question may be raised whether the Epic or Tragic mode of imitation is the higher. If the more refined art is the higher, and the more refined in every case is that which appeals to the better sort of audience, the art which imitates anything and everything is manifestly most unrefined. The audience is supposed to be too dull to comprehend unless something of their own is thrown in by the performers, who therefore indulge in restless movements. Bad flute-players twist and twirl if they have to represent "the quoit-throw," or hustle the coryphaeus when they perform the *Scylla*. Tragedy, it is said, has this same defect. We may compare the opinion that the older actors entertained of their successors. Mynniscus used to call Callippides "ape" on account of the extravagance of his action, and the same view was held of Pindarus. Tragic art, then, as a whole, stands to Epic in the same relation as the younger to the elder actors. So we are told that Epic poetry is addressed to a cultivated audience, who do not need gesture; Tragedy, to an inferior public. Being then unrefined, it is evidently the lower of the two.

Now, in the first place, this censure attaches not to the poetic but to the histrionic art; for gesticulation may be equally overdone in epic recitation, as by Sosistratus, or in lyrical competition, as by Mnasitheus the Opuntian. Next, all action is not to be condemned—any more than all dancing—but only that of bad performers. Such was the fault found in Callippides, as also in others of our own day, who are censured for representing degraded women. Again, Tragedy like Epic poetry produces its effect even without action; it reveals its power by mere reading. If, then, in all other respects it is superior, this fault, we say, is not inherent in it.

And superior it is, because it has all the epic elements—it may even use the epic meter—with the music and spectacular effects as important accessories; and these produce the most vivid of pleasures. Further, it has vividness of impression in reading as well as in representation. Moreover, the art attains its end within narrower limits; for the concentrated effect is more pleasurable than one which is spread over a long time and so diluted. What, for example, would be the effect of the *Oedipus* of Sophocles, if it were cast into a form as long as the *Iliad?* Once more, the Epic imitation has less unity; as is shown by this, that any Epic poem will furnish subjects for several tragedies. Thus if the story adopted by the poet has a strict unity, it must either be concisely told and appear truncated; or, if it conform to the Epic canon of length, it must seem weak and watery. <Such length implies some loss of unity,> if, I mean, the poem is constructed out of several actions, like the *Iliad* and the *Odyssey,* which have many such parts, each with a certain magnitude of its own. Yet these poems are as perfect as possible in structure; each is, in the highest degree attainable, an imitation of a single action.

If, then, Tragedy is superior to Epic poetry in all these respects, and, moreover, fulfills its specific function better as an art—for each art ought to produce, not any chance pleasure but the pleasure proper to it, as already stated—it plainly follows that Tragedy is the higher art, as attaining its end more perfectly.

Thus much may suffice concerning Tragic and Epic poetry in general; their several kinds and parts, with the number of each and their differences; the causes that make a poem good or bad; the objections of the critics and the answers to these objections.

COISLINIAN TRACTATE

This fragmentary manuscript, dating from about the tenth century A.D., was discovered in 1839 in the Bibliothèque Nationale in Paris. The manuscript itself appears to be a copy of materials that may be considerably older, perhaps as early as the first century B.C. This possibility lends even more interest to the contents, since it brings it relatively close in time to Aristotle's *Poetics,* which the *Tractate* is obviously designed to parallel. The translation and interpolations in the passage below are from Lane Cooper's *An Aristotelian Theory of Comedy* (1922).

Coislinian Tractate

Poetry is either (I) non-mimetic or (II) mimetic.

(I) Non-mimetic poetry is divided into (A) historical, (B) instructive. (B) Instructive poetry is divided into (1) didactic, (2) theoretical.

(II) Mimetic poetry is divided into (A) narrative, (B) dramatic and [directly] [1] presenting action. (B) dramatic poetry, or that [directly] presenting action, is divided into (1) comedy, (2) tragedy, (3) mimes, (4) satyr-dramas.

Tragedy removes the fearful emotions of the soul

---

[1] The words in brackets and the other editorial marks are Professor Cooper's.

---

through compassion and terror. And [he says] that it aims at having a due proportion of fear. It has grief for its mother.

Comedy is an imitation of an action that is ludicrous and imperfect, of sufficient length, [in embellished language,] the several kinds [of embellishment being] separately [found] in the [several] parts [of the play]; [directly presented] by persons acting, and not [given] through narrative; through pleasure and laughter effecting the purgation of the like emotions. It has laughter for its mother.

Laughter arises (I) from the diction [= expression] (II) from the things [= content].

(I) From the diction, through the use of—
    (A) Homonyms
    (B) Synonyms
    (C) Garrulity
    (D) Paronyms, formed by
        (?1) addition and
        (?2) clipping
    (E) Diminutives
    (F) Perversion
        (1) by the voice
        (2) by other means of the same sort
    (G) Grammar and syntax

(II) Laughter is caused by the things—
    (A) From assimilation, employed
        (1) toward the worse
        (2) toward the better
    (B) From deception
    (C) From the impossible
    (D) From the possible and inconsequent
    (E) From the unexpected
    (F) From debasing the personages
    (G) From the use of clownish (pantomimic) dancing
    (H) When one of those having power, neglecting the greatest things, takes the most worthless
    (I) When the story is disjointed, and has no sequence

Comedy differs from abuse, since abuse openly censures the bad qualities attaching [to men], whereas comedy requires the so-called emphasis [? or "innuendo"].

The joker will make game of faults in the soul and in the body.

As in tragedies there should be a due proportion of fear, so in comedies there should be a due proportion of laughter.

The substance of comedy consists of (1) plot, (2) *ethos,* (3) *dianoia,* (4) diction, (5) melody, (6) spectacle.

The comic plot is the structure binding together the ludicrous incidents.

The characters [*ethe*] of comedy are (1) the buffoonish, (2) the ironical, and (3) those of the imposters.

The parts of the *dianoia* are two: (A) opinion and (B) proof. [Proofs (or "persuasions") are of] five [sorts]: (1) oaths, (2) compacts, (3) testimonies, (4) tortures ["tests" or "ordeals"], (5) laws.

The diction of comedy is the common, popular language. The comic poet must endow his personages with his own native idiom, but must endow an alien with the alien idiom.

Melody is the province of the art of music, and

hence one must take its fundamental rules from that art.

Spectacle is of great advantage to dramas in supplying what is in concord with them.

Plot, diction, and melody are found in all comedies, *dianoia, ethos,* and spectacle in few.

The [quantitative] parts of comedy are four: (1) prologue, (2) the choral part, (3) episode, (4) exode. The prologue is that portion of a comedy extending as far as the entrance of the chorus. The choral part [choricon] is a song by the chorus when it [the song] is of adequate length. An episode is what lies between two choral songs. The exode is the utterance of the chorus at the end.

The kinds of comedy are: (1) Old, with a superabundance of the laughable; (2) New, which disregards laughter, and tends toward the serious; (3) Middle, which is a mixture of the two.

medleys, was the performer of his own compositions, as all were at that time. And it is said that once he had been recalled for too many encores and lost his voice; so, after begging indulgence, he set a boy to singing before the flute player, while he himself acted out the song with somewhat more vigorous gestures since he was not burdened by the use of his voice. So began the practice of singing to the movements of the actors, while the latter used their voices only in the dialogue. Later, because of this convention, the substance of the plays changed from laughter and loose joking, and drama gradually took an artistic turn; the young folk then left the performance of plays to the actors, while they took to tossing jokes woven into verses among themselves, as in the ancient fashion. Hence they were later called "afterpieces" (*exodia*) and for the most part added to the Atellan farces. This form of play, which had been taken from the Oscans, the younger generation cherished and never allowed it to become contaminated by the actors.

LIVY (59 B.C.–A.D. 17)

Livy's great work is *Ab Urbe Condita Libri* (*From the Founding of the City*), a history of Rome. In the selection reprinted (7.2) he sketches a brief history of the Roman theater. Particularly worthy of note is the observation that stage plays were originally conceived as propitiations to angry gods, a view that anticipates some modern theories of the ritual origins of drama. The translation is by Cedric H. Whitman.

from *Ab Urbe Condita Libri*

Both in this and in the following year . . . there was a plague. . . . And since the violence of the disease was alleviated neither by human devices nor by divine aid, the people's minds were caught by superstition, and it is said that among other things stage plays were also introduced as a propitiation of the wrath of heaven—an innovation for a warlike people whose only spectacle had been the circus. Its beginnings, like most beginnings, were modest, and the plays themselves were of foreign origin. Players were imported from Etruria, who danced to the strains of a flautist without singing or pantomime, producing very graceful gestures after the Tuscan manner. Thereafter the younger people began to imitate them, at the same time exchanging jokes among themselves in rude verses, and their gestures matched their words. And so the practice was accepted and was encouraged by repeated performance. And since the Tuscan word for actor is *hister,* the name *histriones* was given to the artists though they were native Romans. And these did not, as formerly, take turns at flinging out rough verses similar to the Fescennine, but acted out medleys (*saturae*) full of music, and with the songs now written down to the flute accompaniment and gestures appropriate to it.

After some years, Livius Andronicus, who was the first to attach a plot to his play, instead of writing

QUINTILIAN

(c. A.D. 35–c. 99)

A great rhetorician, Quintilian is best known as the author of *De Institutione Oratoria* (*On the Training of an Orator*). The passage reprinted below, from *De Institutione* (10.1.65–72 and 10.1.97–100), provides a number of interesting observations on classical drama viewed as examples of effective rhetoric. The translation is by Cedric H. Whitman.

from *De Institutione Oratoria*

Old Comedy not only is almost alone in preserving the pure grace of Attic speech, but also is of the most eloquent freedom of expression; although it is particularly suitable for chastising vice, nonetheless it has a great deal of power in its other parts also. For it is grand, elegant, and charming, and I wonder if there is any form of poetry, after Homer (of whom, like Achilles, it is always right to make an exception), more akin to the orators or more apt for training them. Its authors were rather numerous, but Aristophanes, Eupolis, and Cratinus are especially eminent. Aeschylus was the first to bring tragedy to distinction; he is lofty, solemn, and grandiloquent, often even to a fault, but rough in many places and unpolished. For this reason the Athenians allowed later poets to edit his plays and produce them in the contests, and many won the prize in that way. But Sophocles and Euripides embellished this genre with greater glory, and there is widespread controversy as to which of these two poets, each with his different mode of expression, is the better. For my part, since it is irrelevant to the subject in hand, I pass over the matter without giving an opinion. But this no one can possibly deny: that Euripides will be far more useful for those who are preparing themselves for pleading in court. For his diction more nearly approaches the genre of oratory (a fact for which he is blamed by those who find greater elevation in the solemnity, majestic style, and resonance of Sophocles). Euripides abounds in apophthegms; in those observations which have been handed down by the philosophers he is almost their equal, and he can be compared, both in statement and rebuttal, with any one of those who have proved eloquent in the forum. He is remarkable for his portrayal of all emotions; but for those involving pity he is easily supreme. Menander, as he often demonstrates, admired him in the extreme and imitated him, though in a different form; and Menander, if carefully read, would, in my opinion, suffice quite by himself to realize the sum total of my instruction, so complete a picture of life did he create, so rich was his invention and ability to express it, so apt is he in all matters of action, character, and emotion. As a matter of fact, those who think that those speeches that are published under the name of Charisius were written by Menander have shown no little insight. But it seems to me that he proves himself an orator far more in his own comedies, unless, forsooth, those legal debates in *The Arbitrants, The Heiress,* and *The Locrians* are failures, or unless every mode of oratory is not perfected in the declamations in *The Timid Man, The Lawgiver,* or *The Supposititious Child.* Yet for my part I think that he has something more still that will be helpful to speech makers, insofar as they must, according to the circumstances of their disputes, assume numerous roles —fathers, sons, soldiers, peasants, the rich, the poor, the angry, the supplicating, the mild, the harsh. In all these roles this poet has marvelously observed propriety. Indeed, he has stolen the reputation away from all the other writers in this form, and, so to speak, his splendid flash has turned them to shadows. Still, there are other comic poets also who, if read with indulgence, have something by which you may profit, especially Philemon, who, in accord with the low taste of his time, was often preferred to Menander, but is now generally agreed to have deserved second place.

Of the early writers of tragedy, Accius and Pacuvius are the most distinguished for profundity of ideas, weightiness of diction, and convincing character. The times, rather than the men themselves, seem to have been deficient in polish and the finishing touch. More force is attributed to Accius; Pacuvius is the more learned, in the opinion of those who affect learning. Next, Varius' *Thyestes* can be compared with any of the ones written in Greek. Ovid's *Medea* strikes me as showing to what extent that man could have excelled, had he preferred to rule his genius rather than indulge it. Of those who lived when I might see them, by far the chief is Pomponius Secundus; my elders thought him not tragic enough, though they granted that he excelled in polish and erudition. We are extremely feeble in comedy, even though Várro, quoting [his teacher] Aelius Stilo, said that the Muses would have spoken the language of Plautus had they wished to speak Latin, and though the ancients loaded Caecilius with praise and attributed the writings of Terence to Scipio Africanus. Still, Ter-

ence's works are the most elegant in this form, and would have even more grace if they had confined themselves to trimeter verse. We barely achieve an insubstantial semblance, so that to me the Latin language itself seems not to have been endowed with that beauty which was granted to those alone who spoke Attic; for not even the Greeks gained it in any other dialect. In the *togata* Afranius excels; would that he had not fouled his plots with ugly pederasty, a confession of his own habits.

AELIUS DONATUS

(fl. A.D. 333)

Donatus was a Roman grammarian who wrote literary commentaries on Terence and Vergil. The excerpt below, translated by George Miltz, is taken from the fragment *De Comoediaet Trageodia,* which was the best-known theoretical statement about the nature of drama throughout the middle ages and early Renaissance. Particularly interesting is the indication of the highly formalized categories of comic types and characters.

A Fragment on Comedy and Tragedy

Comedy is a fable [*fabula*] involving diverse arrangements of civic and private concerns, in which one learns what is useful in life and what on the contrary is to be avoided. The Greeks define it in this way: "Comedy is a harmless arrangement of private and civil deeds." Cicero says that comedy is an imitation of life, a mirror of custom, an image of truth.

Comedies are so called from an ancient custom. In the beginning, songs of this kind were sung among the Greeks in hamlets. There is a comparable custom in Italy in the shows at the festivals of the crossroads, where measured speech was added to entertain the audience while the acts were changing. Or, from the *komai,* that is, from the way of life of men who live in hamlets because of a mediocre fortune; not of those who live in palaces of kings, like the characters of tragedy. Comedy, because it is a poem composed as an imitation of life and a likeness of character, consists in gesture and speech. While there is doubt who first invented comedy among the Greeks, among the Latins it is certain. Livius Andronicus was the first to found comedy and *Tragoedia Togata;* he says that "comedy is a mirror of daily life," and not wrongly. For just as in gazing at a mirror we easily gather the features of truth through images, so also in the reading of comedy we see the reflection of life and custom without difficulty. An explanation of its origin is to be found in foreign states and customs. The Athenians, who preserved Attic elegance, would joyfully and gleefully come together from all places into the hamlets [*kome*] and crossroads when they wished to censure those who were living evilly. There, using names, they would make public the lives of various individuals. This is where the name of comedy is derived. These songs were at first conducted in gentle meadows. Rewards were not lacking to stir the talents of learned men to writing, and gifts were offered to the actors in order that they might more willingly use a pleasing modulation of voice to gain the sweetness of praise. A goat [*tragos*] was given as the gift, and from this the name of tragedy has arisen. Some preferred that the name of tragedy be derived from the watery dregs of oil—a watery humor. When these games were carried on in honor of Father Liber, the writers of tragedies and comedies themselves also began to cultivate and honor the divinity of this god as a father. A probable reason exists for this: these imperfect songs were so produced that his praises and glorious deeds were evidently honored and made public. Then little by little the reputation of this art increased. Thespis first brought forward these writings to the notice of all. Afterward Aeschylus, following his example, made them public. Horace speaks of this in the *Ars Poetica:*

> Thespis is said to have invented an unknown genus of tragic poetry, and to have carried his poems in carts; these poems were sung and acted by people whose faces were smeared with lees. After him came Aeschylus, the founder of tragic costume and upright character. He also laid a stage on a modest scaffolding. He also taught lofty speaking and walking in buskins. After these men came Old Comedy, and not without much praise; but its liberty fell into a fault and force that needed regulation by law. A law was enacted, and the chorus shamefully became silent, after its right to harm was taken away. Our poets have left nothing untried. Those who dared to take away Greek vestiges have not gained any real glory; this is also true of those who honored domestic deeds, or of those who taught the *fabula praetexta* [tragedy] or *fabula togata* [national drama].

Fable is the general name, and there are two parts of it, tragedy and comedy. If the arguing is Latin, tragedy is called *praetextata.* Comedy has many species. Either Greek characters are introduced in Greek dress (*comoedia palliata*), or Roman subjects are treated (*comoedia togata*), or it is low comedy (*comoedia tabernaria*), or it is farce (*comoedia Attellana*), or it is mime, or tragedy is travestied (*comoedia Rhintonica*), or it is "low-footed." Fable is called "low-footed" on account of the lowness of its argument, and the baseness of the actors, who do not use the buskin or sock on the stage or platform, but use a low shoe; or the reason is that it does not contain the business of those living in towers and upper floors but of those living in a low and humble place. Cincius and Faliscus are said to be the first to have acted comedy while masked; for tragedy Minutius and Prothonius were the first.

The writings of all comedies are taken from four things, namely, name, place, deed, and outcome.

Those taken from name are like *Phormio, Hecyra, Curculio, Epidicus.* From place, like *Andria, Leucadia, Brundusina.* From deed, like *Eunuchus, Asinaria, Captivi.* From outcome, *Commorientes, Adelphi, Heauton Timorumenos.*[1] There are three forms of comedy. One is *comoedia palliata,* in which Greek costume is worn; some call this *tabernaria.* In *comoedia togata,* called so according to the type of the characters, the costume of togas is desired. *Comoedia Attellana* is composed of witticisms and jokes, which in themselves have an old elegance.

Comedy is divided into four parts, prologue, protasis, epitasis, catastrophe. The prologue is the first speech, called by the Greeks *prologos,* i.e., a speech preceding the true composition of the fable. There are four species of it: *susatikos,* or praising—in this the fable or poet is praised; *anaphorikos,* or relative—because either curses are *related* to the adversary or thanks expressed to the people; *hupothetikos,* or argumentative—it sets forth the argument of the fable; *miktos,* or mixed—it contains all the above in itself. Some have wished that there be this difference between "prologue" and "prologium": that "prologue" is a kind of preface to the fable, in which alone something besides the argument is said to the audience, either from the poet, or due to the needs of the fable itself or the needs of an actor. But in the "prologium" only the argument is spoken of. The protasis is the first action in the beginning of the drama, in which part of the argument is unfolded and part is kept back to hold the expectation of the people. The epitasis is the increase and advance of the disturbance, and as I said the tangling of the maze. Catastrophe is the change of the situation to a pleasant outcome, a change made clear to all through the knowledge of what has happened.

In some fables the names of the fables are put first, before the names of the poets. In some the names of the poets are put before the names of the fables. This diversity of custom has a basis in antiquity. For when some first published fables, they put the names of the fables before the name of the poet, lest any should be turned away from the writing because they disliked the poet. However, when some authority was gained for the poet after the publication of many fables, then the names of the poets were again put first, in order that attention might be given to the fables because they were the writing of *these* poets.

It is manifest that acts are assigned to diverse games. For there are four species of games, which the Curule Aediles attend to as a public duty. The games in honor of Magna Mater are consecrated to the great ones of god; the Greeks call these games "megalesious." Funeral games were instituted to hold the people back while the funeral procession decreed in honor of a patrician was fully arranged. Plebeian games are put on for the welfare of the people. The

---

[1] *Phormio, Hecyra (The Mother-in-law), Andria, Eunuchus (The Eunuch), Adelphi (The Brothers),* and *Heuton Timorumenos (The Self-Tormentor)* are by Terence. *Curculio, Epidicus, Asinaria (The Ass Comedy), Captivi (The Captives),* and *Commorientes (The Dying-Together)* are by Plautus. *Leucadia* is by Turpilius and *Brundusina* by Lucius Afranius.

Apollonian games are consecrated to Apollo. Two altars used to be put on stage: the one on the right of Liber, the one on the left of the god whose games were being held; whence Terence says in *Andria:* "Take the sacred boughs from this altar."

From here they always bring on stage Ulysses, clothed in a Greek cloak. This is either because one time he pretended insanity, when he wished that he was ruled [rather than ruler] so that he would not be recognized and forced to go off to war, or because of his singular wisdom, under the cover and protection of which he was very helpful to his allies. This was his excellence: namely, to have the talent of always being deceptive. Some relate that the inhabitants of Ithaca, like the Locrians, usually were clothed in cloaks. The characters of Achilles and Neoptolemus have diadems, although they never held royal scepters. An argument given for this scenic representation is that they had never sworn to an oath of military service together with the rest of the young men of Greece to wage war with the Trojans, nor were they ever under the command of Agamemnon.

White clothing is worn by old men in comedy because it is said to be the eldest. Clothing of varied colors is given to young men. Comic slaves are covered with a thin mantle, either because of their former poverty or in order that they might act without impediment. Parasites wear twisted cloaks. To the joyful man white clothing is given, and worn-out clothing to the troubled man. Royal purple is given to the rich man, reddish-purple to the pauper, a purple mantle to the soldier, and to a girl foreign clothing. The procurer uses a cloak of many colors. Golden-yellow is given to the whore to designate greed. These garments are called *syrmata,* or robes with a train, because they are dragged; this institution comes from the luxury of the stage. The same garments on grieving characters show neglect of self through carelessness. Woven curtains are also hung on the stage, because the decoration that was brought from the Attalic kingdom to Rome was painted; in place of these a later age used *siperia,* or smaller curtains. Moreover, there is a farcical veil, which is hung in front of the people while the acts of the production are being changed.

The actors usually deliver the dialogue. The songs usually are arranged in measures not by the poet but by one skilled in the doings of the musical art. For not all songs are presented in the same measures or meters, but in measures and meters frequently changed; . . . [text obscure]. Those who made measures of that kind usually put their names at the beginning of the fable above both the writer and the actor. These songs were so made for flutes that when they were heard many of the people could learn which fable the players would act, before the antecedent title was declared to these spectators. The songs, moreover, were played on "equal" and "unequal" flutes, and on right- and left-handed ones. The right-handed and Lydian flutes by their gravity announce the serious style of comedy. The left-handed and Serranan flutes by a light prick point to the joke in comedy. Where, however, the acted fable was written for right- and left-handed flutes, mixed jokes and seriousness are announced.

ANTONIO RICCOBONI

(1541–1599)

Riccoboni was one of the legion of sixteenth-century Italian commentators who were devoted followers of Aristotle. The essay printed below, translated by George Miltz, originally appeared in Riccoboni's translation of, and commentary on, the *Poetics.* It is a good example of the prevailing neoclassical attempt to apply Aristotle's analysis of tragedy to comedy.

from *The Comic Art* (1585)

PART III: RESEMBLANCES AND DIFFERENCES BETWEEN COMEDY AND OTHER IMITATIONS

Comedy resembles epic in genus only; for both are imitations. It resembles tragedy in genus, instruments, time, manner, and parts of quality and quantity; for both are imitations, both use the rhythm of dancing, harmony, and conversational language or meter, both are enclosed in one circuit of the sun or vary just a little from that, both have an active manner of imitation, and both have the same parts of quality—fable, character, thought, diction, melody, and spectacle—and the same parts of quantity—prologue, choric part, episode, and exodus. Comedy resembles flute-playing, lyre-playing, the imitation of pipes, and danced imitation in genus only. It resembles dithyramb and nome in genus and number of instruments. Comedy differs from epic in instrument, manner, matter, and time; first of all, comedy uses a threefold instrument, but epic uses only a simple instrument, namely, meter. Comedy has an active manner [of imitation], while epic has an expositive manner. Comedy's matter is simple, namely, inferior men, but the matter of epic is better, inferior, and similar men. Comedy is realized in one circuit of the sun, or varies a little from that; epic is indefinite in time. Furthermore, not all the parts of quality and quantity which are fitting to comedy are found in epic. Comedy differs from tragedy in matter, for the matter of comedy is inferior men, but tragedy's matter is better men. It differs from dithyramb and nome in the use of instruments, for dithyramb and nome used to use all the instruments at the same time; comedy, however, uses all the instruments at diverse times. Comedy differs from flute-playing, lyre-playing, the imitation of pipes, and danced imitation in the number of instruments, for comedy makes use of all the instruments, but these do not make use of all.

PART IV: DEFINITION OF COMEDY

We will pass over that definition of comedy which is based on praise, namely that it is an imitation of life, a mirror of custom, or an image of truth; the ancients defined it as a secure understanding [*complexio*] of private and civil affairs. Nevertheless Julius Caesar Scaliger thus criticized this definition: they erred, when they made this definition, namely, that comedy is an understanding of private persons and civil business without danger. First of all, this is true of some other nondramatic fables, which can be recited in simple narrative. Then there is always danger in comedy, for otherwise the conclusion would be dull. Now what else is danger than the approach of imminent evil or a temptation? Besides, not only dangers but even losses are suffered by pimps, rivals, slaves, and masters: consider how roughly the masters are handled in the *Asinaria* and in the *Mustellaria*. In addition, it is not possible to call obscene characters by name in the play under this definition, for they are not real private persons. Finally, this definition also fits mime and dramatic satire. These are the comments of this very learned man. Aristotle, however, defined comedy as an imitation of inferior men, not in every genus of vice, but only in that which is ridiculous. By considering the remarks made above that were based on his teaching, we can form this definition: namely, that comedy is an imitation, which by rhythm, harmony, and meter at diverse times imitates inferior men through an active manner. And so it is a species of imitation: insofar as it uses all the instruments it is distinguished from flute-playing, lyre-playing, the imitation of pipes, and the danced imitation; insofar as they are used at diverse times comedy is distinct from the dithyramb and nome; insofar as it imitates inferior men is it distinct from tragedy, and insofar as it imitates through an active manner is it distinct from epic. Yet another definition has come to our attention: Comedy is a low type of poetry with ridiculous elements, and with abuse that tends to be ridiculous. Accordingly it is distinct from hymns, encomia, epic, and tragedy, which are serious forms of poetry. Also it is distinct from the old vituperations, which were without ridiculous elements. It is distinct from iambic poetry, which indeed used to have ridiculous elements, but which proposed more abuse than ridicule. But if in imitation of Aristotle's definition of tragedy we wish to make a definition of comedy, we would bring in still another. For just as tragedy is an imitation, so also is comedy an imitation; the former is an imitation of an upright action, while the latter is an imitation of an immoral and base [1] action. Both are imitations of completed action, both are of "just" magnitude, and both have pleasant speech; both use single forms of instruments at diverse times. Both are carried on in an active manner. Tragedy through pity and fear, and comedy through pleasure from the ridiculous induces a purgation of minds. We accordingly arrive at this definition: Comedy is an imitation of a base action in that genus of vice which causes laughter; it is an imitation of a completed action and of one having a just magnitude; it accomplishes the imitation through pleasant speech, through individual forms of instruments acting at diverse times, through an active manner, and through inducing a

purgation of minds by the pleasure derived from the ridiculous element. It is an imitation, because all poetry belongs in the category of imitation. It is truly an imitation of a base action in that genus of vice which causes laughter. Not all baseness is appropriate to comedy, but only that which is ridiculous. And so since there are two kinds of poetry, one more serious, and one lower, comedy is in the lower genus; also its matter is people who are inferior, not generally, but in that genus of vice which is ridiculous. Thus it is separated from tragedy, which is an imitation of better men; also from epic and dithyramb, which are imitations of better, inferior, and like men. It is called an imitation of a perfect or completed action, i.e., a whole and integral action. To say that it is an imitation of an action having a just magnitude means that it, just as tragedy, can be contained in one circuit of the sun, give or take a little either way. Thus it is distinguished from epic, which is indefinite in time. It uses pleasant speech, concerning which Aristotle speaks as follows: "I call that speech pleasant which has rhythm, harmony, and melody—i.e., the rhythm of dancing, the harmony of sound, the melody of song," or rather the rhythm of dancing, the harmony of sound and song, and the melody of meter, as we have explained elsewhere. And this is especially made use of in choruses, for in the other parts bare speech and bare meter are used. And so since comic imitation uses a threefold instrument, it is distinguished from epic imitation, which uses speech only; it is also distinct from danced imitation, which uses rhythm only; and also from flute-playing, lyre-playing, and the imitation of pipes, which uses rhythm and harmony. Now since the first instrument of comedy is speech, the question arises whether it can laudably be an imitation if it uses prose. Admittedly, just as Sophron, Xenarchus, and Plato made imitations in prose, so also is it likely that comedy can be an imitation without verse. To this question there are two answers, the one taken from experience, the other from reason. For Aristotle, in the beginning of the *Poetics*, when he was treating of epic, gave the answer that it was not common, i.e., commonly accepted, that poetry can be made in prose. Wherefore if it had been commonly accepted he seemed to affirm that it could be admitted. Since in our times it has been commonly accepted that comedy can be made in prose, it follows that it can be admitted. However, this is not really so, for many have represented and do represent comedies in verses. Accordingly I have followed a man generally excellent in poetic art and in poetry, Giovanni Georgio Trissino, and advised that it is better not to leave verse out. For if we attend to reason, it certainly seems that comedy and all poetry ought to be made in verse, not because verse constitutes the nature of poetry, but because it is its proper instrument: this point has been explained by many when they treated of the threefold instrument of poetry and of what the fable of its action could be. Prose is less suited for the stage because of its sinking quality; verse, however, is more suited because of its rising quality, as we have written elsewhere. Besides speech and meter, harmony and the rhythm of dancing are also used, especially in the choruses, which we shall treat below. They are used in single forms acting separately. The philosopher makes this point as follows:

---

[1] As in Maggi's treatise *On the Ridiculous,* Latin *turpitudo,* etc., is here translated as "baseness" or "ugliness," depending on the context.

they are used in forms acting separately, because some things are known only through meter, and others through melody. For the same man teaches that three instruments are used in comedy and tragedy, not at the same time, as in the poetry of dithyrambs and nomes, where rhythm, harmony and speech are made use of at the same time; but at diverse times, so that speech is used sometimes by itself, as in various characters, and sometimes mixed, as in the choruses. Comedy takes place through an active manner, and by this it is distinguished from dithyramb and epic, which have an expositive manner, sometimes changing itself. Through pleasure from the ridiculous, comedy induces a purgation of minds; for through getting accustomed to pleasure of this kind the mind is prepared for thoroughly enjoying such pleasure, and also the mind is thoroughly purged in the sense that through ridiculous deceptions it learns well to avoid deceptions of this kind.

PART V: QUALITATIVE PARTS

In comedy and tragedy the same parts are beheld: fable, character, thought, diction, harmony, and spectacle. It is satisfactorily established that fable is the putting together of things which imitate the actions of men; that character is that according to which we say agents are of a certain kind; that thought is that which shows something or declares the mind, of which there are three functions: (1) to affirm or deny something, (2) to prepare the affections, and (3) to amplify or diminish; that diction is the composition of meters; that harmony is the composition of song and sound; that spectacle is that which attracts minds from the distant view. We shall now see how fable—the beginning, end, and soul of poetry—will be designated, and how eight properties are required in it.

PART VI: ON FABLE

It ought to be whole. But here is a little problem. In comedy the whole of a certain action does not seem to be represented, but only the part which takes place in one day. For example, the following is a whole action. The Sicilian merchant, having twin sons, Menaechmus and Sosicles, set out for Tarentum with Menaechmus; Menaechmus was seized and taken away to Epidamnus. There he was adopted by the man who seized him, and when he died Menaechmus became his heir; the natural father of Menaechmus also dies at Tarentum. When this news was brought to Menaechmus' grandfather, he changed Sosicles' name to Menaechmus; this brother visited all shores in search of the real Menaechmus. Finally he came to Epidamnus, where he was taken for the true Menaechmus by his whore, his wife, and his father-in-law. Now the whole of this action is not represented in the *Menaechmi* of Plautus, but only the part of the day on which the brothers met and recognized one another. The same can be said about the actions of other comedies, which are represented not in their entirety, but partially. Since various responses can be brought forward to this problem, we especially approve of the view that the whole is twofold; in one way it is great, like a human body, but in another way it is small, like the head. Thus in comic action that whole is understood which is small, so

that not the whole action of many days is represented, but rather the whole action of the last day, in which nevertheless the beginning, middle, and end are preserved; whatever is put in from the great whole are the episodes.

Fable ought to have a fitting magnitude, so as to be neither too small nor too large, but fitted to a viewing of that length of time which is within the spectators' interest. Their interest must be kept in mind, for they must leave the theater after a few hours. Accordingly, the time of the comic fable is thought to be suitable if it is not of one or two hours, for then the people would be gathered for too short a time, or if it does not long surpass one circuit of the sun, for then it would be an impediment to the people, and that Plautinian remark would fit: "The loins grieve from sitting, and the eyes from watching." The suitable time would be what could be understood in one circuit of the sun, give or take a little either way.

The fable ought to be one. Even if sometimes two actions seem to be expressed, as in the *Andria* of Terence there is the action of Pamphilus loving Glycerius and another action of Charinus loving Philumena, still one is principal and the other adventitious and added in the place of an episode. Brevity of time and narrowness of place neither in tragedy nor in comedy admit a multitude of actions. Besides this, the reason of beauty alone demands one action, as is also the case in epic.

The fable ought to be of such a kind as would be possible to happen, and ought to be verisimilar. This verisimilitude is seen in universals, in particular instances, and in names. For universals are perceived by considering the extent to which it is fitting for certain persons to do certain things from verisimilitude or necessity. Particulars are understood in instances, and can be considered universal insofar as they come from many causes in many ways. Poetry is concerned with these universals and particular instances considered universally, and puts many of them together on the basis of verisimilitude. One posits names also from verisimilitude, depending on the quality of character: e.g., one calls the greedy man Chremetes, the cheerful man Phoedria, the prudent man Sophrona, the kind man Mitio, the madman Demea, the daring man Thraso, and many others in a similar way. In allotting these names it is fitting to pay attention to the custom of the place which is represented. Wherefore we can hardly approve of those poets to whom any novelty of name is usually pleasing; still in the adaptations of comedies they change the names for verisimilitude, and use those which are used in that language into which the adaptation was made; they also change the place. It is perhaps a little lacking in verisimilitude to show Greek characters speaking Latin among themselves in the Greek cities which are represented, as in Plautus and Terence. Unless perhaps we were to say that the people is posited as so uncultivated that it thinks that all peoples and countries use one language. This could be more approved of if the comedy were not carried on in cities in which various languages are daily heard.

Fable ought not to be episodic, i.e., contaminated by superfluous episodes. Here by episodes we mean all things invented for showing the nature of the action, which is known only in instances. Unless these elements are connected by verisimilitude or necessity, they make the fable episodic and reprehensible; if they are well connected they do not make it episodic, but praiseworthy. For example, in the *Menaechmi* of Plautus it was known in instances that Menaechmus Sosicles at Epidamnus recognized his brother, who had been carried off. Indeed the elements which were invented to show the nature of this action are called episodes, which were connected by Plautus either from verisimilitude or necessity. First Peniculus speaks: here comes the Menaechmus who was carried away, reproaching his wife; then Erotium the whore goes out, and sends Cylindrus to buy some food; afterward when Menaechmus Sosicles comes up with a slave, and is falsely received by Cylindrus, then by Erotium, then by Peniculus, then by the servant girl, the series ends when he is mistakenly accepted by the wife. Thus in the various parts there is a progression, which is so connected by verisimilitude or necessity that the fable is not to be called episodic.

The fable ought to be surprising, in order that through a ridiculous deception it will induce a purgation of that deception. The wonder at wicked and shameful things, which are mocked and censured in comedies, warns the spectators not to fall into them. If we compare them, we see that in tragedy wonder is caused by wretched and fearful things, while in comedy it is caused by base and laughable things. For example, in the *Adelphi* of Terence, Demea the father is deceived, and believes that his one son, Ctesipho, is upright, and that Aeschinus, the other son, is wicked; from a deception of this kind arises wonder which gives full warning to the spectators not to be deceived in the same way. This purgation is proper to comedy.

The fable ought to be complicated, for that which has a change from adversity to prosperity will be most beautiful. Now, that fable is simple which progresses in one line of fortune, so that the action would always be happy, just as the *Prometheus* of Aeschylus was fashioned as wholly unhappy. That fable is complicated which has a change of fortune through change in fortune and recognition; this can take place six ways, as in tragedy: (1) through signs, (2) through the fiction of the poet, (3) through memory, (4) through syllogism, (5) through paralogism, (6) through a succession of matters, as was explained above.

The fable ought not to have the suffering which tragedy has—that is, according to the definition of Aristotle, the action of a violent death, or of some great trouble. Even so, it will not lack some evil and some disturbances, though without murder, and some wounds, but all of these are converted into weddings, joy, and tranquillity; it will contain some dangers, without which the ending would be very dull. However, in place of tragic evils it ought to contain the ridiculous.

PART XX: ON THE RIDICULOUS

The ridiculous is defined by Aristotle as a certain fault, and ugliness without pain, lacking a destructive force; an example would be a face immediately ridiculous, ugly, and distorted without pain. In this definition the first thing to be understood is the laughter which is caused by the ridiculous. The most learned men have said that it is a sign of joy, and that the

mind makes it through a dilation of the heart from the liberation of the spirits, which cannot be held in once the image of the joyful thing conquers. And so laughter appears by nature. It is apparent how it is aroused, i.e., what its efficient cause is, for it is joy and pleasure. It is apparent where laughter is; for it is in the mind, as in the principal place, which receives the laughter, and in the heart, as it were the instrument of the mind. It is apparent how it comes into being, namely through the liberation of the spirits. It is apparent how the sides, mouth, veins, countenance, and eyes are busied once the image of the joyful thing conquers that force which contains the spirits; the effect of this image is seen first in the thorax, then in the face, and finally in the brain, where the effect is that its humidity breaks out from the eyes, and this is called a tear. Whence Syrus says about Demea: "Tears of joy fall from that man, as from a boy." The truth is that not everything that causes laughter is ridiculous, for certain dear persons and things cause laughter. People whom we meet, such as mothers, fathers, sons, lovers, friends, and the like, cause laughter either right away or after a little time; things like honors, magistracies, precious stones, possessions, joyful messages, and all things which are obtained after a strong and long desire cause laughter. It is for this reason that the ridiculous is defined as a certain fault and baseness, which in Plato's *Sophist* is called a kind of withdrawal from that which is fitting to the nature of something. Now baseness or ugliness either is with pain and causes pity, or it is without pain. Again, if it is without pain, either it is of the body, or of the mind, or of things posited extrinsically. . . .

PART XXI: ON THE UGLINESS OF CHARACTER THAT OUGHT TO BE SEEN

Just as in tragedy—which is an imitation of better men—it is necessary that the poets imitate the good contrivers of forms, who, when they make the proper form, make their subjects more beautiful, as Polignotus did; so also in comedy, which is an imitation of inferior men, it is also necessary that the poets imitate those painters who painted men uglier, as Pauson was said to do. The poets of comedy ought to do this in order to fashion an example of ugliness in that genus of vice which arouses laughter.

BEN JONSON (1573–1637)

The first of the great English poet-critics, Jonson was a neoclassicist whose theory as well as practice was enlivened and enlarged through contact with the broad popular tradition of English drama. The Prologue to *Volpone*, like the play itself, is a reflection of his determination to mix instruction with pleasure. But his fidelity to neoclassical principles enhances rather than constricts the vitality and rhythm of his best plays, providing them with a unifying purpose and design.

from *Volpone* (1607)

DEDICATORY EPISTLE
TO
THE MOST NOBLE AND MOST EQUAL SISTERS,
THE TWO FAMOUS UNIVERSITIES,
FOR THEIR LOVE AND ACCEPTANCE
SHOWN TO HIS POEM IN THE PRESENTATION,
BEN JONSON,
THE GRATEFUL ACKNOWLEDGER,
DEDICATES BOTH IT AND HIMSELF.

There follows an epistle, if you dare venture on the length:

Never, most equal Sisters, had any man a wit so presently excellent as that it could raise itself, but there must come both matter, occasion, commenders, and favourers to it. If this be true, and that the fortune of all writers doth daily prove it, it behoves the careful to provide well toward these accidents, and, having acquired them, to preserve that part of reputation most tenderly, wherein the benefit of a friend is also defended. Hence is it that I now render myself grateful, and am studious to justify the bounty of your act; to which, though your mere authority were satisfying, yet, it being an age wherein poetry and the professors of it hear so ill on all sides, there will a reason be looked for in the subject. It is certain, nor can it with any forehead be opposed, that the too much licence of poetasters in this time hath much deformed their mistress; that every day their manifold and manifest ignorance doth stick unnatural reproaches upon her. But, for their petulancy, it were an act of the greatest injustice, either to let the learned suffer, or so divine a skill (which, indeed, should not be attempted with unclean hands) to fall under the least contempt.

For if men will impartially, and not asquint, look toward the offices and function of a poet, they will easily conclude to themselves the impossibility of any man's being the good poet, without first being a good man. He that is said to be able to inform young men to all good disciplines, inflame grown men to all great virtues, keep old men in their best and supreme state, or, as they decline to childhood, recover them to their first strength; that comes forth the interpreter and arbiter of nature, a teacher of things divine, no less than human, a master in manners; and can alone, or with a few, effect the business of mankind—this, I take him, is no subject for pride and ignorance to exercise their railing rhetoric upon. But it will here be hastily answered that the writers of these days are other things; that not only their manners but their natures are inverted, and nothing remaining with them of the dignity of poet but the abused name, which every scribe usurps; that now, especially in dramatic, or—as they term it—stage poetry, nothing but ribaldry, profanation, blasphemy, all licence of offence to God and man, is practised. I dare not deny a great part of this, and am sorry I dare not, because in some men's abortive features (and would they had never boasted the light!) it is over-true. But that all are embarked in this bold adventure for Hell, is a most uncharitable thought and, uttered, a more malicious slander.

For my particular, I can, and from a most clear conscience, affirm that I have ever trembled to think toward the least profaneness; have loathed the use of such foul and unwashed bawdry as is now made the food of the scene. And howsoever I cannot escape, from some, the imputation of sharpness, but that they will say I have taken a pride, or lust, to be bitter, and not my youngest infant but hath come into the world with all his teeth; I would ask of these supercilious politics, what nation, society, or general order, or state I have provoked? what public person? whether I have not, in all these, preserved their dignity, as mine own person, safe? My works are read, allowed—I speak of those that are entirely mine. Look into them. What broad reproofs have I used? Where have I been particular? Where personal, except to a mimic, cheater, bawd, or buffoon, creatures for their insolencies worthy to be taxed? Yet to which of these so pointingly, as he might not either ingenuously have confessed or wisely dissembled his disease? But it is not rumour can make men guilty, much less entitle me to other men's crimes. I know that nothing can be so innocently writ or carried, but may be made obnoxious to construction. Marry, whilst I bear mine innocence about me, I fear it not. Application is now grown a trade with many; and there are, that profess to have a key for the deciphering of everything. But let wise and noble persons take heed how they be too credulous, or give leave to these invading interpreters to be over-familiar with their fames, who cunningly, and often, utter their own virulent malice under other men's simplest meanings.

As for those that will (by faults which charity hath raked up, or common honesty concealed) make themselves a name with the multitude, or, to draw their rude and beastly claps, care not whose living faces they intrench with their petulant styles; may they do it without a rival, for me. I choose rather to live graved in obscurity, than share with them in so preposterous a fame. Nor can I blame the wishes of those severe and wiser patriots who, providing the hurts these licentious spirits may do in a state, desire rather to see fools and devils and those antique relics of barbarism retrieved, with all other ridiculous and exploded follies, than behold the wounds of private men, of princes, and nations. For, as Horace makes Trebatius speak, among these

> . . . *sibi quisque timet, quamquam est intactus, et odit.*

And men may justly impute such rages, if continued, to the writer, as his sports. The increase of which lust in liberty, together with the present trade of the stage in all their misc'line interludes, what learned or liberal soul doth not already abhor? where nothing but the filth of the time is uttered, and that with such impropriety of phrase, such plenty of solecisms, such dearth of sense, so bold prolepses, so racked metaphors, with brothelry able to violate the ear of a pagan, and blasphemy to turn the blood of a Christian to water. I cannot but be serious in a cause of this nature, wherein my fame, and the reputations of divers honest and learned, are the question; when a name so full of authority, antiquity, and all great mark is, through their insolence, become the lowest scorn of the age; and those men subject to the petulancy of every vernaculous orator, that were wont to be the care of kings and happiest monarchs.

This it is that hath not only rapt me to present indignation, but made me studious heretofore, and by all my actions, to stand off from them. Which may most appear in this my latest work (which you, most learned arbitresses, have seen, judged, and, to my crown, approved), wherein I have laboured, for their instruction and amendment, to reduce not only the ancient forms, but manners of the scene: the easiness, the propriety, the innocence, and last the doctrine, which is the principal end of poesy, to inform men in the best reason of living. And though my catastrophe may, in the strict rigour of comic law, meet with censure, as turning back to my promise; I desire the learned and charitable critic to have so much faith in me, to think it was done of industry. For with what ease I could have varied it nearer his scale, but that I fear to boast my own faculty, I could here insert. But my special aim being to put the snaffle in their mouths, that cry out we never punish vice in our interludes, &c., I took the more liberty; though not without some lines of example drawn even in the ancients themselves, the goings-out of whose comedies are not always joyful, but oft-times the bawds, the servants, the rivals, yea, and the masters are mulcted. And fitly, it being the office of a comic poet to imitate justice and instruct to life, as well as purity of language, or stir up gentle affections. To which I shall take the occasion elsewhere to speak.

For the present, most reverenced Sisters, as I have cared to be thankful for your affections past, and here made the understanding acquainted with some ground of your favours, let me not despair their continuance to the maturing of some worthier fruits. Wherein, if my Muses be true to me, I shall raise the despised head of Poetry again, and, stripping her out of those rotten and base rags wherewith the times have adulterated her form, restore her to her primitive habit, feature, and majesty, and render her worthy to be embraced and kissed of all the great and master spirits of our world. As for the vile and slothful, who never affected an act worthy of celebration, or are so inward with their own vicious natures, as they worthily fear her, and think it a high point of policy to keep her in contempt, with their declamatory and windy invectives; she shall, out of just rage, incite her servants (who are *genus irritabile*) to spout ink in their faces, that shall eat farther than their marrow, into their fames. And not Cinnamus the Barber, with his art, shall be able to take out the brands, but they shall live and be read, till the wretches die, as things worst deserving of themselves in chief, and then of all mankind.

PIERRE CORNEILLE

(1606–1684)

One of the greatest of dramatists, Corneille is also one of the great formulators of neoclassical dramatic theory. His major critical statements are found in his three *Discourses* (1660). The excerpt below is taken from the second of these, the *Discourse on Tragedy*. Although heavily indebted to Aristotelian principles, Corneille never hesitates to disagree with the master, particularly when the disagreement involves a defense of Corneille's own practices as a playwright. This translation is by Henry Hitch Adams and Baxter Hathaway.

Discourse on Tragedy

AND OF THE METHODS OF TREATING IT, ACCORDING TO PROBABILITY [1] AND NECESSITY [1660]

Besides the three uses of a dramatic poem of which I have spoken in the discourse I used as a preface for the first part of this collection, tragedy has this one in particular, "that through pity and fear it purges such passions." [2] These are the terms which Aristotle uses in his definition and which teach us two things: one, that it arouses pity and fear; the other, that by their means it purges such passions. He explains the first at sufficient length, but says nothing about the latter, and of all the terms which he employs in this definition, it is the only one he does not clarify at all. He shows, however, in the last chapter of his *Politics* an intention of speaking of it at a great length in this treatise [the *Poetics*], and it is that which makes most of his interpreters feel that we do not have it complete, because we see nothing at all on this subject.[3] Whatever it might have been, I believe that it is to the point to talk on what he has said before making an effort to divine what he wished to say. The maxims which he establishes for us could lead us to some conjecture on the other [idea of purgation], and on the certainty of what remains we can form a probable opinion of that which has not come down to us.

"We have pity," he says, "for those whom we see suffering a misfortune which they do not deserve, and we fear that a similar misfortune will befall us when we see people like ourselves suffering." [4] This pity concerns the interest of the person whom we see suffering, the fear which follows it concerns our own person, and this passage alone gives us enough opening to find the manner in which the purging of pas-

---

[1] The word "probability" is the closest English word to the French *vraisemblable,* which is sometimes taken over intact, or translated as "verisimility," by the seventeenth- and eighteenth-century critics. Cf. Dryden's *Essay of Dramatic Poesy.*

[2] Pertinent quotations from Aristotle are given in these notes from the modern translation of Bywater.

". . . with incidents arousing pity and fear, wherewith to accomplish its catharsis of such emotions."—Chap. 6, Ingram Bywater, *Aristotle on the Art of Poetry* (Oxford, 1909), p. 17.

[3] Modern scholars are now of the opinion that one or two books of the *Poetics* have been lost, and that Aristotle covered the subject of comedy in one of the missing treatises, but Corneille undoubtedly believed that such a work was never written.

[4] ". . . pity is occasioned by undeserved misfortune, and fear by that of one like ourselves."—Chap. 13, Bywater, p. 35.

sions in tragedy is done. The pity for a misfortune, where we see the fall of people similar to ourselves, brings to us a fear of a similar one. This fear brings us to a desire of avoiding it, and this desire to purging, moderating, rectifying, and even eradicating in ourselves the passion which, before our eyes, plunges into this misfortune the persons we pity; for this common, but natural and indubitable reason, that to avoid the effect it is necessary to remove the cause. This explanation will not please those who attach themselves to the commentators of this philosopher. They are troubled by this passage and agree so little with each other that Paul Beny [5] notes twelve or fifteen different opinions which he refutes before giving us his own. His conforms to this one in the reasoning, but differs on this point, that it applies the effect only to kings and princes, perhaps for this reason, that the tragedy can make us fear only the evils which we see happening to those like us, and, in making them happen only to kings and princes, this fear can affect only those of their rank. But, without doubt, he has too literally understood the phrase, *those similar to us,* and has not sufficiently considered that there were no kings in Athens when the poems from which Aristotle takes his examples were shown, and on which he bases his rules. This philosopher would not care to have this thought attributed to him, and would not have used in tragedy a thing whose effect could function so rarely and whose use could be limited to so few people. It is true that ordinarily only kings are introduced for leading characters in tragedy, and the audience has no sceptres with which to resemble them, so that it can have the opportunity of fearing the misfortunes which overtake them; but these kings are men just as the members of the audience, and fall into those misfortunes through the force of passions of which the audience is capable. They even lend an easy argument for making the least of the greatest, and the spectator can easily conceive that if a king, through abandoning himself too much to ambition, to love, to hate, to vengeance, falls into so great disaster that he makes himself pitied in such proportion, he who is only a common man ought to keep these passions in check for fear of falling into a like misfortune. Besides, it is not necessary to put only the misfortunes of kings in the theatre. Those of other men will find a place if any calamities sufficiently famous and important to deserve it happen to them, and if history takes enough care to teach them to us. Scédase was only a peasant from Leuctres; and I would not hold his woes unworthy of appearing if the purity of our scene could allow that we speak of the effective violation of his two daughters, after the idea of prostitution could not be endured in the person of a saint who had been preserved from it.[6]

[5] Paul Beny, or Paolo Beni, an Italian critic of Aristotle.

[6] Voltaire writes on Scédase:
"Kings, emperors, princes, generals of armies, principal heads of republics, it really does not matter. But tragedy must always contain men elevated above common men, not only because the destiny of states depends on the lot of these important persons, but because the ill-fortunes of illustrious men exposed to the regard of nations makes a deeper impression on us than the misfortunes of common men.
"I very much doubt that a peasant of Leuctres,

To facilitate for us the methods of giving birth to this pity and this fear which Aristotle requires of us, it helps us to choose the characters and the events which can excite both. Also I suppose that it is true that our audience is composed neither of very evil men nor of saints, but people of ordinary goodness, who are not so severely restrained by exact virtue that they are not susceptible to passions but are exposed to the dangers in which passions engage those who yield completely to them. Supposing this, let us examine those characters whom the philosopher excludes from tragedy, in order that we agree with him on those in whom he makes his perfection consist. In the first place, he does not desire "that a completely virtuous man fall from good fortune into bad," and maintains "that this produces neither pity nor fear because this is a completely unjust event." [7] Some interpreters extend the meaning of this Greek word, μιαρόν,[8] which he uses as a name for this happening, to translate it as "abominable"; to which I add that such a success excites more indignation and hate against the man who causes the suffering than pity for the one who suffers, and thus this feeling, which is not the right one for tragedy, at least unless well managed, can suffocate the feeling it ought to produce and leave the hearer discontented by the anger which he carries away and which is mingled with compassion which would please him if he took that alone away with him.

Neither does he want "a bad man to pass from disaster to good fortune, because not only can no pity or fear arise from such a success, but it cannot even touch us with the natural feeling of joy with which the prosperity of the first act fills us, to whom our favor attaches itself." [9] The fall of a bad man into misfortune has the material to please us through the aversion which we take for him; but since it is only a just punishment, it does not make us pity, and does not impress fear upon us, in as much as we are not as bad as he, and thus incapable of his crimes, and so cannot fear an equally disastrous outcome.

It remains, therefore, to find a mean between these two extremes, through the choice of a man who is neither entirely good nor entirely bad and who, through a fault or human frailty, falls into a misfor-

Scédase, by name, whose two daughters had been raped, would be as good a subject for tragedy as Cinna and Iphigenia. Rape, moreover, always has something of the ridiculous, and rarely can be played except among good families, where Corneille pretends that *Théodore* was set, supposing that this Théodore ever existed, and that the Romans had condemned their women to this form of punishment, which assuredly was neither in their laws nor their customs."

Théodore, by Corneille (1645), failed in production, and was banned because it presented the idea of prostitution.

[7] "A good man must not be seen passing from happiness to misfortune. . . . The . . . situation is not fearimposing or piteous, but simply odious to us."—Chap. 13, Bywater, p. 35.

[8] This word implies an offense to our moral or religious feelings. Cf. Bywater, p. 214.

[9] "Nor on the other hand should an extremely bad man be seen falling from happiness into misery. Such a story may arouse the human feeling in us, but it will not move us to either pity or fear."—Chap. 13, Bywater, p. 35.

tune which he does not deserve. Aristotle gives as examples Oedipus and Thyestes, and I really do not understand his thought at all. The first appears to me to contain no error, even though he kills his father, because he does not know him, and he only contests the way as a man of gallant soul against an unknown who attacks him with superior force. Nevertheless, although the meaning of the Greek word ἁμάρτημα [10] may extend to a simple error of misunderstanding, such as his was, let us admit the example with this philosopher, although I cannot see what passion there is to purge, nor how we can correct ourselves by this example. But, as for Thyestes, I cannot discover this common guilt or error without crime which plunges him into his misfortune. If we look at him before the tragedy which carries his name, he is a committer of incest who violates the wife of his brother; if we consider him in the tragedy, he is a man of good faith who takes the word of his brother with whom he is reconciled. In this first state, he is very much a criminal; in the latter, very much a virtuous man. If we attribute his misfortune to his incest, it is a crime of which the spectators are not capable, and the pity which they will feel for him will not include this fear which purges, because they do not resemble him in the least. If we lay his disaster to his good faith, some fear could follow the pity which we will have, but this fear could purge only the easy confidence in the word of a reconciled enemy, which is more the quality of an honest man than a vicious habit; and this purgation would only banish the sincerity of reconciliations. I admit frankly, therefore, that I do not understand the application of this example at all.

I will admit something else. If the purging of passions is accomplished in tragedy, I hold that it works in the way that I have explained, but I doubt that it ever happens, even in those tragedies which have the conditions which Aristotle demands. These conditions are met in *Le Cid* [11] and caused its great success. Rodrigue and Chimène there have this guilt subject to passions, and these passions cause their misfortune since they are unfortunate only to the extent of their passion for each other. They fall into unhappiness by this human weakness which we share with them. Their misfortune causes pity; this is sure, and that it has wrung many tears from the spectators there is no contesting. This pity ought to give us fear of falling into a like misfortune and purge in us this excess of love which causes their misfortune and makes us feel sorry for them; but I do not know if it gives us this fear, nor if it purges it, and I greatly fear that the reasoning of Aristotle on this point is nothing but a good idea which, in truth, never has its effect. I refer to those who have seen the representation. They can demand an accounting of the secret of their heart, and re-examine that which has touched them in the theatre, to determine whether they have come by that to this reflected fear, and whether they have rectified in themselves the passion which has

caused the disgrace which they have pitied. One of the interpreters of Aristotle [12] says that he spoke of this purging of passions in the tragedy only because he wrote after Plato, who banished tragic poets from his republic, because they stirred the people up too strongly. Since he wrote to contradict him and to show that it is not to the point to banish them from civilized states, he wished to find the usefulness in these agitations of the soul, to make them desirable through the same reason that the other uses to banish them. The qualities that give birth to the impressions which provide the force of the example were not available to him: the punishment of evil actions, the reward of good ones was not the usage of his century as we have made it for ours, and except for those sentences and the didactic discourses which tragedy can pronounce according to its judgment, there is not to be found a solid utility; he has substituted one which is perhaps only imaginary. At least, to produce it requires the conditions it demands; they are met with so rarely that Robertello [13] finds them only in the *Oedipus*, maintaining that this philosopher has not prescribed them to us as so necessary that the lack of them will render a work defective, but only as concepts of perfection in tragedies. Our century has seen these things in *Le Cid*, but I do not know if it has seen them in many others; and if we wish to glance again at that rule, we acknowledge that success has justified many plays in which it is not observed.

The exclusion of completely virtuous persons who fall into misfortune banishes martyrs from our theatre. Polyeucte is a success against this maxim, and Héraclius and Nicomède [14] have pleased even though they impart only pity and give us nothing of fear, nor any passion to purge, since we see them oppressed and near death without any fault on their part from which we can by their example correct ourselves.

The misfortune of a very evil man excites neither pity nor fear; it is unworthy of the former and, as the spectators are not evildoers like him, they do not feel the latter in view of his punishment; but it would be apropos to place some distinction between the crimes. There are those of which honest people are capable by violence of passion, of which the evil outcome can have an effect in the soul of the hearer. An honest man does not go to the edge of the woods to steal, nor commit an assassination in cold blood; but if he is very much in love he may practice deceit on his rival, he may fly into a passion of rage and kill on a first impulse, and ambition may engage him in a crime or in a guilty action. There are few mothers who would murder or poison their children from fear of their making their way in the world as Cléopâtre in *Rodogune*; [15] but there are many who would like to do so, and desist only with reluctance, and at the last possible moment. Even though they are not capable of so black and so unnatural an action as that

---

[10] This word in Aristotle probably refers to an error of judgment. By the New Testament times it has come to mean sin, but the consensus of scholars is that it did not have moral connotations in Aristotle's time.

[11] Corneille's most famous play, produced in 1636 or early 1637.

[12] A fairly common statement, to be found as early as Minturnus' *De Poeta*, 1559.

[13] A famous sixteenth-century critic of Aristotle.

[14] The heroes of three famous plays by Corneille. *Polyeucte* (1642 or 1643), *Héraclius* (1646), and *Nicomède* (1651).

[15] *Rodogune* (1644). Cléopâtre is not the famous lover of Antony, but Queen of Syria, who murders her own children.

of the Queen of Syria, there are those among them who have some tincture of that principle, and the view of the just punishment which she receives from it can make them fear, not a like misfortune, but one proportional to that which they are capable of committing. It is thus concerning several other crimes which are not within the scope of our audience. The reader can make the investigation and application on that principle.

However, even with such difficulty as there is in finding this effective and lively purgation of passions by means of pity and fear, it is easy to reconcile ourselves with Aristotle. We have only to say that by that manner of expressing himself, he did not understand that these two means always operate together; and that it sufficed according to him that one of the two make this purgation, with this difference always, that pity *cannot* come without fear, while fear *can* be aroused without pity. The death of the Count does not do this in *Le Cid,* and can many times better purge in us that sort of envious pride of the glory of others than all the compassion we have for Rodogune and for Chimène [16] can purge the affection for this violent love which causes them to pity each other. The hearer can have commiseration for Antiochus,[17] for Nicomède, for Héraclius, but if he continues in it, and if he cannot believe in his falling into a like misfortune, he is not cured of any passion. On the contrary, he has none for Cléopâtre, nor for Prusias,[18] nor for Phocas;[19] but the fear of a similar or approaching adversity can purge a stubborn mother from dispossessing the well-being of her children, a husband from great deference toward a second woman to the prejudice of that of his first bed, everyone from the avidity of usurping by violence the well-being or dignity of others; and all that proportional to the condition of each, and as far as he is capable of understanding. The griefs and irresolutenesses of Auguste in *Cinna* [20] can cause the last effect by pity and fear together; but, as I have already said, it does not always happen that those we pity are unfortunate from their own faults. When they are innocent, our pity for them inspires no fear, and if we conceive a situation which purges our passions, it is by the means of another person than the one whom we pity, and we owe it all to the force of the example.

This explanation finds authorization from Aristotle himself if we wish to weigh well the reason that he gives for the exclusion of events of which he disapproves in tragedy. He never says, "This is not proper because it does not excite pity, and does not give birth to fear, and this other is insupportable because it does not excite fear, and does not give birth to pity," but he rejects them, "because," he says, "they excite neither pity nor fear" [21] thereby making us understand that, because of the lack of the one and the other, they do not please him, and that if they produce one of the two, he does not in the least withhold his approbation.

[16] Chimène and Rodogune are the heroines of Corneille's *Le Cid* and of *Rodogune.*
[17] Antiochus, a character in *Rodogune.*
[18] Prusias, a character in *Nicomède.*
[19] Phocas, a character in *Héraclius.*
[20] *Cinna* (1640).
[21] ". . . will not move us to either pity or fear."— Chap. 13, Bywater, p. 35.

The example of *Oedipus* which he advances confirms me in this thought. If we accept it, it has all the conditions requisite to tragedy; however, his unhappiness excites only pity, and I do not think that, of those who have seen it played, anyone who has pitied has advised himself to fear killing his father or marrying his mother. If this representation can impress some fear, and that fear is capable of purging in us some guilty or vicious inclination, it also purges the curiosity to know the future and prevents us from having recourse to predictions which ordinarily only serve to make us fall into the misfortune predicted to us, by the very pains which we take to avert it; because it is certain that he would not have killed his father nor married his mother, if his father and mother, on hearing the oracle's prediction, had not exposed their fear that this would happen. Moreover, not only would Laïus and Jocasta alone experience this fear, but it would occur merely as the shadow of a crime they had committed forty years before the action presented, and would be impressed on us only by a secondary actor, and by an action outside the tragedy.

To bring this discourse together before passing on to another matter, let us establish for a maxim that the perfection of tragedy consists indeed in exciting pity and fear by means of the leading actor, as Rodrigue in *Le Cid* and Placide in *Théodore,* [22] but that it is not a necessity so absolute that divers persons cannot be used to arouse the two feelings, as in *Rodogune;* and even to bring but one of the two to the audience, as in *Polyeucte,* where the representation forces only pity and no fear. That granted, let us find some moderation in the rigidity of the Rules of the philosopher, or at least some favorable interpretation, so as not to be required to condemn most of the poems we have seen succeed in our theatres.

Aristotle does not in the least desire that a completely innocent man should fall into misfortune, because that would be abominable; it excites greater indignation against the persecuter than pity for the misfortunes. No more does he desire that a completely evil man fall into misfortune, because this man cannot evoke pity for a calamity which he deserves; nor arouse fear of a like disaster in the spectators, who do not resemble him; but while the two judgments leave [room for] the example of a good man whose sufferings excite pity greater than our indignation against the one who causes them, or where the punishment of a great crime can correct in us some imperfection which is similar to his. I consider that it is not necessary to raise objections to exposing on the scene very virtuous or very evil men in calamity. Here are two or three ways of doing this, which perhaps Aristotle did not think to anticipate because he saw no examples of them in the theatres of his time.

The first is, when a very virtuous man is persecuted by a very evil one and escapes from the peril while the villain is caught in it, as in *Rodogune* and in *Héraclius;* this could not have been endured if Antiochus and Rodogune had perished in the first, and if Héraclius, Pulchèrie, and Martian in the other, and Cléopâtre and Phocas had triumphed. Their misfortune stirs a pity which is not in the least stifled by aversion to-

[22] *Théodore* (1645).

ward their oppressors, because it is hoped always that some happy turn will prevent them from succumbing, and, even though the crimes of Phocas and Cléopâtre are great enough to cause the audience to fear committing like ones, the unhappy outcome may have the effects upon the audience of which I have already spoken. It can happen, besides, that a very virtuous man may be persecuted and may even perish at the command of another man, who is not evil enough to arouse much indignation and who shows more weakness than villainy in the persecution which he enforces. If Félix has his son-in-law, Polyeucte, killed, it is not because of an enraged hate toward the Christians which would render him execrable to us, but only because of a shameful timidity that keeps him from daring to save him [Polyeucte] in the presence of Sévère, whose hate and vengeance he [Félix] fears, after the contempt he had shown for him during his ill fortune. We have some aversion for him; we disapprove of his method of working, but this aversion does not remove the pity we have for Polyeucte, and does not prevent his miraculous conversion at the end of the play from reconciling him fully with the audience. We can say the same thing of Prusias in *Nicomède* and of Valeus in *Théodore.* The one mistreats his son, although he is very virtuous, and the other is the cause of the ruin of his, who is no less good, but both have only the weaknesses which do not quite become crimes; and far from exciting an indignation which stifles the pity we have for a generous son, the cowardice of their abasement under the powers they dread, and which they must brave to do well, makes us only have some compassion for them and for their political shame.

To facilitate for us the means of exciting this pity which creates such fine effects in our theatres, Aristotle gives us a clue. "All action," he says, "takes place either between friends, or between enemies, or between people who are indifferent to each other. If an enemy kills or wishes to kill his enemy, that will not produce any commiseration, except in so far as we are moved to learn of or to see the death of a man such as he. When a stranger kills a stranger, that scarcely touches us any further, as long as it does not excite any strife in the soul of him who performs the action; but when these things happen between people whose birth or affection binds them together in interest, as when husband kills or is ready to kill his wife, a mother her children, a brother his sister, it is that which is marvelously suited to tragedy." [23] The reason for this is clear. The opposition of the feelings of nature to the transports of passion, or to the severity of duty, forms powerful emotions which are received

with pleasure by the audience; and the audience is easily disposed to pity an unfortunate man oppressed or persecuted by a person who ought to be interested in his salvation and who oftentimes seeks his ruin only with sorrow or, at the least, with repugnance. Horace and Curiace [24] would not be at all to be pitied if they had not been friends and brothers-in-law; nor Rodrigue if he had been persecuted by another than his mistress; and the unhappiness of Antiochus would touch us much less if some other than his mother had demanded the blood of his mistress, or some other than his mistress had demanded the blood of his mother; or if, after the death of his brother, which makes him subject to the fear of a similar thing happening to his own person, he had had to defy others than his mother and his mistress.

The proximity of blood and the intimacy of love or friendship between the persecutor and persecuted, the hunter and the hunted, the one who causes suffering and the one who suffers is, therefore, a great advantage for exciting pity, but there is some evidence that this condition is not as absolute as that of which I have just spoken, and that it concerns only perfect tragedies and nothing more. At least, the Ancients did not always observe it; I do not see it at all in the *Ajax* of Sophocles, nor in his *Philoctetes,* and anyone who wishes to run over that which remains to us of Æschylus and Euripides can find some examples to join to these. When I say that the two conditions are only for perfect tragedies, I do not mean to say that those in which we do not find them are imperfect; that would make it an absolute necessity, and make me contradict myself. But by the phrase "perfect tragedy" I mean the most sublime and moving of the type, so that those which lack one of these two conditions, or both of them, provided that they are regular with this exception, do not fail of being perfect of their type, even though they remain in a less exalted rank, and do not approach the beauty and splendor of the others if they borrow the pomp of verse, or the magnificence of spectacle, or some other agreement which comes with the subject.

In these tragic actions which happen between relatives, it is necessary to consider whether the one who wishes to cause the death of the other recognizes him or does not recognize him, and if he achieves his goal or does not achieve it. The various combinations of these two manners of proceeding form four kinds of tragedy, to which our philosopher attributes varying degrees of perfection. "A person recognizes the one whom he wishes to kill, and actually has him killed, as Medea kills her children, Clytemnestra her husband, Orestes his mother"; and the least kind is this. "A person has another killed without recognizing him, and then recognizes him with grief after having had him killed, and that," he says, "either before the tragedy, or in the tragedy, as the *Alcmeon* of Astydamas, and Telegonus in *Ulysses Wounded,*" two plays which time has not allowed to come to us; and the second kind, according to him, is more elevated than the first. The third is in the highest degree of excellence, "when a person is ready to have one of his relatives killed without knowing him soon enough to save him, as Iphigenia recognizes Orestes for her brother, but must sacrifice him to Diana, and escapes

[23] "Let us see, then, what kinds of incident strike one as horrible, or rather as piteous. In a deed of this description the parties must necessarily be either friends, or enemies, or indifferent to one another. Now when enemy does it on enemy, there is nothing to move us to pity either in his doing or in his meditating the deed, except so far as the actual pain of the sufferer is concerned; and the same is true when the parties are indifferent to one another. When the tragic deed, however, is done within the family—when murder or the like is done or meditated by brother on brother, by son on father, by mother on son, or son on mother—these are the situations the poet should seek after."—Chap. 14, Bywater, p. 39.

[24] Characters in Corneille's *Horace* (1640).

with him." He cites again two examples of this, of Merope in *Cresphontes* and of *Helle,* of which we know nothing. He entirely condemns the fourth species, in which people recognize, undertake, and complete nothing, which he says has something of evil and nothing of tragedy, and gives for example Haemon, who draws his sword against his father in the *Antigone* and uses it only to kill himself,[25] but unless this condemnation is a little modified, it would extend a little far and would envelop not only *Le Cid,* but *Cinna, Rodogune, Héraclius,* and *Nicomède.*

Let us say, then, that this condemnation is only to be understood of those who recognize the person they wish to ruin and desist because of a simple change of will, without any notable happening which obliges their changing, and without any lack of power on their part. I have already indicated this type of denouement as vicious; but when they have done on their side all that they can, and when they are prevented by a superior power from bringing about the result, or by some change in fortunes which causes them to perish, or puts them in the power of those whom they would ruin, it is beyond doubt that such constitutes tragedy, perhaps more sublime than the three kinds Aristotle approves; and if he has not spoken of this type at all, it is only because he saw no examples in the theatres of his own time, or it was not the custom to save the good by the ruin of the wicked, unless they have soiled themselves with some crime, as in the case of Electra, who delivers herself from oppression by the death of her mother, encouraging her brother in the crime and facilitating the means for him.

The action of Chimène [26] is then not defective be-

[25] "The deed of horror may be done by the doer knowingly and consciously, as in the old poets, and in Medea's murder of her children in Euripides. Or he may do it, but in ignorance of his relationship, and discover that afterwards, as does the Oedipus in Sophocles. Here the deed is outside the play; but it may be within it, like the act of the Alcmeon in Astydamas, or that of Telegonus in *Ulysses Wounded.* A third possibility is for one meditating some deadly injury to another, in ignorance of his relationship, to make the discovery in time to draw back. . . .

"The worst situation is when the personage is with full knowledge on the point of doing the deed, and leaves it undone. It is odious and also (through the absence of suffering) untragic; hence it is that no one is made to act thus except in some few instances, e.g. Haemon and Creon in Antigone. Next after this comes the actual perpetration of the deed meditated. A better situation than that, however, is for the deed to be done in ignorance, and the relationship discovered afterwards, since there is nothing odious in it, and the Discovery will serve to astound us. But the best of all is the last; what we have in *Cresphontes,* for example, where Merope, on the point of slaying her son, recognizes him in time; in *Iphigenia,* where sister and brother are in a like position; and in *Helle,* where the son recognizes his mother when on the point of giving her up to her enemy."—Chap. 14, Bywater, p. 41.

Cresphontes is a lost play by Euripides; *Ulysses Wounded* was by Sophocles; nothing is known of *Helle;* Astydamas was a tragedian who wrote some 240 tragedies, of which 15 took prizes. He was first produced in B.C. 395.

[26] Characters in *Le Cid.*

cause, after undertaking to ruin Rodrigue, she does not do so even though she could, and all the justice she can obtain from the king is a combat wherein the victory of this deplorable lover imposes silence on her. Cinna and his Émilie do not sin at all against the Rules in not killing Auguste, because the discovered conspiracy makes them impotent, and, if such an unexpected clemency did not dissipate all their hate, it would reveal them as having no tincture of humanity. Who spares Cléopâtre for the ruin of Rodogune? Who forgets Phocas for ridding himself of Héraclius? And if Prusias had remained the master, would not Nicomède have had to go to serve as hostage at Rome, which would have been to him a greater punishment than death? The first two receive punishment for their crimes and fail in their enterprises without recanting; and the last is forced to admit his injustice, after the insurrection of his people and the generosity of that son whom he wished to exalt at the expense of the eldest have prevented it from succeeding.

It is not to refute Aristotle that the writer finds so happy this fourth manner of proceeding, which the philosopher condemns, finds it indeed a new type of tragedy finer than the three which he recommends, and which he would doubtless have preferred had he known it. It is to give honor to our century without impinging in the least on the authority of this philosopher; however, I do not know how to conserve this authority and reverse the order of preference which he established among the three types. Nevertheless, I think it to be well founded in experience to question whether that which he esteems the least of the three is not really the best, and if that which he holds for the best is not the least. The reason is that the last cannot excite pity. A father wishes to kill his son without recognizing him, and regards him only as a stranger and perhaps as an enemy. Let him be accepted as one or the other, his peril is not worth any commiseration, according to Aristotle himself, and causes the audience to feel only a certain inner movement of trepidation, to fear that the son will perish before the error is discovered and to wish that it be discovered soon enough for him to escape from death: that which divides interest never prevents us from being interested in the fortune of a man virtuous enough to make himself loved; and when this recognition occurs, it produces only a sentiment of pleasure when we see happen the thing we have wished.

When this recognition is accomplished only after the death of a stranger, the pity excited by the sorrows of the one who causes him to be killed can have no great depth because it is deferred and is confined in the catastrophe; but when it concerns a discovered face, and they know by whom it is desired, the combat of passions contrary to nature, or of duty against love, occupies the best part of the poem; and from that, brings to birth great and powerful emotions, which renew themselves each moment and redouble the pity. To justify this reasoning by experience, we see that Chimène and Antiochus excite the audience more than does Oedipus in his own person. I say in his own person, because the entire poem excites them perhaps more than *Le Cid* or *Rodogune;* but it owes a part to Dircé, and that which she arouses is only pity borrowed from an episode.

I know that agnition [27] is a fine ornament in tragedies: Aristotle says so, but it is certain that it has its inconveniences. The Italians affect it in the greater part of their poems, and sometimes lose, by the attachment they have for it, many occasions for pathetic sentiments which would have considerable beauties. This manifests itself in *The Death of Crispian,* written by one of their best wits, Jean-Baptiste Ghirardelli, and printed at Rome in the year 1653.[28] The author was at pains to conceal his hero's birth from Constantin, and to make him solely a great captain, who is recognized as the son of Constantin only after the latter has had him put to death. This entire play is so full of wit and fine sentiments that it had enough success to oblige others to write against the author and to censure it as soon as it appeared. But how that birth, hidden without necessity, and contrary to the truth of a known history, has robbed him of finer things than the brilliant ones which he has scattered in his work! The pains, the confusion, the irresolutions, and the griefs of Constantin would have been different in pronouncing a stay of death for his son than for a soldier of fortune. The injustice of his preoccupation would have been more sensible to Crispian on the part of a father than on the part of a master; and the quality of the son, augmenting the grandeur of the crime which had been imposed on him, would at the same time have augmented the grief of seeing a father persuaded. Even Faust [29] would have had more internal struggle in undertaking an incest than in resolving on an adultery; his remorse would have been more living, and his despair more violent. The author has renounced all these advantages by having disdained to treat this subject as P. Stephonius, Jesuit,[30] treated it in our time, and as our Ancients have treated that of Hippolytus; and far from believing that he has elevated it to a type higher than those according to the thought of Aristotle, I am not sure that he has not made it fall below the level I have just named.

There is great probability that what this philosopher has said concerning the various degrees of perfection of tragedy had entire justification for his own time and in the presence of his compatriots; I do not wish to question it at all; but I cannot help saying that the taste of our century is not that of his on his preference of one type to the other, or at least that that which pleased his Athenians in the highest degree is not equally pleasing to us French; and I do not know any other method of finding my doubts supportable

and remaining completely in the veneration which we owe to all that he has written on poetry.

Before leaving this matter, let us examine his feeling on two questions touching these subjects between related people; the one, if the poet can invent them; the other, if he can change anything in those which he takes from history or fable.

For the first, it is unquestionable that the Ancients took so little liberty with history that they limited their tragedies to a few families because deeds of this kind occurred in so few families; that made this philosopher say that fortune furnished the subjects, not art.[31] I believe I said this in another discourse. It seems, however, that he accords poets full right to invention by these words: "They must use what they have received or invent it themselves." [32] These terms would decide the question if they were not so general; but as he has posed three kinds of tragedies, according to the varying times of recognition and the different methods of working, we can review all three to judge if it is not apropos to make some distinction which will restrain that liberty. I have given my opinion on it, however, very boldly, that it may not be imputed to me that I have contradicted Aristotle, provided that I have left completely some one of the three.

I think then in the first place that when it is proposed to have someone killed who is recognized, whether this is achieved or whether it is prevented, the author is not at liberty to invent the principal action, but ought to draw it from history or fable. These enterprises against blood relations are always so criminal and so contrary to nature that they are not credible unless supported by one or the other; and they never have the probability without which invented actions cannot be played.

I dare not decide upon the second type so absolutely. When a man takes up a quarrel with another, and having killed him, comes to recognize him for his father or for his brother and falls into despair, that can be only probable, and by consequence can be invented; however, this circumstance of killing one's father or one's brother without knowing him is so extraordinary and so shocking that we have the right to say that history cannot fail of remembering it when it happens among illustrious persons, and to refuse completely to believe it when history does not record it. The ancient theatre has furnished us only the example of Oedipus, and I do not remember having seen any other among our historians. I know that this event is better suited to fable than to history, and that by consequence, it may have been invented, at least in part, but the history and fable of antiquity have been so mixed that, to escape the danger of making a false distinction, we grant them equal authority in our theatres. It suffices that we invent nothing which is not probable, and when invented long

[27] *Agnition* means recognition. Corneille uses this word several times in this meaning, taking it from the Greek word, ἀναγνώρισις. The usual translation is *discovery.*

[28] Very little is known about Giovanni-Battista Filippo Ghirardelli. Voltaire mentions him in a note to this discourse. His only surviving work is a tragedy, *Il Costantino,* in prose.

[29] Corneille is referring to a French translation of *The History of the Damnable Life & Deserved Death of Dr. John Faustus* (1588–94). This work was first published in Paris, translated by Victor Palma Cayet, in 1592. Fifteen editions appeared in the next two hundred years.

[30] Corneille errs in his recording of this name. Bernardus Stephonius, a Jesuit, wrote a tragedy, *Crispus,* in 1634.

[31] "It was accident rather than art that led the poets in quest of subjects to embody this kind of incidents in their Plots."—Chap. 14, Bywater, p. 41.

[32] "In Tragedy . . . they still adhere to the historic names . . . and there are some without a single known name."—Chap. 9, Bywater, pp. 27–29. This is a bad misreading of Aristotle on Corneille's part, for Aristotle says several times that the poet should invent and change for the sake of probability and necessity.

since, it must be so well established in the consciousness of the audience that, on the stage, it does not shock the sight. All the *Metamorphoses* of Ovid are manifestly invention; we can draw from them the subjects of tragedy, but we may not invent on their models unless we take episodes of the same character. The reason is that while we can invent only that which is probable, and that these fabulous subjects, such as Andromeda and Phaeton, are not so at all, to invent these episodes is not so much to invent them as it is to add to those which have already been invented; and the episodes find a type of probability in their relation to the principal action, so that one can say that if this could have been done, it must have been done as the poet describes it.

Yet such episodes would not be proper to a historical subject or one of pure invention, because they lack that relation to the principal action and would be less probable than it is. The appearance of Venus and Eolus were well received in *Andromède;* [33] but if I had made Jupiter descend to reconcile Nicomède with his father, or Mercury reveal the conspiracy of Cinna to Augustus, I would have made all my audience revolt, and this miracle would have destroyed all the belief which the rest of the action had obtained. Denouements by gods from a machine are very frequent among the Greeks in tragedies which resemble histories and which are very probable, with that exception. Aristotle does not completely condemn them, and contents himself with preferring those denouements which come from the subject.[34] I do not know what decided the Athenians who were the judges, but the two examples I have just mentioned show sufficiently that it would be dangerous for us to imitate them in this sort of liberty. It has been said to me that these apparitions should not please us because we manifestly know their falsity, and that they would offend our religion, which was not the case among the Greeks. I admit that it is necessary to accommodate oneself to the customs of the audience, and so much the more to its credibility; but it must be conceded to me that we have at least as much faith in the apparition of angels and saints as the Ancients had in their Apollo and their Mercury; but would it be said that I should have used an angel to make Héraclius quarrel with Martian after the death of Phocas? The poem concerns Christians, and this apparition would have been as fitting there as the gods of antiquity were in those [plays] of the Greeks; it would have been, however, an infallible device for rendering the action ridiculous, and it is necessary only to have a little common sense to keep it in accord. Let me be permitted to say with Tacitus: *Non omnia apud priores meliora, sed nostra quoque aetas multa laudis et artium imitanda posteris tulit.*

I return to tragedies of the second type, where a person does not recognize a father or a son until after he has had him killed; and to conclude in two words after this digression, I would never condemn anyone for having invented it, but I have never allowed it for myself.

Those of the third type admit no difficulty; not only can they be invented, but everything is probable and follows the common manner of natural affections, but I suspect that to oblige poets to take their subjects from history would serve to ban them from the theatres. We do not see anything of that nature among the Greeks which has not the aspect of being invented by their authors. It may be that their story had already been taken from someone. I do not have eyes penetrating enough to pierce such thick obscurities and to determine if the *Iphigenia in Tauris* is the invention of Euripides as his *Helen* and his *Ion,* or if he has taken it from another; but I believe I may say that it is very difficult to find them in history, since such events occur only rarely, and since they do not have enough fame to merit a place. That of Theseus, recognized by the King of Athens, his father, at the time he was about to be killed, is the only one I can remember. Be that as it may, those who love to put them on the stage can invent them without fear of censure. They can thus produce some agreeable suspension in the understanding of the audience, but they need not hope to draw many tears.

The other question, whether it is permitted to change something in the subjects one has drawn from history or fable, seems to be decided in precise enough terms by Aristotle when he says, "that it is not permitted to change subjects as received, and that Clytemnestra ought not to be killed by another than Orestes, nor Eriphyle by another than Alcmeon." [35] This decision, however, is subject to some distinction and some tempering. It is an established fact that these circumstances, or if you like it better, the means of forwarding the action, remain in our power. History does not often note them, or reports them so little that it is necessary to supply them to fill out the poem; and there is the likelihood of presuming that the memory of the auditor, who has read these things elsewhere, will not have them so strongly in his mind that he will notice the change we have made and so accuse us of the sin; this he would not fail to do if he saw that we had changed the principal action. This falsification would cause him to have no faith in all the rest; as, on the contrary, he easily believes all the rest when he sees it lead to the result he knows to be true, when the history has left a strong impression upon him. The example of the death of Clytemnestra can serve to prove what I have just put forward. Sophocles and Euripides have both treated it, but each with a twist and a denouement completely different from the other, and it is this difference which keeps it from being the same play, even though it is the same subject whose principal action they have conserved. It is necessary to conserve this principal action as they did, but it is necessary at the same time to examine it to see if it is so painful or so difficult to represent that it can detract from the belief that the audience owes to the story and that they want to give to the fable by putting it in its place for those who have considered it true. When this inconvenience is to be feared, it is well to hide the outcome from sight, and to make it known by a recitation which shocks less than the spectacle and which impresses us more easily.

It is for this reason that Horace wished that Medea

---

[33] *Andromède* (1650).
[34] "The Denouement also should arise out of the plot itself, and not depend on stage-artifices, as in *Medea*."— Chap. 15, Bywater, p. 43.

[35] "The traditional stories, accordingly, must be kept as they are, e.g., the murder of Clytemnestra by Orestes and that of Eriphyla by Alcmeon." — Chap. 14, Bywater, p. 39.

had not killed her children and that Atreus had not roasted those of Thyestes in the sight of the audience.[36] The horror engenders a repugnance to believe these actions as well as the metamorphosis of Progne into a bird and of Cadmus into a serpent, of which the almost impossible representation excites the incredibility when it is hazarded before the eyes of the spectator:

Quodcumque ostendis mihi sic, incredulus odi.

I go on further, and to weaken or alleviate this dangerous horror in a historical action, I would make it happen without the participation of the protagonist, for whom we must always secure the favor of the audience. After Cléopâtre had killed Séleucus, she presented poison to her other son, Antiochus, on his return from the hunt, and this prince, suspecting what it was, constrained her to take it, and forced her to poison herself.[37] If I had made this action visible without changing it, I would have punished a parricide by another parricide; [38] the audience would have taken an aversion for Antiochus, and it was more pleasant to arrange it that she herself, seeing her shame and black perfidity about to be discovered, poisons herself in her despair, with the design of enveloping the two lovers in her ruin, in removing from them all occasion for caution. This creates two effects. The punishment of this pitiless mother presents a very strong example, because it demonstrates the justice of heaven and not the vengeance of men; on the other hand, Antiochus does not lose anything of the pity and friendly feeling we have for him, which increases more than it diminishes; and finally the action of the history is conserved in spite of the change, since Cléopâtre dies by the same poison which she presents to Antiochus.

Phocas was a tyrant, and slaying him was not a crime; however, it would doubtless have been more suitable to have it happen by the hand of Exupère than by that of Héraclius. We must take care to preserve our heroes from crime so long as it is possible and even to exempt them from drenching their hands in blood except in a just combat. I was very daring in *Nicomède:* Prusias, his father, wanted to have Nicomède assassinated in his army; according to the advice that the latter has had from the assassins themselves, he enters his father's kingdom, seizes it, and compels his unfortunate father to hide in a cavern where the son kills him. I have not pushed history up to that point; and after having drawn Nicomède as too virtuous to indulge in parricide, I believed that I could content myself with making him master for life of those who had persecuted him, without carrying the matter any further.

I would not hide a refinement which I made in the death of Clytemnestra,[39] whom Aristotle proposes to us as an example whose actions ought not to be changed. I believe indeed, with him, that she must die only at the hand of her son Orestes, but I cannot suffer with Sophocles that this son has formed the design of stabbing her while she is on her knees before

him and imploring him to let her live. I cannot even pardon Electra, who passes for oppressed virtue in the rest of the play, for the inhumanity with which she encourages her brother in this matricide. He is a son who avenges his father, but it is on his mother that he avenges him. Séleucus and Antiochus have as much right to do the same thing in *Rodogune;* but I did not dare give them the least thought of it. Also, our maxim of making protagonists loved was not the usage of the Ancients; these republicans had such a strong hatred of kings that they witnessed with pleasure the crimes committed by the most innocent of their breed. To correct this subject to our fashion, it is necessary that Orestes have a plot only against Ægisthus; that a remnant of respectful tenderness toward his mother makes him leave her punishment to God; that this queen insist on protecting her lover, and that she thrust herself between him and her son in so unfortunate a manner that she receive the blow which the prince meant to deal to the assassin of his father. Thus she perishes by the hand of her son as Aristotle wishes it, without the barbarity of Orestes filling us with horror as in Sophocles, nor does his action require the vengeful furies to torment him, since he remains innocent.

Aristotle himself authorizes us to work in this manner when he teaches us that "the poet is not obliged to treat things as they happen, but as they could or may have happened, according to probability or necessity." [40] He often repeats these last words and never explains them. I have tried to supply this explanation as best I can, and I hope I will be forgiven if I am mistaken.

I say first that this liberty which he allows us of embellishing historical actions by probabilities [41] does not bestow upon us any defense for setting aside probability when we are in distress. It is a privilege he gives us, and not a servitude he imposes upon us. That is clear from his own words. If we can treat things according to probability or according to necessity, we can leave probability to follow necessity; and this alternative supplies the choice of serving that of the two which we judge the more fitting.

This liberty of the poet is found again in more precise terms in the twenty-fifth chapter, which contains the excuses, or rather justifications, he provides against censure. "It is necessary," he says, "that the poet follow one of the three ways of treating things, and that he represent them as they were, or as it is said they were, or as they ought to have been"; [42] by which he gives the poet the choice either of true history, or of the common opinion on which the fable is founded, or of the probability. He adds then: "If a poet is charged that he has not written things according to truth, let him answer that he has written things as they ought to have been; if they impute to him that

---

[36] Horace, *Ars poetica,* ll. 182–87.
[37] *Rodogune.*
[38] Corneille obviously uses this word to mean any killing of any relative.
[39] *Oreste* (1659).

[40] "From what we have said, it will be seen that the poet's function is to describe, not the thing that has happened, but a kind of thing that might happen, i.e., what is possible as being probable or necessary."—Chap. 9, Bywater, p. 27.
[41] See note 1, above.
[42] "The poet . . . must necessarily in all instances represent things in one or other of three aspects, either as they were or are, or as they are said or thought to be or to have been, or as they ought to be."—Chap. 25, Bywater, p. 81.

he has done neither the one nor the other, let him defend himself on that which is common public opinion, as they have been told of the gods, of which a great deal is not probable." [43] And a little further down, "Often it is better that these things should not be made to happen as they have been described, even though they have happened effectively in that manner," [44] and by consequence, such an alteration is beyond fault. This last passage shows that we are not obliged to set aside truth to give a better form to the actions of tragedy by ornaments of probability, and it shows all the more strongly that it can be taken for granted, according to the second of these three passages, that common opinion suffices to justify us when we do not have the truth, and that we can make some improvement in what we write if we seek for the beauties of this probability. We run by this some risk of a lesser success; but we sin only against the care which we owe to our reputations, and not against the Rules of the theatre.

I will make a second remark on these terms, probability and necessity, whose order is often found reversed in this philosopher, who often says, "according to necessity or probability," and sometimes "according to probability and necessity." From which I draw an inference that there are occasions when probability is to be preferred to necessity, and others when necessity is to be preferred to probability. The reason is that when we employ the latter of these alternative propositions, it is used as a makeshift with which we are forced to content ourselves when we cannot arrive at the other, and that we must make an effort at the first before being reduced to the second, to which we have the right to recourse only in default of the first.

To clarify this mutual preference for probability to necessity, and for necessity to probability, we must distinguish two things in the actions which make up a tragedy. The first consists of these actions in themselves together with the inseparable circumstances of time and place; the other in their mutual relationship, which makes the one give birth to the other. In the first, probability is to be preferred to necessity; and necessity to probability in the second.

We must place the actions where it is easier and more fitting that they should happen, and make them take place at a reasonable leisure, without accelerating them extraordinarily unless the necessity of confining them to one place and within one day obliges us to do so. I have already made it clear in another Discourse that to conserve the unity of place we often make people who would probably converse in a room talk in a public place; that if the things I have set forth in *Le Cid,* in *Polyeucte,* in *Pompée,* or in *le Menteur* [45] were told in a romance, a little more than one day would have been given to prolong the difficulty. The obeisance which we owe to the Rules of

the Unity of Time and Place exempts us sometimes from probability, even though it does not permit us the impossible; but we do not always fall into that necessity; and *La Suivante,* [46] *Cinna, Théodore,* and *Nicomède* have no need of dispensing with probability in time as do these other poems.

This reduction of tragedy to romance [47] is the touchstone for disentangling necessary actions from probable ones. We are limited in the theatre by place, by time, and by the difficulties of the representation, which entirely prevent us from exposing to sight many persons lest they remain without action, or hamper the action of the others. A romance has none of these constraints: it gives the actions which it describes all the leisure necessary for enactment; it places speaker, doer, or dreamer, in a room, in a forest, in a public place—wherever is most appropriate for the particular action; it has an entire palace, an entire city, an entire realm, all the world, where they may perform; and if something happens or is told in the presence of thirty people, the author can describe the various opinions one after the other. It is for this reason that he has no liberty whatever to depart from probability, because he has no legitimate reason or excuse for giving it up.

As the theatre leaves us little facility to reduce everything to probability, because nothing is made known to us except by characters put before us briefly, it exempts us from probability that much more easily. One can maintain that it does not so much exempt as permit us a larger probability; but since Aristotle authorizes us to treat things according to necessity, I would rather say that whatever happens in a way different from the way it happens in a romance, even though well done, has no probability and ought to be counted among necessary actions.

Horace can furnish us several examples of this: the unity of place is exact. Everything takes place in a room. But if we were to write a romance with the same particulars from scene to scene which I have employed, would we make everything transpire in that room? At the end of the first act, Curiace and Camille, his mistress, wish to rejoin the rest of the family, who must be in another room; between the two acts, they receive the news of the election of the three Horaces; at the beginning of the second, Curiace appears in that same room to congratulate them. In the romance, the author would have had these congratulations given in the same place that the news was received, in the presence of all the family; it is not probable that these two would withdraw for their rejoicing, but it is necessary for the theatre; and at least for presenting the sentiments of the three Horaces, of their father, of their sister, of Curiace, and of Sabine, they must all appear together. Romance, which makes nothing visible, easily arrives at the goal; but on the stage, it is necessary to separate the family, to put them in some order and take them one after the other, and to commence with these two, whom I was forced to place in that room at the expense of probability. That having happened, the remainder of the act is completely probable, and nothing need take place in a manner different from the

[43] "If the poet's description be criticised as not true to fact, one may urge perhaps that the object ought to be as described. . . . If the description, however, be neither true nor of the thing as it ought to be, the answer must be then, that it is in accordance with opinion."—Chap. 25, Bywater, p. 83.

[44] "Of other statements in poetry one may perhaps say, not that they are better than the truth, but that the fact was so at the time."—Chap. 25, Bywater, p. 83.

[45] *Le Menteur* (1643).

[46] *La Suivante* (1637).

[47] The French word is *roman,* which usually means *novel* today, but romance is used here as more descriptive of the kind of work Corneille is describing.

romance. At the end of this act, Sabine and Camille, beside themselves with sorrow, retire from that room in a transport of grief; with probability, they would confine their tears to their room, where the romance makes them remain to receive the news of the battle. However, because of the necessity of having the spectators see these things, Sabine leaves her room at the beginning of the third act and continues to display her sad uneasiness in that room where Camille has found her. After that, the remainder of the act is as probable as the other; and if you wanted to examine the first scenes of the last two with this rigor, you would, perhaps, find the same thing—that if they had once gone out, as they leave at the end of each act, the characters would have been shown in romance elsewhere than in that room.

These examples suffice to explain how an actior can be treated according to necessity when it cannot be treated according to probability—which ought always to be preferred to necessity when one considers only the actions themselves.

The connection [48] which makes the one come from the other does not work that way; necessity is, in this case, to be preferred to probability, not that this connection ought not always to be probable, but because it is much better that it be probable and necessary together. The reason for this is easy to conceive. When the connection is only probable without being necessary, the poem can get by with it and it is of no great importance; but when it is probable and necessary, it must be an essential part of the poem, which cannot otherwise exist. You will find in *Cinna* examples of these two kinds of connections: I call this the manner with which one action is produced by another. His conspiracy against Auguste is caused necessarily by the love which he has for Émilie, because he wishes to marry her, and because she will not give herself to him except on that condition. Of these two actions one is true, the other is probable, and their connection is necessary. The benevolence of Auguste gives remorse and irresolution to Cinna: this remorse and irresolution are made to appear probable only by this benevolence, and have a connection with it that is probable only because Cinna can remain firm and arrive at his goal, which is to marry Émilie. He consults her in his irresolution: this consultation is only probable, but it is a necessary effect of his love, because if he had broken off the conspiracy without her consent, he would never have arrived at the goal which he had set for himself, and by consequence there is a necessary connection between two probable actions, or, if you prefer, a necessary creation of a probable action by another equally probable one.

Before coming to definitions and divisions of probability and necessity, I think again of the actions which compose tragedy, and I find that we can set off three kinds: some follow history; others interpolate history; the third falsify history. The first are true, the second sometimes probable and sometimes necessary, and the last must always be necessary.

When they are true, it is not necessary to take any

pains with probability; they have no need of our help. "All that has happened is manifestly possible," says Aristotle, "because if it could not have happened, it would not have happened." [49] That which we interpolate into history, when it is not approved by this authority, has not this prerogative.

"We have a natural propensity," this philosopher goes on to say, "to believe that what has not happened could not have happened"; [50] and it is because of this that we invent a need of a probability more exact than is required to make it credible.

To weigh these two passages well, I believe that I am not violating his thought in the least when I dare say in definition of probability, that it is a thing manifestly possible with propriety, and that it is neither manifestly true nor manifestly false. We can make two divisions, the one of general and particular probability, and the other of ordinary and extraordinary.

General probability is that which is possible and can be rightly done by a king, a general of an army, a lover, an ambitious person, and so on. The particular is that which can or ought to be done by Alexander, Caesar, Alcibiades, compatible with what history tells us of their actions. Thus everything that violates history departs from this probability because it is manifestly false; and it is not probable that Caesar, after the battle of Pharsalia, should remain in good favor with Pompey, or Augustus with Antony after that of Actium, even though, to speak in general terms, it is probable that after a great battle in a civil war the heads of the opposing parties would be reconciled to each other, principally because they are both generous.

This manifest falsity, which destroys probability, can even be encountered in plays which are completely invented. We can falsify history because it has no communication with us, but there are circumstances, times, and places which can convict an author of falsity when he is gross in his violations. If I introduced a king of France or of Spain under an imaginary name, and if I chose for the time of my action a century of history for which we know the true kings of these two countries, the falsity would be apparent; and it would be even more obvious if I were to place Rome two leagues from Paris so that it would be possible to go there and return in the same day. These are the things over which the poet has no right. He can take some license with history, even regarding particular actions, as those of Caesar or Augustus, and attribute to them actions which they have not performed, or have things happen in a way that they did not do them; but he cannot confuse chronology to make Alexander live in the time of Caesar, and even less can he change the location of places, or the names of kingdoms, provinces, cities, mountains, and notable rivers. The reason is that these provinces, these mountains, these rivers, are permanent things. What we know of their situation was so at the beginning of the world; we can presume that they have not changed—at least if they have,

[48] The French word is *liaison*. Dryden uses it without translation. It means the continuity of the action. *Liaison des scènes* refers to the device used so that the stage was never empty. At least one person of a scene would remain to be a character in the next. Cf. Dryden's *Essay of Dramatic Poesy*, pp. 53, 58–59.

[49] ". . . that which has happened is manifestly possible, else it would not have come to pass."—Chap. 9, Bywater, p. 29.

[50] ". . . we are not yet sure as to the possibility of that which has not happened. . . ."—Chap. 9, Bywater, p. 29.

that history has noted it—and geography teaches us all the ancient and modern names. Thus a man would be ridiculed for imagining that, in the time of Abraham, Paris was at the foot of the Alps, or that the Seine crossed Spain, and for mixing like grotesque things in an invented play. But history is those things which happen and which succeed each other, each only a moment in duration; and many of these moments escape the knowledge of those who write history. Also we cannot show any history which contains all that happened in the places mentioned, nor all that was done by those whose lives it describes. I do not even except the *Commentaries* of Caesar, who wrote his own history and must have know it completely. We know what countries the Rhone and the Seine flowed through before he went among the Gauls; but we do not know very much, and perhaps nothing at all, of the things that happened there before his arrival. Thus we can indeed place those actions which we pretend took place before that time, but not, under the pretext of poetic fiction and remoteness of the times, change there the natural distance of one place from another. This is the system which Barclay has used in his *Argenis* [51] in which he names no city or river of Sicily, or of our provinces, except by its true name, even though all the persons which he places on his tapestry, and their actions, are entirely his invention.

Aristotle seems most indulgent on this subject even though he finds "the poet inexcusable who sins against another art than his, as against medicine or astrology." To which I answer, "he is excusable only under this condition, that he arrives thereby at the goal of his own art, at which he cannot arrive otherwise"; also he goes on to say, "that he sins in that case, and it is better not to sin at all." [52] For my own part, if it is necessary to receive this excuse, I would make a distinction between the arts which can be ignored without shame (because the occasions when it is necessary to speak of them in the theatre happen so rarely), those such as medicine and astrology, which I have just named, and the arts without whose complete or partial cognizance the dramatists cannot establish truth in the play, such as geography and chronology. As he does not know how to represent any action without placing it in some place and in some time, it is inexcusable to make his ignorance

apparent in the choice of this place and this time.

I will go on to the other division of probability, ordinary and extraordinary: the ordinary is an action which happens often, or at least as often as its opposite; the extraordinary is an action which happens, in truth, less often than its opposite, but does not fail of having its possibility feasible enough so as not to approach either the miraculous or those rare events which serve as material for bloody tragedies, because of the support they have in history and common opinion, and which can offer an example only for those events which they embody, because they are not believable without having this support. Aristotle gives two ideas or general examples of this extraordinary probability: the one of a subtle and adroit man who finds himself deceived by one less subtle than he; the other of a weak man who fights against one stronger than he and who gains the victory,[53] which never fails to be well received when the cause of the simpler or the weaker is the more just. It then seems that the justice of heaven has presided at the success, which finds, accordingly, a much easier belief and satisfies the sympathies of the audience, who always take the part of those whose conduct is the better. Thus the victory of the Cid against the Count is found in this extraordinary probability, though it ought not to be true. "It is probable," says our teacher, "that many things may take place against probability"; [54] and since he thus acknowledges that these extraordinary effects happen against probability, I prefer to call them simply believable and to place them under necessity, expecting that they never be used without necessity.

It can be objected that the same philosopher says "that in regard to poetry, the believable impossible ought to be preferred to the incredible possible," [55] and a critic may conclude thereby that I have little reason for requiring the probable, by the definition which I have just made, when it is manifestly possible for it to be believable, since, according to Aristotle, there are impossible things which are believable.

To resolve this difficulty, and to discover the nature of this impossible-believable, which he does not illustrate, I answer that there are things impossible in themselves which, when looked at in another manner, appear easily possible, and by consequence, believable. These are all those cases wherein we falsify history. It is impossible that they could have happened as we represent them, because they happened otherwise and because it is not in the power of God Himself to change anything which has happened; but they appear manifestly possible when they are within general probability, provided that we look at them detached from history, wishing to forget for the time that history has said the opposite from our invention. All that transpires in *Nicomède* is impossible because

---

[51] The *Argenis* is an allegorical romance written by John Barclay (1582–1621) dealing with the dangers of political intrigue.

[52] "There is, however, within the limits of poetry itself a possibility of two kinds of error, the one directly, the other only accidentally connected with the art. If the poet meant to describe the thing correctly, and failed through lack of power of expression, his art itself is at fault. But if it was through his having meant to describe it in some incorrect way (e.g. to make the horse in movement have both right legs thrown forward) that the technical error (one in a matter of, say, medicine or some other special science, or impossibilities of whatever kind they may be), have got into his description, his error in that case is not in the essentials of the poetic art.

"If, however, the poetic end might have been as well or better attained without sacrifice of technical correctness in such matters, the impossibility is not to be justified, since the description should be, if it can, entirely free from error."—Chap. 25, Bywater, p. 55.

[53] "Yet in their Peripeties, as also in their simple plots, the poets I mean show wonderful skill in aiming at the kind of effect they desire—a tragic situation that arouses the human feeling in one, like the clever villain (e.g. Sisyphus) deceived, or the brave wrongdoer worsted."—Chap. 18, Bywater, p. 55.

[54] ". . . there is a probability of things happening against probability."—Chap. 25, Bywater, p. 87.

[55] "For the purposes of poetry, a convincing impossibility is preferable to an unconvincing possibility."—Chap. 25, Bywater, p. 87.

history tells us that he had his father killed without seeing him, and that his brothers of the second marriage were hostages in Rome while he seized the kingdom. All that happens in *Héraclius* is not less so, because he was not the son of Maurice, and even though he had long passed for that of Phocas, and was brought up as such by that tyrant, he comes to overwhelm him by force from the shores of Africa, of which he was governor, and which he perhaps never saw. Nevertheless, we do not consider the incidents of these two tragedies unbelievable; and those who know the departure from history disregard the departure and are pleased at these productions, because they have general probability even though they lack the particular.

All that fable tells us of the gods and their metamorphoses is again impossible and is not allowed by common opinion to be believable, but by this old tradition we have been accustomed to hear them spoken. We even have the right to invent on this model and to join incidents equally impossible to those which the ancient errors have lent us. The hearer is not deceived in his expectations when the title of the poem prepares him to see nothing but the impossible; he finds all completely believable; and, granting this first premise that these are the gods and that they take an interest in and have business with humans, by which all is resolved, he has no difficulty in persuading himself of the remainder.

After having attempted to explain what probability is, it is time that I hazarded a definition of necessity, of which Aristotle speaks so much and which alone authorizes us to change history and exempts us from probability. I say then that necessity, as regards poetry, is nothing other than "the need of the poet to arrive at his goal or to make his actors get there." This definition has its foundation in the diverse interpretations of the Greek word ἀναγχαῖν, which does not always signify that which is absolutely necessary, but also sometimes that which is only useful to bring about something.

The goal of the actors is diverse, according to the varying designs which the variety of subjects gives them. A lover has that of possessing his mistress; an ambitious person, that of seizing a crown; a wronged man, of revenging himself; and so on. The things they must do to bring these ends about constitute the necessity which must be preferred to probability, or to speak more justly, which must be added to probability in the connection of the actions and their dependence on each other. I think that I have already explained myself enough on that above; I will say no more.

The goal of the poet is to please according to the rules of his art. To please, he sometimes has need to heighten the splendor of good actions, and to lessen the horror of disastrous ones. These are the necessities of embellishment when he can violate *particular* probability by some alteration in history, but can only rarely dispense with the *general,* and for things which are of the greatest beauty and so brilliant that they dazzle. Above all, he must not push them beyond extraordinary probability because these ornaments which he adds to his invention are not an absolute necessity, and he does better to give them up entirely than to make his poem appear against every sort of probability. To please according to the rules

of his art, he has need to confine his action to the unities of time and place; and as that is an absolute and indispensable necessity, he is permitted more for these two articles than for embellishments.

It is so difficult to find in history or in the imagination of men enough of these events, both illustrious and worthy of tragedy, in which the deliberation and the execution can happen in the same place and on the same day without doing a little violence to the common order of things, that I believe this kind of violence cannot be completely damnable, provided it does not extend to the impossible. There are fine subjects where it cannot be avoided, and a scrupulous author would deprive himself of a fine occasion of glory and the public of much satisfaction if, out of fear of seeing himself forced to make something happen more quickly than probability would permit, he did not venture to put them in the theatre. I would give him in that case advice which perhaps he would find salutary: that is, to prefix no specific time to his poem, and no set place in the location of his actors. The imagination of the audience has greater liberty to go along with the action if it is not fixed by these marks, and the audience would not notice the rapidity of the action if not reminded of it, and thus in spite of itself, the audience would not apply its own knowledge. I have always repented having made the King in *Le Cid* say that he wished Rodrigue would wait an hour or two after having defeated the Moors before fighting Don Sanche: I have thus emphasized that the play takes place in twenty-four hours, and this serves only to advertise to the spectators the difficulties I had in reducing the action to that limit. If I had resolved the conflict without designation of the hour, perhaps they would not have noticed.

I do not think that in comedy the poet is free to compress his action under the necessity of reducing it to the Unity of Time. Aristotle desires that all the actions which go on there be made entirely probable,[56] and does not add the phrase, "or necessary," as for tragedy. Moreover, there is a very great difference between the actions of one and those of the other. Those of comedy show ordinary persons [57] and consist only in intrigues of love and in deceits which develop easily in a day, and very often in Plautus and Terence the time of their duration scarcely exceeds that of their representation; but in tragedy, public affairs are ordinarily combined with the particular interests of the illustrious persons who are made to appear; great battles take place, the capture of cities, great perils, revolutions of states; and all this ill befits the speed which the Rule obliges us to give to what passes on the stage.

If you were to ask me where to extend this liberty of a poet to go against truth and against probability by consideration of his need, I would have trouble in giving you a precise answer. I have made it apparent that there are things over which we have no rights; and for those to which this privilege may apply, it

[56] "It is only when their plot is already made up of probable incidents that they give it a basis of proper names instead of writing like the old iambic poets about particular persons."—Chap. 9, Bywater, p. 27.

[57] The old commonplace Renaissance distinction between tragedy and comedy. Corneille attacks this idea in his preface to *Don Sanche d'Aragon* (1650), which is a court comedy.

must be more or less reserved according to how well or how little known the subjects are. It is much less permissible in *Horace* and in *Pompée*,[58] of whose history no one is ignorant, than in *Rodogune* and in *Nicomède*, whose names few people knew before I put them into the theatre. The sole rule which can be drawn is that all that is added to history, and all that is changed, should be no more incredible than that which is conserved in the same poem. It is thus that we must understand the verse of Horace touching the fabrication of ornament:

Ficta voluptatis causa sint proxima veris,

and cannot, outside of the subject which he treats, carry the significance of those for which some example can be opened in history or in fable. The same Horace decides the question, in so far as it can be decided, by this other verse with which I finish this discourse:

. . . Dabiturque licentia sumpta pudenter.

Let us furnish it then with discretion, but without qualms; and if possible, let us not furnish it at all; it is more worthy not to have need of grace than to receive it.

MOLIÈRE (1622–1673)

Rarely given to theorizing about his work, Molière was provoked into a reply when his *Tartuffe* was attacked on the grounds of being blasphemous and antireligious. Since the hypocrisy behind the attack was of the very same type that he had satirized in the play, he was able to draw an unusually clear connection between the relationship of drama to life and to underscore his assertion of the moral function of comedy. The Preface is translated by Henri Van Laun.

Preface to *Tartuffe* (1669)

This is a comedy about which there has been a great deal of noise, which has been for a long time persecuted; and the people whom it holds up have well shown that they are the most powerful in France of all those whom I have hitherto portrayed. The marquises, the blue stockings, the cuckolds and the doctors, have quietly suffered themselves to be represented, and have pretended to be amused, in common with all the world, at the sketches which I have made of them; but the hypocrites have not taken the joke. At first they were somewhat amazed, and found it strange that I should have had the presumption to make free with their grimaces, and wish to decry a trade much indulged in by honest people. It is a crime which they could not pardon me, and they

have all risen up in arms against my comedy with a terrible fury. They took particular care not to attack it from the point of view where it wounded them— they have too much policy for that, and are too knowing to lay bare the bottoms of their hearts. In accordance with their laudable customs, they have concealed their interest beneath the cloak of God's cause; and to listen to them, *The Tartuffe* is a piece that offends piety. It is, from beginning to end, full of abominations, and nothing is found in it but what deserves the fire. Every syllable in it is impious; the gesticulations themselves are criminal; and the least glance of the eye, the slightest shake of the head, the smallest step to the right or left, conceal mysteries which they find means to explain to my disadvantage.

Of little avail was it to submit it to the criticism of my friends, and to the censorship of the public; the corrections which I have made, the judgment of the King and the Queen, who have seen it; the approbation of the great princes and gerous by introducing them on the stage; that they are likely to receive any authority from the lips of a scoundrel? There is not the least indication of that; and one ought to approve the comedy of *Tartuffe,* or condemn all comedies wholesale.

It is that which people have attacked furiously of late; and never has the stage been so fiercely tilted at. I cannot deny that there have been Fathers of the Church who have condemned comedy; but neither can it be denied to me that there have been some who have treated it more leniently. Thus the authority upon which people seek to found their censorship is destroyed by this division; and all that can be deduced from this diversity of opinions in equally enlightened minds, is that they have regarded comedy from a different point of view, and that while some have looked at it in its purifying influence, others have considered it in its corrupting tendency, and confounded it with those vile spectacles, rightly named exhibitions of turpitude.

And in fact, since we have to argue upon things, and not upon words; and that the majority of contradictions cannot well be reconciled, and that the same word often envelops two opposite meanings, we have but to lift the veil of the equivocal, and to look what comedy is in itself, to see whether it is to be condemned. It is, doubtless, well known that, being nothing else but an ingenious poem, which, by its agreeable teaching, seeks to point out the faults of mankind, it does not deserve to be so unjustly censured; and if we may listen on that point to the testimony of antiquity, it will tell us that her most famous philosophers have eulogised comedy; they who professed such austere wisdom, and who were incessantly decrying the vices of their age. It will show us that Aristotle devoted many of his vigils to the theatre, and took the trouble to reduce to precept the art of constructing comedies. It will teach us that her greatest men, foremost in dignity, have gloried in composing some themselves; that there were others who did not disdain to recite in public those which they had composed; that Greece proclaimed her appreciation of that art by the glorious prizes she awarded to, and the magnificent theatres she built in honour of it; and lastly, that in Rome this same art was crowned with extraordinary honours. I do not say in debauched Rome, under the licentious emperors, but in disci-

---

[58] *Le Morte de Pompée* by Corneille (1633–34).

plined Rome, under the wisdom of her consuls, and at the most vigorous period of Roman virtue.

I admit that there have been times in which comedy became corrupt. And what is there in this world that does not become corrupt every day? There is nothing so pure but what mankind can bring crime to bear upon it; no art so salutary but what they can reverse its intentions; nothing so good in itself but what they can turn to a bad use. Medicine is a profitable art, and every one esteems it as one of the most excellent things in existence; and yet there have been periods in which it has made itself odious, and has often been used to poison people. Philosophy is a gift of Heaven; it was given to us to lead our minds to the knowledge of God by the contemplation of nature's wonders; still we are not unaware that it has often been diverted from its use, and employed openly to support impiety. Even the most sacred things are not safe from men's corruption; and we see the greatest scoundrels daily abusing piety, and wickedly making it the tool for the most abominable crimes. But for all that, we do not fail to make those distinctions which it is right we should make. We do not envelop in the same warp of a false deduction the good of the thing corrupted with the malice of the corrupter. We always separate the bad use from the honest intention of art, and no more than we would dream of defending the banishment of medicine from Rome, or the public condemnation of philosophy at Athens, ought we to put a veto upon comedy for having been censured at certain times. This censuring had its reasons which have no existence here. It confined itself strictly to what it saw; and we ought, therefore, not to drag it beyond the limits which it has adopted, extend it farther than necessary, or make it class the guilty with the innocent. The comedy which it designed to attack is not at all the comedy which we wish to defend. We must take good care not to confound the one with the other. They are two persons whose morals are totally opposed. They bear no relation to each other except the resemblance of the name; and it would be a crying injustice to wish to condemn Olympia, who is an honest woman, because there was another Olympia, who was a loose character.[1] Such verdicts would, doubtless, produce a great disorder in the world. Everything would be open to condemnation; and, since this rigour is not carried out with reference to all other things which are daily abused, we ought to extend the same grace to comedy, and approve those plays in which instruction and honesty are made manifest.

I am well aware that there are certain minds whose delicacy can tolerate no comedy whatsoever; who say that the most honest ones are the most dangerous; that the passions which they depict are so much the more touching because they are full of virtue; and that people are too much affected by this kind of representations. I do not see any great crime in becoming affected at the sight of an honourable passion: or that the complete state of insensibility to which they

would elevate our feelings would indicate a high standard of virtue. I am inclined to doubt whether such great perfection be in the power of human nature, and whether it would not be better to endeavour to rectify and mollify men's passions, than to eliminate them altogether. I admit that there are places which it would be more salutary to frequent than theatres; and if we take it for granted that all things that do not directly concern God and our salvation are reprehensible, then it becomes certain that comedy should be one of them, and I for one could not object that it should be condemned among the rest. But let us suppose, as it is true, that there must be intervals to pious devotions, and that we have need of amusement during that time, then I maintain that nothing more innocent than comedy could be found. I have digressed too far. Let me wind up with the remark of a great prince [2] on the comedy of *Tartuffe*. A week after it had been forbidden, there was performed before the court a piece entitled *Scaramouch a hermit*,[3] and the King, coming out of the theatre, said to the prince of whom I have just spoken, "I should like to know why the people, who are so very much shocked at the comedy of Molière, do not say a word about *Scaramouch*," to which the prince answered, "The reason of that is, that the comedy of *Scaramouch* makes game of Heaven and religion, about which these gentlemen care very little; but Molière's makes game of them; it is that which they cannot tolerate."

DAVID HUME

(1711–1776)

Consistent with the philosophical empiricism with which he is associated, David Hume's *Of Tragedy* is oriented in terms of the psychology of the audience. In focusing on one's reaction to tragedy, he is careful to choose examples from real life and to see in the tragic experience the same conditions that exist in ordinary experience.

Of Tragedy
[1757]

It seems an unaccountable pleasure, which the spectators of a well-written tragedy receive from sorrow, terror, anxiety, and other passions, that are in themselves disagreeable and uneasy. The more they are touched and affected, the more are they de-

---

[1] It has been said that Molière, in mentioning the name of Olympia, wished to hit at Olympia Maldachini, a sister-in-law of Pope Innocent X. This Pope died in 1655, and was the author of the bull against the five propositions of Jansenius. The life of the lady, who was far from a saint, had only lately been translated from the Italian into French.

[2] The Prince de Condé.

[3] The farce of *Scaramouch a hermit* contained many indecent situations; amongst others, that of a monk entering by the balcony into the house of a married woman, and reappearing from time to time before the public, saying, *"Questo e per morti ficar la carne."*

lighted with the spectacle; and as soon as the uneasy passions cease to operate, the piece is at an end. One scene of full joy and contentment and security is the utmost that any composition of this kind can bear; and it is sure always to be the concluding one. If, in the texture of the piece, there be interwoven any scenes of satisfaction, they afford only faint gleams of pleasure, which are thrown in by way of variety, and in order to plunge the actors into deeper distress by means of that contrast and disappointment. The whole art of the poet is employed in rousing and supporting the compassion and indignation, the anxiety and resentment of his audience. They are pleased in proportion as they are afflicted and never are so happy as when they employ tears, sobs, and cries to give vent to their sorrow and relieve their heart, swollen with the tenderest sympathy and compassion.

The few critics who have had some tincture of philosophy have remarked this singular phenomenon and have endeavored to account for it.

L'Abbé Du Bos, in his reflections on poetry and painting, asserts that nothing is in general so disagreeable to the mind as the languid, listless state of indolence into which it falls upon the removal of all passion and occupation.[1] To get rid of this painful situation, it seeks every amusement and pursuit; business, gaming, shows, executions; whatever will rouse the passions and take its attention from itself. No matter what the passion is: let it be disagreeable, afflicting, melancholy, disordered; it is still better than that insipid languor which arises from perfect tranquillity and repose.

It is impossible not to admit this account as being, at least in part, satisfactory. You may observe, when there are several tables of gaming, that all the company run to those where the deepest play is, even though they find not there the best players. The view, or at least imagination, of high passions arising from great loss or gain affects the spectator by sympathy, gives him some touches of the same passions, and serves him for a momentary entertainment. It makes the time pass the easier with him and is some relief to that oppression under which men commonly labour when left entirely to their own thoughts and meditations.

We find that common liars always magnify, in their narrations, all kinds of danger, pain, distress, sickness, deaths, murders, and cruelties; as well as joy, beauty, mirth, and magnificence. It is an absurd secret which they have for pleasing their company, fixing their attention, and attaching them to such marvellous relations by the passions and emotions which they excite.

There is, however, a difficulty in applying to the present subject, in its full extent, this solution, however ingenious and satisfactory it may appear. It is certain that the same object of distress which pleases in a tragedy, were it really set before us, would give the most unfeigned uneasiness, though it be then the most effectual cure for languor and indolence. Monsieur Fontenelle seems to have been sensible of this difficulty and accordingly attempts another solution of the phenomenon, at least makes some addition to the theory above mentioned.[2]

[1] See Du Bos, p. 253.
[2] *Refléxions sur la poétique* [see p. 289].

"Pleasure and pain," says he, "which are two sentiments so different in themselves, differ not so much in their cause. From the instance of tickling, it appears that the movement of pleasure pushed a little too far becomes pain, and that the movement of pain a little moderated becomes pleasure. Hence it proceeds that there is such a thing as a sorrow soft and agreeable: it is a pain weakened and diminished. The heart likes naturally to be moved and affected. Melancholy objects suit it, and even disastrous and sorrowful, provided they are softened by some circumstance. It is certain that, on the theatre, the representation has almost the effect of reality; yet it has not altogether that effect. However we may be hurried away by the spectacle, whatever dominion the senses and imagination may usurp over the reason, there still lurks at the bottom a certain idea of falsehood in the whole of what we see. This idea, though weak and disguised, suffices to diminish the pain which we suffer from the misfortunes of those whom we love, and to reduce that affliction to such a pitch as converts it into a pleasure. We weep for the misfortune of a hero to whom we are attached. In the same instant we comfort ourselves by reflecting that it is nothing but a fiction. And it is precisely that mixture of sentiments, which composes an agreeable sorrow, and tears that delight us. But as that affliction which is caused by exterior and sensible objects is stronger than the consolation which arises from an internal reflection, they are the effects and symptoms of sorrow that ought to predominate in the composition."

This solution seems just and convincing, but perhaps it wants still some new addition in order to make it answer fully the phenomenon which we here examine. All the passions, excited by eloquence, are agreeable in the highest degree, as well as those which are moved by painting and the theatre. The epilogues of Cicero are, on this account chiefly, the delight of every reader of taste, and it is difficult to read some of them without the deepest sympathy and sorrow. His merit as an orator no doubt depends much on his success in this particular. When he had raised tears in his judges and all his audience, they were then the most highly delighted and expressed the greatest satisfaction with the pleader. The pathetic description of the butchery made by Verres of the Sicilian captains is a masterpiece of this kind. But I believe none will affirm that the being present at a melancholy scene of that nature would afford any entertainment. Neither is the sorrow here softened by fiction, for the audience were convinced of the reality of every circumstance. What is it then which in this case raises a pleasure from the bosom of uneasiness, so to speak, and a pleasure which still retains all the features and outward symptoms of distress and sorrow?

I answer: this extraordinary effect proceeds from that very eloquence with which the melancholy scene is represented. The genius required to paint objects in a lively manner, the art employed in collecting all the pathetic circumstances, the judgment displayed in disposing them: the exercise, I say, of these noble talents, together with the force of expression and beauty of oratorial numbers, diffuse the highest satisfaction on the audience and excite the most delightful movements. By this means, the uneasiness of the melancholy passions is not only overpowered and effaced by something stronger of an opposite kind, but the whole impulse of those passions is converted into pleasure and swells the delight which the eloquence raises in us. The same force of oratory, employed on an uninteresting subject, would not please half so much, or rather would appear altogether ridiculous; and the mind, being left in absolute calmness and indifference, would relish none of those beauties of imagination or expression which, if joined to passion, give it such exquisite entertainment. The impulse, or vehemence, arising from sorrow, compassion, indignation, receives a new direction from the sentiments of beauty. The latter, being the predominant emotion, seize the whole mind and convert the former into themselves, at least tincture them so strongly as totally to alter their nature. And the soul, being at the same time roused by passion and charmed by eloquence, feels on the whole a strong movement which is altogether delightful.

The same principle takes place in tragedy; with this addition, that tragedy is an imitation, and imitation is always of itself agreeable. This circumstance serves still further to smooth the motions of passion and convert the whole feeling into one uniform and strong enjoyment. Objects of the greatest terror and distress please in painting, and please more than most beautiful objects that appear calm and indifferent.[3]

The affection, rousing the mind, excites a large stock of spirit and vehemence, which is all transformed into pleasure by the force of the prevailing movement. It is thus the fiction of tragedy softens the passion, by an infusion of a new feeling, not merely by weakening or diminishing the sorrow. You may by degrees weaken a real sorrow till it totally disappears; yet in none of its gradations will it ever give pleasure, except, perhaps, by accident to a man sunk under lethargic indolence, whom it rouses from that languid state.

To confirm this theory, it will be sufficient to produce other instances where the subordinate movement is converted into the predominant and gives force to it, though of a different, and even sometimes though of a contrary nature.

Novelty naturally rouses the mind and attracts our attention, and the movements which it causes are always converted into any passion belonging to the object and join their force to it. Whether an event excite joy or sorrow, pride or shame, anger or goodwill, it is sure to produce a stronger affection when new or unusual. And though novelty of itself be agreeable, it fortifies the painful as well as agreeable passions.

Had you any intention to move a person extremely by the narration of any event, the best method of in-

creasing its effect would be artfully to delay informing him of it and first to excite his curiosity and impatience before you let him into the secret. This is the artifice practised by Iago in the famous scene of Shakespeare, and every spectator is sensible that Othello's jealousy acquires additional force from his preceding impatience and that the subordinate passion is here readily transformed into the predominant one.

Difficulties increase passions of every kind; and by rousing our attention and exciting our active powers, they produce an emotion which nourishes the prevailing affection.

Parents commonly love that child most whose sickly, infirm frame of body has occasioned them the greatest pains, trouble, and anxiety in rearing him. The agreeable sentiment of affection here acquires force from sentiments of uneasiness.

Nothing endears so much a friend as sorrow for his death. The pleasure of his company has not so powerful an influence.

Jealousy is a painful passion; yet without some share of it, the agreeable affection of love has difficulty to subsist in its full force and violence. Absence is also a great source of complaint among lovers and gives them the greatest uneasiness; yet nothing is more favorable to their mutual passion than short intervals of that kind. And if long intervals often prove fatal, it is only because through time men are accustomed to them and they cease to give uneasiness. Jealousy and absence in love compose the *dolce peccante* of the Italians, which they suppose so essential to all pleasure.

There is a fine observation of the elder Pliny which illustrates the principle here insisted on. "It is very remarkable," says he, "that the last works of celebrated artists, which they left imperfect, are always the most prized, such as the Iris of Aristides, the Tyndarides of Nicomachus, the Medea of Timomachus, and the Venus of Appelles. These are valued even above their finished productions. The broken lineaments of the piece and the half-formed idea of the painter are carefully studied; and our very grief for that curious hand, which had been stopped by death, is an additional increase to our pleasure." [4]

These instances (and many more might be collected) are sufficient to afford us some insight into the analogy of Nature and to show us that the pleasure which poets, orators, and musicians give us, by exciting grief, sorrow, indignation, compassion, is not so extraordinary or paradoxical as it may at first sight appear. The force of imagination, the energy of expression, the power of numbers, the charms of imitation—all these are naturally, of themselves, delightful to the mind. And when the object presented lays hold also of some affection, the pleasure still rises upon us by the conversion of this subordinate movement into that which is predominant. The passion, though, perhaps, naturally, and when excited by the simple appearance of a real object, it may be painful, yet is so smoothed and softened and mollified when raised by the finer arts that it affords the highest entertainment.

To confirm this reasoning, we may observe that if the movements of the imagination be not predom-

---

[3] Painters make no scruple of representing distress and sorrow as well as any other passion, but they seem not to dwell so much on these melancholy affections as the poets, who, though they copy every emotion of the human breast, yet pass very quickly over the agreeable sentiments. A painter represents only one instant, and if that be passionate enough, it is sure to affect and delight the spectator. But nothing can furnish to the poet a variety of scenes and incidents and sentiments except distress, terror, or anxiety. Complete joy and satisfaction is attended with security and leaves no further room for action.

[4] Book XXXV, Chap. 11.

inant above those of the passion, a contrary effect follows, and the former, being now subordinate, is converted into the latter and still farther increases the pain and affliction of the sufferer.

Who could ever think of it as a good expedient for comforting an afflicted parent to exaggerate with all the force of elocution the irreparable loss which he has met with by the death of a favourite child? The more power of imagination and expression you here employ, the more you increase his despair and affliction.

The shame, confusion, and terror of Verres no doubt rose in proportion to the noble eloquence and vehemence of Cicero. So also did his pain and uneasiness. These former passions were too strong for the pleasure arising from the beauties of elocution and operated, though from the same principle, yet in a contrary manner to the sympathy, compassion, and indignation of the audience.

Lord Clarendon, when he approaches towards the catastrophe of the royal party,[5] supposes that his narration must then become infinitely disagreeable, and he hurries over the king's death without giving us one circumstance of it. He considers it as too horrid a scene to be contemplated with any satisfaction, or even without the utmost pain and aversion. He himself, as well as the readers of that age, were too deeply concerned in the events and felt a pain from subjects which an historian and a reader of another age would regard as the most pathetic and most interesting, and, by consequence, the most agreeable.

An action represented in tragedy may be too bloody and atrocious. It may excite such movements of horror as will not soften into pleasure, and the greatest energy of expression bestowed on descriptions of that nature serves only to augment our uneasiness. Such is that action represented in *The Ambitious Stepmother* where a venerable old man, raised to the height of fury and despair, rushes against a pillar, and striking his head upon it, besmears it all over with mingled brains and gore.[6] The English theatre abounds too much with such shocking images.

Even the common sentiments of compassion require to be softened by some agreeable affection in order to give a thorough satisfaction to the audience. The mere suffering of plaintive virtue under the triumphant tyranny and oppression of vice forms a disagreeable spectacle and is carefully avoided by all masters of the drama. In order to dismiss the audience with entire satisfaction and contentment, the virtue must either convert itself into a noble courageous despair, or the vice receive its proper punishment.

Most painters appear in this light to have been very unhappy in their subjects. As they wrought much for churches and convents, they have chiefly represented such horrible subjects as crucifixions and martyrdoms, where nothing appears but tortures, wounds, executions, and passive suffering, without any action or affection. When they turned their pen-

[5] Edward Hyde, first Earl of Clarendon (1609–74), *History of the Rebellion* (1702–4). A well-known history of the Civil Wars in England.

[6] Nicholas Rowe, *The Ambitious Stepmother* (published in 1700/1701).

cil from this ghastly mythology, they had commonly recourse to Ovid, whose fictions, though passionate and agreeable, are scarcely natural or probable enough for painting.

The same inversion of that principle which is here insisted on displays itself in common life as in the effects of oratory and poetry. Raise so the subordinate passion that it becomes the predominant, it swallows up that affection which it before nourished and increased. Too much jealousy extinguishes love. Too much difficulty renders us indifferent. Too much sickness and infirmity disgusts a selfish and unkind parent.

What so disagreeable as the dismal, gloomy, disastrous stories with which melancholy people entertain their companions? The uneasy passion being there raised alone, unaccompanied with any spirit, genius, or eloquence, conveys a pure uneasiness and is attended with nothing that can soften it into pleasure or satisfaction.

OLIVER GOLDSMITH

(1728–1774)

Goldsmith's famous attack on sentimental comedy, "A Comparison between Laughing and Sentimental Comedy," touches on more fundamental matters than the ephemeral drama that is his ostensible target. What Goldsmith is really attempting is to establish a claim for a mode of comedy located between the "comedy of manners" of the Restoration period and the comedy of sentiment popular in his own day. In so doing, he was aligning himself with the tradition of Shakespeare's romantic comedies, a tradition to which he made two notable contributions, *The Good-Natur'd Man* (1768) and *She Stoops to Conquer* (1773).

"A Comparison between Laughing and Sentimental Comedy" (1773)

The theatre, like all other amusements, has its fashions and its prejudices; and when satiated with its excellence, mankind begin to mistake change for improvement. For some years tragedy was the reigning entertainment; but of late it has entirely given way to comedy, and our best efforts are now exerted in these lighter kinds of composition. The pompous train, the swelling phrase, and the unnatural rant are displaced for that natural portrait of human folly and frailty of which all are judges, because all have sat for the picture.

But as in describing nature it is presented with a double face, either of mirth or sadness, our modern writers find themselves at a loss which chiefly to copy from; and it is now debated whether the exhibition of human distress is likely to afford the mind more entertainment than that of human absurdity.

Comedy is defined by Aristotle to be a picture of the frailties of the lower part of mankind, to distinguish it from tragedy, which is an exhibition of the misfortunes of the great. When comedy therefore ascends to produce the characters of princes or generals upon the stage, it is out of its walk, since low life and middle life are entirely its object. The principal question, therefore, is, whether in describing low or middle life an exhibition of its follies be not preferable to a detail of its calamities? Or, in other words, which deserves the preference—the weeping sentimental comedy, so much in fashion at present, or the laughing and even low comedy, which seems to have been last exhibited by Vanbrugh and Cibber?

If we apply to authorities, all the great masters in the dramatic art have but one opinion. Their rule is, that as tragedy displays the calamities of the great, so comedy should excite our laughter by ridiculously exhibiting the follies of the lower part of mankind. Boileau, one of the best modern critics, asserts that comedy will not admit of tragic distress:

"Le comique, ennemi des soupirs et des pleurs,
N'admet point dans ses vers de tragiques
douleurs."

[The comic, enemy of sighs and tears,
Excludes from its verse tragic woe.]

Nor is this rule without the strongest foundation in nature, as the distresses of the mean by no means affect us so strongly as the calamities of the great. When tragedy exhibits to us some great man fallen from his height, and struggling with want and adversity, we feel his situation in the same manner as we suppose he himself must feel, and our pity is increased in proportion to the height from whence he fell. On the contrary, we do not so strongly sympathize with one born in humbler circumstances, and encountering accidental distress: so that while we melt for Belisarius, we scarce give halfpence to the beggar who accosts us in the street. The one has our pity, the other our contempt. Distress, therefore, is the proper object of tragedy, since the great excite our pity by their fall; but not equally so of comedy, since the actors employed in it are originally so mean that they sink but little by their fall.

Since the first origin of the stage, tragedy and comedy have run in distinct channels, and never till of late encroached upon the provinces of each other. Terence, who seems to have made the nearest approaches, yet always judiciously stops short before he comes to the downright pathetic; and yet he is even reproached by Cæsar for wanting the *vis comica*. All other comic writers of antiquity aim only at rendering folly or vice ridiculous, but never exalt their characters into buskined pomp, or make what Voltaire humorously calls "a tradesman's tragedy."

Yet notwithstanding this weight of authority, and the universal practice of former ages, a new species of dramatic composition has been introduced under the name of *sentimental comedy,* in which the virtues of private life are exhibited, rather than the vices exposed; and the distresses rather than the faults of mankind make our interest in the piece. These comedies have had of late great success, perhaps from their novelty, and also from their flattering every man in his favorite foible. In these plays almost all the characters are good, and exceedingly generous; they are lavish enough of their *tin* money on the stage; and though they want humor, have abundance of sentiment and feeling. If they happen to have faults or foibles, the spectator is taught not only to pardon, but to applaud, them, in consideration of the goodness of their hearts; so that folly, instead of being ridiculed, is commended, and the comedy aims at touching our passions, without the power of being truly pathetic. In this manner we are likely to lose one great source of entertainment on the stage; for while the comic poet is invading the province of the tragic muse, he leaves her lovely sister quite neglected. Of this, however, he is no way solicitous, as he measures his fame by his profits.

But it will be said that the theatre is formed to amuse mankind, and that it matters little, if this end be answered, by what means it is obtained. If mankind find delight in weeping at comedy, it would be cruel to abridge them in that or any other innocent pleasure. If those pieces are denied the name of comedies, yet call them by any other name, and if they are delightful, they are good. Their success, it will be said, is a mark of their merit, and it is only abridging our happiness to deny us an inlet to amusement.

These objections, however, are rather specious than solid. It is true that amusement is a great object of the theatre; and it will be allowed that these sentimental pieces do often amuse us; but the question is, whether the true comedy would not amuse us more? The question is, whether a character supported throughout a piece, with its ridicule still attending, would not give us more delight than this species of bastard tragedy, which only is applauded because it is new?

A friend of mine, who was sitting unmoved at one of the sentimental pieces, was asked how he could be so indifferent? "Why, truly," says he, "as the hero is but a tradesman, it is indifferent to me whether he be turned out of his countinghouse on Fish Street Hill, since he will still have enough left to open shop in St. Giles's."

The other objection is as ill-grounded; for though we should give these pieces another name, it will not mend their efficacy. It will continue a kind of mulish production, with all the defects of its opposite parents, and marked with sterility. If we are permitted to make comedy weep, we have an equal right to make tragedy laugh, and to set down in blank-verse the jests and repartees of all the attendants in a funeral procession.

But there is one argument in favor of sentimental comedy which will keep it on the stage in spite of all that can be said against it. It is of all others the most easily written. Those abilities that can hammer out a novel are fully sufficient for the production of a sentimental comedy. It is only sufficient to raise the characters a little: to deck out the hero with a ribbon or give the heroine a title; then to put an insipid dialogue, without character or humor, into their mouths; give them mighty good hearts, very fine clothes; furnish a new set of scenes; make a pathetic scene or two, with a sprinkling of tender melancholy conversation through the whole; and there is no doubt but all the ladies will cry and all the gentlemen applaud.

Humor, at present, seems to be departing from the stage; and it will soon happen that our comic players will have nothing left for it but a fine coat and a song. It depends upon the audience whether they will actually drive those poor merry creatures from the stage, or sit at a play as gloomy as at the tabernacle. It is not easy to recover an art when once lost; and it would be but a just punishment that when, by our being too fastidious, we have banished humor from the stage, we should ourselves be deprived of the art of laughing.

GOTTHOLD EPHRAIM LESSING

(1729–1781)

One of the greatest and most influential dramatists and critics of the eighteenth century, Lessing played a pioneering role in the German revolt against French neoclassicism. Lessing's finest practical dramatic criticism is his *Hamburg Dramaturgy* (1767). Perhaps a better presentation of his early theories, however, is reflected in his *Correspondence with Nicolai and Moses Mendelssohn,* an excerpt from which is printed below. Lessing's comments reflect the movement away from the simple didacticism that demanded that drama teach a moral lesson. He sees the morality of drama residing in the emotion of pity it implants in the audience. This translation is by Henry Hitch Adams and Baxter Hathaway.

Correspondence with Nicolai and Moses Mendelssohn [1756–1757; excerpts]

LESSING TO NICOLAI, NOVEMBER 13, 1756

. . . It may be that we are indebted to the principle that tragedy should improve us for many a miserable but well-intentioned play; it *may* be, I say, for your observations sound a little too witty for me to be assured that they are true. However, this I know to be true, that no principle, if it is widely disseminated, can help to beget better tragedies than this: tragedy should rouse passions.

Consider for a moment that the first principle may be just as true as the other; likewise, adequate reasons can be given to show why in practice the former must have the worse and the latter better consequences. But the former leads to bad results not because it is a false principle but because it is less immediate, because it merely provides us with the end and the latter with the means. If I have the means, I have the

end also, but not the other way around. You ought, consequently, to have stronger reasons for disagreeing with Aristotle, and I wish you had given me a little more light on that subject; but you may attribute it to this omission that you must here read my ideas, since I believe that the teachings of the ancient philosopher ought to be understood and since I think that tragedy can improve us through its rousing of the passions.

The most important question then is: what passions does tragedy raise? In its characters it brings into play all possible passions that are in keeping with the dignity of the material. But are all these passions likewise aroused in the spectator? Does he become joyful? Enamored? Angry? Revengeful? I do not ask whether the poet brings him to the point where he is conscious of the presence of these passions in the actor, but whether he brings him to the point where he himself feels these passions, and is not merely sensible that someone else feels them?

To be brief, I find no other passion that tragedy raises in the spectator except pity. You will say: does it not arouse terror? does it not arouse admiration also? In my opinion, terror and admiration are not passions? What then? If in your description you have made clear what terror is, *eris mihi magnus Apollo;* and if you have made clear what admiration is, *Phyllida solus habeto.*[1]

Sit here on the judges' bench, Sirs Nicolai and Moses. I will tell you what my conception is of both.

Terror in tragedy is nothing more than the sudden surprising of pity, whether I do or do not know the object of my pity. For example, the priest at last speaks forth: "You, Oedipus, are the murderer of Laius"; I am terrified, for all at once I see the righteous Oedipus unfortunate, and immediately my pity is aroused. Another example: a ghost appears; I am terrified; the thought comes that he would not have appeared if he were not bringing misfortune to someone or other. The shadowy representation of this misfortune, whether I know or not whom it concerns, surprises my pity, and this surprised pity is called terror. Teach me a better idea if I am wrong.

Now for admiration! Admiration! In tragedy—to express myself in oracle-like fashion—admiration is pity that has become transmuted. The hero is unfortunate, but he is so far exalted above his misfortune and is so proud that the terrible part begins to disappear from my thoughts and I may more envy than pity him. The steps are thus these: terror, pity, admiration. The whole ladder, however, is to be called pity; and terror and admiration are only rungs, the beginning and the end of pity. For instance, I hear suddenly: "Cato is about to be killed by Caesar."[2] Terror! But then I become acquainted with the noble character of Cato and after that with his misfortune.

---

[1] From Virgil's *Third Eclogue,* ll. 104–7. Two shepherds in the poem are asking riddles of one another. One tells the other that, if he answers, "You will be my great Apollo." The other answers with another riddle and remarks that if the first answers, "You will have Phyllis for yourself."

[2] The fame of Addison's *Cato* had spread throughout Europe and the reference is quite possibly to that version. However, the story of Cato appeared many times in neo-classical tragedy. Another likely reference is the version by Gottsched.

Terror is dissipated into pity. But now I hear him say to himself, "The world that serves Caesar is no longer worthy of me." Admiration sets limits to pity. The poet uses terror to bring pity into being and admiration as relief from it. The road to pity would be too long for the spectator if he were not made attentive by the terror that precedes it; and pity would wear itself out if it were not transformed into admiration. Therefore, if it is true that the whole art of the tragic poet rests on the certain raising and maintaining of pity alone, I can merely add that the purpose of tragedy is this: it should extend our disposition to feel pity. It should not merely teach us to feel pity in connection with this or that unfortunate man, but it should increase our sympathies to the point that our feelings are aroused for the unfortunate of all times and all places and that we adopt their troubles for our own. And now I call to mind a statement, the truth of which Herr Moses may demonstrate for you if you choose to doubt it in opposition to your own feelings. The best man is the man who pities most, the one who is the most outstanding in all social virtues and most disposed to generosity. Therefore, whoever makes us sympathetic, makes us better and more virtuous; and tragedy, which does that, does this too, or it does that in order to do this. Apologize to Aristotle for this, or show me my error.[3]

I deal with comedy in a similar way. It should increase our disposition to perceive all kinds of ridiculous things easily. Whoever possesses this disposition will seek to avoid all kinds of foolishness in his behavior and will become in that way an excellent man of parts. And in this way is the usefulness of comedy likewise justified.

The usefulness of both, of tragedy as well as comedy, cannot be separated from pleasure, since a full half of pity and laughter is pleasure, and it is a great advantage for the dramatic poet that he can be neither profitable nor pleasant unless he is both.

I am now so taken by this whimsy of mine that if I were to write a dramatic poem I would prefix to it an extensive treatise on pity and laughter. I would compare both with one another. I would show that weeping depends as much on a mixture of sadness and joy as laughter on a mixture of pleasure and displeasure. I would show how laughter can be converted into tears, in which pleasure in joy on one side and on the other displeasure in sadness are allowed to develop together in a continual mixing. I would—you would hardly believe all I would do.

I will now give you a few further proofs of how easily and happily one can derive from my principles not only the most famous known Rules but also a flock of new ones where formerly one has had to be content with mere vague feelings.

Tragedy should arouse as much pity as it can; consequently, all characters who are left in misfortunes must have good qualities; it will follow also that the best character will be the most unfortunate, and desert and misfortune will stand in integral relation together. That is, the poet must present no wretches bereft of all good qualities. The hero or the character of most virtue must not, like a god, survey his own virtues calm and undisturbed—a mistake of

Canute's,[4] as you have noticed in another connection. Notice well, however, that I am not here speaking about the conclusion of a tragedy, since I consider it within the poet's province to decide whether he would rather have virtue shine out in a happy ending or be more interesting to us in an unhappy one. I ask only that the characters to whom I am most attached should be the most unfortunate during the duration of the play. The conclusion, however, is not part of this duration.

Terror, I have said, is suddenly surprised pity; I will say here a few words in addition in respect to the suddenly surprised and undeveloped pity: for what purpose should it be suddenly surprised if it is not developed? A tragedy full of terror without pity is lightning without thunder. So many flashes, so many thunderclaps if the flashes are not soon to become matters of no concern to us, so that we come to gape at them with only a childish pleasure. Admiration, as I have expressed myself, is pity that has become transmuted. Since, however, pity is the principal object, it must as rarely as possible be transmuted. The poet must not make his hero too much or too continuously an object of mere admiration; and Cato as a Stoic is to my way of thinking a bad tragic hero. The admired hero is the subject of an epic, the pitied hero the subject of a tragedy. Can you remember a single place in Homer, or Virgil, or Tasso, or Klopstock in which the hero arouses pity? or a single place in one of the tragedies of the Ancients in which the hero is more admired than pitied . . . ?

Pity furnishes no more tears as soon as unpleasant emotions gain the ascendency. I distinguish three levels of pity, of which the middle one is the weeping pity, and perhaps I can distinguish the three kinds with the words sensibility, tears, oppression. Pathetic sensibility occurs when I consider neither the virtues nor the misfortunes of the object, clearly, but have only a vague idea of both. For instance, I am touched by the sight of a beggar. He brings tears to my eyes only when he reveals to me more his good qualities than his misfortune, and both of them bound up together, which is the real secret of arousing tears. Unless he makes me acquainted first with his good qualities and afterwards with his troubles, or first with the latter and afterwards with the former, the emotion, though stronger, will not become strong enough to bring forth tears. Suppose, for example, that I ask the beggar about his circumstances and he answers, "I have been out of a job for three years; I have a wife and children; they are either too sick or too small to provide for themselves; I myself have been up from my sickbed only for a few days." That is his misfortune! But who are you then? I ask further. "I am such and such, of whose ability in this or that public office you have probably heard; I clothed my position with the highest trust; I could return to it any day if I would prefer to be the creature of a Minister to an honest man." These are his virtues! No one can weep over a tale like that. But if the unfortunate will have my tears, he must put together both parts. He must say, "I have been removed from my posi-

---

[3] Lessing is clearly referring to the "catharsis" clause in Aristotle's definition of tragedy in Chapter 6 of the *Poetics.*

[4] Johann Elias Schlegel wrote *Canut, ein Trauerspiel.* It was first performed in 1746 and published in 1747.

tion because I was too honest and made myself hated by the Minister on that account. I am hungry, and with me in hunger is my sick, loving wife, and also hungry are my children who were once promising but are now weakened by poverty, and we will certainly have to be hungry still longer. Yet I would rather be hungry than base; also my wife and children would rather be hungry and receive their bread direct from God, that is, from the hand of a generous man, than to know that their father and husband were wicked." (I do not know whether you understand me. You must fill out my explanation with your own reflections.) For such a tale I always have tears in readiness. Misfortune and desert are always here in balance. But allow the weight to increase in either one scale or the other and watch what happens. Let us first put an addition onto the side of the virtues. The poor man may continue, "But if I and my sick wife once more recover, things will be different. We shall live by the work of our hands; we are not ashamed to do anything; all ways of earning bread are fitting for an honest man—woodcutting or sitting at the helm of State. It is no matter how useful he *is* but how useful he *wants* to be." Now my weeping stops; admiration has stifled it. And in such a way that I hardly recognize that the admiration has had its origin in pity. Let us now make a trial with the other scale. The honest beggar has reason to believe that through some miracle or supernatural rarity his wants are to be taken care of through the generosity of man or straight from the hand of God. But his hopes are dashed with positive insults; on this account his distress is increased, and with it his perplexity. Finally he becomes mad and kills his wife, his children, and himself. Do you weep now? Here the painfulness stifles the tears but not the pity, as admiration did. . . .

LESSING TO MENDELSSOHN, DECEMBER 18, 1756

. . . In my first letter to Herr Nicolai concerning this matter, I wrote: "In a tragedy admiration must be only the relief from pity." Have you correctly understood me? Herr Nicolai set up as his second category of tragedies that kind by which admiration is raised by means of terror and pity. In this category, then, admiration becomes the principal emotion; that is, the misfortune that befalls the hero should not so much move us as provide the hero with the opportunity to show off his extraordinary virtues, the intuitive perception of which arouses in us the pleasant feeling which you call admiration.

I say that such a tragedy becomes an epic poem in dialogue and not a tragedy. The admired hero, as I have expressed myself to Herr Nicolai, is material for an epic poem. You would indeed give me credit in that connection of believing that an epic poem (a poem full of admiration) can be a beautiful poem, but I cannot understand how you would attribute so much blame to me as to suppose that I would want to rob admiration of everything that is beautiful or pleasant. It is a pleasant feeling—good, but does it deserve for that reason the foremost place in a tragedy? Tragedy, says Aristotle (Chapter XIV), should not provide us with every kind of pleasure without distinction, but only that kind of pleasure which is characteristic of it.

Why do you want to confuse the art of poetry unnecessarily and let the boundaries of one kind overlap another? Just as in an epic poem admiration is the principal emotion and all other emotions, pity especially, are subordinated to it, so likewise in tragedy pity is the chief emotion, and all other emotions, admiration especially, ought to be subordinated to it; that is, ought to serve only as an aid in arousing pity. The epic poet allows the hero to be unfortunate in order to bring his virtues into the light. The writer of tragedy brings the virtues of his hero into the light in order to make his misfortune all the more painful to us.

A great pity cannot exist unless there are great virtues in the object of the pity, and there cannot be great virtues, well-expressed, without admiration. However, in tragedy these great virtues should never be unaccompanied by great misfortunes; they should at all times be closely associated with them; and should therefore arouse, not admiration alone, but admiration and pain; that is, pity. And that is what I mean to say. Admiration is thus not to be found in tragedy as a separate emotion, but only as a part of pity. And in this view I was also right to explain it not as a separate emotion but only in connection with its relation to pity.

And in this regard I still say it ought to be the relief from pity, namely there where it should be effective for itself alone. Since you bring up the example of Mithridates here for the second time,[5] I am forced to believe that you have understood my words to mean that I want this relief to help allay pity. However, I don't mean that at all, but just the opposite. Now listen to me!

We are not able to remain for a long time in a state of strong emotion; thus we cannot sustain for a long time even a strong pity; it loses its force. Even mediocre poets have noticed this and have saved the strong pity until the end. But I hate the French tragedies which do not cause my tears to be shed before the end of the fifth act. The true poet scatters pity throughout the whole of his tragedy. He introduces situations throughout in which he shows the virtues and the misfortunes of his hero in moving combination; that is, he arouses tears. Since, however, the whole play cannot be a continuous parade of such situations, he mixes situations with them in which the virtues of his character are alone portrayed, and in these places admiration prevails as admiration. What are these places except a kind of relief in which the spectator catches his breath for the new pity? The former pity should not be quenched in this part; that thought has never come into my mind and would be completely contrary to my system.

. . . Read the 13th Chapter of Aristotle's *Poetics*. The philosopher says there that the hero of a tragedy must be a middle sort of character; he must neither be too villainous nor too virtuous. If he is too villainous and deserves his misfortunes on account of his crimes, we can feel no pity for him; and should he be entirely virtuous and still encounter misfortune, the pity is turned to horror and aversion.

I would like to know how Herr Nicolai would reconcile this rule with the qualities of his hero that

[5] Racine, *Mithridate* (1673).

arouse admiration—but that is not what I want to write about now.

I myself am against Aristotle here, who it seems to me founded his idea on a false explanation of pity. And if I am closer to the truth, I have to thank for it your better concept of the act of pitying. Is it true that the misfortune of an entirely virtuous man arouses horror and aversion? If it is true, horror and aversion must be the highest degree of pity, and of course they are not. The pity that would grow in precisely those circumstances in which virtue and misfortune grow would cease for me to be pleasant and would become all the more unpleasant the greater the virtue on one side and the misfortune on the other.

In the meanwhile it is, however, still true that there must be in the hero a certain *hamartia,* a certain flaw, through which he has brought his misfortune upon himself. But why that kind of *hamartia* that Aristotle described? Perhaps because without it he would be perfect and the misfortune of a perfect man would arouse abhorrence? Certainly not. I think I have found the only real reason. It is this: that without the flaw that leads him into misfortune his character and his misfortune would not comprise a unity, that the one would not be based in the other and we would consider the two of them as two plays. An example will make my meaning clear. Canute may be an example of perfect goodness. Then if he is to arouse pity, I must let him, because of his failure to govern his goodness with prudence, by overwhelming Ulfo with kindnesses, whom he should merely pardon, bring a great misfortune upon himself. Ulfo must take him prisoner and murder him. Pity in the highest degree! But suppose I do not let Canute perish because of his abused goodness but be struck by lightning suddenly or be crushed when his palace collapses on him. Horror and aversion without pity! Why? because there is not the least connection between his goodness and the lightning or the collapsing palace, between his virtue and his misfortune. These are two different things which cannot bring about a single common effect such as pity is, but each of them has its own effect. Another example! Think of the old cousin in *The London Merchant.*[6] When Barnwell chokes him, the spectator is horrified without being compassionate because the good character of the old man contains nothing that can provide a basis for this misfortune. But as soon as he is heard praying to God for his murderer and cousin, the horror is converted into a very rapturous pity, and entirely naturally because this generous act proceeds from his misfortune and has its foundation in it. . . .

MENDELSSOHN TO LESSING, JANUARY, 1757

. . . In the very beginning you assign the tragic passions, admiration and pity, to different provinces and want the one to lord it over the territory of the epic poem and the other over the stage. On this occasion you ask, "Why do we wish to confuse the different kinds of poetry needlessly and allow the boundaries of one kind to overlap upon the other?" Here you let a prejudice run away with you, a kind of behavior that I have often heard you yourself condemn.

On what are these fancied lines of demarcation based? In observation of the works of Nature, it has been decided in the last century that they have not been divided by their mistress into special and separate classes. Why do we not want to let art be in this respect also an imitator of Nature? If word usage, the authority of the Ancients, the division of the arts into their special kinds, and a thousand other prejudices have allowed only such dramatic plays to be given the name of tragedy which particularly arouse pity, the philologist can content himself with this recipe. However, Reason speaks otherwise. It considers any great and worthy event as the subject matter of tragedy only if it is capable of imitation of an important action through a lively presentation. (See my enclosed ideas on aesthetic illusion.) Therefore, do not bar any single passion from the theatre. To the extent that the imitated passion can convince the perceiver of the excellence of the imitation, it deserves to be performed on the stage. Even hate and aversion can, in spite of Aristotle and his followers, be pleasing on the stage, because it is sufficient if the imitated passion can convince us that the imitation is like the original. . . .

Let us however come somewhat nearer together. I will concede to you that pity can more easily give us an intuitive illusion than admiration can. I mean that it is easier to convince us by means of an imitated pity that the imitation is similar to the original than it is to get the same kind of result through admiration. You must agree, however, that art reveals its full splendor when it tries to imitate the finest traits of Nature, to set before us a great soul in its brightest light, if it presents a hero who courageously stands upright under the weight of oppression, his head raised up to the skies, who undaunted hears the thunder crackling around his feet, and who pulls us close together with him in our anxiety for him. The way is hard, very hard, and only the great genius can hope to tread it with success. I grant it, but when has my Lessing worried about the roads on which ordinary souls ought to travel? . . .

Do not apologize for your expression, "Admiration may be relief from pity." Surely, the analysis of the virtues that adorn the hero, or, much more, the revelations of his character, can frequently fill out a secondary scene and provide a relief from pity. However, this is not admiration but esteem, a lesser degree of admiration, which sustains us a while; just as in comedy, so that we will not be laughing all the time, we introduce touching scenes. But where admiration is supposed to be the chief emotion, it must have something more than this kind of menial employment in a Cato, a Brutus,[7] a Grandison,[8] and—why should I not say it?—in a Theophanes.[9] It is in general the fate of all theatrical passions that they are scarcely recognizable any longer if they appear as attendants on other passions. Love, for instance, is a raging and terrible passion when it is given the major emphasis, as in *Hippolytus.* How childish and ridicu-

---

[6] George Lillo, *George Barnwell; or, The London Merchant* (1731), a well-known English domestic tragedy.

[7] Brutus was a common figure in neoclassical tragedy.

[8] The reference is to the chief character in Samuel Richardson's *Sir Charles Grandison,* a character considered by sentimentalists of the eighteenth century to be the example of perfect male virtue.

[9] A character in Lessing's *Der Freigeist* (1749).

lous it is, however, in a thousand French plays in which it fills up only a few secondary scenes. I will not pardon Polyeucte.[10] When you compare him with the fellow who is supposed to cast himself down from the tower, I think the jumper has lost the *tertium comparationis*. The hero must consider the moral good a distinctly greater treasure than the physical good. When pain, fetters, slavery, and death are opposed to a duty, he must not hesitate to hasten to meet all these evils in order to keep his innocence unspotted. This internal victory which his godlike soul wins over his body delights us and creates in us a feeling in which no sensuous delight accompanies the pleasure. The mere admiration of corporeal skill, which you allow to your wheelbarrow-pusher, is without emotion, is without that internal feeling and that warmth of the bowels (if I may so express myself) with which we admire the greatness of, for instance, an Orestes and Pylades. (In passing, I remember that these are probably the only characters of the Ancients who arouse a true admiration.) I am being silent about a certain situation in a Chinese tragedy which you used to admire. At the command of a tyrant an old man is terribly beaten by his friend—by that particular friend for whose benefit he will not reveal a certain secret. He looks back with half angry glances at that man who is carrying out the commands of the tyrant on his back. Now should he open his mouth and utter a single word he can free himself from the terrible pain. But no! He looks at his friend. He calls to mind his duty and the gruesome power which compels his friend to become his tormentor. His anger is converted to sadness. He groans and remains faithful to his duty. Here is magnanimity, here is constancy, here is inner struggle, and the most lordly victory ever won by mortals!

If Reason approves of the emulation that is created in us by means of admiration, you will attribute the effect not to the admiration but to the clear knowledge. I, however, have shown in the pages that accompany this that the intuitive perception must increase the quantity of the motive if the virtuous resolution is to achieve actuality, and in my opinion nothing increases this quantity so much as admiration.

If Herr Nicolai claims that poetry is not concerned with the improvement of morals, he is clearly wrong, and I show the opposite in the pages that are enclosed. If he claims, however, that the improvement of morals cannot be the chief end of tragedy because the imitation can still be perfect, even if the underlying morality is not in full accord with Reason, then I think that the most zealous defender of poetry must agree with him. The aesthetic illusion really depends upon the temporary silencing of the higher mental powers, as I have made reasonably clear in my "Thoughts on Illusion." However, it is made clear from what I have said about moral sensibility that even the readiness to feel pity . . . does not in itself always have a good effect. Our moral sensibility without the assistance of judgment only renders our emotionality weaker and incites us to search for both true and apparent good with greater desire. Your ideas on physical dexterity and the admiration that it

arouses please me uncommonly, and you shame me when you complain about your inability to express your thoughts correctly. How can I answer you here without paying you a return compliment.

Do not exalt admiration for physical dexterity at the expense of the soul! You are uncommonly mistaken if you believe that generosity in specific single cases excites in us merely a wish to act generously in similar cases. In my "Thoughts on the Control of the Affections" you may see how useful it may be to virtue if general abstract ideas were reduced to single cases. This reduction can take place through experience, through example, or even through fiction. Our symbolic understanding always becomes converted into a contemplative understanding; the force of the motive becomes animated, and its quantity becomes greater with the increase in quantity of the sensuous pleasure that opposes it. . . .

JOHANN WOLFGANG VON GOETHE

(1749–1832)

Goethe's observations on the distinctions between epic and dramatic poetry provide some useful insights into the nature of drama. His characterization of tragedy as representing "man thrown in upon himself" provides a terse summary of much of modern drama. Similarly, his assertion that "no claim may be made" upon the imagination of the audience provides an interesting anticipation of the naturalist theater.

"Epic and Dramatic Poetry" [1]
(1797)

The epic poet and the dramatic poet are both subject to the general laws of poetry, and especially to the laws of unity and of progression. Furthermore, they deal with subjects that are similar, and they can avail themselves of motives of either kind. The great and essential difference between them, however, lies in the fact that, whereas the epic poet describes an action as being altogether past and completed, the dramatic poet represents it as actually occurring. The best way of deducing the laws in detail, according to which both have to act, from the nature of man, is to picture to ourselves a rhapsodist and a stage-player, both as poets, the former surrounded by a quiet and attentive circle of listeners, the latter by a crowd impatiently waiting to see and hear him. Nor would it be a difficult matter to explain what is of the greatest

---

[10] Polyeucte is the chief character, a Christian martyr, in Corneille's *Polyeucte* (1640).

[1] Reprinted, complete, from W. B. Rönnfeldt's *Criticisms, Reflections, and Maxims of Goethe* (London, n. d.).

use to each of these respective forms of poetry; what subjects each one will preferably adopt; of what motives it will preferably avail itself. I say *preferably;* for, as I pointed out at the commencement, neither of them can lay exclusive claim to anything.

The subjects of epic poetry and of tragedy should be altogether human, full of significance and pathos. The characters will appear to the greatest advantage if they are represented as having attained a certain stage of development, when self-activity or spontaneity makes them still appear dependent upon themselves alone, and when their influence makes itself felt, not morally, politically, or mechanically, but in a purely personal way. The legends from the heroic times of the Greeks were in this sense especially favorable to their poets.

The epic poem represents above all things circumscribed activity, tragedy, circumscribed suffering. The epic poem gives us man working outside of and beyond himself: battles, wanderings, enterprises of all kinds which demand a certain sensuous breadth. Tragedy gives us man thrown in upon himself, and the actions of genuine tragedy therefore stand in need of but little space.

Of motives I distinguish five different varieties:

1. *Progressive,* which further the action, and are for the most part employed in drama.

2. *Retrogressive,* which draw the action away from its goal; these are almost exclusively confined to epic poetry.

3. *Retardative,* which delay the course or lengthen the way; these are used in both kinds of poetry with the greatest advantage.

4. *Retrospective,* by means of which events that have happened previously to the epoch of the poem are introduced into it.

5. *Anticipatory,* which anticipate that which will happen after the epoch of the poem; the epic poet, as also the dramatic poet, uses both kinds in order to create a perfect poem.

The worlds which are to be represented to view are common to both. They are:

1. The physical; and firstly, that most nearly approaching the one to which the persons represented belong, and by which they are surrounded. Here the dramatist as a rule confines himself strictly to one single point; the epic poet has more freedom of motion and his range of locality is much greater. Secondly, there is the remoter world, in which I include the whole of nature. This one the epic poet, who, generally speaking, has recourse to the imagination, seeks to bring nearer to us by means of similes or comparisons, of which the dramatist avails himself with less frequency.

2. The moral world is equally common to both, and is most happily represented in all its physiological and pathological simplicity.

3. The world of phantasies, presentiments, apparitions, accidents, and fatalities. This lies open to both, it being of course understood that it must approximate to the world of sensuous perception. Hence there arises a special difficulty for the moderns, because, much as we may desire it, we cannot easily find a substitute for the miraculous creatures, the gods, soothsayers, and oracles of the ancients.

With regard to the treatment as a whole, we shall deem the rhapsodist who describes that which belongs altogether to the past, to be a man of wisdom surveying with a calm recollection the things which have happened. His description will tend so to compose his hearers that they find pleasure in listening to him for a long space of time. He will distribute the interest equally throughout, since he is not able to counterbalance any unduly vivid impression with the necessary rapidity. He will turn about and wander to and fro according to the impulse of his fancy; and wherever he goes, he will be closely followed, for he has to deal with the imagination alone, which fashions its own pictures and which is to a certain degree indifferent as to what pictures it summons up. The rhapsodist should not himself appear in his poem as a kind of superior being. The best method for him would be to read from behind a screen, so that his hearers might turn aside their thoughts from all personality and imagine they heard the voice of the muses in general and nothing more.

With the stage-player, on the other hand, the position is exactly reversed. He comes before us as a distinct and determined individual. He wants us to interest ourselves exclusively in him and his immediate surroundings; he wants us to share his mental and bodily sufferings, to feel his perplexities, and to forget ourselves in following him. He too will, indeed, set to work in a gradual manner; but he can venture upon far more powerful effects, because in the case of sensuous presence even an unusually strong impression may be dispelled by means of a weaker one. The contemplative listener is in reason bound to remain in a state of constant sensuous exertion; he must not pause to meditate, but must follow in a state of passionate eagerness; his fancy is entirely put to silence; no claims may be made upon it, and even that which is narrated must be so placed before the eyes of the spectator as though it were actually taking place.[2]

[2] An interesting note on *Dramatic Form,* written about 1775:

"It is well-nigh time that people ceased talking about the form of dramatic compositions, about their length and shortness, their unities, their beginning, middle, and end, and all the rest of it; and that we now began to go straightway to their contents, which hitherto, it seems, have been left to take of themselves.

"There is, however, one form which is as distinct from the other as the internal sense from the external; a form which is not tangible but requires to be felt. Our head must be able to overlook that which the head of another can grasp; our heart must be able to feel that which the heart of another can feel. The intermingling of the rules will not give rise to looseness; and, though the example should prove dangerous, yet it is at bottom better to make a confused piece than a cold one.

"Indeed, if only more persons were alive to this inner form, which comprehends within itself all forms, we should not be disgusted by so many abortive productions of the intellect; writers would not think of expanding every tragic event into a drama and of slicing up every novel into a play. I wish that some clever individual would parody this twofold nuisance by arranging, say, the Aesopian fable of the Wolf and the Lamb in the form of a tragedy in five acts.

"Every form, even that which admits of the greatest amount of feeling, has in it something that is untrue. Yet the form is invariably the glass through which we collect the holy rays of extended nature and throw them upon the heart of humanity as their focus. But as for the glass—he to whom it is not given, will not succeed

AUGUST WILHELM VON SCHLEGEL

(1767–1845)

Schlegel is deservedly well known for his fine translations into German of Shakespeare, which were of primary importance in the establishment of Shakespeare's appeal to German audiences. His *Lectures on Dramatic Art and Literature* (pub. 1809–1811), an excerpt of which is here translated by John Black, were also instrumental in the acceptance of the principles of Romanticism in drama. One particular aspect of this distinction was the elevation of comedy to a position equal to tragedy in the seriousness of its representation of life.

from *Lectures on Dramatic Art and Literature* (1808)

The importance of our subject is, I think, fully proved. Let us now enter upon a brief consideration of the two kinds into which all dramatic poetry is divided, the *tragic* and *comic,* and examine the meaning and import of each.

The three principal kinds of poetry in general are the epic, the lyric, and the dramatic. All the other subordinate species are either derived from these, or formed by combination from them. If we would consider these three leading kinds in their purity, we must go back to the forms in which they appeared among the Greeks. For the theory of poetical art is most conveniently illustrated by the history of Grecian poetry; for the latter is well entitled to the appellation of systematical, since it furnishes for every independent idea derived from experience the most distinct and precise manifestation.

It is singular that epic and lyric poetry admit not of any such precise division into two opposite species, as the dramatic does. The ludicrous epopee has, it is true, been styled a peculiar species, but it is only an

---

in obtaining it, do what he will. Like the mysterious stone of the alchemists, it is both husk and matter, both fire and cooling draught; it is so simple, so common, it lies before every door, and yet so wonderful a thing, that just those people who possess it can as a rule make no use thereof.

"He who would work for the stage should, moreover, study the stage, the effects of scenography, of lights and rouge and other coloring matter, of glazed linen and spangles. He should leave nature in her proper place, and take careful heed not to have recourse to anything but what may be performed by children with puppets upon boards and laths, together with sheets of cardboard and linen."

---

accidental variety, a mere parody of the epos, and consists in applying its solemn staidness of development, which seems only suitable to great objects, to trifling and insignificant events. In lyric poetry there are only intervals and gradations between the song, the ode, and the elegy, but no proper contrast.

The spirit of epic poetry, as we recognise it in its father, Homer, is clear self-possession. The epos is the calm quiet representation of an action in progress. The poet relates joyful as well as mournful events, but he relates them with equanimity, and considers them as already past, and at a certain remoteness from our minds.

The lyric poem is the musical expression of mental emotions by language. The essence of musical feeling consists in this, that we endeavour with complacency to dwell on, and even to perpetuate in our souls, a joyful or painful emotion. The feeling must consequently be already so far mitigated as not to impel us by the desire of its pleasure or the dread of its pain, to tear ourselves from it, but such as to allow us, unconcerned at the fluctuations of feeling which time produces, to dwell upon and be absorbed in a single moment of existence.

The dramatic poet, as well as the epic, represents external events, but he represents them as real and present. In common with the lyric poet he also claims our mental participation, but not in the same calm composedness; the feeling of joy and sorrow which the dramatist excites is more immediate and vehement. He calls forth all the emotions which the sight of similar deeds and fortunes of living men would elicit, and it is only by the total sum of the impression which he produces that he ultimately resolves these conflicting emotions into a harmonious tone of feeling. As he stands in such close proximity to real life, and endeavours to endue his own imaginary creations with vitality, the equanimity of the epic poet would in him be indifference; he must decidedly take part with one or other of the leading views of human life, and constrain his audience also to participate in the same feeling.

To employ simpler and more intelligible language: the *tragic* and *comic* bear the same relation to one another as *earnest* and *sport.* Every man, from his own experience, is acquainted with both these states of mind; but to determine their essence and their source would demand deep philosophical investigation. Both, indeed, bear the stamp of our common nature; but earnestness belongs more to its moral, and mirth to its animal part. The creatures destitute of reason are incapable either of earnest or of sport. Animals seem indeed at times to labour as if they were earnestly intent upon some aim, and as if they made the present moment subordinate to the future; at other times they seem to sport, that is, they give themselves up without object or purpose to the pleasure of existence: but they do not possess consciousness, which alone can entitle these two conditions to the names of earnest and sport. Man alone, of all the animals with which we are acquainted, is capable of looking back towards the past, and forward into futurity; and he has to purchase the enjoyment of this noble privilege at a dear rate. Earnestness, in the most extensive signification, is the direction of our mental powers to some aim. But as soon as we begin to call ourselves to account for our actions, reason compels us to fix this aim higher and higher, till we come at last to the highest end of our existence: and here that longing for the infinite which is inherent in our being, is baffled by the limits of our finite existence. All that we do, all that we effect, is vain and perishable; death stands everywhere in the back ground, and to it every well or ill-spent moment brings us nearer and closer; and even when a man has been so singularly fortunate as to reach the utmost term of life without any grievous calamity, the inevitable doom still awaits him to leave or to be left by all that is most dear to him on earth. There is no bond of love without a separation, no enjoyment without the grief of losing it. When, however, we contemplate the relations of our existence to the extreme limit of possibilities: when we reflect on its entire dependence on a chain of causes and effects, stretching beyond our ken: when we consider how weak and helpless, and doomed to struggle against the enormous powers of nature, and conflicting appetites, we are cast on the shores of an unknown world, as it were, shipwrecked at our very birth; how we are subject to all kinds of errors and deceptions, any one of which may be our ruin; that in our passions we cherish an enemy in our bosoms; how every moment demands from us, in the name of the most sacred duties, the sacrifice of our dearest inclinations, and how at one blow we may be robbed of all that we have acquired with much toil and difficulty; that with every accession to our stores, the risk of loss is proportionally increased, and we are only the more exposed to the malice of hostile fortune: when we think upon all this, every heart which is not dead to feeling must be overpowered by an inexpressible melancholy, for which there is no other counterpoise than the consciousness of a vocation transcending the limits of this earthly life. This is the tragic tone of mind; and when the thought of the possible issues out of the mind as a living reality, when this tone pervades and animates a visible representation of the most striking instances of violent revolutions in a man's fortunes, either prostrating his mental energies or calling forth the most heroic endurance—then the result is *Tragic Poetry.* We thus see how this kind of poetry has its foundation in our nature, while to a certain extent we have also answered the question, why we are fond of such mournful representations, and even find something consoling and elevating in them? This tone of mind we have described is inseparable from strong feeling; and although poetry cannot remove these internal dissonances, she must at least endeavour to effect an ideal reconciliation of them.

GEORG WILHELM FRIEDRICH HEGEL

(1770–1831)

Hegel's speculations on drama in general and tragedy in particular have had a profound effect upon modern theory. His definition of tragedy as the ethical conflict between two partial goods has been adopted and transformed by a host of later students of the subject. The excerpt from *The Philosophy of Fine Art* reprinted below is translated by F. P. B. Osmaston.

from *The Philosophy of Fine Art*

The genuine content of tragic action subject to the *aims* which arrest tragic characters is supplied by the world of those forces which carry in themselves their own justification, and are realized substantively in the volitional activity of mankind. Such are the love of husband and wife, of parents, children, and kinsfolk. Such are, further, the life of communities, the patriotism of citizens, the will of those in supreme power. Such are the life of churches, not, however, if regarded as a piety which submits to act with resignation, or as a divine judicial declaration in the heart of mankind over what is good or the reverse in action; but, on the contrary, conceived as the active engagement with and demand for veritable interests and relations. It is of a soundness and thoroughness consonant with these that the really tragical *characters* consist. They are throughout that which the essential notion of their character enables them and compels them to be. They are not merely a varied totality laid out in the series of views of it proper to the epic manner; they are, while no doubt remaining also essentially vital and individual, still only the one power of the particular character in question, the force in which such a character, in virtue of his essential personality, has made himself inseparably coalesce with some particular aspect of the capital and substantive life-content we have indicated above, and deliberately commits himself to that. It is at some such elevation, where the mere accidents of unmediated individuality vanish altogether, that we find the tragic heroes of dramatic art, whether they be the living representatives of such spheres of concrete life or in any other way already so derive their greatness and stability from their own free self-reliance that they stand forth as works of sculpture, and thus the lofty tragic characters of the Greeks also interpret the essentially more abstract statues and figures of gods more completely than is possible for any other kind of elucidation or commentary.

Broadly speaking, we may, therefore, affirm that the true theme of primitive tragedy is the godlike. But by godlike we do not mean the Divine, as implied in the content of the religious consciousness simply as such, but rather as it enters into the world, into individual action, and enters in such a way that it does not forfeit its substantive character under this mode of realization, nor find itself converted into the contradiction of its own substance. In this form the spiritual substance of volition and accomplishment is ethical life. For what is ethical, if we grasp it, in its direct consistency—that is to say, not exclusively from the standpoint of personal reflection as formal morality—is the divine in its secular or world realization, the substantive as such, the particular no less than the essential features of which supply the changing content of truly human actions, and in such action itself render this their essence explicit and actual.

These ethical forces, as also the characters of the action, are *distinctively defined* in respect to their content and their individual personality, in virtue of the principle of differentiation to which everything is subject, which forms part of the objective world of things. If, then, these particular forces, in the way presupposed by dramatic poetry, are attached to the external expression of human activity, and are realized as the determinate aim of a human pathos which passes into action, their concordancy is cancelled, and they are asserted *in contrast* to each other in interchangeable succession. Individual action will then, under given conditions, realize an object or character, which, under such a presupposed state, inevitably stimulates the presence of a pathos opposed to itself, because it occupies a position of unique isolation in virtue of its independently fixed definition, and, by doing so, brings in its train unavoidable conflicts. Primitive tragedy, then, consists in this, that within a collision of this kind both sides of the contradiction, if taken by themselves, are *justified;* yet, from a further point of view, they tend to carry into effect the true and positive content of their end and specific characterization merely as the negation and *violation* of the other equally legitimate power, and consequently in their ethical purport and relatively to this so far fall under *condemnation.*

I have already adverted to the general ground of the necessity of this conflict. The substance of ethical condition *is,* when viewed as concrete unity, a totality of *different* relations and forces, which, however, only under the inactive condition of the gods in their blessedness achieve the works of the Spirit in enjoyment of an undisturbed life. In contrast to this, however, there is no less certainly implied in the notion of this totality itself an impulse to move from its, in the first instance, still abstract ideality, and transplant itself in the real actuality of the phenomenal world. On account of the nature of this primitive obsession, it comes about that mere difference, if conceived on the basis of definite conditions of individual personalities, must inevitably associate with contradiction and collision. Only such a view can pretend to deal seriously with those gods which, though they endure in their tranquil repose and unity in the Olympus and heaven of imagination and religious conception, yet, in so far as they are actual, viewed at least as the energic in the definite pathos of a human personality, participate in concrete life, all other claims notwithstanding, and, in virtue of their specific singularity and their mutual opposition, render both blame and wrong inevitable.

As a result of this, however, an unmediated contradiction is posited, which no doubt may assert itself in the Real, but, for all that, is unable to maintain itself as that which is wholly substantive and verily real therein; which rather discovers, and only discovers, its essential justification in the fact that it is able to *annul* itself as such contradiction. In other words, whatever may be the claim of the tragic final purpose and personality, whatever may be the necessity of the tragic collision, it is, as a consequence of our present view, no less a claim that is asserted— this is our *third* and last point—by the tragic resolution of this division. It is through *this* latter result that Eternal Justice is operative in such aims and in-

dividuals under a mode whereby it restores the ethical substance and unity in and along with the downfall of the individuality which disturbs its repose. For, despite the fact that individual characters propose that which is itself essentially valid, yet they are only able to carry it out under the tragic demand in a manner that implies contradiction and with a one-sidedness which is injurious. What, however, is substantive in truth, and the function of which is to secure realization, is not the battle of particular unities, however much such a conflict is essentially involved in the notion of a real world and human action; rather it is the reconciliation in which definite ends and individuals unite in harmonious action without mutual violation and contradiction. That which is abrogated in the tragic issue is merely the *one-sided* particularity which was unable to accommodate itself to this harmony, and consequently in the tragic course of its action, through inability to disengage itself from itself and its designs, either is committed in its entire totality to destruction or at least finds itself compelled to fall back upon a state of resignation in the execution of its aim in so far as it can carry this out. We are reminded of the famous dictum of Aristotle that the true effect of tragedy is to excite and purify *fear* and *pity.* By this statement Aristotle did not mean merely the concordant or discordant feeling with anybody's private experience, a feeling simply of pleasure or the reverse, an attraction or a repulsion, that most superficial of all psychological states, which only in recent times theorists have sought to identify with the principle of assent or dissent as ordinarily expressed. For in a work of art the matter of exclusive importance should be the display of that which is conformable with the reason and truth of Spirit; and to discover the principle of this we have to direct our attention to wholly different points of view. And consequently we are not justified in restricting the application of this dictum of Aristotle merely to the emotion of fear and pity, but should relate it to the principle of the *content,* the appropriately artistic display of which ought to purify such feelings. Man may, on the one hand, entertain fear when confronted with that which is outside him and finite; but he may likewise shrink before the power of that which is the essential and absolute subsistency of social phenomena. That which mankind has therefore in truth to fear is not the external power and its oppression, but the ethical might which is self-defined in its own free rationality, and partakes further of the eternal and inviolable, the power a man summons against his own being when he turns his back upon it. And just as fear may have two objectives, so also may compassion. The first is just the ordinary sensibility—in other words, a sympathy with the misfortunes and sufferings of another, and one which is experienced as something finite and negative. Your countrified cousin is ready enough with compassion of this order. The man of nobility and greatness, however, has no wish to be smothered with this sort of pity. For just to the extent that it is merely the nugatory aspect, the negative of misfortune which is asserted, a real depreciation of misfortune is implied. True sympathy, on the contrary, is an accordant feeling with the ethical claim at the same time associated with the sufferer—that is, with what is necessarily implied in his condition as affirmative and substantive. Such a pity as this is not, of course, excited by ragamuffins and vagabonds. If the tragic character, therefore, just as he aroused our fear when contemplating the might of violated morality, is to awake a tragic sympathy in his misfortune, he must himself essentially possess real capacity and downright character. It is only that which has a genuine content which strikes the heart of a man of noble feeling, and rings through its depths. Consequently we ought by no means to identify our interest in the tragic *dénouement* with the simple satisfaction that a sad story, a misfortune merely as misfortune, should have a claim upon our sympathy. Feelings of lament of this type may well enough assail men on occasions of wholly external contingency and related circumstance, to which the individual does not contribute, nor for which he is responsible, such cases as illness, loss of property, death, and the like. The only real and absorbing interest in such cases ought to be an eager desire to afford immediate assistance. If this is impossible, such pictures of lamentation and misery merely rack the feelings. A veritable tragic suffering, on the contrary, is suspended over active characters entirely as the consequence of their own act, which as such not only asserts its claim upon us, but becomes subject to blame through the collision it involves, and in which such individuals identify themselves heart and soul.

Over and above mere fear and tragic sympathy we have therefore the feeling of *reconciliation*, which tragedy affords in virtue of its vision of eternal justice, a justice which exercises a paramount force of absolute constringency on account of the relative claim of all merely contracted aims and passions; and it can do this for the reason that it is unable to tolerate the victorious issue and continuance in the truth of the objective world of such a conflict with and opposition to those ethical powers which are fundamentally and essentially concordant. Inasmuch as then, in conformity with this principle, all that pertains to tragedy pre-eminently rests upon the contemplation of such a conflict and its resolution, dramatic poetry is—and its entire mode of presentation offers a proof of the fact—alone able to make and completely adapt the tragic, throughout its entire course and compass, to the principle of the art product. And this is the reason why I have only now found occasion to discuss the tragic mode of presentation, although it extends an effective force, if no doubt one of subordinate degree, in many ways over the other arts.

In the tragic drama we are now considering, the general basis or background for tragic action is supplied, as was also the case in the Epos, by that world-condition which I have already indicated as the *heroic*. For only in heroic times, when the universal ethical forces have neither acquired the independent stability of definite political legislation or moral commands and obligations, can they be presented in their primitive jocundity as gods, who are either opposed to each other in their personal activities, or themselves appear as the animated content of a free and human individuality. If, however, what is intrinsically ethical is to appear throughout as the substantive foundation, the universal ground, shall we say, from which the growth of personal action arrests our

attention with equal force in its disunion, and is no less brought back again from such divided movement into unity, we shall find that there are two distinct modes under which the ethical content of human action is asserted.

First, we have the simple consciousness, which, in so far as it wills its substantive content wholly as the unbroken identity of its particular aspects, remains in undisturbed, uncriticized, and neutral tranquillity on its own account and as related to others. This undivided and, we may add, purely formal state of mind in its veneration, its faith, and its happiness, however, is incapable of attaching itself to any definite action; it has a sort of dread before the disunion which is implied in such, although it does, while remaining itself incapable of action, esteem at the same time that spiritual courage which asserts itself resolutely and actively in a self-proposed object, as of nobler worth, yet is aware of its inability to undertake such enterprise, and consequently considers that it can do nothing further for such active personalities, whom it respects so highly, than contrast with the energy of their decision and conflict the object of its own wisdom, in other words, the substantive ideality of the ethical Powers.

The *second* mode under which this ethical content is asserted is that of the individual pathos, which urges the active characters with moral self-vindication into opposition to others, and brings them thereby into conflict. The individuals subject to this pathos are neither what, in the modern use of the term, we describe as characters, nor are they mere abstractions. They are rather placed in the vital midway sphere between both, standing there as figures of real stability, which are simply that which they are, without aught of collision in themselves, without any fluctuating recognition of some other pathos, and in so far—in this respect a contrast to our modern irony—elevated, absolutely determinate characters, whose definition, however, discovers its content and basis in a particular ethical power. Forasmuch as, then, the tragic situation first appears in the *antagonism* of individuals who are thus empowered to act, the same can only assert itself in the field of actual human life. It results from the specific character of this alone that a particular quality so affects the substantive content of a given individual, that the latter identifies himself with his entire interest and being in such a content, and penetrates it throughout with the glow of passion. In the blessed gods, however, it is the divine Nature, in its indifference, which is what is essential; in contrast to which we have the contradiction, which in the last instance is not treated seriously, rather is one which, as I have already noticed when discussing the Homeric Epos, becomes eventually a self-resolving irony. These two modes or aspects—of which the one is as important for the whole as the other—namely, the unsevered consciousness of the godlike, and the combating human action, asserted, however, in godlike power and deed, which determines and executes the ethical purpose—supply the two fundamental elements, the mediation of which is displayed by Greek tragedy in its artistic compositions under the form of *chorus* and *heroic figures* respectively.

In modern times, considerable discussion has been raised over the significance of the Greek chorus, and the question has been raised incidentally whether it can or ought to be introduced into modern tragedy. In fact, the need of some such substantial foundation has been experienced; but critics have found it difficult to prescribe the precise manner in which effect should be given to such a change, because they failed to grasp with sufficient penetration the nature of that in which true tragedy consists and the necessity of the chorus as an essential constituent of all that Greek tragedy implies. Critics have, no doubt, recognized the nature of the chorus to the extent of maintaining that in it we find an attitude of tranquil meditation over the whole, whereas the characters of the action remain within the limits of their particular objects and situations, and, in short, receive in the chorus and its observations a standard of valuation of their characters and actions in much the same way as the public discovers in it, and within the drama itself, an objective representative of its own judgment upon all that is thus represented. In this view we have to this extent the fact rightly conceived, that the chorus is, in truth, there as a substantive and more enlightened intelligence, which warns us from irrelevant oppositions, and reflects upon the genuine issue. But, granting this to be so, it is by no means, like the spectator, a wholly disinterested person, at leisure to entertain such thoughts and ethical judgments as it likes which, uninteresting and tedious on its own account, could only be attached for the sake of such reflections. The chorus is the actual substance of the heroic life and action itself: it is, as contrasted with the particular heroes, the common folk regarded as the fruitful earth, out of which individuals, much as flowers and towering trees from their native soil, grow and whereby they are conditioned in this life. Consequently, the chorus is peculiarly fitted to a view of life in which the obligations of State legislation and settled religious dogmas do not, as yet, act as a restrictive force in ethical and social development, but where morality only exists in its primitive form of directly animated human life, and it is merely the equilibrium of unmoved life which remains assured in its stability against the fearful collisions which the antagonistic energies of individual action produces. We are made aware of the fact that an assured asylum of this kind is also a part of our actual existence by the presence of the chorus. It does not, therefore, practically co-operate with the action; it executes no right, actively, as against the contending heroes; it merely expresses its judgment as a matter of opinion; it warns, commiserates, or appeals to the divine law, and the ideal forces imminent in the soul, which the imagination grasps in external guise as the sphere of the gods that rule. In this self expression it is, as we have already seen, lyrical; for it does not act and there are no events for it to narrate in epical form. The content, however, retains at the same time the epic character of substantive universality; and its lyric movement is of such a nature that it can, and in this respect in contrast to the form of the genuine ode, approach at times that of the paean and the dithyramb. We must lay emphatic stress upon this position of the chorus in Greek tragedy. Just as the theatre itself possesses its external ground, its scene and environment, so, too, the chorus, that is the general community, is the spiritual scene; and we may compare it to the architectural temple which sur-

rounds the image of the god, which resembles the heroes in the action. Among ourselves, statues are placed under the open sky without such a background, which also modern tragedy does not require, for the reason that its actions do not depend on this substantive basis, but on the personal volition and personality, no less than the apparently external contingency of events and circumstances.

In this respect it is an entirely false view which regards the chorus as an accidental piece of residuary baggage, a mere remnant from the origins of Greek drama. Of course, it is incontestable that its source is to be traced to the circumstance that, in the festivals of Bacchus, so far as the artistic aspect is concerned, the choral song was of most importance until the introduction and interruption of its course by one reciter, whose relation finally was transformed into and exalted by the real figures of dramatic action. In the blossoming season of tragedy, however, the chorus was not by any means merely retained in honour of this particular phase of the festival and ritual of the god Bacchus; rather it became continuously more elaborate in its beauty and harmonious measures by reason of the fact that its association with the dramatic action is essential and, indeed, so indispensable to it that the decline of tragedy is intimately connected with the degeneration of the choruses, which no longer remain an integral member of the whole, but are degraded to a mere embellishment. In contrast to this, in romantic tragedy, the chorus is neither intrinsically appropriate nor does it appear to have originated from choric songs. On the contrary, the content is here of a type which defeats from the first any attempt to introduce choruses as understood by Greek dramatists. For, even if we go back to the most primitive of those so-called mysteries, morality plays, and farces of a similar character, from which the romantic drama issued, we find that these present no action in that original Greek sense of the term, no outbreak, that is, of opposing forces from the undivided consciousness of life and the godlike. To as little extent is the chorus adapted to the conditions of chivalry and the dominion of kings, in so far as, in such cases, the attitude of the folk is one of mere obedience, or it is itself a party, involved together with the interest of its fortune or misfortune in the course of the action. And in general the chorus entirely fails to secure its true position where the main subject-matter consists of particular passions, ends, and characters, or where any considerable opportunity is admitted to intrigue.

In contrast to the chorus, the *second* fundamental feature of dramatic composition is that of the *individuals* who act in *conflict* with each other. In Greek tragedy it is not at all bad will, crime, worthlessness, or mere misfortune, stupidity, and the like, which act as an incentive to such collisions, but rather, as I have frequently urged, the ethical right to a definite course of action. Abstract evil neither possesses truth in itself, nor does it arouse interest. At the same time, when we attribute ethical traits of characterization to the individuals of the action, these ought not to appear merely as a matter of opinion. It is rather implied in their right or claim that they are actually there as essential on their own account. The hazards of crime, such as are present in modern drama, the useless, or quite as much the so-called noble criminal, with his empty talk about fate, we meet with in the tragedy of ancient literature, rarely, if at all, and for the good reason that the decision and deed depends on the wholly personal aspect of interest and character, upon lust for power, love, honour, or other similar passions, whose justification has its roots exclusively in the particular inclination and individuality. A resolve of this character, whose claim is based upon the content of its object, which it carries into execution in one restricted direction of particularization, violates, under certain circumstances, which are already essentially implied in the actual possibility of conflicts, a further and equally ethical sphere of human volition, which the character thus confronted adheres to, and, by his thus stimulated action, enforces, so that in this way the collision of powers and individuals equally entitled to the ethical claim is completely set up in its movement.

The sphere of this content, although capable of great variety of detail, is not in its essential features very extensive. The principal source of opposition, which Sophocles in particular, in this respect following the lead of Aeschylus, has accepted and worked out in the finest way, is that of the *body politic,* the opposition, that is, between ethical life in its social universality and the family as the natural ground of moral relations. These are the purest forces of tragic representation. It is, in short, the harmony of these spheres and the concordant action within the bounds of their realized content, which constitute the perfected reality of the moral life. In this respect I need only recall the "Seven before Thebes" of Aeschylus and, as a yet stronger illustration, the "Antigone" of Sophocles. Antigone reverences the ties of blood-relationship, the gods of the nether world. Creon alone recognizes Zeus, the paramount Power of public life and the commonwealth. We come across a similar conflict in the "Iphigenia in Aulis," as also in the "Agamemnon," the "Choephorae," and "Eumenides" of Aeschylus, and in the "Electra" of Sophocles. Agamemnon, as king and leader of his army, sacrifices his daughter in the interest of the Greek folk and the Trojan expedition. He shatters thereby the bond of love as between himself and his daughter and wife, which Clytemnestra retains in the depths of a mother's heart, and in revenge prepares an ignominious death for her husband on his return. Orestes, their son, respects his mother, but is bound to represent the right of his father, the king, and strikes dead the mother who bore him.

A content of this type retains its force through all times, and its presentation, despite all difference of nationality, vitally arrests our human and artistic sympathies.

Of a more formal type is that second kind of essential collision, an illustration of which in the tragic story of Oedipus the Greek tragedians especially favoured. Of this Sophocles has left us the most complete example in his "Oedipus Rex," and "Oedipus at Colonus." The problem here is concerned with the claim of alertness in our intelligence, with the nature of the obligation implied in that which a man carries out with a volition fully aware of its acts as contrasted with that which he has done in fact, but unconscious of and with no intention of doing what he has done under the directing providence of the gods. Oedipus slays his father, marries his mother, begets

children in this incestuous alliance, and nevertheless is involved in these most terrible of crimes without active participation either in will or knowledge. The point of view of our profounder modern consciousness of right and wrong would be to recognize that crimes of this description, inasmuch as they were neither referable to a personal knowledge or volition, were not deeds for which the true personality of the perpetrator was responsible. The plastic nature of the Greek on the contrary adheres to the bare fact which an individual has achieved, and refuses to face the division implied by the purely ideal attitude of the soul in the self-conscious life on the one hand and the objective significance of the fact accomplished on the other.

For ourselves, to conclude this survey, other collisions, which either in general are related to the universally accepted association of personal action to the Greek conception of Destiny, or in some measure to more exceptional conditions, are comparatively speaking less important.

In all these tragic conflicts, however, we must above all place on one side the false notion of *guilt* or *innocence.* The heroes of tragedy are quite as much under one category as the other. If we accept the idea as valid that a man is guilty only in the case that a choice lay open to him, and he deliberately decided on the course of action which he carried out, then these plastic figures of ancient drama are guiltless. They act in accordance with a specific character, a specific pathos, for the simple reason that they are this character, this pathos. In such a case there is no lack of decision and no choice. The strength of great characters consists precisely in this that they do not choose, but are entirely and absolutely just that which they will and achieve. They are simply themselves, and never anything else, and their greatness consists in that fact. Weakness in action, in other words, wholly consists in the division of the personal self as such from its content, so that character, volition and final purpose do not appear as absolutely one unified growth; and inasmuch as no assured end lives in the soul as the very substance of the particular personality, as the pathos and might of the individual's entire will, he is still able to turn with indecision from this course to that, and his final decision is that of caprice. A wavering attitude of this description is alien to these plastic creations. The bond between the psychological state of mind and the content of the will is for them indissoluble. That which stirs them to action is this very pathos which implies an ethical justification and which, even in the pathetic aspects of the dialogue, is not enforced in and through the merely personal rhetoric of the heart and the sophistry of passion, but in the equally masculine and cultivated objective presence, in the profound possibilities, the harmony and vitally plastic beauty of which Sophocles was to a superlative degree master. At the same time, however, such a pathos, with its potential resources of collision, brings them to deeds that are both injurious and wrongful. They have no desire to avoid the blame that results therefrom. On the contrary, it is their fame to have done what they have done. One can in fact urge nothing more intolerable against a hero of this type than by saying that he has acted innocently. It is a point of honour with such great characters that they are guilty. They have no desire to excite pity or our sensibilities. For it is not the substantive, but rather the wholly personal deepening of the personality which stirs our individual pain. His securely strong character, however, coalesces entirely with his essential pathos, and this indivisible accord inspires wonder, not compassion. The drama of Euripides marks the transition to that.

The final result, then, of the development of tragedy conducts us to this issue and only this, namely, that the twofold vindication of the mutually conflicting aspects is no doubt retained, but the *one-sided* mode is cancelled, and the undisturbed ideal harmony brings back again that condition of the chorus, which attributes without reserve equal honour to all the gods. The true course of dramatic development consists in the annulment of *contradictions* viewed as such, in the reconciliation of the forces of human action, which alternately strive to negate each other in their conflict. Only so far is misfortune and suffering not the final issue, but rather the satisfaction of spirit, as for the first time, in virtue of such a conclusion, the necessity of all that particular individuals experience, is able to appear in complete accord with reason, and our emotional attitude is tranquillized on a true ethical basis; rudely shaken by the calamitous result to the heroes, but reconciled in the substantial facts. And it is only in so far as we retain such a view securely that we shall be in a position to understand ancient tragedy. We have to guard ourselves therefore from concluding that a *dénouement* of this type is merely a moral issue conformably to which evil is punished and virtue rewarded, as indicated by the proverb that "when crime turns to vomit, virtue sits down at table." We have nothing to do here with this wholly personal aspect of a self-reflecting personality and its conception of good and evil, but are concerned with the appearance of the affirmative reconciliation and the equal validity of both powers engaged in conflict, if the collision is complete. To as little extent is the necessity of the issue a blind destiny, or in other words a purely irrational, unintelligible fate, identified with the classical world by many; rather it is the rationality of destiny, albeit it does not as yet appear as self-conscious Providence, the divine final end of which in conjunction with the world and individuals appears on its own account and for others, depending as it does on just this fact that the highest Power paramount over particular gods and mankind cannot suffer this, namely, that the forces, which affirm their self-subsistence in modes that are abstract or incomplete, and thereby overstep the boundary of their warrant, no less than the conflicts which result from them, should retain their self-stability. Fate drives personality back upon its limits, and shatters it, when it has grown overweening. An irrational compulsion, however, an innocence of suffering would rather only excite indignation in the soul of the spectator than ethical tranquillity. From a further point of view, therefore, the reconciliation of *tragedy* is equally distinct from that of the *Epos*. If we look at either Achilles or Odysseus in this respect we observe that both attain their object, and it is right that they do so; but it is not a continuous happiness with which they are favoured; they have on the contrary to taste in its bitterness the feeling of finite condition, and are forced to fight wearily through difficulties, losses and sacrifices. It is in fact a univer-

sal demand of truth that in the course of life and all that takes place in the objective world the nugatory character of finite conditions should compel attention. So no doubt the anger of Achilles is reconciled; he obtains from Agamemnon that in respect of which he had suffered the sense of insult; he is revenged upon Hector; the funeral rites of Patroclus are consummated, and the character of Achilles is acknowledged in all its glory. But his wrath and its reconciliation have for all that cost him his dearest friend, the noble Patroclus; and, in order to avenge himself upon Hector for this loss, he finds himself compelled to disengage himself from his anger, to enter once more the battle against the Trojans, and in the very moment when his glory is acknowledged receives the prevision of his early death. In a similar way Odysseus reaches Ithaca at last, the goal of his desire; but he does so alone and in his sleep, having lost all his companions, all the war-booty from Ilium, after long years of endurance and fatigue. In this way both heroes have paid their toll to finite conditions and the claim of nemesis is evidenced in the destruction of Troy and the misfortunes of the Greek heroes. But this nemesis is simply justice as conceived of old, which merely humiliates what is everywhere too exalted, in order to establish once more the abstract balance of fortune by the instrumentality of misfortune, and which merely touches and affects finite existence without further ethical signification. And this is the justice of the Epic in the field of objective fact, the universal reconciliation of simple accommodation. The higher conception of reconciliation in tragedy is on the contrary related to the resolution of specific ethical and substantive facts from their contradiction into their true harmony. The way in which such an accord is established is asserted under very different modes; I propose therefore merely to direct attention to the fundamental features of the actual process herein involved.

First, we have particularly to emphasize the fact, that if it is the one-sidedness of the pathos which constitutes the real basis of collisions this merely amounts to the statement that it is asserted in the action of life, and therewith has become the unique pathos of a particular individual. If this one-sidedness is to be abrogated then it is this individual which, to the extent that his action is exclusively identified with this isolated pathos, must perforce be stripped and sacrificed. For the individual here is merely this single life, and, if this unity is not secured in its stability on its own account, the individual is shattered.

The most complete form of this development is possible when the individuals engaged in conflict relatively to their concrete or objective life appear in each case essentially involved in one whole, so that they stand fundamentally under the power of that against which they battle, and consequently infringe that, which, conformably to their own essential life, they ought to respect. Antigone, for example, lives under the political authority of Creon; she is herself the daughter of a king and the affianced of Haemon, so that her obedience to the royal prerogative is an obligation. But Creon also, who is on his part father and husband, is under obligation to respect the sacred ties of relationship, and only by breach of this can give an order that is in conflict with such a sense. In consequence of this we find immanent in the life of both that which each respectively combats, and they are seized and broken by that very bond which is rooted in the compass of their own social existence. Antigone is put to death before she can enjoy what she looks forward to as bride, and Creon too is punished in the fatal end of his son and wife, who commit suicide, the former on account of Antigone's death, and the latter owing to Haemon's. Among all the fine creations of the ancient and the modern world—and I am acquainted with pretty nearly everything in such a class, and one ought to know it, and it is quite possible—the "Antigone" of Sophocles is from this point of view in my judgment the most excellent and satisfying work of art.

The tragic issue does not, however, require in every case, as a means of removing both overemphasized aspects and the equal honour which they respectively claim, the downfall of the contestant parties. The "Eumenides" ends, as we all know, not with the death of Orestes, or the destruction of the Eumenides, these avenging spirits of matricide and filial affection, as opposed to Apollo, who seeks to protect unimpaired the worth of and reverence for the family chief and king, who prompted Orestes to slay Clytemnestra, but with Orestes released from the punishment and honour bestowed on both divinities. At the same time we cannot fail to see in this adjusted conclusion the nature of the authority which the Greeks attached to their gods when they presented them as mere individuals contending with each other. They appear, in short, to the Athenian of everyday life merely as definite aspects of ethical experience which the principles of morality viewed in their complete and harmonious coherence bind together. The votes of the Areopagus are equal on either side. It is Athene, the goddess, the life of Athens, that is, imagined in its essential unity, who adds the white pebble, who frees Orestes, and at the same time promises altars and a cult to the Eumenides no less than Apollo. As a contrast to this type of objective reconciliation the settlement may be, *secondly,* of a more personal character. In other words, the individual concerned in the action may in the last instance surrender his onesided point of view. In this betrayal by personality of its essential pathos, however, it cannot fail to appear destitute of character; and this contradicts the masculine integrity of such plastic figures. The individual, therefore, can only submit to a higher Power and its counsel or command, to the effect that while on his own account he adheres to such a pathos, the will is nevertheless broken in its bare obstinacy by a god's authority. In such a case the knot is not loosened, but, as in the case of Philoctetes, it is severed by a *deus ex machina.*

But as a *further* and final class, and one more beautiful than the above rather external mode of resolution, we have the reconciliation more properly of the soul itself, in which respect there is, in virtue of the personal significance, a real approach to our modern point of view. The most perfect example of this in ancient drama is to be found in the ever admirable "Oedipus at Colonos" of Sophocles. The protagonist here has unwittingly slain his father, secured the sceptre of Thebes, and the bridal bed of his own mother. He is not rendered unhappy by these unwitting crimes; but the power of divination he has

of old possessed makes him realize, despite himself, the darkness of the experience that confronts him, and he becomes fearfully, if indistinctly, aware of what his position is. In this resolution of the riddle in himself he resembles Adam, losing his happiness when he obtains the knowledge of good and evil. What he then does, the seer, is to blind himself, then abdicate the throne and depart from Thebes, very much as Adam and Eve are driven from Paradise. From henceforward he wanders about a helpless old man. Finally a god calls the terribly afflicted man to himself, the man, that is, who refusing the request of his sons that he should return to Thebes, prefers to associate with the Erinyes; the man, in short, who extinguishes all the disruption in himself and who purifies himself in his own soul. His blind eyes are made clear and bright, his limbs are healed, and become a treasure of the city which received him as a free guest. And this illumination in death is for ourselves no less than for him the more truly visible reconciliation which is worked out both in and for himself as individual man, in and through, that is, his essential character. Critics have endeavoured to discover here the temper of the Christian life; we are told we have here the picture of a sinner, whom God receives into His grace; and the fateful misfortunes which expire in their finite condition are made good with the seal of blessedness in death. The reconciliation of the Christian religion, however, is an illumination of the soul, which, bathed in the everlasting waters of salvation, is raised above mortal life and its deeds. Here it is the heart itself, for in such a view the spiritual life can effect this, which buries that life and its deed in the grave of the heart itself, counting the recriminations of earthly guilt as part and parcel of its own earthly individuality; and which, in the full assuredness of the eternally pure and spiritual condition of blessedness, holds itself in itself calm and steadfast against such impeachment. The illumination of Oedipus, on the contrary, remains throughout, in consonance with ancient ideas, the restoration of conscious life from the strife of ethical powers and violations to the renewed and harmonious unity of this *ethical content itself.*

SAMUEL TAYLOR COLERIDGE (1772–1834)

Coleridge was probably a greater critic than he was a poet. His comments on Shakespeare, for example, are commonly considered the finest criticism of the dramatist ever recorded. In the selection reprinted here, Coleridge provides an important distinction between stage illusion and "delusion." The latter is his term for the mistaken conception that the purpose of drama is to convince the audience that the events onstage are occurring in real life. This impulse, as he points out, emphasizes the immediate pleasure of the theatrical experience at the expense of the more significant impact that great drama pro-. vides.

"Progress of the Drama"
(1818)

A theater, in the widest sense of the word, is the general term for all places of amusement through the ear or eye, in which men assembled in order to be amused by some entertainment presented to all at the same time and in common. Thus, an old Puritan divine says:—"Those who attend public worship and sermons only to amuse themselves, make a theater of the church, and turn God's house into the devil's. *Theatra æ des diabololatricæ*." The most important and dignified species of this *genus* is, doubtless, the stage, (*res theatralis histrionica*), which, in addition to the generic definition above given, may be characterized in its idea, or according to what it does, or ought to, aim at, as a combination of several or of all the fine arts in an harmonious whole, having a distinct end of its own, to which the peculiar end of each of the component arts, taken separately, is made subordinate and subservient,—that, namely, of imitating reality—whether external things, actions, or passions—under a semblance of reality. Thus, Claude imitates a landscape at sunset, but only as a picture; while a forest-scene is not presented to the spectators as a picture, but as a forest; and though, in the full sense of the word, we are no more deceived by the one than by the other, yet are our feelings very differently affected; and the pleasure derived from the one is not composed of the same elements as that afforded by the other, even on the supposition that the *quantum* of both were equal. In the former, a picture, it is a condition of all genuine delight that we should not be deceived; in the latter, stage-scenery, (inasmuch as its principal end is not in or for itself, as is the case in a picture, but to be an assistance and means to an end out of itself) its very purpose is to produce as much illusion as its nature permits. These, and all other stage presentations, are to produce a sort of temporary half-faith, which the spectator encourages in himself and supports by a voluntary contribution on his own part, because he knows that it is at all times in his power to see the thing as it really is. I have often observed that little children are actually deceived by stage-scenery, never by pictures; though even these produce an effect on their impressible minds, which they do not on the minds of adults. The child, if strongly impressed, does not indeed positively think the picture to be the reality; but yet he does not think the contrary. As Sir George Beaumont was shewing me a very fine engraving from Rubens, representing a storm at sea without any vessel or boat introduced, my little boy, then about five years old, came dancing and singing into the room, and all at once (if I may so say) *tumbled in* upon the print. He instantly started, stood silent and motionless, with the strongest expression, first of wonder and then of grief in his eyes and countenance, and at length said, "And where is the ship? But that is sunk, and the men are all drowned!" still keeping his eyes fixed on the print. Now what pictures are to little children, stage illusion is to men, provided they retain any part of the child's sensibility; except, that in the latter in-

stance, the suspension of the act of comparison, which permits this sort of negative belief, is somewhat more assisted by the will, than in that of a child respecting a picture.

The true stage-illusion in this and in all other things consists—not in the mind's judging it to be a forest, but, in its remission of the judgment that it is not a forest. And this subject of stage-illusion is so important, and so many practical errors and false criticisms may arise, and indeed have arisen, either from reasoning on it as actual delusion, (the strange notion, on which the French critics built up their theory, and on which the French poets justify the construction of their tragedies), or from denying it altogether, (which seems the end of Dr. Johnson's reasoning, and which, as extremes meet, would lead to the very same consequences, by excluding whatever would not be judged probable by us in our coolest state of feeling, with all our faculties in even balance), that these few remarks will, I hope, be pardoned, if they should serve either to explain or to illustrate the point. For not only are we never absolutely deluded—or anything like it, but the attempt to cause the highest delusion possible to beings in their senses sitting in a theater, is a gross fault, incident only to low minds, which, feeling that they cannot affect the heart or head permanently, endeavor to call forth the momentary affections. There ought never to be more pain than is compatible with co-existing pleasure, and to be amply repaid by thought.

Shakespeare found the infant stage demanding an intermixture of ludicrous character as imperiously as that of Greece did the chorus, and high language accordant. And there are many advantages in this;—a greater assimilation to nature, a greater scope of power, more truths, and more feelings;—the effects of contrast, as in Lear and the Fool; and especially this, that the true language of passion becomes sufficiently elevated by your having previously heard, in the same piece, the lighter conversation of men under no strong emotion. The very nakedness of the stage, too, was advantageous,—for the drama thence became something between recitation and representation; and the absence or paucity of scenes allowed a freedom from the laws of unity of place and unity of time, the observance of which must either confine the drama to as few subjects as may be counted on the fingers, or involve gross improbabilities, far more striking than the violation would have caused. Thence, also, was precluded the danger of a false ideal,—of aiming at more than what is possible on the whole. What play of the ancients, with reference to their ideal, does not hold out more glaring absurdities than any in Shakespeare? On the Greek plan a man could more easily be a poet than a dramatist; upon our plan more easily a dramatist than a poet.

GEORGE MEREDITH
(1828–1909)

Meredith's "Essay on Comedy" was originally given as a lecture under the title *The Idea of the*

Comedy and the Uses of the Comic Spirit in 1877, two years before the publication of his novel *The Egoist*. Theory and practice here coalesced in the expression of Meredith's comic ideal, which is finally the ideal of an ordered, structured society governed by the intellect and rooted in tolerance. It has frequently been pointed out that Meredith's "comedy" is really a characterization of high comedy or of the comedy of manners and that it fails to acknowledge the claims of comedy as diverse as that of Shakespeare and Dickens. Nevertheless, within its limits it provides an original and penetrating insight into that phenomenon that provokes "thoughtful laughter."

from "An Essay on Comedy"

There are plain reasons why the comic poet is not a frequent apparition, and why the great comic poet remains without a fellow. A society of cultivated men and women is required, wherein ideas are current, and the perceptions quick, that he may be supplied with matter and an audience. The semi-barbarism of merely giddy communities, and feverish emotional periods, repel him; and also a state of marked social inequality of the sexes; nor can he whose business is to address the mind be understood where there is not a moderate degree of intellectual activity.

Moreover, to touch and kindle the mind through laughter demands, more than sprightliness, a most subtle delicacy. That must be a natal gift in the comic poet. The substance he deals with will show him a startling exhibition of the dyer's hand, if he is without it. People are ready to surrender themselves to witty thumps on the back, breast, and sides; all except the head—and it is there that he aims. He must be subtle to penetrate. A corresponding acuteness must exist to welcome him. The necessity for the two conditions will explain how it is that we count him during centuries in the singular number. . . . Life, we know too well, is not a comedy, but something strangely mixed; nor is comedy a vile mask. The corrupted importation from France was noxious, a noble entertainment spoilt to suit the wretched taste of a villainous age; and the later imitations of it, partly drained of its poison and made decorous, became tiresome, notwithstanding their fun, in the perpetual recurring of the same situations, owing to the absence of original study and vigor of conception. Scene 5, Act 2, of the *Misanthrope,* owing, no doubt, to the fact of our not producing matter for original study, is repeated in succession by Wycherley, Congreve, and Sheridan, and, as it is at second hand, we have it done cynically—or such is the tone—in the manner of "below stairs." Comedy thus treated may be accepted as a version of the ordinary worldly understanding of our social life; at least, in accord with the current dicta concerning it. The epigrams can be made; but it is uninstructive, rather tending to do disservice. Comedy justly treated, as you find it in Molière, whom we so clownishly mishandled—the comedy of Molière throws no infamous reflection upon life. It is deeply conceived, in the first place, and therefore it cannot be impure. Meditate on that statement. Neither did man wield so shrieking a scourge upon vice; but his consummate self-mastery is not shaken while administering it. Tartuffe and

Harpagon, in fact, are made each to whip himself and his class—the false pietists, and the insanely covetous. Molière has only set them in motion. He strips Folly to the skin, displays the imposture of the creature, and is content to offer her better clothing, with the lesson Chrysale reads to Philaminte and Bélise. He conceives purely, and he writes purely, in the simplest language, the simplest of French verse. The source of his wit is clear reason; it is a fountain of that soil, and it springs to vindicate reason, common sense, rightness, and justice—for no vain purpose ever. The wit is of such pervading spirit that it inspires a pun with meaning and interest. His moral does not hang like a tail, or preach from one character incessantly cocking an eye at the audience, as in recent realistic French plays, but is in the heart of his work, throbbing with every pulsation of an organic structure. If life is likened to the comedy of Molière, there is no scandal in the comparison.

Congreve's *Way of the World* is an exception to our other comedies, his own among them, by virtue of the remarkable brilliancy of the writing, and the figure of Millamant. The comedy has no idea in it, beyond the stale one that so the world goes; and it concludes with the jaded discovery of a document at a convenient season for the descent of the curtain. A plot was an afterthought with Congreve. By the help of a wooden villain (Maskwell), marked gallows to the flattest eye, he gets a sort of plot in *The Double-Dealer.* His *Way of the World* might be called "The Conquest of a Town Coquette"; and Millamant is a perfect portrait of a coquette, both in her resistance to Mirabell and the manner of her surrender, and also in her tongue. The wit here is not so salient as in certain passages of *Love for Love,* where Valentine feigns madness, or retorts on his father, or Mrs. Frail rejoices in the harmlessness of wounds to a woman's virtue, if she keeps them "from air." In *The Way of the World,* it appears less prepared in the smartness, and is more diffused in the more characteristic style of the speakers. Here, however, as elsewhere, his famous wit is like a bullyfencer, not ashamed to lay traps for its exhibition, transparently petulant for the train between certain ordinary words and the powder-magazine of the improprieties to be fired. Contrast the wit of Congreve with Molière's. That of the first is a Toledo blade, sharp, and wonderfully supple for steel; cast for dueling, restless in the scabbard, being so pretty when out of it. To shine, it must have an adversary. Molière's wit is like a running brook, with innumerable fresh lights on it at every turn of the wood through which its business is to find a way. It does not run in search of obstructions, to be noisy over them; but when dead leaves and viler substances are heaped along the course, its natural song is heightened. Without effort, and with no dazzling flashes of achievement, it is full of healing, the wit of good breeding, the wit of wisdom.

"Genuine humor and true wit," says Landor, "require a sound and capacious mind, which is always a grave one." . . . The life of the comedy is in the idea. As with the singing of the skylark out of sight, you must love the bird to be attentive to the song, so in this highest flight of the comic Muse, you must love pure comedy warmly to understand the *Misanthrope;* you must be receptive of the idea of comedy. And to love comedy you must know the real world, and know men and women well enough not to expect too much of them, though you may still hope for good. . . .

Now, to look about us in the present time, I think it will be acknowledged that, in neglecting the cultivation of the comic idea, we are losing the aid of a powerful auxiliar. You see Folly perpetually sliding into new shapes in a society possessed of wealth and leisure, with many whims, many strange ailments and strange doctors. Plenty of common sense is in the world to thrust her back when she pretends to empire. But the first-born of common sense, the vigilant Comic, which is the genius of thoughtful laughter, which would readily extinguish her at the outset, is not serving as a public advocate.

You will have noticed the disposition of common sense, under pressure of some pertinacious piece of light-headedness, to grow impatient and angry. That is a sign of the absence, or at least of the dormancy, of the comic idea. For Folly is the natural prey of the Comic, known to it in all her transformations, in every disguise; and it is with the springing delight of hawk over heron, hound after fox, that it gives her chase, never fretting, never tiring, sure of having her, allowing her no rest.

Contempt is a sentiment that cannot be entertained by comic intelligence. What is it but an excuse to be idly-minded, or personally lofty, or comfortably narrow, not perfectly humane? If we do not feign when we say that we despise Folly, we shut the brain. There is a disdainful attitude in the presence of Folly, partaking of the foolishness to comic perception; and anger is not much less foolish than disdain. The struggle we have to conduct is essence against essence. Let no one doubt of the sequel when this emanation of what is firmest in us is launched to strike down the daughter of Unreason and Sentimentalism—such being Folly's parentage, when it is respectable.

Our modern system of combating her is too long defensive, and carried on too ploddingly with concrete engines of war in the attack. She has time to get behind entrenchments. She is ready to stand a siege, before the heavily-armed man of science and the writer of the leading article or elaborate essay have primed their big guns. It should be remembered that she has charms for the multitude; and an English multitude, seeing her make a gallant fight of it, will be half in love with her, certainly willing to lend her a cheer. Benevolent subscriptions assist her to hire her own man of science, her own organ in the press. If ultimately she is cast out and overthrown, she can stretch a finger at gaps in our ranks. She can say that she commanded an army, and seduced men, whom we thought sober men and safe, to act as her lieutenants. We learn rather gloomily, after she has flashed her lantern, that we have in our midst able men, and men with minds, for whom there is no pole-star in intellectual navigation. Comedy, or the comic element, is the specific for the poison of delusion while Folly is passing from the state of vapor to substantial form. . . .

The comic poet is in the narrow field, or enclosed square, of the society he depicts; and he addresses the still narrower enclosure of men's intellects, with reference to the operation of the social world upon their characters. He is not concerned with beginnings or endings or surroundings, but with what you are now weaving. To understand his work and value it, you must have a sober liking of your kind, and a sober estimate of our civilized qualities. The aim and business of the comic poet are misunderstood, his meaning is not seized nor his point of view taken, when he is accused of dishonoring our nature and being hostile to sentiment, tending to spitefulness and making an unfair use of laughter. Those who detect irony in comedy do so because they choose to see it in life. Poverty, says the satirist, 'has nothing harder in itself than that it makes men ridiculous.' But poverty is never ridiculous to comic perception until it attempts to make its rags conceal its bareness in a forlorn attempt at decency, or foolishly to rival ostentation. Caleb Balderstone, in his endeavor to keep up the honor of a noble household in a state of beggary, is an exquisitely comic character. In the case of "poor relatives," on the other hand, it is the rich, whom they perplex, that are really comic; and to laugh at the former, not seeing the comedy of the latter, is to betray dulness of vision. Humorist and satirist frequently hunt together as ironists in pursuit of the grotesque, to the exclusion of the comic. That was an affecting moment in the history of the Prince Regent, when the First Gentleman of Europe burst into tears at a sarcastic remark of Beau Brummell's on the cut of his coat. Humor, satire, irony, pounce on it altogether as their common prey. The Comic Spirit eyes, but does not touch, it. Put into action, it would be farcical. It is too gross for comedy.

Incidents of a kind casting ridicule on our unfortunate nature, instead of our conventional life, provoke derisive laughter, which thwarts the comic idea. But derision is foiled by the play of the intellect. Most of doubtful causes in contest are open to comic interpretation, and any intellectual pleading of a doubtful cause contains germs of an idea of comedy.

The laughter of satire is a blow in the back or the face. The laughter of comedy is impersonal and of unrivaled politeness, nearer a smile—often no more than a smile. It laughs through the mind, for the mind directs it; and it might be called the humor of the mind.

One excellent test of the civilization of a country, as I have said, I take to be the flourishing of the comic idea and comedy; and the test of true comedy is that it shall awaken thoughtful laughter.

FRIEDRICH NIETZSCHE
(1844–1900)

Nietzsche's *The Birth of Tragedy* (1872), an excerpt of which is here translated by William Haussman, is one of the most celebrated statements in the history of dramatic theory. It argues that Greek tragedy grew out of the worship of the god Dionysus and that tragedy is in essence Dionysian, that is, a celebration of the instinctive, emotional, and irrational elements in human nature. This is in contrast to what Nietzsche characterizes as the Apollonian ideal, that vision of man and nature that idealizes harmony, moderation, and reason. The latter is present in Greek tragedy, particularly in the choral songs, but, argues Nietzsche, it is merely the superstructure, the external form of that tremendous will to live, which is at the core of the experience. Thus, tragedy is the product of the tension between the Apollonian and Dionysian drives in man.

from *The Birth of Tragedy*

We now approach the real purpose of our investigation, which aims at acquiring a knowledge of the Dionyso-Apollonian genius and his artwork, or at least an anticipatory understanding of the mystery of the aforesaid union. Here we shall ask first of all where that new germ which subsequently developed into tragedy and dramatic dithyramb first makes itself perceptible in the Hellenic world. The ancients themselves supply the answer in symbolic form, when they place *Homer* and *Archilochus* as the forefathers and torch-bearers of Greek poetry side by side on gems, sculptures, etc., in the sure conviction that only these two thoroughly original compeers, from whom a stream of fire flows over the whole of Greek posterity, should be taken into consideration. Homer, the aged dreamer sunk in himself, the type of the Apollonian naïve artist, beholds now with astonishment the impassioned genius of the warlike votary of the muses, Archilochus, violently tossed to and fro on the billows of existence: and modern æsthetics could only add by way of interpretation, that here the "objective" artist is confronted by the first "subjective" artist. But this interpretation is of little service to us, because we know the subjective artist only as the poor artist, and in every type and elevation of art we demand specially and first of all the conquest of the Subjective, the redemption from the "ego" and the cessation of every individual will and desire; indeed, we find it impossible to believe in any truly artistic production, however insignificant, without objectivity, without pure, interestless contemplation. Hence our æsthetics must first solve the problem as to how the "lyrist" is possible as an artist: he who according to the experience of all ages continually says "I" and sings off to us the entire chromatic scale of his passions and desires. This very Archilochus appals us, alongside of Homer, by his cries of hatred and scorn, by the drunken outbursts of his desire. Is not just he then, who has been called the first subjective artist, the non-artist proper? But whence then the reverence which was shown to him—the poet—in very remarkable utterances by the Delphic oracle itself, the focus of "objective" art?

Schiller has enlightened us concerning his poetic procedure by a psychological observation, inexplicable to himself, yet not apparently open to any objection. He acknowledges that as the preparatory state to the act of poetising he had not perhaps before him or within him a series of pictures with co-ordinate causality of thoughts, but rather a *musical mood.* ("The perception with me is at first without a clear and definite object; this forms itself later. A certain musical mood of mind precedes, and only after this does the poetical idea follow with me.") Add to this

the most important phenomenon of all ancient lyric poetry, *the union,* regarded everywhere as natural, *of the lyrist with the musician,* their very identity, indeed,—compared with which our modern lyric poetry is like the statue of a god without a head,—and we may now, on the basis of our metaphysics of æsthetics set forth above, interpret the lyrist to ourselves as follows. As Dionysian artist he is in the first place become altogether one with the Primordial Unity, its pain and contradiction, and he produces the copy of this Primordial Unity as music, granting that music has been correctly termed a repetition and a recast of the world; but now, under the Apollonian dream-inspiration, this music again becomes visible to him as in a *symbolic dream-picture.* The formless and intangible reflection of the primordial pain in music, with its redemption in appearance, then generates a second mirroring as a concrete symbol or example. The artist has already surrendered his subjectivity in the Dionysian process: the picture which now shows to him his oneness with the heart of the world, is a dream-scene, which embodies the primordial contradiction and primordial pain, together with the primordial joy, of appearance. The "I" of the lyrist sounds therefore from the abyss of being: its "subjectivity," in the sense of the modern æsthetes, is a fiction. When Archilochus, the first lyrist of the Greeks, makes known both his mad love and his contempt to the daughters of Lycambes, it is not his passion which dances before us in orgiastic frenzy: we see Dionysus and the Mænads, we see the drunken reveller Archilochus sunk down to sleep—as Euripides depicts it in the Bacchæ, the sleep on the high Alpine pasture, in the noonday sun:—and now Apollo approaches and touches him with the laurel. The Dionyso-musical enchantment of the sleeper now emits, as it were, picture sparks, lyrical poems, which in their highest development are called tragedies and dramatic dithyrambs.

The plastic artist, as also the epic poet, who is related to him, is sunk in the pure contemplation of pictures. The Dionysian musician is, without any picture, himself just primordial pain and the primordial re-echoing thereof. The lyric genius is conscious of a world of pictures and symbols—growing out of the state of mystical self-abnegation and oneness,—which has a colouring causality and velocity quite different from that of the world of the plastic artist and epic poet. While the latter lives in these pictures, and only in them, with joyful satisfaction, and never grows tired of contemplating them with love, even in their minutest characters, while even the picture of the angry Achilles is to him but a picture, the angry expression of which he enjoys with the dream-joy in appearance—so that, by this mirror of appearance, he is guarded against being unified and blending with his figures;—the pictures of the lyrist on the other hand are nothing but *his very* self and, as it were, only different projections of himself, on account of which he as the moving centre of this world is entitled to say "I": only of course this self is not the same as that of the waking, empirically real man, but the only verily existent and eternal self resting at the basis of things, by means of the images whereof the lyric genius sees through even to this basis of things. Now let us suppose that he beholds *himself* also among these images as non-genius, *i.e.,* his subject, the whole throng of subjective passions and impulses of the will directed to a definite object which appears real to him; if now it seems as if the lyric genius and the allied non-genius were one, and as if the former spoke that little word "I" of his own accord, this appearance will no longer be able to lead us astray, as it certainly led those astray who designated the lyrist as the subjective poet. In truth, Archilochus, the passionately inflamed, loving and hating man, is but a vision of the genius, who by this time is no longer Archilochus, but a genius of the world, who expresses his primordial pain symbolically in the figure of the man Archilochus: while the subjectively willing and desiring man, Archilochus, can never at any time be a poet. It is by no means necessary, however, that the lyrist should see nothing but the phenomenon of the man Archilochus before him as a reflection of eternal being; and tragedy shows how far the visionary world of the lyrist may depart from this phenomenon, to which, of course, it is most intimately related.

Schopenhauer, who did not shut his eyes to the difficulty presented by the lyrist in the philosophical contemplation of art, thought he had found a way out of it, on which, however, I cannot accompany him; while he alone, in his profound metaphysics of music, held in his hands the means whereby this difficulty could be definitely removed: as I believe I have removed it here in his spirit and to his honour. In contrast to our view, he describes the peculiar nature of song as follows [1] (*Welt als Wille und Vorstellung,* I. 295):—"It is the subject of the will, *i.e.,* his own volition, which fills the consciousness of the singer; often as an unbound and satisfied desire (joy), but still more often as a restricted desire (grief), always as an emotion, a passion, or an agitated frame of mind. Besides this, however, and along with it, by the sight of surrounding nature, the singer becomes conscious of himself as the subject of pure will-less knowing, the unbroken, blissful peace of which now appears, in contrast to the stress of desire, which is always restricted and always needy. The feeling of this contrast, this alternation, is really what the song as a whole expresses and what principally constitutes the lyrical state of mind. In it pure knowing comes to us as it were to deliver us from desire and the stress thereof: we follow, but only for an instant; for desire, the remembrance of our personal ends, tears us anew from peaceful contemplation; yet ever again the next beautiful surrounding in which the pure will-less knowledge presents itself to us, allures us away from desire. Therefore, in song and in the lyrical mood, desire (the personal interest of the ends) and the pure perception of the surrounding which presents itself, are wonderfully mingled with each other; connections between them are sought for and imagined; the subjective disposition, the affection of the will, imparts its own hue to the contemplated surrounding, and conversely, the surroundings communicate the reflex of their colour to the will. The true song is the expression of the whole of this mingled and divided state of mind."

Who could fail to see in this description that lyric poetry is here characterised as an imperfectly attained art, which seldom and only as it were in leaps

[1] *World as Will and Idea,* I. 323, 4th ed. of Haldane and Kemp's translation. Quoted with a few changes.

arrives at its goal, indeed, as a semi-art, the essence of which is said to consist in this, that desire and pure contemplation, *i.e.,* the unæsthetic and the æsthetic condition, are wonderfully mingled with each other? We maintain rather, that this entire antithesis, according to which, as according to some standard of value, Schopenhauer, too, still classifies the arts, the antithesis between the subjective and the objective, is quite out of place in æsthetics, inasmuch as the subject, *i.e.,* the desiring individual who furthers his own egoistic ends, can be conceived only as the adversary, not as the origin of art. In so far as the subject is the artist, however, he has already been released from his individual will, and has become as it were the medium, through which the one verily existent Subject celebrates his redemption in appearance. For this one thing must above all be clear to us, to our humiliation *and* exaltation, that the entire comedy of art is not at all performed, say, for our betterment and culture, and that we are just as little the true authors of this art-world: rather we may assume with regard to ourselves, that its true author uses us as pictures and artistic projections, and that we have our highest dignity in our significance as works of art—for only as an *æsthetic phenomenon* is existence and the world eternally *justified:*—while of course our consciousness of this our specific significance hardly differs from the kind of consciousness which the soldiers painted on canvas have of the battle represented thereon. Hence all our knowledge of art is at bottom quite illusory, because, as knowing persons we are not one and identical with the Being who, as the sole author and spectator of this comedy of art, prepares a perpetual entertainment for himself. Only in so far as the genius in the act of artistic production coalesces with this primordial artist of the world, does he get a glimpse of the eternal essence of art, for in this state he is, in a marvellous manner, like the weird picture of the fairy-tale which can at will turn its eyes and behold itself; he is now at once subject and object, at once poet, actor, and spectator.

With reference to Archilochus, it has been established by critical research that he introduced the *folk-song* into literature, and, on account thereof, deserved, according to the general estimate of the Greeks, his unique position alongside of Homer. But what is this popular folk-song in contrast to the wholly Apollonian epos? What else but the *perpetuum vestigium* of a union of the Apollonian and the Dionysian? Its enormous diffusion among all peoples, still further enhanced by ever new births, testifies to the power of this artistic double impulse of nature: which leaves its vestiges in the popular song in like manner as the orgiastic movements of a people perpetuate themselves in its music. Indeed, one might also furnish historical proofs, that every period which is highly productive in popular songs has been most violently stirred by Dionysian currents, which we must always regard as the substratum and prerequisite of the popular song.

First of all, however, we regard the popular song as the musical mirror of the world, as the original melody, which now seeks for itself a parallel dream-phenomenon and expresses it in poetry. *Melody is therefore primary and universal,* and as such may admit of several objectivations, in several texts.

Likewise, in the naïve estimation of the people, it is regarded as by far the more important and necessary. Melody generates the poem out of itself by an ever-recurring process. *The strophic form of the popular song* points to the same phenomenon, which I always beheld with astonishment, till at last I found this explanation. Any one who in accordance with this theory examines a collection of popular songs, such as "Des Knaben Wunderhorn," will find innumerable instances of the perpetually productive melody scattering picture sparks all around: which in their variegation, their abrupt change, their mad precipitance, manifest a power quite unknown to the epic appearance and its steady flow. From the point of view of the epos, this unequal and irregular pictorial world of lyric poetry must be simply condemned: and the solemn epic rhapsodists of the Apollonian festivals in the age of Terpander have certainly done so.

Accordingly, we observe that in the poetising of the popular song, language is strained to its utmost *to imitate music;* and hence a new world of poetry begins with Archilochus, which is fundamentally opposed to the Homeric. And in saying this we have pointed out the only possible relation between poetry and music, between word and tone: the word, the picture, the concept here seeks an expression analogous to music and now experiences in itself the power of music. In this sense we may discriminate between two main currents in the history of the language of the Greek people, according as their language imitated either the world of phenomena and of pictures, or the world of music. One has only to reflect seriously on the linguistic difference with regard to colour, syntactical structure, and vocabulary in Homer and Pindar, in order to comprehend the significance of this contrast; indeed, it becomes palpably clear to us that in the period between Homer and Pindar the *orgiastic flute tones of Olympus* must have sounded forth, which, in an age as late as Aristotle's, when music was infinitely more developed, transported people to drunken enthusiasm, and which, when their influence was first felt, undoubtedly incited all the poetic means of expression of contemporaneous man to imitation. I here call attention to a familiar phenomenon of our own times, against which our æsthetics raises many objections. We again and again have occasion to observe how a symphony of Beethoven compels the individual hearers to use figurative speech, though the appearance presented by a collocation of the different pictorial world generated by a piece of music may be never so fantastically diversified and even contradictory. To practise its small wit on such compositions, and to overlook a phenomenon which is certainly worth explaining, is quite in keeping with this æsthetics. Indeed, even if the tone-poet has spoken in pictures concerning a composition, when for instance he designates a certain symphony as the "pastoral" symphony, or a passage therein as "the scene by the brook," or another as the "merry gathering of rustics," these are likewise only symbolical representations born out of music—and not perhaps the imitated objects of music—representations which can give us no information whatever concerning the *Dionysian* content of music, and which in fact have no distinctive value of their own alongside of other pictorial expressions. This process of a discharge of music in pictures we have

now to transfer to some youthful, linguistically productive people, to get a notion as to how the strophic popular song originates, and how the entire faculty of speech is stimulated by this new principle of imitation of music.

If, therefore, we may regard lyric poetry as the effulguration of music in pictures and concepts, we can now ask: "how does music *appear* in the mirror of symbolism and conception?" *It appears as will,* taking the word in the Schopenhauerian sense, *i.e.,* as the antithesis of the æsthetic, purely contemplative, and passive frame of mind. Here, however, we must discriminate as sharply as possible between the concept of essentiality and the concept of phenomenality; for music, according to its essence, cannot be will, because as such it would have to be wholly banished from the domain of art—for the will is the unæsthetic-in-itself;—yet it appears as will. For in order to express the phenomenon of music in pictures, the lyrist requires all the stirrings of passion, from the whispering of infant desire to the roaring of madness. Under the impulse to speak of music in Apollonian symbols, he conceives of all nature, and himself therein, only as the eternally willing, desiring, longing existence. But in so far as he interprets music by means of pictures, he himself rests in the quiet calm of Apollonian contemplation, however much all around him which he beholds through the medium of music is in a state of confused and violent motion. Indeed, when he beholds himself through this same medium, his own image appears to him in a state of unsatisfied feeling: his own willing, longing, moaning and rejoicing are to him symbols by which he interprets music. Such is the phenomenon of the lyrist: as Apollonian genius he interprets music through the image of the will, while he himself, completely released from the avidity of the will, is the pure, undimmed eye of day.

Our whole disquisition insists on this, that lyric poetry is dependent on the spirit of music just as music itself in its absolute sovereignty does not *require* the picture and the concept, but only *endures* them as accompaniments. The poems of the lyrist can express nothing which has not already been contained in the vast universality and absoluteness of the music which compelled him to use figurative speech. By no means is it possible for language adequately to render the cosmic symbolism of music, for the very reason that music stands in symbolic relation to the primordial contradiction and primordial pain in the heart of the Primordial Unity, and therefore symbolises a sphere which is above all appearance and before all phenomena. Rather should we say that all phenomena, compared with it, are but symbols: hence *language,* as the organ and symbol of phenomena, cannot at all disclose the innermost essence of music; language can only be in superficial contact with music when it attempts to imitate music; while the profoundest significance of the latter cannot be brought one step nearer to us by all the eloquence of lyric poetry.

We shall now have to avail ourselves of all the principles of art hitherto considered, in order to find our way through the labyrinth, as we must designate *the origin of Greek tragedy.* I shall not be charged with absurdity in saying that the problem of this origin has as yet not even been seriously stated, not to say solved, however often the fluttering tatters of ancient tradition have been sewed together in sundry combinations and torn asunder again. This tradition tells us in the most unequivocal terms, *that tragedy sprang from the tragic chorus,* and was originally only chorus and nothing but chorus: and hence we feel it our duty to look into the heart of this tragic chorus as being the real proto-drama, without in the least contenting ourselves with current art-phraseology—according to which the chorus is the ideal spectator, or represents the people in contrast to the regal side of the scene. The latter explanatory notion, which sounds sublime to many a politician—that the immutable moral law was embodied by the democratic Athenians in the popular chorus, which always carries its point over the passionate excesses and extravagances of kings—may be ever so forcibly suggested by an observation of Aristotle: still it has no bearing on the original formation of tragedy, inasmuch as the entire antithesis of king and people, and, in general, the whole politico-social sphere, is excluded from the purely religious beginnings of tragedy; but, considering the well-known classical form of the chorus in Æschylus and Sophocles, we should even deem it blasphemy to speak here of the anticipation of a "constitutional representation of the people," from which blasphemy others have not shrunk, however. The ancient governments knew of no constitutional representation of the people *in praxi,* and it is to be hoped that they did not so much as "anticipate" it in tragedy.

Much more celebrated than this political explanation of the chorus is the notion of A. W. Schlegel, who advises us to regard the chorus, in a manner, as the essence and extract of the crowd of spectators,—as the "ideal spectator." This view, when compared with the historical tradition that tragedy was originally only chorus, reveals itself in its true character, as a crude, unscientific, yet brilliant assertion, which, however, has acquired its brilliancy only through its concentrated form of expression, through the truly Germanic bias in favour of whatever is called "ideal," and through our momentary astonishment. For we are indeed astonished the moment we compare our well-known theatrical public with this chorus, and ask ourselves if it could ever be possible to idealise something analogous to the Greek chorus out of such a public. We tacitly deny this, and now wonder as much at the boldness of Schlegel's assertion as at the totally different nature of the Greek public. For hitherto we always believed that the true spectator, be he who he may, had always to remain conscious of having before him a work of art, and not an empiric reality: whereas the tragic chorus of the Greeks is compelled to recognise real beings in the figures of the stage. The chorus of the Oceanides really believes that it sees before it the Titan Prometheus, and considers itself as real as the god of the scene. And are we to own that he is the highest and purest type of spectator, who, like the Oceanides, regards Prometheus as real and present in body? And is it characteristic of the ideal spectator that he should run on the stage and free the god from his torments? We had believed in an æsthetic public, and considered the individual spectator the better qualified the

more he was capable of viewing a work of art as art, that is, æsthetically; but now the Schlegelian expression has intimated to us, that the perfect ideal spectator does not at all suffer the world of the scenes to act æsthetically on him, but corporeo-empirically. Oh, these Greeks! we have sighed; they will upset our æsthetics! But once accustomed to it, we have reiterated the saying of Schlegel, as often as the subject of the chorus has been broached.

But the tradition which is so explicit here speaks against Schlegel: the chorus as such, without the stage,—the primitive form of tragedy,—and the chorus of ideal spectators do not harmonise. What kind of art would that be which was extracted from the concept of the spectator, and whereof we are to regard the "spectator as such" as the true form? The spectator without the play is something absurd. We fear that the birth of tragedy can be explained neither by the high esteem for the moral intelligence of the multitude nor by the concept of the spectator without the play; and we regard the problem as too deep to be even so much as touched by such superficial modes of contemplation.

An infinitely more valuable insight into the signification of the chorus had already been displayed by Schiller in the celebrated Preface to his Bride of Messina, where he regarded the chorus as a living wall which tragedy draws round herself to guard her from contact with the world of reality, and to preserve her ideal domain and poetical freedom.

It is with this, his chief weapon, that Schiller combats the ordinary conception of the natural, the illusion ordinarily required in dramatic poetry. He contends that while indeed the day on the stage is merely artificial, the architecture only symbolical, and the metrical dialogue purely ideal in character, nevertheless an erroneous view still prevails in the main: that it is not enough to tolerate merely as a poetical licence *that* which is in reality the essence of all poetry. The introduction of the chorus is, he says, the decisive step by which war is declared openly and honestly against all naturalism in art.—It is, methinks, for disparaging this mode of contemplation that our would-be superior age has coined the disdainful catchword "pseudo-idealism." I fear, however, that we on the other hand with our present worship of the natural and the real have landed at the nadir of all idealism, namely in the region of cabinets of wax-figures. An art indeed exists also here, as in certain novels much in vogue at present: but let no one pester us with the claim that by this art the Schiller-Goethian "pseudo-idealism" has been vanquished.

It is indeed an "ideal" domain, as Schiller rightly perceived, upon which the Greek satyric chorus, the chorus of primitive tragedy, was wont to walk, a domain raised far above the actual path of mortals. The Greek framed for this chorus the suspended scaffolding of a fictitious *natural state* and placed thereon fictitious *natural beings.* It is on this foundation that tragedy grew up, and so it could of course dispense from the very first with a painful portrayal of reality. Yet it is not an arbitrary world placed by fancy betwixt heaven and earth; rather is it a world possessing the same reality and trustworthiness that Olympus with its dwellers possessed for the believing Hellene. The satyr, as being the Dionysian chorist, lives in a religiously acknowledged reality under the sanction of the myth and cult. That tragedy begins with him, that the Dionysian wisdom of tragedy speaks through him, is just as surprising a phenomenon to us as, in general, the derivation of tragedy from the chorus. Perhaps we shall get a starting-point for our inquiry, if I put forward the proposition that the satyr, the fictitious natural being, is to the man of culture what Dionysian music is to civilisation. Concerning this latter, Richard Wagner says that it is neutralised by music even as lamplight by daylight. In like manner, I believe, the Greek man of culture felt himself neutralised in the presence of the satyric chorus: and this is the most immediate effect of the Dionysian tragedy, that the state and society, and, in general, the gaps between man and man give way to an overwhelming feeling of oneness, which leads back to the heart of nature. The metaphysical comfort,—with which, as I have here intimated, every true tragedy dismisses us—that, in spite of the perpetual change of phenomena, life at bottom is indestructibly powerful and pleasurable, this comfort appears with corporeal lucidity as the satyric chorus, as the chorus of natural beings, who live ineradicable as it were behind all civilisation, and who, in spite of the ceaseless change of generations and the history of nations, remain for ever the same.

With this chorus the deep-minded Hellene, who is so singularly qualified for the most delicate and severe suffering, consoles himself:—he who has glanced with piercing eye into the very heart of the terrible destructive processes of so-called universal history, has also into the cruelty of nature, and is in danger of longing for a Buddhistic negation of the will. Art saves him, and through art life saves him—for herself.

For we must know that in the rapture of the Dionysian state, with its annihilation of the ordinary bounds and limits of existence, there is a *lethargic* element, wherein all personal experiences of the past are submerged. It is by this gulf of oblivion that the everyday world and the world of Dionysian reality are separated from each other. But as soon as this everyday reality rises again in consciousness, it is felt as such, and nauseates us; an ascetic will-paralysing mood is the fruit of these states. In this sense the Dionysian man may be said to resemble Hamlet: both have for once seen into the true nature of things, —they have *perceived,* but they are loath to act; for their action cannot change the eternal nature of things; they regard it as shameful or ridiculous that one should require of them to set aright the time which is out of joint. Knowledge kills action, action requires the veil of illusion—it is this lesson which Hamlet teaches, and not the cheap wisdom of John-a-Dreams who from too much reflection, as it were from a surplus of possibilities, does not arrive at action at all. Not reflection, no!—true knowledge, insight into appalling truth, preponderates over all motives inciting to action, in Hamlet as well as in the Dionysian man. No comfort avails any longer; his longing goes beyond a world after death, beyond the gods themselves; existence with its glittering reflection in the gods, or in an immortal other world is abjured. In the consciousness of the truth he has perceived, man now sees everywhere only the awfulness of the absurdity of existence, he now understands the symbolism in the fate of Ophelia, he now discerns the wisdom of the sylvan god Silenus: and loathing seizes him.

Here, in this extremest danger of the will, *art* approaches, as a saving and healing enchantress; she alone is able to transform these nauseating reflections on the awfulness or absurdity of existence into representations wherewith it is possible to live: these are the representations of the *sublime* as the artistic subjugation of the awful, and the *comic* as the artistic delivery from the nausea of the absurd. The satyric chorus of dithyramb is the saving deed of Greek art; the paroxyms described above spent their force in the intermediary world of these Dionysian followers.

The satyr, like the idyllic shepherd of our more recent time, is the offspring of a longing after the Primitive and the Natural; but mark with what firmness and fearlessness the Greek embraced the man of the woods, and again, how coyly and mawkishly the modern man dallied with the flattering picture of a tender, flute-playing, soft-natured shepherd! Nature, on which as yet no knowledge has been at work, which maintains unbroken barriers to culture—this is what the Greek saw in his satyr, which still was not on this account supposed to coincide with the ape. On the contrary: it was the archetype of man, the embodiment of his highest and strongest emotions, as the enthusiastic reveller enraptured by the proximity of his god, as the fellow-suffering companion in whom the suffering of the god repeats itself, as the herald of wisdom speaking from the very depths of nature, as the emblem of the sexual omnipotence of nature, which the Greek was wont to contemplate with reverential awe. The satyr was something sublime and godlike: he could not but appear so, especially to the sad and wearied eye of the Dionysian man. He would have been offended by our spurious tricked-up shepherd, while his eye dwelt with sublime satisfaction on the naked and unstuntedly magnificent characters of nature: here the illusion of culture was brushed away from the archetype of man; here the true man, the bearded satyr, revealed himself, who shouts joyfully to his god. Before him the cultured man shrank to a lying caricature. Schiller is right also with reference to these beginnings of tragic art: the chorus is a living bulwark against the onsets of reality, because it—the satyric chorus—portrays existence more truthfully, more realistically, more perfectly than the cultured man who ordinarily considers himself as the only reality. The sphere of poetry does not lie outside the world, like some fantastic impossibility of a poet's imagination: it seeks to be the very opposite, the unvarnished expression of truth, and must for this very reason cast aside the false finery of that supposed reality of the cultured man. The contrast between this intrinsic truth of nature and the falsehood of culture, which poses as the only reality, is similar to that existing between the eternal kernel of things, the thing in itself, and the collective world of phenomena. And even as tragedy, with its metaphysical comfort, points to the eternal life of this kernel of existence, notwithstanding the perpetual dissolution of phenomena, so the symbolism of the satyric chorus already expresses figuratively this primordial relation between the thing in itself and phenomenon. The idyllic shepherd of the modern man is but a copy of the sum of the illusions of culture which he calls nature; the Dionysian Greek desires truth and nature in their most potent form;—he sees himself metamorphosed into the satyr.

The revelling crowd of the votaries of Dionysus rejoices, swayed by such moods and perceptions, the power of which transforms them before their own eyes, so that they imagine they behold themselves as reconstituted genii of nature, as satyrs. The later constitution of the tragic chorus is the artistic imitation of this natural phenomenon, which of course required a separation of the Dionysian spectators from the enchanted Dionysians. However, we must never lose sight of the fact that the public of the Attic tragedy rediscovered itself in the chorus of the orchestra, that there was in reality no antithesis of public and chorus: for all was but one great sublime chorus of dancing and singing satyrs, or of such as allowed themselves to be represented by the satyrs. The Schlegelian observation must here reveal itself to us in a deeper sense. The chorus is the "ideal spectator"[2] in so far as it is the only *beholder*,[3] the beholder of the visionary world of the scene. A public of spectators, as known to us, was unknown to the Greeks. In their theatres the terraced structure of the spectators' space rising in concentric arcs enabled every one, in the strictest sense, to *overlook* the entire world of culture around him, and in surfeited contemplation to imagine himself a chorist. According to this view, then, we may call the chorus in its primitive stage in proto-tragedy, a self-mirroring of the Dionysian man: a phenomenon which may be best exemplified by the process of the actor, who, if he be truly gifted, sees hovering before his eyes with almost tangible perceptibility the character he is to represent. The satyric chorus is first of all a vision of the Dionysian throng, just as the world of the stage is, in turn, a vision of the satyric chorus: the power of this vision is great enough to render the eye dull and insensible to the impression of "reality," to the presence of the cultured men occupying the tiers of seats on every side. The form of the Greek theatre reminds one of a lonesome mountain-valley: the architecture of the scene appears like a luminous cloud-picture which the Bacchants swarming on the mountains behold from the heights, as the splendid encirclement in the midst of which the image of Dionysus is revealed to them.

Owing to our learned conception of the elementary artistic processes, this artistic proto-phenomenon, which is here introduced to explain the tragic chorus, is almost shocking: while nothing can be more certain than that the poet is a poet only in that he beholds himself surrounded by forms which live and act before him, into the innermost being of which his glance penetrates. By reason of a strange defeat in our capacities, we modern men are apt to represent to ourselves the æsthetic proto-phenomenon as too complex and abstract. For the true poet the metaphor is not a rhetorical figure, but a vicarious image which actually hovers before him in place of a concept. The character is not for him an aggregate composed of a studied collection of particular traits, but an irrepressibly live person appearing before his eyes, and differing only from the corresponding vision of the painter by its ever continued life and action. Why is it that Homer sketches much more vividly[4] than all the other poets? Because he contemplates[5] much more. We talk so abstractly about poetry, because we are all wont to be bad poets. At bottom the æsthetic phenomenon is simple: let a man but have the faculty of perpetually seeing a lively play and of constantly living surrounded by hosts of spirits, then he is a poet: let him but feel the impulse to transform himself and to talk from out the bodies and souls of others, then he is a dramatist.

The Dionysian excitement is able to impart to a whole mass of men this artistic faculty of seeing themselves surrounded by such a host of spirits, with whom they know themselves to be inwardly one. This function of the tragic chorus is the *dramatic* proto-phenomenon: to see one's self transformed before one's self, and then to act as if one had really entered into another body, into another character. This function stands at the beginning of the development of the drama. Here we have something different from the rhapsodist, who does not blend with his pictures, but only sees them, like the painter, with contemplative eye outside of him; here we actually have a surrender of the individual by his entering into another nature. Moreover this phenomenon appears in the form of an epidemic: a whole throng feels itself metamorphosed in this wise. Hence it is that the dithyramb is essentially different from every other variety of the choric song. The virgins, who with laurel twigs in their hands solemnly proceed to the temple of Apollo and sing a processional hymn, remain what they are and retain their civic names: the dithyrambic chorus is a chorus of transformed beings, whose civic past and social rank are totally forgotten: they have become the timeless servants of their god that live aloof from all the spheres of society. Every other variety of the choric lyric of the Hellenes is but an enormous enhancement of the Apollonian unit-singer: while in the dithyramb we have before us a community of unconscious actors, who mutually regard themselves as transformed among one another.

This enchantment is the prerequisite of all dramatic art. In this enchantment the Dionysian reveller sees himself as a satyr, *and as satyr he in turn beholds the god,* that is, in his transformation he sees a new vision outside him as the Apollonian consummation of his state. With this new vision the drama is complete.

According to this view, we must understand Greek tragedy as the Dionysian chorus, which always disburdens itself anew in an Apollonian world of pictures. The choric parts, therefore, with which tragedy is interlaced, are in a manner the mother-womb of the entire so-called dialogue, that is, of the whole stage-world, of the drama proper. In several successive outbursts does this primordial basis of tragedy beam forth the vision of the drama, which is a dream-phenomenon throughout, and, as such, epic in character: on the other hand, however, as objectivation of a Dionysian state, it does not represent the Apol-

---

[2] Zuschauer.
[3] Schauer.

[4] Anschaulicher.
[5] Anschaut.

Ionian redemption in appearance, but, conversely, the dissolution of the individual and his unification with primordial existence. Accordingly, the drama is the Apollonian embodiment of Dionysian perceptions and influences, and is thereby separated from the epic as by an immense gap.

The *chorus* of Greek tragedy, the symbol of the mass of the people moved by Dionysian excitement, is thus fully explained by our conception of it as here set forth. Whereas, being accustomed to the position of a chorus on the modern stage, especially an operatic chorus, we could never comprehend why the tragic chorus of the Greeks should be older, more primitive, indeed, more important than the "action" proper,—as has been so plainly declared by the voice of tradition; whereas, furthermore, we could not reconcile with this traditional paramount importance and primitiveness the fact of the chorus being composed only of humble, ministering beings; indeed, at first only of goatlike satyrs; whereas, finally, the orchestra before the scene was always a riddle to us; we have learned to comprehend at length that the scene, together with the action, was fundamentally and originally conceived only as a *vision,* that the only reality is just the chorus, which of itself generates the vision and speaks thereof with the entire symbolism of dancing, tone, and word. This chorus beholds in the vision its lord and master Dionysus, and is thus for ever the *serving* chorus: it sees how he, the god, suffers and glorifies himself, and therefore does not itself *act.* But though its attitude towards the god is throughout the attitude of ministration, this is nevertheless the highest expression, the Dionysian expression of *Nature,* and therefore, like Nature herself, the chorus utters oracles and wise sayings when transported with enthusiasm: as *fellow-sufferer* it is also the *sage* proclaiming truth from out the heart of Nature. Thus, then, originates the fantastic figure, which seems so shocking, of the wise and enthusiastic satyr, who is at the same time "the dumb man" in contrast to the god: the image of Nature and her strongest impulses, yea, the symbol of Nature, and at the same time the herald of her art and wisdom: musician, poet, dancer, and visionary in one person.

Agreeably to this view, and agreeably to tradition, *Dionysus,* the proper stage-hero and focus of vision, is not at first actually present in the oldest period of tragedy, but is only imagined as present: *i.e.,* tragedy is originally only "chorus" and not "drama." Later on the attempt is made to exhibit the god as real and to display the visionary figure together with its glorifying encirclement before the eyes of all; it is here that the "drama" in the narrow sense of the term begins. To the dithyrambic chorus is now assigned the task of exciting the minds of the hearers to such a pitch of Dionysian frenzy, that, when the tragic hero appears on the stage, they do not behold in him, say, the unshapely masked man, but a visionary figure, born as it were of their own ecstasy. Let us picture Admetes thinking in profound meditation of his lately departed wife Alcestis, and quite consuming himself in spiritual contemplation thereof—when suddenly the veiled figure of a woman resembling her in form and gait is led towards him: let us picture his sudden trembling anxiety, his agitated comparisons, his instinctive conviction—and we shall have an analogon to the sensation with which the spectator,

excited to Dionysian frenzy, saw the god approaching on the stage, a god with whose sufferings he had already become identified. He involuntarily transferred the entire picture of the god, fluttering magically before his soul, to this masked figure and resolved its reality as it were into a phantasmal unreality. This is the Apollonian dream-state, in which the world of day is veiled, and a new world, clearer, more intelligible, more striking than the former, and nevertheless more shadowy, is ever born anew in perpetual change before our eyes. We accordingly recognise in tragedy a thoroughgoing stylistic contrast: the language, colour, flexibility and dynamics of the dialogue fall apart in the Dionysian lyrics of the chorus on the one hand, and in the Apollonian dream-world of the scene on the other, into entirely separate spheres of expression. The Apollonian appearances, in which Dionysus objectifies himself, are no longer "ein ewiges Meer, ein wechselnd Weben, ein glühend Leben," [6] as is the music of the chorus, they are no longer the forces merely felt, but not condensed into a picture, by which the inspired votary of Dionysus divines the proximity of his god: the clearness and firmness of epic form now speak to him from the scene, Dionysus now no longer speaks through forces, but as an epic hero, almost in the language of Homer.

Whatever rises to the surface in the dialogue of the Apollonian part of Greek tragedy, appears simple, transparent, beautiful. In this sense the dialogue is a copy of the Hellene, whose nature reveals itself in the dance, because in the dance the greatest energy is merely potential, but betrays itself nevertheless in flexible and vivacious movements. The language of the Sophoclean heroes, for instance, surprises us by its Apollonian precision and clearness, so that we at once imagine we see into the innermost recesses of their being, and marvel not a little that the way to these recesses is so short. But if for the moment we disregard the character of the hero which rises to the surface and grows visible—and which at bottom is nothing but the light-picture cast on a dark wall, that is, appearance through and through,—if rather we enter into the myth which projects itself in these bright mirrorings, we shall of a sudden experience a phenomenon which bears a reverse relation to one familiar in optics. When, after a vigorous effort to gaze into the sun, we turn away blinded, we have dark-coloured spots before our eyes as restoratives, so to speak; while, on the contrary, those light-picture phenomena of the Sophoclean hero,—in short, the Apollonian of the mask,—are the necessary productions of a glance into the secret and terrible things of nature, as it were shining spots to heal the eye which dire night has seared. Only in this sense can we hope to be able to grasp the true meaning of the serious and significant notion of "Greek cheerfulness"; while of course we encounter the misunderstood notion of this cheerfulness, as resulting from a state of unendangered comfort, on all the ways and paths of the present time.

The most sorrowful figure of the Greek stage, the hapless Œdipus, was understood by Sophocles as the

[6] An eternal sea, A weaving, flowing, Life, all glowing. *Faust,* trans. of Bayard Taylor.

noble man, who in spite of his wisdom was destined to error and misery, but nevertheless through his extraordinary sufferings ultimately exerted a magical, wholesome influence on all around him, which continues effective even after his death. The noble man does not sin; this is what the thoughtful poet wishes to tell us: all laws, all natural order, yea, the moral world itself, may be destroyed through his action, but through this very action a higher magic circle of influences is brought into play, which establish a new world on the ruins of the old that has been overthrown. This is what the poet, in so far as he is at the same time a religious thinker, wishes to tell us: as poet, he shows us first of all a wonderfully complicated legal mystery, which the judge slowly unravels, link by link, to his own destruction. The truly Hellenic delight at this dialectical loosening is so great, that a touch of surpassing cheerfulness is thereby communicated to the entire play, which everywhere blunts the edge of the horrible presuppositions of the procedure. In the "Œdipus at Colonus" we find the same cheerfulness, elevated, however, to an infinite transfiguration: in contrast to the aged king, subjected to an excess of misery, and exposed solely as a *sufferer* to all that befalls him, we have here a supermundane cheerfulness, which descends from a divine sphere and intimates to us that in his purely passive attitude the hero attains his highest activity, the influence of which extends far beyond his life, while his earlier conscious musing and striving led him only to passivity. Thus, then, the legal knot of the fable of Œdipus, which to mortal eyes appears indissolubly entangled, is slowly unravelled—and the profoundest human joy comes upon us in the presence of this divine counterpart of dialectics. If this explanation does justice to the poet, it may still be asked whether the substance of the myth is thereby exhausted; and here it turns out that the entire conception of the poet is nothing but the light picture which healing nature holds up to us after a glance into the abyss. Œdipus, the murderer of his father, the husband of his mother, Œdipus, the interpreter of the riddle of the Sphinx! What does the mysterious triad of these deeds of destiny tell us? There is a primitive popular belief, especially in Persia, that a wise Magian can be born only of incest: which we have forthwith to interpret to ourselves with reference to the riddle-solving and mother-marrying Œdipus, to the effect that when the boundary of the present and future, the rigid law of individuation and, in general, the intrinsic spell of nature, are broken by prophetic and magical powers, an extraordinary counter-naturalness—as, in this case, incest—must have preceded as a cause; for how else could one force nature to surrender her secrets but by victoriously opposing her, *i.e.,* by means of the Unnatural? It is this intuition which I see imprinted in the awful triad of the destiny of Œdipus: the very man who solves the riddle of nature—that double-constituted Sphinx—must also, as the murderer of his father and husband of his mother, break the holiest laws of nature. Indeed, it seems as if the myth sought to whisper into our ears that wisdom, especially Dionysian wisdom, is an unnatural abomination, and that whoever, through his knowledge, plunges nature into an abyss of annihilation, must also experience the dissolution of nature in

himself. "The sharpness of wisdom turns round upon the sage: wisdom is a crime against nature": such terrible expressions does the myth call out to us: but the Hellenic poet touches like a sunbeam the sublime and formidable Memnonian statue of the myth, so that it suddenly begins to sound—in Sophoclean melodies.

. . . .

Greek tragedy had a fate different from that of all her older sister arts: she died by suicide, in consequence of an irreconcilable conflict; accordingly she died tragically, while they all passed away very calmly and beautifully in ripe old age. For if it be in accordance with a happy state of things to depart this life without a struggle, leaving behind a fair posterity, the closing period of these older arts exhibits such a happy state of things: slowly they sink out of sight, and before their dying eyes already stand their fairer progeny, who impatiently lift up their heads with courageous mien. The death of Greek tragedy, on the other hand, left an immense void, deeply felt everywhere. Even as certain Greek sailors in the time of Tiberius once heard upon a lonesome island the thrilling cry, "great Pan is dead": so now as it were sorrowful wailing sounded through the Hellenic world: "Tragedy is dead! Poetry itself has perished with her! Begone, begone, ye stunted, emaciated epigones! Begone to Hades, that ye may for once eat your fill of the crumbs of your former masters!"

But when after all a new Art blossomed forth which revered tragedy as her ancestress and mistress, it was observed with horror that she did indeed bear the features of her mother, but those very features the latter had exhibited in her long death-struggle. It was *Euripides* who fought this death-struggle of tragedy; the later art is known as the *New Attic Comedy*. In it the degenerate form of tragedy lived on as a monument of the most painful and violent death of tragedy proper.

This connection between the two serves to explain the passionate attachment to Euripides evinced by the poets of the New Comedy, and hence we are no longer surprised at the wish of Philemon, who would have got himself hanged at once, with the sole design of being able to visit Euripides in the lower regions: if only he could be assured generally that the deceased still had his wits. But if we desire, as briefly as possible, and without professing to say aught exhaustive on the subject to characterise what Euripides has in common with Menander and Philemon, and what appealed to them so strongly as worthy of imitation: it will suffice to say that the *spectator* was brought upon the stage by Euripides. He who has perceived the material of which the Promethean tragic writers prior to Euripides formed their heroes, and how remote from their purpose it was to bring the true mask of reality on the stage, will also know what to make of the wholly divergent tendency of Euripides. Through him the commonplace individual forced his way from the spectators' benches to the stage itself; the mirror in which formerly only great and bold traits found expression now showed the painful exactness that conscientiously reproduces even the abortive lines of nature. Odysseus, the typical Hellene of the Old Art, sank, in the hands of the new poets, to the figure of the Græculus, who, as the good-naturedly cunning domestic slave, stands henceforth in the centre of dramatic interest. What Euripides takes credit for in the Aristophanean "Frogs," namely, that by his household remedies he freed tragic art from its pompous corpulency, is apparent above all in his tragic heroes. The spectator now virtually saw and heard his double on the Euripidean stage, and rejoiced that he could talk so well. But this joy was not all: one even learned of Euripides how to speak: he prides himself upon this in his contest with Æschylus: how the people have learned from him how to observe, debate, and draw conclusions according to the rules of art and with the cleverest sophistications. In general it may be said that through this revolution of the popular language he made the New Comedy possible. For it was henceforth no longer a secret, how—and with what saws —the commonplace could represent and express itself on the stage. Civic mediocrity, on which Euripides built all his political hopes, was now suffered to speak, while heretofore the demigod in tragedy and the drunken satyr, or demiman, in comedy, had determined the character of the language. And so the Aristophanean Euripides prides himself on having portrayed the common, familiar, everyday life and dealings of the people, concerning which all are qualified to pass judgment. If now the entire populace philosophises, manages land and goods with unheard-of circumspection, and conducts law-suits, he takes all the credit to himself, and glories in the splendid results of the wisdom with which he inoculated the rabble.

It was to a populace prepared and enlightened in this manner that the New Comedy could now address itself, of which Euripides had become as it were the chorus-master; only that in this case the chorus of spectators had to be trained. As soon as this chorus was trained to sing in the Euripidean key, there arose that chesslike variety of the drama, the New Comedy, with its perpetual triumphs of cunning and artfulness. But Euripides—the chorus-master—was praised incessantly: indeed, people would have killed themselves in order to learn yet more from him, had they not known that tragic poets were quite as dead as tragedy. But with it the Hellene had surrendered the belief in his immortality; not only the belief in an ideal past, but also the belief in an ideal future. The saying taken from the well-known epitaph, "as an old man, frivolous and capricious," applies also to aged Hellenism. The passing moment, wit, levity, and caprice, are its highest deities; the fifth class, that of the slaves, now attains to power, at least in sentiment: and if we can still speak at all of "Greek cheerfulness," it is the cheerfulness of the slave who has nothing of consequence to answer for, nothing great to strive for, and cannot value anything of the past or future higher than the present. It was this semblance of "Greek cheerfulness" which so revolted the deep-minded and formidable natures of the first four centuries of Christianity: this womanish flight from earnestness and terror, this cowardly contentedness with easy pleasure, was not only contemptible to them, but seemed to be a specifically anti-Christian sentiment. And we must ascribe it to its influence that the conception of Greek antiquity, which lived on for centuries, preserved with almost enduring persistency that peculiar hectic colour of cheerfulness—as

if there had never been a Sixth Century with its birth of tragedy, its Mysteries, its Pythagoras and Heraclitus, indeed as if the art-works of that great period did not at all exist, which in fact—each by itself—can in no wise be explained as having sprung from the soil of such a decrepit and slavish love of existence and cheerfulness, and point to an altogether different conception of things as their source.

The assertion made a moment ago, that Euripides introduced the spectator on the stage to qualify him the better to pass judgment on the drama, will make it appear as if the old tragic art was always in a false relation to the spectator: and one would be tempted to extol the radical tendency of Euripides to bring about an adequate relation between art-work and public as an advance on Sophocles. But, as things are, "public" is merely a word, and not at all a homogeneous and constant quantity. Why should the artist be under obligations to accommodate himself to a power whose strength is merely in numbers? And if by virtue of his endowments and aspirations he feels himself superior to every one of these spectators, how could he feel greater respect for the collective expression of all these subordinate capacities than for the relatively highest-endowed individual spectator? In truth, if ever a Greek artist treated his public throughout a long life with presumptuousness and self-sufficiency, it was Euripides, who, even when the masses threw themselves at his feet, with sublime defiance made an open assault on his own tendency, the very tendency with which he had triumphed over the masses. If this genius had had the slightest reverence for the pandemonium of the public, he would have broken down long before the middle of his career beneath the weighty blows of his own failures. These considerations here make it obvious that our formula —namely, that Euripides brought the spectator upon the stage in order to make him truly competent to pass judgment—was but a provisional one, and that we must seek for a deeper understanding of his tendency. Conversely, it is undoubtedly well known that Æschylus and Sophocles during all their lives, indeed, far beyond their lives, enjoyed the full favour of the people, and that therefore in the case of these predecessors of Euripides the idea of a false relation between art-work and public was altogether excluded. What was it that thus forcibly diverted this highly gifted artist, so incessantly impelled to production, from the path over which shone the sun of the greatest names in poetry and the cloudless heaven of popular favour? What strange consideration for the spectator led him to defy the spectator? How could he, owing to too much respect for the public—disrespect the public?

Euripides—and this is the solution of the riddle just propounded—felt himself, as a poet, undoubtedly superior to the masses, but not to two of his spectators: he brought the masses upon the stage; these two spectators he revered as the only competent judges and masters of his art: in compliance with their directions and admonitions, he transferred the entire world of sentiments, passions, and experiences, hitherto present at every festival representation as the invisible chorus on the spectators' benches, into the souls of his stage-heroes; he yielded to their demands when he also sought for these new characters the new word and the new tone; in their voices alone he heard the conclusive verdict on his work, as also the cheering promise of triumph when he found himself condemned as usual by the justice of the public.

Of these two spectators the one is—Euripides himself, Euripides *as thinker,* not as poet. It might be said of him, that his unusually large fund of critical ability, as in the case of Lessing, if it did not create, at least constantly fructified a productively artistic collateral impulse. With this faculty, with all the clearness and dexterity of his critical thought, Euripides had sat in the theatre and striven to recognise in the masterpieces of his great predecessors, as in faded paintings, feature and feature, line and line. And here had happened to him what one initiated in the deeper arcana of Æschylean tragedy must needs have expected: he observed something incommensurable in every feature and in every line, a certain deceptive distinctness and at the same time an enigmatic profundity, yea an infinitude, of background. Even the clearest figure had always a comet's tail attached to it, which seemed to suggest the uncertain and the inexplicable. The same twilight shrouded the structure of the drama, especially the significance of the chorus. And how doubtful seemed the solution of the ethical problems to his mind! How questionable the treatment of the myths! How unequal the distribution of happiness and misfortune! Even in the language of the Old Tragedy there was much that was objectionable to him, or at least enigmatical; he found especially too much pomp for simple affairs, too many tropes and immense things for the plainness of the characters. Thus he sat restlessly pondering in the theatre, and as a spectator he acknowledged to himself that he did not understand his great predecessors. If, however, he thought the understanding the root proper of all enjoyment and productivity, he had to inquire and look about to see whether any one else thought as he did, and also acknowledged this incommensurability. But most people, and among them the best individuals, had only a distrustful smile for him, while none could explain why the great masters were still in the right in face of his scruples and objections. And in this painful condition he found *that other spectator,* who did not comprehend, and therefore did not esteem, tragedy. In alliance with him he could venture, from amid his lonesomeness, to begin the prodigious struggle against the art of Æschylus and Sophocles—not with polemic writings, but as a dramatic poet, who opposed *his own* conception of tragedy to the traditional one.

AUGUST STRINDBERG
(1849–1912)

Strindberg's Foreword to *Miss Julie,* translated here by Elizabeth Sprigge, is widely regarded as the major manifesto of the naturalist movement in drama. Other pronouncements, such as Émile Zola's

Le Naturalisme au théâtre, were more elaborately detailed, but none of them contained the most convincing argument of all—intimate association with a play of undeniable greatness. Equally important is the flexibility of Strindberg's employment of naturalist principles. Thus, he incorporates into his credo the defense of such theatrical techniques as mime, monologue, and ballet and views the naturalist ideas of heredity and environment within the larger context of a Darwinian struggle for survival.

Foreword to *Miss Julie* (1888)

Theatre has long seemed to me—in common with much other art—a *Biblia Pauperum,* a Bible in pictures for those who cannot read what is written or printed; and I see the playwright as a lay preacher peddling the ideas of his time in popular form, popular enough for the middle-classes, mainstay of theatre audiences, to grasp the gist of the matter without troubling their brains too much. For this reason theatre has always been an elementary school for the young, the semi-educated and for women who still have a primitive capactiy for deceiving themselves and letting themselves be deceived—who, that is to say, are susceptible to illusion and to suggestion from the author. I have therefore thought it not unlikely that in these days, when that rudimentary and immature thought-process operating through fantasy appears to be developing into reflection, research and analysis, that theatre, like religion, might be discarded as an outworn form for whose appreciation we lack the necessary conditions. This opinion is confirmed by the major crisis still prevailing in the theatres of Europe, and still more by the fact that in those countries of culture, producing the greatest thinkers of the age, namely England and Germany, drama—like other fine arts—is dead.

Some countries, it is true, have attempted to create a new drama by using the old forms with up-to-date contents, but not only has there been insufficient time for these new ideas to be popularized, so that the audience can grasp them, but also people have been so wrought up by the taking of sides that pure, disinterested appreciation has become impossible. One's deepest impressions are upset when an applauding or a hissing majority dominates as forcefully and openly as it can in the theatre. Moreover, as no new form has been devised for these new contents, the new wine has burst the old bottles.

In this play I have not tried to do anything new, for this cannot be done, but only to modernize the form to meet the demands which may, I think, be made on this art today. To this end I chose—or surrendered myself to—a theme which claims to be outside the controversial issues of today, since questions of social climbing or falling, of higher or lower, better or worse, of man and woman, are, have been and will be of lasting interest. When I took this theme from a true story told me some years ago, which made a deep impression, I saw it as a subject for tragedy, for as yet it is tragic to see one favoured by fortune go under, and still more to see a family heritage die out, although a time may come when we have grown so developed and enlightened that we shall view with indifference life's spectacle, now seeming so brutal, cynical and heartless. Then we shall have dispensed with those inferior, unreliable instruments of thought called feelings, which become harmful and superfluous as reasoning develops.

The fact that my heroine rouses pity is solely due to weakness; we cannot resist fear of the same fate overtaking us. The hyper-sensitive spectator may, it is true, go beyond this kind of pity, while the man with belief in the future may actually demand some suggestion for remedying the evil—in other words some kind of policy. But, to begin with, there is no such thing as absolute evil; the downfall of one family is the good fortune of another, which thereby gets a chance to rise, and, fortune being only comparative, the alternation of rising and falling is one of life's principal charms. Also, to the man of policy, who wants to remedy the painful fact that the bird of prey devours the dove, and lice the bird of prey, I should like to put the question: why should it be remedied? Life is not so mathematically idiotic as only to permit the big to eat the small; it happens just as often that the bee kills the lion or at least drives it mad.

That my tragedy depresses many people is their own fault. When we have grown strong as the pioneers of the French revolution, we shall be happy and relieved to see the national parks cleared of ancient rotting trees which have stood too long in the way of others equally entitled to a period of growth—as relieved as we are when an incurable invalid dies.

My tragedy *The Father* was recently criticised for being too sad—as if one wants cheerful tragedies! Everybody is clamouring for this supposed "joy of life," and theatre managers demand farces, as if the joy of life consisted in being ridiculous and portraying all human beings as suffering from St. Vitus's dance or total idiocy. I myself find the joy of life in its strong and cruel struggles, and my pleasure in learning, in adding to my knowledge. For this reason I have chosen for this play an unusual situation, but an instructive one—an exception, that is to say, but a great exception, one proving the rule, which will no doubt annoy all lovers of the commonplace. What will offend simple minds is that my plot is not simple, nor its point of view single. In real life an action—this, by the way, is a somewhat new discovery—is generally caused by a whole series of motives, more or less fundamental, but as a rule the spectator chooses just one of these—the one which his mind can most easily grasp or that does most credit to his intelligence. A suicide is committed. Business troubles, says the man of affairs. Unrequited love, say the women. Sickness, says the invalid. Despair, says the down-and-out. But it is possible that the motive lay in all or none of these directions, or that the dead man concealed his actual motive by revealing quite another, likely to reflect more to his glory.

I see Miss Julie's tragic fate to be the result of many circumstances: the mother's character, the father's mistaken upbringing of the girl, her own nature, and the influence of her fiancé on a weak degenerate mind. Also, more directly, the festive mood of Midsummer Eve, her father's absence, her monthly indisposition, her pre-occupation with animals, the excitement of dancing, the magic of dusk, the strongly aphrodisiac influence of flowers, and finally the chance that drives the couple into a room alone —to which must be added the urgency of the excited man.

My treatment of the theme, moreover, is neither exclusively physiological nor psychological. I have not put the blame wholly on the inheritance from her mother, nor on her physical condition at the time, nor on immorality. I have not even preached a moral sermon; in the absence of a priest I leave this to the cook.

I congratulate myself on this multiplicity of motives as being up-to-date, and if others have done the same thing before me, then I congratulate myself on not being alone in my "paradoxes," as all innovations are called.

In regard to the drawing of the characters, I have made my people somewhat "characterless" for the following reasons. In the course of time the word character has assumed manifold meanings. It must have originally signified the dominating trait of the soul-complex, and this was confused with temperament. Later it became the middle-class term for the automaton, one whose nature had become fixed or who had adapted himself to a particular rôle in life. In fact a person who had ceased to grow was called a character, while one continuing to develop—the skilful navigator of life's river, sailing not with sheets set fast, but veering before the wind to luff again— was called characterless, in a derogatory sense, of course, because he was so hard to catch, classify and keep track of. This middle-class conception of the immobility of the soul was transferred to the stage where the middle-class has always ruled. A character came to signify a man fixed and finished: one who invariably appeared either drunk or jocular or melancholy, and characterization required nothing more than a physical defect such as a club-foot, a wooden leg, a red nose; or the fellow might be made to repeat some such phrase as: "That's capital!" or: "Barkis is willin'!" This simple way of regarding human beings still survives in the great Molière. Harpagon is nothing but a miser, although Harpagon might have been not only a miser, but also a first-rate financier, an excellent father and a good citizen. Worse still, his "failing" is a distinct advantage to his son-in-law and his daughter, who are his heirs, and who therefore cannot criticise him, even if they have to wait a while to get to bed. I do not believe, therefore, in simple stage characters; and the summary judgments of authors—this man is stupid, that one brutal, this jealous, that stingy, and so forth— should be challenged by the Naturalists who know the richness of the soul-complex and realise that vice has a reverse side very much like virtue.

Because they are modern characters, living in a period of transition more feverishly hysterical than its predecessor at least, I have drawn my figures vacillating, disintegrated, a blend of old and new. Nor does it seem to me unlikely that, through newspapers and conversations, modern ideas may have filtered down to the level of the domestic servant.

My souls (characters) are conglomerations of past and present stages of civilization, bits from books and newspapers, scraps of humanity, rags and tatters of fine clothing, patched together as is the human soul. And I have added a little evolutionary history by making the weaker steal and repeat the words of the stronger, and by making the characters borrow ideas or "suggestions" from one another.

Miss Julie is a modern character, not that the half-woman, the man-hater, has not existed always, but because now that she has been discovered she has stepped to the front and begun to make a noise. The half-woman is a type who thrusts herself forward, selling herself nowadays for power, decorations, distinctions, diplomas, as formerly for money. The type implies degeneration; it is not a good type and it does not endure; but it can unfortunately transmit its misery, and degenerate men seem instinctively to choose their mates from among such women, and so they breed, producing offspring of indeterminate sex to whom life is torture. But fortunately they perish, either because they cannot come to terms with reality, or because their repressed instincts break out uncontrollably, or again because their hopes of catching up with men are shattered. The type is tragic, revealing a desperate fight against nature, tragic too in its Romantic inheritance now dissipated by Naturalism, which wants nothing but happiness—and for happiness strong and sound species are required.

But Miss Julie is also a relic of the old warrior nobility now giving way to the new nobility of nerve and brain. She is a victim of the discord which a mother's "crime" has produced in a family, a victim too of the day's complaisance, of circumstances, of her own defective constitution, all of which are equivalent to the Fate or Universal Law of former days. The Naturalist has abolished guilt with God, but the consequences of the action—punishment, imprisonment or the fear of it—he cannot abolish, for the simple reason that they remain whether he is acquitted or not. An injured fellow-being is not so complacent as outsiders, who have not been injured, can afford to be. Even if the father had felt impelled to take no vengeance, the daughter would have taken vengeance on herself, as she does here, from that innate or acquired sense of honour which the upper-classes inherit—whether from Barbarism or Aryan forebears, or from the chivalry of the Middle Ages, who knows? It is a very beautiful thing, but it has become a danger nowadays to the preservation of the race. It is the nobleman's *hara-kiri,* the Japanese law of inner conscience which compels him to cut his own stomach open at the insult of another, and which survives in modified form in the duel, a privilege of the nobility. And so the valet Jean lives on, but Miss Julie cannot live without honour. This is the thrall's advantage over the nobleman, that he lacks this fatal preoccupation with honour. And in all of us Aryans there is something of the nobleman, or the Don Quixote, which makes us sympathize with the man who commits suicide because he has done something ignoble and lost his honour. And we are noblemen enough to suffer at the sight of fallen greatness littering the earth like a corpse—yes, even if the fallen rise again and make restitution by honourable deeds. Jean, the valet, is a race-builder, a man of marked characteristics. He was a labourer's son who has educated himself towards becoming a gentleman. He has learnt easily, through his well-developed senses (smell, taste, vision)—and he also has a sense of beauty. He has already bettered himself, and is thick-skinned enough to have no scruples about using other people's services. He is already foreign to his associates, despising them as part of the life he has turned his back on, yet also fearing and fleeing from them because they know his secrets, pry into his plans, watch his rise with envy, and look forward with pleasure to his fall. Hence his dual, indeterminate character, vacillating between love of the heights and hatred of those who have already achieved them. He is, he says himself, an aristocrat; he has learned the secrets of good society. He is polished, but vulgar within; he already wears his tails with taste, but there is no guarantee of his personal cleanliness.

He has some respect for his young lady, but he is frightened of Kristin, who knows his dangerous secrets, and he is sufficiently callous not to allow the night's events to wreck his plans for the future. Having both the slave's brutality and the master's lack of squeamishness, he can see blood without fainting and take disaster by the horns. Consequently he emerges from the battle unscathed, and probably ends his days as a hotel-keeper. And even if *he* does not become a Roumanian Count, his son will doubtless go to the university and perhaps become a county attorney.

The light which Jean sheds on a lower-class conception of life, life seen from below, is on the whole illuminating—when he speaks the truth, which is not often, for he says what is favourable to himself rather than what is true. When Miss Julie suggests that the lower-classes must be oppressed by the attitude of their superiors, Jean naturally agrees, as his object is to gain her sympathy; but when he perceives the advantage of separating himself from the common herd, he at once takes back his words.

It is not because Jean is now rising that he has the upper hand of Miss Julie, but because he is a man. Sexually he is the aristocrat because of his virility, his keener senses and his capacity for taking the initiative. His inferiority is mainly due to the social environment in which he lives, and he can probably shed it with his valet's livery.

The slave mentality expresses itself in his worship of the Count (the boots), and his religious superstition; but he worships the Count chiefly because he holds that higher position for which Jean himself is striving. And this worship remains even when he has won the daughter of the house and seen how empty is that lovely shell.

I do not believe that a love relationship in the "higher" sense could exist between two individuals of such different quality, but I have made Miss Julie imagine that she is in love, so as to lessen her sense of guilt, and I let Jean suppose that if his social position were altered he would truly love her. I think love is like the hyacinth which has to strike roots in darkness *before* it can produce a vigorous flower. In this case it shoots up quickly, blossoms and goes to seed all at the same time, which is why the plant dies so soon.

As for Kristin, she is a female slave, full of servility and sluggishness acquired in front of the kitchen fire, and stuffed full of morality and religion, which are her cloak and scape-goat. She goes to church as a quick and easy way of unloading her household thefts on to Jesus and taking on a fresh cargo of guiltlessness. For the rest she is a minor character, and I have therefore sketched her in the same manner as the Pastor and the Doctor in "The Father," where I wanted ordinary human beings, as are most country pastors and provincial doctors. If these minor characters seem abstract to some people this is due to the fact that ordinary people are to a certain extent abstract in pursuit of their work; that is to say, they are without individuality, showing, while working, only one side of themselves. And as long as the spectator does not feel a need to see them from other sides, there is nothing wrong with my abstract presentation.

In regard to the dialogue, I have departed somewhat from tradition by not making my characters catechists who ask stupid questions in order to elicit a smart reply. I have avoided the symmetrical, mathematical construction of French dialogue, and let people's minds work irregularly, as they do in real life where, during a conversation, no topic is drained to the dregs, and one mind finds in another a chance cog to engage in. So too the dialogue wanders, gathering in the opening scenes material which is later picked up, worked over, repeated, expounded and developed like the theme in a musical composition.

The plot speaks for itself, and as it really only concerns two people, I have concentrated on these, introducing only one minor character, the cook, and keeping the unhappy spirit of the father above and behind the action. I have done this because it seems to me that the psychological process is what interests people most today. Our inquisitve souls are no longer satisfied with seeing a thing happen; we must also know how it happens. We want to see the wires themselves, to watch the machinery, to examine the box with the false bottom, to take hold of the magic ring in order to find the join, and look at the cards to see how they are marked.

In this connection I have had in view the documentary novels of the brothers de Goncourt, which appeal to me more than any other modern literature.

As far as the technical side of the work is concerned I have made the experiment of abolishing the division into acts. This is because I have come to the conclusion that our capacity for illusion is disturbed by the intervals, during which the audience has time to reflect and escape from the suggestive influence of the author-hypnotist. My play will probably take an hour and a half, and as one can listen to a lecture, a sermon or a parliamentary debate for as long as that or longer, I do not think a theatrical performance will be fatiguing in the same length of time. As early as 1872, in one of my first dramatic attempts, *The Outlaw,* I tried this concentrated form, although with scant success. The play was written in five acts, and only when finished did I become aware of the restless, disjointed effect that it produced. The script was burnt and from the ashes rose a single well-knit act —fifty pages of print, playable in one hour. The form of the present play is, therefore, not new, but it appears to be my own, and changing tastes may make it timely. My hope is one day to have an audience educated enough to sit through a whole evening's entertainment in one act, but one would have to try this out to see. Meanwhile, in order to provide respite for the audience and the players, without allowing the audience to escape from the illusion, I have introduced three art forms: monologue, mime and ballet. These are all part of drama, having their origins in classic tragedy, monody having become monologue and the chorus, ballet.

Monologue is now condemned by our realists as unnatural, but if one provides motives for it one makes it natural, and then can use it to advantage. It is, surely, natural for a public speaker to walk up and down the room practicing his speech, natural for an actor to read his part aloud, for a servant girl to talk to her cat, a mother to prattle to her child, an old maid to chatter to her parrot, and a sleeper to talk in his sleep. And in order that the actor may have a chance, for once, of working independently, free from the author's direction, it is better that the monologue should not be written, but only indicated. For since it is of small importance what is said in one's sleep or to the parrot or to the cat—none of it influences the action—a talented actor, identifying himself with the atmosphere and the situation, may improvise better than the author, who cannot calculate ahead how much may be said or how long taken without waking the audience from the illusion.

Some Italian theatres have, as we know, returned to improvisation, thereby producing actors who are creative, although within the bounds set by the author. This may well be a step forward, or even the beginning of a new art-form worthy to be called *productive.*

In places where monologue would be unnatural I have used mime, leaving here an even wider scope for the actor's imagination, and more chance for him to win independent laurels. But so as not to try the audience beyond endurance, I have introduced music —fully justified by the Midsummer Eve dance—to exercise its powers of persuasion during the dumb show. But I beg the musical director to consider carefully his choice of compositions, so that conflicting moods are not induced by selections from the current operetta or dance show, or by folktunes of too local a character.

The ballet I have introduced cannot be replaced by the usual kind of "crowd-scene," for such scenes are too badly played—a lot of grinning idiots seizing the opportunity to show off and thus destroying the illusion. And as peasants cannot improvise their taunts, but use ready-made phrases with a double meaning, I have not composed their lampoon, but taken a little-known song and dance which I myself noted down in the Stockholm district. The words are not quite to the point, but this too is intentional, for the cunning, i.e. weakness, of the slave prevents him from direct attack. Nor can there be clowning in a serious action, or coarse joking in a situation which nails the lid on a family coffin.

As regards the scenery, I have borrowed from impressionist painting its asymmetry and its economy; thus, I think, strengthening the illusion. For the fact that one does not see the whole room and all the furniture leaves scope for conjecture—that is to say imagination is roused and complements what is seen. I have succeeded too in getting rid of those tiresome exits through doors, since scenery doors are made of canvas, and rock at the slightest touch. They cannot even express the wrath of an irate head of the family who, after a bad dinner, goes out slamming the door behind him, "so that the whole house shakes." On the stage it rocks. I have also kept to a single set, both in order to let the characters develop in their métier and to break away from over-decoration. When one has only one set, one may expect it to be realistic; but as a matter of fact nothing is harder than to get a stage room that looks something like a room, however easily the scene painter can produce flaming volcanoes and water-falls. Presumably the walls must be of canvas; but it seems about time to dispense with painted shelves and cooking utensils. We are asked to accept so many stage conventions that we might at least be spared the pain of painted pots and pans.

I have set the back wall and the table diagonally so that the actors may play full-face and in half-profile when they are sitting opposite one another at the table. In the opera *Aïda* I saw a diagonal background, which led the eye to unfamiliar perspectives and did not look like mere reaction against boring straight lines.

Another much needed innovation is the abolition of foot-lights. This lighting from below is said to have the purpose of making the actors' faces fatter. But why, I ask, should all actors have fat faces? Does not this underlighting flatten out all the subtlety of the lower part of the face, specially the jaw, falsify the shape of the nose and throw shadows up over the eyes? Even if this were not so, one thing is certain: that the lights hurt the performers' eyes, so that the full play of their expression is lost. The footlights strike part of the retina usually protected—except in sailors who have to watch sunlight on water—and therefore one seldom sees anything other than a crude rolling of the eyes, either sideways or up towards the gallery, showing their whites. Perhaps this too causes that tiresome blinking of the eyelashes, especially by actresses. And when anyone on the stage wants to speak with his eyes, the only thing he can do is to look straight at the audience, with whom he or she then gets into direct communication, outside the framework of the set—a habit called, rightly or wrongly, "greeting one's friends."

Would not sufficiently strong side-lighting, with some kind of reflectors, add to the actor's powers of expression by allowing him to use the face's greatest asset:—the play of the eyes?

I have few illusions about getting the actors to play *to* the audience instead of *with* it, although this is what I want. That I shall see an actor's back throughout a critical scene is beyond my dreams, but I do wish crucial scenes could be played, not in front of the prompter's box, like duets expecting applause, but in the place required by the action. So, no revolutions, but just some small modifications, for to make the stage into a real room with the fourth wall missing would be too upsetting altogether.

I dare not hope that the actresses will listen to what I have to say about make-up, for they would rather be beautiful than life-like, but the actor might consider whether it is to his advantage to create an abstract character with greasepaints, and cover his face with it like a mask. Take the case of a man who draws a choleric charcoal line between his eyes and then, in this fixed state of wrath, has to smile at some repartee. What a frightful grimace the result is! And equally, how is that false forehead, smooth as a billiard ball, to wrinkle when the old man loses his temper?

In a modern psychological drama, where the subtlest reactions of a character need to be mirrored in the face rather than expressed by sound and gesture, it would be worth while experimenting with powerful side-lighting on a small stage and a cast without make-up, or at least with the minimum.

If, in addition, we could abolish the visible orchestra, with its distracting lamps and its faces turned toward the audience; if we could have the stalls raised so that the spectators' eyes were higher than the players' knees; if we could get rid of the boxes (the centre of my target), with their tittering diners and supper-parties, and have total darkness in the auditorium during the performance; and if, first and foremost, we could have a *small* stage and a *small* house, then perhaps a new dramatic art might arise, and theatre once more become a place of entertainment for educated people. While waiting for such a theatre it is as well for us to go on writing so as to stock that repertory of the future.

I have made an attempt. If it has failed, there is time enough to try again.

MAX SCHELER (1874–1928)

One of the great social scientists and philosophers of the modern period, Max Scheler was also an astute student of literature. His analysis of tragedy is important in its attempts to make fundamental distinctions about the relationship between tragedy and guilt. In arguing for the principle of "guiltless guilt," he offers a new perspective in dealing with the moral dimension of tragedy. The essay "On the Tragic," reprinted below, is translated by Bernard Stambler.

"On the Tragic"

In the following we will speak of no particular art in which the tragic is portrayed. It is impossible to arrive at the phenomenon of the tragic through the art product alone, although the results of examining its extant forms might be most fruitful in discovering what it really is. The tragic is rather an essential element of the universe itself. The material made use of by the art product and the tragedian must contain beforehand the dark strain of this element. To determine what makes a tragedy genuine we must first have as precise a notion as possible of the phenomenon.

It is doubtful whether the tragic is essentially an esthetic phenomenon. We are speaking of life and history in general without placing ourselves in any particular esthetic circumstance, no matter how unusually full of tragic events and circumstances. The question of how the tragic works on our emotions or of how we come to "enjoy" the tragic in some art form we are purposely avoiding. These things can not tell us what the tragic is. The usual "psychological" method of observation, proceeding from the investigation of the experiences of one observing a tragic incident to its "objective understanding," tries to discover and describe the evocations of these experiences. Such a method avoids the issue rather than clarifies it.[1] It tells us only what the tragic does, not what it is. The tragic is above all a property which we observe in events, fortunes, characters, and the like, and which actually exists in them. We might say that it is given off by them like a heavy breath, or seems like an obscure glimmering that surrounds them. In it a specific feature of the world's makeup appears before us, and not a condition of our own ego, nor its emotions, nor its experience of compassion and fear. What goes on in the observer of the tragic as he feels this heavy breath and sees this shimmering darkness that encircles the head of the "tragic hero" is not related to his ability to understand this phenomenon by using his own symbolical way of looking at this feature in the world's makeup. There are people who are blind, or half blind, to the tragic—like Raphael, Goethe, and Maeterlinck.[2] One must know what the tragic is to depict this experience. Moreover, the experience is historically far more variable than the tragic itself. A tragedy of Aeschylus arouses entirely different emotions today than in his time, although the tragic is just as perceptible to both ages.

The mental processes of understanding the tragic, the inner perception of how it is brought to us, are to be distinguished from what one experiences in observing the tragic. This is not the same as the "experience" theory of the tragic. It has nothing to do with depicting the way it works on us psychologically. However, the former places the problem close to the essence of the tragic and its essential manifestations. Consequently, it should not be disregarded.

How then should we proceed? Should we indiscriminately gather together examples of the tragic, selecting those events that impress men as being such, and then ask what they possess in common? This would be a method of induction that would lend itself well to experimental support. Yet this would bring us only to the observation of our own ego when the tragic works upon us. What right have we to trust men when they call something tragic? A plurality of opinion does not help here. Without knowledge of what the tragic is, must we be forced to decide between the opinions that have weight and those which do not? But even taking this for granted, we would still have to justify ourselves. We would have a confused mass that we would call tragic. What would the common element be that would justify this judgment of ours? Nothing more than the fact that they are all called tragic.

All induction would presuppose that one knows beforehand what the essence of the tragic is, and not just what events are tragic. Our method of procedure will be different. The few examples and statements of others that may be given are not to serve as the basis for abstracting by induction a concept of the tragic. They will rather give us some rough draft in which to see the basic use of the word and the phenomenon expressed therein, without taking into account who uses the word and to what intent. They will provide the basis for seeing in what experience this phenomenon comes to its given state. We do not assume that the examples are facts in which the tragic adheres as a property. They are only something which will contain the basic manifestations of the tragic. They will provide us with the opportunity of searching out these manifestations and finally of arriving at the tragic itself. It is not a question here of proofs but of indications or signs.

One should also guard against treating the tragic as a phenomenon with its own metaphysical, religious, and otherwise speculative interpretations. The tragic is not the result of an interpretation of the world and the important events of the world. It is a fixed and powerful impression that certain things make and one which can itself be subjected to many different interpretations. Theories like that which Maeterlinck proposes, basically the theory of every Rationalism and Pantheism, are totally wrong. According to these theories the tragic is the result of a false and unstable interpretation of the world. The tragic is attributed to the ways of thinking in uncivilized times with uncontrolled emotions. Or it is a sort of sudden bewilderment in the face of the defects of the world against which one knows of no help, or—what is the simple consequence of this as stated by Maeterlinck—no helper is at hand, no helper to put the matter in order. They obscure rather than clarify the essence of the tragic; their own outlook and times prevent them from seeing it. We, however, reason that these interpretations of the world are wrong because they have no place for the undeniable fact of the tragic and that any age which does not perceive it is insignificant.

Metaphysical interpretations of the tragic are most interesting. But the phenomenon itself is taken for granted by them. Certain metaphysicians like Eduard von Hartmann make God Himself the tragic hero. Others think the tragic lies only on the surface of things and that underneath all tragedies lies an imperceptible harmony, into which they are finally resolved. But to know where the tragic has its source, whether in the basic structure of existence or in human passions and unrest, is to know already what the tragic is.

Every interpretation fails before the inflexibility of reality which reduces it to silence.

This question of the tragic is only one example of the importance of contrasting the changing whims of the times with the facts of reality.

THE TRAGIC AND VALUES

All that can be called tragic is contained within the realm of values and their relationships.

In a universe free of values, such as that constructed by mechanical physics, there are no tragedies.

Only where there is high and low, nobleman and peasant, is there anything like a tragic event.

The tragic is not a value like beautiful, ugly, good, or bad. The tragic appears in objects only through the interplay of their inherent values.

It is always founded on values or connected with values. To repeat, it is found only in that realm where there are objects of value and where these work in one way or another on each other.

Serenity, sadness, grandeur, and earnestness can be classified among the more tranquil values. The tragic is absent here. It appears in the realm of changing values and circumstances. Something must happen

---

[1] Even the famous definition of Aristotle: The tragic is that which arouses pity and fear.

[2] Cf. Maeterlinck's *La Sagesse et la Destinée.*

for it to appear. There must be a period of time in which something is lost or destroyed.

In empty space—Schiller notwithstanding—dwells much sublimity, but not the tragic. In a spaceless world the tragic might be possible, but never in a timeless world. In its basic connotations the tragic always implies a determined effectiveness in doing and in suffering. The tragic "character" remains such only as long as he has the necessary dispositions for tragic acting and suffering. Even a situation calling for opposition of forces or their reconciliation is only tragic as long as it contains this effectiveness. If the tragic is to appear, however, this effectiveness must take on a definite direction, a direction toward the annihilation of a positive value in a determined hierarchy. The strength which annihilates it must possess this value itself.

To belong to the category of the tragic some value must be destroyed. With regard to man it does not have to be his existence or his life. But at least something of his must be destroyed—a plan, a desire, a power, a possession, a faith. The destruction as such is not tragic. It is rather the course that an object of lower or equal positive values, never of higher values, is able to force upon it. We can hardly call it tragic for a good man to defeat and bring about the downfall of an evil man, nor for a nobleman to do the same to a peasant. Moral approval precludes a tragic impression here. This much is certain. It is also certain that it must be an object of high positive value that destroys a value. (Values such as the honest with respect to the wicked, the good with regard to the bad, and the beautiful compared to the ugly, are here called positive. All values have this opposition and duality, even excluding their degree of "higher" and "lower.") The tragic is apparent only where the strength to destroy a higher positive value proceeds from an object possessing this positive value. The manifestation is, moreover, purest and clearest where objects of equally high value appear to undermine and ruin each other. Those tragedies most effectively portray the tragic phenomenon in which, not only is every one in the right, but where each person and power in the struggle presents an equally superior right, or appears to fulfill an equally superior duty. If an object of higher positive value, let us take for example a good, just man, is overpowered by some insignificant evil object, the tragic is at once senseless and irrational. In place of arousing tragic pity, it arouses painful indignation. Tragic pity can never fall completely into the depths of pain and disgust, but must maintain some semblance of coolness and calmness.

The tragic is first of all a struggle that is occasioned in an object of high positive value, i.e., of a high moral nature, generally treating of the family, marriage, or the state. The tragic is a "conflict" which takes place between the positive value and the very object which possesses it. The great art of the tragedian is to set each value of the conflicting elements in its fullest light, to develop completely the intrinsic rights of each party.

ON THE TRAGIC AND GRIEF

It is true that in some way all tragic events are sad, but in a very definite sense. This is precisely what fate is, an event surrounded by this quality of sadness.[3] On the other hand it arouses sorrow in the feelings of men. It makes the soul sad.

Not all sad persons are tragic characters, however. Every death is sad and makes those left behind sad as well, but assuredly not every death is tragic. Let us disregard for a moment that type of grief that is produced in us independently of any perception of values, almost as if caused by a "neutral" feeling. We would rather consider the "grieved over something." The nature of a certain event arouses our sentiments and produces this feeling in us. It should not appear to be caused by our individual wishes or aims, but only by the worth of the object. The tragic grief has a double characteristic, one rooted in itself, the other in its subject.

This kind of grief is free from all indignation, anger, reproach, and that accompanying the desire "if it had only been otherwise." It is a calm, quiet fullness; a special kind of peace and composure is characteristic of it.

The atmosphere of tragic grief will be absent if we are aroused to do something about it. Once the event has been completed and brought to its climax, any indication of a compromise or of some chance to avert the catastrophe makes tragic grief impossible.

Tragic grief contains a definite composure. It is thus distinguished from all specifically personal griefs, those which come from a personal experience of being "sad about something." It comes to us from the outside through the soul; it is occasioned by events that are "tragic." The tragedies of Aeschylus show especially well how to awaken this atmosphere of grief in its utmost purity.

We will not point out the twofold characteristic feature of the tragic which causes this atmosphere. One is the very nature of the world's makeup; every individual sad event is thus determined. The other is based on the appearance of an uncompromising inevitability of the destruction of a value, a species of destruction which every tragedy must contain.

In every genuine tragedy we see more than just the tragic event. We see over and above it the permanent factors, associations, and powers which are in the very makeup of the world. It is these which make such a thing possible.[4] In every tragic event we are directly confronted with a definite condition of the world's makeup without deliberation or any sort of "interpretation." This confronts us in the event itself; it does not result from what it does to the things which brought it about. It is only momentarily connected with the event and is independent of the elements that make it up. It is present in the form of a slight presentiment.

Every objective grief like that of a tragic event has its own depth. (I take the word here in a transferred meaning like the "depth" of a room.) It has its own immensity, too, which distinguishes it from a very limited, determined event. The depth is brought about by the fact that its subject is twofold. One is the

---

[3] That the quality of the sad is definitely not a "feeling," nor a so-called "empathic feeling," cf. the essay, "Idole der Selbsterkenntnis."

[4] We mean "such a thing" in the sense of "a so-constituted value."

element of the event that has been seen by us. The other is that point in the world's makeup that is exemplified by the event and of which the event is but an example. Grief seems to pour out from the event into unlimited space. It is not a universal, abstract world-makeup that would be the same in all tragic events. It is rather a definite, individual element of the world's construction. The remote subject of the tragic is always the world itself, the world taken as a whole which makes such a thing possible. This "world" itself seems to be the object immersed in sorrow. In the foreground of this darkness of sorrow we see the specific event and fate standing out all the more clearly.

The element in the world's makeup which produces these situations seems to do so without any warning. In producing them it ignores the peculiarities of the causes of the event and even its normal effects. It is this which causes the second essential element of the tragic, its inevitability.

We will clarify this later. Right now we are interested in the peculiar atmosphere which it lends to the tragedy.

There is a whole category of feelings and affections that can be connected with the destroying of a value. Their essence is in being "preventable," even if in a particular case they may or may not have been prevented. It doesn't matter what these feelings might be—dread, fear, anger, horror, or the like; they all have in general the characteristic of "excitement." Thinking about the possibility of its turning out otherwise, or even better, causes this excitement. In men it is more frequently caused by the thought, "If so and so had only acted differently." This excitement is able to take hold of a man only because he is a practical being and, as it were, the potential actor in any event.

It softens when the inevitability is seen as an impossibility. The grief does not cease to be what it is, but it assumes the character of the feelings of dissatisfaction, excitement, and pain. These are taken in the same narrow sense as the physical feelings of fear, horror, and the like.

Tragic grief is pure, without physical arousement. In a certain sense even a feeling of "contentment" is joined with it.

There is no desire to do away with the event which led to the destruction of some value. This is abolished by seeing its inevitability.

We see that the tragic seems to have its ultimate roots in the essential makeup of the world itself. It is this which clears away all sense of culpability or responsibility. When we see this in the nature of the event a certain reconciliation takes place. It is a species of reconciliation which fills us with peace and rest and with resignation. This resignation banishes the weakness and pain that would come from contemplating a better-made world.

Thus the specific sadness of the tragic is really an objective character of the event itself. It is independent of the individual circumstances of the beholder. It is free from the feelings provoked by excitement, indignation, blame, and the like. It has a depth and immensity. It is not accompanied by physical feelings or by what can be called real pain. It has a definite resignation, contentment, and a species of reconciliation with the existence which it chances to have.

THE TRAGIC KNOT

We asserted previously that in the tragic a struggle takes place between two objects possessing high positive value and that one of them must be overcome. There is one case where this is fulfilled to the highest degree. It happens when the objects are not different events, persons, or things, but coincide in one event, person, or thing; even better, in one and the same quality, power, or ability.

It would be most tragic if the same power which has brought either itself or another object to a very high positive value becomes its destroyer—especially if this takes place in the very act of its achievement.

If we are observing a certain action which is realizing a high value, and then see in that same action that it is working towards the undermining of the very existence of the being it is helping, we receive the most complete and the clearest of tragic impressions.

The same tragic impression occurs when a special courage or boldness which permits a man to accomplish an heroic deed undermines him because it exposes him to a danger that a moderately prudent man would avoid—"If only I were prudent enough I would not be called Tell." Another example is the man with high ideals toward a spiritual goal who permits them to become shipwrecked on the little things of life. Everyone according to Madame de Staël's dictum has the mistakes of his virtue: the same traits of character which permitted a man to do his best have brought him to catastrophe.

We don't have to talk only of human beings here. An art gallery can be destroyed by the very fire that was kindled to preserve the picture. The event has a sharp tragic character. The flight of Icarus is tragic. The very wax which glued his wings to him melts in the same degree as he flies toward the sun.

The use of the phrase, "the tragic knot," is a pertinent metaphor. It illustrates the inner entanglement between the creation of a value and the destruction of a value as they take place in the unity of the tragic action and the tragic event.

Something else can be deduced from the aforesaid. It is not the relationship between values that constitutes the "stage" for the tragic event, nor is it the connection of causal events which it contains. It is rather a special reference of the value relationships to the causal relationships. It is an essential characteristic of our world—and thus of every world—that the course of the causal events disregards completely the value of things. The exigencies of values as they develop toward a unity or as they unfold themselves toward their ideal fulfillment is not taken into account by the causal series. The simple fact that the sun shines on the good and bad alike makes tragedy possible. At times it may happen that the causal relationships simultaneously coincide with an increase of the values. This is accepted as only accidental. It is not occasioned by intrinsic determination. Nor is it occasioned by a consideration of what the values need to reach their fulfillment or that the causality is at hand to produce them.

Without this basic condition there can be no tragedy.

There would be no tragedy in a world which operated on an established system of laws whereby each thing had the powers and capabilities commensurate with its values, and whereby its activity was directed only towards the exigencies of developing or unifying these values. Tragedy would likewise be impossible in a world operating on a system of laws whereby the powers would be directed against the exigencies of these values, purposely opposing them. The tragic would thrive in a satanic world as well as in a divine —a fact that Schopenhauer forgot in his discussion of the tragic.

We see the tragic only when in one glance we embrace both the causality of things and the exigencies of their immanent values. In this unified glance the mind tries to synthetize the conditions in which it finds these values so as to arrive at the unity it is trying to achieve. Then it follows the course of events in their causal sequence. The result is a clear insight into the independence of these two things. It is here that we may see the formal "background" of all tragedies.

Obviously, it is not in the mere knowledge of this circumstance that the tragic exists. The tragic comes into sight only when this independence of the two elements becomes embodied in a concrete event.

What has just been said casts new light on our definition. For never is our insight so clear and so concentrated as when we see that the same action may in some places produce a high value and in others— quite indifferently—destroy this value.

Here then—where we are able to see the unity of an action at a single glance and not by discursive connection, limb by limb—here is a circumstance known previously only by concept which has now come tangibly within our grasp.

What do we mean when we say that in the tragic the destruction of value is "necessary"? Surely not the destruction of causality in general!

Is the question then one of "causal" necessity or is it likely to be one of quite another kind of necessity? Here one might begin to discriminate and say that it is indeed causal necessity but of a particular kind, that is, "inner necessity," and consequently a necessity which depends not on influences breaking in from the outer world but rather on the eternal nature of things and men. Only as such can things and men undergo the tragic fate. Actually, this concept of the tragic—widely held though it may be—is not borne out by the facts.

When a man who seems destined for a certain fate, either by congenital disease or by any sort of natural predisposition, is brought low the first time that external circumstance has a chance to work upon him —such an event does not seem tragic to us even if the highest values inhered in him, values independent of this natural predisposition. Thus Ibsen, with all his artistic genius, has not succeeded in making of Oswald, in *Ghosts,* a tragic figure, since the worm of destruction gnawing at Oswald is the result of a disease he has inherited from his father. We miss here something that belongs to the essence of the tragic hero: that the evil which drives the hero to his downfall pertains to those against whom the struggle is being waged, and also that such a struggle be actually waged.

Both these requirements are missing in *Ghosts.* Nor is the tragic hero to be found in him who imme-

diately surrenders to the inimical, and who at the first dismissive word, immediately abnegates and resigns himself. The "necessity" of which we are now speaking must rather be of such a kind as to take its course even after the performance of all the "free" actions that may be tried in an attempt at flight. When we see the catastrophe opposed by all free efforts of will and means, and can still trace its irruption as "necessary"; when we can even trace, through the turmoil and anguish of this struggle to avert the catastrophe, a species of transcendent necessity: then and then only do we have an example before us of tragic "necessity."

Tragic necessity is not the necessity of the course of nature, a necessity which lies beneath freedom and the power of the will and which may be conceived as the free essence which permits the best linking of events in nature. Rather is tragic necessity of such a kind that it lies *above* freedom: it is to be found only in the conclusion of free acts or of "free causes" in the total sphere of causality, in which may be found even "unfree causes," that is, those which are the results of prior causes.

Wherever men are presented as "milieu-defined," as completely determined by "relationships," as in the naturalist "drama," we have a much less likely source of the tragic than in the drama which gives us the impression that consciously free choices are clearly and conclusively driving the events of the play to its catastrophe. Consequently neither naturalism and determinism on the one hand nor the rationalistic thesis of a "freedom of the human will" limited only by the chances of nature can provide a comprehension of the tragic, or anything more than the beginning of such comprehension. Both these views of the world have no place for the tragic since they make no provision for essential necessity reaching out above the qualities of nature and free choice.

There is still another reason why it is inadequate to define as "inner" that species of necessity we are here discussing. Immanent cause is that which in a thing or in a person exists as latent predisposition, or capacity, or skill, which functions at the inception of true relationships to other things or situations or persons. Wherever we encounter a strictly defined predisposition to the decline of value we must recognize an absence of the true development, of the veridical renewal, of the inner historicity which is needed for the tragic event: in such a situation the catastrophe itself would be predictable if we had a firm and exact picture of the character. The tragic however contains this paradox that when we behold the destruction of value it seems completely "necessary" and at the same time completely "unpredictable." Though the catastrophe may come closer and closer, driven by all the contributory factors (whether free or not), and each new event is visibly pregnant with danger, yet there must still remain one moment when everything —even by ideal calculation—could still turn out quite differently: whereupon from all this complexity is brought forth a deed which resolves these lurking factors into the unity of one species of reality by a means not rationally predictable.

The seemingly "propitious turn of events" just before the catastrophe, which so many tragic poets have been fond of, is a special means to exclude from the audience even the slightest appearance of "predictability." Even the increase of tension, which every tragedy must arouse, would not be possible if the catastrophe did not seem to us to be well founded from the beginning in the latent inner qualities of the characters and their relationships. It is *concrete* causality, which has nothing to do with "natural law," which governs tragic events as it also governs the irreversible motions of the constellations in their consummation of causality—that species of causality which is rightly called the truly "historical." For this we must return to the assertion of Schopenhauer that tragedy never exhibits true "character development" but only "character revelation," revelation of what was previously latent as disposition and character.

Even the tragic transformation of a character, the alteration of disposition and mentality, the essential and latent diversion from the previous course of life —even this transformation is seldom either the catastrophe itself or even an important part of it. A specifically tragic phenomenon is to be seen in the interruption—even in the midst of external victories—of a course of life directed towards certain values as goals. Tragic necessity is to be seen above all in the essence and essential relations of the inevitability and inescapability of things founded in society.

Even these negative definitions indicate that the species of "necessity" we have been talking about becomes apparent only when every conceivable kind of skill seems to be brought into play to halt the destruction of value and to preserve the value in question. Consequently two species of value-destruction are essentially untragic: first, those instances which are tinged with guilt because someone has failed in a duty definitely assigned to him; second, those instances which might have been avoided by the use of available techniques and means. In general, then, the quality of the tragic is lacking when the question "Who is guilty?" has a clear and definite answer.

Only where no such answer can be given does the stuff of tragedy begin to appear. We may use the term "tragic" only when we feel that everyone concerned in the story has hearkened to the demands of his duty with the utmost of his capabilities, and yet the disaster has had to occur. The tragic consists—at least in human tragedies—not simply in the absence of "guilt" but rather in the fact that the guiltiness can not be localized. Wherever we can substitute, in place of a man who plays a role in the unfolding of a catastrophe, another man who is like the first but morally better—that is, one who has a finer sympathy for moral opportunities as well as a greater energy of the moral will—to the extent that we can perform such substitution the growth of a feeling of tragedy is stunted by the amount of blame we can pin on the responsible person.

In such an instance "necessity" is missing as a quality of the tragic phenomena. Consider, for example, the death of Christ; suppose we were able to have the idea that his death, instead of being an essential relationship between His divine purity and the profaneness and opposition of an obdurate "world," had been brought about by the particular moral laxity of Pontius Pilate, or by the wickedness of an individual named Judas, or by the inimical deeds of the Jews. If we were then able to imagine Jesus of Nazareth surrounded not by these men but by a group morally "better," or if we could place him in a different historical context where he would come to higher recognition and repute—if we could do these things the impression of the tragic would vanish.

The death of Jesus is tragic only when it is presented—everywhere and forever—as the consistent adherence to the higher duty of all the parties concerned. An execution, for example, can never have a tragic culmination. The tragic appears when the idea itself of "justice" appears as leading to the destruction of higher value. An execution, if it is unavoidable, awakens deep sympathy; if it were avoidable it might arouse deep anger or irritation, but never tragic sympathy.[5]

If it is true that a disaster becomes tragic only when everyone has done his duty and, in the usual sense of the word, no one has incurred "guilt," it becomes part of the essence of tragic conflict that this conflict be guiltless and unavoidable even before judges who approach the ideal in wisdom and virtue. The tragic misdeed is even definable as that which silences all possible moral and legal powers of judgment; and, on the other hand, every conflict is essentially untragic when by moral and legal lights it is seen to be obvious and simple. Every essential confusion of the bounds of right and wrong, of good and evil, in the unity of action; every maze of threads, of motives, of views, of duties, so presented as to seem to lead equally well to a judgment of "right" or "wrong"; every complication which is not based on necessary moral and legal wisdom but which instead produces from the circumstances alone an absolute confusion of our moral and legal powers of judgment —every such complication pertains to the subjective side of tragic feeling and thereby transposes us completely from the realm of possible "right" and "wrong," from possible "accusation" and "indignation." "Tragic guilt" is of a kind for which no one can be blamed and for which no conceivable "judge" can be found.

Out of this error of our moral judgments, out of this pardonable search for a subject upon whom to pin this "guilt," a guilt which appears to us as such with crystal clarity—only out of this appears that specific tragic grief and tragic sympathy of which we have been speaking, along with its unique peace and reconciliation of the emotions. Now too the shifting of that which is to be feared to the cosmos itself appears as the essence of the reconciliation of the individual men and wills with the culminating deeds and events in which they have been taking part.

In this way, tragic guilt becomes something other than definable "right" and "wrong," or than "obeying obligation" or "defying obligation."

But individual men have quite different microcosms of values, dependent on the extent of their actual moral awareness and even on the extent of their possible moral awareness. Only on these bases can be measured their possible "duties" and areas of duty—quite independently of all the peculiarities of

---

[5] It is for this reason that Aeschylus, in his *Eumenides,* furnishes the judges of the Areopagus with both black and white marbles to indicate the guilt or innocence of Orestes.

their empirical real situations. If every individual does his "duty," to the extent that he does this he behaves *morally*; not otherwise can he do something of equal *value* or *be* in any way of equal value. How deep his gaze thereby penetrates into the macrocosm of moral value, which contains the entire extent of the realm of possible good and evil, and how deep a hold he takes within this macrocosm, are in no way to be decided by the extent to which each individual dutifully produces the "best" of the realm of values with which he has been endowed. It is not duty and the performance of it that "ennoble"—as the Kantian, short-sighted ethic puts it—but rather "noblesse oblige": this is the original nobility of man, which establishes for him quite varied arrays of possible duties—duties which stand in varied relationships to the moral world and are variously "significant" for it.

It makes a difference whether the man doing his duty is a grocer or a noble king; the first one in a vague way obeys a few moral value-distinctions, doing his "duty" with a couple of poor concepts of choice, while the other, living in the fullness of manifold human and other moral relationships, with a finely articulated and higher realm of moral value-distinctions before his eyes, does his "duty" while he demonstrates the highest value given to him, and in will and deed realizes this value. The latter man in this action must conduct himself as occasionally opposed to duty, while the man blind to value blandly performs *his* "duty." If we were now to say that in a true tragic presentation everyone must do his "duty," or at least that it would be prudent so to do, and that—even if everyone has done his duty—the destruction of value and the consequent lessening of the total moral value of the world must nevertheless take place, we would thereby still not know how to exclude this quite different dimension of the moral value-distinction of the individual and of his being taking part in the tragedy. It is rather a quite different species of the tragic which, in this dimension of being, bruises "noble" individuals against the strongly articulated "duties" of the mob. And it appears to be a particular melancholy-ironic glory of this kind of tragedy that the noble individual should accept a moral guilt that his companions do not accept. To the extent that the noble person can more easily become "guilty" than the ignoble—in accord with his richer and higher realm of duties—he is susceptible to a moral "risk" which ever bears with it something potentially tragic, as this risk simultaneously praises and blames his noble nature. The Prometheus of technic, who stole fire from Zeus, is a tragic figure; but even more tragic are the moral Prometheuses in whose eyes a moral world comes with the brilliance of lightning, a moral world that never previously existed. . . . While they are realizing values and acquiring duties which the vulgar do not yet know how to see as value or to feel as duty, the vulgar are themselves only doing their "duty" while the noble see as "evil" what may still be "good" for the vulgar. Here is one instance of the tragic "fall" for the "noble," in that his every eventual moral disapproval of the vulgar must necessarily remain silent—to the extent that only through "good consciences" can his sacred "duty" be accomplished.

We can now penetrate more deeply into "tragic guilt" if we are careful to remain clear on the matter of what, in such a case, is the completion of the duty of the noble. Let it be a proposition here—with no attempt at proof—that moral "good" is the relation by which we realize or tend to realize in a given action that a preference indicates a more highly conceived value.[6] To prefer the higher value is always equivalent to depreciating the lower value, that is, to discontinue the realization of this lower value. However, all "moral norms," i.e., all imperative rules of a general type, are only exercises in what to will and what to do, as suggested by the average levelling of values in any given epoch resulting from the "situations" which are typical of and regularly recurring in this epoch; still, even this levelling of values provides "higher" values which must be realized. Every material rule of morality contains the presuppositions of the particular positive world of good appropriate to its level of civilization. What happens then when the "noble" man perceives a value which is higher than the average, a value which is generally trodden under in the levelling of values, and accomplishes his advance in the moral cosmos of value, an advance that the vulgar are not yet ready to grasp? In such a case it must be obvious to him that what appears "good" and "dutiful" according to the ruling morality now becomes wicked and evil—and by the same token becomes for him "opposed to duty." And this realization is not avoidable but rather—to use a term of Kant's—a "necessary perception" (*"notwendiger Schein"*). And since everything that can be generally a "moral law"—even to the most complete codification and strongly logical presentation of these laws—inevitably exhibits the positive material world of values of the "time," the "time" itself being determined by the prevailing system of value-levelling—such a man must violate the prevailing moral precept and also violate everything in the moral world that comes into the orbit of such precepts. He must necessarily appear "guilty" even before the fairest judge, when he is in fact guiltless and is so seen by God alone. That this is so is not an irregularity but rather part of the essence of all moral development. Here I mean to point out the root of that necessary and "guiltless guilt," which has hitherto been expressed in this paradoxical form only with a feeling for the justice of it. What is essential here is the necessity of the deception into which the most just moralist must blunder when confronted with the "tragic hero." Although the tragic hero with moral awareness[7] is obviously essentially the opposite of a sinner, he can not be distinguished from a sinner by the age in which he lives. Only to the extent that his newly experienced value becomes established and becomes the prevailing "morality" can he be seen and known—and then only in historical retrospect—as a moral hero. And so there are no present tragedies—there are only tragedies of the past. The tragic man necessarily goes his way in his "present" quiet and speechless. He strides unrecognized through the mob; he may even be there considered a sinner. The error of an instance which separates

[6] Cf. my book, *Der Formalismus in der Ethik und die materiale Wertethik*, vol. I, Niemeyer, Halle, 1914.

[7] We are speaking here only of this kind and not of the tragic hero in general.

genius from sinner is here not an accidental but a necessary error. Here, in this tragic fate of the moral genius we can perhaps grasp, in a single species and fashion, the nerve of fate, the complete unpredictability of moral development in man. And even in the absolutely inevitable "fate" and the related, absolute loneliness of the moral genius we can see a moment of the type of the tragic, as it may have happened to Jesus in Gethsemane. Here likewise appears the total fate of the world as it appears compressed into the experience of one man, as though in this moment he were standing alone and yet in the "middle," in the center of all the forces that animate the universe. His experience is as though whole epochs of history occurred in him, yet with no one else being aware of his experience—as though everything lay unified in his hand. And perhaps through this something more may become clear: the tragic hero of this kind is not guilty of his guilt, but rather it "happens" to him: this justifiable circumlocution repeats a very characteristic moment of "tragic guilt." That is: that the "guilt" comes to him and not he to the guilt! . . . *"Ihr führt ins Leben ihn hinein. . . ."*

Nevertheless this "fall" into guilt does not mean that the tragic hero, either through immoderate passion or through stress and a drive in one direction, is so moved that this drive becomes the central point of his ego and his will consequently is impelled in this same direction. This is also the case in the usual moral guiltiness—at least in great measure; and quantities cannot here serve as a basis for differentiation. Even in the midst of the most powerful stresses the will which "follows" such a direction remains a new action, an action not entirely determined by this stress! The tragic guilt into which the hero "falls" is much more accurately characterized by calling it a "guilty" doing or renunciation of doing which darkens the areas of his possible choices and so makes a certain kind of guilt unavoidable, since the choice of the "best" meaning is necessarily in error.

Moral or "guilty guilt" is based on the act of choice; tragic or unguilty guilt is rather based on the sphere of choice! The act of choice is consequently for the tragic hero free of guilt—just the reverse of what obtains in moral guilt, in which the sphere of choice also entails objectively guiltless possibilities, and only the guilt of the act is important. And so the tragic hero "becomes guilty" while doing a guiltless thing.

The consequence of what has been said is the absurdity of the schoolmasters' theory that a moral guiltiness is to be sought in tragedies, and that the tragic poet instead of being a respectable performer of a tragic phenomenon is made into a moral judge over his heroes, whom he punishes for their deeds while at the same time he animates them to perform those deeds. Only total blindness for the phenomenon of tragedy could hatch out this silliest of all theories.

But we should also fall into error if we should try to make the correct concept of tragic guilt serve as the complete definition of the tragic phenomenon. However, since from its earliest presentations the tragic has been a universal phenomenon, not one specifically human or limited to static will, such a definition is self-destructive. However, note this: where a "tragic guilt" is actually portrayed—and it is not the deed of the hero which brings the guilt

upon him or is involved in the "catastrophe," nor is his downfall the bearer of the tragic phenomenon, but rather the "guilt of error" itself, and consequently the fact that purity of will falls into guilt—here is the very bearer and root of the tragic.

In this way it is tragic that Othello falls into the guilt of having to kill his beloved, and that guiltless Desdemona should be killed by her beloved who loves her. In his own words, "For, in my sense, 'tis happiness to die," the death of Othello is not punishment for his deed, which as "punishment" must terminate a conscious evil; rather is it deliverance. Tragic guilt is therefore not a condition of the tragic phenomenon—which would indeed be a *circulus in demonstrando,* if the guilt had to be not any sort of "guilt" but only "tragic" guilt—but it is a species of the tragic itself, and to the extent that we are here dealing with moral value, it is therefore a species of absolute value—so to speak, the culminating point of the tragic. Neither death nor any other mischance but only his "fall into guilt" constitutes the tragic fate of the hero.

SUSANNE LANGER
(1895–   )

Professor emeritus of philosophy at Connecticut College, Susanne Langer has had a distinguished career as an analyst of the philosophical aspects of language and art. She is the author of *Philosophy in a New Key* (1942) and *Feeling and Form* (1953). The excerpt below is reprinted from the latter work. Particularly interesting in her presentation is the thesis that the unity of the dramatic experience derives from "the illusion of Destiny," the appearance of the future in the arts of the present.

from *Feeling and Form*

Most theoretical treatments of literature draw their material and evidence as much from drama as from lyric and narrative works. A serious analysis of literary art with only an occasional, passing mention of Shakespeare may have seemed to many readers a curious innovation. The reason for it, however, is simple enough, and has been suggested above: Shakespeare is essentially a dramatist, and drama is not, in the strict sense, "literature."

Yet it is a poetic art, because it creates the primary illusion of all poetry—virtual history. Its substance is an image of human life—ends, means, gains and losses, fulfillment and decline and death. It is a fabric of illusory experience, and that is the essential product of poesis. But drama is not merely a distinct literary form; it is a special poetic mode, as different from genuine literature as sculpture from pictorial art, or either of these from architecture. That is to say, it makes its own basic abstraction, which gives it a way of its own in making the semblance of history.

Literature projects the image of life in the mode of virtual memory; language is its essential material; the sound and meaning of words, their familiar or unusual use and order, even their presentation on the printed page, create the illusion of life as a realm of events—completed, lived, as words formulate them —events that compose a Past. But drama presents the poetic illusion in a different light: not finished realities, or "events," but immediate, visible responses of human beings, make its semblance of life. Its basic abstraction is the act, which springs from the past, but is directed toward the future, and is always great with things to come.

In using common words, such as "event" or "act," as analytic terms, one runs the danger of suggesting far less general concepts, and indeed a variety of them, all equally inadequate to the purpose in hand. "Event" [is here] used in the sense given it by Whitehead, to cover all space-time occurrence, even the persistence of objects, the repetitious rhythms of life, the occasion of a thought as well as of an earthquake. Similarly, by "act" I mean any sort of human response, physical or mental. The word is commonly used, of course, in more specialized senses. It may mean one of the major divisions of a play—Act I, Act II, etc.; or it may refer to overt behavior, rushing about, laying hands on someone, taking or surrendering an object, and so forth; or it may mean a piece of dissembling, as when one says of a person that he feels one way and acts another. In the general sense here employed, however, all *reactions* are acts, visible or invisible; so in drama, any illusion of physical or mental activity is here called an "act," and the total structure of acts is *a virtual history in the mode of dramatic action.*

An act, whether instinctive or deliberate, is normally oriented toward the future. Drama, though it implies past actions (the "situation"), moves not toward the present, as narrative does, but toward something beyond; it deals essentially with commitments and consequences. Persons, too, in drama are purely agents—whether consciously or blindly, makers of the future. This future, which is made before our eyes, gives importance to the very beginnings of dramatic acts, i.e. to the motives from which the acts arise, and the situations in which they develop; the making of it is the principle that unifies and organizes the continuum of stage action. It has been said repeatedly that the theater creates a perpetual present moment [1]; but it is only a present filled with its own future that is really dramatic. A sheer immediacy, an imperishable direct experience without the ominous forward movement of consequential action, would not be so. As literature creates a virtual past, drama creates a virtual future. The literary mode is the mode of Memory; the dramatic is the mode of Destiny.

[1] For example, R. E. Jones in *The Dramatic Imagination,* p. 40, says: "This is drama; this is theatre—*to be aware of the Now.*" And Thornton Wilder, in "Some Thoughts on Playwriting," lists as one of the "four fundamental conditions of the drama" that "its action takes place in a perpetual present time."—"On the stage it is always now." (*The Intent of the Artist,* p. 83.) [Notes throughout are by the author]

The future, like the past, is a conceptual structure, and expectation, even more obviously than memory, is a product of imagination. The "now" created by poetic composition is always under the aegis of some historical vision which transcends it; and its poignancy derives not from any comparison with actuality, but from the fact that the two great realms of envisagement—past and future—intersect in the present, which consequently has not the pure imaginative form of either memory or prophecy, but a peculiar appearance of its own which we designate as "immediacy" or "now."

In actual life the impending future is very vaguely felt. Each separate act is forward-looking—we put on a kettle expecting it to boil, hand someone a bill and expect to be given change, board a bus with casual confidence that we shall leave it again at an intended point, or board an airplane with somewhat more conscious interest in our prospective exit from its inside. But we do not usually have any idea of the future as a total experience which is coming because of our past and present acts; such a sense of destiny arises only in unusual moments under peculiar emotional stress.

In drama, however, this sense of destiny is paramount. It is what makes the present action seem like an integral part of the future, howbeit that future has not unfolded yet. The reason is that on the stage, every thought expressed in conversation, every feeling betrayed by voice or look, is determined by the total action of which it is a part—perhaps an embryonic part, the first hint of the motive that will soon gather force. Even before one has any idea of what the conflict is to be (i.e. before the "exposition" has been given), one feels the tension developing. This tension between past and future, the theatrical "present moment," is what gives to acts, situations, and even such constituent elements as gestures and attitudes and tones, the peculiar intensity known as "dramatic quality."

In a little-known volume, bearing the modest, impersonal title: *Essays by Divers Hands* (a volume of "Transactions" of the Royal Society of Literature in England),[2] there is a very thoughtful philosophical essay by Charles Morgan, called "The Nature of Dramatic Illusion," in which he seems to me to have both stated and answered the question of what is created in the full-fledged work of dramatic art— the enacted play.

"With every development of dramatic technique," he wrote there, "and every departure from classical structure, the need increases for a new discussion which . . . shall establish for the stage not indeed a formal rule but an aesthetic discipline, elastic, reasoned, and acceptable to it in modern circumstances.

"It is my purpose, then, to discover the principle from which such a discipline might arise. This principle I call the principle of illusion." [3]

"Illusion, as I conceive it, is form in suspense . . . In a play form is not valuable *in itself;* only the suspense of form has value. In a play, form is not and cannot be valuable in itself, because until the play is over form does not exist. . . .

[2] N. S. Vol. 12, ed. by R. W. Macan, 1933. The article in question covers pp. 61–77.

[3] *Ibid.,* p. 61.

"A play's performance occupies two or three hours. Until the end its form is latent in it. . . .

"This suspense of form, by which is meant the incompleteness of a known completion, is to be clearly distinguished from common suspense—suspense of plot—the ignorance of what will happen, . . . for suspense of plot is a structural accident, and suspense of form is, as I understand it, essential to the dramatic form itself . . .

"What form is chosen . . . matters less than that while the drama moves *a* form is being fulfilled." [4]

"Fulfilled" is here the key word to the idea of dramatic form. Everything, of course, has a form of some sort: the famous million monkeys playing a million typewriters for a million years, turning out chance combinations of letters, would be rendering countless phonetic forms (though some of these might not encourage pronunciation); similarly, the most aimless conglomerate of events, acts, utterances, or what not, would *produce* a form when taken together; but before such collections were complete (which would be simply when, for any reason, one stopped collecting), no one could imagine their form. There has to be a sense of the whole, some anticipation of what may or even must come, if the production of new elements is to give the impression that "a form is being fulfilled."

Dramatic action is a semblance of action so constructed that a whole, indivisible piece of virtual history is implicit in it, as a yet unrealized form, long before the presentation is completed. This constant illusion of an imminent future, this vivid appearance of a growing situation before anything startling has occurred, is "form in suspense." It is a human destiny that unfolds before us, its unity is apparent from the opening words or even silent action, because on the stage we see acts in their entirety, as we do not see them in the real world except in retrospect, that is, by constructive reflection. In the theatre they occur in simplified and completed form, with visible motives, directions, and ends. Since stage action is not, like genuine action, embedded in a welter of irrelevant doings and divided interests, and characters on the stage have no unknown complexities (however complex they may be), it is possible there to see a person's feelings grow into passions, and those passions issue in words and deeds.

We know, in fact, so little about the personalities before us at the opening of a play that their every move and word, even their dress and walk, are distinct items for our perception. Because we are not involved with them as with real people, we can view each smallest act in its context, as a symptom of character and condition. We do not have to find what is significant; the selection has been made—whatever is there is significant, and it is not too much to be surveyed *in toto*. A character stands before us as a coherent whole. It is with characters as with their situations: both become visible on the stage, transparent and complete, as their analogues in the world are not.[5]

But what really assures the artistic unity Morgan called "form in suspense," is the illusion of Destiny itself that is given in drama, and that arises chiefly from the way the dramatist handles circumstance. Before a play has progressed by many lines, one is aware not only of vague conditions of life in general, but of a special situation. Like the distribution of figures on a chessboard, the combination of characters makes a strategic pattern. In actual life we usually recognize a distinct situation only when it has reached, or nearly reached, a crisis; but in the theater we see the whole setup of human relationships and conflicting interests long before any abnormal event has occurred that would, in actual life, have brought it into focus. Where in the real world we would witness some extraordinary act and gradually understand the circumstances that lie behind it, in the theater we perceive an ominous situation and see that some far-reaching action must grow out of it. This creates the peculiar tension between the given present and its yet unrealized consequent, "form in suspense," the essential dramatic illusion. This illusion of a visible future is created in every play—not only in very good plays, but in everything we recognize as a play, and not as dance, pageantry, or other non-dramatic "theater art."[6] It is the primary illusion of poetry, or virtual history, in the mode peculiar to drama. The future appears as already an entity, embryonic in the present. That is Destiny.

Destiny is, of course, always a virtual phenomenon—there is no such thing in cold fact. It is a pure semblance. But what it "resembles" (or, in the Aristotelian language which has lately been revived, what it "imitates") is nonetheless an aspect of real experience, and, indeed, a fundamental one, which distinguishes human life from animal existence: the sense of past and future as parts of one continuum, and therefore of life as a single reality.

This wide awareness, which we owe to our peculiarly human talent of symbolic expression, is rooted, however, in the elementary rhythms which we share with all other organisms, and the Destiny which dramatic art creates bears the stamp of organic process—of predeterminate function, tendency, growth, and completion. The abstraction of those vital forms by means of art has already been considered in Chapter 4, with reference to primitive design. In every art it is differently achieved; but in each one,

---

[4] *Ibid.*, pp. 70–72.

[5] A German critic, Peter Richard Rohden, saw this difference in our understanding of illusory and actual persons, respectively, as something of a paradox. "What," he wrote, "distinguishes a character on stage from a

'real' person? Obviously the fact that the former stands before us as a fully articulated whole. Our fellowmen we always perceive only in fragmentary fashion, and our power of self-observation is usually reduced, by vanity and cupidity, to zero. What we call 'dramatic illusion' is, therefore, the paradoxical phenomenon that we know more about the mental processes of a Hamlet than about our own inner life. For the poet-actor Shakespeare shows not only the deed, but also its motives, and indeed more perfectly than we ever see them together in actual life." (See "Das Schauspielerische Erlebnis," in Ewald Geissler's collection of essays, *Der Schauspieler* p. 36.)

[6] On this point Mr. Morgan might not agree with me. Having stated that "form in suspense" is the dramatic illusion itself, and the suspense of form something "without which drama is not," he speaks elsewhere of the dramatic illusion as a rare experience, "the highest reward of playgoing." I do not know whether he uses two concepts or only one, somewhat different from mine.

I think, it is equally subtle—not a simple reference to natural instances of that form, but a genuinely abstractive handling of its reflection in non-living or even non-physical structures. Literally, "organic process" is a biological concept; "life," "growth," "development," "decline," "death"—all these are strictly biological terms. They are applicable only to organisms. In art they are lifted out of their literal context, and forthwith, in place of organic processes, we have dynamic forms: instead of metabolism, rhythmic progression, instead of stimulus and response, completeness, instead of maturation, fulfillment, instead of procreation, the repetition of the whole in the parts—what Henry James calls "reflection" in the parts,[7] and Heinrich Schenker "diminution,"[8] and Francis Fergusson "analogy."[9] And in lieu of a law of development, such as biology sets up, in art we have destiny, the implicit future.

The purpose of abstracting vital forms from their natural exemplifications is, of course, to make them available for unhampered artistic use. The illusion of growth, for instance, may be made in any medium, and in numberless ways: lengthening or flowing lines, that represent no live creatures at all; rhythmically rising steps even though they divide or diminish; increasing complexity of musical chords, or insistent repetitions; a centrifugal dance; poetic lines of gradually deepening seriousness; there is no need of "imitating" anything literally alive in order to convey the appearance of life. Vital forms may be reflected in any elements of a work, with or without representation of living things.

In drama the *situation* has its own "organic" character, that is to say, it develops, or grows, as the play proceeds. That is because all happenings, to be dramatic, must be conceived in terms of acts, and acts belong only to life; they have motives rather than causes, and in turn motivate further and further acts, which compose integrated *actions*. A situation is a complex of impending acts. It changes from moment to moment, or rather, from move to move, as the directly imminent acts are realized and the future beyond them becomes distinct and fraught with excitement. In this way, the *situation* in which characters act differs from their "environment"—a term with which it is sometimes confused, through the influence of the social sciences that invaded the theater a generation ago and bred a teeming, if shortlived progeny of sociological plays, with a few real dramas among them. The environment wherein characters have developed, and whereby they are stunted or hardened, refined or falsely veneered, is almost always implicit (*almost* always, i.e. except where it becomes a conscious factor of interest to someone in the play). The situation, on the other hand, is always explicit. Even in a vague romantic world like that of Pelléas and Mélisande, removed from all actual history, and so ungeographical that the environment is really just castle walls and a forest, without population (the chorus of women in the death-scene simply springs up *ex nihilo*—there were no inhabitants in the background before, as there are in Shakespeare's castles), the situation that elicits the action is clear. The situation is, indeed, part of the action; it is

[7] *The Art of Fiction*, p. 170.
[8] Cf. Chap. 8, p. 129 [*Feeling and Form*].
[9] *The Idea of a Theater*, p. 104.

conceived entirely by the dramatist, and is given by him to the actors to understand and enact, just as he gives them the words to be spoken. The situation is a created element in the play; it grows to its climax, often branching out into elaborate detail in the course of its development, and in the end it is resolved by the closing of the action. . . .

Drama is more variable, more tolerant of choices made by performing artists, than any other art and mode. For this reason, the "commanding form," which is established by the playwright, must be clear and powerful. It has to govern the crisscross of many imaginative minds, and hold them all—the director, the actors, the designers of sets and lights and costumes—to one essential conception, an unmistakable "poetic core." But the poet must give his interpreters scope, too; for drama is essentially an enacted poem, and if the acting can only duplicate what the lines already effect, there will be unintended redundancy, and an apparent clutter of superfluous elements that makes the total form impure and opaque (such failures of clear conception, not the use of materials "belonging" to other arts, nor bold secondary illusions, are the source of impurity in a work; if the commanding form is organic and its realization economical, the most abnormal materials will be assimilated, the most intense effects of abstracted space, time, or power will become part of the pure dramatic work).

If drama is not made of words as a piece of literature is, how can the poet, who composes only the "lines," be said to create the commanding form? "Lines" in a play are only the stuff of speeches; and speeches are only some of the acts that make drama.

They are, however, acts of a special sort. Speech is a highly specialized activity in human life, and its image in all modes of poetry, therefore, has peculiar and powerful uses. Verbal utterance is the overt issue of a greater emotional, mental, and bodily response, and its preparation in feeling and awareness or in the mounting intensity of thought is implicit in the words spoken. Speech is like a quintessence of action. Edith Wharton described its relation to the rest of our activities very aptly, when she indicated its use in her own poetic medium, prose fiction: "The use of dialogue in fiction . . . should be reserved for the culminating moments, and regarded as the spray into which the great wave of narrative breaks in curving toward the watcher on the shore."[10]

Mrs. Wharton's metaphor of the wave is more apt than her literal statement, because one naturally thinks of "culminating moments" as rare moments, high points of the story, whereas the culmination of thought and feeling in speech is a frequent occurrence, like the culmination and breaking of each wave in a constant surf.

If, moreover, one contemplates the metaphor a little more deeply, it conveys a further relation of speech to the poetic elements that surround it, namely: that it is always of the same nature as they, subject to the basic abstraction of the mode in which it is used. In narrative it is an event, like all the events that compose the virtual Past—the private events that culminate in "direct discourse," the public events that intersect in the speaker's experience,

[10] *The Writing of Fiction*, p. 73.

and those which the speech, as a new event, engenders. In drama speech is an act, an utterance, motivated by visible and invisible other acts, and like them shaping the oncoming Future.

A playwright who writes only the lines uttered in a play marks a long series of culminating moments in the flow of the action. Of course he indicates the major non-verbal acts, but that may be done with the fewest possible words: *enter So-and-so, exit So-and-so,* or such laconic directions as: *dies, they fight, excursions and alarums.* Modern playwrights sometimes write pages of instructions to the actors, even describing the heroine's figure and face, or the style of some character's motions and postures (Strindberg tells the leading actor in *Miss Julia* to look like a half-educated man!). Such "stage directions" are really literary treatments of the story—what Clayton Hamilton called, "the sort of stage-directions which, though interesting to the reader, are of no avail whatever to the actor," [11] because they do not partake of the dramatic form. Ibsen prefaced his opening scenes with minute descriptions of persons and set; but his greatest interpreters have always made free with them. The lines of the play are the only guide a good director or actor needs. What makes the play the author's work is that the lines are really the highlights of a perpetual, progressive action, and determine what can be done with the piece on stage.

Since every utterance is the end of a process which began inside the speaker's body, an enacted utterance is part of a virtual act, apparently springing at the moment from thought and feeling; so the actor has to create the illusion of an inward activity issuing in spontaneous speech, if his words are to make a dramatic and not a rhetorical effect. As a very interesting German writer, Ferdinand Gregori, expressed it, "Gesture is older than words, and in the actor's dramatic creation, too, it must be their herald. Whether it is visible to the audience or not, it must always be the pacemaker. Anyone who starts with the words and then hunts for the appropriate gesture to accompany them, lies to the face of art and nature both." [12]

The need of preparing every utterance by some elements of expression and bearing that foreshadow it, has led many theorists and almost all naïve spectators to the belief that an actor must actually undergo the emotive experiences he renders—that he must "live" his part, and produce speech and gesture from a genuine passion. Of course the stage-occurrence is not his own life, but (according to this view) he must pretend to be the individual he represents, until he actually feels the emotions he is to register. Oddly enough, people who hold this belief do not ask whether the actor must also actually have the motives and desires of his alter ego—that is, whether he must really intend or at least wish to kill his antagonist, or to divulge a secret.

The imputation of bona fide feelings and emotions to the actor on stage would be only a negligible popular error, were it not part and parcel of a broader fallacy—the confusion of theatrical representation with "make-believe," or pretense, which has always

led both playwrights and directors to misconceive the relation of the audience to the play, and saddled them with the gratuitous and silly problem of the spectator's credulity. The classic expression of this concern is, of course, Castelvetro's warning in his *Poetics,* published in 1570: "The time of the representation and that of the action presented must be exactly coincident. There is no possibility of making the spectators believe that many days and nights have passed, when they themselves obviously know that only a few hours have actually elapsed; they refuse to be so deceived." [13] Corneille, a generation later, still accepted the principle, though he complained that to limit a dramatic action quite strictly to one room and the time span of a theater visit often "is so awkward, not to say impossible, that some enlargement of place must of necessity be found, as also of time." [14]

An art principle that cannot be fully and wholeheartedly applied, but requires compromises and evasions, should be immediately suspect; yet the principle of making the spectators believe that they are witnessing actual happenings has been accepted down to our own day, [15] and though most theorists have seen its error, it still crops up in contemporary criticism, and—worse yet—in theater practice. We have fairly well recovered from the epidemic of naturalism, the stagecraft that sought to dispense with all artifice, and consequently borrowed living material from the actual world—"drugstore clerks drafted to impersonate themselves in real drugstores transferred bodily to the stage," as Robert Edmond Jones described this sort of dramaturgy. Now it is true that real art *can* be made with such devices; no device in itself is taboo, not even putting stage-beggars in clothes begged from real beggars (Edward Sothern, in his autobiography, recalls his acquisition of one such unalluring treasure). But the theory that a play is a game of "make-believe" designed by the poet, carried on by the actors, and supported by an audience willing to pretend that the stage history is actual, which still persists, and with it its practical counterpart—the principle of deluding the audience, aiding the public "make-believe" by making the play seem as real as possible—is another story.

The whole conception of theater as delusion is

---

[11] *The Theory of the Theatre,* p. 307. A few paragraphs later he remarked on Granville-Barker's plays: "Barker's printed stage-directions are little novels in themselves."

[12] "Die Vorbildung des Schauspielers," in Ewald Geissler's collection *Der Schauspieler.* See p. 46.

[13] Reprinted in *The Great Critics, An Anthology of Literary Criticism,* edited by J. H. Smith and E. W. Parks. See p. 523.

[14] *Ibid.,* p. 531. From *A Discourse on the Three Unities.*

[15] Strindberg, for instance, was convinced that the spectators in the theater let themselves be deluded, tricked into believing or making-believe that what they saw was actual life going on in their presence, and he was seriously afraid of what popular education, and the general enlightenment it was expected to bring, would do to people's credulity. In the famous preface to *Miss Julia* he observes that "the theater has always served as a grammar school to young people, women, and those who have acquired a little knowledge, all of whom retain the capacity for deceiving themselves and being deceived," but that "in our time, when the rudimentary, incomplete thought-processes operating through our fancy seem to be developing into reflection, research, and analysis, the theater might stand on the verge of being abandoned as a decaying form, for the enjoyment of which we lack the requisite conditions."

closely linked with the belief that the audience should be made to share the emotions of the protagonists. The readiest way to effect this is to extend the stage action beyond the stage in the tensest moments, to make the spectators feel themselves actually present as witnesses of the scene. But the result is artistically disastrous, since each person becomes aware not only of his own presence, but of other people's too, and of the house, the stage, the entertainment in progress. Rosamond Gilder reported such an experience in her comment on Orson Welles' staging of *Native Son;* describing the scene wherein Bigger Thomas is cornered by his pursuers, she said: "Here flashing lights, gunplay, shouting and shooting converge on the stage from balcony and boxes. The theatrical illusion, far from being increased, is shattered, and the scene becomes nothing more than a nineteen-forty-one version of Eliza crossing the ice." [16]

I, too, remember vividly to this day the terrible shock of such a recall to actuality: as a young child I saw Maude Adams in *Peter Pan.* It was my first visit to the theater, and the illusion was absolute and overwhelming, like something supernatural. At the highest point of the action (Tinkerbell had drunk Peter's poisoned medicine to save him from doing so, and was dying) Peter turned to the spectators and asked them to attest their belief in fairies. Instantly the illusion was gone; there were hundreds of children, sitting in rows, clapping and even calling, while Miss Adams, dressed up as Peter Pan, spoke to us like a teacher coaching us in a play in which she herself was taking the title role. I did not understand, of course, what had happened; but an acute misery obliterated the rest of the scene, and was not entirely dispelled until the curtain rose on a new set.

The central fallacy in such play production, and in the concept of drama that it assumes, is the total disregard of what Edward Bullough, in an essay that has become deservedly famous,[17] called "psychical Distance." All appreciation of art—painting, architecture, music, dance, whatever the piece may be—requires a certain detachment, which has been variously called the "attitude of contemplation," the "aesthetic attitude," or the "objectivity" of the beholder. As I pointed out in an early chapter of this book,[18] it is part of the artist's business to make his work elicit this attitude instead of requiring the percipient to bring an ideal frame of mind with him. What the artist establishes by deliberate stylistic devices is not really the beholder's attitude—that is a by-product—but a relation between the work and its public (including himself). Bullough terms this relationship "Distance," and points out quite rightly that "objectivity," "detachment," and "attitudes" are complete or incomplete, i.e. perfect or imperfect, but do not admit of degrees. "Distance, on the contrary, admits naturally of degrees, and differs not only according to the nature of the *object,* which may impose a greater or smaller degree of Distance, but

varies also according to the *individual's capacity* for maintaining a greater or lesser degree." [19]

He describes (rather than defines) his concept, not without resort to metaphor, yet clearly enough to make it a philosophical asset:

"Distance . . . is obtained by separating the object and its appeal from one's own self, by putting it out of gear with practical needs and ends. . . . But it does not mean that the relation between the self and the object is broken to the extent of becoming 'impersonal' . . . On the contrary, it describes a *personal* relation, often highly emotionally colored, but *of a peculiar character.* Its peculiarity lies in that the personal character of the relation has been, so to speak, filtered. It has been cleared of the practical, concrete nature of its appeal. . . . One of the best-known examples is to be found in our attitude towards the events and characters of the drama. . . ." [20]

This relation "of a peculiar character" is, I believe, our natural relation to a symbol that embodies an idea and presents it for our contemplation, not for practical action, but "cleared of the practical, concrete nature of its appeal." It is for the sake of this remove that art deals entirely in illusions, which, because of their lack of "practical, concrete nature," are readily distanced as symbolic forms. But delusion —even the quasi-delusion of "make-believe"— aims at the opposite effect, the greatest possible nearness. To seek delusion, belief, and "audience participation" in the theater is to deny that drama is art.

There are those who do deny it. There are very serious critics who see its essential value to society not in the sort of revelation that is proper to art, but in its function as a form of ritual. Francis Fergusson and T. S. Eliot have treated drama in this vein,[21] and several German critics have found in the custom of hand clapping a last vestige of the audience participation·that is really the public's lost birthright.[22] There are others who regard the theater not as a temple, but primarily as an amusement hall, and demand of drama that it shall please, delude us for a while, and incidentally teach morals and "knowledge of man." Brander Mathews extended the demand for amusement—any or every sort of amusement—to all the arts; but as his renown rests entirely on his dramatic criticism and teaching, his view of "art" is really a view of the theater casually extended to all other realms. "The primary purpose of all the arts is to entertain," said Mathews, "even if every art has also to achieve its own secondary aim. Some of these enter-

[16] "Glamor and Purpose," in *Theatre Arts,* May, 1941, pp. 327–335.

[17] "'Psychical Distance' as a Factor in Art and an Aesthetic Principle," *British Journal of Psychology,* June, 1912.

[18] Chap. 4.

[19] *Op. cit.,* p. 94.

[20] *Op. cit.,* p. 91. The attitude referred to is, of course, the famous "aesthetic attitude," here treated as an index to the proper degree of distance.

[21] Cf. Francis Fergusson, *The Idea of a Theater.* A book so full of ideas, scholarship and discernment that even in taking issue with it I would recommend it to every reader.

T. S. Eliot, in "A Dialogue on Dramatic Poetry" (in *Selected Essays, 1917–1932*), p. 35, lets "E." say, "The only dramatic satisfaction that I find now is in a High Mass well performed."

[22] E.g., Theodor Wiesengrund-Adorno, "Applaus," *Die Musik,* 23 (1930–31), p. 476; also A. E. Günther, "Der Schauspieler und wir," in Geissler's *Der Schauspieler,* p. 144.

tainments make their appeal to the intellect, some to the emotions, and some only to the nerves, to our relish for sheer excitement and for brute sensation; but each of them in its own way seeks, first of all, to entertain. They are, every one of them, to be included in the show business." [23]

Here we have certainly two extremes of dramatic theory; and the theory I hold—that drama is art, a poetic art in a special mode, with its own version of the poetic illusion to govern every detail of the performed piece—this theory does not lie anywhere between these extremes. Drama is neither ritual nor show business, though it may occur in the frame of either one; it is poetry, which is neither a kind of circus nor a kind of church.

Perhaps the greatest snare in the course of our thinking about theater is its free trafficking with the standard materials of all the other arts. People are so used to defining each art by its characteristic medium that when paint is used in the theater they class the result as "the painter's art," and because the set requires building, they regard the designer of it as an architect. Drama, consequently, has so often been described as a synthesis of several or even all arts that its autonomy, its status as a special mode of a great single art, is always in jeopardy. It has been treated as essentially dance, by confusion with pantomimic dances that have a dramatic plot; it has been conceived as tableau and pageantry heightened by speech and action (Gordon Craig held that the designer of its visual aspects was its real creator), and as poetic recitation accompanied by gestures, sometimes by dance-gestures. This last view is traditional in India, where it is supported by the obvious epic sources of Hindu plays (as usual, finding the source of a phenomenon is supposed to reveal its "real" nature). Hindu aestheticians, therefore, regard drama as literature, and judge it by literary standards.[24] Nietzsche found its origin in "the spirit of music" and consequently regarded its true nature as musical. Thornton Wilder describes it as an exalted form of narrative: "The theater," he writes, "carries the art of narration to a higher power than the novel or the epic poem. . . . The dramatist must be by instinct a story-teller." [25]

But story-telling, narration, is something quite different from story-enactment in a theater. Many first-rate story-tellers cannot make a play, and the highest developments of narration, such as the modern novel and short story, show devices of their own that have no meaning for the stage. They project a history in retrospect, whereas drama is history coming. Even as performed arts, narration and dramatization are distinct. The ancient rhapsodist, for all his gesticula-

tions and inflections, was not an actor, and today, too, people who are known as good readers of poetry or prose need not therefore have any aptitude for the theater.

The concept of drama as literature embellished with concurrent appeals to the sense of sight is belied most convincingly in the very society where it enjoys its traditional vogue; the fact that in India the classic drama survived as a popular art for centuries after both the Sanskrit and the various Prakrits in which it was composed had become dead languages, understood only by scholars, proves that the stage action was no mere accompaniment, but was instinctively developed by the actors to the point of self-sufficiency, making the precise word meanings of the speeches dispensable; that this drama is, in fact, what Cocteau called "a poetry of the theater," as well as "poetry in the theater."

As for dance, though it probably preceded drama on the boards, and though it uses dramatic plots after its own fashion, it does not give rise to drama—not even to true pantomime. Any direct dramatic action tends to suspend the balletic illusion. The fact that Greek drama arose amidst ritual dancing has led several art historians to consider it as a dance episode; but the dance was, in fact, only a perfect framework for the development of an entirely new art; the minute the two antagonists stepped out of the choric ensemble and addressed not the deity, nor the congregation, but each other, they created a poetic illusion, and drama was born in midst of the religious rite. The choric dance itself was assimilated to the world of the virtual history they presented.

Once we recognize that drama is neither dance nor literature, nor a democracy of various arts functioning together, but is poetry in the mode of action, the relations of all its elements to each other and to the whole work become clear: the primacy of the script, which furnishes the commanding form; the use of the stage, with or without representational scenery, to delimit the "world" in which the virtual action exists; the need of making the scene a "place," so that often the designer produces a plastic illusion that is secondary here, but primary in the art of architecture; [26] the use of music and sometimes of dance to keep the fictitious history apart from actuality and insure its artistic abstraction; [27] the nature of dramatic time, which is "musical" instead of practical time, and sometimes becomes strikingly evident— another secondary illusion in poetry, but the primary one of music. The guiding principle in the use of so many transient borrowed illusions is the making

[23] *A Book About the Theater,* p. 6.

[24] Cf. Sylvain Lévi, *Le théâtre indien,* p. 257: "They [Indian theorists] are wont to consider drama as the juxtaposition of two arts, which simultaneously pursue their respective ends, namely poetry and mimetic dance. . . . Dance and mummery, stagecraft and scenery combine to heighten the illusion and pleasure by appealing to several senses. Representation, therefore, surpasses reading by a quantitative difference of emotion; there is no qualitative difference between them." See also A. B. Smith, *The Sanskrit Drama,* pp. 294–295.

[25] "Some Thoughts on Playwrighting," p. 86.

[26] Cf. Jones, *op. cit.,* p. 75: "The energy of a particular play, its emotional content, its aura, so to speak, has its own definite physical dimensions. It extends just so far in space and no farther. The walls of the setting must be placed at precisely this point."

George Beiswanger, in a little article entitled "Opera for the Eye" (*Theatre Arts,* January, 1943, p. 59), makes a similar remark: "Each opera has its own ideal dimensions, and their illusion must be created whether the actual stage be large or small."

[27] Schiller, in his famous preface to *Die Braut von Messina,* called the Greek chorus, which he revived in this play, "a living wall" to preserve the Distance of the work.

of an *appearance,* not under normal circumstances, like a pretense or social convention, but under the circumstances of the play. Its total emotional tone is like the "palette" of a picture, and controls the intensity of color and light, the sober or fantastic character of the sets, the requirements such as overture, interludes, and what not.

Above all, that emotional tone guides the style of the actors. The actors are the chief interpreters—normally, the only indispensable ones—of the poet's incomplete but commanding creations. An actor does not express his emotions, but those of a fictitious person. He does not undergo and vent emotions; he conceives them, to the smallest detail, and enacts them. . . .

As every act and utterance set down in the poet's script serves to create a perceptible destiny, so all plastic, choreographic, or musical elements that are added to his play in the theater must support and enhance that creation. The dramatic illusion is poetic, and where it is primary—that is to say, where the work is a drama—it transmutes all borrowings from other arts into poetic elements. As Mr. Jones says in *The Dramatic Imagination,* "In the last analysis the designing of stage scenery is not the problem of an architect or a painter or a sculptor or even a musician, but of a poet." [28] It is the painter (or architect, or sculptor) turned poet who understands the commanding form which the author has composed by writing the lines of the play, and who carries this form to the further state of visibility, and it is the actor-poet who takes the whole work—words, setting, happenings, all—through the final phase of its creation, where words become utterances and the visible scene is fused into the occurrence of the virtual life.

Histrionic imagination is the same fundamental talent in the playwright, the leading actors, the performers of even the smallest parts in so far as they are genuine actors, the scene and light designer, the costumer, the light controller, the composer or selector of incidental music, the ballet master, and the director who surveys the whole to his satisfaction or despair. The work on which they are engaged is one thing—an apparition of Destiny.

"From the Greeks to Ibsen the actor has represented, by elocution as well as by movement, human character and human destiny. . . . When drama takes on the abstract character of music or pure dance it ceases to be drama. . . .

"The dramatist . . . is a writer, a poet, before he is a musician or a choreographer. Wagner of course showed that many dramatic elements can be embodied in orchestral music; silent movies showed how much can be done with the visual element alone; but if you add Wagner to Eisenstein and multiply by ten you still do not have a Shakespeare or an Ibsen. This does not say that drama is better than music, dancing, or the visual arts. It is different.

"The defenders of the arts of the theater must be infected by the commodities of the theater if they can forget that all 'theater arts' are means to one end: the correct presentation of a poem." [29]

[28] P. 77.
[29] From E. R. Bently, "The Drama at Ebb," *Kenyon Review,* VII, 2 (Spring, 1945), 169–184.

ANTONIN ARTAUD

(1896–1948)

Actor and director Artaud is best known as the founder of the "theater of cruelty," which attempts to restore to the theater the primitive, animal vitality lacking in the modern theater. The audience would not be passive spectators in this conception, but virtual participants. Artaud put his theories into practice in 1935 in the production of his play *Les Cenci,* but the production was not a success. He subsequently succumbed to mental illness, recovering his sanity shortly before his death. Artaud's theories have had considerable influence in the modern theater, particularly among French directors and playwrights such as Jean Genet and Albert Camus. The selection reprinted below, "The Theatre and Cruelty" from *The Theatre and Its Double* (1933), is translated by Mary Caroline Richards.

"The Theatre and Cruelty"

An idea of the theatre has been lost. And as long as the theatre limits itself to showing us intimate scenes from the lives of a few puppets, transforming the public into Peeping Toms, it is no wonder the elite abandon it and the great public looks to the movies, the music hall or the circus for violent satisfactions, whose intentions do not deceive them.

At the point of deterioration which our sensibility has reached, it is certain that we need above all a theatre that wakes us up: nerves and heart.

The misdeeds of the psychological theatre descended from Racine have unaccustomed us to that immediate and violent action which the theatre should possess. Movies in their turn, murdering us with second-hand reproductions which, filtered through machines, cannot *unite with* our sensibility, have maintained us for ten years in an ineffectual torpor, in which all our faculties appear to be foundering.

In the anguished, catastrophic period we live in, we feel an urgent need for a theatre which events do not exceed, whose resonance is deep within us, dominating the instability of the times.

Our long habit of seeking diversion has made us forget the idea of a serious theatre, which, overturning all our preconceptions, inspires us with the fiery magnetism of its images and acts upon us like a spiritual therapeutics whose touch can never be forgotten.

Everything that acts is a cruelty. It is upon this idea of extreme action, pushed beyond all limits, that theatre must be rebuilt.

Imbued with the idea that the public thinks first of all with its senses and that to address oneself first to its understanding as the ordinary psychological theatre does is absurd, the Theatre of Cruelty proposes to resort to a mass spectacle; to seek in the agitation of tremendous masses, convulsed and hurled against each other, a little of that poetry of festivals and crowds when, all too rarely nowadays, the people pour out into the streets.

The theatre must give us everything that is in crime, love, war, or madness, if it wants to recover its necessity.

Everyday love, personal ambition, struggles for status, all have value only in proportion to their relation to the terrible lyricism of the Myths to which the great mass of men have assented.

This is why we shall try to concentrate, around famous personages, atrocious crimes, superhuman devotions, a drama which, without resorting to the defunct images of the old Myths, shows that it can extract the forces which struggle within them.

In a word, we believe that there are living forces in what is called poetry and that the image of a crime presented in the requisite theatrical conditions is something infinitely more terrible for the spirit than that same crime when actually committed.

We want to make out of the theatre a believable reality which gives the heart and the senses that kind of concrete bite which all true sensation requires. In the same way that our dreams have an effect upon us and reality has an effect upon our dreams, so we believe that the images of thought can be identified with a dream which will be efficacious to the degree that it can be projected with the necessary violence. And the public will believe in the theatre's dreams on condition that it take them for true dreams and not for a servile copy of reality; on condition that they allow the public to liberate within itself the magical liberties of dreams which it can only recognize when they are imprinted with terror and cruelty.

Hence this appeal to cruelty and terror, though on a vast scale, whose range probes our entire vitality, confronts us with all our possibilities.

It is in order to attack the spectator's sensibility on all sides that we advocate a revolving spectacle which, instead of making the stage and auditorium two closed worlds, without possible communication, spreads its visual and sonorous outbursts over the entire mass of the spectators.

Also, departing from the sphere of analyzable passions, we intend to make use of the actor's lyric qualities to manifest external forces, and by this means to cause the whole of nature to re-enter the theatre in its restored form.

However vast this program may be, it does not exceed the theatre itself, which appears to us, all in all, to identify itself with the forces of ancient magic.

Practically speaking, we want to resuscitate an idea of total spectacle by which the theatre would recover from the cinema, the music hall, the circus, and from life itself what has always belonged to it. The separation between the analytic theatre and the plastic world seems to us a stupidity. One does not separate the mind from the body nor the senses from the intelligence, especially in a domain where the endlessly renewed fatigue of the organs requires intense and sudden shocks to revive our understanding.

Thus, on the one hand, the mass and extent of a spectacle addressed to the entire organism; on the other, an intensive mobilization of objects, gestures, and signs, used in a new spirit. The reduced role given to the understanding leads to an energetic compression of the text; the active role given to obscure poetic emotion necessitates concrete signs. Words say little to the mind; extent and objects speak; new images speak, even new images made with words. But space thundering with images and crammed with sounds speaks too, if one knows how to intersperse from time to time a sufficient extent of space stocked with silence and immobility.

On this principle we envisage producing a spectacle where these means of direct action are used in their totality; a spectacle unafraid of going as far as necessary in the exploration of our nervous sensibility, of which the rhythms, sounds, words, resonances, and twitterings, and their united quality and surprising mixtures belong to a technique which must not be divulged.

The images in certain paintings by Grunewald or Hieronymus Bosch tell enough about what a spectacle can be in which, as in the brain of some saint, the objects of external nature will appear as temptations.

It is in this spectacle of a temptation from which life has everything to lose and the mind everything to gain that the theatre must recover its true signification.

Elsewhere we have given a program which will allow the means of pure staging, found on the spot, to be organized around historic or cosmic themes, familiar to all.

And we insist on the fact that the first spectacle of the Theatre of Cruelty will turn upon the preoccupations of the great mass of men, preoccupations much more pressing and disquieting than those of any individual whatsoever.

It is a matter of knowing whether now, in Paris, before the cataclysms which are at our door descend upon us, sufficient means of production, financial or otherwise, can be found to permit such a theatre to be brought to life—it is bound to in any case, because it is the future. Or whether a little real blood will be needed, right away, in order to manifest this cruelty.

NORTHROP FRYE

(1912–   )

Professor of English and principal of Victoria College at the University of Toronto, Northrop Frye is best known for his *Anatomy of Criticism* (1957), the most provocative and noteworthy of recent attempts to present a comprehensive analysis of the nature of literature. The essay reprinted here (from *English Institute Essays,* 1948) is a particularly imaginative and illuminating application of Frye's critical principles.

"The Argument of Comedy"

The Greeks produced two kinds of comedy, Old Comedy, represented by the eleven extant plays of Aristophanes, and New Comedy, of which the best known exponent is Menander. About two dozen New Comedies survive in the work of Plautus and Terence. Old Comedy, however, was out of date before Aristophanes himself was dead; and today, when we speak of comedy, we normally think of something that derives from the Menandrine tradition.

New Comedy unfolds from what may be described as a comic Oedipus situation. Its main theme is the successful effort of a young man to outwit an opponent and possess the girl of his choice. The opponent is usually the father (*senex*), and the psychological descent of the heroine from the mother is also sometimes hinted at. The father frequently wants the same girl, and is cheated out of her by the son, the mother thus becoming the son's ally. The girl is usually a slave or courtesan, and the plot turns on a *cognitio* or discovery of birth which makes her marriageable. Thus it turns out that she is not under an insuperable taboo after all but is an accessible object of desire, so that the plot follows the regular wishfulfillment pattern. Often the central Oedipus situation is thinly concealed by surrogates or doubles of the main characters, as when the heroine is discovered to be the hero's sister, and has to be married off to his best friend. In Congreve's *Love for Love*, to take a modern instance well within the Menandrine tradition, there are two Oedipus themes in counterpoint: the hero cheats his father out of the heroine, and his best friend violates the wife of an impotent old man who is the heroine's guardian. Whether this analysis is sound or not, New Comedy is certainly concerned with the maneuvering of a young man toward a young woman, and marriage is the tonic chord on which it ends. The normal comic resolution is the surrender of the *senex* to the hero, never the reverse. Shakespeare tried to reverse the pattern in *All's Well That Ends Well,* where the king of France forces Bertram to marry Helena, and the critics have not yet stopped making faces over it.

New Comedy has the blessing of Aristotle, who greatly preferred it to its predecessor, and it exhibits the general pattern of Aristotelian causation. It has a material cause in the young man's sexual desire, and a formal cause in the social order represented by the *senex,* with which the hero comes to terms when he gratifies his desire. It has an efficient cause in the character who brings about the final situation. In classical times this character is a tricky slave; Renaissance dramatists often use some adaptation of the medieval "vice"; modern writers generally like to pretend that nature, or at least the natural course of events, is the efficient cause. The final cause is the audience, which is expected by its applause to take part in the comic resolution. All this takes place on a single order of existence. The action of New Comedy tends to become probable rather than fantastic, and it moves toward realism and away from myth and romance. The one romantic (originally mythical) fea-

ture in it, the fact that the hero or heroine turns out to be freeborn or someone's heir, is precisely the feature that trained New Comedy audiences tire of most quickly.

The conventions of New Comedy are the conventions of Jonson and Molière, and a fortiori of the English Restoration and the French rococo. When Ibsen started giving ironic twists to the same formulas, his startled hearers took them for portents of a social revolution. Even the old chestnut about the heroine's being really the hero's sister turns up in *Ghosts* and *Little Eyolf.* The average movie of today is a rigidly conventionalized New Comedy proceeding toward an act which, like death in Greek tragedy, takes place offstage, and is symbolized by the final embrace.

In all good New Comedy there is a social as well as an individual theme which must be sought in the general atmosphere of reconciliation that makes the final marriage possible. As the hero gets closer to the heroine and opposition is overcome, all the right-thinking people come over to his side. Thus a new social unit is formed on the stage, and the moment that this social unit crystallizes is the moment of the comic resolution. In the last scene, when the dramatist usually tries to get all his characters on the stage at once, the audience witnesses the birth of a renewed sense of social integration. In comedy as in life the regular expression of this is a festival, whether a marriage, a dance, or a feast. Old Comedy has, besides a marriage, a *komos,* the processional dance from which comedy derives its name; and the masque, which is a by-form of comedy, also ends in a dance.

This new social integration may be called, first, a kind of moral norm and, second, the pattern of a free society. We can see this more clearly if we look at the sort of characters who impede the progress of the comedy toward the hero's victory. These are always people who are in some kind of mental bondage, who are helplessly driven by ruling passions, neurotic compulsions, social rituals, and selfishness. The miser, the hypochondriac, the hypocrite, the pedant, the snob: these are humors, people who do not fully know what they are doing, who are slaves to a predictable self-imposed pattern of behavior. What we call the moral norm is, then, not morality but deliverance from moral bondage. Comedy is designed not to condemn evil, but to ridicule a lack of self-knowledge. It finds the virtues of Malvolio and Angelo as comic as the vices of Shylock.

The essential comic resolution, therefore, is an individual release which is also a social reconciliation. The normal individual is freed from the bonds of a humorous society, and a normal society is freed from the bonds imposed on it by humorous individuals. The Oedipus pattern we noted in New Comedy belongs to the individual side of this, and the sense of the ridiculousness of the humor to the social side. But all real comedy is based on the principle that these two forms of release are ultimately the same: this principle may be seen at its most concentrated in *The Tempest.* The rule holds whether the resolution is expressed in social terms, as in *The Merchant of Venice,* or in individual terms, as in Ibsen's *An Enemy of the People.*

The freer the society, the greater the variety of individuals it can tolerate, and the natural tendency of comedy is to include as many as possible in its final festival. The motto of comedy is Terence's "Nothing human is alien to me." This may be one reason for the traditional comic importance of the parasite, who has no business to be at the festival but is nevertheless there. The spirit of reconciliation which pervades the comedies of Shakespeare is not to be ascribed to a personal attitude of his own, about which we know nothing whatever, but to his impersonal concentration on the laws of comic form.

Hence the moral quality of the society presented is not the point of the comic resolution. In Jonson's *Volpone* the final assertion of the moral norm takes the form of a social revenge on Volpone, and the play ends with a great bustle of sentences to penal servitude and the galleys. One feels perhaps that the audience's sense of the moral norm does not need so much hard labor. In *The Alchemist,* when Lovewit returns to his house, the virtuous characters have proved so weak and the rascals so ingenious that the action dissolves in laughter. Whichever is morally the better ending, that of *The Alchemist* is more concentrated comedy. *Volpone* is starting to move toward tragedy, toward the vision of a greatness which develops *hybris* and catastrophe.

The same principle is even clearer in Aristophanes. Aristophanes is the most personal of writers: his opinions on every subject are written all over his plays, and we have no doubt of his moral attitude. We know that he wanted peace with Sparta and that he hated Cleon, and when his comedy depicts the attaining of peace and the defeat of Cleon we know that he approved and wanted his audience to approve. But in *Ecclesiazusae* a band of women in disguise railroad a communistic scheme through the Assembly, which is a horrid parody of Plato's *Republic,* and proceed to inaugurate Plato's sexual communism with some astonishing improvements. Presumably Aristophanes did not applaud this, yet the comedy follows the same pattern and the same resolution. In *The Birds* the Peisthetairos who defies Zeus and blocks out Olympus with his Cloud-Cuckoo-Land is accorded the same triumph that is given to the Trygaeus of the *Peace* who flies to heaven and brings a golden age back to Athens.

Comedy, then, may show virtue her own feature and scorn her own image—for Hamlet's famous definition of drama was originally a definition of comedy. It may emphasize the birth of an ideal society as you like it, or the tawdriness of the sham society which is the way of the world. There is an important parallel here with tragedy. Tragedy, we are told, is expected to raise but not ultimately to accept the emotions of pity and terror. These I take to be the sense of moral good and evil, respectively, which we attach to the tragic hero. He may be as good as Caesar, and so appeal to our pity, or as bad as Macbeth, and so appeal to terror, but the particular thing called tragedy that happens to him does not depend on his moral status. The tragic catharsis passes beyond moral judgment, and while it is quite possible to construct a moral tragedy, what tragedy gains in morality it loses in cathartic power. The same is true of the comic catharsis, which raises sympathy and ridicule on a moral basis, but passes beyond both.

Many things are involved in the tragic catharsis, but one of them is a mental or imaginative form of the sacrificial ritual out of which tragedy arose. This is the ritual of the struggle, death, and rebirth of a God-Man, which is linked to the yearly triumph of spring over winter. The tragic hero is not really killed, and the audience no longer eats his body and drinks his blood, but the corresponding thing in art still takes place. The audience enters into communion with the body of the hero, becoming thereby a single body itself. Comedy grows out of the same ritual, for in the ritual the tragic story has a comic sequel. Divine men do not die: they die and rise again. The ritual pattern behind the catharsis of comedy is the resurrection that follows the death, the epiphany or manifestation of the risen hero. This is clear enough in Aristophanes, where the hero is treated as a risen God-Man, led in triumph with the divine honors of the Olympic victor, rejuvenated, or hailed as a new Zeus. In New Comedy the new human body is, as we have seen, both a hero and a social group. Aristophanes is not only closer to the ritual pattern, but contemporary with Plato; and his comedy, unlike Menander's, is Platonic and dialectic: it seeks not the entelechy of the soul but the Form of the Good, and finds it in the resurrection of the soul from the world of the cave to the sunlight. The audience gains a vision of that resurrection whether the conclusion is joyful or ironic, just as in tragedy it gains a vision of a heroic death whether the hero is morally innocent or guilty.

Two things follow from this: first, that tragedy is really implicit or uncompleted comedy; second, that comedy contains a potential tragedy within itself. With regard to the latter, Aristophanes is full of traces of the original death of the hero which preceded his resurrection in the ritual. Even in New Comedy the dramatist usually tries to bring his action as close to a tragic overthrow of the hero as he can get it, and reverses this movement as suddenly as possible. In Plautus the tricky slave is often forgiven or even freed after having been threatened with all the brutalities that a very brutal dramatist can think of, including crucifixion. Thus the resolution of New Comedy seems to be a realistic foreshortening of a death-and-resurrection pattern, in which the struggle and rebirth of a divine hero has shrunk into a marriage, the freeing of a slave, and the triumph of a young man over an older one.

As for the conception of tragedy as implicit comedy, we may notice how often tragedy closes on the major chord of comedy: the Aeschylean trilogy, for instance, proceeds to what is really a comic resolution, and so do many tragedies of Euripides. From the point of view of Christianity, too, tragedy is an episode in that larger scheme of redemption and resurrection to which Dante gave the name of *commedia*. This conception of *commedia* enters drama with the miracle-play cycles, where such tragedies as the Fall and the Crucifixion are episodes of a dramatic scheme in which the divine comedy has the last word. The sense of tragedy as a prelude to comedy is hardly separable from anything explicitly Christian. The serenity of the final double chorus in the St. M. thew Passion would hardly be attainable if compo· and audience did not know that there was more to the story. Nor would the death of Samson lead to "calm of mind all passion spent" if Samson were not a prototype of the rising Christ.

New Comedy is thus contained, so to speak, within the symbolic structure of Old Comedy, which in its turn is contained within the Christian conception of *commedia*. This sounds like a logically exhaustive classification, but we have still not caught Shakespeare in it.

It is only in Jonson and the Restoration writers that English comedy can be called a form of New Comedy. The earlier tradition established by Peele and developed by Lyly, Greene, and the masque writers, which uses themes from romance and folklore and avoids the comedy of manners, is the one followed by Shakespeare. These themes are largely medieval in origin, and derive, not from the mysteries or the moralities or the interludes, but from a fourth dramatic tradition. This is the drama of folk ritual, of the St. George play and the mummers' play, of the feast of the ass and the Boy Bishop, and of all the dramatic activity that punctuated the Christian calendar with the rituals of an immemorial paganism. We may call this the drama of the green world, and its theme is once again the triumph of life over the waste land, the death and revival of the year impersonated by figures still human, and once divine as well.

When Shakespeare began to study Plautus and Terence, his dramatic instinct, stimulated by his predecessors, divined that there was a profounder pattern in the argument of comedy than appears in either of them. At once—for the process is beginning in *The Comedy of Errors*—he started groping toward that profounder pattern, the ritual of death and revival that also underlies Aristophanes, of which an exact equivalent lay ready to hand in the drama of the green world. This parallelism largely accounts for the resemblances to Greek ritual which Colin Still has pointed out in *The Tempest*.

The Two Gentlemen of Verona is an orthodox New Comedy except for one thing. The hero Valentine becomes captain of a band of outlaws in a forest, and all the other characters are gathered into this forest and become converted. Thus the action of the comedy begins in a world represented as a normal world, moves into the green world, goes into a metamorphosis there in which the comic resolution is achieved, and returns to the normal world. The forest in this play is the embryonic form of the fairy world of *A Midsummer Night's Dream*, the Forest of Arden in *As You Like It*, Windsor Forest in *The Merry Wives of Windsor*, and the pastoral world of the mythical sea-coasted Bohemia in *The Winter's Tale*. In all these comedies there is the same rhythmic movement from normal world to green world and back again. Nor is this second world confined to the forest comedies. In *The Merchant of Venice* the two worlds are a little harder to see, yet Venice is clearly not the same world as that of Portia's mysterious house in Belmont, where there are caskets teaching that gold and silver are corruptible goods, and from whence proceed the wonderful cosmological harmonies of the fifth act. In *The Tempest* the entire action takes place in the second world, and the same may be said of *Twelfth Night*, which, as its title implies, presents a carnival society, not so much a green world as an evergreen one. The second world is absent from the so-called problem comedies, which is one of the things that makes them problem comedies.

The green world charges the comedies with a symbolism in which the comic resolution contains a suggestion of the old ritual pattern of the victory of summer over winter. This is explicit in *Love's Labor's Lost*. In this very masque-like play, the comic contest takes the form of the medieval debate of winter and spring. In *The Merry Wives of Windsor* there is an elaborate ritual of the defeat of winter, known to folklorists as "carrying out Death," of which Falstaff is the victim; and Falstaff must have felt that, after being thrown into the water, dressed up as a witch and beaten out of a house with curses, and finally supplied with a beast's head and singed with candles while he said, "Divide me like a brib'd buck, each a haunch," he had done about all that could reasonably be asked of any fertility spirit.

The association of this symbolism with the death and revival of human beings is more elusive, but still perceptible. The fact that the heroine often brings about the comic resolution by disguising herself as a boy is familiar enough. In the Hero of *Much Ado About Nothing* and the Helena of *All's Well That Ends Well*, this theme of the withdrawal and return of the heroine comes as close to a death and revival as Elizabethan conventions will allow. The Thaisa of *Pericles* and the Fidele of *Cymbeline* are beginning to crack the conventions, and with the disappearance and revival of Hermione in *The Winter's Tale,* who actually returns once as a ghost in a dream, the original nature-myth of Demeter and Proserpine is openly established. The fact that the dying and reviving character is usually female strengthens the feeling that there is something maternal about the green world, in which the new order of the comic resolution is nourished and brought to birth. However, a similar theme which is very like the rejuvenation of the *senex* so frequent in Aristophanes occurs in the folklore motif of the healing of the impotent king on which *All's Well That Ends Well* is based, and this theme is probably involved in the symbolism of Prospero.

The conception of a second world bursts the boundaries of Menandrine comedy, yet it is clear that the world of Puck is no world of eternal forms or divine revelation. Shakespeare's comedy is not Aristotelian and realistic like Menander's, nor Platonic and dialectic like Aristophanes', nor Thomist and sacramental like Dante's, but a fourth kind. It is an Elizabethan kind, and is not confined either to Shakespeare or to the drama. Spenser's epic is a wonderful contrapuntal intermingling of two orders of existence, one the red and white world of English history, the other the green world of the Faerie Queene. The latter is a world of crusading virtues proceeding from the Faerie Queene's court and designed to return to that court when the destiny of the other world is fulfilled. The fact that the Faerie Queene's knights are sent out during the twelve days of the Christmas festival suggests our next point.

Shakespeare too has his green world of comedy and his red and white world of history. The story of the latter is at one point interrupted by an invasion from the comic world, when Falstaff *senex et parasitus* throws his gigantic shadow over Prince Henry, assuming on one occasion the role of his father. Clearly, if the Prince is ever to conquer France he must reassert the moral norm. The moral norm is duly reasserted, but the rejection of Falstaff is not a comic resolution. In comedy the moral norm is not morality but deliverance, and we certainly do not feel delivered from Falstaff as we feel delivered from Shylock with his absurd and vicious bond. The moral norm does not carry with it the vision of a free society; Falstaff will always keep a bit of that in his tavern.

Falstaff is a mock king, a lord of misrule, and his tavern is a Saturnalia. Yet we are reminded of the original meaning of the Saturnalia, as a rite intended to recall the golden age of Saturn. Falstaff's world is not a golden world, but as long as we remember it we cannot forget that the world of *Henry V* is an iron one. We are reminded too of another traditional denizen of the green world, Robin Hood, the outlaw who manages to suggest a better kind of society than those who make him an outlaw can produce. The outlaws in *The Two Gentlemen of Verona* compare themselves, in spite of the Italian setting, to Robin Hood, and in *As You Like It* Charles the wrestler says of Duke Senior's followers: "There they live like the old Robin Hood of England: they say many young gentlemen flock to him every day, and fleet the time carelessly, as they did in the golden world."

In the histories, therefore, the comic Saturnalia is a temporary reversal of normal standards, comic "relief" as it is called, which subsides and allows the history to continue. In the comedies, the green world suggests an original golden age which the normal world has usurped and which makes us wonder if it is not the normal world that is the real Saturnalia. In *Cymbeline* the green world finally triumphs over a historical theme, the reason being perhaps that in that play the incarnation of Christ, which is contemporary with Cymbeline, takes place offstage, and accounts for the halcyon peace with which the play concludes. From then on in Shakespeare's plays, the green world has it all its own way, and both in *Cymbeline* and in *Henry VIII* there may be suggestions that Shakespeare, like Spenser, is moving toward a synthesis of the two worlds, a wedding of Prince Arthur and the Faerie Queene.

This world of fairies, dreams, disembodied souls; and pastoral lovers may not be a "real" world, but, if not, there is something equally illusory in the stumbling and blinded follies of the "normal" world, of Theseus' Athens with its idiotic marriage law, of Duke Frederick and his melancholy tyranny, of Leontes and his mad jealousy, of the Court Party with their plots and intrigues. The famous speech of Prospero about the dream nature of reality applies equally to Milan and the enchanted island. We spend our lives partly in a waking world we call normal and partly in a dream world which we create out of our own desires. Shakespeare endows both worlds with equal imaginative power, brings them opposite one another, and makes each world seem unreal when seen by the light of the other. He uses freely both the heroic triumph of New Comedy and the ritual resurrection of its predecessor, but his distinctive comic resolution is different from either: it is a detachment of the spirit born of this reciprocal reflection of two illusory realities. We need not ask whether this brings us into a higher order of existence or not, for the question of existence is not relevant to poetry.

We have spoken of New Comedy as Aristotelian, Old Comedy as Platonic and Dante's *commedia* as Thomist, but it is difficult to suggest a philosophical spokesman for the form of Shakespeare's comedy. For Shakespeare, the subject matter of poetry is not life, or nature, or reality, or revelation, or anything else that the philosopher builds on, but poetry itself, a verbal universe. That is one reason why he is both the most elusive and the most substantial of poets.

FRIEDRICH DÜRRENMATT

(1921–   )

For Dürrenmatt, "the world . . . stands as something monstrous, an enigma of calamity that has to be accepted but to which there must be no surrender." That vision has informed a number of notable plays and a group of essays from which the excerpt below, translated by Gerhard Nellhaus, is taken. As with many contemporary playwrights, Dürrenmatt insists that the age-old distinctions between the tragic and the comic are no longer viable. Thus, the seriousness of the dramatist's response to the sense of chaos in modern life is accurately reflected in his commitment to comic forms in his plays.

from Preface to *Four Plays*

Of course, the theatre has never dealt only with kings and generals; in comedy the hero has always been the peasant, the beggar, the ordinary citizen—but this was always in comedy. Nowhere in Shakespeare do we find a comic king; in his day a ruler could appear as a bloody monster but never as a fool. In Shakespeare the courtiers, the artisans, the working people are comic. Hence, in the evolution of the tragic hero we see a trend towards comedy. Analogously the fool becomes more and more of a tragic figure. This fact is by no means without significance. The hero of a play not only propels an action on, he not only suffers a certain fate, but he also represents a world. Therefore we have to ask ourselves how we should present our own questionable world and with what sort of heroes. We have to ask ourselves how the mirrors which catch and reflect this world should be ground and set.

Can our present-day world, to ask a concrete question, be represented by Schiller's dramatic art? Some writers claim it can be, since Schiller still holds audiences in his grip. To be sure, in art everything is possible when the art is right. But the question is if an art valid for its time could possibly be so even for our day. Art can never be repeated. If it were repeatable, it would be foolish not just to write according to the rules of Schiller.

Schiller wrote as he did because the world in which he lived could still be mirrored in the world his writing created, a world he could build as an historian.

But just barely. For was not Napoleon perhaps the last hero in the old sense? The world today as it appears to us could hardly be encompassed in the form of the historical drama as Schiller wrote it, for the reason alone that we no longer have any tragic heroes, but only vast tragedies staged by world butchers and produced by slaughtering machines. Hitler and Stalin cannot be made into Wallensteins. Their power was so enormous that they themselves were no more than incidental, corporeal and easily replaceable expressions of this power; and the misfortune associated with the former and to a considerable extent also with the latter is too vast, too complex, too horrible, too mechanical and usually simply too devoid of all sense. Wallenstein's power can still be envisioned; power as we know it today can only be seen in its smallest part for, like an iceberg, the largest part is submerged in anonymity and abstraction. Schiller's drama presupposes a world that the eye can take in, that takes for granted genuine actions of state, just as Greek tragedy did. For only what the eye can take in can be made visible in art. The state today, however, cannot be envisioned, for it is anonymous and bureaucratic; and not only in Moscow and Washington, but also in Berne. Actions of state today have become *post-hoc* satyric dramas which follow the tragedies executed in secret earlier. True representatives of our world are missing; the tragic heroes are nameless. Any small-time crook, petty government official or policeman better represents our world than a senator or president. Today art can only embrace the victims, if it can reach men at all; it can no longer come close to the mighty. Creon's secretaries close Antigone's case. The state has lost its physical reality, and just as physics can now only cope with the world in mathematical formulae, so the state can only be expressed in statistics. Power today becomes visible, material only when it explodes as in the atom bomb, in this marvelous mushroom which rises and spreads immaculate as the sun and in which mass murder and beauty have become one. The atom bomb cannot be reproduced artistically since it is mass-produced. In its face all man's art that would recreate it must fail, since it is itself a creation of man. Two mirrors which reflect one another remain empty.

But the task of art, in so far as art can have a task at all, and hence also the task of drama today, is to create something concrete, something that has form. This can be accomplished best by comedy. Tragedy, the strictest genre in art, presupposes a formed world. Comedy—in so far as it is not just satire of a particular society as in Molière—supposes an unformed world, a world being made and turned upside down, a world about to fold like ours. Tragedy overcomes distance; it can make myths originating in times immemorial seem like the present to the Athenians. But comedy creates distance; the attempt of the Athenians to gain a foothold in Sicily is translated by comedy into the birds undertaking to create their own empire before which the gods and men will have to capitulate. How comedy works can be seen in the most primitive kind of joke, in the dirty story, which, though it is of very dubious value, I bring up only because it is the best illustration of what I mean by creating distance. The subject of the dirty story is the purely sexual, which because it is purely sexual, is formless and without objective distance. To give form the purely sexual is transmuted, as I have already mentioned, into the dirty joke. Therefore this type of joke is a kind of original comedy, a transposition of the sexual on to the plain of the comical. In this way it is possible today, in a society dominated by John Doe, to talk in an accepted way about the purely sexual. In the dirty story it becomes clear that the comical exists in forming what is formless, in creating order out of chaos.

The means by which comedy creates distance is the conceit. Tragedy is without conceit. Hence there are few tragedies whose subjects were invented. By this I do not mean to imply that the ancient tragedians lacked inventive ideas of the sort that are written today, but the marvel of their art was that they had no need of these inventions, of conceits. That makes all the difference. Aristophanes, on the other hand, lives by conceits. The stuff of his plays are not myths but inventions, which take place not in the past but the present. They drop into their world like bombshells which, by throwing up huge craters of dirt, change the present into the comic and thus scatter the dirt for everyone to see. This, of course, does not mean that drama today can only be comical. Tragedy and comedy are but formal concepts, dramatic attitudes, figments of the aesthetic imagination which can embrace one and the same thing. Only the conditions under which each is created are different, and these conditions have their basis only in small part in art.

Tragedy presupposes guilt, despair, moderation, lucidity, vision, a sense of responsibility. In the Punch-and-Judy show of our century, in this backsliding of the white race, there are no more guilty and also, no responsible men. It is always, "We couldn't help it" and "We didn't really want that to happen." And indeed, things happen without anyone in particular being responsible for them. Everything is dragged along and everyone gets caught somewhere in the sweep of events. We are all collectively guilty, collectively bogged down in the sins of our fathers and of our forefathers. We are the offspring of children. That is our misfortune, but not our guilt: guilt can exist only as a personal achievement, as a religious deed. Comedy alone is suitable for us. Our world has led to the grotesque as well as to the atom bomb, and so it is a world like that of Hieronymus Bosch whose apocalyptic paintings are also grotesque. But the grotesque is only a way of expressing in a tangible manner, of making us perceive physically the paradoxical, the form of the unformed, the face of a world without face; and just as in our thinking today we seem to be unable to do without the concept of the paradox, so also in art, and in our world which at times seems still to exist only because the atom bomb exists: out of fear of the bomb.

But the tragic is still possible even if pure tragedy is not. We can achieve the tragic out of comedy. We can bring it forth as a frightening moment, as an abyss that opens suddenly; indeed, many of Shakespeare's tragedies are already really comedies out of which the tragic arises.

After all this the conclusion might easily be drawn that comedy is the expression of despair, but this conclusion is not inevitable. To be sure, whoever realizes the senselessness, the hopelessness of this world might well despair, but this despair is not a result of this world. Rather it is an answer given by an individual to this world; another answer would be not to despair, would be an individual's decision to endure this world in which we live like Gulliver among the giants. He also achieves distance, he also steps back a pace or two who takes measure of his opponent, who prepares himself to fight his opponent or to escape him. It is still possible to show man as a courageous being.

In truth this is a principal concern of mine. The blind man, Romulus, Übelohe, Akki, are all men of courage. The lost world-order is restored within them; the universal escapes my grasp. I refuse to find the universal in a doctrine. The universal for me is chaos. The world (hence the stage which represents this world) is for me something monstrous, a riddle of misfortunes which must be accepted but before which one must not capitulate. The world is far bigger than any man, and perforce threatens him constantly. If one could but stand outside the world, it would no longer be threatening. But I have neither the right nor the ability to be an outsider to this world. To find solace in poetry can also be all too cheap; it is more honest to retain one's human point of view. Brecht's thesis, that the world is an accident, which he developed in his *Street Scene* where he shows how this accident happened, may yield—as it in fact did—some magnificent theatre; but he did it by concealing most of the evidence! Brecht's thinking is inexorable, because inexorably there are many things he will not think about.

And lastly it is through the conceit, through comedy, that the anonymous audience becomes possible as an audience, becomes a reality to be counted on, and also one to be taken into account. The conceit easily transforms the crowd of theatre-goers into a mass which can be attacked, deceived, outsmarted into listening to things it would otherwise not so readily listen to. Comedy is a mouse-trap in which the public is easily caught and in which it will get caught over and over again. Tragedy, on the other hand, predicated a true community, a kind of community whose existence in our day is but an embarrassing fiction. Nothing is more ludicrous, for instance, than to sit and watch the mystery plays of the Anthroposophists when one is not a participant.

Granting all this, there is still one more question to be asked: is it permissible to go from a generality to a particular form of art, to do what I just did when I went from my assertion that the world was formless to the particular possibility for writing comedies today. I doubt that this is permissible. Art is something personal, and something personal should never be explained with generalities. The value of a work of art does not depend on whether more or less good reasons for its existence can be found. Hence I have also tried to avoid certain problems, as for example the argument which is quite lively today, whether or not plays ought to be written in verse or in prose. My own answer lies simply in writing prose, without any intention of thereby deciding the issue. A man has to choose to go one way, after all, and why should one way always be worse than another? As far as my con-

cepts of comedy are concerned, I believe that here, too, personal reasons are more important than more general ones that are always open to argument. What logic in matters of art could not be refuted! One talks best about art when one talks of one's own art. The art one chooses is an expression of freedom without which no art can exist, and at the same time also of necessity without which art cannot exist either. The artist always represents his world and himself. If at one time philosophy taught men to arrive at the particular from the general, then—unlike Schiller, who started out believing in general conclusions—I cannot construct a play as he did when I doubt that the particular can ever be reached from the general. But my doubt is mine and only mine, and not the doubt and problems of a Catholic for whom drama holds possibilities non-Catholics do not share. This is so even if, on the other hand, a Catholic who takes his religion seriously, is denied those possibilities which other men possess. The danger inherent in this thesis lies in the fact that there are always those artists who for the sake of finding some generalities to believe in accept conversion, taking a step which is the more to be wondered at for the sad fact that it really will not help them. The difficulties experienced by a Protestant in writing a drama are just the same difficulties he has with his faith. Thus it is my way to mistrust what is ordinarily called the building of the drama, and to arrive at my plays from the unique, the sudden idea or conceit, rather than from some general concept or plan. Speaking for myself, I need to write off into the blue, as I like to put it so that I might give critics a catchword to hang on to. They use it often enough, too, without really understanding what I mean by it.

But these matters are my own concerns and hence it is not necessary to invoke the whole world and to make out that what are my concerns are the concerns of art in general (lest I be like the drunk who goes back to Noah, the Flood, original sin and the beginning of the world to explain what is, after all, only his own weakness). As in everything and everywhere, and not just in the field of art, the rule is: No excuses, please!

Nevertheless the fact remains (always keeping in mind, of course, the reservations just made) that we now stand in a different relationship to what we have called our material. Our unformed, amorphous present is characterized by being surrounded by figures and forms that reduce our time to a mere result, even less, to a mere transitional state, and which give excessive weight to the past as something finished and to the future as something possible. This applies equally well to politics. Related to art it means that the artist is surrounded by all sort of opinions about art and by demands on him which are based not upon his capacities, but upon the historical past and present forms. He is surrounded therefore by materials which are no longer materials, that is possibilities, but by materials which have already taken on shape, that is some definitive form. Caesar is no longer pure subject matter for us; he has become the Caesar whom scholarship made the object of its researches. And so it happened that scholars, having thrown themselves with increasing energy not only upon nature but also upon intellectual life and upon art, establishing in the process intellectual history, literary scholarship, philology and goodness knows what else, have created a body of factual information which cannot be ignored (for one cannot be conscious of these facts and at the same time pretend to be so naïve that one need pay no attention to the results of scholarship). In this way, however, scholars have deprived the artist of materials by doing what was really the artist's task. The mastery of Richard Feller's *History of Berne* precludes the possibility of an historical drama about the city of Berne; the history of Berne was thus given shape before some literary artist could do it. True, it is a scholastic form (and not a mythical one which would leave the way open for a tragedian), a form that severely limits the field for the artist, leaving to art only psychology which, of course, has also become a science. To rewrite such a history in a creative literary manner would now be a tautology, a repetition by means which are not suitable or fitting, a mere illustration of scholarly insight; in short, it would be the very thing science often claims literature to be. It was still possible for Shakespeare to base his Caesar upon Plutarch, for the Roman was not an historian in our sense of the word but a story-teller, the author of biographical sketches. Had Shakespeare read Mommsen he could not have written his Caesar because he would of necessity have lost the supremacy over his materials. And this holds true now in all things, even the myths of the Greeks which, since we no longer live them but only study, evaluate, investigate them, recognizing them to be mere myths and as such destroying them, have become mummies; and these, bound tightly round with philosophy and theology, are all too often substituted for the living thing.

Therefore the artist must reduce the subjects he finds and runs into everywhere if he wants to turn them once more into real materials, hoping always that he will succeed. He parodies his materials, contrasts them consciously with what they have actually been turned into. By this means, by this act of parody, the artist regains his freedom and hence his material; and thus material is no longer found but invented. For every parody presupposes a conceit and an invention. In laughter man's freedom becomes manifest, in crying his necessity. Our task today is to demonstrate freedom. The tyrants of this planet are not moved by the works of the poets. They yawn at a poet's threnodies. For them heroic epics are silly fairy-tales and religious poetry puts them to sleep. Tyrants fear only one thing: a poet's mockery. For this reason, then, parody has crept into all literary genres, into the novel, the drama, into lyrical poetry. Much of painting, even of music, has been conquered by parody, and the grotesque has followed, often well camouflaged, on the heels of parody: all of a sudden the grotesque is there.

But our times, up to every imaginable trick there is, can handle all that and nothing can intimidate it: the public has been educated to see in art something solemn, hallowed and even pathetic. The comic is considered inferior, dubious, unseemly; it is accepted only when it makes people feel as bestially happy as a bunch of pigs. But the very moment people recognize the comic to be dangerous, an art that exposes, demands, moralizes, it is dropped like a hot potato, for art may be everything it wants to be so long as it remains *gemütlich*.

We writers are often accused of art that is nihilistic. Today, of course, there exists a nihilistic art, but not every art that seems nihilistic is so. True nihilistic art does not appear to be nihilistic at all; usually it is considered to be especially humane and supremely worthy of being read by our more mature young people. A man must be a pretty bungling sort of nihilist to be recognized as such by the world at large. People call nihilistic what is merely uncomfortable. Then also people say, the artist is supposed to create, not to talk; to give shape to things, not to preach. To be sure. But it becomes more and more difficult to create "purely" or however people imagine the creative mind should work. Mankind today is like a reckless driver racing ever faster, ever more heedlessly along the highway. And he does not like it when the frightened passengers cry out, "Watch out" and "There's a warning sign! Slow down," or "Don't kill that child!" What is more, the driver hates it even worse when he is asked, "Who is paying for the car?" or "Who's providing the petrol and oil for this mad journey?," to say nothing of what happens when he is asked for his driver's licence. What unpleasant facts might then come to light! Maybe the car was stolen from some relatives, the petrol and oil squeezed from the passengers, and really not petrol and oil but the blood and sweat of us all; and most likely he wouldn't even have a driver's licence and it would turn out that this was his first time driving. Of course, it would be embarrassing if such personal questions were to be asked. The driver would much prefer the passengers to praise the beauty of the countryside through which they are travelling, the silver of the river and the brilliant reflection of the ice-capped mountains in the far distance, would even prefer to have amusing stories whispered into his ear. Today's author, however, can no longer confine himself with good conscience to whispering pleasant stories and praising the beautiful landscape. Unfortunately, too, he cannot get out of this mad race in order to sit by the wayside, writing the pure poetry demanded of him by all the non-poets. Fear, worry, and above all anger open his mouth wide.